THE COMPLETE WORD STUDY DICTIONARY

NEW TESTAMENT

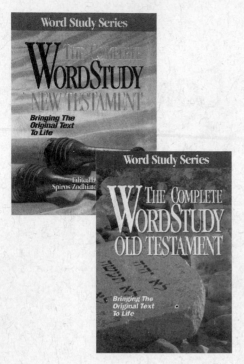

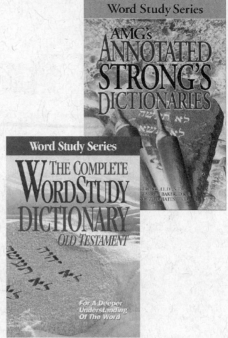

AMG Publishers is committed to helping you understand the meaning of every word in the original biblical languages. The Strong's numbering system is the easiest and best way to facilitate this endeavor. Enhance your study of the Bible today! AMG's Complete Word Study Series is a comprehensive set of tools for understanding the Hebrew Old Testament and Greek New Testament *without* having to learn the languages.

The Complete Word Study Old Testament (ISBN: 978-089957-665-7) provides a grammatical code and Strong's number right on the words of the English text of the Old Testament. Tools provided at the back of the book allow you to use these codes and numbers to learn more about the words of the Old Testament.

The Complete Word Study Dictionary: Old Testament (ISBN: 978-089957-667-1) is organized by Strong's number and gives extended definitions for each Hebrew/Aramaic word. Also included is a concordance of all the Old Testament verses where the word(s) represented by each Strong's number occurs in the Hebrew Old Testament. Excerpts from this dictionary were used to enhance the *Annotated Strong's Hebrew Dictionary of the Old Testament* contained in this volume.

The Complete Word Study New Testament (ISBN: 978-089957-651-0) gives a grammatical code and Strong's number right on the English text of the New Testament. Also included is a concordance of all the New Testament verses where the word(s) represented by each Strong's number occur in the Greek New Testament. Tools provided at the back of the book allow you to use these codes and numbers to learn more about the words of the New Testament.

AMG's Annotated Strong's Dictionaries (ISBN: 978-089957-710-4) is an updated, easy-to-read, larger print edition of Strong's orignal language dictionaries. For key entries, AMG has added materials taken from our Compete Word Study Dictionaries for the Old Testament and the New Testament.

W THE COMPLETE
WORD STUDY
DICTIONARY
NEW TESTAMENT

Based on the lexicon of Edward Robinson (as revised by
Alexander Negris and John Duncan), with constant reference to
and citations from the works of John Parkhurst and Hermann
Cremer. Greek words in the text are transliterated and coded
throughout according to the numbering system found in James
Strong's *Exhaustive Concordance of the Bible.*

General Editor
Spiros Zodhiates, Th.D.

Managing Editor
Warren Baker, D.R.E.

Associate Editor
Rev. George Hadjiantoniou, Ph.D.

AMG
PUBLISHERS

Chattanooga, TN

THE COMPLETE WORD STUDY DICTIONARY: NEW TESTAMENT

ISBN-13: 978-089957-663-3

ISBN-10: 0-89957-663-X

Printed in China
18 17 16 15 14 13 –CK– 18 17 16 15 14 13

*To my beloved wife, Joan, who spent
as much time editing the manuscripts
as I did preparing them*

Preface

We at AMG Publishers are doing our best to make every word of the New Testament understandable to the English reader by reference to the original manuscript. *The Complete Word Study Dictionary: New Testament* is a result of the desire to see this accomplished.

Our first effort was in providing the *Hebrew Greek Key Study Bible*, available in the King James Version or the New American Standard, thus making it possible for all to benefit by referring to the original Hebrew and Greek words. This Bible, however, contains only the explanations of certain key words.

The next step was to provide *The Complete Word Study New Testament* in the King James Version. This work gives every word a grammatical code which explains its structure as it is used in the Greek text. In addition, a number over each word identifies it by the numbering system of James Strong's *Exhaustive Concordance of the Bible*. This New Testament also contains a Greek concordance and has a section indicating all the Greek words which an English word represents in translation. Word studies expound upon key words, and footnotes explain key passages.

With that basic word and grammar identification, we are now proud to present the ultimate tool for in–depth Bible study. This lexicon of the Greek New Testament, created as a companion for *The Complete Word Study New Testament*, is a complete dictionary of every Greek New Testament word.

This volume is based on *A Greek and English Lexicon of the New Testament* by Edward Robinson, as revised by Alexander Negris and John Duncan, with extensive quotations from *The Greek and English Lexicon* by John Parkhurst. I used these two basic works because I found them the most adequate in their presentation, although changes were made as deemed necessary. I felt, for example, that much additional information was needed in the discussion of the theology of some words, as well as the inclusion of derivatives, synonyms, and antonyms of words when such exist. I know of no other New Testament dictionary which contains these additions.

The greatest benefit of this dictionary will undoubtedly be realized by the person who has taken the time and exercised the discipline and diligence to study the Greek grammar and language of the New Testament. However, the student of the Word of God need not know Greek grammar or even the Greek alphabet to be greatly helped by this unique dictionary. Every Greek word is transliterated and identified by Strong's number, followed by the meaning or meanings in English. We have tried to make this dictionary as accurate as possible; however, some mistakes may still exist. Please let us know if you find any.

May God bless you in your endeavors to study and fully understand His Word.

SPIROS ZODHIATES

Acknowledgements

My beloved wife Joan worked equally as hard editing the material with painstaking diligence. If it were not for her help, you would not be holding this valuable reference work in your hands.

Other people who deserve my great gratitude are:

Rev. George A. Hadjiantoniou, Ph.D., who has taught theology, Greek grammar, and exegesis in seminaries and universities in Europe and Canada. He is the author of *A Basic Grammar of the New Testament* which is the best available grammar for self–study of the language of the New Testament. Dr. Hadjiantoniou carefully read the text of this dictionary making valuable contributions.

Dr. Warren Baker, former seminary assistant professor, now the managing editor of AMG Publishers and director of AMG's special projects department, who acted as general supervisor in the editing and coordination of this work.

Employees of the special projects department who helped in producing this work: David Gray, Joel Kletzing, Kim Knicely, Mark Oshman, Trevor Overcash, Sam Wallace, and Todd Williams.

The typists who prepared the manuscripts.

Volunteers who assisted in proofreading, checking the correctness of the Strong's numbers, Scripture references, Greek adjuncts, and English grammar: Dorothy Boyse, George Clark, Tom Crook, Jim Gee, Mr. and Mrs. Don Chapman, Philip Hise, Sandy Jennings, Mr. and Mrs. Gordon Peters, and Alma Stewart.

Table of Contents

Abbreviations

abl. (ablative)
acc. (accusative)
act. (active)
adj. (adjective, adjectival)
adv. (adverb, adverbial, adverbially)
ant. (antonym)
aor. (aorist [2 aor. for second aorist])
art. (article)
a.t. (author's translation)
attrib. (attributive)
AV (Authorized Version)
cf. (compare, comparison)
chap. (chapter)
Class. Gr. (Classical Greek)
coll. (collective)
comp. (compound, compounds)
conj. (conjunction, conjunctive)
dat. (dative)
def. (definite)
deriv. (derivative[s], derivation)
e.g. (for example)
Eng. (English)
etc. (and so forth)
f. (following)
ff. (following in the plural)
fem. (feminine)
fut. (future)
gen. (genitive)
Gr. (Greek)
Hebr. (Hebrew)
ibid. (in the same place)
i.e. (that is)
imper. (imperative)
imperf. (imperfect)
indef. (indefinite, indefinitely)
indic. (indicative)
inf. (infinitive)
intens. (intensive)
intrans. (intransitive)
KJV (King James Version)
Lat. (Latin)
masc. (masculine)

mid. (middle)
Mod. Gr. (Modern Greek)
MS (manuscript)
MSS (manuscripts)
MT (Masoretic text)
NASB (New American Standard Bible)
n.f. (not found in the NT)
NIV (New International Version)
NKJV (New King James Version)
NT (New Testament)
neg. (negative)
neut. (neuter)
nom. (nominative)
obj. (object, objective[ly])
OT (Old Testament)
opt. (optative)
p. (page), pp. (pages)
part. (participle, participial)
pass. (passive)
perf. (perfect)
pl. (plural)
pluperf. (pluperfect)
poss. (possessive)
prep. (preposition)
pres. (present)
priv. (privative)
pron. (pronoun)
RSV (Revised Standard Version)
Sept. (Septuagint)
sing. (singular)
subst. (substantive)
subj. (subject, subjective)
s.v. (under the word)
syn. (synonym, synonymous)
TR (Textus Receptus)
trans. (transitive, transitively)
UBS (United Bible Society)
v. (verse), vv. (verses)
voc. (vocative)
vol. (volume)
WH (Westcott & Hort)

Books of the Bible

The Old Testament

Genesis	Gen.	Ecclesiastes	Eccl.
Exodus	Ex.	Song of Solomon	Song
Leviticus	Lev.	Isaiah	Is.
Numbers	Num.	Jeremiah	Jer.
Deuteronomy	Deut.	Lamentations	Lam.
Joshua	Josh.	Ezekiel	Ezek.
Judges	Judg.	Daniel	Dan.
Ruth	Ruth	Hosea	Hos.
1 Samuel	1 Sam.	Joel	Joel
2 Samuel	2 Sam.	Amos	Amos
1 Kings	1 Kgs.	Obadiah	Obad.
2 Kings	2 Kgs.	Jonah	Jon.
1 Chronicles	1 Chr.	Micah	Mic.
2 Chronicles	2 Chr.	Nahum	Nah.
Ezra	Ezra	Habakkuk	Hab.
Nehemiah	Neh.	Zephaniah	Zeph.
Esther	Esth.	Haggai	Hag.
Job	Job	Zechariah	Zech.
Psalms	Ps.	Malachi	Mal.
Proverbs	Prov.		

The New Testament

Matthew	Matt.	1 Timothy	1 Tim.
Mark	Mark	2 Timothy	2 Tim.
Luke	Luke	Titus	Titus
John	John	Philemon	Phile.
Acts	Acts	Hebrews	Heb.
Romans	Rom.	James	James
1 Corinthians	1 Cor.	1 Peter	1 Pet.
2 Corinthians	2 Cor.	2 Peter	2 Pet.
Galatians	Gal.	1 John	1 John
Ephesians	Eph.	2 John	2 John
Philippians	Phil.	3 John	3 John
Colossians	Col.	Jude	Jude
1 Thessalonians	1 Thess.	Revelation	Rev.
2 Thessalonians	2 Thess.		

Books that have only one chapter are normally referenced by book name and verse (e.g., Jude 27). However, for the sake of indexing on the computer, etc., we have included a chapter number when referencing them (e.g., Jude 1:27).

Explanation of General Format

The Complete Word Study Dictionary: New Testament is the second in a series of Bible study tools which are designed to make the original languages of the Bible accessible to every student of the Word of God. This lexicon is a companion volume for *The Complete Word Study New Testament*, and together they compose the New Testament portion of this series. *The Complete Word Study Old Testament* and *The Complete Word Study Dictionary: Old Testament* are forthcoming.

Both the student who does not have a working knowledge of Greek as well as the one who does can benefit from *The Complete Word Study Dictionary: New Testament*. Special features of this unique dictionary make it usable for the English reader, allowing him to gain insights into the meaning of the Greek. The use of Strong's numbering system permits the student to locate the Greek words easily. An English transliteration is given along with the Greek word for each entry, and transliteration is used throughout the text. Gender and part-of-speech identifications are given in English instead of the usual Greek designations. In addition to the meaning or meanings for each word, a discussion of the implications of some Greek words for the interpretation of more difficult passages has been given.

Studying the Greek text is made simple when this dictionary is used with its companion volume. *The Complete Word Study New Testament* places the grammatical code and Strong's number of the Greek words above the corresponding words of the English text. Using the GRAMMATICAL CODES section of the New Testament, the student can understand the sense of the Greek grammar. And using the Strong's number, the student can look up the meaning of the Greek words in this dictionary. Since nearly ninety percent of the dictionary entries include all the New Testament references for the word, a complete Greek word study is already done for most of the words. In this manner, the student can understand the Greek behind the English.

STUDY HELPS are included to assist the user:

GUIDES TO TRANSLITERATION for both the Hebrew and the Greek are included.

A TRANSLATIONAL REFERENCE INDEX of the New Testament lists almost every word of the King James Text followed by the Strong's number for each Greek word that is translated by that English word.

SPECIAL FEATURES include:

GENERAL ENTRIES with the Strong's number, Greek word, transliteration, forms needed to conjugate or decline the word, identification, derivation, definition and references. The designation masc.–fem. indicates that there is only one determination for both masculine and feminine forms of the adjective.

MULTIPLE SPELLINGS AND ROOTS have often been placed under the same number by Strong. We have distinguished between the two by using a comma between multiple spellings (e.g., ἐκτινάσσω *ektinássō*, ἐκτινάττω *ektináttō*) and using "and" between multiple roots (e.g., ὀμνύω *omnúō* and ὄμνυμι *ómnumi*). Differences of people, places, or usage and extended discussions are handled under regular outline divisions.

MIDDLE FORMS of the verbs were listed by Strong's when they were the only form which appear in the New Testament. We have listed these verbs in the active form. Only deponent verbs have been listed in middle forms.

SEPTUAGINT citations occur frequently; however, all references are English Bible references. The designation Sept. has been used to indicate that the Greek word appears in the corresponding verse or verses of the Septuagint. The text used as a standard was *Septuaginta* (Greek OT, ed. Alfred Rahlfs).

DERIVATIVES are listed when they occur. When more than two derivatives occur for a word not found in the New Testament, the derivatives have been placed under one of the derivatives and the others have been referred to it. When two occur, they are cross-referenced to each other.

SYNONYMS AND ANTONYMS are included when such exist. It is important to understand the nature of these categories as used in this work.

Each category represents the broadest possible range of meaning which might feasibly be placed under its heading. Synonyms are those words which share a relevant semantic affinity with the entry word. Antonyms are those words which bear a semantically inverse or antithetical relationship to the entry word. These categories are, therefore, pedagogical and not technical in design. The author has attempted to place words more closely related first, and the lists are not intended to be exhaustive. Occasionally, the more obvious choices may have been overlooked and conversely may have included less preferable or qualified terms under the two categories.

Extensive research by scholars in the field of semantics in biblical studies since the appearance of James Barr's *The Semantics of Biblical Language* in 1961 has resulted in significant developments in this area. Recent publications include those by J. P. Louw, *Semantics of New Testament Greek*, 1982, Moises Silva, *Biblical Words and Their Meaning: An Introduction to Lexical Semantics*, 1983, and the innovative two–volume lexicon by J. P. Louw and Eugene Nida, *Greek–English Lexicon of the New Testament Based on Semantic Domains*, 1990. These works are recommended to the reader interested in a more detailed study of semantic distinctions and the nature of relationships between words.

A SCRIPTURE INDEX to this work is now available.

We trust that *The Complete Word Study Dictionary*: *New Testament* will enrich your study of the Word of God and help to deepen your knowledge of God.

GUIDE TO THE TRANSLITERATION AND PRONUNCIATION OF HEBREW CONSONANTS

Consonant	Hebrew Name	Trans–literation	Phonetic Sound	Example
א	Aleph	'	Silent	Similar to h in honor
בּ	Beth	b	b	as in boy
ב	Veth	v	v	as in vat
גּ	Gimel	g	g	as in get
ג	Gimel	gh	g	as in get
דּ	Daleth	d	d	as in do
ד	Daleth	dh	d	as in do
ה	Hē	h	h	as in hat
ו	Waw	w	w	as in wait
ז	Zayin	z	z	as in zip
ח	Cheth	ch	ch	Similar to ch in the German *ach*
ט	Teth	<u>t</u>	t	as in time
י	Yodh	y	y	as in you
כּ	Kaph	k	k	as in kit
כ	Chaph	kh	ch	Similar to ch in the German *ach*
ל	Lamed	l	l	as in lit
מ	Mem	m	m	as in move
נ	Nun	n	n	as in not
ס	Samekh	<u>s</u>	s	as in see
ע	Ayin	'	Silent	Similar to h in honor
פּ	Pē	p	p	as in put
פ	Phē	ph	f	as in phone
צ	Tsadde	ts	ts	as in wits
ק	Qoph	q	q	as in Qatar
ר	Resh	r	r	as in run
שׂ	Sin	s	s	as in see
שׁ	Shin	sh	sh	as in ship
תּ	Taw	t	t	as in time
ת	Thaw	th	th	as in this

GUIDE TO THE TRANSLITERATION AND PRONUNCIATION OF HEBREW VOWELS

Vowel	Hebrew Name	Position	Transliteration	Sound	Example
ְ	Shewa (Silent)	מְ	Not transliterated nor pronounced		
ְ	Shewa (Vocal)	מְ	e	u	as in but
ַ	Pathah	מַ	a	a	as in lad
ֲ	Hateph Pathah	מֲ	a	a	as in lad
ָ	Qamets	מָ	ā	a	as in car
ֳ	Hateph Qamets	מֳ	ā	a	as in car
ֵי	Sere Yodh	מֵי	ē	ey	as in prey
ֵ	Sere	מֵ	ē	ey	as in prey
ֶ	Seghol	מֶ	e	e	as in set
ֱ	Hateph Seghol	מֱ	e	e	as in set
ִי	Hiriq Yodh	מִי	ī	i	as in machine
ִ	Hiriq	מִ	i	i	as in pin
ָ	Qamets Qatan	מָ	o	o	as in hop
ֹ	Holem	מֹ	ō	o	as in go
וֹ	Holem	מוֹ	ō	o	as in go
ֻ	Qubbuts	מֻ	u	u	as in put
וּ	Shureq	מוּ	ū	u	as in tune

GUIDE TO THE TRANSLITERATION
AND MODERN PRONUNCIATION
OF THE GREEK ALPHABET

Capital Letter	Small Letter	Greek Name	Trans-literation	Phonetic Sound	Example
Α	α	alpha	*a*	a	as in father
Β	β	bēta	*b*	v	as in victory
Γ	γ	gamma	*g*	y	as in yell (soft gutteral)
Δ	δ	delta	*d*	th	as in there
Ε	ε	epsilon	*e*	e	as in met
Ζ	ζ	zēta	*z*	z	as in zebra
Η	η	ēta	*ē*	ee	as in see
Θ	θ	thēta	*th*	th	as in thin
Ι	ι	iōta	*i*	i	as in machine
Κ	κ	kappa	*k*	k	as in kill (soft accent)
Λ	λ	lambda	*l*	l	as in land
Μ	μ	mē	*m*	m	as in mother
Ν	ν	nē	*n*	n	as in now
Ξ	ξ	xi	*x*	x	as in wax
Ο	ο	omicron	*o*	o	as in obey
Π	π	pi	*p*	p	as in pet (soft accent)
Ρ	ρ	ro	*r*	r	as in courage
Σ	σ, ς	sigma	*s*	s	as in sit
Τ	τ	tau	*t*	t	as in tell (soft accent)
Υ	υ	ēpsilon	*u*	ee	as in see
Φ	φ	phi	*ph*	ph	as in graphic
Χ	χ	chi	*ch*	h	as in heel
Ψ	ψ	psi	*ps*	ps	as in ships
Ω	ω	omega	*ō*	o	as in obey

*At the end of words

SPECIAL RULES FOR THE TRANSLITERATION AND MODERN PRONUNCIATION OF THE GREEK LANGUAGE

COMBINATIONS OF CONSONANTS

Small Letter	Greek Names	Trans-literation	Phonetic Sound	Example
γγ	gamma + gamma	gg	g	as in go
γκ	gamma + kappa	gk	g	as in go
γχ	gamma + chi	gch	gh	as in ghost
μπ	mē + pi	mp	b	as in boy
ντ	nē + tau	nt	d	as in dog
τζ	tau + zēta	tz	g	as in gym

DIPHTHONGS (DOUBLE VOWELS)

Small Letter	Greek Names	Trans-literation	Phonetic Sound	Example
αι	alpha + iōta	ai	ai	as in hair
αυ	alpha + ēpsilon	au	af, av	as in waft or lava
ει	epsilon + iōta	ei	ee	as in see
ευ	epsilon + ēpsilon	eu	ef, ev	as in effort or every
ηυ	ēta + ēpsilon	ēu	eef, eev	as in reef or sleeve
οι	omicron + iōta	oi	ee	as in see
οε	omicron + ēpsilon	ou	ou	as in group
ει	ēpsilon + iōta	ui	ee	as in see

BREATHINGS (Occur only with initial vowels)

(’)   Smooth, not transliterated or pronounced.
When words begin with vowels, it may occur at the beginning of words with every vowel or double vowel (diphthong). ἔργον—*érgon*, work; εὐχή←*euchḗ*, vow.

(‘)   Rough = h.
When words begin with vowels, it may occur at the beginning of words with every vowel or double vowel (diphthong). No distinction in pronunciation from the smooth breathing. To indicate the rough breathing we use "h" in the transliteration.

(ῥ)   Rho = r.
(ὑ)   Eepsilon = u.
When these begin a word, they always have the rough breathing. There they are transliterated rh, hu, respectively. ῥέω—*rhéō*, flow; ὑπομονή—*hupomonḗ*, patience.

Translational Reference Index

This index lists most of the English words used in the King James Version of the New Testament, along with their various forms and endings. Following the English word in each entry are the Strong's numbers for all the Greek words which that English word represents in this translation. Finally, the scripture references (in italics) given for certain entries list each verse where that English word occurs.

A

a; an — 1520, 3391: *John 1:6; Rev. 9:13*

Aaron — 2: *Luke 1:5; Acts 7:40; Heb. 5:4; 9:4; 7:11*

Abaddon — 3: *Rev. 9:11*

abased; abasing (see **humble**) — 5013: *Matt. 23:12; Luke 14:11; 18:14; 2 Cor. 11:7; Phil. 4:12*

Abba — 5: *Mark 14:36; Rom. 8:15; Gal. 4:6*

Abel — 6: *Matt. 23:35; Luke 11:51; Heb. 11:4; 12:24*

abhor -rest — 655, 948: *Rom. 2:22; 12:9*

Abia; Abijah — 7: *Matt. 1:7; Luke 1:5*

Abiathar — 8: *Mark 2:26*

abide -ing -eth; abode — 63, 390, 835, 1304, 1804, 1961, 2476, 2650, 3306, 3438, 3887, 4160, 4357, 5278

Abilene — 9: *Luke 3:1*

ability; able — 1410, 1411, 1415, 1840, 2141, 2192, 2425, 2427, 2479, 2480

Abiud — 10: *Matt. 1:13*

aboard — 1910: *Acts 21:2*

abolished — 2673: *2 Cor. 3:13; Eph. 2:15; 2 Tim. 1:10*

abominable; abomination -s — 111, 946, 947, 948

abound -ed -eth -ing — 4052, 4121, 4129, 5248

about — 1330, 1722, 1909, 1994, 2021, 2212, 2596, 2943, 2944, 2945, 3163, 3195, 3329, 3840, 3936, 3985, 4012, 4013, 4015, 4016, 4017, 4019, 4022, 4024, 4029, 4034, 4037, 4038, 4043, 4060, 4064, 4066, 4225, 4314, 4762, 5418, 5613, 5616

above — 507, 509, 511, 1883, 1909, 3844, 4012, 4117, 4253, 5228, 5231

Abraham — 11

abroad — 864, 1096/5456, 1232, 1255, 1287, 1289, 1290, 1310, 1330, 1519/5318, 1632, 1831, 4496, 4650, 5318

absence; absent — 548, 553, 666, 817

abstain; abstinence — 567, 776

abundant -ly; abundance — 100, 1411, 4050, 4051, 4052, 4053, 4054, 4055, 4056, 4121, 4146, 4183, 5236, 5250

abuse -ers -ing — 733, 2710: *1 Cor. 6:9; 7:31; 9:18*

accept -able -ably -ation -ed -est -eth -ing — 587, 588, 594, 1184, 1209, 2101, 2102, 2144, 2983, 4327, 5487

access — 4318: *Rom. 5:2; Eph. 2:18; 3:12*

accompany -ied — 2192, 4311, 4862, 4902, 4905: *Acts 10:23; 11:12; 20:4, 38; Heb. 6:9*

accomplish -ed -ing -ment — 1604, 1822, 2005, 4130, 4137, 5055

accord — 830, 844, 3661, 4861

according — 2526, 2530, 2531, 2596, 4314, 5613

account -ed -ing — 1380, 1677, 2233, 2661, 3049, 3056:

accursed — 331: *Rom. 9:3; 1 Cor. 12:3; Gal. 1:8, 9*

accuse -ation -ed -er(s) -eth -ing — 156, 1225, 1228, 1458, 1722/2724, 1908, 2722, 2723, 2920, 4811

Aceldama — 184: *Acts 1:19*

Achaia (see **Greece**) — 882

Achaicus — 883: *1 Cor. 16:17*

Achaz — 881: *Matt. 1:9*

Achim — 885: *Matt. 1:14*

acknowledge -ed -eth -ing -ment — 1921, 1922

acquaintance — 1110, 2398: *Luke 2:44; 23:49; Acts 24:23*

act — 1888: *John 8:4*

Adam — 76

add -ed -eth — 1928, 2007, 2018, 2023, 4323, 4369

Addi — 78: *Luke 3:28*

addicted — 5021: *1 Cor. 16:15*

adjure — 1844, 3726: *Matt. 26:63; Mark 5:7; Acts 19:13*

administered; administration -s — 1247, 1248: *1 Cor. 8:19, 20; 12:5; 2 Cor. 9:12*

admired; admiration — 2295, 2296: *2 Thess. 1:10; Jude 1:16; Rev. 17:6*

admonish -ed -ing; admonition — 3559, 3560, 3867, 5537

ado — 2350: *Mark 5:39*

adoption — 5206: *Rom. 8:15, 23; 9:4; Gal. 4:5; Eph. 1:5*

adorn -ed -ing — 2885, 2889

Adramyttium — 98: *Acts 27:2*

Adria — 99: *Acts 27:27*

adultery -ies -ers -ess(es) -ous — 3428, 3429, 3430, 3431, 3432

advantage -ed -eth — 3786, 4053, 4122, 5622, 5623: *Luke 9:25; Rom. 3:1; 1 Cor. 15:32; 2 Cor. 2:11; Jude 1:16*

adventure — 1325: *Acts 19:31*

adversary -ies — 476, 480, 5227

adversity — 2558: *Heb. 13:3*

advice; advised — 1012/5087, 1106: *Acts 27:12; 2 Cor. 8:10*

advocate — 3875: *1 John 2:1*

Aeneas — 132: *Acts 9:33, 34*

Aenon — 137: *John 3:23*

afar — 3112, 3113, 3467, 4207

affairs — 2596, 4012, 4230

affect -ed — 2206, 2559: *Acts 14:2; Gal. 4:17, 18*

affection -ately -ed -s — 794, 2442, 3804, 3806, 4698, 5387, 5426

affirm -ed — 1226, 1340, 5335, 5346

afflicted; affliction -s — 2346, 2347, 2552, 2553, 2561, 3804, 4777, 4797, 5003

affrighted (see **afraid**) — 1568, 1719: *Mark 16:5, 6; Luke 24:37; Rev. 11:13*

afoot — 3978, 3979: *Mark 6:33; Acts 20:13*

afore -hand -time — 4218, 4270, 4279, 4282, 4301

afraid — 1168, 1630, 1719, 5141, 5399

afresh — 388: *Heb. 6:6*

after -ward(s) — 516, 1207, 1208, 1223, 1230, 1377, 1519/3195, 1534, 1567, 1722, 1836, 1887, 1894, 1899, 1909, 1934, 1938, 1971, 2089, 2517, 2547, 2596, 2614, 2628, 3195, 3326, 3326/5023, 3347, 3693, 3694, 3753, 3765, 3779, 4023, 4137, 4329, 4459, 5225, 5305, 5613, 5615

Agabus — 13: *Acts 11:28; 21:10*

again — 313, 321, 326, 330, 344, 364, 375, 386, 450, 467, 470, 479, 483, 488, 509, 518, 523, 560, 591, 600, 618, 654, 1208, 1364, 1453, 1515, 1537/1208, 1880, 1994, 3326, 3825, 3825/509, 4388, 4762, 5290

against — 210, 368, 470, 471, 481, 483, 495, 497, 561, 1519, 1727, 1693, 1715, 1722, 1909, 2018, 2019, 2596, 2620, 2649, 2691, 2702, 2713, 2729, 3326, 3844, 4012, 4314, 4366, 5396

age -ed -s — 165, 1074, 2244, 2250, 4246, 4247, 5046, 5230

ago — 575, 3819, 4253

agony — 74: *Luke 22:44*

agree -ed -ment -eth — 800, 1106, 1526, 2132, 2470, 3662, 3982, 4783, 4856, 4934

Agrippa — 67

aground — 2027: *Acts 27:41*

ah — 3758: *Mark 15:29*

air — 109, 3722

alabaster — 211: *Matt. 26:7; Mark 14:3; Luke 7:37*

alas — 3759: *Rev. 18:10, 16, 19*

albeit — 2443: *Phile. 1:19*

Alexander — 223: *Mark 15:21; Acts 4:6; 19:33; 1 Tim. 1:20; 2 Tim. 4:14*

Alexandria -ns — 221: *Acts 6:9; 18:24; 27:6; 28:11*

alienated — 526: *Eph. 4:18; Col. 1:21*

aliens — 245, 526: *Eph. 2:12; Heb. 11:34*

alive (see **quick**) — 326, 2198, 2227

all — 537, 1273, 2178, 2527, 3122, 3364, 3367, 3650, 3654, 3745, 3762, 3779, 3829, 3832, 3837, 3843, 3956, 4219, 5033

alleging — 3908: *Acts 17:3*

allegory — 238: *Gal. 4:24*

alleluia — 239: *Rev. 19:1, 3, 4, 6*

allow -ed -eth — 1097, 1381, 4327, 4909: *Luke 11:48; Acts 24:15; Rom. 7:15; 14:22; 1 Thess. 2:4*
allure (see **tempt**) — 1185: *2 Pet. 2:18*
almighty — 3841
almost — 1722/3641, 3195, 4975
alms; almsdeeds — 1654
aloes — 250: *John 19:39*
alone — 863, 1439, 2596/1438, 2596/2398, 2651, 3440, 3441
aloud — 310: *Mark 15:8*
Alpha — 1: *Rev. 1:8, 11; 21:6; 22:13*
Alpheus — 256: *Matt. 10:3; Mark 2:14; 3:18; Luke 6:15; Acts 1:13*
already — 2235, 4258, 5348
also — 260, 1161, 1211, 2504, 2528, 2532, 2546, 2547, 2548, 2579, 4828, 4879, 4901, 5037
altar -s — 1041, 2379
altered — 2087: *Luke 9:29*
although — 2532/1487, 2543: *Mark 14:29; Heb. 4:3*
altogether — 1722/4183, 3650, 3843: *John 9:34; Acts 26:29; 1 Cor. 5:10; 9:10*
always — 104, 1223/3956, 1275, 1539, 1722/3956/2540, 3839, 3842, 3956/2250
am; art; be; been; being; is; was; wast; were — 1096, 1304, 1488, 1498, 1510, 1511, 2070, 2075, 2076, 2192, 2258, 4160, 5607
amazed; amazement — 1096/2285, 1568, 1605, 1611, 1611/2983, 1839, 2284, 4423
ambassador -s — 4242, 4243: *Luke 14:32; 2 Cor. 5:20; Eph. 6:20*
Amen — 281
amend — 2192/2866: *John 4:52*
amethyst — 271: *Rev. 21:20*
Aminadab — 284: *Matt. 1:4; Luke 3:33*
amiss — 824, 2560: *Luke 23:41; James 4:3*
Amon — 300: *Matt. 1:10*
among — 303/3319, 1223, 1519, 1537, 1722, 1722/3319, 1722/5216, 1909, 2596, 3319, 3326, 3844, 4045, 4314, 5259
Amos — 301: *Luke 3:25*
Amphipolis — 295: *Acts 17:1*
Amplias — 291: *Rom. 16:8*
Ananias — 367
anathema — 331: *1 Cor. 16:22*

anchor -s — 45: *Acts 27:29, 30, 40; Heb. 6:19*
Andrew — 406
Andronicus — 408: *Rom. 16:7*
angel -s (see **archangel**) — 32, 2465
anger; angry — 3709, 3710, 3711, 3949, 5520
anguish — 2347, 4730, 4928: *John 16:21; Rom. 2:9; 2 Cor. 2:4*
anise — 432: *Matt. 23:23*
ankle — 4974: *Acts 3:7*
Anna — 451: *Luke 2:36*
Annas — 452: *Luke 3:2; John 18:13, 24; Acts 4:6*
anoint -ed -ing — 218, 1472, 2025, 3462, 5545, 5548
anon — (see **forthwith; immediately; straightway**) 2112, 2117: *Matt. 13:20; Mark 1:30*
another — 240, 243, 245, 246, 1438, 1520, 2087, 3588, 3739, 4299, 4835
answer -ed -est -eth -ing -s — 470, 483, 611, 612, 626, 627, 1906, 2036, 4960, 5274, 5538
antichrist -s — 500: *1 John 2:18, 22; 4:3; 2 John 1:7*
Antioch — 490, 491
Antipas — 493: *Rev. 2:13*
Antipatris — 494: *Acts 23:31*
any — 1520, 1536, 2089, 3361, 3364, 3367, 3379, 3381, 3387, 3588, 3762, 3763, 3765, 3956, 4218, 4455, 4458, 5100
apart — 659, 2596/2398
Apelles — 559: *Rom. 16:10*
apiece (see **each**) — 303: *Luke 9:3; John 2:6*
Appolonia — 624: *Acts 17:1*
Apollos — 625
Apollyon — 623: *Rev. 9:11*
apostle -s -ship — 651, 652, 5570
apparel -ed — 2066, 2440, 2441, 2689
appeal -ed — 1941: *Acts 25:11, 12, 21, 25; 26:32; 28:19*
appear -ance -ed -eth -ing — 82, 398, 602, 1491, 1718, 2014, 2015, 2064, 3700, 3799, 4383, 5316, 5318/5600, 5319
appeased — 2687: *Acts 19:35*
Apphia — 682: *Phile. 1:2*
Appii — 675: *Acts 28:15*
appoint -ed — 322, 606, 1299, 1303,

1935, 2476, 2525, 2749, 4160, 4287, 4384, 4929, 5021, 5087

apprehend -ed — 2638, 4084: *Acts 12:4; 2 Cor. 11:32; Phil. 3:12, 13*

approach -eth -ing — 676, 1448: *Luke 12:33; 1 Tim. 6:16; Heb. 10:25*

approve -ed -est -ing — 584, 1381, 1384, 4921: *Phil. 1:10; 2 Tim. 2:15; Heb. 10:25*

apron -s — 4612: *Acts 19:12*

apt — 1317: *1 Tim. 3:2; 2 Tim. 2:24*

Aquila — 207

Arabia -ns — 688, 690: *Acts 2:11; Gal. 1:17; 4:25*

Aram — 689: *Matt. 1:3, 4; Luke 3:33*

archangel (see **angel**) **—** 743: *1 Thess. 4:16; Jude 1:9*

Archelaus — 745: *Matt. 2:22*

Archippus — 751: *Col. 4:17; Phile. 1:2*

Areopagite — 698: *Acts 17:34*

Areopagus — 697: *Acts 17:19*

Aretas — 702: *2 Cor. 11:32*

Arimathea — 707: *Matt. 27:57; Mark 15:43; Luke 23:51; John 19:38*

arise -eth; arose — 305, 393, 450, 906, 1096, 1326, 1453, 1525

Aristarchus — 708

Aristobulus — 711: *Rom. 16:10*

ark — 2787

arm -ed -s — 43, 1023, 1723, 2528, 3695

Armageddon — 717: *Rev. 16:16*

armor — 3696, 3833: *Luke 11:22; Rom. 13:12; 2 Cor. 6:7; Eph. 6:11, 13*

army -ies — 3925, 4753, 4760

Arphaxad — 742: *Luke 3:36*

array -ed — 1746, 2441, 4016

arrived — 2668, 3846: *Luke 8:26; Acts 20:15*

Artemas — 734: *Titus 3:12*

arts — 4021: *Acts 19:19*

as — 5613

Asa — 760: *Matt. 1:7, 8*

ascend -ed -eth -ing — 305

ashamed — 153, 422, 1788, 1870, 2617

Asher — 768: *Luke 2:36; Rev. 7:6*

ashes — 4700, 5077: *Matt. 11:21; Luke 10:13; Heb. 9:13, 2 Pet. 2:6*

Asia — 773, 775

aside — 402, 565, 659, 863, 1824, 2596/2398, 5087, 5298

ask -ed -est -eth -ing — 154, 350, 523, 1833, 1905, 2065, 3004, 4441

asleep — 879, 2518, 2837

asps — 785: *Rom. 3:13*

ass — 3678, 3688, 5268

assault -ed — 2186, 3730: *Acts 14:5; 17:5*

assembled; assembling; assembly — 1096, 1577, 1997, 3831, 4863, 4864, 4871, 4905

assented — 4934: *Acts 24:9*

assist — 3936: *Rom. 16:2*

Assos — 789: *Acts 20:13, 14*

assure -ance -ed -edly — 806, 3982, 4102, 4104, 4136, 4822

astonished; astonishment — 1605, 1611, 1839, 2284, 4023/2285

astray — 4105: *Matt. 18:12, 13; 1 Pet. 2:25; 2 Pet. 2:15*

asunder — 673, 1288, 1371, 2997, 4249, 5562

Asyncritus — 799: *Rom. 16:14*

at — 345, 575, 630, 1065, 1223, 1369, 1448, 1451, 1519, 1531, 1537, 1715, 1722, 1847, 1848, 1909, 2527, 2596, 2621, 2919, 3195, 3379, 3762, 3763, 3844, 4012, 4218, 4314, 4363, 4455, 4873

Athens; Athenians — 116, 117

athirst — 1372: *Matt. 25:44; Rev. 21:6; 22:17*

atonement (see **propitiation**) **—** 2643: *Rom. 5:11*

attain -ed — 2638, 2658, 2983, 3877, 5348

Attalia — 825: *Acts 14:25*

attempted; attempting — 3984/2983, 3985, 3987: *Acts 9:26; 16:7; Heb. 11:29*

attend -ance -ed -ing — 2145, 4337, 4342

attentive — 1582: *Luke 19:48*

audience — 189, 191

aught — 5100, 3762

Augustus — 828: *Luke 2:1; Acts 25:21, 25; 27:1*

austere — 840: *Luke 19:21, 22*

author — 159, 747: *Heb. 5:9; 12:2*

authority -ies — 831, 1413, 1849, 1850, 2003, 2715, 5247

availeth — 2480: *Gal. 5:6; 6:15; James 5:16*

avenge -ed -er — 1556, 1558, 2919/

3588/2917, 4160/1557, 4160/3588/
1557

avoid -ing — 1223, 1578, 1624, 3868,
4026, 4724

await — 1917: *Acts 9:24*

awake; awoke — 1235, 1326, 1453,
1594, 1852

aware — 1097, 1492, 4894, 5442

away — 115, 142, 337, 343, 520, 522,
565, 577, 580, 595, 617, 628, 630,
645, 646, 649, 654, 657, 659, 665,
667, 683, 726, 851, 863, 868, 1294,
1544, 1593, 1599, 1601, 1602, 1808,
1813, 1821, 1831, 1854, 2210, 2673,
3179, 3334, 3350, 3351, 3895, 3911,
3928, 4014, 4879, 5217

axe — 513: *Matt. 3:10; Luke 3:9*

Azor — 107: *Matt. 1:13, 14*

Azotus — 108: *Acts 8:40*

B

Baal — 896: *Rom. 11:4*

babbler; babblings — 2757, 4691:
Acts 17:18; 1 Tim. 6:20; 2 Tim. 2:16

babe -s — 1025, 3516

Babylon (see **Chaldeans**) — 897

back — 617, 650, 3557, 3694, 4762,
5288, 5289, 5290

backbiters; backbitings — 2636,
2637: *Rom. 1:30; 2 Cor. 12:20*

backside — 3693: *Rev. 5:1*

backward — 3694: *John 18:6*

bad — 2556, 4190, 4550: *Matt. 13:48;
22:10; 2 Cor. 5:10*

bade — 657, 2036, 2564

bag -s — 905, 1101: *Luke 12:33; John
12:6; 13:29*

Balaam — 903: *2 Pet. 2:15; Jude 1:11;
Rev. 2:14*

Balak — 904: *Rev. 2:14*

balances — 2218: *Rev. 6:5*

band -ed -s — 1199, 2202, 4160/
4963, 4686, 4886

bank — 5132: *Luke 19:23*

banquetings — 4224: *1 Pet. 4:3*

**baptize -ed -est -eth -ing; bap-
tism(s); Baptist** — 907, 908, 909,
910

Barabbas — 912

Barachias — 914: *Matt. 23:35*

Barak — 913: *Heb. 11:32*

barbarian -s; barbarous — 915: *Acts*

28:2, 4; *Rom. 1:14; 1 Cor. 14:11; Col.
3:11*

Bar–jesus — 919: *Acts 13:6*

Bar–jona (see **Jona**) — 920: *Matt. 16:17*

barley — 2915, 2916: *John 6:9, 13; Rev.
6:6*

barn -s — 596: *Matt. 6:26; 13:30; Luke
12:18, 24*

Barnabas — 921

barren — 692, 4723: *Luke 1:7, 36; 23:29;
Gal. 4:27; 2 Pet. 1:8*

Barsabas — 923: *Acts 1:23; 15:22*

Bartholomew (see **Nathanael**) —
918: *Matt. 10:3; Mark 3:18; Luke 6:14;
Acts 1:13*

Bartimaeus (see **Timaeus**) — 924:
Mark 10:46

base -er (see **vile**) — 36, 60, 5011:
Acts 17:5; 1 Cor. 1:28; 2 Cor. 10:1

basin — 3537: *John 13:5*

basket -s — 2894, 4553, 4711

bastards — 3541: *Heb. 12:8*

battle — 4171: *1 Cor. 14:8; Rev. 9:7, 9;
16:14; 20:8*

beam — 1385: *Matt. 7:3-5; Luke 6:41, 42*

bear -est -eth -ing; bare -est —
142, 399, 430, 503, 715, 941, 1080,
1131, 1627, 2592, 3114, 3140, 4064,
4160, 4722, 4828, 4901, 5041, 5088,
5297, 5342, 5409, 5576

beast -s — 2226, 2341, 2342, 2934,
4968, 5074

beat -en -eth -ing — 1194, 1911,
4350, 4363, 4366, 4463, 5180

beautiful — 5611: *Matt. 23:27; Acts
3:2, 10; Rom. 10:15*

became; become -eth — 516, 889,
1096, 1402, 1986, 2289, 2412, 2673,
3154, 3471, 4241

because — 473, 575, 1063, 1223, 1360,
1537, 1722, 1893, 1894, 1909, 2443,
2530, 3704, 3754, 3757/1752, 4314,
5484

beckoned; beckoning — 1269, 2656,
2678, 3506

bed -s — 2825, 2845, 2895, 4766

Beelzebub — 954

befall -en; befell — 1096, 4819, 4876:
Matt. 8:33; Mark 5:16; Acts 20:19, 22

before -hand -time (see **afore; ere**)
— 509, 561, 575, 1519/4383, 1715,
1725, 1726, 1773, 1799, 1909, 2596,
2713, 2714, 2192, 3319, 3362/4386,

3764, 3844, 3908, 3936, 4250, 4253, 4254, 4256, 4257, 4264, 4267, 4270, 4271, 4275, 4277, 4278, 4280, 4281, 4282, 4283, 4293, 4294, 4295, 4296, 4299, 4300, 4301, 4302, 4303, 4305, 4308, 4309, 4310, 4313, 4314, 4315, 4363, 4384, 4386, 4391, 4401, 4412, 4413

beg -gar -garly -ged -ging — 154, 1871, 4319, 4434

begat; begotten — 313, 616, 1080, 3439, 4416

begin -ner -ing(s); began; begun — 509, 746, 746/2983, 756, 1728, 2020, 2129, 2691, 3195, 4278, 4412, 4413

beguile -ed -ing (see **guile**) — 1185, 1818, 2603, 3884: *2 Cor. 11:3; Col. 2:4, 18; 2 Pet. 2:14*

behalf — 1909, 3313, 4012, 5228

behave -ed -eth -ior — 390, 807, 812, 1096, 2688, 2887

behead -ed — 607, 3990: *Matt. 14:10; Mark 6:16, 27; Luke 9:9; Rev. 20:4*

behind — 2641, 3693, 3694, 5278, 5302

behold -est -eth -ing; beheld — 333, 816, 991, 1492, 1689, 1896, 2029, 2300, 2334, 2396, 2400, 2657, 2734, 3708

behooved (see **necessary; ought**) — 1163, 3784: *Luke 24:46; Heb. 2:17*

Belial — 955: *2 Cor. 6:15*

believe -ed -ers -est -eth -ing; belief — 544, 569, 571, 3982, 4100, 4102, 4103, 4135

belly -ies — 1064, 2836

belong -ed -eth -ing — 1510

beloved — 25, 27

beneath — 2736: *Mark 14:66; John 8:23; Acts 2:19*

benefit; benefactors — 18, 210, 2108, 5485: *Luke 22:25; 2 Cor. 1:15; 1 Tim. 6:2; Phile. 1:14*

benevolence — 2133: *1 Cor. 7:3*

Benjamin — 958: *Acts 13:21; Rom. 11:1; Phil. 3:5; Rev. 7:8*

Berea — 960: *Acts 17:10, 13; 20:4*

Bernice — 959: *Acts 25:13, 23; 26:30*

berries — 1636: *James 3:12*

beryl — 969: *Rev. 21:20*

beseech -ing; besought — 1189, 2065, 3870

beset — 2139: *Heb. 12:1*

beside -s — 846, 1839, 1909, 3063, 3105, 4359, 4862, 5565

best — 2909, 4413: *Luke 15:22; 1 Cor. 12:31*

bestow -ed — 1325, 2872, 4060, 4863, 5595

Bethabara — 962: *John 1:28*

Bethany — 963

Bethesda — 964: *John 5:2*

Bethlehem — 965: *Matt. 2:1, 5, 6, 8, 16; Luke 2:4, 15; John 7:42*

Bethphage — 967: *Matt. 21:1; Mark 11:1; Luke 19:29*

Bethsaida — 966

betray -ed -eth -est -ers — 1212/ 4160, 3860, 4273

better -ed — 1308, 2570, 2573, 2909, 3081, 4052, 4284, 4851, 5242, 5543, 5623

between — 303/3319, 1537, 1722, 3307, 3326, 3342, 4314

bewail -ed — 2799, 2875, 3996: *Luke 8:52; 23:27; 2 Cor. 12:21; Rev. 18:9*

beware — 991, 4337, 5442

bewitched — 940, 1839: *Acts 8:9, 11; Gal. 3:1*

beyond — 1537, 1900, 2596/5236, 4008, 4053, 5228, 5233, 5236, 5238, 5239, 5249

bid -den -deth; bade — 479, 657, 2036, 2564, 2753, 3004, 4367

bier — 4673: *Luke 7:14*

bill — 975, 1121: *Mark 10:4; Luke 16:6, 7*

bind -ing; bound — 332, 1195, 1196, 1210, 2611, 3784, 4019, 4029, 4385, 4887, 5265

bird -s — 3732, 4071, 4421

birth — 1079, 1083, 5605: *Matt. 1:18; Luke 1:14; John 9:1; Gal. 4:19; Rev. 12:2*

birthday — 1077: *Matt. 14:6; Mark 6:21*

birthright — 4415: *Heb. 12:16*

bishop -ric -s — 1984, 1985

bite — 1143: *Gal. 5:15*

Bithynia — 978: *Acts 16:7; 1 Pet. 1:1*

bits — 5469: *James 3:3*

bitter -ly -ness — 4087, 4088, 4089, 4090

black -ness — 1105, 2217, 3189: *Matt. 5:36; Heb. 12:18; Jude 1:13; Rev. 6:5*

blade — 5528: *Matt. 13:26; Mark 4:28*

blame -ed -less — 273, 274, 298, 299, 338, 410, 483, 2607, 3469

blaspheme -ed -er(s) -est -eth -ies -ing -ous(ly) -y — 987, 988, 989

Blastus — 986: *Acts 12:20*

blaze — 1310: *Mark 1:45*

blemish -es — 299, 3470: *Eph. 5:27; 1 Pet. 1:19; 2 Pet. 2:13*

bless -ed -edness -ing(s) — 1757, 2127, 2128, 2129, 3106, 3107, 3108

blind -ed -ness — 4456, 4457, 5185, 5186

blindfolded — 4028: *Luke 22:64*

blood -y — 129, 130, 131, 1420

blot -ted -ting — 1813: *Acts 3:19; Col. 2:14; Rev. 3:5*

blow -eth; blew — 1920, 4154, 5285

Boanerges — 993: *Mark 3:17*

boards — 4548: *Acts 27:44*

boast -ed -eth -ing(s) -er — 212, 213, 2620, 2744, 2745, 2746, 3004, 3166

boat -s — 4142, 4627: *John 6:22, 23; Acts 27:16, 30, 32*

Boaz — 1003: *Matt. 1:5; Luke 3:32*

body -ies -ily — 4430, 4954, 4983, 4984, 4985, 5559

boisterous — 2478: *Matt. 14:30*

bold -ly -ness (see **courage**; **emboldened**) — 662, 2292, 3954, 3955, 5111, 5112

bond -age -s — 254, 1198, 1199, 1210, 1397, 1398, 1401, 1402, 2615, 4886

bondmaid; bondman; bondwoman — 1401, 3814: *Gal. 4:22, 23, 30, 31; Rev. 6:15*

bone -s — 3747, 4974

book -s — 974, 975, 976

border -s — 2899, 3181, 3725: *Matt. 4:13; 23:5; Mark 6:56; 7:24; Luke 8:44*

born — 313, 1080, 1084, 1085, 1626, 5088

borne — 142, 941, 1418, 5409: *John 5:37; 3 John 1:6*

borrow — 1155: *Matt. 5:42*

bosom — 2859: *Luke 6:38; 16:22, 23; John 1:18; 13:23*

Bosor — 1007: *2 Pet. 2:15*

both — 297, 1417, 1538, 2532, 5037

bottle — 779: *Matt. 9:17; Mark 2:22; Luke 5:37, 38*

bottom -less — 12, 2736

bought — 59, 5608

bounds — 3734: *Acts 17:26*

bounty -ifully -ifulness — 572, 2129: *2 Cor. 9:5, 6, 11*

bow -ed -ing — 1120, 2578, 2827, 4781, 4794, 5087, 5115

bowels — 4698

box — 211: *Matt. 26:7; Mark 14:3; Luke 7:37*

braided — 4117: *1 Tim. 2:9*

bramble — 942: *Luke 6:44*

branch -es — 902, 2798, 2814, 4746

brass; brazen — 5470, 5473, 5474, 5475

brawler -s — 269: *1 Tim. 3:3; Titus 3:2*

bread — 740

breadth — 4114: *Eph. 3:18; Rev. 20:9; 21:16*

break -er -ing; broke -en — 827, 1284, 1358, 1575, 1846, 2608, 2622, 2800, 2801, 2806, 3089, 3847, 3848, 4486, 4917, 4919, 4937, 4977

breast -s — 4738: *Luke 18:13; 23:48; John 13:25; 21:20; Rev. 15:6*

breastplate -s — 2382: *Eph. 6:14; 1 Thess. 5:8; Rev. 9:9, 17*

breath -ed -ing — 1709, 1720, 4157: *John 20:22; Acts 9:1; 17:25*

bride — 3565: *John 3:29; Rev. 18:23; 21:2, 8; 22:17*

bridechamber — 3567: *Matt. 9:15; Mark 2:19; Luke 5:34*

bridegroom — 3566

bridle -eth -s — 5468, 5469: *James 1:26; 3:2; Rev. 14:20*

briefly — 346, 1223/3641: *Rom. 13:9; 1 Pet. 5:12*

briers — 5146: *Heb. 6:8*

bright -ness — 541, 796, 2015, 2986, 2987, 5460

brim — 507: *John 2:7*

brimstone — 2303, 2306

bring -est -eth -ing; brought — 71, 114, 163, 321, 363, 397, 399, 518, 520, 616, 654, 667, 985, 1080, 1096, 1295, 1325, 1396, 1402, 1521, 1533, 1544, 1625, 1627, 1806, 1863, 1898, 2018, 2036, 2049, 2064, 2097, 2164, 2592, 2601, 2609, 2615, 2673, 2865, 2989, 3350, 3860, 3920, 3930, 3936, 4160, 4254, 4311, 4317, 4374, 4851, 4992, 5013, 5062, 5088, 5142, 5179, 5342, 5461

broad — 2149, 4115: *Matt. 7:13; 23:5*
broiled — 3702: *Luke 24:42*
brokenhearted — 4937/2588: *Luke 4:18*
brood — 3555: *Luke 13:34*
brook — 5493: *John 18:1*
brother -hood -ly; brethren — 80, 81, 5360, 5361, 5569
brow — 3790: *Luke 4:29*
bruise -ed -ing — 2352, 4937: *Matt. 12:20; Luke 4:18; 9:39; Rom. 16:20*
brute — 249: *2 Pet. 2:12; Jude 1:10*
budded — 985: *Heb. 9:4*
buffet -ed — 2852: *Matt. 26:67; 1 Cor. 4:11; 2 Cor. 12:7; 1 Pet. 2:20*
build -ed -est -eth -ing(s) -er(s); built (see **rear**) — 456, 1739, 2026, 2680, 2937, 3618, 3619, 4925, 5079
bulls — 5022: *Heb. 9:13; 10:4*
bundle -s — 1197, 4128: *Matt. 13:30; Acts 28:3*
burden -ed -s -some — 4, 916, 922, 1117, 1722/922, 2347, 2599, 2655, 5413
burn -ed -eth -ing -t — 1572, 1714, 2370, 2545, 2618, 2740, 2742, 3646, 4448, 4451
burst — 2997, 4486: *Mark 2:22; Luke 5:37; Acts 1:18*
bury -ial -ied -ing — 1779, 1780, 2290, 4916, 5027
bush — 942: *Mark 12:26; Luke 6:44; 20:37; Acts 7:30, 35*
bushel — 3426: *Matt. 5:15; Mark 4:21; Luke 11:33*
business — 2398, 4229, 4710, 5532: *Luke 2:49; Acts 6:3; Rom. 12:11; 16:2; 1 Thess. 4:11*
busybody -ies — 244, 4020, 4021: *2 Thess. 3:11; 1 Tim. 5:13; 1 Pet. 4:15*
but (see **nevertheless**) — 235, 1161, 3305, 4133
buy -eth — 59, 1710
by — 1223, 1537

C

Caesar — 2541
Caesarea — 2542
cage — 5438: *Rev. 18:2*
Caiaphas — 2533
Cain — 2535: *Heb. 11:4; 1 John 3:12; Jude 1:11*

Cainan — 2536: *Luke 3:36, 37*
calf; calves — 3447, 3448
call -ed -est -eth -ing — 154, 363, 1458, 1528, 1941, 1951, 2028, 2036, 2046, 2564, 2821, 2822, 2840, 2919, 2983, 3004, 3106, 3333, 3343, 3603, 3686, 3687, 3870, 4316, 4341, 4377, 4779, 4867, 5455, 5537, 5581
calm — 1055: *Matt. 8:26; Mark 4:39; Luke 8:24*
Calvary — 2898: *Luke 23:33*
camel — 2574
camp — 3925: *Heb. 13:11, 13; Rev. 20:9*
can; could -est — 102, 1097, 1410, 1415, 1492, 1735, 2192, 2480, 2489, 5342
Cana — 2580: *John 2:1, 11; 4:46; 21:2*
Canaan; Canaanite — 2581, 5471, 5478: *Matt. 10:4; 15:22; Mark 3:18; Acts 7:11*
Candace — 2582: *Acts 8:27*
candle — 3088
candlestick -s — 3087
canker -ed — 1044, 2728: *2 Tim. 2:17; James 5:3*
cannot — 176, 180, 215, 368, 551, 761, 893, 2076/3756, 3361, 3361/1410, 3756, 3756/1410, 3756/1492, 3756/1735, 3756/2192, 3756/2480
Capernaum — 2584
Cappadocia — 2587: *Acts 2:9; 1 Pet. 1:1*
captain -s — 747, 4755, 4759, 5506
captive -ity -s — 161, 162, 163, 164, 2221
carcass -es — 2966, 4430: *Matt. 24:28; Heb. 3:17*
care -ed -est -eth -s — 1959, 3199, 3308, 3309, 4710, 5426
careful -ly -ness — 275, 1567, 3309, 4708, 4710, 5426, 5431
carnal -ly — 4559, 4561: *Rom. 7:14; Heb. 7:16*
carpenter — 5045: *Matt. 13:55; Mark 6:3*
Carpus — 2591: *2 Tim. 4:13*
carriages — 643: *Acts 21:15*
carry -ied -ieth -ing — 71, 142, 399, 520, 667, 941, 1308, 1580, 1627, 1643, 3346, 3350, 3351, 4046, 4064, 4216, 4792, 4879, 5342
case -s — 156, 3364: *Matt. 5:20; 19:10; John 5:6; 1 Cor. 7:15*

cast -eth -ing — 114, 577, 580, 641, 656, 683, 906, 1000, 1260, 1544, 1601, 1614, 1620, 1685, 1911, 1977, 2210, 2598, 2630, 2975, 3036, 3679, 3860, 4016, 4406, 4496, 5011, 5020
castaway — 96: *1 Cor. 9:27*
castle — 3925: *Acts 21:34, 37; 22:24; 23:10, 16, 32*
Castor — 1359: *Acts 28:11*
catch -eth; caught — 64, 726, 1949, 2221, 2340, 2983, 4084, 4815, 4884, 2983, 4084, 4815, 4884
cattle — 2353, 4165: *Luke 17:7; John 4:12*
cause -ed -eth -s — 156, 158, 846, 873, 1223/5124, 1352, 1432, 1500, 1752, 2289, 2358, 2716, 3056, 3076, 3588/2596, 4160, 5484
cave -s — 3692, 4693: *John 11:38; Heb. 11:38*
cease -ed -eth -ing — 83, 89, 180, 1257, 1618, 2270, 2664, 2673, 2869, 3973
Cedron — 2748: *John 18:1*
celestial — 2032: *1 Cor. 15:40*
Cenchrea — 2747: *Acts 18:18; Rom. 16:1*
censer — 2369, 3031: *Heb. 9:4; Rev. 8:3, 5*
centurion -s — 1543, 2760
Cephas (see **Peter; Simon**) — 2786
certain -ly -ty; certify — 444, 790, 803, 804, 1107, 1212, 1520, 3689, 4225, 5100
chaff — 892: *Matt. 3:12; Luke 3:17*
chain -s — 254, 1199, 4577
chalcedony — 5472: *Rev. 21:19*
Chaldeans — 5466: *Acts 7:4*
chamber -s — 5009, 5253: *Acts 9:37, 39; 20:8*
chambering — 2845: *Rom. 13:13*
chamberlain — 3623: *Acts 12:20; Rom. 16:23*
chance — 4795, 5177: *Luke 10:31; 1 Cor. 15:37*
change -ed — 236, 3328, 3331, 3337, 3339, 3345, 3346
changers (see **moneychangers**) — 2773, 2855: *John 2:14, 15*
charge -able -ed -ing -s — 77, 916, 1159, 1263, 1291, 1462, 1690, 1781, 1909, 1912, 2004, 2008, 2476,

2655, 3049, 3146, 3726, 3800, 3852, 3853
charger — 4094: *Matt. 14:8, 11; Mark 6:25, 28*
chariot -s — 716, 4480: *Acts 8:28, 29, 38; Rev. 9:9; 18:13*
charity; charitably (see **love**) — 26, 2596/26
chaste — 53: *2 Cor. 11:2; Titus 2:5; 1 Pet. 3:2*
chasten -ed -eth -ing; chastise -ment — 3809, 3811
cheek — 4600: *Matt. 5:39; Luke 6:29*
cheer -ful -fully -fulness — 2114, 2115, 2293, 2431, 2432
cherisheth — 2282: *Eph. 5:29; 1 Thess. 2:7*
cherubims — 5502: *Heb. 9:5*
chicken -s — 3556: *Matt. 23:37*
chief -est -ly — 204, 749, 750, 752, 754, 758, 775, 2233, 3122, 4410, 4411, 4412, 4413, 5228/3029, 5506
child -ish -less; children; child-bearing — 815, 1025, 1471, 1722/1064/2192, 3439, 3515, 3516, 3808, 3812, 3813, 3816, 5040, 5041, 5042, 5043, 5044, 5206, 5207
Chios — 5508: *Acts 20:15*
Chloe — 5514: *1 Cor. 1:11*
choice; choose -ing; chose -en — 138, 140, 1586, 1588, 1589, 1951, 4400, 4401, 4758, 550
choke -ed — 638, 4155, 4846
Chorazin — 5523: *Matt. 11:21; Luke 10:13*
Christ (see **God; Jesus**) — 5547, 5580
Christian -s — 5546: *Acts 11:26; 26:28; 1 Pet. 4:16*
chrysolite — 5555: *Rev. 21:20*
chrysoprasus — 5556: *Rev. 21:20*
church -es — 1577, 2417
Chuza — 5529: *Luke 8:3*
Cilicia — 2791
cinnamon — 2792: *Rev. 18:13*
circumcise -ed -ing -ion (see **con-cision**) — 203, 4059, 4061
circumspectly — 199: *Eph. 5:15*
city -ies — 4172
citizen -s — 4177: *Luke 15:15; 19:14; Acts 21:39*
clamor — 2906: *Eph. 4:31*
Clauda — 2802: *Acts 27:16*
Claudia — 2803: *2 Tim. 4:21*

Claudius — 2804: *Acts 11:28; 18:2; 23:26*

clay — 4081: *John 9:6, 11, 14, 15; Rom. 9:21*

clean; cleanse -ed -eth -ing — 2511, 2512, 2513, 3689

clear -ing -ly — 53, 627, 1227, 2513, 2529, 2929, 2986, 5081

cleave -ed -eth — 2853, 4347

clemency — 1932: *Acts 24:4*

Clement — 2815: *Phil. 4:3*

Cleopas — 2810: *Luke 24:18*

Cleophas — 2832: *John 19:25*

climbed; climbeth — 305: *Luke 19:4; John 10:1*

cloak — 1942, 2440, 4392, 5341

close -ed — 788, 2576, 4428, 4601

closet -s — 5009: *Matt. 6:6; Luke 12:3*

cloth — 4470, 4616: *Matt. 9:16; 27:59; Mark 2:21; 14:51, 52*

clothe -ed -ing -s (see **raiment**) — 294, 1463, 1737, 1742, 1746, 1902, 2066, 2439, 2440, 3608, 4016, 4683, 4749, 5509

cloud -s — 3507, 3509

cloven — 1266: *Acts 2:3*

clusters — 1009: *Rev. 14:18*

Cnidus — 2834: *Acts 27:7*

coals — 439, 440: *John 18:18; 21:9; Rom. 12:20*

coast -s — 3313, 3725, 3864, 3882, 5117, 5561

coat -s — 1903, 5509

cock — 220

cockcrowing — 219: *Mark 13:35*

cold — 5592, 5593, 5594

collection — 3048: *1 Cor. 16:1*

colony — 2862: *Acts 16:12*

Colosse — 2857: *Col. 1:2*

color -ed — 4392: *Acts 27:30; Rev. 17:3, 4*

colt — 4454

come -est -eth -ing -ers; came -est — 191, 305, 565, 576, 602, 864, 1096, 1204, 1205, 1224, 1237, 1330, 1448, 1511, 1525, 1529, 1531, 1607, 1660, 1684, 1764, 1831, 1834, 1880, 1904, 1910, 1975, 1998, 1999, 2049, 2064, 2113, 2186, 2240, 2597, 2658, 2673, 2718, 3195, 3719, 3854, 3918, 3928, 3936, 3952, 4130, 4301, 4137, 4331, 4334, 4365, 4370, 4845, 4863, 4872, 4905, 4940, 5302, 5342, 5348, 5562

comely -iness — 2157, 2158, 4241: *1 Cor. 7:35; 11:13; 12:23, 24*

comfort -ed -eth -er -less — 2174, 2293, 3737, 3870, 3874, 3875, 3888, 3889, 3890, 3931, 4837

command -ed -est -eth -ing -ment(s) — 1291, 1297, 1299, 1778, 1781, 1785, 2003, 2004, 2036, 2750, 2753, 3852, 3853, 4367, 4483

commend -ed -eth -ing -ation — 1867, 3908, 3936, 4921, 4956

commit -ted -teth; commission — 764, 1325, 1439, 2011, 2038, 2416, 3429, 3431, 3860, 3866, 3872, 3908, 4100, 4160, 4203, 4238, 5087

commodious — 428: *Acts 27:12*

common -ly — 442, 1219, 1310, 2839, 2840, 3654, 4183, 4232

commonwealth — 4174: *Eph. 2:12*

commotions — 181: *Luke 21:9*

communed; communion — 1255, 2842, 3656, 4814

communicate -ed -ion(s) — 148, 394, 2841, 2842, 2843, 3056, 3657, 4790

compacted — 4822: *Eph. 4:16*

companion -s — 2844, 4791, 4898, 4904: *Acts 19:29; Phil. 2:25; Heb. 10:33; Rev. 1:9*

company -ies — 2398, 2828, 2853, 3461, 3658, 3792, 3793, 4128, 4849, 4874, 4923

compare -ed -ing -ison — 3846, 3850, 4793: *Mark 4:30; 1 Cor. 2:13; 2 Cor. 10:12*

compass -ed — 2944, 4013, 4029, 4033

compassion — 1653, 3356, 3627, 4697, 4834, 4835

compel -led -lest — 29, 315

complainers; complaints — 157, 3202: *Acts 25:7; Jude 1:16*

complete — 4137: *Col. 2:10; 4:12*

comprehend -ed — 346, 2638: *John 1:5; Rom. 13:9; Eph. 3:18*

conceits — 1438: *Rom. 11:25; 12:16*

conceive -d — 1080, 2602, 2845/ 2192, 4815, 5087

concern -ing — 1519/3056, 2596, 3754, 4012, 4314, 5228

concision (see **circumcise**) — 2699: *Phil. 3:2*

conclude **-ed** — 2919, 3049, 4788: *Acts 21:25; Rom. 3:28; 11:32; Gal. 3:22*

concord — 4857: *2 Cor. 6:15*

concourse — 4963: *Acts 19:40*

concupiscence — 1939: *Rom. 7:8; Col. 3:5; 1 Thess. 4:5*

condemn **-ed** **-est** **-eth** **-ing** **-ation** — 176, 843, 2607, 2613, 2631, 2632, 2633, 2917, 2919, 2920, 5272

condescend — 4879: *Rom. 12:16*

conditions — 4314: *Luke 14:32*

conduct **-ed** — 2525, 4311: *Acts 17:15; 1 Cor. 16:11*

conferred; conference — 4323, 4814, 4820: *Acts 4:15; 25:12; Gal. 1:16; 2:6*

confess **-ed** **-eth** **-ing** **-ion** — 1843, 3670, 3671

confidence; confident **-ly** — 1340, 2292, 3954, 3982, 4006, 5287

confirm **-ed** **-ing** **-ation** — 950, 951, 1991, 2964, 3315, 4300

conflict — 73: *Phil. 1:30; Col. 2:1*

conformed; conformable — 4832, 4964: *Rom. 8:29; 12:2; Phil. 3:10*

confound **-ed; confused; confusion** — 181, 2617, 4797, 4799

congregation — 4864: *Acts 13:43*

conquer **-ing** **-ors** — 3528, 5245: *Rom. 8:37; Rev. 6:2*

conscience **-s** — 4893

consecrated — 1457, 5048: *Heb. 7:28; 10:20*

consent **-ed** **-ing** — 1962, 4334, 4784, 4852, 4859, 4909

consider **-ed** **-est** **-eth** **-ing** — 333, 357, 1260, 1492, 2334, 2648, 2657, 3539, 4648, 4894, 4920: *Mark 6:52; Rom. 4:19*

consist **-eth** — 2076, 4921: *Luke 12:15; Col. 1:17*

consolation — 3874

consorted — 4345: *Acts 17:4*

conspiracy — 4945: *Acts 23:13*

constantly — 1226, 1340: *Acts 12:15; Titus 3:8*

constrain **-ed** **-eth** **-t** — 315, 317, 3849, 4912

consultation; consulted; consulteth — 1011, 4823, 4824: *Matt. 26:4; Mark 15:1; Luke 14:31; John 12:10*

consume **-ed** **-ing** — 355, 1159,

2654: *Luke 9:54; Gal. 5:15; 2 Thess. 2:8; Heb. 12:29; James 4:3*

contain **-ed** **-ing** — 1467, 4023, 5562

contemptible — 1848: *2 Cor. 10:10*

contend **-ed** **-ing** — 1252, 1864: *Acts 11:2; Jude 1:3, 9*

content **-ment** — 714, 841, 842, 2425/4160

contention **-s; contentious** — 73, 2052, 2054, 3948, 5380

continue **-ance** **-ed** **-eth** **-ing; continual** **-ly** — 88, 1096, 1265, 1273, 1275, 1300, 1304, 1519/5056, 1696, 1725, 1961, 2476, 2523, 3306, 3887, 3905, 4160, 4342, 4357, 4839, 4842, 5281

contradicting; contradiction — 483, 485: *Acts 13:45; Heb. 7:7; 12:3*

contrariwise — 5121: *2 Cor. 2:7; Gal. 2:7; 1 Pet. 3:9*

contrary — 480, 561, 1727, 3844, 3891, 5227

contribution — 2842: *Rom. 15:26*

controversy — 3672: *1 Tim. 3:16*

convenient **-ly** — 433, 2119, 2121, 2122, 2520, 2540

conversation — 390, 391, 4175, 4176, 5158

convert **-ed** **-eth; conversion** — 1994, 1995, 4762

conveyed — 1593: *John 5:13*

convicted — 1651: *John 8:9*

convince **-ed** **-eth** — 1246, 1651, 1827

cool — 2711: *Luke 16:24*

Coos — 2972: *Acts 21:1*

coppersmith — 5471: *2 Tim. 4:14*

corban — 2878: *Mark 7:11*

cords — 4979: *John 2:15*

Corinth **-ians** — 2881, 2882

corn — 2848, 4621, 4702, 4719

Cornelius — 2883

corner **-s** — 204, 746, 1137

corpse — 4430: *Mark 6:29*

corrected; correction — 1882, 3810: *Heb. 12:9; 2 Tim. 3:16*

corrupt **-ed** **-eth** **-ible** **-ion** — 853, 862, 1311, 1312, 2585, 2704, 4550, 4595, 5349, 5351, 5356

Cosam — 2973: *Luke 3:28*

cost **-liness** **-ly** — 1160, 4185, 4186, 5094: *Luke 14:28; John 12:3; 1 Tim. 2:9; Rev. 18:19* couch -es — 2826, 2895: *Luke 5:19, 24; Acts 5:15*

council -s — 4824, 4892, 4894

counsel -or -s — 1010, 1011, 1012, 4823, 4824, 4825

count -ed -eth — 515, 1075, 2192, 2233, 2661, 3049, 3106, 4860, 5585

countenance (see face) — 2397, 3799, 4383, 4659

country -ies — 68, 589, 1085, 1093, 3968, 4066, 5561

countrymen — 1085, 4853: *2 Cor. 11:26; 1 Thess. 2:14*

courage (see bold; emboldened) — 2294: *Acts 28:15*

course — 165, 1408, 2113, 2183, 3313, 4144, 5143, 5164

court -s — 833, 933: *Luke 7:25; Rev. 11:2*

courteous -ly — 5364, 5390, 5391: *Acts 27:3; 28:7; 1 Pet. 3:8*

cousin -s — 4773: *Luke 1:36, 58*

covenant -ed -s — 1242, 2476, 4934

covenant breakers — 802: *Rom. 1:31*

cover -ed -eth -ing — 1943, 2572, 2596, 2619, 4018, 4028, 4780

covet -ed -ous -ousness — 866, 1937, 2206, 3713, 4123, 4124, 5366

craft; craftsman; craftsmen — 1388, 2039, 3313, 3673, 5078, 5079

crafty -iness — 3834, 3835: *Luke 20:23; 1 Cor. 3:19; 2 Cor. 4:2; 12:16; Eph. 4:14*

craved — 154: *Mark 15:43*

created; creation; Creator; creature -s — 2936, 2937, 2938, 2939

creditor — 1157: *Luke 7:41*

creek — 2859: *Acts 27:39*

creep -ing; crept — 1744, 2062, 3921: *Acts 10:12; 11:6; Rom. 1:23; 2 Tim. 3:6; Jude 1:4*

Crescens — 2913: *2 Tim. 4:10*

Crete -s -ians — 2912, 2914

crime -s — 156, 1462: *Acts 25:16, 27*

cripple — 5560: *Acts 14:8*

Crispus — 2921: *Acts 18:8; 1 Cor. 1:14*

crooked — 4646: *Luke 3:5; Phil. 2:15*

cross — 4716

crow; crew — 5455

crown -ed -edst -s — 1238, 4735, 4737

crucify -ied — 388, 4362, 4717, 4957

crumbs — 5589: *Matt. 15:27; Mark 7:28; Luke 16:21*

cry -eth -ied -ies -ing — 310, 349, 863, 994, 995, 1916, 2019, 2896, 2905, 2906, 5455

crystal — 2929, 2930: *Rev. 4:6; 21:11; 22:1*

cubit -s — 4083, 4088: *Matt. 6:27; Luke 12:23; John 21:8; Rev. 21:17*

cumbered; cumbereth — 2673, 4049: *Luke 10:40; 13:7*

cumi — 2891: *Mark 5:41*

cummin — 2951: *Matt. 23:23*

cunning -ly — 4221, 4679: *Eph. 4:14; 2 Pet. 1:16*

cup -s — 4221

cure -ed -s — 2323, 2392

curious — 4021: *Acts 19:19*

curse -ed -edst -eth -ing — 332, 685, 1944, 2551, 2652, 2653, 2671, 2672

custom -s — 1480, 1485, 1486, 4914, 5056, 5058

cut -ting — 609, 851, 1282, 1371, 1581, 2629, 2875, 4932

cymbal — 2950: *1 Cor. 13:1*

Cyprus — 2954

Cyrene -ian(s) — 2956, 2957

Cyrenius — 2958: *Luke 2:2*

D

daily — 1967, 2184, 2522, 2596/2250, 2596/1538/2250, 2596/3956/2250

dainty — 3045: *Rev. 18:14*

Dalmanutha — 1148: *Mark 8:10*

Dalmatia — 1149: *2 Tim. 4:10*

damage — 2209, 2210: *Acts 27:10; 2 Cor. 7:9*

Damaris — 1152: *Acts 17:34*

Damascus; Damascenes — 1153, 1154

damnation; damnable; damned — 684, 2917, 2919, 2920, 2632

damsel — 2877, 3813, 3814

danced; dancing — 3738, 5525: *Matt. 11:17; 14:6; Mark 6:22; Luke 7:32; 15:25*

danger -ous — 1777, 2000, 2793: *Matt. 5:21, 22; Mark 3:29; Acts 19:27, 40; 27:9*

Daniel — 1158: *Matt. 24:15; Mark 13:14*

dare; durst — 5111

dark -ened -ly -ness — 850, 1722/ 135, 2217, 4652, 4653, 4654, 4655

dart -s — 956, 1002: *Eph. 6:16; Heb. 12:20*

dash — 4350: *Matt. 4:6; Luke 4:11*

daughter -s — 2364, 2365, 5043

daughter-in-law — 3565

David — 1138

dawn — 1306, 2020: *Matt. 28:1; 2 Pet. 1:19*

day -s (see **midday; today**) — 737, 827, 839, 1773, 1887, 2250, 4594

dayspring — 395: *Luke 1:78*

daystar — 5459: *2 Pet. 1:19*

deacon -s — 1247, 1249: *Phil. 1:1; 1 Tim. 3:8, 10, 12, 13*

dead -ly -ness — 581, 599, 2258, 2286, 2287, 2288, 2289, 2348, 2837, 3498, 3499, 3500, 4430, 4880, 5053

deaf — 2974: *Matt. 11:5; Mark 7:32, 37; 9:25; Luke 7:22*

deal -eth -ings -t — 1793, 2686, 3307, 4054, 4160, 4374, 4798

dear — 26, 27, 1784, 5093

dearth — 3042: *Acts 7:11; 11:28*

death -s — 336, 337, 520, 599, 615, 1935, 2079, 2288, 2289, 5054

debate -s — 2054: *Rom. 1:29; 2 Cor. 12:20*

debt -or(s) -s — 1156, 3781, 3782, 3783, 3784, 5533

Decapolis — 1179: *Matt. 4:25; Mark 5:20; 7:31*

decayeth — 3822: *Heb. 8:13*

decease -ed — 1841, 5053: *Matt. 22:25; Luke 9:31; 2 Pet. 1:15*

deceive -ableness -ed -eth -ing(s) -er(s); deceit -ful -fully -fulness — 538, 539, 1386, 1387, 1388, 1389, 1818, 3884, 4105, 4106, 4108, 5422, 5423

decently — 2156: *1 Cor. 14:40*

decked — 5558: *Rev. 17:4; 18:16*

declare -ation -ed -ing — 312, 394, 518, 1107, 1213, 1229, 1334, 1335, 1555, 1718, 1732, 1834, 2097, 2605, 3724, 3853, 5319, 5419

decreased — 1642: *John 3:30*

decree -ed -s — 1378, 2919: *Luke 2:1; Acts 16:4; 17:7; 1 Cor. 7:37*

dedicated; dedication — 1456, 1457: *John 10:22; Heb. 9:18*

deed -s — 1411, 2041, 2108, 2735, 4162, 4234, 4238, 4334

deemed — 5282: *Acts 27:27*

deep -ly -ness — 12, 389, 899, 900, 901, 1037

defamed — 987: *1 Cor. 4:13*

defended; defense — 292, 626, 627: *Acts 7:24; 19:33; 22:1; Phil. 1:7, 17*

deferred — 306: *Acts 24:22*

defile -ed -eth — 733, 2839, 2840, 3392, 3435, 4695, 5351

defraud -ed — 650, 4122

degree — 898, 5011: *Luke 1:52; 1 Tim. 3:13; James 1:9*

delay -eth — 311, 3635, 5549: *Matt. 24:48; Luke 12:45; Acts 9:38; 25:17*

delicacies — 4764: *Rev. 18:3*

delicately — 5172: *Luke 7:25*

deliciously — 4763: *Rev. 18:7, 9*

delight — 4913: *Rom. 7:22*

deliver -ance -ed -edst -er -ing — 325, 525, 591, 629, 859, 1080, 1325, 1560, 1659, 1807, 1929, 2673, 3086, 3860, 4506, 5088, 5483

delusion — 4106: *2 Thess. 2:11*

demanded — 1905, 4441: *Matt. 2:4; Luke 3:14; 17:20; Acts 21:33*

Demas — 1214: *Col. 4:14; 2 Tim. 4:10; Phile. 1:24*

Demetrius — 1216: *Acts 19:24, 38; 3 John 1:12*

demonstration — 585: *1 Cor. 2:4*

den -s — 4693: *Matt. 21:13; Mark 11:17; Luke 19:46; Heb. 11:38; Rev. 6:15*

deny -ied -ieth -ing — 483, 533, 720

depart -ed -eth -ing -ure — 321, 359, 360, 402, 565, 630, 672, 673, 867, 868, 1316, 1330, 1607, 1633, 1826, 1831, 1841, 2718, 3327, 3332, 3855, 4198, 5217, 5562

depth -s — 899, 3989

deputy -ies — 446: *Acts 13:7, 8, 12; 18:12; 19:38*

Derbe — 1191: *Acts 14:6, 20; 16:1; 20:4*

derided — 1592: *Luke 16:14; 23:35*

descend -ed -eth -ing; descent — 35, 1075, 2597, 2600, 2718

describeth — 1125, 3004: *Rom. 4:6; 10:5*

desert -s — 2047, 2048

desire -ed -edst -eth -ing -ous -s — 154, 515, 1809, 1905, 1934, 1937, 1939, 1971, 1972, 1974, 2065,

2107, 2206, 2212, 2307, 2309, 2442, 2755, 3713, 3870

desolate -ion — 2048, 2049, 2050, 3443

despair -ed — 1820: *2 Cor. 1:8; 4:8*

despise -ed -est -eth -ers -ing — 114, 818, 820, 865, 1848, 2706, 2707, 3643, 4065

despite -ful -fully — 1796, 1908, 5195, 5197: *Matt. 5:44; Luke 6:28; Acts 14:5; Rom. 1:30; Heb. 10:29*

destitute — 650, 3007, 5302: *1 Tim. 6:5; Heb. 11:37; James 2:15*

destroy -ed -er -est; destruction — 622, 684, 1311, 1842, 2506, 2507, 2647, 2673, 3089, 3639, 3644, 3645, 4199, 4938, 5351, 5356

determinate; determined — 1011, 1956, 2919, 3724, 4309, 5021

device -s — 1761, 3540: *Acts 17:29; 2 Cor. 2:11*

devil -ish -s — 1139, 1140, 1141, 1142, 1228

devised — 4679: *2 Pet. 1:16*

devotions — 4574: *Acts 17:23*

devour -ed -eth — 2068, 2666, 2719

devout — 2126, 2152, 4576

Diana — 735: *Acts 19:24, 27, 28, 34, 35*

Didymus (see **Thomas**) — 1324: *John 11:16; 20:24; 21:2*

die -ed -eth; dying — 599, 622, 684, 3500, 4880, 5053

differ -eth -ing -ence(s) — 1243, 1252, 1293, 1308, 1313, 3307

dig -ged — 2679, 3736, 4626

dignities — 1391: *2 Pet. 2:10; Jude 1:8*

diligent -ly; diligence — 199, 1567, 1960, 2039, 4704, 4705, 4706, 4707, 4708, 4709, 4710

diminishing — 2275: *Rom. 11:12*

dine -ed; dinner — 709, 712: *Matt. 22:4; Luke 11:37, 38; 14:12; John 21:12, 15*

Dionysius — 1354: *Acts 17:34*

Diotrephes — 1361: *3 John 1:9*

dip -ped -peth — 911, 1686

direct — 2720: *1 Thess. 3:11; 2 Thess. 3:5*

disallowed — 593: *1 Pet. 2:4, 7*

disannul -leth -ling — 114, 115, 208: *Gal. 3:15, 17; Heb. 7:18*

discern -ed -er -ing — 350, 1252, 1253, 1381, 2924

disciple -s — 3100, 3101, 3102

discouraged — 120: *Col. 3:21*

discovered — 398, 2657: *Acts 21:3; 27:39*

discreet -ly — 3562, 4998: *Mark 12:34; Titus 2:5*

disease -ed -s — 769, 770, 2192/2560, 3119, 3553, 3554

disfigure — 853: *Matt. 6:16*

dish — 5165: *Matt. 26:23; Mark 14:20*

dishonesty — 152: *2 Cor. 4:2*

dishonor -est -eth — 818, 819, 2617

dismissed — 630: *Acts 15:30; 19:41*

disobedience; disobedient — 506, 543, 544, 545, 3876

disorderly — 812, 814: *2 Thess. 3:6, 7, 11*

dispensation — 3622: *1 Cor. 9:17; Eph. 1:10; 3:2; Col. 1:25*

dispersed — 1287, 1290, 4650: *John 7:35; Acts 5:37; 2 Cor. 9:9*

displeased — 23, 2371: *Matt. 21:15; Mark 10:14, 41; Acts 12:20*

disposed; disposition — 1014, 1296, 2309: *Acts 7:53; 18:27; 1 Cor. 10:27*

disputed; disputer; disputing -s; disputation -s — 1253, 1256, 1260, 1261, 3859, 4802, 4803, 4804

dissembled — 4942: *Gal. 2:13*

dissension — 4714: *Acts 15:2; 23:7, 10*

dissimulation — 505, 5272: *Rom. 12:9; Gal. 2:13*

dissolved — 2647, 3089: *2 Cor. 5:1; 2 Pet. 3:11, 12*

distinction — 1293: *1 Cor. 14:7*

distraction — 563: *1 Cor. 7:35*

distress -ed -es — 318, 4729, 4730, 4928

distribute -ed -ing -ion — 1239, 2130, 2841, 2842, 3307

ditch — 999: *Matt. 15:14; Luke 6:39*

divers — 1313, 4164, 4187, 5100

diversities — 1085, 1243: *1 Cor. 12:4, 6, 28*

divide -ed -er -eth -ing — 873, 1096, 1239, 1244, 1266, 2624, 3307, 3311, 3312, 3718, 4977

divine — 2304, 2999: *Heb. 9:1, 2; 2 Pet. 1:3, 6*

divination — 4436: *Acts 16:16*

division -s — 1267, 1370, 4978

divorced; divorcement — 630, 647: *Matt. 5:31, 32; 19:7; Mark 10:4*

do -ers -es -est -eth -ing -ne -st -th; did -est — 14, 15, 16, 17, 91, 92, 387, 1096, 1107, 1286, 1398, 1731, 1754, 2005, 2038, 2041, 2109, 2140, 2192, 2480, 2554, 2557, 2569, 2673, 2698, 2716, 3000, 3930, 4163, 4238, 4374, 4704, 4982

doctor -s — 1320, 3547: *Luke 2:46; 5:17; Acts 5:34*

doctrine -s — 1319, 1322, 3056

dog -s — 2952, 2965

dominion -s — 2634, 2904, 2961, 2963

door -s — 2374, 2377

Dorcas (see **Tabitha**) — 1393: *Acts 9:36, 39*

doting — 3552: *1 Tim. 6:4*

double — 1362, 1363: *1 Tim. 5:17; Rev. 18:6*

double-minded — 1374: *James 1:8; 4:8*

double-tongued — 1351: *1 Tim. 3:8*

doubt -ed -eth -ful -ing -less — 142/5590, 639, 686, 1063, 1065, 1211, 1252, 1261, 1280, 1365, 3304, 3349, 3843

dove -s — 4058

down — 345, 347, 377, 387, 1308, 1581, 1931, 2504, 2506, 2507, 2521, 2523, 2524, 2596, 2597, 2598, 2601, 2609, 2621, 2625, 2630, 2647, 2662, 2667, 2673, 2679, 2701, 2718, 2736, 2778, 2875, 3879, 3935, 4098, 4496, 4776, 4781, 4782, 4952, 5011, 5294, 5465

dragging — 4951: *John 21:8*

dragon — 1404

draught — 61, 856: *Matt. 15:17; Mark 7:19; Luke 5:4, 9*

draw -eth -ing -n; drew — 307, 385, 501, 502, 645, 868, 1096, 1670, 1828, 2020, 4264, 4317, 4334, 4358, 4685, 4951, 5288, 5289

dream -ers -s — 1797, 1798, 3677

dressed; dresser — 289, 1090: *Luke 13:7; Heb. 6:7*

drink -eth -ing -s; drank; drunk -en — 4095, 4188, 4213, 4222, 4608, 4844, 5202

drive -en -eth; drove — 416, 556, 1308, 1544, 1643, 1856, 1929, 5342

drops — 2361: *Luke 22:44*

dropsy — 5203: *Luke 14:2*

drown -ed — 1036, 2666, 2670: *Matt. 18:6; 1 Tim. 6:9; Heb. 11:29*

drunk -en -eness; drunkard -s — 3178, 3182, 3183, 3184, 5435

Drusilla — 1409: *Acts 24:24*

dry -ied — 504, 3583, 3584

due -s — 514, 2398, 3782, 3784

dull — 917, 3576: *Matt. 13:15; Acts 28:27; Heb. 5:11*

dumb — 216, 880, 2974, 4623

dung — 906/2874, 2874, 4657: *Luke 13:8; 14:35; Phil. 3:8*

dust — 2868, 5522

duty — 3784: *Luke 17:10; Rom. 15:27*

dwell -ers -est -eth -ing -t — 1460, 1774, 2521, 2730, 2731, 3306, 3611, 3940, 4039, 4637, 4924

dwelling place — 790: *1 Cor. 4:11*

E

each — 240, 303, 1538: *Luke 13:15; Acts 2:3; Phil. 2:3; 2 Thess. 1:3; Rev. 4:8*

eagle -s — 105: *Matt. 24:28; Luke 17:37; Rev. 4:7; 12:14*

ear -s — 189, 191, 3775, 4719, 5621

early — 260/4404, 3719, 3721, 3722, 4404, 4405, 4406

earnest -ly — 603, 728, 816, 1617, 1864, 1971, 1972, 2206, 4056, 4335, 4710

earth -en -ly -y — 1093, 1919, 2709, 3625, 3749, 5517

earthquake -s (see **quake**) — 4578

ease -ed — 373, 425: *Luke 12:19; 2 Cor. 8:13*

east — 395

Easter (see **Passover**) — 3957: *Acts 12:4*

easy; easier — 2123, 2138, 2154, 5543

eat -en -eth -ing; ate — 977, 1035, 1089, 2068, 2192/3542, 2719, 2880, 3335, 4662, 4906, 5176, 5315

edge -s — 1366, 4750: *Luke 21:24; Heb. 11:34; Rev. 2:12*

edify -ied -ieth -ing -ication — 3618, 3619

effect -ual -ually — 208, 1601, 1753, 1754, 1756, 2673, 2758

egg — 5609: *Luke 11:12*

Egypt; Egyptian -s — 124, 125

eight; eighth — 3590, 3637, 3638
eighteen — 1176/2532/3638: *Luke 13:4, 11, 16*
either — 2228
Elamites — 1639: *Acts 2:9*
elder -s; eldest — 3187, 4244, 4245, 4850
Eleazar — 1648: *Matt. 1:15*
elect -ed -ion — 1588, 1589, 4899
elements — 4747: *Gal. 4:3, 9; 2 Pet. 3:10, 12*
eleven -th — 1733, 1734
Eli (see **Eloi**) — 2241: *Matt. 27:46*
Eliakim — 1662: *Matt. 1:13; Luke 3:30*
Eliezer — 1663: *Luke 3:29*
Elijah — 2243
Elisabeth — 1665: *Luke 1:5, 7, 13, 24, 36, 40, 41, 57*
Elisha — 1666: *Luke 4:27*
Eliud — 1664: *Matt. 1:14, 15*
Elmodam — 1678: *Luke 3:28*
Eloi (see **Eli**) — 1682: *Mark 15:34*
eloquent — 3052: *Acts 18:24*
else — 1490, 1893, 2087, 2532
Elymas — 1681: *Acts 13:8*
emboldened (see **bold**) — 3618: *1 Cor. 8:10*
embraced; embracing — 782, 4843: *Acts 20:1, 10; Heb. 11:13*
emerald — 4664, 4665: *Rev. 4:3; 21:19*
Emmaus — 1695: *Luke 24:13*
empty — 2756, 4980: *Matt. 12:44; Mark 12:3; Luke 1:53; 20:10, 11*
emulation -s — 2205, 3863: *Rom. 11:14; Gal. 5:20*
enabled — 1743: *1 Tim. 1:12*
enclosed — 4788: *Luke 5:6*
encountered — 4820: *Acts 17:18*
end -ed -ing -less -s — 165, 179, 206, 562, 1096, 1519, 1545, 2078, 3796, 4009, 4137, 4930, 4931, 5049, 5055, 5056
endeavor -ed -ing — 2212, 4704: *Acts 16:10; Eph. 4:3; 1 Thess. 2:17; 2 Pet. 1:15*
endued — 1746, 1990: *Luke 24:49; James 3:13*
endure -ed -eth -ing — 430, 2076, 2553, 2594, 3114, 3306, 5278, 5281, 5297, 5342
enemy -ies (see **adversary; foes**) — 2190

engender -eth — 1080: *Gal. 4:24; 2 Tim. 2:23*
engrafted (see **graft**) — 1721: *James 1:21*
engraven — 1795: *2 Cor. 3:7*
enjoin -ed — 1781, 2004: *Phile. 1:8; Heb. 9:20*
enjoy — 619, 5177: *Acts 24:2; 1 Tim. 6:17; Heb. 11:25*
enlarge -ed — 3170, 4115: *Matt. 23:5; 2 Cor. 6:11, 13; 10:15*
enlightened — 5461: *Eph. 1:18; Heb. 6:4*
enmity — 2189: *Luke 23:12; Rom. 8:7; Eph. 2:15, 16; James 4:4*
Enoch — 1802: *Luke 3:37; Heb. 11:5; Jude 1:14*
Enos — 1800: *Luke 3:38*
enough — 566, 713, 714, 2425, 2880, 4052
enriched — 4148: *1 Cor. 1:5; 2 Cor. 9:11*
ensue (see **follow**) — 1377: *1 Pet. 3:11*
entangle -ed -eth — 1707, 1758, 3802: *Matt. 22:15; Gal. 5:1; 2 Tim. 2:4; 2 Pet. 2:20*
enter -ed -eth -ing; entrance — 305, 1524, 1525, 1529, 1531, 1684, 1910, 2064, 3922
entertain -ed — 3579, 5381: *Heb. 13:2*
enticed; enticing — 1185, 3981, 4086: *1 Cor. 2:4; Col. 2:4; James 1:14*
entire — 3648: *James 1:4*
entreat -ed -y (see **exhort**) — 818, 2065, 2138, 2559, 3868, 3870, 3874, 5195, 5530
envy -ies -ieth -ing(s) -ious — 2205, 2206, 5354, 5355
Epaenetus — 1866: *Rom. 16:5*
Epaphras — 1889: *Col. 1:7; 4:12; Phile. 1:23*
Epaphroditus — 1891: *Phil. 2:25; 4:18*
Ephesus; Ephesian -s — 2180, 2181
Ephphatha — 2188: *Mark 7:34*
Ephraim — 2187: *John 11:54*
Epicureans — 1946: *Acts 17:18*
epistle -s — 1992
equal -ity -s — 2465, 2470, 2471, 4915
Er — 2262: *Luke 3:28*
Erastus — 2037: *Acts 19:22; Rom. 16:23; 2 Tim. 4:20*

ere (see **afore; before**) — 4250: *John 4:49*

err **-ed** **-or(s)** — 51, 635, 795, 4105, 4106

Esau — 2269: *Rom. 9:13; Heb. 11:20; 12:16*

escape **-ed** — 668, 1295, 1309, 1545, 1628, 1831, 5343

eschew — 1578: *1 Pet. 3:11*

Esli — 2069: *Luke 3:25*

especially — 3122

espoused — 718, 3423: *Matt. 1:18; Luke 1:27; 2:5; 2 Cor. 11:2*

Esrom — 2074: *Matt. 1:3; Luke 3:33*

establish **-ed** — 950, 2476, 3549, 4732, 4741

estate **-s** — 4012

esteem **-ed** **-eth** **-ing** — 1848, 2233, 2919, 3049

eternal — 126, 165, 166

Ethiopia **-ns** — 128: *Acts 8:27*

Eubulus — 2103: *2 Tim. 4:21*

Eunice — 2131: *2 Tim. 1:5*

eunuch **-s** — 2134, 2135: *Matt. 19:12; Acts 8:27, 34, 36, 38, 39*

Euodias — 2136: *Phil. 4:2*

Euphrates — 2166: *Rev. 9:14; 16:12*

Euroclydon — 2148: *Acts 27:14*

Eutychus — 2161: *Acts 20:9*

evangelist **-s** — 2099: *Acts 21:8; Eph. 4:11; 2 Tim. 4:5*

Eve — 2096: *2 Cor. 11:3; 1 Tim. 2:13*

even — 737, 891, 1063, 1161, 2089, 2193, 2504, 2531, 2532, 2536, 2548, 3303, 3483, 3676, 3739/5158, 3761, 3779, 5037, 5613, 5615, 5618

even **-ing** **-tide** — 2073, 3796, 3798, 3798/1096, 3798/5610

ever **-lasting** **-more** — 104, 126, 165, 166, 1336, 3745, 3842, 4218, 4253

every — 303, 376, 537, 1330, 1538, 2596, 3650, 3836, 3837, 3840, 3956, 5100, 5101

evidence; evident **-ly** — 1212, 1650, 1732, 2612, 4270, 4271, 5320

evil **-s** **-doer(s)** — 92, 987, 988, 1426, 2549, 2551, 2554, 2555, 2556, 2557, 2559, 2560, 2635, 2636, 4190, 4190/4487, 5337

exact — 4238: *Luke 3:13*

exalt **-ed** **-eth** — 1869, 5229, 5251, 5311, 5312

examine **-ation** **-ed** **-ing** — 350, 351, 426, 1381, 3985

example **-s** — 1164, 3856, 5179, 5261, 5262

exceed **-ing** **-ingly** — 1519/5236, 1613, 1630, 2596/5236, 3029, 3173/5401, 3588/2316, 4036, 4052, 4056, 4057, 4970, 4971, 5228, 5228/1537/4053, 5235, 5248, 5250

excel **-leth** **-lency** **-lent** — 1308, 1313, 2903, 3169, 4052, 4119, 5235, 5236, 5242, 5247

except **-ed** — 1508, 1509, 1622, 2228, 3362, 3923, 4133

excess — 192, 401, 810, 3632: *Matt. 23:25; Eph. 5:18; 1 Pet. 4:3, 4*

exchange **-ers** — 465, 5133: *Matt. 16:26; 25:27; Mark 8:37*

exclude **-ed** — 1576: *Rom. 3:27; Gal. 4:17*

excuse **-ed** **-ing** — 379, 626, 3868: *Luke 14:18, 19; Rom. 1:20; 2:15; 2 Cor. 12:19*

execute **-ed** **-ioner** — 2407, 4160, 4688: *Mark 6:27; Luke 1:8; John 5:27; Jude 1:15*

exercise **-ed** **-eth** — 778, 1128, 1129, 1850, 2634, 2715, 2961, 4160

exhort **-ation** **-ed** **-eth** **-ing** (see **entreat**) — 3867, 3870, 3874, 4389

exorcists — 1845: *Acts 19:13*

expectation; expecting — 603, 1551, 4328, 4329

expedient — 4851

expelled — 1544: *Acts 13:50*

experience; experiment — 1382: *Rom. 5:4; 2 Cor. 9:13*

expert — 1109: *Acts 26:3*

expired — 4137, 5055: *Acts 7:30; Rev. 20:7*

expounded — 1329, 1620, 1956: *Mark 4:34; Luke 24:27; Acts 11:4; 18:26; 28:23*

express **-ly** — 4490, 5481: *1 Tim. 4:1; Heb. 1:3*

extortion **-er(s)** — 724, 727: *Matt. 23:25; Luke 18:11; 1 Cor. 5:10, 11; 6:10*

eye **-s** — 3442, 3659, 3788, 5168, 5169

eye salve — 2854: *Rev. 3:18*

eyeservice — 3787: *Eph. 6:6; Col. 3:22*

eyewitnesses — 845, 2030: *Luke 1:2; 2 Pet. 1:16*

Ezekias — 1478: *Matt. 1:9, 10*

F

fables — 3454: *1 Tim. 1:4; 4:7; 2 Tim. 4:4; Titus 1:14; 2 Pet. 1:16*

face -s (see **countenance**) — 1799, 3799, 4383, 4750

fade -eth — 262, 263, 3133: *James 1:11; 1 Pet. 1:4; 5:4*

fail -eth -ing — 413, 674, 1587, 1601, 1952, 2673, 4098, 5302

fain — 1937: *Luke 15:16*

faint -ed — 1573, 1590, 2577

fair — 791, 2105, 2129, 2146, 2568: *Matt. 16:2; Acts 7:20; 27:8; Rom. 16:18; Gal. 6:12*

faith -ful -fully -less — 571, 1680, 3640, 4102, 4103

fall -en -eth -ing; **fell** — 634, 646, 679, 868, 1096, 1601, 1706, 1911, 1968, 2064, 2597, 2667, 2702, 2837, 3895, 3900, 4045, 4098, 4363, 4417, 4431, 4625

false -ly — 1228, 4811, 5569, 5570, 5571, 5572, 5573, 5574, 5575, 5576, 5577, 5578, 5580, 5581

fame — 189, 1310, 2279, 3056, 5345

family — 3965: *Eph. 3:15*

famine -s — 3042

fan — 4425: *Matt. 3:12; Luke 3:17*

far -ther — 891, 1519/5236, 2193, 2436, 3112, 3113, 3117, 4008, 4054, 4183, 4183/3123, 4206, 4260, 4281, 5231

fare -ed -well — 657, 2165, 4517, 5463

farm — 68: *Matt. 22:5*

farthing -s — 787, 2835: *Matt. 5:26; 10:29; Mark 12:42; Luke 12:6*

fashion -ed -ing — 1491, 3778, 4383, 4832, 4964, 4976, 5179

fast — 472, 805, 2722

fast -ed -est -ing(s) — 777, 3521, 3522, 3523

fastened; fastening — 816, 2510: *Luke 4:20; Acts 3:4; 11:6; 28:3*

Father; father -less -s — 540, 3737, 3962, 3964, 3967, 3970, 3971, 3995

fathoms — 3712: *Acts 27:28*

fatlings; fatness; fatted — 4096, 4618, 4619: *Matt. 22:4; Luke 15:23, 27, 30; Rom. 11:17*

fault -less -s — 156, 158, 264, 273, 299, 1651, 2275, 3201, 3900

favor -ed — 5485, 5487: *Luke 1:28, 30; 2:52; Acts 2:47; 7:10, 46; 25:3*

fear -ed -eth -ful -ing -s — 870, 1167, 1169, 1630/1510, 2124, 2125, 5398, 5399, 5400, 5401, 5401/2192

feast -s — 755, 1173, 1408, 1456, 1858, 1859, 4910

feeble — 772, 3886: *1 Cor. 12:22; Heb. 12:12*

feebleminded — 3642: *1 Thess. 5:14*

feed -eth -ing; **fed** — 1006, 4165, 4222, 5142, 5526, 5595

feel -ing; **felt** — 524, 1097, 3958, 4834, 5584: *Mark 5:29; Acts 17:27; 28:5; Eph. 4:19; Heb. 4:15*

feign -ed — 4112, 5271: *Luke 20:20; 2 Pet. 2:3*

Felix — 5344

fellow -s — 435, 2083, 3353

fellow citizens — 4847: *Eph. 2:19*

fellow disciples — 4827: *John 11:16*

fellow heirs — 4789: *Eph. 3:6*

fellow helper -s; **fellow laborer** -s — 4904

fellow prisoner -s — 4869: *Rom. 16:7; Col. 4:10; Phile. 1:23*

fellow servant -s — 4889

fellowship — 2842, 2844, 3352, 4790

fellow soldier — 4961: *Phil. 2:25; Phile. 1:2*

fellow workers — 4904: *Col. 4:11*

female — 2338: *Matt. 19:4; Mark 10:6; Gal. 3:28*

fervent -ly — 1618, 1619, 2204, 2205

Festus — 5347

fetch -ed — 1806, 4022: *Acts 16:37; 28:13*

fetters — 3976: *Mark 5:4; Luke 8:29*

fever — 4445, 4446

few — 1024, 3641, 4935

fidelity — 4102: *Titus 2:10*

field -s — 68, 5561, 5564

fierce -ness — 434, 2001, 2372, 4642, 5467

fiery — 4442, 4448, 4451: *Eph. 6:16; Heb. 10:27; 1 Pet. 4:12*

fifteen -th — 1178, 4002, 4003: *Luke 3:1; John 11:18; Acts 7:14; 27:28; Gal. 1:18*

fifty -ies — 4002/3461, 4004

fig -s — 3653, 4808, 4810
fight -ings; **fought** — 73, 75, 119, 2313, 2314, 2341, 3163, 3164, 4170, 4171, 4438
figure -s — 499, 3345, 3850, 5179
fill -ed -eth -ing — 378, 466, 1072, 1705, 2767, 4130, 4137, 4138, 4845, 5055, 5526
filth -y -iness — 147, 148, 150, 151, 168, 766, 3436, 4027, 4507, 4509, 4510
finally — 3063, 5056
find -eth -ing; **found** — 421, 429, 1096, 2147, 2638
fine — 4585
finger -s — 1147
finish -ed -er — 535, 658, 1096, 1274, 1615, 2005, 4931, 5047, 5048, 5055
fire — 4442, 4443, 4447, 4448, 5394, 5457
firkins — 3355: *John 2:6*
firm — 949: *Heb. 3:6*
first — 509, 746, 1207, 3391, 4276, 4295, 4386, 4412, 4413
first begotten; firstborn — 4416
firstfruit -s — 536
fish -es -ing -er(s) -ermen — 231, 232, 1903, 2485, 2486, 3795
fit -ly -ted — 433, 2111, 2520, 2675, 4883
five; fifth — 3991, 3999, 4000, 4001, 4002
fixed — 4741: *Luke 16:26*
flame -ing — 5395
flattering — 2850: *1 Thess. 2:5*
flax — 3043: *Matt. 12:20*
flee -eth; **fled** — 1628, 2703, 5343
flesh -ly -y — 2907, 4559, 4560, 4561
flock — 4167, 4168
flood -s — 2627, 4132, 4215, 4216
floor — 257: *Matt. 3:12; Luke 3:17*
flour — 4585: *Rev. 18:13*
flourished — 330: *Phil. 4:10*
flow — 4482: *John 7:38*
flower — 438, 5230: *1 Cor. 7:36; James 1:10, 11; 1 Pet. 1:24*
flux — 1420: *Acts 28:8*
fly -ing; **flight** — 4072, 5437
foal — 5207: *Matt. 21:5*
foameth; foaming — 875, 876, 1890: *Mark 9:18, 20; Luke 9:39; Jude 1:13*
foes (see **adversary; enemy**) — 2190: *Matt. 10:36; Acts 2:35*

fold — 1667: *Heb. 1:12*
fold (see **sheepfold**) — 833, 4167: *John 10:16*
follow -ed -ers -eth -ing — 190, 1096, 1205/3694, 1377, 1811, 1836, 1872, 1887, 1966, 2071, 2076/3326, 2192, 2517, 2614, 2628, 3326/5023, 3401, 3402, 3877, 4831, 4870
food — 1035, 1304, 5160: *Acts 14:17; 2 Cor. 9:10; 1 Tim. 6:8; James 2:15*
fool -s -ish -ishly -ishness; **folly** — 453, 454, 781, 801, 876, 877, 878, 1722/877, 3471, 3472, 3473, 3474, 3912
foot; feet — 939, 2662, 3979, 4158, 4228
footstool — 5286, 5286/3588/4228
for — 1063, 5228
forasmuch (see **forsomuch; insomuch**) — 1487, 1893, 1894, 1895, 5607
forbear -ance -ing — 430, 447, 463, 3361, 4722, 5339
forbid -den -deth -ding; **forbade** — 209, 1254, 2967, 3361/1096
force — 726, 949: *Matt. 11:12; John 6:15; Acts 23:10; Heb. 9:17*
forefathers — 4269: *2 Tim. 1:3*
forehead -s — 3359
foreigners — 3941: *Eph. 2:19*
foreknow -ledge; **foreknew** — 4267, 4268: *Acts 2:23; Rom. 8:29; 11:2; 1 Pet. 1:2*
foreordained — 4267: *1 Pet. 1:20*
forepart — 4408: *Acts 27:41*
forerunner — 4274: *Heb. 6:20*
foreship — 4408: *Acts 27:30*
foretell; foretold — 4280, 4293, 4302: *Mark 13:23; Acts 3:24; 2 Cor. 13:2*
forever -more — 165, 2250/165, 3588/165
forewarn -ed — 4277, 5263: *Luke 12:5; 1 Thess. 4:6*
forget -ful -teth -ting; **forgotten** — 1585, 1950, 1953, 3024/2983
forgive -en -eth -ing -ness; **forgave** — 630, 859, 863, 5483
form -ed — 3444, 3445, 3446, 4110, 4111, 5179, 5296
former — 4386, 4387, 4413: *Acts 1:1; Eph. 4:22; Heb. 10:32; 1 Pet. 1:4; Rev. 21:4*

fornication -s; fornicator -s — 1608, 4202, 4203, 4205

forsake -en -eth -ing; forsook — 646/575, 657, 863, 1459, 2641

forseeing; foresaw — 4275, 4308: *Acts 2:25; Gal. 3:8*

forsomuch (see **forasmuch; insomuch**) — 2530: *Luke 19:9*

forswear — 1964: *Matt. 5:33*

forth — 321, 392, 584, 616, 649, 669, 985, 1032, 1080, 1544, 1554, 1584, 1599, 1600, 1607, 1614, 1627, 1631, 1632, 1731, 1754, 1804, 1806, 1821, 1831, 1854, 1901, 1907, 1911, 2164, 2564, 2592, 2604, 2609, 3004, 3319, 3855, 3860, 3908, 3928, 4160, 4198, 4254, 4261, 4270, 4311, 4388, 4393, 4486, 5087, 5088, 5319, 5348

forthwith (see **anon; immediately; straightway**) — 2112, 2117, 3916

Fortunatus — 5415: *1 Cor. 16:17*

forty — 5062, 5063

forum — 675: *Acts 28:15*

forward -ness — 2309, 4261, 4281, 4288, 4311, 4704, 4707, 4710

foul — 169, 5494: *Matt. 16:3; Mark 9:25; Rev. 18:2*

founded; foundation -s — 2310, 2311, 2602

fountain -s — 4077

four -th -fold — 5064, 5066, 5067, 5070, 5071, 5072, 5073

four–footed — 5074: *Acts 10:12; 11:6; Rom. 1:23*

fourscore — 3589: *Luke 2:37; 16:7*

foursquare — 5068: *Rev. 21:16*

fourteen -th — 1180, 5065: *Matt. 1:17; Acts 27:27, 33; 2 Cor. 12:2; Gal. 2:1*

fowls — 4071, 3732

fox -es — 258: *Matt. 8:20; Luke 9:58; 13:32*

fragments — 2801

framed — 2675, 4883: *Eph. 2:21; Heb. 11:3*

frankincense — 3030: *Matt. 2:11; Rev. 18:13*

frankly — 5435: *Luke 7:42*

free -dom (see **liberty**) **-ed -ly** — 1344, 1432, 1658, 1659, 3326/3954, 3955, 4174, 5486

freeman — 558: *1 Cor. 7:22*

freewoman — 1658: *Gal. 4:22, 23, 30*

frequent — 4056: *2 Cor. 11:23*

fresh — 1099: *James 3:12*

friend -s -ship — 2083, 3588/3844, 3982, 4674, 5373, 5384

fro — 2831: *Eph. 4:14*

frogs — 944: *Rev. 16:13*

froward — 4646: *1 Pet. 2:18*

fruit -ful -s — 175, 1081, 2590, 2592, 2593, 3703, 5062, 5352

frustrate — 114: *Gal. 2:21*

fulfill -ed -ing — 378, 1096, 1603, 4137, 4138, 4160, 4931, 5048, 5055

full -ness -y — 1072, 1073, 1705, 2880, 3324, 3325, 3877, 4130, 4134, 4135, 4136, 4137, 4138, 4845, 5046, 5460, 5526

fuller — 1102: *Mark 9:3*

furlongs — 4712: *Luke 24:13; John 6:19; 11:18; Rev. 14:20; 21:16*

furnace — 2575: *Matt. 13:42, 50; Rev. 1:15; 9:2*

furnished — 1822, 4130, 4766: *Matt. 22:10; Mark 14:15; Luke 22:12; 2 Tim. 3:17*

further -ance -more — 1161, 1339, 1534, 1909/4118, 2089, 3063, 4206, 4297

G

Gabbatha — 1042: *John 19:13*

Gabriel — 1043: *Luke 1:19, 26*

Gad — 1045: *Rev. 7:5*

Gadarenes — 1046: *Mark 5:1; Luke 8:26, 37*

gain -ed -s — 1281, 2039, 2770, 2771, 4122, 4160, 4200, 4333

gainsay -ers -ing — 369, 471, 483, 485: *Luke 21:15; Acts 10:29; Rom. 10:21; Titus 1:9; Jude 1:11*

Gaius — 1050: *Acts 19:29; 20:4; Rom. 16:23; 1 Cor. 1:14; 3 John 1:1*

Galatia -ns — 1052, 1053, 1054

Galilean -s — 1057

Galilee — 1056

gall — 5521: *Matt. 27:34; Acts 8:23*

Gallio — 1058: *Acts 18:12, 14, 17*

Gamaliel — 1059: *Acts 5:34; 22:3*

garden -er — 2779, 2780: *Luke 13:19; John 18:1, 26; 19:41; 20:15*

garlands — 4725: *Acts 14:13*

garment -s — 1742, 2067, 2440, 4158, 4749, 5509

garner — 596: *Matt. 3:12; Luke 3:17*

garnish -ed — 2885: *Matt. 12:44; 23:29; Luke 11:25; Rev. 21:19*
garrison — 5432: *2 Cor. 11:32*
gate -s — 2374, 4439, 4440
gather -ed -eth -ing — 346, 1865, 1996, 1997, 3048, 3792, 4816, 4822, 4863, 4867, 4896, 4962, 5166
gay — 2986: *James 2:3*
Gaza — 1048: *Acts 8:26*
gazing — 1689: *Acts 1:11*
gazingstock — 2301: *Heb. 10:33*
genealogies — 1076: *1 Tim. 1:4; Titus 3:9*
general — 3831: *Heb. 12:23*
generation -s — 1074, 1078, 1081, 1085
Gennesaret — 1082: *Matt. 14:34; Mark 6:53; Luke 5:1*
Gentile -s — 1483, 1484, 1672
gentle -ness — 1932, 1933, 2261, 5544:
Gergesenes — 1086: *Matt. 8:28*
get; gotten — 645, 1684, 1826, 1831, 2147, 2597, 4122, 5217
Gethsemane — 1068: *Matt. 26:36; Mark 14:32*
Ghost; ghost — 1606, 1634, 4151
Gideon — 1066: *Heb. 11:32*
gift -s — 334, 1390, 1394, 1431, 1434, 1435, 1445, 3311, 5485, 5486
gird -ed -edst; girt; girdle -s — 328, 1241, 2223, 2224, 4024
give -ing -en -er -eth; gave -est — 402, 437, 591, 632, 1096, 1239, 1291, 1325, 1377, 1394, 1395, 1402, 1433, 1502, 1547, 1781, 1788, 1907, 1929, 2010, 2014, 2227, 2468, 2702, 2753, 3004, 3140, 3330, 3548, 3844, 3860, 3923, 3930, 3936, 3943, 4160, 4222, 4272, 4337, 4342, 4369, 4823, 4980, 5087, 5461, 5483, 5524
glad -ly -ness — 20, 21, 780, 2097, 2165, 2167, 2234, 2236, 5463, 5479
glass — 2072, 2734, 5193, 5194
glistering — 1823: *Luke 9:29*
glorify -ied -ing — 1392, 1740, 4888
glory -ieth -ing -ious — 1223/1391, 1391, 1392, 1722/1391, 1741, 2620, 2744, 2745, 2746, 2755, 2811
gluttonous — 5314: *Matt. 11:19; Luke 7:34*
gnashed; gnasheth; gnashing — 1030, 1031, 5149

gnat — 2971: *Matt. 23:24*
gnawed — 3145: *Rev. 16:10*
go -est -eth -ing -ne; went -est — 33, 71, 305, 402, 424, 549, 565, 576, 589, 630, 863, 1276, 1279, 1330, 1339, 1353, 1524, 1525, 1578, 1607, 1684, 1821, 1826, 1831, 1910, 1931, 1994, 2021, 2064, 2212, 2597, 2718, 3327, 3596, 3597, 3854, 3899, 3928, 3985, 4013, 4043, 4105, 4108, 4198, 4254, 4260, 4281, 4313, 4320, 4334, 4344, 4570, 4782, 4848, 4897, 4905, 5055, 5217, 5221, 5233, 5298, 5342, 5562
goats — 2055, 2056, 5131: *Matt. 25:32, 33; Heb. 9:12, 13, 19; 10:4*
goatskins — 122/1192: *Heb. 11:37*
God; Godward — 2316, 2962, 4314/2316
god -s — 1140, 2316
goddess — 2299: *Acts 19:27, 35, 37*
Godhead — 2304, 2305, 2320: *Acts 17:29; Rom. 1:20; Col. 2:9*
godly -iness — 516/2316, 2150, 2152, 2153, 2316, 2317, 2596/2316
Godspeed — 5463: *2 John 1:10, 11*
Gog — 1136: *Rev. 20:8*
gold -en — 5552, 5553, 5554, 5557
Golgotha — 1115: *Matt. 27:33; Mark 15:22; John 19:17*
Gomorrah — 1116: *Matt. 10:15; Mark 16:11; Rom. 9:29; 2 Pet. 2:6; Jude 1:7*
good -ly -ness — 14, 15, 18, 515, 865, 979, 2095, 2097, 2106, 2107, 2108, 2109, 2133, 2140, 2162, 2163, 2425, 2480, 2565, 2567, 2570, 2573, 2750, 2986, 3112, 4851, 5358, 5542, 5543, 5544
goodman — 3611: *Matt. 20:11; 24:43; Mark 14:14; Luke 12:39; 22:11*
goods — 18, 3776, 4147, 4632, 4674, 5223, 5224
gorgeous -ly — 1741, 2986: *Luke 7:25; 23:11*
gospel — 2097, 2098, 4283
government -s — 2941, 2963: *1 Cor. 12:28; 2 Pet. 2:10*
governor -s — 755, 1481, 2116, 2230, 2232, 2233, 3623
grace -ious — 2143, 5485, 5543
graft -ed (see **engrafted**) **—** 1461: *Rom. 11:17, 19, 23, 24*
grain — 2848

grandmother — 3125: *2 Tim. 1:5*
grant -ed — 1325, 2036, 5483
grapes — 4718: *Matt. 7:16; Luke 6:44; Rev. 14:18*
grass — 5528
grave -ity (see **sober**) — 4586, 4587: *1 Tim. 3:4, 8, 11; Titus 2:2, 7*
grave -s (see **sepulcher**) — 86, 3418, 3419
graveclothes — 2730: *John 11:44*
graven — 5480: *Acts 17:29*
great -er -est -ly -ness — 1568, 1569, 1971, 1974, 2245, 2425, 3029, 3112, 3123, 3166, 3167, 3170, 3171, 3173, 3174, 3175, 3176, 3186, 3187, 3745, 3819, 3827, 4055, 4080, 4118, 4119, 4183, 4185, 4186, 4214, 4970, 5082, 5118, 5246, 5479
Greece; Grecians; Greek -s (see **Achaia**) — 1671, 1673, 1674, 1675, 1676
greedy -ily -iness — 146, 866, 1632, 4124: *Eph. 4:19; 1 Tim. 3:3, 8; Jude 1:11*
green — 5200, 5515: *Mark 6:39; Luke 23:31; Rev. 8:7; 9:4*
greet -eth -ing -s — 782, 783, 5463
grieve -d -ous -ously; grief — 926, 1171, 1278, 1418, 2560, 3076, 3077, 3636, 4190, 4360, 4727, 4818
grind -ing — 229, 3039: *Matt. 21:44; 24:41; Luke 17:35; 20:18*
groan -ed -eth -ing(s) — 1690, 4726, 4727, 4959
gross — 3975: *Matt. 13:15; Acts 28:27*
ground -ed — 68, 1093, 1474, 1475, 1477, 2311, 5476, 5561, 5564
grow -eth -n; grew — 305, 837, 1096, 2064, 3373, 4886, 5232
grudge -ing -ingly — 1112, 1537/ 3077, 4727: *2 Cor. 9:7; James 5:9; 1 Pet. 4:9*
guard — 4759: *Acts 28:16*
guest -s — 345, 2647: *Matt. 22:10, 11; Luke 19:7*
guestchamber — 2646: *Mark 14:14; Luke 22:11*
guide -s — 2720, 3594, 3595, 3616
guile (see **beguile**) — 1388
guiltless; guilty — 338, 1777, 3784, 5267
gulf — 5490: *Luke 16:26*
gushed — 1632: *Acts 1:18*

H

habitation -s — 1886, 2732, 2733, 3613, 4633
Hagar — 28: *Gal. 4:24, 25*
hail — 5463, 5464
hair -s — 2359, 2863, 2864, 4117, 5155
hale -ing — 2694, 4951: *Luke 12:58; Acts 8:3*
half — 2253, 2255, 2256
hall — 833, 4232
hallowed (see **sanctify**) — 37: *Matt. 6:9; Luke 11:2*
halt (see **lame**) — 5560: *Matt. 18:8; Mark 9:45; Luke 14:21; John 5:3*
Hamor — 1697: *Acts 7:16*
hand -s — 849, 886, 1448, 1451, 1764, 2021, 2186, 2902, 4084, 4475, 5495, 5496, 5497, 5499
handkerchiefs — 4676: *Acts 19:12*
handle -ed -ing — 821, 1389, 2345, 5584: *Mark 12:4; Luke 24:39; 2 Cor. 4:2; Col. 2:21; 1 John 1:1*
handmaid -en(s) — 1399: *Luke 1:38, 48; Acts 2:18*
handwriting — 5498: *Col. 2:14*
hang -ed -eth — 519, 2910, 3935, 4029
haply — 686, 3379, 3381: *Mark 11:13; Luke 14:29; Acts 5:39; 17:27; 2 Cor. 9:4*
happen -ed — 1096, 4819
happy -ier — 3106, 3107
Haran — 5488: *Acts 7:2, 4*
hard -en -ened -eneth -ly -ness — 1421, 1422, 1423, 1425, 2553, 3425, 3433, 4456, 4457, 4641, 4642, 4643, 4645, 4927
harlot -s — 4204
harm -less — 172, 185, 824, 2556, 2559, 4190, 5196
harp -ed -ers -ing -s — 2788, 2789, 2790
harvest — 2326
haste -ed -ily -ing — 4692, 4710, 5030
hate -ed -ers -est -eth -ful -ing; hatred (see **despise**) — 2189, 2319, 3404, 4767
have -ing; had -st; hast; hath (see **retain**) — 474, 568, 1096, 1526, 1699, 1746, 1751, 2071, 2076, 2192,

2258, 2722, 2983, 3335, 3844, 3918, 5224, 5225, 5607

haven -s — 2568, 3040: *Acts 27:8, 12*

havoc — 3075: *Acts 8:3*

hay — 5528: *1 Cor. 3:12*

hazarded — 3860: *Acts 15:26*

head -s — 2776

headlong — 2630, 4248: *Luke 4:29; Acts 1:18*

heady — 4312: *2 Tim. 3:4*

heal -ed -ing(s) -th — 1295, 2322, 2323, 2386, 2390, 2392, 4982, 4991, 5198

heap -ed — 2002, 2343, 4987: *Rom. 12:20; 2 Tim. 4:3; James 5:3*

hear -er(s) -est -eth -ing -d — 189, 191, 201, 202, 1233, 1251, 1522, 1873, 1874, 4257

hearken -ed — 191, 1801, 3980, 5219

heart -s — 674, 2588, 2589, 4641, 5590

heartily — 1537/5590: *Col. 3:23*

heat — 2329, 2738, 2741, 2742

heathen — 1482, 1484

heaven -ly -s — 1537/3772, 2032, 3321, 3770, 3771, 3772

heavy -lness — 85, 916, 926, 2726, 3076, 3077

Heber — 1443: *Luke 3:35*

Hebrew -s — 1444, 1445, 1446, 1447

hedge -ed -s — 5418, 4969/5418: *Matt. 21:33; Mark 12:1; Luke 14:23*

heed — 433, 991, 1907, 3708, 4337, 4648

heel — 4418: *John 13:18*

heifer — 1151: *Heb. 9:13*

height — 5311, 5313: *Rom. 8:39; Eph. 3:18; Rev. 21:16*

heir -s — 2816, 2818, 4789

Heli — 2242: *Luke 3:23*

hell — 86, 1067, 5020

helm — 4079: *James 3:4*

helmet — 4030: *Eph. 6:17; 1 Thess. 5:8*

help -ed -eth -ing -s -er(s) — 482, 484, 996, 997, 998, 1947, 4815, 4820, 4878, 4903, 4904, 4943

hem — 2899: *Matt. 9:20; 14:36*

hen — 3733: *Matt. 23:37; Luke 13:34*

hence -forth -forward — 534, 575/3588/3568, 575/737, 737, 1782, 1821, 2089, 3063, 3226/5025, 3371, 3568, 3765, 5025, 5217

herbs — 1008, 3001

herd — 34: *Matt. 8:30–32; Mark 5:11, 13; Luke 8:32, 33*

here -after -by -in -of -tofore -unto — 575/737, 575/3568, 848, 1519/5124, 1537/5127, 1722/5129, 1759, 2089, 3195, 3326/5023, 3370, 3778, 3918, 3936, 4258, 4840, 5602

heresy -ies; heretic — 139, 141: *Acts 24:14; 1 Cor. 11:19; Gal. 5:20; Titus 3:10; 2 Pet. 2:1*

heritage — 2819: *1 Pet. 5:3*

Hermas — 2057: *Rom. 16:14*

Hermes — 2060: *Rom. 16:14*

Hermogenes — 2061: *2 Tim. 1:15*

Herod — 2264

Herodians — 2265: *Matt. 22:16; Mark 3:6; 12:13*

Herodias — 2266

Herodion — 2267: *Rom. 16:11*

hewn — 1581, 2991, 2998

hide -eth; hid -den — 613, 614, 1470, 2572, 2927, 2928, 2990, 3871, 4032

Hlerapolis — 2404: *Col. 4:13*

high -er -est -ly — 507, 511, 749, 1537/4053, 2032, 2371, 2409, 3173, 4410, 4411, 5242, 5251, 5252, 5308, 5310, 5311, 5313

highminded — 5187, 5309: *Rom. 11:20; 1 Tim. 6:17; 2 Tim. 3:4*

highway -s — 1327/3598, 3598: *Matt. 22:9, 10; Mark 10:46; Luke 14:23*

hill -s — 697, 1015, 3714, 3735

hinder — 4403: *Mark 4:38; Acts 27:41*

hinder -ed (see **restrained**) **— 348, 1465, 1581, 2967, 5100/1464/1325**

hire -ed -ling — 3407, 3408, 3409, 3410, 3411

hither — 1204, 1759, 3333, 5602: *Mark 11:3; Rev. 4:1*

hitherto — 891/1204, 2193/737, 3768: *John 5:17; 16:24; Rom. 1:13; 1 Cor. 3:2*

hoisted — 1869: *Acts 27:40*

hold -en -est -eth -ing; held — 472, 1907, 1949, 2192, 2258, 2270, 2476, 2722, 2902, 2983, 4160, 4601, 4623, 4912, 5083, 5084, 5392, 5438

holes — 5454: *Matt. 8:20; Luke 9:58*

holy -iest -ily -iness — 37, 38, 39, 40, 41, 42, 1859, 2150, 2412, 2413, 3741, 3742, 3743

home — 1438, 1736, 2398, 3614, 3624, 3626

honest -ly -y — 2156, 2570, 2573, 4586, 4587

honey — 3192: *Matt. 3:4 Mark 1:6; Rev. 10:9, 10*

honeycomb — 3193/2781: *Luke 24:42*

honor -able -ed -eth — 820, 1391, 1392, 1741, 1784, 2158, 5091, 5092, 5093

hook — 44: *Matt. 17:27*

hope -ed -eth -ing — 560, 1679, 1680

horn -s — 2768

horse -s — 2462

horsemen — 2460, 2461: *Acts 23:23, 32; Rev. 9:16*

hosanna — 5614: *Matt. 21:9, 15; Mark 11:9, 10; John 12:13*

Hosea — 5617: *Rom. 9:25*

hospitality — 5381, 5382: *Rom. 12:13; 1 Tim. 3:2; Titus 1:8; 1 Pet. 4:9*

host — 3581, 3830, 4756: *Luke 2:13; 10:35; Acts 7:42; Rom. 16:23*

hot — 2200, 2743: *1 Tim. 4:2; Rev. 3:15, 16*

hour -s — 734, 2256, 5610

house -s -hold -holder -top(s) — 1430, 2322, 3609, 3610, 3613, 3614, 3615, 3616, 3617, 3624, 3832

how — 2245, 2531, 3704, 3745, 3754, 4012, 4080, 4212, 4214, 4219, 4459, 5101, 5613

howbeit — 235, 1161, 3305

howl — 3649: *James 5:1*

humble -ed -ness -eth — 5011, 5012, 5013

humility; humiliation — 5012, 5014

hundred -s -fold — 1250, 1540, 1541, 1542, 3461, 4001, 5071, 5145, 5516

hunger -ed; hungry — 3042, 3983, 4361

hurt -ful — 91, 983, 984, 2559, 5196

husband -s — 435, 5220, 5362

husbandman; husbandmen; husbandry — 1091, 1092

husks — 2769: *Luke 15:16*

Hymenaeus — 5211: *1 Tim. 1:20; 2 Tim. 2:17*

hymn -s — 5214, 5215: *Matt. 26:30; Mark 14:26; Eph. 5:19; Col. 3:16*

hypocrisy -ies; hypocrite -s — 505, 5272, 5273

hyssop — 5301: *John 19:29; Heb. 9:19*

I

Iconium — 2430: *Acts 13:51; 14:1, 19, 21; 16:2; 2 Tim. 3:11*

idle — 692, 3026

idol -s -ater(s) -atry -atries — 1493, 1494, 1495, 1496, 1497, 2712

Idumea — 2401: *Mark 3:8*

if — 1437, 1487, 1489, 1490, 1499, 1512, 1513, 1535, 2579, 3379

ignorant -ly; ignorance — 50, 52, 56, 2399, 2990

ill — 2556: *Rom. 13:10*

illuminated — 5461: *Heb. 10:32*

Illyricum — 2437: *Rom. 15:19*

image — 1504, 5481

imagine -ation(s) — 1261, 1271, 3053, 3191: *Luke 1:51; Acts 4:25; Rom. 1:21; 2 Cor. 10:5*

Immanuel — 1694: *Matt. 1:23*

immediately (see **anon; forthwith; straightway**) — 1824, 2112, 2117, 3916

immortal -ity — 110, 861, 862: *Rom. 2:7; 1 Cor. 15:53, 54; 1 Tim. 1:17; 6:16; 2 Tim. 1:10*

immutable; immutability — 276: *Heb. 6:17, 18*

impart -ed — 3330: *Luke 3:11; Rom. 1:11; 1 Thess. 2:8*

impediment — 3424: *Mark 7:32*

impenitent — 279: *Rom. 2:5*

implacable — 786: *Rom. 1:31*

implead — 1458: *Acts 19:38*

importunity — 335: *Luke 11:8*

imposed — 1945: *Heb. 9:10*

impossible — 101, 102, 418

impotent — 102, 770, 772: *John 5:3, 7; Acts 4:9; 14:8*

imprisoned; imprisonment(s) — 5438, 5439: *Acts 22:19; 2 Cor. 6:5; Heb. 11:36*

impute -ed -eth -ing — 1677, 3049

inasmuch — 1909/3745, 2526, 2596/3745

incense — 2368, 2370: *Luke 1:9, 11; Rev. 8:3, 4*

incontinency; incontinent — 192, 193: *1 Cor. 7:5; 2 Tim. 3:3*

incorruptible; incorruption (see **uncorruptible**) — 861, 862

increase -ed -eth -ing — 837, 838, 1743, 4052, 4121, 4147, 4298, 4369

incredible — 571: *Acts 26:8*

indebted — 3784: *Luke 11:4*

indeed — 230, 235, 1063, 2532, 3303, 3689

indignation — 23, 24, 2205, 2372, 3709

inexcusable — 379: *Rom. 2:1*

infants — 1025: *Luke 18:15*

inferior — 2274: *2 Cor. 12:13*

infidel — 571: *2 Cor. 6:15; 1 Tim. 5:8*

infirmity -ies — 769, 771, 3554

informed — 1718, 2727: *Acts 21:21, 24; 24:1; 25:2, 15*

inhabitants; inhabiters — 2730: *Rev. 8:13; 12:12; 17:2*

inherit -ance -ed — 2816, 2817, 2819, 2820

iniquity -ies — 92, 93, 458, 3892, 4189

injured; injurious — 91, 5197: *Gal. 4:12; 1 Tim. 1:13*

ink — 3188: *2 Cor. 3:3; 2 John 1:12; 3 John 1:13*

inn — 2646, 3829: *Luke 2:7; 10:34*

inner — 2080, 2082: *Acts 16:24; Eph. 3:16*

innocent — 121: *Matt. 27:4, 24*

innumerable — 382, 3461: *Luke 12:1; Heb. 11:12; 12:22*

inordinate — 3806: *Col. 3:5*

inquire -ed -y — 198, 1231, 1331, 1567, 1833, 1934, 2212, 4441, 4802

inscription — 1924: *Acts 17:23*

insomuch (see **forasmuch; forsomuch**) — 1519, 5620

inspiration — 2315: *2 Tim. 3:16*

instant -ly — 1945, 2186, 4342, 4705, 5610

instruct -ed -or(s) -ing -ion — 2727, 3100, 3453, 3807, 3809, 3810, 3811, 4264, 4822

instruments — 3696: *Rom. 6:13*

insurrection — 2721, 4714, 4955: *Mark 15:7; Acts 18:12*

intend -ing — 1011, 1014, 2309, 3195: *Luke 14:28; Acts 5:28, 35; 12:4; 20:13*

intent -s — 1771, 2443, 3056

intercession -s — 1783, 1793, 5241: *Rom. 8:26, 27, 34; 11:2; 1 Tim. 2:1; Heb. 7:25*

interpret -ation -ed -er — 1328, 1329, 1955, 2058, 2059, 3177

into — 891, 1519, 1531, 1722, 1909, 2080, 2596, 3350, 5259

intruding — 1687: *Col. 2:18*

inventors — 2182: *Rom. 1:30*

invisible — 517: *Rom. 1:20; Col. 1:15, 16; 1 Tim. 1:17; Heb. 11:27*

inward -ly — 1722/2927, 2080, 2081, 4698

iron — 4603, 4604

Isaac — 2464

Isaiah — 2268

Iscariot — 2469

island; isle — 3519, 3520

Israel -ite(s) — 2474, 2475

Issachar — 2466: *Rev. 7:7*

issue -ed — 131, 1607, 4511, 4690

Italy -ian — 2482, 2483: *Acts 10:1; 18:2; 27:1, 6; Heb. 13:24*

itching — 2833: *2 Tim. 4:3*

itself — 846, 1438, 5565

Ituraea — 2484: *Luke 3:1*

ivory — 1661: *Rev. 18:12*

J

jacinth — 5191, 5192: *Rev. 9:17; 21:20*

Jacob — 2384

jailer — 1200: *Acts 16:23*

Jairus — 2383: *Mark 5:22; Luke 8:41*

Jambres — 2387: *2 Tim. 3:8*

James — 2385

jangling — 3150: *1 Tim. 1:6*

Janna — 2388: *Luke 3:24*

Jannes — 2389: *2 Tim. 3:8*

Jared — 2391: *Luke 3:37*

Jason — 2394: *Acts 17:5-7, 9; Rom. 16:21*

jasper — 2393: *Rev. 4:3; 21:11, 18, 19*

jealous -y — 2205, 2206: *Rom. 10:19; 11:11; 1 Cor. 10:22; 2 Cor. 11:2*

Jechonias — 2423: *Matt. 1:11, 12*

jeopardy — 2793: *Luke 8:23; 1 Cor. 15:30*

Jephthah — 2422: *Heb. 11:32*

Jeremiah — 2408: *Matt. 2:17; 16:14; 27:9*

Jericho — 2410

Jerusalem — 2414, 2419

Jesse — 2421: *Matt. 1:5, 6; Luke 3:32; Acts 13:22; Rom. 15:12*

jesting — 2160: *Eph. 5:4*

Jesus — 2424

Jew -ess -ish -s — 2450, 2451, 2452, 2453

Jewry — 2449: *Luke 23:5; John 7:1*

Jezebel — 2403: *Rev. 2:20*

Joanna — 2489: *Luke 3:27; 8:3; 24:10*

Joatham — 2488: *Matt. 1:9*

Job — 2492: *James 5:11*

Joel — 2493: *Acts 2:16*

John — 2491

join -ed — 2675, 2853, 4347, 4801, 4883, 4927

joint -s — 719, 860: *Eph. 4:16; Col. 2:19; Heb. 4:12*

joint heirs — 4789: *Rom. 8:17*

Jona; Jonah (see **Bar-jona**) — 2495

Jonan — 2494: *Luke 3:30*

Joppa — 2445

Joram — 2496: *Matt. 1:8*

Jordan — 2446

Jorim — 2497: *Luke 3:29*

Josaphat — 2498: *Matt. 1:8*

Jose — 2499: *Luke 3:29*

Joseph — 2501

Joses — 2500

Josiah — 2502: *Matt. 1:10, 11*

jot — 2503: *Matt. 5:18*

journey -ed -ing(s) — 589, 590, 1279, 2137, 3593, 3596, 3597, 3598, 4197/4160, 4198, 4922

joy -ed -ing -ous; **joyful** -ly -ness — 20, 21, 2167, 2744, 3326/5479, 3685, 5463, 5479, 5485

Judah; Judas; Jude — 2448, 2455

Judea — 2449, 2453

judge -ed -est -eth -ing -ment(s) -s — 144, 350, 968, 1106, 1252, 1341, 1345, 1348, 1349, 2233, 2250, 2917, 2919, 2920, 2922, 2923, 4232

Julia — 2456: *Rom. 16:15*

Julius — 2457: *Acts 27:1, 3*

Junia — 2458: *Rom. 16:7*

Jupiter — 1356, 2203: *Acts 14:12, 13; 19:35*

jurisdiction — 1849: *Luke 23:7*

just -ly — 1342, 1346, 1738

justify -ication -ied -ier -ieth — 1344, 1345, 1347

Justus — 2459: *Acts 1:23; 18:7; Col. 4:11*

K

keep -er(s) -est -eth -ing; **kept** — 71, 650, 1006, 1096, 1200, 1301, 1314, 1858, 2192, 2343, 2377, 2621, 2722, 2853, 2902, 2967, 3557, 3626, 3930, 4160, 4238, 4601, 4874, 4912, 4933, 5083, 5084, 5288, 5299, 5432, 5441, 5442

key -s — 2807

kick — 2979: *Acts 9:5; 26:14*

kid — 2056: *Luke 15:29*

kill -ed -est -eth -ing — 337, 615, 1315, 2289, 2380, 4969, 5407

kin -sfolk -sman -smen — 4773

kind -s — 1085, 5100, 5449

kind -ly -ness — 5360, 5363, 5387, 5541, 5543, 5544

kindled; kindleth — 381, 681: *Luke 12:49; 22:55; Acts 28:2; James 3:5*

kindred -s — 1085, 3965, 4772, 5443

king -dom(s) -s — 932, 933, 935, 936, 937

Kish — 2797: *Acts 13:21*

kiss -ed — 2705, 5368, 5370

knee -s — 1119

kneeled; kneeling — 1120, 5087/1119

knit — 1210, 4822: *Acts 10:11; Col. 2:2, 19*

knock -ed -eth -ing — 2925

know -est -eth -ing -ledge -n; **knew** -est (see **wist**) — 50, 56, 319, 1097, 1107, 1108, 1110, 1231, 1232, 1492, 1921, 1922, 1987, 1990, 2467, 2589, 3877, 4135, 4267, 4892, 4907, 5318

Korah — 2879: *Jude 1:11*

L

labor -ed -er(s) -eth -ing -s — 75, 2038, 2040, 2041, 2872, 2873, 4704, 4866, 4904, 5389

lack -ed -est -eth -ing — 170, 1641, 1729, 3007, 3361/2192, 3361/3918, 5302, 5303, 5332

lad — 3808: *John 6:9*

lade -ed -en -ing — 2007, 4987, 5412, 5414: *Matt. 11:28; Luke 11:46; Acts 27:10; 28:10; 2 Tim. 3:6*

lady — 2959: *2 John 1:1, 5*

lake — 3041
lama — 2982: *Matt. 27:46; Mark 15:34*
lamb -s — 286, 704, 721
lame (see **halt**) — 5560
Lamech — 2984: *Luke 3:36*
lament -ation -ed — 2354, 2355, 2870, 2875
lamp -s — 2985
land -s — 68, 1093, 3584, 5561, 5564
landed; landing — 2609, 2718: *Acts 18:22; 21:3; 28:12*
lanes — 4505: *Luke 14:21*
language — 1258: *Acts 2:6*
lanterns — 5322: *John 18:3*
Laodicea -ns — 2993, 2994
large — 2425, 3173, 4080, 5118: *Matt. 28:12; Mark 14:15; Luke 22:12; Gal. 6:11; Rev. 21:16*
lasciviousness — 766
Lasea — 2996: *Acts 27:8*
last — 2078, 4218, 5305
latchet — 2438: *Mark 1:7; Luke 3:16; John 1:27*
late -ly — 3568, 4373: *John 11:8; Acts 18:2*
Latin — 4513: *Luke 23:38; John 19:20*
latter — 2078, 3797, 5305
laud — 1867: *Rom. 15:11*
laugh -ed -ter — 1070, 1071, 2606
launch -ed — 321, 1877: *Luke 6:4; 8:22; Acts 21:1; 27:2, 4*
law -ful -fully -less -s — 60, 458, 459, 460, 1772, 1832, 1833, 2917, 2919, 3544, 3545, 3547, 3548, 3549, 3551, 3565, 3891, 3994, 3995
lawgiver — 3550: *James 4:12*
lawyer -s — 3544
lay -eth -ing; **lie** -eth; **laid; lain; lying** — 347, 597, 606, 659, 863, 906, 991, 1458, 1462, 1474, 1748, 1911, 1917, 1936, 1945, 1949, 1968, 2007, 2192, 2343, 2476, 2598, 2621, 2698, 2749, 2827, 3049, 3180, 4160, 4369, 5087, 5294, 5342
Lazarus — 2976
lead -ers -eth; **led** -dest — 71, 162, 163, 321, 399, 520, 1236, 1521, 1533, 1806, 3594, 3595, 4013, 4863, 4879, 5342, 5496, 5497
leaned; leaning — 345, 377: *John 13:23; 21:20*
leap -ed -ing — 242, 1814, 2177, 4640

learn -ed -ing — 1121, 1319, 3129, 3811
least — 1646, 1647, 1848, 2534, 2579, 3398
leather — 1193: *Matt. 3:4*
leave -ing -eth; **left** — 447, 620, 657, 782, 863, 1439, 1459, 1544, 2010, 2641, 3973, 4051, 4052, 5275, 5277
leaven -ed -eth — 2219, 2220
leaves — 5444: *Matt. 21:19; 24:32; Mark 11:13; 13:28; Rev. 22:2*
Lebbaeus (see **Thaddeus**) — 3002: *Matt. 10:3*
left — 710, 2176
legs — 4628: *John 19:31–33*
legion -s — 3003: *Matt. 26:53; Mark 5:9, 15; Luke 8:30*
leisure — 2119: *Mark 6:31*
lend — 1155, 5531: *Luke 6:34, 35; 11:5*
length — 3372, 4218: *Rom. 1:10; Eph. 3:18; Rev. 21:16*
leopard — 3917: *Rev. 13:2*
leper -s; **leprosy** — 3014, 3015
less — 253, 820, 1640, 1647, 2276, 3398
lest — 1519/3588/3361, 3361, 3363, 3379, 3381
let -test -teth — 630, 863, 1439, 1554, 1832, 1929, 2010, 2524, 2722, 2967, 5465
letter -s — 1121, 1989, 1992
Levi (see **Matthew**) — 3017, 3018
Levite -s -ical (see **priest**) — 3019, 3020: *Luke 10:32; John 1:19; Acts 4:36; Heb. 7:11*
lewd -ness — 4190, 4467: *Acts 17:5; 18:14*
liberal -ity -ly — 572, 574, 5485: *1 Cor. 16:3; 2 Cor. 8:2; 9:13; James 1:5*
libertines — 3032: *Acts 6:9*
liberty — 425, 630, 859, 1657, 1658, 1849, 2010
Libya — 3033: *Acts 2:10*
license — 2010, 5117: *Acts 21:40; 25:16*
licked — 621: *Luke 16:21*
lie -ed -s; **liar** -s; **lying** — 893, 5571, 5573, 5574, 5579, 5582, 5583
life -time; **lives** — 72, 895, 979, 981, 982, 2198, 2222, 2227, 4151, 5590
lift -ed -ing — 142, 352, 450, 461, 1453, 1458, 1869, 5188, 5312
light -ed -eth -ing -s; **lighten** -ed

-eth — 272, 602, 681, 797, 1645, 2014, 2017, 2064, 2545, 2893, 2985, 2989, 3088, 4098, 5035, 5338, 5457, 5458, 5460, 5461, 5462

lightly; lightness — 1644, 5035: *Mark 9:39; 2 Cor. 1:17*

lightning -s — 796

like -ed -ened -ness — 407, 499, 871, 1381, 1503, 2470, 2472, 2504, 2532, 2596/3665, 3663, 3664, 3666, 3667, 3779, 3945, 3946, 4832, 5024, 5108, 5613, 5615, 5616, 5618

likeminded — 2473, 3588/846/5426: *Rom. 15:5; Phil. 2:2, 20*

likewise — 36, 437, 2532, 3668, 3779, 3898, 5615

lilies — 2918: *Matt. 6:28; Luke 12:27*

limiteth — 3724: *Heb. 4:7*

line — 2583: *2 Cor. 10:16*

lineage — 3965: *Luke 2:4*

linen — 1039, 1040, 3043, 3608, 4616

lingereth — 691: *2 Pet. 2:3*

Linus — 3044: *2 Tim. 4:21*

lion -s — 3023

lips — 5491

listed; listeth — 2309, 3730/1014: *Matt. 17:12; Mark 9:13; John 3:8; James 3:4*

little — 974, 1024, 1646, 2365, 2485, 3357, 3397, 3398, 3640, 3641, 3813, 4142, 5040, 5177

live -ed -est -eth -ing — 326, 390, 979, 980, 1236, 1514, 2068, 2071/3118, 2198, 2225, 4176, 4800, 5171, 5225

lively — 2198: *Acts 7:38; 1 Pet. 1:3; 2:5*

lo — 2396, 2400

loaf; loaves — 740

locusts — 200: *Matt. 3:4; Mark 1:6; Rev. 9:3, 7*

lodge -ed -eth -ing — 835, 2647, 2681, 3578, 3579, 3580

loins — 3751

Lois — 3090: *2 Tim. 1:5*

long -ed — 1971, 1973: *Rom. 1:11; 2 Cor. 9:14; Phil. 1:8; 2:26; 4:1*

long -er — 1909, 1909/4119, 2089, 2118, 2193, 2425, 2863, 3114, 3117, 3370, 3752, 3756/3641, 3819, 4119, 4183, 4214, 5118, 5550

longsuffering — 3114, 3115

look -ed -eth -ing — 308, 352, 553, 816, 872, 991, 1492, 1551, 1561, 1689, 1896, 1914, 1980, 1983, 2300, 2334, 3700, 3706, 3879, 4017, 4327, 4328, 4329, 4648

loose -ed -ing — 142, 321, 447, 630, 2673, 3080, 3089

Lord — 1203, 2960, 2961, 2962, 4462

lord -s -ship — 2634, 2961, 2962, 3175

lose -eth; loss; lost — 358/1096, 580, 622, 2209, 2210, 3471

lot -s — 2624, 2819, 2975

Lot — 3091: *Luke 17:28, 29, 32; 2 Pet. 2:7*

loud — 3173

love -ed -edst -er(s) -est -eth -ly — 25, 26, 2309, 4375, 5358, 5360, 5361, 5362, 5363, 5365, 5367, 5368, 5369, 5377, 5382, 5383, 5388

low -er -est — 1642, 2078, 2737, 5011, 5013, 5014

lowering — 4768: *Matt. 16:3*

lowly; lowliness — 5011, 5012: *Matt. 11:29; Eph. 4:2; Phil. 2:3*

Lucius — 3066: *Acts 13:1; Rom. 16:21*

lucre — 146, 147, 866, 2771: *1 Tim. 3:3, 8; Titus 1:7, 11; 1 Pet. 5:2*

Luke — 3065: *Col. 4:14; 2 Tim. 4:11; Phile. 1:24*

lukewarm — 5513: *Rev. 3:16*

lump — 5445: *Rom. 9:21; 11:16; 1 Cor. 5:6, 7; Gal. 5:9*

lunatic — 4583: *Matt. 4:24; 17:15*

lust -ed -eth -s — 1511/1938, 1937, 1939, 1971, 2237, 3715, 3806

Lycaonia — 3071: *Acts 14:6, 11*

Lycia — 3073: *Acts 27:5*

Lydia — 3070: *Acts 16:14, 40*

Lydda — 3069: *Acts 9:32, 35, 38*

Lysanias — 3078: *Luke 3:1*

Lysias — 3079: *Acts 23:26; 24:7, 22*

Lystra — 3082: *Acts 14:6, 8, 21; 16:1, 2; 2 Tim. 3:11*

M

Maath — 3092: *Luke 3:26*

Macedonia -n — 3109, 3110

mad -ness — 454, 1519/3130, 1693, 3105, 3913

Magdala — 3093: *Matt. 15:39*

Magdalene — 3094

magistrate -s — 746, 758, 3980, 4755

magnificence — 3168: *Acts 19:27*

magnify -ied — 1392, 3170

Magog — 3098: *Rev. 20:8*
maid -s -en(s) — 2877, 3814, 3816
maimed — 376, 2948: *Matt. 15:30, 31; 18:8; Mark 9:43; Luke 14:13, 21*
mainsail — 736: *Acts 27:40*
maintain — 4291: *Titus 3:8, 14*
majesty — 3168, 3172: *Heb. 1:3; 8:1; 2 Pet. 1:16; Jude 1:25*
make -er -est -eth -ing; made -est — 142, 208, 272, 319, 347, 387, 393, 461, 591, 626, 770, 805, 871, 886, 1080, 1096, 1107, 1165, 1189, 1215, 1217, 1232, 1239, 1252, 1295, 1303, 1308, 1325, 1392, 1402, 1510, 1511, 1517, 1519, 1586, 1642, 1659, 1710, 1743, 1770, 1793, 1839, 1861, 2005, 2049, 2090, 2092, 2116, 2134, 2146, 2165, 2227, 2301, 2350, 2390, 2427, 2433, 2476, 2511, 2525, 2559, 2617, 2625, 2673, 2675, 2680, 2721, 2722, 2744, 2749, 2758, 2841, 2936, 3021, 3076, 3182, 3421, 3447, 3471, 3489, 3666, 3670, 3753, 3822, 3856, 3868, 3903, 3982, 4052, 4062, 4087, 4115, 4121, 4122, 4135, 4137, 4147, 4148, 4160, 4062, 4161, 4170, 4198, 4222, 4294, 4336, 4364, 4400, 4483, 4679, 4692, 4732, 4766, 4776, 4820, 4832, 4921, 4931, 4955, 4977, 4982, 5014, 5048, 5055, 5087, 5241, 5293, 5319, 5461, 5487, 5499, 5567
Malchus — 3124: *John 18:10*
male — 730: *Matt. 19:4; Mark 10:6; Luke 2:23; Gal. 3:28*
malefactor -s — 2555, 2557: *Luke 23:32, 33, 39; John 18:30*
Maleleel — 3121: *Luke 3:37*
malice; malicious -ness — 2549, 4190
malignity — 2550: *Rom. 1:29*
mammon — 3126: *Matt. 6:24; Luke 16:9, 11, 13*
man; men — 407, 435, 442, 444, 730, 1538, 2478, 3367, 3494, 3495, 3762, 3956, 4753, 5046, 5100
Manaen — 3127: *Acts 13:1*
Manasses — 3128: *Matt. 1:10; Rev. 7:6*
manger — 5336: *Luke 2:7, 12, 16*
manifest -ation -ed -ly — 602, 852, 1212, 1552, 1717, 1718, 4271, 5318, 5319, 5321
manifold — 4164, 4179, 4182: *Luke 18:30; Eph. 3:10; 1 Pet. 1:6; 4:10*

manna — 3131: *John 6:31, 49, 58; Heb. 9:4; Rev. 2:17*
manner -s — 72, 195, 442, 686, 981, 1483, 1485, 1486, 2239, 3592, 3634, 3697, 3779, 4012, 4169, 4187, 4217, 4458, 5158, 5159, 5179, 5615
mansions — 3438: *John 14:2*
manslayers — 409: *1 Tim. 1:9*
many — 2425, 3745, 4119, 4182, 4183, 4214, 5118
Maranatha — 3134: *1 Cor. 16:22*
marble — 3139: *Rev. 18:12*
Mark — 3138
mark -ed -s — 1907, 4648, 4649, 4742, 5480
market -place(s) -s — 58
marred — 622: *Mark 2:22*
marrow — 3452: *Heb. 4:12*
marry -iage -ied -ieth -ing — 1060, 1061, 1062, 1096, 1547, 1548, 1918
Mars — 697: *Acts 17:22*
Martha — 3136
martyr -s — 3144: *Acts 22:20; Rev. 2:13; 17:6*
marvel -ed -ous — 2296, 2298
Mary — 3137
master -s — 1203, 1320, 1988, 2519, 2942, 2962, 3617, 4461
masterbuilder — 753: *1 Cor. 3:10*
mastery -ies — 75, 118: *1 Cor. 9:25; 2 Tim. 2:25*
Mattatha — 3160: *Luke 3:31*
Mattathias — 3161: *Luke 3:25, 26*
matter -s — 244, 1308, 1646, 2087, 2596, 3056, 4229, 5130, 5208
Matthan — 3157: *Matt. 1:5*
Matthat — 3158: *Luke 3:24, 29*
Matthew — 3156: *Matt. 9:9; 10:3; Mark 3:18; Luke 6:15; Acts 1:13*
Matthias — 3159: *Acts 1:23, 26*
may -est; might -est — 1410, 1411, 1832, 2479, 2480, 2481
meal — 224: *Matt. 13:33; Luke 13:21*
mean — 767, 3342
mean -eth -ing -t — 1411, 1498, 2076, 2309/1511, 3195, 4160
means — 1096, 3361, 3364, 3843, 4458, 4459, 5158
measure -ed -ing -s — 280, 488, 943, 2884, 3354, 3358, 4053, 4057, 4568, 5234, 5236, 5249, 5518
meat -s — 1033, 1034, 1035, 4371, 4620, 5132, 5160, 5315

meat market — 3111: *1 Cor. 10:25*

Medes — 3370: *Acts 2:9*

mediator — 3316

meditate — 3191, 4304: *Luke 21:14; 1 Tim. 4:15*

meek -ness — 4235, 4236, 4239, 4240

meet (see **fit**) — 514, 1163, 1342, 2111, 2173, 2425, 2427, 2570

meet; met — 296, 528, 529, 4820, 4876, 4877, 5221, 5222

Melchi — 3197: *Luke 3:24, 28*

Melchizedek — 3198

Melea — 3190: *Luke 3:31*

Melita — 3194: *Acts 28:1*

melody — 5567: *Eph. 5:19*

melt — 3089, 5080: *2 Pet. 3:10, 12*

member -s — 3196

memory -ial — 3422: *Matt. 26:13; Mark 14:9; Acts 10:4; 1 Cor. 15:2*

Menan — 3104: *Luke 3:31*

mending — 2675: *Matt. 4:21; Mark 1:19*

menpleasers — 441: *Eph. 6:6; Col. 3:22*

menservants — 3816: *Luke 12:45*

menstealers — 405: *1 Tim. 1:10*

mention — 3417, 3421: *Rom. 1:9; Eph. 1:16; Phile. 1:4; 1 Thess. 1:2; Heb. 11:22*

merchandise — 1117, 1711, 1712: *Matt. 22:5; John 2:16; 2 Pet. 2:3; Rev. 18:11, 12*

merchant -s — 1713: *Matt. 13:45; Rev. 18:3, 11, 15, 23*

Mercurius — 2060: *Acts 14:12*

mercy -iful -ies — 448, 1653, 1655, 1656, 2433, 2436, 3628, 3629, 3741: *Rom. 12:1; Jude 1:2, 21*

mercyseat — 2435: *Heb. 9:5*

merry — 2114, 2165

Mesopotamia (see **Aram**) — 3318: *Acts 2:9; 7:2*

message; messenger -s — 31, 32, 652, 1860, 4242

Messiah — 3323: *John 1:41; 4:25*

mete — 3354: *Matt. 7:2; Mark 4:24; Luke 6:38*

Methuselah — 3103: *Luke 3:37*

Michael — 3413: *Jude 1:9; Rev. 12:7*

midday — 2250/3319: *Acts 26:13*

middle; midst — 3319, 3320, 3321, 3322

midnight — 3317, 3319/3571: *Matt. 25:6; Mark 13:35; Luke 11:5; Acts 16:25; 20:7; 27:27*

Midian — 3099: *Acts 7:29*

might -ier -ily -y — 972, 1410, 1411, 1413, 1414, 1415, 1722/1411, 1722/2479, 1754, 2159, 2478, 2479, 2480, 2596/2904, 2900, 3168, 3173, 5082

mile — 3400: *Matt. 5:41*

Miletum, Miletus — 3399: *Acts 20:15, 17; 2 Tim. 4:20*

milk — 1051: *1 Cor. 3:2; 9:7; Heb. 5:12, 13; 1 Pet. 2:2*

mill — 3459: *Matt. 24:41*

millstone — 3037/3457, 3458, 3458/3684: *Matt. 18:6; Mark 9:42; Luke 17:2; Rev. 18:21, 22*

mind -ed -ful -ing -s — 363, 1011, 1014, 1106, 1271, 1374, 1771, 1878, 3195, 3403, 3421, 3540, 3563, 3661, 3675, 4288, 4290, 4993, 4995, 5012, 5279, 5426, 5427, 5590

mingled — 3396: *Matt. 27:34; Mark 15:23; Luke 13:1; Rev. 8:7; 15:2*

minister -ed -eth -ing -s; ministration; ministry — 1247, 1248, 1249, 1325, 2023, 2038, 2418, 3008, 3009, 3010, 3011, 3930, 5256, 5257, 5524

minstrels — 834: *Matt. 9:23*

mint — 2238: *Matt. 23:23; Luke 11:42*

miracle -s — 1411, 4592

mire — 1004: *2 Pet. 2:22*

mischief — 4468: *Acts 13:10*

misery -able -ably -ies — 1652, 2560, 5004: *Matt. 21:41; Rom. 3:16; 1 Cor. 15:19; James 5:1; Rev. 3:17*

mist — 887, 2217: *Acts 13:11; 2 Pet. 2:17*

mite -s — 3016: *Mark 12:42; Luke 12:59; 21:2*

Mitylene — 3412: *Acts 20:14*

mixed; mixture — 194, 3395, 4786: *John 19:39; Heb. 4:2; Rev. 14:10*

Mnason — 3416: *Acts 21:16*

mock -ed -ers -ing(s) — 1701, 1702, 1703, 3456, 5512

moderation — 1933: *Phil. 4:5*

modest — 2887: *1 Tim. 2:9*

moisture — 2429: *Luke 8:6*

Moloch — 3434: *Acts 7:43*

moment — 823, 3901, 4743: *Luke 4:5; 1 Cor. 15:52; 2 Cor. 4:17*

money — 694, 2772, 3546, 4715, 5365, 5475, 5536: *1 Tim. 6:10*

moneychangers — 2885: *Matt. 21:12; Mark 11:15*

month -s — 3376, 5072, 5150

moon — 3561, 4582

more — 197, 243, 316, 414, 1065, 1308, 1508, 1617, 1833, 2001, 2089, 2115, 2596/5236, 3122, 3123, 3185, 3187, 3370, 3745, 3761, 3765, 3844, 4053, 4054, 4055, 4056, 4057, 4119, 4179, 4325, 4369, 4707, 5112, 5228, 5245

moreover — 235/2532, 1161, 1161/2532, 2089, 2532, 3739/1161/3063

morning — 3720, 4404, 4405, 4407

morrow (see **tomorrow**) — 839, 1836, 1887

morsel -1035: *Heb. 12:16*

mortal -ity — 2349: *Rom. 6:12; 8:11; 1 Cor. 15:53, 54; 2 Cor. 4:11; 5:4*

mortify — 2289, 3499: *Rom. 8:13; Col. 3:5*

Moses — 3475

most — 40, 2236, 2903, 3122, 4118, 4119, 5310

mote — 2595: *Matt. 7:3-5; Luke 6:41, 42*

moth, eaten — 4597: *Matt. 6:19, 20; Luke 12:33*

motheaten — 4598: *James 5:2*

mother -s — 282, 3384, 3389, 3994

motions — 3804: *Rom. 7:5*

mount -ain(s) — 3735

mourn -ed -ing — 2354, 2875, 3602, 3996, 3997

mouth -s — 1993, 3056, 4750

move -ed -er -ing — 23, 383, 761, 2125, 2206, 2795, 2796, 3056/4160, 3334, 4525, 4531, 4579, 4697, 5342

much — 23, 1280, 2425, 2470, 2579, 3123, 3366, 3383, 3386, 3433, 3588, 3745, 3761, 4055, 4056, 4124, 4180, 4183, 4214, 5118, 5248

multiply -ied -ing — 4129

multitude -s — 3461, 3793, 4128

murder -er(s) -s — 443, 3389, 3964, 4607, 5406, 5407, 5408

murmur -ed -ers -ing(s) — 1111, 1112, 1113, 1234, 1690

mused — 1260: *Luke 3:15*

music -ians — 3451, 4858: *Luke 15:25; Rev. 18:22*

must — 318, 1163, 2192, 2443, 3784

mustard — 4615: *Matt. 13:31; 17:20; Mark 4:31; Luke 13:19; 17:6*

mutual — 1722/240: *Rom. 1:12*

muzzle — 5392: *1 Cor. 9:9; 1 Tim. 5:18*

my -self; **mine** — 846, 1683, 1691, 1698, 1699, 1700, 3427, 3450

Myra — 3460: *Acts 27:5*

myrrh — 4666, 4669: *Matt. 2:11; Mark 15:23; John 19:39*

Mysia — 3465: *Acts 16:7, 8*

mystery -ies — 3466

N

Naaman — 3497: *Luke 4:27*

Naasson — 3476: *Matt. 1:4; Luke 3:32*

Nagge — 3477: *Luke 3:25*

Nahor — 3493: *Luke 3:34*

nailing; nails — 2247, 4338: *John 20:25; Col. 2:14*

Nain — 3484: *Luke 7:11*

naked -ness — 1130, 1131, 1132

name -ed -eth -s — 2564, 3004, 3686, 3687

namely — 1722: *Mark 12:31; Acts 15:22; Rom. 13:9*

Naphtali — 3508: *Matt. 4:13, 15; Rev. 7:6*

napkin — 4676: *Luke 19:20; John 11:44; 20:7*

Narcissus — 3488: *Rom. 16:11*

narrow — 2346: *Matt. 7:14*

Nathan — 3481: *Luke 3:31*

Nathanael (see **Bartholomew**) — 3482: *John 1:45-49; 21:2*

nation -s — 246, 1074, 1085, 1484

nature; natural -ly — 1078, 1083, 1103, 2596/5449, 5446, 5447, 5449, 5591

naught — 557, 1432, 1847, 1848, 2049, 2647, 2673, 3762

naughtiness — 2549: *James 1:21*

Naum — 3486: *Luke 3:25*

Nazarene -s — 3480: *Matt. 2:23; Acts 24:5*

Nazareth — 3478

Neapolis — 3496: *Acts 16:11*

near -er; **nigh** — 316, 1448, 1451, 1452, 3844, 3897, 4139, 4314, 4317

necessary; necessity -ies — 316, 318, 1876, 4314/3588/5532, 5532

neck -s — 5137

need -ed -est -eth -ful -s — 316, 318, 422, 1163, 2006, 2076/318,

2121, 2192/318, 2192/5532, 3784,
3843, 4326, 5532, 5535

needle — 4476: *Matt. 19:24; Mark 10:25;
Luke 18:25*

neglect -ed -ing; negligent — 272,
857, 3865, 3878

neighbor -s — 1069, 4040, 4139

neither — 2228, 2532, 3361, 3364,
3366, 3383, 3756, 3761, 3777

nephews — 1549: *1 Tim. 5:4*

Nereus — 3517: *Rom. 16:15*

Neri — 3518: *Luke 3:27*

nests — 2682: *Matt. 8:20; Luke 9:58*

net -s — 293, 1350, 4522

never — 3361, 3364/1519/165, 3364/
4218, 3364/4455, 3368, 3756, 3756/
1519/3588/165, 3761, 3762, 3763,
3764

nevertheless — 235, 1161, 2544,
3305, 3676, 4133

new -ness — 46, 1098, 2537, 2538,
3501, 3561, 4372

newborn — 738: *1 Pet. 2:2*

next — 839, 1206, 1836, 1887, 1966,
2064, 2087, 2192, 3342

Nicanor — 3527: *Acts 6:5*

Nicodemus — 3530: *John 3:1, 4, 9;
7:50; 19:39*

Nicolaitan(e)s — 3531: *Rev. 2:6, 15*

Nicolas — 3532: *Acts 6:5*

Nicopolis — 3533: *Titus 3:12*

Niger — 3526: *Acts 13:1*

night -s — 1273, 3571, 3574

nine; ninth — 1766, 1767, 1768

ninety — 1768: *Matt. 18:12, 13; Luke
15:4, 7*

Nineveh; Ninevites — 3535, 3536:
Matt. 12:41; Luke 11:30, 32

no; nay — 209, 235, 269, 686, 790,
1063, 1487, 3304, 3361, 3364,
3361/5100, 3367, 3756, 3761, 3762,
3765, 3777, 3780

Noah — 3575

noble — 2104, 2903: *Acts 17:11; 24:3;
26:25; 1 Cor. 1:26*

nobleman — 937, 2104/444: *Luke
19:12; John 4:46, 49*

noise -ed — 191, 1096/5408, 1255,
2350, 4500, 5456

noisome — 2556: *Rev. 16:2*

none — 208, 677, 1601, 2673, 2758,
3361, 3367, 3387, 3756, 3762, 3777,
5100/3361

noon — 3314: *Acts 22:6*

nor — 2228, 2532, 3361, 3364, 3366,
3383, 3756, 3761, 3761/3364, 3777

north — 1005, 5566: *Luke 13:29; Acts
27:12; Rev. 21:13*

note -able — 1110, 1978, 2016, 4593:
*Matt. 27:16; Acts 2:20; 4:16; Rom. 16:7;
2 Thess. 3:14*

nothing — 3114, 3361, 3361/1537/
846, 3367, 3385, 3756, 3756/5101,
3762, 3777, 3956, 3956/4487/3756,
5100/3361

notice — 4293: *2 Cor. 9:5*

notwithstanding — 235, 4133

nought (see **naught**)

**nourished; nourisheth; nourish-
ment** — 397, 1625, 1789, 2023,
5142

novice — 3504: *1 Tim. 3:6*

now — 737, 1160, 1161, 1211, 2235,
2236, 2532, 3063, 3568, 3570, 3765,
3767

number -ed — 705, 706, 1469, 2639,
2674, 3049, 3793, 4785

nurse — 5162: *1 Thess. 2:7*

nurture — 3809: *Eph. 6:4*

Nymphas — 3564: *Col. 4:15*

O

oath — 332, 3727, 3728

Obed — 5601: *Matt. 1:5; Luke 3:32*

obey -ed -ing; obedience; obedient
— 544, 3980, 1096/5255, 3982,
5218, 5219, 5255, 5293

object — 2723: *Acts 24:19*

observe -ation -ed — 3906, 3907,
4160, 4933, 5083, 5442

obtain -ed -ing — 1653, 2013, 2147,
2638, 2816, 2820, 2902, 2932, 2975,
2983, 3140, 4047, 5177

occasion — 874, 1223, 4625

occupation — 5078: *Acts 18:3; 19:25*

occupy -ied -ieth — 378, 4043, 4231:
Luke 19:13; 1 Cor. 14:16; Heb. 13:9

odor -s — 2368, 3744: *John 12:3; Phil.
4:18; Rev. 5:8; 18:13*

off — 114, 554, 568, 575, 595, 609,
631, 659, 660, 851, 1537, 1562, 1575,
1581, 1601, 1621

offend -ed -er; offense -s — 91,
264, 266, 677, 3900, 4348, 4349,
4417, 4624, 4625

offer -ed -ing(s) — 321, 399, 1325,
1435, 1494, 1929, 3646, 3930, 4374,
4376, 4689
office -er(s) — 1247, 1248, 1984,
2405, 2407, 4233, 4234, 5257
offscouring — 4067: *1 Cor. 4:13*
offspring — 1085: *Acts 17:28, 29; Rev.
22:16*
oft -en -entimes -times — 3740,
4178, 4183, 4183/5550, 4212, 4435,
4437
oil — 1637
ointment -s — 3464
old -ness — 744, 1088, 1094, 1095,
1126, 1332, 1541, 1597, 3819, 3820,
3821, 3822, 4218, 4245, 4246, 5550
olive -s — 65, 1636, 2565
Olivet — 1638: *Acts 1:12*
Olympas — 3652: *Rom. 16:15*
Omega — 5598: *Rev. 1:8, 11; 21:6; 22:13*
omitted — 863: *Matt. 23:23*
omnipotent — 3841: *Rev. 19:6*
once — 530, 2178, 3366, 3826, 4218
on — 575, 991, 1519, 1537, 1677, 1716,
1720, 1722, 1745, 1746, 1760, 1782,
1883, 1896, 1904, 1909, 1911, 1913,
1936, 1941, 1945, 1949, 1968, 2007,
2020, 2510, 2596, 3326, 3779, 3840,
3979, 4012, 4016, 4060, 4342, 5228,
5265, 5311, 5476
one -s — 240, 243, 846, 1438, 1520,
2087, 3303, 3391, 3442, 3588/3303,
3661, 3675, 3739, 3739/3303, 3956,
4861, 5100, 5129
Onesimus — 3682
Onesiphorus — 3683: *2 Tim. 1:16; 4:19*
only — 1520, 3439, 3440, 3441
open -ed -eth -ing -ly — 71, 343,
380, 455, 457, 1219, 1272, 1717,
1722/3588/5318, 1722/3954, 3856,
3954, 4271, 4977, 5136, 5320
operation -s — 1753, 1755: *1 Cor.
12:6; Col. 2:12*
opportunity — 170, 2120, 2540: *Matt.
26:16; Luke 22:6; Gal. 6:10; Phil. 4:10;
Heb. 11:15*
oppose -ed -eth -itions — 475, 477,
480, 498: *Acts 18:6; 2 Thess. 2:4;
1 Tim. 6:20; 2 Tim. 2:25*
oppress -ed — 2616, 2669: *Acts 7:24;
10:38; James 2:6*
or — 1161, 1508, 1535, 2228, 2532,
3383, 4253, 5037

oracles — 3051: *Acts 7:38; Rom. 3:2;
Heb. 5:12; 1 Pet. 4:11*
oration; orator — 1215, 4489: *Acts
12:21; 24:1*
ordain -ed — 1096, 1299, 2525, 2680,
2919, 3724, 4160, 4270, 4282, 4304,
5021, 5087, 5500
order -ly — 1299, 1930, 2517, 4748,
5001, 5010
ordinance -s — 1296, 1345, 1378,
1379, 2937, 3862
other -s — 237, 240, 243, 244, 245,
492, 846, 1520, 1565, 1622, 2084,
2087, 2548, 3062, 3588, 3739, 4008
otherwise — 243, 247, 1490, 1893,
2085, 2088
ought -est — 1163, 3784, 5534
outer; outside — 1623, 1855, 1857
outward -ly — 1722/3588/5318, 1722/
5318, 1854, 1855, 4383
outrun — 4370/5032: *John 20:4*
outwent — 4281: *Mark 6:33*
oven — 2823: *Matt. 6:30; Luke 12:28*
over — 481, 495, 561, 1224, 1276,
1277, 1330, 1537, 1537/1727, 1608,
1722, 1883, 1909, 1924, 2596, 2634,
2713, 3346, 3860, 3928, 4008, 4012,
4052, 4121, 4291, 5055, 5228, 5231,
5240
overcharge -ed — 925, 1912: *Luke
21:34; 2 Cor. 2:5*
overcome -eth; overcame — 2274,
2634, 3528
overflowed — 2626: *2 Pet. 3:6*
overlaid — 4028: *Heb. 9:4*
overmuch — 4055: *2 Cor. 2:7*
overseers; oversight — 1983, 1985:
Acts 20:28; 1 Pet. 5:2
overshadow -ed — 1982: *Matt. 17:5;
Mark 9:7; Luke 1:35; 9:34; Acts 5:15*
overtake -n — 2638, 4301: *Gal. 6:1;
1 Thess. 5:4*
overthrow -n; overthrew — 390,
396, 2647, 2690, 2692, 2693
owe -ed -est -eth — 3781, 3784,
4359
own -eth — 830, 848, 849, 1103, 1438,
1683, 1699, 2076, 2398, 2596, 4572
owner -s — 2962, 3490: *Luke 19:33;
Acts 27:11*
ox -en — 1016, 5022
Ozias — 3604: *Matt. 1:8, 9*

P

pain -ed -fulness -s — 928, 3449, 4192, 5604

pair — 2201, 2218: *Luke 2:24; Rev. 6:5*

palace — 833, 4232

pale — 5515: *Rev. 6:8*

palm -s (see **hand**) — 4474, 4475: *Matt. 26:67; Mark 14:65; John 18:22*

palm -s (see **tree**) — 5404: *John 12:13; Rev. 7:9*

palsy -ies — 3885, 3886

Pamphylia — 3828: *Acts 2:10; 13:13; 14:24; 15:38; 27:5*

paper — 5489: *2 John 1:12*

Paphos — 3974: *Acts 13:6, 13*

paps — 3149: *Luke 11:27; 23:29; Rev. 1:13*

parable -s — 3850, 3942

paradise — 3857: *Luke 23:43; 2 Cor. 12:4; Rev. 2:7*

parcel — 5564: *John 4:5*

parchments — 3200: *2 Tim. 4:13*

parents — 1118, 3962, 4269

Parmenas — 3937: *Acts 6:5*

part -ly -s — 1161, 2819, 2825, 3307, 3310, 3313, 3313/5100, 5124/3303

partakest; partaker -s — 482, 1096/ 4791, 2841, 2844, 3310, 3335, 3348, 3353, 4777, 4790, 4791, 4829, 4830

parted — 1266, 1339: *Matt. 27:35; Mark 15:24; Luke 23:34; 24:51; John 19:24; Acts 2:45*

Parthians — 3934: *Acts 2:9*

partial -ity — 87, 1252, 4346: *1 Tim. 5:21; James 2:4; 3:17*

particular -ly — 1520/1538/2596, 2596/3313, 3313, 3588/1520: *Acts 21:19; 1 Cor. 12:27; Eph. 5:33; Heb. 9:5*

partition — 5418: *Eph. 2:14*

partner -s — 2844, 3353: *Luke 5:7, 10; 2 Cor. 8:23; Phile. 1:17*

pass -ed -eth -ing; past — 390, 421, 492, 524, 565, 1096, 1224, 1230, 1276, 1279, 1330, 1353, 2064, 3327, 3819, 3844, 3855, 3881, 3899, 3928, 3944, 4266, 4281, 4302, 5230, 5235, 5242

passion -s — 3663, 3958: *Acts 1:3; 14:15; James 5:17*

passover — 3957

pastors — 4166: *Eph. 4:11*

pasture — 3542: *John 10:9*

Patara — 3959: *Acts 21:1*

paths — 5147, 5163: *Matt. 3:3; Mark 1:3; Luke 3:4; Heb. 12:13*

patient -ly; patience — 420, 1933, 3114, 3115, 3116, 5278, 5281

Patmos — 3963: *Rev. 1:9*

patriarch -s — 3966: *Acts 2:29; 7:8, 9; Heb. 7:4*

Patrobas — 3969: *Rom. 16:14*

pattern -s — 5179, 5262, 5296: *1 Tim. 1:16; Titus 2:7; Heb. 8:5; 9:23*

Paul; Paulus (see **Saul**) — 3972

Pavement — 3038: *John 19:13*

pay -ment; paid — 586, 591, 1183, 5055

peace -able -ably -makers — 1515, 1516, 1517, 1518, 2270, 2272, 4601, 4623, 5392

pearl -s — 3135

peculiar — 1519/4047, 4041: *Titus 2:14; 1 Pet. 2:9*

Peleg — 5317

pen — 2563: *3 John 1:13*

pence; penny -worth — 1220

Pentecost — 4005: *Acts 2:1; 20:16; 1 Cor. 16:8*

penury — 5303: *Luke 21:4*

people -s — 1218, 1484, 2992, 3793

peradventure — 3379, 5029: *Rom. 5:7; 2 Tim. 2:25*

perceive -ed -est -ing — 143, 991, 1097, 1492, 1921, 2147, 2334, 2638, 2657, 3539, 3708

perdition — 684

perfect -ed -ing -ion -ly -ness — 195, 197, 199, 739, 1295, 2005, 2675, 2676, 2677, 3647, 4137, 5046, 5047, 5048, 5050, 5051, 5052

perform -ance -ed — 591, 1096, 2005, 2716, 4160, 5050, 5055

Perga — 4011: *Acts 13:13, 14; 14:25*

Pergamos — 4010: *Rev. 1:11; 2:12*

perhaps — 686, 3381, 5029: *Acts 8:22; 2 Cor. 2:7; Phile. 1:15*

peril -ous -s — 2794, 5467: *Rom. 8:35; 2 Cor. 11:26; 2 Tim. 3:1*

perish -ed -eth — 599, 622, 684, 853, 1311, 1498, 1519, 2704, 4881, 5356

perjured — 1965: *1 Tim. 1:10*

permit -ted; permission — 2010,

4774: *Acts 26:1; 1 Cor. 7:6; 14:34; 16:7; Heb. 6:3*

pernicious — 684: *2 Pet. 2:2*

perplexed; perplexity — 639, 640, 1280: *Luke 9:7; 21:25; 24:4; 2 Cor. 4:8*

persecute -ed -est -ing -ion(s) -or — 1375, 1376, 1377, 1559, 2347

perseverance — 4343: *Eph. 6:18*

Persis — 4069: *Rom. 16:12*

person -s — 678, 4380, 4381, 4382, 4383, 5287

persuade -ed -est -eth -ing; persuasion — 374, 3982, 3988, 4135

pertain -eth -ing — 3348, 4012

pervert -eth -ing; perverse — 654, 1294, 3344, 3859

pestilences; pestilent — 3061: *Matt. 24:7; Luke 21:11; Acts 24:5*

Peter (see **Cephas; Simon**) — **4074**

petitions — 155: *1 John 5:15*

Phalec — 5317: *Luke 3:35*

Phanuel — 5323: *Luke 2:36*

Pharaoh — 5328: *Acts 7:10, 13; Rom. 9:17*

Phares — 5329: *Matt. 1:3; Luke 3:33*

Pharisee -s — 5330

Phenice — 5405: *Acts 27:12*

Philadelphia — 5359: *Rev. 1:11; 3:7*

Philemon — 5371: *Phile. 1:1*

Philetus — 5372: *2 Tim. 2:17*

Philip — 5376

Philippi — 5375

Philippians — 5374: *Phil. 4:15*

Philologus — 5378: *Rom. 16:15*

philosophers; philosophy — 5385, 5386: *Acts 17:18; Col. 2:8*

Phlegon — 5393: *Rom. 16:14*

Phoebe — 5402: *Rom. 16:1*

Phoenicia — 5403: *Acts 11:19; 15:3; 21:2*

Phrygia — 5435: *Acts 2:10; 16:6; 18:23*

Phygellus — 5436: *2 Tim. 1:15*

phylacteries — 5440: *Matt. 23:5*

physician -s — 2395

piece -s — 1288, 1406, 1915, 3313, 4138

pierce -ed -ing — 1330, 1338, 1574, 3572, 4044

piety — 2151: *1 Tim. 5:4*

pigeons — 4058: *Luke 2:24*

Pilate — 4091

pilgrims — 3927: *Heb. 11:13; 1 Pet. 2:11*

pillar -s — 4769: *Gal. 2:9; 1 Tim. 3:15; Rev. 3:12; 10:1*

pillow — 4344: *Mark 4:38*

pineth — 3583: *Mark 9:18*

pinnacle — 4419: *Matt. 4:5; Luke 4:9*

pipe -d -ers — 832, 834, 836: *Matt. 11:17; Luke 7:32; 1 Cor. 14:7; Rev. 18:22*

Pisidia — 4099: *Acts 13:14; 14:24*

pit — 999, 5421

pitched — 4078: *Heb. 8:2*

pitcher — 2765: *Mark 14:13; Luke 22:10*

pity -iful — 1653, 2155, 4184: *Matt. 18:33; James 5:11; 1 Pet. 3:8*

place -s — 201, 402, 1502, 1564, 1786, 3692, 3699, 3837, 4042, 5117, 5562, 5564, 5602

plague -s — 3148, 4127

plain -ly -ness — 1718, 3723, 3954

plain — 5117/3977: *Luke 6:17*

plaited; plaiting — 1708, 4120: *Matt. 27:29; Mark 15:17; John 19:2; 1 Pet. 3:3*

plant -ed -eth — 4854, 5451, 5452

platter — 3953, 4094: *Matt. 23:25, 26; Luke 11:39*

play — 3815: *1 Cor. 10:7*

please -ed -ing; pleasure -s — 699, 700, 701, 2100, 2101, 2106, 2107, 2237, 2307, 2309, 3588/1380, 4684, 4909, 5171, 5485, 5569

plentifully; plenteous — 2164, 4183: *Matt. 9:37; Luke 12:16*

plow -eth -ing — 722, 723: *Luke 9:62; 17:7; 1 Cor. 9:10*

pluck -ed — 726, 1288, 1544, 1610, 1807, 1808, 1846, 5089

poets — 4163: *Acts 17:28*

point -s — 2079, 3195: *Mark 5:23; John 4:47; Heb. 4:15; James 2:10*

poison — 2447: *Rom. 3:13; James 3:8*

polluted; pollutions — 234, 2840, 3393: *Acts 15:20; 21:28; 2 Pet. 2:20*

Pollux — 1359: *Acts 28:11*

pomp — 5325: *Acts 25:23*

pondered — 4820: *Luke 2:19*

Pontius — 4194: *Matt. 27:2; Luke 3:1, Acts 4:27; 1 Tim. 6:13*

Pontus — 4195: *Acts 2:9; 18:2; 1 Pet. 1:1*

pool — 2861: *John 5:2, 4, 7; 9:7, 11*

poor — 3993, 3998, 4433, 4434

porch -es — 4259, 4440, 4745

Porcius — 4201: *Acts 24:27*

porter — 2377: *Mark 13:34; John 10:3*

portion — 3313, 4620: *Matt. 24:51; Luke 12:42, 46; 15:12*

possess -ed -eth -ing -ion(s) -ors — 1139, 2192, 2697, 2722, 2932, 2933, 2935, 4047, 5224, 5564

possible — 102, 1410, 1415

pot -s; potter — 2763, 2764, 3582, 4713

potentate — 1413: *1 Tim. 6:15*

pound -s — 3046, 3414

pour -ed -eth -ing — 906, 1632, 2708, 2767

poverty — 4432: *2 Cor. 8:2, 9; Rev. 2:9*

powder — 3039: *Matt. 21:44; Luke 20:18*

power -ful -s — 746, 1325, 1410, 1411, 1415, 1756, 1849, 1850, 2478, 2479, 2904, 3168

Praetorium — 4232: *Mark 15:16*

praise -ed -ing -s — 133, 134, 136, 703, 1391, 1867, 1868, 2127, 5214

prating — 5396: *3 John 1:10*

pray -ed -er(s) -est -eth -ing — 1162, 1189, 1783, 2065, 2171, 2172, 3870, 4335, 4336

preach -ed -er -est -eth -ing — 189, 1229, 1256, 2097, 2605, 2782, 2783, 2784, 2980, 3954, 4137, 4283, 4296

precept — 1785: *Mark 10:5; Heb. 9:19*

precious — 927, 1784, 2472, 4185, 5092, 5093

predestinate -ed — 4309: *Rom. 8:29, 30; Eph. 1:5, 11*

preeminence — 4409, 5383: *Col. 1:18; 3 John 1:9*

preferred; preferring — 1096, 4285, 4299: *John 1:15, 27, 30; Rom. 12:10; 1 Tim. 5:21*

premeditate — 3191: *Mark 13:11*

prepare -ation -ed -ing — 2090, 2091, 2092, 2675, 2680, 3903, 3904, 4282

presbytery — 4244: *1 Tim. 4:14*

presence — 561, 1715, 1799, 2714, 3952, 4383

present -ed — 2476, 3936, 4374

present -ly — 737, 1736, 1764, 1824, 2186, 3306, 3568, 3854, 3873, 3916, 3918, 4840

preserve -ed — 2225, 4933, 4982, 5083

press (see **multitude**) — 3793: *Mark 2:4; 5:27, 30; Luke 8:19; 19:3*

press -ed -eth — 598, 916, 971, 1377, 1945, 1968, 4085, 4912

presumptuous — 5113: *2 Pet. 2:10*

pretense — 4392: *Matt. 23:14; Mark 12:40; Phil. 1:18*

prevail -ed — 2480, 2729, 3528, 5623

prevent -ed — 4399, 5348: *Matt. 17:25; 1 Thess. 4:15*

price -s — 4185, 4186, 5092

pricked; pricks — 2669, 2759: *Acts 2:37; 9:5; 26:14*

priest -hood -s — 748, 749, 2405, 2406, 2407, 2409, 2420

prince -s — 747, 758, 2232

principal -ity -ities — 746, 2596/1851

principles — 746, 4747: *Heb. 5:12; 6:1*

print — 5179: *John 20:25*

Prisca — 4251: *2 Tim. 4:19*

Priscilla — 4252: *Acts 18:2, 18, 26; Rom. 16:3; 1 Cor. 16:19*

prison -er(s) -s — 1198, 1200, 1201, 1202, 3612, 3860, 5084, 5438

private -ly — 2398, 2596/2398

privy -ily — 2977, 3918, 3922, 4894

prize — 1017: *1 Cor. 9:24; Phil. 3:14*

proceed -ed -eth -ing — 1607, 1831, 4298, 4369

Prochorus — 4402: *Acts 6:5*

proclaimed; proclaiming — 2784: *Luke 12:3; Rev. 5:2*

profane — 952, 953

profess -ed -ing -ion — 1861, 3670, 3671, 5335

profit -able -ed -eth -ing — 2173, 3786, 4297, 4298, 4851, 5539, 5622, 5623, 5624, 5624/2076

promise -ed -s — 1843, 1860, 1861, 1862, 3670, 4279

proof -s — 1382, 1732, 4135, 5039

proper — 791, 2398: *Acts 1:19; 1 Cor. 7:7; Heb. 11:23*

prophecy -ies — 4394, 4397

prophesy -ied -ieth -ing(s) — 4394, 4395

prophet -ess -s — 4396, 4397, 4398, 5578

propitiation — 2434, 2435: *Rom. 3:25; 1 John 2:2; 4:10*

proportion — 356: *Rom. 12:6*

proselyte -s — 4339: *Matt. 23:15; Acts 2:10; 6:5; 13:43*

prosper -ed -eth -ous — 2137: *Rom. 1:10; 1 Cor. 16:2; 3 John 1:2*

protest — 3513: *1 Cor. 15:31*

proud; pride — 212, 5187, 5243, 5244

prove -ed -ing — 584, 1381, 3936, 3985, 4256, 4822

proverb -s — 3850, 3942: *Luke 4:23; John 16:25, 29; 2 Pet. 2:22*

provide -ed -ing; provision — 2090, 2932, 3936, 4160, 4265, 4306, 4307

providence — 4307: *Acts 24:2*

province — 1885: *Acts 23:34; 25:1*

provoke -ed -ing; provocation — 653, 2042, 3863, 3893, 3894, 3947, 3948, 3949, 4292

prudent; prudence — 4908, 5428: *Matt. 11:25; Luke 10:21; Acts 13:7; 1 Cor. 1:19; Eph. 1:8*

psalm -s — 5567, 5568

Ptolemais — 4424: *Acts 21:7*

public -ly — 1219, 3856: *Matt. 1:19; Acts 18:28; 20:20*

publican -s — 754, 5057

publish -ed — 1096, 1308, 2784

Publius — 4196: *Acts 28:7, 8*

Pudens — 4227: *2 Tim. 4:21*

puffed; puffeth — 5448

pull -ed -ing — 385, 726, 1288, 1544, 2506, 2507

punish -ed -ment — 1349, 1557, 2009, 2849, 2851, 5097, 5098, 5099/ 1344

purchase -ed — 2932, 4046, 4047: *Acts 1:18; 8:20; 20:28; Eph. 1:14; 1 Tim. 3:13*

pure -ness -ity — 47, 53, 54, 1506, 2513

purge -ed -ing -eth — 1245, 1571, 2508, 2511, 2512, 4160/2512

purify -ied -ieth -ing -ication — 48, 49, 2511, 2512, 2514

purloining — 3557: *Titus 2:10*

purple — 4209, 4210, 4211

purpose -ed -eth — 1011, 1013, 1096/1106, 4160, 4255, 4286, 4388, 5087

purse -s — 905, 2223: *Matt. 10:9; Mark 6:8; Luke 10:4; 22:35, 36*

put -teth -ting — 115, 142, 337, 363, 506, 520, 554, 555, 595, 615, 630, 649, 654, 659, 683, 782, 863, 906,

1096, 1252, 1325, 1453, 1544, 1614, 1631, 1677, 1688, 1745, 1746, 1749, 1808, 1878, 1911, 1936, 2007, 2289, 2507, 2638, 2673, 3004, 3089, 3179, 3335, 3348, 3856, 3860, 3908, 3982, 4016, 4060, 4160, 4261, 4374, 5087, 5279, 5293, 5294, 5392, 5562

Puteoli — 4223: *Acts 28:13*

Q

quake — 1790, 4579: *Matt. 27:51; Heb. 12:21*

quarrel — 1758, 3437: *Mark 6:19; Col. 3:13*

quarter -s — 1137, 3836, 5117: *Mark 1:45; Acts 9:32; 16:3; 28:7; Rev. 20:8*

Quartus — 2890: *Rom. 16:23*

quaternions — 5069: *Acts 12:4*

queen — 938: *Matt. 12:42; Luke 11:31; Acts 8:27; Rev. 18:7*

quench -ed — 762, 4570

question -ed -ing -s — 1458, 1905, 2213, 2214, 2919, 3056, 4802

quick; quicken -ed -eth -ing — 2198, 2227, 4806

quickly — 1722/5034, 5030, 5032, 5035

quicksands — 4950: *Acts 27:17*

quiet -ness — 1515, 2263, 2270, 2271, 2272, 2687

quit — 407: *1 Cor. 16:13*

R

Rabbi — 4461

Rabboni — 4462: *John 20:16*

Raca — 4469: *Matt. 5:22*

race — 73, 4712: *1 Cor. 9:24; Heb. 12:1*

Rachel — 4478: *Matt. 2:18*

rage -ing — 66, 2830, 5433: *Luke 8:24; Acts 4:25; Jude 1:13*

Rahab — 4460, 4477: *Matt. 1:5; Heb. 11:31; James 2:25*

railed; railer; railing -s — 987, 988, 989, 3059, 3060

raiment — 1742, 2066, 2440, 2441, 4629

rain -ed — 1026, 1026/5205, 1028, 5205

rainbow — 2463: *Rev. 4:3; 10:1*

raise -ed -ing -eth — 386, 450, 1326, 1453, 1817, 1825, 1892, 4160/1999, 4891

Ramah — 4471: *Matt. 2:18*

ranks — 4237: *Mark 6:40*

ransom — 487, 3083: *Matt. 20:28; Mark 10:45; 1 Tim. 2:6*

rashly — 4312: *Acts 19:36*

rather — 2228, 2309, 3123, 3304, 4056, 4133

ravening — 724, 727: *Matt. 7:15; Luke 11:39*

ravens — 2876: *Luke 12:24*

reach -ed -ing — 190, 1901, 2185, 5342

read -est -eth -ing — 314, 320

ready -iness — 1451, 2090, 2092, 2093, 2130, 3195, 3903, 4288, 4289, 4689

reap -ed -ers -est -eth -ing — 270, 2325, 2327

rear — 1453, 1846: *John 2:20*

reason -able -ed -ing — 701, 1223, 1256, 1260, 1261, 1537, 1752, 3049, 3050, 3056, 4802, 4803, 4817

Rebecca — 4479: *Rom. 9:10*

rebuke -ed -ing — 298, 1651, 1969, 2008, 2192/1694

receive -ed -edst -eth -ing; receipt — 308, 324, 353, 354, 568, 588, 618, 1183, 1209, 1325, 1523, 1653, 1926, 2210, 2865, 2983, 3028, 3335, 3336, 3549, 3858, 3880, 4327, 4355, 4356, 4687, 4732, 5058, 5264, 5274, 5562

reckon -ed -eth — 3049, 4868/3056

recommended — 3860: *Acts 14:26; 15:40*

recompense -ed — 467, 468, 489, 591, 3405

reconcile -ed -iation -ing — 604, 1259, 2433, 2643, 2644

record — 3140, 3141, 3143, 3144

recover -ing — 309, 366, 2192/2573: *Mark 16:18; Luke 4:18; 2 Tim. 2:26*

red — 4449, 4450: *Matt. 16:2, 3; Rev. 6:4; 12:3*

Red Sea — 2281: *Acts 7:36; Heb. 11:29*

redeem -ed -ing; redemption — 59, 629, 1805, 3084, 3085, 4160/3085

redound — 4052: *2 Cor. 4:15*

reed — 2563

reformation — 1357: *Heb. 9:10*

refrain — 868, 3973: *Acts 5:38; 1 Pet. 3:10*

refresh -ed -ing — 373, 403, 404, 1958/5177, 4875

refuge — 2703: *Heb. 6:18*

refuse -ed — 579, 720, 3868

regard -ed -est -eth -ing — 272, 991, 1788, 1914, 3851, 4337, 5426

regeneration — 3824: *Matt. 19:28; Titus 3:5*

region -s — 2825, 4066, 5561

rehearsed — 312, 756: *Acts 11:4; 14:27*

reign -ed -eth — 757, 936, 2192/932, 2231, 4821

reins — 3510: *Rev. 2:23*

reject -ed -eth — 96, 114, 593, 1609, 3868

rejoice -ed -eth -ing — 21, 2165, 2620, 2744, 2745, 2746, 4796, 5463

release -ed — 630

relieve -ed; relief — 1248, 1884: *Acts 11:29; 1 Tim. 5:10, 16*

religion; religious — 2356, 2357, 2454, 4576

remain -ed -est -eth -ing — 620, 1265, 3062, 3306, 3588/3063, 4035, 4052

remember -ed -est -eth -ing; remembrance — 363, 364, 3403, 3415, 3417, 3418, 3421, 5179, 5279, 5280, 5294

remit -ted; remission — 859, 863, 3929

remnant — 2640, 3005, 3062: *Matt. 22:6; Rom. 9:27; 11:5; Rev. 11:13; 12:17; 19:21*

remove -ed -ing — 142, 2795, 3179, 3327, 3331, 3346, 3351, 3911

Remphan — 4481: *Acts 7:43*

rend; rent — 1284, 4048, 4486, 4682, 4977, 4978

render -ing — 467, 591

renew -ed -ing — 340, 341, 342, 365

renounced — 550: *2 Cor. 4:2*

repay — 467, 591, 661: *Luke 10:35; Rom. 12:19; Phile. 1:19*

repent -ance -ed -eth — 278, 3338, 3340, 3341

repetitions — 945: *Matt. 6:7*

repliest — 470: *Rom. 9:20*

report -ed — 189, 191, 312, 518, 987, 1310, 1426, 2162, 2163, 3140, 3141

reproach -ed -es -est -fully — 819, 3059/5484, 3679, 3680, 3681, 5195, 5196, 5484

reprobate -s — 96: *Rom. 1:28; 2 Cor. 13:5-7; 2 Tim. 3:8; Titus 1:16*

reprove -ed; reproof — 1650, 1651

reputation — 1380, 1784, 2758, **5093**: *Acts 5:34; Gal. 2:2; Phil. 2:7, 29*

request -s — 155, 1162, 1189: *Rom. 1:10; Phil. 1:4; 4:6*

require -ed -ing — 154, 155, 523, 1096, 1567, 2212, 4238

requite — 287/591: *1 Tim. 5:4*

rescued — 1807: *Acts 23:27*

resemble — 3666: *Luke 13:18*

reserve -ed — 2641, 5083

residue — 2645, 3062: *Mark 16:13; Acts 15:17*

resist -ed -eth — 436, 478, 496, 498

resolved — 1097: *Luke 16:4*

resort -ed — 2064, 4848, 4863, 4905

respect -er — 578, 678, 1914, 2596, 3313, 3382, 4380, 4381, 4382

rest -ed -eth -s — 372, 373, 425, 1515, 1879, 1954, 1981, 2192/372, 2270, 2663, 2664, 2681, 2838, 3062, 4520

restitution — 605: *Acts 3:21*

restore -ed -eth — 591, 600, 2675

restrained — 2664: *Acts 14:18*

resurrection — 386, 1454, 1815

retain -ed — 2192, 2722, 2902: *John 20:23; Rom. 1:28; Phile. 1:13*

return -ed -ing — 344, 360, 390, 844, 1877, 1880, 1994, 5290

Reu — 4466: *Luke 3:35*

Reuben — 4502: *Rev. 7:5*

reveal -ed; revelation -s — 601, 602, 5537

revellings — 2970: *Gal. 5:21; 1 Pet. 4:3*

revenge -er (see **vengeance;**

avenge) — 1556, 1557, 1558: *Rom. 13:4; 2 Cor. 7:11; 10:6*

reverence — 127, 1788, 5399

revile -ed -ers -est — 486, 987, 3058, 3060, 3679

revived — 326: *Rom. 7:9; 14:9*

reward -ed -er — 469, 514, 591, 2603, 3405, 3406, 3408

Rhegium — 4484: *Acts 28:13*

Rhesa — 4488: *Luke 3:27*

Rhoda — 4498: *Acts 12:13*

Rhodes — 4499: *Acts 21:1*

rich -es -ly — 4145, 4146, 4147, 4148, 4149, 5536

right — 1188

right -ly — 1342, 1849, 2117, 3723, 4993

righteous -ly -ness — 1341, 1342, 1343, 1344, 1345, 1346, 2118

ring — 1146, 5554: *Luke 15:22; James 2:2*

ringleader — 4414: *Acts 24:5*

riot -ing -ous — 810, 811, 2970, **5172**: *Luke 15:13; Rom. 13:13; Titus 1:6; 1 Pet. 4:4; 2 Pet. 2:13*

ripe — 187, 3583: *Rev. 14:15, 18*

rise -en -eth -ing; rose — 305, 386, 393, 450, 1453, 1817, 1881, 4891, 4911

river -s — 4215

roareth; roaring — 2278, 3455, **5612**: *Luke 21:25; 1 Pet. 5:8; Rev. 10:3*

robbed; robber -s -y — 725, 2417, 3027, 4813

robe -s — 2066, 2440, 4749, 5511

Roboam — 4497: *Matt. 1:7*

Rock; rock -s — 4073, 5138/5117

rod -s — 4463, 4464

roll -ed — 617, 1507, 4351

Roman -s — 4514

Rome — 4516

roof — 4721: *Matt. 8:8; Mark 2:4; Luke 7:6*

room -s — 473, 508, 1240, 4411, 5117, 5253, 5562

root -ed -s — 1610, 4491, 4492

ropes — 4979: *Acts 27:32*

rough — 5138: *Luke 3:5*

round — 2943, 2944, 3840, 4015, 4017, 4026, 4033, 4034, 4038, 4039, 4066

rowed; rowing — **1643**: *Mark 6:48; John 6:19*

royal — **934, 937**: *Acts 12:21; James 2:8; 1 Pet. 2:9*

rubbing — **5597**: *Luke 6:1*

rudder — **4079**: *Acts 27:40*

rude — **2399**: *2 Cor. 11:6*

rudiments — **4747**: *Col. 2:8, 20*

rue — **4076**: *Luke 11:42*

Rufus — **4504**: *Mark 15:21; Rom. 16:13*

ruin -s — **2679, 4485**: *Luke 6:49; Acts 15:16*

rule -er(s) -eth -ing — **746, 752, 755, 757, 758, 1018, 2232, 2233, 2525, 2583, 2888, 4165, 4173, 4291**

rumor -s — **189, 3056**: *Matt. 24:6; Mark 13:7; Luke 7:17*

run -neth -ning; ran — **1530, 1532, 1632, 1998, 2027, 2701, 3729, 4063, 4370, 4390, 4890, 4936, 5143, 5240, 5295**

rushed; rushing — **3729, 5342**: *Acts 2:2; 19:29*

rust — **1035, 2447**: *Matt. 6:19, 20; James 5:3*

Ruth — **4503**: *Matt. 1:5*

S

sabachthani — **4518**: *Matt. 27:46; Mark 15:34*

Sabaoth — **4519**: *Rom. 9:29; James 5:4*

sabbath — **4315, 4521**

sackcloth — **4526**: *Matt. 11:21; Luke 10:13; Rev. 6:12; 11:3*

sacrifice -ed -s — **1494, 2378, 2380**

sacrilege — **2416**: *Rom. 2:22*

sad — **4659, 4768**: *Matt. 6:16; Mark 10:22; Luke 24:17*

Sadducees — **4523**

Sadoc — **4524**: *Matt. 1:14*

safe -ly -ty — **803, 806, 809, 1295, 5198**

sail -ed -ing -ors — **321, 636, 1020, 1276, 1277, 1602, 3492, 3881, 3896, 4126, 4144, 4632, 5284**

saint -s — **40**

sake -s — **1722, 1752**

Salah — **4527**: *Luke 3:35*

Salamis — **4529**: *Acts 13:5*

Salem (see **Jerusalem**) — **4532**: *Heb. 7:1, 2*

Salim — **4530**: *John 3:23*

Salmon — **4533**: *Matt. 1:4, 5; Luke 3:32*

Salmone — **4534**: *Acts 27:7*

Salome — **4539**: *Mark 15:40; 16:1*

salt -ed -ness — **217, 233, 251, 252, 1096/358**: *Matt. 5:13; Mark 9:49, 50; Luke 14:34; Col. 4:6; James 3:12*

salute -ation(s) -ed -eth — **782, 783**

Samaria; Samaritan -s — **4540, 4541**

same; selfsame — **846, 846/5124, 1565, 2532, 3673, 3778, 4954, 5023, 5026, 5126, 5129, 5615**

Samos — **4544**: *Acts 20:15*

Samothracia — **4548**: *Acts 16:11*

Samson — **4546**: *Heb. 11:32*

Samuel — **4545**: *Acts 3:24; 13:20; Heb. 11:32*

sanctify -ication -ied -ieth — **37, 38**

sanctuary — **39**: *Heb. 8:2; 9:1, 2; 13:11*

sand — **285**: *Matt. 7:26; Rom. 9:27; Heb. 11:12; Rev. 13:1; 20:8*

sandals — **4547**: *Matt. 6:9; Acts 12:8*

Sapphira — **4551**: *Acts 5:1*

sapphire — **4552**: *Rev. 21:19*

Sarah — **4564**: *Rom. 4:19; 9:9; Heb. 11:11; 1 Pet. 3:6*

sardine (see **sardius**) — **4555**: *Rev. 4:3*

Sardis — **4554**: *Rev. 1:11; 3:1, 4*

sardius (see **sardine**) — **4556**: *Rev. 21:20*

sardonyx — **4557**: *Rev. 21:20*

Sarepta — **4558**: *Luke 4:26*

Satan — **4567**

satisfy -ing — **4140, 5526**: *Mark 8:4; Col. 2:23*

Saul (see **Paul**) — **4569**

save -ing (see **except**) — **235, 1508, 2228, 3844, 3924, 4133**

save -ed -ing; Savior; salvation — **1295, 3924, 4047, 4982, 4990, 4991, 4992, 5442**

savor -est — **2175, 3471, 3744, 5426**

sawn — 4249: *Heb. 11:37*
say -est -ing(s); said -st; saith —
471, 669, 2036, 2046, 2980, 2981,
3004, 3056, 3058, 4280, 4483,
4487, 5335, 5346
scales — 3013: *Acts 9:18*
scarce -ly — 3433: *Acts 14:18; 27:7;
Rom. 5:7; 1 Pet. 4:18*
scarlet — 2847: *Matt. 27:28; Heb.
9:19; Rev. 17:3, 4; 18:12, 16*
scattered; scattereth — 1262,
1287, 1289, 1290, 4496, 4650
scepter — 4464: *Heb. 1:8*
Sceva — 4630: *Acts 19:14*
schism — 4978: *1 Cor. 12:25*
school — 4981: *Acts 19:9*
schoolmaster — 3807: *Gal. 3:24, 25*
science — 1108: *1 Tim. 6:20*
scoffers — 1703: *2 Pet. 3:3*
scorch -ed — 2739: *Matt. 13:6; Mark
4:6; Rev. 16:8, 9*
scorn — 2606: *Matt. 9:24; Mark 5:40;
Luke 8:53*
scorpion -s — 4651: *Luke 10:19;
11:12; Rev. 9:3, 5, 10*
scourge -ed -eth -ing(s) — 3146,
3147, 3148, 3164, 5416, 5417
scribe -s — 1122
scrip — 4082: *Matt. 10:10; Mark 6:8;
Luke 9:3; 10:4; 22:35, 36*
Scripture -s — 1121, 1124
scroll — 975: *Rev. 6:14*
Scythian — 4658: *Col. 3:11*
sea -s — 1337, 1724, 2281, 3864,
3882, 3989
seal -ed -ing -s — 2696, 4972,
4973
seam — 729: *John 19:23*
search -ed -eth -ing — 350, 1830,
1833, 2045
seared — 2743: *1 Tim. 4:2*
season -ed — 741: *Mark 9:50; Luke
14:34; Col. 4:6*
season -s — 171, 2121, 2540, 3641,
4340, 5550, 5610
seat -s — 968, 2362, 2382, 2515,
4410
second -arily — 1207, 1208
secret -ly -s — 614, 2926, 2927,
2928, 2931, 2977, 4601, 5009
sect — 139: *Acts 5:17; 15:5; 24:5; 26:5;
28:22*
Secundus — 4580: *Acts 20:4*

secure -ity — 2425, 4160/275: *Matt.
28:14; Acts 17:9*
sedition -s — 1370, 4714: *Luke
23:19, 25; Acts 24:5; Gal. 5:20*
seduce -ing -ers — 635, 1114,
4105, 4108: *Mark 13:22; 1 Tim. 4:1;
2 Tim. 3:13; 1 John 2:26; Rev. 2:20*
see -ing -est -eth; saw -est —
308, 542, 990, 991, 1063, 1227,
1492, 1512, 1689, 1893, 1894,
1897, 2147, 2300, 2334, 2396,
2400, 2477, 2529, 3070, 3467,
3700, 3708, 3754, 4275, 4308,
5316, 5461
seed -s — 4687, 4690, 4701, 4703
seek -est -eth -ing; sought —
327, 1567, 1934, 2212
seem -ed -eth — 1096/2107, 1380,
5316
seize — 2722: *Matt. 21:38*
Seleucia — 4581: *Acts 13:4*
self — 846, 1683, 4572: *John 5:30;
17:5; 1 Cor. 4:3; Phile. 1:19; 1 Pet.
2:24*
selfwilled — 829: *Titus 1:7; 2 Pet.
2:10*
sell -er -eth; sold — 591, 1710,
4097, 4211, 4453
selves — 846, 1438, 5367
Semei — 4584: *Luke 3:26*
senate — 1087: *Acts 5:21*
send -eth -ing; sent — 375, 628,
630, 649, 652, 657, 863, 906, 1026,
1032, 1544, 1599, 1821, 3343,
3992, 4882
senses — 145: *Heb. 5:14*
sensual — 5591: *James 3:15; Jude
1:19*
sentence — 610, 1948, 2919: *Luke
23:24; Acts 15:19; 2 Cor. 1:9*
separate -ed — 873, 5562
sepulcher -s — 3418, 3419, 5028
Sergius — 4588: *Acts 13:7*
sergeants — 4465: *Acts 16:35, 38*
serpent -s — 2062, 3789
Serug — 4562: *Luke 3:35*
servant -s — 1249, 1401, 1402,
3407, 3411, 3610, 3816, 5257
serve -ed -eth -ice -ing — 1247,
1248, 1398, 2324, 2999, 3000,
3009, 5256
set -ter -teth -ting — 321, 345,
377, 392, 461, 584, 630, 649, 816,

968, 1299, 1325, 1369, 1416, 1847,
1848, 1913, 1930, 1940, 2007,
2064, 2350, 2476, 2521, 2523,
2525, 2604, 2749, 3326, 3908,
4060, 4270, 4295, 4388, 4741,
4776, 4900, 4972, 5002, 5021,
5087, 5394, 5426
Seth — 4589: *Luke 3:38*
settle -ed — 1476, 2311, 5087: *Luke
21:14; Col. 1:23; 1 Pet. 5:10*
seven -th — 1442, 2033, 2034, 2035
seventy — 1440, 1441: *Matt. 18:22;
Luke 10:1, 17*
sever — 873: *Matt. 13:49*
several -ly — 303/1520, 2398: *Matt.
25:15; 1 Cor. 12:11; Rev. 21:21*
severity — 663: *Rom. 11:22*
seweth — 1976: *Mark 2:21*
shadow -ing — 644, 2683, 4639
shake -n; shook — 660, 1621,
4531, 4579
shame -facedness -fully — 127,
149, 152, 808, 818, 819, 821, 1788,
1791, 2617, 3856, 5195
shape -s — 1491, 3667: *Luke 3:22;
John 5:37; Rev. 9:7*
Sharon — 4565: *Acts 9:35*
sharp -er -ly -ness — 664, 3691,
5114
shave -n — 3587: *Acts 21:24; 1 Cor.
11:5, 6*
Shealtiel — 4528: *Matt. 1:12; Luke
3:27*
shearer; shorn — 2751: *Acts 8:32;
18:18; 1 Cor. 11:6*
sheath — 2336: *John 18:11*
Shechem — 4966: *Acts 7:16*
shed -ding — 130, 1632
sheep — 4262, 4263
sheepfold — 833/4263: *John 10:1*
sheepskins — 3374: *Heb. 11:37*
sheet — 3607: *Acts 10:11; 11:5*
Shem — 4590: *Luke 3:36*
shepherd -s — 750, 4166
shewbread — 740/4286, 4286/740:
*Matt. 12:4; Mark 2:26; Luke 6:4; Heb.
9:2*
shield — 2375: *Eph. 6:16*
shine -ed -eth -ing; shone — 796,
797, 826, 1584, 2989, 4015, 4034,
4744, 5316
ship -ping -s — 3490, 3491, 4142,
4143

shipmaster — 2942: *Rev. 18:17*
shipmen — 3492: *Acts 27:27, 30*
shipwreck — 3489: *2 Cor. 11:25;
1 Tim. 1:19*
shivers — 4937: *Rev. 2:27*
shoes; shod — 5265, 5266
shoot -eth — 4160, 4261: *Mark 4:32;
Luke 21:30*
shore — 123, 4358, 5491
short -ened — 2856, 3641, 4932,
4958, 5302, 5610
shortly — 1722/5034, 2112, 5030,
5031, 5032
should -est — 1163, 3195, 3784
shoulders — 5606: *Matt. 23:4; Luke
15:5*
shout — 2019, 2752: *Acts 12:22;
1 Thess. 4:16*
show -ed -est -eth -ing — 312,
322, 323, 518, 584, 1165, 1166,
1213, 1325, 1325/1717/1096,
1334, 1653, 1718, 1731, 1754,
1804, 1925, 2097, 2146, 2151,
2605, 2698, 3004, 3056, 3170,
3377, 3700, 3930, 3936, 4160,
4293, 4392, 5263, 5319
shower — 3655: *Luke 12:54*
shrines — 3485: *Acts 19:24*
shun -ned — 4026, 5288: *Acts 20:27;
2 Tim. 2:16*
shut -teth — 608, 2623, 2808, 4788
sick -ly -ness(es) — 732, 769, 770,
772, 2192/2560, 2577, 3554, 3885,
4445
sickle — 1407: *Mark 4:29; Rev.
14:14–19*
side — 492, 1188, 1782, 3313, 3840,
3844, 4008, 4125
Sidon — 4605
sift — 4617: *Luke 22:31*
sighed — 389, 4727: *Mark 7:34; 8:12*
sight -s — 308, 309, 991, 1491,
1715, 1726, 1799, 2714, 2335,
3705, 3706, 3788, 3844, 5324,
5400
sign -s — 1770, 3902, 4592
signify -ied -ieth -ing -ication —
880, 1213, 1229, 1718, 4591
Silas (see **Silvanus**) — 4609
silence — 2271, 4601, 4602, 5392
silk — 4596: *Rev. 18:12*
silly — 1133: *2 Tim. 3:6*
Siloam — 4611: *Luke 13:4; John 9:7, 11*

Silvanus (see **Silas**) — 4610: *2 Cor.
1:19; 1 Thess. 1:1; 2 Thess. 1:1; 1 Pet.
5:12*

silver — 693, 694, 696, 1406

silversmith — 695: *Acts 19:24*

Simeon — 4826

similitude — 3665, 3667, 3669:
Rom. 5:14; Heb. 7:15; James 3:9

Simon — 4613

simple; simplicity — 172, 185, 572:
Rom. 12:8; 16:18, 19; 2 Cor. 1:12; 11:3

sin -ful -ned -ner(s) -neth -s (see
transgress) — 264, 265, 266, 268,
361, 3781, 3900, 4258

Sinai — 4614: *Acts 7:30, 38; Gal. 4:24,
25*

since — 575, 575/3739, 1537, 1893,
1894, 3326, 5613

sincere -ity -ly — 55, 97, 861,
1103, 1505, 1506

sing -ing; sang; sung — 103, 5214,
5567

single -ness — 572, 573, 858: *Matt.
6:22; Luke 11:34; Acts 2:46; Eph. 6:5;
Col. 3:22*

sink; sunk — 1036, 2670, 2702,
5087: *Matt. 14:30; Luke 5:7; 9:44;
Acts 20:9*

sir -s — 435, 2962

sister -s — 79, 431

sit -test -teth -ting; sat — 339,
345, 347, 377, 1910, 2516, 2521,
2523, 2621, 2625, 3869, 4775,
4776, 4873

six -th — 1803, 1812, 1835

sixteen — 1440/1803: *Acts 27:37*

sixty -fold (see **threescore**) —
1835: *Matt. 13:8, 23; Mark 4:8, 20*

skin — 1193: *Mark 1:6*

skull — 2898: *Matt. 27:33; Mark 15:22;
John 19:17*

sky — 3772: *Matt. 16:2, 3; Luke 12:56;
Heb. 11:12*

slack -ness — 1019, 1022: *2 Pet. 3:9*

slanderers; slanderously — 987,
1228: *Rom. 3:8; 1 Tim. 3:11*

slaughter — 2871, 5408, 4967: *Acts
8:32; 9:1; Rom. 8:36; Heb. 7:1; James
5:5*

slaves — 4983: *Rev. 18:13*

slay; slain; slew — 337, 615, 1315,
1722/5408/599, 2380, 2695, 4968,
4969, 5407

sleep -est -eth -ing; slept —
1852, 1853, 2518, 2837, 5258

sleight — 2940: *Eph. 4:14*

slip — 3901: *Heb. 2:1*

slothful — 3576, 3636: *Matt. 25:26;
Rom. 12:11; Heb. 6:12*

slow -ly — 692, 1021: *Luke 24:25;
Acts 27:7; Titus 1:12; James 1:9*

slumber -ed -eth — 2659, 3573:
Matt. 25:5; Rom. 11:8; 2 Pet. 2:3

small -est — 1646, 2485, 3398,
3641, 3795, 4142, 4979

smell -ing — 2175, 3750: *1 Cor.
12:17; Phil. 4:18*

smite -est -eth; smitten; smote
— 851, 1194, 1325/4475, 3817,
3960, 4141, 4474, 5180

smoke -ing — 2586, 5187

smooth — 3006: *Luke 3:5*

Smyrna — 4667, 4668: *Rev. 1:11; 2:8*

snare — 1029, 3803

snow — 5510: *Matt. 28:3; Mark 9:3;
Rev. 1:14*

so -ever — 686, 1161, 1437, 1519,
2443, 2504, 2532, 3123, 3303,
3365, 3366, 3383, 3483, 3634,
3668, 3704, 3745/302, 3761, 3767,
3779, 4819, 5023, 5037, 5082,
5118, 5124, 5613, 5615, 5620

sober -ly -ness; sobriety —
1519/4993, 3524, 3525, 4993,
4994, 4996, 4997, 4998

Sodom — 4670

soft -ly — 3120, 5285: *Matt. 11:8;
Luke 7:25; Acts 27:13*

sojourn -ed -ing — 1510/3941,
3939, 3940: *Acts 7:6; Heb. 11:9;
1 Pet. 1:17*

soldier -s — 4753, 4754, 4757, 4758

solitary — 2048: *Mark 1:35*

Solomon — 4672

**some -body -thing -time(s) -
what** — 243, 575/3313, 1161,
1520, 2087, 3381, 3588,
3588/3303, 4218, 5100, 5207

Son; son -s — 431, 3816, 5043,
5206, 5207

song -s — 5603: *Eph. 5:19; Col. 3:16;
Rev. 5:9; 14:3; 15:3*

soon -er — 1096, 2112, 3711, 3752,
3753, 3916, 5030, 5032

soothsaying — 3132: *Acts 16:16*

sop — 5596: *John 13:26, 27, 30*

Sopater — 4986: *Acts 20:4*
sorcerer -s; sorcery -ies — 3095, 3096, 3097, 5331, 5332, 5333
sore -er — 23, 1568, 1630, 2425, 2560, 3029, 3173, 4183, 4970, 5501
sore -s — 1668, 1669: *Luke 16:20, 21; Rev. 16:2, 11*
sorrow -ed -ful -ing -s; sorry — 253, 3076, 3077, 3600, 3601, 3997, 4036, 5604
sort — 516, 3313, 3697
Sosipater — 4989: *Rom. 16:21*
Sosthenes — 4988: *Acts 18:17; 1 Cor. 1:1*
soul -s — 5590
sound -ness — 3647, 4995, 5198, 5199
sound -ed -ing -s — 1001, 1096, 1837, 2278, 2279, 4537, 5353, 5456
south — 3047, 3314, 3558
sow -ed -er -est -eth -n — 4687, 5300
space — 575, 1024, 1292, 1339, 1909, 4158, 5550
Spain — 4681: *Rom. 15:24, 28*
spare -ed -ing — 4052, 5339
sparingly — 5340: *2 Cor. 9:6*
sparrows — 4765: *Matt. 10:29, 31; Luke 12:6, 7*
speak -er -est -eth -ing(s); spake; spoken — 226, 312, 368, 400, 483, 626, 653, 669, 987, 988, 1097, 1256, 2036, 2046, 2551, 2605, 2635, 2636, 2980, 3004, 3056, 4180, 4277, 4280, 4354, 4369, 4377, 4483, 4814, 5350, 5537, 5573
spear — 3057: *John 19:34*
spearmen — 1187: *Acts 23:23*
special — 3756/3858/5177: *Acts 19:11*
spectacle — 2302: *1 Cor. 4:9*
speech -es -less — 1769, 2129, 2974, 2981, 3056, 3072, 3424, 5392
speed -ily — 1722/5034, 5463, 5613/5033: *Luke 18:8; Acts 17:5; 2 John 1:10, 11*
spend -est; spent — 1159, 1230, 1550, 2119, 2827, 4160, 4298, 4321, 4325, 5551

spew — 1692: *Rev. 3:16*
spices — 759: *Mark 16:1; Luke 23:56; 24:1; John 19:40*
spikenard — 3487/4101: *Mark 14:3; John 12:3*
spilled — 1632: *Mark 2:22; Luke 5:37*
spin — 3514: *Matt. 6:28; Luke 12:27*
Spirit; spirit -s -ual -ually — 3588/4151, 4151, 4152, 4153, 5326
spit -ted; spat; spittle — 1716, 4427, 4429
spitefully — 5195: *Matt. 22:6; Luke 18:32*
spoil -ed -ing -s — 205, 554, 724, 1283, 4661, 4812
sponge — 4699: *Matt. 27:48; Mark 15:36; John 19:29*
sporting — 1792: *2 Pet. 2:13*
spot -s -ted — 299, 784, 4694, 4695, 4696
spread — 1268, 1310, 1831, 4766, 5291
spring -ing; sprang; sprung — 242, 305, 393, 985, 1080, 1530, 1816, 4855, 5453
sprinkled; sprinkling — 4378, 4472, 4473: *Heb. 9:13, 19, 21; 10:22; 11:28; 12:24; 1 Pet. 1:2*
spy -ies — 1455, 2684, 2685: *Luke 20:20; Gal. 2:4; Heb. 11:31*
Stachys — 4720: *Rom. 16:9*
staff; staves — 3586, 4464
staggered — 1252: *Rom. 4:20*
stairs — 304: *Acts 21:35, 40*
stall — 5336: *Luke 13:15*
stand -est -eth -ing; stood — 450, 639, 1453, 1510, 2186, 2192/4714, 2476, 2944, 3306, 3936, 4026, 4739, 4836, 4921
star -s — 792, 798, 5459
state — 3588/2596, 3588/4012
stature — 2244: *Matt. 6:27; Luke 2:52; 12:25; 19:3; Eph. 4:13*
staunched — 2476: *Luke 8:44*
stayed — 1907, 2722: *Luke 4:42; Acts 19:22*
stead — 5228: *2 Cor. 5:20; Phile. 1:13*
steadfast -ly -ness — 816, 949, 1476, 4342, 4731, 4733, 4740, 4741
steal; stole — 2813
steep — 2911: *Matt. 8:32; Mark 5:13; Luke 8:33*

Stephanas — 4734: *1 Cor. 1:16; 16:15, 17*
Stephen — 4735
stepped; steppeth; steps — 1684, 2487, 2597: *John 5:4, 7; Rom. 4:12; 2 Cor. 12:18; 1 Pet. 2:21*
stern — 4403: *Acts 27:29*
steward -ship -s — 2012, 3621, 3622, 3623
sticks — 5434: *Acts 28:3*
stiffnecked — 4644: *Acts 7:51*
still — 2089, 2476, 4357, 5392
sting -s — 2759: *1 Cor. 15:55, 56; Rev. 9:10*
stinketh — 3605: *John 11:39*
stir -red -reth — 329, 383, 1326, 1892, 3947, 3951, 4531, 4787, 4797, 5017
stock — 1085: *Acts 13:26; Phil. 3:5*
stocks — 3586: *Acts 16:24*
Stoics — 4770: *Acts 17:18*
stomach — 4751: *1 Tim. 5:23*
stone -ed -s -est -y — 2642, 2991, 3034, 3035, 3036, 3037, 4074, 4075, 5586
stoop -ed -ing — 2955, 3879
stop -ped — 1993, 4912, 5420: *Acts 7:57; Rom. 3:19; 2 Cor. 11:10; Titus 1:11; Heb. 11:33*
store — 597, 2343: *1 Cor. 16:2; 1 Tim. 6:19; 2 Pet. 3:7*
storehouse — 5009: *Luke 12:24*
storm — 2978: *Mark 4:37; Luke 8:23*
straight — 461, 2113, 2116, 2117, 3717
straightway — 1824, 2112, 2117, 3916
strain — 1368: *Matt. 23:24*
strait -ened -est -ly — 196, 547, 4183, 4728, 4729, 4912
strange -er -ers — 241, 245, 1854, 1927, 2087, 3579, 3580, 3581, 3861, 3927, 3939, 3940, 3941, 5381
strangled — 4156: *Acts 15:20, 29; 21:25*
stream — 4215: *Luke 6:48, 49*
street -s — 58, 4113, 4505
strength -en -ened -eneth -ening — 772, 1411, 1412, 1743, 1765, 1849, 1991, 2479, 2480, 2901, 2904, 4599, 4732, 4741

stretch -ed -ing — 1600, 1614, 1911, 5239
strewed — 1287, 4766: *Matt. 21:8; 25:24, 26; Mark 11:8*
strike -er -eth; struck; stricken — 906, 1325/4475, 3817, 3960, 4131, 4260, 5180, 5465
string — 1199: *Mark 7:35*
stripes — 3468, 4127
stripped — 1562: *Matt. 27:28; Luke 10:30*
strive -ed -eth -ing(s); strove; strife -s — 75, 118, 464, 485, 1264, 2051, 2052, 2054, 3054, 3055, 3163, 3164, 4865, 4866, 5379, 5389
strong -er — 1415, 1743, 1753, 2478, 2901, 3173, 3794, 4608, 4731, 4732
stubble — 2562: *1 Cor. 3:12*
stuck — 2043: *Acts 27:41*
study — 4704, 5389: *1 Thess. 4:11; 2 Tim. 2:15*
stuff — 4632: *Luke 17:31*
stumble -ed -eth -ing — 4350, 4417, 4625
stumblingblock; stumbling- stone — 3037/4348, 4348, 4625
subdue -ed — 2610, 5293: *1 Cor. 15:28; Phil. 3:21; Heb. 11:33*
subject -ed -ion — 1379, 1396, 1777, 3663, 5292, 5293
submit -ted -ting — 5226, 5293
suborned — 5260: *Acts 6:11*
substance — 3776, 5223, 5224, 5287: *Luke 8:3; 15:13; Heb. 10:34; 11:1*
subtlely; subtlety — 1388, 2686, 3834: *Matt. 26:4; Acts 7:19; 13:10; 2 Cor. 11:3*
subvert -ed -ing — 384, 396, 1612, 2692: *Acts 15:24; 2 Tim. 2:14; Titus 1:11; 3:11*
succor -ed -er — 997, 4368: *Rom. 16:2; 2 Cor. 6:2; Heb. 2:18*
such — 1170, 3588, 3592, 3634, 3748, 3778, 5023, 5107, 5108, 5125, 5128, 5130
suck -ed -lings — 2337
sudden -ly — 160, 869, 1810, 1819, 5030
sue — 2919: *Matt. 5:40*
suffer -ed -est -eth -ing(s) —

430, 818, 863, 971, 1325, 1377,
1439, 2010, 2210, 2552, 2553,
2558, 2967, 3114, 3804, 3805,
3958, 4310, 4330, 4722, 4778,
4841, 5159, 5254, 5278, 5302
suffice -eth -iency -ient — 713,
714, 841, 2425, 2426
sum — 2774, 5092: *Acts 7:16; 22:28;
Heb. 8:1*
summer — 2330: *Matt. 24:32; Mark
13:28; Luke 21:30*
sumptuously — 2983: *Luke 16:19*
sun — 2246
sunder — 1371: *Luke 12:46*
sundry — 4181: *Heb. 1:1*
sup -ped -per — 1172, 1173
superfluity; superfluous — 4050,
4053: *2 Cor. 9:1; James 1:21*
superscription — 1923: *Matt. 22:20;
Mark 12:16; 15:26; Luke 20:24; 23:38*
superstition — 1175: *Acts 25:19*
superstitious — 1174: *Acts 17:22*
supplication -s — 1162, 2428: *Acts
1:14; Eph. 6:18; Phil. 4:6; 1 Tim. 2:1;
5:5; Heb. 5:7*
supply -ied -ieth — 378, 2024,
4137, 4322
support — 472, 482: *Acts 20:35;
1 Thess. 5:14*
suppose -ed -ing — 1380, 2233,
3049, 3543, 3633, 5274, 5282
supreme — 5242: *1 Pet. 2:13*
sure — 804, 805, 949, 1097, 1492,
4103, 4731
surely — 230, 2229, 3483, 3843,
4135
surety — 230, 1450: *Acts 12:11; Heb.
7:22*
surfeiting — 2897: *Luke 21:34*
surmisings — 5283: *1 Tim. 6:4*
surname -ed — 1941, 2007/3686,
2564
Susanna — 4677: *Luke 8:3*
sustenance — 5527: *Acts 7:11*
swaddling — 4683: *Luke 2:7, 12*
swallow -ed — 2666: *Matt. 23:24;
1 Cor. 15:54; 2 Cor. 2:7; 5:4; Rev.
12:16*
swear -eth; swore; sworn — 3660
sweat — 2402: *Luke 22:44*
sweep; swept — 4563: *Matt. 12:44;
Luke 11:25; 15:8*
sweet — 1099, 2175

sweetsmelling — 2175: *Eph. 5:2*
swelling -s; swollen — 4092, 5246,
5450: *Acts 28:6; 2 Cor. 12:20; 2 Pet.
2:18; Jude 1:16*
swerved — 795: *1 Tim. 1:6*
swift — 3691, 5031, 5036: *Rom. 3:15;
James 1:19; 2 Pet. 2:1*
swim — 1579, 2860: *Acts 27:42, 43*
swine — 5519
sword -s — 3162, 4501
sycamine — 4807: *Luke 17:6*
sycamore — 4809: *Luke 19:4*
Sychar — 4965: *John 4:5*
synagogue -s — 656, 752, 4864
Syntyche — 4941: *Phil. 4:2*
Syracuse — 4946: *Acts 28:12*
Syria -n — 4947, 4948
Syrophenician — 4949: *Mark 7:26*

T

tabernacle -s — 4633, 4634, 4636,
4638
Tabitha (see **Dorcas**) — 5000: *Acts
9:36, 40*
table -s — 345, 2825, 4093, 4109,
5132
tackling — 4631: *Acts 27:19*
tail -s — 3769: *Rev. 9:10, 19; 12:4*
take -en -est -eth -ing; took —
142, 259, 321, 337, 353, 520, 522,
589, 618, 642, 643, 657, 726, 851,
941, 1011, 1096, 1209, 1325, 1405,
1544, 1562, 1684/1519, 1723,
1869, 1921, 1949, 1959, 2018,
2021, 2192, 2221, 2507, 2639,
2722, 2902, 2938, 2983, 3880,
3911, 4014, 4084, 4160, 4301,
4327, 4338, 4355, 4648, 4815,
4823, 4838, 4868, 4912
talent -s — 5006, 5007
tales — 3026: *Luke 24:11*
Talitha — 5008: *Mark 5:41*
talk -ed -ers -est -eth -ing —
2980, 3056, 3151, 3473, 3656,
4814, 4926
Tamar — 2283: *Matt. 1:3*
tame -ed — 1150: *Mark 5:4; James
3:7, 8*
tanner — 1038: *Acts 9:43; 10:6, 32*
tares — 2215: *Matt. 13:25–27, 29, 30,
36, 38, 40*
tarry -ied -iest — 1019, 1304,

1551, 1961, 2523, 3195, 3306, 4160, 4328, 4357, 5278, 5549

Tarsus — 5018, 5019: *Acts 9:11, 30; 11:35; 21:39; 22:3*

taste -ed — 1089

tattlers — 5397: *1 Tim. 5:13*

taverns — 4999: *Acts 28:15*

taxed; taxing — 582: *Luke 2:1–3, 5; Acts 5:37*

teach -er(s) -est -eth -ing; taught — 1317, 1318, 1319, 1320, 1321, 1322, 2085, 2312, 2567, 2605, 2727, 3100, 3547, 3811, 4994, 5572

teareth; tore; torn — 4486, 4682, 4952: *Mark 1:26; 9:18, 20; Luke 9:39, 42*

tears — 1144

tedious — 1465: *Acts 24:4*

tell -eth; told — 226, 312, 518, 1285, 1334, 1492, 1583, 1650, 1834, 2036, 2046, 2980, 3004, 3377, 4277, 4280, 4302

temperance; temperate — 1466, 1467, 1468, 4998

tempered — 4786: *1 Cor. 12:24*

tempest -uous — 2366, 2978, 4578, 5189, 5492, 5494

temple -s — 2411, 3485, 3624

temporal — 4340: *2 Cor. 4:18*

tempt -ation(s) -ed -er -eth -ing — 551, 1598, 3985, 3986

ten -th — 1176, 1181, 1182, 3461, 3463

tender — 527, 3629, 4698: *Matt. 24:32; Mark 13:28; Luke 1:78; James 5:11*

tenderhearted — 2155: *Eph. 4:32*

tentmakers — 4635: *Acts 18:3*

Terah — 2291: *Luke 3:34*

terrestrial — 1919: *1 Cor. 15:40*

terrible — 5398: *Heb. 12:21*

terrify -ied — 1629, 4422, 4426: *Luke 21:9; 24:37; 2 Cor. 10:9; Phil. 1:28*

terror — 5401: *Rom. 13:3; 2 Cor. 5:11; 1 Pet. 3:14*

Tertius — 5060: *Rom. 16:22*

Tertullus — 5061: *Acts 24:1, 2*

testament — 1242

testator — 1303: *Heb. 9:16, 17*

testify -ied -ieth -ing — 1263,

1957, 3140, 3142, 3143, 4303, 4828

testimony — 3140, 3141, 3142

tetrarch — 5075, 5076: *Matt. 14:1; Luke 3:1, 19; 9:7; Acts 13:1*

Thaddaeus (see **Lebbaeus**) — 2280: *Matt. 10:3; Mark 3:18*

than — 1508, 1883, 2228, 2260, 3844, 4133, 5228, 5245

thank -ed -ful -fulness -ing -s — 437, 1843, 2168, 2169, 2170, 2192/5485, 3670, 5485

thanksgiving -s — 2169

thankworthy — 5485: *1 Pet. 2:19*

theater — 2302: *Acts 19:29, 31*

thefts — 2809, 2829: *Matt. 15:19; Mark 7:22; Rev. 9:21*

themselves — 240, 830, 848, 1438, 3441

theirs — 846, 3588/1565: *Matt. 5:3, 10; 1 Cor. 1:2; 2 Tim. 3:9*

then — 686, 1161, 1534, 1899, 2532, 3063, 3303, 3766, 3767, 5037, 5119, 5119/1161/2532, 5119/3767

thence -forth — 1537/5127, 1564, 2089, 3606

Theophilus — 2321: *Luke 1:3; Acts 1:1*

there (see **thither; yonder**) — 847, 1563, 1564, 1566, 1722/846, 1759, 1927, 5602

thereabout — 4012/5127: *Luke 24:4*

thereat; thereby — 1223/846, 1223/5026, 1722/846

therefore — 235, 473/5607, 686, 686/3767, 1063, 1160, 1211, 1223/5124, 1352, 1360, 1519/5124, 3767, 5105, 5106, 5620

therein -to — 1519/846, 1722/846, 1722/5129, 5125

thereof — 846, 1538/846

thereon; thereupon — 846, 1722/846, 1883/846, 1909/846, 1911, 1913, 1924, 1945, 2026

thereto; thereunto — 1519/846/5124, 1519/5124, 1928, 4334

therewith — 1722/846, 1909/5125, 5125: *Phil. 4:11; 1 Tim. 6:8; James 3:9; 3 John 1:10*

these; those — 846, 1565, 3588, 3588/846, 3745, 3778, 5023, 5025, 5118, 5128, 5130

Thessalonica; Thessalonians — 2331, 2332

Theudas — 2333: *Acts 5:36*

thief; thieves — 2812, 3027

thigh — 3382: *Rev. 19:16*

thine; thyself — 846, 1438, 2398, 4572, 4671, 4674, 4675

thing -s — 18, 846, 1520, 3056, 4110, 4229, 4487, 5023, 5313

think -est -eth; thought -s — 1260, 1261, 1270, 1380, 1760, 1761, 1911, 1963, 2106, 2233, 2919, 3049, 3053, 3309, 3539, 3540, 3543, 3633, 4305, 5252, 5282, 5316, 5426

third -ly — 5152, 5154

thirst -y — 1372, 1373

thirty -fold — 5144

this — 737, 2235, 3127, 3568, 3588, 3592, 3778, 3779, 4594, 5023, 5026, 5124, 5125, 5126, 5127, 5129, 5602

thistles — 5146: *Matt. 7:16*

thither -ward (see **there; yonder**) **—** 1563, 1904, 3854, 4370

Thomas (see **Didymus**) **—** 2381

thongs — 2438: *Acts 22:25*

thorn -s — 173, 174, 4647

though — 1223, 1437, 1499, 1512, 2532, 2532/1487, 2539, 2544, 2579, 3676, 3754

thousand -s — 1367, 2035, 3461, 3463, 4000, 5070, 5153, 5505, 5507

threaten -ed -ing(s) — 546, 547, 4324

three — 5140, 5145, 5148, 5150, 5151, 5153

threescore (see **sixty**) **—** 1440, 1835

thresheth — 248: *1 Cor. 9:10*

threw; thrown — 906, 2647, 4496, 4952

thrice — 5151

throat — 2995, 4155: *Matt. 18:28; Rom. 3:13*

throne -s — 968, 2362

throng -ed -ing — 2346, 4846, 4912, 4918: *Mark 3:9; 5:24, 31; Luke 8:42, 45*

through -ly -out — 303, 1223, 1223/3650, 1224, 1245, 1279, 1330, 1358, 1519, 1537, 1653,

1722, 1722/3956, 1822, 1909, 2596, 2700, 4044, 4063

thrust — 683, 906, 1544, 1877, 2601, 2700, 3992

thunder -ed -ings -s — 1027, 1027/1096

thus — 2532, 2596/5023, 3592, 3779, 5023, 5124, 5127

Thyatira — 2363: *Acts 16:14; Rev. 1:11; 2:18, 24*

thyine — 2367: *Rev. 18:12*

Tiberias — 5085: *John 6:1, 23; 21:1*

Tiberius — 5086: *Luke 3:1*

tidings — 2097, 3056, 5334

tied — 1210: *Matt. 21:2; Mark 11:2, 4; Luke 19:30*

tiling — 2766: *Luke 5:19*

till — 891, 891/3757, 1508/3752, 1519, 2193, 3360

Timaeus (see **Bartimaeus**) **—** 5090: *Mark 10:46*

time -s — 744, 1074, 1208, 1441, 1597, 1909, 2034, 2119, 2121, 2235, 2250, 2540, 3195, 3379, 3568, 3819, 3999, 4218, 4287, 4340, 4455, 5119, 5151, 5550, 5610

Timon — 5096: *Acts 6:5*

Timothy — 5095

tinkling — 214: *1 Cor. 13:1*

tip — 206: *Luke 16:24*

tithe -s — 586, 1181, 1183: *Matt. 23:23; Luke 11:42; 18:12; Heb. 7:5, 6, 8, 9*

title — 5102: *John 19:19, 20*

tittle — 2762: *Matt. 5:18; Luke 16:17*

Titus — 5103

today — 4594

together — 240, 260, 346, 1794, 1865, 1909/3588/846, 1996, 1997, 1998, 2086, 2596/3588/846, 2675, 3326/240, 3674, 4314/240, 4776, 4779, 4786, 4789, 4794, 4801, 4802, 4806, 4811, 4816, 4822, 4831, 4837, 4851, 4853, 4854, 4856, 4863, 4865, 4866, 4867, 4873, 4883, 4886, 4888, 4890, 4891, 4904, 4936/1909/846, 4896, 4897, 4899, 4903, 4905, 4911, 4925, 4943, 4944

toil -ed -ing — 928, 2872: *Matt. 6:28; Mark 6:48; Luke 5:5; 12:27*

token — 1730, 1732, 4592, 4593:

Mark 14:44; Phil. 1:28; 2 Thess. 1:5; 3:17

tolerable — 414: *Matt. 10:15; 11:22, 24; Mark 6:11; Luke 10:12, 14*

tomb -s — 3418, 3419, 5028

tomorrow (see **morrow**) — 839

tongue -s — 1100, 1258, 1447, 2084

too — 1174: *Acts 17:22*

tooth; teeth — 3599, 3679

top — 206, 509: *Matt. 27:51; Mark 15:38; John 19:23; Heb. 11:21*

topaz — 5116: *Rev. 21:20*

torches — 2985: *John 18:3*

torment -ed -ors -s — 928, 929, 930, 931, 2558, 2851, 3600

tortured — 5178: *Heb. 11:35*

tossed — 928, 2831, 4494, 5492: *Matt. 14:24; Acts 27:18; Eph. 4:14; James 1:6*

touch -ed -eth -ing — 680, 1909, 2345, 2596, 2609, 4012, 4379, 4834, 5584

toward — 1519, 1722, 1909, 2596, 4314, 5228

towel — 3012: *John 13:4, 5*

tower — 4444: *Matt. 21:33; Mark 12:1; Luke 13:4; 14:28*

town -s — 2968, 2969

town clerk — 1122: *Acts 19:35*

Trachonitis — 5139: *Luke 3:1*

trade -ed -ing — 1281, 2038: *Matt. 25:16; Luke 19:15; Rev. 18:17*

tradition -s — 3862

traitor -s — 4273: *Luke 6:16; 2 Tim. 3:4*

trample — 2662: *Matt. 7:6*

trance — 1611: *Acts 10:10; 11:5; 22:17*

transferred — 3345: *1 Cor. 4:6*

transfigured — 3339: *Matt. 17:2; Mark 9:2*

transformed; transform -ing — 3339, 3345: *Rom. 12:2; 2 Cor. 11:13–15*

transgress -ed -eth -ion(s) -or(s) — 458/4160, 459, 3845, 3847, 3848, 3928

translated; translation — 3179, 3331, 3346: *Col. 1:13; Heb. 11:5*

transparent — 1307: *Rev. 21:21*

trap — 2339: *Rom. 11:9*

travail -est -eth -ing — 3449, 4944, 5088, 5604, 5605

travel -ed -ing — 589, 1330, 4898:

Matt. 25:14; Acts 11:19; 19:29; 2 Cor. 8:19

tread -eth; trod; trodden — 248, 2662, 3961

treasure -s -est — 1047, 2343, 2344

treasury — 1049, 2878

treatise — 3056: *Acts 1:1*

tree -s — 65, 1186, 2565, 3586, 4808, 4809

tremble -ed -ing — 1719/1096, 1790/1096, 2192/5156, 5141, 5156, 5425

trench — 5482: *Luke 19:43*

trespass -es — 264, 3900

trial — 1382, 1383, 3984: *2 Cor. 8:2; Heb. 11:36; 1 Pet. 1:7; 4:12*

tribe -s — 1429, 5443

tribulation -s — 2346, 2347

tribute — 1323, 2778, 5411

trimmed — 2885: *Matt. 25:7*

triumph -ing — 2358: *2 Cor. 2:14; Col. 2:15*

Troas — 5174

Trogyllium — 5175: *Acts 20:15*

Trophimus — 5161: *Acts 20:4; 21:29; 2 Tim. 4:20*

trouble -ed -s -est -eth -ing — 387, 1298, 1613, 1776, 2346, 2347, 2350, 2360, 2553, 2873, 2873/3930, 3926, 3930/2873, 4660, 5015, 5015/1438, 5016, 5182

trucebreakers — 786: *2 Tim. 3:3*

true -ly; truth (see **verily; verity**) — 225, 226, 227, 228, 230, 686, 1103, 1161, 1909/225, 3303, 3483, 3689, 4103

trump; trumpet -ers -s — 4536, 4537, 4538

trust -ed -eth — 1679, 3982, 4006, 4100, 4276

try -ing; tried; trieth — 1381, 1383, 1384, 3985, 4314/3986, 4448

Tryphena — 5170: *Rom. 16:12*

Tryphosa — 5173: *Rom. 16:12*

tumult -s — 181, 2351

turn -ed -ing — 344, 387, 402, 576, 654, 665, 1096, 1294, 1624, 1824, 1994, 2827, 3179, 3329, 3344, 3346, 4762, 5077, 5157, 5290

turtledoves — 5167: *Luke 2:24*

tutors — 2012: *Gal. 4:2*

twelve; twelfth — 1177, 1427, 1428, 1429
twenty — 1501
twice — 1364: *Mark 14:30, 72; Luke 18:12; Jude 1:12*
twinkling — 4493: *1 Cor. 15:52*
two -fold; twain — 296, 1250, 1322, 1332, 1337, 1366, 1367, 1417
two–edged — 1366: *Heb. 4:12; Rev. 1:16*
Tychicus — 5190: *Acts 20:4; Eph. 6:21; Col. 4:7; 2 Tim. 4:12; Titus 3:12*
Tyrannus — 5181: *Acts 19:9*
Tyre — 5183, 5184

U

unawares — 160, 2990, 3920, 3921: *Luke 21:34; Gal. 2:4; Heb. 13:2; Jude 1:4*
unbelief; unbelievers; unbelieving — 543, 544, 570, 571
unblamable; unblamably — 274, 299: *Col. 1:22; 1 Thess. 2:10; 3:13*
uncertain -ly — 82, 83: *1 Cor. 9:26; 14:8; 1 Tim. 6:17*
unchangeable — 531: *Heb. 7:24*
uncircumcised; uncircumcision — 203, 203/2192, 564, 1722/203, 1986
unclean -ness — 167, 169, 2839, 2840, 3394
unclothed — 1562: *2 Cor. 5:4*
uncomely — 807, 809: *1 Cor. 7:36; 12:23*
uncondemned — 178: *Acts 16:37; 22:25*
uncorruptible; uncorruptness (see **incorruptible**) — 90, 862: *Rom. 1:23; Titus 2:7*
uncovered — 177, 648: *Mark 2:4; 1 Cor. 11:5, 13*
unction — 5545: *1 John 2:20*
undefiled — 283: *Heb. 7:26; 13:4; James 1:27; 1 Pet. 1:4*
under — 332, 506, 1640, 1722, 1909, 2662, 2709, 2736, 5259, 5270, 5273, 5284, 5293, 5295, 5299
undergirding — 5269: *Acts 27:17*
understand -est -eth -ing; understood — 50, 191, 801, 1097, 1107, 1271, 1425, 1492, 1987,

2154, 3129, 3539, 3563, 3877, 4441, 4907, 4920, 5424, 5426
undone — 863: *Matt. 23:23; Luke 11:42*
unequally — 2086: *2 Cor. 6:14*
unfeigned — 505: *2 Cor. 6:6; 1 Tim. 1:5; 2 Tim. 1:5; 1 Pet. 1:22*
unfruitful — 175
ungodly -iness — 763, 764, 765
unholy — 462, 2839: *1 Tim. 1:9; 2 Tim. 3:2; Heb. 10:29*
unity — 1775: *Eph. 4:3, 13*
unjust — 91, 93, 94
unknown — 50, 57
unlade — 670: *Acts 21:3*
unlawful — 111, 459: *Acts 10:28; 2 Pet. 2:8*
unlearned — 62, 261, 521, 2399: *Acts 4:13; 1 Cor. 14:16, 23, 24; 2 Tim. 2:23; 2 Pet. 3:16*
unleavened — 106
unless — 1622/1508: *1 Cor. 15:2*
unloose — 3089: *Mark 1:7; Luke 3:16; John 1:27*
unmarried — 22: *1 Cor. 7:8, 11, 32, 34*
unmerciful — 415: *Rom. 1:31*
unmoveable — 277, 761: *Acts 27:41; 1 Cor. 15:58*
unprepared — 532: *2 Cor. 9:4*
unprofitable -ness — 255, 512, 888, 889, 890
unquenchable — 762: *Matt. 3:12; Luke 3:17*
unreasonable — 249, 824: *Acts 25:27; 2 Thess. 3:2*
unrebukable — 423: *1 Tim. 6:14*
unreprovable — 410: *Col. 1:22*
unrighteous -ness — 93, 94, 458
unruly — 183, 506, 813: *1 Thess. 5:14; Titus 1:6, 10; James 3:8*
unsearchable — 419, 421: *Rom. 11:33; Eph. 3:8*
unseemly — 808: *Rom. 1:27; 1 Cor. 13:5*
unskillful — 552: *Heb. 5:13*
unspeakable — 411, 412, 731: *2 Cor. 9:15; 12:4; 1 Pet. 1:8*
unspotted — 784: *James 1:27*
unstable — 182, 793: *James 1:8; 2 Pet. 2:14; 3:16*
untaken — 3361/343: *2 Cor. 3:14*
unthankful — 884: *Luke 6:35; 2 Tim. 3:2*

until — 891, 1519, 2193, 3360

untimely — 3653: *Rev. 6:13*

untoward — 4646: *Acts 2:40*

unwashen — 449: *Matt. 15:20; Mark 7:2, 5*

unwise — 453, 878: *Rom. 1:14; Eph. 5:17*

unworthy -ily — 370, 371, 3756/514: *Acts 13:46; 1 Cor. 6:2; 11:27, 29*

upbraid -ed -eth — 3679: *Matt. 11:20; Mark 16:14; James 1:5*

upholding — 5342: *Heb. 1:3*

upper — 508, 510, 5250, 5253

uppermost — 4410, 4411: *Matt. 23:6; Mark 12:39; Luke 11:43*

upright -ly — 3716, 3717: *Acts 14:10; Gal. 2:14*

uproar — 387, 2350, 2351, 4714, 4797

upside — 387: *Acts 17:6*

Urbane — 3773: *Rom. 16:9*

urge — 1758: *Luke 11:53*

Uriah — 3774: *Matt. 1:6*

use -ed -eth -ing -s — 390, 1096/1722, 1247, 1838, 1908, 2192, 3348, 5195, 5382, 5383, 5530, 5532, 5540

usurp — 831: *1 Tim. 2:12*

usury — 5110: *Matt. 25:27; Luke 19:23*

us–ward — 2248: *Eph. 1:19; 2 Pet. 3:9*

utmost; uttermost — 206, 1231, 2078, 3838, 4009, 5056

utter -ance -ed — 215, 669, 1325, 2044, 2980, 3004, 3056

utterly — 2618, 2704, 3654: *1 Cor. 6:7; 2 Pet. 2:12; Rev. 18:8*

V

vagabond — 4022: *Acts 19:13*

vain -ly -glory; vanity -ies — 1432, 1500, 2754, 2755, 2756, 2757, 2758, 2761, 3150, 3151, 3152, 3153, 3154, 3155

valiant — 2478: *Heb. 11:34*

valley — 5327: *Luke 3:5*

value -ed — 1308, 5091: *Matt. 10:31; 27:9; Luke 12:7*

vanish -ed -eth — 853, 854, 1096/855, 2673: *Luke 24:31; 1 Cor. 13:8; Heb. 8:13; James 4:14*

vapor — 822: *Acts 2:19; James 4:14*

variableness — 3883: *James 1:17*

variance — 1369, 2054: *Matt. 10:35; Gal. 5:20*

vaunteth — 4068: *1 Cor. 13:4*

vehement -ly — 1171, 1537/4053, 1972, 2159, 4366: *Luke 6:48, 49; 11:53; 23:10; 2 Cor. 7:11*

veil — 2571, 2665

vengeance — 1349, 1557, 3709

verily — 230, 281, 1063, 1222, 2532, 3303, 3304, 3483, 3689

verity — 225: *1 Tim. 2:7*

very — 85, 230, 662, 846, 927, 957, 1565, 1582, 1646, 1888, 2236, 2532, 2566, 2735, 3029, 3827, 4036, 4118, 4119, 4184, 4185, 4186, 4708, 4970, 5228

vessel -s — 30, 4632

vesture — 2440, 2441, 4018: *Matt. 27:35; John 19:24; Heb. 1:12; Rev. 19:13, 16*

vex -ed — 928, 1139, 2559, 2669, 3791, 3958

vial -s — 5357

victory — 3528, 3529, 3534

victuals — 1033, 1979: *Matt. 14:15; Luke 9:12*

vigilant — 1127, 3524: *1 Tim. 3:2; 1 Pet. 5:8*

vile — 819, 4508, 5014: *Rom. 1:26; Phil. 3:21; James 2:2*

village -s — 2968

vine — 288

vineyard — 289, 290

vinegar — 3690

violence; violent -ly — 970, 971, 973, 1286, 1411, 3731

viper -s — 2191: *Matt. 3:7; 12:34; 23:33; Luke 3:7; Acts 28:3*

virgin -s — 3933

virginity — 3932: *Luke 2:36*

virtue — 703, 1411: *Mark 5:30; Luke 6:19; 8:46; Phil. 4:8; 2 Pet. 1:3, 5*

vision -s — 3701, 3705, 3706

visible — 3707: *Col. 1:16*

visit -ed -est — 1980

visitation — 1984: *Luke 19:44; 1 Pet. 2:12*

vocation — 2821: *Eph. 4:1*

voice -s — 5456, 5586

void — 677, 2763, 2758: *Acts 24:16; Rom. 3:31; 4:14; 1 Cor. 9:15*

volume — 2777: *Heb. 10:7*

voluntary — 2309: *Col. 2:18*
vomit — 1829: *2 Pet. 2:22*
vow — 2171: *Acts 18:18; 21:23*
voyage — 4144: *Acts 27:10*

W

wages — 3408, 3800: *Luke 3:14; John 4:36; Rom. 6:23; 2 Cor. 11:8; 2 Pet. 2:15*
wagging — 2795: *Matt. 27:39; Mark 15:29*
wail -ed -ing — 214, 2805, 2875, 3996
wait -ed -eth -ing — 362, 553, 1096/1917, 1551, 1747, 1748, 1917, 3180, 4037, 4160/1747, 4327, 4328, 4332, 4342
wake — 1127: *1 Thess. 5:10*
walk -ed -edst -est -eth -ing — 1330, 1704, 3716, 4043, 4198, 4748
wall -s — 5038, 5109
wallowed; wallowing — 2946, 2947: *Mark 9:20; 2 Pet. 2:22*
wandered; wandering — 4022, 4105, 4107: *1 Tim. 5:13; Heb. 11:37, 38; Jude 1:13*
want -ed -ing -s — 3007, 5302, 5303, 5304, 5532
wanton -ness — 766, 2691, 4684: *Rom. 13:13; 1 Tim. 5:11; James 5:5; 2 Pet. 2:18*
war -fare -reth -ring -s — 497, 4170, 4171, 4752, 4753, 4754
ward — 5438: *Acts 12:10*
warmed; warming — 2328: *Mark 14:54, 67; John 18:18, 25; James 2:16*
warn -ed -ing — 3560, 5263, 5537
wash -ed -ing(s) — 628, 633, 637, 907, 909, 1026, 3067, 3068, 3538, 4150
wast — 2258, 5607
waste -ed — 684, 1287, 4199: *Matt. 26:8; Mark 14:4; Luke 15:13; 16:1; Gal. 1:13*
watch -ed -eth -ful -ing(s) — 69, 70, 1127, 2892, 3525, 3906, 5083, 5438
water -ed -eth -ing -s — 504, 4215, 4222, 5202, 5204
waterpot -s — 5201: *John 2:6, 7; 4:28*
wave -s — 2830, 2949, 4535

wavereth; wavering — 186, 1252: *Heb. 10:23; James 1:6*
wax -ed -eth -ing — 1095, 1096, 2691, 2901, 3822, 3955, 3975, 3982, 4147, 4298, 5594
way -s — 296, 684, 1545, 1624, 1722, 3112, 3319, 3598, 3938, 4105, 4197, 4206, 4311, 5158
weak -er -ness — 102, 769, 770, 772
wealth — 2142: *Acts 19:25; 1 Cor. 10:24*
weapons — 3696: *John 18:3; 2 Cor. 10:4*
wear -eth -ing; wore — 1737, 2827, 4025, 5409
weary -ied -iness — 1573, 2577, 2872, 2873, 5299
weather — 2105, 5494: *Matt. 16:2, 3*
wedding — 1062: *Matt. 22:3, 8, 10–12; Luke 12:36; 14:8*
week — 4521
weep -est -ing; wept — 1145, 2799, 2805
weight -ier -y — 922, 926, 3591, 5006
well — 15, 16, 17, 18, 957, 1510/2101, 1921, 2095, 2100, 2101, 2106, 2509, 2532, 2569, 2573, 3140, 3184, 4260, 4982
well -s — 4077, 5421: *John 4:6, 11, 12, 14, 17; 2 Pet. 2:17*
well-beloved — 27: *Matt. 12:6; Rom. 16:5; 3 John 1:1*
wellpleasing — 2101: *Phil. 4:18; Heb. 13:21*
wert — 1498: *Rom. 11:17, 24; Rev. 3:15*
west — 1424, 3047, 5566
whale — 2785: *Matt. 12:40*
what — 1063, 2228, 2245, 3588, 3634, 3697, 3699, 3739, 3745, 3748, 3779, 4169, 4214, 4217, 4459, 5100, 5101, 5101/686
whatsoever — 1221, 3588, 3588/3739, 3697/4219, 3739, 3739/302, 3739/1437, 3739/1437/5100, 3745, 3745/302, 3745/1437, 3748/302, 3956, 3956/3754/5100, 5100
wheat — 4621
when -soever — 1437, 1722/3588, 1722/3739, 1875, 1893, 2259,

2531, 3326, 3698, 3704, 3752,
3753, 3753/3588, 3757, 4218,
5613, 5613/1437
whence — 3606, 3739, 4159
where -soever — 296, 1330, 1337,
1722/3739, 1722/3956, 1722/5117,
2596, 3606, 3699, 3699/302,
3699/1437, 3757, 3837, 4226, 5101
whereas — 1722/3759, 3699, 3748
whereby — 1223/3739, 1722/3739,
2596/5101, 3588, 4012/3757,
4314, 4314/3739
wherefore — 686, 686/1065, 1161,
1223/3739, 1223/5124, 1302,
1352, 1355, 1519/3739,
1519/5101, 1909/3739, 2443/5101,
3606, 3739/5484, 3767, 5101,
5101/1752, 5105, 5484/5101, 5620
wherein -soever — 1223/3757,
1519/3739, 1519/3757, 1722/3739,
1722/3739/302, 1722/3757,
1909/3739, 1909/3757, 3757,
4012/3739
whereof — 1537/3739, 1909/3739,
3739, 4012/3739, 4012/5101
whereon; whereupon —
1722/3739, 1909/3739, 3606
whereto; whereunto — 1519/3739,
3739, 5101
wherewith -al — 1722/5101, 3739,
3745, 5101
whether — 1487, 1535, 2273,
3379/1520, 3739, 4220, 5037, 5101
which — 846, 1352, 2076, 2532,
3588, 3739, 3634, 3745, 3748,
4169, 5101
while -s -st — 891/3739,
1722/3588, 1722/3739, 2193,
2193/3755, 2250, 2540, 3153,
3397, 3588, 3641, 3752, 3753,
3819, 4340, 5550, 5550/5099, 5613
whisperers — 5588: *Rom. 1:29*
whisperings — 5587: *2 Cor. 12:20*
whit — 3367, 3650: *John 7:23; 13:10;
2 Cor. 11:5*
white -ed — 2867, 2986, 3021, 3022
whither — 3226, 3699, 3757
whithersoever — 3699/302,
3699/1437, 3757/1437
**who; whom -soever; whose;
whoso -ever** — 846, 1437/5100,
1536, 2532, 2532/846, 3588, 3739,
3739/302, 3739/1437, 3745/302,

3746, 3748, 3748/302, 3778, 3956,
3956/3588, 3956/3739,
3956/3739/302, 5100, 5101
whole -some; wholly — 537, 1295,
1510/1722, 2390, 2480, 3390,
3648, 3650, 3651, 3956, 4982,
5198, 5199
whore — 4204: *Rev. 17:1, 15, 16; 19:2*
whoremonger(s) — 4205: *Eph. 5:5;
1 Tim. 1:10; Heb. 13:4; Rev. 21: 8;
22:15*
why — 1063, 1302, 1519/5101, 2444,
2444/5101, 3754, 5101
wicked -ness — 113, 459, 2549,
2556, 4189, 4190, 4191, 5129/824
wide — 4116: *Matt. 7:13*
widow -s — 5503
wife; wives — 1126, 1134, 1135,
3994
wild — 65, 66, 2342
wilderness — 2047, 2048
wiles — 3180: *Eph. 6:11*
**will -eth -fully -ing -ingly; wilt;
would -est** — 210, 830, 1012,
1013, 1014, 1096, 1106, 1479,
1596, 1635, 2106, 2107, 2133,
2172, 2307, 2308, 2309,
2596/1596, 2843, 3195, 3785,
4288, 4289
win; won — 2770: *Phil. 3:8; 1 Pet. 3:1*
wind -s — 416, 417, 4154, 4157
window — 2376: *Acts 20:9; 2 Cor.
11:33*
wine — 1098, 3631, 3632, 3943
winebibber — 3630: *Matt. 11:19;
Luke 7:34*
winepress — 3025, 3025/3631:
Matt. 21:33; Rev. 14:19, 20; 19:15
wine vat — 5276: *Mark 12:1*
wings — 4420: *Matt. 23:37; Luke
13:34; Rev. 4:8; 9:9; 12:14*
winked — 5237: *Acts 17:30*
winter -ed — 3914, 3915, 3916,
5494
wipe -ed — 631, 1591, 1813
wisdom — 4678, 5428
wise -ly -er — 3097, 3588/3838,
3779, 3843, 4679, 4680, 4920,
5429, 5430
wish -ed — 2172: *Acts 27:29; Rom.
9:3; 2 Cor. 13:9; 3 John 1:2*
wist; wit; wot (see **know**) — 1107,
1492, 5613

witchcraft — 5331: *Gal. 5:20*

withal — 260

withdraw -n; withdrew — 402, 645, 868, 4724, 5288, 5298

withered; withereth — 3583, 3584, 5352

withholdeth — 2722: *2 Thess. 2:6*

within — 1223, 1722, 1787, 2080, 2081, 2082, 4314

without — 35, 77, 87, 88, 89, 112, 175, 186, 194, 267, 275, 278, 280, 282, 298, 299, 361, 369, 379, 427, 448, 459, 460, 504, 505, 540, 563, 677, 678, 729, 772, 784, 794, 801, 815, 817, 820, 866, 870, 880, 886, 895, 1432, 1500, 1618, 1622, 1854, 1855, 2673, 3361, 3672, 3924, 5565

withstand; withstood — 436, 2967

witness -ed -es -eth -ing — 267, 1263, 2649, 3140, 3141, 3142, 3144, 4828, 4901, 5575, 5576, 5577

woe -s — 3759

wolf; wolves — 3074: *Matt. 7:15; 10:16; Luke 10:3; John 10:12; Acts 20:29*

woman; women — 1133, 1135, 1658, 2338, 4247

womb -s — 1064, 2836, 3388

wonder -ed -ful -ing -s — 1411, 1569, 1839, 2285, 2296, 2297, 3167, 4592, 5059

wont (see **custom**) — 1486, 2596/1485, 3543: *Matt. 27:15; Mark 10:1; Luke 22:39; Acts 16:13*

wood — 3585, 3586: *1 Cor. 3:12; 2 Tim. 2:20; Rev. 9:20; 18:12*

wool — 2053: *Heb. 9:19; Rev. 1:14*

word -s — 518, 2036, 3050, 3054, 3055, 3056, 4086, 4487, 5542

work -ers -eth -ing -man(ship) -men -s — 1411, 1753, 1754, 1755, 2038, 2039, 2040, 2041, 2716, 3056, 3433/2480, 4160, 4161, 4229, 4234, 4903

workfellow — 4904: *Rom. 16:21*

world -s — 165, 166, 1093, 2889, 3625

worldly — 2886: *Titus 2:12; Heb. 9:1*

worm -s — 4662, 4663: *Mark 9:44, 46, 48; Acts 12:23*

wormwood — 894: *Rev. 8:11*

worse — 1640, 2276, 5302, 5501

worship -ed -er(s) -eth -ing — 1391, 1479, 1799, 2151, 2318, 2323, 2356, 3000, 3511, 4352, 4353, 4573, 4574, 4576

worthy — 414, 515, 516, 2425, 2570, 2661, 2735

wound — 1210, 4958: *John 19:40; Acts 5:6*

wound -ed -s — 4127, 4127/2007, 4969, 5134, 5135, 5180

woven — 5307: *John 19:23*

wrapped — 1750, 1794, 4683

wrath -s; wroth — 2372, 2373, 3709, 3710, 3949, 3950

wrest — 4761: *2 Pet. 3:16*

wrestle — 2076/3823: *Eph. 6:12*

wretched — 5005: *Rom. 7:24; Rev. 3:17*

wrinkle — 4512: *Eph. 5:27*

write -ing(s); written; wrote — 583, 975, 1121, 1123, 1125, 1449, 1924, 1989, 4093, 4270

wrong -ed -fully — 91, 92, 93, 95

wrought (see **do; make; work**) — 1096, 1754, 2038, 2716, 4160, 4903

Y

yea; yes — 235, 1161, 2228, 2532, 3304, 3483

year -s — 1096/3173, 1332, 1333, 1541, 1763, 2094, 2250, 4070, 5063, 5148

yesterday — 5504: *John 4:52; Acts 7:28; Heb. 13:8*

yet — 188, 235, 1063, 1065, 1161, 2089, 2236, 2532, 2579, 2596, 3195, 3305, 3364, 3369, 3380, 3764, 3765, 3768

yield -ed -eth — 591, 863, 1325, 1634, 3936, 3982, 4160

yoke -ed — 2086, 2201, 2218

yokefellow — 4805: *Phil. 4:3*

yonder — 1563: *Matt. 17:20; 26:36*

your -s -selves — 240, 846, 1438, 2398, 2596/5209, 3588, 3844/1438, 5209, 5210/846, 5212, 5213, 5213/846, 5216, 5216/846

youward — 1519/5209, 4314/5209: *2 Cor. 1:12; 13:3; Eph. 3:2*

young -er — 1025, 1640, 2365, 3494,

3495, 3501, 3502, 3678, 3813, 3816

youth -ful — 3503, 3512

Z

Zacchaeus — 2195: *Luke 19:2, 5, 8*
Zacharias — 2197
Zara — 2196: *Matt. 1:3*
zeal -ous -ously — 2205, 2206, 2207

Zebedee — 2199
Zebulun — 2194: *Matt. 4:13, 15; Rev. 7:8*
Zechariah (the prophet) — 2197: *Matt. 23:35; Luke 11:51*
Zelotes — 2208: *Luke 6:15; Acts 1:13*
Zenas — 2211: *Titus 3:13*
Zion — 4622
Zorobabel — 2216: *Matt. 1:12, 13; Luke 3:27*

A

1. α *a*; indeclinable, neut. noun. Alpha, The first letter of the Greek alphabet which corresponds in name, order, and power to the Hebr. *aleph*.

(I) *A* is used as a prefix in compound words as a particle to denote:

(A) Negation or privation from *áter* (817), apart from, without or *áneu* (427), without. In such instances, *a* is called the alpha privative (e.g., *asebḗs* [765], ungodly, from the neg. *a* and *sébomai* [4576], to worship; *aóratos* [from the priv. *a* and *horatós* {3707}, visible], invisible). When the priv. *a* is compounded with words which begin with a vowel, it frequently takes a *n* (*nē*), after it for the sake of euphony (e.g., *anamártētos* [361], sinless).

(B) Intensity increasing the meaning of the simple word. In such a case, it is called an intens. or augmentative *a* (e.g., *atenízō* [816], to look at intensely).

This meaning is probably derived from *ágan* (n.f.), very much, as in *aganaktéō* (23), to be indignant, from *ágan*, very much, and *áchthos* (n.f.), grief.

(C) Collectiveness or assembling from *háma* (260), same, together, with. The *a* then is called collative (e.g., *hápas* [537], everyone, from the collative *a* and *pás* [3956], every; *adelphós* [80], brother, from the collative *a* and *delphós*, a womb, or one who came from the same womb).

(II) Alpha is used with the last letter of the Gr. alphabet (*ōméga* [5598]) in the expression "alpha and omega, the first and the last," which is applied to God the Father or Christ (Rev 1:8, 11; 21:6; 22:13). The Hebrews, the Greeks, and the Romans all used their alphabetical letters as numerals, which accounts for the ease with which alpha and omega also represented first and last.

(A) The meaning of the expression "alpha and omega" is explained by the accompanying words: "the beginning [*archḗ* (746)] and the end [*télos* (5056)], the first [*prṓtos* (4413)] and the last [*éschatos* (2078)]." The "first" does not mean "the first created," but rather the one who brought everything into existence. The meaning is similar to *archḗ* used in an act. sense as the cause of the creation, not the first created being (Rev 3:14). Also equal to *prṓtos* as pertaining to Christ being the cause and the preeminent one (John 1:15, 30; Rev 1:17; 2:8). The same meaning is to be ascribed to *prōtótokos* (4416), firstborn (Luke 2:7; Rom 8:29; Heb 11:28), but when it speaks of Christ it refers to His preeminence over those who are born (Col 1:15, 18). Thus in Revelation, alpha indicates that He is the one who brought all things into existence, and omega that He is the one who will bring them to their determined end (2 Pet 3:10–13; Rev 21:1). The expression means that the whole of existence from beginning to end is attributable to God the Father or Jesus Christ (John 1:3; Rom 11:36; Eph 1:10; Rev 3:14).

(B) In addition, *a* signifies the eternal, creative existence of God (cf. Isa 44:6) as well as, eschatologically, the redemptive activity of Christ (cf. Rev 2:8).

(C) The fact that the expression "the alpha and omega" is applied to Christ is another proof of the deity of the Lord Jesus Christ and His coeternity with the Father. That Jesus Christ is the Son does not imply that He was generated from the Father.

2. Ἀαρών *Aarṓn*; masc. proper noun transliterated from the Hebr. *'Aharōn* (175, OT). Aaron. In the narratives of the Book of Exodus, Aaron is, after Moses, the most prominent figure, the priest and the head of the Israelite priesthood. He was probably the oldest son of Amram and Jochebed and three years older than his brother Moses (Ex 6:20; 7:7). When God sent Moses on his mission to the Israelites, Aaron was appointed to be Moses' spokesman to the people because of his fluency (Ex 4:14–16). In the account of the plagues, Aaron occupies a subordinate place, being the silent companion of his brother Moses who is sent to Pharaoh to announce the coming plagues (Ex 7:14ff.; 8:1ff., 20ff.; 9:1ff., 13ff.). Aaron is summoned four times along with Moses to entreat for their removal (Ex 8:8, 25; 9:27; 10:16). Aaron, in particular, was anointed that he might be set apart for the sacred office of the high priest (Lev 8). He was thus the spiritual leader of Israel. Both Moses and Aaron were excluded from entering the Promised Land (Num 20:12). Aaron died on Mount Hor, his garments first being taken from him and put on his son and successor Eleazar (Num 20:28 [cf. Num 33:38, 39; Deut 10:6]).

In the NT, three of the five references to Aaron are historical references only: Luke 1:5 identifying Elisabeth as one "of the daughters of Aaron"; Acts 7:40 referring to the Israelites' request that Aaron make them gods; Heb 9:4 speaking of "Aaron's rod that budded." The other two passages refer to Aaron's office as high priest and are directly concerned with the Christian doctrine of the priesthood of Christ: "And no man taketh this honor unto himself, but he that is called of God, as was Aaron" (Heb 5:4); "that another priest should rise after the order of Melchizedek" who should "not be called after the order of Aaron" (Heb 7:11).

3. Ἀβαδδών *Abaddōn*; masc. noun transliterated from the Hebr. *'Abaddōn* (11, OT). Wound, destruction. The Hebr. *'Abaddōn* designates the abode of unbelievers following death and is synonymous with *Sheʿōl* (7585, OT) which is expressed by destruction and loss (Sept.: Job 21:30; 31:12). In Job 26:6; Prov 15:11; 27:20 it occurs in conjunction

with Sheol; in Ps 88:11 mistakenly with the grave. *Hádēs* (86) or Sheol was the place of the departed spirits, while the grave (*táphos* [5028]; *mnēmeíon* [3419]) was the depository of the dead body. In Job 28:22, it is linked with death and personified in the same way as death in Dan 4:23; Rev 6:8, where death and Hades are companions.

In the NT found only in Rev 9:11 where it is used as the proper name of the prince of the infernal regions and explained by the word *Apollúōn* (623), destroyer.

4. ἀβαρής *abarḗs*; gen. *abaroús*, masc.-fem., neut. *abarés*, adj. from the priv. *a* (1), without, and *báros* (922), weight, burden. Not burdensome. Occurs only in 2 Cor 11:9 where Paul states that he did not become an economic and physical burden to the Corinthians. He was indeed needy, but his need was apparently met by brethren who came from Macedonia and brought him help. "I have kept myself from being burdensome unto you, and so will I keep myself," he tells the affluent Corinthians. This verse ought to be read in conjunction with 2 Cor 8:1–5 in which he states that the Macedonians had proved themselves more generous in their poverty than had the Corinthians in their abundance. Paul did not want to be a burden even to those who could afford to give sustenance to God's servants.

Syn.: *elaphrós* (1645), light.
Ant.: *barús* (926), heavy.

5. ἀββᾶ *abbá*; transliterated from the Aramaic *'Abba'* (2, OT). Father, my father. In the NT, it is always used to address God and is followed immediately by the translation (Mark 14:36; Rom 8:15; Gal 4:6). This double expression was common in the early church.

6. Ἄβελ *Ábel*; masc. proper noun transliterated from the Hebr. *Hebel* (1893, OT). Abel, the second son of Adam and Eve. By occupation a herdsman

(Gen 4:2), Abel offered to God a more excellent sacrifice than Cain (Heb 11:4).

Abel is mentioned in two of the gospels (Matt 23:35 and Luke 11:51) where his death is recorded as one whose innocent blood was shed. He is referred to in Matt 23:35 as "righteous," and this idea reappears in Heb 11:4. In Heb 12:24, the blood of Abel is contrasted with the "blood of sprinkling," under the new dispensation. The blood of sprinkling is the blood shed in ratification of a new covenant, whose mediator is Jesus Christ.

7. Ἀβιά *Abiá*; masc. proper noun transliterated from the Hebr. *'Abiyyāh* (29, OT), Jehovah is my father. Abijah or Abia, the son of Rehoboam by Maachah (2 Chr 11:20). He reigned over Judah from about 913–910 B.C., and the impressions he made are given in 1 Kgs 15:3 and 2 Chr 13:4–22. His name appears in the royal line of Jesus (Matt 1:7).

8. Ἀβιάθαρ *Abiáthar*; masc. proper noun transliterated from the Hebr. *'Ebyāthār* (54, OT), the great one is father. Abiathar, the son of Ahimelech. He alone escaped from the massacre of his family by Saul and joined David at Keilah, bringing with him an ephod (1 Sam 22:20–22; 23:6, 9). He helped to take the ark to Jerusalem where he was one of David's counselors (1 Chr 15:11; 27:34). When David fled from Absalom, Abiathar remained in Jerusalem with his son Jonathan to act in King David's interests (2 Sam 15:35ff.; 17:15). At the close of David's reign, Abiathar conspired to make Adonijah king and was expelled from office by Solomon (1 Kgs 1; 2). Abiathar may have been high priest during David's reign; he seems to have been senior to Zadok (1 Kgs 2:35 [cf. Mark 2:26]). It is uncertain whether he had a son Ahimelech or whether the two names have been transposed in 2 Sam 8:17; 1 Chr 24:6.

9. Ἀβιληνή *Abilēnḗ*; gen. *Abilenḗs*, fem. proper noun. Abilene, a district of which Lysanias was Tetrarch in the fifteenth year of Tiberius (Luke 3:1). It is said to be modern Suk, about twenty miles northwest of Damascus. The name Abilene comes from its capital Abila on the river Barada which is derived from the Hebr. *ábel* (58, OT), meadow. Little is known of the history of the people of Abilene at the time referred to by Luke. However, we do know that ten years after Tiberius died in A.D. 37, a tetrarchy of Lysanias was bestowed by Caligula on Herod Agrippa I. This grant was confirmed in A.D. 41 by Claudius. On the death of Agrippa I (A.D. 44), his dominions passed into the charge of Roman procurators. In A.D. 53 some parts of them, including Abilene, were granted by Claudius to Agrippa II and remained in his possession until his death in A.D. 100.

10. Ἀβιούδ *Abioúd*; masc. proper noun transliterated from the Hebr. *'Abīhūd* (31, OT). A son of Zerubbabel or Zorobabel (only in Matt 1:13 [cf. 1 Chr 8:3]).

11. Ἀβραάμ *Abraám*; masc. proper noun transliterated from the Hebr. *'Abrāhām* (85, OT). Abraham. In the Synoptic Gospels, the name Abraham appears often (e.g., Matt 1:1, 2, 17; 3:9; 8:11; 22:32; Mark 12:26; Luke 1:55, 73; 3:8, 34; 13:16, 28; 16:22–25, 29, 30; 19:9; 20:37). In John's gospel his name appears only in John 8:33, 37, 39, 40, 52, 53, 56–58.

The first three gospels present him as the ancestor of the Jews, holding a unique place in their reverence and affections. He is their father, and they are his children (Matt 3:9; Luke 3:8; 13:16; 16:24, 30; 19:9). In the Song of Mary and the Song of Zacharias, Abraham is the forefather of the race (Luke 1:55, 73), the recipient of the divine promises of mercy and goodwill to himself and his descendants (Luke 1:72, 73 [cf. Acts 7:17; Rom 4:13; Gal 3:16, 18; Heb 6:13]). Abraham's name is a pledge that God will not overlook or cease to care for His children (Luke 1:55).

To be with Abraham and his great sons, to "sit down with Abraham, and Isaac, and Jacob, in the kingdom of heaven" (Matt 8:11), was the desire and reward of the faithful Israelite. This reward, however, is not confined to the Jews, the sons of Abraham according to the flesh, and still less is it an inheritance to which they have a right by virtue of mere physical descent from him. It is a reward that will be enjoyed by many faithful ones from other lands, even to the exclusion of the sons of the kingdom if they prove themselves to be faithless and unworthy (Luke 13:28).

The expression "Abraham's bosom" (Luke 16:22) is equivalent to *parádeisos* (3857), paradise (Luke 23:43).

In Matt 1:2, Abraham stands at the head of the genealogy of Jesus. Luke, however, carries the Lord's genealogy back in an uninterrupted chain to its ultimate source in God, and the patriarch Abraham is but one link (Luke 3:34). It thus indicates the different standpoints of Jewish and Gentile thought.

Abraham is presented as existing in the days of Christ, indicating that death does not put an end to human personality (Matt 22:32; Mark 12:26; Luke 16:22; 20:37).

In John 8:58, Abraham is mentioned in the very important statement that "before Abraham came into being [*genésthai*, the second aor. inf. of *gínomai* {1096}, to become] I am [*egố eimí* (*egố* {1473} I, myself; *eimí* {1510} am)]." (a.t.). While Abraham came into being at a particular time, Christ has always been self-existent, uncreated, and the cause of creation (John 1:1–4; Col 1:16, 17; Rev 3:14). This was the Lord's answer to the question of the Pharisees, "Whom makest thou thyself?" (John 8:53).

Paul in his epistles is anxious to strike down the view that God's choice of Abraham was due to any righteous works on his part. Abraham's faith is not presented as merely one of "the works of the law" (Gal 3:5). The Jews believed that God's choice of Abraham was due

to his obedience exemplified in his willingness to sacrifice Isaac (Gen 22:12, 18; 26:5). Paul's response was that Abraham's faith preceded his works since he would not have obeyed had he not first believed God's promise. Paul quotes Gen 15:6: "Abraham believed God, and it was counted unto him for righteousness" (Rom 4:3 [cf. Gal 3:6]). God's covenant with Abraham preceded the giving of the Law by 430 years (Gal 3:17); thus Abraham's righteousness was not of law, but of faith (Rom 4:13).

Abraham was "justified" or counted righteous while still uncircumcised, circumcision being the seal of the righteousness and faith which he had while he was still uncircumcised (Rom 4:11). Although circumcision itself, the sign and seal of Abraham's covenant (Gen 17:11, 14), had become the proud token of Jewish nationalism, Paul viewed it as nothing less than a pledge of the eventual admission of the Gentiles to the status and privileges of Abraham's seed (Rom 4:12).

God did not choose the Jews as an elect nation for special privileges as if He were rejecting other nations, but that His will for the salvation of all mankind might be realized through Israel: "In thy seed shall all the nations of the earth be blessed" (Gen 22:18). Ex 19:5f. reveals the purpose of the covenant of Sinai: since the earth is Jehovah's, Israel is to be "a kingdom of priests, and an holy nation" (Ex 19:6f.). The true seed of Abraham now includes all who believe in Christ—whether circumcised or uncircumcised. Circumcised Jews who reject Christ are no longer the seed of Abraham (Rom 9:7 and context). God's promise to Abraham is fulfilled in Christ: "And the Scripture, foreseeing that God would justify the heathen by faith, preached before the gospel unto Abraham, saying, In thee shall all the nations be blessed. So then they which be of faith are blessed with faithful Abraham" (Gal 3:8, 9 [cf. Rom 4:18–25]). Upon the Gentiles has come the blessing of Abraham in Christ Jesus (Gal 3:14).

12. ἄβυσσος *ábussos*; gen. *abússou*, fem. noun from *a* (1), an intens., and *buthós* (1037), deep. Abyss, an extremely deep place. It occurs only twice outside the book of Revelation (Rom 10:7, simply the abode of the dead; Luke 8:31, the prison destined for evil spirits). In Rev 9:1, 2; 11:7; 17:8; 20:1, 3, it is a prison in which evil powers are confined and out of which they can at times be let loose. It is not the lake of fire (Rev 20:2, 10); nor is Satan regarded as being cast into this prison forever, but only to be so cast for one thousand years (Rev 20:1, 2).

13. Ἄγαβος *Ágabos*; gen. *Agábou*, masc. proper noun. Agabus, a Christian prophet living at Jerusalem (Acts 11:27–30; 21:10–11). Though the prophets were not essentially predictors of the future, the case of Agabus shows that their functions sometimes did include the actual prediction of coming events. At Antioch, Agabus foretold a famine over all the world in the days of Claudius. Both Suetonius and Eusebius date a famine in the fourth year of Claudius, A.D. 45; and since Judea as well as Greece suffered, it is probably this famine to which Agabus referred. The other prophecy of Agabus followed the OT method of symbolism and has a close parallel in John 21:18. He foretold to Paul his imprisonment in Jerusalem, but did not thereby divert him from the journey (Acts 21:10, 11).

14. ἀγαθοεργέω *agathoergéō*; contracted *agathoergṓ*, fut. *agathoergḗsō*, from *ágathoergós* (n.f.), doing good, which is from *agathós* (18), benevolent, and *érgon* (2041), work. To do good to others, to work good, i.e., to act for someone's advantage or benefit.

In 1 Tim 6:18, Paul admonishes the rich to "do good" (*agathoergeín*, pres. inf. of *agathoergéō*) with their riches. Believers are not to become conceited and trust in their riches but are to trust God and be benevolent, otherwise riches can be a curse instead of a blessing. Rather than striving for material wealth, believers are

to be "rich in good [*kalós* (2570), things good in themselves, instead of *agathós* (18), benevolent] works."

Agathoergéō is similar in meaning to *agathopoiéō* (15), to do good. In Acts 14:17, the UBS text has *agathourgón* instead of *agathopoión* as in the TR. *Agathopoiéō* denotes not simply the doing of good works, as expressed by *agathoergéō*, but also the benefit of those works to others (Luke 6:9, 33, 35). God is said to do good (*agathoergeín*). God does good (*agathoergeí*) because it is His nature to do so; He cannot do evil. However, man may not necessarily benefit by that good due to his own sinfulness. The good which God does sometimes turns out to man's detriment because of man's attitude. Thus God's *agathoergía* (the fem. noun of *agathoergéō*) does not always turn out to be His *agathopoiḯa* (the fem. noun of the verb *agathopoiéō*), good that benefits others. *Agathopoiéō* in Acts 14:17 (TR) would speak of God's intended benevolence and not only a demonstration of His character, *agathoergéō* (UBS).

Syn.: *sumphérō* (4851), to cause things to be brought together for the glory of God and the benefit of oneself and others; *kalopoiéō* (2569), to do well and thus show one's good nature; *euergetéō* (2109), to do acts of benevolence instead of just having a benevolent attitude.

Ant.: *kakóō* (2559), to mistreat; *kakopoiéō* (2554), to do evil, harm; *thlíbō* (2346), to afflict; *talaipōréō* (5003), to make miserable; *adikéō* (91), to wrong, do injustice, hurt; *bláptō* (984), to injure; *ochléō* (3791), to disturb, trouble; *basanízō* (928), to torment.

15. ἀγαθοποιέω *agathopoiéō*; contracted *agathopoiṓ*, fut. *agathopoiḗsō*, from *agathós* (18), benevolent, and *poiéō* (4160), to make or do. To do good to others (Mark 3:4; Luke 6:9, 33, 35; Acts 14:17; 1 Pet 2:15, 20; 3:6, 17; 2 John 1:11).

Deriv.: *agathopoiïa* (16), benevolence; *agathapoiós* (17), one that does well.

Syn.: *agathoergéō* (14), to do good works; *kalopoiéō* (2569), to do well or show one's good nature by doing good; *euergetéō* (2109), to do an act of benevolence; *sumphérō* (4851), to cause things to be brought together for the glory of God and the benefit of oneself and others.

Ant.: *kakóō* (2559), to mistreat; *kakopoiéō* (2554), to do evil, harm; *thlíbō* (2346), to afflict; *talaipōréō* (5003), to make miserable; *adikéō* (91), to wrong, do injustice, hurt; *bláptō* (984), to injure; *ochléō* (3791), to disturb, trouble; *basanízō* (928), to torment.

16. ἀγαθοποιΐα *agathopoiïa*; gen. *agathopoiïas*, fem. noun from *agathopoiéō* (15), to do good works. Well-doing, found only in 1 Pet 4:19 where Peter speaks about those who suffer according to the will of God. The suffering referred to here is not as a consequence for some wrong committed, but suffering because one is a believer. The verb used in relation to the believer's response to this suffering is *paratithésthōsan*, the 3d person pl. pres. imper. mid. of *paratíthēmi* (3908), to present, to deposit as a trust. The verb implies that God Himself places believers where they are; it is God who permits the suffering. Knowing that God is faithful and that as Creator He is in control, believers can entrust their souls to Him and do good despite the outcome.

Ant.: *ponēría* (4189), iniquity, wickedness; *kakía* (2549), naughtiness, evil, malice; *kakoḗtheia* (2550), mischievousness, malignity.

17. ἀγαθοποιός *agathopoiós*; gen. *agathopoioú*, masc.-fem., neut. *agathapoión*, adj. from *agathopoiéō* (15), to do good works. Virtuous, he that does well, an adj. which can be used substantively that speaks not only of the acts of well-doing, but of the character of the

one who performs the acts. Found only in 1 Pet 2:14

Ant.: *kakopoiós* (2555), evildoer; *ponērós* (4190), hurtful, evil.

18. ἀγαθός *agathós*; fem. *agathḗ*, neut. *agathón*, adj. Good and benevolent, profitable, useful.

(I) Good, excellent, distinguished, best, of persons (Matt 19:16, 17; Mark 10:17, 18; Luke 18:18, 19; Sept.: 1 Sam 9:2); of things (Luke 10:42; John 1:46; 2 Thess 2:16; Sept.: Ezra 8:27).

(II) Good, i.e., of good character, disposition, quality.

(A) Of persons: upright, virtuous (Matt 5:45; 12:35; 25:21, 23; Luke 6:45; 19:17; 23:50; John 7:12; Acts 11:24; Sept.: 2 Chr 21:13; Prov 13:2, where *agathós* is used as opposed to *paránomos*, unlawful; Prov 15:3; Isa 63:7, a benevolent judge). Of their external conditions, appearance, dress (Matt 22:10).

(B) Of things: **(1)** in a physical sense, e.g., a tree (Matt 7:17, 18); ground (Luke 8:8; Sept.: Ex 3:8). **(2)** in a moral sense, good, upright, virtuous; e.g., heart (Luke 8:15); commandment (Rom 7:12); word (2 Thess 2:17); will of God (Rom 12:2); the Spirit (Sept.: Neh 9:20; Ps 143:10); good conscience, i.e., conscious of integrity (Acts 23:1; 1 Tim 1:5, 19; 1 Pet 3:16, 21); good works, deeds, virtue, rectitude (Rom 2:7; 13:3; Eph 2:10; Col 1:10; 2 Tim 2:21; 3:17; Titus 1:16; 3:1; Heb 13:21; Sept.: 1 Sam 19:4).

(C) Of abstract things: *agathón* (sing.) and *agathá* (pl.), meaning virtue, rectitude, love of virtue (Matt 12:34, 35; 19:16; Luke 6:45; John 5:29; Rom 2:10; 3:8; 7:18, 19; 9:11; 12:9; 13:3; 16:19; 2 Cor 5:10; 1 Pet 3:11, 13; 3 John 1:11). In Rom 7:13 *tó agathón* means that which is in itself good; Rom 14:16, the good cause, the gospel of Christ; Sept.: Ps 34:14; 53:1, 3.

(III) Good, in respect to operation or influence on others, i.e., useful, beneficial, profitable.

(A) Of persons: benevolent, beneficent (Matt 20:15; Rom 5:7; 1 Thess 3:6;

Titus 2:5; 1 Pet 2:18; Sept.: 2 Chr 30:19; Ps 73:1).

(B) Of things: e.g., *dómata* (1390), gifts (Matt 7:11; Luke 11:13); *dósis* (1394), gift (James 1:17); work (Phil 1:6); conduct (1 Pet 3:16); fruit (James 3:17); fidelity (Titus 2:10); benevolent way (Sept.: 1 Sam 12:23); benevolent commandments (Sept.: Neh 9:13). Benevolent treasure or treasure of good things (Matt 12:35; Luke 6:45); good deeds, benefits (Acts 9:36; 2 Cor 9:8; 1 Tim 2:10; 5:10). With the meaning of suitable or adapted to (Rom 15:2; Eph 4:29, word suitable for education).

(C) Of abstract things: *tó agathón*, something useful and profitable, beneficial (Rom 8:28; 12:21; 13:4; Gal 6:10; Eph 4:28; 6:8; 1 Thess 5:15; Phile 1:6, 14). In the pl. *tá agathá*, things good and useful, benefits, blessings (Matt 7:11; Luke 1:53; 16:25; Gal 6:6; Heb 9:11; 10:1). With the meaning of goods, wealth (Luke 12:18, 19; Sept.: Gen 24:10; 45:18, 20; Deut 6:11).

(IV) Good in respect to the feelings, excited, i.e., pleasant, joyful, happy (1 Pet 3:10; Rom 10:15, blessed times; Sept.: Ps 34:12; Zech 8:19).

Deriv.: *agathopoiéo* (15), to do good to others; *agathōsúnē* (19), goodness; *philágathos* (5358), love of good men.

Syn.: *kalós* (2570), constitutionally good but not necessarily benefiting others; *chrēstós* (5543), useful, kind.

Ant.: *ponērós* (4190), malevolent; *aphilágathos* (865), not a lover or a friend of good.

19. ἀγαθωσύνη *agathōsúnē*; gen. *agathōsúnēs*, fem. noun from *agathós* (18), benevolent. Active goodness.

(I) Of disposition and character, virtue (Rom 15:14; Eph 5:9; 2 Thess 1:11; Sept.: 2 Chr 24:16).

(II) Beneficence, in Gal 5:22 referred to as goodness, but the Eng. word includes several pleasing qualities whereas the Gr. word refers to one particular quality. It is more than *chrēstótēs* (5544), gentleness, kindness, a mellowing of character. It is

character energized, expressing itself in *agathón* (18), benevolence, active good. There is more activity in *agathōsúnē* than in *chrēstótēs*. *Agathōsúnē* does not spare sharpness and rebuke to cause good (*agathón*) in others. A person may display his *agathōsúnē*, his zeal for goodness and truth, in rebuking, correcting, or chastising. Christ's righteous indignation in the temple (Matt 21:13) showed His *agathōsúnē*, goodness, but not His *chrēstótēs*, gentleness. See Rom 15:14; Eph 5:9; 2 Thess 1:11.

Syn.: *euergesía* (2108), good deed; *cháris* (5485), grace, benefit; *tó agathón* (from *agathós* [18], benevolent), the good action or deed, benefit; *eúnoia* (2133), that which is owed to someone; *eupoiḯa* (2140), the good deeds done; *philanthrōpía* (5363), love for human beings, philanthropy.

Ant.: *kakía* (2549), evil, malice; *kakoḗtheia* (2550), mischievousness, malignity; *ponēría* (4189), iniquity, wickedness.

20. ἀγαλλίασις *agallíasis*; gen. *agalliáseōs*, fem. noun from *agalliáō* (21), to exult. Exultation, exuberant joy. Not found in Gr. writers but often meaning joy, exultation (Sept.: Ps 30:5; 45:15; 65:12, rejoicing with song, dancing. See Ps 126:2, 6); great joy (Ps 45:7; 51:8, 12). In the NT, joy, gladness, rejoicing (Luke 1:14, 44; Acts 2:46; Heb 1:9 from Ps 45:7, oil of gladness with which guests were anointed at feasts, where used as an emblem of the highest honors [cf. Jude 1:24]).

Syn.: *chará* (5479), joy, delight, the feeling experienced in one's heart, especially a result of God's grace (*cháris* [5485]), whereas *agallíasis* is the demonstration of that joy; *euphrosúnē* (2167), good cheer, joy.

Ant.: *aischúnē* (152), shame; *aschēmosúnē* (808) unseemliness; *lúpē* (3077), grief; *entropḗ* (1791), shame, the feeling of withdrawal into oneself; *atimía* (819), lack of sense of honor; *phóbos* (5401), fear; *deilía* (1167), fearfulness, lack of courage; *phóbētron* (5400), terror.

21. ἀγαλλιάω *agalliáō*; contracted *agalliṓ*, fut. *agalliásō*, aor. *ēgallíasa*, from *ágan* (n.f.), much, and *hállomai* (242), to leap. To exult, leap for joy, to show one's joy by leaping and skipping denoting excessive or ecstatic joy and delight. Hence in the NT to rejoice, exult. Often spoken of rejoicing with song and dance (Sept.: Ps 2:11; 20:5; 40:16; 68:3). Usually found in the mid. deponent *agalliáomai*.

(I) Used in an absolute sense (Acts 2:26, "my tongue was glad," meaning I rejoiced in words, sang aloud; Luke 10:21; Acts 16:34). It is sometimes put after *chaírō* (5463), to rejoice, which is of less intense significance, and produces an expression meaning to rejoice exceedingly (Matt 5:12; 1 Pet 4:13; Rev 19:7; see Ps 40:16; 90:14).

(II) With a noun of the same significance in an adv. sense (1 Pet 1:8 with *chará* [5479], joy, "rejoice with joy unspeakable").

(III) Followed by *hína* (2443), so that, with the subjunctive (John 8:56, "he rejoiced that he should see my day" [a.t.]).

(IV) Followed by *epí* (1909), upon, with the dat. (Luke 1:47).

(V) Followed by *en* (1722), in, with the dat. where a simple dat. might stand (John 5:35; Acts 16:34; 1 Pet 1:16; Sept.: Ps 13:5; 89:16).

Deriv.: *agallíasis* (20), exultation.

Syn.: *euphraínō* (2165), to cheer, gladden; *chaírō* (5463), to rejoice; *kaucháomai* (2744), to boast, glory, rejoice; *katakaucháomai* (2620), to glory against.

Ant.: *lupéō* (3076), to grieve; *stenázō* (4727), to groan; *diaponéō* (1278), to be sorely grieved; *prosochthízō* (4360), to be vexed with something, irksome; *adēmonéō* (85), to be troubled; *baréō* (916), to burden; *odunáō* (3600), to cause pain.

22. ἄγαμος *ágamos*; gen. *agámou*, masc.-fem., adj. from the priv. *a* (1), and *gámos* (1062), marriage, wedding. Unmarried. Used only in 1 Cor chapter seven to refer to those who are not currently married, whether they have never been married or were once married and have been widowed or, by extension, divorced (1 Cor 7:8, 11, 32, 34).

Ant.: *húpandros* (5220), married.

23. ἀγανακτέω *aganaktéō*; fut. *aganaktḗsō*, from *ágan* (n.f.), very much, and *áchthos* (n.f.), pain, grief. To be oppressed in mind, grieved, resentful. The spiritual significance of being indignant (Matt 20:24; 21:15; 26:8; Mark 10:14, 41; 14:4; Luke 13:14).

Deriv.: *aganáktēsis* (24), indignation.

Syn.: *prosochthízō* (4360), to be sorely vexed; *thumomachéō* (2371), to fight with great anger.

Ant.: *hēsucházō* (2270), to be at rest; *anapaúō* (373), to rest; *eudokéō* (2106), to be well-pleased; *suneudokéō* (4909), to have pleasure in; *anéchomai* (430), to put up with, tolerate.

24. ἀγανάκτησις *aganáktēsis*; gen. *aganaktḗseōs*, from *aganaktéō* (23), to be indignant or under a great burden which results in indignation. Indignation (2 Cor 7:11).

Syn.: *orgḗ* (3709), wrath; *thumós* (2372), anger; *zḗlos* (2205), jealousy, zeal.

Ant.: *eirḗnē* (1515), peace; *hēsuchía* (2271), quietness; *anochḗ* (463), self-restraint, forbearance, tolerance.

25. ἀγαπάω *agapáō*; contracted *agapṓ*, fut. *agapḗsō*. To esteem, love, indicating a direction of the will and finding one's joy in something or someone. It differs from *philéō* (5368), to love, indicating feelings, warm affection, the kind of love expressed by a kiss (*phílēma* [5370]).

(I) To love, to regard with strong affection (Luke 7:42; John 3:35; 8:42; 21:15; 2 Cor 9:7; Rev 3:9; Sept.: Gen 24:67; Ruth

4:15). With the acc. of the corresponding noun, "his great love wherewith he loved us" (Eph 2:4 [cf. 2 Sam 13:15]). Perf. pass. part. *ēgapēménos*, beloved (Eph 1:6; Col 3:12).

(II) As referring to superiors and including the idea of duty, respect, veneration, meaning to love and serve with fidelity (Matt 6:24; 22:37; Mark 12:30, 33; Luke 16:13; Rom 8:28; Sept.: 1 Sam 18:16). The pres. act. part. used substantively of those loving the Lord, meaning faithful disciples or followers of the Lord (Eph 6:24; James 1:12; 2:5; Sept.: Ex 20:6; Deut 5:10).

(III) To love, i.e., to regard with favor, goodwill, benevolence (Mark 10:21; Luke 7:5; John 10:17). In other passages the effects of benevolence are expressed as to wish well to or do good to. To love one's neighbor, one's enemies (Matt 5:43; 19:19; 22:39; Luke 6:32). The fut. imper., *agapéseis*, especially in regard to one's enemies, should not necessarily be taken to mean doing that which will please them, but choosing to show them favor and goodwill (Matt 5:43, 44). One should realize the need of people to be changed through Christ's grace, and do everything possible to bring them to a knowledge of the Lord. This may involve expressions of benevolence or even discipline and punishment, all as the outworking of this love. In 2 Cor 12:15 it means, "even if, having conferred greater benefits on you, I receive less from you" (a.t.).

(IV) Spoken of things, to love, i.e., to delight in (Luke 11:43; John 3:19; Heb 1:9; 1 John 2:15). The expression "not to love" means to neglect, disregard, condemn (Rev 12:11, meaning they condemned their lives even unto death, i.e., they willingly exposed themselves to death). Other references: Matt 5:44, 46; Mark 12:31; Luke 6:27, 35; 7:47; 10:27; John 3:16; 11:5; 12:43; 13:1, 23, 34; 14:15, 21, 23, 24, 28, 31; 15:9, 12, 17; 17:23, 24, 26; 19:26; 21:7, 16, 20; Rom 8:37; 9:13, 25; 13:8, 9; 1 Cor 2:9; 8:3; 2 Cor 11:11; Gal 2:20; 5:14; Eph 5:2, 25,

28, 33; Col 3:19; 1 Thess 1:4; 4:9; 2 Thess 2:13, 16; 2 Tim 4:8, 10; Heb 12:6; James 2:8; 1 Pet 1:8, 22; 2:17; 3:10; 2 Pet 2:15; 1 John 2:10; 3:10, 11, 14, 18, 23; 4:7, 8, 10–12, 19–21; 5:1, 2; Rev 1:5; 20:9.

(V) Contrast with *philéō* (5368), to be content with, denoting common interests, hence to befriend. Most scholars agree that *agapáō* is used of God's love toward man and vice versa, but *philéō* is rarely used by God of the love of men toward Him. In John 21:15, 16, it is a statement by Peter to Jesus and in verse seventeen it is only a question by Jesus to Peter. In verses fifteen and sixteen while Jesus was asking Peter, *Agapás me?* "Do you love me?" (a.t.) Peter was answering, *Philố se*, "I am your friend" (a.t.). In verse seventeen for the third time Jesus asked Peter, but this time He said, *Phileís me?*, "Are you my friend?" (a.t.). Jesus indeed makes us His friends in His great condescension, but for us to call ourselves His friends is somewhat of a presumption.

In the first question of Jesus to Peter in John 21:15, there is the comparison of love (*agápē*) toward Himself versus love toward material things, possibly the fish and bread which all were eating. The expression "more than these" may very well refer to the love of the other disciples present (John 21:2). Jesus was asking whether Peter's love was greater than that of the other disciples. In this question of Jesus to Peter in John 21:15 there is also the comparison of love (*agápē*) toward Himself versus the love of the other disciples present (John 21:2). Again Jesus was asking whether Peter's love was greater than that of the other disciples. Peter in his answer used the expression *sú oídas hóti philố se*, "thou knowest [*oída* (1492), to know intuitively] that I am your friend [*philéo* (5368)]" (a.t.). That was an upgrading by Peter of his devotion to Christ. The Lord, however, intuitively knew that Peter had not accepted His determination to die while He could avoid death (Matt 16:22, 23). Not only did Peter not acknowledge Jesus as his friend, but denied that he even knew

Him (Matt 26:69–75), even as Jesus had predicted Peter would (Matt 26:31–35). The Lord did not accept Peter's self-upgraded love from *agápē* (26) to *philía* (5373), friendship. We love (*agapáō*) God because He first loved us (1 John 4:10). But none of us, especially Peter, earn the right to declare ourselves friends (*phílos* [5384]) of God. He alone can declare us as such, even as He did Abraham (James 2:23).

The second question Jesus asked Peter was not the same as the first. It was not a question of comparison. He did not ask Peter, "Do you love [*agapáō*] me more than these?" but simply "Do you love me [*agapáō*]?" (author's translations). The Lord would be pleased with a personal statement of reciprocation of His love without a comparison of oneself to others. Jesus, being God incarnate, has intuitive knowledge of each one of His children. Thus the Lord would not accept Peter's confession of personal attachment to Himself as that of friendship. Jesus intuitively knew that Peter was not always His devoted friend, for He knew that Peter would deny Him. Some have suggested that in this passage Christ was providing an opportunity for Peter to "redeem" himself from the earlier denial of the Lord.

The third question of Jesus to Peter was different, "Do you love me [*philéō*, Are you my friend]?" (a.t.). Are your interests, now that you have seen Me risen from the dead, different than before the resurrection? Peter became sorrowful because he understood the deeper meaning of Jesus' question (John 21:17). His answer utilized two similar, but distinct verbs, *oída*, to know intuitively, and *ginóskō* (1097), to know experientially: "Lord, thou knowest, [*oídas*, intuitively] all things. Thou knowest [*gínóskeis*, know experientially] that I love thee [*philó*, that I am now your friend]." When it comes to the expression of the love of the Father God to the Son God, both verbs, *agapáō* and *philéō*, are used. John 3:35 states, "The Father loveth [*agapá*]

the Son and hath given all things into his hand." In John 5:20 we read, "For the Father loveth [*phileí*] the Son, and showeth him all things that himself doeth."

Agapáō and never *philéō* is used of love toward our enemies. The range of *philéō* is wider than that of *agapáō* which stands higher than *philéō* because of its moral import, i.e., love that expresses compassion. We are thus commanded to love (*agapáō*) our enemies, to do what is necessary to turn them to Christ, but never to befriend them (*philéō*) by adopting their interests and becoming friends on their level.

Deriv.: *agápē* (26), love; *agapētós* (27), beloved, dear.

Syn.: *philéō* (5368), to befriend, love.

Ant.: *miséō* (3404), to hate.

26. ἀγάπη *agápē*; gen. *agápēs*, fem. noun from *agapáō* (25), to love. Love, affectionate regard, goodwill, benevolence. With reference to God's love, it is God's willful direction toward man. It involves God doing what He knows is best for man and not necessarily what man desires. For example, John 3:16 states, "For God so loved [*ēgápēsen*] the world, that he gave." What did He give? Not what man wanted, but what God knew man needed, i.e., His Son to bring forgiveness to man.

In the pl., *agápai*, love feasts, public banquets of a frugal kind instituted by the early Christian church and connected with the celebration of the Lord's Supper. The provisions were contributed by the more wealthy individuals and were made common to all Christians, whether rich or poor, who chose to partake. Portions were also sent to the sick and absent members. These love feasts were intended as an exhibition of that mutual love which is required by the Christian faith, but as they became subject to abuses, they were discontinued.

(I) Generally, love as in 1 Cor 4:21, "Shall I come unto you with a rod, or in love," means full of love, all love; Col 1:13, "the kingdom of his dear Son [the Son of His love]," is the same as *ho agapētós*, beloved son. Spoken more especially of good will toward others, the love of our neighbor, brotherly affection, which the Lord Jesus commands and inspires (John 15:13; 17:26; Rom 13:10; 1 Cor 13:1; Heb 6:10; 1 John 4:7). In 2 Cor 13:11, "the God of love" means the author and source of love, who Himself is love. In Rom 15:30, "the love of the Spirit" means that love which the Spirit inspires. Followed by *eis* (1519), unto, with the acc. (2 Cor 2:4, 8; 2 Thess 1:3, love unto others; 1 Pet 4:8). Followed by *en* (1722), in, with the dat. (John 13:35, "love one to another"; 2 Cor 8:7).

(**II**) *Hē agápē toú Theoú* or *toú Christoú*, specifically "the love of God" or "of Christ." Here the gen. is sometimes subj. or act. and sometimes obj. or pass.

(**A**) Subj. or act. means the love which God or Christ exercises towards Christians. The love that is derived from God (Rom 5:5; Eph 2:4; 2 Thess 3:5). Followed by *eis* (1519), unto someone (Rom 5:8), and by *en* (1722), in someone (1 John 4:9, 16). The love of Christ means the love which is derived from Christ (2 Cor 5:14).

(**B**) Obj. or pass., that love of which God or Christ is the object in the hearts of Christians. Of God (Luke 11:42; John 5:42; 1 John 2:5). Also used in an absolute sense (1 John 4:16, 18; 2 John 1:6). Of Christ (John 15:10; Rom 8:35). Instead of the gen. *mou*, mine, we find in John 15:9 *en tē agápē tē emē* meaning "in the love, the one of mine" (a.t.).

(**C**) Metaphorically, the effect or proof of love, benevolence, benefit conferred (Eph 1:15; 3:19; 1 John 3:1; 2 Thess 2:10, "the love of the truth," meaning the true love, the true and real benefits conferred by God through Christ).

Syn.: *philía* (5373), friendship based on common interests; *philanthrōpía* (5363), love for man, philanthropy; *agápai heortē* (1859), a feast or festival; *deípnon* (1173), the chief meal of the day, dinner; *dochē* (1403), a reception, feast, banquet.

Ant.: *échthra* (2189), hatred, enmity.

27. ἀγαπητός *agapētós*; fem. *agapētē*, neut. *agapētón*, adj. from *agapáō* (25), to love. Beloved, dear. In the NT, it is used with the force of the perf. pass. part., *ēgapēménos*, beloved, dear.

(**I**) Beloved, dear, but spoken only of Christians as united with God or with each other in the bonds of holy love. *Agapētoí*, the pl. (Acts 15:25; Rom 12:19; 2 Cor 7:1; 12:19; Col 1:7; 4:14; 1 Thess 2:8; 1 Tim 6:2; Heb 6:9; 1 Pet 2:11; 4:12; 2 Pet 3:1, 8, 14, 15, 17; 1 John 3:2, 21; 4:1, 7, 11; 2 John 1:1, 5, 11; Jude 1:3, 17, 20), meaning conjoined in the bonds of faith and love. In 1 Cor 15:58, "beloved brethren," i.e., Christians. See Eph 6:21; Phil 4:1; Col 4:7, 9; Phile 1:1, 2, 16; James 1:16, 19; 2:5. *Agapētoí Theoú*, beloved of God, means chosen by Him to salvation (Rom 1:7; 11:28; Eph 5:1). *Agapētoí sou*, your beloved, refers to the worshipers of God (Sept.: Ps 60:5; 108:6; 127:2). Paul seems to apply the term particularly to those converted under his ministry when he speaks of *Epaíneton tón agapētón mou* in Rom 16:5. Also see Rom 16:8, 9, 12, "Timotheus, who is my beloved son . . . in the Lord" (cf. 1 Cor 4:17; 2 Tim 1:2). Spoken also of a whole church gathered by Paul (1 Cor 4:14, "My beloved sons"). See 1 Cor 10:14; Phil 2:12.

(**II**) The phrase *huiós agapētós* (*huiós* [5207], son; *agapētós*, inherently beloved) means the only son as being the object of peculiar love. In the NT, spoken only of Christ, the Son beloved of God (Matt 3:17; 12:18; 17:5; Mark 1:11; 9:7; Luke 3:22; 9:35; 2 Pet 1:17). In Mark 12:6, "one son, his well-beloved," meaning his only son. See Luke 20:13; Sept.: Gen 22:2, 12. The phrase *pénthos agapētoú* (*pénthos* [3997], mourning; *agapētoú*, of a beloved one) means mourning for an only son, i.e., deep sorrow (Jer 6:26; Amos 8:10; Zech 12:10).

Ant.: *stugētós* (4767), hateful; *theostugēs* (2319), hateful to God.

28. Ἄγαρ *Ágar*; proper noun transliterated from the Hebr. *Hāgār* (1904, OT). Hagar. The name of the Egyptian bondservant in Abraham's household, handmaid to Sarah, probably acquired during their sojourn in Egypt. With the passing years, Abraham felt keenly the lack of a son and heir yet earnestly believed God's promise that he would indeed have a son (Gen 15:2–6). As time progressed, Abraham and Sarah had doubts and sought to gain an heir by their own unsanctioned efforts. A custom at that time, as attested in tablets from Ur and Nuzi, moved childless Sarah to urge Abraham to have a son by her servant Hagar. Thus Ishmael was born, the son of a bondwoman (Gen 16 [cf. Gal 4:24, 25]).

29. ἀγγαρεύω *aggareúō*; fut. *aggareúsō*. To press into service, to send off an *ággaros* or public courier. This word is of Persian origin, and after being received into the Gr. language, passed also into use among the Jews and Romans. The *ággaroi*, couriers, had authority to press into their service men, horses, ships or anything which came in their way and which might serve to hasten their journey. Afterwards *aggareúō* came to mean to press into service for a journey in the manner of *ággaros*. In the NT used as a trans. verb meaning to compel, to press, to accompany one (Matt 5:41; 27:32; Mark 15:21).

Syn.: *anagkázō* (315), to constrain, whether by threat, entreaty, force or persuasion.

Ant.: *eleutheróō* (1659), to make free, to deliver; *apallássō* (525), to release.

30. ἀγγεῖον *aggeíon*; gen. *aggeíou*, neut. noun, a diminutive of *ággos* (n.f.), pail. Vessel (Sept.: Gen 42:25; Num 4:9). A vessel or container which could be used for solid substances such as fish (Matt 13:48, in some texts *ággos*) or liquids such as oil (Matt 25:4). The vessel was made of wood, clay, shell, gold, silver, or copper. In Class. Gr., it meant the body of man in contrast to his soul. It is syn. with *skeúos* (4632), which in the NT is also translated a "vessel," "equipment," or "goods."

31. ἀγγελία *aggelía*; gen. *aggelías*, fem. noun from *ággelos* (32), messenger. Message (1 John 3:11; Sept.: Prov 12:25).

Syn.: *akoḗ* (189), the thing heard; *kḗrugma* (2782), proclamation, preaching.

32. ἄγγελος *ággelos*; gen. *aggélou*, masc. noun. Messenger, one sent to announce or proclaim.

(I) A messenger, one who is sent in order to announce, teach, perform, or explore anything (Matt 11:10; Luke 7:24; 9:52; Gal 4:14; James 2:25; Sept.: Josh 6:17; Mal 2:7). In 1 Cor 11:10, *aggélous*, acc. pl., is interpreted variably as spies or angels, good or evil, even demons. The angels of the seven churches are probably the bishops or pastors of those churches, the delegates or messengers of the churches of God (Rev 1:20; 2:1, 8, 12, 18; 3:1, 7, 14). Heb 13:2 may have reference to itinerate preachers rather than angels.

(II) An angel, a celestial messenger, a being superior to man. God is represented as surrounded by a host of beings of a higher order than man. These He uses as His messengers and agents in administering the affairs of the world and in promoting the welfare of humans (Matt 1:20; 18:10; 22:30; Acts 7:30). As to the numbers of the angels, see Heb 12:22; Rev 5:11. See *archággelos* (743), archangel. In 2 Peter 2:4; Jude 1:6, some of the angels that sinned are said to have been cast down to hell. They are called the angels of the devil or Satan (Matt 25:41; 2 Cor 12:7; Rev 12:9). In Rev 9:11, the angel of the bottomless pit is the destroying angel *Abaddṓn* (3), Abaddon.

Deriv.: *aggelía* (31), message; *archággelos* (743), archangel; *isággelos* (2465), like or equal to an angel.

Syn.: *apóstolos* (652), apostle, messenger.

33. ἄγε *áge*; the imper. of *ágō* (71), to lead away, to bring, to go. Go, intimating compulsion and can be translated come, come now (James 4:13; 5:1).

34. ἀγέλη *agélē*; gen. *agélēs*, fem. noun from *ágō* (71), to lead, to drive. A herd. In the NT, it is used only of swine (Matt 8:30–32; Mark 5:11, 13; Luke 8:32, 33).

35. ἀγενεαλόγητος *agenealógētos*; gen. *agenealogḗtou*, masc.-fem., neut. *agenealógēton*, adj. from the priv. *a* (1), without, and *genealogéō* (1075), to trace a genealogy. Without a genealogy or pedigree. Melchizedek was said to be without genealogy. He was not from any sacerdotal family, as the Levitical priests were from Aaron (Ex 40:15; Num 3:10; Heb 7:3), which might prove his right to the priesthood.
Syn.: *amḗtōr* (282), without the record of a mother; *apátōr* (540), without the record of a father.

36. ἀγενής *agenḗs*; gen. *agenoús*, masc.-fem., neut. *agenés*, adj. from the priv. *a* (1), and *génos* (1085), nation, offspring, race. Ignoble, base, one who does not live up to the expectation of his stock, race or nation. In the NT, it is found only in 1 Cor 1:28.
Syn.: *tapeinós* (5011), low, humble, of lowly degree.
Ant.: *eugenés* (2104), noble; *agathós* (18), benevolent.

37. ἀγιάζω *hagiázō*; fut. *hagiásō*, from *hágios* (40), holy. To make holy, sanctify.
(I) To make clean, render pure.
(A) Particularly in Heb 9:13.
(B) Metaphorically, to render clean in a moral sense, to purify, sanctify (Rom 15:16, "being sanctified by the Holy Ghost," meaning by the sanctifying influences of the Holy Spirit on the heart. See 1 Cor 6:11; Eph 5:26; 1 Thess 5:23; 1

Tim 4:5; Heb 2:11; 10:10, 14, 29; 13:12; Rev 22:11). *Hoi hēgiasménoi*, those who are sanctified, is a reference to Christians in general (Acts 20:32; 26:18; 1 Cor 1:2; Jude 1:1). In 1 Cor 7:14, the perf. tense *hēgíastai*, has been sanctified, refers to an unbelieving husband or wife who is sanctified by a believing spouse. The word "sanctification" here should not be construed to mean salvation. The unbelieving partner is set apart on account of the believing partner. The unbeliever comes under a special and direct spiritual influence and benefits from divine favor in the life of the believer. As long as there is contact, there is hope that the unbeliever will turn to faith in Jesus Christ. The point of the passage is that in such a marriage the believer is not defiled by the unbeliever, rather the unbeliever is sanctified by the believer.
(II) To consecrate, devote, set apart from a common to a sacred use since in the Jewish ritual, this was one great object of the purifications.
(A) Spoken of things (Matt 23:17; 23:19; 2 Tim 2:21; Sept.: Lev 8:10f., 30).
(B) Spoken of persons, to consecrate as being set apart of God and sent by Him for the performance of His will (John 10:36, "whom the father hath sanctified, and sent into the world"; 17:17, "Sanctify them through [or in the promulgation of] thy truth" [cf. John 17:18, 19]).
(III) To regard and venerate as holy, to hallow (Matt 6:9; Luke 11:2; 1 Pet 3:15; Sept.: Isa 8:13; 10:17; 29:23). Thus the verb *hagiázō*, to sanctify, when its object is something that is filthy or common, can only be accomplished by separation (*aphorízō* [873]) or withdrawal. It also refers to the withdrawal from fellowship with the world and selfishness by gaining fellowship with God.
Deriv.: *hagiasmós* (38), sanctification.
Ant.: *koinóō* (2840), to profane, call common or unclean; *miaínō* (3392), to stain, pollute; *molúnō* (3435), to besmear,

defile; *spilóō* (4695), to make a stain or spot, defile; *phtheírō* (5351), to corrupt.

38. ἁγιασμός *hagiasmós*; gen. *hagiasmoú*, masc. noun from *hagiázō* (37), to sanctify. Sanctification, translated "holiness" (Rom 6:19, 22; 1 Thess 4:7; 1 Tim 2:15; Heb 12:14). Separation unto God (in 1 Cor 1:30, cause or author of sanctification; 2 Thess 2:13, "sanctification of the Spirit," meaning produced by the Holy Spirit; 1 Pet 1:2). The resultant state, the behavior befitting those so separated (1 Thess 4:3, 4, resulting in abstention from fornication). There are two other Gr. words which are translated "holiness" but they must be distinguished from *hagiasmós*, sanctification. They are *hagiótēs* (41), the attribute of holiness, and *hagiōsúnē* (42), the state of being sanctified, i.e., sanctification not as a process but as the result of a process. *Hagiasmós* is similar to *dikaíōsis* (1347), justification, which denotes not only the act of God's free grace in justifying sinners, but also the result of that justification upon the sinner in making him just and equipping him to recognize the rights of God on his life. *Hagiasmós* refers not only to the activity of the Holy Spirit in setting man apart unto salvation and transferring him into the ranks of the redeemed, but also to enabling him to be holy even as God is holy (2 Thess 2:13).
   Syn.: *hosiótēs* (3742), the quality of ceremonial conformity; *eusébeia* (2150), piety, godliness; *eilikríneia* (1505), sincerity.
   Ant.: *míasma* (3393), pollution, defilement; *miasmós* (3394), the act of defiling, the process in contrast to *míasma*, the defiling element; *molusmós* (3436), the action whereby a person or thing is defiled; *phthorá* (5356), corruption; *akatharsía* (167), moral uncleanness.

39. ἅγιον *hágion*; neut. of the adj. *hágios* (40), holy. Used of those structures set apart for God.
   (I) Of the tabernacle in the wilderness (Heb 9:1). It is sometimes used specifically of the inner part of the tabernacle, the Holy of Holies, the holiest of all (Heb 9:3, 8, 24, 25). In Heb 9:3, *hágia*, pl. without the art., appears in the expression *Hágia Hagíōn*, Holy of Holies. *Hágia* is probably intended to fix attention on the character of the sanctuary as being holy. The pl. suggests the idea of the sanctuary with all its parts. *En tópō hagíō* (*en* [1722], in; *tópō* [5117] place, dat. without the art.; *hagíō*, holy, the dat.), in the holy place (Matt 24:15).
   (II) *Hagíōn* in Heb 8:2 refers to heaven itself, the immediate presence of God and His throne. Heaven is designated as the true tabernacle (Heb 8:2; 9:12; 10:19).
   Syn.: *naós* (3485), the inner part of the temple in Jerusalem; *hierón* (2411), a sacred place, the entire area of the temple.
   Ant.: *koinós* (2839), common, defiled; *spílos* (4696), a spot, a moral blemish.

40. ἅγιος *hágios*; fem. *hagía*, neut. *hágion* (39), adj. from *hágos* (n.f.), any matter of religious awe, expiation, sacrifice. Holy, set apart, sanctified, consecrated, saint. It has a common root, *hág-*, with *hagnós* (53), chaste, pure. Its fundamental idea is separation, consecration, devotion to the service of Deity, sharing in God's purity and abstaining from earth's defilement.
   (I) Pure, clean, ceremonially or morally clean, including the idea of deserved respect, reverence.
   (A) It particularly means perfect, without blemish (Rom 12:1).
   (B) Metaphorically it means morally pure, upright, blameless in heart and life, virtuous, holy. **(1)** Generally (Mark 6:20; Rom 7:12; 1 Cor 7:34; Eph 1:4; 5:27; 1 Pet 1:16; Sept.: Lev 11:44). **(2)** Spoken of those who are purified and sanctified by the influences of the Spirit. This is assumed of all who profess the Christian name, hence *hágios*, saint, *hágioi*, saints, Christians (Acts 9:13, 14, 32, 41; 26:10; Rom 1:7; 8:27; 1 Thess 3:13). Spoken of those who are to be in any way included in the Christian community (1 Cor 7:14). Holy kiss means the sacred Christian kiss,

the pledge of Christian affection (Rom 16:16; 1 Cor 16:20; 2 Cor 13:12).

(II) Consecrated, devoted, sacred, holy, meaning set apart from a common to a sacred use; spoken of places, temples, cities, the priesthood, men (Matt 4:5; 7:6; 24:15; 27:53; Acts 6:13; 7:33; Rom 11:16, of firstfruit); of a male opening the womb (Luke 2:23); of apostles (Eph 3:5); of prophets (Luke 1:70; Acts 3:21; 2 Pet 1:21); of angels (Matt 25:31).

(III) Holy, hallowed, worthy of reverence and veneration:

(A) Of God (John 17:11; Rev 4:8; 6:10; Sept.: Isa 5:16; 6:3).

(B) Of His Name (Luke 1:49; Sept.: Lev 22:2).

(C) Of the Holy Spirit (Matt 1:18).

(D) Of holy covenant (Luke 1:72).

(E) Of the Holy Scriptures (Rom 1:2; Sept.: Dan 11:28, 30).

The *hiereús* (2409), priest, although he may not always be *hágios*, holy, performs priestly duties or ordinances and is sacred or consecrated (*hósios* [3741]).

Deriv.: *hagiázō* (37), to sanctify; *hagiótēs* (41), holiness; *hagiōsúnē* (42), holiness, the quality of sanctification.

Syn.: *hieroprepḗs* (2412), a fitting sanctity; *eusebḗs* (2152), godly, pious; *hósios* (3741), pure from evil contact, ceremonially pure; *áspilos* (784), without spot; *hierós* (2413), sacred, outwardly associated with God; *eilikrinḗs* (1506), sincere, pure.

Ant.: *koinós* (2839), common, defiled; *akáthartos* (169), unclean.

41. ἁγιότης hagiótēs; gen. *hagiótētos*, fem. noun from *hágios* (40), holy. Holiness. In the NT, it occurs only in Heb 12:10. *Hagiótēs* as moral holiness is to be distinguished from *hosiótēs* (3742), sanctity that conforms to religious traditions, which is related to *hósios* (3741) as contrasted with *hágios*. *Hagiótēs*, inherent or acquired moral holiness, is also to be distinguished from *hagiasmós*, sanctification, specifically the act of sanctification as effected by God and passed on to the character of man.

Syn.: *hagiōsúnē* (42), the attribute of holiness.

✓**42. ἁγιωσύνη hagiōsúnē**; gen. *hagiōsúnēs*, fem. noun from *hágios* (40), holy. Sanctity or holiness. *Hagiōsúnē* and *hagiótēs* (41) are qualities of character for which there need not be any proof; but for *hagiasmós* (38), the process of sanctification and the result of that process upon the individual, proof is necessary at each stage of its progressive achievement.

Hagiōsúnē occurs in only three places in the NT: In Rom 1:4, it refers to the holiness of God pervading and molding the scheme of redemption and finally being made manifest in and by Christ. The contrast between "according to the flesh" and "according to the spirit of holiness" is not of natural and moral qualities, but of human and divine relationship or dependence. The expression here is not *pneúma hágion* (*pneúma* [4151], spirit; *hágion* [39], holy) Holy Spirit, but *pneúma hagiōsúnēs*, spirit of sanctity or holiness. This does not refer to something Christ achieved but what Christ was in Himself, holy. In His flesh the Lord Jesus did not achieve holiness, but manifested the holiness that was His forever. 2 Cor 7:1 is an exhortation to believers to perfect holiness, to live a virtuous life in the fear of God. 1 Thess 3:13 speaks of the holiness of man, a life that is pleasing to God. See Eph 1:4; 5:27; Col 1:22.

Syn.: *hagiasmós* (38), sanctification; *hosiótēs* (41), the quality of ceremonial compliance; *eusébeia* (2150), piety, godliness.

Ant.: *akatharsía* (167), uncleanness; *miasmós* (3394), the act of defilement; *míasma* (3393), defilement; *molusmós* (3436), the act of defiling; *spílos* (4696), moral blemish; *phthorá* (5356), corruption.

43. ἀγκάλη agkálē; gen. *agkálēs*, fem. noun from *agkḗ* (n.f.), an arm. The arm when bent, found only in Luke 2:28.

Syn.: *brachíōn* (1023), the shorter part of the arm from the shoulder to the elbow, used metaphorically to denote strength.

44. ἄγκιστρον *ágkistron*; gen. *agkístrou*, neut. noun akin to *ágkos* (n.f.), a bend, curve, hence the Eng. "angle," formed by the arm when bent. A hook, found only in Matt 17:27; Sept.: 2 Kgs 19:28; Job 40:20; Isa 19:8; Ezek 32:3; Hab 1:15.

45. ἄγκυρα *ágkura*, gen. *agkúras*, fem. noun. That which forms a bend and can stabilize the thing to which it is attached, hence an anchor (Acts 27:29, 30, 40). Metaphorically applied to the hope generated by faith in the gospel, enabling the believer to stand firm and immovable in the face of temptations, calamities and storms (Heb 6:19).

46. ἄγναφος *ágnaphos*; gen. *agnáphou*, masc.-fem., neut. *ágnaphon*, adj. from the priv. *a* (1), without, and *gnáptō* (n.f.), to smooth fibers by carding. (A card is a wire-toothed brush or similar implement used in disentangling and combing out fibers of wool, flax, etc., preparatory to spinning.) Not carded, new, occurs only in Matt 9:16 and Mark 2:21 where it refers to an unsewn piece of cloth. See Luke 5:36. Related word: *gnapheús* (1102), fuller.

47. ἀγνεία *hagneía*; gen. *hagneías*, fem. noun from *hagnós* (53), pure from defilement, not contaminated. Purity, referring to chastity. Used only in 1 Tim 4:12; 5:2. In the latter reference, it refers to one's moral attitude toward younger sisters in Christ and denotes the chastity which shuts out any impurity of spirit or manner that might defile.

Syn.: *katharótēs* (2514), the state of remaining clean; *katharismós* (2512), the act or process of cleansing, corresponding to *hagnismós* (49), ceremonial purification.

Ant.: *míasma* (3393), defilement occasioned by one's contact with the world;

miasmós (3394), the act or process of becoming defiled; *molusmós* (3436), defilement; *spílos* (4696), a spot, a moral blemish.

48. ἀγνίζω *hagnízō*; fut. *hagnísō*, from *hagnós* (53), pure. To make clean, purify.

(I) To consecrate, purify, lustrate. Purification was required in priests for divine service (Num 8:21; 2 Chr 29:5, 34), and indeed in all who belonged to the chosen people (Ex 19:10, 11; Josh 3:5). It was to prepare oneself by participating in the sacred festivals in visiting the temple, offering up prayers, abstaining from certain kinds of food, washing the clothes, bathing, or shaving the head (John 11:55 [cf. Sept.: Ex 19:10, 14ff.; 2 Chr 29:16, 18]).

(II) It is used in the mid., *hagnízomai*, perf. and aor. pass. *hḗgnismai*, *hēgnísthēn* with mid. meaning to live as one under a vow of abstinence, i.e., like a Nazarite (Acts 21:24, 26; 24:18). The Jews were accustomed, when under a vow of this kind, to abstain for a certain time from the better kinds of food, to let their hair grow, to keep themselves from all pollution, and so forth. When this time had expired, they were freed from the obligation of their vow by a particular sacrifice (Num 6:2–21).

(III) Metaphorically, to render pure in a moral sense, to reform (James 4:8; 1 Pet 1:22; 1 John 3:3). Used not only with the meaning of purifying or cleansing, but also with the collateral meaning of consecration.

Deriv.: *hagnismós* (49), ceremonial purification.

Syn.: *katharízō* (2511), to cleanse; *kathaírō* (2508), to cleanse, purge; *ekkathaírō* (1571), to cleanse out, purge from; *diakatharízō* (1245), to cleanse thoroughly.

Ant.: *koinóō* (2840), to make common, unholy, defile; *molúnō* (3435), to besmear as spoken of moral defilement resulting from contact with the world; *spilóō* (4695), to spot, besmear; *phtheírō*

(5351), to corrupt; *miaínō* (3392), to stain, of ceremonial and moral defilement.

49. ἁγνισμός hagnismós; gen. *hagnismoú*, masc. noun from *hagnízō* (48), to consecrate. Act of consecration, purification of the Levites (Num 8:7; 31:23; see 6:9–13). In the NT only in Acts 21:26.

Syn.: *katharismós* (2512), the act of cleansing; *katharótēs* (2514), the result or state of cleansing.

50. ἀγνοέω agnoéō; contracted *agnoṓ*, fut. *agnoḗsō*, from the priv. *a* (1), not, and *noéō* (3539), to perceive, understand. Not to recognize or know.

(I) To be ignorant of, unacquainted with, followed by the acc. (Acts 17:23; Rom 10:3; 11:25; 2 Cor 2:11); with the prep. *perí* (4012), concerning, meaning to be in ignorance concerning anything (1 Cor 12:1; 1 Thess 4:13); followed by *hóti* (3754), that (Rom 1:13 "I would not have you ignorant," i.e., be well assured; 2:4; 6:3; 7:1; 11:25; 1 Cor 10:1; 2 Cor 1:8). In the pass., to be unknown, unrecognized, rejected (2 Cor 6:9). It came to mean to be ignorant, to have no discernment of, not to understand (Mark 9:32; Luke 9:45; Rom 10:3; Acts 13:27 [cf. Acts 17:23; 1 Cor 2:8; 14:38 "let him be ignorant [voluntarily]," of foolish action; 1 Tim 1:13]).

(II) To err, to commit a fault or faults arising from the want of discernment, knowledge, or insight, denoting conduct of which the result and importance is unperceived by the agent (Heb 5:2; 2 Pet 2:12; Sept.: Lev 4:13; 5:18). The idea that sin can be done ignorantly and involuntarily is not found in the NT.

Deriv.: *agnóēma* (51), mistake, oversight, sin resulting from ignorance; *ágnoia* (52), ignorance.

Syn.: *lanthánō* (2990), to be hidden, concealed, unknown.

Ant.: *noéō* (3539), to perceive; *katanoéō* (2657), to perceive clearly; *eídō* (1492), to consider; *suneidéō* (4894), to have mental perception; *manthánō*

(3129), to learn; *katamanthánō* (2648), to learn thoroughly; *ginṓskō* (1097), to know by experience and observation; *epiginṓskō* (1921), to have full knowledge, to accept the knowledge of revelation; *katalambánō* (2638), to apprehend; *dokéō* (1380), to think; *logízomai* (3049), to reckon; *nomízō* (3543), to suppose; *phronéō* (5426), to have in mind, think; *krínō* (2919), to make a judgment, an evaluation; *suníēmi* (4920), to perceive; *epístamai* (1987), to know well; *punthánomai* (4441), to inquire; *gnōrízō* (1107), to make known.

51. ἀγνόημα agnóēma; gen. *agnoḗmatos*, neut. noun from *agnoéō* (50) not to know, ignore. Error (Sept.: Gen 43:12). The word is found in the NT only in Heb 9:7. The *agnoḗmata*, for which the high priest offered sacrifice on the great Day of Atonement, were not specifically willful transgressions or presumptuous sins, but the sins of the nation as a whole.

Syn.: *hamartía* (266), sin.

Ant.: *gnôsis* (1108), knowledge; *epígnōsis* (1922), full or additional knowledge, hence revelation.

52. ἄγνοια ágnoia; gen. *agnoías*, fem. noun from *agnoéō* (50), not to know. Want of knowledge, ignorance which leads to mistaken conduct and forbids unconditional imputation of the guilt of the acts performed (Acts 3:17; 1 Pet 1:14 [cf. Luke 23:34; 1 Cor 2:8]). According to Paul this *ágnoia* or ignorance is the characteristic of heathendom (Acts 17:30; Eph 4:18 [cf. Eph 4:17]) and is a state which renders repentance necessary (Acts 17:30). Thus it eventually furnishes ground for blame (Eph 4:18), or otherwise for forbearance.

Ant.: *gnôsis* (1108) knowledge.

53. ἁγνός hagnós; fem. *hagnḗ*, neut. *hagnón*, adj. Freedom from defilements or impurities. In a more restricted sense, not only chaste but also virginal. Akin to *hágios* (40), holy.

(I) Innocent, pure, blameless (2 Cor 7:11; Phil 4:8; 1 Tim 5:22).

(II) Modest, chaste (2 Cor 11:2; Titus 2:5; 1 Pet 3:2).

(III) Pure, perfect, holy. Of God (1 John 3:3); of His wisdom (James 3:17; Sept.: Ps 12:1; 19:11).

Deriv.: *hagneía* (47), purity, cleanliness; *hagnízō* (48), to make clean, purify; *hagnótēs* (54), cleanness, pureness; *hagnṓs* (55), purely, sincerely.

Syn.: *alēthinós* (228), true; *gnḗsios* (1103), genuine; *apseudḗs* (893), true; *ádolos* (97), unadulterated; *katharós* (2513), clean; *amíantos* (283), undefiled; *áspilos* (784), unspotted; *haploús* (573), single, clear; *eilikrinḗs* (1506), sincere; *akéraios* (185), harmless, innocent; *ádolos* (97), without deceit.

Ant.: *dólios* (1386), deceitful; *akáthartos* (169), dirty; *rhuparós* (4508), wicked, vile; *bébēlos* (952), profane, wicked; *ponērós* (4190), evil; *kakós* (2556), bad; *plastós* (4112), false, feigned.

54. ἀγνότης *hagnótēs*; gen. *hagnótētos*, fem. noun from *hagnós* (53), pure. Purity, sincerity (2 Cor 6:6). In 2 Cor 11:3 UBS *hagnótēs* occurs with *haplótēs* (572), sincerity, simpleness, the opposite of duplicity, whereas the TR has only *haplótēs*. *Haplótēs* refers to sincerity, *eilikríneia* (1505), as part of the character of a person and not necessarily its influence on others.

Syn.: *hagneía* (47), purity; *katharótēs* (2514), cleanness, purification.

Ant.: *aischrótēs* (151), shamefulness, filthiness; *akatharsía* (167), filthiness; *rhuparía* (4507), dirtiness; *anaídeia* (335), impudence; *entropḗ* (1791), shame, withdrawal; *ponēría* (4189), depravity, wickedness; *kakía* (2549), badness; *hupókrisis* (5272), hypocrisy.

55. ἀγνῶς *hagnṓs*; adv. from *hagnós* (53), chaste. Purely, sincerely. In Phil 1:16, it refers to the simplicity of spirit with the absence of selfish motives.

Therefore, *hagnṓs* can really mean without duplicity.

Syn.: *haplṓs* (5740, simply, without duplicity).

56. ἀγνωσία *agnōsía*; gen. *agnōsías*, fem. noun from the priv. *a* (1), without, and *gnôsis* (1108), knowledge. Ignorance. In Class. Gr., it meant not being acquainted with something. In the NT, it is not merely an intellectual ignorance but a moral defect or fault, a willful ignorance or blindness (1 Cor 15:34 [cf. Eph 2:12; 1 Pet 2:15; Sept.: Job 35:16]).

Syn.: *ágnoia* (52), ignorance.

Ant.: *sophía* (4678), wisdom; *gnôsis* (1108), knowledge.

57. ἄγνωστος *ágnōstos*; gen. *agnṓstou*, masc.-fem., neut. *ágnoston*, adj. from the priv. *a* (1), not, and *gnōstós* (1110), known. Unknown. In the Class. Gr., not knowable, withdrawing oneself from being known, unrecognizable. In Acts 17:23, it is used with a pass. meaning, the unknown god, or the god who did not make himself known to man. In the pantheon of Athenian gods, there were those who the Greeks thought did not reveal themselves to man. The altars were to these unknown deities and not to the true God. The Apostle Paul revealed to them the true God whom, likewise, they did not know.

Syn.: *apókruphos* (614), hidden, kept secret; *kruptós* (2927), private, concealed secret; *ádēlos* (82), indistinct, uncertain; *aphanḗs* (852), unapparent; *árrētos* (731), unsaid, unspeakable, inexpressible

Ant.: *gnōstós* (1110), known; *phanerós* (5318) and *emphanḗs* (1717), manifest; *lamprós* (2986), bright, clear; *dḗlos* (1212), evident, manifest.

58. ἀγορά *agorá*; gen. *agorás*, fem. noun from *ageírō* (n.f.), to collect, gather. A place in which the people assemble, assembly.

(I) The place of meeting, a public place, a broad street, and so forth (Matt 11:16; 20:3; 23:7; Mark 6:56; 12:38;

Luke 7:32; 11:43; 20:46; see Sept.: Eccl 12:4, 5).

(II) A forum, a market place where things were exposed for sale and where assemblies and public trials were held (Mark 7:4; Acts 16:19; 17:17).

Deriv.: *agorázō* (59), to buy; *agoraíos* (60), relating to the market place, a vulgar person.

Syn.: *plateía* (4113), broadway, square; *ámphodon* (296), an open place where two streets meet, the open street.

59. ἀγοράζω *agorázō*; fut. *agorásō*, from *agorá* (58), market place. To buy. With the acc., to buy a thing (Matt 13:44, 46; 14:15; 25:9, 10; 27:7; Mark 6:36, 37; 15:46; 16:1; Luke 9:13; 14:18, 19; 22:36; John 4:8; 6:5; Sept.: Gen 41:57; Isa 24:2). With the gen. it indicates the value of something (Mark 6:37). In the pass. in 1 Cor 6:20; 7:23, declaring that believers "are bought with a price" or "for a price" (a.t.). The consequence of something or someone having been bought is that the buyer has the right of possession. In the redemptive work of Christ the idea is that Christ, by offering Himself for us as due satisfaction, freed us from our liability in paying it ourselves (1 Cor 6:20; 7:23; Gal 3:13; 2 Pet 2:1; Rev 5:9; 14:3, 4). He, having paid the price, binds us to Himself. Other references: Mark 11:15; Luke 17:28; 19:45; John 13:29; 1 Cor 7:30; Rev 3:18; 13:17; 18:11.

Deriv.: *exagorázō* (1805), to buy out, especially to purchase a slave for his freedom.

Syn.: *ōnéomai* (5608), to buy; *emporeúomai* (1710), to trade, both buying and selling; *ktáomai* (2932), to obtain; *peripoiéō* (4046), to gain, possess, purchase; *lutróō* (3084), to release on receipt of ransom, redeem.

Ant.: *pōléō* (4453), to sell; *pipráskō* (4097), to carry across the sea for selling; *apodídōmi* (591), to give up or back, to sell.

60. ἀγοραῖος *agoraíos*; gen. *agoraíou*, masc.-fem., neut. *agoraíon*, adj. from

agorá (58), a marketplace. Belonging to the marketplace. Found only in the pl. in the NT. In Acts 17:5 used to describe loose, profligate fellows who spent their time idly in the marketplace (cf. Matt 20:3). In Acts 19:38, it refers to the courts to which various matters were referred for solution by representatives of the law. These courts were held in the forum or public place, i.e., the marketplace.

Syn.: *agenḗs* (36), one of low birth, ignoble; *tapeinós* (5011), low, insignificant; *koinós* (2839), common.

Ant.: *eugenḗs* (2104), noble; *krátistos* (2903), most noble; *euschḗmōn* (2158), noble.

61. ἄγρα *ágra*; gen. *ágras*, fem. noun. A capture or catching, a catch of fish (Luke 5:4, 9).

Deriv.: *agreúō* (64), to catch.

62. ἀγράμματος *agrámmatos*; gen. *agrammátou*, masc.-fem., neut. *agrámmaton*, adj. from *a* (1), without, and *grámma* (1121), a letter, learning. Unlearned, illiterate (Acts 4:13).

Syn.: *amathḗs* (261), unlearned; *apaídeutos* (521), uninstructed; *idiṓtēs* (2399), unlearned, ignorant.

Ant.: *euschḗmōn* (2158), well-informed; *lógios* (3052), eloquent; *didaktós* (1318), instructed; *didaktikós* (1317), instructive.

63. ἀγραυλέω *agrauléō*; contracted *agraulṓ*, fut. *agraulḗsō*, from *agrós* (68), field, and *aulízomai* (835), to remain in the fields. To live in the field or outdoors, usually spending the night there. Found only in Luke 2:8 (cf. Gen 31:40).

Syn.: *ménō* (3306), to stay, abide.

Ant.: *metatíthēmi* (3346), move; *metakinéō* (3334), to remove; *methístēmi* (3179), to transfer; *astatéō* (790), not to have a permanent place to stay or stand; *ekchōréō* (1633), to depart out; *metoikízō* (3351), to transfer residence.

64. ἀγρεύω *agreúō*; fut. *agreúsō*, from *ágra* (61), a catch. To hunt, to take or catch animals, birds, or fish. Figuratively in Mark 12:13, to catch or ensnare with words.

Deriv.: *zōgréō* (2221), to take alive.

Syn.: *thēreúō* (2340), to hunt or catch wild beasts; *piázō* (4084), to capture, apprehend.

Ant.: *apóllumi* (622), to lose.

65. ἀγριέλαιος *agriélaios*; gen. *agrielaíou*, masc. noun from *ágrios* (66), wild, and *elaía* (1636), olive tree, olive. Wild olive tree. Found only in Rom 11:17, 24.

Ant.: *kalliélaios* (2565), a cultivated olive tree.

66. ἄγριος *ágrios*; fem. *agría*, neut. *ágrion*, adj. from *agrós* (68), field. Belonging to the field, wild. Applied to honey which in Judea was frequently found in hollow trees or the clefts of rocks (Matt 3:4; Mark 1:6 [cf. Deut 32:13; Judg 14:8; 1 Sam 14:25, 26; Ps 81:16]). This is why Palestine is often called a land flowing with honey. Wild, turbulent, tempestuous (Jude 1:13).

Deriv.: *agriélaios* (65), a wild olive tree.

Syn.: *anémeros* (434), savage, fierce; *bárbaros* (915), barbarian.

Ant.: *hḗremos* (2263), tranquil; *práos* (4235), gentle, meek; *eugenḗs* (2104), noble.

67. Ἀγρίππας *Agríppas*; gen. *Agríppa*, masc. proper noun. Agrippa.

(I) Herod Agrippa the elder or Herod the king (Acts 12:1, 6, 11, 19–21; 23:35), otherwise known as Agrippa. He was a son of Aristobulus and grandson of Herod the Great and Mariamne. After his father's execution in 7 B.C., he was sent to Rome with his mother Bernice and lived on terms of intimacy with the imperial family. On the accession of Caligula he received with the title of king the provinces which before belonged to his uncle Philip and to Lysanias. To these were added those of Herod Antipas. In A.D. 43, Claudius gave him further all those parts of Judea and Samaria which belonged to Herod the Great. He died suddenly and miserably at Caesarea in A.D. 44 (Acts 12:21–23).

(II) Herod Agrippa the younger, born in A.D. 27, called Agrippas (Acts 25:13, 22–24, 26; 26:1, 2, 7, 19, 27, 28, 32). He was the son of the elder Herod Agrippa. At his father's death he received from Claudius the kingdom of Chalcis, which belonged to his uncle Herod. He was then seventeen years old. In A.D. 53, he was given the title of king and was transferred to the provinces which his father at first possessed, i.e., Batanea, Trachonitis, Auranitis, and Abilene. These territories north and northwest of Palestine were enlarged by Nero in A.D. 56. He changed the name of his capital from Caesarea Philippi to Neronias as a compliment to the Emperor Nero. From A.D. 48–66 he had the prerogative of appointing the Jewish high priests. He did his best to prevent the outbreak of the Jewish war against Rome in A.D. 66. When his efforts failed, he remained loyal to Rome and was rewarded with a further expansion of his kingdom. He died childless about A.D. 100. He is best known in the NT for hearing Paul's defense (Acts 25:13; 26:32).

68. ἀγρός *agrós*; gen. *agroú*, masc. noun. Field (Matt 6:28, 30); an area of cultivated ground (Matt 13:24, 27, 44; 27:7, 8). In the pl., lands, fields (Matt 19:29; Mark 10:30; Luke 15:15); the country in distinction from cities or villages (Mark 5:14; 6:56; Luke 8:34; 9:12). See Matt 13:31, 36, 38; 22:5; 24:18, 40; 27:10; Mark 6:36; 10:29; 13:16; 15:21; 16:12; Luke 12:28; 14:18; 15:25; 17:7, 31, 36; 23:36; Acts 4:37.

Deriv.: *agrauléō* (63), to live outdoors; *ágrios* (66), wild.

Syn.: *patrís* (3968), one's native country; *chṓra* (5561), country, region, land; *méros* (3313), place, country; *gḗ* (1093), earth, land; *édaphos* (1475), ground.

69. ἀγρυπνέω agrupnéō; agrupnṓ, fut. agrupnḗsō, from the priv. a (1), without, and húpnos (5258), sleep. To abstain totally from sleep, to watch, wake, be awake. Spiritually, to be watchful and attentive to spiritual things (Mark 13:33; Luke 21:36; Eph 6:18; Heb 13:17).

Deriv.: agrupnía (70), sleeplessness or watchfulness.

Syn.: dianuktereúō (1273), to remain awake all night; grēgoréō (1127), to watch, keep awake, be vigilant; néphō (3525), to abstain from wine or to be morally alert, sober. With the sense of alertness: blépō (991), to take heed; horáō (3708), to watch; proséchō (4337), to give heed, turn one's attention to; epéchō (1907), to take heed; phulássomai (5442), to beware.

Ant.: aphupnóō (879), to fall asleep; koimáō (2837), to sleep.

70. ἀγρυπνία agrupnía; gen. agrupnías, fem. noun from agrupnéō (69), to stay awake. Total abstinence from sleep, watchfulness (2 Cor 6:5; 11:27).

Ant.: koímēsis (2838), sleeping, repose; húpnos (5258), sleep.

71. ἄγω ágō; imper. áge (33), fut. áxō, aor. pass. ḗchthēn, 2d aor. ḗgagon. To lead, lead along, bring, carry, remove.

(I) Trans. or in an absolute sense, to lead, conduct, bring.

(A) Used in a variety of modifications which are determined by adjuncts. **(1)** Ágō éxō (1854) out, to lead out, bring forth (John 19:4, 13). **(2)** Followed by héōs (2193), until (Luke 4:29; Acts 17:15). **(3)** Used with epí (1909), upon, with the acc. of person or place, to lead or conduct, bring before (Matt 10:18; Luke 21:12; 23:1; Acts 17:19; 18:12; Sept.: Ex 22:13; Jer 25:9; Ezek 43:1). See in Acts 8:32, epí sphagḗn (sphagḗn [4967], slaughter), for the purpose of slaughtering, in fulfillment of Isa 53:7. **(4)** Followed by hṓde (5602), hither, to bring hither (Luke 19:27; Sept.: Judg 18:3). **(5)** To lead or bring to anyone, followed by prós (4314), toward

(Luke 4:40; 18:40; 19:35; John 1:42; 8:3; 9:13; Acts 9:27; 23:18; Sept.: Gen 2:19, 22). Used in the same sense with the dat. in Matt 21:2, agageté moi, bring to me. The verb is also used by itself in the same sense as to bring (Matt 21:7; Mark 11:2, 7; Luke 19:30; John 7:45; 10:16; Acts 5:21, 26, 27; 19:37; 20:12; 25:6, 17, 23). **(6)** To bring with one (Acts 21:16, "brought with them one Mnason"; 1 Thess 4:14, "will God bring with him" meaning into heaven, see 1 Thess 4:17; 2 Tim 4:11, "bring him with thee"). **(7)** To lead out or away; either simply (Mark 13:11; Luke 22:54; 23:32); or followed by eis (1519), unto, with the acc. of place, and so forth, lead away to, conduct to (Luke 4:1, 9; 10:34; John 18:28; Acts 6:12; 9:2; 11:26; 21:34; 22:5; 23:10, 31). Acts 17:5, "to bring them out to the people"; Heb 2:10, "unto glory." Followed by epí (1909), upon, unto (Acts 9:21, "bring them bound unto the chief priests"). **(8)** Similar to the Hebr. bō (935, OT), to bring forth, i.e., to cause to come, cause to arise as in Acts 13:23 UBS, "raised unto Israel a Savior, Jesus," instead of ḗgeire, the aor. of egeírō (1453), to raise, as in the TR. Also Sept.: Isa 46:11; Zech 3:8.

(B) Metaphorically, to lead, induce, incite, guide (Rom 2:4, "to repentance"; 1 Cor 12:2, "even as ye were led," meaning to idolatry, the figure being drawn from pastoral life [cf. Ex 3:1; Isa 11:6]). Also, to be led by the Spirit of God (Rom 8:14; Gal 5:18); by lusts (2 Tim 3:6).

(II) Trans. spoken of time.

(A) To pass, to spend. Luke 24:21, "today is the third day," where ágei is either impersonal or the word chrónos (5550), time, is implied.

(B) To celebrate, hold, e.g., a birthday (Matt 14:6); judicial days (Acts 19:38), which were held in the marketplace; see Sept.: Esth 9:18, 19, 21, 22.

(III) Intrans. or reflexively, to go, depart, with hēmás heautoús implied meaning "Let us go" (Mark 14:42 [cf. Matt 26:46; John 11:16]). Followed by enteúthen (1782), hence, from here (John 14:31); followed by eis (1519), unto

(Mark 1:38; John 11:7); followed by *prós* (4314), toward (John 11:15).

Deriv.: *agélē* (34), a herd; *agōgḗ* (72), course of life, manner of leading or spending it; *anágō* (321), to bring, lead, carry, or take up; *áxios* (514), to estimate or value; *apágō* (520), to lead, carry or take away; *diágō* (1236), to lead one's life, to live; *doulagōgéō* (1396), to bring into subjection; *eiságō* (1521), to bring in, introduce; *exágō* (1806), to lead forth or bring out; *epágō* (1863), to bring upon; *hēgéomai* (2233), to lead, consider; *katágō* (2609), to bring down; *metágō* (3329), to turn about; *parágō* (3855), to depart, pass away; *periágō* (4013), to lead about; *proágō* (4254), to go before, lead, precede; *proságō* (4317), to bring or come to, to bring; *stratēgós* (4755), the leader, commander of an army; *sulagōgéō* (4812), to lead off as prey; *sunágō* (4863), to bring together, assemble; *hupágō* (5217), to depart, go away; *chalinagōgéō* (5468), to bridle; *cheiragōgós* (5497), one who leads another by the hand.

Syn.: *phérō* (5342), to carry, bear, lead; *hodēgéō* (3594), to lead the way, guide; *komízō* (2865), to receive, bring in; *aírō* (142), to take away; *anaphérō* (399), to offer up; *eisphérō* (1533), to carry or bring in.

Ant.: *kataleípō* (2641), to leave behind, abandon; *egkataleípō* (1459), to leave behind, desert, forsake; *paraitéomai* (3868), to refuse, shun reject; *aphíēmi* (863), to forsake, omit, lay aside.

72. ἀγωγή *agōgḗ*; gen. *agōgḗs*, fem. noun from *ágō* (71), to lead. A way of life, the manner of leading or spending life (2 Tim 3:10).

Syn.: *bíōsis* (981), manner or means of life; *bíos* (979), life in regard to a period of time, moral conduct, or means of livelihood; *anastrophḗ* (391), behavior, conduct; *éthos* (2239), custom of life, ethical conduct.

73. ἀγών *agṓn*; masc. noun. Strife, contention, contest for victory or mastery such as was used in the Greek games of running, boxing, wrestling, and so forth. Paul applies the word to the evangelical contest against the enemies of man's salvation (1 Tim 6:12; 2 Tim 4:7 [cf. 1 Cor 9:24]). A race, a place to run (Heb 12:1). A struggle, contest, contention (Phil 1:29, 30; Col 2:1; 1 Thess 2:2). In the NT, it is presented as the life task of the Christian.

Deriv.: *agōnía* (74), agony; verb: *agōnízomai* (75), to contend.

Syn.: *áthlēsis* (119), combat, contest of athletes, a struggle or fight; *pólemos* (4171), war; *máchē* (3163), a fight, strife; *pálē* (3823), wrestling; *kópos* (2873), labor, weariness; *móchthos* (3449), painfulness, travail; *talaipōría* (5004), misery.

Ant.: *eirḗnē* (1515), peace; *táxis* (5010), order; *asphália* (803), security, safety; *hēsuchía* (2271), stillness, quietness; *anápausis* (372), inner rest.

74. ἀγωνία *agōnía*; gen. *agōnías*, fem. noun from *agōn* (73), contest, but more abstract and eclectic giving prominence to the pain and labor of the conflict. Combat, from which the Eng. "agony" is derived. It is used to refer to the trembling excitement and anxiety produced by fear or tension before a wrestling match or a fight. In the NT, it is used denoting not the fear which draws back and flees, but the fear which trembles in the face of the issue yet continues on to the end (Luke 22:44 [cf. Matt 26:37, 38; John 12:27]).

Syn.: *stenochōría* (4730), anguish, distress; *sunochḗ* (4928), anxiety, anguish; *phóbos* (5401), fear; *tarachḗ* (5016), disturbance, trouble; *súgchusis* (4799), riotous disturbance, confusion; *thórubos* (2351), disturbance, uproar; *anágkē* (318), distress.

Ant.: *galḗnē* (1055), tranquility, calm.

75. ἀγωνίζομαι *agōnízomai*; fut. *agonísomai*, mid. deponent from *agṓn* (73), conflict. To contend for victory in the public games (1 Cor 9:25). It generally came to mean to fight, wrestle (John 18:36). Figuratively, it is the task of faith in persevering amid temptation and opposition (1 Tim 6:12; 2 Tim 4:7). It also came to mean to take pains, to wrestle as in an award contest, straining every nerve to the uttermost towards the goal (Luke 13:24 [cf. 1 Cor 9:25; Phil 3:12ff.; Heb 4:1]). Special pains and toil (Col 1:29; Col 4:12). Implies hindrances in the development of the Christian life.

Deriv.: *antagōnízomai* (464), to antagonize, strive against; *epagōnízomai* (1864), to contend; *katagōnízomai* (2610), to subdue; *sunagōnízomai* (4865), to struggle in company with, strive together with.

Syn.: *epilambánomai* (1949), to lay hold upon, take hold of, help; *kópiáō* (2872), to toil, feel fatigue; *ergázomai* (2038), to work; *kóptomai* (2875), to beat the breast in grief, lament; *máchomai* (3164), to fight, strive; *poleméō* (4170), to carry on a war, fight; *athléō* (118), to contend in competitive games, strive; *strateúomai* (4754), to contend, be a soldier, go to war; *hoplízomai* (3695), to equip with weapons, arm oneself.

Ant.: *anapaúō* (373), to repose, rest; *anapsúchō* (404), to refresh; *eirēnopoiéō* (1517), to make peace; *aníēmi* (447), to relax, loosen; *dialássō* (1259), to conciliate, reconcile; *katapaúō* (2664), to settle down; *hēsucházō* (2270), to quiet.

76. Ἀδάμ *Adám*; masc. proper noun transliterated from the Hebr. *'Ādām* (121, OT). Adam. The name occurs nine times in the NT, eight times with reference to the first man (Luke 3:38; Rom 5:14, twice; 1 Cor 15:22, 45; 1 Tim 2:13, 14; Jude 1:14), and once with reference to Christ (1 Cor 15:45). In addition there are allusions to Adam, the first man, though the name does not occur (Matt 19:4–8; Mark 10:6–8; Rom 5:12, 15–17, 19). Adam is represented as the first existing man (1 Cor 15:45, 47). Adam is called the son of God not having come by human generation (Luke 3:38).

Through Adam, man fell, but through Christ, man can be restored (1 Cor 15:45–49; Rom 5:12–19). Sin and death entered into the world by Adam, whose sin constitutes the first sin of humanity (Rom 5:12, 14). In Adam all men sinned and died (Rom 5:19), the judgment of condemnation is passed upon all men (Rom 5:16, 18), and death reigns over humanity (Rom 5:15, 17; 1 Cor 15:22). When a person receives Christ as Lord and Savior, his union with Adam is terminated and he possesses righteousness, justification, and life (Rom 5:15–19; 1 Cor 15:22, 45, 49).

There can be no doubt about the historicity of the account of Adam in Genesis. If this was a mere myth, it would not be used as the basis of NT theology. In 1 Cor 15:45, 47 allusion is made to Gen 2:7; in Jude 1:14 to Gen 5:3–18; in 1 Tim 2:13 to Gen 2:20–23; in 1 Tim 2:14 to Gen 3:1–6, 13; in Matt 19:4; Mark 10:6 to Gen 1:27; in Matt 19:5, 6; Mark 10:7, 8 (cf. Eph 5:31) to Gen 2:24; in Rom 5:12–19; 1 Cor 15:22 to Gen 2:17; 3:19. All of these references of the NT assume the historicity of Adam and the events pertaining to him as well as the authenticity of the Genesis record.

77. ἀδάπανος *adápanos*; gen. *adapanou*, masc.-fem., neut. *adápanon*, adj. from the priv. *a* (1), without, and *dapánē* (1160), expense. Without expense or charge, not chargeable (1 Cor 9:18). Paul does not teach here that a minister of Christ is not entitled to compensation (1 Cor 9:13, 14). It was Paul's right to be paid, but he decided to forego this right voluntarily so that his preaching of the gospel might be more effective among the Corinthians.

78. Ἀδδί *Addí*; proper noun, the Gr. form of the Hebr. *'Iddō* (5714, OT). Addi, an ancestor of Jesus Christ (Luke 3:28).

79. ἀδελφή *adelphḗ*; gen. *adelphḗs*, the fem. of *adelphós* (80), brother. A sister by the same mother (Luke 10:39, 40; John 11:1, 3); a sister in general (Matt 19:29; Mark 10:29, 30); a near kinswoman, a cousin (Matt 13:56; Mark 6:3 [cf.

Matt 12:50; Mark 3:35]); a sister in the common faith, a Christian woman (Rom 16:1; 1 Cor 7:15; 9:5; James 2:15). Compare *adelphós*, a brother in the common faith, a son of God through Christ and co-heir of eternal life (1 John 2:9–11). See John 11:5, 28, 39; 19:25; Acts 23:16; Rom 16:15; 2 John 1:13.

80. ἀδελφός *adelphós*; gen. *adelphoú*, fem. *adelphḗ* (79), masc. noun from the collative *a* (1), denoting unity, and *delphús* (n.f.), a womb. A brother. *Adelphós* generally denotes a fellowship of life based on identity of origin, e.g., members of the same family (Matt 1:2; Luke 3:1, 19; 6:14); members of the same tribe, countrymen, and so forth (Acts 3:22; 7:23; Rom 9:3). One of the same nature, a fellow man was regarded as a brother (Matt 5:22–24, 47). *Adelphós* also came to designate a fellowship of love equivalent to or bringing with it a community of life (Matt 12:50; Mark 3:35; 10:29, 30; Acts 12:17). In this manner Jesus speaks of His brethren (Matt 25:40; 28:10; John 20:17; Rom 8:29; Heb 2:11, 17). The members of the same Christian community are called brothers (John 21:23; Acts 9:30; Rom 16:14; 1 Cor 7:12).

The Hebr. word *'āch* (251, OT) encompassed more distant relatives (Gen 14:16; 29:12, 15); therefore, some argue that this ought to be taken into consideration where brothers and sisters of the Lord Jesus are referred to (Matt 12:46, 47; 13:55; Mark 3:31, 32; 6:3; Luke 8:19, 20; John 2:12; Acts 1:14). However, the only passage where the brothers of Jesus are not conjoined with His mother is John 7:3, 5, 10. The conjoined mention of the mother of Jesus appears to imply that children of the same mother are meant.

Deriv.: *adelphótēs* (81), brotherhood; *philádelphos* (5361), one who loves his brother; *pseudádelphos* (5569), false brother.

Syn.: *súntrophos* (4939), companion; *suggenḗs* (4773), relative.

Ant.: *xénos* (3581), stranger; *pareísaktos* (3920), one who was smuggled in; *parepídēmos* (3927) alien, foreigner.

81. ἀδελφότης *adelphótēs*; gen. *adelphótētos*, fem. noun from *adelphós* (80), brother. Brotherhood, a brotherly or sisterly relationship. Occurs only in 1 Pet 2:17; 5:9. Equivalent to *philadelphía* (5360), brotherly love (Rom 12:10; 1 Thess 4:9; Heb 13:1; 1 Pet 1:22; 2 Pet 1:7) and *philádelphos* (5361), friend of brethren (as an adj. in 1 Pet 3:8). While *adelphótēs* is used in the NT and by ecclesiastical writers, it is not used by Class. Gr. writers who used *philadelphía* to denote only the love of siblings to each other. In Christianity *adelphótēs* is a brotherhood or sisterhood which has been made possible by Jesus Christ. Since all believers are given the new birth, it is by virtue of that spiritual birth that men and women are truly brothers and sisters.

82. ἄδηλος *ádēlos*; gen. *adḗlou*, masc.-fem., neut. *ádēlon*, adj. from the priv. *a* (1), without, and *dḗlos* (1212), manifest. Not manifest, not apparent, concealed. As applied to graves, meaning overgrown with grass or weeds and thus concealed, as the graves of the poor frequently were in contrast to those of the rich which might have been kept and beautified (Luke 11:44 [cf. Num 19:16]). Not manifest, uncertain (1 Cor 14:8).

Deriv.: *adēlótēs* (83), uncertainty; *adḗlōs* (84), uncertainly.

Syn.: *kruptós* (2927), concealed, secret; *apókruphos* (614), hidden; *ágnōstos* (57), unknown.

Ant.: *bébaios* (949), certain; *asphalḗs* (804), sure; *pródēlos* (4271), manifest; *phanerós* (5318) and *emphanḗs* (1717), apparent; *dḗlos* (1212), evident.

83. ἀδηλότης *adēlótēs*; gen. *adēlótētos*, fem. noun from *ádēlos* (82), uncertain. Uncertainty, inconstancy (1 Tim 6:17).

Ant.: *aspháleia* (803), certainty, safety; *bebaíōsis* (951), the act of confirmation;

stērigmós (4740), stability; *hupóstasis* (5287), confidence, substance, basis.

84. ἀδήλως *adḗlōs*; adv. from *ádēlos* (82), uncertain. Uncertainly, irresolutely, without attending to the prescribed marks or lines, without exposure to the spectators who are there to judge the race or the performance (1 Cor 9:26).

Ant.: *óntōs* (3689), verily, certainly; *asphalṓs* (806), assuredly, safely.

85. ἀδημονέω *adēmonéō*, contracted *adēmonṓ*, fut. *adēmonḗsō*. To faint, be depressed and almost overwhelmed with sorrow or burden of mind (Matt 26:37; Mark 14:33; Phil 2:26).

Syn.: *lupéō* (3076), to grieve; *baréomai* (916), to be heavy-hearted, burdened; *tarássomai* (5015), to be troubled; *thlíbomai* (2346), to be afflicted; *ochléomai* (3791), to be vexed; *enochléomai* (1776) and *parenochléomai* (3926), to be annoyed; *skúllō* (4660), to vex, annoy; *anastatóō* (387), to stir; *thorubéō* (2350), to make an uproar; *throéō* (2360), to make an outcry; *thorubázō* (2350), to disturb, trouble; *diaponéō* (1278), to be sore troubled; *embrimdomai* (1690), to groan, murmur against; *stenázō* (4727), to groan, sigh.

Ant.: *hēsucházō* (2270), to be quiet, at rest; *katastéllō* (2687), to quiet, appease; *anapaúomai* (373), to refresh, rest; *epanapaúomai* (1879), to be at rest upon; *eirēneúō* (1514), to be at peace; *katapaúō* (2664), to rest.

86. ᾅδης *hádēs*; gen. *hádou*, masc. noun from the priv. *a* (1), not, and *ideín*, the inf. of the 2d aor. *eídō* (1492), to see. In Homer and Hesiod the word is spelled *Haïdés* meaning obscure, dark, invisible. Hades, the region of departed spirits of the lost (Luke 16:23).

It corresponds to *Sheol* in the OT which occurs 59 times. In the NT, *Hádēs* occurs only 10 times. It is found nowhere in John's gospel, the epistles of Paul, the Epistle to the Hebrews, or the General Epistles. Three of the occurrences are on Christ's lips (Matt 11:23 [with Luke 10:15]; 16:18; Luke 16:23). In two of these, the words are obviously used in a figurative sense: in the case of Capernaum to express an absolute overthrow, a humiliation as deep as the former loftiness and pride had been great; in the case of the Church, to express a security which shall be proof against death and destruction. The third occurrence, in the story of the rich man and Lazarus (Luke 16:19–31), is of a different kind and has even been taken to put our Lord's confirmation on the Jewish idea of two compartments in Hades, distinct from and yet near one another. In Acts 2:27, 31, the word *Hádēs* occurs in a quotation from Ps 16:10 in an application of OT faith in the advent of Christ, His death, and His resurrection. Therefore, it has again the meaning of the world of the departed into which Christ passed like other men, but only to transform its nature from a place accommodating both believers and unbelievers to one for unbelievers only (Matt 11:23; 16:18; Luke 10:15; 1 Cor 15:55; Rev 1:18; 6:8; 20:13, 14).

In all the NT passages except Matt 11:23; Luke 10:15, Hades is associated with death. It expresses the general concept of the invisible world or abode into which the spirits of men are ushered immediately after death. The prevalent idea connected with it in its association with death are those of privation, detention, and just recompense. The thought of the relative reward of good is subordinate, if expressed at all, to the retribution of evil and to the penal character pertaining to Hades as the minister of death. In none of the passages in which the word itself occurs have we any disclosures or even hints of purgatorial fires, purifying processes, or extended operations of grace.

The state of human beings in Hades is immediate and irreversible after death, although it does not constitute the eternal state, for Hades itself later becomes the exclusive place for unbelievers. It is cast into the lake of fire (Rev 20:14), while the reign of the just becomes paradise

(Luke 23:43; 2 Cor 12:4; Rev 2:7) which is ultimately absorbed into the final heaven (Rev 21:1). Our Lord conclusively teaches in the story of the rich man and Lazarus that there is no possibility of repentance after death. It is in this light that 1 Pet 3:18–20 should be viewed (cf. *phulakē* [5438], prison).

Unfortunately, both the OT and NT words have been translated in the KJV as "hell" (Ps 16:10) or the "grave" (Gen 37:35) or the "pit" (Num 16:30, 33). Hades never denotes the physical grave nor is it the permanent region of the lost. It is the intermediate state between death and the ultimate hell, Gehenna (*Géenna* [1067]). Christ declares that He has the keys of Hades (Rev 1:18). In Rev 6:8 it is personified with the meaning of the temporary destiny of the doomed; it is to give up those who are in it (Rev 20:13), and is to be cast into the lake of fire (Rev 20:14).

Syn.: *Géenna* (1067), the final destiny of the wicked, hell; *tartaróō* (5020), the prison of the fallen angels or evil spirits; *ábussos* (12), abyss, the place where the dragon (*drákōn* [1404]), i.e., Satan, is bound during the millennial reign (cf. Luke 8:31; Rev 9:11); *límnē* (3041) and *toú purós* (4442), lake of fire, the place into which the beast and the false prophet are cast after their defeat by Christ. An additional statement in Rev 21:8 describes those who have their part in the lake of fire, compare the description of those who are outside the city (Rev 22:15).

Ant.: *parádeisos* (3857), paradise; *kólpos Abraám* (*kólpos* [2859], bosom; *Abraám* [11], Abraham), Abraham's bosom; *ouranós* (3772), heaven.

87. ἀδιάκριτος *adiákritos*; gen. *adiakrítou*, masc.-fem., neut. *adiákriton*, adj. from *a* (1), without, and *diakrínō* (1252), to separate, distinguish, judge. Indistinguishable, making no partial distinctions, free from partial regards, impartial (James 3:17).

Syn.: *díkaios* (1342), just.

Ant.: *kritikós* (2924), discerning; *prosōpolếptēs* (4381), one exhibiting partiality.

88. ἀδιάλειπτος *adiáleiptos*; gen. *adialeíptou*, masc.-fem., neut. *adiáleipton*, adj. from *a* (1), without, and *dialeípō* (1257), to intermit, leave an interval or gap. Unceasing, continual, without intermission (Rom 9:2; 2 Tim 1:3). This, however, must not be taken as referring to unbroken continuity. In Rom 9:2, Paul speaks of the distress he experiences for the unrepentance of Israel on every occasion he thinks of his people. In 2 Tim 1:3, he tells Timothy that on every occasion of praying for individuals, he remembers him in particular. The word *déēsis* (1162), particular supplication, occurs in this verse giving it the above meaning.

Deriv.: *adialeíptōs* (89), unceasingly, continually, permanently.

Syn.: *akatápaustos* (180), incessant.

Ant.: *ephếmeros* (2184), ephemeral, daily, occasional.

89. ἀδιαλείπτως *adialeíptōs*; adv. from *adiáleiptos* (88), permanent, without ceasing. Continually, without intermission. In Rom 1:9, Paul tells the believers in Rome that they are constantly in his mind, not meaning, however, that other things were excluded. Whenever Paul encountered evidence of their faith, he did not fail to pray for them. In 1 Thess 1:3, he mentions constantly remembering the believers' work of faith, labor of love, and patience of hope. Their example left a permanent example for him. In 1 Thess 2:13, he mentions his constant thanksgiving on behalf of the Thessalonians. In 1 Thess 5:17, we find Paul's injunction to incessantly pray, which means to pray every time an opportunity presents itself and to be in a constant attitude of dependence upon God (Luke 18:1; Rom 12:12; Eph 6:18). This does not imply that the believer should neglect everything else and should utter unending prayer, or that he should abstain from work and cloister himself in a monastery where he can constantly pray. The word for "pray" here is *proseúchomai* (4336), a word which never refers to praying to men, but always to God. Therefore Paul's injunction means that one should be constantly conscious of his full dependence upon God.

Syn.: *nuchthḗmeron* (3574), night and day; *pántote* (3842), always; *aeí* (104), always, ever; *diá pantós*, forever (*diá* [1223], for; *pantós*, the gen. of the neut. of *pás* [3956], all).

Ant.: *oudépote* (3763), not even at any time, never at all, used with more absoluteness than *mēdépote* (3368), never, or not even ever, which is more subjective and relative.

90. ἀδιαφθορία *adiaphthoría*; gen. *adiaphthorías*, fem. noun from *adiáphthoros* (n.f.), incorrupt, which is from the priv. *a* (1), without, and *diaphtheírō* (1311), to corrupt. Incorruptibility, integrity, freedom from corruptible mixtures or adulterations (Titus 2:7). Titus was advised not to mix in his teaching (*didaskalía* [1319]) anything that would in any way deprive Christian teaching of its eternal value and cause it to be relegated to second place. After the word *didaskalía*, we have *adiaphthoría* or *aphthoría*, without admixture. This means that the content of Christian teaching must be without adulteration. In this verse, Paul mentions several ways in which this unadulterated teaching should be done. One is with *semnótēs* (4587), dignity, venerableness, modesty, reverence, not casually as if it were just another thing to do (cf. 1 Tim 2:2; 3:4). It refers not only to the manner of teaching, but also to the apparel of the teacher. And then follows a word very similar to *adiaphthoría*. It is *aphtharsía* (861), used also in Rom 2:7; 1 Cor 15:42, 50, 53, 54; Eph 6:24; 2 Tim 1:10. In Titus 2:7, this word is translated "sincerity," but it should be incorruption, referring to the nature of Christian teaching. It is impossible that it lose its inherent value, no matter how much it may be corrupted by

some. There will always be the inherent incorruption or incorruptibility to genuine Christian teaching.

Syn.: *aphtharsía* (861), incorruption, genuineness, imperishability; *aphthoría* instead of *adiaphthoría* is found in some texts (see Titus 2:7); *aúxēsis* (838), growth, increase.

Ant.: *phthorá* (5356), decay, corruption; *diaphthorá* (1312), utter decay.

91. ἀδικέω *adikéō*; contracted *adikṓ*, fut. *adikḗsō*, from *ádikos* (94), unjust. To do wrong, hurt, damage.

(I) Intrans.: to act unjustly, do wrong (Acts 25:11; 2 Cor 7:12; Col 3:25; Rev 22:11; Sept.: 1 Kgs 8:47; 2 Chr 26:16; Ps 106:6; Jer 37:18).

(II) Trans.: to act unjustly, to do wrong to or injure someone (Matt 20:13; Acts 7:24–27; 25:10; 1 Cor 6:8; 2 Cor 7:2; Gal 4:12; Phile 1:18).

(III) By metonymy, to hurt, damage, harm (Luke 10:19; Rev 2:11; 6:6; 7:2, 3; 9:4, 10, 19; 11:5; Sept.: Lev 6:2; Isa 3:15; 10:20; 51:23).

Deriv.: *adíkēma* (92), a misdeed, an injury.

Syn.: *bláptō* (984), to injure, damage; *kakóō* (2559), to harm; *kakouchéō* (2558), to mistreat; *parabaínō* (3845), to transgress; *paranoméō* (3891), to act contrary to law; *zēmióō* (2210), to suffer loss; *lumaínomai* (3705), to cause havoc; *páschō* (3958), to suffer.

Ant.: *dikaióō* (1344), to justify; *eulogéō* (2127), to bless, speak well of; *makarízō* (3106), to declare blessed; *euergetéō* (2109), to do good; *ōpheléō* (5623), to profit; *lusiteléō* (3081), to benefit.

92. ἀδίκημα *adíkēma*; gen. *adikḗmatos*, neut. noun from *adikéō* (91), to act unjustly. That which results from *adikía* (93), an injustice, a crime, a criminal act (Acts 18:14; 24:20; Rev 18:5; Sept.: 1 Sam 20:1; 26:18; 2 Sam 22:49; Isa 59:12).

Syn.: *adikía* (93), wrong, the act of injustice; *húbris* (5196), injurious treatment, hurt; *tó kakón* (the neut. of *kakós* [2556] with the art.), an evil thing, harm; *anomía* (458), violation of law.

Ant.: *euergesía* (2108), good deed; *cháris* (5485), grace, benefit; *tó agathón* (the neut. of *agathós* [18] with the art.), the good, the benefit; *eúnoia* (2133), benevolence; *tó sumphéron* (from *sumphérō* [4851], to profit, benefit), the benefit, common good; *epieíkeia* (1932), mildness, clemency, gentleness; *boétheia* (996), assistance; *epikouría* (1947), service; *epieíkeia* (1932), mildness, clemency, gentleness.

93. ἀδικία *adikía*; gen. *adikías*, fem. noun from *ádikos* (94), unjust. Injustice. What is not conformable with justice, what ought not to be, that which is wrong. Related to *ádikos* (94), unjust, that which is out of harmony with *díkē*, established usage, what is right and fit, hence injustice, unrighteousness. There is *adikía* only because there is *alḗtheia* (225), truth, which occupies the place of *díkē*, justice. In 1 John 5:17, it is written that "all unrighteousness [*adikía*] is sin [*hamartía* (266)]." (See also 1 John 3:4.) Whatever does not meet God's justice is missing God's goal for us. What is wrong in man's relationship to man is also wrong in man's relationship to God. The result of *adikía*, unrighteousness, is *adíkēma* (92), evil doing (Acts 18:14).

(I) Wrong, injustice.

(A) Generally as in Luke 18:6, the unjust judge or literally the judge of injustice, meaning the judge to whom people accused of injustice are brought. The character of this judge is detailed in Luke 18:2 as one who did not fear God nor regard man. In Rom 9:14, an axiomatic statement is made concerning God that there is no unrighteousness with Him, which means that He cannot treat anyone unjustly (Sept.: Deut 32:4).

(B) Wrong or injury as done to others (2 Cor 12:13; Sept.: Ps 7:3; Mic 3:10).

(II) As related to *dikaiosúnē* (1343), righteousness which is often used of life and conduct. Thus *adikía* takes by

antithesis the sense of impropriety, iniquity, unrighteousness, wickedness (Luke 13:27, "the workers of iniquity," meaning wicked men; Acts 1:18; Rom 1:29; 3:5; 6:13; 2 Tim 2:19; Heb 8:12; 2 Pet 2:13; 1 John 5:17). In 1 John 1:9 where the sense is that God, who Himself is righteous (*díkaios* [1342]), would not only pardon sin, but also render man righteous. Justification is not a mere legal pronouncement of the elimination of guilt, but it is the transformation of the repentant sinner. In James 3:6, "a world of iniquity," means that the tongue is capable of all kinds of wickedness. (See also Sept.: Gen 6:11, 13; 1 Sam 3:13, 14; Ps 11:5; Zech 3:9). This wickedness is seen more particularly in the neglect of the true God and His laws and in an adherence to the world or to idolatry; hence, *adikía* means impiety, ungodliness, contempt of God, as opposed to *alḗtheia* (225), truth or piety toward God. In Rom 1:18, those "who hold the truth in unrighteousness," i.e., iniquity, are those who impede the worship of the true God by their obstinate adherence to worldliness or to idolatry (Rom 2:8; 2 Thess 2:10, 12; 2 Pet 2:15).

(III) Fraud, deceit, guile (John 7:18).

(IV) Money, as in the context of the parable of Luke 16:1–9. In verse eight, it stands for money as leading to unrighteousness. In this verse, the "steward of unrighteousness [a.t.]" should be understood as the steward of money since he was entrusted with the handling of the rich man's money and apparently did nothing wrong in collecting at a discount rate bad debts which were owed to his master. He was still acting as a steward when he was fired by the rich man having not been investigated first to see if he had done anything wrong. The accusation against the steward before the rich man was a false accusation as the verb *diabállō* (1225) in verse one should be understood, coming from the noun *diábolos* (1228), the devil, who is a false accuser. The steward was dismissed on devilish hearsay or false accusation. The rich man was therefore unjust. The steward who tried to recover money owed to his master by forgiving a certain percentage of the debt, without keeping any of it, was not unjust. This parable illustrates how Christians should behave on earth so that they may find a welcome in the eternal habitations (v. 9). Thus the steward could not be accused as being an unjust steward, but as a steward of that which is used in the world unjustly, namely money. "The mammon of unrighteousness" in verse nine is the god of money. The word *adikía*, unrighteousness or iniquity, here stands for money because primarily it is used for unrighteous purposes. In Euripides, Helen 911 and Electra 943, we have the term *ploútos ádikos*, unrighteous wealth, which refers to wicked or iniquitous money. In Acts 8:23, Peter was speaking to Simon the sorcerer, and said to him, "For I perceive that thou art in the gall of bitterness, and in the bond of iniquity [*adikías*]." Simon was trying to buy the gift of the Holy Spirit by offering money. The "bond of iniquity" mentioned here is the *súndesmos* (4886), the connection of *adikía*, unrighteousness, referring to money. 1 Cor 13:6 could be taken as those material things that could be acquired through the employment of falsehood in defrauding others instead of telling the truth. In Hos 12:7, "He is a merchant, the balances of deceit are in his hand: he loveth to oppress," the word "deceit" (4820, OT) means ill-gotten wealth and is translated in the Sept. as *adikía*. See also Ezek 28:18, "the iniquity of thy traffic" which means making money through false merchandising. See also Deut 19:18; Mic 6:12.

Syn.: *hamartía* (266), sin, missing the mark, *ponería* (4189), wickedness; *kríma* (2917), condemnation, judgment; *égklēma* (1462), crime; *anomía* (458), lawlessness; *paranomía* (3892), transgression, iniquity.

Ant.: *euergesía* (2108), good work, benevolence; *eupoiïa* (2140), well-doing; *euthútēs* (2118), rectitude; *cháris* (5485), benefit; *tó agathón* (the neut. of *agathós* [18], benevolent), the benevolence;

eúnoia (2133), good mind, disposition, will; *dikaiosúnē* (1343), justice; *díkē* (1349), the principle of justice; *tó díkaion* (1342), that which is just, right; *tó orthón* (3717), that which is upright; *óphelos* (3786), profit, advantage; *ōphéleia* (5622), benefit.

94. ἄδικος *ádikos*; gen. *adíkou*, masc.-fem., neut. *ádikon*, adj. from the priv. *a* (1), without, and *díkē* (1349), justice. Unjust, unrighteous.

(I) Unjust, unrighteous, falling short of the righteousness required by divine laws (1 Pet 3:18).

(II) Lacking the imputed righteousness of faith and the inherent righteousness wrought by the Spirit of God (Matt 5:45; Acts 24:15; 1 Cor 6:1, 9; 2 Pet 2:9; Sept.: Ex 23:1; Job 16:11; Prov 15:26; Ezek 21:3).

(III) Unjust toward others (Luke 18:11; Rom 3:5; Heb 6:10).

(IV) As *adikía* (93) means idolatry (Rom 1:18; 2:8; 2 Thess 2:10, 12; 2 Pet 2:13, 15), *ádikos* also means an idolater, a pagan (1 Cor 6:1, 9).

(V) Fraudulent, false, deceitful (Luke 16:10, 11; Sept.: Deut 19:18; Jer 5:31; 29:9).

Deriv.: *adikéō* (91), to act unjustly; *adikía* (93), injustice; *adíkōs* (95), unjustly.

Syn.: *athémitos* (111), unlawful; *skoliós* (4646), warped; *dólios* (1386), deceitful; *ponērós* (4190), evil; *kakós* (2556), bad; *phaúlos* (5337), foul, trivial; *hamartōlós* (268), sinful.

Ant.: *euthús* (2117), level, true, straight; *díkaios* (1342), fair, just; *éndikos* (1738), conformable to right within the law; *eusebés* (2152), devout, godly; *asebés* (765), impious, ungodly, irreverent.

95. ἀδίκως *adíkōs*; adv. from *ádikos* (94), unjust. Unjustly, wrongly, undeservedly (1 Pet 2:19; Sept.: Prov 1:11, 17).

Ant.: *dikaíōs* (1346), justly; *orthős* (3723), rightly; *alēthős* (230), truly.

96. ἀδόκιμος *adókimos*; gen. *adokímou*, masc.-fem., neut. *adókimon*, adj. from the priv. *a* (1), without, and *dókimos* (1384), acceptable. Unapproved, unworthy, spurious, worthless. In a pass. sense meaning disapproved, rejected, cast away (1 Cor 9:27; 2 Cor 13:5–7; Heb 6:8 [cf. 2 Tim 3:8; Titus 1:16]). With an act. usage meaning undiscerning, not distinguishing, void of judgment (Rom 1:28); although in this text it may be understood in the pass.: a reprobate abominable mind, a mind to be abhorred by God and man. Spoken of metals such as silver (Prov 25:4; Isa 1:22).

Syn.: *anáxios* (370), unworthy; *dólios* (1386), deceitful; *pseudḗs* (5571), false; *ásēmos* (767), mean, ignoble, one not bearing the mark; *koinós* (2839), common; *eleeinós* (1652), pitiable, miserable; *apóblētos* (579), cast away, rejected one; *achreíos* (888), useless; *áchrēstos* (890), inefficient.

Ant.: *dókimos* (1384), approved; *áxios* (514), worthy; *polútimos* (4186), valuable; *eklektós* (1588), chosen, elect; *chrḗsimos* (5539), serviceable, profitable; *tímios* (5093), valuable.

97. ἄδολος *ádolos*; gen. *adólou*, masc.-fem., neut. *ádolon*, adj. from the priv. *a* (1), without, and *dólos* (1388), guile. Without deceit, sincere. Only in 1 Pet 2:2. It indicates the absence of fraud and deceit (cf. John 1:47).

Syn.: *alēthinós* (228), true; *apseudḗs* (893), veracious, incapable of lying; *haploús* (573), single, without duplicity; *ákakos* (172), constitutionally harmless; *akéraios* (185), without admixture; *gnḗsios* (1103), true, genuine; *eilikrinḗs* (1506), sincere; *hagnós* (53), pure, undefiled.

Ant.: *dólios* (1386), deceitful; *plános* (4108), one leading astray; *phrenapátēs* (5423), mind-deceiver; *plastós* (4112), molded, plastic, artificial, false; *nóthos* (3541), spurious, illegitimate; *pseudḗs* (5571), false.

98. Ἀδραμυττηνός *Adramuttēnós*; fem. *Adramuttēnḗ*, neut. *Adramuttēnón*, adj. Of Adramyttium, a seaport in Mysia, northwest of Asia Minor, on the Aegean Sea (Acts 27:2).

99. Ἀδρίας *Adrías*; gen. *Adríou*, masc. proper noun. The Adriatic Sea including the whole Ionian Sea, between the island of Crete and Sicily (Acts 27:27).

100. ἀδρότης *hadrótēs*; gen. *hadrótetos*, fem. noun from *hadrós* (n.f.), thick, fat, full-grown, rich. Bounty (2 Cor 8:20). Bountiful giving or opulent offering and not just mere abundance.

Syn.: *perisseía* (4050), overflowing, and *perísseuma* (4051), abundance; *huperbolḗ* (5236), exceeding greatness; *eulogía* (2129), a blessing; *haplótēs* (572), bountifulness, liberality.

Ant.: *pleonexía* (4124), greediness.

101. ἀδυνατέω *adunatéō*; contracted *adunatṓ*, fut. *adunatḗsō*, impersonal verb from *adúnatos* (102), weak, unable. To be impossible (Matt 17:20; Luke 1:37).

Syn.: *asthenéō* (770), to be weak.

Ant.: *dúnamai* (1410), I am able; *dunatós eimí* (*dunatós* [1415], able, possible; *eimí* [1510], I am), I am able; *ischúō* (480), I am able.

102. ἀδύνατος *adúnatos*; gen. *adunátou*, masc.-fem., neut. *adúnaton*, adj. from the priv. *a* (1), without, and *dunatós* (1415), possible, able, or powerful. In an act. sense, impotent, weak (Acts 14:8; Rom 8:3; 15:1, in the mind, judgment). In a neut. or pass. sense meaning impossible, not to be done (Matt 19:26; Mark 10:27; Luke 18:27; Heb 6:4, 18; 10:4; 11:6).

Deriv.: *adunatéō* (101), to be impossible.

Syn.: *anéndektos* (418), inadmissible; *asthenḗs* (772), without strength, feeble; *árrōstos* (732), sick; *malakós* (3120), soft, effeminate.

Ant.: *dunatós* (1415), powerful, possible; *hikanós* (2425), sufficient, competent; *ischurós* (2478), strong, having inherent and moral power; *krataiós* (2900), one with relative and manifest power; *megaleíos* (3167), wonderful, showing oneself great; *mégas* (3173), great, mighty; *tēlikoútos* (5082), of so extreme a degree.

103. ᾄδω *ádō*, contracted from *aeídō*, fut. *ásō*. To sing, used trans. always of praise to God (intrans. in Eph 5:19; Col 3:16; Sept.: Ex 15:21; 1 Chr 16:23; trans. in Rev 5:9; 14:3; 15:3; Sept.: Ex 15:1; Num 21:17).
Deriv.: *ōdḗ* (5603), a song.
Syn.: *psállō* (5567), to rub or touch the surface, to play on a stringed instrument; *humnéō* (5214), to sing a hymn.

104. ἀεί *aeí*; adv. Always, ever, continually, at all times (Acts 7:51: 2 Cor 6:10); always or ever in a restrained sense, i.e., at some stated time (Mark 15:8, "as he always did" [a.t.], meaning customarily; Sept.: Judg 16:20); very frequently, continually (2 Cor 4:11; 2 Pet 1:12, assiduously). From this is derived the Eng. "aye," "ever." See also Titus 1:12; Heb 3:10; 1 Pet 3:15; Sept.: Isa 51:13; Ps 95:10.
Deriv.: *aḯdios* (126), eternal.
Syn.: *diapantós* (1275), through all time; *pantḗ* (3839) and *pántote* (3842), always; *eis tó diēnekés* (*eis* [1519], unto; *tó* [3588], the; *diēnekés* [1336], continuously), forever; *hekástote* (1539), each time, always; the phrases with *aiṓn* (165), age, time: *eis tón aiṓna*, forever; *eis toús aiṓnas*, unto the ages; *eis toús aiṓnas tṓn aiṓnōn*, unto the ages of the ages; *eis tón aiṓna toú aiṓnos*, unto the age of the age or forever and ever; *toú aiṓnos tṓn aiṓnōn*, of the age of the ages, forever and ever; *eis pántas* (3956) *toús aiṓnas*, unto all the ages; *eis hēméran* (2250) *aiṓnos*, unto a day of an age, forever.
Ant.: *oudépote* (3763), never with an absoluteness; *mēdépote* (3368), never, but more subjective and conditional, not as strong as *oudépote*; *oudépō* (3764), not yet; *pṓpote* (4455), not at any time.

105. ἀετός *aetós*; gen. *aetoú*, masc. noun. An eagle or vulture, a species of rapacious birds represented as preying on dead bodies where some species of vulture is probably intended (Matt 24:28; Luke 17:37; Rev 4:7; 12:14; Sept.: Job 39:27, see Job 39:30; Ps 103:5; Prov 30:17).

106. ἄζυμος *ázumos*; gen. *azúmou*, masc.-fem., neut. *ázumon*, adj. from the priv. *a* (1), without, and *zúmē* (2219), leaven. Unleavened, metaphorically undefiled. In the NT used of the Feast of the Passover (Matt 26:17; Mark 14:1, 12; Luke 22:1, 7; Acts 12:3; 20:6; Lev 2:4; Num 6:15; 1 Chr 23:29). Figuratively meaning unpenetrated by evil (1 Cor 5:7, 8).
Syn.: *alēthinós* (228), true; *gnḗsios* (1103), genuine; *apseudḗs*, (893), without falsehood; *ádolos* (97), without deceit.

107. Ἀζώρ *Azṓr*; masc. proper noun transliterated from the Hebr. 'Azzur (5809, OT). Azor, an ancestor of the Lord Jesus (Matt 1:13, 14).

108. Ἄζωτος *Ázōtos*; gen. *Azótou*, fem. proper noun. A city in Israel called Ashdod, eighteen miles northeast of Gaza (Josh 13:3; 1 Sam 6:17; Acts 8:40). Its early occupation was noted by Joshua (Josh 11:22) when it withstood attempts by Judah to conquer it and settle there (Josh 13:3; 15:46, 47). It was one of the principal ports and strongholds of the Philistines with the temple of Dagon to which the ark was taken (1 Sam 5:1ff.). Defeated by Sargon II in 711 B.C., (Amos 1:8; Isa 20:1). By the time of Jeremiah the city was weak (Jer 25:20) and gradually became more derelict (Zeph 2:4; Zech 9:6). It was partially repopulated after the exile (Neh 4:7; 13:24), but its continued idolatry provoked several attacks by the Maccabees. Azotus again flourished after its restoration by Herod.

109. ἀήρ aér; gen. *aéros*, masc. noun from *áō* (n.f.), to blow. Air, the celestial air surrounding the earth. The Greeks believed it to be the substance that filled the space between the earth and moon. They considered it to be thick and misty in contrast to the very pure, higher substance which they called *aithér*, ether.

(**I**) The space above us (Acts 22:23; 1 Thess 4:17; Rev 16:17).

(**II**) The space around us in which we may engage in useless and aimless activity as in the expressions "beateth the air" (1 Cor 9:26), "speak into the air" (1 Cor 14:9).

(**III**) Eschatologically: In Rev 9:2 it refers to the atmospheric air as it will be affected by God's judgment in the darkening of the sun and the moon (Matt 24:29; Mark 13:24, 25; Luke 21:25), and in Rev 16:17 the seventh angel pours his bowl of wrath into the air. In 1 Thess 4:17 Christ at His *parousía* (3952), coming, meets the believers in the air, designated to be the area immediately above the earth. The air is not designated by the Jews as the dwelling place of angels, but of Satan and his demons. It is in this context that Paul designates Satan as being the ruler of the power of the air (Eph 2:2 [cf. 6:12]). The Lord will penetrate this area in order to deliver His own from the earth.

110. ἀθανασία athanasía; gen. *athanasías*, fem. noun from *athánatos* (n.f.), immortal, which is from the priv. *a* (1), without, and *thánatos* (2288), death. Rendered "immortality" in 1 Cor 15:53, 54 of the glorified body of the believer. In the NT it expresses the nature not of life itself, but strictly speaking, only a quality of life such as the quality of the life of God and the resurrection body of the believer. Our bodies are subject to death, mortal (related to *thnētós* [2349], to die). Used in Rom 6:12 of the body where it is called "mortal," not simply because it is liable to death but because it is the organ in and through which death carries on its fatal activities.

The only other place where *athanasía* occurs is 1 Tim 6:16 where the word is used in reference to the Lord Jesus Christ in His manifestation as the God-Man. It is true that He suffered death, His physical body and His spirit separated one from the other, but they did not remain separated. He brought them together once again with an incorruptible body that had all the characteristics that our resurrection body will have. The Lord Jesus Himself, however, has inherent *athanasía*, immortality, in that no one could permanently separate His body from His spirit. He raised His body and joined it together with His spirit which temporarily had been committed to the Father. Thus He is the only One who inherently has always had immortality. The phrase here is as it is found in Gr.: "the only one having immortality" (a.t.), meaning that He always had it. He never gave it up and He still has it. Therefore, *athanasía* always refers to the nonseparation of the spirit. This is the quality of having the spirit attached to the resurrection body, while *aphtharsía* refers to the incapacity of the new resurrection body to deteriorate. This is a quality, however, that our present bodies do not have but will have in the resurrection.

Syn.: *aphtharsía* (861), incorruptibility as pertains to the body.

Ant.: *thnētós* (2349), mortal.

111. ἀθέμιτος athémitos; gen. *athemítou*, masc.-fem., neut. *athémiton*, adj. from the priv. *a* (1), not, and *themitós* (n.f.), lawful. Unlawful, forbidden (Acts 10:28; 1 Pet 4:3).

Syn.: *ánomos* (459), lawless; *áthesmos* (113), lawless; *bdeluktós* (947), abominable; *ádikos* (94), unjust; *ponērós* (4190), evil; *kakós* (2556), bad; *phaúlos* (5337), foul.

Ant.: *énnomos* (1772), lawful.

112. ἄθεος átheos; gen. *athéou*, masc.-fem., neut. *átheon*, adj. from the priv. *a*

(1), without, and *Theós* (2316), God. In Class. Gr. it primarily and actively meant godless, destitute of God, without God, and consequently *álogos* (249), devoid of reason, thus denoting a person who was forgetful of God. It also refers to one who did not care about the existence of the gods and consequently did not honor them. In the NT it occurs only in Eph 2:12 in the pass. meaning without divine help, forsaken by God, excluded from communion with God. "Without God" does not really convey the full meaning. It means more than not knowing God, it means neglectful of God. See also 1 Thess 4:5.

Syn.: *asebés* (765), impious, ungodly; *anósios* (462), unholy, profane.

Ant.: *eusebés* (2152), pious, godly.

113. ἄθεσμος *áthesmos*; gen. *athésmou*, masc.-fem., neut. *áthesmon*, adj. from the priv. *a* (1), without, and *thesmós* (n.f.), a law, custom, which is from *títhēmi* (5087), to set, place. Lawless, unprincipled, not in conformity to acceptable custom. The noun *thesmós*, used in the pl. in Class. Gr., did not refer to a law enacted by a body of lawmakers but that which became prevalent by custom and was expected to be observed as if it were a law. Akin to *éthos* (1485), a custom, and *éthō* (1486), to use by habit, to be accustomed. The homosexuals of Sodom and Gomorrah are called *áthesmoi* in 2 Pet 2:7, which is rendered in the KJV as "wicked." In the NIV it is rendered "lawless men." It occurs also in 2 Pet 3:17. In both instances it refers to those who deviate from conduct that is accepted as good and adopted as a law or rule of custom, i.e., *thesmós*. A better translation of the word would be nefarious, that which is contrary to what is right, i.e., illegal.

Syn.: *ponērós* (4190), evil, malevolent, wicked; *kakós* (2556), inherently bad in oneself; *ánomos* (459), lawless.

Ant.: *dektós* (1184), accepted; *apodektós* (587), acceptable; *euárestos* (2101), well acceptable.

114. ἀθετέω *athetéō*; fut. *athetḗsō*, from *áthetos* (n.f.), not placed, which is from the priv. *a* (1), without, and *thetós* (n.f.), placed. To displace, to abrogate, abolish, get rid of. In the NT:

(I) To make void, render null, such as the commandment in Mark 7:9, or one's will in Luke 7:30; 1 Cor 1:19 (cf. Gal 2:21; 3:15; Sept.: Ps 33:10; Isa 24:16; Ezek 22:26). Hence, not to keep, to cast off as the first faith (1 Tim 5:12; Sept.: Ps 132:11; Jer 3:20).

(II) To deny, despise, condemn, such as Moses' law (Heb 10:28); of persons (Mark 6:26). See Luke 10:16; John 12:48; 1 Thess 4:8; Jude 1:8; Sept.: Ex 21:8; 1 Sam 2:17; Isa 1:2.

Deriv.: *athétēsis* (115), disannulment, cancellation.

Syn.: *katargéō* (2673), to abolish; *ekpíptō* (1601), to fall from one's position; *aporríptō* (641), to cast off; *kathairéō* (2507), to cast down, demolish; *exouthenéō* (1848), to make of no account; *kataphronéō* (2706), to despise, look down on; *periphronéō* (4065), to think around someone or something with the idea of despising him or it; *atimázō* (818), to dishonor; *oligōréō* (3643), to care little for, have little regard; *logízomai eis oudén*, (*logízomai* [3049], to count; *eis* [1519], unto; *oudén* [3762], nothing) to reckon as nothing; *akuróō* (208), to void, cancel out; *kenóō* (2758), to empty, make of no effect; *exoudenóō* (1847), to treat as nothing; *katalúō* (2647), to overthrow, come to naught; *apodokimázō* (593), to reject; *paraitéomai* (3868), to beg off.

Ant.: *stērízō* (4741), to make fast, set, establish; *stereóō* (4732), to make firm; *hístēmi* (2476), to cause to stand; *bebaióō* (950), to confirm; *epistērízō* (1991), to strengthen, support; *kuróō* (2964), to make valid, ratify.

115. ἀθέτησις *athétēsis*; gen. *athetḗseōs*, fem. noun from *athetéō* (114), to abrogate. Cancellation, disannulling. In Heb 7:18, it refers to the natural abrogation or annulment of the commandment for the sacrifice of animals in that it was weak and unprofitable. Such sacrifice was set aside by the death of Christ which could not only justify the sinner before God, but also render the sinner just. Christ's death changed the character of the sinner (Rom 5:19). In Heb 9:26, it is used similarly, indicating the putting away or the abolition of the animal sacrifices since their benefit was not permanent. The death of Jesus Christ is presented as a once-and-for-all sacrifice with permanent effect and thus naturally to be preferred. One cannot accept the permanent sacrifice of Christ and keep the recurring sacrifices of animals. The one naturally replaced the other.

Syn.: *anaíresis* (336), the act of killing or abrogating.

Ant.: *stērigmós* (4740), sustaining.

116. Ἀθῆναι *Athênai*; gen. *Athenôn*, pl. fem. proper noun of *Athēná*.

(**I**) Athena, the Greek goddess of wisdom, arts, and industries and prudent warfare, identified by the Romans with Minerva.

(**II**) Athens (Acts 17:15, 16; 18:1; 1 Thess 3:1). After the Roman conquest, Athens (pl.) became a federated city entirely independent of the governor of *Achaïa* (882), Achaia, who paid no taxes to Rome and had internal judicial autonomy. The Athenians were said to possess the keenest minds among the Greeks, and the University of Athens was the most important school, ahead of those of Tarsus and Alexandria. The Athenians were religious but not spiritual and indulged in lasciviousness at the festival of Dionysus, the god of wine. They had great love of human slaughter in the gladiatorial games.

117. Ἀθηναῖος *Athēnaíos*; fem. *Athēnaía*, neut. *Athēnaíon*, adj. Of Athens, used subst., Athenian, a native of Athens (Acts 17:21, 22). See *Athênai* (116, II).

118. ἀθλέω *athléō*; contracted *athlô*, fut. *athlēsō*, from *áthlos* (n.f.), a contest either in war or sport, especially a contest for a prize. To contend, to be a champion in public games such as boxing, throwing the disc, wrestling, running (2 Tim 2:5).

Deriv.: *áthlēsis* (119), a contest, fight; *sunathléō* (4866), to strive together.

Syn.: *epagōnízomai* (1864), to contend earnestly; *agōnízomai* (75), to contend; *máchomai* (3164), to fight, quarrel; *antagōnízomai* (464), to struggle against; *sunagōnízomai* (4865), to strive together with; *diamáchomai* (1264), to fight fiercely.

Ant.: *hēsucházō* (2270), to live quietly; *katastéllō* (2687), to quiet, appease; *eirēneúō* (1514), to bring to peace, reconcile; *eirēnopoiéō* (1517), to make peace; *anapaúō* (373), to give rest.

119. ἄθλησις *áthlēsis*; gen. *athléseōs*, a fem. noun from *athléō* (118), to contest. Contest or exercise, as opposed to the result of a contest. Translated "fight" (KJV) and "contest" (NIV), it denotes the act of meeting a difficult situation which necessitates a fight and exercise of one's power. The word occurs only in Heb 10:32, "the enlightenment [*phōtisthéntes* (5461), aor. pass. part.] of the Lord after a great fight of afflictions." These believers became recipients of the light given to them by God. This did not exempt them from sufferings brought about by someone else which is indicated by the word *pathēmátōn*, the gen. pl. of *páthēma* (3804), suffering. Such sufferings did not crush these believers, indicated by the aor. *hupemeínate* from *hupoménō* (5278), to remain under. Suffering in the life of a believer does not cause him to merely be passive, remaining under them, but produces in him the determination to resist Satan by exercising every power in his spiritual being.

Syn.: *agōn* (73), conflict, fight, contest.

Ant.: *eirēnē* (1515), peace, quietness; *hēsuchía* (2271), quietness.

120. ἀθυμέω athuméō; contracted athumṓ, fut. athumḗsō, from áthumos (n.f.), without heart or spirit, which is from the priv. a (1), without, and thumós (2372), fierceness, passion. To be despondent, disturbed in mind, lose courage (Col 3:21; Sept.: 2 Sam 6:8).

    Syn.: barúnō (925), to burden; baréō (916), to weigh down.

    Ant.: euthuméō (2114), to be in a good mood; euphraínomai (2165), to be merry; paramuthéomai (3888), to encourage, comfort; parakaléō (3870), to comfort; tharséō (2293), to have courage.

121. ἀθῷος athôos; gen. athôou, masc.-fem., neut. athôon, adj. from the priv. a (1), without, and thôḗ (n.f.), penalty, which is from títhēmi (5087), to place. Having never been punished, innocent, free from guilt. In Matt 27:4 it describes the blood of Christ as innocent. In Matt 27:24 it is used with the gen. apó toú haímatos (apó [575], from; toú [3588], the; haímatos [129], blood), from the blood, or of the blood, or in regard to the blood of Christ that was about to be shed. Pilate thus declared himself innocent. See Sept.: Gen 24:41; 2 Sam 3:28.

    Syn.: ákakos (172), innocent, unable to think of others as evil; anaítios (338), blameless.

    Ant.: énochos (1777), guilty; hupódikos (5267), brought to trial, under judgment, suspicious, subject to judgment; aítios (159), one to be blamed.

122. αἴγειος aígeios; fem. aigeía, neut. aígeion, adj. from aíx (n.f.), a goat. Belonging to a goat as in Heb 11:37. The goat was second in importance only to the sheep. The reference to it in the story of Jacob and Esau (Gen 27:9) points out its value as meat. However, only the kids were killed and eaten. The she-goats provided milk. Skins were used for leather and bottles. The hair of some varieties was woven into cloth. Over half of the many references in the OT have to do with the goat's sacrificial use. In the NT,

Gr. words for goat are ériphos (2056) (Matt 25:32; Luke 15:29); eríphion (2055), a diminutive of ériphos (Matt 25:33); trágos (5131), a he-goat (Heb 9:12, 13, 19; 10:4).

123. αἰγιαλός aigialós; gen. aigialoú, from aḯssō (n.f.), to rush, and háls (n.f., see below), sea. The coast of a sea, lake, or bay (Matt 13:2, 48; John 21:4; Acts 21:5; 27:39, 40; Sept.: Judg 5:17).

    Deriv. of háls (n.f.), sea: halieús (231), a fisherman; enálios (1724), belonging in the sea, marine; thálassa (2281), sea.

124. Αἰγύπτιος Aigúptios; fem. Aiguptía, neut. Aigúption, adj. Of Egypt, used subst., Egyptian (Acts 7:22, 24, 28; Heb 11:29). In Acts 21:38, an Egyptian Jew who set himself up in Jerusalem as a prophet and had many followers who were dispersed and killed by Felix.

125. Αἴγυπτος Aíguptos; gen. Aigúptou, fem. proper noun. Egypt. The whole region was known to the Jews by the name Mizraim. Egypt became a place of refuge for great numbers of Jews after the captivity. See Matt 2:13–15, 19; Acts 2:10; 7:9–12, 15, 17, 34, 36, 39, 40; 13:17; Heb 3:16; 8:9; 11:26, 27; Jude 1:5. In Rev 11:8 the word is used symbolically of the Jews.

126. ἀΐδιος aḯdios; gen. aïdíou, masc.-fem., neut. aḯdion, adj. from aeí (104), ever, always. Eternal, without beginning or end, hence self-existent (Rom 1:20). Perpetual, without end (Jude 1:6).

    Syn.: aiṓnios (166), eternal, primarily without end but possibly with a beginning such as eternal life.

    Ant.: próskairos (4340), temporal.

127. αἰδώς aidṓs; gen. aidoús, fem. noun. Modesty, an innate moral repugnance to a dishonorable act or fashion. Aidṓs is grief due to the personal sense of evil. Aidṓs finds its motive in itself. It implies reverence for the good as good, not merely as that to which honor and reputation are attached. Only in 1 Tim 2:9; Heb 12:28, reverence, veneration.

Syn.: *entropḗ* (1791), withdrawal into oneself, recoiling; *aischúnē* (152) is subjective confusion, a feeling of shame felt by oneself or by others; *eulábeia* (2124), reverence.

Ant.: *atimía* (819), dishonor; *aschēmosúnē* (808), shame, indecency.

128. Αἰθίοψ *Aithíops*; gen. *Aithíopos*, masc. proper noun from *aíthomai* (n.f.), to burn, and *óps* (n.f.), face. Ethiopian. In Hebr., a Cushite. Found twice in Acts 8:27. The Ethiopia referred to here, as in Isa 18:1; Jer 13:23; Ezek 30:4, 5, 9, is what is called Upper Ethiopia or Habesh, lying south of Egypt on the Nile, and including the island of Meroe.

129. αἷμα *haíma*; gen. *haímatos*, neut. noun. The blood of the human or animal body (Mark 5:25, 29; Luke 8:43, 44; 13:1).

(I) Blood as the substantial basis of the individual life (John 1:13; Acts 17:26). Although the OT contains nothing parallel to these two passages, the expression corresponds to the idea contained in Lev 17:11, "For the life of the flesh is in the blood."

(II) With *sárx* (4561), flesh and blood conjoined to indicate the natural human body, mortal man (Heb 2:14). Flesh and blood designates mankind insofar as it owes its distinctive character to the material aspect of its being (Eph 6:12). The expression means the physical origin of man in Matt 16:17; 1 Cor 15:50; Gal 1:16. The physical and the spiritual natures of man are contrasted in Eph 6:12 (cf. Heb 2:14).

(III) *Haíma* by itself serves to denote life passing away in bloodshed, and generally life taken away by force (Matt 23:30, 35; 27:4, 6, 8, 24; Luke 11:50, 51; Acts 1:19; 22:20; Rom 3:15; Heb 12:4; Rev 6:10; 16:6; 18:24; 19:2; Sept.: Gen 4:10; 9:6; 37:22; 2 Sam 16:7; Ezek 18:10; 24:6, 9). The expression "to shed blood" (*haíma ekchéō* [1632]) emphasizes not

so much the manner of slaying, but rather the fact of the forcible taking away of life, whether produced by or only accompanied by the shedding of blood (Matt 26:28; Mark 14:24; Luke 22:20; Acts 22:20).

(IV) Related to the forcible taking away of life, *haíma* is used to denote life given up or offered as an atonement since, in the ritual of sacrifice, special emphasis is laid upon it as the material basis of the individual life. The life of the animal offered for propitiation appears in the blood separated from the flesh which the Jews were forbidden to eat (Gen 9:4; Lev 3:17; 17:10–14; Deut 12:23; Heb 9:7–13, 18–25; 11:28; 13:11). This life is, on the one hand, in the blood, presented to God; on the other hand by sprinkling, appropriated to man (Heb 9:7, 19, 20). This blood thus becomes the blood of the covenant or testament (see *diathḗkē* [1242]) which God commanded to us (Heb 9:20).

(V) The same is true of the blood of Christ (Heb 10:29); the blood of the testament (Matt 26:28; Mark 14:24; Luke 22:20; Heb 13:20); "the new testament in my blood" (1 Cor 11:25; 1 Pet 1:2) which designates the life of Christ offered for an atonement contrasted with the blood of beasts slain in sacrifice (Heb 9:12 [Heb 9:14, 25]).The blood of Christ, therefore, represents the life that He gave for our atonement (Matt 26:28; Acts 20:28; Rom 3:25; 5:9; 1 Cor 10:16; 11:27; Eph 1:7; 2:13; Col 1:14, 20; 5:6, 8; Heb 9:12, 25; 10:19; 13:12; 1 Pet 1:19; 1 John 1:7; 5:6, 8; Rev 1:5; 5:9; 7:14; 12:11). This shedding of Christ's blood was necessary for the satisfaction of God's justice. Man's sin could not go without expiation (*hilasmós* [2434]), a means whereby sin is covered and remitted objectively, the act of propitiation.

(VI) The most important use of the word "blood" in the NT is in connection with the death of Jesus Christ and the simultaneous manifestation of His blood being shed from the wound inflicted in His side by Roman soldiers (John 19:34 in fulfillment of the prophecy of

Zech 12:10). Therefore, the cross of Jesus Christ involves the shedding of His blood as the expression of His death. That He actually shed His blood, which was in the flesh and which He took upon Himself in His incarnation as the eternal *Lógos* (John 1:1, 14), is a historical event. That physical, historical fact was the due punishment for man's sin. Christ's death was not merely spiritual but also physical. He shed His blood as the God-Man, i.e., He poured out His life as a sacrifice in a real, physical death. At that time when He was made sin for us (2 Cor 5:21), He indeed felt spiritually forsaken by His Father (Matt 27:46; Mark 15:34). However, this forsaking was concomitant with His physical death as the unique God-Man. His physical death and His instantaneous forsaking by the Father demonstrated that the wages of sin is indeed death, both physical and spiritual (Rom 6:23). Jesus Christ became the permanent fulfillment of the purpose for which the high priest entered once a year into the Holy of Holies. What the high priest could not accomplish because he was only man and a sinner himself, Jesus Christ accomplished because He was the God-Man and consequently sinless (Heb 4:15; 5:1, 3). As the sacrifice made by the high priest was physical, having a spiritual purpose and goal, so the sacrifice of the Lord Jesus Christ was also physical with a spiritual purpose and goal. With the sacrifice by the high priest, God did not provide *áphesis* (859), forgiveness or subjective deliverance from sin in the life of the individual such as Christ provides, but *páresin* (3929), which is the word used in Rom 3:25, which is wrongly translated "remission," for it actually means toleration or overlooking or by-passing. Thus these sacrifices were repeated yearly since they were not remedies for sin, but only reminders of it (Heb 10:3, 4). The shedding of the blood of Christ, which was absolutely necessary for the remission of our sins, had two purposes to it. One purpose was the satisfaction of the righteousness and holiness of God (1 John 2:2); the other was the transformation of and the giving of the new birth to the individual and making him a partaker of the divine nature (John 3:3, 5; 2 Pet 1:4).

There are two words used in Rom 5:9, 10 which distinguish the two purposes involved in the shedding of Christ's blood. The first is the verb *dikaióō* (1344), to justify, found in verses one and nine. In both of these verses, the grammatical form is *dikaiōthéntes*, which is the aor. pass. part. of *dikaióō*. The aor. tense indicates that this action took place at a particular time in the past. It was when Jesus Christ died on the cross shedding His blood for us. The basic meaning of this verb is to proclaim that a person is without guilt or, if guilty, that justice was satisfied because someone other than himself adequately bore the condemnation of that guilt. It refers basically and principally to the satisfaction of justice. This is what the Son, the Lord Jesus Christ, came into the world to do—to shed His blood in order to satisfy the justice or righteousness of God. This was for the same purpose as the sacrifices offered by the high priest in the sprinkling of the blood of the animal on the sacred utensils, especially on the mercy seat (*hilastérion*). The spiritual accomplishment of this physical act is expressed by the technical term *hilasmós* (2434), expiation, propitiation, atonement. This physical shedding of the blood of the animal typified what Christ's blood was going to accomplish spiritually for all eternity. In 1 John 2:2, we have Christ presented as the propitiation (*hilasmós*) for sins: "And he is the propitiation for our sins: and not for ours only, but also for the sins of the whole world." "Ours only" refers to those of us who have by faith accepted the fact of the historical sacrifice of Christ on our behalf. It refers to those who have believed, and all those who will believe. "But also for the sins of the whole world" means those who have not as yet by faith accepted Christ's work on the cross. Therefore, the shedding of the blood of Christ on the cross has a universal sufficiency without temporal limitations.

The fact that the blood (His life poured out in sacrifice) of the God-Man, the Lord Jesus Christ, was not mere human blood, but divine, and that its accomplishment was a supernatural cleansing is clearly demonstrated in Acts 20:28, "Take heed therefore unto yourselves, and to all the flock, over the which the Holy Ghost hath made you overseers, to feed the church of God, which he hath purchased with his own blood." This statement that God purchased the church with "his own blood" does not, of course, teach that God has blood or that the material blood in the person of Christ was divine. Such an idea would imply the transfer of properties in the person of Christ, a doctrine clearly rejected by the orthodox Christological formula of Chalcedon. Rather, the thought is that it was at the cost of the life of the incarnate Second Person of the Godhead that the elect people of God were redeemed.

The shedding of Christ's blood is a historical event never to be repeated. It has regenerated those who received it. For those who did not receive it, it is still the only way whereby they may obtain salvation, i.e., through the exercise of faith in Christ's substitutionary death. It is the acceptance of the sacrifice of Christ which makes the potential actual. The phrase, "shedding of His blood", depicts Christ's death in OT sacrificial language in order to show that it was the fulfillment of the sprinkling of the blood of the animals upon the covering of the tabernacle in execution of His divine promise. It provides an all-important theological qualification to Christ's death by linking it with the OT and defining it as sacrificial in nature. The tabernacle contained the testament of God to His people, and the sprinkling of the blood was done on behalf of all the people. In the same manner, in Christ's blood there is complete expiation since His sacrifice was acceptable to the Father as satisfaction of His justice. On Calvary's cross, Jesus Christ

justified man before His Father (Rom 5:1, 9), but His justification is only potentially effective for those who have not yet believed. If His justification is not fulfilled in the individual, it is because of unbelief and not due to an insufficiency or inadequacy of the work of Christ.

The second word, found in Rom 5:10, is katēllágēmen, the aor. pass. indic. of katallássō (2644), to reconcile. This word derives from the prep. katá (2596), an intens. in this instance, and allássō (236), to change. It means to change a person for the purpose of being able to have fellowship together. The verb katallássō is found only in Rom 5:10; 1 Cor 7:11; 2 Cor 5:18–20, and the subst. katallagḗ (2643) is found in Rom 5:11; 11:15; 2 Cor 5:18, 19. The word implies two people who are at variance with each other and who are brought together because of a change that occurs. When the words are used in reference to the variance that exists between God and man, the change never occurs in God, but always in man who is the sinner. This is the meaning of the verb in Rom 5:10, "We were reconciled to God by the death of his Son; much more, being reconciled we shall be saved by his life." Such a reconciliation to God necessitates His changing us, through the new birth (John 1:12; 3:3). It is also the meaning of the subst. in Rom 5:11, "And not only so, but we also joy in God through our Lord Jesus Christ, by whom we have now received the atonement [katallagḗ, reconciliation]."

With the exception of 1 Cor 7:11 where the variance is between two married people, a husband and wife who are a part of each other (one flesh, Matt 19:6; Mark 10:8), all the cases involve man who, being sinful, is changed because of Christ and brought into friendship and fellowship with God. There is no more separation between man and God. If man does not accept the work of Christ on the cross, he does not personally realize the crossing over into spiritual life with Christ and the light (1 John 1:6, 7); he does not walk in the way of faith, the light provided by Christ.

We see that the terms Christ's blood and Christ's death are interchangeable and synonymous in Paul's use of these phrases in Rom 5:9, 10: "Much more then, being now justified by his blood, we shall be saved from wrath through him. For if, when we were enemies, we were reconciled [katēllágēmen] to God by the death of his Son; much more, being reconciled [katallagéntes, having been reconciled and now being in that state] we shall be saved by his life" (Rom 5:10). Faith in the death of Christ causes us to cross over into spiritual life with Christ, and thereafter we walk with Him as friends by living in Him and He in us (Rom 8:10).

Then in Rom 5:11 we have the substantive used, "And not only so, but we also joy in God through our Lord Jesus Christ, by whom we have now received the atonement [katallagḗ]." The word translated "atonement" is exactly the same word as katallagéntes used verbally in verse ten and translated "reconciled." It would have been better if the word katallagḗ in verse eleven were also translated "reconciliation" so that the English reader would immediately identify it as the same word. The NKJV, NASB, and NIV have all changed the translation to "reconciliation." In Rom 11:15 the Apostle Paul speaks of the casting away of Israel because of Israel's rejection of Christ and says, "For if the casting away of them [Israel] be the reconciling [katallagḗ] of the world, what shall the receiving of them be, but life from the dead?" This means that even the evil of Israel's rejection of Christ brought about His acceptance by the Gentiles. Nevertheless, God is not finished with Israel for they, too, will accept Him; and when Israel accepts Christ, then they will have fellowship with God in Christ as a result of the change that will come in them. That change will be equal to their being resurrected from the dead. This will also prove God's promise true.

Except for Rom 5:10 which deals with man being reconciled to God through Christ's death, and 1 Cor 7:11 which deals with two marital partners at variance being reconciled, the only other place that the verb is used is 2 Cor 5:18–20 where it is used twice as a substantive and once as an imperative. In the previous context of these verses, it is not the blood of Christ that is mentioned, but His death, "For the love of Christ constraineth us; because we thus judge, that if one [Christ] died for all, then were all dead" (2 Cor 5:14). And then in 2 Cor 5:15 Paul continues, "And that *he* [Christ] *died* for all, that they which live should not henceforth live unto themselves, but unto him which *died* for them, and rose again" (italics added). It is in this context in which is found the verse, "Therefore, if any man be in Christ, he is a new creature [kainḗ (2537), qualitatively new]: old things are passed away; behold all things are become new [kainá]" (2 Cor 5:17).

The Apostle John in 1 John 1:7 describes the work that the blood which Christ shed on the cross does for man: "And the blood of Jesus Christ his Son cleanseth us from all sin." The verb in Gr. is katharízei (2511), cleanses, which is in the pres. indic. indicating continuity. There is a beginning and there is a continuing cleansing. All this is because Jesus Christ once and for all shed His blood on Calvary's cross and fully satisfied God the Father. Thus there is an initial cleansing of the defiled heart of the sinner effecting a new birth. We are not to imagine that Christ's physical blood is somehow mystically applied as though it were the actual agent of cleansing. To be sure, the blood of Christ was actually shed and served as the visible, historical expression of His soul being offered in sacrifice for sin. However, when John says that Christ's blood cleanses us, He means that the benefit of forgiveness wrought by sacrificial death of Christ, vividly symbolized by the word blood, remains efficacious. If the real and physical death of Christ was not necessary, then why was it necessary for the Word, (*Lógos* [3056]) to become flesh (John 1:1, 14)? This historical fact has spiritual effects for those who believe the true meaning of the event. For those who disbelieve, it has a condemning effect (John 3:18). The cleansing is not automatic for all, but it is available for all. And to show that this blood is the same means of forgiveness for all, John says in 1 John 1:9, "If we confess our sins, he is faithful and just [God's justice has been satisfied through the shedding of Christ's blood] to forgive us our sins, and to cleanse us from all unrighteousness." To forgive is *aphḗ* (the aor. subjunctive of *aphíēmi* [863]), meaning to remove our sins or cause them to stand away from us. To cleanse us is *katharísē*, (the aor. subjunctive of *katharízō* [2511]), which means to cleanse us from the particular sin that we have committed and have confessed in our lives as believers no matter what the sin. From the above, it is evident that the expression shedding of blood is a theologically nuanced metonym for the death of Jesus Christ. In order to accomplish both the satisfaction of the justice of God and, to demonstrate His love, to reconcile man to God, Christ had to shed His blood and to die (Heb 9:22). Jesus could have died without shedding His blood, and He could merely have shed His blood without dying. However, He did both because the death of Christ includes the shedding of His blood as the visible expression, historical proof and theological qualification of it.

In Rom 5:8 Paul makes the statement that Christ died for us while we were yet sinners. His death was the result of this love for us. His death reconciled us to the Father and made us friends. Observe, however, that v. 9 begins with "much more then, having been justified by means of His blood" (a.t.). These then are the two distinct results accomplished by two acts of Christ: our justification through the shedding of His blood declaring us free from guilt before His Father, and our reconciliation to the Father

through Christ's death. Thus from enemies we become friends of God. Our reconciliation was dependent on our justification before the Father; hence we are no more enemies, but friends. Therefore the two terms, the blood and the death, can be considered as synonymous effecting one and the same purpose. The former term defines and lends theological significance to the latter.

Nor should we confuse the sacrifices of the OT by equating the work of the high priest with the offerings which the people brought and which the priests daily accepted. The work of the high priest always involved the sacrifice of an animal, but only the priests could accept the substitutionary gifts of the poor in lieu of those involving the shedding of blood (Lev 5). The work of Christ is not equated to the work of priests, but to the work of the high priest (Heb 2:17; 3:1; 4:14, 15; 5:5, 10; 6:20; 7:26–28; 8:1, 3; 9:7, 11, 25; 10:11 which refers to the frequency of priestly sacrifices; 13:11). Whenever the word "priest" is ascribed to Jesus Christ, it is because, as the priests daily received the offerings of the people, both sacrificial offerings which involved the shedding of blood and oblations which did not involve the shedding of blood, we also must come daily to Jesus Christ, for He is not only our exclusive high priest, but also our priest. In fact, to indicate that He has made us what He is, *makárioi* (3107), blessed, through His high priestly function, He has also made us priests (Rev 1:6; 5:10; 20:6). None of us, however, has been made the High Priest that He is. He has made us priests, giving us not only the privilege of direct communion with God (Rom 5:2), but also the privilege of engaging in the work of reconciliation (2 Cor 5:18, 19) and the work of intercession for others who need God's forgiveness (1 Tim 2:1; 4:5).

Other references to *haíma*: John 6:53–56; Acts 2:19, 20; 5:28; 15:20, 29; 18:6; 20:26; 21:25; Heb 10:4; 11:28; 12:24; 13:11; Rev 8:7, 8; 11:6; 14:20; 16:3, 4; 17:6; 18:24; 19:13.

Deriv.: *haimatekchusía* (130), shedding of blood; *haimorroéō* (131), to hemorrhage.

130. αἱματεκχυσία *haimatekchusía*; gen. *haimatekchusías*, fem. noun from *haíma* (129), blood, and *ekchéō* (1632), to pour out. Shedding of blood. Strictly speaking, it is the bringing of the blood to the altar, the application of the blood for objective expiation (Ex 29:16; Lev 8:15; 9:9; Deut 12:27; 2 Kgs 16:15) whose correlative is *rhantismós* (4473), sprinkling, the application of the atonement to its object. *Haimatekchusía* does not include the shedding of blood, the slaying of a victim, nor the sprinkling of that blood on the object to be expiated. The question dealt with in Heb 9:22 is not the manner, but the means of propitiation (*hilasmós* [2434]) which is through the *haíma*, blood (see Heb 9:18, 19, 22, 25), denoting only a part of the act of atonement (*lútrōsis* [3085], Luke 1:68; 2:38; Heb 9:12) or redemption (*apolútrōsis* [629], Luke 21:28; Rom 3:24; 8:23; 1 Cor 1:30; Eph 1:7, 14; 4:30; Col 1:14; Heb 9:15; 11:35). As such it would exclude the sprinkling upon the people (Heb 9:19), for it could not include this sprinkling and at the same time the sprinkling of the holy vessels (Heb 9:21). Thus the shedding of blood denotes only the shedding of the blood as the act of killing. The ritualistic act of blood outpouring always required additional demonstrations at the altar (Lev 8:15; 9:9) or on the altar (2 Kgs 16:15). The verb *proschéō* and the noun *próschusis* ([4378], Heb 11:28 [cf. Ex 12:7, 22]) are commonly used and should not be translated as sprinkling but as shedding forth or toward. Therefore, *haimatekchusía* means blood shedding and not the actual pouring out of the blood, the expression employed concerning the blood of Christ (Luke 22:20) which for our sakes was poured out. The word means only blood shedding, slaying, killing, and not the application of it.

131. αἱμορροέω *haimorroéō*; contracted *haimorroó*, fut. *haimorroésō*, from *haíma* (129), blood, and *rhéō* (4482), to flow. To have a flow or issue of blood (Matt 9:20). This is the word from which the Eng. "hemorrhage" is derived.

132. Αἰνέας *Ainéas*; gen. *Ainéou*, masc. proper noun. Aeneas, the name of a man whom Peter healed (Acts 9:33, 34).

133. αἴνεσις *aínesis*; gen. *ainéseōs*, fem. noun from *ainéō* (134), to praise. The act of praise (Heb 13:15).

   Syn.: *húmnos* (5215), hymn; *psalmós* (5568), a sacred ode or poem, music accompanied with the voice, harp, or other instrument; *ōdḗ* (5603), a religious metrical composition, a song; *eulogía* (2129), blessing, praise.

   Ant.: *ará* (685), malediction, cursing; *katára* (2671), a curse; *anáthema* (331), anathema, sacrificial offering, ill-favor; or *katanáthema* (2652, *katáthema* in the UBS), the object cursed.

134. αἰνέω *ainéō*; contracted *ainó*, fut. *ainḗsō* or *ainésō*. To sing praises. In the NT, it only refers to praising God (Luke 2:13, 20; 19:37; 24:53; Acts 2:47; 3:8, 9; Rom 15:11; Rev 19:5; Sept.: Gen 49:8; 1 Chr 16:4, 10; Ps 100:4).

   Deriv.: *aínesis* (133), the act of praise; *aínos* (136), a tale or narration which came to denote praise; *epainéō* (1867), to commend; *parainéō* (3867), to exhort, admonish.

   Syn.: *humnéō* (5214), to laud, to sing a hymn; *psállō* (5567), to twitch or twang as a bowstring, to play a stringed instrument with the fingers; *eulogéō* (2127), to speak well of, praise.

   Ant.: *anathematízō* (332), to utterly curse; *katanathematízō* (2653 [TR]) or *katathematízō* (UBS), to imprecate, curse; *kataráomai* (2672), to wish evil against; *kakologéō* (2551), to speak evil; *epikatáratos* (1944), accursed, the same as *epáratos* in some MSS of John 7:49.

135. αἴνιγμα aínigma; gen. *ainígmatos*, neut. noun from *ainíssomai* (n.f.), to hint obscurely, which is from *aínos* (136), discourse. An enigma, riddle, an obscure saying in which one thing answers to, corresponds to, or represents another, which is in some respect similar to it. See Sept.: 1 Kgs 10:1; Prov 1:6. In 1 Cor 13:12, "now [in this life] we see as by means of a mirror reflecting the images of heavenly and spiritual things [*en ainígmati*, in an enigmatic manner, since invisible things are represented by the visible, spiritual by the natural, eternal by the temporal], but then [in the life to come] we shall see face to face" (a.t.). From *ainíssomai*, to hint, intimate, signify with some degree of obscurity.

Syn.: *mustērion* (3466), mystery.
Ant.: *haplótēs* (572), simplicity.

136. αἶνος aínos; gen. *aínou*, masc. noun from *ainéō* (134), to praise. Praise returned for benefits received or expected (Matt 21:16; Luke 18:43; Sept.: Ps 8:3).

Deriv.: *épainos* (1868), approval, commendation.

137. Αἰνών Ainōn; fem. noun transliterated from the Hebr. '*Ēnāwān* (not found in the OT). Aenon, the area or fountain on the west side of Jordan near Salem where John was baptizing because water was plentiful (John 3:23).

138. αἱρέω hairéō; fut. *hairēsomai*, 2d aor. *heilómēn*. To take. In the NT, only in the mid. *hairéomai*, to take for oneself, i.e., to choose, elect, prefer (Phil 1:22; 2 Thess 2:13; Heb 11:25; Sept.: 2 Sam 15:15; Job 34:4).

Deriv.: *haíresis* (139), heresy; *hairetízō* (140), to choose, akin to *hairetós*, that which may be taken; *hairetikós* (141), heretic; *anairéō* (337), to take up or away, abolish; *authaíretos* (830), of one's own accord; *aphairéō* (851), to take away; *diairéō* (1244), to separate, divide, distribute; *exairéō* (1807), to tear out, in the mid. to select, figuratively

to release, deliver, pluck out, rescue; *kathairéō* (2507), to take down; *periairéō* (4014), to take away that which surrounds; *proairéomai* (4255), prefer, propose, intend, purpose.

Syn.: *eklégomai* (1586), to choose out, elect; *epilégomai* (1951), to be called or named.

Ant.: *apodokimázō* (593), to reject after investigation; *athetéō* (114), to do away with; *paraitéomai* (3868), to resign, ask to be excused.

139. αἵρεσις haíresis; gen. *hairéseōs*, fem. noun from *hairéō* (138), to choose, select. Heresy, a form of religious worship, discipline, or opinion (Acts 5:17; 15:5; 24:5, 14; 26:5; 28:22; 1 Cor 11:19; Gal 5:20; 2 Pet 2:1).

In contrast to *schísma* (4978), schism which is an actual tearing apart, *haíresis* may represent a divergent opinion but still be part of a whole. One can hold different views than the majority and remain in the same body, but he is a heretic (*hairetikós* [141]). However, when he tears himself away (*schízō* [4977]), then he is schismatic. Heresy may lead to schism which is when actual tearing off and separation occur.

140. αἱρετίζω hairetízō; fut. *hairetísō*, from *hairéō* (138), to take. To choose, only in Matt 12:18 related to the verbal adj. *hairetós*, that which may be taken. To take, with the implication that what is taken is eligible or suitable, to choose by reason of its suitability.

Syn.: *chōrízō* (5563), to separate; *anadeíknumi* (322), to indicate, appoint; *egkrínō* (1469), to accept as approved; *eklégomai* (1586), to choose because of love; *epilégomai* (1951), to select; *hairéomai* (138), to take for oneself, prefer; *aírō* (142), to take up or away.

Ant.: *aporríptō* (641), to reject; *apobállō* (577), to cast away; *periphronéō* (4065), to despise; *arnéomai* (720), to refuse; *apōthéomai* (683), to put away; *apophérō* (667), to bear off.

141. αἱρετικός *hairetikós*; gen. *hairetikoú*, masc. noun from *hairéō* (138), to take. Heretic, pertaining to choice, capable of choice in an act. sense. In ecclesiastical Gr., heretical (Titus 3:10). See Rom 16:17 where one still belongs to the fellowship, but whom the fellowship eventually had to exclude.

Syn.: *ápistos* (571), unfaithful.

Ant.: *pistós* (4103), faithful.

√**142. αἴρω** *aírō*; fut. *arṓ*, aor. *éra*, perf. *ḗrka* (Col 2:14), perf. pass. *ḗrmai* (John 20:1). To take up. Trans:

(I) To take up, to lift up, to raise.

(A) Particularly, as stones from the ground (John 8:59); serpents (Mark 16:18); anchors (Acts 27:13); the hand (Rev 10:5); see also Sept.: Deut 32:40; Isa 49:22. Pass. *árthēti* (Matt 21:21).

(B) Figuratively, to raise, elevate; the eyes (John 11:41; see also Sept.: Ps 121:1; 123:1); the voice, meaning, to cry out, to sing (Luke 17:13; Acts 4:24; see also Sept.: Judg 21:2; 1 Sam 11:4). To hold the mind (*psuchē* [5590]) or soul of someone suspended, i.e., in suspense or doubt (John 10:24).

(II) To take up and place on oneself, to take up and bear, meaning to bear, carry (Matt 4:6, "they shall bear you" [a.t.] in the hands. See also Sept.: Ps 91:12); my yoke (Matt 11:29; see also Sept.: Lam 3:27); the cross (Matt 16:24; 27:32; Mark 15:21); to take or carry with one (Mark 6:8; Luke 9:3; see also Sept.: Gen 44:1; 2 Kgs 7:8).

(III) To take up and carry away, meaning to take away, to remove by carrying, spoken of a bed (Matt 9:6; John 5:8); a dead body, a person, and so forth (Matt 14:12; 22:13; Acts 20:9); bread with the idea of laying up, making use of (Matt 14:20; 15:37; Mark 8:8, 19, 20). Generally (Matt 17:27; Acts 21:11). Pass. *árthēti*, "be thou removed" (Matt 21:21). In a metaphorical sense, to take away sin, meaning the imputation or punishment of sin (John 1:29; 1 John 3:5; 1 Sam 15:25); to bear the punishment of sin (Lev 5:17; Num 5:31; 14:33); to take away by taking upon oneself (Matt 8:17; 1 Pet 2:24).

(IV) To take away, remove, with the idea of lifting away from, usually with the idea of violence and authority.

(A) Particularly (Luke 6:29, 30; 11:22). The new piece tears away still more of the old garment (Matt 9:16; Mark 2:21). Of branches, meaning to cut off, prune (John 15:2); Spoken of persons, meaning to take away or remove from a church, excommunicate (1 Cor 5:2, in some MSS *exarthḗ* [1808]). To take away or remove out of the world by death, and so forth (Matt 24:39). In His humiliation and oppression was His sentence; He was torn away, meaning hurried away to death (Acts 8:33; Isa 53:8; 57:1, 2). In the imper. *aíre* or *áron*, away with, meaning put out of the way, kill (Luke 23:18; John 19:15; Acts 21:36; 22:22).

(B) Figuratively (John 11:48, "and take away [destroy] our city and nation" [a.t.]; 1 Cor 6:15, taking away wrongfully the members which belong to Christ). With the meaning of to deprive of the kingdom of heaven (Matt 21:43); the word of God (Mark 4:15; Luke 8:12, 18); gifts (Mark 4:25); joy (John 16:22; see also Sept.: Isa 16:10). Spoken of vices, to put away (Eph 4:31); of a law, to abrogate (Col 2:14).

Deriv.: *apaírō* (522), to lift off; *exaírō* (1808), to put away from the midst; *epaírō* (1869), to lift up, as in the eyes, the head, the hands or the heel; *sunaírō* (4868), to take up together, to reckon; *huperaírō* (5229), to be exalted above measure.

Syn.: *bastázō* (941), to bear; *phérō* (5342), to bring, carry; *methístēmi* (3179), to remove; *lambánō* (2983), to take, lay hold of; *piázō* (4084), to lay hold of forcefully; *airéō* (138), to take; *komízō* (2865), to bring.

Ant.: *kataleípō* (2641), to leave behind; *hupoleípō* (5275), to leave remaining; *hupolimpánō* (5277), to leave behind, bequeath.

143. αἰσθάνομαι *aisthánomai*; fut. *aisthḗsomai*, 2d aor. *hēsthómēn*, a mid. deponent from *aíō* (n.f.), to perceive.

To perceive, primarily with the external senses. Figuratively of spiritual perception: to become conscious of, observe, understand, used more of immediate knowledge than that arrived at by reasoning (Luke 9:45; Sept.: Job 23:5; Prov 24:14).

Deriv.: *aísthēsis* (144), perception, discernment; *aisthētērion* (145), organ of perception.

Syn.: *krínō* (2919), to judge, conclude; *suníēmi* (4920), to comprehend; *sōphronéō* (4993), to exercise a sound mind; *diakrínō* (1252), to discern.

Ant.: *paralogízomai* (3884), to reason falsely; *paraphronéō* (3912), to misthink, to think as a fool.

144. αἴσθησις *aísthēsis*; gen. *aisthḗseōs*, fem. noun from *aisthánomai* (143), to perceive with the external senses. Perception, with the senses as well as the mind. Pass., to become cognizant of, to make oneself observed by someone. Involves knowledge based upon experience. In Phil 1:9 contrast *epígnōsis* (1922), the insight obtained by penetrating knowledge, going down to the foundation. *Aísthēsis*, however, is experiential knowledge which is or becomes naturally manifold, and therefore has the addition of *pása*, the fem. of *pás* (3956), all (Phil 1:9).

Syn.: *krísis* (2920), decision, judgment, evaluation; *gnṓmē* (1106), opinion, purpose.

145. αἰσθητήριον *aisthētērion*; gen. *aisthētēríou*, neut. noun from *aisthánomai* (143), to perceive with the external senses. Organ of sense. In the NT, used figuratively (Heb 5:14).

146. αἰσχροκερδής *aischrokerdḗs*; gen. *aischrokerdoús*, contracted *aischrokerdoús*, masc.-fem., neut. *aischrokerdés*, adj. from *aischrós* (150), indecent, dishonorable, and *kérdos* (2771), gain. A person who is eager to gain even if such gain degrades his moral character. Occurs only in 1 Tim 3:3 (TR), 8; Titus 1:7.

A bishop, elder, or deacon must not go after gain that would dishonor his character.

Deriv.: *aischrokerdōs* (147), in a manner that demonstrates desire for sordid gain.

Syn.: *pleonéktēs* (4123), covetous; *philárguros* (5366), lover of money.

Ant.: *tímios* (5093), honest; *éntimos* (1784), honorable; *euthús* (2117), straight; *chrēstós* (5543), useful, moral.

147. αἰσχροκερδῶς *aischrokerdōs*; adv. from the adj. *aischrokerdés* (146), eager of sordid gain. For the sake of dishonorable gain, sordidly. Occurs only in 1 Pet 5:2 indicating the manner in which an elder of a local congregation should behave, i.e., not using his position for personal gain. This does not refer exclusively to material gain such as the demand of a salary which gives the impression that an elder serves primarily from his desire for selfish purposes rather than his desire to be of service. It may also refer to gaining popularity by adulterating the gospel to attract more people to the congregation, and showing special favors and consideration to the rich and the influential in order to gain personal advantage and profit. It stands in antithesis to *prothúmōs* (4290) which means serving willingly because of the worthiness of the ministry rendered, instead of the gain acquired as a result of the ministry. An *aischrokerdés* has as his philosophy: "The ministry is my profession; I have to do it because that is my living." The one ministering (*prothúmōs* [4290]) says: "I am in the ministry because I am needed and am going to serve regardless of the compensation."

148. αἰσχρολογία *aischrología*, gen. *aischrologías*, fem. noun from *aischrologéō* (n.f.), to be foul-mouthed, which is from *aischrós* (150), filthy or improper, and *légō* (3004), to say. Vile conversation. It occurs only in Col 3:8 where it refers to shameful words coming out of the mouth, implying that the person who has been redeemed by Christ (Col 3:1) should never utter improper or filthy words which he may have uttered in his life of unbelief. A Christian ought to have a changed vocabulary, and the genuineness of one's Christianity can be discerned by his vocabulary.

Ant.: *euphēmía* (2162), good language; *épainos* (1868), praise; *eulogía* (2129), speaking well.

149. αἰσχρόν aischrón; gen. *aischroú*, neut. of the adj. *aischrós* (150). Shameful. It occurs in 1 Cor 11:6 referring to the shame that a woman brings upon herself if she cuts off or shaves her hair, because such was the custom of lewd women, especially the prostitutes serving at the temple of Aphrodite on Acrocorinth. A decent woman always was distinguished by hair which covered the head well, a sign of decorum and propriety. In this instance, *aischrón* indicates the assumption of the role that does not belong to a decent woman. It is equivalent to Paul's saying, "Don't adorn your hair, shear it, or shave it, for that indicates that you belong to a base and vile class of women." The word also occurs in 1 Cor 14:35, referring again to wives (*gunaixín*, dat. pl. of *gunē* [1135], in this context meaning wife or wives, not "women" as the KJV has it). Paul says that it is shameful or vile for wives to speak in church and cause confusion. The word for "speak" is *laleín*, the inf. of *laléō* (2980) which in the context of 1 Cor 14 means to speak in such a way as to cause confusion, in contrast to *légō* (3004) which means to speak intelligently and understandably. (In other contexts, it means to repeat exactly as received [John 3:11, 34] or to declare without necessarily explaining [Acts 2:31; 3:24] or to simply utter [1 Cor 12:3; Heb 1:1].) It is the duty of husbands to prevent their wives from disorderly speaking. If a wife has a question which she needs to have clarified, she must not ask in church and embarrass her husband, but she should ask her husband at home. It should be borne in mind that at the time of Paul's injunction, it was rare for a woman to be educated. Neither should a wife speak in church in such a way as to usurp authority (*authentéō* [831]) over her husband (1 Tim 2:11, 12). *Aischrón* also occurs in Eph 5:12 indicating that activities of which one would be ashamed are usually done in secret. Paul intimates that shameful things done in secret should not be aired in public by Christians. It is the duty of the Christian, however, to allow the light of the gospel to shine upon the evil things that are perpetrated in darkness, but always in redemptive consideration of the vile person. Every revelation of the light should be for the redemption of the one who acts in darkness.

Syn.: *phaúlos* (5337), foul, evil, trifling; *kakós* (2556), bad; *ponērós* (4190), evil.

Ant.: *agathós* (18), good, benevolent; *kalós* (2570), good; *áxios* (514), worthy; *arestós* (701), pleasing; *euárestos* (2101), well-pleasing.

150. αἰσχρός aischrós; fem. *aischrá*, neut. *aischrón* (149), adj. Indecent, indecorous, dishonorable. It refers to the inappropriate conduct of the elder of the local church, that he be not given to improper gain for selfish purposes (only in Titus 1:11). The expression, *aischroú kérdous*, for improper gain, is equivalent to *aischrokerdēs* (146), fond of dishonest or unscrupulous gain of which the bishop is prohibited in 1 Tim 3:3, 8 and the elder in Titus 1:7. The joining of *aischrós* with *kérdos* (2771), gain or profit as a way of life, is to be avoided by the bishop and the elder for it constitutes a great danger and temptation in the local church. Such leaders can so easily take advantage of the people served for personal, selfish gain that warnings against it are issued in all the pertinent passages advising the proper conduct of the minister of a local church.

Deriv.: *aischrokerdēs* (146), sordidly eager of gain; *aischrótēs* (151), impropriety.

151. αἰσχρότης *aischrótēs*; gen. *aischrótetos*, fem. noun from *aischrós* (150), indecent. Impropriety, a summarizing improper conduct whether in action or word or even thought and intent; indecorum of any kind; conduct which when exposed by the light makes the person ashamed of himself; ugly, shameful conduct of any kind; conduct which is contrary to a person who follows after God (only in Eph 5:4). Attachment and conformity to God requires a conduct of which God is not ashamed and which could not bring shame to the person when it is brought to light.

Syn.: *ponēría* (4189), evil; *atimía* (819), dishonor; *kakoḗtheia* (2550), bad character, malignity; *molusmós* (3436), a stain, immorality, filthiness; *asélgeia* (766), incontinence, unable to have sufficient pleasure.

Ant.: *aretḗ* (703), virtue; *chrēstótēs* (5544), excellence in character; *euprépeia* (2143), good behavior, gracefulness.

152. αἰσχύνη *aischúnē*; gen. *aischúnēs*, fem. noun from *aíschos* (n.f.), shame. Disgrace, shame.

(I) Subjectively meaning a sense of shame resulting from exposure of one's weaknesses or sins. It is that feeling which leads one to shun what is unworthy out of the prospect and anticipation of dishonor, fear of disgrace (Luke 14:9).

(II) Objectively meaning disgrace, reproach (Heb 12:2; Sept.: Job 8:22; Ps 69:20; Isa 50:6).

(III) Cause of shame, i.e., a shameful thing or action, disgraceful conduct. Hidden things of shame, clandestine conduct of which the disciples of Christ should be ashamed (2 Cor 4:2). See also Phil 3:19; Heb 12:2; Jude 1:13. "Shameful nakedness" (Rev 3:18 [a.t.]). See also Sept.: 1 Sam 20:30.

Syn.: *atimía* (819), dishonor; *entropḗ* (1791), hidden shame which causes a person to withdraw within himself; *aschēmosúnē* (808), unseemliness, shame; *aidṓs* (127), shame that is objective because of conviction with regard to others, which is stronger than *aischúnē*. *Aidṓs* would restrain a good man from an unworthy act, but *aischúnē* may sometimes restrain even a bad one.

Ant.: *kaúchēma* (2745), boast; *kaúchēsis* (2746), boasting.

153. αἰσχύνω *aischúnō*; fut. *aischunṓ*, from *aíschos* (n.f.), shame. To shame, put to shame. In the pass., to be put to shame, be made ashamed (2 Cor 10:8; Phil 1:20; 1 John 2:28, "that we be not put to shame before him" [a.t.]; Sept.: Jer 22:22). In the mid., *aischúnomai*, to shame oneself, to feel ashamed, dishonored (Luke 16:3; 1 Pet 4:16; Sept.: Ps 25:3; 119:80).

Deriv.: *epaischúnomai* (1870), to be mortified, humiliated; *kataischúnō* (2617), to put to shame.

Syn.: *entrépō* (1788), to put to shame, and *entrépomai*, to be ashamed resulting in withdrawal; *atimázō* (818), to dishonor, put to shame; *paradeigmatízō* (3856), to set forth as an example; *atimázō* (818), to render infamous; *atimóō* (821), to handle shamefully.

Ant.: *kaucháomai* (2744), to boast; *epaíromai* (1869), to exalt oneself.

154. αἰτέω *aitéō*; fut. *aitḗsō*. Ask, request, beg. The seeking by the inferior from the superior (Acts 12:20); by a beggar from the giver (Acts 3:2); by the child from the parent (Matt 7:9); by man from God (Matt 7:7; James 1:5; 1 John 3:22).

(I) To ask, with the acc. of thing in *pará* (3844), from (with the gen. of person).

(II) Generally (Matt 5:42; 7:9, 10; Mark 6:22–25; Luke 11:9–13; 1 John 5:14–16; Sept.: Josh 15:18; 19:50). Spoken in respect to God, to supplicate, to pray for (Matt 6:8; 7:11; 18:19; James 1:5, 6). With the word *Theós* (2316), God, implied (Matt 7:7, 8; Col 1:9; James 4:2, 3; Sept.: Isa 7:11, 12). In His requests to the Father, the Lord never uses *aitéō*, to beg, but *erōtáō*, to ask as an equal of the Father on behalf of Himself or His disciples (John 14:16; 16:26; 17:9, 15, 20).

(III) To ask or call for, require, demand (Luke 1:63; 12:48; 23:23; Acts 3:14; 25:15; 1 Pet 3:15; Sept.: Job 6:22; Dan 2:49).

(IV) To desire (Acts 7:46; Sept.: 1 Kgs 19:4; Eccl 2:10; Deut 14:26).

Deriv.: *aítēma* (155), request, petition; *aitía* (156), an accusation; *apaitéō* (523), to require; *exaitéomai* (1809), to ask to have; *epaitéō* (1871), to beg; *paraitéomai* (3868), to refuse, give up; *prosaitéō* (4319), to ask earnestly.

Syn.: *punthánomai* (4441), to ask by way of inquiry; *zētéō* (2212), to seek; *parakaléō* (3870), to beseech; *déomai* (1189), to make a specific request; *epithuméō* (1937), desire, long; *epizētéō* (1934), to demand; *diṓkō* (1377), to pursue; *erōtáō* (2065), ask.

155. αἴτημα *aítēma*; gen. *aitḗmatos*, neut. noun from *aitéō* (154), to ask. Petition, request, a thing asked or an asking. Occurs twice in the NT (Phil 4:6; 1 John 5:15) in the sense of a petition of men to God, both times in the pl. They are particular requests of which prayer (*proseuchḗ* [4335]) may consist, e.g., in the Lord's Prayer there are seven *aitḗmata*, petitions, although some have regarded the first three as *euchaí* (2171), wishes. *Aítēma* is used in Luke 23:24 in the sense of petition by the Jews for releasing Barabbas.

Syn.: *déēsis* (1162), supplication or prayer for particular benefits; *énteuxis* (1783), intercession; *eucharistía* (2169), thanksgiving; *hiketēría* (2428), entreaty, supplication; *boúlēma* (1013), will, purpose; *boulḗ* (1012) will; *epithumía* (1939), a longing; *thélēma* (2307), volition, determination; *paráklēsis* (3874), request, imploration.

156. αἰτία *aitía*; gen. *aitías*, fem. noun from *aitéō* (154), to ask or require because an accusation or crime is that for which one is required to appear before a judge to be questioned. A cause, reason,

incitement (cf. *aítios* [159], a causator, author).

(I) Efficient cause, motive, reason, ground (Matt 19:3; Luke 8:47; Acts 22:24; 28:20; 2 Tim 1:6, 12; Titus 1:13; Heb 2:11).

(II) In the sense of affair, matter, case (Acts 10:21; 23:28). In Matt 19:10, "if such is the case" (a.t.). With the meaning of thing, affair (Gen 20:8; Eccl 7:8); case, manner (Deut 15:2; 19:4; 1 Kgs 9:15).

(III) In a forensic sense, cause.

(A) An accusation of crime, charge (Matt 27:37; Mark 15:26; Acts 25:18, 27).

(B) Fault, guilt, crime (John 18:38; 19:4, 6; Acts 13:28; 28:18; Sept.: Gen 4:13; Prov 28:17).

Deriv.: *anaítios* (338), innocent.

Syn.: *katēgoría* (2724), an accusation; *lógos* (3056), reason.

157. αἰτίαμα *aitíama*; gen. *aitiámatos*, neut. noun from *aitiáomai* (n.f.), to charge, accuse, which is from *aitía* (156), cause. A thing charged, complaint. In the pl. in Acts 25:7 it refers to the actual charges brought against Paul by the Jews who came from Jerusalem to Caesarea to accuse him before Festus. In the usage of *aitía* or *aitíama*, the accusation made against one as being true or false is not implied explicitly. This is decided by the context. In Matt 27:37 it is evident that *aitía*, the accusation brought against the Lord Jesus, was false. The same can be said for the *aitiámata* of Acts 25:7, which should be translated "trumped-up charges" (a.t.), as the forms in which they were presented imply.

Syn.: *momphḗ* (3437), blame; *lógos* (3056), reason; *aphormḗ* (874), occasion, excuse; *élegchos* (1650) in 2 Tim 3:16; Heb 11:1, implies not merely the charge, but the truth of the charge and the conviction in the heart of the one so charged.

Ant.: *ékbasis* (1545), result; *karpós* (2590), fruit.

158. αἴτιον *aítion*; gen. *aitíou*, neut. of *aítios* (159), adj. The reason for which something takes place implying the motivation for which something is done in contrast to its happening by chance or as a result of an inescapable situation, the reason for doing something. Used in Luke 23:4 by Pilate in his attempt to exonerate Jesus. Used here as a noun, although it is an adj., to indicate a criminal charge or purposeful crime which Jesus had done to warrant His crucifixion. Similarly used in Luke 23:14. In Luke 23:22 it is used with the gen. *thanátou* (2288), of death, which means a crime deserving death. In Acts 19:40 it is used by the town clerk of Ephesus when declaring that there was no cause for the commotion made by Demetrius and the silver craftsmen.

159. αἴτιος *aítios*; fem. *aitía*, neut. *aítion* (158), adj. used subst. in the NT. Cause or source, as of eternal salvation (only in Heb 5:9 of Melchizedek as a type of Jesus Christ). The translation of *aítios* as "author" does not fully convey the meaning. Jesus is spoken of as having reached the goal that He set for man's salvation (*teleiōtheís*, the aor. pass. part. of *teleióō* [5048], to finish properly in moral perfection), having brought salvation and consequent obedience to those who believed on Him. Such believers on looking back could see only the reason for their salvation and the basis of it, Jesus Christ. We have here the retroactive appreciation of the reason for their salvation and their obedience (cf. *aitía* [156], cause, without any implication of good or evil).

Syn.: *arché* (746), the active cause, beginning; *téktōn* (5045), producer, craftsman.

160. αἰφνίδιος *aiphnídios*; gen. *aiphnidíou*, masc.-fem., neut. *aiphnídion*, adj. from *aíphnēs* (n.f.), unexpected, sudden. Sudden, unexpected, unforeseen, something that one cannot anticipate nor understand how it happened. The word occurs twice in the NT. In Luke 21:34 it is used as a predicate of *hēméra* (2250),

day, giving it the meaning of an adv., suddenly. In 1 Thess 5:3 it is used in relation to the day of judgment spoken of in 1 Thess 5:2 where it is an adj. of the noun *ólethros* (3639), destruction. Here it means the sudden, unexpected, unforeseen destruction accompanying the tribulation. Also from *aíphnēs* (n.f.): *exaíphnēs* (1810), suddenly, a comp. of the same root.

Syn.: *áphnō* (869), suddenly; *exápina* (1819), suddenly, unexpectedly; *tachéōs* (5030), quickly, hastily; *en táchu* (*en* [1722], in; *táchu* [5035], suddenly), in a sudden manner.

Ant.: *bradús* (1021), slow; *argós* (692), slow.

161. αἰχμαλωσία *aichmalōsía*; gen. *aichmalōsías*, fem. noun from *aichmálōtos* (164), a captive. The state of being captive or of taking someone captive by the force of the spear. In Eph 4:8 *aichmalōsía* is used with the verb *aichmalōtízō* (163), to take captive, meaning a captive multitude. Quoted from Ps 68:18, it is a prophecy of the distribution of gifts (*charísmata* [5486]) to believers. What the Lord Jesus received from the Father (Matt 28:19, 20) at the time of His ascension, He distributed as gifts to His own to enable them to continue His work. The use of both the verb and the noun, "He captivated captivity" (a.t. [Eph 4:8]), indicates that the ascended Lord was in full possession of all believers and that their destiny was absolutely in His hands, no matter what difficulties they would encounter in the execution of their task of spreading the gospel. Distributing gifts was Christ's confirmation of the captivity of the captives who were to serve Him through the exercise of the gifts. In exercising these gifts they were never to forget that He was in full control. The word also occurs in Rev 13:10 where the KJV says, "He that leadeth into captivity shall go into captivity." In the Gr. text there is only one verb, *hupágei* (5217), to go. The literal translation is: "If anyone has captivity, he goes" (a.t.). The meaning assumed for the first clause cannot be different from the meaning of the second clause. It means that since one has chosen to become a captive of Jesus Christ, he moves on into captivity because he has tasted that the captivity is not for his harm but for his good. To be a captive of Jesus Christ is the greatest freedom that one can experience. Rev 13 speaks of the activity of the Antichrist. At that time on earth, there will be the believers who have placed themselves under the protective captivity of Jesus Christ and will be maintained by Him and will not in any way succumb to the pressures of the Antichrist. The endurance and the faith of the believers is spoken about in verse ten. Therefore, the word *aichmalōsía* here refers to the state of the captivity of the believers even as does Eph 4:8 which regards the multitude of the believers as the "captivity." In Ephesians we have the captives and in Revelation we have the state of the captives or the captivity itself.

Syn.: *zōgréō* (2221), to take men alive.

Ant.: *eleuthería* (1657), freedom; *ánesis* (425), a loosening, liberty, a lifting up; *áphesis* (859), release.

162. αἰχμαλωτεύω *aichmalōteúō*; fut. *aichmalōteúsō*, from *aichmálōtos* (164), a captive. To capture. A verb basically similar to *aichmalōtízō* (163), to lead captive. Verbs that end in *ízō*, very common in Mod. Gr., do not necessarily represent repetition or intensity. They sometimes have a causative idea and, then again, lose even that distinctive note and supplant the older form of the word. For instance, *baptízō* (907), baptize, has supplanted *báptō* (911), dip. Used in Eph 4:8 in the aor., *ēchmalóteusen*, it is translated periphrastically as "led captive," but in reality the verb means captivated, or asserts the captivity already accomplished. When Jesus Christ ascended into heaven, He did not forsake those who became His willing captives, but He asserted His protective captivity over them. The

TR in 2 Tim 3:6 has *aichmalōteúontes* from *aichmalōteúō* (162), while the UBS in the same verse has *aichmalōtízontes* from *aichmalōtízō* (163), designating one of the characteristics of the last days, namely, the deceptive ability of men to penetrate homes and to captivate women loaded with sins. Thus, *aichmalōteúō* in this text has the meaning of taking captive by deception, while in Eph 4:8 it has a benevolent meaning.

Syn.: *sullambánō* (4815), to capture; *pagideúō* (3802), to ensnare; *katalambánō* (2638), to apprehend, seize; *piázō* (4084), to seize.

Ant.: *apolúō* (630), to release; *epitrépō* (2010), to permit; *aníēmi* (447), to loosen, to let up; *aphíēmi* (863), to let go, dismiss.

163. αἰχμαλωτίζω *aichmalōtízō*; fut. *aichmalōtísō*, from *aichmálōtos* (164), a prisoner, captive. To lead captive. Pass., to be carried away captive (Luke 21:24; Sept.: 1 Kgs 8:46). In the sense of to captivate (2 Tim 3:6). By implication, to subdue, bring into subjection (Rom 7:23; 2 Cor 10:5).

164. αἰχμάλωτος *aichmálōtos*; gen. *aichmalōtou*, masc.-fem., neut. *aichmáloton*, adj. from *aichmḗ* (n.f.), a spear, and *halōtós* (n.f.), to be taken, conquered. Taken by the sword, used subst. meaning a captive. Occurs only in Luke 4:18 referring to those who have become captives of the devil (John 8:44; Acts 10:38; 2 Tim 2:26; 1 Pet 5:8; Sept.: Isa 61:1; Ezek 12:4).

Deriv.: *aichmalōsía* (161), captivity; *aichmalōteúō* (162), to capture; *aichmalōtízō* (163), to lead captive; *sunaichmálōtos* (4869), fellow-prisoner.

Syn.: *désmios* (1198), prisoner; *desmṓtēs* (1202), a captive, prisoner; *doúlos* (1401), bondslave, servant.

Ant.: *eleútheros*, (1658), free man; *apeleútheros* (558), freed-man, one who was captive but has been freed.

165. αἰών *aiṓn*; gen. *aiṓnos*, masc. noun. Age, referring to an age or time in contrast to *kósmos* (2889), referring to people or space. Denotes duration or continuance of time, but with great variety.

(I) Age, an indefinitely long period or lapse of time, perpetuity, ever, forever, eternity.

(A) Spoken of time future in the following phrases: **(1)** *Eis tón aiṓna* (*eis* [1519] into, unto; *tón* [3588], the; *aiṓn* [165], age), forever, without end, to the remotest time (Mark 11:14; Luke 1:55; John 6:51, 58; 8:35; 12:34; 13:8; 14:16; 1 Cor 8:13; Heb 5:6, 21; 1 Pet 1:25; 2 John 1:2); spoken of Christ (Heb 6:20; 7:17; 7:24, 28); spoken of the blessedness of the righteous (Jn 6:51, 58; 2 Cor 9:9; 1 John 2:17; 2 Pet 2:17); of the punishment of the wicked (Jude 1:13). With a neg., meaning never (Matt 21:19; Mark 3:29; John 4:14; 8:51, 52; 10:28; 11:26; Sept.: Deut 29:29; Isa 28:28; 40:8; 51:6, 8; Jer 50:39). *Eis hēméran aiṓnos* (*eis* [1519], unto; *hēméran* [2250], day), of the age, meaning forever. See also Sept.: Ex 14:13; Isa 13:20. **(2)** The phrase *eis toús aiṓnas*, unto the ages, meaning ever, forever, to all eternity (Matt 6:13; Luke 1:33; Rom 16:27; Heb 13:8), spoken of God (Rom 1:25; 9:5; 11:36; 2 Cor 11:31); of Christ (Luke 1:33 as explained by the statement "of His kingdom there shall be no end"; Heb 13:8; Sept.: Ps 77:8). **(3)** The phrase *eis toús aiṓnas tṓn aiṓnōn*, unto the ages of the ages, being an intens. form meaning forever and ever (2 Tim 4:18; Heb 13:21; 1 Pet 4:11; Rev 1:6, 18; 4:9, 10; 5:13; 7:12; 10:6; 11:15; 15:7; 19:3; 20:10; 22:5). Spoken of God (Gal 1:5; Phil 4:20; 1 Tim 1:17; 1 Pet 5:11). Without the art. *eis aiṓnas aiṓnōn*, unto the ages of the ages (Rev 14:11). Also in the expression *eis pásas tás geneás toú aiṓnos tṓn aiṓnōn* (*pása*, the fem. pl. of *pás* [3956], every, all; *geneás* [the acc. pl. of *geneá* {1074}, generation]) as in Eph 3:21 meaning throughout all ages and literally unto all generations of the age of

the ages. Spoken of Christ (2 Pet 3:18; Rev 1:18; 5:13; 11:15); of the blessedness of the saints (Rev 22:5); of the punishment of the wicked (Rev 14:11; 19:3; 20:10). In the Sept. the phrase *eis aiṓna aiṓnos*, literally means unto the age of the age (Ps 19:9; 110:3, 10).

(B) Spoken of time past as *ap' aiṓnos apó* (*apó* [575], from), meaning of old, from everlasting (Luke 1:70; Acts 3:21; 15:18). *Apó tṓn aiṓnōn* meaning from the ages (Eph 3:9; Col 1:26). Also *ek toú aiṓnos ou* (*ek* [1537], from; *ou* [3756], not) meaning literally from the ages not, i.e., never (John 9:32); *pró tṓn aiṓnōn* (*pró* [4253], before) literally from the ages, meaning before time began, from eternity (1 Cor 2:7). See also Gen 6:4; Ps 90:2; Jer 2:20; Sept.: Ps 55:19).

(II) With the meaning of the world or the people that live at a certain time. *Aiṓn* is to be distinguished from *kósmos* (2889), world, which refers to people. *Aiṓn* also is to be distinguished from *oikouménē* (3625), the inhabited earth.

(A) This world and the next. **(1)** As implying duration (Matt 12:32, "neither in this world nor the next" [a.t.], meaning never) (Mark 10:30; Luke 18:30). **(2)** The present world, with its cares, temptations, and desires; the idea of evil, both moral and physical, being everywhere implied (Matt 13:22; Luke 16:8; 20:34; Rom 12:2; 1 Cor 1:20; 2:6, 8; 2 Tim 4:10; Titus 2:12). Hence this world is called *aiṓn ponērós* (4190), evil, meaning evil world (Gal 1:4). Satan is called the "god of this world" (2 Cor 4:4; Sept.: Eccl 3:11). **(3)** By metonymy, the men of this world, wicked generation, and so forth (Eph 2:2). *Huioí toú aiṓnos toútou* (*huioí*, the pl. of *huiós* [5207], son; *toútou* [5127], of this) sons of this generation, the people of this world (Luke 16:8; 20:34). **(4)** By metonymy, the world itself as an object of creation and existence (Matt 13:40; 24:3; 1 Tim 1:17; Heb 1:2; 11:3).

(B) Spoken in reference to the advent of the Messiah, meaning age: **(1)** The age or world before the Messiah, the Jewish dispensation (1 Cor 10:11, "the ends of the world"). **(2)** The age or world after the Messiah, the gospel dispensation, the kingdom of the Messiah (Eph 2:7; Heb 6:5; see also Heb 2:5).

Deriv.: *aiṓnios* (166), eternal.

Syn.: *geneá* (1074), generation, the people of a certain period of time; *hēlikía* (2244), the age or height of an individual; *hēméra* (2250), day or period of time. For the various prep. phrases with *aiṓn*, see *aeí* (104), forever, always.

Ant.: *chrónos* (5550), time; *kairós* (2540), season; *stigmḗ* (4743), moment; *diástēma* (1292), an interval, space.

166. αἰώνιος *aiṓnios*; gen. *aiōníou*, masc.-fem., neut. *aiṓnion*, adj., also fem. *aiōnía*, neut. *aiṓnion*, from *aiṓn* (165), age. Eternal, perpetual, belonging to the *aiṓn* (165), to time in its duration, constant, abiding. When referring to eternal life, it means the life which is God's and hence it is not affected by the limitations of time. *Aiṓnios* is specially predicated of the saving blessings of divine revelation, denoting those things which are not transitory. Meanings:

(I) Spoken chiefly of future time:

(A) Of God (Rom 16:26; 1 Tim 6:16; Sept.: Gen 21:33; Isa 40:28).

(B) Of the blessedness of the righteous (Matt 19:29; 25:46; Mark 10:30; John 3:15, 16, 36; Rom 2:7; 2 Cor 4:17). In some passages this *zōḗ aiṓnios* (*zōḗ* [2222], life), life eternal which is equivalent to the kingdom of God, and the entrance into life, means the entrance into the kingdom (John 3:3, 5, 15; Matt 19:16; Acts 13:46).

(C) Of the punishment of the wicked (Matt 18:8; 25:41, 46; Mark 3:29; 2 Thess 1:9; Heb 6:2; Jude 1:7; Sept.: Dan 12:2).

(D) Generally (2 Cor 4:18; 5:1; Heb 9:14; 13:20; 1 John 1:2; Rev 14:6; in Phile 1:15 *aiṓnion*, an adv. meaning forever, always). In the Sept.: *diathḗkē aiṓnios* (1242), testament, covenant, meaning eternal covenant (Gen 9:16; 17:7).

(II) Spoken of time past (Rom 16:25), *chrónois aiōníois* (from *chrónos* [5550],

time) meaning times eternal, ancient ages, of old (2 Tim 1:9; Titus 1:2 meaning before time was, from eternity [cf. Sept.: Ps 24:7, 9]).

Other references for this word include: Mark 10:17; Luke 10:25; 16:9; 18:18, 30; John 4:14, 36; 5:24, 39; 6:27, 40, 47, 54, 68; 10:28; 12:25, 50; 17:2, 3; Acts 13:48; Rom 5:21; 6:22, 23; Gal 6:8; 2 Thess 2:16; 1 Tim 1:16; 6:12, 19; 2 Tim 2:10; Titus 3:7; Heb 5:9; 9:12, 15; 1 Pet 5:10; 2 Pet 1:11; 1 John 2:25; 3:15; 5:11, 13, 20; Jude 1:21.

(III) Spoken of endless duration. The expression *zōḗ aiṓnios* (*zōḗ* [2222], life), life eternal. Whenever it is used for the life which God gives to those who believe in Christ (Matt 19:16, 29; 25:46; Mark 10:30; Luke 10:25; 18:18, 30; John 3:15, 36; 4:14, 36; 5:24, 39; 6:27, 40, 47, 68; 10:28; 12:25, 50; 17:2, 3; Acts 13:46, 48; Rom 2:7; 5:21; 6:22, 23; Gal 6:8; 1 Tim 6:12, 19; Titus 1:2; 3:7; 1 John 1:2; 2:25; 3:15; 5:11, 13, 20; Jude 1:21), it is to be understood as referring not only to duration, but more so to quality. That is, it is not merely a life that is eternal in duration, but is primarily something different from the natural life of man, i.e., the life of God. Since it is His life God gives to the believer through Christ, and He is endless, His life imparted must be endless, although the life He gives to the believer has a beginning. The word which indicates no beginning and no end is *aḯdios* (126), eternal.

The expression *aiōníous skēnás* (4633), tabernacles, tents, houses, eternal tents, habitations, means heaven (Luke 16:9).

There is *aiṓnion púr* (4442), eternal fire, which means punishment brought about by God (Matt 18:8; 25:41); *kólasis aiṓnios* (*kólasis* [2851], punishment, torment), eternal punishment, refers to God-given punishment lasting forever (Matt 25:46).

Ólethros aiṓnios (*Ólethros* [3639] ruin, punishment), destruction which is eternal (2 Thess 1:9) or everlasting destruction, is destruction or a state which is imposed by God forever. *Kríma aiṓnion* (*kríma* [2917], judgment), eternal judgment (Heb 6:2) means the sentence imposed by God forever. All of these designations of punishment stand in contrast to eternal life as the inherent punishment for those who reject Christ's salvation in that they will be separated from the life of God which they rejected. As to the duration of what is designated as *aiṓnios* when it comes to punishment, it is only proper to assign it the same duration or endlessness as to the life which is given by God.

Syn.: *aḯdios* (126), having no beginning and no ending, everlasting.

Ant.: *próskairos* (4340), temporal, for a season; *ephḗmeros* (2184), for a day, transient. In *prós hṓran* (*prós* [4314], for; *hṓran* [5610], hour) for the hour, meaning temporarily.

167. ἀκαθαρσία *akatharsía*; gen. *akatharsías*, fem. noun from *akáthartos* (169), unclean. Uncleanness or filth in a natural or physical sense (Matt 23:27; Sept.: 2 Sam 11:4); moral uncleanness, lewdness, incontinence in general (Rom 6:19; Eph 4:19; 5:3; 1 Thess 2:3 of avarice; 4:7); any kind of uncleanness different from whoredom (2 Cor 12:21); any unnatural pollution, whether acted out by oneself (Gal 5:19; Col 3:5), or with another (Rom 1:24 [cf. Rom 1:26, 27]; Sept.: Ezek 22:15; 36:25).

Syn.: *miasmós* (3394), a defilement; *rhúpos* (4509), dirt, filth; *aischrótēs* (151), obscenity, impurity; *rhuparía* (4507), moral defilement; *molusmós* (3436), a soiling, defilement; *asélgeia* (766), lasciviousness, wantonness; *miasmós* (3394), contamination, uncleanness; *míasma* (3393), foulness, pollution; *spílos* (4696), stain, blemish defect, spot; *stígma* (4742), stigma, mark scar.

Ant.: *hagnótēs* (54), pureness, purity; *hagneía* (47), cleanliness, purity; *katharismós* (2512), a cleansing; *katharótēs* (2514), cleanness, purification.

168. ἀκαθάρτης *akathártēs*; gen. *akathártētos*, a shortened form of *akatharótēs*, fem. noun from the priv. *a* (1), without, and *katharótēs* (2514), cleanness. Unclean-ness, filthiness (Rev 17:4).

Syn.: *akatharsía* (167), uncleanness.

Ant.: *katharótēs* (2514), cleanness; *hagnótēs* (54), cleanness, pureness.

169. ἀκάθαρτος *akáthartos*; gen. *akathártou*, masc.-fem., neut. *akátharton*, adj. from the priv. *a* (1), without, and *kathaírō* (2508), to cleanse. Unclean.

(I) Unclean by legal or ceremonial standards (Acts 10:14, 28; 11:8; Rev 18:2 [cf. Lev 5:2; 11:4, 25; 13:45; Deut 14:7]) whereas in the Sept. it compares with 2 Cor 6:17 where *akáthartos* seems ultimately to refer to all idolatrous worship and heathen impurity.

(II) Unclean, unfit to be admitted to the peculiar rights and privileges of the church and particularly to baptism (1 Cor 7:14; Sept.: Isa 52:1; Amos 7:17).

(III) Unclean by unnatural pollution (Eph 5:5).

(IV) Unclean as applied to the devils who are frequently called unclean spirits in the NT because, having lost their original purity, they are become unclean themselves and through their solicitations have polluted mankind with all uncleanness and every abomination which the Lord hates (Mark 5:2, 8, 13. See also Matt 10:1; 12:43; Mark 1:23, 26, 27; 3:11, 30; 6:7; 7:25; 9:25; Luke 4:33, 36; 6:18; 8:29; 9:42; 11:24; Acts 5:16; 8:7; Rev 16:13).

Deriv.: *akatharsía* (167), uncleanness.

Syn.: *bébēlos* (952), profane; *rhuparós* (4508), vile; *ponērós* (4190), evil, but sometimes used as unclean; *koinós* (2839), common, defiled.

Ant.: *katharós* (2513), clean, pure; *hagnós* (53), pure from defilement; *eilikrinḗs* (1506), sincere, pure; *ámemptos* (273), irreproachable; *gnḗsios* (1103), genuine, true.

170. ἀκαιρέομαι *akairéomai*; contracted *akairoúmai*, fut. *akairésomai*, from the priv. *a* (1), without, and *kairós* (2540), opportune time, season. To lack opportunity (only in Phil 4:10).

Ant.: *eukairéō* (2119), to have time or opportunity.

171. ἀκαίρως *akaírōs*; adv. from *ákairos* (n.f.), unseasonable, which is from the priv. *a* (1), without, and *kairós* (2540), season or time involving opportunity, i.e., opportune time. Only in 2 Tim 4:2 meaning inopportunely, unseasonably, in contrast to the opposite *eukaírōs* (2122), conveniently or in season. The two prefixes, the priv. *a* (1), without, and *eu*, good or well, stand in opposition to each other. We are to preach God's Word both when we believe that it is appropriate to do so and when it is inconvenient.

172. ἄκακος *ákakos*; gen. *akákou*, masc.-fem., neut. *ákakon*, adj. from the priv. *a* (1), without, and *kakós* (2556), constitutionally bad. Harmless, void of evil, blameless (Rom 16:18; Heb 7:26).

Syn.: *haploús* (573), single or without duplicity; *ádolos* (97), without guile; *akéraios* (185), without any foreign matter or without admixture; *athóos* (121), unpunished, innocent; *kalós* (2570), good; *agathós* (18), benevolent; *chrēstós* (5543), gentle, mellow.

Ant.: *kakós* (2556), bad; *ponērós* (4190), malevolent; *phaúlos* (5337), bad, evil, worthless.

173. ἄκανθα *ákantha*; gen. *akánthēs*, fem. noun from *akḗ* (n.f.), a point or prick. A thorn or brier which abounds with pricks (Matt 7:16; 13:7, 22; 27:29; Mark 4:7, 18; Luke 6:44; 8:7, 14; John 19:2; Heb 6:8).

Deriv.: *akánthinos* (174), made of thorns.

Syn.: *skólops* (4647), something pointed, a stake, thorn.

174. ἀκάνθινος *akánthinos*; fem. *akanthínē*, neut. *akánthinon*, adj. from *ákantha* (173), thorn. Made of thorns, thorny (Mark 15:17; John 19:5). The suffix *inos* refers to what something is made out of instead of behavior, which is indicated by the suffix *ikós*. See *sárkinos* (4560) (2 Cor 3:3) and *sarkikós* (4559) (Rom 7:14; 15:27; 1 Cor 3:1, 3, 4; 9:11; 2 Cor 1:12; 10:4; Heb 7:16; 1 Pet 2:11).

175. ἄκαρπος *ákarpos*; gen. *akárpou*, masc.-fem., neut. *ákarpon*, adj. from the priv. *a* (1), without, and *karpós* (2590), fruit, produce. Unfruitful, bearing no fruit (Jude 1:12 [cf. Matt 13:22; Mark 4:19; Titus 3:14; 2 Pet 1:8]; Sept.: Jer 2:6). Unprofitable, producing bad fruit (1 Cor 14:14; Eph 5:11).

Syn.: *achreíos* (888), useless, unprofitable.

Ant.: *karpophóros* (2593), fruit-bearing; *eúchrēstos* (2173) and *Onḗsimos* (3682), profitable.

176. ἀκατάγνωστος *akatágnōstos*; gen. *akatagnṓstou*, masc.-fem., neut. *akatágnoston*, adj. from the priv. *a* (1), without, and *kataginṓskō* (2607), condemn. Irreprehensible, not worthy of condemnation, not to be condemned or blamed (Titus 2:8).

177. ἀκατακάλυπτος *akatakáluptos*; gen. *akatakalúptou*, masc.-fem., neut. *akatakálupton*, adj. from the priv. *a* (1), without, and *katakalúptō* (2619), to cover, hide, veil. Uncovered, used only in 1 Cor 11:5, 13 in relation to a woman prophesying and praying. The verb *katakalúptomai* is also used in the same relationship in 1 Cor 11:6, 7. The prophesying and praying are in the environment of the local church. Since the praying and prophesying are an either / or question in 1 Cor 11:5, it must refer to the public prayer or prophesying in the sense of telling forth that which one knows of the Lord publicly and audibly. Paul stresses that what is spoken by a woman, whether in public prayer or in prophecy, must be an outward demonstration of her inward saintliness. A woman who had her hair cut short was styled in the same manner as a prostitute or one of low morals. Such were the priestesses at the temple of Aphrodite at Acrocorinth. If one of these was saved and came into the local congregation of believers, she was not to speak with her short hair, but to cover her head as a substitute for the long hair which would take some time to grow. This is why in 1 Cor 11:15 the long or womanly hair is considered in lieu of a wrapping called *peribólaion* (4018).

Syn.: *anakalúptō* (343), to unveil; *apokalúpto* (601), to uncover.

Ant.: *kekalumménos*, the pres. part. pass., covered, from *kalúptō* (2572), to cover.

178. ἀκατάκριτος *akatákritos*; gen. *akatakrítou*, masc.-fem., neut. *akatákriton*, adj. from the priv. *a* (1), without, and *katakrínō* (2632), to condemn. Uncondemned or not having gone through a legal trial. Used by Paul as he speaks to sergeants who were sent by the magistrates (generals) to the prison at Philippi to set Paul and Silas free (Acts 16:37), and when addressing the chief Roman captain before whom he was brought in Jerusalem (Acts 22:25).

Syn.: *akatágnōstos* (176), not to be condemned; *dókimos* (1384), approved; *áxios* (514), worthy; *ámemptos* (273), irreproachable; *anepíleptos* (423), blameless; *amṓmētos* (298), unblamable; *ámōmos* (299), unblemished; *áspilos* (784), unspotted.

Ant.: *autokatákritos* (843), self-condemned; *adókimos* (96), unapproved.

179. ἀκατάλυτος *akatálutos*; gen. *akatalútou*, masc.-fem., neut. *akatáluton*, adj. from the priv. *a* (1), without, and *katalúō* (2647), to dissolve. Indissoluble, an adj. used of the life of Christ and translated as "endless life" (Heb 7:16). The word, however, has nothing to do with time but with the indissoluble character

of life. The life of Christ is declared as distinct from the life of someone else, life that was not acquired and that cannot be done away with. The lives of animals sacrificed by the priests ceased to exist, but when Jesus Christ sacrificed Himself as the Lamb of God, His life did not cease. This adj. *akatálutos*, referring to the inherent life of Christ, agrees fully with John 1:4 which states that in Him was or had been (*én* [the imperf. of *eimí* {1510}, to be]) life. His life has no derivation and is interminable.

Syn.: *apérantos* (562), interminable, endless; *adiáleiptos* (88), permanent.

Ant.: *próskairos* (4340), temporary and *phthartós* (5349), corruptible.

180. ἀκατάπαυστος *akatápaustos*; gen. *akatapaústou*, masc.-fem., neut. *akatápauston*, adj. from the priv. *a* (1), without, and *katapaúō* (2664), to quiet down. Unable to desist, that which cannot be restrained. Used only in 2 Pet 2:14 and translated "that cannot cease" from sin. A better translation would be "unable to cease" (a.t.) from sin, taking the gen. *hamartías* (266), sin, as abl. gen. or gen. of separation. It describes the eyes of the unrighteous (2 Pet 2:9) seeing every and any woman as an object with whom they could satisfy their lust, their eyes being unable to be separated from sin.

Syn.: *adiáleiptos* (88), unceasing, continual; *ektenḗs* (1618), stretched out, earnest, fervent; *eis télos* (*eis* [1519], unto, and *télos* [5056], end) unto the end, continual; *diá pantós*, throughout or during which something is done, continually (*diá* [1223], throughout, *pantós*, the gen. neut. of *pás* [3956], all); *eis tó diēnekés* (*eis* [1519], unto; *tó*, the; *diēnekés* [1336], something that is carried through to the end), forever; *aiṓnios* (166), unending, eternal; *aḯdios* (126), everlasting, without beginning.

Ant.: *próskairos* (4340), for a season, temporary, temporal.

181. ἀκαταστασία *akatastasía*; gen. *akatastasías*, fem. noun from *akatástatos*

(182), unstable. Commotion, tumult (Luke 21:9; 1 Cor 14:33; 2 Cor 6:5, "uncertainty of residence" [a.t.], i.e., exile [KJV, "tumults"]; 2 Cor 12:20; James 3:16; Sept.: Prov 26:28).

Syn.: *súgchusis* (4799), confusion; *thórubos* (2351), noise, tumult; *tarachḗ* (5016), disturbance.

Ant.: *eirḗnē* (1515), peace, tranquility; *hēsuchía* (2271), quietness; *apokatástasis* (605), restoration; *táxis* (5010), order.

182. ἀκατάστατος *akatástatos*; gen. *akatastátou*, masc.-fem., neut. *akatástaton*, adj. from the priv. *a* (1), not, and *kathístēmi* (2525), to settle. Unsettled, unsteady, unstable (James 1:8).

Deriv.: *akatastasía* (181), instability.

Syn.: *akatáschetos* (183), one that cannot be restrained; *astḗriktos* (793), unstable; *átaktos* (813), insubordinate, unruly.

Ant.: *kósmios* (2887), decent, modest, orderly; *taktós* (5002), arranged, set; *euschḗmōn* (2158), honorable, comely.

183. ἀκατάσχετος *akatáschetos*; gen. *akataschétou*, masc.-fem., neut. *akatáscheton*, adj. from the priv. *a* (1), without, and *katéchō* (2722), to retain. Untameable, not to be restrained. Referring to the tongue as unruly, evil, or an evil that cannot be restrained (James 3:8).

Syn.: *anupótaktos* (506), unruly, disobedient; *átaktos* (813), disorderly.

Ant.: *kósmios* (2887), orderly, decent, modest; *taktós* (5012), arranged, set; *euschḗmōn* (2158), honorable, comely.

184. Ἀκελδαμά *Akeldamá* (TR); *Akeldamách* (UBS), transliterated from the Aramaic *haqal dᵉmā'*, meaning "field of blood." The field purchased with the money for which Judas betrayed Jesus (Acts 1:19), previously known as the Potter's Field. It has been equated with the Potter's House (Jer 18:2) in the Hinnom Valley. The traditional site has long been used for burials.

185. ἀκέραιος *akéraios*; gen. *akeraíou*, masc.-fem., neut. *akéraion*, adj. from the priv. *a* (1), without, and *keránnumi* (2767), to mix. Without any mixture of deceit, without any defiling material (Matt 10:16; Rom 16:19; Phil 2:15).

Syn.: *euschḗmōn* (2158), comely, honorable; *téleios* (185), perfect, one who has reached the goal; *ártios* (739), complete; *holóklēros* (3648), entire, whole; *plḗrēs* (4134), complete full; *tímios* (5093), honest; *éntimos* (1784), reputable, honorable; *euthús* (2117), straight; *chrēstós* (5543), of good and useful morals; *áxios* (514), worthy; *ákakos* (172), without being constitutionally bad; *ádolos* (97), without any guile; *haploús* (573), without wrinkles or duplicity, single or simple.

Ant.: *dólios* (1386), deceitful; *átimos* (820), without honor; *plános* (4108), deceiver, seducer; *phrenapátēs* (5423), a mind-deceiver; *anáxios* (370), unworthy.

186. ἀκλινής *aklinḗs*; gen. *aklinoús*, masc.-fem., neut. *aklinés*, adj. from the priv. *a* (1), without, and *klínō* (2827), to incline. Steady, without inclining or giving way, used to describe the testimony of our hope (Heb 10:23). The KJV gives this steadiness to "our faith" while the TR and UBS have the word *elpís* (1680), hope, which fits much better exegetically. Having spoken of the assurance of faith (Heb 10:22), the Apostle wants the believers to have a testimony of unwavering hope because their faith is certain.

Syn.: *bébaios* (949), secure, steadfast, firm; *hedraíos* (1476), morally stable; *stereós* (4731), firm, steadfast; *pistós* (4103), faithful, sure, dependable; *ametamélētos* (278), irrevocable.

Ant.: *ápistos* (571), untrustworthy.

187. ἀκμάζω *akmázō*; fut. *akmásō*, from *akmḗ* (n.f.), the point of a weapon. To flourish, ripen, be in one's prime. Intrans. in Rev 14:18.

Syn.: *prokóptō* (4298), to advance; *auxánō* (837), to increase; *anathállō* (330), to revive, flourish again; *pro-*

ágomai (4254), to go before, advance; *probibázomai* (4264), to move forward, force forward; *anaptússomai* (380), to unroll and move forward.

Ant.: *xēraínomai* (3583), to dry up, wither; *maraínomai* (3133), to fade away; *katapíptō* (2667), to fall down.

188. ἀκμήν *akmḗn*; adv., acc. of *akmḗ* (n.f.), point or edge of a sharp instrument or a point of time. The most fitting time. In the NT, the acc. *akmḗn* in Matt 15:16 is used adv. for the expression *kat' akmḗn* (*katá* [2596], according to), meaning at this point of time, yet, still, even now.

Syn.: *nún* (3568), now.

Ant.: *metépeita* (3347), afterward.

189. ἀκοή *akoḗ*; gen. *akoḗs*, fem. noun from *akoúō* (191), to hear. Hearing, the faculty of hearing (Rom 10:16, 17 [cf. Matt 13:14; Acts 28:26; Gal 3:2, 5]; Sept.: Ex 15:26; 19:5); the sense of hearing (1 Cor 12:17; Heb 5:11); the organ or instrument of hearing, the ear (Mark 7:35; Acts 17:20; 2 Tim 4:3, 4); something which is or may be heard, a rumor, report (Matt 4:24; 14:1; 24:6; Mark 1:28; 13:7; Luke 7:1; John 12:38; Rom 10:16; Gal 3:2, 5, doctrine taught and received with faith; 1 Thess 2:13; 2 Tim 4:3; Heb 4:2; 2 Pet 2:8; Sept.: Isa 53:1; 2 Sam 13:30).

Syn.: *oús* (3775), ear; *ōtíon* (5621), a diminutive of *oús*, ear; *phḗmē* (5346), fame, report; *lógos* (3056), a word, report, account; *échos* (2279), noise, sound, rumor, echo; *aggelía* (31), a message, proclamation, news; *presbeía* (4242), embassy, a message, messengers; *kḗrugma* (2782), proclamation, preaching; *marturía* (3141), witness, report; *diágnōsis* (1233), diagnosis, hearing for the purpose of discerning; *akroatḗrion* (201), a place of hearing.

Ant.: *parakoḗ* (3876), not hearing, disobedience; *hēsuchía* (2271), silence.

190. ἀκολουθέω *akolouthéō*; contracted *akolouthṓ*, fut. *akolouthḗsō*, from *akólouthos* (n.f.), attendant, follower, which is from the coll. *a* (1), together, and *kéleuthos* (n.f.), a way. To attend, to accompany, to go with or follow a teacher (Matt 4:20, 22, 25; 9:9; 19:27, 28; 27:55; Mark 1:18; 9:38; John 1:41; 12:26; Sept.: 1 Kgs 19:20, 21; Isa 45:14). Generally (Matt 8:1; 9:19, 27; Mark 5:24; 10:32; Luke 22:54; John 11:31; 1 Cor 10:4; Sept.: Ruth 1:14; 1 Sam 25:42). The individual calling to follow Jesus involved abiding fellowship with Him, not only for the sake of learning as a scholar from his teacher (Matt 8:19), but also for the sake of the salvation known or looked for which presented itself in such fellowship (Matt 19:21; Luke 9:61). The first thing involved in following Jesus is a cleaving to Him in believing trust and obedience. Those cleaving to Him must also follow His leading and act according to His example (John 8:12; 10:4, 5, 27). Hence constant stress is laid by the Lord Jesus upon the need of self-denial and fellowship of the cross (Matt 8:19, 20, 22; 10:38; Mark 8:34; John 8:12; 12:26). Following Jesus thus denotes a fellowship of faith as well as a fellowship of life, sharing in His sufferings not only inwardly, but outwardly if necessary (Matt 9:9, 19, 27). Such outward fellowship with Jesus, however, could not continue without inner moral and spiritual fellowship, without a life resembling His and a self-denying sharing of His cross. The expression "follow the Lamb (Jesus)" occurs only in Rev 14:4. In John 8:12; 10:4, 5, 27; 12:26, following Jesus appears as an independent concept apart from any outward act or momentary circumstances of time and place which union with Him might involve. See also Matt 8:10, 22, 23; 12:15; 14:13; 19:2; 20:29, 34; 21:9; 26:58; Mark 2:14, 15; 3:7; 6:1; 10:21, 28, 52; 11:9; 14:13, 51, 54; 15:41; Luke 5:11, 27, 28; 7:9; 9:11, 49, 59; 18:22, 28, 43; 22:10, 39; 23:27; John 1:37, 38, 40, 43; 6:2; 13:36, 37; 18:15; 20:6; 21:19, 20, 22; Acts 12:8, 9; 13:43; 21:36; Rev 6:8; 14:13; 19:14. With reference to time, *akolouthéō* means to follow thereupon (Rev 14:8, 9, to follow in succession, succeed; 14:13, their good deeds accompany them to the judgment seat of God). Figuratively it refers to spiritual or moral relationships (Matt 10:38; 16:24; Mark 8:34; Luke 9:23; John 8:12; 12:26).

Deriv.: *exakolouthéō* (1811), to follow up, to continue to the end; *epakolouthéō* (1872), to follow after, close upon; *katakolouthéō* (2628), to follow behind or intently after; *parakolouthéō* (3877), to follow close up or side by side, hence to accompany, conform to, follow intending to practice; *sunakolouthéō* (4870), to follow along with, to accompany a leader.

Syn.: *hupakoúō* (5219), to obey; *diṓkō* (1377), to pursue without hostility, to follow; *miméomai* (3401), to imitate; *epioúsios* (1967), the following.

Ant.: *hēgéomai* (2233), to lead; *proágō* (4254), to go before; *hysteréō* (5302), to come late, to fall short, linger behind; *aphístēmi* (868), to stand off; *kataleípō* (2641), to leave, leave behind; *egkataleípō* (1459), to forsake, abandon; *aphíēmi* (863), to forsake, the same word as to forgive, for to forgive means to remove the sins from somebody; *apotássō* (657), to place in the proper category away from someone.

191. ἀκούω *akoúō*; fut. *akoúsō*, aor. pass. *ēkoústhēn*, perf. *akékoa*, perf. pass. *ékousmai*. To hear. It governs a gen. either of the person or thing, to hear someone or something, or more usually an acc. of the thing.

(I) To hear in general (Matt 2:3, 9, 18; 9:12; 10:27; 11:5; 12:19; Mark 7:25; 10:41; 14:64; Luke 7:3, 9; John 3:8; Sept.: Gen 3:8, 10).

(II) To hear with attention, hearken or listen to (Mark 4:3; 7:14; 12:29, 37; Luke 5:1; 10:39; 11:31; Acts 2:22; 15:7); in respect to a teacher (Mark 6:20; Luke 15:1; 19:48); *hoi akoúontes* (pres. part. pl. as part. noun), these hearing, i.e., disciples to understand, hear with the ear of the mind (Matt 11:15; John 8:43, 47; 1 Cor 14:2);

(III) Intrans., to have the faculty of hearing, spoken of the deaf (Matt 11:5;

Mark 7:37; Rom 11:8, "ears unable to hear" [a.t.]; Matt 13:14, "hearing ye shall hear"; Acts 28:26; Sept.: Ex 15:26; 19:5; Matt 13:15, to be "dull of hearing"). Used trans. and either absolutely or constructed with the acc. or gen. of the thing heard and usually with gen. of the person from whom one hears. Instead of the gen. of thing we find *perí* (4012), about, followed by the gen. (Mark 5:27; Acts 9:13); instead of the gen. of person, we have *apó* (575), from, followed by the gen. (Acts 9:13; 1 John 1:5); *pará* (3844), from, followed by the gen. (John 8:26); *ek* (1537), from, out of, followed by the gen. (2 Cor 12:6). To hear, perceive with the ears. To hear effectually or so as to perform or grant what is spoken, to obey (Matt 10:14; 17:5; 18:15, 16; Mark 6:11; John 9:31; 11:41; Acts 3:22, 23; 4:4, 19; 1 John 4:5, 6; 5:14, 15).

(IV) To obey (Luke 10:16; 16:29, 31 [cf. John 5:24; 8:47; 18:37; Acts 3:22, 23; 4:19; 1 John 4:5, 6]; Sept.: Gen 3:17; Ex 16:20; Deut 11:27; 2 Chr 20:14; Isa 48:18). Here belongs the phrase "he who hath ears, let him hear," i.e., give heed, obey (Matt 11:15; 13:9, 13 [cf. the phrase, "he who has a mind" in Rev 13:18 {a.t.}; see also 2:7, 11, 17, 29; 3:6, 13, 22; 13:9; 17:9, "he who has wisdom" {a.t.}]). In the writings of John as spoken of God, meaning to heed, regard, i.e., to hear and answer prayer (John 9:31; 11:41, 42; 1 John 5:15; Sept.: Ps 10:17, *eisakoúō* [1522], to listen to).

(V) To hear, i.e., to learn by hearing, be informed, know. Generally (Matt 2:3, 22; 4:12; 5:21, 27; 11:2; Mark 5:27; 6:14; Acts 14:14; 15:24). Followed by *hóti* (3754), that (Matt 20:30; Mark 2:1; 10:47; John 14:28; Sept.: Gen 41:15; 42:2). Spoken of instruction, doctrines (John 8:40; 15:15; Acts 1:4; 4:20; Rom 10:14, 18; Heb 2:1; 1 John 2:7, 24). Pass. meaning, to be heard of, to be reported (Matt 28:14; Mark 2:1; Luke 12:3; Acts 11:22; 1 Cor 5:1; Sept.: 2 Chr 26:15).

(VI) To hear in a forensic sense as a judge or magistrate, to try, examine judicially (Acts 25:22; John 7:51).

(VII) To understand, comprehend
(Mark 4:33; John 6:60; 1 Cor 14:2; Gal
4:21; Sept.: Gen 11:7; 42:23). See also
Matt 5:33, 38, 43; 7:24, 26; 8:10; 11:4;
12:24, 42; 13:20, 22, 23, 43; 14:1, 13;
15:10, 12; 17:6; 19:22, 25; 20:24; 21:16,
33, 45; 22:7, 22, 33, 34; 24:6; 26:65;
27:13, 47; Mark 2:17; 3:8, 21; 4:9, 12,
15, 16, 18, 20, 23, 24; 5:36; 6:2; 6:29, 55;
7:16; 8:18; 9:7; 11:14, 18; 12:28; 13:7;
14:11, 58; 15:35; 16:11; Luke 1:41, 58,
66; 2:18, 20, 46, 47; 4:23, 28; 5:15; 6:17,
47, 49; 7:22, 29; 8:8, 10, 12–15, 18, 21,
50; 9:7, 9, 35; 10:24; 11:28; 14:15, 35;
15:25; 16:2, 14; 18:6, 22, 23, 26, 36;
19:11; 20:16; 21:9, 38; 22:71; 23:6, 8;
John 1:37, 40; 3:29, 32; 4:1, 42, 47; 5:25,
28, 30, 37; 6:45; 7:32, 40; 8:9; 9:27, 32,
35, 40; 10:3, 8, 16, 20, 27; 11:4, 6, 20,
29; 12:12, 18, 34; 14:24; 16:13; 18:21;
19:8, 13; 21:7; Acts 2:6, 8, 11, 33, 37;
4:4, 24; 5:5, 11, 21, 24, 33; 6:11, 14; 7:2,
12, 34, 37, 54; 8:6, 14, 30; 9:4, 7, 13, 21,
38; 10:22, 33, 44, 46; 11:1, 7, 18; 13:7,
16, 44, 48; 14:9; 15:7, 13; 16:14, 38;
17:8, 21, 32; 18:8, 26; 19:2, 5, 10, 26, 28;
21:12, 20, 22; 22:1, 2, 7, 9, 14, 15, 22, 26;
23:16; 24:4, 22, 24; 26:3, 14, 29; 28:15,
22, 26–28; Rom 15:21; 1 Cor 2:9; 11:18;
2 Cor 12:4; Gal 1:13, 23; Eph 1:13, 15;
3:2; 4:21, 29; Phil 1:27, 30; 2:26; 4:9; Col
1:4, 6, 9, 23; 2 Thess 3:11; 1 Tim 4:16; 2
Tim 1:13; 2:2, 14; 4:17; Phile 1:5; Heb
2:3; 3:7, 15, 16; 4:2, 7; 12:19; James
1:19; 2:5; 5:11; 2 Pet 1:18; 1 John 1:1, 3,
5; 2:18; 3:11; 4:3; 2 John 1:6; 3 John 1:4;
Rev 1:3, 10; 3:3, 20; 4:1; 5:11, 13; 6:1,
3, 5–7; 7:4; 8:13; 9:13, 16, 20; 10:4, 8;
11:12; 12:10; 14:2, 13; 16:1, 5, 7; 18:4,
22, 23; 19:1, 6; 21:3; 22:8, 17, 18.
Deriv.: *akoé* (189), hearing; *diakoúō*
(1251), to hear through, hear fully; *eisakoúō* (1522), to listen to, to hear and obey;
epakoúō (1873), to listen to, hear with favor on an occasion; *parakoúō* (3878), to
overhear or hear amiss; *proakoúō* (4257),
to hear before; *hupakoúō* (5219), to obey.
Syn.: *epakroáomai* (1874), to listen attentively to; *enōtízomai* (1801), to
give ear to, to listen; *peitharchéō* (3980),

to obey one in authority, be obedient;
peíthomai (3982), to be persuaded.
Ant.: *homiléō* (3656), to talk; *parakoúō*
(3898), disobey; *apeithéō* (544), to disobey.

192. ἀκρασία *akrasía*; gen. *akrasías*,
fem. noun from *akratḗs* (193), incontinent. Lack of strength, want of power to
regulate one's appetites, intemperance,
incontinence (Matt 23:25; 1 Cor 7:5, the
latter referring to sexual incontinence).
Syn.: *hēdonḗ* (2237), lust, pleasure;
kraipálē (2897), debauchery, drunkenness; *anáchusis* (401), a pouring out,
overflowing; *asōtía* (810), prodigality, profligacy; *asélgeia* (766), lasciviousness, an immoral life; *oinophlugía*
(3632), drunkenness, debauchery, excess
of wine.
Ant.: *egkráteia* (1466), continence,
temperance, self-restraint.

193. ἀκρατής *akratḗs*; gen. *akratoús*,
masc.-fem., neut. *akratés*, adj. from the
priv. *a* (1), without, and *krátos* (2904),
strength. Unable to govern one's appetites, incontinent (2 Tim 3:3).
Deriv.: *akrasía* (192), incontinence.
Syn.: *ékdotos* (1560), given over.
Ant.: *egkratḗs* (1468), continent, to
have self-control; *nēphálios* (3524), sober, temperate; *sṓphrōn* (4998), sober,
one who voluntarily places limitations on
his own freedom; *egkrateúomai* (1467),
to show continency, be temperate.

194. ἄκρατος *ákratos*; gen. *akrátou*,
from *a* (1), without, and *keránnumi*
(2767), to mix. Pure wine unmixed with
water; used in a figurative sense in Rev
14:10.
Syn.: *hagnós* (53), pure from defilement, not contaminated; *katharós* (2513),
cleansed; *eilikrinḗs* (1506), unalloyed,
sincere.
Ant.: *mígma* (3395), a mixture.

195. ἀκρίβεια *akríbeia*; gen. *akribeías*,
fem. noun from *akribḗs* (n.f.), accurate.
Accuracy, exactness (Acts 22:3). In the

neut. *akribésteron* means more accurately, exactly (Acts 18:26; 23:15, 20; 24:22).

Deriv. of *akribḗs* (n.f.): *akribóō* (198), to inquire exactly; *akribṓs* (199), exactly, accurately.

Syn.: *alḗtheia* (225), truth.

Ant.: *pseúdos* (5579), falsehood; *apátē* (539), deceit; *plánē* (4106), delusion, error.

196. ἀκριβέστατος *akribéstatos*; the superlative of *akribḗs* (n.f.), accurate. Only in Acts 26:5 referring to the most accurate or exact sect of the Pharisees, i.e., strictly adhering to its rules and regulations.

197. ἀκριβέστερον *akribésteron*; the acc. comparative of *akribḗs* (n.f.), accurate. More accurate or exact. In the acc. and neut. used as an adv. meaning more accurately or exactly (Acts 18:26; 23:15, 20; 24:22).

198. ἀκριβόω *akribóō*; contracted *akribṓ*, fut. *akribṓsō*, from *akribḗs* (n.f., see *akríbeia* [195]), accurate. To know or do something accurately, to inquire accurately, diligently (Matt 2:7, 16). In Matt 2:8, *exetásate*, aor. imper. of *exetázō* (1833), to inquire, *akribṓs* (199), accurately, inquire exactly or accurately.

Syn.: *orthopodéo* (3716), to walk uprightly.

Ant.: *ptaíō* (4417), to err.

199. ἀκριβῶς *akribṓs*; adv. from *akribḗs* (n.f., see *akríbeia* [195]), accurate. Diligently, accurately, exactly (Matt 2:8; Luke 1:3; Acts 18:25; Eph 5:15, "circumspectly"; 1 Thess 5:2).

Syn.: *spoudaíōs* (4709), diligently; *epimelṓs* (1960), carefully, diligently; *orthṓs* (3723), rightly.

Ant.: *kakṓs* (2560), badly; *adíkōs* (95), unjustly.

200. ἀκρίς *akrís*; gen. *akrídos*, fem. noun. Locust. Practiced in many nations of Asia and Africa, the eating of locusts of various species was permitted by the Mosaic Law (Lev 11:21, 22) and thus was common in Judea also (See Matt 3:4; Mark 1:6; Rev 9:3, 7). The rabbis believed that there were 800 varieties of locusts. They are migratory, but their migrations do not take place at fixed seasons of the year nor at definite intervals. Their swarms are driven along by the wind, as they have little power to guide their own flight, usually invading Palestine from the Arabian Desert on the south or southeast. They devour all vegetation on which they alight. Nine different Hebr. words are used in the OT where the locust is intended. The most common, *'arbeh* (697, OT) the general term, occurs fourteen times. It is usually connected with the root *rābah* (7231, OT), to multiply. It is used of the Egyptian plague (Ex 10:4–6) and is listed as one of four insects in Lev 11:22. The other three are also members of the locust family. Two occur only in this verse: *sāl'ām* (5556, OT), "bald-locust," from a rabbinical statement that its head was bald in front, and *hārgōl* (2728, OT), incorrectly translated "beetle". The fourth word, *hāgāb* (2284, OT), grasshopper, occurs five times. Its root meaning is to hide, and the illusion is perhaps to its concealing the sun with its swarms. Three other words are used in a list in Joel 1:4. They are either different kinds of locusts or locusts in different stages of development (*gāzām* [1501, OT] from a root meaning to cut off; *yeleq* [3218, OT], perhaps from a root meaning to lick; *hāsīl* [2625, OT] from a root meaning to consume, ravage). Other words used are *tsᵉlātsal* (6767, OT) (Deut 28:42), from a root meaning to whir, and *gōb* (1462, OT), from a root meaning to dig (Nah 3:17), literally meaning a swarm. A plague of locusts is sometimes interpreted as a visitation of God's wrath.

201. ἀκροατήριον *akroatḗrion*; gen. *akroatēríou*, neut. noun from *akroáomai* (n.f.), to hear. A place of hearing, audience or an audience chamber (Acts 25:23).

202. ἀκροατής akroatḗs; gen. *akroatoú*, masc. noun from *akroáomai* (n.f.), to hear. A hearer (Rom 2:13; James 1:22, 23, 25). In Class. Gr., the alternate *akroázomai*, to hear and the deriv. *akróama* meant something heard, especially with pleasure, such as a piece read, recited, played, or sung. In the NT, it has the meaning of one just listening without practicing what one hears.

203. ἀκροβυστία akrobustía; gen. *akrobustías*, fem. noun from *ákron* (206), the extreme, and *búō* (n.f.), to cover. The foreskin (Acts 11:3); uncircumcision (Sept.: Gen 17:11, 14; Lev 12:3). In the NT, and especially the Pauline writings, the word is never applied to moral and spiritual things. Col 2:13; 3:11 only seem to hint of such a figurative application. To label someone as uncircumcised means to designate somebody as not being a Jew and, therefore, outside of the promises (Rom 2:25, 26; 1 Cor 7:18, 19; Gal 5:6; 6:15; Col 2:13). That this refers to the external rite and to the state of a Gentile is shown by the addition of *sárx* (4561), flesh, in Eph 2:11, and not to the circumcision of the heart (Deut 10:16). By metonymy, uncircumcised means the Gentile pagans, as opposed to circumcision (*peritomḗ* [4061]) which refers to the Jews (Rom 2:26, 27; 3:30; 4:9–12; Gal 2:7; Eph 2:11; Col 3:11). The Jews in scorn called all other nations "uncircumcised" (Judg 14:3; 15:18; Isa 52:1).

Syn.: *aperítmētos* (564), uncircumcised; verb: *epispáomai* (1986), to draw over, to become uncircumcised, as if to efface Judaism.

Ant.: *peritomḗ* (4061), circumcision.

204. ἀκρογωνιαῖος akrogōniaíos; fem. *akrogōniaía*, neut. *akrogōniaíon*, from *ákron* (206), extreme, and *gōnía* (1137), corner. The foundation cornerstone, applied figuratively to Christ who not only sustains the whole structure of the Church, but also unites Jews and Gentiles into one mystical building (Eph 2:20; 1 Pet 2:6 [cf. Job 38:6; Ps 118:22; Isa 28:16]).

Syn.: *themélios* (2310), foundational.

Ant.: *potapós* (4217), unimportant.

205. ἀκροθίνιον akrothínion; gen. *akrothiníou*, neut. noun from *ákron* (206), the extreme, and *thís* (n.f.), a heap. The top of the heap, the best of choice parts, the firstfruits of the field, of booty. In this sense the word is used by Homer, and from this use comes the application denoting a heap of something, particularly of corn. In Class. Gr., it meant the top of a heap of corn, hence the firstfruits of corn because these were usually taken from the top of the heap. In Heb 7:4, it means the best of warfare spoils. Abraham gave Melchizedek tithes not only of the chief spoils (Heb 7:2; Gen 14:20), but that which he gave as a tenth of all was of the chief and best of the spoils. The writer does not say a tenth of the chief spoils but a tenth of all taken from the chief spoils. The Greek writers Herodotus, Thucydides and Xenophon call that part of the spoil which was dedicated to Greek gods *akrothínia*, the pl. of *akrothínion*.

206. ἄκρον ákron; fem. *ákra*, neut. *ákron*, adj., the acc. of *ákros*, from *akḗ* (n.f.), a sharp point. The top or tip (Luke 16:24; Heb 11:21), used substantively with the neut. art. *tó ákron*. Extreme, extremity, end (Matt 24:31; Mark 13:27; Luke 16:24; Heb 11:21 [cf. Ex 29:20; Deut 4:32; Isa 13:5]).

Deriv.: *akrobustía* (203), uncircumcision; *akrogōniaíos* (204), cornerstone, foundation; *akrothínion* (205), top of the heap, firstfruits.

207. Ἀκύλας Akúlas; gen. *Akúla*, masc. proper noun. Aquila. Aquila and his wife, *Príska* (4251), Priscilla, are mentioned in Acts 18:2, 18, 26; Rom 16:3; 1 Cor 16:19; 2 Tim 4:19. In Paul's eyes, they were people of importance. The careful description of Aquila as a Jew, a man of Pontus by race (Acts 18:2), implies that Priscilla, his wife, was not a Jewess. Perhaps Priscilla was a converted Roman, there being evidence that she came from a distinguished Roman family. The historian Harnack describes the couple, mentioning Priscilla first as "Prisca, the missionary, with her husband Aquila." Perhaps influenced in Rome by Christian teaching, they came from Italy to Corinth (Acts 18:2). They were apparently people of means, and they maintained a house-church at Ephesus and at Rome. When Paul went to Ephesus, Aquila and Priscilla went with him and remained there to do pioneer work while he visited Jerusalem. Thus much of the initial work in Ephesus was done by Aquila and Priscilla. During this time, Apollos came to Ephesus and was instructed by them in the Scriptures (Acts 18:26). Aquila and Priscilla seem to have fulfilled their mission with skill and courage; and when a church was gathered, the members met in their house (1 Cor 16:19). A little later we met them in Rome, where, most probably, they were sent by Paul to prepare the way for his going there. They were very special to Paul as indicated by Rom 16:3, 4. They later returned to Ephesus (2 Tim 4:19).

208. ἀκυρόω akuróō; contracted *akurṓ*, fut. *akurṓsō*, from the priv. *a* (1), without, and *kuróō* (2964), to confirm. To cancel. In Matt 15:6, the Lord tells the Pharisees that they revoked (*ēkurṓsate*, aor. 2d person pl. of *akuróō*) the Word of God, or "You made God's law of no effect for the sake of your tradition" (a.t.). He did not mean that it ceases to be the law of God, but that it had no value, worth, or lordship over them. All these are indicated by the word *kúros* (from which *kúrios* [2692], lord, is derived), authority. Used similarly in Mark 7:13. In Gal 3:17, we have two words from the same root, *kuróō*, to confirm. The first referring to covenant

or testament is *prokekurōménēn*, from *prokuróomai* (4300), to confirm before (or having received authority before), and the verb *akuróō*, translated "annul." It would have been better to translate the first "having been confirmed in advance [perf. tense]" and the second "unconfirmed," i.e., a testament that has been confirmed in advance by God. This means that the law that has come 430 years later does not annul so as to make the promise of no effect.

Syn.: *athetéō* (114), to annul, nullify, thwart; *katargéō* (2673), to reduce to inactivity; *kenóō* (2758), to make empty, of no effect; *katalúō* (2647), dissolve; *dialúō* (1262), to dissolve completely; *metakaléō* (333), to recall elsewhere.

Ant.: *poiéō* (4160), to do, execute; *kuróō* (2964), to confirm; *kathístēmi* (2525), to constitute.

209. ἀκωλύτως akōlútōs; an adv. from the priv. *a* (1), without, and *kōlúō* (2967), to hinder. Without hindrance, not hindered. In Acts 28:31, it refers to Paul's preaching in Rome under house arrest and yet preaching without hindrance, prohibition, or impediment.

Ant.: *duskólōs* (1423), with difficulty; *anagkastós* (317), by constraint.

210. ἄκων ákōn; a contracted form of *aékōn*, from the priv. *a* (1), without, and *hekṓn* (1635), willing. Unwillingly, against one's will, forced. Occurs only in 1 Cor 9:17.

Syn.: *akousíōs*, unwillingly, often used in the Sept., but not in the NT; *anagkastós* (317), by compulsion.

211. ἀλάβαστρον alábastron; gen. *alabástrou*, neut. noun of *alábastros*. Alabaster, a vessel to hold ointment or perfume, so-called because it was made of alabaster stone, a valuable marble found in Thebes in Egypt, in Damascus in Syria, as well as in Italy and Cappadocia (Matt 26:7; Mark 14:3; Luke 7:37).

212. ἀλαζονεία *alazoneía*; gen. *alazoneías*, fem. noun from the adj. *alazón* (213), a boaster. Ostentation, boasting about what one is not or does not possess. Someone going about with empty and boastful professions of cures and other feats. An *alazón* shows off that which he thinks or pretends he possesses. An ostentatious quack. A boast or boasting (James 4:16). As joined with *bíos* (979), life, it means the period of extension or duration of life as contrasted to *zōḗ* (2222) which means the breath of life. Therefore, *alazoneía toú bíou* in 1 John 2:16 means showing off to fellow mortals; the pride, pomp, or manner of life; the ambitious or vainglorious pursuit of the honors, glories, and splendors of this life; the luxury of life for the purpose of showing off, whether in dress, house, furniture, servants, food.

Syn.: *kenodoxía* (2754), the act of pretending to be what one is not; *kaúchēsis* (2746), the act of boasting in a good or bad sense; *kaúchēma* (2745), the boast itself in a good or bad sense; *huperēphanía* (5243), pride, the desire to show off what one may be or have in comparison with others, thus appearing above them.

Ant.: *tapeinophrosúnē* (5012), lowliness of mind; *tapeínōsis* (5014), humiliation; *euschēmosúnē* (2157), decorousness, comeliness, showing one's proper shape.

213. ἀλαζών *alazón*; gen. *alazónos*, masc. noun from *álē* (n.f.), a wandering about. A boaster. (Rom 1:30; 2 Tim 3:2; Sept.: Hab 2:5).

Deriv.: *alazoneía* (212), vaunting in those things one does not possess.

Syn.: *huperḗphanos* (5244), proud, one who shows himself above his fellows; *hubristḗs* (5197), insolent wrongdoer to others for the pleasure which the affliction imparts.

Ant.: *tapeinós* (5011), humble, one who places himself on the ground floor; *eleeinós* (1652), miserable.

214. ἀλαλάζω *alalázō*; fut. *alaláxō*, from *alalḗ* (n.f.), the military shout of the Greeks before a battle. To shout, to utter a loud sound. It was originally an invocation of the Greeks to their gods to assist them. Even today the Muslims when entering upon action still cry out, "Allah! Allah!" which is the Arabic name for God. It was also the acclamation of the chorus in the hymns of Apollo, *alalaí*, from which we have the Eng. exclamation of grief, "alas!" To raise the cry of battle (Sept.: Josh 6:20; Judg 15:14). To utter a loud cry, e.g., of rejoicing, to shout (Sept.: Ps 46:2; 65:1). In the NT, to utter a loud but mournful sound, to wail, lament aloud. Used intrans. in Mark 5:38; Sept.: Jer 4:8; 29:2; 30:3; 32:20; 47:2. To make a disagreeable, inarticulate noise, spoken of a cymbal, to tinkle, clang (1 Cor 13:1).

Syn.: *kóptō* (2875), to beat the breast in grief, wail; *penthéō* (3996), to mourn; *thrēnéō* (2354), lament; *klaíō* (2799), to weep; *ololúzō* (3649), to howl; *ōdínō* (5605), to travail in birth; *dakrúō* (1145), to shed tears.

215. ἀλάλητος *alálētos*; gen. *alalḗtou*, masc.-fem., neut. *alálēton*, adj. from the priv. *a* (1), without, and *laléō* (2980), to speak, utter, make noise. Unutterable, not to be expressed in words. In Rom 8:26, describing groanings which are not capable being adequately expressed in words.

Syn.: *áphōnos* (880), voiceless, soundless, having reference to the voice, whereas *álalos* (216) has reference to words.

216. ἄλαλος *álalos*; gen. *alálou*, masc.-fem., neut. *álalon*, adj. from the priv. *a* (1), without, and *laléō* (2980), to speak, utter sounds. Not speaking, unable to speak, dumb, incapable of making any noise with the mouth (Mark 7:37). In Mark 9:17, 25, "dumb spirit" is a malignant spirit, dumb or silent through obstinacy or imposed by a higher power which is contrary to one's usual character (see Mark 1:24, 34; 5:7), hence Christ says this type of demon is difficult to be cast out (Mark 9:29).

Syn.: *alálētos* (215), having no possibility of being expressed audibly while *álalos* refers to words even if they are meaningless or speechless; *áphōnos* (880), voiceless, dumb.

217. ἅλας *hálas*; gen. *hálatos*, neut. noun, equivalent to *háls* (251). Salt.

(I) Natural salt which purifies, cleanses, and preserves from corruption (Luke 14:34; Sept.: Lev 2:13; Judg 9:45). In Matt 5:13 and Mark 9:50 applied spiritually to the disciples of Christ who were to circulate among and purify the corrupted mass of mankind by their heavenly doctrines and holy examples.

(II) Metaphorically used of wisdom and prudence (Matt 5:13; Mark 9:50 [cf. Acts 15:9; Col 4:6; 1 Pet 1:4; 1 John 3:3]).

218. ἀλείφω *aleíphō*; fut. *aleípsō*. To rub, to cover over, besmear (Matt 6:17; Mark 6:13; 16:1; Luke 7:38, 46; John 11:2; 12:3; James 5:14; Sept.: Gen 31:13; Ezek 13:10–12). Contrast *chríō* (5548), anoint as pertaining to the sacred and religious. *Aleíphō* is used indiscriminately of either oil or ointment (*aleiphḗ* in Mod. Gr.) in all actual anointings. The Jew was accustomed not only to rubbing his head with oil or ointment at feasts in token of joy, but also both the head and the feet of those whom he wished to distinguish by special honor. In the case of sick persons and also of the dead, they rubbed the whole body (see Gen 50:2; Ps 23:5; 45:7; 104:15; Eccl 9:8; Luke 7:37, 38; John 19:40). This was also done by the Greeks and Romans. Sometimes this rubbing was used for physical relaxation after washing (Sept.: Ruth 3:3; 2 Sam 12:20; Dan 10:3; Mic 6:15). In the NT, the product used was either oil or ointment (Luke 7:38, 46). It is also used of rubbing a pillar (Sept.: Gen 31:13), or captives (Sept.: 2 Chr 28:15), or daubing a wall with mortar (Sept.: Ezek 13:10–12, 14, 15), and in the sacred sense of

anointing priests (Sept.: Ex 40:13; Num 3:3). In James 5:14, the word is used in the aor. part. *aleípsantes* which means that the rubbing with oil was the medicinal means applied prior to prayer.

Deriv.: *exaleíphō* (1813), to blot out, wipe away.

Syn.: *chríō* (5548), more limited in its use of sacred and symbolical anointings; *murízō* (3642), to anoint the body for burial.

219. ἀλεκτοροφωνία *alektorophōnía*; gen. *alektorophōnías*, fem. noun from *aléktōr* (220), a rooster, and *phōnḗ* (5456), voice. The crowing of a rooster or cock (Mark 13:35).

220. ἀλέκτωρ *aléktōr*; gen. *aléktoros*, masc. noun. A rooster (Matt 26:34, 74, 75; Mark 14:30, 68, 72; Luke 22:34, 60, 61; John 13:38; 18:27).

Deriv.: *alektorophōnía* (219), the crowing of a rooster.

221. Ἀλεξανδρεύς *Alexandreús*; gen. *Alexandréōs*, masc. adj. An Alexandrian, one born or living in Alexandria (Acts 6:9; 18:24). Alexandria was frequented by the Jews. During the apostolic period, Egypt had a large Jewish population of about one million.

Syn.: *Alexandrinós* (222), one who belongs to Alexandria, but not necessarily born or living there.

222. Ἀλεξανδρῖνος *Alexandrínos*; gen. *Alexandrinoú*, masc. adj. Belonging to Alexandria but not necessarily born or living there, as denoted by *Alexandreús* (221). Spoken of a ship in Acts 27:6; 28:11.

223. Ἀλέξανδρος *Aléxandros*; gen. *Alexándrou*, masc. proper noun. Alexander, helper of men. Found in the NT in five different connections, possibly designating different individuals:

(I) The son of Simon of Cyrene who bore the cross to Calvary (Mark 15:21) and the brother of Rufus. He and his brother were well-known and honored men in the church of Rome (Rom 16:13) to which the Gospel of Mark was addressed. Mark identifies the father by a reference to the sons.

(II) A leader of the priestly party in Jerusalem subsequent to the death of Christ. After the healing of the impotent man, Alexander was present at a meeting of the Jewish authorities along with Annas, Caiaphas, and John, and "as many as were of the kindred of the high priest" (Acts 4:6).

(III) A leading member of the Jewish community at Ephesus (Acts 19:33) who was put forward by the Jews at the time of the Ephesian riot to clear themselves of any complicity with Paul or his teaching, but whom the mob refused to hear.

(IV) A Christian convert and teacher who, along with Hymenaeus and others, ended in spiritual wreckage and was delivered to Satan by the Apostle Paul and condemned to physical suffering (1 Tim 1:19, 20).

(V) Alexander the coppersmith who did much evil to Paul and whom the latter desired that he be rewarded according to his works (2 Tim 4:14, 15). This Alexander has been identified with either of the men mentioned under III and IV above. We are able to gather certain facts regarding him which would seem to connect him under III: his trade was that of a coppersmith, a worker in metal, originally brass, but subsequently any other metal which might associate him with the craftsmen of Ephesus. The statement regarding him was addressed to Timothy who was settled in Ephesus. On the other hand, we are told that Alexander greatly withstood Paul's words, which seems to indicate a bitter personal hostility as well as controversial disputes on matters of doctrine which might rather connect him under IV, the associate of Hymenaeus. It is possible that the men listed under III, IV, and V may be the same person, but Alexander was a very common name, and data is insufficient to allow any certain identification.

224. ἄλευρον áleuron; gen. *aleúrou*, neut. noun from *aléō* (n.f.), to grind. Flour, fine meal (Matt 13:33; Luke 13:21; Sept.: Num 5:15; Judg 6:19).

225. ἀλήθεια alḗtheia; gen. *alētheías*, fem. noun from *alēthḗs* (227), true. Truth, reality; the unveiled reality lying at the basis of and agreeing with an appearance; the manifested, the veritable essence of matter.

(I) Truth, verity, reality. The reality pertaining to an appearance (Rom 1:18, 25).

(A) Truth as evidenced in relation to facts, therefore, *alḗtheia* denotes the reality clearly lying before our eyes as opposed to a mere appearance, without reality (Mark 5:33; John 5:33; 16:7; Acts 26:25; Rom 9:1; 2 Cor 6:7, "by the word of truth"; 12:6; Eph 4:25; 1 Tim 2:7; Sept.: 1 Kgs 22:16; 2 Chr 18:15). Prefixed by *epí* (1909), upon, followed by the gen., *epí alētheías*, of a truth, as the fact or event shows (Luke 4:25; 22:59; Acts 4:27; 10:34; Sept.: Job 9:2; Isa 37:18).

(B) Spoken of what is true in itself, purity from all error or falsehood (Mark 12:32; Acts 26:25; Rom 2:20; "the form of knowledge and of the truth in the law"; 2 Cor 7:14; 12:6; Col 1:6; 2 Tim 2:18; 3:7, 8; 4:4). "The truth of the gospel" (Gal 2:5) means the verity of the gospel. "The word of truth" means the true doctrine (Eph 1:13; Col 1:5; 2 Tim 2:15; James 1:18); "thy commandments are faithful" (Ps 119:86); "the word of truth" (Ps 119:43).

(II) Truth, love of truth, both in words and conduct, meaning sincerity, veracity (Matt 22:16; Mark 12:14; Luke 20:21; John 4:23, 24, with a sincere mind, with sincerity of heart, not merely with external rites; John 8:44, "there is no truth in him," meaning he is a liar and loves not the truth [Rom 2:2; 3:7; 15:8; 1 Cor 5:8; 2 Cor 7:14; 11:10, as I truly, sincerely, follow Christ]; Eph 4:24, in true and sincere holiness; 5:9; 6:14; Phil 1:18; 1 John 1:6, we do not act in sincerity, equivalent to *pseudómetha* [5547], we are lying, behaving in a hypocritical way, 1 John 1:8; 2:4; 3:18, 19; 5:6, "the Spirit is truth," meaning true, veracious; 2 John 1:3; 3 John 1:3; Sept.: Josh 2:14; 1 Sam 12:24; 2 Sam 2:6; 1 Kgs 2:4; 3:6; 2 Chr 19:9; Ps 35:6).

(III) In the NT especially, divine truth or the faith and practice of the true gospel is called "truth" either as being true in itself and derived from the true God, or as declaring the existence and will of the one true God, in opposition to the worship of false idols. Hence divine truth, gospel truth, as opposed to heathen and Jewish fables (John 1:14, 17; 8:32, "ye shall know the truth"; 8:40, 45, 46; 16:13; 17:17, 19; 18:37, everyone who loves divine truth; 18:38; Rom 1:18, 25; 2 Cor 4:2; 13:8; Gal 3:1; 5:7; 2 Thess 2:10, 12, 13; 1 Tim 2:4, 7; 3:15; 2 Tim 2:25; Titus 1:1, 14; Heb 10:26; James 1:18; 3:14; 1 Pet 1:22; 2 Pet 1:12; 2:2; 1 John 2:21; 2 John 1:2, 4; 3 John 1:8). Hence the Lord Jesus is called the truth, meaning truth incarnate, the teacher of divine truth (John 14:6). "The Spirit of truth" means one who declares or reveals divine truth (John 14:17; 15:26; 16:13;). "They that have known the truth" (a.t.) means those who know the truth, are disciples of Christ (1 Tim 4:3). In the Sept., truth means the true religion (Ps 24:5; 25:3; 85:11).

(IV) Conduct conformed to the truth, integrity, probity, virtue, a life conformed to the precepts of the gospel. In John 3:21, *ho poión tén alétheian* means he who lives in the truth, who does what is true, from *poiéō* (4160), to make or to do. In opposition to it we have John 3:20, *ho phaúla prássōn*, one doing evil things, from *phaúla* (5337), foul, trivial, evil things, and *prássō* (4238), to perform. John 3:21 thus stands in contrast to verse twenty. In John 8:44, "he did not remain in his integrity" (a.t.). In Rom 2:8 and 1 Cor 13:6, *alétheia* stands in opposition to *adikía* (93), unrighteousness, wrong (Eph 4:21; 1 Tim 6:5; James 5:19; 3 John 1:3, 4, 12; Sept.: Ps 119:30; Prov 28:6; Isa 26:10).

(V) Truth as opposed to types, emblems, shadows (John 1:14, 17 [cf. John 4:23, 24; 14:6; Col 2:17]).

(VI) Integrity, rectitude of nature (John 8:44 [cf. Eph 4:24]).

Syn.: *hupóstasis* (5287), substance; *bebaíōsis* (951), confirmation; *plērōma* (4138), fulfillment.

Ant.: *pseúdos* (5579), falsehood, lie; *dólos* (1388), guile; *pseúsma* (5582), a falsehood or an acted lie; *epiboulḗ* (1917), a plot; *phantasía* (5326), spectre, spirit; *optasía* (3701), vision.

226. ἀληθεύω *alētheúō*; fut. *alētheúsō*, from *alēthḗs* (227), real, actual, not counterfeit. To act genuinely, truly. In Eph 4:15, the expression "speaking the truth in love" is *alētheúontes*, meaning to endeavor to express the truth in a loving manner. In Gal 4:16 not only speaking the truth but presenting an action as the truth and not counterfeit (Sept.: Gen 42:16; Prov 21:3).

Syn.: *bebaióō* (950), to confirm; *plēróō* (4137), to accomplish.

Ant.: *pseúdomai* (5574), to lie, deceive by lies, speak falsely; *planáō* (4105), to lead astray, deceive; *dolióō* (1387), to use deceit; *dolóō* (1389), to handle deceitfully; *diastréphō* (1294), to pervert; *sugkalúptō* (4780), to conceal in collusion.

227. ἀληθής *alēthḗs*; gen. *alēthoús*, masc.-fem., neut. *alēthés*, adj. from the priv. *a* (1), without, and *léthō*, an older form of *lanthánō* (2990), to be hid, unawares. True, one who cannot lie.

(I) True, real, conformed to the nature and reality of things (John 8:16; 19:35; Acts 12:9; Sept.: Prov 22:21). In John 4:18, "This you have spoken true" (a.t.), means truly (cf. 1 John 2:8). Hence also true as shown by the result or event (John 10:41; Titus 1:13; 2 Pet 2:22), thus credible, not to be rejected as a witness (John 5:31, 32; 8:13, 14, 17; 21:24; 2 Cor 6:8, a teacher; 1 Pet 5:12, grace; 1 John 2:27; 3 John 1:12; Sept.: Job 42:7, 8; Dan 8:26).

(II) True, loving truth, sincere, veracious (Matt 22:16; Mark 12:14; John 3:33; 8:26; Rom 3:4).

(III) True in conduct, sincere, upright, honest, just (John 7:18; Phil 4:8; Sept.: Isa 41:26).

Deriv.: *alḗtheia* (225), truth; *alētheúō* (226), to deal faithfully or truly; *alēthinós* (228), real, ideal, genuine (*alēthḗs* denotes the reality of the thing while *alēthinós* defines the relation of the concept to the corresponding thing, genuine.); *alēthṓs* (230), truly, surely, indeed.

228. ἀληθινός *alēthinós*; gen. *alēthinoú*, fem. *alēthinḗ*, neut. *alēthinón*, from *alēthḗs* (227), true, one who cannot lie. Real, genuine. *Alēthinós* defines the relation of the concept to the corresponding thing.

(I) True, conformed to truth (John 4:37; 19:35). In the sense of real, unfeigned, not fictitious (John 17:3, meaning the only true God, not feigned like idols; 1 Thess 1:9; 1 John 5:20; Rev 3:7; Sept.: 2 Chr 15:3; Isa 65:16). Spoken of what is true in itself, genuine, real, as opposed to that which is false, (*pseudḗs* [5571]), pretended (John 1:9; 4:23; 1 John 2:8); of the vine (John 15:1; Sept.: Jer 2:21); of Jerusalem (Sept.: Zech 8:3); of the bread coming down from heaven (John 6:32, of which the manna was the type); *skēnḗ alēthinḗ* (*skēnḗ* [4633], tabernacle) means the heavenly temple, after the model of which the Jews regarded the temple of Jerusalem as built (Heb 8:2). *Tá alēthiná hágia* (39), sanctuary (Heb 9:24), as opposed to the earthly copy. See Rev 11:19; 15:5. In Luke 16:11, "that which is true" (a.t.) refers to the real, genuine, and good, as opposed to the earthly, material goods of this world.

(II) True, i.e., loving truth, veracious and hence worthy of credit (John 7:28; Rev 3:14; 19:9, 11; 21:5; 22:6; Sept.: Prov 12:19, of lips).

(III) True, i.e., sincere, upright of the heart (Heb 10:22; Sept.: Job 2:3; 8:6; 27:17; Isa 38:3); of a judge or judgment, meaning upright, just (Rev 6:10; 15:3;

16:7; 19:2; Sept.: Deut 25:15; Isa 25:1; 59:4).

Syn.: *gnḗsios* (1103), true, genuine, sincere; *pistós* (4103), faithful, true; *ádolos* (97), sincere, without guile; *apseudḗs* (893), veracious, one who cannot lie; *eilikrinḗs* (1506), sincere, tested as genuine.

Ant.: *pseudḗs* (5571), false; *dólios* (1386), deceitful; *plános* (4108), one who leads astray; *phrenapátēs* (5423), a mind-deceiver; *plastós* (4112), fictitious; *nóthos* (3541), illegitimate.

229. ἀλήθω *alḗthō*; fut. *alḗsō*, equivalent to *aléō* (n.f.), to grind, akin to *áleuron* (224), flour, cornmeal. To grind (Matt 24:41; Luke 17:35; Sept.: Judg 16:21; Eccl 12:3). The grinding of corn was done by slaves with a hand mill.

230. ἀληθῶς *alēthṓs*; adv. from *alēthḗs* (227), true. Truly, really, in truth, certainly (Matt 14:33; 26:73; 27:54; Mark 14:70; 15:39; John 1:47; 4:18, 42; 6:14, 55; 7:26, 40; 8:31; 17:8; Acts 12:11; 1 Thess 2:13; 1 John 2:5). In Luke 9:27, "*légō* (3004) . . . *alēthṓs*" means "I speak with certainty" (a.t.; see also Luke 12:44; 21:3; Sept.: Gen 20:12).

Syn.: *óntōs* (3689), really, actually, indeed; *gár* (1063), verily; *kaí* (2532), and, followed by *gár*, for, *kaí gár*, and in fact, for also; *allá* (235), but, followed by *kaí*, *allá kaí*, but even, and indeed; *kaí* (2532) preceded by the particle *ge* (1065), doubtless, at least, ever indeed; *mḗti* (1509), if not indeed, unless indeed; *pántōs* (3843), at all events, doubtless; *naí* (3483), yea, surely; *gnēsíōs* (1104), sincerely, truly, genuinely; *amḗn* (281), amen, verily; *dḗpou* (1222), of course, verily.

Ant.: *tácha* (5029), peradventure, perhaps; *ára* (686), perhaps; *mḗpōs* (3381), lest somehow, by some means, haply; *pṓs* (4459), how.

231. ἁλιεύς *halieús*; gen. *haliéōs*, masc. noun from *háls* (n.f., see *aigialós* [123]), sea. A fisherman (Matt 4:18, 19; Mark

1:16, 17; Luke 5:2; Sept.: Isa 19:8; Jer 16:16; 51:41; Ezek 47:10).

Deriv.: *halieúō* (232), to fish.

232. ἀλιεύω *halieúō*; fut. *halieúsō*, from *halieús* (231), fisherman. To fish, catch fish (John 21:3; Sept.: Jer 16:16).

Syn.: *agreúō* (64), to catch alive, entrap; *pagideúō* (3802), to entrap, entangle; *deleázō* (1185), entrap, allure.

233. ἀλίζω *halízō*; fut. *halísō*, from *háls* (251), salt. To sprinkle with salt, to preserve by salting. Pass. in Mark 9:49, every sacrifice offered to God was to be sprinkled with salt (cf. Sept.: Lev 2:13). Hence, metaphorically everyone shall be seasoned or tried with fire, i.e., the wicked with eternal fire (Mark 9:47, 48), while every Christian shall be tried or perfected by suffering so as to become acceptable in the sight of God, just as every animal was prepared for sacrifice by being sprinkled with salt. See also Matt 5:13, which asks of salt which has become insipid, how can it be a preservative itself?

Deriv.: *sunalízō* (4871), to gather a throng together.

234. ἀλίσγημα *alísgema*; gen. *alisgématos*, neut. noun from *alisgéō* (n.f.), to pollute. Pollution by unclean (i.e., forbidden) food. Occurs only in Acts 15:20, in which what is expressed as "pollutions of idols" and in Acts 15:29 is called *eidōlóthuta* (1494), "meats offered to idols." The verb *alisgéō* is used to refer particularly to pollution by meats or drinks (Sept.: Dan 1:8; Mal 1:7, 12). The Apostle Paul alludes to the customs of heathen nations among whom, after sacrifice had been completed and a portion of the animal given to the priests, the remaining part was either displayed by the owner for sale in the market or became the occasion of a banquet either in the temple or at the owner's house (1 Cor 8).

Syn.: *míasma* (3393), pollution, defilement; *miasmós* (3394), contamina-tion, uncleanness; *molusmós* (3436), a stain, filthiness.

Ant.: *katharismós* (2512), purification; *hagnismós* (49), cleansing, lustration.

235. ἀλλά *allá*; an adversative particle originally the neut. pl. of *állos* (243), other. A particle implying in speech some diversity or superaddition to what preceded. It serves, therefore, to mark opposition, antithesis, or transition. It is less frequent in the Sept. than the NT as there is no corresponding particle in Hebr. In the NT, it means "but" in various modifications:

(I) But, as denoting antithesis or transition.

(A) In direct antithesis after the neg. particle *ou* (3756), not, followed by *mónon* (3440), only, in the contrasting phrase *ou mónon—allá kaí* (2532), and, meaning not only—but also (John 5:18; 11:52; 12:9).

(B) In an emphatic antithesis after a full negation, meaning but, but rather, but on the contrary (Luke 1:60; 13:5; 18:13; John 7:12; Acts 16:37; 19:2; Rom 3:27, 31; 7:7). Also in the beginning of a clause which asserts the contrary of what precedes (Luke 14:10, 13; Acts 2:16; 1 Cor 12:22; 1 Pet 2:20; Sept.: Job 32:8). Also followed by *ou* (3756), not, *all' ou* or *all' ouchí* (3780), not, used interrogatively, meaning "not rather?" (Luke 17:8; Heb 3:16).

(C) Often and chiefly used where the discourse or train of thought is broken off or partially interrupted. **(1)** By an objection (Rom 10:18, 19; 1 Cor 15:35; Sept.: Job 11:5). **(2)** By a correction or limitation of what precedes (Mark 14:36, 49; John 11:11, 15, 22; Rom 11:4; 1 Cor 8:7; Phil 2:27; Sept.: Ezra 10:13). **(3)** By some phrase modifying or explaining what precedes: especially after *mén* (3303), a particle of affirmation or concession; *gár* (1063), a particle assigning a reason, e.g., as, because; *dé* (1161), a particle expressing continuance or the opposite, e.g., and, but (Matt 24:6; Mark 9:13; Luke 21:9; John 11:30; 12:42; 16:20;

Acts 5:13; 1 Cor 4:4; 7:7; 14:17). Frequently *mén* is omitted (John 3:8; 8:37; 16:33; Rom 10:2; 1 Cor 3:6; 6:12; 2 Cor 4:8, 9; Sept.: 1 Sam 15:30; 29:9). **(4)** By an interrogation (Matt 11:8, 9; Luke 7:25). **(5)** By a phrase of incitement, urging where it is followed by an imper. (Matt 9:18; Mark 9:22; 16:7; Luke 22:36; Acts 10:20, "Arise therefore, and get thee down, and go with them"; Acts 26:16; Sept.: Job 12:7; 36:21). **(6)** *Allá* is employed to mark a transition to something else without direct antithesis, e.g., Mark 14:28; John 16:7; Acts 20:24; 1 Cor 8:6; 9:12; 10:5; 2 Cor 1:9; Sept.: Job 36:10; Isa 43:17. Also after an interrogation implying a neg. (John 7:49; Rom 8:35–37; 1 Cor 10:20; Sept.: Job 14:4).

(II) But, used as a continuative, but now, but indeed, but further, moreover.

(A) Generally, as marking a transition in the progress of discourse (Mark 13:24; Luke 6:27; 11:42; John 6:36, 64; Rom 10:16; Gal 2:14; Eph 5:24; Rev 10:7; Sept.: 1 Sam 16:6). Followed by *ei* (1487), if, *all' ei*, but if, but if indeed (1 Cor 7:21; 1 Pet 3:14). Also followed by *ou* (3756), not, *all' ou*, neither, but neither (John 10:8).

(B) As an emphatic where there is a gradation in the meaning, but still more, yea, even, and with a neg., no, not even (Luke 12:7; 16:21; 23:15; John 16:2; 2 Cor 7:11; Phil 3:8, "yea indeed, and therefore I count" [a.t.]).

(III) Yet, nevertheless, at least, yet assuredly, in an apodosis (conclusion) after the conditional particles *ei* (1487), if; *eán* (1437), if, (Rom 6:5, meaning yet assuredly, also; 1 Cor 4:15; 9:2). See also Mark 14:29; 2 Cor 5:16; 11:6; Col 2:5. Sometimes the protasis (condition) must be supplied, e.g., Acts 15:11, i.e., "[although we observe the law only in part], yet we hope to be saved even as they" (a.t.); Rom 5:13, 14, "[but] sin is not imputed when there is no law. Nevertheless death reigned."

(IV) *All' é* (2228), or, after a neg. meaning other than, except, unless (1 Cor 3:5). See Luke 12:51; 2 Cor 1:13; Sept.:

Num 13:29; 23:13; Deut 4:12; 2 Chr 18:30; 19:3; 21:17; Dan 10:7, 21.

Syn.: With the meaning of nay, no: *ou* (3756), no, not; *ouchí* (3780), not indeed; *menoúnge* (3304), no rather, no but, yet verily, yes doubtless, in some instances rendered as *mén* (3303), followed by *oún* (3767), not therefore. With the meaning of not withstanding: *plén* (4133), howbeit, yet, except that. With the meaning of rather, used as a conj.: *perissotérōs* (4056), the more exceedingly. With the meaning of yea, yes: *naí* (3483), yes, a particle of affirmation; *kaí* (2532), and, even; *mén oún* (3303, 3767), in some texts *menoúnge* (3304), yea, rather.

236. ἀλλάσσω *allássō*, **ἀλλάττω** *alláttō*; fut. *alláxō*, from *állos* (243), other, another. To change.

(I) To change the form or nature of a thing, to transform the voice or tone (Gal 4:20). To change for the better, in the pass. (1 Cor 15:51, 52; Sept.: Jer 13:23). To change for the worse, to corrupt, cause to decay, e.g., the heavens (Heb 1:10–12, meaning the heavens shall grow old, lose their splendor, decay [cf. Ps 102:26; Isa 51:6]). In Acts 6:14, to "change the customs," i.e., do away with them (Sept.: Ezra 6:11, 12).

(II) To change one thing for another, to exchange (Rom 1:23, "they changed the glory of the incorruptible God for an image" [a.t.], i.e., set up an image in place of the true God; Sept.: Gen 41:14, of garments; Lev 27:10, 33; 2 Sam 12:20; Ps 106:20).

Deriv.: *apallássō* (525), to change, to free from, release, deliver; *diallássō* (1259), to reconcile in cases of mutual hostility yielding to mutual concession; *katallássō* (2644), to reconcile to God in His relationship to sinful man; *metallássō* (3337), exchange one thing for another or into another.

Syn.: *metabállō* (3328), change; *metastréphō* (3344), to turn about; *katargéō* (2673), to abolish; *rhúomai* (4506), to rescue from; *antibállō* (474), to exchange, spoken usually of words that can be exchanged one with another.

Ant.: *tēréō* (5083), to preserve, keep; *diatēréō* (1301), to keep carefully; *suntēréō* (4933), to preserve, keep safe; *phulássō* (5442), to guard, watch; *diaphulássō* (1314), to guard thoroughly; *kratéō* (2902), to keep, hold; *kataleípō* (2641), to leave behind or remaining, reserve.

237. ἀλλαχόθεν *allachóthen*; adv. from *allachoú*, elsewhere, from *állos* (243), other, and the suffix *then*, denoting from a place. From elsewhere (John 10:1; Sept.: Esth 4:14).

Ant.: *enteúthen* (1784), hence; *ekeíthen* (1564), thence.

238. ἀλληγορέω *allēgoréō*; contracted *allēgorō̂*, fut. *allēgorḗsō*, from *állos* (243), another, and *agoreúō* (n.f.), to speak in a place of assembly, which is from *agorá* (58), market place. To allegorize, to speak allegorically where the thing spoken of is emblematic or representative (Gal 4:24, "which things are said allegorically" [a.t.], or in a mystical sense).

Syn.: *túpos* (5179), type; *múthos* (3454), a fable; *analogía* (356), analogy; *mustérion* (3466), mystery. All these may be classified as allegorical or figurative, insofar as they point to a meaning different from that contained in the word or words used.

239. ἀλληλούϊα *allēlloúia*, ἀλληλοϊά *hallēloïa*, a transliteration of the Hebr. *halᵉlū* (1984, OT), to praise, and *yāh* (3050, OT), Yah. Hallelujah, literally, praise ye Yah. Yah is the shortened form of Yahweh, Jehovah, or God, which occurs 24 times in the Psalter. With one exception (Ps 135:3), *allēlloúia* is always found at the beginning or end of psalms, suggesting that it was a standardized call to praise in the temple worship. In the NT, only in Rev 19:1, 3, 4, 6, all related to the judgment of God and His glory (cf. Ps 104:35).

240. ἀλλήλων *allélōn*; gen. pl. of a reciprocal pron. *allélous*, one another; dat. masc. pl. *allélois*; fem. *allélais*; neut. *allélois*, from *állos* (243), another. One another. This pron. has no nom. and no sing. Used only in the acc., gen., and dat.: *allélous*, one another; *allélōn*, of one another; *allélois*, for, in, to one another (Matt 24:10; John 15:12, 17).

241. ἀλλογενής *allogenḗs*; gen. *allogenoús*, masc.-fem., neut. *allogenés*, adj. from *állos* (243), other, and *génos* (1085), a nation, race. Used as a subst., one of another nation, a stranger, foreigner (Luke 17:18, see Luke 17:16; Sept.: Ex 12:43; 29:33; Job 15:19; Isa 56:3, 6).

Syn.: *allóphulos* (246), one of another race, nation; *xénos* (3581), stranger, foreigner; *allótrios* (245), stranger; *pároikos* (3941), a pilgrim; *héteros* (2087), another of a different kind, a stranger; *parepídēmos* (3927), pilgrim or sojourner.

Ant.: *oikeíos* (3609), relative; *sumpolítēs* (4847), fellow-citizen.

242. ἄλλομαι *hállomai*; fut. *haloúmai*, aor. *hēlámēn*. To leap, leap up, jump, spring. Intrans.: Acts 3:8; 14:10; Sept.: Job 6:10. To spring up, bubble up, as water from a spring (John 4:14).

Deriv.: *agalliáō* (21), to exult, leap for joy; *exállomai* (1814), to leap up; *ephállomai* (2177), to leap upon.

Syn.: *skirtáō* (4640), to leap for joy; *eispēdáō* (1530), to spring or leap in; *ekpēdáō*, to spring forth, (Acts 14:14 [UBS]).

Ant.: *píptō* (4098), to fall; *strónnumi* (4766), to strew, make a bed; *katákeimai* (2621), to recline; *kataklínō* (2625), to take a place at table.

243. ἄλλος *állos*; fem. *állē*, neut. *állon*, adj. Another, numerically but of the same kind in contrast to *héteros* (2087), another qualitatively, other, different one.

(I) Without the art., meaning other, another, some other (Matt 2:12; 13:33;

26:71; 27:42; Gal 1:7); another of the same kind (Mark 7:4, 8; John 21:25); another besides (Matt 25:16, 17; Mark 12:32; 15:41; John 6:22; 14:16, "another Comforter [*paráklētos* {3875}]"). Marking succession, i.e., in the second or third place (Mark 12:4, 5; Rev 12:3; 13:11). In John 20:30, not only these, but also others. See Sept.: Num 23:13; 1 Kgs 13:10.

(II) Distributively, when repeated or joined with other pronouns, e.g., *hoútos—állos* (*hoútos* [3778], this one), meaning this or that, one or another (Matt 8:9); *hoi mén—álloi dé* (*mén dé* [3303, 1161], on the one hand or on the other), some or others (Matt 16:14); *álloi—álloi*, some or others (Matt 13:5–8; Mark 4:7, 8; 6:15; 8:28; 1 Cor 12:8–10); *állos prós állon* (*prós* [4314], to), one to another (Acts 2:12); *álloi mén oún állo ti ékrazon* (*oún* [3767] therefore; *ti* [5100], something; *krázō* [2896], to cry), "Some therefore cried one thing, and some another" (Acts 19:32).

(III) With the art., *ho állos*, the other (Matt 5:39; 10:23; 12:13; John 18:16; Rev 17:10, "the other," the remaining one). *Hoi álloi*, the others, the rest (John 21:8; 1 Cor 14:29).

Deriv.: *allá* (235), but; *allássō / alláttō* (236), to change; *allachóthen* (237), from another place; *allēgoréō* (238), to allegorize; *allélōn* (240), of one another; *allogenḗs* (241), one of another nation; *allótrios* (245), another's; *allóphulos* (246), one of another race or nation; *állōs* (247), an adv. meaning otherwise.

Syn.: *diáphoros* (1313), different.

Ant.: *autós* (846), same; *ídios* (2398), same.

244. ἀλλοτριοεπίσκοπος *allotrioepískopos*; gen. *allotrioepiskópou*, masc. noun from *allótrios* (245), another's, and *epískopos* (1985), superintendent, overseer, bishop. An inspector of foreign or strange things, one who busies himself with what does not concern him, a busybody. See *állos* (243) for the basic meaning as an adj. (in NT, only in 1 Pet 4:15).

245. ἀλλότριος *allótrios*; fem. *allotría*, neut. *allótrion*, from *állos* (243), other. Belonging to another, not one's own.

(I) When used in the pl. *tá allótria*, it means others' goods (Luke 16:12).

(II) Spoken of a country, strange, foreign, belonging to other people (Acts 7:6; Heb 11:9; Sept.: Ex 2:22; 18:3); persons who do not belong to one's own family, strangers (Matt 17:25, 26; Sept.: Ps 49:11).

(III) By implication, meaning hostile, an enemy; with the idea of impiety, heathen, enemy, Gentile (Heb 11:34; Sept.: 1 Kgs 8:41; Ezra 10:2; Ps 54:3).

Deriv.: *allotrioepískopos* (244), busybody.

Syn.: Distinguished from *allóphulos* (246), one of another race or nation; *allogenḗs* (241), one of another nation, not a Jew, a stranger, foreigner (Luke 17:18); *héteros* (2087), another of a different kind; *xénos* (3581), alien, foreign, foreigner; *parádoxos* (3861), contrary to prevailing opinion or custom.

Ant.: *oikeíos* (3609), relative; *oikétēs* (3610), a fellow resident, a menial domestic servant; *polítēs* (4177), citizen; *sumpolítēs* (4847), fellow citizen; *hēméteros* (2251), ours.

246. ἀλλόφυλος *allóphulos*; gen. *allophúlou*, masc.-fem., neut. *allóphulon*, adj. from *állos* (243), other, and *phulḗ* (5443), a tribe or race. Not a Jew, one of another race or nation (Acts 10:28; Sept.: 2 Kgs 8:28; Isa 2:6; 61:5).

Syn.: *éthnos* (1484), nation, not Jewish; *ethnikós* (1482), Gentile, non-Jewish; *allogenḗs* (241), of another nation or race; *allótrios* (245), belonging to another.

247. ἄλλως *állōs*; adv. from *állos* (243), other. Otherwise (1 Tim 5:25, "which are otherwise" [a.t.] or not good works; Sept.: Job 11:12; Esth 1:19; 9:27).

Syn.: *hetérōs* (2088), otherwise, of a different frame of mind; *ei dé mḗge* (1490), not indeed, otherwise.

Ant.: *homoíōs* (3668), likewise; *hōsaútōs* (5615), in like manner, a strengthened form of *hōs* (5613), as; *kaí* (2532), and, even, likewise; *paraplēsíōs* (3898), nearby, nearly; *hoútōs* (3779), thus, so; *oún* (3767), therefore, likewise.

248. ἀλοάω *aloáō*; contracted *aloó*, fut. *alḗsō*. To tread out corn, to force corn from the husks by treading. In the NT, to drive around in a circle, especially oxen, upon grain in order to thresh it; to thresh with oxen (1 Cor 9:9, 10; 1 Tim 5:18; Sept.: Deut 25:4; Isa 41:15; Jer 51:33).

    Syn.: *patéō* (3961), to tread; *katapatéō* (2662), to tread down, trample under foot.

249. ἄλογος *álogos*; gen. *álogou*, masc.-fem., neut. *álogon*, adj. from the priv. *a* (1), without, and *lógos* (3056), reason. Unendowed with reason, irrational, brute (2 Pet 2:12; Jude 1:10); unreasonable, absurd (Acts 25:27). Contrast with *álalos* (216), without words (even if they are meaningless), *lógos* being reason and the expression in words of what one thinks, while *laliá* (2981) is prattle, loquacity, accent in speaking (Matt 26:73; Mark 14:70), as also *laléō* (2980), simply to talk, express sounds as contrasted to *légō*, to speak expressing thought.

    Syn.: *átopos* (824), out of place, hence unreasonable; *anóētos* (453), without understanding; *áphrōn* (878), without reason; *asúnetos* (801), without discernment; *mōrós* (3474), stupid, foolish.

    Ant.: *logikós* (3050), reasonable; *sunetós* (4908), prudent, one who can put things together; *sophós* (4680), wise; *orthós* (3717), right; *sṓphrōn* (4998), of sound mind; *phrónimos* (5429), prudent.

250. ἀλόη *alóē*; gen. *alóēs*, fem. noun. Aloe, the name of a tree which has highly aromatic wood. Used by the Orientals as a perfume and by the Egyptians for embalming purposes (John 19:39; Sept.: Num 24:6; Prov 7:17).

251. ἅλς *háls*; gen. *halós*, masc. noun. The sea, which may be derived from the Gr. verb *hállomai* (242), to leap, on account of the impetuous motion of its waters. Salt (Mark 9:49; Sept.: Gen 14:3; Lev 2:13). Related to *hálas* (217), salt, and *halukós* (252), salty.

    Deriv.: *hakízō*, (233), to sprinkle with salt; *halukós* (252), salt; *ánalos* (358), without salt; *parálios* (3882), near the sea.

    Syn.: *potamós* (4215), river.
    Ant.: *gē̂* (1093), land.

252. ἀλυκός *halukós*; fem. *halukḗ*, neut. *halukón*, from *háls* (251), salt. Of the sea, hence brackish, salty, bitter. Only in James 3:12; Sept.: Num 34:3, 12.

253. ἀλυπότερος *alupóteros*; the comparative of *álupos*, from the priv. *a* (1), without, and *lúpē* (3077), sorrow. More free from sorrow or grief. "That I may be the less sorrowful" (Phil 2:28).

254. ἅλυσις *hálusis*; gen. *halúseōs*, fem. noun. Chains for the hands or feet, manacles, shackles (Mark 5:3, 4; Luke 8:29; Acts 12:6, 7). Figuratively, meaning bonds, imprisonment, state of custody (Eph 6:20; 2 Tim 1:16; Rev 20:1). Acts 21:33 and 28:20 may allude to the custom of the Romans who usually (as we learn from Josephus, Seneca, and Athenaeus) confined prisoners not only by shutting them up in prison, but also by chaining their right arm to the left arm of a soldier who guarded them (Acts 28:16).

    Syn.: *desmós* (1199), bond; *seirá* (4577), a cord, rope, band, chain (2 Pet 2:4).

255. ἀλυσιτελής *alusitelḗs*; gen. *alusiteloús*, masc.-fem., neut. *alusitelés*, adj. from the priv. *a* (1), without, and *lusitelḗs* (n.f.), profitable, which is from *lúō* (3089), to loose, and *télos* (5056), end. Yielding no gain, unprofitable, and by implication exceedingly harmful or dangerous (Heb 13:17).

Syn.: *achreíos* (888), unprofitable; *áchrēstos* (890), unserviceable; *anōphelés* (512), not beneficial.

Ant.: *chrḗsimos* (5539), useful; *eúchrēstos* (2173), serviceable; *ōphélimos* (5624), profitable, useful; *súmphoros* (from *sumphérō* [4851], to bring together, to be an advantage, profitable, expedient), profit, expedience, profitable (found in some MSS in 1 Cor 7:35; 10:33).

256. Ἀλφαῖος *Alphaíos*; gen. *Alphaíou*, masc. proper noun. Alphaeus.

(I) The father of Levi, the tax collector (Mark 2:14) who is generally identified as the Apostle Matthew.

(II) The father of the Apostle James the less who is called "the son of Alphaeus" (Matt 10:3; Mark 3:18; Luke 6:15; Acts 1:13). James' title here was to distinguish the Apostle James from James the son of Zebedee. For further discussion on James, see *Iákōbos* (2385). Alphaeus was the husband of Mary, who was the sister of our Lord's mother (Mark 15:40; John 19:25 where he is called Cleophas [cf. Matt 27:56; Luke 24:10]).

257. ἅλων *hálōn*; gen. *hálōnos*, also *hálōs*, masc., fem. noun. A threshing floor or area where grain is threshed and winnowed (Sept.: Gen 50:10, 11). In the NT, the produce of the threshing floor, corn, grain (Matt 3:12; Luke 3:17; Sept.: Ex 22:6; Judg 15:5; Ruth 3:2; Job 39:12).

258. ἀλώπηξ *alópēx*; gen. *alópekos*, fem. noun. A fox (Matt 8:20; Luke 9:58; Sept.: Judg 15:4; Ezek 13:4). Metaphorically of a crafty, cunning, malicious person (Luke 13:32), applied to Herod the Tetrarch.

259. ἅλωσις *hálōsis*; gen. *hálōseōs*, from *halískō* (n.f.), to capture. Taking, catching (2 Pet 2:12; Sept.: Jer 50:46). Also from *halískō* (n.f.): *analískō* (355), to take away, destroy.

Syn.: *aichmalōsía* (161), captivity.

Ant.: *eleuthería* (1657), liberty.

260. ἅμα *háma*; an adv. and prep. Together, together with. When spoken of time:

(I) As an adv.: at the same time (Acts 24:26; 27:40; Col 4:3; 1 Tim 5:13; Phile 1:22); of persons meaning together, in company (1 Thess 4:17, where it is used with *sún* [4862], with, *autoís*, them, leaving no doubt that the believers who are alive at the time of the *parousía*, the coming of the Lord for His saints, will be caught up together with the resurrected dead [1 Thess 5:10]); "they are altogether become unprofitable" (a.t.; Rom 3:12, cf. Gen 13:6; 22:6; Ps 14:3).

(II) As a prep.: with, together with; with a dat.: "lest together with them" (a.t.; Matt 13:29; Sept.: Deut 33:5; Jer 31:24). With the dawn, "early in the morning" (Matt 20:1; Sept.: Neh 7:3; Mic 2:1).

Deriv.: *amáō* (270), to collect, gather; *hápas* (537), all, the whole.

Syn.: *homoú* (3674), together; *hótan* (3752), when; *hóte* (3753), when; *hopóte* (3698), when; *hopótan* (3698), when; *tóte* (5119), then; *póte* (4219), when.

Ant.: *poté* (4218), never; *mḗpote* (3379), never (subj. conditional); *oudépote* (3764), never (used in an absolute sense).

261. ἀμαθής *amathḗs*; gen. *amathoús*, masc.-fem., neut. *amathés*, adj. from *a* (1), without, and *manthánō* (3129), to learn. Unlearned, uninstructed (2 Pet 3:16).

Syn.: *agrámmatos* (62), unlettered, illiterate; *apaídeutos* (521), uninstructed; *idiṓtēs* (2399), unlearned, ignorant.

Ant.: *lógios* (3052), intelligent, fluent; *euschḗmōn* (2158), noble.

262. ἀμαράντινος *amarántinos*; fem. *amarantínē*, neut. *amarántinon*, adj. corresponding to *amárantos* (263), unfading. Made of amaranths, a fabled flower that did not fade away. Used in 1 Pet 5:4 and should not be translated "fadeth not." The word is *amarántinos* and does not refer to the quality of the heavenly inheritance as not fading away, but rather to the makeup of the crown itself as being of amaranths, unfading flowers.

Syn.: *amárantos* (263), unfading; *áphthartos* (862), incorruptible; *amíantos* (283), unsoiled, undefiled.

263. ἀμάραντος *amárantos*; gen. *amarántou*, masc.-fem., neut. *amáranton*, adj. from the priv. *a* (1), without, and *maraínō* (3133), to fade. Unfading, only in 1 Pet 1:4. Our heavenly inheritance is not something beautiful which lasts only for a while and then fades away. It is of unfailing loveliness, reserved for the faithful in heaven. The fabled flower that did not fade away was an amaranth (*amárantos*) in contrast to the ordinary grass (*chórtos* [5528]) which fades, falls away, and dies quickly (Job 14:2; Ps 37:2; 103:15; Isa 40:6, 7; Matt 6:30; James 1:11; 1 Pet 1:24). Another Gr. word, *amarántinos* (262), is unfortunately translated "that fadeth not away" (1 Pet 5:4) which corresponds more to the meaning of *amárantos*, spoken of the quality of the crown of glory. The suffix *-inos* in *amarántinos* indicates the substance of which something is made and not the quality of it as does *amárantos*. The crown of glory will be *amarántinos*, made up of amaranths or the fabled, unfading flowers. The heavenly inheritance of the believer does not decay for it is *amárantos*. Corruption cannot touch it or ever wear out its freshness, brightness, and beauty. See also *amíantos* (283), undefiled.

264. ἀμαρτάνω *hamartánō*; fut. *hamartḗsō*, aor. *hēmártēsa*; 2d aor. *hḗmarton*. To sin, to miss a mark on the way, not to hit the mark. One who keeps missing the mark in his relationship to God is *hamartōlós* (268), sinner.

(I) To err, swerve from the truth, go wrong, used in an absolute sense in 1 Cor 15:34, meaning to beware lest one be drawn into errors pertaining to faith, of which the Apostle is speaking (Titus 3:11).

(II) To err in action, in respect to a prescribed law, i.e., to commit errors, to do wrong, sin.

(A) Generally, to sin, spoken of any sin, used in an absolute sense (Matt 27:4; John 5:14; 8:11; 9:2, 3; Rom 2:12; 3:23; 5:12, 14, 16; 6:15; 1 Cor 7:28, 36; Eph 4:26; 1 Tim 5:20; Heb 3:17; 10:26; 1 Pet 2:20; 2 Pet 2:4; 1 John 1:10; 2:1; 3:6, 8, 9; 5:16, 18. In 1 John 5:16, to sin a sin. Sept.: Ex 32:30; Lev 4:14, 23, 28).

(B) With *eis* (1519), unto, with the acc. to sin against anyone, to offend, wrong (Matt 18:15, 21; Luke 15:18, 21; 17:3, 4; Acts 25:8; 1 Cor 6:18; 8:12; Sept.: Gen 20:6, 9; 43:9; 1 Sam 2:25).

(C) To "sin before someone" means to do evil in the sight of anyone, to sin against, to wrong (Luke 15:21; Sept.: Gen 39:9; Deut 1:41; 20:18; 1 Sam 7:6; 12:23; 14:33, 34). See *hamartía* (266), sin, which has many syn. listed; *hamártēma* (265), an individual deed or sin; *anamártētos* (361), without sin; *proamartánō* (4258), to sin previously.

Deriv.: *amártēma* (265), sin; *hamartía* (266), sin, sinful; *hamartōlós* (268), a sinner; *anamártētos* (361), without sin; *proamartánō* (4258), to sin previously.

Syn.: *ptaíō* (4417), to stumble, offend; *adikéō* (91), to do wrong; *skandalízō* (4624), to offend, be a stumblingblock to someone, trip someone; *astochéō* (795), to miss the goal; *parabaínō* (3845), to transgress; *píptō* (4098), to fall; *parapíptō* (3895), to fall away; *paranoméō* (3891), to go contrary to law; *peripíptō* (4045), to fall by the side; *planáomai* (4105), to go astray.

Ant.: *orthopodéō* (3716), to walk uprightly; *akolouthéō* (190), to follow.

265. ἁμάρτημα *hamártēma*; gen. *hamartḗmatos*, neut. noun from *hamartánō* (264), to sin. Deed of disobedience to a divine law, a mistake, miss, error, transgression, sin (Mark 3:28; 4:12; Rom 3:25; 1 Cor 6:18; Sept.: Gen 31:36; Isa 58:1). Nouns ending in *-ma* indicate the result of a certain action, in this case *hamartía* (266), sin. *Hamártēma* is sin as an individual act.

Syn.: *paráptōma* (3900), the deed of trespassing, a trespass; *adíkēma* (92), a wrong, an iniquity perpetrated; *agnóēma* (51), shortcoming, error, a thing ignored; *opheílēma* (3783), that which one owes, a debt; *héttēma* (2275), a loss, defeat, defect; *plánē* (4106), deceit, delusion.

Ant.: *akríbeia* (195), exactness; *aspháleia* (803), safety; *alḗtheia* (225), truth; *epanórthōsis* (1882), rectification, correction.

266. ἀμαρτία *hamartía*; gen. *hamartías*, fem. noun from *hamartánō* (264), to sin. Sin, missing the true end and scope of our lives, which is God. An offense in relation to God with emphasis on guilt.

(I) Aberration from the truth, error (John 8:46 where it stands as the opposite of *alḗtheia* [225], truth. See also John 16:8, 9).

(II) Aberration from a prescribed law or rule of duty, whether in general or of particular sins.

(A) Generally (Matt 3:6; 9:2, 5, 6; Mark 1:4, 5; 1 Cor 15:3; Heb 4:15; Sept.: Gen 15:16; 18:20; Isa 53:5). "Thou art wholly born in sin" (a.t.; John 9:34) means thou art a sinner from the womb (cf. Ps 51:5; 58:3; Isa 48:8). To "commit sin" (a.t.; 2 Cor 11:7; 1 Pet 2:22; 1 John 3:9) means the same thing as to work sin (James 2:9). In 1 John 5:16, to "sin a sin" means to commit any sin. In the gen. after another noun, *hamartía* often supplies the place of an adj. meaning sinful, wicked, impious. In 2 Thess 2:3, the "man of sin" means the Antichrist. In Rom 7:5, "the passions of sins" (a.t.) means sinful desires. In Heb 10:6, 8 and 13:11, "concerning sin" (a.t.) refers to sacrifice for sin. In Heb 10:26, "offering for sin" (a.t.) refers to those who sin willfully (see also Heb 10:18; Sept.: Lev 5:8; Ps 40:7).

(B) Spoken of particular sins, e.g., of unbelief (John 8:21, 24); of lewdness (2 Pet 2:14); of defection from the gospel of Christ (Heb 11:25; 12:1).

(C) By metonymy, of abstraction for concrete, *hamartía* for *hamartōlós* (268), sinner meaning sinful, i.e., either as causing sin (Rom 7:7, "Is the law the cause of sin?" [a.t.]) or as committing sin (2 Cor 5:21 meaning He has been treated as if He were a sinner). In Heb 12:4, it refers to the adversaries of the gospel.

(D) By metonymy, the practice of sinning, habit of sin (Rom 3:9; 5:12, 20, 21; Gal 3:22).

(E) By metonymy, proneness to sin, sinful desire or propensity (John 8:34; Rom 6:1, 2, 6, 12, 14; 7:7ff.; Heb 3:13, "the deceitfulness of our sinful propensities" [a.t.]).

(III) The imputation or consequences of sin, the guilt and punishment of sin as in the phrase "to take away [or bear] sin" (a.t.), i.e., the imputation of it (John 1:29; Rom 11:27; Heb 9:26; 10:11; 1 Pet 2:24; 1 John 3:5). To remit (*aphíēmi* [863]) sins and the remission (*áphesis* [859]) of sins means to remove the guilt, punishment, and power of sin (Matt 9:2, 5, 6; 26:28; Luke 7:47–49; John 20:23; Heb 10:4). In John 9:41, "your sin remains" (a.t.) means your guilt and exposure to punishment remain (cf. John 15:22, 24; 1 John 1:9). In 1 Cor 15:17, "ye are yet in your sins" means you are still under the guilt and power of your sins. In Heb 9:28, "without sin" means He shall appear the second time but not for the putting away of the consequences of sin (Heb 9:26; Sept.: Lev 22:9; Num 9:13; Prov 10:16; Isa 5:18; 53:6, 11; Lam 3:39; Ezek 3:20; Zech 14:19). See *hamártēma* (265), sin as an individual act, a determination of the nature of man as a personal power and also used of individual acts. Used in an absolute or relative sense. Individual sins do not annul the general character or the actions of the regenerate. "There is a sin [*hamartía* (266)] unto death" (1 John 5:16) refers to willful and intentional sin (see also Heb 10:26, 29) and physical death (Acts 5:1–11; 1 Cor 5:5; 11:30), and there is a sin not unto death. The sins of the regenerate are regrettably unavoidable in view of their present unredeemed body (Rom 8:2, 3) and the environment in which they live (1 John 2:2). The sinfulness of sin depends on the innate or acquired knowledge of God's expectations (James 4:17).

Syn.: *agnóēma* (51), a sin of ignorance; *opheílēma* ([3783] akin to *opheilē* [3782], a debt), that which is legally due; *adikía* (93), unrighteousness; *adíkēma* (92), a wrong, an injury; *ponēría* (4189), wickedness; *paranomía* (3892), lawbreaking; *anomía* (458), lawlessness; *parábasis* (3847), violation, transgression; *kríma* (2917), condemnation; *églēma* (1462), crime which is tried in court; *sunōmosía* (4945), a plot, conspiracy; *asébeia* (763), impiety, ungodliness; *parakoē* (3876), disobedience; *apeítheia* (543), obstinate rejection of God's will; *paráptōma* (3900), a false step, a blunder; *ptōsis* (4431), a fall; *apostasía* (646), a standing away from, although not necessarily a departure from a position in which one stood; *aitía* (156) and *aítion* (158), a crime, a legal ground for punishment, fault; *hēttēma* (2275), a loss, defeat, defect; *hamártēma* (265), an act of sin or disobedience to divine requirement and expectation.

Ant.: *sōtēría* (4991), salvation; *dikaiosúnē* (1343), righteousness; *áphesis* (859), forgiveness, removal of sin; *cháris* (5485), grace; *hagiōsúnē* (42), the state of holiness; *hagiótes* (41), inherent holiness.

267. ἀμάρτυρος *amárturos*; gen. *amartúrou*, masc.-fem., neut. *amárturon*, adj. from the priv. *a* (1), without, and *mártus* (3144), a witness. Without a witness (Acts 14:17).

268. ἀμαρτωλός *hamartōlós*; gen. *hamartōloú*, masc.-fem., neut. *hamartōlón*, adj. from *hamartánō* (264), to deviate, miss the mark, sin. Erring from the way or mark. In the NT, metaphorically used as an adj. or subst.

(I) As adj., erring from the divine law, sinful, wicked, impious.

(A) Generally: a sinful generation (Mark 8:38); a sinful man, a sinner (Luke 5:8; 19:7; 24:7; John 9:16, 24); a sinful woman (Luke 7:37, 39; Sept.: Num 32:14; Isa 1:4); "more wicked than all others" (a.t.; Luke 13:2); a sinner (Luke 18:13; Rom 3:7); sinful, sinners (Rom 5:8; Gal 2:17; James 4:8).

(B) Oblivious to the consequences of sin, guilty and exposed to punishment: (Rom 5:19, many became exposed to the punishment of sin; 7:13; Gal 2:15; Jude 1:15, ungodly persons deserving of punishment).

(II) As subst., a sinner, transgressor, impious person.

(A) Generally (Matt 9:10, 11, 13; 11:19; Mark 2:15–17; Luke 5:30, 32; 6:32–34; 7:34; 15:1, 2, 7, 10; John 9:25, 31; 1 Tim 1:9, 15; Heb 7:26; 12:3; James 5:20; 1 Pet 4:18; Sept.: Ps 1:1, 5; 37:12, 20; Isa 13:9; Ezek 33:8, 19; Amos 9:8).

(B) The Jews called the Gentiles sinners or despisers of God and considered them heathen or pagan, *tá éthnē* (1484), the nations (Matt 26:45 [cf. Matt 20:19; Mark 10:33; Luke 18:32; Sept.: Isa 14:5]).

(C) Often connected with *telṓnes* (pl. [5077]), publicans or tax collectors (Matt 9:10, 11; 11:19; Mark 2:15, 16; Luke 7:34; 15:1) who were in bad repute among Jews and Greeks. See also Matt 26:45; Mark 14:41; Luke 5:30; 6:33, 34; 7:39; 13:2; 15:2, 7, 10; 18:13; 19:7; John 9:16, 24, 25, 31; Rom 3:7; Gal 2:15, 17; Heb 12:3; James 4:8; 5:20; 1 Pet 4:18.

Syn.: *asebēs* (765), impious, ungodly; *ápistos* (571), an unbeliever; *opheilétēs* (3781), a debtor; *énochos* (177), guilty of something; *aítios* (159), one to be blamed; *ádikos* (94), unjust.

Ant.: *athōos* (121), innocent; *anaítios* (338), guiltless; *anamártētos* (361), one without sin; *ákakos* (172), one without malice; *díkaios* (1342), just, one who recognizes that God has rights upon his life. He submits himself to be God's rightful possession and, therefore, acquires God's nature and performs his duty toward God.

One who exercises first his duties and then his rights toward God.

269. ἄμαχος *ámachos*; gen. *amáchou*, masc.-fem., neut. *ámachon*, adj. from the priv. *a* (1), without, and *máchē* (3163), battle, controversy. Not disposed to fight, not contentious or quarrelsome (1 Tim 3:3; Titus 3:2).

Syn.: *eucháristos* (2170), pleasant; *sumpathḗs* (4835), sympathetic; *agapētós* (27), beloved; *eirēnikós* (1516), peaceful; *eirēnopoiós* (1518), peacemaker; *hēsúchios* (2272), quiet.

Ant.: *pároinos* (3943), tarrying at wine and consequently becoming quarrelsome; *philóneikos* (5380), one loving to quarrel, contentious; *anósios* (462), unholy; *stugnētós* (4767), hateful; *bdeluktós* (947), detestable.

270. ἀμάω *amáō*; contracted *amṓ*, fut. *amḗsō*, from *háma* (260), together. To collect, gather, reap, mow, cut down (James 5:4; Sept.: Lev 19:9; 25:11; Deut 24:21).

Syn.: *therízō* (2325), to harvest, reap.

Ant.: *skorpízō* (4650), to scatter; *diaskorpízō* (1287), to scatter abroad, to waste; *diaspeírō* (1289), to scatter seed; *likmáō* (3039), to winnow.

271. ἀμέθυστος *améthustos*; masc. noun from the priv. *a* (1), without, and *methúō* (3184), to get drunk. Amethyst, a gem of a deep purple or violet color (Rev 21:20; Sept.: Ex 28:19). It was assigned this name because although it comes close to the color of wine, it falls short of it and stops at a violet color. Others propose it is called amethyst, something that cannot lead to drunkenness because its color resembles wine mixed with water, or diluted wine. Others suggest that it was given the name because it was thought to have a remedial virtue against drunkenness.

272. ἀμελέω *ameléō*; contracted *amelṓ*, fut. *amelḗsō*, from *amelḗs* (n.f.), careless, which is from the priv. *a* (1), without,

and *mélei* (3199), to show concern, to care. Not to care for, to neglect (Matt 22:5; 2 Pet 1:12). With the gen. (1 Tim 4:14; Heb 2:3; 8:9; Sept.: Jer 4:17).

Syn.: *paratheōréō* (3865), to overlook, neglect; *oligōréō* (3643), to regard lightly.

Ant.: *blépō* (991), to look with close attention; *epiblépō* (1914), to look upon, supervise; *proséchō* (4337), to give heed to; *phrontízō* (5431), to care for; *merimnáō* (3309), to exercise anxious care; *epimeléomai* (1959), to care for; *pronoéō* (4306), to consider in advance, provide; *peripoiéomai* (4046), to show concern and care; *diakonéō* (1247), to minister; *thálpō* (2282), to cherish, brood.

273. ἄμεμπτος *ámemptos*; gen. *amémptou*, masc.-fem., neut. *ámempton*, adj. from the priv. *a* (1), without, and *mémphomai* (3201), to find fault. Blameless (Luke 1:6; Phil 2:15; 3:6; 1 Thess 3:13; Heb 8:7).

Deriv.: *amémptōs* (274), unblamably.

Syn.: *ámōmos* (299), unblemished, unspotted. The *ámōmos*, the unblemished, may be *ámemptos*, unblamed; *áspilos* (784), without spot; *anégklētos* (410), legally irreproachable; *anepílēptos* (423), irreprehensible, one who cannot be caught and accused; *anaítios* (338), guiltless, blameless; *ádolos* (97), without guile; *ákakos* (172), without being bad in oneself; *akéraios* (185), without foreign mixture, sincere, harmless; *haploús* (573), single, without duplicity; *amṓmētos* (298), without blemish.

Ant.: *énochos* (1777), liable to a charge or action at law or in court; *hupódikos* (5267), liable to trial; *hamartōlós* (268), sinner.

274. ἀμέμπτως *amémptōs*; adv. from *ámemptos* (273) blameless. Blamelessly, faultlessly (1 Thess 2:10; 5:23).

275. ἀμέριμνος *amérimnos*; gen. *amerímnou*, masc.-fem., neut. *amérimnon*, adj. from the priv. *a* (1), without, and *mérimna* (3308), care or anxiety. Secure. Used in Matt 28:14 indicating that the soldiers who were told to lie in regard to the resurrection of the body of Christ, claiming that it was stolen, should not worry or be anxious about being caught in their falsehood. In 1 Cor 7:32, Paul argues about unselfish anxiety that pertains to a married person for his family. The general principle in the NT regarding the word *mérimna*, anxiety, is that when it is worry about self or the common material things of life, it is sinful anxiety (Matt 6:25–34), but when it is reasonable concern about others, such as one's family, it is not anxiety but healthy concern (1 Cor 7:32). Such healthy concern is the responsibility of every married person for his family. The use of the verb *merimnáō* (3309), meaning to care for with reasonable concern, is illustrated in the use of the word in 1 Cor 12:25 in regard to the care and concern which one member of the body of Christ ought to demonstrate for fellow members.

Syn.: *hēsúchios* (2272), tranquil; *hḗremos* (2263), quiet, undisturbed; *eirēnikós* (1516), peaceful; *makários* (3107), blessed.

Ant.: *émphobos* (1719), alarmed, afraid; *éntromos* (1790), terrified.

276. ἀμετάθετος *ametáthetos*; gen. *ametathétou*, masc.-fem., neut. *ametátheton*, adj. from the priv. *a* (1), without, and *metatíthēmi* (3346), to change condition or place, transfer. Immovable, immutable, sure, unchangeable. Spoken of God's constitutional will (*boulē* [1012]) in Heb 6:17. See the verb *boúlomai* (1014) as contrasted with *thélō* (2309), to will, indicating the power to execute in addition to the determination in oneself, and the noun *thélēma* (2307), executive will. Also used in Heb 6:18, where the author speaks about two immutable things, one being God's promise and the other His oath in regard to the absolute truthfulness of His word.

Syn.: *ametakínetos* (277), immovable; *asáleutos* (761), immovable; *stereós*

(4731), stable; *aklinḗs* (186), not leaning, firm; *hedraíos* (1476), firm, steadfast.

Ant.: *próskairos* (4340), temporal.

277. ἀμετακίνητος *ametakínētos*; gen. *ametakinḗtou*, masc.-fem., neut. *ametakínēton*, adj. from the priv. *a* (1), without, and *metakinéō* (3334) to move away. Unmovable, firm (1 Cor 15:58).

Syn.: *asáleutos* (761), immovable; *bébaios* (949), firm, secure; *hedraíos* (1476), steadfast; *stereós* (4731), firm; *ametáthetos* (276), immovable.

278. ἀμεταμέλητος *ametamélētos*; gen. *ametamelḗtou*, masc.-fem., neut. *ametamélēton*, adj. from the priv. *a* (1), without, and *metamélomai* (3338), to change one's mind. Without repentance. Used in regard to the gifts and calling of God unto salvation (Rom 11:29). The translation of *ametamélētos* "without repentance" is very inadequate. It would have been better translated "without regret" (a.t.). What the apostle is saying here is that when God has given gifts to men and has extended His salvation to them, He never regrets the extension of His grace or changes His mind as having made a mistake because of the behavior of the ones that He saved and gifted. Salvation should never be considered as merely man's decision to follow Christ, but also God's acceptance of the genuineness of that decision and the birth and existence of faith.

The second time that this word is used is in 2 Cor 7:10: "For godly sorrow worketh repentance to salvation not to be repented of: but the sorrow of the world worketh death." Here *ametamélēton* is used as a verbal adj., but in its translated form, it is not clear as to whether it is related to the repentance or to the salvation spoken about. We must exclude its relation to salvation, for how can a person who is saved ever look at the results of his salvation and regret it? This adj. must therefore be connected with repentance; thus we have the adj. *ametamélēton* and the noun *metánoia* (3341), repentance.

Metánoia is true repentance, changing of one's mind and asking God to change his heart that he may sin no more. *Metaméleia*, the noun derived from *metaméllomai* (3338), means to regret the results of one's decision and action. A thief may regret having stolen because he was caught and punished. However, if the thief is convicted in his heart that stealing is wrong and sinful, he will repent of his sin, not because he was caught, but because of his conviction that sin is contrary to God's will and his own good. Thus he is contrite and asks God to take away the guilt of his sin and to make him a righteous person, one who hates stealing and all other sin. What Paul is therefore speaking about here is unregrettable repentance. No one would regret his repentance because of the consequence of that repentance which is salvation. The adj. *ametaméleton* is placed after *sotería* (4991), salvation, because the whole phrase, "repentance unto salvation" must be taken together. "Unto salvation" qualifies the kind of repentance, and *ametaméleton*, unregrettable, qualifies the repentance unto salvation. It is not to be regretted because it has led unto salvation (Num 23:19; 1 Sam 15:29).

Syn.: *ametanóetos* (279), impenitent, unrepentant.

279. ἀμετανόητος *ametanóetos*; gen. *ametanoétou*, masc.-fem., neut. *ametanóeton*, adj. from the priv. *a* (1), without, and *metanoéo* (3340), to repent or change one's mind. Unrepenting, impenitent (Rom 2:5).

Syn.: *ametaméletos* (278), not to be concerned after an act has been committed (Rom 11:29; 2 Cor 7:10).

280. ἄμετρος *ámetros*; gen. *amétrou*, masc.-fem., neut. *ámetron*, adj. from the priv. *a* (1), without, and *métron* (3358), measure. Without measure (only in 2 Cor 10:13, 15). Paul states to the Corinthians among whom there had arisen some self-proclaimed "super" apostles (2 Cor 11:5; 12:11) who believed that their achievements were one hundred percent of what God expected them to do, that he was not behind them. Paul argues, however, that although they accomplished what they themselves thought was their duty to do, yet what needed to be done was immeasurable, *ámetron*. How could one boast of what he has done when he knows that what needs to be done is without measure? Our achievements in the work of the Lord seem so small and inconsequential when they are compared to what needs to be done, which is indeed without the possibility of measuring. When it comes to the immeasurable, unaccomplished task, no one has a right to boast.

Syn.: *aríthmetos* (382), innumerable.

281. ἀμήν *amén*; transliterated from the Hebr. *'ámen* (543, OT). Amen, to be firm, steady, truthworthy. Rendered also as "truth" (Isa 65:16, "God of amen"; Jer 11:5, "So be it"). The Gr. word is a transliteration of the Hebr. and is rendered "verily" in the frequently recurring formula, "Verily, verily, I say unto you."

(I) In the OT used often at the end of a sentence as an adv. meaning truly, surely, certainly. It thus confirms the preceding words and invokes their fulfillment: "so be it," equivalent to the Gr. *génoito*, the 2d aor. opt. of *gínomai* (1096), to be, to become.

(II) Used also in oaths or imprecations being equivalent to a binding promise (Neh 5:13; Deut 27:15–26, in the Sept. rendered *génoito*). A response of praise by the people when listening to a choir (Ps 41:13, 14; 72:19; 89:52 [cf. 1 Chr 16:36; Neh 8:6; Ps 106:48]).

(III) In the Sept., *génoito* is used also by individuals as an imprecation (Num 5:22) or in response to a command (1 Kgs 1:36). More rarely in the OT, it stands at the beginning of a sentence for the sake of emphasis, i.e., assuredly, verily, in truth; equivalent to *alethós* ([230] Sept.: Josh 7:20).

(IV) In the NT, it indicates affirmation, in truth, verily, it is so (Matt 5:18, 26; 6:2 [cf. 2 Cor 1:20]). Equivalent to *alēthôs* (230), truly, verily (cf. Matt 16:28; Luke 9:27).

(V) In the entire NT, only the Lord Jesus uses *amén* at the beginning of a sentence as a word of affirmation. Throughout the Gospel of John, the Lord uses the word *amén*, doubled in John 1:51, "Amen, amen, I say unto you," or "Verily, verily, I say unto you," which could be rendered, "I who am the Amen [Truth itself] tell you as a most certain and infallible truth" (a.t.). See also Matt 6:5, 16; 8:10; 10:15, 23, 42; 11:11; 13:17; 17:20; 18:3, 13, 18; 19:23, 28; 21:21, 31; 23:36; 24:2, 34, 47; 25:12, 40, 45; 26:13, 21, 34; 28:20; Mark 3:28; 6:11; 8:12; 9:1, 41; 10:15, 29; 11:23; 12:43; 13:30; 14:9, 18, 25, 30; 16:20; Luke 4:24; 12:37; 13:35; 18:17, 29; 21:32; 23:43; 24:53; John 3:3, 5, 11; 5:19, 24, 25; 6:26, 32, 47, 53; 8:34, 51, 58; 10:1, 7; 12:24; 13:16, 20, 21, 38; 14:12; 16:20, 23; 21:18, 25; Rom 16:24; 1 Cor 16:24; Gal 1:5; 6:18; Eph 3:21; 6:24; Phil 4:20, 23; Col 4:18; 1 Thess 5:28; 2 Thess 3:18; 1 Tim 6:16; 2 Tim 4:18; Phile 1: 25; Heb 13:21, 25; 1 Pet 4:11; 5:11; 2 Pet 3:18; Jude 1:25; Rev 1:6; 5:14; 7:12; 19:4; 22:20. Each of the four gospels ends with *amén*.

(VI) It also means consent or desire, so be it, and as such it concludes prayers (Matt 6:13; Rom 15:33; 2 Cor 13:14). It expresses thanksgiving (Rom 11:36; 16:27 [cf. 1 Cor 14:16]); used to express both affirmation and thanksgiving (Rom 1:25; 9:5); used both for affirmation and supplication (Rev 1:7; 22:21); as a noun referring to the Lord Jesus with the implication of His faithfulness and true witness (Rev 3:14).

Syn.: *génoito*, let it be, 2d aor. opt. of *gínomai* (1096), to be, become; *naí* (3483), yea, verily; the particle *mén* (3303), indeed; and in Acts 26:9, combined with *oún* (3767), therefore, meaning yea.

Ant.: *mḗ génoito* (*mḗ* [3361], not; *génoito* [2d aor. opt. of *gínomai* {1096},

to be], become), let it not be, "God forbid"; *mḗpote* (3379), not ever; *mḗpō* (3380), not yet; and the more absolute *oudépote* (3763) and *oudépō* (3764), never.

282. ἀμήτωρ amétōr; gen. *amétoros*, masc.-fem., adj. from the priv. *a* (1), without, and *métēr* (3384), mother. Without the record of a mother. This is predicated of the king-priest Melchizedek, "a priest forever after the order of Melchizedek" (Ps 110:4). The background of this acclamation is provided by David's conquest of Jerusalem in 1000 B.C., by virtue of which David and his house became heirs to Melchizedek's dynasty of priest-kings. The king so acclaimed was identified by the Lord Jesus and His contemporaries as the Davidic Messiah (Mark 12:35ff.). If Jesus is the Davidic Messiah, He must be the "priest forever after the order of Melchizedek."

This is developed in the Epistle to the Hebrews with our Lord's heavenly priesthood presented on the basis of Ps 110:4, expounded in the light of Gen 14:18ff., where Melchizedek appears and disappears suddenly. Nothing is said about his birth or death, ancestry or descent, which declares his superiority to Abraham and, by implication, to the Aaronic priesthood descended from Abraham. The superiority of Christ in His new order to the Levitical order of OT times is thus established (Heb 5:6–11; 6:20—7:28). Of Melchizedek, it is said in Heb 7:3 that he was "without father [*apátōr* (540)], without mother (*amétōr*), without descent." This does not mean that Melchizedek did not have a mother or a father, but that there was no record of any of his ancestors. Yet in spite of the lack of his genealogy, he was a priest: "one who has been made like the Son of God" (a.t.). It is to be noted that what is translated "has been made like" is the Gr. part. *aphōmoiōménos* (871) in the perf. tense which indicates that not only was he made like the Son of God, but that he continues to be so. This does not imply in any way that Jesus

Christ did not have a mother as the God-Man incarnate. It refers rather to who He was, the eternal King-Priest, who did not depend on His human genealogy, especially as far as His priesthood was concerned. The genealogies of Jesus, that of His legal father (in Matthew) and of His physical mother (in Luke), extend back to the royal family of David. Before that, the legal line extends to Abraham and the physical line to Adam, and nowhere are there any priestly ancestors. His tribe is that of Judah and not of Levi. Melchizedek is presented as a type of Christ, the King-Priest, who stands alone and unique in His priesthood and is absolutely distinct from the long Aaronitic succession of priests.

283. ἀμίαντος *amíantos*; gen. *amiántou*, masc.-fem., neut. *amíanton*, adj. from the priv. *a* (1), not or without, and *miaínō* (3392), to defile. That which has nothing in it that defiles, unpolluted, unstained, unsoiled, undefiled by sin (Heb 7:26); of marriage (Heb 13:4), chaste; of the worship of God (James 1:27), pure, sincere; of the heavenly inheritance (1 Pet 1:4), inviolate.

Syn.: *hagnós* (53), pure from defilement; *katharós* (2513), cleansed; *eilikrinḗs* (1506), sincere, unalloyed; *hágios* (40), holy as being free from admixture of evil; *hósios* (3741), one who observes duties toward God, Godlike; *tímios* (5093), honorable; *hierós* (2413), sacred, outwardly associated with God.

Ant.: *koinós* (2839), common with the idea of coming in contact with everything, defiled in a ceremonial sense; *akáthartos* (169), unclean, impure; *anósios* (462), unholy, profane; *asebḗs* (765), impious, ungodly; *bébēlos* (952), wicked, profane; *rhuparós* (4508), dirty, vile; *theostugḗs* (2319), impious, hater of God.

284. Ἀμιναδάβ *Aminadáb*; proper noun, transliterated from the Hebr. ʿAmmīnādāb (5992, OT). Aminadab, an ancestor of our Lord (Matt 1:4; Luke 3:33).

285. ἄμμος *ámmos*; gen. *ámmou*, fem. noun. Sand (Rev 20:8; Sept.: Gen 22:17; Ex 2:12; Isa 10:22). Used also to convey the idea of weight (Sept.: Job 6:3) and instability (Matt 7:26). A somewhat obscure illusion (Deut 33:19) speaks of "treasures hid in the sand," perhaps a reference to the manufacture of glass from sand. In the NT, sand indicates a large quantity because it is usually collected together and cannot be counted (Rom 9:27; Heb 11:12; Rev 13:1).

286. ἀμνός *amnós*; gen. *amnoú*, masc. noun. Lamb for sacrifice. After John 1:29, 36, "Behold the Lamb of God" (*amnós* and not *arníon*, [721]), it became usual to designate Christ as *amnós*. In later Gr., the term *arnós* or *arníon* was adopted through-out the Book of the Revelation, where it is never *amnós* but always *arníon*. In fact, *amnós* is found only in John 1:29, 36; Acts 8:32; 1 Pet 1:19; Sept.: Ex 12:5, *arnós* is used for the Paschal Lamb; cf. Lev 14:10ff.; Num 6:12; Ex 29:38ff., the expression *ho amnós*, the lamb, *toú Theoú*, of God, means the lamb provided by God (see Gen 22:8). The Lord Jesus is called the *Amnós* of God because He sacrificed Himself at the time of the Passover (see John 2:13; 1 Cor 5:7). His deliverance of sinners is likened to the deliverance of Israel out of Egypt. Thus John the Baptist recognized in Jesus Christ the One Who was to bring deliverance in that day. The lamb during the Exodus was the means of sparing the people, and on account of it, destruction passed them by. In like manner, Jesus is now the means of sparing those who are willing to apply His blood in order that the judgment of God may bypass them. *Amnós* designates more often the sacrifice of the Lamb (1 Pet 1:19), referring to the Paschal Lamb or a lamb given up to death in the service of God.

A sheep is *próbaton* (4263) and a young goat is *ériphos* (2056) while its diminutive is *eríphion* (2065), a young kid.

287. ἀμοιβή *amoibé*; gen. *amoibés*, fem. noun from *ameíbō* (n.f.), to change. Change, exchange. In 1 Tim 5:4, recompense. In the KJV, translated "requite," which in Eng. has an evil connotation. In the NT, however, it is used in the positive sense of returning the good which children and grandchildren have received in childhood from their parents.

Syn.: *misthós* (3408), reward, wages; *opsṓnion* (3800), soldier's pay, wages; *antapódoma* (468), recompense; *antapódosis* (469), the act of compensating; *antimisthía* (489), a commensurate reward; *misthapodosía* (3405), a recompense; *épainos* (1868), praise.

Ant.: *timōría* (5098), vindication, penalty; *kólasis* (2851), punishment; *krísis* (2920), judgment; *kríma* (2915), condemnation; *katákrima* (2631), an adverse verdict; *katákrisis* (2633), the act of condemnation.

288. ἄμπελος *ámpelos*; gen. *ámpelou*, fem. noun. A vine (Matt 26:29; Mark 14:25; Luke 22:18; James 3:12). Metaphorically, Jesus calls Himself the true vine (John 15:1, 4, 5) since a spreading and fruitful vine is the emblem of prosperity and blessings (cf. Ezek 17:6; 19:10; Ps 80:8–10; 128:3). In Rev 14:19, "the vine of the earth" denotes the prosperous enemies of the Messiah who are to be cut off as grapes are gathered and cast into the winepress (cf. Isa 63:2, 3; Lam 1:15). *Ámpelos* may be derived from a Hebr. word meaning to send forth shoots as the vine does.

Deriv.: *ampelourgós* (289), a vine-dresser; *ampelṓn* (290), a vineyard.

289. ἀμπελουργός *ampelourgós*; gen. *ampelourgoú*, mas., fem. noun from *ámpelos* (288), vine, and *érgon* (2041), work. A vine-dresser, one who tends a vineyard (Luke 13:7; Sept.: 2 Chr 26:10; Isa 61:5).

290. ἀμπελών *ampelṓn*; gen. *ampelṓnos*, masc. noun from *ámpelos* (288), a vine. A vineyard, a place planted with vines (Matt 20:1, 2, 4, 7, 8). Figuratively, the vineyard of God's Church (Matt 21:28, 33, 39–41; Mark 12:1, 2, 9; Luke 13:6; 20:9, 10, 13, 15, 16; 1 Cor 9:7; Sept.: Gen 9:20; in Isa 5:1–7 *ámpelos*).

291. Ἀμπλίας *Amplías*; gen. *Amplíou*, masc. proper noun. Amplias, a friend of Paul whom he affectionately greets in Rom 16:8. The name is found in inscriptions of Caesar's household (cf. Phil 4:22). It was a common name, sometimes called Ampliatus.

292. ἀμύνω *amúnō*; fut. *amunṓ*. To defend. In the Class. Gr., *amúnomai* (this form only is found in the NT), the mid. of *amúnō*, meant to avert from oneself, resist, repel, to defend oneself (Acts 7:24, to aid, assist, defend; Sept.: Isa 59:16, to deliver).

Syn.: *antilambánomai* (482), to help; *sullambánomai* (4815), to assist; *sunantilambánomai* (4878), to help; *boēthéō* (997), to come to the aid of; *sumbállō* (4820), to contribute in benefiting others; *sunupourgéō* (4943), to serve with anyone as an underworker; *parístēmi* (3936), to stand by to help; *agōnízomai* (75), to struggle.

Ant.: *adikéō* (91), to hurt, to wrong; *bláptō* (984), to injure, damage; *kakóō* (2559), to harm; *paradídōmi* (3860), to give up or over; *kámptō* (2578), to bend, bow; *hupochōréō* (5298), to withdraw; *hupeíkō* (5226), to surrender; *paraitéomai* (3868), to beg off; *egkataleípō* (1459), to forsake; *hupotássomai* (5293), to submit.

293. ἀμφίβληστρον *amphíblēstron*; gen. *amphiblḗstrou*, neut. noun from *amphibállō* (n.f.), to throw around, which is from the prefix *amphí*, round about, and *bállō* (906), to throw. A casting net. When skillfully thrown from over the shoulder by one standing on the shore or in a boat, it spreads out into a circle (*amphibállō*) as it falls upon the water, sinking swiftly by the weight of the leads attached to it and enclosing whatever is below it (Matt 4:18; Mark 1:16; Sept.: Ps 141:10; Eccl 9:12; Hab 1:15–17).

Syn.: *díktuon* (1350), a general term for net; *sagénē* (4522), a dragnet; *ágkistron* (44), a hook.

294. ἀμφιέννυμι *amphiénnumi*, fut. *amphiésō*, from the prefix *amphí*, round about, and *énnumi* (n.f.), to invest. To enrobe, wrap clothes around oneself (Matt 6:30; 11:8; Luke 7:25; 12:28). *Amphí* does not occur separately but with other words making comp. such as *amphíblēstron* (293), a net thrown around; *Amphípolis* (295), a city in Macedonia surrounded by a river.

Syn.: *endúō* (1746), to sink into a garment, clothe; *peribállō* (4016), to throw all around.

Ant.: *apobállō* (577), to put off; *apekdúō* (554), to put off; *ekdúō* (1562), to unclothe.

295. Ἀμφίπολις *Amphípolis*; gen. *Amphipóleōs*, fem. proper noun. Amphipolis, an important strategic and commercial center at the north of the Aegean, situated on the river Strymon, about three miles inland. This important Macedonian city commanded the entrance to a pass leading through the mountains into the great Macedonian plains. It was almost encircled by the river, as its name *amphí*, about or around, and *pólis* (4172), a city, indicates. The Romans made it a free city and the capital of the first of four districts into which they divided Macedonia. It lay on the Via Egnatia, which connected Dyrrachium with the Hellespont. From Philippi, it was thirty-two miles to the southwest. It was on the way from Philippi to Thessalonica, and apparently the Apostle Paul and his fellow travelers remained in *Amphípolis* overnight, the next day going on to Apollonia (Acts 17:1). It belongs to Greece and the village near it is called Neochori, new village.

296. ἄμφοδον *ámphodon*; gen. *amphódou*, neut. noun from *ámphō* (n.f.), both, the two, and *hodós* (3598), a way. A

place where two roads meet (Sept.: Jer 17:27). Used in the neut. in Mark 11:4.

297. ἀμφότερος *amphóteros*; fem. *amphotéra*, neut. *amphóteron*, from *ámphō* (n.f.), both, the two. Each of two. In the pl. *amphóteroi*, fem. *amphóterai*, neut. *amphótera*. Both. Spoken only of two (Matt 9:17; 13:30; 15:14; Luke 1:6, 7; 5:7, 38; 6:39; 7:42; Acts 8:38; Eph 2:14, 16, 18). In Acts 23:8, *tá amphótera*, both, meaning the resurrection and the existence of angels and spirits (Sept: Gen 21:27; Ex 12:11).

Syn.: *zeúgos* (2201), pair, yoke.

Ant.: *hékastos* (1538), each one; *mónos* (3441), alone, as a unit; *pás* (3956), each of a group; *heís* (1520), one.

298. ἀμώμητος *amómētos*; gen. *amómētou*, masc.-fem., neut. *amómēton*, adj. from *a* (1), without, and *mōmáomai* (3469), to censure, blame. Irreproachable, one who cannot be blamed because he is *ámōmos* (299), without blame (Phil 2:15; 2 Pet 3:14).

Amómētos occurs in Phil 2:15 to describe the nature of the children of God. In the expression, "the sons of God, without rebuke," the word "sons" should have been translated "children" (*tékna* [5043]), referring to the fact of the new birth and not of the development of the child of God into being a son (*huiós* [5207]). Phil 2:15 beautifully delineates the duty of the believer to work out the salvation which he has been given by God. Earlier, in Phil 2:13, 14, Paul reminds us that unless God works in us, we cannot show any outward manifestation of His salvation, then tells us how we should externalize our salvation. And then verse fifteen says: "That ye may be blameless [*ámemptoi* (273)] and harmless [*akéraioi* (185)], the sons [children] of God, without rebuke [*amómēta*]." The pl. adj. *amómēta* tells us what kind of children of God we are. It does not use the syn. *ámōma* (299), meaning without the actuality of a blemish or blame. This is what we call a verbal adj. with the suffix *-tos* added to the adj. *amōmos*, making it *amómētos*. A characteristic of such a verbal adj. is that it expresses possibility. In this case, because of the preceding neg. (*amómētos*), it expresses the impossibility of *mómos*, which means reproach or blame in a moral sense.

An obedient child of God for whom God has bought his salvation externalizes His salvation. Those around him will recognize that he has become a compliant child of God and as such it is impossible to bring upon him a reproach for moral blame which will cancel out his belonging to God's family as His child (*téknon*). The world should not find any possibility of blaming God's work in us.

The word *amómētos* is clearly used in 2 Pet 3:14: "be diligent that ye may be found of Him in peace, without spot, and blameless [*amómētoi*]." Here Peter says it should be our utmost concern that we be found not only without the actuality of blame, but also without even the possibility of moral blame.

Syn.: *amíantos* (283), undefiled; *ámōmos* (299), spotless, without blemish; *dókimos* (1384), approved, acceptable; *áxios* (514), worthy; *akatákritos* (178), uncondemned; *ámemptos* (273), unblamable; *anaítios* (338), guiltless; *anepíleptos* (423), irreproachable; *anégklētos* (410), not liable to be brought to law or court; *áspilos* (784), unspotted, unstained.

Ant.: *adókimos* (96), rejected, reprobate, castaway; *potapós* (4217), not good for much; *anáxios* (370), unworthy; *ásēmos* (767), mean; *koinós* (2839), common, defiled; *eleeinós* (1652), miserable.

299. ἄμωμος *ámōmos*; gen. *amómou*, masc.-fem., neut. *ámōmon*, adj. from the priv. *a* (1), without, and *mómos* (3470), spot, blemish. Spotless, without blemish. In Class. Gr., used as a technical word to designate the absence of something amiss in a sacrifice or something which would render it unworthy to be offered (Sept.: Ex 29:1; Num 6:14; Ezek 43:22). Of Christ as a lamb; used in conjunction with *áspilos* (784), without spot,

unspotted (1 Pet 1:19; see Lev 1:10; 22:19–22; Heb 9:14). In this case, *ámōmos* would be used metaphorically indicating the absence of internal blemish, and *áspilos*, that of external spot. Metaphorically (Eph 1:4; 5:27; Col 1:22; Heb 9:14; Jude 1:24; Rev 14:5). Used in Col 1:22 with *anégklētos* (410), legally unaccused, and Eph 1:4 and 5:27 with *hágios* (40), holy. Therefore, *ámōmos* is the unblemished (cf. *ámemptos* [273], unblamed).

Ámōmos occurs in Eph 1:4 speaking of the ones that God had chosen before the foundation of the world to be without blemish, deserved or undeserved. The word here has the same meaning as *katákrima* (2631), condemnation, as in Rom 8:1.

In Eph 5:27, Paul speaks of the church in its glorification being presented as holy and without blemish (*ámōmos*). The Church is the aggregate of the believers and therefore there is a connection between Eph 1:4 and 5:27. The same is true in the use of the word in Col 1:22.

In Heb 9:14, it refers to Jesus Christ as being without spot in His sacrifice for our sins. Actually, it would have been better to translate this "without blame, without any deficiency whatsoever" (a.t.). This speaks of the uniqueness of Jesus Christ's sinlessness as man and the exclusion of anyone else's sinlessness.

1 Pet 1:19 speaks of the blood of Christ as *ámōmon*, without blemish, without any deficiency. No one could ever say that it was not what God expected it to be.

In Jude 1:24, we are told of the power of God to keep us without the actuality of blemish that would hinder us from appearing in the presence of His glory eternally. Rev 14:5 speaks of the believers of the tribulation as being without blemish or reproach in spite of all the judgment of God around them during the tribulation.

Christ was *ámōmos* in that there was no spot or blemish in Him, and He could say, "Which of you convinceth me of sin?" (John 8:46). But strictly, He was not *ámemptos*, unblamed. This adj. is never attributed to Him in the NT seeing that He endured the contradiction of sinners against Himself who slandered Him and laid to His charge things that He knew not (*anégklētos* [410]) without any legal charge or accusation brought against Him. While *ámōmos* means without the presence of a blemish, blame, or spot, *amṓmētos* (298) means without the possibility of *mṓmos*, blame or blemish. Here we must note that, in Class. Gr., *mṓmos* was a censure either derived from the attitude of the subject being censorious or the deficiency found in the object.

Syn.: *ámemptos* (273), unblamable, related to *mémphomai* (3201), to blame, find fault; *anaítios* (338), guiltless; *anepílēptos* (423), irreproachable; *anégklētos* (410), not chargeable in court; *díkaios* (1342), just; *euthús* (2117), straight; *orthós* (3717), straight, upright; *akatákritos* (178), uncondemned; *anepaíschuntos* (422), irreprehensible.

Ant.: *ádikos* (94), unrighteous; *ánomos* (459), lawless, transgressor; *potapós* (4217), what possible sort; *anáxios* (370), unworthy; *koinós* (2839), common, unclean; *eleeinós* (1652), miserable.

300. Ἀμών *Amṓn*; masc. proper noun transliterated from the Hebr. *'Āmōn* (526, OT). Amon, a son of Manasseh and king of Judah about 640 B.C. See 2 Kgs 21:18ff.; 2 Chr 33:20ff. Mentioned in the Lord's genealogy in Matt 1:10.

301. Ἀμώς *Amṓs*; masc. proper noun transliterated from the Hebr. *'Āmōts* (531, OT). Amos, meaning strong. One of the progenitors of Jesus (Luke 3:25).

302. ἄν *án*; particle used with the opt., subjunctive, and indic. moods; sometimes properly rendered by "perhaps"; more commonly not expressed in Eng. by any corresponding particle, but only giving to a proposition or sentence a stamp of uncertainty and mere possibility, and indicating a dependence on circumstances. In this way it serves to modify or strengthen the intrinsic force of the opt.

and subjunctive while it can also, similarly, affect the meaning of the indic. (the pres. and perf. excepted) and other verbal forms. This particle stands after one or more words in a clause and is thus distinguished from *án* for *eán* (1437), if. (See III for the contrast of the two particles, *án* and *eán*). In the NT, the use of *án* is generally the same as that of Class. Gr. writers, but sometimes not.

(I) As conformed to Class. Gr. usage:

(A) With the opt., in an independent clause, it indicates that the supposition or possibility expressed by the simple opt., under the circumstances implied by *án*, will be realized. **(1)** In vows, wishes as in Acts 26:29, meaning I could pray to God, and under the circumstances do pray to Him. **(2)** In interrogations, direct or indirect, where the thing inquired about is possible, or certain, but the inquirer is uncertain when or how it is to take place. Luke 1:62, "how he might wish him to be called" (a.t.), i.e., since he was to have a name, what that name should be. See also Luke 9:46; John 13:24; Acts 2:12; 5:24; 17:18; 21:33.

(B) With the subjunctive in relative clauses and connected with relative words which are thus rendered more general and indicate mere possibility, the Class. Gr. writers use *án* in contrast to sacred writers who use *eán*. **(1)** With relative pron. or particles where *án* implies some condition or uncertainty whether or where the thing will take place, equivalent to ever, soever. Thus in **(a)** *Hós án* (*hós* [3739], he who, a relative pron.), whoever, whosoever (Matt 5:21, 31, 32; 10:11; 12:32; Mark 3:29; John 1:33; Sept.: Dan 3:5, 6). **(b)** *Hóstis án* (*hóstis* [3748], which) whosoever (Matt 10:33; Luke 10:35; John 2:5; Acts 3:23). **(c)** *Hósos án* (*hósos* [3745], as much, great, long), whosoever (Matt 7:12; 21:22; Mark 3:28; John 11:22; Acts 2:39). **(d)** *Hópou án* (*hópou* [3699], where, at whichever spot), wheresoever (Mark 9:18; 14:9; Luke 9:57; Rev 14:4). **(e)** *Hós án* (*hós* [5613], as, in which manner) as, in whatever manner (1 Thess 2:7). **(2)** With particles of time, conj.: **(a)** *Héōs án* (*héōs*

[2193], until), until, with the time being indefinite (Matt 2:13; 5:18, 26; 10:11, 23; Mark 6:10; Luke 20:43; Acts 2:35). In 1 Cor 11:26; 15:25, *áchris hoú án* (*áchris* [891], until, with the idea of a termination; *hoú* [the gen. of *hós* {3739, a}, the masc. relative pron., with *chrónou* [the gen. of *chrónos* {5550}, time implied]), meaning until such time as. **(b)** *Hēníka án* (*hēníka* [2259], at which time), whenever, as soon as, indefinite (2 Cor 3:16; Sept.: Deut 7:12). **(c)** *Hṓs án* (*hṓs* [5613], as), when, as soon as, indefinite (1 Cor 11:34, meaning, when I shall come, i.e., but I do not know when this will be; Phil 2:23). **(d)** *Hosákis án* (*hosákis* [3740], as many times as), so often as, however often, as often or as many times as (1 Cor 11:25 which does not indicate frequency, but that whenever you drink the cup, you should remember that this is the cup of the NT in Christ's blood. Therefore do not do it meaninglessly). **(3)** With the illative (introducing an inference) particle *hópōs* (3704), that, in order that; *hópōs án*, that at some time or other, that sooner or later (Luke 2:35; Acts 3:19; 15:17; Rom 3:4; Sept.: Ps 51:4).

(C) With the indic. in the historical tenses (but not in the primary ones), *án* is used in the apodosis (the result) of a conditional sentence in which *ei* ([1487], if) precedes and indicates that the thing in question would have taken place, if that contingency which is the subject of the protasis (the proposition) had also taken place; but that in fact neither the one nor the other has taken place. In Matt 11:21, it means that if these miracles had been done in Tyre, they would have repented; but the miracles were not done, and they did not repent (see also Luke 10:13; John 4:10; 9:41; Heb 4:8; John 8:42, where the meaning is, if God were your Father, you would love me; however, neither is true [similarly in Matt 11:23; 12:7; 23:30; 24:22, 43; Mark 13:20; John 11:21; Rom 9:29; 1 Cor 2:8; 11:31; Gal 1:10; 1 John 2:19]).

(II) The following are departures from Class. Gr. usage:

(A) When, in relative clauses, a relative pron. with *án* is followed by the indic., Class. Gr. writers employ the subjunctive or opt. This occurs in the NT when a thing is spoken of as actually taking place, not at a definite time or in a definite manner, but as often as opportunity arises. It is thus found only with a preterite, a verb tense that indicates action in the past without reference to duration, continuance, or repetition. Used in Mark 6:56, meaning, "as many as" or "however many"; Acts 2:45; 4:35; 1 Cor 12:2, meaning led away to idol worship, just as he happened to be led, i.e., I do not say by whom or how; see also Sept.: Gen 2:19; Lev 5:3. Once with the pres. indic. in Mark 11:24, where some MSS have the indic. verb *aiteísthe* in the subjunctive (*aitḗsthe*, from *aitéomai* [154], to ask, beg). See also Luke 8:18; 10:8.

(B) As an adv. or in a false construction, meaning perhaps, possibly. Used once before an inf. (2 Cor 10:9, "as if I would terrify you"); also once without any mood (1 Cor 7:5, meaning "unless perhaps by mutual consent" [a.t.]).

(III) *'An* used as a conj., contrasted from *eán* (1437), if, and distinguished from the basic *án* as discussed above, by being put at the beginning of a proposition or clause (John 20:23).

303. ἀνά *aná*; prep. On, upon.

(I) In the NT, with the acc., it forms a periphrases (a longer phrasing in place of a possible shorter and plainer form of expression) for an adv.; e.g., *aná méros* ([3313], part), by turns, alternately (1 Cor 14:27); *aná méson* ([3319] followed by the gen.), in the midst of, through the midst of, between.

Spoken of place (Matt 13:25; Mark 7:31; Rev 7:17; Sept.: Isa 57:5; 2 Kgs 16:14).

Spoken of persons (1 Cor 6:5). In Matt 20:9, 10 *aná dēnárion* (*aná* [303], to each, *dēnárion* [1220], dinar), "to each a dinar" (a.t.).

(II) With numerical words it marks distribution (Mark 6:40; Luke 9:3, 14;

10:1; John 2:6; Rev 4:8; see Isa 6:2). In Rev 21:21, "each one of the gates" (a.t.).

(III) In composition with other words forming a comp.:

(A) *Aná* denotes up or upward, as *anabaínō* (305), I go up.

(B) Back or again, equal to the Eng. prefix re-, implying repetition, increase, intensity, as *anakainízō* (340), to renew; *anachōréō* (402), to depart; *anaginōskō* (314), to know again, to read.

304. ἀναβαθμός anabathmós; gen. *anabathmoú*, masc. from *anabaínō* (305), to come up. The act of ascending, the means of ascent, i.e., steps, stairs (Acts 21:35, 40, of the stairs leading from the fortress Antonia to the temple; Sept.: 1 Kgs 10:19, 20). It is also used in the titles of the Songs of Ascent or degrees (Sept.: Ps 120—134).

305. ἀναβαίνω anabaínō; fut. *anabḗsomai*, 2d aor. *anébēn*, 2d. aor. imper. *anábēthi* and *anába* (Rev 4:1); from *aná* (303), up, and *baínō* (n.f., see *apobaínō* [576]), to go. To go or come up, to ascend, cause to ascend from a lower to a higher place. Construed with *apó* (575), from, and *ek* (1537), out of, followed by the gen. of place, meaning whence, from where, and with *eis* (1519), to, *epí* (1909), upon, *prós* (4314), toward, followed by the acc. of place meaning whither, to which, or *hóde* (5602), here or hither (Rev 4:1).

(I) Spoken of persons, animals (Matt 5:1; Mark 3:13; Luke 5:19; Sept.: Gen 49:4). In Luke 19:4, it means to climb; in Mark 6:51 and Sept.: Jon 1:3, to enter into a boat, to embark; in John 10:1, climbing up or entering some other way; in Acts 8:31, to get up into a chariot; in Matt 3:16, from the water; Acts 8:39, out of the water, from the water, upon the land (see Acts 8:38). In another case, the phrase "coming out of the river" (a.t.) is used (Sept.: Gen 41:3, 18, 27). Spoken of fish (Matt 17:27, "the fish that first comes up," or "is brought up" [author's translations]); of those who go from a lower to a higher region of country, e.g., from Galilee or Caesarea to Judea (Luke 2:4; Acts 18:22) and especially to Jerusalem (Matt 20:17, 18; John 7:8, 10; 12:20; Sept.: 1 Kgs 12:27, 28; Ezra 2:1; 7:6, 7; Neh 7:6); of those who ascend into heaven or to the height, either to have communion with God or to dwell there (John 3:13; 6:62; 20:17; Rom 10:6; Eph 4:8–10; Rev 4:1; 11:12). Used in the phrase, "to go up into heaven," (Sept.: Deut 30:12; Ps 139:8 [cf. Job 38:19–38]; Prov 30:4; Isa 14:13, 14; Jer 51:53). Spoken of angels who are said to ascend and descend upon the Son of man (John 1:51; see Sept.: Gen 28:12, i.e., they minister continually to the Lord [cf. Matt 4:11; Mark 1:13]).

(II) Spoken also of inanimate things which are said to go up, ascend, rise, e.g., smoke (Rev 8:4; 9:2; 14:11; 19:3; Sept.: Ex 19:18; Isa 34:10); of plants, fruit, to spring up, grow (Matt 13:7; Mark 4:8, 32; Sept.: Isa 5:24; 32:13; 55:13); of a rumor (Acts 21:31, a word was brought up to the chief captain in the fortress Antonia); of thoughts, actions, which come up into one's mind, to spring up, arise in the heart (Luke 24:38); upon the heart (Acts 7:23; 1 Cor 2:9); prayers as a memorial (Acts 10:4). See also Isa 65:17; Jer 3:16; 32:35; 44:21.

Deriv.: *anabathmós* (304), the act of ascending; *prosanabaínō* (4320), to go up higher; *sunanabaínō* (4872), to come up with.

Syn.: *eisérchomai* (1525), to go in; *anatéllō* (393), to arise, spring up; *érchomai* (2064), to come or go; *exérchomai* (1831), to come out or go out; *epérchomai* (1904), to come or go upon; *prosérchomai* (4334), to come or go near to; *apérchomai* (565), to come away or from; *paragínomai* (3854), to arrive or to be present; *hḗkō* (2240), to come or be present; *aphiknéomai* (864), to arrive at a place; *enístēmi* (1764), to stand in or set in; *ephístēmi* (2186), to stand by or over; *katantáō* (2658), to come to; *phérō* (5342), to carry; *phthánō* (5348), to come sooner than expected, arrive, precede; *ekporeúomai* (1607), to depart, emanate; *prosporeúomai* (4365), to come near to; *proseggízō* (4331), to come near; *eisporeúomai* (1531), to go into; *eíseimi* (1524), to go into; *poreúomai* (4198), to go on one's way; *ágō* (71), to bring, lead; *hupágō* (5217), to go away or go slowly away, depart; *ápeimi* (548), to be away; *anachōréō* (402), to withdraw, depart; *éxeimi* (1826), to go out; *ápeimi* (549), to go away; *anérchomai* (424), to go up; *peripatéō* (4043), to walk; *phúō* (5453), to germinate, spring up, sprout; *blastánō* (985), to sprout; *hállomai* (242), to leap, spring, referring to water or figuratively to the Holy Spirit.

Ant.: *katabaínō* (2597), to come down.

306. ἀναβάλλω anabállō; fut. *anabalō̇* from *aná* (303), back, and *bállō* (906), to cast. To cast back, to put off, defer (Acts 24:22; Sept.: Ps 78:21).

Deriv.: *anabolē̇* (311), delay.

Syn.: *bradúnō* (1019), to delay; *husteréō* (5302), to come behind; *kathusteréō* (5302), to delay.

Ant.: *speúdō* (4692), to hasten; *biázō* (971), to force, be violent, seize; *grēgoréō* (1127), to be vigilant, watchful.

307. ἀναβιβάζω anabibázō; fut. *anabibásō*, from *aná* (303), up, and *bibázō* (n.f., see *embibázō* [1688]), to make, go up, to come, lift up. To draw up, to cause to ascend, mount, to drag to the shore or land (Matt 13:48; Sept.: Gen 37:28; Ex 3:17; Lam 2:10).

Syn.: *egeírō* (1453), to raise; *hupsóō* (5312), to lift; *epaírō* (1869), to raise up; *huperaíromai* (5229), to exalt self; *anaphérō* (399), to bring up; *anágō* (321), to lead or bring up to; *helkúō* (1670), to draw; *súrō* (4951), to pull, drag; *spáō* (4685), to draw or pull a sword from its sheath; *anaspáō* (385), to draw or pull up; *apospáō* (645), to draw away from; *antléō* (501), to draw water in any way; *exélkō* (1828), to draw away; *anatássomai* (392), to arrange in order, to draw up.

Ant.: *katágō* (2609), to lead down; *hupostéllō* (5288), to withdraw.

308. ἀναβλέπω anablépō; fut. *anablépsō*, from *aná* (303), up or again, and *blépō* (991), to see or look. To look up, see.

(I) To look up or upwards, to look upon (Matt 14:19; Mark 6:41; 7:34; Luke 9:16; 19:5; Acts 22:13); to look up, raise the eyes from the ground (Mark 8:24; Luke 21:1; Sept.: Gen 13:14; 18:2; Deut 4:19).

(II) To see again, receive sight again (Matt 11:5; 20:34; Mark 10:51, 52; Luke 7:22; 18:41–43; Acts 9:12, 17, 18; 22:13).

(III) To see or receive sight which one never had before (John 9:11, 15, 18, cf. John 9:1, 2; Sept.: Isa 42:18; 61:1).

(IV) To look again or attentively, examine (Mark 16:4).

Deriv.: *anáblepsis* (309), recovery of sight.

Ant.: *tuphlóō* (5186), to blind.

309. ἀνάβλεψις anáblepsis; gen. *anablépseōs*, from *anablépō* (308), to see again. Recovery of sight (Luke 4:18).

310. ἀναβοάω anaboáō; contracted, *anaboō̇*, fut. *anaboḗsō*, from *aná* (303), an emphatic, and *boáō* (994), to cry out. To cry out loud, exclaim (Matt 27:46; Mark 15:8; Luke 9:38; Sept.: Num 20:16; Isa 36:13; Ezek 11:13).

Syn.: *krázō* (2896), to cry out; *kraugázō* (2905), to shout; *anakrázō* (349), to cry out loudly; *phōnéō* (5455), to utter a loud sound, cry; *epiphōnéō* (2019), to shout.

Ant.: *phimóō* (5392), to keep silence, to muzzle, to be still or speechless; *sigáō* (4601), to be silent; *siōpáō* (4623), to keep silent.

311. ἀναβολή anabolḗ; gen. *anabolḗs*, from *anabállō* (306), to defer. Delay (Acts 25:17).

Syn.: *bradútēs* (1022), tardiness, slackness.

Ant.: *bía* (970), hurry; *spoudḗ* (4710), haste; *táchu* (5035), speed, suddenness.

312. ἀναγγέλλω *anaggéllō*; fut. *anaggelṓ*, aor. *anḗggeila*, 2d aor. pass. *anēggélēn*, from *aná* (303), on, upon, and *aggéllō* (n.f., see below), to tell, declare, which is from *ággelos* (32), messenger. To announce, make known, declare, tell of things done, events (Mark 5:14, 19; Acts 14:27; 15:4; 16:38; 2 Cor 7:7). To bring word, inform (John 5:15); of things fut., to show beforehand, foretell (John 16:13; Sept.: Isa 41:22, 23; 46:10); of the Christian doctrine, to declare, show forth, teach (John 4:25; 16:14, 15, 25; Acts 20:20, 27; Rom 15:21; 1 Pet 1:12; 1 John 1:5; Sept.: Deut 8:3; 26:3; Dan 2:9); of evil deeds, meaning to declare, confess (Acts 19:18; Sept.: Job 33:23; Ps 38:18; Isa 3:8)

Deriv. of *angéllō* (n.f.): *apaggéllō* (518), to announce; *diaggéllō* (1229), to declare; *exaggéllō* (1804), to publish, show forth; *epaggéllō* (1861), to proclaim; *kataggéllō* (2605), to declare plainly, *paraggéllō* (3853), charge, command.

Syn.: *diēgéomai* (1334), to relate in full; *ekdiēgéomai* (1555), to narrate in full; *exēgéomai* (1834), to make known, explain, declare; *dēlóō* (1213), to make plain; *phrázō* (5419), to explain, declare; *gnōrízō* (1107), to make known; *emphanízō* (1718), to declare plainly; *phaneróō* (5319), to manifest; *anatíthēmi* (394), to make known, to place before, declare to someone; *marturéō* (3140), to testify; *diaphēmízō* (1310), to spread abroad; *mēnúō* (3377), to disclose, make known; *légō* (3004), to tell; *laléō* (2980), to speak; *apophthéggomai* (669), to speak forth, give utterance; *prosphōnéō* (4377), to address, call to; *eréō* (2046), to speak; *dialégomai* (1256), to discuss, reason, speak; *chrēmatízō* (5537), to warn, instruct as if through an oracle; *apologéomai* (626), to make a defense; *eklaléō* (1583), to speak out; *diasaphéō* (1285), to make clear.

Ant.: *phimóō* (5392), to muzzle, put to silence; *sigáō* (4601), to be silent; *siōpáō* (4623), to keep silent; *krúptō* (2928), to hide; *apokrúptō* (613), to keep secret from; *sugkalúptō* (4780), to cover up; *egkrúptō* (1470), to hide in.

313. ἀναγεννάω *anagennáō*; fut. *anagennḗsō*, from *aná* (303), again, and *gennáō* (1080), to beget. To beget again, regenerate. In the pass. *anagennáomai*, to be begotten again, regenerated (1 Pet 1:3, 23). It is equivalent to being a child of God (Gal 3:26) or to be born of God (John 1:12, 13; 1 John 3:9) or to be born from above (*anóthen* [509], John 3:3), or becoming a qualitatively new (*kainós* [2537]) creation or creature (*ktísis* [2937]), as in 2 Cor 5:17. The subst. *anagénnēsis*, new birth, never occurs in the NT. However, *paliggenesía* (3824), restoration, becoming something new, is the closest to *anagénnēsis*, new birth. *Paliggenesía* comes from *pálin* (3825), once more, again, and *gínomai* (1096), to become.

Syn.: *apokuéō* (616), to give birth to, from *kuéō*, to be pregnant, used metaphorically of spiritual birth (James 1:18) and of death as the offspring of sin (James 1:15); *tíktō* (5088), to bring forth.

Ant.: *apothnḗskō* (599), to die.

314. ἀναγινώσκω *anaginṓskō*; fut. *anagnṓsomai*, 2d aor. *anégnōn*, perf. pass. *anégnōsmai*, aor. first pass. *anegnṓsthēn*, from *aná* (303), an emphatic, and *ginṓskō* (1097), to know. To perceive accurately. Later it came to mean to recognize. In Attic Gr., it usually meant to read and always so in the NT and the Sept. The consequential meaning is to know by reading (Matt 12:3, 5; 19:4; 21:16, 42; 22:31; 24:15; Mark 2:25; 12:10, 26; 13:14; Luke 6:3; 10:26; John 19:20; Acts 8:28, 30, 32; 15:31; 23:34; 2 Cor 1:13; Eph 3:4; Rev 1:3; 5:4; Sept.: Deut 17:19; 2 Kgs 5:7; Isa 29:11, 12). To read aloud before others (Luke 4:16; Acts 13:27; 15:21; 2 Cor 3:15; Col 4:16; 1 Thess 5:27; Sept.: Deut 31:11; 2 Kgs 22:11; Neh 13:1). Metaphorically in 2 Cor 3:2, "our letter . . . read of all men" (a.t.), i.e., open, manifest.

Deriv.: *anágnōsis* (320), reading.

315. ἀναγκάζω *anagkázō*; fut. *anagkásō*, from *anágkē* (318), necessity. To force, compel by external violence (Acts 26:11; Gal 2:3; 6:12). To force, compel in a moral sense as by authoritative command (Matt 14:22; Mark 6:45); by importunate persuasion (Luke 14:23); by prevalent example (Gal 2:14); by injustice (Acts 28:19).

Syn.: *aggareúō* (29), to press into service; *parabiázomai* (3849), to employ force contrary to nature and right, to compel by using force; *sunéchō* (4912), to constrain.

Ant.: *apolúō* (630), to set at liberty; *apostéllō* (649), to send away, set at liberty; *epitrépō* (2010), to allow, leave; *aporríptō* (641), to reject, hurl off.

316. ἀναγκαῖος *anagkaíos*; gen. *anagkaíou*, adj., fem. *anagkaía*, neut. *anagkaía*, adj. from *anágkē* (318), necessity. Necessary by a physical need (1 Cor 12:22, cf. Titus 3:14); necessary by a moral or spiritual need (Acts 13:46; 2 Cor 9:5; Phil 1:24; 2:25; Heb 8:3); near, intimate, closely connected (Acts 10:24).

Syn.: *epitḗdeios* (2006), suitable, convenient, necessary; *eúkairos* (2121), timely, seasonable; *chrḗsimos* (5539), useful; *eúchrēstos* (2173), serviceable; *ōphélimos* (5624), profitable.

Ant.: *áchrēstos* (890), unprofitable, useless; *hekoúsios* (1596), voluntary, used in the neut. acc. with the art., *tó hekoúsion* (1595), as an adv., meaning voluntarily (Phile 1:14).

317. ἀναγκαστῶς *anagkastós*; adv. from *anágkē* (318), necessity. Of necessity, by constraint. *Anágkē* stands for several Hebr. words which denote the afflictions and distresses of illness, persecution, enmity, which were often considered by the Israelites to indicate God's alienation from them. In the same aspect, however, the OT presents Jehovah alone as the One who can save men from *anágkē* (Ps 25:17), or even lead a person into it (Job 20:22). In the NT, the noun *anágkē* occurs 17 times, the adj. *anagkaíos*, 8 times, and the verb *anagkázō*, 9 times, all by Paul. The verb *anagkázō* in the NT, both in the act. and pass., describes a compulsion or a being compelled which does not rest on the use of outward force (Matt 14:22; Acts 28:19; Gal 2:3). Luke 14:23 does not intimate the use of force. The adj. *anagkaíos* refers once to close friends as in the sense of those to whom one is bound (Acts 10:24), but is otherwise used predicatively, meaning necessary. In Acts 13:46 it stands as equivalent to *dei* (1163), must (Luke 24:7, 26; Acts 1:16, 22). *Anágkē* intimates divine providence consequent to salvation as in Matt 18:7; Rom 13:5; 1 Cor 9:16. *Anágkē* is also used almost as an alternative to *thlípsis* (2347), tribulation or persecution, in describing the tribulations which continually recur and break in upon believers from outside (1 Cor 7:26; 2 Cor 6:4; 12:10; 1 Thess 3:7). It is in this sense that the distress spoken of in Luke 21:23 should be understood. The only place where the adv. is used is 1 Pet 5:2, standing in contrast to *hekousíōs* (1596), voluntarily or willfully. Both words occur in this verse referring to the motive of the service as a spiritual shepherd. One should exercise the task of pastor not because of any outward or inward constraint but voluntarily. No one should be a pastor because he is hired to be one, but because he has been called of God to be one whether he is paid or not.

318. ἀνάγκη *anágkē*, gen. *anágkēs*, fem. noun. Necessity, compelling force, as opposed to willingness (*tó hekoúsion* [1595]; 1 Cor 7:37; 2 Cor 9:7; Phile 1:14); moral necessity (Matt 18:7; Heb 7:12, 27; 9:16, 23) which means that as a result of the depravity and wickedness of men, there is a moral inevitability that offenses should come (also Luke 14:18; 23:17); spiritual or religious necessity (Rom 13:5; 1 Cor 9:16; Jude 1:3); distress, affliction (Luke 21:23; 1 Cor 7:26; 2 Cor 6:4; 12:10; 1 Thess 3:7).

Deriv.: *anagkázō* (315), to force; *anagkaíos* (316), needful; *anagkastós* (317), of necessity, by constraint; *epánagkes* (1876), of necessity.

Syn.: *stenochōría* (4730), narrowness of place, distress; *thlípsis* (2347), affliction; *sunochḗ* (4928), a compressing together, distress, anguish; *chreía* (5532), a need, necessity; *deí* (1163), it is necessary; *déon*, from *déomai* (1189), to petition, related to *deí* (1163), it is necessary, used as a noun meaning that which is needful, due, proper; *prépō* (4241), I must; *epitagḗ* (2003), an injunction, decree, commandment.

319. ἀναγνωρίζω *anagnōrízō*; fut. *anagnōrísō*, from *aná* (303), again, and *gnōrízō* (1107), to know. To know again. Pass.: *anagnōrízomai*, to be made known again (Acts 7:13; Sept.: Gen 45:1); *anegnōrísthēn*, aor. pass. with reflexive meaning, to make oneself known.

Syn.: the phrase *phanerós gínomai* (*phanerós* [5318], manifest; *gínomai* [1096], become), to become manifest; *epiginṓskō* (1921), to fully know; *epístamai* (1987), to understand; *manthánō* (3129), to learn; *homologéō* (3670), to acknowledge, confess; *paradéchomai* (3858), to admit; *apodéchomai* (588), approve, accept; *egkrínō* (1469), approve; *sumphōnéō* (4856), to agree with.

Ant.: *agnoéō* (50), not to know; *lanthánō* (2990), to forget; *arnéomai* (720), to contradict, deny; *antitássomai* (498), to oppose, resist; *aporríptō* (641), to reject; *periphronéō* (4065), to despise.

320. ἀνάγνωσις *anágnōsis*; gen. *anagnṓseōs*, fem. noun from *anaginṓskō* (314), to know certainly and hence to read, particularly the Scriptures. Reading (Acts 13:15; 2 Cor 3:14) and especially the public reading of Holy Scriptures (Sept.: Neh 8:8). In 1 Tim 4:13, it refers to the public reading of the OT Scriptures or of the portion of Scripture appointed to be read in public which is called *anágnōsma*. The readers in the church upon whom originally devolved the duty of reading and expounding or application of that portion chosen were called *anagnṓstai*, the public readers.

321. ἀνάγω *anágō*; fut. *anáxō*, 2d aor. *anḗgagon*, aor. pass. *anḗchthēn* with mid. sense, from *aná* (303), up, again, or away, and *ágō* (71), to bring or lead. To bring, lead, carry, or take up (Luke 2:22; 4:5; 22:26; Acts 7:41; 9:39; 12:4; 16:34 [cf. Matt 4:1]; Rom 10:7; Heb 13:20; Sept.: Gen 50:24; Ex 8:5; Lev 14:20; 1 Kgs 3:15; Job 1:5; Ps 30:4; 71:20; Isa 57:6). To bring or offer up as a sacrifice (Acts 7:41). The pass. *anágomai*, to be carried up, used as a term of navigation meaning to put out to sea, set sail (Luke 8:22; Acts 13:13; 16:11; 18:21; 20:3, 13; 21:1, 2; 27:2, 4, 12, 21; 28:10, 11). To bring back (Rom 10:7; Heb 13:20).

Deriv.: *epanágō* (1877), to thrust out, return.

Syn.: *anaphérō* (399), to bring up; *anabibázō* (307), to cause to ascend; *hélkō* (1670), to draw; *súrō* (4951), to drag; *spáō* (4685), to draw or pull; *anaspáō* (385), to draw up; *antléō* (501), to draw up water; *epanágō* (1877), to lead up upon; *aníēmi* (447), to send back or upwards; *aírō* (142), to take up, remove; *analúō* (360), to depart, especially from this life; *pléō* (4126), to sail; *apopléō* (636), to sail away; *ekpléō* (1602), to sail from; *diapléō* (1277), to sail across; *analambánō* (353), to take up; *anairéō* (337), to take up.

Ant.: *apoleípō* (620), to leave behind; *egkataleípō* (1459), to leave behind in, forsake; *hupoleípō* (5275), to leave remaining; *perileípō* (4035), to leave on the side; *aphiēmi* (863), to send forth.

322. ἀναδείκνυμι *anadeíknumi*; fut. *anadeíxo*, aor. *anédeixa*, from *aná* (303), an emphatic, and *deiknúō* or *deíknumi* (1166), show. To show plainly or openly (Acts 1:24); to mark out, appoint to an office by some outward sign (Luke 10:1).

Deriv.: *anádeixis* (323), showing.

Syn.: *kathístēmi* (2525), to appoint a person to a position; *títhēmi* (5087), to put, used of appointment to any form of service; *tássō* (5021), to place in order, arrange, appoint; *cheirotonéō* (5500), to stretch out the hands and appoint, usually elders in the apostolic church; *horízō* (3724), to mark by a limit, to ordain; *poiéō* (4160), to make, appoint; *eklégō*, see *eklégomai* (1586), to choose; *epilégō* see *epilégomai* (1951), to select; *chōrízō* (5563), to separate.

Ant.: *kōlúō* (2967), prevent, hinder; *aporríptō* (641), to reject; *periphronéō* (4065), to despise; *apobállō* (577), to throw off; *apokrúptō* (613), to hide; *krúptō* (2928), to conceal.

323. ἀνάδειξις *anádeixis*; gen. *anadeíxeōs*, fem. noun from *anadeiknúō* or *anadeíknumi* (322), to show plainly or openly. The secular usage is that of the choice, institution, or proclamation of officials. Etymologically, it means appearance or manifestation. Found only in Luke 1:80, in relation to the appearance and proclamation of John the Baptist in his official character as the forerunner of Jesus Christ.

Syn.: *phanérōsis* (5321) and *epipháneia* (2015), manifestation; *apokálupsis* (602), revelation.

324. ἀναδέχομαι *anadéchomai*; fut. *anadéxomai*, aor. *anedexámēn*, from *aná* (303), an emphatic, and *déchomai* (1209), to receive. To undertake, take upon oneself. Used in Heb 11:17, "He who had taken up" (a.t.), or undertaken, not merely "received." The verb implies the seizing or laying hold upon that which is presented. In Acts 28:7, to receive hospitably.

Syn.: *lambánō* (2983), to receive as a self-prompted action whereas *déchomai* (1209) may signify a favorable reception; *analambánō* (353), to take to oneself, receive; *apolambánō* (618), to receive from another either as one's due or not; *hupolambánō* (5274), to receive.

Ant.: *apostréphō* (654), to turn or put back; *apolúō* (630), to set free; *aphíēmi* (863), to put away; *aírō* (142), to remove;

katargéō (2673), to abolish; *kathairéō* (2507), to put down; *apostéllō* (649), to send forth; *apōthéomai* (683), to reject; *lúō* (3089), to loose; *apotrépō* (665), to cause to turn away; *methístēmi* (3179), to turn away; *ekklínō* (1578), to turn aside.

325. ἀναδίδωμι *anadídōmi*; fut. *anadṓsō*, from *aná* (303), an emphatic, and *dídōmi* (1325), to give. To present, deliver over, yield (Acts 23:33).

Syn.: *chorēgéō* (5524), to supply, give; *paréchō* (3930), to supply, give.

Ant.: *phulássō* (5442), to keep; *kratéō* (2902), to hold; *nosphízō* (3557), to keep back.

326. ἀναζάω *anazáō*; contracted *anazṓ*, fut. *anazḗsō*, aor. *anézēsa*, from *aná* (303), again, and *záō* (2198), to live. To live again, to revive (Luke 15:24, 32; Rom 7:9; 14:9; Rev 20:5).

Syn.: *akmázō* (187), to be fully ripe; *prokóptō* (4298), to increase, grow; *proágomai* (4254), to lead forward; *probibázomai* (4264), to move to the front; *anaptússomai* (380), to develop; *anathállō* (330), to flourish anew, revive; *egeírō* (1453), to raise from a sitting or lying position because of sickness or death, revive; *anístēmi* (450), to rise from a lying position of sleep or death, to stand up alive or generally to stand up; *diagrēgoréō* (1235), to become fully awake; *zōogonéō* (2225), to rescue from death; *zōopoiéō* (2227), to make alive.

Ant.: *apokteínō* (615), to kill; *phoneúō* (5407), to murder; *thanatóō* (2289), to put to death; *apothnḗskō* (599), to die; *thnḗskō* (2348), to die; *ekleípō* (1587), to cease to live, die; *teleutáō* (5053), to finish life, expire; *methístēmi* (3179), to transfer from this world to the next; *apodēméō* (589), to go to a foreign country, die; *ekdēméō* (1553), to vacate this life; *ekpnéō* (1606), to give up the spirit; *nekróō* (3499), to deaden.

327. ἀναζητέω *anazētéō*; contracted *anazētṓ*, fut. *anazētḗsō*, from *aná* (303), an emphatic, and *zētéō* (2212), to seek.

To seek diligently (Luke 2:44; Acts 11:25; Sept.: Job 3:4; 10:6).

Syn.: *zēlóō* (2206), to seek zealously; *ereunáō* (2045), to seek, investigate; *exereunáō* (1830), to explore; *epizētéō* (1934), to seek after; *agreúō* (64), to entrap; *thēreúō* (2340), to hunt.

Ant.: *ameléō* (272), to neglect; *paratheōréō* (3865), to overlook; *agnoéō* (50), to be ignorant of; *lanthánō* (2990), to forget; *amérimnos* (275), not anxious; *epilanthánomai* (1950), to neglect; *oligōréō* (3643), to despise.

328. ἀναζώννυμι anazṓnnumi; fut. *anazṓsō*, from *aná* (303), up, and *zṓnnumi* (2224), to gird. To gird up. Occurs only in 1 Pet 1:13, where it is applied to the mind being held in constant preparation. It is taken from the custom of the eastern nations who, when they had occasion to exert themselves (as in journeying, running, etc.), used to bind up their long-flowing garments by a girdle or belt about their hips (see Ex 12:11; 1 Kgs 18:46; 2 Kgs 4:29; 9:1).

Syn.: *hetoimázō* (2090), to make ready; *ergázomai* (2038), to labor; *douleúō* (1398), to work as a slave; *philotiméomai* (5389), to be earnest in doing something.

Ant.: *argéō* (691), to be idle; *koimáomai* (2837), to fall asleep; *oknéō* (3635), to be slow, lazy; *scholázō* (4980), to be at leisure; *katheúdō* (2518), to fall asleep.

329. ἀναζωπυρέω anazōpuréō; contracted *anazōpurṓ*, fut. *anazōpurḗsō*, from *aná* (303), again, and *zōpuréō* (n.f.), to revive a fire. To revive, stir up as a fire (2 Tim 1:6; Sept.: Gen 45:27).

Syn.: *diegeírō* (1326), to stir up; *epegeírō* (1892), to stir up; *paroxúnō* (3947), to provoke; *anáptō* (381), to kindle; *phlogízō* (5394), to inflame; *puróō* (4448), to kindle, burn; *zēlóō* (2206), to be zealous.

Ant.: *sbénnumi* (4570), to quench; *katakaíō* (2618), to burn down, consume completely; *katastéllō* (2687), to put down; *psúchō* (5594), to cool, chill; *katapsúchō* (2711), to cool down; *anapsúchō* (404), to cool off.

330. ἀναθάλλω anathállō; fut. *anathalṓ*, from *aná* (303), again, and *thállō* (n.f.), to thrive, flourish. To thrive or flourish again as trees or plants which, though they seem dead in the winter, revive and flourish again in spring. In Phil 4:10, the verb is used trans.: "Ye have caused your care of me to thrive [or flourish] again" (a.t.). See also Sept.: Ezek 17:24.

Syn.: *anazáō* (326), to live again.

Ant.: *thnḗskō* (2348), to die; *apothnḗskō* (599), to die off or out; *katheúdō* (2518), to fall asleep; *teleutáō* (5053), to end, die; *koimáō* (2837), to lie down, die; *apogínomai* (581), to die out; *apóllumi* (622), to perish. See also ant. of *anazáō* (326), to live again.

331. ἀνάθεμα anáthema; gen. *anathématos*, neut. noun from *anatíthēmi* (394), to place, lay up. A gift given by vow or in fulfillment of a promise, and given up or devoted to destruction for God's sake (Sept.: Num 21:1–3; Deut 13:16–18); therefore, given up to the curse and destruction, accursed (1 Cor 12:3; 16:22; Gal 1:8, 9). In Rom 9:3, estrangement from Christ and His salvation. The word does not denote punishment intended as discipline but being given over or devoted to divine condemnation. It denotes an indissoluble vow. See also Acts 23:14; Gal 1:9. *Anáthema* is not to be confused with *anáthēma* (334), a votive offering or an offering not involving sacrifice, something consecrated in the temple, a gift, an offering (Luke 21:5).

Deriv.: *anathematízō* (332), to declare anathema, to curse; *katanáthema* (2652), an accursed thing.

Syn.: *ará* (685), a malediction, cursing; *katára* (2671), a curse.

Ant.: *aínos* (136), praise; *épainos* (1868), commendation; *aínesis* (133), the act of praising; *aretḗ* (703), virtue, praise; *dóxa* (1391), glory, praise; *húmnos* (5215), hymn, praise; *eulogía* (2129), eulogy, speaking well of, blessing; *euché* (2171), vow, good wish.

332. ἀναθεματίζω *anathematízō*; fut. *anathematísō*, from *anáthema* (331), a curse. To bind by a curse (Acts 23:12, 14, 21) or simply to curse (Mark 14:71).
Deriv.: *katanathematízō* (2653), to utterly curse.
Syn.: *kataráomai* (2672), to pray or wish evil against a person or thing; *kakologéō* (2551), to speak evil.
Ant.: *ainéō* (134), to speak in praise of; *epainéō* (1867), to commend; *humnéō* (5214), to laud; *psállō* (5567), to sing praise; *eulogéō* (2127), to speak well of.

333. ἀναθεωρέω *anatheōréō*; contracted *anatheōrṓ*, fut. *anatheōrḗsō*, from *aná* (303), an emphatic, and *theōréō* (2334), to view. To view or behold attentively (Acts 17:23). To consider attentively, contemplate (Heb 13:7).
Syn.: *horáō* (3708), to see, perceive, take heed; *blépō* (991), to see, perceive, beware, heed; *emblépō* (1689), to look earnestly; *theáomai* (2300), to contemplate with amazement; *epopteúō* (2029), to witness as a spectator, oversee; *atenízō* (816), to gaze intently; *suneidéō* (4894), to become conscious as the result of mental perception; *katamanthánō* (2648), to consider well, learn; *noéō* (3539), to perceive; *katanoéō* (2657), to perceive clearly; *logízomai* (3049), to take account of; *analogízomai* (357), to take into account, consider; *skopéō* (4648), to heed, look at accurately, mark; *suníēmi* (4920), to understand; *dialogízomai* (1260), to deliberately consider; *ginṓskō* (1097), to come to know, recognize; *oída* from the same root as *eídō* (1492), to know intuitively; *epiginṓskō* (1921), to observe, fully perceive; *epístamai* (1987), to know, understand; *gnōrízō* (1107), to come to know, discover; *diagnōrízō* (1232), to make known publicly; *anagnōrízō* (319), to make oneself known.
Ant.: *agnoéō* (50), not to know, to neglect knowing; *ameléō* (272), to neglect; *lanthánō* (2990), to forget, not to learn.

334. ἀνάθημα *anáthēma*; gen. *anathḗmatos*, from *anatíthēmi* (394), to separate, lay up. A consecrated gift hung up or laid up in a temple (Luke 21:5). Such gifts, called votive offerings (*anathḗmata*), were distinguished from sacrificial offerings (*anathémata* [331]). They were dedicated to God for the honor of the people offering them as well as for God's glory. Such offerings could be shields, chaplets, golden chains, and candlesticks. Such were and still are common in heathen temples. The same custom was imitated in the Jewish temple as even in some so-called Christian churches today.
Syn.: *dṓron* (1435), a gift; *dōreá* (1431), a gift conveying the meaning of the freeness of the gift; *dṓrēma* (1434), that which is given as a gift, boon; *dóma* (1390), a gift as such without any benefit necessarily derived from it; *dósis* (1394), the act of giving; *chárisma* (5486), the gift resulting from grace or *cháris* (5485); *prosphorá* (4376), an offering; *holokaútōma* (3646), a burnt offering.

335. ἀναίδεια *anaídeia*; gen. *anaideías*, fem. noun from *anaidḗs* (n.f.), impudent, which is from the priv. *a* (1), without, and *aidṓs* (127), shame. Recklessness, audacity, shamelessness, insolence. Recklessness or disregard of consideration by the one making the request (Luke 11:8).
Syn.: *atimía* (819), shame, disgrace, dishonor; *aschēmosúnē* (808), unseemliness, shame.
Ant.: *aischúnē* (152), a sense of shame due to the exposure of one's weaknesses or sins; *entropé* (1791), a withdrawal into oneself in aversion to evil; *aidṓs* (127), modesty.

336. ἀναίρεσις *anaíresis*; gen. *anairéseōs*, fem. noun from *anairéō* (337), to take away. Murder, taking up or away of dead bodies for burial (Acts 8:1; 22:20 [TR]; Sept.: Num 11:15).

Syn.: *thánatos* (2288), death; *teleuté* (5054), an end, limit, death; *análusis* (359), departure from life.

Ant.: *paliggenesía* (3824), renovation, restoration; *génnēsis* (1083), birth.

337. ἀναιρέω *anairéō*; contracted *anairṓ*, fut. *anairésō*, from *aná* (303), an emphatic or up, and *hairéō* (138), to take. To take away, abolish (Heb 10:9); to slay, murder, take off (Matt 2:16; Acts 5:36; 7:28; 9:23, 24, 29; 16:27; 23:15, 21, 27; 25:3); spoken of public execution (Luke 23:32; Acts 2:23; 10:39; 12:2; 13:28; 22:20; 26:10; Sept.: Ex 21:29; 2 Sam 10:18; Isa 37:36; Dan 2:13, 14); to take up (Acts 7:21).

Deriv.: *anaíresis* (336), death.

Syn.: *thanatóō* (2289), to put to death; *apágō* (520), to lead away, put to death; *apokteínō* (615), to kill; *phoneúō* (5407), to murder; *spháttō* or *spházō* (4969), to butcher, slay; *thúō* (2380), to sacrifice; *analúō* (360), to depart from life.

Ant.: *zōogonéō* (2225), to revive from death; *gennáō* (1080), to give birth; *tíktō* (5088), to bear, bring forth.

338. ἀναίτιος *anaítios*; gen. *anaitíou*, masc.-fem., neut. *anaítion*, adj. from the privative *a* (1), without, and *aitía* (156), a crime. Not criminal, guiltless, innocent (Matt 12:5, 7; Deut 19:10, 13; 21:8, 9).

Syn.: *ámemptos* (273), without blame, faultless; *ámōmos* (299), without blemish or shortcoming; *amṓmētos* (298), one who cannot have blemish; *anepílēptos* (423), irreproachable; *anégklētos* (410), blameless insofar as being chargeable before a court of law; *athṓos* (121), innocent; *ákakos* (172), harmless; *díkaios* (1342), righteous.

Ant.: *énochos* (1777), guilty; *hupódikos* (5267), liable for trial; *ádikos* (94), unjust.

339. ἀνακαθίζω *anakathízō*; fut. *anakathísō*, from *aná* (303), up, and *kathízō* (2523), to sit. To sit up (Luke 7:15; Acts 9:40).

Syn.: *anákeimai* (345), to sit down or recline; *anaklínō* (347), to cause to recline, to make to sit down; *kataklínō* (2625), to sit down; *anapíptō* (377), to fall back, to lean.

Ant.: *anístēmi* (450), to raise, and intrans., to arise; *hístēmi* (2476), to stand upright; *egeírō* (1453), to raise, rouse, rise.

340. ἀνακαινίζω *anakainízō*; fut. *anakainísō*, from *aná* (303), again, and *kainízō* (n.f.), to renew, which is from *kainós* (2537), qualitatively new. To renew. Occurs only in Heb 6:6, *anakainízein eis metánoian* (*eis* [1619], unto; *metánoian*, the acc. of *metánoia* [3341], repentance), meaning to have a new or qualitatively different kind of repentance which would see the person who had it through to the very end. Also from *kainízō* (n.f.): *egkainízō* (1457), to dedicate, consecrate.

Syn.: *ananeóō* (365), to renew in the sense of making young or replacing numerically. See both *néos* (3501), new, either numerically or one coming later, and *kainós* (2537), qualitatively new.

Ant.: *diatēréō* (1301), to keep carefully; *suntēréō* (4933), to preserve; *phulássō* (5442), to keep, watch; *diaphulássō* (1314), to keep carefully.

341. ἀνακαινόω *anakainóō*; contracted *anakainṓ*, fut. *anakainísō*, from *aná* (303), again, and *kainóō* (n.f.), to make new, which is from *kainós* (2537), qualitatively new. To be renewed completely by God. Used only in the pass. (2 Cor 4:16; Col 3:10, cf. Eph 4:23). Refers to the redemptive activity of God corresponding to the creation of man, which, by putting an end to man's existing corrupt state, establishes a new beginning. It is qualitatively different than the past in agreement with the meaning of the word *kainós* (2537), qualitatively new as contrasted to *néos* (3501), numerically another or a new one. Used in the act. voice in Heb 6:6, *anakainízō* (340) means that man himself must have a new and qualitatively different kind of repentance if the first repentance did not see him through to its desired purpose of eternal redemption.

Deriv.: *anakaínōsis* (342), renewal.

Syn.: *ananeóō* (365), to reform, renew with the same kind of experience as in the past; *neótēs* (3503), youth with reference simply to age and not quality of life.

Ant.: *palaióō* (3822), to make worn out, old.

342. ἀνακαίνωσις *anakaínōsis*; gen. *ankainóseōs*, fem. noun from *anakainóō* (341), to renew qualitatively. Therefore, a renewing or a renovation which makes a person different than in the past. Occurs in Rom 12:2; Titus 3:5 (cf. John 3:5). See also *anakainízō* (340), to renew qualitatively.

Syn.: *paliggenesía* (3824), rebirth, renewal.

Ant.: *palaiótēs* (3821), oldness.

343. ἀνακαλύπτω *anakalúptō*; fut. *anakalúpsō*, from *aná* (303), back again, and *kalúptō* (2572), to hide, cover, veil. To unveil, to remove a veil or covering, understand through one's own ability, discover (2 Cor 3:14, 18; Sept.: Job 33:16; Isa 3:12; 22:14; Dan 2:22).

Syn.: *apokalúptō* (601), to take off the cover and make understandable, reveal.

Ant.: *kalúptō* (2572), to cover.

344. ἀνακάμπτω *anakámptō*; fut. *anakámpsō*, from *aná* (303), back again, and *kámptō* (2578), to bend. To go back to one's course, to return (Matt 2:12; Luke 10:6; Acts 18:21; Heb 11:15; Sept.: Ex 32:27; Isa 45:23; 55:11).

Syn.: *analúō* (360), to depart; *anastréphō* (390), to turn back; *epanágō* (1877), to return, bring back; *epistréphō* (1994), to return; *epanérchomai* (1880), to come back again; *epanágō* (1877), to launch out, return.

Ant.: *ménō* (3306) and *diaménō* (1265), to remain throughout; *anorthóō* (461), to set straight, set up; *poreúomai* (4198), to depart; *methístēmi* (3179), turn

away; *ápheimi* (548), to go away; *exeími* (1826), to go out; *apérchomai* (565), to go off; *exérchomai* (1831), to get out; *aphístēmi* (868), to withdraw self; *ekporeúomai* (1607), to proceed out of; *probaínō* (4260), to walk forward.

345. ἀνάκειμαι *anákeimai*; fut. *anakeísomai*, from *aná* (303), an emphatic, and *keímai* (2749), to lie down. To lie as a dead person (Mark 5:40). To lie down, recline, which was the posture used in eating at a table by the Jews, Greeks, and Romans (Matt 9:10; 26:7, 20; Mark 14:18; 16:14; John 13:23, 28). In Luke 7:37, we have the Lord reclining at meat in the Pharisee's house with His face toward the table and His feet toward the outside on the couch. In John 13:23, the Lord's last supper, one of His disciples was reclining on Jesus bosom. In Luke 22:27, the word is used as a part. noun meaning the persons lying at table, hence guests (Matt 22:10, 11; John 6:11).

Deriv.: *sunanákeimai* (4873), to recline, to sit with.

Syn.: *káthēmai* (2521), to sit down; *kathézomai* (2516), to sit; *kataklínomai* (2625) and *katákeimai* (2621), to recline at a meal; *parakathízō* (3869), to sit down near; *anapíptō* (377), to fall back; *epipíptō* (1968), to fall upon, lie down; *kathízō* (2523), to sit down.

Ant.: *anístēmi* (450), to stand up; *egeírō* (1453), to raise; *anabaínō* (305), to go up; *anachōréō* (402), to withdraw self.

346. ἀνακεφαλαιόω *anakephalaióō*; contracted *anakephalaió*, fut. *anakephaleósō*, from *aná* (303), an emphatic meaning again, and *kephalaióō* (2775), to sum up, recapitulate. To sum up, gather together in one. In the mid. voice, to gather together again in one, to reunite under one head (Eph 1:10, "to bring all things into one in Christ" [a.t.]; to introduce a unity of feeling and of expectation among all beings both in heaven and on earth by means of the Christian dispensation, especially between Jews and Gentiles [cf. Eph 2:14, 15]). In the pass., to be summed up, be comprised (Rom 13:9, summed up in this one precept of love).

Ant.: *diēgéomai* (1334), to relate fully; *exēgéomai* (1834), to unfold, explain.

347. ἀνακλίνω *anaklínō*; fut. *anaklinṓ*, from *aná* (303), an emphatic, and *klínō* (2827), to lay down. To lay down (Luke 2:7); in the act. voice, to make to recline, put in a posture of reclining, which in biblical times was used in eating (cf. *anákeimai* [345] as in Mark 6:39; Luke 9:15; 12:37). In the pass., to lean sideways, recline, or be reclined (Matt 14:19; Luke 7:36, cf. Matt 8:11; Luke 13:29, spoken of the feast or banquet in the kingdom of heaven [under which image the later Jews were accustomed to describe the happiness of the righteous in the Messiah's kingdom {cf. Matt 22:1ff.; 25:1ff.; 26:29; Mark 14:25; Luke 14:15ff.; 22:16, 18, 30}]). For syn. and ant. see *anákeimai* (345), to lie down.

348. ἀνακόπτω *anakóptō*; fut. *anakópsō*, from *aná* (303), back, and *kóptō* (2875), to strike, impel. To beat or drive back, hinder (Gal 5:7). It is an Olympic expression related to a race, meaning to come across the course in such a manner as to jostle and throw a participant out of the way.

Syn.: *kōlúō* (2967), to restrain, hinder; *diakōlúō* (1254), to hinder thoroughly; *epéchō* (1907), to detain.

Ant.: *prokóptō* (4298), to cut forward, advance; *auxánō* (837), to increase; *probaínō* (4260), to walk forward; *proágō* (4254), to lead forth or forward.

349. ἀνακράζω *anakrázō*; fut. *anakráxō*, from the emphatic *aná* (303) and *krázō* (2896), to cry. To cry out, exclaim (Mark 1:23; 6:49; Luke 4:33; 8:28; 23:18; Sept.: Josh 6:5; Judg 7:20; 1 Kgs 22:32; Joel 4:16).

Syn.: *phōnéō* (5455), to utter a loud sound or cry; *epiphōnéō* (2019), to

acclaim or shout against; *anaphōnéō* (400), to exclaim; *boáō* (994), to shout; *anaboáō* (310), to cry out; *ololúzō* (3649), to howl; *phthéggomai* (5350), to speak, proclaim.

Ant.: *hēsucházō* (2270), to be still; *katastéllō* (2687), to quiet; *siōpáō* (4623), to hush; *sigáō* (4601), to keep silence.

350. ἀνακρίνω *anakrínō*; fut. *anakrinṓ*, from the emphatic *aná* (303) and *krínō* (2919), to judge. To discern, judge (1 Cor 2:14, 15; 4:3, 4; 9:3; 14:24); to examine or question in order to pass a judicial sentence (Luke 23:14; Acts 4:9; 12:19; 24:8; 28:18); to examine accurately or carefully (Acts 17:11); to inquire, ask questions in general (1 Cor 10:25, 27).

Deriv.: *anákrisis* (351), a judicial examination.

Syn.: *erōtáō* (2065), to ask; *eperōtáō* (1905), to question; *punthánomai* (4441), to ask by way of inquiry; *dokimázō* (1381), to test, prove; *anetázō* (426), to examine judicially; *peirázō* (3985), to try, examine; *ereunáō* (2045), to search, examine; *exereunáō* (1830), to search out; *exetázō* (1833), to examine closely, inquire carefully; *akribóō* (198), to ascertain.

Ant.: *aphíēmi* (863), to let go; *apolúō* (630), to dismiss; *ameléō* (272), to neglect.

351. ἀνάκρισις *anákrisis*; gen. *anakríseōs*, fem. noun from *anakrínō* (350), to examine. A judicial examination (Acts 25:26).

Syn.: *zétēsis* (2214), a searching, questioning.

Ant.: *páreisis* (3929), toleration; *áphesis* (859), forgiveness, remission.

352. ἀνακύπτω *anakúptō*; fut. *anakúpsō*, from *aná* (303), back again, and *kúptō* (2955), to bend. To lift or raise up oneself from a bending posture (Luke 13:11; John 8:7, 10; Sept.: Job 10:15). To lift oneself up or look up, as a person in hope (Luke 21:28).

Syn.: *egeírō* (1453), to awaken, raise up; *aírō* (142), to take up, lift; *epaírō*

(1869), to lift up the eyes; *hupsóō* (5312), to lift or raise up; *anístēmi* (450), to arise; *anorthóō* (461), to set upright.

Ant.: *káthēmai* (2521), to sit in a natural posture; *anákeimai* (345), to recline at a table; *katákeimai* (2621), to lie down; *anaklínō* (347), to cause to recline, make to sit down; *kataklínō* (2625), to make to recline, sit down; *kathízō* (2523), to cause to sit down, to set; *kathézomai* (2516), to sit.

353. ἀναλαμβάνω *analambánō*; fut. *analépsomai*, aor. pass. *aneléphthēn*, 2d aor. *anélabon*, from *aná* (303), up, and *lambánō* (2983), to take. To take up (Mark 16:19; Acts 1:2, 11, 22; 7:43, with the accessory idea of bearing; Acts 10:16; 20:13, 14; 23:31; Eph 6:13, 16; 1 Tim 3:16; 2 Tim 4:11; Sept.: Gen 24:61; 45:18; 48:1; Deut 1:41; Num 25:7; Judg 19:28; Josh 4:8; 2 Kgs 2:9, 10; Amos 5:26).

Deriv.: *análēpsis* (354), ascension, taking up.

Syn.: *déchomai* (1209), to receive by deliberate and ready reception whatever is offered; *anadéchomai* (324), to receive gladly; *apodéchomai* (588), to welcome, accept gladly; *lagchánō* (2975), to obtain by lot; *apaírō* (522), to lift off; *exaírō* (1808), to take away; *epaírō* (1869), to lift, raise; *anairéō* (337), to take up; *aphairéō* (851), to take away; *piázō* (4084), to lay or take hold of forcefully.

Ant.: *apōthéomai* (683), to push off; *aníēmi* (447), to let up; *anairéō* (337), to take up; *exouthenéō* (1848), to set at naught; *apolúō* (630), to dismiss.

354. ἀνάληψις *análēpsis*; gen. *analépseōs*, fem. noun from *analambánō* (353), to receive up. A receiving up, ascension. The act of being taken up (only in Luke 9:51).

Syn.: *húpsōma* (5313), altitude; *anaíresis* (336), the act of taking up, death.

Ant.: *katábasis* (2600), descent.

355. ἀναλίσκω *analískō*; fut. *analôsō*, aor. *anélōsa*, from *aná* (303), away, and *halískō* (n.f.), to take. To take away, destroy, consume (Luke 9:54; Gal 5:15; 2 Thess 2:8; Sept.: Gen 41:30; Prov 23:28; Jer 50:7; Ezek 15:4, 5). Also from *analískō* (n.f.): *hálōsis* (259), catching.

Deriv.: *katanalískō* (2654), to consume utterly; *prosanalískō* (4321), to expend further.

Syn.: *aphanízō* (853), to cause to disappear, put out of sight; *dapanáō* (1159), to spend; *diatríbō* (1304), to spend time, abide; *diágō* (1236), to spend in.

Ant.: *tēréō* (5083), to preserve, keep; *diatēréō* (1301), to keep carefully; *suntēréō* (4933), to preserve, keep safe; *phulássō* (5442), to keep; *diaphulássō* (1314), to keep carefully; *kratéō* (2902), to hold fast; *nosphízō* (3557), to keep back in the sense of embezzling (mid. *nosphízomai*).

356. ἀναλογία *analogía*; gen. *analogías*, fem. noun from *aná* (303), denoting distribution, and *lógos* (3056), account. Proportion. Analogy means the right relation. In Aristotle it meant arithmetical or geometric proportion. The "proportion of faith" in Rom 12:6 concerns the faith of the individual as God has made it available in a certain measure (Rom 12:3). The gift of prophecy must not be exercised assuming a measure of faith which the individual does not possess. Since it is God who has given both faith and prophecy (v. 3), the same God gives the prophecy in direct relationship and proportion to one's apportioned faith.

Syn.: *métron* (3358), measure.

Ant.: *ámetros* (280), without measure.

357. ἀναλογίζομαι *analogízomai*; fut. *analogísomai*, from *aná* (303), denoting distribution, distinction, or repetition, and *logízomai* (3049), to reckon, think. To consider accurately and distinctly or again and again (Heb 12:3).

Syn.: *eídō* (1492), used as the aor. tense of *horáō* (3708), to consider; *suneídō* (4894), to be conscious as the result of mental conception; *katamanthánō* (2648), to learn thoroughly; *noéō* (3539), to perceive with the mind, ponder; *katanoéō* (2657), to perceive clearly, consider carefully; *theōréō* (2334), to behold; *anatheōréō* (333), to consider carefully; *epístamai* (1987), to understand; *epiginóskō* (1921), to perceive; *paratēréō* (3906), to observe, watch.

Ant.: *agnoéō* (50), not know; *paraphronéō* (3912), to think mistakenly, think like a fool; *paralogízomai* (3884), to reckon mistakenly, delude oneself; *paralégomai* (3881), to sail past, not to reckon; *paraporeúomai* (3899), to go by, not to pay attention; *parérchomai* (3928), to neglect; *paríēmi* (3935), to let by; *parabouleúomai* (3851), to disregard; *paratheōréō* (3865), to disregard, neglect.

358. ἄναλος *ánalos*; gen. *análou*, masc.-fem., neut. *ánalon*, adj. from the priv. *a* (1), without, and *hals* (251), salt. Without saltiness, not having the taste of salt (Mark 9:50).

Syn.: *mōrós* (3474), useless.
Ant.: *halukós* (252), salty.

359. ἀνάλυσις *análusis*; gen. *analúseōs*, fem. noun from *analúō* (360), to return. Departure or return, death (2 Tim 4:6 [cf. verb in Phil 1:23]).

Syn.: *éxodos* (1841), exodus, departure; *teleutḗ* (5054), death; *thánatos* (2288), death; *anaíresis* (336), taking up or off, putting to death.

Ant.: *génnēsis* (1083), birth; *áphixis* (867), literally, arrival; but in the NT, departure.

360. ἀναλύω *analúō*; fut. *analúsō*, from *aná* (303), back again or denoting separation, and *lúō* (3089), to loose. The ancient Greeks used the word to indicate loosing the anchor of a ship in order to sail from a port. In the NT, to return (Luke 12:36); to depart by loosing anchor, as it were, and

setting sail to a better and a more blessed world, to die (Phil 1:23).

Deriv.: *análusis* (359), departure, death.

Syn.: *apopléō* (636), to set sail; *anágō* (321), to lead up; *hupágō* (5217), to go, depart; *apérchomai* (565), to go away; *poreúomai* (4198), to go, journey; *anachōréō* (402), to go back; *metabaínō* (3327), to depart; *apolúō* (630), to set free, loose; *aníēmi* (447), to send back or up.

Ant.: *ménō* (3306), to stay, abide; *diaménō* (1265), to remain throughout; *apoleípō* (620), to remain; *perileípō* (4035), to leave over, remain around; *epéchō* (1907), to wait or stay in a place; *kōlúō* (2967), to hinder.

361. ἀναμάρτητος *anamártētos*; gen. *anamartḗtou*, masc.-fem., neut. *anamártēton*, adj. from the priv. *a* (1), without, and *hamartánō* (264), to sin, miss the mark. Without sin, sinless, but not absolutely, only in a particular case. Occurs only in John 8:7; not to be confused with *téleios* (5046), perfect, reaching one's goal.

Syn.: *ámemptos* (273), unblamable; *athóos* (121), innocent; *anaítios* (338), blameless, guiltless; *anepílēmptos* or *anepíleptos* (423), irreproachable; *hágios* (40), saint, holy; *díkaios* (1342), righteous.

Ant.: *hamartōlós* (268), a sinner; *énochos* (1777), guilty; *ádikos* (94), unrighteous.

362. ἀναμένω *anaménō*; fut. *anamenō*, from *aná* (303), an emphatic, and *ménō* (3306), to remain, wait. To wait for, await, expect (1 Thess 1:10; Sept.: Job 7:2; Isa 59:11).

Syn.: *ekdéchomai* (1551), to expect; *apekdéchomai* (553), to wait or expect eagerly; *prosdéchomai* (4327), to look for with a view of receiving favorably; *prosdokáō* (4328), to await; *proskarteréō* (4342), to continue steadfastly.

Ant.: *paraitéomai* (3868), to give up, refuse; *apochōréō* (672), to resign; *egkataleípō* (1459), to forsake.

363. ἀναμιμνήσκω *anamimnḗskō*; fut. *anamnḗso*, from *aná* (303), again, and *mimnḗskō* (3403), to put in mind, remind. In the act., to put in mind again, remind (1 Cor 4:17; 2 Tim 1:6, with the implied meaning of to exhibit). In the mid., to call to mind again, remember (Mark 11:21; 14:72; 2 Cor 7:15; Heb 10:32; Sept.: Gen 8:1; Num 15:39).

Deriv.: *anámnēsis* (364), remembrance; *epanamimnḗskō* (1878), to remind.

Syn.: *enthuméomai* (1760), to ponder; *analogízomai* (357), to contemplate, consider; *historéō* (2477), to recall as history, interview; *entupóō* (1795), to engrave; *sēmeióō* (4593), to note; *mnēmoneúō* (3421), to recall, remember.

Ant.: *lanthánō* (2990), to escape notice, forget; *epilanthánomai* (1950), to forget or neglect; *eklanthánomai* (1585), to forget completely; *lḗthē* (3024), forgetfulness; *epilēsmonḗ* (1953), complete forgetfulness.

364. ἀνάμνησις *anámnēsis*; gen. *anamnḗseōs*, fem. noun from *anamimnḗskō* (363), to remind. Remembrance. A commemoration (Heb 10:3). A memorial (Luke 22:19; 1 Cor 11:24, 25), as applied to the Lord's Supper. "In remembrance of me" means that the participant should remember Christ and the expiatory sacrifice of His death. The memory of the greatness of the sacrifice should cause the believer to abstain from sin. See Sept.: Num 10:10; Ps 38:1.

365. ἀνανεόω *ananeóō*; fut. *ananeósō*, mid. *ananeóomai* or *ananeoúmai*, from *aná* (303), again, and *neóō*, to renew (n.f.), which is from *néos* (3501), new, another. To renew, make young. Used in Eph 4:23, *ananeóomai*, and is to be taken in the pass. mid. To be renewed insofar as spiritual vitality is concerned.

Syn.: *anakainízō* (340) and *anakainóō* (341), to make qualitatively new; *kainós* (2537), qualitatively new.

Ant.: *palaióō* (3822), to make worn out, old.

366. ἀνανήφω *ananḗphō*; fut. *ananḗpsō*, from *aná* (303), again, and *nḗphō* (3525), to be sober. To awake out of a drunken sleep and become sober, to become sober (2 Tim 2:26). This word may refer to a practice in which sowers scattered seeds impregnated with drugs intended to put birds to sleep that a net might be drawn over them to capture them.

Syn.: *egkrateúomai* (1467), to exercise self-restraint; *nēsteúō* (3522), to fast; *elégchō* (1651), to check; *chalinagōgéō* (5468), to bridle; *damázō* (1150), to tame; *katastéllō* (2687), to put down; *apéchō* (568), to abstain; *sōphronéō* (4993), to exercise a sound mind, to be sober-minded, exercise self-control.

Ant.: *ataktéō* (812), behave in a disorderly manner; *paralúō* (3886), to enfeeble; *methúskō* (3182), to be drunk; *methúō* (3184), to get drunk; *euthuméō* (2114), to be merry.

367. Ἀνανίας *Ananías*; gen. *Anania*, masc. proper noun from the Hebr. *Chananᵉyāh* (2608, OT), Hananiah. Ananias which means Jehovah has dealt graciously.

(I) A member of the apostolic church of Jerusalem whose contribution to the common fund was less than he pretended, and due to this sin he fell dead when his dishonesty was exposed (Acts 5:1ff.).

(II) Another personality with the name Ananias appears in Acts 9:10ff., a follower of Jesus in Damascus, "a devout man according to the law" (a.t.), who befriended Saul of Tarsus immediately after his conversion and conveyed Christ's commission to him (Acts 9:10–17; 22:12).

(III) There is yet a third personality by the name of Ananias who was the son of Nedebaeus (Acts 23:2; 24:1). He was the high priest (A.D. 47–58) and president of the Sanhedrin when Paul was brought before it, notorious for his greed, and killed by Zealots in A.D. 66 for his pro-Roman sympathies.

368. ἀναντίρρητος *anantírrētos*; gen. *anantirrḗtou*, masc.-fem., neut. *anantírrēton*, adj. from the priv. *a* (1), without, *antí* (473), against, and *eréō* (2046), to speak. Not to be spoken against or contradicted, indisputable (Acts 19:36).
Deriv.: *anantirrḗtōs* (369), indisputably.
Syn.: *bébaios* (949), sure; *asphalḗs* (804), certain; *pistós* (4103), dependable.
Ant.: *ádēlos* (82), uncertain; *astḗriktos* (793), unfounded; *episphalḗs* (2000), insecure, dangerous.

369. ἀναντιρρήτως *anantirrḗtōs*; adv. from *anantírrētos* (368), indisputable. Indisputably, without gainsaying or disputing (Acts 10:29).
Syn.: *asphalṓs* (806), assuredly; *akribṓs* (199), exactly.
Ant.: *adḗlōs* (84), uncertainly.

370. ἀνάξιος *anáxios*; gen. *anaxíou*, masc. adj. from the priv. *a* (1), without, and *áxios* (514), worthy. Unworthy (1 Cor 6:2).
Deriv.: *anaxíōs* (371), unworthily.
Syn.: *énochos* (1777), guilty, liable; *ásēmos* (767), not worthy of notice; *koinós* (2839), common; *eleeinós* (1652), pitiable, miserable.
Ant.: *áxios* (514), worthy; *hikanós* (2425), worthy, capable; *polútimos* (4186), valuable; *eklektós* (1588), favorite, chosen; *spoudaíos* (4705), significant.

371. ἀναξίως *anaxíōs*; adv. from *anáxios* (370), unworthy. Unworthily, irreverently, in an unbecoming manner (1 Cor 11:27, 29), treating the Lord's Supper as a common meal without attributing to it and its elements their proper value.
Ant.: *eusebṓs* (2153), piously, reverently.

372. ἀνάπαυσις *anápausis*; gen. *anapaúseōs*, fem. noun from *anapaúō* (373), act., to give rest. Rest, inward tranquility while one performs necessary labor (Matt 12:43; Luke 11:24; Rev 4:8; 14:11). In Matt 11:28, 29, the Lord promises *anápausis* (inner tranquility) to the weary and heavy laden who come to Him while they are engaged in necessary labor.
Syn.: *anápsuxis* (403), recovery of breath; *ánesis* (425) implies the relaxing or letting down of chords or strings which have been strained or drawn tight (Acts 24:23; 2 Cor 2:13; 7:5; 8:13; 2 Thess 1:7); *katápausis* (2663), rest, cessation of labor, referring to God or man's; *sabbatismós* (4520), a sabbath keeping, sabbath rest; *koímēsis* (2838), a resting, reclining, natural sleep and therefore rest; *eirḗnē* (1515), inner peace with the meaning of rest.
Ant.: *móchthos* (3449), toil, travail; *kopetós* (2870), lamentation; *paideía* (3809), chastening; *talaipōría* (5004), misery; *phthorá* (5356), corruption, fatigue resulting from physical corruptibility.

373. ἀναπαύω *anapaúō*; fut. *anapaúsō*, from *aná* (303), again, and *paúō* (3973), to cease, give rest. To give rest, quiet, recreate, refresh (Matt 11:28; 1 Cor 16:18; Phile 1:20); in the mid. / pass. form, to be refreshed (2 Cor 7:13; Phile 1:7, 20; Sept.: Prov 29:17; Isa 14:3; Ezek 34:15). In the mid., *anapaúomai*, to rest oneself, to take one's rest (Matt 26:45; Mark 6:31; 14:41; Luke 12:19; 1 Pet 4:14; Rev 6:11; 14:13; Sept.: Deut 33:20; Esth 9:16; Job 10:20; Prov 21:16; Isa 13:20, 21; 27:10; Mic 4:4). In relation to 1 Pet 4:14, compare the Sept. of Isa 11:2, where *anapaúomai* is also applied to the Holy Spirit resting upon Christ.
Deriv.: *anápausis* (372), inner rest; *epanapaúō* (1879), to cause to rest; *sunanapaúomai* (4875), to rest with or together.

Syn.: *aníēmi* (447), to loosen, relax, take up; *anapsúchō* (404), to refresh, relax; *hēsucházō* (2270), to be at peace or rest; *kopázō* (2869), to relax, cease.

Ant.: *kopiáō* (2872), to toil; the expression *kópous paréchō* (*kópous*, pl. of [2873], troubles, followed by *paréchō* [3930], present, provide), to trouble, vex (Matt 26:10; Mark 14:6; Luke 11:7; 18:5; Gal 6:17); *kóptō* (2875), to beat the breast in grief; *kataponéō* (2669), to wear down with toil; *katabállō* (2598), to wear down; *talaiporéō* (5003), to be wretched, miserable; *paideúō* (3811), to chasten; *basanízō* (928), to torment.

374. ἀναπείθω *anapeíthō*; fut. *anapeísō*, from *aná* (303), an emphatic, and *peíthō* (3982), to persuade. To persuade earnestly (Acts 18:13; Sept.: Jer 29:8).

Syn.: *plērophoréō* (4135), to assure; *protrépō* (4389), to recommend; *sumbouleúō* (4823), to consult; *parotrúnō* (3951), to stimulate, stir up.

Ant.: *apotrépō* (665), to dissuade; *metanoéō* (3340), to repent; *metaméllomai* (3338), to change course.

375. ἀναπέμπω *anapémpō*; fut. *anapémpsō*, from *aná* (303), again, and *pémpō* (3992), to send. To send again or send back again (Luke 23:11; Phile 1:12); to remit (Luke 23:7, 15).

Syn.: *apostéllō* (649), to send forth; *exapostéllō* (1821), to dispatch; *exágō* (1806), to lead forth; *ekkomízō* (1580), to carry out; *aphairéō* (851), to remove; *ekbállō* (1544), to cast out; *apobállō* (577), to put away; *apospáō* (645), to draw away; *metágō* (3329), to transfer.

Ant.: *eiságō* (1521), to lead in; *embállō* (1685), to cast into; *eisdéchomai* (1523), to take into one's favor; *eispēdáō* (1530), to rush in; *eisérchomai* (1525), to enter.

376. ἀνάπηρος *anápēros*; gen. *anapérou*, masc. adj. from *aná* (303), up, or used as a distributive, and *pērós* (n.f.), maimed, disabled in a limb. Maimed, having lost a limb or some part of the body (Luke 14:13, 21).

Syn.: *kúllos* (2948), crippled, halt; *chōlós* (5560), lame; *asthenḗs* (772), infirm, weak, sick.

Ant.: *hugiḗs* (5199), whole, healthy, sound; *holóklēros* (3648), whole, entire.

377. ἀναπίπτω *anapíptō*; fut. *anapesoúmai*, aor. mid. *anepesámēn*, 2d aor. *anépeson*, from *aná* (303), an intens. and *píptō* (4098), to fall. To fall down, to lie down in order to eat. Although the literal meaning of the word, to fall down, is used by the Class. Gr. writers and in the Sept. (Gen 49:9), the meaning in the NT was always to lie down in order to eat. This was either on the ground as indicated in Matt 15:35; Mark 6:40; 8:6; Luke 14:10; 17:7, in the aor. mid. imper. *anápesai* or *anápeson*, *anápese* (TR); 22:14; John 6:10; 13:12; on sofas, as indicated in Luke 11:37; 22:14; John 21:20, reclined upon the breast of Jesus, i.e., next to Him on the three-seat divan (John 13:23, 25).

Syn.: *anákeimai* (345), to recline; *kathízō* (2523), to cause to sit down, mid. *kathízomai*, to sit down; *kathézomai* (2516), to sit down; *káthēmai* (2521), to sit in a natural position; *katákeimai* (2621), to lie down; *anaklínō* (347), to cause to recline; *kataklínō* (2625), to make recline.

Ant.: *hístēmi* (2476), to stand; *anístēmi* (450), to rise; *stḗkō* (4739), to stand fast; *ménō* (3306), to remain; *egeírō* (1453), to raise.

378. ἀναπληρόω *anaplēróō* or *anaplērṓ*; fut. *anaplērṓsō*, from *aná* (303), up, or as an emphatic, and *plēróō* (4137), to fill. To fill the place of anyone (1 Cor 14:16, he who fills the place of an unlearned person, or who himself is such); to fill up, complete, as spoken of a measure (1 Thess 2:16); to fill up or supply a deficiency, make good (1 Cor 16:17; Phil 2:30); to fulfill a prophecy (Matt 13:14), a law (Gal 6:2; see also John 13:34); in 1 Thess 2:16, "to make the measure of sin quite full" (a.t.), distinguishing it from *plēróō* meaning just to make it full (Matt

22:32). See also Gen 15:16; Dan 8:23. The word is stronger than *plēróō* and means to make very full, to the very end, to perfection. Thus *plēróō* emphasizes the act while *anaplēróō* emphasizes the measure.

Deriv.: *antanaplēróō* (466), to fill up, supplement; *prosanaplēróō* (4322), to supply abundantly.

Syn.: *pímplēmi* (4130), to fill; *empíplēmi* (1705), to fill full; *gemízō* (1072), to fill or load full; *korénnumi* (2880), to fill or to satisfy; *mestóō* (3325), to fill full; *teléō* (5055), to fulfill, to bring to its intended end; *suntelḗō* (4931), to complete; *teleióō* (5048), to bring to an end with an element of moral behavior.

Ant.: *kenóō* (2758), to make void.

379. ἀναπολόγητος *anapológētos*; neut. *anapológētou*, masc.-fem., neut. *anapológēton*, adj. from the priv. *a* (1), without, and *apologéomai* (626), to apologize, excuse. Without apology or excuse, inexcusable (Rom 1:20; 2:1).

Syn.: *álalos* (216), mute; *ádikos* (94), unjust, treacherous.

Ant.: *díkaios* (1342), innocent, just; *athóos* (121), innocent, not guilty.

380. ἀναπτύσσω *anaptússō*; fut. *anaptúxō*, from *aná* (303), back again, and *ptússō* (4428), to roll up. To roll or fold back, unroll, as a volume or roll of a book. See Sept.: Deut 22:17. The word refers to the form of books used among the Jews which did not, like ours, consist of distinct leaves bound together, but were long scrolls of parchment rolled upon two sticks and written in columns (Luke 4:17), as copies of the OT now are used in the Jewish synagogues. This word is also used with the meaning of spreading out (Sept.: 2 Kgs 19:14).

Syn.: *anoígō* (455), to open; *dianoígō* (1272), to open up completely; *anakalúptō* (343), to unveil, open.

Ant.: *sustréphō* (4962), to twist together, collect, gather; *kammúō* (2576), to close down, to shut the eyes; *sigáō* (4601), to be silent as contrasted with

anaptússō, meaning to open up or explain with words; *kleíō* (2808), to shut up.

381. ἀνάπτω *anáptō*; fut. *anápsō*, from *aná* (303), an intens. and *háptō* (681), touch, fasten or bind to. To light up, kindle, from the fact that it was through fastening and rubbing things together that fire was produced. To produce fire or kindle (Luke 12:49; Acts 28:2); in a figurative sense (James 3:5).

Syn.: *puróō* (4448), to kindle; *kaíō* (2545), to kindle, burn; *phlogízō* (5394), to inflame, set on fire; *anazōpuréō* (329), to rekindle.

Ant.: *sbénnumi* (4570), to quench.

382. ἀναρίθμητος *anaríthmētos*; gen. *anarithmḗtou*, masc.-fem., neut. *anaríthmēton*, adj. from the priv. *a* (1), without, and *arithmós* (706), to number. Not to be numbered, innumerable (Heb 11:12; Sept.: Job 21:33; 22:5; Prov 7:26).

Syn.: *muriás* (3461), myriad, ten thousand or an indefinite number; in the pl. *muriádes*, innumerable; *pleonázōn* (the pres. part. of *pleonázō* [4121], to superabound), superabundant; *ámetros* (280), without measure.

Ant.: *olígos* (3641), small or little in quantity; *mikrós* (3398), little, small; *brachús* (1024), short of number or quantity.

383. ἀνασείω *anaseíō*; fut. *anaseísō*, from *aná* (303), an emphatic, and *seíō* (4579), to move. To move or stir up. In the NT used only with reference to stirring up the multitude or people (Mark 15:11; Luke 23:5; Sept.: Job 2:3).

Syn.: *kinéō* (2795), to set in motion, move; *epegeírō* (1892), to stir up; *diegeírō* (1326), to stir up, arise; *sugkinéō* (4787), to stir up, excite; *sugchéō* (4797), to confound; *paroxúnō* (3947), to provoke; *erethízō* (2042), to stir, provoke; *anastatóō* (387), to excite, unsettle.

Ant.: *eirēneúō* (1514), to pacify; *eirēnopoiéō* (1517), to make peace; *siōpáō* (4623), to keep silence, peace;

hēsucházō (2270), to cease, to be quiet, render quiet; *phimóō* (5392), to muzzle.

384. ἀνασκευάζω *anaskeuázō*; fut. *anaskeuásō*, from *aná* (303), back, and *skeuázō* (n.f., see below), to prepare, which is from *skeúos* (4632), a vessel, furniture. To pack up baggage, and so forth, in order to remove, hence to subvert or unsettle (Acts 15:24).
    Deriv. of *skeuázō* (n.f.): *aposkeuázō* (643), to remove; *kataskeuázō* (2680), to prepare fully; *paraskeuázō* (3903), to make ready, prepare.
    Syn.: *anastatóō* (387), to disturb (e.g., Gal 5:12); *anatrépō* (396), to overthrow; *ekstréphō* (1612), to turn inside out; *diastréphō* (1294), to distort; *metastréphō* (3344), to transform into something of an opposite character.
    Ant.: *oikodoméō* (3618), to build up; *anoikodoméō* (456), to build again; *epoikodoméō* (2026), to build upon; *kataskeuázō* (2680), to establish; *stērízō* (4741), to strengthen; *stereóō* (4732), to make firm; *bebaióō* (950), to confirm, establish.

385. ἀνασπάω *anaspáō*; contracted *anaspṓ*, from *aná* (303), up or back again, and *spáō* (4685), to draw. To draw up or back again (Luke 14:5; Acts 11:10).
    Syn.: *anabibázō*, to make go up, cause to ascend; *súrō* (4951), to drag; *harpázō* (726), to snatch away; *ekbállō* (1544), to pull out; *helkúō* or *hélkō* (1670), to draw.
    Ant.: *eiságō* (1521), to bring in; *embállō* (1685), to cast into; *eispēdáō* (1530), to rush in; *eisdéchomai* (1523), to receive.

386. ἀνάστασις *anástasis*; gen. *anastáseōs*, fem. noun from *anístēmi* (450), to stand up. Resurrection, recovery.
    (I) A standing on the feet again or rising as opposed to falling; used figuratively in Luke 2:34.
    (II) Resurrection of the body from death, return to life.

    (A) Spoken of individuals who have returned to life (Heb 11:35; Sept.: 1 Kgs 17:17f.; 2 Kgs 4:20f.). Of the resurrection of Jesus (Acts 1:22; 2:31; 4:33; 17:18; Rom 1:4; 6:5; Phil 3:10; 1 Pet 1:3; 3:21).
    (B) Spoken of the future resurrection (John 11:24; Acts 17:32; 24:15, 21; 26:23; 1 Cor 15:12, 13, 21, 42; Heb 6:2); resurrection unto life or unto condemnation (John 5:29). In Heb 11:35, "that they might obtain a better resurrection," i.e., than that just before spoken. Resurrection denied by the Sadducees (Matt 22:23, 28, 30, 31; Mark 12:18, 23; Luke 20:27, 33; Acts 23:8); by certain others (2 Tim 2:18).
    (C) Spoken of the resurrection of the righteous (Matt 22:30; Luke 14:14; 20:35, 36); the first resurrection (Rev 20:5, 6, see discussion below. Cf. 1 Cor 15:23, 24; 1 Thess 4:16).
    (D) By metonymy, the author of resurrection (John 11:25).
    In Rev 20:4–6 we read of two distinct resurrections of the dead, with 1,000 years between, in which risen saints reign with Christ. By those who spiritualize most of Rev, it is claimed that since verse four speaks of the souls of the saints and not of their bodies, this must refer to the spiritual resurrection when a believer is resurrected from his old life of sin to a new life of regeneration. The verb used in relation to these souls is "beheaded" (*pepelekisménoi*, the pl. perf. pass. part. of *pelekízō* [3990], to behead, from *pélekos*, an axe), and the reference is to the souls which have been beheaded. The word *pelekízō* is used only here and it cannot be spiritualized. This is a literal resurrection of the body since the word "resurrection" is used in referring to the body, for the most part, and only once figuratively in Luke 2:34.
    The condition indicated in Rev 20:4, however, is not that of a spiritual regeneration from spiritual death, but of actual death of the body. The vision of Rev chapter twenty speaks about disembodied spirits or souls. These are the souls of those who died, death being interpreted as

the separation of the spirit from the material body. There is only one way that we can interpret the reviving of the souls and that is their reunion with their separated bodies. Therefore, the resurrection actually is when the departed spirit is joined together with a new body. In verse four, we read that these disembodied souls or spirits "lived" (*ézēsan*, the aor. indic. of *záō* [2198], which word is never applied in any instance in the NT to the souls in their disembodied state). However, it is constantly used to describe that reanimation by which the soul is united again to its tabernacle of the flesh. The souls from their disembodied existence receive again an identifiable existence but in a different form.

All throughout 1 Cor 15 the verb *zōopoiéō* (1 Cor 15:22, 36, 45), translated "to quicken," without any doubt whatsoever means the resurrection of the body from the dead. The word in these instances means to make alive, to make a new living person which is achieved by raising the body to be united with the separated soul-spirit. Thus we affirm that the verb *ézēsan*, they lived, in the latter part of Rev 20:4, must refer to the resurrection of the body and the reunification of that resurrected body with the spirit-soul of those who were dead. To affirm that this is so in verse six we have a definitive reference that this is the first resurrection, or as the Gr. has it, "the resurrection, the first one [*hē anástasis hē prótē*]" (a.t.).

Of the forty-two times in the NT that the word *anástasis* occurs, with the exception of Luke 2:34, it always means the resurrection of the body. It is never used with the meaning of spiritual regeneration or quickening. Furthermore, the two resurrections contrasted cannot be one spiritual and the other physical for there is a chronological separation between the two.

The entire scene revealed here is that of judgment (Rev 20:12), and it is the dead, small and great, standing before the Lord to be judged. It is a contrast between the people who were not adequately and completely judged during their lifetime on earth but are being judged in the afterlife in their reconstituted personalities. Thus the meaning is clear that the souls spoken of in Rev 20:4 are those whose bodies are resurrected and joined with their souls as indicated in verse twelve.

In 1 Thess 4:16, we have the prediction of Christ's return to raise His saints. In Rev 20:1, we have a similar expression of the angel descending from heaven, even as the Lord will descend from heaven. It is apparent that, in 1 Thess 4:16, the Lord is accompanied by an archangel who sounds his trumpet and then the dead in Christ shall rise first. The two scenes must refer to the same event, for although Rev 20:1 refers only to an angel, 1 Thess 4:16 refers to both the Lord and an angel. Since there is no doubt that this latter verse deals with the resurrection of the bodies of the believers, Rev 20:1 must also refer to the same.

In 1 Cor 15:23, the Apostle Paul speaks of the resurrection of Christ and then of those who are Christ's at His coming. There is no doubt whatsoever that these are the same saints described as those who constitute the first resurrection in Rev 20:5.

In Rev 20:12 the dead spoken of are in contrast to the blessed and saints (Rev 20:6). They are unbelievers who appear before the Great White Throne to be judged. These are the "rest of the dead" referred to in Rev 20:5. These "rest of the dead" who are being judged are separated in their rising and destiny from the believers who live and reign with Christ for 1,000 years (Rev 20:4), and sit with Christ on His throne and reign with Him. On the other hand, the rest of those who are unbelievers are the dead who stand before the throne to be judged.

The first group have incorruptible and immortal bodies, according to 1 Cor 15:51–54. Over these the second death has no power (Rev 20:6). As believers, they will never be separated from God and their resurrection body will never be separated from their spirits as occurred with their first death. The other dead unbelievers, whose names are not in the Book of Life, acquire corruptible bodies as their resurrection bodies. These are subject to change since they are cast into the lake of fire. Clearly there is 1,000 years existing between these two resurrections (Rev 20:5). The chronological order of the resurrection is also detailed in 1 Cor 15:21–25. Verse twenty-two says, "As in Adam all die [in the Gr. it is the pres. indic., indicating that they are in the process of dying], even so in Christ shall all be made alive [zōopoiēthḗsontai, fut. pass. of zōopoiéō, which indicates a punctiliar action in the fut., referring to the resurrection of the bodies of all, believers and unbelievers]." This is a statement of the universality of the resurrection although it does not mean that this is simultaneous. Immediately Paul goes on, however, to designate the order of this universal resurrection by saying, "But every man in his own order" (v. 23). The word "order" is tágma (5001), mentioned only here. This intimates that there are several such bands or groups of those who are being resurrected. The first one, the firstfruits of the resurrection, is Jesus Christ. What is translated as "firstfruits" in the phrase "Christ the firstfruits" is the word aparchḗ (536), which means the One who starts it off, the One making a beginning. Paul in Col 1:18 calls Him the prōtótokos (4416), the first born from the dead, or the first One given up by the world of the dead. The Lord Jesus leads this group who are His: "Afterward they that are Christ's at his coming" (1 Cor 15:23). "Afterward" (épeita [1899]) here indicates chronological time. These are believers referred to in 1 Thess 4:16 as "the dead in Christ" who shall rise first. They are the same blessed and holy ones who shall be raised first to reign with Christ for 1,000 years.

Between the resurrection of Jesus Christ and those that are Christ's, the believers, there has been a long time (at least 2,000 years). 1 Cor 15:24 begins with a correlative word of épeita, namely eíta (1534), which means afterward, after, or after that. Etymologically, since in our historical perspective we see that about 2,000 years have elapsed since the resurrection of Jesus Christ and the present time, is it not consistent to believe that there can be 1,000 years between the resurrection of the believers and the resurrection of the unbelievers?

What then, according to Paul, is the next chronological event after the resurrection of the believers? This is stated in 1 Cor 15:24 which begins with eíta, afterward, in the phrase "Afterward, the end" (a.t.). Télos (5056), end, does not indicate the termination of the world, but the goal, the expected purpose, the event which will spell the conclusion of the mediatorial work of the Lord Jesus Christ— "When he shall have delivered up the kingdom to God, even the Father, when he shall have put down all rule, and all authority and power." This is the conclusion of the present dispensation, which is called the consummation (suntéleia [4930]), of the age (aiṓn, [165]). This expression, suntéleia toú aiōnos, occurs in Matt 13:39, 40, 49; 24:3; 28:20; Heb 9:26. It is evident that this consummation completes the work which the Lord Jesus came to do for those who would believe on Him that He would raise them from the dead, give them an incorruptible body, and cause them to reign with Him forever. He also puts an end to death. These believers will never die again as they did when they were in their Adamic body.

Consequent to Christ's completion of His work for the believers, He subjugates the unbelievers as expressed in 1 Cor 15:27. The rest of the dead (Rev 20:5) do not live (in other words, are not resurrected) until the 1,000 years of Christ's reign on earth with the believers is finished. It is at that time that death and Hades give up the dead that are in them and every man is judged according to his works. We see that there is absolute harmony between the teaching of Rev chapter twenty and 1 Cor chapter fifteen, one explaining the other. The Scriptures teach that God's actions are not capriciously eclectic, but according to His foreknowledge (Rom 8:29). Jesus Christ came to save all and His salvation is offered to all, but only those are saved who believe on Him (1 Tim 4:10). They are a separate group of people within the world who are going to be treated in a distinct manner, different from those who do not believe (1 Thess 5:9). The believers, therefore, are from within the world and are called out of the world. However, they still live in the world and the day will come when they shall be, if dead, resurrected first. Then those who are Christ's and are still alive at the coming of the Lord will be changed so that their bodies will become congruous to the new environment that will be created by God for them to live in (Rom 8:19–23; 1 Thess 4:14–16; Rev 21:1).

In the same manner, the Lord is going to call the believers from among the dead. Luke 20:35 says, "But they which shall be accounted worthy to obtain that world, and the resurrection from the dead, neither marry, nor are given in marriage." The expression "the resurrection from the dead" in Gr. is *tḗs anastáseōs tḗs ek nekrṓn*, meaning "the resurrection, the one from among the dead" (a.t.). This indicates that there are some who will be raised and others who will not be. Here we have once again God's eclecticism, the scriptural teaching of election that as some are chosen in the world to be saved from the world spiritually because they believed on the Lord Jesus Christ, so those who believed are going to be chosen out from among the dead.

Since the redemption provided by Christ, there has always been a believing and an unbelieving group dealt with by God separately, not capriciously, but according to their own choice of God's sacrifice in and through Christ. This is very clearly demonstrated in Phil 3:8, 11 where Paul says, "I count all things but loss . . . if by any means I might attain unto the resurrection out from among the dead" (a.t.). The expression is the same

as that in Luke 20:35, *tḗn exanástasin tḗn ek nekrṓn*, which literally means the resurrection out from among the dead ones. The word used here is not *anástasis*, resurrection, but *exanástasis* (1815), used only here and which is made from the prep. *ek*, from out of, and *anástasis* (386), resurrection. This is an eclectic resurrection, a separation and quickening to life from among the dead. Paul intimated that this was an express and intense desire on his part to strive to attain this resurrection, to belong to this first group of those who were going to be resurrected. If the resurrection is one general, inevitable resurrection, there is absolutely no reason why Paul should strive for it since it is going to come anyway. And why should our Lord speak of those who shall be "accounted worthy to obtain that age and the resurrection out from among the dead" ([a.t.] Luke 20:35) if there were not those who are counted unworthy and are not going to obtain this resurrection? This eclectic resurrection is referred to also in OT passages such as Dan 12:2, being a Messianic eschatological portion in which we read, "And many of them that sleep in the dust of the earth shall awake, some to everlasting life, and some to shame and everlasting contempt." It is evident that some awake at one time and others at another, which agrees with the NT declarations, especially that of Rev chapter twenty.

Is there any Scripture which supports a simultaneous resurrection of the just and the unjust? Some quote John 5:25, "Verily, verily, I say unto you, The hour is coming, and now is, when the dead shall hear the voice of the Son of God: and they that hear shall live." Likewise, in verse twenty-eight we read, "Marvel not at this: for the hour is coming, in the which all that are in the graves shall hear his voice." The dead here may refer only to those who belong to Christ because it is only they that can recognize His voice. In John 10:27 we read, "My sheep hear my voice," which indicates that those who are not His sheep do not hear His voice.

This is all in the context of the resurrection. Rom 8:11 makes it amply clear that it is the Holy Spirit within us that causes us to recognize Christ's voice when He shall speak to us and our bodies shall be raised: "But if the Spirit of him that raised up Jesus from the dead dwell in you, he that raised up Christ from the dead shall also quicken your mortal bodies by his Spirit that dwelleth in you." That Spirit is the bond of life between Christ and all that sleep in Him and the pledge of their redemption from the grave (Rom 8:23). The unbelievers will not hear His voice and will not be raised at the same time as the believers. Therefore, the passage in John 5:25, 28 refers only to the resurrection of the believers. This is given to them as a distinct inheritance.

Another Scripture verse of significance is 2 Tim 4:1, "I charge thee therefore before God, and the Lord Jesus Christ, who shall judge the quick and the dead at his appearing and his kingdom." As we see in 2 Tim 4:2, the charge was for Timothy to preach the word of God. Reference here is to the judgment by Christ of the living ones at the time when He shall come for that purpose and the dead ones who will be raised who are among the rest of the dead of Rev 20:5, 12. Here the word "living" does not refer to the believers and "the dead" to the unbelievers, but rather to both unbelieving groups, i.e., those who would be alive at that time and those who would be dead.

There is no doubt that John 5:28, 29 and Luke 20:36 have reference to the literal rising of the body from the grave. Apply these to Rev 20:1–6 and you will find them perfectly fitting the words of our Lord, "Marvel not at this: for the hour is coming, in the which all that are in the graves shall hear his voice, and shall come forth; they that have done good, unto the resurrection of life" (John 5:28, 29). "And they lived and reigned with Christ" (Rev 20:4); this is the first resurrection (Rev 20:6). In Luke 20:35, 36 we read, "They which shall be accounted worthy to obtain that world, and the resurrection from the dead, neither marry, nor are given in marriage, neither can they die any more"; and in Rev 20:6, "On such [who have experienced the first resurrection] the second death hath no power." Thus, "They which shall be accounted worthy to obtain . . . the resurrection from the dead" in Luke 20:35 are the believers in Rev 20:6 who are called "blessed and holy" and who have part in the first resurrection. John 5:29, "They that have done evil, unto the resurrection of damnation," corresponds to Rev 20:12, "And the dead were judged . . . according to their works." These texts, although found in different places, must be fitted together for us to get the panorama of the resurrection of both the believers and the unbelievers.

Syn.: *égersis* (1454), a rousing, resurrection (Matt 27:53).

387. ἀναστατόω *anastatóō*; contracted *anastató*, fut. *anastatósō*, from *anástatos* (n.f.), made to rise up and depart, which is from *anístēmi* (450), to stand up. To disturb, disquiet, unsettle (Acts 17:6; Gal 5:12); to excite, stir up to sedition (Acts 21:38).

Syn.: *epegeírō* (1892), to stir up; *diegeírō* (1326), to arouse or stir up; *anaseíō* (383), to shake out, move to and fro, stir up; *saleúō* (4531), to shake, stir up; *paroxúnō* (3947), to provoke; *erethízō* (2042), to stir up, provoke; *tarássō* (5015), to trouble; *diatarássō* (1298), to agitate greatly, and *ektarássō* (1613), to throw into great trouble; *enochléō* (1776), to disturb, vex; *parenochléō* (3926), to annoy, trouble; *skúllō* (4660), to annoy; *thorubéō* (2350), to make noise or an uproar; *throéō* (2360), to make an outcry; *thorubéō* (2350), to disturb, trouble, or *turbázō* (5182), to trouble.

Ant.: *hēsucházō* (2270), to be still; *katastéllō* (2687), to appease; *eirēneúō* (1514), to bring to peace; *eirēnopoiéō* (1517), to make peace; *sigáō* (4601), to be silent; *siōpáō* (4623), to be silent or still; *phimóō* (5392), to muzzle.

388. ἀνασταυρόω *anastauróō*; contracted *anastaurṓ*, fut. *anastaurṓsō*, from *aná* (303), again or up, and *stauróō* (4717), to crucify. To crucify again or afresh (Heb 6:6).

389. ἀναστενάζω *anastenázō*; fut. *anastenáxō*, from *aná* (303), an emphatic, and *stenázō* (4727), to groan. To give forth a deep-drawn sigh, to sigh or groan deeply (Mark 8:12).

  Syn.: *embrimáomai* (1690), to snort with anger, to fret, be moved painfully, express indignation, murmur against, groan; *goggúzō* (1111), to murmur; *ōdínō* (5605), to experience pain in childbearing.

  Ant.: *geláō* (1070), to laugh; *agalliáō* (21), to rejoice greatly; *chaírō* (5463), to rejoice; *euphraínomai* (2165), to be merry, glad, rejoice.

390. ἀναστρέφω *anastréphō*; fut. *anastrépsō*, aor. pass. *anestráphēn*, from *aná* (303), again, and *stréphō* (4762), to turn. To overturn, return.

  (I) To turn up, overturn (John 2:15).

  (II) To turn back again, intrans. mid., to return (Acts 5:22; 15:16; Sept.: Gen 8:7, 9; 14:7, cf. Amos 9:11). Generally meaning to restore, set up again.

  (III) Mid. *anastréphomai*, and *anestráphēn*, 2d aor. pass., to turn oneself around, to be turned around, followed by *en* (1722), in, and the dat.:

  (A) Of place, to move about in a place, to sojourn, dwell in (Matt 17:22; 2 Cor 1:12; Sept.: Josh 5:5; Ezek 19:6); of a state, a thing, to be occupied with, to be in, live in (2 Pet 2:18).

  (B) Of persons, literally to move about, among, i.e., to live with, be conversant with, and hence generally to live or pass one's time, to conduct oneself (Eph 2:3; 1 Tim 3:15; Heb 10:33; 13:18; 1 Pet 1:17; Sept.: Prov 20:7; Ezek 22:7).

  Syn.: *politeúomai* (4176), to conduct oneself as a citizen worthy of his country; *bióō* (980), to spend one's life; *epanágō* (1877), to bring back.

  Ant.: *anatrépō* (396), to turn up or over; *katalúō* (2647), to overthrow; *katargéō* (2673), to abolish.

391. ἀναστροφή *anastrophḗ*; gen. *anastrophḗs*, fem. noun from *anastréphō* (390), to turn up, to move about. A turning about. In the NT, mode of life, conduct, behavior, deportment (Gal 1:13; Eph 4:22; 1 Tim 4:12; James 3:13; 1 Pet 2:7; 3:11); life, as made up of actions (Heb 13:7; 1 Pet 1:15).

  Syn.: *agōgḗ* (72), mode of living; *bíos* (979), living, livelihood; *zōḗ* (2222), life; *katástēma* (2688), demeanor; *trópos* (5158), a manner of living; *políteuma* (4175), the behavior of a citizen; *bíōsis* (981), the spending of one's life; *éthos* (1485), custom; *ḗthos* (2239), moral conduct, used usually in the pl. meaning morals.

392. ἀνατάσσομαι *anatássomai*; fut. *anatáxomai*, from *aná* (303), an intens., and *tássō* (5021), to place in one's proper category. To compose in an orderly manner. Only in Luke 1:1.

  Syn.: *horízō* (3724), to determine, define; *títhēmi* (5087), to place; *paratíthēmi* (3908), to place alongside; *apokathístēmi* (600), to restore.

  Ant.: *ménō* (3306), to remain; *apókeimai* (606), to await; *parákeimai* (3873), to lie near.

393. ἀνατέλλω *anatéllō*; fut. *anatelṓ*, aor. *anéteila*, perf. *anatétalka*, from *aná* (303), up, and *téllō* (n.f.), to set out for a goal. to rise, cause to rise. Intrans. to rise, spring, spring up as the sun (Matt 4:16; 13:6; Mark 4:6; 16:2; James 1:11, cf. 2 Pet 1:19; Sept.: Gen 32:31; Ex 22:3; Judg 9:33; Isa 58:10). Trans. to cause to rise (Matt 5:45; Sept.: Gen 3:18; Isa 61:11). To rise, spring, as the Lord Jesus Christ who stands for the true light arose from the tribe of Judah (Heb 7:14). To rise as a cloud (Luke 12:54). Also used to refer to the idea of spring forth or spread upon as the light (Sept.: Job 3:9; Isa 14:12).

Deriv.: *anatolḗ* (395), east; *exanatéllō* (1816), to spring up out of.

Syn.: *phúō* (5453), to spring up, grow; *blastánō* (985), to sprout; *anabaínō* (305), to go up; *hállomai* (242), to leap; *anístēmi* (450), to stand up; *exanístēmi* (1817), to rise up out of; *egeírō* (1453), to raise; *anabaínō* (305), to go up.

Ant.: *dúnō* (1416), to set as spoken of the sun; *kathízō* (2523), to set, to cause to sit down.

394. ἀνατίθημι *anatíthēmi*; mid *anatíthemai* fut. mid. *anathḗsomai*, from *aná* (303), an emphatic, and *títhēmi* (5087), to place. To lay up, suspend, as a gift in a temple (Sept.: Lev 27:28; 1 Sam 31:10). In the mid. and 2d aor., *anethémēn*, to propose, place before, communicate, declare, make known (Acts 25:14; Gal 2:2; Sept.: Mic 7:5).

Deriv.: *anáthema* (331), accursed; *anáthēma* (334), a gift; *prosanatíthēmi* (4323), to confer.

Syn.: *bállō* (906), to place; *aggareúō* (29), to compel; *phortízō* (5412), to load, burden.

Ant.: *apokleíō* (608), to exclude.

395. ἀνατολή *anatolḗ*; gen. *anatolḗs*, fem. noun from *anatéllō* (393), to rise. The dayspring or dawn, used only in a spiritual sense (Luke 1:78). The word in the sing. or the pl. also refers to that region or those parts of the heaven or earth where the solar light first springs up and appears, the east, the dayspring, dawn, the rising sun (Matt 2:1, 2, 9; 8:11; 24:27; Luke 13:29; Rev 7:2; 16:12; 21:13; Sept.: Isa 9:2; 60:1, 3). A shoot (Jer 23:5; Zech 3:8; 6:12). In the pl. *anatolaí* (Sept.: Gen 2:8; Num 32:19; Deut 3:27).

Syn.: *augḗ* (827), dawn; *órthros* (3722), dawn.

Ant.: *dusmḗ* (1424), sunset.

396. ἀνατρέπω *anatrépō*; fut. *anatrépsō*, from *aná* (303), again or used as an emphatic, and *trépō* (n.f., see below), to turn. To subvert, overturn (2 Tim 2:18; Titus 1:11; Sept.: Ps 118:13; Prov 10:3).

Deriv. of *trépō* (n.f.): *apotrépō* (665), to turn away or from; *ektrépō* (1624), to turn out or away, avoid; *entrépō* (1788) to withdraw, invert; *epitrépō* (4062), to overturn; *tropḗ* (5157), a turning, turning back; *trópos* (5158), turn direction; *portrépō* (4389), to turn forward.

Syn.: *katastréphō* (2690), to turn down or over, to destroy; *anastréphō* (390), to overthrow; *kataláō* (2647), to destroy; *katastrónnumi* (2693), to prostrate, overthrow.

Ant.: *antilambánomai* (482), to help; *antéchomai* (472), to support.

397. ἀνατρέφω *anatréphō*; fut. *anathrépsō*, from *aná* (303), an emphatic, and *tréphō* (5142), to nourish, nurse. To nourish up, nurse, bring up, educate (Acts 7:20, 21; 22:3).

Syn.: *ektréphō* (1625), to nurture, rear children; *entréphō* (1789), to train up; *chortázō* (5526), to satisfy; *korénnumi* (2880), to eat enough; *diatēréō* (1301), to keep; *suntēréō* (4933), to sustain, preserve; *psōmízō* (5595), to supply food; *paideúō* (3811), to train up.

Ant.: *peináō* (3983), to famish; *nēsteúō* (3522), to fast.

398. ἀναφαίνω *anaphaínō*; fut. *anaphanō*, from *aná* (303), an emphatic, and *phaínō* (5316), to show. The mid. / pass. *anaphaínoma*, to be shown, appear openly (Luke 19:11; Acts 21:3; Sept.: Job 11:18).

Syn.: *optánomai* and *óptomai* (3700), to allow oneself to be seen.

Ant.: *krúptō* (2928), to conceal; *apokrúptō* (613), to keep secret; *egkrúptō* (1470), to hide in something as leaven hidden in meal (Matt 13:33); *perikrúptō* (4032), to hide by placing something around; *kalúptō* (2572), to cover; *lanthánō* (2990), to escape notice, to be hidden from.

399. ἀναφέρω *anaphérō*; fut. *anoísō*, aor. *anénegka*, 2d aor. *anénegkon*, from *aná* (303), up, and *phérō* (5342), to carry, bring, bear. To carry, bring up.

(I) To carry or bring up (Matt 17:1; Mark 9:2; Luke 24:51; Sept.: 1 Sam 17:54; 1 Chr 15:3, 12, 14; 2 Chr 5:1, 3, 4; 29:31).

(II) To offer sacrifices by bringing them up to the altar (Heb 7:27 [cf. James 2:21]; Sept.: Gen 8:20; Lev 6:26; 14:19; Num 23:2; Judg 11:31; 2 Chr 1:6). Spiritually (Heb 13:15, referring to spiritual sacrifices which Christians are to offer in and through Him; 1 Pet 2:5).

(III) To take up and bear sins by imputation as typified by the ancient sacrifices, to take away (Heb 9:28; 1 Pet 2:24 [cf. Ex 29:10; Lev 1:4; 16:21, 22; Isa 53:6, 12]).

Syn.: *bastázō* (941), to support as a burden; *aírō* (142), to raise up, lift; *poiéō* (4160), to do, reduce, bear; *ágō* (71), to lead, see also its deriv.; *komízō* (2865), to bring, receive; *paréchō* (3930), to offer, furnish, supply; *dídōmi* (1325), to give; *spéndō* (4689), to pour out as a drink offering; *epidídōmi* (1929), to give; *thúō* (2380), to sacrifice by slaying a victim.

Ant.: *kratéō* (2902), to keep, retain; *epilambánōmai* (1949), to lay hold of; *nosphízōmai* (3557), to set apart for oneself, keep back in the sense of embezzling.

400. ἀναφωνέω *anaphōnéō*; contracted *anaphōnṓ*, fut. *anaphōnḗsō*, from *aná* (303), an emphatic, and *phōnéō* (5455), to cry out. To speak out (Luke 1:42).

Syn.: *epiphōnéō* (2019), to shout against or in acclamation; *boáō* (994), to raise a cry and its deriv.: *krázō* (2896), to cry out; *kraugázō* (2905), to shout; *anakrázō* (349), to cry out loudly; *anaboáō* (310), to cry out.

Ant.: *phimóō* (5392), to muzzle, put to silence; *sigáō* (4601), to be silent; *siōpáō* (4623), to hush.

401. ἀνάχυσις *anáchusis*; gen. *anachúseōs*, fem. noun from *anachéō* (n.f.), to pour forth, which is from *aná* (303), an intens., and *chéō* (n.f., see *epichéō*

[2022]), to pour out. A profusion, effusion, gulf, or pool of water, but not used in this sense in the NT. In a figurative sense, a sewer of vice or debauchery (1 Pet 4:4).

Syn.: *asōtía* (810), prodigality; *kṓmos* (2970), rioting; *truphḗ* (5172), luxuriousness.

Ant.: *sōphrosúnē* (4997), soberness.

402. ἀναχωρέω *anachōréō*; fut. *anachōrḗsō*, from *aná* (303), back again or an emphatic, and *chōréō* (5562), to go, depart. To go or turn back again (Matt 2:12, 13; 4:12; 27:5). To depart (Matt 9:24; 12:15; 14:13; 27:5 [cf. Matt 15:21]). To withdraw, retire (Matt 2:14, 22; Mark 3:7; John 6:15; Acts 23:19; 26:31).

Syn.: *hupágō* (5217), to go, depart; *poreúomai* (4198), to depart from one place to another; *chōrízomai* (5563), to separate oneself; *analúō* (360), to depart, especially from this life; *éxeimi* (1826), to go out; *metaírō* (3332), to depart; *aphístēmi* (868), to stand off, to depart from anyone; *metabaínō* (3327), to depart; *ápeimi* (548), to go away; *apérchomai* (565), to go away; *apodēméō* (589), to go to another country; *paragínomai* (3854), to go; *hodoiporéō* (3596), to go or be on a journey; *epistréphō* (1994), return; *aphístēmi* (868), to withdraw oneself, stand away from.

Ant.: *paragínomai* (3854), to come near, be present; *ménō* (3306), to remain, and its comp. *paraménō* (3887), to remain beside; *prosménō* (4357), to continue with; *diatríbō* (1304), to spend time with, to stay; *aulízomai* (835), to lodge; *agrauléō* (63), to lodge in a fold in a field; *hístēmi* (2476), to stand, to abide.

403. ἀνάψυξις *anápsuxis*; gen. *anapsúxeōs*, fem. noun from *anapsúchō* (404), to refresh. A refreshing, being refreshed. In Acts 3:19, we have the times of refreshing (*anapsúxeōs*), relating to the blessings of Christ's first coming and His kingdom of grace (cf. Matt 11:29) and the restitution (*apokatástasis* [605], Acts 3:21) referring to the state of righteousness which will be brought by His Second Coming beginning the kingdom of glory.

Syn.: *anápausis* (372), inner rest, refreshment; *katápausis* (2663), cessation involving rest; *ánesis* (425), relief; *sabbatismós* (4520), a Sabbath rest; *koímēsis* (2838), a resting through sleep; *eirénē* (1515), peace.

Ant.: *thlípsis* (2347), affliction; *tarachḗ* (5016), agitation, disturbance; *stenochōría* (4730), narrowness of place, distress, anguish; *sunochḗ* (4928), a compressing, distress; *anágkē* (318), a necessity; *móchthos* (3449), travail, labor, involving painful effort; *ōdín* (5604), birth pang; *lúpē* (3077), grief, sorrow; *odúnē* (3601), pain, sorrow; *básanos* (931), torment.

404. ἀναψύχω *anapsúchō*; fut. *anapsúxō*, from *aná* (303), again, and *psúchō* (5594), to breathe, wax cold. To make cool, refresh. Cooling again, refrigerating or refreshing with cool air as the body when overheated. Intrans. in Sept.: Ex 23:12; Judg 15:19; Ps 39:13; 1 Sam 16:23. Not used in the NT in this sense, but used figuratively, meaning to refresh, to relieve when under distress (2 Tim 1:16).

Deriv.: *anápsuxis* (403), refreshing.

Syn.: *anapaúō* (373), to give inner rest; *sunanapaúonai* (4875), to rest with; *katapaúō* (2664), to cause to rest by ceasing from labor; *hēsucházō* (2270), to be still, rest from labor; *epanapaúomai* (1879), to rest upon; *aniēmi* (447), to refresh.

Ant.: *tarássō* (5015), to trouble, disturb; *diatarássō* (1298), to agitate greatly and *ektarássō* (1613), to throw into great trouble, agitate; *thlíbō* (2346), to afflict; *enochléō* (1776), to throng, trouble, vex; *parenochléō* (3926), to annoy; *skúllō* (4660), to vex, annoy; *anastatóō* (387), to upset; *thorubéō* (2350), to cause noise or an uproar; *throéō* (2360), to make an outcry; *thorubázō* (2350) or *turbázō* (5182), to disturb, trouble; *adēmonéō* (85), to be bewildered; *diaponéō* (1278), to work out

with toil; *kópous paréchō* (*kópous* [2873], troubles, fatigue; *paréchō* [3930], to supply), to cause trouble; *ōdínō* (5605), to be in birth pangs.

405. ἀνδραποδιστής *andrapodistḗs*; gen. *andrapodistoú*, masc. noun from *andrapodízō* (n.f.), to enslave, which is from *andrápodon* (n.f.), a slave. A man stealer, kidnapper, one who steals men to make them slaves or sell them into slavery. *Andrapodistḗs* is not only he who by deceit reduces free men to slavery, but also seduces slaves from their masters in order to convey them elsewhere and sell them. Both activities are prohibited for Christians (1 Tim 1:10). *Andrápodon* is a captive slave, while *doúlos* (1401), which originally was the lowest term in the scale of servitude, is a bond-slave.

Syn.: verbal: *doulóō* (1402), *doulagōgéō* (1396) and *katadoulóō* (2615), to make a slave of, bring into bondage,.

Ant.: *lutrōtḗs* (3086), redeemer.

406. Ἀνδρέας *Andréas*; gen. *Andréou*, proper noun. Andrew, a native of Bethsaida (John 1:44) shared the same house at Capernaum (Mark 1:21, 29) with his better known brother Simon Peter. By trade he was a fisherman (Matt 4:18), but attracted by all that he had heard or seen of John the Baptist, he, for a time at least, left his work and followed John the Baptist into the wilderness. There he came to be recognized as one of John's disciples (John 1:35, 40). When Christ came, He found Andrew with a heart ready and eager to welcome Him. No sooner did Andrew meet the Lord than he went in search of his brother Peter (John 1:35–42). Later, Jesus met Andrew by the sea along with his three companions and called them to follow Him (Matt 4:18ff.). Andrew was later appointed to a place in the apostolic group (Matt 10:2ff.). His place must have been a place of honor for his name always occurs in the first group of four, and it is with Peter, James and John that he is again associated in the private inquiries to Jesus regarding the time of the last things (Mark 13:3). He appears in the story of the feeding of the 5,000 (John 6:5ff.) and again in John 12:20ff. when the Greeks came to see Jesus. He is especially associated with Philip, the only other apostle who bore a Greek name. It is generally believed that he was martyred at Patrae in Achaia, Greece, being bound but not nailed to a cross in order to prolong his sufferings. He was not only the first home missionary (John 1:41), but also the first foreign missionary (John 12:22).

407. ἀνδρίζω *andrízō*; fut. *andrísō*, from *anḗr* (435), a man or husband. To behave oneself with the wisdom and courage of a man, as opposed to a babe or child in Christ (1 Cor 16:13; Sept.: Deut 31:6, 7; Josh 1:6, 9; 10:25). To behave courageously.
    Ant.: *nēpiázō* (3515), to be or act as a baby.

408. Ἀνδρόνικος *Andrónikos*; gen. *Androníkou*, proper noun. Andronicus, a Greek name saluted by Paul in Rom 16:7, and coupled with that of Junias or Junia. It is impossible, as this name occurs in the acc. case, to determine whether it is masc. or fem. The pair are described as "my kinsmen" by Paul, by which may be meant fellow Jews (Rom 9:3), possibly members of the same tribe, almost certainly not relatives. The only relatives of Paul known to us are a sister and a nephew (Acts 23:16). Andronikos and Junias are also described as Paul's fellow prisoners. They may have shared imprisonment with Paul, possibly in Philippi (Acts 16:23). It is possible, however, that they were not in prison together with Paul, but that they may have suffered imprisonment even as Paul did. They are also described as "of note among the apostles" which means notable or distinguished among the apostles (Rom 16:7). They were apparently Christians even before Paul became one (Rom 16:7).

409. ἀνδροφόνος *androphónos*; gen. *androphónou*, masc. noun from *anḗr* (435), a man, and *phónos* (5408), murder. A manslayer, murderer (1 Tim 1:9).
    Syn.: *phoneús* (5406), a murderer; *olothreutḗs* (3644), destroyer; *anthrōpoktónos* (443), a manslayer, murderer; *patrolóas* (3964), a murderer of one's father; *sikários* (4607), an assassin; *mētralóas* (3389), a murderer of mothers.
    Ant.: *lutrōtḗs* (3086), redeemer; *sōtḗr* (4990), savior.

410. ἀνέγκλητος *anégklētos*; gen. *anegklḗtou*, masc.-fem., neut. *anégklēton*, adj. from the priv. *a* (1), without, and *egkaléō* (1458), to accuse in court. Not merely unaccusable but unaccused, free from any legal charge. Occurs in 1 Cor 1:8; Col 1:22; 1 Tim 3:10; Titus 1:6, 7.
    Syn.: *ámemptos* (273), unblamable; *ámōmos* (299), unblemished; *anepílēptos* (423), irreproachable; *áspilos* (784), unspotted; *amṓmētos* (298), without blemish; *anaítios* (338), guiltless.
    Ant.: *énochos* (1777), liable to a charge in court; *hupódikos* (5267), one under judgment; *kategnōsménos*, condemned, the perf. part. of *kataginṓskō* (2607), to blame, condemn.

411. ἀνεκδιήγητος *anekdiḗgētos*; gen. *anekdiēgḗtou*, masc.-fem., neut. *anekdiḗgēton*, adj. from the priv. *a* (1), without, and *ekdiēgéomai* (1555), to relate particularly. Incapable of being adequately expressed or uttered, unspeakable, inexpressible, unutterable, ineffable (2 Cor 9:15).
    Syn.: *aneklálētos* (412), unable to be told out; *árrhētos* (731), incapable of being spoken, unspeakable.
    Ant.: *graptós* (1123), written.

412. ἀνεκλάλητος *aneklálētos*; gen. *aneklalḗtou*, masc.-fem., neut. *aneklálēton*, adj. from the priv. *a* (1), without, and *eklaléō* (1583), to utter. Unutterable, inexpressible (1 Pet 1:8).

Syn.: *anekdiḗgētos* (411), inexpressible; *árrētos* (731), unspoken.
Ant.: *graptós* (1123), written.

413. ἀνέκλειπτος *anékleiptos*; gen. *anekleíptou*, masc.-fem., neut. *anékleipton*, adj. from the priv. *a* (1), without, and *ekleípō* (1587), to fail. That which does not fail, unfailing (Luke 12:33).
Syn.: *bébaios* (949), sure.

414. ἀνεκτότερος *anektóteros*; gen. *anektotérou*, masc. adj., the comparative of *anektós*, tolerable, from *anéchō* (430), to bear. More tolerable, easier to be borne (Matt 10:15; 11:22, 24; Mark 6:11; Luke 10:12, 14).
Syn.: *epieikḗs* (1933), gentle, tolerant; *makrothumía* (3115), longsuffering toward people; *anexíkakos* (420), forbearing evil.
Ant.: *austerós* (840), austere; *sklērós* (4642), stern, hard.

415. ἀνελεήμων *aneleḗmōn*; gen. *aneleḗmonos*, masc.-fem., neut. *aneleḗmon*, adj. from the priv. *a* (1), without, and *eleḗmōn* (1655), merciful. Unmerciful, not compassionate (Rom 1:31).
Syn.: *aníleōs* (448), unmerciful, merciless.
Ant.: *eleḗmōn* (1655), merciful; *híleōs* (2436), propitious, merciful, a quality of God toward undeserving man; *eúsplagchnos* (2155), compassionate, sympathetic; *chrēstós* (5543), gracious, kind, benevolent.

416. ἀνεμίζω *anemízō*; fut. *anemísō*, from *ánemos* (417), wind. In the mid. pass. *anemízomai*, to be impelled or driven by the wind, spoken of the waves (James 1:6).

417. ἄνεμος *ánemos*; gen. *anémou*, masc. noun. Wind (Matt 7:25, 27; 8:26; 11:7; 14:24, 30, 32; Mark 4:37, 39, 41; 6:48, 51; Luke 7:24; 8:23–25; John 6:18; Acts 27:4, 7, 14, 15; James 3:4; Jude 1:12; Rev 6:13; Sept.: Job 21:18; Isa 41:16 [cf.

Eph 4:14, metaphorically as the emblem of instability, i.e., empty doctrine, unstable opinion {Job 15:2}]). The four winds are used for the four cardinal points, or the North, South, East, and West (Matt 24:31; Mark 13:27; Rev 7:1 [cf. Luke 13:29]; Sept.: 1 Chr 9:24; Jer 49:36; Dan 11:4).
Deriv.: *anemízō* (416), to toss or drive with the wind.
Syn.: *pnoḗ* (4157), breath, used of the rushing wind at Pentecost (Acts 2:2); *pneúma* (4151), spirit (John 3:8); *thúella* (2366), tempest; *laílaps* (2978), whirlwind.

418. ἀνένδεκτος *anéndektos*; gen. *anendéktou*, masc.-fem., neut. *anéndekton*, adj. from the priv. *a* (1), without, and *endéchetai* (1735), it is possible. Impossible (Luke 17:1), not allowed.
Syn.: *adúnatos* (102), inadmissible.
Ant.: *dunatós* (1415), possible; *éxesti* (1832), it is permissible.

419. ἀνεξερεύνητος *anexereúnētos*; gen. *anexereunḗtou*, masc.-fem., neut. *anexereúnēton*, adj. from the priv. *a* (1), without, and *exereunáō* (1830), to search out. Not capable of being searched out, inscrutable (Rom 11:33). See Prov 25:3; Jer 17:9.
Syn.: *anexichníastos* (421), impossible to trace out, unsearchable.
Ant.: *phanerós* (5318), apparent, and its syn.

420. ἀνεξίκακος *anexíkakos*; *anexíkákou*, masc.-fem., neut. *anexíkakon*, adj. from *anéchō* (430), to bear, and *kakós* (2556), bad. Patient, describing one who bears evil, sorrow, ill. Occurs only in 2 Tim 2:24.
Syn.: *epieikḗs* (1933), tolerant. This stresses the positive attitude in contrast to *anexíkakos*, which stresses the neg. attitude of being patient regarding wrong; *anektóteros* (414), more tolerable.
Ant.: *aneleḗmōn* (415), merciless.

421. ἀνεξιχνίαστος *anexichníastos*; gen. *anexichniástou*, masc.-fem., neut. *anexichníaston*, adj. from the priv. *a* (1), without, and *exichniázō* (n.f.), to explore. Impossible to be traced out, untraceable, unsearchable (Rom 11:33; Eph 3:8; Sept.: Job 5:9; 9:10; 34:24).

Syn.: *anexereúnētos* (419), search diligently, impossible to be searched out, unsearchable. *Anexereúnētos* is generally impossible to search out, while *anexichníastos* has the meaning of impossible to trace step-by-step.

Ant.: *phanerós* (5318), manifest.

422. ἀνεπαίσχυντος *anepaíschuntos*; gen. *anepaischúntou*, masc.-fem., neut. *anepaíschunton*, adj. from the priv. *a* (1), without, and *epaischúnomai* (1870), to be ashamed. Not to be ashamed, irreproachable (2 Tim 2:15).

Ant.: *aischrós* (150), shameful, base, filthy.

423. ἀνεπίληπτος *anepílēptos*; gen. *anepilḗptou*, masc.-fem., neut. *anepílēpton*, adj. from the priv. *a* (1), without, and *epilambánō* (1949), to seize. One who has nothing which an adversary could seize upon with which to base a charge. Rendered in 1 Tim 3:2; 5:7 "blameless" and in 1 Tim 6:14 "unrebukable." "Irreprehensible" is a closer translation, giving the true meaning of the word.

Syn.: *anégklētos* (410), legally unaccused. *Anepílēptos* demonstrates a higher morality on which no blame can be found to base an accusation, while *anégklētos* indicates that one cannot be legally charged; *ámōmos* (299), without blemish; *amṓmētos* (298), unblamable; *ámemptos* (273), one in whom no fault can be found; *eúphēmos* (2163), of good report; *anaítios* (338), guiltless; *akatákritos* (178), uncondemned; *áspilos* (784), unspotted; *dókimos* (1384), approved; *áxios* (514), worthy.

Ant.: *potapós* (4217), awful; *adókimos* (96), unapproved.

424. ἀνέρχομαι *anérchomai*; fut. *aneleúsomai*, aor. *anḗlthon*, from *aná* (303), up, and *érchomai* (2064), to come. To go up (John 6:3; Gal 1:17, 18). See Sept.: Judg 21:8; 1 Kgs 13:12.

Deriv.: *epanérchomai* (1880), to return.

Syn.: *anabaínō* (305), to ascend; *hupsóō* (5312), to lift; *epaíromai* (1869), to raise oneself up; *meteōrízō* (3349), to suspend.

Ant.: *katérchomai* (2718), to come down; *katabaínō* (2597), to go down; *píptō* (4098), to fall; *rhíptomai* (4496), to throw oneself down; *katapíptō* (2667), to fall down completely.

425. ἄνεσις *ánesis*; gen. *anéseōs*, fem. noun from *aníēmi* (447), to loose. Liberty, rest.

In 2 Thess 1:7, Paul is speaking about the revelation of the Lord Jesus Christ from heaven, which is the same event described by him in 1 Thess 4:13–18. This event commonly known as the rapture of the resurrected believers and the changed living ones is provided as a basis for not sorrowing (1 Thess 4:13) and providing comfort (1 Thess 4:18). In 2 Thess 1:7, the *ánesis* is provided as a comforting prospect for those who were being afflicted (*thliboménois*, from *thlíbomai* [2346], to suffer affliction, from *thlípsis* [2347], tribulation, applied among other tribulations to the time of the Tribulation that the remaining unbelievers will suffer when the Lord comes for His own). Therefore, in 2 Thess 1:7, the word *ánesis* must be viewed as the loosening from the earth which believers will experience, whether under the ground as their bodies will be if they are dead, or on the ground if they are alive. They will be taken up and thus loosed from their affliction and tribulation. This rest or relaxation through ascent to be with Christ is what is meant by the Day of Christ or "the day of the Lord Jesus" (1 Cor 1:8; 5:5; 2 Cor 1:14; Phil 1:6, 10; 2:16; 2 Thess 2:2).

In Acts 24:23, to have *ánesin* means to be freed from bonds, to give liberty, and so forth A good translation of *ánesis* in 2 Cor 8:13 would be "not that others may be freed from the duty of contributing" (a.t.). *Ánesis* also means rest, quiet, either internal as in 2 Cor 2:13 or external as in 2 Cor 7:5; also in 2 Thess 1:7 by being taken up from this earth as explained above.

Syn.: *anápausis* (372), inward rest while laboring, whereas *ánesis* indicates a relaxation brought about by a source other than oneself; *chará* (5479), joy; *agallíasis* (20), exuberance; *euphrosúnē* (2167), rejoicing; *áphesis* (859), release, liberty, forgiveness; *eleuthería* (1657), freedom; *katápausis* (2663), rest by ceasing to work.

Ant.: *thlípsis* (2347), affliction; *lúpē* (3077), sorrow; *stenochōría* (4730), distress; *pónos* (4192), pain; *anágkē* (318), distress.

426. ἀνετάζω *anetázō*; fut. *anetásō*, from *aná* (303), an emphatic, and *etázō* (n.f.), to examine. To examine strictly, thoroughly or forensically, to examine by scourging (Acts 22:24, 29; Sept.: Judg 6:29). Also from *etázō* (n.f.): *exetázō* (1833), to verify, explore.

Syn.: *exereunáō* (1830), to explore; *anakrínō* (350), to investigate, carry on an inquiry, forensically to examine by torture; *dokimázō* (1381), to test, approve; *peirázō* (3985), to tempt, try; *exetázō* (1833), to search out.

Ant.: *aphíēmi* (863), to let go; *apolúō* (630), to dismiss; *ameléō* (272), to neglect.

427. ἄνευ *áneu*; prep. governing a gen. Without, not with. Spoken of things, e.g., of an instrument, without the help of (1 Pet 3:1; Sept.: Ex 21:11; Isa 55:1; Dan 2:34); of manner (1 Pet 4:9, "without grumblings" [a.t.]; Sept.: 1 Sam 6:7, meaning their calves being left at home); of persons, without the knowledge or will of (Matt 10:29, without the Father's knowledge; see Sept.: Amos 3:5).

Syn.: *chōrís* (5565), apart from; *parektós* (3924), besides, in addition; *oú metá* (3757, 3326), without.

Ant.: *sún* (4862), with; *metá* (3326), with; *pará* (3844), near, expressing immediate vicinity.

428. ἀνεύθετος *aneúthetos*; gen. *aneuthétou*, masc.-fem., neut. *aneútheton*, adj. from the priv. *a* (1), without, and *eúthetos* (2111), fit, opportune. Unfit, inconvenient, not appropriate (Acts 27:12).

Syn.: *átopos* (824), improper.

Ant.: *eúthetos* (2111), opportune; *epitḗdeios* (2006), requisite.

429. ἀνευρίσκω *aneurískō*; fut. *aneurḗsō*, 2d aor., *aneúron*, from *aná* (303), an emphatic, and *heurískō* (2147), to find. To find out by diligent seeking (Luke 2:16; Acts 21:4). While *aneurískō* in the pres. tense means to seek diligently, yet in the 2d aor., *aneúron* (in Luke 2:16) means to find out by diligent seeking.

Syn.: *anakalúptō* (343), to discover; *epiginṓskō* (1921), to become fully acquainted.

Ant.: *apóllumi* (622), to lose; *aphanízō* (853), to vanish away.

430. ἀνέχω *anéchō*; fut. *anéxō*, from *aná* (303), in, and *échō* (2192), to have. To hold up or back from falling, e.g., the rain (Sept.: Amos 4:7). To hold in or back, restrain, stop. In the NT, only in the mid., *anéchomai*; fut. *anéxomai*; imperf. *aneichómēn*, or with double augment in *ēneichómēn* in TR (2 Cor 11:1, 4); 2d aor. *ēneschómēn* (cf. Acts 18:14). To hold oneself upright, to bear up, hold out, endure.

(**I**) Spoken of things, to endure, bear patiently, with the gen. as afflictions (2 Thess 1:4). See Sept.: Isa 42:14. Used in an absolute sense (1 Cor 4:12; 2 Cor 11:20).

(**II**) Spoken of persons, to bear with, have patience with in regard to the errors or weaknesses of anyone (Matt

17:17; Mark 9:19; Luke 9:41; 2 Cor 11:1, 19; Eph 4:2; Col 3:13; Sept.: Isa 46:4; 63:15).

(III) By implication, to admit, receive, i.e., to listen to, with the gen., spoken of persons as in Acts 18:14. In 2 Cor 11:4, of doctrine. See 2 Tim 4:3; Heb 13:22; Sept.: Job 6:26.

Deriv.: *anektóteros* (414), more tolerable; *anexíkakos* (420), forbearing; *anochḗ* (463), forbearance, tolerance.

Syn.: *bastázō* (941), to support, carry, take up; *phérō* (5342), to bring or bear; *hupophérō* (5297), to bear up under, endure; *phoréō* (5409), to bear or endure habitually; *tropophoréō* (5159), to bear as a matter of permanent attitude; *stégō* (4722), to bear up against, provide a roof over; *metriopathéō* (3356), to treat with mildness or moderation, bear gently with; *karteréō* (2594), to be steadfast, patient (Heb 11:27); *kakopathéō* (2553), to suffer evil; *páschō* (3958), to suffer; *hupéchō* (5254), to hold under; *hupoménō* (5278), to endure as far as things or circumstances are concerned; *maktrothuméō* (3114), enduring or being longsuffering toward people.

Ant.: *krínō* (2919), to judge.

431. ἀνεψιός *anepsiós*; gen. *anepsioú*, masc. noun. A cousin or nephew (Col 4:10; Sept.: Num 36:11).

432. ἄνηθον *ánēthon*; gen. *anḗthou*, neut. noun. Dill, an herb (Matt 23:23).

433. ἀνήκω *anḗkō*; fut. *anéxō*, from *aná* (303), up, and *hḗkō* (2240), to come. To come up, come to, reach to, pertain, belong to. As an impersonal verb, *anékei*: it belongs, it is fit, proper, becoming (Col 3:18). What is fit, becoming (Eph 5:4; Phile 1:8).

Syn.: *prépō* (4241), to befit; *kathḗkō* (2520), to be fitting; *katartízō* (2675), to equip, make fit, prepare; *harmózō* (718), to fit.

434. ἀνήμερος *anḗmeros*; gen. *anēmérou*, masc.-fem., neut. *anḗmeron*,

adj. from the priv. *a* (1), without, and *hḗmeros*, mild. Not mild, ungentle, fierce (2 Tim 3:3).

Syn.: *chalepós* (5467), hard, difficult, fierce, grievous; *sklērós* (4642), hard, rough, fierce.

Ant.: *ḗremos* (2263), quiet, tranquil; *hēsúchios* (2272), tranquil because of an attitude within oneself; *ḗpios* (2261), mild, gentle; *eirēnikós* (1516), peaceful.

435. ἀνήρ *anḗr*; gen. *andrós*, masc. noun. Man, husband.

(I) A man, i.e, an adult male person.

(A) Males as distinguished from females (Matt 14:21; 15:38; Luke 1:34). Spoken of men in various relations and circumstances where the context determines the proper meaning; e.g., husband (Matt 1:16; Mark 10:2, 12; Luke 2:36; Rom 7:2, 3; 1 Cor 7:2–4, 10, 11, 13, 14, 16, 34, 39; 11:3, 4, 7–9, 11, 12; 14:35; 2 Cor 11:2; Gal 4:27; Eph 5:22–25, 28, 33; Col 3:18, 19; 1 Tim 2:8, 12; 3:2, 12; 5:9; Titus 1:6; 2:5; 1 Pet 3:1, 5, 7; Sept.: Gen 2:23; 3:6); a bridegroom betrothed (Matt 1:19; Rev 21:2; Sept.: Deut 22:23); a soldier (Luke 22:63). In the voc. in a direct address, in the pl. *ándres*, men (Acts 14:15; 19:25; 27:10, 21, 25). When it is desired to express respect meaning a man of weight, importance (Luke 24:19; John 1:30; James 2:2), syn. *tó árchōn* (758), chief, leader.

(B) Joined with an adj. or noun, it forms a periphrasis for a subst. In Luke 5:8 joined with the adj. *hamartōlós* (268), sinner (cf. Matt 7:24, 26; Acts 3:14). With *Ioudaíos* (2453), Jewish, meaning a Jew (Acts 10:28; see Matt 12:41; Acts 8:27; 11:20; 16:9). With other adj. in a direct address, men, meaning Athenians (Acts 17:22); Ephesians (Acts 19:35); Israelites (Acts 2:22; 3:12; 5:35; 13:16; 21:28); Galileans (Acts 1:11); brethren (Acts 1:16).

(C) A man of mature understanding as opposed to a child (1 Cor 13:11; Eph 4:13).

(II) A man, one of the human race, a person, syn. with *ánthrōpos* (444), a human being (Mark 6:44; Luke 5:12, 18; 8:27; 9:38; 11:29, 31, meaning the people of this generation; Acts 6:11; James 1:8, 20, 23; 3:2; Sept.: Prov 16:27–29; Neh 4:18). In Rom 4:8, "Blessed is the man," meaning blessed is he. Also James 1:12; Sept.: Ps 1:1; 112:5. Men of the place, meaning inhabitants (Matt 14:35; Luke 11:32; Sept.: 1 Sam 5:7).

(III) A husband, as one who plays a role in conceiving a child (John 1:13). John's gospel being written to prove Christ's deity, it is inconceivable that it would not refer to His virgin birth. John 1:13 may be that reference. In John 1:13, there is a variant reading which is supported by a detailed treatise by the Roman church father Tertullian (A.D. 155–222). This verse is presented as beginning with the sing. masc. relative pron. *hós* (3739), who, referring to "the Word" of verses one and fourteen. "In the beginning was the Word . . . and the Word was made [*egéneto* [1096], became] flesh" (a.t.). Apparently the copyists were tempted to change the *s* (sigma) at the end of the sing. relative pron. *hós* to *i* (iota) making it the pl. *hoi* to agree with *hósoi* (the pl. of *hósos* [3745], whosoever) with which verse twelve begins. It is thus made to refer back to "as many as," meaning those who receive "the Word," Jesus Christ, rather than to the *Lógos*, the Word, the One existing before becoming "flesh." In other words, if we take the relative pron. *hós* in the sing. (he who), it must refer to the eternal Christ Who from the very beginning had always been with "the God" of John 1:1, meaning the Father.

A grammatical reason in support of the acceptance of the MS in which verse thirteen begins with *hós* in the sing. is that there is no connective conj. between verses twelve and thirteen. Therefore verse thirteen must not be made to refer to verse twelve, which deals with those who receive Christ. It must rather deal with Christ Himself who, being the active cause (*arché* [746], Rev 3:14) of everything (John 1:2, 3), became flesh (John 1:14). Verse thirteen thus should be taken

as referring to the manner in which Christ became flesh.

This MS also has the last verb of verse thirteen in the 3d person sing. *egennḗthē* (aor. pass. of *gennáō* [1080], to give birth to), He was born, referring to Christ, the *Lógos*, the incorporeal One. He who was the First Cause of everything was born into the world as a material human being. John 1:13, therefore, would read *hós . . . egennḗthē*, "who (the Word) . . . was born" (a.t.) and not *hósoi . . . egennḗthēsan*, "those born." Again it was easy for the copyists to change the sing. third person *egennḗthē*, referring to "the Word," to *egennḗthēsan* by simply adding -*san* to make it pl. referring to those who receive the Word of verse twelve.

The determinative as to which MS should be accepted is the meaning of the word *andrós*, the gen. sing. of *anḗr*. Does it mean "man" as is commonly translated or "husband?" We believe it refers to a "husband," as we thoroughly examine John 1:1–18.

The verse would therefore read, "Who [the Word of v. 1] was born not of bloods [the word in all the MSS is the pl. gen. *haimátōn* and not the sing. *haímatos* (129) as most of the translations render it], nor of the will of the flesh, nor of the will of a husband, but of [*ek* (1537), out of] God [*Theoú*, no def. art. is before the word as in John 1:1b, thus meaning of deity] He was born" (a.t.). Any serious student of the Word of God can easily see that all the elements of this birth are material: bloods, those of a wife and a husband; the will of the flesh, the determination of the mind resulting in the marital relationship involving the flesh; the will of a husband (*andrós*). The word *anḗr* cannot possibly be conceived of as referring to the generic word *ánthrōpos* (444), man, anyone of the human race, male or female. There was only a woman involved, impregnated mystically and supernaturally by the Holy Spirit, Himself one of the three persons of the Trinity or Godhead (*Theoú*). It was the role of a husband that the Holy Spirit played.

The incarnation of the Word was not the result of a conjugal relationship as originally instituted by God in the beginning. Jesus Christ was born of a virgin and did not come into the physical world in the same manner that every other human being did; hence, He indeed became the only God-Man on earth.

(IV) A husband, in reference to the bonding relationship between husband and wife in marriage as illustrated by Paul in Rom 7:1–3. The principles enunciated here are:

(A) In verse two, the wife is *húpandros* (5220), under a husband. The word is translated "the woman which hath an husband" (KJV); "the married woman" (NASB, NIV). *Húpandros* derives from the prep. *hupó* (5259), under, and *andrós*, the gen. of *anér*, husband. A wife is under her husband. Here a husband is *anér* and a wife is *gunḗ* (1135). In contrast to these two specific words stands *ánthrōpos* (444), man in its generic sense in verse one, referring to both man and woman. The wife is said to be under her husband which indicates that a married woman ceases to be independent. She comes under the protection of her husband. The opposite of *húpandros* is *ágamos* (22), not married.

(B) A wife remains under the jurisdiction of her husband as long as he is alive. When he dies, she is freed from the law of her husband.

(C) This bond is not only by virtue of God's ordinance, but also legal.

(D) If a wife under a husband, while he is alive, marries another, she becomes an adulteress. This does not take into account particular circumstances discussed by Christ in Matt 5:27–32; 19:3–10; Mark 10:2–12; Luke 16:18. See also: *apolúō* (630), to dismiss; *chōrízō* (5563), to separate; *apostásion* (647), bill of divorce, certificate of innocence, separation paper; *porneía* (4202), fornication, sexual sin of any kind; *porneúō* (4203), to commit fornication; *pórnē* (4204), a harlot; *pórnos* (4205), a fornicator; *moicháō* (3429) or *moicheúō* (3431), to commit adultery; *moicheía* (3430), adultery; *moichós* (3432), an adulterer; *moichalís* (3428), an adulteress; *gaméō* (1060), to marry a wife; *gamískō* (1061), to give in marriage; *gámos* (1062), marriage; *chḗra* (5503), widow.

(V) Husband, generally (Luke 1:27, 34; 2:36; 16:18; John 1:13; 4:16–18; Acts 5:9, 10; 2 Cor 11:2; Gal 4:27). Man, male (Matt 7:24, 26; 12:41; 14:21 [adult males; 15:38; Mark 6:44; Luke 9:14; John 4:4; 6:10]; Mark 6:20; Luke 5:8, 18; 6:8; 7:20; 8:38, 41; 9:30, 32; 14:24; 17:12; 19:2, 7; 22:63; 23:50; 24:4, 19; John 1:30; Acts 1:10, 11, 16, 21; 2:5, 14, 22, 29, 37; 3:2, 12, 14; 5:1, 14, 25, 35, 36; 6:3, 5, 11; 7:2, 26; 8:2, 3, 9, 12, 27; 9:2, 7, 12, 13, 38; 10:1, 5, 17, 19, 21, 22, 28, 30; 11:3, 11, 12, 20, 24; 13:6, 7, 15, 16, 21, 22, 26, 38; 14:8, 15; 15:7, 13, 22, 25; 16:9; 17:5, 12, 22, 31, 34; 18:24, 27; 19:7, 25; 19:35, 37; 20:30; 21:11, 23, 26, 28, 38; 22:1, 3, 4, 12; 23:1, 6, 21, 27, 30; 24:5; 25:5, 14, 17, 23, 24; 27:10, 21, 25; 28:17; Rom 11:4; 1 Cor 11:4, 7–9, 11, 12, 14; 1 Tim 2:8; James 2:2).

(VI) With the verb *apolúō* (630), to dismiss unjustifiably (Mark 10:2, it is not permissible for a husband to dismiss a wife or vice versa in 10:12; Luke 16:18, he who marries a wife who has dismissed herself from her husband commits adultery).

(VII) With the verb *chōrízō* (5563), to separate (1 Cor 7:10, a wife should not separate herself from her husband).

(VIII) With the verb *aphíēmi* (863), to send forth, forsake, leave (1 Cor 7:1, a husband should not leave his wife; 7:13, and a wife whose unbelieving husband consents to live with her, should not leave him).

In Matt 19:29, the Lord Jesus said, "And every one that hath forsaken houses, or brethren, or sisters, or father, or mother, or wife, or children, or lands, for my name's sake, shall receive an hundredfold and shall inherit everlasting life." The verb translated "hath forsaken" is *aphéken*, the perf. third person sing. of *aphíēmi*, to let stand away from.

The meaning of *aphíēmi* here is equal to *apotássomai* (657), to place in one's proper category away from oneself.

(IX) With the verb *katallássō* (2644), to reconcile when the fault is hers for leaving her husband (1 Cor 7:11, "let her remain unmarried, or be reconciled to her husband"). See the verb in its contrast to *diallássō* (1259), to reconcile when the fault lies with both.

(X) The duties of a husband toward his wife:

(A) To love (*agapáō* [25]) her, to discern her needs as a wife and meet them as only a husband can (Eph 5:25, "Husbands love your very own wives, even as Christ loved the church and gave Himself for her" [a.t.]. The church is imperfect and yet Christ loves and serves her, even as a husband should an imperfect wife.) The verb *agapáte* is in the pres. imper. which indicates continuous loving. This is presented as a duty, a debt in Eph 5:28, "So ought men [husbands] to love their wives as their own bodies. He that loveth his wife loveth himself." The verb translated "ought" is *opheílō* (3784), to be under obligation. No husband can ever turn to his wife and tell her he does not love her. Marriage for a husband creates a duty to love his wife. In Col 3:19, Paul says, "Husbands, love your wives, and be not bitter against them."

There is an obligation which marital partners owe to each other as expressed in 1 Cor 7:3, 4, "Let the husband render unto the wife due benevolence: and likewise also the wife unto the husband. The wife hath not power of her own body, but the husband: and likewise also the husband hath not power of his own body, but the wife." The expression "due benevolence" is *tēn opheiloménēn eúnoian* (*opheílō* is the same verb as in Eph 5:28 translated "ought"). Benevolence is *eúnoia* (2133) which means a good mindset. Good disposition is an absolute must, a debt to each other for a husband and wife. The other word which is important in 1 Cor 7:4 is what is translated "have power." It is *exousiázō* (1850), to have

authority over, to have the right and power over. If this admonition were to be adhered to, very much heartache would be avoided in marriage.

(B) The wife must take her proper place under her husband. The verb which indicates such positioning is *hupotássomai* (5293), to submit, be obedient, be in subjection. It derives from *hupó* (5259), under, and *tássomai* (5021), to arrange oneself in an orderly fashion, to place oneself in one's proper position. In the following passages this verb is used and it is the wife who takes the initiative to place herself in the proper position under the protection and guidance of her husband. No husband is to put his wife where he thinks she belongs. The verb is never used in the act. voice (*hupotássō*) indicating that the husband can subject his wife. That is not his prerogative. **(1)** In Col 3:18 (KJV), it is a command to wives: "Wives, submit yourselves [*hupotássesthe*, the pres. continuous mid. voice]." In the NASB, "be subject to your husbands"; NIV, "submit to your husbands." This is the response of a wife to the love shown by the husband. She finds her place under her husband because that is the thing she wants to do. She is *húpandros* (5220, IV, A), under a husband. The Greek text says *hōs anēken en Kuríō* (*hōs* [5613], as; the impersonal *anēken*, from *anēkō* [433], to come up to, from *aná* [303], again, and *hēkō* [2240], to come, to be here; *en* [1722], in; *Kuríō* [2962], Lord, implying the strong one), "as it is fit in the Lord." This is how things have been arranged by the Lord. Woman was created from man and she finds her fulfillment in one man whom the Lord gives to her for life (Gen 2:21–24). **(2)** Eph 5:22, "Women, place yourselves in the proper position under your very own husbands [*hupotássesthe*], as unto the Lord" (a.t.). This is God's order for a wife to place herself under her husband. In Eph 5:24 Paul says she should do this as the Church *hupotássetai*, finds her place under Christ. Christ's love and sacrifice redeem human beings who become His Church. The submission of the Church is not brought about by subjugation. It is through the wooing of the Holy Spirit. It is a mysterious, mystical union between an individual who believes in God and responds to His love. Christ, then, through the Holy Spirit, joins that individual to His body (1 Cor 12:13). The two become one unit. The submission of the believer to Christ is a voluntary act resulting from what God makes the believer to be. A regenerated, saved individual is given by Christ a submissive nature. The believer recognizes who God is in his life and how he fits in Christ. He must be the Head. Such is what happens in marriage. The love of the husband wins the wife who finds her natural shelter under her husband. (3) Titus 2:5, "obedient to their own husbands" (KJV); "subject" (NASB, NIV). The Gr. text is the pres. part. mid. voice *hupotassoménas*, placing themselves in their proper order under their husbands. It is a natural, voluntary attitude by the wife who finds her proper fulfillment in the love of her husband. She is not commanded there by her husband, but is wooed to his bosom. This is a constant, abiding attitude. (4) 1 Pet 3:1, "Likewise, ye wives, be in subjection to your own husbands" (KJV); "be submissive" (NASB, NIV). The Gr. text says *hupotassómenai*, placing yourselves in your proper position under your husbands. Again it is a natural, voluntary, continuous attitude. (5) 1 Pet 3:5, "for after this manner in the old time the holy women also, who trusted in God, adorned themselves, being in subjection [*hupotassómenai*] unto their own husbands." In the NASB and NIV, "being submissive," "were submissive." The Gr. text is "as they submitted themselves," or "placed themselves in their proper place under their husbands" (author's translations), the Lord having instituted that order of existence. Again, the verb is the pres. mid. part., indicating that the wives voluntarily submitted themselves to their husbands. (6)

This verb *hupotássomai*, to submit oneself under or place oneself under in one's proper order is not the same as the verb *hupakoúō* (5219), to obey or listen attentively in order to conform to or command authority. It derives from *hupó* (5259), under, and *akoúō* (191), to hear with the expectation of an affirmative response. The verb *hupakoúō* involves a command to which there must be obedience without personal concurrence. It is used of disturbed physical forces such as the wind and the stormy sea obeying Christ (Matt 8:27; Mark 4:4, 41; Luke 8:25); of demons or unclean spirits indwelling humans coming out (Mark 1:27); a sycamore tree being uprooted and planted in the sea (Luke 17:6). These, the wind, storms, demons, and a tree, do not voluntarily conform to the one commanding, but are overpowered by a superior will. Such power is never granted for a husband to exercise over his wife. It never says in the NT that the wives must *hupakoúō*, blindly, involuntarily obey their husbands as Sarah wrongly obeyed Abraham in whose case the verb used is *hupakoúō* (1 Pet 3:6). The verb is used in regard to slaves (Rom 6:16; Eph 6:5; Col 3:22) obeying their masters, and children (*tékna* [5043], those born to natural parents) (Col 3:20, "Children obey your parents in all things: for this is well-pleasing unto the Lord"). We are never told, however, that the *huioí* ([5207], the grown-up sons who are not merely children, but conform to the will of their family) should *hupakoúō*, obey blindly. They are like the wives who find themselves voluntarily placing themselves under their husbands. We, therefore, never read that wives should *hupakoúoun*, blindly obey their husbands, but only *hupotássontai*, voluntarily place themselves in their proper position and that is under their husbands.

(C) With the verb *authentéō* in 1 Tim 2:12, "But I suffer not a woman to teach, nor to usurp authority [*authenteín*, the pres. inf. of *authentéō* [831], to act as an absolute master] . . . " From this word we derive our Eng. word "authentic" which means genuine, with its own inherent value evident in itself. The Gr. word derives from *autós* (846), oneself, and the *éntea*, armor, arms. An *authéntēs*, therefore, was one who took the arms in his own hands and exercised the power to kill himself or others. It is one who exercises absolute authority. Such exercise of authority is forbidden by a wife over her husband in 1 Tim 2:12. Nor is a husband permitted to be an autocrat over his wife. In the KJV *authentéō* is translated "to usurp authority" meaning to take it by force; in the NASB "to exercise authority"; in the NIV "to have authority over a man." The argument here is that if a wife teaches indiscriminately, especially men, she may be so puffed up that she may be tempted to put a ring through her husband's nose and master him. The moral here is that a wife should avoid any activity which will in any way adversely affect her marital relationship. No teaching in the church or in the world is worth the price of a wrecked marriage. A wife cannot boss her husband, nor can a husband boss his wife. His love must voluntarily make her seek protection under him.

(D) With the verb *phobéomai* (5399), to be afraid, revere, fear, and also *phóbos* (5401), fear, reverence, respect. In Eph 5:33, "Nevertheless, let every one of you in particular so love his wife even as himself; and the wife see that she reverence her husband" (KJV); "respect" (NASB, NIV). If the proper position of a wife is under her husband, then at all times she should look up to him and the husband should stand so high as to give his wife someone to really look up to with the greatest respect. The verb *phobéomai* does not mean paralyzing fear, but respect which is the response to abundant, sincere love of the husband toward his wife, for "there is no fear in love" (1 John 4:18).

(E) What does the expression "the husband of one wife" mean (1 Tim 3:2, 12)? The gen. *miás gunaikós*, of one wife, is attributive, a husband who pays attention only to his wife and not to others, a one-woman husband. This has nothing to do with having been the husband at any time in the past of a woman other than one's present wife. The opposite expression is found in 1 Tim 5:9 and is in reference to a widow worthy of the church's help, "having been the wife of one man," not having been flirtatious while her husband was alive.

(F) The husband is the head of the wife (1 Cor 11:3; Eph 5:23). It must be remembered that in marriage the two individuals, the husband and the wife, are joined together into one body (Matt 19:5). The unity is such that unless the one body has one head it will be a dicephalous monstrosity. Therefore, since there can be only one head on one body, the husband is that head. This, however, does not mean superiority and independence of his body, but a functional union and cooperation. Injury to the body of one means disfunction of the two made into one body. The body cannot live without the cooperation between the head and the body. (1) The husband is the head of the wife in the same manner that "the head of Christ is God" (1 Cor 11:3). The Gr. text says *kephalḗ dé Christoú ho Theós*, and the head of Christ the God. Here distinction is made in the two personalities of the Triune God, the Son and the Father. The word *Theós* (2316), God, has the def. art. in front of it which indicates that it refers to God the Father. For the Son the word *Christós* (5547) is used which refers to the anointed One, the preincarnate Son of the Father (John 1:18). In the preincarnate state of the Son there was a distinction of personalities (John 1:1b), but they are both God (John 1:1). The Father and the Son in their eternal state have always been equal in their essence, but not so positionally and functionally. The Lord Jesus confessed to this relationship of His with the Father in John 10:29, "My Father, which gave them me, is greater than all; and no man is able to pluck them [the believers] out of my

Father's hand." Observe two things. In the statement of 1 Cor 11:3, "and the head of Christ *is* God," the word "is" is in italics in the KJV. This indicates it is not in the original Gr. text which means that there is no chronological limitation to this relationship. There has always been this relationship of the eternal Father and the eternal Son, the Father being the head of Christ. Nevertheless, the Son is no less God than the Father, "and the Word was God" (John 1:1); "I and my Father are one" (John 10:30). The verb *esmén*, we are (from *eimí* [1510], to be) is used by the Lord Jesus to indicate that even in His incarnation He was one (*hén*, the neut. indicating essential oneness and not identity of personality which would have been indicated by *heís* [1520] one unit, one in number) with the Father. The Father is God and so is the Son. (2) What Paul teaches in 1 Cor 11:3 is that the institution of marriage is as inseparable as the eternal unity of Christ and the Father. When God joins together two distinct individuals, they become one body (*hén*) although they are two. But that does not mean that because the husband is the head of the two-in-one that he is a superior human being than the wife. The distinction is in leadership and function, the husband is the head of the body even as the Father is the head of Christ. And as Christ and the God (the Father) have always been One and the Father has always been the head, so the two married persons when unified in the mystery of marriage (Eph 5:31–33) are indeed one, equal before God (Gal 3:28; 1 Pet 3:7). In the conjugal union there can be only one head and that is the husband. (3) But the husband is the proper head of the married couple only if Christ is the head of the husband. No one can be without authority over him. Observe that "the head of *every man* is Christ" (italics added [1 Cor 11:3]). The husband who independently exercises authority over his wife without himself being under the authority of Christ is a travesty in marriage. See also *kephalē* (2776), head.

When a Christian couple is married, it is as if they had never been apart even as the Son and the Father in their eternal separate and yet united existence were never apart. In the execution, however, of the redemptive work of Christ, the Son received authority from the Father (Matt 28:18), which He on completion of His work will deliver as "the Kingdom" established by Him, back to the Father (1 Cor 15:24–28). It is indeed interesting that the verbs used in verses twenty-seven and twenty-eight a total of six times and translated "put under," "subdue," "be subject" are all forms of the verb *hupotássō* (5293), to place under in proper order, and the noun *hupotagḗ* (5292), subjection or the putting under in proper order. The verb *hupakoúō* (5219), to obey, is never used in any of its forms in this passage. We have already seen that *hupotássomai* in its various forms are the very words used in the delineation of the conjugal relationship of the wife toward the husband. It is not *hupakoúō* meaning to obey by virtue of subjugation (cf. XI, B, 5).

Deriv.: *andrízō* (407), to act manly; *androphónos* (409), murderer; *húpandros* (5220), one married or under the authority of a husband.

Syn.: *árrēn* (730), male; *téleios* (5046), perfect, one of mature or ripe age; *súzugos* (4805), a yokefellow, hence a husband or wife.

Ant.: *país* (3816), a child as an immature human being; *paidíon* (3813), child, a diminutive of *país paidárion* (3808), one acting like a child; *népios* (3516), childish, babyish or baby.

436. ἀνθίστημι *anthístēmi*; fut. *antistḗsō*, perf. *anthéstēka*, 2d aor. *antéstēn*, imperf. mid. *anthistámēn*, from *antí* (473), against, and *hístēmi* (2476), to stand. To stand against, resist, whether in deed or word (Matt 5:39; Luke 21:15; Acts 6:10; 13:8; Rom 9:19; 13:2; Gal 2:11; Eph 6:13; 2 Tim 3:8; 4:15; James 4:7; 1 Pet 5:9; Sept.: 2 Chr 13:7, 8; Josh

1:5; 23:9; Job 9:19; Ps 76:7; Jer 49:18; 50:24; Dan 4:32).

Syn.: *antikathístēmi* (478), to stand firm against; *antitássō* (498), to set oneself against, resist, oppose; *antipíptō* (496), to fall against or upon, resist; *kōlúō* (2967), to forbid, hinder, withstand.

Ant.: *sumphōnéō* (4856), to be in accord, agree; *suntíthēmi* (4934), to assent; *sugkatatíthēmi* (4784), to consent; *eunoéō* (2132), to agree with; *peíthō* (3982), to persuade; *epineúō* (1962), to nod to, approve, consent; *súmphēmi* (4852), to express agreement with; *suneudokéō* (4909), to approve of, assent, consent.

437. ἀνθομολογέομαι *anthomologéomai*; fut., *anthomologḗsomai*, from *antí* (473), in turn, and *homologéō* (3670), to confess, acknowledge. To utter mutually the same things; hence spoken of two parties, to make an accord. Also alternately or mutually to confess or profess. In the NT, to profess publicly, i.e., to praise, to celebrate alternately, as in the temple worship. With the dat. in Luke 2:38, "and she likewise praised the Lord" (a.t.), i.e., as Simeon had just done before (Sept.: Ezra 3:11; Ps 79:13).

Syn.: *eucharistéō*, to give thanks.

Ant.: *antilégō* (483), to speak against.

438. ἄνθος *ánthos*; gen. *anthéos* or *ánthous*, neut. noun. A flower or an herb (James 1:10, 11; 1 Pet 1:24; Sept.: Num 17:8; Job 15:33; Isa 5:24).

439. ἀνθρακιά *anthrakiá*; gen. *anthrakiás*, fem. noun from *ánthrax* (440), a burning coal. A heap or fire of live coals (John 18:18: 21:9; Ezek 1:13).

440. ἄνθραξ *ánthrax*; gen. *ánthrakos*, masc. noun. A burning or live coal. Rom 12:20 borrowed from Prov 25:22. To "heap coals of fire on his head," means to excite in him feelings of painful regret.

Deriv.: *anthrakiá* (439), a heap of live coals.

441. ἀνθρωπάρεσκος *anthrōpáreskos*; gen. *anthrōparéskou*, masc.-fem., neut. *anthrōpáreskon*, adj. from *ánthrōpos* (444), man, and *aréskō* (700), to please. To try to please men and not God. Denotes one who endeavors to please all (Eph 6:6; Col 3:22).

442. ἀνθρώπινος *anthrṓpinos*; fem. *anthrōpínē*, neut. *anthrṓpinon*, adj. from *ánthrōpos* (444), man. Human, belonging to man, i.e., his manners, custom, nature or condition.

(I) In nature or kind (1 Cor 2:4, 13, human wisdom; James 3:7, human nature, i.e., man; Sept.: Num 19:16; Job 10:5).

(II) In respect to origin or adaptation: human day of trial, i.e., a day in court (1 Cor 4:3); human ordinance (1 Pet 2:13); human temptation, i.e., common to men, not peculiar (1 Cor 10:13); "I speak after the manner of men" (Rom 6:19), i.e., in a manner adapted to human weakness.

Syn.: *kat' ánthrōpon* (*katá* [2596], according; *ánthrōpos* [444], man), according to the manner of men.

443. ἀνθροποκτόνος *anthrōpoktónos*; gen. *anthrōpoktónou*, masc.-fem., neut. *anthropoktónon*, adj. from *ánthrōpos* (444), man and *kteínō* (n.f.). Homicidal, used subst. manslayer, one who commits homicide (John 8:44; 1 John 3:15). Also from *kteínō* (n.f.): *apokteínō* (615), to kill, put to death.

Syn.: *phoneús* (5406), murderer, a more general word; *sikários* (4607), an assassin; *patrolṓas* (3964), a murderer of one's father; *mētralṓas* (3389), a murderer of one's mother.

Ant.: *lutrōtḗs* (3086), redeemer; *sōtḗr* (4990), savior.

444. ἄνθρωπος *ánthrōpos*; gen. *anthrṓpou*, masc., fem. noun. Man, a generic name in distinction from gods and the animals. In the NT, used to make the distinction between sinful man, whose conduct, way, or nature is opposed to God, and *anḗr* (435), male or husband.

(**I**) A man or woman, an individual of the human race, a person.

(**A**) Generally and universally (Matt 4:19; 12:12; Mark 7:21; Luke 2:52; 5:10; John 1:4; 1 Cor 4:9). In a direct address, "O man" (*ō ánthrōpe*) implies an inferior or common person (Luke 5:20; 12:14; 22:58, 60; Rom 2:1, 3; 9:20; James 2:20; Sept.: Isa 2:9; 5:15). In Rev 9:10, 15, 18, 20, *hoi ánthrōpoi*, men, i.e., the living, are those with whom we live, people (Matt 5:13, 16, 19; 6:1; 8:27; 13:25; Mark 8:24, 27), or men of this world or generation, wicked men (Matt 10:17; 17:22; Luke 6:22, 26). In Matt 6:5, 14–16; 7:12; 19:12; 23:4; Luke 6:31; 11:46, other men, others. See also Sept.: Judg 16:7; 18:28.

(**B**) Spoken in reference to his human nature, a man, i.e., a human being, a mortal. (**1**) As in Phil 2:7; 1 Tim 2:5; James 5:17; Rev 4:7; 9:7. Here is included the idea of human infirmity and imperfection, especially when spoken in contrast to God and divine things (1 Cor 1:25; 3:21). In Gal 1:11, 12, *katá* (2596), according, *ánthrōpon*, and *pará* (3844), from, *anthrṓpou*, of human origin. To speak (*légō* [3004], or *laló* or *laléō* [2980]), *katá ánthrōpon*, means to speak after the manner of men, i.e., in accordance with human views, and so forth, to illustrate by human example or institutions, to use a popular manner of speaking (Rom 3:5; 1 Cor 9:8; Gal 3:15). In 1 Cor 15:32, "if according to man's will" (a.t.), i.e., not according to God (see 2 Cor 7:9, 11; 11:17). The gen. *anthrṓpou* stands also instead of the adj. *anthrṓpinos* (442), as in 2 Pet 2:16, "with a human voice" (a.t.). "A man's number" (a.t. [Rev 13:18]) means an ordinary number. "Human measure" (a.t. [Rev 21:17]) means common measure (cf. Sept.: Isa 8:1). (**2**) Metaphorically used of the internal man, meaning the mind, soul, the rational man (Rom 7:22; Eph 3:16). In 1 Pet 3:4, "the hidden man of the heart," to which is opposed the outward or external visible man (2 Cor 4:16). The old man (*ho palaiós* [3820])

means the old man or the former unrenewed disposition of heart, and the new man (*kainós*, 2537) means the disposition or attitude which is created and cherished by the new nature that Jesus Christ gives to the believer (Rom 6:6; Eph 2:15; 4:22, 24; Col 3:9).

(**C**) Spoken with reference to the character and condition of a person and applied in various senses according to the context: (**1**) A man, a male person of maturity and ripe age (Matt 8:9; 11:8; 25:24; Mark 3:3; Luke 19:21; John 1:6; 3:1; Acts 4:13). The expression "man of God" (*ánthrōpos toú Theoú*) means a minister or messenger of God, one devoted to His service (1 Tim 6:11; 2 Tim 3:17; 2 Pet 1:21; Sept.: 1 Kgs 13:1; 2 Kgs 1:9–13; 4:7, 9, 21). In 2 Thess 2:3, the "man of sin" means that impious man referring to the Antichrist (so named in 1 John 2:18, 22; 4:3; 2 John 1:7). (**2**) A husband as contrasted to a wife (Matt 19:3, 10; 1 Cor 7:1; Sept.: Deut 22:30). (**3**) A son as contrasted to a father (Matt 10:35), or a male child generally (John 7:23; 16:21). (**4**) A master as contrasted to servants (Matt 10:36). (**5**) A servant (Luke 12:36). In Rev 18:13, "souls of men" means male and female slaves. See also Sept.: Ezek 27:13. (**6**) In John 4:28, "the men" in the city means citizens, inhabitants.

(**II**) Used with *tis* (5100), an enclitic indef. pron. meaning any man, a certain man, i.e., one, someone, anyone.

(**A**) Generally *ánthrōpós tis*, a certain man (Luke 10:30; 12:16; 14:2; John 5:5). Without *tis* as in Matt 9:9, "he saw a man . . . sitting." See Matt 12:10; 13:31; 16:26; 21:28; Mark 4:26; 5:2; 10:7; 12:1; Luke 6:48, 49; John 3:4, 27; Sept.: Lev 13:2, 9. *Heís* (1520), one, *ánthrōpos*, for, *heís tis* as in John 11:50 and 18:14, meaning a man, anyone out of a number. In Rom 3:28, "a man is justified by faith" means anyone who has faith, irrespective of who he is (see also 1 Cor 11:28). With a neg., no man, no one (Matt 19:6; John 5:7; 7:46; Sept.: Ex 33:20).

(**B**) Joined with an adj. or noun, it forms a periphrase for a subst. as in Matt

11:19, "a man, a glutton and winebibber" (a.t.). *Ánthrōpos émporos* (1713), a merchant (Matt 13:45); *ánthrōpos oikodespótēs* (3617), "a despot [or master] of the house" (a.t. [Matt 13:52]), means the head of a family or a business (cf. Matt 18:23; 21:33; Luke 2:14; Titus 3:10); *ánthrōpos Rōmaíos* (4514), means a Roman (Acts 22:25); those men (Acts 16:37); *Ánthrōpos Ioudaíos* ([2453] a Judean) means a Jew (Acts 21:39; see also Sept.: Ex 2:11). See *ho ánthrōpos* with the art. meaning every man or person, no matter who (Matt 4:4; 12:35; 15:11, 18; Mark 7:15, 18, 20; Luke 4:4; 6:45; Rom 7:1; 14:20; Sept.: Gen 8:21; Lev 5:4; Deut 8:3).

(III) *Ho ánthrōpos* with the art., meaning this or that man, he (Matt 12:13, 45; 26:72), this man of whom you speak (Mark 14:71. See Mark 3:3, 5; 14:21; Luke 6:10; 23:4, 6; John 4:50; 19:5; Sept.: Gen 24:29, 30, 32). Sometimes *ekeínos* (1565), that one, is added, as in Matt 26:24, *ho ánthrōpos ekeínos* (Mark 14:21; James 1:7).

(IV) *Huiós* (5207), son, *toú anthrṓpou*, son of man, means:

(A) *Ánthrōpos*, a man; sons of men are simply men (Mark 3:28). In Matt 12:31, "sons of men" (a.t.) is expressed simply with the dat. pl. *toís anthrṓpois*. In Heb 2:6, in the first clause, we have *ti*, the neut. of *tis* (5101), who, *estín* (the third person sing. of *eimí*, [1510], to be) *ánthrōpos*; while in the second clause we have *ē* ([2228], or) *huiós*, son, *anthrṓpou*, of man, which indicates that the second clause (the son of man) stands for man himself. In Rev 1:13, *hómoion* (3664), like, *huiṓ*, the dat. of *huiós*, *anthrṓpou*, "like unto the Son of man," means like a man. See Sept.: Gen 11:5; Ps 4:2; 8:4; Eccl 2:8; 3:18, 19; 8:11.

(B) The designation, the Son of man, was used by the Lord Jesus to designate His Messiahship. It is found 81 times in the gospels: Matt 8:20; 9:6; 10:23; 11:19; 12:8, 32, 40; 13:37, 41; 16:13, 27, 28; 17:9, 12, 22; 19:28; 20:18, 28; 24:27, 30 (twice), 37, 39, 44; 25:31; 26:2, 24

(twice), 45, 64, making a total of 30 times in Matthew; Mark 2:10, 28; 8:31, 38; 9:9, 12, 31; 10:33, 45; 13:26; 14:21 (twice), 41, 62, making a total of 14 times in Mark; Luke 5:24; 6:5, 22; 7:34; 9:22, 26, 44, 58; 11:30; 12:8, 10, 40; 17:22, 24, 26, 30; 18:8, 31; 19:10; 21:27, 36; 22:22, 48, 69; 24:7; John 1:51; 3:13, 14; 6:27, 53, 62; 8:28; 12:23, 34 (twice); 13:31, making a total of 11 times in John.

Apart from the gospels, it is found only in Acts 7:56 (cf. Luke 22:69). In Rev 1:13 and 14:14, the expression used, though akin, is not the same: it is "one [sitting] like unto the Son of man," which is a precise reproduction of the phrase in Dan 7:13. The title itself is really not found in Dan 7:13. Daniel describes a vision in which four great beasts come up from the sea: a lion, a bear, a leopard, and a beast with four horns. These are judged by the "Ancient of days" and their dominion is taken from them. Thereupon the prophet said, "I saw in the night visions, and, behold, one like the Son of man came with the clouds of heaven, and came to the Ancient of days, and they brought him near before him." Daniel does not regard "the saints of the most high" (Dan 7:18) as coming down from heaven. They are already upon the earth suffering the oppression of the tyrant symbolized by the "little horn" (Dan 7:8) and awaiting deliverance and reversal of conditions, which come when the Most High sits for judgment.

With but one exception, the name as found in the gospels is used only by our Lord Himself. The exception is John 12:34, and even there it is presupposed that Jesus had spoken of Himself as "the Son of man." "The multitude therefore answered him, We have heard out of the law that the Christ abideth forever; and how sayest thou, The Son of man must be lifted up? Who is this Son of man?" (a.t.). The multitude was familiar with the title "the Son of man." To them it was a designation of the Messiah. Their difficulty was to reconcile Messiahship with exaltation through death. The fact that both friends and enemies were acquainted with the representation of the title as to Messiahship is confirmed by the fact that not a trace of inquiry is presented either by the disciples or the wider public as to the meaning of the title. They were not perplexed by the designation.

"The Son of man" was a title of self-designation by our Lord Himself. It was a messianic title before our Lord used it. A speaker usually applies a title to himself with an obvious purpose which his hearers would discern. Taking the first occurrences in Matt 9:6; Mark 2:10; Luke 5:24, we conclude that Jesus used this title in the presence of hostile scribes. The scribes were charging Jesus with blasphemy because He assumed to pronounce the forgiveness of sins which is God's prerogative. In Matt 9:8, we read that the multitudes "glorified God which had given such power unto men."

Our Lord adopted this title more fully and consistently, most probably consequent to Peter's confession at Philippi Caesarea (Matt 16:13; Luke 9:18–20). We are not precisely told why our Lord used this designation in preference to any other messianic title, but it was a title which did not possess the limitations of other messianic designations. It allowed the concept of the Suffering Servant to be integrated with that of the Messianic King. Daniel did not identify the suffering Messiah before the Triumphant One who was going to come in glory, but since it is an event that follows, what precedes cannot be precluded. What Daniel failed to disclose, the suffering Messiah, Jesus revealed (Mark 9:9, 12, 31; 10:33; 14:21, 41). Only when the crucifixion and the resurrection were accomplished facts, in the light of which His disciples might discern how false and misleading had been their narrow concept of what Messiahship could be, does Jesus speak to them of Himself in other terms: "Behooved it not the Christ to suffer these things?" and again: "Thus it is written that the Christ should suffer" (author's translations [Luke 24:26, 46]).

If "the Son of man" was a title capable of being associated with suffering and death, it was a title already associated with the glorious coming of One who should have everlasting rule over a world in which the powers of evil should no more have sway (Matt 25:31ff.; Mark 8:38; 13:26; 14:62). In John 5:27 He declared that He was going to be the Judge. The Son of man spoke of Christ's descent from heaven which indicated a close association with God more than any other current messianic title that could have been used.

But it also spoke of a closer association with man universally and not only with Israel, which would have been indicated if He designated Himself as "the son of David." When Jesus attached the concept of suffering to His Messiahship, He did so in order to make it clear that the entrance upon His sovereignty was still far distant (Matt 16:16, 21, 22). This is why He used the title most frequently when speaking of His suffering (Matt 17:9 paralleled with Mark 9:9, 12; Matt 17:22 paralleled with Mark 9:31 and Luke 9:44; Matt 20:18 paralleled with Mark 10:33 and Luke 18:31; Matt 26:24 paralleled with Mark 14:21 and Luke 22:22; Matt 26:45 paralleled with Mark 14:41).

After the crucifixion and the resurrection, Jesus began to speak to them of Himself as the Christ (Luke 24:26, 46). The utterances concerning the return of "the Son of man" in glory and the predictions that the Son of man must suffer and die are in strict correlation.

Why did not Jesus' followers, except Stephen (Acts 7:56), apply this title to Him? It was because Paul wrote primarily for Greeks who would most likely not understand by the title "the Son of man" what the Jews understood. The Gentiles would have taken the title to refer simply to a man. The use of this title would have led the Gentiles to an undue and, therefore, misleading stress about our Lord's humanity. To the Jew, "the Son of man" suggested the Lord from heaven; not so to the Gentile. When the association of the name with heavenly origin and majesty could not be assumed, there the Apostles adopted other terms as they spoke or wrote of their risen and ascended Lord and proclaimed Him as "the Christ, the Son of God" (John 20:31).

The Church refused to refer to Jesus as "the Son of man" because He had already sat upon the throne of God and was, in fact, no longer merely a man but the ruler of heaven and earth. For instance, the term "the Lord" occurs 24 times in 1 Thess and 22 times in 2 Thess. It is the Lord who comes with the clouds of heaven (1 Thess 4:16, 17; 2 Thess 1:7).

The new designation as "Lord" indicates the widening range of the Church's appeal beyond the confines of Judaism. In John 12:34 "the Son of man" and "the Christ" are interchanged. In Luke 22:69, 70 "the Son of man" and "the Son of God" are also interchanged. In Matt 16:13, 16, 20 "the Son of God," "the Son of man," and "the Christ" all are used. By using this name before His judges, Jesus openly professed Himself to be the Messiah and was so understood by all present (Matt 26:64; Mark 14:62; Luke 22:69, 70; John 1:52; 5:27).

Deriv.: *anthrōpáreskos* (441), man-pleaser; *anthrṓpinos* (442), human; *anthrōpoktónos* (443), murderer.

445. ἀνθυπατεύω *anthupateúō*; fut. *anthupateúsō*, from *anthúpatos* (446), a proconsul. To have proconsular authority, to be proconsul (Acts 18:12).

446. ἀνθύπατος *anthúpatos*; gen. *anthupátou*, from *antí* (473), for, instead of, and *húpatos* (n.f.), a consul, so-called by the Greek writers because after the expulsion of the kings, the consuls had the supreme or highest authority in the Roman government. A proconsul, a person sent as governor into a Roman province with consular power which was very intensive. Augustus, at the beginning of his reign, divided the provinces into two parts; one of which he gave wholly over

to the people, and the other which he reserved for himself. After this, the governors who were sent into the first division bore the name of proconsuls though they were denied the whole military power, and so fell short of the old proconsuls. This title of proconsul was given by Luke to Sergius Paulus (Acts 13:7, 8, 12). Gallio was also called proconsul (Acts 19:38).

Deriv.: *anthupateúō* (445), to be a proconsul.

447. ἀνίημι *aníēmi*; fut. *anḗsō*, 2d aor. *anḗn*, aor. pass. *anéthēn*, from *aná* (303), back, and *híēmi* (n.f., see *iós* [2447]), to send. To send up or forth, to let up, let go, relax, loosen (Acts 16:26; 27:40). To dismiss, let alone, forbear, cease from threatening (Eph 6:9). To dismiss, leave, neglect (Heb 13:5; Sept.: Deut 31:6; 1 Sam 9:5; Isa 5:6).

Deriv.: *ánesis* (425), loosening, taking up, relaxation of strain.

Syn.: *anéchomai* (430), to endure, forbear; *pheídomai* (5339), to spare; *stégō* (4722), to bear up under, provide a roof over; *aphíēmi* (863), to let, permit, forgive; *eleutheróō* (1659), to free; *chōrízō* (5563), to separate; *kataleípō* (2641), to leave behind; *apoleípō* (620), to leave behind; *egkataleípō* (1459), to abandon; *hupoleípō* (5275), to leave remaining; *perileípō* (4035), to leave over; *eáō* (1439), to let, permit; *anágō* (321), to bring up; *lúō* (3089), to loose, release; *apolúō* (630), to set free, release; *eklúō* (1590), to relax.

Ant.: *déō* (1210) to bind; *sundéō* (4887), to bind together; *peridéō* (4019), to bind around; *desméō* (1196), to shackle.

448. ἀνίλεως *aníleōs*, gen. *aníleōn*, masc.-fem., neut. *aníleō*, adj. from *a* (1), not, and *híleōs* (2436), merciful. Unmerciful, uncompassionate. The Class. Gr. form would be *anēleés*, without mercy. Occurs only in James 2:13, where it means that in the day of the judgment of the believer's works, he will not be shown mercy if he did not perform works of mercifulness on earth. A leniency of the judge is expressed in proportion to one's mercifulness on earth.

Syn.: *aneleḗmōn* (415), without mercy.

Ant.: *eleéō* (1653), to feel sympathy toward another; *oikteírō* (3627), to show pity; *oiktírmōn* (3629), pitiful, compassionate for the ills of others.

449. ἄνιπτος *ániptos*; gen. *aníptou*, masc.-fem., neut. *ánipton*, adj. from *a* (1), without, and *níptō* (3538), to wash. Not washed (Matt 15:20; Mark 7:2, 5).

Syn.: *akáthartos* (169), dirty; *rhuparós* (4508), filthy.

Ant.: *katharós* (2513), clean.

450. ἀνίστημι *anístēmi*; fut. *anastḗsō*, aor. *anéstēsa*, 2d aor. *anéstēn*, imper. *anástēthi* or *anásta*, from *aná* (303), again, and *hístēmi* (2476), to stand. To stand again. This verb may have a trans. or an intrans. meaning, as *hístēmi*.

(I) Trans. in the pres., imperf., fut., and aor. of the act., meaning to cause to rise up, to raise up, cause to stand.

(A) Spoken of those lying down (Acts 9:41; Sept.: Lev 26:1; Num 7:1); of the dead, meaning to raise up, recall to life (John 6:39, 40, 44, 54; Acts 2:32; 13:33); *ek nekrṓn* (*ek* [1537], out of; *nekrṓn* [3498], of the dead [pl.]) as in Acts 13:34; 17:31.

(B) Metaphorically, to raise up, to cause to exist, cause to appear (Matt 22:24 [cf. Gen 38:8]; Acts 2:30; 3:22, 26; 7:37; Sept.: Deut 18:18); pass. (Heb 7:11, 15).

(II) Intrans. in the perf., pluperf., and 2d aor. act. and in the mid. meaning to rise up, arise.

(A) Particularly spoken of those who are sitting or lying down (Matt 26:62; Mark 5:42; 9:27; 14:60; Luke 4:16; 5:25; 6:8; 22:45); rising up from prayer, i.e., from a kneeling or recumbent posture (Luke 17:19); rising from bed or from sleep (Luke 11:7, 8; 22:46); arising from the dead, returning to life (Matt 17:9; Mark 9:9, 10; Luke 16:31; John

20:9; Acts 17:3); without *ek nekrṓn* from among the dead (Matt 20:19; Mark 8:31; 9:31; 10:34; Luke 9:8, 19; 18:33: 1 Thess 4:14, 16). Metaphorically in Eph 5:14, to arise from the death of sin and put on the new man in Christ.

(B) Metaphorically, to arise, come into existence, to be (Acts 7:18; 20:30; Sept.: Ex 1:8; Dan 8:22; 11:2).

(C) Meaning to stand forth, come forward, appear (Matt 12:41; Mark 14:57; Luke 10:25; 11:32; Acts 5:36, 37; 6:9; Sept.: 2 Chr 20:5). Followed by *epí* (1909), upon, meaning to rise up against any one, assault (Mark 3:26; Sept.: Gen 4:8; 2 Chr 24:13).

(D) Followed by verbs of going or doing (Matt 9:9, "he arose, and followed him"; Mark 1:35; 2:14; 7:24; 10:1, 50; Luke 1:39; 5:28; 15:18, 20; Acts 8:26, 27; 9:6, 11; Sept.: 1 Sam 24:5; 2 Sam 13:31. See Rom 15:12 [cf. Isa 11:10]; 1 Cor 10:7 [cf. Ex 32:6]).

Deriv.: *anástasis* (386), resurrection; *exanístēmi* (1817), to rise out of or from among; *epanístamai* (1881), to rise up or against, to arise.

Syn.: *egeírō* (1453), to raise; *anatéllō* (393), to arise; *aírō* (142), to raise, take up, lift; *epaírō* (1869), to lift up, raise; *hupsóō* (5312), to lift or raise up; *anorthóō* (461), to set upright; *anakúptō* (352), to lift oneself up; *exegeírō* (1825), to raise up from; *sunegeírō* (4891), to raise together; *epegeírō* (1892), to rouse up, excite; *stḗkō* (4739), to stand fast.

Ant.: *keímai* (2749), to lie; *katákeimai* (2621), to lie down; *anákeimai* (345), to be laid up; *anapíptō* (377), to fall back; *epipíptō* (1968), to fall upon; *apothnḗskō* (599), to die.

451. Ἄννα *Anna*; gen. *Ánnēs*, fem. proper noun. Anna, an aged widow, daughter of Phanuel of the tribe of Asher (Luke 2:36–38). She and Simeon "were waiting for the consolation of Israel." They attended regularly morning and evening the services at the temple. On hearing Simeon's words at the presentation of Jesus, she commended the child as the "long-awaited Messiah" (a.t.) and praised God for the fulfillment of His promises.

452. Ἄννας Ánnas; gen. Ánna, masc. proper noun. Annas, the son of Sethi, appointed high priest by Quirinius in A.D. 6 or 7, retaining office till he was deposed by Valerius Gratus in A.D. 15. He had five sons who all held the office of high priest. From John 18:13, we learn that Joseph Caiaphas, the high priest at the date of the crucifixion, was a son-in-law of Annas. His removal from office in A.D. 15 did not by any means diminish his influence. Being extremely wealthy, he was able to exert the powers of high priest long after he was deposed. Other references: Luke 3:2; John 18:13, 24; Acts 4:6.

453. ἀνόητος anóētos; gen. anoḗtou, masc.-fem., neut. anóēton, adj. from the priv. a (1), without, and noéō (3539), to comprehend. Lacking intelligence, foolish; one who does not govern his lusts, one without noús (3563), mind, the highest power of knowledge in man, the organ by which divine things are comprehended and known or ignored, being the ultimate seat of error (Luke 24:25; Rom 1:14; Gal 3:1, 3; 1 Tim 6:9; Titus 3:3; Sept.: Deut 32:31; Ps 49:13; Prov 15:21; 17:28).
Syn.: áphrōn (878), without reason; mōrós (3474), foolish; asúnetos (801), without discernment; ásophos (781), unwise.
Ant.: sophós (4680), wise; phrónimos (5429), prudent, sensible; sunetós (4908), understanding, intelligent, sagacious.

454. ἄνοια ánoia; gen. anoías, fem. noun from ánous (n.f.), mad, foolish, from the priv. a (1), without, and noús (3563), mind, understanding. Madness, folly, lack of understanding (Luke 6:11; 2 Tim 3:9).
Syn.: mōría (3472), foolishness; aphrosúnē (877), senselessness; manía (3130), madness, mania; paraphronía (3913), mind aberration.

Ant.: phrónēsis (5428), prudence; súnesis (4907), understanding; sophía (4678), wisdom.

455. ἀνοίγω anoígō; fut. anoíxō, aor. anéōxa or énoixa, 2d perf. anéōga, perf. pass. anéōgmai and ēnéōgmai, aor. pass. aneṓchthēn, later ēnoíchthēn and ēneṓchthēn, 2d aor. pass. ēnoígēn, fut. pass. anoigḗsomai, from aná (303), again, and oígō, to open. To open.
(I) Spoken of what is closed by a cover or door (Matt 2:11, referring to treasures, i.e., boxes, caskets; Sept.: Jer 50:26, "storehouses"). Sepulchers which were closed by large stones (Matt 27:52). See also Matt 27:60, 66; 28:2; Mark 16:3, 4; Sept.: Ezek 37:12, 13. Metaphorically the throat of wicked men is called táphos (5028), a tomb, aneōgménos, an open sepulcher (Rom 3:13), as bringing forth noisome slanders against God and the righteous (Ps 5:10). Most frequently with thúra (2374), a door or gate (Acts 5:23; 16:26, 27; Rev 4:1), so that one may enter (Matt 25:11; Luke 12:36; 13:25; John 10:3), or go out (Acts 5:19, or view the interior, as the naós (3485), temple (Rev 11:19; 15:5) or the pit of the abyss (Rev 9:2) since in the East pits or wells were closed with large stones (cf. Gen 29:2). "Door" is implied before "shall be opened" in Matt 7:7, 8; Luke 11:9, 10, meaning the door shall be opened to receive you as a guest. Metaphorically to open the door, i.e., heart, meaning to receive willingly (Rev 3:20); to open the door of faith or of the kingdom of heaven, and so forth, meaning to afford an opportunity of embracing the gospel of Christ (Acts 14:27; Rev 3:7, 8); to open the door for the gospel, for a teacher, meaning to give opportunity to publish the gospel and make converts (1 Cor 16:9; 2 Cor 2:12; Col 4:3 [cf. Sept.: Isa 45:1]).
(II) Spoken of the heavens, to open the heavens or to have the heavens opened or divided so that celestial things become manifest (Matt 3:16; Luke 3:21; John 1:51; Acts 7:56; 10:11; Rev 19:11; Sept.: Isa 64:1; Ezek 1:1; Ps 78:23).

(III) Spoken of a book, i.e., a volume, rolled up and sealed (Rev 5:2–5; 10:2, 8; 20:12); of the seals of a book (Rev 5:9; 6:1, 3, 5, 7, 9, 12; 8:1).

(IV) Spoken of the mouth, to open the mouth of a fish (Matt 17:27; see also Ps 22:13); in order to speak, i.e., to hold forth, speak at length, discourse (Matt 5:2; 13:35; Acts 8:35; 10:34; 18:14; Rev 13:6; Sept.: Judg 11:35, 36; Dan 10:16). In the sense of to pour out one's mind, to open one's heart, i.e., to speak fully and frankly (2 Cor 6:11). Not to open one's mouth, i.e., not to utter complaints (Acts 8:32; see also Ps 38:14; 39:9; Isa 53:7). Spoken of the dumb, to have the mouth opened, means to recover the power of speech (Luke 1:64; see also Num 22:28). Spoken of the earth, to open her mouth, means to open or form a chasm (Rev 12:16; see also Num 16:30; 26:10; Deut 11:6; Ps 106:17).

(V) Spoken of the eyes, to open the eyes means either one's own eyes (Acts 9:8, 40) or those of another, meaning to cause to see, restore sight (Matt 9:30; 20:33; John 9:10, 14, 17, 21, 26, 30, 32; 10:21; 11:37; Sept.: Isa 35:5; 37:17; 42:7). Metaphorically, to open the eyes means the understanding of the mind, to cause to perceive and understand, as in Acts 26:18.

Deriv.: *ánoixis* (457), an opening; *dianoígō* (1272), to open up completely.

Syn.: *anaptússō* (380), to unroll.

Ant.: *kammúō* (2576), to close the eyes; *ptússō* (4428), to fold, double up.

456. ἀνοικοδομέω *anoikodoméō*; contracted *anoikodomṓ*, fut. *anoikodomḗsō*, from *aná* (303), again, and *oikodoméō* (3618), to construct, build a house. To build up again, rebuild, trans. in Acts 15:16; Sept.: Amos 9:11.

Syn.: *ktízō* (2936), to fabricate, make, create, found; *egeírō* (1453), to erect.

Ant.: *apóllumi* (622), to destroy utterly; *lúō* (3089), to loose, demolish, destroy; *katalúō* (2647), to destroy utterly; *kathairéō* (2507), to pull down.

457. ἄνοιξις *ánoixis*; gen. *anoíxeōs*, fem. noun from *anoígō* (455), to open. The act of opening (Eph 6:19), where (in the subsequent clause) *en* (1722), in, *anoíxei*, opening, *toú stómatos* (4750), of the mouth, corresponds to *en parrēsía* (3954), with confidence, boldly.

458. ἀνομία *anomía*; gen. *anomías*, from *ánomos* (459), lawless. Lawlessness. In most cases in the NT it means not the absence of the Law, but the violation of Law, i.e., transgression or lawlessness. In the NT, it places stress, not in a subjective law that we ourselves create for our convenience, but chiefly in a divinely instituted Law.

(I) In 1 John 3:4, we have a statement which relates *hamartía* (266), the general word for sin, and *anomía*. A literal translation of this verse is: "Whosoever commits the sin [on a continual basis] also commits [continuously] lawlessness [*anomían*], and the sin is the lawlessness" (a.t.). Sin (*hamartía*) is missing the mark ordained by God and not by us. God has placed in our hearts an innate knowledge of what is good and evil. There may not be any specific law which we violate when we sin, but that does not make sin any less sinful. Crucial to the understanding of all this is Rom 2:15, " . . . the work of the law written in their hearts, their conscience also bearing witness, and their thoughts the mean while accusing or else excusing one another." The nonexistence of a specific law forbidding an act or a life of sinfulness does not absolve a person from being lawless.

(II) By implication, therefore, *anomía* is sin, iniquity, unrighteousness (Matt 23:28; 24:12; Rom 4:7; see Sept.: Ps 32:1, where *anomía* is paralleled with *hamartía*). Rom 6:19: " . . . for as ye have yielded your members servants to uncleanness and to iniquity [*anomía*] unto iniquity [*anomían*]" means you were obedient to depraved desires so as to work iniquity. There may not be a specific law against depraved or lustful desires, but nevertheless they are sin (2 Cor 6:14;

Titus 2:14). In Heb 1:9: "Thou hast . . . hated iniquity [*anomían*, used collectively]." In Heb 8:12 and 10:17, the sins and iniquities (*anomíai*) are coupled together (also Sept.: Jer 31:34). He who works or does iniquity (*anomían*) is a worker of iniquity, meaning a wicked, impious person (Matt 7:23; 13:41; Sept.: Job 31:3; Ps 5:6). In 2 Thess 2:7, we have the phrase, "The mystery of iniquity [*anomías*]," meaning the resistance of people to come to Christ. Their resistance, however, will not hinder Christ in executing His plan in making His appearance visible (2 Thess 2:8). See also Sept.: Ex 34:7; Isa 6:7; Ezek 8:6; 18:12, 20; 33:12.

Syn.: *paranomía* (3892), transgression; *hamártēma* (265), individual sin; *hamartía* (266), sin; *kríma* (2917), condemnation; *opheílēma* (3783), debt; *égklēma* (1462), indictable crime; *athétēsis* (115), acting contrary to accepted custom; *adikía* (93), unrighteousness *adíkēma* (92), a wrong, injury, misdeed; *ponēría* (4189), wickedness, *ho ponērós* (4190) one of the designations of the devil; *parábasis* (3847), an overstepping, transgression; *paráptōma* (3900), sidestepping; *plánē* (4106), a wandering or forsaking of the right path; *agnóēma* (51), a sin of ignorance; *hamártēma* (265), evil deed; *asébeia* (763), impiety; *parábasis* (3847), transgression.

Ant.: *tó díkaion* (1342), that which is just; *dikaiosúnē* (1343), righteousness; *euthútēs* (2118), righteousness; *dikaíōsis* (1347), the act of justifying; *dikaiokrisía* (1341), righteous judgment.

459. ἄνομος *ánomos*; gen. *anómou*, masc.-fem., neut. *ánomon*, adj. from the priv. *a* (1), without, and *nómos* (3551), law. Without law, lawless. Not having, knowing or acknowledging the law (1 Cor 9:21); lawless in the sense of transgressing the law, a transgressor, wicked (Mark 15:28; Luke 22:37; Acts 2:23; 2 Thess 2:8; 1 Tim 1:9; 2 Pet 2:8; Sept.: Isa 53:12; 55:7; Ezek 18:24; 33:8, 12).

Deriv.: *anomía* (458), lawlessness; *anómōs* (460), lawlessly.

Syn.: *ékthetos* (1570), exposed to perish, cast out; *ádikos* (94), unjust; *athémitos* (111), contrary to accepted customs; *anósios* (462), wicked, unholy, the strongest term denoting presumptuous and wicked self-assertion.

Ant.: *énnomos* (1772), lawful; *éndikos* (1738), just, equitable.

460. ἀνόμως *anómōs*; adv. from *ánomos* (459), without law, lawless. Lawlessly, in a manner which acts as if there were no law, being against law. Only in Rom 2:12 (twice), those who have sinned not being subject to the Law (referring to the Law of Moses) will be condemned, not by the Law of Moses, but by the moral law (see Rom 2:14, 15).

Syn.: *adíkōs* (95), unjustly.

Ant.: *euthéōs* (2112), straightly; *orthós* (3723), rightly; *dikaíōs* (1346), justly; *nomímōs* (3545), lawfully.

461. ἀνορθόω *anorthóō*; fut. *anorthṓsō*, from *aná* (303), again or up, and *orthóō* (n.f.), to erect, which is from *orthós* (3717), right, upright, erect. To make straight or upright again. Aor. pass. *anōrthṓthēn* with mid. significance, to stand erect (Luke 13:13; Sept.: Ps 20:8). In the sense of to confirm, strengthen, establish (Heb 12:12 quoted from Isa 35:3; Sept.: 2 Sam 7:13, 16; Ps 145:14; 146:8; Jer 33:2). To erect again (Acts 15:16).

Syn.: *egeírō* (1453), to raise up; *stḗkō* (4739), to stand fast, persevere; *exanístēmi* (1817), to raise or rise up; *exegeírō* (1825), to raise up; *aírō* (142), to raise or take up, lift; *epaírō* (1869), to raise, used of lifting up the eyes; *hupsóō* (5312), to lift or raise up; *anístēmi* (450), to lift or raise up; *anakúptō* (352), to lift oneself up.

Ant.: *dolóō* (1389), to corrupt morally; *atimázō* (818), to dishonor; *anaklínō* (347), to sit down; *strónnumi* (4766), to spread out; *píptō* (4098), to fall down; *kataklínō* (2625), to recline down; *katákeimai* (2621), to sit down; *keímai* (2749), to lie outstretched.

462. ἀνόσιος anósios; gen. *anosíou*, masc.-fem., neut. *anósion*, adj. from the priv. *a* (1), without, and *hósios* (3741), consecrated, hallowed, holy, righteous, unpolluted with wickedness. Unholy, ungodly, no regard of duty to God or man (1 Tim 1:9; 2 Tim 3:2).

Syn.: *koinós* (2839), common, defiled; *asebés* (765), impious; *bébēlos* (952), profane; *theostugés* (2319), impious, hater of God; *stugnētós* (4767), odious, hateful; *bdeluktós* (947), detestable.

Ant.: *amíantos* (283), undefiled; *eusebés* (2152), pious, devout; *hierós* (2413), sacred; *hágios* (40), holy; *theíos* (2304), divine; *hósios* (3741), consecrated; *tímios* (5093), honorable.

463. ἀνοχή anochḗ; gen. *anochḗs*, from *anéchō* (430), to bear with, suffer. Forbearance, indulgence, temporary longsuffering, as in Rom 3:25. God's attitude toward sin is demonstrated in Rom 3:25 where the word *páresis* (3929), bypassing, is used which does not mean remission of sins. *Páresis* was temporary. God winked at the sins of the people because of their animal sacrifices. That was the *páresis* of verse twenty-five, the overlooking, which in this verse is also called *anochḗ*, forbearance or temporary suspension of His wrath. The sacrifice of Christ provides *áphesis* (859), remission, the forgiveness of sins which is once and for all, taking them away, and is more than *páresis*, bypassing or skirting their sins. Redemption through Christ's blood, however, provided permanent satisfaction of His justice (Rom 5:9).

Syn.: *epieíkeia* (1932), clemency; *hupomonḗ* (5281), patience; *makrothumía* (3115), longsuffering toward people.

Ant.: *aganáktēsis* (24), indignation; *orgḗ* (3709), wrath; *zḗlos* (2205), indignation or jealousy.

464. ἀνταγωνίζομαι antagōnízomai; fut. *antagōnísomai*, from *antí* (473), against, and *agōnízomai* (75), to fight against a person. To be in conflict with someone (Heb 12:4).

Syn.: *pukteúō* (4438), to box, fight; *máchomai* (3164), to fight, strive; *poleméō* (4170), to war; *diamáchomai* (1264), to struggle against; *erízō* (2051), to wrangle, strive; *athléō* (118), to contend in games, wrestle.

Ant.: *antilambánomai* (482), to help, support; *sullambánō* (4815), to assist; *sunantilambánomai* (4878), to take hold alongside, assist, take a share in, help in bearing; *boēthéō* (997), to come to the aid of anyone; *sumbállomai* (4820), to help or benefit; *sunupourgéō* (4943), to help together, join in helping; *sunergéō* (4903), to help in work, cooperate; *parístēmi* (3936), to assist.

465. ἀντάλλαγμα antállagma; gen. *antallágmatos*, neut. noun from *antallássō* (n.f.), to exchange, barter, which is from *antí* (473), against or instead of, and *allássō* (236), to change, make other than it is. That which is exchanged for anything, compensation, equivalent, generally the price paid for something (Matt 16:26; Mark 8:37, the price of his life, meaning deliverance from death, which phrase is borrowed from the redemption of a slave; Sept.: Ruth 4:7; Jer 15:13; Job 28:15).

Syn.: *antapódosis* (469), reward.

Ant.: *hustérēsis* (5304), a falling short, deprivation; *hustérēma* (5303), a deficit, lack.

466. ἀνταναπληρόω antanaplēróō; fut. *antanaplērósō*, from *antí* (473), in turn or correspondent to, and *anaplēróō* (378), to fulfill. To fill up instead of, to make good. Trans. as in Col 1:24, meaning I fill up or make good what is yet wanting to me of afflictions for Christ, i.e., instead of any deficiency, I endure a fullness of afflictions for Christ. Compared with Acts 9:4, 5, it would mean that as Christ once suffered for believers (and for myself in particular), and declared that in this world His disciples or members should have tribulation, so I in my turn fill up; or as Christ once suffered in the flesh many afflictions, so I

(in conformity to His example) am filling up in my own flesh what is lacking in
such sufferings as He endured.
Syn.: *antikathístēmi* (478), to set as a
replacement; *apoteléō* (658), to complete
entirely.
Ant.: *hustereō* (5302), to come short;
hupoleípomai (5275), to be left behind,
under.

467. ἀνταποδίδωμι *antapodídōmi*; fut.
antapodḗsō, from *antí* (473), in turn, and
apodídōmi (591), to render. To give back
in return for something received, repay,
requite.
(I) In a good sense meaning to recompense or to reward (Luke 14:14; Rom
11:35; 1 Thess 3:9; Sept.: 1 Sam 24:18; 2
Sam 22:21; Isa 63:7).
(II) To repay with evil, requite, avenge
(Rom 12:19; 2 Thess 1:6; Heb 10:30;
Sept.: Gen 44:4; 50:15; Judg 1:7; 1 Sam
24:18; 25:21; Ps 103:10).
Deriv.: *antapódoma* (468), what is
given back in return; *antapódosis* (469),
the action of recompensing.
Syn.: *apotínō / apotíō* (661), to pay in
full.
Ant.: *aposteréō* (650), to deprive, rob,
defraud; *hustereō* (5302), to come short
of; *leípō* (3007), to forsake, be left destitute; *pleonektéō* (4122), to take advantage of, want more for oneself.

468. ἀνταπόδομα *antapódoma*; gen.
antapodómatos, neut. noun from *antapodídōmi* (467), to recompense, repay. That
which is offered or given as recompense,
retribution in a good sense (Luke 14:12);
in an evil sense, retribution (Rom 11:9;
Sept.: Ps 28:4; 137:8; Joel 3:4). With the
suffix *-ma*, *antapódoma* stresses the recompense itself while *antapódosis* (469)
stresses the action.
Syn.: *antállagma* (465), something given in exchange; *antimisthía*
(489), a reward in a good or bad sense;
misthapodosía (3405), a reward in a good
or bad sense.
Ant.: *pleonexía* (4124), covetousness.

469. ἀνταπόδοσις *antapódosis*; gen.
antapodóseōs, fem. noun from *antapodídōmi* (467), to recompense or reward.
Reward, stressing the action. Only in Col
3:24, in a good sense.
Syn.: *antimisthía* (489), a reward or
requital; *misthapodosía* (3405), a recompense of reward or punishment.
Ant.: *hustérēsis* (5304), a deprivation.

470. ἀνταποκρίνομαι *antapokrínomai*; aor. pass. *antapekríthēn*, from *antí*
(473), against, and *apokrínomai* (611),
to answer. With mid. meaning, to answer
against (Luke 14:6). To reply to something, make a declaratory and argumenta-
tive reply, dispute (see Rom 9:20; Sept.:
Judg 5:29; Job 16:8; 32:12).
Syn.: *apologéomai* (626), to apologize, to speak for oneself; *antilégō* (483),
to speak against.
Ant.: *phimóō* (5392), to hold speechless; *sigáō* (4601), to be silent; *siōpáō*
(4623), to keep silence.

471. ἀντέπω *antépō*; 2d aor. *anteípon*,
from *antí* (473), against, and *épō* (2036),
to say, To gainsay, contradict (Luke
21:15; Acts 4:14; Sept.: Gen 24:50; Job
20:2; 32:1).
Syn.: *suzētéō* (4802), to dispute;
apologéomai (626), to plea for oneself,
make self-defense; *anthístēmi* (436), to
resist; *antitássō* (498), to oppose; *enístēmi*
(1764), to be prepared for self-defense;
antilégō (483), to contradict, say against,
gainsay; *antilogía* (485), gainsaying or
saying in opposition.
Ant.: *sumphōnéō* (4856), to sound together, agree; *suntíthēmi* (4934), to agree,
assent to; *sugkatatíthēmi* (4784), to consent; *eunoéō* (2132), to agree with; *peíthō*
(3982), to persuade; *suntássomai* (4929),
to agree; *sumbállomai* (4820), to join in.

472. ἀντέχω *antéchō*; fut. *anthéxō*, from
antí (473), against or to, and *échō* (2192),
have. In the mid. voice *antéchomai*, to
hold firmly, cleave to (Matt 6:24; Luke
16:13); of holding to the faithful word

(Titus 1:9); to support (1 Thess 5:14; Sept.: Prov 3:18; 4:6; Isa 56:2, 4, 6; Jer 2:8; 8:2; Zeph 1:6).

Syn.: *kratéō* (2902), to take hold of, keep, retain; *epilambánomai* (1949), to take hold of; *antilambánomai* (482), to help, support; *tēréō* (5083), to keep, give heed to, observe; *phulássō* (5442), to guard, hold.

Ant.: *kataleípō* (2641), to leave behind; *egkataleípō* (1459), to forsake; *aphíēmi* (863), to forgive, forsaking; *apotássō* (657), to set apart or in its proper category.

473. ἀντί *antí*; prep. with the general meaning of over against, in the presence of, in lieu of. Spoken metaphorically either in a hostile sense, meaning against, or by way of comparison, where it implies something of equivalent value, and denotes substitution, exchange, requital. In the NT used in the following:

(I) By way of substitution, in place of, instead of (Luke 11:11; 1 Cor 11:15; James 4:15). As implying succession (Matt 2:22, the one king succeeding the other). In John 1:16, trans. with "for" in the phrase "and grace for grace," meaning grace upon grace, most abundant grace, one favor in place of or after another. God's grace is not given once-and-for-all, but there is a renewal of it that is constant.

(II) By way of exchange, requital, equivalent, meaning in consideration of, on account of, spoken:

(A) Of price, meaning for (Heb 12:16; Sept.: Num 18:21, 31).

(B) Of persons, for whom or for the sake of whom, in behalf of (Matt 17:27; 20:28; Mark 10:45).

(C) Of retribution, meaning for (Matt 5:38; Rom 12:17; 1 Thess 5:15; 1 Pet 3:9).

(D) Of the cause, motive, occasion meaning on account of, because of (Luke 12:3, on account of which things, wherefore; Eph 5:31, "for this cause," "that is, because of this" [a.t.]; Heb 12:2, "on account of the joy" [a.t.]. See also Sept. for

Jer 11:17). The expression *anth' hōn* (pl. gen. of the relative pron. *hós* [3739]) is more commonly a causative particle for *antí toútou* (the gen. sing. of *toúto* [5124], this) followed by *hóti* (3754), that—*antí toútou hóti*, meaning on this account that, because that, or simply because. This is found in Luke 1:20 in the expression *anth' hōn ouk epísteusas*, translated simply as "because you did not believe" (a.t.). See Luke 19:44; Acts 12:23; 2 Thess 2:10; Sept.: Gen 22:18; 26:5; 2 Sam 12:6; Deut 28:62; Jer 22:9.

(III) In composition *antí* denotes:

(A) Over against, as *antitássomai* (498), to resist, oppose.

(B) Contrary to, as *antilégō* (483), to gainsay or speak against.

(C) Reciprocity, as *antapodídōmi* (467), to recompense or requite.

(D) Substitution, as *anthúpatos* (446), a deputy, proconsul.

(E) Similarity or correspondence, as *antíthesis* (477), opposition.

Deriv.: *antikrú* (481), opposite to, over against.

474. ἀντιβάλλω *antibállō*; fut. *antibalō̂*, from *antí* (473), reciprocally, and *bállō* (906), to cast. To cast or toss from one to the other, such as a ball; may be applied to a conference or mutual discussion of a subject through speech; to exchange thoughts (Luke 24:17).

Syn.: *koinōnéō* (2841), to communicate; *sugkrínō* (4793), to compare; *parabállō* (3846), to place side by side; *paromoiázō* (3945), to resemble; *homoióō* (3666), to liken.

Ant.: *kratéō* (2902), to keep, and its syn.

475. ἀντιδιατίθημι *antidiatíthēmi*; fut. *antidiathḗsō*, from *antí* (473), against, and *diatíthēmi* (1303), to dispose. In the NT, mid. *antidiatíthēmai* to place oneself over against, to oppose oneself, be adverse, used as a part. noun in 2 Tim 2:25 meaning either those who directly oppose the gospel or those who are ill-disposed toward or unaffected by it. The latter meaning seems preferable because the Apostle directs Timothy to treat the *antidiatitheménous*, those whose attitudes are contrary or ill-disposed to the gospel, in a very different manner from the *anthistaménous* (436), opposers, those actually opposing the gospel, from whom he was to turn away (2 Tim 3:5, 8). The difference is between *diáthesis*, disposition, and *thésis*, position (from which *anthístēmi* [436] is derived). It is disposition versus position. In Eng., writing a thesis is presenting one's position on a certain subject.

Syn.: *antíkeimai* (480), to stand against; *diaphérō* (1308), to differ; *antitássō* (498), setting oneself against; *diḯstēmi* (1339), to stand apart; *aporríptō* (641), to reject; *antilégō* (483), to gainsay.

Ant.: *sumphōnéō*, (4856), to agree; *homologéō* (3670), to acknowledge, confess; *sumbibázō* (4822), to put together, compromise; *suntássō* (4929), to put in order, together, edit; *summorphóō* (4833), to shape together; *diallássō* (1259), to reconcile; *katallássō* (2644), to befriend by changing the character of one of two parties.

476. ἀντίδικος *antídikos*; gen. *antidíkou*, masc., fem. noun from *antí* (473), against, and *díkē* (1349), a cause or suit at law. An adversary, enemy, or opponent in a lawsuit (Matt 5:25; Luke 12:58). In Luke 18:3, it is equivalent to *echthrós* (2190), enemy. It is applied to the devil, the great adversary of man and accuser of the brethren (1 Pet 5:8 [cf. Job 1:6; Zech 3:1; Rev 12:10]; Sept.: 1 Sam 2:10; Isa 41:11; Jer 50:34; 51:36).

Syn.: *hupenantíos* (5227), one who is contrary to; *ho antikeímenos* (480), the one lying in opposition, the adversary; *diábolos*, the devil, the false accuser; *Satanás* (4567), the adversary, Satan; *ho ponērós* (4190), the wicked one, the devil.

Ant.: *phílos* (5384), friend; *hetaíros* (2083), one who pretends to be a friend for selfish purposes.

477. ἀντίθεσις *antíthesis*; gen. *antithéseōs*, fem. noun from *antitíthēmi* (n.f.), to oppose, which is from *antí* (473), against, and *títhēmi* (5087), to place. Opposition, opposite opinions, contrary positions or doctrine (1 Tim 6:20). Equivalent to the Eng. word "antithesis," which is derived from this Greek word.

Syn.: *antilogía* (485), contradiction; *zétēsis* (2214), dispute; *dichostasía* (1370), dissension; *diastolḗ* (1293), difference, distinction; *éris* (2054), contention.

Ant.: *sugkatáthesis* (4783), agreement; *sumphōnía* (4858), symphony, agreement.

478. ἀντικαθίστημι *antikathístēmi*; fut. *antikatastḗsō*, from *antí* (473), against, and *kathístēmi* (2525), to place. To put in place of another (Sept.: Josh 5:7). To place against or in opposition to (Sept.: Deut 31:21). In the NT, in the 2d aor. intrans., to stand firm against, resist (Heb 12:4).

Syn.: *anthístēmi* (436), to set against; *antitássō* (498), to set oneself against, especially in battle, to oppose; *antipíptō* (496), to resist.

Ant.: *sumphōnéō* (4856), to sound together, agree; *suntíthēmi* (4934), to put together, assent; *sugkatatíthēmi* (4784), to consent with; *eunoéō* (2132), to be well disposed.

479. ἀντικαλέω *antikaléō*; fut. *antikalésō*, from *antí* (473), in return, and *kaléō* (2564), to call. To call or invite in turn to a feast, to bid again (Luke 14:12).

Syn.: *keleúō* (2753), to bid.

Ant.: *aporríptō* (641), to reject, cast off.

480. ἀντίκειμαι *antíkeimai*; fut. *antikeísomai*, from *antí* (473), against, and *keímai* (2749), to be placed, to lie. To oppose, with the dat. in Gal 5:17; 1 Tim 1:10. *Ho antikeímenos*, in the pres. part., the one lying against, an adversary, opposer, followed by the dat. as in Luke

13:17; 21:15; 1 Cor 16:9; 1 Tim 5:14;
Sept.: Ex 23:22; Job 13:25; Isa 66:6;
Zech 3:1.
  Syn.: *antitássomai* (498), to set oneself against; *antidiatíthemai* (475), to
have an opposite attitude.
  Ant.: *antilambánomai* (482), to support; *sunantilambánomai* (4878), to take
hold of at the side for assisting; *boēthéō*
(997), to help; *sunupourgéō* (4943), to
help together or to serve with anyone as
an underworker; *sunergéō* (4903), to help
in work, cooperate.

481. ἀντικρύ *antikrú*; adv. governing a
gen. from *antí* (473), against. Opposite
to, over against (Acts 20:15).
  Syn.: *katenópion* (2714), directly in
front of, before; *énanti* (1725), in front
of, before; *enantíon* (1726), in the presence of, before; *émprosthen* (1715), in
front of.
  Ant.: *ópisthen* (3693), behind, at the
back, *opísō* (3694), to the back.

482. ἀντιλαμβάνω *antilambánō*; fut.
antilépsomai, from *antí* (473), mutually or against, and *lambánō* (2983), to
take, to hold. Used in the mid. pass. form
antilambánomai, to take hold of another mutually as by the hand, hence figuratively to support from falling as by the
hand, to support, help, assist (Luke 1:54;
Acts 20:35); to take hold, as it were, on
the opposite side (1 Tim 6:2), which refers to taking hold of the glorious benefit
of Christ's redemption on the other side,
properly denoting to support a burden
with another person on the other side. In
this view, the expression beautifully represents the masters as laying hold of the
benefit of the gospel on one side while
their slaves also, who are now the Lord's
free men, have hold of it in similar manner on the other side. In Class. Gr. writings, however, *antilambánomai* often
means to partake of, receive, enjoy, and
would explain 1 Tim 6:2 as "but rather
let them do service, because they who receive the benefit of their service are be-

lievers, and beloved" (a.t. [cf. Eph 6:8;
Phile 1:16]).
  Deriv.: *antílēpsis* (484), a help, assistance; *sunantilambánō* (4878), to help.
  Syn.: *sunantilambánomai* (4878), to
take hold of; *boēthéō* (997), aid, help,
succor; *sumbállō* (4820), to throw together, helping or benefiting; *sunupourgéō*
(4943), to help together, to serve with
anyone; *sunergéō* (4903), to help in
work, cooperate; *parístēmi* (3936), to
stand by for help; *antéchomai* (472), to
support, hold.
  Ant.: *adikéō* (91), to do hurt; *bláptō*
(984), to injure; *kakóō* (2559), to harm.

483. ἀντιλέγω *antilégō*; fut. *antiléxō*,
from *antí* (473), against, and *légō* (3004),
to speak. To speak against.
  (I) To contradict (Acts 13:45; 28:19,
22). Followed by *mḗ* (3361), not, with the
inf., to deny (Luke 20:27).
  (II) To oppose, disobey, revile (Luke
2:34; John 19:12; Rom 10:21; Titus 1:9;
2:9; Sept.: Isa 50:5; 65:2; Hos 4:4).
  Deriv.: *antilogía* (485), contradiction.
  Syn.: *katalaléō* (2635), to speak
against; *kakologéō* (2551), to speak evil.
  Ant.: *sumphōnéō* (4856), to agree,
speak in agreement with; *suntíthēmi*
(4934) to make an agreement, assent
to; *sugkatatíthemai* (4784), to consent;
eunoéō (2132), to be well-minded; *peíthō*
(3982), to persuade, agree.

484. ἀντίληψις *antílēpsis*; gen.
antilépseōs, fem. noun from *antilambánō*
(482), help, relief. Literally the receiving of remuneration. It came to mean a
laying hold of anything, the holding of
that which one has, perception, apprehension. In NT Gr., used like the verb
antilambánomai (482), to receive in return for, render assistance, help. It is in
this way that we must understand the
meaning of the word "helps" as one of
the gifts of the Spirit (1 Cor 12:28), implying duties toward the poor and sick
even as the deacons were appointed to
give attention to (Acts 6; Rom 16:1). If
we take it as manual services associated

with the office of the deacon, then the kubérnēsis (2941), translated "government," must be attributed to the elders. See Ps 22:19.

Syn.: boétheia (996), help; epikouría (1947), help or assistance; ōphéleia (5622), usefulness; euergesía (2108), well-doing; eupoiïa (2140), benefiting others; chrēstótes (5544), usefulness, kindness; sumphéron (4851), benefit.

Ant.: epiboulḗ (1917), a plot to hurt others; zēmía (2209), damage, detriment.

485. ἀντιλογία antilogía; gen. antilogías, fem. noun from antilégō (483), to contradict. Contradiction.

(I) Controversy, question, strife (Heb 6:16; 7:7). Spoken of a controversy before a judge (Sept.: Ex 18:16; Deut 25:1; 2 Sam 15:4).

(II) Reproach (Heb 12:3 [cf. Matt 26:60; 27:22, 29, 40–49]; Acts 13:45; Jude 1:11). Rebellion or strife or reproach (Sept.: Num 20:13; Deut 21:5; Ps 80:6).

Syn.: suzḗtēsis (4803), mutual questioning, discussion, disputation; dialogismós (1261), disputation; logomachía (3055), a dispute about words; paradiatribḗ (3859), wrangling.

Ant.: sumphṓnēsis (4857), sounding together, agreement, concord; sumphōnía (4858), symphony, a sounding together, agreement.

486. ἀντιλοιδορέω antiloidoréō; fut. antiloidorḗsō, from antí (473), in return, and loidoréō (3058), to revile. To revile again or in return (1 Pet 2:23).

Syn.: oneidízō (3679), to reproach, upbraid; blasphēméō (987), to speak profanely, blaspheme; kakologéō (2551), to revile; mémphomai (3201), to blame.

Ant.: eulogéō (2127), to bless, speak well of; eneulogéomai (1757), to bring blessing upon someone; makarízō (3106), to pronounce as indwelt by God because of Jesus Christ and, therefore, perfectly satisfied.

487. ἀντίλυτρον antílutron; gen. antilútrou, neut. noun from antí (473),

in return, or correspondence, and lútron (3083), a ransom. A ransom, a price of redemption. The "ransom for many" used in Matt 20:28; Mark 10:45 (lútron) is here called antílutron in order to stress the fact of Christ's coming and suffering in the place of all and for their advantage (hupér [5228]). There is a reference to expiation in 1 Pet 1:18, 19 where giving Himself denotes self-surrender to death (see Titus 2:14; Gal 1:4).

Syn.: eleuthería (1657), freedom; sōtería (4991), salvation; sōtḗrion (4992), means of salvation.

Ant.: ólethros (3639), ruin, destruction; phthorá (5356), corruption; súntrimma (4938), a crushing, complete destruction.

488. ἀντιμετρέω antimetréō; fut. antimetrḗsō, from antí (473), in turn, and metréō (3354), to measure. To measure or to measure back again or in turn (Matt 7:2; Luke 6:38). Metaphorically, to repay, requite, to render like for like.

Ant.: sunergéō (4903), to cooperate; boēthéō (997), to help.

489. ἀντιμισθία antimisthía; gen. antimisthías, fem. noun from antí (473), in return, and misthós (3408), a reward. A recompense, either in a good or bad sense, retribution (Rom 1:27; 2 Cor 6:13).

Syn.: antapódoma (468), that which is given back in return; antapódosis (469), giving back in return; misthapodosía (3405), a payment of wages, recompense.

490. Ἀντιόχεια Antiócheia; gen. Antiocheías, fem. proper noun. Antioch. There were places called Antioch established by Seleucus, the first Nicator, in honor of his father. The most celebrated was Antioch of Syria founded about 300 B.C. Cicero commended Antioch for its distinguished culture. Close by the city were the renowned groves of Daphne in a sanctuary dedicated to Apollo where orgiastic rites were celebrated in the name of religion.

Despite the bad moral tone, life in Antioch at the beginning of the Christian era was rich and varied. Next to Jerusalem, this city was most intimately connected with the beginnings of Christianity. Acts 6:5 records that a certain Nicolas had abandoned Greek paganism and had become a member of the Jewish synagogue at Antioch. During the persecution which followed the death of Stephen, some of the disciples went as far north as Antioch (Acts 11:19), about 300 miles from Jerusalem, and preached to the Jews. Later, Christianity spread also to the Greeks there. The church in Jerusalem sent Barnabas to Antioch, who, after assessing the situation, went to Tarsus and brought Saul back with him. They both taught there for over a year. The church in Antioch was a benevolent church, having sent alms to the church in Jerusalem when famine struck (Acts 11:27–30).

It is indeed noteworthy that the place where the first Gentile church was founded and where the Christians were first given that characteristic name should be the birthplace of Christian foreign missions (Acts 13:1). Paul and Barnabas set out from the seaport of Antioch and sailed for Cyprus. This first journey into Asia Minor concluded when Paul and Barnabas returned to Antioch and reported to the assembled church. When Jews in the church of Antioch taught the necessity of circumcision of Gentiles, the matter was referred to the Jerusalem church through a delegation headed by Paul and Barnabas (Acts 15:22–26). Paul began and ended his second missionary journey at Antioch from which he also began his third missionary journey. Today, the city in Turkey is called Antakya and about 20 ruined churches have been unearthed dating from the fourth century A.D.

There is yet another Antioch, which is in Pisidia. It was established as an important trading route between Ephesus and Cilicia and was a prominent center of Hellenism. Jewish colonists received Paul kindly there on his first missionary journey (Acts 13:14). Under the Roman Empire, Pisidian Antioch was included in the province of Galatia (in the region Phrygia Galatica). The Emperor Augustus gave it the status of a Roman colony. In Phrygia, women enjoyed considerable prestige and sometimes occupied civic offices. The opponents of Paul enlisted some of these influential persons (Acts 13:50) to attain his expulsion from the city. The ruined site is near Yalovach in modern Turkey. Other references: Acts 11:20, 22, 26; 14:19, 21, 26; 15:30, 35; 18:22; Gal 2:11; 2 Tim 3:11.

491. Ἀντιοχεύς *Antiocheús*; gen. *Antiochéōs*, masc. noun. A citizen of *Antiócheia* (490), Antioch (Acts 6:5).

492. ἀντιπαρέρχομαι *antiparérchomai*; fut. *antipareleúsomai*, from *antí* (473), over against, and *parérchomai* (3928), to pass by. To pass by on the opposite side, to turn out of the way and so pass by (Luke 10:31, 32, where in the parable of the Good Samaritan the priest and the Levite are presented by the Lord as turning out of the way at the sight of the wounded and half-dead man).

Syn.: *paraporeúomai* (3899), to go past, pass by.

Ant.: *ephístēmi* (2186), to stand upon or by, to be present; *parístēmi* (3936), to stand by or beside; *periΐstēmi* (4026), to stand around; *paragínomai* (3854) and *sumparagínomai* (4836), to come up to assist.

493. Ἀντίπας *Antípas*; masc. proper noun. Antipas, a shorter form of Antipater, otherwise unknown. He is mentioned in Rev 2:13. Later, Greek tradition made him bishop of Pergamum, martyred under Domitian by being thrown into a heated brazen bull which stood at the temple of Diana and so being roasted alive. The name has been allegorized as *antí* (473), against, and *pás* (3596), all. The two words would mean against all. The character of the Revelation, again, admits the hypothesis that the name refers to the god Pan. Pan was worshiped at Ephesus and in many cities in Asia Minor—though no record of his worship at Pergamum is in existence—under the strong influences of Arcadian and Peloponnesian cults. It is possible, therefore, that the church at Pergamum is praised for its opposition to the heathen Pan. See *Balaám* (903), Balaam; *Nikolaïtēs* (3531), Nicolaitans.

494. Ἀντιπατρίς *Antipatrís*; gen. *Antipatrídos*, fem proper noun. Antipatris, a Hellenistic town of Palestine at the eastern edge of the Plain of Sharon where the military road from Jerusalem to Caesarea left the hills. Under the protection of a body of Roman cavalry and infantry, Paul was brought here by night, and from here with a diminished escort, he was taken to Caesarea by the sea (Acts 23:31, 32). Being a border town between Judaea and Samaria, it was thought that after Paul reached there, he would be in less danger of a Jewish attack.

495. ἀντιπέραν *antipéran*; adv. from *antí* (473), against, and *péran* (4008), beyond, on the farther side. On the opposite shore, over against (Luke 8:26).
    Syn.: *katenópion* (2714), directly in front of; *énanti* (1725), in front; *antikrú* (481), opposite, over against; *émprosthen* (1715), in front of.
    Ant.: *ópisthen* (3692), behind; *opísō* (3694), to the back.

496. ἀντιπίπτω *antipíptō*; fut. *antipesoúmai*, from *antí* (473), against, and *píptō* (4098), to fall. To fall or rush against or upon in a hostile manner, assault, resist by force and violence, fall or strive against (Acts 7:51; Sept.: Num 27:14).
    Syn.: *anthístēmi* (436), to set against; *antikathístēmi* (478), to stand firm against; *antitássō* (498), to rage in battle against.
    Ant.: *antilambánomai* (482), to support; *sunantilambánomai* (4878), to help in bearing one's burden; *boēthéō* (997), to help, succor; *sumbállō* (4820), to

help or benefit; *sunupourgéō* (4943), to help together by being an underworker; *sunergéō* (4903), to help in work by cooperating; *parístēmi* (3936), to stand by for help.

497. ἀντιστρατεύομαι *antistrateúomai*; mid. deponent from *antí* (473), against, and *strateúomai* (4754), to war. To war or lead an army against. In Rom 7:23, metaphorically, to war against, oppose.
    Syn.: *poleméō* (4170), to fight, make war; *agōnízomai* (75), to contend, strive, fight; *pukteúō* (4438), to box, fight with one's hands; *máchomai* (3164), to strive; *diamáchomai* (1264), to struggle against; *antagōnízomai* (464), to struggle or strive against.
    Ant.: *sumphōnéō* (4856), to agree, and its syn.

498. ἀντιτάσσω *antitássō*; fut. *antitáxō*, from *antí* (473), against, and *tássō* (5021), to arrange. To set an army in array against, to arrange in battle order. In the NT, *antitássomai* is used metaphorically to set oneself in opposition to or in array against, to resist (Acts 18:6; Rom 13:2; James 4:6; 5:6; 1 Pet 5:5; Sept.: Prov 3:34).
    Syn.: *antíkeimai* (480), to place oneself against; *antidiatíthemai* (475), to have a disposition against; *anthístēmi* (436), to resist, set against; *antikathístēmi* (478), to stand firm against; *antipíptō* (496), to fall against or upon.
    Ant.: *sumphōnéō* (4856), to agree.

499. ἀντίτυπον *antítupon*; the neut. of the masc. adj. *antítupos*, gen. *antítupou*, from *antí* (473), against, instead of, corresponding to, and *túpos* (5179), a type, model, figure, form, impression, print. In the NT, *antí* (473) in composition implies resemblance, correspondence; hence, formed after a type or model, like unto, corresponding. Used in the neut. *antítupon* as a subst. meaning antitype, that which corresponds to a type (Heb 9:24), used in the pl. and translated "figures" as representing the holy places where sacrifices were offered, being not the real things but the antitypes or representations of the real things.

In 1 Pet 3:21, baptism is referred to as an antitype or figure of salvation or a physical act corresponding to the spiritual reality of salvation. According to Rom 6:3–14 baptism is a symbol of Christ's death and resurrection. The word *antítupon*, antitype, explains the word "baptism" being in apposition to it. It is a copy or an impression of something that has reality, standing instead of the real thing. In this passage baptism does not refer to the water at all, but to the ark in which Noah and his family found their salvation through the water. The water in the case of the flood symbolizes not salvation, but the means of destruction used by God, even as the fire will be the means of destruction in the end times (2 Pet 3:6, 7, 10). Therefore, baptism, which is a symbol of our having been rescued by God through our voluntary entrance into the ark of His salvation, is here called the symbol that saves us. However, it is not the symbol itself which saves us, but what it symbolizes which is the death and resurrection of Jesus Christ. The one who appropriates Christ's death and resurrection is saved even as the people in the days of Noah who entered the ark.

In the ancient Christian church, they called the bread and wine in the communion the *antítupa* (pl.) of Christ's body and blood. The antitype mysteries of the body and blood of Christ represented the bread and wine.

Syn.: *parabolḗ* (3850), a parable; *hupódeigma* (5262), a pattern that is placed under for tracing; *homoíōma* (3667), something which is made to resemble something else; *eikṓn* (1504), an image representing something which has reality; *deígma* (1164), sample, example; *homoíōsis* (3669), making something to look like something else; *homoiótēs* (3665), likeness.

Ant.: *diaíresis* (1243), difference, diversity, division; *diastolḗ* (1293)

distinction; *diákrisis* (1253), distinction; *parallagḗ* (3883), transmutation, variableness.

500. ἀντίχριστος *antíchristos*; gen. *antichrístou*, masc. noun from *antí* (473), instead of or against, and *Christós* (5547), Christ, anointed. Antichrist, literally an opposer of Christ or one who usurps the place of Christ, found only in John's epistles and collectively meaning all who deny that Jesus is the Messiah and that the Messiah is come in the flesh (1 John 2:18, 22; 4:3; 2 John 1:7). We do not know exactly whom John had in mind, but most probably Jewish opposers to the Messiah-ship of Christ. It occurs nowhere else in the NT. Paul's reference to the same person is called "the man of sin," "son of perdition," "wicked one" (*ánomos* [459], lawless) as in 2 Thess 2:3, 8. He is the one opposing Christ (*antikeímenos* [480]) as in 2 Thess 2:4, asserting the fulfillment of God's Word in himself and therefore seeking to establish his own throne. *antíchristos* (Matt 24:24; Mark 13:22) is to be distinguished from *pseudóchristos* (5580), a false christ, the *antíchristos* does not deny the existence of Christ, but takes advantage of the fact of the expectation of the appearance of Christ. He thus deceives the people in believing that he is "the Christ," whereas the antichrist denies the existence of the true God.

In the OT, we have the intimation of someone who will be opposed to the Lord and His anointed (Ps 2; Ezek 38; 39; Zech 12—14; see Dan 7:8, 20f.; 8:24; 11:28, 30, 36f., which read in conjunction with 2 Thess 2:4 and Rev 13:1–8).

In His Olivet Discourse, our Lord warns against "the false christs" and "the false prophets" (Matt 24:24; Mark 13:22).

In 2 Thess 2:1–12, Paul asserts that, before the day of Christ (the day of the rapture of the Church described in 1 Thess 4:13–17), there must come first an apostasy or a standing off, and the man of sin, the Antichrist, will be revealed. He will sit in the new temple yet to be rebuilt under his own direction during the first three and one-half years of the seven-year period of the tribulation. He will demonstrate great satanic power and will perform signs and lying wonders. The Lord will slay this Antichrist at His second coming (Rev 20:10). In 1 John 2:18, attention is drawn to the antichrists already existing and working against Christ, but the real Antichrist whose coming was erroneously expected by the early Church was not included here (see 1 John 2:22; 4:3; 2 John 1:7).

Rev 17:8 refers to the beast which should be connected with the beast of Dan 7—8. He claims and wins respect equal to that of God and makes war on God's people. He rules for three and one-half years over the earth and is finally destroyed by the Lord in a great battle.

Syn.: *pseudóchristos* (5580), a false christ.

501. ἀντλέω *antléō*; contracted *antlṓ*, fut. *antlḗsō*, from *ántlos* (n.f.), the hold of a ship. To bail out, dip water, to draw out, such as water or wine; to empty a sink, as used by the Class. Gr. writers. In the NT, to draw out as water out of a well (John 2:9; 4:7, 15; Sept.: Gen 24:13, 20; Ex 2:16, 19) or wine from a jar (John 2:8).

Deriv.: *ántlēma* (502), a bucket for drawing water by a rope.

Syn.: *kenóō* (2758), to empty; *ekchéō* (1632), to pour out.

Ant.: *gémō* (1073), to fill, swell out; *plēróō* (4137), to fill up.

502. ἄντλημα *ántlēma*; gen. *antlḗmatos*, neut. noun from *antléō* (501), to draw up or out. In the NT, a bucket, any vessel for drawing water (John 4:11).

503. ἀντοφθαλμέω *antophthalméō*; contracted *antophthalmṓ*, fut. *antophthalmḗsō*, from *antí* (473), against, and *ophthalmós* (3788), eye. To direct the eye against another who observes him, to look a person in the face, as used by the

Classics. In the NT, it applies to a ship, meaning to bear up against the wind, to look the storm in the face as it were (Acts 27:15). On the prow of the ancient ships was placed a round piece of wood, sometimes called *ophthalmós*, the eye of the ship, because it was fixed in its foredeck.

504. ἄνυδρος *ánudros*; gen. *anúdrou*, masc.-fem., neut. *ánudron*, adj. from the priv. *a* (1), without, and *húdōr* (5204), water. Without water, dry. *Ánudroi tópoi* (5117), dry places, barren, sandy, desert (Matt 12:43; Luke 11:24). The Jews supposed that the abode of evil spirits was in deserts (cf. Rev 18:2; Sept.: Isa 41:19; 43:19, 20; 44:3; Hos 2:3). Spoken of boastful deceivers and seducers who are called *pēgaí* (4077), fountains, *ánudroi*, waterless and *nephélai* (3507), clouds, fountains or clouds that promise much water but deceive those who rely on them (2 Pet 2:17; Jude 1:12).

Syn.: *xērós* (3584), dry.

Ant.: *hugrós* (5200), wet, moist.

505. ἀνυπόκριτος *anupókritos*; gen. *anupokrítou*, masc.-fem., neut. *anupókriton*, adj. from the priv. *a* (1), without, and *hupokrínomai* (5271), to pretend, simulate. Originally it meant inexperienced in the art of acting. In the NT, it came to mean one without hypocrisy or pretense, unfeigned, genuine, real, true, sincere (Rom 12:9; 2 Cor 6:6; 1 Tim 1:5; 2 Tim 1:5; 1 Pet 1:22; James 3:17).

Syn.: *ádolos* (97), pure, sincere; *gnésios* (1103), genuine; *eilikrinḗs* (1506), pure, sincere; *hagnós* (53), pure, chaste.

Ant.: *hupokritḗs* (5273), a hypocrite; *pseudḗs* (5571), false, and their syn.

506. ἀνυπότακτος *anupótaktos*; gen. *anupotáktou*, from the priv. *a* (1), without, and *hupotássō* (5293), to subject, sit under in an orderly manner. Not subject (Heb 2:8); disobedient to authority, disorderly (1 Tim 1:9; Titus 1:6, 10).

Syn.: *apeithḗs* (545), unwilling to be persuaded, disobedient.

Ant.: *hupékoos* (5255), obedient, giving ear to; *eupeithḗs* (2138), obedient.

507. ἄνω ánō; adv. Above, in a higher place (Acts 2:19; Rev 5:3, Majority Text). With the neut. pl. art. *tá*, *tá ánō*, the place above (John 8:23 [cf. 3:13, 31; 6:38]; Col 3:1, 2); with the sing. fem. art. *hē ánō*, that which is above (Gal 4:26); *hē ánō klḗsis* ([2821], calling), the upper or heavenly calling (Phil 3:14, equivalent to Heb 3:1. See Sept.: Ex 20:4; Deut 4:39; Josh 2:11; Isa 7:3). With *héōs* (2193), as far as, up to the brim (John 2:7; Sept.: 2 Chr 26:8). Upwards (John 11:41; Heb 12:15; Sept.: 1 Chr 22:5; Eccl 3:21; Isa 8:21; 37:21).

Deriv.: *anógeon* (508), an upper room or chamber; *ánōthen* (509), from above, from the beginning, again; *epánō* (1883), above, more than; *huperáno* (5231), high above.

Syn.: *hupsēlós* (5308), high, lofty; *húpsistos* (5310), most high; *mégas* (3173), great, high; *húpsos* (5311), height; *húpsōma* (5313), high thing or height.

Ant.: *kátō* (2736), below; *hupokátō* (5270), under, underneath; *katōtérō* (2736) under, below; *elássōn* (1640), less.

508. ἀνώγεον anógeon; gen. *anōgéou*, neut. noun from *ánō* (507), up, and *gaía* (n.f.), ground, earth. An upper room or chamber (Mark 14:15; Luke 22:12).

Syn.: *huperóon* (5253), upper, an upper chamber.

509. ἄνωθεν ánōthen; adv. from *ánō* (507), above, and the suffix -*then* denoting from. From above.

(I) Of place: from above, from a higher place (Matt 27:51; Mark 15:38; John 19:23). Used in substitution of *ouranóthen* (3771), from heaven, or *ek toú ouranoú* (*ek* [1537], from; *toú ouranoú* [3772], the heaven), from the heaven, from God since God dwells in heaven. In John 3:3, 7, 31; 19:11; James 1:17, the meaning is from God, implied in the "from above." The wisdom from above in James 3:17 is

the heavenly or divine wisdom (cf. James 3:15; Sept.: Ex 28:27; Job 3:4).

(II) Of time:

(A) From the first, from the beginning (Luke 1:3; Acts 26:5, knowing me from the first [*ánōthen*], from the earliest age; Gal 4:9, again, from the very beginning, as if you had never been a Christian).

(B) Again, another time as in John 3:3, 7, "be born again." This could also be translated "to be born from above." Both meanings are correct since this is a birth from God and it is a new birth. In John 3:4, Nicodemus clearly takes it to mean to be born a second time (*deúteron* [1208]).

Syn.: *dís* (1364), twice; *pálin* (3825), again; *próteron* (4386), before, first; *prótos* (4413), first; *próton* (4412), firstly, of time; *en archḗ* (*en* [1722], in; *archḗ* [746], beginning) from the beginning; *ap' archḗs* (*apó* [575], from, *archḗs* [n.f.], beginning), from the beginning.

510. ἀνωτερικός anōterikós; fem. *anōterikḗ*, neut. *anōterikón*, adj. from *anóteros* (511), upper, higher. Upper, higher as in Acts 19:1 meaning higher up in the country, further in the inland parts of Asia Minor or more distant from the sea referring to the districts of Phrygia and Galatia.

511. ἀνώτερος anóteros; fem. *anōtéra*, neut. *anóteron*, adj., the comparative of *ánō* (507), up or upward, above; adv. in the neut. *anóteron*. The higher, superior, upper. Higher, to a higher place (Luke 14:10). Above, previously (Heb 10:8).

Deriv.: *anōterikós* (510), upper.

Ant.: *katóteros* (2737), inferior; *kátō* (2736), beneath, down, the lower; *elássōn/eláttōn* (1640), less, under; *éschatos* (2078), last in time or place; *hústeros* (5306), latter, terminal.

512. ανωφελής anōphelḗs; gen. *anōpheléos* contracted *anōpheloús*, masc.-fem., neut. *anōphelés*, adj. from the priv. *a* (1), without, and *ōpheléō* (5623), to profit. Unprofitable, serving no purpose, and hence injurious, noxious (Titus 3:9; Sept.: Prov 28:3; of idols in Jer 2:8; Isa 44:10). Used as a subst. in the neut., *tó anōphelés*, the unprofitable thing, unprofitableness (Heb 7:18).

Syn.: *achreíos* (888), useless, unprofitable; *alusitelḗs* (255), not advantageous in the sense of not being spent or used profitably; *áchrēstos* (890), unserviceable, unprofitable.

Ant.: *ōphélimos* (5624) and *chrḗsimos* (5539), profitable, useful; *eúchrēstos* (2173), profitable, capable of being put to good use.

513. ἀξίνη *axínē*; gen. *axínēs*, fem. noun from *ágnumi* (n.f.), to break. An axe (Matt 3:10; Luke 3:9; Sept.: Deut 19:5; 1 Sam 13:20). Also from *ágnumi*: (n.f.): *katágnumi* (2608), to break down.

514. ἄξιος *áxios*; fem. *axía*, neut. *áxion*, adj. from *ágō* (71), to weigh. An estimate or value. Some believe it refers to a set of scales where the weights bring or draw down (*ágousi*) the beam to a horizontal level when the weights are equal on each side. Worthy, indicating inherent value as contrasted to *tímios* (5093), worthy from attributed value.

(I) Of equal value, similar worth, comparable (Rom 8:18, "the sufferings of this present time are not worthy to be compared with the [future] glory"; Sept. Prov 3:15; 8:11 [cf. Gen 23:9; 1 Chr 21:22, 24]).

(II) Worthy or deserving of either good or evil.

(A) Of good, referring to persons meaning worthy, useful, deserving (Matt 10:10, 11, 13; 22:8; Luke 7:4; 10:17; Acts 13:46; 1 Tim 5:18; 6:1; Rev 3:4); things (1 Tim 1:15; 4:9; Sept.: Esth 7:4). With the gen. of person (Matt 10:37, 38, "worthy of me," worthy to be my friend or to be cherished by me or anyone; Heb 11:38); with the aor. inf. (Luke 15:19, 21, "no more worthy to be called thy son"; Acts 13:25; Rev 4:11; 5:2, 4, 9, 12); with *hína* (2443), in order that (John 1:27, "I

am not worthy to unloose the strap of his shoe" [a.t.]).

(B) Of evil, deserving of in an absolute sense (Rev 16:6). With the gen. *plēgṓn* (4127), stripes (Luke 12:48, "worthy of stripes" or deserving of punishment; 23:15, "worthy [or deserving] of death"; Acts 23:29; 25:11, 25; 26:31; Rom 1:32).

(III) By implication, suitable, congruent, corresponding to, with the gen. as fruits worthy of repentance, meaning congruent or suitable to repentance (Matt 3:8; Luke 3:8; 23:41; Acts 26:20). With the verb *estí*, is, the 3d person sing. of *eimí* (1510), I am, meaning it is suitable, proper (2 Thess 1:3).

Deriv.: *anáxios* (370), unworthy; *axióō* (515), to think or count worthy, to deem oneself entitled to; *axíōs* (516), worthily.

Syn.: *ídios* (2398), one's own or that which is due to someone; *hikanós* (2425), sufficient; *kalós* (2570), good, meet; *eúthetos* (2111), well-placed, fit; *díkaios* (1342), just, right, equal to.

Ant.: *anáxios* (370), unworthy; *ádikos* (94), unjust, wrong.

515. ἀξιόω *axióō*; contracted *axió*, fut. *axiṓsō*, from *áxios* (514), worthy. To esteem, count or reckon worthy or deserving (Luke 7:7; 1 Tim 5:17; Heb 3:3; 10:29; Sept.: Gen 31:28); to think fit, suitable or proper (Acts 15:38 [cf. 28:22]); to count worthy or fit, to account or accept as worthy (2 Thess 1:11); to desire, wish, hence demand (Sept.: Esth 4:8; Dan 1:8; 2:16, 23).

Deriv.: *kataxióō* (2661), to count worthy indeed.

Syn.: *epithuméō* (1937), to desire earnestly; *erōtáō* (2065), to ask on an equal basis between the one who asks and the one from whom something is asked; *aitéō* (154), to ask, having the connotation of an inferior asking from a superior; *thélō* (2309), to will, wish, with the determination to act as contrasted to *boúlomai* (1014), to will deliberately, without necessarily effecting that which one wills; *zētéō* (2212), to seek, and the more emphatic *epizētéō* (1937), to seek earnestly; *epipothéō* (1971), to long after; *exaitéomai* (1809), to desire intensely; *parakaléō* (3817), to beseech.

Ant.: *kataleípō* (2641), to leave, forsake; *egkataleípō* (1459), to leave behind; *aphíēmi* (863), to let go or be separated from; *apotássō* (657), to forsake or to set in order away from oneself.

516. ἀξίως *axíōs*; adv. from *áxios* (514), worthy. Worthily, suitably, properly (Rom 16:2; Eph 4:1; Phil 1:27; Col 1:10; 1 Thess 2:12; 3 John 1:6). Verb: *axióō* (515), to esteem.

Syn.: *dikaíōs* (1346), justly.

Ant.: *anaxíōs* (371), unworthily; *adíkōs* (95), unjustly, wrongfully.

517. ἀόρατος *aóratos*; gen. *aorátou*, masc.-fem., neut. *aóraton*, adj. from the priv. *a* (1), without, and *horáō* (3708), to see. Invisible, that which cannot be seen with the physical eyes (Rom 1:20; Col 1:15, 16; 1 Tim 1:17; Heb 11:27; Sept.: Gen 1:2).

Syn.: *kruptós* (2927), concealed, private but possible to be discovered; *apókruphos* (614), secret, hidden; *kekalumménos*, the hidden one, from *kalúptō* (2572), to cover, hide; *ádēlos* (82), indistinct, uncertain; *ágnōstos* (57), unknown.

Ant.: *phanerós* (5318), apparent; *apokekalumménos*, the revealed one, from *apokalúptō* (601), to reveal; *epiphanḗs* (2016), conspicuous, manifest.

518. ἀπαγγέλλω *apaggéllō*; fut. *apaggelṓ*, imperf. *apḗggellon*, 2d aor. pass. *apēggélēn*, from *apó* (575), from, and *aggéllō* (n.f., see *anaggéllō* [312]), to tell, declare. To announce.

(I) To bring a message from any person or place.

(A) To relate, inform, tell what has occurred, with the dat. of person (Matt 14:12; 28:8, 10, 11; Mark 6:30; 16:10, 13; Luke 7:18; 8:20, 36; 9:36; 13:1; 18:17; 24:9; John 4:51; 20:18; Acts 11:13; Sept.: Judg

13:10); with acc. (Matt 8:33; Acts 4:23; 1 Thess 1:9). With the prep. *eis* (1519), into or to (Mark 5:14; Luke 8:34, into or in the town and in the fields; Sept.: Amos 4:13).

(B) To announce, make known, declare, tell what is done or to be done (Matt 12:18; Acts 5:25; 12:14, 17; 15:27; 16:36; 23:16, 17, 19; 28:21; Heb 2:12, "I shall declare [or make known] your name to my brethren" [a.t.]; 1 John 1:2, 3; Sept.: Gen 24:49; 29:15; Josh 2:2; Judg 13:6; Ps 78:4, 6 quoted from 22:23). To praise, celebrate (Ps 89:1; 105:1). To exhort, with the inf. (Acts 26:20, "repent and turn to God"). By implication to confess (Luke 8:47; 1 Cor 14:25; Sept.: Gen 12:18).

(II) To bring back word from anyone, report, with the dat. of person with or without the acc. of thing (Matt 2:8; 11:4; Luke 7:22; 14:21; Acts 22:26; Sept.: Gen 27:42; 29:12).

Syn.: *diēgéomai* (1334), to narrate, relate; *ekdiēgéomai* (1555), to narrate in full; *exēgéomai* (1834), to lead out, make known, rehearse; *dēlóō* (1213), to declare; *phrázō* (5419), to express, declare; *gnōrízō* (1107), to make known; *marturéō* (3140), to testify; *diaphēmízō* (1310), to report to the public; *phaneróō* (5319), to make manifest; *légō* (3004), to tell; *laléō* (2980), to speak; *eklaléō* (1583), to speak out; *eréō* (2046), to say; *diasaphéō* (1285), to make clear; *mēnúō* (3377), to show or make known.

Ant.: *krúptō* (2928), to cover, hide; *apokrúptō* (613), to conceal, keep secret; *egkrúptō* (1470), to hide in anything; *perikrúptō* (4032), to hide by placing something around; *kalúptō* (2572), to cover, conceal; *parakalúptō* (3871), to cover with a veil, conceal; *lanthánō* (2990), to escape notice, be hidden from.

519. ἀπάγχω *apágchō*; fut. *apágxō*, from *apó* (575), an intens., and *ágchō* (n.f.), to strangle. Found only in the mid. *apágchomai*, to strangle oneself by hanging (Matt 27:5; Sept.: 2 Sam 17:23 [cf. Acts 1:18, speaking of Judas who, having hanged himself and the cord perhaps having broken, fell with such violence as to dash out his bowels]).

Syn.: *kremánnumi* (2910), to hang; *ekkremánnumai* (1582) or *ekkrémamai*, in the mid. voice, to hang from or upon.

Ant.: *anapsúschō* (404), to revive; *anazáō* (326), to recover life.

520. ἀπάγω apágō; fut. *apáxō*, aor. pass. *apéchthēn*, 2d aor., *apégagon*, from *apó* (575), from, and *ágō* (71), to carry, lead. To lead away. Used trans.:

(I) Generally, to lead (Luke 13:15); with *prós* (4314), toward, indicating direction (Sept.: Gen 31:18; Deut 28:36, 37; 1 Kgs 1:38). In the NT mainly in a judicial sense, to lead away or bring before a judge or to prison (Matt 27:2; Mark 14:44; 15:16; Acts 23:17; 24:7); with *prós* (4314), toward, or *eis* (1519), into (Matt 26:57; Mark 14:53; John 18:13); to punishment (Matt 27:31; Luke 23:26; John 19:16). When used in an absolute sense it means to be put to death (Acts 12:19). Of a prisoner, *apagómenos*, the one being carried away (Sept.: Gen 39:22; 40:3; 42:16).

(II) Of a way, with *eis* (1519), into (Matt 7:13, 14, the way which leads to perdition or to life).

(III) In the mid. *apágomai*, literally to lead oneself away, go away, used metaphorically meaning to go astray, be seduced (1 Cor 12:2, "unto these dumb idols," meaning unto the worship of idols).

Deriv.: *sunapágō* (4879), to carry away with.

Syn.: *apophérō* (667), to carry forth; *ekbállō* (1544), to cast out; *ekkomízō* (1580), to carry out; *aírō* (142), to lift and carry away; *thanatóō* (2289), to put to death; *phoneúō* (5407), to murder; *spháttō* / *spházō* (4969), to butcher; *anairéō* (337), to take or lift up or away, to put to death; *apokteínō* (615), to kill; *thúō* (2380), to sacrifice; *phérō* (5342), to carry; *hodēgéō* (3594), to lead the way; *anaphérō* (399), to carry or lead up; *planáō* (4105), to lead astray; *apoplanáō*

(635), to cause to go astray; *apaírō* (522), to lift up; *paraphérō* (3911), to bear away.

Ant.: *aphíēmi* (863), to leave alone, forsake, neglect; *aníēmi* (447), to let go; *kataleípō* (2641) and *egkataleípō* (1459), to leave behind; *apoleípō* (620), to allow to remain; *hupoleípō* (5275), to leave under, remaining; *perileípō* (4035), to leave around or over; *eáō* (1439), to let, permit; *hupolimpánō* (5277), to leave; *ménō* (3306), to stay, abide; *diaménō* (1265), to remain throughout; *anéchomai* (430), to bear with.

521. ἀπαίδευτος apaídeutos; gen. *apaideútou*, masc.-fem., neut. *apaídeuton*, adj. from the priv. *a* (1), without, and *paideúō* (3811), to instruct, chastise, correct. Unlearned, untaught, ignorant, stupid, foolish. Of persons (Sept.: Prov 8:5; 15:15; 17:21). Only in 2 Tim 2:23 referring to nonsensical, i.e., inept, trifling, absurd disputations.

Syn.: *agrámmatos* (62), unlettered, unlearned; *amathḗs* (261), unlearned, ignorant; *idiṓtēs* (2399), a private citizen, an ignorant person; *áphrōn* (878), without reason; *anóētos* (453), without understanding; *mōrós* (3474), dull, sluggish in understanding; *asúnetos* (801), without discernment; *agoraíos* (60), one relating to the market-place, a commoner.

Ant.: *didaktós* (1318), one who can be taught; *theodídaktos* (2312), God-taught; *epistḗmōn* (1990), one who knows; *sunetós* (4908), intelligent, understanding, prudent; *sophós* (4680), wise; *polítēs* (4177), a townsman, one belonging to the city, hence cultured.

522. ἀπαίρω apaírō; fut. *aparṓ*, from *apó* (575), from, and *aírō* (142), to take away. Trans., to take away, remove. Intrans., to go away, depart (Sept.: Gen 12:9; 13:11). In the NT only in aor. pass. *apḗrthen*, to be taken away from (Matt 9:15; Mark 2:20; Luke 5:35).

Syn.: *aphairéō* (851), to remove; *harpázō* (726), to seize, snatch away; *lambánō* (2983), to take; *apágō* (520), to take away; *methístēmi* (3179), to cause to remove; *metatíthēmi* (3346), to remove a person or thing from one place to another; *apochōrízō* (673), to separate; *kinéō* (2795), to move. In the mid. voice it is a syn. of *metabaínō* (3327), to pass over from one place to another; *metoikízō* (3351), to remove oneself to a new abode.

Ant.: *tēréō* (5083), to preserve, keep; *diatēréō* (1301), to keep carefully; *phrouréō* (5432) and *phulássō* (5442), to guard, keep; *diaphulássō*, to guard thoroughly; *échō* (2192), to hold, have; *kratéō* (2902), to hold fast; *nosphízomai* (3557), to keep back implying deceit; *apérchomai* (565), to go away; *poreúomai* (4198), to go on one's way; *anachōréō* (402), to depart, retire.

523. ἀπαιτέω *apaitéō*; contracted *apaitṓ*, fut. *apaitḗsō*, from *apó* (575), again, and *aitéō* (154), to ask. To recall, demand back, legal exaction of a demand or legitimate claim (Deut 15:2, 3). To require, ask again (Luke 6:30, our Lord teaches here that it is better to be master of your emotions than of your possessions). To require, demand again in Luke 12:20 is in the 3d person pl., *apaitoúsin*, "they require thy soul of thee" (a.t.). The phrase "they require" must be understood as a reference to the three Persons of the Triune God (Luke 6:38; 12:48; Sept.: Deut 32:39; 1 Sam 2:6; 2 Kgs 5:7). Life must be viewed as a loan from God due to be returned to Him at death.

Syn.: *zētéō* (2212), to seek, inquire, desire; *epizētéō* (1934), to seek after or for; *ekzētéō* (1567), to seek out.

Ant.: *aphíēmi* (863), to remit, forgive; *charízomai* (5483), to provide grace or forgiveness of debt; *apolúō* (630), to let loose from, release; *leípō* (3007), to leave; *apoleípō* (620), to leave behind; *perileípō* (4035), to leave all around.

524. ἀπαλγέω *apalgéō*; contracted *apalgṓ*, fut. *apalgḗsō*, from *apó* (575), denoting privation, and *algéō* (n.f.), to feel pain. To grow or become insensible,

void of or past feeling. In Eph 4:19 used metaphorically meaning to be insensible to honor or shame. This is the word from which the Eng. "analgesic" is derived, meaning that which takes away pain.

Syn.: *pōróō* (4456), to make callous, insensitive; *sklērúnō* (4645), to render stubborn, harden.

Ant.: *aisthánomai* (143), to apprehend by the senses, to feel, perceive; *pónos* (4192), pain.

525. ἀπαλλάσσω *apallássō*, ἀπαλλάττω *apalláttō*; fut. *apalláxō*, from *apó* (575), from, and *allássō* (236), to change. To transfer from one state to another, to remove from. Strictly to change by separating, therefore, to break up an existing connection and set the one part into a different state or relation, to set free, make loose. In the mid. voice, intrans. *apallássomai*, to escape (Acts 19:12); act. voice, to set free, dismiss, trans. (Heb 2:15); pass., to be freed, get loose (Luke 12:58). *Apallássō* is also a technical term to denote the satisfaction of the plaintiff by the defendant, especially of the creditor by the debtor.

Syn.: *eleutheróō* (1659), to set free, deliver; *apolúō* (630), to loose from; *aphíēmi* (863), to remit, forgive; *lutróō* (3084), to ransom, redeem; *apolúō* (630), to release.

Ant.: *déō* (1210), to bind; *desmeúō* / *desméō* (1195), to put in fetters or to place a burden upon a person.

526. ἀπαλλοτριόω *apallotrióō*; contracted *apallotrió*, fut. *apallotriósō*, from *apó* (575), from, and *allotrióō* (n.f.), to alienate. To estrange, alienate entirely (Eph 2:12; 4:18; Col 1:21). It denotes the state prior to man's reconciliation to God. See Sept.: Job 21:29; Ps 58:3; Ezek 14:5.

Ant.: *katallássō* (2644), to reconcile, to change from enmity to friendship; *apokatallássō* (604), to reconcile completely; *diallássō* (1259), to reconcile.

527. ἁπαλός hapalós; fem. *hapalḗ*, neut. *hapalón*, adj. Yielding to the touch, soft, tender (Matt 24:32; Mark 13:28; Sept.: Gen 18:7; Isa 47:1).

Ant.: *sklērós* (4642), hard.

528. ἀπαντάω apantáō; contracted *apantṓ*, fut. *apantḗsō*, from *apó* (575), from, and *antáō* (n.f., see *katantáō* [2658]), to meet. To come from another place into the presence of, to meet from opposite directions (Matt 28:9; Mark 5:2; 14:13; Luke 17:12; John 4:51; Acts 16:16; Sept.: 1 Sam 10:5). Spoken of a hostile encounter (Mark 5:2; Luke 14:31; Sept.: Judg 8:21; 2 Sam 1:15).

Deriv.: *apántēsis* (529), a meeting.

Ant.: *apérchomai* (565), to come or go away; *anachōréō* (402), to retire, go away; *apochōréō* (672), to depart from; *ekchōréō* (1633), to depart out of, leave a place; *chōrízō* (5563), to put apart, separate; *apochōrízō* (673), to separate off; *diachōrízō* (1316), to separate completely; *analúō* (360), to depart from life; *aphístēmi* (868), to stand away from, depart.

529. ἀπάντησις apántēsis; gen. *apantḗseōs*, fem. noun from *apantáō* (528), to meet coming from different directions. A meeting (Matt 25:1, 6; Acts 28:15). In 1 Thess 4:17, the expression *eis* (unto) *apántēsin* (meeting) indicates that the Lord will be coming from one direction and we shall be coming from another to meet together in the air. See Sept.: 1 Sam 9:14; 1 Chr 12:17; Jer 41:6.

Syn.: *sunántēsis* (4877), meeting with; *énteuxis* (1783), meeting at one place, interview, supplication.

Ant.: *apostasía* (646), standing apart, separation; *apostásion* (647), divorce, separation.

530. ἄπαξ hápax; adv. of time. Once.

(I) One time (2 Cor 11:25; Heb 9:7, 27; 12:26, 27; 1 Pet 3:18; Sept.: Ex 30:10; Lev 16:34). In Phil 4:16; 1 Thess 2:18; Sept.: Neh 13:20, *hápax kaí dís* (*kaí*

[2532], and; *dís* [1364], twice), once and again, several times.

(II) Once for all, already, formerly (Heb 6:4; 9:26, 28; 10:2; Jude 1:3, 5; Sept.: Ps 62:12; 89:36). The word *hápax* with the meaning of once and for all is stressed in Heb 9:26 in regard to the sacrifice of the Lord Jesus Christ as contrasted by the appearance of the high priest every year in the Holy of Holies (Heb 9:25). *Hápax* in this sense means that this was the first and last time that Christ's offering was made, and it was made for the once-and-for-all removal of sin. In verse twenty-seven the death of Christ is compared with man's death, which occurs only once. In verse twenty-eight the fact that Christ cannot die twice is stressed, for it is not only that Christ sacrificed Himself once and for all, but also His sacrifice for sin is never to be repeated (Heb 10:12, 14).

The word *hápax* is also used in Heb 6:4, 5 and applies to all the part. in these verses: *phōtisthéntas* (5461), having been enlightened; *geusaménous* (1089), having tasted; *genēthéntas* (1096), having been made; and again *geusaménous*, used in regard to the Word of God. The *hápax* here refers to the once-and-for-all experience of salvation which begins with God's enlightenment, with man's being made a partaker of the Holy Spirit and tasting that the Word of God is good. This does not refer to the continuous experience by the believer of God's enlightenment, but to the once-and-for-all enlightenment and the reception of such unto salvation. Once a person has been saved, if he falls away (the part. here is a suppositional part., Matt 16:26; Luke 9:25), it is impossible to renew (*anakainízein* [340], to renew qualitatively) his salvation experience, or to have a new kind of repentance, because this would involve a recrucifixion of the Son of God. This is impossible since He died once and for all and it would disparage His death as having been non-efficacious.

The meaning of *hápax* is made clear by the use of the comp. *ephápax* (2178), from *epí* (1909), upon, at, and *hápax*, once (Rom 6:10; Heb 7:27; 9:12; 10:10). See *ephápax* in Heb 7:27 where it is used of Christ's offering in contrast to the daily sacrifices. Jesus Christ is pictured here as both the priest and the offering for sin. It indicates the impossibility of the repetition of His sacrifice and the sufficiency of Christ's offering of Himself.

Therefore, both the *hápax* and the *ephápax* are equivalent in meaning to *aiōnios* (166), eternal, which indicates not only the source, God, but also the duration of the life He gives. The word *aiōnios* is used in relation to eternal life, the life God gives to repentant, sinful man (Matt 19:29; Mark 10:17, 30; Luke 10:25; 18:18, 30; John 4:36), as well as to eternal salvation (Heb 5:9) also given by God forever.

Deriv.: *ephápax* (2178), once for all.

Syn.: *poté* (4218), once upon a time, formerly, at one time.

Ant.: *oudépote* (3763), not at any time, never; *mēdépote* (3368), never; *oudépō* (3764) and *oúpō* (3768), not yet; *ou mē eis tón aiōna* (*ou mē* [3364], not at all; *eis* [1519], unto; *tón aiōna* [165], the age), never; *ouk* (not) *eis tón aiōna*, never; *ou mē poté*, by no means ever, "never"; *ou mē . . . pópote*, by no means, not ever at any time; *oudeís pópote* (*oudeís* [3762], no one; *pópote* [4455], at no time, never yet) no man ever yet.

531. ἀπαράβατος *aparábatos*; gen. *aparabátou*, masc.-fem., neut. *aparábaton*, adj. from the priv. *a* (1), without, and *parabaínō* (3845), to go beyond, transgress. Unchangeable. Only in Heb 7:24, speaking of the unchangeable, eternal priesthood of Christ. Contrasted to the Jewish high priesthood which was passed from father to son and successor and was liable to be violated and transgressed (Heb 7:11), Christ's priesthood cannot be transferred to another; it is final.

Syn.: *hedraíos* (1476) and *ametakínētos* (277), immovable; *ametáthetos* (276), unchangeable; *stereós* (4731),

solid, stable, steadfast; *bébaios* (949), firm.

Ant.: *episphalḗs* (2000), insecure.

532. ἀπαρασκεύαστος *aparaskeúastos*; gen. *aparaskeuástou*, masc., fem adj. from the priv. *a* (1), without, and *paraskeuázō* (3903), to prepare. Unprepared, not ready (2 Cor 9:4). In 2 Cor 9:2f., the Christians of Achaia are said to have been prepared (*paraskeúastai*) since the previous year to take the collection to the poor in Jerusalem. Corinth belonged to Achaia, yet Paul was afraid lest these Corinthians would be found *aparaskeúastoi*, unprepared, for this particular benevolent offering and thus be unfavorably exposed to the Macedonians (those of northern Greece) who had shown such generosity in the midst of their poverty (2 Cor 8:1–5).

Ant.: *hétoimos* (2092), ready.

533. ἀπαρνέομαι *aparnéomai*; contracted *aparnoúmai*, fut. *aparnḗsomai*, fut. pass. 1st person *aparnēthḗsomai*, from *apó* (575), from, and *arnéomai* (720), to deny, refuse. A mid. deponent. To abnegate, deny.

(I) Of Christ and what He stands for (Matt 26:34, 35, 75; Mark 14:30, 31, 72; Luke 22:34 [TR], 61; John 13:38 [TR]).

(II) Followed by the reflex. pron. *heautón* (1438), oneself, to deny oneself, meaning to disown and renounce self and to subjugate all works, interests and enjoyments (Matt 16:24; Mark 8:34; Luke 9:23 [{TR} cf. Phil 3:7, 8]).

(III) Of those whom the Lord will deny (Luke 12:9 [cf. Sept.: Isa 31:7]). In Luke 12:9, the protasis, "But he that denieth me before men," uses the verb *arnēsámenos*, aor. mid. part., but with act. meaning, (a deponent verb). The aor. is constantive and may have in view an isolated point in time meaning "he that denied me once, not necessarily continuously" (a.t.). However, the constantive force of the aor. can also have in view the conduct of one's entire life (cf. John 2:20, the aor. pass. *oikodomḗthē* {[3618], to build}, "was built," an action occurring over forty years). In this case Jesus' words mean "he that did not spend his life denying me" (a.t.). Such a person is no doubt an unbeliever. The apodosis, "before men, shall be denied," uses *aparnēthḗsetai*, fut. pass. 3d person. If the action is viewed as punctiliar, then it indicates a definite denial by the Son of Man before the angels of God. In order for us to understand this verse, it is necessary to go back to Luke 12:8 where we see that the ant. of *arnéomai* (720), to deny, is *homologéō* (3670), to confess or to speak in agreement with. The Lord here is speaking to His friends (Luke 12:4), encouraging them to withstand persecution from those who would kill them because of their testimony (Luke 12:5). Then in verse six He says that God would not even let the sparrow fall without His will and that even the hairs of the believer's head are counted (Luke 12:6, 7). What follows in verse eight may be interpreted as an assurance that every time a believer confesses or externalizes his faith in spite of danger, there will be an equivalent recognition in the day of the judgment of the believer's works (2 Cor 5:10). (Again, however, Jesus may be speaking of hypocrites who once professed faith but who, under persecution, genuinely repudiate Him. Their failure to persevere reveals their true character and dooms them to the sentence of eternal destruction to be issued from the mouth of Jesus Himself.)

An opposite result is also true. The Lord Jesus recognizes that it is possible for the believer to deny Him, even as Peter did (Matt 26:34, 35, 75; Mark 14:30, 31, 72; Luke 22:34, 61; John 13:38). In every one of these references where Peter's denial by Christ is involved, the verb is the comp. *aparnéomai*, although the basic verb *arnéomai* also occurs in Matt 26:70, 72; Mark 14:68, 70; Luke 22:57; John 18:25, 27. Basically, the words can thus be said to convey the same meaning, although the comp. *aparnéomai* in Luke 12:9 is presented as the corresponding

denial of Jesus Christ because of the initial denial by His disciples.

The fact that the Son of Man (in Matt 10:32, 33, the Lord uses the personal pron. *kagṓ* [2504], and I) promises to confess or deny the worthy or unworthy disciples "before the angels of God" (Luke 12:8, 9) or "before my Father, which is in heaven" (Matt 10:32, 33) implies that this scene is in heaven. Therefore the denial indicated by the basic verb *arnéomai* or *aparnéomai* can refer to the rejection by the Lord of an unbeliever denying him entrance into heaven, or to the privation of rewards for a believer. If the latter interpretation is assumed, then the passage is teaching that our rewards will be in proportion to our faithfulness or unfaithfulness to the Lord Jesus in each instance that either is demonstrated.

Syn.: *antilégō* (483), to speak against, contradict; *paraitéomai* (3868), to avoid, reject; *apodokimázō* (513), to reject, disapprove; *athetéō* (114), to make void, nullify, disallow; *anthístēmi* (436), to set against; *antikathístēmi* (478), to stand firm against; *antitássō* (498), to set oneself against, oppose; *antipíptō* (496), to strive against, resist.

Ant.: *déchomai* (1209), to receive willingly; *apodéchomai* (528), to receive heartily; *prosdéchomai* (4327), to accept favorably; *lambánō* (2983), to take; *homologéō* (3670), to confess.

534. ἀπάρτι *apárti*; adv. of time, from *apó* (575), from, and *árti* (737), now. From this time, henceforth, hereafter (Matt 23:39; 26:29, 64; John 1:51 [cf. *apó toú nún* {*apó* (575), from; *toú* (3588), the; *nún* (3568), now}]), from the now (Luke 1:48; 5:10; 12:52; Acts 18:6), equal to *árti* (737), now, but stronger meaning at this very time, even now (John 13:19; 14:7; Rev 14:13, "Blessed [even now] are the dead").

Syn.: *tó loipón* (3063), for the remaining time; *héōs árti* (*héōs* [2193], until; *árti* [737], now), until now, hitherto; *áchri toú deúro* (*áchri* [891], until;

toú deúro [1204], here), until now or the present; *nún* (3568), now, present.

Ant.: *oukéti* (3765), not yet; *mēkéti* (3371), no longer; *oúpō* (3768), not yet.

535. ἀπαρτισμός apartismós; gen. *apartismoú*, masc. noun from *apartízō* (n.f.), to perfect, which is from *apó* (575), an intens., and *artízō* (n.f.), to perfect, finish. The act of completion, finishing, perfecting (Luke 14:28).

Syn.: *teleíōsis* (5050), fulfillment, completion, perfection; *suntéleia* (4930), consummation, an appointed climax.

Ant.: *aparaskeúastos* (532), unprepared.

536. ἀπαρχή aparchḗ; gen. *aparchḗs*, fem. noun from *apárchomai* (n.f.), from *apó* (575), from, and *árchomai* (756), to begin. Firstfruits (but in the Gr. always sing.), the first of the ripe fruits (Sept.: Ex 25:2, 3, "offering"; 2 Chr 30:24 KJV; 2 Chr 35:7, 9). Such firstfruits were usually offered to God (Sept.: Ex 23:19; Lev 23:10). Applied to Christ risen from the dead (1 Cor 15:20, 23); to the gifts of the Holy Spirit as a foretaste of the believer's eternal inheritance (Rom 8:23 [cf. Eph 1:14]; Heb 6:5); to believers first converted in any particular place or country (Rom 16:5; 1 Cor 16:15); to believers in general consecrated to God from among the rest of mankind (James 1:18; Rev 14:4); to the patriarchs and ancestors of the Jewish people (Rom 11:16). The OT ordinance was to give a heave offering of dough as firstfruits (Num 15:20f.).

Syn.: *prṓtos* (4413), beginning, first.

Ant.: *hústeros* (5306), later, at the end; *télos* (5056), termination, end.

537. ἅπας hápas; fem. *hápasa*, neut. *hápan*, adj. from *háma* (260), together, and *pás* (3956), all, but stronger than the basic *pás*. All, the whole, universally (Matt 6:32; 24:39; Mark 16:15; Luke 9:15; 17:27, 29; 21:4; 23:1; Acts 2:1, 4; Sept.: Ps 22:23; Jer 18:23). Spoken also indef. of a large number without

necessarily including every individual of that number (Mark 8:25; 11:32; Luke 3:21; 8:37; 19:48; see also Matt 28:11; Mark 5:40; 16:15; Luke 2:39; 3:16; 4:6; 5:11, 26, 28; 7:16; 15:13; 17:27, 29; 19:7, 48; 21:12; Acts 2:14, 44; 4:31, 32; 5:12, 16; 6:15; 10:8; 13:29).

In 1 Tim 1:16 we have *hápasan* (UBS), *pásan* (TR), *makrothumían* (3115), longsuffering, in the acc., translated in KJV as "all long-suffering" which is literal, but which leaves out the def. art. *tḗn* (*makrothumía*, long-suffering in Gr. is fem., therefore, the fem. def. art.). The literal translation would be "the all longsuffering." Long-suffering is not exactly the same as patience. Long-suffering is one's attitude toward humans while patience (*hupomonḗ* [5281]) is one's enduring attitude toward things and circumstances. The NASB has "his perfect patience"; the NIV, "his unlimited patience." The translation of *makrothumía* as "patience" is inadequate, but it is noteworthy that *hápasan* or *pásan* is translated "perfect" and "unlimited." Of course, Paul refers to the demonstration of Christ's long-suffering, first of all to Paul as a great sinner and then to all humanity. In Christ's long-suffering we have the ultimate demonstration of long-suffering, all of the virtue in its various aspects fully demonstrated. The adj. "all" here should be taken as the virtue in all its inclusiveness, therefore, the ultimate long-suffering.

In 1 Pet 3:20 it is called "the long-suffering of God," indirectly affirming the deity of Christ in that the long-suffering of Christ is the long-suffering of God. See 2 Tim 4:2. Therefore, where *hápas* or *pás* is preceded by an art. as in 1 Tim 1:16, *tḗn pásan* or *hápasan*, and followed by a noun as *makrothumían*, it means the whole of God's long-suffering or the fruits of His long-suffering.

Syn.: *hólos* (3650), the whole, all; *hékastos* (1538), each.

Ant.: *oudeís* (3762), not even one; *mēdeís* (3367), not even one; *oudeís métis* (3385), no one.

538. ἀπατάω *apatáō*; contracted *apatṓ*, fut. *apatḗsō*, from *apátē* (539), deceit. To deceive, bring, or seduce into error (Eph 5:6; 1 Tim 2:14; James 1:26; Sept.: Gen 3:13; Ex 22:16; 2 Kgs 18:32; as a device to mislead another, Judg 14:15; 16:5).

The base verb *apatáō* is used twice in the TR (KJV) in 1 Tim 2:14, but in the UBS it is used only of Adam having been deceived. When it comes to Eve, the woman, it is *exapatētheísa*, the aor. pass. part. fem. of *exapatáō* (1818) to deceive completely. In 2 Cor 11:3 both in the TR and UBS, speaking of the serpent deceiving Eve directly, it is the comp. verb that is used, *exēpátēsen*, thoroughly deceived. In the mind of Paul, when Satan directly deals with man, he endeavors to thoroughly deceive. This Satan did to Eve while she simply deceived (*ēpátēsen*) her husband in persuading him to eat of the fruit of the forbidden tree. Thus in the three instances where the word *apatáō* occurs, we can say that we can be deceived by the vain, empty, or idle words of others (Eph 5:6), by Satan (1 Tim 2:14), or by vain, external, empty religiosity (James 1:26).

Deriv.: *exapatáō* (1818), to deceive completely.

Syn.: *planáō* (4105), to lead astray; *planáomai*, to go astray; *apoplanáō* (635), to lead astray from, seduce; *paralogízomai* (3884), to deceive by false reasoning, delude; *deleázō* (1185), to catch by a bait, entice, allure; *emplékō* (1707), to entangle; *enedreúō* (1748), to lay wait for, lay a trap, plot for assassination; *dolóō* (1389), to ensnare; *dolióō* (1387), to lure; *kapēleúō* (2585), to huckster, to sell anything for unwarranted personal gain.

Ant.: *stērízō* (4741), to fix, make fast, confirm; *epistērízō* (1991), to make to lean upon, to strengthen; *stereóō* (4732), to make firm, establish; *bebaióō* (950), to make firm, secure; *kuróō* (2964), to make valid, ratify; *prokuróō* (4300), to confirm or ratify before; *hístēmi* (2476), to cause to stand, establish.

539. ἀπάτη *apátē*; gen. *apátēs*, fem. noun. Deceit, delusion. In the pass. sense spoken of anything which is deceptive, seducing (Matt 13:22; Mark 4:19; Col 2:8; 2 Thess 2:10). In Heb 3:13 connected with sin, meaning the deceitfulness of our sinful propensities. In 2 Pet 2:13, the word "sin" is to be understood as following the dat. pl. *apátais*, deceivings, i.e., the deceptive involvements of sin. In Eph 4:22, *epithumías* (1939), desires of deceit, means deceitful propensities which seduce to sin and lead to disappointment.

Deriv.: *apatáō* (538), to deceive.

Syn.: *dólos* (1388), a bait, snare, guile; *plánē* (4106), deceit, error, wandering, leading or being led astray; *panourgía* (3834), craftiness, subtlety; *pseúdos* (5579), falsehood, lie; *ponēría* (4189), malice; *epiboulḗ* (1917), a plan against someone, a plot; *rhadioúrgēma* (4467), crafty behavior, lewdness; *rhadiourgía* (4468), acting mischievously, mischief; *enédra* (1747), ambush; *kubeía* (2940), fraud, deception; *methodeía* (3180), craft, trickery.

Ant.: *bebaíōsis* (971), confirmation; *stērigmós* (4740), steadfastness; *alḗtheia* (225), truth; *eilikríneia* (1505), sincerity.

540. ἀπάτωρ *apátōr*; gen. *apátoros*, masc. noun from the priv. *a* (1), without, and *patḗr* (3962), father. Literally, without a father meaning without the record or genealogy of the father. Used only in Heb 7:3 with reference to Melchizedek's being "without father," indicating that the Bible completely ignores Melchizedek's genealogy. He did not inherit nor did he transmit his priesthood, although it was royal. It did not depend on any previous or any following connection but was inherent in his person only, and was entirely independent of any connection other than that of God. Melchizedek's genealogy is not to be found anywhere in spite of the fact that genealogies were very carefully kept in those days. Yet, it seems that Abraham bows to his priesthood. Melchizedek therefore becomes a symbol of the priesthood of Jesus Christ, which priesthood was not dependent on any genealogy. Jesus Christ was a priest in Himself to whom all must bow.

541. ἀπαύγασμα apaúgasma; gen. *apaugásmatos*, neut. noun from *apaugázō* (n.f.), to emit light or splendor, which is from *apó* (575), from, and *augázō* (826), to shine. Effulgence, light, or splendor emitted or issuing from a luminous body.

The word is found only in Heb 1:3 and refers to the person of Jesus Christ. The Son is the effulgence or shining forth of God's glory and the likeness of the Father. Being the effulgence of the eternal light (John 1:4–5), the Lord Jesus must also be Himself eternal. The all-glorious divinity of the Son of God is essentially one with the Father's, but the Son is a personality distinct from that of the Father. Observe that the verb used is *hōn*, being, the masc. pres. part. of *eimí* (1510), to be. This means that there has never been a time when Jesus Christ has not been the effulgence of God's glory, even in His incarnation when He purged our sins. To distinguish the meaning of *apaúgasma* with the word *charaktḗr* (5481), character, found in the same verse and translated "the express image," see the discussion under *charaktḗr* and *eikṓn* (1504), image, in contrast to *homoíōma* (3667), similitude, or *homoíōsis* (3669), likeness.

Syn.: *phṓs* (5457), light; *phéggos* (5338), brightness, lustre.

Ant.: *skótos* (4655), darkness; *zóphos* (2217), the gloom of the underworld, blackness.

542. ἀπεῖδον apeídon; the 2d aor. of *aphoráō* (872), to consider attentively, aor. subjunctive *aphídō*, from *apó* (575), an intens., and *eídō* (1492), to see. To look away from one thing toward another, to see to an end or perceive clearly (Phil 2:23 [see *aphoráō* {872} in Heb 12:2]).

543. ἀπείθεια apeítheia; gen. *apeítheias*, fem. noun from *apeithḗs* (545), disobedient. Disobedience, unwillingness to be persuaded, willful unbelief, obstinacy. In the NT, it corresponds in its use with the verb *apistéō* (569), to be unbelieving, opposing the gracious word and purpose of God; a stronger term than the syn. *apistía* (570), disbelief, unbelief (Heb 3:12, 19); hence we have the sons of *apeitheías*, disobedience, unbelievers, i.e., heathen, pagans (Rom 11:30, 32; Eph 2:2; 5:6; Col 3:6; Heb 4:6, 11).

Syn.: *parakoḗ* (3876), hearing amiss, hence disobedience; *apistía* (570), unbelief; *parábasis* (3847), transgression; *paranomía* (3892), law-breaking.

Ant.: *hupakoḗ* (5218), obedience; *hupotagḗ* (5292), subjection.

544. ἀπειθέω apeithéō; contracted *apeithḗ*, fut. *apeithḗsō*, from *apeithḗs* (545), disobedient. Not to allow oneself to be persuaded or believe, to disbelieve, be disobedient.

(I) Spoken of disbelievers in Christ (Acts 14:2; 17:5; 19:9; Rom 15:31; 1 Pet 2:8); of those who are disobedient to God (Rom 10:21; 11:31; Heb 3:18; 1 Pet 3:20; Sept.: Deut 9:7; Isa 50:5; 63:10; 65:2). In Heb 11:31 *hoi apeithḗsantes*, those who did disobey, unbelievers, heathen. See Sept.: Isa 66:14.

(II) With the dat. of person or thing, the one being disobedient to the Son (John 3:36); to God (Rom 11:30; Sept.: Num 14:43); to the truth (Rom 2:8); to the Word (1 Pet 2:8; 3:1); to the gospel (1 Pet 4:17 [cf. Deut 1:26; 9:23; 32:51]).

Syn.: *apistéō* (569), to disbelieve; *parakoúō* (3878), to hear imperfectly and thus to disobey; *parabaínō* (3845), to transgress; *anthístēmi* (436), to stand against; *exanístēmi* (1817), to object; *epanístamai* (1881), to rise up against; *aphístēmi* (868), to stand afar, desist; *ataktéō* (812), to behave in a disorderly manner.

Ant.: *hupakoúō* (5219), to listen, obey; *peíthomai* (3982), to be persuaded;

pisteúō (4100), to believe; *peitharchéō* (3980), to obey one in authority; *hupotássomai* (5293), to be in subjection; *summorphóomai* (4833), to become conformed; *akolouthéō* (190), to follow.

545. ἀπειθής *apeithḗs*; gen. *apeithoús*, masc.-fem., neut. *apeithés*, adj. from the priv. *a* (1), without, and *peíthō* (3982), to persuade. Unwilling to be persuaded, unbelieving, disobedient (Luke 1:17; Acts 26:19; Rom 1:30; 2 Tim 3:2; Titus 1:16; 3:3).

Deriv.: *apeítheia* (543), disobedience; *apeithéō* (544), to be disobedient.

Syn.: *anupótaktos* (506), disobedient; *átaktos* (313), unruly; *sklērós* (4642), hard, not pliable.

Ant.: *eupeithḗs* (2138), easily persuaded; *hupḗkoos* (4255), submissive, obedient; *peithós* (3981), persuasive.

546. ἀπειλέω *apeiléō*; contracted *apeilō̂*, fut. *apeilḗsō*. To threaten, menace (Acts 4:17), to reproach (1 Pet 2:23; Sept.: Isa 66:14; Nah 1:4).

Deriv.: *apeilḗ* (547), a threat; *prosapeiléō* (4324), to threaten further.

Ant.: *pistóō* (4104), to trust or give assurance to; *plērophoréō* (4135), to fully assure; *peíthō* (3982), to persuade; *bebaióō* (50), to confirm, assure; *epistērízō* (1991), to strengthen; *kuróō* (2964), to ratify.

547. ἀπειλή *apeilḗ*; gen. *apeilḗs*, fem. noun from *apeiléō* (546), to threaten. A threat, threatening, menace (Acts 4:17, 29; 9:1); reproach, upbraiding (Eph 6:9; Sept.: Prov 13:8; 17:10; 19:12; Hab 3:12).

Ant.: *pístis* (4102), assurance, guarantee; *plērophoría* (4136), full confidence; *bebaíōsis* (971), confirmation.

548. ἄπειμι *ápeimi*; from *apó* (575), from, and *eimí* (1510), to be. To be absent (1 Cor 5:3; 2 Cor 10:1, 11; 13:2, 10; Phil 1:27; Col 2:5).

Deriv.: *apousía* (666), absence.

Syn.: *aphístēmi* (868), to stand away from, desist; *ekdēméō* (1553), to vacate, exit, be absent; *analúō* (360), to depart; *chōrízomai* (5563), to separate oneself.

Ant.: *enístēmi* (1764), to be present now; *ephístēmi* (2186), to stand over or be present; *paragínomai* (3854), to come and be present; *parákeimai* (3873), to lie beside, be present; *endēméō* (1736), to be present or at home; *ménō* (3306), to abide; *parístēmi* (3936), to show oneself present; *hḗkō* (2240), to arrive, be present.

549. ἄπειμι *ápeimi*; imperf. *apéein*, from *apó* (575), from, and *eími* (n.f., see below), to go. To go away, depart, intrans. (Acts 17:10).

Deriv.: of *eími*, to go (n.f.): *eíseimi* (1524), to enter into; *éxeimi* (1826), to go out; *súneimi* (4896), to gather together.

Syn.: *ágō* (71), to go; *hupágō* (5217), to go away; *metabaínō* (3327), to go from one place to another; *apérchomai* (565), to go away; *anachōréō* (402), to withdraw, depart; *apodēméō* (589), to go to another country; *exérchomai* (1831), to go out; *paragínomai* (3854), to go; *ekporeúomai* (1607), to go out of; *apolúō* (630), to release, dismiss.

Ant.: *érchomai* (2064) and *gínomai* (1096), to come; *epanérchomai* (1880), to come back again; *paragínomai* (3854), to come and be present; *hḗkō* (2240), to come, be present; *aphiknéomai* (864), to arrive; *enístēmi* (1764), to be present, at hand; *ephístēmi* (2136), to stand by or come up; *parístēmi* (3936), to stand by or near, be present; *phthánō* (5348), to arrive; *proseggízō* (4331), to come near.

550. ἀπεῖπον *apeípon*; mid. *apeipómēn*, from *apó* (575), from, and *eípon*, I said, the 2d aor. of *épō* (2036), to speak. Literally, to speak out against, to hold to the end, to refuse, deny, renounce, disown with aversion (2 Cor 4:2; Sept.: Job 10:3).

Syn.: *apotássō* (657), to set in its proper category away from oneself; *arnéomai*

(720), to deny; *aparnéomai* (533), to deny utterly; *antilégō* (483), to contradict.

Ant.: *sumphōnéō* (4856), to be in accord; *suntíthēmi* (4934), to assent to; *sugkatatíthēmi* (4784), to consent; *eunoéō* (2132), to set one's mind in agreement with; *peíthō* (3982), to assure; *homologéō* (3670), to agree with, to speak the same thing.

551. ἀπείραστος *apeírastos*; masc.-fem., neut. *apeíraston*, adj. from the priv. *a* (1), without, and *peirázō* (3985), to tempt or test. Only in James 1:13 where it means incapable of being tempted to do evil.

552. ἄπειρος *ápeiros*; gen. *apeírou*, masc.-fem., neut. *ápeiron*, adj. from the priv. *a* (1), without, and *peíra* (3984), experience. Inexperienced, unskillful (Heb 5:13), ignorant of true doctrine. See Sept.: 1 Sam 17:39; Zech 11:15.

553. ἀπεκδέχομαι *apekdéchomai*; fut. *apéxomai*, mid. deponent from *apó* (575), an intens., and *ekdéchomai* (1551), to expect, look for. To wait for, used as a suitable expression for the Christian's hope which includes the two elements of hope and patience (Rom 8:25). In Rom 8:23 the obj. of this fut. expectation is the *huiothesía*, the adoption, as will be realized in the redemption of the body (Rom 8:19; 1 Cor 1:7; Gal 5:5; Phil 3:20; Heb 9:28 [cf. 1 Pet 3:20]).

Syn.: *prosdokáō* (4328), to await, expect; *prosdéchomai* (4327), to expect, look for; *anaménō* (362), to wait for with patience and confident expectancy; *periménō* (4037), to wait around for the fulfillment of an event; *proskarteréō* (4342), to wait around looking forward to the fulfillment of something one expects to take place; *elpízō* (1679), to hope; *prosménō* (4357), to tarry, wait with patience and steadfastness; *apoblépō* (578), to look away from all else at one object, to look steadfastly.

Ant.: *exaporéomai*, to be without a way of escape, despair; *apelpízō* (560), to give up in despair.

554. ἀπεκδύομαι *apekdúomai*; fut. *apekdúsomai*, mid. deponent of *apekdúō*, from *apó* (575), from, and *ekdúō* (1562), strip. To put off, to strip or put off clothes, as figuratively applied in the NT to putting off the old man or the corrupt nature we derive from fallen Adam (Col 3:9). To strip, divest of power or authority (Col 2:15), to deprive of power.

Deriv.: *apékdusis* (555), the act of putting off.

Syn.: *apobállō* (577), to cast away; *ekbállō* (1544), to cast out, from, forth; *aporríptō* (641), to cast off; *apotíthēmi* (659), to put off; *apōthéō* (683), to thrust away; *kathairéō* (2507), to cast down, demolish; *athetéō* (114), to cast out.

Ant.: *endúō* (1746) to clothe oneself; *amphiénnumi* (294), to put clothes around or on oneself; *endidúskō* (1737), to wear; *ependúō* (1902) and *himatízō* (2439), to put on clothes; *peribállō* (4016), to put on around; *enkombóomai* (1493), to wrap oneself with something; *peritíthēmi* (4060), to put around or on; *bállō* (906), to put.

555. ἀπέκδυσις *apékdusis*; gen. *apekdúseos*, fem. noun from *apekdúomai* (554), to put off from oneself. A putting or stripping off (Col 2:11).

Syn.: *apóthesis* (595), the act of putting off or away; *athétēsis* (115), the act of annulling; *gumnótēs* (1132), nakedness.

Ant.: *éndusis* (1745), the act of putting on clothing.

556. ἀπελαύνω *apelaúnō*; contracted *apeláō*, aor. *apélasa*, from *apó* (575), from, and *elaúnō* (1643), to drive. To drive away from (Acts 18:16; Sept.: Ezek 34:12).

Syn.: *ekbállō* (1544), to cast forth; *exōthéō* (1856), to thrust out; *apōthéō* (683), to thrust away; *pémpō* (3992), to send; *diōkō* (1377), to drive away;

ekdiōkō (1559), to drive out; *aphorízō* (873), to mark off by boundaries, to separate; *apodiorízō* (592), to mark off; *chōrízō* (5563), to separate.

Ant.: *proskaléō* (4341), to bid to come; *epikaléō* (1941), to call upon.

557. ἀπελεγμός *apelegmós*; gen. *apelegmoú*, masc. noun from *apelégchō* (n.f.), to refute, from *apó* (575), an intens., and *elégchō* (1651), to reprove, refute. Refutation, used by the Class. Gr. writers. Disgrace (Acts 19:27).

Syn.: *aítion* (158), a legal ground or cause for punishment; *aitía* (156), fault; *héttēma* (2275), a loss, fault; *paráptōma* (3900), a trespass; *mômos* (3470), a blemish, moral disgrace; *oneidismós* (3680), a reproach, defamation; *óneidos* (3681), a disgrace; *atimía* (819), dishonor; *húbris* (5196), injury.

Ant.: *aínos* (136), a message of praise; *épainos* (1868), approbation, commendation, praise; *aínesis* (133), the act of praise; *aretḗ* (703), virtue, excellence; *dóxa* (1391), glory, praise.

558. ἀπελεύθερος *apeleútheros*; gen. *apeleuthérou*, masc. noun from *apó* (575), from, and *eleútheros* (1658), free. A freedman, an emancipated slave. Found only in 1 Cor 7:22 and indicates that the slavery which may be a part of relations on earth does not exist in the new sphere of the divine calling.

Ant.: *doúlos* (1401), a slave.

559. Ἀπελλῆς *Apellḗs*; gen. *Apelloú*, masc. proper noun. Apelles, the name of a tested Christian greeted by Paul in Rom 16:10. Origen expresses the opinion that *Apellḗs* may have been used for *Apollṓs* of Acts 18:24; 19:1.

560. ἀπελπίζω *apelpízō*; from *apó* (575), from, and *elpízo* (1679), to hope. To cease to hope, renounce or give up a thing or a person, to despair. With the acc., to give up what one does not expect to keep, to give up in despair.

This word occurs only in Luke 6:35 in the phrase *mēdén apelpízontes*, "hoping for nothing again." The phrase indicates that reward should be expected from God only. Christ has already indicated that men are likely to do good to someone who might do good to them in return. Likewise, it is easy to lend to those who will repay and to love those who love us. The height of Christian virtue, however, is to love those that despise us most or those whom we despise most, i.e., our enemy. To be like Him, we must be "kind unto the unthankful and the evil" (v. 35b). Some MSS have *mēdéna* (masc.) instead of *mēdén* so that the phrase must be "not hoping for anyone" (a.t.). Thus the phrase would speak of those from whom we might hope to recompense rather than what might be given for the same.

Some would render the word "to despair." While this is philologically admissible, it does not agree with the context. It requires one to add an unfounded idea of causation to the meaning of the word, as "causing no one to despair" (a.t.).

Syn.: *exaporéō* (1820), to be wholly without resource, to despair utterly; *aporéō* (639), despair or be perplexed.

Ant.: *prosdokáō* (4328) and *ekdéchomai* (1551), to look for or expect; *apekdéchomai* (553), to expect eagerly; *anaménō* (362), to wait for.

561. ἀπέναντι *apénanti*; adv. from *apó* (575), from, and *énanti* (1725), before, over against, in the presence of. Opposite to, over against. Before, in the presence of, spoken of persons (Matt 21:2; 27:24; Acts 3:16; Sept.: Gen 21:16; Ex 14:2; Num 7:10; Judg 19:10; Hos 7:2); of place (Matt 27:61; Sept.: Ezek 40:47; Neh 7:3). In Rom 3:18 quoted from Ps 36:2, "There is no fear of God before their eyes," means in their minds.

Syn.: *émprosthen* (1715), before, in front, in the sight of a person; *enṓpion* (1799), in the sight of or presence; *katenṓpion* (2614), right over against, opposite.

Ant.: *makrán* (3112), far off, and its syn.

562. ἀπέραντος *apérantos*; gen. *aperántou*, masc.-fem., neut. *apéranton*, adj. from *peraínō* (n.f.), to bring to an end, which is from the priv. *a* (1), without, and *péras* (4009), a boundary, end, limit. Endless, unlimited (1 Tim 1:4), interminable genealogies.

Syn.: *mégas* (3173), great; *polús* (4183), much, great; *hikanós* (2425), large in number.

Ant.: *eláchistos* (1646), least; *mikrós* (3398), small, little; *olígos* (3641), little, few in number; *brachús* (1024), short of time.

563. ἀπερισπάστως *aperispástōs*; adv. from *aperíspastos* (n.f.), without distraction, which is from the priv. *a* (1), without, and *perispáō* (4049), to distract or be distracted. Without distraction or distracting care in regard to earthly things (1 Cor 7:35).

Syn.: *epimelôs* (1960), carefully, diligently; *akribôs* (199), accurately, exactly, circumspectly.

564. ἀπερίτμητος *aperítmētos*; gen. *aperitmétou*, masc.-fem., neut. *aperítmēton*, adj. from the priv. *a* (1), without, and *peritémnō* (4059), to circumcise. Uncircumcised. In Acts 7:51, "uncircumcised in heart and ears" means being callous or perverse so that they do not listen or obey God's Word. See Sept.: Gen 17:14; Ex 12:48; Lev 26:41; Jer 6:10; 9:26; Ezek 44:7, 9.

565. ἀπέρχομαι *apérchomai*; fut. *apeleúsomai*, 2d aor. *apélthon*, perf. *apelélutha*, from *apó* (575), from, and *érchomai* (2064), to come or go. To go, go away, depart (cf. *ápeimi* [549], to go away).

(I) Generally to go away, depart (Matt 8:21; 13:25, 28; 16:4; 18:30; Mark 5:20, 24; 6:27); followed by *apó* (Mark 5:17; Luke 1:38; 2:15; 8:37; Sept.: Gen 15:15; 19:2; 21:14). Metaphorically spoken of things, such as leprosy (Mark 1:42; Luke 5:13); fruits (Rev 18:14); the earth (Rev 21:1 [TR]); woe (Rev 9:12, "is past," is over; 11:14).

(II) To go away to a place, depart for, set off, journey, with *ekeí* (1563), there, yonder (Matt 2:22); with *hópou* (3699), wheresoever or where (Matt 8:19); followed by *eís* (1519), unto (Matt 8:32, 33; 10:5; 14:15; 25:46); by *prós* (4314), toward (Matt 14:25; Mark 3:13; Rev 10:9); spoken of a passage by water (Matt 8:18; Mark 6:32; John 6:1, 22); metaphorically of rumor, to go forth, spread abroad (Matt 4:24; 9:26, *exélthen* instead of *apélthen*). In Luke 23:33 with *epí* (1909), upon, at, when they arrived at the place; Sept.: Gen 42:21.

(III) To go after someone, to follow as companions or disciples (Luke 17:23); with *opísō* (3694), after or following (Mark 1:20; John 12:19; in Jude 1:7, having become devotees of other flesh, i.e., fornication). See Judg 2:12; 1 Sam 6:12 where the Sept. has *poreúomai* (4198), to go, *opísō*, after. Similarly with *prós* (4314), unto, followed by the acc. (John 6:68).

(IV) To withdraw, go apart (Matt 26:36; Acts 4:15).

(V) Spoken of those who turn or go back, return, followed by *eís* (1519), unto (Matt 9:7; Luke 1:23; John 4:3; Sept.: Gen 3:19; 31:13; Josh 1:15; 6:14; Job 1:21); by *eis ta opísō* (*tá* [3588], the, pl. neut. art.; *opísō* [3694], backward), to turn back, return (John 6:66; 18:6).

Syn.: *exérchomai* (1831) and *éxeimi* (1826), to go out; *apobaínō* (576) and *ápeimi* (548), to go away; *ekporeúomai* (1607), to go out of, proceed; *hupágō* (5217), to go; *poreúomai* (4198), to depart from one place to another; *apochōréō* (672), to depart from; *analúō* (360), to unloose, to depart; *apolúō* (630), to let go, depart; *aphístēmi* (868), to stand away from; *metabaínō* (3327) and *anágomai* (321), to depart, go; *ágō* (71), to lead, go; *apodēméō* (589), going into another country; *parágō* (3855), to pass by, to go apart.

Ant.: *epérchomai* (1904), to come upon; *paragínomai* (3854), to go and be present; *prosporeúomai* (4365), to go near to; *eisérchomai* (1525), to come into; *epanérchomai* (1880), to come back again; *embaínō* (1684), to go into; *hḗkō* (2240) and *enístemi* (1764), to come, be present; *aphiknéomai* (864), to arrive at a place; *ephístēmi* (2186), to come upon; *katantáō* (2658), to come to; *phthánō* (5348), to arrive, come before; *proseggízō* (4331), to come near.

566. ἀπέχει *apéchei*; used impersonally, from the verb *apéchō* (568), to have, receive. Literally, "to have off or out," meaning to have all that is one's due so as to cease from demanding or having any more. Thus, the impersonal *apéchei* means it is enough as in Mark 14:41, meaning you have slept enough (cf. Luke 22:45, 46 [also Luke 22:38, *hikanón estí* {*hikanón* (2425), sufficient; *estí*, the 3d person sing of *eimí* (1510), to be, is}]), it is enough.
Ant.: *prosdokáo* (5328), to anticipate.

567. ἀπέχομαι *apéchomai*; fut. *aphéxomai*, the mid. voice of *apéchō* (568), to keep oneself from. To abstain or refrain (Acts 15:20, 29; 1 Thess 4:3; 5:22; 1 Tim 4:3; 1 Pet 2:11; Sept.: Job 1:1, 8; Prov 23:4).
Syn. *egkrateúomai* (1467), to exercise self-restraint; *néphō* (3525), to be sober; *sōphronéō* (4993), to exercise soundness of mind, to think soberly, use self-control.
Ant.: *aschēmonéō* (807), to behave badly.

568. ἀπέχω *apéchō*; fut. *aphéxō*; from *apó* (575), from, and *échō* (2192), to have, be. To hold off from, as a ship from the shore, to avert, restrain (Sept.: Prov 3:27). The mid. *apéchomai* (567), to hold back oneself from, abstain, refrain. Intrans. use meaning to be distant from, absent (Luke 7:6; 15:20; 24:13; Sept.: Isa 55:9).

To have received in full; spoken of reward or wages in regard to the person who for show gives alms, prays, and fasts (Matt 6:2, 5, 16). If a person does all these things in order to be admired by people and receives the admiration, he should not expect any further reward from the Lord. The same applies to pleasure in Luke 6:24. When one seeks all the physical comforts on earth at the detriment of the work of Christ and what He came to accomplish on earth, he ought not to expect to receive his comfort in heaven also. In Phil 4:18 the verb *apéchō* in the 1st person sing., followed by *pánta*, the acc. neut. pl. of *pás* (3956), all things or simply all, means that I have everything that I need and surplus; therefore, I do not expect more (Phile 1:15; Sept.: Gen 43:23; Num 32:19).

Metaphorically spoken of the heart (Matt 15:8; Mark 7:6, "their heart is far from me," they do not reverence nor regard Me, quoted from Isa 29:13). Used impersonally, *apéchei* (566), to have all that is one's due so as to cease from having any more.
Deriv.: *apéchei* (566), it is enough.
Syn.: *aphístēmi* (868), to desist, stand off; *apotrépomai* (665), to turn away from.
Ant.: *proseggízō* (4331), to approach near and its syn.

569. ἀπιστέω *apistéō*; contracted *apistṓ*, fut. *apistḗsō*, from *ápistos* (571), untrustworthy. To put no confidence in, to disbelieve (Mark 16:11, 16; Luke 24:11, 41; Acts 28:24; Rom 3:3). To be unfaithful, to doubt or not to acknowledge as in 2 Tim 2:13 where it is opposed to *pistós* (4103), faithful.
Syn.: *apeithéō* (544), to refuse to be persuaded or believe.
Ant.: *pisteúō* (4100), to believe; *peíthō* (3982), to persuade.

570. ἀπιστία *apistía*; gen. *apistías*, fem. noun from *ápistos* (571), untrustworthy. Faithlessness or uncertainty, distrust, unbelief. In the NT, the lack of acknowledgment of Christ (Matt 13:58; Mark 6:6); want of confidence in Christ's power (Matt 17:20; Mark 9:24; 16:14). In general, a want of trust in the God of promise (Rom 3:3; 4:20; 11:20, 23; 1 Tim 1:13; Heb 3:12, 19).

Syn.: *apeítheia* (543), disobedience; *parakoḗ* (3876), hearing amiss, an act of disobedience.

Ant.: *plērophoría* (4136), full assurance, entire confidence; *hupóstasis* (5287), substance, confidence; *hupakoḗ* (5218), obedience; *hupotagḗ* (5292), subjection, placing oneself in one's proper category.

571. ἄπιστος *ápistos*; gen. *apístou*, masc.-fem., neut. *ápiston*, adj. from *a* (1), without, and *pistós* (4103), believing, faithful. Not worthy of confidence, untrustworthy. In the NT in a pass. sense, a thing not to be believed, incredible (Acts 26:8); in an act. sense, not believing (Matt 17:17; Mark 9:19; Luke 9:41; 12:46; John 20:27). Denotes one who disbelieves the gospel of Christ, an unbeliever, infidel (1 Cor 6:6; 7:12–15; 10:27; 14:22–24; 2 Cor 4:4; 6:14, 15; 1 Tim 5:8; Titus 1:15; Rev 21:8; Sept.: Isa 17:10).

Deriv.: *apistéō* (569), to disbelieve; *apistía* (570), unbelief.

Syn.: *apeithḗs* (545), spurning belief, disobedient; *anupótaktos* (506), insubordinate, disobedient.

Ant.: *bébaios* (949), firm, steadfast; *stereós* (4731), firm, solid; *hupḗkoos* (5255), obedient.

572. ἁπλότης *haplótēs*; gen. *haplótētos*, fem. noun from *haplóos* contracted *haploús* (573), single, not having an ulterior or double motive. Simplicity, purity, sincerity, faithfulness, plenitude (Rom 12:8; Sept.: 2 Sam 15:11; Prov 19:1). In the NT used only in a moral sense as the opposite of duplicity meaning sincerity, faithfulness toward others, manifest in helpfulness and giving assistance to others. Equivalent to being faithful and benevolent. Although in some portions (2 Cor 8:2; 9:11, 13) translated liberality or

bountifulness, it is not exactly so. It is rather faithful benevolence out of proper motivation. Eph 6:5, "in singleness of your heart" means in sincerity; Col 3:22; Sept.: 1 Chr 29:17. In 2 Cor 11:3, "the simplicity that is in Christ" means frankness, integrity, fidelity.

Syn.: *aphelótēs* (858), simplicity, singleness; *eulogía* (2129), a blessing, indicating abundance; *cháris* (5485), grace, with the meaning of bounty; *hadrótēs* (100), fatness, indicating abundance; *perisseía* (4050), an exceeding measure; *huperbolḗ* (5236), beyond measure.

Ant.: *apátē* (539), deceit or deceitfulness; *dólos* (1388), guile; *plánē* (4106), error, wandering, deceit; *panourgía* (3834), craftiness.

573. ἁπλόος *haplóos*; contracted *haploús*, fem. *haplḗ*, neut. *haploún*. Only in Matt 6:22; Luke 11:34 translated single, i.e., not complex, easy, used of the eye as not seeing double as when it is diseased. When the eye accomplishes its purpose of seeing things as they are, then it is *haploús*, single, healthy, perfect. Singleness, simplicity, absence of folds. This, however, does not involve stupidity on the part of the Christian, but rather *phrónēsis* (5428), prudence, knowing how to deal with fellow humans and the circumstances of life. Thus the Christian is supposed to be not only *haploús*, single and without duplicity, but also *phrónimos* (5429), prudent (Matt 10:16; Rom 16:19).

Deriv.: *haplótēs* (572), singleness; *haplṓs* (574), bountifully.

Syn.: *ákakos* (172), harmless, unwilling to do harm; *akéraios* (185), harmless; *ádolos* (97), without guile; *gnḗsios* (1103), sincere, genuine; *eilikrinḗs* (1506), pure, sincere; *agathós* (18), benevolent; *kalós* (2570), good; *chrēstós* (5443), kindly.

Ant.: *dólios* (1386), deceitful; *plános* (4108), one leading astray; *phrenapátēs* (5423), a mind deceiver; *kakós* (2556), bad; *ponērós* (4190), evil, malevolent; *phaúlos* (5337), slight, trivial.

574. ἀπλῶς haplṓs; adv. *haploús* (573), sincere, uncompounded, clear, without duplicity. Bountifully, liberally (James 1:5).

Syn.: *ep' eulogíais* (*epí* [1909], upon; and *eulogía* [2129], blessing, well-speaking), well-doing, abundance.

Ant.: *pheidoménōs* (5340), sparingly.

575. ἀπό apó; prep. primarily meaning from. It governs the gen. and expresses what is strictly the idea of the gen. case itself like *ek* (1537), out of; *pará* (3844), near, beside; and *hupó* (5259), under. It basically means the going forth or proceeding of one object from another. *Apó* indicates the separation of a person or an object from another person or an object with which it was formerly united but is now separated. See Luke 16:18, *apoleluménēn* (630), "dismissed from a husband" (a.t.), indicates a wife who is separated from her husband without the permissible justification of fornication having been committed by her. However, if one object or person was previously in another, then the prep. for the separation of the two is not *apó*, but *ek* (1537), out of. Therefore, the meanings that *apó* can have are from, away from, of. Specific indications are as follows:

(I) Of place implying:

(A) Motion, i.e., from, away from. **(1)** After words, indicating departure from a place or person (Matt 8:34; 13:1; 20:29; 24:1; Mark 16:8; Luke 4:1; 9:33; 24:31, 51; Acts 1:4; 12:19; 13:13, 14; 15:38); metaphorically (Mark 1:42; Acts 19:12; 21:21; Rom 16:17; 1 Tim 6:5, 10; James 5:19; Rev 18:14). After words indicating any kind of motion, meaning away from a place or person (Matt 5:29; 26:39; 28:2; Mark 7:33; 14:36; Luke 9:5; John 18:28); metaphorically (Acts 8:22; 2 Thess 2:2; Heb 6:1; 1 John 3:17). With the idea of down as from a mountain (Matt 8:1; Luke 9:37; Acts 9:18; 13:29). **(2)** Indicating the place where something comes from or sets off from (Acts 12:20; 15:33; 28:21; 1 Thess 3:6). Corresponding to

méchri (3360), till, until, up to a certain point (Rom 15:19); to *héōs* (2193), until (Matt 1:17). Put after verbs of coming, following, setting off (Matt 2:1; 3:16 where *anébē* [305] *apó toú húdatos* [5204], water, would be better translated "went up . . . away from the water" (a.t.) than "went up . . . out of the water"; 4:25; 8:11; Mark 1:9; 6:33; Luke 12:54; Acts 13:31; Rom 1:18). With *elthṓn*, the aor. part. of *érchomai* (2064), to come, implied (Mark 7:4; Luke 22:43). Prefixed to an adv. meaning the same, such as *ánōthen* (509), from above (*apó ánōthen*) (Matt 27:51). Indicating order or succession, *árchomai* (756), I begin, *apó* followed by the gen. meaning to begin from (Matt 20:8; Luke 23:5; John 8:9; Acts 8:35). With *arxámenos*, the aor. part. of *árchomai*, having begun, implied (Acts 17:2; 28:23). In Matt 2:16, "from two years old and under," or downwards; 23:34.

(B) The separation or removal of one thing from another, and put after words which denote this in any way. The separation or removal is indicated by the gen. construction of such verbs, but the addition of *apó* can then be construed as emphatic or for the sake of clarity. **(1)** After verbs implying separation (Matt 25:32; Rom 8:35, 39; 1 Thess 2:17). In Rom 9:3 connected with a wish in the phrase "accursed from Christ," means excluded from God's favor, separated from Christ and the benefits of His death, and doomed to eternal destruction. In 2 Cor 11:3 the connection is with fear in the phrase, "so your minds should be corrupted from the simplicity that is in Christ," and means that the separation from Christ involves duplicity. In 2 Thess 1:9 we have punishment involved. The phrase "destruction from the presence of the Lord" means a destruction that results from the separation from the Lord and not the destruction imposed by the Lord. In Col 2:20, "from the rudiments of the world," means separated from the elements of the world. **(2)** After verbs of depriving, removing, taking

away (Matt 9:15: 13:12; Luke 10:42). In
Luke 6:29, it is connected with the idea
of being deprived by someone. *Apó* in
composition is also used where the idea
of loss or privation is implied as in Rev
18:14 in the word *apélthen*, the 2d aor.
mid. indic. of *apérchomai* (565), depart,
pass away (Sept.: Jer 18:18). After verbs
of hiding, concealing in which removal is
implied (Matt 11:25; Luke 9:45; 19:42;
Sept.: Gen 4:14; 2 Kgs 4:27). After
husteróō or *husteréō* (5302), to fall behind (Heb 12:15), meaning to fall behind
from the supply of grace that God makes
available. (**3**) After verbs of demanding,
desisting, abstaining, restraining, with
apaitéō (523), to demand (Luke 6:30);
with *ekzētéō* (1567), to seek after (Luke
11:51); with *aphístēmi* (868), to stand
apart (Acts 5:38); with *apéchomai* (567),
to refrain (Acts 15:20); with *katapaúō*
(2664), to cease (Heb 4:4); with *ekdikéō*
(1556), to punish, avenge, bring out justice (Rev 6:10). (**4**) After verbs of loosing
such as *lúō* (3089), to loose, and *apolúō*
(630), to dismiss, let loose from oneself
(Luke 13:15; 16:18; 1 Cor 7:27). With the
verb *katargéō* (2673), to put away, render inactive (Rom 7:2, 6, meaning that a
widow is not bound by the law of her de-
ceased husband and thus restricted, even
as the believer in Christ is not bound by
the law of the old self which has died to
sin). Similarly after verbs of freeing, purifying from, healing, and also after similar adj. In Matt 1:21, after *sōzō* (4982),
to save, "shall save his people from their
sins" means will loose them from their
sins by removing their sins from them;
with the verb *therapeúō* (2323), cure,
heal (Luke 5:15); with *iáomai* (2390), to
heal (Luke 6:17); with *dikaióō* (1344),
to justify (Acts 13:39); with *eleutheróō*
(1659), to liberate (Rom 6:18, 22); with
rhúomai (4506), to deliver (Rom 15:31);
with *katharízō* (2511), to purge, purify
(2 Cor 7:1; 2 Tim 2:21); with *rhantízō*
(4472), to sprinkle (Heb 10:22); with
loúō (3068), to wash (Acts 16:33; Rev
1:5). By implication in Heb 11:34. After the adj. *athóos* (121), innocent (Matt

27:24); *hugiés* (5199), sound, whole,
healthy (Mark 5:34); *katharós* (2513),
clean (Acts 20:26); *eleútheros* (1658),
free (Rom 7:3); *áspilos* (784), unspotted
(James 1:27). With verbs of redeeming as
agorázō (59), to buy, redeem (Rev 14:3,
4). (**5**) After verbs implying fear, caution, avoidance, as *phobéomai* (5399), to
be afraid (Matt 10:28; Luke 12:4; Sept.:
Jer 10:2); *phulássō* (5442), to beware
(Luke 12:15; 2 Thess 3:3; 1 John 5:21);
proséchō (4337), to take heed (Matt
7:15; 10:17; Luke 12:1; 20:46; Sept.: 2
Chr 35:21); *blépō* (991), take heed, beware (Mark 8:15; 12:38); *pheúgō* (5343),
to escape, flee, avoid (1 Cor 10:14).
   (**C**) Distance of one object from another meaning gone from, as away from the
serpent (Rev 12:14); far from (Matt 8:30;
Sept.: Ex 33:7). After *apéchō* (568), to
be distant from (Luke 7:6; 24:13). *Apó* is
prefixed to the noun of measure, marking the distance (John 11:18, "about the
distance of fifteen furlongs" [a.t.]; 21:8;
Rev 14:20); before an adv. of distance,
such as *makróthen* (3113), from far (Matt
26:58; Rev 18:10; Sept.: Ps 138:6; Ezra
3:13).
   (**D**) Sometimes found instead of *ek*
(1537), although *ek* is used to indicate
the separation of something that is in another thing and *apó* is used to indicate
separation from something or someone
else. *Apó* is used after comp. verbs with
the prep. *ek*, such as *ekbállō* (1544), to
take or cast out of (Matt 7:4 where the
prep. used is *apó*, while in Matt 7:5 the
prep. is *ek*). In Acts 13:50, *apó* is used
after the verb *ekbállō* (1544), to cast out
of. In John 2:15, the prep. used with the
same verb is *ek*. In Luke 9:5 *apó* is used
with *exérchomai* (1831), to come out of.
In John 4:30 *ek* is used. In Matt 17:18,
the same verb is used with *apó*, while
in Mark 1:25, 26 *ek* is used. *Apó* is also
used metaphorically of thoughts, purposes. In Mark 7:15 *apó* is used, while in
Mark 7:20 we have *ek*, as in Matt 15:11,
18, 19. In Matt 18:35 we have *apó*, while
Mark 12:30, 33, *ek*. In many instances such verbs imply external departure

and are then properly construed with *apó* (Luke 5:8), see I, A, 1. *Ek* also occurs after the verbs *egeírō* (1453), to rise, and *diegeírō* (1326), to stir up. In Matt 1:24; 14:2; 27:64; 28:7 *apó* is used. In Mark 6:14, 16; John 12:1, 9; Acts 3:15; 13:30; Rom 13:11, *ek* is used. Both prep., *apó* and *ek*, may be used in the following senses: when referring to time (Matt 11:12, "from the days of John the Baptist"; John 9:1 where *ek* is used to indicate the time of birth); when the cause is indicated (Matt 18:7, "Woe unto the world because [*apó*] of offenses"; Luke 19:3, "and could not see because [*apó*] of the crowd" [a.t.]; Acts 12:14, "she opened not the gate for [*apó*] gladness"; 22:11, "and when I could not see for [*apo*] the glory"; however, in John 4:6, "being wearied with [*ek*, because of] his journey"; Rev 16:10, "for" [*ek*], because of pain; 16:11, "because [*ek*] of their pains"); when the meaning is instrumental (Matt 11:19, "justified of [*apó*, by means of] her children"; Luke 7:35, "But wisdom is justified of [*apó*, by means of] all her children"; 16:9, "make to yourselves friends of [*ek*, by means of or using] the mammon of unrighteousness," meaning money; John 6:65, "except it were given unto him of [*ek*] my Father"); when used adv. (2 Cor 1:14, "As also ye have acknowledged us in part" [*apó mérous*, partially]; 2:5, "but in part" [*apó mérous*, partially]; however, in 9:7, "not grudgingly" [*mē ek lúpēs*, not sorrowfully]). When the prep. denotes a place of origin, both *apó* and *ek* may be used together (John 1:44, "now Philip was of [*apó*] Bethsaida, the city of [*ek*] Andrew and Peter"; 11:1, "of [*apó*] Bethany, the town of [*ek*] Mary"); also when indicating membership (Acts 6:9, "certain of [*ek*] the synagogue," meaning members of the synagogue; 12:1, "certain of [*apó*] the church," meaning the members). In Mark 1:10, *apó* is used referring to the baptism of Jesus: "and straightway coming up [*anabaínōn* (305)] out of the water [*apó toú húdatos* or away from the water, and not out of the water]." The

fact that Jesus was in the water is indicated by the verb *anabaínō* (305), to go up. Therefore, both actions, up and out, are indicated in this verse. However, in Matt 3:16, "went up [*anébē*]" is used. In Acts 8:38, 39 *apó* refers to the baptism of the Ethiopian eunuch by Phillip, "and they went down [*katabaínō* (2597)], both into [*eis*, (1519)], the water." The prep. *eis* indicates that they went somewhere from which they would come up (*anabaínō*). Mark 1:10 UBS has with the prep. *ek*, in which case we conclude that Mark emphasizes only the coming out of the water and does not include the going away from the water which Matt 3:16 makes evident.

(II) Of time, from any time onwards, since any time.

(A) Before a noun (Matt 9:22; 11:12; Luke 1:70; 8:43; Acts 23:23; 1 John 1:1); with the names of persons (Matt 1:17; Rom 5:14); before events or circumstances (Matt 1:17; 13:35; Luke 2:36; Acts 11:19).

(B) Before a pron., e.g., a relative pron., *aph' hḗs*, from which, fem. (Luke 7:45, "since the time," when or from; Acts 24:11; 2 Pet 3:4); with *hēméras* (2250), day (Acts 20:18; 24:11; Col 1:6, 9). With the noun *chrónou* (5550), time understood as following the relative pron. *hoú*, as *aph' hoú*, meaning from what time, since (Luke 13:25; 24:21; Rev 16:18; Sept.: Ex 5:23).

(C) Before an adv. of time, with or without *toú*, of, as *apó toú nún* (3568), now, from now, henceforth (Luke 1:48; Acts 18:6); *ap' árti* (737), now, present, from now, from the present (Matt 23:39); "From that time" (Matt 4:17); "from morning" (Acts 28:23); since a year ago (2 Cor 8:10; 9:2).

(III) Of the origin or source of anything where *apó* marks the secondary, indirect, mediate origin; while *ek* denotes the primary, direct, ultimate source; and *hupó* (5259), by, the immediate efficient agent. Spoken of:

(A) The place or quarter from which anyone is derived or where he belongs, with the art. (Matt 15:1; 21:11 "the prophet of [*ho apó* (the one from)] Nazareth"; Mark 15:43; John 1:45; Acts 6:9); without the art. (Mark 8:11, "a sign from heaven"; Luke 9:38, "a man of the company"; Acts 2:5; Gal 4:24, the Mount Sinai covenant; Heb 7:13).

(B) The source, meaning the person or thing from which anything proceeds or is derived (Matt 24:32, the parable drawn from the fig tree; 1 Thess 2:6, "glory, neither of you, nor yet of others," referring to human applause; 2 Tim 1:3, whom I worship with a devotion inherited from my ancestors or in the manner of my ancestors). Spoken of persons from whom one hears, learns, asks anything (Matt 11:29; Mark 15:45; Luke 22:71; Acts 9:13; Col 1:7); of any source of knowledge (Matt 7:16, 20). **(1)** Before the incidental cause, from, by reason of, on account of, because of, in consequence of (Matt 18:7; Luke 19:3; John 21:6; Acts 20:9; 22:11; 2 Cor 7:13; Heb 5:7; Sept.: Ex 6:9; 2 Chr 5:6; 20:9). **(2)** Before the inciting cause or motive, especially an emotion (Matt 13:44; 14:26; 28:4; Luke 21:26; 24:41; Acts 12:14; 2 Cor 2:3). **(3)** Before the secondary efficient cause or that which produces, exhibits, bestows anything (Matt 12:38, "we would see a sign from thee," meaning exhibited by you, but wrought ultimately by [*hupó* (5259)] God; Acts 23:21, "a promise from thee," meaning to be given, made by you; 2 Cor 3:18; Gal 1:1; 1 John 2:28, "and not be ashamed before him at his coming"). After verbs of having or receiving anything from the author (1 Cor 6:19; 1 Tim 3:7; 1 John 2:20, 27; 4:21); *apó Theoú*, from God, or *apó Kuríou*, the Lord as the author or bestower (Rom 1:7; 13:1; 1 Cor 1:3, 30; 4:5; 2 Cor 1:2; Gal 1:3; Eph 1:2; Phil 1:2, 28). Of oneself or one's own accord or authority (Luke 12:57; 21:30; John 5:19; 15:4). *Ap' emautoú* (1683), of myself (John 5:30; 7:17, 28; 14:10). *Ap' emoú* (1700), of myself, by my own authority. **(4)** Put after neut. and pass. verbs to mark the author and source of

the action, but not where the author is to be conceived of as personally and immediately active, this latter idea being expressed by *hupó* (5259), by, and *pará* (3844), by, e.g., Matt 16:21, "and suffer many things of the elders," does not mean that the elders were the immediate instigators of His sufferings, but the ones who were responsible for them; Acts 2:22, "a man approved of God," means confirmed by God from heaven without involving direct confirmation; Acts 10:17, 21, "which were sent from Cornelius," means sent from Cornelius' household, not necessarily from him personally (cf. 11:11 where we read "sent from Caesarea"); Luke 1:26 "the angel . . . sent from [*hupó*]," while John 1:6 has *pará*, and James 1:13 has *apó*, "from God I am tempted" (a.t.), or from heaven (cf. *hupó*, Matt 4:1); Luke 4:2, "by the devil" (a.t.), indicating direct temptation where Satan is represented as the immediate agent of temptation. See Matt 11:19; 20:3; Luke 7:35; Jude 1:23; Rev 12:6. *Apó* would also seem, in a few instances in the NT, to be used less definitely where *hupó* might be expected (Mark 8:31; Luke 9:22; 17:25 [cf. 1 Pet 2:4 where it is *hupó*]).

(C) The manner or mode in which anything is done: to forgive from the heart, meaning heartily, fully (Matt 18:35); *apó mérous* (3313), out of a part, meaning in part, partly (Rom 11:25; 15:15; 2 Cor 1:14); *apó miás*, "with one consent" (Luke 14:18), the noun *phōnḗs* (5456), voice, being understood, meaning with one voice; in the manner of one's ancestors (2 Tim 1:3; Sept.: Gen 11:1; Ex 24:3).

(D) The instrument or instrumental source, from, by means of, with (Luke 8:3, "ministered unto him of their substance," or by means of their belongings; 15:16; Rev 18:15).

(E) The material, from or of (Matt 3:4, "raiment of camel's hair").

(F) Dependence from or on any person or thing, attachment to or connection with anyone (Acts 12:1, "certain of the church" or attached to the church; 15:5, "certain of the sect of the Pharisees"; 27:44, "some on boards . . . of the ship").

(G) Implying a part in relation to or from the whole meaning from, of. After *esthíō* (2068), to eat, and *pínō* (4095), to eat or drink of anything meaning a part of it (Matt 15:27; Mark 7:28; Luke 22:18). In Mark 7:4, *apó agorás* (58), marketplace, means returning from somewhere in the marketplace. See Luke 22:16; John 4:14; 1 John 4:13; Sept.: Lev 11:40; Jer 51:7. So also after other verbs, where an acc. would imply the whole. In Mark 6:43, *apó* with the gen. implies from the whole, part of the whole; 12:2; Luke 20:10; 24:42; John 21:10; Acts 2:17, 18; 5:2, 3; Rev 22:19. Spoken of a class or number of persons from which one is selected or of which he forms part (Matt 27:9, 21; Luke 16:30; 19:39; Heb 7:2).

(IV) In composition, *apó* implies:

(A) Separation from or off as in the verb *apolúō* (630) made up of *apó* and *lúō*, to dismiss or to set loose from oneself.

(B) Removal away from as *apobállō* (577), from *apó* and *bállō*, (906), to throw. To cast from oneself.

(C) Abatement or cessation, as *apalgéō* (524), from *apó* and *algéō* (to sting), to reduce pain.

(D) Completion in full as *apéchō* (568), from *apó* and *échō* (2192), to have completely.

(E) Restitution, as *apodídōmi* (591), from *apó* and *dídōmi* (1325, to give), to give back.

(F) Like a priv., it removes the force of the simple word as *apodokimázō* (593), from *apó* and *dokimázō* (1381, to approve), to disallow, not to permit.

(V) Paul's use of *apó* in 1 Cor 11:23, "For I have received of [*apó*] the Lord," indicates that the institution of the Lord's Supper was originally due to the Lord Himself. It does not mean that Paul claims that he directly received it from the Lord, but that it originated directly with the Lord. The reading of one manuscript with *pará*, which would indicate

the immediate reception by Paul of this tradition, must be rejected in view of the fact that Paul did not receive this directly from the Lord. Paul emphasizes that this ordinance of the Lord's Supper did not come to him through intermediaries, but that he wanted the Corinthians to realize that this ordinance of the Lord's Supper was something which originated with the Lord. He emphasizes only that which can be traced directly.

576. ἀποβαίνω *apobaínō*; fut. *apobḗsomai*, 2d aor. *apébēn*, from *apó* (575), from, out of, and *baínō* (n.f., see below), to go, come. To go or come out of the ship, to disembark (Luke 5:2; John 21:9). Metaphorically, to happen, to come or turn out (Luke 21:13; Phil 1:19; Sept.: Ex 2:4; Job 13:5, 16).

Deriv. of *baínō* (n.f.), to go, walk, step: *anabaínō* (305), to go or come up; *bathmós* (898), a degree, rank; *básis* (939), a step, peace, foot, base; *bébaios* (949), fixed, sure; *bébēlos* (952), unhallowed, profane; *bēma* (968), a step, pace, footstep; *bōmós* (1041), a step, base, an idol; *diabaínō* (1224), to pass over, through; *embaínō* (1684), to go in, enter; *epibaínō* (1910), to go upon; *katabaínō* (2597), to descend; *metabaínō* (3327), to pass; *parabaínō* (3845), to transgress, violate; *probaínō* (4260), to go forward, advance; *sumbaínō* (4819), to happen together, come to pass; *huperbaínō* (5233), to go or pass over.

Syn.: *exérchomai* (1831), to come out; *apérchomai* (565), to come away; *hupágō* (5217), to go away, withdraw; *ekporeúomai* (1607), to go out of; *ágō* (71), to go; *hupágō* (5217) and *ápeimi* (548), to go away; *anachōréō* (402), to withdraw; *éxeimi* (1826), to go out.

Ant.: *epibaínō* (1910), to come to or into; *embaínō* (1684) or *eíseimi* (1524), to go into; *hḗkō* (2240), to come; *eisporeúomai* (1531), to enter, go in.

577. ἀποβάλλω *apobállō*; fut. *apobalō*, 2d aor. *apébalon*, from *apó* (575), from, and *bállō* (906), to cast. To cast off or away, spoken of a garment (Mark 10:50; Sept.: Isa 1:30); to lay aside (Heb 10:35, meaning to lose confidence).

Deriv.: *apóblētos* (579), that which is to be rejected; *apobolḗ* (580), casting away, loss.

Syn.: *ekbállō* (1544), to cast out of; *aporríptō* (641), to cast off; *apōthéō* (683), to thrust away; *lúō* (3089) and *apotíthēmi* (659), to put off; *apekdúō* (554), to strip off clothes or arms; *periairéō* (4014), to take away entirely.

Ant.: *epitíthēmi* (2007), to put on or upon; *endúō* (1746), to put on clothes; *endidúskō* (1737), to dress oneself, to wear; *ependúō* (1902), to dress, put on clothes; *himatízō* (2439), to put on clothes; *peribállō* (4016), to put on or around; *egkombóomai* (1463), to enwrap or clothe oneself.

578. ἀποβλέπω *apoblépō*; fut. *apoblépsō*, from *apó* (575), an intens., and *blépō* (991), to see, look. To behold or look toward something, to fix the eyes earnestly or attentively (Heb 11:26; Sept.: Ps 11:4; Hos 3:1).

Syn.: *emblépō* (1689), to look penetratingly; *atenízō* (816), to gaze, look steadfastly; *theōréō* (2334), to behold.

579. ἀπόβλητος *apóblētos*; gen. *apoblḗtou*, masc.-fem., neut. *apóblēton*, verbal adj. from *apobállō* (577), to cast off. Rejected (1 Tim 4:4).

Syn.: *adókimos* (96), not standing the test, rejected.

Ant.: *dektós* (1184), acceptable; *apodektós* (587), acceptable and well-pleasing; *euprósdektos* (2144), acceptable, with great favor; *euárestos* (2101), well-pleasing, and the basic *arestós* (701), agreeable; *klētós* (2822), called, invited; *eklektós* (1588), chosen, elect.

580. ἀποβολή *apobolḗ*; gen. *apobolḗs*, fem. noun from *apobállō* (577), to cast off. A casting off, rejection (Rom 11:15); a loss (Acts 27:22).

Syn.: *apóleia* (864), loss; *kathaíresis* (2506), a pulling down; *ólethros* (3639),

ruin, destruction; *phthorá* (5356), corruption; *ekbolḗ* (1546), a throwing overboard; *anáthema* (331), excommunicated, accursed.

Ant.: *klḗsis* (2821), invitation, calling; *eklogḗ* (1589), choice, election; *apodochḗ* (594), acceptance with approval; *cháris* (5485), grace, acceptance.

581. ἀπογενόμενος *apogenómenos*; 2d aor. mid. part. of *apogínomai* (n.f.), from *apó* (575), from, and *gínomai* (1096), to become. To be afar off, separated, take no part in. Later it came to mean to cease to be what one was before, to die (1 Pet 2:24, corresponding with Rom 6:11). Denotes not a legal, but a moral relation to sin, which is here represented according to its individual manifestations (Rom 6:2; 7:6; Col 2:20), and indeed a relation of such a kind that the molding by sin of the character of the person ceases.

Syn.: *thnḗskō* (2348), to die; *apothnḗskō* (599), to die off; *teleutáō* (5053), to end one's life; *ekleípō* (1587), to cease, die; *suntríbō* (4937), to break in pieces; *sbénnumi* (4570), to extinguish; *apóllumi* (622), to destroy, die, lose; *leípō* (3007), to be wanting, lacking; *apoleípō* (620), to leave behind; *phtheírō* (5351), to corrupt, destroy.

Ant.: *poiéō* (4160), to make.

582. ἀπογραφή *apographḗ*; gen. *apographḗs*, fem. noun from *apográphō* (583), to enroll, register. An enrollment in a public register, a census, an enumeration of property and persons (Luke 2:2; Acts 5:37).

583. ἀπογράφω *apográphō*; fut. *apográpsō*, from *apó* (575), from, and *gráphō* (1125), to write. To write down, enroll, register in a census (Luke 2:1ff.); in the mid. *apográphomai*, to cause oneself to be enrolled, to give one's name to the census. To be registered, enrolled in a figurative and spiritual sense, an allusion to the Book of Life (Heb 12:23 [cf. Ps 69:28]).

Deriv.: *apographḗ* (582), an enroll-ment.

Syn.: *eggráphō* (1449), to write in.

Ant.: *exaleíphō* (1813), to obliterate, wipe away.

584. ἀποδείκνυμι *apodeíknumi*; the obs. *apodeíkō* fut. *apodeíxō*, from *apó* (575), an intens., and *deiknúmi* (1166), to show. To show, demonstrate, exhibit.

(I) To designate, constitute, appoint in relation to any office or station. In 1 Cor 4:9, "That God hath set forth [trans. aor. act. *apédeixen*, set forth, meaning at-tested, proven] us the apostles last." The apostles are described as *éschatoi* (2078), last in the social scale, but God proved them and because they proved accept-able, He set them forth. In 2 Thess 2:4, "showing himself that he is God" means designating himself that he is God.

(II) To show by argument, to demonstrate, prove. In Acts 2:22 *apodedeigménon*, perf. pass. part. mean-ing approved, confirmed of God through miracles, wonders, and signs (*dunámeis* [1411], miracles or powers; *térasi* [5059], wonders, things out of the or-dinary; *semeíois* [4592], signs) which is indicative of the fact that the miracu-lous demonstrations which Jesus did dur-ing His lifetime were for the purpose of proving Him confirmed of God. They showed that He had power to accomplish anything He chose to, i.e., anything out of the ordinary (actually the word *téras* means wonder as viewed by the human point of view), and that what He did was a sign as to who He really was, the Mes-siah, the One approved of God. In Acts 25:7, charges which they were not able to prove.

Deriv.: *apódeixis* (585), demonstra-tion.

Syn.: *dokimázō* (1381), *parístēmi* (3936), *sumbibázō* (4822), and *sunístēmi/ sunistánō* (4921), to prove; *bebaióō* (950), to confirm; *peirázō* (3985), to test in order to prove; *kuróō* (2964), to rati-fy; *prokuróō* (4300), to confirm or rati-fy before; *marturéō* (3140), to witness;

martúromai (3143), to affirm solemn-ly; *epimarturéō* (1957), to testify fully; *emphanízō* (1718), to declare, signify; *dēlóō* (1213), declare, show.

Ant.: *apodokimázō* (593), to repudiate; *aporríptō* (641), to reject; *krúptō* (2928), hide, keep secret; *apokrúptō* (613), to conceal away or keep secret; *kalúptō* (2572), to cover up, hide; *sugkalúptō* (4780), to conceal altogether; *anairéō* (377), to abolish; *elégchō* (1651), to re-buke, reprove.

585. ἀπόδειξις *apódeixis*; gen. *apo-deíxeōs*, fem. noun from *apodeíknumi* (584), to prove. Manifestation, demon-stration, proof (1 Cor 2:4).

Syn.: *dokimḗ* (1382), proof of genu-ineness; *dokímion* (1383), the means of proving genuineness; *éndeixis* (1732), the act of proving or demonstrating; *éndeigma* (1730), the means of demon-stration or proving; *tekmḗrion* (5039), a positive proof; *bebaíōsis* (971), confir-mation; *martúrion* (3142), evidence, wit-ness; *deígma* (1164), specimen, example in the process of proving something; *sēmeíon* (4592), token, wonder, sign.

Ant.: *anaíresis* (336), death, killing, disproof; *élegchos* (1650), reproof, con-viction.

586. ἀποδεκατόω *apodekatóō*; con-tracted *apodekatō̃*, fut. *apodekatḗsō*, from *apó* (575), from, and *dekatóō* (1183), to tithe. To tithe from. Trans., to tithe, levy tithe, e.g., of persons (Heb 7:5; Sept.: 1 Sam 8:15, 17). To pay or give tithes of (Matt 23:23; Luke 11:42; 18:12; Sept.: Gen 28:22; Deut 14:22).

Ant.: *nosphízomai* (3557), to purloin, keep back that which does not belong to oneself.

587. ἀπόδεκτος *apódektos*; gen. *apodéktou* or *apodektoú*, masc.-fem., neut. *apódekton*, adj. from *apodéchomai* (588), to welcome. Acceptable (1 Tim 2:3; 5:4), pleasing, grateful.

Syn.: *euárestos* (2101), well-pleas-ing; *euprósdektos* (2144), acceptable, favorable; *dókimos* (1384), approved, acceptable.

Ant.: *apóblētos* (579), rejected; *adókimos* (96), not standing the test.

588. ἀποδέχομαι *apodéchomai*; fut. *apodéxomai*, mid. deponent from *apó* (575), an intens., and *déchomai* (1209), to take from another for oneself, to receive. Used only by Luke, of persons, to receive kindly or hospitably (Luke 8:40; Acts 15:4; 18:27); of God's Word, to receive or embrace heartily (Acts 2:41); of benefits, to receive or accept gratefully (Acts 24:3).

Deriv.: *apódektós* (587), acceptable; *apodochḗ* (594), a receiving back.

Syn.: *lambánō* (2983), to receive without necessarily indicating a favorable reception; *paralambánō* (3880), to receive from another; *apolambánō* (618), to receive from another as one's due; *proslambánō* (4355), to take to oneself; *eudokéō* (2106), to approve; *sugkatatíthemai* (4784), to consent; *euarestéō* (2100), to please or be pleased; *paradéchomai* (3858), to accept with delight, receive; *prosdéchomai* (4327), to accept, to look for; *egkrínō* (1469), to reckon on, approve; *homologéō* (3670), to assent, confess, accept, accept together.

Ant.: *apodokimázō* (593), to reject by disapproving; *athetéō* (114), to do away with; *ekptúō* (1609), to spit out or reject; *paraitéomai* (3868), to beg off, ask to be excused; *arnéomai* (720), to deny, renounce; *parakoúō* (3878), to refuse to hear, disobey; *apobállō* (577), to cast away; *aporríptō* (641), to reject; *apōthéomai* (683), to put away from oneself; *aparnéomai* (533), to deny utterly; *apotássomai* (657), to renounce or to place in its proper category away from oneself; *apopheúgō* (668), to escape, avoid; *apodokimázō* (593), to disapprove.

589. ἀποδημέω *apodēméō*; contracted *apodēmō̃*; fut. *apodēmḗsō*, from *apódēmos* (590), emigrant. To go away from one's own people or country, to travel abroad or into a foreign country, to emigrate (Matt 21:33; 25:14, 15; Mark 12:1; Luke 15:13; 20:9).

Syn.: *metoikízō* (3351), transfer as a settler.

Ant.: *endēméō* (1736), to be among one's people; *ménō* (3306), to remain, abide.

590. ἀπόδημος *apódēmos*; gen. *apodḗmou*, masc.-fem., neut. *apódēmon*, adj. from *apó* (575), from, and *dḗmos* (1218), people. One gone abroad, absent in a foreign country (Mark 13:34).

Deriv.: *apodēméō* (589), to emigrate.

Syn.: *xénos* (3581), stranger; *allótrios* (245), foreigner; *allogenḗs* (241), one from another race or people or nation; *pároikos* (3941), a sojourner; *parepídēmos* (3927), pilgrim; *allóphulos* (246), foreigner, one belonging to another nation.

Ant.: *polítēs* (4177), citizen.

591. ἀποδίδωμι *apodídōmi*; fut. *apodṓsō*, aor. *apédōka* (Luke 9:42), 2d aor. *apédōn*, opt. *apodóē* (2 Tim 4:14), from *apó* (575), from, and *dídōmi* (1325), to give. To give or to do something necessary in fulfillment of an obligation or expectation. To give, bestow (2 Tim 4:8 [cf. Rom 2:6]). Of testimony or witness, to give, bear (Acts 4:33). In the mid. *apodídomai*, to sell, give from oneself for a price (Acts 5:8; 7:9; Heb 12:16; Sept.: Gen 25:33; 37:27, 35; Deut 2:8; Amos 2:6). To reward, recompense, render, whether in a good or bad sense (Matt 6:4, 6; 16:27; Rom 2:6; 12:17; 1 Tim 5:4; 2 Tim 4:14). To repay, restore, return (Luke 4:20; 9:42; 10:35; 19:8); a debt (Matt 18:25, 26); tribute (Matt 22:21; Rom 13:7); hire (Matt 20:8). *Apodídōmi lógon* (3056), to give or render an account (Matt 12:36; Luke 16:2; Acts 19:40; Heb 13:17; 1 Pet 4:5); *apodídōmi hórkous* (3727), to keep or perform one's oaths (Matt 5:33). Other references: Matt 5:26; 6:18; 18:28–30, 34; 21:41; 27:58; Mark 12:17; Luke 7:42; 12:59; 20:25; 1 Cor 7:3; 1 Thess 5:15; Heb 12:11; 1 Pet 3:9; Rev 18:6; 22:2, 12.

Deriv.: *antapodídōmi* (467), to give back as an equivalent, to recompense with the idea of complete return.

Syn.: *apotínō* or *apotíō* (661), to pay off a fine or whatever is due; *apokathístēmi* (600), to restore to a former condition of health or divine favor; *chorēgéō* (5524), to supply.

Ant.: *kratéō* (2902), to keep back; *aposteréō* (650), to deprive; *nosphízomai* (3557), to keep back implying deceit.

592. ἀποδιορίζω *apodiorízō*; fut. *apodiorísō*, from *apó* (575), from, and *diorízō* (n.f.), to divide, separate. To separate (only in Jude 1:19, to separate from or cause divisions among the Christian community).

Syn.: *aphorízō* (873), to mark off by bounds; *chōrízō* (5563), to separate.

Ant.: *sunéchō* (4912), to hold together; *sundéō* (4887), to bind with; *suzeúgnumi* (4801), to yoke together, conjoin.

593. ἀποδοκιμάζω *apodokimázō*; fut. *apodokimásō*, from *apó* (575), from, and *dokimázō* (1381), to prove. To reject as the result of examination and testing of one's qualification for an office. Later it came to mean to put out of office or place, to reject, disapprove, refuse (Matt 21:42; Mark 8:31; 12:10; Luke 9:22; 17:25; 20:17; Heb 12:17, of Esau being refused; 1 Pet 2:4, 7, of the rejection of Christ; Sept.: Jer 6:30; 7:28; 14:19; 31:36).

Syn.: *athetéō* (114), to make void, nullify, reject; *ekptúō* (1609), to spit out, spurn; *paraitéomai* (3868), to refuse; *akuróō* (208), to disannul, render of no effect; *aporríptō* (641), to reject.

Ant.: *apodeíknumi* (584), to prove by demonstration; *prosdéchomai* (4327), to admit, accept; *sunístēmi* (4921), to commend; *déchomai* (1209), to accept; *apodéchomai* (588), to approve.

594. ἀποδοχή *apodochḗ*; gen. *apodochḗs*, fem. noun from *apodéchomai* (588), to receive from. Recognition, acknowledgment, approval, or more ex-actly, ready or willing acknowledgment (only in 1 Tim 1:15; 4:9).

Syn.: *sugkatáthesis* (4783), agreement; *eudokía* (2107), good pleasure; *homología* (3671), acknowledgment, confession; *bebaíōsis* (951), confirmation; *anochḗ* (463), forbearance.

Ant.: *athétēsis* (115), abolition, disannulling.

595. ἀπόθεσις *apóthesis*; gen. *apothéseōs*, fem. noun from *apotíthēmi* (659), to put away. Putting off, laying aside. Metaphorically (1 Pet 3:21; 2 Pet 1:14).

Syn.: *apobolḗ* (580), casting off, rejection, and its syn.; *ekbolḗ* (1546), ejection.

Ant.: *apodochḗ* (594), acceptance; *lḗpsis* (3028), receipt, receiving.

596. ἀποθήκη *apothḗkē*; gen. *apothḗkēs*, fem. noun from *apotíthēmi* (659), to put away. A place where anything is laid up, repository of arms or arsenal, a treasury (Sept.: 1 Chr 29:8). In the NT spoken of grain, a granary, storehouse, barn (Matt 3:12; 6:26; 13:30; Luke 3:17; 12:18, 24; Sept.: Prov 3:10 [*tameía*, pl. (5009), treasury, closet]; Jer 50:26).

Syn.: *tameíon* (5009), treasury, closet, a chamber on the ground floor or interior of an oriental house, generally kept for privacy; *krúptē* (2926), a cellar, crypt, secret place; *koitṓn* (2846), a bedroom.

597. ἀποθησαυρίζω *apothēsaurízō*; fut. *apothēsaurísō*, from *apó* (575), away, from, and *thēsaurízō* (2343), to store treasure. To treasure, lay up in store, used metaphorically (1 Tim 6:19).

Syn.: *sullégō* (4816), to collect, gather together; *sunágō* (4863), take, lead in, gather together; *apotíthemi* (659), to lay aside.

Ant.: *dapanáō* (1159), to spend; *prosanalískō* (4321), to spend additionally; *analískō* (355), to consume; *katanalískō* (2654), to consume utterly; *diagínomai* (1230), used of time meaning to elapse; *chronotribéō* (5551), to spend time with purposeful delay.

598. ἀποθλίβω *apothlíbō*; fut. *apothlípsō*, from *apó* (575), from or an intens., and *thlíbō* (2346), to squeeze, press around, trouble. To press from every side, to crowd. Used in an absolute sense (Luke 8:45; Sept.: Num 22:25).

Syn.: *tarássō* (5015), to trouble; *enochléō* (1776), to crowd in, annoy; *sugchéō* (4797), to perplex, confuse; *ochléō* (3791), to harass; *adēmonéō* (85), to be in distress; *thorubéō* (2350), to set in an uproar.

Ant.: *anapaúō* (373), to rest; *hēsucházō* (2270), to be quiet, rest; *anapsúchō* (404), to cool off, refresh.

599. ἀποθνήσκω *apothnḗskō*; fut. *apothanoúmai*, 2d aor. *apéthanon*, from *apó* (575) an intens., and *thnḗskō* (2348), to die. Literally, to die off, but used with the simple meaning of to die, although stronger than *thnḗskō*. To die a natural death, applied to both men and animals (Matt 8:32; 22:24, 27; 26:35; Heb 9:27); to be dead to sin, as the truly regenerate are, by having renounced and abandoned it in consequence of their conformity with Christ in His death (Rom 6:2 [cf. Col 3:3]); when applied to Christ, to die for or on account of sin, i.e., to make an atonement and satisfaction for it (Rom 6:10 [cf. Heb 9:26–28]); to be dead to the Law, i.e., to have no more dependence upon mere legal righteousness for justification and salvation than a dead man would have, as being self-crucified and dead together with Christ (Gal 2:19 [cf. Rom 6:4; Col 2:20]). Other references: Matt 9:24; Mark 5:35, 39; 9:26; 12:19–22; 15:44; Luke 8:42, 52, 53; 16:22; 20:28–32, 36; John 4:47, 49; 6:49, 50, 58; 8:21, 24, 52, 53; 11:14, 16, 25, 26, 32, 37, 50, 51; 12:24, 33; 18:32; 19:7; 21:23; Acts 7:4; 9:37; 21:13; 25:11; Rom 5:6–8, 15; 6:7–9; 7:2, 3, 6, 9; 8:13, 34; 14:7–9, 15; 1 Cor 8:11; 9:15; 15:3, 22, 31, 32, 36; 2 Cor 5:14, 15; 6:9; Gal 2:21; Phil 1:21; 1 Thess 4:14; 5:10; Heb 7:8;

10:28; 11:4, 13, 21, 37; Jude 1:12; Rev 3:2; 8:9, 11; 9:6; 14:13; 16:3.

Deriv.: *sunapothnḗskō* (4880), to die with.

Syn.: *teleutáō* (5053), to end one's life; *koimáō* (2837), to fall asleep, figuratively, to die; *apogínomai* (581), to be away from, to die; *apóllumi* (622), to destroy, die.

Ant.: *záō* (2198), to live; *bióō* (980), to spend one's existence; *hupárchō* (5225), to exist; *anístēmi* (450), to stand up, rise from the dead; *egeírō* (1453), to rise from the dead.

600. ἀποκαθίστημι *apokathístēmi*; fut. *apokatastḗsō*, from *apó* (575), back again, and *kathístēmi* (2525), to constitute. To restore, e.g., to health or soundness (Matt 12:13; Mark 3:5; 8:25; Luke 6:10; Sept.: Ex 4:7; Lev 13:16). To put back into a former state, restore, reform, applied to the reformation brought about by the preaching and ministry of John the Baptist (Matt 17:11; Mark 9:12 [cf. Mal 4:6; Luke 1:16, 17]). To restore lost dominion or authority (Acts 1:6; Sept.: Ezek 16:55). In the pass., to be restored, brought or sent back again (Heb 13:19; Sept.: Jer 16:15; 24:6).

Deriv.: *apokatástasis* (605), restitution of a thing to its former condition.

Syn.: *epistréphō* (1994) and *epanágō* (1877), to return; *epanérchomai* (1880), to come again; *therapeúō* (2323), to cure, restore health.

Ant.: *apóllumi* (622), to destroy utterly; *apothnḗskō* (599), to die, perish; *aphanízō* (853), to cause to disappear; *katargéō* (2673), to abolish; *kathairéō* (2507), to destroy, pull down; *lúō* (3089), to loose, dissolve; *katalúō* (2647), to destroy utterly; *olothreúō* (2645), to destroy; *exolothreúō* (1842), to destroy utterly; *porthéō* (4199), to cause havoc.

601. ἀποκαλύπτω *apokalúptō*; fut. *apokalúpsō*, from *apó* (575), from, and *kalúptō* (2572), to cover, conceal. Literally, to remove a veil or covering exposing to open view what was before hidden.

To make manifest or reveal a thing previously secret or unknown (Luke 2:35; 1 Cor 3:13). Particularly applied to supernatural revelation (Matt 11:25, 27; 16:17; 1 Cor 2:10). See Matt 10:26; Luke 17:30; John 12:38; Rom 1:17, 18; 8:18; 1 Cor 14:30; Gal 1:16; 3:23; Eph 3:5; Phil 3:15; 2 Thess 2:3, 6, 8; 1 Pet 1:5, 12; 5:1.

Deriv.: *apokálupsis* (602), disclosure, revelation.

Syn.: *chrēmatízō* (5537), to give divine instruction; *apostegázō* (648), to unroof, uncover; *anakalúptō* (343), to unveil, discover, open up; *emphanízō* (1718), to manifest; *anaptússō* (380), to unroll, open up.

Ant.: *epikalúptō* (1943), to conceal, cover; *perikalúptō* (4028), to cover all around; *peribállō* (4016), to clothe around; *ependúō* (1902), to place clothing upon, to invest upon oneself; *sugkalúptō* (4780), to cover or conceal closely; *krúptō* (2928), to hide; *apokrúptō* (613), to hide from someone.

602. ἀποκάλυψις *apokálupsis*; gen. *apokalúpseōs*, fem. noun from *apokalúptō* (601), to reveal. Revelation, uncovering, unveiling, disclosure. One of three words referring to the Second Coming of Christ (1 Cor 1:7; 2 Thess 1:7; 1 Pet 1:7, 13). The other two words are *epipháneia* (2015), appearing (1 Tim 6:14), and *parousía* (3952), coming, presence (2 Thess 2:1). *Apokálupsis*, a grander and more comprehensive word, includes not merely the thing shown and seen but the interpretation, the unveiling of the same. The *epipháneiai* (pl.), appearances, are contained in the *apokálupsis*, revelation, being separate points or moments therein. Christ's first coming was an *epipháneia* (2 Tim 1:10); the second, an *apokálupsis*, will be far more glorious.

(I) Spoken of the removal of ignorance and darkness by the communication of light and knowledge, illumination, instruction (Luke 2:32; Sept.: Isa 42:6).

(II) In the sense of revelation, disclosure, manifestation of that which becomes evident by the event. In Rom 2:5, "the day of manifestation of God's wrath" (a.t.), i.e., when it will be manifested; 8:19, "the manifestation of the sons of God," means the revelation of the glory (Rom 8:18, 21) which they will experience. The true worth of the believers as they experience suffering is not made manifest now, but it will be when the Lord comes again and the glory of each believer will be proportionate to his suffering and sacrifice for Christ. The revelation of the mysteries refers to divine purposes and doctrines which before were unknown and concealed (Rom 16:25 [TR]; 1 Cor 14:6, 26). Of revelations from God the Father or Christ (2 Cor 12:1, 7; Gal 1:12; 2:2; Eph 3:3). In Eph 1:17 "a spirit of . . . revelation" means a spirit which can fathom and unfold the deep things of God. Spoken of future events (Rev 1:1), where it forms part of the title of the book.

Syn.: *gumnótēs* (1132), nakedness; *phanérōsis* (5321), manifestation; *éleusis* (1660), coming (Acts 7:32).

Ant.: *peribólaion* (4018), something that covers around, a veil; *sképasma* (4629), a covering, roofing; *stégē* (4721), roof, covering; *éndusis* (1745), putting on; *kálumma* (2571), a cover, veil.

603. ἀποκαραδοκία *apokaradokía*; gen. *apokaradokías*, fem. noun from *apokaradokéō* (n.f.), to expect earnestly. Attentive or earnest expectation or looking for, as with the neck stretched out and the head thrust forward (Rom 8:19; Phil 1:20, where it is *karadokía* in some MSS; Sept.: Ps 37:7).

Syn.: *prosdokía* (4329), expectation; *ekdochḗ* (1561), the looking for, expectation.

Ant.: *léthē* (3024), forgetfulness; *agnóēma* (51), a thing ignored; *epilēsmonḗ* (1953), forgetfulness, negligence.

604. ἀποκαταλλάσσω *apokatallássō*, **ἀποκαταλλάττω** *apokatalláttō*; fut. *apokatalláxō*, from *apó* (575), from, indicating the state to be left behind, and *katallássō* (2644), to reconcile. *Apokatallássō* is the stronger term for reconcile, differing from *katallássō* (2644), to reconcile, to set up a relationship of peace not existing before, in that *apokatallássō* is the restoration of a relationship of peace which has been disturbed (Eph 2:16; Col 1:20, 21). See Eph 1:10 where the verb is *anakephalaiṓsasthai*, the aor. inf. mid. of *anakephalaióō* (346), to gather together in one or under one head, which refers to the eschatological bringing together of Jews and Gentiles.

Syn.: *diallássō* (1259), to reconcile in cases of mutual hostility; *eirēnopoiéō* (1517), to make peace; *sumbibázō* (4822), to drive together.

Ant.: *dicházō* (1369), to set at variance; *erízō* (2051), to strive; *diamáchomai* (1264), to fight, strive; *diḯstēmi* (1339), to be parted; *logomachéō* (3054), strive about words.

605. ἀποκατάστασις *apokatástasis*; gen. *apokatastáseōs*, fem. noun from *apokathístēmi* (600), to restore. A restitution of a thing to its former condition.

Occurs only in Acts 3:21 where the restitution of all things is to be understood as the day of judgment and of the consummation of the age when the Lord will return. The relative pron. *hṓn*, translated "which" in the phrase "Whom the heaven must receive until the times of restitution of all things, which God hath spoken by the mouth of all his holy prophets since the world began," does not refer to *pántōn*, "of all things." If it did, it would limit *pántōn*, i.e., this restoration would concern not all things, but only those things spoken by God through the mouth of His saints. The relative pron. *hṓn* in the masc. gen. pl. must, therefore, refer to the times of restoration and be taken as its attribute. An understandable translation then would be "whom [the ascended Christ] the heaven must receive until the times of restitution of all things, of which [times of restitution] God spoke by the mouth of all His holy prophets" (a.t.). See also Acts 1:11; 1 Cor 14:2, 3; Col 4:3; Heb 2:3.

It is at that time that life will be restored to the bodies of the dead, and the image of God in man, defaced by Adam's fall, will be perfectly renewed in righteousness. This is a restoration not only of the image of God in man, but also of the recognition of God in nature and by man for all that He rightly is, a wise God who governs the affairs of men. God's power and justice will be recognized once again. He will then render to each person according to his works (2 Cor 5:10). At that time the veracity of God's predictions will be proven (2 Pet 3:3, 4).

Apokatástasis may be taken as syn. with *paliggenesía* (3824), regeneration, in its application (Matt 19:28). Although the believer enjoys Christ's salvation on this earth, it is not complete in view of the fact that man is still in his mortal body and the environment in which he lives has been tainted by sin. Both the body and the environment will one day be changed completely for this restoration to take place (Rom 8:23; Rev 21:1) when a qualitatively new (*kainḗ* [2537]) heaven and earth (*gḗ* [1093]) are going to be created.

606. ἀπόκειμαι *apókeimai*; fut. *apokeísomai*, from *apó* (575), from, away, and *keímai* (2749), to lie, to be laid up, set away. To be laid up or away for preservation (Luke 19:20). Metaphorically, with the dat. of person to be in store for, to await someone. Spoken of rewards (Col 1:5, the hope that awaits you in heaven; 2 Tim 4:8, a crown); death (Heb 9:27).

Syn.: *apotíthēmi* (659), to put away, lay apart; *periménō* (4037), *anaménō* (362) and *prosdéchomai* (4327), to await; *períkeimai* (4029), to lie all around; *epiménō* (1961), to persevere; *prosménō* (4357), to stay on looking forward; *epéchō* (1907), to pay attention to; *diatríbō* (1304), to continue; *dialeípō* (1257), to intermit; *ekdéchomai* (1551), to expect; *hupodéchomai* (5264), to receive.

Ant.: *apéchomai* (567), to hold back oneself, abstain, and the impersonal *apéchei* (566), to have in full what is one's due; *lanthánomai* (2990), to be ignorant of; *epilanthánomai* (1950), to neglect.

607. ἀποκεφαλίζω *apokephalízō*; fut. *apokephalísō*, from *apó* (575), from, and *kephalḗ* (2776), head. To behead. Trans. (Matt 14:10; Mark 6:16, 27; Luke 9:9).

Syn.: *phoneúō* (5407), to murder, slay; *apokteínō* (615), to put to death, kill.

Ant.: *anazáō* (326), to recover life, revive.

608. ἀποκλείω *apokleíō*; fut. *apokleísō*, from *apó*, from, away, and *kleíō* (2808), to shut up. To close up, shut, make fast the door (Luke 13:25; Sept.: Gen 19:10; Judg 3:23; 2 Sam 13:17, 18).

Syn.: *exairéō* (1807), to exclude, pluck out; *perileípo* (4035), to leave around; *kataleípo* (2641), to leave behind.

Ant.: *sumperilambánō* (4843), to include together.

609. ἀποκόπτω *apokóptō*; fut. *apokópsō*, from *apó* (575), from, away, and *kóptō* (2875), to cut down, chop. To cut off, amputate. Trans. (Mark 9:43, 45; John 18:10, 26; Acts 27:32; Sept.: Deut 25:12; 1 Sam 31:9). In the mid. *apokópsomai* (Gal 5:12) as spoken of Judaizing teachers. Paul wished that in their case they would not only circumcise, but even cut off the parts usually circumcised (Chrysostom), meaning to emasculate themselves (Sept.: Deut 23:1). Metaphorically, to separate themselves from the Christian community.

Syn.: *katakóptō* (2629), to chop down, cut; *dichotoméō* (1371), to bisect; *apospáō* (645), to draw away.

Ant.: *epispáomai* (1986), to draw over, to efface the mark of circumcision, become uncircumcised; *kolláō* (2853), to cleave, glue, join; *proskolláō* (4347), to cleave to, glue onto, adhere.

610. ἀπόκριμα *apókrima*; gen. *apokrímatos*, neut. noun from *apokrínomai* (611), to answer. Answer, not the act of answering (*apókrisis* [612]), but the answer itself. Used in 2 Cor 1:9 as syn. with *katákrima* (2631), condemnation, in the sense of those who have been rejected or pronounced guilty, sentenced to death in the opinions and minds of others.

Syn.: *chrēmatismós* (5538), a divine response through an oracle; *apología* (627), a verbal defense; *eperótēma* (1906), a legal questioning or appeal; *katadíkē* (UBS) or *díkē* (TR) (1349), a judicial sentence, condemnation; *katákrisis* (2633), sentencing adversely.

Ant.: *áphesis* (859), forgiveness; *hilasmós* (2434), atonement, propitiation; *cháris* (5485), grace; *dikaíōsis* (1347), justification; *dikaíōma* (1345), a right; *apolútrōsis* (629), redemption; *lúsis* (3080), a loosening.

611. ἀποκρίνομαι *apokrínomai*; fut. pass. *apokrithḗsomai*, aor. mid. *apekrinámēn*, aor. pass. *apekríthēn*, mid. deponent verb from *apó* (575), from, and *krínō* (2919), to separate, discern, judge. To answer or return answer which ought to be done with discretion (Matt 3:15; 4:4; 26:23; 27:12); to take occasion to speak or say, not strictly in answering but in relation or reference to preceding circumstances (Matt 11:4; 12:38; 17:4; 22:1; 26:25, 63; Mark 9:5, 17; Luke 7:40).

Deriv.: *antapokrínomai* (470), to answer in contradiction, to answer back; *apókrima* (610), answer or judicial sentence; *apókrisis* (612), the act of answering.

Syn.: *hupolambánō* (5274), to catch up in speech, to answer; *apologéomai* (626), to speak back, to answer in making a defense for oneself; *antilégō* (483), to speak or answer against; *proslaléō* (4354), to speak to; *phthéggomai* (5350), to utter a sound or voice; *apophthéggomai* (669), to speak forth; *chrēmatízō* (5537), to utter an oracle.

Ant.: *phimóō* (5392), to muzzle; *sigáō* (4601), to voluntarily keep silent; *hēsucházō* (2270), to hold one's peace; *siōpáō* (4623), to keep silence involuntarily, unable to speak.

612. ἀπόκρισις *apókrisis*; gen. *apokríseōs*, fem. noun from *apokrínomai* (611), answer. Decision or answer (Luke 2:47; 20:26; John 1:22; 19:9; Sept.: Deut 1:22; Job 32:5; Ps 15:1). For syn. and ant. see *apókrima* (610), answer, sentence. The distinction between *apókrisis* and *apókrima* is that the first is the act of answering and the second is the answer itself.

613. ἀποκρύπτω *apokrúptō*; fut. *apokrúpsō*, from *apó* (575), from, away, and *krúptō* (2928), to hide. To hide away, conceal. Trans., the money (Matt 25:18). Metaphorically, to hide, not to reveal, followed by *apó* with the gen. of person (Matt 11:25; Luke 10:21); used in an absolute sense (1 Cor 2:7; Eph 3:9; Col 1:26; Sept.: 2 Kgs 4:27; Ps 119:19).

Apokrúptō is to hide with a benevolent purpose, either because of the incapacity of the receiver to understand or because of the knowledge of the revealer that such revelation of hidden things would not benefit the receiver. This is the word used by God in not revealing all that He knows, that which man cannot receive, in the same manner that a parent does not reveal all that he knows to his child because of the child's immaturity to comprehend or the relative unimportance of the information.

Deriv.: *apókruphos* (614), secret, treasured.

Syn.: *kalúptō* (2572), to cover up; *krúptō* (2928), to hide; *apokrúptō* (613), to conceal from; *egkrúptō* (1470), to hide in something; *parakalúptō* (3871), to cover with a veil, hide; *lanthánō* (2990), to escape notice.; *stégō* (4722), to provide a roof over; *egkrúptō* (1470), to conceal in.

Ant.: *apokalúptō* (601), to reveal; *chrēmatízō* (5537), to give divine instruction; *apostegázō* (648), to unroof, uncover; *anakalúptō* (343), to unveil, discover, open up; *emphanízō* (1718), to manifest; *anaptússō* (380), to unroll, open up; *deiknúō* (1166), to show; *dēlóō* (1213), to make plain; *emphanízō* (1718), to exhibit, disclose; *marturéō* (3140), to give evidence; *phaneróō* (5319), to render apparent; *probállō* (4261), to put forth; *apodeíknumi* (584), to exhibit, prove, set forth; *phaínō* (5316), to appear, show.

614. ἀπόκρυφος *apókruphos*; gen. *apokrúphou*, masc.-fem., neut. *apókruphon*, adj. from *apokrúptō* (613), to conceal. Hidden away, concealed. Metaphorically (Mark 4:22; Luke 8:17; Sept.: Dan 2:22). By implication, laid up in store, metaphorically (Col 2:3; Sept. Isa 45:3; Dan 11:43).

Syn.: *kruptós* (2927), concealed, inward, hidden by virtue of its nature, while *apókruphos* is something purposely hidden by another; *mustérion* (3466), mystery.

Ant.: *phanerós* (5318), apparent, manifest; *emphanḗs* (1717), manifest; *ékdēlos* (1552), wholly evident, manifest; *gnōstós* (1110), known; *dḗlos* (1212), evident; *pródēlos* (4271), evident, manifest beforehand, clearly evident; *katádēlos* (2612), quite manifest, evident; *éxōthen* (1855), outward; *dēmósios* (1219), public, open.; *eilikrinḗs* (1506), sincere, genuine; *ékdēlos* (1552), wholly evident, manifest; *epiphanḗs* (2016), conspicuous, notable.

615. ἀποκτείνω *apokteínō*, also *apokténō* or *apokténnō*; fut. *apoktenṓ*, aor. *apékteina*, aor. pass. *apektánthēn* (Matt 16:21; Mark 8:31), from *apó* (575), an intens., and *kteíno* (n.f.), to slay. To kill outright, put to death. Trans. (Matt 10:28; Luke 12:4; Rev 9:5; Sept.: Hab 1:17; Dan 2:13). Also from *kteíno* (n.f.): *anthrōpoktónos* (443), murderer.

(I) Particularly, to put to death in any manner (Matt 14:5; 16:21; 21:35, 38, 39; Mark 6:19; John 18:31; Rev 6:8; Sept.:

Gen 4:8; 18:25; Ex 4:24; Josh 11:10; Judg 9:5; 1 Sam 17:46). With the reflexive *heautón* (1438), himself, to kill oneself (John 8:22); pass. to be slain, meaning to die, perish (Rev 9:18, 20).

(II) Metaphorically, to kill eternally, to bring under eternal condemnation of death, to kill the soul, equivalent to causing the soul to perish in Gehenna (Matt 10:28; Luke 12:5 [cf. Rom 7:11; 2 Cor 3:6]).

(III) Metaphorically, to destroy or abolish the enmity (Eph 2:16; Sept.: Ps 78:47).

Syn.: *thanatóō* (2289), to put to death; *phoneúō* (5407), to murder; *thúō* (2380), to slay; *spházō* (4969), to butcher, slaughter, kill, slay; *apóllumi* (622), to destroy fully, kill, die; *kathairéō* (2507), to demolish, destroy.

Ant.: *anazáō* (326), to recover life, revive; *akmázō* (187), to be fully ripe; *prokóptō* (4298), to increase, grow; *proágomai* (4254), to lead forward; *probibázomai* (4264), to move to the front; *anaptússomai* (380), to develop; *anathállō* (330), to flourish anew, revive; *egeírō* (1453), to raise from a sitting or lying position because of sickness or death, revive; *anístēmi* (450), to rise from a lying position of sleep or death, to stand up alive or generally to stand up; *diagrēgoréō* (1235), to become fully awake; *zōopoiéō* (2227), to make alive; *zōogonéō* (2225), to rescue from death, to engender alive; *anazōpuréō* (329), to rekindle, stir up; *anístēmi* (450), to arise from the dead; *egeírō* (2564), to raise from the dead.

616. ἀποκυέω *apokuéō*, contracted *apokuố*; fut. *apokuếsō*, from *apó* (575), from, and *kuéō* (n.f.), to swell, be pregnant. To beget, bear (James 1:18 [cf. 1 Cor 4:15; 1 Pet 1:3, 23]). To bring forth, as sin brings death (James 1:15).

Deriv.: of *kúō*, to swell (n.f.): *égkuos* (1471), pregnant; *kúma* (2949), a wave.

Syn.: *tíktō* (5088), to bring forth; *gennáō* (1080), to beget, give birth.

Ant.: *sullambánō* (4815), to conceive, take, catch.

617. ἀποκυλίνδω *apokulíndō*, **ἀποκυλίω** *apokulíō* fut. *apokulísō*, from *apó* (575), from, and *kulíō* (2947), to roll about. To roll away (Matt 28:2; Mark 16:3, 4 [*anakulíō*, to roll up or back, in some MSS in v. 4]; Luke 24:2; Sept.: Gen 29:3, 8, 10).

618. ἀπολαμβάνω *apolambánō*; fut. *apolếpsomai*, 2d aor. *apélabon*, from *apó* (575), from, and *lambánō* (2983), to receive, take. To receive fully.

(I) To receive in full what is one's due, syn. with *apéchō* (568), to have in full (Luke 16:25). Also generally, to obtain (Gal 4:5; Sept.: Num 34:14).

(II) To receive back, obtain again, such as money (Luke 6:34; 15:27). Spoken of reward or retribution (Luke 18:30; 23:41; Rom 1:27; Col 3:24; 2 John 1:8).

(III) To take to oneself from another place or person, i.e., either to receive as a friend or guest (3 John 1:8) or to take aside (Mark 7:33).

Syn.: *déchomai* (1209), to receive, take; *prosdéchomai* (4327), to receive favorably; *apodéchomai* (588), to accept gladly; *ekdéchomai* (1551), to accept, expect; *hupodéchomai* (5264), to admit under one's roof, entertain hospitably; *paradéchomai* (3858), to accept near, admit; *hupolambánō* (5274), to take from below, carry upward, take up, assume; *paralambánō* (3880), to take unto; *proslambánō* (4355), to take to oneself, receive, take.

Ant.: *arnéomai* (720), to deny, renounce; *paraitéomai* (3868), to refuse; *apodokimázō* (593), to reject; *aporríptō* (641), to reject; *apostréphomai* (654), to turn away from; *apodokimázō* (593), to disapprove.

619. ἀπόλαυσις *apólausis*; gen. *apolaúseōs*, fem. noun from *apolaúō* (n.f.), to enjoy. It denotes the cleaving or adherence of the mind or affection to an object. Enjoyment.

(I) The act of enjoying (1 Tim 6:17).

(II) The source of enjoyment, advantage, profit, pleasure (Heb 11:25; Sept.: Ps 119:143).

Syn.: *euphrosúnē* (2167), joyfulness; *hēdoné* (2237), pleasure; *eudokía* (2107), good pleasure; *chará* (5479), joy; *cháris* (5485), grace.

Ant.: *anágkē* (318), distress; *thlípsis* (2347), suffering, tribulation; *lúpē* (3077), grief, sorrow; *odúnē* (3601), pain, distress; *ōdín* (5604), birth pang; *pénthos* (397), mourning; *stenochōría* (4730), distress; *báros* (922), burden, weight; *pónos* (4192), pain.

620. ἀπολείπω *apoleípō*; fut. *apoleípsō*, 2d aor. *apélipon*, from *apó* (575), from, and *leípō* (3007), to lack. To leave behind.

(I) Leave, leave behind, trans. (2 Tim 4:13, 20). Pass., to be left behind, remain (Sept.: Ex 14:28). Metaphorically in Heb 4:6, 9; 10:26, *apoleípetai*, "there remaineth."

(II) To desert, renounce (Jude 1:6; Sept.: Prov 2:17; 9:6).

Syn.: *aphíēmi* (863), to leave, forsake; *aníēmi* (447), to loosen, forbear, relieve; *kataleípō* (2641), to leave behind; *egkataleípō* (1459), to leave behind in; *hupoleípō* (5275), to leave remaining; *perileípō* (4035), to leave over, remain; *hupolimpánō* (5277), to leave.

Ant.: *lambánō* (2983), to take; *paralambánō* (3880), to receive; *proslambánō* (4355), to take to oneself; *aírō* (142) or *aphairéō* (851), to take away.

621. ἀπολείχω *apoleíchō*; fut. *apoleíxō*, from *apó* (575), from, and *leíchō* (n.f.), to lick. To lick off (Luke 16:21).

622. ἀπόλλυμι *apóllumi* or *apolúō*; fut. *apolésō*, 2d aor. *apōlómēn*, perf. *apolóleka*, 2d perf. *apólōla*, mid. fut. *apoloúmai*, from *apó* (575) an intens., the mid. *óllumi* (n.f.), to destroy. The force of *apó* here is away or wholly; therefore, the verb is stronger than the simple

óllumi. To destroy, mid. be destroyed, perish. Also from *óllumi* (n.f.): *ólethros* (3639), rain, destruction.

(I) Act. form:

(A) To destroy, cause to perish, trans.: **(1)** Spoken of things figuratively (1 Cor 1:19, meaning to bring to naught, render void the wisdom of the wise, quoted from Isa 29:14). **(2)** Of persons, to destroy, put to death, cause to perish. **(a)** Spoken of physical death (Matt 2:13; 12:14; 21:41; 22:7; Mark 3:6; 9:22; 11:18; 12:9; Luke 6:9 [TR]; 17:27, 29; 19:47; 20:16; John 10:10; Jude 1:5; Sept.: Gen 20:4; Deut 11:4; Esth 4:9; 9:16); in a judicial sense to sentence to death (Matt 27:20; James 4:12). **(b)** Spoken of eternal death, i.e., future punishment, exclusion from the Messiah's kingdom. In this sense it has the same meaning as *apothnḗskō* (599), to die (Matt 10:28; Mark 1:24; Luke 4:34; 9:56). This eternal death is called the second death (Rev 20:14). In Luke 9:25, to "destroy himself" (a.t.) means to subject himself to eternal death, which is the opposite of eternal life (John 6:50, 51, 58). Physical and eternal death are to be distinguished (John 8:21, 24; 11:25, 26; Rom 7:10; 8:13).

(B) To lose, be deprived of, trans. of such things as reward (Mark 9:41); a sheep (Luke 15:4); a drachma or coin (Luke 15:8, 9). See John 6:39; 2 John 1:8; Sept.: Prov 29:3. To lose one's life or soul (Matt 10:39; 16:25; Mark 8:35; Luke 9:24; 17:33; John 12:25).

(II) Mid. and pass. forms as also 2d perf. *apólōla*.

(A) To be destroyed, perish, intrans. Spoken of: **(1)** Things (Matt 5:29, 30; 9:17; Mark 2:22; Luke 5:37; John 6:27; James 1:11; 1 Pet 1:7). In all these instances the verb must not be thought of as indicating extinction, but only change from one state of being to another. Nothing actually becomes extinct, but everything changes. In Heb 1:11, "even these heavens will perish" (a.t.) quoted from Ps 102:27; Jer 9:11; 48:8; Ezek 29:8; 35:7, means that these present heavens will be qualitatively changed as well as the earth

(Rev 21:1). The new, redeemed creation and physically redeemed creatures, especially the presently redeemed men with their redeemed bodies, will have a congruous environment in which to live (Rom 8:19–23). (2) Persons, to be put to death, to die, perish, relating to physical death (Matt 8:25; 26:52; Mark 4:38; Luke 8:24; 11:51; 13:33; 15:17; John 18:14; Acts 5:37; 1 Cor 10:9, 10; 2 Cor 4:9; 2 Pet 3:6; Jude 1:11; Sept.: Lev 23:30; Esth 9:12). Relating to eternal death (see I, A, 2, b), to perish eternally, i.e., to be deprived of eternal life (Luke 13:3, 5; John 3:15, 16; 10:28; 17:12; Rom 2:12; 1 Cor 15:18; 2 Pet 3:9). Those who perish (*hoi apolluménoi*, who are perishing) means those who are exposed to eternal death (1 Cor 1:18; 2 Cor 2:15; 4:3; 2 Thess 2:10).

(B) To be lost to the owner, such as hair (Luke 21:18), anything (John 6:12). Spoken of those who wander away and are lost, e.g., the prodigal son (Luke 15:24); sheep straying in the desert (Luke 15:4, 6). Metaphorically (Matt 10:6; 15:24; Sept.: Ps 119:176; Jer 50:6; Ezek 34:4).

Deriv.: *Apollúōn* (623), destroyer; *apóleia* (684), destruction; *sunapóllumi* (4881), to destroy with.

Syn.: *katargéō* (2673), abolish; *kathairéō* (2507), to cast down; *lúō* (3089), to loose; *katalúō* (2647), to destroy utterly; *olothreúō* (2645), to destroy; *exolothreúō* (1842), to destroy utterly; *phtheírō* (5351), to corrupt; *porthéō* (4199), to ruin by laying waste, to make havoc; *thnḗskō* (2348), to die; *apothnḗskō* (599), to die off or out; *teleutáō* (5053), to end, to die; *apogínomai* (581), to die, to become something else.

Ant.: *auxánō* (837), to increase; *záō* (2198), to live; *zōogonéō* (2225), to become alive, quicken; *kerdaínō* (2770), to gain; *ōpheléō* (5623), to profit; *prokóptō* (4298), to advance.

623. Ἀπολλύων *Apollúōn*; gen. *Apollúonos*, masc. part. from *apóllumi* (622), to destroy, corrupt. The destroyer (Rev 9:11). A Greek name for the demon of the abyss (*ábussos* [12]). The Hebr. name is transliterated *Abaddṓn* (3).

Syn.: *olothreutḗs* (3644), a destroyer.

Ant.: *sōtḗr* (4990), savior.

624. Ἀπολλωνία *Apollōnía*; proper noun. Apollonia, meaning belonging to Apollo. A Greek city through which Paul passed (Acts 17:1). Apollonia is on the Egnatian Road between Philippi and Thessalonica in Macedonia, located about thirty-six miles east of Thessalonica and thirty miles southwest of Amphipolis.

625. Ἀπολλώς *Apollṓs*; proper noun. Apollos, one of John's disciples, born at Alexandria, Egypt, of Jewish parents, and described as an eloquent man and mighty in the Scriptures (Acts 18:24). He had been instructed in the elements of the Christian faith, but coming to Ephesus in A.D. 54, during the temporary absence of Paul, he was more fully taught the doctrines of the Gospel by Aquila and Priscilla. They had themselves been favored with the company and instruction of Paul at Corinth and on a voyage from that city to Ephesus. Apollos afterwards preached with great success in Achaia and Corinth. Paul had already been instrumental in establishing a church there, to the care of which Apollos succeeded (1 Cor 3:6). The members of the church in Corinth were divided into parties, some being particularly partial to Paul, others to Apollos, and still others to Cephas or Peter. When Paul wrote his first epistle to the Corinthians, probably at Ephesus in A.D. 57, it is likely Apollos was either with him or near him. From 1 Cor 16:12 we learn that in consequence of these dissensions, Apollos absolutely declined to go to Corinth. The contentions between the friends and admirers of Paul and those of Apollos had no effect on the two men's love and respect for each other. They both refrained from visiting the church while it was distracted with such prejudices and partialities, though a worldly ambition might have selected it as the field and the season of self-aggrandizement. Apollos is last mentioned very affectionately by Paul in Titus 3:13. Since Apollos was an extremely brilliant individual, some scholars attribute the authorship of the Epistle to the Hebrews to him.

626. ἀπολογέομαι *apologéomai*; contracted *apologoúmai*, fut. *apologḗsomai*, a mid. deponent from *apó* (575), from, and *lógos* (3056), speech. To defend or speak or plead for oneself before a tribunal or elsewhere (Luke 21:14; Acts 25:8; 26:1; Rom 2:15). Followed by a dat. of person (Acts 19:33; 2 Cor 12:19 meaning to or against whom). With *prós* (4314), toward someone (Sept.: Jer 12:1). Followed by *epí* (1909), before, and the gen. (Acts 26:2); by *perí* (4012), concerning, with an acc. implying manner (Luke 12:11; Acts 26:24).

    Deriv.: *anapológētos* (379), indefensible, inexcusable; *apología* (627), defense, answer.

    Syn.: *apokrínomai* (611), to give an answer to a question; *antapokrínomai* (470), to answer by contradiction; *antilégō* (483), to speak against; *apophthéggomai* (669), to speak forth.

    Ant.: *phimóō* (5392), to muzzle; *sigáō* (4601), to be silent; *siōpáō* (4623), to keep silent.

627. ἀπολογία *apología*; gen. *apologías*, fem. noun from *apologéomai* (626), to give an answer or speech in defense of oneself. A plea, defense before a tribunal or elsewhere (Acts 22:1; 2 Tim 4:16). Generally (2 Cor 7:11; Phil 1:7, 17). Followed by dat. of person, against whom (1 Cor 9:3; 1 Pet 3:15); by *perí* (4012), concerning, and the gen. (Acts 25:16); with *prós* (4314), toward, and the acc. (Acts 22:1).

    Syn.: *apókrisis* (612), the act of answering; *apókrima* (610), an answer, sentence; *eperṓtēma* (1906), an answer in the form of an interrogation.

    Ant.: *sigḗ* (4602), silence; *hēsuchía* (2271), quietness.

628. ἀπολούω *apoloúō*; fut. *apoloúsō*, from *apó* (575), from, and *loúō* (3068), to wash, bathe. To wash away. In the mid. *apoloúomai*, to wash oneself clean from, to be freed from sin. In Acts 22:16 it gives prominence to the cleansing from sin connected with salvation. The part. *epikalesámenos* (*epikaléomai* [1941], to call upon) which is translated "calling on," is not a pres. part. but is an aor. part. which, if taken as antecedent to the action of the main verb (an aor. part. used with an aor. main verb can denote either antecedent or contemporaneous action), places the calling upon the name of the Lord as prior to both baptism and washing away. Unfortunately, the KJV, NASB, and NIV translate it "calling on," instead of "having called" or "since you called upon" His name, or the name of the Lord (Majority Text). In 1 Cor 6:11, a confounding of the outward with the inward cleansing is guarded against by the use of *apeloúsasthe* "you were washed" (a.t.), instead of *ebaptísthēte* "you were baptized" (a.t.). The former to the inner cleansing of the heart coupled with "ye are sanctified . . . ye are justified in the name of the Lord Jesus." See Sept.: Job 9:30 (cf. Ps 51:4, 9; Isa 1:16; Jer 4:14).

    Syn.: *níptō* (3538), to wash part of the body; *aponíptō* (633), to wash off; *plúnō* (4150), to wash inanimate objects; *apoplúnō* (637) used of garments and figuratively; *rhantízō* (4472), to sprinkle; *bréchō* (1026), to wet; *baptízō* (907), to baptize.

    Ant.: *koinóō* (2840), to make common or unclean; *miaínō* (3392), to stain, defile; *molúnō* (3435), to besmear, soil, the latter not used in a ritual or ceremonial sense; *spilóō* (4695), to make a stain or spot, defile; *miaínō* (3392), to defile, pollute.

629. ἀπολύτρωσις *apolútrōsis*; gen. *apolutrṓseōs*, fem. noun from *apolutróō* (n.f.), to let go free for a ransom, which is from *apó* (575), from, and *lutróō* (3084), to redeem. Redemption. The recalling of captives (sinners) from captivity (sin) through the payment of a ransom for them, i.e., Christ's death. Sin is presented as slavery and sinners as slaves (John 8:34; Rom 6:17, 20; 2 Pet 2:19). Deliverance from sin is freedom (John 8:33, 36; Rom 8:21; Gal 5:1).

(I) Deliverance on account of the ransom paid as spoken of the deliverance from the power and consequences of sin which Christ procured by laying down His life as a ransom (lútron [3083]) for those who believe (Rom 3:24; 1 Cor 1:30; Eph 1:7, 14; Col 1:14; Heb 9:15 [cf. Matt 20:28; Acts 20:28]).

(II) Deliverance from calamities and death without the idea of a ransom being paid (Luke 21:28; Heb 11:35). So also of the soul from the body as its prison (Rom 8:23 at the coming of the Lord; Eph 4:30 [cf. Rom 7:24]).

Syn.: áphesis (859), remission, forgiveness; hilasmós (2434), propitiation; katallagé (2643), reconciliation, atonement.

Ant.: míasma (3393), defilement; miasmós (3394), the act of defiling; molusmós (3436), defilement.

630. ἀπολύω apolúō; fut. apolúsō; from apó (575), from, and lúō (3089), to loose. To let loose from, to loose or unbind a person or thing.

(I) To free from, relieve from, with the gen. of sickness (Luke 13:12).

(II) To release, let go free, set at liberty, such as a debtor (Matt 18:27) or persons accused or imprisoned (Matt 27:15; Mark 15:6; Luke 22:68; John 19:10; Acts 4:21; 26:32; 28:18). Metaphorically, to overlook, forgive (Luke 6:37).

(III) Spoken of a wife, to let go free, put away, dismiss, with the presupposition that the dismissed wife is innocent and, according to Deut 24:1–4, deserves a bill of divorcement which was equivalent to a certificate of innocence (Matt 5:31, 32; 19:3). So also of a husband in Mark 10:12. In the case of Matt 1:19 with Joseph wanting to dismiss Mary secretly, she was indeed not guilty of having had any relations with someone else, although in the mind of Joseph there was a suspicion. This the Lord made clear to him through an angelic message. The perf. pass. part. fem., apoleluménēn, in Matt 5:32 refers to an innocent, unjustifiably dismissed wife who, because she was not given a bill of divorcement, i.e., a certificate of innocence, had to bear the stigma of guilt as if she were an adulteress. Thus someone marrying her has adultery committed against himself (moichátai). The same is the case with apoleluménēn of Matt 19:9. This one is also an innocent, unjustifiably dismissed wife who carries on her the stigma of adultery because her dismissing husband did not give her a bill of divorcement. However, the same part. in Luke 16:18 refers to a guilty wife who unjustifiably dismissed herself from (apó [575]) her husband who did nothing to warrant this dismissal. Therefore, he who marries such a woman, a definite bearer of the guilt of adultery in unjustifiably dismissing her husband, commits adultery. The verb in Luke 16:18 is moicheúei, the act. pres. tense and not the mid. pass., moichátai, as in Matt 5:32.

(IV) To dismiss, simply to let go, send away, trans. (Matt 14:15, 22, 23; 15:32, 39; Luke 8:38; 9:12; 14:4; Acts 13:3; 15:30; 19:41; 23:22). Mid. apolúomai, to depart, go away (Acts 15:33; 28:25; Sept.: Ex 33:11).

(V) To dismiss from life, let depart, die, trans. (Luke 2:29; Sept.: Num 20:29).

Syn.: chōrízō (5563), to put apart, separate; apochōrízō (673), to separate off; diachōrízomai (1316), to be separated through or completely; analúō (360), to depart, unloose; aphístēmi (868), to cause to depart; aphíēmi (863), to send away; ápeimi (548), to go away; aniēmi (447), to let up, forbear.

Ant.: déō (1210), to bind; sundéō (4887), to unite together; desmeúō (1195), to bind together; suzeúgnumi (4801), to join together; sumbibázō (4822), to coalesce, to join or knit together; doulóō (1402), to bring into bondage.

631. ἀπομάσσω *apomássō*; fut. *apomáxō*, from *apó* (575), from, and *mássō* (n.f., see *ekmássō* [1591]), to wipe off. To wipe off. In Luke 10:11, to wipe the dust off from oneself.

Syn.: *exaleíphō* (1813), to wipe out or away.

632. ἀπονέμω *aponémō*; fut. *aponemṓ*, from *apó* (575), from, and *némō* (n.f., see below), to give, attribute. To allot, give, apportion, assign (Sept.: Deut 4:19). In the NT, to assign, bestow, trans. (1 Pet 3:7, assigning honor).

Deriv. of *némō* (n.f.), to give, attribute: *dianémō* (1268), to distribute throughout; *klēronómos* (2818), an heir, distributing the inheritance; *nómos* (3551), something parceled out, law; *oikonómos* (3623), an administrator.

Syn.: *merízō* (3307), to distribute; *dídōmi* (1325), to give; *apodídōmi* (591), to restore, to give what is due; *chorēgéō* (5524), supply, give.

Ant.: *aposteréō* (650), to defraud, deprive.

633. ἀπονίπτω *aponíptō*; fut. *aponípsō*, from *apó* (575), from, and *níptō* (3538), to wash. Mid. *aponíptomai*, to wash off oneself, the hands (Matt 27:24; Sept.: 1 Kgs 22:38; Prov 30:12). This was a symbolic action to signify one's innocence (Deut 21:6, 7).

Syn.: *loúō* (3068), to bathe, implying the whole body; *apoloúō* (628), to wash off; *katharízō* (2511), to cleanse; *kathaírō* (2508), to purge; *plúnō* (4150), to wash inanimate objects; *rhantízō* (4472), to sprinkle; *bréchō* (1026), to wet; *baptízō* (907), to baptize.

Ant.: *rhupóō* (4510), to soil; *molúnō* (3435), to defile; *spilóō* (4695), to spot; *miaínō* (3392), to defile, pollute.

634. ἀποπίπτω *apopíptō*; fut. *apopesoúmai*, 2d aor. *apépeson*, from *apó* (575), from, and *píptō* (4098), to fall. To fall off from (Acts 9:18; Sept.: Job 29:24).

Syn.: *rhíptomai* (4496), to throw oneself; *katabibázomai* (2601), to bring down; *hupostéllomai* (5288), to withhold under; *katágomai* (2609), to lead down.

Ant.: *anágō* (321), to bring up; *egeírō* (1453), to raise; *hupsóō* (5312), to lift up; *anabaínō* (305), to come up; *anabibázō* (307), to cause to go up; *aírō* (142), to take up; *apaírō* (522), to lift off; *epaírō* (1869), to raise up.

635. ἀποπλανάω *apoplanáō*; contracted *apoplanṓ*, fut. *apoplanḗsō*, from *apó* (575), from, and *planáō* (4105), to seduce. To lead astray from, seduce, deceive, draw aside from the right course (Mark 13:22; Sept.: Jer 50:6). Pass., to go astray from, swerve from (1 Tim 6:10; Sept.: Prov 7:21; 2 Chr 21:11).

Syn.: *astochéō* (795), to miss the mark, fail; *apágō* (520), to lead away; *ektrépō* (1624), to turn aside or out of the way; *emplékō* (1707), to entangle; *parapíptō* (3895), to fall aside; *deleázō* (1185), to entice; *apatáō* (538), to beguile, deceive; *paralogízomai* (3884), to deceive, delude.

Ant.: *cheiragōgéō* (5496), to lead by the hand; *poimaínō* (4165), to shepherd; *kateuthúnō* (2720), to guide, direct; *phōtízō* (5461), to enlighten; *hupodeíknumi* (5263), to admonish, warn.

636. ἀποπλέω *apopléō*; contracted *apoplṓ*, fut. mid. *apopleúsomai*, from *apó* (575), from, and *pléō* (4126), sail. To sail away, depart by ship, intrans. (Acts 13:4; 14:26; 20:15; 27:1).

Syn.: *anágō* (321), to lead up; *diaperáō* (1276), to cross over by ship (Acts 21:2).

Ant.: *déō* (1210), to bind, tie; *kathístēmi* (2525), to set, place down.

637. ἀποπλύνω *apoplúnō*; fut. *apoplunṓ*, from *apó* (575), from, and *plúnō* (4150), to wash out, to rinse. To wash nets (Luke 5:2; Sept.: 2 Sam 19:24; Ezek 16:9).

Syn.: *aponíptō* (633), to wash off; *apoloúō* (628), to wash off, implying the whole body.

Ant.: *rhupóō* (4510), to soil; *koinóō* (2840), to profane, make unclean; *molúnō* (3435), to defile; *bebēlóō* (953), to desecrate; *spilóō* (4695), to spot; *miaínō* (3392), to defile, pollute.

638. ἀποπνίγω apopnígō; fut. *apopníxō*, from *apó* (575), an intens., and *pnígō* (4155), to choke. To choke or suffocate (Matt 13:7; Luke 8:7, 33). In these first two passages it is applied to plants choked by thorns. One must remember that all trees and plants owe their vegetation and life to the element of air.

Syn.: *nekróō* (3499), to deaden; *ekpnéō* (1606), to expire; *thanatóō* (2289), to put to death.

Ant.: *zōopoiéō* (2227), to make alive; *zōogonéō* (2225), to preserve.

639. ἀπορέω aporéō; contracted *aporō̂*, fut. *aporḗsō*, mid. / pass. *aporéomai*, from *áporos* (n.f.), without resource. Figuratively, to doubt, hesitate, be perplexed, not knowing how to proceed, determine, speak or act (John 13:22; Acts 25:20; 2 Cor 4:8; Gal 4:20; Sept.: Gen 32:8; Jer 8:18).

Deriv.: *aporía* (640), perplexity; *diaporéō* (1280), to be thoroughly perplexed; *exaporéomai* (1820), to despair.

Syn.: *distázō* (1365), to hesitate; *meteōrízomai* (3349), to be like a meteor, hang in the air; *diakrínō* (1252), to waver; *exístēmi* (1839), to become astounded, astonished; *peripíptō* (4045), to fall around not knowing where one is; *periágomai* (4013), to walk around without any direction.

Ant.: *peíthō* (3982), to assure; *bebaióō* (950), to confirm; *pistóō* (4104), to assure; *pisteúō* (4100), to believe; *paradéchomai* (3858), to admit; *dokéō* (1380), to recognize, think; *stērízō* (4741), to confirm one's mind; *themelióō* (2311), to establish.

640. ἀπορία aporía; gen. *aporías*, fem. noun from *aporéō* (639), to be perplexed. Perplexity (Luke 21:25), uncertain dis-

quiet, as to an event (Sept.: Lev 26:16; Isa 8:22).

Syn.: *dialogismós* (1261), questioning hesitation.

Ant.: *pepoíthēsis* (4006), confidence, trust; *pístis* (4102), faith, conviction, assurance; *bebaíōsis* (951), confirmation, assurance; *ékbasis* (1545), a way out, exit; *dógma* (1378), doctrine, something that one can believe in; *thársos* (2294), boldness, courage.

641. ἀπορρίπτω aporríptō; fut. *aporrípsō*, from *apó* (575), from, and *rhíptō* (4496), to cast. To cast off or out, to cast aside (Acts 27:43). With the reflexive pron. implied (*heautoús* [1438], themselves) it means throwing or letting themselves off or down from the ship into the water (Sept.: Ex 22:31).

Syn.: *ekpíptō* (1601), to cast; *apobállō* (577), to throw off from; *ekbállō* (1544), to cast out from; *apōthéō* (683), to thrust away; *apotíthēmi* (659), to put off.

Ant.: *eklégō* (1586), to choose; *epilégomai* (1951), to select, choose; *proorízō* (4309), to determine before, ordain; *proairéomai* (4255), to choose for oneself before another thing.

642. ἀπορφανίζω aporphanízō; fut. *aporphanísō*, mid./pass. *aporphanízomai*, from *apó* (575), from, and *orphanós* (3737), an orphan. To bereave of parents. In 1 Thess 2:17, as disciples deprived of a teacher, as children bereaved of their father, helpless.

Syn.: *apochōrízō* (673), to separate; *egkataleípō* (1459), to leave behind.

Ant.: *huiothesía* (5206), adoption (subst.).

643. ἀποσκευάζω aposkeuázō; fut. *aposkeuásō*, mid. / pass. *aposkeuázomai*; from *apó* (575), from, and *skeuázō* (n.f., see *anaskeuázō* [384]), to prepare. In the mid. literally to divest oneself of baggage, to remove, put out of the way (Acts 21:15; Sept.: Lev 14:36). To divest oneself of baggage, perhaps leaving part of it behind for the sake of greater speed. The above *aposkeuasámenoi* is in the TR while in the WH, the Majority Text and the UBS it is *episkeuasámenoi*, which is entirely the opposite from the verb *episkeuázō* which means to furnish with things necessary, and in the mid. voice, *episkeuázomai*, to furnish for oneself, used of equipping beasts of burden for a journey. In such a case it should be translated "we took our baggage" instead of "we left our baggage behind."

644. ἀποσκίασμα *aposkíasma*; gen. *aposkiásmatos*, neut. noun from *apó* (575), from, and *skiázō* (n.f., see below), to shade. Metaphorically, the slightest trace, or degree (James 1:17).
   Deriv. of *skiázō* (n.f.): *episkiázō* (1982), to cast a shadow upon; *kataskiázō* (2683), to throw a shadow upon.

645. ἀποσπάω *apospáō*; contracted *apospṓ*; fut. *apospásō*, from *apó* (575), from, and *spáō* (4685), to draw or pull. To draw from or out as a sword from its sheath (Matt 26:51). Spoken of persons, to draw away disciples from another to oneself (Acts 20:30). In the pass. to be withdrawn, retire, to depart, go away (Luke 22:41; Acts 21:1).
   Syn.: *anachōréō* (402), to withdraw, depart; *aphístēmi* (868), to withdraw oneself; *chōrízō* (5563), to separate; *apochōrízō* (673), to separate from; *diairéō* (1244), to separate, divide; *merízō* (3307), to divide; *aphairéō* (851), to cut off, take away; *apokóptō* (609), to cut off.
   Ant.: *sundéō* (4887), to bind together; *súneimi* (4896), to assemble, gather together; *proskolláō* (4347), to join together, glue together; *sunéchō* (4912), to hold together.

646. ἀποστασία *apostasía*; gen. *apostasías*, fem. noun from *aphístēmi* (868), to depart. Departure, apostasy. Occurs in Acts 21:21 translated "forsake" and in 2 Thess 2:3, "a falling away"; Sept.: 2 Chr 29:19; Jer 29:32. In Acts 21:21 the new Christian believers among the Jews, having departed from Moses and coming

to Jesus Christ, decided that they should stay apart from Moses, i.e., their Judaistic practices, for they were in a new dispensation. They were not Judaizing Christians, but Christians standing apart from Moses. In 2 Thess 2:3 the word *apostasía* does not refer to genuine Christians who depart from the faith, but mere professors who, without divine grace, succumb to the Satanic deception of the Antichrist. If those who are truly Christ's and through the Holy Spirit have become members of His body (1 Cor 12:13) could be detached, then the assurances Jesus gave that His own will not perish would be made null and void (John 10:28, 29). See Sept.: 2 Chr 29:19.

647. ἀποστάσιον *apostásion*; gen. *apostasíou*, neut. noun from *aphístēmi* (868), to depart or stand away from. A departure, a divorce or dismissal of a woman from her husband, the deed or instrument of such divorce (Matt 5:31; see also 19:7). In Mark 10:4, *biblíon* (975), a book or document, *apostasíou*, of dismissal. This is a reference to the document spoken about in Deut 24:1–4 which the dismissing husband was required to give to an innocent, dismissed wife in whom the husband was finding a pretext for dismissal. It is equivalent to a certificate of innocence because the husband who was instructed to issue it in divorcing his guiltless wife and sending her away from his house was, in fact, the guilty person. If the woman had committed fornication, she would have been dismissed and never permitted to remarry as this woman was: "And when she is departed out of his house, she may go and be another man's wife" (Deut 24:2). In fact, the guilty dismissed spouse (see Deut 22:21) was to be stoned to death which was rarely, if ever, practiced. The teaching of our Lord was that, although contrary to God's will and purpose, if a man decided to put away his wife or a wife her husband (Mark 10:12), the innocent spouse was to be given a bill of divorcement or a certificate of innocence which would free him or her of the stigma of being considered as having committed adultery. The word "divorce" as understood in our modern society and which is issued by a judge without reference to the guilt or innocence of either party, does not have its real equivalent in the OT or NT. The *apostásion*, then, was supposed to be given by a guilty husband to an innocent wife, or vice versa (Mark 10:12), whom he or she wanted to dismiss, since it was through such a certificate of innocence that the dismissed one had the possibility of remarrying. The teaching of our Lord in Matt 5:32; 19:3–12; Mark 10:2–12, is that a woman dismissed without a bill of divorcement carries the stigma of adultery, and if someone marries her, that stigma passes on to him. This is conveyed by the mid. / pass. verb *moichátai* (Matt 5:32; 19:9; Mark 10:12).

648. ἀποστεγάζω *apostegázō*; fut. *apostegásō*, from *apó* (575), from, and *stegázō* (n.f.), to cover. To uncover, remove a covering as in Mark 2:4 in which we find *apestégasan tēn stégēn* (*stégē* [4721], roof), "they unroofed the roof" (a.t.), or "they opened the trap door" (a.t.) which used to be on the top of the flat-roofed houses in Judea (2 Kgs 1:2; Deut 22:8) and which, lying even with the roof, was a part of it when it was let down and shut.

Syn.: *apokalúptō* (601), to take off the cover.

Ant.: *kalúptō* (2572), to cover; *epikalúptō* (1943), to cover up or over; *perikalúptō* (4028), to cover around; *sugkalúptō* (4780), to cover completely; *katakalúptō* (2619), to cover up completely; *stégō* (4722), to cover with, roof over.

649. ἀποστέλλω *apostéllō*; fut. *apostelō*, aor. *apésteila*, 2d aor. *apestálēn*, perf. *apéstalka*, perf. pass. *apéstalmai*, from *apó* (575), from, and *stéllō* (4724), to withdraw from, avoid. To send off, forth, out. Distinguished from *pémpō* (3992), to send, in that *apostéllō* is to send forth on a certain mission such as to preach (Mark 3:14; Luke 9:2); speak (Luke 1:19);

bless (Acts 3:26); rule, redeem, propitiate (Acts 7:35; 1 John 4:10); save (1 John 4:14). The expression that Jesus was sent by God (John 3:34) denotes the mission which He had to fulfill and the authority which backed Him. The importance of this mission is denoted by the fact that God sent His own Son. In the NT, to send forth from one place to another, to send upon some business or employment (Matt 2:16; 10:5; 20:2); to send away, dismiss (Mark 12:3, 4); to send or thrust forth as a sickle among corn (Mark 4:29). Other references: Matt 10:16, 40; 11:10; 13:41; 14:35; 15:24; 21:1, 3, 34, 36, 37; 22:3, 4, 16; 23:34, 37; 24:31; 27:19; Mark 1:2; 3:31; 5:10; 6:7, 17, 27; 8:26; 9:37; 11:1, 3; 12:2, 5, 6, 13; 13:27; 14:13; Luke 1:26; 4:18, 43; 7:3, 20, 27; 9:48, 52; 10:1, 3, 16; 11:49; 13:34; 14:17, 32; 19:14, 29, 32; 20:10, 20; 22:8, 35; 24:49; John 1:6, 19, 24; 3:17, 28; 4:38; 5:33, 36, 38; 6:29, 57; 7:29, 32; 8:42; 9:7; 10:36; 11:3, 42; 17:3, 8, 18, 21, 23, 25; 18:24; 20:21; Acts 3:20; 5:21; 7:14, 34; 8:14; 9:38; 10:8, 17, 20, 21, 36; 11:11, 13, 30; 13:15, 26; 15:27; 16:35, 36; 19:22; 26:17; 28:28; Rom 10:15; 1 Cor 1:17; 2 Cor 12:17; 2 Tim 4:12; Heb 1:14; 1 Pet 1:12; 1 John 4:9; Rev 1:1; 5:6; 22:6; Sept.: Gen 31:4; 32:3; 41:8, 14; Ex 4:28; 9:15, 28; Lev 25:21; Josh 24:9.

This word is to be distinguished from *pémpō* (3992), to send, a more general term than *apostéllō*. The two terms, however, are used interchangeably and yet the distinction is discernible in passages such as John 5:23, 24, 30, 37 where the word used is *pémpō* (cf. with John 5:33, 36, 38 where the word *apostéllō* is used). *Pémpō* is also used in John 6:38, 39, 40, 44 and *apostéllō* in 6:29, 57. In John 17, *apostéllō* is used six times, while *pémpō* is not used at all in this high priestly prayer of Christ.

Deriv.: *apostolē* (651), dispatching or sending forth; *apóstolos* (652), one sent, apostle, ambassador; *exapostéllō* (1821), to send away, forth; *sunapostéllō* (4882), to send along with.

Syn.: *ekbállō* (1544), to send out; *apotássomai* (657), to send forth; *ekpémpō* (1599), to send forth; *pémpō* (3992), to send.

Ant.: *kaléō* (2564), to call; *proskaléomai* (4341), to summon, invite.

650. ἀποστερέω *aposteréō*; contracted *aposterṓ*; fut. *aposterḗsō*, from *apó* (575), from, and *steréō* (4732), to deprive. To deprive, wrong, or defraud another of what belongs to him (Mark 10:19; 1 Cor 6:8; 7:5; Sept.: Ex 21:10). In the mid., *aposteréomai*, to suffer oneself to be defrauded, as spoken of persons (1 Cor 6:7); to be kept back by fraud, as spoken of a thing (James 5:4, wages held back by fraud; Sept.: Deut 24:16; Mal 3:5). The pass. joined with a gen., to be destitute of, devoid of (1 Tim 6:5, "defrauding themselves" [a.t.], i.e., "destitute of the truth" [cf. 1 Cor 7:5 in respect to conjugal intercourse]).

Deriv.: *aphusteréō*, used in some MSS in James 5:4 instead of *aposteréō*.

Syn.: *aporphanízomai* (642), to be rendered an orphan, bereaved of the company of; *pleonektéō* (4122), to defraud, take advantage of; *leípō* (3007), to leave, forsake; *elattonéō* (1641), to be less.

Ant.: *katéchō* (2722), to hold fast; *ktáomai* (2932), to acquire; *hupárchō* (5225), to be or to have; *apolambánō* (618), to receive.

651. ἀποστολή *apostolḗ*; gen. *apostolḗs*, fem. noun from *apostéllō* (649), to send. Dispatching or sending forth, also that which is sent, e.g., a present. In the NT, apostleship (Acts 1:25; Rom 1:5; 1 Cor 9:2; Gal 2:8).

Syn.: *presbeía* (4242), persons sent as ambassadors.

652. ἀπόστολος *apóstolos*; gen. *apostólou*, masc. noun from *apostéllō* (649), to send. Used as a subst., one sent, apostle, ambassador. Sometimes used syn. with *presbeutḗs*, ambassador, related to *presbeúō* (4243), to act as an ambassador (2 Cor 5:20; Eph 6:20). The messenger or ambassador (Phil 2:25 [see also 4:18]) can never be greater than the one who sends him (John 13:16; Sept.: 1 Kgs 14:6). The Lord chose the term *apóstoloi* to indicate the distinctive relation of the Twelve Apostles whom He chose to be His witnesses because in Class. Gr. the word was seldom used (Luke 6:13; Acts 1:2, 26). Therefore, it designates the office as instituted by Christ to witness of Him before the world (John 17:18). It also designates the authority which those called to this office possess. See the verb *apostéllō* in Rom 10:15. Paul combines both these meanings (Rom 1:1; 11:13; 1 Cor 1:1; 9:1, 2; 15:9; 2 Cor 1:1; 12:12; Gal 1:1). It was the distinctive name of the Twelve Apostles originally (Matt 10:2; Luke 6:13; 9:10; 22:14; Rev 21:14) or the eleven later, with whom Paul himself was reckoned, as he says in 1 Cor 15:7, 9; Acts 1:26. Paul justified his being counted as an apostle by the fact that he had been called to the office by Christ Himself.

However, the denomination seems from the very beginning to have been applied, in a much wider sense, to all who ministered as colleagues of the Twelve and bore witness of Christ (Acts 14:4, 14 of Paul and Barnabas; 15:2; Rom 16:7 of Andronicus and Junias; 2 Cor 8:23) and even by Paul (2 Cor 11:13; 1 Thess 2:6). This general meaning of the word held its place alongside its special and distinctive application.

There is no continuity of the office of an apostle since in no place were the churches instructed to ordain apostles.

The term is applied to Christ once in Heb 3:1 who was sent by the Father into the world, not to condemn it but to save it (John 3:17; 17:3, 8, 21, 23; 20:21).

In Corinth there were what Paul calls *hoi huperlían apóstoloi* (2 Cor 11:5; 12:11), translated "the very chiefest apostles." The adj. *huperlían* derives from the prep. *hupér* (5228), more, beyond, super, above, and the adv. *lían* (3029), exceedingly. These were those who claimed to be exceedingly above the other apostles whose words, they insisted, should be heard above the authentic apostolic teaching.

Other references: Mark 6:30; Luke 11:49; 17:5; 24:10; Acts 2:37, 42, 43; 4:33, 35–37; 5:2, 12, 18, 29, 34, 40; 6:6; 8:1, 14, 18; 9:27; 11:1; 15:4, 6, 22, 23, 33; 16:4; Rom 11:13; 16:7; 1 Cor 4:9; 9:5; 12:28, 29; Gal 1:17, 19; Eph 1:1; 2:20; 3:5; 4:11; Col 1:1; 1 Tim 1:1; 2:7; 2 Tim 1:1, 11; Titus 1:1; 1 Pet 1:1; 2 Pet 1:1; 3:2; Rev 2:2; 18:20.

Deriv.: *pseudapóstolos* (5570), a false apostle.

Syn.: *ággelos* (32), a messenger, an angel.

653. ἀποστοματίζω *apostomatízō*; fut. *apostomatísō*, from *apó* (575), from, and *stóma* (4750), mouth. To draw or force words, as it were, from the mouth of another, to incite or provoke to speak, to question as in a court (Luke 11:53, to prepare questions to be answered off-hand, to ensnare by questions).

Syn.: *prokaléō* (4292), to call forth.

Ant.: *apologéomai* (625), to make a defense, speak in behalf of someone.

654. ἀποστρέφω *apostréphō*; fut. *apostrépsō*, from *apó* (575), from or back again, and *stréphō* (4762), to turn. To turn away from (Luke 23:14, turning away the people from Caesar, i.e., exciting to rebellion [Sept.: Job 33:17]; Acts 3:26; Rom 11:26, "to put away . . . from" [a.t.], to remove [quoted from Isa 59:20]; 2 Tim 4:4, "to turn away the ears from the truth" [a.t.]; Sept.: Josh 22:16, 18; Job 33:17; Prov 4:27); to return, put back (Matt 26:52); to return, bring back (Matt 27:3; Sept.: Gen 24:5, 6; 28:15); in the pass., *apostréphomai* with an acc. following, to turn or be turned away from, to reject (Matt 5:42, refuse; 2 Tim 1:15, to forsake, desert [Sept.: Jer 15:6]; Titus 1:14; Heb 12:25; Sept.: Hos 8:3; Zech 10:6).

Syn.: *apotíthēmi* (659), to put away; *apōthéō* (683), to thrust away; *apobaínō* (576), to turn out, to go; *metatíthēmi* (3346), to change, remove; *ektrépō*

(1624), to cause to turn aside; *apotrépō* (665), to cause to turn away; *ekklínō* (1578), to turn aside; *anachōréō* (402), to withdraw; *apéchomai* (567), to hold oneself off, refrain; *bdelússomai* (948), to detest, abhor.

Ant.: *sumpathéō* (4834), to feel sympathy.

655. ἀποστυγέω *apostugéō*; contracted *apostugṓ*; fut. *apostugḗsō*, from *apó* (575), from, or an intens., and *stugéō* (n.f., see below), to hate. To hate, abhor, detest with horror (Rom 12:9).

Deriv. of *stugéō* (n.f.): *theostugḗs* (2319), haters of God; *stugētós* (4767) hateful, detestable.

Syn.: *apostréphomai* (654), to turn away from; *apotrépō* (665), to deflect; *apophérō* (667), to bear off; *apéchomai* (567), to hold oneself off, refrain; *bdelússomai* (948), to abhor, detest; *phríssō* (5425), to shudder; *apōthéomai* (683), to push off.

Ant.: *sumpathéō* (4834), to have compassion, be touched with the feeling of.

656. ἀποσυνάγωγος *aposunágōgos*; gen. *aposunagṓgou*, masc.-fem., neut. *aposunágōgon*, adj. from *apó* (575), from, and *sunagōgḗ* (4864), synagogue. Separated from the synagogue, excommunicated. Only in John 9:22; 12:42; 16:2. There were three degrees of excommunication or banishment among the Jews. The first was only a temporary exclusion from the congregation and a restriction against communication with others for thirty days. The second step was an exclusion from the congregation and from all communication with others for an indefinite period or forever. John 16:2, in particular, hardly allows us to suppose a mere temporary exclusion such as the first step involved, which might be proposed and even decreed for the rejected person, without consultation with the Sanhedrin. This did not necessarily mean exclusion from attendance on and participation in the synagogue worship, but exclusion from the fellowship of the congregation and their blessings and privileges. The third was a perpetual exclusion from all rights and privileges of the Jewish people both civil and religious. Thus *aposunágōgos* denotes one who has been excommunicated from the commonwealth of the people of God and is given over to the curse. See Luke 6:22 where it uses the term *aphorízō* (873), to put out of bounds or to excommunicate.

Syn.: *apóblētos* (579), a rejected or cast off one.

Ant.: *dókimos* (1384), approved.

657. ἀποτάσσω *apotássō*, **ἀποτάττω** *apotáttō*; fut. *apottáxō*, from *apó* (575), from, and *tássō* (5021), to place in order. To assign to different places, allot. In the NT, only in the mid. meaning to take leave of, bid farewell; to dismiss, forsake, or renounce. Translated "forsaketh" in Luke 14:33 and carries the notion of putting something aside (perhaps in its correct priority) to prevent it from being a hindrance or gaining excessive control. In Luke 9:61 the man who expressed the desire to follow Jesus wanted first to see that his own family was well cared for. Jesus knew that by the time he did that, he would have forgotten his promise to Him. In other references it means separating oneself from others, places, or things (Mark 6:46; Acts 18:18, 21; 2 Cor 2:13).

Syn.: *kataleípō* (2641), to leave behind; *egkataleípō* (1459), to abandon, leave; *aphíēmi* (863), to leave, forsake; *aníēmi* (447), to let go, to go up; *apoleípō* (620), to leave behind; *apaspázomai* in Acts 21:6 (UBS) and *aspázomai* (782 [TR]) to enfold in the arms, embrace, take leave.

Ant.: *analambánō* (353), to take up; *apolambánō* (618), to receive; *paralambánō* (3880), to take to oneself; *proslambánō* (4355), to receive; *prosdéchomai* (4327), to receive favorably; *eudokéō* (2106), to approve, approbate; *paradéchomai* (3858), to receive with delight; *homologéō* (3670), to assent, confess.

658. ἀποτελέω *apoteléō*; contracted *apotelō*; fut. *apotelésō*, from *apó* (575), an intens., and *teléō* (5055), to complete. To perfect, accomplish, achieve the natural purpose as in James 1:15, to be of full stature.

Syn.: *gínomai* (1096), to become; *katergázomai* (2716), to perform; *teleióō* (5048), to complete, fulfill; *ekteléō* (1615), to finish out; *epiteléō* (2005), to bring through to another end; *sunteléō* (4931), to bring to fulfillment; *dianúō* (1274), to finish a journey or life; *teleutáō* (5053), to finish life; *kleíō* (2808), to shut; *sumplēróō* (4845), to accomplish, fill up, fully come; *katartízō* (2675), to repair, complete, make fit.

Ant.: *árchomai* (756), to commence, begin; *epilambánomai* (1949), to take charge, take hold of; *epicheiréō* (2021), to put the hand upon, undertake.

659. ἀποτίθημι *apotíthēmi*; fut. *apothḗsō*, from *apó* (575), from, and *títhēmi* (5087), to lay. Used in the NT only in the middle voice, *apotíthemai*. To renounce, lay off or down (Acts 7:58; Sept.: Ex 16:33, 34; Lev 16:23). To lay aside, put off in a figurative sense (Rom 13:12, "cast off the works of darkness"; Eph 4:22, 25; Col 3:8; Heb 12:1; James 1:21; 1 Pet 2:1).

Deriv.: *apóthesis* (595), a laying aside; *apothḗkē* (596), barn, garner.

Syn.: *apobállō* (577), to throw off from, lay aside, cast away; *ekbállō* (1544), to cast out of, from, forth; *aporríptō* (641), to cast off; *apōthéomai* (683), to thrust away; *apókeimai* (606), to be laid away or up; *apolúō* (630), to let go; *aphíēmi* (863), to send away; *katargéō* (2673), to put away; *apekdúō* (554), to strip off clothes or arms.

Ant.: *títhēmi* (5087), to place; *embállō* (1685), to cast into; *eiságō* (1521), to bring in; *paratíthēmi* (3908), to put forth, set before; *parabállō* (3846), to throw alongside; *tássō* (5021), to place in order; *diatássō* (1299), to arrange thoroughly; *apokathístēmi* (600), to reconstitute, restore; *thēsarízō* (2343), to lay up or store up.

660. ἀποτινάσσω *apotinássō*; fut. *apotináxō*, from *apó* (575), from, and *tinássō* (n.f.), to shake loose or free. To shake off (Luke 9:5; Acts 28:5; Sept.: 1 Sam 10:2; Lam 2:7). Also from *tinássō* (n.f.): *ektinássō* (1621), to shake off.
Ant.: *stereóō* (4732), to make strong, establish.

661. ἀποτίνω *apotínō*, **ἀποτίω** *apotíō* fut. *apotísō*, from *apó* (575), again, and *tínō* (5099), to pay. To pay off, repay, make good (Phile 1:19; Sept.: Ex 21:19; 22:17; Lev 24:18).
Syn.: *apodídōmi* (591), to give back, repay; *antapodídōmi* (467), to give in return for, recompense; *antimetréō* (488), to mete out in return.
Ant.: *hysteréō* (5302), to be in want; *leípō* (3007), to be wanting, lacking.

662. ἀποτολμάω *apotolmáō*; contracted *apotolmṓ*; fut. *apotolmḗsō*, from *apó* (575), an intens., and *tolmáō* (5111), to dare. To dare very much, be very bold (Rom 10:20), to speak out boldly, boldly declare.
Syn.: *tharréō* (2292), to be bold, courageous; *parrēsiázomai* (3955), to speak boldly.
Ant.: *phobéomai* (5399), to be afraid; *sunéchomai* (4912), to be restrained; *trémō* (5141), to tremble; *ptoéomai* (4422), to be frightened or scared; *sustéllomai* (4958), to draw together, be afraid; *phríssō* (5425), to shudder.

663. ἀποτομία *apotomía*; gen. *apotomías*, fem. noun from *apotémnō* (n.f.), to cut off. A cutting off, severing, as of a man cutting off dead or useless boughs from a fruit tree (Rom 11:22 [cf. Rom 11:19, 20, 24]). Also from *apotémnō* (n.f.): *apotómōs* (664), severely, abruptly.
Syn.: *apheidía* (857), severity, austerity; *sklērótēs* (4643), hardness.

Ant.: *chrēstótēs* (5544), goodness, kindness; *philanthrōpía* (5363), the love shown toward men; *epieíkeia* (1932), gentleness, toleration; *praütēs* (4240), meekness, clemency.

664. ἀποτόμως *apotómōs*; adv. from *apotémnō* (n.f.), to cut off. Severely, abruptly, curtly, in a manner that cuts, cutting off (2 Cor 13:10 [cf. 1 Cor 5:1–5; Titus 1:13]). Also from *apotémnō* (n.f.): *apotomía* (663), a cutting off.
Syn.: *exaíphnēs* (1810), unexpectedly.

665. ἀποτρέπω *apotrépō*; fut. *apotrépsō*, from *apó* (575), from, and *trépō* (n.f., see *anatrépō* [396]), to turn. In the mid. *apotrépomai*, to turn away from, avoid, shun (2 Tim 3:5).
Syn.: *apostréphō* (654), to cause to turn away, remove; *methístēmi* (3179), to turn away; *ekklínō* (1578), to turn aside; *apōthéō* (683), to push off.
Ant.: *helkúō* (1670), to draw; *súrō* (4951), to drag, draw.

666. ἀπουσία *apousía*; gen. *apousías*, fem. noun from *ápeimi* (548), to be absent. Absence (Phil 2:12).
Ant.: *parousía* (3952), presence, coming.

667. ἀποφέρω *apophérō*; fut. *apoísō*, aor. *apḗnegka*, aor. pass. *apēnéchthēn*, 2d aor. *apḗnegkon*, from *apó* (575), from, and *phérō* (5342), to carry, bear. To carry away (Mark 15:1; Luke 16:22; 1 Cor 16:3; Rev 17:3; 21:10; Sept.: 2 Chr 36:7; Job 21:32; Hos 10:6).
Syn.: *apágō* (520), to bring forth; *apokuéō* (616), to bring forth; *gennáō* (1080), to beget, bring forth; *ekkomízō* (1580), to carry out; *aírō* (142), to carry away.
Ant.: *phérō* (5342), to bear, carry, bring; *komízō* (2865), to receive, bring in.

668. ἀποφεύγω *apopheúgō*; fut. *apopheúxō*, from *apó* (575), from, and *pheúgō* (5343), to flee. To flee away from, escape (2 Pet 1:4; 2:18, 20).

Syn.: *diapheúgō* (1309), to flee through; *exérchomai* (1831), to come or go out of a place; *apotrépō* (665), to avoid, turn away.

Ant.: *ekzētéō* (1567), to search out; *zētéō* (2212), to seek; *agreúō* (64), to entrap, catch; *halieúō* (232), to fish; *thēreúō* (2340), to hunt; *diasṓzō* (1295), to bring safely.

669. ἀποφθέγγομαι *apophthéggomai*; fut. *apophthégxomai*, from *apó* (575), from, and *phthéggomai* (5350), to utter. To utter, declare, speak, particularly pithy and remarkable sayings (Acts 2:4, 14; 26:25; Sept.: 1 Chr 25:1; Ezek 13:9). This is the verb used to indicate the discernable utterance of the "other tongues" in which the Holy Spirit enabled the believers to speak at Pentecost. Acts 2:4 says, "as the Spirit gave them utterance." The word "utterance" is the inf. *apophthéggesthai*, to form the sounds of the words. They were the sounds of known dialects (Acts 2:6, 8) understood by the people present. Therefore, the "other tongues" that the Holy Spirit enabled the believers to speak at Pentecost were meaningful words and not something which could not be understood. They were not incoherent babblings resulting from a state of ecstasy, but they were deliberate, understandable words energized directly by the Holy Spirit. They were entirely different from *glóssa* (1100), the unknown tongue (in the sing.), practiced among the Corinthians (1 Cor 14:2, 4, 13, 19, 26, 27). In the Corinthian context, whenever the word *glóssa*, tongue, is in the pl. with a sing. personal pron., *glóssai*, it means languages (1 Cor 14:5, 6, 18, 22, 23), even as in Acts 2:4. The verb *apophthéggomai*, to utter intelligible and meaningful words, is used also in Acts 2:14 when Peter preached to those present in the upper room. In Acts 2:14 *apephthégxato* is translated "said" while in Acts 2:4 *apophthéggesthai* is translated "gave them utterance." That the verb refers to meaningful speech is made clear

in Acts 26:25 in Paul's comments to Festus who thought Paul to be mad because of his boldness: "I am not mad . . . but speak [*apophthéggomai*] forth the words of truth and soberness."

Syn.: *légō* (3004), to speak; *phēmí* (5346), to declare, usually used in quoting the words of another; *eréō* (2046), to speak; *prosphōnéō* (4377), to call or address to; *dialégomai* (1256), to discuss, reason; *apologéomai* (626), to make a defense in answer to; *anaggéllō* (312), to declare; *laléō* (2980), to say, to break silence, repeat words or sounds.

Ant.: *siōpáō* (4623), to hush, to maintain silence; *sigáō* (4601), to refuse to speak; *lanthánomai* (2990), to lie hid, to escape attention.

670. ἀποφορτίζομαι *apophortízomai*; fut. *apophortísomai*, mid. deponent from *apó* (575), from, and *phortízō* (5412), to load. To unload, a ship (Acts 21:3).

Syn.: *kenóō* (2758), to empty.

Ant.: *gémō* (1073), to make full; *epitíthēmi* (2007), to lay upon.

671.   ἀπόχρησις *apóchrēsis*; gen. *apochrēseōs*, fem. noun from *apochráomai* (n.f.), to use up completely, consume by use, to use, which is from *apó* (575), from, and *chráomai* (5530), to use. Consumption in full (Col 2:22 [cf. Mark 7:18, 19; 1 Cor 6:13]). *Apóchrēsis* is not mere "using" as some versions render the word (e.g., Col 2:22 KJV). Using or use is *chrēsis*. *Apóchrēsis* is using up something so that nothing remains, complete consumption. There were, at the time Paul wrote to the Colossians, men's ordinances against certain foods (Col 2:20), and it was commonly being said, "Touch not; taste not; handle not" (Col 2:21). And then Paul expounds upon these things, "which all are for the purpose of consumption [*eis* {1519}, unto, for the purpose of; *phthorá* {5356}, corruption or consumption] by using them up [*tē apochrḗsei*]" (a.t.). Food, therefore, is for the purpose of using until it is consumed (see John 6:27). Paul teaches that we should not allow the commandments and doctrines of men (*entálmata* [1778], humanly instituted religious injunctions) to hinder us from using food which God has provided.

Ant.: *apéchō* (568), to abstain.

672. ἀποχωρέω apochōréō; contracted *apochōró*; fut. *apochōrḗsō*, from *apó* (575), from, and *chōréō* (5562), to go. Used intrans. meaning to depart, go from (Matt 7:23; Luke 9:39; Acts 13:13; Sept.: Jer 46:5).

Syn.: *hupágō* (5217), to go, depart; *apérchomai* (565), to go away; *exérchomai* (1831), to go out of; *poreúomai* (4198), to go on one's way, depart; *anachōréō* (402), to depart, go back; *apochōrízomai* (673), to separate oneself; *analúō* (360), to depart; *éxeimi* (1826), to go out; *aphístēmi* (868), to stand off, to depart from someone; *metabaínō* (3327), to depart; *apéchō* (568), to keep oneself away, be distant; *apéchomai* (567), to hold oneself off; *apospáomai* (645), to draw oneself away.

Ant.: *sunéchomai* (4912), to keep oneself together, hold oneself together; *proseggízō* (4331), to approach near, come near; *thiggánō* (2345), to handle, touch; *prostíthēmi* (4369), to add to, annex; *proskolláō* (4347), to join oneself to, glue to; *phthánō* (5348), to anticipate, arrive at, catch up with; *prophthánō* (4399), to catch up with; *prolambánō* (4301), to catch up with, surprise, overtake.

673. ἀποχωρίζω apochōrízō; fut. *apōchorísō*, mid. *apochōrízomai*, from *apó* (575), from, and *chōrízō* (5563), to separate. To designate, appoint, depart (Sept.: Ezek 43:21). In the NT, to separate, disjoin. In Rev 6:14 in the pass., the heaven was separated or disjoined, meaning the firmament (Gen 1:6) was separated, torn apart, and the parts rolled away as a scroll (cf. Isa 34:4). In the mid., to separate oneself as in Acts 15:39, "so that they separated one from another" (a.t.). Intrans. the same as *apochōréō* (672), to depart.

Syn.: With the trans. meaning of to separate: *diḯstēmi* (1339), to set apart, separate; *apospáō* (645), to draw off; *aírō* (142), to take up; *kinéō* (2795), to move.

Ant.: *suzeúgnumi* (4801), to yoke together; *sunbállō* (4820), to combine; *sunarmologéō* (4883), to fit together; *sundéō* (4887), to bind together; *sunistáō* (4921), to set together; *suntássō* (4929), to place together.

674. ἀποψύχω apopsúchō; fut. *apopsúxō*, from *apó* (575) denoting privation, and *psúchō* (5594), to breathe, wax cold. In the NT, to be faint of heart due to fear or terror as in Luke 21:26 (cf. Matt 28:4).

Syn.: *kámnō* (2577), to faint or be weary as a result of continuous labor.

Ant.: *thermaínō* (2328), to heat, warm; *anathállō* (330), to revive, flourish again; *kaíō* (2545), to burn; *puróō* (4448), to burn.

675. Ἄππιος Áppios; gen. *Appíou* masc. proper noun. The Roman Appius Claudius Caesar, a celebrated magistrate of Rome who built the Appian Way from Rome to Brundusium. In Acts 28:15, *Appíou Phórou*, Appii Forum, is a small town on the Appian Way, forty-three miles from Rome.

676. ἀπρόσιτος aprósitos; gen. *aprosítou*, masc.-fem., neut. *aprósiton*, adj. from the priv. *a* (1), without, and *próseimi* (n.f.), to approach, which is from *prós* (4314), unto, and *eimí* (1510), to be, go, or come. That which cannot be approached, inaccessible, unapproachable, hence unapproachable light (1 Tim 6:16 [cf. Ps 104:1–3; Ezek 1:4, 13, 26–28]).

Syn.: *pórrō* (4206), at a distance; *makrán* (3112), at a distance; *makróthen* (3113), from a distance or afar.

Ant.: *geítōn* (1069), a neighbor; *parakeímenos*, the part. adj. from *parákeimai* (3873), to lie near; *pároikos* (3941), a dweller nearby, an alien resident; *plēsíon* (4139), near; *eggús* (1451), at hand, near.

677. ἀπρόσκοπος *apróskopos*; gen. *aproskópou*, masc.-fem., neut. *apróskopon*, adj. from the priv. *a* (1), not, and *proskóptō* (4350), to strike at, to trip. Not taking or giving offense. Intrans., not stumbling or falling, figuratively speaking, in the path of duty and religion (Phil 1:10). Applied to the conscience, not stumbling over or impinging upon anything for which our heart condemns us (Acts 24:16 [cf. Acts 23:1; 1 Cor 4:4; 2 Cor 1:12; 2 Tim 1:3]). Trans., not causing others to stumble, not giving occasion to fall into sin (1 Cor 10:32 [cf. 2 Cor 6:3]).

Syn.: *áptaistos* (679), not stumbling; *eleútheros* (1658), free, at liberty.

678. ἀπροσωπολήπτως *aprosōpolēptōs*; adv. from the priv. *a* (1), without, and *prosōpolēptéō* (4380), to have respect for persons. Without respect of persons, impartially (1 Pet 1:17).

Syn.: *dikaíōs* (1346), equitably, justly.
Ant.: *adíkōs* (95), unjustly, wrongfully.

679. ἄπταιστος *áptaistos*; gen. *aptaístou*, masc.-fem., neut. *áptaiston*, adj. from the priv. *a* (1), without, and *ptaíō* (4417), to stumble. Free from stumbling, blameless. It occurs only in the benediction, of Jude 1:24 "Now unto him that is able to keep you from falling [*aptaístous*]." Is Jude promising that we shall live our lives without ever stumbling? James 3:2 says that we all stumble in many things. Yet, 2 Pet 1:10 assures us that we will never fall. The word "falling," then, seems ambiguous and poses an interpretive dilemma. If the stumbling in view concerns the daily sins of God's children, then Jude's words are meant to be an encouragement telling us that God's grace is sufficient to keep us from sin. However, if the stumbling refers to an utter fall into perdition (as in 2 Pet 1:10), then Jude's confession is a promise of eternal security. The rhetorical question Paul asks in Rom 11:11 is "Have

they stumbled that they should fall?" Here the definite distinction is drawn between *ptaíō* (4417), to stumble, and *píptō* (4098), to fall. To stumble is not necessarily to fall. This refers to the Jews who did not receive Jesus Christ as the Messiah. In James 2:10 we find that *ptaíō*, to stumble, is used in connection with the keeping of the Law. The mere stumbling or faltering over one precept is like faltering or stumbling over the whole of the Law.

In James 3:2 the word used is *ptaíō*, but is translated "offend": "For in many things we offend all." This means that we all stumble over many things and none of us is exempt. James goes on to say that the most likely stumbling is with our tongue: "If any man offend not in word, the same is a perfect man." Is, therefore, Jude's wish in verse twenty-four that we be kept *áptaistoi*, without stumbling or blameless, an empty wish? No. Here he is not referring to us but to the ability of the Lord to keep us from stumbling. He is not saying that we shall live through our lives without any stumbling in contradiction to James 3:2, but that the Lord is able to keep us from stumbling. That is His part and His activity in our lives. We never stumble because of Him, but because we live in a body that is corruptible and liable to stumble in a world which is yet unredeemed and full of traps (see Rom 8:18–28). See also *amōmous* (299), without blemish, which also occurs in Jude 1:24: "and to present you faultless [*amōmous*], before the presence of his glory with exceeding joy." What is translated "to present you" in Gr. is *stēsai*, the aor. inf. act. of *hístēmi* (2476), to stand. "The Lord who is able to keep us from stumbling is going to cause us to stand before His glory" (a.t.). This refers to the glorification of Jesus Christ and our glorification, the demonstration and the revelation of what we are, in and through Christ. He is going to present us *amōmous* (299), translated "faultless," meaning without *mōmos* (3470), spot or blemish. Jesus Christ came before God as *ámōmos*, unblemished, to shed His blood for us. That was the word that was used for the spotlessness or unblemished character of the sacrifices that were made in the OT. It is His blood that causes us also to be *ámōmoi* (Eph 1:4; 5:27; Col 1:22). The shedding of Christ's blood (i.e., His sacrificial death) makes the sinner blameless before the Lord at the time of His glorification. It will be a time of great rejoicing (*agallíasis* [20]) to discover that in spite of our *ptaísmata*, stumblings, we are not going to be deprived of the privilege of being glorified with Him, being washed with His blood and being made without internal blemish and thus proper candidates for glorification.

Syn.: *ámōmos* (299), without blemish; *amṓmētos* (298), without rebuke; *pistós* (4103), faithful; *ámemptos* (273), without blame.

Ant.: *hamartōlós* (268), sinner, sinful, one who has missed the mark; *ádikos* (94), unjust, unrighteous.

680. ἅπτομαι *háptomai*; fut. *hápsomai*, mid. deponent from *háptō* (681), to connect, bind. To apply oneself to, to touch. Refers to such handling of an object as to exert a modifying influence upon it or upon oneself. The same effect may be conveyed by the verb *thiggánō* (2345). These words sometimes may be exchanged one for the other (e.g., Sept.: Ex 19:12). Both words are used together in Col 2:21. *Háptomai* is usually stronger than *thiggánō* (1 John 5:18; Sept.: Ps 104:15). *Thiggánō* is correctly translated in Col 2:21 as "handle not," but the basic meaning is touching for the purpose of manipulating. Distinguished from *psēlapháō* (5584), which actually only means to touch the surface of something (Luke 24:39; 1 John 1:1). In 2 Cor 6:17, "touch no unclean thing" (a.t.), means have no dealings with the heathen (cf. Isa 52:11). In 1 Cor 7:1, "to touch a woman" is not to be taken literally, but is a euphemism for sexual intercourse. However, in the context of this verse, Paul seems to be referring to the whole idea of the sanctity of the marriage relationship. See Sept.:

Gen 20:4, 6. By implication in 1 John 5:18, to harm, injure. See 1 Chr 16:22; Job 5:19. Other references: Matt 8:3, 15; 9:20, 21, 29; 14:36; 17:7; 20:34; Mark 1:41; 3:10; 5:27, 28, 30, 31; 6:56; 7:33; 8:22; 10:13; Luke 5:13; 6:19; 7:14, 39; 8:44–47; 18:15; 22:51; John 20:17.

Syn.: *prospsaúō* (4379), to touch upon, touch slightly (Luke 11:46); *eggízō* (1448), to come near; *piázō* (4084), to lay hand on; *kolláō* (2853), to glue; *proseggízō* (4331), to approach.

Ant.: *apéchomai* (567), to hold oneself off; *egkrateúomai* (1467), to exercise self-restraint; *néphō* (3525), to be sober; *sōphronéō* (4993), to exercise soundness of mind, to think soberly, use self-control.

681. ἅπτω *háptō*; fut. *hápsō*. To handle an object so as to exert a modifying influence upon it, to fasten to. As a trans. verb when spoken of fire as applied to things, it means to set fire to, kindle, light (Luke 8:16; 11:33; 15:8; 22:55). In Luke 22:55, *periáptō* is found in some MSS instead of *háptō*.

Háptō is to be distinguished from *thiggánō* (2345). *Háptō* involves a self-conscious effort to touch, which is always absent from *thiggánō*. Col 2:21 should rather be translated, "Handle not, taste not, touch not" (a.t.); thus *háptomai* is "handle" and *thígō* is "touch."

Deriv.: *anáptō* (381), to light up, kindle; *háptomai* (680), to touch; *aphḗ* (860), a joint; *katháptō* (2510), to bind, fasten.

Syn.: with the meaning of to light: *phōtízō* (5461), to shine, give light; *epiphaúō* (2017), to shine forth; *lámpō* (2989), to give forth the light of a torch; *epiphaínō* (2014), to show forth; *kaíō* (2545), to burn, a light. With the meaning to touch: *thiggánō* (2345), to touch.

Ant.: with the meaning to kindle, light: *sbénnumi* (4570), to extinguish; *skotízō* (4654), to darken. With the meaning to touch: *apéchomaí* (567), to hold oneself off.

682. Ἀπφία *Apphía*; gen. *Apphias*, proper noun. Apphia, Christian woman addressed by Paul in Phile 1:2. Her name stands immediately after Philemon's which leads to the reasonable conjecture that she was Philemon's wife.

683. ἀπωθέω *apōthéō*; contracted *apōthṓ*, fut. *apésō*, aor. *apōsámēn*, from *apó* (575), from, and *ōthéō* (n.f.), to push, thrust, drive. To thrust away from oneself, cast off, repel, reject (Acts 7:27, 39; 13:46; Rom 11:1, 2; 1 Tim 1:19; Sept: Ezek 5:11; 11:16; Hos 9:17; 2 Kgs 17:18, 20; Jer 6:19; Jon 2:5). Also from *ōthéō* (n.f.): *exōthéō* (1856), to expel, drive.

Syn.: *apobállō* (577), to throw off from, cast away; *ekbállō* (1544), to cast out of, from, forth; *aporríptō* (641), to cast off; *apotíthēmi* (659), to put off; *chōrízō* (5563), to separate; *apostréphomai* (654), to turn oneself away; *apotrépō* (665), to turn away.

Ant.: *helkúō* (1670), to draw; *súrō* (4951), to drag, pull; *anaspáō* (385), to take up or extricate.

684. ἀπώλεια *apōleia*; gen. *apōleías*, fem. noun from *apóllumi* (622), to destroy fully. Used trans. the losing or loss (Matt 26:8), intrans. perdition, ruin. In the NT, *apóleia* refers to the state after death wherein exclusion from salvation is a realized fact, wherein man, instead of becoming what he might have been, is lost and ruined. Destruction, either temporal (Acts 25:16, death; Sept.: Deut 4:26; Esth 7:4; Prov 6:15; Isa 34:5), or the second death which is eternal exclusion from Christ's kingdom, equivalent to *apothnḗskō* (599), to die (Matt 7:13; Acts 8:20; Rom 9:22; Phil 1:28; 3:19; 1 Tim 6:9; Heb 10:39; 2 Pet 2:1, 3; 3:7, 16; Rev 17:8, 11). "Heresies of destruction" (a.t.) in 2 Pet 2:1 means fatally destructive heresies. In John 17:12; 2 Thess 2:3, "the son of perdition," an allusion to the Antichrist, means one determined to remain spiritually lost. See *huiós* (5207), son. Destruction or waste (Mark 14:4; Sept.: Lev 6:3, 4). *Apóleia*

and the verb *apóllumi* (622), to destroy, lose, perish, must never be construed as meaning extinction. One dies physically when his spirit and his body separate. Neither the body becomes extinct, nor the spirit. The body decomposes and ceases to exist in the form it was. Its constituent parts, however, continue to exist in a noncohesive form. The spirit takes a new existence, separate from its previous existence joined with the body. The lost sheep which was wandering away from the shepherd and the rest of the flock is called *apolōlós* (Luke 15:4, 6), also the coin which the woman lost (Luke 15:9, *apólesa* [the aor. of *apóllumi* {622}, to lose]) and the prodigal son who was lost (Luke 15:24, 32), but none of them ceased to exist. They simply were lost to the relationship which they had before and which was desired again by the owner.

In 1 Tim 6:9 the words *ólethros* and *apóleia* occur together referring to those who determine to be rich. In this instance, *ólethros* refers to the actual physical death of those who desire to be rich by any means such as Judas, Ananias and Sapphira. *Apóleia*, on the other hand, refers to separation from God Himself in fulfillment of our Savior's warnings that the rich enter the kingdom of heaven with difficulty (Matt 19:23, 24; Mark 10:25). *Ólethros* speaks more of the way in which destruction comes than of the state in which a lost person is found. It refers specifically to the destruction of the flesh (1 Cor 5:5). *Apóleia*, on the other hand, refers to the destruction or the perishing of the whole personality as is indicated by the opposite of *apóllumi* which is *sōzomai* (4982), to be saved, "that the spirit may be saved." Thus we can conclude that for the flesh there is *ólethros* while for the spirit there is salvation. Yet salvation may be taken as the ant. of both *apóllumi* and *ólethros*. In the latter case the word "salvation" must be taken as the healing of the body (James 5:15 where the word translated "saved" is the Gr. word *sōzō* [4982], to save). In the spiritual realm, however, *sōzō* is also the opposite of *apóllumi*, to perish. Thus *sōtēría* (4991), salvation or deliverance, can be taken as the exact opposite of *apóleia*.

Syn.: *phthorá* (5356), destruction that comes with corruption, consumption by using up; *súntrimma* (4938), a breaking in pieces; *thánatos* (2288), death; *anaíresis* (336), a taking up or off, usually used in regard to life; *teleuté* (5054), an end of life, death; *zēmía* (2209), loss; *apobolé* (580), a casting away; *héttēma* (2275), defeat, loss, defect; *kathaíresis* (2506), a taking or pulling down, hence destruction; *ólethros* (3639), an eschatological destruction surprising people like labor pains coming upon a pregnant woman.

Ant.: *aiōnios zōé* ([166], [2222]), eternal life; *bíos* (979), the present state of existence, life, living; *kérdos* (2771), gain; *porismós* (4200), a providing, procuring, a means of gain.

685. ἀρά *ará*; gen. *arás*, fem. noun. Originally it meant prayer, but came to mean more often an imprecation, a curse which the deity was to execute, the opposite of *euché* (2171), wish, vow. *Ará* is the basic word from which *katára* (2671), a curse against, is derived. Finally the word came to mean the evil invoked, the mischief itself, the realized curse. Used only in Rom 3:14 while the comp. *katára* is used more frequently (Gal 3:10, 13; Heb 6:8; James 3:10; 2 Pet 2:14); the verb *kataráomai* (2672), to curse, pray against, wish evil against a person or thing; the adj. *epikatáratos* ([1944] see Gal 3:10, 13 [TR]) or *epáratos*, accursed (John 7:49 [UBS]).

Deriv.: *katára* (2671), a curse.

Syn.: *anáthema* (331), a curse, disfavor of God; *katanáthema* (2652), an accursed thing.

Ant.: *eulogía* (2129), blessing; *chrēstología* (5542), fair speech, good words; *makarismós* (3108), the declaration of the blessed state of an individual; *euché* (2171), wish.

686. ἄρα *ára*; inferential particle. Then or therefore, and indicating an interrogative.

In Class. Gr. it stands after other words in a clause and is always written *ára*, then, therefore. As an interrogative, it stands first in a clause, and in prose and the epic poets is written *ára*. In other poets, if the first syllable is long it is written *ára*; if short, *ára*.

As an inferential particle *ára* means therefore, then, now, consequently, marking a transition to what naturally follows from the words preceding.

(I) In Rom 7:21, "I find then a law" (also Rom 8:1; 1 Cor 15:14; Gal 3:7). In 1 Cor 5:10; 7:14, preceded by *epeí* (1893), since, since then; *epeí ára* meaning since in that case.

(II) Where it does not directly refer to anything expressed, but still the idea "according to nature or custom" lies at the basis and means then, now, indeed, perhaps, and so forth, but often not to be expressed in Eng. Preceded by *tis* (5101), it means "Who now?" "Who then?" or simply "Who?" (Matt 18:1; 19:25; 24:45; Mark 4:41; Luke 8:25; 12:42; 22:23). Preceded by *ti* (the neut. of *tis* [5100], who), it means "What then?" or simply "What?" (Matt 19:27; Luke 1:66; Acts 12:18). Preceded by *ei* (1487), if, *ei ára* means if perhaps (Mark 11:13; Acts 8:22). Preceded by *eíper* (1512), if perhaps, *eíper ára* means if indeed (1 Cor 15:15; Sept.: Gen 18:3; Num 22:11; Ps 58:11). Preceded by *ouk* (3756), not, it means not then as in Acts 21:38: "Art not thou [then] that Egyptian?" Preceded by *méti* (3385), whether at all, not, *méti ára* as in 2 Cor 1:17, "Did [lest] I use lightness?"

(III) Contrary to Class. Gr. usage, *ára* is used in the NT as an inferential particle at the beginning of a clause, and without interrogation meaning therefore, consequently (Luke 11:48; Rom 10:17; 2 Cor 7:12; Heb 4:9; Sept.: Ps 139:11). When *ei* (1487), if, precedes *ára* constituting a protasis, proposition, *ára*, being in the apodosis (the conclusion), may be rendered "it follows that" (Matt 12:28; Luke 11:20; 1 Cor 15:18; 2 Cor 5:14; Gal 2:21; 3:29; 5:11; Heb 12:8). In this case and use, *ára* is sometimes strengthened by other particles such as *oún* (3767), therefore; *ára oún* making it "therefore then," "so then," "wherefore," which is a favorite expression of Paul in Rom 5:18; 7:3, 25; 8:12; 9:16, 18; 14:12, 19; Gal 6:10; Eph 2:19; 1 Thess 5:6; 2 Thess 2:15. *Ára* followed by *ge* (1065), a particle of emphasis, means "therefore then," "so then" (Matt 7:20; 17:26; Acts 11:18). After *ei* (1487), if, whether, *ei ára ge*, it means "if perhaps" (Acts 17:27).

Syn.: *pántōs* (3843), doubtless; *mépote* (3379), lest ever, lest perhaps; *mépōs* (3381), lest in any way, or *mépou* (UBS) in Acts 27:29; *houtō* (3779), thus; *hōsaútōs* (5615), a strengthened form of *hōs* (5613), just so, likewise; *homoíōs* (3668), likewise; *pōs* (4459), how, after what manner; *tácha* (5029), perhaps, peradventure; *tóte* (5119), then, therefore; *eíta* (1534), then, next, furthermore; *épeita* (1899), thereupon, thereafter, then; *loipón* (3063), then, finally; *oún* (3767), then; *oukoún* (3766), so then; *toínun* (5106), accordingly, then, therefore; *dé* (1161), but; *gár* (1063), for; *kaí* (2532), and; *te* (5037), and, then; *hóthen* (3606), thereupon, therefore; *óntōs* (3689), indeed.

687. âpa *ára*; adv. Whether. A question to which a neg. answer is required. See *ára* (686) followed by *oún* (3767 I, C), therefore, and followed by *ge* (1065 II), a particle of emphasis. For syn. see *ára* (686).

As an interrogative, *ára* at the beginning of a clause, serves merely to denote a question and it cannot be expressed in Eng. It requires the answer to be neg. as in Luke 18:8, "Nevertheless [*ára*], when the Son of man cometh, shall he find faith on the earth?" The answer must be "no." The same in Gal 2:17; Sept.: Gen 18:3; 4:2. When strengthened by *ge* (1065), a particle of emphasis as *ára ge*, it means whether indeed (Acts 8:30; Sept.: Gen 26:9; Jer 4:10).

688. Ἀραβία *Arabía*; gen. *Arabías*, fem. proper noun. Arabia, meaning arid,

sterile. A large peninsula in the southwestern part of Asia between the Red Sea, the Indian Ocean, and the Persian Gulf. Its extreme length from north to south is about 1300 miles, and its greatest breadth is about 1500 miles, though from the northern point of the Red Sea to the Persian Gulf it is only about 900 miles. The Sinaitic Peninsula is a small triangular region in the northwestern part, or corner, of Arabia. Arabia in the early history of Israel was a small tract of country south and east of Palestine, probably the same as that called Kedem, or "the East" (Gen 10:30; 25:6; 29:1). It was about the same area in NT times (Gal 1:17; 4:25). The main inhabitants were known as Ishmaelites, Arabians, Idumeans, Horites, and Edomites. In Scripture there are many references both to the country and to the people who lived there. Some suggest that Job dwelt in Arabia. The forty years of wandering by the Israelites under Moses were in Arabia. Solomon received gold from there (1 Kgs 10:15; 2 Chr 9:14) and Jehoshaphat received flocks (2 Chr 17:11). Some of its people were in Jerusalem at the Pentecost (Acts 2:11). The prophecies of Isaiah and Jeremiah frequently refer to it (Isa 21:11–13; 42:11; 60:7; Jer 25:24; 49:18, 29). According to Paul's own testimony (Gal 1:17), he visited Arabia, but we do not know what part of it and for how long. Luke, who gives the details of his conversion and his presence in Damascus and his departure from there, does not give us any detailed information, but Paul's trip to Arabia may well fit into Acts 9:20–27.

689. Ἀράμ *Arám*; proper noun from the Hebr. *Rām* (OT 7410), meaning high (Sept.: 1 Chr 2:10). A man in Matt 1:3, 4; Luke 3:33.

690. Ἄραψ *Áraps*; gen. *Árabos*, masc. noun. An Arab (Acts 2:11).

691. ἀργέω *argéō*; contracted *argṓ*, fut. *argḗsō*, from *argós* (692), idle. To do nothing. Only in 2 Pet 2:3, to be inactive, to rest (Sept.: Ezra 4:24).

Deriv.: *katargéō* (2673), entirely idle, abolish, cease.

Syn.: *scholázō* (4980), to be at leisure.

Ant.: *ergázomai* (2038), to work; *katergázomai* (2716), to complete a work; *ekteléō* (1615), to complete fully; *douleúō* (1398), to serve; *hupēretéō* (5256), to serve, minister; *energéō* (1754), to be at work; *poiéō* (4160), to produce, make; *prássō* (4238), to perform, accomplish.

692. ἀργός argós; fem. *argḗ*, neut. *argón*, adj. from the priv. *a* (1), without, and *érgon* (2041), work. Not at work, idle, not employed, inactive (Matt 20:3, 6, with the idea that they chose to be idle; 1 Tim 5:13; Titus 1:12, "slow bellies," lazy gluttons; 2 Pet 1:8, with the idea of indolent, slothful in Christian duty). Idle, insincere, false, unprofitable (Matt 12:36, "idle word," insincere language of a person who speaks one thing and means another [cf. 2 Pet 1:8]).

Deriv.: *argéō* (691), to be idle.

Syn.: *bradús* (1021), slow; *oknērós* (3636), indolent, slothful.

Ant.: *tachús* (5036), swift.

693. ἀργύρεος argúreos; contracted *arguroús*; fem. *arguréa* contracted *argurá*, neut. *arguréon* contracted *arguroún*, adj. from *árguros* (696), silver. Made of silver (Acts 19:24; 2 Tim 2:20; Rev 9:20; Sept.: Gen 24:53; Ex 3:22).

694. ἀργύριον argúrion; gen. *arguríou*, neut. noun from *árguros* (696), silver. Silver, a piece of silver (Acts 3:6; 20:33; 1 Pet 1:18). A piece of silver money (Matt 26:15; 27:3, 5, 6, 9; Acts 19:19 [cf. Ex 21:32; Zech 11:12, 13]). Money in general (Matt 25:18, 27; 28:12, 15; Mark 14:11; Luke 9:3; 19:15, 23; 22:5; Acts 7:16; 8:20), because silver seems to have been the most ancient form of money. Until the captivity the Jews had no coins, the shekel being properly a weight and all money being reckoned by weight and assigned value (Gen 23:15, 16; Ex 21:32;

Josh 7:21). In the time of the Maccabees silver coins were first struck with the inscription "Shekel of Israel," which were equal to four Attic *drachmaí* or *drachmḗ* (1406) or one *statḗr* (4715). The drachma was equivalent to sixteen cents American money, but this does not represent its purchasing power. In the year 300 B.C., a sheep could be bought with it. With five drachmae, an ox could be purchased. The *drachmḗ* is mentioned only in Luke 15:8f. where in the pl. it is translated "pieces of silver." The *dídrachmon* (1323), two *drachmaí* which was one coin, was used among the Jews for the half-shekel required for the annual temple tax (Matt 17:24). This regulation derived from the atonement money prescribed in Ex 30:11–16, which, according to Maimonides, later developed into a regular annual poll tax. After the fall of Jerusalem and the destruction of the temple, this tax had to be paid into the Roman treasury. The *statḗr* (4715) was a coin of four *drachmaí* (Matt 17:27) which would pay the temple tax for both Jesus Christ and Peter. In Matt 28:12, 13, *argúria hikaná* (2425), competent, ample, most probably does not refer to the size of the coins but to the sufficiency of them. There were one hundred silver *drachmaí* to the *mná*, translated "pound" and referred to in Luke 19:11–27, the parable of the pounds. The talent was not a coin, but a unit of monetary reckoning. Its value was always high, though it varied with the different metals involved and the different monetary standards. In the parables of the Lord, the talents referred to were most probably silver talents (Matt 18:24; 25:15–28, where in verse eighteen it is referred to as *argúrion*, a silver piece which suggests that our Lord had the silver talent in mind). The silver *dēnárion* (1220), denarius or dinar, was a Roman coin, twenty-five of which made a gold dinar. The smallest Roman coin was the quadrans, in Gr. *kodrántēs* (2835), usually translated "farthing," and it was made of copper (see Mark 12:42 where the widow's two *leptá* [3016], translated "mite," were equivalent to a quadrans). Matt

5:26 uses *kodrántēs* (2835), farthing, for the smallest coin, which had to be paid to clear a debt in full, while in the TR of Luke 12:59, *leptón* (3016), mite, is used, except for the Western text which agrees with Matthew.

Another copper coin used among the Roman was the *assárion* (787), also translated "farthing," which was one sixteenth of the silver dinar (Matt 10:29; Luke 12:6). This was the price at which two sparrows were sold. Luke has five sparrows for two farthings. The dinar or *dēnárion* (1220), usually and unfortunately translated "penny" thus giving the idea of insignificance, was so-called because the word means ten at a time, and it was the equivalent in silver to ten copper *assária* which in today's money is worth sixteen cents. However, remember that it could buy a sheep. From the parable of Matt 20:1–16, it appears to have been the daily wages of a laborer (see also Luke 10:35 which tells us that it was what the good Samaritan gave to the innkeeper). The silver *dēnárion* (1220) was apparently the coin used in attempting to trick Jesus in the question concerning the payment of tribute money (Matt 22:19; Mark 12:15; Luke 20:24). Acts 19:19, referring to the 50,000 pieces of silver, does not make it clear whether they are Jewish, Greek, or Roman silver pieces. However, it could range in equivalent American dollars from $7,000 to $28,000. This would place a high price on books and these were priced so highly because they were books prepared by magicians, and they did not represent the ordinary value of books.

Syn.: *chrḗma* (5536), a thing that one uses, money, riches; *chalkós* (5475), copper or copper coin, money; *kérma* (2772), a small coin, change; *nómisma* (3546), the current coin of the state, currency; *statḗr* (4715), a coin; *drachmḗ* (1406), drachma; *dídrachmon* (1323), a double drachma.

695. ἀργυροκόπος *argurokópos*; gen. *argurokópou*, masc. noun from *árguros* (696), silver, and *kóptō* (2875), to cut,

beat out. A silversmith (Acts 19:24; Sept.: Judg 17:4; Jer 6:29).

696. ἄργυρος *árguros*; gen. *argúrou*, masc. noun from *argós* (n.f.), white, shining, bright, glistening. Silver (Rev 18:12 [cf. Acts 17:29]); silver money (Matt 10:9; James 5:3). Figuratively meaning good works such as will endure the fire of God's final judgment (1 Cor 3:12).

Deriv.: *argúreos* (693), made of silver; *argúrion* (694), silver, money; *argurokópos* (695), one who cuts or makes silver coins, a silversmith; *philárguros* (5366), lover of money or silver, covetous.

697. Ἄρειος Πάγος *Áreios Págos*. Areopagus or Mars Hill (Acts 17:19), a hill in Athens with an open place where the Court of the Areopagus sat (Acts 17:22–34). This was the supreme tribunal of justice instituted by Solon. Today the Supreme Court of Greece is called *Áreios Págos*.

698. Ἀρεοπαγίτης *Areopagítēs*; gen. *Areopagítou*, masc. proper noun. A judge sitting at the Court of Areopagus. Occurs only in Acts 17:34. Mars Hill is situated in the middle of Athens, opposite the Acropolis. Here the famous Senate, or Court of the Areopagites, used to assemble. The names of both the place and court were probably derived from a famous judgment there passed on *Árēs*, a Thessalian prince, whom these judges acquitted from punishment though he had killed Hallirothius, son of Neptune, a neighboring prince, in revenge for the latter's having violated his daughter Alcippa. Although this tribunal did indeed take notice of religious matters, it does not appear that Paul was carried to the place of their assembly in order to undergo a formal trial, but only to satisfy the curiosity of those who wanted to inquire about that strange doctrine he taught (Acts 17:19, 22). The same name is used in Greece today of a judge appointed to the Supreme Court.

699. ἀρέσκεια aréskeia; gen. *areskeías*, fem. noun from *aréskō* (700), to please. An endeavor to please, sometimes referring to an excessive desire to please in a bad sense. In a good sense, to please God. Only in Col 1:10; Sept.: Prov 31:30.

Syn.: *hēdonḗ* (2237), pleasure; *eudokía* (2107), good pleasure; *thélēma* (2307), will, pleasure, favor; *euphrosúnē* (2167), joyfulness, gladness; *chará* (5479), joy; *apólausis* (619), enjoyment; *agallíasis* (20), exuberance.

Ant.: *anágkē* (318), distress; *lúpē* (3077), sorrow; *pikría* (4088), bitterness; *stenochōría* (4730), anguish, distress; *cholḗ* (5521), gall.

700. ἀρέσκω aréskō; fut. *arésō*, aor. *éresa*, from *árō* (n.f., see *podērēs* [4158]), to fit, adapt, please. To make one inclined to, to be content with, soften one's heart towards another. In the NT, the meaning has evolved from the pass. "being pleased" to the active "to please," i.e., passing from a relationship to behavior (Matt 14:6; Mark 6:22; Rom 8:8; 1 Cor 7:32–34; Gal 1:10; 1 Thess 2:15; 4:1; 2 Tim 2:4; Sept.: Josh 22:30, 33; Esth 2:4; 5:14). In Acts 6:5 "to please in the sight of someone" (a.t.) means to be acceptable to him (Sept.: Deut 1:23; 2 Sam 3:36). In Rom 15:1–3; Gal 1:10; 1 Thess 2:4 it means to seek to please or gratify, to accommodate oneself to. The pres. and imper. tenses denote intentional, deliberate, and continuous conduct and have nothing to do with verbs denoting states or relationships; yet the word involves a relationship prior to behavior. It is actually satisfying or behaving properly toward one with whom one is related. In 1 Cor 10:33 the expression *pánta pásin aréskō* (*pánta* [3956], everyone; *pásin* [3956], in each thing), means I seek to accommodate myself to each one without discrimination in order to win as many as possible to Christ (1 Cor 9:3, 4, 19–25).

Deriv.: *anthrōpáreskos* (441), one who endeavors to please men; *aréskeia* (699), the endeavor to please; *arestós* (701),

dear, pleasant, well-pleasing; *euárestos* (2101), pleasing, agreeable.

Syn.: *eudokéō* (2106), to think well of; *thélō* (2309), to wish, desire; *dokimázō* (1381), to approve; *eucharistéō* (2168), to express gratitude, give thanks; *apolambánō* (618), to receive; *entrupháō* (1792), to revel in; *euphraínō* (2165), to rejoice, make glad.

Ant.: *lupéō* (3076), to cause grief; *pikraínō* (4087), to make bitter; *stenochōréō* (4729), to distress; *choláō* (5520), to be irritable, angry.

701. ἀρεστός arestós; fem. *arestḗ*, neut. *arestón*, adj. from *aréskō* (700), to please or to be content with. To be dear, pleasant, well-pleasing as in Acts 12:3 but elsewhere used only of God's will (John 8:29; Sept.: Deut 12:28); doing that which pleases somebody. It is in this sense that it is used in 1 John 3:22, distinguishing between claim or requirement and satisfaction, the claim being the commandments and the satisfaction being those things that we do out of the love that we have for God (see Sept.: Ex 15:26; Deut 6:18; 12:25; Ezra 10:11; Isa 38:3). In Acts 6:2 reference is not made to the apostles but to that which is pleasing to God. In Acts 12:3 reference is made to pleasing the Jews.

Syn.: *eúthetos* (2111), fit, proper; *kalós* (2570), good; *sumpathḗs* (4835), sympathetic; *euprósdektos* (2144), well-received, approved, favorable; *glukús* (1099), sweet; *dektós* (1184), approved, referring to relationship. *Arestós* presupposes man's relationship with God, but it also tells about God's judgment to man's conduct.

Ant.: *chalepós* (5467), perilous, fierce; *kakós* (2556), evil.

702. Ἀρέτας Arétas; gen. *Aréta*; masc. proper noun. Aretas, a king of Arabia Petraea whose daughter was once the wife of Herod Antipas. About A.D. 39 or 40 Aretas had possession of Damascus for a short time. Mentioned only once in 2 Cor 11:32.

703. ἀρετή aretḗ; gen. aretḗs, fem. noun. Superiority or being pleasing to God, or the superiority of God revealed in the work of salvation. Aretḗ denotes in a moral sense what gives man his worth, his efficiency. In the NT: virtue, moral excellency, perfection, goodness of action. In 1 Pet 2:9, aretás (pl.) is translated "praises." The virtues as a force or energy of the Holy Spirit accompanying the preaching of the glorious gospel. In 2 Pet 1:3 it stands next to dóxa (1319), glory. Human virtue in general (Phil 4:8); courage, fortitude, resolution (1 Pet 2:9; 2 Pet 1:5 [cf. 1 Cor 16:13]); moral excellence.

Syn.: huperbolḗ (5236), a throwing beyond, surpassing, an excellence; huperochḗ (5247), the act of overhanging, hence superiority, preeminence, excellency; aínos (136), praise; épainos (1868), approbation, commendation; dóxa (1391), glory; dúnamis (1411), power; chárisma (5486), gift; ōphéleia (5622), usefulness, benefit.

Ant.: hustérēma (5303), lack, want; tó phaúlon (5337), that which is light, wicked or evil; páthos (3806), passion, lust; tó kakón (2556), that which is bad in itself; tó ponērón (4190), evil, malevolence.

704. ἀρήν arḗn; gen. arnós or arénos. Lamb (Luke 10:3; Sept.: Gen 30:32; Lev 1:10; Isa 11:6; 40:11; 65:25; Jer 51:40).

Deriv.: arníon (721), lamb, a diminutive of arnḗn.

Syn.: amnós (286), a lamb expected to be sacrificed; próbaton (4263), a sheep.

705. ἀριθμέω arithméō; contracted arithmṓ, fut. arithmḗsō, from arithmós (706), number. To number, reckon by number (Matt 10:30; Luke 12:7; Rev 7:9; Sept.: Gen 15:5; Job 14:16).

Deriv.: katarithméō (2674), to number, enroll.

Syn.: logízomai (3049), to reckon; katalégō (2639), to place among; metréō (3354), to estimate, measure.

706. ἀριθμός arithmós; gen. arithmoú, masc. noun. A number (Luke 22:3; John 6:10; Acts 4:4; 5:36; 6:7; 11:21; 16:5; Rom 9:27; Rev 5:11; 7:4; 9:16; 13:17, 18; 15:2; 20:8; Sept.: Num 1:49; 1 Sam 6:4; 1 Kgs 18:31; 1 Chr 7:2; Hos 1:10).

Deriv.: anaríthmētos (382), innumerable; arithméō (705), to number.

707. Ἀριμαθαία Arimathaía; gen. Arimathaías, fem. proper noun. Arimathea meaning heights. A town in Judea and the home of Joseph who begged the body of Jesus for burial (Matt 27:57; Mark 15:43; Luke 23:51; John 19:38). Its exact location is uncertain, but the church historian Eusebius and church Father Jerome identified it with Ramah or Ramathaim, the birthplace of Samuel (1 Sam 1:1, 19).

708. Ἀρίσταρχος Arístarchos; gen. Aristárchou, masc. proper noun. Aristarchus, a native of Thessalonica who became the companion of Paul. He was seized in the tumult at Ephesus and was afterwards carried with Paul as a prisoner to Rome (Acts 19:29; 20:4; 27:2; Col 4:10; Phile 1:24).

709. ἀριστάω aristáō or aristṓ; fut. aristḗso from áriston (712), breakfast. To breakfast but also to dine. To take any meal before the principal one or supper (deípnon [1173]). See Luke 11:37; John 21:12, 15; Sept.: Gen 43:25; 1 Sam 14:24.

Syn.: esthíō (2068), to eat; phágō (5315), to eat, consume; trṓgō (5176), to chew, eat; bibrṓskō (977), to devour, eat.

Ant.: peináō (3983), to hunger; nēsteúō (3522), to fast.

710. ἀριστερός aristerós; fem. aristerá, neut. aristerón, adj. The left as opposed to the right. Referring to weapons of righteousness in the pl. aristerón, on the left (2 Cor 6:7). Used in the fem., hē aristerá, with the noun cheír (5495), hand, being understood, it means the left hand

(Matt 6:3). In the pl. gen. with *ek* ([1537], from), on the left-hand side (Luke 23:33). The Greeks believed that the left side was unlucky and an evil omen.

Ant.: *dexiós* (1188), right, opposite to the left.

711. Ἀριστόβουλος *Aristóboulos*; gen. *Aristoboúlou*, masc. proper noun. Aristobulus, a Christian (Rom 16:10).

712. ἄριστον *áriston*; neut. noun. An abbreviation of *aóriston*, without boundaries, indefinite, because it was a meal taken at no particular time. Among the Jews it was a meal corresponding sometimes to our breakfast and sometimes to our lunch. Their principal meal was the *deípnon* (1173), supper, in the early part of the evening when the heat of the day was gone. The *áriston* was a light refreshment taken sometimes in the morning, a little before noon, or just afternoon as circumstances might vary, hence it was called an uncertain meal, *aóriston*, which then became *áriston* (Luke 11:38; 14:12). In Matt 22:4 it is made unnecessarily to be the same as *deípnon*. In Homer the *áriston* is taken about sunrise; in later times it corresponded to the midday meal. See also 2 Sam 24:15.

Deriv.: *aristáō* (709), to eat breakfast or dinner.

Syn.: *brósis* (1035), the act of eating; *prosphágion* (4371), primarily a delicacy or relish, especially cooked fish to be eaten with bread; *bróma* (1033), food; *sitométrion* (4620), a measured portion of food; *trophé* (5160), food, nourishment.

Ant.: *limós* (3042), famine, hunger; *nēsteía* (3521), a fast.

713. ἀρκετός *arketós*; from *arkéō* (714), to be sufficient. Sufficient, enough (Matt 6:34; 10:25; 1 Pet 4:3). This verb indicates that to be personally content is helpful to others, and furthermore, when one helps others he senses his own sufficiency.

Syn.: *hikanós* (2425), enough, sufficient, fit; *autárkeia* (841), self-sufficiency,

contentment; *perissós* (4053), having an abundance and therefore sufficient for oneself; *eparkéō* (1884), to be strong enough and therefore capable of relieving others.

Ant.: *olígos* (3641), little, insufficient; *endeés* (1729), lacking; *anagkaíos* (316), necessary, needful.

714. ἀρκέω *arkéō*; contracted *arkō̄*, fut. *arkésō*. To suffice, be sufficient, satisfy, and by implication to be strong and able to assist someone (Matt 25:9; John 6:7; 14:8, "It sufficeth us"; 2 Cor 12:9, "My grace is sufficient for thee"). In the mid. or pass., *arkéomai* or *arkoúmai* governing the dat., to be satisfied, content with (Luke 3:14; 1 Tim 6:8; Heb 13:5); followed by the prep. *epí* (1909) (3 John 1:10, "and not content therewith").

Deriv.: *arketós* (713), sufficient; *autárkēs* (842), self-sufficient, content; *eparkéō* (1884), to be sufficient.

Syn.: *suneudokéō* (4909), to consent, to be content (1 Cor 7:12); *apéchō* (566), to have in full and therefore to have sufficient; *hikanóō* (2427), to make sufficient, fit; *eparkéō* (1884), to be sufficient, therefore able to help.

Ant.: *leípō* (3007), to lack; *epileípō* (1952), to be insufficient for, fail; *hupoleípō* (5275), to leave under or fall behind; *aphíēmi* (863), to send forth, to forsake, let alone, omit.

715. ἄρκτος *árktos*, **ἄρκος** *árkos*; gen. *árktou*, masc., fem. noun. A bear (Rev 13:2).

716. ἅρμα *hárma*; gen. *hármatos*, neut. noun. A chariot or vehicle (Acts 8:28, 29, 38; Rev 9:9; Sept.: Gen 41:43; Joel 2:5).

Syn.: *rhéda* (4480), a wagon with four wheels, used usually for traveling purposes, while *hárma* was used for military purposes.

717. Ἀρμαγεδδών *Armageddón*; presumed to be from the Hebr. words *har* (2022, OT), a mountain and *Me̓giddō̄* (4023, OT), Megiddo. Armageddon, or the mountain of Megiddo (Rev 16:16), a place famous in the history of the OT for destruction and slaughter (Judg 5:19; 2 Kgs 9:27; 2 Chr 35:22) and pertaining to the tribe of Manasseh. Here Israel was victorious over the kings of Canaan, which might be taken as typical of the triumph of God and His kingdom over hostile world powers. The defeat and death of Saul and Jonathan at the eastern extremity of the plain of Megiddo (1 Sam 31:1ff.); the disastrous struggle of Josiah on the same field against Pharaoh Necho (2 Kgs 23:29; 2 Chr 35:22), and Zechariah's reference to the "mourning of Hedadrimmon in the valley of Megiddon" (Zech 12:11), suggest a great day of overthrow and destruction. Ezekiel prophesies the destruction of Gog and Magog in this area (Ezek 38:8, 21; 39:2, 4, 17). It is there that the overthrow of Satan and his hosts takes place according to Rev 20:8.

718. ἁρμόζω *harmózō*; fut. *harmósō*, from *harmós*, (719), joint. To adjust, fitly join as used in the Gr. writers and in Sept.: Prov 17:7, but not in the NT. In Sept.: Prov 19:14, the verb *harmózō* is used to indicate a father's betrothing his daughter to a man to join in wedlock. In the mid. *harmózomai*, intrans., to contract, marry, espouse, or betroth (2 Cor 11:2).

    Syn.: *sunistáō* (4921), to set together; *suntássō* (4929), to arrange jointly; *katartízō* (2675), to join together; *sundéō* (4887), to bind with; *sunarmologéō* (4883), to fit together; *mnēsteúō* (3423), to woo and win, espouse or promise in marriage; *gaméō* (1060), to marry; *ekgamízō* (1547) and in some MSS *gamízō*, *ekgamískō* (1548), or *gamískō* (1061), to give out in marriage; *epigambreúō* (1918), to take to wife or marry a deceased husband's next of kin.

    Ant.: *lúō* (3089), to loose; *dialúō* (1262), to dissolve completely; *chōrízō* (5563), to separate.

719. ἁρμός *harmós*; gen. *harmoú*, masc. noun from *árō* (n.f., see *podérēs* [4158]),

to adjust, join properly together. A joint (Heb 4:12).

    Deriv.: *harmózō* (718), to adjust.

    Syn.: *haphḗ* (860), a joint.

720. ἀρνέομαι *arnéomai*; contracted *arnoúmai*, fut. *arnḗsomai*, deponent. To deny.

    (I) To deny, refuse (Heb 11:24).

    (II) Related to previous meaning with the acc. of person, to refuse someone, not to know or recognize him, to reject him either in the face of a former relationship or better knowledge. To deny, decline, reject, give up (Matt 10:33; 2 Tim 2:12, 13, to renounce one's own character, to be inconsistent with oneself; 1 John 2:22, 23, denying God to be the Father of Christ and Christ to be the Son of God). It can include the idea of falsehood or contradiction, not only with reference to the obj. but on the part of the subj. against himself (Matt 10:33; Luke 12:9; 22:57, denying that he had any connection with him; Acts 3:13, 14; 7:35; 2 Pet 2:1; 1 John 2:22; Jude 1:4).

    (III) As used with something as its obj., to reject anything, retract, renounce, deny, disown depending on the context (1 Tim 5:8; 2 Tim 3:5; Titus 1:16, to deny by actions that there is a God; Titus 2:12; Rev 2:13; 3:8). Used in an absolute sense in 2 Tim 2:12.

    (IV) To gainsay without further specification of the obj. (Luke 8:45; John 1:20; Acts 4:16; Titus 1:16). Falsely to deny, disown (Matt 26:70, 72; Mark 14:68, 70; John 18:25, 27). Opposite of *homologéō* (3670), to confess or say together (Matt 10:33; John 1:20; Titus 1:16).

    How will the Lord Jesus deny believers? In Matt 10:33, "him will I also deny [*arnḗsomai*, the fut. indic. of *arnéomai*] before my Father which is in heaven." This may refer to the rewards of the believers, since the word here does not necessarily mean an utter denial as the case will be in the day of judgment for those who acted as would-be Christian miracle workers. To these the Lord will say, "I never knew you" (Matt 7:21–23). In

Matt 10:33, however, we find the believers before the Father who is in heaven being recognized for their consistency and fidelity in witnessing while on earth. The teaching here is that the recognition in heaven will be proportionate to the confession (*homología* [3671], acknowledgment or witnessing) on earth.

A similar statement is found in Luke 12:8, and then in verse nine we read, "But he that denieth me before men shall be denied before the angels of God." The first verb "denieth" is *arnēsámenos*, the aor. part. of *arnéomai*, which should literally translate "he who did deny me" (a.t.). The aor. is constantive and possibly has in view any single moment in one's lifetime (although we cannot be dogmatic because the constantive could also be considering the entirety of one's lifespan). Here the word *arnéomai* stands in contrast to *homologéō* (3670), to acknowledge, witness, confess, which verb in verse eight is also in the subjunctive aor. which refers to acts of the acknowledgment of Jesus Christ before men. The second time the verb is used in regard to the Son of man, it is *homologései*, which is the fut. indic. and which again refers to the occasion of the acknowledgment by Christ of those times in which the believer confessed Him before men. In verses eight and nine this acknowledgment by the Lord Jesus Christ of the confessing or the denying believer is said to be made before the angels of God. This is in heaven for only there are the angels of God. It is difficult to imagine that these angels and the believers would be found in the eternal fire which was prepared for the devil and his angels (Matt 25:41). The angels referred to in Luke 12:8, 9 are God's unfallen angels, while in Matt 25:41 reference is made to the devil's messengers, those angels who became demons because of their disobedience to God (Isa 14:12–15; Job 4:18; 2 Pet 2:4; Jude 1:6; Rev 12:9). In Luke 12:9 the verb used in regard to the denial is not *arnéomai* but the comp. *aparnēthḗsetai*, the fut. pass. of *aparnéomai* (533), which could be taken as meaning that the denial

by the Lord Jesus Christ, the *apárnēsis*, is in direct proportion to the *árnēsis*, man's denial.

In 2 Tim 2:12 we have another occurrence of the denial by Jesus Christ in the future: "if we deny him, he also will deny us." The verb "deny" in Gr. is *arnēsómetha*, which is the fut. indic. with punctiliar meaning, again perhaps referring to occasions of refusing to confess Jesus Christ. In the proportion that we refuse to confess Him, He will also deny (*arnḗsetai*) us, again in the fut. indic. which refers to occasions of not confessing before His Father and His angels as indicated in Matt 10:33; Luke 12:9. The expression in 2 Tim 2:13 "he cannot deny himself" has the verb *arnḗsasthai*, the aor. inf. This again refers to occasions of denying Himself, meaning not to live up to His character of justice of reward proportionate to our witnessing for Him on earth. At no time will the Lord show Himself inconsistent in His judgment of our works, i.e., confessing Jesus Christ before men as well as our lack of such confession which is denying Him. It is indeed noteworthy that in 1 John 2:22, 23 the verb is in the pres. part. three times, *arnoúmenos*, which indicates a life of continuous denial that Jesus is the Christ and the Son of the Father. He who constantly denies the Lord Jesus Christ cannot be a believer. He is called an antichrist. The same is true in Jude 1:4 where the word "denying" is again *arnoúmenoi*, constantly denying. These, of course, are called ungodly men, worthy of condemnation.

Deriv.: *aparnéomai* (533), to deny.

Syn.: *antitássomai* (498), to place oneself against, oppose, resist; *aporríptō* (641), to hurl off, reject; *aposteréō* (650), to despoil, keep back; *periphronéō* (4065), to despise, depreciate; *apōthéomai* (683), to reject, push away; *apotrépō* (665), to deflect, avoid, turn away; *apophérō* (667), to bear off, carry away; *aparnéomai* (533), to deny completely; *apotássomai* (657), to renounce; *paraitéomai* (3868), to avoid, reject; *apodokimázō* (593), to disapprove;

athetéō (114), to break faith with, reject; *ekptúō* (1609), to spit out.

Ant.: *homologéō* (3670), to confess, witness, say in agreement with; *prosdéchomai* (4327), to accept; *paréchō* (3930), to present, to bring; *sunaírō* (4868), to reckon, agree together; *egkrínō* (1469), to judge in, count among; *apodéchomai* (588), to take fully, welcome, approve; *euarestéomai* (2100), to be pleased, gratified entirely; *eudokéō* (2106), to approve, think well of, be pleased; *paradéchomai* (3858), to admit, delight in, receive; *anagnōrízō* (319), to recognize.

721. ἀρνίον *arníon*; gen. *arníou*, neut. noun. Lamb (John 21:15; Rev 13:11). Designation of the exalted Christ in Rev 5:6, 8, 12, 13; 6:1, 16; 7:9, 10, 14, 17; 12:11; 13:8; 14:1, 4, 10; 15:3; 17:14; 19:7, 9; 21:9, 14, 22, 23, 27; 22:1, 3. The Lamb is contrasted to the Lion of the tribe of Judah in Rev 5:5 (see Acts 8:32), the words *hōs* (5613), as, *epí sphagén* (*epí* [1909], upon; *sphagḗ* [4967], slaughter), to be slaughtered, point to His death (see also Jer 11:19; 50:45; Ps 114:4, 6). *Spházō* (4969) is the usual expression in the Class. Gr. and the Sept. meaning to kill for sacrifice. *Arníon* denotes sacrificial death as demonstrated in Rev 7:14; 12:11; 14:4. See also Heb 9:26; 1 Pet 1:19, 20; 1 John 1:7. Later the term *arníon* became syn. with *amnós* (286), the sacrificial lamb. *Arníon* is a diminutive of *arḗn* (704), lamb.

722. ἀροτριάω *arotriáō*; contracted *arotriṓ*, fut. *arotriásō*. To plow, cultivate the earth by plowing (Luke 17:7; 1 Cor 9:10; Sept.: Deut 22:10; Isa 28:24).

723. ἄροτρον *árotron*; gen. *arótrou*, neut. noun from *aróō* (n.f.), to plow. A plow (Luke 9:62; Sept.: Isa 2:4; Joel 3:10).

724. ἀρπαγή *harpagḗ*; gen. *harpagḗs*, from *harpázō* (726), to seize upon with force. Robbery, plundering, in the act. sense as in Luke 11:39 (TR), although the reference to the contents of the cup as in Matt 23:25 may make it pass. In combination with *akrasía* (192), incontinency, it denotes an attribute, and the partial explanation of the figure of Luke is in favor of the act. meaning. The word *harpagḗ* is not used in reference to the rapture of the Church but the verb is used in 1 Thess 4:17, *harpagēsómetha*, in the fut. indic. showing punctiliar action.

Syn.: *pleonexía* (4124), covetousness, extortion; *skúlon* (4661), in the pl. meaning spoils, arms stripped from an enemy; *akrothínion* (205), the top of a heap, the choicest spoils in war.

Ant.: *agathopoiḯa* (16), well-doing, benevolence; *chrēstótēs* (5544), goodness, kindness; *agathōsúnē* (19), the quality of being benevolent; *eupoiḯa* (2140), beneficence.

725. ἀρπαγμός *harpagmós*; gen. *harpagmoú*, masc. noun from *harpázō* (726), to seize upon with force. Occurs only in Phil 2:6: "Who [Christ], being in the form of God, thought it not robbery [*harpagmón*] to be equal with God." His truly being in the form of God could not render His claim of equality with God as robbery. The Lord did not esteem being equal with God as identical with the coming forth or action of a robber (*hárpax* [727]). The trans. meaning of *harpagmós*, robbery, is necessary here. This is clear from the fact that the expression "to be equal with God" cannot be taken as the obj. of *hēgḗsato* (aor. of *hēgéomai* [2233], to consider), not to be considered a robbery. If it were the obj. of the verb, then it must be essentially different from *morphḗ Theoú* (form of God), which it can no more be than "and was made in the likeness of man" can be essentially different from "took upon him the form of a servant." The "form of a servant" includes "being made in the likeness of man." Similarly, the "form of God" includes the "being equal with God." Certainly the two expressions do not in both cases denote in an absolute sense the same thing; they differ: absolute divine existence is indicated by *hupárchōn* (5225), being, in the form of God. The part. *hupárchōn* means that Jesus continued to be in the form of God, which is what He was before He became man and had always been, for in essence He has always been God. His divine existence in relation to the world is indicated by the phrase, "He did not think being equal with God a robbery" (a.t.) as He was God among men. He was always God (John 1:1), and He became flesh (John 1:14), and thus on earth He was the God-Man. In *schḗma* (4976), outer appearance, He was man. In essence (*morphḗ* [3444]) He was God. When He became man, He truly took the form (*morphḗ* [3444], essence) of a servant. He esteemed not His equality with God as something requiring an act of force against the world or a thing to be forced upon the world. In *harpagmós* we may see the action of robbing, while in *harpagḗ* the result of the action.

Syn.: *klopḗ* (2829), theft; *klémma* (2809), a thing stolen.

Ant.: *euergesía* (2108), beneficence; *eudokía* (2107), delight, good pleasure, kindness.

726. ἀρπάζω *harpázō*; fut. *harpásō*, aor. pass. *hērpásthēn*, 2d aor. pass. *hērpágēn*. To seize upon, spoil, snatch away. In Class. Gr., the fut. pass. *harpázomai* is used more often than in the NT. Literally, to seize upon with force, to rob; differing from *kléptō* (2813), to steal secretly. It denotes an open act of violence in contrast to cunning and secret stealing. Though generally *harpázō* denotes robbery of another's property, it is not exclusively used thus, but sometimes used generally meaning forcibly to seize upon, snatch away, or take to oneself (Matt 13:19; John 6:15; 10:12, 28, 29; Acts 23:10; Jude 1:23). Especially used of the rapture (Acts 8:39; 2 Cor 12:2, 4; 1 Thess 4:17; Rev 12:5); to use force against one (Matt 11:12).

Deriv.: *harpagḗ* (724), robbery, plundering; *harpagmós* (725), robbery; *hárpax* (727), a rapacious person; *diarpázō* (1282), to seize, plunder; *sunarpázō*

(4884), to seize or grasp with great violence.

Syn.: *paralambánō* (3880), to receive; *proslambánō* (4355), to receive unto; *apospáō* (645), to draw away; *aphairéō* (851), to remove; *exaírō* (1808), to take away; *exairéō* (1807), to pluck out, deliver, rescue; *aníēmi* (447), to let go; *apotássō* (657), to take away from and place in proper order.

Ant.: *aphíēmi* (863), to leave; *kataleípō* (2641), to leave behind; *apoleípō* (620), to leave away from oneself or behind; *egkataleípō* (1459), to leave behind; *hupoleípō* (5275), to leave remaining; *perileípō* (4035), to leave around; *eáō* (1439), to leave; *hupolimpánō* (5277), to leave.

727. ἀρπαξ *hárpax*; gen. *hárpagos*, masc., fem. noun from *harpázō* (726), to seize upon. A rapacious person or animal, as wolves (Matt 7:15; Sept.: Gen 49:27). Rapacious, given to rapacity or extortion, an extortioner (Luke 18:11; 1 Cor 5:10, 11; 6:10).

Syn.: *biastḗs* (973), a forceful one, one who is violent; *kléptēs* (2812), thief, one who steals secretly and deliberately; *lēstḗs* (3027), robber, one who robs publicly. *Hárpax*, however, has the connotation of sudden and unexpected action.

Ant.: *euergétēs* (2110), benefactor; *agathopoiós* (17), a well-doer; *agathós* (18), benevolent; *kalós* (2570), good; *chrēstós* (5543), kindly.

728. ἀρραβών *arrabṓn*; gen. *arrabṓnos*, masc. noun transliterated from the Hebr. 'arabōn (6162, OT). Earnest money, a pledge, something which stands for part of the price and paid beforehand to confirm the transaction. Used in the NT only in a figurative sense and spoken of the Holy Spirit which God has given to believers in this present life to assure them of their future and eternal inheritance (2 Cor 1:22; 5:5; Eph 1:14).

Syn.: *aparchḗ* (536), translated "firstfruits"; *parakatathḗkē* (3872), a deposit.

729. ἄρραφος árraphos; gen. *arráphou*, masc., fem adj. from the priv. *a* (1), without, and *rháptō* (n.f.), to sew. Without seam, having no seam (John 19:23, not made of two pieces, but woven whole, and having no seams on the sides or shoulders. Such was the tunic of the high priest). Also from *rháptō* (n.f.): *epirráptō* (1976), to sew upon.

730. ἄρσην ársēn; gen. *ársenos*, neut. *ársen*, an older form of *árrēn*., masc. adj. Male (Matt 19:4; Mark 10:6; Luke 2:23; Rom 1:27; Gal 3:28; Rev 12:5, 13; Sept.: Gen 1:27; Lev 1:3; 3:1; 27:7).
   Deriv.: *arsenokoítēs* (733), a homosexual.
   Syn.: *anḗr* (435), male, husband.
   Ant.: *thḗlus* (2338), female.

731. ἄρρητος árrētos; gen. *arrḗtou*, masc.-fem., neut. *árrēton*, adj. from the priv. *a* (1), without, and *rhētós* (4490), utterable. Not utterable, not to be uttered, not possible or lawful to be uttered, unspeakable (2 Cor 12:4).
   Syn.: *anekdiḗgētos* (411), inexpressible; *aneklálētos* (412), unutterable.

732. ἄρρωστος árrōstos; gen. *arrṓstou*, masc.-fem., neut. *árrōston*, adj. from *a* (1), without, and *rhónnumi* (4517), to strengthen. Infirm, sick, invalid (Matt 14:14; Mark 6:5, 13; 16:18; 1 Cor 11:30; Sept.: Mal 1:8). Used in ancient Greece to indicate moral weakness or slackness. The noun form is *arróstia* (n.f.), weakness, sickness, a lingering ailment, bad state of health. For a discussion on the relationship of the three words meaning weakness or sickness (*nósēma* [3553], *nósos* [3554], and *arróstia* including *árrōstos* [732]), see *asthéneia* (769), weakness.
   Syn.: *asthenḗs* (772), without strength, feeble, hence sick.
   Ant.: *hugiḗs* (5199), healthy; *holóklēros* (3648), whole, all the constituent parts of the personality holding together; *holotelḗs* (3651), complete, each mem-

ber of the personality accomplishing its purpose.

733. ἀρσενοκοίτης arsenokoítēs; gen. *arsenokoítou*, masc. noun, from *ársēn* (730), a male, and *koítē* (2845), a bed. A man who lies in bed with another male, a homosexual (1 Cor 6:9; 1 Tim 1:10 [cf. Lev 18:22; Rom 1:27]).

734. Ἀρτεμᾶς Artemás; gen. *Artemá*, masc. proper noun. Artemas, a Christian friend of Paul (Titus 3:12). It is the masc. form of the ancient Greek goddess, Artemis or Diana.

735. Ἄρτεμις Ártemis; gen. *Artémidos* or *Artémios*, fem. proper noun. Artemis, the Greek name of Diana, the goddess of hunting. She was the twin sister of Apollo. Her temple at Ephesus was one of the seven wonders of the world. She was worshiped as the "virgin goddess" and was considered as a mother goddess of Asia Minor. Her temple was supported on one hundred massive columns. Tradition claims that her image fell there from the sky (Acts 19:35) and is thought to refer to a meteorite. Her statues today present her with many breasts. Her silversmiths who made small pottery shrines caused a riot when Paul was at Ephesus (Acts 19:23 to 20:1). Their cry, "Great is Diana of the Ephesians" (Acts 19:28, 34), and inscriptions found at Ephesus indicate that she was indeed called "Artemis the Great."

736. ἀρτέμων artémōn; gen. *artémonos*, masc. noun from *artáō* (n.f.), to suspend, hoist, hang up. The meaning of this word is unclear, but it seems to denote either a sail in the forepart of the ship, or the top sail which hung toward the top of the mast (Acts 27:40).

737. ἄρτι árti; adv. of time. Now.
   (I) Now, at present, at this moment (Matt 3:15, "Suffer it to be so now," for the present; 26:53; John 9:19, 25; 13:7, 33, 37; 16:12, 31; 1 Cor 13:12; 16:7; Gal 1:9, 10; 4:20; 2 Thess 2:7; 1 Pet 1:6, 8). In

1 Cor 4:11, "the present time" (a.t.). See also John 2:10; 16:24; 1 Cor 4:13; 8:7; 15:6; 1 John 2:9.

(II) Now, already, spoken of a time just elapsed (Matt 9:18; Rev 12:10).

(III) Now, lately (1 Thess 3:6).

(IV) *héōs árti* (*héōs* [2193], until), meaning until now, to this present time (Matt 11:12, "until now," up to the present moment; John 5:17).

(V) *ap' árti* from *apó* (575), from this present time, henceforward (Matt 23:39; 26:29; John 1:51).

Deriv.: *apárti* (534), henceforth; *artigénnētos* (738), just born; *ártios* (739), complete, perfect.

Syn.: *tó loipón* (*tó* [3588], the; *loipón* [3063], remainder), for the remaining time; *apó toú nún*, (*apó* [575], from; *toú nún* [3568], the now), from the now; *áchri toú deúro* (*áchri* [891], until; *toú deúro* [1204], hitherto), until the present; *nún* (3568), now present, present; *nuní* (3570), just now; *ḗdē* (2235), already; *apárti* (534), from now.

Ant.: *ékpalai* (1597), of old, of a long time; *ap' archḗs* (575, 746), from the beginning; *pántote* (3842), always; *apó ktíseōs*, (*apó* [575], from, *ktíseōs* [2937], creation), from the creation.

738. ἀρτιγέννητος *artigénnētos*; gen. *artigennḗtou*, masc.-fem., neut. *artigénnēton*, adj. from *árti* (737), now, lately, and *gennētós* (1084), born. Lately born, newborn; occurs only in 1 Pet 2:2.

Syn.: *neossós* (3502), a youngling, used only of birds.

739. ἄρτιος *ártios*; gen. *artíou*, fem. *artía*, neut. *ártion*, adj. from *árti* (737), now, exactly. Complete, sufficient, completely qualified (2 Tim 3:17). More closely syn. with *holóklēros* (3648), one in which all the parts are complete or whole and what they are supposed to be, so that they might serve their destined purpose.

Syn.: *téleios* (5046), perfect, complete; *pantelḗs* (3838), entire, complete; *akéraios* (185), unmixed, blameless, without guile;

plḗrēs (4134), complete; *ámemptos* (273), faultless, blameless; *áptaistos* (679), not stumbling, without sin; *holotelḗs* (3651), complete to the end.

Ant.: *anápēros* (376), crippled, maimed; *chōlós* (5560), lame; *endeḗs* (1729), lacking.

740. ἄρτος *ártos*; gen. *ártou*, masc. noun. Bread.

(I) Bread, a loaf, pl. *ártoi*, loaves (Matt 4:3, 4; 7:9; 14:17, 19; 15:34, 36; Mark 6:41; John 21:9, 13; Sept.: Gen 14:18). Spoken of the shewbread (Matt 12:4; Heb 9:2; Sept.: Lev 24:7; 1 Sam 21:4, 6); of the bread in the Last Supper (Matt 26:26; Mark 14:22; Luke 22:19; 1 Cor 10:16, 17; 11:23, 26–28); metaphorically meaning the bread from heaven, i.e., that divine spiritual nourishment presented as the life and soul of Christians in the person of the Son of God (John 6:31–58, particularly vv. 51–56; hence compared with manna in vv. 49, 58; see Ps 78:24, 25; Prov 9:5).

(II) Anything for the sustenance of the body of which bread is a principal part (Matt 6:11; Mark 6:8, 36; Luke 11:3; 2 Cor 9:10; Sept.: Ex 16:4, 15, 29; Isa 58:7). In Matt 15:26 and Mark 7:27, "the bread of the children" (a.t.) means food destined for the children. In Matt 15:2; Mark 3:20; 7:5, 27; Luke 14:1, 15, to "eat bread" means to take food, eat a meal (cf. Sept.: Gen 37:25; 39:6; 1 Sam 20:34; 1 Kgs 13:8–23). In John 13:18, "who eats bread with me" (a.t.) means who is my familiar friend, quoted from Ps 41:9. In 2 Thess 3:8, to eat the bread of someone means to be supported by someone (cf. 2 Sam 9:7, 10). In 2 Thess 3:12, to eat one's own bread means to support oneself. Other references: Matt 16:5, 7–10; Mark 2:26; 6:37, 38, 44, 52; 7:2; 8:4–6, 14, 16, 17, 19; Luke 4:3, 4; 6:4; 7:33; 9:3, 13, 16; 11:5, 11; 15:17; 24:30, 35; John 6:5, 7, 9, 11, 13, 23, 26; Acts 2:42, 46; 20:7, 11; 27:35.

741. ἀρτύω *artúō*; fut. *artúsō*. To fit, prepare, set in order, as used in Class. Gr. To prepare with seasoning, to season as with salt (Mark 9:50; Luke 14:34, to restore to salt its pungency; Col 4:6, metaphorically a word or discourse "seasoned with salt" means appropriate, proper).

742. Ἀρφαξάδ *Arphaxád*; masc. proper noun, transliterated from the Hebr. *'Arpakhshad* (775, OT). Arphaxad, a son of Shem (Luke 3:36 [cf. Gen 10:22, 24; 11:10, 12]).

743. ἀρχάγγελος *archággelos*; gen. *archaggélou*, masc. noun from *árchōn* (758), chief, and *ággelos* (32), angel or messenger. The first or highest angel, the archangel, leader of the angels. See Dan 10:13; 12:1. Of these angels there are said to be seven who stand immediately before the throne of God (Luke 1:19; Rev 8:2), who have authority over other angels (Rev 12:7), and are the patrons of particular nations (Dan 10:13; 12:1). The names of two only are found in the Scriptures: Michael, the patron of the Jewish nation (Dan 10:13, 21; 12:1; Jude 1:9; Rev 12:7), and Gabriel (Dan 8:16; 9:21; Luke 1:19, 26). The term "archangel" denotes a definite rank by virtue of which one is qualified for special work and service. The archangel, head or ruler of the angels, sometimes denotes Christ being the God-Man (1 Thess 4:16 [cf. John 5:25–27]; Jude 1:9 [cf. Zech 3:2]).

744. ἀρχαῖος *archaíos*; fem. *archaía*, neut. *archaíon*, adj. from *archē* (746), beginning. Old, expressing that which was from the beginning. Contrast to *palaiós* (3820), old, as having existed a long period of time (*pálai* [3819], time past). Since there may be many later beginnings of time, it is quite possible to conceive of the *palaiós* as older than *archaíos*. *Archaíos* reaches back to a beginning, whenever that beginning may have been. *Archaíos*, disciple (Acts 21:16), not necessarily an elderly disciple but one who had been such from the beginning of the faith, from the day of Pentecost (Acts 2). See also Matt 5:21, 27, 33; Luke 9:8, 19; Acts

15:7, 21; 2 Cor 5:17; 2 Pet 2:5; Rev 12:9; 20:2; Sept.: 1 Kgs 4:30; Isa 37:26; 43:18.

Syn.: *progínomai* (4266), to be already or to have previously come to exist; *patroparádotos* (3970), traditional; *patrōos* (3971), hereditary.

Ant.: *néos* (3501), new, chronologically or quantitatively; *kainós* (2537), new, qualitatively; *prósphatos* (4372), a recent one, new, newly slain; *chlōrós* (5515), green.

745. Ἀρχέλαος *Archélaos*; gen. *Archeláou*, masc. proper noun. Archelaus, meaning prince of the people, a son of Herod the Great by a Samaritan woman. He and his brother Antipas (493) were brought up in Rome. On the death of his father, 4 B.C., the same year that Christ was born, he succeeded to the government of Idumea, Samaria and Judea, with the title of ethnarch (1481), governor of the nation. His character was cruel and revengeful. Therefore, Joseph and Mary, on their return from Egypt, naturally feared to live under his government (Matt 2:22). In the tenth year of his reign, he was deposed by the emperor for cruelty on charges brought against him by his brothers and subjects. He was banished to Vienne in France (Gaul) where he died.

746. ἀρχή *archē*; gen. *archēs*. Beginning. *Archē* denotes an act. cause, as in Col 1:18; Rev 3:14 (cf. Rev 1:8; 21:6; 22:13). Christ is called "the beginning" because He is the efficient cause of the creation; "the head" because He is before all things, and all things were created by Him and for Him (John 1:1–3; Col 1:16–17; Heb 1:10). *Archē* may also mean the pass. beginning of something, as the beginning of a line, road, and so forth The line or road is conceived in one's mind, but where he touches the paper to draw the line is the pass. beginning of the line (Matt 19:8; Mark 1:1; 10:6; 13:8). *Archē* also means the extremity or outermost point (Acts 10:11; 11:5); rule, authority, dominion, power (Luke 20:20; 1 Cor 15:24).

(I) When it refers to time, it means the beginning, commencement, relative to an event or a situation such as in Matt 24:8, "the beginnings of sorrows"; Mark 1:1, "beginning of the gospel"; 13:8, "beginning of sorrows"; Heb 7:3, "beginning of days"; Sept.: Job 40:14; Hos 1:2. When it does not refer to a restrictive event, situation or time, it is used in an absolute sense as in John 1:1, "In the beginning was the Word." It does not delineate what beginning. Here it means before there was any beginning whatsoever, the Word had been. There is no art. before the word archḗ. Before the creation of the world there had been the Creator, the Word (Lógos [3056], which primarily means intelligence and the expression of that intelligence in making the world, the creation). See also the use of archḗ in an absolute manner (John 1:2 [without the art. as also in 1 John 1:1; 2:13, 14]; Rev 21:6; 22:13). Other references with the use of archḗ as a relative beginning: Phil 4:15, "the beginning of the gospel"; 2 Pet 3:4, "the beginning of the creation"; 1 John 2:7, 24; 3:8, 11; 2 John 1:5, 6; Jude 1:6. In Heb 2:3, archḗn laboúsa, "which at the first began [lambánō {2983}, to take]," having taken or made a beginning, means began. In John 2:11, "The beginning of signs" (a.t.) means the first miracle. In Heb 3:14, "the beginning of our confidence [hupostáseōs {5287}]," the ground beneath or something on which one can base himself, hence "confidence" means our first confidence, our faith as at the beginning. In Heb 5:12, "the first principles" or elements of faith as also in Heb 6:1.

(II) With a prep. preceding: apó (575), from, ap' archḗs, from the beginning:

(A) Of all things, from everlasting (Matt 19:4, 8; John 8:44; 1 John 3:8), or ap' archḗs toú kósmou, or tḗs ktíseōs, from the beginning of the world or creation (Matt 24:21; Mark 10:6; 13:19; 2 Pet 3:4; Sept.: Isa 43:13; Eccl 3:11; Hab 1:12).

(B) Of any particular thing, e.g., of the gospel dispensation or of Christian experience meaning from the first (Luke 1:2; John 15:27; Acts 26:4, "of life"; 2 Thess 2:13; 1 John 1:1; 2:7, 13, 14, 24; 3:11; 2 John 1:5, 6).

(III) With the prep. en (1722), in, with the dat. archḗ, en archḗ, in the beginning of all things, of the world (John 1:1, 2; Sept.: Gen 1:1); or of any particular thing, e.g., of the gospel dispensation or Christian experience, meaning at the first (Acts 11:15; Phil 4:15).

(IV) With the prep. ex (1537) (the k [kappa] in the prep. ek changes to x [chi] because archḗ begins with a vowel), meaning from the beginning, from the first, as of Christ's ministry (John 6:64; 16:4).

(V) With the prep. katá (2596), at or about, with the acc. pl. archás, kat' archás, meaning at the beginning of all things, of old (Heb 1:10).

(VI) In the acc. with the art., tḗn archḗn, used adv., meaning at the beginning, at first (Sept.: Gen 43:18, 20; Dan 8:1). In the NT, it means from the very beginning on, i.e., throughout, wholly (John 8:25, "Wholly that which I also say unto you" [a.t.]).

(VII) Spoken by metonymy of persons indicating not time but priority and preeminence (Col 1:18, "who is the beginning," meaning the ruler). See prōtótokos (4416), firstborn; Sept.: Gen 49:3; Deut 21:17. In Rev 1:8; 21:6; 22:13, "the beginning and the end" means the first and the last indicating the One who created the beginning and the One who will bring about the end of what He originally created, not through elimination but change. In Rev 3:14, "the beginning of the creation" means the active beginning of the creation, the One who caused the creation, referring to Jesus Christ not as a created being, but the One who created all things (John 1:3).

(VIII) Spoken of place, it means the extremity, corner, e.g., of a sheet (Acts 10:11; 11:5).

(IX) Spoken of dignity, meaning the first place, power, dominion (Luke 20:20; Sept.: Gen 1:16; Jer 34:1; Mic 4:8). In the sense of preeminence, precedence, rulership (Jude 1:6, "angels who did not keep their own eminence" [a.t.] or original status). See also Sept.: 1 Chr 26:10 (cf. Gen 6:2). By metonymy meaning rulers, magistrates, princes, i.e., persons of influence and authority such as civil rulers (Luke 12:11; Titus 3:1; Sept.: Mic 3:1). Spoken of the princes or chiefs among angels (Eph 1:21; 3:10; Col 2:10); among demons (1 Cor 15:24; Eph 6:12; Col 2:15); the powers of the other world (Rom 8:38; Col 1:16 [cf. *exousía* {1849}, authority].

Deriv.: *archaíos* (744), of old, original; *archēgós* (747), a leader; *árchō* (757), to be first or to rule; *patriárchēs* (3966), patriarch, progenitor.

Syn.: *gōnía* (1137), corner; *prótos* (4413), first, preeminent; *dúnamis* (1411), ruling power; *exousía* (1849), authority; *krátos* (2904), dominion; *hēgemón* (2232), a leader, ruler; *megistán* (3175), used usually in the pl. *megistánes* meaning, great ones, magnates, chiefs; with the meaning rule or regulation: *kanón* (2583), a rule; with the meaning of ruler: *kosmokrátōr* (2888), a ruler of this world; *pantokrátōr* (3841), universal ruler or ruler of all things, sovereign; *politárchēs* (4173), a ruler of a city; *architríklinos* (755), a superintendent of a banquet.

Ant.: *tó méllon*, (*méllō* [3195], I shall; *télos* [5056], end, goal) the future; *éschatos* (2078), last; *péras* (4009), an extremity, end; *teleuté* (5054), end, death; *ōméga* (5598), the last letter of the Gr. alphabet, end; *ákron* (206), end, tip, extremity; *hórion* (3725), boundary; *ékbasis* (1545), an exit, way to escape.

747. ἀρχηγός *archēgós*; gen. *archēgoú*, masc. noun from *arché* (746), beginning or rule, and *ágō* (71), to lead. Originator, founder, leader, chief, first, prince, as distinguished from simply being the cause. One may be the cause of something but not the beginning. *Arché*, like *archēgós*, denotes the founder as the first cause, ruler, dispenser; e.g., Jesus Christ is called the *archēgós* of life (Acts 3:15) because He is *hē arché*, the beginning or the originator of God's creation (Rev 3:14). This excludes Him from Himself being a product of that beginning. Jesus Christ is called *archēgós*, the originator of faith in Heb 12:2. This may mean that Jesus is the one who initiates (and completes) faith in the souls of men. However, because faith is actually articular (*tēs písteōs*) it may be best to understand it objectively referring to what is believed. In the context faith is treated as a way of life. The author summons a "cloud of witnesses" whose lives testify to the reward of the life of faith. Jesus stands as the chief witness for it was He who blazed the trail and gave us the ideal model of "the faith." This is why the author urges his readers to fix their sights on Jesus. He is also called the firstfruits, *aparché*, of them that sleep, the originator of the resurrection of those who are going to be raised from the dead. *Archēgós* occurs also in Acts 5:31, a leader, chief (cf. Acts 2:36; Eph 1:20; Sept.: Isa 30:4; Judg 5:15; 2 Chr 23:14).

Syn.: *aítios* (159), he who causes something, the author; *chilíarchos* (5506), commander of a thousand soldiers; *stratēgós* (4755), commander of an army; *stratopedárchēs* (4759), camp commander; *árchōn* (758), he who rules but may not be a ruler per se, *hēgemón* (2232), a leader, ruler; *megistánes* (3175), the great ones, princes, lords.

Ant.: *idiótēs* (2399), a private person; *dēmósios* (1219), a public or common person; *leitourgós* (3011), a public servant, a worshiper, minister.

748. ἀρχιερατικός *archieratikós*; fem. *archieratikē*, neut. *archieratikón*, adj. from *archiereús* (749), chief priest. Belonging to the chief priest(s) (Acts 4:6).

749. ἀρχιερεύς *archiereús*; gen. *archieréōs*, masc. noun from *archí-*, denoting rank or degree, and *hiereús* (2409), a priest. A high priest, chief priest (Sept.: Lev 4:3); more usually called the great priest (Sept.: Lev 21:10; Num 35:25).

(I) The high priest of the Jews (Matt 26:3, 62, 63, 65; Mark 2:26; Luke 22:50).

The president of the Sanhedrin during the trial of the Lord Jesus was a high priest (Caiaphas [2533], also Matt 26:57, 62, 63, 65; Mark 14:60, 61, 63, 66; John 18:19, 22, 24). Besides Caiaphas, those chief priests which are named are Abiathar (8), Mark 2:26; Ananias (367), Acts 23:2; 24:1; Annas (452), Luke 3:2; John 18:13, 24; Acts 4:6; Sceva (4630), Acts 19:14. The pl. is used in the NT to denote members of the Sanhedrin who belonged to high priestly families. Besides the ruling high priest, to the group were added ex–high priests whose number varied with the frequent changes of appointment made by the Roman authorities.

The high priest acquired much of the dignity that had formerly belonged to the king. In 520 B.C., the high priest Joshua and the Davidic governor Zerubbabel were placed side by side as equals (Hag 1:1, 12, 14; 2:2, 4). They began rebuilding the temple together (Ezra 3:1ff.; Hag chaps. 1,2). They shared the rule of the community as the "two anointed" (Zech 4:14; 6:9–15). In the temple, however, it was the high priest who was supreme (Zech 3:6, 7). Later the high priest became the undisputed head of the Jewish state, supreme both in civil and ecclesiastical matters. After the deposition of Abiathar by Solomon (1 Kgs 2:26, 27), the high priestly line descended from Eleazar, the son of Aaron. The office was ordinarily hereditary and conferred for life (Num 3:32; 25:11ff.; 35:25, 28).

The installation of a high priest was an elaborate ceremony lasting seven days (Ex 29:1–37; Lev 8:5–35). Technically the high priests were confined at first to the heads of the 24 courses; but the term was convenient and fluid, and when used loosely, embraced any priest whose character or status gave them a certain recognized authority. In the time of the Romans, the office was something that would go to the highest bidder. The term of office was also no longer for life, and thus there were often several persons living at one time who had borne the office and still retained the title of high priest.

There appears also to have been a sort of substitute for the high priest to perform his duties on certain occasions. Such a substitute is not expressly mentioned in the Scriptures, though such a person seems to be implied in 2 Kgs 25:18 and Jer 52:24. In one of these senses, Annas is called high priest in Luke 3:2; John 18:13; Acts 4:6.

For the distinctive high priestly clothing see Ex 28:4–39; 39:1–31; Lev 8:7–9. These vestments symbolized the mediatorial office of the high priest—the colored materials, gold, and precious stones representing the glory of God; and the breastplate, or breastpiece, inscribed with the names of the twelve tribes representing Israel as a whole. When, however, the high priest entered the Holy of Holies on the day of atonement, he laid aside his ceremonial robes and wore only linen garments—coat or tunic, breeches, girdle, and turban (Lev 16:4, 23, 32). On the Day of Atonement, only the high priest could enter the Holy of Holies and sprinkle the Mercy Seat with the blood of the sin offerings for himself and his house, and for the people (Lev 16:1–25). He also made atonement both for himself and for the people as a whole by sprinkling the blood of other sin offerings before the sanctuary and applying it to the horns of the altar (Lev 4:3–21 [cf. Lev 9:8ff.]).

The high priest was also expected to share in the general duties of the priesthood (Ex 27:21; Lev 6:19–22). There were strict moral codes that were placed upon the high priest (Lev 21:10–15). As far as his own sins are concerned, there were special sin offerings that he was required to make (Lev 4:3–12). The title also went to the holders of priestly offices such as treasurer, captain of police. We thus find the word in the pl., chief priests, with rulers (árchontes [758]) (Luke 23:13; 24:20); with scribes (grammateís [1122]), (Matt 2:4; 20:18; 21:15; Mark 10:33; 11:18; 14:1; 15:31; Luke 20:19; 22:2, 66; 23:10); with elders (presbúteroi [4245]) (Matt 21:23; 26:3, 4; 27:1, 3, 12, 20; Acts 4:23; 23:14; 25:15); with scribes and elders (Matt 16:21; 27:41; Mark 8:31; 11:27; 14:43, 53; 15:1; Luke 9:22); followed by "and all the council" (*pás* [3956], all; *tó sunédrion* [4892], the council) (Matt 26:59; Mark 14:55; Acts 22:30). *Hoi archiereís*, the high priests, without any further designation, means the Sanhedrin (Acts 9:14).

(II) A chief priest, as spoken of those who were at the head of the twenty-four classes of priests mentioned in 1 Chr 24 and who are there called *árchontes* (758), rulers of the families of priests. (1 Chr 24:6 [cf. Matt 2:4; 26:3; Mark 14:1; Luke 22:2]).

(III) Christ is presented in Heb 2:17; 3:1 as the high priest who has made atonement for the sins of men and also as the apostle (*apóstolos* [652]; Heb 5:10; 6:20; 7:26; 8:1; 9:11). In Heb 4:14 He is called the great (*mégas* [3173]) high priest.

To show His priestly function, He is also called a priest (Heb 5:6; 7:3, 11, 15, 17, 21), but His titles of high priest and great priest (Heb 10:21) show His eminence in the priestly character. Here we must determine just what is a priest in order to find the function of the Lord Jesus. In the Epistle to the Hebrews the priest is the person through whom and through whose ministry people draw near to God, through which they are "sanctified," i.e., made a people of God and enabled to worship. The apostle finds it impossible to conceive of the Jewish religion without a priest and without sacrifices. Men are presented as sinful people, and without mediation of some kind they cannot draw near to God at all. The people of God had mediators under the OT, and they have a Mediator under the NT, Christ Jesus.

Through Christ as the Mediator between God and man, man's sin is effectually removed and the way into the Holiest is opened for all. The system of the OT priesthood and the priests' sacrifices were indeed of God, but that system was not the true and final one, for the simple reason that the priesthood was imperfect. The priests were mortal men and could not continue because of death. They were

sinful men, too, and had to offer for their own sins before they could offer for those of the people. The sanctuary was imperfect, "a worldly sanctuary" (Heb 9:1), not the real dwelling place of God. The sacrifices were imperfect; the blood of bulls and goats and other animals, whatever its virtue, could not make the worshipers perfect touching the conscience, i.e., it could not bring them to the desired goal of a fearless peace toward God. The very repetition of the sacrifices showed that the work of removing sin had not really, once and for all been achieved. Man's access to God was imperfect. The priest had no access at all into the Holiest Place and when the high priest did enter on one day in the year, it was no abiding entrance; the communion of the people with God, which his presence there symbolized, was lost as soon as he came out from the shrine and the veil closed behind him.

Everything in the old religion had imperfection written upon it—the imperfection involved in the nature of its priests (Heb 7:19) and sacrifices. It is in contrast to this that Christ's priesthood is set forth. Christ is the perfect priest. "Thou art a priest forever after the order of Melchizedek" (Ps 110:4). A permanent fellowship with God has been won by our High Priest forever. The word that characterizes the work of this High Priest, Christ, is "eternal," *aiōnios* (166).

Inasmuch as He is the true priest, Christ's blood (i.e., His sacrificial death) is the blood of an eternal covenant (Heb 13:20). He offered Himself through His eternal spirit (Heb 9:14) and has become the Author of eternal salvation (Heb 5:9). He has obtained eternal redemption (Heb 9:12) and enables men to receive of the eternal inheritance (Heb 9:15; 13:20). All these are ways of indicating the perfection and finality of His priesthood, i.e., of His function to mediate between the Holy God and sinful men, and to enable those sinful men to realize a complete and abiding fellowship with God. His commission was divine (Heb 5:5f.; Ps 2:7; 110:4). He proved Himself a merciful and trustworthy high priest (Heb 2:17) by becoming one with those whom He represents before God, in having become like them a partaker of flesh and blood (Heb 2:14), by being tempted in all points like us, yet without sin (Heb 4:15). He learned obedience by the things which He suffered (Heb 5:8) knowing what it is to worship with others and to wait upon God (Heb 2:12f.), and, at last, tasting death. He was tempted like all mankind, yet sin is alien to Him (Heb 4:15). Hence, in virtue of His nature and His experience, He can sympathize with us through suffering especially. He has been made "perfect," i.e., been made all that He ought to be as a priest to stand before God for sinful men, able truly to enter into their case. The word translated "perfect" or "to perfect" is the verb *teleióō* (5048) meaning to bring to a successful conclusion, to accomplish (Heb 2:10; 5:9; 7:28; 10:14; 12:23).

The Law and the old sacrifices could not accomplish anything that was conclusive and permanent insofar as the restoration of man to God was concerned (Heb 7:19; 9:9; 10:1). Every priest was appointed to offer gifts and sacrifices (Heb 8:3) for sins (Heb 5:1), but our High Priest, Christ, offered Himself because He was perfect and, therefore, the work that He accomplished was also perfect. Heb 10:4–9, quoted from Ps 40:6–8, shows Christ's work as "doing the will of God" in contrast with sacrifices and offerings and whole burnt offerings and sin offerings, indicating that the work of the priests has been put away in order to establish the work of Christ. Indeed, we have been sanctified through the offering of the body of Jesus Christ once and for all (Heb 10:10).

What the Lord did away with was not sacrifice and obedience in themselves, but the OT sacrifices in which the victims were involuntary and the offering, therefore, morally imperfect. Christ's willing sacrifice of Himself, as a voluntary act of obedience to the Father, had a significance and a moral worth which no animal sacrifice could have. But the obedience involved in it was not simply the obedience required of man as such; it was the obedience required of the Son whom the Father had commissioned to be the mediator of a new covenant, the restorer of fellowship between Himself and sinful men. In other words, it was the obedience of the Priest who was to "annul sin by the sacrifice of himself" ([a.t.] Heb 9:26); to be "offered once for all to bear the sins of many" ([a.t.] Heb 9:28); to enter into the sanctuary "through his own blood" ([a.t.] Heb 9:12); and "by one offering to perfect forever them that are being sanctified" ([a.t.] Heb 10:14). In short, it is not sacrifice and obedience alone that are blankly contrasted here, but unintelligent and involuntary animal sacrifice compared to the sacrificial obedience of the Priest who willingly dies to make an atonement for sins (Heb 1:3).

As the perfect high priest, Christ made once and for all the perfect sacrifice for sin, and thus the Levitical sacrifices have passed away. What Jesus Christ did on earth in shedding His blood for us in some way purified the heavens (Heb 4:14; 9:23, 24). Our High Priest is now seated with God the Father in heaven to intercede for us (Heb 4:16). The title of high priest is never attributed to any believer, nor any of the special functions involved in the unique priesthood of Christ.

In the NT, we do not have any Christian believers acting as a human high priest or chief priest. All Christian believers, however, are called a holy priesthood (1 Pet 2:5); a royal priesthood (1 Pet 2:9); kings and priests (Rev 1:6; 5:10); priests of God and of Christ (Rev 20:6). This is why we as believers at any time can draw near with boldness into the presence of God (Eph 2:17; Heb 4:16). Because of our High Priest, Christ, we as Christians have access directly to God (Rom 5:2), and our sonship in our relationship to God through Christ has made us also priests enjoying all the privileges of the priesthood. We are acceptable to God (Rom 12:1). There is no such thing in the NT as a sacrifice for sin by us as priests of God and Jesus Christ. We need no sacrifice for sin except the sacrifice which Christ offered once for all. Paul speaks of himself in Rom 15:16 as "ministering the gospel of God." The word translated "ministering" is *hierourgoúnta*, the pres. part. of *hierourgéō* (2418), which means to officiate as a priest, perform the function of a priest. This by no stretch of the imagination should cause us to conceive that Paul claims that he himself is a Christian priest making sacrifice for sin and mediating again in the Aaronic fashion between God and man. What he is doing here is contrasting the gospel to the sacrifices. The sacrifices of old were imperfectly valid only for the Jews, but now the gospel is also for the Gentiles, and because of the sufficiency of the gospel for the Gentiles too, he declares himself *leitourgón* (3011), a public servant, translated "minister" in the KJV. The second time that this verb occurs in this verse, however, it is *hierourgoúnta*, "ministering," performing the function of a priest. Paul presents the Gentiles as an offering to God, acceptable to Him not because of any of the old sacrifices, but because of the preaching of the gospel. Other occurrences of *archiereús*: Matt 21:45; 26:14, 51, 58; 27:6, 62; 28:11; Mark 14:10, 47, 54; 15:3, 10, 11; Luke 19:47; 20:1; 22:4, 52, 54; 23:4, 23; John 7:32, 45; 11:47, 49, 51, 57; 12:10; 18:3, 10, 15, 16, 26, 35; 19:6, 15, 21; Acts 5:17, 21, 24, 27; 7:1; 9:1, 21; 22:5; 23:4, 5; 25:2; 26:10, 12.

Deriv.: *archieratikós* (748), highpriestly.

750. ἀρχιποίμην *archipoímēn*; gen. *archipoiménos*, masc. noun from *archí-*, denoting rank or degree, and *poimḗn* (4166), a shepherd. Chief shepherd, applied to Christ (1 Pet 5:4; cf. Heb 13:20).

Syn.: *archiereús* (749), chief priest; *árchōn* (758), a ruler; *archisunágōgos* (752), a ruler of a synagogue.

751. Ἄρχιππος *Árchippos*; gen. *Archíppou*, masc. proper noun. Archippus, meaning master of the horse, a Christian teacher addressed by Paul in Col 4:17 and Phile 1:2. Some think that Archippus was Philemon's son.

752. ἀρχισυνάγωγος *archisunágōgos*; gen. *archisunagṓgou*, masc. noun from *archí-*, denoting rank or degree, and *sunagōgḗ* (4864), a synagogue. Ruler of the synagogue. As there were several elders in each synagogue, one of them was chosen, or appointed, ruler or rector of the synagogue. He governed all its affairs, such as preserving order, and selecting and inviting persons to read or speak in the assembly. The presiding elder was called *archisunágōgos*, though the name is sometimes applied to all elders (Matt 5:22, 35, 36, 38; Luke 8:49; 13:14; Acts 13:15; 18:8, 17). We do not know how many such rulers were in each synagogue, but it seems that there were more than one. Multiple rulers of the synagogue are mentioned in Mark 5:22 (cf. Acts 13:15).

Syn.: *archiereús* (749), a chief priest; *archipoimḗn* (750), a chief shepherd; *árchōn* (758), one who rules.

753. ἀρχιτέκτων *architéktōn*; gen. *architéktonos*, masc. noun from *archí-*, denoting rank or degree, and *téktōn* (5045), a workman, builder. A head or master workman or builder, an architect (1 Cor 3:10; Sept.: Isa 3:3).

754. ἀρχιτελώνης *architelṓnēs*; gen. *architelṓnou*, masc. noun from *archí-*, denoting rank or degree, and *telṓnēs* (5057), a publican. A chief publican or head collector of public revenues (Luke 19:2).

755. ἀρχιτρίκλινος *architríklinos*; gen. *architriklínou*, masc. noun from *archí-*, denoting rank or degree, and *tríklinos*, with three couches, which is from *treís*, three, and *klínē* (2825), a couch. A ruler, governor, or the master of a feast, the person who had the direction of the entertainment, arrangement of the guests, and so forth (John 2:8, 9). The *architríklinos*, (so named because among the Romans, three couches were usually set around one square table in the dining room, the remaining fourth side of the table being left free for access by the servants) was required to remain strictly sober at all times as he directed the affairs of the feast, tasted the wine first lest the drunken guests thought they were drinking wine while they were drinking water. The Greeks called such a ruler *sumposíarchos* (the ruler of a *sumpósion* [4849], a drinking party or symposium) or *trapezopoiós* (the one who makes or arranges a *trápeza* [5132], a table or tables for eating).

Syn.: *oikonómos* (3623), one who rules a house, a superior servant.

756. ἄρχομαι *árchomai*; fut. *árxomai*, aor. *ērxámēn*, the mid. of *árchō* (757), to rule, govern. It means:

(I) To begin, used intrans. and followed by an inf. expressed or implied (Matt 4:17; 11:7, 20; 12:1; 14:30; 16:21, 22; 18:24; 24:49; 26:22, 37, 74; Mark 1:45; 2:23; 4:1; 5:17, 20; 6:2, 34, 55; 8:11, 31, 32; 10:41, 47; 11:15; 12:1; 13:5; 14:19, 33, 65, 69, 71; 15:8, 18; Luke 3:23, "and Jesus was beginning [entering upon the age of] to be about thirty years" [a.t.]; 4:21; 5:21; 7:15, 24, 38, 49; 9:12; 11:29, 53; 12:1, 45; 13:25, 26; 14:9, 18, 29, 30; 15:14, 24; 19:37, 45; 20:9; 21:28; 22:23; 23:2, 30; John 13:5; Acts 1:1; 2:4; 11:4, 15; 18:26; 24:2; 27:35; 2 Cor 3:1).

(II) To attempt to undertake, to venture (Mark 6:7; 10:28, 32; Luke 3:8; Sept.: Judg 10:18).

(III) Aor. part. *arxámenos* and *apó* (575), from, with the gen., meaning beginning from, expressing the point of beginning in a narration, transaction, and so forth (Matt 20:8; Luke 23:5; 24:27, 47; John 8:9; Acts 1:22; 8:35; 10:37; Sept.: Gen 44:12). In 1 Pet 4:17, "time to begin the judgment starting from the house of God" ([a.t.] Sept.: Ezek 9:6).

Deriv.: *enárchomai* (1728), to begin, commence.

Syn.: *anatéllō* (393), to rise, spring up.

Ant.: *teleióō* (5048), to accomplish, finish; *teléō* (5055), to conclude, achieve

the goal, perform; *teleutáō* (5053), to finish life, expire; *kleíō* (2808), to close; *epiteléō* (2005), to fulfill further, to terminate; *sumplēróō* (4845), to complete; *ekpnéō* (1606), to expire; *katantáō* (2658), to arrive at, attain; *apobaínō* (576), to eventuate.

757. ἄρχω *árchō*; fut. *árxō*, from *archḗ* (746), beginning, first. To be first in rank, hence, to rule, govern (Mark 10:42; Rom 15:12; Sept.: Gen 1:18; Deut 15:6). In the Gr. writers, the verb *árchō* in the act. voice and *árchomai* in the mid. voice meant to begin, but in the NT, *árchomai* (756) is used only in this sense in Matt 4:17; 11:7; 12:1 (see 756). Also, in Luke 24:47, *arxámenon* is an impersonal part. and may be rendered as a beginning being made, in making a beginning, or so that a beginning be made.

Deriv.: *árchomai* (756), beginning; *Asiárchēs* (775), a ruler of Asia; *ethnárchēs* (1481), the governor of a district; *hekatontárchēs* (1543), centurion; *politárchēs* (4173), ruler of the city; *stratopedárchēs* (4759), captain of the guard; *tetrárchēs* (5076), tetrarch; *hupárchō* (5225), to behave, live; *chilíarchos* (5506), captain.

Syn.: *basileúō* (936), to reign; *hēgemoneúō* (2230), to act as a ruler; *hēgéomai* (2233), to lead; *oikodespotéō* (3616), to rule a house; *proḯstēmi* (4291), to stand before, to rule; *poimaínō* (4165), to act as a shepherd; *exousiázō* (1850), to exercise authority upon; *katexousiázō* (2715), to exercise full authority; *kurieúō* (2961), to exercise lordship over; *katakurieúō* (2634), to lord it over completely; *prōteúō* (4409), to be first.

Ant.: *akolouthéō* (190), to follow; *miméomai* (3401), to imitate, follow; *summorphóomai* (4833), to become conformable to.

758. ἄρχων *árchōn*; gen. *árchontos*, masc. part. of *árchō* (757), to rule. A ruler, chief, prince, magistrate (Matt 9:34; 20:25; John 14:30; Acts 7:27; Rev 1:5). It should seem from a comparison of John

3:1 with John 7:45–50 that the *árchōn* of the Jews in the former passage means a member of the Jewish Sanhedrin, though it is plain from comparing Matt 9:18, 23 with Mark 3:22 and Luke 8:41 that *árchōn* in those texts of Matthew means only a ruler of a synagogue. Generally a leader, a chief person (Matt 20:25; Acts 4:26; Rom 13:3; 1 Cor 2:6, 8; Sept.: Gen 49:20; Num 23:21; Isa 14:5. See also Gen 12:15; 25:16; 2 Chr 8:9). Spoken of the Messiah as King of kings (Rev 1:5); of Moses as a ruler and leader of Israel (Acts 7:27, 35); of magistrates of any kind such as the high priest (Acts 23:5); of civil judges (Luke 12:58; Acts 16:19); of persons of weight and influence among the Pharisees and other sects at Jerusalem who also were members of the Sanhedrin (Luke 14:1; 18:18; 23:13, 35; 24:20; John 3:1 [cf. 7:45, 50; John 7:26, 48; 12:42; Acts 3:17; 4:5, 8; 13:27; 14:5]); of magnates (Sept.: Neh 5:7); of the chief of the fallen angels, Satan, the chief of demons (Matt 9:34; 12:24; Mark 3:22; Luke 11:15), called "the ruler of this world," which means Satan ruling in the hearts of worldly and wicked men (John 12:31; 14:30; 16:11), also the prince or ruler of "the power of the air" (Eph 2:2). Contrast to *archēgós* (747), which also means leader. However, while *árchōn* is one who temporarily acts as a leader, *archēgós* has an inherent right to be a leader with the meaning of being the author or source, translated in Acts 3:15; 5:31 as "prince"; in Heb 2:10 as "captain"; in 12:2 as "author." In every one of these instances, it refers to the person of Jesus Christ as the author of life, salvation, and our faith. He was not One who assumed leadership, but was indeed the author of all these things.

Deriv.: *archággelos* (743), archangel.

Syn.: *stratēgós* (4755), captain, magistrate; *megistán* (3175), a great man; *kosmokrátōr* (2888), a ruler of the world; *pantokrátōr* (3841), almighty; *politárchēs* (4173), a ruler of a city; *architríklinos* (755), superintendent of a banquet; *hēgemṓn* (2232), a leader.

Ant.: *doúlos* (1401), bondman; *diákonos* (1249), deacon, servant; *hupērétēs* (5257), servant, an underrower; *oikétēs* (3610), a house servant; *therápōn* (2324), an attendant; *místhios* (3407), hired servant; *misthōtós* (3411), a wage earner, hired servant; *dēmósios* (1219), a public servant; *idiṓtēs* (2399), a private person; *leitourgós* (3011), a public servant, usually in the temple.

759. ἄρωμα *árōma*; gen. *arṓmatos*, neut. noun. An aromatic, a spice such as myrrh, *múron* (3464), and aloe, *alóē* (250). Mark 16:1; Luke 23:56; 24:1; John 19:40; Sept.: 2 Kgs 20:13; 2 Chr 9:1, 9.

Syn.: *kinámōmon* (2792), a fragrant spice (Rev 18:13), cinnamon; *euōdía* (2175), fragrance; *osmḗ* (3744), odor; *thumíama* (2368), fragrant powder burnt in religious services, incense; *líbanos* (3030), incense, frankincense, and also *libanōtós* (3031), frankincense, but also the censer itself in which incense is burnt.

760. Ἀσά *'Asá*; masc. proper noun, transliterated from the Hebr. *'Āṣā'* (609, OT), meaning physician. Asa, son and successor of Abijam on the throne of Judah (955–914 B.C.). He reigned forty-one years. He was decidedly opposed to idolatry and purified his kingdom from it (Matt 1:7, 8; see 1 Kgs 15:9–24; 2 Chr chaps. 14—16).

761. ἀσάλευτος *asáleutos*; gen. *asaleútou*, masc.-fem., neut. *asáleuton*, adj. from the priv. *a* (1), without, and *saleúō* (4531), to agitate, shake. Not to be shaken, unshaken, immovable, Acts 27:41; in Heb 12:28, used metaphorically meaning firm, enduring.

Syn.: *ametakínētos* (277), firm, immovable; *aklinḗs* (186), not leaning, firm; *stereós* (4731), solid, stable, steadfast; *hedraíos* (1476), immovable, settled; *asphalḗs* (804), certain, safe, sure; *bébaios* (949), firm, stable.

Ant.: *astḗriktos* (793), vacillating, unstable.

762. ἄσβεστος *ásbestos*; gen. *asbéstou*, masc.-fem., neut. *ásbeston*, adj. from the priv. *a* (1), without, and *sbénnumi* (4570), to quench. Not to be quenched, unquenchable, inextinguishable (Matt 3:12; Mark 9:43, 45; Luke 3:17 [cf. Matt 18:8]). In all three instances, it describes the fire that burns the chaff separated from the wheat, the chaff therefore being useless and worthy only of burning (Matt 3:12). This fire is representative of the means of punishment for those who will not believe, represented by the phrase *kaí* (2532), and, and *purí*, the dat. of *púr* (4442), fire, *kaí purí*, "and with fire." Here first are presented those who will be baptized in the Holy Spirit, meaning those who will be accepted by Christ and baptized by Him with the Holy Spirit into His body (1 Cor 12:13). Those who are not baptized into the body of Christ are the unbelievers and their fate will be punishment by fire, even as befalls the chaff. The verb used in Matt 3:12 for this burning is *katakaíō* (2618), to burn down completely. Lest the misunderstanding occur that this verb *katakaíō* (in the fut. indic., *katakaúsei*, will burn completely at an indef. time in the future) means annihilation of the unbelievers, and not a permanent and changed state of being involving punishment and pain, the adj. *asbéstō*, unquenchable, is added to explain the verb. It thus characterizes the fire as unquenchable, i.e., inextinguishable. Thus, if the fire burns inextinguishably, then the punishment is without end. In Matt 3:10, the statement is "and is cast into the fire." This does not intimate that the unfruitful tree is annihilated. In Mark 9:43, 45, the expression, "the fire inextinguishable" (a.t.) definitely refers to and qualifies Gehenna (*Géenna* [1067]) as the place of everlasting punishment. The expression in Luke 3:17 is similar to the one in Matt 3:12.

Syn.: *diēnekés* (1336), perpetual, forever.

Ant.: *próskairos* (4340), for a season, temporal; *brachús* (1024), short; *ephḗmeros* (2184), for a day.

763. ἀσέβεια *asébeia*; gen. *asebeías*, fem. noun from *asebḗs* (765), impious, ungodly, wicked. Impiety toward God, ungodliness, lack of reverence (Rom 1:18); wickedness in general, neglect or violation of duty toward God, our neighbor or ourselves, joined with and springing from impiety toward God (Rom 11:26; 2 Tim 2:16; Titus 2:12; Jude 1:15, 18; Sept.: Prov 4:17; Eccl 8:8; Jer 5:6; Ezek 16:58; 21:24).

Syn.: *adikía* (93), injustice, unrighteousness, iniquity; *anomía* (458), illegality, violation of law, wickedness; *hamartía* (266), sin; *ponēría* (4189), wickedness, malevolence; *kakía* (2549), wickedness, badness; *paranomía* (3892), law breaking; *anaídeia* (335), impudence, insolence; *kakoḗtheia* (2550), mischievousness, depravity of heart.

Ant.: *eusébeia* (2150), piety; *eulábeia* (2124), religious reverence; *theosébeia* (2317), devoutness, piety, godliness.

764. ἀσεβέω *asebéō*; contracted *asebṓ*, fut. *asebḗsō*, from *asebḗs* (765), impious, ungodly, wicked. To act impiously, to sin against anything which should be considered sacred. Without an obj., to trespass, commit an offense. In the Scriptures it occurs in a very strong reference to sinfulness in 2 Pet 2:6 and Jude 1:15.

Syn.: *adikéō* (91), to be unjust, to do wrong; *hamartánō* (264), to sin, offend; *kataphronéō* (2706), to despise; *periphronéō* (4065), to depreciate, not to give due respect.

Ant.: *sébomai* (4576), to reverence, worship; *eulabéomai* (2125), to religiously reverence; *sebázomai* (4573), to worship; *proskunéō* (4352), to crouch before, reverence, adore, worship; *timáō* (5091), to honor, value, revere; *latreúō* (3000), to worship while serving, to render religious service; *leitourgéō* (3008), to serve God; *eusebéō* (2151), to show respect, act reverently.

765. ἀσεβής *asebḗs*; gen. *aseboús*, masc.-fem., neut. *asebés*, adj. from the priv. *a* (1), without, and *sébomai* (4576), to worship, venerate. Basically it means godless, without fear and reverence of God. It does not mean irreligious, but one who actively practices the opposite of what the fear of God demands. *Asebés* is one characterized by immoral and impious behavior. Often opposite of *díkaios* (1342), just (Rom 4:5; 5:6). *Asebés* also occurs in 2 Pet 2:5; 3:7; Jude 1:4, 15.

Deriv.: *asébeia* (763), impiety; *asebéō* (764), to act impiously.

Syn.: *hamartōlós* (268), sinful, sinner; *anósios* (462), wicked, unholy; *bébēlos* (952), wicked, profane; *theostugḗs* (2319), impious, hater of God; *hubristḗs* (5197), an insulter.

Ant.: *eusebḗs* (2152), pious; *sebastós* (4575), august; *semnós* (4586), respectful, worthy of respect; *hieroprepḗs* (2412), becoming to a sacred place or person; *eulabḗs* (2126), devout.

766. ἀσέλγεια *asélgeia*; gen. *aselgeías*, fem. noun, from *aselgḗs* (n.f.), licentious, brutal. Lasciviousness, license, debauchery, sexual excess, absence of restraint, insatiable desire for pleasure. Mark 7:22, arrogance, insolence referring to words; 2 Cor 12:21, wantonness, lustfulness, excessive pleasure (also Rom 13:13; Gal 5:19; 2 Pet 2:7, 18); Eph 4:19, debauchery, perversion in general; 1 Pet 4:3; 2 Pet 2:7; Jude 1:4.

Syn.: *asōtía* (810), wastefulness and riotous excess; *epithumía* (1939), lust; *aischrótēs* (151), impropriety, all that is contrary to purity; *rhuparía* (4507), filth; *molusmós* (3436), defilement; *strḗnos* (4764), insolent luxury; *porneía* (4202), fornication; *akrasía* (192), lack of self-restraint, incontinency; *hēdoné* (2237), lust, pleasure; *kraipálē* (2897), debauchery, glut, drunkenness.

Ant.: *egkráteia* (1466), self-control; *sōphrosúnē* (4997), sobriety, the ability to limit one's freedom; *élegchos* (1650), conviction, restriction, control; *aidṓs* (127), modesty, reverence.

767. ἄσημος *ásēmos*; gen. *asḗmou*, masc.-fem., neut. *ásēmon*, adj. from the priv. *a* (1), without, and *séma* (n.f., see below), a mark, a sign. Not remarkable, inconsiderable (Acts 21:39; Sept.: Gen 30:42; Job 42:11).

Deriv. of *séma* (n.f.): *epísēmos* (1978), having a mark upon; *eúsēmos* (2154), well-expressed, easily understood; *parásēmos* (3902), the sign or ensign of a ship; *sēmaíno* (4591), to signify; *sússēmon* (4953), a signal.

Syn.: *anáxios* (370), unworthy, of little value; *aphanḗs* (852), not apparent; *koinós* (2839), common; *eláchistos* (1646), least; *éschatos* (2078), lowest, last.

Ant.: *spoudaíos* (4705), energetic, hence one who makes his mark; *sēmaínōn* (4591), notable; *mégas* (3173), great; *prôtos* (4413), foremost, first, chief; *gnōstós* (1110), known; *epiphanḗs* (2016), conspicuous; *aidṓs* (127), modesty, reverence.

768. Ἀσήρ *Asḗr*; masc. proper noun transliterated from the Hebr. *'Ashēr* (836, OT). Asher, meaning blessed, the eighth son of Jacob (Luke 2:36; Rev 7:6 [cf. Gen 30:13]).

769. ἀσθένεια *asthéneia*; gen. *astheneías*, fem. noun from *asthenḗs* (772), weak, sick. Weakness, sickness. In the NT, this word and related words, *asthenḗs* (772), weak, sick, and *asthenéō* (770), to be sick or weak, are the most common expressions for illness and are used in the comprehensive sense of the whole man. However, it can also refer to a special form of bodily weakness or sickness. Figuratively, *asthéneia* can mean general impotence, weakness (Rom 8:26). The noun occurs only seven times in the gospels. In Matt 8:17, a quotation from Isa 53:4, He (Christ on the cross) took our infirmities (*astheneías*), which means that, in His manhood, He took upon Himself the consequences of our sins without sinning Himself. He became mortal so that He could die for us. That is the first meaning.

There is, however, a second word in Matt 8:17, *nósous* (the pl. of *nósos* [3554], the sicknesses themselves), which must be considered. Here *asthéneia* may be said to be the result of illness since it indeed deprives us of the strength that we would enjoy if it were not for sickness. The Lord on the cross took upon himself not only the consequences of sickness (*astheneías*), but sicknesses (*nósous*) themselves, both being basically the result of man's disobedience to God (Gen 2:17). Christ's death provided the redemptive means for our spirits which is realized by the believer immediately. This regeneration of the human spirit is called "the firstfruits of the Spirit" in Rom 8:23. The redemption of the body, however, is something that the Christian looks forward to and which will be realized at the believer's resurrection when the Lord comes for His own (Rom 8:23; 1 Cor 15:50–51; 1 Thess 4:14–17).

An expression with a similar meaning is *kakós échō* (*kakós* [2560], badly, and *échō* [2192], to have), to have it bad. This expression is followed by *nósois*, the dat. pl. of *nósos* in Mark 1:34: "and he healed many that were sick (*kakós échontas*) of diverse (*poikílais* [4164], various, manifold) diseases (*nósois*)." It was the diseases that made them have it bad or be weak (*astheneías*). A similar expression is found in Luke 4:40, using both the pres. part. *asthenoúntas* and *nósois*, meaning that they were sick because of diseases as in Luke 5:15. *Asthéneiai*, sicknesses, may refer to physical weaknesses due to specific diseases (*nósous*), or the corruptibility (*phthorá* [5356]) of the human body from which no one is exempt, for all die. The indef. nature of *asthéneia* appears from the use of the adj. *asthenḗs* (Acts 4:9); *asthéneia* (Acts 28:9); and the verb *asthenéō* (James 5:14), which are used syn. with *adúnatos* (102), impotent, weak (see Acts 14:8; Rom 15:1).

In 1 Cor 11:30, the adj. *astheneís* (pl.), weak, and its syn. *árrōstoi* (732), sick, are used together, indicating that there must be a difference between the two terms. *Astheneís* here must refer to those

suffering from weakness of any kind, i.e., physical, psychosomatic, emotional, economic, relational, or whatever causes a person to state, "I don't feel well." The Greeks had and still have a word for this, *athumía*, faintheartedness, despondency. The noun does not occur in the NT, but the verb *athuméō* (120), to be spiritless, disheartened, dismayed, occurs in Col 3:21. In Gal 4:13 Paul refers to the physical weakness (*asthéneian tḗs sarkós*) that resulted from what he calls "a thorn in the flesh" (2 Cor 12:7) which must have been the illness (*nósos* [3554]) or the lingering illness of the *arrōstía*. The two words which more definitively refer to the results of *nósos* and *arrōstía* are *nósēma* (3553) in John 5:4 and *arrōstēma*, not occurring in the NT.

The adj. *árrōstoi* is derived from the priv. *a* (1) and the noun *rhōsis* (n.f.), strength, and the verb *rhōnnumi* (4517), to strengthen. The verb *anarrōnnumi*, to recover, and the noun *annárrōsis*, recovery, are used in connection with *nósoi* (3554), diseases (Plutarch and Hesychius), which would tend to indicate actual physical sickness. This viewpoint can be sustained by the fact that such are said to lead to death. The noun *arrōstía*, which is used commonly in Mod. Gr., according to lexicographers Liddell and Scott, especially refers to a lingering ailment, a bad state of health (Aristotle).

The use of the word *árrōstoi*, sick, in Matt 14:14 would sustain this particular meaning. On learning that Jesus had arrived by boat, the people brought to Him for healing those who were suffering from lingering sicknesses.

In Nazareth, Jesus' hometown, the Lord "laid his hands upon a few sick folk, and healed them" (Mark 6:5). The word for "sick" here is *arrōstois* (the dat. pl. of *árrōstos*). The Lord must have healed only some of those who were sick a long time from lingering illnesses to cause them to believe, but they would not. This is why He "marveled because of their unbelief. And he went round about the villages, teaching."

The third instance of the use of *árrōstoi* is in Mark 6:13, which also sustains the view that these were physical sufferers. There were two kinds of sufferers, those who were possessed by demons and those who were bodily ill. "And they [the Twelve Apostles] cast out many devils [*daimónia* {1140}, little demons] and anointed [*éleiphon* rubbed, the imperf. of *aleíphō* (218), to rub] with oil many that were sick [*arróstous*, the acc. pl. of *árrōstos*] and healed them." Here we have the same verb *aleíphō* used in James 5:14 which refers to the application of the then-existing and acceptable medicinal means of treatment, rubbing with oil and simultaneously exercising the apostolic power of healing.

The fourth occurrence of *árrōstoi* is in the disputed passage of Mark 16:18, where we read, "they shall lay hands on the sick, and they shall recover." If this action of laying on of hands referred to ceremonial anointing, the specific religious verb *chríō* (5548), to anoint, would have been used. But the action expected of the disciples is "they shall lay hands on" (Mark 16:18). The same expression is used in Mark 6:5. They were to use their hands to rub them with oil which, transferred to the context of our culture, is to apply whatever medicinal means exist in order to heal the physically sick. *Asthéneia*, therefore, may refer rather to the symptoms of *nósos* (3554) or *arróstia*, sickness, whatever that may be.

That evil spirits or demons can cause such bodily weakness is evident from Luke 8:2; 13:11, 12. In these passages these women were probably suffering physical results of a spiritual or attitudinal cause, such a disease being psychosomatic, as we say today. In John 5:5, the stress is on the man who for thirty-eight years was paralyzed, being in his *asthéneia* unable to move. This was the consequence of his sickness, which in John 5:4 is called *nósēma* (3553). This is the only place where it occurs in the NT and means the result of *nósos*, sickness. The result in itself is *asthéneia*, with the difference that

the *nósēma* is *asthéneia*, which is pinpointed as having its cause in a *nósos*. The patient at the Bethesda Pool was suffering from some definite sickness. The only other place where *asthéneia* occurs in the gospels is in John 11:4, referring to the infirmity of Lazarus, "This sickness [*asthéneia*] is not unto death." The Lord is not diagnosing the disease of Lazarus, but simply saying that the infirmity or weakness from which he suffered was not going to result in permanent death but that He, Christ, was going to be glorified and would prevail.

It is indeed noteworthy that, in the apostolic writings, only five particular kinds of diseases are specified: palsy (Acts 8:7; 9:33); impotence (Acts 3:2); a digestive trouble (1 Tim 5:23); dysentery (Acts 28:8); and abdominal disease associated with worms (Acts 12:21ff.). In addition, we have those suffering from nervous disorders (Acts 5:16 [cf. Acts 16:16–18; 19:12]). Individuals are, in general terms, "sick" (Acts 9:37, Dorcas who became ill [*asthenḗsasan*]; Phil 2:26, 27, Epaphroditus became ill [*ēsthénēse*]; 2 Tim 4:20, Trophimus being ill [*asthenoúnta*, being ill]). In these cases, no specific symptoms are mentioned by which the nature of the illness may be defined. In Acts 28:9, those who were brought to the Apostle Paul on the island of Malta are said to have had *astheneías*, weaknesses or infirmities, but without any reference to the particular diseases. The only allusion to account for the cause of any sickness is by Paul in his advice to the Corinthians concerning the Lord's Supper in 1 Cor 11:30: "For this cause many are weak [*astheneís* {772}] and sickly [*árrōstoi* {732}] among you." This weakness of the body refers to sickness inflicted by God as an act of judgment due to the flagrant abuse of the Lord's Supper.

A connection between sin and sickness is suggested by the Lord Jesus in John 5:14. Evil spirits are reported as going out from those whom they had possessed (Acts 19:12), a particular instance of which is in Acts 16:16–18.

The use of medicinal means is intimated in James 5:14 where the verb *aleípsantes*, the aor. part. of *aleíphō* (218), to rub with oil, is used. It is also used in Mark 6:13. This verb should be distinguished from the sacred use of the verb *chríō* (5548), to anoint. Believers, however, are not to set their whole trust on medicinal means, but they are to pray, for it is the prayer (*euchḗ* [2171], wish) of faith that counts much in the healing of the believer (James 5:15). In the case of unbelievers, God uses means in spite of the possible nonexistence of the influence of prayer. He executes His will whether or not man through prayer shows his dependence upon God. Other references to weaknesses resulting from physical causes are in 1 Tim 5:23; Heb 4:15; 5:2; 7:28; 11:34.

In Rom 6:19, the expression, "the infirmity [*asthéneia*] of your flesh" means the resident weakness of the flesh due to sin which must always be recognized by the believer and who must seek to fight it (Rom 8:13). In Rom 8:26, "Likewise the Spirit also helpeth our infirmities," refers to the resident weakness of the flesh. In 1 Cor 2:3, "and I was with you in weakness [*astheneía*], and in fear, and in much trembling," means the realization of the fact that the body has not been redeemed yet. In this instance it also refers to timidity. In 1 Cor 15:43, *asthéneia* stands in contrast to *dúnamis* (1411) and could be said to be a syn. of *adunamía* (n.f.), lack of strength or power (see *adunatéō* [101], to be unable).

The human body is sown in weakness (*astheneía*) (1 Cor 15:43) which refers to its corruptibility, but it is raised in power (*dunámei* [1411]). It is absolutely wrong to claim that the body now has incorruptibility and, therefore, a Christian should expect exemption from sickness and death. That exemption will come only with the resurrection body (1 Cor 15:53, 54).

In 2 Cor 11:30; 12:5, 9, 10, Paul speaks of his weaknesses (*astheneías*) referring to the results of Adamic sin which, however, in no way should be overwhelming because the power of God is made manifest through our weaknesses (Rom 4:20; Eph 6:10; Phil 4:13; 1 Tim 1:12; 2 Tim 2:1; 4:17).

Syn.: *árrōstos* (732), infirm, without robustness; *Malakía* (3119), weakness, softness; *nósos* (3554), disease, malady.

Ant.: *dúnamis* (1411), strength; *ischús* (2479), inherent ability, might, strength; *íama* (2386), a means of healing; *íasis* (2392), the process of healing; *sōtēría* (4991), healing, health, physical salvation in addition to its more frequent meaning of spiritual salvation; *therapeía* (2322), healing, with the meaning of service.

770. ἀσθενέω *asthenéō*; contracted *asthenō̂*, fut. *asthenḗsō*, from *asthenḗs* (772), without strength, powerless, sick. To lack strength, be infirm, weak, feeble.

(I) To be weak (Rom 8:3; 2 Cor 13:3; Sept.: 1 Sam 2:5; 2 Sam 3:1; Lam 2:8). In 2 Cor 13:4, 9, to be considered weak. Christ is not to be considered inherently powerless when He does not immediately impose the proper punishment.

(II) Specifically, to be infirm in the body, i.e., to be sick, to suffer from disease or the consequences thereof (Matt 10:8; 25:36; Mark 6:56; Luke 4:40; 7:10 where *asthenōn*, the weak one, is contrasted to one who is healthy or *hugiaínōn* [5198] from which we derive the Eng. word "hygiene"). See Luke 9:2, where the corresponding verb for healing is *iáomai* (2390). In John 4:46 and 5:3, it is clear that *asthenoúntōn*, "impotent people," refers to those who were weak, this being the symptom of their actual sicknesses or ailments, i.e., blindness, lameness, stiffness (dryness). In John 6:2, *ho asthenōn* (sing.) or *hoi asthenoúntes* (pl.), the sick one or ones, refers to any of these people who may have been suffering from various diseases. In John 11:1–3, 6, observe that the Lord did not probe to discover the specific disease from which Lazarus was suffering. In Acts 9:37 and 19:12, observe that Dorcas (who was described as *asthenḗsasan*), and those who were weak or sick (*asthenoúntas*), were suffering from diseases (*nósous* [3554]) which departed from them. But there were also those who were weak or sick from being indwelt by evil spirits. The adj. part. *asthenoúntas* is applied to both those who were physically sick with different diseases and those who were affected by the evil spirits (2 Tim 4:20).

(III) Figuratively of the mind, to be feebleminded, fainthearted, timid (2 Cor 11:21; Sept.: Isa 7:4); to doubt, hesitate, vacillate, as meaning weak or doubleminded, spoken of those whose minds are easily disturbed (Rom 14:2, 21; 1 Cor 8:9, 11, 12); to be weak or unsettled in the faith (Rom 4:19), or in opinion (Rom 14:1; Sept.: Ps 27:2; Jer 50:32; Hos 14:2).

(IV) By implication, to be afflicted, distressed as by want, oppression, calamity, and so forth (Acts 20:35; 2 Cor 11:29; 12:10; Sept.: Job 4:4; Dan 11:33–35). For a full discussion see *asthéneia* (769), infirmity, weakness, sickness.

Deriv.: *asthénēma* (771), infirmity.

Syn.: *noséō* (3552), to be sick; *échō kakṓs* (*échō* [2192], to have; *kakṓs* [2560], badly), to have it badly, to be ill; *páschō* (3958), to suffer; *hupophérō* (5297), to endure, to bear from underneath; *basanízō* (928), to suffer pain; *phtheírō* (5351), to pine or waste away, to corrupt in the sense of degeneration; *sunéchō* (4912), to be sick, confined.

Ant.: *anakúptō* (352), to unbend, to recover; *therapeúomai* (2323), to be healed; *iáomai* (2390), to be healed, to be made whole, to be rid of the cause of the sickness; *sṓzō* (4982), to save with the meaning of to make whole, heal; *hugiaínō* (5198), to be healthy; *sthenóō* (4599), to strengthen.

771. ἀσθένημα *asthénēma*; gen. *asthenḗmatos*, neut. noun from *asthenéō* (770), to be weak or powerless. The result of being weak, as indicated by the suffix *-ma* (Rom 15:1, in the pl., referring to the scruples which arise by being weak in the faith [cf. 2 Cor 11:29]).

772. ἀσθενής *asthenḗs*; gen. *asthenoús*, masc.-fem., neut. *asthenés*, adj. from the priv. *a* (1), without, and *sthénos* (n.f.), strength. Without strength, powerless. Weak, powerless, without physical ability (Matt 26:41, "the flesh is weak," impotent, i.e., unequal to the task; Mark 14:38; 1 Pet 3:7; Sept.: Num 13:19; Job 4:3; Ezek 17:14). Including the idea of imperfection (1 Cor 12:22; Gal 4:9; Heb 7:18). In 1 Cor 1:25 as a subst., "the weakness of God" means the weak but godly person; in 1 Cor 1:27 "the weak things of the world," spoken of men who are naturally weak. Infirm, sick, sickly, diseased (Matt 25:39, 43, 44; Luke 10:9; Acts 4:9; 5:15, 16; 1 Cor 11:30); without strength or weak in a spiritual sense, weak with regard to spiritual things (2 Cor 10:10 [cf. 1 Cor 2:3; 2 Cor 11:21]). Implying a want of decision and firmness of mind, weakminded, i.e., doubting, hesitating, vacillating in opinion or in faith (1 Cor 8:7, 10; 9:22; 1 Thess 5:14). By implication, meaning afflicted, distressed by oppression, calamity, and so forth (1 Cor 4:10 [cf. 1 Cor 4:9, 11f.]; Sept.: Prov 22:22). In a moral sense, wretched, diseased, i.e., in a state of sin and wretchedness (Rom 5:6, equivalent to sinners). Also from *sthénos* (n.f.): *sthenóō* (4599), to strengthen.

Deriv.: *asthéneia* (769), lack of strength, powerlessness, weakness; *asthenéō* (770), to be weak or powerless, sick.

Syn.: *árrōstos* (732), sick, without strength or robustness; *adúnatos* (102), weak, without strength.

Ant.: *dunatós* (1415), strong, able, powerful; *ischurós* (2478), inherently strong; *hugiḗs* (5199), healthy.

773. Ἀσία *Asía*; gen. *Asías*, fem. proper noun. Asia. In the NT, referring to the Roman province of Asia, the western part. Many Jews lived in Asia Minor (Acts 19:26, 27; 21:27; 24:18; 27:2). It was used also to refer to the region of Ionia of which Ephesus was the capital (Acts 2:9; 6:9; 16:6; 19:10, 22; 20:4, 16, 18). See also 1 Cor 16:19; 2 Cor 1:8; 2 Tim 1:15; 1 Pet 1:1; Rev 1:4, 11.

774. Ἀσιανός *Asianós*; gen. *Asianoú*, masc.-fem., adj. Asiatic, belonging to "the province of Asia" (Acts 20:4).

775. Ἀσιάρχης *Asiárchēs*; gen. *Asiárchou*, masc. noun from *Asía*, (773), Asia, and *árchō* (757), to rule. A chief of Asia (Acts 19:31). These were officers of a religious nature who presided over the public games instituted in honor of the heathen gods.

776. ἀσιτία *asitía*; gen. *asitías*, fem. noun from *ásitos* (777), without food. Abstinence from food, fasting (Acts 27:21).
Syn.: *nēsteía* (3521), fasting.
Ant.: *trophḗ* (5160), food; *diatrophḗ* (1305), sustenance; *brṓsis* (1035), eating; *brṓma* (1033), food.

777. ἄσιτος *ásitos*; gen. *asítou*, masc.-fem., neut. *ásiton*, adj. from the priv. *a* (1), without, and *sítos* (4621), corn, wheat, food. Without food regularly taken, fasting (Acts 27:33).
Deriv.: *asitía* (776), abstinence from food.
Syn.: *nḗstis* (3523), fasting, abstinent from food.

778. ἀσκέω *askéō*; contracted *askṓ*, fut. *askḗsō*. To exercise oneself, to exert all one's diligence, study and industry, to endeavor, strive (Acts 24:16).
Syn.: *morphóō* (3445), to formulate, form; *anaptússō* (380), to unroll, develop, open; *paideúō* (3811), to instruct; *proágō* (4254), to lead forward; *katartízō* (2675), to fit, prepare; *stoichéō* (4748), to arrange in a regular line, to conform to virtue and piety; *gumnázō* (1128), to exercise; *phrontízō* (5431), to care for, to exercise thought; *anatréphō* (397), to nourish, bring up; *suntēréō* (4933), to maintain, preserve, keep; *proetoimázō* (4282), to prepare ahead of time.
Ant.: *argéō* (691), to be idle; *scholázō* (4980), to be at leisure.

779. ἀσκός *askós*; gen. *askoú*. A container usually used for liquids. A bottle, and particularly in the NT, a leather bottle or vessel such as was used to hold wine (Matt 9:17; Mark 2:22; Luke 5:37, 38; Sept. Josh 9:4, 13; Jer 13:12). A goat skin in its entirety was made into a large container, which was filled with wine or other liquids. They were tanned with acacia bark. The hair remained on the outside. If the wine was new, it would ferment and break an old skin (cf. Josh 9:4, 13; Job 32:19). If these goat skins were hung in the smoke to dry, they would shrivel (Ps 119:83).
Syn.: *thḗkē* (2336), a receptacle, usually one which held a sword, a sheath; *sákkos* (4526), a sack; *péra* (4082), a pouch, usually for food; *spurís* (4711), a hamper, basket; *kóphinos* (2894), a small basket; *kibōtós* (2787), ark; *phiálē* (5357), a broad shallow cup.

780. ἀσμένως *asménōs*; adv. from *hēsménos*, the perf. pass. part. of *hḗdomai* (n.f.), to delight. Gladly, joyfully (Acts 2:41; 21:17 [cf. Luke 8:13]). Also from *hḗdomai* (n.f.): *authádēs* (829), self-complacent.
Syn.: *prothúmōs* (4290), willingly; *en spoudḗ* (1722, 4710), in speed, speedily, eagerly, with diligence; *euthéōs* (2112), immediately.
Ant.: *oudamṓs* (3760), by no means.

781. ἄσοφος *ásophos*; gen. *asóphou*, masc.-fem., neut. *ásophon*, adj. from the priv. *a* (1), without, and *sophós* (4680), wise. Unwise, foolish (Eph 5:15), not walking as God expects one to walk.
Syn.: *áphrōn* (878), mindless, stupid, unmindful of the consequence of a thought or action; *mōrós* (3474), foolish; *asúnetos* (801), unintelligent, unable to reason logically and arrive at proper conclusions.
Ant.: *sophós* (4680), wise, able to know and regulate a relationship with God; *phrónimos* (5429), prudent, sensible, able to regulate relationships with fellow humans; *sunetós* (4908), intelligent, able to reason logically; *logikós* (3050), logical, rational; *sṓphrōn* (4998), of sound mind,

discreet,; *nēpháleos* / *nēphálios* (3524), circumspect, sober; *néphōn* (3525), discreet, sober, abstaining from the abuse of alcohol.

782. ἀσπάζομαι *aspázomai*; fut. *aspásomai*, mid. deponent verb. To embrace, to salute, trans. spoken of those who meet or separate (OT references with the meaning of greeting: Judg 19:20; Ruth 2:4; 1 Sam 25:6; 2 Sam 20:9; Dan 10:19). Equivalent to the NT "Peace be unto you" of those who meet (Luke 24:36; John 20:19; also coll. Matt 10:12; Luke 10:5). Also spoken of those who separate (Judg 18:6; 2 Sam 15:9); equivalent to the NT "Go in peace" (Mark 5:34).

(I) Of those who meet or are present, to salute, welcome, greet (Matt 10:12; Mark 9:15; Luke 1:40; 10:4; Acts 21:19; Sept.: Ex 18:7). Including the idea of to visit, pay one's respects to (Acts 18:22; 21:7; 25:13). To salute with a kiss (Rom 16:16; 1 Cor 16:20; 2 Cor 13:12; 1 Pet 5:14). Spoken of the salute given to a king, homage accompanied with prostration (Mark 15:18, 19).

(II) Of those who separate, take leave of, bid goodbye (Acts 20:1; 21:6).

(III) Of greetings sent by letter or other means (Rom 16:3, 5–16, 21–23; 1 Cor 16:19, 20; 2 Cor 13:12; Phil 4:21, 22; Col 4:10, 12, 14, 15; 1 Thess 5:26; 2 Tim 4:19, 21; Titus 3:15; Phile 1:23; Heb 13:24; 1 Pet 5:13; 2 John 1:13; 3 John 1:14).

(IV) By implication, to love, treat with affection (Matt 5:47).

(V) Spoken of things, to welcome, embrace, receive gladly (Heb 11:13 referring to the promises).

Deriv.: *aspasmós* (783), greeting, salutation.

Syn.: *philéō* (5368), to love, be friendly, kiss, envelop with affection; *enagkalízomai* (1723), to take in one's arms, embrace; *hupodéchomai* (5264), to admit into one's group, receive, offer hospitality.

Ant.: *katakrínō* (2632), to condemn; *krínō* (2919), to judge; *elégchō* (1651), reprove; *apodokimázō* (593), to

repudiate; *katadikázō* (2613), to condemn; *mémphomai* (3201), to blame, find fault; *diabállō* (1225), to accuse falsely; *kakologéō* (2551), to speak evil of; *katalaléō* (2635), to slander; *katēgoréō* (2723), to accuse; *epikrínō* (1948), to bring judgment upon.

783. ἀσπασμός *aspasmós*; from *aspázomai* (782), to salute. A salutation, greeting, either orally or by letter (Matt 23:7; Mark 12:38; Luke 1:29, 41, 44; 11:43; 20:46; 1 Cor 16:21; Col 4:18; 2 Thess 3:17).

Syn.: *phílēma* (5370), a kiss.

Ant.: *apobolé* (580), casting away; *ekbolé* (1546), a throwing overboard or putting out; *apotomía* (663), severity; *ará* (685) and *katára* (2671), a curse.

784. ἄσπιλος *áspilos*; gen. *aspílou*, masc.-fem., neut. *áspilon*, adj. from the priv. *a* (1), without, and *spílos* (4696), spot. Without blemish or spot, free from spot, unblemished, pure. Spoken of Christ in 1 Pet 1:19; of doctrine in 1 Tim 6:14; of moral conduct in James 1:27; 2 Pet 3:14.

In 1 Pet 1:19, the Lord Jesus is referred to as the lamb that is *ámōmon* (299), without any internal blemish or sin for He was sinless in Himself, and *áspilos* in that He did not have any external spot or sin, for having no sin in Himself, He never sinned in relation to others. In 2 Pet 3:14 the apostle commands that we should be diligent that we may be found without spot (*áspiloi*), without external sin, and *amṓmētoi* (298), not allowing ourselves to become sinful through evil internal attitudes and iniquity. *Ámemptos* (273), means one against whom there can be no blame or reproach. Although our Lord in 1 Pet 1:19 is called *ámōmos*, without internal sinfulness and spot, and *áspilos*, without external sin or spot, He is never said to be *ámemptos*, without accusation or reproach, as He Himself taught in Luke 6:26: "Woe unto you, when all men shall speak well of you." Although He Himself was without internal and external spot or blemish, yet there were those who spoke evil of Him or who brought *momphḗ* (3437), blame, against Him which led to His death. We, however, are admonished to walk and live in such a manner that we will not justifiably elicit the reproach of others (Luke 1:6; Phil 2:15; 3:6; 1 Thess 3:13).

Anégklētos (410) means unaccused, such as the believer who will stand before the ultimate Judge, but no accusation against him will exclude him from the kingdom if he has been justified before God through Jesus Christ by the exercise of a living and effective faith (Rom 8:1. See 1 Cor 1:8; Col 1:22; 1 Tim 3:10; Titus 1:6, 7). *Anégklētos* is an entirely legal term.

Anepílēptos (423) or *anepílēmptos*, a qualification the Apostle Paul recommends that a bishop or elder should have (1 Tim 3:2; 5:7), means beyond reproach, i.e., that he ought to live in such a way that reproach will not come to him justifiably when he stands under the scrutiny of judicial examination by God; hence he is unindictable. This is found also in 1 Tim 6:14, spoken of God's commandments grouped together as one commandment. We should incorporate in our lives God's commandments in such a way that the spoken word and the life of the speaker may not bring the commandment under indictment as being either faulty or ineffective.

Syn.: *katharós* (2513), clean, pure; *amíantos* (283), pure, undefiled; *hagnós* (53), clean, chaste; *kalós* (2570), good; *chrēstós* (5543), useful, kind, gracious; *hierós* (2413), sacred, holy; *hágios* (40), holy, blameless; *hósios* (3741), consecrated, holy; *tímios* (5093), valuable, honored, of good reputation.

Ant.: *anósios* (462), wicked, unholy; *bébēlos* (952), wicked, profane; *theostugḗs* (2319), hateful of God, impious; *kakós* (2556), bad; *phaúlos* (5337), foul, evil; *aischrós* (150), shameful, filthy; *átimos* (820), without honor; *achreíos* (888), useless, unprofitable; *rhuparós* (4508), vile, cheap, shabby, morally wicked; *akáthartos* (169), unclean, impure.

785. ἀσπίς *aspís*; gen. *aspídos*, fem. noun. An asp, a species of a deadly serpent which rolls itself up in a spiral form, possibly so-named because of the sound of the serpent's hissing (Rom 3:13 from Ps 140:3; Deut 32:33; Isa 30:6; 59:5). In the Sept. and Gr. writers, also a shield.

Syn.: *óphis* (3789), snake, metaphorically a malicious person; *échidna* (2191), a poisonous snake, viper; *skorpíos* (4651), a scorpion.

786. ἄσπονδος *áspondos*; gen. *aspóndou*, masc.-fem., neut. *áspondon*, adj. from the priv. *a* (1), without, and *spondḗ* (n.f.), libation or drink offering. The absolutely irreconcilable person who, being at war, refuses to lay aside his enmity or to listen to terms of reconciliation. Implacable, in a state of war (Rom 1:31; 2 Tim 3:3). See *asúnthetos* (802), covenant breaker (Rom 1:31).

Syn.: *asúmphōnos* (800), one not agreeing; *philóneikos* (5380), quarrelsome, born of strife.

Ant.: *eirēnikós* (1516), peaceable; *homóphrōn* (3675), of the same mind.

787. ἀσσάριον *assárion*; gen. *assaríou*, neut. noun. A Roman brass coin equal to the tenth part of the dinar (*dēnárion* [1220]) or drachma (*drachmḗ* [1406]) which was the usual pay for a day's labor. Used in the NT to denote the most trifling value, like our penny (Matt 10:29; Luke 12:6). See *argúrion* (694), silver.

788. ἆσσον *ásson*; adv., the comparative of *ágchi* (n.f.), near. Nearer, next, very near, close (Acts 27:13).

Syn.: *eggús* (1451), near; *eggúteron* (1452), nearer; *plēsíon* (4139), close by.

Ant.: *makrán* (3112), far off; *péran* (4008), beyond, across, farther; *pórrō* (4206), at a distance; *epékeina* (1900), on the further side of, beyond.

789. Ἄσσος *Ássos*; gen. *Ássou*, proper noun. Assos, a city of Mysia in Asia Minor, 19 miles southeast of Troas and on the Mediterranean Sea. Extensive ruins of buildings, citadels, tombs, and a gateway still exist there. Paul visited it (Acts 20:13, 14). It was also called *Apollonía*.

790. ἀστατέω *astatéō*; contracted *astatố*, fut. *astatḗsō*, from *ástatos* (n.f.), unstable, which is from the priv. *a* (1), not, and *hístēmi* (2476), to stand, be fixed. To be unsettled, have no certain or fixed abode (1 Cor 4:11).

Syn.: *kinéō* (2795), to move; *metakinéō* (3334), to remove.

Ant.: *paraménō* (3887), to be permanent; *ménō* (3306), to abide.

791. ἀστεῖος *asteíos*; gen. *asteíou*, masc.-fem., neut. *asteíon*, adj. from *ástu* (n.f.), a city. One who dwells in a city and by consequence is well-bred, polite, eloquent, as the inhabitants of cities may be in comparison with those of the country. Used only of Moses, meaning elegant in external form (Acts 7:20; Heb 11:23). The Greeks used to call the opposite of *asteíos*, the urban person, the *agroíkos*, the one who comes from *agrós* (68), field or country-side. Therefore, *asteíos* came to be assumed as one who is fair to look on and attractive, a suggestion of beauty but not generally of a high character.

Asteíos may mean the same thing as *hōraíos*, fair or beautiful, but they reach that beauty by paths which are entirely different, resting as they do on different images. *Asteíos* belongs to art and to it are attributed the notions of neatness, symmetry, and elegance. *Hōraíos* receives its hour of beauty by nature which may be brief but which constitutes the season of highest perfection

Another word, *kalós* (2570), occurs many times in the NT and usually is translated "good." It may be used, however, to mean beautiful, but its beauty is contemplated from a point of view which is especially dear to the Greek mind, namely, as the harmonious completeness, the balance, proportion and measure of all the parts with one another.

Syn.: *hōraíos* (5611), beautiful; *kalós* (2570), good, beautiful.

792. ἀστήρ *astḗr*; gen. *astéros*, masc. noun. A star (Matt 2:2, 7, 9, 10; 1 Cor 15:41; Rev 6:13; 8:12). A luminous body resembling a star such as the wise men saw in the sky leading them to Bethlehem (Matt 2:2, 7, 9, 10). We can assume that the motion of that luminous body which appeared to the wise men was different from any of the other stars. It differed also by possibly appearing in the daytime since they may have been traveling during the day. No doubt its light was much more intense than the others, though inferior to that light which was above the brightness of the sun and which shone around Paul and those that journeyed with him (Acts 26:13).

Metaphorically, Jude 1:13 speaks of false and impious teachers as star planets, wandering stars, meteors.

The angels or messengers of churches are figuratively denoted as stars who, having received for themselves light from the Sun of Righteousness, wrought by their example both in purity of doctrine and in integrity of life to give light to others (Rev 1:16, 20; 2:1, 28; 3:1). In the eschatological discourse of our Lord in Matt 24:29 and Mark 13:24, 25, we are told that the sun shall be darkened, the moon shall not give its acquired light (*phéggos* [5338]) and the stars of the heaven shall be falling. This will be at the end of the Great Tribulation, when the Lord Jesus comes back to earth in triumph and glory to establish a new heaven (*ouranón* [3772], *kainón* [2537]) and a new earth. The first heaven and the first earth will have passed away. If someone doubts the possibility of this, he should remember the statement of John 1:4, in which we are told that in Jesus Christ there has always been life and that life has always been the light of men. In reality, neither life nor light are dependent on the present sun, since the sun and the moon were created after God created lights in the firmament of the heaven (Gen 1:14, 16).

As there must have been life and light prior to the creation of the sun and the moon and naturally the stars, so shall there be after their destruction as referred to in 2 Pet 3:10. The Bible treats the stars as the work of the Creator (Job 25:5; Ps 8:3; 19:1), insisting on their brightness (Dan 12:3), their height above the earth (Job 22:12; Isa 14:13; Obad 1:4), and especially their number (Gen 15:5; 22:17; 26:4; Ex 32:13; Deut 1:10; 10:22; 28:62; Neh 9:23; Jer 33:22; Heb 11:12). They are sometimes poetically represented as living beings (Job 38:7, "the morning stars sang together"; Judg 5:20, "the stars . . . fought against Sisera"), and the darkening of the stars is treated as a sign of coming distress (Isa 13:10; 34:4; Ezek 32:7, 8; Joel 2:10; 3:15; Matt 24:29; Mark 13:25; Luke 21:25). But they were created by God (Gen 1:14; Job 9:7; Ps 74:16; 136:7; Amos 5:8) to give light (Gen 1:16; Jer 31:35); He gave them their paths according to fixed laws (Job 38:33; Jer 33:25); and they are subject to Him (Job 9:7; Ps 147:4; Isa 45:12) Who calls them by their names (Isa 40:26).

It follows that star-worship is rigorously forbidden (Deut 4:19; 17:2, 3), though introduced by Manasseh (2 Kgs 21:3 [cf. 2 Kgs 23:4, 5, 11]). Amos 5:26 does not necessarily imply its existence at an earlier date, and it is several times mentioned at a later date (Jer 7:18; 19:13; 44:17; Zeph 1:5). It is always referred to with reprobation (cf. 2 Kgs 17:16; Jer 44:25–27). In Acts 7:43 Stephen refers to the star of the god Remphan as he castigates the idolatry of the Israelites. This is a quotation from the Sept. of Amos 5:26. The Hebr. has *Chiun* (3594, OT), which may have been read as Kewan and changed into Remphan. Stephen wanted to show that foreign idolatrous planet worship had crept in and brought about apostasy from the true worship of Jehovah. This is the degeneracy of worshiping the creature instead of the Creator that Paul mentions in Rom 1:25. No matter how majestic and how high a creature is, it should never be worshiped as if it were the creator.

In 1 Cor 15:41, where Paul speaks of the glory of the resurrection, and particularly of the resurrected bodies of the believers, he says, "There is one glory of the sun, and another glory of the moon, and another glory of the stars; for one star differeth from another star in glory." What Paul is saying that as we look at the sun, the moon, and the stars, and know them, so believers in their resurrection bodies will be recognized for the glory that they have won through their life of sacrifice and compliance with Christ. Not all believers will enjoy heaven equally, nor will they shine with equal splendor.

Turning to the use of the word "star" in Revelation, we find in the vision of the Son of Man that "he had in his right hand seven stars" (Rev 1:16) and that "The seven stars are the angels of the seven churches" (v. 20). Some interpret the angels of the churches as being their pastors or rulers. Some consider these to be earthly messengers, ancient postal carriers, who acted as couriers dispatching messages across the empire. Others attribute to these angels the literal meaning of the spiritual superhuman ministering beings standing in some intimate relationship to the churches. If the latter is taken as the true meaning, then why would letters be written to heavenly beings since it is earthly matters that are taken up in these portions of Scriptures? The Son of Man is pictured here as holding in His hands the seven stars, and these stars are simultaneously presented on earth to show that in the hand of the Son of Man are both the actual messengers (*ággeloi*) and the records of their performance on earth which are kept in heaven. The messengers of the churches are called stars because the message which they proclaimed is a message from on high, from the heavens (Rev 2:1; 3:1).

In Rev 2:28, the promise is given to the overcomer at the church of Thyatira, "And I will give him the morning star." What is this morning star which will be given to the overcomer? In Rev 22:16 the Lord Jesus says, "I am the root and the offspring of David, and the bright and morning star." It is evident that the Lord Jesus in His glory equates Himself with the bright and morning star. In the gospels, the Lord Jesus is spoken of as the light (Luke 2:32; John 1:4, 5, 7–9; 3:19; 8:12; 9:5; 12:35) and also the sun (Matt 17:2). But never as a star. In Revelation, however, Christ calls Himself the morning star as the herald and introducer of a new age, the age not of His humiliation nor of His enlightening as unto salvation, but rather the age of His glory, the dawn of a brighter day and a new existence. In 2 Pet 1:19, Peter discusses the effect produced by the transfiguration of the Lord Jesus and says that by it "We have also a more sure word of prophecy." The glorification of Christ on the Mount of Transfiguration was not only a partial fulfillment of Messianic prediction, but was in itself the earnest of a complete glorification when the Lord Jesus is indicated as the bright and morning star. All this is connected with the eschatological coming of the Lord Jesus in glory.

In 2 Pet 1:19, we have the prophetic word presented as "a light that shineth in a dark place." The word translated "light" here is *lúchnos* (3088), a candle, lantern. What is translated "a dark place" is a Gr. word used only here, *auchmērós tópos* (850, 5117) meaning a dismal, murky, squalid place. This is a description of the world in the last days when the day will dawn and the daystar arise. The word that is translated "daystar" here is *phōsphóros* (5459), which means something which bears light, light-bearing. The Eng. word "phosphorus" is actually a transliteration of the Gr. word. Basically this verse speaks of Jesus Christ as the light of the world coming into the dark soul or heart of man, for it says, "As unto a light that shineth in a dark place, until the day dawn, and the daystar arise in your hearts." This is the first manifestation of Christ as the light of the world in the human heart. He turns the thickest darkness into light. The word "star" is not in the word *phōsphóros*, but this light-bearing is spoken of as coming with the dawn. The verb "dawn" is *anatélē*, the fut. subjunctive of *anatéllō* (393), which means to rise

as the rising of the sun. The word *anatolé* (395) means east where the sun rises. The first appearance of light is from the east as the sun rises in the east. When Christ visited this world with His salvation, it is said that "the dayspring from on high hath visited us" (Luke 1:78). 1 Pet 2:9 says of Christ that He has called us "out of darkness into His marvelous light." There are two daysprings in the world's past and future history. One is when Jesus Christ came into the world to shine His light in our hearts. The second will be when He will come again in glory as the bright and morning star. We shall then be indeed as shining stars of varying degrees (1 Cor 15:41).

Rev 6:13; 8:10–12; 9:1; 12:4 refer to the cosmic disturbances in the heavens alluded to by our Lord in Matt 24:29 and Mark 13:25 (see also Isa 13:10; Ezek 32:7; Joel 2:10; 3:15). Rev 12:1 represents the glorified community of the believers in heaven while the earth and the heavens are shaking (Luke 21:11, 25; Acts 2:19).

Syn.: *ástron* (798), a constellation, but also used for a single star.

793. ἀστήρικτος *astēriktos*; gen. *astēríktou*, masc.-fem., neut. *astērikton*, adj. from the priv. *a* (1), without, and *stērízō* (4741), to confirm, establish. Unsettled, unstable, unsteady (2 Pet 2:14; 3:16).

Syn.: *akatástatos* (182), unstable, restless; *ádēlos* (82), indistinct, uncertain.

Ant.: *hedraíos* (1476), settled; *tethemeliōménos* from *themelióō* (2311), to lay a basis, to ground, settle; *asphalés* (804), certain, safe, sure; *bébaios* (949), stable, steadfast.

794. ἄστοργος *ástorgos*; gen. *astórgou*, masc.-fem., neut. *ástorgon*, adj. from the priv. *a* (1), without, and the noun *storgé* (n.f.), family love. Without family love (Rom 1:31; 2 Tim 3:3). Also from *storgé* (n.f.): *philóstorgos* (5387), family love.

Syn.: *aphilágathos* (865), hostile to benevolence; *stugnētós* (4767), odious, hateful.

Ant.: *prosphilés* (4375), friendly, lovely; *philádelphos* (5361), fond of brethren; *philóstorgos* (5387), fond of natural relatives.

795. ἀστοχέω *astochéō*; contracted *astochṓ*, fut. *astochḗsō*, from *ástochos* (n.f.), one who misses his aim (*stóchos*, aim, target). To err, deviate in a figurative and spiritual sense, not to reach one's goal (1 Tim 1:6; 6:21; 2 Tim 2:18). More distinctively, the verb does not mean to miss achieving the aim that one has set, but not to set the proper aim at which one ought to aim. It is not focusing on the right goal instead of not achieving one's set aim. Naturally if one specializes in the proclamation of something that is not essential and central, he will inevitably neglect that which is central and important. The verb does not mean what is conceived by some as "to fall from grace."

Syn.: *hamartánō* (264), to miss the mark set by God for each individual; *planáō* (4105), to lead astray, deceive, and the comp. *apoplanáō* (635), to lead astray from; *nauagéō* (3489), to suffer shipwreck which must not be taken as necessarily involving the loss of life, either physical or spiritual.

Ant.: *epitugchánō* (2013), to attain, obtain; *euodóō* (2137), to prosper, succeed; *prokóptō* (4298), to advance; *kerdaínō* (2770), to gain; *nikáō* (3528), to overcome, prevail; *karpophoréō* (2592), to bear fruit; *telesphoréō* (5052), to bring to completion; *teleióō* (5048), to carry through completely, to accomplish; *epiteléō* (2005), to perfect, complete; *katartízō* (2675), to make one what he ought to be.

796. ἀστραπή *astrapḗ*; gen. *astrapḗs*, fem. noun. Lightning.

(I) The physical phenomenon of lightning (Rev 4:5; 8:5; 11:19; 16:18; Sept.: Ex 19:16; Jer 10:13).

(II) By implication, brightness, splendor (Matt 28:3; Luke 11:36; Sept.: Deut 32:41; Dan 10:6). God is generally represented as sending lightning, and the lack of the power to do so is one proof of the weakness of man (Job 38:35). Lightning is associated with theophanies or appearances of God, as at Sinai (Ex 19:16; 20:18), in Ezekiel's vision (Ezek 1:13, 14), and in various stages of the Revelation (Rev 4:5; 8:5; 11:19; 16:18). It is regarded as an instrument of God's judgment (Ps 144:6). In Zech 9:14, God's "arrows" of destruction are compared to lightning, which seems also to be spoken of as His "sword" in Deut 32:41, and as His "spear" in Hab 3:11. Lightning is a figure for brightness of countenance (Dan 10:6; Matt 28:3) and of raiment (Luke 24:4), for the suddenness of the Second Coming (Matt 24:27; Luke 17:24), and for the swift completeness of Satan's overthrow (Luke 10:18). In some passages, fire evidently refers to lightning, as when fire and hail are mentioned together (Ex 9:23; Ps 105:32; 148:8), and when fire from heaven is spoken of either as an agency of destruction (2 Kgs 1:10, 12, 14; Job 1:16) or as a token of God's acceptance of a sacrifice (1 Kgs 18:38; 1 Chr 21:26).

(III) As the symbol of speed (Matt 24:27; Luke 10:18; 17:24; Sept.: Nah 2:4).

Deriv.: *astráptō* (797), to lighten, flash.

Syn.: *phṓs* (5457), light; *phéggos* (5338), light of the moon.

Ant.: *skotía* (4653) and *skótos* (4655), darkness; *gnóphos* (1105), blackness; *zóphos* (2217), gloom, the blackness of the darkness.

797. ἀστράπτω *astráptō*; fut. *astrápsō*, from *astrapḗ* (796), lightning. To lighten, flash or shine as lightning (Luke 17:24; 24:4 [cf. Matt 28:3; Sept.: Ps 144:6]).

Deriv.: *exastráptō* (1823), to flash like lightning; *periastráptō* (4015), to flash around.

Syn.: *phaínō* (5316), to give light, shine; *epiphaínō* (2014), to appear; *lámpō* (2989), to shine as a torch; *stílbō* (4744), to shine, glisten; *eklámpō* (1584), to shine forth; *perilámpō* (4034), to shine around; *epiphaúō* (2017), to shine forth; *augázō*

(826), to shine forth, especially referring to dawn; *phōtízo* (5461), to give light.

Ant.: *skotízō* (4654), to darken; *episkiázō* (1982), to cast a shade upon, overshadow.

798. ἄστρον *ástron*; gen. *ástrou*, neut. noun. A constellation consisting of several stars but also used for a single star (Luke 21:25; Acts 7:43, the star god, an image of Saturn in the form of a star; 27:20; Heb 11:12; Sept.: Ex 32:13; Job 38:7).

799. Ἀσύγκριτος *Asúgkritos*; gen. *Asugkrítou*, masc. proper noun. Asyncritus, incomparable, one without comparison, a Christian whom Paul saluted (Rom 16:14).

800. ἀσύμφωνος *asúmphōnos*; from the priv. *a* (1), without, and *súmphōnos* (4859), agreeing in speech. Dissonant, harshly discordant, disagreeing (Acts 28:25).

Syn.: *diáphoros* (1313), differing.

Ant.: *súmphōnos* (4859), agreeing; *homóphrōn* (3675), like-minded.

801. ἀσύνετος *asúnetos*; gen. *asunétou*, masc.-fem., neut. *asúneton*, adj. from the priv. *a* (1), without, and *sunetós* (4908), sagacious. Without insight or understanding (*súnesis* [4907]), unintelligent, foolish. In Matt 15:16, Christ characterized Peter and the other disciples as being *asúnetoi*, since they were unable to reason out the practical application of His parabolic teaching (see Ps 92:7; Mark 7:18). In Rom 1:21, Paul calls unredeemed man's heart *asúnetos*, because of its inability to conclude from the observable creation that there must be a Creator. This is in spite of the fact that, by nature of His essence as spirit (John 4:24) and His necessarily being greater than His creation, God may not be observable by man or any limited created being (John 1:18a). Fallen man cannot figure out creation, therefore he propounds foolish theories. In Rom 1:31, Paul ascribes the adj.

asunétous (pl.) to fallen men. In Rom 10:19, the believing Gentiles were considered by the unbelieving Jews as being illogical, and thus accepting Jesus as the Messiah. See Sept.: Deut 32:21 (cf. Job 2:10; Ps 14:1).

Syn.: *áphrōn* (878), without reason, mental insanity; *mátaios* (3152), vain; *anóētos* (453), thinking incorrectly; *mōrós* (3474), stupid, morally worthless, sluggish.

Ant.: *hugiḗs* (5199), sound, healthy, with particular application to the mind; *sunetós* (4908), able to reason logically and arrive at the proper conclusions, the only direct ant. of *asúnetos*; *sophós* (4680), wise, able to regulate relationships with God; *phrónimos* (5429), prudent, sensible, able to regulate relationships with his others; *nēpháleos* or *nēphálios* (3524), circumspect, sober, free from the influence of intoxicants and avoiding them; *sṓphrōn* (4998), self-controlled, sober-minded; *epistḗmōn* (1990), intelligent.

802. ἀσύνθετος *asúnthetos*; gen. *asunthétou*, masc.-fem., neut. *asúntheton*, adj. from the priv. *a* (1), not, and the pass. of *suntíthēmi* (4934), to consent, make agreement. Not put together nor made up of several parts. In the NT, a breaker of a covenant or agreement, faithless, treacherous (Rom 1:31; Sept.: Jer 3:7, 8, 10, 11). Paul, however, uses it with an act. sense referring to those who, being in covenant and treaty with others, refuse to abide by their agreements.

Syn.: *áspondos* (786), implacable (although *asúnthetos* presupposes a state of peace or an agreement interrupted by the unrighteous, while *áspondos* presupposes a broken treaty and a state of war involving a refusal to terminate the hostilities); *asúnetos* (801), foolish, without insight.

Ant.: *pistós* (4103), dependable, faithful.

803. ἀσφάλεια *aspháleia*; gen. *asphaleías*, fem. noun from *asphalḗs* (804), safe. Firmness, security, safety (Acts

5:23; 1 Thess 5:3, security from peril; Sept.: Deut 12:10; Lev 26:5; Ps 104:5; Isa 18:4); certainty (Luke 1:4).

Syn.: *sōtēría* (4991), salvation, safety; *bebaíōsis* (951), confirmation, making sure; *élegchos* (1650), evidence; *apódeixis* (585), demonstration, proof; *ochúrōma* (3794), something such as a castle which provides safety, a stronghold, fortress.

Ant.: *áspondos* (786), implacable (Rom 1:31; 2 Tim 3:3); *adēlótēs* (83), uncertainty.

804. ἀσφαλής *asphalḗs*; gen. *asphaloús*, masc.-fem., neut. *asphalés*, adj. from the priv. *a* (1), without, and *sphállō* (n.f.), to supplant, throw down. Firm, that which cannot be thrown down as used in the Class. Gr. Firm, sure, steady, immovable (Heb 6:19 of an anchor; see Sept.: Prov 8:28), safe, secure from peril (Phil 3:1), certain (Acts 25:26). When used in the neut. with the art. *to* (3588), certainty, truth, in which case the adj. neut. is used as a subst. (Acts 21:34; 22:30). Also from *sphállō* (n.f.): *episphalés* (2000), ready to fall, insecure.

Deriv.: *aspháleia* (803), security, safety; *asphalízō* (805), to render secure, safe; *asphalōs* (806), safely.

Syn.: *pistós* (4103), faithful, trustworthy; *stereós* (4731), solid, sure; *dēlos* (1212), certain, evident, visible; *bébaios* (949), certain.

Ant.: *ádēlos* (82), uncertain; *episphalés* (2000), insecure; dangerous; *chalepós* (5467), perilous.

805. ἀσφαλίζω *asphalízō*; fut. *asphalísō*, from *asphalḗs* (804), safe. To make safe, fast, secure against enemies (Matt 27:64–66; Sept.: Isa 41:10); to secure the feet fast as in wood or stocks (Acts 16:24; Sept.: Neh 3:15).

Syn.: *bebaióō* (950), to establish, confirm, stabilize; *apodeíknumi* (584), to prove; *phrouréō* (5432), to guard, protect; *phulássō* (5442), to watch, guard; *skopéō* (4648), to watch over; *teréō* (5083), to guard, keep.

Ant.: *kinduneúō* (2793), to be in danger.

806. ἀσφαλῶς *asphalōs*; adv. from *asphalḗs* (804), safe. Safely (Mark 14:44; Acts 16:23; Sept.: Gen 34:25), certainly, assuredly (Acts 2:36).

Syn.: *óntōs* (3689), verily, actually, certainly; *pántōs* (3843), altogether; *alēthōs* (230), truly; *mén* (3375), assuredly.

807. ἀσχημονέω *aschēmonéō*; fut. *aschēmonēsō*, from *aschēmōn* (809), uncomely, indecent. To behave in an ugly, indecent, unseemly or unbecoming manner (1 Cor 13:5). To be disgraced, suffer reproach (1 Cor 7:36, "if any man thinks himself exposed to disgrace in respect to his virgin" [a.t.], i.e., if he has fear of her being seduced; Sept.: Deut 25:3). The "any man" is not the would-be groom, but the father of the unmarried virgin who realizes that he unfairly kept her at home and she could not marry. The exact opposite of the noun derived from *aschēmonéō* is found in 1 Cor 7:35, *tó euschēmon*, that which is comely or constitutes proper behavior. See also *schēma* (4976), fashion, appearance, outward behavior. In 1 Cor 13:5, the verb is used as a neg. qualification of true love which is *agápē* (26), benevolent love, translated "charity . . . doth not behave itself unseemly [*ouk aschēmoneí*]," which succinctly means that love in its speech and action seeks to contain no evil, but seeks to change the evildoer.

Syn.: *atimázō* (818), to dishonor; *atimóō* (821), to maltreat; *entrépomai* (1788), to withdraw because of public shame; *kataischúnō* (2617), to put to shame; *paradeigmatízō* (3856), to set forth as a public example.

808. ἀσχημοσύνη *aschēmosúnē*; gen. *aschēmosúnēs*, fem. noun from *aschēmōn* (809), uncomely, indecent. Deformity, indecency, obscenity (Rom 1:27); nakedness, shame, shameful parts (Rev 16:15; Sept.: Ex 20:26; Lev 18:6, 7).

Syn.: *atimía* (819), dishonor; *aischúnē* (152), shame, embarrassment; *entropḗ* (1791), inward shame, withdrawal.

Ant.: *aidṓs* (127), modesty resulting from inner conviction, a sense of respect toward the moral character of others, shamefacedness, a good moral quality; *euprépeia* (2143), gracefulness; *egkráteia* (1466), self-control, temperance; *semnótēs* (4587), decency, uprightness.

809. ἀσχήμων *aschḗmōn*; gen. *aschḗmonos*, adj. from the priv. *a* (1), without, and *schḗma* (4976), outward shape, figure. Uncomely, indecent (1 Cor 12:23, Sept.: Gen 34:7; Deut 24:3 [cf. Rev 16:15]).
Deriv.: *aschēmonéō* (807), to behave indecently; *aschēmosúnē* (808), an indecency.
Syn.: *agenḗs* (36), ignoble; *átopos* (824), out of place, improper; *aischrós* (150), shameful.
Ant.: *eugenḗs* (2104), noble; *kósmios* (2887), orderly, decorous, modest; *euschḗmōn* (2158), comely, decorous; *semnós* (4586), honorable; *dókimos* (1384), approved, acceptable.

810. ἀσωτία *asōtía*; gen. *asōtías*, fem. noun from *ásōtos* (n.f.), a prodigal, which is from the priv. *a* (1), and *sṓzō* (4982), to save. Having no hope of safety; extravagant squandering, dissoluteness, prodigality (Eph 5:18; Titus 1:6; 1 Pet 4:4; Sept.: Prov 28:7). An *ásōtos*, a prodigal, is one who spends too much, who slides easily under the fatal influence of flatterers and the temptations with which he has surrounded himself into spending freely on his own lusts and appetites. *Asōtía* is a dissolute, debauched, profligate manner of living. Cf. *asélgeia* (766), lawless insolence and unmanageable caprice (Mark 7:22; Rom 13:13; 2 Cor 12:21; Gal 5:19; Eph 4:19; 1 Pet 4:3; 2 Pet 2:7, 18; Jude 1:4). See also *asōtōs* (811), dissolutely, riotously.
Syn.: *akrasía* (192), lack of self-restraint; *hēdonḗ* (2237), lust, pleasure; *kraipálē* (2897), drunkenness,

debauchery; *dapánē* (1160), expense, prodigality.
Ant.: *egkráteia* (1466), confidence, temperance; *sōphrosúnē* (4997), soberness, the ability to place limitations on one's liberty.

811. ἀσώτως *asṓtōs*; adv. from *ásōtos* (n.f.), prodigal. Profligately, riotously, prodigally (Luke 15:13). See also *asōtía* (810), prodigality.
Ant.: *sōphrónōs* (4996), with sound mind, moderately, soberly, with restraint.

812. ἀτακτέω *ataktéō*; fut. *ataktḗsō*, from *átaktos* (813), one out of order. To break the ranks (as of soldiers), to behave irregularly or in a disorderly manner, to neglect one's duties (2 Thess 3:7).
Syn.: *apeithéō* (544), to disbelieve, be disobedient; *anthístēmi* (436), to oppose, resist; *parabaínō* (3845), to transgress; *epanístamai* (1881), to rise up against; *parakoúō* (3878), to disobey, neglect to hear.
Ant.: *summorphóō* (4833), to assimilate, obey; *chalinagōgéō* (5468), to bridle; *peitharchéō* (3980), to submit to authority; *hupokoúō* (5219), to obey, heed.

813. ἄτακτος *átaktos*; gen. *atáktou*, masc.-fem., neut. *átakton*, adj. from the priv. *a* (1), and *tássō* (5021), to set in order. Disorderly, irregular (1 Thess 5:14, neglectful of duties).
Deriv.: *ataktéō* (812), to behave irregularly; *atáktōs* (814), irregularly and in a disorderly fashion.
Syn.: *akatástatos* (182), inconstant, unstable; *apeithḗs* (545), disobedient; *anupótaktos* (506), insubordinate.
Ant.: *taktós* (5002), appointed or stated, set; *hupḗkoos* (5255), obedient.

814. ἀτάκτως *atáktōs*; adv. from *átaktos* (813), disorderly. In a disorderly manner, irregularly (2 Thess 3:6, 11).
Ant.: *en táxei* (*en* [1722], in; *táxei*, the dat. of *táxis* [5010], order, rank, succession), in order or rank.

815. ἄτεκνος *áteknos*; gen. *atéknou*, from the priv. *a* (1), without, and *téknon* (5043), a child. Having no child, childless (Luke 20:28–30; Sept.: Gen 15:2; Lev 20:20; Isa 49:21; Jer 18:21).

Syn.: *steíros* (4723), sterile, barren.

Ant.: *goneús* (1118), a parent.

816. ἀτενίζω *atenízō*; fut. *atenísō*, from *atenés* (n.f.), strained, intent, which is from the intens. *a* (1), and *teínō* (n.f.), stretch, strain. To look fixedly, gaze intently (Luke 4:20; 22:56; Acts 1:10; 3:4, 12; 6:15; 7:55; 10:4; 11:6; 13:9; 14:9; 23:1; 2 Cor 3:7, 13).

Syn.: *horáō* (3708), to perceive, see; *blépō* (991), to look, see,; *emblépō* (1689), to look earnestly; *theōréō* (2334), to carefully observe; *theáomai* (2300), to look with wonder; *elpízō* (1679), to hope; *prosdokáō* (4328), to expect, look for; *apekdéchomai* (553), to expect fully, look for; *anaménō* (362), to wait for; *skopéō* (4648), to look at, take heed.

Ant.: *apelpízō* (560), to give up hope, despair; *kammúō* (2576), to close the eyes.

817. ἄτερ *áter*; adv. Without, not with, not having (Luke 22:35); in the absence of (Luke 22:6).

Syn.: *áneu* (427), without; *chōrís* (5565), apart from; *parektós* (3924), besides.

Ant.: *metá* (3326), with; *sún* (4862), with; *homoú* (3674), together; *apó koinoú* (*apó* [575], from; *koinós* [2839], common) together, jointly; *homothumadón* (3661), unanimously; *pará* (3844), by the side of, with.

818. ἀτιμάζω *atimázō*; fut. *atimásō*, from *átimos* (820), without honor. To dishonor, treat with indignity (Luke 20:11, to abuse; John 8:49; Acts 5:41; Rom 1:24; 2:23; James 2:6; Sept.: Gen 16:4, 5; Mic 7:6).

Syn.: *exouthenéō* (1848), to make of no account; *kataphronéō* (2706), to despise; *periphronéō* (4065), to despise; *athetéō* (114), to set aside, reject; *oligōréō* (3643),

to care little for, regard lightly; *kataischúnō* (2617), to dishonor; *entrépomai* (1788), to turn in upon, withdraw because of public shame; *paradeigmatízō* (3856), to set forth as an example; *logízomai eis oudén* (*logízomai* [3049], to count; *eis* [1519], unto; *oudén* [3762], nothing), to reckon as nothing; *loidoréo* (3058), to heap abuse upon; *blasphēméō* (987), to revile, blaspheme.

Ant.: *timáō* (5091), to honor; *doxázō* (1392), to glorify, honor; *kaucháomai* (2744), to boast, to vaunt in a good sense; *sebéomai* (4576), to respect.

819. ἀτιμία *atimía*; gen. *atimías*, fem. noun from *átimos* (820), without honor. Dishonor, disgrace, ignominy (Rom 1:26, "shameful passions" [a.t.]; 2 Cor 6:8; 11:21; Sept.: Prov 12:9; Job 12:21; Jer 23:40). In the sense of dishonor (Rom 9:21; 1 Cor 11:14, improperly; 15:43, vileness, dishonor; 2 Tim 2:20, for a dishonorable use; Sept.: Prov 11:2; 13:18; Jer 20:11).

Syn.: *aischúnē* (152), public shame; *entropḗ* (1791), shame; *aschēmosúnē* (808), unseemliness; *oneidismós* (3680), reproach; *óneidos* (3681), disgrace; *húbris* (5196), insolence, injury, reproach.

Ant.: *timḗ* (5092), value, honor; *dóxa* (1391), glory, honor; *kaúchēma* (2745), boasting, glorying; *kaúchēsis* (2746), the act of boasting.

820. ἄτιμος *átimos*; gen. *atímou*, masc.-fem., neut. *átimon*, adj. from the priv. *a* (1), without, and *timḗ* (5092), honor. Dishonored, without honor (Matt 13:57, of low character or reputation; Mark 6:4; 1 Cor 4:10; 12:23; Sept.: Isa 3:5).

Deriv.: *atimázō* (818), to dishonor; *atimía* (819), dishonor; *atimóō* (821), to dishonor.

Syn.: *aphilágathos* (865), hostile to virtue; *ádikos* (94), unjust, wicked.

Ant.: *éntimos* (1784), honorable; *tímios* (5093), honest, honorable; *euschḗmōn* (2158), honorable; *kalós* (2570), good, honorable; *semnós* (4586), honorable, venerable; *éndoxos* (1741), glorious, honorable, of high reputation; *díkaios* (1342), just, right.

821. ἀτιμόω *atimóō*; contracted *atimṓ*, fut. *atimṓsō*, from *átimos* (820), without honor. To dishonor, treat with indignity (Mark 12:4; Sept.: 1 Sam 10:27; 2 Sam 10:5; Jer 22:28).
   Syn.: *atimázō* (818), to dishonor.
   Ant.: *timáō* (5091), to honor; *sebéomai* (4576), to respect.

822. ἀτμίς *atmís*; gen. *atmídos*, fem. noun. Vapor, exhalation (James 4:14). Also spoken of dense smoke (Acts 2:19 quoted from Joel 2:30). In the Sept., this word corresponds to the Hebr. word meaning a cloud, namely of incense (Lev 16:13; Ezek 8:11; see also Gen 19:28).

823. ἄτομος *átomos*; gen. *atómou*, masc.-fem., neut. *átomon*, adj. from the priv. *a* (1), without, and *tomḗ* (n.f.), a cut, which is from *témnō* (n.f.), to cut, divide. Indivisible. This is the word from which "atom" is derived (*to átomon*), that which cannot be divided. When referring to time, it means an indivisible point of time, an instant, a moment (1 Cor 15:52). Also from *tomḗ* (n.f.): *dichotoméō* (1371), to cut asunder.
   Syn.: *stigmḗ* (4743), a moment.
   Ant.: *chrónos* (5550), a season, period of time.

824. ἄτοπος *átopos*; gen. *atópou*, masc.-fem., neut. *átopon*, adj. from *a* (1), without, and *tópos* (5117), place. Without place or having no place. Inconvenient, prejudicial, hurtful, evil, improper (Acts 28:6). Of persons: absurd, unreasonable (2 Thess 3:2); of conduct: inconvenient, unsuitable, improper, wrong (Luke 23:41; Sept.: Job 4:8; 11:11).
   Syn.: *kakós* (2556), bad; *ponērós* (4190), evil; *álogos* (249), unreasonable; *áthesmos* (113), not according to custom; *ánomos* (459), lawless; *parádoxos* (3861), contrary to expectation; *mōrós* (3474), foolish, absurd; *anóētos* (453), nonintelligent; *asúnetos* (801), foolish,

unintelligent; *áphrōn* (878), mindless, foolish; *aneúthetos* (428), inconvenient.
   Ant.: *kalós* (2570), good; *agathós* (18), benevolent; *chrēstós* (5543), gracious, useful; *eúkairos* (2121), well-timed; *logikós* (3050), logical, reasonable; *sunetós* (4908), sagacious, one who reasons things out; *sophós* (4680), wise; *orthós* (3717), right; *prépōn* (4241), becoming; *epitḗdeios* (2006), serviceable, needful; *eúthetos* (2111), well-placed, appropriate.

825. Ἀττάλεια *Attáleia*; gen. *Attaleías*, fem. proper noun. Attalia, a maritime city of Pamphylia (Acts 14:25) named for its founder Attalus Philadelphus, King of Pergamus.

826. αὐγάζω *augázō*; fut. *augásō*, from *augḗ* (827), dawn. Used trans.: to illuminate; intrans.: to shine (2 Cor 4:4; irradiate, beam, shine forth; Sept.: Lev 13:24–26, 28).
   Deriv.: *diaugázō* (1306), to shine through.
   Syn.: *phaínō* (5316), to cause to appear, to shine; *epiphaínō* (2014), to shine upon, give light; *lámpō* (2989), to shine as a torch; *eklámpō* (1584), to shine forth; *astráptō* (797), to flash as lightning; *periastráptō* (4015), to flash around; *epiphaúskō* or *epiphaúō* (2017), to shine forth; *phōtízō* (5461), to illuminate; *anáptō* (381), to kindle, light.
   Ant.: *skotízō* (4654), to darken; *episkiázō* (1982), to cast a shadow upon; *skotóō* (4656), to cover with darkness.

827. αὐγή *augḗ*; gen. *augḗs*, fem. noun. Brightness, light, splendor, as used by the Class. Gr. In the NT, the dayspring, daybreak, first appearance of daylight (Acts 20:11, "till dawn" [a.t.]; Sept.: Isa 59:9).
   Deriv.: *augázō* (826), to shine.
   Syn.: *órthros* (3722), dawn.
   Ant.: *núx* (3571), night; *skótos* (4655), darkness; *zóphos* (2217), blackness, darkness, mist; *hespéra* (2073), evening; *opsé* (3796), after the close of the day, the beginning of the evening.

828. Αὔγουστος *Aúgoustos*; gen. *Augoústou*, masc. proper noun. Augustus, meaning venerable. A surname conferred by the Senate on Octavianus, the first Roman emperor in 27 B.C., his full name being Caius Julius Caesar Octavianus (62 B.C. to A.D. 14). He was the grand nephew of Julius Caesar. It was he who gave the order for the enrollment which was the human cause of the Bethlehemic birth of Jesus (Luke 2:1). He was one of the second so-called Triumvirate, with Mark Antony and Lepidus. After the removal of Lepidus, he fought and defeated Antony at Actium in 31 B.C. For this reason the Roman Senate conferred upon him the title of Augustus. He is found in the NT in connection with Herod, whom he had greatly honored and reinstated in his kingdom, although Herod had espoused the cause of Antony. At Herod's death, Augustus divided his kingdom in accordance with his will and even educated two of his sons, since their relations had been very intimate. He reigned 44 years as sole sovereign, or 56 years reckoning from his first entrance into public life. He was succeeded by Tiberius Caesar (Luke 3:1).

829. αὐθάδης *authádēs*; gen. *authádous*, masc.-fem., neut. *authádes*, adj. from *autós* (846), himself, and *hédomai* (n.f.), to please. One who is pleased with himself and despises others, insolent, surly, the contrast of courteous or affable. A person who obstinately maintains his own opinion or asserts his own rights but is reckless of the rights, feelings, and interests of others. He regulates his life with no respect to others (Titus 1:7; 2 Pet 2:10; Sept.: Gen 49:3, 7; Prov 21:24). Also from *hédomai* (n.f.): *asménōs* (780): gladly, with joy.

Syn.: *phílautos* (5367), loving self, selfish; *propetḗs* (4312), precipitous, headlong, heady, rash; *hubristḗs* (5197), an insulter.

Ant.: *semnós* (4586), venerable, honorable; *epieikḗs* (1933), appropriate, gentle, tolerant; *eugenḗs* (2104), noble; *chrēstós* (5543), gracious.

830. αὐθαίρετος *authaíretos*; gen. *authairétou*, masc.-fem., neut. *authaíreton*, adj. from *autós* (846), himself, and *hairéō* (138), to choose. Choosing or willing of oneself or of one's own accord (2 Cor 8:3, 17); spontaneous, voluntary.

Syn.: *autómatos* (844), spontaneous, automatic.

Ant.: *anagkastōs* (317), compulsorily; *anagkaíos* (316), necessary, needful; *bíaios* (972), resulting from force; *opheilétēs* (3781), one who owes.

831. αὐθεντέω *authentéō* contracted *authentō̂*; fut. *authentḗsō*, from *authéntēs* (n.f.), murderer, absolute master, which is from *autós* (846), himself, and *éntea* (n.f.) arms, armor. A self-appointed killer with one's own hand, one acting by his own authority or power. Governing a gen., to use or exercise authority or power over as an autocrat, to domineer (1 Tim 2:12). See *anḗr* (435, XI, C), husband.

Syn.: *exousiázō* (1850), to exercise the right and power to rule; *katexousiázō* (2715), to exercise full authority over; *kurieúō* (2961), to lord it over, rule over as lord, and the more intens. *katakurieúō* (2634), to lord it over completely; *basileúō* (936), to rule, reign; *hēgemoneúō* (2230), to act as the ruler, to govern.

Ant.: *hupēretéō* (5256), to serve, be a subordinate; *douleúō* (1398), to be a slave to, to serve; *diakonéō* (1247), to be an attendant, to minister.

832. αὐλέω *auléō* contracted *aulō̂*; fut. *aulḗsō*, from *aulós* (836), a pipe or flute. To pipe, play on a pipe or flute (Matt 11:17; Luke 7:32; 1 Cor 14:7). The word is used in the parable that the Lord Jesus gave of children first playing their flutes, as if at a wedding, while other children would not respond to their rejoicing. Then they cried, but again the other children would not join in with them. The lesson is that there was no participation from others no matter what they did. Likewise, no matter what we do as believers on behalf of the kingdom of God, not all will follow us and do the same thing. The Lord Jesus wanted to portray the unresponsiveness of those around us to what we do, for He has likened us to children, and, unless we become as children, we cannot enter into the kingdom of heaven (Matt 18:3). The Lord then parallels the life of John as one of privation, but not all followed him. In fact, they killed him. The Lord followed a different way, that of socialization, eating and drinking with sinners and publicans, but again they did not accept His way and they killed Him. To summarize, no matter what we do as believers in Jesus, we can't please all, nor can we attract all (Luke 6:26). The concluding sentence, "and justified was wisdom by her works" (a.t. [Matt 11:19]), indicates that we should do that which pleases God regardless of its acceptance or rejection by men. See also Luke 7:31–35.

Deriv.: *aulētēs* (834), a flute player.

833. αὐλή *aulḗ*; gen. *aulḗs*, fem. noun. An enclosed space exposed to the open air, a sheepfold, a place where sheep are housed (John 10:1, 16). The exterior courtyard before a dwelling or edifice (Rev 11:2). Such courtyards served as places of reception for company (Matt 26:3, 58, 69; Mark 14:54, 66; 15:16; Luke 22:55; John 18:15; Sept.: Ex 27:9; Neh 8:16; Esth 1:5). A palace or edifice because they were usually built with an open court around them, also a part of the whole, the courtyard for the house, mansion, palace (Matt 26:3; Luke 11:21; Sept.: Isa 34:13).

Deriv.: *aulízomai* (835), to lodge; *proaúlion* (4259), gateway, vestibule.

Syn.: *basíleion* (933), king's court (Luke 7:25); *praitórion* (4232), common hall, judgment hall, palace; *phragmós* (5418), hedge round about.

834. αὐλητής *aulētēs*; gen. *aulētoú*, from *auléō* (832), to pipe. A player on a pipe or flute (Rev 18:22). Cf. Matt 9:23 with Jer 48:36, which indicates that Jewish

funerals, as early as the time of Jeremiah, were accompanied with the music of pipes or flutes for mourning (2 Chr 35:25; Jer 9:17). At such times the Jews employed women who would mourn by piping and singing.

835. αὐλίζομαι *aulízomai*; fut. *aulísomai*, mid. deponent from *aulḗ* (833), a sheepfold. To be put or remain in a field or stable as sheep or other cattle. Used in this sense in the Class. Gr. Spoken of men: to lodge at night, to take a night's lodging (Matt 21:17; Luke 21:37; Sept.: Josh 6:11; 8:9; Judg 19:6, 10, 15, 20).

Deriv.: *agrauléō* (63), to live in the fields or outdoors.

Syn.: *ménō* (3306), to stay, abide; *diatríbō* (1304), to spend or pass time, tarry; *agrauléō* (63), to lodge in a fold in a field, from *agrós* (68), field, and *aulḗ* (833), a courtyard, fold; *kataskēnóō* (2681), to pitch one's tent; *katalúō* (2647), to lodge; *xenízomai* (3579), to lodge, remain as a stranger.

Ant.: *hupágō* (5217), to depart; *apérchomai* (565), to go away; *poreúomai* (4198), to go forth; *anachōréō* (402), to depart; *apochōréō* (672), to depart from; *éxeimi* (1826), to go out; *metaírō* (3332), to depart; *aphístēmi* (868), to stand away from or to depart; *metabaínō* (3327), to depart.

836. αὐλός *aulós*; gen. *auloú*, masc. noun. A pipe or flute (1 Cor 14:7; Sept.: 1 Sam 10:5; Isa 5:12).

Deriv.: *auléō* (832), to play on a pipe.

837. αὐξάνω *auxánō*, **αὔξω** *aúxō*; fut. *auxḗsō*, aor. *ēúxēsa*, aor. pass. *ēuxéthēn*. To grow, increase, to augment (1 Cor 3:7; Eph 2:21; Col 2:19). Used both trans. and intrans.To grow, increase, add to something.

(I) Trans.: to give increase, cause to grow, enlarge (1 Cor 3:6, 7); in number (2 Cor 9:10; Sept.: Gen 17:20; 26:22; Josh 4:14; Job 42:10).

(II) Intrans.: *auxánō* and *aúxō*, and in later writers in the mid. *auxánomai*, fut.

auxḗsomai, aor. pass. with mid. sense *ēuxḗthēn*, meaning to exceed, increase, grow.

(A) Mid. in Matt 13:32; 1 Pet 2:2. Metaphorically in 2 Cor 10:15; Col 1:10; Sept.: Gen 1:22, 28; 21:8; Ex 1:7; Num 24:7; Judg 13:24.

(B) In the act. form in Matt 6:28; Mark 4:8; Luke 1:80; 2:40; 12:27; 13:19; John 3:30; Acts 6:7; 7:17; 12:24; 19:20; Eph 2:21; 4:15; Col 2:19; 2 Pet 3:18.

For someone or something to grow (*auxánō*), it must be acted upon by an outside power or have the element of life within him or it. This is seen clearly in the use of the verb *auxánō*. For example, the lilies grow (Matt 6:28; Luke 12:27); the seed is grown (Matt 13:32); the fruit comes from the seeds (Mark 4:8); the mustard seed grew to a tree. In all these instances, it was something living that could grow because of the element of life within it. This growth, however, was not because of any special ability of the seeds, but because of the quality of life so implanted by God Himself. However, the verb *prokóptō* (4298) has in it the character of human achievement. It is advancement, either of good or evil, not because of the inevitability of its constitution, but because of conscious effort which is particularly manifested in the use of *prokopḗ* (4297), advancement, the subst. of *prokóptō* in Phil 1:25; 1 Tim 4:15. In Gal 1:14, where Paul says, "And profited [*proékopton*]," he is saying that he was consciously advancing in the Jewish religion above many of his equals. In 2 Tim 2:16, there is the conscious advancement unto more ungodliness; in 2 Tim 3:9 there is the proceeding (*prokópsousin*) no further in their folly; and in 2 Tim 3:13, what is translated "shall wax worse" is also *prokópsousin*. Man is held responsible in this advancement of evil.

Both the words *auxánō* and *prokóptō* are used in relation to the human growth of the Lord Jesus as a child. *Auxánō* is used in Luke 2:40: "And the child grew [*ēuxane*, the imperf. of *auxánō*], and waxed strong in spirit, filled [*plēroúmenon*, the pres. part. pass. of *plēróō* {4137}, to fill] with wisdom; and the grace of God was upon him." *Prokópto* is used in Luke 2:52. The word *ēuxane* means that the child Jesus, just like any other child, was growing into human maturity because He was a living person, and His spirit, i.e., His human spirit, was being strengthened constantly, being filled with wisdom and grace or divine favor. His physical growth was equal to the growing realization of His divine nature. In verse fifty-two, however, we read, "And Jesus increased [*proékopte*, the imperf. of *prokóptō*, which indicated His self-motivated and conscious advancement in wisdom and human maturity as well as in favor with God and with men]." In other words, Jesus was growing in His humanity because there was a living human spirit in Him just in the same manner as there is a human spirit in all of mankind, but He also exercised a conscious advancement in His growth, and that is *prokopḗ*.

Deriv.: *auíxesis* (838), growth, increase; *sunauxánō* (4885), to grow together; *huperauxánō* (5232), to grow abundantly.

Syn.: *mēkúnomai* (3373), to grow long; *phúō* (5453), to spring up in regard to the seed coming up; *sumphúō* (4855), to grow together or to come up together (Luke 8:7); in the sense of increase, *perisseúō* (4052), to abound; *pleonázō* (4121), to make to abound, to increase abundantly; *plēthúnō* (4129), to multiply *prokóptō* (4298), progress, advance by one's own effort.

Ant.: *elattóō* (1642), to decrease; *kóptō* (2875), to cut down.

838. αὔξησις *auíxēsis*; gen. *auxéseōs*, fem. noun from *auíxō* (837), to grow. Growth, increase, applied spiritually only (Eph 4:16; Col 2:19). It is God who gives the growth or increase. This is further indication of the distinction between the verb *auxánō*, growth caused by factors outside oneself or by the element of life placed there by God Himself, and *prokóptō* (4298), to advance by one's conscious effort. Thus *aúxēsis* is growth or increase brought about by God, while *prokopḗ* (4297), is a conscious advancement through exertion.

Syn.: *prokopḗ* (4297), advancement.

839. αὔριον *aúrion*; adv. Time immediately after or succeeding, soon after. Tomorrow (Matt 6:30; Luke 12:28; Acts 23:15, 20; 25:22; 1 Cor 15:32; Sept.: Ex 8:10, 23; 9:5, 18; 2 Sam 11:12); with *hēméra* (2250), day explicit or implied, it means the morrow, the next day (Matt 6:34; Luke 10:35; Acts 4:3, 5; James 4:14). In Luke 13:32, 33, the expression *sḗmeron kaí aúrion kaí tḗ trítē* (*sḗmeron* [4594], today; *kaí* [2532], and; *tḗ* [5037], and; *trítē* [5154], third) "today and tomorrow and the third day," means for a definite time. In James 4:13, "today or tomorrow" means for a period of time as if time were their possession.

Deriv.: *epaúrion* (1887), tomorrow, the next day.

Ant.: *nún* (3568), now; *sḗmeron* (4594), today.

840. αὐστηρός *austērós*; fem. *austērá*, neut., *austērón*, adj. Austere (Luke 19:21, 22). Contrast *sklērós* (4642), hard as related to the touch. *Austērós* is often associated with honor, meaning earnest and severe, but not so with *sklērós* which always conveys a harsh, inhuman character (Matt 25:24; John 6:60; Acts 9:5; James 3:4; Jude 1:15).

Syn.: *chalepós* (5467), difficult, furious, perilous; *oxús* (3691), sharp; *pikrós* (4089), bitter.

Ant.: *epieikḗs* (1933), appropriate, mild, gentle, tolerant; *ḗpios* (2261), affable, mild, kind, gentle; *práos* (4235), meek; *eugenḗs* (2272), gentle.

841. αὐτάρκεια *autárkeia*; gen. *autarkeías*, fem. noun from *autárkēs* (842), self-sufficient, content. Self-sufficiency in a good sense, sufficiency with oneself as spoken of a satisfied mind or disposition. Spoken of the necessities of life (2 Cor 9:8); contentment (1 Tim 6:6).

Ant.: *gumnótēs* (1132), nudity, hence need; *limós* (3042), scarcity of food, famine, hunger; *hustérēma* (5303), deficit, want, lack,; *anágkē* (318), need, distress.

842. αὐτάρκης *autárkēs*; gen. *autárkous*, masc.-fem., neut. *autárkes*, adj. from *autós* (846), himself, and *arkéō* (714), to suffice. Self-sufficient in a good sense, sufficient, adequate, as used in the Class. Gr. Content, satisfied with one's lot (Phil 4:11).

Deriv.: *autárkeia* (841), self-sufficiency, contentment.

Syn.: *arketós* (713), enough, satisfactory; *hikanós* (2425), competent, sufficient, worthy; *plḗrēs* (4143), full; *mestós* (3324), full, replete.

Ant.: *penichrós* (3998), needy, poor; *ptōchós* (4434), poor, helpless; *olígos* (3641), little in quantity.

843. αὐτοκατάκριτος *autokatákritos*; gen. *autokatakrítou*, masc.-fem., neut. *autokatákriton*, adj. from *autós* (846), himself, and *katakrínō* (2632), to condemn. Self-condemned, condemned by one's own decision (Titus 3:11), meaning passing sentence upon oneself. This is either voluntarily cutting oneself off from the church in open revolt, or, by renouncing his faith, rendering himself incapable of receiving the privileges and blessings to which he has been entitled. He is actually judging or declaring himself unworthy of the blessings tendered by the church. Such are the *asebeís* (765), ungodly ones.

Ant.: *athṓos* (121), not guilty, innocent; *akatágnōstos* (176), not to be condemned; *akatákritos* (178), not condemned; *anaítios* (338), blameless.

844. αὐτόματος *autómatos*; gen. *automátou*, neut. *autómaton*, masc., fem. noun from *autós* (846), himself, and *máō* (n.f.), to be excited, eager, ready. Spontaneous, of its own accord (Mark 4:28; Acts 12:10; Sept.: Lev 25:5, 11). In Mark 4:28, *automátē*, is an adj. which in Eng. can only be translated as the adv.

"automatically." The earth is presented as bearing fruit by being the medium of the living powers of the seed. The earth could not bring fruit if it were not for the seed. Therefore, it may be misleading to translate *automátē* in reference to the earth as bringing forth fruit of itself (although Mark may be using the language of appearance). It is the seed that bears the element of life, and such is present and energized because of God. Here we have a parable of how God's Word is divinely energized in the human heart. It does not need other elements such as heat and moisture. These by themselves would not avail to bring forth fruit without the living seed. (See 1 Cor 3:4–6.) God is the One who gives the increase and He is the One who provides even the contributory means for vegetation. Concurrently, there are natural causes of vegetation, i.e., heat and moisture (see Job 14:8, 9; 2 Sam 23:4), which work together with the assistance and cultivation of man. This is the word from which "automatic" comes.

Syn.: *authaíretos* (830), self-chosen, voluntary. It is different from *autómatos* in that in *authaíretos* there is the personal conscious choice of action according to the predetermined possibility of development.

845. αὐτόπτης *autóptēs*; gen. *autóptou*, masc. noun from *autós* (846), himself, and *óptomai* (3700), to see. One who has seen with his own eyes, an eyewitness (Luke 1:2).

Syn.: *mártus* (3144), witness.

846. αὐτός *autós*; fem. *autḗ*, neut. *autó.*, pron. Self; him, her, it; the same (with the art. preceding it).

(**I**) Self, in all the persons, i.e., myself, thyself, himself.

(**A**) Self, used as an intens. for emphasis. It sets the individual apart from everything else. (**1**) With proper names: Mark 6:17, "Herod himself"; 12:36, 37; Luke 20:42 "David himself"; 24:15 "Jesus himself" in distinction from His disciples; John 4:2; 2 Cor 10:1, "Now I Paul myself." With other nouns: Rom 8:26, "the Spirit itself"; 1 Cor 15:28, "the Son also himself"; Gal 6:13, "For neither they themselves . . . the circumcised ones" (a.t.); 1 Thess 4:16; Heb 9:23; 3 John 1:12; Rev 21:3, "God himself." With a personal pron. as *autós egṓ* (*egṓ* [1473], I), Luke 24:39; Acts 10:26, "I myself"; Rom 15:14, I myself; Mark 6:31, "you yourselves" (a.t.); John 3:28, "yourselves," you or you yourselves; 1 Cor 11:13. The same with other pron. as *autoí hoútoi* (*hoútoi* [3778], these), Acts 24:15, 20, themselves, meaning they themselves; Matt 27:57; Mark 15:43, "who also himself" (a.t.). See also Sept.: 1 Sam 10:19. (**2**) With the meaning of even, implying comparison and distinction: 1 Cor 11:14, "Does not even nature herself teach?" (a.t.); 2 Cor 11:14, "for even Satan himself" (a.t.). See also Rom 8:21; Heb 11:11. (**3**) As marking the strongest emphasis and prominence, the very: John 5:36, "The very works which I do" (a.t.); Heb 9:24, "unto the very heaven" (a.t.). (**4**) As marking the exclusion of all else, self alone: 2 Cor 12:13, "I alone" (a.t.), meaning exclusive of the other Apostles; Rev 19:12, "except himself alone" (a.t.). With *mónos* (3441), alone, subjoined as in John 6:15, "himself alone." (**5**) Of oneself, of one's own accord, voluntarily: John 16:27, "the Father himself [of His own accord, without compulsion] loveth you." See 1 Pet 2:24.

(**B**) Used alone with the personal pron. being omitted or implied, mainly in the nom. for "I myself," "he himself," with various degrees of emphasis; in the oblique cases (any cases except the nom. and voc.) only at the beginning of the construction. (**1**) Generally and often having *kai* (2532), and. In the nom. in Luke 6:42, "thyself not seeing the beam" (a.t.), and so forth; 11:4, "for we also forgive"; 11:46, 52; 15:14; John 7:4; 9:21; Acts 2:34; 13:14; 17:25; 21:24; Phil 2:24, "that I also myself shall come shortly"; Col 1:17; 1 John 1:7. Also in the oblique cases (any except the nom. and voc.) at the beginning of a construction: Luke 24:24, "but him they saw not"; John 9:21, "ask him." **(2)** For special emphasis when used for a person distinguished from all others, whom all know and respect, and so forth. Of Jesus, i.e., He, as used for the Master, the Lord, and so forth; Matt 8:24, "but he was asleep"; Mark 4:38; 6:47; 8:29; Luke 5:16, 17; 8:54; 9:51; 10:38; 11:17; 14:1. Of God as in Heb 13:5.

(C) Where several words intervene between the subj. and verb., *autós* is put emphatic instead of repeating the subj. itself. **(1)** In the sense of *hoútos* (3778), this one, or *ekeínos* (1565), that one, and often to be expressed in Eng. by an emphatic "he," "she," "it," "they," and so forth: Matt 1:21, "for he [and no other] shall save his people from their sins"; 5:4, "for they [of all others] shall be comforted" (see the same in Matt 5:5–10). Matt 6:4, "[He] shall reward thee openly"; 11:14, "this is Elias" (a.t.); 12:50 (cf. Mark 3:35, where *hoútos* [3778], this, occurs); Matt 25:17; Mark 1:8; 14:15; Luke 1:17, 36; 11:14; John 14:10; Acts 10:42; Heb 8:9; 1 John 2:2; Sept.: Ps 19:6; Isa 53:5, 7, 12. **(2)** With ordinals, *autós* implies oneself with the others included in the number. Rev 17:11, "he is the eighth," i.e., he was with the seven and is one of them (cf. 2 Pet 2:5).

(II) Used instead of the personal pron. of the 3d person, i.e., him, her, it, them, but only in the oblique cases and not at the beginning of construction.

(A) As referring to a def. subj. or antecedent expressed. **(1)** Generally and simply as in Matt 3:16, "and, lo, the heavens were opened unto him [*autṓ*], and he saw the Spirit of God descending . . . upon him [*autón*]"; 6:26; 8:1f.; 11:25; 26:71; Mark 3:33; Luke 1:21, 22; John 1:5, 6; Acts 7:21. Irregularities: **(a)** A transition is made from the 1st person to the 3d person, as in Luke 1:44, 45; or from the 2d person to the 3d person, as in Rev 18:22–24. **(b)** Sometimes *autón, autoú,* refer not to the nearest subj., but to a remote one. Mark 8:22, "and besought him [Jesus], to touch him [the blind man]." See also Mark 9:27, 28; Sept.: Gen 16:6, 7. **(2)** For

the sake of distinction, *autón* is sometimes inserted after an antecedent by way of repetition, usually in the same case. Matt 4:16 (TR), "to them which sat . . . light is sprung up unto them" (a.t.); 5:40, "if any man will . . . let him"; 25:29, "from him that hath not shall be taken away"; John 15:2; Rev 1:5, 6; 2:7, "to him overcoming I shall give unto him" (a.t.); 6:4. In a different case, Matt 12:36; Sept.: Gen 16:3. This especially takes place after a relative pron. as in Mark 7:25, "A certain woman, whose [*hḗs,* of which, fem.] young daughter [*autḗs,* of her] had an unclean spirit." Also Mark 1:7; John 1:27; Acts 15:17; Eph 2:10; Rev 7:2, 9; Sept.: Ex 4:17; Lev 18:5; Num 11:21; Judg 18:5, 6; 1 Kgs 13:10. Of the same kind of clauses commencing with the relative pron., where the writer falls out of the construction and proceeds with *autoú,* 2 Pet 2:3, *hoís,* whose, *autón* for *hṓn.* Also in Rev 2:18, *autoú* instead of *hoú.* See also Rev 17:2. Of a different kind are those constructions where *autón,* and so forth, is put after a relative pron. epexegetically. Matt 3:12, "Whose fan is in his hand"; Rev 7:9; Sept.: Gen 24:3; Judg 6:10.

(B) Where no def. subj. or antecedent is directly expressed, but *autón* is understood by the construction of the sentence. **(1)** As referring to names, places, countries, in which is likewise included the collective idea of their inhabitants. Matt 4:23, "teaching in their synagogues," where "their" stands for "of the Galileans"; 9:35; Luke 4:15; Acts 8:5 where *autoís* stands for the Samaritans; 20:2; 2 Cor 2:13; 1 Thess 1:8, 9. **(2)** As referring to an abstract noun implied in a preceding concrete one, and vice versa. John 8:44, "he is a liar, and the father of it," meaning of lying; Rom 2:26, "if the uncircumcision . . . not his uncircumcision," means of such a one who is not circumcised. In Luke 5:17, *autoús* means the sick ones; see Luke 5:15. **(3)** As referring to an antecedent implied in a preceding verb: Acts 12:21, "and made an oration unto them," meaning, of course, unto the *dḗmos* (1218), the public, which word is used in Acts 12:22. See also 1 Pet 3:14 where *autṓn*, their, refers to the terror of those that will harm you of 1 Pet 3:13. (4) Where there is no grammatical reference whatever to the preceding context, but the antecedent is merely presupposed as in Luke 1:17, where "before him" refers to the Messiah. Also 1 John 2:12; 2 John 1:6; Luke 2:22, where *autṓn*, their, purification in the Gr. text refers to the mother and child; Acts 23:28, "unto their counsel," referred to by *autṓn*, means those who constituted the Sanhedrin, the counselors, the high priests and the scribes, see Acts 23:6 (cf. John 7:47, 50; 20:15, together with John 20:13); Acts 4:5, referring to the people meaning the Jews; also Matt 11:1; 12:9; Heb 8:8, where *autoís*, with them, means to those who had the first covenant.

(C) Sometimes *autoú*, *autón* is found where we might expect the reflexive *heautoú* (1438), of him, or *hautoú* (848), of him, and so forth. Matt 21:45 where *perí autón* stands for *perí hautṓn*. John 1:48; 4:47 where *autoú* stands for *hautoú*. In such cases, the sentiment is expressed in the person of the writer, not in that of the subj.; see Sept.: Gen 16:3.

(D) Sometimes, though not often, *autón* is omitted where it must be supplied in thought. Acts 13:3 where *autoús* must be understood; Mark 6:5; Eph 5:11; 2 Thess 3:15; 1 Tim 6:2.

(III) With the art. preceding *ho autós*, *hē autḗ*, *tó autó*, meaning the same.

(A) Generally it means the same, not different objectively. Mark 14:39, "the same word" (a.t.); Luke 6:38, "with the same measure"; Rom 9:21, "of the same lump"; 10:12, "the same Lord over all"; 1 Cor 12:4, 6, 8, 9; Phil 1:30; Sept.: Ex 36:7; Job 31:15. *Tó autó*, *tá autá*, the same, the same things, like things (Matt 5:46; Luke 6:33; Acts 15:27; Rom 2:1; 1 Cor 1:10; Eph 6:9). The following are adv. phrases: (1) *Tó autó*, the same, in the same manner, in like manner (Matt 27:44; 1 Cor 12:25). (2) *Epí* (1909), upon, *tó autó*, spoken of place or time. Spoken of place, meaning in the same place, in one place (Matt 22:34; Acts 2:1, 44; 4:26; 1 Cor 11:20; Sept.: 2 Sam 10:15; Ps 2:2). Spoken of time, meaning at the same time, together (Luke 17:35; Acts 3:1; Sept.: Deut 32:10; 2 Sam 21:9; Ps 37:38). (3) *Katá* (2596), at, *tó autó*, meaning at the same time, together (Acts 14:1; Sept.: 1 Sam 31:6; 2 Sam 2:16).

(B) Spoken subjectively, meaning always the same, i.e., not changing, immutable (Heb 1:12 quoted from Ps 102:28). See also Heb 13:8; Sept.: Isa 41:4.

(C) Constructed with a dat., meaning the same with, the same as if (1 Cor 11:5; 1 Pet 5:9).

Deriv.: *authádēs* (829), self-complacent; *authaíretos* (830), voluntary; *autárkēs* (842), self-sufficient, content; *autokatákritos* (843), self-condemned; *autómatos* (844), spontaneous; *autóptēs* (845), an eyewitness; *autócheir* (849), with one's own hands, personally; *emautoú* (1683), myself; *tautá* (5024), the same things; *phílautos* (5367), one who loves himself more than he ought; *hōsaútos* (5615), likewise.

Syn.: *hómoios* (3664), similar.

Ant.: *héteros* (2087), another of a different kind; *diáphoros* (1313), different.

847. αὐτοῦ *autoú*; the gen. neut. of *autós* (846), he. Used as an adv. for *autóthi*, here, there, in this or that place (Matt 26:36; Acts 15:34; 18:19; 21:4; Sept.: Ex 24:14; Num 22:19; 32:6; Deut 5:31; 2 Sam 20:4).

848. αὐτοῦ *hautoú*; fem. *hautḗs*, neut. *hautoú*, the contracted form of *heautoú* (1438), of his own. Himself, herself, itself (Matt 1:21; 3:12; Luke 5:25; 9:14; 2 Tim 2:19; Rev 16:17). For *autoú* instead of *hautoú*, see *autós* (846, II, C), he or self.

849. αὐτόχειρ *autócheir*; gen. *autócheiros*, masc.-fem., adj. from *autós* (846), himself, and *cheír* (5495), hand. Accomplished with one's own hands Used adverbially in Acts 27:19, "we cast out with our own hands."

850. αὐχμηρός *auchmērós*; fem. *auchmerá*, neut. *auchmerón*, adj. from *auchmós* (n.f.), drought, dust, filth as where water is evaporated by drought. Miry, filthy, murky, dismal, dark (2 Pet 1:19).

Syn.: *skoteinós* (4652), full of darkness.

Ant.: *phōteinós* (5460), bright, full of light; *lamprós* (2986), bright.

851. ἀφαιρέω *aphairéō* contracted *aphairṓ*; fut. *aphairḗsō*, 2d aor. *apheílon*, 2d aor. mid. *apheilómēn*, from *apó* (575), from, and *hairéō* (138), to take. To take off or away, to remove. In Luke 1:25, referring to the reproach. See Sept.: Gen 30:23. Rom 11:27, to "take away their sins," i.e., to procure the forgiveness of sin. See also Heb 10:4; Sept.: Ex 34:7, 9; Lev 10:17; Isa 6:7; 27:9; Zech 3:4. With *apó* (575), from, followed by the gen., to take away from anyone (Rev 22:19). In the mid. (Luke 16:3); in the pass. (Luke 10:42). See also Sept.: Gen 31:31; Lev 4:10; Num 11:17; Deut 12:32; Prov 4:16. Used in place of "to cut off," such as the ear (Matt 26:51; Mark 14:47; Luke 22:50; Sept.: 1 Sam 17:51; Isa 9:14; 18:5).

Syn.: *kóptō* (2875), to cut; *apospáō* (645), to take off or away; *exaírō* (1808), to take away; *elattóō* (1642), to lessen; *aphíēmi* (863), to remit, pardon; *lúō* (3089), to loose, free; *eleutheróō* (1659), to set free, emancipate, liberate.

Ant.: *plēthúnō* (4129), to multiply; *prostíthēmi* (4369), to add; *mēkúnō* (3373), to lengthen, increase.

852. ἀφανής *aphanḗs*; gen. *aphanoús*, masc.-fem., neut. *aphanés*, adj. from the priv. *a* (1), without, or *phaínō* (5316), to appear. Not appearing, not manifest (Heb 4:13, hidden, concealed).

Deriv.: *aphanízō* (853), to vanish away, perish.

Syn.: *kruptós* (2927), hidden, secret; *apókruphos* (614), hidden away for a purpose; *aóratos* (517), invisible.

Ant.: *emphanḗs* (1717), manifest; *phanerós* (5318), open to sight, visible; *dḗlos* (1212), evident; *ékdēlos* (1552), quite evident; *pródēlos* (4271), evident beforehand; *katádēlos* (2612), manifest clearly; *horatós* (3707), visible; *diaphanḗs* (1307), transparent.

853. ἀφανίζω *aphanízō*; fut. *aphanísō*, from *aphanḗs* (852), hidden. To remove out of sight. In the pass., to be removed out of sight, disappear, vanish away (James 4:14); metaphorically, to faint with terror, to expire from fear (Acts 13:41 quoted from Hab 1:5. See Sept.: Ezek 30:9); to destroy, corrupt, spoil, as does the moth or canker (Matt 6:19, 20 [cf. Luke 12:33 where *diaphtheírō* {1311}, destroy utterly, is used]); to deform, disfigure, as the hypocritical Pharisees deformed their countenances when they fasted (Matt 6:16). The word *aphanízō* as well as its syn. should never be taken to mean annihilation. Nothing is annihilated but simply changes from one state to another. Destruction means the cessation of being what a person or thing is and taking another form of existence.

Deriv.: *aphanismós* (854), disappearance.

Syn.: *analískō* (355), to use up or destroy; *katanalískō* (2654), to consume entirely; *dapanáō* (1159), to expend, consume; *katargéō* (2673), abolish; *phtheírō* (5351), to corrupt, degenerate; *diaphtheírō* (1311), to corrupt entirely; *kataphtheírō* (2704), to corrupt or pull down, destroy; *sḗpō* (4595), to putrify; *apóllumi* (622), to destroy, perish; *apothnḗskō* (599), to die, perish.

Ant.: *tugchánō* (5177), to happen; *parístēmi* (3936), to be present; *paratugchánō* (3909), to happen by, to meet with; *emphanízō* (1718), to exhibit; *prosérchomai* (4334), to come near; *anaphaínomai* (398), to appear; *emphanízomai* (1718), to appear; *epiphaínō* (2014), to shine upon, to appear; *phaneróō* (5319), to manifest; *proságō* (4317), to bring forth; *probállō* (4261), to put forward; *proteínō* (4385), to stretch forward; *epideíknumi* (1925), to show, exhibit.

854. ἀφανισμός *aphanismós*; gen. *aphanismoú*, masc. noun from *aphanízō* (853), to vanish away, destroy. A disappearing or vanishing away (Heb 8:13).

Syn.: *apousía* (666), absence; *apóleia* (684), perdition; *ólethros* (3639), ruin, destruction; *phthorá* (5356), corruption, degeneration; *súntrimma* (4938), shattering; *lúsis* (3080), a loosening.

Ant.: *apokálupsis* (602), revelation; *epipháneia* (2015), a shining forth; *parousía* (3952), presence; *phanérōsis* (5321), manifestation.

855. ἄφαντος *áphantos*; gen. *aphántou*, masc.-fem., neut. *áphanton*, adj. from the priv. *a* (1), without, and *phaínō* (5316), to appear. Not appearing, invisible (Luke 24:31).

Syn.: *aphanḗs* (852), not apparent; *aóratos* (517), invisible.

Ant.: *emphanḗs* (1717), manifest; *phanerós* (5318), apparent; *horatós* (3707), visible; *dḗlos* (1212), evident, manifest; *diaphanḗs* (1307), transparent.

856. ἀφεδρών *aphedrṓn*; gen. *aphedrṓnos*, masc. noun from *apó* (575), from, denoting separation, and *hédra* (n.f., see below), a seat, stool. A privy, a separate or private place where people sit to relieve themselves or empty their bowels (Matt 15:17; Mark 7:19; Sept.: Lev 15:19, 20, 25).

Deriv. of *hédra* (n.f.), a seat, stool: *hedraíos* (1476), settled, steady; *enédra* (1747), an ambush, a lying in wait.

857. ἀφειδία *apheidía*; from *apheidḗs* (n.f.), not sparing, from the priv. *a* (1), without, and *pheídomai* (5339), to spare. Not sparing, severity, austerity (Col 2:23 refers to ascetic discipline, courageous exposure to hardship).

Syn.: *perisseía* (4050), abundance; *ploútos* (4149), riches, wealth; *hadrótēs* (100), liberality.

Ant.: *ptōcheía* (4432), poverty.

858. ἀφελότης *aphelótēs*; gen. *aphelótetos*, fem. noun from *aphelḗs* (n.f.), without a stone, level, simple, without guile and duplicity. Simplicity, sincerity, purity of intention (Acts 2:46). Also *aphéleia* in Class. and Mod. Gr.

Syn.: *haplótēs* (572), singleness and hence liberality; *agathōsúnē* (19), beneficence; *eilikríneia* (1505), purity, sincerity.

Ant.: *hupókrisis* (5272), hypocrisy.

859. ἄφεσις *áphesis*; gen. *aphéseōs*, fem. noun. from *aphíēmi* (863), to cause to stand away, to release one's sins from the sinner. Forgiveness, remission. This required Christ's sacrifice as punishment of sin, hence the putting away of sin and the deliverance of the sinner from the power of sin, although not from its presence, which will come later after the resurrection when our very bodies will be redeemed (Rom 8:23). See Matt 26:28; Mark 1:4; 3:29; Luke 1:77; 3:3; 4:18; 24:47; Acts 2:38; 5:31; 10:43; 13:38; 26:18; Eph 1:7; Col 1:14; Heb 9:22; 10:18; Sept.: Lev 25:11; Deut 15:3; Esth 2:18; Isa 61:1. Distinguished from *páresis* (3929), the temporary bypassing of sin (only in Rom 3:25).

Of the 17 times *áphesis* occurs in the NT, it is followed on 12 occasions by the word *hamartiṓn* (266), of sins; therefore, sins are the cords whereby man is bound away from God. Man became a slave of sin because of the fall of Adam (Rom 5:12; 6:17, 20), and thus in his fallen state is presented as a prisoner. In Luke 4:18, where the Lord Jesus declared His ministry on earth, quoted from Isa 61:1, man is presented as *aichmálōtos* (164), a prisoner of war, a captive. His captivity is due to the sin of Adam and to his own sin in that he continues in sinfulness.

It is interesting indeed that in Luke 4:18, the word *áphesis* is used without any designation of what this deliverance or forgiveness is from. The Lord said: "He hath anointed me to . . . preach deliverance to the captives [the word is the same, *áphesis*] . . . to set at liberty [again the word is the same, *en* {1722}, in; *aphései*, at freedom]." The work of

Christ, therefore, is designated as deliverance from everything that holds man a prisoner away from God. However, setting sinful man free would have been a very dangerous thing if God did not simultaneously change man's nature (2 Cor 5:17; 2 Pet 1:4). Man's freedom is not one that permits him to continue in sin (1 John 3:6), but binds him in Christ. What Christ does is not simply to take man from prison and set him free, but also to change him radically (*katallássei* [2644]), giving him power over sin.

Áphesis involves the new birth of man spiritually or in his inner self (John 3:1–12). Man's spirit, therefore, is transformed through faith in Jesus Christ (Rom 5:1). Man with a new spirit within him is given the ability to have power over sin, having been delivered from the guilt of sin: "But God be thanked, that ye were the servants of sin, but ye have obeyed from the heart that form of doctrine which was delivered you. Being then made free from sin, ye became the servants of righteousness" (Rom 6:17, 18).

Áphesis is part of a larger process which does not involve simply the freedom of the sinner, but the change of the sinner from being a slave of sin to becoming a slave of God. With that freedom from sin, he acquires freedom of action because of his changed nature and spirit. He acquires that ability to follow after God instead of fleeing from God, the desire to flee from sin and pursue it. Forgiveness, therefore, must never be understood as the permission for the sinner to continue in his sinful condition.

In the same manner, we must not misunderstand the use of the verb *aphíemi* (863), to forgive on the part of the Christian in regard to another, as meaning the forgiving Christian is supposed to allow the sinner to continue in his sinful condition. Forgiveness is not condoning sin but rather doing everything possible to see that the particular sin or sins of the sinner are removed from him by God who is the only One who can deliver and cleanse him. Forgiveness, therefore, is never

freedom *in* sin but freedom *from* sin by God (italics added).

Heb 9:22 contains an absolute statement, "without shedding of blood is no remission [*áphesis*]." As animal sacrifices gave OT sinners relief from the guilt of sin, so Jesus Christ's shed blood (His sacrificial death) gives believers not only freedom from the guilt of sin, which in the NT is called justification (*dikaíōsis* [1347]) (Rom 4:25; 5:18), but also *katharismós* (2512), cleansing or purification (Heb 1:3; 2 Pet 1:9). This is why in Rom 3:25 in speaking of the OT sacrifices, Paul calls the result *páresis* (3929), which unfortunately is translated "remission," as if it were the same as *áphesis*. If Paul meant it to be *áphesis*, the permanent remission of sins without the need of further sacrifices, he would have called it that. The blood of Christ provided the removal of the guilt of sin as well as the cleansing from sin on a permanent basis. *Páresis* (3929), occurring only in Rom 3:25, must be translated the "bypassing" of sin and not the "remission" of sin, for where there is forgiveness of sins there is no more offering for sin (Heb 10:18).

Syn.: *apolútrōsis* (629), redemption; *ánesis* (425), a relaxing, letting loose; *aníēmi* (441), to stand up or to provide liberty or rest; *eleuthería* (1657), freedom, which is the resultant effect of forgiveness or *áphesis*; *hilasmós* (2434), atonement, propitiation; *cháris* (5485), grace (indicating the disposition of the one forgiving, while *áphesis* expresses the result of the acceptance of that grace); *sōtēría* (4991), salvation, deliverance; *dikaíōsis* (1347), justification, being more than acquittal since it also renders a person just.

Ant.: *kríma* (2917), verdict pronounced; *katákrima*, condemnation, sentence followed by a suggested punishment; *krísis* (2920), the process of judging, judgment; *katákrisis* (2633), the act of condemnation.

860. ἀφή *haphḗ*; gen. *haphḗs*, fem. noun from *háptō* (681), to connect, adjoin, apply. A joint by which other members of the body are connected together (Eph 4:16). Indeed, the Lord joins us to His body (1 Cor 12:13) and to each other, but every member must make its own contribution to the welfare of the whole body. Joints or parts of contact are very important among the members of Christ's body even as the joints are to the body (Col 2:19). Spiritually, these joints receive their nourishment from the Head, Christ (Col 1:18), but how we are joined together with other members of Christ's body affects the whole body of Christ, the Church.

Syn.: *harmós* (719), a joint.

861. ἀφθαρσία aphtharsía; gen. *aphtharsías*, fem. noun from *áphthartos* (862), incorruptible. Incorruption, incorruptibility, incapacity for corruption. 1 Cor 15:42, 50, 53, 54 strictly refer to the resurrection body of believers compared to the corruptibility of the present body.

In Rom 2:7, *aphtharsía* should be translated "incorruptibility," for it speaks of the future incorruptible body which will be part of the believer's glorification while unbelievers amass unto themselves wrath in the day of wrath (Rom 2:5). The resurrected bodies of unbelievers will not be glorious incorruptible bodies, but those which will continue to have the evidence on them of God's wrath and judgment even as man's present body bears the marks of sin. *Aphtharsía* also means incorruptible in a moral or spiritual sense, i.e., freedom from corrupt doctrines or designs. In Eph 6:24, *en* (1722), in, *aphtharsía*, translated "in sincerity," actually refers to the peace, love and grace given by God to the believer. See Rom 5:1–5 where all three qualities are given through faith in Jesus Christ. These are not subject to deterioration, but maintenance and growth. The word should be better translated "nondeteriorating." These qualities, peace, love, and grace, given by God to the believer, do not deteriorate. They are so constituted as to grow, for they are living.

In 2 Tim 1:10, *aphtharsía* is translated in Rom 2:7, "immortality." It should

again be translated "incorruptibility" referring to the revelation by the gospel as to what God is going to do to our present vile or humiliated body as revealed by Paul in Phil 3:21. He will reshape it and give it not immortality, the absence of death (*athanasía* [110]), but incorruptibility. Paul, facing imminent death as he wrote 2 Timothy, realized that his body was indeed corruptible and could be executed, but the body which he was going to receive on the resurrection day would be incorruptible, and no one could cause any deterioration or death. Paul is definitely speaking here of physical death. In 2 Tim 1:10, that which is translated "appearing" is the word *epipháneia* (2015), made up of the prep. *epí* (1909), over, on top, again, and *phaínō* (5316), to appear, to illuminate, give light. In the instances where this word *epipháneia* is used (2 Thess 2:8; 1 Tim 6:14; 2 Tim 4:1, 8; Titus 2:13), it is clearly used in connection with the Second Coming of the Lord Jesus. That truly will be the *epipháneia*, the coming again to shine in glory. The only place where it seems that it refers to both His first and second coming is 2 Tim 1:10. In His first coming, that which God had foreordained (see 2 Tim 1:9) became a reality, and with His first coming He foreordained His second coming which would be the coming in glory. The first coming was a revelation of what is yet to be, the *aphtharsía*, the incorruptibility of the body. The Lord brought life to light, i.e., the spiritual life which we receive now and which controls our present corruptible body, but He also revealed that this corruptible body is going to be clothed with incorruption. All this comes through the knowledge of the gospel.

In Titus 2:7 (UBS) we have only *aphthorían*, which means incorruption or incapacity to decay, and thus metaphorically means integrity. However, in the TR we have *adiaphthoría* (90), indicating that total corruption is impossible. Paul says to Titus that he should present teaching that is completely and utterly incorruptible, which is impossible to change and degenerate. It is evident that here we have the metaphorical use of the word. The Majority Text also adds *aphtharsía*, which means incorruptibility. The difference between *adiaphthoría* and *aphtharsía* is that the first indicates that it is constitutionally impossible to change the teaching of Christ and still have it produce the same results as the pure doctrine of the gospel, whereas the second refers to constitutional incorruptibility and that no matter what people do, they cannot change the doctrine of Christ.

Syn.: *amarántinos* (262), used in reference to the crown of glory which is going to be made, as it were, of an unfading flower called *amárantos*; *athanasía* (110), immortality (*aphtharsía* referring to the incorruptibility of the resurrection body but *athanasía* referring to the future impossibility of its separation from its spirit).

Ant.: *phthorá* (5356), corruptibility; *diaphthorá* (1312), thorough and utter corruptibility.

862. ἄφθαρτος *áphthartos*; gen. *aphthártou*, masc.-fem., neut. *áphtharton*, adj., from the priv. *a* (1), not, and *phthartós* (n.f.), corruptible, which is from *phtheírō* (5351), to corrupt. Incorruptible, not capable of corruption. See 1 Cor 9:25; 15:52; 1 Pet 1:23. The word is not found in the Sept. In Rom 1:23, Paul calls God *áphthartos*, incorruptible, an attribute of deity that even the heathen recognize. The KJV, in 1 Tim 1:17, incorrectly renders *áphthartos* as immortal. It should be rendered as incorruptible, distinguished from *athánatos*, immortal and as the one having *athanasían* (110), immortality (1 Tim 6:16). When predicated on God, *áphthartos* means that He is exempt from the wear, waste, and final perishing which characterize the present body of man. Therefore, *phthorá* (5356), corruptibility, is the characteristic of the perishability of the body of man as presently constituted. This body which is now corruptible will receive God's *aphtharsía* (861), incorruptibility, on the day of the resurrection (1 Cor 15:52; Heb 1:10–12). Therefore, the two words *athanasía* (110), immortality, and *aphtharsía*, incorruption, as referred to in Scripture, have nothing to do with the spiritual makeup of man, but only with his physical makeup, his body. In 1 Pet 1:4, the inheritance of the believer is called *áphthartos*, incorruptible, not like the body that is going to be done away with. It is something that the believer receives in this life and will continue to have after this life is over. It is not subject to the same kind of deterioration as the present body in which the believer suffers. See *amíantos* (283), undefiled, and *amárantos* (263), unfading.

Deriv.: *aphtharsía* (861), incorruptibility.

Syn.: *akatálutos* (179), indissoluble, permanent, endless; *aiṓnios* (166), eternal, perpetual; *akéraios* (185), unmixed, unaffected.

Ant.: *phthartós* (5349), corruptible, perishable; *skōlēkóbrōtos* (4662), worm-eaten; *saprós* (4550), bad, corrupted by age, worn out.

863. ἀφίημι *aphíēmi*; fut. *aphḗsō*, fut. pass. *aphethḗsomai*; aor. pass. *aphéthēn*, perf. *apheíka* irregular forms: pres. 2d person *apheís*, imperf. *ḗphion*, perf. pass. 3d person pl. *aphéōntai*; from *apó* (575), from, and *hiēmi* (n.f., see *iós* [2447]), to send. To send forth or away, let go from oneself. Used trans.:

(I) To dismiss, e.g., the multitudes (Matt 13:36); of a wife, to put her away (1 Cor 7:11–13). In Matt 27:50, "he gave up the spirit" (a.t.), expired. See also Gen 35:18. In Mark 15:37, "when Jesus let forth a loud cry" (a.t. [Sept.: Gen 45:2]).

(II) To let go from one's power, possession, to let go free, let escape (Matt 24:40, 41; Luke 17:34–36; Sept.: Prov 4:13). Metaphorically, to let go from obligation toward oneself, to remit, e.g., a debt, offense, with the dat. of person (Matt 18:27, 32, 35; Mark 11:25; Sept.: Deut 15:2). Of sins, to remit the penalty of sins, i.e., to pardon, forgive, with the dat. of person, e.g., *opheilḗmata* (3783), debts, faults (Matt 6:12); *hamartías* (266), sins (Matt 9:2, 5, 6; 12:31; Mark 2:5, 7, 9, 10); *blasphēmían* (988), blasphemy, evil speaking (Matt 12:31, 32); *paraptōmata* (3900), trespasses, offenses (Matt 6:14, 15; Mark 11:25); *hamartémata* (265), individual sins (Mark 3:28; 4:12); *anomías* (458), iniquities, acts of lawlessness (Rom 4:7). Also Sept.: Gen 50:17; Ex 32:32; Lev 4:20; 5:10, 13; Ps 25:18; 32:5; Isa 22:14; 55:7. The expression "to forgive sins" or to remit sins means to remove the sins from someone. Only God is said to be able to do this (Mark 2:10). To forgive sins is not to disregard them and do nothing about them, but to liberate a person from them, their guilt, and their power. We are to ask God to forgive our sins, remove them away from us so that we do not stand guilty of them or under their power. We are never expected to forgive the sins of others toward God because we have no power to do so, but we are expected to forgive others for the sins done to us ("Forgive us our debts, as we forgive our debtors" or those who are our debtors [Matt 6:12]). To forgive others does not mean to separate them from us, but to allow them through our contact to know God who can free them from their sins. Thus we should do everything in our power to see that the sins of others are removed from them through the grace and power of Jesus Christ which we make known to them.

(III) To let go from one's further notice, care, attendance, occupancy, i.e., to leave or let alone.

(A) Spoken of persons, to quit, forsake or abandon (Matt 4:11; 8:15; 15:14; 26:44, 56; Mark 4:36; John 10:12). Of things, the nets (Matt 4:20); the house (Mark 13:34); Judea (John 4:3); all things (Matt 19:27, 29). See also Sept.: 1 Sam 17:20, 28; Jer 12:7. To leave in any place or state, let remain (Matt 5:24; 18:12; Mark 1:20; Luke 10:30; John 4:28; 8:29, "hath not left me"; 14:18, 27; 16:32; Acts 14:17; Sept.: Gen 42:33; Ex 9:21; 2 Sam 15:16; 1 Kgs 19:3; 1 Chr 16:21). To leave to anyone, i.e., to let him have or take (Matt 5:40, "let him

have thy cloak"). To leave behind as at death (Matt 22:25; Mark 12:19–22; Sept.: Ps 17:14; Eccl 2:18). To leave remaining, and in the pass., to be left, remain (Matt 23:38; 24:2, "There shall not be left here one stone upon another"; Mark 13:2; Luke 13:35; 19:44; 21:6; Heb 2:8; Sept.: Judg 2:23; 3:1).

(B) Metaphorically, in various senses, to leave, desert, quit (Rom 1:27, "the natural use"; Rev 2:4). To omit, pass by (Heb 6:1, leaving the word of the beginning). To neglect, to omit (Matt 23:23, "the weightier matters of the law"; Mark 7:8; Luke 11:42; Sept.: Eccl 11:6).

(IV) To let go, i.e., to let pass, permit, suffer, with the acc. followed by the inf. expressed or implied (Matt 8:22; 13:30; 19:14; Mark 1:34; 5:37). See also Matt 3:15; Mark 5:19; 11:6; Luke 13:8; John 11:48; 12:7; Rev 2:20 (*apheís* or *eás*) "your [wife] Jezebel to teach" (a.t.); Sept.: Ex 12:23; Num 22:13; Judg 16:26; 2 Sam 16:11. Followed by *hína* (2443), so that, with the subjunctive after verbs of command (Mark 11:16). The imper. *áphes* (sing.) and *áphete* (pl.) are followed by the subjunctive without *hína*, e.g., *áphes ídōmen* (first person pl. 2d aor. subjunctive of *horáō* [3708], to see, let us see, suffer us to see [Matt 27:49; Mark 15:36]); Matt 7:4, "Let me pull out"; Luke 6:42.

Deriv.: *áphesis* (859), remission, forgiveness.

Syn.: *paúō* (3973), to stop, quit; *katapaúō* (2664), to cease; *katargéō* (2673), to render inactive; *charízomai* (5483), to bestow a favor, to forgive; *apolúō* (630), to release, dismiss; *kataleípō* (2641), to leave behind; *egkataleípō* (1459), to forsake, abandon; *apotássō* (657), to place in order away from oneself; *apotíthēmi* (659), to put off from oneself; *apoleípō* (620), to remain; *perileípō* (4035), to leave around; *eáō* (1439), to let, permit; *hupolimpánō* (5277), a late form of *leípō* (3007), to leave; *epitrépō* (2010), to permit; *apotíthēmi* (659), to put away; *chōrízō* (5563), to separate; *apostréphō* (654), to turn away; *apothéomai* (683), to thrust away; *lúō* (3089), to loose; *pémpō* (3992), to send.

Ant.: *kratéō* (2902), to retain; *lambánō* (2983), to take; *ekdikéō* (1556), to bring justice out, vindicate; *déō* (1210), to bind.

864. ἀφικνέομαι *aphiknéomai*; contracted *aphiknoúmai*, fut. *aphíxomai*, mid. deponent from *apó* (575), from, and *hiknéomai* (n.f., see *diïknéomai* [1338]), to come. To come from one place to another, to arrive, reach (Rom 16:19).

Deriv.: *áphixis* (867), arrival; in the NT, departure.

Syn.: *érchomai* (2064), to come; *epérchomai* (1904), to arrive at; *prosérchomai* (4334), to come near to; *paragínomai* (3854), to arrive; *hékō* (2240), to come and be present; *enístēmi* (1764), to set in, be present; *ephístēmi* (2186), to come upon; *phthánō* (5348), to arrive; *prosporeúomai* (4365), to come near to.

Ant.: *poreúomai* (4198), to proceed from one place to another; *ágō* (71), to go; *hupágō* (5217), to go away; *ápeimi* (548), to go away; *metabaínō* (3327), to go from one place to another; *apérchomai* (565), to go away; *anachōréō* (402), to withdraw, go away, depart; *hupochōréō* (5298), to go back; *apobaínō* (576), to go away from; *apodēméō* (589), to go to another country.

865. ἀφιλάγαθος *aphilágathos*; gen. *aphilagáthou*, masc.-fem., neut. *aphilágathon*, adj. from the priv. *a* (1), and *philágathos* (5358), a lover of being good. Unfriendly, hostile, a person who may have pity but does not necessarily do anything to relieve the suffering of another through self-denial. Only in 2 Tim 3:3, meaning hostile to good men.

Syn.: *kakós* (2556), bad; *phaúlos* (5337), foul, trivial; *aischrós* (150), shameful; *átimos* (820), without honor; *achreíos* (888), useless, unprofitable; *kataphronētḗs* (2707), a despiser.

Ant.: *agathós* (18), benevolent; *kalós* (2570), good; *chrēstós* (5543), useful;

ákakos (172), harmless; *philágathos* (5358), a lover of doing good.

866. ἀφιλάργυρος *aphilárguros*; gen. *aphilargúrou*, masc.-fem., neut. *aphilárguron*, adj. from the priv. *a* (1), without, and *philárguros* (5366), lover of money. Not fond of money or covetous (1 Tim 3:3; Heb 13:5).

Ant.: *philarguría* (5365), avarice, love of money; *phílautos* (5367), loving oneself; *pleonéktēs* (4123), avaricious, covetous.

867. ἄφιξις *áphixis*; gen. *aphíxeōs*, fem. noun from *aphiknéomai* (864), to arrive, reach. Literally, to arrive; in the NT, meaning going away, departure (Acts 20:29).

Syn.: *éleusis* (1660), advent, coming.

Ant.: *análusis* (359), an unloosing, departure; *poreía* (4197), travel.

868. ἀφίστημι *aphístēmi*; from *apó*, from, and *hístēmi* (2476), to stand, to place. Trans.: to put away, remove, as in Acts 5:37, he seduced the people to follow him (Sept.: Deut 7:4; 13:10). Intrans.: to withdraw, remove oneself, forsake, desert, retire, cease from something (Luke 2:37; 4:13; 13:27 quoted from Ps 6:8 [see Matt 7:23 where *apochōreíte* (672) means to depart from]; Acts 5:38; 12:10; 15:38; 19:9; 22:29; 2 Cor 12:8; 1 Tim 6:5; Sept.: Num 12:10; 1 Sam 18:12; Lam 4:15; Ezek 23:17, 18). In all of the above, the verb is followed by the prep. *apó* followed by the gen. from someone or something. Transferred to moral conduct in 2 Tim 2:19, it is followed by *apó adikías* (*apó* [575], from; *adikías* [93], unrighteousness), from unrighteousness; in Heb 3:12, "from the living God" (Sept.: Gen 14:4; 2 Chr 26:18; 28:19, 22; Ezek 20:8; Dan 9:9). This latter expression does not mean that at one time they belonged to God and now they no longer belong to Him, but rather that they stood away from God, never having belonged to Him. The same is true with 1 Tim 4:1, in which the word is translated "depart," meaning they stood away from believing. This does not refer to those who had at one time been believers, but to those who refuse to believe, who stand aloof, alone (Heb 3:12). The word is also used in Luke 8:13 in connection with the interpretation of the seed that falls on stony ground. The seed finds a little soil on top of the stone, but it is not enough to take root and so the growth is only seasonal. When testing comes, there is no root to hold it down. The word *aphístantai* here does not indicate uprooting because there never was a root; the temporary plant stood by itself. The union with the soil was only an apparent union, never a true foundation with roots capable of holding up the plant.

Deriv.: *apostasía* (646), apostasy, staying away from; *apostásion* (647), separative, divorce.

Syn.: *apolúō* (630), to depart, dismiss; *apospáō* (645), to draw away; *apochōrízō* (673), to separate, depart from; *apochōréō* (672), to depart from; *hupágō* (5217), to depart, go; *apérchomai* (565), to depart; *apopíptō* (634), to fall from.

Ant.: *proseggízō* (4331), to approach; *eggízō* (1448), to approach.

869. ἄφνω *áphnō*; adv., contracted form of *aphanōs*. Suddenly, unexpectedly, unforeseeably (Acts 2:2; 16:26; 28:6; Sept.: Josh 10:9; Eccl 9:12).

Syn.: *exaíphnēs* (1810), suddenly; *exápina* (1819), suddenly, unexpectedly; *tachéōs* (5030), suddenly, hastily; *apotómōs* (664), abruptly; *táchos* (5034), swiftly.

870. ἀφόβως *aphóbōs*; adv. from *áphobos* (n.f.), fearless, which is from the priv. *a* (1), and *phóbos* (5401), fear. Without fear, fearlessly (Luke 1:74; 1 Cor 16:10; Phil 1:14; Jude 1:12; Sept.: Prov 1:33).

Syn.: *parrēsía* (3954), with boldness.

Ant.: *adēlōs* (84), uncertainly.

871. ἀφομοιόω *aphomoióō*; contracted *aphomoiō̂*, fut. *aphomoiōsō*, from *apó* (575), an intens. and *homoióō* (3666), to make like, liken. Only in Heb 7:3, meaning to make very much like.

Syn.: *eíkō* (1503), to be like, resemble; *paromoiázō* (3945), to resemble.

Ant.: *diaphérō* (1308), differ from, to differ, discern; *diastéllomai* (1291), to set oneself apart, to distinguish; *chōrízō* (5563), to place room between, separate.

872. ἀφοράω *aphoráō*; contracted *aphorō̂*, fut. *apópsomai*, from *apó* (575) an intens., and *horáō* (3708), to look. To look away steadfastly or intently toward a distant object. Metaphorically, to behold in the mind, to fix the mind upon (Phil 2:23; Heb 12:2).

Syn.: *blépō* (991), to look; *apoblépō* (578), to intently regard; *proséchō* (4337), turn one's attention to; *epéchō* (1907), to give attention to; *skopéō* (4648), to look, mark, take heed; *theōréō* (2334), to behold, perceive.

Ant.: *agnoéō* (50), to ignore; *kataphronéō* (2706), to despise.

873. ἀφορίζω *aphorízō*; fut. *aphoriō̂*, from *apó* (575), from, and *horízō* (3724), to define. To separate locally (Matt 13:49; 25:32 [cf. Acts 19:9]; 2 Cor 6:17; Gal 2:12; Sept.: Lev 20:25; Isa 56:3); to separate from or cast out of society as wicked and abominable, to excommunicate (Luke 6:22); to separate, select to some office or work (Acts 13:2; Rom 1:1; Gal 1:15). The Pharisees, the sect to which Paul belonged before his conversion (Acts 23:6; 26:5; Phil 3:5), got their names from this word, which meant to separate (*aphōrisménoi*, separated ones). This is probably what Paul alludes to in Rom 1:1 where he who was before separated unto the law, or to the study of it, now says of himself that he is separated to the gospel.

Syn.: *diakrínō* (1252), to separate; *chōrízō* (5563), to separate; *apodiorízō* (592), to mark off, separate; *katargéō* (2673), to reduce to inactivity; *diachōrízō* (1316), to remove completely; *arnéomai* (720), to disavow; *antitássō* (498), to oppose; *aporríptō* (641), to reject; *periphronéō* (4065), despise; *apothéomai*

(683), to push off, reject; *periphronéō* (4065), to depreciate, despise; *apotrépō* (665), to avoid, turn away; *apophérō* (667), to bear off; *aparnéomai* (533), to deny utterly, disown; *apotássomai* (657), to put in one's proper category away from self.

Ant.: *prosdéchomai* (4327), to receive to oneself; *paréchō* (3930), to hold near; *egkrínō* (1469), to count among, approve, to judge in; *apodéchomai* (588), to welcome approvingly; *euarestéō* (2100), to gratify entirely, please; *eudokéō* (2106), to approve; *paradéchomai* (3858), to accept near, admit; *anagnōrízō* (319), to recognize.

874. ἀφορμή *aphormḗ*; gen. *aphormḗs*, fem. noun from *apó* (575), from, and *hormḗ* (3730), a rushing on, onset, impetus, violent tendency. An occasion, an opportunity or casual circumstance producing a tendency toward something else (Rom 7:8, 11; 2 Cor 5:12; 11:12; Gal 5:13; 1 Tim 5:14).

Syn.: *lógos* (3056), reason; *archḗ* (746), beginning, cause; *pēgḗ* (4077), source, supply; *rhíza* (4491), root; *aitía* (156), cause, reason. *Aphormḗ*, however, means an excuse rather than the real cause which *aitía* signifies.

Ant.: *ékbasis* (1545), way of escape; *karpós* (2590), fruit, result.

875. ἀφρίζω *aphrízō*; fut. *aphrísō*, from *aphrós* (876), foam, froth. To foam or froth at the mouth (Mark 9:18, 20).

Deriv.: *epaphrízō* (1890), to foam out or up, metaphorically to externalize.

876. ἀφρός *aphrós*; gen. *aphroú*, masc. noun. Used only in Luke 9:39 of human foam, indicating sudden foaming.

Deriv.: *aphrízō* (875), to foam, froth.

877. ἀφροσύνη *aphrosúnē*; gen. *aphrosúnēs*, fem. noun from *áphrōn* (878), unwise. Folly, foolishness, lack of sense (2 Cor 11:1, 17, 21; Sept.: Prov 18:13; 19:3; 26:4, 5). Want of true wisdom, sense, proper use of one's logical mind (Mark

7:22; Sept.: Deut 22:21; Job 4:6; Eccl 7:26). Opposite of spiritual wisdom and sobriety which is *sōphrosúnē* (4997).

In Mark 7:21, 22, *aphrosúnē* appears as the last in the list of vices, probably indicating that it is basic to the other sins mentioned, mainly evil thoughts, adulteries, fornications, murders, thefts, covetousness, wickedness, deceit, lasciviousness, an evil eye, blasphemy, pride. The final sin is *aphrosúnē*, as if to say that all of these are the result of not being able to think properly and arrive at adequate conclusions. However, verse twenty-one establishes *aphrosúnē*, foolishness or the inability to think properly according to God's intended gift of mind, as caused by the heart, "from within, out of the heart of men." The mind becomes corrupt, unable to think properly when the heart is sinful and unregenerate. It can only function according to God's intent and purpose as the heart becomes purified by Him, for as the Lord said, "Blessed are the pure in heart: for they shall see God" (Matt 5:8). The mind sees nothing correctly if the heart is not pure.

In 2 Cor 11:1, Paul admits that it is not possible for a Christian to always have the proper judgment in all things. Therefore, he asks the Corinthians for toleration "in my folly [*aphrosúnē*]." This means not that he is *áphrōn*, foolish in nature, but occasionally demonstrates a lack of proper judgment in certain things. The Christian indeed possesses God's wisdom (*sophía* [4678], the ability to regulate his relationship with God) and His *phrónēsis* (5428), God's ability given to man to regulate his relationships with his environment and his fellow humans according to His intents and purposes. But in his contact with his fellowman, man sometimes shows *aphrosúnē*. He misses the mark and does not accomplish the intended purpose even as the Christian commits acts of sin but is not an inveterate sinner (1 John 2:1; 3:4–9).

Paul uses the word *aphrosúnē* in 2 Cor 11:17, 21 in the same manner as he uses it in verse one. In 2 Cor 11:16, he definitely states that he is not a fool and that he should not be thought of as one: "Let no man think me a fool [*áphrona* {878}, foolish]." He insists that even if he were to be thought of as such, he would still have to be received by those to whom he ministered ("Yet as a fool receive me") because of his appointment as an apostle of Jesus Christ (1 Cor 9:1). Paul states that the reason for being thought of as a fool was that he was boasting, but he proceeds to explain that the Corinthians are to examine not the boasting itself, but the basic reason for the boasting (*hupóstasis* [5287], the underlying ground on which something stands, translated "confidence," v. 17). He then goes on with a touch of sarcasm to say that they sweetly tolerate fools while they themselves are *phrónimoi* (5429), prudent. Paul definitely refuses to call himself and other fellow believers as *áphrones*, fools. However, he states the Corinthians were committing an act of *aphrosúnē*, foolishness, by accepting the boasting of foolish people while not allowing him the privilege of boasting when it was based on spiritual realities, Jesus Christ and His cross (Rom 2:17; 5:2, 11; 1 Cor 1:17, 18, 31; 2 Cor 10:8, 13, 15, 17; 11:30; Phil 3:3; James 1:9). Paul admits in 2 Cor 11:21 that his boasting in the things that God has done could be taken as an element of foolishness, but he dares do it because such boasting glorifies God. Thus Paul's conclusion is that we should boast in the cross of Jesus Christ and the things that He has done for us, in spite of the fact that we may appear as foolish in so doing (Rom 2:17, 23; 5:2, 11; 1 Cor 1:31; Gal 6:14).

Syn.: *paraphronía* (3913), insanity, foolhardiness; *mōría* (3472), foolishness.

Ant.: *phrónēsis* (5428), prudence; *súnesis* (4907), understanding, the ability to put it together; *noús* (3563), mind; *diánoia* (1271), the faculty of knowing, understanding; *phrónēma* (5427), thought in the mind, mind-set; *sophía* (4678), wisdom; *logismós* (3053), reasoning; *sōphrosúnē* (4997), soundness

of mind; *sōphronismós* (4995), causing self-control, discipline.

878. ἄφρων *áphrōn*; gen. *áphronos*, masc.-fem., neut. *áphron*, adj. from the priv. *a* (1), without, and *phrḗn* (5424), understanding Unwise, imprudent, inconsiderate, foolish. In Luke 11:40, Jesus calls the ritualistic Pharisees fools (*áphrones*) because they thought that, by doing something external, they could automatically gain favor with God. In Luke 12:20, Jesus calls the rich, successful farmer a fool, *áphrōn*, because he mistook success to be having all that he could get without thought of others or what his own destiny would be after death. In 1 Cor 15:36, Paul calls a fool the person who considers death the terminal point of existence, while death, as in the case of a seed, is necessary to a better and richer life as the case is with the death of the believer in Christ. In 2 Cor 11:16, 19, Paul claims that it is possible for a Christian to be accused of being a fool as he boasts, and yet such an accusation needs to be accepted since the believer stands on something which is worthy of boasting (see *aphrosúnē* [877]). In 2 Cor 12:6, 11, Paul claims that proper boasting on the things of the Lord is not being foolish as long as it is not intended to cause others to think of the boaster more highly than he is. See also Sept.: Prov 10:1; 11:29; Eccl 2:19. In the sense of misinstructed, unlearned, ignorant as to the truth of the gospel (Rom 2:20; Eph 5:17; 1 Pet 2:15; Sept.: Ps 92:6).

Syn.: *anóētos* (453), not applying his right mind; *mōrós* (3474), dull, sluggish; *asúnetos* (801), without discernment, senseless, one who cannot put things together; *ásophos* (781), unwise.

Ant.: *phrónimos* (5429), prudent; *sōphrōn* (4998), self-controlled, of sound mind; *sophós* (4680), wise; *sunetós* (4908), intelligent, understanding; *logikós* (3050), reasonable.

879. ἀφυπνόω *aphupnóō* contracted *aphupnṓ*; fut. *aphupnṓsō*, from *apó*

(575), an intens., and *hupnóō* (n.f.), to fall asleep, which is from *húpnos* (5258), sleep. To fall into a deep and prolonged sleep (Luke 8:23). See Matt 8:24 and Mark 4:38, where *katheúdō* (2518), to fall asleep, is used.

Syn.: *koimáomai* (2837), to sleep naturally, but also used of the believer's dying as going to sleep; *katheúdō* (2518), to fall asleep.

Ant.: *exupnízō* (1852), to awaken; *egeírō* (1453), to raise, to awake; *exegeírō* (1825), to raise out of; *exanístēmi* (1817), to rise out of; *anístēmi* (450), to arise; *stékō* (4739), to stand. In a metaphorical sense, *diegeírō* (1326), to stir up.

880. ἄφωνος *áphōnos*; gen. *aphṓnou*, masc.-fem., neut. *áphōnon*, adj. from the priv. *a* (1), without, and *phōnḗ* (5456), voice. Voiceless, dumb, not having the power of speech. Spoken of beasts (2 Pet 2:16); of idols (1 Cor 12:2 [cf. Ps 115:5; Hab 2:18, 19]). Mute, silent, as in patient suffering (Acts 8:32 quoted from Isa 53:7). Metaphorically, meaning unexpressive, i.e., without expression, not having the power of voice (1 Cor 14:10, 11).

Syn.: *álalos* (216), speechless; *hēsúchios* (2272), quiet.

881. Ἀχαζ *Achaz*; masc. proper noun transliterated from the Hebr. *'Āchāz* (271, OT). Ahaz, meaning possessor (Matt 1:9). A king of Judah (2 Kgs 16; 2 Chr 28); a son of Jotham (2 Kgs 15:38; 2 Chr 27:9) and father of Hezekiah (2 Kgs 16:20; 2 Chr 28:27).

882. Ἀχαΐα *Achaía*; gen. *Achaías*, fem. proper noun. Achaia, meaning trouble. A Roman province in NT times nearly coextensive with the southern part of modern Greece. Augustus divided the whole country into two proconsular provinces, Macedonia to the north, and Achaia to the south. Achaia included Peloponnesus and the city of Corinth, which was its capital and the residence of the proconsul. Paul visited the churches in Achaia (Acts 18:12, 27; 19:21; Rom 15:26; 16:5; 1 Cor 16:15; 2 Cor 1:1; 9:2; 11:10; 1 Thess 1:7, 8).

883. Ἀχαϊκός *Achaïkós*; gen. *Achaïkoú*, masc. proper noun. Achaicus, meaning belonging to *Achaia* (882). A Christian mentioned in 1 Cor 16:17.

884. ἀχάριστος *acháristos*; gen. *acharístou*, masc.-fem., neut., adj. from the priv. *a* (1), without, and *charízomai* (5483), to show favor or kindness. Unthankful, ungrateful (Luke 6:35; 2 Tim 3:2).

Ant.: *eucháristos* (2170), gracious, thankful.

885. Ἀχείμ *Acheím*; masc. proper noun from the Hebr. *Yāchīn*, a contraction of *Yᵉhōwyākyīn*, meaning the Lord will establish. Achim, an ancestor of Christ (Matt 1:14).

886. ἀχειροποίητος *acheiropoíētos*; gen. *acheiropoiḗtou*, masc.-fem., neut. *acheiropoíēton*, adj. from the priv. *a* (1), without, and *cheiropoíētos* (5499), made with hands. Not made with hands, made or performed without hands (Mark 14:58; 2 Cor 5:1; Col 2:11).

887. ἀχλύς *achlús*; gen. *achlúos*, fem. noun. A thick mist. A collection of heavy vapors which diverts the rays of light by turning them out of their direct course. Hence a certain disorder of the eye is called *achlús* and those who are afflicted with it seem to see through a thick mist or fog. Found only in Acts 13:11, where Elymas the sorcerer was miraculously punished by Paul with a disorder of this kind previous to his total blindness.

Syn.: *skótos* (4655), darkness; *gnóphos* (1105), a thick dark cloud; *zóphos* (2217), thick darkness resulting from foggy weather or smoke; *néphos* (3509), cloud; *nephélē* (3507), a definitely shaped cloud.

Ant.: *eudía* (2105), a clear sky.

888. ἀχρεῖος *achreíos*; fem. *achreía*, neut. *achreíon*, adj. from the priv. *a* (1), without, and *chreía* (5532), utility, usefulness. Unprofitable, one who has been set aside and is no longer useful (Matt 25:30, slothful, wicked [see Matt 25:26]; Luke 17:10, humble, of little value; Sept.: 2 Sam 6:22).

Deriv.: *achreióō* (889), to render useless, to become unprofitable.

Syn.: *áchrēstos* (890), unprofitable, useless; *alusitelés* (255), not advantageous, not useful; *anōphelés* (512), not serviceable, unprofitable, useless; *kenós* (2756), empty, vain; *mátaios* (3152), vain, empty, profitless; *adókimos* (96), unapproved, unfit; *alusitelés* (255), unprofitable, useless.

Ant.: *eúchrēstos* (2173), profitable, useful; *ōphélimos* (5624), helpful, profitable; *chrḗsimos* (5539), serviceable, useful; *anagkaíos* (316), necessary, needful; *polútimos* (4186), very valuable.

889. ἀχρειόω *achreióō*; contracted *achreiṓ*, fut. *achreiṓsō*; from *achreíos* (888), useless, unprofitable. To make unprofitable; in the mid. *achreióomai*, to become unprofitable, vile (Rom 3:12). See also Sept.: 2 Kgs 3:19; Jer 11:16.

Ant.: *chráomai* (5530), to use; *ōpheléō* (5623), to profit, benefit.

890. ἄχρηστος *áchrēstos*; gen. *achrḗstou*, masc.-fem., neut. *áchrēston*, adj., neut. *áchrēston*, from the priv. *a* (1), without, and *chrēstós* (5543), profitable. Unprofitable, useless (Phile 1:11 [see Phile 1:18]).

Syn.: *achreíos* (888), unprofitable.

891. ἄχρι *áchri*; *áchris* if before a vowel, adv. of time (in the NT also of place). Continually; with the gen. as a prep., continually until, i.e., during, until; with verbs as a conj., so long as until, i.e., until, followed in the NT only by the subjunctive mood implying uncertainty.

(**I**) As a prep. with the gen.:

(**A**) With nouns: (**1**) Of time, as *áchri kairoú* (2540), time, season, meaning during a season (Luke 4:13; Acts 2:29, "till the day" [a.t.]; 3:21, "until the times"; 20:11, till dawn; 22:22, till this word; 23:1, "until this day"; 26:22; Rom 5:13; 1 Cor 4:11; 2 Cor 3:14; Gal 4:2; Phil 1:6; Heb 6:11; Rev 2:26). In Acts 20:6, "in five days" or until on the fifth day. Of a point of time, e.g., until death (Acts 22:4; Rev 2:10; 12:11). (**2**) Of place, Acts 11:5, up to where I am; 13:6, "up to Paphos," as in 20:4. See also Acts 28:15; 2 Cor 10:13, 14; Rev 14:20; 18:5.

(**B**) With a relative pron. either with a noun of time (Matt 24:38, "until the day that"; Luke 1:20; 17:27; Acts 1:2). With the relative pron. *hoú* it has the nature of a conj. (Acts 7:18, "until another king arose" [a.t.]; 27:33; Rom 11:25; 1 Cor 11:26; 15:25; Gal 3:19; 4:19; Rev 2:25; 7:3). With a verb in the pres., *áchris hoú* means so long as, while (Heb 3:13).

(**C**) Before particles as in Rom 1:13, *áchri toú deúro* (*toú* [3588], the; *deúro* [1204], here), until the hither, until now. In Rom 8:22, *áchri toú nún* (*nún* [3568], now), now, until the present. See Phil 1:5.

(**II**) As a conj. before verbs in the subjunctive (Luke 21:24; Rev 15:8; 17:17; 20:3).

Syn.: *héōs* (2193), until; *méchri* or *méchris* (3360), until, referring to terminal time.

Ant.: *poté* (4218), never, and its syn.

892. ἄχυρον *áchuron*; gen. *achúrou*, neut. noun. Chaff, the husks and refuse of wheat separated by thrashing and winnowing which have no steadiness but are easily disturbed or put in motion by every blast of air (Matt 3:12; Luke 3:17; Sept.: Gen 24:25, 32; Judg 19:19; Isa 30:24). Such chaff or straw was used by the Jews as fodder and for burning (Ex 5:7; Luke 12:28).

893. ἀψευδής *apseudḗs*; gen. *apseudoús*, masc.-fem., neut. *apseudés*, adj. from the priv. *a* (1), without, and *pseudḗs* (5571), false, a liar. That which cannot lie or deceive (Titus 1:2).

Ant.: *alēthḗs* (227), true to fact; *alēthinós* (228) and *gnḗsios* (1103), genuine; *pistós* (4103), faithful, trustworthy; *eilikrinḗs* (1506), genuine, sincere.

894. ἄψινθος *ápsinthos*; gen. *apsínthou*, fem. noun. Wormwood, as the emblem of poisonous bitterness (Rev 8:11; whereas the name of the star, it is the masc. *ho Ápsinthos*). In Sept.: Prov 5:4 *cholḗ* (5521), gall or bile. The figure of waters converted into bitter poison in this way is perhaps drawn from Jer 9:15; 23:15; Lam 3:15, 19 (cf. Ex 15:23; Deut 29:18; Heb 12:15).

895. ἄψυχος *ápsuchos*; gen. *apsúchou*, masc.-fem., neut. *ápsuchon*, adj. from the priv. *a* (1), without, and *psuchḗ* (5590), soul or the breath of life. Lifeless (1 Cor 14:7). In Class. Gr. it means without character, spiritless, cowardly.

Syn.: *adúnatos* (102), weak; *asthenḗs* (772), without strength, sick; *nekrós* (3498), dead.

Ant.: *dunatós* (1415), strong.

B

896. Βάαλ *Báal*; masc. proper noun transliterated from the Hebr. *Ba'al* (1168, OT), meaning master, a heathen idol. A ruler, but also the sun as the great independent ruler of nature which was worshiped by idolaters of several nations. In Hebr., it was properly the name of one of the chief gods of the Phoenicians and Babylonians representing either the sun or, more probably, the planet Jupiter. See Rom 11:4 quoted from 1 Kgs 19:18. The Israelites were often seduced to the worship of Baal (Judg 2:11, 13; 3:7; 8:33; 1 Kgs 16:31).

897. Βαβυλών *Babulōn*; gen. *Babulōnos*, fem. proper noun. Babylon, the capital of Chaldea (Matt 1:11, 12, 17; Acts 7:43). A symbolical name for heathen Rome (Rev 14:8; 16:19; 17:5; 18:2, 21), which took the place of ancient Babylon as a persecuting power (cf. Isa 21:9; Jer 50:35; 51:7, 8). This is also the sense given to Babylon in 1 Pet 5:13 by the church fathers and many commentators, but others believe it to be Babylon in Asia, since it is quite possible that Peter labored for a while in that city where there was at that time a large Jewish colony. Still others maintain that Babylon in Egypt, now called Old Cairo, is what is being referred to.

898. βαθμός *bathmós*; gen. *bathmoú*, masc. noun from *baínō* (n.f., see *apobaínō* [576]), to go. Literally it means a step, but as such is not used in the NT. A degree, rank. Some scholars have cited its usage in 1 Timothy 3:13 as evidence that a form of hierarchy was present in the primitive church.

899. βάθος *báthos*; contracted *báthous*, gen. *bathéos* neut. noun from *bathús* (901), deep. Depth.

(I) A deep (Matt 13:5; Mark 4:5; Luke 5:4; Rom 8:39; Sept.: Isa 51:10; Ezek 27:34; 31:14, 18; Zech 10:11). Depth in a figurative sense, as poverty (2 Cor 8:2, deep, abject poverty).
(II) Metaphorically meaning greatness, immensity, as riches (Rom 11:33; Sept.: Prov 18:3). Depth, profoundness, inscrutability, abstruseness (1 Cor 2:10, "the secret, unrevealed purposes of God" [a.t.]; Eph 3:18; Rev 2:24 [TR], of Satan; Sept.: Eccl 7:25 [cf. Ps 92:5; Dan 2:22]).
Syn.: *pélagos* (3989), deep or open sea.
Ant.: *epipháneia* (2015), surface.

900. βαθύνω *bathúnō*; fut. *bathunṓ*, from *bathús* (901), deep. To deepen (Luke 6:48, "he dug deep" [a.t.]; Sept.: Ps 92:5; Jer 49:8).

901. βαθύς *bathús*; fem. *batheía*, neut. *bathú*, adj. Deep (John 4:11; Sept.: Job 11:8; Prov 22:14). Deep, in a metaphorical sense, as sleep (Acts 20:9). As spoken of the morning, early, very early (Luke 24:1), literally deep twilight, earliest dawn, the same as *lían prōΐ* (*lían* [3029], much, exceeding; *prōΐ* [4404], morning), early in the morning (Mark 16:2). Also *órthros* (3722), dawn. In Rev 2:24 (TR), the deep things, secret purposes of Satan.
Deriv.: *báthos* (899), depth; *bathúnō* (900), to deepen.

902. βάϊον *báïon*; gen. *báïou*, pl. *tá baía*, neut. noun from *báïs* (n.f.), a palm branch. Palm branches, a word of Egyptian origin frequently used in papyri writings (John 12:13; Sept.: Lev 23:40).
Syn.: *kládos* (2798), branch; *klḗma* (2814), a tender, flexible branch, especially the shoot of a vine, a vine sprout; *stoibás* (4746), a layer of leaves, reeds, twigs, or straw serving for a bed.

903. Βαλαάμ *Balaám*; transliterated from the Hebr. *Bil'ām* (1109, OT), foreigner. Balaam, the son of Beor or Bosor and a native of Pethor, a village of Mesopotamia. He had a great reputation as a prophet or soothsayer, and appears to have been a worshiper of the one God having come from the country of Abraham where it is in every way probable that remnants of the primitive monotheism existed to his day. He was hired by Balak, king of the Moabites, to curse the Israelites. His history is given in Num 22—24, 31; Deut 23:4; Josh 24:9. In the NT used as the symbol of false and seducing teachers (2 Pet 2:15; Jude 1:11; Rev 2:14). See *Nicolaĭtēs* (3531), Nicolaitans.

904. Βαλάκ *Balák*; masc. proper noun transliterated from the Hebr. *Bālāk* (1111, OT), meaning spoiler or vacant. Balak, the king of Moab who hired *Balaám* (903) to curse Israel (Rev 2:14; Num 22—24; Josh 24:9; Judg 11:25; Mic 6:5).

905. βαλάντιον *balántion*; gen. *balántiou*, neut. noun. A purse or pouch, a money bag (Luke 10:4; 12:33; 22:35, 36; Sept.: Job 14:17; Prov 1:14).
    Syn.: *glōssókomon* (1101), originally a case in which the mouthpiece of a wind instrument was kept or a small box for any purpose, but especially a purse to keep money in; *zṓnē* (2223), a girdle or belt which also served as a purse for money.

906. βάλλω *bállō*; fut. *baló*, fut. pass. *blēthḗsomai*, 2d aor. *ébalon.*, aor. pass. *eblḗthēn*, perf. *béblēka*, perf. pass. *béblēmai*. To cast off or to bring, to carry. The verb in all its applications retains the idea of impulse. To cast, throw.
    (I) To cast lots (Matt 27:35; Mark 15:24; Luke 23:25; Sept.: 1 Sam 14:42; Neh 10:34; 11:1). Spoken of a tree, to cast its fruit (Rev 6:13). To cast oneself, and with *kátō* (2736), down, to cast oneself

down (Matt 4:6; Luke 4:9). Followed by the dat. as in Matt 15:26; Mark 7:27, to cast to or before anyone; Matt 25:27, to put out or place out money with the brokers. When used with different prep. and particles, the meaning is altered accordingly, but with the idea of throwing always maintained.
    (A) Followed by *apó* (575), from, to throw from one, cast away (Matt 5:29; 18:8, 9).
    (B) Followed by *ek* (1537), out of, to cast out of the mouth, to vomit (Rev 12:15, 16).
    (C) Followed by *éxō* (1854), away, forth, out, out of, to cast out or throw away, reject (Matt 5:13; 13:48; Luke 14:35; John 15:6).
    (D) Followed by *eis* (1519), into, with the acc. of place, meaning where it is cast, to cast into, i.e., a bed (Rev 2:22); the fire (Matt 3:10; 5:29; 6:30; 13:42; Mark 9:22, 45; Sept.: Dan 3:21, 24); the sea (Matt 21:21; Mark 11:23; Rev 18:21); of nets, to cast into or let down into the sea (Matt 4:18; 13:47; Sept.: Isa 19:8); cast into prison (Matt 18:30; Luke 12:58; Acts 16:37); to cast contributions of money into a treasury (Mark 12:41, 43; Luke 21:1, 4); to deposit (Matt 27:6); of a sword, to thrust into the sheath, to put away (John 18:11); of a sickle (Rev 14:19); the finger, hand, to thrust into, put into (Mark 7:33; John 20:27 [cf. Sept.: Job 28:9]; Dan 11:42 [*ekteínō* {1614}, to stretch forth]); to put or place bits in horses' mouths (James 3:3). Spoken of liquids as wine and water where we can only translate by saying to put or pour into (Matt 9:17; Mark 2:22; Luke 5:37; John 13:5; Sept.: Judg 6:19). Metaphorically, to put into one's heart, suggest to one's mind (John 13:2).
    (E) Followed by *émprosthen* (1715), in front of, or *enṓpion* (1799), before, and the gen. meaning to cast before anyone or anything (Matt 7:6; Rev 2:14; 4:10).
    (F) Followed by *epí* (1909), upon, to cast upon, as the seed upon the earth, to sow, scatter seed (Mark 4:26; Sept.: Ps 126:6); to cast stones at anyone (John 8:7, 59; Sept.: Eccl 3:5; Isa 37:33; Ezek

21:22); to send peace upon the earth (Matt 10:34); to put upon, impose (Rev 2:24). Spoken of a sickle, to thrust in (Rev 14:16). Spoken of liquids, to pour (Matt 26:12 [see also Matt 26:7]).

(II) Perf. and pluperf. pass., *béblēmai*, to be cast, meaning to be laid down, to lie, equivalent to *keímai* (2749), to lie outstretched (Matt 8:6, a paralytic was lying in the house [see Matt 8:14]); laid on a bed (Matt 9:2; Mark 7:30) laid at a gate (Luke 16:20).

(III) With the acc. of person, to throw at anyone (Mark 14:65, "they throw at him with blows" [a.t.], means they gave him blows). See Sept.: 2 Chr 26:15; Ps 78:9.

(IV) Intrans. or with *heautón* (1438), himself implied, means to cast oneself, to rush forward; as spoken of a wind, to blow (Acts 27:14).

Deriv.: *anabállō* (306), to defer, put off; *antibállō* (474), to have; *apobállō* (577), to throw off from, lay aside; *bélos* (956), a missile; *blētéos* (992), that which one must put out; *bolé* (1000), a throw; *bolís* (1002), dart; *diabállō* (1225), to throw in between; *ekbállō* (1544), to cast out of or from; *embállō* (1685), to cast into; *epibállō* (1911), to cast upon; *katabállō* (2598), to cast down or around; *lithoboléō* (3036), to cast stones; *metabállō* (3328), to throw over, change mind; *parabállō* (3846), to arrive, compare; *peribállō* (4016), to cast about; *probállō* (4261), to put forward; *sumbállō* (4820), to confer, encounter; *huperbállō* (5235), to excel, pass; *hupobállō* (5260), to suborn.

Syn.: With the meaning of to cast: *rhíptō* (4496), to throw with a certain motion; *apōthéō* (683), to thrust away; *apotíthēmi* (659), to put off; *ektíthēmi* (1620), to expose, cast out; *kathairéō* (2507), to cast down, demolish. With the meaning of to lay down: *títhēmi* (5087), to put or place, set; *anaklínō* (347), to lay down; *keímai* (2749), to lie; *apókeimai* (606), to be laid away or up, as money in a box or purse; *katákeimai* (2621), to lie down; *epíkeimai* (1945), to lie upon;

epipíptō (1968), to fall upon; *anákeimai* (345), to be laid up, to lie. With the meaning of to pour as liquids: *katachéō* (2708), to pour down upon; *ekchéō* (1632), to pour out of; *ekchúnō* (1632), to pour out, shed; *epichéō* (2022), to pour upon. With the meaning of to put: *títhēmi* (5087), to place, lay, set; *apolúō* (630), to let go, dismiss; *aphíēmi* (863), to send away; *periairéō* (4014), to take away; *exaírō* (1808), to put away from; *apekdúō* (554), to strip off clothes or arms; *methístēmi* (3179), to remove; *anágō* (321), to lead or bring up; *endúō* (1746), to put on oneself; *embibázō* (1688), to put in; *probibázō* (4264), to put forward; *apostréphō* (654), to turn away, remove; *ekteínō* (1614), to stretch forth; *lúō* (3089), to loose. With the meaning of to send: *apostéllō* (649), to send forth; *pémpō* (3992), to send; *apotássomai* (657), to place in a proper order away from oneself. With the meaning of thrust: *katatoxeúō* (2700), to strike down with an arrow; *exōthéō* (1856), to drive out.

Ant.: *lambánō* (2983), to receive; *déchomai* (1209), to receive gently; *anístēmi* (450), to rise; *egeírō* (1453), to rise.

907. βαπτίζω baptízō; fut. *baptísō*, from *báptō* (911), to dip. Immerse, submerge for a religious purpose, to overwhelm, saturate, baptize (John 1:25).

(I) Washing or ablution was frequently by immersion, indicated by either *baptízō* or *níptō* (3538), to wash. In Mark 7:3, the phrase "wash their hands" is the translation of *níptō* (3538), to wash part of the body such as the hands. In Mark 7:4 the verb wash in "except they wash" is *baptízomai*, to immerse. This indicates that the washing of the hands was done by immersing them in collected water. See Luke 11:38 which refers to washing one's hands before the meal, with the use of *baptízomai*, to have the hands baptized. In the Sept.: 2 Kgs 5:13, 14 we have *loúō* (3068), to bathe and *baptízomai*. See also Lev 11:25, 28, 40, where *plúnō* (4150), to wash clothes by dipping, and *loúō*

(3068), to bathe are used. In Num 19:18, 19, *bápho*, to dip, and *plúno*, to wash by dipping are used.

(II) To baptize or immerse in or wash with water in token of purification from sin and spiritual pollution (Matt 3:6, 11; Mark 1:4, 5, 8, 9; Luke 3:7, 12, 16, 21; 7:30; John 1:25, 28; 3:22, 23, 26; 4:1, 2; 10:40; Acts 2:38, 41; 8:12, 13, 36, 38; 9:18; 10:47; 16:15, 33; 18:8; 22:16; 1 Cor 1:14, 16, 17). In Mark 6:14, "John the baptizing one [*ho baptízon*]" (a.t.). In Luke's writings with a dat. of the instrument or material employed, *húdati*, the dat. of *húdor* (5204), water, means with water (Luke 3:16; Acts 1:5; 11:16). Elsewhere, however, the prep. *en* (1722), in, is used, *en húdati*, in water (Matt 3:11; Mark 1:8; John 1:26, 31, 33 (cf. "in the Jordan" [a.t. {Matt 3:6}]). In Mark 1:9, *eis* (1519), into, "into the Jordan" (a.t.).

(III) The adjuncts mark the object and effect of baptism: especially *eis* (1519), into, unto, with the acc., to baptize or to be baptized into anything means into the belief, profession or observance of anything (Matt 3:11, "unto repentance"; Acts 2:38, "unto remission of sins" [a.t.]; 19:3, "Unto John's baptism," meaning the repentance unto which John baptized or the baptism related to John's preaching; Rom 6:3, "unto death" [a.t.] means that those who are baptized do so in relation to Jesus Christ's bearing their sins through His sacrifice and atonement on the cross; 1 Cor 12:13, "unto one body" [a.t.] that we may become parts of the body of Christ and parts of each other). With *eis* followed by the acc. of person, it means to baptize or be baptized into a profession of faith or into anyone, in sincere obedience to him. Also in 1 Cor 10:2, "unto Moses"; Gal 3:27, "unto Christ" (a.t.); also "into the name of someone"(a.t.) means to be identified with what the name of that one stands for (Matt 28:19; Acts 8:16; 19:5; 1 Cor 1:13, 15). The same sense is understood when the prep. *epí* (1909), upon, or *en* (1722), in, followed by the dat., *onómati* (3686), upon the name of, is used (Acts 2:38, *epí* 10:48, *en*). With

hupér (5228), on behalf of or for (1 Cor 15:29, those being "baptized for [or on account of] the dead," i.e., on a belief of the resurrection of the dead).

(IV) Metaphorically and in direct allusion to the practice of water baptism (Matt 3:11; Luke 3:16), to baptize in or with the Holy Spirit and in or with fire, the baptism in the Holy Spirit being the spiritual counterpart of the water baptism. This Spirit baptism is referred to in 1 Cor 12:13 as an act performed by God in joining all true believers to the body of the Lord Jesus. To be baptized in fire (Matt 3:11 [TR]; Luke 3:16) stands in contrast to the baptism in the Spirit. Those who refuse to be joined into the body of Christ through the energy of the Holy Spirit will suffer the consequent punishment (Matt 3:12; Luke 3:17). In regard to the Spirit baptism, see also Mark 1:8; John 1:33; Acts 1:5; 11:16, where the baptism in the Holy Spirit occurs as a specific phrase indicating what happened at Pentecost in joining the Jews who believed to the body of Christ (Acts 2). This is explained by Peter in Acts 11:15, 16 indicating that the Gentiles of Caesarea were also baptized in the Holy Spirit. A third group was the disciples of John in Acts 19:6. This Spirit baptism was characterized by the phenomenon of speaking in languages never learned by those who were baptized in or with the Spirit (see Acts 2:4 [language], 6, 8 [dialect], 11 [languages]; 10:46 [languages]; 19:6 [languages]). Thus the baptism in the Holy Spirit is Christ's attachment of those who genuinely believe as members of His body. In 1 Cor 12:13 the verb *ebaptísthemen* refers to all believers of all times. It is something that God did in forming the spiritual body of Jesus Christ or the body of all believers, the Church. It fulfills the promise of Christ to send into the world in a special way the Holy Spirit or the *Parákletos* (3875), the Paraclete, Comforter, Intercessor, Consoler (John 16:7–14).

(V) Metaphorically, the verb *baptízo*, to baptize, and the noun *báptisma*, baptism, are used in connection with calamities as in Matt 20:22, 23; Mark 10:38, 39, meaning to be overwhelmed with sufferings as the life of Jesus Christ was characterized. A similar expression is in Isa 21:4 in the Sept., "lawlessness baptizes me" (a.t.) or "overwhelms me" (a.t.). In 1 Cor 15:29, "What shall those being baptized for the dead do?" (a.t.); "Why therefore are they baptized on their behalf?" (a.t.) means if the dead do not rise, why expose ourselves to so much danger and suffering in the hope of a resurrection? This is an argument which Paul presents in order to prove the reality of the resurrection (cf. 1 Cor 15:30, 31 where the verbs *kinduneúō* [2793], to undergo danger, and *apothnḗskō* [599], to die, used instead of *baptízomai*, to be baptized).

(VI) In contrast to the verb *baptízō*, to dip, immerse, is the verb *rhantízō* (4472), to sprinkle, which must not be taken as equivalent to *baptízō*. *Rhantízō* is used in Mark 7:4 in the WH instead of *baptísōntai*. *Baptísōntai*, however, of the TR and the UBS texts, is to be preferred in agreement with *baptismoús* (pl. [909]) occurring in the same verse referring to the ceremonial washings of utensils. *Baptismós*, the ceremonial washing, should never be confused with *báptisma* which is a distinct practice related to the work of the Lord Jesus Christ. *Baptismós* as mere cleansing of instruments was equated with *rhantismós* (4473), sprinkling (found only in Heb 12:24; 1 Pet 1:2), because this word was used to indicate the cleansing in symbolism done by the priest of the OT. Such ceremonial cleansing symbolized by sprinkling (Heb 9:19, 21; 10:22; 12:24; 1 Pet 1:2) had no permanent value nor did it actually cleanse the consciences of individual people. The verb *rhantízō*, to sprinkle, is found in Heb 9:13 where the contrast between the sprinkling is symbolic of the cleansing of the flesh. However, in Heb 9:14, the blood of Jesus Christ will *katharieí* (the same as *katharísei*), cleanse (from the verb *katharízō* [2511], purify or cleanse) the conscience of man or his inner being. The high priest never

baptized anyone in the way that Christian believers are baptized. He merely sprinkled the blood of animals. Therefore, the sprinkling has nothing to do with baptism but simply with ceremonial cleansing (Heb 9:21). Since, according to Heb 9:22, there can be no remission of sins without the "shedding of blood," Jesus Christ did indeed shed His blood (i.e., lay His life down as a sacrifice for sin). Thus it is not through some magical sprinkling of that blood upon our bodies or souls that we are saved, but when through faith we have our hearts "sprinkled" (the application of the benefits of Christ's death) from an evil conscience and our bodies washed (*lelouménoi*, the perf. pass. part. of *loúō* [3068], to bathe) with clean water (Heb 10:22). The verb *loúō*, bathe, must be definitely differentiated from the verb *níptō* (3538), to wash part of the body, usually feet, hands, or face, which can be used syn. with *baptízō*, as the verb of *baptismós*, ceremonial ablution (Luke 11:38), but never equivalent to the NT technical term of *baptízō*. The two great cleansing ceremonies of the OT, sprinkling and washing, typified the true work of salvation in Jesus Christ. The former perhaps signifying forgiveness (the cleansing of sin's guilt) and the latter probably betokening regeneration (the washing away of sin's defilement). Because believers have received the antitypical reality of these ceremonies in Christ, the writer can say that we have indeed had our consciences sprinkled and our bodies washed.

Deriv.: *báptisma* (908), baptism, the result of baptizing; *baptismós* (909), the ceremonial washing of articles; *baptistḗs* (910), baptist, used of John to qualify him as one baptizing.

Syn.: *buthízō* (1036), to sink, but not necessarily to drown; *katapontízō* (2670), to plunge down, submerge; *embáptō* (1686), to dip.

Ant.: *pléō* (4126), to sail upon the water.

908. βάπτισμα *báptisma*; gen. *baptís-matos*, neut. noun from *báptō* (911), to dip. Baptism.

(I) The suffix *-ma* indicates the result of the act of dipping. In contrast, *báptisis* with the suffix *-is* indicates the act of baptism, while *baptismós* (909) with the suffix *-os* indicates the completed act. *Báptisma* must not be confused with *baptismós* (909), ceremonial washing.

(II) The term *báptisma* is a technical NT term. It begins with John's baptism in or with water (Matt 3:7; 21:25; Mark 1:4; 11:30; Luke 3:3; 7:29; 20:4; Acts 1:22; 10:37; 13:24; 18:25; 19:3, 4). In all these instances, this baptism is called the baptism of John or the baptism of repentance. This was a distinct baptism associated with John, the forerunner of Jesus Christ (Acts 19:4). It was known as "baptism of repentance" relating it to repentance. It was also known as John's baptism (Luke 7:29). It should not be taken as the same as the baptism of Jesus or the baptism in the name of Jesus (Acts 19:5) or the Father, the Son and the Holy Spirit (Matt 28:19). It is said in Acts 18:25 that Apollos knew only the baptism of John. When the believers at Ephesus, including Apollos, were found to have been baptized only unto John's baptism (Acts 19:3), they were not told by Paul that such was sufficient nor that it was identical with the baptism "in the name of the Lord Jesus" (Acts 19:5). It was then that they were truly baptized into the body of Christ according to 1 Cor 12:13. Almost concurrently Paul placed his hands upon these disciples of John just baptized in the name of the Lord Jesus, and the Holy Spirit came upon them, and they spoke with languages or tongues and prophesied. This was the unique demonstration of the baptism with the Holy Spirit, and this was the third time that it occurred confirming that Jews first were baptized with the Holy Spirit and became members of the body of Christ. In Acts 11:15, 16 Peter speaks to Cornelius and the other Gentiles of Caesarea telling them that as the Jews had the Holy Spirit come upon them at first and they spoke with languages (tongues) unknown to them according to Acts 10:44–46, so the same Holy Spirit came also upon the Gentile believers. As the Jews in Acts 2 spoke with other languages or dialects according to Acts 2:4, 6, 8, 11, so the Gentiles, too, would do the same, which they did (Acts 10:46).

(III) We thus conclude that in Acts 2 there was the first demonstration of the baptism in the Holy Spirit; the second was at Caesarea, and the third was at Ephesus. Thus three distinct groups, as far as their religious backgrounds were concerned, were introduced into the body of Jesus Christ, namely Jews, Gentiles, and the disciples of John the Baptist. The baptism of John was a baptism of repentance, a water baptism which was related to the act of repentance on the part of those who sought and received it. If, however, John's baptism was characterized by the repentance of those who were baptized by him, why did the Lord Jesus seek John's baptism (Matt 3:13–17; Mark 1:9–11; Luke 3:21–22)?

(IV) The spiritual meaning of baptism is identification with a person in what the name of that person stands for or what he has come to do. For instance, in 1 Cor 10:2, those who came out of Egypt are said to have been "baptized unto Moses" which means they were identified with the character and the purpose of Moses.

(V) When the Lord Jesus sought to be baptized by John the Baptist, it was not a baptism of repentance for Him, but it was a baptism that meant His identification with the claims of John that he was surely the forerunner of the Messiah and that men did indeed need to repent and turn from their sins. John's baptism was thus declared to be a step toward the work which Jesus Christ came to do immediately following that of John. John did not understand the purpose of Jesus in seeking to be baptized by him, and this is why he remonstrated with Him. Jesus answered, "For thus it becometh us [both you and me] to fulfill all righteousness"

(Matt 3:15), which caused John to become willing to baptize Him. The word for "righteousness" here is *dikaiosúnē* (1343), which comes from the basic word *díkē* (1349), justice. The Lord Jesus told John that it was proper (justice fulfilled) for him to have the right to baptize Him in spite of the fact that he had confessed that he was not worthy to untie the Lord's shoes (Mark 1:7) being so inferior to Jesus. John the Baptist responded to the call to become the forerunner of Jesus and his identifying himself with Jesus by baptizing Him was a rightful, just act, and not a presumption. On the other hand, by seeking to be baptized by John, Jesus did not identify Himself as a sinner who had repented as all the others had, but as indeed confirming that He was the One to whom John had pointed, saying, "Behold the Lamb of God, which taketh away the sin of the world" (John 1:29). Thus we must clearly understand that John's baptism was not the same as the baptism in the Name of Christ (Acts 19:5), nor the baptism in the Name of the Father, and of the Son and of the Holy Spirit (Matt 28:19), which was to be practiced by the disciples who heeded the Great Commission to go and preach the gospel and make disciples of all nations.

John's baptism was to cease while the baptism in the name of Christ or of the triune Godhead was to continue as a practice in the Christian church. The baptism in the name of the Lord Jesus in the case of the believing disciples of John in Acts 19:5 is shorthand for, and identical with, the baptism in the name of the triune God in Matt 28:19; Mark 16:16; Acts 2:38. This baptism is unto the remission of sins because of the sacrifice of Jesus Christ on Calvary's cross.

(VI) The baptism instituted by the Lord Jesus is spoken of in Rom 6:4 which illustrates and demonstrates the inner work of salvation. A person is buried and raised with Christ, not because of the physical act of baptism, but because of the identification with the death and resurrection of Christ through faith (Rom 5:1; 6:7).

A person does not die unto sin because he is baptized in water, but before he is baptized. Before the discussion of baptism in Rom 6:3–8, he is said to have already died unto sin: "How shall we, that are dead to sin, live any longer therein?" (Rom 6:2). In this verse, that which is translated "that are dead to sin" is the verb *apethánomen*, we died, the aor. indic. of the verb *apothnḗskō* (599), to die. The teaching here is that only those who did die to sin are to be baptized, and this dying to sin can only take place as the Holy Spirit works in the heart of a sinner and causes him to be justified by Christ through faith and makes him just (2 Cor 5:21). Dying to sin is not through an outward physical act such as baptism, but it is by Jesus Christ through faith as Rom 5:1 unmistakably declares. The dipping into the water is symbolic of our already having died and being buried unto sin, and our rising up from the water is symbolic of the new life, the life of the resurrection that Jesus Christ gives. Even the repentant thief on the cross received this life in spite of the fact that he had no opportunity to receive water baptism. Thus the teaching is that water baptism, when it is by immersion into the water and rising out of the water, is a perfect symbol of the death and resurrection of the believer in Jesus Christ. Rom 6:7 reads, "For he that is dead [*ho apothanṓn*, the aor. part. of *apothnḗskō* {599}, to die, he who died] is freed [*dedikaíōtai*, the perf. pass. indic. of *dikaióō* {1344}, to justify, meaning has been justified] from sin." If that justification is the result of both faith in Jesus Christ and the act of water baptism, then Rom 5:1 cannot be true.

(VII) That there is a definitive distinction between the Spirit baptism and water baptism is clearly demonstrated by what happened in Caesarea, described in Acts 10:44, 45. These Gentile believers could not have spoken in other languages and magnified God had they not been saved and spiritually baptized into the body of Christ, according to 1 Cor 12:13.

(VIII) In the Acts of the Apostles, the speaking in languages other than one's own is always in demonstration of the baptism in the Holy Spirit. It was after this Spirit baptism that Peter suggested that they should be also baptized in water (Acts 10:47): "Can any man forbid water, that these should not be baptized, which have received the Holy Ghost as well as we?" No one can claim that these people were not saved unless he also claims that Peter too was unsaved. They received (*élabon*, the aor. act. indic. 3d person pl. of *lambánō* [2983], to receive) the Holy Spirit. This is a definite act of acceptance pertaining to both Peter and also these believers. Observe Acts 11:15: "And as I [Peter] began to speak, the Holy Ghost fell on them, as on us at the beginning." That included Peter at Pentecost. They received the Holy Spirit and thus they were believers before they were baptized in water. Therefore, the distinction between the Spirit baptism and the water baptism is definitely conclusive.

(IX) In Matt 20:22, 23; Mark 10:38, 39, a pair of Hebrew disciples, James and John, who desired a special place of rulership in Christ's glory, were told that they should be willing to be baptized with the baptism with which the Lord Jesus was being baptized. The meaning of baptism in these verses is identification with suffering. The words "baptize" and "baptism" both occur in these verses and have nothing to do with water baptism but merely mean identification.

In Luke 12:50, the Lord Jesus speaks of a similar baptism, not water baptism, but identification with death which He was about to experience shortly.

(X) In Eph 4:5 there is no indication as to which baptism Paul refers. The whole paragraph, Eph 4:1–5, is indicative of Paul's desire that there should be unity of the Spirit in the body of Christ. No reference is made to water baptism at all. The verse says, "One Lord, one faith, one baptism." This baptism must be, therefore, the spiritual baptism, the baptism in the Spirit that was promised by John the Baptist that the One coming after him would accomplish (Matt 3:11; Mark 1:8; Luke 3:16; John 1:33) and Jesus Christ Himself promised in Acts 1:5. This took place in Acts 2 and was followed by the resultant speaking with other tongues; also in Caesarea in Acts 11:16–18; 10:44–46 and in Ephesus with the same manifestation of speaking in other languages (Acts 19:1–7). The purpose of this Spirit baptism is shown in 1 Cor 12:13 as the incorporation of all believers into the body of Christ, the Church (Eph 1:22, 23). When believers are disunited, the whole body of Christ feels it. We must all remember that we were all baptized into one body and that the same Lord belongs to all and that He owns all of us.

(XI) In Col 2:12, baptism occurs again, "Buried with him in baptism, wherein also ye are risen with him through the faith of the operation of God, who hath raised him from the dead." Here there is no clear delineation as to which baptism is referred to, the spiritual baptism by Christ with the Holy Spirit which makes us members of the body of Christ (1 Cor 12:13) or water baptism. The phrase *en autṓ*, in Him, occurs in Col 2:9, 10 referring to Jesus Christ, e.g., "And ye are complete in him." This means that each one of us finds his proper position in the body of Christ. In Col 2:11, we have the phrase *en hṓ*, the *hṓ* being the relative pron. in the dat. referring to *autṓ*, Him. The reference again is to Jesus Christ. And then verse eleven says, "Ye are circumcised with the circumcision made without hands." The verb is *perietmḗthēte*, you were circumcised, the aor. pass. indic. of *peritémnō* (4059), to circumcise. Here reference is made to an act of God, i.e., you were circumcised at a specific time in the past by Jesus Christ Himself. This could not refer to the circumcision that any Jewish believer may have been subjected to since it is stated as having been circumcision performed by Jesus Christ Himself. In order to exclude the possibility of this circumcision being thought of as the severing of the foreskin, a physical act, the Apostle designates it as *acheiropoiḗtō* (886), not made by hand. If it was not made by hand, then it was spiritually wrought. Paul goes on to describe the effect of such spiritual circumcision, "in putting off the body of the sins of the flesh." This is the old man whom Jesus Christ crucified together with Him, "that the body of sin might be destroyed" (Rom 6:6). This is indicated as a work of Christ. When He circumcises our hearts with the circumcision that is spiritual (Rom 2:29) He saves us, which is called in Col 2:11 "the circumcision of Christ." This does not refer to the circumcision Christ underwent when He was an infant, but the circumcision which Christ brings about, the circumcision not made with hands, i.e., the circumcision of the heart. Such circumcision precedes water baptism, even as in Acts 10:44–46 the spiritual baptism preceded the water baptism in Acts 10:47. This spiritual baptism took place in the hearts of all believers whether physically circumcised as the Jews were or uncircumcised as the Gentiles were. Paul told us in Rom 6:6 that the body of sin is crucified together with Christ. It is part and parcel of our salvation. Crucifixion leads to burial. Here in Col 2:12 we have a parallel statement, "Buried with him in baptism." What is translated "buried with him" in Gr. is *suntaphéntes*, the aor. pass. part. of *suntháptō* (4916), to bury together. Not only were we crucified together with Christ, but we were buried together with Him and by Him through His death and burial. When our faith is identified with Him in the purpose of His crucifixion and burial and resurrection, a revolution takes place in our personality. The old body is crucified and buried (Rom 6:6) as if it were an old garment. The body of sin which enslaved us to sin is now itself enslaved. That is what our spiritual identification with Christ and His death does to us through faith. Paul in Col 2:12 says, *en tṓ baptísmati*, "in the baptism" (a.t.) or by means of the baptism, but he does not qualify which baptism. However, it is evident that this baptism is not strictly

the NT counterpart of the OT circumcision, which identified the individual with the race of Israel and not with Abraham whose righteousness was not due to his physical circumcision but to his faith. "Abraham believed God, and it was imputed unto him for righteousness" (a.t. [Rom 4:3; James 2:23]). No Jew became the child of God or the friend of God (as Abraham) through circumcision alone. The Jew is only the physical and not the spiritual seed of Abraham as anyone who is only physically baptized without faith in Jesus Christ is not a child of God. It is impossible, therefore, that this baptism in Col 2:12 refers to water baptism apart from faith, even as physical circumcision does not indicate acceptance into the family of God. The verse proceeds with the phrase *en hṓ*, which until now referred to the person of Jesus Christ (Col 2:9, 10, *en autṓ*, "in him"; in v. 11, *en hṓ*, "in whom"; and again in v. 12, *en hṓ*). The question that we must determine is whether the *en hṓ* in verse twelve refers to the word "baptism" which it follows or whether it refers to Jesus Christ. Unfortunately, the KJV and the NASB connect *en hṓ* with the baptism, which can be done grammatically but not exegetically. The NIV is much better as it translates the phrase thus, "having been buried with him [Christ] in baptism." From the grammatical point of view, the relative pron. *hṓ* with *en*, in, could really refer to either Christ or baptism, for *hṓ* can be the dat. of the masc. word *Christós*, Christ, or the neut. word *báptisma*. It therefore could apply to either. Grammatically it very well may refer to either Christ or to the baptism in the Holy Spirit that He administers. Remember that in Matt 3:11; Mark 1:8; Luke 3:16; John 1:33, John the Baptist most definitively declared that the One who was going to baptize in the Spirit or with the Spirit was going to be Jesus Christ Himself. So here in Col 2:12 we have the declaration of the agent of baptism, which is the Holy Spirit and also the means. The Holy Spirit baptism itself is the means of the attachment of individual believers to the body of Christ according to 1 Cor 12:13. So that there could be absolutely no misunderstanding regarding the kind of baptism spoken about here, we have the results that ensue from this Spirit baptism. It is not simply being crucified with Christ and dying with Him, but it is being raised with Him to live in victory and in the energy of God. "In whom also ye are risen with him" (a.t. [Col 2:12]). It is by means of Christ that we are raised into newness of life. If en hố refers to baptism, it must refer to the spiritual baptism with which Christ baptizes us by means of the Holy Spirit. The verb here is sunēgérthēte, the aor. pass. indic. of sunegeírō (4891), to rise up together, to rise with. No one who understands the NT doctrine of salvation could claim that such joint resurrection of the believer with Christ can be achieved through the physical water baptism. This resurrection unto new life with the body of the old man put away as a filthy garment is achieved "through the faith of the operation of God, who hath raised him from the dead" (Col 2:12). The exact translation of the Gr. text here is, "through the faith of the energy of God who raised him from out among the dead ones." (a.t.). Col 2:13 makes it amply evident that all this work is done through Jesus Christ and not through water baptism. When verse thirteen says, "And you, being dead in your sins and the uncircumcision of your flesh, hath he quickened together with him, having forgiven you all trespasses," it does not refer to baptism, but to Jesus Christ. Therefore, we conclude after this detailed study that the word báptisma, baptism, in this context refers to the baptism in the Holy Spirit by Jesus Christ Himself.

(XII) There remains only one more occurrence of the word báptisma in the NT and that is 1 Pet 3:21. This verse must be studied in its context. 1 Pet 3:18 speaks of Christ having suffered once and for all for our sins, the righteous on behalf of the unrighteous ones. It is clearly stated that it is Jesus who brings us before God, having been put to death in the flesh and made alive in the spirit. In 1 Pet 3:19 we have the spirit of Jesus Christ which He delivered to the Father upon dying, going to make a declaration to the spirits who were kept in prison. This must not be taken as evangelizing the spirits of the past who disobeyed God. The verb is ekēruxen, preached or made a declaration. These disobedient souls were those to whom the longsuffering of God extended itself for a protracted time.

Peter brings the example of those who did not heed Noah while he was preparing the ark. Only eight were saved. Although technically it was not the water that saved them, but the ark, the water in a sense did serve to deliver Noah and his family. By destroying the wicked and reprobate generation in which Noah's family lived, the flood rescued them from the vexation of the presence and influence such ungodliness. The water here was the medium both of destruction and salvation. In fact, the destruction of the wicked was the salvation of the godly. It is not odd, then, that Peter speaks of Noah and his family as having been saved by the water. Peter employs the prep. diá (1223), through, and not én (1722), with. Both are used instrumentally but the former has a wider connotation than the latter and includes the circumstances of an occasion. In this case, as explained, the attending circumstance is the ungodly being swept away in judgment of the flood. Peter connects this OT event of salvation history with the NT rite of baptism. Verse twenty-one begins with the relative pron. ho (the which). The antecedent is strictly húdōr (5204), water, or broadly the whole preceding idea of Noah and his family being delivered by water. Either way, Peter makes the point that his readers have also been delivered by the water of divine judgment. The water in view is identified as that contained in Christian baptism. Peter says, "which [water] also . . . now saves you, namely, baptism." Peter says this because he sees a correspondence between baptism and the flood. The word rendered "like figure" (KJV) is *antítupon* (499), counterpart, likeness, or as an adj., corresponding to. As the waters of the flood removed the old world of wickedness from the godly, so the waters of baptism remove the filth of the old man (i.e., sin) from him. The flood is a macrocosm of what takes place in baptism.

Some have concluded from this that Peter is teaching sacramental salvation. However, Peter is careful to qualify his words to avoid being misunderstood. He explains that baptism is not the washing away of the sins of the flesh. That is, baptism is not simply a ceremony. Rather, it is occasioned by the repentance and faith of one who has turned to Christ. Most significantly baptism is "the pledge of a good conscience toward God" (a.t.). The term "pledge" is *eperótēma* (1906). It originally meant to inquire or make a request, and was used to denote the exchange between parties entering into a contract. By inclusion, the word signified not only the questions asked in such negotiations but also the promises or pledges given to uphold the terms or affirm the facts of the contract. Therefore, Peter is saying that baptism is the response of the soul to God in which it affirms faith in Jesus Christ and recognizes God's covenant claim upon him. Baptism is a sign and seal of salvation and is ineffectual without faith.

Finally, Peter adds that salvation is "through the resurrection of Jesus Christ." No question need remain concerning the means or ground of salvation. According to Peter, salvation is by the grace of God in Christ Jesus and is received by faith alone. Baptism is a means of that grace and is effectual only in those who demonstrate personal faith and repentance.

(XIII) Because the baptism of John and Christian baptism involve water, it does not necessarily follow that the mere mention of water (*hudōr* [5204]) must involve water baptism. The term *en húdati*, in water, follows the verb "baptize" in Matt 3:11; John 1:33. Just the dat. *húdati* without the prep. *en* (1722), in or with,

conveys the same idea that the element in which baptism takes place is water. Water is a cleansing element that we use in bathing, and since baptism indicates outwardly the inward cleansing of the human heart, God designated it as the element of baptism. In contrast to that, the baptism promised by John as a ministry to be performed by the Lord Jesus was the baptism in the Holy Spirit (*en Pneúmati Hagíō* [Matt 3:11; Mark 1:8; Luke 3:16; John 1:33]). Thus we see that the element of physical baptism was and is water, as it was in the case of the baptism of John the Baptist.

In Acts 1:5 we also have the statement that John baptized (*húdati*, the dat. of *húdōr*) in or with water, but that the disciples were going to be baptized in or with the Holy Spirit. This was the promise that the Lord Jesus gave the disciples after His resurrection and before His ascension. The Lord Jesus was baptized by John the Baptist in the waters of the Jordan River (Matt 3:13; Mark 1:9). The Pharisees had spread the false rumor that Jesus was baptizing more disciples than John. Since this took place in Judea, and since John was baptizing in the River Jordan, Jesus' disciples were quite likely also baptizing in the River Jordan.

Water is mentioned in the discourse of the Lord Jesus to Nicodemus in John 3:5, the mention of which has given some the idea that the Lord Jesus was speaking of baptism. Such a presumption, however, is unjustified. Water in this verse stands for the physical element of the birth of man. The Lord Jesus said, "Except a man be born of water and of the Spirit, he cannot enter into the kingdom of God." The verb "be born" in Gr. is *gennēthé*, the aor. pass. subjunctive of *gennáō* (1080), to give birth. This verb is never used in the NT in connection with baptism as if baptism physically introduces a person into the kingdom of God. Paul very clearly states in 1 Cor 15:50 "that flesh and blood cannot inherit the kingdom of God." This means that there is no physical means whereby man can enter this spiritual kingdom of God. The kingdom of God here means that spiritual kingdom which Jesus Christ established in the hearts of believing persons as He Himself said in Luke 17:21, "Behold, the kingdom of God is within you." Jesus Christ does not become the King of our hearts and live in us through water baptism. Nowhere in the Scriptures is anything of the kind stated. The prep. that is used in connection with the gen. case (húdatos in John 3:5) is ex, the same as ek (1537), out of, which becomes ex because the word húdōr begins with a vowel. The literal translation of ex, therefore, is not "of," but "out of." In every instance that the prep. is used in connection with the water that is used in the baptisms by John the Baptist or the disciples, it is always en (1722), in or with. Baptism naturally involves going into the water before coming out of it.

In John 3:5, however, the statement is "if a man be born out of water" (a.t.), not "in and out" (a.t.). Yet the prep. ek is used when the reference is to coming out of the womb of the mother as in Matt 19:12, "For there are some eunuchs, which were so born from [ek] their mother's womb." In Luke 23:29 we read, "Blessed are the barren, and the wombs that never bare [egénnēsan, the aor. of gennáō {1090}, gave birth to], and the paps which never gave suck." Clearly, birth here is associated with a woman's womb. In the very context of John 3:1–12, it is evident that the spiritual birth which is out of the Spirit is contrasted with the physical birth out of water which is the water in which an embryo develops in a woman's womb. The one birth is earthly as explained by the Lord Himself in verse twelve: "If I have told you earthly things, and ye believe not." The "out of the water" (a.t.) birth is earthly and the "out of the Spirit" (a.t.) birth is heavenly. "How shall ye believe, if I tell you of heavenly things?" (v. 12). In verse six, it is further confirmed that the "out of the water" (a.t.) birth is the physical birth, for "that which is born of the flesh is flesh," meaning that which

comes out of the water is a physical human being, man, constituted of spirit, soul, and body (1 Thess 5:23). That, however, which is born out of the Spirit is spirit. The Holy Spirit energizes man's spirit, and only man has spirit which is the medium of communicating with God, and the result is the birth from above spoken about by Jesus in John 3:3. The translation says "again" for ánothen (509) which may also mean "from above." Nicodemus understood the word to mean "again." It can also mean "from the beginning" (Luke 1:3; Acts 26:5; Gal 4:9). So we have birth as an earthly thing, the flesh, the physical personality (v. 12), and we have the birth from above (v. 3) which is a heavenly thing (v. 12).

It is interesting that the prep. ex in verse five occurs only once. It is ex húdatos kaí Pneúmatos, out of water and Spirit. Correctly the KJV has the second "of" in italics. The prep. ek does not occur twice, but only once, before húdatos, of water. The prep. belongs to both the words "water" and "Spirit." This indicates that no one can be born out of the Holy Spirit who has not first been born out of water. The Lord Jesus through the Holy Spirit saves only those who have had physical birth. He does not save incorporeal spirits but only the spirits that dwell in human bodies. This is the reason we never read of the salvation of angels who are spirit beings. Angels were all created good, but some fell of their own accord and became demons (Rev 12:7–12). The Lord Jesus is never said to have died for fallen demons, and nowhere in Scripture do we find even a hint of redemption offered to them. The angels who did not fall continue to be God's ministering spirits. See Satanás (4567), Satan; daímōn (1142), demon, and ággelos (32), angel. Even Nicodemus in his lack of knowledge understood the birth out of water to be physical birth for he said, "How can a man be born when he is old? Can he enter the second time into his mother's womb? [koilía {2836}, the same word found in Matt 19:12; Luke 23:29 relating to physical birth]." If the

Lord meant to convey the idea of water baptism here, He would have said so. He does not in any shape or form refer to baptism, however, but to the physical birth of man. This confirms that the misunderstanding by Nicodemus was in regard to the existence of only one earthly birth, out of a mother's womb, and not a birth from above, a heavenly birth which emanates from the Holy Spirit. Thus we conclude that the word "water" or "out of water" (a.t.) in John 3:5 does not refer to water baptism.

(XIV) There is another word which is misunderstood as referring to water baptism and that is *loutrón* (3067), bath, to which unfortunately Strong in his dictionary attributes the figurative meaning of baptism, although he does give to it the literal meaning of washing.

(A) *Loutrón* occurs in Eph 5:26; Titus 3:5: "That he might sanctify and cleanse it [the Church] with the washing of water by the word." Some claim that the expression "with the washing of water" refers to water baptism. Studying the context will help us to understand what this expression means. From Eph 5:22 on, Paul explains how spouses should behave between themselves, and that the husband ought to be the head even as Christ is the Head of the Church. It is about the Church that he is speaking (v. 26). The Church is composed of repentant, redeemed, and saved individuals. Even as Paul has indicated how a wife submits herself to the care of her husband, so the Church ought to submit herself to the care of Christ. The literal translation of this verse is, "so that he may sanctify her [*hagiásē*, the aor. subjunctive of *hagiázō* {37}, to consecrate, sanctify] since he did cleanse her by means of the bath of the water in the utterance" (a.t.). Here Paul speaks of what the Church experienced, i.e., cleansing. The part. used is *katharísas*, which is the aor. part. of *katharízō* (2511), to cleanse, purge, purify. This is what Christ already did. He cleansed the Church, i.e., the individuals who make up the Church. He

purified each one, otherwise they could not be members of the Church.

(B) The expressions translated "with the washing of water by the word" provides the means, the element whereby the individuals making up the Church were cleansed. The word *tō loutrō*, being in the dat., provides the means whereby this purification was accomplished. *Loutrón* (3067) means a laver or basin used for washing (or bathing), or metonymically the washing (or bathing) itself, and is used only here and in Titus 3:5. The cleansing of the Church involved giving her a bath or washing as the only means whereby a body can be cleansed. The only element of physical washing is water, and thus we have the washing or the bath of water or with water.

(C) Now the question is, can this bath of water referred to here mean baptism? Is the human heart cleansed by Christ as a result of the administration of the rite of baptism? All throughout the Scriptures we find that physical bathing does not cleanse the human heart. It is the blood of Jesus Christ that cleanseth us from all sin (Heb 9:22; 1 John 1:7, 9). We are never told in the Scriptures that the physical act of water baptism has the ability to do that which the blood of Christ only can do, to cleanse us from sin. If baptism is the necessary element whereby we are cleansed or saved, then the thief on the cross could not have been saved in spite of the assurance of Christ that he was going to be with Him in paradise that day. We are saved through faith in Jesus Christ plus nothing (Rom 4:5, 9, 22, 25). Not one word in the entire NT is said that we are justified, we are saved, we are cleansed through the physical act of baptism. In fact, nowhere are we given the idea that by performing something external, an act of the body, can we have a change of heart and spiritual salvation. In the NT, baptism is spoken of as the external testimony of that which the Holy Spirit did internally in cleansing the individual from sin. Baptism must be preceded by faith, and whenever the word is spoken by itself as saving (1 Pet 3:21, see the exegesis of it above), it must include living faith in Christ (Mark 16:16; Acts 2:38).

(D) Never do we find in Scripture that he who is not baptized is condemned, but we do find in many places that he who believes not is condemned already (Mark 16:16b; John 3:18). The righteousness of God is unto all who believe, not unto all who are baptized (Rom 3:22). In Mark 16:16 we read, "He that believeth and is baptized shall be saved; but he that believeth not shall be damned." The literal translation of this verse is, "He who did believe and was baptized shall be saved; but he who did not believe shall be condemned" (a.t.). It is possible, therefore, to be condemned for not having believed, but it is not possible to be saved by just having been baptized without believing.

(E) We conclude, therefore, that the *loutrón*, bath or washing of water, cannot be physical baptism but is a symbol of the cleansing of the soul, even as water is used for the cleansing of the body. And so that there may be no mistake that this is symbolism, Paul adds the qualifying dat. with the prep. *en* (1722), in or with, *rhḗmati* (4487), utterance. *Rhéma* is that which God speaks or utters in contrast to *lógos* (3056), intelligent word, either spoken or written. It is not a physical bath with physical water that is spoken of here, but it is *en rhḗmati*, in word or with word. This concerns God's Word. He said salvation would come when we believe in Christ. No explanation is necessary or needed which is indicated by the use of *rhéma*, utterance, instead of *lógos* (3056), intelligence spoken out. *Rhéma* stands for what God said which allows us, when we believe, to be born again. As the water cleanses our body when we bathe, so the Holy Spirit applies God's Word when we believe it unto salvation. If man believes what God has said, he is saved and he is cleansed. Eph 5:26 begins with the phrase, "That he might sanctify her [the Church]" (a.t.). This is a telic phrase meaning for the purpose of

sanctifying her. The verb *hagiásē* is in the aor. subjunctive which indicates a definitive act to be accomplished once and for all for the purpose of setting the Church apart, having cleansed her by means of the washing of water, i.e., with the Word. The verb *hagiázō* here and in many other portions of Scripture indicates the behavior of the believers who constitute the Church. Once Jesus Christ cleanses us from sin, He sets us apart to live a life of honor to the One who cleansed us.

(F) Consider 1 Thess 4:3 where sanctification is the abstention from fornication. Such must be the behavior of the believers who have been sanctified, and the behavior of every true believer toward his or her spouse. Once a person is married, he or she separates himself or herself to the one and only one to whom he or she belongs. There must be no fornication. Therefore, Paul presents here the behavior of spouses to each other as an example of how the Church ought to behave toward the Lord to whom she is married. There is absolutely nothing about water baptism in this portion of Scripture.

(G) The other Scripture where the word *loutrón* occurs is Titus 3:5. It describes how Christ saved us: "Not by works of righteousness which we have done [and in this the OT people could include circumcision as part of the works and in the NT we could include the rite of baptism without living faith in Jesus Christ], but according to his mercy he saved us, by the washing [*loutroú*] of regeneration, and renewing of the Holy Ghost." Is the washing of regeneration representative of water baptism? The word for "regeneration" is *paliggenesía* (3824), which is made up of *pálin* (3825), again, and *genesía* (1077), birthday, coming from *génesis* (1078), generation, genesis. Here Paul is not speaking of a bath or physical washing that brings new birth or regeneration to the heart of man, but a washing which is regeneration. In other words, he is saying that we were saved by Christ according to His mercy by regenerating us, which regeneration is a cleansing, a washing. Even as the body gets cleansed with water, we are cleansed by what Paul describes following the word "regeneration": "And renewing of the Holy Ghost." Without this renewing of the Holy Spirit, there could be no regeneration, and regeneration is a bath of cleansing of our total personality made up of spirit, soul, and body (1 Thess 5:23).

The word "renewing" is *anakaínōsis* (342), from the prep. *aná*, which in composition can mean again or up, and *kainós* (2537), which means qualitatively new. Therefore, the comp. verb *anakainóō* (341) means to make something or someone qualitatively new, and that new nature is due to the activity from above, even as Jesus told Nicodemus, "You must be born from above [*ánōthen* {509}]" (a.t.), which Nicodemus, however, took to mean to be born again from the womb of his mother (John 3:3, 4). Paul tells us how this birth from above makes man a qualitatively new (*kainē*) creation (2 Cor 5:17). It is a renewing by the Holy Spirit. He is the only one who can do this and no physical act of baptism has the power to change an individual from a sinner to a saint and make him a new creature.

How this regeneration is accomplished is explained further in Titus 3:6, "Which he shed on us abundantly through Jesus Christ our Savior." It is not water baptism, but Jesus Christ who does it all. And Titus 3:7 continues the claim that this is all done through Jesus Christ, "being justified by his grace." Therefore, we have here the affirmation that the word *loutrón* is not water baptism, but it is a washing of the sinner, if he or she wants to be cleansed from sin, even as water cleanses a dirty body. The Holy Spirit and the Lord Jesus Christ are the only Ones who can bring spiritual cleansing to the believing sinner. Observe how the Holy Spirit and Jesus Christ are spoken of as both active in the work of the sinner's justification and his becoming an heir of eternal life. And this is all by faith "that they which have believed in God might be careful to maintain good works" (Titus 3:8).

909. βαπτισμός *baptismós*; gen. *baptismoú*, masc. noun from *baptízō* (907), to baptize. Ceremonial washing. In Heb 9:10 the word translated "divers [various] washings," is not *baptísmata*, pl. of *báptisma*, baptism, but the pl. of *baptismós*, i.e., *baptismoí*, washings, as constituents of the rites of OT law. *Baptismós* denotes the act as a fact, and *báptisma* the result of the act; hence the former word is suitable as a designation of the institution (Mark 7:4, 8; Heb 6:2; Lev 11:32; also 11—15; Num 19). This word must not be confused with *báptisma* (908), baptism, a technical term in the NT referring to the water baptism by John the Baptist and as instituted by Christ to be administered by His disciples.

Syn.: *loutrón* (3067), a bath, metaphorically meaning the Word of God which, when believed, brings spiritual cleansing.

910. βαπτιστής *baptistḗs*; gen. *baptistoú*, masc. noun from *baptízō* (907), to baptize. A baptizer or baptist, referring to John the Baptist (Matt 3:1; 11:11, 12; 14:2, 8; 16:14; 17:13; Mark 6:24, 25; 8:28; Luke 7:20, 28, 33; 9:19). A name given to John, suggested by the function committed to and exercised by him (Matt 21:25; Mark 11:30; Luke 20:4; John 1:33).

911. βάπτω *báptō*; fut. *bápsō*. To immerse, dip, trans. (Luke 16:24 of the thing touched; John 13:26). To dye by dipping (Rev 19:13, to tinge, dye). As a comp. with the prep. *en*, in, *embáptō* (1686), to dip in (Matt 26:23; Mark 14:20; Sept.: Lev 4:6; 14:6; Num 19:18; Ruth 2:14; 2 Kgs 8:15; Job 9:31).

Deriv.: *baptízō* (907), to baptize; *embáptō* (1686), to dip in.

912. Βαραββᾶς *Barabbás*; gen. *Barabbá*, masc. proper noun transliterated from the Aramaic *bar* (1247, OT) and *'ab* (2), father, meaning son of Abba. Barabbas, a noted criminal at Jerusalem in confinement for sedition and murder when Christ was condemned (Matt 27:16, 17, 20, 21, 26; Mark 15:7, 11, 15; Luke 23:18; John 18:40). The Jews were permitted at the time of the Jewish Passover to choose a prisoner whom the Romans would release, and when the choice lay between Barabbas and Christ, they chose the robber (Matt 27:21; Mark 15:6–11; Luke 23:18; John 18:40; Acts 3:14). Pilate was anxious to save Christ, but under pressure from the Jews, he released Barabbas.

913. Βαράκ Barák; masc. proper noun transliterated from the Hebr. *Bārāk* (1301, OT), lightning. Barak, the son of Abinoam, distinguished for his share in the conquest of Sisera and the deliverance of Israel from a long and severe oppression. A history of the transaction and a copy of their sublime triumphal song are given in Judg 4, 5. Barak's was probably a contemporary of Shamgar and is mentioned as a hero of the faith in Heb 11:32.

914. Βαραχίας Barachías; gen. *Barachíou*, masc. proper noun, transliterated from the Hebr. *Berekyah* (1296), blessing of Yah. Barachias, one whom Jehovah has blessed (Matt 23:35; Zech 1:7). Barak was probably the same person as Jehoida (2 Chr 24:2, 20), as the Jews often had two names.

915. βάρβαρος bárbaros; gen. *barbárou*, masc. noun. A barbarian, i.e., a man who speaks a foreign or strange language, a foreigner (1 Cor 14:11; Sept.: Ps 114:1). The inhabitants of Melita (Malta) were called barbarians because they spoke a dialect of the Phoenician language (Acts 28:2, 4). In Rom 1:14, "to the Greeks, and to the barbarians," Paul refers to those who were not Greeks as barbarians. In Col 3:11, *bárbaros* seems to refer to those nations of the Roman Empire which did not speak Gr. such as the Jews, Romans, or Spaniards. The Greeks generally called the Romans and Jews

barbarians. The Egyptians also referred to non-Egyptians as Berbers.

916. βαρέω baréō; contracted *barṓ*, fut. *barḗsō*, from *báros* (922), weight, burden. To burden, load, weigh down. In the pass. *baréomai*, to be oppressed, weighed down, heavy, as the eyes or body with sleep (Matt 26:43; Mark 14:40; Luke 9:32; Sept.: 1 Sam 3:2). To be oppressed, burdened, weighed down with affliction or calamity (2 Cor 1:8; 5:4). To be burdened or charged with expense (1 Tim 5:16).
Deriv.: *epibaréō* (1912), to burden heavily; *katabaréō* (2599), to weigh down.
Syn.: *katanarkáō* (2655), to be burdensome with the sense of being numbed or in a stupor, to be a dead weight; *phortízō* (5412), to load up; *barúnō* (925), to burden.

917. βαρέως baréōs; adv. from *barús* (926), heavy. Heavily, dully, metaphorically with difficulty (Matt 13:15; Acts 28:27 quoted from Isa 6:10; Sept.: Gen 31:35).

918. Βαρθολομαῖος Bartholomaíos; gen. *Bartholomaíou*, masc. proper noun transliterated from the Aramaic *bar* (1247, OT) and *talmay* (8526, OT), Tolmai, meaning ridged. Bartholomew, meaning son of Tolmai. He is supposed to be the same person elsewhere called Nathanael. This conjecture rests in part upon the fact that Philip and Nathanael are associated together by John, and in the parallel passages of the other evangelists Philip and Bartholomew are associated; and further, that Bartholomew is not mentioned in John's list of the Twelve, nor is Nathanael in the list of the other evangelists. It is therefore very likely that he bore two names as many others did. We know nothing of his history except for the fact of his conversion (John 1:45–51) and his presence on the Lake of Tiberias where the risen Lord appeared to him and other disciples (John 21:2). See also

Matt 10:3; Mark 3:18; Luke 6:14; Acts 1:13.

919. Βάρ-ιησοῦς *Bar-iēsoús*, Βαριησοῦς *Bariēsoús*; gen. *Bar-iēsoú*, masc. proper noun, transliterated from the Aramaic *bar* (1247, OT) and *yᵉhōwshūwa'* (3091, OT), Joshua, meaning Jehovah-saved. Bar-jesus, meaning son of Joshua, a magician who resided with Sergius Paulus at Paphos on the island of Cyprus when Paul and Barnabas were there (Acts 13:6), also known by his Arabic designation of Elymas the magician. Sergius Paulus was an officer of high rank under the Roman government and was anxious to receive religious instruction from the two missionaries. But Bar-jesus, seeing that his occupation and influence would cease wherever the light of the gospel should come, opposed Paul and tried to dissuade Paulus from giving heed to his preaching. Paul gave him a severe reproof, immediately after which the wicked man was struck with temporary blindness as a rebuke from God.

920. Βάρ-ιωνᾶς *Bar-iōnás*, Βαριωνᾶ *Bariōná*; gen. *Bariōná*, masc. proper noun transliterated from the Aramaic *bar* (1247, OT) and *yōnāh* (3124, OT), Jonah, meaning a dove. Bar-jonas, meaning son of Jonas or Jonah, used in Matt 16:17 for Peter.

921. Βαρνάβας *Barnábas*, masc. proper noun transliterated from the Aramaic *bar* (1247, OT) and *nᵉbīy'* (5029, OT), Nabas, meaning prophet, consolation. Barnabas, meaning son of consolation. A Levite of Cyprus and an early convert to the Christian faith (Acts 4:36). His original name was Joses, but he derived his unusual title from his remarkable powers of exhorting the people and ministering consolation to the afflicted (Acts 4:36). Barnabas was one of those who gave up all their worldly substance and all their strength and influence to the support and spread of the gospel. He introduced Paul to the disciples on the latter's visit to

Jerusalem, three years after his conversion (Acts 9:27). Afterward he brought Paul from Tarsus to Antioch, and they labored together for two years with great success (Acts 11:22, 25, 30; 12:25; 13:1, 2, 7, 43, 46, 50; 14:12, 14, 20; 1 Cor 9:6). They attended together the Council of Jerusalem (Acts 15:2, 12, 22, 25, 35–37, 39; Gal 2:1, 9, 13). After-ward they separated and Barnabas went on an independent missionary tour with Mark (Acts 15). Some ascribe to him the Epistle to the Hebrews. We have under his name an epistle which is not included in the Canon.

922. βάρος *báros*; gen. *bárous*. Burdensome, weight in reference to its pressure, burden, load (Matt 20:12, where "the burden . . . of the day" means the heavy labor of the day). Used in Acts 15:28; Rev 2:24 to designate precepts which are burdensome to observe; to indicate sinful conduct and its consequences resulting in trouble and sorrow (Gal 6:2); in a pecuniary sense (1 Thess 2:6) meaning to be burdensome. In 2 Cor 4:17 "eternal weight [*báros*] of glory," here "weight" refers to greatness, abundance, fullness.

Deriv.: *abarḗs* (4), not burdensome; *baréō* (916), to weigh down.

Syn.: *phortíon* (5413), freight, load, something to be merely borne without reference to its weight in contrast to *báros* which always suggests that which is heavy or burdensome; *phortós* (5414), the cargo of a ship; *gómos* (1117), signifying full, e.g., the freight of a ship.

923. Βαρσαβᾶς *Barsabás*; gen. *Barsabá*, masc. noun transliterated from the Aramaic *bar* (1247, OT) and *tsᵉbā'* (6633, OT), Saba, meaning to summon. Barsabas, meaning son of Saba, the name of two men.

(I) Joseph Barsabas, surnamed Justus, was one of the two candidates for the vacancy in the apostleship occasioned by the defection of Judas (Acts 1:23). Some identify him with Joses Barnabas, the companion of Paul (Acts 4:36).

(II) Judas Barsabas (Acts 15:22) who was appointed to accompany Paul and Barnabas from Jerusalem to Antioch on an important mission. He is called one of the "chief men among the brethren," but is otherwise unknown. Some commentators infer from the surname that he was a brother of Joseph Barsabas.

924. Βαρτίμαιος *Bartímaios*; gen. *Bartimaíou*, masc. proper noun transliterated from the Aramaic *bar* (1247, OT) and *tāmē'* (2931, OT), unclean, defiled. Bartimaeus, meaning son of Timaeus, who was instantly cured of blindness by the Lord in the vicinity of Jericho (Mark 10:46).

925. βαρύνω *barúnō*; fut. *barunó*, from *barús* (926), heavy. To be heavy, used only in Luke 21:34 in the aor. pass. *ebarúnthēn*. Metaphorically, to be oppressed, dull, stupid.
   Syn.: *baréō* (916), to burden.
   Ant.: *kouphízō* (2893), to unload, lighten; *kenóō* (2758), to make empty.

926. βαρύς *barús*; fem. *bareía*, neut. *barú*. Burdensome, in the pl. heavy burdens, spoken metaphorically of burdensome precepts (Matt 23:4; see Sept.: 2 Chr 10:4, 11; Ps 38:4). Weighty, i.e., important (Matt 23:23 [cf. Acts 25:7 where it means not trivial but severe]; see Sept.: Dan 2:11). In 2 Cor 10:10 a "weighty" epistle means not to be made light of, stern, severe. Grievous, meaning oppressive, hard to be borne, referring to precepts (1 John 5:3; Sept.: Neh 5:18). In the sense of being afflictive, violent (Acts 20:29, "fierce wolves").
   Deriv.: *baréōs* (917), heavily; *barúnō* (925), to load heavily, overcharge; *barútimos* (927), very precious.
   Syn.: *dusbástaktos* (1419), heavy, oppressive.
   Ant.: *elaphrós* (1645), light.

927. βαρύτιμος *barútimos*; gen. *barutímou*, masc.-fem., neut. *barútimon*, adj. from *barús* (926), heavy, and *timé*

(5092), value, price. Of great price, very precious or valuable (Matt 26:7).
   Syn.: *tímios* (5093), valuable; *áxios* (514), worthy.
   Ant.: *anáxios* (370), unworthy; *átimos* (820), dishonor, without (attributed) value.

928. βασανίζω *basanízō*; fut. *basanísō* from *básanos* (931), an examination by torture, torment. To torture, afflict with pain, vex, harass (2 Pet 2:8); used metaphorically meaning to examine, scrutinize, either by words or physical torment (Rev 9:5); vex physically with toil (Mark 6:48); of a vessel tossed by the waves (Matt 14:24); spoken of disease (Matt 8:6); of the pains of giving birth (Rev 12:2); of punishment (Matt 8:29; Mark 5:7; Luke 8:28; Rev 11:10 [see also Rev 11:6; 14:10; 20:10]).
   Deriv.: *basanismós* (929), torment; *basanistés* (930), tormentor.
   Syn.: *kakouchéō* (2558), to treat in an evil manner; *odunáō* (3600), to be in anguish; *tumpanízō* (5178), literally to beat a drum, hence to torture by beating; *talaipōréō* (5003), to cause misery; *timōréō* (5097), to punish; *paideúō* (3811), to chasten; *kataponéō* (2669), to oppress; *aganaktéō* (23), to be indignant; *lumaínomai* (3075), to insult, mistreat, make havoc of; *mastízō* (3147), to scourge; *dérō* (1194), to thrash, smite; *páschō* (3958), to suffer, vex; *hupophérō* (5297), literally to bear from underneath, endure; *dokimázō* (1381), to test; *cheimázomai* (5492), to be tossed with tempest; *kakopathéō* (2553), to endure affliction; *aganaktéō* (23), to be indignant; *pnígō* (4155), to choke, strangle, drown; *enochléō* (1776), to crowd in, to annoy, trouble; *tarássō* (5015), to agitate.
   Ant.: *eunoéō* (2132), to be well minded, agreeable; *euthuméō* (2114), to cheer up; *eupsuchéō* (2174), to be of good comfort.

929. βασανισμός *basanismós*; gen. *basanismoú*, masc. noun from *basanízō* (928), to vex, torture. Examination, especially by torture; a torture, torment (Rev 14:11). Referring to the torture of smoke, meaning the smoke of the fire in which one is tormented (Rev 18:7, 10, 15).

Syn.: *odúnē* (3601), grief, sorrow; *ōdín* (5604), a pang of childbirth; *dokimḗ* (1382), proof, trial; *talaipōría* (5004), wretchedness, calamity, misery; *paideía* (3809), chastening; *páthēma* (3804), hardship, pain, suffering; *stenochōría* (4730), anguish, distress; *báros* (922), burden; *phortíon* (5413), freight, burden.

Ant.: *heortḗ* (1859), feast; *sumpósion* (4849), a drinking party; *panḗguris* (3831), festal gathering.

930. βασανιστής basanistḗs; gen. *basanistoú*, masc. noun from *basanízō* (928), to vex, torture. One who applies torture, an inquisitor. In the NT a prison keeper, jailer (Matt 18:34).

Syn.: *desmophúlax* (1200), a prison keeper; *túrannos* (5181), tyrant.

Ant.: *euergétēs* (2110), benefactor.

931. βάσανος básanos; gen. *basánou*, fem. noun. A touchstone, a black siliceous stone used to test the purity of gold, silver and other metals, hence any test or criterion by which the qualities of a thing are tried. Metaphorically meaning instrument of torture by which one is forced to divulge the truth, examination, trial by torture. In the NT, torment, pain from disease (Matt 4:24; Sept.: Ezek 12:18); also used of punishment (Luke 16:23, 28).

Syn.: *basanismós* (929), torture; *élegchos* (1650), reproof; *dokimḗ* (1382), proof, trial; *talaipōría* (5004), calamity; *kákōsis* (2561), maltreatment; *paideía* (3809), chastisement; *kakopátheia* (2552), hardship; *martúrion* (3142), martyrdom.

Ant.: *makarismós* (3108), blessedness; *eudokía* (2107), good pleasure; *euergesía* (2108), beneficence.

932. βασιλεία basileía; gen. *basileías*, fem. noun from *basileús* (935), king.

Royal dominion, kingdom (Matt 4:8). *Basileía tṓn ouranṓn* "the kingdom of heaven" or of the heavens, a phrase peculiar to Matthew (Matt 3:2; 4:17; 5:3, 10, 19, 20; 7:21; 8:11; 10:7; 11:11, 12; 13:11, 24, 31, 33, 44, 45, 47, 52; 16:19; 18:1, 3, 4, 23; 19:12, 14, 23; 20:1; 22:2; 23:14; 25:1) for which the other evangelists use *basileía toú Theoú*, "the kingdom of God" (Mark 1:15; 4:11, 26, 30; 9:1, 47; 10:14, 15, 23–25; 12:34; 14:25; 15:43; Luke 4:43; 6:20; 7:28; 8:1, 10; 9:2, 11, 27, 60, 62; 10:9; 11:20; 13:18, 20, 28, 29; 14:15; 16:16; 17:20, 21; 18:16, 17, 24, 25, 29; 19:11; 21:31; 22:16, 18; 23:51; John 3:3, 5), which Matthew also uses in 12:28; 19:24; 21:31, 43. Essentially the two terms mean the same and are interchangeable (Matt 19:23, 24). Spiritually the kingdom of God is within the human heart (Luke 17:21). Both expressions also refer to the prophecies of Dan 2:44; 7:13f. and denote the everlasting kingdom which God the Father will give to Christ the Son, namely, the spiritual and eternal kingdom which is to subsist first in more imperfect circumstances on earth, but afterwards will appear complete in the world of glory (Matt 25:31ff.; Mark 13:26f.; Luke 21:27f,). In some verses the kingdom of heaven more particularly signifies God's rule within us while we are on this earth (Matt 13:41, 47; 20:1); at other times it indicates only the state of glory (1 Cor 6:9, 10; 15:50; Gal 5:21).

(I) Dominion, reign, the exercise of kingly power (Matt 6:13; Luke 1:33; 19:12, 15; Heb 1:8; Rev 17:12, 17, 18; Sept.: 1 Sam 10:16, 25; 13:13; 28:17). In Rev 1:6, the TR has *basileís* (935), kings.

(II) Dominions, realm, i.e., a people in a territory under kingly rule (Matt 4:8; 12:25, 26; 24:7; Mark 3:24; 6:23; 13:8; Luke 4:5; 11:17, 18; 21:10; Heb 11:33; Rev 11:15; 16:10; Sept.: Gen 10:10; Num 32:33; Josh 11:10; Esth 2:3).

(III) The phrases *hē basileía toú Theoú* (2316), "the kingdom of God" (Matt 6:33; Mark 1:15; Luke 4:43; 6:20; John

3:5); "his kingdom," referring to Christ (Matt 13:41 [cf. 20:21]); "the kingdom of our father David" (Mark 11:10); "the kingdom of Christ and of God" (Eph 5:5); "the kingdom . . . of Jesus Christ" (Rev 1:9); "heavenly kingdom" (2 Tim 4:18); and *he basileía*, "the kingdom" (Matt 8:12; 9:35) are all syn. in the NT and mean the divine spiritual kingdom, the glorious reign of the Messiah. The idea of the kingdom has its basis in the prophecies of the OT where the coming of the Messiah and His triumphs are foretold (e.g., Ps 2; 110; Isa 2:1–4; 11:1ff.; Jer 23:5ff.; 31:31ff.; 32:37ff.; 33:14ff.; Ezek 34:23ff.; 37:24ff.; Mic 4:1ff., and especially Dan 2:44; 7:14, 27; 9:25ff.). His reign is described as a golden age when true righteousness will be established, and with it the theocracy will be established bringing peace and happiness. Prior to the visible manifestation of this kingdom and its extension to the material and natural realms of the world, it exists spiritually in the hearts of men, and thus it was understood by Zacharias (Luke 1:67ff.); Simeon (Luke 2:25ff.); Anna (Luke 2:36ff.); Joseph (Luke 23:50, 51).

The Jews, however, generally gave to these prophecies a temporal meaning and expected a Messiah who should come in the clouds of heaven. As king of the Jewish people, He was expected to restore the ancient Jewish religion and worship, reform the corrupt morals of the people, make expiation for their sins, give freedom from the yoke of foreign dominion, and at length reign over the whole earth in peace and glory.

The concept of the kingdom in the OT is partly fulfilled in the NT. First we have the Christian dispensation. The kingdom of heaven or God on earth, consisting of the community of those who receive Jesus as their Savior, and who, through the Holy Spirit, form His Church with Him as its head. This spiritual kingdom has both an internal and external form. As internal, it already exists and rules in the hearts of all Christians and is therefore present. As

external, it is either embodied both in the visible and invisible Church, and thus is present and progressive; or it is to be perfected in the coming of the Son of Man to judge and reign in bliss and glory. This is the further realization of the kingdom of God in the future.

However, these different aspects are not always distinguished. The expression often embraces both the internal and external kingdom and refers both to its commencement in this world and its completion in the world to come. Hence, in the NT we find it spoken about in the Jewish temporal sense by Jews and the Apostles before the day of Pentecost (Matt 18:1; 20:21; Luke 17:20; 19:11; Acts 1:6); in the Christian sense as announced by John, where perhaps something of the Jewish view was intermingled (Matt 3:2 [cf. Luke 23:51]); as announced by Jesus and others (Matt 4:17, 23; 9:35; 10:7; Mark 1:14, 15; Luke 10:9, 11; Acts 28:31); in the internal spiritual sense (Rom 14:17, "For the kingdom of God is not meat and drink; but righteousness, and peace, and joy in the Holy Ghost." See also Matt 6:33; Mark 10:15; Luke 17:21; 18:17; John 3:3, 5; 1 Cor 4:20); in the external sense, i.e., as embodied in the visible church and the universal spread of the gospel (Matt 6:10; 12:28; 13:24, 31, 33, 44, 47; 16:28; Mark 4:30; 11:10; Luke 13:18, 20; Acts 19:8); as perfected in the future world (Matt 13:43; 16:19; 26:29; Mark 14:25; Luke 22:29, 30; 2 Pet 1:11; Rev 12:10). In this latter view it denotes especially the bliss of heaven which is to be enjoyed in the Redeemer's kingdom, i.e., eternal life (Matt 8:11; 25:34; Mark 9:47; Luke 13:28, 29; Acts 14:22; 1 Cor 6:9, 10; 15:50; Gal 5:21; Eph 5:5; 2 Thess 1:5; 2 Tim 4:18; Heb 12:28; James 2:5). The kingdom spoken of generally (Matt 5:19). In Matt 8:12, "the sons of the kingdom" (a.t.) means the Jews who thought that the Messiah's reign was destined only for them and that by ancestry alone, which claimed belief in the God of Abraham, they had the right to be called the sons of the kingdom (John 8:33, 37, 39).

However, "the children of the kingdom" in Matt 13:38 are the true citizens of the kingdom of God. See also Matt 11:11, 12; 13:11, 19, 44, 45, 52; 18:4, 23; 19:12, 24; 20:1. Spoken also generally of the privileges and rewards of the divine kingdom, both here and hereafter (Matt 5:3, 10, 20; 7:21; 18:3; Col 1:13; 1 Thess 2:12).

Syn.: *hēgemonía* (2231), reign; *thrónos* (2362), throne, and by implication the power that the throne represents, kingdom; *aulḗ* (833), palace, as standing for kingdom; *krátos* (2904), dominion; *archḗ* (746), rule; *exousía* (1849), authority.

933. βασίλειον *basíleion*; gen. *basileíou*, neut. of *basíleios* (934), royal, used as a subst. with the neut. sing. art. *tó basíleion* pl. *tá basíleia*. Used only in Luke 7:25 in the pl. as a subst. meaning royal houses, palaces (Sept. pl.: Esth 1:9; 2:13; Nah 2:6; sing.: Prov 18:19).

Syn.: *aulḗ* (833), palace.

934. βασίλειος *basíleios*; gen. *basileíou*, masc.-fem., neut. *basíleion*, adj. Royal, belonging to, appointed, suitable for the king. "Royal priesthood" (*basíleion*, neut. in 1 Pet 2:9 quoted from Ex 19:6) suggests a priesthood called to royal dominion or clothed with royal dignity, i.e., in a distinguished manner (see Rev 1:6).

Syn.: *baslikós* (937), royal.

935. βασιλεύς *basileús*; masc. noun. A king, monarch.

(I) Of David (Matt 1:6; Acts 13:22); of Pharaoh (Acts 7:10, 18; Heb 11:23, 27); of the Roman emperor (John 19:15); of ancient Jewish kings (Luke 10:24); of Jesus as the Messiah who is often called King, King of Israel or of the Jews (Matt 2:2; 21:5; 25:34, 40; Luke 19:38; John 1:49; 12:13, 15; Sept.: Ps 2:6); spoken of God (1 Tim 1:17; 6:15; Rev 15:3; 17:14, "King of kings" by way of emphasis; Sept.: Ps 5:2; 29:10; 47:2; 95:3). "The city of the great King" (Matt 5:35) means of God, Jerusalem as the seat of His worship (Ps 47:2).

(II) In a more general and lower sense, as a title of distinguished honor, e.g., viceroy, prince, leader, chief. Herod the Great and his successors had the title of king, but were dependent for the name and power on the Romans (Matt 2:1, 3, 9; Luke 1:5; Acts 12:1; 25:13ff.; 26:2ff.), and Herod Antipas was in fact only a tetrarch, meaning ruler of only a fourth of the kingdom (Matt 14:1; Luke 3:1, 19; 9:7), though he is called "king" in Matt 14:9; Mark 6:14. See also Aretas, king of Arabia, Petraea (2 Cor 11:32). Also used when joined with *hēgemónes* (2232), leaders, rulers (Matt 10:18; Mark 13:9; Luke 21:12; Sept.: Ps 2:2; 102:15). Generally (Matt 17:25; 18:23; Acts 9:15; 1 Tim 2:2; 1 Pet 2:13, 17; Rev 9:11). Figuratively spoken of Christians as about to reign with the Messiah over the nations (Rev 1:6 [{TR} cf. 5:10; 20:6]).

Deriv.: *basileía* (932), kingdom; *basíleios* (934), royal, kingly in nature; *basileúō* (936), to reign; *basilikós* (937), belonging to a king, such as a courtier or something kingly; *basílissa* (938), queen.

Syn.: *árchōn* (758), ruler; *politárchēs* (4173), ruler of a city; *despótēs* (1203), despot, an absolute ruler; *kúrios* (2962), lord; *pantokrátōr* (3841), the all-ruling, almighty, omnipotent; *hēgemṓn* (2232), a leader, ruler, governor; *Kaísar* (2541), Caesar, a title of the Roman emperor; *dunástēs* (1413), mighty potentate.

Ant.: *idiṓtēs* (2399), private person, also means ignorant, rude, unlearned in the proper context; *polítēs* (4177), a citizen.

936. βασιλεύω *basileúō*; fut. *basileúsō*, from *basileús* (935), a king. To reign, rule, be king, intrans. (Matt 2:22; Luke 1:33 of the Messiah; 19:14, 27; 1 Cor 4:8, to enjoy the honor and prosperity of kings; 1 Tim 6:15; Sept.: Judg 9:8, 10; 1 Sam 8:9, 11). Applied to God (Rev 11:15, 17; 19:6; Ps 93:1; 96:10; 97:1; 99:1); to Christ (1 Cor 15:25); those who belong to Christ (Rev 5:10; 20:4, 6; 22:5). Paul's usage: to reign or have predominance (Rom 5:14, 17, 21; 6:12).

Deriv.: *sumbasileúō* (4821), to reign with someone.

Syn.: *huperéchō* (5242), to hold oneself above, be superior; *proéchō* (4284), to excel; *diakrínomai* (1252), to distinguish oneself as superior; *prōteúō* (4409), to have preeminence; *kurieúō* (2961), to exercise lordship, have dominion over; *árchō* (757), to reign, rule over; *sumbasileúō* (4821), to reign together; *hēgéomai* (2233), to rule over; *hēgemoneúō* (2230), to act as a ruler.

Ant.: *husteréō* (5302), to be inferior; *hupoleípomai* (5275), to leave under; *hupobállō* (5260), to throw under; *aphanízomai* (853), to vanish away; *hupotássomai* (5293), to obey, to subject oneself in an orderly fashion.

937. βασιλικός basilikós; fem. *basilikḗ*, neut. *basilikón*, adj. from *basileús* (935), king. Kingly, belonging to a king (Acts 12:20, a territory; John 4:46, 49, a nobleman, a person attached to a court; Sept.: Num 20:17; 21:22; 2 Sam 14:26; Esth 8:15). Befitting a king, of kingly dignity (Acts 12:21, a robe; James 2:8, noble, excellent, preeminent, referring to law).

Syn.: *basíleios* (934), royal.

938. βασίλισσα basílissa; gen. *basilíssēs*, fem. noun from *basileús* (935), king. A queen (Matt 12:42; Luke 11:31; Acts 8:27; Rev 18:7; Sept.: 1 Kgs 10:1; Esth 1:9, 11, 12, 15–17).

939. βάσις básis; gen. *báseōs*, fem. noun from *baínō* (n.f., see *apobaínō* [576]), to go, tread. A basis, base or foundation from its steadiness (Sept.: Ex 30:18). The sole of the foot, or in a more general meaning, the foot of a man, which is, as it were, the basis on which he stands or goes (Acts 3:7).

Deriv.: *bastázō* (941), to take up, bear.

Syn.: *poús* (4228), foot; *kathédra* (2515), bench, seat, as something which is stationary; *thrónos* (2362), seat, throne,

as something immovable; *hupóstasis* (5287), substance; *édaphos* (1475), a basis, ground; *themélios* (2310), substructure, foundation.

940. βασκαίνω baskaínō; fut. *baskanō*. To bewitch as with the eye, to cast an evil eye. A Greek commentator on the work of the poet Theocritus observes that the noun *báskanos* means one who with his eyes kills or destroys. Superstitious people believed that great harm might result from the "evil eye" or from being looked upon with envious and malicious stares. *Baskaínō* and its deriv. are frequently used in the Class. Gr. authors for envy, and the Sept. and Apocryphal writers apply the words with the same meaning. In the NT, it means to utter foolish babble, i.e., to mislead by pretenses as if by magic arts, to bewitch (Gal 3:1).

Syn.: *exístēmi* (1839), translated "bewitch" in Acts 8:9, but really meaning to confuse, amaze; *mageúō* (3096), to practice magic, use sorcery.

941. βαστάζω bastázō; fut. *bastásō*, from *básis* (939), basis, foot. To raise upon a basis, to support. In the NT, generally it means to take up and hold, to bear.

(I) Trans.: to take up and hold, especially in the hands (John 10:31). To take up and bear, take up and bear away or take away (John 20:15; Acts 21:35). To take upon oneself and bear (Matt 8:17, sickness, relating to Isa 53:4).

(II) To bear, carry in the hands or on the shoulders (Matt 3:11, "whose shoes I am not worthy to bear," which was the duty of a servant; Mark 14:13; Luke 22:10, "a pitcher of water"). Luke 14:27; John 19:17 refer to carrying the cross. See also Luke 7:14; John 12:6; Acts 3:2; 15:10; Gal 6:5; Rev 17:7. In Acts 9:15, "to bear my name" means to announce, publish. Used in Rom 11:18 in the sense of to bear up, support. Metaphorically it means to bear, support, endure, i.e., labors, sufferings (Matt 20:12, burden or weight, implied in Rev 2:3). The punishment incurred by being foolish (Gal 5:10). To bear patiently (Rom 15:1; Gal 6:2; Rev 2:2). Metaphorically in the sense of to receive, understand (John 16:12).

(III) To bear or carry about as attached to one's person (Acts 15:10; Gal 6:17) as a syn. to *hupéchō* (5254), to endure with patience (Luke 11:27, "the womb which bore thee" [a.t.]). In the sense of to wear for which Class. Gr. writers use *phoréō* (5409), to bear, wear (Luke 10:4).

Deriv.: *dusbástaktos* (1419), hard to be borne, oppressive.

Syn.: *hupophérō* (5297), to endure; *tropophoréō* (5159), to endure the manners of someone; *aírō* (142), to raise up, to lift and carry away; *anéchomai* (430), to tolerate, forbear; *stērízō* (4741), to strengthen, steady; *epistērízō* (1991), to support further, strengthen, confirm; *themelióō* (2311), to lay a basis, foundation; *phérō* (5342), to carry, bear.

Ant.: *kinéō* (2795), to move; *metakinéō* (3334), to move something away; *seíō* (4579), to shake; *saleúō* (4531), to stir up, render insecure; *saínō* (4525), to wag the tail, shake, disturb; *anaseíō* (383), to shake to and fro.

942. βάτος *bátos*; gen. *bátou*, fem. noun. A thornbush or bramble (Mark 12:26; Luke 6:44; 20:37; Acts 7:30, 35; Sept.: Ex 3:2–4; Deut 33:16).

943. βάτος *bátos*; gen. *bátou*, pl. *bátoi*, masc. noun. A bath which is a Jewish measure for wine and oil equal to the ephah for dry measure (Luke 16:6). According to Josephus (Antiquities 8.2.9.) it contained 72 *xéstai* or *sextárii*; but the *sextárius*, which at Rome was equal to 1.5 pints and would thus make the bath equal to 13.5 gallons, varied much in different places. The more usual estimate for the capacity of the bath is 7.5 or 9 gallons. See *kóros* (2884), a measure equal to 10 baths (*bátoi*) or ephahs (cf. 1 Kgs 7:26, 38; Ezek 45:10, 11, 14).

944. βάτραχος *bátrachos*; gen. *batráchou*, masc. noun. A frog (Rev 16:13; Sept.: Ps 78:45; 105:30).

945. βαττολογέω *battologéō*; contracted *battologṓ*, fut. *battologḗsō*, from *báttos* (n.f.), a proverbial stammerer, and *lógos* (3056), word. To speak foolishly, babble, chatter (see Lev 5:4; Job 11:2, 3; Isa 16:6; 44:25). Not to be confused with *battarízō*, to stutter. Characterizes *polulogía* (4180), wordiness. Much talk without content, repeating the same thing over and over again (Matt 6:7), useless speaking without distinct expression of purpose as contrasted to succinct, knowledgeable speech, thus foolish speaking or indiscrete vowing in prayer.

Syn.: *phluaréō* (5396), to be a babbler; *phlúaros* (5397), to be a tattler or one who talks unnecessarily and too much; *mōrología* (3473), foolish talking.

946. βδέλυγμα *bdélugma*; gen. *bdelúgmatos*, neut. noun from *bdelússō* (948), to emit a foul odor, to turn away through loathing or disgust, abhor. Abomination.

(I) Generally that which is detestable to God (Luke 16:15; Sept.: Prov 11:1; 15:8, 9; 20:23; 21:27).

(II) That which was unclean in the Jewish tradition and especially of impure idol worship; hence, idolatry, licentiousness, abominable impurity (Rev 17:4, 5; 21:27; Sept.: 2 Kgs 16:3; 21:2 [cf. Lev 18:22; also Lev 11:10, 12, 13; Jer 11:15]).

(III) In connection with (II) is the expression "the abomination of desolation" (*to bdélugma tḗs erēmṓseōs* [2050], desolation, spoliation, desolation, emptying out). This expression is found in the Olivet Discourse of our Lord (Matt 24:15; Mark 13:14) in connection with the Second Coming of the Lord. In Luke 21:20, only the word *erḗmōsis*, desolation as referring to Jerusalem, is mentioned, but it refers to the same event. This destruction of Jerusalem is associated with the desecration of the temple and the forsaking of it by the Jews. The destruction was foretold by the Lord in Matt 24:2; Mark 13:2; Luke 21:6. There is a historical fulfillment of the destruction of Jerusalem and the temple in A.D. 70 by the Roman legions under Titus. This destruction, however, was a mere forerunner to the destruction that is yet future and associated by our Lord with His *parousía* (3952), His coming presence (Matt 24:3). This destruction of Jerusalem and the abomination of the temple are also connected with "the consummation of the age" (*suntéleia* [4930], entire completion or consummation; *toú aiṓnos* [165], age, a period of time). See the word *suntéleia* which refers to the consummation or the end of this dispensation of grace or the dispensation of the Church for further elucidation. Such destruction of Jerusalem and the abomination of desolation in regard to the temple in Jerusalem in relation to the Second Coming and the consummation of this dispensation of grace have not yet occurred. It is connected furthermore with the Antichrist (1 John 2:18, 22; 2 John 1:7) or as Paul calls him in 2 Thess 2:3, "the man of sin, the son of perdition." He is associated in 2 Thess 2:1 with the coming of the Lord. This Antichrist or "the man of sin" in prophecy is called the "little horn" (Dan 7:8; 8:9); "a king of fierce countenance" (Dan 8:23); the Roman "prince" (Dan 9:26); the willful king (Dan 11:36). In connection with the destruction of Jerusalem, the abomination of desolation of the temple and the coming of the Lord are also connected very clearly. A period of tribulation as the world has never known is described in Matt 24:6–28; Mark 13:5–27; Luke 21:8–28. That such a period of tribulation has never visited this earth is made clear by the words of the Lord Jesus, "For then shall be great tribulation, such as was not since the beginning of the world to this time, no, nor ever shall be" (Matt 24:21; Mark 13:19). It is evident that our Lord taught that immediately after such tribulation there will be events that our world has never yet seen

and will see only once: "Immediately after the tribulation of those days shall the sun be darkened, and the moon shall not give her light, and the stars shall fall from heaven, and the powers of the heavens shall be shaken" (Matt 24:29; Mark 13:24, 25; Luke 21:25, 26). It is clear, therefore, that although there has been a destruction of Jerusalem and a desolation of the temple, yet there is going to be another one in connection with the Second Coming of the Lord, the appearance of the Antichrist, the Great Tribulation period, and the great unprecedented and once-and-for-all events that are to ensue in the heavenly bodies.

Ant.: *hagiótēs* (41), sanctity, holiness; *hagiōsúnē* (42), sacredness; *theiótēs* (2305), divinity; *hosiótēs* (3742), piety, ceremonial holiness.

947. βδελυκτός *bdeluktós*; fem. *bdeluktḗ*, neut. *bdeluktón* adj. from *bdelússō* (948), to abominate. Abominable, detestable (Titus 1:16; Sept.: Prov 17:15). That which is an abomination to God. Does not occur in Class. Gr.

Syn.: *anósios* (462), unholy; *bébēlos* (952), wicked, profane; *theostugḗs* (2319), impious, hater of God; *stugnētós* (4767), odious.

Ant.: *hierós* (2413), holy, sacred; *hágios* (40), holy; *hósios* (3741), sacred; *tímios* (5093), honorable.

948. βδελύσσω *bdelússō*; mid. *bdelússomai*, to render foul, from *bdéō* (n.f.), to stink. To cause to be abhorred, to turn oneself away from a stench, to feel disgust, detest (Rom 2:22; Rev 21:8, polluted with crimes; Sept.: Lev 26:11; Deut 23:7; Amos 5:10). In the perf. pass. part. *ebdelugménos*, abominable, detestable, i.e., polluted with crimes (Sept.: Lev 18:30; Job 15:16; Prov 8:7; Isa 14:19; Hos 9:10).

Deriv.: *bdélugma* (946), an abomination; *bdeluktós* (947), abominable.

Syn.: *apostréphō* (654), to turn away.

Ant.: *sumpathéō* (4834), to sympathize; *hēlkúō* (1670), to attract.

949. βέβαιος *bébaios*; fem. *bebaía*, neut. *bébaion*, firm, adj. from *baínō* (n.f., see *apobaínō* [576]), to go. Fixed, sure, certain. Figuratively that upon which one may build, rely, or trust (see Rom 4:16; 2 Cor 1:7; Heb 2:2; 3:6, 14; 9:17; 2 Pet 1:10, 19). In the NT not used of persons but objects (Heb 6:19), that which does not fail or waver, immovable, and on which one may rely.

Deriv.: *bebaióō* (950), to establish.

Syn.: *alēthés* (227), true; *asphalḗs* (804), safe, sure; *pistós* (4103), faithful, trustworthy; *hedraíos* (1476), steadfast, equivalent to *stereós* (4731), fast, firm, hard.

Ant.: *ádēlos* (82), uncertain; *astḗriktos* (793), unstable; *akatástatos* (184), unstable.

950. βεβαιόω *bebaióō*; contracted *bebaiṓ*, fut. *bebaiṓsō*, from *bébaios* (949), sure, fixed. To make firm or reliable so as to warrant security and inspire confidence, to strengthen, make true, fulfill (Mark 16:20; Rom 15:8; 1 Cor 1:6; Heb 2:3). In the NT used with or without the personal obj. and signifying the confirmation of a person's salvation, preservation in a state of grace (1 Cor 1:8; 2 Cor 1:21; Col 2:7; Heb 13:9; Sept.: Ps 41:13; 119:28).

Deriv.: *bebaíōsis* (951), confirmation; *diabebaióomai* (1226), to make firm.

Syn.: *stērízō* (4741), to set steadfastly; *epistērízō* (1991), to strengthen; *kuróō* (2964), to make valid, ratify; *stereóō* (4732), to make firm; *marturéō* (3140), to testify; *dēlóō* (1213), to declare; *apodeíknumi* (584), to prove.

Ant.: *distázō* (1365), to waver, doubt; *exístēmi* (1839), to wonder; *aporéō* (639), to be at a loss, perplexed; *diaporéō* (1280), to be thoroughly perplexed.

951. βεβαίωσις *bebaíōsis*; gen. *bebaiṓseōs*, fem. noun from *bebaióō* (950), to establish. Ratification, confirmation, corroboration (Phil 1:7; Heb 6:16).

Syn.: *stērigmós* (4740), stability; *aspháleia* (803), certainty, safety; *pepoíthēsis* (4006), confidence, trust; *apódeixis* (585), manifestation; *plērophoría* (4136), entire confidence, assurance.

Ant.: *adēlótēs* (83), uncertainty; *apistía* (570), unfaithfulness, disbelief; *hupónoia* (5283), suspicion; *mustḗrion* (3466), a mystery; *aporía* (640), quandary, perplexity; *súgchusis* (4799), confusion.

952. βέβηλος *bébēlos*; gen. *bebḗlou*, masc.-fem., neut. *bébēlon*, adj. from *baínō* (n.f., see *apobaínō* [576]), to go, and *bēlós* (n.f.), a threshold, particularly of a temple, so that *bébēlos* properly denoted one who either was or ought to have been debarred from the threshold or entrance of a temple. Unhallowed, the opposite of *hierós* (2413), sacred (1 Tim 4:7; 6:20; 2 Tim 2:16). Profane, void of religion or piety (Sept.: Lev 10:10; 1 Sam 21:4, 5; Ezek 22:26). Applied to persons (1 Tim 1:9; Heb 12:16; Sept.: Ezek 21:25). *Bébēlos* lacks all relationship or affinity to God.

Deriv.: *bebēlóō* (953), to profane, pollute.

Syn.: *anósios* (462), unholy; *theostugḗs* (2319), hateful to God, impious.

Ant.: *hágios* (40), holy; *theíos* (2304), divine; *hósios* (3741), sacred, holy; *tímios* (5093), honorable.

953. βεβηλόω *bebēlóō* or *bebēlṓ*; fut. *bebēlṓsō*, from *bébēlos* (952), profane. To profane, to cross the threshold (Matt 12:5; Acts 24:6, Sept.: Ex 31:14; Lev 19:8, 12; Ezek 43:7, 8).

Syn.: *miaínō* (3392), to taint, contaminate, defile; *molúnō* (3435), to soil; *asebéō* (764), to act impiously; *hierosuléō* (2416), to be a temple-robber, commit sacrilege; *blasphēméō* (987), to blaspheme, revile, speak evil; *koinóō* (2840), to defile, pollute; *spilóō* (4695), to stain, soil, spot.

Ant.: *hagiázō* (37), to make holy, sanctify; *eulogéō* (2127), to speak well of, bless; *eusebéō* (2151), to be pious, to worship; *eulabéomai* (2125), to reverence.

954. Βεελζεβούλ *Beelzeboúl*; masc. noun, transliterated from the Hebr. *Ba‘al Zᵉbūb* (1176, OT). Beelzebub, the name properly should be Beelzebul in all NT passages (Matt 10:25; 12:24, 27; Mark 3:22; Luke 11:15, 18, 19). In the OT, Beelzebub meant lord of flies or fly-god (2 Kgs 1:2) and was in common use among the Jews in Christ's day as the title of Satan as the prince of the demons.
Syn.: *Satanás* (4567), Satan; *diábolos* (1228), devil; *daímōn* (1142), demon; *ponērós* (4190), evil, hurtful.
Ant.: *agathós* (18), benevolent.

955. Βελίαλ *Belíal*; masc. noun transliterated from the Hebr. *Bᵉlīyya‘al* (1100, OT) meaning wickedness (1 Sam 25:25). Belial, a word applied by the sacred writers to such lewd, profligate, and vile persons as seem to regard neither God nor man (Deut 13:13; Judg 19:22; 1 Sam 2:12). Used as an appellation of Satan by the Apostle Paul in 2 Cor 6:15 to the citizens of Corinth known for their lewdness and profligacy, "What concord hath Christ with Belial?" who is the prince of licentiousness and corruption.

956. βέλος *bélos*; gen. *beléos*, *bélous*, a neut. noun from *bállō* (906), to cast. A missile weapon, e.g., a dart, arrow. In the NT used only figuratively for Satanic temptations (Eph 6:16) where the expression, "the fiery darts," seems an evident allusion to those arrows or javelins which were sometimes used in sieges in battles. Sometimes they were missiles fitted with combustibles, and so forth (Sept.: 2 Sam 22:15; Ps 18:15; 144:6).
Syn.: *tóxon* (5115), a bow.

957. βελτίων *beltíon*; gen. *beltínos*, masc.-fem., neut. *béltion*, adj., an irregular comparative of *agathós* (18), good. Better, well enough, very well. In 2 Tim 1:18 used adv.: you know better, implying to be followed by "than I can write."

Syn.: *kreíttōn* (2909), better.
Ant.: *cheírōn* (5501), worse; *hḗtton* (2276), worse.

958. Βενιαμίν *Beniamín*; transliterated from the Hebr. *Binyāmīn* (1144, OT), meaning son of the right hand, i.e., of fortune. Benjamin, the youngest son of Jacob and Rachel. His mother died immediately upon his birth which took place near Bethlehem when the family was on their journey from Padan-Aram to Canaan. With her dying breath she called him *Benōnī* ([1126, OT] "the son of my sorrow"), but his father gave him the name he bore (Gen 35:16–18). The relationship between Benjamin and Jacob was always very tender, particularly after Joseph's supposed death, but we know nothing about him personally. The tribe formed from his descendants exhibited the traits of courage, cunning, and ambition as foretold by the dying Jacob (Gen 49:27). It has its portion of the Promised Land adjoining Judah, and when ten of the tribes revolted, Benjamin continued steadfast in its attachment to Judah and formed a part of that kingdom (1 Kgs 12:17, 23). Saul, the first king, and Paul were descendants of this tribe (1 Sam 10:21; Phil 3:5). In the NT, it occurs in Acts 13:21; Rom 11:1; Phil 3:5; Rev 7:8.

959. Βερνίκη *Berníkē*; gen. *Berníkēs*, fem. proper noun meaning victorious. Bernice, the eldest daughter of Agrippa, surnamed the Great, and sister to the younger Agrippa, who were both kings of the Jews (Acts 25:13, 23; 26:30). Her first husband was her uncle Herod, the king of Chalcis. She appears in Acts in connection with her brother, Agrippa the Second, with whom she lived in an incestuous relationship after Herod's death, A.D. 48. To put an end to the scandal, she married Polemo, king of Cilicia, whom she persuaded to be circumcised. This union being soon dissolved, she returned to her brother and afterwards became mistress of Vespasian (A.D. 9–79),

Roman emperor from A.D. 70–79, and his son Titus (A.D. 40 or 41 to 81), a Roman emperor (A.D. 79–81).

960. Βέροια *Béroia*; gen. *Beroías*, fem. proper noun. Berea, a city of Macedonia, Greece (Acts 17:10, 13) on the eastern side of the Olympian Mountains, a fair-sized city still in existence today.

961. Βεροιαῖος *Beroiaíos*; fem. *Beroiaía*, neut. *Beroiaíon*, adj. A Berean or a native of *Béroia* (960) (Acts 20:4).

962. Βηθαβαρά *Bēthabará*; gen. *Bēthabarás*, fem. proper noun transliterated from the Hebr. *bayith* (1004, OT), house and *'abārāh* (5679, OT), crossing place, ferry. Bethabara, meaning house of the ford, a place beyond Jordan (John 1:28). Some of the best MSS read Bethany, same as Bethabara; possibly at Beth-nimrah or Nimrin, but more probably at Abarah, a leading stream of the Jordan on the road to Gilead.

963. Βηθανία *Bēthanía*; gen. *Bēthanías*, fem. proper noun transliterated from the Hebr. *bayith* (1004, OT), house and *'anīyyāh* (6041, OT), depressed. Bethany, house of depression or misery. A village on the eastern slope of Mt. Olivet about one and one half to two miles east of Jerusalem (Luke 19:29; 24:50; John 11:1, 18) toward Jericho. It was the hometown of Lazarus, Mary, and Martha where Jesus often stayed (Matt 21:17; Mark 11:1, 11, 12) and where Lazarus was raised from the dead (John 11:18); also the home of Simon the leper (Matt 26:6; Mark 14:3; John 12:1). Today a small hamlet inhabited by Muslim Arabs, Bethany is called in Arabic *El-Azariyeh*, "a place of Lazarus." Some MSS read "Bethabara" (John 1:28). It was here that John baptized. See *Bethabará* (962).

964. Βηθεσδά *Bēthesdá*, fem. proper noun transliterated from the Hebr. *bayith* (1004, OT), house and *chēsēd* (2617, OT), lovingkindness, mercy. Bethesda, house of mercy or flowing water. A pool in Jerusalem near the sheep-gate or market with a building over or near it for the accommodation of the sick (John 5:2).

965. Βηθλεέμ *Bēthleém*; fem. proper noun, transliterated from the Hebr. *Bēth Lechem* (1035, OT). Bethlehem, meaning house of bread. A town in the hill-country about 6 miles south of Jerusalem situated on a narrow eastward ridge which breaks down in abrupt terraced slopes to the deep valleys below and is 2,527 feet above sea level. It is referred to over 40 times in the Bible and is one of the oldest towns in Palestine having existed for over 4,000 years. It was Rachel's burial place called Ephrath (Gen 35:19); the home of Naomi, Boaz, and Ruth (Ruth 1:19); birthplace of David (1 Sam 17:12); burial place of Joab's family (2 Sam 2:32); taken by the Philistines and the site of a noted well (2 Sam 23:14, 15); fortified by Rehoboam (2 Chr 11:6); foretold as the birthplace of Christ (Mic 5:2); the birthplace of Jesus (Matt 2:1); visited by the shepherds (Luke 2:15–17) and the magi (Matt 2). The Church of the Nativity still existing there is the oldest church in Christendom built in A.D. 330 by the Empress Helena and is reputed to be the place of our Lord's birth. The chapel beneath the church was the study of St. Jerome where he spent 30 years on his great work, the Lat. version of the Bible called the *Vulgate*, which is still the standard version in the Roman Catholic church. In the courtyard of the church stands his statue.

966. Βηθσαϊδά *Bēthsaïdá*, **Βηθσαϊδάν** *Bēthsaïdán*; fem. proper noun transliterated from the Hebr. *bayith* (1004, OT), house and *tsayād* (6719, OT), hunter. Bethsaida, meaning place of fishing or hunting, city of Galilee near Capernaum (Matt 11:21; Mark 6:45; 8:22; Luke 9:10; 10:13; John 1:44; 12:21 [cf. John 6:17]). Eusebius says only that it lay on the sea of Gennesareth, i.e., the western shore of Galilee, as its name would also imply.

There was but one Bethsaida which was built on both sides of the Jordan at the site where the Jordan empties into the sea of Galilee. The eastern part was beautified by Philip the Tetrarch and called Bethsaida Julias (in honor of a daughter of the Emperor Augustus) to distinguish it from the western Bethsaida in Galilee. It was the home of Philip, Andrew, and Peter (John 1:44). In the desert tract near Bethsaida, the Lord Jesus miraculously fed the five thousand and then departed by ship to the other side of the lake (Mark 6:31ff.; Luke 9:10 [cf. Matt 14:13ff.; John 6:1, 2, 5ff., 17, 22, 24; see also Mark 8:22]).

967. Βηθφαγή *Bēthphagé*; fem. proper noun transliterated from the Hebr. *bayith* (1004, OT), house and *pag* (6291, OT), unripe. Bethphage, meaning house of green figs, a village near Bethany, east of the Mount of Olives (Matt 21:1; Mark 11:1; Luke 19:29).

968. βῆμα *bḗma*; gen. *bḗmatos*, neut. noun from *baínō* (n.f., see *apobaínō* [576]), I go. A step, i.e., a pace or footstep (Acts 7:5; Sept.: Deut 2:5). By implication any elevated place to which the ascent is by steps, e.g., a stage or pulpit for a speaker or reader (Sept.: Neh 8:4). An elevated seat like a throne in the theater at Caesarea on which Herod sat (Acts 12:21). More commonly it means a tribunal, especially of a judge or magistrate (Matt 27:19; John 19:13; Acts 18:12, 16, 17; 25:6, 10, 17; Rom 14:10; 2 Cor 5:10). In the NT, the word is translated "judgment seat." The judge invariably sat on a special seat or throne. Jerusalem and the smaller cities alike had their thrones for judgment (Judg 4:5; 1 Kgs 7:7; Ps 122:5). In Rome, magistrate and jury were seated together on the raised tribunal or bench. The custom extended also to the provinces. In the NT, *kritéria* (2922), tribunals, is used of law courts generally (1 Cor 6:2, 4; James 2:6), while *bḗma* is applied to the judgment seat not only of the Emperor (Acts 25:10) but also of the governors:

Pilate (Matt 27:19; John 19:13), Gallio (Acts 18:12, 16f.), Festus (Acts 25:6, 17). *Bḗma* is even used metaphorically in reference to Christ (Rom 14:10; 2 Cor 5:10) in which cases the word has eschatological meaning. We must, therefore, consider these two terms as interchangeable. Both refer to the judgment after death found in Heb 9:27, "It is appointed unto men once to die, but after this the judgment." There is absolutely no way whereby the doctrine of the opportunity of salvation after death can be scripturally sustained. James 4:12 presents God as the lawgiver who can save and destroy. The word for destroy is *apolésai*, the aor. act. inf. of *apóllumi* (622), from the prep. *apó* (575), from, and *óllumi*, to lose or perish. The word *apóllumi* stands in contrast to *sṓzō* (4982), to save, which indicates not only salvation from peril, but also keeping near oneself. One of the greatest values of salvation is the deliverance from sin and consequent fellowship which Christ provides for us. He lives in us and we live in Him. Those who are perishing continue to be in their lost condition as a result of Adam's sin. This condition of salvation or lostness, of having Christ or not having Him, will be ultimately confirmed in the day of judgment by God Himself. He is so presented as the Judge in Heb 12:23; Acts 10:42; 2 Tim 4:8. Paul declared on Mars Hill, "God . . . will judge the world in righteousness by that man whom he hath ordained," which means Jesus Christ (Acts 17:31).

Who is said to be judged before the judgment seat of Christ? It is evident from the context of Rom 14:1–13; 2 Cor 5:1–11 that this is the judgment of the believers connected with the *parousía* (3952), the coming presence of the Lord Jesus. This concerns the evaluation of our life on earth and its character and works (see especially 2 Cor 5:10). This does not imply that when the believer dies and is with Christ (2 Cor 5:8; Phil 1:23), he loses his identity and his past life is forgotten. When we leave this tabernacle of our present body, we go to be with Christ which constitutes the greatest reward and gain for the believer. The believer does not become an unidentifiable spirit in heaven where Christ is (Acts 1:11), but puts on a new garment (*ependúomai* [1902], to put clothing on, only in 2 Cor 5:2, 4). We are not told what this garment will be, but it must be a garment of identity of the bodiless spirit immediately after death. This is identified in 2 Cor 5:2 as the *oikētḗrion* (3613), translated "house," and in Jude 1:6 where it is translated "habitation." Etymologically, all we can say concerning the word *oikētḗrion* is that it is a dwelling place and pertains to a house where one actually lives. However, its contextual meaning is that it refers to the clothing which we as spirits shall put on after death. In Jude 1:6 it refers to the habitation or dwelling place which the fallen angels had left. This indicates that *oikētḗrion* is a dwelling place of angelic beings who are spirits.

The parallel word to *oikētḗrion* is *katoikētḗrion* (2732) (Eph 2:22), which is presented as a habitation of God through the Spirit or in the Spirit. Here it is presented as a dwelling place of God who is spirit. In Rev 18:2 it is presented as the habitation of devils who also are spirits. We conclude, therefore, that both *oikētḗrion* and *katoikētḗrion* are the habitation of spirits or spirit beings. There is going to be a distinct garment or housing for each believer which he or she receives immediately after death. But the implication that it is not going to be the same for all believers is found in 2 Cor 5:1: "For we know that, if our earthly house of this tabernacle were dissolved, we have a building of God, a house not made with hands, eternal in the heavens." The word translated "house" is *oikodomḗn* (3619), which means a building in the process of being constructed. What is stated here by the Apostle Paul is that while we are here on earth there is a house being built for us into which we shall move, and this is presented also as clothing which we are eager to put on (2 Cor 5:2). The building

and the clothing are in accordance with our works of faith here on earth, whether good or bad (2 Cor 5:10). This is in full accord with the teaching of Rom 2:1–16 in regard to the righteous judgment of God for all people, believers and unbelievers. See also Rom 14:10–23; 1 Cor 3:13; 4:5.

The complete and final evaluation of the believer's life, however, is going to be connected with the *Parousía*, the Second Coming of the Lord as explained in the Olivet Discourse (Matt 24; 25; Mark 13; Luke 21). According to 1 Thess 4:13–18, the dead in Christ will be resurrected first, and believers who are still alive will be changed to receive a body conformable to that of those who had already risen. In Luke 14:14, the Lord makes it very plain that the rewards are going to be distributed in the resurrection of the just which must precede the resurrection of the unjust (Rev 20:5). See *anástasis* (386), resurrection, and our discussion of the first and second resurrections.

The unbelievers will be judged consequent to their resurrection, and this judgment is identified as the Great White Throne Judgment (Rev 20:11). It can be taken as a term parallel to the *bḗma* of God or of Christ. Up until now the judgments of God and of Christ were temporary, intermediary, but the throne indicates a final judgment which will also include the believers of the Tribulation period. It is designated to be a white throne because white is the color of light, the symbol of purity, innocence, holiness and, therefore, absolute justice. A hypocrite has no white robe. He is only like a whitewashed wall (Acts 23:3 [cf. Matt 23:27]). However, the elders (Rev 4:4), the martyrs (Rev 6:11), and the great multitude that come out of the Tribulation (Rev 7:9) are all clothed in white raiment. Their robes were not always white, but they washed them and made them white in the blood of the Lamb (Rev 7:14).

This judgment of the great white throne is the absolute revelation of all that both believers and unbelievers of all

times ever did in their lives and the just
apportionment of punishments and rewards. We believe that the great white
throne does not involve only unbelievers,
but also believers, both of the period pri-
or to the Great Tribulation described in
Rev 6—19 and the saints who were saved
during the time of the Tribulation.

After the Church of Jesus Christ is
raptured into heaven (1 Thess 4:13–17),
there is going to be a great multitude of
those who remain behind and go through
the Tribulation who will be saved as de-
lineated in Rev 7:14. These are the elect
spoken of by our Savior in Matt 24:22,
24, 31; Mark 13:20, 22, 27. These elect
ones of the Tribulation will not worship
the Antichrist because their names have
been written in the Book of Life of the
Lamb (Rev 13:8). There has to be a time
for the reward of these Tribulation believers and that time is the Great White
Throne Judgment. This is why in the pertinent passage of Rev 20:11–15 we have
the books with the works of both believers and unbelievers written in them.

There is, however, only one book
called the Book of Life in which the
names of the believers are written. It is
in connection with this final judgment
that our Lord spoke in Matt 25:31–46.
This is the time for the reward of those
who gallantly resisted the Antichrist, that
great beast (Rev 20:4). It is interesting indeed that here the word "throne" is used
in the pl. There are thrones for the judges. These thrones must include Christ and
His Apostles (Matt 19:28) and the saints
of God of the dispensation of grace (1
Cor 6:3). In Rev 4:4; 11:16 the elders are
on the thrones round about the throne of
God. There will also be the judgment of
the saints of God of all ages as they live
during the millennial reign of Christ on
earth (Rev 20:1–6).

It is to be noted also that after the millennial reign of Christ, Satan will be released, but after that he will experience
his final destiny and be cast into the lake
of fire (Rev 20:10, 14, 15) along with
those who resisted the gospel (Rev 21:8).

The beast or the Antichrist and the false
prophet who were active during the Tribulation will have already been cast into
the lake of fire (Rev 19:20).

969. βήρυλλος *bḗrullos*; gen. *bērúllou*,
masc., fem. noun. Beryl, a precious stone
of a sea-green color (Rev 21:20).

970. βία *bía*; gen. *bías*, fem. noun.
Strength, especially of the body. In
the NT, force, impetus, violence (Acts
5:26; 21:35; 24:7; 27:41; Sept.: Ex 1:14;
14:25).

Deriv.: *biázō* (971), to press, suffer violence; *bíaios* (972), violent.

Syn.: *hórmēma* (3731), a rush; *dúnamis*
(1411), power, violence; *ischús* (2479),
forcefulness; *harpagḗ* (724), extortion;
harpagmós (725), plunder, robbery.

Ant.: *hupomonḗ* (5281), patience;
anochḗ (463), tolerance; *epieíkeia* (1932),
clemency; *makrothumía* (3115), longsuffering, forbearance towards people.

971. βιάζω *biázō*; fut. *biásō*, from *bía*
(970), violence. To overpower, impel,
but also to rush into. In Matt 11:12 used
in the pass. but with mid. meaning, i.e.,
the kingdom of God *biázetai*, is sought
with eagerness, haste. It is not carefully
thought of as to its consequences which
may not be pleasant, such as persecution by one's very own household (Matt
10:36). In the mid. voice, meaning that
one presses himself in to seize the kingdom with his own energy as if the kingdom could be had as something to be
grasped. We see this today as people eagerly and flippantly come forward to "accept Christ" without having experienced
repentance of sin or having counted the
cost of their acceptance (Matt 16:24–28).
Luke 16:16 implies the thoughtless eagerness with which the gospel was seized
(*harpázō* [726], grasp in Matt 11:12) in
the agitated state of men's minds (cf.
Matt 11:12; Sept.: Ex 19:24).

Deriv.: *biastḗs* (973), a person who is
violent; *parabiázomai* (3849), to coerce,
persuade.

Syn.: *hormáō* (3729), to rush.

Ant.: *bradúnō* (1019), to delay; *anabállō* (306), to put off; *hupoménō* (5278), to bear under.

972. βίαιος *bíaios*; fem. *biaía*, neut. *bíaion* adj. from *bía* (970), violence. Violent, vehement, spoken of the wind (Acts 2:2; Sept.: Ex 14:21; Isa 59:19).

Ant.: *epieikḗs* (1933), patient; *eirēnikós* (1516), peaceable; *anexíkakos* (420), enduring of ill, forbearance.

973. βιαστής *biastḗs*; gen. *biastoú*, masc. noun from *biázō* (971), to suffer violence, but also to hurry into or press into without proper thought and repentance. A violent person, one who uses force, but also one who hurries to appropriate something that seems good without measuring the consequences of such action. In Matt 11:12 it refers to those who heard the preaching of John the Baptist and came to him to be baptized without truly repenting of their sins. They must have said to themselves, "Let's hurry to be baptized; let's accept the advantages by the mere physical act of baptism," But they never repented and believed in Christ. They were rushing into the kingdom and as such they were *biastaí*, those who speedily pushed their way in. That is why they are said to *harpázousin* (726), seize by force, the kingdom of God. They may seize by their own energy, but they are not saved unless they repent, believe, and are accepted by Christ (1 Cor 12:13). It is spoken of one who has a vehement desire for anything (Matt 11:12).

974. βιβλαρίδιον *bibliarídion*; gen. *bibliaridíou*, a neut. diminutive of *bíblos* (976), book. A small roll or volume, a little scroll (Rev 10:2, 8–10).

975. βιβλίον *biblíon*; gen. *biblíou*, neut. noun, a diminutive of *bíblos* (976), book. A roll, volume, as was the form of ancient books (Luke 4:17, 20; John 20:30; 21:25; Gal 3:10; 2 Tim 4:13; Rev 5:1–5, 7–9; 6:14; 22:7, 9, 10, 18, 19; Sept.: Ex 17:14; Josh 24:26). In the pl., the books of judgment (Rev 20:12). In Rev 1:11 and perhaps 2 Tim 4:13, it refers to letters or epistles which were also rolled up. Spoken of documents, e.g., a Jewish bill of divorce (Matt 19:7; Mark 10:4; Sept.: Deut 24:1, 3); the Mosaic Law or Pentateuch (Heb 9:19; 10:7; Sept.: Ps 40:8); the Book of Life (Rev 17:8; 20:12; 21:27).

Biblíon is used interchangeably with *bíblos* (976) in reference to the Book of Life, the book where the names of those who believe on the Lord Jesus will be recorded. Because of God's omniscience, they are said to have been written before the foundation of the world (Rev 17:8). In view of Rev 17:8, the term "from the foundation of the world" (Rev 13:8) should refer to those whose names were written in the Book of Life rather than to the Lamb that was slain. In both instances, the verb *gégraptai*, the perf. pass. indic. of *gráphō* (1125), to write, is used. This indicates that they were written at a certain time by God Himself or Christ, and they are still there and no one can erase them. If that were possible, it would prove someone to be stronger than Christ and Christ as having been deceived by thinking people were saved while they were not.

One can note that in Rev 13:8 only those whose names have not been written in the Book of Life will bow and worship the Antichrist. In Rev 17:8, it is stated that the saints of the Tribulation whose names are written in the Book of Life will not bow down to the beast. In Rev 3:5 it seems to appear as if it were possible for the names written in the Book of Life to be erased, but in reality the opposite is stated: "He that overcometh, the same shall be clothed in white raiment; and I will not blot out his name out of the book of life, but I will confess his name before my Father and before his angels." A double neg. is used before the words "blot out" (*ou mḗ* [3756, 3361]), indicating that it is impossible, i.e., *No*, never! (author's italics) Here it is Christ speaking and saying, "It is impossible that I blot his name out of the book of life" (a.t.). And then this truth is stated with the Lord saying, "But I will confess his name before my Father, and before his angels." The truths stated in this verse are that each member of the true Church of Jesus Christ who is baptized into His body (1 Cor 12:13) is victorious. His name is written in the Book of Life, and it will be declared before the Father and the angels.

In Rev 20:12, the Book of Life is distinguished from the "books" which constitute the records of the works of both believers and unbelievers. This indicates that there will be varying degrees of rewards for the believers and varying degrees of punishment for the unbelievers. No one, however, whose name is not written in the Book of Life has entrance into the eternal heaven which is also called the Holy City in Rev 22:19 where the expression "the book of life" does not occur. The Majority Text as well as the UBS and later editions of the TR in this verse have *apó* (575), from, *toú xúlou* (3586), the wood, *tēs zōēs* (2222), of life. Only in the older TR editions is there the word *biblíou* instead of *xúlou*. The NASB and the NIV have translated *xúlou* as the "tree of life" which is incorrect, because *xúlon* (3586) is the word used for dry wood which indicates the cross on which Christ was crucified (Acts 5:30; 10:39; 13:29; Gal 3:13; 1 Pet 2:24). The word for tree in Gr. is *déndron* (1186), which never refers to the cross of Christ. The term "the wood of life" is what we have in Rev 2:7; 22:2, 14, as well as in 22:19. This expression refers to the symbolic source of rewards according to the investments the believers made while on earth in being crucified with Christ and bearing the consequences of such a crucifixion. Since the cross of Jesus Christ is called *xúlon*, wood, for those who stood and suffered for the cross of Christ, there will be a recompense derived from the wood of life in the eternal heaven. The Scripture teaches that our glorification will be proportionate to our suffering for

Christ and His cross (Rom 5:1–5; 8:18; 1 Cor 2:7; 2 Cor 3:7, 18; 4:4–17). In Phil 4:3, two particular women who labored together with Paul are said to have their names in the Book of Life. In Rev 21:27 we are told who is not going to find entrance into the new Jerusalem which is equated with the final, blissful heaven for the believer: "And there shall in no wise enter into it anything that defileth [the word here is *koinón* {2839} meaning that which is in himself defiled], neither whatsoever worketh abomination or maketh a lie [the verb here is the continuous pres. part. *ho poión* {4160}, the one who continuously works abomination and lying], but they which are written in the Lamb's book of life." The verb translated "which are written" is *gegramménoi*, the perf. pass. part. of *gráphō* (1125), to write. This means that in all instances we have concerning the writing of the names in the Book of Life, no one writes in his own name. It is written by God Himself, and when God writes one's name in the Book of Life even before the foundation of the world, there is no one on earth who can erase it. Our Lord confirmed this in John 10:28: "And I give unto them eternal life, and they shall never perish, neither shall any man pluck them out of my hand."

976. βίβλος *bíblos*; gen. *bíblou*, fem. noun. Paper made from Egyptian papyrus. In the NT, a roll, volume, scroll, i.e., a book (Mark 12:26, "in the book of Moses" meaning the Law; Luke 3:4; 20:42; Acts 1:20; 7:42; 19:19; Sept.: Josh 1:8; 1 Sam 10:25; Ezra 6:18). Spoken of a genealogical table or catalog (Matt 1:1; Sept.: Gen 5:1). The phrase, "the book of life [*bíblos tēs zōēs* {2222}, life]" is equal in the Sept. to the book of the living ones (Ps 69:28 [cf. Ex 32:32, 33]), where God is shown as having the names of the righteous who are to inherit eternal life inscribed in a book. See also Phil 4:3; Rev 3:5; 20:15. This is the same phrase as *tó biblíon* (975), a diminutive of *bíblos* (Rev 17:8; 20:12; 21:27; Sept.: Dan

12:1). Different from this is the book in which God has from eternity inscribed the destinies of men (Ps 139:16 [cf. Job 14:5]). The pl. and the diminutive *biblía* are twice mentioned in Rev 20:12 referring to the books of judgment in which the actions of men are recorded (see Dan 7:10).

Deriv.: *bibliarídion* (974), a little scroll; *biblíon* (975), a roll, scroll.

977. βιβρώσκω *bibrṓskō*; fut. *brṓsomai*, perf. *bébrōka*. To eat (John 6:13; Sept.: Josh 5:12; 1 Sam 30:12; Ezek 4:14).

Deriv.: *brṓma* (1033), meat, food; *brṓsis* (1035), eating, food; *sētóbrōtos* (4598), moth-eaten; *skōlēkóbrōtos* (4662), eaten by worms.

Syn.: *esthíō* (2068), to eat; *katesthíō / kataphágō* (2719), to devour; *sunesthíō* (4906), to eat with or in the company of; *trṓgō* (5176), to gnaw, chew, stressing the slow process; *geúō* (1089), to cause to taste, and *geúomai*, the mid., to taste; *korénnumi* (2880), to satiate, satisfy with food, be filled; the expression *nomḗn échō* (*nomḗn* [3542], pasturage; *échō* [2192], have), to find pasture; *metalambánō* (3335), to partake of, share, eat; *phágō* (5315), to eat, devour, consume.

Ant.: *peináō* (3983), to hunger; *nēsteúō* (3522), to fast.

978. Βιθυνία *Bithunía*; gen. *Bithunías*, fem. proper noun. Bithynia, a province of Asia Minor on the Euxine Sea and Propontis, bounded on the west by Mysia, south and east by Phrygia and Galatia, and east also by Paphlagonia (Acts 16:7; 1 Pet 1:1).

979. βίος *bíos*; gen. *bíou*, masc. noun. Life, but not as in *zōḗ* (2222), life, in which is meant the element or principle of the spirit and soul. *Bíos*, from which the word "biography" is derived, refers to duration, means, and manner of life. See Mark 12:44; Luke 8:14, 43; 15:12, 30; 21:4; Sept.: Job 7:6; 8:9; Prov 31:14; 1 Tim 2:2; 2 Tim 2:4; 1 Pet 4:3; 1 John 2:16; 3:17, possessions or wealth.

Deriv.: *bióō* (980), to live, to pass one's life without reference to its quality.

Syn.: with the meaning of goods, wealth: *húparxis* (5223), subsistence, goods, and also as a pl. part. noun, *tá hupárchonta*; *skeúos* (4632), primarily a vessel, but also goods; *psuchḗ* (5590), with the meaning of natural life, breath of life, the seat of personality; *agōgḗ* (72), a manner of life, conduct; *anastrophḗ* (391), behavior, conduct.

Ant.: *thánatos* (2288), death; *nékrōsis* (3500), deadness, impotency; *teleutḗ* (5054), decease, death; *limós* (3042), famine, hunger; *apóleia* (684), loss; *anaíresis* (336), killing, death.

980. βιόω *bióō*; contracted *biṓ*; fut. *biṓsō*, from *bíos* (979), manner, possessions of life, living. To live, to pass one's life (1 Pet 4:2). See also *záō* (2198), to live, possess life.

Deriv.: *bíōsis* (981), manner of life.

Syn.: *anastréphomai* (390), to conduct oneself, behave, live; *diágō* (1236), to pass a life; *politeúō* or *politeúomai* (4176), to live or behave as a citizen; *hupárchō* (5225), to be in existence.

Ant.: *apothnḗskō* (599), to die; *apérchomai* (565), to pass away; *ekleípō* (1587), to cease to be, to die; *teleutáō* (5053), to finish life; *analúō* (360), to depart; *apodēméō* (589), to go abroad, which can also mean to die; *ekdēméō* (1553), to emigrate, to go from this world to the next; *methístēmi* (3179), to go from here to there, to metastasize, to go from this world to the next; *ekpnéō* (1606), to expire; *paradídōmi* (3860), to give up, followed by *tó pneúma* (4151), spirit, to give up the spirit; *thnḗskō* (2348), to die; *nekróō* (3499), to deaden; *phoneúō* (5407), to murder; *koimáomai* (2837), to sleep with the meaning of die.

981. βίωσις *bíōsis*; gen. *biṓseōs*, fem. noun from *bióō* (980), to live. Life, the way in which one lives, the manner of life (Acts 26:4).

Deriv.: *biōtikós* (982), pertaining to this life.

Syn.: *bíos* (979), life, the manner of life.

982. βιωτικός *biōtikós*; gen. *biōtikoú*, fem. *biōtikḗ*, neut. *biōtikón*, adj. from *bíōsis* (981), manner of life. Pertaining to this life (Luke 21:34; 1 Cor 6:3, 4). The earlier Greeks used *biōtikós* instead of the earlier form *toú bíou*, of life.

983. βλαβερός *blaberós*; fem. *blaberá*, neut. *blaberón*, adj. from *bláptō* (984), to injure, hurt. Hurtful, noxious (1 Tim 6:9; Sept.: Prov 10:26).

Syn.: *kakós* (2556), bad, wicked, injurious; *ponērós* (4190), hurtful.

Ant.: *athôos* (121), innocent, not guilty; *ákakos* (172), harmless.

984. βλάπτω *bláptō*; fut. *blápsō*. To hurt, disable, injure, weaken, impede (Mark 16:18; Luke 4:35).

Deriv.: *blaberós* (983), injurious.

Syn.: *adikéō* (91), to do wrong, hurt; *kakóō* (2559), to do evil to anyone, to harm; *zēmióō* (2210), to suffer loss; *katastréphō* (2690), to turn upside down, upset, overthrow; *phtheírō* (5351), to wither, corrupt, ruin; *diaphtheírō* (1311), to destroy, corrupt completely; *analískō* (355), to destroy, consume; *bibrṓskō* (977), to eat up as if to finish it; *katastrēniáō* (2691), to live in pleasurable rebellion against.

Ant.: *pheídomai* (5339), to treat leniently, forbear, spare; *phrontízō* (5431), to care for; *phulássō* (5442), to keep, guard, protect.

985. βλαστάνω *blastánō*; fut. *blastḗsō*, from *blastós* (n.f.), germ. To germinate, put forth. Trans., to cause to spring up, produce, yield (James 5:18; Sept.: Gen 1:11; Num 17:8). Intrans., to sprout, spring up (Matt 13:26; Mark 4:27; Heb 9:4; Sept.: Num 17:8; Joel 2:22).

Syn.: *gínomai* (1096), to become, to spring up; *gennáō* (1080), to generate, beget; *anatéllō* (393), to arise, spring up;

phúō (5453), to bring forth, spring up, grow; *anabaínō* (305), to spring up.

Ant.: *erēmóō* (2049), to desolate, bring to nothing; *ekpíptō* (1601), to fall off; *maraínō* (3133), to fade away.

986. Βλάστος *Blástos*; gen. *Blástou*, masc. proper noun. Blastus, the chamberlain of Herod Agrippa I (Acts 12:20). Such persons usually had great influence with their masters.

987. βλασφημέω *blasphēméō*; contracted *blasphēmô̄*; fut. *blasphēmḗsō*, from *blásphēmos* (989), blasphemous or a blasphemer. To blaspheme, revile. To hurt the reputation or smite with reports or words, speak evil of, slander, rail (Mark 3:28; 15:29; Luke 23:39; John 10:36; Acts 18:6; 19:37; 26:11 [cf. Acts 26:9]; Rom 3:8; 14:16; 1 Cor 4:13; 10:30; 1 Tim 1:20; 6:1; Titus 3:2; James 2:7; 1 Pet 4:4, 14; 2 Pet 2:2, 10, 12; Jude 1:8, 10; Sept.: 2 Kgs 19:6, 23). To speak with impious irreverence concerning God Himself or what stands in some particular relation to Him, to blaspheme, a transliteration of the Gr. word *blasphēméō* (Matt 9:3; 26:65; Acts 13:45; Rom 2:24; Titus 2:5; Rev 16:9, 11, 21). In the NT generally syn. with *oneidízō* (3679), revile, and *loidoréō* (3058), to reproach (Matt 27:39; Mark 15:29; Luke 22:65; 23:39; Rom 3:8; 14:16; 1 Cor 4:13; Titus 3:2; 2 Pet 2:10; Jude 1:8); especially to revile God and divine things (Rev 13:6). Reviling against the Holy Spirit (Mark 3:29; Luke 12:10) means to resist the convicting power of the Holy Spirit unto repentance.

Syn.: *hēttáō* (2274), to make inferior; *hubrízō* (5195), to insult; *kataráomai* (2672), to curse; *anathematízō* (332), to curse with an oath; *asebéō* (764), to be impious, disrespectful; *hierosuléō* (2416), to commit sacrilege.

Ant.: *eusebéō* (2151), to revere; *eulabéomai* (2125), to show reverence; *eúchomai* (2172), to vow, to offer a wish that is good; *eulogéō* (2127), to speak well of, bless.

988. βλασφημία *blasphēmía*; gen. *blasphemías*, fem. noun from *blásphēmos* (989), blasphemous or a blasphemer. Blasphemy, verbal abuse against someone which denotes the very worst type of slander mentioned in Matt 15:19 with false witnesses; wounding someone's reputation by evil reports, evil speaking. See Mark 7:22; Eph 4:31; Col 3:8; 1 Tim 6:4 [cf. 2 Pet 2:11]; Jude 1:9 (*blásphēmos* [989], a blasphemer); Rev 2:9; Sept.: Ezek 35:12. Used especially in a religious sense meaning blasphemy toward or against God (Matt 26:65; Mark 2:7; 14:64; Luke 5:21; John 10:33; Rev 13:5, 6); against the Holy Spirit (Matt 12:31; Mark 3:28; Luke 12:10 using *blasphēméō* [987]) including the resistance against the convicting power of the Holy Spirit. The expression stands for names of blasphemy (Rev 13:1; 17:3; Dan 3:29).

Syn.: *katalalía* (2636), evil speaking, backbiting; *loidoría* (3059), abuse, railing, reviling; *apistía* (570), unbelief; *asébeia* (763), impiety; *húbris* (5196), insult, hurt, reproach; *dusphēmía* (1426), defamation.

Ant.: *eulábeia* (2124), reverence, piety; *eusébeia* (2150), piety, godliness; *theosébeia* (2317), devotion, godliness; *pístis* (4102), faith.

989. βλάσφημος *blásphēmos*; gen. *blasphḗmou*, masc.-fem., neut. *blásphēmon*, adj. from *bláx* (n.f.), sluggish, slow, stupid, and *phḗmē* (5345), rumor, fame. To be abusive, reviling, destroying one's good name (2 Tim 3:2, a slanderer, blasphemer in respect to men); blasphemous, a blasphemer (Acts 6:11, 13, of words uttered against God and divine things; 1 Tim 1:13, a subst. meaning a blasphemer in respect to God; 2 Pet 2:11, of words against men, slanderous).

Deriv.: *blasphēméō* (987), to blaspheme; *blasphēmía* (988), blaspheming abuse against someone.

Syn.: *loídoros* (3060), reviling, railing, or a railer; *hubristḗs* (5197), an insulter; *empaíktēs* (1703), a derider, mocker.

Ant.: *eusebḗs* (2152), devout; *alēthḗs* (227), true; *eulabḗs* (2126), pious.

990. βλέμμα *blémma*; gen. *blémmatos*, neut. noun from *blépō* (991), to see. The act of seeing or the object seen (2 Pet 2:8, "seeing and hearing," i.e., with what he saw and heard).

Syn.: *theōría* (2335), spectatorship, a spectacle, sight, with the sense of amazement thus making it a gaze; *eídos* (1491), an external appearance, form or shape; *hórama* (3705), that which is seen, a spectacle, sight, vision; *ophthalmós* (3788), an eye; *hórasis* (3706), the sense of sight; *optasía* (3701), vision, a coming into view; *ópsis* (3799), the act of seeing; *théatron* (2302), a theater, spectacle.

Ant.: *skótos* (4655), obscurity, darkness.

✓**991. βλέπω** *blépō*; fut. *blépsō* / *ópsomai* (the fut. of *optánomai* [3700], to see). Used in the NT 137 times, mostly in the pres. tense.

(I) To see.

(A) To be able to see, i.e., to have the faculty of sight, and as spoken of the blind, to recover sight. Intrans. (Matt 12:22). In Acts 9:9, "without sight" means blind. See Rev 3:18; 9:20; Sept.: Ex 4:11; 23:8; 1 Sam 3:2; Ps 69:23. The pres. inf. with the neut. art. *tó blépein*, used as a subst. means sight, the faculty of seeing (Luke 7:21). Figuratively in John 9:39: "that they which see not might see; and that they which see might be made blind" or may not see (cf. John 9:41). The expression "seeing ye shall see" in Matt 13:14 means ye shall indeed see. Also Mark 4:12; Acts 28:26 (cf. Isa 6:9).

(B) In the sense of to perceive as with the eyes meaning to discern, to understand. Trans. (Matt 7:3, "Why beholdest thou the mote that is in thy brother's eye?" signifies the diligence needed to discern the mote). See Matt 11:4; 14:30; 24:2; Mark 8:24; Luke 11:33; John 1:29; 21:9; Sept.: 2 Kgs 9:17; Amos 8:1. In Rev 1:12, "to see the voice," means to see where it came from. Construed with an acc. and part. instead of a subjunctive or inf. as in Matt 15:31, "seeing the dumb speaking [*blépontas*, seeing; *kōphoús* {2974}, the dumb; *laloúntas* {2980}, speaking]" (a.t.); Mark 5:31; John 5:19 (the part. *ónta*, the neut. pl. acc. of *ón* [5607], being, or *prássonta*, the pres. part. acc. of *prássō* [4238], to do or to make, making). Intrans. or in an absolute sense (Matt 6:4, 6, 18). By implication, to have before the eyes as spoken of what is present (Rom 8:24, meaning what one has before his eyes, i.e., present, how can he yet hope for it? [cf. Rom 8:25]). Hence, the part. *blepómenos*, seeing, means present. Rom 8:24 means that hope which is realized can no longer be hope. *Tá blepómena*, things seen, means present things; and those things not seen means future things (2 Cor 4:18; Heb 11:1, 7). Spoken of a vision, to see in vision (Rev 1:11; 6:1, 3, 5, 7 [TR], where other texts read *íde*, the imper. of *eídō* [1492], to see). In Sept.: of 1 Sam 9:9, *ho blépōn*, the seeing one or the seer.

(C) Metaphorically to perceive with the mind, be aware of, observe (Rom 7:23; Heb 10:25; Sept.: Neh 2:17). Followed by *hóti*, that (2 Cor 7:8; Heb 3:19; James 2:22).

(II) To look, i.e., to look at or upon, to direct the eyes upon, to behold. Trans. and intrans.:

(A) Spoken of persons followed by the acc. (Matt 5:28 referring to constant fixation of the eyes upon; Rev 5:3, 4, to look into the book, meaning to examine it; Sept.: Hag 2:4). In Matt 18:10, "their angels do always behold the face of my Father," i.e., in accordance with the customs of oriental monarchs, they have constant access to him, are admitted to his privacy as his friends. See 2 Kgs 25:19; Esth 1:14; Jer 52:25. Followed by *eis* (1519), unto, with the acc. meaning to look upon, behold (Acts 3:4, "Look on us"). In John 13:22; Luke 9:62, *eis* (1519), unto, *tá opísō* (3694), behind, to look back (Sept.: Gen 19:17). Spoken of a place, to look, i.e., to be situated, followed by *katá* with

the acc. (Acts 27:12; Sept.: 2 Chr 4:4; Ezek 40:6, 21–23, 46; 46:1, 13, 20).

(B) Metaphorically, to look to, direct the mind upon, consider, take heed; followed by the acc. (1 Cor 1:26; 10:18; Col 2:5, joyfully beholding; Gen 39:23; Ps 37:37; Isa 22:11; Phil 3:2 take heed to, keep an eye upon, and thus by implication, meaning beware of). Followed by *eis* (1519), unto, with the acc. (Matt 22:16, "thou regardest not," has not respect to the external appearance of men). Followed by *ti*, what, an obj., and *pós* (4459), how (Mark 4:24; Luke 8:18; 1 Cor 3:10; Eph 5:15). Followed by *hína* (2443), so that (1 Cor 16:10; Col 4:17; 2 John 1:8). Spoken by way of caution, in the imper. *blepétō* or *blépete*, look to it, take heed, be on the watch, beware (Mark 13:23, 33); followed by *heautoús* (1438), yourselves (Mark 13:9; 2 John 1:8). Also *blépete mé* (3361), not, meaning watch out, take heed lest, followed by the aor. subjunctive (Luke 21:8; Acts 13:40; 1 Cor 10:12; Gal 5:15). Followed by *mépōs* (3381), lest (1 Cor 8:9), followed by the fut. indic. (Col 2:8); by *mépote* (3379), lest at any time (Heb 3:12). Followed by *apó* (575), from, meaning look away from, avoid, beware of (Mark 8:15; 12:38).

(III) It is critical to observe the slightly different shades of meaning between *blépō* and other words in its domain. Notice *horáō* (3708), with its aor. form *eídon*. The former occurs 113 times and the latter 350 times in the gospels and the books of Acts and the Revelation. The meanings of these two words are broader than *blépō*. The fut. is *ópsomai* in the mid. voice. These verbs in their different tenses indicate bodily vision (John 6:36); mental vision or perception (Matt 8:4); it is said of Christ as seeing the Father (John 6:46), and of what He had seen with the Father (John 8:38). It indicates the direction of the thought to the object seen; also the meaning of seeing to or caring for a thing (Matt 27:4); to take heed (Matt 16:6; 18:10). *Blépō*, however, denotes ability to see as distinct from blindness (Matt 12:22; 15:31; Mark 8:23, 24; Luke 7:21; John 9:7, 15, 19, 21, 25). In Rev 5:3, 4 it has the meaning of not only seeing the book but also reading it; *theōréō* (2334), used 58 times, from *theōrós*, a spectator, to look at a thing with interest and with care for details (Mark 15:47; Luke 10:18; 23:35; John 20:6, 12, 14). In John 8:51; 17:24, it means to experience or partake; *theáomai* (2300), which occurs 22 times, to behold, view attentively, contemplate with wonder and loving interest. *Theáomai* is never used of the sight of God by man; rather it is the word *horáō* which is so used (John 1:18). It is a careful and deliberate vision which gives meaning to what one sees (Luke 23:55; John 1:14, 32; Acts 1:11; 1 John 1:1). In Matt 28:1, speaking of the two Marys who came to the sepulcher, the verb *theōréō* is used indicating their intent to observe the details about the tomb of Christ and for the purpose of meditating upon the holy event. These women expected to be affected by the event of the death and the entombment of Christ. In John 14:17 the verb *theōréō* is used in relation to seeing the Spirit of truth, which means being affected by the Spirit of truth. In John 14:19, "the world seeth me no more [*theōreí*]" or does not have me around to scrutinize, "but ye see me [*theōreíte*]," means you are affected by my presence. In John 16:10, 16, 17, 19, the verb *theōréō* is used for the physical presence of Jesus Christ and for the comprehension that his physical presence gave the disciples. However, in verse nineteen it is the verb *ópsesthe* that is used in the latter phrase, "but ye shall see me" (a.t.) which refers to the physical presence of Jesus Christ after His resurrection. In John 20:5, speaking of John who ran to the sepulcher faster than Peter and stooping down and looking into the sepulcher, the word *blépei* is used. It indicates a mere glance in regard to the grave clothes, not an examination and not necessarily being affected by the sight. In John 20:6, however, when Simon Peter came to the sepulcher and entered, we read, "and seeth [*theōreí*]," i.e., he looks at them in greater detail and is affected by the sight. Then when John entered the sepulcher, we read in John 20:8, "he saw [*eíden*, the aor. of *horáō* {3708}]." This means not only careful, physical vision, but also mental perception which resulted in believing or being persuaded that indeed the Lord Jesus had risen from the dead.

Deriv.: *anablépō* (308), to look up, and when spoken of the blind, to receive their sight; *apoblépō* (578), to look away from all else and toward one object, to look steadfastly; *blémma* (990), a look, glance, sight; *diablépō* (1227), to see clearly or to see through; *emblépō* (1689), to look earnestly, with the object of learning lessons of faith from, e.g., the birds; *epiblépō* (1914), to look upon or with favor; *periblépō* (4017), to look around; *problépō* (4265), to foresee, provide.

Syn.: *atenízō* (816), to gaze upon, behold earnestly; *katoptrízō* (2734), to look in a mirror; *aphoráō* (872), to look away from one thing so as to see another; *kathoráō* (2529), to look down upon, discern clearly. With the meaning of to heed: *proséchō* (4337), to pay attention to, beware; *phulássō* (5442), to guard, watch; *epéchō* (1907), to give attention to; *skopéō* (4648), to take heed; *muōpázō* (3467), to be shortsighted; *phaínō* (5316), to cause to appear.

Ant.: *tuphlóō* (5186), to make blind.

992. βλητέος *blētéos*; fem. *blētéa*, neut. *blētéon*, adj. from *bállō* (906), to send, thrust. A verbal adj. implying necessity, propriety, that which is to be cast, to be put (Mark 2:22 [TR]; Luke 5:38).

993. Βοανεργές *Boanergés*; transliterated from the Aramaic *běn* (1123, OT), son and *regesh* (7285, OT), tumult, thunder. Boanerges, meaning sons of thunder. It was the name given to James and John implying that they would be powerful instruments accomplishing mighty things for God by persevering in their inspired preaching and miraculous powers in spite of all opposition (Mark 3:17).

994. βοάω boáō; contracted *boó*, fut. *boésō*, from *boé* (995), cry. To cry aloud, exclaim (Luke 18:38; Acts 17:6; 21:34; Sept.: 1 Sam 24:8; 2 Kgs 2:12; Isa 5:30). An exclamation of joy (Gal 4:27 quoted from Isa 54:1; Sept.: Isa 14:7; 44:23). The cry as a result of terror or pain (Mark 15:34; Acts 8:7; Sept.: Gen 39:15, 18; 1 Kgs 8:18; Isa 15:5 [cf. 2 Kgs 18:28; Neh 9:4]). A command or exhortation given with a loud voice as by a herald (Matt 3:3; Mark 1:3; Luke 3:4; John 1:23 [cf. Isa 40:3, 6]). A cry for help (Luke 18:7; Sept.: Gen 4:10; Num 12:13; Judg 15:18; Hos 7:14; Joel 1:19).
Deriv.: *anaboáō* (310), to cry out; *epiboáō* (1916), to exclaim vehemently.
Syn.: *krázō* (2896), to cry out; *anakrázō* (349), to cry out loudly; *kraugázō* (2905), to make an outcry; *phōnéō* (5455), to utter a loud sound; *epiphōnéō* (2019), to shout aloud against; *thorubéō* (2350), to make a noise; *ololúzō* (3649), to howl.
Ant.: *phimóō* (5392), to muzzle, put to silence; *sigáō* (4601), to be silent.

995. βοή boé; gen. *boés*, fem. noun. A cry, outcry, exclamation as for help (James 5:4; Sept.: Ex 2:24; 1 Sam 9:16).
Deriv.: *boáō* (994), to cry; *boēthéō* (997), to help.
Syn.: *kraugé* (2906), clamor; *thórubos* (2351), noise, uproar.
Ant.: *sigé* (4602), silence; *hēsuchía* (2271), quietness; *galénē* (1055), tranquility; *psithurismós* (5587), whispering.

996. βοήθεια boétheia; gen. *boētheías*, fem. noun from *boēthéō* (997), to help. Help, aid, succor (Heb 4:16; Sept.: Judg 5:23; Ps 38:22; 121:1; 124:8). In the pl. meaning helps, means of help, e.g., ropes, chains, and so forth (Acts 27:17).
Syn.: *antílēpsis* (484), relief, laying hold of; *epikouría* (1947), assistance by an ally or a helper.
Ant.: *próskomma* (4348), stumblingblock; *phragmós* (5418), a fence,

hindrance; *egkopé* (1464), an impediment, a hindrance.

997. βοηθέω boēthéō; contracted *boēthō*, fut. *boēthésō*; from *boé* (995), a cry, exclamation, and *théo* (n.f.), to run. To run on hearing a cry, to give assistance. Generally meaning to succor, help, aid. Used with the dat. (Matt 15:25; Mark 9:22, 24; Acts 16:9; 2 Cor 6:2; Heb 2:18; Rev 12:16; Sept.: Gen 49:25; Josh 10:6; 2 Sam 8:5).
Deriv.: *boétheia* (996), a help; *boēthós* (998), a helper.
Syn.: *antilambánomai* (482), to uphold, help; *sullambánō* (4815), to assist, take part with; *sunantilambánomai* (4878), to take hold with at the side for assistance; *sumbállō* (4820), to throw together; *sunupourgéō* (4943), to join in helping, serve with anyone as an underworker; *sunergéō* (4903), to help in work, cooperate; *parístēmi* (3936), to stand or place oneself beside, to stand by, be at hand; *problépō* (4265), to foresee, provide; *pronoéō* (4306), to take thought for, provide.
Ant.: *egkóptō* (1465), to detain a person unnecessarily, hinder; *anakóptō* (348), to hinder; *ekkóptō* (1581), to cut out, frustrate; *kōlúō* (2967), to hinder, forbid, restrain; *diakōlúō* (1254), to thoroughly hinder.

998. βοηθός boēthós; gen. *boēthoú*, masc. noun from *boēthéō* (997), to help. A helper (Heb 13:6; Sept.: Ps 18:3; 71:7; Job 29:12).
Syn.: *sunergós* (4904), a helper, fellow worker.

999. βόθυνος bóthunos; gen. *bothúnou*, masc. noun. A pit or ditch as an emblem of destruction (Matt 15:14; Luke 6:39; Sept.: Isa 24:18; Jer 48:43, 44 [cf. Ps 40:2]). In the case of a cistern in Matt 12:11, equal to *phréar* (5421), a well (Luke 14:5).
Syn.: *ábussos* (12), abyss, something with a bottomless pit; *hupolénion* (5276),

a vessel or trough beneath a wine press to receive the juice.

1000. βολή bolḗ; gen. *bolḗs*, fem. noun from *bállō* (906), to cast. A cast, a throw, spoken of distance (Luke 22:41) indicating about a stone's throw.

1001. βολίζω bolízō; fut. *bolísō*, from *bolís* (1002), a weapon, a javelin or dart. Intrans. to cast or let down a line and plummet in order to test the depth of water, to sound, fathom (Acts 27:28).

1002. βολίς bolís; gen. *bolídos*, from *bállō* (906), to cast. Something thrown as the plummet in measuring the depth of the sea. A weapon, a javelin or dart (Heb 12:20; Sept.: Num 24:8; Neh 4:17; Ezek 5:16).
 Deriv.: *bolízō* (1001), to sound; *tríbolis* (5146), three-pointed, three-pronged.

1003. Βοόζ Boóz; proper noun transliterated from the Hebr. *Bō'az* (1162, OT) meaning lovely. Boaz, a descendant of Judah (Ruth 2:1) through whom is traced the regular succession of Jewish kings (Matt 1:5; Luke 3:32). Boaz was a man of wealth and great respectability. He married Ruth and begat Obed, the father of Jesse, the father of David.

1004. βόρβορος bórboros; gen. *borbórou*. Dirt, mire, filth, such as the manure where animals are kept, therefore, dung (2 Pet 2:22 where the expression is proverbial). Sept.: Jer 38:6 of the mire in the dungeon into which Jeremiah was cast.
 Syn.: *skúbalon* (4657), refuse, either of the body or that which is thrown away from a table to the dogs; *kopría* (2874), manure or dunghill.

1005. βορρᾶς borrás; gen. *borrá*, contracted from *boréas* (n.f.), the north, masc. noun. The north wind, used metonymically as the northern quarter of the heavens (Luke 13:29; Rev 21:13; Sept.: Gen 13:14; Job 37:22). Other directions

of the horizon: *nótos* (3558), south; *anatolḗ* (395), east; *dusmḗ* (1424), west; *mesēmbría* (3314), noon or when the sun is directly overhead.

1006. βόσκω bóskō; fut. *boskḗsō*. To feed sheep, to pasture or tend while grazing, trans. Mid. *bóskomai* (Matt 8:30, 33; Mark 5:11, 14; Luke 8:32, 34; 15:15; Sept.: Gen 29:7, 9; 37:12, 16; Ezek 34:2, 3, 8, 10f.; John 21:15, 17 used metaphorically of a Christian teacher meaning to instruct).
 In John 21:15–17, the Lord commands Peter to feed (*bóske*) first the lambs (*arníon* [721]) and secondly the sheep (*próbaton* [4263]), perhaps representing the young and old, both of whom need feeding, although it is also possible to understand the latter as a term of endearment used to intensify Jesus' appeal to Peter. In verse sixteen, however, the Lord did not use the same word for "feed [*bóske*]," but "shepherd [*poímaine*]" my sheep, which involves total care. In the spiritual realm the Lord wanted to teach Peter that caring for older Christians involves much more than caring for lambs, representative of younger Christians. In verse seventeen the Lord repeated the commandment *bóske*, feed, because He wanted to make sure that the feeding is included in the shepherding. Compare the meanings of *agapáō* (25), to love for the sake of meeting another's need, and *philéō* (5368), to be a friend of and consequently to adopt the same interests as the one befriended. Peter did not want to come down to the level of confessing that he simply loved Jesus for the sake of having his needs met by Him, but that he elected to be His friend (contrary to his earlier behavior, Matt 26:69–75) and adopt for himself the same interests as the Lord Jesus had. It was because of this higher confession of Peter that the Lord commanded him both to feed and to shepherd, for those were the interests of the Lord Jesus in coming into the world.
 Deriv.: *botánē* (1008), herbage, plants.

Syn.: *poimaínō* (4165), to shepherd, to act as shepherd, tend, involving much more than feeding

1007. Βοσόρ *Bosór*; masc. proper noun, transliterated from the Hebr. *B⁽ᵉ⁾ōwr* (1160, OT). Beor, the father of Balaam. 2 Pet 2:15; see Num 22:5; Josh 13:22).

1008. βοτάνη *botánē*; gen. *botánēs*, fem. noun from *bóskō* (1006), to graze. Pasturage, meaning the herbage, grass, plants (Heb 6:7; Sept.: Gen 1:11, 12; Ex 9:22, 25).
Syn.: *láchanon* (3001), a garden herb, a vegetable in contrast to wild plants; *chórtos* (5528), a feeding enclosure, a garden, but the word later came to mean grass for feeding cattle, green grass, hay.

1009. βότρυς *bótrus*; gen. *bótruos*, masc. noun. A cluster, especially of grapes (Rev 14:18; Sept.: Gen 40:10; Num 13:25).
Syn.: *staphulé* (4718), a bunch of grapes, the ripe cluster, stressing the grapes themselves.

1010. βουλευτής *bouleutés*; gen. *bouleutoú*, masc. noun from *bouleúō* (1011), to consult, to purpose. A councilman, senator, spoken of a member of the Jewish Sanhedrin (Mark 15:43; Luke 23:50).
Ant.: *idiótēs* (2399), a private person.

1011. βουλεύω *bouleúō*; fut. *bouleúsō*, from *boulé* (1012), counsel, will. To resolve in council, to decree. In the NT, only in the mid., *bouleúomai*, fut. *bouleúsomai*, to take counsel, with the meaning of to consult, determine, deliberate with oneself or with one another in counsel.
(I) To consult, to deliberate as spoken of a single person (Luke 14:31; Sept.: 1 Kgs 12:28; Neh 5:7).
(II) To resolve, determine, purpose after deliberation in particular, used with the acc. (2 Cor 1:17; Sept.: Isa 14:26, 27; 19:17; 46:10; 14:26, 27; 19:17); used with the aor. inf. (Acts 5:33; 15:37;

27:39; Sept.: Esth 3:6). Followed by *hína* (2443), so that (John 12:10).
Deriv.: *bouleutés* (1010), a councilman, a member of a council; *parabouleúomai* (3851), to disregard; *sumbouleúō* (4823), to counsel with someone.
Syn.: *thélō* (2309), to will, which means not only to wish and decide but also to have the power to execute.

1012. βουλή *boulé*; gen. *boulḗs*, fem. noun. Will, purpose, intention as the result of reflection; counsel, decree, aim or estimation as it denotes deliberation and reflection; the assembly of the council. In Mod. Gr., parliament is called *boulé*. Distinguished from *thélēma* (2307) which stands also for the commanding and executing will of God. The will (*boulé*) of God refers only to God's own purpose. *Thélēma* signifies the will urging on to action, while *boulé*, the counsel preceding the resolve, signifies the decision. Therefore, Eph 1:11 should be translated "according to the decision [or plan] of His will" (a.t.). The apostle not only gives prominence to the absolute freedom of the decision of the divine will, but calls attention to the saving plan lying at the basis of the saving will as it manifests itself. In some instances *boulé* and *thélēma* are perfectly syn. *Boulé* is also used to denote the divine decree concerning redemption (Luke 7:30; Acts 2:23; 4:28, purpose, plan; 5:38; 13:36; 20:27; 27:42; Heb 6:17; Sept.: Ezra 4:5; Neh 4:15). Referring to the decisions of men (Luke 23:51; Acts 27:12; Sept.: Prov 19:21; Isa 5:19; Jer 49:20, 30); secret thoughts, purpose (1 Cor 4:5; Sept.: Job 5:12; Isa 55:7, 8 [cf. Ezra 6:22]), equal to *kardía* (2588), heart, meaning its thoughts, desires.
Deriv.: *bouleúō* (1011), to take counsel; *epiboulé* (1917), a plot, conspiracy; *súmboulos* (4825), a councilman, council member.
Syn.: *gnṓmē* (1106), the faculty of knowledge, reason, opinion, resolve, purpose; *krísis* (2920), judgment, decision; *kritérion* (2922), a tribunal or the place or assembly where a judgment or decision

is made; *phrónēma* (5427), thought or the object of thought; *phrónēsis* (5428), the ability to make a decision, prudence; *próthesis* (4286), purpose.

1013. βούλημα *boúlēma*; neut. noun from *boúlomai* (1014), to will. The thing willed, the intention, purpose (Acts 27:43). It denotes plan or purpose, resolve, especially when it refers to God's purpose (*boúlēma*) as in Rom 9:19 when the meaning is that nobody can resist God's purpose as described in Rom 9:18. On the other hand, God's *boulḗ* is the content of the apostolic message (Acts 20:27; Eph 1:1ff.). Contrast *thélēma* (2307) which is not only a will or a wish, but also the execution of it or the desire to execute it. *Thélēma* gives prominence to the element of wish or inclination (1 Pet 4:3 [TR]).

1014. βούλομαι *boúlomai*; 2d person sing. *boúlei*, imperf. *eboulómēn*; aor. pass. *eboulḗthēn*, and with augment *ēboulḗthēn*, mid. deponent. To will, be willing, wish, desire. *Boúlomai* expresses a merely passive desire, propensity, willingness, while *thélō* (2309) expresses an active volition and purpose. *Boúlomai* expresses also the inward predisposition and bent from which active volition proceeds; hence it is never used of evil people. In speaking of the gods, Homer uses *boúlomai* in the sense of *thélō* (2309). In the NT followed by an inf. expressed or implied, either of the aor. or pres. tense; once also with the subjunctive (John 18:39).

(I) As spoken of men, to be willing, inclined, disposed (Mark 15:15; Acts 17:20; 18:27; 19:30; 22:30; 23:28; 25:22; 27:43; 28:18; Phile 1:13; 3 John 1:10; Sept.: Lev 26:21; Deut 25:7, 8; Job 9:3; 39:9). Meaning to intend, purpose, have in mind (Matt 1:19; Acts 5:28; 12:4; 2 Cor 1:15; Sept.: Ezra 4:5). Also in a stronger sense meaning to desire, to aim at (1 Tim 6:9; James 4:4). With the meaning of to choose, prefer, decide (John 18:39; Acts 18:15; 25:20; James 3:4; 2 John 1:12). As

implying command or direction, to will, that is, to direct, followed by the acc. and the inf. (Phil 1:12, "It is my will" [a.t.]; 1 Tim 2:8; 5:14; Titus 3:8; Jude 1:5, "I will that ye call to mind" [a.t.]).

(II) Spoken of God, equivalent to *thélō* (2309), to will, that is, to please, appoint, decree (Luke 22:42; Heb 6:17; James 1:18; 2 Pet 3:9); of Jesus as the Son of God (Matt 11:27; Luke 10:22); of the Spirit (1 Cor 12:11). *Boúlomai* denotes the unconscious willing or an inner decision or thinking while *thélō* indicates conscious willing and denotes a more active resolution urging on to action.

Deriv.: *boúlēma* (1013), purpose, will.

Syn.: *axióō* (515), to desire worthily; *epithuméō* (1937), to desire earnestly stressing an inward impulse rather than an object desired, equivalent to covet; *orégomai* (3713), to long after something; *epizētéō* (1934), to seek earnestly; *epipothéō* (1971), to long after, usually in a bad sense meaning to lust; *parakaléō* (3870), to beseech; *bouleúō* (1011), to take counsel; *eúchomai* (2172), to wish.

Ant.: *distázō* (1365), to waver, doubt, hesitate.

1015. βουνός *bounós*; gen. *bounoú*, masc. noun. Hill, rising ground (Luke 3:5; 23:30; Sept.: Ex 17:9, 10; Isa 40:4; 55:12).

Syn.: *óros* (3735), hill, mountain.

Ant.: *pháragx* (5327), a ravine or valley, figuratively a condition of loneliness and danger.

1016. βοῦς *boús*; gen. *boós*, masc., fem. noun. Ox, cow, an animal of the bovine family (Luke 13:15; 14:5, 19; John 2:14, 15; 1 Cor 9:9; 1 Tim 5:18; Sept.: Gen 13:5; 41:2–4).

Syn.: *taúros* (5022), a bull.

1017. βραβεῖον *brabeíon*; gen. *brabeíou*, neut. noun from *brabeúō* (1018), to assign the prize in a public game. A prize such as a wreath or garland bestowed on victors in the contests of the Greeks (1

Cor 9:24). Metaphorically, refers to the rewards of virtue in the future life (Phil 3:14).

Syn.: *amoibḗ* (287), recompense; *stéphanos* (4735), prize, crown.

1018. βραβεύω *brabeúō*; fut. *brabeúso*. To be a *brabeús*, an umpire, director or arbiter in the public Greek games. In the NT, to rule, govern, and metaphorically to prevail, abound. Used intrans. (Col 3:15, "the peace of God rule in your hearts").

Deriv.: *brabeíon* (1017), prize; *katabrabeúō* (2603), to lay down the reward or that which is due as a result of winning.

Syn.: *árchō* (757), to rule; *perisseúō* (4052), abound; *pleonázō* (4121), to superabound; *huperéchō* (5242), to excel.

Ant.: *timōréō* (5097), to punish; *kolázō* (2849), to chastise, punish; *katakrínō* (2632), to condemn; *aphorízō* (873), to set off, excommunicate; *paradeigmatízō* (3856), to make a public example, put to open shame; *katadikázō* (2613), to condemn.

1019. βραδύνω *bradúnō*; from *bradús* (1021), slow. To be slow, to delay, used intrans. referring to the fact that the Lord will not be tardy or slack in respect to His promise (1 Tim 3:15; 2 Pet 3:9), or it may be interpreted that the Lord of the promise will not be slack to fulfill that promise.

Syn.: *anakóptō* (348), to beat back, check, hinder; *chronízō* (5549), to delay, tarry.

Ant.: *speúdō* (4692), to hasten; *tréchō* (5143), to run; *grēgoréō* (1127), to be vigilant, watchful; *elaúnō* (1643), to push, drive.

1020. βραδυπλοέω *braduploéō*; from *bradús* (1021), slow, and *pléō* (4126), to sail. To sail slowly (Acts 27:7).

1021. βραδύς *bradús*; fem. *bradeía*, neut. *bradú*, adj. Slow as opposed to *tachús* (5036), swift or quick (Luke

24:25, "slow of understanding" [a.t.]; James 1:19 used twice meaning not hasty).

Deriv.: *bradúnō* (1019), to be slow, delay; *braduploéō* (1020), to sail slowly; *bradútēs* (1022), slackness.

Syn.: *nōthrós* (3576), sluggish; *argós* (692), inactive; *oknērós* (3636), shrinking, irksome.

1022. βραδύτης *bradútēs*; gen. *bradútētos*, fem. noun from *bradús* (1021), slow. Slowness, tardiness (2 Pet 3:9 in that the Lord does not delay in respect to His promise).

Syn.: *chronotribéō* (5551), to procrastinate, linger.

Ant.: *táchos* (5034), a brief space of time; *spoudḗ* (4710), haste.

1023. βραχίων *brachíōn*; gen. *brachíonos*, masc. noun, comparative of *brachús* (1024), short. The shorter part of the arm from the shoulder to the elbow. The arm in general, because the arm of man is the principal organ or instrument with which he exerts his strength. Used figuratively meaning the strength or power of God (Luke 1:51; John 12:38; Acts 13:17; Sept.: Deut 5:15; Isa 44:12; 51:5).

1024. βραχύς *brachús*; fem. *bracheía*, neut. *brachú*, adj. Short, small, as spoken of:

(**I**) Time (Luke 22:58, "a little after" [a.t.]; Acts 5:34; Sept.: Ps 94:17).

(**II**) Place (Acts 27:28 meaning having gone a little further; Sept.: 2 Sam 16:1). Figuratively of rank or dignity (Heb 2:7, 9, "a little lower than the angels," referring to the Lord Jesus during His earthly life as quoted from Ps 8:6).

(**III**) Of quantity or number meaning small, few (John 6:7), a little. In few words, briefly (Heb 13:22; Sept.: Deut 26:5; 28:62).

Ant.: *makrós* (3117), long; *hikanós* (2425), much, sufficient, long; *polús* (4183), much; *tosoútos* (5118), so long; *pósos* (4214), how much, how long; *hósos* (3745), how much, usually qualifying time; *diēnekés* (1336), perpetual; *adiáleiptos* (88), permanent, continual; *ektenés* (1618), without ceasing.

1025. βρέφος *bréphos*; gen. *bréphous*, neut. noun. Babe, an unborn child (Luke 1:41, 44); a newborn child or an older infant (Luke 2:12, 16; 18:15; Acts 7:19; 2 Tim 3:15 meaning from infancy, from the cradle). Used metaphorically of those who have just embraced the Christian religion (1 Pet 2:2 [cf. 1 Cor 3:2; Heb 5:12, 13]) from *phérbos* which is from *phérbō*, to feed, nourish, from *phérō* (5342), to bring, and *bíos* (979), sustenance. By transposition from *phérbō*, to feed, nourish, because babies are nourished in the womb and when born require frequent nourishment.

Syn.: *népios* (3516), a little child; *tekníon* (5040), a little child; *téknon* (5043), child; *paidíon* (3813), a little or young child, an infant just born; *país* (3816), child; *paidárion* (3808), a little boy or girl; *korásion* (2877), a little girl, damsel; *paidískē* (3814), a little girl.

Ant.: *néos* (3501), young but usually after the adolescent age; *gérōn* (1088), an old person; *anér* (435), a man, a mature person; *gunḗ* (1135), a mature woman; *presbútēs* (4246), an old man; *presbútis* (4247), an aged woman; *neanías* (3494), a youth up to about forty years; *neanískos* (3495), a youth under forty years.

1026. βρέχω *bréchō*; fut. *bréxō*. To wet, moisten, trans. as with a shower (Luke 7:38, 44; Rev 11:6; Sept.: Ps 6:7; Isa 34:3; Ezek 22:24). To rain, to cause to rain (Sept.: Isa 5:6; Joel 2:23). Used in an absolute sense in Matt 5:45; Sept.: Gen 2:5; Amos 4:7; with the acc. in Luke 17:29; Sept.: Gen 19:24; Ex 9:23; Ezek 38:22. With the subject implied, meaning it rains (James 5:17).

Deriv.: *brochḗ* (1028), rain.

Ant.: *xēraínō* (3583), to dry up, wither.

1027. βροντή *brontḗ*; gen. *brontḗs*, fem. noun. Thunder (Mark 3:17, "sons of thunder"); see *boanergés* (993), which means

sons of thunder, a surname applied by the Lord to James and John because of their lively, impetuous spirits (John 12:29; Rev 4:5; 6:1; 8:5; 10:3, 4; 11:19; 14:2; 16:18; 19:6; Sept.: Job 26:14; Ps 77:18).

1028. βροχή *brochḗ*; gen. *brochḗs*, fem. noun from *bréchō* (1026), to wet, moisten. Rain (Matt 7:25, 27; Sept.: Ps 68:9; 105:32). Used in the Sept. for a Hebr. verb meaning to bless which often applied to rain, dew or moisture (Gen 49:25; Deut 28:12; Isa 44:3).

Syn.: *huetós* (5205), rain, shower; *ómbros* (3655), a thunderstorm, shower.

1029. βρόχος *bróchos*; gen. *bróchou*, masc. noun. A snare, noose (1 Cor 7:35, "not that I would cast a noose over you" [a.t.], meaning impose on you anything that you do not desire; Sept.: Prov 6:5; 7:21; 22:25).

Syn.: *pagís* (3803), a trap; *ágra* (61), a catching; *thḗra* (2339), a hunting game; *enédra* (1747), a trap.

Ant.: *phugḗ* (5437), escape.

1030. βρυγμός *brugmós*; gen. *brugmoú*, masc. noun from *brúchō* (1031), to grind, gnash, crunch the teeth together. A grating or gnashing of the teeth (Matt 8:12; 13:42, 50; 22:13; 24:51; 25:30; Luke 13:28). The image is drawn from a person in a fit of envy, rage, pain, and so forth (Acts 7:54; Sept.: Prov 19:12, spoken of the roar or growl of the lion).

Syn.: *kraugḗ* (2906), clamor, cry.

Ant.: *psithurismós* (5587), a whispering; *sigḗ* (4602), silence, hush.

1031. βρύχω *brúchō*; fut. *brúxō*. To grind, gnash, or crunch the teeth together, as a person in violent rage or anger (Acts 7:54). It is applied to mad dogs and lions and seems to be a word formed from the sound, as the Eng. "crunch."

Deriv.: *brugmós* (1030), gnashing of teeth.

Syn.: *trízō* (5149), originally meaning to chirp or squeak, and later to grind the teeth.

Ant.: *siōpáō* (4623), to hush; *sigáō* (4601), to keep silent.

1032. βρύω *brúō*; fut. *brúsō*. To be full, abound, overflow. Used intrans. in the Class. Gr. In the NT however, it is used trans. meaning to pour forth, emit voluminously. Spoken of a fountain (James 3:11).

Syn.: *ekchúnō / ekchéō* (1632), to pour forth.

Ant.: *sullégō* (4816), to gather together or up; *sunágō* (4863), to collect.

1033. βρῶμα *brṓma*; gen. *brṓmatos*, neut. noun from *bibrṓskō* (977), to eat. That which is chewed such as meat or vegetables in opposition to milk which is liquid (1 Cor 3:2). Used with its primary meaning as food (Matt 14:15; Mark 7:19; Luke 3:11; 9:13; 1 Cor 6:13; Sept.: Gen 6:21; 41:35ff.; Deut 2:28; 2 Chr 9:4). Spoken of meats permitted by the Mosaic Law (Heb 9:10; 13:9); of meats against which Jewish Christians observed certain scruples in eating (Rom 14:15, 20; 1 Cor 8:8, 13; 1 Tim 4:3). It denotes sustenance, nourishment (John 4:34) or that by which one lives. Used for spiritual food, manna, as an emblem of spiritual nourishment or instruction (1 Cor 3:2; 10:3).

Syn.: *trophḗ* (5160), food, nourishment; *diatrophḗ* (1305), sustenance, food; *sitométrion* or *sitómetron* (4620), a measured portion of food; *sítos* (4621), grain, wheat; *mánna* (3131), manna, food.

Ant.: *nēsteía* (3521), a fast.

1034. βρώσιμος *brṓsimos*; gen. *brosímou*, masc.-fem., neut. *brṓsimon*, adj. from *brṓsis* (1035), food. Edible (Luke 24:41, "Have ye here any meat?" meaning anything edible; Sept.: Lev 19:23; Ezek 47:12).

1035. βρῶσις *brṓsis*; gen. *brṓseōs*, fem. noun from *bibrṓskō* (977), to eat. Eating. Spoken of:

(I) The act of eating (1 Cor 8:4; 2 Cor 9:10) with the prep. *eis* (1519), unto or for, meaning bread to eat as in Isa 55:10; Mal 3:11; Sept.: Deut 32:24. Figuratively it means erosion, corrosion in an abstract or complete manner (Matt 6:19, 20, moth and corrosion, corroding rust [cf. James 5:2, 3]).

(II) That which is eaten, food, equivalent to *brṓma* (1033) (John 6:27; "food that perishes" [a.t.], food for the body; Heb 12:16; Sept.: Gen 47:24; 2 Sam 19:42; 1 Kgs 19:8; Jer 7:33; 19:7). In Rom 14:17, "the kingdom of God is not [solid] meat and drink" means that the experience of the kingdom of God does not consist of eating or drinking, or through an act that is physical because the kingdom of God is spiritual and experienced by faith (Col 2:16). Metaphorically it means nourishment (John 4:32. In John 6:27, 55, *brṓsis* is used in the sense of food for the soul, meaning spiritual nourishment from above which is offered to Christians through Christ.

Deriv.: *brṓsimos* (1034), edible.

Syn.: *brṓma* (1033), food.

Ant.: *nēsteía* (3521), a fast.

1036. βυθίζω *buthízō*; fut. *buthísō*, from *buthós* (1037), the depth. To sink in the deep or to cause to sink. Used in the pass. meaning to sink (Luke 5:7), metaphorically (1 Tim 6:9) followed by *eis* (1519), unto, *ólethron* (3639), ruin, destruction, and *apóleian* (684), ruin or loss. These two words do not mean annihilation or cessation of existence, but change of constitutional existence.

Syn.: *katapontízō* (2670), to sink, drown; *kataphérō* (2703), to bear down, sink down; *embáptō* (1686), to dip in; *báptō* (911), to cover fully with fluid, dip; *baptízō* (907), to baptize, immerse.

Ant.: *pléō* (4126), to float or sail.

1037. βυθός *buthós*; gen. *buthoú*. Depth, the deep, referring to the bottom of the sea as in 2 Cor 11:25.

Deriv.: *ábussos* (12), abyss, the deep; *buthízō* (1036), to sink, drown.

Ant.: *epipháneia* (2015), visible surface, that which is seen on top.

1038. βυρσεύς *burseús*; gen. *burséōs*, masc. noun from *búrsa* (n.f.), a skin or hide of a beast when separated or flayed off from its body. A tanner, leather dresser (Acts 9:43; 10:6, 32).

1039. βύσσινος *bússinos*; fem. *bussínē*, neut. *bússinon*, adj. from *bússos* (1040), a type of fine linen. Made of fine linen or cotton (Sept.: Gen 41:42; 1 Chr 15:27; Rev 18:12 and in later editions also in Rev 18:16; 19:8, 14).

1040. βύσσος *bússos*; gen. *bússou*, fem. noun. A type of fine linen or sometimes cotton highly prized in ancient times (Luke 16:19; Rev 18:12 [TR]).

In Egypt and Syria it was used to wrap mummies (Ezek 27:7, 16, see also 1 Chr 4:21; 2 Chr 3:14 [cf. Ex 26:31]). It was of different colors, the Jews preferring yellow and sometimes purple or crimson (Luke 16:19). White is mentioned in Rev 19:8, 14.

Deriv.: *bússinos* (1039), fine linen.

1041. βωμός *bōmós*; gen. *bōmoú*, masc. noun from *baínō* (n.f., see *apobaínō* [576]), to go, step. A step, base, pedestal. In the NT, it is used of idolatrous altars (Acts 17:23; Sept.: Ex 34:13; Num 23:1). Contrast *thusiastérion* (2379), an altar of the true God.

Γ

1042. Γαββαθα̂ *Gabbathá*; fem. noun transliterated from the Aramaic *gab* (1355, OT) Gabbatha, a raised or elevated place, tribunal, stage or scaffold (John 19:13). In Gr. it is explained as *lithóstrōton* (3038), stone pavement.

1043. Γαβριήλ *Gabriḗl*; masc. proper noun transliterated from the Hebr. *Gabrīy'ēl* (1403, OT), man of God. Gabriel, an angel especially entrusted with the message to Zacharias concerning the birth of John, and to Mary concerning the birth of Christ (Luke 1:19–26). At an earlier period, he was sent to Daniel to unfold a vision (Dan 8:16; 9:21). One of the two angels referred to in the Bible, the other being Michael the archangel (Jude 1:9) who is the warrior angel, *ággelos* (32), angel.

1044. γάγγραινα *gággraina*; gen. *gaggraínēs*, fem. noun from *gráō* or *graínō* (n.f.), to devour, corrode, consume, eat away. Gangrene or mortification which, unless properly treated, spreads from the place affected and eats away or consumes the neighboring parts of the body and at length destroys the whole body (2 Tim 2:17).

1045. Γάδ *Gád*; proper noun transliterated from the Hebr. *Gād* (1410, OT), good fortune. Gad, a tribe of Israel. The territory given to the tribe of Gad lay east of the Jordan, north of that allotted to Reuben, and south of that given to Manasseh on that side of the river. It extended from the Jordan eastward to Aroer (Josh 13:25) including half of Mount Gilead and half of Ammon (Deut 3:12; Josh 13:25). Its chief cities were Ramoth-gilead, Mahanaim, Hashbon, and Aroer. Two famous men came from Gad: Barzillai (2 Sam 17:27) and Elijah (1 Kgs 17:1). See Rev 7:5.

1046. Γαδαρηνός *Gadarēnós*; gen. *Gadarēnoú*, masc. proper noun. A Gadarene, an inhabitant from a town east of the Jordan called Gadara. Gadara was the fortified capital of Peraea, or the region east of the Jordan. It was situated by Tiberias and Scythopolis, in or near the range of mountains bordering the eastern shore of Lake Galilee and the valley of the Jordan. It is supposed that it was on the site of the present village Om Keis which lies southeast from the southern extremity of the lake and not far from the river Hieromax. Josephus calls Gadara a Greek city with many wealthy inhabitants. When first taken from the Jews, it was annexed by the Romans to Syria. Augustus gave it to Herod the Great, but it was restored to Syria after Herod's death. See Mark 5:1; Luke 8:26, 37. In some MSS it appears also in Matt 8:28 called "the country of the Gergesenes" (see *Gerasēnó*, 1086).

1047. γάζα *gáza*; gen. *gázēs*, fem. noun. A treasury, especially of a king of state (Acts 8:27). The word is of Persian origin (Sept.: Ezra 5:17; 6:1; Esth 4:7).

Deriv.: *gazophulákion* (1049), a treasury.

1048. Γάζα *Gáza*; gen. *Gázēs*; fem. proper noun transliterated from the Hebr. 'Azzah (5804, OT), strong. Gaza, the chief of the five cities of the Philistines, fifty miles southeast of Jerusalem, three miles from the Mediterranean and ten miles from Ashkelon. It is one of the oldest cities in the world. Peopled by the descendants of Ham (Gen 10:19) and by the Anakin (Josh 11:22); given to Judah (Josh 15:47); traversed by Samson (Judg 16); ruled by Solomon and called Azzah (1 Kgs 4:24). It was smitten by Egypt (Jer 47:1, 5) and prophesied against (Amos 1:6, 7; Zeph 2:4; Zech 9:5). In the NT it occurs only in Acts 8:26, "And the angel of the Lord spake unto Philip, saying, Arise, and go toward the south unto the way that goeth down from Jerusalem unto Gaza, which is desert," where he met the Ethiopian eunuch. Some take the expression "which is desert" as meaning that which leads through the desert where Philip met the eunuch. Others refer the desert to Gaza itself, and suppose the later city to have been built on a different site. As, however, Gaza was sacked and destroyed in A.D. 65 during an insurrection of the Jews, we may perhaps regard the expression, "which is desert," as the words not of the angel, but of Luke, implying that the city was desolate at the time he wrote. In the intertestamental period it appears the city was standing, but about 95 B.C., Alexander Jannaeus took it after a siege of a year and destroyed it. Gabinius afterwards rebuilt it, and Augustus bestowed it on Herod the Great, after whose death it was annexed to Syria. The city was a chief stronghold of pantheism and the worship of the god Marnas (Dagon) whose temples were destroyed in A.D. 400; taken by the Arabs, in A.D. 634; restored by the Crusaders in A.D. 1149; plundered by Saladin in A.D. 1170, and again in A.D. 1187; and taken by Napoleon in 1799.

1049. γαζοφυλάκιον *gazophulákon*; gen. *gazophulakíou*, neut. noun from *gáza* (1047), a treasure or treasury, and *phulakḗ* (5438), a place where something is guarded. A treasury, a place of deposit for the public treasure. Among the Jews this was the sacred treasury kept in one of the courts of the temple (Neh 10:37, 38; 13:4, 5, 7, 8; Esth 3:9). According to the Talmudists, the treasury was in the court of the women where stood thirteen chests, called from their shape "trumpets," into which the Jews cast their offerings (Ex 30:13f. In the NT in Mark 12:41, 43; Luke 21:1). Spoken of the court itself in John 8:20.

Syn.: *thēsaurós* (2344), treasury, storehouse, also treasure.

1050. Γάϊος *Gáios*; gen. *Gaḯou*, masc. proper noun. Gaius, a Macedonian (Acts 19:29) who was Paul's host at Corinth when the Epistle to the Romans was written (Rom 16:23) and was baptized with his household by Paul (1 Cor 1:14). He accompanied Paul to Ephesus and was seized by the mob (Acts 19:29). The association of his name with that of *Arístarchos* (708) seems to identify him with the Gaius of Derbe (1191) (Acts 20:4). The Apostle John addresses his third Epistle to someone by that name, but we do not know whether it is the same person or not.

1051. γάλα *gála*; gen. *gálaktos*, neut. noun. Milk (1 Cor 9:7). Figuratively, the sincere and sweet word of Christ by which believers grow in grace and are nourished to life eternal (1 Pet 2:2). The rudiments of Christianity are to nourish the babes in Christ (1 Cor 3:2; Heb 5:12, 13). In its metaphorical sense syn. with *stoicheía* (4747), spiritual elements of Christian instruction (Heb 5:12).

1052. Γαλάτης *Galátēs*; gen. *Galátou*, masc. proper noun. A Galatian, an inhabitant of Galatia (Gal 3:1).

1053. Γαλατία *Galatía*; gen. *Galatías*, fem. proper noun. Galatia, a central province of Asia Minor subject to Roman rule, bounded by Bithynia and Paphlagonia on the north, Pontus on the east, Cappadocia and Lycaonia on the south, and Phrygia on the west. Its boundaries, however, were often changed. In Ptolemy's time it extended to the Euxine or Black Sea, and at one time included Lycaonia on the south. Its capitals were Tavium, Pessinus, and Ancyra. The country was chiefly a high tableland between the two rivers Halys and Sangarius. The Galatians were originally Gauls or Celts who, 300 years before Christ, moved from the regions of the Rhine back toward the east and there mingled with Greeks and Jews. They combined quick temper, prompt action, inconstancy, and changeableness. Thus these attributes appeared in Paul's epistle to them. Galatia was a part of Paul's missionary field. He visited it once with Silas and Timothy (Acts 16:6), and again on his third tour he "went over all the country of Galatia" (Acts 18:23) and received a collection for the saints from its churches (1 Cor 16:1). Crescens also appears to have been sent there near the close of Paul's life (2 Tim 4:10).

1054. Γαλατικός *Galatikós*; fem. *Galatikḗ*, neut. *Galatikón*, adj. Galatian (Acts 16:6; 18:23, the Galatian land meaning Galatia).

1055. γαλήνη *galḗnē*; gen. *galḗnēs*, fem. noun. A calmness, tranquility or quietness of the sea (Matt 8:26; Mark 4:39; Luke 8:24).

Syn.: *hēsuchía* (2271) stillness, quietness; *eudía* (2105), fine or fair weather.

Ant.: *tarachḗ* (5016), disturbance; *klúdōn* (2830), a surge of the sea, raging wave; *kúma* (2949), wave; *ánemos* (417), wind; *thúella* (2366), storm, tempest; *laílaps* (2978), storm; *sálos* (4535), billow, wave; *pnoḗ* (4157), wind.

1056. Γαλιλαία *Galilaía*; gen. *Galilaías*, fem. proper noun. Galilee meaning circle, circuit. A name in the OT for a small district in the northern mountains of Naphtali, around Kedesh-naphtali, and including twenty towns given by Solomon to Hiram, king of Tyre (Josh 20:7; 21:32; 1 Kgs 9:11; 2 Kgs 15:29; Isa 9:1, called "Galilee of the nations"). Devastated during the wars of the captivity, it was repeopled by strangers. In the time of the Maccabees, they probably outnumbered the Jewish population, and gave their new name to a much wider district.

In the time of Christ, Palestine was divided into three provinces of which Galilee was the most northern. It included the whole region from the Plain of Jezreel to the Leontes River, being about fifty miles long and twenty to twenty-five miles wide. The northern part was known as Upper and the southern part as Lower Galilee. These included the territories given to Asher, Naphtali, Zebulon, and Issachar. The area was fertile with rich pastures and fine forests. The portion west of the lake was the most beautiful. In the Roman period the population was dense, between two to three million as estimated by Josephus, although that seems to be an exaggerated number. It had a mixed population of Gentiles and Jews. The latter, having a strong, if not dominant, influence, were less strict and less acquainted with the law than their southern Judaean neighbors by whom they were little esteemed.

The noted mountains of Galilee were Carmel, Gilboa, and Tabor; the towns were Nazareth, Cana, Tiberias, Chorazin, Bethsaida, and Capernaum.

The Lord Jesus spent the greater portion of His life and ministry in Galilee. Many of His most remarkable miracles, teachings, and labors were within this province of Galilee. Many of the teachings and miracles of our Lord took place in Galilee including the sermon on the Mount (Matt 5—7), the raising of the widow's son (Luke 7:11–15), the stilling of the tempest (Matt 8:26), the feeding of the five thousand (Mark 6:44), the transfiguration (Mark 9:2), the marriage feast (John 2:1), the draught of fishes (Luke 5:6), the mountain refuge for secret prayer (Matt 14:23), the little child in the Savior's arms (Mark 9:36), and the marvelous explanation of the bread of life (John 6).

Galilee gallantly resisted in the war with Rome (A.D. 67–70). The hardest fighting of the war was done on the soil of Galilee, and in that terrible year 150,000 of her people perished. From the days of Joshua to those of Bar-Cochba, no Jewish army had shown greater valor than did the compatriots of Jesus of Nazareth, the men from the homeland of Christ.

The body of water in Galilee appears under different names. Although today it is called the lake of Tiberias, the term is never used in the NT. Luke 5:1 is the only place where the name "lake of Gennesaret" occurs. In four instances it is referred to as "the lake" (Luke 5:2; 8:22, 23, 33). In several others it is called "the sea" (John 6:11–25). In John 6:1; 21:1, John calls it the "sea of Tiberias." But in the first case, he had already mentioned in a natural way the sea of Galilee, and immediately explained for his Gentile readers that it was the same as the sea of Tiberias. "Sea of Galilee" would seem to be the best known and most appropriate name, and this is used five times (Matt 4:18; 15:29; Mark 1:16; 7:31; John 6:1). In the OT, it is called the "sea of Chinnereth" (Num 34:11, defining the boundary of the land; Josh 13:27, defining the border of the territory of Gad). "Sea of Chinnereth" is given in describing the territory of Sihon that was conquered by Moses (Josh 12:3). Chinnereth means harp and is used once in Deut 3:17 and once as Chinneroth in Josh 11:2, both referring to the sea of Galilee. Once Chinneroth is used for a district conquered by Benhadad (1 Kgs 15:20), and Chinnereth appears in Josh 19:35 as a "fenced city." It is perfectly consistent with oriental usage for a city, a district and a body of water adjoining it, to be called by the same name, although it is quite possible that Deut 3:17; Josh 11:2; 19:35 all refer to the city Chinnereth or Chinneroth. It is also known as Gennesareth. Gennesareth may be derived from Gan and Sar, meaning princess garden, applied, of course, to the land of Gennesareth, from which the sea of Galilee is once called the "lake of Gennesareth" (Luke 5:1).

The sea of Galilee is thirteen miles long and a little less than seven miles wide in the widest part. Its greatest depth is less than 200 feet. It is not quite oval in form, although it appears to be so when looked at from the surrounding heights. It is more pear-shaped, having the small end at the south. Its level below the Mediterranean Sea is about 700 feet. On the east side the mountain rises from its shore to an elevation of 2,000 feet. On the south the lake touches the plain of the Jordan valley.

The rabbis used to say, "Although God has created seven seas, yet He has chosen this one as His special delight." From the shore of the sea of Galilee, if we add its depression of 700 feet to the elevation of Mount Hermon to the north, we look up to its summit at a sheer height of over 10,000 feet.

The storm recorded in Matt 8:24, when Christ stilled the waters, was no infrequent occurrence. This was due partly to the difference of temperature about the lake from that of the mountains or tableland so far above it.

The River Jordan enters the lake at the northern end, and exits at the southern end. It brings down so much sediment at times that it appears like a very dirty stream; still the water of the lake itself is always clear, sweet, and cool. There are hot springs near the sea.

The fish of this lake have always been held in highest appreciation. Bethsaida on the north was known as a "house of fish" indicating the abundance of fish found in the lake. Tarichea on the south was a fish factory. The Jews distinguished sharply between clean and unclean fish, a fact no doubt alluded to in our Lord's parable of the net where the good were gathered into baskets and the bad were cast away (Matt 13:47, 48).

There were plenty of boats engaged in fishing or traffic with a lucrative shipbuilding business in the area. Some of the boats must have been of a large size since many of the soldiers and citizens of Tarichea, of whom 4,000 to 6,000 were slain, took refuge in ships during the war with the Romans.

The word used for boats around Galilee is usually *ploíon* (4143). In John 21:8 the diminutive *ploiárion* (4142) is used, which must have been a smaller boat frequently towed after a large ship.

The Lord Jesus made His home in Capernaum (Matt 4:13) and spent the greatest part of His life in the area. Here He called the fishermen, Peter, Andrew, James, and John, to be fishers of men (Matt 4:18–22) and also Matthew from the receipt of custom (Mark 2:13–17). Here multitudes came to Jesus "to be healed of their diseases" and He "healed them all" (Luke 6:17–19). Among them were the nobleman's son (John 4:46–54), the centurion's servant (Matt 8:5–13), Jairus' daughter (Matt 9:18–26), the paralytic who was let down through the uncovered roof (Mark 2:1–12), the demoniac in the synagogue at Capernaum (Mark 1:21–28), the demoniac of Gadara on the eastern shore (Luke 8:26–40), the blind man at Bethsaida (Mark 8:22–26), and Peter's mother-in-law (Matt 8:14–17). It is to some or all of these acts that Christ Himself alludes as "mighty works" (Matt 11:20–24) which would have moved the people of Tyre, or even those of Sodom, could they have witnessed them.

Two of the incidents which illustrate our Lord's character and His life in Galilee are His walking on the water and calming the tempest (Matt 14:22–36) and His feeding of the five thousand (Matt 14:13–21).

Some of the important and representative conversations and warnings of our Lord were made here. In "the leaven of the Pharisees" (Luke 12:1), hypocrisy was rebuked; in the innocence of childhood, humility was praised (Luke 9:46–48); at the feast with Levi, social courtesies were observed (Mark 2:15); in the paying of the tribute money, patriotism was upheld (Matt 17:24–27); and from the signs in the sky as well as the sower in the field, valuable truths were taught (Matt 13:1–15; 16). It was here in Galilee that the foundational principles of Christianity were first promulgated and the nature of the bread of life unfolded (Matt 5:1–14; John 6).

The Lord chose Capernaum as His residential city, not simply because it was a commercial one, but because it was a center of news. Roads extended from there to Damascus and Euphrates, to the cities of the Mediterranean coast which were in touch with Europe, to the southwest by Gaza and from there to Egypt, to the south along the great mountain range

of Shechem, Jerusalem, and Hebron, to the Jordan Valley and the rich and populous country of Peraea. People of all kinds from everywhere passed through this place for business or pleasure. The news of this startling teacher, healer, and exhibitor of great wisdom would be carried very rapidly in every direction. Christ chose His residence where He could reach the most people. Yet the record simply says, "Leaving Nazareth, he ... dwelt in Capernaum" (Matt 4:13). If the Lord Jesus had cloistered Himself away from people, we would have been deprived of the exhibition of His interest, power, and concern.

1057. Γαλιλαῖος *Galilaíos*; fem. *Galilaía*, neut. *Galilaíon*, adj. Galilean, a native or inhabitant of Galilee (Matt 26:69; Mark 14:70; Luke 13:1; 22:59; John 4:45; Acts 1:11; 2:7; 5:37). The Galileans were brave and industrious, though the other Jews regarded them as stupid, unpolished, and seditious, and therefore, proper objects of contempt (John 1:47; 7:52). They had a peculiar dialect by which they were easily distinguished from the Jews of Jerusalem (Mark 14:70).

1058. Γαλλίων *Gallíōn*; gen. *Gallíōnos*, masc. proper noun. Gallio, a Roman proconsul of Achaia (Acts 18:12) and brother of Seneca, the famous philosopher. Seneca describes him as a man of great mildness and simplicity. Paul was brought before his tribunal at Corinth. Gallio dismissed the case as one not recognized by a Roman court, deeming the offense at best a trivial one (Acts 18:12–16). Like his brother Seneca, Gallio was executed at the command of Nero.

1059. Γαμαλιήλ *Gamaliēl*; masc. proper noun, transliterated from the Hebr. *Gamliy'ēl* (1583, OT), reward of God. Gamaliel, the son of Simeon and grandson of the celebrated liberal rabbi, Hillel. He was a doctor of the law and a member of the Sanhedrin. He represented the liberal wing of the Pharisees, the school of Hillel, as opposed to that of Shammai. He spoke up at the trial of the apostles (Acts 5:34), probably because for thirty-two years he was the Sanhedrin's president. He was Paul's teacher at Jerusalem (Acts 22:3).

1060. γαμέω gaméō; contracted *gamṓ*, fut. *gamḗsō*, imperf. *egámoun*, aor. *égēma*, and in later Gr. *egámēsa*, aor. pass. *egamḗthēn*, perf. *gegámēka*, from *gámos* (1062), marriage. To marry, take as a wife, to enter into the conjugal state, with the acc. (Matt 19:10; 22:25, 30; 24:38; Mark 6:17; 10:11; 12:25; Luke 17:27; 20:34, 35; 1 Cor 7:28, 33). Used trans. of the man (Matt 5:32; 19:9; Mark 6:17; 10:11; Luke 14:20; 16:18); intrans. (Luke 20:34, 35; 1 Cor 7:28, 33); used trans. applying to the woman (1 Cor 7:28, 34, 36; 1 Tim 5:11, 14); spoken of both sexes (1 Cor 7:9, 10; 1 Tim 4:3). In 1 Cor 7:39 the verb is used in the aor. pass. inf. with the dat. meaning to enter into marriage. In Mark 10:12 it is used in the subjunctive aor. meaning, "and if she, when she dismisses her own husband, marries another, she commits adultery against herself" (a.t.).
Syn.: *epigambreúō* (1918), to marry.

1061. γαμίσκω gamískō; fut. *gamísō*, from *gámos* (1062), marriage. To give in marriage (Mark 12:25 [TR]). The same as *gamízō*.
Deriv.: *ekgamískō* (1548), to give in marriage.

1062. γάμος gámos; gen. *gámou*, masc. noun. Marriage, a wedding feast (Matt 22:10–12; Luke 14:8; John 2:1, 2); the actual joining of a husband and wife (Heb 13:4). Used also of the wedding festivities in the pl., *gámoi* (Luke 12:36; Matt 22:2–4, 9, alternately with the sing., Matt 22:8, 10–12; 25:10 *gámous*). The expression, "the wedding feast of the Lamb" (a.t. [Rev 19:7, 9]), and also certain parables (Matt 22:2ff.; 25:1–10), refer to the "husband-wife" relationship of God to Israel as presented in Isa 54:4 ff; Hosea

2:19. This relationship of Jehovah to His people in the OT, Israel, was to be fully realized in the Messianic era (to which the expression in John 3:29, and perhaps Matt 9:15, points) and is parlayed into Christ's relation to His redeemed bride, the Church, in the NT (2 Cor 11:2; Eph 5:26, 27; Rev 21:2; 22:17). The marriage of the Lamb is the consummation of salvation to be ushered in by the *parousía* (3952), the appearing of the Lord.
Deriv.: *ágamos* (22), unmarried; *gaméō* (1060), to marry; *gamískō* (1061), to give in marriage.

1063. γάρ gár; a causative particle standing always after one or more words in a clause and expressing the reason for what has been before, affirmed or implied. For, in the sense of because, and so forth.
(I) When it stands by itself:
(A) After an antecedent sentence expressed (Matt 1:20), the antecedent sentence expressed being "fear not to take unto thee Mary thy wife: for [*gár*] that which is conceived in her." Matt 1:21, "Thou shalt call his name Jesus: for [*gár*] he shall save," also Mark 1:22; 6:18; Luke 1:15. After a clause of prohibition or caution (Matt 3:9; 24:5; Luke 7:6). *Gár* is also put after two words in a clause (Matt 2:6; Mark 1:38; Luke 6:23; John 12:8; Acts 4:20). *Gár* is often found in two consecutive clauses where the same idea is expressed twice, that is, affirmatively and negatively or generally and specifically (John 8:42; 1 Cor 16:7; 2 Cor 11:19), or where the latter clause is dependent on the former (Matt 10:20; Mark 6:52; John 5:21, 22; Acts 2:15), or where two different causes are assigned (Matt 6:32; 18:10, 11; Rom 16:18, 19). In similar circumstances *gár* is also found in three consecutive clauses (Matt 16:25–27; Mark 9:39–41; Luke 9:24–26; Acts 26:26). In Matt 26:10, 12 the phrases, "for she hath wrought a good work" (v. 10) and "for in that she hath poured" (v. 12) refer to the act of the woman, but in Matt 26:11 in the phrase "for ye have the poor always" refers to the objection of the disciples. The

gár is also sometimes repeated where the writer again takes on the sentence which began with *gár* and was interrupted (Rom 15:26, 27; 2 Cor 5:2, 4).

(B) Elliptically, where the clause to which it refers is omitted and is to be supplied in thought. In this case it assigns the motive for an opinion or judgment as in Matt 2:2, "Where is he that is born King of the Jews? [He must be born] for we have seen his star"; in Matt 27:23, "for what evil hath he done?" (a.t.); Mark 8:37, 38, "what can the man give in exchange for his soul? [a vain hope!]"; Mark 12:23; Luke 22:37; John 4:43, 44, "he departed . . . into Galilee [not indeed into Nazareth His own country] for Jesus himself testified" (cf. Luke 4:16ff.; Acts 13:36; 21:13; 22:26); Rom 2:25; 8:14, 18 "If we suffer with him that we may also be glorified together. For [*gár*] I reckon" (a.t. [see also Rom 14:10; 1 Cor 1:18]). In a quotation where the preceding clause is omitted (Acts 17:28), *kaí* (2532), and, *gár*, *kaí gár* (Matt 8:9; Luke 7:8, This I know by comparing my own case "for [*gár*] I, too, am" [a.t.]). Matt 15:27, "yes [or true], Lord; yet still help me for even [*kaí gár*] the dogs" [a.t.]). Also *ou* (3756) *gár*, for not (Matt 9:13; Acts 4:20).

(C) Elliptically and in common usage *gár* is also simply intens. and merely serves to strengthen a clause, like the Eng. "then" and "truly." (1) In questions where a preceding "No!" may perhaps be supplied (Matt 27:23; John 7:41, "Shall [then] Christ come out of Galilee?"; Acts 8:31, "How can I [then]?"; Acts 19:35, "what man [then] is there?"; Rom 3:3; Phil 1:18, *tí* [5101] *gár*, "What then?" See also 1 Cor 11:22). (2) In a strong affirmation or negation (John 9:30, "truly herein [or, herein then] is a strange thing" [a.t.]; 1 Pet 4:15, "let [then] none of you suffer"; Acts 16:37, "No then! No indeed!"). (3) In exclamations, as of wishing, with the opt. (2 Tim 2:7, "may the Lord then give thee" [a.t.]). Used more commonly with *ei* (1487), if, followed by *gár*, *ei gár* meaning Oh that! (Sept.: Job 6:2, 8).

(D) Put by way of explanation or demonstration: (1) Where it merely takes up a preceding annunciation and continues or explains it like the Eng. "namely," "to wit," "that is," though it is often not to be rendered in Eng. So also after *hoútōs* (3779), thus (Matt 1:18, "the birth of Jesus Christ was [thus, that is] His mother being espoused" [a.t.]). (2) In a less strict sense, where it introduces by way of explanation the ground or motive of what precedes, for, that is, since, and so forth (Matt 6:7, 16; 10:35; 15:4; 24:7; 1 Cor 11:26). In this sense it serves to introduce parenthetic clauses (Mark 5:42; 6:14; 14:40; 16:4; John 4:8; Acts 13:8; 2 Cor 5:7; Eph 6:1).

(II) With other particles where, however, each retains its own separate force and meaning; e.g., *eán* (1437) *gár*, *ei gár*, if, for if (Matt 5:46; 6:14). Preceded by *ei* (1487), if, meaning for if (Rom 3:7; 4:14). Preceded by *idoú* (2400), behold, *idoú gár* meaning "For behold" or "for lo!" (Luke 1:44, 48; 2:10). Preceded by *kaí* (2532), and, *kaí gár* meaning for also or for even (Matt 26:73; Mark 10:45; Luke 6:32; John 4:45). Also followed by *kaí*, and, *gár kaí*, meaning for also (Acts 17:28; 2 Cor 2:9). Preceded by *kaí*, and, and followed by *ouk* (3756), not, *kaí gár ouk*, meaning for neither (1 Cor 11:9). *Men* (3303) *gár*, followed by *dé* (1161), on the one hand and on the other, two particles of contrast *men gár dé* meaning for indeed (Acts 13:36; 23:8; Rom 2:25). Also where the clause with the contrasting particle *dé* (1161) is altogether omitted (Rom 3:2; 1 Cor 11:18) or is readily supplied (Heb 6:16 [Heb 6:13]). Followed by *allá* (235), but (Acts 4:16, 17). *Mḗ* (3361), not, followed by *gár*, *mḗ gár* meaning for not (James 1:7). *Ou* (3756), not, followed by *gár*, *ou gár* meaning for not (Matt 9:13; Mark 6:52; Luke 8:17; Rom 4:13). Preceded by *oudé* (3761), neither, *oudé gár* meaning for neither (John 5:22; 7:5; 8:42). Preceded by *oúte* (3777), neither, followed by *gár*, *oúte gár*, for neither (Luke 20:36; Acts 4:12; 1 Cor 8:8; 1 Thess 2:5).

1064. γαστήρ *gastḗr*; gen. *gastéros*, pl. *gastéres*. The belly (Sept.: Num 5:22; Job 40:11).

(I) Particularly the stomach (Sept.: Job 15:2; 20:23) and metaphorically, appetite, excessive eating. In the NT, a glutton (Titus 1:12), "The Cretians are always . . . slow bellies," meaning lazy gormandizers or gluttons. Such in ancient Greece were called *gastródouloi*, slaves of their stomachs. Our Eng. gastritis and gastric are derived from *gastḗr*.

(II) The womb (Luke 1:31; Sept.: Gen 25:23; Ps 58:3). To be pregnant with child is expressed as *en gastrí échein*, in the womb to have (Matt 1:18, 23; 24:19; Mark 13:17; Luke 21:23; 1 Thess 5:3; Rev 12:2; Sept.: Gen 16:4; 38:25; 2 Kgs 8:12).

Syn.: *koilía* (2836), hollow, belly, or the entire physical cavity, most frequently used to denote the womb and metaphorically meaning the innermost part of man, the soul, heart; *phágos* (5314), a glutton; *mḗtra* (3388), the womb.

1065. γε *ge*; an enclitic particle. Serves to strengthen or render more emphatic the word to which it is appended by placing it in opposition to other words and thus fixing the attention upon it; e.g., a part in reference to a whole, a single object in reference to many, a less infrequency to a greater, and vice versa. Often it cannot be translated adequately in Eng., but it must be rendered by some emphatic instrument.

(I) Used alone.

(A) As marking a lesser in reference to a greater, at least (Luke 11:8, "though he will not give him, because he is his friend [the greater reason] yet at least because of his importunity but [the lesser reason] he will rise" [a.t.]; Luke 18:5). See also 1 Cor 4:8, "I could wish at least" [a.t.]; Sept.: Job 30:24).

(B) As marking a greater in reference to a lesser. Even, indeed (Rom 8:32, who even).

(II) In connection with other particles. **(1)** Preceded by *allá* (235), but, *allá ge* or in one word *állage*, meaning yet at least, yet surely (1 Cor 9:2). In Luke 24:21, but indeed, moreover. **(2)** Preceded by *ára* (686), therefore, making it either one word *árage* or two words *ará ge*, meaning therefore. **(3)** Preceded by *ei* (1487), if, making it *eíge*, meaning if at least, if indeed, if so be, followed by the indic. and spoken of what is taken for granted (Eph 3:2; 4:21; Col 1:23; Sept.: Job 16:4). Also *eíge*, followed by *kaí* (2532), and, *eíge kaí*, meaning if indeed also, as applying only to what is taken for granted, but may be given by since, although (Gal 3:4, since [in this case] it is in vain). In 2 Cor 5:3, although being now clothed, we shall not (cf. with 2 Cor 5:4 and 1 Cor 15:51ff.). For, preceded by *ei* (1487), if, *dé* (1161), a particle of contrast and combined with *mḗ* (3361), not, in the expression *ei dé mḗge*, equivalent to *ei dé mḗ*, but stronger, meaning but if not indeed, if otherwise indeed, and serving to annul the preceding proposition, whether affirmative or negative. So after an affirmation it means, but if not, otherwise (Matt 6:1; Luke 10:6; 13:9). After a negation, where it consequently affirms, if otherwise, else, and so forth (Matt 9:17; Luke 5:36, 37; 14:32; 2 Cor 11:16). **(4)** Preceded and joined to *kaí* (2532), and, *kaíge*, and at least, and even, yes, yes even (Acts 2:18). **(5)** Preceded by *kaítoi* (2543), nevertheless, making it *kaítoige*, equal to *kaítoi*, but stronger, meaning though indeed (John 4:2; Acts 14:17; 17:27). **(6)** Preceded by *menoún* (3304), making *menoúnge*, equal to *menoún*, but stronger, yes indeed, yes truly (Luke 11:28; Rom 9:20; 10:18; Phil 3:8). **(7)** Preceded by *mḗti* (3385), whether at all, but stronger, meaning not to say, then, much more then (1 Cor 6:3).

1066. Γεδεών *Gedeṓn*; masc. proper noun, transliterated from the Hebr. *Gidʻōn* (1439, OT), a hewer. Gideon, the son of Joash and fifth judge of Israel. He first comes into notice when an angel appears to him under the oak in Ophrah and assures him of God's special favor (Judg 6:11, 12). Subsequently, God commanded him to offer as a sacrifice to the Lord the bullock which his father had set apart for Baal and to destroy the altar of Baal. He did both, but only escaped the murderous wrath of his fellow citizens through the wily intervention of his father (Judg 6:31). The great works of Gideon's life were the abolition of idolatry (Judg 8:33) and the deliverance of the land from the invasions of the Midianites. Before undertaking the latter enterprise, he secured a pledge of the divine favor in the phenomena of the dew and the fleece (Judg 6:36–40). God, desirous of showing the victory to be the immediate result of supernatural agency, diminished Gideon's army from 32,000 to 300. With this small force, Gideon completely terrified and successfully routed the enemy in an assault by night (Judg 7:15–21). Gideon refused the crown (Judg 8:23) from the whole nation, which his son, Abimelech, afterward received from a part of the people. Gideon judged Israel for forty years (Judg 8:28), and the nation enjoyed peace and engaged in the worship of God (Judg 8:33). He was one of her greatest rulers and is honorably mentioned in Heb 11:32.

1067. γέεννα **géenna**; gen. *geénnēs*, fem. noun. Hell, the place or state of the lost and condemned (Matt 5:29, 30; 10:28 [cf. 23:15; James 3:6]). Represents the Hebr. *gā-Hinnom* (the Valley of Tophet) and a corresponding Aramaic word. Found twelve times in the NT, eleven of which are in the Synoptic Gospels and in every instance spoken by the Lord Himself. Many times the word *Hádēs* (86) is wrongly translated "hell" or "grave." Terms descriptive of hell are found in Matt 13:42; 25:46; Phil 3:19; 2 Thess 1:9; Heb 10:39; 2 Pet 2:17; Jude 1:13; Rev 2:11; 19:20; 20:6, 10, 14; 21:8. The word *Gehenna* is derived from the Hebr. expression, *gāHinnom*, Valley of Hinnom (Josh 15:8; Neh 11:30) which is an abbreviated form of "valley of the son of Hinnom" (2 Kgs 23:10; 2 Chr 28:3; 33:6; Josh 18:16; Jer 7:31, 32; 19:2, 6). In the Sept. this name appears variously as *pháragx* (5327), ravine, *Onom* or *Ennom* (Josh 15:8); *gaienna* (Josh 18:16); *Gaibenthom* or *Gēbeennom* (2 Chr 28:3); *ge Bane Ennom* or *ge Beennom* (2 Chr 33:6). Elsewhere we find generally *pháragx*, ravine, of the son of Hinnom.

This place became so notorious through its evil associations that it was simply called "the valley" (Jer 2:23; 31:40), and the gate of Jerusalem leading toward it "the valley gate" (2 Chr 26:9; Neh 2:13, 15; 3:13). This valley lay to the south and southwest of Jerusalem. Topographically, it provided the boundary between Judah and Benjamin (Josh 15:8; 18:16) and the northern limit of the district occupied by the tribe of Judah after the captivity (Neh 11:30), and it lay in front of the gate Harsith of Jerusalem (Jer 19:2).

Religiously it was a place of idolatrous and human sacrifices. These were first offered by Ahaz and Manasseh who made their children to "pass through the fire" to Molech in this valley (1 Kgs 16:3; 2 Kgs 21:6; 2 Chr 28:3; 33:6). These sacrifices were probably made on the "high places of Tophet which is in the valley of the son of Hinnom" (Jer 7:31 [cf. Jer 32:15]). In order to put an end to these abominations, Josiah polluted it with human bones and other corruptions (2 Kgs 23:10, 13, 14). But this worship of Molech was revived under Jehoiakim (Jer 11:10–13; Ezek 20:30). In consequence of these idolatrous practices in the Valley of Hinnom, Jeremiah prophesied that one day it would be called the "valley of slaughter" and that they should "bury them in Tophet, till there be no place to bury" (Jer 7:32; 19:11).

It is also referred to as a place of punishment for rebellious or apostate Jews in the presence of the righteous. Gehinnom or Gehenna is not actually mentioned with this meaning in the OT, but it is this and no other place that is implied in Isa 50:11, "in a place of pain shall ye lie down" (a.t.). Furthermore, in Isa 66:24 it bears this new connotation and the punishment of the apostate Jews is conceived of as eternal: "They . . . shall look upon the carcasses of the men that have transgressed against me: for their worm shall not die, neither shall their fire be quenched; and they shall be an abhorring unto all flesh." The punishment of Gehenna is implied also in Dan 12:2, "some to shame and everlasting abhorrence" (a.t.). This particular word "abhorrence" occurs in these two passages only, and the reference in both is to Gehenna. Therefore, Gehenna was always conceived of as a place of both corporeal and spiritual punishment, not only for the Jews, but for all the wicked in the presence of the righteous.

In the NT Gehenna is presented always as the final place of punishment into which the wicked are cast after the last judgment. It is a place of torment both for body and soul as indicated in Matt 5:29, 30, "It is profitable for thee that one of thy members should perish, and not that thy whole body go into Gehenna" (a.t.). The Lord Jesus did not have the living in mind here, but the dead, for it is not until after the final judgment that the wicked are cast into Gehenna. At the resurrection, the spirit and the body are united. Both are punished in Gehenna. Gehenna as the last punishment was conceived of also as the worst. It slays both soul (the incorporeal spiritual part of man) and body (the corporeal)—not in the absolute sense of annihilation, but relatively in that it permitted a change of state that could suffer the pain and punishment of Gehenna. Thus in Matt 10:28, "Fear him which is able to destroy both soul and body in Gehenna" (a.t. [cf. Luke 12:5]). Gehenna is conceived of as a fire (Matt 5:22; 18:9); an unquenchable fire (Mark 9:45); a place where "their worm dieth not, and the fire is not quenched" (Mark 9:48); a "furnace of fire" (Matt 13:42, 50); "the outer darkness" (Matt 8:12; 22:13; 25:30); a "lake of fire" (Rev 19:20; 20:10, 14, 15; 21:8). Because fire is often used as an apocalyptic symbol of judgment (especially eschatological judgment) it is difficult to insist that the flames are material. Nevertheless, such a symbol clearly represents a real and painful judgment. Hades, the place of the disembodied wicked spirits, is finally cast into it (Rev 20:14). In the NT, Hades and Gehenna seem never to be confused together. See *Hádēs* (86), the place of the departed souls often translated "hell," but mistakenly so; *ábussos* (12), abyss, bottomless pit; *tartaróō* (5020), to incarcerate in eternal torment, spoken of the fallen angels.

1068. Γεθσημανῆ *Gethsēmanē*; fem. proper noun transliterated from the Aramaic *gath* (1660, OT), a press and *shemen* (8081, OT), oil. Gethsemane, meaning oil press, a place across the Kedron and at the foot of the Mount of Olives, noted as the scene of our Lord's agony (John 18:1; Mark 14:26; Luke 22:39). A garden or orchard was attached to it and Jesus frequently resorted to this place (Matt 26:36; Mark 14:32; John 18:2).

1069. γείτων *geítōn*; gen. *geítonos*, pl. *geítones*, masc., fem. noun. A neighbor, one of the same country, a countryman (Luke 14:12; 15:6, 9; John 9:8; Sept.: Job 26:5; Jer 6:21). It is always used in the pl.

Syn.: *períoikos* (4040), meaning dwelling around; *plēsíon* (4139), the one near.

1070. γελάω *geláō*; contracted *gelô*, fut. *gelásō*. To laugh, be merry (Luke 6:21, 25; Sept.: Gen 17:17; 18:12, 13, 15).

Deriv.: *gélōs* (1071), laughter; *katageláō* (2606), to laugh scornfully.

Ant.: *klaíō* (2799), to weep, accompanied by a loud expression of grief; *dakrúō* (1145), to shed tears; *thrēnéō* (2354), to mourn in a formal lamentation; *alalázō* (214), to wail; *stenázō* (4727), to groan; *odurmós* (3602), mourning, to lament audibly.

1071. γέλως *gélōs*; gen. *gélōtos*, masc. noun from *geláō* (1070), to laugh. Laughter, particularly of joy or triumph (James 4:9; Sept.: Gen 21:6; Job 8:21).

Ant.: *klauthmós* (2805), weeping, crying; *odurmós* (3602), mourning; *dákru* (1144), tear; *thrḗnos* (2355), lamentation.

1072. γεμίζω gemízō; fut. *gemísō*, from *gémō* (1073), to be full. To make full, to fill. Used trans. and with the gen. of thing (Mark 15:36; John 2:7; 6:13); with *apó* (575), from (Luke 15:16); with *ek* (1537), from, denoting origin (Rev 8:5; 15:8; Lev 9:17; Ps 127:5; Jer 51:34); used in an absolute sense (Mark 4:37; Luke 14:23). For deriv., syn., and ant. see *gémō* (1073), to be full.

Ant.: *kenóō* (2758), to empty.

1073. γέμω gémō; fut. *gemṓ*. To be full, stuffed. Used intrans. (Matt 23:27; Luke 11:39; Rev 4:6, 8; 5:8; 15:7; 17:3, 4; 21:9). See also Rom 3:14 quoted from Ps 10:7. With *ek* (1537), from, denoting origin (Matt 23:25).

Deriv.: *gemízō* (1072), to fill; *gómos* (1117), merchandise, burden.

Syn.: *plēróō* (4137), to make full, to fill up; *anaplēróō* (378), to fill up completely; *antanaplēróō* (466), to fill up in turn or on one's part; *sumplēróō* (4845), to fill completely with; *pímplēmi / plḗthō* (4130), to fill; *empíplēmi* (1705), to fill full, to satisfy; *chortázō* (5526), to fill or satisfy with food; *korénnumi* (2880), to satisfy as used of spiritual things; *mestóō* (3325), to fill full.

Ant.: *kenóō* (2758), to empty; *scholázō* (4980), to take leisure.

1074. γενεά geneá; gen. *geneás*, fem. coll. noun from *gínomai* (1096), to become. Originally meaning generation, i.e., a multitude of contemporaries. In NT Gr. *geneá* literally means space of time, circle of time, which only in a derived sense signifies the meaning of a time, a race; then generally in the sense of affinity of communion based upon the sameness of stock. Race or posterity (Acts 8:33, "who shall declare his posterity?" [a.t.] i.e., the number of His followers as spoken of the Messiah and quoted from Isa 53:8; Sept.: Gen 17:12; Num 13:22; Esth 9:28). A descent or genealogical line of ancestors or descendants. Generation (Matt 1:17; Sept.: Gen 15:16; 25:13; Deut 23:3) as used in special reference to the physical or moral circumstances of a particular period, just as we speak of an age or time referring to the spiritual state of its society (Heb 3:10 [cf. Luke 7:31; 11:31; Acts 13:36]). The connection alone must decide whether the sense is limited to the state of society at a certain time or whether the word refers simply to race or stock. Spoken of the period of time from one descendant to another, that is, the average duration of human life, reckoned apparently by the ancient Jews at one hundred years (cf. Gen 15:16 with Ex 12:40, 41); by the Greeks at three generations for every one hundred years, that is, thirty-three and a half years each. Hence, in the NT of a less definite period, an age, time, period, day, as ancient generations, that is, times of old (Luke 1:50, "generation to generation," i.e., to the remotest ages [cf. Rev 1:6; Acts 14:16; 15:21; Eph 3:5, 21, of future ages; Col 1:26. See Sept.: Gen 9:12; Ps 72:5; Prov 27:24; Isa 34:17; Joel 3:20]). In Luke 16:8, "in their very own generation" (a.t.), means they are wiser in their day, so far as it concerns this life. Metaphorically spoken of the people of any generation or age, those living in any one period, a race or class, e.g., "this generation" means the present generation (Matt 11:16; 12:39, 41, 42, 45; 16:4; 17:17; 23:36; 24:34; Mark 8:12, 38; 9:19; 13:30; Luke 7:31; 9:41; 11:29–32, 50, 51; 17:25; 21:32; Acts 2:40; Phil 2:15). Spoken of a former generation (Acts 13:36; Heb 3:10); of the future (Luke 1:48; Sept.: Deut 32:5, 20; Ps 12:8; 14:5; 24:6; 78:6, 8). The word *geneá* in Matt 24:34 may have had reference to the kind of Jew with whom Jesus was conversing during that particular time (Matt 21:23; 23:29). He was telling them that this generation or type, such as the Sadducees and Pharisees of that day, would not pass away until all these things occurred and until His coming again in His *parousía* (3952), Second Coming, which has proven to be true. He was prophesying the destruction of their nation (Matt 24:15–28). Others have understood Jesus to be saying that the generation present immediately preceding His return, who witness the events signaling His coming, will not pass away. Christ's return will not be thwarted.

Deriv.: *genealogéō* (1075), to reckon by generations; *genetḗ* (1079), from his birth or the beginning of his life.

Syn.: *génos* (1085), kind, family, generation; *génnēma* (1081), generation, but with the idea of having had birth from; *éthnos* (1484), nation or people of the same kind; *aiṓn* (165), an age, era.

1075. γενεαλογέω *genealogéō*; contracted *genealogṓ*, fut. *genealogḗsō* from *geneá* (1074), generation, and *légō* (3004), to reckon. In the NT in the mid. / pass., *genealogéomai* or *genealogoúmai*, fut. *genealogḗsomai*, to be traced or inscribed in a genealogy, to be reckoned by descent (Heb 7:6, to trace one's descent or to derive one's origin; Sept.: 1 Chr 5:1; 9:1; Ezra 2:61).

Deriv.: *agenealógētos* (35), one without recorded pedigree or genealogy; *genealogía* (1076), genealogy.

1076. γενεαλογία *genealogía*; gen. *genealogías*, fem. noun from *genealogéō* (1075), to make a genealogical register. Genealogy. The expression in 1 Tim 1:4 denotes busying oneself about traditions of the past based upon the slightest historical hints which diverted the heart from God's truth. This, as it appears from Titus 1:10, was a practice of Jewish false teachers though this is not implied in the expression itself (see also Titus 3:9). These Jews were turning the entire historical substance into mere myth. The genealogies were not treated primarily as historical documents but instead were subjected to a highly symbolic interpretive scheme. Names, dates and places supposedly contained hidden meanings which became the basis for esoteric doctrines.

1077. γενέσια *genésia*; gen. *genesíōn*, neut. noun from *génesis* (1078), generation. A birthday, the celebrations and tokens of joy observed on a birthday (Matt 14:6; Mark 6:21). Used only in the pl. *tá genésia*. Some earlier Gr. writers use the word *genéthlia* which also meant the solemn rites for the dead. This word is used in Mod. Gr. for birthday.

1078. γένεσις *génesis*, gen. *genéseōs*, fem. noun from *gínomai* (1096), to form. Origin, rise. In Matt 1:18; Luke 1:14 (TR), we have *génnēsis* (1083), birth, or the coming of Christ as a human being in contrast to *génesis* which means origination, the beginning of His temporary existence as the God-Man. In John 1:14 "And the Word became [*egéneto* from *gínomai*, to become] flesh" (a.t.). He began His life in the body at Bethlehem, but this was not His origination as a personality. He had been as the *Lógos* (3056), Word, spiritual and immaterial (John 4:24) prior to His becoming flesh (man). In the pass., *génesis* means race, lineage, equivalent to *geneá* (1074), genealogy, book of genealogy (Matt 1:1). It also means generation, kind, species, as well as being, existence (James 1:23 [*prósōpon tḗs genéseōs*], the face of birth, meaning native or natural face; Sept.: Gen 31:13; 32:9). A book of descent, genealogy table (Matt 1:1; Sept.: Gen 5:1; 2:4; 10:1, 32).

Deriv.: *genésia* (1077), birthday; *paliggenesía* (3824), regeneration.

1079. γενετή *genetḗ*; gen. *genetḗs*, fem. noun from *geneá* (1074), generation, birth. Birth. Used with *ek* (1537), from, and the gen. *genetḗs*, that is, *ek genetḗs* denoting origin, from birth (Sept.: Lev 25:47).

1080. γεννάω *gennáō*; contracted *gennṓ*, fut. *gennḗsō*, from *génos* (1085), generation, kind, offspring. To beget as spoken of men; to bear as spoken of women; pass., to be begotten or be born.

(I) In the act. sense:

(A) Spoken of men, to beget (Matt 1:2–16; Acts 7:8, 29; Sept.: Gen 5:3ff.). Metaphorically, to generate, to occasion, e.g., strifes (2 Tim 2:23).

(B) Spoken in the Jewish manner of the relation between a teacher and his disciples, to beget in a spiritual sense, to be the spiritual father of someone, that is, the instrument of his conversion to a new spiritual life (1 Cor 4:15; Phile 1:10).

(C) Spoken of God begetting in a spiritual sense which consists in regenerating, sanctifying, quickening anew, and ennobling the powers of the natural man by imparting to him a new life and a new spirit in Christ (1 John 5:1). Hence, Christians are said to be born of God and to be the sons of God (Rom 8:14; Gal 3:26; 4:6). Spoken of the relationship between God and the Messiah, called His Son. The designation of this relationship by words with a temporal notion has troubled theologians, who have proffered various explanations. Origen understood this as referring to the Son's relationship within the Trinity and was the first to propose the concept of eternal generation. The Son is said to be eternally begotten by the Father. Others have viewed the language more figuratively and connected it with Christ's role as Messiah. Upon Christ's exaltation to the Father's right hand, God is said to have appointed, declared or officially installed Christ as a king (Acts 13:33; Rom 1:4; Heb 1:5; 5:5; Sept.: Ps 2:6–8 [cf. huiós {5207}, son]).

(D) Spoken of women, to bear, bring forth (Luke 1:13, 57; 23:29; John 16:21; figuratively Gal 4:24; Sept.: Gen 46:15; Ex 6:20; Ezra 10:44).

(II) In the pass. sense gennáomai, contracted gennōmai.

(A) To be begotten (Matt 1:20, "that which is conceived in her" or begotten, i.e., in her womb, the fetus; Heb 11:12).

(B) To be born as used generally (Matt 2:1, 4; 19:12; 26:24; Mark 14:21; John 3:4, blind; 9:2, 19, 20, 32; 16:21, "into the world"; Acts 7:20; 22:28, I have been born a Roman; Rom 9:11; Heb 11:23; Gal 4:23, 29, "after the flesh," in the course

of nature). With eis (1510), unto, denoting finality, destination (John 18:37; 2 Pet 2:12). In Matt 1:16, "of whom [fem. gen.]" meaning of the mother. See Luke 1:35. In John 3:6, with ek (1537), "out of the flesh" (a.t.), indicating the source. See also John 8:41. With en (1722), in, and the dat. of place (Acts 22:3). With the dat. of state or condition (John 9:34, in the state of sinfulness or sins). In Acts 2:8, "wherein we were born," meaning the dialect, the native tongue. Metaphorically, ek (1537), out of God or of the Spirit, only in the writings of John, meaning to be born of God or of the Spirit, in a spiritual sense, to have received from God a new spiritual life. See also John 1:13; 3:5, 6, 8; 1 John 2:29; 3:9; 4:7; 5:1, 4, 18, and to be "born again" or from above which is equivalent to be born of God (John 3:3, 7); also ánōthen (509), from above.

Deriv.: anagennáō (313), to give new birth; génnēma (1081), offspring; génnēsis (1083), birth; gennētós (1084), born.

Syn.: apokuéō (616), to give birth to, bring forth. Used in a spiritual sense: tíktō (5088), to bring forth, give birth to a child, also used metaphorically in regard to sin in James 1:15.

Ant.: thanatóō (2289), to put to death; anairéō (337), to take or lift up or away, put to death; apágō (520), to put to death; apokteínō (615), to kill; thúō (2380), to sacrifice; phoneúō (5407), to kill; spházō (4969), to slaughter.

1081. γέννημα génnēma; gen. gennḗmatos, neut. noun from gennáō (1080), to give birth to, beget, involving generation from gínomai (1096), to become. That which is born or produced. Spoken of men it means offspring, progeny (Matt 3:7), progeny of vipers (Matt 12:34; 23:33; Luke 3:7). Spoken of trees the variant génema means fruit, produce (Matt 26:29; Mark 14:25; Luke 22:18). In Luke 12:18 génema is used in a special sense common to later writers. Metaphorically spoken of the rewards of Christian virtue (2 Cor 9:10 [TR]). *Strong's Dictionary* does not make the distinction between *génnēma*, offspring, and *génēma*, fruit, produce, which results in great confusion.

1082. Γεννησαρέτ *Gennēsarét*; fem. proper noun, transliterated from the Hebr. *Kinnereth* (3672, OT). Gennesaret, also called Gennesareth. Found three times in the NT: the Lake of Gennesaret (Luke 5:1), also called Sea of Galilee; and the land of Gennesaret (Matt 14:34; Mark 6:53), a small crescent-shaped strip of country on the northwest side of the Sea of Galilee. It extends along the lake for three or four miles and inland a mile or more where it is shut in by the hills. The plain was formerly very rich and fruitful, according to Josephus, and supposedly is the scene of the parable of the sower (Matt 13:1–8). Its three important cities are Capernaum, Bethsaida, and Chorazin, although the latter two were supposed to have been farther north. Also, Magdala, from whence came Mary Magdalene, was a town in the plain. See *Galilaía* (1056), Galilee.

1083. γέννησις *génnēsis*; gen. *gennēseōs*, fem. noun from *gennáō* (1080), to give birth to, beget. Birth, nativity (Matt 1:18; Luke 1:14 [TR], where other texts have *génesis* [1078], generation; see *geneá* [1074], generation).

Ant.: *análusis* (359), departure (from life); *thánatos* (2288), death; *anaíresis* (336), the taking up or off, another word for death; *teleutḗ* (5054), an end, termination.

1084. γεννητός *gennētós*; fem. *gennētḗ*, neut. *gennētoú*, adj. from *gennáō* (1080), to give birth to, beget. Born, brought forth (Matt 11:11; Luke 7:28, "among those born of women"; Sept.: Job 14:1; 15:14; 25:4).

Deriv.: *artigénnētos* (738), newborn.

1085. γένος *génos*; gen. *génous*, neut. noun from *gínomai* (1096), to become. Offspring, posterity (Acts 17:28, 29; Rev 22:16; Sept.: Jer 36:31). Family, lineage, stock (Acts 4:6 where some translate it

as "sect" or "order"; Sept.: Jer 41:1; Acts 7:13; 13:26; Phil 3:5); nation, people (Mark 7:26; Acts 4:36; 7:19; 18:2, 24; 2 Cor 11:26; Gal 1:4; 1 Pet 2:9; Sept.: Gen 11:6; Esth 2:10); kind, sort, species (Matt 13:47; 17:21; Mark 9:29; 1 Cor 12:10, 28; 14:10; Sept.: Gen 6:20; 7:14; 2 Chr 4:13).

Deriv.: *agenḗs* (36), base things; *allogenḗs* (241), stranger; *gennáō* (1080), to give birth; *eugenḗs* (2104), more noble, nobleman; *monogenḗs* (3439), only begotten; *suggenḗs* (4773), countryman.

Syn.: *phulḗ* (5443), tribe, kindred; *patriá* (3965), paternal descent, family; *éthnos* (1484), nation, people of the same country. See also *geneá* (1074).

Ant.: *allóphulos* (246), of another race or nation.

1086. Γεργεσηνός *Gergesēnós*; gen. *Gergesēnoú*, masc. proper noun. A Gergesene, person belonging to the country of the Gergesenes or Gergesa (Sept.: Gen 15:21; Deut 7:1; Josh 24:11; Matt 8:28), probably the same as Gadarenes (Mark 5:1; Luke 8:26) on the east side of the Sea of Galilee where the miracle of the casting out of the demons took place. Origen says that a city called Gergesa stood on the eastern shore of the Lake Tiberias, and that the precipice was still pointed out down which the swine rushed. Some take the readings in the above passages to be *Gerasēnós*, referring to one of the cities of the Decapolis, Jerrash as it is called today, which is the same as the ancient Gerasa. It is improbable, however, that Gerasa is referred to in the above passages being so far away from the Sea of Galilee.

1087. γερουσία *gerousía*; gen. *gerousías*, fem. noun from *gérōn* (1088), an old person. An assembly of elders or old men, a senate, a council. The Sept. frequently uses the same phrase for the Jewish Sanhedrin (Ex 3:16, 18; 12:21; 24:9; Deut 27:1). In Acts 5:21 it means the Sanhedrin, the whole senate of Israel or the elders of Israel in general, that is, persons of age and influence who were invited to sit with the Sanhedrin, or as Acts 4:8 calls them, the "elders of Israel" (see also Acts 25:15).

Syn.: *sunédrion* (4892), council.

Ant.: *idiótēs* (2399), a private citizen, unlearned;

1088. γέρων gérōn; gen. *gérontos*, masc. noun. An old man, used by Nicodemus in referring to himself (John 3:4; see also Sept.: Prov 17:6).

Deriv.: *gerousía* (1087), senate.

Syn.: *presbútēs* (4246), an old man.

Ant.: *néos* (3501), young man; *neanías* (3494), a young man; *neanískos* (3495), a diminutive of *neanías* (3494), a young man; *bréphos* (1025), a baby.

1089. γεύω geúō; fut. *geúsō*, mid. *geúomai*, fut. *geúsomai*. To cause to taste, to let taste (Sept.: Gen 25:30). Standing by itself (Matt 27:34). Followed by the acc. (John 2:9; Sept.: 1 Kgs 4:29; Job 12:11; 34:3). With the meaning of to eat, partake, used in an absolute sense (Acts 10:10; 20:11). Followed by the gen. (Luke 14:24; Acts 23:14; Sept.: 1 Sam 14:24 of bread; 2 Sam 3:35). Metaphorically, to experience, prove, partake of. With the acc. (Heb 6:5). With a gen. following, to taste of death, that is, to die (Matt 16:28; Mark 9:1; Luke 9:27; John 8:52; Heb 2:9). When used in this connection, it gives prominence to what is really involved in dying. In Heb 6:4, "who have tasted of the heavenly gift." It is not wise to press the distinction between the use of the gen. and acc. with this word as is often done where they occur in Heb 6:4, 5. Followed by *hóti* (3754), that. See also Sept.: Ps 34:9.

Syn.: With the meaning of to eat: *esthíō* (2068), to eat; *phágō* (5315), to eat, devour, consume; *trṓgō* (5176), to chew, eat; *bibrṓskō* (977), to eat, devour.

Ant.: *néphō* (3525), to abstain, especially of wine.

1090. γεωργέω geōrgéō; fut. *geōrgḗsō*, from *geōrgós* (1092), farmer. To cultivate or till the earth. In the pass. *geōrgéomai*,

to be cultivated, tilled as the earth (Heb 6:7; Sept.: 1 Chr 27:26).

Ant.: *ameléō* (272), to be negligent.

1091. γεώργιον geórgion; gen. *geōrgíou*, neut. noun from *geōrgós* (1092), a farmer A tilled field, farm (Sept.: Prov 24:30; 31:16). Used metaphorically of Christians (1 Cor 3:9).

Syn.: *agrós* (68), a cultivated field; *chṓra* (5561), land, country, field; *chōríon* (5564), a piece of land, field.

1092. γεωργός geōrgós; gen. *geōrgoú*, masc. noun from *gē* (1093), ground, earth, land, and *érgon* (2041), work. A farmer, husbandman, one who tills the earth or ground (2 Tim 2:6; James 5:7; Sept.: Jer 14:4; 31:24; 51:23). Used syn. with *ampelourgós* (289), a vine dresser, one who cultivates vines (Matt 21:33–35, 38, 40, 41; Mark 12:1, 7, 9; Luke 20:9, 10, 14, 16); metaphorically of God (John 15:1 [cf. Isa 5:1ff.]).

Deriv.: *geōrgéō* (1090), to cultivate the earth; *geórgion* (1091), a tilled field, farm.

1093. γῆ gē; gen. *gēs*, fem. noun. Earth, land.

(I) In reference to its vegetative power, earth, soil (Matt 13:5, 8, 23; Mark 4:5, 8, 20; Luke 14:35; John 12:24; Gen 1:11, 12; 3:14, 19; Sept.: Gen 4:2, 3).

(II) As that on which we tread, the ground (Matt 10:29; 15:35; Luke 6:49; 22:44; 24:5; John 8:6, 8; Acts 9:4, 8; Sept.: Ex 3:5; 9:33; 1 Sam 26:7, 8; 2 Sam 17:12).

(III) In distinction from the sea or a lake, the land, solid ground (Mark 4:1; 6:47; John 6:21; Acts 27:39, 43, 44; Sept.: Gen 8:7, 9; Jon 1:13).

(IV) Of a country, region, territory, as the land of Israel (Matt 2:20, 21); Canaan (Acts 13:19); Egypt (Acts 7:11, 36, 40; 13:17); Judah (Matt 2:6); Zebulon (Matt 4:15); Gennesareth (Matt 14:34; Mark 6:53). Of the country adjacent to any place or city (Matt 9:26, 31). With a gen. of person, one's native land (Acts 7:3).

Spoken particularly of and used in an absolute sense of the land of the Jews, Palestine (Matt 23:35; 27:45; Mark 15:33; Luke 4:25; 21:23; Rom 9:28; James 5:17; Isa 10:23). Also in the expression, to "inherit the earth" (Matt 5:5 quoted from Ps 37:11; see Ps 37:9, 22, 29; 25:13; Isa 60:21 [cf. Lev 20:24; Deut 16:20]). Figuratively used for the inhabitants of a country (Matt 10:15; 11:24).

(V) The earth. In distinction from *ho ouranós* (3772), heaven (Matt 5:18, 35; 6:10, 19; Luke 2:14; Acts 2:19; 7:49; Sept.: Gen 1:1, 2; 2:4; 4:11; 7:4; 1 Chr 16:30); hence, "all things . . . that are in heaven, and that are in earth" means the universe (Col 1:16, 20). "A new earth" (2 Pet 3:13; Rev 21:1) means qualitatively new (*kainé* [2537]), not just another earth.

(VI) Spoken of the habitable earth (*hē oikouménē* [3625]) (Luke 11:31; 21:35; Acts 10:12; 11:6; 17:26; Heb 11:13; Rev 3:10; Sept.: Gen 6:1, 5, 7, 11, 12; Isa 24:1), hence the expression *tá epí tēs gēs* (*tá epí* [1909], those upon; *tēs gēs*, of the earth), upon earthly things or pertaining to this life (Col 3:2); "all the earth" (Rom 9:17; 10:18); "upon the earth" (Col 3:5); the inhabitants of the earth, men (Rev 6:8; 11:6; 13:3; 19:2; Sept.: Gen 9:19; 11:1; 19:31). Also where things are said to be done or take place on earth, which have reference chiefly to men (Matt 5:13; 6:10; 10:34; Luke 12:49; John 17:4). In John 3:31, "he being of the earth" (a.t.), means he who is of human birth and speaks only of worldly things.

Deriv.: *geōrgós* (1092); a farmer; *epígeios* (1919), of this earth, earthly.

Syn.: *agrós* (68), a field; *patrís* (3968), native country or one's fatherland; *chóra* (5561), country, land; *períchōros* (4066), country round about; *oikouménē* (3625), the inhabited earth; *katachthónios* (2709), under the earth; *choïkós* (5517), of the soil or earthy; *édaphos* (1475), the ground; *chōríon* (5564), a piece of land; *kósmos* (2889), the earth, but primarily the people who dwell on the earth.

1094. γῆρας gḗras; gen. *gḗratos*, neut. noun. Old age (Luke 1:36 [TR], in later additions *en gḗrei*; Sept.: Gen 15:15; 1 Chr 29:28).

Deriv.: *gēráskō* (1095), to get old.
Syn.: *palaiótēs* (3821), oldness.
Ant.: *neótēs* (3503), youth; *kainótēs* (2538), renewal, newness; *anakaínōsis* (342), a qualitative renewal.

1095. γηράσκω gēráskō; fut. *gērásō*, from *gḗras* (1094), old age. To be old, become old. Intrans. in John 21:18; Heb 8:13; Sept.: Gen 18:13; 27:1.

Syn.: *palaióō* (3822), to make or declare old.
Ant.: *anazáō* (326), to live again; *anathállō* (330), to revive; *anapsúchō* (404), to refresh; *anakainóō* (341), to make new qualitatively; *anakainízō* (340), to restore, renew; *anaeóō* (365), to renew in the sense of another of the same quality or another in number, but not of different quality as the previous two words infer.

1096. γίνομαι gínomai; fut. *genḗsomai*, 2d aor. *egenómēn*, perf. part. *gegenēménos*, 2d perf. *gégona*, 2d pluperf. *egegónein*, aor. pass. *egenḗthēn* for *egenómēn*. This verb is mid. deponent intrans. primarily meaning to begin to be, that is, to come into existence or into any state; and in the aor. and 2d perf. to have come into existence or simply to be. Thus *egenómēn*, *egenḗthēn*, and *gégona* serve likewise as the past tenses of to be (*eínai* [1511]).

(I) To begin to be, to come into existence as implying origin (either from natural causes or through special agencies), result, change of state, place, and so forth.

(A) As implying origin in the ordinary course of nature. (1) Spoken of persons, to be born (John 8:58; James 3:9), followed by *ek* (1537), out of, followed by the gen., to be born of, descended from (Rom 1:3; Gal 4:4; 1 Pet 3:6; Sept.: Gen 21:3, 5). (2) Of plants and fruits, to be produced, grow (Matt 21:19; 1 Cor 15:37). (3) Of the phenomena, occurrences of nature to arise, to come on, occur, e.g., *seismós* (4578), earthquake (Matt 8:24); *laílaps* (2978), storm, tempest (Mark 4:37); *galénē* (1055), tranquillity (Matt 8:26; Mark 4:39); *skótos* (4655), darkness (Matt 27:45; Mark 15:33); *nephélē* (3507), cloudiness (Mark 9:7; Luke 9:34); *brontḗ* (1027), thunder (John 12:29). So also of a voice or cry, tumult as *phōnḗ* (5456), voice (John 12:30); *kraugḗ* (2906), clamor, cry (Matt 25:6); *thórubos* (2351), disturbance, uproar (Matt 26:5; 27:24); *stásis* (4714), an uprising (Luke 23:19); *schísma* (4978), division (John 7:43); *zḗtēsis* (2214), questioning (John 3:25); *sigḗ* (4602), silence (Acts 21:40; Rev 8:1). Also of emotions as *thlípsis* (2347), tribulation, affliction (Matt 13:21; see also Luke 15:10; 22:24; 1 Tim 6:4). **(4)** Spoken of time such as day, night, evening to come or come on, approach (Matt 8:16; 14:15, 23; 27:1; Mark 6:2; 11:19; 15:33; Luke 22:14; John 6:16; 21:4; Acts 27:27).

(II) As implying origin through an agency specially exerted, to be made, created, equal to *poioúmai*, the mid. pass. of *poiéō* (4160), to make or to do.

(A) Spoken of the works of creation (John 1:3, 10; 1 Cor 15:45; Heb 4:3; 11:3; Sept.: Gen 2:4; Isa 48:7).

(B) Of works of art (Acts 19:26, "with hands").

(C) Of miracles and the like, to be wrought, performed (Matt 11:20; Acts 4:22; 8:13); with *diá*, through or with (Mark 6:2; Acts 2:43; 4:16); with *hupó* (5259), by (Luke 9:7; 13:17).

(D) Of a promise, plot to be made (Acts 26:6; 20:3); of waste, *apóleia* (684), loss, waste (Mark 14:4).

(E) Of the will or desire (*thélēma* [2307]) of someone, to be done, fulfilled; (Matt 6:10; 26:42; Luke 11:2; Acts 21:14); *aítēma* (155), petition, request (Luke 23:24).

(F) Of a meal, to be prepared, made ready (John 13:2); of a judicial investigation, to be made, initiated (Acts 25:26); so also of a change of law (Heb 7:12, 18).

(G) Of particular days, festivals to be held or celebrated (Matt 26:2; John 2:1; 10:22; Sept.: 2 Kgs 23:22).

(H) Of persons advanced to any station or office, to be made, constituted, appointed (1 Cor 1:30; Col 1:23, 25; Heb 5:5; 6:20); so also with *epánō* (1883), upon (Luke 19:19).

(I) Of customs, institutes to be appointed, instituted (Mark 2:27, the Sabbath; Gal 3:17, the existing law).

(J) Of what is done to or in someone (Luke 23:31, "what shall be done in the dry?"; Gal 3:13, "being [himself] made a curse for us," i.e., suffering the penalty to which we were subject).

(III) As implying a result, event to take place or come to pass, occur, be done:

(A) Generally (Matt 1:22, "And all this took place" [a.t.]; Mark 5:14; Luke 1:20, "until these things take place" [a.t.]; 2:15; John 3:9; Acts 4:21; 5:24; 1 Cor 15:54; 1 Thess 3:4; Rev 1:19). In Heb 9:15, "death having taken place" (a.t.), that is, through His death. See also Matt 18:31; Luke 8:34; James 3:10; 2 Pet 1:20. So also in the phrase *mḗ génoito* (*mḗ* [3361], not; *génoito* [1096], it be), let it not happen, God forbid, an exclamation of aversion (Luke 20:16; Rom 3:4, 6, 31; 6:2, 15; 7:7 [cf. Sept.: Gen 44:7, 17; Josh 22:29; 1 Kgs 21:3]).

(B) With the dat. of person, to happen to someone (Mark 9:21; Luke 14:12; John 5:14; 1 Pet 4:12). With the inf. as subj. (Acts 20:16; Gal 6:14; Sept.: Gen 44:7, 17). With an adv. of manner (Mark 5:16; Eph 6:3).

(C) With a prep. in the same sense as *eis* (1519), unto, followed by *tiná*, someone (Acts 28:6). In Mark 5:33, *epí* (1909), upon, with the dat. *tiní*, someone.

(D) With an inf. and acc. expressed or implied, to come to pass that (Matt 18:13, "if it comes to pass that he find it" [a.t.]; Mark 2:23; Acts 27:44, "it came to pass, that they escaped"; 28:8).

(E) *Kai* (2532), and, with *egéneto*, and it came to pass, sometimes followed by *dé* (1161), a contrasting particle corresponding to "and it came to pass that," always with the notation of time, introduced by *hóte* (3753), when, *hōs* (5613), until, *en* (1722), in, an absolute gen., and followed by a finite verb with or without *kaí* (2532), and, with *kaí* repeated (Matt 9:10, "And as Jesus sat at meat in the house . . . and behold" [a.t.]; Mark 2:15, "And it came to pass . . . and many" [a.t.]; Luke 2:15, *kaí egéneto hōs . . . kaí hoi ánthrōpoi*, "and it came to pass that . . . and the men, the shepherds" [a.t.]; 5:1, 12, 17; 8:1, 22; 9:28; 14:1; 17:11; 19:15; 24:4, 15; Sept.: Gen 39:7, 13, 19, 43).

(**F**) Without *kaí* repeated (Matt 7:28; 13:53; 19:1; 26:1; Mark 1:9; 4:4; Luke 1:8; 2:1; 6:12; Sept.: Gen 22:1).

(**IV**) As implying a change of state, condition, or the passing from one state to another, to become, to enter upon any state, condition.

(**A**) Spoken of persons or things which receive any new character or form. (**1**) Where the predicate is a noun (Matt 4:3, "that these stones become bread" [a.t.]; 5:45, "that ye may become the sons of the father" [a.t.]; 13:32, "becomes a tree" [a.t.]; Mark 1:17, "that you may become fishers of men" [a.t.]; Luke 4:3; 6:16; 23:12; John 1:12, 14; 2:9; Acts 12:18, "what was become of Peter"; 26:28; Rom 4:18; Heb 2:17; Rev 8:8). (**2**) Construed with *eis* (1519), unto something as the predicate (Matt 21:42, He "became unto a cornerstone" [a.t.] or "He became a cornerstone" [a.t.]; Mark 12:10; Luke 13:19; John 16:20; Acts 5:36; Sept.: Gen 2:7; 1 Sam 30:25). (**3**) When the predicate is an adj. (Matt 6:16, "do not . . . become of a sad countenance" [a.t.], do not put on or affect sadness; 10:16, "therefore become prudent" [a.t.]; 12:45, "last . . . shall be worse" [a.t.]; 13:22, "becomes fruitless" [a.t.]; 23:26; 24:32, 44, become ready, prepare yourselves; John 9:39; Acts 7:32; 10:4; Rom 3:19). With a particle of manner (Matt 10:25, "so that he become as his teachers" [a.t.]; 18:3; 28:4, "they became as if they were dead" [a.t.]). In 1 Cor 9:20, 22, with the dat. of person, for or in respect to whom. (**5**) With the gen. of possession or relation (Luke 20:14, "that the

inheritance become ours" [a.t.]; 20:33; Rev 11:15). (**6**) With the dat. of person as possessor (Rom 7:3, 4, to become married to another man; Sept.: Lev 22:12; Jer 3:1).

(**B**) Construed with prep. or adv. implying motion, it denotes change or transition to another place, to come. (**1**) With the prep. *eis* (1519), unto, to come to or into, to arrive at (Acts 20:16; 21:17; 25:15). Figuratively, the voice (Luke 1:44); the blessing (Gal 3:14); the gospel (1 Thess 1:5); sore or ulcer (Rev 16:2). (**2**) With *ek* (1537), out of, to come from a place, as the voice (Mark 1:11; Luke 3:22; 9:35), but *ek mésou* (3319), from the midst, with *gínomai* is to be put out of the way (2 Thess 2:7). (**3**) With *en* (1722), in, used metaphorically (Acts 12:11, "being come to himself" [a.t. {cf. Luke 15:17}]). (**4**) With *epí* (1909), upon, to come upon, arrive at (Luke 22:40; John 6:21; Acts 21:35). With the acc. (Luke 1:65, fear; 4:36; 24:22; Acts 8:1); of an oracle (Luke 3:2). (**5**) With *katá* (2596), upon, with the gen., to come throughout (Acts 10:37); with the acc., to come to (Luke 10:32; Acts 27:7). (**6**) With *prós* (4314), toward, with the acc., to come to (2 John 1:12); of oracles (Acts 7:31; 10:13; Sept.: Gen 15:1, 4; Jer 1:2, 4). (**7**) With the adv. *eggús* (1451), near, to come or draw near (John 6:19; metaphorically Eph 2:13); *hōde* (5602), hither (John 6:25); *ekeí* (1563), thither (Acts 19:21).

(**V**) In the aor. and perf., to have begun to be, to have come into existence, meaning simply to be, to exist.

(**A**) Generally, to be, to exist (John 1:6, "there came to be a man" [a.t.]; Rom 11:5; 1 John 2:18). With *en* (1722), in (2 Pet 2:1); *émprosthen* (1715), before someone (John 1:15, 30); *epí* (1909), upon the earth (Rev 16:18).

(**B**) As a copula connecting a subj. and predicate. (**1**) Of quality, with the nom. (Luke 1:2, those who "from the beginning became eyewitnesses . . . of the word" [a.t.]; 2:2; John 14:22; Acts 4:4; 1 Cor 4:16; 2 Cor 1:18, 19; 1 Thess 2:8; Titus 3:7). With the dat. of advantage, to be anything to, for, or in behalf of (Acts

1:16; Luke 11:30; Col 4:11; 1 Thess 1:7). With an adv. (1 Thess 2:10). With a gen. of age (Luke 2:42; 1 Tim 5:9). **(2)** Implying propriety (Matt 11:26; Luke 10:21, "such was thy good pleasure" [a.t.]). **(3)** Joined with the part. of another verb, it forms patterns like *eínai* (1511), to be, a periphrasis for a finite tense of that verb (Mark 1:4, literally, "it came to be John baptizing," which really stands for the verb "was baptizing"; see also 9:3, 7; Heb 5:12; Rev 16:10; Sept.: Neh 1:4.

(C) Joined with a prep. it implies locality or state, disposition of mind **(1)** With *en* (1722), in, spoken of place, to be in a place (Matt 26:6, "when Jesus was in Bethany"; Mark 9:33, "in the house"; Acts 13:5; 2 Tim 1:17; Rev 1:9). Spoken of condition or state, to be in any state (Luke 22:44, "when he came to be in agony" [a.t.]; Acts 22:17, "in ecstasy" [a.t.]; Rom 16:7, "in Christ," i.e., to be in the number of Christ's followers, Christians; Phil 2:7, "having become the likeness" [a.t.], equal to "having likened himself" [a.t.]; 1 Tim 2:14, "having placed herself in the state of the transgression" [a.t.]; Rev 1:10; 4:2). **(2)** With *metá* (3326), with, followed by the gen. of person, to be with someone (Acts 9:19; 20:18). In Mark 16:10, "those who had been with him" (a.t.), means His friends, companions. **(3)** Followed by *prós* (4314), to or toward, with an acc., to be towards, that is, disposed towards someone (1 Cor 2:3; 16:10). **(4)** Followed by *sún* (4862), with, to be with (Luke 2:13). In John 1:1–18, a distinct usage of two verbs is made, that of *ḗn*, the imperf. of *eimí* (1510), to be, and *gínomai*, to come to existence. Whenever reference is made to the existence of the *Lógos*, the preincarnate Christ, always the verb *ḗn* is used to indicate that He always was and never ceased to be what He was, even in the incarnation. Even before the beginning of creation, the *Lógos* was self-existent and, therefore, in our opinion the best translation that we could give to that verb in that context would be, "He had been." In contrast to a beginning in time and space is the verb *gínomai*. The

verb *ḗn* is used in verses one and two, and the translation of these two verses would provide more adequate understanding of the preexistence of the *Lógos* if it was thus: "Before there was any beginning the Word had been, and the Word had been toward God [the Father], and God had been the Word. He Himself was before there was any beginning toward God [the Father]" (a.t.). Immediately afterwards in verse three, we come to created beings and things and, therefore, the verb *egéneto* is used. It is not in the imperf. tense but in the aor., which indicates the coming into existence of the particular person or thing within time and space at an undefined yet definite time. All things (people, animals, the whole creation), this verse tells us, came to be through Him, and without Him not one single item which exists, came to be. In verse four we go back to the use of the verb *ḗn* because it refers to the life not acquired, but inherent. It had always been with the Word: "In him had been life, and the life had been the light of men" (a.t.).

Verse six deals with the coming into existence of John the Baptist, and therefore, *egéneto*, came to be, is used. In verse eight, in order not to confuse John with the One who had always been the light, it says, "He had not been the light" (a.t.). John just became *a* light when he came into the world, but he was not the original light. But in verse nine referring to the preexistent Christ, the verb *ḗn* is used, "He hath been the light, the true one" (a.t.). In other words, no one was ever enlightened without Jesus Christ, either in His preincarnate state or His incarnate state or His post-incarnate state. This is the reason why the verb "lighteth [*phōtízei*]" is the pres. tense verb *phōtízō* (5461), to enlighten. It indicates that no man has ever come into the world who has not in some way received the light of Jesus Christ, nor will there be any who will yet come who will be able to excuse themselves that they have not received the light that came, comes, and will come from Jesus Christ.

Of course, this light comes in different forms as it pleases God Himself in Christ.

Then in verse ten the use of *én* is observed. This tells us that there has never been a time that Jesus Christ was not in the world, although in His incarnation He came into the world in a human form that He was not in previously. He had been in the world and the world through Him came to be (*egéneto*). Christ as spirit had always been in the world that He created. He came to visit it for a definite time in the form of the God-Man and He is in the world now in His post-incarnate form.

In verse eleven when it speaks of a definite historical coming into the world to affect the humanity that He created and particularly His own people, the Jews, the verb *élthe* is used. This is the 2d aor. indic. of *érchomai* (2064), to come. He had always been in the world that He made, but within a particular time and space He came into it in a different form from that in which He had always been. In verse fourteen we have the incarnation of the Word in time and space as the God-Man and, therefore, the verb *egéneto* is again used. In verse fifteen, speaking again about the eternal existence of the Lord Jesus, the verb *én* is used.

In verse seventeen when it speaks of the grace of God becoming available through Christ, the verb *egéneto* is also used. The grace of God became available to man in a particular way through Jesus Christ because of His virgin birth, His supernatural life, His unique death, the shedding of His blood, and His resurrection.

Then in verse eighteen, in order to indicate that there has never been a time of separation between the two personalities of the Triune God as eternity, infinity, and essential spirit, it is the pres. part. of *eimí* that is used, *ho ón*, "who, being in the bosom of the Father" (a.t.). He has always been in the bosom of the Father, and even when He became incarnate, God the Father as spirit and God the Son as spirit never separated. Jesus Christ simply took upon Himself another form and came into the world as the God-Man. He could thus speak to us in the language that we as humans could understand in order to reveal to us the character of God which is impossible for man on his own to discover. That which man could not discover God had to reveal in an understandable fashion. He had to become man without ever ceasing to be God.

Deriv.: *geneá* (1074), age, generation, nation; *génesis* (1078), generation, nature; *génos* (1085), generation, kind, offspring; *goneús* (1118), a parent; *diagínomai* (1230), to intervene, to elapse, pass; *epigínomai* (1920), to spring up, blow; *paragínomai* (3854), to be present; *progínomai* (4266), to happen before.

Syn.: *érchomai* (2064), to come; *apérchomai* (565), to come away from; *hékō* (2240), to come, be present; *aphiknéomai* (864), to arrive at a place; *eRístēmi* (1764), to stand in, be present; *ephístēmi* (2186), to stand by or over; *katantáō* (2658), to come to, over against; *parístēmi* (3936), to stand by or near; *phérō* (5342), to come, to bring; *phthánō* (5348), to come upon, arrive at; *proseggízō* (4331), to come near; *diateléō* (1300), to bring through to an end; *ménō* (3306), to abide; *epioúsa* (1966), the next day, used as a verb meaning to come, arrive; *auxánō* (837), to grow or increase, to become something that one was not; *phúō* (5453), to produce, grow; *hupárchō* (5225), to exist, to continue to be what one was before; *eimí* (1510), to be; *diérchomai* (1330), to pass through or over; *apérchomai* (5656), to go away; *diabaínō* (1224), to step across or over; *metabaínō* (3327), to pass over from one place to another; *parágō* (3855), to pass by or away; *diaperáō* (1276), to pass over; *diodeúō* (1353), to travel through or along; *chōráō* (5562), to pass, retire; *katargéō* (2673), to do away with, abolish; *paroíchomai* (3944), to have passed by, be gone; *anachōréō* (402), to withdraw; *chōréō* (5562), to have place; *phthánō* (5348), to arrive, catch up; *parístēmi* (3936), to be pressed, arrive; *sumbaínō* (4819), to come to pass; *prokóptō* (4298), to advance from within.

Ant.: *paúō* (3973), to stop, make an end; *dialeípō* (1257), to leave between or an interval; *hēsucházō* (2270), to be quiet, still; *kopázō* (2869), to cease, to be tired; *aphíēmi* (863), to let go, cease to be; *katapaúō* (2664), to cease; *katargéō* (2673), to render inactive; *parérchomai* (3928), to pass by, in regard to time.

1097. γινώσκω *ginóskō*; fut. *gnósomai*, 2d aor. *égnōn*, perf. *égnōka*, fut. pass. *gnōsthḗsonai*, aor. pass. *egnṓsthēn*, perf. pass. *égnōsmai*. To know, in a beginning or completed sense.

(I) To know, in a beginning sense, that is, to come to know, to gain or receive a knowledge of, where again the perf. implies a completed action and is often to be taken in the pres. sense, to know. In the pass., to become known.

(A) Generally: **(1)** Followed by the acc. of thing (Matt 12:7; John 8:32, "you will know the truth" [a.t.]; Luke 12:47; Acts 1:7; 1 Cor 4:19, "And I shall know, not the speech . . . , but the power" [a.t.]; 2 Cor 2:9). With an acc. implied (Mark 6:38; 1 Cor 13:9; Sept.: 1 Sam 20:3; 21:2; 2 Sam 24:2). Followed with *ek* (1537), from or of and the gen. (Matt 12:33, to know from or by anything; Luke 6:44; 1 John 3:24; 4:6). Followed by *en* (1722), by means of, and the dat. (John 13:35, to know by means of anything; 1 John 3:16, 19, 24; 4:13; 5:2; Sept.: Gen 24:14; 42:33). Also with *hóthen* (3606), whence (1 John 2:18). With *katá* (2596), according to, followed by the acc. *ti*, what (Luke 1:18; Sept.: Gen 15:8). **(2)** With the acc. of person (John 14:7, "If ye had known me"; Luke 24:35; 19:15; Rom 1:21; 2 Cor 5:16; Gal 4:9, *gnóntes*, "since you knew God" [a.t.]; 1 John 2:3; 3:1; Sept.: 1 Sam 3:7). Also with an acc. and *hóti* (3754), that (Matt 25:24, *égnōn se*, "I knew you [*hóti*] that you are a hard man" [a.t.]; John 5:42; Sept.: 1 Sam 20:32). **(3)** With *hóti* (3754), that, instead of an acc. and inf. (John 6:69, *egnṓkamen hóti sú eí ho Christós*, "we have known that you are the Christ" [a.t.]; 7:26; 8:52; 19:4; James

2:20; Sept.: Gen 8:11; 42:34). **(4)** Pass., to be known or distinguished (1 Cor 14:7).

(B) In a judicial sense, to know by trial, to inquire into or examine the reason or cause (John 7:51; Acts 23:28).

(C) In the sense of to know from others, learn, find out. In the pass., to be made known, disclosed (Matt 10:26; Acts 9:24). With the acc. of thing expressed or implied (Mark 5:43; Acts 21:34; Col 4:8; Matt 9:30; Luke 9:11; Sept.: 1 Sam 21:2). With *hóti* (3754), that (John 4:1; Acts 24:11; Sept.: 1 Sam 4:6). Also with *apó* (575), from, with the gen. (Mark 15:45).

(D) In the sense of to perceive, observe, be aware of, with the acc. expressed or implied (Matt 16:8; 22:18, "their wickedness"; 26:10; Sept.: Ruth 3:4). With *hóti* (3754), that (Mark 5:29, *égnō tō̄ sṓmati hóti*, knew in her body; John 4:53; 6:15; Acts 23:6; Sept.: 1 Sam 20:33). With the acc. and part. (Luke 8:46, "I knew that power came out of me" [a.t.]).

(E) In the sense of to understand or comprehend, with the acc. expressed or implied (Matt 13:11, the mysteries; Mark 4:13, parables; Luke 18:34; John 3:10; 7:49, the law; 1 Cor 2:8, 14; John 10:6; 12:16; 13:12; Acts 8:30; Rom 11:34; Sept.: 1 Sam 20:39; Prov 1:2).

(F) By euphemism, to lie with a person of another sex as spoken of a man or men (Matt 1:25; Sept.: Gen 4:1, 17; 24:16); of a woman or women (Luke 1:34; Sept: Gen 19:8; Num 31:17, 35).

(II) To know in a completed sense, that is, to have the knowledge of.

(A) Generally: **(1)** As in Matt 6:3, "let not your left hand know what your right hand does" (a.t.); see 24:50; Luke 2:43; 7:39; 16:15; John 2:25; Rom 2:18; 10:19; 2 Cor 5:21; 1 John 3:20. Also the imper. *ginṓskete*, know, be assured of with the acc. (Matt 24:43; Luke 10:11; 12:39). Also *íste ginṓskontes toúto*, you are knowing this (Eph 5:5; Sept.: Job 20:4; Eccl 8:7; Jer 3:13). With the acc. and *hóti* (3754), that, by attraction, "the Lord knoweth the thoughts of the wise" (1 Cor 3:20). With the acc. and part. (Acts 19:35, "who does not know how that the city of the Ephesians is [oúsan, being] a worshiper" [a.t.]; Heb 13:23). With the adv. (Acts 21:37, "Do you know Greek?" [a.t. {cf. Sept.: Neh 13:24}]). (2) With the acc. of person, to know as by sight or person (John 1:48; 2 Cor 5:16); to know one's character (John 1:10; 2:24; 14:7, 9; 16:3; Acts 19:15; Sept.: Deut 34:10; Ps 87:4; 139:1). (3) With hóti (3754), that, instead of an acc. and inf. (John 21:17; James 1:3). (4) With the inf. alone (Matt 16:3).

(B) In the sense of to know, as being what one is or professes to be, to acknowledge, with the acc. (Matt 7:23). Pass. (1 Cor 8:3; Gal 4:9; Sept.: Isa 33:13; 61:9; 63:16).

(C) With the idea of volition or good will, to know and approve or love, to care for, with the acc. of person (John 10:14, 15, 27; 1 Tim 2:18, "The Lord knoweth them that are his [toús óntas autoú]"; Sept.: Ps 144:3; Amos 3:2; Nah 1:7); of men (Ps 36:11; Hos 8:2). With the acc. of thing (Rom 7:15, "That which I do, I do not know" [a.t.], meaning I do not approve, or as the KJV has it, "allow not"; Sept.: Ps 1:6).

Sometimes there can be no distinction between the two verbs ginōskō and epiginōskō (Mark 2:8; 8:17; Mark 5:30; Luke 8:46). In both cases the meaning is to perceive, while epiginōskō may also mean to learn (Luke 7:37), understand (2 Cor 1:13, 14), or to know (Acts 25:10). Sometimes, however, epiginōskō suggests advanced knowledge or special appreciation (Rom 1:32, "when they knew full well" [a.t.], while Rom 1:21 "they knew God" [ginōskō] simply suggests that they could not avoid the perception of God). In the Gospel of John, ginōskō denotes personal fellowship with God or Christ and also between the Father and the Son (John 10:14, 15, 27). Since the Father and the Son know each other they love each other (John 3:35). The same relationship exists between the Lord Jesus and His disciples (John 13:1). To know (ginōskō) the Father and the Son, since They have life, is to have Their life which is eternal life (John 5:26; 17:3). To know God is to be directed by love (1 John 4:7, 8) and is, therefore, followed by a life of love and the execution of Christ's commandments (1 John 2:3ff.). See also John 15:9; 13:34. Thus, it could be said that ginōskō means to believe, for it is through faith that we come to love the Lord. Knowing God is certainly more than just knowing about Him (John 6:42; 7:28). It is knowing the relation that He has with the Father (John 10:38; 14:31ff.). He who knows God sees Him (John 14:7ff.). He who believes also knows (John 5:24; 6:60ff.) and he who knows believes (John 10:38; 14:20). Without faith one cannot know either initially or progressively (John 16:30; 17:7, 8). Sometimes epiginōskō implies a special participation in the object known and gives greater weight to what is stated (John 8:32), in which it is equivalent to believing and then knowing the truth. In 1 Tim 4:3 the word epiginōskō stresses the participation in the truth, not simply believing it. Epiginōskō indicates a closer relationship resulting from a fuller knowledge (see Col 1:6). In 1 Cor 13:12 the two words are used together, ginōskō as our knowledge here on earth, and epiginōskō as our knowledge in our perfect state in heaven, even as we are known (epiginōskō) in a fuller way by Him here on earth. Epiginōskō also has the sense of to discover, ascertain, determine (Luke 7:37; 23:7; Acts 9:30; 19:34; 22:29; 28:1). Epígnōsis (1922), meaning full knowledge, as well as the verb epiginōskō, have a particular object in mind, that is, almost a technical meaning, e.g., the conversion to Christianity (1 Tim 2:4; 2 Tim 2:25; Titus 1:1). Gnōsis (1108), knowledge, as well as the verb ginōskō, may have a more general meaning. In Rom 1:28 the epígnōsis is the same as gnōsis. Epígnōsis may refer rather to edification than learning (Rom 15:14; 1 Cor 14:6).

The contrast between ginōskō and oída (1492), is that the first often suggests an acquired knowledge, but oída suggests intuitive knowledge, that is, I know what I know because I am what I am. Man, for example, does not have the intuitive knowledge or instinct that an animal has because he is not an animal, and vice versa. In the same sense, man cannot know as God knows because he is not God. This is made clear in John 8:55, "Yet ye have not known [egnṓkate] him, but I know [oída] him." Man cannot know the Father experientially, but the Lord Jesus knows the Father intuitively because He and the Father are one, of the same essence. In John 13:7 the Lord Jesus said to Peter, "What I do [the washing of his feet] you do not know [intuitively because you are not what you will one day be in order to understand the deeper significance of My actions] now, but thou shalt know hereafter [gnṓsē, it will be shown to you, it will be explained to you and then you will understand]" (a.t.). In Mark 4:13 the Lord Jesus said to His disciples: "Know ye not [oídate {1492}, you have not intuitively perceived in spite of the fact that you are My disciples, which you should have been able to perceive] this parable? And how then will ye know [gnṓsesthe, know by observation even if somebody tells you and explains it] all parables?" In Matt 7:23, "And then will I profess [homologḗsō {3670}, confess or I shall agree] unto them, I never knew you [égnōn {1097}, came to observe you as having experienced Me]." However, in Matt 25:12 the Lord spoke to the unprepared virgins, "I know you not [ouk oída, I do not intuitively know you as being my own, I do not recognize you intuitively]." The unprepared virgins were not rejected because they did not have oil in their lamps, but because they were not related to Jesus Christ. And in Matt 26:13 our Lord said, "for ye know [oídate, intuitively know because you are still in the imperfect body and God's revelation to you is only partly known by you {1 Cor 13:9}]."

Deriv.: anaginṓskō (314), to read; gnṓmē (1106), cognition; gnṓsis (1108), knowledge; gnṓstēs (1109), a knower, expert; gnōstós (1110), well-known, acquaintance; diaginṓskō (1231), to know thoroughly; epiginṓskō (1921), to

observe, fully perceive, notice attentively, discern; kardiognṓstēs (2589), heart-knower; kataginṓskō (2607), to blame condemn; proginṓskō (4267), to know beforehand.

Syn.: epístamai (1987), to know or acquire knowledge; sunoída (4894), to know together, be conscious of; theōréō (2334), to be a spectator and thus to understand or perceive; aisthánomai (143), to perceive with the senses, while ginṓskō is to perceive through the mind; noéō (3539), to perceive with the mind, to understand; katanoéō (2657), to understand more fully; katalambánō (2638), to lay hold of, apprehend, perceive; blépō (991), to see and perceive; suníēmi (4920), to mentally put it together, to perceive, understand; punthánomai (4441), to inquire in order to know; parakolouthéō (3877), to follow, observe, understand; gnōrízō (1107), to come to know, know; diagnōrízō (1232), to make known widely; gnōstós (1110), known; ágnōstos (57), unknown; agnōsía (56), ignorance; kardiognṓstēs (2589), one who knows the heart; anagnōrízō (319), to recognize, to make oneself known; diagnōrízō (1232), to make known; diaginṓskō (1231), to determine by thorough examination; gnōrízō (1107), to make known, understand.

Ant.: agnoéō (50), to be ignorant; lanthánō (2990), to fail to know, to be lacking or missing as far as understanding is concerned.

1098. γλεῦκος gleúkos; gen. gleúkous, neut. noun from glukús (1099), sweet. Must, sweet wine (Acts 2:13; Sept.: Job 32:19). Some believe that it is what distills of its own accord from the grapes which is the sweetest and smoothest. It was mentioned at Pentecost (Acts 2:13) indicating that the ancients may have had a method of preserving the sweetness, and by consequence retarding the inebriating effect of the oínos (3631), wine. Yet those full of gleúkos were considered drunk, which indicates that gleúkos was indeed intoxicating. In instituting the Lord's Supper, the Lord speaks of the contents of the cup as neither wine (*oínos* [3631]), nor *gleúkos*, but as the "fruit [*génnēma* {1081}] of the vine [*tēs ampélou* {288}]" (Matt 26:29; Mark 14:25; Luke 22:18) employing a double metonymy. The word *génnēma* also means offspring (e.g., Matt 3:7; 12:34), but in connection with *ámpelos*, vine, it means fruit or produce.

1099. γλυκύς glukús; fem. *glukeía*, neut. *glukú*, adj. Sweet, as honey (Rev 10:9, 10). Water is called sweet, meaning potable (James 3:11, 12), in contrast to salty (*halukós* [252]) (Sept.: Judg 14:14; Isa 5:20).

    Deriv.: *gleúkos* 1098), sweet wine.
    Syn.: *ánalos* (358), saltless.
    Ant.: *pikrós* (4089), bitter.

1100. γλῶσσα glōssa; gen. *glōssēs*, fem. sing. noun. Tongue.

    (I) An organ of the body (Rev 16:10); as of taste (Luke 16:24); of speech (Mark 7:33, 35; Luke 1:64; 1 Cor 14:9; James 3:5, 6); personified (Rom 14:11; Phil 2:11, "every tongue" means every person [cf. Acts 2:26; Sept.: Isa 45:23 {see also Ps 16:9}). To bridle the tongue (James 1:26; 3:8; 1 Pet 3:10; Sept.: Judg 7:5; Job 29:10; 33:2).

    (II) Metaphorically, speech or language.

    (A) Generally (1 John 3:18, "Let us not love in word nor speech only" [a.t.]; Sept.: Prov 25:15; 31:26).

    (B) Of a particular language or dialect as spoken by a particular people (Acts 2:11; 1 Cor 13:1; Sept.: Gen 10:5, 20; Dan 1:4). Used for the people who speak a particular language, e.g., tribes, people, and tongues (Rev 5:9; 7:9; 10:11; 11:9; 13:7; 14:6; 17:15; Sept.: Isa 66:18; Dan 3:4, 7, 30, 32).

    (C) In the phrases *glōssais hetérais* (2083), tongues others or different, meaning different than their own native tongues. Also *glōssais kainaís* (2537), qualitatively new, to speak languages not known to them before, means to speak in or with tongues other than their own

native tongue (Mark 16:17; Acts 2:4; 10:46; 19:6; 1 Cor 12:30; 14:2, 4–6, 13, 18, 23, 27, 39).

    In 1 Cor 14:19, *lógoi* (3056), words or discourses in a tongue (sing.), or an unknown language spoken by Paul in Corinth but not immediately understood by the hearers. In 1 Cor 12:10, 28, *génē* (1085), kinds, families of languages, refers to actual ethnic languages. In 1 Cor 13:8; 14:20 *glōssai* (pl.) tongues, means ethnic languages.

    To "pray in a tongue [sing.]" (a.t.) in 1 Cor 14:14 means in an unknown tongue as practiced in Corinth, not immediately understood by others but in an ecstasy. In 1 Cor 14:26, 27 where it appears in the sing., Paul refers to the Corinthian practice of speaking in an ecstatic language in public, and he gives regulations that it may not get out of hand. In 1 Cor 14:2, 4, it is *glōssa*, sing. which refers to the Corinthian practice of speaking in an unknown ecstatic tongue. It is clear from the study of the NT that there were two distinct uses of the word "tongue." **(1)** One was the promised gift of languages (*glōssai*) other than one's own native language. This gift was for those who were going to be baptized in the Holy Spirit into the body of Jesus Christ and which gift they were to use to affirm the gospel as happened in the historical context of Jerusalem at Pentecost (Acts 2:3, 4 [*diálektos* (1258), Acts 2:6, 8], 11) and involving Jewish believers. It was also exhibited at Caesarea Maritime (Acts 10:44–46; 11:15–18) involving Gentile believers and in Ephesus (Acts 19:1–6) involving the disciples of John. These were foreign languages which the speakers had not learned, but yet they were enabled to speak as a result of the supernatural intervention of the Holy Spirit in what the NT calls specifically "the baptism in the Holy Spirit" (a.t.) by Jesus Christ (Matt 3:11; Mark 1:8; Luke 3:16; John 1:33; Acts 1:5; 11:16; 1 Cor 12:13). See *baptízō* (907); *báptisma* (908).

    Promise of this event was given in Mark 16:17. In connection with this verse, it should be noted that these signs were not for believers of generations to come, but for previous believers since the part. *pisteúsasi* is in the aor. tense indicating those who at some time in the past had believed. These were all languages unknown to the speakers, spoken at that particular time in demonstration of their being baptized into the body of Jesus Christ (1 Cor 12:13).

Observe that the baptism in the Holy Spirit is an event which includes all believers. These are the same languages demonstrated as *charísmata* (the results of the grace of God in the human heart) mentioned by Paul in 1 Cor 12:10, 30; 14:5, 6, 18, 22, 39.

It is then to be observed that whenever the word *glóssa* is used in the pl. (*glóssai*) with a sing. pron. or subj., it refers to dialects (Acts 2:3f., 8, 11) which were not learned by the individual concerned. Such an individual was enabled instantly and temporarily by the Holy Spirit to speak in a language other than his native tongue. In 1 Cor 14:6, 18, Paul himself refers to speaking in *glóssais*, languages or tongues. By this he meant languages which he already knew or the ones that he was enabled to speak by the Holy Spirit when and if needed. The pl. *glóssai* with a sing. pron. or subj. refers to known, understandable languages, and not to an unknown tongue as practiced in Corinth. But even when utilizing these gifts, one should be sure he is understood by those who hear him, otherwise he will be taken as a maniac (*maínomai* [3105], beside oneself, mad) (1 Cor 14:23). (2) Whenever the word *glóssa* in the sing. with a sing. subj. or pron. is used, translated in the KJV "unknown tongue" (1 Cor 14:2, 4, 13, 14, 19, 26, 27), it refers to the Corinthian practice of speaking in an unknown tongue not comprehended by someone and, therefore, not an ordinarily-spoken language. Such was the unknown language of the priestesses spoken in the oracles at Delphi. For example, 1 Cor 14:26 may refer to a language foreign to the hearers and uninterpreted.

The expression in 1 Cor 13:1, "the tongues of men and of angels," means the languages which humans and angels speak. The language or languages of angels cannot be interpreted as being the same as the unknown tongue spoken in Corinth which was different from any intelligible ethnic language. Whenever the angels spoke to humans as God's messengers, they always spoke in an understandable language, needing no interpreter, as to the shepherds (Luke 2:10–12), the Virgin Mary (Luke 1:28), and many others. Never did God or any angel He sent speak to someone in a language which that person could not understand. Even the fish, when Jonah was in its belly, understood when God spoke to it. Speech has as its direct object the understanding of the words uttered. The phrase probably denotes inspired utterances. Angels were often the *vehicula* of divine revelation and the bearers of holy oracles. Hebrews 2:2 characterizes the OT as "the word spoken by angels."

Deriv.: *glōssókomon* (1101), a bag, case; *heteróglōssos* (2084), a person speaking a tongue other than one's native tongue.

Syn.: *diálektos* (1258), dialect, an ethnic language.

1101. γλωσσόκομον *glōssókomon*; gen. *glōssokómou*, neut. noun from *glōssa* (1100), tongue, and *koméō* (n.f.), to keep, preserve. A case, purse, box in which to keep the tongues or reeds used in playing wind instruments. Generally it means any box, case, bag, for money (John 12:6; 13:29); the little chest or coffer in which the Philistines put the golden mice and emerods (Sept.: 1 Sam 6:11; 2 Chr 24:8, 10, 11). Also from *koméō* (n.f.): *komízō* (2865), to take care of, provide for.

Syn.: *balántion* (905), bag, purse; *zṓnē* (2223), a girdle or belt which served as a purse.

1102. γναφεύς *gnapheús*; gen. *gnaphéōs*, masc. noun from *gnáphos* (n.f.), a card or teasle. A fuller, one who bleaches and dresses new material or washes and scrubs soiled garments (Mark 9:3; Sept.: 2 Kgs 18:17; Isa 7:3; 36:2 meaning washer). Related word: *ágnaphos* (46), new cloth that has not been washed.

1103. γνήσιος gnḗsios; gen. *gnēsíou*, fem. *gnēsía*, neut. *gnḗsion*, adj. from *génos* (1085), born. Of children meaning legitimate, lawfully born. In the NT, it means genuine, true, not degenerate, as in Phil 4:3. Spoken of the relation of a disciple to his teacher, genuine (1 Tim 1:2; Titus 1:4). As a subst. in the neut. *tó gnḗsion*, genuineness, sincerity (2 Cor 8:8).
    Deriv.: *gnēsíōs* (1104), genuinely, really.
    Syn.: *ádolos* (97), guileless, pure, sincere; *eilikrinḗs* (1506), sincere, pure; *hagnós* (53), chaste, clean, pure; *alēthḗs* (227), unconcealed, manifest; *alēthinós* (228), real, genuine; *apseudḗs* (983), one that cannot lie.
    Ant.: *pseudḗs* (5571), false; *nóthos* (3541), illegitimate.

1104. γνησίως gnēsíōs; adv. from *gnḗsios* (1103), legitimate. Sincerely (Phil 2:20).
    Syn.: *hagnós* (55), with pure motives; *alēthṓs* (230), truly, indeed; *óntōs* (3689), certainly, truly.

1105. γνόφος gnóphos; gen. *gnóphou*, neut. noun from *néphos* (3509), a cloud. A thick dark cloud (Heb 12:18; Sept.: Ex 20:21; Deut 4:11; 5:22; 2 Sam 22:10).
    Syn.: *skótos* (4655), darkness; *zóphos* (2217), darkness, foggy weather, smoke which is used to imply infernal darkness; *achlús* (887), a thick mist or a fog.
    Ant.: *eudía* (2105), fine weather, clear sky.

1106. γνώμη gnṓmē; gen. *gnṓmēs*, fem. noun from *ginṓskō* (1097), to discern, know. Generally it means capacity of judgment, faculty of discernment as far as conduct is determined.
    (I) As implying will, in the sense of accord, consent (Phile 1:14). In the sense of purpose, counsel, determination (Acts 20:3; Rev 17:17).
    (II) As implying opinion, judgment, in reference to oneself (1 Cor 7:40, "according to my opinion" [a.t.]). In reference to others, advice (1 Cor 7:25; 2 Cor 8:10).
    With the meaning of bent, inclination, desire (1 Cor 1:10; Rev 17:13, the same mind or will). In 1 Cor 1:10 used in conj. with *noús* (3563), mind. These two words *noús* and *gnṓmē*, although connected, must be distinguished. The distinction cannot be that of the organ being *noús*, mind, and *gnṓmē*, its function. *Gnṓmē* includes the direction by the subject to a certain object, or the determining of the subject by some object. It is discernment which determines conduct. *Noús* refers only to thinking without direction. It signifies consciousness, mind, opinion, thought. *Gnṓmē* can be syn. with will, as in Rev 17:13 which must be taken in conj. with Rev 17:17, meaning God's direction, inclination. *Gnṓmē*, when referring to pleasure or purpose means decision as in Acts 20:3. It is judgment, conviction, opinion in the sense of *dokéō* (1380), to think or recognize, indicating purely subjective opinion as in 1 Cor 7:25, 40; 2 Cor 8:10 where Paul gives an entirely subjective view of the matter. By using this word, Paul indicates that he expects the counsel he gives will be recognized without a command on his part. For deriv. see *ginṓskō* (1097), to know, understand.
    Syn.: *boulḗ* (1012), a counsel or piece of advice being the result of determination, while *gnṓmē* is the result of knowledge; *krísis* (2920), decision, judgment, but from the legal point of view, while *gnṓmē* indicates the judgment of the mind with direction; *kríma* (2917), condemnatory judgment; *aísthēsis* (144), perception resulting from the senses; *phrónēma* (5427), thought existing in the mind without externalizing it while *gnṓmē* implies externalization of that which one thinks; *phrónēsis* (5428), the thought process, understanding; *boúlēma* (1013), deliberate intention or purpose; *thélēma* (2307), a desire expressive of the will; *próthesis*

(4286), purpose; *thélēsis* (2308), the act of willing or wishing; *eudokía* (2107), good pleasure or will; *eúnoia* (2133), good will; *diánoia* (1271), intelligence, understanding; *dianóēma* (1270), something thought through, a thought, consideration.

Ant.: *agnóēma* (51), ignorance, unwitting error; *agnōsía* (56), ignorance, willfulness implied.

1107. γνωρίζω gnōrízō; fut. *gnōrísō* Attic fut. *gnōriō*. To make known, trans. and with the dat. or *prós* (4314), toward or to someone (*tiná*, acc.) as in Phil 4:6.

(I) To others:

(A) Generally to make known, declare, reveal (Rom 9:22, 23); with the dat. (Luke 2:15; Acts 2:28 quoted from Ps 16:11; Eph 3:3, 5, 10; Col 1:27; Gal 1:11); with the prep. *pros* (4314), to (Phil 4:6; Sept.: 1 Sam 16:3; 1 Chr 16:8; Ps 25:4).

(B) In the sense of to narrate, tell, inform (Eph 6:21; Col 4:7, 9; 2 Cor 8:1).

(C) Spoken of a teacher who unfolds divine things, to announce, declare, proclaim (John 15:15; 17:26; Rom 16:26; Eph 1:9; 6:19; 2 Pet 1:16; Sept.: Ezek 20:11).

(D) In the sense of to put in mind of, impress upon, confirm (1 Cor 12:3; 15:1).

(II) To make known to oneself, to ascertain, find out (Phil 1:22; Sept.: Job 34:25).

Deriv.: *anagnōrízomai* (319), to make known; *diagnōrízō* (1232), to tell abroad.

Syn.: *epístamai* (1987), to know, understand; *apokalúptō* (601), to reveal.

Ant.: *apokrúptō* (613), to hide, keep secret; *kríptō* (2928), to hide.

1108. γνῶσις gnṓsis; gen. *gnṓseōs*, fem. noun from *ginṓskō* (1097), to know. Knowledge. Present and fragmentary knowledge as contrasted with *epígnōsis* (1922), clear and exact knowledge which expresses a more thorough participation in the object or knowledge on the part of the knowledgeable subject. Present intuitive knowledge is often expressed by the verb *oída* or *eídō* (1492) (Luke 1:77; 11:52; Rom 11:33; 1 Cor 13:2; Col 2:3; 2 Pet 1:5, 6).

(I) The power of knowing, intelligence, comprehension (Rom 8:35; 1 Cor 12:31; 13:2; Eph 3:19, "the love of Christ surpassing comprehension" [a.t.]).

(II) Subjectively spoken of what one knows, knowledge (Luke 1:77; Rom 11:33; Phil 3:8; Sept.: Ps 73:11; 139:6; Hos 4:6). Of the knowledge of Christianity generally (Rom 15:14; 1 Cor 1:5; 8:1; 2 Pet 3:18). Of a deeper and better Christian knowledge, both theoretical and experimental (1 Cor 8:7, 10, 11; 2 Cor 11:6). Spoken of practical knowledge, discretion, prudence (2 Cor 6:6; 1 Pet 3:7; 2 Pet 1:5, 6; Sept.: Prov 13:16).

(III) Objectively spoken of what is known, the object of knowledge, generally knowledge, doctrine, science (2 Cor 2:14; 4:6; Col 2:3; Sept.: Dan 1:4; Mal 2:7); of religious knowledge, i.e., doctrine, science as spoken of Jewish teachers (Luke 11:52; Rom 2:20; 1 Tim 6:20); of a deeper Christian knowledge, Christian doctrine (1 Cor 12:8, "word of knowledge" meaning the faculty of unfolding and expounding theoretically the deeper knowledge or fundamental principles of the Christian religion, equivalent to what in Luke 11:52 is called the "key of knowledge"; 1 Cor 13:2, 8; 14:6; 2 Cor 8:7). Hence in 2 Cor 10:5, "against the true doctrine of God" (a.t.), i.e., against the Christian religion. From *gnōsis* is derived "gnosticism," a cult of pre-Christian and early Christian centuries distinguished by the conviction that matter is evil and that emancipation comes through *gnōsis*, knowledge.

Deriv.: *agnōsía* (56), without knowledge.

1109. γνώστης gnṓstēs; gen. *gnōstoú*, masc. noun, from *ginṓskō* (1097), to know. One who knows (Acts 26:3).

1110. γνωστός gnōstós; gen. *gnōstoú*, fem. *gnōstḗ*, neut. *gnōstón*, adj. from *ginṓskō* (1097), to know. Known.

(I) Generally and followed by the dat. (John 18:15, 16; Acts 1:19; 15:18;

19:17; 28:22). Followed with *katá* (2596), throughout, with the gen. of place (Acts 9:42; Sept.: Isa 19:21; 66:14). *Gnōstón éstō* (pres. imper. of *eimí* [1510], to be), be it known, with the dat. (Acts 2:14; 4:10; 13:38; 28:28; Sept.: Ezek 36:32; Ezra 4:12, 13). In the sense of knowable, *tó gnōstón toú Theoú*, what may be known of God or the knowledge of God, equal to *gnōsis* (1108) as in Rom 1:19. God is knowable or known by man because of the demonstration of His power in His creation. Here reference is made not to the knowledge possessed by God, but to man's knowledge of God (Sept.: Gen 2:9). In an emphatic sense, known of all, i.e., notable, incontrovertible (Acts 4:16).

(**II**) As a subst. with the art. *ho gnōstós*, it means an acquaintance (Luke 2:44; 23:49; Sept.: 2 Kgs 10:11; Ps 88:8, 18). A specific syn. is *phanerós* (5318), visible, manifest, known.

Deriv.: *ágnōstos* (57), unknown.

1111. γογγύζω *goggúzō*; fut. *goggúsō*. A onomatopoeic word derived from the sound made when murmuring or muttering in a low and indistinct voice with the idea of complaint. To murmur, mutter, used in an absolute sense in 1 Cor 10:10 with the idea of complaint, also Sept.: Num 11:1. With *katá* (2596), against, with the gen. in Matt 20:11; Sept.: Ex 16:7. With *perí* (4012), about, and the gen. in John 6:41, 61; Sept.: Num 14:27. With *prós* (4314), toward, and the acc. in Luke 5:30. With *met' allḗlōn* (*met'* [3326], with; *allḗlōn* [240], each other), with each other (John 6:43).

Deriv.: *goggusmós* (1112), grumbling, murmuring; *goggustḗs* (1113), grumbler, murmurer; *diagoggúzō* (1234), to murmur throughout, constantly complain indignantly.

Syn.: *embrimáomai* (1690), to murmur against; *stenázō* (4727), to murmur, sigh.

Ant.: *eulogéō* (2127), to speak well of, bless; *makarízō* (3106), to declare as blessed or having been indwelt by God and thus fully satisfied; *eucharistéō* (2168), to give thanks.

1112. γογγυσμός *goggusmós*; gen. *goggusmoú*, masc. noun from *goggúzō* (1111), to grumble, murmur. Grumbling, grudging, murmuring. Murmuring or muttering in general (John 7:12). Murmuring from discontent, grumbling (Acts 6:1). In Phil 2:14 without murmurings, meaning cheerfully (also 1 Pet 4:9; Sept.: Ex 16:7, 8, 12; Isa 58:9). For deriv. and syn. see *goggúzō* (1111), to grumble, murmur.

Ant.: *eulogía* (2129), blessing, when God or others speak well of us or we do the same thing for others; *makarismós* (3108), an inscription of blessedness that one is indwelt by God and consequently is fully satisfied.

1113. γογγυστής *goggustḗs*; gen. *goggustoú*, masc. noun from *goggúzō* (1111), to grumble, murmur. A grumbler, murmurer (Jude 1:16; Sept.: Prov 26:21, *loídoros* [3060], a railer, reviler).

1114. γόης *góēs*; gen. *góētos*, masc. noun. A conjurer, an enchanter. Plato mentions *góēs* in company with *pharmakeús* (5332) which word is akin to pharmacist or druggist, meaning an enchanter with drugs, and *sophistḗs*, a cunning cheat. In the NT, by implication *góēs* is a deceiver, an impostor (2 Tim 3:13).

Syn.: *plános* (4108), one who leads astray, a seducer; *phrenapátēs* (5423), a mind deceiver.

1115. Γολγοθᾶ *Golgothá*; proper noun transliterated from the Aramaic *Gulgultá'*, skull. Golgotha, the name of the place where Jesus was crucified (Matt 27:33). Syn. with Calvary (*kraníon* [2898]), it was the place in Jerusalem where criminals were commonly executed (Mark 15:22; John 19:17).

1116. Γόμορρα *Gómorra*; gen. *Gomórras*, fem. proper noun. Hebr. 'Amōrāh (6017, OT). Gomorrah meaning submersion. One of the five cities in the valley

of Siddim (Gen 14:2–11) destroyed for
its wickedness (Gen 18:20; 19:24, 28);
made a warning by Moses (Deut 29:23;
32:32); referred to by Isaiah (1:9, 10); by
Jeremiah (23:14; 49:18; 50:40); by Amos
(4:11); by Zephaniah (2:9); by the Lord
Jesus (Matt 10:15; Mark 6:11); by Paul,
quoting Isaiah (Rom 9:29); by Peter and
Jude (2 Pet 2:6; Jude 1:7). The site is disputed, some placing it at the southern end,
and others at the northern end of the Dead
Sea. A valley known as Wadi Ammorrhat
is now found at the southwest side of the
Dead Sea.

1117. γόμος gómos; gen. *gómou*, masc.
noun from *gémō* (1073), to be full. The
burden or load of an animal (Sept.: Ex
23:5); a ship (Acts 21:3). Merchandise
brought by sea (Rev 18:11, 12).
    Syn.: *báros* (922), weight; *phortíon*
(5413), something carried, load.

1118. γονεύς goneús; gen. *gonéōs*,
masc. noun from *gínomai* (1096), to generate. A parent, whether father or mother.
In the NT only pl., *goneís*, parents (Matt
10:21; Mark 13:12; Luke 2:27, 41; 8:56;
18:29; 21:16; John 9:2, 3, 18, 20, 22, 23;
Rom 1:30; 2 Cor 12:14; Eph 6:1; Col
3:20; 2 Tim 3:2).
    Syn.: *patḗr* (3962), father; *mḗtēr*
(3384), mother.
    Ant.: *téknon* (5043), a child; *tekníon*
(5040), a little child; *huiós* (5207), a son,
indicating conformity with the parents;
país (3816), a child in relation to descent,
a boy; *paidíon* (3813), a little child, one
subject to education, training; *paidárion*
(3808), a lad; *népios* (3516), a baby.

1119. γόνυ gónu; gen. *gónatos*, neut.
noun. The knee. Pl. *tá gónata*, the knees
(Heb 12:12; Sept.: Gen 30:3; 48:12).
    Deriv.: *gonupetéō* (1120), to fall on
the knees.

1120. γονυπετέω gonupetéō; contracted *gonupetṓ*, fut. *gonupetḗsō*, from *gónu*
(1119), knee, and *píptō* (4098), to fall. To
fall down on the knees or kneel before

another in supplication (Matt 17:14;
Mark 1:40); in reverence (Mark 10:17);
in mock homage (Matt 27:29). To kneel
down in prayer or supplication (Luke
22:41; Acts 7:60; 9:40; 20:36; 21:5); in
mockery by the soldiers who were crucifying Jesus (Matt 27:29). In Luke 5:8, the
expression, "fell down at Jesus' knees,"
means embraced them by way of supplication (see also Rom 11:4; Eph 3:14; Phil
2:10). To bend the knee or knees to someone, means to kneel in homage, adoration
(Rom 14:11 quoted from Isa 45:23).

1121. γράμμα grámma; gen. *grámmatos*,
neut. noun from *gráphō* (1125), to write.
That which is written, a letter of the alphabet, a book, letter, bond, and so forth. NT
meanings: a letter or character of literal
writing where reference is made to what
Moses wrote, versus the verbal utterances of the Lord Jesus, making *grámma* to
stand in contrast to *rhḗma* (4487) (Luke
23:38 [cf. 2 Cor 3:7; Gal 6:11]); a writing (John 5:47); a bill, an account (Luke
16:6, 7); the letter of the law, i.e., the literal sense and outward ordinances of
the law (Rom 2:27, 29; 7:6; 2 Cor 3:6,
7); a letter, an epistle (Acts 28:21). Pl.:
grámmata, letters, with the def. art. *ta*
(3588) meaning learning, erudition gained
from books (John 7:15; Acts 26:24); also
hierá (2413), holy, *grámmata*, letters, or
the Holy Scriptures (2 Tim 3:15 [cf. John
5:47]). *Tá hierá grámmata* is an expression distinct from *hē graphḗ*, the writing. *Tá hierá grámmata* describes the
letters of the alphabet as used in Scripture as the object of study or knowledge,
whereas *graphḗ* (1124) describes them
as an authority. It cannot be proved that
tá grámmata, writings without the qualifying word *hierá*, holy, means Holy
Scriptures; at least there is no sufficient
reason for taking it thus in the single passage of John 7:15 where it occurs without
the article: "How knoweth this man letters [*grámmata*], having never learned?"
The expression means knowledge contained in writings, learning, or usually the
elements of knowledge. At a later period

it meant science. The Jews simply said, "How has this man attained knowledge or science without pursuing the usual course of study?" (a.t.). The word in Acts 26:24 means, "Thou hast studied too much" (a.t.). In the letters of Paul we have the antithesis between *grámma*, letter, and *pneúma* (4151), spirit (Rom 2:29; 7:6; 2 Cor 3:6). This antithesis may be explained thus: *grámma* denotes the law in its written form whereby the relation of the law to the man whom it concerns is the more inviolably established (Rom 2:27; 2 Cor 3:7). It is the external, fixed, and governing law; whereas the *pneúma*, the spirit, is the inner, effective, energizing, and divine principle of life (Rom 7:6).

Deriv.: *agrámmatos* (62), unlearned.

Syn.: *biblíon* (975), a small book, any scroll or sheet on which something is written; *didaskalía* (1319), teaching instruction, doctrine; *epistolé* (1992), epistle, letter; *pinakídion* (4093), a tablet on which one can write.

Ant.: *lógos* (3056), a word; *rhḗma* (4487), an utterance, a saying; *laliá* (2981), speech.

1122. γραμματεύς grammateús; gen. *grammatéos*, masc. noun from *gráphō* (1125), to write. A scribe or writer. Such was in public service among the Greeks and acted as the reader of legal and state papers; hence, scholar (Ezra 7:11, 12). The king's "scribe" meant the secretary of state (2 Sam 8:17; 20:25, military clerk; 2 Kgs 25:19; 2 Chr 26:11).

In the Sept. *grammateús* is frequently used for a political officer who assisted kings or magistrates by keeping written accounts of public acts and occurrences or royal revenues (2 Kgs 12:10). Used for one skilled in the Mosaic Law (Ezra 7:6, 11, 12, 21; Jer 36:26) and commonly used in the same sense in the NT (Matt 13:52; 23:34; 1 Cor 1:20); especially for those who sat in Moses' seat, explaining the law in the schools and synagogues. Thus it became syn. with public instructors (cf. Neh 8:4); hence, *nomodidáskalos*, teacher or doctor of the law, or *nomikós*, lawyer. It was one well-versed in the law, i.e., in the Holy Scriptures, a lawyer, a clever scribe (cf. Ezra 7:6; Neh 8:1; Mark 9:11, 14, 16), and who expounded them (Matt 7:29; 8:19; 9:3; 17:10; 23:2, 13–34; Mark 1:22; 2:6). He also had the charge of transcribing them. Many were members of the Sanhedrin, and we often find them mentioned with the elders and chief priests (Matt 2:4; 5:20; 7:29; 12:38; 16:21; 20:18; 21:15; 26:3; 27:41; Mark 7:5; 8:31; 10:33; 11:18, 27; 14:43, 53; 15:1, 31; Luke 9:22; 19:47; 20:1, 19, 39, 46; Acts 4:5; 6:12). The scribes were supposed to be acquainted with the interpretation of God's saving purpose (Matt 13:52; 23:34), but in the time of Jesus they opposed His offer of salvation (Mark 12:28, 32, 35, 38). Where they appear clothed with special authority or side by side with those in authority (Matt 2:4; 20:18; 23:2; 26:57; Mark 3:22; 7:1; 14:1; Luke 22:2, 66; 23:10), they can hardly be regarded as in legal possession of such authority. Their authority seems to have been granted to them in a general way only by virtue of their occupation (Matt 13:52; John 8:3) and did not include decisive power. Authorities allied themselves with the scribes for the sake of the respect attached to them by the Jewish people due to their knowledge of the Law.

Syn.: *nomikós* (3544), lawyer; *nomodidáskalos* (3547), teacher of the law, one instructed, a scholar, a learned teacher of religion.

1123. γραπτός graptós; fem. *graptḗ*, neut. *graptón*, adj. from *gráphō* (1125), to write. Written, inscribed (Rom 2:15).

1124. γραφή graphḗ; gen. *graphḗs*, fem. noun from *gráphō* (1125), to write. Used in the pl. in the NT for the Holy Scriptures, or in the sing. (30 times) for a part of it (Matt 21:42; 22:29; Mark 12:10, 24; 15:28; John 5:39; 10:35; Acts 1:16; 8:32; Rom 1:2; 9:17; James 2:23; Sept.: Ezra 6:18). The terms are almost invariably preceded by the def. art., the only exceptions being in John 19:37 and 2 Tim

3:16 where the art. before *graphḗ* is replaced by *hetéra* (2087), another, and *pása* (3956), all of it together and every part of the whole respectively. See Rom 1:2; 16:26; 1 Pet 2:6; 2 Pet 1:20 where *graphḗ* has become a proper noun synonymous with "Scripture." In these verses the Scriptures are explicitly characterized as *graphaí hágiai* (pl. [407]), Scriptures holy ones, or Holy Scriptures, and *graphaí prophētikaí* (4397), prophetic ones, prophetic Scriptures. In 2 Tim 3:15, another designation is used, *hierá grámmata* (*hierá* [4313], sacred; *grámmata* [1121], writings). The distinction between *hágios* and *hierós* must be born in mind. The Scriptures (*graphaí*) being holy (*hágiai*) refers to their established authority whose purpose produces holiness, separation from sin and unto God. No sinner can long read the Scriptures without a change taking place in his or her life. Either he or she will change in a supernatural way or the Scriptures will not be read for long. The Scriptures are an authoritative document of God which produces holiness. The word *grámmata*, writings, in 2 Tim 3:15, "And that from a child thou hast known the Holy Scriptures," is *tá hierá grámmata*, the sacred writings which were sacred for religious training versus mundane learning. Timothy is reminded by Paul of his training (*émathes*, "thou hast learned" in 2 Tim 3:14, being the aor. of *manthánō* [3129], indicating not only being taught but actually learning). In 2 Tim 3:16 Paul uses *pása* (3956), all, meaning every part of the whole and all of it together, and *graphḗ*, Scripture, and not *grámmata* as he used in verse fifteen. It is as if Paul were to say to Timothy, "From your babyhood up you were exposed to and learned the available religions and sacred [*hierá*] writings, but now we have the Scripture [the *graphḗ*], that which has been written once and for all and constitutes the final authority of God's revelation" (a.t.). We thus conclude that *grámmata* should never be taken as the Holy Scripture, i.e., *graphḗ* in the sing. or *graphaí* in the pl. In 2 Tim

3:16 they are called "God-breathed" (a.t.) or "inspired," and in Matt 26:54, 56; Luke 4:21; Rom 16:26, "Scriptures prophetic" (a.t.). Matt 26:56 and Rom 16:26 have reference to the prophetic Scriptures within the totality of Scriptures. The Holy Scriptures are everywhere termed as *hē*, the, *graphḗ*, Scripture, giving it authoritativeness. The word "Scripture" may refer to a single text (Mark 12:10; Luke 4:21; John 13:18; 17:12; 19:24, 28, 36, 37; Acts 1:16; 8:35; 17:2, 11; 18:24, 28; James 2:8, 23; 4:5; 1 Pet 2:6) or to the whole (Mark 14:49; Luke 24:27, 32, 45; John 2:22; 7:38, 42; 10:35; 20:9; Acts 8:32; Rom 4:3; 10:11; 11:2; 1 Cor 15:3, 4; Gal 3:8, 22; 4:30; 1 Tim 5:18; 2 Pet 1:20). Some theologians think that in 2 Pet 3:16 the writings of Paul and other apostles are meant. In the Sept. of 1 Chr 15:15; 2 Chr 30:5, the Holy Scripture is indicated when the written Law or statute is referred to. Paul in Rom 1:2 refers to the Scriptures as *graphaís hagíais*, holy. They are called "holy" because they separate man unto God.

1125. γράφω *gráphō*; fut. *grápsō*. To engrave, write (Mark 10:4; Luke 1:63; John 21:25; Gal 6:11; 2 Thess 3:17). The ancient Greeks equated *gráphō* with *xéō*, to carve. They carved figures with meaning on wooden tablets and later replaced these when letters were developed. The engraved tablet was covered with another, and being tied together and sealed, constituted the form of an ancient letter. The Sept. several times applies the word in this sense of engraving, carving, or cutting out (1 Kgs 6:29; Isa 22:16 [cf. Job 19:23, 24]). From Ex 31:18; 32:16; 2 Cor 3:7 we deduce that the first literal writing was of this kind. Thus originally the word meant to cut in, make an incision. Later, with the invention of the parchment and paper, it came to mean to write, to delineate literal characters on a tablet, parchment, or paper (Luke 1:63; 16:6, 7; John 8:6; 19:19; Acts 23:25; 3 John 1:13). It also came to mean to describe in writing (John 1:45; Rom 10:5); to write a law, command in writing, as would a legislator (Mark 12:19). The writing of names in heaven emphasizes that God remembers and will not forget, since by writing, the name of a person is fixed. The use of the word *gégraptai*, it is written, in the perf. tense refers authoritatively to what is found written in Holy Scripture and denotes legislative act or enactment. In the sphere of revelation, the written records hold this authoritative position, and *gégraptai* always implies an appeal to the indisputable and legal authority of the passage quoted (Matt 4:4, 6, 7, 10; 11:10). It is completed by additions such as "in the law" (Luke 2:23; 10:26); "in the book of the words of Isaiah" (Luke 3:4); "in the prophets" (John 6:45).

(I) To form letters with a stylus so that the letters were cut in or engraved on material such as the ground as in the case of Jesus in John 8:6, 8. Also 2 Thess 3:17, "thus I write" (a.t.), means this is my handwriting. In the sense of to write upon, meaning to fill with writing as in Rev 5:1, a book filled on the inside and the outside, means filled with writing all over and is equivalent to the comp. verb *epigráphō* (1924), to write on or over.

(II) To write, to commit to writing, express by writing with the acc. expressed or implied: Pilate's expression, *hó gégrapha*, the perf. indic. of *gráphō*, meaning that which I have written has been written or stands (John 19:21, 22); "which have not been committed to writing [*há ouk ésti gegramména* {the perf. part. of *gráphō*}]" (a.t.), refers to those signs or miracles which the Lord Jesus did which have not been committed to writing (John 20:30), and then in John 20:31, "but these things have been written [*taúta* {5023}], these; *dé* {1161}, but; *gégraptai*, the perf. pass. indic.]" (a.t.), or they have been committed to writing; "the disciple which . . . wrote these," or committed them to writing (John 21:24), and in John 21:25, the subjunctive, "if they were to be written" (a.t.), or committed to writing (*tá graphómena*, the pres. pass. part., i.e., those written). See also Luke 1:63; 16:6,

7; Rom 16:22; Rev 1:11; 10:4; 14:1; Sept.: Ex 24:4; 1 Sam 10:25. Spoken of what is written or contained in the Scriptures (Mark 1:2; John 8:17; Luke 3:4). Thus *gégraptai*, the perf. pass. indic. meaning has been written, and *tó gegramménon*, the neut. perf. pass. part. meaning that which has been written or it is written, is used as a formula of citation (Matt 4:4, 6, 7, 10; 26:31; Luke 4:4, 8, 10; Rom 1:17; 2:24). *Tó gegramménon* stands in contrast to *tó eirēménon*, the perf. pass. part. neut. of *rhéō* (4483), to say. When reference was made to a saying, the aor. pass. part. neut. was used as in *tó rhēthén* (Matt 1:22; 2:15, 17, 23; 3:3; 4:14; 12:17; 21:4; 22:31; 27:9). The aor. is used because that which was said is not the same as that which has been written and which exists in the form that it was written. Whenever the perf. pass. part. *eirēménon* (2046) is used (Luke 2:24; Acts 2:16; 13:40; Rom 4:18 quoting Gen 15:5), it has reference to the Law of God, to the prophets, or to a specific saying written down. This difference in tenses indicates that what is said is spoken of in a historic context and does not have present indisputable existence as that which also has a written form to it, as the *gegramménon*, written would indicate. *Gégraptai*, it has been written, constructed with a prep. such as *diá* (1223), through or by someone (Matt 2:5; Luke 18:31); with the prep. *epí* (1909) followed by the acc. (Mark 9:12, 13; John 12:16); with *epí*, followed by the dat. it means of or concerning someone as also with the prep. *perí* (4012), about (Matt 11:10; 26:24; John 5:46); with the dat. of person, meaning of or concerning whom (Luke 18:31). In a similar sense, to write about, describe, with the acc. (John 1:45; Rom 10:5; Sept.: Ezra 3:2; Neh 10:34, 36).

(III) To write, to compose or prepare in writing such as *biblíon* (975), a book or a document, *apostasíou* (647), separation, thus a document of separation which was to be issued by a guilty husband divorcing his innocent wife in order that she might be able to marry again (Mark 10:4; Deut 24:1–4). This document was to be in writing and not simply in spoken word in order that the dismissed person could have evidence of innocence when dismissed unjustifiably by the marital partner. To write an epistle, *epistolén* (1992) (Acts 23:25; 2 Pet 3:1; Sept.: Ezra 4:6, 8).

(IV) To write to someone, i.e., to make known by writing, with the acc. and dat. (Rom 15:15; 2 Cor 1:13, "We do not write other things to you" [a.t.]; 2:4; Phil 3:1 with the dat.; 2 John 1:12; Rev 2:1). With the dat. and *hóti* (3754), that (1 John 2:12–14). Used in an absolute sense (2 Cor 2:9; Sept.: Esth 3:12). Also of written directions, instructions, information (Acts 15:23; 18:27; 25:26; 1 Cor 5:9; 7:1; 14:37; 2 Cor 9:1); 1 Thess 4:9, "you have no need that I write to you" (a.t.); 5:1, "I do not need to write to you" (a.t.). To write a commandment to someone means to prescribe (Mark 10:5; 1 John 2:7). Used in an absolute sense in Mark 12:19; Luke 20:28. In Luke 2:23, *gégraptai* means it is prescribed (Sept.: 2 Kgs 17:37; Ezra 3:4).

(V) To inscribe, e.g., one's name in a book, register (Luke 10:20; Rev 13:8; 17:8). See *bíblos* (976), book, and *biblíon* (975), a diminutive of *bíblos*, a small book. See Ps 69:28; 139:16.

Deriv.: *apográphō* (583), to write, tax; *grámma* (1121), bill, letter, Scripture; *grammateús* (1122), scribe, town clerk; *graptós* (1123), written; *graphḗ* (1124), Scripture; *eggráphō* (1449), engrave; *epigráphō* (1924), to inscribe; *prográphō* (4270), to write previously, before ordain; *cheirógraphon* (5498), handwriting.

1126. γραώδης graṓdēs; gen. *graṓdous*, masc.-fem., neut. *graṓdes*, adj. from *graús* (n.f.), an old woman. Of or belonging to old women (1 Tim 4:7) meaning silly, e.g., old wives' tales.

1127. γρηγορέω grēgoreúō; fut. *grēgorḗsō*, from *egeírō* (1453) to arise, arouse. To watch, to refrain from sleep. It was transferred in meaning from the physical to the moral religious sphere (Matt 26:38, 40, 41). It denotes attention (Mark 13:34) to God's revelation or to the knowledge of salvation (1 Thess 5:6); a mindfulness of threatening dangers which, with conscious earnestness and an alert mind, keeps it from all drowsiness and all slackening in the energy of faith and conduct (Matt 26:40; Mark 14:34, 37, 38; 1 Thess 5:6; 1 Pet 5:8). It denotes the caution needed against anxiety resulting from the fear of the loss of one's salvation (1 Cor 16:13; Col 4:2; Rev 16:15); the worry over the salvation and preservation of others (Acts 20:31; Rev 3:2, 3). The general attitude of alertness on the part of the Christian believer, in view of actual or imminent tests of his spiritual life, is inculcated through the verb *grēgoréō* (1127) (Matt 24:42, 43; 25:13; 26:38, 40, 41; Mark 13:35; 14:34, 37, 38; Luke 12:37, 39). This involves the duty of vigilance combined with prayer in regard either to a certain day or hour when the Son of man shall arrive, or to some actual crisis or trial (especially the agony of Gethsemane), or as a preparation for some impending temptation. In Acts 20:31 it is found in the exhortation by Paul to the elders at Miletus in view of the apostasy that has taken place or may be repeated under the influence of "fierce wolves" (a.t.). The duty of alertness as opposed to a slack or sleepy spirit is proclaimed in 1 Cor 16:13; Col 4:2; 1 Thess 5:6; 1 Pet 5:8; Rev 3:2, 3; 16:15. In 1 Thess 5:6 and 1 Pet 5:8, the verb "to watch" is combined with *néphō* (3525), to exercise discretion or to be sober, which in 2 Tim 4:5 and 1 Pet 4:7 is translated, "be watchful" or "watch." However, *néphō* means to be temperate or sober (originally to avoid intoxication, the abuse [not proper use] of alcohol). It conveys the sense of calmness or coolness prepared for any emergency and arising out of abstinence from what will excite rather than the more general self-control of *egkráteia* (1466), continence, and *sōphrosúnē* (4997), soberness or sobriety or the limitation of one's freedom. Watchfulness or watching indicates that the Christian is alert or vigilant in order to defend himself against a spiritual foe. He is properly prepared for any surprise or sudden change in his circumstances, and above all, in order that his fellowship with God in prayer may be undistracted and efficacious.

Deriv.: *diagrēgoréō* (1235), to be awake.

Syn.: *agrupnéō* (69), keep awake; *blépō* (991), to take heed, beware; *horáō* (3708), behold, take heed; *proséchō* (4337), turn one's attention to, take heed; *epéchō* (1907), to give attention to, give heed; *skopéō* (4648), to watch, look, take heed; *phulássō* (5442), to guard.

Ant.: *katheúdō* (2518), to sleep, fall asleep; *koimáomai* (2837), to sleep; *ameléō* (272), to neglect.

1128. γυμνάζω *gumnázō*; fut. *gumnásō*, from *gumnós* (1131), naked. To train naked, as the Greek athletes. Generally to exercise, train. Thus *gumnásion*, gymnasium, is a place of exercising. Metaphorically to train in godliness (1 Tim 4:7; Heb 5:14; 12:11); training in covetousness (2 Pet 2:14).

Deriv.: *gumnasía* (1129), exercise.

Syn.: *askéō* (778), to exercise by training or discipline; *katartízō* (2675), to fit; *stoichéō* (4748), to keep step, metaphorically to conform to virtue and piety; *phrontízō* (5431), to exercise thought; *anatréphō* (397), to rear, to bring or nourish up; *suntēréō* (4933), to preserve; *agōnízomai* (75), to strive; *athléō* (118), to contend in competitive games, to exercise.

1129. γυμνασία *gumnasía*; gen. *gumnasías*, fem. noun from *gumnázō* (1128), to exercise. Exercise of the body by severities such as fasting, abstinence, or watching (1 Tim 4:8 in antithesis with 1 Tim 4:7, i.e., ascetic training, mortification of bodily appetites as described in 1 Tim 4:3[cf. Rom 14:17; 1 Cor 8:8; Col 2:23]).

1130. γυμνητεύω *gumnēteúō*; fut. *gumnēteúsō*, from *gumnós* (1131), naked. To be naked with the implied meaning of to be poorly clothed (1 Cor 4:11).

1131. γυμνός *gumnós*; fem. *gumnḗ*, neut. *gumnón*, adj. Naked. Stark naked (Mark 14:51, 52 [cf. Rev 17:16]; Sept.: Gen 3:1; 3:7, 10, 11; Job 1:21); comparatively naked or ill-dressed (Matt 25:36, 38, 43, 44; James 2:15; Sept.: Job 31:19; 24:7; Isa 58:7 [cf. 2 Cor 5:3, our souls will not strictly be found naked, but our bodies will be glorified {cf. 2 Cor 5:4 and 1 Cor 15:51}]); naked or stripped of the upper garment (John 21:7; Acts 19:16; Sept.: 1 Sam 19:24; Isa 20:2); naked, open, uncovered, manifest (Heb 4:13, uncovered, open, manifest [cf. Job 26:6]); naked, bare, mere (1 Cor 15:37, "bare grain"); naked of spiritual clothing, i.e., the imputed righteousness of faith (Rev 3:17; 16:15).

Deriv.: *gumnázō* (1128), to exercise; *gumnēteúō* (1130), to be naked or scantily clothed; *gumnótēs* (1132), nakedness, lack of sufficient clothing, metaphorically lack of spirituality.

1132. γυμνότης *gumnótēs*; gen. *gumnótetos*, fem. noun from *gumnós* (1131), naked. Nakedness, destitute of convenient or decent clothing (Rom 8:35; 2 Cor 11:27; Sept.: Deut 28:48); spiritual nakedness, being destitute of the spiritual clothing of the righteousness which is by faith (Rev 3:18; Sept.: Gen 9:22, 23). Verb: *gumnēteúō* (1130), to be naked or scantily clad.

Syn.: *apobolḗ* (580), a casting off; *apékdusis* (555), a divestment, putting off.

Ant.: *éndusis* (1745), a putting on of clothing; *esthḗs* (2066), clothing, apparel; *himatismós* (2441), a coll. noun meaning clothing, raiment; *katastolḗ* (2689), a garment let down; *peribólaion* (4018), clothing or anything that is wrapped around; *stolḗ* (4749), a costume; *énduma* (1742), anything put on; *chitṓn* (5509), an inner vest or undergarment; *himátion* (2440), an outer garment, a mantle; *phelónēs* (5341), a cloak for traveling.

1133. γυναικάριον *gunaikárion*; gen. *gunaikaríou*, neut. noun, a diminutive of *gunḗ* (1135), woman, wife. A foolish woman; one who displays immaturity and a lack of dignity. (2 Tim 3:6).

1134. γυναικεῖος *gunaikeíos*; fem. *gunaikeía*, neut. *gunaikeíon*, adj. from *gunḗ* (1135), woman, wife. Female, feminine, womanly (1 Pet 3:7; Sept.: Lev 18:22; Deut 22:5).
Ant.: *ársēn* (730) or *árrēn*, male.

1135. γυνή *gunḗ*; gen. *gunaikós*, fem. noun. Woman, wife (Matt 14:21; 15:38; Acts 22:4; 1 Cor 11:12; Sept.: Gen 2:22, 23).

(I) Spoken of a young woman, maiden, damsel (Luke 22:57; Gal 4:4; Sept.: Esth 2:4); of an adult woman (Matt 5:28; 9:20, 22; 11:11; Rev 12:1, 4).

(II) In Rom 7:2, *húpandros* (5220), under a man, implies relation to a particular man. One betrothed or engaged but not necessarily yet married and engaging in sexual relations (Matt 1:20, 24 [cf. Matt 1:18]; Luke 2:5; Sept.: Lev 19:20; Deut 22:24 [see Deut 22:23]). See *anḗr* (435, IV), husband, man.

(III) Used of the Church as the Bride of Christ (Rev 19:7; 21:9).

(IV) Of a married woman, wife (Matt 5:31, 32; 14:3; 18:25; Mark 6:18; Luke 1:18, 24; 8:3; Rom 7:2; 1 Cor 7:2; Sept.: Gen 24:3f.); as stepmother (1 Cor 5:1; Sept.: Lev 18:8); a widow (Matt 22:24; Mark 12:19; Luke 20:29), with *chḗra* (5503), widow (Luke 4:26).

(V) In the voc. *ō̄* (5599) *gúnai* as an address expressive of kindness or respect (Matt 15:28 [cf. 9:22 where *thugátēr* {2364}, daughter, is used]; Luke 13:12; John 2:4; 4:21; 20:13, 15; 1 Cor 7:16).

(VI) Whether a female or a wife is meant depends on context.

(A) Additionally a woman or women in Matt 13:33; 15:22, 39; 19:10; 26:7, 10; 27:55; 28:5; Mark 5:25, 33; 7:25, 26; 14:3; 15:40; Luke 1:28, 42; 4:26; 7:28, 37, 39, 44, 50; 8:2, 43, 47; 10:38; 11:27; 13:11, 12, 21; 14:20; 15:8; 23:27, 49, 55; 24:22, 24; John 2:4; 5:7, 9; 4:11, 15, 17, 19, 21, 25, 27, 28, 39, 42; 8:3, 4, 9, 10; 16:21; 19:26; 20:13, 15; Acts 1:14; 5:14; 8:3, 12; 9:2; 13:50; 16:1, 13, 14; 17:4, 12, 34; 21:5; 1 Cor 7:1, 34; 9:5; 11:5, 6, 8, 9, 13, 15 (see X, B); Rev 2:20; 9:8; 12:6, 13–17; 14:4; 17:3, 4, 6, 7, 9, 18.

(B) Additionally wife or wives (Matt 19:3, 5, 8, 9, 29; 22:25, 27, 28; 27:19; Mark 6:17; 10:2, 7, 11; 12:20, 22, 23; Luke 1:5, 13; 3:19; 14:26; 16:18; 17:32; 18:29; 20:28, 32, 33; Acts 5:1, 2, 7; 24:24; 1 Cor 7:3, 4, 10–14, 16, 27, 29, 33, 39; 11:3, 7, 10, 11; 14:34, 35 (see X, B); Eph 5:22–25, 28, 31, 33; Col 3:18, 19; 1 Tim 2:9–12, 14; 3:2, 11, 12; 5:9; Titus 1:6; Heb 11:35; 1 Pet 3:1, 5.)

(VII) In the sight of God there is no essential difference between a male (*ársen* [730]) and a female (*thḗlu* [2338]) in regard to their ontological spiritual status (Gal 3:28). Women do not form any inferior part of Christ's body; they are entitled to God's promises as much as men. Therefore, a wife should be treated as an equal recipient of God's grace (1 Pet 3:7) with her husband. She should not be treated as inferior, but as only physically weaker, which weakness is to be complemented in the husband's strength. A woman and a man, whether or not they are husband or wife, must acknowledge their common source which is the Lord; and if they are husband and wife, their mutual interdependence one on the other (1 Cor 11:11, 12) and both under God, with the husband as head since in their marital status they are one body.

(VIII) The word *gunaíkas* in 1 Tim 3:11 should be translated "wives" and should be understood to be referring to the wives of the deacons of 1 Tim 3:8 and not "women" as the NASB translates it. The NIV and NKJV translate it correctly as "wives." The whole discussion is the responsibility of male deacons (and perhaps the overseer) to have wives whose dress, conduct, and speech are exemplary and befitting their position as wives of deacons.

(IX) (A) The confusion regarding the word *gunḗ* being translated "woman" instead of "wife" is primarily related to whether they should speak in a local assembly of believers. Is a woman supposed to be totally silent during a Christian worship service? Paul discusses this in 1 Cor 14:33–40. His concern in this discussion is not whether a woman should remain totally silent in the worship service and only men should speak, but whether confusion and improper behavior could result from excessive participation by women. See how the discussion begins with verse thirty-three, "For God is not the author of confusion, but of peace, as in all churches of the saints," and also how the discussion closes in verse forty, "Let all things be done decently and in order." Here, however, he does not speak about women in general, but about the wives of husbands who were together with them in the assembly of believers worshiping Christ. In verse thirty-four the translation should not be "Let your women keep silence in the churches," but "Let your wives be silent in the churches" (a.t.). No man as such has authority to forbid a woman to speak, but a husband has authority over his wife when he sees that disorder may result from her speaking. The command, therefore, is given to husbands worshiping with their wives in a local assembly because only they are the head of the home. Taken in the total context, it seems that women were starting to speak in an unknown tongue as practiced in Corinth, and it was the duty of their husbands to restrain them. Husbands were the only ones who had the right to do so. (We are speaking of direct and personal authority over a woman. A man acting in the capacity of an elder would have *ex officio* authority to govern the assembly.) The concern of the Apostle Paul is expressed in 1 Cor 14:23, "If therefore the whole church be come together into one place, and all speak with tongues, and there come in those that are unlearned, or unbelievers, will they not say that ye are mad (*maínesthe* [3105])?" The admonition of Paul is that no wife who worships with her husband in a local congregation should give the impression to those present that Christians behave improperly.

(B) As further substantiation that 1 Cor 14:34–35 does not refer to women in general, but to wives, two things must be pointed out: **(1)** The use of the verb *hupotássomai* (5293), to be subject, to take one's proper place under, in verse thirty-four, "Let your women [wives, for only one's wife can be spoken of as one's woman] keep silence in the churches: for it is not permitted unto them to speak [*laléō* {2980}, to speak, 1 Cor 14:2, 4, 5, 6, 9, 11, 13, 18, 19, 21, 23, 27, 28, 29, 34, 39, a word used to form *glossolalía* which was prevalent in Corinth and a verb which stands in contrast to *légō* {3004}, to speak intelligently], but they are commanded to be under obedience as also saith the law." The phrase "they are commanded to be under obedience" is translated from one Gr. word, *hupotássesthai*, the pres. inf. mid. of *hupotássomai*, which is the term explicitly used in the wife / husband relationship (Eph 5:22; Col 3:18; Titus 2:5; 1 Pet 3:1, 5) meaning to take one's proper position under. See *anér* (435, XI, B), man, husband. **(2)** There is an explicit reference to husbands and wives in verse thirty-five, "And if they will learn any thing, let them ask their husbands at home: for it is a shame for women to speak in the church." The particular reference to *gunaixín*, the pl. dat. of *gunḗ*, must refer to the wives spoken of in the first part of the verse, and by natural extension to women in general. The logic of this is as follows: If married women are to wait until they get home to ask their husbands to explain certain items of concern, who are the single women to ask? The implication is that regardless of who they ask they are not to ask publicly in church, but to ask in private. Not to ask in a public worship service is part of the decorum of church gathering. As women should not ask during public worship, men also should learn in silence. Interruption by anyone, man or woman, married or unmarried, of a church service is improper and brings confusion. A woman's abrupt interruption of the service was disorderly not merely because of its disruptive effect upon the order of the church meeting, but also because such action represented a clear transgression of her divinely ordained role of submission. So it was especially important that she speak only when recognized by those controlling the meeting. No one should create confusion; and in order to control this at least partially, the husbands must instruct their wives not to speak out of turn in public worship. As for women in public worship who may not have husbands worshiping with them, they must adhere to the same rules of order as the male worshipers.

(C) The translation of *ándras* or *anḗr* (435) in 1 Cor 14:35 as "husbands," "And if they will learn anything, let them ask their "husbands" (a.t.) at home: for it is a shame for "women" (a.t.) to speak in the church," was correct. However, the translators were correct only partially when they translated *gunaixín*, the dat. pl. of *gunḗ*, as "wives" in the first occurrence, as they should have similarly translated it "wives" also in the second occurrence (see X, B). It should be "wives" and women by extension since wives are women. The corresponding word to "husband" is not "woman," but "wife." Although the teaching of the NT is that we do not have women as bishops, elders, or deacons in a local church, yet it is not forbidden for women, under the authority of the elders, to participate categorically in praying or prophesying in the local assembly. The restrictions of public worship found in 1 Cor 14:26–33 apply to single women as contrasted with men, being equal in the sight of God (1 Pet 3:7). A woman per se is not inferior to a man in a relationship with God. However, as a unit of one body made up of husband and wife, the wife is under the husband in her proper order of creation and function.

(D) 1 Tim 2:12 should not be interpreted as a prohibition by Paul for any woman to teach, but only for a wife when that teaching may be construed by those who hear her to think that she is dominant in her relationship with her husband. "But I suffer not a woman [*gunaikí*, which should be translated a wife or a woman in her relationship as a wife] to teach [*didáskein*, the pres. inf. of *didáskō* {1321}, to teach, indicating continuity of teaching which may be interpreted as lording it over her husband]." If this were a prohibition of a woman teaching men, it would have said *authentéō* (831), to usurp authority over men, *andrṓn* (435), the pl. gen. instead of the sing. gen., instead of *andrós*, in the sing. meaning over man, referring to her own husband. (It must be conceded, however, that the sing. noun could be collective.) Paul is anxious to make very clear here that no woman through her teaching should give the impression that she is the boss and lording it over her husband. If any such impression is given at any time, then she should keep quiet (*hēsuchía* [2271], be undisturbed and not disturbing others. The word *hēsuchía* is the ant. of *taraché* [5016], disturbance). The word does not mean silence, which would have been indicated by *sigḗ* (4602), silence, the verbal form of which is used in 1 Cor 14:34. The relationship expressed in 1 Tim 2:13 is not that of Adam and Eve as man and woman, but rather as husband and wife.

To understand the whole teaching of the Lord Jesus on the subjects of marriage, divorce, and remarriage, see the words *anḗr* (435), husband; *apolúō* (630), to dismiss; *kephalḗ* (2776), head; *moicháō* (3429) and *moicheúō* (3431), to commit adultery; *moicheía* (3420), adultery; *moichós* (3432), adulterer; *moichalís* (3428), adulteress; *porneúō* (4203), to commit fornication or any immoral sexual act; *porneía* (4202), fornication; *pórnē* (4204), a harlot; *pórnos* (4205), a fornicator, whoremonger; *gaméō* (1060), to marry; *gamískō* (1061), to give a daughter in marriage; *gámos* (1062), marriage; *suzeúgnumi* (4801), to yoke together, conjoin in marriage; *chōrízō* (5563), to separate.

Deriv.: *gunaikárion* (1133), a foolish woman; *gunaikeíos* (1134), female, womanly.

Syn.: *thêlus* (2338), female, woman.

Ant.: *anêr* (435), male or husband; *árrēn* or *ársēn* (730), male.

1136. Γώγ *Gōg*; proper noun transliterated from the Hebr. *Gōg* (1463, OT). Gog, mentioned in Ezek 38:2 as "Gog, the land of Magog, the chief prince," also referred to as the prince of Rosh, believed by many to refer to Russia. The Sept. translators understood Magog as a people, not as a country. The ancients understood Magog to refer to the northern nations which they also called *Skúthai* (4658), Scythians. In Rev 20:8 we find Gog and Magog after the millennium coming in great military power against the holy city, the New Jerusalem.

1137. γωνία *gōnía*; gen. *gōnías*, fem. noun. An angle, corner. An outward corner as of a street (Matt 6:5); a corner of a building in which it has reference only to the spiritual building of God, namely to the church consisting of Jews and Gentiles of which Christ is said to be the head (Ps 118:22); the headstone or the keystone of the corner which means the upper cornerstone, which not only unites and strengthens the whole building but is also at the very summit of it. Being so high, in falling it is able to grind people to powder (cf. Zech 4:7). The stone that is at the head of the corner (*kephalê* [2776], head; *gōnías* Matt 21:42; Mark 12:10; Luke 20:17; Acts 4:11; 1 Pet 2:7) is not the same as the *akrogōniaíos* (204), belonging to the extreme corner, in Eph 2:20; 1 Pet 2:6. The *akrogōniaíos* is the foundation cornerstone, applied figuratively to Christ who not only sustains the whole structure of the church, but also unites the Jews and Gentiles into this one mystical structure. *Gōnía* is also used to refer to an inner corner which indicates a secret or private place, even as we use the expression today for secrecy (Acts 26:26). It also refers to an extremity (Rev 7:1; 20:8) as the four corners of the earth, meaning the four extremities of the earth. See Sept.: Ex 27:2; Ezek 43:20.

Deriv.: *akrogōniaíos* (204), cornerstone; *tetrágōnos* (5068), four-cornered.

1138. Δαβίδ Dabíd; masc. proper noun transliterated from the Hebr. *Dāwīd* (1732, OT), beloved. David, the famous king of the Jews (1055–1015 B.C.). His life is described in the books of 1 and 2 Sam; 1 Chr 12—30; referred to in the NT in Matt 1:6, 17; 12:3; 22:43, 45. The "book of David" means the Psalms (Heb 4:7; see Ps 95:7). The "son of David" means the descendant of David (Matt 1:20, spoken of Joseph, the husband of Mary). Often applied to Jesus as a title of the expected Messiah (Matt 9:27; 12:23; 15:22; 20:30, 31; Mark 10:47, 48). It does not occur in John's writings. The "root of David" means the ancestry of David (Rev 5:5; 22:16; see Isa 11:1, 10). The kingdom or reign of the Messiah is designated as the "kingdom of David" (a.t. [Mark 11:10]); the "throne of David" (a.t. [Luke 1:32]); the "tent of David" (a.t. [Acts 15:16 {cf. Amos 9:11}]); the "key of David" (Rev 3:7 [cf. Isa 22:22; Matt 16:19]) means the key of the Messianic kingdom.

1139. δαιμονίζομαι daimonízomai; fut. *daimonísomai*, from *daímōn* (1142), demon. The Class. Gr. form *daimonáō*, to be violently possessed by, to be in the power of a demon.

(I) Possessed by a demon or a devil (Matt 8:16, 28, 33; 9:32; 12:22; 15:22; Mark 1:32; 5:15, 16, 18; Luke 8:36; John 10:21, see John 10:20); having a demon (John 7:20). The *daimonizómenoi*, those violently possessed by demons, are distinguished from other sick folk in Matt 4:24; Mark 1:32. In addition to the term *daimonizómenos*, the pres. mid. part. of the verb meaning demon-possessed (Matt 4:24), there are other expressions used in the Gospels such as *daimonistheís*, the aor. pass. part. indicating a definite entrance into a person (Mark 5:18; Luke 8:36); also a man with an unclean spirit (Mark 1:23; 5:2) where the prep. *en* (1722) refers to being in the power of demons; having demons (Luke 8:27); a man having a spirit or an unclean demon (Luke 4:33); disturbed by unclean spirits (Luke 6:18); driven of a demon (Luke 8:29); and the verb *selēniázomai* (4583), to be moonstruck, a lunatic. Most of those who are said to be possessed are adult men; the few exceptions are certain women who had been healed of evil spirits such as Mary Magdalene (Luke 8:2), the woman who had been bound by Satan for eighteen years (Luke 13:11, 16), and the little daughter of the Syro-Phoenician woman (Mark 7:25). It is, however, probable that others besides men are included in such passages as Mark 1:32ff.; Luke 7:21. The signs of possession designated as *selēniázomai* (Matt 4:24) are distinguished from the *daimonizómenoi*, which would also appear to have been regarded as a sign of possession. A man who is "mad," in the modern sense of being out of his mind, is said to have a demon, this being an accusation against John the Baptist (Matt 11:18) and Christ (John 10:20).

(II) A demoniac is spoken of as the dwelling-place of a demon, and a number of demons can dwell in one person (Matt 12:45; Mark 5:9; Luke 8:2).

(III) Sometimes the demon is differentiated from the man possessed (Mark 1:23, 24); at other times the two are identified (Mark 3:11); in Mark 5:1–20 the demon acts both as part of the man and independently of the man. Differentiation is strongly marked when an expression such as that in Luke 6:18 is used, "They that were vexed [*enochloúmenoi*, {UBS (1776); *ochloúmenoi*, TR (3791)}, to annoy, to trouble] with unclean spirits."

(IV) The same outward signs are at one time spoken of as possession, at another as an ordinary sickness (Matt 4:24; 17:15). One of Christ's chief works on earth was to annihilate the power of demons; the demons themselves realized this (Mark 1:24; Luke 4:34 [cf. 1 John 3:8]). The destruction of their kingdom is necessary for the establishment of the kingdom of God.

(V) With the exception of the case of the woman bound by Satan for eighteen years in Luke 13:11, 16, no instance is recorded of Jesus laying His hands upon or in any way coming in direct contact with one who is possessed by a demon. On the other hand, His words are never severe when addressing the possessed.

(VI) Very remarkable, moreover, is the fact that even when He speaks to the demon itself, Christ's words are never angry. He "rebukes" the demon (Mark 1:25; Luke 4:35), but the words of rebuke are simply, "Hold thy peace, and come out of him," or a command that He should not be made known (Mark 3:12, contrast Luke 8:39). On one occasion the request of demons is granted (Matt 8:31, 32; Mark 5:12, 13; Luke 8:32).

(VII) The power which Christ has over demons is absolute, for they are wholly subject unto Him and are compelled to yield to Him obedience (Mark 1:27; Luke 4:41). That it is an unwilling obedience is obvious, and this is graphically brought out, for example, when it is said of a demon that before coming out of a man it threw him down in the midst (Luke 4:35).

(VIII) The recognition of Christ by demons is of a kind which is very striking, for He is not only recognized as Jesus of Nazareth, i.e., as one born of men, but is also addressed as the "Holy One of God" (Luke 4:34) and as the "Son of God" (Luke 4:41), i.e., as one of Divine nature. This latter title is emphasized by their knowledge of His power to cast them into the abyss (Luke 8:31), which also accounts for their fear of Him.

(IX) The power of Christ over demons was regarded as something new called *hē didachē hē kainē* (*didachē* [1322], teaching; *kainē* [2537], qualitatively new), "new doctrine" (Mark 1:27). This was because a method of exorcism which was familiar to the Jews until then was the pronouncing of a magical formula over the possessed. In the Gospels, as a rule, the casting out of a demon is stated without specifying by what means it was done (Mark 1:34; Luke 7:21; 8:2), but we learn the methods used from a number of other passages: by a word (Matt 8:8); in the Spirit of God (Matt 12:28); with the finger of God (Luke 11:20); through rebuking (*epitimáō* [2008]) (Matt 17:18); through simply saying "Go" (Matt 8:32); through saying "Come out" (Mark 5:8; Luke 4:35). On one occasion the words are addressed to the mother of a child who is possessed, "Be it as thou wantest" (a.t. [Matt 15:28; Mark 7:29]), the possessed child not being in His presence (Mark 7:30), thus His power did not depend on His visible personality.

(X) In view of the fact that Jesus Christ has absolute power over the demons, it is impossible for a demon to possess a believer in whose heart Christ dwells. In Mark 3:22 the scribes say of Christ that "He hath Beelzebub," and in Mark 3:30 occur the words, "Because they said, He hath an unclean spirit." It is evident that Beelzebub, the "prince of the demons," and "unclean spirit" are syn. with "demon." In John 7:20 the Jews accused Christ of being possessed by a demon because He said they sought to kill Him (John 8:48, 49).

(XI) Christ bestowed this power of casting out demons on His Twelve Apostles (Matt 10:1; Mark 3:14, 15; Luke 9:1). When demons were cast out it was by virtue of the power of His Name (Matt 7:22; Luke 10:17). Following the Trans-figuration, Christ's disciples were not able to do this because of lack of faith on their part (Matt 17:20). We read, however, in Mark 9:38, 39 of one who was not a follower of Christ but who was, nevertheless, able to cast out demons in His name (cf. Matt 12:27; Luke 11:19).

(XII) Some forms of possession were regarded as mental derangement. Christ speaks of John the Baptist having been looked upon as possessed (Matt 11:18; Luke 7:33). He was so regarded because his mode of life seemed to be somewhat eccentric. The man who was possessed was despised because he spoke what was deemed nonsense. The supposed connection between possession and mental derangement is pointedly brought out in John 10:20, "He hath a devil [*daimónion* {1140}, demon] and is mad." While intimated in the Synoptic Gospels that the possession has no direct connection with moral standing, this is brought forth more clearly in the above verse. In addition, the verb *maínetai* (3105), is mad, is also used in 1 Cor 14:23 in regard to the persons who utter ecstatic utterances in the church.

1140. δαιμόνιον *daimónion*; gen. *daimoníou*, the neut. of *daimónios*, from *daímōn* (1142), a demon. Generally, a god, deity, spoken of the heathen gods (Acts 17:18); used with the Jewish meaning of a demon, an evil spirit, devil, subject to Satan (Matt 9:34), implying him to be a fallen angel. See *ággelos* (32), angel.

(I) In Luke 8:29 Satan is made equal to an unclean spirit (see Luke 8:30). These spirits wandered in desolate places (Sept.: Isa 13:21; 34:14 [cf. Matt 12:43]) and also dwelt in the air or atmosphere (cf. Eph 2:2). They were thought to have the power of working miracles, but not for good (Rev 16:14, see John 10:21).

(II) The demons were hostile to mankind (John 8:44). They uttered the heathen oracles (cf. Acts 16:16, 17) and lurked in the idols of the heathen which are thus called *daimónia*, devils (1 Cor 10:20, 21; Rev 9:20 [cf. Sept.: Deut 32:17; Ps 91:6; 106:37]). They are spoken of as the authors of moral evil to mankind, (1 Tim 4:1; James 2:19 [cf. Eph 6:12]), and also as entering into a person and rendering him a demoniac and afflicting him with various diseases (Luke 8:30, 33), implied in the verb *daimonízomai* (1139), to be possessed with demons.

(III) The expression "to have a devil" means to be a demoniac (Luke 4:33; 8:27). This was the accusation of the Jews against Jesus (John 7:20; 8:48, 49, 52; 10:20); also against John the Baptist (Matt 11:18; Luke 7:33). These demons came out of people (Matt 17:18; Mark 7:29, 30; Luke 4:35, 41; 8:2, 33, 35, 38; 11:14). The demons are spoken of as being cast out (Matt 7:22; 9:34; 10:8; 12:24, 27, 28; Mark 1:34, 39; 3:15, 22; 6:13; 7:26; 9:38; 16:9, 17; Luke 9:49; 11:14, 15, 18–20; 13:32). Used in the pass. (Matt 9:33). The casting out of devils was done by Christ in His own divine authority and by the Apostles in His name (Luke 9:1; 10:17; 11:15 [cf. Acts 19:13ff.]), but the Jews charged Him with doing it by the authority of Satan who is called the prince of the demons or the ruler (*árchōn* [758]) of the demons (Matt 9:34; 12:24; Mark 3:22; Luke 11:15). The actions of persons are ascribed to demons who are said to dwell in them (Mark 1:34; Luke 9:42; 10:17; John 10:21).

A number of Hebr. expressions are tied up with demons: evil spirits (Judg 9:23; 1 Sam 16:14); spirit of perverseness (Isa 19:14); demons (Deut 32:17; Ps 106:37; Isa 13:21; 34:14); vain gods, (Lev 17:7).

Satan stands at the head of the demons. When the seventy came back to Jesus saying, "Lord, even the devils [*daimónia*] are subject unto us through thy name" (Luke 10:17), His answer related these demons to Satan himself: "And he said unto them, I beheld Satan as lightning fall from heaven" (Luke 10:18 [cf. Rev 12:7–12; Isa 14:12–15; Ezek 28:11–19]).

In the story of the creation we do not find any particular mention of the creation of demons. Possibly this is because the narrative of the creation from Gen 1:2–2:25 is the creation of the physical world. Yet in Gen 3:1 we find the physical representation of Satan or the devil in a serpent. (See Rev 12:9; 20:2.) And yet we know from the total study of the OT and NT that the devil was a spiritual being who was created to dwell in heaven from where, according to the Lord Jesus in Luke

10:18, he fell like lightning. In Jude 1:6 we read "and the angels which kept not their first estate [original, *archḗ* {746}], but left their own habitation." The devil must have been created as one among the angels who fell from heaven and that creation must be incorporated in Gen 1:1 for, "In the beginning God created the heaven and the earth." How God created the heaven and populated it we are not told. We are only told of His dealings with the earth. Since Satan and the demons were first heavenly beings from whence they fell, they must have been created, not as evil spirits, but as good spirits prior to the creation of the physical world. The angels were created by God and were witnesses to the creation of the material universe (Job 38:7). Satan rebelled against God, and he fell from His favor along with the demons. It is his aim to mislead men into evil and then to accuse them before God, hence, the further name *katḗgoros* (2725), the accuser (Rev 12:10 [cf. Zech 3:1]).

Satan is at liberty to enter the divine presence (cf. Job 1:6) and accuse men before God.

The kingdom of Satan (cf. Mark 3:23ff.) consists of himself as head and an innumerable horde of angels or messengers who do his will. The very term *ággelos* (32), angel, is used in 2 Cor 12:7, "the messenger of Satan." This is the exact antithesis of the kingdom of God. These constitute the first grade of demons, those who were created as angels. They were originally in the service of God, but rebelled against Him (cf. Luke 10:18).

Demons are designated by various names in the Gospels such as *daimónion* (Matt 10:8). *Daímōn* (1142), translated "devil," used only in Matt 8:31; Mark 5:12; Luke 8:29; Rev 16:14; 18:2, would imply a more definite personality.

In Matthew *daimónion* is almost always used. In Mark both *daimónion* and *pneúma akátharton* (Mark 1:23, 26, 27; 3:11, 30; 5:2, 8, 13; 6:7; 7:25; 9:25) occur frequently. In Luke there is a more varied usage. In John the few references to a demon (the pl. does not occur) are always

accusations against Christ, and the word used is always *daimónion* (John 7:20; 8:48, 49, 52; 10:20, 21). In the vast majority of cases these expressions are used in the pl. form. In the Gospels, Satan, Beelzebub, and the "prince of the demons" are one and the same.

The phrase in 1 John 3:8, "For the devil sinneth from the beginning," means that ever since he fell and became a devil, he has been sinning, not that he was created a fallen angel.

In Rev 12:9; 20:2 the old serpent of Gen 3:1 is identified as the personification of the devil who was originally created a spiritual being.

Demons are regarded as morally evil. Possession is frequently mentioned in the same category as ordinary sickness (e.g., Matt 10:1); dumbness is said to be due to possession (Matt 9:33; Luke 11:14), as is lunacy (*selēniázomai* [4583], to be moonstruck) (Matt 17:15) and blindness (Matt 12:22). Of course, demons may occasionally be responsible for such diseases, but it does not mean that they are the only cause of them.

Demons are spoken of as taking up their abode in a man without his having any apparent choice in the matter (Mark 5:1ff.). They cannot do so, however, in a Christian believer because Christ indwells the believer. No demon can be conceived as stronger than Christ and able to oust Him from a believer's heart. It is noteworthy, however, that the wicked, such as Pharisees, publicans, and sinners, are never spoken of as being possessed (e.g., Luke 11:39ff.; 15:1). The possessed are permitted to enter the synagogue (Mark 1:23; Luke 4:33), which would hardly have been the case had they been regarded as notoriously evil. On the other hand, the evidence is stronger for possession having been regarded as a moral as well as a physical disorder. Some are referred to as being morally as well as physically harmful (Luke 8:2, *pneumátōn* [4151] *ponērōn* [4190], evil or malevolent; 11:26). Demons are directly referred to as evil spirits (Luke 7:21; 8:2). There are degrees of evil among them (Matt 12:45), some being merely malignant, and some being more harmful physically than others as in Matt 15:22 where the expression *kakόs* (2560), badly, and *daimonízetai* (1139), is possessed and acting as a demon, implies some specially virulent form of possession. In one case a demon is such that it can only be expelled by prayer (Mark 9:29), which implies that in the generality of cases this was not necessary, and, indeed, we find this to be the case, since in every other recorded instance the Word was sufficient.

Beelzebub, the prince of the demons, is identified with Satan (Matt 12:24–30; Mark 3:22–30; Luke 11:15–19 [cf. Rev 16:14]), and Satan himself is by name reckoned among the demons in Luke 10:17–29. He is the originator of sin in man as shown by the temptation, the parable of the tares (Matt 13:24ff.), and the sin of Judas (see especially Luke 22:3).

The demons are intangible, incorporeal and invisible. Luke 10:18, where the Lord speaks of seeing Satan coming down or falling from heaven as lightning, indicates that the Lord in His preincarnate essence as Spirit saw Satan who was also spirit. The word "lightning" indicates the rapidity of his fall in the account of the temptation in Luke 4:5ff. The devil appears in physical form as if he were temporarily assuming a form in which he could utilize the same language that the God-Man was utilizing since one of the temptations to be presented to the Lord Jesus was the challenge to make bread out of stones, both of which are material.

The demon enters (*eisérchetai* [1525], enters in) a man at will and he goes out (*exérchetai* [1831], goes out) at will (Luke 11:24), but in most cases he goes out only on compulsion (*ekbállō* [1544], to cast out).

A demon is also able to take possession of animals (Mark 5:13).

From the terminology used in Mark 4:39 where the word *epitimáō* (2008), to rebuke, is used for bringing calm to the turbulent sea and in Mark 1:25 where the Lord uses the same word to cast out an unclean spirit, it is evident that demons can also bring physical storms.

Demons have a preference for desolate places, such as the desert (Luke 8:29) or mountainous regions (Mark 5:5) or among tombs (Mark 5:2) and waterless places (Luke 11:24), i.e., places to which men come only in small numbers or singly.

They are represented as congregating together (Mark 5:9; Luke 8:30), sometimes in sevens (Luke 8:2; 11:26 [cf. Rev 1:4]), and thus for this reason the pl. form is usually used. In Mark 5:10 the demons beseech Christ not to send them out of the country. They are thus able to speak, or at least to overpower their victim as to make his faculties their own (Mark 1:26).

Nothing is said in the Gospels directly as to where the permanent home of the demons is, but the abyss (*ábussos* [12], bottomless pit) is spoken of apparently as a place from which they could not return if once banished there. This would account for their request not to be banished there in Luke 8:31. They clearly realized that a time of torment was coming for them (Matt 8:29) and that this torment might take place before the appointed time (Mark 5:7; Luke 8:28), and thus the sight of Christ filled them with dread.

Deriv.: *daimoniốdēs* (1141), proceeding from or resembling a demon, demoniac.

Syn.: *diábolos* (1228), false accuser, the devil; *katḗgoros* (2725), accuser; *pneúma* (4151), spirit.

1141. δαιμονιώδης *daimoniốdēs*; gen. *daimoniốdous*, masc.-fem., neut. *daimoniốdes*, adj. from *daimónion* (1140), devil. Demon-like. Originally this could be used with a good sense as godlike, but in NT demonic, devilish (James 3:15; Sept.: Ps 91:6, *daimoníou*). See *daimonízomai* (1139), to be possessed by a demon; *daimónion* (1140), demon; *daímōn* (1142), demon, devil.

Syn.: *ponērós* (4190), evil, wicked.

1142. δαίμων *daímōn*; gen. *daímonos*, masc., fem. noun. Demon (Matt 8:31; Mark 5:12; Luke 8:29; Rev 16:14 [TR]; 18:2 [TR]). Elsewhere in the NT instead of *ho daímōn* we have the diminutive *tó daimónion* (1140), in the neut. but with the same sense. The Greeks gave the word *daímōn* the same meaning as "god." What they meant, however, by the word is still a conjecture. They may have related a demon with *daémon* as knowing, experienced in a thing, or they may have derived the word from *daíomai*, to assign or award one's lot in life (*diaítetaí kaí dioikētaí tōn anthrōpōn*, the arbitrators or umpires and governors of men). They conceived of them as those who rule and direct human affairs, not as a personality, but primarily as a destructive power. Thus they called the happy or lucky person *eudaímōn*, one who is favored by this "divine" power. The adj. *daimónios* was used for one who demonstrated power irrespective of whether it was saving or destructive. The Greek tragic poets use *daímōn* to denote fortune or fate, frequently bad fortune, but also good fortune if the context represents it so. Thus, *daímōn* is associated with the idea of a destiny independent of man, gloomy and sad, coming upon and prevailing over him. Consequently, *daímōn* and *túchē*, luck, are often combined, and the doctrine of demons developed to become a beneficent or evil power in the lives of people. The diminutive *tó daimónion*, being abstract and generally less used than *daímōn*, fell into disuse as a belief in or doctrine of demons became more defined and concrete. *Daímōn* implies more of a personality, even as *diábolos* (1228), the devil, and *Satanás* (4567), Satan.

In NT Gr., on the contrary, the use of *daimónion* prevailed probably for the same reason that strange gods were called *daimónia* (not *daímones*) instead of *theoí*, gods, the nature of the evil spirits thus designated being obscure to human knowledge and alien to human life. The Sept. does not use *daímōn*. In Plutarch and Xenophon, the verb *daimonáō* (in the NT *daimonízomai* [1139]) to be deranged, a syn. of *paraphronéō* (3912), to act insanely, was used.

Daímōn or *daimónion* was applied especially to evil spirits (Ps 78:49; Prov 16:14). They were considered unclean, wicked, or evil spirits (Mark 3:20 [cf. 3:22; 5:2, 8]; Luke 4:33; 8:2, 29; Rev 16:13, 14; 18:2). They make their appearance in connection with Satan (Matt 12:24ff.; Mark 3:22ff.; Luke 10:17, 18; 11:18 [cf. Matt 9:34; 12:24, 26; Mark 3:22; Luke 11:15]). These are put into opposition with God (Deut 32:17 [cf. 1 Tim 4:1; James 2:19; Rev 9:20]; 1 Cor 10:20, 21). While in some parts of the NT *daimónia* are viewed in their morally destructive influence (1 Cor 10:20f.; 1 Tim 4:1; Rev 9:20; 16:14), they appear in the Gospels as special powers of evil, as spirits (Luke 10:17, 20) in the service of Satan (Matt 12:26–28), influencing both the spiritual and physical life of individuals so that the man is no longer master of himself (Luke 13:11, 16). Demoniacal possession is attributed as the reason for unexpected peculiar behavior (Matt 11:18; Luke 7:33; John 7:20; 8:48–52; 10:20, 21). The demoniacal violent overpowering of men indicated by *katadunasteuoménous* (2616), those against whom dominion was exercised (Acts 10:38), essentially differs from satanic influence exercised on Judas (John 13:2, 27) wherein he became, like the demons, in the range of human activity analogously the instrument of Satan. The kingdom of God, including all divine influences obtained by Christ's mediation, testifies effectually against demoniacal violence as the worst form of human suffering produced by Satan's agency (1 John 3:8; see Matt 12:28; 7:22; 9:33, 34; 10:8; Mark 1:34, 39; 3:15; 6:13; 7:26; 9:38; 16:9, 17; Luke 9:49; 11:14, 15, 18–20; 13:32).

Deriv.: *daimonízomai* (1139), to be possessed of a demon; *daimónion* (1140), a little demon.

1143. δάκνω *dáknō*; fut. *dḗxomai*. To bite, sting. Used metaphorically meaning to thwart, vex, irritate (Gal 5:15).

1144. δάκρυ *dákru*, **δάκρυον** *dákruon*; gen. *dákrous* and *dakrúou* respectively, neut. noun. A tear which flows from the eyes (Rev 7:17; 21:4). In the pl. (Luke 7:38, 44); with the meaning of weeping (2 Tim 1:4); with the prep. *diá* (1223), through (2 Cor 2:4); with the prep. *metá* (3326), with (Mark 9:24; Acts 20:19, 31; Heb 5:7; 12:17; Sept.: Ps 6:6, 7; Lam 2:11).
Deriv.: *dakrúō* (1145), to weep, shed tears.

1145. δακρύω *dakrúō*; fut. *dakrúsō*, from *dákru* (1144), tear. To shed tears, weep. Intrans. (John 11:35).
A distinction must be drawn between *dakrúō* and *klaíō*. Unfortunately, *dakrúō* is translated "wept" in John 11:35, whereas it should be translated, "He shed a tear" (a.t.) or "tears" (a.t.). The verb weep as a loud expression of grief is *klaíō*, and is man's reaction toward death (Mark 5:38, 39; 16:10; Luke 7:13; 8:52; John 11:31; 20:11, 13; Acts 9:39). In all these instances we have man's reaction toward death in weeping, wailing, loudly crying. When the Lord, however, stood before the tomb of Lazarus, He simply shed a tear as if to say to those around Him that He was Master of the situation, even if that situation was death. Our Lord is never said to have wept aloud as if wailing, except when He stood over unrepentant Jerusalem in Luke 19:41, "And when he was come near, he beheld the city, [being unrepentant and having rejected Him] and wept [*éklausen* {2799}, wept aloud] over it." Before the dead Lazarus He simply shed a tear, but before unrepentant Jerusalem He shows deep, loud grief in crying. Nothing makes the Lord Jesus more sorrowful than when He is rejected as the Savior that He came to be.
Syn.: *klaíō* (2799), to weep as a loud expression of grief especially in mourning

for the dead; *thrēnéō* (2354), to mourn formally, lament; *alalázō* (214), to wail; *stenázō* (4727), to groan; *penthéō* (3996), to mourn; *kóptō* (2875), to lament.
Ant.: *geláō* (1070), to laugh; *agalliáō* (21), to exult, rejoice; *chaírō* (5463), to rejoice; *euphraínomai* (2165), to be merry.

1146. δακτύλιος *daktúlios*; gen. *daktulíou*, masc. noun from *dáktulos* (1147), finger. A finger ring (Luke 15:22) given as a mark of honor (cf. Gen 41:42; Esth 8:2).
Deriv.: *chrusodaktúlios* (5554), a golden finger ring.

1147. δάκτυλος *dáktulos*; gen. *daktúlou*, masc. noun. A finger (Matt 23:4; Mark 7:33; Luke 11:46; 16:24; John 8:6; 20:25, 27; Sept.: Lev 4:6). The finger of God in Luke 11:20 refers to the power of God (cf. with Matt 12:28, "the Spirit of God" which is indicative of the power of God). We should never interpret Scripture in an anthropomorphic manner, thinking that God has fingers, as if He were man, for God is spirit. He is presented as man having bodily members in order to make Him more understandable and related to us. See also Ex 8:19; 31:18; Ps 8:3.
Deriv.: *daktúlios* (1146), a finger-ring.

1148. Δαλμανουθά *Dalmanouthá*; fem. proper noun. Dalmanutha, a city or village near Magdala in Galilee (Matt 15:39; Mark 8:10). The town was situated on the western shore of the Lake of Galilee, a little north of Tiberias.

1149. Δαλματία *Dalmatía*; gen. *Dalmatías*, fem. proper noun. Dalmatia, a province of Europe on the east of the Adriatic Sea forming part of Illyricum and near Macedonia. Here Paul sent Titus to spread the knowledge of the gospel (2 Tim 4:10).

1150. δαμάζω *damázō*; fut. *damásō*. To reduce to stillness or quietness, from which we derive the Eng. "tame." To subdue, tame (Mark 5:4; James 3:7, 8; Dan 2:40).

Deriv.: *dámalis* (1151), a tame heifer.

1151. δάμαλις *dámalis*; gen. *damáleōs*; from *damázō* (1150), to tame. A heifer old enough to be tamed to the yoke (Heb 9:13; Sept: Num 19:2; Isa 7:21; 15:5; Hos 4:16).

1152. Δάμαρις *Dámaris*; gen. *Damáridos*, fem. proper noun. Damaris, a woman of Athens who was led by Paul's preaching to embrace Christianity (Acts 17:34).

1153. Δαμασκηνός *Damaskēnós*; fem. *Damaskēnḗ*, neut. *Damaskēnón*. Belonging to Damascus, a Damascene (2 Cor 11:32).

1154. Δαμασκός *Damaskós*; gen. *Damaskoú*, fem. proper noun. Damascus, a famous city of Syria first mentioned in Gen 14:15, 133 miles northeast of Jerusalem at the base of the Anti-Lebanon mountains. In the days of Paul the city was so thronged by Jews that, according to Josephus, ten thousand of them were put to death at once, and most of the Syrian females of the city became converts to Judaism. At this period the city was under Roman dominion but was held for a time by Aretas, a Nabataean king. It was conquered by the Arabs in A.D. 635; attacked by the Crusaders in A.D. 1126; several times besieged; taken by the Mongols in A.D. 1260; plundered by the Tartars in A.D. 1300; attacked by Timour in A.D. 1399 to whom it paid one million pieces of gold; became a provincial capital of the Turkish Empire in A.D. 1516 and is now the capital of Syria, an independent Muslim country. In A.D. 1860, six thousand Christians were massacred by the Muslims in cold blood. The most remarkable building is the Blue Mosque which was once a Byzantine church dedicated to John the Baptist. The main street known as Sultany, or Queens Street, runs in nearly a straight line from east to west and is supposed to be the same as the street called "Straight" in Acts 9:11. The traditional sites of the houses of Naaman and Ananias and the place in the wall where Paul was let down in a basket are still pointed out.

1155. δανείζω *daneízō*; fut. *daneísō*, from *dáneion* (1156), debt. To lend, in the NT without interest. Generally (Luke 6:34, 35; Sept.: Deut 28:44; Prov 19:17). In the mid. voice, *daneízomai*, to borrow money (Matt 5:42; Sept.: Neh 5:4).

Deriv.: *daneistḗs* (1157), creditor.

Syn.: *chráō* (5531), to lend what is needful as distinguished from *daneízō*, to lend on security or return.

1156. δάνειον *dáneion*; gen. *daneíou*, neut. of the noun *dáneios*, from *dános* (n.f.), a gift or loan, something that is lent. A debt of money lent (Matt 18:27; Sept.: Deut 24:11).

Deriv.: *daneízō* (1155), to lend.

Syn.: *opheilḗ* (3782), that which is due, a debt; *opheílēma* (3783), debt in the sense of that which is legally due.

1157. δανειστής *daneistḗs*; gen. *daneistoú*, masc. noun from *daneízō* (1155), to borrow, lend. A creditor (Luke 7:41), a lender (Sept.: 2 Kgs 4:1; Ps 108:11).

Ant.: *opheilétēs* (3781), debtor; *chreōpheilétēs* (5533), a debt-ower, a stronger word than *opheilétēs*.

1158. Δανιήλ *Daniḗl*; masc. proper noun transliterated from the Hebr. *Dāniyē'l* (1840, OT), God is my judge. Daniel. One of the four major prophets, probably born in Jerusalem (Dan 1:3; 9:24). In his early youth he was taken captive by Nebuchadnezzar to Babylon together with three other Jewish youths of rank, Hananiah, Mishael, and Azariah in 604 B.C. They were trained for royal service in the palace (Dan 1:1–4). The prince of the eunuchs changed all their names, calling them respectively Belteshazzar, meaning prince of Bel, Shadrach, Meshach and

Abednego. They refused to eat the king's meat and to drink his wine. Nevertheless, in spite of their simple food, they were in better physical condition than the heathen courtiers. After three years of training Daniel displayed his learning and wisdom to Nebuchadnezzar by interpreting one of the dreams the king had forgotten (Dan 2). As a result, Daniel was made "ruler over the whole province of Babylon, and chief of the governors over all the wise men of Babylon" (Dan 2:48). This gave him great fame (Ezek 14:14, 20; 28:3). He explained faithfully to the king the intention of God to punish him for his pride (Dan 4). Darius the Mede made Daniel the first of the "three presidents" of the empire (Dan 6:2). His enemies obtained a command from Darius forbidding all prayer except unto the king for thirty days. But Daniel did not stop praying and, being discovered, was cast into the den of lions which was the punishment for a violation of the king's order. However, God delivered him, and he retained his office. In the reign of Cyrus he likewise prospered but seems to have left Babylon. When and where he died is uncertain.

Daniel at the court of Babylon resembles Joseph at the court of Pharaoh. Both were involuntary exiles from their country and people; became great statesmen; maintained the purity of their religion and their personal character though surrounded by idolatry and corruption; rose by their wisdom and integrity from slavery to a high dignity in a heathen empire; and grew to be shining examples of loyalty to God and to virtue. Daniel's name is in Matt 24:15 and Mark 13:14 referring to his prophecy found in Dan 9:27. The abomination of desolation prophesied by the Lord Jesus occurred in the context of the Roman occupation of Palestine under Titus in A.D. 70. There will be another one which is definitely connected with the *suntéleia toú aiōnos*, the consummation (*suntéleia* [4930]) of the age (*aiōnos* [165], referring to the dispensation of grace) and the *parousía* (3952), coming

presence or the Second Coming of the Lord Jesus, as clearly expressed in Matt 24:3. These events are placed in conjunction with the great tribulation period (Seventieth week of Daniel, beginning with the middle of the week or the seven year period [Dan 9:27]). This tribulation period is definitive and unique (Matt 24:21), and its closing is associated with an unprecedented disturbance of the heavenly bodies such as the sun, the moon and the stars (Matt 24:29). Certainly these predicted events are not part of history. Rather, they are forthcoming and in connection with the appearance of Antichrist in the context of a renewed Roman empire and an Israel to whom unprecedented peace and safety are granted for a time (Ezek 38:8–11). It is then that the temple will be rebuilt and desecrated by the one who will have built it. To this "abomination of desolation" is the prophetic reference of Dan 9:27.

1159. δαπανάω *dapanáō*; contracted *dapanō*; fut. *dapanēsō*, from *dapánē* (1160), expense. To spend, expend. Trans. in Mark 5:26 and in an absolute sense in 2 Cor 12:15. In Acts 21:24 it means to be at the expense of their sacrifices in connection with the completion of a vow. In a neg. sense it means to waste, consume. Used trans. (Luke 15:14) and in an absolute sense (James 4:3).

Deriv.: *ekdapanáō* (1550), to spend, expend; *prosdapanáō* (4325), to spend in addition or besides.

Syn.: *prosanalískō* (4321), to spend additionally; *analískō* (355), to consume; *katanalískō* (2654), to consume utterly; *diagínomai* (1230), used of time meaning to elapse; *chronotribéō* (5551), to spend time with purposeful delay.

Ant.: *kerdaínō* (2770), to gain; *apolambánō* (618), to receive; *ōpheloúmai* (5623), to profit.

1160. δαπάνη *dapánē*; gen. *dapánēs*, fem. noun. Expense, cost (Luke 14:28; Sept.: Ezra 6:4, 8).

Deriv.: *adápanos* (77), free of charge, without expense; *dapanáō* (1159), to expend, incur cost.

Syn.: *apóleia* (684), loss; *zēmía* (2209), detriment, loss.

Ant.: *kérdos* (2771), profit; *óphelos* (3786), benefit; *ōphéleia* (5622), advantage; *sumphéron* (4851), benefit, mutual advantage.

1161. δέ *dé*; a particle standing after one or two words in a clause, strictly adversative, but more frequently denoting transition or conversion, and serving to introduce something else, whether opposed to what precedes or simply continuative or explanatory. Generally it has the meaning of but, and, or also, namely.

(I) Adversative, meaning but, on the contrary, on the other hand.

(A) Simply (Matt 6:6, see also Matt 6:14–17; Luke 12:9, 10; John 1:12; 15:24; Acts 12:9; Rom 6:22; 2 Cor 6:10; 2 Tim 2:16; Heb 4:15). Before answers implying contradiction (Luke 12:14; 13:8; Acts 12:15; 19:2, 3, 4).

(B) In the formula with *mén* (3303), on the one hand, preceding it: *mén . . . dé*, meaning indeed . . . but, though often not to be rendered at all in Eng. (Acts 9:7; 23:8; Rom 2:7, 8; 1 Cor 1:12; 15:39; 2 Cor 10:1). See also *mén* (3303), on the one hand.

(II) Continuative, meaning but, now, and, also, and the like.

(A) Generally and after introducing a new paragraph or sentence (Matt 1:18; 2:9; 3:1; Mark 16:9; Luke 12:11, 16; 13:6, 10; 15:11, 17; Acts 6:1, 2, 8, 9; 9:7, 8; 1 Cor 14:1; 15:17; 16:1). In this way it is sometimes emphatic, especially in interrogative clauses (2 Cor 6:14–16; Gal 4:20, "I could wish indeed" [a.t.]).

(B) Where it takes up and carries on a thought which had been interrupted, meaning then, therefore (Matt 6:7; John 15:26; Rom 5:8; 2 Cor 10:2; James 2:15). Also consequentially after *ei* (1487), if, for *epeí* (1893), seeing that, since (Acts 11:17).

(C) As marking something added by way of explanation or example meaning but, and, namely, e.g., to wit (Mark 4:37, "and the waves," meaning so that the waves; 16:8, "trembling also seized them" [a.t.]; John 6:10, "Now there was [or there being] much grass"; Acts 23:13; Rom 3:22; 1 Cor 10:11; 15:56).

(D) *Kaí* (2532), and, together with *dé*, i.e., *kaí dé*, and also. With *kaí*, it always has the meaning of also, and also (Mark 4:36, "And . . . also . . . other little ships"; John 15:27; Acts 5:32).

1162. δέησις *déēsis*; gen. *deéseōs*, fem. noun from *déomai* (1189), to make known one's particular need. Want, need. In the NT, supplication or prayer for particular benefits, petition for oneself (Luke 1:13; Phil 4:6; Heb 5:7; 1 Pet 3:12; Sept.: Job 27:9; Ps 39:12; 40:2; 1 Kgs 8:28, 30); in behalf of others (Phil 1:19; James 5:16); with *hupér* (5228), on behalf of (Rom 10:1; 2 Cor 1:11; 9:14; Phil 1:4; 1 Tim 2:1); with *perí* (4012), concerning (Eph 6:18); generally spoken of any prayer (Luke 2:37; 5:33; Acts 1:14; Eph 6:18; Phil 1:4; 1 Tim 5:5; 2 Tim 1:3; Sept.: 1 Kgs 8:45; 2 Chr 6:40).

Syn.: *proseuchḗ* (4335), a more general word for prayer to God in particular which is a more sacred word than *déēsis*; *euchḗ* (2171), translated "prayer," but in reality meaning a vow or wish; *énteuxis* (1783), intercession, a petition to a superior; *aítēma* (155), something asked for, request as if it were from an inferior to a superior; *hiketēría* (2428), originally an olive branch carried by a suppliant.

Ant.: *autárkeia* (841), self-sufficiency.

1163. δεῖ *deí*; imperf. *édei*, inf. *deín*, impersonal verb. Needs, is necessary, has need of, is inevitable in the nature of things. In the NT only with an inf. pres. or aor. expressed or implied and with or without an acc., meaning needs, is necessary, is inevitable.

(I) That which must be done from a sense of duty. In Matt 16:21 the Lord was speaking to His disciples telling them that "it was necessary" (a.t.) for Him to go to Jerusalem and to suffer because that was the very purpose for which He came and it was His duty to fulfill that purpose (Matt 26:35; Mark 14:31; Luke 2:49; 4:43; John 3:7, 30; 1 Cor 11:19 should rather be translated "inevitable" instead of "must be" for divisions are really not necessary, but inevitable because of the imperfection of the Christian human character; Heb 9:26). In John 3:14 it was necessary for Jesus to go to the cross in order to fulfill God's plan for the redemption of man. In John 20:9 it was absolutely necessary that Jesus rise from the dead, that necessity involving inevitability due to His divine nature. In Acts 4:12 there is only one way whereby it is inevitable for people to be saved. Here the inevitability is not inferring that all will be saved, but propounds the necessity of the method whereby someone may be saved. Also in Acts 14:22 we have the inevitability of suffering in the Christian life. In Matt 24:6, of things unavoidable, translated "must come to pass" which, however, would have been better rendered, "unavoidably, all these things must come to pass" (a.t.). See also Mark 13:7; Acts 1:16; 9:16; Rom 1:27; 2 Cor 11:30.

(II) Spoken of what is right and proper in itself or prescribed by law, duty, custom. It is right or proper, one must, it ought, it should (Matt 18:33; 25:27; Mark 13:14; Luke 13:14, 16; John 4:20; Acts 5:29; 2 Tim 2:6; Sept.: Job 15:3). Also that which prudence would dictate (Acts 27:21).

We also have *déon*, the part. of *deí* used impersonally and meaning necessary, proper, inevitable from the circumstances or nature of the case (1 Pet 1:6). With the meaning, in accordance with what is right and proper, (Acts 19:36). In 1 Tim 5:13 *tá mḗ déonta* (*tá* [3588], the [pl.]; *mḗ* [3361], not; *déonta*, the pl. of *déon* in the acc.), those things unnecessary, in which case it would be equivalent to *tá mḗ préponta*, those things that are not proper, from *prépō* (4241).

Syn.: *opheílō* (3784), morally obliged or personally obliged; *chrḗzō* (5535), to need; *chrē* (5534), if needs be; *opheilḗ* (3782), obligation, duty; *áxios* (514), worthy, fit; *hikanós* (2425), sufficient, competent, fit; *kalós* (2570), proper, meet; *eúthetos* (2111), correct, well-placed; *díkaios* (1342), just, meet; *anagkaíos* (316), necessary; *anágkē* (318), a necessity; *epánagkes* (1876), of necessity; *chreía* (5532), a need; *kathḗkon*, that which is necessary, becoming; *kathḗkō* (2520), to reach down to do what is right and necessary.

Ant.: *átopos* (824), improper; *aneúthetos* (428), inconvenient; *astochéō* (795), to miss the mark, to err; *hamartánō* (264), to sin, miss the mark; *parabaínō* (3845), to transgress.

1164. δεῖγμα *deígma*; gen. *deígmatos*, neut. noun from *deíknúō* (1166), to show. An example, specimen, sample, a display of things sold, occurring only in Jude 1:7 making the suffering of Sodom and Gomorrah an example of the future suffering of God's judgment (cf. 2 Pet 2:6).

Deriv.: *deigmatízō* (1165), to make a show.

Syn.: *túpos* (5179), pattern, model, impression; *hupódeigma* (5262), example, copy; *hupotúpōsis* (5296), an outline, sketch, pattern; *hupogrammós* (5261), an underwriting, an example; *aparchḗ* (536), firstfruit.

Ant.: *prôtos* (4413), foremost; *archē* (746), active beginning.

1165. δειγματίζω *deigmatízō*; fut. *deigmatísō*, from *deígma* (1164), an example. To make a public show or spectacle as the Romans did when they exposed their captives and the spoils of the conquered enemies to public view in their triumphal processions. Occurs only in Col 2:15: putting into open and painful shame the principalities and powers which previously held Christians captive.

Deriv.: *paradeigmatízō* (3856), to expose to public shame.

Syn.: *ektíthēmi* (1620), to expose.

Ant.: *epainéō* (1867), to commend, praise.

1166. δεικνύω *deiknúō* and δείκνυμι *deíknumi* fut. *deíxō*. To show, used trans.:

(I) To point out, present to the sight, to cause to see (Matt 4:8; Luke 4:5, "all the kingdoms of the world"; John 5:20; 14:8, 9). In Matt 8:4, "show yourself to the priest" (a.t.), present yourself for inspection; Mark 1:44; Luke 5:14; Sept.: Ex 15:25; Deut 34:1, 4; Judg 4:22; of what is shown in visions (Rev 1:1; 4:1; 17:1; 21:9, 10; 22:1, 6, 8).

(II) To offer to view, exhibit, display (John 20:20, "showed them the hands" [a.t.]; Heb 8:5; Sept.: Ex 25:9, 40); of deeds (John 2:18; 10:32; 1 Tim 6:15; Sept.: Mic 7:15, *ópsesthe* [3700] see); of inward things meaning to manifest, prove, (James 2:18; 3:13 [cf. Sept.: Ps 60:5; 71:20]).

(III) To show or assign as for use, e.g., a great upper room (Mark 14:15; Luke 22:12; Sept.: Ex 13:21).

(IV) Metaphorically to show by words, meaning to teach, direct (Matt 16:21; Acts 7:3; 10:28; 1 Cor 12:31; Sept.: Deut 4:5; 1 Sam 12:23; Isa 48:17).

Deriv.: *anadeíknumi* (322), to show plainly or openly; *apodeíknumi* (584), to demonstrate, prove; *deígma* (1164), example; *endeíknumi* (1731), to show forth, prove; *epideíknumi* (1925), to exhibit, display; *hupodeíknumi* (5263), to show plainly, instruct.

Syn.: *mēnúō* (3377), to disclose, tell, make known; *parístēmi* (3936), to show; *paréchō* (3930), to show; *exaggéllō* (1804), to proclaim abroad; *anaggéllō* (312), to declare; *kataggéllō* (2605), proclaim; *phaneróō* (5319), to manifest; *dēlóō* (1213), to make plain; *diēgéomai* (1334), to recount, declare; *emphanízō* (1718), to manifest; *apaggéllō* (518), to announce.

Ant.: *krúptō* (2928), to hide and its synonyms.

1167. δειλία *deilía*; gen. *deilías*, fem. noun from *deilós* (1169), fearful, timid. Cowardice, timidity, reticence, fearfulness (2 Tim 1:7, "a spirit of timidity" [a.t.], i.e., a fearful spirit; Sept.: Ps 54:5).

Syn.: *Deilía* is always in a bad sense as contrasted with *phóbos* (5401), fear. *Phóbos* lies in between *deilía*, cowardice, and *eulábeia* (2124), religious reverence.

Ant.: *thársos* (2294), by transposition akin to *thrásos*, daring, boldness.

1168. δειλιάω *deiliáō*; contracted *deilió*, fut. *deiliásō*, from *deilós* (1169), fearful, timid. To be timid, afraid. Used in an absolute sense (John 14:27, "Do not be afraid of anything" [a.t.]; Sept.: Deut 1:21; Josh 10:25; Isa 13:7). In Class. Gr. writers, *apodeiliáō*. Subst.: *deilía* (1167), cowardice, timidity.

Syn.: *trémō* (5141), to tremble, fear; *phobéomai* (5399), to be afraid; *ptoéō* (4422), in the mid. voice, *ptoéomai*, to be scared.

Ant.: *andrízomai* (407), to act manly; *tolmáō* (5111), to dare.

1169. δειλός *deilós*; fem. *deilē*, neut. *deilón*, adj. from *deídō* (n.f.), to fear. Timid, fearful (Matt 8:26; Mark 4:40; Rev 21:8; Sept.: Deut 20:8; Judg 7:3).

Deriv.: *deilía* (1167), timidity; *deiliáō* (1168), to be afraid.

Syn.: *oligópsuchos* (3642), fainthearted, with a small soul, little spirited; *émphobos* (1719), fearful.

Ant.: *tolmētḗs* (5113), daring.

1170. δεῖνα *deína*; gen. *deínos*, dat. *deíni*, acc. *deína*, sometimes indeclinable, indef. pron., used for all genders. Someone, such an one; spoken of a person or thing whom one does not know or does not wish to name (Matt 26:18).

1171. δεινῶς *deinōs*; adv. from *deinós* (n.f.), terrible, vehement. Vehemently (Matt 8:6; Luke 11:53).

Syn.: *kakōs* (2560), badly, grievously; *eutónōs* (2159), vigorously; *megálōs*

(3171), much, greatly; *lían* (3029), exceeding, great; *sphódra* (4970), vehemently, exceedingly; *sphodrós* (4971), exceedingly, very much.

Ant.: *olígos* (3641), a little; *eláchistos* (1646), least.

1172. δειπνέω *deipnéō*; contracted *deipnó*, fut. *deipnḗsō*, from *deípnon* (1173), dinner or supper. To eat or to have dinner. Used intrans. in Luke 17:8; Sept.: Prov 23:1. Spoken of the paschal supper (Luke 22:20; 1 Cor 11:25). In the sense of to eat, to banquet, as figurative of Christ's kingdom (Rev 3:20). See *gámos* (1062), marriage, wedding.

Syn.: *esthío* (2068), to eat; *phágō* (5315), to eat, consume; *trṓgō* (5176), to eat, gnaw, chew; *geúomai* (1089), to taste; *bibrṓskō* (977), to eat, devour.

Ant.: *nēsteúō* (3522), to fast.

1173. δεῖπνον *deípnon*, gen. *deípnou*, neut. noun. In Homer, breakfast. In Attic writers and the NT, dinner or supper.

(I) The chief meal of the Jews, Greeks and Romans taken at or towards evening and often prolonged into the night; hence, usually an evening banquet or a feast in general (Matt 23:6; Mark 6:21; 12:39; Luke 14:12, 16, 17, 24; 20:46; John 12:2; Sept.: Dan 5:1).

(II) Spoken of the paschal supper (John 13:2, 4; 21:20); of the Lord's Supper (1 Cor 11:20) with which was associated the *agápē* (26) feast, the love feast.

(III) Food taken at supper (1 Cor 11:21; Sept.: Dan 1:16).

Deriv.: *deipnéō* (1172), to eat dinner or supper.

Syn.: *áriston* (712), a light refreshment taken sometimes in the morning or a little before or just after noon as circumstances might dictate; *heortḗ* (1859), a feast or festival; *dochḗ* (1403), a reception, feast, banquet; *gámos* (1062), a wedding or especially a wedding feast; *agápē* (26), love feast.

1174. δεισιδαιμονέστερος *deisidaimonésteros*; the comparative of *deisi-*

daímōn (n.f.), fearing the gods. Religiously disposed (Acts 17:22). The subst. *deisidaimonía* (1175), piety that leads to fear instead of worship (Acts 25:19) in contrast to *deilía* (1167) which is the fear of demon-gods (*daimónia* [1140]). The recognition of God or the gods mingled with more fear than trust, which often leads to superstition.

Syn.: *eusebḗs* (2152), godly; *theosebḗs* (2318), devout, godly; *eulabḗs* (2126), pious; *thrḗskos* (2357), religious.

Ant.: *asebḗs* (765), impious, ungodly; *anósios* (462), unholy, impious.

1175. δεισιδαιμονία *deisidaimonía*; gen. *deisidaimonías*, fem. noun from *deisidaímōn* (n.f.), fearing the gods. Reverence towards deity or fear of God. In this sense it may be used in Acts 25:19. It indicates a dread of the gods, usually in a condemnatory or contemptuous sense.

Syn.: *thrēskeía* (2356), religion in its external aspect, religious worship, especially the ceremonial service of religion; *theosébeia* (2317), reverential worship of God; *eusébeia* (2150), piety; *eulábeia* (2124), the devotion arising from godly fear.

Ant.: *asébeia* (763), ungodliness; *anomía* (458), lawlessness or defiance of God's laws.

1176. δέκα *déka*; indeclinable, used for all genders, cardinal number. Ten (Matt 20:24; Mark 10:41). Often put for any specific number (Matt 25:1, 28; Luke 15:8; 19:13, 17; Sept.: Amos 5:3). Rev 2:10, "tribulation of ten days" [a.t.] indicating a short time (Sept.: Dan 1:12; 1 Sam 25:38).

Deriv.: *héndeka* (1733), eleven; *dekadúō* (1177), twelve; *dekapénte* (1178), fifteen; *dekatéssares* (1180), fourteen; *dṓdeka* (1427), twelve.

1177. δεκαδύω *dekadúō*; indeclinable, used for all genders, cardinal number from *déka* (1176), ten, and *dúo* (1417), two. Twelve (Acts 19:7; 24:11; Sept.: Ex

28:21; 1 Chr 15:10). The more usual form is *dṓdeka* (1427), twelve.

1178. δεκαπέντε *dekapénte*; indeclinable, used for all genders, cardinal number from *déka* (1176), ten, and *pénte* (4002), five. Fifteen (John 11:18; Acts 27:28; Gal 1:18). Another form is *pentekaídeka* (Sept.: Gen 7:20).

1179. Δεκάπολις *Dekápolis*; gen. *Dekápoleōs*, fem. proper noun. Decapolis, meaning ten cities. A Roman region of ten cities, all of which, except Scythopolis, lay east of the Jordan River. Pliny and Ptolemy agree as to eight of these ten cities: Scythopolis, Hippos, Gadara, Dion, Pella, Gerasa, Philadelphia, Canatha. To these Pliny adds Damascus and Raphana, but Ptolemy includes Capitolias. Josephus includes Damascus when he calls Scythopolis the largest city of the Decapolis. Decapolis is mentioned in Matt 4:25; Mark 5:20; 7:31.

1180. δεκατέσσαρες *dekatéssares*; gen. *dekatessárōn*, used for both masc. and fem., neut. *tá dekatéssara*, cardinal numeral from *déka* (1176), ten, and *téssares* (5064), four. Fourteen (Matt 1:17; 2 Cor 12:2; Gal 2:1).

1181. δεκάτη *dekátē*; gen. *dekátēs*, the fem. of *dékatos* (1182). A tithe (Heb 7:8, 9 [cf. Gen 14:20]). The fem. noun *merís* (3310), portion, is understood as following it. A tenth part (Heb 7:2, 4). The Jewish law required that a tenth be paid both from the produce of the earth and the increase of the flocks to the Lord (Lev 27:30–32). The payment of tithe was a widespread practice among the Semitic and non-Semitic people. Besides Abraham paying tithes of the spoil to Melchizedek (Gen 14), Jacob at Bethel also made a conditional vow to pay God a tenth of all that He gave to him (Gen 28:22).

The cattle were tithed by letting them pass out of an enclosure, under a rod held by some person who touched every tenth beast. This thereupon became the property of the Levites so that, if the animal was changed, both the original and the substitute were forfeited (Lev 27:32, 33). It does not appear that a tithe of herbs was demanded. The Pharisees, however, tithed their mint, anise, cummin, and rue. However, it was not for this that our Savior condemned them, but for neglecting more important things, such as mercy, judgment, and faith, while they were so scrupulously exact in matters of little importance (Matt 23:23).

In the NT, the tithe is not stressed because in the OT it was compulsory and was considered a means of earning favor with God. The Jews were prone to do the external and material while neglecting the expression of the inner qualities of the spirit (Luke 11:37–42). The Christian, however, is urged to give voluntarily (2 Cor 9:7) without neglecting the development of spiritual qualities. Noteworthy is Luke 11:41: "But rather give alms of such things as ye have." The word here is *enónta*, from *éneimi* (1751), to be within, meaning those things which are inside you, i.e., the spiritual qualities. The Christian is also to be a joyous (*hilarós* [2431], cheerful) giver, propitious of mercy.

In the OT, the Lord's tithe (Lev 27:30), the festival tithe (Deut 12:10, 11), and the tithe for the poor (Deut 14:28, 29), were all compulsory. In addition to these, however, there was voluntary giving which included the firstfruits giving and freewill offerings. An Israelite who loved God voluntarily gave the firstfruits of his crop to Him. He did this before he had harvested the entire crop and did not yet know how much he would reap. Firstfruits giving was giving the best to God and trusting Him to provide a harvest. It was giving by faith. See Ex 25:2 as to how Moses built the tabernacle. Such voluntary giving has a promise attached to it (Prov 3:9, 10). 2 Cor 8:1–7; 9:6–9 deal with this voluntary grace of Christian giving as well as Jesus' promise in Luke 6:38. Christian giving is characterized by what Paul wrote to Philemon, "That thy benefit should not be as it were of necessity, but willingly" (Phile 1:14).

Deriv.: *dekatóō* (1183), to pay tithes.

1182. δέκατος dékatos; fem. *dekátē* (1181), neut. *dékaton*, adj. from *déka* (1176), ten. Tenth (John 1:39; Rev 11:13; 21:20). When used with the def. art. *tó dékaton*, it means the tenth part, the tithe (Sept.: Lev 5:11; 27:32; Ezek 45:11). See *dekátē* (1181) for the discussion of the tithe in the OT and the teaching of giving in the NT.

Deriv.: *pentekaidékatos* (4003), the fifteenth; *tessareskaidékatos* (5065), fourteenth.

1183. δεκατόω dekatóō; contracted *dekatṓ*, fut. *dekatṓsō*, from *dekátē* (1181), a tenth. To tithe. Trans., to receive tithes from (Heb 7:6, 9), equal to "to receive tithes" (*dekátas lambánōn* [2983], receiving tithes). Pass., to be tithed, to pay tithes (Heb 7:9, *dedekátōtai* Sept.: Neh 10:37). Unknown to the Class. Gr. writers who used *dekateúō*. For the doctrine of tithing see *dekátē* (1181), tithe.

Deriv.: *apodekatóō* (586), to tithe.

1184. δεκτός dektós; fem. *dektḗ*, neut. *dektón*, a verbal adj. from *déchomai* (1209), to accept, decide favorably. Elected, acceptable, one of whom there is or has been a favorable decision of the will. Particularly used of the sacrifice although not to distinguish it from unacceptable sacrifices, but to specify it as the object of divine approval (Phil 4:18; Sept.: Lev 1:3, 4; Prov 11:1; 14:35; Isa 56:7; Mal 2:13). Equal to *arestós* (701), fit. Used with elements of time such as *kairós* (2540), season, and *eniautós* (1763), year, meaning a time in which God has pleasure, and which He Himself has chosen (Luke 4:19; 2 Cor 6:2). When spoken of men (Luke 4:24), it means well-liked or valued men (Acts 10:35).

Syn.: *euárestos* (2101), well-pleasing, acceptable.

Ant.: *adókimos* (96), not standing the test, rejected; *apóblētos* (579), cast away, rejected, refused.

1185. δελεάζω deleázō; fut. *deleásō*, from *délear* (n.f.), bait. To bait, entrap. In the NT metaphorically to entice, beguile. Trans. (James 1:14; 2 Pet 2:14, 18).

Syn.: *apatáō* (538), to deceive; *exapatáō* (1818) as used of Satan's deception of Eve to beguile thoroughly; *paralogízomai* (3884), to deceive by false reasoning; *pagideúō* (3802), to ensnare; *agreúō* (64), to entrap; *thēreúō* (2340), to stalk an animal, to hunt; *enedreúō* (1748), to lurk, lay wait for.

Ant.: *eleutheróō* (1659), to liberate and its syn.

1186. δένδρον déndron; gen. *déndrou*, neut. noun. A tree (Matt 3:10; 7:17–19; 12:33; 21:8; Mark 11:8; Luke 3:9; 6:43, 44; 21:29; Jude 1:12; Rev 7:1, 3; 8:7; 9:4; Sept.: Gen 18:4, 8). In Matt 13:32; Luke 13:19, "to become a tree" (a.t.) means become like a tree in size (cf. Mark 4:32). In Mark 8:24, "I see men as trees" means not distinctly, in an unnatural size.

1187. δεξιολάβος dexiolábos; gen. *dexiolábou*, masc. noun from *dexiós* (1188), right, and *lambánō* (2983), to receive. One who takes the right hand; hence, probably a guard or bodyguard. The word was unknown to Class. Gr. writers and was probably the name of some type of light-armed soldiers (Acts 23:23). Spearmen.

1188. δεξιός dexiós; fem. *dexiá*, neut. *dexión*, adj. Right as opposed to left, right hand or side. When giving or receiving is spoken about, preference is given to the right hand (Matt 6:3; Luke 6:6; Rev 5:7). In the case of division and apportionment, the right hand is chosen as that which comes first (Matt 5:29, 30, 39; Rev 10:2), both when the division is unimportant (Matt 20:21, 23; Mark 10:37, 40; 15:27; Luke 23:33; 2 Cor 6:7 [cf. Sept.: 2 Sam 16:6; 1 Kgs 22:19; 2 Chr 18:18]), and when preference is clearly given to one side (Matt 25:33, 34). In all-important transactions when action must be resolute and involves full participation by the doer, and also when energy and emphasis are intended, the right hand is used (Rev 1:16, 17, 20; 2:1; 5:1, 7). Not only in the case of the actor, but also in that of the person acted upon, the right hand or side is preferred (Acts 3:7), hence God is said to be at the right hand of the person whom He helps as the enemy is to the right of him whom he seeks to overcome and the accuser to the right of the accused. By the right hand the whole man is claimed, whether in action or in suffering (Ps 109:6, 31; Acts 2:25 quoted from Ps 16:8; see also Ps 73:23; 110:5; 121:5; Isa 41:13; Zech 3:1). A person of high rank who puts someone on his right hand gives him equal honor with himself and recognizes him as of equal dignity (Matt 20:21, 23; 22:44; 26:64; 27:38; Mark 12:36; 14:62; 16:19; Luke 20:42; 22:69; Acts 2:33, 34; 5:31; 7:55, 56; Rom 8:34; Eph 1:20; Col 3:1; Heb 1:3, 13; 8:1; 10:12; 12:2; 1 Pet 3:22; 1 Kgs 2:19; Ps 45:9). In Gal 2:9, "they gave . . . the right hands of fellowship," in confirmation of a promise or agreement (cf. Ezek 17:18). See also Matt 27:29; Mark 16:5; Luke 1:11; 22:50; John 18:10; 21:6; Rev 13:16.

Deriv.: *dexiolábos* (1187), spearman, bodyguard.

Ant.: *aristerós* (710), left side, with the word "hand" sometimes understood; *euónumos* (2176), left.

1189. δέομαι *déomai*; fut. *deésomai*, aor. pass. *edeéthēn*, with mid. sense (Luke 8:38), deponent. *Déomai*, by some construed as pass. and meaning to be reduced to want, is perhaps more correctly to be regarded as in the mid. voice, meaning to lack for oneself, to need. Hence in the NT to make one's need known, to beseech, ask. *Déēsis* (1162), prayer for a particular need, supplication. Used with the gen. of the person (Luke 8:38; 9:40 [cf. Acts 26:3; 2 Cor 10:2]). With the acc. (2 Cor 8:4). Followed by *hópōs* (3704),

so that (Matt 9:38; Luke 10:2 [cf. Acts 8:24]). Followed by *hína* (2443), in order (Luke 9:40 [cf. Luke 21:36; 22:32]). Followed by *mḗ* (3378), an interrogative neg. meaning never, not (Luke 8:28). Spoken of prayer to God in general (Acts 8:22, with the gen. of God, "I beseech of God" [a.t.]; 10:2). With the prep. *prós* (4314), and the acc. *tón Kúrion* ([3588], [2962]), the Lord (Acts 8:24). Used in an absolute sense in Luke 21:36; 22:32; Acts 4:31; 1 Thess 3:10; Sept.: Dan 6:11; Job 8:5; Ps 30:8; Isa 37:4. Used generally and in an absolute sense in Rom 1:10, "making request"; 2 Cor 5:20. Followed by the gen. of person (Luke 5:12; 9:38, 40; Acts 8:34, "I pray thee"; 21:39; 26:3; Gal 4:12; Sept.: Deut 3:23; 2 Kgs 1:13; Prov 26:25). Followed by the acc. of thing or inf. for acc. (2 Cor 8:4; 10:2). While *proseuché* (4335) refers to prayer in general, *déēsis* refers to a particular need for which one prays. Thus *déomai* is related to *aitéō* (154), to make a request, ask as an inferior of a superior.

Deriv.: *déēsis* (1162), prayer, request; *prosdéomai* (4326), to require additionally.

Syn.: *chrḗzō* (5535), to have need; *parakaléō* (3870), literally to call to one's side, hence to call to one's aid, being the most commonly used word with this sense; *erōtáō* (2065), to beseech, to ask with the idea of equality between the one who asks and the one of whom he asks, as for instance in the prayers of the Lord Jesus to His Father; *eúchomai* (2172), translated "pray," but in reality it means to wish.

Ant.: *chráomai* (5530), to furnish what is needed; *therapeúō* (2323), to relieve.

1190. Δερβαῖος *Derbaíos*; gen. *Derbaíou*, masc. proper noun. A Derboean or an inhabitant of Derbe (Acts 20:4).

1191. Δέρβη *Dérbē*; gen. *Derbḗs*, fem. proper noun. Derbe, a city of Lycaonia (Acts 14:6, 20; 16:1), about twenty miles from Lystra.

1192. δέρμα dérma; gen. *dérmatos*, neut. noun from *dérō* (1194), to flay, strip off the skin and hence to scourge, beat. A skin of an animal (Heb 11:37; Sept.: Lev 13:48).

Deriv.: *dermátinos* (1193), made of leather.

1193. δερμάτινος dermátinos; fem. *dermatínē*, neut. *dermátinon*, adj. from *dérma* (1192), skin, and the suffix *-inos* meaning made of, in contrast to the suffix *-ikós* which means with a tendency to show one's nature. Made of skin or leather (Matt 3:4; Mark 1:6; Sept.: 2 Kgs 1:8).

1194. δέρω dérō; fut. *derṓ*, 2d fut. pass. *darésomai*, aor. *édeira*, 2d aor. pass. *edárēn*. To skin, flay (Sept.: 2 Chr 29:34). In the NT, to beat or scourge so as to take off the skin (Matt 21:35; Mark 12:3, 5; Luke 20:10, 11; Acts 16:37; 22:19). In John 18:23 we have the question of Jesus to the high priest, "Why smitest thou me?" This verb corresponds to the *rhápisma* (4475) of John 18:22, the blow with the open hand. Therefore, *dérō* in verse twenty-three must be translated to "hit or slap me with the palm" (a.t.). In 2 Cor 11:20, "If a man smite you on the face," means if a man treats you with contempt. In Luke 22:63 *dérontes* is the pres. part. attached to the principle verb *enépaizon*, the imperf. of *empaízō* (1702), to mock, deride. They were mocking Christ, but how? The answer is *dérontes*, by smiting Him either on the face or on His body. Such was the treatment received by our Lord prior to His crucifixion.

In Acts 5:40 the same verb is used about the treatment received by the disciples from the Sanhedrin. The verb *deírantes* here, however, is in the aor. part. This indicates an act or a series of acts within a time frame and not the pres. part. *dérontes* as in Luke 22:63 which characterized the treatment of our Savior. In Acts 5:40 it is "and when they had called the apostles, and beaten them," which was a characteristic act of intimidation to cause them to quit witnessing for Christ. In the pass., it is *darésesthe*, "You will be smitten in synagogues" (a.t. [Mark 13:9]).

Whenever there were several synagogues in an area, representatives of these synagogues gathered together to form the *sunédrion* (4892), a joint session of an official body constituting a tribunal. In such cases, the tribunal was made of twenty-three members. If, however, there was only one synagogue in the area, then it was a local body of officials made up usually of seven, called the elders of the Jews (Luke 7:3) or the rulers (*árchontes* [758]); see Matt 9:18, 23; Luke 8:41. These elders or rulers exercised a wide jurisdiction. For minor offenses the penalty was scourging (*mastigóō* [3146], whipping; Matt 10:17; 23:34). Scourging (*mastízō* [3147], the verb of *mástix* [3148], a whip) was one method of *dérō*, to smite, as indicated in Acts 22:19. This smiting, however, was not to be confused with the Roman penalty of scourging (Matt 20:19; John 19:1 [cf. 2 Cor 11:24]) and administered in the synagogue. Excommunication was the punishment for offenses which were thought to imperil the stability of the Jewish community (Luke 6:22; John 9:22; 12:42; 16:2).

The verb *dérō* is also used in the parable of the faithful and the bad servants in Luke 12:35–48. The first observation we must make is that this is a judgment of service and not of salvation. Those servants who proved faithful in the execution of their master's investment in them will be rewarded accordingly, and those servants who did not take their responsibility seriously will be dealt with accordingly. This is proof that not all believers are going to enjoy heaven equally. The entrance into heaven is due to the acceptance by faith of the work which Christ did on the cross, but the enjoyment of heaven will depend on how faithfully a servant honored Christ on earth and the trust that Christ was able to put in him. Both rewards and punishments are graded according to the servant's faithfulness and fruitfulness.

Deriv.: *dérma* (1192), skin.

Syn.: *rhapízō* (4474), to slap, smite; *mastízō* (3147), to whip, scourge.

Ant.: *eulogéō* (2127), to bless; *philéō* (5368), to kiss; *aspázomai* (782), to embrace; *enagkalízomai* (1723), to embrace.

1195. δεσμεύω *desmeúō*; fut. *desmeúsō*, from *desmós* (1199), a bond, chain. To bind, trans. as a prisoner, with cords, chains (Acts 22:4; Sept.: Judg 16:11). To bind together as a bale or bundle; with *phortía* (5413), burdens (Matt 23:4 used metaphorically for the burdensome precepts of the Pharisees); of sheaves (Sept.: Gen 37:7).

Syn.: *sunéchō* (4912), to hold together; *sundéō* (4887), to bind with; *peridéō* (4019), to bind around; *hupodéō* (5265), to bind under; *katadéō* (2611), to bind or tie down; *doulóō* (1397), to enslave.

Ant.: *lúō* (3089), to loose; *chaláō* (5465), to dissolve, let down; *chōrízō* (5563), to put asunder; *eleutheróō* (1659), to set free; *apallássō* (525), to release; *dialúō* (1262), to dissolve, scatter; *apolúō* (630), to dismiss, let go free; *eklúō* (1590), to set free from.

1196. δεσμέω *desméō*; contracted *desmṓ*, fut. *desmḗsō*, from *desmós* (1199), bond, chain. To bind as with chains, equal in meaning with *desmeúō* (1195). Only in Luke 8:29.

Deriv.: *désmios* (1198), a prisoner.

Syn.: *sunéchō* (4912), to hold together; *sundéō* (4887), to bind with; *peridéō* (4019), to bind around; *hupodéō* (5265), to bind under; *katadéō* (2611), to bind or tie down; *doulóō* (1397), to enslave.

Ant.: *lúō* (3089), to loose; *chaláō* (5465), to dissolve, let down; *chōrízō* (5563), to put asunder; *eleutheróō* (1659), to set free; *apallássō* (525), to release; *dialúō* (1262), to dissolve, scatter; *apolúō* (630), to dismiss, let go free; *eklúō* (1590), to set free from.

1197. δέσμη *désmē*; gen. *désmēs*, fem. noun from *déō* (1210), to bind. A bundle, sheaf (Matt 13:30; Sept.: Ex 12:22).

Ant.: *méros* (3313), a part, portion of a whole; *merís* (3310), a part or portion.

1198. δέσμιος *désmios*; gen. *desmíou*, masc. noun from *desméō* (1196), to bind. One who is bound, a prisoner, captive (Matt 27:15, 16; Mark 15:6; Acts 16:25, 27; 23:18; 25:14, 27; 28:16, 17; Heb 13:3). Of Paul, a prisoner of Christ or in confinement for the sake of Jesus (Eph 3:1; 4:1; 2 Tim 1:8; Phile 1:9; Heb 10:34; Sept.: Eccl 4:14; Zech 9:11, 12).

Syn.: *aichmálōtos* (164), literally one taken by the spear, usually a captive of war; *doúlos* (1401), slave.

Ant.: *eleútheros* (1658), a free person; *apeleútheros* (1658), someone who was a prisoner or a slave before and has been freed, a freed man; *polítēs* (4177), a citizen, meaning a free person.

1199. δεσμὸς *desmós*; gen. *desmoú*, masc. noun from *déō* (1210), to bind. Band, bond, ligament.

(I) In the sing., spoken of a ligament or whatever matter may cause some member of the body such as the tongue to be impeded (Mark 7:35); or the limbs (Luke 13:16, see also Luke 13:11; Sept.: Judg 15:13; Dan 4:12).

(II) In the pl. *oi desmoí*, and Attic *ta desmá* (neut. pl.), bonds, imprisonment, for example:

(A) *Hoi desmoí* in Phil 1:13 and probably elsewhere in the writings of Paul (Phil 1:7, 14, 16; Col 4:18; 2 Tim 2:9; Phile 1:10, 13, in bonds or imprisonment for the sake of the gospel; Heb 10:34; 11:36; Jude 1:6; Sept.: Judg 15:14; Job 39:5; Ps 2:3; Jer 27:2).

(B) In the neut. pl. *tá desmá*. In Luke's writings (Luke 8:29; Acts 16:26; 20:23; 22:30; 23:29; 26:29, 31) meaning that which holds someone bound, without freedom.

Deriv.: *desmeúō* (1195), to bind, chain; *desméō* (1196), to bind with chains; *desmophúlax* (1200), a prison-keeper.

Syn.: *súndesmos* (4886), something that binds closely; *zeuktēría* (2202), that which yokes; *speíra* (4686), anything wound, a twisted rope, a body of men at arms; *sustrophḗ* (4963), a secret coalition, riotous crowd forming a conspiracy; *hálusis* (254), a chain.

Ant.: *eleuthería* (1657), freedom.

1200. δεσμοφύλαξ *desmophúlax*; gen. *desmophúlakos*, masc. noun from *desmós* (1199), bond, prison, chain, and *phúlax* (5441), keeper. A prison-keeper (Acts 16:23, 27, 36; see Sept.: Gen 39:21–23, *archidesmophúlax*, the chief keeper of the prison).

1201. δεσμωτήριον *desmōtḗrion*; gen. *desmōtēríou*, neut. noun from *desmóō* (n.f.), to bind. A prison (Matt 11:2; Acts 5:21, 23; 16:26; Sept.: Gen 40:3). Also from *desmóō* (n.f.): *desmṓtēs* (1202), a prison. The prison in Jerusalem (Acts 5:18ff.) was controlled by the priests and probably attached to the high priest's palace or the temple. Paul was imprisoned at Jerusalem in the Fort Antonia (Acts 23:10); at Caesarea by the sea in Herod's Praetorium (Acts 23:35); and probably his final imprisonment was in Rome at the Tullianum dungeon or Mamertine consisting of a larger, oblong, upper story and a smaller, circular, underground dungeon.

Syn.: *phulakḗ* (5438), a prison, a guard, period during which a watch is kept; *tḗrēsis* (5084), a watching, guarding, a place of keeping; *oíkēma* (3612), a tenement used as a prison.

1202. δεσμώτης *desmṓtēs*; gen. *desmṓtou*, masc. noun from *desmóō* (n.f.), to bind. A prisoner (Acts 27:1, 42). Equivalent in meaning to *désmios* (1198), a prisoner (Acts 28:16; Sept.: Gen 39:20). Also from *desmóō* (n.f.): *desmōtḗrion* (1201), a prisoner.

1203. δεσπότης *despótēs*; gen. *despótou*, masc. noun. Master, one who possesses supreme authority, despot. More commonly used as a comp. noun with *oíkos* (3624), house, household, i.e., *oikodespótēs* (3617), master in respect to

his slaves (1 Tim 6:1; 2 Tim 2:21; 1 Pet 2:18).

(I) As opposed to a servant, the head of a family (1 Tim 6:1, 2; 2 Tim 2:21; Titus 2:9; 1 Pet 2:18).

(II) By implication as denoting supreme authority in which case equal to Lord, spoken of God (Luke 2:29; Acts 4:24); of Christ (2 Pet 2:1; Jude 1:4; Rev 6:10; Sept.: Gen 15:2, 8; Job 5:8; Prov 29:26; Isa 1:24).

Deriv.: *oikodespótēs* (3617), householder, master of the house.

Syn.: *megistán* (3175), great, denoting chief men, nobles; *hēgemṓn* (2232), a chief person, ruler; *prōtótokos* (4416), in the sense of being the first over, supreme, in which case it is equivalent to *prōteúōn* (4409), having the preeminence; *árchōn* (758), chief ruler, prince; *kubernḗtēs* (2942), captain, master of a ship; *dunástēs* (1413), a ruler or officer, potentate, one who possesses great power (*dúnamis* [1411]). *Kúrios* (2962), lord, master. *Despótēs* wields unlimited authority, while *kúrios* exercises morally restricted authority for good. Jesus is predominantly called *Kúrios*, Lord, because of His omnipotent concern. God is *Kúrios*, Lord, because He is *despótēs* of all things (cf. Job 5:8ff.).

Ant.: *doúlos* (1401), slave, servant; *diákonos* (1249), deacon, minister, servant; *país* (3816), child, an attendant, servant; *oikétēs* (3610), a house servant; *hupērétēs* (5257), servant; *therápōn* (2324), an attendant, servant; *místhios* (3407) and *misthōtós* (3411), hired servant.

1204. δεῦρο *deúro*; adv. both of place meaning here, hither, to this place, and time meaning unto this time. In the NT when referring to place, it is used only in calling or encouraging and may be translated "come," "come hither" as an exclamation or imperative (Mark 10:21; Luke 18:22). Pl. *deúte* (1205), come hither. In John 11:43 *deúro éxō* (1854), out, come forth. In Acts 7:3, "come into the land"; Sept.: 1 Kgs 1:53; 2 Kgs 9:1. With an imper., "Come and follow me" (Matt 19:21; Mark 10:21; Luke 18:22; Sept.: Judg 9:10, 12; 2 Sam 13:11; 2 Kgs 5:5). With the fut. indic. (Acts 7:34; Rev 17:1; 21:9; Sept.: Judg 19:11, 13; 1 Sam 16:1). Of time, with the neut. art. *áchri toú deúro* (*áchri* [891], up to; *toú deúro* implying *chrónou* [550], time), meaning unto this time, hitherto, up to this time (Rom 1:13).

1205. δεῦτε *deúte*; adv., the pl. of *deúro* (1204), here, hither, up to this time. Come, come hither. With the prep. *eis* (1519), into or to, come to (Matt 22:4; Mark 6:31). With the prep. *prós* (4314), toward, come to (Matt 11:28). With *opísō* (3694), behind or after, come after, follow me (Matt 4:19; Mark 1:17; Sept.: 2 Kgs 6:19). With an imper. (Matt 21:38; Mark 12:7; Luke 20:14; Sept.: Gen 37:19). Come see (Matt 28:6; John 4:29; Sept.: 2 Kgs 7:14; Ps 66:5). See also Matt 25:34; John 21:12; Rev 19:17.

1206. δευτεραῖος *deuteraíos*; fem. *deuteraía*, neut. *deuteraíon*, adj. from *deúteros* (1208), second. On the second day, marking succession of days and used only in an adv. sense (Acts 28:13).

1207. δευτερόπρωτος *deuteróprōtos*; gen. *deuteroprṓtou*, masc.-fem., neut. *deuteróprōton*, adj. from *deúteros* (1208), second, and *prṓtos* (4413), first. The second-first, found only in Luke 6:1, the second-first Sabbath, the first Sabbath after the second day of unleavened bread connected with the Passover. The paschal lamb was to be killed and eaten on the eve of the fourteenth day of Nisan (Lev 23:5); on the fifteenth was the first day of the festival of unleavened bread, a day of rest or Sabbath (Lev 23:6, 7), and, when coinciding with the weekly Sabbath, called a great day of Sabbath or high festival (John 19:31); on the morrow of this Sabbath, or the sixteenth of Nisan, the sheaf of the firstfruits was to be presented (Lev 23:10, 11); and from this sixteenth day were to be counted seven full weeks to the Day of Pentecost (Lev 23:15, 16). The Sabbath of the first of these weeks was probably the Sabbath *deuteróprōton*, the second-first, being the first of the seven, but the second in respect to the first day or Sabbath of unleavened bread. Some translate this word as the first of two Sabbaths, and refer it to a time when two Sabbatical days would immediately succeed each other; e.g., when the first or last day of unleavened bread (Lev 23:7, 8) fell on the day before the weekly Sabbath, the former would then be a Sabbath *deuteróprōton*.

1208. δεύτερος *deúteros*; fem. *deutéra*, neut. *deúteron*, adj. Second in number (Matt 22:26; John 4:54; Titus 3:10); in order (Matt 22:39; Acts 13:33; 1 Cor 15:47; Rev 4:7); in place (Acts 12:10; Heb 9:3); in time (Acts 7:13, "at the second time"). Used in the neut. adv. with the def. art. *tó deúteron*, the second time, again (2 Cor 13:2; Jude 1:5; Sept.: Gen 41:5; Lev 13:5). Without the art., *deúteron* in the neut. indicates either the second time or again (John 3:4; Rev 19:3). With *pálin* (3825), again (John 21:16), or secondly (1 Cor 12:28; Sept.: Gen 22:15; Jer 33:1). With the prep. *ek* (1537), and, with the gen., *ek deutérou*, the second time, again (Mark 14:72; John 9:24; Acts 11:9; Heb 9:28); with *pálin* (3825), again (Matt 26:42; Acts 10:15; Sept.: Josh 5:2; Jer 1:13).

Deriv.: *deuteraíos* (1206), on the second day; *deuteróprōtos* (1207), the second-first.

1209. δέχομαι *déchomai*; fut. *déxomai*, perf. *dédegmai* (Acts 8:14 with mid. meaning, has received to herself), mid. deponent. To accept an offer deliberately and readily. To take to oneself what is presented or brought by another, to receive. Trans.:

(I) Of things:

(A) To take, receive, receive into one's hands (Luke 2:28 implying from his parents; Luke 16:6, 7, "take thy bill" implying back from me; Luke 22:17, "when he received the cup from an attendant" [a.t.]; Eph 6:17, "and take the helmet of salvation"; Sept.: 2 Chr 29:16, 22).

(B) Generally to receive, accept, e.g., letters (Acts 22:5; 28:21); the grace or the collection (2 Cor 8:4); whatever was sent from the Philippians (Phil 4:18). See Sept.: Gen 33:10; Ex 29:25; 32:4.

(C) Metaphorically to receive the kingdom of God (Mark 10:15; Luke 18:17); living words (Acts 7:38); the grace of God (2 Cor 6:1; Sept.: Jer 9:20; 17:23). Also of what is received by the ear, to hear of, learn, as the gospel (2 Cor 11:4). To receive, admit with the mind and heart, i.e., by implication to approve, embrace, follow (Matt 11:14, in an absolute sense; Luke 8:13, "receive the word"; Acts 8:14; 11:1; 17:11; 1 Thess 1:6; 2:13; James 1:21); the things of the Spirit (1 Cor 2:14); the exhortation or teaching (2 Cor 8:17); the love of the truth (2 Thess 2:10). Also Sept.: Prov 10:8; Zeph 3:7.

(II) Of persons, to receive, admit, accept. To receive kindly, welcome as a teacher, friend, or guest into the house (Luke 16:4); into the eternal habitations or heaven (Luke 16:9; Acts 7:59). In Acts 3:21, "whom the heaven must receive." Generally in Matt 10:14, 40, 41; 18:5; Mark 6:11; 9:37; Luke 9:5, 48, 53; 10:8, 10; John 4:45; Acts 21:17; 2 Cor 7:15; Gal 4:14; Col 4:10; Heb 11:31. In the sense of to admit to one's presence, to the house where one is, as the multitudes (Luke 9:11). By implication in 2 Cor 11:16, to bear with.

Deriv.: *anadéchomai* (324), to entertain anyone hospitality; *apodéchomai* (588), to receive heartily, welcome; *dektós* (1184), accepted, acceptable, agreeable; *diadéchomai* (1237), to come after; *dókimos* (1384), to prove, try; *doché* (1403), a feast, acceptance, reception; *eisdéchomai* (1523), to receive into; *ekdéchomai* (1551), to take or receive from, to await, expect; *endéchomai* (1735), to accept; *epidéchomai* (1926), to receive; *paradéchomai* (3858), to receive, to admit; *prosdéchomai* (4327), to take, accept, receive, expect; *hupodéchomai* (5264), to entertain hospitably.

Syn.: Distinguished from *lambánō* (2983) which sometimes means to receive as merely a self-prompted action without necessarily signifying a favorable reception (Gal 2:6); *apéchō* (568), to have in full, to have received all that is due; *chōréō* (5562), to make room for, receive with the mind; *lagchánō* (2975), to obtain by lot.

Ant.:   *dídōmi* (1325),   to   give; *charízomai* (5483), to show favor or kindness, to grant, give freely; *paréchō* (3930), to furnish, provide, supply; *dōréō* (1433), to bestow, make a gift, grant, with the emphasis on what is given; *aponémō* (632), to assign, distribute, give; *chorēgéō* (5524), to supply, render, give; *apobállō* (577), to cast away; *aporríptō* (641), to hurl off; *apotíthemai* (659), to put off; *apōthéomai* (683), to cast away, repel; *ekbállō* (1544), to put out; *ekptúō* (1609), to spit out.

1210. δέω *déō*; fut. *déso*, aor. *édēsa*, perf. *dédeka*, perf. pass. *dédemai*. To bind, trans.:

(I) Of things, to bind together or to anything, to bind around, fasten (Matt 13:30; 21:2; Mark 11:2, 4; Luke 19:30; Acts 10:11; Sept.: Josh 2:21; Judg 15:4). Spoken of dead bodies which are bound or wound around with graveclothes (John 11:44; 19:40). Here also belongs the interpretation of the word found in Matt 16:19, "whatsoever [*ho* {3739}, that which, the neut. sing. def. art.] thou shalt bind on earth shall be bound in heaven," and in Matt 18:18, "those things which" (a.t. [*hósa* {neut. pl. of *hósos* (3745)}]). This means that we as believers on earth can only confirm what has already been decided in heaven. Heaven does not have to confirm our pronouncements. The use of the pl., which includes other believers, indicates that this was not an exclusive prerogative of Peter, "whatsoever ye [pl.] shall bind on earth . . . and whatsoever ye [pl.] shall loose." The word "church" appears for the first time in Matt 16:18 and, therefore, this authority the Lord Jesus gave to all His disciples was the necessary apostolic authority for the establishment of the truth in the church. It has to do with individuals in regard to forgiveness or judgment. The privilege of the forgiveness of sins, which means their removal from the sinner and his regeneration, is the unique privilege of God (Mark 2:7). Here the kingdom, or church, of the Lord is compared to an edifice to which the Apostles have the keys (Matt 16:19; Isa 22:22; Rev 3:7). Accordingly, as they shut or open the door to anything that should be believed or rejected in the church on earth, it must be in agreement with what God has already ordained in heaven. The allusion here is to the ancient manner of binding together the twin doors of houses with a chain to which a padlock was sometimes suspended. In this connection see also the word *aphíēmi* (863), to forgive, in relation to John 20:23. That this binding and loosing had to do only with the doctrine and government of the local church is demonstrated by the leadership Peter assumed consequent to this experience. He acted as chairman of the group of disciples in Jerusalem even before the coming of the Holy Spirit (Acts 1:15–26). At Pentecost he was the one who preached when three thousand souls believed (Acts 2:14–41). It was Peter also who brought the gospel to the Gentiles at Caesarea by the sea (Acts 10:34–48). It is evident that what the council at Jerusalem did had been ratified in heaven by the Holy Spirit (Acts 15:8, 9). "Binding and loosing" were idiomatic expressions among the rabbis denoting what these rabbis permitted the people to do or not to do. The disciples were acting in a similar manner as the rabbis for the Jews, but they were acting on behalf of all believers. Such authority was given to all the disciples as Matt 18:18 makes clear. It was Peter who disciplined Ananias and Sapphira, and his decision received ratification from heaven (Acts 5:1–11). We have a similar experience with Paul in 1 Cor 5 when discipline was needed. Paul said to the Corinthians that when they were assembled, and his spirit was present, with the power of the Lord Jesus,

then the judgment of God would be made manifest in a practical way (1 Cor 5:3–5). It was at the apostolic council in Jerusalem that it was said, "it seemed good to the Holy Ghost, and to us" (Acts 15:28). What was bound on earth had first been bound in heaven.

(II) Of persons, to bind the hands, feet, to put in bonds, i.e., to deprive of liberty (Mark 5:3, 4; Acts 12:6; 21:33; Sept.: Judg 16:7, 8; 2 Chr 36:6). Generally to bind someone (Matt 12:29; 14:3; 22:13, "Bind him hand and foot"; Matt 27:2; Mark 3:27; 6:17, had cast him bound into prison; Mark 15:1; John 18:12; Acts 9:14; 21:11; 22:29; Rev 20:2). In the pass. *déomai*, to be bound, to be in bonds, in prison (Mark 15:7; John 18:24; Acts 9:2, 21; 21:13; 22:5; 24:27; Col 4:3; Rev 9:14; Sept.: Gen 42:24; 2 Sam 3:34; 2 Kgs 17:4). Metaphorically in Luke 13:16, "whom Satan hath bound," i.e., deprived of the use of her limbs (see also Luke 13:11), Satan being here represented as the author of physical evil. See also *daimónion* (1140), a demonic being, devil. In 2 Tim 2:9, "the word of God is not bound," means the preaching of the Word was not hindered or restrained because Paul was in bonds.

(III) The perf. pass. *dédemai*, to be bound, used metaphorically when spoken of the conjugal bond, to be bound to anyone (Rom 7:2; 1 Cor 7:27, 39). In Acts 20:22, "bound in the spirit" means impelled in mind, compelled (cf. 18:5).

Deriv.: *désmē* (1197), a bundle; *desmós* (1199), a band, bond, fetter; *katadéō* (2611), to bind or tie down; *peridéō* (4019), to bind around; *sundéō* (4887), to bind together; *hupodéō* (5265), to bind underneath, used of binding of sandals.

Syn.: *sunistáō* or *sunístēmi* (4921), to set or hold together; *suntássō* (4929), to arrange jointly; *katartízō* (2675), to fit, join together; *sunéchō* (4912), to hold together.

Ant.: *lúō* (3089), to loosen, loose, break up; *dialúō* (1262), to dissolve utterly, scatter; *apóllumi* (622), to lose, to send away; *apogínomai* (581), to be away from;

aphorízō (873), separate; *chōrízō* (5563), to put asunder, separate; *apodiorízō* (592), to mark off; *diamerízō* (1266), to partition thoroughly, divide; *kláō* (2806), to break; *katalúō* (2647), to loosen, dissolve; *chaláō* (5465), to let down; *eklúō* (1590), to relax, to allow to go from; *eleutheróō* (1659), to liberate, deliver.

1211. δή dé; adv. Used as a particle giving to a sentence an expression of certainty and reality in opposition to mere opinion or conjecture meaning indeed, then, now. Used as an affirmative meaning of truly, in truth, really (Matt 13:23; 2 Cor 12:1 in the sense of doubtless; Sept.: Job 15:17). With the meaning of exhorting, by all means (Luke 2:15; Acts 15:36 [cf. 13:2]); with the meaning of inference or conclusion, therefore (1 Cor 6:20, "glorify then God" [a.t.]; Sept.: Gen 18:4). This, however, includes the meaning of affirmation and wish giving it the meaning of therefore truly, or therefore by all means.

Deriv.: *dépote* (1221), whatever; *dépou* (1222), indeed, verily.

Syn.: *oún* (3767), therefore, so then; *dé* (1161), but, and, now, often implying an antithesis; *kaí* (2532), and, now, sometimes, but; *ára* (686), then, expressing a more informal inference, so then.

1212. δῆλος délos; fem. *délē*, neut. *délon*, adj. Plain, evident, manifest (Matt 26:73). With the verb *estí* (2076), is, and the acc., it is evident (1 Cor 15:27; Gal 3:11; 1 Tim 6:7).

Deriv.: *ádēlos* (82), uncertain, hidden; *dēlóō* (1213), to make plain; *ékdēlos* (1552), quite evident; *katádēlos* (2612), abundantly manifest; *pródēlos* (4271), manifest beforehand.

Syn.: *phanerós* (5318), outwardly or openly manifest, visible; *emphanḗs* (1717), manifest openly or outwardly; *eilikrinḗs* (1506), sincere.

Ant.: *kruptós* (2927), secret, hidden; *apókruphos* (614), hidden.

1213. δηλόω dēlóō; contracted *dēló*, fut. *dēlṓsō*, from *délos* (1212), manifest. To make manifest, known. Used trans. and spoken of things past, to tell, relate (1 Cor 1:11; Col 1:8; Sept.: Esth 2:22); of things future or hidden, to reveal, show, bring to light (1 Cor 3:13; Heb 9:8; 1 Pet 1:11; 2 Pet 1:14; Sept.: Ex 6:3; 1 Sam 3:21; Dan 4:15); of words, to imply, signify (Heb 12:27).

Syn.: *anaggéllō* (312), to announce, report; *apaggéllō* (518), to announce or report from a person or place; *diaggéllō* (1229), to announce thoroughly or to declare fully; *kataggéllō* (2605), to declare; *paraggéllō* (3853), to charge; *poiéō* (1804), to make, bring forth; *diēgéomai* (1334), to narrate; *ekdiēgéomai* (1555), to narrate in full; *exēgéomai* (1834), to declare the meaning of; *horízō* (3724), to mark off by boundaries, to declare; *phrázō* (5419), to explain, declare; *gnōrízō* (1107), to make known; *emphanízō* (1718), to declare plainly; *phaneróō* (5319), to manifest; *anatíthemai* (394), to communicate with the meaning of showing; *deiknúō* (1166), exhibit; *anadeíknumi* (322), to show forth, declare; *endeíknumi* (1731), to show forth, prove; *epideíknumi* (1925), to display demonstrate; *hupodeíknumi* (5263), to show secretly; *mēnúō* (3377), to disclose, make known in a legal sense, to take to court; *parístēmi* (3936), to present; *apodeíknumi* (584), to demonstrate; *paréchō* (3930), to afford or bring; *exaggéllō* (1804), to tell out, proclaim abroad; *kataggéllō* (2605), to proclaim; *euaggelízō* (2097), to bring glad tidings; *katatíthēmi* (2698), to lay up, deposit; *légō* (3004), to tell, signify; *sēmaínō* (4591), to indicate.

Ant.: *krúptō* (2928), to cover, conceal, keep secret; *apokrúptō* (613), to conceal from; *egkrúptō* (1470), to hide in anything; *perikrúptō* (4032), to hide by placing something around; *kalúptō* (2572), to cover, conceal, so that no trace of it can be seen; *parakalúptō* (3871), to cover with a veil; *lanthánō* (2990), to escape notice, be hidden from.

1214. Δημᾶς Dēmás; gen. *Dēmá*, masc. proper noun. Demas, a zealous disciple and fellow laborer with Paul (Phile 1:24; Col 4:14) who afterward left him through inordinate love of the world (2 Tim 4:10).

1215. δημηγορέω *dēmēgoréō*; contracted *dēmēgorṓ*, fut. *dēmēgorḗsō*, from *dḗmos* (1218), people, and *agoreúō* (n.f.), to speak, which is from *agorá* (58), a marketplace. To speak or address a public assembly, to harangue the people, make a public oration (Acts 12:21; Sept.: Neh 8:4).

1216. Δημήτριος *Dēmḗtrios*; gen. *Dēmētríou*, masc. proper noun. Demetrius.

(I) A silversmith who resided at Ephesus and manufactured silver shrines or small portable temples and images of Diana (in Gr., *Ártemis* [735], Acts 19:24, 38). These were purchased by foreigners who either could not come to Ephesus to worship or else desired a memento of the city and a model of its famous temple. In a city where Diana was worshiped, this was a profitable business which began to suffer with the spread of the gospel, and thus Demetrius tried his best to dissuade the people from believing. Calling a meeting of those who worked at the trade, he inflamed the passion of his fellow craftsmen who excited the multitude until the whole city of Ephesus was thrown into an uproar. This was finally quelled by the advice of the town clerk (Acts 19).

(II) A disciple of high reputation and, as some suppose, although without warrant, the Demetrius of Ephesus converted to the faith of the gospel (3 John 1:12).

1217. δημιουργός *dēmiourgós*; gen. *dēmiourgoú*, adj. from *dḗmos* (1218), a people, and *érgon* (2041), work. Used as a subst. to denote one who works for the public or performs public works such as an architect. Applied to God, the architect of that continuing and glorious city which Abraham looked for (Heb 11:10). It brings out the power of the divine creator expressing God's manifold wisdom, the infinite variety and beauty of the works of His hand (Acts 19:24, 38; Heb

11:10; Rev 18:22) in contrast to *technítēs* (5079) which comes from *téchnē* (5078), trade, and *teúchō*, to fabricate, meaning an artificer, craftsman, workman.

Syn.: *ktístēs* (2939), founder of a city, creator. Both *dēmiourgós* and *ktístēs* are used only once in the NT. They identify God as the creator, along with *technítēs* mentioned conjointly with *dēmiourgós* in Heb 11:10. The word *technítēs* is the Gr. word from which our Eng. words "technology" and "technical" are derived, indicating a specialty in the formulation of particular things. The predominant word used is the verbal deriv. of *ktístēs* which is *ktízō* (2936) which was used of building cities (Mark 13:19; Rom 1:25; 1 Cor 11:9; Eph 2:10, 15; 3:9; 4:24; Col 1:16; 3:10; 1 Tim 4:3; Rev 4:11; 10:6). Class. Gr. did not note the actual erection of a building but the basic and decisive resolve to establish, institute or found, which is indicated by *dēmiourgéō* (n.f.), to create. However, it must be noted that *ktízō* was also used for the administration of a building. Moreover, *ktízō* (2936) involved the idea of proprietorship or a builder. In the case of a city, it involved the rulership of that city by the one who had built it. *Dēmiourgéō*, however, refers to the technical manual process, while *ktízō* has in it the intellectual and volitional process involved in its design. In the NT *ktízō* is the most common word used to indicate the creative act of God. The verb *ktízō* and deriv. are used in the NT only of God's creation. Other syns. in the NT which indirectly refer to a creator are *lógos* (3056) in John 1:1, 14 where the Lord Jesus is called *ho Lógos* which basically means intelligence. He is called that in order to show us that He, as the Creator of the world (John 1:3), exercised intelligence and planning in the creation, the *archḗ* (746), the active beginning as the cause (Rev 3:14) referring to the Lord Jesus Christ. The second most common word is *poiéō* (4160) (Acts 4:24; 17:24). The other words related to *ktízō* are *ktísis* (2937), creation, creature (Mark 10:6; 13:19; 16:15; Rom

1:20, 25; 8:19–22, 39; 2 Cor 5:17; Gal 6:15; Col 1:15, 23; Heb 4:13; 9:11; 1 Pet 2:13; 2 Pet 3:4; Rev 3:14) and *ktísma* (2938), an original formation, created thing, creature (1 Tim 4:4; James 1:18; Rev 5:13). The cognate words of *poiéō* (4160), to create or make, are *poíēma* (4161), a product, a thing which is made, workmanship (Rom 1:20; Eph 2:10); *poíēsis* (4162), the act of doing (James 1:25); *poiētḗs* (4162), a poet (Acts 17:28), a maker, doer (Rom 2:13; James 1:22, 23, 25; 4:11). So, although the verb *poiéō* means create, yet the cognates do not. Another word meaning to make or form is *plássō* (4111), translated "formed" in Rom 9:20; 1 Tim 2:13. The noun *plásma* (4110) occurs only in Rom 9:20 and is translated "the thing formed" or the thing that has been manipulated by hand, referring to what is made from clay. The word *plástēs*, a molder, an artist who works in clay or wax, does not occur in the NT although Philo does refer to it as a creator. Instead of *plástēs* in the NT, we have it expressed through the aor. part. of *plássō* (4111), to shape, form, fabricate, the One who formed or made it with his hands as in Rom 9:20, *tō plásanti* (4111). There are two more words that are used only in their verbal form which are syn. of *dēmiourgéō*, to create. They are *kataskeuázō* (2680), which in Heb 3:4 is translated "builded" and is used in a play on words referring to man, and "built" which refers to God as the builder. Basically, the word means to prepare (Matt 11:10; Mark 1:2; Luke 1:17; 7:27). In Heb 3:3 it is translated "hath builded"; in Heb 9:2 as "made"; in Heb 9:6 as "ordained"; and in Heb 11:7 and 1 Pet 3:20, as "prepared and preparing." A final word could qualify, the verb *themelióō* (2311) in Heb 1:10, translated "hast laid the foundation." The other occurrences of this verb are Matt 7:25; Luke 6:48; Eph 3:17, 18; Col 1:23; 1 Pet 5:10, translated "founded, grounded, settled."

Ant.: There is no exact opposite of *dēmiourgós*, creator, in the NT which

would indicate one who would put an end to what exists. However, there are cognate words such as the verbs *katastréphō* (2690), literally to turn upside down, upset, destroy; *ho apollúōn* (623), destroyer; *olothreutḗs* (3644), a destroyer; *exolothreúō* (1842), to destroy completely. Verbs: *katargéō* (2673), to abolish; *kathairéō* (2507), to pull down by force, destroy; *lúō* (3089), to loose, dissolve, and *dialúō* (1262), to dissolve utterly; *katalúō* (2647), to destroy, dissolve; *phtheírō* (5351), to destroy, corrupt; *olothreúō* (3645), to destroy.

1218. δῆμος *dḗmos*; gen. *dḗmou*, masc. noun from *déō* (1210), to bind. A people, so-called because they are united by laws and ties of a society (Acts 12:22; 17:5; 19:30, 33). From this word is derived "democracy" where the people or the public rules.

Deriv.: *apódēmos* (590), taking a far journey; *dēmēgoréō* (1215), to make an oration; *dēmiourgós* (1217), maker; *dēmósios* (1219), public, common.

Syn.: *laós* (2992), people; *óchlos* (3793), a crowd, throng; *éthnos* (1484), a nation; *kósmos* (2889), world, people; *koinōnía* (2842), partnership, communion, fellowship.

Ant.: *ánthrōpos* (444), man; *prósōpon* (4383), person; *plēsíon* (4139), a neighbor; *polítēs* (4177), citizen; *idiótēs* (2399), a private person.

1219. δημόσιος *dēmósios*; fem. *dēmosía*, neut. *dēmósion*, adj. from *dḗmos* (1218), people. Public, belonging to the public, for public use (Acts 5:18). In the dat., *dēmosía* meaning publicly; used adv. meaning in a public place (Acts 16:37; 18:28; 20:20).

Syn.: with the meaning of common or for public use: *koinós* (2839), common, shared by all; *parrēsía* (3954), with boldness; *phanerós* (5320), manifestly. A periphrastic syn. is *en tō phanerō* (5319), in the open, publicly, or with the adv. *phanerōs* (5320), publicly, openly.

Ant.: *ídios* (2398), one's own, private; *kat' idían* (2596, 2398), privately; *láthra* (2977), secretly, covertly, unnoticed.

1220. δηνάριον *dēnárion*; gen. *dēnaríou*, a neut. noun formed from the Latin *denarius*, which denotes the Roman penny. It was a silver coin equivalent in value to the Greek drachma. Denarius, or the *dēnárion* rendered as "penny," is the most frequently mentioned coin in the gospels (Matt 18:28; 20:2, 9, 10, 13; 22:19; Mark 6:37; 12:15; 14:5; Luke 7:41; 10:35; 20:24; John 6:7; 12:5; Rev 6:6). It was the most important Roman coin which circulated throughout the empire and with which all public accounts were tallied. In Mark 14:5; John 12:5 the ointment with which Mary anointed our Lord is valued at three hundred denarii, which sum probably represents at least the annual income of a laborer of those days. This appears from the parable of the laborers in the vineyard in Matt 20:1–15 where a denarius is evidently considered liberal pay for a day's work of twelve hours beginning at 6 a.m. and ending at 6 p.m. In the parable of the Good Samaritan (Luke 10:30–37), two denarii are given to the innkeeper as a reasonable payment in advance for the upkeep of the wounded traveler for a day or two, to be supplemented, if necessary, on the return of the Samaritan. Of special interest is the reference to the denarius in Matt 22:19; Mark 12:15; Luke 20:24 in connection with the Pharisees' question as to the lawfulness of paying tribute to Caesar. The denarius was the money of the tribute or tax (Matt 22:19). It bore upon it the name and title of the reigning emperor, along with the effigy either of himself or of some member of the imperial family, i.e., the "image and superscription" to which our Lord alluded. It was issued by imperial authority, the Roman Senate only having the right to mint copper coins. Thus the *dēnárion* could appropriately be spoken of as "that which is Caesar's."

Syn.: *argúrion* (694), silver, money; *chréma* (5536), money, wealth; *chalkós*

(5475), copper or copper coin; *kérma* (2772), a small coin; *nómisma* (3546), currency, money; *statér* (4715), the equivalent of four *drachmaí* (1406), the temple tax for two persons.

1221. δήποτε *dépote*; adv. from *dé* (1211), a particle of emphasis meaning truly, and *poté* (4218), ever. Whatever. Subjoined to the relative pron. it strengthens the idea of generality and comprehensiveness (John 5:4). Indeed, or whatsoever (John 5:4).

1222. δήπου *dépou*; adv. from *dé* (1211), a particle of emphasis or explicitness, and *pou* (4226), where. Indeed, truly, verily (only in Heb 2:16).

1223. διά *diá*; prep., governing the gen. and acc. Through, throughout

(**I**) With the gen. meaning of through:

(**A**) Of place implying motion, through a place, and used after verbs of motion, e.g., of going, coming (Matt 2:12). With the *diabaínō* (1224), to pass through (Heb 11:29). With the *diaporeúomai* (1279), to travel through (Luke 6:1). With the *diérchomai* (1330), to walk through (Matt 12:43; 19:24). With the *eisérchomai* (1525), to go in (John 10:1, 9). With *ekporeúomai* (1607), to proceed from, depart (Matt 4:4). With *érchomai* (2064), to come, go (Mark 10:1). With *paraporeúomai* (3899), to travel near (Mark 2:23; 9:30). With *parérchomai* (3928), to go by (Matt 8:28). With *hupostréphō* (5290), to return (Acts 20:3). In Rom 15:28; 2 Cor 1:16, to go out of or through your city. With many other verbs implying motion as in 2 Cor 8:18 implying *diaggéllō* (1229), to announce. Also after *blépō* (991), to see (1 Cor 13:12). After *diaphérō* (1308), transport (Mark 11:16; Acts 13:49). With *kathíēmi* (2524), to let down (Luke 5:19). With *chaláō* (5465), to let down (2 Cor 11:33). In 1 Cor 3:15, "saved; yet so as by fire" meaning as if passing through fire.

(**B**) Of time: (**1**) Continued time, time indefinite, meaning through, throughout, during (Luke 5:5, "all the night," i.e., during the whole night; Acts 1:3, "during forty days" [a.t.]; Heb 2:15, "during their whole life" [a.t.]. Also *diapantós* (1275), through all the time, continually, used adv.). Also Acts 23:31. Spoken of time, meaning when, i.e., of an indefinite time, during a longer interval such as *diá tḗs nuktós* (3571), during the night, i.e., at some time of the night, by night (Acts 5:19; 16:9; 17:10). (2) Of time elapsed, meaning after (Mark 2:1, "after some days"; Acts 24:17, "after many years," i.e., many years having elapsed; Gal 2:1, "after fourteen years" [a.t.]; Sept.: Deut 9:11; 15:1).

(C) Of the instrument or intermediate cause; that which intervenes between the act of the will and the effect, and through which the effect proceeds, meaning through, by, by means of: (1) Of things, meaning through, by, by means of, as in Mark 16:20, "by means of signs" (a.t.); John 11:4; 17:20; Acts 3:18, 21, "through the mouth of the holy prophets" (a.t.); Acts 5:12, "through the hands of the apostles" (a.t.); 8:18; 10:43, "through a profession of faith in His name" (a.t.); 11:30; 15:32; 19:26; 20:28, "through the intervention of His blood" (a.t.); Rom 3:20, "through [or by means of] the law" (a.t.); 3:27; 5:10; 8:3; 1 Cor 3:5; 4:15; 2 Cor 1:4; 10:9; Gal 2:16; 3 John 1:13. Also meaning by virtue of, in consequence of (Rom 12:3, "by virtue of the grace given me" [a.t.]; Gal 1:15; Phile 1:22). In exhortations, meaning through (Rom 12:1, "through the mercies of God" [a.t.]; 15:30; 1 Cor 1:10; 2 Cor 10:1). (2) Of persons through whose hands anything would pass, through or by whose agency or ministry an effect takes place or is produced, the efficient cause as in Matt 1:22, "through the prophet" (a.t.); 2:5, 15, 23; Luke 18:31; John 1:17; Acts 2:22, "signs which God did through Him" (a.t.); 2:43; 4:16; 12:9; Rom 2:16; 5:5; 1 Cor 2:10; 8:6; Heb 1:2, 3. Also Rom 1:5; 5:1; 1 Cor 11:12, "the man through the woman" (a.t.); Gal 1:1; 2 Tim 2:2; Heb 2:2; 7:9. Also through the fault of (Matt 18:7; 26:24; Rom 5:12, 16, 19; 1 Cor

15:21; Sept.: 2 Chr 29:5; Esth 1:15; Isa 37:24). In this construction *diá* may also refer to the author or first cause, when the author does anything through himself instead of another, e.g., of God (Rom 11:36, "of [or out of] Him and through Him and unto Him all things" [a.t.]; 1 Cor 1:9, "God, through whom you were called" [a.t.]; Heb 2:10). Also of Christ (John 1:3 "All things were made by him"; Col 1:16, "all things through Him and unto Him have been created" [a.t.]). In protestings and exhortations (Rom 15:30; 1 Thess 4:2; 2 Thess 3:12).

(D) Of the mode, manner, state, or circumstances through which anything, as it were, passes, i.e., takes place, is produced: (1) Of manner where *diá* with its gen. forms a periphrasis for the corresponding adv. (Luke 8:4, "He spake through a parable" [a.t.], meaning by means of a parable which could have been expressed with the adv. *parabolikṓs*, parabolically; Acts 15:27, "through [or by] word" [a.t.], meaning orally; Rom 8:25; 14:20, "so as to give offense" [a.t.]; 2 Cor 10:11; Gal 5:13; Eph 6:18; Heb 12:1, through or "with patience," i.e., patiently). Also John 19:23, *di' hólou* (3650), whole, meaning throughout as also in Acts 15:32, "with many words"; Heb 13:22, *diá brachéōn* (1024), and 1 Pet 5:12 *di' olígōn* (3641), both implying *lógōn* (3056), words, meaning briefly. In 2 Cor 1:11 *diá pollṓn* (4183), many, implying persons, meaning "by the means of many persons." (2) Of the state, circumstances, emotions, through, in, with which or on occasion of which anything exists, is produced or done. The verbs *eimí* (1510), to be, *gínomai* (1096), to become, *érchomai* (2064), to come, and the like being usually expressed or implied as in Rom 2:27; 4:11, believers who are not circumcised; 14:14, "through itself" (a.t.), i.e., in and of its own nature; 15:32, "that I may come unto you through the will of God" (a.t.); 1 Cor 1:1; 14:19; 2 Cor 2:4, "with many tears," i.e., weeping; 3:11, "glorified" (a.t.); 5:7, "we walk by faith [in Christ], not by sight," i.e., we are Christians through and in a state of faith in Christ, not of sight or of personal contact with Him; 5:10; 6:7; 8:5, 8, on occasion of, because of; Gal 1:15, "and called me through his grace" (a.t.); Phil 1:20, "whether I live or die" (a.t.); 2 Thess 2:2, "as if it were ours" (a.t.); Heb 9:12, "through his own blood" (a.t.), i.e., offering Himself as sacrifice; 2 Pet 1:3, "through glory and virtue" (a.t.), i.e., the highest glory and virtue of God being thus conspicuously exhibited; 1 John 5:6, "he came by [through] water and blood" (a.t.), i.e., He received baptism and suffered death which were testimonials of His mission.

(II) With the acc. meaning through, by, by means of, or more generally on account of.

(A) Spoken of: (1) The instrument, the intermediate or efficient cause (see I, C above); through, by, by means of. (2) Of things as in John 15:3, "by means of the word" (a.t.); Heb 5:14, "through use" (a.t.); Rev 12:11; 13:14, "deceives through [by means of] those miracles" (a.t.); also Heb 5:12, "through the time spent" (a.t.), i.e., the time spent should have made you already teachers; 2 Pet 3:12, "the day of God, wherein the heavens." (3) Of persons. (See I, C, 2 above [John 6:57; Rom 8:11, 20; Heb 6:7; Sept.: Isa 50:11]). (4) Of emotions, through which or from which one is led to do anything (Matt 27:18; Mark 15:10; Luke 1:78; Eph 2:4; Phil 1:15).

(B) Of the ground or motive, the moving or impelling cause of anything, "on account of" or "because of." (1) Generally in Matt 10:22, "on account of my name" (a.t.); 13:21, "because of the word"; 13:58; Mark 2:4; Luke 8:47; John 4:39, 41; 12:11; Acts 22:24; 28:2; Sept.: Gen 43:18; Deut 15:10. Diá with the acc. indicates a more act. cause and motivation than the more pass. héneken (1752) or heíneken, on account of, with the gen. (Matt 24:9 [cf. 5:10, 11]). Also before an inf. with the neut. art. to, the (Mark 5:4; Luke 11:8; 23:8, "on account of hearing many things" [a.t.]; Acts 4:2; 18:3, "because he was of the same trade" [a.t.];

Sept.: Deut 1:36). Also in phrases, e.g., diá followed by the indef. enclitic pron. tí (5100), that (neut.), meaning on what account? wherefore? why? (Matt 9:11; Luke 5:30, 33; John 13:37). Also written as one word, diatí (1302), why? (Matt 13:10; 15:2; Mark 2:18; 7:5; Luke 19:23; John 7:45; Acts 5:3; Sept.: Ex 2:18; Num 11:11; Deut 29:23). Also diá toúto (5124), this, on this account, for this cause or reason, therefore (Matt 6:25; Mark 6:14; Acts 2:26; Rom 1:26; 2 Cor 4:1; Rev 18:8; Sept.: Isa 49:4; Mic 3:12). Also diá toúto followed by hóti (3754), that, meaning on this account, because (John 5:16; 8:47; 15:19). (2) Meaning for the sake of, on behalf of, as marking the purpose or object of an action (Matt 14:3; 24:22, "for the elect's sake"; Mark 2:27; 6:17; John 11:15; Acts 16:3; Rom 11:28). Also diá toúto, for the sake of this, for this purpose (John 12:27, "for this purpose I came to suffer death" [a.t.]; 1 Cor 4:17). With hína (2443), so that, in order that (John 1:31; 1 Tim 1:16). Hópōs (3704), so that (Heb 9:15). (3) As marking the occasion of anything, the occasion or cause, that on occasion, on account of, because of which anything takes place (Matt 27:19; John 7:43; 10:19; Rom 2:4; 15:15, "because of," by virtue of; 2 Pet 2:2).

(C) Of the manner or state, meaning through or during which anything takes place (Gal 4:13, "through infirmity," i.e., during bodily weakness [cf. I, D]). This sense of diá is rare with the acc. and comes from the general idea of duration.

(III) In composition diá mostly retains its meaning and refers to space and time as through, throughout, implying transition, continuance, as diabaínō (1224), to come over or pass through; diapléō (1277), to sail through; diagínomai (1230), to be past, to have elapsed; diágō (1236), to pass time or life. Metaphorically meaning through to the end, marking completeness and thus becoming intensive as diablépō (1227), to look through, to recover full vision; diaginṓskō (1231), to know thoroughly. It may refer to distribution, diffusion, as throughout, among, everywhere, as *diaggéllō* (1229), to declare thoroughly. It also can refer to mutual or alternate effects or endeavors as through or between or among one another, to and fro, as *diakrínomai* (1252), to distinguish oneself; *diamáchomai* (1264), to fight fiercely; *diairéō* (1244), to divide, separate; *dialúō* (1262), to dissolve; *diarréssō* (1284), to tear asunder or to break up.

1224. διαβαίνω diabaínō; fut. *diabēsomai*, from *diá* (1223), through, and *baínō* (n.f., see *apobaínō* [576]), to go. To pass through or over (Luke 16:26 followed by *prós* [4314] toward, with the acc.; Acts 16:9 followed by *eis* [1519], to; Heb 11:29 followed by the acc. of thing; Sept.: Gen 31:21; 1 Sam 13:7).
    Syn.: *diérchomai* (1330), to pass through or over; *diaporeúomai* (1279), to pass across, journey through; *diaperáō* (1276), to pass or cross over; *diodeúō* (1353), to travel through or along.
    Ant.: *ménō* (3306), to remain.

1225. διαβάλλω diabállō; fut. *diabalō*, from *diá* (1223), through, and *bállō* (906), to cast, throw. To accuse falsely. Used only in Luke 16:1, in the pass. voice. The translation "he was falsely accused" (a.t.) would make this difficult parable more easily understood.
    Deriv.: *diábolos* (1228), false accuser.
    Syn.: *egkaléō* (1458), to bring a charge against, usually in court; *epēreázō* (1908), to insult, misuse, treat despitefully; *katēgoréō* (2723), to accuse; *sukophantéō* (4811), to accuse wrongfully; *proaitiáomai* (4256), to bring a previous charge against; *katalaléō* (2635), to speak against; *kakologéō* (2551), to speak evil.
    Ant.: *epainéō* (1867), to praise, commend; *eulogéō* (2127), to praise, speak well of, bless.

1226. διαβεβαιόομαι diabebaióomai; contracted *diabebaioúmai*, deponent from *diá* (1223), an intens., and *bebaióō* (950),

to confirm. To assure firmly, affirm, make firm (1 Tim 1:7; Titus 3:8).
    Syn.: *diïschurízomai* (1340), to assert vehemently; *pháskō* (5335), to show or make known one's thoughts, to affirm by way of alleging or professing.
    Ant.: *arnéomai* (720), to deny; *aparnéomai* (533), to deny utterly; *antilégō* (483), to speak against, contradict; *paraitéomai* (3868), avoid, refuse; *apologéomai* (626), to talk oneself out of, to defend oneself; *katalaléō* (2635), to speak against; *kakologéō* (2551), to speak evil.

1227. διαβλέπω diablépō; fut. *diablépsō*, from *diá* (1223) an intens., and *blépō* (991), to see. To look through, view attentively, see clearly or fully (Matt 7:5; Luke 6:42).
    Syn.: *theáomai* (2300), to view attentively, see with admiration; *theōréō* (2334), to carefully examine with attention to details; *horáō* (3708), to see, to exercise mental perception, take heed; *emblépō* (1689), to look intensively or earnestly; *epopteúō* (2029), to oversee; *atenízō* (816), to behold steadfastly; *katanoéō* (2657), to behold and conceive with the mind that which one ought to be taught by what he sees.
    Ant.: *muōpázō* (3467), to be shortsighted; *tuphlóō* (5186), to blind; *pōróō* (4456), to observe carefully.

1228. διάβολος diábolos; gen. *diabólou*, masc., fem. noun from *diabállō* (1225), to accuse. A false accuser, used for the devil.
    (I) One who falsely accuses and divides people without any reason. He is an accuser, a slanderer (1 Tim 3:11; 2 Tim 3:3; Titus 2:3; Sept.: Esth 7:4; 8:1).
    (II) With the art. *ho diábolos*, the Devil. Satan is called by that name because originally he accused or slandered God in paradise, being averse to the increase of man's knowledge and happiness (Gen 3:5; John 8:44, the children of the devil).
    In Rev 12:10 Satan is called *ho katégoros* (2725), the accuser, as if he

were standing in a court of law. The devil still slanders God by false and blasphemous suggestions and because he is also the accuser of the brethren before God (Rev 12:9, 10 [cf. Job 1—2]). He is called our adversary (*antídikos* [476]) or opponent. *Diábolos* is used either for the prince of devils (Matt 4:1; Rev 12:9; 20:2) or for evil spirits in general (Acts 10:38; Eph 4:27; 6:11). The Lord Jesus calls Judas *diábolos* (John 6:70) because under the influence of this evil spirit he would be Christ's accuser and betrayer (cf. Matt 16:23; Mark 8:33 where the Lord calls Peter *Satanás* [4567], Satan or adversary, and not *diábolos*, devil). This prince of the devils is called *diábolos* thirty-eight times, and *Satanás* thirty-four times in the NT. Other references to *diábolos*: Matt 4:5, 8, 11; 13:39; 25:41; Luke 4:2, 3, 5, 6, 13; 8:12; John 13:2; Acts 13:10; 1 Tim 3:6, 7; 2 Tim 2:26; Heb 2:14; James 4:7; 1 Pet 5:8; 1 John 3:8, 10; Jude 1:9; Rev 2:10; 12:12; 20:10; Sept.: 1 Chr 21:1; Job 1:6f.; 2:1f.; Zech 3:1, 2. The devil is also identified in the NT as Beelzebub or Beelzebul, the prince of the devils (Matt 12:24–29 [cf. 10:25; Mark 3:22; Luke 11:15–19]). He is also called *ho ponērós* (4190), the evil, malignant or hurtful one (Matt 13:19, 38; 2 Thess 3:3, and perhaps in the Lord's Prayer in Matt 6:13); *óphis ho archaíos* ([3789], serpent; [744], old or original), the old serpent (Rev 12:9; 20:2); *ho echthrós* ([2190] from *échthō*, to hate), the enemy, the hateful one, the adversary (Matt 13:39); *ho toú kósmou árchōn* ([2889] of the world; [758], the first, chief, ruler), the prince of this world (John 12:31; 14:30; 16:11); *árchōn tṓn daimoníōn* ([1140], of the demons), the prince of the devils (Matt 9:34; 12:24; Mark 3:22; Luke 11:15); *ho árchōn tḗs exousías* ([1849], authority, power) *toú aéros* ([109], of the air), "the prince of the power of the air" (Eph 2:2).

Jesus felt Himself in the presence of demons belonging to a kingdom of evil ruled over by a supreme personality, Satan, the devil or Beelzebub. These personal agencies of the devil work every form of physical and moral calamity. They recognize, however, the might of the Lord Jesus, the Messiah, gifted with the power of God to destroy the works of Satan and all his personal subordinates (Mark 1:24, 34; 3:11, 12, 15, 23–27; 6:7; Luke 10:17–20; 11:14–22; 13:32). Jesus fully recognized the existence and power of the kingdom of Satan which resists the establishment of the kingdom of God (Matt 12:26; Mark 3:24).

In the narrative of the temptation, the world is regarded as ruled by Satan (cf. John 14:30); but in Luke 4:6, Satan confesses that his authority is not original and fundamental. He is given limited authority, but never to cancel God's overall plan and purpose. This power which he falsely claims to have he is willing to transfer to Jesus upon condition of His allegiance. The narrative illustrates the character of cunning that belongs to Satan as the tempter of mankind (Gen 3:1), for he quotes Ps 91:11, 12 for his own purposes (Matt 4:6) and applies the words to the Messiah.

Jesus warns His disciples against this subtle deceit. Satan is eager to sift Simon as wheat (Luke 22:31) and enters like a demon into Judas (Luke 22:3).

Christ acknowledged that physical maladies could be caused by the direct agency of evil spirits. This demonic power that works physical havoc is under the control of Satan and is ascribed to him in the case of the afflicted woman (Luke 13:16). In the expulsion of demons by His disciples, Christ sees the overthrow of Satan's power (Luke 10:18 in which utterance our Lord refers to the well-known passage in Isa 14:12f.).

Satan's power is definitely set under the control of God's righteous rule, whereby a definite term is determined for Satan's sway. Nevertheless, Satan sets up a rival kingdom with himself as a quasi-god (cf. 2 Cor 4:14). This evil is intellectual, moral, and physical. The devil takes the seed of the divine Word out of the heart of man (Matt 13:19, 39; Mark 4:15) and plants the spurious wheat (*zizánia* [2215], tares).

He blinds the thoughts of the unbeliever so that they are unable to behold the gospel light of Christ's glory (2 Cor 4:4). In Rom 8:38; 1 Cor 15:24 the Apostle Paul refers to *archaí* (746), powers, principalities, *exousíai* (1849), authorities, jurisdictions, and *dunámeis* (1411), powers. All are in the pl. Perhaps the *archaí* are to be identified with the *árchontes* (758), magistrates, rulers of this world in 1 Cor 2:6.

The gods of the heathen are not absolutely nonexistent but are evil spirits and have a subordinate potency in heathen religions as *theoí* (2316), gods, and *kúrioi* (2962), lords (1 Cor 8:4–6 [cf. 12:2]). These supernatural "princes of this world" have a certain wisdom of their own (1 Cor 2:6, 8), to whom the eternal wisdom revealed by God's Spirit to simple faith appears to be folly. Their "wisdom" will be brought to naught (cf. 2 Cor 10:5).

To these lords and gods may correspond the *stoicheía* (4747), elements or principles of the world which may be considered to be an abstraction standing in place of the personal concrete names (cf. *archaí*, *exousíai*, *thrónoi* [2362], thrones, and *kuriótētes* [2963], dominions, governments), or principles which represent the sphere of their personal activity. These are called the *kosmokrátores* (2888), the world-rulers of the dark spiritual world against which the Christian is to arm himself (Eph 6:12) and over which the Lord Jesus triumphed on the cross (Col 2:15).

Satan reigns over all this world of evil energy, and all his collective power for evil is gathered up in his personality. He is the tempter (*ho peirázōn*, the tempter, the pres. part. of *peirázō* [3985], to tempt) (1 Cor 7:5; 1 Thess 3:5 [cf. Matt 4:1–3]). Bodily diseases are ascribed to him just as in Luke 13:16.

In one remarkable passage, 1 Cor 5:4, 5, we even see Satan utilized for the advantage of the individual and the church. The offender in a solemn church assembly is to be delivered over to Satan for the destruction of the flesh in order that the spirit of the sinner may be saved in the day of the Lord's appearing. Satan, as the inflicter of physical malady, is apparently identified with the destroyer (Sept.: Ex 12:23; *ho olothreúōn*, from *ólethros* [3639], destruction, hence the destroyer, see word and also *apollúōn* [623], the destroyer, Num 16:21ff., to which 1 Cor 10:10 evidently alludes [cf. also the destroying angel of 2 Sam 24:16; 2 Kgs 19:35]). According to the Apostle Paul, man's surrender to Satan brought death as the ultimate consequence imposed by God (1 Cor 5:5; 2 Cor 2:11). In John 8:44 Satan is called *anthrōpoktónos* (443), a man-slayer, "murderer from the beginning" (cf. Gen 3:19). The Lord Jesus destroyed this power by His death (Heb 2:14).

The Apostle Paul ascribed his own physical maladies to Satan's agency. He called "a thorn in the flesh" (*skólops* [4647]) "the messenger of Satan" (2 Cor 12:7). The phrase *en astheneía* (769), weakness in 2 Cor 12:9, followed by *en astheneíais* (pl.), clearly points to some bodily affliction, possibly chronic fever. Here again, Satan is made subordinate to God's purposes of grace. He becomes a servant to moral discipline which the Apostle Paul was strengthened to bear, though he prayed frequently to be delivered from it. See also 1 Cor 5:4, 5; 1 Tim 1:20. The Apostle Paul, like his contemporaries, did not think of the demons as inhabiting subterranean regions. The angels of God have their residence in the higher regions of the heavens, and even Satan and his retinue did not dwell beneath the earth (their final destination after the last judgment), but in the lower atmospheric realm. Thus in Eph 2:2 Satan is called "the prince of the power of the air" (cf. Eph 6:12, "We wrestle . . . against principalities, against powers, against the rulers of the darkness of this world, against spiritual wickedness in high places [*epouraníois* {2032}, in places above the heavens or the sky])." In Luke 10:18, Jesus states that he witnessed Satan falling (*pesónta*, aor. part. of *píptō* [4098]) from heaven. This pronouncement occurred immediately following the disciples' report that they were successful in subduing even demonic spirits. This is the beginning and an adumbration of the defeat of Satan and his kingdom by Jesus and His kingdom. The decisive blow is dealt to the devil by Jesus through His death, resurrection and session.

Beliar or Belial is also apparently identified by the Apostle Paul in 2 Cor 6:15 with Satan. Paul identifies Satan with the serpent which tempted Eve. This clearly corroborates Rom 16:20, "The God of peace shall bruise Satan under your feet," obviously based on Gen 3:15 (cf. 1 Tim 2:14; Rev 12:9; 20:2).

In the Book of Revelation we see a war carried on in heaven between God with His angels of light against Satan, or the dragon, the "old serpent," the deceiver of the whole world (Rev 12:9), and the hosts of darkness. After the last great overthrow of the beast and the kings of the earth (Rev 19), Satan is imprisoned in the bottomless pit one thousand years (Rev 20:2). (The meaning of this is widely disputed by Christian scholars. Some treat this as formally literal believing that Satan will actually be bound with some kind of restraining device at Christ's return and will remain in an abyss during a future, earthly millennial reign of Christ. Others, because of the highly symbolic nature of apocalyptic literature, feel compelled to interpret this as materially literal and suggest this scene depicts the utter defeat of Satan in his effort to hinder the gospel [and hence Christ's kingdom] from reaching all nations.) After this he is loosed and deceives the nations, but at length is finally cast into the lake of fire and brimstone where the beast and false prophet are (Rev 20:10 [cf. 2 Pet 2:4]).

In the Gospel of John and his epistles we find Satan and Christ mutually opposed. Satan cannot touch him who is born of God (1 John 5:18). The devil is the ruler of this world and has nothing in Christ (John 14:30; 16:11 [cf. 12:31]). Sin enslaves through the power of the devil (John 8:34) and this bondage is established, as John and Paul alike taught,

through the flesh which is the organic point of human attachment to the world.

Satan sinned from the beginning (1 John 3:8) and was the cause of death (John 8:44) as a predetermined consequence of disobedience set by God Himself. Falsehood is his special realm (John 8:44). Jesus stands outside the world that is ruled by Satan (John 8:23; 17:14, 16) and gradually wins individuals from him into the kingdom of God. Christ's own disciples were rescued from Satan's worldly dominion (John 15:19; 17:12, 14). Only Judas, however, abandoned himself to the devil, to his own ruin (John 6:70).

The world is at present in hostility to Jesus and His disciples (John 14:17, 19, 22; 15:18, 19; 16:8; 17:9; 1 John 2:15–17), but we are assured of Christ's final conquest of the world (John 16:33 [cf. 17:21, 23]). The Son of God was manifested for the express purpose of destroying the works of the devil (1 John 3:8). This is in harmony with Christ's own teaching respecting Satan's overthrow reported in Luke 10:18. In John 16:11 the judgment and condemnation of the devil are indicated according to the tense usage of *kékritai*, the perf. pass. indic. of *krínō* (2919), to judge, meaning he has been judged. In other words, there was a specific time in which he was condemned, and he still exists in this state of condemnation. It frequently occurs in the NT as having been already accomplished (John 12:31).

Syn.: *ho katḗgoros* (2725), the accuser; *Satanás* (4567), Satan or adversary; *apollúōn* (623), the destroyer.

1229. διαγγέλλω *diaggéllō*; fut. *diaggelṓ*, from *diá* (1223), through, and *aggéllō* (n.f., see *anaggéllō* [312]), to tell, declare. To herald thoroughly, declare, preach.

(I) To announce, declare fully or far and wide (Luke 9:60; Rom 9:17, pass.; Sept.: Ex 9:16; Ps 2:7).

(II) To declare plainly, fully, exactly (Acts 21:26; Sept.: Josh 6:10).

Syn.: *diēgéomai* (1334), to conduct a narration through to the end; *ekdiēgéomai* (1555), to narrate in full; *exēgéomai* (1834), to lead out, make known, declare; *dēlóō* (1213), to make plain, declare plainly; *phrázō* (5419), to declare by making it clear; *gnōrízō* (1107), to make known; *emphanízō* (1718), to declare plainly; *phaneróō* (5319), to manifest; *kērússō* (2784), to preach; *parrēsiázomai* (3955), to be bold in speech, to preach boldly; *laléō* (2980), to speak; *dialégomai* (1256), to give a reasoned discourse or to discuss.

Ant.: *phimóō* (5392), to muzzle, put to silence; *sigáō* (4601), to be silent; *siōpáō* (4623), to be silent or still, keep silence; *hēsucházō* (2270), to be still, silent.

1230. διαγίνομαι *diagínomai*; fut. *diagenēsomai*, 2d aor. *diegenómēn*, from the prep. *diá* (1223), through, and *gínomai* (1096), to become, to be. Of time: to be through, meaning to be past, to have elapsed, passed over (Mark 16:1; Acts 25:13; 27:9).

Syn.: *dapanáō* (1159), to expend or spend; *ekdapanáō* (1550), to spend out; *prosdapanáō* (4325), to spend besides; *prosanalískō* (4321), to expend, to spend besides, consume; *analískō* (355), to expend, consume.

Ant.: *ménō* (3306), to stay; *diaménō* (1265), to remain throughout; *perileípō* (4035), to leave over; *apoleípō* (620), to be reserved, to remain; *perisseúō* (4052), to abound, to be over and above, remain over.

1231. διαγινώσκω *diaginōskō*; fut. *diagnōsomai*, from *diá* (1223), denoting separation or emphasis, and *ginōskō* (1097), to know experientially. To discuss, examine thoroughly (Acts 23:15; 24:22; Sept.: Deut 2:7). Generally it means to perceive clearly or discriminatingly, discern, distinguish, decide, investigate in a judicial sense.

Deriv.: *diágnōsis* (1233), discernment.

Syn.: *oída* (1492), to know intuitively, to perceive; *epístamai* (1987), to understand; *suníēmi* (4920), to bring or set together, to put it together, understand; *noéō* (3539), to perceive with the mind; *punthánomai* (4441), to inquire, to understand; *gnōrízō* (1107), to make known; *manthánō* (3129), to learn; *phronéō* (5426), to mind, understand; *parakolouthéō* (3877), to follow up, to trace, have understanding; *plērophoréō* (4135), used in the pass., to be fully assured; *anagnōrízō* (319), to recognize; *diagnōrízō* (1232), to make known; *krínō* (2919), to be of an opinion, to determine; *horízō* (3724) to declare, determine, specify; *epilúō* (1956), to solve.

Ant.: *agnoéō* (50), not to know, to be ignorant; *lanthánō* (2990), to make a mistake, to be unlearned.

1232. διαγνωρίζω *diagnōrízō*; fut. *diagnōrísō*, from *diá* (1223), denoting separation, and *gnōrízō* (1107), to know. To know by distinguishing. In Luke 2:17, to make known through a district, spread abroad the tidings.

Syn.: *plērophoréō* (4135), to make fully known; *diaggéllō* (1229), to declare fully; *exaggéllō* (1804), to tell out, proclaim abroad; *diēgéomai* (1334), to relate in full; *anaggéllō* (312), to report, declare; *phaneróō* (5319), to manifest; *dēlóō* (1213), to make plain; *apaggéllō* (518), to announce, declare.

Ant.: *krúptō* (2928), to hide; *phimóō* (5392), to muzzle, put to silence; *sigáō* (4601), to be silent.

1233. διάγνωσις *diágnōsis*; gen. *diagnōseōs*, fem. noun from *diaginōskō* (1231), to know thoroughly. Discernment or distinguishing (Eng. diagnosis), only in Acts 25:21.

Syn.: *diákrisis* (1253), a distinguishing, a decision, discerning.

Ant.: *ágnoia* (52), want of knowledge or perception, ignorance; *agnōsía* (56), willful ignorance; *agnóēma* (51), a sin of ignorance, hence error.

1234. διαγογγύζω *diagoggúzō*; fut. *diagoggúsō*, from *diá* (1223), an intens., and *goggúzō* (1111), to grumble, murmur. To murmur greatly or to keep murmuring, associated with the idea of complaint, to express a grumbling attitude (Luke 15:2; 19:7; Sept.: Ex 15:24; 16:2, 8).

Syn.: *embrimáomai* (1690), to express indignant displeasure; *stenázō* (4727), to murmur.

Ant.: *ainéō* (134), to speak in praise of; *eulogéō* (2127), to bless, speak well of; *makarízō* (3106), to declare blessed; *eucharistéō* (2168), to thank.

1235. διαγρηγορέω *diagrēgoréō*; contracted *diagrēgorṓ*, fut. *diagrēgorḗsō*, from *diá* (1223), through or an intens., and *grēgoréō* (1127), to awake. To stay awake through the night or to be fully awake (Luke 9:32).

Syn.: *paratēréō* (3906), to observe, watch; *agrupnéō* (69), to be sleepless and hence watchful; *nḗphō* (3525), to abstain from alcoholic drinks and, therefore, to watch, be sober; *merimnáō* (3309), to be anxious, take thought, be careful; *mélei* (3199), the 3d person sing. of *mélō* used impersonally and meaning to be concerned; *phrontízō* (5431), to be thoughtful, careful; *epimeléomai* (1959), to take care of, exercise forethought and provision; *phronéō* (5426), to be careful, take thought; *episkopéō* (1983), to oversee; *exupnízo* (1852), to wake up, awaken.

Ant.: *amérimnos* (275), to be without anxiety or concern; *koimáomai* (2837), to sleep, fall asleep; *katheúdō* (2518), to fall asleep, lie down to rest.

1236. διάγω *diágō*; fut. *diáxō*, from *diá* (1223), through, and *ágō* (71), to lead. To lead or pass through or over. Spoken of time meaning to bring through, to pass, lead a quiet life (1 Tim 2:2; Titus 3:3).

Syn.: *záō* (2198), to live; *bióō* (980), to exist or pass one's life; *politeúomai* (4176), to live as a citizen.

Ant.: *thnḗskō* (2348), to die; *apothnḗskō* (599), to die off or out; *teleutáō* (5053),

to end one's life; *analúō* (360) to depart, die.

1237. διαδέχομαι *diadéchomai*; fut. *diadéxomai*, from *diá* (1223), denoting transition, and *déchomai* (1209), to receive. To receive by succession from another or former possessor (Acts 7:45).

Deriv.: *diádochos* (1240), a successor.

Syn.: *akolouthéō* (190), to follow, come after.

Ant.: *proēgéomai* (4285), to go on before, put before himself; *proporeúomai* (4313), to go before; *protréchō* (4390), to precede, run ahead; *proágō* (4254), to go before.

1238. διάδημα *diádēma*; gen. *diadḗmatos*, neut. noun from *diadéō* (n.f.), to bind around, which is from the prep. *diá* (1223), around, and *déō* (1210), to bind. Diadem, not a crown but a filament of silk, linen, or some such thing tied around the head as a symbol of royal dignity. Used in Rev 12:3; 13:1; 19:12; Sept.: Esth 1:11; 2:17; Isa 62:3.

Syn.: *stéphanos* (4735), crown.

1239. διαδίδωμι *diadídōmi*; fut. *diadṓsō*, from *diá* (1223) denoting transition or dispersion, and *dídōmi* (1325), to give. To deliver through, especially from hand to hand in succession, to deliver over in succession. Used trans. in Rev 17:13 (TR). To deal out, divide out, distribute, used trans. or in an absolute sense in Luke 11:22; 18:22; John 6:11; Acts 4:35.

Syn.: with the meaning of give: *paréchō* (3930), to provide; *dōréō* and particularly in the mid. voice, *dōréomai* (1433), to grant; *aponémō* (632), to assign or apportion; *légō* (3004), to give out. With the meaning of distribute: *merízō* (3307), to apportion; *koinōnéō* (2841), to have in common; *diairéō* (1244), to divide into parts; *diamerízō* (1266), to divide up.

Ant.: with the meaning of to deliver: *tēréō* (5083), to preserve, keep; *diatēréō* (1301), to keep carefully; *phulássō* (5442), to guard, keep; *diaphulássō* (1314), to guard thoroughly; *kratéō* (2902), to hold; *nosphízō* (3557), to keep back.

1240. διάδοχος *diádochos*; gen. *diádochou*, masc., fem. noun from *diadéchomai* (1237), to succeed, follow after. A successor in Acts 24:27.

Syn.: *hústeros* (5306), latter; *opísō* (3694), one who follows.

Ant.: *próteros* (4387), former; *palaiós* (3820), old one; *proēgoúmenos* (4285), one coming before; *proporeuómenos* (4313), one preceding; *protréchōn* (4390), one running before; *pródromos* (4274), forerunner; *prógonos* (4269), ancestor.

1241. διαζώννυμι *diazṓnnumi*; fut. *diazṓsō*, from *diá* (1223), about, and *zṓnnumi* (2224), to gird. To gird about or around, meaning firmly. Used trans. in John 13:4. With the mid. meaning to gird anything around oneself (John 21:7; Sept.: Ezek 23:15) used in reference to the flowing robes of Orientals. In the aor. pass. with mid. meaning in John 13:5.

Syn.: *peribállō* (4016), to enwrap in clothing; *endúō* (1746), to clothe.

Ant.: *apolúō* (630), to loose from oneself; *lúō* (3089), to loose, put off; *apekdúomai* (554), to put off; *ekdúō* (1562), to take off from; *apobállō* (577), to put off.

1242. διαθήκη *diathḗkē*; gen. *diathḗkēs*, fem. noun from *diatíthēmi* (1303), to set out in order, to dispose in a certain order. Testament, covenant. In Class. Gr. it always meant the disposition which a person makes of his property in prospect of death, i.e., his testament, and used either in the sing. or pl. See discussion which follows. The pl. also means the testamentary arrangements of a person.

(I) A solemn disposition, institution, or apportionment of God to man (Heb 9:16–18) to which our word "dispensation" answers adequately, e.g., for the religious dispensation or institution which God appointed to Abraham and the patriarchs (Acts 3:25); the dispensation from Sinai (Heb 8:9); the dispensation of faith and free justification of which Christ is the mediator (Heb 7:22; 8:6) and which is called "new [*kainḗ*, {2537}, qualitatively new]" in that it is a dispensation of faith in respect to the old, the old being the Sinaitic one related to the Law (2 Cor 3:6; Heb 8:8, 10; 9:15).

On the other hand, the old dispensation is called *palaiá diathḗkē* (*palaiá* [3820]) and should be distinguished from *archaía* (744), initial, first, old which is related to *archḗ* (746) referring to the beginning. *Palaiá*, which relates to the OT, is not the original testament and dispensation of God but is simply the old contrasted to the new and refers to the dispensation contained in the books of Moses (2 Cor 3:14).

(II) A covenant, but not in the sense that God came to an agreement or compromise with fallen man as if signing a contract. Rather, it involves the declaration of God's unconditional promise to make Abraham and his seed the recipients of certain blessings (Gen 13:14–17; 15:18; 17:7–8, 19–21; 21:12, 14; 22:2, 12). God is bringing about His prearranged disposition in regard to Israel in spite of the fact that Israel has not yet believed in the Messiah. The Sinaitic *diathḗkē* to Moses, however, was a conditional dispensation or series of promises (Ex 19:5–8, 20–23; Heb 12:18–21) which God made for the Jews only if they obeyed. In the NT, God provided His Son in the execution of His plan and dispensation but not as a result of the obedience to any rule that He preset. However, the giving of eternal life to individuals depends on their acceptance of that sacrifice of the Son of God.

(III) A divine promise conditioned on obedience, a solemn disposition or appointment of man and God's covenants with men (Luke 1:72; 22:20; Acts 7:8; Rom 9:4; 11:27; Gal 3:17; 4:24; Eph 2:12; Heb 9:4; 10:16; Rev 11:19). The term "the covenant of the new testament" may be understood as referring personally to Christ (Matt 26:28; Mark 14:24; Luke 22:20; 1 Cor 11:25; 2 Cor 3:6; Heb 10:29; 12:24; 13:20). This testament is called "new [kainḗ, {2537}, qualitatively new]" (Heb 9:15), equivalent to "the second" (Heb 8:7), or "the better one" (Heb 7:22). The same meaning would pertain to the blood of His covenant which would be the blood of His promise, the blood of Christ (i.e., His sacrificial death) (Heb 9:20; 10:29).

(IV) Will. There is ample evidence in the papyri that this is the ordinary meaning in the NT. To the Apostle Paul the word meant the same as the Gr. word in the Sept., i.e., a unilateral enactment, in particular a will or testament. The corresponding Hebr. word, bᵉrîth (1285, OT), is always rendered "covenant." In some instances, e.g., 1 Sam 18:3; 23:18; 1 Kgs 20:34, the word indisputably meant covenant in the full sense, i.e., a mutual relationship between two parties. In others, the idea of the mutual relationship is wanting, as in 1 Sam 11:1. However, the idea of setting up a relationship, which may be done by the free act or choice of one person, is always present. It is in this latter sense that we understand the divine bᵉrîth or covenant. This is a divine order or agreement which is established without any human cooperation and springing from the choice of God Himself whose will and determination account for both its origin and its character. The word "covenant," however, in its Eng. meaning gives to the word a possible misunderstanding. In the Eng. language we do not possess a word which exactly conveys the meaning of the divine *berith*. Why did the Sept. choose and adhere to the Gr. word *diathḗkē* as the rendering of bᵉrîth? It is because the Gr. word *diathḗkē* had the meaning of will or testament. It is claimed that there is only one instance of its use in the sense of covenant in the whole of Gr. literature, namely in Aristophanes. In the early part of the third century B.C., no better word was available to express the OT idea of a solemn and irrevocable disposition made by God Himself of His own gracious choice and meant to secure a religious inheritance to His chosen people.

The meaning of bᵉrîth, referring for the most part to a solemn promise or undertaking by God, is that which is unilateral. The dilemma that we face in the NT with the meaning of the word *diathḗkē* is the determination of whether the word refers to the unilateral disposition of God toward man as a symbol of His grace or to any other meaning. The only way to determine this is to examine the passages in the NT which bring out the various meanings of the word.

Heb 9:16–18 is the first passage. The word *diathḗkē* occurs once each in verses sixteen and seventeen, and it is implied but not explicitly stated in verse eighteen. Also the part. *diatheménou* in verse sixteen and *diathémenos* in verse seventeen, translated "testator," do occur. Both of these part. are in the 2d aor. mid. referring to the one who makes the will. The one who makes the will does not ask the recipient of the will whether it is acceptable or not. It is a unilateral demonstration of the will of the testator. The KJV translates the words as "testament" and "testator," while the NASB translates the noun and the part. as "covenant" and "the one who made it." The NIV translates the words "a will" and "the one who made it." In verse eighteen, however, the translators insert the word "covenant" without italicizing it, but in reality the word is not there in the Gr. at all. It is a mere presumption that the word implied in verse eighteen is different than the word *diathḗkē* explicitly translated "a will." Undoubtedly in verse seventeen the word *diathḗkē* refers to a human will, which becomes a document of value only when the one who prepared it dies. No will is of any value while the one who made it is still alive. The most lucid translation of verse seventeen is that of the NIV: "Because a will [an ordinary will as we know it today and as they knew it then] is in force only when somebody has died; it never takes effect while the one who made it is living." The question that confronts us is whether the prior usage of the word in verse sixteen means the same as in verse seventeen or has a different meaning. Our conclusion is that it means the same thing as in verse seventeen and should be translated in the manner that the NIV translates it: "In case of a will, it is necessary to prove the death of the one who made it." The effort of the Apostle here is to prove that we do not have a bilateral agreement through the word *diathḗkē*, but the expression of the disposition of God toward humanity. Verse eighteen must also imply the same word with the same meaning as a will made by God for the benefit of man. It is unfortunate that the NIV reverts to the word "covenant" which could be misunderstood as a bilateral agreement between God and man in verse eighteen. The NIV should have retained the same translation or no translation at all since the word does not even occur. Thus it would have read, "This is why even the first will was not put into effect without blood" (a.t.).

We are not going to fully comment on the word *egkekaínistai* translated "was not put into effect" except to say that this is the form in which the TR, the UBS, and the Majority Text have it. It is the perf. pass. of the verb *egkainízō* (1457), to renew qualitatively, found only in Heb 9:18; 10:20 meaning to make qualitatively new or to initiate its qualitatively different effect or to innovate or begin its operation. From Heb 10:20 it is evident that this refers to the qualitatively new way initiated through the sacrifice of Jesus Christ at which time the veil in the temple which stood as a barrier to the most holy place was rent in twain from above downward. This indicated that this was a new way of approach to God which He willed for man. It came down from God to man, not upward from man to God. This, however, only became effective at the sacrifice of the Lord Jesus Christ which was the death of the Testator. This is another implicit proof of the deity of Jesus Christ in His providing the death of the Testator. The fact that the word *egkekaínistai* is in the perf. pass. indicates that there was a historical start for this effective testament that God made for man. This beginning

was at the time when the Lord Jesus died on the cross. However, it affects those who believe at any time in the history of the world. This was entirely an act of God. Everyone in the OT who was saved as was Abraham, was saved in the prospect of that sacrifice of the Testator (John 8:56). The eternal God brought Himself in the person of His Son into the world of time and space to die within history so that His covenant of grace might apply to all who believe, regardless of when they lived. This death of the Testator, the Lord Jesus Christ, was foreshadowed even at the time when the first testament or will was given, which, as the whole argument of the epistle shows, looked forward to His perfect sacrifice. This Testator was a distinct personality from God the Father (John 1:1b), yet He as the Word was God (John 1:1c).

The question now arises as to why the Testator, Jesus Christ, is called the mediator of the new (*kainḗs* [2537], qualitatively new) will, or *diathḗkē*. We must make clear that the word is the same in Heb 9:15. It should be understood as having the same meaning as in verses sixteen through eighteen, namely a will or that document which one prepares unilaterally and which becomes effective at the death of the one who makes it, what we today understand as a last will and testament. If the word here is translated "covenant," it may give the misunderstanding that it is a bilateral agreement, while it is in fact a unilateral expression of God's desire and disposition for man. It is not a *sunthḗkē*, a bilateral agreement, a covenant, but it is a *diathḗkē*, a will, testament. The KJV translates Heb 9:15 as follows: "And for this cause he is the mediator of the new testament [better than the NIV which states a new covenant], that by means of death, for the redemption of the transgressions that were under the first testament [the word is the same here, *diathḗkē*], they which are called might receive the promise of eternal inheritance."

The question is, how can the testator be also the mediator? Does a will require a mediator? The word *mesítēs* (3316), mediator, does not always mean the one that stands between two parties and is accepted by both parties, but as in Heb 7:22 Jesus is called the "surety [*égguos* {1450}]," or a guarantee. In the NASB and NIV it is translated "of a better covenant" in the sense that He is called the mediator of the new (*kainés*) and better covenant (*kreíttonos* [2909]). God expressed His will toward man by making known His disposition and plan of redemption for man. In order that this promise of God might be guaranteed, He offered Jesus Christ as that guarantee. Right from the beginning in the first gospel declaration in Gen 3:15, God pledged Jesus Christ as the guarantee for the effectiveness of what He promised. For the understanding of the word "mediator" in that sense, we go to the use of the verbal form *mesiteúō* in Heb 6:17: "Wherein God, willing more abundantly to show unto the heirs of promise [*epaggelías* {1860}, which is here equivalent to *diathḗkē*, a promise that has a guaranteed fulfillment in its expression] the immutability [*ametátheton* {276}, the unchangeableness] of his counsel, confirmed it by an oath." Jesus Christ, in other words, is the confirmation of the veracity and the effectiveness of the promise or the will or testament of God. God gave His promise directly to Abraham and placed Jesus Christ as the guarantee of that promise before He, actually being the Word, became flesh (John 1:1, 14).

The same meaning of a unilateral will or testament should also be ascribed to Heb 9:20; 10:29; 13:20 as also in Heb 7:22; 12:24. The references in Heb 8:6ff., being mostly quotations from Jer 31:31–34, use the word *diathḗkē*. It is sometimes used as the unconditional promise of God to Israel and sometimes as God's dealing with them if they did not obey the conditions that His testament indicated for a corresponding fulfillment of His promises.

We need also to examine Paul's treatment of the word in Gal 3:15–17. Here the Apostle Paul declares that he is about to speak "after the manner of men" (Gal 3:15). By this he means that he is going to use the word *diathḗkē* (vv. 15, 17) as ordinary people understand it and not in the bilateral concept as a covenant. It is interesting that the word *epaggelía* (1860), promise, in the sing. and pl., is used three times in verses sixteen through eighteen. It is used as syn. with the human understanding of testament as a will left by a testator. This testament belongs to Abraham and to his seed. It comes by way of a gift and invests those taking part in it with the rights of inheritance. The testator designates his heir and arranges that at a predetermined time he shall receive the specified promise (Gal 4:2). The word "will" or "testament" to the Apostle Paul suggested a human document which no one could set aside; how much more, therefore, must God's testament remain unalterable (Gal 3:15).

In Rom 9:4; Eph 2:12 the idea of "will" seems most probable. In these verses, the use of the pl. of *diathḗkē* to express the sing., meaning "will," is equivalent to promises and is very frequent in Gr., referring to either the different provisions or the will as a whole. It is quite possible, however, that the Apostle is thinking of the oft-renewed promises made to the fathers.

In Gal 4:24 the word is used twice. Once it is applied to the *diathḗkē* of promise given to Abraham and fulfilled through Christ, and once to the *diathḗkē* of God's conditional promise made at Sinai.

The Law of Moses, which in Gal 3:19 appeared only as a supplement to the testament of promise, delaying its operation but not cancelling it, is here spoken of as an inferior testament. In essence, Paul was saying, "If you insist that it is a testament and choose to come under its provisions, it will bring you an inheritance of slavery."

When our Lord, as recorded and reported by the Apostle Paul in 1 Cor 11:25, said, "This cup is the new testament in my blood," the word was used as will or promise. It was the fulfillment of His promise. Our Lord here was almost in the very presence of death and, in view of that death which activated the will or the promise, vividly promised to His disciples a share in His inheritance (Luke 22:29). It is only as we understand 1 Cor 11:25 that we can understand 2 Cor 3:6, 14. These verses indicate the willful ignorance of the Jews toward the messianic work of Christ.

Acts 3:25 refers to Abraham and to the inheritance that he and his seed would receive.

In Acts 7:8 the word *diathékē* stands for the seal which accompanied the establishment of the new relationship.

1243. διαίρεσις *diaíresis*; gen. *diairéseōs*, fem. noun from *diairéō* (1244), to divide. Division, distribution, classification or separation. Used only in 1 Cor 12:4–6 in regard to the gifts, services and results of energies or operations. Apportionments or distributions in a pass. sense. Here the Apostle does not merely mean the Spirit bestows different gifts, but bestows certain gifts to certain people, not the same to all. The possessors of these gifts are exhorted to a mutual communication and fellowship (Sept.: 2 Chr 8:14; Ezra 6:18).

Syn.: *diastolé* (1293), a setting asunder, distinction; *merismós* (3311), division, partition, distribution.

Ant.: *episunagōgé* (1997), a gathering together; *logía* (3048), collection, gathering.

1244. διαιρέω *diairéō*; contracted *diairṓ*, fut. *diairḗsō*, from *diá* (1223), through or denoting separation, and *hairéō* (138), to take, grasp, seize. To take from, divide, partition, apportion, assign. In the NT, it means to distribute among (Luke 15:12; 1 Cor 12:11; Sept.: Josh 18:5; 1 Chr 23:6).

Deriv.: *diaíresis* (1243), diversity.

Syn.: *aphorízō* (873), to mark off by boundaries, separate, divide; *apodiorízō* (592), to mark off, make separations or divisions; *diadídōmi* (1239), to deal out, distribute; *diakrínō* (1252), to separate, discriminate; *merízō* (3307), to divide

into; *diamerízō* (1266), to divide up; *kataklērodotéō* (2624), to distribute lots; *chōrízō* (5563), to separate; *apochōrízō* (673), to separate, tear apart; *schízō* (4977), to split or sever.

Ant.: *sunéchō* (4912), to hold together.

1245. διακαθαρίζω *diakatharízō*; fut. *diakathariṓ*, from *diá* (1223), an intens., and *katharízō* (2511), to cleanse. To cleanse thoroughly or throughout. Used trans. in Matt 3:12; Luke 3:17, to cleanse the threshing floor.

Syn.: *hagnízō* (48), to purify, cleanse, spoken of ceremonially as cleansing and metaphorically referring to moral cleansing.

Ant.: *koinóō* (2840), to defile; *miaínō* (3392), to stain, pollute, usually used of ceremonial or moral defilement; *molúnō* (3435), to besmear, defile, but not of ceremonial defilement; *spilóō* (4695), to make a stain or spot, defile.

1246. διακατελέγχομαι *diakatelégchomai*; fut. *diakatelégxomai*, from *diá* (1223), an intens., and *katelégchō* (n.f.), to dispute, which is from *katá* (2596), against, and *elégchō* (1651), to convict. To overcome thoroughly in disputation (Acts 18:28).

Syn.: *epitimáō* (2008), to rebuke; *epiplḗssō* (1969), to strike at, to rebuke; *mōmáomai* (3469), to find fault with; *mémphomai* (3201), to find fault; *kataginṓskō* (2607), to condemn.

Ant.: *ainéō* (134), to speak in praise of; *epainéō* (1867), to commend; *humnéō* (5214), to praise; *eulogéō* (2127), to bless, speak well of.

1247. διακονέω *diakonéō*; contracted *diakonṓ*, fut. *diakonḗsō*, aor. *diēkónēsa*, from *diákonos* (1249), servant, deacon. To serve, wait upon, with emphasis on the work to be done and not on the relationship between lord and servant. In *doúlos* (1401), slave, the work is involuntary, and also to a lesser degree in *hupērétēs* (5257), servant, one working under a superior in contrast to the voluntary service of *therápōn* (2324), attendant.

(I) In its narrowest sense, *diakonéō* means to serve by waiting on a table, serving a dinner (Matt 8:15; 20:28; 27:55; Mark 1:31; 10:45; 15:41; Luke 4:39; 10:40; 12:37; 17:8; 22:26, 27; John 12:2). With the dat. alone in Acts 6:2, "to serve money tables" (a.t.), i.e., to have charge of the alms and other pecuniary matters.

(II) Generally it means to do anyone a service, care for someone's needs (Matt 4:11; 25:44; Mark 1:13; Luke 8:3), and is an inferred service rendered, bringing advantage to others, to help. One may work, *douleúō* (1398), and not help anybody, but when *diakonéō* is used, then helping someone directly is involved (Luke 22:27, John 12:26; Acts 19:22; 1 Tim 3:10, 13; Phile 1:13).

(III) Used also of the alms collected by the churches, the distribution of alms (Rom 15:25; Heb 6:10; 1 Pet 4:11). Such alms were called *cháris* (5485), literally grace, meaning to administer, distribute (2 Cor 8:19, 20).

(IV) In the sense of being the attendant or assistant of anyone as Timothy and Erastos were said to be ministering to Paul (Acts 19:22). Those in the early church who fulfilled the duties of the office of a deacon (*diákonos*) were those who served being in charge of the poor and the sick (1 Tim 3:10, 13).

(V) Of things, followed by the acc. of manner and the dat. expressed or implied. Spoken of prophets who minister, i.e., announce, deliver the divine will (1 Pet 1:12). Also in the pass. with the meaning of to minister anything to anyone, to administer, provide (2 Cor 3:3, "ministered by us," meaning written by our aid or ministry; 2 Tim 1:18). By implication to minister to one's wants (1 Pet 4:10).

Syn.: *leitourgéō* (3008), to render public service; *hupēretéō* (5256), to toil, render service; *therapeúō* (2323), to wait upon menially, relieve, cure; *hierourgéō* (2418), to minister in priestly service; *ergázomai* (2038), to work; *prosedreúō* (4332), to attend as a servant; *proskarteréō*

(4342), to serve in a close personal relationship.

Ant.: *bláptō* (984), to harm; *zēmióō* (2210), to cause loss; *katastréphō* (2690), to destroy; *anatrépō* (396), to turn upside down, upset, overthrow; *phtheírō* (5351), to corrupt.

1248. διακονία *diakonía*; gen. *diakonías*, fem. noun from *diákonos* (1249), deacon, servant. Service, attendance, ministry. Verb, *diakonéō* (1247), to minister, serve.

(I) Service towards a master or guest, at table or in hospitality (Luke 10:40; 1 Cor 16:15).

(II) Ministry, ministration, i.e., the office of ministering in divine things, spoken chiefly of apostles and teachers (Acts 1:17, 25; 6:4; 20:24; 21:19; Rom 11:13; 1 Cor 12:5; 2 Cor 3:7–9; 4:1; 5:18; 6:3; Eph 4:12; Col 4:17; 1 Tim 1:12; 2 Tim 4:5, 11). Used once of the office of a *diákonos* (1249), deacon (Rom 12:7). Some, however, take this to have a wider sense as above.

(III) In the sense of aid meaning relief as spoken of alms, contributions (Acts 11:29; Rom 15:31 [see Rom 15:26]; 2 Cor 8:4; 9:1, 13; 11:8; Rev 2:19). Spoken of the distribution or ministration of alms collected (Acts 6:1; 12:25, see 11:30; 2 Cor 9:12). *Diakonía* involves compassionate love towards the needy within the Christian community (Acts 6:1, 4; 2 Cor 8:4; 9:12, 13; Rev 2:19). Every business, every calling, so far as its labor benefits others, is a *diakonía*. In this sense Paul and Luke in the Acts use the word to designate the vocation of those who preach the gospel and have the care of the churches (Acts 20:24; Rom 11:13; 1 Cor 12:5; Col 4:17; 1 Tim 1:12; 2 Tim 4:5). Therefore, *diakonía* is an office or ministration in the Christian community viewed with reference to the labor needed for others, both in the case of individuals (1 Cor 12:5), and generally as a total concept including all branches of service (Rom 12:7; 2 Cor 4:1; 6:3; Eph 4:12; 1 Tim 1:12).

Syn.: ōphéleia (5622), advantage, profit; euergesía (2108), benevolence; chrēstótēs (5544), usefulness, kindness; sumphéron (4851), profit, expedience; therapeía (2322), attendance, service or healing with tenderness; leitourgía (3009), a sacred or priestly ministration; latreía (2999), primarily hired service; episkopé (1984), inspection, the office of a bishop, visitation; episústasis (1999), responsibility for oversight based upon authority; prónoia (4307), forethought, provision, providence; epiméleia (1958), kind attention, care.

Ant.: zēmía (2209), loss; kópos (2873), toil; phthorá (5356), corruption, ruin; katastrophḗ (2692), catastrophe, overthrow.

1249. διάκονος diákonos; gen. diakónou, masc., fem. noun. A minister, servant, deacon. The derivation is uncertain. According to some it comes from diakónis, in the dust laboring, or running through dust. Others derive it from diákō, the same as diékō, to hasten, related to diókō, to pursue.

Also used in the NT as a technical term side by side with epískopos (1985), bishop or overseer (1 Tim 3:8, 12; Phil 1:1). The deacons in this sense were helping or serving the bishops or elders, and this is why they were probably called deacons. They did not, though, possess any ruling authority as did the elders. Tychicus was called a deacon in his relation to Paul (Eph 6:21; Col 4:7 [cf. Acts 19:22]). The origin of this relationship is likely found in Acts 6:1–4. Stephen and Philip were deacons and were first chosen as distributors of alms and other forms of aid, but soon appeared alongside the Apostles and as their helpers and as evangelists (Acts 6:8–10; 8:5–8). The care of the churches fell upon the deacons as the helpers of the elders who held distinct offices.

The only passage in which special officials of the church are mentioned is 1 Tim 3:8–12. In verse eight it speaks of diakónous which undoubtedly refers to male deacons because the adjectives that are used in the verse such as semnoús (4586), grave, are in the masc. pl. and not in the fem. In verse eleven the KJV gives an interpretation and not a translation when it says, "Even so must their wives be grave." The Gr. says, "women likewise grave" (a.t.). The NIV also has that translation. The NASB has the preferred translation, "Women [must] likewise [be] dignified [or grave]." It is impossible to determine whether the Apostle Paul is speaking of women in general in verse eleven or the wives of the deacons.

The only possible reference to a woman as a deacon is Rom 16:1, 2, although the word diákonon may just as well be translated "servant." In this regard we must note that the story of the early church significantly begins with the inclusion of women in the apostolic meetings for prayer (Acts 1:14). Their presence and activity are clearly illustrated by the references to Tabitha (Acts 9:36), Mary the mother of John Mark (Acts 12:12), Lydia (Acts 16:14), Damaris (Acts 17:34), and Priscilla (Acts 18:2). The story of Sapphira (Acts 5:7f.) implies the comparatively independent membership and responsibility of women within the Christian community. Priscilla illustrates their active evangelism (Acts 18:26). Attention is expressly called to the "multitudes" of women converts added to the church (Acts 5:14). In Phil 4:2, 3, Euodias and Syntyche (both women) are spoken of as fellow laborers of the Apostle Paul, and in 1 Cor 1:11 Chloe is mentioned as having reported to Paul the condition of the church at Corinth. In Rom 16:1–3, 6, 12, 13, 15 we have numerous salutations to women. Nevertheless, aside from the normal and expected involvement of women in a wide range of church activities and auxiliary ministries, they are never found to be holding ordained offices or engaging in the work of those positions.

In 1 Cor 14:34 Paul forbids women to speak in the churches, but that must be taken in the context in which it was spoken which refers to speaking in unknown tongues in the sense of the Corinthian practice. It is in such a context that it must be considered in view of the fact that the prophesying of the four daughters of Philip the evangelist are also mentioned in Acts 21:9. That women served as deaconesses of local churches is inconclusive. See *gunế* (1135), woman; *didáskō* (1321), to teach.

Deriv.: *diakonéō* (1247), to minister, adjust, regulate, set in order; *diakonía* (1248), ministry, service.

Syn.: *doúlos* (1401), a slave; *therápōn* (2324), attendant; *hupērétēs* (5257), servant; *leitourgós* (3011), a public servant, usually one serving at the temple or one who performs religious public duties; *místhios* (3407) and *misthōtós* (3411), a hired servant; *oikétēs* (3610), a household servant; *país* (3816), basically a child, but it also an attendant; *epískopos* (1985), a bishop, supervisor, one who serves as a leader in a church.

Ant.: *kúrios* (2962), lord; *despótēs* (1203), despot, absolute ruler; *oikodespótēs* (3617), master of the house; *árchōn* (758), ruler, magistrate; *pantokrátōr* (3841), almighty; *hēgemốn* (2232), governor, ruler; *kaísar* (2541), caesar, emperor.

1250. διακόσιοι *diakósioi*; fem. *diakósiai*, neut. *diakósia*, cardinal number from *dís* (1364), twice, and *hekatón* (1540), a hundred. Two hundred (Mark 6:37; John 6:7; 21:8; Acts 23:23; 27:37; Rev 11:3; 12:6).

1251. διακούω *diakoúō*; fut. *diakoúsomai*, from *diá* (1223), an intens., and *akoúō* (191), to hear. To hear thoroughly or fully in a judicial sense, to provide a legal hearing. Used with the gen. in Acts 23:35; Sept.: Deut 1:16

Syn.: *enōtízomai* (1801), to listen, hearken; *epakoúō* (1873), to hearken.

Ant.: *parakoúō* (3878), to mishear, disobey; *kataphronéō* (2706), despise; *agnoéō* (50), to ignore.

1252. διακρίνω *diakrínō*; fut. *diakrinố*, from *diá* (1223), denoting separation, and *krínō* (2919), to distinguish, decide, judge.

To separate throughout, completely, used trans. In the mid., to separate oneself. Particularly, to separate oneself from.

(I) "And on some [i.e., those not Christians] have compassion, making a difference [*diakrinómenoi*]" (a.t. [Jude 1:22 {TR}]), exercise discernment.

(II) If we take the verb in the part. nom. 1st person pl., *diakrinómenoi* (TR, Majority Text), it refers to those exercising mercy, that they should be discreet and discriminating with those whom they help. If the word is in the part. acc. 3d person pl., *diakrinoménous*, then it refers to those on whom Christians show mercy, that they should be those who are needy. The context makes *diakrinómenoi* a preferable reading.

(III) By implication, to distinguish, make a distinction, cause to differ (Acts 15:9; 1 Cor 11:29, "not distinguishing the body of the Lord" [a.t.] from common food). In the mid. in James 2:4, "Do you not then make a distinction in yourselves?" (a.t.), i.e., are you not partial? (see V). With the idea of preference or prerogative (1 Cor 4:7 "who then distinguishes you" [a.t.], or makes you different?). Figuratively it means to distinguish, discern clearly, note accurately (Matt 16:3; 1 Cor 11:31, "if we took a proper view" [a.t.], or formed a just estimate of ourselves; 14:29, equivalent to *dokimázō* [1381], to examine; 1 John 4:1; Sept.: Job 12:11).

(IV) In the sense of to consider accurately, judge, decide (1 Cor 6:5; Sept.: Ex 18:16; 1 Kgs 3:9; Ps 50:4; Prov 31:9).

(V) In the mid. *diakrínomai*, aor. pass. *diekríthēn* with mid. meaning. To separate oneself from, i.e., to contend with. In the NT used metaphorically.

(A) To contend or strive with, dispute with, followed by a dat. (Jude 1:9). Followed by *prós* (4314), toward, with the acc. (Acts 11:2). In the Sept. followed by the dat. (Jer 15:10); followed by *prós*, to (Ezek 20:35).

(B) To be in strife with oneself, i.e., to doubt, hesitate, waver (Matt 21:21; Mark 11:23; Rom 4:20; 14:23; James 1:6; 2:4 without taking it as a question, "and if you do this without hesitation" [cf. II]). In Acts 10:20 *mēdén* (3367), nothing, *diakrinómenos*, the pres. mid. part. meaning without hesitation, confidently, also Acts 11:12.

Deriv.: *adiákritos* (87), undistinguished, without partiality; *diákrisis* (1253), a distinguishing.

Syn.: *epagōnízomai* (1864), to contend; *diaginōskō* (1231), to distinguish, judge; *diaphérō* (1308), to be different from or superior to; *dokimázō* (1381), to test, prove; *aporéō* (639), to be in doubt, perplexity; *diaporéomai* (1280), to be in utter perplexity; *distázō* (1365), to hesitate, to stand at a crossroad with uncertainty as to which way to take; *meteōrízō* (3349), to be in midair like a meteor; *apostréphomai* (654), to withdraw; *apōthéomai* (683), to thrust oneself away; *lúō* (3089), to loose.

Ant.: *apatáō* (538), to beguile, deceive; *exapatáō* (1818), to deceive thoroughly; *dolóō* (1389), to ensnare; *planáō* (4105), to cause to go astray; *paralogízomai* (3884), to think wrongly.

1253. διάκρισις *diákrisis*; gen. *diakríseōs*, fem. noun from *diakrínō* (1252), to distinguish, decide, judge. A distinguishing, discerning clearly, i.e., spoken of the act or power (1 Cor 12:10; Heb 5:14). By implication Rom 14:1, literally meaning not for scrutinizing of thoughts, i.e., not with searching out and pronouncing judgment on their opinions (cf. Rom 14:5, 13). This also could be rendered as doubts, scruples.

Syn.: *diágnōsis* (1233), diagnosis, judgment, thorough understanding; *gnōmē* (1106), opinion.

Ant.: *apátē* (539), deceit; *plánē* (4106), delusion, error; *agnóēma* (51), ignorance.

1254. διακωλύω *diakōlúō*; fut. *diakōlúsō*, from *diá* (1223), an intens., and *kōlúō* (2967), to hinder. To hinder throughout, i.e., to impede or forbid utterly; trans. in Matt 3:14, spoken in the imperf. of a continued action.

Syn.: *egkóptō* (1465), to cut into, to impede, hinder; *kolobóō* (2856), to abridge,

shorten; *phrássō* (5420), to block up, stop; *anakóptō* (348), to check, hinder; *anastréphō* (390), to overthrow; *sunéchō* (4912), to constrain; *mataióō* (3154), to bring to nothing; *desmeúō* (1195), to bind; *déō* (1210), to bind, tie.

Ant.: *antilambánō* (482), to help support; *boēthéō* (997), to come to the aid of anyone; *sunergéō* (4903), to cooperate; *parístēmi* (3936), to stand by for help; *antéchomai* (472), to support.

1255. διαλαλέω *dialaléō*; contracted *dialalō*, fut. *dialalēsō*, from *diá* (1223), denoting dispersion or transition, and *laléō* (2980), to speak. To talk, converse (Luke 6:11, meaning they communed, consulted). To announce everywhere or tell abroad, divulge. Used trans. and in a pass. construction in Luke 1:65.

Syn.: *diaphēmízō* (1310), to advertise, spread abroad; *phaneróō* (5319), to manifest; *plērophoréō* (4135), to make fully known; *dēlóō* (1213), to declare; *apokalúptō* (601), to reveal; *diasaphéō* (1285), to declare.

Ant.: *paríēmi* (3935), to let by; *parérchomai* (3928), to go by; *kalúptō* (2572), to cover up; *sugkalúptō* (4780), to conceal altogether; *siōpáō* (4623), to keep silent; *sigáō* (4601), to keep secret; *apokrúptō* (613), to hide.

1256. διαλέγομαι *dialégomai*; fut. *dialéxomai*, aor. pass. *dieléchthēn* with mid. meaning, mid. deponent from *diá* (1223), denoting transition or separation, and *légō* (3004), to speak. To speak back and forth or alternately, to converse with, reason, present intelligent discourse.

(I) Of an argument meaning to dispute, discuss. Used intrans. followed by the dat. as in Jude 1:9 with the prep. *prós* (4314), toward or with, and the acc. *allélous* (240), each other (Mark 9:34 [see Mark 9:33]; Sept: Isa 1:18; Judg 8:1).

(II) To teach publicly, discourse, present intelligent arguments, akin to *lógos* (3056), intelligence, word, to discuss or argue, used intrans. and in an absolute sense (Acts 18:4; 19:8, 9; 20:9; 24:25);

followed by a dat. (Acts 17:2, 17; 18:19; 20:7); followed by *prós* (4314), toward, with the acc. (Acts 24:12; Sept.: Ex 6:27; Isa 63:1). Figuratively of an exhortation meaning to address, to speak to, followed by a dat. (Heb 12:5).

Deriv.: *diálektos* (1258), language, tongue.

Syn.: *suzētéō* (4802), to discuss; *apologéomai* (626), to make a verbal defense; *homiléō* (3656), to speak, talk; *laléō* (2980), to talk.

Ant.: *siōpáō* (4623), to keep silent; *sigáō* (4601), to keep silent.

1257. διαλείπω *dialeípō*; fut. *dialeípsō*, from *diá* (1223), between, and *leípō* (3007), to leave. To intermit, desist, cease, leave an interval whether of space or time (Luke 7:45, "she has not ceased kissing my feet" [a.t.]; Sept.: Jer 17:8; 44:18).

Deriv.: *adiáleiptos* (88), unceasing, continual.

Syn.: *paúō* (3973), to stop, make an end, rest; *hēsucházō* (2270), to be quiet, still, at rest; *kopázō* (2869), to stop raging; *aphíēmi* (863), to let go; *katapaúō* (2664), to rest, cease.

Ant.: *ménō* (3306), abide; *diaménō* (1265), to continue throughout without interruption; *emménō* (1696), to abide in, continue; *epiménō* (1961), to remain on, abide; *paraménō* (3887), to remain by or near, abide; *proskarteréō* (4342), to endure in; *parateínō* (3905), to extend, stretch.

1258. διάλεκτος *diálektos*; gen. *dialéktou*, fem. noun from *dialégomai* (1256), to dispute, discourse, reason. Language spoken by a people or province, ethnic language, dialect, or a peculiar idiom (Acts 1:19; 2:6, 8; 21:40; 22:2; 26:14). It is apparent that the word in Acts 2:6, 8 is syn. with *glōssais* (1100, pl.), tongues or languages in Acts 2:11 (cf. Acts 2:4 where it definitely means language).

1259. διαλλάσσομαι *diallássomai*, **διαλλάττομαι** *dialláttomai*; fut. *dialláxō*, from *diá* (1223), denoting transition,

and *allássō* (236), to change. To change one's own feelings towards, to reconcile oneself, become reconciled. In the mid. voice, *diallássomai* or *dialáttomai*, to be reconciled, only in Matt 5:24. Applies to a quarrel in which the fault may be two-sided or one-sided. The context must show which side the active enmity is on. *Katallássō* (2644) is more frequent in later Gr. and differs from *diallássō* (act.) only in that in the same construction the acc. may denote either of the parties.

Syn.: *eirēnopoiéō* (1517), to cause a state of peace or reconciliation between two persons.

Ant.: *diḯstēmi* (1339), to stand apart, be parted; *erízō* (2051), to wrangle, strive; *diaphérō* (1308), to differ.

1260. διαλογίζομαι *dialogízomai*; fut. *dialogísomai*, from *diá* (1223), an intens., and *logízomai* (3049), to reckon, reason. To reckon through, to settle an account. In the NT to consider, reason, discourse, whether in silence by oneself (Matt 21:25; Mark 2:6, 8; Luke 1:29; 3:15; 5:21, 22; 12:17; see Sept.: Ps 77:6; 119:59) or by discourse with others to consider together, deliberate, debate (Matt 16:7, 8; Mark 8:16, 17; Luke 20:14); to consider (John 11:50); to dispute (Mark 9:33).

Deriv.: *dialogismós* (1261), word, account, reasoning.

Syn.: *noéō* (3539), to perceive; *katanoéō* (2657), to perceive clearly, consider carefully; *analogízomai* (357), to consider; *skopéō* (4648), to mark, consider, focus; *suníēmi* (4920), understand, put things together; *suzētéō* (4802), to discuss, examine together; *sullogízomai* (4817), to reason, compute; *dokéō* (1380), to think; *hēgéomai* (2233), to account, consider; *huponoéō* (5282), to surmise; *nomízō* (3543), to suppose; *phronéō* (5426), to think; *sōphronéō* (4993), to exercise sound mind or judgment; *krínō* (2919), to reckon, judge.

1261. διαλογισμός *dialogismós*; gen. *dialogismoú*, masc. noun from *dialo-*

gízomai (1260), to reason. Thoughts and directions.

(I) Generally (Luke 2:35; 5:22; 6:8; 9:47; James 2:4, "judges having evil thoughts" [a.t.], unjust, partial; Sept.: Ps 92:6; Isa 59:7; Dan 2:29, 30). Reasoning, opinion (Rom 1:21; 1 Cor 3:20; Rom 14:1; Sept.: Ps 94:11). Mind, purpose, intention (Luke 6:8). Especially evil thoughts, purposes. (Matt 15:19; Mark 7:21; Sept.: Ps 56:6, evil; Isa 59:7), doubts (Luke 24:38, doubtful thoughts, suspense).

(II) In the sense of dispute, debate, contention (Mark 9:33, 34 in its verbal form; Luke 9:46; Phil 2:14; 1 Tim 2:8).

Syn.: *suzétēsis* (4803), a dispute, questioning; *antilogía* (485), contradiction, gainsaying; *logismós* (3053), a thought suggestive of evil intent, imagination; *enthúmēsis* (1761), deliberation, device; *epínoia* (1963), a design of the mind; *nóēma* (3540), a perception, thought; *dianóēma* (1270), a thought, plot, machination, sentiment.

1262. **διαλύω** *dialúō*; fut. *dialúsō*, from *diá* (1223), denoting separation, and *lúō* (3089), to loose. To dissolve, dissipate, disperse, break up. Used only in Acts 5:36 with the meaning of dispersing or breaking up a group of people.

Syn.: *skorpízō* (4650), to scatter; *diaskorpízō* (1287), to scatter abroad, dissipate, waste; *diaspeírō* (1289), to sow or scatter throughout; *likmáō* (3039), to winnow or grind to powder.

Ant.: *sullégō* (4816), to collect, gather together; *sunágō* (4863), to bring together; *episunágō* (1996), to gather together in one place; *sustréphō* (4962), to twist together; *sunathroízō* (4867), to assemble together.

1263. **διαμαρτύρομαι** *diamartúromai*; fut. *diamarturoúmai*, mid. deponent from *diá* (1223), an intens., and *martúromai* (3143), to witness, bear witness. To bear witness, testify earnestly or repeatedly, or to charge as it were before witnesses, to affirm (Acts 20:23; Heb 2:6). Attesting to facts and truths of redemption or the Word of the Lord, of Christ, the gospel, the kingdom of God (Acts 2:40; 8:25; 10:42; 18:5; 20:21, 24; 23:11; 28:23; 1 Thess 4:6). To charge anyone, exhort earnestly (1 Thess 4:6; 2 Tim 2:14; 4:1). Followed by *hína*, so that (Luke 16:28; 1 Tim 5:21).

Syn.: *diastéllomai* (1291), to admonish, literally to draw asunder; *embrimáomai* (1690), to charge strictly; *egkaléō* (1458), to accuse; *entéllomai* (1781), to command, give charge; *epitimáō* (2008), to rebuke; *paraggéllō* (3853), to command, give charge; *dierōtáō* (1331), to question so as to make sure.

Ant.: *pistóō* (4104), to give assurance; *peíthō* (3982), to persuade; *epainéō* (1867), to applaud, commend; *eulogéō* (2127), to speak well of, bless.

1264. **διαμάχομαι** *diamáchomai*; fut. *diamachésomai*, mid. deponent from *diá* (1223), an intens., and *máchomai* (3164), to contend, fight. To fight together. Used in Acts 23:9 metaphorically meaning to contend with words or to dispute earnestly.

Syn.: *agōnízomai* (75), to contend; *erízō* (2051), to wrangle; *antagōnízomai* (464), to struggle against; *sunagōnízomai* (4865), to strive together with; *sunathléō* (4866), to strive together; *athléō* (118), to contend in games, wrestle.

Ant.: *eirēneúō* (1514), to bring to peace or be at peace, reconcile; *eirēnopoiéō* (1517), to make peace; *hēsucházō* (2270), to be still, hold one's peace.

1265. **διαμένω** *diaménō*; fut. *diamenō*, from *diá* (1223), an intens., and *ménō* (3306), to remain. To remain permanently or to continue in the same place. Spoken of state, condition, circumstances, meaning to remain the same, continue, endure, not to change (Gal 2:5; Heb 1:11 a quotation of Ps 102:27; 2 Pet 3:4 [cf. Ps 119:90; Luke 1:22; 22:28, to remain constant towards anyone]).

Syn.: *diateléō* (1300), to continue right through; *proskarteréō* (4342), to persevere in; *apoleípō* (620), to remain.

Ant.: *anágō* (321), to set sail, depart; *epanágō* (1877), to return; *hupágō* (5217), to go, depart; *apérchomai* (565), to come or go away; *exérchomai* (1831), to go out; *katérchomai* (2718), to come down, depart; *poreúomai* (4198), to depart from one place to another; *ekporeúomai* (1607), to go out from; *anachōréō* (402), to depart; *apochōréō* (672), to depart from; *ekchōréō* (1633), to leave a place; *chōrízomai* (5563), to separate oneself; *diachōrízomai* (1316), to separate oneself from; *analúō* (360), to depart from life, to die; *éxeimi* (1826), to go out; *aphístēmi* (868), to depart from anyone; *metabaínō* (3327), to depart.

1266. διαμερίζω *diamerízō*; fut. *diamerísō*, from *diá* (1223), denoting separation, and *merízō* (3307), to divide. To separate into parts or divide up. In the pass. part. meaning divided flames or divided out to each person from one common source (Acts 2:3). In the mid. in a reciprocal sense, to divide up for oneself or with one another (Matt 27:35; Luke 23:34; John 19:24; Sept.: Gen 10:25; 1 Chr 1:19 [cf. Deut 32:8]). To distribute (Luke 22:17; Acts 2:45; Sept.: Judg 5:30; 2 Sam 6:19). As used in a pass. sense meaning to be divided into parties (Luke 12:52). With the prep. *epí* (1909), over, against, meaning to be divided against, be at discord with (Luke 11:17, 18; 12:53).

Deriv.: *diamerismós* (1267), division.

Syn.: *dianémō* (1268), to disseminate, spread; *aphorízō* (873), to mark off by boundaries, divide, separate; *diairéō* (1244), to divide into parts; *aponémō* (632), to apportion; *klēróō* (2820), to allot; *merízō* (3307), to apportion; *diadídōmi* (1239), to distribute; *diakrínō* (1252), to discriminate; *orthotoméō* (3718), to rightly divide; *kataklērodotéō* (2624), to divide by lot; *diḯstēmi* (1339), to set apart, separate; *apospáō* (645), to draw off or tear away.

Ant.: *déō* (1210), to bind; *sundéō* (4887), to bind together; *proskolláō* (4347), to glue to; *sunarmologéō* (4883), to

fit together; *sumbállō* (4820), to combine; *sunantáō* (4876), to meet with; *sunéchō* (4912), to hold together; *sugkoinōnéō* (4790), to communicate.

1267. διαμερισμός *diamerismós*; gen. *diamerismoú*, masc. noun from *diamerízō* (1266), to divide up. Division, apportionment, portion. Used metaphorically meaning dissension (Luke 12:51).

Syn.: *dichostasía* (1370), division, dissension; *schísma* (4978), division, rent, schism; *diaíresis* (1243), division.

Ant.: *súndesmos* (4886), uniting, bond; *henótēs* (1775), unity; *zugós* (2218), yoke, a balancing out as it joins.

1268. διανέμω *dianémō*; fut. *dianemṓ*, from *diá* (1223), denoting dispersion, and *némō* (n.f., see *aponémō* [632]), to give. To distribute throughout. In the pass. meaning to divulge, spread abroad (Acts 4:17).

Syn.: *strōnnúō* or *strṓnnumi* (4766), to spread; *hupostrōnnúō* or *hupostrṓnnumi* (5291), to spread under; *ekpetánnumi* (1600), to spread out; *skorpízō* (4650), to scatter throughout; *diaskorpízō* (1287), to scatter; *diaspeírō* (1289), to scatter abroad as if it were seed; *likmáō* (3039), to winnow; *dialúō* (1262), to dissolve, disperse.

1269. διανεύω *dianeúō*; fut. *dianeúsō*, from *diá* (1223), an intens., and *neúō* (3506), to signal or beckon. To nod or wink repeatedly or to make signs with the head or eyes (Luke 1:22; Sept.: Ps 35:19).

Syn.: *kataseíō* (2678), to shake down or to wave.

1270. διανόημα *dianóēma*; gen. *dianoēmatos*, neut. noun from *dianoéomai* (n.f.), to agitate in mind, which is from *diá* (1223), denoting separation, and *noéō* (3539), to think over. A thought or reflection with an evil connotation (Luke 11:17; Sept.: Isa 55:9). See *noús* (3563), mind. The basic subj. is *nóēma* (3540), a device of the mind or thought without the evil connotation that is in *dianóēma*.

While *dianóēma* refers to a particular evil thought and *epínoia* (1963) refers to a thought by way of design.

Syn.: *enthúmēsis* (1761), an inward reasoning, generally evil surmising or supposition, device, usually imaginary; *énnoia* (1771), thoughtfulness, denoting inward intentions that involve moral understanding without any evil connotations; *logismós* (3053), the art of reckoning, reasoning; *dialogismós* (1261) refers to a more thorough reflection, thought, thinking something through; *phrónēsis* (5428), mental action or activity, intellectual insight, prudence; *phrónēma* (5427), that which one has in the mind, thought, an object of thought with a bad or good connotation.

Ant.: *aphrosúnē* (877), senselessness.

1271. διάνοια *diánoia*; gen. *dianoías*, fem. noun from *dianoéomai* (n.f.), to agitate in mind, which is from *diá* (1223), denoting separation, and *noéō* (3539), to think over. Understanding, intellect, intellectual faculty, thought, mind.

(I) By metonymy the mind, thoughts, intellect, i.e., the thinking faculty (Matt 22:37; Mark 12:30; Luke 10:27; Eph 1:18, only in some MSS; 4:18; Heb 8:10; 10:16 quoted from Jer 31:33; 1 Pet 1:13; 2 Pet 3:1; Sept.: Gen 17:17; 24:45).

(II) Intelligence, insight (1 John 5:20; Sept.: Ex 35:25; 36:1).

(III) Mind, i.e., mode of thinking and feeling, the feelings, affections, disposition of mind (Eph 2:3; Col 1:21). In Luke 1:51, the proud in the mental disposition of their hearts. The comp. verb *dianoéomai* does not occur in the NT, but the basic verb *noéō* (3539), to perceive with the mind, does occur. *Noús* (3563) and *diánoia* mean almost the same thing, *noús* being the faculty of thinking, and *diánoia*, the mind activated; while *énnoia* (1771) (Heb 4:12; 1 Pet 4:1) is the meaning that the mind attaches to persons or things. Outside the Pauline Epistles, *noús* (3563), the specific word for mind, occurs only in Luke 24:45; Rev 13:18; 17:9. In Acts 14:2 what is translated "minds" is

psuchás (5590), souls, and not *dianoías*. The same is true in Phil 1:27; Heb 12:3. In Phile 1:14; Rev 17:13 "mind" stands for *gnṓmē* (1106), opinion, judgment, and in Rom 8:27 for *phrónēma* (5427) which denotes not the mental faculty itself, but its thoughts and purposes.

Syn.: *lógos* (3056), reason, intelligence; *phrónēma* (5427), the thought of the mind and the process of thinking and understanding; *phrónēsis* (5428), prudence; *epínoia* (1963), a thought or design for evil purposes; *nóēma* (3540), the product of the mind or thought; *dianóēma* (1270) an evil device; *enthúmēsis* (1761) a thought that involves the agitation of passion; *thumós* (2372), wrath; *logismós* (3053), the working out of the mind, imagination; *dialogismós* (1261), the results of the thorough exercise of the mind. While *noús* and *diánoia* may denote the faculty of reflective consciousness, the organ of moral thinking and knowing is *súnesis* (4907), a peculiar force or accurateness in the exercise of the mind.

Ant.: *ánoia* (454), without understanding, folly; *manía* (3130), frenzy, madness; *paraphronía* (3913), being beside oneself, mad; *aphrosúnē* (877), imprudence, folly; *mōría* (3472), foolishness, being a moron, foolish.

1272. διανοίγω *dianoígō*; fut. *dianoíxō*, from *diá* (1223), through, and *anoígō* (455), to open. To open what before was closed, open as the firstborn opens the womb (Luke 2:23; Sept.: Ex 13:2; 34:19). To open the ears, eyes, understanding, heart (Mark 7:34, 35; Isa 35:5; Luke 24:31), to open the eyes of anyone, i.e., to cause to see what was not seen before (Sept.: 2 Kgs 6:17), to open the mind, the heart, i.e., to make able and willing to understand, receive (also Acts 16:14; Sept.: Hos 2:15), to open the Scriptures, to explain, expound.

Syn.: *anaptússō* (380), to unroll.

Ant.: *kammúō* (2576), to close, used usually for shutting the eyes; *ptússō* (4428), to fold, double up as used of a scroll; *kleíō* (2808), to shut; *apokleíō*

(608), to shut fast with the idea of hindering entrance after closing; *katakleíō* (2623), to shut down or to shut up in confinement; *sugkleíō* (4788), to enclose.

1273. διανυκτερεύω *dianuktereúō*; fut. *dianuktereúsō*, from *diá* (1223), through, and *nuktereúō* (n.f.), to pass the night, which is from *núx* (3571), night. To pass the whole night. Intrans. in Luke 6:12; Sept.: Job 2:9.
    Syn.: *diatríbō* (1304), to stay; *aulízomai* (835), to lodge; *agrauléō* (63), to lodge in a fold in a field; *ménō* (3306), to abide.
    Ant.: *pheúgō* (5343), to run away, go away; *hupágō* (5217), to depart; *apérchomai* (565), to go away; *apochōréō* (672), to depart from; *ekchōréō* (1633), to depart out of a place; *metabaínō* (3327), to depart.

1274. διανύω *dianúō*; fut. *dianúsō*, from *diá* (1223), an intens., and *anúō* (n.f.), to perform. To bring through to an end or to complete, finish (Acts 21:7, the sailing).
    Syn.: *teléō* (5055), to bring to an end; *teleióō* (5048), to bring to an end with a sense of moral accomplishment, complete; *ekteléō* (1615), to finish out; *epiteléō* (2005), to bring through to an end; *sunteléō* (4931), to bring to fulfillment; *apoteléō* (658), to complete entirely.
    Ant.: *egkóptō* (1465), to hinder; *suntémnō* (4932), to condense by cutting, to cut short.

1275. διαπαντός *diapantós*; adv. from *diá* (1223), through, and *pantós* (3956), through all. The whole time, continually, always (Mark 5:5, Acts 2:25; 24:16; Rom 11:10). Used in Luke 24:53 of what is done at all stated or proper times, (Acts 10:2; Heb 9:6; Sept.: Deut 11:12; Ps 34:1; 119:44).
    Syn.: *adialeíptōs* (89), uninterruptedly; *aeí* (104), perpetually, incessantly and successively; *pántē* (3839), all, always, with *chrónō*, the dat. of *chrónos* (5550), time, or *kairō̂*, the dat. of *kairós* (2540), time, implying opportune time; *hekástote* (1539), at every time; *pásas tás hēméras*

(*pásas*, the fem. pl. acc. of *pás* [3956]; *tás*, the fem. pl. acc. of the def. art.; *hēméras*, the acc. pl. of *hēméra* [2250], day), all the days, at all seasons; *pántote* (3842), at all times, always; *diēnekḗs* (1336), unbroken, continuous, and used also periphrastically with the expression *eis tó diēnekés* (*eis* [1519], unto, followed by the neut. *tó diēnekés*), meaning perpetually, forever (Heb 7:3; 10:1, 12, 14); the expression *eis télos* (*eis* [1519], unto; *télos* [5056], end, goal), unto the end, i.e., continually until the end is reached (Matt 10:22; 24:13; Mark 13:13; John 13:1; 1 Thess 2:16). The word *télos* is also used with the prep. *héōs* (2193), until, i.e., *héōs télous*, until the end (1 Cor 1:8; 2 Cor 1:13); *méchri* (3360), until, in the expression *méchri télous* (Heb 3:6, 14) or with *áchri* (891), until, in the expression *áchri télous*, until the end or the goal (Heb 6:11; Rev 2:26). The expression *diá pantós* (*diá* [1223], through; *pantós* [3956], the gen. sing. of *pás*) refers to a period throughout or during which anything is done (Matt 18:10; Mark 5:5; Luke 24:53; Acts 10:2; 24:16; Rom 11:10; 2 Thess 3:16; Heb 9:6; 13:15).
    Ant.: *próskairos* (4340), temporal, for a season; *olígon* (the neut. of *olígos* [3641]), for a short duration.

1276. διαπεράω *diaperáō*; contracted *diaperō̂*, fut. *diaperásō*, from *diá* (1223), denoting transition, and *peráō* (n.f.), to pass. To cross entirely or over (Matt 9:1; 14:34; Mark 5:21; 6:53; Luke 16:26; Acts 21:2; Sept.: 2 Sam 19:15; Isa 23:2).
    Syn.: *diérchomai* (1330), to pass through or over; *diabaínō* (1224), to step across, cross over; *diaporeúomai* (1279), to pass across; *diodeúō* (1353), to travel through.
    Ant.: *ménō* (3306), to stay, abide; *diaménō* (1265), to remain throughout.

1277. διαπλέω *diapléō*; fut. *diapleúsō*, from *diá* (1223), through, and *pléō* (4126), to sail. To sail through or over (Acts 27:5).

Syn.: *anágō* (321), to lead up; *diaperáō* (1276), to cross over.

Ant.: *ágkura* (45), anchor.

**1278. διαπονέω *diaponéō*; contracted *diaponṓ*, fut. *diaponḗsō*, from *diá* (1223), through or an intens., and *ponéō* (n.f.), to labor, which is from *pónos* (4192), toil, pain. To labor through, produce with labor. In the pass. with the mid. meaning *diaponéomai*, to grieve oneself, to be tired by labor, become wearied or grieved at the continuance of anything (Acts 4:2; 16:18). In the aor. pass. *dieponḗthēn*. There are a number of syn. indicating grief and trouble, but none as a result of labor indicating fatigue.

Ant.: *anapaúomai* (373), to rest; *hēsucházō* (2270), to be still, to rest from labor; *epanapaúomai* (1879), to rest upon, to find rest; *anapsúchō* (404), to refresh with the metaphorical meaning of to relax.

**1279. διαπορεύομαι *diaporeúomai*; fut. *diaporeúsomai*, deponent from *diá* (1223), through, and *poreúomai* (4198), to go. To go or pass through (Luke 6:1; 13:22; 18:36; Acts 16:4; Rom 15:24; Sept.: Gen 24:62; Job 2:2; Zeph 2:15).

Syn.: *hodoiporéō* (3596), to travel, journey; *hodeúō* (3593), to journey, be on the way; *apodēméō* (589), to go on a journey to another country.

Ant.: *ménō* (3306), to stay, abide; *diaménō* (1265), to remain throughout; *kataménō* (2650), to remain where one is found; *diatríbō* (1304), to tarry; *aulízomai* (835), to lodge; *agrauléō* (63), to lodge in a fold in a field.

**1280. διαπορέω *diaporéō*; contracted *diaporṓ*, fut. *diaporḗsō*, from *diá* (1223), through, and *aporéō* (639), to be perplexed. To be thoroughly perplexed, to be in much doubt, hesitate greatly (Luke 9:7; 24:4; Acts 2:12; 5:24; 10:17).

Syn.: *distázō* (1365), to stand at a crossroad, hesitate, be double-minded; *meteōrízō* (3349), to stand in midair, to be uncertain; *diakrínō* (1252), to discriminate, contend, doubt; *dialégomai* (1256), to think different things, dispute; *dialogízomai* (1260), to reason; *suzētéō* (4802), to seek to examine, to discuss; *apistéō* (569), to disbelieve; *agnoéō* (50), not to know.

Ant.: *pistóō* (4104), to trust or give assurance; *plērophoréō* (4135), in the mid. meaning to be fully assured; *pisteúō* (4100), to believe, be persuaded of; *peíthō* (3982), to persuade; *ginóskō* (1097), to know experientially; *oída* (1492), to know intuitively; *epiginṓskō* (1921), to know fully; *epístamai* (1987), to know with understanding; *gnōrízō* (1107), to come to know, discover, to make known.

**1281. διαπραγματεύομαι *diapragmateúomai*; fut. *diapragmateúsomai*, deponent from *diá* (1223), through or an intens., and *pragmateúomai* (4231), to negotiate, trade, gain by trading. To gain by negotiating or business (Luke 19:15). *Pragmateutḗs* means a businessman, merchant, and *pragmateía* (4230), a transaction or negotiation.

Syn.: *emporeúomai* (1710), to trade.

**1282. διαπρίω *diapríō*; fut. *diaprísō*, from *diá* (1223), through, and *príō* (n.f.), to saw, cut with a saw. To saw through or asunder, to divide by a saw (Sept.: 1 Chr 20:3). In the NT only in the mid., *diapríomai*, used metaphorically meaning to be enraged, moved with anger, to be cut or torn emotionally (Acts 5:33; 7:54).

Syn.: *kóptō* (2875) to cut; *katakóptō* (2629), to cut down; *dichotoméō* (1371), to cut into two parts.

Ant.: *epirráptō* (1976), to sew on, stitch.

**1283. διαρπάζω *diarpázō*; fut. *diarpásō*, from *diá* (1223), an intens. or denoting separation, and *harpázō* (726), to snatch. To seize, plunder, snatch asunder, spoil (Matt 12:29; Mark 3:27; Sept.: Gen 34:27, 29; Deut 28:29; 1 Sam 23:1; Nah 2:9).

**1284. διαρρήσσω *diarrḗssō* and διαρρήγνυμι *diarrḗgnumi*; fut.

diarrḗxō, from *diá* (1223), denoting separation, and *rhḗssō / rhḗgnumi* (4486), to tear, break, rend. To tear through, rend asunder, such as clothing (Matt 26:65; Acts 14:14); a garment (Mark 14:63); a net (Luke 5:6); chains (Luke 8:29; Sept.: Gen 37:29, 34; 2 Sam 23:16; Ps 2:3). The Jews in expressing grief or indignation used to tear their garments from their chest to the waist (Gen 37:29, 33, 34; 44:13; Num 14:6; Josh 7:6; 2 Sam 3:31).

Syn.: *schízō* (4977), to split or rend open.

1285. διασαφέω *diasaphéō*; contracted *diasaphṓ*, fut. *diasaphḗsō*, from *diá* (1223), an intens., and *saphéō* (n.f.), to manifest. To make fully manifest or known (Matt 18:31; Sept.: Deut 1:5).

Syn.: *exēgéomai* (1834), to declare, bring out the meaning; *dēlóō* (1213), to make plain, evident; *sēmaínō* (4591), to indicate, signify, express by signs; *emphanízō* (1718), to manifest, make apparent; *diaggéllō* (1229), to announce by making plain what is said.

Ant.: *skotízō* (4654), to make dark; *skotóō* (4656), to cover with darkness, to darken used of the heavenly bodies and also of the mind; *en ainígmati* (*en* [1722], in; *ainígmati* [135], enigma, riddle), in an enigma or darkly, something that has to be figured out.

1286. διασείω *diaseíō*; fut. *diaseísō*, from *diá* (1223), an intens., and *seíō* (4579), to shake. To shake thoroughly, used trans. meaning to cause to shake vehemently (Sept.: Job 4:14). Used metaphorically and trans. meaning to harass, oppress, extort from (Luke 3:14).

Syn.: *phobéō* (5399), to cause to fear or marvel; *biázō* (971), to press, suffer violence; *hormáō* (3729), to rush.

Ant.: *antilambánomai* (482), to help; *antéchomai* (472), to support, hold; *boēthéō* (997), to come to the aid of anyone, succor; *sunupourgéō* (4943), to help together, to serve as an underworker; *sunergéō* (4903), to help in work, co-

operate; *parístēmi* (3936), to stand by, to help.

1287. διασκορπίζω *diaskorpízō*; fut. *diaskorpísō*, from *diá* (1223), an intens. or denoting separation, and *skorpízō* (4650), to dissipate. To scatter abroad, disperse, used of chaff being scattered to the wind on the threshing floor, meaning to winnow (Matt 25:24, 26; Sept. using *likmáō* [3039], to winnow: in Ruth 3:2; Isa 30:24). Used trans. meaning to disperse (Luke 1:51); in the pass. (Matt 26:31; Mark 14:27; John 11:52; Acts 5:37; Sept.: Deut 30:1, 3; Ezek 5:2; Neh 1:8). Used metaphorically meaning to dissipate, squander (Luke 15:13; 16:1).

Syn.: *diasporá* (1290), dispersion; *diaspeírō* (1289), to sow seed by scattering it; *rhíptō* (4496), to throw, cast; *likmáō* (3039), to winnow or scatter as dust; *dialúō* (1262), to dissolve or disperse.

Ant.: *sunágō* (4863), to gather or bring together; *episunágō* (1996), to gather together in one spot; *sullégō* (4816), to collect, gather up or out; *trugáō* (5166), to gather in as spoken of harvest; *sunathroízō* (4867), to convene together; *epathroízō* (1865), to gather together in one place.

1288. διασπάω *diaspáō*; contracted *diaspṓ*, fut. *diaspásō*, from *diá* (1223), denoting separation, and *spáō* (4685), to draw, pull. To pull up, asunder, or tear to pieces. Used trans. and in the pass. (Mark 5:4; Acts 23:10; Sept.: Judg 16:9, 12; Job 19:10; Hos 13:8).

Syn.: *tíllō* (5089), to pluck; *harpázō* (726), to seize, snatch; *exairéō* (1807), to take out or pluck out; *exorússō* (1846), to dig out or up; *ekrizóō* (1610), to pluck up by the roots; *ekbállō* (1544), to cast out or pluck out; *diarrḗssō* (1284), to break asunder; *perirrḗgnumi* (4048), to tear off all around; *schízō* (4977), to split, rend open; *diachōrízō* (1316), to separate one from the other; *dicházō* (1369), to put apart, set at variance; *dichotoméō* (1371), to bisect, cut asunder; *apochōrízō* (673), to rend apart, separate.

Ant.: *déō* (1210), to bind; *sundéō* (4887), to bind together; *proskolláō* (4347), to cleave, glue together; *sunarmologéō* (4883), to fit or join together; *sunéchō* (4912), to hold together.

1289. διασπείρω *diaspeírō*; fut. *diasperṓ*, from *diá* (1223), denoting separation, and *speírō* (4687), to sow, scatter. To sow here and there or to scatter as seed, disperse, spoken of persons in the pass. (Acts 8:1, 4; 11:19; Sept.: Gen 11:9; Ex 5:12; Lev 26:33; Ezek 12:15).
Deriv.: *diasporá* (1290), a dispersion.
Syn.: *skorpízō* (4650), to disperse; *diaskorpízō* (1287), to scatter abroad; *rhíptō* (4496), to throw or cast down; *likmáō* (3039), to winnow or scatter as dust.
Ant.: *sunágō* (4863), to gather or bring together; *episunágō* (1996), to gather together in one place; *sullégō* (4816), to collect, gather up or out; *trugáō* (5166), to gather in the harvest; *sunathroízō* (4867), to gather together.

1290. διασπορά *diasporá*; gen. *diasporás*, a fem. noun from *diaspeírō* (1289), to scatter abroad. A scattering or dispersion, spoken of the state of dispersion in which many of the Jews lived after the captivity, in Chaldea, Persia, and chiefly in Egypt, Syria and Asia Minor (Sept.: Jer 34:17). In the NT, it refers to the dispersion of the Jews (James 1:1; 1 Pet 1:1). In John 7:35 "the dispersed among the Gentiles" means the Jews dwelling either among the Gentiles generally, or among nations that used the Greek language, e.g., in Egypt and Asia Minor, the Hellenists (Sept.: Ps 147:2).
Ant.: *episunagōgḗ* (1997), a gathering together; *sunagōgḗ* (4864), synagogue, assembly; *ekklēsía* (1577), an assembly, church.

1291. διαστέλλω *diastéllō*; fut. *diastelṓ*, from *diá* (1223), denoting transition, and *stéllō* (4724), to send. In the NT only in the mid. *diastéllomai*, to give a charge, command, enjoin upon (Acts 15:24).

Used in an absolute sense in Heb 12:20. Followed by a neg. clause, it may be rendered to forbid, prohibit (Matt 16:20; Mark 5:43; 7:36; 8:15; 9:9; Sept.: Ezek 3:18, 21; Mal 3:11).
Deriv.: *diastolḗ* (1293), difference, distinction.
Syn.: *diamartúromai* (1263), to bear a solemn protest, charge earnestly, testify; *diatássō* (1299), to order; *embrimáomai* (1690), to charge strictly; *egkaléō* (1458), to charge in court or legally, to accuse; *entéllomai* (1781), to command, enjoin; *epitimáō* (2008), to rebuke.

1292. διάστημα *diástēma*; gen. *diastēmatos*, a neut. noun from *diístēmi* (1339), to part, separate. Distance, space, interval, referring to time (Acts 5:7).
Syn.: *chrónos* (5550), time; *tópos* (5117), space.

1293. διαστολή *diastolḗ*; gen. *diastolḗs*, fem. noun from *diastéllō* (1291), to put asunder, set apart. Distinction, difference (Rom 3:22; 10:12; 1 Cor 14:7).
Syn.: *diaíresis* (1243), a distinction, division, difference, variety; *diákrisis* (1253), discernment, disputation.

1294. διαστρέφω *diastréphō*; fut. *diastrépsō*, perf. pass. *diéstrammai*, from *diá* (1223), denoting separation, and *stréphō* (4762), to turn. To turn or twist throughout or to distort, pervert. Used metaphorically meaning to pervert; trans. spoken of persons meaning to turn away, seduce, mislead (Luke 23:2; Acts 13:8; Sept.: Ex 5:4; 1 Kgs 18:17, 18). Of things, meaning to pervert, wrest, corrupt (Acts 13:10, "to turn aside divine truth" [a.t.]; Sept.: Prov 10:9; Mic 3:9). The perf. pass. part. *diestramménos*, perverted or perverse, corrupt, vicious (Matt 17:17; Luke 9:41; Acts 20:30; Phil 2:15).
Syn.: *ektrépō* (1624), to cause to turn aside; *apotrépō* (665), to cause to turn away; *peritrépō* (4062), to turn about; *methístēmi* (3179), to remove; *anastatóō* (387), to stir up, unsettle; *ekklínō* (1578), to turn aside; *klínō* (2827), to turn.

1295. διασώζω *diasṓzō*; fut. *diasṓsō*, from *diá* (1223), through, and *sṓzō* (4982), to save. To save through, to bring safely through danger, sickness, to preserve, used trans. (Acts 27:43; 28:1, 4; 1 Pet 3:20, "were brought safely through the waters" [a.t.]; Sept.: Num 10:9; Deut 20:4; Job 29:12; Dan 11:41). With the idea of motion, to bring safely through to any place or person; in the pass., to come to or reach safely (Acts 23:24; Acts 27:44; Sept.: Gen 19:19; Isa 37:38). Of the sick, to bring safely through, to heal (Matt 14:36; Luke 7:3; Sept.: Jer 8:20).

Syn.: *exairéomai* (1807), to rescue; *diaphulássō* (1314), to protect; *rhúomai* (4506) to rescue; *peripoiéomai* (4046), to preserve; *therapeúō* (2323), to care for the sick, heal; *iáomai* (2390), to heal.

Ant.: *leípō* (3007), to fail; *aphanízō* (853), to consume, disappear, perish; *ekleípō* (1587), to cease to be, to die, fail; *dialúō* (1262), to dissolve utterly; *katalúō* (2647), to loosen down, demolish, destroy; *teleutáō* (5053), to expire; *analískō* (355), to consume.

1296. διαταγή *diatagḗ*; gen. *diatagḗs*, fem. noun from *diatássō* (1299), to appoint. Order, a disposition, ordinance, appointment (Acts 7:53; Rom 13:2). The verb *tássō*, meaning to arrange in an orderly manner and thus to assign, ordain, set appropriately, is essential to the adequate comprehension of the many comp. of the word. The subst. of *tássō* is *táxis* (5010), regular arrangement, proper setting and thus order.

The verb *diatássō* from which *diatagḗ* derives is not simply to command or give an order, but to penetrate into a certain situation. This is suggested by the prep. *diá*, through or thoroughly, and *tássō*, to arrange in an orderly manner, e.g., when a person determines the proper arrangement of things or situations, he orders or commands that such arrangements be executed. Note also the deriv. *tágma* (5001), anything arranged in an orderly fashion as a body of troops, a band of soldiers, order,

succession of the resurrection as in 1 Cor 15:23; also the adj. *taktós* (5002), an arranged or proper day as in Acts 12:21 referring to the set day in which Herod sat on his speaking platform. This detailed understanding of the basic word *tássō* and its cognates is necessary if we are to properly understand *diatássō* not as a mere capricious ordering or commanding and *diatagḗ* not as an arbitrary commandment, order, ordinance, disposition or appointment, but something that is thought out and proposes orderliness and method.

In Acts 7:53 we have the condemnatory words of Stephen at the hour of his martyrdom, spoken to the Jews who were executing him, "Who [*hoítines*, pl. of *hóstis* {3748}, referring to the "you" {*humeís*}, Acts 7:51] have received the law." Stephen up to here states two facts: **(1)** that it was God who gave the Law and **(2)** that they received the Law realizing it was for them. The implication of the verb "ye received [*elábete*, the aor. of *lambánō* {2983}]" denotes not only privilege, but responsibility. Stephen's accusation is that they accepted the privilege, but not the responsibility. The second difficult part of the verse stresses how inexcusable the Jews were in their rejection of Jesus Christ for whom Stephen was martyred. That Law given to them and received by them was properly ordained or administered by angels who are God's ministering spirits from God to man (Heb 1:14). Stephen said to the unbelieving Jews: "[You] who have received the law by the disposition of angels, and have not kept it." The phrase is *eis diatagás aggélōn* (*eis* [1519], *diatagás* [1296], *aggélōn* [32]), literally meaning "unto arrangements of angels." The difficulty of the exegesis of this can be easily detected from the variety of the translations other than the above KJV. The NKJV has it "by the direction of angels"; the NASB as "ordained by angels"; and the NIV as "that was put into effect through angels." If we review what actually took place when the Law was given, we may be able to arrive at the proper meaning of Stephen's statement. In Deut 33:2 we find no angels mentioned except for the material messengers of God which accompanied the giving of the Law; namely, fire, light, a cloud and thick darkness (Ex 19:18; Deut 4:11; 5:22, 26; 33:2; Hab 3:3). As the people experienced these material agents of God, they also heard the audible voice of God (Deut 5:22). In Deut 33:2 we read that the Lord "came with ten thousands of saints." The word for "saints" is "holy ones" (NASB, NIV). Some believe that this is a reference to angels, based in part on a variant reading in the Sept., which interprets the Hebrew words translated "fiery law" or "flashing lightning" as a singular word for "angels." It is believed that these were angels assigned by God to minister the Law to the Israelites at the foot of the mountain when Moses descended with the Ten Commandments. The angels could have acted as exegetes of God's commandments, placing them in orderly arrangements (*eis diatagás*, Acts 7:53). The angels could have explained the commandments to them. It is quite possible that the angels explained to the Jews the temporary aspects of the Law given them until the coming of the Just One, Jesus Christ (Acts 7:52). However, the Jews killed the one who fulfilled the Law and God instituted the dispensation of grace. This is clearly stated in Gal 3:19, "Wherefore then serveth the law? It was added because of transgressions till the seed [Christ] should come to whom the promise was made; and it was ordained [*diatageís*] by angels in the hand of a mediator." In this verse we have the verb *diatássō*, used in the aor. pass. part. which means "was properly arranged" or ordered. What is translated "by angels" in Gr. is *di' aggélōn*, which should be translated "through angels," which fully substantiates our interpretation of Acts 7:53, that angels explained to the Jews the details of the purposes of the Law. The mediator spoken of here is not Christ, but Moses. In Deut 5:5 he said, "I stood between the Lord and you at that time, to show you the word of the Lord: for ye

were afraid by reason of the fire, and went not up into the mount." Thus at the giving of the Law, we have Moses the mediator between God and Israel and the ministering angels until Christ came who became the new mediator (1 Tim 2:5) and made us His angels or messengers (Rev 2:1, 8, 12, 18; 3:1, 7, 14) of the word of reconciliation (2 Cor 5:18, 19). "The word spoken by angels" referred to in Heb 2:2 also substantiates the interpretation of Acts 7:53.

The second occurrence of *diatagḗ* is in Rom 13:2 where Paul speaks about human governments. In Rom 13:1 he says, "the powers that be are ordained of God." That word translated "ordained" is *tetagménai*, basically from the same root word *tássō*, to set in order in the perf. pass. part. Governments exist not simply because they choose to, but because God has allowed them to fulfill some purpose in the execution of His eternal plan. This may be applied to the worst possible government at the time, that of Nero. We must never forget the truth of Ps 76:10, "Surely the wrath of man shall praise thee: the remainder of wrath shalt thou restrain." And then in Rom 13:2 the word *diatagḗ*, the noun of *diatássō*, is used and translated "ordinance": "Whosoever therefore resisteth the power, resisteth the ordinance [*diatagḗ*] of God." It is that which God has arranged to accomplish His purpose. Nothing that God permits is purposeless in the life of the believer.

Syn.: *diátagma* (1297), an arrangement, edict, mandate, the result of *diatagḗ*.

1297. διάταγμα *diátagma*; gen. *diatágmatos*, neut. noun from *diatássō* (1299), to command, arrange in its proper order. The order, commandment, or edict itself. Only in Heb 11:23 of the decree of the king (Sept.: Ezra 7:11).

1298. διαταράσσω *diatarássō*, **διατάραττω** *diataráttō*; fut. *diataráxō*, from *diá* (1223), through, and *tarássō* (5015), to agitate, trouble. To stir up throughout. Spoken of the mind, and elsewhere, to disturb, agitate. Used in the pass. in Luke 1:29.

1299. διατάσσω *diatássō*, **διατάττω** *diatáttō*; fut. *diatáxō*, from *diá* (1223), through, and *tássō* (5021), to appoint, order. To arrange throughout, to dispose in order as trees, troops. In the NT: to command, used in connection with what was appointed for tax officials to collect (Luke 3:13); of the tabernacle as appointed by God for Moses to make (Acts 7:44); of arrangements made by Paul (Acts 20:13); of what the Apostle ordained in the churches in regard to marital conditions (1 Cor 7:17); of what the Lord ordained in regard to the support of those who proclaim the gospel (1 Cor 9:14); of the Law as administered through angels by Moses (Gal 3:19; see *diatagē* [1296], order by arrangement). In Titus 1:5 it refers to the ordination of church officers. Additional references: Matt 11:1; Luke 8:55; 17:9, 10; Acts 18:2; 23:31; 24:23; 1 Cor 11:34; 16:1; Sept.: Ezek 21:19, 20; Dan 1:5.

Deriv.: *diatagē* (1296), an ordinance; *diátagma* (1297), that which is imposed by decree or law; *epidiatássomai* (1928), to arrange, appoint.

1300. διατελέω *diateléō*; contracted *diatelō*, fut. *diatelésō*, from *diá* (1223), through or an intens., and *teléō* (5055), to finish. To bring through to a completed end, to finish fully, completely. To continue throughout, to remain, used in an absolute sense (Acts 27:33).

1301. διατηρέω *diatēréō*; contracted *diatērō*, fut. *diatērésō*, from *diá* (1223), an intens., and *tēréō* (5083), to guard, watch. To keep carefully, as the mother of Jesus kept His saying in her heart (Luke 2:51; Sept.: Gen 37:11); the command of the apostles (Acts 15:29, to guard or keep oneself wholly from anything, i.e., to abstain completely; Sept.: Isa 56:2).

Syn.: *phulássō* (5442), to guard; *diaphulássō* (1314), guard thoroughly or carefully; *phrouréō* (5432), to keep as if with a military guard; *kratéō* (2902), to hold fast.

Ant.: *lanthánō* (2990), to forget; *epilanthánomai* (1950), to forget altogether with the implication of neglect; *eklanthánomai* (1585), to forget utterly.

1302. διατί *diatí*; adv. from *diá* (1223), on account of, and *tí* (5101), what, which. On what account? Wherefore? Why? (Matt 9:11, 14; 15:3; 17:19; 21:25; Mark 11:31; Luke 5:30, 33; 19:31; 20:5; 24:38; John 8:43, 46; 12:5; 13:37; Rom 9:32; 1 Cor 6:7; 2 Cor 11:11; Rev 17:7). In the above instances the two words *diá* and *tí* are separated. In the following verses (TR) they are joined together as one word: Matt 13:10; 15:2; Mark 2:18; 7:5; Luke 19:23; John 7:45; Acts 5:3.

1303. διατίθεμαι *diatíthemai*; fut. *diathēsomai*, mid. of *diatíthēmi*, from *diá* (1223), an intens., and *títhēmi* (5087), to place. To dispose or arrange for oneself (Acts 3:25; Heb 8:10, a testament for Israel but not a covenant with Israel's consent and participation. The prep. used in Acts 3:25 and Heb 10:16 is not *metá* [3326], with, but *prós* [4314], unto, toward. The KJV, NASB, NKJV, and the NIV all have wrongly translated the prep. *prós* "with." The Sept. in Deut 5:3 has the dat. pl. *toís patrásin*, to your fathers, followed by *prós humás*, unto you; Heb 9:16, 17, a testator; Heb 10:16; Sept.: Ex 24:8; Deut 5:2, 3; Josh 9:6, 7; 2 Sam 3:13). Commonly it means to arrange and dispose of one's effects by will and testament. Followed by the dat. of the person, to bequeath a thing to anyone (Luke 22:29), allow or assign. As a verb it is important in its bearing upon the scriptural use of the subst. *diathēkē* (1242), testament.

Deriv.: *antidiatíthēmi* (475), to set oneself opposite; *diathēkē* (1242), a contract, covenant.

Syn.: *protíthemai* (4388), to propose, purpose; *skopéō* (4648), to aim, look at, mark; *apoblépō* (578), to intensely regard; *atenízō* (816), to set eyes on; *bouleúomai*

(1011), to purpose; *thélō* (2309), to will; *logízomai* (3049), to reckon; *proorízō* (4309), to determine before.

1304. διατρίβω diatríbō; fut. *diatrípsō*, from *diá* (1223), through or an intens., and *tríbō* (n.f., see below), to wear, spend. To rub continually, to wear away or consume by rubbing and other means. In the NT spoken only of time, meaning to spend or pass the time. Used trans., to pass, spend time (Acts 14:3, 28), days (Acts 16:12; 20:6; 25:6, 14; Sept.: Lev 14:8). Used in an absolute sense or with time implied, meaning to remain in a place, abide, with an adv. or other adjunct of place (John 3:22; 11:54; Acts 12:19; 15:35; Sept.: Jer 35:7).
Deriv. of *tríbō* (n.f.): *tríbos* (5147), a beaten pathway, highway; *chronotribéō* (5551), to spend time.
Syn.: with the meaning of abide: *ménō* (3306), to stay, remain; *epiménō* (1961), to continue to stay; *kataménō* (2650), to reside constantly; *paraménō* (3887), to continue near; *aulízomai* (835), to lodge in a courtyard, in the open air or a house; *agrauléō* (63), to lodge in a fold in a field. With the meaning of continue: *diateléō* (1300), to bring through to an end; *diaménō* (1265), to continue throughout; *emménō* (1696), to remain or abide in. With the meaning of tarry: *chronízō* (5549), to delay; *bradúnō* (1019), to slow down or tarry.
Ant.: *apérchomai* (565), to go away; *poreúomai* (4198), to go on one's way, depart from one place to another; *ekporeúomai* (1607), to go out; *anachōréō* (402), to depart, withdraw; *apochōréō* (672), to depart from; *analúō* (360), to unloose, depart; *metabaínō* (3327), to depart.

1305. διατροφή diatrophḗ; gen. *diatrophḗs*, fem. noun from *diatréphō* (n.f.), to maintain, which is from *diá* (1223), an intens., and *tréphō* (5142), to nourish. Food, nourishment (1 Tim 6:8).

Syn.: *trophḗ* (5160), food; *mánna* (3131), manna, food; *sítos* (4621) wheat, grain.

1306. διαυγάζω diaugázō; fut. *diaugásō*, from *diá* (1223), through, and *augázō* (826), to shine. To shine through; spoken of daylight, to break forth, to dawn, used intrans. in 2 Pet 1:19.
Syn.: *epiphṓskō* (2020), to shine light upon.
Ant.: *skotízō* (4654), to deprive of light, to make dark; *skotóō* (4656), to darken.

1307. διαφανής diaphanḗs; gen. *diaphanoús*, masc.-fem., neut. *diaphanés*, adj. from *diaphaínō* (n.f.), to shine through, which is from *diá* (1223), through, and *phaínō* (5316), to shine. Transparent, manifest. It is the Gr. word from which our Eng. "diaphanous," transparent, is derived (Rev 21:21 [TR]) and in other MSS *diaugḗs* from *diaugázō* (1306), to glimmer through.
Syn.: *emphanḗs* (1717), manifest, open; *phanerós* (5318), apparent; *dḗlos* (1212), evident, manifest; *horatós* (3707), visible.
Ant.: *skoteinós* (4652), dark; *auchmērós* (850), murky, dark; *aóratos* (517), invisible; *aphanḗs* (852), non-apparent; *kruptós* (2927), concealed; *apókruphos* (614), secret, hidden.

1308. διαφέρω diaphérō; fut. *dioísō*, 2d aor. *diénegkon*, from *diá* (1223), denoting transition or separation, and *phérō* (5342), to carry, bear.
(I) To carry through, to bear in relation to a place (Mark 11:16).
(II) Trans. in the pass. construction. To bear asunder, to carry different ways.
(A) Spoken metaphorically of doctrine in the pass. voice meaning to be divulged, published abroad (Acts 13:49). Spoken of a ship in the pass. meaning to be borne here and there, to be driven about (Acts 27:27).
(B) Intrans. or reflexively with *heautoú* (1438), himself implied, meaning to bear oneself apart, separate oneself from

others, to differ. **(1)** In Rom 2:18; Phil 1:10, *tá diaphéronta*, things different, has the meaning of distinguishing things that are different. **(2)** When used impersonally, *diaphérei*, it differs, it makes a difference, with the dat. (Gal 2:6). **(3)** Followed by the gen., to differ from, be other than, rarely in a lesser degree, i.e., to be inferior, hence to be superior or better than, to surpass (Matt 6:26; 10:31; Luke 12:7); followed by the dat. *pósō* (from *pósos* [4214]), how great, meaning how much more superior (Matt 12:12; Luke 12:24); by *oudén* the neut. of *oudeís* (3762), nothing (Gal 4:1).

Deriv.: *diáphoros* (1313), different, diverse; *diēnekḗs* (1336), carried through, extended.

Syn.: with the meaning of to be better or superior: *perisseúō* (4052), to be over or above; *lusiteléō* (3081), to indemnify or pay expenses, hence to be useful, advantageous, to be better; *huperbállō* (5235), to exceed; *huperéchō* (5242), to hold or have above, to be superior, better; *proéchomai* (4284), to be surpassed. With the meaning to be different: *diakrínō* (1252), to separate throughout, make a distinction.

Ant.: *ísos* (2470), equal; *homoióō* (3666), to compare, liken; *eíkō* (1503), to be alike, resemble; *paromoiázō* (3945), to liken; *aphomoióō* (871), to liken.

1309. διαφεύγω *diapheúgō*; fut. *diapheúxō*, from *diá* (1223), an intens., and *pheúgō* (5343), to escape. To flee through, to escape by flight, used in an absolute sense in Acts 27:42; Sept.: Josh 8:22; Prov 19:5.

Syn.: *diasṓzō* (1295), to bring safely through a danger.

1310. διαφημίζω *diaphēmízō*; fut. *diaphēmísō*, from *diá* (1223), denoting dispersion, and *phēmízō* (n.f.), to speak. To rumor abroad, divulge, advertise (Matt 28:15; Mark 1:45). Spoken of a person and meaning to spread one's fame abroad (Matt 9:31).

Syn.: *koinóō* (2840), to communicate, make common; *apaggéllō* (518), to report, announce, declare; *anaggéllō* (312), to bring back word, declare; *diaggéllō* (1229), to proclaim; *exaggéllō* (1804), to publish, show forth.

Ant.: *phimóō* (5392), to muzzle, put to silence; *sigáō* (4601), to be silent; *siōpáō* (4623), to be silent; *krúptō* (2928), to keep secret.

1311. διαφθείρω *diaphtheírō*; fut. *diaphtherṓ*, from *diá* (1223), as an intens., and *phtheírō* (5351), to defile, destroy, corrupt. To corrupt throughout. Used trans. and in the pass. it means to decay wholly, to perish (Luke 12:33; 2 Cor 4:16; Rev 8:9; 11:18). Metaphorically and in a moral sense, to corrupt wholly, pervert (1 Tim 6:5, meaning men of perverse minds). In the pres. part. acc. *toús diaphtheírontas*, "those corrupting the earth" (a.t.) in Rev 11:18, it means those seducing the nations to idolatry (Sept.: Judg 2:19).

Deriv.: *adiaphthoría* (90), uncorruptness; *diaphthorá* (1312), corruption.

Syn.: *palaióō* (3822), to make old; *apóllumi* (622), to destroy utterly; *katargéō* (2673), to abolish; *kathairéō* (2507), to pull down by force; *lúō* (3089), to dissolve or loose; *katalúō* (2647), to loosen, take apart, to destroy utterly; *olothreúō* (3645), to destroy, especially in the sense of slaying; *exolothreúō* (1842), to destroy utterly.

Ant.: *tēréō* (5083), to preserve; *suntēréō* (4933), to keep; *zōogonéō* (2225), to preserve alive; *phulássō* (5442), to preserve; *sṓzō* (4982), to save, preserve.

1312. διαφθορά *diaphthorá*; gen. *diaphthorás*, fem. noun from *diaphtheírō* (1311), to corrupt, destroy, perish. Corruption, destruction in a moral sense. Used in relation to the death of the body (Acts 2:27, 31; 13:35–37; Sept.: Ps 16:10). To die no more (Acts 13:34 [cf. Job 33:28; Ps 30:9; Isa 51:14]). It does not refer to extinction but to the change of the present constitution of the body or the change of the moral makeup of a person.

Syn.: *bórboros* (1004), mire, mud (metaphorically meaning moral degradation); *akatharsía* (167), impurity, uncleanness.

Ant.: *térēsis* (5084), keeping; *sōtēría* (4991), deliverance, preservation, salvation; *therapeía* (2322), healing, attendance; *íasis* (2392), cure, healing; *anakaínōsis* (342), renovation, renewing; *aphtharsía* (861), incorruption as pertains to the body; *adiaphthoría* (90), incorruptibility.

1313. διάφορος *diáphoros*; gen. *diaphórou*, masc.-fem., neut. *diáphoron*, adj. from *diaphérō* (1308), to be different, superior. Different. Distinct meanings: diverse, various (Rom 12:6; Heb 9:10; Sept.: Deut 22:9); to be superior, better (Heb 1:4; 8:6).

Syn.: *héteros* (2087), other, but qualitatively different in contrast to *állos* (243), numerically another; *poikílos* (4164), something which can take a variety of colors, manifold; *polupoíkilos* (4182), manifold; *krátistos* (2903), superior, corresponding to that particular meaning of the word.

Ant.: *hómoios* (3664), like, resembling; *parómoios* (3946), much like; *ísos* (2470), equal; *autós* (846), the same.

1314. διαφυλάσσω *diaphulássō*, **διαφυλάττω** *diaphuláttō*; fut. *diaphuláxō*, from *diá* (1223), an intens., and *phulássō* (5442), to guard, keep. To guard thoroughly, protect, meaning to preserve carefully (Luke 4:10; Sept.: Gen 28:15; Ps 91:11).

Syn.: *phrouréō* (5432), to keep with a military guard; *kratéō* (2902), to hold fast; *grēgoréō* (1127), to watch; *tēréō* (5083), to keep; *suntēréō* (4933), to preserve, keep, save; *sunéchō* (4912), to hold together.

Ant.: *apóllumi* (622), to destroy; *katargéō* (2673), to abolish; *kathairéō* (2507), to cast down; *lúō* (3089), to loose, dissolve; *katalúō* (2647), to destroy utterly;

olothreúō (3645), to destroy, especially in the sense of slaying; *exolothreúō* (1842), to destroy utterly; *phtheírō* (5351), to corrupt; *diaphtheírō* (1311), to corrupt thoroughly; *porthéō* (4199), to make havoc of, destroy, waste.

1315. διαχειρίζω *diacheirízō*; fut. *diacheirísō*, from *diá* (1223), an intens., and *cheirízō* (n.f.), to handle. In the NT, only in the mid. *diacheirízomai*, to lay hands upon, to kill, slay; used trans. in Acts 5:30; 26:21.

Syn.: *apokteínō* (615), to kill, used both physically and metaphorically; *anairéō* (337), to take up with the meaning of to kill; *analískō* (355), to consume; *thúō* (2380), to sacrifice by slaying a victim; *phoneúō* (5407), to murder; *thanatóō* (2289), to put to death, kill; *spházō* (4969), to slay or slaughter.

Ant.: *sốzō* (4982), to save from danger, suffering, or death; *diasốzō* (1295), to bring safely through, to rescue; *phulássō* (5442), to keep, guard, preserve.

1316. διαχωρίζω *diachōrízō*; fut. *diachōrísō*, from *diá* (1223), denoting separation, and *chōrízō* (5563), to separate throughout or wholly (Sept.: Gen 1:4, 6, 7). In the NT, only in the mid. *diachōrízomai*, to separate oneself wholly from or to depart, to go away from someone (Luke 9:33; Sept.: Gen 13:9, 11).

Syn.: *aphorízō* (873), to mark off by bounds, separate; *apodiorízō* (592), to mark off; *apospáō* (645), to draw away from; *apotássomai* (657), to go one's own way; *dicházō* (1369), to set at variance, draw apart; *dichotoméō* (1371), to bisect, cut asunder; *schízō* (4977), to rend, split, sever; *diairéō* (1244), to separate, divide; *merízō* (3307), to disunite, apportion, divide; *dialúō* (1262), to dissolve utterly, scatter.

Ant.: *déō* (1210), to bind, knit; *sundéō* (4887), to bind or join with; *proskolláō* (4347), to glue together; *sunarmologéō* (4883), to fit together; *sunantáō* (4876), to meet with; *sunéchō* (4912), to hold together; *sugkoinōnéō* (4790), to co-participate in, communicate with, be partaker of.

1317. διδακτικός *didaktikós*; fem. *didaktikḗ*, neut. *didaktikón*, adj. from *didáskō* (1321), to teach. Didactic, able to communicate Christian teaching, apt or skilled in teaching. A quality named as a requisite for a bishop (*epískopon* [1985] 1 Tim 3:2) or elder (*presbúteron* [4245]), the terms being synonymous (Acts 20:17, 28). This quality of being willing and ready to teach is not mentioned as one of the qualities of deacons in 1 Tim 3:8–13. In 2 Tim 2:24 the quality of being a teacher is urged upon Timothy as a special delegate of Paul (Acts 19:21, 22; Phil 2:19, 20) which reference is to Christian teaching. *Didaktikós* is to be contrasted with *didaktós* (1318), teachable, in John 6:45 a quote from Isa 54:13, "all . . . shall be taught of the Lord," and in 1 Cor 2:13 where Paul points out that what he taught was of the Holy Spirit and not with words of human wisdom.

1318. διδακτός *didaktós*; fem. *didaktḗ*, neut. *didaktón*, verbal adj. from *didáskō* (1321), to teach. Taught, used with the gen. of the agent as in John 6:45, "taught of God," meaning having the inherent possibility of being taught by God and therefore bearing personal responsibility. In 1 Cor 2:13 it refers to things or lessons taught or imparted or suggested by the Holy Spirit as contrasted to the things taught by words of human wisdom. There are things that are not taught by human wisdom but by God's Spirit, and the possibility of that learning is with everybody as the word "all" makes clear in John 6:45. To be distinguished from *didaktikós* (1317) which means communicative, didactic or able and apt to teach as in 1 Tim 3:2; 2 Tim 2:24 as one of the qualities of a bishop or elder, but not of a deacon (1 Tim 3:8–13).

1319. διδασκαλία *didaskalía*; gen. *didaskalías*, fem. noun from *didáskō*

(1321), to teach. Teaching or instruction as spoken of:

(I) The art or manner of teaching (Rom 12:7; 1 Tim 4:13, 16; 5:17; Titus 2:7). With the meaning of warning (Rom 15:4; 2 Tim 3:16 [cf. 1 Cor 10:11]).

(II) The thing taught, instruction, precept, doctrine: as coming from men, perverse (Matt 15:9; Mark 7:7; Eph 4:14; Col 2:22; 1 Tim 4:1; Sept.: Isa 29:13); from God meaning divine teaching (1 Tim 1:10; 4:6; 6:1, 3; 2 Tim 3:10; 4:3; Titus 1:9; 2:1, 10). A distinction must be made between the process of teaching and the subject matter of teaching. The Eng. word "teaching" may mean either the act of imparting truth or the body of truth imparted. Sometimes the biblical usage includes both meanings by way of double entendre.

(III) The NT employs two terms for teaching, *didachḗ* (1322), and *didaskalía*. Generally speaking, *didachḗ* means the substance of teaching and *didaskalía* the act of teaching. In the KJV this distinction is not made so apparent since both *didachḗ* (Matt 7:28; 16:12) and *didaskalía* (Eph 4:14; 1 Tim 4:1) are usually rendered "doctrine." Both *didachḗ* and *didaskalía* are used in the act. and pass. senses, i.e., the act of teaching and what is taught. The pass. is predominant in *didachḗ* which always means the act, and in many instances both the act and the content of Christian instruction. It also stresses the authority of the teacher while the latter, *didaskalía*, stresses the act of teaching and literally means that which belongs to the teacher (*didáskalos* [1320]). The content of teaching suggested by this term is apparent from such phrases like "precepts and doctrines" (Col 2:22), "sound doctrine" (1 Tim 1:10; 2 Tim 4:3; Titus 1:9), and without any qualification "the doctrine" (1 Tim 6:1, 3; Titus 2:10). *Didachḗ* occurs sixteen times and *didaskalía* occurs seventeen times in the NT.

(IV) Teaching (*didaskalía*) was numbered among the *charísmata* (5486), spiritual gifts of grace, which resulted from the bestowal of the Holy Spirit and which included such gifts as prophesying, healing, working of miracles, and tongues (Rom 12:7; 1 Cor 12:10f.).

(V) Teaching and preaching are mentioned in close association. The gift of teaching was regarded as conferring on its recipient a distinct function in the ministry of the Word. In the Gospels our Lord is described first as "preaching" the glad tidings of the kingdom (Mark 1:14) and then as "teaching" His disciples the inner meaning and principles of the gospel (Mark 4:1). In the early church preaching was distinguished from teaching, although in certain instances they were often combined (Matt 4:23; Acts 5:42; 28:31). Preaching was primarily the proclamation of the good news of salvation through Jesus Christ, whereas teaching was the systematic instruction in the details of Christian truth and duty which followed the summons to repentance and saving faith. While preaching and teaching were distinct as functions, they might, in some cases at least, be united in the ministry of one person (1 Tim 2:7; 2 Tim 1:11), especially as the content both of the preaching and the more elaborate instruction was necessarily often the same (Acts 5:42; 15:35; Col 1:28). Teachers are mentioned after apostles and prophets (1 Cor 12:28f.; Eph 4:11), and in a less formal list of spiritual functions, teaching is mentioned after prophecy (Rom 12:6f.). However, in 1 Corinthians "the word of wisdom" and "the word of knowledge," which together constituted the gift of teaching, are placed before prophecy (1 Cor 12:8, 10), and "a teaching" comes before "a revelation" (1 Cor 14:26).

(VI) Prophecy was a specialized form of teaching. The differences between the two apparently lay in the fact that while prophecy was the utterance of a revelation received directly from God, teaching was the utterance of that which one had gained by thought and reflection. The teacher must be led and guided by the Spirit to be a true teacher and have genuine spiritual teaching, but what he said was in a real sense his own. Some prophets were able also to teach, but not all teachers were able to prophesy.

(VII) The apostles might also teach. Paul speaks of himself as appointed to be both an apostle and a teacher (1 Tim 2:7; 2 Tim 1:11). Teachers, like apostles and prophets, traveled about from place to place, being greatly honored. They were not officials appointed by a church body. Teaching was not an office, for even as late as the fifth century laymen are called teachers (Apostolic Constitutions VIII, XXII). Local congregations tested both the message and the moral character of these visiting instructors.

(VIII) Teachers were more like the apostles, prophets and evangelists who were itinerant up to and during the post-apostolic period unlike pastors. At a later stage it was one of the qualifications of a bishop that he should be "apt to teach" (1 Tim 3:2) as teaching is a major part of his ministry.

(IX) Instruction was often given collectively, in public or in private, in the temple and at home (Acts 5:42), in the Christian congregation (Acts 11:26), and more generally in the meeting for edification such as Paul describes in detail in 1 Cor 14. According to this chapter, teaching came between the "psalm [or hymn of praise]" and the prophetic "revelation" (1 Cor 14:26). Supplementary teaching was given privately "from house to house" (Acts 20:20) or to individuals (Acts 18:26).

(X) Individuals instructed were to contribute toward the support of their teacher (Gal 6:6). In later times many churches came to have regular schools for the teaching of individuals, that of Alexandria being especially famous. The teaching was mostly oral. As time progressed, however, the epistles were also used for teaching. The teaching consisted of mainly a recital of the facts concerning the life, death, and resurrection of Jesus Christ (Rom 1:3f.; 1 Cor 15:1ff.; Gal 4:4f.). Also Christian ordinances (or, sacraments) were explained (1 Cor 11:23f.).

(XI) Meaningful instruction was to be conveyed through "hymns and spiritual songs" (Col 3:16) which could include admonition (Col 1:28), exhortation (1 Tim 4:13; 6:2), and even reproof and rebuke (2 Tim 4:2). The administration of these called for patience and longsuffering.

(XII) The Christian teacher taught "in the name of Jesus" (Acts 4:18; 5:28). He used the doctrines of the OT inasmuch as they bore witness of Christ. He repeated the teaching given by Christ with the formula "remember the words of the Lord Jesus" (Acts 20:35). He continued "in the apostles' doctrine" (Acts 2:42), and as occasion arose he applied the principles underlying the teaching of Jesus and relating to the doctrinal and ethical problems that arose within the church. In the later epistles a conservative tendency is noticeable. The content of Christian teaching came to be fixed and authoritative. It was called "the teaching" (1 Tim 6:1; 2 John 1:9 [cf. Rev 22:18f.]) or "sound doctrine" (2 Tim 4:3). Paul warns the Romans against departing from "the doctrine which ye learned" (Rom 16:17). Later Timothy is called a good minister because he had been "nourished up in the words of faith, and of good doctrine" (1 Tim 4:6), and in which he continued. The content of the teaching may be inferred from the fact that it is described in 1 Cor 12:8 as the "word of wisdom" and as the "word of knowledge." The word of wisdom was an acquaintance with "God's wisdom" (1 Cor 1:21) or the divine plan of redemption which Paul calls elsewhere "the mystery of God" (Col 2:2). The knowledge (gnósis [1108]) came by intuition and consisted of insight into truth through spiritual illumination but must not be taken as apokálupsis (602), revelation. Wisdom enabled the teacher to explain the truth, and knowledge as a divine gift qualified him to interpret it.

Syn.: paideía (3809), education or training; kḗrugma (2782), preaching; lógos (3056), word, speech, utterance, doctrine, precept, teaching; parádosis

(3862), delivery, the act of delivering over from one to another, that delivery being in some instances instruction, teaching, precept, ordinance.

1320. διδάσκαλος *didáskalos*; gen. *didaskálou*, masc. noun from *didáskō* (1321), to teach. Instructor, master, teacher.

(I) A teacher (Rom 2:20; Heb 5:12). The term occurs fifty-eight times in the NT, forty-eight times in the Gospels, forty-one refer to Jesus (twenty-nine in direct address). There are *didáskaloi* in the churches (Acts 13:1; 1 Cor 12:28, 29; Eph 4:11). Paul calls himself a teacher (1 Tim 2:7; 2 Tim 1:11). It correlates with *mathētḗs* (3101), a learner, pupil, disciple (Matt 10:24, 25; 12:38; 19:16; 22:16, 24, 36; Mark 4:38; 9:17, 38; 10:17, 20; 10:35; 12:14, 19, 32; 13:1; Luke 3:12; 6:40; 7:40; 9:38; 10:25; 11:45; 12:13; 18:18; 19:39; 20:21, 28, 39; 21:7; John 8:4; 20:16). When used in addressing Jesus (Matt 22:16; John 1:38), it is meant as a name of respect as given to the Jewish scribes (Luke 2:46) as was the custom of the time. Jesus assumed the absolute title of being called *Ho Didáskalos*, "The Teacher" (a.t. [Matt 26:18]).

(II) Acts 13:1 refers to *didáskaloi*, teachers, with *prophḗtai* (4396), prophets. From this it is concluded that in the Christian church the *didáskaloi*, teachers, appear as having a special function (Acts 13:1; 1 Cor 12:28, 29; Eph 4:11; James 3:1). These *didáskaloi* answer to the Jewish *grammateís* (pl.) (1122), scribes, and are to be viewed as in a special sense acquainted with and interpreters of God's salvation (Matt 13:52; Luke 2:46). To them fell the duty of giving progressive instruction of God's redeeming purpose, a function which, according to Eph 4:11, may have been united with *poimḗn* (4166), pastor, in one person. Notwithstanding, linguists have debated the precise relationship between teachers and pastors in that text. There is a growing consensus that pastors are a sub-group within the larger body of teachers. This seems to be true also for the expression "apostles and prophets."

(III) A comparison of Acts 13:1 with Rom 12:7; 2 Tim 1:11; 4:3; James 3:1 shows that teachers (*didáskaloi*) included not only those men who held the office of teacher but also those endowed with the teaching gift who ministered in an unofficial capacity. As distinct from the exhortations of prophets, the instruction given by teachers would be an exposition of the OT and of the words and acts of Christ.

(IV) Teachers were inferior to prophets and were connected with pastors (1 Cor 12:28, 29; Eph 4:11). Apostles and pastors always had the gift of teaching; prophets usually possessed it; but men might have it without belonging to any of these classes. Paul called himself, besides *kḗrux* (2783), preacher, an *apóstolos* (652), apostle in a restrictive sense having the same authority as the Twelve and with the special emphasis of *didáskalos ethnṓn* (pl. gen. of *éthnos* [1484], nation, Gentile), teacher of nations or the Gentiles (1 Tim 2:7; 2 Tim 1:11; see John 3:10; Gal 2:7ff.; Eph 3:8, 9). Spoken of Jesus (Matt 8:19; 9:11; 17:24; 23:8 [TR], in UBS, *kathēgētḗs* [2519], guide; 26:18; Mark 5:35; 14:14; Luke 6:40; 8:49; 22:11; John 3:2; 11:28; 13:13, 14 [cf. the *hēgoúmenoi* {2233}, leaders in Heb 13:7, 17]).

(V) The *poiménes* (4166), pastors or shepherds, and the *didáskaloi*, teachers, seem to have been members of the presbytery (Acts 20:28; 1 Tim 3:2; 2 Tim 2:24). The *didáskalos*, while certainly a *kḗrux* (2783), preacher, was distinct from an *euaggelistḗs* (2099), the evangelist (Eph 4:11; 1 Tim 2:7).

(VI) Side by side with them we find false teachers appearing, not only outside, but probably within the presbytery (1 Tim 1:3; 2 Tim 4:3) called *pseudodidáskaloi* (5572), false teachers (2 Pet 2:1), and *heterodidaskaléō* (2085), teaching a qualitatively different doctrine (1 Tim 1:3; 6:3).

Deriv.: *heterodidaskaléō* (2085), to teach another doctrine; *kalodidáskalos* (2567), good teacher or teacher of good things; *nomodidáskalos* (3547), an expounder or teacher of the Jewish law; *pseudodidáskalos* (5572), a false teacher indicating falsehood both in character and in the content of the teaching.

1321. διδάσκω *didáskō*; fut. *didáxō*, from *dáō* (n.f.), to know or teach. Teach, instruct by word of mouth (Matt 28:15, 20; Luke 11:1; 12:12; Acts 15:1; 1 Cor 11:14; Rev 2:14).

(I) Generally and in an absolute sense (Matt 4:23; 9:35; Mark 1:21; Luke 4:15; 1 Cor 4:17; 11:14; Eph 4:21). Construed with the acc. of person or thing or both: of person (Matt 5:2; Mark 9:31; Luke 4:31; John 7:35; Sept.: Job 13:23; 37:19; Prov 4:4); of thing (Matt 15:9; 1 Tim 4:11; Titus 1:11; Sept.: Isa 9:15; Eccl 12:9); of both person and thing (John 14:26; Heb 5:12). In the pass. construction, *edidáchthēte*, you were taught (2 Thess 2:15; Sept.: Deut 11:19; Judg 3:2; Prov 4:11; 22:21). Instead of the acc. of a thing it is sometimes followed by the inf. (Matt 28:20; Luke 11:1; Rev 2:14 [TR]; Sept.: Deut 4:1; 20:18; Job 10:2); or by *hóti* (3754), that (Mark 8:31); by *perí* (4012), regarding, with the gen. of a thing (1 John 2:27). With the dat. of person (acc. in [TR]; Rev 2:14; see Deut 33:10; Job 21:22).

(II) In the sense of to tutor, direct, advise, put in mind (Matt 28:15; John 9:34; Acts 21:21; Heb 8:11; Rev 2:20). Other references: Matt 7:29; 21:23; 22:16; 26:55; Mark 1:22; 2:13; 4:1, 2; 6:2, 6, 30, 34; 7:7; 11:17; 12:14, 35; 14:49; Luke 5:3, 17; 6:6; 13:10, 22, 26; 19:47; 20:21; 21:37; 23:5; John 6:59; 7:14, 28; 8:2, 20, 28; Acts 1:1; 4:2, 18; 5:21, 25, 28; 18:11, 25; 20:20; 21:28; 28:31; Rom 2:21; Gal 1:12; Col 2:7; 3:16; 1 Tim 2:12; 6:2; 2 Tim 2:2.

(III) In Col 1:28; 3:16 *didáskō* occurs with *nouthetéō* (3560), to admonish or to set the mind right. In this connection as well as in 1 Tim 4:11; 6:2; 2 Tim 2:2; Titus 1:11, *didáskō* is used in a pastoral and moral connection.

(IV) *Didáskō* has inherent in it the intent to influence the understanding of the person who is taught. Its counterparts are *akoúō* (191), to hear for the purpose of understanding, and *manthánō* (3129), to learn, from which *mathētḗs* (3101), learner, pupil, disciple, is derived. The one *didáskei*, teaches, and the other *mathēteúei* (3100), learns or assimilates what he learns as part of himself (Matt 10:24, 25; Luke 6:40; 19:39). *Kērússō* (2784), to preach or proclaim, does not have inherent the same expectation of learning and assimilation as that which is being taught (*didáskō*) (Matt 4:23; 9:35; 11:1; 13:54; Luke 20:1; Acts 5:42; 15:35). The thing aimed at when one teaches (*didáskō*) is the shaping of the will of the one taught by the communication of knowledge (Matt 5:19; Acts 21:21; Col 1:28). It is used in an absolute sense of Christ's teaching (Mark 9:31; 10:1; John 8:20; Col 1:28), and as instruction in the Christian faith and teaching (Acts 11:26; Rom 12:7; Col 1:28; Heb 5:12).

Deriv.: *didaktikós* (1317), instructive, didactic, skilled in teaching, communicative; *didaktós* (1318), capable of being taught, instructed; *didaskalía* (1319), instruction, teaching, either the manner of teaching or the content of teaching; *didáskalos* (1320), a teacher; *didachḗ* (1322), doctrine, instruction, the act or content of teaching which depends on the context in which it is found; *theodídaktos* (2312), taught by God.

Syn.: *paideúō* (3811), to instruct with discipline; *katēchéō* (2727), to teach orally, the word from which we derive our Eng. "catechize" and "catechism" which is religious instruction; *mathēteúō* (3100), to disciple, teach with the expectation of one's learning and appropriating; *muéō* (3453), to initiate into certain mysteries, learn a secret.

1322. διδαχή *didachḗ*; gen. *didachḗs*, fem. noun from *didáskō* (1321), to teach. In an act. sense it means the act of teaching, instructing, tutoring (Mark 4:2; 12:38; 1 Cor 14:6, 26; 2 Tim 4:2); in a pass. sense, teaching which is given, that which anyone teaches, the manner or

character of one's teaching (Matt 7:28; 22:33; Mark 1:22, 27; 11:18; Luke 4:32). In an absolute sense, it denotes the teaching of Jesus (2 John 1:9, 10); the Lord (Mark 11:18; John 18:19; Acts 13:12); the Apostles (Acts 2:42; 5:28; Titus 1:9); the things taught, precept, doctrine (Matt 16:12; John 7:16, 17; Acts 17:19; Rom 6:17; 16:17; Heb 6:2; 13:9). Other doctrines: of Balaam, magic, gnosticism (Rev 2:14 [cf. 2 Pet 2:15; Jude 1:11]); of the Nicolaitans, similar to that of Balaam (Rev 2:15 [cf. Rev 2:6]); of Jezebel, adultery, idolatry (Rev 2:24). Essentially *didachḗ* is the same as *didaskalía* (1319), sometimes meaning the manner of teaching and sometimes the content of teaching. Both are used in the act. and pass. senses, i.e., the act of teaching and the content of what is taught. However, it is to be noted that the pass. sense is predominant in *didachḗ* and the act. sense in *didaskalía*. In *didachḗ*, we have incorporated the authority of that which is taught, and *didaskalía* predominates in the act or art of teaching. *Didachḗ* is used only twice in the Pastoral Epistles (2 Tim 4:2; Titus 1:9) while *didaskalía*, with a stress on the art of teaching, occurs fifteen times.

Syn.: *lógos* (3056), word, doctrine or a discourse.

Ant.: *ágnoia* (52), want of knowledge or perception; *agnōsía* (56), willful ignorance; *agnóēma* (51), a sin of ignorance; *idiṓtēs* (2399), a person who is unskilled, unlearned; *agrámmatos* (62), unlearned.

1323. δίδραχμον *dídrachmon*; gen. *didráchmou*, neut. noun from *dís* (1364), twice, and *drachmḗ* (1406), a drachma, a Greek silver coin equal in value to the Roman denarius or *dinar dēnárion* (1220) which represented an average pay for one twelve-hour day's work (Matt 20:2). Didrachma, a double drachma. Each Jew used to pay yearly to God a *dídrachmon* into the temple treasury at Jerusalem, the sum which Moses ordered to be paid by every Israelite whenever the people were mustered (Ex 30:12, 13). This same tax was required for the repair of the temple in the reign of Joash (2 Chr 24:6, 9). Therefore, this became a type of voluntary tribute paid annually by every Jew. See Matt 17:24 when the collectors of the *dídrachma* (pl.) said to Peter, "Does not your master pay the *dídrachma*?" (a.t.). They did not intimate that Christ should pay more than a *dídrachmon* for Himself, but that He should also pay for His disciples. This He did, in fact, by having Peter give a *statếr* (4715), a coin equal to two *dídrachma*, or four Roman denarii for Himself and Peter (Matt 17:27).

Syn.: see *argúrion* (694), silver, money.

1324. Δίδυμος *Dídumos*; gen. *Didúmou*, masc. proper noun. Didymus, meaning twain, twin (Sept.: Gen 25:24), double. Given as a surname of the Apostle Thomas, the twin (John 11:16; 20:24; 21:2). See *Thốmás* (2381), Thomas.

1325. δίδωμι *dídōmi*; fut. *dốsō*, aor. *édōka*, 2d aor. *édōn*, perf. *dédōka*, pluperf. *ededốkein*, pres. 3d person pl. *didóasi* (Rev 17:13 UBS); aor. subjunctive 3d person. sing. *dốsē* (John 17:2); 2d aor. opt. 3d person. *dốē* (Rom 15:5; Eph 1:17); pluperf. *dedốkei*, without augment (Mark 14:44; John 11:57 *dedốkeisan*). To give of one's own accord and with good will. Used trans., with the acc. and dat. expressed or implied.

(I) To give, bestow upon.

(A) Generally (Matt 4:9, "all these things will I give thee"; 13:12; 25:8; Mark 2:26; 10:21; Luke 6:4; 12:33; John 4:5 [cf. Gen 48:22; Sept.: Gen 24:53; 25:5, 6; 1 Sam 30:11, 12]).

(B) Spoken of sacrifice, homage, meaning to offer, present (Luke 2:24; Rev 4:9).

(C) Spoken of a person who does anything to or for another, one from whom anything is received, the source, author or cause of a favor, benefit to anyone; to give, grant, permit, present, cause. **(1)** Generally (Matt 21:23, "who gave thee this authority?"; John 4:12; Acts 8:19; 1 Cor 7:25; 2 Cor 8:10). In Luke 14:9, "give this man place" means make way, give way, yield

(also Eph 4:27). Also with an acc. where the idea may often also be expressed by the verb cognate with the noun, e.g., to give praise to God meaning to praise (Luke 18:43); to give an answer or to answer (John 1:22); to give occasion (2 Cor 5:12). See also 1 Tim 5:14. To give glory to God means to glorify, praise, honor (Luke 17:18; John 9:24; Acts 12:23; Sept.: Josh 7:19; Jer 13:16); to give hindrance or hinder (1 Cor 9:12); to give commandment or command (John 11:57; 12:49); to give offense or offend (2 Cor 6:3); to give a strike or to hit (John 18:22); to give a mark or engrave (Rev 13:16); to give a word easily understood or speak distinctly (1 Cor 14:9). **(2)** Spoken of God or of Christ as the author or source of what one has or receives; to give, grant, bestow, impart (Matt 6:11, "give us [or grant us] this day our daily bread"; 9:8, "God who gave power unto men" [a.t.]; 12:39; Mark 13:11; Luke 12:32; John 3:27; 17:22, 24; Acts 7:5; 11:17; 2 Cor 9:9; Gal 3:22; Eph 4:8; 2 Tim 2:7; Rev 2:28). To give grace, to grant a favor, or confer a benefit (Rom 12:3, 6; 1 Cor 3:10; Eph 3:8; James 4:6). In Rev 2:21, "I gave her space," granted her time. Also of rulers (Acts 13:20, 21). In various constructions as with the gen. of part, "To him . . . will I give to eat of the hidden manna" (Rev 2:17). In 1 John 4:13, "he hath given us of his Spirit." Followed by *eis* (1519), into, their mind or their hearts (Heb 8:10; see also 10:16; Rev 17:17). Construed often with the dat. and an inf. as a neut. subj. instead of an acc. (Matt 13:11, "unto you it is given [granted] to know" [a.t.]; John 5:26; Acts 2:4; Rom 15:5; 2 Tim 1:18; Rev 6:4). This inf. is sometimes implied (Matt 19:11; John 19:11; Rev 11:3). With *hína* (2443), so that, used instead of the inf. (Mark 10:37). With an acc. and inf. meaning to permit, suffer, grant (Acts 2:27; 10:40; 13:35; 14:3). In Rev 3:8, "I have given before you an open door" (a.t.), meaning I have granted or caused an open door to be before you. Spoken of evil or punishment divinely inflicted, meaning to give, inflict

(2 Thess 1:8; Rev 18:7). In 2 Cor 12:7, "a thorn in the flesh was given me" (a.t.).

(D) Metaphorically, of things which are the cause, source or occasion of anything, meaning to give, impart, cause (Acts 3:16, "and the faith gave him strength" [a.t.]). With an acc. where the idea may also be expressed by the cognate verb (Matt 24:29, "and the moon shall not give her light" instead of the verb *phéggō*, to shed light; 1 Cor 14:7, 8; James 5:18, "and the heaven gave rain" instead of rained).

(II) To give with the particular meaning of to give up, deliver over, present, commit to, i.e., to put into the hands, power, or possession of anyone.

(A) Generally of a person (Matt 5:31; 14:8, 9; 19:7; 24:45; Mark 6:41; Luke 7:15, "and he gave him [or delivered him] to his mother" [a.t.]; 11:7, 8; John 6:51; 18:11; Rev 15:7). In Acts 9:41, "and having given her the hand" (a.t.). In Acts 1:26, "they gave in their lots" (a.t.). See also Sept.: Lev 16:8. In Luke 15:22, "give [or bring] a ring for his hand" (a.t.). With the dat. of person and the inf., to give unto them to eat and to drink (Matt 14:16; Luke 8:55; 15:16; John 4:7; 6:31; Rev 16:6). In Matt 7:6, "give . . . unto the dogs."

(B) In the sense of to commit or trust to the charge or care of anyone, as spoken of things (Matt 16:19; 25:15; Mark 12:9; Luke 12:48; 16:12; 20:16; John 3:35; 5:22; 13:3); of works to be done (John 5:36; 17:4); of instruction given (John 17:8; Acts 7:38); spoken of persons delivered over, committed to one's charge, teaching (John 10:29; 17:6, 9, 11, 12, 24; Heb 2:13).

(C) To give oneself, deliver oneself, meaning to consecrate or devote oneself (2 Cor 8:5). Followed by *hupér* (5228), on behalf of, for (Gal 1:4, to give or devote oneself to death for anyone; see also Titus 2:14). In 1 Tim 2:6, "gave himself a ransom for all." See also Luke 22:19; John 6:51. In Matt 20:28, "to give his life a ransom for [*antí* {473}, instead, for]." Also Mark 10:45. Construction with *eis* (1519), unto, with the acc. of place, to go to any place (Acts 19:31, to give oneself to, to go to).

(III) To give, i.e., to give forth, render up, yield, especially in return for anything bestowed, e.g., as a gift, labor, attention, hence often found where *apodídōmi* (591), to give over, might have been used.

(A) Generally of persons (Rev 20:13, "the sea gave up the dead which were in it"); of things (Luke 6:38). Metaphorically, "shall render an account of himself to God" (a.t. [Rom 14:12]).

(B) Spoken of what is given as a reward or recompense for labor, meaning to give, reward, pay (Matt 20:4, 14; Mark 14:11; Rev 11:18); of the price of anything, tribute, tithes (Matt 16:26; 22:17; 27:10; Mark 8:37; Luke 20:22; 23:2; Heb 7:4; Sept.: Zech 11:12).

(C) Spoken of the earth, to give forth, yield fruit (Matt 13:8; Mark 4:7, 8; Sept.: Zech 8:12).

(IV) To place or to put.

(A) With the acc. and followed by *epí* (1909), upon, as in Luke 19:23, to place money upon the table (cf. Matt 25:27, i.e., to place at interest [cf. Sept.: Lev 25:37; Rev 8:3, meaning to offer in sacrifice]). In Luke 15:22 with *eis* (1519), in, with the meaning of put, apply effort, endeavor (Luke 12:58, "give diligence").

(B) Spoken of miracles, meaning to do, perform, exhibit (Matt 24:24; Acts 2:19 quoted from Joel 2:30; Sept.: Ex 7:9; Deut 13:1).

(C) With a double acc. of person, meaning to appoint, constitute, where the last acc. is by apposition (Eph 1:22, "and gave him [the 1st acc.] head [the 2d acc.] over all things" [a.t.]; see also Eph 4:11). In the Sept. *títhēmi* (5087), to place (Gen 17:5; Ex 7:1).

(D) Spoken of a law or ordinance meaning to give, i.e., to ordain, institute, prescribe (John 7:19; 7:22, circumcision; Acts 7:8, testament or covenant of circumcision; Gal 3:21, law; Sept.: Num 25:12; Lev 26:46; Josh 24:25; Ezra 9:11, to give a testament or covenant). See also Gen 17:2; Lev 26:1 where the Sept. has *títhēmi*.

Deriv.: *anadídōmi* (325), to deliver, hand over; *apodídōmi* (591), to pay back, reward; *diadídōmi* (1239), to deliver over in succession; *dóma* (1390), gift; *dósis* (1394), gift, giving; *dótēs* (1395), giver; *dōreá* (1431) and *dōron* (1435), gift, primarily a cultic offering; *ekdídōmi* (1554), to give forth; *epidídōmi* (1929), to give over, deliver to, give, offer; *metadídōmi* (3330), to impart; *paradídōmi* (3860), to deliver from hand to hand, from one to another; *prodídōmi* (4272), to give before.

Syn.: *dōréomai* (1433), to give freely, emphasizing the free aspect; *metadídōmi* (3330), to impart or give from one to another. With the meaning of add: *epichorēgéō* (2023), to supply, minister; *charízomai* (5483), to grant, bestow; *paréchō* (3930), to provide, supply; *aponémō* (632), to assign, apportion.

Ant.: *lambánō* (2983), to take, lay hold of; *aírō* (142), to lift, carry, take up or away; *déchomai* (1209), to receive; *prosdéchomai* (4327), to receive favorably; *drássomai* (1405), to grasp with the hand; *katéchō* (2722), to hold, take; *piázō* (4084), to lay or take hold of forcefully.

1326. **διεγείρω** *diegeírō*; fut. *diegerō*, from *diá* (1223), an intens., and *egeírō* (1453), to raise, rouse. To wake up fully, arouse, used trans. of persons as from sleep (Matt 1:24; Mark 4:38, 39; Luke 8:24); of things such as the sea, to agitate, in the pass. (John 6:18); of the mind, to excite, incite, stir up (2 Pet 1:13; 3:1).

Syn.: *eknéphō* (1594), to become sober; *exupnízō* (1852), to rouse a person out of sleep; *diagrēgoréō* (1235), to watch, being fully awake; *anazōpuréō* (329), to kindle afresh, revive; *parotrúnō* (3951), to urge on; *sugkinéō* (4787), to move together, excite; *sugchéō* (4797), to pour together or mix up; *paroxúnō* (3947), to provoke; *erethízō* (2042), to stir up; *anastatóō* (387), to unsettle.

Ant.: *hēsucházō* (2270), to be still; *katastéllō* (2687), to quiet.

1327. διέξοδος *diéxodos*; gen. *diexódou*, fem. noun from *diá* (1223), through, and *éxodos* (1841), a way out. A highway, a place where several ways or streets divide or where there is an opening out of them. In the NT, a thoroughfare, a place in a city where several streets meet, an intersection (Matt 22:9).

Syn.: *hodós* (3598), a road, highway.

1328. **διερμηνευτής** *diermēneutḗs*; gen. *diermēneutoú*, masc. noun from *diermēneúō* (1329), to interpret fully. An interpreter (1 Cor 14:28).

1329. **διερμηνεύω** *diermēneúō*; fut. *diermēneúsō*, from *diá* (1223), an intens., and *hermēneúō* (2059), to interpret, translate. To explain clearly and exactly (Luke 24:27); to interpret, translate, explain from one language into another (Acts 9:36; 1 Cor 12:30; 14:5, 13, 27).

Deriv.: *diermēneutḗs* (1328), an interpreter.

1330. **διέρχομαι** *diérchomai*; fut. *dieleúsomai*, from *diá* (1223), through, and *érchomai* (2064), to come, go.

(I) To come or go through, to pass through (Matt 12:43; 19:24; Mark 10:25 [TR]; Luke 4:30; 9:6; 11:24; 17:11; 19:1, 4; John 4:4; 8:59; Acts 8:4, 40; 9:32; 12:10; 13:6; 14:24; 15:3, 41; 16:6; 18:23; 19:1, 21; 20:2; 1 Cor 10:1; 16:5; 2 Cor 1:16; Heb 4:14, "who has passed through the heavens" [a.t.], i.e., all the heavens, right up to the throne of God [cf. 2 Cor 12:2, 4; Eph 4:10; Heb 7:26; Sept.: Gen 41:46; Josh 18:4; 1 Sam 30:31; 2 Chr 23:15; Ezek 9:4; 29:11; 44:2]). In Acts 8:4, 40, the surrounding areas (see also Acts 10:38; 17:23; 20:25). To go or travel through the country as far as (Acts 11:19, 22), or simply to go or pass a place; followed by *héōs* (2193), until (Luke 2:15; Acts 9:38). Metaphorically in Rom 5:12, "death passed upon all men." See Sept.: 2 Sam 17:24; Jon 2:4. Spoken of things such as a sword, to pierce through (Luke 2:35). Metaphorically, of a rumor meaning to go out through the country, to be spread abroad (Luke 5:15).

(II) Spoken of those who pass over the river, lake, sea (Mark 4:35; Luke 8:22; Acts 13:14, passing over by water from Perga to Antioch [cf. Acts 13:13; 18:27]; Sept.: Deut 4:21; Jer 2:10; 48:32).

Syn.: *poreúomai* (4198), to journey, walk; *diaporeúomai* (1279), to go through; *periágō* (4013), to lead or go about; *diodeúō* (1353), to travel throughout; *periérchomai* (4022), to go around or about; *diaperáō* (1276), to pass through; *hodoiporéō* (3596), to go on a journey; *peripatéō* (4043), to walk.

Ant.: *ménō* (3306), to abide, stay; *epiménō* (1961), to abide in; *kataménō* (2650), to abide with the concept of continuous residence; *paraménō* (3887), to remain or continue near; *prosménō* (4357), to abide still longer; *diatríbō* (1304), to spend or pass time, to stay; *aulízomai* (835), to lodge; *agrauléō* (63), to stay in a fold in a field.

1331. διερωτάω *dierōtáō*; contracted *dierōtṓ*, fut. *dierōtḗsō*, from *diá* (1223), an intens., and *erōtáō* (2065), to ask, inquire. To inquire diligently or repeatedly (Acts 10:17).

Syn.: *punthánomai* (4441), to learn by inquiry; *zētéō* (2212), to seek; *exetázō* (1833), to examine, seek out; *epizētéō* (1934), to seek after; *ekzētéō* (1567), to search after; *diaginṓskō* (1231), to ascertain exactly; *akribóō* (198), to learn by diligent or exact inquiry; *ereunáō* (2045), to search, examine; *exereunáō* (1830), to search diligently.

Ant.: *apokrínomai* (611), to give an answer to a question; *antapokrínomai* (470), to reply against; *apologéomai* (626), to answer by way of making a defense; *antilégō* (483), to speak against, to answer back.

1332. διετής *dietḗs*; gen. *dietoús*, masc.-fem., neut. *dietés*, adj. from *dís* (1364), twice, and *étos* (2094), year. Of two years continuance or two years old (Matt 2:16,

"from the child of two years old and under" [a.t.]; Sept.: Ezra 3:8).

Deriv.: *dietía* (1333), a space of two years.

1333. διετία *dietía*; gen. *dietías*, fem. noun from *dietḗs* (1332), two years old or of two years. A period of two years (Acts 24:27; 28:30).

1334. διηγέομαι *diēgéomai*; contracted *diēgoúmai*, fut. *diēgésomai*, from *diá* (1223), through or an intens., and *hēgéomai* (2233), to lead. To conduct a narration through to the end. To recount, relate in full (Mark 5:16; 9:9; Luke 8:39; 9:10; Acts 8:33 [quoted from Isa 53:8]; 9:27; 12:17; Heb 11:32).

Deriv.: *diḗgēsis* (1335), a narrative and not a declaration; *ekdiēgéomai* (1555), to recount, rehearse or relate particularly.

Syn.: *anaggéllō* (312), to announce, report; *apaggéllō* (518), to announce or report from a person or place, declare; *diaggéllō* (1229), to announce thoroughly, declare fully; *kataggéllō* (2605), to proclaim; *dēlóō* (1213), to make plain, declare; *phrázō* (5419), to declare; *gnōrízō* (1107), to make known; *emphanízō* (1718), to declare plainly; *phaneróō* (5319), to manifest; *anatíthemai* (394), to declare, communicate; *mēnúō* (3377), to disclose something before unknown; *exaggéllō* (1804), to tell out, proclaim abroad; *légō* (3004), to tell; *megalúnō* (3170), to magnify; *exēgéomai* (1834), to declare by making plain; *diasaphéō*, (1285) to make clear.

Ant.: *krúptō* (2928), to hide; *sigáō* (4601), to keep silent; *siōpáō* (4623), to be mute, hold one's peace.

1335. διήγησις *diḗgēsis*; gen. *diēgéseōs*, fem. noun from *diēgéomai* (1334), to declare, relate. A narration, history (Luke 1:1).

Ant.: *sigḗ* (4602), silence.

1336. διηνεκές *diēnekés*; gen. *diēnekoús*, neut. of *diēnekḗs*, adj. from *diaphérō* (1308), to bear through. Continual, perpetual, protracted. *Tó diēnekés* used as a subst. meaning continuity, in the expression *eis* (1519), unto, *tó diēnekés*, continually (Heb 7:3), refers to Jesus Christ who became our priest before God. Having become Man and the mediator between God and man (2 Tim 2:5), He will ever be; i.e., we shall never need another priest, as in the OT, to stand between us and God. Heb 10:1 refers to the sacrifices of the OT that had to be offered repeatedly until Jesus Christ offered Himself, a lamb without blemish and without spot (Heb 10:10, 12; 1 Pet 1:19).

Syn.: *eis télos* (*eis* [1519], unto; *télos* [5056], end), unto the end, continual; *diá pantós* (*diá* [1223], throughout; *pantós* [3843] the gen. neut. of *pás* [3956], every), at all times, always; *adialeíptōs* (89), continually, unceasingly; *pántote* (3842), at all times, always; *aeí* (104), perpetually; *aiónios* (166), used as an adv. meaning forever, always.

Ant.: *próskairos* (4340), for a season; *olígos* (3641), brief.

1337. **διθάλασσος** *dithálassos*; gen. *dithalássou*, masc.-fem., neut. *dithálasson*, adj. from *dís* (1364), twice, and *thálassa* (2281), sea. Where two seas meet, between two seas. In the NT, it probably refers to a shoal or sandbank at the confluence of two opposite currents (Acts 27:41).

1338. **διϊκνέομαι** *diïknéomai*; contracted *diïknoúmai*, fut. *diïxomai*, from *diá* (1223), through, and *hiknéomai* (n.f., see below), to come. To stand apart, go or pass through, pierce through (Heb 4:12).

Deriv. of *hiknéomai* (n.f.): *aphiknéomai* (864), to arrive; *ephiknéomai* (2185), to arrive at, reach; *hikanós* (2425), sufficient; *íchnos* (2487), footstep.

Syn.: *nússō* (3572), to pierce; *diérchomai* (1330), to go through; *ekkentéō* (1574), to pierce; *peripeírō* (4044), to put on a spit, hence, to pierce.

1339. **διΐστημι** *diḯstēmi*; fut. *diastḗsō*, aor. *diéstēsa*, from *diá* (1223), denoting

separation, and *hístēmi* (2476), to stand. Trans., to separate, place asunder. Intrans., to separate oneself, go away. In the NT, spoken of place used intrans. meaning to depart from (Luke 24:51; Acts 27:28 where the meaning is departing a little or going a little further); spoken of time, to pass away, to elapse (Luke 22:59).

Deriv.: *diástēma* (1292), distance, space.

Syn.: *ápeimi* (548), to go away; *metabaínō* (3327), to go or pass over from one place to another; *apérchomai* (565), to go away; *anachōréō* (402), to withdraw, depart; *hupochōréō* (5298), to go back, retire; *éxeimi* (1826), to depart; *apodēméō* (589), to go to another country.

Ant.: *ménō* (3306), to stay, abide; *diaménō* (1265), to remain throughout; *apoleípō* (620), to remain; *perileípō* (4035), to leave over; *hístēmi* (2476), to stand, stay, abide.

1340. **διϊσχυρίζομαι** *diïschurízomai*; fut. *diischurísomai*, mid. deponent from *diá* (1223), an intens., and *ischurízomai* (n.f.), to corroborate, confirm, affirm, which is from *ischurós* (2478), firm, strong. To affirm or assert strongly or vehemently. Used in an absolute sense in Luke 22:59; Acts 12:15.

Syn.: *diabebaióomai* (1226), to make sure, affirm confidently; *pháskō* (5335), to affirm by way of alleging or professing; *phēmí* (5346), to say with affirmation.

Ant.: *aporéō* (639), to be in doubt or perplexity; *diaporéō* (1280), to be perplexed; *diakrínō* (1252), to doubt, foresee difficulties; *distázō* (1365), to doubt, waver; *arnéomai* (720), to deny; *aparnéomai* (533), to deny utterly.

1341. **δικαιοκρισία** *dikaiokrisía*; gen. *dikaiokrisías*, fem. noun from *díkaios* (1342), just, righteous, and *krísis* (2920), judgment. A judgment which renders justice and produces right. Righteous judgment (Rom 2:5 [cf. Hos 6:5; 2 Thess 1:5]).

Ant.: *prosōpolēpsía* (4382), partiality, favoritism; *pseúdos* (5579), falsehood.

1342. δίκαιος *díkaios*; fem. *dikaía*, neut. *díkaion*, adj. from *díkē* (1349), right, just. Righteous, just. Used in the neut. *tó díkaion*, that which is right, conformable to right, pertaining to right, that which is just. This is expected by the one who sets the rules and regulations whereby man must live, whether that be society or God. Therefore, it means that which is expected as duty and which is claimed as a right because of one's conformity to the rules of God or society.

When used in the masc. or fem. adjectivally of persons, it refers to the one who acts conformably to justice and right without any deficiency or failure. Thus it is applied to God (John 17:25; Rom 3:26); Christ as the God-Man (Matt 27:19, 24; Luke 23:47; Acts 3:14; 7:52; 22:14; 1 Pet 3:18; 1 John 1:9; 2:1; Rev 16:5).

Being *díkaios*, just, means that one conforms in his actions to his constitutionally just character. The rules are self-imposed. When this absolute justice is applied to man, it is stated that there is no man who in his behavior can fully meet the expectations of God in his life (Rom 3:10).

Díkaios may also apply to the person who establishes his own rules of life. Such were the Pharisees whom the Lord exposed as righteous in their own eyes (Matt 9:13; 23:28; Luke 18:9). Having set up and kept, or pretended to keep certain standards, they called themselves righteous or just in the sight of God. Most of these rules and regulations, however, were not those of inner holiness and conformity to God, but mere performance of external ceremonial ordinances (Rom 10:3).

The nonbelievers, the heathen, call others righteous or just as they compare them with their own standards, such as social virtues. It has more of a social than a divine reference. Plato designated *dikaiosúnē* (1343), righteousness, as inseparably linked with *sōphrosúnē* (4997), soberness or sobriety, the expression of a sound mind, the ability to place restrictions on one's freedom in action. In the heathen mind, a *díkaios* is one who neither selfishly nor forgetfully transgresses the bounds fixed for him. He gives to everyone his due, yet still desires what is his and may not in the least withdraw an assertion of his own claims. Christianity must continually combat such a view. The heathen say, "My right is my duty," whereas the Christian says, "My duty is my right."

The OT righteous were those whose conduct was made conformable to God and whose justification was made possible through their faith in the promised Redeemer (Hab 2:4; Gal 3:11 [cf. Gen 6:9; Heb 11:7]).

In the NT those that are called righteous (*díkaioi*) are those who have conditioned their lives by the standard which is not theirs, but God's (Rom 2:13; 5:7; 1 Tim 1:9). They are the people related to God and who, as a result of this relationship, walk with God (Matt 1:19; 5:45; 10:41; 13:17, 49; 23:29, 35; 25:37; Mark 2:17; 6:20; Luke 1:6, 17; 2:25; 5:32; 15:7; 20:20; 23:50; Acts 10:22; 24:15; Rom 1:17; Titus 1:8; Heb 10:38; 12:23; James 5:6; 1 Pet 3:12; 4:18; 2 Pet 1:13; 2:7, 8; 1 John 3:7; Rev 22:11). A righteous person is one justified by faith and showing forth his faith by his works (James 2:14–26; 1 John 3:12).

Díkaios is equivalent to *eusebés* (2152), pious (Acts 10:2), and fearing God (v. 22). Peter spoke of Cornelius as having a fear of God and his righteousness as being accepted by God (Acts 10:35). This coincides with the Pauline doctrine of justification. A person is just or righteous with the righteousness which is through the faith of Christ, the righteousness which is of God by faith (Phil 3:9). He is justified through faith (Rom 5:19) and brings forth the fruits of righteousness or justification (Phil 1:11; see Matt 13:43; 25:46; Luke 14:14; Heb 11:4).

The word *díkaios* is also used of dispositions, judgments, things to indicate their just, right, or conformable relation to justice or righteousness (Matt 20:4, 7; Luke 12:57; John 5:30; 7:24; Acts 4:19; Rom 7:12; Eph 6:1; Phil 1:7; 4:8; Col 4:1; 2

Thess 1:5, 6; 2 Tim 4:8; Rev 15:3; 16:7; 19:2).

Deriv.: *dikaiokrisía* (1341), righteous judgment; *dikaiosúnē* (1343), righteousness; *dikaióō* (1344), to justify; *dikaíōs* (1346), justly.

Syn.: *agathós* (18), good, i.e., one whose goodness and works of goodness are transferred to others; yet *díkaios* is a concept of a relation and presupposes a norm, whereas the subject of *agathós*, good and doing good, is its own norm. Therefore, *agathós* includes the predicate of *díkaios*. In the NT, *díkaios* stands in opposition to *paránomos*, unlawful (related to *paranomía* [3892], transgression of the law). In 1 Pet 3:12 the righteous stand as the opposite of those who do evil; in 1 Pet 4:18 as contrary to the ungodly and the sinner; in 2 Pet 2:7 as the opposite of *áthesmos* (113), translated "wicked" but actually meaning "without an acceptable standard"; and in 2 Pet 2:8 contrasted to *ánomos* (459), lawless. See 1 Tim 1:9. In most instances *díkaios* stands in opposition to *ádikos* (94), unrighteous; *hágios* (40), holy in the sense of blameless in character; *hósios* (3741), sacred, the performer of the ordinances. See *dikaiosúnē* (1343), righteousness, and *euthús* (2117), straight, true.

1343. δικαιοσύνη *dikaiosúnē*; gen. *dikaiosúnēs*, fem. noun from *díkaios* (1342), just, righteous. Justice, righteousness. It is the essence of *tó díkaion*, that which is just, or *díkaios*, of him who is just or righteous. The *súnē* ending makes this an abstraction. Righteousness fulfills the claims of *díkē*, which, in the case of the believer, are God's claims; and in the case of the nonbeliever, the claims of that higher authority which a person adopts as his own standard. *Dikaiosúnē*, righteousness, is thus conformity to the claims of higher authority and stands in opposition to *anomía* (458), lawlessness.

In both the OT and NT, righteousness is the state commanded by God and standing the test of His judgment (2 Cor 3:9; 6:14; Eph 4:24). It is conformity to

all that He commands or appoints. Since God Himself is the standard of the believers, the righteousness of God means the righteousness which belongs to God or to oneself from God, or God-like righteousness (Matt 6:33; James 1:20). Thus righteousness, in general, is God's uprightness or standard, without reference to any particular form of its embodiment, to which man is expected to conform.

The righteousness of God is the claim which God has upon man. In order for man to recognize and fully submit to that claim of God upon his life, he must receive God as He offers Himself and His righteousness to him as a gift (Rom 5:17). Man can only accept the claims of God upon his life as he repents of his sin and receives Christ as His Savior by faith. He thus becomes a child of God, realizing God's claims upon him by the miraculous regenerating action of the Holy Spirit (John 1:12; Rom 4:11–13; 5:21; 6:16; 8:10; 9:30; 10:6; 2 Cor 6:7, 14; Eph 4:24; 6:14; 2 Pet 1:1).

The recognition and acceptance of God's claim upon man, realized through faith, stands in opposition to the righteousness which is of the Law (Rom 10:5; Gal 3:21) and which is man's acceptance of the claims of the Law upon his life. Man in his natural, fallen condition tends rather to accept his own set of standards, creating his own righteousness (Rom 10:3; Phil 3:6). In reality, however, such a set of standards is not righteousness (Rom 10:3, 5; Gal 3:21) and does not satisfy God. God's righteousness is imputed and imparted as a gift to man and not earned. It results in God's act of justification by faith through Christ.

(I) Doing alike to all, that which is equal, that which is equitable, impartial; spoken of a judge (Acts 17:31; Rev 19:11). In Heb 11:33, "wrought righteousness" means dispensed justice to the nations. See Rom 9:28 quoted from Isa 10:22; Ps 9:8; 35:24; Isa 5:16; 9:7.

(II) Character, conduct, the being just as one should be, i.e., rectitude, uprightness, righteousness, virtue, equivalent to the adj. *díkaios* (1342), just, righteous.

(A) Of actions, duties, equivalent to *tó díkaion*, what is right, proper, fit (Matt 3:15).

(B) Of disposition or conduct in common life (Eph 5:9; 1 Tim 6:11; 2 Tim 2:22; Heb 1:9; 7:2; Rev 19:11; Sept.: 1 Sam 26:23; Job 29:14; Ps 15:2; 50:6; Prov 8:18, 20). Including the idea of kindness, benignity, liberality (2 Cor 9:9, 10; 2 Pet 1:1 [cf. *díkaios*, just, righteous]). Equal to alms (Matt 6:1, in later MSS; Sept.: Gen 20:13; 21:23; 1 Sam 12:7; Ps 24:5; Isa 63:7; Mic 6:5).

(C) Spoken of that righteousness which has regard to God and the divine law: **(1)** Merely external and consisting of the observance of external precepts as righteousness of the law (Phil 3:6, 9 where it is contrasted with righteousness which is through faith). **(2)** Internal, where the heart is right with God, piety toward God, and hence righteousness, godliness, i.e., faith acceptable to God (Matt 5:6, 10, 20; 6:33; 21:32; Luke 1:75; Acts 10:35; 24:25; Rom 6:16, 18f.; Heb 1:9; 5:13; James 3:18; Sept.: Gen 18:19; 1 Kgs 3:6; Ps 17:15; Ezek 14:14). To count or impute as righteousness, i.e., to regard as evidence of piety (Rom 4:3, 5, 6, 9, 22; Gal 3:6; James 2:23, all quoted from Gen 15:6), hence the righteousness which is of (*ek* [1537], out of) or through (*diá* [1223]) faith in Christ, i.e., where faith is counted or imputed as righteousness or as evidence of piety (Rom 9:30; 10:6; Phil 3:9; Heb 11:7). Christ is presented as the source or author of righteousness (1 Cor 1:30). Thus the righteousness of God, spoken of objectively, means the righteousness which God approves, requires, bestows (Rom 1:17; 3:21, 22, 25, 26). Those on whom God bestows His righteousness become righteous before God (2 Cor 5:21; Sept.: Ps 5:8). **(3)** In the highest and most perfect sense, of God subjectively, i.e., as an attribute of His character (Rom 3:5); of Christ (John 16:8, 10).

(III) By metonymy, in the sense of being regarded as just, i.e., imputation

of righteousness, justification, *dikaíōsis* (1347) being the act of justification (Rom 5:17, 21; 10:4, 5; 2 Cor 3:9), the ministration of righteousness being the opposite of the ministration of condemnation. See Gal 2:21; 3:21; 5:5. Rom 10:3 refers to the mode or the way of justification.

(IV) In Class. Gr., righteousness is chiefly a social virtue. In the NT, however, righteousness is, above all things, a religious concept. It is righteousness according to divine standard, conformity to the will and nature of God Himself. In the NT, the character of God is presented as absolute moral perfection. Therefore, righteousness in men becomes a name for that disposition and method of life which aligns itself with God's holy will. In short, righteousness is Godlikeness or godliness. The adj. *díkaios* (1342) occurs with nearly equal frequency in the Synoptic Gospels and the Pauline Epistles.

(V) The noun *dikaiosúnē* occurs six times in Matthew, once in Luke, and not at all in Mark, and is more frequently used by Paul than by all the other NT writers combined. To understand more fully the NT doctrine of righteousness, examine the Synoptic Gospels.

In Matt 5:20, the Lord Jesus differentiated between what He meant by righteousness and what the Pharisees meant by it. The popular Jewish idea of righteousness grew out of the then-current concept of God and of His revelation. Righteousness was thought to consist of obedience to commandments, and the nature of the divine commands was viewed quite superficially. The rich young man who came to Jesus asking what he should do to inherit eternal life is an illustration of the view which the Jews took of the OT commandments (Matt 19:16ff.). This young man said that he had kept them all. His concept evidently was that to refrain from the outward sins which they forbade, i.e., stealing, lying, Sabbath-breaking and the like, was to keep the commandments. Only a superficial concept of the importance and obedience to the commandments could have permitted him to make the claim that he had kept them all from his youth.

The same faulty notion of the real moral requirements of the Law lay at the root of the proud self-righteousness of the Pharisees. They were able to think themselves righteous only because they measured themselves by an imperfect standard, an inadequate idea of the high demands which the Law made upon the inner life. Righteousness was thus placed too much in externals and too little in the state of the heart. It exaggerated the ritual features of religion and overlooked its deeper spiritual requirements upon conduct and life. According to the Lord Jesus, a correct action had to overflow from the love of the heart. In the writings of Paul, the righteousness of God is used to denote an attribute of God.

(VI) In Rom 3:5, Paul asks this rhetorical question: "But if our unrighteousness commend the righteousness of God, what shall we say?" The context shows that the "righteousness of God" here means essentially the same as the faithfulness or truthfulness of God (cf. Rom 3:3, 4). God's righteousness is His faithfulness to His own nature and promises.

(VII) In Rom 3:25, 26, Paul speaks of the éndeixis (1732), the indication of His righteousness, which God the Father has made in the death of Christ and which should prevent men from supposing that because God treated leniently the sins of men in past times, He is indifferent to sin or disregards it. God's leniency in the past is demonstrated by the use of the word páresis (3929), which unfortunately is translated "remission," but in reality is tolerance, the passing by of sins. Here, then, the righteousness of God must denote that self-respecting quality of holiness in God, that reaction of His nature against sin, which must find expression in condemnation of it. Righteousness, in this sense, expresses itself in divine wrath, which is the reaction of God's holy nature against sin.

With Paul, righteousness meant the state of acceptance with God into which one enters by faith. This is the meaning in Rom 1:17: "For therein [in the gospel] is revealed the righteousness of God by faith unto faith; as it is written . . . the righteous shall live by faith" (a.t.); also in Rom 3:21, 22. This righteousness of God is available through faith in Jesus Christ unto all that believe. Faith, in Paul's view, is a personal relationship with God mediated through Christ. It involves, by its very nature, spiritual union with God, obedience to His will, and increasing likeness of character to His. There is thus a close connection between the righteous character of God and the righteous status which He reckons as belonging to believers.

(VIII) There are two distinct words in the theology of Paul. These are dikaiosúnē (1343), righteousness or the inherent righteousness of God, the nature and quality of His character, and dikaíōsis (1347) which is the act of justification, God making man what He is, righteous. To justify (dikaióō [1344]), in Pauline language, means to regard and treat one as righteous, i.e., to declare one accepted by God.

This judgment of justification God pronounces upon condition of faith. The fact or truth that faith is reckoned for righteousness (logízomai [3049], reckon; eis [1519], for, unto; dikaiosúnē [1343], righteousness) in Rom 4:3, 5, 6, 9, 11, 22 is actually a periphrasis for "to justify," dikaióō, to declare righteous upon condition of faith, meaning the same as to reckon faith for righteousness. Thus faith is the necessary condition of a gracious salvation. Salvation is a free gift; faith is its humble and thankful acceptance.

This justification, however, is part of a salvation which consists of not merely a legal transaction between God and man. It involves also a spiritual renewal for man. Salvation gives not only the gift of righteousness which is the basis of justification, but it also imparts a vital righteousness through the Holy Spirit, a new principle of life. Man does not simply receive the righteousness of God, but he is made righteous and acquires the nature of God (Rom 5:21; 2 Pet 1:4). This is the miracle of regeneration—man is not only declared righteous but he has begun to be made righteous; from an enemy of God he becomes a friend of God.

(IX) In the writings of John, there is demonstrated the righteous treatment of God toward those who have been reconciled to Him through faith in Christ. God treats His own in a very special way and that can never be considered as unfair. Only in one passage in John's Gospel is the word *díkaios* (1342), just or righteous, applied to God. John 17:25 reads, "O righteous Father, the world hath not known thee: but I have known thee." What is inherent in God's righteousness here appears to be that quality which prevents Him from passing the same judgment upon Christ's disciples which He passes upon the sinful world. Upon this equitableness of God, the Lord Jesus bases His confidence in asking that special blessing be conferred upon His disciples. The thought is similar in John 17:11, where the Father is designated as *hágios* (40), holy. As the one who is absolutely good—wholly separate from all that is sinful and wrong—God is besought to guard from evil those whom He has given to His Son. In both of these cases, the righteousness or holiness of God is not conceived of as a forensic or retributive quality, but as God's own moral self-consistency, His faithfulness to His own equity.

In 1 John 1:9; 2:29, God is described as *díkaios*, righteous, and, in both cases, in a sense closely akin to that which we have found in the gospel. "If we confess our sins, he is faithful [*pistós* {4103}, trustworthy, unfailing] and just [*díkaios*, righteous] to forgive us our sins. . . . " The correlation of the word *díkaios*, righteous, with the word *pistós*, faithful or trustworthy, as well as the entire context, shows that righteousness here is that quality of God which would certainly lead Him to forgive those who repent. It would be inconsistent for God—and contrary both to His promises and to His nature—not to forgive the penitent and to exert upon his

life the purifying influence of His grace because of His covenant promise. In the remaining passage of 1 John 2:29, the term "righteous" has a broader meaning and designates the moral perfection of God in general as the type and ideal of all goodness in man. "If ye know that he [God] is righteous, ye know that every one that doeth righteousness is born of him." Since God is inherently righteous, those who are begotten of Him must also be righteous.

A similar thought is presented in 1 John 3:7, but in the reverse order: "He that doeth righteousness is righteous, even as he [Christ] is righteous." Opposing the gnostic over-emphasis on knowledge, the Apostle insists that the mere intellectual possession of truth is not enough. Truth, or righteousness, is not merely something to be known, but something to be done (1 John 1:6; 3:12). The man is righteous who walks in the truth as his native element (2 John 1:4; 3 John 1:3, 4); in whom the truth dwells, controlling and guiding him (John 8:44; 1 John 2:4); who belongs to the truth and draws from it the strength and inspiration of his life (John 18:37; 1 John 2:21; 3:19). Doctrine and life are inseparable. Both Hebrews and James allude to righteousness in the sense of the gift of God on condition of faith (Heb 11:7; James 2:23), but both these epistles generally speak of it as that good life which the Christian loves and seeks.

(X) In the epistles of Peter, righteousness is the holy life in contrast to sin as in 1 Pet 2:24, "that we, having died unto sins, should live unto righteousness" (a.t.). In Revelation righteousness is predicated on the judgment (Rev 19:11 [cf. 15:4]), and is said to be "done" (cf. 1 John 3:7) by those who are righteous in the world to come (Rev 22:11). Thus we conclude that in the NT righteousness is presented in two ways: (1) as a quality of God's nature and action, and (2) as the character which God requires of man. What God requires is grounded in what God is.

(XI) In the NT, righteousness is sometimes used more comprehensively to denote the equity or uprightness of God in general. Through His Son, the Lord Jesus Christ, God imputes His righteousness to those who receive Christ. These having become His friends, He treats justly, as one would his friends. He does, however, discriminate against those who prefer to remain His enemies by not believing on the Lord Jesus Christ (John 3:18). Therefore, the exercise of His justice is toward those who appropriated His righteousness by faith as well as those who rejected it by rejecting the Lord Jesus. See all the cognate words for their interrelationships and their syn. and ant. under *díkē* (1349), justice.

Syn.: *euthútēs* (2118), rectitude, righteousness.

Ant.: *adikía* (93), unrighteousness, injustice; *adíkēma* (92), a wrong, a wrongdoing; *ponēría* (4189), wickedness; *anomía* (458), lawlessness; *paranomía* (3892), law-breaking, iniquity; *kakía* (2549), depravity.

1344. δικαιόω *dikaióō*; contracted *dikaiô*, fut. *dikaiṓsō*, from *díkaios* (1342), just, righteous. To justify. Verbs which end in *-óō* generally indicate bringing out that which a person is or that which is desired, but not usually referring to the mode in which the action takes place. In the case of *dikaióō*, it means to bring out the fact that a person is righteous.

In Class. Gr., *dikaióō* could also mean to make anyone righteous by permitting such a one to bear for himself his condemnation, judgment, punishment, or chastisement. Such action of guilt upon one being tried in court would have been better expressed by the verb *dikázō* (which does not occur in the NT), although the subst. *dikastḗs* (1348), a judge, does occur (Luke 12:14; Acts 7:27, 35 [TR]). The more common word referring to the condemning of a guilty person examined in court is *katadikázō* (2613), to condemn (Matt 12:7, 37; Luke 6:37; James 5:6). The noun *katadíkē* does not occur in the NT, but it does in Class. Gr. and means a judgment given against one, a sentence.

The verb is used in Matt 12:37, "For by thy words thou shalt be justified, and by thy words thou shalt be condemned [*katadikasthḗsē*]" (2613). Thus *katadikázō* stands as a direct opposite of *dikaióō*. The examination of a case, whether favorable (1 Cor 4:3, 4) or unfavorable (1 Cor 9:3; 14:24), is expressed by the investigative verb *anakrínō* (350).

It must be clearly understood that in the NT the verb *dikaióō*, to justify, never means to make anyone righteous or to do away with his violation of the law, by himself bearing the condemnation and the imposed sentence. In the NT, man in his fallen condition can never do anything in order to pay for his sinfulness and thus be liberated from the sentence of guilt that is upon him as it happens in the mundane world; i.e., when a guilty person has paid the penalty of a crime, he is free from condemnation.

In the NT, *dikaióō* in the act. voice means to recognize, to set forth as righteous, to declare righteous, to justify as a judicial act. This is clear from Luke 10:25 in which a lawyer who came to Jesus asked Him how he could inherit eternal life. "Willing to justify himself" (Luke 10:29) means that he wanted to establish himself as righteous. So also the Pharisees to whom the Lord said in Luke 16:15, "Ye are they which justify yourselves before men," i.e., you have set yourselves forth as righteous, as if there is nothing wrong with you if you were to stand in a court of justice. Used in the same sense in Luke 7:29 stating that the people recognized that God acted justly in sending John the Baptist to preach repentance. This was an indirect recognition that indeed man needed to repent.

In the OT, in some instances (such as Ps 73:13 KJV), the Sept. translation of *edikaíōsa*, "I justified my heart" really means "I cleansed my heart." Elsewhere, when used in regard to a thing or a person, it means to find anything as right, to recognize or acknowledge anyone as just, to set forth as right or just.

(I) As a matter of right or justice, to absolve, acquit, clear from any charge or imputation. In Matt 12:37, *dikaióō* stands in direct opposition to *katadikázō* (2613), to condemn, to sentence (see 1 Cor 4:4, where the Apostle Paul speaks of God's favorable judgment upon him, after having examined or investigated him and his actions in life). This investigative process is expressed by the verb *anakrínō* (350). See 1 Cor 9:3; 14:24 where the verb *anakrínomai* (the pass. form) is used as a parallel of *elégchomai* (1651), to be reproved, convicted of one's error and condemned. The Apostle Paul, therefore, does not use the word *dikaióō*, to declare right by a capricious judge, but rather that he declares a person right or wrong after the process of investigation and the finding of guilt or innocence.

In Acts 13:39, it is used with the prep. *apó* (575), from, referring to all those things from which the Mosaic Law could not liberate us. In this instance, therefore, as well as in Rom 6:7 where *apó* is used with the word "sin," "from sin" (see also Rom 6:18), it refers to our liberation from something, i.e., sin which holds man a prisoner, a slave. The verb *dikaióō*, therefore, is used in a similar vein as the verb *eleutheróō* (1659), to deliver, set free. Thus *dikaióō* does not mean the mere declaration of innocence, but the liberation from sin which holds man a prisoner (see Sept.: Ex 23:7; Deut 25:1; 1 Kgs 8:32).

When used with *heautón* (1438) in the acc., himself or oneself, it means to justify or excuse oneself. This meaning must definitely be distinguished from the use of the verb with God as Judge and man the object of His judgment. God never excuses man for being wrong, since He has His own perfect standard of judgment. Man, on the contrary, being perverse, due to the fall of Adam, judges himself by his own standard and excuses himself. That was what the young lawyer who came to Jesus did, "But he, willing to justify himself . . . " (Luke 10:29). The word *dikaióō*, to justify, here did not mean that he kept the commandments that he quoted in Luke 10:27, but that he excused himself from keeping them.

In the Class. Gr. writers, the word is used more widely meaning to do justice to or to defend the right of anyone, irrespective of whether such a defense may prove the person guilty or innocent.

(II) Spoken of character, *dikaióō* means to declare to be just as it should be, to pronounce right; of things, to regard as right and proper. It means to have the right to own or to claim things. In the NT, however, it is used only of persons meaning to acknowledge and declare anyone to be righteous, virtuous, good, *díkaios* (1342), just; therefore it means:

(A) By implication, to vindicate, approve, honor, glorify, and in the pass. to receive honor, and so forth. In Luke 7:29, the people who heard Jesus "justified God," meaning they declared that God was right and that they approved of what He was saying. In Matt 11:19, "wisdom is justified of her children" means wisdom was approved by wise people. One has to be wise to recognize wisdom and declare it worthwhile (cf. Luke 7:35). To understand 1 Tim 3:16 with the same meaning of approval see below. In Rom 3:4, "that thou mightest be justified in thy sayings" (from Ps 51:4), means acknowledged to be just and righteous in His sentence. This implies that when God is the judge, He exhibits the righteousness of His character, while man judges to exhibit the guilt or innocence of the accused. What God says proves what He is (Sept.: Ezek 16:52).

(B) In relation to God and the divine Law, it means to declare righteous, to regard as pious. In Luke 16:15 the Lord Jesus castigates the Pharisees for presenting themselves to be righteous and pious before men, no matter what God thought of them. Their interest was in their appearance before men. Spoken especially of the justification bestowed by God upon men through Christ, through the instrumentality of faith (Rom 3:26, 30; 4:5; 8:30, 33; Gal 3:8); in the pass. in Rom 3:28; 5:1; Gal 2:16; 3:24 where faith is stressed as the means of being justified; with the phrase "of works" (*ex érgōn* [1537, 2041]), or with the neg. *ouk* (3756), not (*ouk ex érgōn*) as in Rom 3:20; 4:2; Gal 2:16; James 2:21, 24, 25); with the expression "not by law," i.e., not by means of law (Gal 3:11 [cf. Rom 2:13; 3:24; 5:9; 1 Cor 6:11; Gal 2:17; Titus 3:7]).

(III) In the sense of to make or cause to be upright. In the mid., to make oneself upright, i.e., to be upright, virtuous. In Rev 22:11, in the aor. pass. imper. with mid. meaning, "he that is upright, let him be upright still" (TR).

(IV) Everywhere in the OT, the root meaning of *dikaióō* is to set forth as righteous, to justify in a legal sense (Ezek 16:51, 52).

Ex 23:7 is noteworthy: "Keep thee far from a false matter; and the innocent [*athóon* {121}] and righteous [*díkaion* {1342}] slay thou not: for I will not justify, the wicked" or as the Sept. has it, "thou shall not justify" because of receiving gifts (Ex 23:8). In other words, no man can declare someone righteous because of the gifts he receives from him or from anybody else. *Dikaióō* is one aspect of judicial activity as demonstrated in the Sept. by the expression *díkaion*, just, and the verb *krínō* (2919), which in the Bible is the main verb referring to judicial activity, deciding whether a person is guilty or not. "He that justifieth the wicked, and he that condemneth the just, even they both are abomination to the Lord" (Prov 17:15). In this verse *díkaion* is translated "just," and *ádikon* (94) "the wicked," which really means unjust.

(V) In the NT, *dikaióō* means to recognize, set forth as righteous, justify as a judicial act (Luke 10:29; 16:15). It has the same meaning in the pass., to be recognized, found, set forth as righteous, justified (Matt 12:37; Rom 2:13; 3:20). A comment is necessary on Rom 2:13: "For not the hearers of the law are just before God, but the doers of the law shall be justified." Here there is a contrast between the hearers (*akroataí* [202]), and the doers (*poiētaí* [4163]). The verb used here is *dikaiōthḗsontai*, fut. pass. punctiliar,

which indicates that at a particular time in the future they will be judicially declared as righteous. The first part of the verse could be better translated: "For the hearers of the law [are] not just alongside or before God" (a.t.). There is no verb at all which makes the statement true without any time limitation. What it declares is a timeless truth, i.e., the mere hearers of the law have never been and never will be considered by God as just. If, however, they change from mere hearers to doers of the law by believing in Him who became the fulfillment of the law (Matt 3:15; 5:17; Rom 8:21; Gal 4:4–7; Col 2:14), only then will God pronounce them as just. No one can become a doer of the law without believing on Christ. This verse declares a standard, a norm, that not he who knows the law but he who is a doer of the law in Christ can be declared just before the Judge.

Compare this verse with Rom 3:20 where seemingly a contradictory statement is given: "Therefore by the deeds of the law there shall no flesh be justified in his sight: for by the law is the knowledge of sin." The explanation is that, whereas Rom 2:13 affirms the norm that the doer will be declared just, a matter-of-fact declaration is made in Rom 3:20 that by the deeds of the law no man can be justified, inasmuch as the deeds of the law are only possible in and through Christ. Even if man is able to do the works of the law, he still cannot be justified since a person can be legally correct but morally wrong. He may conform to a certain law in spite of the fact that he may hate it, but if he did not fear the consequences of transgression, he might never obey it. No law can make a person morally right, although he can be proven legally conforming to the law if he does the works that are detailed by it.

Therefore, *dikaiōthḗsontai*, shall be justified, in the first phrase of Rom 2:13 must be interpreted as not to be made or found righteous in character, but simply to appear as righteous because of having conformed to the directions of the law. This is made clear in Rom 4:2: "For if Abraham were justified by works, he hath whereof to glory; but not before God." Here the verb *edikaióthē*, was justified, does not have the meaning of being declared righteous in reality, but only in appearance. No law could condemn a person who keeps it, but that does not mean that God will assume that a person, legally right before Him, recognizes His (God's) rightful ownership of himself. Abraham, although he obeyed the law, could not stand before God as righteous and boast about it. His declaration of his righteousness by the law was not equal to God's declaration of righteousness. Paul says in 1 Tim 3:16 that Jesus Christ was not declared righteous by the law, but in the Spirit. This means that His high claims of being the Son of God, the Messiah, the Redeemer, were justified or proven true by the descent of the Holy Spirit upon Him at His baptism, by the miracles that He performed, the life that He lived, and finally through His resurrection from the dead (Rom 1:4; 1 Pet 3:18).

(VI) The NT tells how being justified by God and declared just before Him may be achieved in the lives of men. We are justified before God by Christ's grace through faith (Gal 2:16; 3:11; Titus 3:6, 7). When we receive Christ, we recognize God's right over us, and then we are made just (Rom 5:19). With our justification God simultaneously performs the miracle of regeneration and changes our character. We do not then obey God because we are afraid of the consequences of our disobedience, but because His grace has changed our character and made us just. When we become the children of God, we exercise rights toward God and act as His children. We are thus liberated from the guilt and power of sin, but not from the presence of it. That will come later (Rom 8:23).

In 1 Tim 3:16, it is said of Jesus Christ, God incarnate, that He was justified in (*en* [1722]) the Spirit or by means of the Spirit. In the appearance of the Spirit upon Jesus, there was the confirmation of the claims of the Son of God that He was the Messiah, the King of Israel, the Redeemer of mankind. This refers to the descent of the Holy Spirit upon Him at His baptism and through the miracles which He performed in full agreement with the Spirit and with God the Father. The justification of His claims, however, was through His resurrection (Rom 1:4; 1 Pet 3:18).

The two phrases in 1 Tim 3:16 must be taken together: "God was manifest in the flesh." That was His incarnation. And then immediately after that we read, "justified in the Spirit." This means that through the manifestation of the Holy Spirit which came upon Him, His claims for Himself as the God-Man were confirmed. "He was justified" refers to the Godhead: God the Father, God the Son in His preincarnate state, and God the Holy Spirit. Note that the word *Theós* (2316), God, has no definite article before it and refers to the triune God who was by the Second Person the incarnate Christ, the God-Man (Col 2:9). He was confirmed as such by the descent and testimony of the Holy Spirit. Later Christ proved His deity by His works, death, and resurrection. What Christ left behind with the Father when He became the God-Man was His glory (*dóxa* [1391]), the recognition He received in heaven for all that He was. This glory He regained as He ascended to the Father (John 17:5). His deity was proven by His words (Matt 7:29; John 7:46), His works (John 2:11; 3:2; 14:11), and His resurrection (Acts 2:27; Rom 1:4).

(VII) According to the Apostle Paul man is justified by God's grace (Rom 3:24; 4:5; Eph 2:8; Titus 3:7). God's grace arouses man's faith (Acts 13:39; Rom 5:1). Thus grace is the principle on God's side which involves the free and unmerited love of God (Rom 3:24), and faith on man's side (Rom 1:17; 4:5). As proceeding from the divine grace, justification by faith is totally opposed to justification by works, which depends on merit (Rom 4:4). Instead of attaining a righteousness by his own efforts, the believer submissively receives a righteousness which is wholly of God and is His gift (Rom 5:17; 10:3; Phil 3:9).

Thus faith is the method by which the grace of God is subjectively appropriated. Faith is therefore to be conceived of as obedience (Rom 10:3) emanating from devotion and love, not self-righteousness. Paul speaks of obedience of faith (Rom 1:5).

A revelation of the divine grace which awakens faith takes place, according to Paul, in the person of Christ (2 Cor 5:17), in His work, His death, and also His resurrection. Christ's death was the work of divine grace, in that God ordained it as an expiatory sacrifice for sin. Christ was dying on behalf of sinners, that in the act of justification He might not be misconstrued as being indulgent of sin (Rom 3:25 [cf. Rom 5:8; 2 Cor 5:21]). Christ's resurrection is also included in the revelation by which God's grace is made known to sinners (Rom 4:25; 8:34; 10:9; 1 Cor 15:17).

Grace represents the divine activity in justification and faith represents the human activity. Thus it is a justification of the ungodly (Rom 4:5; 2 Cor 5:19). It is not by works of the law (Rom 3:20; Gal 3:11), or of the law written in the heart of Gentiles apart from their uncircumcision (Rom 2:15). It is for remission of sins (Rom 3:25), peace with God, access into grace, and hope of glory (Rom 5:1, 2), righteousness (Rom 3:22; 4:22; 5:17; 2 Cor 5:21; Eph 4:24; Phil 3:9), and for life (Rom 5:18), which means it is a justification resulting in life, which is through the body of Christ (Rom 7:4) and by His Spirit (Rom 5:5; 8:2, 4, 6, 10, 11; Eph 2:18).

Deriv.: *dikaíōma* (1345), judgment, ordinance; *dikaíōsis* (1347), justification.

Syn.: Inasmuch as *dikaióō* means to declare righteous by making a sinner righteous through faith in Christ, it can be said to have the following syn.: *aphíēmi* (863), to forgive, to take sins away from the individual sinner and make him free through and in Christ; *charízomai* (5483), to pardon, from *cháris* (5485), grace, with

the meaning of to remit, forgive, not to exact the due punishment (Luke 7:42, 43, involving a debt; 2 Cor 2:7, 10; 12:13; Eph 4:32; Col 2:13; 3:13 which refers to wrong or sin, meaning to forgive, not to punish); *charitóō* (5487), also related to the basic word *cháris* meaning to grace, supply with grace, make acceptable. In the NT, this is spoken only of the divine favor which is offered, not in condemnation of sin, but in redemption from sin as the word *cháris*, grace, always implies. In Luke 1:28 we have the angel speaking to the virgin Mary in the annunciation saying, "Hail, thou that art highly favored." The word in the Gr. here is *kecharitōménē* which is the perf. pass. part. of *charitóō*. It means, someone who has been graced or honored, who has been the recipient of God's grace at a particular time and has a present possession of that grace. The verb *charitóō* is also found in Eph 1:6, "To the praise of the glory of his grace, wherein he hath made us accepted [*echarítōsen*, the aor. of *charitóō*] in the beloved," meaning with which grace He hath graced us, or in which grace He has richly imparted that grace unto us in relation to the forgiveness of our sins.

Additional syn: *sṓzō* (4982), to save from the guilt and power of sin, equivalent to giving eternal life; *apallássō* (525), to deliver in a legal sense from the claims of an opponent; *lutróō* (3084), to redeem by paying ransom; *lúō* (3089), to loose, let go, and the comp. *apolúō* (630), to dismiss, forgive, set at liberty; *rhúomai* (4506), to rescue. For further syn., see *dikaiosúnē* (1343), righteousness.

Ant.: *krínō* (2919), to judge, determine; *anakrínō* (350), to examine, investigate for the purpose of judging whether a person is innocent or guilty; *katakrínō* (2632), to condemn, sentence; *diakrínō* (1252), to discern, judge; *katadikázō* (2613), to pronounce judgment, condemn; *kataginṓskō* (2607), to know something against, condemn; *mōmáomai* (3469), to find fault with; *diaginṓskō* (1231), to ascertain exactly, determine.

1345. δικαίωμα *dikaíōma*; gen. *dikaiómatos*, neut. noun from *dikaióō* (1344), to justify. The product or result of being justified by God. The rights or claims which one has before God when he becomes His child by faith through Christ. In Rev 19:8, *dikaiōmata* is translated "the righteousness" of saints, and in Heb 9:1 "ordinances" of divine service, which word actually means legal rights of the saints. See Luke 1:6, a law, ordinance, precept; Rom 1:32; 2:26; 8:4; Heb 9:10; Sept.: Ex 15:25, 26; 21:1; Lev 25:18; Num 36:13; Deut 30:16. In Rom 5:16, acquittal as opposed to *katákrima* (2631), an adverse sentence; Rev 15:4, condemnation, implying punishment (Sept.: Ps 119:75, 137, *kríma* [2917], judgment); Rev 19:8, righteousness, virtue, piety toward God, e.g., of saints; Rom 5:18, of Christ as manifested in His obedience, equal to *hupakoḗ* (5218), obedience, in Rom 5:19.

Syn.: *diatagḗ* (1296), ordinance; *dógma* (1378), decree.

1346. δικαίως *dikaíōs*; adv. from *díkaios* (1342), just. Justly, conformable to justice (1 Pet 2:23; Sept.: Deut 1:16; Prov 31:9); honestly, without injuring anyone (1 Thess 2:10; Titus 2:12); deservedly (Luke 23:41); as it is fit, proper, right (1 Cor 15:34).

Syn.: *euthéōs* (2112), straightly; *orthôs* (3723), rightly.

Ant.: *adíkōs* (95), unjustly.

1347. δικαίωσις *dikaíōsis*; gen. *dikaióseōs*, from *dikaióō* (1344), to justify. The act which declares a right or just person as such; justification, but as an act and not as the essence or character of justice which is *dikaiosúnē* (1343).

Of the two places that the word occurs in the NT, the first is Rom 4:25: "Who was delivered for our offenses, and was raised again for our justification [*dikaíōsin*]." The resurrection of Jesus Christ must not be thought of simply as evidence of His death. The stress here is that the resurrection of Jesus Christ is necessary to justification, not merely because of the difference it makes to us as certifying the atoning efficacy of His death and thus evoking our faith in Him, but also because of the difference it makes for Christ Himself. It marks the point at which His sovereign power as Lord is made effective. Our justification, the basis of which has been laid in the death, becomes an accomplished fact and effective reality only through Christ's rising again.

By faith we are united to a living Christ whose death was essential for our redemption. That which redeems is not Christ's atoning death apart from His living person into whose union we are brought by faith. We cannot separate the propitiatory work of Christ from Christ Himself. We are saved, not by believing the fact that Christ died for our sins, but by union with the crucified and risen, exalted Savior. Only through union with a living Savior who has in Him the virtue of His atoning death do justification, forgiveness, and all the blessings of redemption become ours: "In whom we have redemption through his blood" (Eph 1:7; Col 1:14). We are accepted "in the beloved" (Eph 1:6). "There is therefore now no condemnation to them which are in Christ Jesus" (Rom 8:1).

Justification is ours as we are "in Christ" in such living union with Him that His life becomes identified with ours and ours with His. Because of this identification or incorporation, Christ's acts are repeated in us so that in His death we die to sin, "crucified with Christ" (Gal 2:20), and in His life we live to righteousness. But it is only by His risen life that Christ can come into such living union with men as thus to effect their redemption. The apostolic thought in Rom 4:25 accordingly is this: "He was delivered up [to death] on account of our trespasses [to make atonement for them]; and he was raised on account of our justification [that it might become an accomplished fact]" (a.t.). His rising again was the necessary antecedent of His applying to His elect the virtue of the atonement which His death wrought for all men. He died to purchase what He rose again to apply. So it is that in a sense the resurrection of Christ is referred to as the cause of justification.

It is doubtlessly true that Paul did not make an abstract separation between Christ's death and His resurrection, as if the death and the resurrection either had different motives or served ends separable from each other. Christ's work is one and its end is one. He both died and was raised for our justification, but the end effect was only through the resurrection (cf. Rom 8:34: "Who is he that condemneth? It is Christ that died, yea rather, that was raised from the dead" [a.t.]; Rom 5:10, "saved by his life"; 1 Cor 15:17, "If Christ be not risen, your faith is futile; you are still in your sins" [a.t.]).

In Hebrews, the same truth is presented from the point of view of the priesthood of Christ. In OT ritual, only when the high priest took the blood within the veil and sprinkled it upon the Mercy Seat was the offering for sin completed and the covenant-fellowship with God established. In the same way, Christ's offering for sin was not completed until, in the heavenly sanctuary, He presented Himself "through his own blood" (a.t. [Heb 9:12]), i.e., with the virtue of His atoning death in Him. Only then is the new covenant (i.e., fellowship between God and sinners) established. It is in Him as the living, prevailing High Priest, and not merely through something which He did in the past, that we have peace with God. He is now always at the right hand of God interceding for us (Rom 8:34).

The second verse in which the word *dikaíōsis* occurs is Rom 5:18 which has to do with the life He gives us through His resurrection and the sharing of His life with us: "Therefore, as by the offense of one judgment came upon all men to condemnation; even so by the righteousness of one the free gift came upon all men unto justification (*dikaíōsin*) of life."

Syn.: *áphesis* (859), remission; *lútrōsis* (3085), redemption, deliverance from the guilt and power of sin; *apolútrōsis* (629), a releasing on payment of ransom;

hilastḗrion (2435), propitiation, referring to the blood of Christ (His atoning death) sprinkled for our sins in satisfaction of the justice of God. The word, however, does not fully convey the meaning of *dikaíōsis* which includes the subjective part of Christ's propitiation as applied to the sinner which makes him a child of God. The same also with *hilasmós* (2434), expiation, Christ's shedding His blood to satisfy God's justice for sin, but not necessarily the application of that blood for the cleansing of man in a subjective manner; *sōtēría* (4991), salvation from sin which involves more the subjective part of the application of Christ's work in the sinner, liberating him from sin and causing him to be attached to God.

Ant.: *krísis* (2920), the process of investigation and, in the case of guilt, the act of sentencing; *katákrisis* (2633), condemnation, with the suggestion of the process leading to it, the process of condemnation; *díkē* (1349), judgment, the execution of justice; *katákrima* (2631), condemnation.

1348. δικαστής *dikastḗs*; gen. *dikastoú*, masc. noun from *dikázō* (n.f.), to give judgment, which is from *díkē* (1349), justice. A judge (Luke 12:14; Acts 7:27, 35; Sept.: Ex 2:14; 1 Sam 8:1). One who executes *díkē* one who maintains law and equity. Because he arrives at a conclusion and gives final judgment, the judge is called *kritḗs* (2923), a more general term for judge, while *dikastḗs* is a judge who is nominated or elected to become part of a tribunal and arrive at a conclusion concerning a person or a case.

1349. δίκη *díkē*; gen. *díkēs*, a fem. noun. Originally *díkē* meant manner, tendency. Gradually it became the designation for the right of established custom or usage. The basic meaning of the word involves the assertion by human society of a certain standard expected by its people which, if not kept, can bring forth ensuing judgment. Thus it can be said that *díkē* is expected behavior or conformity, not according to one's own standard, but according to an imposed standard with prescribed punishment for nonconformity. It refers to legitimate custom.

(I) A penalty, punishment (Acts 25:15 [TR]; 2 Thess 1:9; Jude 1:7).

(II) Justice, personified as *Díkē*, the daughter of the mythological Greek god Zeus and goddess Themis (Acts 28:4).

(III) Distinctions: the basic noun *díkē* (1349) occurs only four times (Acts 25:15; 28:4; 2 Thess 1:9; Jude 1:7), and means punishment; *díkaios* (1342), just, righteous, when applied to Jesus Christ as the Messiah refers to inherent righteousness in complete accord with God's will (Acts 3:14; 7:52). It also applies to those who by faith receive the righteousness of Christ (1 John 2:29), the OT patriarchs (Matt 23:35) and saints (2 Pet 2:7), the prophets (Matt 13:17) and martyrs (Matt 23:35). The parents of John the Baptist are called righteous (Luke 1:6), as are Simeon (Luke 2:25) and Cornelius (Acts 10:22). It stands in contrast to *hamartōlós* (268), sinful, or *ádikos* (94), unjust or unrighteous. The word *díkaioi* stands in contrast to *ponēroí* (4190), evil ones (Matt 13:49).

Dikaíōma (1345), anything justly or rightly done; hence, right, justice, equity from the favorable standpoint; but condemnation or judgment from the unfavorable standpoint (see Rom 5:16; Rev 15:4). It also means ordinance or precept (Luke 1:6; Rom 8:4; Heb 9:1). In the technical, Pauline sense in Rom 5:16, 18 it is the act of justification regarded as complete, while *dikaíōsis* (1347), which occurs only twice (Rom 4:25; 5:18), is the act in process.

Dikaiosúnē (1343), righteousness, refers to the inherent righteousness of God in that He is justice personified and cannot be anything else. The phrase "the righteousness of God [*dikaiosúnē* {1343}; *Theoú* {2316}]" constantly referred to, especially in Romans, must never be taken as meaning an acquired righteousness as if He needed such righteousness. *Dikaiosúnē* also refers to the imputed

righteousness of man through faith in Christ which causes man to stand before God with boldness and to claim his rights in view of a Father-son relationship with God through Christ. Man's recognition of God's rights over him is naturally missing because of man's fall in Adam (Rom 5:12), but His standard of integrity should characterize the life of the man who acknowledges God's claims upon him and permits Christ, by the Holy Spirit, to work in him.

Dikaiosúnē should be clearly distinguished from *dikaíōsis* (1347), the first being the position of high command, inherent righteousness, and the other an action which establishes righteousness or which makes a person righteous (*díkaion*). Hence, the first should be translated "righteousness" and the second "justification."

When *díkē*, as expected conformity, becomes judgment for violation, it becomes in Gr. *katadíkē* (found only in the UBS text), used in the NT only in a verbal form, *katadikázō* (2613), to condemn (Matt 12:7, 37; Luke 6:37; James 5:6). In all instances when *díkē* occurs in the NT (Acts 25:15; 28:4; 2 Thess 1:9; Jude 1:7), it is used with the sense of *katadíkē*, judgment, to render justice, and refers to those who suffer punishment in order that the acceptable behavior or custom violated by them might be reestablished.

From the basic word comes *dikaíōma* (1345), a legitimate claim. The person adhering to the expectations of his society has certain legitimate claims (*dikaiōmata*) of which a stranger or one violating the standard of expectation is deprived. The enjoyment of one's right in a society presupposes the acceptance of duties by that citizen. In this is the total idea of the use of this whole group of words emanating from *díkē*. In the Scriptures, God is presented as expecting a certain conformity of man to His principles. They are man's duties toward God. When they are accepted and conformed to, God gives man certain rights which do not belong to those who do not recognize His authority or their duties.

Deriv.: *ádikos* (94), unjust or unrighteous; *antídikos* (476), an opponent, adversary; *díkaios* (1342), just; *ékdikos* (1558), a punisher or one who carries out the verdict of an issue, an avenger; *éndikos* (1738), one who acts within his rights, fair, just; *hupódikos* (5267), under sentence, one who comes judgment.

1350. δίκτυον *díktuon*; gen. *diktúou*, neut. noun. A net. A general name for all nets including the hunting net, the net with which birds are taken, and the fishing net (Matt 4:20, 21; Mark 1:18, 19; Luke 5:2, 4–6; John 21:6, 8, 11). Other names for nets: *amphíblēstron* (293), a casting net which, when skillfully cast from over the shoulder by one standing on the shore or in a boat, spreads out into a circle (*amphibálletai*) as it falls upon the water and then sinks swiftly by the weight of the leads attached to it enclosing whatever is below (Matt 4:18; Mark 1:16 [cf. Eccl 9:12]); *sagḗnē* (4522), a sweep-net, the ends of which are carried out in boats so as to cover a large extent of open sea and are then drawn together and all which is enclosed can then be taken (Matt 13:47 [cf. Isa 19:8; Ezek 19:8; 26:5, 14]).

1351. δίλογος *dílogos*; gen. *dilógou*, masc.-fem., neut. *dílogon*, adj. from *dís* (1364), twice, and *légō* (3004), to speak. Double-tongued, two-faced, deceitful in one's words (1 Tim 3:8)

1352. διό *dió*; conj. from *diá* (1223), for, and the neut. rel. pron. *ho* from *hós* (3739), which. For which, wherefore, therefore (Matt 27:8; Luke 1:35; 7:7; Heb 3:7).
  Deriv.: *dióper* (1355), wherefore, truly.

1353. διοδεύω *diodeúō*; fut. *diodeúsō*, from *diá* (1223), through, and *hodeúō* (3593), to journey. To travel or pass through (Luke 8:1; Acts 17:1).
  Syn.: *poreúomai* (4198), to go on one's way; *ágō* (71), to go with the idea of leading; *hupágō* (5217), to go away, depart; *ápeimi* (548), to go away;

metabaínō (3327), to go or pass from one place to another; *apérchomai* (565), to go away; *periérchomai* (4022), to go around; *diabaínō* (1224), to pass through; *diaporeúomai* (1279), to pass across, to journey through; *diaperáō* (1276), to pass over, cross.
  Ant.: *ménō* (3306), to stay, abide; *diaménō* (1265), to remain throughout; *epiménō* (1961), to abide in, to persevere, to continue; *kataménō* (2650), to remain constantly at; *paraménō* (3887), to remain beside or to continue near; *diatríbō* (1304), to spend or pass time, to stay.

1354. Διονύσιος *Dionúsios*; gen. *Dionusíou*, masc. proper noun. Dionysius, a member of the court of the Areopagus on Mars Hill, who was converted under the preaching of Paul at Athens (Acts 17:34). In Greek mythology, *Dionúsios* was the god of wine; therefore, the name meant reveller or one who drank.

1355. διόπερ *dióper*; conj. from *dió* (1352), therefore, wherefore, and *per* (4007), a particle expressing emphasis. Wherefore, truly, wherefore by all means, or especially (1 Cor 8:13; 10:14; 14:13).
  Syn.: *di' hḗn aitían* (the acc. of *aitía* [156], reason; *diá* [1223], for; *hḗn*, the rel. pron.), for which reason; *hóthen* (3606), whence, wherefore; *héneka* (1752), because; *chárin hoú* (*chárin* [5484], grace; the gen. of *hós* [3739], a relative pron. meaning which), because of whom or which; *eis tí* (*eis* [1519], unto; the neut. of *tis* [5101], an interrogative meaning what), why, for which reason; *eis hó* (*eis* [1519], unto; the neut. sing. of *hós* [3739] meaning which), for which reason; *ára* (687), therefore; *hína tí* (*hína* [2443], in order that; the neut. sing. of *tís* [5101], what), wherefore, why, for what reason; *toigaroún* (5105), wherefore; *oún* (3767), a particle expressing sequence or consequence; *hṓste* (5620), so that, wherefore.

1356. διοπετής *diopetḗs*; gen. *diopetoús*, masc.-fem., neut. *diopetés*, adj. from *Diós*

(2203), the chief god of the Greeks, also called Jupiter, and *pétō* (n.f.), to fall. An image which fell from the statue of Jupiter (Acts 19:35) and was worshiped in the temple of Diana at Ephesus.

1357. διόρθωσις *diórthōsis*; gen. *diorthṓseōs*, fem. noun from *diorthóō* (n.f.), to correct, amend. Amendment, correction, reformation, only in Heb 9:10, the time of a new and better dispensation under the Messiah.

Syn.: *táxis* (5010), order; *euprépeia* (2143), good suitableness.

Ant.: *akatastasía* (181), confusion.

1358. διορύσσω *diorússō*, **διορύττω** *diorúttō*; fut. *diorúxō*, from *diá* (1223), through, and *orússō* (3736), to dig. To dig or break through, as the walls of a house which in the East are built of clay, earth (Matt 6:19, 20; 24:43; Luke 12:39; Sept.: Job 24:16; Ezek 12:7).

Syn.: *lúō* (3089), to break up, loose; *diarrḗgnumi* or *diarrḗssō* (1284), to burst asunder, rip open; *skáptō* (4626), to dig.

1359. Διόσκουροι *Dióskouroi*; gen. *Diokoúrōn*, masc. pl. proper noun. Castor and Pollux, who in mythology were the sons of Zeus by Leda, and the patron deities of sailors (Acts 28:11).

1360. διότι *dióti*; conj. made up from *diá* (1223), for, and *hóti* (3754), that. On account of this or that, for this reason, that, simply because, for (Luke 1:13; 2:7; 21:28; Acts 10:20; 17:31; 18:10; 22:18; Rom 1:19, 21; 3:20; 8:7; 1 Cor 15:9; Gal 2:16; Phil 2:26; 1 Thess 2:8; 4:6; Heb 11:5, 23; James 4:3; 1 Pet 1:16, 24).

Syn.: *hóti* (3754), because; *epeidḗ* (1894), inasmuch; *diá* (1223), because of; *héneka* (1752), on account of, for the sake of; *dió* (1352), for this cause.

1361. Διοτρεφής *Diotrephḗs*; gen. *Diotrephoús*, masc. proper noun. Diotrephes, the head of a church in Asia Minor of which we do not know much (3 John 1:9), to which *Gáïos* (1050), Gaius,

belonged. John rebukes Diotrephes for his arbitrary use of authority and resistance to the higher powers.

1362. διπλοῦς *diploús*; fem. *diplḗ*, neut. *diploún*, adj. from *dís* (1364), twice, and the suffix -*ploús*, denoting times or fold. Double or twice as much, used of honor (1 Tim 5:17; Sept.: Gen 43:15; Ex 16:5; Jer 16:18); of punishment (Rev 18:6). Comparative, *diplóteron*, as an adv. meaning two-fold more (Matt 23:15).

Deriv.: *diplóō* (1363), to double.

1363. διπλόω *diplóō*; contracted *diplṓ*, fut. *diplṓsō*, from *diploús* (1362), two-fold, double. To double, render back two-fold punishment (Rev 18:6), literally "double to her double" (a.t.).

1364. δίς *dís*; adv. from *dúo* (1417), two. Twice (Mark 14:30, 72; Luke 18:12; Phil 4:16 "once and twice" [a.t.], meaning again or often; 1 Thess 2:18; Jude 1:12, "twice dead," i.e., utterly dead).

Deriv.: *diakósioi* (1250), two hundred; *dídrachmon* (1323), a double drachma, tribute; *dietḗs* (1332), two years old; *dithálassos* (1337), between two seas; *dílogos* (1351), double-tongued; *diploús* (1362), double; *distázō* (1365), to doubt; *dístomos* (1366), two-edged; *dischílioi* (1367), two thousand; *dípsuchos* (1374), double-minded.

Syn.: *pálin* (3825), again, for the second time.

1365. διστάζω *distázō*; fut. *distásō*, from *dís* (1364), twice, two ways. To doubt, waver, hesitate, be uncertain. Used intrans. in Matt 14:31; 28:17. It is a figurative word taken either from a person standing where two ways meet and not knowing which to choose (inclining sometimes to one, sometimes to the other), or from the quivering motion of a balance when the weights on either side are approximately equal (when first one side, then the other, seems to be predominate). In Matt 28:17, the verb in the aor. *edístasan* translated "some doubted" should rather be translated "they hesitated" (a.t.). This refers not to the doubt of the disciples concerning the identity of the risen Christ because they recognized Him fully. However, they hesitated in regard to their responsibility to preach the gospel to the world knowing that Jesus in His resurrection body was no longer going to be on earth.

Syn.: *aporéō* (639), to be in perplexity; *diaporéō* (1280), to be perplexed and in despair; *meteōrízomai* (3349), to waver.

Ant.: *pistóō* (4104), to trust or give assurance to; *plērophoréō* (4135), to bring in full measure, be fully assured; *peíthō* (3982), to persuade, assure.

1366. δίστομος *dístomos*; gen. *distómou*, masc.-fem., neut. *dístomon*, adj. from *dís* (1364), twice, and *stóma* (4750), an edge. Cutting on both sides, two-edged (Heb 4:12; Rev 1:16; 2:12; Sept.: Ps 149:6; Prov 5:4 [cf. Isa 49:2]).

1367. δισχίλιοι *dischílioi*; fem. *dischíliai*, neut. *dischília*, cardinal number from *dís* (1364), twice, and *chílioi* (5507), a thousand. Two thousand (Mark 5:13).

1368. διυλίζω *diulízō*; fut. *diulísō*, from *diá* (1223), through, and *hulízō* (n.f.), to filter, percolate, strain. To filter or strain as with a sieve or strainer. Used trans. in Matt 23:24.

Syn.: *exetázō* (1833), to test thoroughly; *ereunáō* (2045), to investigate; *exereunáō* (1830), to search diligently.

1369. διχάζω *dicházō*; fut. *dichásō*, from *dícha* (n.f.), separately, which is from *dís* (1364), twice. To divide in two, set at variance. Figuratively meaning to incite one against another (Matt 10:35 [cf. Luke 12:52, 53]).

Syn.: *diachōrízō* (1316), to separate thoroughly; *schízō* (4977), to tear; *chōrízō* (5563), to separate; *merízō* (3307), to apportion; *apochōrízō* (673), to separate from; *dialúō* (1262), to dissolve; *diaspáō* (1288), to pluck asunder.

Ant.: *déō* (1210), to bind; *sundéō* (4887), to bind together; *proskolláō* (4347), to glue onto; *sunarmologéō* (4883), to fit together; *sumbállō* (4820), to put together; *sunéchō* (4912), to hold together.

1370. διχοστασία *dichostasía*; gen. *dichostasías*, fem. noun from *dícha* (n.f.), separately, and *stásis* (4714), dissension. A separate faction, division, separation (Rom 16:17; 1 Cor 3:3; Gal 5:20).

Syn.: *diamerismós* (1267), dissension, division, discord; *schísma* (4978), schism, division, tearing apart; *haíresis* (139), heresy, disunion; *merismós* (3311), a division, partition, separation.

Ant.: *henótēs* (1775), unity.

1371. διχοτομέω *dichotoméō*; contracted *dichotomṓ*, fut. *dichotomḗsō*, from *dícha* (n.f.), separately, and *tomḗ* (n.f.), cut. To cut in two or asunder. If this word is understood in its primary and literal sense, it must denote that most horrible punishment of being cut in two while alive. There is a tradition that the prophet Isaiah thus died, and the Apostle is thought to allude to this in Heb 11:37, "they were sawn asunder"; see 1 Sam 15:33; 2 Sam 12:31; Dan 2:5; 3:29. This was a manner of execution of criminals practiced at that time. In the NT used figuratively meaning to scourge with the utmost severity, to cut asunder as it were by scourging (Matt 24:51; Luke 12:46). Scourging was usually inflicted upon idle and negligent servants among the Jews. In Matthew, the servant must endure great punishment, and in Luke 12:47 the explanation is given that the unfaithful servant should be beaten with many stripes. These parables refer to the Master's rewards and punishments for faithful or unfaithful service by those who claim to be His servants. The Lord's words should induce us to awesome thoughtfulness as to what we do with our lives on earth. The evidence that one is a true servant of Jesus Christ is found in how he responds to the duties which his Lord imposes upon him. Accordingly, how we live our lives in this life becomes the basis of reward and punishment in the next. God's true servants will be rewarded for their faithfulness and good works while hypocrites will be punished for their evil works and unfaithfulness. Also from *tomé* (n.f.): *átomos* (823), indivisible.

Syn.: *kóptō* (2875), to cut; *katakóptō* (2629), to cut down; *diapríō* (1282), to saw asunder.

1372. διψάω *dipsáō*; contracted *dipsṓ*, fut. *dipsḗsō*. To be dry or thirsty (Matt 25:35, 37, 42, 44; John 4:15; 19:28; Rom 12:20; 1 Cor 4:11; Rev 7:16). To thirst in a figurative sense, desire ardently (Matt 5:6; John 4:13, 14; 6:35; 7:37; Rev 21:6; 22:17 [cf. Isa 41:17; 55:1; Sept.: Ps 42:2; 63:1]). See Sept.: Judg 15:18; Prov 25:21).

Deriv.: *dípsos* (1373), thirst.
Ant.: *sbénnumi* (4570), to quench.

1373. δίψος *dípsos*; gen. *dípsous*, neut. noun from *dipsáō* (1372), to thirst. Thirst (2 Cor 11:27).

1374. δίψυχος *dípsuchos*; gen. *dipsúchou*, masc.-fem., neut. *dípsuchon*, adj. from *dís* (1364), twice, and *psuchḗ* (5590), soul, mind. Double-minded, doubtful. In James 1:8, referring to the doubter or waverer which corresponds to *diakrínō* (1252); in the pl., in a general sense as an unstable person (James 4:8). Such a person suffers from divided loyalties. On the one hand, he wishes to maintain a religious confession and desires the presence of God in his life; on the other hand, he loves the ways of the world and prefers to live according to its mores and ethics.

Syn.: *akatástatos* (182), unstable.
Ant.: *bébaios* (949), certain.

1375. διωγμός *diōgmós*; gen. *diōgmoú*, masc. noun from *diṓkō* (1377), to follow, persecute, pursue, press toward. Pursuit, particularly of enemies, persecution, hostile prosecution (Matt 13:21; Mark 4:17;

10:30; Acts 8:1; 13:50; Rom 8:35; 2 Cor 12:10; 2 Thess 1:4; 2 Tim 3:11; Sept.: Prov 11:19).

Syn.: *thlípsis* (2347), tribulation, persecution.
Ant.: *stégē* (4721), roof, covering, indicating protection; *epikouría* (1947), assistance.

1376. διώκτης *diṓktēs*; gen. *diṓktou*, masc. noun from *diṓkō* (1377), to pursue, press forward, persecute. A persecutor (1 Tim 1:13).

Ant.: *prostátis* (4368), a patroness; *sōtḗr* (4990), savior, deliverer.

1377. διώκω *diṓkō*; fut. *diṓxō*, from *díō* (n.f.), to pursue, prosecute, persecute, but also to pursue in a good sense. To prosecute, persecute, pursue with repeated acts of enmity (Matt 5:10–12, 44; 10:23; 23:34; Luke 21:12; John 5:16; 15:20; Acts 7:52; 9:4, 5; 22:4, 7, 8; 26:11, 14, 15; Rom 12:14; 1 Cor 15:9; 2 Cor 4:9; Gal 1:13, 23; 4:29; 5:11; 6:12; Phil 3:6; 2 Tim 3:12; Rev 12:13). To follow after (Luke 17:23). To follow or press hard after, to pursue with earnestness and diligence in order to obtain, to go after with the desire of obtaining (Rom 9:30, 31; 12:13; 14:19; 1 Cor 14:1; Phil 3:12, 14; 1 Thess 5:15; 1 Tim 6:11; 2 Tim 2:22; Heb 12:14; 1 Pet 3:11).

Deriv.: *diōgmós* (1375), persecution; *diṓktēs* (1376), a persecutor; *ekdiṓkō* (1559), to drive out; *katadiṓkō* (2614), to search persistently.

Syn.: *thlíbō* (2346), to press, distress, trouble; *apothlíbō* (598), to press, crush; *biázō* (971), to press violently or force one's way into; *sunéchō* (4912), to constrain; *enéchō* (1758), to set oneself against; *epíkeimai* (1945), to press upon; *epipíptō* (1968), to fall upon, press upon.

Ant.: *phulássō* (5442), to guard, watch, keep; *diaphulássō* (1314), to guard carefully, defend; *phrouréō* (5432), to keep under guard; *sṓzō* (4982), to deliver; *diasṓzō* (1295), to bring safely through; *tēréō* (5083), to watch over, preserve; *diatēréō* (1301), to keep carefully.

1378. δόγμα dógma; gen. *dógmatos*, neut. noun from *dokéō* (1380), to think. Opinion, conclusion, ordinance, proposition, dogma. With the meaning of conclusion (Acts 16:4); as a decree or command (Luke 2:1; Acts 17:7); of the Mosaic Law, i.e., external precepts (Eph 2:15; Col 2:14; Sept.: Dan 2:13; 3:10; 6:8, 13, 15). Used concerning Christianity, it means views, doctrinal statements, principles.

Deriv.: *dogmatízō* (1379), to decree.

Syn.: *diatagé* (1296), ordinance; *parádosis* (3862), tradition, that which has been handed down; *arché* (746), principle; *kanōn* (2583), rule, canon; *nómos* (3551), law; *alétheia* (225), truth; *pístis* (4102), faith.

1379. δογματίζω dogmatízō; fut. *dogmatísō*, from *dógma* (1378), decree, ordinance. To conclude, ordain, establish as a dogma, conclusion or ordinance. In the mid. voice, *dogmatízomai*, to let oneself fall into a certain order, subject oneself to ordinances (Col 2:20).

Syn.: *kuróō* (2964), to ratify, confirm.

Ant.: *kataginōskō* (2607), to condemn.

1380. δοκέω dokéō; contracted *dokō*, fut. *dóxō*, aor. *édoxa*. To think, imagine, consider, appear. Expresses the subjective mental estimate or opinion formed by man concerning a matter.

(I) With a reflexive pron. expressed or implied, *dokō emautō* ([1683], dat., to think in myself) or (*heautō* [1438], dat., in oneself), meaning to seem to oneself, i.e., to be of opinion, to think, suppose, believe, followed by the inf. (Acts 26:9, "I verily thought with myself, that I ought to do many things").

(A) Followed by the inf. with the same subject, e.g., with inf. pres. expressing a continued action (Matt 3:9, "think not," presume not to say; Luke 8:18; 24:37; John 5:39; 16:2, "will think that he doeth God service"; Acts 12:9; 1 Cor 3:18; 7:40; 14:37; Gal 6:3; James 1:26). With the perf. inf. implying an action completed in reference to the present time (Acts

27:13 "supposing that they had obtained their purpose"; 1 Cor 8:2; Phil 3:4).

(B) Followed by the inf. with a different subj. in the acc. (Mark 6:49, "they supposed it had been a spirit"; 1 Cor 12:23; 2 Cor 11:16; Sept.: Gen 38:15).

(C) Followed by *hóti* (3754), that, instead of the acc. and inf. (Matt 6:7, "they think that they shall be heard"; 26:53; Luke 12:51; 13:2, 4; 19:11; John 5:45; 11:13; 13:29; 20:15; 1 Cor 4:9; 2 Cor 12:19; James 4:5).

(D) Used in an absolute sense (Matt 24:44; Luke 12:40; 17:9, "I think not" [a.t.]). In Heb 10:29 with *pósō* (4214), how much.

(II) In reference to others:

(A) To seem, appear, followed by the dat. and inf. (Luke 10:36, "Who do you think has become a neighbor unto him" [a.t.]). Without the dat. but followed by the inf. of the same subj., which then takes the adjuncts in the nom. (Acts 17:18, "He seemeth to be a setter forth of strange gods"; see 1 Cor 12:22; 2 Cor 10:9; Heb 12:11).

(B) Spoken of those who consider themselves rulers (Mark 10:42; Luke 22:24; Gal 2:9). In Gal 2:6, "who seem to be something" (a.t.), i.e., who are persons of note, distinguished (cf. Gal 2:9); thus *hoi dokoúntes*, those "who seemed to be pillars" means the chiefs, leaders (see Gal 2:2).

(III) Impersonally, *dokeí moi* ([3427], to me), it seems to me, that is:

(A) Personally to think, suppose. Interrogatively, *tí soí dokeí* (*tí* [5101], what; *soí* [4671], to thee, or in the pl. *humín* [5213], to you), what do you think?, sing. and pl. (Matt 17:25; 18:12; 21:28; 22:17, 42; 26:66; John 11:56). Without interrogatives (Acts 25:27, "it seemeth to me unreasonable").

(B) It seems good to me, it is my pleasure, equivalent to "personally determine," "resolve," followed by the inf. (Luke 1:3, "It seemed good to me"). See Acts 15:22, 25, 28, 34. As a part. with the art. *tó dokoún autois* ([846], to them), what seems good to them, i.e., what seems their pleasure or will (Heb 12:10, "as they thought best" [a.t.]).

Deriv.: *dógma* (1378), a decreed ordinance; *dóxa* (1391), glory, esteem; *eudokéō* (2106), to think well of.

Syn.: *nomízō* (3543), to consider, suppose, think; *hupolambánō* (5274), to suppose; *huponoéō* (5282), to suspect, conjecture; *oíomai* (3633), to expect, imagine, suppose; *logízomai* (3049), to reckon, suppose; *hēgéomai* (2233), to account, to think; *noéō* (3539), to perceive, understand; *phronéō* (5426), to think; *ginōskō* (1097), to come to know, recognize; *oída* (1492), to perceive; *epístamai* (1987), to know, understand; *gnōrízō* (1107), to discover, know.

Ant.: *agnoéō* (50), to be ignorant, lacking in knowledge; *lanthánō* (2990), to be ignorant of.

1381. δοκιμάζω *dokimázō*; fut. *dokimásō*, from *dókimos* (1384), tested, approved. To try, prove, discern, distinguish, approve. It has the notion of proving a thing whether it is worthy or not.

(I) Metaphorically, to make trial of, put to the proof, examine, e.g., by fire (1 Cor 3:13; 1 Pet 1:7; Sept.: Prov 17:3; Zech 13:9); other things, by use (Luke 14:19); generally, by any method (Rom 12:2; 1 Cor 11:28; 2 Cor 8:8, 22; 13:5; Gal 6:4; Eph 5:10; 1 Thess 2:4, "our hearts"; 5:21; 1 Tim 3:10; 1 John 4:1; Sept.: Ps 17:3; 139:1, 23; Jer 11:20). By implication, to examine and judge, i.e., to estimate, distinguish (Luke 12:56; see Matt 16:3; Rom 2:18; Phil 1:10; Sept.: Zech 11:13). Spoken with reference to God meaning to put to the proof, i.e., to tempt, which is equivalent to *peirázō* (3985), to tempt, but with the meaning of to try or test (Heb 3:9 [cf. Mal 3:15]). *Dokimázō*, to prove to bring forth the good in us or to make us good, is at times contrasted with *peirázō*, to tempt to make us fall. *Dokimázō* could not be used of Satan since he never wants us to experience God's approval. He always tempts (*peirázei*) us with the intent to make us fall.

(II) In the sense of to have proved, i.e., to hold as tried, to regard as proved, and generally to approve, judge fit and proper, e.g., persons (1 Cor 16:3; 1 Thess 2:4); things (Rom 14:22), followed by the inf. (Rom 1:28).

Deriv.: *apodokimázō* (593), to disapprove, reject.

Syn.: *apodeíknumi* (584), to show forth, approve; *anakrínō* (350), to investigate, usually judicially; *diakrínō* (1252), to discriminate, determine, decide.

Ant.: *apodokimázō* (593), to reject as the result of examination and disapproval; *athetéō* (114), to do away with what has been laid down, make void, nullify, disannul; *ekptúō* (1609), to spit out, loathe; *arnéomai* (720), to deny, renounce, reject.

1382. δοκιμή *dokimē̄́*; gen. *dokimē̄́s*, fem. noun from *dókimos* (1384), approved, tried. Proof of genuineness, trustworthiness. Distinguish between a pres. and past, an act. and a pass. meaning for this word which has a reflexive sense. Hence, it must be either the experience itself or the fact that one has proved oneself true or the act of proving himself true (Rom 5:4; 2 Cor 2:9, "Whether you prove yourselves true" [a.t.]; 13:3 meaning, "You desire proof that Christ is speaking through me" [a.t.]; Phil 2:22, "How he has proved himself true" [a.t.]). One who conducts himself nobly in trial is approved (*dókimos* [1384]). If the result of the testing is unsatisfactory, he is reprobate (*adókimos* [96]). It includes the process of proving (2 Cor 8:2; 9:13) and thus incorporating the trial itself as proof; also the effect of proving, in which case the meaning is approval.

Syn.: *éndeigma* (1730), the result of proving, the token; *tekmē̄́rion* (5039), the mark or sign which provides positive proof of the trial.

Ant.: *athétēsis* (115), disannulling, cancellation, rejection; *apobolē̄́* (580), rejection, casting away from oneself.

1383. δοκίμιον *dokímion*; gen. *dokimíou*, neut. noun from *dókimos* (1384), approved, tried. The means of proving, a criterion or test by which anything is proved or tried, as faith by afflictions (James 1:3). In 1 Pet 1:7 the meaning is slightly different. Here it reflects an adjectival sense which means genuine or approved. In NT times it was used of metals that were without alloy. Peter uses the word as a subst. referring to the genuineness of faith.

1384. δόκιμος *dókimos*; gen. *dokímou*, masc.-fem., neut. *dókimon*, adj. from *déchomai* (1209), to accept, receive. Proved, receivable, tried as metals by fire and thus be purified (Sept.: Gen 23:16; 1 Chr 29:4; 2 Chr 9:17). Hence to be approved as acceptable men in the furnace of adversity (James 1:12 [cf. Rom 16:10]); be approved or accepted (Rom 14:18). Approval does not mean self-commendation, but the commendation of the Lord (2 Cor 10:18). Doing that which is honorable brings a person real approval, as distinguished from seeming approval (2 Cor 13:7). A workman needing not to be ashamed is approved unto God (2 Tim 2:15 [cf. 1 Cor 11:19]).

Deriv.: *adókimos* (96), unapproved, reprobate; *dokimázō* (1381), to prove, try; *dokimḗ* (1382), trial, proof; *dokímion* (1383), test. *Dokímion* by some is considered to be the equivalent of *dokímeion*, the instrument which is used for testing something, in which case it would be equivalent to *dokimḗ*, the whole experience and not only the means utilized to test or prove something.

Syn.: *áxios* (514), worthy; *hikanós* (2425), able; *eklektós* (1588), chosen; *akatákritos* (178), uncondemned; *ámemptos* (273), unblamable; *anepíleptos* (423), blameless; *amṓmetos* (298), unblamable; *ámōmos* (299), faultless; *áspilos* (784), spotless.

Ant.: *adókimos* (96), unapproved; *anáxios* (370), unworthy.

1385. δοκός *dokós*; gen. *dokoú*, fem. noun. A beam or rafter used in building, a joist (Matt 7:3–5; Luke 6:41, 42; Sept.: Gen 19:8).

Syn.: *sanís* (4548), plank; *xúlon* (3586), timber, stick.

Ant.: *kárphos* (2595), a dry twig, straw.

1386. δόλιος *dólios*; fem. *dolía*, neut. *dólion*, adj. from *dólos* (1388), deceit. Deceitful (2 Cor 11:13).

Syn.: *plános* (4108), a deceiver; *phrenapátēs* (5423), mind deceiver (Titus 1:10); *panoúrgos* (3835), crafty; *pseudḗs* (5571), erroneous, false; *saprós* (4550), corrupt.

Ant.: *ádolos* (97), without guile; *ákakos* (172), without evil, guileless; *akéraios* (185), sincere, harmless; *haploús* (573), single, without duplicity, sincere; *athṓos* (121), innocent; *agathós* (18), benevolent; *chrēstós* (5543), good, mellow; *semnós* (4586), venerable, honest; *euschḗmōn* (2158), comely, honorable; *eilikrinḗs* (1506), sincere.

1387. δολιόω *dolióō*; contracted *dolió*, fut. *doliṓsō*, from *dólos* (1388), deceit. To lure as by bait, use deceit or guile to deceive, used intrans. (Rom 3:13 quoted from Ps 5:9; Sept.: Num 25:18). Akin to *dolóō* (1389), to adulterate or handle deceitfully.

Syn.: *apatáō* (538), to beguile, deceive; *exapatáō* (1818), to beguile thoroughly or deceive wholly; *phrenapatáō* (5422), to deceive the mind; *planáō* (4105), to wander, lead astray; *paralogízomai* (3884), to beguile; *kapēleúō* (2585), to corrupt by huckstering, to do anything for sordid personal gain, while *dolóō* or *dolióō* involves only deceitful dealing without necessarily personal gain which is involved in *kapēleúō*; *deleázō* (1185), to catch with bait, beguile; *pseúdomai* (5574), to deceive by falsehood.

Ant.: *alētheúō* (226), to speak the truth, be honest.

1388. δόλος *dólos*; gen. *dólou*, masc. noun from *délō* (n.f.), to bait. Bait, metaphorically and generally fraud, guile, deceit (Matt 26:4; Mark 7:22; 14:1; John 1:47; Acts 13:10; Rom 1:29; 2 Cor 12:16; 1 Thess 2:3; 1 Pet 2:1, 22; 3:10; Rev 14:5; Sept.: Gen 27:35; Job 13:7; Ps 32:2; Isa 53:9).

Deriv.: *ádolos* (97), without guile; *dólios* (1386), deceitful; *dolióō* (1387), to deceive; *dolóō* (1389), to adulterate or handle deceitfully.

Syn.: *apátē* (539), deceit or deceitfulness; *panourgía* (3834), craftiness; *pseúdos* (5579), a lie; *plánē* (4106), deceit.

Ant.: *alḗtheia* (225), truth, honesty; *eilikríneia* (1505), sincerity; *hagnótēs* (54), cleanness, pureness, and metaphorically without guile; *aphtharsía* (861), incorruptness, sincerity.

1389. δολόω *dolóō*; contracted *dolṓ*, fut. *dolṓsō*, from *dólos* (1388), deceit. To adulterate. Mixing human traditions with the pure word of the gospel. Contrast *kapēleúō* which always includes *dólos*, deceit, but *dolóō* never extends to *kapēleúō* which, in addition to adulterating, has the notion of unjust lucre, gain, profit, advantage.

Syn.: *apatáō* (538), to beguile, deceive; *exapatáō* (1818), to beguile thoroughly, deceive wholly; *phrenapatáō* (5422), to cause deceit in the mind; *planáō* (4105), to cause to go astray, wander; *paralogízomai* (3884), to deceive by false reasoning; *deleázō* (1185), to catch by a bait (*délear*); *apoplanáō* (635), to cause to wander away from, lead astray.

Ant.: *alētheúō* (226), to speak the truth, be honest.

1390. δόμα *dóma*; gen. *dómatos*, neut. noun from *dídōmi* (1325), to give. A gift (Eph 4:8; Phil 4:17; see Sept.: Gen 25:6; Ps 68:18; Prov 18:16; Dan 2:48); lends greater emphasis to the character of the gift than to its beneficent nature; a good gift from man to man (Matt 7:11; Luke 11:13) irrespective of the character of the giver which may be evil. In Eph 4:8, the pl. *dómata* means the actual gifts proving Christ's generous character (referred to by *dōreá* in Eph 4:7) at the time His spirit left His God-Man personality. In Phil 4:17, *dóma* refers to the material gifts the Philippians repeatedly sent to Paul for his needs. For a full discussion of all the cognate words see *dóron* (1435), a gift.

Ant.: *chreía* (5532), need, lack; *hustérēsis* (5304), the act of going without; *anágkē* (318), necessity.

1391. δόξα *dóxa*; gen. *dóxēs*, fem. noun from *dokéō* (1380), to think, recognize. Glory.

A look at the root word of *dóxa*, i.e., *dokéō* (1380), to think or suppose, is necessary. Etymologically, the word primarily means thought or opinion, especially favorable human opinion, and thus in a secondary sense reputation, praise, honor (true and false), splendor, light, perfection, rewards (temporal and eternal). Thus the *dóxa* of man is human opinion and is shifty, uncertain, often based on error, and its pursuit for its own safety is unworthy. But there is a glory of God which must be absolutely true and changeless. God's opinion marks the true value of things as they appear to the eternal mind, and God's favorable opinion is true glory. This contrast is well seen in John 5:44 as the Lord speaks of the glory that the people were receiving among themselves and the only glory that comes from God (see John 12:43). Glory, therefore, is the true apprehension of God or things. The glory of God must mean His unchanging essence. Giving glory to God is ascribing to Him His full recognition. The true glory of man, on the other hand, is the ideal condition in which God created man. This condition was lost in the fall and is recovered through Christ and exists as a real fact in the divine mind. The believer waits for this complete restoration. The glory of God is what He is essentially; the glory of created things including man is what they are meant by God to be, though not yet perfectly attained (Heb 2:10; Rom 8:18–21).

(I) Spoken of honor due or rendered, i.e., praise, applause (Luke 14:10; John 5:41, 44; 7:18; 8:50, 54; 2 Cor 6:8; 1 Thess 2:6); of God, e.g., to the honor and glory of God, i.e., that God may be honored, glorified (John 11:4; Rom 3:7; 15:7; Phil 1:11). In Rev 4:11, "to receive the glory" (a.t.) means to be extolled in praises. In ascriptions of glory or praise to God (Luke 2:14; Rom 11:36; Gal 1:5; 1 Pet 4:11; Sept.: 1 Chr 16:28, 29 [cf. Ps 29:9; 104:35; 106:48]). By metonymy, spoken of the ground, occasion or source of honor or glory (1 Cor 11:15; 2 Cor 8:23; Eph 3:13; 1 Thess 2:20).

(II) In the NT, spoken also of that which excites admiration or to which honor is ascribed.

(A) Of external conditions meaning dignity, splendor, glory (Heb 2:7 quoted from Ps 8:5; 1 Pet 1:24). By metonymy that which reflects, expresses or exhibits dignity (1 Cor 11:7). Spoken of kings, regal majesty, splendor, pomp, magnificence, e.g., the expected temporal reign of the Messiah (Mark 10:37 [cf. Matt 20:21 where the word *basileía* {932}, kingdom, is used]); of the glory of His Second Coming (Matt 19:28; 24:30; Mark 13:26; Luke 9:26; 21:27; Titus 2:13; Sept.: 1 Sam 2:8; 1 Chr 29:25; Isa 8:7; Dan 11:21); of the accompaniments of royalty, e.g., splendid apparel (Matt 6:29; Luke 12:27; Sept.: Ex 28:2, 36; Esth 5:1; Isa 61:3); of wealth, treasures (Matt 4:8; Luke 4:6; Rev 21:24, 26; Sept.: Gen 31:1; Isa 10:3). By metonymy spoken in the pl. of persons in high honor, e.g., *dóxai*, dignities, i.e., kings, princes, magistrates (2 Pet 2:10; Jude 1:8 [cf. Isa 5:13]).

(B) Of an external appearance as luster, brightness, dazzling light: "The glory of that light" (Acts 22:11); the sun, stars (1 Cor 15:40, 41); Moses' face (2 Cor 3:7; Sept.: Ex 34:29, 30, 35); the celestial light which surrounds angels (Rev 18:1), or glorified saints (Luke 9:31, 32; 1 Cor 15:43; Phil 3:21; Col 3:4). Spoken especially of the celestial splendor in which God sits enthroned and His divine effulgence, dazzling majesty, radiant glory (2 Thess 1:9; 2 Pet 1:17; Rev 15:8; 21:11, 23 [cf. 22:5]); as visible to mortals (Luke 2:9; John 12:41, see Isa 6:1; Acts 7:55); as manifested in the Messiah's Second Coming (Matt 16:27; Mark 8:38; Sept.: Ex 16:10; 24:17; 1 Kgs 8:11 [cf. Ps 104:1ff.; Ezek 1:26–28]). In Heb 9:5, "cherubim of glory" means the representatives of the Divine Presence (cf. Ex 25:22; Num 7:89; 2 Sam 6:2).

(C) Of internal character, i.e., glorious moral attributes, excellence, perfection. As spoken of God, infinite perfection, divine majesty and holiness (Acts 7:2; Rom 1:23; Eph 1:17, "the Father of glory" means the One possessing infinite perfections; Heb 1:3); of the divine perfections as manifested in the power of God (John 11:40; Rom 6:4; 9:23; Eph 1:12, 14, 18; 3:16; Col 1:11; 2 Pet 1:3); of Jesus, as the brightness (*apaúgasma* [541]) of the divine character (John 1:14; 2:11; Heb 1:3); of things in place of an adj. as excellent, splendid, glorious (2 Cor 3:7–9; Eph 1:6).

(D) Of that exalted state of blissful perfection which is the portion of those who dwell with God in heaven. As spoken of Christ and including the idea of His royal majesty as Messiah (Luke 24:26; John 17:5, 22, 24; 2 Thess 2:14; 1 Tim 3:16; 1 Pet 1:11); of glorified saints, i.e., salvation, eternal life (Rom 2:7, 10; 8:18; 1 Cor 2:7; 2 Cor 4:17; 1 Thess 2:12; 2 Tim 2:10; Heb 2:10; 1 Pet 5:1). In Rom 5:2; 1 Pet 5:10, the glory of God means the glory which God will bestow. By metonymy, the author or procurer of this glory for anyone, i.e., the author of salvation (Luke 2:32), the same as the Lord of glory (1 Cor 2:8 [see v. 7]). Other references: Matt 6:13; 25:31; Luke 17:18; 19:38; Acts 12:23; Rom 4:20; 9:4; 16:27; 1 Cor 10:31; 2 Cor 1:20; 3:10, 11, 18; 4:4, 6, 15; 8:19; Eph 3:21; Phil 2:11; 3:19; 4:19, 20; Col 1:27; 1 Tim 1:11, 17; 2 Tim 4:18; Heb 2:9; 3:3; 9:5; 13:21; James 2:1; 1 Pet 1:7, 21; 4:13; 5:11; 2 Pet 3:18; Jude 1:24, 25; Rev 1:6; 4:9; 5:12, 13; 7:12; 11:13; 14:7;

16:9; 19:1, 7. In brief, *dóxa* can mean appearance, reputation, glory.

(III) Basically, in the Bible it refers to the recognition, honor or renown belonging to a person. When we read in Rom 3:23 that they "come short of [or lack] the glory of God," it means they are not what God intended them to be. They lack His image and character. The predominant meaning of the noun *dóxa* in Scripture is recognition. It may denote form, aspect, or that appearance of a person or thing which catches the eye, attracts attention, or commands recognition. It is thus equivalent to splendor, brilliance, glory attracting the gaze, which makes it a strong syn. of *eikón* (1504), image (Rom 1:23).

(IV) *Dóxa* embraces all which is excellent in the divine nature, coinciding with God's self-revelation. It comprises all that God will manifest Himself to be in His final revelation to us (Luke 2:9; Rom 5:2; 6:4; Rev 21:23). God's glory revealed itself in and through Jesus Christ (John 1:14; 2 Cor 4:6; Heb 1:3).

(V) His Second Coming is spoken of as the blessed hope and the appearing of His glory. It is not "the glorious appearing" as the translation has it, but *epiphaneia* (2015) *tēs* ([3588], the) *dóxēs*, "the appearance of the glory of the great God and our Savior Jesus Christ" (a.t. [Titus 2:13]). Then, at Christ's Second Coming, He will be truly recognized for all that He is. The glory of the Son of Man in Matt 19:28; 25:31; Mark 10:37 (cf. Luke 9:32; 24:26) is to be understood in contrast with His earthly manifestation (John 17:22, 24; Phil 3:21). It is brought by Christ Himself in connection with the *dóxa*, glory, which He had before His humiliation in the incarnation (John 17:5 [cf. 12:41; Phil 2:11]).

(VI) Heb 1:3 equates the glory of Jesus to God's glory, being the self-revelation of God in the economy of redemption. In this sense, future glory is the hope of Christians. More specifically, *dóxa* means not merely the outward glorious appearance attracting attention to the person or thing itself, but inner glory outwardly manifested, e.g., splendor, glory, brightness, adornment (Matt 4:8; Luke 4:6).

(VII) The NT idea of *dóxa* is represented in the OT by the word *kabod* (3519, OT) with the root idea of heaviness (i.e., weight) and, metaphorically, worthiness. When it is ascribed to men, it refers to their splendor or reputation. When the glory of Jehovah is spoken about, it refers to the revelation of God's person, nature, and presence to mankind, sometimes with visible phenomena. The glory of Jehovah went with His people out of Egypt and was shown in the cloud which led them through the wilderness (Ex 16:7, 10). The cloud rested on Mt. Sinai where Moses saw God's glory (Ex 24:15–18). No man could see God's face and live (Ex 33:20), but some vision of His glory was granted (Ex 33:21–23; 34:5–8). Thus we have the glory appearing to Israel at Sinai (Ex 24:16, 17); at the door of the tent (Lev 9:23; Num 14:10; 16:19); at the dedication of Solomon's temple (1 Kgs 8:10, 11); in the visions of Isaiah (Isa 6:1–3) and Ezekiel (Ezek 1:28; 3:23; 8:4). Similarly the messianic hopes of Israel are expressed under the figure of glory dwelling in the land (Ps 85:9). The glory of God also filled the tabernacle (Ex 40:34, 35) and appeared especially in the hour of sacrifice (Lev 9:6, 23; see Num 14:21, 22; Ps 96:3; Isa 6:1–4; 40:4, 5; 60:1–3; Ezek 1:28). In the NT, the same concept of glory is seen in Luke's account of the nativity (Luke 2:9) and of the transfiguration (Luke 9:28ff.) where the glory of Christ shines forth visibly in the dazzling brightness of His countenance. It encompasses the forms of Moses and Elijah (Luke 9:30), and even transfigures material objects like Christ's clothing (Luke 9:29). With this passage may be compared the visions of Stephen (Acts 7:55); Saul of Tarsus (Acts 9:3; 22:6–11; 26:13); and the Apostle John in Patmos (Rev 1:13–16).

(VIII) What is meant by the glory and the glorifying of Jesus Christ? It means the revelation of His essential deity, that which He is in the mind of the Father,

though veiled from man by the limitations of the incarnation (John 17:5; 1 Cor
2:8; Heb 1:3; James 2:1). When in John
17:1, 5, 24 the Lord Jesus prayed for His
glorification by the Father, He was looking forward to the splendor of His passion
as issuing in the resurrection, wherein His
true nature and redemptive work are recognized and celebrated by the faithful.
That was only the partial meaning ascribed to the word "glorified," for there
is a glory which is yet to come. This will
complete the present glory of the spiritual resurrection of believers with all that
is involved in the future resurrection and
glorification (John 17:24).

(IX) As to the glorification of the believer spoken of by Paul and Peter, it involves the obtaining of the glory of our
Lord Jesus Christ (2 Thess 2:14). The
present invisible glory of the believer through his union with Christ by the
Spirit is greater than the visible glory recorded in the OT (2 Cor 3:7–11).
The glory of God recognized in Christ
by the believer is a new creation of life
(2 Cor 4:6). Present limitations and sufferings will be abundantly compensat-
ed in the full, future revelation of glory
(2 Cor 4:17 [cf. Rom 8:18ff.]). The glorification of the believer is already ideally complete (Rom 8:30), but it will be
visibly completed in the resurrection of
the body (Phil 3:21 [cf. 1 Pet 5:1, 4]).
In the majority of cases in which glory is predicated of Christ, of Christians,
and of the environment of their life, the
sense is distinctly eschatological. The
sufferings of Christ and of believers are
contrasted with the glories which will
follow (Phil 3:21; 2 Thess 2:14; 1 Pet
1:11, 21; 4:13). Glory is a technical term
for the state of final salvation, the heavenly kingdom in which Christ now lives
and which is to be brought to man by
His *parousía* (3952), presence or Second
Coming. This is the coming glory (Rom
8:18) about to be revealed (1 Pet 5:1),
the inheritance of God and His saints
(Eph 1:18) unto which they are prepared
beforehand (Rom 9:23), called (1 Pet

5:10), led by Christ (Heb 2:10). It is their
unfading crown (1 Pet 5:4), the manifestation of their true nature (Col 3:4),
their emancipation from all evil limitations (Rom 8:21). It is the new heaven
and earth and all of the promised blessings associated with them. In the hope of
it they rejoice (Rom 5:2); for it they are
made meet by the indwelling Christ (Col
1:27) and by the discipline of the present
(2 Cor 4:17).

Deriv.: *doxázō* (1392), to glorify;
éndoxos (1741), glorious; *kenódoxos*
(2755), self-conceited; *parádoxos* (3861),
strange, contrary to expected appearance,
equivalent to a miraculous manifestation.

Syn.: *agallíasis* (20), exultation;
chará (5479), joy; *euphrosúnē* (2167),
having a joyful attitude; *kléos* (2811),
renown; *kaucháomai* (2744), to boast;
kaúchēsis (2746), the act of boasting;
kaúchēma (2745), the boast or the reason for boasting.

Ant.: *atimía* (819), dishonor; *aischúnē*
(152), shame; *entropḗ* (1791), a recoiling
resulting from shame; *aidós* (127), modesty, reverence, a sense of moral repugnance; *aschēmosúnē* (808), that which is
unseemly; *alazoneía* (212), vainglory, appearing to be what one is not.

1392. δοξάζω *doxázō*; fut. *doxásō*, from
dóxa (1391), glory. To glorify. The consequential meaning from the opinion which
one forms is to recognize, honor, praise,
invest with dignity, give anyone esteem
or honor by putting him into an honorable
position.

(I) To ascribe glory or honor to anyone,
praise, celebrate (Matt 6:2; Luke 4:15;
John 8:54; Acts 13:48; Heb 5:5; Rev 18:7;
Sept.: 2 Sam 6:22; Lam 1:8). To glorify
God, meaning to render glory to Him, recognize Him for Who and What He is, to
celebrate with praises, worship, adoration
(Matt 5:16; 9:8; 15:31; Mark 2:12; Luke
2:20; 5:25, 26; 7:16; 13:13; 17:15; 18:43;
23:47; John 13:31, 32; 14:13; 15:8; 17:4;
21:19; Acts 4:21; 11:18; 21:20; Rom
1:21; 15:6, 9; 1 Cor 6:20; 2 Cor 9:13; Gal
1:24; 1 Pet 2:12; 4:11, 16); the name of

God (John 12:28; Rev 15:4). See Sept.: Ps 22:23; 86:9, 12; Isa 42:10.

(II) To honor, bestow honor upon, exalt in dignity, render glorious.

(A) Used generally (1 Cor 12:26; 2 Thess 3:1; Sept.: 1 Chr 19:3; Esth 6:6, 7, 9, 11; Prov 13:18); with the meaning of to render excellent, splendid, and, in the pass. voice, to be excellent, splendid, glorious (Rom 11:13; 2 Cor 3:10; 1 Pet 1:8; Sept.: Ex 34:29, 30, 35).

(B) Spoken of God and Christ, meaning to glorify, i.e., to render conspicuous and glorious the divine character and attributes; e.g., of God as glorified by the Son (John 12:28; 13:31, 32; 14:13; 17:1, 4); by Christians (John 15:8; 21:19); of Christ as glorified by the Father (John 8:54; 13:32; 17:1, 5; Acts 3:13); by the Spirit (John 16:14); by Christians (John 17:10); generally (John 11:4; 13:31; Sept.: Ex 15:6, 11; Lev 10:3; Isa 5:16).

(C) Spoken of Christ and His followers, to glorify. In John 7:39, "because that Jesus was not yet glorified" refers to the passion and the resurrection of Jesus which was going to make evident to all that He was indeed God incarnate, all that He claimed to be. To fully clarify this would be the privilege of the coming Holy Spirit at Pentecost. See John 12:16, "These things understood not his disciples at the first: but when Jesus was glorified, then remembered they that these things were written of him." This refers to the definite time of the crucifixion and the resurrection of Christ when He proved His words about Himself which the disciples had found hard to understand. Similar is the meaning of John 12:23 (cf. Isa 52:13), and of Rom 8:30, the latter verse referring to the change that came about in the lives of those whom Jesus Christ justified before His Father.

Deriv.: *sundoxázō* (4888), to glorify together.

Syn.: *timáō* (5091), to honor; *megalúnō* (3170), to make great, magnify.

Ant.: *atimázō* (818), to dishonor, insult; *exouthenéō* (1848), to make of no account; *kataphronéō* (2706), to despise; *periphronéō* (4065), to reject in one's mind; *athetéō* (114), to set aside, reject; *oligōréō* (3643), to have little regard for; the expression *logízomai eis oudén* (*logízomai* [3049]; *eis* [1519]; *oudén* [3762]), "to reckon as nothing" (a.t.); *kataischúnō* (2617), put to shame; *aischúnomai* (153), to be ashamed; *epaischúnomai* (1870), to be ashamed of; *entrépō* (1788), to put to shame, cause to recoil.

1393. Δορκάς *Dorkás*; gen. *Dorkádos*, fem. proper noun. Dorcas, a woman at Joppa known also as Tabitha, meaning gazelle. She was an exemplary disciple of Christ, and her deeds of benevolence had greatly endeared her to the people. After she was dead and her body prepared for the grave, she was miraculously restored to life through the instrumentality of Peter (Acts 9:36–40).

1394. δόσις *dósis*; gen. *dóseōs*, fem. noun from *dídōmi* (1325), to give. Gift, the act of human or divine giving (Phil 4:15; James 1:17). For a full discussion of all the cognate words see *dóron* (1435), a gift.

1395. δότης *dótēs*; gen. *dótou*, masc. noun from *dídōmi* (1325), to give. A giver, a human giver to God and His work (2 Cor 9:7; Sept.: Prov 22:9). For a full discussion of all the cognate words see *dóron* (1435), a gift.

1396. δουλαγωγέω *doulagōgéō*; contracted *doulagōgṓ*, fut. *doulagōgḗsō*, from *doúlos* (1401), servant, and *ágō* (71), to lead, bring. To bring into servitude or subjection (1 Cor 9:27).

Syn.: *doulóō* (1402), to make a slave, enslave; *katadoulóō* (2615), to bring into bondage; *hupotássō* (5293), to subject.

Ant.: *eleutheróō* (1659), to make free; *dikaióō* (1344), to justify and consequently to set free in view of the change in the one who is justified by God; *apallássō* (525), to deliver; *rhúomai* (4506), to rescue from, deliver; *sōzō* (4982), to save, rescue.

1397. δουλεία *douleía*; gen. *douleías*, fem. noun from *douleúō* (1398), to be a slave, to serve. Servitude, dependence, the state of a *doúlos* or slave. That state of man in which he is prevented from freely possessing and enjoying his life, a state opposed to liberty. In the NT, used only figuratively as a slavish spirit, in contrast to the spirit of sonship (Rom 8:15); of the condition of those who are subject to death (Rom 8:21); of those under the Mosaic Law (Gal 4:24; 5:1); of those subject to the fear of death (Heb 2:15).

Deriv.: *ophthalmodouleía* (3787), eyeservice, implying an outward service only.

Ant.: *eleuthería* (1657), liberty, freedom; *politeía* (4174), citizenship as opposed to the lack of privilege for slaves to become citizens; *áphesis* (859), release; *exousía* (1849), authority.

1398. δουλεύω *douleúō*; fut *douleúsō*, from *doúlos* (1401), servant. To be in the position of a servant and act accordingly; to be subject and serve in subjection or bondage. Used of actions which are directed by others in contrast to *doulóō* (1402) which means to make someone a slave or to be held in bondage without necessarily the idea of serving. Subjugated, reduced to bondage under someone (John 8:33; Acts 7:7; Rom 9:12). Used in the absolute sense, it means to be deprived of freedom (Gal 4:25); to be under the law (see Gal 4:21); serve in bondage, put one's dependence into effect, i.e., to obey (Matt 6:24; Luke 15:29; 16:13; Eph 6:7; 1 Tim 6:2); metaphorically, to be a slave to things such as pleasures (Titus 3:3).

(I) Spoken of involuntary service (Matt 6:24; Luke 16:13; Eph 6:7; 1 Tim 6:2; Sept.: Lev 25:39; Deut 15:12); of a people meaning to be subject to (John 8:33; Acts 7:7; Rom 9:12, see Gen 25:23; 27:40; Sept.: Gen 14:4; Judg 3:8,

14). Metaphorically, of those subject to the Mosaic Law (Gal 4:25).

(II) Metaphorically spoken of voluntary service, to obey, be devoted to (Luke 15:29; Rom 12:11, doing what the occasion demands; Gal 5:13; Phil 2:22; Sept.: Gen 29:15, 18, 20, 25, 30). In a moral sense, to obey or be devoted to God or Christ, (Matt 6:24; Luke 16:13; Acts 20:19; Rom 7:6; 1 Thess 1:9); to Christ (Rom 14:18; 16:18; Col 3:24); to the law of God (Rom 7:25; Sept.: Deut 13:4; Judg 2:7; Mal 3:18). Spoken of false gods (Gal 4:8; Sept.: Ex 23:33); of things, to obey, follow, indulge in, e.g., mammon (Matt 6:24; Luke 16:13); sin (Rom 6:6); the belly, i.e., one's appetite (Rom 16:18); the elements (Gal 4:9). To indulge in one's lusts (Titus 3:3).

Deriv.: *douleía* (1397), slavery, bondage.

Syn.: *diakonéō* (1247), to minister; *leitourgéō* (3008), to render public service, do service to the gods; *latreúō* (3000), to serve for hire, spoken of the service of both priests and people and distinguished from *leitourgéō* in that the latter speaks of the fulfillment of an office or the discharge of a function; *hupēretéō* (5256), to serve as an underling; *hierourgéō* (2418), to minister in priestly service; *ergázomai* (2038), to work.

Ant.: *argéō* (691), to be idle; *scholázō* (4980), to be at leisure.

1399. δούλη *doúlē*; gen. *doúlēs*, the fem. of *doúlos* (1401), bondservant. A female servant, a handmaid (Acts 2:18; Sept.: Lev 25:44; 1 Sam 8:16). Used instead of the personal pron. in the oriental style by a female when addressing a superior. (Luke 1:38, 48; Sept.: 1 Sam 25:41; 2 Sam 14:6; 1 Kgs 1:13, 17; 2 Kgs 4:2, 16).

Ant.: *eleuthéra*, the fem. of *eleútheros* (1658), free person.

1400. δούλον *doúlon*; the acc. sing. of *doúlos* (1401). A male bond servant, only in Rom 6:19.

1401. δοῦλος *doúlos*; gen. *doúlou*, masc. noun. A slave, one who is in a permanent relation of servitude to another, his will being altogether consumed in the will of the other (Matt 8:9; 20:27; 24:45, 46). Generally one serving, bound to serve, in bondage (Rom 6:16, 17).

(I) A slave, servant, spoken of involuntary service, e.g., a slave as opposed to a free man (*eleútheros* [1658]; 1 Cor 7:21; Gal 3:28; Col 3:11; Rev 6:15). Also generally a servant (Matt 13:27, 28; John 4:51; Acts 2:18; Eph 6:5; 1 Tim 6:1; Sept.: Lev 25:44; Josh 9:23; Judg 6:27). In Phil 2:7, having taken "the form of a servant," means appearing in a humble and despised condition.

(II) Metaphorically spoken of voluntary service, a servant, implying obedience, devotion (John 15:15; Rom 6:16). Implying modesty (2 Cor 4:5); in praise of modesty (Matt 20:27; Mark 10:44). Spoken of the true followers and worshipers of God, e.g., a servant of God, either of agents sent from God, as Moses (Rev 15:3; see Josh 1:1) or prophets (Rev 10:7; 11:18; Sept.: Josh 24:29; Jer 7:25), or simply of the worshipers of God (Rev 2:20; 7:3; 19:5; Sept.: Ps 34:22; 134:1); the followers and ministers of Christ (Eph 6:6; 2 Tim 2:24); especially applied to the Apostles (Rom 1:1; Gal 1:10; 2 Pet 1:1; Jude 1:1). Used instead of the personal pron. in the oriental style of addressing a superior (Luke 2:29; Acts 4:29; Sept.: 1 Sam 3:9, 10; Ps 19:12). In respect of things, one such as the servant of sin who indulges in or is addicted to something (John 8:34; Rom 6:16, 17; 2 Pet 2:19).

(III) In the sense of minister, attendant, spoken of the officers of an oriental court (Matt 18:23, 26–28, 32; 22:3, 4, 6, 8, 10).

Deriv.: *doulagōgéō* (1396), to be a slave driver; *douleúō* (1398), to be a slave to, to serve; *doulóō* (1402), to make a slave or bring someone into slavery; *súndoulos* (4889), fellow slave.

Syn.: *diákonos* (1249), a deacon, servant, minister; *país* (3816), literally "a

child," but also an attendant, servant; *oikétēs* (3610), a house servant; *hupērétēs* (5257), a servant; *therápōn* (2324), a healer who also cares, an attendant servant; *místhios* (3407) and *misthōtós* (3411), a hired servant.

Ant.: *hodēgós* (3595), a leader on the way, a guide; *kúrios* (2962), lord, master; *despótēs* (1203), despot, an absolute ruler; *proïstámenos* (the mid. part. of *proḯstēmi* [4291]), to stand before or in rank above, person ranking ahead or above; *oikodespótēs* (3617), householder, head of a family or master of the house; *eleútheros* (1658), a free man; *dunástēs* (1413), ruler, potentate.

1402. δουλόω *doulóō*; contracted *doulô*, fut. *doulōsō*, perf. pass. *dedoúlōmai* with the pres. meaning to be a slave, to serve, from *doúlos* (1401), slave. To make a slave or servant, to subject, subjugate (Acts 7:6; 1 Cor 9:19; Sept.: Gen 15:13); in the pass., to be subjugated, subdued (Rom 6:18, 22); in the perf. tense, to be dependent (Gal 4:3). It denotes not so much a relation of service as primarily one of dependence upon, or bondage to, something (Titus 2:3; 2 Pet 2:19). In 1 Cor 7:15 the verb refers to a brother or sister being bound by law.

Deriv.: *katadoulóō* (2615), to enslave.

Syn.: *kurieúō* (2961), to exercise lordship over.

Ant.: *eleutheróō* (1659), to liberate; *charízomai* (5483), to deliver; *apolúō* (630), to set free, dismiss.

1403. δοχή *dochḗ*; gen. *dochḗs*, fem. noun from *déchomai* (1209), to receive. A reception, entertainment, banquet (Luke 5:29; 14:13; Sept.: Gen 26:30; Esth 1:3; 5:4).

Syn.: *heortḗ* (1859), a feast or festival; *deípnon* (1173), the chief meal of the day, dinner or supper; *gámos* (1062), a wedding or a wedding feast; *agápē* (26), a love feast.

Ant.: *apobolḗ* (580), a casting away, and its syn.

1404. δράκων drákōn; gen. *drákontos*, masc. noun from *dérkomai* (n.f.), to look at, behold. A dragon, a huge serpent, so-called because of his sight which is very acute (cf. *óphis* [3789], a serpent). The Greeks called the dragon a species of serpent because he could see so well. In the NT, *drákōn* is used only symbolically for Satan (Rev 12:3, 4, 7, 9, 13, 16, 17; 13:2, 4, 11; 16:13; 20:2 [cf. Gen 3:1ff.]).

1405. δράσσομαι drássomai, δράττομαι dráttomai; fut. *dráxomai*. Used only in the mid. voice *drássomai*, to grasp with the hand, to seize, take (1 Cor 3:19 [cf. Job 5:13; Sept.: Num 5:26]).
  Deriv.: *drachmḗ* (1406), drachma.
  Syn.: *lambánō* (2983), to take, lay hold of; *epilambánō* (1949), to lay hold of; *katalambánō* (2638), to apprehend.
  Ant.: *aphíēmi* (863), to let go; *aníēmi* (447), to let go, loosen, let up; *kataleípō* (2641), to leave behind; *apoleípō* (620), to remain; *egkataleípō* (1459), to leave behind in; *apotássomai* (657), to send away from oneself to the proper place.

1406. δραχμή drachmḗ; gen. *drachmḗs*, fem. noun, *drássomai* (1405), to grasp. A drachma, i.e., something after which people grasped. A Greek coin of silver equal to a quarter of the Jewish shekel, and to the Roman denarius or dinar which was the average pay for a twelve-hour work day (Luke 15:8, 9 [cf. Matt 20:2]).
  Deriv.: *dídrachmon* (1323), tribute.
  Syn.: *argúrion* (694), a piece of silver, a silver coin.

1407. δρέπανον drépanon; gen. *drepánou*, neut. noun from *drépō* (n.f.), to pluck, crop, cut off. A sickle, a reaping hook (Mark 4:29; Rev 14:14–19. See Sept.: 1 Sam 13:20; Joel 3:13).

1408. δρόμος drómos; gen. *drómou*, masc. noun from *drameín*, 2 aor. inf. of *tréchō* (5143), to run. A running, a race (Sept.: 2 Sam 18:27; Eccl 9:11), or a place of running, a stadium. In the NT, used metaphorically meaning course, career, or one's life, ministry (Acts 13:25; 20:24; 2 Tim 4:7 [cf. Sept.: Jer 23:10]).
  Syn.: *poreía* (4197), travel, journey, career, course; *hodós* (3598), way, route, journey; *tríbos* (5147), path.
  Ant.: *stásis* (4714), a standing.

1409. Δρουσίλλα Drousílla; gen. *Drousíllēs*, proper noun. Drusilla, the youngest daughter of Herod Agrippa I, sister of the younger Agrippa and Bernice, celebrated for her beauty (Acts 24:24). She was first engaged to Epiphanes, prince of Comagena, but was afterwards married to Azizus, King of Emessa, whom Felix persuaded her to abandon so she could become his wife. This was done through a sorcerer, Simon of Cyprus. She was present at the hearing of the Apostle Paul before her husband at Caesarea.

1410. δύναμαι dúnamai; imperf. *edunámēn* (Matt 22:46), with double augment *ēdunámēn* (Matt 26:9; Luke 1:22), fut. *dunḗsomai*, aor. *ēdunḗthēn* (Matt 17:16, 19), pres. indic. 2d person sing. *dúnē* for *dúnasai* (Rev 2:2), mid. deponent. To be able, have power, whether by virtue of one's own ability and resources (Rom 15:14), through a state of mind or favorable circumstances (1 Thess 2:6), by permission of law or custom (Acts 24:8, 11), or simply to be able, powerful (Matt 3:9; 2 Tim 3:15).
  (I) Followed by the inf. expressed:
  (A) Of the pres., as expressing continued action (Matt 6:24; 7:18; Mark 2:7, 19; Luke 6:39; John 5:19, 30; 6:60; Acts 27:15; Rom 15:14; 1 Cor 10:21; 1 Thess 2:6; Sept.: Gen 37:4; 43:32).
  (B) More commonly of the aor., implying transient or momentary action, either past or pres. (Matt 3:9; 10:28; Mark 1:45; 6:5; Luke 5:12; 8:19; John 7:34, 36; 10:35; Acts 4:16; 17:19; 1 Cor 2:14; James 4:2; Rev 3:8; 13:4; Sept.: Gen 15:5; 19:19). Also where the action in itself might be expressed either as continued or transient, but the writer chooses to express it as tran-

sient (Matt 5:14; Luke 1:20, 22; John 3:3; Acts 13:39; Heb 9:9; Rev 2:2).

(II) With an inf. implied which is readily suggested by the context (Matt 16:3; Mark 6:19; Luke 9:40; Acts 27:39; 1 Cor 3:2; Sept.: 1 Kgs 22:22). Construction with the acc. and the inf. *poieín* (4160), to do, which is implied, or an acc. of manner (Mark 9:22; 2 Cor 13:8).

Deriv.: *dúnamis* (1411), power, ability, strength; *dunástēs* (1413), ruler; *dunatós* (1415), powerful, strong.

Syn.: *ischúō* (2480), to be strong, prevail, but indicating a more forceful strength or ability than is involved in *dúnamai*; *exischúō* (1840), to be thoroughly strong; *katischúō* (2729), to overpower, prevail; *éxesti* (1832), it is permitted, and, in question form, "May I?"; *krataióō* (2901), to strengthen, sustain; *sthenóō* (4599), to strengthen.

Ant.: *adunatéō* (101), to be unable.

1411. δύναμις *dúnamis*; gen. *dunámeōs*, fem. noun from *dúnamai* (1410), to be able. Power, especially achieving power. All the words derived from the stem *dúna-* have the meaning of being able, capable. It may even mean to will. Contrast *ischús* (2479) which stresses the factuality of the ability, not necessarily the accomplishment.

(I) Spoken of intrinsic power, either physical or moral, as in the verb *dúnamai*.

(A) Of the body (1 Cor 15:43, "in power" stands in opposition to "in weakness"; Heb 11:11; Sept.: Job 39:19, *dúnamis*; Job 40:11, *ischús*; Ps 29:4, *ischús* [2479], strength).

(B) Generally (Matt 25:15; Acts 6:8; 1 Cor 15:56; 2 Tim 1:7) a spirit of strength, meaning manly vigor in opposition to a spirit of cowardice (*deilías* [1167]) (Heb 1:3, "His powerful word" [a.t.]; 7:16; 11:34; Rev 1:16; Sept.: 2 Kgs 18:20; 1 Chr 13:8; 29:2; Ezra 2:69; 10:13; Job 12:13). Also in various constructions with *katá* (2596), according to one's strength, meaning as far as one can (2 Cor 8:3). With *hupér* (5228), beyond, above one's

strength (2 Cor 1:8; 8:3). With *en* (1722), in, and the dat. *dunámei* meaning with power or powerfully, mightily (Col 1:29; 2 Thess 1:11). With the dat. only (Acts 4:33). In Eph 3:16; Col 1:11, the dat. *dunámei* means with power.

(C) Spoken of God, the Messiah, the great power of God, meaning His almighty energy (Matt 22:29; Mark 12:24; Luke 1:35; 5:17; Rom 1:20; 9:17; 1 Cor 6:14; 2 Cor 4:7; 13:4; Eph 1:19; 3:7, 20; 2 Tim 1:8; 1 Pet 1:5; 2 Pet 1:3). Joined with *dóxa* (1391), glory, it implies the greatness, omnipotence, and majesty of God (Rev 15:8. See Matt 26:64; Mark 14:62; Luke 22:69, "on the right hand of the power of God"; Heb 1:3, "on the right hand of the Majesty"). By metonymy spoken of a person or thing in whom the power of God is manifested, i.e., the manifestation of the power of God (Acts 8:10; see Rom 1:16; 1 Cor 1:18, 24). With the gen. phrase "of God" it expresses the source, i.e., power imparted from God (1 Cor 2:5; 2 Cor 6:7). Spoken of Jesus as exercising the power to heal (Mark 5:30; Luke 6:19; 8:46; 2 Cor 12:9). In Rom 1:4, "in power [*en dunámei*]" (a.t.) stands for the gen. *toú dunatoú*, the Son of God, the powerful One. In the sense of power, omnipotent majesty (Matt 24:30; Mark 9:1; 13:26; Luke 21:27, "with power and great glory"; 2 Thess 1:7, "with angels of His power" [a.t.] means the angels who are the attendants of His majesty; 2 Pet 1:16); as spoken of the power of the Spirit meaning the power imparted by the Spirit (Luke 4:14; Rom 15:13, 19); of prophets and apostles as empowered by the Holy Spirit (Luke 1:17; 24:49; Acts 1:8 [cf. Acts 2:4]).

(D) Spoken of miraculous power, "the mighty power of signs and wonders" (a.t.) means the power of working miracles (Rom 15:19, explained by the power of the Spirit in the next clause; see Acts 10:38; 1 Cor 2:4; 2 Cor 12:12; 2 Thess 2:9). By metonymy of effect for cause, the pl. *dunámeis*, powers, is often used for mighty deeds, miracles (Matt 7:22; 11:20, 21, 23; 13:54, 58; 14:2; Mark 6:2,

5, 14; Luke 10:13; 19:37; Acts 2:22; 8:13; 19:11; 1 Cor 12:10; 2 Cor 12:12; Gal 3:5; Heb 2:4; Sept.: Job 37:14; Ps 106:2). The abstract for the concrete, meaning a worker of miracles (1 Cor 12:28, 29).

(E) Spoken of the essential power, true nature or reality of something (Phil 3:10, "the power of his resurrection"; 2 Tim 3:5). As opposed to *lógos* (3056), speech (1 Cor 4:19, 20; 1 Thess 1:5). Metaphorically of language, the power of a word, i.e., meaning, significance (1 Cor 14:11, "the power of the voice" [a.t.]).

(II) Spoken of power as resulting from external sources and circumstances:

(A) Power, authority, might (Luke 4:36; 9:1; Acts 3:12; 2 Pet 2:11; Rev 13:2; 17:13). Spoken of omnipotent sovereignty as due to God, e.g., in ascriptions (Matt 6:13; Rev 4:11; 5:12; 7:12; 11:17; 12:10; 19:1; Sept.: 1 Chr 29:11). Joined with *ónoma* (3686), name (Acts 4:7; 1 Cor 5:4, meaning warrant). In Rom 8:38 "powers" stands for persons in authority, the mighty, the powerful ones (see 1 Cor 15:24; Eph 1:21; 1 Pet 3:22; Sept.: Esth 2:18).

(B) With the meaning of number, quantity, abundance, wealth (in Rev 3:8, a small number of members or perhaps true believers [cf. Rev 18:3]). Metaphorically for enjoyment, happiness (Heb 6:5).

(C) Of warlike power, meaning force, i.e., host, army (Luke 10:19, over the whole host of Satan [see Luke 10:20]; Sept.: Ex 14:28; 15:4; 2 Sam 10:7; 17:25; 20:23). The powers of the heavens means the hosts of heaven, i.e., the sun, moon, and stars (Matt 24:29; Mark 13:25; Luke 21:26 [cf. Rev 6:13; Sept.: Isa 34:4; Dan 8:10]).

Deriv.: *dunamóō* (1412), to strengthen. **Syn**.: *ischús* (2479), strength, ability, force, somewhat stronger than *dúnamis*; *krátos* (2904), dominion, enduring strength; *exousía* (1849), authority; *archḗ* (746), rule, power; *megaleiótēs* (3168), majesty; with the meaning of miracle: *sēmeíon* (4592), sign, token; *téras* (5059), something strange, a marvel, wonder; *megaleíon* (3167), a great

work; *éndoxon* (1741), a glorious work; *parádoxon* (3861), a strange work; *thaumásion* (2297), a marvelous work; *thaúma* (2295), a wonder, marvel; *érgon* (2041), work when referring to Christ's work.

Ant.: *asthéneia* (769), feebleness, infirmity, disease.

1412. δυναμόω *dunamóō*; contracted *dunamṓ*, fut. *dunamṓsō*, from *dúnamis* (1411), strength. To strengthen. In the NT, used in the pass., to be strengthened, grow strong morally (Col 1:11 [cf. Eph 3:16]).

Deriv.: *endunamóō* (1743), to make strong.

Syn.: *ischúō* (2480), to have strength; *enischúō* (1765), to strengthen; *krataióō* (2901), to strengthen; *sthenóō* (4599), to strengthen; *stereóō* (4732), to establish; *epistērízō* (1991), to establish, confirm; *stērízō* (4741), to establish, strengthen.

Ant.: *asthenéō* (770), to lack strength, be weak; *échō kakṓs* or *kakṓs échō* (*échō* [2192], have; *kakṓs* [2560], badly), to have badly, be ill; *kámnō* (2577), to work, to be sick from much labor; *sunéchomai* (4912), to be seized or afflicted by ills; *noséō* (3552), to be sick.

1413. δυνάστης *dunástēs*; gen. *dunástou*, masc. noun from *dúnamai* (1410), to be able. Possessor of power or authority, one who occupies high position (Acts 8:27; Sept.: Gen 50:4; Lev 19:15; Jer 34:19), especially of independent rulers of territories (Luke 1:52). Referring to the Lord as the absolute ruler (1 Tim 6:15; Sept.: Prov 8:15; 23:1).

Syn.: *dunatós* (1415), powerful, mighty, and *ischurós* (2478), strong; *krataiós* (2900), one who has dominion; *kúrios* (2962), lord, master; *despótēs* (1203), despot, master, lord; *megistán* (3175), great man, prince, lord.

Ant.: *boēthós* (998), a helper; *idiótēs* (2399), a private person; *polítēs* (4177), a citizen.

1414. δυνατέω *dunatéō*; contracted *dunató*, fut. *dunatéso*, from *dunatós* (1415), strong, able, a mighty person. To show oneself able, mighty (2 Cor 13:3). Akin to *dúnamai* (1410), to be able, to have power whether by virtue of one's own ability and resources (Rom 15:14), or through a state of mind or favorable circumstances (1 Thess 2:6), or through the enablement by law or custom (Acts 24:8, 11). *Ischúō* (2480), to be strong, to prevail, indicates a more forceful strength or ability than *dúnamai*. See James 5:16. A more common equivalent: *dunamóō* (1412), to enable.

1415. δυνατός *dunatós*; fem. *dunatḗ*, neut. *dunatón*, adj. from *dúnamai* (1410), to be able. Able, strong, powerful. Used in the NT generally of things (Acts 7:22; 2 Cor 10:4); with the def. art. *ho* (3588), the mighty, spoken of God, the Almighty (Luke 1:49). The expression "I am strong [*dunatós*]" (a.t.) means "I am able, I can" (a.t.); followed by the pres. inf. (Titus 1:9; Heb 11:19), and by the aor. inf. (Luke 14:31; Rom 4:21; 11:23; 14:4; 2 Cor 9:8; 2 Tim 1:12; James 3:2, see Acts 11:17). Metaphorically it means strong, firm, fixed, established (Rom 15:1; 2 Cor 12:10; 13:9; Sept.: Num 22:38; Dan 3:17). In the expression *dunatós en* ([1722], in) followed by the dat., powerful in, meaning able, skillful, eminent in work and word (Luke 24:19; Acts 7:22); able in the Scriptures, i.e., eminent in Scripture learning (Acts 18:24). In the pl. (*dunatoí*) used as a noun, the powerful, the mighty as spoken of persons in authority (1 Cor 1:26); of members of the Jewish council or Sanhedrin (Acts 25:5; Sept.: Dan 3:17). In Rev 6:15 (UBS), we have *hoi ischuroí* (2478), the strong ones. Also used in the neut. *dunatón*, meaning able to be done, possible. With the conditional conj. *ei* (1487), if, used in an absolute sense or with *ésti*, the 3d person. sing. of *eimí* (1510), to be, meaning, if possible (*ei dunatón*), if it be possible (Matt 24:24; 26:39; Mark 13:22; 14:35; Rom

12:18; Gal 4:15). With the dat. of person it means possible for or with someone (Mark 9:23; 14:36; Acts 20:16). With *pará* (3844), with, beside, with the dat. it means possible with someone (Matt 19:26; Mark 10:27; Luke 18:27). With the acc. and the inf., *tó dunatón* as a subst. meaning "the power." (Rom 9:22).

Deriv.: *adúnatos* (102), impossible; *dunatéō* (1414), to be efficient, mighty.

Syn.: *hikanós* (2425), able, the one who has sufficiency, to be distinguished from *dunatós*, the one who has power; *autárkēs* (842), sufficient in oneself; *arketós* (713), sufficient; *ischurós* (2478), strong; *bíaios* (972), violent, rushing; *krataiós* (2900), mighty with the connotation of being able to maintain power; *megaleíos* (3167), great; *dunástēs* (1413), potentate; *mégas* (3173), great; *tēlikoútos* (5082), so great.

Ant.: *asthenḗs* (772), without strength, impotent; *adúnatos* (102), without ability, impossible; *árrōstos* (732), feeble, sickly.

1416. δύνω *dúnō*; a form of *dúo* (n.f.), to immerse, to sink, go down, intrans. used of the sun (Mark 1:32; Luke 4:40; Sept.: Gen 28:11; 2 Chr 18:34).

Deriv.: *dusmḗ* (1424), sun set, west; *ekdúō* (1562), to take off, unclothe; *endúnō* (1744), to creep; *endúō* (1746), to array, clothe, endue; *epidúō* (1931), to go down.

Syn.: *kathízō* (2523), to cause to sit down, set.

Ant.: *anatéllō* (393), to rise; *egeírō* (1453), to raise; *anístēmi* (450), to stand up, rise.

1417. δύο *dúo*; indeclinable, used for all genders, cardinal number. Two. The irregular and later dat. *dusí* occurs in Matt 6:24; 22:40. With the nom. noun (Matt 9:27; 20:21; Luke 7:41; John 1:37). With the gen. noun (Matt 18:16; 20:24; Luke 12:6; John 1:40). With the acc. noun (Matt 4:18; Luke 3:11). The phrase "two or three" (Matt 18:20; 1 Cor 14:29) means some, a few. The phrases *aná dúo* (*aná* [303]) and *katá dúo* (*katá* [2596], a distributive prep.) mean by two and two

(Luke 9:3; 10:1; 1 Cor 14:27); *eis dúo* (*eis* [1519], into), means in two parts (Matt 27:51; Mark 15:38); *dúo dúo* means two and two (Mark 6:7; Sept.: Gen 6:20).
Deriv.: *dekadúo* (1177) and *dṓdeka* (1427), twelve.

1418. δυς *dus*; inseparable particle implying difficulty, used as a prefix like the Eng. un-, in-, mis- and dis-. Examples: *dúskolos* (1422), difficult; *dusphēmía* (1426), defamation.
Ant.: *eu* (2095), well.

1419. δυσβάστακτος *dusbástaktos*; gen. *dusbastáktou*, masc.-fem., neut. *dusbástakton*, adj. from *dus* (1418), a particle expressing difficulty, and *bastázō* (941), to bear, carry. Hard to be borne or carried, oppressive, e.g., referring to burdens (Matt 23:4; Luke 11:46; Sept.: Prov 27:3).
Syn.: *barús* (926), heavy, burdensome.
Ant.: *elaphrós* (1645), light in weight, easy to bear.

1420. δυσεντερία *dusentería*; gen. *dusenterías*, fem. noun from *dus* (1418), denoting illness or sickness, and *énteron* (n.f.), a bowel, intestine, which is from *entós* (1787), within. A dysentery, diarrhea (Acts 28:8).

1421. δυσερμήνευτος *dusermḗneutos*; gen. *dusermēneútou*, masc.-fem., neut. *dusermḗneuton*, adj. from *dus* (1418), hard, difficult, and *hermēneúō* (2059), to interpret. Difficult to explain, or hard to understand (Heb 5:11).
Syn.: *dusnóētos* (1425), hard to understand; *dúskolos* (1422), difficult; *sklērós* (4642), hard, austere.
Ant.: *eúsēmos* (2154), easy to understand.

1422. δύσκολος *dúskolos*; gen. *duskólou*, masc.-fem., neut. *dúskolon*, adj. from *dus* (1418), denoting difficulty, and *kólon* (n.f.), food. Difficult about one's food. Figuratively hard to please,

morose, peevish, disagreeable. Difficult, spoken of things hard to accomplish (Mark 10:24).
Deriv.: *duskólōs* (1423), with difficulty, hardly.
Syn.: *sklērós* (4642), hard, austere; *skoliós* (4646), warped, perverse, crooked; *chalepós* (5467), difficult, fierce, dangerous.
Ant.: *elaphrós* (1645), light, metaphorically easy to bear.

1423. δυσκόλως *duskólōs*; adv. from *dúskolos* (1422), hard. With difficulty, hardly (Matt 19:23; Mark 10:23; Luke 18:24).
Syn.: *mólis* (3433), scarcely, with difficulty.
Ant.: *eukopṓteros* (2123), easier; *aperispástōs* (563), without distraction; *hetoímōs* (2093), readily; *prothúmōs* (4290), willingly.

1424. δυσμή *dusmḗ*; gen. *dusmḗs*, fem. noun from *dúnō* (1416), to sink, to set as the sun. Usually only in the pl. *haí dusmaí*, the settings, especially of the sun (Sept.: Gen 15:12; Deut 11:30). In the NT used only by implication meaning the west (Matt 8:11; 24:27; Luke 12:54; 13:29; Rev 21:13; Sept.: Ps 50:1; 75:6; 113:3; Isa 43:5; 59:19; Mal 1:11).
Ant.: *anatolḗ* (395), the rising of the sun, east.

1425. δυσνόητος *dusnóētos*; gen. *dusnoétou*, masc.-fem., neut. *dusnóēton*, adj. from *dus* (1418), hard, and *noētós* (n.f.), understood, which is from *noéō* (3539), to understand. Hard to be understood (2 Pet 3:16).
Syn.: *dusermḗneutos* (1421), difficult to explain, hard to understand; *dúskolos* (1422), difficult; *sklērós* (4642), hard, difficult.
Ant.: *eúchrēstos* (2173), easy to use.

1426. δυσφημία *dusphēmía*; gen. *dusphēmías*, fem. noun from *dus* (1418), badly, and *phḗmē* (5345), rumor, fame, report. Evil speaking, infamy, reproach, ill-report (2 Cor 6:8). The verb *dusphēméō*, to defame or revile (1 Cor 4:13), is used in some MSS.

Syn.: *blasphēmía* (988), blasphemy, evil speaking; *katalalía* (2636), evil speaking, backbiting; *loidoría* (3059), reviling.

Ant.: *euphēmía* (2162), good report. When the report is neither good nor bad, the word used is *akoḗ* (189), hearing.

1427. δώδεκα *dṓdeka*; indeclinable, used for all genders, cardinal number, from *dúō* (1417), two, and *déka* (1176), ten. Twelve (Matt 9:20; 14:20). Used as a noun with the def. art. *hoi dṓdeka*, the Twelve, meaning the Apostles corresponding to the twelve tribes (Matt 26:14, 20, 47; Mark 14:10, 20 [cf. Matt 19:28; Rev 7:5; 21:12; 22:2 {see Sept.: Ex 28:21; Num 17:2; Josh 4:8; 1 Kgs 7:25}]). Other references: Matt 10:1, 2, 5; 11:1; 20:17; 26:53; Mark 3:14; 4:10; 5:25, 42; 6:7, 43; 8:19; 9:35; 10:32; 11:11; 14:17, 43; Luke 2:42; 6:13; 8:1, 42, 43; 9:1, 12, 17; 18:31; 22:3, 14, 30, 47; John 6:13, 67, 70, 71; 11:9; 20:24; Acts 6:2; 7:8; 1 Cor 15:5; James 1:1; Rev 7:6–8; 12:1; 21:14, 16, 21 (cf. *héndeka* [1733], eleven, but sometimes referring to the Twelve Disciples when one of them separated himself from the Twelve).

Deriv.: *dōdékatos* (1428), twelfth; *dōdekáphulon* (1429), twelve tribes.

1428. δωδέκατος *dōdékatos*; fem. *dōdekátē*, neut. *dōdékaton*, adj. from *dṓdeka* (1427), twelve. Twelfth (Rev 21:20).

1429. δωδεκάφυλον *dōdekáphulon*; gen. *dōdekaphúlou*, neut. noun from *dṓdeka* (1427), twelve, and *phulḗ* (5443), tribe. Twelve tribes (Acts 26:7), referring to the people of Israel.

1430. δῶμα *dṓma*; gen. *dṓmatos*, neut. noun from *démō* (n.f.), to build. A house, building, and by deduction a hall, chamber. In the NT, "upon the housetop" means the housetop, roof (Matt 24:17; Mark 13:15; Luke 5:19; 17:31; Acts 10:9). The expression in Matt 10:27; Luke 12:3, "upon the housetops," or the buildings or the roofs, means publicly (cf. Deut 22:8; Josh 2:6, 8; 2 Sam 16:22; Isa 15:3). The roofs of oriental houses were flat and covered with a composition of gravel. The people spent much time upon them to enjoy the breeze and often slept there.

1431. δωρεά *dōreá*; gen. *dōreás*, fem. noun from *dídōmi* (1325), to give. A free gift with emphasis on its gratuitous character. Used in the NT of a spiritual or supernatural gift (John 4:10; Acts 2:38; 8:20; 10:45; 11:17; Rom 5:15, 17; 2 Cor 9:15; Eph 3:7; 4:7, "in proportion to the gift bestowed on us by Christ" [a.t.]; Heb 6:4; Sept.: Dan 2:6). For a full discussion of all the cognate words see *dóron* (1435), a gift.

Deriv.: *dōreán* (1432), freely; *dōréomai* (1433), to make a gift of.

1432. δωρεάν *dōreán*; adv., the acc. of *dōreá* (1431), gift. Freely, gratis, as a free gift (Matt 10:8; Rom 3:24; 2 Cor 11:7; 2 Thess 3:8; Rev 21:6; 22:17; Sept.: Gen 29:15; Num 11:5). In John 15:25, it means undeservedly, without cause; in Gal 2:21, that Christ's sufferings and death has been useless, or in vain. For a full discussion of all the cognate words see *dóron* (1435), a gift.

Syn.: *eikḗ* (1500), in vain, without a cause; *mátēn* (3155), in vain, to no purpose.

1433. δωρέομαι *dōréomai*; fut. *dōrḗsomai*, mid. deponent from *dōreá* (1431), gift. To make a gift of. Used trans. in Mark 15:45 of the body of Christ having been freely given by Pilate to Joseph of Arimathea, implying that Pilate had complete authority over the body. Little did he know that the body of Christ was the most unique corpse which ever existed and which the grave could not hold. In 2 Pet 1:3 it is used to denote the free giving of the power of God resulting in life and godliness. The verb indicates that this

divine power does not give life and godliness because somebody deserves it, but
because it is available to all; it is a free
gift. Also used in 2 Pet 1:4 referring to
the promises of God given to the believers as being initiated by God Himself and
therefore undeserved promises. For a full
discussion of all the cognate words see
dóron (1435), a gift.

Deriv.: *dṓrēma* (1434), gift.

Syn.: *charízomai* (5483), to show favor or kindness; *chorēgéō* (5524), to furnish, give; *apodídōmi* (591), to give away,
deliver; *epichorēgéō* (2023), to supply,
contribute; *paréchō* (3930), to furnish,
provide, supply; *aponémō* (632), to apportion.

Ant.: *apsotéreō* (650), to defraud, deprive; *aphairéō* (851), to take away.

1434. δώρημα *dṓrēma*; gen. *dōrḗmatos*,
neut. noun from *dōréō* (1433), to make a
gift. The thing given (Rom 5:16; James
1:17). The suffix *-ma* makes it the result
of *dósis* (1394), the act of giving. For a
full discussion of all cognate words see
dóron (1435), a gift.

1435. δῶρον *dóron*; gen. *dórou*, neut.
noun from *dídōmi* (1325), to give. Gift.
Used of gifts given as an expression of
honor (Matt 2:11); for support of the temple (Matt 15:5; Mark 7:11; Luke 21:1,
4); to God (Matt 5:23, 24; 8:4; 23:18, 19;
Heb 5:1; 8:3, 4; 9:9; 11:4); as the gift of
salvation (Eph 2:8); for celebrating (Rev
11:10). See Sept.: Gen 4:4; 30:20; Ex
23:8; Lev 1:2, 3; 2:4, 5, 7, 11; 1 Kgs 4:21;
15:19; 1 Chr 16:29; 18:2; Isa 66:20.

There are two verbs which could be
translated "to give": the common *dídōmi*
(1325), to give, which has a variety of
meanings according to the context, and
dōréomai (1433), to grant, with the inherent emphasis on the gratuity of giving, showing the generosity of the giver,
e.g., Pilate in Mark 15:45 regarding Jesus' body, and God in 2 Pet 1:3, 4 referring to His power and promises.

Dōreá (1431), a free gift, stresses its
gratuitous character, while *dóma* (1390),

a gift, emphasizes the gift itself. From
dōreá we have the adv. *dōreán* (1432),
freely, without charge (Matt 10:8; John
15:25; Rom 3:24; 2 Cor 11:7; Gal 2:21;
2 Thess 3:8; Rev 21:6; 22:17). *Dōreá* in
the NT is spoken of as a supernatural gift
(John 4:10; Acts 2:38; 8:20; 10:45; 11:17;
Rom 5:15, 17; 2 Cor 9:15; Eph 3:7; 4:7;
Heb 6:4). Likewise *dṓrēma* (1434), a gift,
refers to the gift that comes from God
(used only in Rom 5:16; James 1:17).
Dóron, however, is used of offerings
to God (Matt 2:11; 5:23, 24; 8:4; 15:5;
23:18, 19; Mark 7:11; Luke 21:1, 4; Heb
5:1; 8:3, 4; 9:9; 11:4; Rev 11:10), except
in Eph 2:8. *Dóma* (1390), except in Eph
4:8, is used of human gifts (Matt 7:11;
Luke 11:13; Phil 4:17). *Dósis* (1394),
stressing the act of giving, may refer to
either a human (Phil 4:15) or a divine gift
(James 1:17). The human who gives to
God is called *dótēs* (1395), giver.

In James 1:17, both *dṓrēma* (1434) and
dósis (1394) are translated "gift" without
distinction between the two words: "Every good gift [*dósis*] and every perfect gift
[*dṓrēma*] is from above." The distinction
between *dṓrēma* and *dósis* is that while
dósis emphasizes simply the act or intent
of giving, *dṓrēma* has in it not only *dósis*,
the act and intent of giving, but also the
result of it, the actual gift resulting from
the benevolent intent. The intent (*dósis*)
according to James should always be benevolent (*agathḗ* [18]), purposing to do
good to others, although it may not always result in actual good in others. The
dṓrēma is described by James as perfect
(*téleion* [5046]), i.e., reaching its goal. In
other words, when the *dósis* reaches its
goal, then it becomes *dṓrēma*.

In Rom 5:16 *tó* ([3588], the) *dṓrēma*
is translated "the gift." It speaks of that
which Christ did for the sinner, justifying him (Rom 5:1). It is called *dṓrēma*
because it is the result of the intent of
Christ's death and resurrection for us, i.e.,
to justify us before God or to declare us
not guilty and to give us His life. His benevolent intent became a tangible change
in us as sinners. If the word *dósis* were

used, it would have meant only the act of giving without its result. If the word *dốron* or *dōreá* were used it would have stressed only the free nature of the gift. *Dốrēma* involves the purposeful act of God's benevolence, in that there should be a way whereby we can be saved without our doing something to gain it except believing, which results in our actual salvation from sin. *Dốrēma* stands in near equivalence to *chárisma* (5486), found in Rom 5:15 and translated "free gift." As *cháris* (5485), grace, stands to *chárisma*, gift, so do *dósis* and (partly) *dōreá* stand to *dốrēma*, which involves the very character of God's intention and the result of the salvation of the sinner. Observe that the word *chárisma* occurs also in Rom 5:16 in the statement, "But the free gift is of many offenses unto justification."

E

1436. ἔα *éa*; interjection, probably for the imper. of *eáō* (1439), to allow, to permit. Let it be. It is a natural exclamation of indignation and grief such as "ah!," "alas!," "oh!" (Mark 1:24; Luke 4:34; Sept.: Job 4:19 [cf. Josh 7:7; Judg 6:22; Joel 1:15]).

1437. ἐάν *eán*; conj. formed by combining *ei* (1487), a conditional particle meaning if, and *án* (302), a particle denoting supposition, wish, possibility or uncertainty. What, where, whither, whosoever. Sometimes *eán* is contracted to *án*. It differs from *ei* in that *ei* expresses a condition which is merely hypothetical, a subjective possibility; *eán* implies a condition which experience must determine, an objective possibility, and thus refers always to something future. In 1 Cor 7:36, we have both conj. used, the first *ei* being purely hypothetical, subjective, "if he thinks in himself" (a.t.), not that he does something uncomely toward his virgin; and the second is *eán*, if she is actually past the age for marriage (see Rev 2:5). *Eán* is usually construed with the subjunctive; in later writers also with the indic., and very rarely in Class. Gr. writers with the opt., involving wishing. In the NT it is used:

(**I**) Alone, i.e., without other particles.

(**A**) With the subjunctive, and implying uncertainty with the prospect of decision. (**1**) With the pres. subjunctive and used as a conclusion or in the apodosis. (**a**) With the indic. fut. (Matt 6:22, 23). In this sentence we have a protasis, a conditional clause, "If therefore thine eye be single," and then the apodosis, the conclusion with the fut. indic. *éstai*, shall be, from the verb *eimí* (1510), to be, "thy whole body shall be full of light." See Luke 10:6; John 7:17; Acts 5:38; Rom 2:26. After *hóti* (3754), that, referring to

a previous clause (1 John 5:14, "that, if we ask"; Sept.: Job 9:15, 20). The future of the apodosis, which in Gr. grammar means conclusion or the whole conclusion, is sometimes to be supplied as in John 6:62 where the protasis, the condition, is expressed in "if ye shall see the Son of man ascend up where he was before." The apodosis or conclusion is not expressed but, referring back to John 6:61, "Does this offend you?" implies "How much more will this offend you?" See also Acts 26:5; 1 Cor 4:15. In Luke 19:31, "And if any man ask you," has the apodosis in the fut. indic. used as an imper., "Thus shall ye say unto him." However, *ou mḗ* (3364), not at all (comprised of *ou* [3756], not, and *mḗ* [3361], not), a double neg., is followed by the aor. subjunctive (*pisteúsēte* instead of the fut. indic. *pisteúsete* as in Acts 13:41). See the discussion of *ou mḗ* in *mḗ* (3361), not, and also in *ou mḗ* (3364), not at all, no never. (**b**) Followed by the pres. imper. (John 7:37; see also Rom 12:20). In Matt 10:13 followed by the aor. imper., *elthétō*, let come, from the verb *érchomai* (2064), to come. See also Mark 9:43. (**c**) Followed by the pres. indic. (John 8:16, "And yet if I judge, my judgment is true"; see also Matt 8:2; John 13:17; 21:22; Rom 2:25; 1 Cor 6:4; 12:15, 16; 2 Tim 2:5). After *hóti* (3754), that (Gal 5:2). Also followed by the perf. indic. with pres. meaning (John 20:23) where *kekrátēntai*, although the perf. indic. pass., has the pres. meaning of "are retained," whereas grammatically it is "hath been retained." (**2**) With the aor. subjunctive and in the apodosis or conclusion. (**a**) Followed by the indic. fut. (Matt 4:9; 5:13; 28:14; Mark 8:3; John 8:36; Rom 10:9; Sept.: Job 8:18; 9:12; 11:10). With the apodosis or the fut. implied as in Mark 11:31, 32 where in verse thirty-one we have the protasis and therefore *eán* is implied before *eípōmen* of verse thirty-two, "but if we shall say, Of men," the fut. apodosis, "ye know what will happen," is implied. See also Rom 11:22. With the fut. for imper. in Matt 21:3, "ye shall say" stands for "say"; also 1 John 5:16. Instead of the fut. indic. is the aor. subjunctive after *ou mḗ*, the double neg. (John 8:51, 52). **(b)** Followed by the pres. imper. (Matt 18:17; 1 Cor 10:28; Gal 6:1), or aor. imper. (Matt 18:15, 17; 1 Cor 7:11; Col 4:10). Also in prohibitions expressed by *mḗ*, followed by the aor. subjunctive instead of the imper. (Matt 24:23; Heb 3:7). **(c)** Followed by the pres. indic. (Matt 18:13; Mark 3:24; 8:36; John 8:31; Rom 7:3; 2 Cor 5:1). Also followed by the perf. indic. with pres. meaning (Rom 7:2; 14:23). **(d)** Followed by the aor. subjunctive (1 Cor 7:28). Also after *hína* (2443), so that, depending on a previous clause (John 9:22; 11:57). Also with *hópōs* (3704), so that (Acts 9:2). **(3)** Sometimes with both pres. and aor. subjunctives in the same clause, followed in the apodosis by the fut. indic. (1 Cor 14:23); by the imper. (Matt 5:24); by the pres. indic. (1 Cor 14:24; James 2:15; 1 John 1:6).

(B) With the indic., but only in later Gr. writers. In the NT only once and with the indic. perf. as pres. in the apodosis (1 John 5:15; Sept.: Job 9:14; 22:3).

(C) Used in respect of certainties as though they were uncertain, and hence equivalent to a particle of time, meaning when, equivalent to *hótan* (3752), when, with the subjunctive as John 12:32 where the translation should have been "and I, when I be lifted up" (a.t.). Also John 14:3; 1 John 3:2; Sept.: Prov 3:24; Isa 24:13; Amos 7:2; also Gen 38:9 where in the Sept. we have *hótan*.

(D) Instead of *án* (302), in the NT and later Gr. writers, used in relative clauses and with relative words. Such words are thus rendered more general, implying mere possibility, and take only the subjunctive, meaning ever, soever. **(1)** *Hós eán* (*hós* [3739], he who, followed by *eán*, if) meaning whoever, whosoever, whatsoever (Matt 5:19; 7:9; 10:14, 42; 12:36;

14:7; 16:19; Sept.: Gen 15:14; 21:22). **(2)** *Hóstis eán* (*hóstis* [3748], whosoever, followed by *eán*, if) meaning whoever, whatsoever (Col 3:23 [TR]). **(3)** *Hósos eán* (*hósos* [3745], how much, followed by *eán*, if) meaning whosoever, as many as (Matt 18:18; Rev 3:19; Sept.: Gen 44:1). **(4)** *Hópou eán* (*hópou* [3699], where, followed by *eán*, if) meaning wheresoever (Matt 8:19; 24:28; Mark 6:10; 14:14). **(5)** *Hou eán* (*hou* [3757], where, followed by *eán*, if) meaning wheresoever (1 Cor 16:6; Sept.: Gen 20:13). **(6)** *Hōs eán* (*hōs* [5613], as, followed by *eán*, if) meaning as if, in whatsoever manner, as when (Mark 4:26); whensoever (Rom 15:24; Sept.: Job 37:10). **(7)** *Kathó eán* (*kathó* [2526], according to which, as, followed by *eán*, if) meaning according to whatsoever (2 Cor 8:12). **(8)** *Hosákis eán* (*hosákis* [3740], whensoever, as many times as, followed by *eán*, if) meaning so often as (Rev 11:6).

(II) In connection with other particles, where, however, for the most part each retains its own power. The following only require to be noted, all with the subjunctive (cf. I, A).

(A) *Eán dé kaí* meaning and if also, but if also (Matt 18:17; 1 Cor 7:11, 28; 2 Tim 2:5 [cf. Sept.: Job 31:14]).

(B) *Eán mḗ* (*eán* followed by *mḗ* [3361], not) meaning if not, i.e., unless, except (Matt 5:20; 6:15; Mark 3:27; 7:4; John 3:2, 5; 15:6; Gal 2:16; Sept.: Ex 3:19; 4:1, 8, 9). In the sense of except, that, but that (Matt 26:42, "so but that I drink" [a.t.]; Mark 4:22, "but that it shall be revealed" [a.t.]; Mark 10:30, "but that he shall receive" [a.t.], i.e., who shall not receive).

(C) *Eán per* (*eán* followed by *per* [4007], a particle significant of abundance or emphasis) meaning if indeed, if now (Heb 3:6, 14; 6:3).

(D) *Eán te* (*eán* followed by the particle *te* [5037] emphasizing connection or addition) meaning if it be, be it that (2 Cor 10:8). Also as repeated *eán te . . . eán te*, meaning whether . . . or (Rom 14:8; Sept.: Ex 19:13; Lev 3:1).

1438. ἑαυτοῦ *heautoú*; contracted *hautoú* (848), fem. *heautḗs* contracted *hautḗs*, neut. *heautoú* contracted *hautoú*, acc. masc. *heautón*, fem. *heautḗn*, neut. *heautó*, a 3d person. reflexive pron. Of himself, herself, or itself.

(I) In the 3d person. sing. and pl. (Matt 8:22; 27:42; Luke 9:25; John 5:18).

(II) As a general reflexive standing also for the 1st and 2d persons. For 1st person pl. *hēmṓn autṓ*, meaning ourselves (Rom 8:23; see also 1 Cor 11:31; 2 Cor 1:9; 10:12, 14; 1 John 1:8). For the 2d person sing. masc. *seautoú*, fem. *seautḗs*, neut. *seautoú*, meaning thyself (Rom 13:9, *hōs heautón*, "as thyself"). Also for 2d person pl., *humṓn autṓn*, yourselves (1 Cor 6:19, *ouk esté heautṓn*). See also Heb 10:34.

(III) Pl. in a reciprocal sense for *allḗlōn*, e.g., *légontes prós heautoús*, i.e., *prós allḗlous*, to one another, one to another (Mark 10:26; John 12:19; Rom 1:24; Col 3:13, 16; Jude 1:20).

(IV) With prep.:

(A) *Aph' heautoú* (*apó* [575, III, B, 3], from), of oneself, meaning of one's own accord, by his own authority (Luke 12:57; 21:30; John 5:19; 15:4).

(B) *Di' heautoú* (with *diá* [1223], through or by itself) meaning through, by itself, in its own nature (Rom 14:14).

(C) *En heautṓ* (*en* [1722], in) meaning in himself, in mind, generally (Matt 13:21; Mark 5:30; 9:50; John 11:38; Acts 10:17; 1 John 5:10). Also *légō en heautṓ* (*légō* [3004], to say, or with the aor. *eípon*, to say or said within oneself), meaning to think (Matt 3:9; 9:3, 21; Sept.: Esth 6:6; Ps 36:1). Also in one's own self, person, nature (John 5:26; 6:53; Eph 2:15). In the phrase *gínomai en heautṓ* (1096), to become in oneself, to become (Acts 12:11), and sometimes with *érchomai* (2064), to come, *eis heautón* (Luke 15:17).

(D) *Ex heautoú* (with *ex* or *ek* [1537], of), meaning of or by oneself (2 Cor 3:5).

(E) *Kath' heautón* (with *katá* [2596], according to or by) meaning by himself, alone (Acts 28:16, see Acts 28:30; James 2:17, faith in itself).

(F) *Meth' heautoú* (with the prep. *metá* [3326], with) meaning with oneself, alone with (Matt 12:45; Mark 8:14).

(G) *Par' heautṓ* (with the prep. *pará* [3844], by, near or with) meaning by himself at home (1 Cor 16:2).

(H) *Prós heautón* (with *prós* [4314], toward) meaning to one's house, home (Luke 24:12; John 20:10; Sept.: Num 24:25). With the meaning of, with, or in himself, i.e., in mind, in thought (Luke 18:11).

1439. ἐάω *eáō*; contracted *eṓ*, imperf. *eíōn*, fut. *eásō*, aor. *eíasa*. To permit, to let be.

(I) To permit, allow, not to hinder; with the acc. and inf. (Matt 24:43; Luke 4:41; Acts 14:16; 27:32; 28:4; 1 Cor 10:13; Rev 2:20 [TR]); with the inf. implied (Acts 16:7; 19:30; Sept.: Gen 38:16; Job 9:18).

(II) To let alone, to leave, followed by the acc. of person (Acts 5:38; Sept.: Judg 11:37). Spoken of things, to let alone, meaning to desist (Luke 22:51, "Desist thus far!" [a.t.] meaning it is enough).

(III) To leave to, commit to: as spoken of persons, to leave in charge (Acts 23:32); of things (Acts 27:40) meaning they committed the ship to sea, i.e., let her sail.

Deriv.: *proseáō* (4330), to permit or allow further.

Syn.: *epitrépō* (2010), to allow; *aphíēmi* (863), to permit.

1440. ἑβδομήκοντα *hebdomḗkonta*; indeclinable, used for all genders, cardinal number from *heptá* (2033), seven. Seventy, seven tens (Acts 7:14; 23:23; 27:37). In Luke 10:1, 17, the "seventy" refers to the seventy disciples sent out by Christ as teachers, equal in number to the Sanhedrin.

Deriv.: *hebdomēkontákis* (1441), seventy times.

1441.ἑβδομηκοντάκις *hebdomēkontákis*; adv. from *hebdomḗkonta* (1440), seventy. Seventy times (Matt 18:22), a frequent general expression for any large number (cf. Gen 4:24).

1442. ἕβδομος *hébdomos*; fem. *hebdómē*, neut. *hébdomon*, ordinal number from *heptá* (2033), seven. An adj., seventh (John 4:52; Heb 4:4; Jude 1:14; Rev 8:1; 10:7; 11:15; 16:17; 21:20).

1443. Ἐβέρ *Ebér*; masc. proper noun transliterated from the Hebr. *ʿḖbēr* (5677, OT), over, beyond. Eber, one of Abraham's ancestors (Luke 3:35 [cf. Gen 10:21, 24, 25]).

1444. Ἑβραϊκός *Hebraïkós*; fem. *Hebraïkḗ*, neut. *Hebraïkón*, adj. Hebrew (Luke 23:38), referring to the Hebr. language.

1445. Ἑβραῖος *Hebraíos*; fem. *Hebraia*, neut. *Hebraíon*. noun. A Hebrew. Applied to Abraham in Gen 14:13 and his descendants, the Israelites generally (Gen 39:14; Ex 1:15; Deut 15:12). In the NT, the Hebrews are the Jews of Palestine who use the Hebr. or Aramaic language, to whom the language and country of their fathers peculiarly belong; the true seed of Abraham in opposition to the *Hellēnistaí* (1675), the Hellenists or Greek-speaking Jews who were born out of Palestine. See 2 Cor 11:22; Phil 3:5. In Acts 6:1, they are Hebrew Christians, in distinction from Hellenistic Christians.

1446. Ἑβραΐς *Hebraḯs*; gen. *Hebraḯdos*, fem. noun. The Hebr. language or dialect, the Hebr. Aramaic or Syro-Chaldaic which was the vernacular language of the Palestinian Jews in the time of Christ and the Apostles (Acts 21:40; 22:2; 26:14).

1447. Ἑβραϊστί *Hebraïstí*; adv. In the Hebr. language (John 5:2; 19:13, 17, 20; Rev 9:11; 16:16). The suffix -*istí* makes this a forceful adv.

1448. ἐγγίζω *eggízō*; fut. *eggísō* (James 4:8) or *eggiṓ* (Attic), from *eggús* (1451), near. To bring near and come near in a trans. and intrans. sense, to approach, as is often the case with verbs of motion such as *ágō* (71), lead (Sept.: Gen 48:10; Isa 5:8). Usually in the NT used intrans., meaning to come near, approach (Luke 7:12; 15:1, 25; 22:47; Acts 10:9), in the perf. *éggika*, to have drawn near, to be near, to be at hand; in the expression *éggiken*, is near, referring to the kingdom of God or heaven (Matt 3:2; 4:17; 10:7; Mark 1:15; Luke 10:11). The verb has reference to space, meaning that something is here.

(I) Spoken of persons (Matt 26:46; Mark 14:42; Luke 12:33; 18:40; 19:37, 41; 24:15; Acts 21:33; 23:15). Followed by the dat. (Luke 7:12; 15:1, 25; 22:47; Acts 9:3; 10:9; 22:6; Sept.: Gen 27:21, 26; Ex 32:19). Followed by *eis* (1519), to, with the acc. (Matt 21:1; Mark 11:1; Luke 18:35; 19:29; 24:28). With *prós* (4314), toward (Sept.: Gen 37:18; 45:4).

(II) Spoken of things, time (Matt 3:2; 4:17; 10:7; 21:34; 26:45; Mark 1:15; Luke 21:8, 20, 28; 22:1; Acts 7:17; Rom 13:12; Heb 10:25; James 5:8; 1 Pet 4:7). Followed by *epí* (1909), upon, with the acc. (Luke 10:9, 11).

(III) Metaphorically (Phil 2:30, "he was nigh unto death"; Sept.: Job 33:22; Ps 88:3; 107:18).

(IV) The expression *eggízō tṓ Theo*, "to draw near to God" means to offer sacrifices in the temple (Sept.: Ex 19:22; Ezek 44:13). In the NT it means to worship God with a pious heart (Matt 15:8; Heb 7:19; James 4:8, quoted from Isa 29:13). God is said to approach men, which means to draw near to Christians, by the aid of His Spirit, grace (James 4:8; Sept.: Deut 4:7 [cf. Ps 145:18]).

Deriv.: *proseggízō* (4331), approaching, coming close to.

Syn.: *paraplēsíon* (3897), near; *plēsíon* (4139), near, neighbor; *pará* (3844), beside, along side, near; *prós* (4314), toward, on the side, near; *ephístēmi* (2186), to come near, be at hand; *prosérchomai* (4334), to draw near; *proságō* (4317), to draw near; *érchomai* (2064), to come, as contrasted to *hḗkō* (2240), to arrive and be present; *paragínomai* (3854), to arrive and be present; *aphiknéomai* (864), to arrive at a place; *katantáō* (2658), to come to; *parístēmi* (3936), to stand by or near; *phthánō* (5348), to come upon, arrive.

Ant.: *ágō* (71), to go, lead the way; *hupágō* (5217), to go away; *ápeimi* (548), to go away; *metabaínō* (3327), to go or pass over from one place to another; *apérchomai* (565), to go away; *anachōréō* (402), to depart; *apobaínō* (576), to go away from; *éxeimi* (1826), to go out; *apodēméō* (589), to go abroad; *exérchomai* (1831), to go out; *ekporeúomai* (1607), to go out of.

1449. ἐγγράφω *eggráphō*; fut. *eggrápsō*, from *en* (1722), in or on, and *gráphō* (1125), to write, engrave, inscribe. Used metaphorically meaning to inscribe, to fix, as in the heart (2 Cor 3:2, 3).

Syn.: *epigráphō* (1924), to inscribe.

Ant.: *exaleíphō* (1813), to blot out.

1450. ἔγγυος *égguos*; gen. *egguóu*, masc.-fem., neut. *égguon*, adj. from *eggúē* (n.f.), pledge, bail, security. Yielding a pledge. In the NT, occurs only in Heb 7:22, which is not to be used in reference to the death of Christ by which He has answered for us, but to His eternal life through which He is surety for the better covenant (cf. Heb 7:21, 24, 25).

Syn.: *bebaíōsis* (951), confirmation; *plērophoría* (4136), assurance; *marturía* (3141), evidence; *apódeixis* (585), proof.

1451. ἐγγύς *eggús*; adv. Close, near.

(I) Of place (John 19:42). With the gen. (John 3:23; 6:19, 23; 11:18, 54; 19:20; Acts 1:12); with the acc. (Luke 19:11; Sept.: Gen 45:10; Ezek 23:12). With the dat. (Acts 9:38; 27:8; Sept. metaphorically: Ps 34:18). Metaphorically meaning near, nigh (Phil 4:5, "the Lord is near" [a.t.] means He is ready

to help [cf. Phil 4:6 {see also Ps 34:18; 145:18}]). With the gen. (Heb 6:8; 8:13). He is near you or close at hand, meaning ready to help (Rom 10:8, quoted from Deut 30:14). Those who are near are the Jews, having the knowledge and worship of the true God, as opposed to those who are far, meaning the Gentiles (Eph 2:17; Sept.: Isa 57:19). To become near to God means to embrace the gospel (Eph 2:13).

(II) Of time (Matt 24:32; Mark 13:28; Luke 21:30). The expression "at the doors" (Matt 24:33; Mark 13:29) means near. The time is near (Matt 26:18; Rev 1:3; 22:10); the Passover (John 2:13; 6:4; 11:55); the feast (John 7:2); the kingdom of God (Luke 21:31); the Lord (Phil 4:5 [cf. Heb 10:37]). The day is at hand (Sept.: Ezek 30:3; Joel 1:15; 2:1).

Deriv.: *eggízō* (1448), to bring near; *eggúteron* (1452), nearer.

Ant.: *makrán* (3112), far, afar off; *makróthen* (3113), from afar; *pórrō* (4206), a great way off; *pórrōthen* (4207), afar off; *porrōtérō* (4208), further.

1452. ἐγγύτερον *eggúteron*; adv., the comparative of *eggús* (1451), near. Nearer, spoken of time (Rom 13:11).

1453. ἐγείρω *egeírō*; fut. *egerṓ*, aor. *ḗgeira*, mid. deponent *egeíromai*, aor. pass. *ēgérthēn*, perf. pass. *egḗgermai*, with mid. meaning. To rise, to have risen.

(I) To rise from sleep, implying also the idea of rising up from the posture of sleep, i.e., from lying down (Matt 8:25, "and the disciples . . . awoke Him" or raised Him up or brought Him to an upright position; 25:7; Mark 4:27; Acts 12:7; Sept.: Gen 41:4, 7; Prov 6:9). Metaphorically, to wake up from sluggishness, lethargy (Rom 13:11 [cf. Eph 5:14]); from death, of which sleep is the emblem (Matt 27:52 [cf. Job 14:12; Dan 12:2]). To raise the dead (Matt 10:8; John 5:21; Acts 26:8; 1 Cor 15:15, 16; 2 Cor 1:9). To rise from the dead (*ek nekrṓn* [1537, 3498]) and in the mid. followed by *apó* (575), from, or *ek* (1537), "out of," "from," to rise from the dead (see John 12:1, 9, 17]; Gal 1:1; 1 Thess 1:10). In the mid. with *apó* (575), from (Matt 14:2; 27:64; 28:7). With *ek* (1537), out of (Mark 6:14, 16; Luke 9:7; John 2:22; see also Matt 16:21; 17:23; 27:63; Mark 16:14; Acts 5:30; Rom 4:25; 2 Cor 4:14; Sept.: 2 Kgs 4:31; Isa 26:19).

(II) The idea of sleep not being involved, it also means to cause to rise up, raise up, set upright, and in the mid. to rise up, arise.

(A) Spoken of persons who are sitting (Acts 3:7) or reclining at a table (John 13:4), or prostrate or lying down (Matt 17:7; Luke 11:8; Acts 9:8; 10:26; Sept.: 2 Sam 12:17); also of sick persons (Matt 8:15; Mark 1:31; 2:12), including the idea of convalescence, to set up again, i.e., to heal (James 5:15).

(B) By an oriental pleonasm prefixed to verbs of going, of undertaking, or doing something. The same as in *anístēmi* (450, II, D), to rise or raise up (Matt 2:13, 14, "having risen take the child" [a.t.]; also Matt 2:20, 21; 9:19; John 11:29; Sept.: 1 Chr 22:19).

(C) Metaphorically of persons, mid., to rise up against as does an adversary, with *epí* (1909), upon or against (Matt 24:7; Mark 13:8; Luke 21:10; Sept.: Isa 10:26; Jer 50:9). Also "to rise in the judgment with this generation" (a.t. [Matt 12:42; Luke 11:31]).

(D) Spoken of things, to raise up, e.g., out of a pit (Matt 12:11 [cf. Luke 14:5]). In John 2:19, 20, to erect, build.

(III) Metaphorically, to raise up, to cause to arise or exist; in the mid. to arise, to appear, Luke 1:69, "raised up a horn of salvation" means a Savior. Also Acts 13:22, 23. In the mid., spoken of prophets (Matt 11:11; 24:11, 24; Mark 13:22; Luke 7:16; John 7:52; Sept.: Judg 3:9, 15; Isa 41:25; 45:13). In the sense of to cause to be born, to create (Matt 3:9; Luke 3:8).

(IV) Intrans. or with *heautón* (1438) in the acc. implied, meaning to awake, to arise; thus to awake from sleep or figuratively from sluggishness (Eph 5:14); also to rise up, arise from a sitting or reclining

posture (Mark 2:9, 11; 3:3; 5:41; 10:49; Luke 5:23, 24; 6:8; John 5:8).

Deriv.: *grēgoréō* (1127), to watch, be vigilant; *diegeírō* (1326), awake from natural sleep; *égersis* (1454), stimulation, erection, awakening; *exegeírō* (1825), to raise from out of; *epegeírō* (1892), to rouse up, excite; *sunegeírō* (4891), to raise together.

Syn.: *diagrēgoréō* (1235), to be fully watchful by being wide awake; *agrupnéō* (69), to be awake, watchful; *agrupnía* (70), sleeplessness; *anístēmi* (450), to stand up or arise. Verbal forms of *anístēmi* and *egeírō* are used interchangeably, occurring consecutively in the same passages as in Mark 12:25, 26; Luke 11:31, 32 or in parallel passages (cf. Matt 16:21; 17:23 with 17:9) without apparent distinction of meaning. *Anastáseōs* (the gen. of *anástasis* [386], resurrection) *tṓn nekrṓn*, of the dead (Matt 22:31). However, in the parallel passages of Mark 12:25, *ek nekrṓn anastṓsin* ("when they shall rise from among the dead" [a.t.]) and Luke 20:35, *tḗs anastáseōs tḗs ek nekrṓn* ("the resurrection from out of the dead" [a.t. {cf. Acts 2:31}]), *ek nekrṓn*, out of the dead, is the phrase used of Christ's predicted resurrection (Matt 17:9; Mark 9:9, 10). It is also used of the supposed resurrection of John the Baptist (Matt 14:2), and of the case of one rising from the dead (Luke 16:31). In the epistles *ek* (1537), out of, is used of Christ's resurrection (1 Pet 1:3); *anástasis tṓn nekrṓn*, resurrection of the dead, is used of resurrection generally (1 Cor 15:12, 13, 21, 42; Heb 6:2). A distinction of usage seems to exist, implying an individual or a non-universal resurrection. The verb *zōopoiéō* (2227), to revitalize, make alive, quicken (John 5:21; 6:63 [cf. Rom 4:17; 8:11; 1 Cor 15:22, 36, 45]) is more of a syn. for *anístēmi* than *egeírō*. Other syn.: *eknḗphō* (1594), to return to one's senses from drunkenness, become sober; *exupnízō* (1852), to arouse a person from sleep (John 11:11); *aírō* (142), to raise, take up, lift; *epaírō* (1869), to lift up, raise; *hupsóō* (5312), to lift or raise up; *anorthóō* (461), to set upright; *anakúptō* (352), to lift oneself up; *anabibázō* (307), to cause to go up or ascend; *exanístēmi* (1817), to raise up from among or to rise up; *anabaínō* (305), to go up; *anatéllō* (393), to rise, speaking of the sun; *katephístēmi* (2721), to rise up as in insurrection; *epanístamai* (1881), to rise up against; *hístēmi* (2476), to cause to stand; *stēkō* (4739), to stand upright; *anakathízō* (339), to set up, intrans. to sit up.

Ant.: *kathízō* (2523), to cause to sit down; *epikathízō* (1940), used trans. meaning to set; *keímai* (2749), to lie, to be laid; *anákeimai* (345), to be laid up; *káthēmai* (2521), to sit down; *anapíptō* (377), to lie down, lean back, fall back, recline for a meal; *katákeimai* (2621), to lie down; *anaklínō* (347), to cause to recline; *kataklínō* (2625), to make to recline, usually for a meal; *sugkathízō* (4776), to make to sit together; *kathézomai* (2516), to sit down; *parakathízō* (3869), to sit down beside.

1454. ἔγερσις *égersis*; gen. *egérseōs*, fem. noun from *egeírō* (1453), to wake up. Resurrection, reanimation of the dead (Matt 27:53).

Syn.: *anástasis* (386), resurrection; *exanástasis* (1815), resurrection out of.

Ant.: *thánatos* (2288), death; *anaíresis* (336), taking away of life; *teleutē* (5054), an end, death; *koímēsis* (2838), a resting, reclining, going to sleep.

1455. ἐγκάθετος *egkáthetos*; gen. *egkathétou*, masc.-fem., neut. *egkátheton*, adj. from *egkathíēmi* (n.f.), which is from *en* (1722), in, and *kathíēmi* (2524), to let down, set in ambush. Sitting in ambush, lying in wait (Sept.: Job 31:9). Used metaphorically of an insidious person, spy (Luke 20:20).

Syn.: *katáskopos* (2685), spy.

1456. ἐγκαίνια *egkaínia*; gen. *egkainíōn*, pl. neut. noun from *en* (1722), in or at, and *kainós* (2537), qualitatively new. Dedication. Occurs only in John 10:22 referring to the Feast of Dedication which was a festive solemnity in memory of the dedication of the temple at Jerusalem or of its purification and making it qualitatively new, as it were, after it had been polluted by heathen idolatries and impurities. This festival was instituted by Judas Maccabaeus to commemorate the purification of the temple and the renewal of the temple worship after the three years of profanation by Antiochus Epiphanes. It was held for eight days, beginning on the twenty-fifth day of the month of Kislev, which began the new moon of December. Josephus calls it *phóta* (5457), i.e., the festival of lights or lanterns.

1457. ἐγκαινίζω *egkainízō*; fut. *egkainísō*, from *en* (1722), in or at, and *kainízō* (n.f.), to make new. To dedicate, consecrate (Heb 9:18; 10:20; Sept.: Deut 20:5; 1 Kgs 8:64 [cf. 1 Sam 11:14]). Also from *kainízō* (n.f.): *anakainízō* (340), to renew.

Syn.: *ananeóō* (365), to renew.

Ant.: *achreióō* (889), to render useless.

1458. ἐγκαλέω *egkaléō*; contracted *egkalō*, fut. *egkalésō*, from *en* (1722), in, and *kaléō* (2564), to call. To bring a charge against, call to account, accuse, arraign (Acts 19:38, 40; 23:28, 29; 26:2, 7; Rom 8:33).

Deriv.: *anégkalētos* (410), unaccused, blameless; *égklēma* (1462), a public accusation.

Syn.: *katēgoréō* (2723), to accuse; *diabállō* (1225), to accuse, defame; *katakrínō* (2632), to condemn; *elégchō* (1651), to reprove; *mémphomai* (3201), to find fault.

Ant.: *dikaióō* (1344), to declare righteous or innocent; *apallássō* (525), to deliver, release; *eleutheróō* (1659), to set free; *exairéō* (1807), to deliver by rescuing from danger, to exempt; *rhúomai* (4506), to rescue from, preserve; *sōzō* (4982), to rescue, save.

1459. ἐγκαταλείπω *egkataleípō*; fut. *egkataleípsō*, from *en* (1722), in, and *kataleípō* (2641), to forsake, desert. To leave behind in any place or state. Used trans. with the soul as the obj. (Acts 2:27 quoted from Ps 16:10). With the meaning of to leave remaining (Rom 9:29 quoted from Isa 1:9). By implication, to leave in the lurch, forsake, desert, abandon, with the acc. (Matt 27:46; Mark 15:34; [Sept.: Ps 22:1]; 2 Tim 4:10, 16; Heb 10:25; 13:5; Sept.: Deut 31:6, 8; Isa 1:8).

Syn.: *aphíēmi* (863), to forsake, forgive; *aphístēmi* (868), to depart from; *apotássō* (657), to separate oneself from; *apoleípō* (620), to leave behind.

1460. ἐγκατοικέω *egkatoikéō*; contracted *egkatoikṓ*, fut. *egkatoikḗsō*, from *en* (1722), in or among, and *katoikéō* (2730), to dwell. To dwell permanently in or among (2 Pet 2:8).

Syn.: *enoikéō* (1774), to inhabit; *oikéō* (3611), to reside, live; *skēnóō* (4637), to reside in a tent, encamp; *paroikéō* (3939), to dwell near, reside as a foreigner; *sunoikéō* (4924), to reside together.

Ant.: *apodēméō* (589), to go and live in a foreign land.

1461. ἐγκεντρίζω *egkentrízō*; fut. *egkentrísō*, from *en* (1722), in, and *kentrízō*, (n.f.), make a puncture, which is from *kéntron* (2759), a prick, sting, to prick. To insert by making a puncture or small opening, to engraft. Used metaphorically in Rom 11:17, 19, 23, 24, in which verses the Apostle observes that it is contrary to nature that a branch of a wild olive tree should be grafted into a good olive tree, although the opposite is done.

1462. ἔγκλημα *égklēma*; gen. *egklḗmatos*, neut. noun from *egkaléō* (1458), to arraign. An accusation made in public but not necessarily before a tribunal (Acts 23:29), complaint, charge (Acts 25:16).

Syn.: *katēgoría* (2724), a criminal charge, an accusation.

1463. ἐγκομβόομαι *egkombóomai*; contracted *egkomboúmai*, fut. *egkombṓsomai*, mid. deponent, from *en* (1722), in, and *kombóō* (n.f.), to gather or tie in a knot, hence to fasten a garment, to clothe. To clothe or girdle oneself. *Egkómbōma* is a long white apron or outer garment with strings worn by slaves. Metaphorically in 1 Pet 5:5, to tie or bind oneself into an *egkómbōma*, meaning to put on, to clothe oneself in, used with the acc. of thing.

Syn.: *amphiénnumi* (294), to put clothes around; *endúō* (1746), to put on clothes; *endidúskō* (1737), to wear; *ependúō* (1902), to put on over; *himatízō* (2439), to put on raiment; *peribállō* (4016), to put around.

Ant.: *apotíthēmi* (659), to put off; *apekdúō* (554), to strip off clothes; *ekdúō* (1562), to undress.

1464. ἐγκοπή *egkopḗ*; gen. *egkopḗs*, fem. noun from *egkóptō* (1465), to impede, hinder, detain. An impediment, hindrance (1 Cor 9:12).

Ant.: *prokopḗ* (4297), progress; *antílēpsis* (484), a help; *boḗtheia* (996), help, succor; *epikouría* (1947), help.

1465. ἐγκόπτω *egkóptō*; fut. *egkópsō*, from *en* (1722), in, and *kóptō* (2875), to cut down, to strike. Metaphorically, to impede or hinder, used trans. in Rom 15:22; Gal 5:7; 1 Thess 2:18. In the sense of delay (Acts 24:4); render fruitless (1 Pet 3:7).

Deriv.: *egkopḗ* (1464), hindrance.

Syn.: *kōlúō* (2967), to hinder, restrain; *diakōlúō* (1254), to hinder completely.

Ant.: *antilambánomai* (482), to help; *boēthéō* (997), to help, succor; *sumbállō* (4820), to assist; *sunupourgéō* (4943), to help together; *sunergéō* (4903), to help in work, cooperate; *parístēmi* (3936), to stand by, assist; *prokóptō* (4298), to advance; *auxánō* (837), to grow.

1466. ἐγκράτεια *egkráteia*; gen. *egkrateías*, fem. noun from *egkratḗs* (1468), temperate, self-controlled. Continence, temperance, self-control (Acts 24:25; Gal 5:23; 2 Pet 1:6).
Syn.: *autárkeia* (841), contentedness, sufficiency; *sōphrosúnē* (4997), soberness.
Ant.: *akrasía* (192), excess, incontinence, self-indulgence; *akratḗs* (193), without self-control, incontinent; *aphrosúnē* (877), senselessness; *asōtía* (810), prodigality; *hēdonḗ* (2237), pleasure; *kraipálē* (2897), drunkenness.

1467. ἐγκρατεύομαι *egkrateúomai*; fut. *egkrateúsomai*, mid. deponent from *egkratḗs* (1468), self-controlled. To be continent, temperate, to have self-control (1 Cor 7:9; 9:25; Sept.: Gen 43:31).
Syn.: *néphō* (3525), to be sober; *apéchomai* (567), to refrain; *sōphronéō* (4993), to be of sound mind, sober.
Ant.: *paralúō* (3886), to become feeble.

1468. ἐγκρατής *egkratḗs*; gen. *egkratoús*, masc.-fem., neut. *egkratés*, adj. from *en* (1722), in, and *krátos* (2904), power, dominion, strength, government. Having power over, being master of. Used metaphorically, meaning self-control, continence (Titus 1:8).
Deriv.: *egkráteia* (1466), self-control; *egkrateúomai* (1467), to be self-controlled.
Syn.: *nēphálios* (3524), sober, temperate; *sōphrōn* (4998), sober-minded.
Ant.: *akratḗs* (193), intemperate; *ékdotos* (1560), given over to; *sarkikós* (4559), fleshly, carnal; *philḗdonos* (5369), lover of pleasure; *áphrōn* (878), mindless.

1469. ἐγκρίνω *egkrínō*; fut. *egkrinō̂*, from *en* (1722), in or among, and *krínō* (2919), to judge, reckon, classify. To judge or classify among. In 2 Cor 10:12, it is joined with *heautoús* (1438), ourselves, and the dat. *tisín* (5100), to some,

thus to judge ourselves to be of a certain number or rank of. In later Gr., it came to mean to approve, esteem as being up to the standard and therefore admissible.
Syn.: *psēphízō* (5585), to compute, count; *logízomai* (3049), to reckon; *katalégō* (2639), to enroll, take into the number; *anagnōrízō* (319), to recognize; *paradéchomai* (3858), to accept, receive.

1470. ἐγκρύπτω *egkrúptō*; fut. *egkrúpsō*, from *en* (1722), in, and *krúptō* (2928), to hide. To hide in something. Trans., as if by covering or mixing (Sept.: Josh 7:21). By implication, it means to mix in, knead in leaven with flour (Matt 13:33; Luke 13:21; Sept.: Ezek 4:12).
Syn.: *kalúptō* (2572), to cover, conceal; *sumperilambánō* (4843), to include.
Ant.: *phaneróō* (5319), to manifest; *emphanízō* (1718), to make manifest; *apokalúptō* (601), to reveal; *apokleíō* (608), to exclude from; *exairéō* (1807), to tear out; *exaírō* (1808), to remove.

1471. ἔγκυος *égkuos*; gen. *egkúou*, masc.-fem., neut. *égkuon*, adj. from *egkúō* (n.f.), which is from *en* (1722), in, and *kúō* (n.f.), to swell, be pregnant. Pregnant, heavy with child (Luke 2:5).
Syn.: the expression *en gastrí* (*gastḗr* [1064], womb), with child in the womb, pregnant.
Ant.: *steíros* (4723), sterile, barren; *áteknos* (815), without a child.

1472. ἐγχρίω *egchríō*; fut. *egchrísō*, from *en* (1722), in, and *chríō* (5548), to anoint. To anoint but with a mundane meaning such as to rub with eye salve (Rev 3:18). While the word *chríō* has primarily a sacred sense, to anoint with symbolic meaning, the comp. *egchríō* and *epichríō* (2025), have the meaning of smearing. In the case of *egchríō*, it is with eyesalve, and in the case of *epichríō*, with mud, as of Christ smearing on the blind man's eyes the mud He made by spitting on the ground (John 9:6, 11). In this sense, these two comp. verbs have the mundane meaning of the verb *aleíphō* (218), to rub (Matt 6:17; Mark 6:13; 16:1; Luke 7:38, 46; John 11:2; 12:3; James 5:14). These two comp. and *aleíphō* can be counted also as syn. with *murízō* (3462), to rub with perfumed ointment, i.e., *múron* (3464), myrrh or perfumed oil.

1473. ἐγώ *egṓ*; gen. *emoú* or *mou*, 1st person sing. personal pron. I. The monosyllabic forms *mou*, *moi*, *me*, are usually enclitic (receive no accent), but have an independent accent after a prep., except in *prós me*. Various forms include *hēmín* (2254), dat. pl. and *ēmṓn* (2257), gen. pl.

(I) Nom. *egṓ*, pl. *hēmeís* (Matt 8:7; 28:14; Mark 14:58 Acts 17:3). With a certain emphasis (Matt 3:11, 14; 5:22, 28, 32, 34; John 4:26). With a mark of distinction (Matt 6:12; 17:19; 19:27). Paul uses this pron. in the sing. sometimes to express the totality of the people he has in mind as if he were their representative, thus he used *egṓ*, I, for *hēmeís* (2249), nom. pl., we (Rom 7:9, 14, 17, 20, 24, 25; 1 Cor 10:30). Sometimes he uses *hēmeís*, we, for *egṓ*, I (1 Cor 1:23; 2:12; 4:8, 10). In the phrases "Behold, I am here Lord" (*idoú* [2400], behold; *egṓ*, I) (Acts 9:10), and "I go sir" (*egṓ Kúrie* [2962]) (Matt 21:30), the word *egṓ* is used in lieu of an affirmative adv., it is well, acceptable with me. See also Sept.: Gen 22:1, 11; 27:24; 1 Sam 3:8; 2 Sam 20:17.

(II) The gen. *mou* (not *emoú*), mine (Matt 2:6; Luke 7:46; John 6:54), and *hēmṓn*, ours (Matt 6:12; Luke 1:55; Rom 6:6), are often used instead of the corresponding poss. pron. *emós*. Also *mou* as pass. or obj. in John 15:10 "in my love" (*en tḗ agápē mou*), meaning in the love of mine or towards me.

(III) In the dat. in the phrase *tí emoí kaí soí*, "What is it to me and thee?" (*tí* [the neut. of *tís* {5100}], what; *emoí* [the sing. dat. of *egṓ*, I]; *kaí*, and; *soí*, sing. dat. meaning thou, you), meaning "What is there common between us? What have I to do with thee?" (a.t. [Matt 8:29; Mark 5:7; Luke 8:28; John 2:4; Sept.: Judg 11:12; 2 Sam 16:10; 19:22]).

1474. ἐδαφίζω *edaphízō*; fut. *edaphísō*, from *édaphos* (1475), ground, soil. To level with the ground, raze, destroy, used trans. in Luke 19:44; Sept.: Hos 14:1; Nah 3:10.

Syn.: *katalúō* (2547), to loosen, dissolve, destroy; *kathairéō* (2507), to pull down; *apóllumi* (622), to destroy fully, perish; *phtheírō* (5351), to ruin, corrupt; *diaphtheírō* (1311), to ruin completely; *analískō* (355), to use up, consume.

Ant.: *hupsóō* (5312), to lift or raise up; *oikodoméō* (3618), to build.

1475. ἔδαφος *édaphos*; gen. *edáphous*, neut. noun. The ground upon which things rest, the base or bottom of a ship or a room, the floor (Sept.: Num 5:17; 1 Kgs 6:15); the earth (Acts 22:7; Sept.: Ezek 41:16, 20).

Deriv.: *edaphízō* (1474), to level with the ground.

Syn.: *gḗ* (1093), earth, but sometimes the ground; *chamaí* (5476), on the ground.

1476. ἑδραῖος *hedraíos*; fem. *hedraía*, neut. *hedraíon*, adj. from *hédra* (n.f., see *aphedrṓn* [856]), seat, chair, base. Settled, steady, steadfast. Used metaphorically in referring to the mind and purpose (1 Cor 7:37; 15:58; Col 1:23. See Prov 4:18).

Syn.: *bébaios* (949), firm, secure; *stereós* (4731), firm, steadfast; *asphalḗs* (804), safe; *asáleutos* (761), unmoved, immovable; *ametakínētos* (277), immovable.

Ant.: *metakinéō* (3334), to move away; *seíō* (4579), to shake; *saleúō* (4531), to shake.

1477. ἑδραίωμα *hedraíōma*; gen. *hedraiṓmatos*, neut. noun from *hedraióō* (n.f.), to make stable. A support, stay, ground, basis, foundation (1 Tim 3:15).

Syn.: *steréōma* (4733), a support, foundation denoting strength; *stērigmós*

(4740), setting firmly, fixedness, steadfastness; *aspháleia* (803), certainty, safety; *bebaíōsis* (951), confirmation.

1478. Ἐζεκίας *Ezekías*; proper noun transliterated from the Hebr. *Chizqīyāh* (2396, OT), strength from Jehovah. Hezekiah, the king of Judah referred to in Matt 1:9, 10, son and successor of the apostate Ahaz. He ascended the throne in 726 B.C. at the age of twenty-five and ruled twenty-nine years until 697 B.C. He was one of the three best kings of Judah, and an eminently godly man (2 Kgs 18:5; 2 Chr 29:2). He restored the Mosaic institutions to honor, accomplished the abolition of idol worship in his kingdom (2 Kgs 18:4, 22), and tore down the high places which had been dedicated to idolatry. He also broke in pieces the brazen serpent of Moses which had become the object of idolatrous regard (2 Kgs 18:4). During his reign, the temple was repaired (2 Chr 29:3ff.) and the Passover celebrated with festivities that had not been equalled for magnificence since the days of Solomon and David (2 Chr 30:26). He held Isaiah the prophet in high esteem and frequently consulted him (2 Kgs 19:3; Isa 37:2). The king became sick unto death and Isaiah uttered his doom in the words, "Thou shalt die, and not live" (2 Kgs 20:1). Turning his face to the wall, he lamented the event and prayed God to avert it. Isaiah, on going into the court, was checked by the word of the Lord and commanded to return and announce the prolongation of the king's life by fifteen years (2 Kgs 20:6). As a sign of the cure the shadow on the sundial was made to go back ten degrees (2 Kgs 20:11). Another event of note in Hezekiah's life was the judgment pronounced upon his house by Isaiah (2 Kgs 20:17) for the display he made of his riches to the messengers of the king of Babylon, who had come to congratulate him upon his recovery. Hezekiah died in honor and was buried in the "chiefest of the sepulchers of the sons of David" (2 Chr 32:33).

1479. ἐθελοθρησκεία *ethelothrēskeía*; gen. *ethelothrēskeías*, fem. noun from *thélō* (2309), to will, and *thrēskeía* (2356), religion or ceremonial observance. Voluntary worship, worship in which one goes beyond what God requires without any particular command (Col 2:23); to be interpreted in an evil sense such as the worship of angels in Col 2:18. It is the religion of self-will or legalism. Man is forbidden to establish his own ceremonial rites and to call it the true worship of God.

1480. ἐθίζω *ethízō*; fut. *ethísō*, from *éthos* (1485), custom. To accustom; in the pass. to be accustomed; of things, to be customary. Used as a perf. pass. part. neut., *tó eithisménon*, what is customary, and as a subst., custom, rite (Luke 2:27).
    Syn.: *éthō* (1486), to be used by habit or custom.

1481. ἐθνάρχης *ethnárchēs*; gen. *ethnárchou*, masc. noun from *éthnos* (1484), nation, people, and *árchō* (757), to reign or rule over. An ethnarch, ruler of a people, chief (2 Cor 11:32).
    Syn.: *árchōn* (758), a ruler, chief; *archḗ* (746), rule, sovereignty, the first one; *kosmokrátōr* (2888), the ruler of the world; *pantokrátōr* (3841), almighty or the ruler of everything; *politárchēs* (4173), ruler of a city; *hēgemṓn* (2232), a leader, governor; *archēgós* (747), leader; *kúrios* (2962), lord; *despótēs* (1203), despot, absolute leader; *oikodespótēs* (3617), master of the house; *basileús* (935), king.

1482. ἐθνικός *ethnikós*; fem. *ethnikḗ*, neut. *ethnikón*, adj. from *éthnos* (1484), nation. National, popular. In the NT, this word answers to the biblical idea of *éthnē* (n.f.), nations, and means heathen, that which pertains to those who are unconnected with the people and the God of salvation (only in Matt 6:7; 18:17). Gentile, not Jewish. In the NT, *Héllēnes*, the pl. of *Héllēn* (1672), Greeks, is sometimes used, especially by Paul, as syn. with "Gentiles" (Rom 2:9; 1 Cor 12:13).

Deriv.: *ethnikós* (1483), in a manner of the Gentiles.

Ant.: *Ioudaíos* (2453), a Jew.

1483. ἐθνικẈς *ethnikós*; adv. from *ethnikós* (1482), a heathen, Gentile. After the manner of the heathen or the Gentiles. Used only in Gal 2:14, meaning to live in a way not in keeping with the manner and customs of Israel.

Ant.: *Ioudaikós* (2452), Judaically, as do the Jews.

1484. ἔθνoς *éthnos*; gen. *éthnous*, neut. noun. A multitude, people, race, belonging and living together.

(I) Generally in Acts 8:9, the people or inhabitants of Samaria (see Acts 8:5). In Acts 17:26, the whole race of mankind. See also 1 Pet 2:9; Sept.: 2 Chr 32:7; Isa 13:4. Spoken of a flock or a swarm in Class. Gr.

(II) In the sense of nation, people, as distinct from all others (Matt 20:25; Mark 10:42; Luke 7:5; John 11:48, 50; Acts 7:7; 10:22; Sept.: Gen 12:2; Ex 1:9; 33:13; Deut 1:28).

(III) In the Jewish sense, *tá éthnē*, the nations, means the Gentile nations or the Gentiles in general as spoken of all who are not Israelites and implying idolatry and ignorance of the true God, i.e., the heathen, pagan nations (Matt 4:15; 10:5; Mark 10:33; Luke 2:32; Acts 4:27; 26:17; Rom 2:14; 3:29; Sept.: Neh 5:8, 9; Isa 9:1; Ezek 4:13; 27:33, 36; 34:13; Jer 10:3).

In the NT, *éthnos* generally designates a non-Jewish nation, but it is also used of the Jewish nation when referred to officially (Luke 7:5; 23:2; John 11:48f.; 18:35; Acts 10:22; 24:2, 10, 17; 26:4; 28:19). Also used of the Christian society (Matt 21:43; Rom 10:19). In 1 Pet 2:9, Christians are called both an elect *génos* (1085), race, offspring, and a holy *éthnos*. In Mark 7:26 and Gal 1:14, it is the word *génos* which is translated "nation," but it should be race. In 1 Cor 10:32, Paul distinguishes three classes of people, Jews (*Ioudaíoi* [2453]); Greeks (*Héllēnes* [1672]), and the church of God which consists of both Gentiles and Jews.

Two pairs of Gr. words draw a similar contrast in relation to God's people. One is *Ioudaíoi* (2453), Jews, which indicates the independence of the Jewish people, a term often used by John who wrote when the Jewish and Christian communities were separated from one another. The other word is *Israél* (2474), Israel, which is used always with a note of affection and pride by those who count themselves as its members, sharers in the divine choice and covenant. There is a similar contrast between the words *éthnos* and *laós* (2992), people, with the former and *éthnē* (the pl. in the phrase "all nations") being used generally of political states. With the definite art. *tá éthnē*, the word has the special meaning "of the Gentiles" or "the non-Jewish people," which gradually took on a bad moral meaning to the extent that *ethnikoí* is translated "heathen" in Gal 1:16; 2:9 (cf. Matt 6:7). However, the common noun which corresponds with Israel is *laós*, people. It conveys the sense of God's possession and purpose, which are symbolic of the national unity maintained by the sacrifices and observances of the Law. As *éthnē* sank down to the meaning of heathen, so *laós* was at length appropriated by the Christian consciousness. A few exceptions to the above rules should be noted. In Luke 7:5; 23:2, and throughout the Gospel of John, *éthnos* is used in the place of *laós*; for, as was just stated, in the later apostolic circles the old prerogatives of Israel were claimed for the "Israel of God," i.e., the Christians. In Luke 2:10, *laós* is translated as if it were *éthnē*. The correct translation should be to "all the people" (a.t.).

Paul employs *éthnē*, the pl. of *éthnos*, nation, in a twofold sense, either as pagan Gentiles as contrasted to the Jews (Rom 2:14; 3:29; Gal 2:8) or as Gentiles in contrast to Jewish Christians (Rom 11:13; Gal 2:12, 14). This double usage is well illustrated by comparing Eph 3:1 with

4:17. In both passages *éthnē* is used, but in the first it is simply a mark of nationality while in the second it has a moral touch. The word "Gentiles" is, therefore, sometimes practically equivalent to heathen (2 Kgs 16:3; 21:2; Ezra 6:21; Ps 2:1, 8; Jer 10:2). From this point of view, *tá éthnē*, the nations outside Israel, have no part in the covenants of promise (Eph 2:12), hence the emphasis which the NT lays upon the new order of things when the mystery of the gospel (Eph 6:19) is made known (Acts 10:45; 11:18; 15:7) and until finally, the difference between Jew and Gentile having disappeared, the word *éthnē* (heathen) may be simply contrasted to the united Christian church made up of Jews and Gentiles (1 Cor 5:1; 10:20; 12:2; 1 Thess 4:5; 1 Pet 2:12). The exclusive attitude of the Jews toward the Gentiles was such that it caused the historian Tacitus (cf. 1 Thess 2:15) and others to call the Jews enemies of the human race. Even to enter the house of a Gentile, and much more to eat with him, involved ceremonial uncleanness (John 18:28; Acts 10:28; 11:3). For three days before and after a heathen festival, it was unlawful to transact business with Gentiles, to lend to or borrow from them, to pay money to or receive it from them. With this attitude of exclusivity, the Jews exercised a great effort at proselytism (Matt 23:15). If the Gentiles hoped to be saved in the same way as the Jews, it was expected of them to enter into salvation through Judaism, an idea that dawned very slowly upon the minds even of some of the Apostles of our Lord. There is ample evidence that this brought about a confrontation between Peter and Paul (see Gal 2).

Deriv.: *ethnárchēs* (1481), the governor of a district; *ethnikós* (1482), a heathen.

1485. ἔθος *éthos*; gen. *éthous*, neut. noun. Custom, usual practice or manner, whether established by law or otherwise (Luke 1:9; 2:42; 22:39; John 19:40; Acts 6:14; 15:1; 16:21; 21:21; 25:16; 26:3; 28:17; Heb 10:25).

Deriv.: *ethízō* (1480), to accustom; *éthos* (2239), manners, custom.

Syn.: *sunétheia* (4914), a custom.

Ant.: *parádoxos* (3861), extraordinary, contrary to expectation.

1486. ἔθω *éthō*; obsolete verb. To be used, to be accustomed. Used only in the pluperf. *eióthei* as imperf. (Matt 27:15; Mark 10:1), and the perf. part. *eiōthós* with *katá* (2596), according, and the definite art., *katá tó eiōthós autó*, according to his custom, as he was used to (Luke 4:16; Acts 17:2; Sept.: Num 24:1).

1487. εἰ *ei*; conditional conj. If. As such it expresses a condition which is merely hypothetical and separate from all experience in indicating a mere subjective possibility and differing from *eán* (1437), if, which implies a condition which experience must determine, i.e., an objective possibility referring always to something future. The conj. *ei* is purely subjective as in 1 Cor 7:36, "But if any man think that he behaveth himself uncomely toward his virgin." It is a thought by the father concerning his unmarried daughter. The *eán*, however, is based on objective reality and for clarification could be translated "because" (a.t.), "because she is overage" (a.t.). *Ei* and *eán* are used together in 1 Cor 7:36. In Rev 2:5 the *ei dé mḗ* (1487, 1161, 3361), but if not, is purely hypothetical, bearing only a subjective possibility with the verb *metanoésēs*, repent, being implied. "But if you do not repent . . . " (a.t.), implies that this is up to them. Irrespective of whether or not they repented they should remember that Jesus was going to come quickly or suddenly (*táchu* [5035]) which would not permit repentance at the last moment. The second conditional phrase is *eán mḗ*, if not, translated "or else," except or unless you repent. The avoidance of the removal of the lamp from its place depends on the repentance advised. *Ei* is construed with the opt. (expressing a wish); more usually with the indic. (a factual statement);

and rarely with a subjunctive (expressing a condition or contingency).

(I) As a conditional particle it is used alone, without other particles.

(A) With the opt., implying that although the thing in question is possible, it is uncertain and problematic, but nonetheless assumed as probable. In the NT, followed by the subjunctive in the apodosis (conclusion), affirming something definite with the pres., as in 1 Pet 3:14, "But and if ye suffer" (*ei páschoite* [pres. opt. of *páschō* {3958}]), "but even if ye suffer [as is most probable] do not be afraid [*mḗ phobēthḗ* {2d person, aor. mid. subjunctive of *phobéō* (5399)}], nor be ye troubled [*tarachthḗte*]" (a.t.). In Gr. grammar, the "if" clause which places the supposition is called the protasis, and the result from the reality of that supposition is called the apodosis, expressed by the "then" clause as in Matt 6:22, 23, "If therefore thine eye be single [the protasis], thy whole body shall be full of light [apodosis]." See also Acts 24:19. In parenthetic clauses such as "if it were possible" (Acts 27:39); "it may be" (1 Cor 14:10); "perhaps" (a.t. [1 Cor 15:37]); "if the will of God be so" (1 Pet 3:17), the apodosis in each case lies in the affirmation.

(B) With the indic., implying possibility without the expression of uncertainty, a condition or contingency as to which there is no doubt. **(1)** With the pres. indic., and in the apodosis followed by the pres. (Matt 19:10; Acts 5:39; Rom 8:25; 1 Cor 9:17); followed by the imper. (Matt 4:3; 19:17; 27:42; John 7:4; 1 Cor 7:9); followed by the fut. (Mark 11:26; Acts 19:39; Rom 8:11; Heb 9:13). With the aor. subjunctive, followed by the fut. indic.: after *ou mḗ* (3364), not, a double neg., instead of the fut. indic., the aor. subjunctive is placed in the apodosis (1 Cor 8:13); followed by the aor. subjunctive in exhortation (1 Cor 15:32; Gal 5:25); followed by the aor. indic. (Matt 12:26, 28; Gal 2:21); followed by the perf. (1 Cor 15:13, 16) which admits the supposition that the dead are not raised. See

also Rom 4:14; 1 Cor 9:17. **(2)** With the fut. indic., and in the apodosis followed by the pres. (1 Pet 2:20); followed by the perf. as pres. (James 2:11); followed by the fut. (Matt 26:33); followed by the imper. after *ei mḗ* (1 Cor 7:17). **(3)** With the perf. indic., and in the apodosis followed by the pres. (Acts 25:11; 1 Cor 15:14, 17, 19; 2 Cor 5:16); followed by the imper. (Acts 16:15); followed by the fut. (John 11:12; Rom 6:5); followed by the perf. (2 Cor 2:5). **(4)** With the aor. indic., and in the apodosis followed by the pres. (Rom 4:2; 15:27; 1 John 4:11); followed by the imper. (John 18:23; Rom 11:17; Col 3:1; Phile 1:18); followed by the fut. (John 13:32; 15:20; Rom 5:10, 17); followed by the aor. (Rom 5:15). **(5)** With the indic. of the historic tenses, and in the apodosis a similar tense with *án*, expressing a previous condition on which depended a certain result but implying that neither has taken place. Followed by the imperf., in the sense of would be, would do; after an imperf. with *ei* (Luke 7:39, "if he were a prophet, he would know" [a.t.]. Also John 5:46; 9:41; 15:19; 1 Cor 11:31). After an aor. with *ei* (Gal 3:21; Heb 4:8); followed by an aor. in the sense of would have been, would have done; after an imperf. with *ei* (John 14:28, "If ye had loved me, ye would have rejoiced" [a.t.]; 18:30; Acts 18:14). After an aor. with *ei* (Matt 11:21, "if these had been done, they would have repented" [a.t.]; 1 Cor 2:8). After a pluperf. with *ei* (Matt 12:7, "if ye had known . . . ye would not have condemned." Followed by the pluperf. in the sense of would have been, after an imperf. with *ei* (John 11:21, "if thou hadst been here, my brother would not have died" [a.t.]; 1 John 2:19). After a pluperf. with *ei* (John 14:7, "If ye had known me, ye would have known my Father also" [a.t.]). In such constructions *án* is sometimes omitted in the apodosis, e.g., Matt 26:24; John 9:33; 15:22; 19:11; Acts 26:32; Rom 7:7; Sept.: Judg 8:19. **(6)** With the indic. sometimes where the opt. would naturally be expected, as where a thing is uncertain, though assumed as probable as in Acts 20:16, "if it were possible for him, to be." Also where there is no probability nor even assumed possibility as in Mark 14:35, "if it were possible, the hour might pass from him." See also Matt 24:24; Mark 13:22. **(7)** *Ei* with the indic. is spoken of things not merely probable, but certain, and dependent on no condition—after *thaumázō* (2296), to marvel—and other verbs signifying an emotion of mind, where it is equivalent to *hóti* (3754), that (Mark 15:44, "Pilate marveled if he were already dead," meaning that He was so soon dead; Luke 12:49; 17:2; Acts 26:8, 23; 2 Cor 11:15; 1 John 3:13); elsewhere also as equivalent to *epeí* (1893), meaning because, since, as, inasmuch as (Matt 6:30, if then the grass, since; 7:11; John 7:23; 13:17; Acts 4:9; Heb 7:15). With the aor. indic. (John 13:14, 32; Acts 11:17; 2 Cor 5:14); in *eí tis*, *eí ti*, if someone or if something, used with a sort of emphasis for *hóstis* (3748), whosoever, whatsoever, everyone who; with the pres. indic. (Mark 9:35; Luke 14:26; 1 Cor 3:12; 8:2, 3; 1 Tim 5:8; 6:3); with the fut. indic. (1 Cor 3:14, 15); with the perf. indic. (2 Cor 7:14; 10:7); with the aor. indic. (Rev 20:15). **(8)** With the indic. before the *aposiópēsis* (or silencing) where the apodosis is not expressed but left to be inferred; the protasis being thus rendered more emphatic (Luke 19:42, "If thou hadst known, even thou, the things belonging unto thy peace!" [a.t.] where the natural apodosis would be, "How much better had it been for thee!" Also Luke 22:42; Acts 23:9; Rom 9:22, "If then God" [a.t.]). In oaths and asseverations, the apodosis or imprecation being omitted, *ei* comes to imply a neg. such as "not" (Mark 8:12; Heb 3:11; 4:3, 5; Sept.: Gen 14:23; Num 14:30; 1 Sam 3:14; 2 Kgs 6:31; Ps 95:11).

(C) With the subjunctive, rarely in NT or early Gr. writers, and only where an action depends on something fut., if, if so be, supposing that, and with a neg., meaning unless, except (cf. *ei mḗ* [Luke 9:13; 1 Cor 14:5]).

(II) As an interrogative particle, whether:

(A) In an indirect question after verbs implying question, doubt, uncertainty, and the like, with the opt. and indic. as in Class. Gr. writers. With the opt. (Acts 17:11, 27, "if perhaps" or "whether perhaps"; 25:20). With the pres. indic. (Matt 26:63; 27:49; Mark 10:2; 15:36; Luke 14:28, 31; John 9:25; Acts 4:19; 10:18; 19:2; 2 Cor 2:9; 13:5). With the fut. indic. (Mark 3:2; 1 Cor 7:16). With the aor. indic. (Mark 15:44; Acts 5:8; 1 Cor 1:16). With the fut. indic., "if perhaps" or "whether perhaps" (Mark 11:13; Acts 8:22).

(B) In a direct question where it implies some doubt or uncertainty in the mind of the interrogator which cannot be expressed in Eng. (Matt 12:10; 19:3; Luke 13:23; 14:3; 22:49; Acts 1:6; 7:1; 21:37; 22:25; Sept.: Gen 17:17; Ruth 1:19; 1 Kgs 1:27; 13:14; Job 6:6; Dan 2:26; 3:14).

(III) In connection with other particles, where, however, for the most part each retains its own power: *ei dé*, where *dé* has its usual adversative or continuative power, "but if," "and if" (Matt 12:7; Luke 11:19; John 10:38). *Ei dé kaí*, and if also (Luke 11:18; 1 Cor 4:7; 2 Cor 4:3; 5:16; 11:6). *Ei dé mḗ*, but if not, properly only after an affirmative clause, of which it then expresses the contrary or neg. (John 14:2, 11; Rev 2:5, 16). Sometimes also after a neg. clause, of which it then necessarily expresses the contrary and, therefore, affirms, "if otherwise," or "else" (Mark 2:21, 22). *Ei kaí*, where *kaí*, and, either refers to the subsequent clause and then each retains its own separate power, in which case it means if also; or *kaí* refers to the condition expressed by *ei*, if, meaning even, though, although, if also (1 Cor 7:21; 2 Cor 11:15); with the subjunctive (Phil 3:12); with the opt. (1 Pet 3:14), if even, meaning though, although, implying the reality and actual existence of that which is assumed thus differing from *ei kaí* and also from *kaí ei*, which leaves it uncertain. Only with the pres. indic. (Luke 18:4; 2 Cor 4:16; 12:11, 15; Phil 2:17; Col 2:5; Heb 6:9); with the imperf. (2 Cor 7:8); fut. (Matt 26:33; Luke 11:8); with the aor. (2 Cor 7:8, 12); *kaí ei*, even if, though, the same as *ei kaí* (Mark 14:29; 1 Pet 3:1); *kaí gár ei* (2 Cor 13:4); *kaí gár eíper* (1 Cor 8:5); *ei mḗ*, if not, meaning unless, except, expressing a neg. condition, supposition, in which *mḗ* refers to the whole clause, thus differing from *ei ou*, where *ou* refers only to some particular word with which it expresses one idea. Before finite verbs with the indic. (Matt 24:22; Mark 13:20; John 9:33; 15:22; 19:11; Acts 26:32). Followed by *hína* (2443), in order that (John 10:10); *hóti* (3754), that (2 Cor 12:13; Eph 4:9); without a following finite verb (Matt 11:27; 12:4, 24, 39; Mark 6:8; Acts 11:19; 1 Cor 7:17; Gal 1:7); followed by an inf. (Matt 5:13; Acts 21:35). With *ektós ei mḗ* (*ektós* [1622], unless; *ei mḗ*, except; 1 Cor 14:5; 15:2; 1 Tim 5:19). *Ei mḗti* (3385), unless perhaps (Luke 9:13; 1 Cor 7:5; 2 Cor 13:5). *Eí per*, if indeed, if so be, assuming the supposition is true whether justly or not. With the indic. (Rom 8:9; 1 Cor 15:15; 1 Pet 2:3). By implication meaning "since," the same as *eíge* ([1489] Rom 8:17; 2 Thess 1:6). With *kaí*, *kaí eíper*, though, although (1 Cor 8:5). *Eí pōs* (1513), if by any means, if possibly, with the opt. (Acts 27:12; Sept.: 2 Sam 16:12). With the fut. indic. (Rom 1:10; 11:14; Phil 3:11; Sept.: 2 Kgs 19:4). *Eíte . . . eíte* (1535), whether . . . or, as including several particulars; followed by a verb in the indic. (1 Cor 12:26; 2 Cor 1:6); or the subjunctive (1 Thess 5:10) or without a verb (Rom 12:6–8; 1 Cor 3:22; 8:5; 13:8; 15:11; 1 Pet 2:13, 14); as expressing doubt (2 Cor 12:2, 3).

Deriv.: *eíte* (1535), and if, ever; *hṓspereí* (5619), just as if, as it were.

1488. εἰ *eí*; pres. act. indic. 2d person sing. of *eimí* (1510), to be. You are.

1489. εἴγε *eíge*; particle from *ei* (1487), if, and *ge* (1065), indeed. A particle of emphasis or qualification meaning if at least, if indeed, if so be, followed by the indic. and spoken of what is taken for granted (Eph 3:2; 4:21; Col 1:23; Sept.: Job 16:4). Followed by *kaí* (2532), and, if indeed also, which as applying only to what is taken for granted, may be expressed by since, although (2 Cor 5:3, "although being now clothed, we shall not" [a.t.]; Gal 3:4 "since it is in vain" [a.t. {cf. 1 Cor 15:51}]).

1490. εἰ δέ μή *ei dé mḗ*, εἰ δέ μή γε *ei dé mḗ ge*; conditional expression from *ei* (1487), if, and *dé* (1161), but, and *mḗ* (3361), not, and *ge* (1065), indeed. But if not indeed, if otherwise indeed, usually only after an affirmative clause of which it then expresses the contrary or neg. (John 14:2, 11; Rev 2:5, 16); however, sometimes also after a neg. clause of which it then necessarily expresses the contrary and thus affirms, i.e., if otherwise, or else (Mark 2:21, 22). It is also equal to *ei dé mḗ* but stronger, meaning "but if not indeed," "if indeed otherwise," and serves to annul the preceding proposition whether affirmative or neg. So also after an affirmation meaning but if not, otherwise (Matt 6:1; Luke 10:6; 13:9). After a negation, where it consequently affirms; "if otherwise," or "else" (Matt 9:17; Luke 5:36, 37; 14:32; 2 Cor 11:16).

1491. εἶδος *eídos*; gen. *eídous*, neut. noun from *eídō* (1492), to see. The act of seeing, the thing seen, external appearance, sight (2 Cor 5:7, metaphorically our future bliss has yet no visible appearance or form); the object of sight, form, appearance (Luke 3:22; 9:29; John 5:37; Sept.: Gen 41:2f.; Ex 24:17; Num 9:16; 1 Sam 25:3; Esth 2:7); manner, kind, species (1 Thess 5:22, Sept.: Jer 15:3). In 2 Cor 5:7, it refers to the visible appearance of things which are set in contrast to that which directs faith, meaning that the believer is guided not only by what he beholds, but by what he knows to be true though invisible. In 1 Thess 5:22, the form of evil.

Deriv.: *eídōlon* (1497), idol; *petrṓdēs* (4075), rock-like, stone-like.

Syn.: *schḗma* (4976), figure, fashion; *morphḗ* (3444), form, makeup; *homoíōma* (3667), likeness; *theōría* (2335), gaze, spectacle; *hórama* (3705), that which is seen, appearance.

1492. εἴδω *eídō*. To see. This verb is obsolete in the pres. act. for which *horáō* (3708), to see with perception, is used. The tenses derived from the meaning of *eídō* form two families, one of which has exclusively the meaning of to see, the other that of to know.

(**I**) To see, 2d aor. *eídon*, opt. *ídoimi*, subjunctive *ídō*, inf. *ideín*, part. *idṓn*; for the imper. *idé* (Rom 11:22; Gal 5:2), later form *íde* (Matt 25:20; Mark 3:34; John 1:29). These forms are all used as the aor. of *horáō* or *eídō* in the sense of "I saw," trans., implying not the mere act of seeing but the actual perception of some object, and thus differing from *blépō* (991), to see.

(**A**) Followed by the acc. of person or thing (Matt 2:2; 5:1; 21:19; Mark 9:9; 11:13, 20; John 1:48; 4:48; Acts 8:39; Heb 3:9; Rev 1:2; Sept.: Gen 9:23). Followed by the acc. with part. (Matt 3:7; 8:14; 24:15; Mark 6:33; Luke 5:2). Also with the part. *ónta*, being, implied, the pres. part. of *eimí* (1510), to be (Matt 25:38, 39). With part. of the same verb by way of emphasis, *idṓn eídon* (Acts 7:34 quoted from Ex 3:7). Followed by *hóti* (3754), that, with the indic. (Mark 9:25; John 6:22; Rev 12:13). Used in an absolute sense in Matt 9:8; Luke 2:17; Acts 3:12. *Hoi idóntes* means the spectators in Mark 5:16; Luke 8:36. Before an indirect question as in Matt 27:49; Mark 5:14; Gal 6:11. Also in various modified senses such as: (**1**) To behold, look upon, contemplate (Matt 9:36; 28:6; Mark 8:33; Luke 24:39; John 20:27; Sept.: Num 12:8). (**2**) To see in order to know, to look at or into, examine (Mark 5:14; 6:38; 12:15; Luke 8:35; 14:18; John 1:39, 46). (**3**) To see face to face, to see and talk with, to visit, i.e., to have personal

acquaintance and relationship with (Luke 8:20; 9:9; John 12:21; Acts 16:40; Rom 1:11; 1 Cor 16:7; Gal 1:19; Phil 1:27; 2:28). Also of a city, such as Rome (Acts 19:21). (**4**) To wait to see, watch, observe (Matt 26:58; 27:49; Mark 15:36). (**5**) To see take place, witness, to live to see (Matt 13:17; 24:33; Mark 2:12). Also "to see one's day" (a.t.) means to witness the events of his life and times as in Luke 17:22; John 8:56.

(**B**) Metaphorically spoken of the mind meaning to perceive by the senses, to be aware of, to remark (Matt 9:2, 4; Luke 17:15; John 7:52; Rom 11:22). Followed by *hóti* (3754), that (Matt 2:16; 27:24; Mark 12:34; Acts 12:3; 16:19; Gal 2:7, 14; Sept.: Josh 8:14; Job 32:5; Eccl 2:12, 13; Isa 6:9).

(**C**) To see, i.e., to experience either good (meaning to enjoy) or evil (meaning to suffer), followed by the acc. referring to death in Luke 2:26; Heb 11:5. Sept.: Ps 89:48, *óptomai*, same as *optánomai* (3700), corruption (Acts 2:27, 31; 13:35; Sept.: Ps 16:10); *pénthos* (3997), grief, mourning (Rev 18:7). In 1 Pet 3:10, "see good days"; Sept.: Ps 34:12. In John 3:3, to see and enjoy the privileges of the divine kingdom (cf. Sept.: Ps 27:13; Eccl 6:6).

(**II**) To know, in the 2d perf. *oída*, subjunctive *eidṓ*, in the inf. *eidénai*, in the part. *eidṓs*, in the pluperf. *ḗdein*, in the fut. *eidḗsō* (Heb 8:11). The pl. forms *oídamen* (John 9:20), *oídate* (1 Cor 9:13), and *oídasi* (Luke 11:44) belong to the later Gr. instead of the forms *íste* (Heb 12:17) and *ísasi* (Acts 26:4). *Oída* strictly means to have seen, perceived, apprehended; hence it takes the pres. meaning of to know, and the pluperf. becomes an imperf.

(**A**) To be acquainted with, followed by the acc., spoken of things (Matt 25:13; Mark 10:19; Luke 18:20; John 4:22; Rom 7:7; 13:11; Jude 1:5, 10; Sept.: Ex 3:7; Job 8:9. See also 1 Cor 16:15; 1 Thess 2:1). Spoken of persons (Matt 25:12; Mark 1:34; John 6:42; Acts 7:18; Heb 10:30; 1 Pet 1:8, "whom having not seen," i.e., by sight, personally). Also followed by the acc. with an adj. the part. *ónta*, being, implied as in Mark 6:20, "knowing him to be a just man" (a.t.). See also Mark 1:24; Luke 13:25; John 7:27; Sept.: 2 Sam 17:8. Followed by the acc. and inf. (Luke 4:41; 1 Pet 5:9). Followed by *hóti* (3754), that, with the indic. instead of the acc. and inf. (Matt 15:12; Mark 12:14; Luke 8:53; Acts 3:17). Followed by *perí* (4012), about, and the gen. (Matt 24:36; Mark 13:32). Used in an absolute sense (Luke 11:44; 2 Cor 11:11). Before an indirect question with the indic. (Matt 24:43; Mark 13:35; Luke 12:39; Col 4:6; 1 Thess 4:2; 2 Thess 3:7). With the subjunctive (Mark 9:6).

(B) In the sense of to perceive, be aware of, understand. Followed by the acc. of thing (Matt 12:25; Mark 4:13; 12:15; Luke 11:17). Followed by *hóti* (3754), that, with the indic. (Mark 2:10; Luke 5:24; John 6:61; 1 John 5:13). Followed by *pós* (4459), how, in what way, with the indic. (1 Tim 3:15). Before an indirect question (Eph 1:18). *Oída*, perf. tense of *eídō*, expresses the knowledge which comes from one's state of being, intuitive knowledge.

In the following verses, the word refers to the absolute knowledge of God the Father or the Lord Jesus Christ: Matt 6:8, "The Father knows intuitively what your needs are" (a.t.), also Matt 6:32; John 6:6, Jesus Christ knew intuitively what He was going to do, which would not be dependent on Philip's answer; John 6:64 indicates the innate knowledge that Jesus Christ had of who would not be true believers. John 8:14 refers to the intuitive knowledge of Jesus Christ as to where He came from and where He was going, indicating the consciousness of His deed. John 11:42 indicates that whenever Jesus Christ was heard praying publicly, it was for the sake of His hearers. He intuitively knew that the Father always heard Him for there was always an identity of purpose between the Father and the Son. In John 13:11, Jesus reveals that He knew all the time who was going to betray Him.

This was not something that was revealed by the experience of a final betrayal by Judas. In John 18:4, we have the indication that Jesus knew intuitively everything that was going to take place against Him and nothing would have happened unless He permitted it. See 2 Cor 11:31; 2 Pet 2:9; Rev 2:2, 9, 13, 19; 3:1, 8, 15.

Spoken of man's knowledge as a result of and only in view of his relationship with God the Father through Jesus Christ. There are certain things that human beings simply cannot know intuitively unless they become the children of God. The verb is used in that respect in Rom 2:2; 3:19; 5:3; 6:9; 7:14, 18; 8:22, 26–28; 1 Thess 1:4, 5; 2:1; 2 Thess 3:7.

Contrasted with *oída*, *ginōskō* (1097), to know experientially, frequently suggests the inception or progress in knowledge, while *oída* suggests fullness of knowledge. The contrast is shown in John 8:55: "Yet ye have not known him [*egnōkate* {perf. act. indic. of *ginōskō*}, you never had the initial experience of knowing Him]; but I know Him [*oída*, I intuitively know Him because I am God as the Father is God]; and if I should say, I know Him not [*ouk oída*, that I do not intuitively know Him], I shall be a liar like unto you: but I know Him [*oída*, I know Him intuitively], and keep His saying." This means that Jesus did the will of His Father not through obedience only but in the identity that He had as God. Jesus Christ here confesses that His knowledge of God was not acquired and progressive, but it was intuitive and full because He and the Father were one (John 10:30) and the Father was in Him and He in the Father (John 14:10, 11). The contrast between *oída* and *ginōskō* is apparent in John 13:7, "Jesus answered and said unto him, What I do thou knowest not now [*ouk oídas*, i.e., you do not intuitively]; but thou shalt know hereafter [*gnōsē*, the fut. mid. indic. of *ginōskō*, to experientially know]." Peter could not believe and perceive on his own that Jesus who was omnipotent would allow Himself to be put to death by others, but he would understand it all when he saw it taking place before his eyes. That one must be attuned to God Himself in order to understand what God teaches is demonstrated by Mark 4:13 where Jesus, speaking to His disciples after the first parable which He realized they did not understand, said to them, "Know ye not [*ouk oídate*, you do not understand intuitively] this parable? And how then will ye know [*gnốsesthe*] all parables [will know the meaning and teaching of each parable in your own experience]?" In Matt 7:23, to the hypocrites who call upon the name of the Lord but who never come to experientially know Him, the Lord said, "And then will I profess unto them, I never knew you [*égnōn* {the 2d aor. indic. act. of *ginốskō*}, there was never a time that I acknowledged a relationship between you and Me]." On the other hand in Matt 25:12, the Lord in speaking to the imprudent five virgins in the parable said, "Verily I say unto you, I know you not [*ouk oída*, you are not related to me]."

(C) By implication, to know how, i.e., to be able, followed by an inf. (Matt 7:11; Luke 12:56; Phil 4:12; 1 Thess 4:4; 1 Tim 3:5; James 4:17; 2 Pet 2:9). With the inf. implied (Matt 27:65).

(D) With the idea of volition, to know and approve or love; hence spoken of men, to care for, take an interest in (1 Thess 5:12; Sept.: Gen 39:6). Of God, to know God, i.e., to acknowledge and adore God (Gal 4:8; 1 Thess 4:5; 2 Thess 1:8; Titus 1:16; Heb 8:11; Sept.: 1 Sam 2:12; Job 18:21; Jer 31:34).

Deriv.: *Hádēs* (86), Hades; *apeídō* (542), to see fully; *eídos* (1491), appearance, shape, sight; *íde* (2396) and *epeídon* (1896), behold, look upon; *idéa* or *eidéa* (2397), aspect, countenance, idea; *ísēmi* (2467), to confirm; *proeídō* (4275), foresee; *suneídō* (4894), to understand together, metaphorically meaning to become aware; *hupereídon* (5237), to overlook.

Syn.: *blépō* (991), to see, to perceive, take heed; *horáō* (3708), to see; *emblépō*

(1689), to look earnestly; *theōréō* (2334), to scrutinize; *theáomai* (2300), to behold with wonder; *epopteúō* (2029), to witness as a spectator or overseer; *atenízō* (816), to gaze upon; *katanoéō* (2657), to comprehend, apprehend, perceive fully; *óptomai* (3700), to see, both objectively and subjectively, sometimes *optánō*, to allow oneself to be seen; *noéō* (3539), to perceive with the mind; *katanoéō* (2657), to perceive clearly; *logízomai* (3049), to consider, use one's mind, take into account; *analogízomai* (357), to consider well; *suníēmi* (4920), to understand, consider; *ginốskō* (1097), to know; *proséchō* (4337), to pay attention to, take heed.

Ant.: *tuphlóō* (5186), to blind; *pōróō* (4456), to harden; *agnoéō* (50), not to know, to ignore; *lanthánō* (2990), to forget, to skip.

1493. εἰδωλεῖον *eidōleíon*; gen. *eidōleíou*, neut. noun from *eídōlon* (1497), idol. An idol temple (1 Cor 8:10).

1494. εἰδωλόθυτον *eidōlóthuton*; gen. *eidōlothútou*, neut. noun from *eídōlon* (1497), idol, and *thúō* (2380), to sacrifice. Whatever is sacrificed or offered to an idol such as flesh or heathen sacrifices (Acts 15:29; 21:25; 1 Cor 8:1, 4, 7, 10; 10:19, 28; Rev 2:14, 20).

1495. εἰδωλολατρεία *eidōlolatreía*; gen. *eidōlolatreías*, fem. noun from *eídōlon* (1497), idol, and *latreía* (2999), service, worship. Idolatry. Used only in the NT and Patristic Gr. (1 Cor 10:14; Gal 5:20; Col 3:5, of covetousness; 1 Pet 4:3).

1496. εἰδωλολάτρης *eidōlolátrēs*; gen. *eidōlolátrou*, masc. noun from *eídōlon* (1497), idol, and *látris* (n.f.), a servant, worshiper. Idolater, a servant or worshiper of idols (1 Cor 5:10, 11; 6:9; 10:7; Eph 5:5 of a covetous person [see Col 3:5]; Rev 21:8; 22:15).

Syn.: *ethnikós* (1482), heathen, Gentile; *proskunētḗs* (4353), worshiper.

Ant.: *theosebḗs* (2318), worshiper of God; *theóphilos* (2321), a friend of God; *philótheos* (5377), a friend of God; *pistós* (4103), faithful.

1497. εἴδωλον *eídōlon*; gen. *eidólou*, neut. noun from *eídos* (1491), a form, appearance. An image or representation whether corporeal or imaginary or some other thing. In Class. Gr., used for a statue of man or even for a concept of the mind, an imaginary deity. In the NT, it stands for an idol or image set up to be worshiped as a god, whether or not intended as a representative of the true God (Acts 7:41) or of a false one (Acts 15:20; 1 Cor 12:2; Rev 9:20; Sept.: 2 Chr 33:22; Isa 30:22). Also stands for a false god, usually worshiped as an image (Rom 2:22; 2 Cor 6:16; 1 Thess 1:9; 1 John 5:21). Paul in 1 Cor 8:4, 7; 10:19 (Sept.: Num 25:2; 2 Kgs 17:12; 21:11, 21) says that although an idol is nothing in the world, it does represent something which is not the true God. Idols may be material, the works of men's hands such as statues of gold, or creations of God Himself such as the sun and moon. However, they have none of the excellency which would merit divine worship or that servile worshipers are pleased to attribute to them (cf. Isa 41:24; Hab 2:18, 19).
Deriv.: *eidōleíon* (1493), idol temple; *eidōlóthuton* (1494), that which is sacrificed to idols; *eidōlolatreía* (1495), idolatry; *eidōlolátrēs* (1496), an idolater; *kateídōlos* (2712), utterly idolatrous, given to idolatry.
Syn.: *eikṓn* (1504), statue, icon, resemblance, image, representation.
Ant.: *Theós* (2316), God; *theótēs* (2320), Godhead.

1498. εἴην *eíēn*; pres. opt. of *eimí* (1510), to be. Might be (Luke 1:29; 3:15; 8:9; 9:46; 15:26; 18:36; 22:23; Acts 8:20; 21:33).

1499. εἰ καί *ei kaí* conditional expression from *ei* (1487), if, and *kaí* (2532), and. If also, even if, if that, though. The *kaí* (2532), and, refers either to the subsequent clause in which case each retains its own separate power, if also, or *kaí* refers to the condition expressed by *ei*, if even, meaning though, although. Generally it means if also, with the indic. (1 Cor 7:21; 2 Cor 11:15); with the opt. (1 Pet 3:14); with the subjunctive (Phil 3:12). It can also mean if even, though, although, implying the reality and natural existence of that which is assumed, thus differing from the above use of *ei kaí*, and also, from *kaí ei* which leaves it uncertain. Only with the pres. indic. (Luke 18:4; 2 Cor 4:16; 12:11, 15; Phil 2:17; Col 2:5; Heb 6:9); with the imper. (2 Cor 7:8); with the fut. (Luke 11:8); with the aor. (2 Cor 7:8, 12). Very rarely *kaí ei*, even if, though, the same as *ei kaí* (Mark 14:29; 1 Pet 3:1), *kaí gár* (1063) *ei* (2 Cor 13:4); *kaí gár eíper* (1512) (1 Cor 8:5).

1500. εἰκῇ *eikḗ*; adv. Without purpose, inconsiderately, groundlessly, without cause (Matt 5:22; Col 2:18); to no purpose, in vain (Rom 13:4; 1 Cor 15:2; Gal 3:4; 4:11).
Syn.: *dōreán* (1432), without a cause; *mátēn* (3155), to no purpose, in vain; *anōphelḗs* (512), unprofitable; *alusitelḗs* (255), gainless; *áchrēstos* (890), useless; *perissós* (4053), superfluous.
Ant.: *ōphélimos* (5624), profitable; *chrḗsimos* (5539), useful; *anagkaíos* (316), necessary, needful.

1501. εἴκοσι *eíkosi*; indeclinable, used for all genders, cardinal number. Twenty (Luke 14:31; Acts 27:28).

1502. εἴκω *eíkō*; fut. *eíxō*. To give place, yield, give way, to obey, submit, with the dat. (Gal 2:5).
Syn.: *ekchōréō* (1633), to give place to; *epitrépō* (2010), to let, allow.
Ant.: *antagōnízomai* (464), to struggle against; *anthístēmi* (436), to resist.

1503. εἴκω *eíkō*; an obsolete form. The 2d perf. *éoika* is used with the meaning of the present, to be like. With the dat. in

James 1:6, 23, to be like, resemble (Sept.: Job 6:25).
   Deriv.: *eikṓn* (1504), likeness; *hupeíkō* (5226), to submit, surrender, yield.
   Syn.: *homoiázō* (3662), to resemble.
   Ant.: *diaphérō* (1308), to differ.

1504. εἰκών *eikṓn*; gen. *eikónos*, fem. noun from *eíkō* (1503), to be like, resemble. A representation, an image, as of a man, made of gold, silver, or other material (Rom 1:23); a monarch's likeness impressed on a coin (Matt 22:20; Mark 12:16; Luke 20:24); image, resemblance, likeness (Rom 8:29; 1 Cor 11:7; 15:49; 2 Cor 3:18; 4:4; Col 1:15; 3:10; Heb 10:1). *Eikṓn* sometimes may be used as syn. with *homoíōma* (3667), and both may refer to earthly copies and resemblances of the archetypal things in the heavens. However, there is a distinction in that *eikṓn*, image, always assumes a prototype, that which it not merely resembles but from which it is drawn (Rev 13:14, 15; 14:9, 11; 15:2; 16:2; 19:20; 20:4; Sept.: Deut 4:16; 2 Kgs 11:18; Isa 40:19, 20; Ezek 23:14). Thus, the reflection of the sun on the water is *eikṓn*. More importantly, the child is *émpsuchos* (possessed of a soul) *eikṓn*, image of his parents. *Homoíōma* is the result, the likeness or resemblance (Rom 1:23; 5:14; 6:5; 8:3; Phil 2:7; Rev 9:7). *Homoíōsis* (3669) is the process or act of producing a likeness or resemblance (James 3:9). However, while in *homoíōma* and *homoíōsis* there is resemblance, it by no means follows that it is derived from what it resembles. There may be a resemblance between two men in no way related to each other. The *eikṓn*, image, includes and involves the resemblance or similitude (*homoíōsis*), but the *homoíōsis* does not involve the image. The Son is the *eikṓn* of God indicating the revelatory character of the incarnation (2 Cor 4:4; Col 1:15). There are two other Gr. words that stand in contrast to *eikṓn* and *homoíōma*. They are *charaktḗr* (5481), character, and *apaúgasma* (541), brightness (used only in Heb 1:3). *Charaktḗr* signifies the image impressed as corresponding to the original pattern. On account of this idea of close resemblance, it has for its syn. *mímēma* (n.f.), imitation, anything imitated, a copy; *eikṓn*, image; *apeikónisma* (n.f.), representation. On the other hand, *apaúgasma* means radiation, not merely reflection. Furthermore, Heb 1:3 uses *charaktḗr*, not *cháragma* (5480), because the latter word was used in a narrower sense and rarely denoted the peculiar characteristics of an individual or a people and always prominently suggested the pass. bearing of the subject spoken about. *Cháragma* occurs in Acts 17:29; Rev 13:16, 17; 14:9, 11; 15:2 (TR); 16:2; 19:20; 20:4 meaning impression, mark, symbol.

1505. εἰλικρίνεια *eilikríneia*; gen. *eilikrineías*, fem. noun from *eilikrinḗs* (1506), pure, sincere. Purity, sincerity, clearness, used metaphorically (1 Cor 5:8; 2 Cor 1:12; 2:17).
   Syn.: *euthútēs* (2118), rectitude; *haplótēs* (572), sincerity.
   Ant.: *pseúdos* (5579), lie; *ponēría* (4189), iniquity, wickedness; *hupókrisis* (5272), hypocrisy; *dólos* (1388), deceit.

1506. εἰλικρινής *eilikrinḗs*; gen. *eilikrinoús*, masc.-fem., neut. *eilikrinés*, adj. from *heílē* (n.f.), the shining or splendor of the sun, and *krínō* (2919), to judge, discern. Sincere, pure, unsullied, free from spot or blemish to such a degree as to bear examination in the full splendor of the sun. In the NT, generally understood to relate to the lives or wills of Christians, since in the Pauline Epistles it seems to refer to *dokimázō* (1381), to discern (Phil 1:10; 2 Pet 3:1). Peter connects it with *diánoia* (1271), understanding, thus indicating that clarity or perspicuity of mind or understanding by which one is able to see all things intelligibly and clearly, and to proceed without mistake. Therefore, *eilikrinḗs* may be rendered clear, clearly discerning, of clear judgment or discernment, i.e., spiritually in all things both of Christian faith and practice. Another Gr. word with which *eilikrinḗs* is frequently associated is *katharós* (2513), pure, clean, free from soil or stain. Also from *heílē* (n.f.): *élios* (2246), sun.

Deriv.: *eilikríneia* (1505), sincerity.

Syn.: *ádolos* (97), guileless, pure; *ákakos* (172), without evil; *gnḗsios* (1103), true, genuine, sincere; *alēthḗs* (227), manifest, unconcealed; *alēthinós* (228), genuine, real; *hagnós* (53), pure; *katharós* (2513), pure, cleansed; *haploús* (573), sincere; *anupókritos* (505), unhypocritical.

Ant.: *hupokritḗs* (5273), hypocrite; *pseudḗs* (5571), false; *dólios* (1386), deceitful.

1507. εἰλίσσω *heilíssō*; fut. *heilíxō*, the Ionian form of *helíssō* (1667), to fold up, roll up, or to gather as a scroll (Rev 6:14).

Deriv.: *eneiléō* (1750), to roll or wrap up in.

1508. εἰ μή *ei mḗ*; neg. conditional or suppositional expression, from *ei* (1487), if, and *mḗ* (3361), not. If not, unless, except. Before finite verbs with the indic. (Matt 24:22; Mark 13:20; John 9:33; 15:22; 19:11; Acts 26:32); followed by *hína* (2443), so that (John 10:10); by *hóti* (3754), that, for, because (2 Cor 12:13; Eph 4:9). Without a following finite verb (Matt 11:27; 12:4, 24, 39; Mark 6:8; 9:9; Acts 11:19; 1 Cor 7:17; Gal 1:7). Followed by the inf. (Matt 5:13; Acts 21:25); preceded by *ektós* (1622), unless, except (1 Cor 15:2; 1 Tim 5:19). The expression *ei dé mḗ*, but if not, always standing elliptically after an affirmative clause, of which it then expresses the contrary or neg. as in John 14:2, "In my Father's house are many mansions: but if it were not so, I would have told you" (a.t. [see John 14:11; Rev 2:5, 16; Sept.: Gen 24:49]). Sometimes also after a neg. clause, of which it then necessarily expresses the contrary and therefore affirms, meaning, if otherwise, or else, as in Mark 2:21, 22.

1509. εἰ μή τι *ei mḗ ti*, neg. conditional or suppositional expression, from *ei* (1487), if, and *mḗ* (3361), not, and *ti* (5100), some. If not somewhat, except, unless perhaps (Luke 9:13; 1 Cor 7:5; 2 Cor 13:5).

1510. εἰμί *eimí*; imperf. *ḗn* (2258), fut. *ésomai* (2071), pres. indic. 2d person sing. *eí* (1488), 3d person. pl. *eisí* (1526), pres. imper. sing. *ísthi* ([2468], Matt 2:13), 3d person. *éstō* ([2468], Matt 5:37), pres. opt. *eíēn* (1498), pres. inf. *eínai* (1511), pres. indic. 3d person sing. *estí* (2076), pres. indic. 1st person pl. *esmén* (2070). Less usual forms are the imperf. 2d person sing. *ēs* ([2258], Matt 25:21, 23) instead of the more usual *éstha* ([2258], Matt 26:69; Mark 14:67), imperf. 1st person sing. *ḗmēn* ([2252], Gal 1:10, 22), imper. sing. *ḗtō* ([2277], 1 Cor 16:22; James 5:12), 2d person pl. *ḗte* for *éste* ([2075], 1 Cor 7:5 [TR], *sunérchesthe* [4905]). *Eimí*, to be, is the usual verb of existence, and also the usual logical copula or link, connecting subj. and predicate.

(I) As a verb of existence, to be, to have existence.

(A) Particularly and generally: **(1)** In the metaphysical sense as in John 1:1, "In the beginning was the Word," meaning it had been before there was any beginning or existed before the beginning of anything; John 8:50, *estín*, in the pres. tense indicating eternal existence, "There has always been one that seeks and judges" (a.t.); John 8:58, *egṓ eimí* (*egō* [1473], I; *eimí* [1510], am), "I am," meaning I have always been; Mark 12:32, *heís estí* (*heís* [1520], one; *estí*, there is), "the one there is" (a.t.), meaning there has always been the one and there is no other, or there has never been another beside Him (Christ). See Acts 19:2; Heb 11:6. Of things as in John 17:5, "before the world came into existence [*eínai* {1511}, the pres. inf.]" (a.t.); 2 Pet 3:5, *ésan ékpalai* (1597), "were [have been] of old," from of old. This indicates that the physical heavens as we know them now have not always been as they were from the beginning, but they were created later and the prophecy is that they will be changed again (2 Pet 3:10; see Matt 24:29; Mark 13:24, 25; Luke 21:25, 26). In Rev 4:11, "for thy pleasure they are" (TR), or were (UBS), meaning they have always been. For the pres. part. ṓn (sing.), tá ónta neut. pl. (see D). Spoken of life, to exist, to live (Matt 2:18; 23:30); in Acts 17:28, "In Him we live and move and have our being," our lives are preserved. (2) Generally, it means to be, exist, to be found, as of persons (Matt 12:11; Luke 4:25, "there were many widows" [a.t.], 27; John 3:1; Rom 3:10, 11). Of things, meaning to be, exist, to have place (Matt 6:30; 22:23; Mark 7:15; Luke 6:43; Acts 2:29; Rom 13:1). Also estí (sing.), there is; eisí (pl.), there are (John 7:12; Acts 27:22; Rom 3:22; 1 Cor 12:4–6; Rev 10:6; 21:4). In John 7:39, literally "for there was not yet Holy Spirit" (a.t.), meaning the giving of the Holy Spirit had not yet occurred. By implication, to be present, the same as páreimi (3918), to be near, but this meaning lies only in the adjuncts as in Matt 12:10, "there was present" (a.t.); Matt 24:6; Mark 8:1. (3) Spoken of time, generally (Mark 11:13; Luke 23:44; John 1:40; Acts 2:15; 2 Tim 4:3); of festivals (Mark 15:42; Acts 12:3).

(B) By implication and by force of the adjuncts, eimí means to come to be, come into existence, equal to gínomai (1096), to come about. (1) To come to pass, take place, occur, be done. The fut. éstai and other tenses also have similar meaning (Luke 12:55 [cf. 21:11, 25; Acts 11:28; 27:25]). In Luke 22:49, tó esómenon means what was about to happen. See Matt 24:3; Luke 1:34. Followed by the dat. of person (Luke 14:10). In Acts 2:17, 21 quoted from Joel 2:28–32, kaí éstai, "and it shall be" (a.t.), or "shall come to pass," followed by the fut.; also Rom 9:26 quoted from Hos 1:10. (2) To become anything as in Matt 19:5; Eph 5:31, where the fut. pl. ésontai, shall be, is implied in the phrase "and they two shall be one flesh," quoted from Gen 2:24. See

Luke 3:5 with reference to Isa 40:4; Acts 13:47 with reference to Isa 49:6; Eph 1:11. Followed by the dat. of person (1 Cor 14:22; 2 Cor 6:18; Heb 8:10; James 5:3).

(C) The 3d person sing. estí followed by the inf. means it is proper, in one's power or convenient (1 Cor 11:20; Heb 9:5, "of which we cannot now speak").

(D) The part. ṓn, masc. sing.; oúsa, fem. sing.; ón, neut. sing., means being. (1) Joined with a noun or pron., it is used in short parenthetical clauses by way of emphasis to indicate an existing state, condition, character, and may be rendered by the case in an absolute sense or by being, as being, as (Matt 7:11, "being evil"; John 3:4; 4:9; 9:25; Acts 16:21, "being Romans"; Rom 5:10; 11:17; Gal 6:3; Eph 2:4; Titus 3:11; James 3:4). (2) With the art. ho ṓn, masc. sing.; tá ónta, neut. pl., it implies real and true existence. Thus in the phrase, ho ṓn kaí ho ḗn kaí ho erchómenos, "the One who is, the One who had been, and the One who is coming" (a.t.), is used as a comp. indeclinable proper name of God, and governed by apó (575), from (Rev 1:4, 8; 11:17; 16:5). In Rom 4:17, "those that are not as those that were" (a.t.), meaning things existing and things not existing. Used metaphorically in 1 Cor 1:28.

(II) As a logical copula or link connecting the subj. and predicate, to be, where the predicate specifies who or what a person or thing is in respect to nature, origin, office, condition, circumstances, state, place, habits, disposition of mind. But this all lies in the predicate and not in the copula, which merely connects the predicate with the subj. The predicate may be made by various parts of speech, thus:

(A) With an adj. as predicate which is strictly the more logical construction. Matt 2:6, "thou Bethlehem . . . art not the least among the princes of Judah," the predicate being elachístē (1646), the least. See Matt 18:8; Mark 1:7; John 4:12; 5:32; Acts 7:6; Rom 8:29; 1 John 1:9. With a neg. adj. oudén (3762), none, meaning it is nothing (Matt 23:16; 1 Cor

7:19; 13:2). With *mēdén*, the neut. of *mēdeís* (3367), none (Gal 6:3). With numerals as in Mark 5:13, "they were about two thousand," "two thousand" being the predicate. Also in the phrase, *heís* (1520), one (masc.) or *hén* (neut.), followed by the inf. *eínai*, spoken of two or more, meaning to be one in mind and purpose (John 10:30; 17:11, 22). To be one in rank, right, (1 Cor 3:8; 12:12; Gal 3:28). In this construction, *eimí* with an adj. sometimes forms a periphrasis for the cognate verb; e.g., *dunatós eimí* (*dunatós* [1415], able), I am able, I can (Luke 14:31; Acts 11:17; Rom 4:21). In 2 Tim 3:9, *ékdēlos* (1552), manifest, followed by *eimí*, means to manifest myself, equivalent to the mid. form of the verb *ekdēloúmai*.

(B) With a noun as predicate, in the same case with the subj. **(1)** Particularly in Matt 3:4, "his meat was locusts." See also Matt 3:17; 15:14; Mark 2:28; 10:47; Acts 2:32; 3:25; 28:6; Rom 8:24; Heb 11:1. In Matt 7:12 "this is the law," means this is contained in the Law. Sometimes the noun or pron. of the predicate is not directly expressed, but only implied as in Matt 14:27, "It is I," I am, meaning I am Jesus. In John 13:13, *eimí gár* (1063), "for," implying the teacher, for I am the teacher; in John 18:5, "I am," implying Jesus. Also *houtós estín* (3778), this one is, implying John in Mark 6:16. See Luke 7:27; John 7:25; 9:9. Followed by the dat. of person or thing for or in respect to whom the predicate is asserted as in Acts 1:8, "and ye shall be witnesses unto me"; 9:15; Rom 1:14; 1 Cor 1:18; 2:14; 9:2, "If I be not an apostle unto others, yet doubtless I am to you." **(2)** Metaphorically and metonymically, the subst. of the predicate often expresses not what the subj. actually is, but what it is like or is accounted to be, by means of comparison, substitution, or cause and effect. Thus *eimí* may be rendered to be accounted, to be like or in place of, to mean as in Matt 5:13, 14, "Ye are the salt of the earth . . . the light of the world"; Matt 12:50, "he is my brother and my sister and my mother" (a.t.), meaning as

my brother, sister, mother; Matt 13:37–39; 19:6; Luke 8:11, "The seed is the word of God"; Luke 12:1; John 1:4, "the life was the light of men" (see John 1:8; 4:34; 6:33, 35, 41, 48, 50, 51, 55; 11:25; 12:50; 15:1, 5; Acts 4:11; 1 Cor 3:10; 4:17; 10:4; Eph 5:8; James 4:14; Rev 4:5; 21:22. In the words of Christ, "This is my body . . . this is my blood" [Matt 26:26, 28; Mark 14:22, 24; Luke 22:19; 1 Cor 11:24]; though Lutherans have strong arguments against this).

(III) *Eimí* with the subst. of the predicate sometimes forms a periphrasis for the corresponding verb as in 1 Cor 10:6 where *epithumētēs* (1938), a craver, is preceded by *eimí* instead of using the verb *epithuméō* (1937), to desire. See 1 Cor 14:12.

(IV) With a pron. as predicate, in the same case with the subj. as *houtos* (3778), this, the following (John 1:19, "this is the testimony" [a.t.]; John 15:12; 17:3). With *autós* (846), this (Luke 24:39; Heb 1:12). With *tís* (5101), who, or the neut. *tí*, indef. meaning someone, anything (1 Cor 10:19). Metaphorically of importance (Acts 5:36, "that he is important" [a.t.]; 1 Cor 3:7). With *tís*, *tí*, the interrogatives meaning who, what (John 5:13; Acts 21:22, "What is it then?" [a.t.] implying what is to be done; Rom 14:4; 1 Cor 9:18; 14:15, 26; Heb 12:7; James 4:12). With *poíos* (4169), who (Mark 12:28). With *pósos* (4214), how much (Mark 9:21). With *potapós* (4217), of what possible kind (Luke 1:29). With *hopoíos* (3697), of the kind that (Acts 26:29). With *hóstis* (3748), whoever (Gal 5:10, 19). With the poss. pron. as *emós* (1699), mine, *sós* (4674), thine (John 17:10). With *huméteros* (5212), your own (Luke 6:20). Metaphorically as with nouns (see B, 2), the predicate often expresses not what the subj. actually is, but what it is accounted to be or means; e.g., as in *tí estin*, *tó*, what that means (Matt 9:13; Mark 1:27, "What is it?" [a.t.]; Mark 9:10; Luke 15:26, "What mean these?" [a.t.]; Luke 20:17; John 18:38, "What is truth?"; Acts 2:12; 10:17; 17:20; Eph 4:9). In Luke 8:9,

"What might this parable be?" *Tout' ésti*, meaning that is (Matt 27:46; Acts 19:4; Rom 1:12).

(V) With a gen. of a noun or pron. as predicate spoken:

(A) Of quality, character (Luke 9:55, "You do not know of what manner of spirit you are" [a.t.]; Acts 9:2; Heb 12:11).

(B) Of age (Mark 5:42, "she was twelve years old" [a.t.]; Acts 4:22).

(C) Of a whole of which the subj. is a part (Acts 23:6, "one part were Sadducees"; 1 Tim 1:15).

(D) Of possession, property (Matt 5:3, 10, "theirs is the kingdom of heaven"; Mark 12:7, 23; Luke 4:7; John 19:24; Acts 21:11). Metaphorically of persons or things to whom the subj. belongs, appertains, or on whom it is in any way dependent; e.g., of God (2 Cor 4:7); of a master, teacher, guide (Acts 27:23; Rom 14:8; 1 Cor 1:12; 3:4, 23; 2 Cor 10:7); of things which one follows after (1 Thess 5:5, 8); implying fitness, propriety (Acts 1:7, "It is not proper for you to know the times" [a.t.]; Heb 5:14, "strong meat belongs to them that are of full age" [a.t.]).

(VI) With the dat. of a noun or pron. as predicate, to be to someone, implying possession, property (Luke 12:20; John 17:9, "for they are thine"; Acts 2:39; 1 Cor 9:16, 18; 1 Pet 4:11). By inverting the construction, it may be rendered "to have" (Luke 7:41, "a certain creditor which had two debtors," as also Luke 6:32–34; John 18:39; Acts 8:21; 21:23; Eph 6:12, "we wrestle not against," i.e., we have not a struggle against), or to receive (Matt 19:27, "what shall we receive?" [a.t.]).

(VII) With a part. of another verb as predicate.

(A) Without the art., *eimí* often forms with the part. a periphrasis for a finite tense of the same verb, expressing, however, a continuance or duration of the action or state, like the corresponding construction in Eng. as in Luke 5:1, *kaí autós én hestó*, "and he was standing" [a.t.], instead of the imperf. *hístē*, he stood. In Matt 24:9, "and ye shall be hated by all" [a.t.]; Mark

2:6, "and there were some sitting" [a.t.]; Mark 2:18; 9:4; 13:25, "the stars shall be falling" [a.t.]; Mark 15:43; Luke 3:23; 5:17; 24:32; Acts 1:10; 2:2, 42. With the part. of the perf. pass. which, however, assumes nearly the nature of an adj. as in Matt 9:36, "they fainted, and were scattered abroad"; Mark 6:52, "their heart was hardened"; 1 John 1:4. Used in impersonals as *déon estín* (*déon* [1163], must), it is necessary (Acts 19:36); *prépon estí* (*prépon* [4241], proper), used instead of *prépei* as (1 Cor 11:13). In some cases the part. is not a predicate and then *eimí* is not thus an auxiliary, e.g., Mark 10:32, "they were in the way going up to Jerusalem" where *en tē hodō*, "in the way," is the predicate and *anabaínontes*, "going up," is an adjunct. See Luke 7:8.

(B) With the art. where the part. may then be regarded as equivalent to a noun, or as an emphatic shorter construction instead of a personal tense of the verb as in Matt 3:3, "he is the one" (a.t.) or the person spoken of, the predicted, where *ho rētheís* instead of *hós erréthē* is used. See Matt 13:19; Mark 7:15, "those are they that defile the man"; John 4:10; Acts 2:16; Rom 3:11; 1 John 5:5; Jude 1:19; Rev 2:23; 14:4, "these are the ones following" (a.t.), which refers to the preceding construction, "these are they which were not defiled."

(VIII) With an adv. as a predicate, e.g., of quality or character, as *houtōs* (3779), thus, as in John 3:8, "thus" (a.t.) or "so is every one"; Matt 19:10; *houtōs éstai*, "so shall . . . be" (Rom 4:18. See Matt 24:27; Luke 17:24, 26). Followed by the dat. (Matt 12:45; Luke 11:30). *Taúta* (5023), these, as an adv. as *houtōs* (3779), so, thus (Luke 17:30; 1 Cor 6:11). *Hōs*, meaning according as (Rev 22:12); of likeness (Matt 22:30; 28:3; Luke 6:40); *hōsper* (5618), just as (Matt 6:5; Luke 18:11). Followed by the dat. (Matt 18:17); of plenty or want, *perissotérōs* (4056), more abundantly (2 Cor 7:15). With *chōrís* (5565), without (Heb 12:8); of place, as a place where, e.g., *eggús* (1451), near (John 11:18; Rom 10:8).

With *ekeí* (1563), there (Matt 18:20; Mark 3:1). With *makrán* (3112), far off (Mark 12:34; John 21:8). With *hópou* (3699), where (Mark 5:40; John 7:34; 18:1). With *pou* (4226), where (Matt 2:2; John 7:11). With *hóde* (5602), in this same spot (Matt 12:6; Rev 13:10). Of place or origin, *póthen* (4159), whence (Matt 21:25; John 2:9; 7:27). With *enteúthen* (1782), hence (John 18:36). Of time, with *eggús* (1451), near (Matt 26:18).

(IX) With a prep. and a noun as predicate.

(A) *Apó* (575), from (John 1:44). See *apó* (575, III, A).

(B) *Eis* (1519), unto, with the acc., as marking that which anything becomes (cf. above in I, B, 2). As denoting direction, object, end, *eis tí* (Luke 5:17, "and the power of the Lord was present to heal them"). Of a person, *eis tína* (1 Pet 1:21, "be [or rest] in God"). Adv. (1 Cor 4:3, "But with me it is a very small thing that I should be judged"). Spoken of place, whither or where (Mark 2:1, "that he was in the house"; Mark 13:16; Luke 11:7; John 1:18).

(C) *Ek* (1537), of or out of with the gen. always implying origin; spoken of place (Mark 11:30; John 1:46, "Out of Nazareth can there come anything good?" [a.t.]; Acts 23:34). Of family, race (Luke 2:4; Acts 4:6). Of persons or things as the source, author, cause (Matt 1:20, "He is of the Holy Spirit" [a.t.]; 5:37; Mark 11:30; John 4:22; 7:17, "his teaching is of God" [a.t.]; 8:23; 15:19; 17:14; Acts 5:38; 19:25; Gal 3:21; 1 John 2:16). Hence, metaphorically of a person on whom one is dependent or to whom he is devoted as a follower (John 8:47, "ye are not of God," i.e., not His followers, adherers. See John 8:44, "Ye are of . . . the devil," i.e. you originate from him; 1 John 3:10; 4:6). Of things such as the truth (John 18:37; 1 John 3:19); "of the works of the law" (Gal 3:10); "the law is not of faith," i.e., it depends not on faith, has no connection with it (Gal 3:12); "of one pearl" (Rev 21:21). Of a whole in relation to a part (1 Cor 12:15, 16, "am I not of the body?" [a.t.] means, Am I not part of the whole body?). Of persons (Matt 26:73, "thou also art one of them" [a.t.]; Luke 22:3, "being of the number of the twelve"; John 1:24; 10:16; 18:17, 25; Col 4:9; 2 Tim 3:6).

(D) *En* (1722), in, with the dat. implying location in a place, thing, person. Spoken of place (Mark 1:3, "in the wilderness"; John 2:23, "in Jerusalem"; Acts 5:12; Rev 9:10). Of things; *en toútō* (5129), in this, i.e., herein (John 9:30; 1 John 4:10); *en toútois ísthi*, "be wholly in these things" (a.t.), occupied with them (1 Tim 4:15); *en sarkí eínai* (1722, 4561), to be in the flesh, i.e., followers of the world, aliens from God (Rom 7:5). In 1 Cor 2:5, "that your faith may not be in the wisdom of men, but in the power of God" (a.t.) means consist in, depend on. Of a state, condition (Mark 5:25, "being in a state of blood flowing" [a.t.]; Luke 23:40; Phil 4:11; 1 John 2:9). Of persons, to be in someone, where the subj. is a thing (John 11:10, "the light is not in him" [a.t.], i.e., in his path, around him; Acts 25:5, what is in or on this man, i.e., in his conduct). Also of faculties, virtues, vices, which are in someone (John 1:4, 48; Acts 4:12; 20:10). Where the subj. is a person, i.e., to be near and in intimate union with, to be one with, as in mind, purpose, feeling: of God and Christ (John 14:10, 11); of Christ in His followers (2 Cor 13:5); of the Spirit in Christians (John 14:17); of Christians in Christ (Rom 16:11; 1 Cor 1:30; 1 John 5:20). Followed by the dat. pl., to be among (Matt 27:56); in the midst of (1 Cor 14:25).

(E) With *epí* (1909), upon, followed by the gen. of place, meaning upon (Luke 17:31; John 20:7). Metaphorically of dignity, station, meaning over (Acts 8:27; Rom 9:5). Followed by the dat. of place, meaning upon, in, at (Matt 24:33; Mark 4:38). Followed by the acc. of place, as *eínai epí tó autó*, to be together (1 Cor 7:5 [3rd ed. UBS], spoken of conjugal relationship). Of persons, *eínai epí* followed by the acc., to be upon someone means to be or rest upon, used metaphorically in Acts 4:33.

(F) With *katá* (2596), against, followed by the gen., to be against someone (Matt 12:30; Gal 5:23); by the acc. of thing, to be according to, in accordance with (Luke 17:30; Rom 2:2; 2 Cor 11:15).

(G) With *metá* (3326), with, followed by the gen., to be with someone, present with, in company with (Matt 17:17; Mark 2:19; Luke 23:43); to be for or on the side of someone as an adherent, helper (Matt 12:30; John 3:2; Acts 7:9; 18:10; Phil 4:9); to be devoted to someone (2 John 1:2, 3).

(H) With *pará* (3844), from, followed by the gen., to be from someone, sent by someone (John 6:46; 7:29); received from someone (John 17:7); by the acc. of place, to be by, on, at (Mark 5:21).

(I) With *pró* (4253), before, followed by the gen. of place, to be before (Acts 14:13). Metaphorically of dignity (Col 1:17).

(J) With *prós* (4314), near, followed by the acc. of place, to be near to, by (Mark 4:1; Luke 24:29). Of persons, to be near, with, among (Matt 13:56; Mark 9:19).

(K) With *sún* (4862), together, followed by the dat., to be with someone, present with, in company with (Luke 24:44; Phil 1:23; Col 2:5; 1 Thess 4:17); as a follower, disciple (Luke 8:38; Acts 4:13); as a partisan (Acts 14:4).

(L) With *hupér* (5228), for, followed by the gen., to be for someone, on his side (Mark 9:40); by the acc. of person, to be above someone (metaphorically in Luke 6:40).

(M) With *hupó* (5259), under, with the acc., to be under, spoken of place (John 1:48; 1 Cor 10:1). Of person or thing, to be subject to (Rom 3:9; Gal 3:10; 1 Tim 6:1).

As a copula or link, the forms of *eimí* are very frequently omitted (Matt 9:37; 13:54; Mark 9:23; 1 Cor 10:26; 11:12).

Deriv.: *ápeimi* (548), to be absent; *éneimi* (1751), to be within; *páreimi*

(3918), to be present; *súneimi* (4895), to be with.

Syn.: *gínomai* (1096), to begin to be, to come to pass; *hupárchō* (5225), to be in existence.

Ant.: *aphanízō* (853), to cause to disappear; *dialúō* (1262), to dissolve; *analískō* (355) and the mid. *analískomai*, to consume, be consumed; *teleutáō* (5053), to finish life, be dead; *sbénnumi* (4570), to extinguish.

1511. εἶναι *eínai*; pres. inf. of *eimí* (1510), to be, to exist.

1512. εἴ περ *eí per* conditional expression from *ei* (1487), if, and *pér* (4007), perhaps. If indeed, if so be, assuming the supposition as true whether justly or not (1 Cor 15:15; 1 Pet 2:3). By implication it means since, equivalent to *eíge* (1489), if indeed, seeing that, unless (Rom 8:9, 17; 1 Cor 8:5; 15:15; 2 Thess 1:6; 1 Pet 2:3). See *ge* (1065, II, 3).

1513. εἴ πως *eí pōs* conditional expression from *ei* (1487), if, and *pós* (4458), how. If by any means, if possibly; with the opt. (Acts 27:12) implying that the thing in question is possible but uncertain and problematical, though assumed as probable (Sept.: 2 Sam 16:12). With the fut. indic. (Rom 1:10; 11:14; Phil 3:11; Sept.: 2 Kgs 19:4).

1514. εἰρηνεύω *eirēneúō*; fut. *eirēneúsō*, from *eirḗnē* (1515), peace. To make peace, be at peace (1 Kgs 22:44). In the NT metaphorically to live in peace, harmony, accord. Used in an absolute sense in 2 Cor 13:11. In 1 Thess 5:13, "be at peace among yourselves"; Mark 9:50, "with each other" (a.t.); Rom 12:18, "with all."

Syn.: *eirēnopoiéō* (1517), to make peace, should be distinguished from *eirēneúō*. The latter causes peace to come to the parties concerned and to prevail while the former indicates merely the cessation of hostilities and emphasizes the condition of the absence of quarrelling or fighting; *sigáō* (4601), to be silent, to hold one's peace; *hēsucházō* (2270), hold one's peace; *phimóō* (5392), to muzzle, hold one's peace.

Ant.: *diatarássō* (1298), to disturb, agitate greatly; *tarássō* (5015), to stir or agitate, trouble; *anastatóō* (387), to disturb, make an uproar; *diegeírō* (1326), to arouse, stir up; *maínomai* (3105), to be mad; *turbázō* (5182), to disturb, trouble; *máchomai* (3162), to fight; *poleméō* (4170), to be in warfare.

1515. εἰρήνη *eirḗnē*; gen. *eirḗnēs*, fem. noun. Peace.

(I) Particularly in a civil sense, the opposite of war and dissension (Luke 14:32; Acts 12:20; Rev 6:4). Among individuals, peace, harmony (Matt 10:34; Luke 12:51; Acts 7:26; Rom 14:19). In Heb 7:2, "King of peace," means a peaceful king. Metaphorically peace of mind, tranquility, arising from reconciliation with God and a sense of a divine favor (Rom 5:1; 15:13; Phil 4:7 [cf. Isa 53:5]).

(II) By implication, a state of peace, tranquility (Luke 2:29; 11:21; John 16:33; Acts 9:31; 1 Cor 14:33; 1 Thess 5:3; Sept.: Judg 6:23; Isa 14:30; Ezek 38:8, 11).

(III) Peace, meaning health, welfare, prosperity, every kind of good. In Luke 1:79, "the way of peace" means the way of happiness; 2:14; 10:6, "son of peace" means son of happiness, i.e., one worthy of it; 19:42; Rom 8:6; Eph 6:15, "gospel of peace" means gospel of bliss, i.e., which leads to bliss; 2 Thess 3:16. "The God of peace" means the author and giver of blessedness (Rom 15:33; 16:20; Phil 4:9; 1 Thess 5:23; Heb 13:20 [cf. Sept.: Isa 9:6, "the Prince of Peace"]. "Your peace" means the good or blessing which you have in Christ and share through salutation and benediction (Matt 10:13; Luke 10:6; John 14:27). The expression "with peace" means with good wishes, benediction, kindness (Acts 15:33; Heb 11:31). Simply "in peace" (1 Cor 16:11; Sept.: Gen 26:29; Ex 18:23). As used in formulas of salutation, either at meeting or parting, see *aspázomai* (782), to embrace, to greet. Thus on meeting, the salutation is "Peace be unto you [*eirḗnē humín*]," meaning every good wish (Luke 24:36; John 20:19, 21, 26; Dan 10:19). Also in letters (Rom 1:7; 2:10; 1 Cor 1:3; 2 Cor 1:2; Gal 1:3). In Luke 10:5, "Peace unto this house" (a.t.) means every good wish for this house; Sept.: Judg 19:20; 1 Chr 12:18. At parting, *húpage* (5217), go, meaning to go away in peace (Mark 5:34; James 2:16). The same with the verb *poreúou* from *poreúomai* (4198), to go in peace (Luke 7:50; 8:48; Acts 16:36; Sept.: Judg 18:6; 1 Sam 1:17; 20:42).

(IV) In the OT the equivalent word *shalom* (7965, OT) meant wholeness, soundness, hence health, well-being, prosperity; more particularly, peace as opposed to war (Judg 4:17; 1 Sam 7:14; Eccl 3:8 [cf. Luke 14:32; Acts 12:20; Rev 6:4]), or concord as opposed to strife (Ps 28:3; Jer 9:8; Obad 1:7 [cf. Matt 10:34; 1 Cor 7:15; Eph 4:3 {see also Acts 24:2; 1 Thess 5:3; Ps 122:7; Isa 52:7; Jer 29:7}]).

(V) God is said to be a God of peace, not as one who needs peace, but one who dispenses peace. He expects peace of His people, meaning the absence of confusion (Rom 14:17; 1 Cor 7:15; 14:33; Eph 4:3; Heb 12:14; Ps 34:14; 35:20; Zech 8:16). He rewards those who practice this peace (James 3:18 [cf. Matt 5:9]), but those who disregard it are punished (Rom 3:17 [cf. Isa 59:8, 9]). Peace is a blessing of which God alone is the author (Job 25:2; Ps 147:14; Isa 45:7). He, being the author of peace, is the only one who can bestow it upon the righteous (Gen 15:15, upon Abraham; 2 Kgs 22:20, upon Josiah; Ps 37:37, upon the perfect man; 119:165, upon those who love God's law; Prov 3:2, upon those who follow divine wisdom [cf. James 3:18; Ps 4:8; Job 5:23; Isa 32:17]). It is a gift which God desires to impart to all His people (Jer 29:11), but which He is often unable to grant because of their sins (Sept.: Isa 48:18; Jer 4:10 [cf. Jer 4:14]). There can be no peace to the wicked (Sept.: Isa 57:19 [cf. Isa 57:20,

21; 48:22]). Those who hope for it, while continuing in their iniquity, are self-deceived (Sept.: Jer 6:14; 8:15 [cf. Jer 8:11; Ezek 13:10, 16]).

(VI) Peace is the paramount blessing that Israel was looking for in the messianic kingdom (Num 25:12; Lev 26:6; Isa 54:10; Ezek 34:25; 37:26; Mal 2:5, 6). The messenger who brings tidings of the coming salvation is one who publishes peace (Isa 52:7; Nah 1:15). The Messiah Himself is the Prince of Peace (Isa 9:6 [cf. Mic 5:5; Zech 6:13]). Of the increase of His government and peace there shall be no end (Isa 9:7). See Ps 29:11; 37:11; 72:3, 7, "In his days the righteous shall flourish; and abundance of peace so long as the moon endureth"; 122:7; Isa 54:13; 60:17; 66:12; Jer 4:10; 6:14; 8:15; 14:13; 23:17; 28:9; 33:6; Hag 2:9. The NT shares with the OT the view of peace as a characteristic of the messianic time (Luke 1:79; 2:14; 19:38; Acts 10:36). The identification of the coming of the Lord Jesus with the coming of the Messiah is often what the disciples meant with their greetings on their missionary journeys (Matt 10:13; Luke 10:5, 6). In His farewell words to His disciples, Jesus names peace as a gift to them from Himself (John 14:27; 16:33, "My peace I give unto you . . . these things I have spoken unto you, that in me ye might have peace").

(VII) Characteristic of the NT is the view of peace as the present possession of the believer. In a single case it is used by Paul of that future blessedness which is to be expected by the righteous and the *Parousía* or Second Coming (Rom 2:10), but in general it denotes the state of the Christian in this present life. It is so used by Jesus in His farewell promise, "My peace I give unto you" (John 14:27). It is thus represented by Paul (Rom 5:1; 8:6; 15:13; 2 Thess 3:16; Col 3:15), in which case peace acquires the technical meaning of the tranquil state of a soul assured of its salvation through Christ, fearing nothing from God and consequently content with its earthly lot, whatever it is.

This is the direct result of redemption by Christ (Eph 2:15, 17) and consists primarily of a state of conscious reconciliation with God (Rom 5:1), although it is often used in a broader sense to denote all the blessings which accompany and flow from that reconciliation (Rom 1:7; 1 Cor 1:3; 2 Thess 3:16).

(VIII) Words with which *eirḗnē* are associated in the NT are as follows: *agápē* (26), love (2 Cor 13:11; Eph 6:23, "Peace . . . and love with faith"); *cháris* (5485), grace (Rom 1:7; 1 Cor 1:3; 2 Cor 1:2; Gal 1:3; Eph 1:2; Phil 1:2; Col 1:2; 1 Thess 1:1; 2 Thess 1:2; 1 Tim 1:2; 2 Tim 1:2; Titus 1:4; Phile 1:3; 1 Pet 1:2; 2 Pet 1:2; 2 John 1:3; Rev 1:4); *dóxa* (1391), glory, and *timḗ* (5092), honor as the eschatological reward for working well (Rom 2:10); *dikaiosúnē* (1343), righteousness; *chará* (5479), joy (Rom 14:17); hope and joy (Rom 15:13); peace and mercy (Gal 6:16) *aspháleia* (803), safety, security, as the opposite of eschatological peril (1 Thess 5:3). The NT concept of peace has nothing to do with the Stoic concept of *apátheia* (n.f.), indifference or apathy, and the Epicurean *ataraxía* (n.f.), selfish nondisturbance. The peace which God gives is never to be identified with selfish unconcern (cf. 1 Cor 7:15; Phil 4:7; Col 3:15). God's peace is independent of outside conditions and is the fruit of an objective, real salvation with God.

Deriv.: *eirēneúō* (1514), to bring peace, reconcile; *eirēnikós* (1516), peaceful; *eirēnopoiéō* (1517), to make peace without necessarily effecting a change in the person or persons involved.

Syn.: *hēsuchía* (2271), quietness; *galḗnē* (1055), tranquility, calm.

Ant.: *pólemos* (4171), war; *agṓn* (73), fight, conflict, an athletic contest; *stenochōría* (4730), narrowness of room, anguish, distress; *sunochḗ* (4928), restrained anxiety; *mérimna* (3308), distraction, anxiety; *phóbos* (5401), fear; *tarachḗ* (5016), disturbance; *súgchusis* (4799), confusion; *thórubos* (2351), disturbance, tumult, uproar; *schísma* (4978), split, division, schism; *máchē* (3163), fight, strife.

1516. εἰρηνικός *eirēnikós*; fem. *eirē-nikḗ*, neut. *eirēnikón*, adj. from *eirḗnē* (1515), peace. Pertaining to peace, peaceable or peaceful (Heb 12:11, healthful, wholesome; James 3:17, peaceful, disposed to peace; Sept.: Deut 2:26; Ps 37:37; 120:7). The reference is to *eirḗnē* (1515), peace, as the blessing of salvation.

    Syn.: *hēsúchios* (2272), quiet, peaceful; *homóphrōn* (3675), harmonious, of one mind; *isópsuchos* (2473), of one soul, agreeable, like-minded; *éremos* (2263), tranquil.

    Ant.: *asúmphōnos* (800), disharmonious; *philóneikos* (5380), quarrelsome, contentious.

1517. εἰρηνοποιέω *eirēnopoiéō*; contracted *eirēnopoiṓ*, fut. *eirēnopoiḗso*, from *eirḗnē* (1515), peace, and *poiéō* (4160), to make. To make peace, reconciliation (Col 1:20; Sept.: Prov 10:10). *Eirēnopoiéō* concerns itself with bringing about a cessation of hostilities while *eirēneúō* (1514) affects the attitudes of those concerned, to be at peace.

    Deriv.: *eirēnopoiós* (1518), peacemaking or a peacemaker.

    Syn.: *diallássō* (1259), to conciliate, reconcile; *katallássō* (2644), to reconcile man to God when the change occurs in man; *apokatallássō* (604), to reconcile fully.

    Ant.: *poleméō* (4170), to fight, make war; *agōnízomai* (75), to fight, strive; *máchomai* (3164), to dispute, fight, strive; *strateúomai* (4754), to contend, go to war; *hoplízomai* (3695), to arm oneself; *antilégō* (483), to dispute, contradict; *antagōnízomai* (464), to antagonize.

1518. εἰρηνοποιός *eirēnopoiós*; gen. *eirēnopoioú*, masc. noun from *eirēnopoiéō* (1517), to make peace. Peacemaker. The one who, having received the peace of God in his own heart, brings

peace to others (only in Matt 5:9). He is not simply one who makes peace between two parties, but one who spreads the good news of the peace of God which he has experienced.

1519. εἰς *eis*; prep. governing the acc. with the primary idea of motion into any place or thing; also of motion or direction to, toward or upon any place, thing. The antithesis is expressed by *ek* (1537), out of.

    (I) Of place, which is the primary and most frequent use, meaning into, to.

    (A) After verbs implying motion of any kind, into or to, toward, upon any place or object, e.g., verbs of going, coming, leading, following, sending, growing, placing, delivering over to and the like (Matt 2:12; 4:8; 5:1; 6:6; 8:18; 12:44; 15:11, 17; 20:17; 21:18; Mark 1:38; 5:21; 6:45; 9:31; 13:14; Luke 8:23, 26; John 1:9; 7:14; 16:21, "is born into the world"; Acts 16:16; 26:14; Rom 5:12; 10:18; Rev 2:22). With the acc. of thing, implying place (Mark 4:22; 13:16; John 1:11; 7:8, 10; 16:32; 18:6; Acts 15:38; 21:6). With an acc. of person, but referring always to the place where the person dwells or is, and implying to, among (Luke 10:36; 21:24; Acts 18:6; 20:29; 22:21; Rom 5:12; 16:19; 2 Cor 9:5; 10:14; 1 Thess 1:5; Rev 16:2). Spoken also of persons meaning into whom demons have entered (Mark 9:25; Luke 8:30 [cf. Matt 8:31; Luke 15:17, "having come to himself" {a.t.}, i.e., to his right mind]).

    (B) After verbs implying duration, upon, or toward any place or object, e.g., verbs of hearing, calling, announcing, showing (Matt 10:27; 22:3, 4; Mark 5:14; 13:10; Luke 7:1; 24:47; John 8:26; Acts 11:22, "hearing in the ears" [a.t.]; 1 Cor 14:9; 2 Cor 8:24; 11:6). Especially after verbs of looking (Matt 5:35, "toward Jerusalem" [a.t.], i.e., turning or looking toward it; Matt 22:16; John 13:22; Acts 1:10, 11; 3:4; Heb 11:26). After nouns (Acts 9:2, "letters [directed] to Damascus"; Rom 15:31, "my service which I have for Jerusalem").

(C) Metaphorically of a state or condition into which one comes, after verbs of motion, duration (Matt 25:46; Mark 5:26; 9:43; Luke 22:33; 24:20; John 4:38; 5:24; 16:13; Acts 26:18; 2 Cor 10:5; Gal 1:6; Phil 1:12; 3:11; 1 Tim 2:4; 3:6; Heb 2:10). To baptize into somebody or into the name of somebody means to baptize into the obligations incumbent on a disciple of someone or to be identified with the character and purposes of such a person (Matt 28:19; Acts 8:16; Rom 6:3, 4). See *baptízō* (907), to baptize.

(II) Of time:

(A) Time meaning when, implying a term, limit, i.e., to, up to, until (Matt 10:22, *eis télos* [5056], the end, meaning accomplishment of the task undertaken; Acts 4:3, "till the morrow" [a.t.]; Acts 13:42; Phil 1:10, "unto the day of Christ" [a.t.], or in expectation of the day of Christ; Phil 2:16; 1 Thess 4:15; 2 Thess 2:6; 2 Pet 2:4; 3:7). With the acc. of person as marking the time when one lives, appears (Gal 3:17, 24, "unto Christ," meaning until Christ came).

(B) Time, meaning "how long" or marking duration (Matt 21:19, "unto the age" [a.t.], forever; Mark 3:29; Luke 1:50, "unto generations of generations" [a.t.]; 12:19, "unto many years" [a.t.]; John 8:35; 1 Tim 6:19; Heb 7:3; 2 Pet 3:18; Rev 9:15).

(III) Figuratively as marking the object or point to or toward which anything ends.

(A) Spoken of a result, effect, consequence, marking that which any person or thing inclines toward or becomes (Matt 13:30, "bind them in bundles"; 27:51, "split in parts" [a.t.]; John 17:23; Acts 2:20; 10:4, "your prayers went up unto remembrance" [a.t.]; Rom 10:10, "with the heart man believeth unto righteousness"; 1 Cor 11:17; 15:54; Eph 2:21, 22; Heb 6:6, 8; 1 Pet 1:22; Rev 11:6). With an inf. as subst. (Rom 7:4, 5; 12:3; 1 Cor 9:18; Gal 3:17; Heb 11:3). Thus *logízomai* (3049), to reckon someone or something unto, when used with *eis*, means to be considered as anything (Acts 19:27; Rom

2:26; 9:8; Sept.: 1 Sam 1:13; Isa 29:17). The expression *logízomai* followed by the dat., in connection with *eis* and the acc., means to reckon or to impute to someone, for, as (Rom 4:3, 5, 9, 22 "unto righteousness" [a.t.]; Gal 3:6 quoted from Gen 15:6; Ps 106:31). Also after verbs of constituting, making, becoming, and the like (Acts 13:22, "he raised up unto them David to be their king" or unto king [see Acts 13:47 {cf. Sept.: Ezek 37:22}]). With *eínai* (1511), to be (Matt 19:5, "they shall be into one flesh" [a.t.], indicating becoming one flesh; see Mark 10:8 [cf. Gen 2:24; Luke 3:5 {cf. Isa 40:4; 1 Cor 14:22; 2 Cor 6:18; Heb 1:5}]). With *gínomai* (1096), to become (Luke 13:19, became into a big tree, instead of became a great tree; John 16:20; Acts 5:36; Rom 11:10 quoted from Ps 69:23; 1 Cor 15:45; Rev 8:11).

(B) Spoken of measure, degree, extent, where *eis* can be translated "even," i.e., guilty even unto Gehenna (Matt 5:22). See *énochos* (1777), guilty of. Chiefly by way of periphrasis for an adv. as in Luke 13:11, *eis tó pantelés* (3838), i.e., entirely. In Heb 7:25, with the idea of perpetuity. In 2 Cor 4:17, *eis huperbolḗn* (5236), hyperbole, exceeding or exceedingly. In 2 Cor 10:13, *eis tá ámetra* (280), those things that cannot be measured means immeasurable, indefinitely extensive. In 2 Cor 13:2, *eis tó pálin* (3825), means simply again. Also *eis kenón* (2756), empty, vain, means in vain (2 Cor 6:1; Gal 2:2; Phil 2:16).

(C) Spoken of a direction of mind, i.e., as marking an object of desire, good will, also aversion **(1)** In a good sense, toward, for, in behalf of (Matt 26:10, "she did a good work for my benefit" [a.t.]; Rom 1:27, "one toward another" of homosexual lust; 10:1, "unto salvation" [a.t.] or for or toward salvation; 12:16; 14:19; 2 Cor 10:1; Phil 1:23, "desire to depart" or to die; 1 Thess 4:10; 5:15; 2 Pet 3:9; Jude 1:21, "unto eternal life"). Also after nouns, e.g., love on behalf of someone (Rom 5:8; 2 Cor 2:4, 8; Eph 1:15); the gift bestowed upon someone or for the good of someone (2 Cor 1:11). After an adj. (Eph 4:32 "kind one to another" [a.t.]; 1 Pet 4:9 "hospitable one to another" [a.t.]). With the verbs *elpízō* (1679), to hope, and *pisteúō* (4100), to believe, with *eis*, usually with a dat., in which case these verbs imply an affection or direction of mind toward a person or thing, i.e., to place hope or confidence in or upon (Matt 18:6, those "which believe [or place confidence] in me"; John 2:11; 5:45; 2 Cor 1:10 [cf. Acts 24:15]). The subst. *elpís* (1680), hope, or *pístis* (4102), faith, *eis* followed by the acc., hope or faith in someone (Acts 20:21; 24:24; 1 Pet 1:21). With *pepoíthēsis* (4006), confidence (2 Cor 8:22). (2) In an unfriendly sense, "against" (Matt 18:15; Mark 3:29; Luke 12:10, "whosoever speaks a word against the Son of man" [a.t.], against the Holy Spirit, indicated by *eis*; Acts 9:1; 1 Cor 6:18, to sin against; Col 3:9). Also after nouns as in Acts 23:30 with *epiboulḗ* (1917), a plan against; Rom 8:7 with *échthra* (2189), enmity against God; Heb 12:3 with *antilogía* (485), contradiction against him.

(D) Spoken of an intention, purpose, aim, end; *eis* final. (1) In the sense of unto, in order to or for, i.e., for the purpose of, for the sake of, on account of (Matt 8:4, 34; 27:7, 10; Mark 1:4; Luke 5:4; 22:19; 24:20; John 1:7; 9:39; Acts 4:30; 11:29; 14:26; Rom 1:16, 17; 5:21; 6:19; 9:21; 10:4; 15:18; 1 Cor 2:7; 2 Cor 2:12; Eph 4:12; 1 Tim 1:16). In Matt 3:11, to "baptize . . . unto repentance" or on account of repentance, could mean that no one has a right to be baptized unless he repents. In 1 Cor 12:13, "we were baptized into one body . . . we were made to drink into one spirit" (a.t.), refers to the spiritual baptism whereby we are made members of the body of Christ through the operation of that one Holy Spirit of which we were made to drink which satisfies our thirst. Therefore, believers, being members of the same body of Christ and participating of the same Holy Spirit, are one in body and spirit. In Matt 18:20, "gathered together in my name," means

on My account, because of Me, for My sake, in order to promote My cause. Also before an inf. with the art., in order to, in order that (Matt 20:19; Mark 14:55; Luke 20:20; Rom 1:11; 11:11; James 1:18). With the acc. meaning to what end? wherefore? why? (Matt 14:31; Mark 15:34). With *toúto* (5124), this, *eis toúto*, meaning to this end, for this purpose, therefore (Mark 1:38; Acts 9:21; Rom 9:17). Followed by the relative pron. *hó*, *eis hó*, meaning to which end, whereunto, (2 Thess 1:11; 1 Pet 2:8). (2) In the sense of to or for, implying use, advantage and equivalent to the dat. of purpose (Matt 5:13; 10:10; 20:1, "to hire workers unto his vineyard" [a.t.] or to serve his vineyard; Mark 8:19, 20; Luke 7:30, "unto themselves" [a.t.], i.e., to their own detriment; 9:13; 14:35, "neither for serving the land nor for the dunghill" [a.t.]; John 6:9; Acts 2:22; Rom 11:36; 15:26; 16:6; 1 Cor 8:6, unto him, for him, i.e., for his honor and glory; 2 Cor 8:6; Gal 4:11; Eph 1:5; 3:2; 1 Pet 1:4).

(E) Generally as marking the obj. of any reference, relation, allusion unto or toward, i.e., with reference to. (1) In accordance with, conformable to (Matt 10:41, 42, "He who receives a prophet in the name of a prophet" [a.t.], means in accordance with the character of a prophet, or as a prophet, or with the honor deserving of a prophet). In Matt 12:41; Luke 11:32, "they repented at [*eis*] the preaching of Jonah," where *eis*, into, means conformable to or at the preaching of Jonah. In Acts 7:53, "received the law by the disposition of angels," *eis* means conformable to or in consequence of the arrangements of angels. See *diatagḗ* (1296), arrangement. (2) In the sense meaning as, as to, in respect to, concerning (Luke 12:21, "not rich toward [*eis*] God" means in respect to God; Acts 2:25, "For David speaketh concerning [*eis*] him"; 25:20, "because I doubted of such manner of questions," *eis tḗn . . . zḗtēsin* [2214], searching, question, where *eis* [TR] means concerning; Rom 4:20; 13:14; 16:5, 19; 2 Cor 2:9; 9:8; Gal

6:4; Eph 3:16; 5:32; 1 Thess 5:18; 2 Tim 2:14; Heb 7:14; 1 Pet 3:21).

(IV) Sometimes *eis* with the acc. is found where the natural construction would seem to require *en* with the dat. as after verbs which imply neither motion nor direction, but simply rest in a place or state. In such cases the idea of a previous coming into that place or state is either actually expressed or is implied in the context (Matt 2:23; Mark 1:38, 39; 2:1, "that he was come into the house" [a.t.]; 13:9, 16; Luke 11:7, as we would say in Eng., my children are in bed, i.e., they had gone there before and they are now in bed; 21:37; John 9:7; Acts 7:4; 8:40; 18:21; 21:12, 13; 23:11). Here belongs also in the NT the apparent construction of *eis* with a gen. through the omission of its noun as *eis hádou*, as found in Acts 2:27, 31; the noun omitted is *oíkon* (3624), house. The expression would be *eis oíkon hádou*, which could have been also stated *eis hádēn*. The phrase in Acts is *egkataleípseis*, the fut. indic. act. of *egkataleípō* (1459), to leave behind or in it, *eis Hádou* (quoted from Ps 16:10), to leave behind in *Hádēs* (86), the realm of the dead. In other instances, *eis* and *en* are used alternately according to the different trend of thought, e.g., in John 20:19, 26, "came Jesus and stood in [*eis*] the midst," but Luke 24:36 uses *en* (1722), in. Here the attention of John is fixed more on Jesus' coming and standing, while that of Luke is on His actual presence. See also John 21:4 (cf. 8:3, 9; Acts 4:7). In Matt 13:2; Mark 13:3 we have *eis*, and in Matt 26:29 we have *en*. See Matt 3:6, *en*, where the attention is fixed upon the act of baptism, while in Mark 1:9, it is also on the coming of Jesus to the Jordan. The expression "Go in peace" can have either *eis* or *en*, go away into peace or in peace (*eirḗnē* [1515], peace). It means into or in the enjoyment of peace, good, the idea being in the final analysis the same, but expressed under different aspects (Mark 5:34; Luke 7:50 [cf. Acts 16:36; James 2:16]).

(V) In composition, *eis* implies motion into, as *eisdéchomai* (1523), to take into one's favor, receive; *eíseimi* (1524), to enter into; *eisérchomai* (1525), to enter in; *eisphérō* (1533), to bring in. Motion or direction, direction to, toward, as *eisakoúō* (1522), to listen to, hear.

(VI) In its relationship with other prep., *prós* (4314), toward, *eis* denotes entry into, while *prós* denotes approach, up to. *Eis* is used with impersonal objects and *prós* with personal (2 Cor 1:15, *prós* twice and *eis* once). In Gal 2:9, "That we should go unto [*eis*] the heathen [the nations, the Gentiles], and they unto [*eis*] the circumcision [the Jews]." Here reference is made to the territories where Jews or Gentiles abounded. Both prepositions may express purpose. In Rom 3:25, "to declare his righteousness [*eis*]," while in Rom 3:26, "to declare [*prós*]." Both prepositions may be used also to express result. In Rom 1:20, "so that they are without excuse [*eis*]"; in 1 John 5:16, "which is not unto death [*prós*]," resulting in death. The prep. *prós* is used in John 1:1, 2, and *eis* in John 1:18, and both figure importantly in the eternal and equal relationship between God the Father and God the Son. "In the beginning was the Word, and the Word was toward [*prós*] the God. The same was in the beginning toward [*prós*] the God" (a.t.). *Prós* here is used to indicate the communion of the Son with the Father. In verse eighteen, to show the role that the Son was going to play in the incarnation, *eis* is used indicating that the Father was in the Lord and the Lord Jesus was in the Father (cf. John 10:38), and that the Son and the Father have always been one (John 10:30). And yet, insofar as the incarnation was concerned, Jesus Christ, the eternal Son, was in (*eis*) the bosom of the Father as if He were someone who could be separated from the Father in His new temporary existence as the God-Man (John 1:1, 14), but never separated in the eternal Father-Son relationship. In John 10:38, to show forcefully the deity of the incarnate Son, the prep. *en* (1722), in, is used, "In me the Father and I in him" (a.t.). When we think of the Father, we see all of deity; and when we see Jesus Christ the Son incarnate, we see God not as spirit (John 4:24), but as a human being with bodily reality (Col 1:19; 2:9).

1520. εἷς heís; fem. *mía*, neut. *hén*; gen. masc. *henós*, fem. *miás* (3391), neut. *henós*. One, the first cardinal numeral.

(I) Without the subst. (Luke 18:19, "No one is good except one, God" [a.t.]; 1 Cor 9:24; Gal 3:20). In Matt 25:15, "to one he gave five talents, to the one two, to the other one [omitting the subst. talent repeated]" (a.t.). With a subst. (Matt 5:41, "one mile" [a.t.]; 6:27, "one cubit"; Mark 10:8, the two into one flesh; John 11:50; Acts 17:26; 1 Cor 10:8. With a neg., equivalent to not one, none (Matt 5:18, "one jot or one tittle shall in no wise pass"; Rom 3:12, "not so much as one" [a.t.], not even one, quoted from Ps 14:3; 53:4; Sept.: Judg 4:16 [cf. Ex 9:7]). The expression *oudé* (3761), nor, followed by *heís* in the masc. or in the neut. *oudé hén*, not one, not even one, more emphatic than *oudeís* (3762), not even one. See Matt 27:14; John 1:3; Acts 4:32; Rom 3:10; 1 Cor 6:5. With the art. *ho heís*, masc., and *tó hén*, neut., the one (Matt 25:18, 24; 1 Cor 10:17). In Matt 5:19, "one of these least commandments"; Mark 6:15, "one of the prophets"; Luke 5:3; John 12:2. Also with *ek* (1537), of, followed by the gen. (Matt 18:12, "one of them"; Mark 9:17; Acts 11:28; Rev 5:5).

(II) Used distributively:

(A) *Heís / heís*, one / one, i.e., one / the other (Matt 20:21; 24:41; 27:38; John 20:12), fem. *mía / mía*. Also with the art. *ho heís / ho heís*, the one / the other (Matt 24:40). In 1 Thess 5:11, *heís tón héna*, one another. In 1 Cor 4:6, *heís hupér* (5228), above, *toú henós*, the one above the other. In Matt 17:4, *mían / mían / mían*, one tent for each of the three, Jesus, Moses, and Elijah. See Mark 4:8; Luke 9:33; Sept.: Lev 12:8; 1 Sam 10:3; 13:17, 18; 2 Chr 3:17. With the art. *ho heís / ho héteros*, the one / the other (Matt 6:24; Luke 7:41;

Acts 23:6). In Rev 17:10, *ho heís / ho állos* (243), other, the one / the other.

(B) *Heís hékastos* (1538), each one, every one (Acts 2:6; 20:31; Col 4:6). Followed by the gen. partitively (Luke 4:40; Acts 2:3; Eph 4:7). In Rev 21:21, *aná* (303), on, upon, *heís hékastos* means each one of the gates. See *aná* (303, II).

(C) The expression *kath' héna* or *kath' hén*, one by one, singly (John 21:25; 1 Cor 14:31). In Eph 5:33, *hoi kath' héna*, every one of you. In Acts 21:19, *kath' hén hékaston*, each one singly, where *kath' hén* here qualifies *hékaston*, each one. The expression *hén kath' hén*, one by one, one after another, singly (Rev 4:8, UBS). The expression *heís kath' heís*, one by one, is irregularly used in the NT for *heís kath' héna* (Mark 14:19; John 8:9). In Rom 12:5, *ho dé kath' heís*, and every one.

(III) Emphatic, one, i.e.:

(A) Even one, one single, only one (Matt 5:36; 21:24; Mark 8:14; 10:21; 12:6; John 7:21; 1 Cor 10:17; 2 Pet 3:8). The expression *apó* (575), from, *miás* in Luke 14:18 means with one accord or voice. In the sense of only, alone (Mark 2:7; James 4:12). In John 20:7, "in only one place" (a.t.).

(B) One and the same (Rom 3:30; 1 Cor 3:8; Gal 3:28; Phil 2:2; Heb 2:11; Rev 17:13; Sept.: Gen 41:25, 26). Fully written, *hén kaí tó autó* (1 Cor 11:5; 12:11).

(IV) Indefinitely meaning one, someone, someone, the same as *tis* (5100), someone (Matt 19:16). With the subst. (Matt 8:19, "a . . . scribe"; Mark 12:42, "a . . . widow"; John 6:9; Rom 9:10). Followed by the gen. partitive, one of many (Luke 5:3; 20:1; Sept.: Gen 22:2; 27:45; 42:16). *Heís tis*, a certain one (Mark 14:51, "a certain young man," followed by the gen. [see Mark 14:47]). Followed by *ek* (1537), of, from (Luke 22:50; John 11:49). In this use, *heís* sometimes has the force of our indef. art. "a" or "an" as in Matt 21:19, "a fig tree"; James 4:13, "a year"; Rev 8:13; 9:13; Sept.: Ezra 4:8; Dan 2:31; 8:3.

(V) As an ordinal, the first, mostly spoken of the first day of the week as in Matt 28:1 where the noun *hēméra* (2250), day, is understood. See Mark 16:2; Luke 24:1; Acts 20:7; 1 Cor 16:2. In the Sept. used for the first of the month (Gen 1:5; 8:13; Ex 40:2, 17). In Rev 9:12, the "one" means the first.

Deriv.: *héndeka* (1733), eleven; *henótēs* (1775), oneness, unity.

1521. εἰσάγω eiságō; fut. *eisáxō*, from *eis* (1519), into, in, and *ágō* (71), to bring. To lead into, to bring in or into, trans. and followed by *eis* (1519), with the acc. of place. Thus of person (Luke 2:27; 14:21; 22:54, "They . . . brought him into"; John 18:16; Acts 9:8; 21:28, 29, 37; Heb 1:6, to produce, to introduce into the world; Sept.: Gen 8:9; 24:67; 2 Kgs 9:2); of things (Acts 7:45).

Deriv.: *pareiságō* (3919), to bring in privily.

Syn.: *phérō* (5342), to bring; *eisphérō* (1533), to bring into; *komízō* (2865), to bring in; *hodēgéō* (3594), to lead, to bring; *pareiságō* (3919), to bring in craftily.

Ant.: *exágō* (1806), to bring out; *ekphérō* (1627), to bring out; *ekbállō* (1544), to cast out; *apokuéō* (616), to bring forth, beget; *apágō* (520), to lead away; *apophérō* (667), to bear away.

1522. εἰσακούω eisakoúō; fut. *eisakoúsomai*, from *eis* (1519), in, and *akoúō* (191), to hear. To give heed to, listen to. To give heed to, obey, with the gen. (1 Cor 14:21; Sept.: Deut 1:43; 4:30). To hear, with the meaning of to hear favorably, to grant, only in the pass. (Matt 6:7; Luke 1:13; Acts 10:31; Heb 5:7; Sept.: Ps 4:1, 3; 6:9; 13:3).

Syn.: *epakroáomai* (1874), to listen attentively to; *enōtízomai* (1801), to give ear to; *peitharchéō* (3980), to obey one in authority; *hupotássō* (5293), to be under obedience; *pisteúō* (4100), to trust.

Ant.: *parakoúō* (3878), to disobey, neglect to hear; *apeithéō* (544), to refuse to be persuaded, to disobey; *apistéō* (569), to disbelieve.

1523. εἰσδέχομαι eisdéchomai; fut. *eisdéxomai*, mid. deponent from *eis* (1519), into, and *déchomai* (1209), to receive. To receive into favor or communion (only in 2 Cor 6:17, "and I will gather you" [a.t.], quoted apparently from Jer 32:37, 38. See Jer 23:3; Ezek 11:17; 20:34, 41 of God gathering the exiles of Israel into their own land).

Syn.: *lambánō* (2983), to receive; *paralambánō* (3880), to receive from another; *prosdéchomai* (4327), to accept favorably; *proslambánō* (4355), to receive, take to oneself; *apodéchomai* (588), to receive gladly.

Ant.: *apodokimázō* (593), to reject, disapprove; *athetéō* (114), to reject; *paraitéomai* (3868), to refuse; *arnéomai* (720), to deny, renounce; *apobállō* (577), to cast away; *aporríptō* (641), to reject.

1524. εἴσειμι eíseimi; imperf. *eisḗein*, from *eis* (1519), in, into, and *eími* (n.f., see *ápeimi* [549]), to go. To go into, to enter followed by the prep. *eis* and the acc. of place (Acts 3:3; 21:26; Heb 9:6); followed by the prep. *prós* (4314), toward, with the acc. of person (Acts 21:18; Sept.: Ex 28:29, 35).

Syn.: *eisérchomai* (1525), to come into; *eisporeúomai* (1531), to go into; *embaínō* (1684), to go in; *ágō* (71), to bring, lead; *hupágō* (5217), to go.

Ant.: *éxeimi* (1826), to go out; *exérchomai* (1831), to go out of; *ekporeúomai* (1607), to proceed from; *ekchōréō* (1633), to depart out; *aphístēmi* (868), to depart; *metabaínō* (3327), to depart.

1525. εἰσέρχομαι eisérchomai; fut. *eiseleúsomai*, 2d aor. *eisḗlthon*, from *eis* (1519), in, and *érchomai* (2064), to come. To go or come into, to enter.

(I) Spoken of persons, followed by *eis* with the acc. of place (Matt 6:6; 24:38; Mark 3:27; Luke 9:34; John 18:28; Acts 11:20; Rev 22:14). Followed by *eis* with the acc. of person (Acts 16:40 [TR], "unto Lydia" [a.t.], meaning into her house, with later editions having *prós* [4314], toward; 19:30, "unto the people" means into the assembly; 20:29, *eis humás*, "among you"). Spoken of Satan or of demons entering into persons (Mark 9:25; Luke 8:30; 22:3); into swine (Mark 5:12, 13; Luke 8:32, 33); with *eis* implied (Matt 12:45; Luke 11:26). Followed by *en* with the dat. of person in Rev 11:11, "life . . . entered into [and remained in] them" ([TR] *epí* [1909], upon); by *pará* (3844), by, with, meaning to enter in by or with someone, to lodge with (Luke 19:7); by *prós* (4314), toward, with the acc. of person, to enter to someone, i.e., into his house (Mark 15:43; Acts 10:3; 17:2; Rev 3:20); by *hupó* (5259), by with the acc. of place, e.g., under the roof (Matt 8:8); by *ésō* (2080), inside (Matt 26:58); by *hópou* (3699), where (Mark 14:14); by *hóde* (5602), hither (Matt 22:12).

(II) Metaphorically of person, followed by *eis* with the acc. of state, condition (Matt 5:20; 18:3, 8, 9, "to enter into life"; 19:24; 25:21, 23, "into the joy of thy Lord"; Mark 9:43, 45, 47); John 3:5 "into the kingdom of God"; Heb 3:11; 4:1, 3, "into my rest"). With both *eis* and the acc. implied (Matt 7:13; 23:13; Luke 11:52; 13:24). In Matt 26:41, enter, to come into or enter into temptation means to fall into temptation. In John 4:38, "ye are entered into their labors," i.e., ye succeed them and reap the fruits of their labors.

(III) Spoken of things, to enter in or into, equivalent to *eisphéromai* (1533), to be brought or put into, e.g., food into the mouth (Matt 15:11; Acts 11:8). Used metaphorically in Luke 9:46, "there arose a dispute among them" (a.t.); James 5:4. Of hope, in Heb 6:19, "entering in" (a.t.), i.e., extending even unto.

(IV) The expression *eisérchomai* and *exérchomai* (1831), to go out or to go in and out, means to perform one's daily duties, spoken of one's daily walk and life, e.g., of Jesus as in Acts 1:21f., *eph' hēmás*, among us, in our company. Metaphorically in John 10:9 (cf. *eisporeúomai* [1531], to enter, and *ekporeúomai* [1607], to go out, in the expression "to go in and out" [a.t. {Acts 9:28; Sept.: Deut 31:2; 1 Sam 18:13, 16; 2 Chr 1:10}]). In the Sept. *eísodos* (1529), entrance, and *éxodos* (1841), exit (1 Sam 29:6; Isa 37:28).

Deriv.: *pareisérchomai* (3922), to come in privily; *suneisérchomai* (4897), to go in with.

Syn.: *gínomai* (1096), to become, to enter or be present; *paragínomai* (3854), to be present; *embaínō* (1684), to go into; *hēkō* (2240), to come, be present; *aphiknéomai* (864), to arrive at a place; *katantáō* (2658), to come to or over against; *suntugchánō* (4940), to come at; *eisporeúomai* (1531), to go into; *eíseimi* (1524), to go into.

Ant.: *exérchomai* (1831), to depart; *ekporeúomai* (1607), to go out; *hupágō* (5217), to go, depart; *apérchomai* (565), to go away; *poreúomai* (4198), to go; *apochōréō* (672), to depart from; *ekchōréō* (1633), to depart out; *éxeimi* (1826), to go out; *aphístēmi* (868), to depart, stand away from; *metabaínō* (3327), to depart; *pheúgō* (5343), to flee; *ekpheúgō* (1628), to flee out of a place; *ápeimi* (548), to go away from; *apobaínō* (576), to go away.

1526. εἰσί *eisí*; pres. indic. 3d person. pl. of *eimí* (1510), I exist or am. They are.

1527. εἷς καθ᾽ εἷς *heís kath' heís* adv. expression from *heís* (1520), one, and *kath' heís*, which is from *katá* (2596), according to or as (as a distributive), and *heís*, one. One by one (Mark 14:19; John 8:9). See *heís* (1520, II, C).

1528. εἰσκαλέω *eiskaléō*; contracted *eiskalô*, fut. *eiskalésō*, from *eis* (1519), in, and *kaléō* (2564), to call. To call or invite into a house. In the mid. *eiskaléomai* contracted *eiskaloúmai*, to invite into one's own house (Acts 10:23).

Syn.: *proskaléō* (4341), to invite.

Ant.: *apolúō* (630), to dismiss; *apostéllō* (649) to send from, commission; *apōthéō*

(683), to push off; *ekbállō* (1544), to cast out; *ekpémpō* (1599), to send forth; *pémpō* (3992), to send; *aphíēmi* (863), to send away.

1529. εἴσοδος *eísodos*; gen. *eisódou*, fem. noun from *eis* (1519), in, and *hodós* (3598), a way. A way in or into, an entrance, a first-coming with the act or power of entering; followed by the prep. *eis* (1519), into, with the acc. of place (2 Pet 1:11); followed by the gen. (Heb 10:19); by *prós* (4314), toward, with the acc. of person, a coming to someone, access (1 Thess 1:9; 2:1). Used in an absolute sense in Acts 13:24; Sept.: 1 Sam 16:4; Mal 3:2.
Syn.: *éleusis* (1660), a coming; *parousía* (3952), a presence denoting both an arrival and a consequent presence with; *áphixis* (867), arrival.
Ant.: *éxodos* (1841), exit, metaphorically to cease; *análusis* (359), unloosing, departure, death.

1530. εἰσπηδάω *eispēdáō*; contracted *eispēdṓ*, fut. *eispēdḗso*, from *eis* (1519), in or into, and *pēdáō* (n.f.), to leap. To leap into, to spring in as among the people (Acts 14:14). Used in an absolute sense in Acts 16:29; Sept.: Amos 5:19.
Syn.: *hormáō* (3729), to rush; *hállomai* (242), to leap, spring; *eistréchō* (1532), to run in.
Ant.: *ménō* (3306), to stay, abide; *diaménō* (1265), to remain throughout; *paraménō* (3887), to remain, continue to remain.

1531. εἰσπορεύομαι *eisporeúomai*; fut. *eisporeúsomai*, mid. deponent from *eis* (1519), in, and *poreúomai* (4198), to go. To go into, enter.
(I) Spoken of persons followed by *eis* with the acc. of place (Mark 1:21; 6:56; 11:2; Acts 3:2); with *eis* (Mark 11:2; Luke 8:16; 11:33; 19:30); followed by *hópou* (3699), where (Mark 5:40); by *hoú*, where (Luke 22:10); by the phrase "from house to house" (a.t. [Acts 8:3]); by *prós* (4314), toward, with the acc. of

person meaning to enter to someone, i.e., into his house (Acts 28:30; Sept.: Gen 44:30; Esth 2:14).
(II) Of things, to enter in (cf. in *eisérchomai* [1525, III], to enter in). Followed by *eis* (Matt 15:17; Mark 7:15, 18, 19). Metaphorically, to arise, to spring up in the mind (Mark 4:19).
(III) From the phrase *eisporeúomai* and *ekporeúomai* (1607), to go out, to go in and out, meaning to perform one's daily duties as spoken of one's daily life and walk (Acts 9:28).
Syn.: *érchomai* (2064), to come; *eisérchomai* (1525), to enter; *paragínomai* (3854), to arrive; *embaínō* (1684), to go into; *hḗkō* (2240), to come, be present; *eíseimi* (1524), to go into.
Ant.: *ekporeúomai* (1607), to depart, to proceed; *apérchomai* (565), to go away; *exérchomai* (1831), to go out; *anachōréō* (402), to retire, depart, withdraw; *apochōréō* (672), to depart from; *ekchōréō* (1633), to depart out; *éxeimi* (1826), to go out.

1532. εἰστρέχω *eistréchō*; 2d aor. *eisédramon*, from *eis* (1519), in, and *tréchō* (5143), to run. To run into a house. In the NT used in an absolute sense meaning to run inside (Acts 12:14).
Syn.: *hormáō* (3729), to rush with violence; *eispēdáō* (1530), to spring in; *biázō* (971), to push oneself in, force, crowd in.
Ant.: *apostréphō* (654), to turn away or back.

1533. εἰσφέρω *eisphérō*; fut. *eisoísō*, aor. *eisénegka*, 2d aor. *eisénegkon*, from *eis* (1519), in or to, and *phérō* (5342), to bring, bear. To bear or bring into, followed by *eis* and the acc. of place (1 Tim 6:7, "we brought nothing into this world"; Heb 13:11). With *eis* (Sept.: Ex 40:21; Num 31:54); with *eis* implied (Luke 5:18, 19). Spoken of persons, followed by *eis* with the acc. of state or condition, meaning to lead into temptation (Matt 6:13; Luke 11:4). In Acts 17:20, to bring into the ears of someone, announce.

Syn.: *anágō* (321), to bring up to; *eiságō* (1521), to bring into; *komízō* (2865), to bring in; *paréchō* (3930), to furnish, supply.

Ant.: *apaírō* (522), to lift off; *exaírō* (1808), to take away; *aphairéō* (851), to take away; *ekbállō* (1544), to cast out; *apágō* (520), to lead away; *exágō* (1806), to lead out; *apophérō* (667), to bring away; *ekphérō* (1627), to bring out.

1534. εἶτα *eíta*; adv. of time or order. Then.

(I) Of time, meaning afterwards, after that (Mark 8:25; Luke 8:12; John 13:5; 19:27; 20:27; James 1:15). By a sort of redundance before a part. (Mark 4:17).

(II) Of order and succession as *prṓton* (4412), first, with *eíta* following (Mark 4:28; 1 Tim 2:13; 3:10). Also after first, second, third (1 Cor 12:28). In 1 Cor 15:7 both *épeita* (1899), after, and *eíta* are used and in 1 Cor 15:24 *eíta* by itself. In 1 Cor 15:5, 6 *eíta*, precedes *épeita*.

(III) The word is also used as a particle of continuation, meaning then, so then, consequently (Heb 12:9).

Syn.: *metépeita* (3347), afterwards; *hústeron* (5305), afterwards, with the suggestion of at length.

Ant.: *prṓton* (4412), first, at first; *próteron* (4386), former time; *prín* (4250), before; *émprosthen* (1715), in front.

1535. εἴτε *eíte*; conj. from *ei* (1487), if or whether, and *te* (5037), and. And if or whether, as including several particulars followed by a verb in the indic. (1 Cor 12:26; 2 Cor 1:6) or subjunctive (1 Thess 5:10) or without a verb (Rom 12:6–8; 1 Cor 3:22; 8:5; 13:8; 15:11; 1 Pet 2:13, 14); as expressing doubt (2 Cor 12:2, 3). It is most often used to set items in contrast or opposition to one another.

1536. εἴ τις *eí tis* conditional expression from *ei* (1487), if, and *tis* (5100), any. If any, if someone, used with the sort of emphasis for *hóstis* (3748), whosoever, whatsoever, everyone who. With

the indic. pres. (Mark 9:35; Luke 14:26; 1 Cor 3:12; 8:2, 3; 2 Cor 5:17; Gal 1:9; 1 Tim 5:8; 6:3); with indic. fut. (1 Cor 3:14, 15; Rev 13:10); with indic. perf. (2 Cor 7:14; 10:7); with indic. aor. (Rev 20:15).

1537. ἐκ *ek*; before a vowel, *ex*. Prep. governing the gen., primarily meaning out of, from, of, as spoken of such objects which were before in another. However, *apó* (575), of or from, is used of such objects as before were on, by or with another, but are now separated from it, i.e., they are not in it, to which *ek* corresponds. If something is in something else, then the separation from it is expressed with *ek*, out of, while if it is near it, on it, with it, then *apó* is used. *Ek* is used either in respect of place, time, source, or origin. It is the direct opposite of *eis* (1519), into or in.

(I) Of place, which is the primary and most frequent use, meaning out of, from.

(A) After verbs implying motion of any kind, out of or from any place or object, e.g., verbs of going, coming, sending, throwing, following, gathering, separating, removing, and the like (Matt 2:6, 15, "Out of Egypt"; 7:5; 13:49, "the evil ones from among the righteous" [a.t. {also Matt 13:52; 17:5; 24:17}]; Mark 1:11, "a voice came out of heaven" [a.t.]; 9:7; 11:8; 13:15, "to take anything out of his house" [also Mark 13:27; 16:3]; Luke 2:4; 10:18; 17:24; 23:55; John 1:19; 2:15; 13:1; Acts 23:10; 27:29, 30; Rom 11:24; 2 Thess 2:7, "be taken away" [a.t.]; Heb 3:16; Rev 2:5). With a gen. of person, out of or from whose presence, number, any person or thing proceeds (Mark 7:20, "that which proceeds out of the man" [a.t.]; John 8:42; Acts 3:22, 23; 19:34; 20:30; 1 Cor 5:13; Heb 5:1; 1 John 2:19). Spoken also of persons out of whom demons are cast or depart (Mark 7:26, 29; 9:25; Luke 4:35). Here it is interchanged with *apó*, as in Luke 4:41; 8:3, 33. In Heb 7:5, "to come forth out of the loins" (a.t.) of someone means to be born to him (see Heb 7:10; Sept.: Gen 35:11; 2 Chr 6:9).

(B) After verbs implying direction, out of or from any place, thus marking the point from which the direction sets off or tends (Luke 5:3, "He taught . . . from out of the boat" [a.t.], i.e., from the boat or while in the boat; Mark 11:20 [cf. Job 28:9; John 19:23; Acts 28:4]). In Rev 19:2, "at her hand" is *ek tḗs cheirós autḗs*, meaning God has avenged or taken vengeance from her. See Sept.: Gen 9:5; 1 Sam 24:16; 2 Sam 18:19; 2 Kgs 9:7. In Rev 15:2, those who become conquerors over the beast. As implying the direction in which one is placed in respect to a person or thing, as to sit, stand, or be *ek dexiás* (1188), right hand side, or *ex euōnúmōn* (2176), the left hand side, where in Eng. we use at or on (Matt 20:21, 23; 22:44; 25:33; 26:64; Mark 10:37; Luke 1:11; Acts 2:25, 34; Heb 1:13; Sept.: Ex 14:22, 29; 1 Sam 23:19, 24; Ps 16:8).

(C) Metaphorically of a state or condition, out of which one comes or is brought. After verbs of motion, direction as in John 10:28, 39, "out of their hand," meaning power; Acts 4:2; 17:3, to "rise again from among the dead" (a.t.), from the state of being dead, 31; Rom 6:4, "Christ rose from among the dead" (a.t.) means from the state of being dead, 9, 13; 7:4, 24, "who shall deliver me from the body of this death?" means from the corruptible influence of the body; 11:15; 13:11, "to arise from sleep" (a.t.) means to become alert; Col 1:18, "the first one to come out from among the dead" (a.t.), or "the first to be born from among the dead" (a.t.) meaning to become alive with a glorified body, a state in which no one else had been. See Luke 1:74; 2 Cor 1:10; 5:8; Gal 3:13. In John 12:27, "save me from this hour," i.e., from the condition that My coming crucifixion is going to bring upon Me, the full acceptance of the divine task by My humanity. In John 17:15, "that thou mayest keep them from the evil one" (a.t.) means that they may not conform to the world by the influence of Satan while they are in the world. See Luke 1:71; Heb 5:7. Metaphorically in John 5:24; Acts 1:25, "the ministry out of

which Judas fell on the side" (a.t.); 15:29; 1 Cor 9:19; 2 Tim 2:26; James 5:20; 1 Pet 1:18; 2:9; 2 Pet 2:21; Rev 2:21, "to repent from out of the state of her fornication" (a.t.), that is to get out of it and not to engage in it anymore; Rev 2:22; 3:10; 9:20, 21; 14:13, "they shall rest from their labors" (a.t.), i.e., from out of their labors.

(II) Of time, of the beginning of a period of time, a point from which onward anything takes place (Matt 19:12, "from their mother's womb," from the time of their conception; 19:20, "from my youth"; Luke 1:15; 8:27, for a "long time" means from many years; John 6:64, "from the beginning"; 9:1, "from his birth," 9:32, "since the age began" [a.t.]; Acts 9:33; 15:21; 24:10; Sept.: Ps 22:10; 71:6). It may sometimes be rendered as after (Rom 1:4, "after the resurrection from the dead" [a.t.]; 2 Pet 2:8, "from day to day" meaning day after day; Rev 17:11, "after the seven," i.e., their successor; Sept.: Gen 39:10 (cf. Lev 25:50; Deut 15:20). With an adj. or pron. it forms sometimes an adv. of time, e.g., *ex autḗs* with *hṓras* (5610), hour, literally from this time or hour, i.e., immediately (John 12:27). *Ex hikanoú* (2425), much, with *chrónou* (5550), "time" understood, meaning of old, long ago, of a long time (Luke 23:8, "from this time" [a.t.], i.e., afterwards; John 6:66). *Ek deutérou* (1208), second, a second time, again (Acts 10:15). *Ek trítou* (5154), third, the third time (Matt 26:44).

(III) Of the origin or source of anything, i.e., the primary, direct, immediate source, in distinction from *apó* (575), which marks the secondary, indirect origin, and *hupó* (5259), by, which denotes the immediate efficient agent. This is strictly the primary sense of the gen. case itself, which is also so used both in the NT and Gr. writers (2 Cor 4:7).

(A) Of persons, of the place, stock, family, condition, meaning out of which one is derived or to which he belongs, e.g.: **(1)** Of the place from which one is, where one resides (Luke 8:27, "a man from the city" [a.t.]; 23:7, "that he belonged originally to the jurisdiction of Herod" [a.t.]; John 1:46; Acts 23:34). In Col 4:9, 12, *ho ex humṓn*, "of you" means of your city; Luke 11:13, *ho patḗr ho ex ouranoú*, "heavenly Father"; elsewhere usually *en* (1722), in, *ouranṓ*, in heaven (Matt 5:45; 6:9; 7:21). (2) Of family, race, ancestors (Luke 1:5, "a . . . priest of the course of Abijah," 27; 2:4, "of the house of David"; Acts 4:6; 13:21; Rom 9:5, 24; Heb 7:14). In Acts 15:23, "brethren those from the nations" (a.t.) means Gentile Christians; Rom 9:6, *hoi ex Israḗl*, means Israelites. See Matt 3:9, "out of the stones to raise children unto Abraham" (a.t.); Acts 17:26; John 3:6. *Ek spérmatos* (4690), seed, followed by the gen., means of or from the seed, i.e., family or race of someone (John 7:42; Rom 1:3; 2 Tim 2:8; Sept.: Ruth 4:12; 1 Kgs 11:14). Followed by the gen., of the mother, to be born of a woman (Matt 1:3, 5, 6, 16; Gal 4:4, 22, 23). (3) Of condition or state (John 8:41, "We have not been born out of fornication" [a.t.], we are not bastards). *Hoi ek peritomḗs* (4061), circumcision, *pistoí* (4103), faithful, meaning believers out from circumcision, or the Jewish Christians (Acts 10:45; Rom 4:12; Gal 2:12).

(B) Of the source, i.e., the person or thing, out of or from which anything proceeds, is derived, or to which it pertains. (1) Used generally (Matt 21:19; Mark 11:30, "The baptism of John, was it out of heaven or from men?" [a.t.]; Luke 1:78; 10:11; John 1:13; 3:25, 27, 31; 4:22, first revealed to the Jews and proceeds from them to others; 7:22; 10:16, 32; Acts 5:38; 19:25; Rom 2:29; 10:17; 12:18, so far as it is of or from you, depends on you; 1 Cor 2:12, "the Spirit, the one out of God" [a.t.], means the divine Spirit; 15:47; 2 Cor 5:2; 8:7; 9:2; Heb 2:11; 7:6; 1 John 4:7; Rev 15:8). Spoken of an affection or state of mind out of which an emotion flows (2 Cor 2:4, "out of much affliction"; 1 Tim 1:5; 1 Pet 1:22); of any source of knowledge (Matt 12:33; Luke 6:44; John 12:34; Rom 2:18); of proof (James 2:18, "I shall show you my faith

with my works" [a.t.] thus proving it; 3:13); of the source from which any judgment is drawn, from, out of, whereas in Eng. we would translate it "by" or "according to" (Matt 12:37, "by thy words thou shalt be justified," meaning you will be judged according to your words; Luke 19:22; Rev 20:12; Sept.: Num 26:56). (2) As marking not only the source and origin, but also the character of any person or thing as derived from that source, implying connection, dependence, adherence, devotion, likeness (John 3:6, 8, "of the flesh"; 3:31, "of the earth"; 7:17, "he shall know of the doctrine, whether it be of God," the character or content of the doctrine will show whether it originates in God; 8:23, of those things from below, of those things from above; 8:44, "of . . . the devil" or out of the devil meaning that the devil is one's father; 8:47, "He that is of God, heareth God's words," means your hearing God's words proves that you have come out of God, i.e., character shows origin; 17:14, 16, "not of the world"; 1 John 2:16, 29; 3:8–10; 4:1–7). Metaphorically of the source of character, quality, implying adherence to, connection with (John 18:37, "whoever is of the truth" [a.t.], i.e., whose source is truth; Gal 3:10, 12, "the law is not of faith," is not born of faith, does not originate in faith; 1 John 2:21; 3:19). Hence, *ek* with its gen. preceded by the art. forms a periphrasis for an adj. or part., e.g., *ho ek písteōs*, literally a person of faith, a believer, the same as the pres. part. noun *ho pisteúōn*, the believing one. (Rom 3:26; 4:16, a person "of Abraham's faith" [a.t.], who believes as he did; Gal 3:7, 9); *ho ek nómou* (3551), law, one of the law, i.e., one under the law, an adherent of it (Rom 4:14, 16). In Rom 2:8, "those out of contention" (a.t.) means the contentious ones; 2:27, the "uncircumcision which is by nature" means the natural state; Titus 2:8.

(C) Of the motive, ground, occasion from whence anything proceeds, the incidental cause, "from," "out of," i.e., by reason of, because of, in consequence of

(John 4:6, being tired as a result of walking; 2 Cor 13:4, "He was crucified because of weakness [physical], but He lives by reason of the power of God" [a.t.]; Phil 1:16, 17, some motivated by love and others by contention; 1 Tim 6:4; Heb 7:12; James 4:1; Rev 8:11, 13; 16:10, 11, 21). With the verb *dikaióō* (1344), to justify, or *dikaioúmai ek písteōs*, to justify or to be justified by, from, on account of, or through faith (Rom 3:30; 5:1; Gal 2:16; 3:24). Elsewhere with the gen. (Rom 3:20; 4:2; Gal 2:16), with the adj. *díkaios* (1342), just or righteous, *ek písteōs*, just or righteous by or on account of faith (Rom 1:17). With the noun *dikaiosúnē* (1343), righteousness, *ek písteōs* (Rom 3:26; 9:30; 10:6, righteousness out of or resulting from faith).

(**D**) Of the efficient cause or agent, that from which any action or thing proceeds, is produced or effected, i.e., from, by (Matt 1:18, 20; John 6:65, "if it is not given unto him by my Father" (a.t.), means if the efficient cause is not the Father; 12:49, *ex emautoú* (1683), "of myself"; Rom 9:10; 1 Cor 8:6; 2 Cor 1:11; 2:2; 7:9; Gal 5:8, "of him that calleth," i.e., of the calling one; Eph 4:16; Phil 1:23; Rev 2:11; 9:2, 18).

(**E**) Of the manner or mode in which anything is done, out of, from, or, as we would express in Eng., in, with (Matt 12:34; Mark 12:30, 33, "to love him with the whole heart . . . and with the whole soul"; Luke 10:27; John 3:31; 8:44; Acts 8:37; Rom 6:17, heartily; 14:23, "not out of faith" [a.t.], i.e., not in or with faith; 2 Cor 8:11, "according to your ability" [a.t.]; 8:14; Eph 6:6, "from [or with] the heart" or "soul" [a.t.]; 1 Thess 2:3; 1 Pet 4:11; 1 John 4:5). In an adv. sense, e.g., *ek perissoú* (4053), abundance, meaning abundantly, exceedingly (Mark 6:51; 14:31); *ek mérous* (3313), part, meaning in part, partly (1 Cor 12:27; 13:9, 10, 12); *ek métrou* (3358), measure, meaning measurably, moderately (John 3:34); *ek sumphṓnou* (4859), agreement, meaning by mutual consent (1 Cor 7:5).

(**F**) Of the means, instrument, instrumental cause, from, i.e., by means of, by, through, with (Luke 16:9, "by means of" [a.t.]; John 3:5, "out of water" [a.t.], through the instrumentality of water as every child is born out of water; 9:6; 1 Cor 9:13, 14, "to live by means of the gospel" [a.t.]; Heb 11:35; Rev 3:18, "gold tried by means of fire [*ek purós* (4442)]" [a.t.]; 17:2, 6; 18:3, 19). Also with verbs of filling, being full, (Matt 23:25; John 12:3; Rev 8:5); also of a price as a means of acquiring anything (Matt 20:2, 13, for one dinar; 27:7, "and by means of them [silver coins] they bought the field" [a.t.]; Acts 1:18, where *ek* with the gen. is equivalent to the simple gen. which is the usual construction).

(**G**) Of the material, of, out of, from (Matt 27:29, "crown made of thorns" [a.t.]; John 2:15; Rom 9:21; 1 Cor 11:8; Eph 5:30; Heb 11:3; Rev 18:12; 21:21).

(**H**) Of the whole in relation to a part, a whole from which a part is spoken of, i.e., partitively (1 Cor 12:15, 16, "I am not [part] of the body"; Acts 10:1.) After *esthíō* (2068) or *phágomai* (5315), to eat, *pínō* (4095), to drink, meaning to eat or drink of anything, i.e., part of it (Matt 26:27, 29; Luke 22:16; John 4:12–14; 6:26; 1 Cor 9:7; 11:28; Rev 2:7; 14:10; 18:3). In Class. Gr. writings, the simple gen. is used. See Sept.: Gen 9:21; 2 Sam 12:3, and similar use of *apó* (575, III, G); also after other verbs where an acc. would imply the whole and where Class. Gr. writers put the simple gen. (Matt 25:8; John 1:16; 6:11; Rev 18:4; Sept.: 1 Chr 29:14). In 1 Cor 10:17, "we all of the one bread partake" (a.t.); also Matt 13:47, "and gathered of every kind," some of every kind. Spoken of a class or number out of which one is separated, of which he forms part (Mark 14:69, "He is out of them" [a.t.], he belongs to them but he is separated from them; Luke 22:3; John 1:24; Acts 6:9; 21:8; Rom 16:10; Phil 4:22; 2 Tim 3:6). See *eimí* (1510, IX, C). After a numeral or pron., e.g., *heís* (1520), one (Matt 10:29, "one of them" [a.t.]; Mark 9:17; Luke 15:4); two (Matt

25:2, "five of them" [a.t.]; Mark 16:12; John 1:35, "two of his disciples" [a.t.]; Acts 26:23, "first of those from the resurrection of the dead" [a.t.]; Heb 7:4, "the tenth of the spoils"). After *tis* (5100), one, indef. (Heb 4:1, "if any of you" [a.t.]); *tinés*, pl. (Luke 11:15; Acts 11:20; Rom 11:14; James 2:16). After *tis* (5101) as an interrogative, who, which (Matt 21:31, "who of the two" [a.t.]; Luke 11:5; John 8:46). After *oudeís* (3762), none (John 7:19). Also with *tis* (sing.) and *tinés* (pl. implied) (Matt 23:34; Luke 21:16; John 9:40; 16:17; Rev 3:9).

(**IV**) In composition *ek* implies:

(**A**) Removal out, from, off, or away, as *ekbállō* (1544), to eject or to put away or out of; *ekphérō* (1627), to bring forth or out.

(**B**) Continuance, as *ekteínō* (1614), to extend, put or stretch forth; *ektréphō* (1625), to nourish, bring up or, literally, to feed so that one can come out of himself as he now is.

(**C**) Completion, meaning "in full" as *ekdapanáō* (1550), to spend everything, all that one has.

(**D**) Indicating intensiveness as *ékdēlos* (1552), wholly evident or manifest; *exapatáō* (1818), to completely deceive; *ektarássō* (1613), to disturb completely.

(**V**) Used in conjunction with other prep.:

(**A**) *Ek / apó* (575). See introduction in respective words. Both prepositions govern the gen. and express strictly the idea of the gen. case itself. *Ek*, however, presupposes the separation of someone or somebody who was part of another or in another. As a direct antithesis of *eis* (1519), in, *apó* indicates the separation of one object from another, the former object before having been on, by, or with another, but now is separated from the latter object.

An instance where we find the two prepositions *apó* and *ek* together is in 2 Cor 3:5, "not that we are sufficient of ourselves [*aph' heautón*] to think anything as of ourselves [*exí heautón*]; but our sufficiency is of God [*ek toú Theoú*]." The

first part of the verse declares that the believer is incapable of thinking only on his own because he is indwelt by the Spirit of God. His thoughts do not originate from himself as if he were an entity apart from that which he became with the indwelling of Christ. The second phrase declares that even that which seems to come out of man only in his depraved humanity does not come out of himself as if Christ were not indwelling him. The third declaration is that the believer's sufficiency is out of God (*ek toú Theoú*) the Father who came to indwell him through Christ (2 Cor 3:4). The indwelling God is the one who expresses Himself in the thoughts of the believer.

The two prep. *ek / hupó* (5259), out of, by, are found in 1 Cor 2:12: "Now we have received, not the spirit of the world, but the Spirit which is of God [*tó ek toú Theoú*]; that we might know the things that are freely given to us of God [*tá hupó toú Theoú*]." The Spirit of God originates from God and comes out of God to us in a partitive way. What comes to us never ceases to exist as an objective reality, becoming for us a subjective entity. The *hupó* indicates the immediate agency of God in giving us all the things that pertain to His grace (*charisthénta*) as from *cháris* (5485). The teaching here is that the Spirit of God comes from God into us and remains in us, but there is also a constant inflow of the gifts that come to us and they come directly from God. The activity of God the Father in our lives is constant in addition to the indwelling Spirit.

Ek / diá (1223), through, is used as instrumental in 1 Cor 11:12, "For as the woman is of the man [*ek toú andrós*, male] even so is the man also by [*diá tés gunaikós*] the female; but all things of God [*ek toú Theoú*]" (a.t.). Here the original creation is referred to. The woman came out of the body of man, she was part of him (Gen 2:21, 22), a female coming out of the male. Since that time, however, man comes through the instrumentality of a female, but all come out of God.

If it were not for God in the beginning, no man or no woman would have been created or would be able to produce anything. All things are out of *the* God, deity (italics added). In 2 Cor 5:18: "And all things are of God [*ek toú Theoú*], who hath reconciled us to himself by Jesus Christ [*diá*], and hath given to us the ministry of reconciliation." Everything comes out of God and is transmitted to us through Jesus Christ.

In John 17:11 our Lord declares that the believers are in (*en* [1722]) the world, part of the physical world. In John 17:15, however, Jesus Christ is asking the Father not to take them physically out of the world (*ek toú kósmou*), but to keep them *ek toú ponēroú* (4190), out of the evil one, separated from his influence. And then in John 17:16, our Lord says "They are not of [*ek*] the world, even as I am not of the world," meaning they do not display the characteristic of their environment, the world in which they live.

1538. ἕκαστος hékastos; fem. *hekástē*, neut. *hékaston*, adj. from *hékas* (n.f.), separate. Each, every one, of any number separately.

(**I**) Generally, as in Matt 16:27, "to each one separately" (a.t. [Luke 6:44; John 7:53; Rom 2:6]). Followed by the gen. pl. (Matt 26:22, "each one of them" [a.t.]; John 6:7; Rom 14:12). This idea of separation or singling out is expressed still more strongly by *heís hékastos*, each one (Acts 20:31; Eph 4:16; Rev 21:21). Followed by the gen. pl. (Luke 4:40; Acts 2:3). In the phrase *kath' hekástēn hēméran*, with the prep. *katá* (2596), a distributive, and *hēméra* (2250), day, we have the strengthened distributive force of *katá* (Heb 3:13; Rev 22:2).

(**II**) Distributively, in construction with pl. verbs where it is in apposition with the pl. noun implied (Matt 18:35; John 16:32; Heb 8:11). Followed by the gen. pl. (Acts 11:29). *Heís hékastos*, each one (Acts 2:6). In apposition, with the pl. noun or pron. expressed (Luke 2:3; Acts 2:8; Eph 5:33). With *heís* (1 Cor 12:18).

Deriv.: *hekástote* (1539), each time, always.

Syn.: *pás* (3956), every one, any and every; *idía*, the dat. of *ídios* (2398), self, individual, individually.

Ant.: *oudeís* (3762), no one, more in an absolute sense and objectively; *mēdeís* (3367), no one, but with the element of subjectiveness and relativity as a prohibition or admonition.

1539. ἑκάστοτε hekástote; adv. of time, from *hékastos* (1538), each, every one. Each time, ever, always (2 Pet 1:15).

Syn.: *aeí* (104), perpetually, invariably; *diapantós* (1275), through all time; *pántē* (3839) and *pántote* (3842), always; the expression *eis tó diēnekés* (1336), continuously.

Ant.: *oudépote* (3763), never; *mēdépote* (3368), never, but with a less strong declarative negation; *oudépō* (3764), not yet, never yet; *oukéti* (3765), no longer; *oúpō* (3768) and *mēdépō*, (3369) not yet; *pópote* (4455), not at any time.

1540. ἑκατόν hekatón; indeclinable, used for all genders, cardinal number. One hundred (Matt 18:12, 28; John 19:39). Adv., a hundredfold (Matt 13:8; Mark 4:8 [cf. Luke 8:8]).

Deriv.: *diakósioi* (1250), two hundred; *hekatontaétēs* (1541), one hundred years old; *hekatontaplasíōn* (1542), a hundred times, hundredfold; *hekatontárchēs / hekatóntarchos* (1543), centurion; *exakósioi* (1812), six hundred; *pentakósioi* (4001), five hundred; *tetrakósioi* (5071), four hundred; *triakósioi* (5145), three hundred.

1541. ἑκατονταέτης hekatontaétēs; gen. *hekatontaétous*, masc.-fem., neut. *hekatontaétēs*, adj. from *hekatón* (1540), one hundred, and *étos* (2094), a year. Of a hundred years, one hundred years old (Rom 4:19; Sept.: Gen 17:17).

1542. ἑκατονταπλασίων hekatontaplasíōn; gen. *hekatontaplasíonos*, masc.-fem., neut. *hekatontaplásion*, adj. from *hekatón* (1540), one hundred, and *plasíon*, used as a numeral termination equivalent to *-plex* in Lat. and *-fold* in Eng. A hundredfold (Matt 19:29; Mark 10:30; Luke 8:8; Sept.: 2 Sam 24:3).

Syn.: *pollaplasíon* (4179), many times more.

1543. ἑκατοντάρχης *hekatontárchēs* and **ἑκατόνταρχος** *hekatóntarchos*; gen. *hekatontárchou*, masc. noun from *hekatón* (1540), one hundred, and *árchō* (757), to command. A centurion, a Roman military officer commanding one hundred men. Ending in *-ēs*, *hekatontárchēs* (Acts 10:1, 22; 24:23; 27:1, 31). Ending in *-os*, *hekatóntarchos* (Matt 8:5, 8, 13; 27:54; Luke 7:2, 6; 23:47; Acts 21:32; 22:25, 26; 23:17, 23; 27:6, 11, 43; 28:16; Sept.: Ex 18:25; Deut 1:15).

1544. ἐκβάλλω *ekbállō*; fut. *ekbalṓ*, 2d aor. *exébalon*; pluperf. without augment *ekbeblḗkein* (Mark 16:9), from *ek* (1537), out, and *bállō* (906), to cast, throw, drive. To cast, throw out.
  (I) Generally and with the idea of force, impulse, followed by *eis* (1519), in or into, with the acc. of place (Matt 8:12; 15:17; 25:30; Acts 27:38; Sept.: Lev 14:40). Followed by *éxō* (1854), out, with the gen. of place (Matt 21:39). Followed by *éxō*, with the gen. implied (Luke 20:15; John 9:34, 35; 12:31 [cf. Sept.: Lev 14:40]). In the sense of to force, thrust, urge or drive out (Mark 1:12, "the Spirit drives him into the desert" [a.t.]; 9:47, the eye; John 10:4, the sheep [cf. *exágo* {1806}, to bring out in John 10:3]). Followed by *ek* (1537), out of, with the gen. of place (John 2:15; 3 John 1:10). Followed by *éxō* with the gen. (Luke 4:29; Acts 7:58); *éxo* with the gen. implied (Luke 8:54; John 6:37, of the kingdom; John 12:31). Followed by *apó* (575), out of or from, with the gen. of place (Acts 13:50). Used in an absolute sense, but from a place implied (Matt 9:25; Luke 19:45; Acts 16:37; Gal 4:30). Spoken of demons, to cast or drive out, expel from the body of someone, e.g.,

apó (Mark 16:9); *ek* (1537), out of followed by the gen., someone (Mark 7:26). Generally (Matt 7:22; Mark 1:34, 39; Luke 9:40). In the sense of to send out as laborers for the harvest (Matt 9:38; Luke 10:2); to send away, send off (James 2:25). Metaphorically in the sense of to cast out, to scorn and reproach, reject (Luke 6:22, i.e., when they shall falsely slander you, the same as when they "shall say all manner of evil against you falsely," in Matt 5:11).
  (II) The idea of force being dropped, to take out, extract, remove (Matt 7:4, 5; Luke 6:42); to bring out or forth (Matt 12:20 quoted from Isa 42:3; Matt 12:35; Luke 10:35); to throw out, i.e., not to include, leave out (Rev 11:2).
  Deriv.: *ekbolḗ* (1546), ejection.
  Syn.: *aírō* (142), to remove; *aníēmi* (447), to let go; *apelaúnō* (556), to drive from; *aporríptō* (641), to cast off; *apospáō* (645), to draw away; *apostéllō* (649), to send forth; *apotássō* (657), to put away from oneself; *apotíthēmi* (659), to put off, lay aside; *apōthéō* or *apóthéō* (683), to thrust or put away; *aphairéō* (851), to take away; *ekdiṓkō* (1559), to chase away; *ekkomízō* (1580), to bear forth, carry out; *ekkóptō* (1581), to cut off; *ekpémpō* (1599), to send away; *ekrizóō* (1610), to pluck up by the root; *ekphúō* (1631), to cause to grow out; *ekchéō* (1632), to gush out; *exágō* (1806), to bring forth; *exairéō* (1807), to take out; *exaírō* (1808), to put away from the midst of; *exōthéō* (1856), to thrust out; *periairéō* (4014), to take away; *chōrízō* (5563), to separate.
  Ant.: *eiságō* (1521), to bring in; *eisdéchomai* (1523), to take receive; *eisérchomai* (1525), to enter in; *eisphérō* (1533), to bring in; *embaínō* (1684), to step in; *embállō* (1685), to cast into.

1545. ἔκβασις *ékbasis*; gen. *ekbáseōs*, fem. noun from *ekbaínō* (n.f.), to go out, escape, which is from *ek* (1537), out, and *baínō* (n.f.), to go. A going out, spoken of a way to escape (1 Cor 10:13); an event, end, outcome or result (Heb 13:7).

Syn.: *péras* (4009), a limit; *suntéleia* (4930), bringing to completion together, consummation; *télos* (5056), an end, goal; *teleíōsis* (5050), completion.

Ant.: *archḗ* (746), beginning; *prṓtos* (4413), first.

1546. ἐκβολή *ekbolḗ*; gen. *ekbolḗs*, fem. noun from *ekbállō* (1544), to cast out. A casting out of the ship's load in order to lighten it (Acts 27:18; Sept.: Jon 1:5).

Syn.: *apobolḗ* (580), casting away.

Ant.: *eísodos* (1529), entrance.

1547. ἐκγαμίζω *ekgamízō*; fut. *ekgamísō*, from *ek* (1537), out, and *gamízō* (an alternate form of *gamískō* [1061]), to give in marriage. To place out in marriage, to give in marriage as a father does with his daughter (Matt 22:30; 24:38; Luke 17:27; 1 Cor 7:38).

Syn.: *ekgamískō* (1548), to give to marriage.

1548. ἐκγαμίσκω *ekgamískō*; from *ek* (1537), out, and *gamískō* (1061), to give in marriage. The same as *ekgamízō* (1547). To give in marriage, in the pass. (Luke 20:34, 35).

1549. ἔκγονος *ékgonos*; gen. *egkánou*, masc.-fem., neut. *ékgonon*, adj. from *ekgínomai* (n.f.), to spring forth, which is from *ek* (1537), out, and *gínomai* (1096), to be or become. A descendant of any kind, a son, daughter, grandchild. In the NT, in the neut. pl. *tá ékgona*, descendants, especially grandchildren (1 Tim 5:4; Sept.: Deut 7:13; 29:11; 31:12; Isa 14:29; 49:15).

Syn.: *thugátēr* (2364), daughter; *thugátrion* (2365), little daughter; *korásion* (2877), a little girl; *sárx* (4561), flesh; *spérma* (4690), seed, offspring; *tekníon* (5040), little child; *téknon* (5043), child; *huiós* (5207), son.

Ant.: *goneús* (1118), parent; *mámmē* (3125), grandmother; *mḗtēr* (3384), mother; *patḗr* (3962), father; *patriárchēs* (3966), patriarch, progenitor; *prógonos* (4269), ancestor.

1550. ἐκδαπανάω *ekdapanáō*; fut. *ekdapanḗsō*, from *ek* (1537), out or entirely, and *dapanáō* (1159), to spend. To spend out or entirely, to consume. In the pass., to be consumed, entirely spent, spoken of one's life, powers (2 Cor 12:15).

Syn.: *analískō* (355), to spend, consume; *diagínomai* (1230), to spend time; *prosanalískō* (4321), to spend besides.

Ant.: *sṓzō* (4982), to save; *tēréō* (5083), to hold fast; *phulássō* (5442), to keep, preserve; *diasṓzō* (1295), to save thoroughly.

1551. ἐκδέχομαι *ekdéchomai*; fut. *ekdéxomai*, from *ek* (1537), out, and *déchomai* (1209), to receive. To watch for, expect, to be about to receive from any quarter (John 5:3; 1 Cor 16:11; Heb 11:10; James 5:7); expect, wait for (Acts 17:16; 1 Cor 11:33; Heb 10:13; 1 Pet 3:20).

Deriv.: *apekdéchomai* (553), to look for, expect fully; *ekdochḗ* (1561), expectation.

Syn.: *anaménō* (362), to wait for in confident expectancy; *apekdéchomai* (553), to await or expect eagerly; *elpízō* (1679), to hope for; *periménō* (4037), to wait for; *prosdokáō* (4328), to watch toward, look for; *paredreúō* (4332), to wait upon with steadfastness; *proskarteréō* (4342), to wait on; *prosdéchomai* (4367), to expect, look for.

Ant.: *apelpízō* (560), despair; *exaporéō* (1820), to be in despair.

1552. ἔκδηλος *ékdēlos*; gen. *ekdḗlou*, masc.-fem., neut. *ékdēlon*, adj. from *ek* (1537), an intens., and *dēlos* (1212), manifest. Quite plain, conspicuous, very evident (2 Tim 3:9).

Syn.: *emphanḗs* (1717), manifest; *pródēlos* (4271), evident beforehand, clearly evident; *phanerós* (5318), visible, manifest.

Ant.: *ádēlos* (82), indistinct, uncertain; *apókruphos* (614), secret; *aphanḗs* (852), unseen, hidden; *kruptós* (2927), secret, hidden.

1553. ἐκδημέω *ekdēméō*; contracted *ekdēmó*, fut. *ekdēméso*, from *ékdēmos* (n.f.), away from home, which is from *ek* (1537), from or out of, and *dēmos* (1218), people. To go abroad, to part as the parting from the body, the earthly abode of the spirit (2 Cor 5:6, 8, 9) or to be away or absent from the body and present with the Lord. Also from *ékdēmos* (n.f.): *sunékdēmos* (4898), absent or traveling.

Syn.: *apogínomai* (581), to be away from; *apodēméō* (589), to go abroad, go away from where one is; *apothnḗskō* (599), to die off or out; *thnḗskō* (2348), to die; *teleutáō* (5053), to reach the end of the present state of being.

Ant.: *endēméō* (1736), to be at home, present.

1554. ἐκδίδωμι *ekdídōmi*; fut. *ekdṓsō*, from *ek* (1537), out, and *dídōmi* (1325), to give. To give out, to publish a book, decree, and so forth. In the NT in the mid. *ekdídomai*, to let out, to hire out for one's own benefit (Matt 21:33, 41; Mark 12:1; Luke 20:9).

Deriv.: *ékdotos* (1560), delivered up or out.

1555. ἐκδιηγέομαι *ekdiēgéomai*; contracted *ekdiēgoúmai*, fut. *ekdiēgésomai*, from *ek* (1537), out, and *diēgéomai* (1334), to recount or declare. To tell forth, relate in full. Trans. in Acts 13:41; 15:3; Sept.: Ezek 12:16.

Deriv.: *anekdiēgētos* (411), unspeakable.

Syn.: *anaggéllō* (312), to announce, report; *apaggéllō* (518), to announce or report; *dēlóō* (1213), to make plain; *diaggéllō* (1229), to announce or declare fully; *exēgéomai* (1834), to bring out the meaning; *kataggéllō* (2605), to proclaim; *kērússō* (2784), to proclaim; *phrázō* (5419), to expound.

Ant.: *krúptō* (2928), to cover, conceal; *apokrúptō* (613), to conceal from; *egkrúptō* (1470), to hide in; *kalúptō* (2572), to cover; *lanthánō* (2990), to escape notice, to hide; *parakalúptō* (3871),

to cover with a veil; *perikrúptō* (4032), to hide by placing something around; *sigáō* (4601), to keep silent, quiet.

1556. ἐκδικέω *ekdikéō*; fut. *ekdikḗsō*, from *ékdikos* (1558), avenger. To execute justice, defend one's cause, maintain one's right (Luke 18:5). In Luke 18:3 where the translation is "Avenge me of my adversary" [a.t.], it means bring out my right or justice so the accusation of my adversary may not stand against me (Sept.: Ps 37:28). To avenge, i.e., to make penal satisfaction as in Rom 12:19 (see Rom 12:17, 20). To take vengeance on, to punish, e.g., in the constructions "avenge the blood on" or "at the hand of" (a.t.) someone as in Rev 6:10; 19:2. See Sept.: 2 Kgs 9:7 (cf. Deut 18:19; Hos 1:4). In the sense of simply to punish in 2 Cor 10:6; Sept.: Ex 21:20.

Deriv.: *ekdíkēsis* (1557), vengeance, the bringing forth of justice.

Syn.: *antapodídōmi* (467), to repay; *apodídōmi* (591), to requite.

Ant.: *aphíēmi* (863), to forgive.

1557. ἐκδίκησις *ekdíkēsis*; gen. *ekdikēseōs*, fem. noun from *ekdikéō* (1556), to execute justice. Execution of right, justice.

(I) Maintenance of right, support, protection, hence, *poiéō ekdíkēsin* (*poiéō* [4160], to do) is the same as *ekdikéō*, to maintain one's right, defend one's cause, followed by the gen. of person, meaning for whom (Luke 18:7, 8). Followed by the dat. of person, meaning against whom (Acts 7:24 [cf. Sept.: Judg 11:36; 2 Sam 22:48]).

(II) Vengeance, i.e., penal retribution (Rom 12:19; Heb 10:30; Sept.: 2 Sam 4:8; Ps 79:10; Jer 11:20; Hos 9:7). In the sense of vindictive justice, punishment (Luke 21:22; 2 Thess 1:8; 1 Pet 2:14). Referring to the evildoer (2 Cor 7:11 [cf. 2 Cor 7:12; Sept.: Mic 5:15]).

Syn.: *epitimía* (2009), penalty, punishment; *kólasis* (2851), punishment; *kríma* (2917), condemnation; *krísis* (2920), judgment; *timōría* (5098), vengeance, punishment which vindicates one's honor.

Ant.: *antimisthía* (489), requital, in a good sense; *brabeíon* (1017), a prize; *misthapodosía* (3405), a payment of wages; *misthós* (3408), pay, wages, reward; *opsónion* (3800), wages, particularly those paid to a soldier.

1558. ἔκδικος *ékdikos*; gen. *ekdíkou*, masc., fem. noun from *ek* (1537), from, out, and *díkē* (1349), justice. Executing right and justice, hence an avenger, punisher. Literally, the one outside of that which is lawful. Lawless, mischievous, opposite of *hósios* (3741), holy. In later Gr., it came to mean he who brings to pass what he believes to be his right, an avenger. Only in the NT in Rom 13:4, translated "revenger," and in 1 Thess 4:6 translated "avenger," referring to the magistrate as being the one who executes justice.

Deriv.: *ekdikéō* (1556), to execute justice.

Syn.: *dikastḗs* (1348), one who brings justice among people; *kritḗs* (2923), judge; *misthapodótēs* (3406), rewarder.

Ant.: *hupódikos* (5267), one under judgment.

1559. ἐκδιώκω *ekdiṓkō*; fut. *ekdiṓxō*, from *ek* (1537), an intens., and *diṓkō* (1377), to pursue, persecute. To chase out, to drive out from a place (Sept.: Deut 6:19; Joel 2:20; Dan 4:22). In the NT, to persecute, used trans. with the meaning of *diṓkō*, to pursue or persecute, but stronger (Luke 11:49; 1 Thess 2:15; Sept.: Ps 119:157).

Syn.: *apelaúnō* (556), to drive from; *ekbállō* (1544), to cast forth; *elaúnō* (1643), to drive, urge on; *exōthéō* (1856), to thrust out.

Ant.: *déchomai* (1209), to receive deliberately; *apéchō* (568), to have in full; *lambánō* (2983), to receive; *paralambánō* (3880), to receive from another; *proslambánō* (4355), to take to oneself; *chōréō* (5562), to have room for.

1560. ἔκδοτος *ékdotos*; gen. *ekdótou*, masc.-fem., neut. *ékdoton*, adj. from *ekdídōmi* (1554), to deliver up. Delivered out or up (Acts 2:23).

1561. ἐκδοχή *ekdochḗ*; gen. *ekdochḗs*, fem. noun from *ekdéchomai* (1551), to expect. A looking for, expectation (Heb 10:27).

Syn.: *apokaradokía* (603), intense anticipation; *prosdokía* (4329), watching for, expectation; *elpís* (1680), hope.

Ant.: *aporía* (640), state of perplexity; *exaporéomai* (1820), to despair; *apelpízō* (560), to give up, be without hope.

1562. ἐκδύω *ekdúō*; fut. *ekdúsō*, from *ek* (1537), out, and *dúō* (1416), to cause to sink, to go or come. To go or come out of, put off, especially clothing, to unclothe. In the NT especially, to put off, to strip one of his clothing, unclothe, with two acc. in Matt 27:31; with the acc. of person in Matt 27:28; Mark 15:20; Luke 10:30. In the mid., to lay off one's clothes, unclothe oneself. Used figuratively of the mortal body in 2 Cor 5:4.

Deriv.: *apekdúomai* (554), to put off, spoil off.

Syn.: *aírō* (142), to remove; *apekdúō* (554), to strip off clothes or weapons; *apotíthēmi* (659), to put away; *apōthéō* (683), to thrust away; *aphairéō* (851), to take away; *ekbállō* (1544), to take off.

Ant.: *endúō* (1746), to put on clothes; *epitíthēmi* (2007), to put on.

1563. ἐκεῖ *ekeí*; adv. of place. In that place, there (Matt 2:13, 15; 5:24; 6:21; 8:12; 12:45; 13:42, 50; 24:51; 25:30; James 2:3). With the def. art. in the pl. *hoi ekeí*, those there, meaning those who were there (Matt 26:71; Sept.: Gen 2:8, 12); with *hópou* (3699), where (Mark 6:55; Rev 12:6, 14; Sept.: Gen 13:4; 1 Sam 9:10). Also spoken of place, meaning whither, thither, to that place, after verbs of motion instead of *ekeíse* (1566), thither, there (Matt 2:22, meaning he was afraid to go there, i.e., for the sake of remaining there. See Matt 17:20; 21:17; Mark 6:33; Luke 12:18; 17:37; John 11:8; 18:3; Sept.: Deut 1:37; 4:42; Judg 18:3; 2 Sam 17:18).

Deriv.: *ekeíthen* (1564), thence; *ekeínos* (1565), that, that one there; *ekeíse* (1566), thither, there.

Ant.: *autoú* (847), here; *hóde* (5602), hither.

1564. ἐκεῖθεν *ekeíthen*; adv. of place, from *ekeí* (1563), there, and the suffix *-then* meaning from a place. Thence, from that place (Matt 4:21; 5:26; 9:9, 27; Acts 13:4; 20:13). With the def. art. in the pl. *hoi ekeíthen*, it means those from there or those who belong there (Luke 16:26; Sept.: Gen 28:2, 6).

Syn.: *hóthen* (3606), whence, from there.

Ant.: *autoú* (847), here; *entháde* (1759), hither.

1565. ἐκεῖνος *ekeínos*; fem. *ekeínē*, neut. *ekeíno*, demonstrative pron. from *ekeí* (1563), there. That one there, and in the pl., *ekeínoi*, those there. When in antithesis or opposition it usually refers to the person or thing more remote or absent; elsewhere to the next preceding, which it thus often renders more definite and emphatic.

(I) In antithesis referring to the more remote subject, e.g., with *hoútos* (3778), this one (Luke 18:14; James 4:15; see Matt 13:11; Mark 16:20; Luke 13:4; 19:4, 27; John 5:35, 47; 8:42; Heb 12:25).

(II) Without antithesis, referring to the person or thing immediately preceding or just mentioned.

(A) Generally in Matt 17:27; Mark 3:24; 16:10, 11, 13; John 4:25; 5:19, 43; 7:45; 13:6, 27; Acts 3:13; Rom 14:14; 2 Cor 8:9; James 1:7; 2 Pet 1:16; 1 John 5:16. With a subst. of time and referring to a time more or less definite (Matt 3:1, "In those days"; 24:19; Mark 1:9; 2:20; Luke 2:1; 4:2). In the sing., in that day (Matt 7:22; 13:1; 22:23; Mark 4:35). With the prep. *apó* (575), from, from that day (Matt 9:22; 22:46), *en* (1722), in, in

that day or hour (Matt 8:13; 10:19; 11:25; 12:1; 22:23), *kata* (2596), at, at that time (Acts 12:1; 19:23).

(B) Used as an emphatic like the Eng. "that" or "he," where the emphasis lies in the construction, and not in the word itself. Thus where it is used instead of repeating the subject (Mark 7:15, 20; John 1:18; 5:11; 9:37; 10:1; 12:48; 14:26; Rom 14:14; 2 Cor 10:18), it also introduces a following clause, e.g., before a relative pron. (John 10:35; 13:26; Rom 14:15; Heb 6:7; 11:15). The neut. *ekeíno* before *hóti* (3754), that (Matt 24:43) is used especially for persons well-known and celebrated (Matt 27:63; 1 John 3:5). In the fem. sing. it also refers to a well-known day, e.g., to the time of Christ's Second Coming (Matt 7:22; 26:29; Acts 2:18).

(III) The gen. fem. *ekeínēs* as an adv. for *ekeínēs hodoú* (3598), that way (Luke 19:4).

Deriv.: *epékeina* (1896), to behold, look upon; *huperékeina* (5238), beyond those parts.

Ant.: *hoútos* (3778), this one.

1566. ἐκεῖσε *ekeíse*; adv. of place, from *ekeí* (1563), there, and *-se* a suffix denoting at a place. Thither, to that place. In the NT used instead of *ekeí*, there, in that place (Acts 21:3; 22:5; Sept.: Job 39:29).

Ant.: *autoú* (847), here; *hóde* (5603), here, in this place; *entháde* (1759), hither.

1567. ἐκζητέω *ekzētéō*; contracted *ekzētó*, fut. *ekzētēso*, from *ek* (1537), out, or an intens., and *zētéō* (2212), to see. To seek out, search diligently for anything lost (Sept.: Ezek 34:10, 11, 12). In the NT used metaphorically, to seek in order to obtain (Heb 12:17; Sept.: 1 Kgs 14:5; Ps 122:9; Mic 6:8) or know (1 Pet 1:10; Sept.: Ps 44:21). To seek diligently or earnestly after, namely God, with a sincere and earnest desire to obtain His favor (Acts 15:17; Rom 3:11; Heb 11:6. See Sept.: Deut 4:29; 2 Chr 15:2, 13; Ps 14:2; Jer 29:13). To require, demand, or exact severely (Luke 11:50, 51. See Gen 9:5; 42:22; 2 Sam 4:11; Ezek 3:18, 20).

Syn.: *aitéō* (154), to ask; *anazētéō* (327), to seek out; *diaginṓskō* (1231), to ascertain; *dierōtáō* (1331), to inquire thoroughly; *exetázō* (1833), to examine; *ereunáō* (2045), to search, investigate; *proséchō* (4337), to give heed, attend. *punthánomai* (4441), to inquire.

Ant.: *ameléō* (272), to neglect; *lanthánō* (2990), to lie hidden; *oligōréō* (3643), to regard or esteem lightly; *paratheōréō* (3865), to overlook.

1568. ἐκθαμβέω *ekthambéō*; contracted *ekthambṓ*, fut. *ekthambḗsō*, from *ékthambos* (1569), astonished. To utterly astonish, greatly amaze. In the NT, in the pass. *ekthambéomai* contracted *ekthamboúmai*, to be greatly amazed or astonished from admiration (Mark 9:15); from terror (Mark 16:5, 6); from distress of mind (Mark 14:33) where it is parallel with *lupéō* (3076), to be sorry (Matt 26:37).

Syn.: *ekplḗssō* (1605), to astonish, amaze; *exístēmi* (1839), to be beside oneself; *ptoéō* (4422), to terrify; *phobéō* (5399), to fear, revere; *ekphobéō* (1629), to frighten away; *ptúrō* (4426), to terrify; *seíō* (4579), to shake; *trémō* (5141), to tremble; *phríssō* (5425), to shudder.

Ant.: *eirēneúō* (1514), to keep peace or to be at peace; *hēsucházō* (2270), to be still, quiet; *katastéllō* (2687), to quiet, appease.

1569. ἔκθαμβος *ékthambos*; gen. *ekthámbou*, masc.-fem., neut. *ékthambon*, adj. from *ek* (1537), out, or an intens., and *thámbos* (2285), astonishment, amazement. Quite astonished, greatly amazed (Acts 3:11).

Deriv.: *ekthambéō* (1568), to amaze.

Syn.: *aiphnídios* (160), unexpected; *áphōnos* (880), dumbfounded; *émphobos* (1719), frightened; *parádoxos* (3861), extraordinary, strange; *phoberós* (5398), fearful, terrible.

1570. ἔκθετος *ékthetos*; gen. *ekthétou*, masc.-fem., neut. *éktheton*, adj. from *ektíthēmi* (1620), to expose. Exposed, cast out, abandoned as an infant (Acts 7:19).

1571. ἐκκαθαίρω *ekkathaírō*; fut. *ekkatharṓ*, from *ek* (1537), out, and *kathaírō* (2508), to purge. To purge out, meaning to cleanse thoroughly. In the NT, used metaphorically with the acc. of person, to cleanse oneself from (2 Tim 2:21; Sept.: Judg 7:4). Followed by the acc. of thing meaning to cleanse out, put away (1 Cor 5:7).

Syn.: *hagnízō* (48), to purify, cleanse from defilement; *katharízō* (2511), to make clean, purge; *diakatharízō* (1245), to cleanse thoroughly.

Ant.: *koinóō* (2840), to make common or ceremonially unclean; *miaínō* (3392), to stain; *molúnō* (3435), to besmear, defile; *spilóō* (4695), to make a stain or spot, to morally defile; *phtheírō* (5351), to corrupt.

1572. ἐκκαίω *ekkaíō*; fut. *ekkaúsō*, aor. pass. *exekaúthēn*, from *ek* (1537), an intens., and *kaíō* (2545), to burn, light, set fire to. To cause to burn or flame up. Trans., meaning to kindle (Sept.: Ex 22:6; Judg 15:5). In the NT, used in the pass. or mid., to burn out, flame up; intrans. meaning to be inflamed, burn furiously; metaphorically with lust (Rom 1:27); anger (Sept.: Deut 29:20; Ps 2:12; Jer 4:4).

Syn.: *emprḗthō* (1714), to burn up, set on fire; *thermaínō* (2328), to heat; *puróomai* (4448), to glow with heat; *phlogízō* (5394), to set on fire, burn up.

Ant.: *anapsúchō* (404), to cool off, metaphorically to relieve, refresh; *katapsúchō* (2711), to cool; *psúchō* (5594), to chill, make cold; *sbénnumi* (4570), to quench.

1573. ἐκκακέω *ekkakéō*; fut. *ekkakḗsō*, from *ek* (1537), out of, or an intens., and *kakós* (2556), bad. To turn out to be a coward, to lose one's courage. In the NT, generally, to be fainthearted, to faint or despond in view of trial, difficulty. Intrans. (2 Cor 4:1, 16; Eph 3:13). In the sense of to be remiss or slothful in duty (Luke 18:1; Gal 6:9; 2 Thess 3:13).

Syn.: *apopsúchō* (674), to lose soul or heart, faint; *eklúō* (1590), to be faint, grow weary; *kámnō* (2577), to be weary.

Ant.: *anazónnumi* (328), to gird up; *anathállō* (330), to flourish again, revive; *tharréō* (2292), to take courage; *parrēsiázomai* (3955), to speak boldly; *tolmáō* (5111), to dare; *apotolmáō* (662), to be very bold.

1574. ἐκκεντέω *ekkentéō*; contracted *ekkentṓ*, fut. *ekkentḗsō*, from *ek* (1537) out, or an intens., and *kentéō* (n.f.), to sting, stab, prick, pierce. To dig out, pierce. Used trans., meaning to pierce through, transfix (John 19:37; Rev 1:7. See Num 22:29; Judg 9:54; Zech 12:10). Also from *kentéō* (n.f.): *kéntron* (2759), goad, prick.

Syn.: *diérchomai* (1330), to pierce through; *diïknéomai* (1338), to penetrate, pierce; *nússō* (3572), to pierce through; *peripeírō* (4044), to put on a spit, used metaphorically meaning to pierce.

1575. ἐκκλάω *ekkláō*; contracted *ekklṓ*, fut. *ekklásō*, aor. pass. *exeklásthēn*, from *ek* (1537), out, or an intens., and *kláō* (2806), to break. To break out or off, as a branch (Rom 11:17, 19, 20; Sept.: Lev 1:17).

1576. ἐκκλείω *ekkleíō*; fut. *ekkleísō*, aor. pass. *exekleísthēn*, from *ek* (1537), out, and *kleíō* (2808), to shut. To shut out, exclude (Rom 3:27; Gal 4:17).

Syn.: *apokleíō* (608), to close fully, shut up.

Ant.: *egkrúptō* (1470), to conceal in, incorporate with; *empíptō* (1706), to be entrapped by; *sumperilambánō* (4843), to take by including together, embrace.

1577. ἐκκλησία *ekklēsía*; gen. *ekklēsías*, fem. noun from *ékklētos* (n.f.), called out,

which is from *ekkaléō* (n.f.), to call out. It was a common term for a congregation of the *ekklētoí* (n.f.), the called people, or those called out or assembled in the public affairs of a free state, the body of free citizens called together by a herald (*kḗrux* [2783]) which constituted the *ekklēsía*. In the NT, the word is applied to the congregation of the people of Israel (Acts 7:38). On the other hand, of the two terms used in the OT, *sunagōgḗ* (4864) seems to have been used to designate the people from Israel in distinction from all other nations (Acts 13:43 [cf. Matt 4:23; 6:2; James 2:2; Rev 2:9; 3:9]). In Heb 10:25, however, when the gathering of Christians is referred to, it is called not *sunagōgḗ*, but *episunagōgḗ* (1997), with the prep. *epí* (1909), upon, translated "the assembling . . . together." The Christian community was designated for the first time as the *ekklēsía* to differentiate it from the Jewish community, *sunagōgḗ* (Acts 2:47 [TR]). The term *ekklēsía* denotes the NT community of the redeemed in its twofold aspect. First, all who were called by and to Christ in the fellowship of His salvation, the church worldwide of all times, and only secondarily to an individual church (Matt 16:18; Acts 2:44, 47; 9:31; 1 Cor 6:4; 12:28; 14:4, 5, 12; Phil 3:6; Col 1:18, 24). Designated as the church of God (1 Cor 10:32; 11:22; 15:9; Gal 1:13; 1 Tim 3:5, 15); the body of Christ (Eph 1:22; Col 1:18); the church in Jesus Christ (Eph 3:21;); exclusively the entire church (Eph 1:22; 3:10, 21; 5:23–25, 27, 29, 32; Heb 12:23). Secondly, the NT churches, however, are also confined to particular places (Rom 16:5; 1 Cor 1:2; 16:19; 2 Cor 1:1; Col 4:15; 1 Thess 2:14; Phile 1:2); to individual local churches (Acts 8:1; 11:22; Rom 16:1; 1 Thess 1:1; 2 Thess 1:1). *Ekklēsía* does not occur in the gospels of Mark, Luke, John, nor the epistles of 2 Timothy, Titus, 1 and 2 John, or Jude.

(I) Of persons legally called out or summoned (Acts 19:39, of the people); and hence also of a tumultuous assembly not necessarily legal (Acts 19:32, 41).

In the Jewish sense, a congregation, assembly of the people for worship, e.g., in a synagogue (Matt 18:17) or generally (Acts 7:38; Heb 2:12 quoted from Ps 22:22; Sept.: Deut 18:16; 2 Chr 1:3, 5).

(II) In the Christian sense, an assembly of Christians, generally (1 Cor 11:18, a church, the Christian church).

(A) A particular church, e.g., in Jerusalem (Acts 8:1; 11:22); Antioch (Acts 11:26; 13:1); Corinth (1 Cor 1:2; 2 Cor 1:1); Asia Minor (1 Cor 16:19); Galatia (Gal 1:2); Thessalonica (1 Thess 1:1; 2 Thess 1:1); Cenchrea (Rom 16:1). Also, "the churches of the nations" (a.t.) means churches of Gentile Christians (Rom 16:4); the church which meets at the house of someone (Rom 16:5; 1 Cor 16:19; Phile 1:2); the churches of Christ (Rom 16:16); the church of God at Corinth (1 Cor 1:2).

(B) The church universal (Matt 16:18; 1 Cor 12:28; Gal 1:13; Eph 1:22; 3:10; Heb 12:23); church of God (1 Cor 10:32; 11:22; 15:9; 1 Tim 3:15 [cf. in the Sept. the church of the Lord {Deut 23:2, 3}]).

(III) The word *ekklēsía* is nowhere used of heathen religious assemblies in Scripture. In the OT, two different words are used to denote gatherings of the chosen people or their representatives: *edah* (5712, OT) meaning congregation and *qahal* (6951, OT), assembly. In the Sept., *sunagōgē* (4864) is the usual translation of *edah* while *qahal* is commonly rendered *ekklēsía*. Both *qahal* and *ekklēsía* by their derivation indicate calling or summoning to a place of meeting, but there is no foundation for the widespread notion that *ekklēsía* means a people or a number of individual men called out of the world or mankind. *Qahal* or *ekklēsía* is the more sacred term denoting the people in relation to Jehovah, especially in public worship. Perhaps for this very reason, the less sacred term *sunagōgē* was more commonly used by the Jews in our Lord's time, and probably influenced the first believers in adopting *ekklēsía* for Christian use. *Sunagōgē*, though used in the early church as a syn. for *ekklēsía*

(James 2:2), quickly went out of use for a Christian assembly, except in sects which were more Jewish than Christian. Owing to the growing hostility of the Jews, it came to indicate opposition to the church (Rev 2:9; 3:9). *Ekklēsía*, therefore, at once suggests the new people of God, the new Israel.

(IV) The terms "the kingdom of God" and "the church" are distinguished in Scripture. The kingdom appears to be a reign rather than a realm, which the church is. These two ideas, however, are complementary, the one implying the other. Sometimes it is hardly possible to distinguish between them. It may be true that by the words "the kingdom of God," our Lord means not so much His disciples, whether individually or as a collective body, but something which they receive or a state upon which they enter. At the same time, the whole history of the growth of the idea of the kingdom led, naturally, to the belief that the kingdom of God about which Christ taught would be expressed and realized in a society. His kingdom is visibly represented in His church, and the church is the kingdom of heaven insofar as it has already come, and it prepares for the kingdom as it is to come in glory. See *basileía* (932), kingdom.

1578. ἐκκλίνω *ekklínō*; fut. *ekklinō̂*, from *ek* (1537), out, and *klínō* (2827), to incline, bend, turn aside or away, recline. To avoid, used metaphorically of those who turn away or swerve from piety and virtue (Rom 3:12 quoted from Ps 14:3; Rom 16:17; 1 Pet 3:11; Sept.: Ps 37:27; Prov 3:7).

Syn.: *ápeimi* (548), to go away; *apérchomai* (565), to go away or aside, depart; *apostréphō* (654), to turn away; *ektrépō* (1624), to turn away or aside; *éxeimi* (1826), to go out or depart; *kámptō* (2578), to bend; *methístēmi* (3179), to remove; *metatíthēmi* (3346), to locate oneself in another place; *paraporeúomai* (3899), to pass by; *stréphō* (4762), to turn aside; *paraphéromai* (3911), to fall aside.

Ant.: *anakúptō* (352), to lift oneself up; *anístēmi* (450), to raise up; *anorthóō* (461), to set up, make straight; *egeírō* (1453), to rise up; *epaírō* (1869), to lift up; *hupsóō* (5312), to lift or raise up.

1579. ἐκκολυμβάω *ekkolumbáō*; contracted *ekkolumbṓ*; fut. *ekkolumbḗsō*, from *ek* (1537), out, and *kolumbáō* (2860), to swim. To swim out toward land (Acts 27:42).

Ant.: *buthízō* (1036), to drown, to sink; *katapontízō* (2670), to sink.

1580. ἐκκομίζω *ekkomízō*; fut. *ekkomísō*, from *ek* (1537), out, and *komízō* (2865), to carry. To bear or carry out, e.g., the dead body out of the city or town for burial. The Jews usually did not bury their dead within the walls of the towns (see 1 Kgs 11:43; 15:8, 24). The Athenians and the Romans even enacted laws to forbid such a practice (Luke 7:12 [cf. Matt 27:60; John 11:31, 38; 19:41]).

Syn.: *ágō* (71), to lead or carry; *aírō* (142), to lift and carry away; *apophérō* (399), to carry away; *apágō* (520), to carry away; *ekbállō* (1544), to cast out; *ekphérō* (1627), to carry forth.

Ant.: *apoleípō* (620), to leave behind; *egkataleípō* (1459), to leave behind in one place; *eáō* (1439), to let, leave; *kataleípō* (2641), to leave behind; *perileípō* (4035), to leave over; *hupoleípō* (5275), to leave remaining; *hupolimpánō* (5277), to leave.

1581. ἐκκόπτω *ekkóptō*; fut. *ekkópsō*, from *ek* (1537), out, and *kóptō* (2875), to cut. To cut off or out, as a branch from a tree (Rom 11:22, 24 making the verb parallel with *ekkláō* [1575], to break off, in Rom 11:17, 19, 20). To cut down a tree (Matt 3:10; 7:19; Luke 3:9; 13:7, 9); the right hand (Matt 5:30; 18:8; Sept.: Jer 6:6; 22:7); one's hand or foot (Matt 18:8). Metaphorically, to cut out or off, meaning to remove (2 Cor 11:12); in 1 Pet 3:7 (TR), "that your prayers be not cut off" (a.t.) or rendered fruitless.

Syn.: *apokóptō* (609), to cut off; *diapríō* (1282), to saw asunder; *dichotoméō* (1371), to cut into two parts; *katakóptō* (2629), to cut down.

1582. ἐκκρέμαμαι *ekkrémamai*; the mid. form of *ekkremánnumi* from *ek* (1537), from, and *krémamai* (2910), to hang. To hang from, used metaphorically of those who listen closely to a person speaking, equal to the Eng. "to hang on the words" of someone. Followed by the gen. of person (Luke 19:48; Sept.: Gen 44:30).

Syn.: *akoúō* (191), to hearken; *diakoúō* (1251), to hear through, fully; *eisakoúō* (1522), to listen to; *enōtízomai* (1801), to give ear to; *epakoúō* (1873), to hearken; *epakroáomai* (1874), to listen attentively to; *peitharchéō* (3980), to be obedient, to obey one in authority; *peíthomai* (3982), to be persuaded; *proséchō* (4337), to take heed; *hupakoúō* (5219), to pay attention to, obey.

Ant.: *ameléō* (272), to be careless, make light of; *paratheōréō* (3865), to overlook, neglect; *parakoúō* (3878), to overhear, to hear amiss or imperfectly.

1583. ἐκλαλέω *eklaléō*; contracted *eklalṓ*, fut. *eklalḗsō*, from *ek* (1537), out, and *laléō* (2980), to speak. To speak out, to tell, disclose; used trans. with the dat. of person in Acts 23:22, where the inf. is used instead of the imper.

Deriv.: *aneklálētos* (412), unutterable.

Syn.: *anaggéllō* (312), to announce; *apaggéllō* (518), to declare; *exēgéomai* (1834), to explain; *mēnúō* (3377), to tell, disclose.

Ant.: *sigáō* (4601), to be silent; *siōpáō* (4623), to be silent; *phimóō* (5392), to put to silence.

1584. ἐκλάμπω *eklámpō*; fut. *eklámpsō*, from *ek* (1537), out, or an intens., and *lámpō* (2989), to shine. To shine forth or out, to be resplendent (Matt 13:43, an allusion to Dan 12:3).

Syn.: *exastráptō* (1823), to shine forth; *epiphaínō* (2014), to shine upon; *epiphaúō* (2017), to shine forth; *periastráptō* (4015), to flash around; *stílbō* (4744), to shine, glisten; *phaínō* (5316), to cause to appear;.

Ant.: *skotízō* (4654), to deprive of light, make dark; *skotóō* (4656), to darken.

1585. ἐκλανθάνω *eklanthánō*; fut. *eklḗsō*, from *ek* (1537), an intens., and *lanthánō* (2990), to forget, lie hidden. To make to forget entirely. In the NT found only in the mid. *eklanthánomai*. In the perf. pass. with mid. meaning, *eklélēsmai*, to forget entirely, followed by the gen. (Heb 12:5).

Syn.: *epilanthánomai* (1950), to forget or neglect.

Ant.: *anamimnḗskō* (363), to call to mind, remember; *epanamimnḗskō* (1878), to remind again; *mimnḗskomai* (3403) and the older form *mnáomai* (3415), to remind, remember; *mnēmoneúō* (3421), to call to mind; *hupomimnḗskō* (5279), to remember, put in mind.

1586. ἐκλέγω *eklégō*; fut. *ekléxō*, from *ek* (1537), out, and *légō* (3004), to select, choose. To choose, select, choose for oneself, not necessarily implying the rejection of what is not chosen, but giving favor to the chosen subject, keeping in view a relationship to be established between the one choosing and the object chosen. It involves preference and selection from among many choices. In the NT found only in the mid. *eklégomai*.

(I) Generally of things (Luke 10:42; 14:7). Followed by *hína* (2443), so that, of purpose (1 Cor 1:27, 28; Sept.: Gen 13:11); of persons followed by the acc. simply (John 6:70; 15:16; Acts 1:2, 24; 6:5; 15:22, 25; Sept.: 1 Sam 8:18; 10:24); followed by *ek* (1537), from, with the gen. (John 15:19); followed by *apó* (575) with a gen. (Luke 6:13). With an inf. implied (James 2:5 where the implied inf. is *eínai* [1511], to be). Followed by *en* (1722), among (Acts 15:7, "God chose

among us . . . that through my mouth" [a.t.]).

(II) By implication, to choose out, with the accessory idea of kindness, favor, love (Mark 13:20; John 13:18; Acts 13:17; Eph 1:4; Sept.: Deut 4:37; Ps 65:4; Zech 3:2). In some MSS, Luke 9:35 (TR) has *eklelegménos*, chosen, instead of *agapētós* (27), beloved.

Deriv.: *eklektós* (1588), chosen, elect.

Syn.: *hairéomai* (138), to prefer; *hairetízō* (140), to prefer, choose; *epilégomai* (1951), to select, choose for oneself.

Ant.: *apobállō* (577), to throw off, cast away; *aporríptō* (641), to reject, cast off; *periphronéō* (4065), to despise.

1587. ἐκλείπω *ekleípō*; fut. *ekleípsō*, from *ek* (1537), out, or an intens., and *leípō* (3007), to fail, to leave out or off. Trans., to relinquish, desert. Intrans., to leave off, to fail, cease (Luke 22:32; Heb 1:12 quoted from Ps 102:27, "and thy years shall not fail"; Sept.: Gen 21:15; Josh 3:13; Jer 7:28). To cease to live, to die (Luke 16:9; Sept.: Gen 49:33; Jer 42:17, 22; Lam 1:19).

Deriv.: *anékleiptos* (413), not left out, inexhaustible.

Syn.: *apothnḗskō* (599), to die; *apotássō* (657), to forsake, to put away from self in one's rightful position; *apopsúchō* (674), literally to breathe out life, to faint; *aphanízō* (853), to disappear, vanish away; *ekdēméō* (1553), to vacate, to die; *egkakéō* or *ekkakéō* (1573), to lose heart; *eklúō* (1590), to grow weary; *kámnō* (2577), to be weary; *katargéō* (2673), to abolish, cease; *paúō* (3973), to make to cease; *teleutáō* (5053), to die; *hupolimpánō* (5277), to leave; *husteréō* (5302), to fall short, fail.

Ant.: *asphalízō* (805), to secure; *bióō* (980), to spend existence, to live; *heurískō* (2147), to find; *záō* (2198), to live.

1588. ἐκλεκτός *eklektós*; fem. *eklektḗ*, neut. *eklektón*, adj. from *eklégō* (1586), to choose, select. Chosen, select. In the group of three important biblical words, *eklektós, eklégō*, and *eklogē* (1589), choice or election, selection involves thoughtful and deliberate consideration.

(I) Select, choice, elect. Used as an adj. in regard to stone as in 1 Pet 2:4, 6 quoted from Isa 28:16; see Ezra 5:8. In both of these instances the stone is the Lord Jesus Christ as the one chosen of God the Father to accomplish the work of redemption for sinful man. Of persons, chosen or distinguished as in 1 Pet 2:9, *génos eklektón* (*génos* [1085], generation), "a chosen generation," referring to the believers in Christ. See Sept.: Isa 43:20. Of angels in 1 Tim 5:21, referring to them as chosen by God to minister to the special needs of believers.

(II) By implication meaning chosen, with the accessory idea of kindness, favor, love, equivalent to cherished, beloved. In Luke 23:35, the enemies of Christ around His cross said, "Let him save himself, if he be Christ, the chosen of God," which means the one cherished and beloved of God and who was selected to accomplish the work of salvation for others. In Rom 16:13, referring to Rufus, "the chosen one in the Lord" (a.t.), meaning the beloved one as in the previous verse referring to Persis. For Paul, Rufus was special in the Lord. He was dearly beloved. In the pl. *hoi eklektoí*, the elect, are those chosen of God unto salvation and who therefore enjoy His favor and lead a holy life in communion with Him. They are also called saints (Rom 1:7; 15:31); Christians (Acts 11:26; 26:28; 1 Pet 4:16). The word is used to differentiate those who believe in Christ from those who do not. They are Christians because God chose them from among the lost world to become His followers. A great deal of confusion, however, will ensue if the term "the elect" is understood as composing only those who constitute the church of Jesus Christ during this dispensation of grace. Therefore, to arrive at the proper conclusion of who the elect are in each instance of its occurrence, the context has to be taken into account. In Matt 24:22, 24 and Mark 13:20, 22 it is evident that the elect are only those who will be saved during the tribulation, not all the saved of all generations. However, the term can refer to believers of all times, including those of the dispensation of grace, the church age, and those who will be saved during the tribulation as in Matt 24:31 and Mark 13:27. Referring to those who are effectively called unto salvation generally (Matt 20:16; 22:14; Rom 8:33; Col 3:12; 2 Tim 2:10; Titus 1:1); of the believers who are discriminated against during their lifetime (Luke 18:7). Generally, with a subst. (1 Pet 1:2; 2 John 1:1, 13) or as a subst. (Rev 17:14).

Deriv.: *suneklektós* (4899), elected together with.

1589. ἐκλογή *eklogē*; gen. *eklogḗs*, fem. noun from *eklégō* (1586), to choose, select. Election, choice, selection.

(I) Generally as in Acts 9:15, a chosen vessel, an instrument of usefulness.

(II) Election, the benevolent purpose of God by which any are chosen unto salvation so that they are led to embrace and persevere in Christ's bestowed grace and the enjoyment of its privileges and blessings here and hereafter. In Rom 11:5 we have clearly demonstrated the motive of God's election being grace. "According to the election of grace" means according to the election which results from grace. In Rom 11:28, "as touching the election" means according to the principle of election which precludes personal worth as in the case of unbelieving Israel. However, they were beloved because of their fathers, such as Abraham who believed God, who rejoiced in seeing the day of Christ (John 8:56). God does not choose unto salvation and bestow His grace because of the worth of any person, but only because of and for the sake of Jesus Christ. In 1 Thess 1:4, "knowing, brethren beloved, your election of God," the verb that is used is *eidótes* (1492), to perceive intuitively. What Paul is saying is that one recognizes that his salvation and conversion is of grace only when he has experienced that grace.

2 Pet 1:10, "to make your calling and election sure," stresses the responsibility of the Christian believer to live conformably to his new nature in Christ Jesus (2 Pet 1:4). Rom 11:7, "What then? Israel hath not obtained [*epétuchen*, the aor. of *epitugchánō* {2013}, to attain one's aim] that which he seeketh for; but the election hath obtained it [*epétuchen*, attained it or succeeded in accomplishing its purpose], and the rest were blinded," indicates that in spite of the corporate rejection of Christ by Israel, yet Christ's election of grace succeeded in saving some Jews. Paul also says in Rom 11:26 that Israel's election unto salvation will yet be accomplished in that "all Israel shall be saved," which refers to Israel as a nation who will, consequent to the great tribulation, acclaim Christ as their Messiah.

(III) By implication meaning free choice, free will, election. In Rom 9:11 we have the expression, "The purpose of God according to election might stand." This means that God's intention (*próthesis* [4286]) was according to the principle of election which is God's free choice without being affected by any outside circumstances or the worth of the individuals concerned. Such free election by God must never be considered as a demonstration of injustice by God as Rom 9:14 declares, "What shall we say then? Is there unrighteousness [*adikía* {93}, injustice] with God? God forbid." God's principle of the exercise of His freedom to choose is always in favor of man as long as there is no violation of God's justice. Man is a fallen creature and deserves God's punishment. Whenever God makes a choice, it is always a choice unto salvation energizing those whom He calls to believe without forbidding those who do not believe to do so.

Rom 9:22 is very helpful in the understanding of the principle of election: "What if God, willing to show his wrath, and to make his power known, endured with much longsuffering the vessels of wrath fitted to destruction." The verb "fitted" in Gr. is *katērtisména* which is the perf. pass. part. with mid. meaning of the verb *katartízō* (2675), prepared or adjusted. These unbelievers were not fitted to become vessels of perdition by God Himself, but *by their own selves* in refusing to believe on the Lord Jesus Christ. Therefore, the whole principle of election is that man may know that his salvation is not because he deserves it, but because of the grace of God. Also, someone who will not accept God's salvation can never face God and claim that He was unjust and had caused his loss.

The subst. *eklogé* is not found in the Sept. Whenever and however the seventeen different Hebr. words that have the root meaning of "choose" are used in the OT, they chiefly describe God's choice of Israel out of all the nations of the world to be His own people (Deut 4:7; 7:7), and of Jerusalem to be the covenant home of worship (Deut 12:5). It is used also of God's choice of individuals to the chief offices in the nation, e.g., His choice of Aaron and his family for the service of the sanctuary, and His choice of the kings, especially David. It is once used of Abraham; and in Isa 40—66, it passes naturally from its use in connection with Israel to the "servant of the Lord," Jesus Christ.

When we think of election as the right of an omnipotent God, we must not limit ourselves only to God's power, but look also at God's love and mercy. The Author of election is also the Author of all knowledge. He is not limited by the element of time. The concept and measurement of time is simply and merely for man's accommodation, man being finite in his comprehension. God does not need to wait until someone believes to write his name in the Book of Life (Rev 13:8; 17:8). By virtue of God's omniscience, it is impossible for Him to make a mistake and write someone's name in the Book of Life from the beginning of the world and then for Him to find out that He has erred and that person is not saved. If God can err, He is no longer God. God's disposition and will is that all men be saved and come to the knowledge of the truth (1 Tim 2:4) and that none be lost (2 Pet 3:9). God cannot go against His own declared will and willfully cancel His plan to save the human race by deliberately and capriciously assigning some to hell. Indeed, none could be saved without the effective calling of God and His election, and whenever any person is saved it is because of that effective calling of God in Christ. No one can be saved on his own, generating his own faith and in his own power approaching God. Man, having fallen in Adam, cannot approach God. God had to approach man in Christ.

Those who are lost are not lost because Christ discriminated against them, but because they did not respond to Christ's offer of grace and salvation. This is why we never have any of the three words in the group (eklégomai [1586], to choose; eklektós [1588], chosen one or ones, or the subst. eklogé [1589]) used with man as the subject and God as the object. The subject is always God and the object is always man when it comes to salvation. Man cannot choose God but God chooses man and makes effectual His call to accomplish His eternal purpose to redeem and save mankind.

In the OT, we find two of the Hebr. words corresponding to eklektós (bachur [970, OT] and bachir [972, OT]) used in the sense of select men (Judg 20:16; 1 Sam 24:2) or persons chosen by God for special service: Moses (Ps 106:23); David (Ps 89:20, 21); the nation Israel (Ps 106:5; Isa 45:4; 65:9, 15); the servant of the Lord (Isa 42:1 [cf. 52:13]).

In the NT, we find the verb eklégomai used always in the mid. voice of our Lord's choice of the Twelve from the company of the disciples (Luke 6:13; John 6:70; 13:18; 15:19; Acts 1:2); of the choice of an apostle in the place of Judas (Acts 1:24); of Stephen and his colleagues (Acts 6:5); of God's choice of the patriarchs (Acts 13:17); and of the choice of delegates to carry the decisions of the Apostolic Council to the Gentile churches (Acts 15:22, 25). It is used of God's choice of the foolish things of the world to put to shame them that are wise, and the weak things to put to shame the things which are strong (1 Cor 1:27); and of His choice of the poor to be rich in faith and heirs of the kingdom promised to them that love Him (James 2:5).

There are two Gr. words that need to be examined in their interrelationship: klētoí (2822), the called ones, and the eklektoí (1588), the chosen ones. No one can be a chosen one unless he is a called one. The initiative always comes from God. In Matt 20:16; 22:14 the words of Christ are "For many are called, but few are chosen." These two terms seem to be coextensive, as two aspects of the same process, klētoí, the called, having special reference to the goal, and eklektoí, referring to the starting point. The same persons are "called" to Christ and "chosen out" from the world. All are called by Christ: "Come unto me, all ye that labor and are heavy laden, and I will give you rest" (Matt 11:28). None is excluded, but not all who are called accept the call, and those who accept are the eklektoí, the chosen ones whom the grace of God puts at the starting point of the newly regenerated life, giving them from that moment on a sense of responsibility and fulfillment of the purpose to which they are called.

He who calls (ho kalōn, the pres. part. of kaléō [2564]) in the epistles is used of God or Christ in the pres. tense (Gal 5:8; 1 Thess 2:12; 5:24). However, the pres. pass. part. of eklégō (ho eklegómenos) is never used, nor the pres. tense of any part of the verb, the aor. being used to describe what depended upon God's eternal purpose (Eph 1:4; 2 Thess 2:13). In Peter's epistles eklektós is found four times, once of elect in "people" (1 Pet 1:2), once of Christians as an "elect race" (a.t. [1 Pet 2:9]), and twice of Christ as the living stone, "chosen" to be the cornerstone (1 Pet 2:4, 6).

Eklogé is spoken of the divine act (Acts 9:15; Rom 9:11; 11:5, 28; 1 Thess 1:4; 2 Pet 1:10), and once as the abstract for the concrete *eklektoí* (Rom 11:7). It is noteworthy that Christ speaks of those who were saved as those whom the Father had given Him (John 6:37, 39; 17:2, 24), to whom He should give life eternal and whom He would keep so that they should never perish (John 10:28).

Not only does God not make a mistake in the choice He makes of sinful men who become His chosen ones, but once He saves them, He does not lose them. If He did, then that would be a declaration of impotence on His part. When the Apostle Paul preached for the first time to Gentiles at Antioch of Pisidia, we read "as many as were ordained to eternal life believed" (Acts 13:48). Paul preached to all who would listen, even as Jesus Christ invited all to come to Him, but only a few heeded the call and believed. Many are called, but few are the chosen ones (Matt 20:16; 22:14). 1 Thess 1:2–10 sets forth the results of their election, i.e., their patient endurance of affliction and the joy they had in their new spiritual life, a joy begotten in them by the Holy Spirit.

The elect know who they are, and their lives indicate a transformation. The choosing by God involves our sanctification and our glorification (2 Thess 2:13–15). In 2 Thess 2:13 a syn. of *eklégō* is used, namely *heíleto* or *heílato*, the aor. mid. of *hairéō* or *hairéomai* (138), to take for oneself, prefer, choose. Again, observe that this choice was made from the beginning indicating the omniscience of God as to who was going to respond to His call. This choice is done by God "from the beginning," from eternity. Therefore, such eternal salvation cannot be attributed to mere circumstances, although God brings about circumstances that lead to salvation. In this case the preaching of the Apostle Paul was the circumstance that God permitted to come to these people.

Although God knows and foreordains the chosen ones, yet as Jesus Christ invited all to come to Him, we also must do likewise since we are totally ignorant of who the elect are. None who refuse to come to the Lord can ever claim that they have not been called and thus they have perished.

In Rom 8:28–30, Paul speaks of the believers as foreknown and predestinated (*proórise*, the aor. of *proorízō* [4309], to determine before, v. 29); called (*ekálese*, the aor. of *kaléō* [2564], to call, v. 30); justified (*edikaíōsen*, the aor. of *dikaióō* [1344], to justify, to declare just and make just or righteous); glorified (*edóxase*, the aor. of *doxázō* [1392], to glorify, v. 30). All that God did for the believer is in the aor. tense (*proégnō*, foreknew; *proórise*, foreordained; *ekálese*, called; *edikaíōsen*, justified; *edóxase*, glorified). Observe, however, that the behavior and action of the called ones is in the pres. tense as indicated by the verb *oídamen* (the perf. of *eídō* [1492], used in the pres. tense) referring to intuitive knowledge of one in whose heart God performed the miracle of regeneration, and *toís agapósi*, those loving, the pres. part. of *agapáō* (25), to love. Therefore, they who intuitively know and love God are identical with "them that are the called according to His purpose" (*toís katá próthesin klētoís*), or those called according to His pre-established position (v. 28). They are "foreordained" so that they may attain the likeness of God's Son, and further, that He may be glorified in them and see the travail of His soul and be satisfied.

God's elect (Rom 8:33) may have the assaults of temptation and trial to face, as well as tribulation, anguish, persecution, famine, nakedness, peril, and suffering to endure; but nothing can separate them from the love of God which is in Christ Jesus. In Eph 1:4–6 the spiritual blessings enjoyed in such abundance by the believers are traced to their election by God, "Even as he chose us in him [Christ] before the foundation of the world, that we should be holy and without blemish before him in love: having foreordained us unto adoption as sons through Jesus Christ unto himself, according to the good pleasure of his will, to the praise of the glory of his grace" (a.t.). The word "adoption" in Gr. is *huiothesía* (5206), which means a more conscious conformity to the will and purpose of God once our nature has been changed (2 Pet 1:4). It is Christ who at all times activates our wills to believe and to obey, and no work which we perform can be said to be truly our work (Eph 2:10). There is in the life of the elect a merging of one's own regenerated will with the will of God to accomplish God's eternal purposes (2 Tim 1:10).

In Rom 9—11, Paul deals with the mystery of the call of the Gentiles to take the place of gainsaying and disobedient Israel. In so doing, he first vindicates God from the accusation that He has departed from His ancient covenant, a reproach which would be well-founded if the covenant people were rejected and the Gentiles put in their place. Such a rejection, Paul contends, would not be altogether out of keeping with God's treatment of His people in the course of their history. God indeed chose Israel, but Israel did not choose God. The "election within the election" (a.t.), Paul argues, is the Christian church—the Israel after the Spirit—and the reproach of the objector falls to the ground (Rom 9:6–9).

The apostle further maintains in Rom 9:10–24 that God, in His electing purpose, is sovereign as is seen in the difference between the two sons of Rebecca; in the divine word to Moses: "I will have mercy on whom I will have mercy"; and in the hardening of the heart of Pharaoh. And after all, if the election were cancelled, the blame would be Israel's own because of unbelief and disobedience. This Moses denounced and Isaiah bewailed when he said, "All the day long did I spread out my hands unto a disobedient and gainsaying people" (a.t. [Rom 10:21]). But, despite appearances, Israel was not cast off. Their rejection was not final. There were believing Israelites, like Paul himself, in all the churches; and he could say, "At this present time also there is a remnant according to the election of

grace" (Rom 11:5). Meanwhile, the problem of Israel's unbelief and of the passing over of spiritual privilege to the Gentiles (Rom 11:11) is to be solved by the Gentiles provoking Israel to jealousy—appreciating and embracing and profiting by the blessings of the Christian salvation to such an extent that Israel will be moved to desire and to possess those blessings for their own. When Jews in numbers come to seek as their own the righteousness and goodness which they see thus manifested in the lives of Christians, and are stirred up to envy and emulation by the contemplation of them, the time will be at hand when all Israel, as a nation, shall be saved. Of that issue Paul has no doubt, for "the gifts and calling of God are without repentance" (Rom 11:29). God has not made a mistake in calling the Gentiles at this present time in view of Israel's rejection. God's election is not conditioned upon any good foreseen in the elect, nor upon any faith or merit which they may exhibit in time (Rom 9:11–13), but is "according to the good pleasure of his will" (Eph 1:5), "according to his own purpose and grace" (2 Tim 1:9), and of God's sovereign purpose and grace (Rom 9:15; 11:5–7). It is carried out "in Christ" (Eph 1:3; 2:10) through the elect being brought into union with Him by faith, that they may receive forgiveness of sins and every spiritual blessing in the heavenly places (Eph 1:3, 5). It issues in sanctification by the Spirit, and assurance of the truth (2 Thess 2:13f.), and heavenly glory (Rom 8:30), and is proved by acceptance of the gospel call and by the trust and peace and joy of believing and obedient hearts (1 Thess 1:4–6).

Syn.: *haíresis* (139), choice.

1590. ἐκλύω *eklúō*; fut. *eklúsō*, from *ek* (1537), out, or an intens., and *lúō* (3089), to loose. To loose out of, set free from. Used in the pass. or mid. *eklúomai*, to be weary, exhausted, to faint (Gal 6:9), a parallel with *ekkakéō* (1573), to faint, be weary; spoken of a body (Matt 9:36

[TR]; 15:32; Mark 8:3; Sept.: 1 Sam
14:28; 2 Sam 16:14; 17:29; 21:15; Lam
2:12, 19); spoken of the mind, to faint, to
be despondent (Heb 12:3, 5; Sept.: Deut
20:3).

Syn.: *apopsúchō* (674), to be out of
breath or faint; *kámnō* (2577), to be fa-
tigued as a result of labor; *paralúō* (3886),
to relax, to cease to be able.

Ant.: *anapsúchō* (404), to cool off, relieve; *tharréō* (2292), to be of good courage; *parrēsiázomai* (3955), to be bold;
tolmáō (5111), to dare; *apotolmáō* (662),
to be very bold.

1591. ἐκμάσσω *ekmássō*, **ἐκμάττω**
ekmáttō; fut. *ekmáxō*, from *ek* (1537),
an intens., and *mássō* (n.f., see below), to
handle, wipe. To wipe off, wipe dry, used
trans. (Luke 7:38, 44; John 11:2; 12:3;
13:5).

Deriv. of *másso* (n.f.): *apomássō*
(631), to wipe off; *massáomai* (3145), to
chew, gnaw.

Syn.: *exaleíphō* (1813), to wipe out or
away; *kathaírō* (2508), to cleanse, purge.

Ant.: *bebēlóō* (953), to desecrate,
profane; *molúnō* (3435), to soil; *rhupóō*
(4510), to soil, become dirty morally;
spilóō (4695), to defile, spot.

1592. ἐκμυκτηρίζω *ekmuktērízō*; fut.
ekmuktērísō, from *ek* (1537), an intens.,
and *muktērízō* (3456), to mock, sneer.
To deride, sneer, or scoff at. Used trans.
(Luke 16:14; 23:35; Sept.: Ps 2:4; 22:7).

Syn.: *katageláō* (2606), to laugh at
scornfully.

Ant.: *dokimázō* (1381), to approve.

1593. ἐκνεύω *ekneúō*; fut. *ekneúsō*,
from *ek* (1537), out, and *neúō* (3506), to
move, tend, incline. To shake off, spoken
of a horse and meaning to toss the head
about. Trans. it means to shake off by
throwing the head about. Used intrans.
meaning to turn aside, turn away (John
5:13). Generally it means to escape, withdraw privately (Sept.: Judg 4:18; 18:26;
2 Kgs 2:24; 23:16).

1594. ἐκνήφω *eknḗphō*; fut. *eknḗpsō*,
from *ek* (1537), out, and *nḗphō* (3525),
to be sober. Intrans. it means to sober up
or become sober from a drunken spell
(Sept.: Gen 9:24; 1 Sam 25:37; Joel 1:5).
Used metaphorically meaning to rouse
up, awake from a state of stupor, ignorance, delusion (1 Cor 15:34; Sept.: Ps
78:65).

Syn.: *diagrēgoréō* (1235), to make
fully awake; *diegeírō* (1326), to arouse;
egeírō (1453), to awaken; *egkrateúomai*
(1467), to exercise self-restraint; *exupnízō*
(1852), to rouse a person out of sleep;
sōphronéō (4993), to act moderately.

Ant.: *methúskō* (3182), to make drunk;
methúō (3184), to be drunk.

1595. ἑκούσιος *hekoúsios*; gen. *hekou-
síou*, fem. *hekousía*, neut. *hekoúsion*, adj.
from *hekṓn* (1635), willingly. Voluntary, willing. Only in Phile 1:14 where
it means willingly, uncompelled, gladly
(Sept.: Num 15:3).

Deriv.: *hekousíōs* (1596), voluntarily.

Syn.: *authaíretos* (830), voluntary,
willing; *hétoimos* (2092), ready; *próthumos* (4289), willing;.

Ant.: *anagkaíos* (316), necessary,
needful; *bíaios* (972), violent; *opheilétēs*
(3781), one owing.

1596. ἑκουσίως *hekousíōs*; adv. from
hekoúsios (1595), voluntary. Voluntarily,
intentionally. Refers to sins committed
willingly, those done designedly and deliberately in the face of better knowledge
(Heb 10:26; 1 Pet 5:2; Sept.: Ps 54:6).

Syn.: *hekṓn* (1635), voluntarily, willingly.

Ant.: *ákōn* (210), unwillingly; *anagkastós* (317), compulsorily.

1597. ἔκπαλαι *ékpalai*; adv. from *ek*
(1537), of, and *pálai* (3819), anciently,
formerly. Of old, long since (2 Pet 2:3;
3:5). To be distinguished from *ex archḗs*
(*ex* [1537], out, from; *archḗs* [746], beginning), from the beginning, from the
first (John 6:64; 16:4), and *ap' archḗs*

(*apó* [575], from; *archḗs* [746], beginning), from the beginning of all things, from everlasting, as spoken of any particular thing (Matt 19:4, 8).

Syn.: *poté* (4218), once, formerly, of old.

Ant.: *apárti* (534), from now, henceforth; *árti* (737), just now; *nún* (3568), now, at present; *nuní* (3570), just now; *metá taúta* (*metá* [3326], after; *taúta* [5023], these things), after these things, henceforth.

1598. ἐκπειράζω *ekpeirázō*; fut. *ekpeiráso*, from *ek* (1537), an intens., and *peirázō* (3985), tempt. Try, prove, tempt, put to the test. Sinners are said to tempt God (Matt 4:7; Luke 4:12; 10:25; Acts 5:9, *peirázō*; 1 Cor 10:9), putting Him to the test, refusing to believe Him or His Word until He has manifested His power (Sept.: Deut 6:16; 8:16; Ps 78:18). When God is said to try (*peirazō*) man (Heb 11:17 [cf. Gen 22:1; Ex 15:25]), in no other sense can He do this (James 1:13) but to train in order to elevate a person as a result of the self-knowledge which may be won through these testings (*peirasmoí* [3986]). Thus, man may emerge from his testings holier, humbler, stronger than when he entered in (James 1:2, 12). *Peirázō* is predominantly used to try someone in order to show he is not approved of God but reprobate, in the hope that he will break down under the proof. *Peirázō* is also used for Satan's solicitations (Matt 4:1; 1 Cor 7:5; Rev 2:10).

Syn.: *peirázō* (3985), to test; *dokimázō* (1381), to test, prove.

1599. ἐκπέμπω *ekpémpō*; fut. *ekpémpsō*, from *ek* (1537), out, and *pémpō* (3992), to send. To send out or forth (Acts 13:4; 17:10; Sept.: Gen 24:54, 56, 59).

Syn.: *apostéllō* (649), to send forth; *exapostéllō* (1821), to send forth.

Ant.: *anadéchomai* (324), to receive gladly; *analambánō* (353), to take up; *apodéchomai* (588), to welcome; *déchomai* (1209), to receive deliberately and readily; *eisdéchomai*

(1523), to receive into; *lambánō* (2983), to receive; *paralambánō* (3880) or *apolambánō* (618), to receive from another; *prosdéchomai* (4327), to receive to oneself; *proslambánō* (4355), to take to oneself; *hupodéchomai* (5264), to receive under one's roof.

1600. ἐκπετάννυμι *ekpetánnumi*; fut. *ekpetásō*, from *ek* (1537), out, and *petánnumi* (n.f.), to stretch out. To spread out, expand, stretch forth, as with the hands in supplication (Rom 10:21 from Isa 65:2; see Ex 9:29, 33).

Syn.: *anaptússō* (380), to unroll, open; *strónnumi* (4766), to spread.

Ant.: *helíssō* (1667), to roll together; *entulíssō* (1794), to roll up; *ptússō* (4428), to fold; *sustéllō* (4958), to draw together, contract, enwrap; *sustréphō* (4962), to gather.

1601. ἐκπίπτω *ekpíptō*; fut. *ekpesoúmai*, aor. *exépesa*, 2d aor. *exépeson*, perf. *ekpéptōka*, from *ek* (1537), from, and *píptō* (4098), to fall. To fall off or from, to fall (Gal 5:4).

(I) Particularly spoken of things, to fall out of or from their place, e.g., stars from heaven (Mark 13:25 [cf. Matt 24:29; Isa 14:12]), flowers (James 1:11; 1 Pet 1:24; Sept.: Isa 28:1, 4), chains from the hands (Acts 12:7), a boat from a ship (Acts 27:32). Of a ship, to fall off or be driven from its course, usually followed by *eis* (1519), to, with the acc. of place, to bring upon (Acts 27:17, 26, 29). Figuratively, to fall from any state or condition, i.e., to lose one's part or interest in that state; followed by the gen. (Gal 5:4; 2 Pet 3:17; Rev 2:5 [TR]).

(II) Metaphorically to fall away, i.e., to fail, be without effect, to be in vain, of love (1 Cor 13:8); of the Word of God (Rom 9:6). See Josh 23:14 and 2 Kgs 6:5.

Syn.: *athetéō* (114), to reject, set aside; *akuróō* (208), to render void, cancel; *exoudenóō* (1847), to set at naught; *kathairéō* (2507), destroy, pull down; *katargéō* (2673), to render useless or inactive; *kenóō* (2758), to make empty; *hustereō* (5302), to come behind in or be inferior.

Ant.: *epiménō* (1961), to abide or continue in; *kataménō* (2650), to continue to remain; *kolláō* (2853), to glue or cement together; *proskolláō* (4347), to stick to; *ménō* (3306), to abide; *paraménō* (3887), to remain beside; *prosménō* (4357), to abide still longer; *hupoménō* (5278), to abide under.

1602. ἐκπλέω *ekpléō*; fut. *ekpleúsomai*, from *ek* (1537), out, and *pléō* (4126), to sail. To sail from a port or harbor (Acts 15:39; 18:18); followed by *apó* (575) from (Acts 20:6).

Syn.: *anágō* (321) to put out to sea; *diaperáō* (1276), to sail over.

Ant.: *proseggízō* (4331), to approach or come near; *prosormízō* (4358), to moor, draw to the shore.

1603. ἐκπληρόω *ekplēróō* contracted *ekplērṓ*; fut. *ekplērṓso*, from *ek* (1537), an intens., and *pleróō* (4137), to fill, fulfill. To fulfill entirely, completely (Acts 13:33, "the promise").

Deriv.: *ekplérōsis* (1604), accomplishment.

Syn.: *anaplēróō* (378), to fill up, fill completely; *empíplēmi* (1705), to fill full; *epiteléō* (2005), to fill further, finish; *plḗthō* (4130), to fill; *sunteléō* (4931), to complete, bring to completion; *teleióō* (5048), to bring to an end, fulfill; *teléō* (5055), to fulfill.

Ant.: *ekleípō* (1587), to leave out, fail; *ekpíptō* (1601), to fall off; *katargéō* (2673), to abolish; *hustereō* (5302), to come behind, fall short, miss.

1604. ἐκπλήρωσις *ekplérōsis*; gen. *ekplērṓseos*, fem. noun from *ekplēróō* (1603), to fulfill. A fulfilling, accomplishment (only in Acts 21:26 announcing the fulfillment [full observance] of the days, i.e., that he was about to keep in full the proper number of days; see Num 6:9).

Syn.: *plḗrōma* (4138), a filling up, fulfillment; *teleíōsis* (5050), performance, fulfillment.

Ant.: *hustérēma* (5303), that which is lacking, wanting; *hustérēsis* (5304), lack, want.

1605. ἐκπλήσσω *ekpléssō*, ἐκπλήττω *ekpléttō*; fut. *expléxō*, 2d aor. pass. *exeplágēn*, from *ek* (1537), an intens., and *plḗssō* (4141), to strike. To strike out, force out by a blow, but found only in the sense of knocking one out of his senses or self-possession, to strike with astonishment, terror, admiration. In the NT only in the pass., to be struck with astonishment, admiration, to be amazed (Matt 13:54; 19:25; Mark 6:2; 7:37; 10:26; Luke 2:48). Followed by *epí* (1909), upon, with the dat. (Matt 7:28; 22:33; Mark 1:22; 11:18; Luke 4:32; 9:43; Acts 13:12).

Syn.: *aporéō* (639), to be at a loss; *ekthambéō* (1568), to greatly astonish; *exístēmi* (1839), to amaze; *thambéō* (2284), to astonish; *phríssō* (5425), to shudder.

1606. ἐκπνέω *ekpnéō*; fut. *ekpneúsō*, from *ek* (1537), from, and *pnéō* (4154), to breathe. To breathe out or forth. Used intrans. meaning to expire, die (Mark 15:37, 39; Luke 23:46).

Syn.: *apogínomai* (581), to die; *apothnḗskō* (599), to die off or out; *thnḗskō* (2348), to die; *koimáomai* (2837), to sleep the sleep of death; *teleutáō* (5053), to end one's life.

Ant.: *anazáō* (326), to live again; *bióō* (980), to pass one's life; *záō* (2198), to live; *zōogonéō* (2225), to quicken; *zōopoiéō* (2227), to give life, make alive.

1607. ἐκπορεύομαι *ekporeúomai*; fut. *ekporeúsomai*, from *ek* (1537), out, and *poreúomai* (4198), to go. To go out, to go or come forth, spoken of:

(I) Persons, followed by *ek* (1537), out of, with the gen. of place, meaning whence (Mark 13:1); by *apó* (575), from (Matt 20:29; Mark 10:46); by *éxō*

(1854), out, with the gen. (Mark 11:19); by *ekeíthen* (1564), thence (Mark 6:11); by *pará* (3844), from, beside, with the gen. of person, from whom (John 15:26). Used in an absolute sense (Luke 3:7; Acts 25:4), as spoken of demons (Matt 17:21); followed by *eis* (1519) with the acc. of place, whither (Mark 10:17; John 5:29); by *epí* (1909), upon, with the acc. of person (Rev 16:14); by *prós* (4314), toward, with the acc. of person (Matt 3:5; Mark 1:5).

(II) Things, to go forth from, proceed out of; followed by *ek* (1537), out of, with the gen. (Matt 15:11, 18; Mark 7:20, 21; Luke 4:22; Eph 4:29); of a sword (Rev 1:16; 19:15, 21); lightning (Rev 4:5); fire (Rev 9:17, 18; 11:5); a river (Rev 22:1). Followed by *apó* (575), from (Mark 7:15); by *diá* (1223), through, with the gen. (Matt 4:4); by *ésōthen* (2081), from within (Mark 7:23); by *eis* (1519), into, with the acc. of place, whither, as of rumor (Luke 4:37). With the sense of to be ejected (Mark 7:19).

(III) In the phrase *eisporeúomai* (1531), to go in, and *ekporeúomai* (1607), to go out, meaning to go in and out, with the sense of performing one's daily duties (Acts 9:28).

Syn.: *ekchōréō* (1633), to depart out of; *exérchomai* (1831), to come forth.

Ant.: *eisérchomai* (1525), to go in.

1608. ἐκπορνεύω *ekporneúō*; fut. *ekporneúsō*, from *ek* (1537), out or from, and *porneúō* (4203), to commit fornication or lewdness. To practice fornication, be given to lewdness, used intrans. in Jude 1:7; Sept.: Gen 38:24; Ex 34:16.

1609. ἐκπτύω *ekptúō*; fut. *ekptúsō*, from *ek* (1537), out, and *ptúō* (4429), to spit. Used metaphorically meaning to loathe, reject, trans. in Gal 4:14 (cf. Rev 3:16).

Syn.: *athetéō* (114), to do away with, make void; *exoudenóō* (1847), to despise; *apodokimázō* (593), to reject.

Ant.: *apodéchomai* (588), to welcome; *déchomai* (1209), accept; *dokimázō* (1381), to prove; *lambánō* (2983), to receive; *prosdéchomai* (4327), to allow, accept.

1610. ἐκριζόω *ekrizóō*; contracted *ekrizṓ*, fut. *ekrizṓsō*, from *ek* (1537), out, and *rhizóō* (4492), to root. To root out or up, used trans. (Matt 13:29; 15:13; Luke 17:6; Jude 1:12; Sept.: Jer 1:10; Zeph 2:4).

Syn.: *exairéō* (1807), to pluck out; *exorússō* (1846), to dig out or up.

Ant.: *rhizóō* (4492), to cause to take root; *phuteúō* (5452), to plant.

1611. ἔκστασις *ékstasis*; gen. *ekstáseōs*, from *exístēmi* (1839), to remove out of its place or state. A putting away, removal of anything out of a place.

(I) An ecstasy in which the mind is for a time carried, as it were, out of or beyond itself and lost. Great astonishment, amazement (Mark 5:42; 16:8; Luke 5:26; Acts 3:10; Sept.: Gen 27:33; Deut 28:28; 2 Chr 14:14; Ezek 27:35).

(II) A trance, sacred ecstasy or rapture of the mind beyond itself when the use of the external senses are suspended and God reveals something in a peculiar manner (Acts 10:10; 11:5; 22:17 [cf. 2 Cor 12:2; Ezek 1:1 {cf. Sept.: Gen 2:21}]).

(III) The Eng. word which would correspond to *ékstasis* is rapture, but not in its exact sense as the act of seizing and carrying away, which would literally correspond to *harpagḗ* (724) and the verb *harpázō* (726), to seize, take by force or catch away upward. *Harpagḗ* and the verb *harpázō* are used trans., while *ékstasis* and the verb *exístēmi* are used as a reaction of the mind to an external cause or an internal feeling. It is not being oneself but, as if it were, one standing outside himself.

(IV) In Class. Gr. *ékstasis* means frenzy. However, in the NT it rarely expresses this high degree of emotion, but may include distraction of mind caused by wonder and astonishment or exceptional joy and rapture. Among the results of the healing of the paralytic by Christ, Luke tells us that amazement (*ékstasis*) took hold on all (Luke 5:26). Mark, in describing the effects of the resurrection upon the minds of the women as they fled from the tomb, states that trembling and astonishment (*ékstasis*) had come upon them (Mark 16:8). In Matt 12:23; Mark 2:12; 6:51 the verb *exístēmi* (1839) in the mid. sense is used in reference to the effects upon the multitude conveyed by the bestowal of the gift of tongues (Acts 2:7, 12), and of the preaching of Paul in the synagogues immediately after his conversion (Acts 9:21).

(V) At Pentecost, it was not those who spoke in languages other than their own as a result of the coming of the Holy Spirit upon them who were ecstatic, but those who heard them speak in languages which they knew were not native to them (see Acts 2:7). The ones who spoke did not speak in what would be termed "the unknown tongue" of the Corinthians. In Acts 2:8 it is not the word tongue (*glóssa* [1100]), that is used, but *diálektos* (1258), dialect or language. This was not an unknown tongue, but each heard in his own native language, and since the hearers knew that their languages were unknown to the speakers, they were amazed. In Acts 2:11 the word is *glóssais*, languages, the languages learned from birth (equal to dialects of Acts 2:8) by the people who were then present. Those who heard them were greatly perplexed (*diēpóroun*, the imperf. of *diaporéō* [1280] which in the KJV is inadequately translated "were in doubt" [Acts 2:12]), not understanding how the believers could speak the languages of those who listened. Although the noun *ékstasis* ecstasy, and the verb *exístēmi*, to be ecstatic, do not occur in relation to the unknown tongue spoken in Corinth, yet it could be termed "ecstatic" for the following reasons stated in 1 Cor 14:2, 9, 11, 14, 19, 23: the unknown tongue is mysterious and does not edify others (v. 2); it has no target, but is as if speaking to the air (v. 9); a person may be considered a barbarian, uncivilized (v. 11); it does not benefit his spirit

(v. 14); it does not enable others to understand what he is saying, and there is an excess of words spoken (v. 19); and others may think that the speakers are maniacs (v. 23). All these reactions indicate ecstasy in speaking the unknown tongue which the Apostle Paul was desperately trying to control in Corinth. On the other hand, the deliberate, clearly enunciated and understood languages which those who were filled by the Holy Spirit at Pentecost spoke were not spoken in ecstasy, but aroused ecstasy or amazement either for (Acts 2:12) or against (Acts 2:13). The verb that indicates the clear, deliberate speech of those who spoke in languages other than their own at Pentecost is *apophthéggomai* (669), which means to enunciate plainly. See Acts 2:4, 14; 26:25.

(VI) The stronger sense of the word *ékstasis*, translated in Eng. as "trance," is found in the description of Peter's vision of the vessel full of unclean animals (Acts 10:10; 11:5). While engaged in prayer in the temple at Jerusalem, Paul fell into an *ékstasis* in which he was warned by the Lord to escape from the city (Acts 22:17–21).

(VII) The OT provides us with instances of undoubted rapture or ecstasy (cf. Num 24:15ff.; 1 Sam 2:27; 9:6ff.; 10:5ff.; 2 Sam 24:11; 2 Kgs 9:11; Jer 29:26; Ezek 3:25, 26). In the NT, to be in ecstasy would mean to have one's spirit recognize spiritual objects beyond himself, such as the Apostle Paul describes in 2 Cor 12:1–6, although he does not refer to the word itself, but rather to visions (*optasías* [3701], visions the spirit received while separated from the body, at which time certain revelations of the Lord were made). Such were the revelations that John received on the island of Patmos in which instance ecstasy is what he describes in Rev 1:10 as "I was in the spirit." It is noteworthy that the word "spirit" is not preceded by the art. in the Gr. and may very well mean that this should be translated "I came to be in the spiritual world," or seeing things with his spirit, even as Paul did, his spirit ascending to the third heaven or paradise.

Syn.: *aporía* (640), bewilderment; *thámbos* (2285), astonishment; *hórasis* (3706), gazing, vision; *phóbos* (5401), fear.

Ant.: *galḗnē* (1055), tranquillity; *eirḗnē* (1515), peace; *hēsuchía* (2271), quiet.

1612. ἐκστρέφω *ekstréphō*; fut. *ekstrépsō*, from *ek* (1537), out, and *stréphō* (4762), to turn. To turn out of a place, used trans. as for a tree or post from the earth, to turn inside out as a garment. Used metaphorically meaning to change for the worse, subvert, pervert (Titus 3:11; Sept.: pass. in Deut 32:20; Amos 6:13).

Syn.: *anaskeuázō* (384), to subvert; *anatrépō* (396), to overthrow.

Ant.: *bebaióō* (950), to confirm, establish; *dunamóō* (1412) and *ischúō* (2480), to strengthen; *endunamóō* (1743) and *epischúō* (2001), to make strong; *epistērízō* (1991), to strengthen, confirm; *hístēmi* (2476), to stand; *krataióō* (2901), to establish, strengthen; *sthenóō* (4599), to make strong; *stērízō* (4741), to settle, confirm; *stereóō* (4732), to make firm, establish.

1613. ἐκταράσσω *ektarássō*, **ἐκταράττω** *ektaráttō*; fut. *ektaráxō*, from *ek* (1537), an intens., and *tarássō* (5015), to trouble, disturb. To stir up completely, to disturb or agitate greatly, used trans. in regard to the city of Philippi (Acts 16:20; Sept.: Ps 18:4; 88:16).

Syn.: *anastatóō* (387), to cause an uproar; *thorubéō* (2350), to cause an uproar or noise; *throéō* (2360), to make an outcry.

Ant.: *eirēneúō* (1514), to bring to peace, reconcile; *eirēnopoiéō* (1517), to make peace; *hēsucházō* (2270), to be still, quiet; *sigáō* (4601), to be silent or put to silence; *siōpáō* (4623), to be silent or still; *phimóō* (5392), to muzzle.

1614. ἐκτείνω *ekteínō*; fut. *ektenō̇*, perf. *tétaka*, from *ek* (1537), out, and *teínō* (n.f., see *parateínō* [3905]), to stretch. To stretch out, extend, such as the neck or the body for sleep.

(I) As spoken of the hand, to stretch forth the hand generally (Matt 12:13; 26:51; Mark 3:5; Luke 6:10; Acts 26:1; Sept.: Gen 19:10; 22:10; Ex 15:12); for the purpose of healing (Matt 8:3; Mark 1:41; Luke 5:13; Acts 4:30); assisting (Matt 14:31); entreaty (John 21:18). Followed by *epí* (1909), upon, with the acc. of person, to stretch out one's hand upon, and generally towards (Matt 12:49); to lay hands upon in a hostile manner (Luke 22:53; Sept.: Ex 7:5; Jer 6:12; Ezek 6:14).

(II) Of an anchor, to let go an anchor with its cable, to cast anchor (Acts 27:30).

Deriv.: *ekténeia* (1616), intenseness or continuance; *ektenḗs* (1618), stretched out, continued; *epekteínō* (1901), to stretch forward; *huperekteínō* (5239), to stretch out beyond.

Syn.: *probállō* (4261), to put forward.

Ant.: *apospáō* (645), to take away from; *aphístēmi* (868), to withdraw oneself; *exélkō* (1828), to draw away; *spáō* (4685), to draw or pull; *stéllō* (4724), to abstain, avoid, withdraw; *súrō* (4951), to drag; *hupostéllō* (5288), to withdraw.

1615. ἐκτελέω *ekteléō*; contracted *ektelō̇*, fut. *ektelésō*, from *ek* (1537), out or an intens., and *teléō* (5055), to finish, bring to an end. To finish out or off, to complete fully (Luke 14:29, 30; Sept.: Deut 32:45).

Syn.: *gínomai* (1096), to become, to finish; *dianúō* (1274), used in relation to finishing a journey or traveling.

Ant.: *kolobóō* (2856), to cut short; *suntémnō* (4932), to cut down, cut short; *sustéllō* (4958), to contract, shorten; *husteréō* (5302), to come behind, fall back, lack.

1616. ἐκτένεια *ekténeia*; gen. *ekteneías*, fem. noun from *ekteínō* (1614), to stretch out. Intenseness, continuance (Acts 26:7). In the dat. with *en* (1722), in, meaning intently, assiduously.

Syn.: *epiméleia* (1958), carefulness.

Ant.: *rhipé* (4493), twinkling, an instant; *stigmé* (4743), instant, moment; *tachú* (5035), suddenly.

1617. ἐκτενέστερον *ektenésteron*; neut. comparative of *ektenés* (1618), without ceasing, fervent. Used adv., more intensely or earnestly (Luke 22:44).

Syn.: *akribôs* (199), exactly, diligently; *epiméleia* (1958), carefulness, attention; *epimelôs* (1960), carefully, diligently; *spoudaiotérōs* (4708), more diligently; *spoudaíōs* (4709), earnestly, diligently.

Ant.: *elachistóteros* (1647), far less, less than the least.

1618. ἐκτενής *ektenḗs*; gen. *ektenoús*, contracted *ektenoús*, masc.-fem., neut. *ektenés*, adj. from *ekteínō* (1614), to stretch out, extend. Stretched out, continual, intense (Acts 12:5 [TR]; 1 Pet 4:8). The comparative: *ektenésteron* (1617), more intensely, earnestly.

Deriv.: *ektenôs* (1619), intensely, earnestly.

Syn.: *adiáleiptos* (88), unceasing; *makrós* (3117), long; *spoudaíos* (4705), diligent, earnest.

Ant.: *amérimnos* (275), not anxious; *átomos* (823), atom, something that cannot be divided, a moment; *brachús* (1024), short; *euthús* (2117), straight, immediate; *stigmé* (4743), an instant, a moment; *tachús* (5036), swift, prompt.

1619. ἐκτενῶς *ektenôs*; adv. from *ektenés* (1618), continual or intense. Intently, earnestly (1 Pet 1:22; Sept.: Jon 3:8).

Syn.: *akribôs* (199), exactly, diligently, carefully; *diēnekôs* (1336), perpetually; *epimelôs* (1960), carefully, diligently; *spoudaíōs* (4708), earnestly, diligently.

Ant.: *suntómōs* (4935), concisely.

1620. ἐκτίθημι *ektíthēmi*; fut. *ekthḗsō*, from *ek* (1537), out, and *títhēmi* (5087), to put. To expose, to place out as an infant (Acts 7:21). In the mid. *ektíthemai*, to set forth or expound, expose oneself, declare (Acts 11:4; 18:26; 28:23; Sept.: Job 36:15).

Deriv.: *ékthetos* (1570), exposed, cast out.

Syn.: *gnōrízō* (1107), to make known; *dēlóō* (1213), to make plain; *diermēneúō* (1329), to interpret fully; *exēgéomai* (1834), to unfold, declare; *epilúō* (1956), to solve, explain; *hermēneúō* (2059), to interpret; *horízō* (3724), to define; *phaneróō* (5319), manifest.

Ant.: *krúptō* (2928), to hide; *sigáō* (4601), to keep secret, silent; *phimóō* (5392), to muzzle.

1621. ἐκτινάσσω *ektinássō*, **ἐκτινάττω** *ektináttō*; fut. *ektináxō*, from *ek* (1537), from, and *tinássō* (n.f.), to shake. To shake from or off, as the dust of one's feet (Matt 10:14; Acts 13:51); "the dust under your feet" (Mark 6:11); garments (Acts 18:6). These were symbolic actions, meaning the total breaking off of all further communication. Also from *tinássō* (n.f.): *apotinássō* (660), to shake off.

Syn.: *apotinássō* (660), to shake off; *seíō* (4579), to shake; *anaseíō* (383), to stir up; *siniázō* (4617), to sift.

Ant.: *kratéō* (2902), to hold fast; *suntēréō* (4933), to preserve, keep safe; *tēréō* (5083), to preserve; *diatēréō* (1301), to keep carefully; *phulássō* (5442), to keep; *diaphulássō* (1314), to guard or keep carefully.

1622. ἐκτός *ektós*; adv. governing a gen. from *ek* (1537), out. Out of, without, of place as opposed to within, (*entós* [1787]) (1 Cor 6:18, sin which is outside the body, i.e., does not pertain to the body, is not physical; 2 Cor 12:2, 3); with the neut. art., *tó ektós*, the outside (Matt 23:26); metaphorically "without," i.e., except, besides; as a prep. with the gen. (Acts 26:22; 1 Cor 15:27; Sept.: Judg 8:26; 1 Kgs 4:23; 10:13; Dan 11:4); *ektós ei mḗ* (*ei* [1487], if; *mḗ* [3361], not), except that, without perhaps, unless (1 Cor 14:5; 15:2; 1 Tim 5:19).

Deriv.: *parektós* (3924), without, except.

Syn.: *áneu* (427), without; *éxōthen* (1855), from without, the outside; *plḗn* (4133), except, *chōrís* (5565), without, with the meaning of except.

Ant.: *sún* (4862), together with, in addition to; *metá* (3326), with; *pará* (3844), near; *homoú* (3674), at the same place or time.

1623. ἕκτος *héktos*; fem. *héktē*, neut. *hékton*, ordinal numeral from *héx* (1803), six. Sixth, as the sixth hour, meaning (in the Jewish reckoning) noon, the first hour being six o'clock in the morning, the beginning of a working day (Matt 20:5; 27:45; Mark 15:33; Luke 1:26, 36; 23:44; John 4:6; 19:14; Acts 10:9; Rev 6:12; 9:13, 14; 16:12; 21:20; Sept.: Gen 1:31; 30:19).

1624. ἐκτρέπω *ektrépō*, fut. *ektrépsō*, from *ek* (1537), from, and *trépō* (n.f., see *anatrépō* [396]), to turn. To turn out or away. Used in the mid. and aor. *exetrápen*, to turn oneself aside or away from a way or course, deflect, to be turned out of the way or aside (Heb 12:13, "Make straight and level paths, that the lame may not be driven to turn aside into other paths, but may be healed" [a.t.], i.e., that those who are wavering in faith may not be led to turn away, but rather be brought back and established). To turn aside in an intrans. sense (1 Tim 1:6; 5:15; 2 Tim 4:4), followed by *epí* (1909), upon; with an acc. of person or thing following, to turn away from, avoid (1 Tim 6:20).

Syn.: *anastatóō* (387), to stir up; *apostréphō* (654) and *apotrépō* (665), to cause to turn away; *diastréphō* (1294), to distort; *ekklínō* (1578), to turn away from; *methístēmi* (3179), to remove, turn away; *metastréphō* (3344), to pervert;

metatíthēmi (3346), to remove; *stréphō* (4762), to turn, convert.

Ant.: *anakámptō* (344), to turn back; *anastréphō* (390), to turn back, return; *epanágō* (1877), to bring back; *epanérchomai* (1880), to come back again; *epistréphō* (1994), to turn about, convert; *hupostréphō* (5290), to turn behind or back.

1625. ἐκτρέφω *ektréphō*; fut. *ekthrépsō*, from *ek* (1537), out or an intens., and *tréphō* (5142), to nourish, rear, feed. To nurture, rear, to bring up to maturity such as children (Sept.: 1 Kgs 12:8, 10; Isa 23:4; 49:21). To nourish or cherish one's own flesh (Eph 5:29; Sept.: Gen 45:11). In the sense of to train or educate, used trans. (Eph 6:4; Sept.: Prov 23:24).

Syn.: *bóskō* (1006), to feed literally or figuratively; *poimaínō* (4165), to shepherd or take general care of; *potízō* (4222), to give to drink; *chortázō* (5526), to feed to satiety, fill, satisfy; *psōmízō* (5595), to feed with morsels.

Ant.: *peináō* (3983), to hunger.

1626. ἔκτρωμα *éktrōma*; gen. *ektrómatos*, neut. noun from *ektitrōskō* (n.f.), to cut or excise out, to cause or suffer abortion, miscarry. An abortion, one born prematurely (1 Cor 15:8; Sept.: Job 3:16; Eccl 6:3). In the Attic, *ámblōma*.

Ant.: *génnēma* (1081), offspring; *génnēsis* (1083), birth.

1627. ἐκφέρω *ekphérō*; fut. *exoísō*, aor. *exénegka*, 2d aor. *exénegkon*, from *ek* (1537), out, and *phérō* (5342), to bring, bear, carry. To bear or carry out, bring forth (Luke 15:22, from its place; Acts 5:15, "out of the houses" [a.t.]; 1 Tim 6:7; Sept.: Gen 14:18; Judg 6:19); to carry out to burial (Acts 5:6, 9, 10). Spoken of the earth, to bring forth, yield, used trans. (Heb 6:8; Sept.: Gen 1:12; Hag 1:11).

Syn.: *ágō* (71), to lead, bring; *anágō* (321), to bring up to; *apágō* (520), to lead away; *apokuéō* (616), to beget; *blastánō* (985), to bud, spring up; *gennáō* (1080), to bring forth, generate; *ekbállō* (1544), to cast out; *ektréphō* (1625), to nourish, bring up; *exágō* (1806), to lead out; *proágō* (4254), to lead forth; *propémpō* (4311), to send forth; *tíktō* (5088), to deliver, bring forth as a child.

Ant.: *apostréphō* (654), to turn back; *eiságō* (1521), to bring into; *eisphérō* (1533) and *komízō* (2865), to bring in; *epágō* (1863), to bring upon; *katágō* (2609), to bring down, to land; *proságō* (4317), to bring to.

1628. ἐκφεύγω *ekpheúgō*; fut. *expheúxomai*, from *ek* (1537), out, and *pheúgō* (5343), to flee. To flee out of a place, used intrans. (Acts 16:27; 19:16). Trans., to flee from, escape, followed by the acc., such as calamities (Luke 21:36; Rom 2:3, God's judgment; 2 Cor 11:33); out of the power of someone, with the acc. implied (1 Thess 5:3; Heb 2:3; Sept.: Job 15:30; Prov 10:19).

Syn.: *apallássō* (525), to release; *apotássomai* (657), to place in order away from oneself; *diasṓzō* (1295), to bring safely through a danger; *eleutheróō* (1659), to set free; *exairéō* (1807), to deliver; *exérchomai* (1831), to come or go out of a place; *rhúomai* (4506), to rescue from; *sṓzō* (4982), to save, rescue.

Ant.: *agreúō* (64), to entrap, catch; *empíptō* (1706), to be entrapped by, to fall among; *emplékō* (1707), to entangle; *zōgréō* (2221), to capture, ensnare, take alive; *katalambánō* (2638), to seize, possess; *pagideúō* (3802), to ensnare; *peripíptō* (4045), to fall into or among something; *piázō* (4084), to seize, capture, arrest, catch; *sullambánō* (4815), to seize, arrest.

1629. ἐκφοβέω *ekphobéō*; contracted *ekphobṓ*, fut. *ekphobḗsō*, from *ek* (1537), an intens., and *phobéō* (5399), to frighten. To frighten greatly, terrify (2 Cor 10:9; Sept.: Lev 26:6; Job 7:14; Zeph 3:13).

Deriv.: *ékphobos* (1630), terrified.

Syn.: *diaseíō* (1286), to shake violently, intimidate; *eulabéomai* (2125), to act with the reverence produced by holy fear;

ptoéō (4422), to terrify; *ptúrō* (4426), to scare; *tarássō* (5015), to stir, agitate.

Ant.: *bebaióō* (950), to establish; *diabebaióomai* (1226), to affirm constantly; *diïschurízomai* (1340), to affirm; *epistērízō* (1991), to strengthen; *tharréō* (2292), to be of good courage, be confident; *kuróō* (2964), to make valid, ratify; *peíthō* (3982), to be confident; *pistóō* (4104), to give assurance to; *plērophoréō* (4135), to fully assure; *stērízō* (4741), to make fast, establish, strengthen; *stereóō* (4732), to make strong, confirm.

1630. ἔκφοβος *ékphobos*; gen. *ekphóbou*, masc.-fem., neut. *ékphobon*, adj. from *ekphobéō* (1629), to greatly frighten. Frightened outright or out of one's senses, greatly terrified (Mark 9:6; Heb 12:21; Sept.: Deut 9:19).

Syn.: *ékthambos* (1569), utterly astounded, greatly wondering; *émphobos* (1719), terrified; *éntromos* (1790), terrified.

Ant.: *eirēnikós* (1516), peaceable; *hēsúchios* (2272), quiet, peaceable; *éremos* (2263), quiet, tranquil.

1631. ἐκφύω *ekphúō*; fut. *ekphúsō*, 2d aor. *exéphun*, from *ek* (1537), out, and *phúō* (5453), to germinate, spring up. To produce, put or thrust forth as a fig tree its leaves (Matt 24:32; Mark 13:28). In both these passages *ekphúō phúlla* (*phúlla* [5444], leaves), may be rendered either trans., put forth leaves, or intrans., spring forth. *Phúlla*, leaves, may be either in the acc. or the nom. case. The first meaning is to be preferred because Luke 21:30 uses *probálōsi* (4261), send forth, which is in the subjunctive aor.

Syn.: *anabaínō* (305), to spring up; *blastánō* (985), to bud; *dídōmi* (1325), to give; *phuteúō* (5452), to plant; *rizóō* (4492), to take root.

1632. ἐκχέω *ekchéō* and **ἐκχύνω** *ekchúnō*; fut. *ekcheó*, fut. pass. *ekchuthḗsomai*, aor. *exéchea* (John 2:15), aor. pass. *exechúthēn*, perf. pass. *ekkéchumai*, from *ek* (1537), out, and *chéō* (n.f., see *epichéō* [2022]), to pour. To pour out.

(I) Particularly in Matt 9:17; Mark 2:22, "the wine is poured out" (a.t.) means spilled; Luke 5:37; John 2:15, "he poured out the money" (a.t.) means he scattered it upon the ground; Acts 1:18, "his bowels gushed out." See Sept.: Ex 4:9; Lev 4:12; 14:41; Judg 6:20; 2 Sam 20:10. In the phrase *haíma* ([129], blood) *ekchéō* (to pour out) means to shed blood and bring about death through the shedding of blood (Acts 22:20; Rom 3:15; Rev 16:6). In Matt 23:35; Luke 11:50 the pres. part. *ekchunómenon* is used, indicating not a continuous pouring out, but that the pouring was before the foundation of the world, planned and destined to be so. Spoken of the blood of Christ (a pregnant theological metaphor for His death) shed or poured out as a sacrifice for sin (Matt 26:28; Mark 14:24; Luke 22:20 [cf. Gen 9:6; Deut 19:10; 1 Sam 25:31; 2 Kgs 21:16; Ps 79:10]). By metonymy, the container for the contents (Rev 16:1–4, 8, 10, 12, 17).

(II) Metaphorically to pour out, shed abroad, give generously; followed by *en* (1722), in, as in Rom 5:5; by *epí* (1909), upon, with the acc. of person, such as the Spirit (Acts 2:17, 18; 10:45; Titus 3:6; Sept.: Joel 2:28, 29; Zech 12:10).

(III) Metaphorically in the pass. or mid., to be poured out, spoken of persons, i.e., intrans., to pour forth, rush tumultuously (cf. Sept.: Judg 9:44; 20:37). In the NT, spoken metaphorically of a passion or direction of the mind, to rush into, give oneself up to (Jude 1:11).

Deriv.: *aimatekchusía* (130), shedding of blood; *huperekchúnō* (5240), to run or spill over.

Syn.: *kataklúzō* (2626), to deluge; *réō* (4483), to pour forth; *spéndō* (4689), to pour out as a libation.

1633. ἐκχωρέω ekchōréō; fut. *ekchōréso*, from *ek* (1537), out, and *chōréō* (5562), to go. To depart out of a place, go away, flee out of (Luke 21:21; Sept.: Amos 7:12).

Syn.: *analúō* (360), to depart from life; *anachōréō* (402), to retire, go away; *apérchomai* (565), to come or go away; *apochōréō* (672), to depart from; *aphístēmi* (868), to stand off, to depart from someone; *éxeimi* (1826), to go out; *exérchomai* (1831), to go out of; *poreúomai* (4198), to depart from one place to another; *hupágō* (5217) and *metabaínō* (3327), to go, depart.

Ant.: *diatríbō* (1304), to continue to stay, tarry; *kataménō* (2650), to remain at the same place; *ménō* (3306), to remain; *paraménō* (3887), to continue to abide.

1634. ἐκψύχω ekpsúchō; fut. *ekpsúxō*, from *ek* (1537), out, and *psúchō* (5594), to breathe. To expire, die, used intrans. (Acts 5:5, 10; 12:23; Sept.: Judg 4:21; Ezek 21:7).

Syn.: *apogínomai* (581), to be away from; *thnḗskō* (2348), to die; *apothnḗskō* (599), to die off or out; *koimáomai* (2837), to fall asleep; *teleutáō* (5053) and *apóllumi* (622) to die, expire. None of the words indicating death in any way suggest extinction of being, but rather the change in the state of existence as the prep. *ek* (1537), out of, and *apó* (575), from, would indicate. When one dies, he goes from one state to another.

Ant.: *anazáō* (326), to live again; *záō* (2198), to live; *zōogonéō* (2225), to bring to life; *zōopoiéō* (2227), to cause to live, quicken; *hupárchō* (5225), to live, to continue to be.

1635. ἑκών hekṓn; fem. *hekoúsa*, neut. *hekón*, adj. Willing, unconstrained, used in an adv. sense meaning gladly, willingly. Usually it stands in opposition to violence or compulsion (only in Rom 8:20; 1 Cor 9:17).

Deriv.: *ákōn* (210), unwillingly; *ekoúsios* (1595), willing, voluntary.

Syn.: *hekousíōs* (1596), willingly.

Ant.: *ákōn* (210), unwilling; *anagkastós* (317), compulsorily; *bíaios* (972), violent; *opheilétēs* (3781), debtor.

1636. ἐλαία *elaía*; gen. *elaías*, fem. noun. The olive tree (Matt 21:1; 24:3; 26:30; Mark 11:1; 13:3; 14:26; Luke 19:29, 37; 21:37; 22:39; John 8:1; James 3:12; Sept.: 2 Sam 15:30; Zech 14:4). The fruit, an olive (James 3:12). Symbolically in Rom 11:17, 24; Rev 11:4; Sept.: Gen 8:11; Judg 9:8, 9; Zech 4:3, 11, 12.

    Deriv.: *agriélaios* (65), wild olive tree; *élaion* (1637), olive oil; *elaiṓn* (1638), an olive orchard; *kalliélaios* (2565), a cultivated or good olive tree.

1637. ἔλαιον *élaion*; gen. *elaíou*, neut. noun from *elaía* (1636), olive tree. Olive oil. Used for lamps (Matt 25:3, 4, 8). As oil is used to give light, so the Holy Spirit enlightens men's hearts concerning their need of God, namely Jesus Christ. In Mark 6:13 and Luke 7:46, the word is used with the verb *aleíphō* (218), the mundane verb meaning to rub or besmear with oil, in contrast to the sacred word *chríō* (5548), to anoint. The same verb *aleíphō* is used in James 5:14 in the aor. part. indicating that medical treatment, in those days equivalent to rubbing with olive oil, was to precede the prayer offered by the elders of the church. In Luke 10:34 the verb used is *epichéō* (2022), to pour upon, which does not involve touching by the hand. In Heb 1:9, *élaion* is used with the verb *chríō* indicating the exhilarating influence of the Holy Spirit typified by oil. Oil was also an article of commerce (Luke 16:6; Rev 18:13; Sept.: Gen 28:18; 1 Sam 16:1, 13). By metonymy and general use, oil is used for the fruit of the tree (Rev 6:6 [cf. Jer 40:10; Hag 1:11]). *Élaion* should be distinguished from *múron* (3464), ointment. Ointment has oil as its base, to which spice or scent or other aromatic ingredients are added. There is evidence that, in ancient times, men were rubbed with oil while women were rubbed with ointment. This distinction clarifies Luke 7:45, 46 in which our Lord is found in the house of the Pharisee telling him, "My head with oil [*élaion*] thou didst not anoint: but this woman hath anointed my feet with ointment [*múron*]." Oil represented the common courtesy that would be extended to a man. It was as if our Lord said to the Pharisee, "You withheld from me a cheap and ordinary courtesy [represented by oil], while this woman bestowed upon me costly and rare homage [represented by *múron*] which she did not put on my head, but on my feet," intimating that even the least honored part, the feet, received the highest honor, anointing with *múron*.

1638. ἐλαιών *elaiṓn*; gen. *elaiṓnos*, masc. noun from *elaía* (1636), olive tree. An olive orchard (Sept.: Ex 23:11; 2 Kgs 5:26). In the NT, it is the name of the Mount of Olives (Acts 1:12), a high ridge lying east of Jerusalem, parallel to the city and separated from it by the Valley of the Kidron. It was formerly planted with olive trees, of which few remain. The Olivet Discourse, or the discourse of our Lord on the Mount of Olives, is His prophetic teaching found in Matt 24, 25; Mark 13; Luke 21.

1639. Ἐλαμίτης *Elamítēs*; gen. *Elamítou*, masc. proper noun. An Elamite, an inhabitant of Elam or Elymais, a region of Persia near the extremity of the Persian Gulf between Media and Babylonia, and forming part of the district of Susiana or the modern Khusistan, of which Susa was the capital (Acts 2:9 [cf. Isa 21:2; Jer 49:34; Dan 8:2]).

1640. ἐλάσσων *elássōn*, ἐλάττων *eláttōn*; gen. *eláttonos*, the comparative of *mikrós* (3398), small. Inferior in worth or quality (John 2:10); in dignity meaning less (Heb 7:7); inferior in age, younger (Rom 9:12; 1 Tim 5:9, adv. meaning less than).

    Deriv.: *elattonéō* (1641), to make less, diminish; *elattóō* (1642), to make less, decrease.

    Syn.: *hḗssōn* (2276), less, worse; *mikróteros* (3398), smaller; *cheírōn* (5501), worse, the comparative degree of *kakós* (2556), bad.

Ant.: *meízon* (3185), in a greater degree; *pleíōn* (4119) or *meízōn* (3187), greater, more.

1641. ἐλαττονέω *elattonéō*; fut. *elattonḗsō*, fut. pass. *elattōthḗsomai*, from *eláttōn* (1640), less, minor. To make less. Trans., to diminish (Sept.: Gen 8:3, 5; Lev 25:16; Prov 14:34). Used intrans., to be less in respect to quantity, i.e., to lack, fall short, used in an absolute sense in 2 Cor 8:15 quoted from Ex 16:18. See Sept.: Ex 30:15, later word used instead of *elattóō* (1642), to decrease.

Syn.: *kolobóō* (2856), to shorten; *kóptō* (2875), to cut down.

Ant.: *auxánō* (837), to grow; *perisseúō* (4052), to increase, abound; *pleonázō* (4121), to make to abound, increase; *plēthúnō* (4129), to multiply; *ploutéō* (4147), to be wealthy; *ploutízō* (4148), to make wealthy; *prokóptō* (4298), to advance, progress.

1642. ἐλαττόω *elattóō*; contracted *elattṓ*, fut. *elattṓsō*, from *eláttōn* (1640), smaller. To diminish, the same as *elattonéō* (1641). To make less, used trans. in regard to dignity (Heb 2:7, 9 quoted from Ps 8:6; Sept.: Num 26:54). Used in the pass. or mid., intrans., meaning to become less, decrease (John 3:30; Sept.: Jer 44:18).

1643. ἐλαύνω *elaúnō*; fut. *elásō*, imperf. pass. *ēlaunómēn*, aor. *élasa*, perf. *elḗlaka*. To drive, impel, urge on. Used trans. of ships and clouds driven about by winds (James 3:4; 2 Pet 2:17). Metaphorically of a person (Luke 8:29). By implication it also means to propel a vessel with oars, to row; used in an absolute sense in Mark 6:48, John 6:19; Sept.: Isa 33:21.

Deriv.: *apelaúnō* (556), to drive from; *sunelaúnō* (4900), to drive together, to set at one again.

Syn.: *apophérō* (667), to carry away; *ekphérō* (1627), to carry forth; *phérō* (5342), to drive, bring.

Ant.: *ménō* (3306), to remain in a place.

1644. ἐλαφρία *elaphría*; gen. *elaphrías*, fem. noun from *elaphrós* (1645), light. Lightness in regard to weight. Used metaphorically of the mind, shallow-minded, inconstant (2 Cor 1:17).

Syn.: in the metaphorical sense: *ánoia* (454), lack of understanding, folly; *aphrosúnē* (877), senselessness, folly; *mōría* (3472), foolishness.

Ant.: *súnesis* (4907), understanding, apprehension; *phrónēsis* (5428), prudence.

1645. ἐλαφρός *elaphrós*; fem. *elaphrá*, neut. *elaphrón*. Light, not heavy, easy to bear (Matt 11:30); metaphorically in 2 Cor 4:17.

Deriv.: *elaphría* (1644), lightness, inconstancy.

Syn.: in the metaphorical sense: *anóētos* (453), without understanding; *asúnetos* (801), without discernment; *áphrōn* (878), without reason; *mōrós* (3474), dull, sluggish, silly.

Ant.: *barús* (926), weighty, grave. In the metaphorical sense: *sophós* (4680), wise; *sunetós* (4908), intelligent, understanding; *sṓphrōn* (4998), of sound mind; *phrónimos* (5429), prudent, sensible.

1646. ἐλάχιστος *eláchistos*; fem. *elachístē*, neut. *eláchiston*, adj., the superlative of *mikrós* (3398), small, of which the comparative is *elássōn* (1640), smaller. The least, minimal in magnitude (James 3:4); in number and quantity (Luke 16:10; 19:17); in rank or dignity (Matt 2:6; 25:40, 45; 1 Cor 15:9; Sept.: 1 Sam 9:21; 2 Kgs 18:24; Job 30:1; Prov 30:24); in weight or importance (Matt 5:19; Luke 12:26; 1 Cor 4:3; 6:2). Comparative degree: *elachistóteros* (1647), lesser than the least.

Ant.: *málista* (3122), most of all, especially; *mállon* (3123), very much, increasingly more; *meizóteros* (3186), the greatest of the great; *meízōn* (3187), greater than; *perissóteros* (4055), excessive, more excessive; *pleístos* (4118), the most; *pleíōn* (4119), more, greater; *hupér* (5228), over, above, more.

1647. ἐλαχιστότερος *elachistóteros*; fem. *elachistóterē*, neut. *elachistóteron*, adj., an unusual comparative formed from the superlative *eláchistos* (1646), least. Less than the least, far less, far inferior (Eph 3:8). Such double comparisons, though used by the poets, are elsewhere found only in the prose of a later age.
Syn.: *elássōn* (1640), smaller.
Ant.: *éti* (2089), more; *málista* (3122), most of all, especially; *mállon* (3123), very much more; *meizóteros* (3186), the greatest of the great; *meízōn* (3187), greater than; *perissóteros* (4055), excessive, more excessive; *pleístos* (4118), the most; *pleíōn* (4119), more, greater; *hupér* (5228), over, above, more.

1648. Ἐλεάζαρ *Eleázar*; masc. proper noun transliterated from Hebr. *'Elíāzār* (499, OT), my God is helper. Eleazar, an ancestor of Joseph (Matt 1:15).

1649. ἔλεγξις *élegxis*, gen. *elégxeōs*, fem. noun from *elégchō* (1651), to convict, reprove. Conviction, reproof (2 Pet 2:16; Sept.: Job 21:4).
Syn.: *dokimḗ* (1382), proof; *krísis* (2920), judgment; *momphḗ* (3437), fault.
Ant.: *apodochḗ* (594), acceptance; *épainos* (1868), commendation, praise; *eúnoia* (2133), approving consideration, benevolence; *euphēmía* (2162), good report, reputation.

1650. ἔλεγχος *élegchos*; gen. *elégchou*, masc. noun from *elégchō* (1651), to convict. Conviction. Metonymically, meaning certain persuasion (Heb 11:1). In the sense of refutation of adversaries (2 Tim 3:16; see Sept.: Job 13:6; 23:4; Hos 5:9). Implies not merely the charge on the basis of which one is convicted, but the manifestation of the truth of that charge

and the results to be reaped; also the acknowledgement, if not outwardly, yet inwardly, of its truth on the part of the accused.
Syn.: *dokimḗ* (1382), proof; *krísis* (2920), judgment; *momphḗ* (3437), fault.
Ant.: *apodochḗ* (594), acceptance; *épainos* (1868), praise; *eulogía* (2129), blessing, good word; *eúnoia* (2133), favorable consideration; *euphēmía* (2162), good repute.

1651. ἐλέγχω *elégchō*; fut. *elégxō*. To shame, disgrace, but only in Class. Gr. In the NT, to convict, to prove one in the wrong and thus to shame him. Trans.:
(I) To convict, to show to be wrong (John 8:9). Followed by *perí* (4012), concerning (John 8:46; 16:8); *hupó*, by (1 Cor 14:24; James 2:9). To convince of error, refute, confute (Titus 1:9, 13; 2:15; Sept.: Job 32:12; Prov 18:17).
(II) By implication, to reprove, rebuke, admonish (Matt 18:15; Luke 3:19; 1 Tim 5:20; 2 Tim 4:2; Sept.: Gen 21:25; Prov 9:8). To reprove by chastisement, correct, chastise in a moral sense (Rev 3:19); with *paideúō* (3811), train (Heb 12:5 from Prov 3:11, 12. See Sept.: Job 5:17; Ps 6:1; 38:1).
(III) By implication spoken of hidden things, to detect, demonstrate, make manifest (John 3:20 where *elegchthḗ* is parallel with *phanerōthḗ* [5319], to manifest in John 3:21 [Eph 5:11, 13]).
Deriv.: *élegxis* (1649), the act of rebuking; *élegchos* (1650), reproof; *exelégchō* (1827), to convict thoroughly.
Syn.: *apodokimázō* (593), to repudiate; *epikrínō* (1948), to adjudge; *kakologéō* (2551), to speak evil of; *katakrínō* (2632) or *katadikázō* (2613), to condemn; *katalaléō* (2635), to slander; *katēgoréō* (2723), to accuse; *krínō* (2919), to judge; *mémphomai* (3201), to find fault.
Ant.: *apodéchomai* (588), to approve; *egkrínō* (1469), to approve; *epitrépō* (2010), to permit; *eulogéō* (2127), to bless.

1652. ἐλεεινός *eleeinós*; fem. *eleeinḗ*, neut. *eleeinón*, adj. from *éleos* (1656), mercy. Worthy of pity, pitiable, full of misery, wretched, miserable. In the NT used only in 1 Cor 15:19; Rev 3:17.

Syn.: *kakós* (2556), bad in character; *ponērós* (4190), evil, harmful; *saprós* (4550), corrupt, rotten; *phaúlos* (5337), slight, trivial.

Ant.: *agathós* (18), beneficial; *anektóteros* (414), more tolerable; *áxios* (514), worthy; *arestós* (701), fit, pleasing; *eklektós* (1588), favorable, chosen; *kalós* (2570), good.

1653. ἐλεέω *eleéō*; contracted *eleó*, fut. *eleḗsō*, from *éleos* (1656), mercy. To show mercy, to show compassion, extend help for the consequence of sin, as opposed to *sklērúnomai* (4645), to be hardened. The general meaning is to have compassion or mercy on a person in unhappy circumstances. Used trans. in the pass., to be pitied, obtain mercy, implying not merely a feeling for the misfortunes of others involving sympathy (*oiktirmós* [3628], pity), but also an active desire to remove those miseries.

(I) Generally (Matt 5:7; 9:27; 15:22; 17:15; 18:33; 20:30, 31; Mark 5:19; 10:47, 48; Luke 16:24; 17:13; 18:38, 39; Phil 2:27; Jude 1:22; Sept.: Deut 13:17; 2 Sam 12:22; 2 Kgs 13:23; Ps 6:2; Isa 13:18). Spoken of those who had charge of the poor (Rom 12:8 [cf. Prov 14:21, 31; 28:8]); of those who are freed from deserved punishment, in the pass., to obtain mercy, be spared (1 Tim 1:13, 16; Sept.: Deut 7:2; Isa 9:19; Ezek 7:4, 9). By implication, to be gracious toward, bestow kindness on (Rom 9:15, 16, 18 quoted from Ex 33:19; Sept.: Gen 43:29).

(II) Spoken of the mercy of God through Christ or salvation in Christ, to bestow salvation on; in the pass., to obtain salvation (Rom 11:30–32; 1 Cor 7:25; 2 Cor 4:1; 1 Pet 2:10).

(III) *Éleos* (1656) specifically means a feeling of empathy, fellow feeling with misery, compassion. In the sense of

God's pity for human woe which manifests itself in His will for man's salvation, *éleos* is found frequently in the apostolic writings (cf. Rom 9:23; 15:9; 2 Tim 1:16, 18; 1 Pet 1:3; Jude 1:21). It is found joined with *agápē* (26), love, in Eph 2:4; with *makrothumía* (3115), long-suffering, in 1 Tim 1:16; and with *cháris* (5485), grace, in Heb 4:16. We find the group "grace, mercy, and peace," in the greetings of 1 Tim 1:2; 2 Tim 1:2; 2 John 1:3; "mercy and peace" together in Gal 6:16; Jude 1:2. The verb *eleéō* is found in a similar sense in Rom 9:15, 16; 11:30, 32; 2 Cor 4:1; 1 Tim 1:13, 16; 1 Pet 2:10. It is also found of the mercy of man toward his fellowman (Rom 12:8; 1 Cor 7:25; Phil 2:27). *Oiktirmós* (3628), pity, also means compassion, mercy, and with the adj. *oiktírmōn* (3629), compassionate, merciful, and the verb *oikteírō* (3627), to have compassion on, is used both of God's compassion for men and of men's compassion for one another. In the NT *oiktirmós* is mostly used in the pl. *Oiktirmós* is used with reference to God in Rom 12:1; Heb 10:28. In 2 Cor 1:3 God is called the Father of mercies, *oiktirmṓn*. *Oiktirmós* is used of human pity in Col 3:12 (cf. *oiktírmōn* [of God] in James 5:11 and *oikteírō* [of God] in Rom 9:15).

Syn.: *hiláskomai* (2433), to be propitious, merciful, make reconciliation for; *lupéō* (3076), to be sad, sorry; *splagchnízomai* (4697), to have bowels of mercy or a yearning heart, feel sympathy, pity; *sumpathéō* (4834), to have sympathy, compassion; *sumpáschō* (4841), to suffer with.

Ant.: *adēmonéō* (85), to distress; *anastatóō* (387), to stir; *diaponéō* (1278), to experience pain as a result of work; *ektarássō* (1613), to trouble greatly; *enochléō* (1776), to vex, and the comp. *parenochléō* (3926), to annoy; *thlíbō* (2346), to afflict; *thorubéō* (2350), to disturb; *throéō* (2360), to make an outcry; *pōróō* (4456), to make hard, callous; *pṓrōsis* (4457), hardness, callousness; *sklērótēs* (4643), hardness; *skúllō* (4660), to trouble; *tarássō* (5015), to agitate; *diatarássō* (1298), to agitate greatly.

1654. ἐλεημοσύνη *eleēmosúnē*; gen. *eleēmosúnēs*, from *eleḗmōn* (1655), merciful. Mercifulness, compassion (Sept.: Prov 21:21; Isa 38:18). In the NT by metonymy of effect for cause, alms, charity, money given to the poor (Matt 6:1 [TR]; 6:2–4; Luke 11:41; 12:33; Acts 3:2, 3, 10; 9:36; 10:2, 4, 31; 24:17; Sept.: Dan 4:24). *Eleēmosúnē* is the expression of mercy to be contrasted with *oiktirmós* (3628), which conveys more the expression of sentiment than the outward manifestation of character. *Oíktos*, from *oikteírō* (3627) and the subst. *oiktirmós*, only mentally expresses pity and emotional agony for a situation or a person, while *éleos* (1656), mercy, *eleéō* (1653), to be merciful, and the subst. *eleēmosúnē* refer to the actual helpful action of the pity. This is the reason why *eleēmosúnē* is consistently translated "alms" or "almsgiving" although it is derived from *éleos*, mercy, while *oiktirmós* is consistently translated "mercy" (Rom 12:1; 2 Cor 1:3; Phil 2:1; Col 3:12; Heb 10:28). In truth, however, *eleēmosúnē* is the result of being *eleḗmōn* (1655), merciful, and it is the outward expression of *éleos*, active compassion or mercifulness. However, *oiktirmós*, although translated "mercy," really has nothing to do with *éleos*, mercy, in its outward manifestation. It is rather inward pity and compassion.

1655. ἐλεήμων *eleḗmōn*; gen. *eleḗmonos*, masc.-fem., neut. *eleḗmon*, adj. from *éleos* (1656), mercy. Compassionate, benevolently merciful involving thought and action. As referring to believers it occurs only in Matt 5:7, "Blessed are the merciful ones" (a.t.), not merely those who express acts of mercifulness, but who have this attribute as a result of the indwelling God, being *makárioi* (3107), blessed, because of Christ; referring to Christ (Heb 2:17). See Sept.: Ex 22:27; Ps 103:8; 145:8; Jer 3:12.

Deriv.: *aneleḗmōn* (415), unmerciful; *eleēmosúnē* (1654), merciful.

Syn.: *oiktírmōn* (3629) feelings of compassion.

1656. ἔλεος *éleos*. Mercy, compassion.

(I) *Ho éleos*, gen. *éleou*, masc. noun.

(A) Mercy, compassion, active pity (Matt 23:23; Titus 3:5; Heb 4:16; Sept.: Isa 60:10).

(B) With the sense of goodness in general, especially piety (Matt 9:13; 12:7 quoted from Hosea 6:6 where *éleos* is parallel to *epígnōsis Theoú* [1922, 2316], knowledge of God), special and immediate regard to the misery which is the consequence of sin.

(II) *To éleos*, gen. *eléous*, neut. noun, found only in the Sept., the NT, and church writers in contrast to the noun in the masc. *ho éleos* which alone is used by Class. Gr. writers. Mercy, compassion, active pity.

(A) Generally (Luke 1:50, 78; Rom 9:23; 15:9; Eph 2:4; 1 Pet 1:3; James 3:17; Sept.: Deut 13:17; Neh 13:22; Ps 51:1; Isa 63:7). With the verb *poiéō* (4160), to do mercy for someone means to show mercy to, equivalent to the verb *eleéō* (1653), to have compassion on, show mercy (Luke 1:72; 10:37; James 2:13; Sept.: Gen 24:12; 1 Sam 15:6). With the verb *megalúnō* (3170), to make great, magnify, show great mercy on someone (Luke 1:58). In the phrase, *mnēsthḗnai eléous*, to remember mercy, from *mimnḗskō* (3403), to remember, (Luke 1:54), means to give a new proof of mercy and favor to Israel, in reference to God's ancient mercies to that people (cf. Ps 25:6; 89:28, 50; Sept.: 2 Chr 6:42; Jer 2:2). Spoken of mercy as passing over deserved punishment (James 2:13 [cf. Sept.: Num 14:19]).

(B) Spoken of the mercy of God through Christ, i.e., salvation in the Christian sense from sin and misery (Jude 1:21, "the mercy of our Lord Jesus Christ" means salvation through Christ; see Rom 11:31). In benedictions, including the idea of mercies and blessings of every kind, e.g., "the Lord give mercy" (2 Tim 1:16, 18). Also joined with *eirḗnē* (1515), peace (Gal 6:16; 1 Tim 1:2; 2 Tim 1:2; Titus 1:4; 2 John 1:3; Jude 1:2).

(III) Contrast *cháris* (5485) which is God's free grace and gift displayed in the forgiveness of sins as offered to men in their guilt. God's mercy (*éleos*) is extended for the alleviation of the consequences of sin. Grace identifies the free nature of salvation, that which is unmerited and without obligation. Mercy is the application of grace and reminds us that redemptive freedom rescued us from the pathetic condition of our sinfulness. Peace (*eirḗnē* [1515]) refers us to the effect of salvation, namely, that we were set free from the condemnation of sin and reconciled to God. This is true not only objectively in that we no longer stand before God as enemies but now as beloved children; but this is also true subjectively in that we have been relieved of the hostility in our hearts toward God and the torment of guilt in our consciences. The lower creation is also an object of God's mercy inasmuch as the burden of man's curse has fallen also upon it (Rom 8:20–23). But man greatly needs God's grace and is capable of receiving it and consequently being changed. In God's mind and in the order of our salvation as conceived therein, God's mercy, His loving and benevolent pity for the misery brought about by our sin, precedes His saving grace and continues to be actively demonstrated after the work of that grace. There may be certain consequences of our past sinfulness which grace cannot eliminate. For these we need God's mercifulness. In John 3:16, God loved in mercy and gave in grace. It is always grace and mercy that we find in the apostolic salutations, for as we experience guilt for our sin and receive God's grace, we also need mercy to alleviate the consequences of our sins which may remain unaffected by grace. The guilt and power of sin must be removed through God's grace before the alleviation of the misery of sin can be experienced. The believer is

to exercise mercifulness, for he can feel compassion for the misery of sin upon others, but he has no power to exercise grace in the same manner as Christ since that is exclusively God's work. "Blessed are the merciful; for they shall obtain mercy" (Matt 5:7; James 2:12, 13).

Deriv.: *eleeinós* (1652), worthy of pity; *eleéō* (1653), to be merciful; *eleḗmōn* (1655), merciful.

Syn.: *oiktirmós* (3628), pity; *lúpē* (3077), sorrow; *splágchnon* (4698), affection, sympathy; *hilasmós* (2434), propitiation.

Ant.: *sklērótēs* (4643), hardness; *pṓrōsis* (4457), hardness, callousness.

1657. ἐλευθερία *eleuthería*; gen. *eleutherías*, fem. noun from *eleútheros* (1658), a free person. Freedom, generosity, independence.

(I) Freedom is presented as a signal blessing of the economy of grace, which, in contrast with the OT economy, is represented as including independence from religious regulations and legal restrictions (1 Cor 10:29; 2 Cor 3:17; Gal 2:4; 2 Pet 2:19). Freedom from the yoke of the Mosaic Law (Gal 5:1, 13); from the yoke of observances in general (1 Pet 2:16); from the dominion of sinful appetites and passions (James 1:25; 2:12); from a state of calamity and death (Rom 8:21). In contrast with the present subjection of the creature to the bondage of corruption, freedom represents the future state of the children of God (Rom 8:20, 21). "The perfect law of liberty" or freedom in James 1:25 is the freedom of generosity, especially in James 2:12 when the Judge shows His generosity in proportion to the mercifulness of the believers on earth.

(II) In the OT, the idea of spiritual freedom is not as prominent as in the NT (Ps 51:2; 54:6; 119:45). "The fear of the Lord" is a common expression for OT religion (Ps 34:11) and is the foundation of OT piety. "Servant" is the distinctive title of the good man (Ps 19:11 [cf. Heb 3:5]). God is thought of chiefly as the supreme, universal sovereign and ruler whose eminence is clearly recognized (Isa 33:22; 57:15). Obedience is the central virtue of religious character to which all blessings are promised (1 Sam 15:22). The OT age was the age of childhood and revealed religion, when children were trained for independence by a course of obedience and subjection to authority (Gal 4:1f.). "The law has been our tutor to bring us unto Christ" (a.t. [Gal 3:24]). The provisions of the OT are called by Paul in Gal 4:9 as "weak and beggarly rudiments" (a.t.). The prevailing spirit was a "spirit of bondage again to fear" (Rom 8:15). At the same time, the emphasis laid on God's work of redemption might have given rise to thoughts of spiritual freedom (Ex 13:14; Deut 7:8; 1 Chr 17:21), and in Isa 61:1 this truth finds glorious expression. The political system of Israel had certain elements of freedom which distinguished it from the despotisms of the day by many humane regulations unknown elsewhere, such as those with regard to slavery (Ex 21:2) and land (Lev 25:10, 23).

(III) Christianity brought, first of all, freedom from the ceremonial restrictions and conditions of OT religion. The Mosaic Law is described as "a yoke . . . which neither our fathers nor we were able to bear" (Acts 15:10). Such reinstatement of lack of freedom is opposed by Paul in Gal 3:24; 5:1ff. The teaching of the Epistle to the Hebrews supports Paul (Heb 9:23; 10:1).

(IV) The NT condemns all attempts to reduce Christianity to a mere system of ritual. It is characterized by inward freedom as the privilege of all believers in Christ. Sin brings one into bondage (John 8:34; Rom 6:16f.), but out of this bondage believers are saved, both negatively and positively. Redemption in and by Christ brings deliverance from a sense of guilt, fear, and condemnation which oppresses and enslaves the soul (Rom 8:2; Titus 2:14). "Ye were the servants of sin . . . ye became the servants of righteousness" (Rom 6:17f.). Knowledge of the truth is the means (John 8:32) and

Christ Himself the source (John 8:36; 2 Cor 3:17) of this highest freedom.

(V) The "spirit of bondage" gives place to the "spirit of adoption" (*huiothesía* [5206], which can very well be designated as a syn. of *eleuthería*) (Rom 8:15; Gal 4:6). Sin, death, and the world are concrete enemies (Rom 8:37–39; 1 Cor 15:55ff.; 1 John 5:4). The exultant sense of power, of present and future triumph enjoyed by the believer, is vividly expressed in passages like Rom 5:2, 10; 6:12, 22; 8:38. Spiritual freedom of believers culminates in their relationship as children to God.

(VI) Freedom is the distinctive privilege of the saved. It is so profound and far-reaching that the believer is conscious of sonship in relation to God, who is his Father in heaven (Matt 5:48; 7:11; John 1:12, 13; Rom 8:16; 1 John 3:1f.). Of the believer Paul says, "Thou art no more a servant, but a son" (Gal 4:7). God is thought of as Father, no longer as merely Ruler. The most distinct exercise of the liberty of the children of God is the boldness with which believers may draw near to Him (Heb 4:16; 10:19). Christians are invested with the full privileges of the priesthood (1 Pet 2:9). Liberty is freedom not license (Gal 5:13; 1 Pet 2:16).

Syn.: *politeía* (4174), citizenship, referring to the fact that a citizen was a free man; *cháris* (5485), grace.

Ant.: *douleía* (1397), bondage, slavery; *zugós* (2218), yoke, servitude, bondage; *desmós* (1199), shackle, band.

1658. ἐλεύθερος *eleútheros*; fem. *eleuthéra*, neut. *eleútheron*, adj. Capable of movement, the free one. In the absolute sense, free, unconstrained, unfettered, independent. One who is not dependent upon another, for the most part in a social and political sense. In a relative sense, free, separate from or independent of (Rom 7:3; 1 Cor 9:19).

(I) In a civil sense:

(A) Freeborn (1 Cor 12:13; Gal 3:28; 4:22, 23, 30, 31; Eph 6:8; Col 3:11; Rev 6:15; 13:16; 19:18). Figuratively of the heavenly Jerusalem, meaning nobler (Gal 4:26; Sept.: Neh 13:17; Eccl 10:17).

(B) Freed, made free (John 8:33; 1 Cor 7:21, 22; Sept.: Ex 21:2, 26, 27).

(C) Free, exempt from an obligation or law (Matt 17:26; Rom 7:3; 1 Cor 7:39 [cf. Sept.: Deut 21:14]); free from external obligations in general so as to act as one pleases (1 Cor 9:1, 19); in respect to the exercise of piety (1 Pet 2:16).

(II) Metaphorically free from the slavery of sin (John 8:36; Rom 6:18 [cf. Rom 6:20, "free from righteousness"].

Deriv.: *apeleútheros* (558) free man; *eleuthería* (1657), freedom; *eleutheróō* (1659), to make free.

Ant.: *doúlos* (1401), slave.

1659. **ἐλευθερόω** *eleutheróō*; contracted *eleutherṓ*, fut. *eleutherṓsō*, from *eleútheros* (1658), free. To make free, liberate from the power and punishment of sin, the result of redemption (John 8:32, 36; Rom 6:18, 22); from a state of calamity and death (Rom 8:2, 21); from the power of condemnation by the Mosaic Law (Gal 5:1). For a full discussion, see *eleuthería* (1657), freedom, liberty.

Syn.: *charízō* (5483), to deliver; *apolúō* (630), to set free; *apallássō* (525), to release.

Ant.: *douleúō* (1398), to serve as a slave; *doulóō* (1402) or *doulagōgéō* (1396), to bring into bondage; *katadoulóō* (2615), to bring into complete bondage.

1660. **ἔλευσις** *éleusis*; gen. *eleúseōs*, fem. noun from *érchomai* (2064), to come. A coming (Acts 7:52).

Syn.: *áphixis* (867), arrival; *parousía* (3952), presence; *apokálupsis* (602), a revelation or appearing; *epipháneia* (2015), appearance. While these last three syn. may refer to the Second Coming of the Lord Jesus, *éleusis* refers only to His first coming.

Ant.: *éxodos* (1841), departure; *análusis* (359), departure from life, death; *phugḗ* (5437), escape.

1661. **ἐλεφάντινος** *elephántinos*; fem. *elephantínē*, neut. *elephántinon*, adj. from *eléphas* (n.f.), an elephant, ivory. Made of ivory (Rev 18:12; Sept.: 1 Kgs 10:18; Amos 3:15).

1662. **'Ελιακείμ** *Eliakeím*; masc. proper noun transliterated from the Hebr. *'Elyāqīm* (471, OT), God-appointed. Eliakim (Matt 1:13; Luke 3:30).

1663. **'Ελιέζερ** *Eliézer*; masc. proper noun transliterated from the Hebr. *'Elīezer* (461, OT), my God is a helper. Eliezer, one of Christ's ancestors (Luke 3:29).

1664. **'Ελιούδ** *Elioúd*; masc. proper noun transliterated from the Hebr. *'El hōd* ('*El* [410, OT], God; *hōd* [1935, OT], praise), my God is praise. Eliud, one of Christ's ancestors (Matt 1:14, 15).

1665. **'Ελισάβετ** *Elisábet*; fem. proper noun transliterated from the Hebr. *'Elīshevaí* (472, OT), my God is an oath. Elizabeth, the wife of Zechariah the priest and mother of John the Baptist (Luke 1:5, 7, 13, 24, 36, 40, 41, 57). Being of priestly descent herself, Elizabeth is described as a cousin, more accurately kinswoman (*suggenḗs* [4773], kin, cousin) of the virgin Mary (Luke 1:36) to whom she addressed the remarkable words of Luke 1:42–45.

1666. **'Ελισσαîος** *Elissaíos*; gen. *Elissaíou*, masc. proper noun transliterated from the Hebr. *'Elīshā* (477, OT), my God is deliverance. Elisha, the disciple and successor of Elijah (Luke 4:27; 1 Kgs 19:16ff.; 2 Kgs 2—9; 13:14–21). Elijah anointed Elisha, by divine command, where he found him plowing. He threw his mantle over him as they stood in the field, thus signifying the service to which he was called. Elisha promptly obeyed the call and, leaving his oxen in the field, took leave of his father and mother and followed Elijah. He did not perform any independent service until Elijah's translation which took place some eight years afterward. Elisha then became the head of the school of the prophets. He was the counselor and friend of successive kings. Elisha was the opposite of Elijah in most things. He lived in the city or with his students, was honored and sought for, a welcome guest in the homes he graced by his presence. He was filled with a double portion of Elijah's spirit both to work miracles and give counsel for present and future emergencies. He multiplied the widow's oil, and when the son of the good Shunammite woman died, he raised him to life. Elisha cured Naaman, smote Gehazi with leprosy, misled the Syrians, foretold abundant food in time of famine, and, when dying, gave the king the promise of victory. He was an active prophet for sixty years, 892–832 B.C.

1667. ἐλίσσω *helíssō*, ἐλίττω *helíttō* fut. *helíxō*, Ionian *heilíssō* (1507), to roll together. To roll or fold up as a garment to be laid away, used metaphorically in relation to the heavens (Heb 1:12 quoted from Ps 102:26 [cf. Isa 34:4]).

Syn.: *entulíssō* (1794), to wrap up, roll up; *sustréphō* (4962), to twist together, collect in a bundle, gather.

Ant.: *anaptússō* (380), to unroll.

1668. ἕλκος *hélkos*; gen. *hélkous*, a neut. noun. An ulcer, a sore (Luke 16:21; Rev 16:2, 11; Sept.: Ex 9:9; Job 2:7).

Deriv.: *helkóō* (1669), to cause to ulcerate.

Syn.: *plēgḗ* (4127), a wound; *traúma* (5134), a wound, by transliteration in Eng. "trauma"; *gággraina* (1044), an ulcer, canker, gangrene.

1669. ἑλκόω *helkóō*; contracted *hélkō*, from *hélkos* (1668), ulcer. To cause to ulcerate. Found only in Luke 16:20.

1670. ἑλκύω *helkúō* and ἕλκω *hélkō*; fut. *helkúsō*, aor. *heílkusa*. To draw toward without necessarily the notion of force as in *súrō* (4951). See Acts 8:3;

14:19; 17:6; Rev 12:4. To drag, although it may be just implied (Acts 16:19, of persons, to drag, force before magistrates; 21:30, "out of the temple"; James 2:6). *Helkúō* is used by Jesus of the drawing of souls unto Him (John 6:44; 12:32, to draw or induce to come). It is the drawing to a certain point as in John 21:6, 11 indicating the drawing of the net while *súrō* (John 21:8) is merely dragging. To draw a sword (John 18:10). See Sept.: 2 Sam 22:17; Ps 10:9; Jer 38:13.

Deriv.: *exélkō* (1828), to draw away.

Ant.: *apōthéomai* (683), to repel, push off; *apostréphō* (654), to turn away from; *apotinássō* (660), to brush or shake off; *apotrépō* (665), to avoid, turn away; *apotássomai* (657), to place in order away from oneself, forsake; *exōthéō* (1856), to expel, drive out.

1671. Ἑλλάς *Hellás*; gen. *Helládos*, fem. proper noun. Greece. Hellas was the name of a city in Thessaly founded by Hellen, the son of Deucalion, then of the adjacent portion of Thessaly inhabited by the Myrmidons, afterwards of the whole central part of continental Greece as far north as to Thesprotia, excluding the Peloponnesus and islands. In this sense it seems to be used in Acts 20:2 where it is distinguished from Macedonia. See *Achaḯa* (882). Elsewhere in Class. Gr., it is also spoken of the whole extent of Greece, including the Peloponnesus, the islands, and Macedonia as opposed to Asia Minor. It sometimes included Ionia where Ephesus is said to have been. The Hebr. name of Greece is *Iōnía* (Sept.: Gen 10:2), but the Sept. also translates it as *Hellás* in Isa 66:19; Ezek 27:13. It is named four times in the OT as Greece or Grecia (Dan 8:21; 10:20; 11:2; Zech 9:13), and once in the NT (Acts 20:2). It or its people are referred to in Hebrew history as Javan (Isa 66:19; Ezek 27:13, 19), and in apostolic history as Achaia (Acts 18:12, 27; 19:21). Some of its cities mentioned in the NT are Athens, Corinth, Cenchrea, Thessalonica, Philippi, Berea, and Nicopolis.

1672. Ἕλλην *Héllēn*; gen. *Héllēnos*, masc. proper noun. Greek. Distinction should be made, however, between the Greeks (*Héllēnes*) and the Grecians (*Hellēnistaí* [1675]). The Greeks were the Greeks by birth (Acts 16:1, 3; 18:17), or else Gentiles as opposed to Jews (Rom 2:9, 10), while the Grecians (*Hellēnistaí*) were foreign Greek-speaking Jews as distinct from those in Palestine who were called Hebrews (Acts 11:20). The Greeks and Hebrews first met when the Tyrians sold the Jews to the Greeks (Joel 3:6). Greece is noted prophetically in Dan 8:21 where the history of Alexander and his successors is rapidly sketched. Zech 9:13 foretells the triumphs of the Maccabees over the Graeco-Syrian Empire, while Isaiah looks forward to the conversion of the Greeks, among other Gentiles, through the instrumentality of Jewish missionaries (Isa 66:19). After the complete subjection of the Greeks by the Romans, and the absorption into the Roman Empire of the kingdoms which were formed out of the dominions of Alexander, the political connection between the Greeks and the Jews as two independent nations no longer existed.

Rom 1:14 speaks of "the Greeks and the barbarians" through which latter word reference is made to all those who are not Greeks. The implication is that the Greeks were sophisticated or wise while the others were ignorant. In Acts 18:17, the Greek inhabitants of Corinth are mentioned in distinction from the Jews. This distinction was often in the broadest sense referring to all those who used the Gr. language and customs whether in Greece, Asia Minor, or other countries. As Gr. was the prevailing language, the name "Greek" was often used to designate as Gentiles all those who were not Jews (Acts 16:1, 3; 19:10, 17; 20:21; 21:28; Rom 1:16; 2:9, 10; 3:9; 10:12; 1 Cor 1:22–24; 10:32; 12:13; Gal 2:3; 3:28; Col 3:11). In Acts 11:20 the TR has *Hellēnistás* (1675), Greek-speaking Jews. In John 7:35, the dispersion of the

Hellḗnōn (Greeks) is the dispersed among the Gentiles (cf. Sept.: Isa 9:11). Greeks are also spoken of as Gentile converts to Judaism or Greek proselytes (John 12:20; Acts 14:1; 17:4; 18:4).

1673. Ἑλληνικός *Hellēnikós*; fem. *Hellēnikḗ*, neut. *Hellēnikón*, adj. Greek or Grecian (Luke 23:38; Rev 9:11; Sept.: Jer 46:16; 50:16). Usually refers to the language.

1674. Ἑλληνίς *Hellēnís*; gen. *Hellēnídos*, the fem. of *Héllēn* (1672), a Greek. A female Greek or Gentile (Mark 7:26; Acts 17:12).

1675. Ἑλληνιστής *Hellēnistḗs*; gen. *Hellēnistoú*, masc. proper noun. A Hellenist, i.e., a Jew by birth or religion who speaks Gr., used chiefly of foreign Jews and proselytes whether converted to Christianity or not (Acts 6:1; 9:29; 11:20 [TR]), and in later editions *Héllēnas*.

1676. Ἑλληνιστί *Hellēnistí*; adv. In the Gr. language (John 19:20; Acts 21:37).

1677. ἐλλογέω *ellogéō*; contracted *ellogṓ*, fut. *ellogḗsō*, from *en* (1722), in, and *lógos* (3056), word. To reckon in, to charge, impute, take into account or consideration (Rom 5:13 metaphorically of sin, to impute; Phile 1:18).

Syn.: *logízomai* (3049), to reckon by calculation or imputation.

Ant.: *aphíēmi* (863), to forgive; *charízomai* (5483), to show grace to, deliver, forgive; *apolúō* (630), to loose from, let go, dismiss.

1678. Ἐλμωδάμ *Elmōdám*; masc. proper noun. Elmodam, an ancestor of Christ (Luke 3:28).

1679. ἐλπίζω *elpízō*; from *elpís* (1680), hope. To hope, expect with desire.

(I) Used trans. and in an absolute sense (2 Cor 8:5); followed by the aor. inf. (Luke 6:34; 23:8; Acts 26:7; Rom 15:24; 1 Cor 16:7; Phil 2:19, 23; 1 Tim 3:14; 2

John 1:12; 3 John 1:14); by the perf. inf. (2 Cor 5:11); by *hóti* (3754), that, instead of an inf. (Luke 24:21). See Acts 24:26; 2 Cor 1:13; 13:6; Phile 1:23. Followed by the acc. of thing, to hope for (Rom 8:24, 25; 1 Cor 13:7).

(II) In the construction meaning to hope in someone, i.e., to trust in, confide in; generally followed by the dat. (Matt 12:21) followed by *eis* (1519) with the acc. (John 5:45; Sept.: Isa 51:5; Ps 145:15); by *epí* (1909), upon, and the dat. (Rom 15:12; 1 Tim 6:17; Sept.: Judg 9:26; Ps 44:6) by *epí*, upon, and the acc. (1 Pet 1:13; Sept.: Judg 20:36; Ps 62:8, 10). Spoken of those who put their trust in God, followed by *eis* (1519), in, with the acc. (2 Cor 1:10); by *epí* (1909), upon, with the dat. (1 Tim 4:10; Sept.: Ps 26:1 [cf. Isa 11:10]); with the acc. (1 Tim 5:5; 1 Pet 3:5; Sept.: Ps 37:3, 5; Isa 11:10). Spoken of trusting in Christ, followed by *en* (1722), in, with the dat. (1 Cor 15:19; Sept.: 2 Kgs 18:5; Ps 33:21).

Deriv.: *apelpízō* (560), to bring to despair; *proelpízō* (4276), to hope before.

Syn.: *prosdokáō* (4328), to expect; *prosménō* (4357), to abide still, with an element of hope; *apekdéchomai* (553), to expect fully; *anaménō* (362), to wait for; *ekdéchomai* (1551), to await, expect, anticipate.

Ant.: *exaporéō* (1820), to be utterly without a way, to despair; *apelpízō* (560), to despair; *athuméō* (120), to be spiritless, dismayed.

1680. ἐλπίς *elpís*; gen. *elpídos*, fem. noun. Hope, desire of some good with expectation of obtaining it.

(I) Generally (Rom 8:24, "in hope are we saved" [a.t.], as yet only an expectation, not an actuality; 2 Cor 10:15; Phil 1:20). With a gen. of the thing hoped for (Acts 27:20). See Acts 16:19; 23:6, "of the hope and resurrection" indicating the hope of the resurrection; 26:6, 7. Of the person hoping (Acts 28:20; 2 Cor 1:7; Sept.: Job 14:7; 17:15; Isa 31:2; Ezek 37:11). With *pará* (3844), against or in spite of, with the acc. *par' elpída*,

against hope, i.e., without ground of hope (Rom 4:18). With *epí* (1909), upon, and the dat., *ep' elpídi*, literally on hope or in hope, i.e., with hope, full of hope and confidence (Acts 2:26; see Rom 4:18; 8:20; 1 Cor 9:10; Sept.: Ps 4:8; 16:9). By metonymy spoken of the object of hope (Rom 8:24, "hope that is seen is not hope" [see *blépō* {991, I, B}, to see]). In 1 Cor 9:10 (TR), "should be partaker of his hope." See Sept.: Job 6:8.

(II) Spoken especially of those who experience the hope of salvation through Christ, eternal life, and blessedness (Rom 5:2, 4, 5; 12:12; 15:4, 13, "the God of hope" means the author and source of hope, not the one who needs hope; see 1 Cor 13:13; 2 Cor 3:12; Eph 2:12; 4:4; 1 Thess 4:13; 5:8; 2 Thess 2:16; Titus 1:2; 3:7; Heb 3:6; 6:11; 10:23; 1 Pet 1:3; 3:15). Followed by the gen. of the thing or person on which this hope rests (Eph 1:18; Col 1:23; 1 Thess 1:3). By metonymy spoken of the object of this hope, i.e., salvation (Col 1:5). The hope or salvation resulting from justification by faith (Gal 5:5; see Titus 2:13; Heb 6:18; 7:19). By metonymy also of the source, ground, author of hope, i.e., Christ (Col 1:27; 1 Tim 1:1). Generally in 1 Thess 2:19.

(III) Of a hope in or on someone, i.e., trust, confidence, followed by *eis* (1519), in (Acts 24:15; 1 Pet 1:21); by *epí* (1909), upon, and the dat. (1 John 3:3).

(IV) The Jews lived in the hope of the coming Messiah. Theirs was a religion of hope. Jesus Christ declared that He was the realization of the hope of Judaism. In Matt 5:17 He declared, "Think not that I am come to destroy the law, or the prophets: I am not come to destroy, but to fulfill." The apostle, writing in Heb 7:19, declared, "For the law made nothing perfect." The word for "made perfect" in Gr. is *eteleíōsen*, the aor. indic. act. of *teleióō* (5048), to bring to fulfillment or the realization of a goal. The Law never realized God's ultimate goal for mankind, for it was only the shadow of things to come (Col 2:17) and acted only as a schoolmaster leading to Christ (Gal 3:24). With

Christ having come and been received by faith, we are no more under the Law (Gal 3:25). Heb 7:19 continues to say, "the law made nothing perfect, but the bringing of a better hope did; by the which we draw nigh unto God." This declares that Christ was the goal of the Law and, when He came, God's purpose of the Law was realized, for Christ is the better hope.

(V) The disciples comprehended, especially after the resurrection of the Lord Jesus, that Christ was indeed the fulfillment of the Law and, therefore, their hope was no more in the future but in the present. They realized that they had the fulfillment of all the prophecies and the Law among them and in them in the person of the Lord Jesus Christ. When the Lord Jesus was brought into the temple as a child and Simeon took Him in his arms, he said in words what Jesus Christ deliberately expressed later when He began His public ministry, "For mine eyes have seen thy salvation, which thou hast prepared before the face of all people; a light to lighten the Gentiles, and the glory of thy people Israel" (Luke 2:30–32). The eighty-year-old Anna, a widow and a prophetess, confirmed that Jesus was the fulfillment of the expectation of the Jews and those others who looked to Jerusalem for redemption.

(VI) Throughout the Gospels we find Jesus calling attention to His own person and not to a coming Messiah. He did not use the word "hope" lest it should hinder His acceptance as the looked-for Messiah, the redemption of Israel and the world. He did not say, "Look forward to that which is coming," but He said in Matt 11:28, "Come unto me." He used specific promises concerning the things that were going to happen in regard to His person and His work. We have the promises of His resurrection, His perpetual spiritual presence, and His final return in glory. We find Peter, for example, speaking of a living hope indicating that Jesus Christ, having been raised from the dead, was indeed not an unknown hope in an unknown future, but the living hope of

believers, and as He lives so shall we live forever (1 Pet 1:3, 21). The hope realized in Jesus Christ was salvation (1 Thess 5:8), eternal life (Titus 1:2; 3:7), the glory of God (Rom 5:2; Col 1:27), the resurrection of the dead (Acts 23:6; 24:15). These blessings are all summed up in Jesus Christ Himself, the hope of the world realized. When we hope in Jesus, all these particular and specific blessings are included. This is why the Apostle Paul calls Him "our hope" (1 Tim 1:1). We speak of our hope being fixed in heaven, for Jesus Christ, who is our hope, is there now. The Apostle Paul speaks of our blessed hope as a coming liberator and King, "Looking for the blessed hope, and the glorious appearing of our great God and Savior Jesus Christ" (Titus 2:13). Our hope is closely tied up in our future transformation when "we shall be like him for we shall see him as he is" (1 John 3:2, 3). Even inanimate nature groans for the coming of our Lord in His *Parousía* (3952), Second Coming, having been subjected to vanity "in hope" (Rom 8:20). Thus the full realization of Christian hope will not be reached until the return of Christ; yet even now we as believers have a foretaste of the bliss that ultimately will be ours. Christ now dwells in us and in this indwelling Christ we have an earnest of final fulfillment of our hope. He is "the hope of glory" (Col 1:27). It is, therefore, clear that to be without Christ is to be without hope (Eph 2:12).

(VII) Hope is one of the most distinctive marks of the Christian life in opposition to the hopelessness of the Gentile world (Eph 2:12 [cf. 1 Thess 4:13]). The conclusion of Paul's hymn of love in 1 Cor 13:13 speaks of hope not as something that is future, but as something that is not going to be needed in the future. "And now abideth faith, hope, charity (love), these three; but the greatest of these is charity." It is evident that the Apostle here speaks of heaven and the graces that will survive our earthly existence. The word "greatest" (*meízōn* [3187]) refers not to the inherent value of love, but to the continuation of its function in the future. Faith and hope, on the other hand, are aspects of the Christian's experience that are exercised only on this earth and will not be needed in heaven. Heaven will be the realization of these attributes to those having experienced the love of Christ and having responded in turn with love. To be with Christ and to know Him even as we are known now (1 John 3:2, 3) will be the finalization of our faith which was the basis of our hope. Faith and hope are based on something now unseen, but historically having existed in the person of Christ. Heaven will make that which is now unseen in the graces of faith and hope to become sight. "These all died in faith" (Heb 11:13) is almost equivalent to "these all died in hope." They "endured as seeing him who is invisible" (Heb 11:27). Curiously, John has only one reference to hope, describing it as a motive to personal sanctification (1 John 3:3). "Fullness of hope" (a.t. [Heb 6:11]) accompanies "fullness of faith" (a.t. [Heb 10:22]) and "fullness of understanding" (a.t. [Col 2:2]). Hope stands sometimes for its object (Eph 1:18; Col 1:5; Titus 2:13).

Deriv.: elpízō (1679), to trust, hope.

Syn.: apokaradokía (603), intense anticipation, earnest expectation; ekdochḗ (1561), expectation. Elpís may be defined as desire for future good, accompanied by faith in its realization. The object both of faith and hope is unseen. Faith (pístis [4102]) has regard equally to past, present, or future, while in Scripture referring mainly to the future. Hope is directed only to the future. Expectation (prosdokía [4329]) differs from hope in referring to either good or evil things, and thus lacks the element of desire. In the NT the noun elpís and the verb elpízō are used always of favorable expectation. In Isa 28:19 in the Sept. we have the expression "evil hope." In Heb 10:23, what is translated "the profession of our faith" is in the Gr. homología (3671), the confession, tḗs elpídos, of the hope. It is indeed noteworthy that in the Gospels

the word elpís, hope, does not occur at all, and the verb elpízō occurs only five times (Matt 12:21 quoting Sept. of Isa 42:1; Luke 6:34; 23:8; 24:21; John 5:45). However, in none of these instances does it refer to the theological virtue of looking ahead with desire for something unseen.

1681. 'Ελύμας Elúmas; gen. Elúma, masc. proper noun. Elymas, or Bar-Jesus (Bariēsoús [919]), a magician or sorcerer who resided with Sergius Paulus at Paphos in Cyprus when Paul and Barnabas were there (Acts 13:6ff.). Elymas, meaning sage, is the Arabic designation of his name. Sergius Paulus was an officer of high rank under the Roman government and was eager to receive religious instruction from the two missionaries. But Bar-Jesus, seeing that his occupational influence would cease wherever the light of the gospel would come, opposed Paul and Barnabas and tried to dissuade Paulus from giving heed to their preaching. Paul gave him a severe reproof, immediately after which the wicked man was struck with temporary blindness as a rebuke from God.

1682. 'Ελωΐ Elōΐ; interjection from the Aramaic 'Elāhh (426, OT), "My God" (Mark 15:34 quoted from Ps 22:2). Our Lord calls God "Eli, Eli" (Matt 27:46), as in Ps 22:1, equivalent to Elōΐ. The "Eli, Eli" of Matt 27:46 represents Hebr. whereas "Elōΐ Elōΐ" of Mark 15:34 represents Aramaic, both meaning "My God" as translated. Matthew's revision conforms to the Hebr. text of Ps 22:1.

1683. ἐμαυτοῦ emautoú; fem. emautḗs, neut. emautoú, reflexive pron. of the 1st person found only in gen., dat., acc. sing. from emoú (1700), of me, and autoú (846), self. Of myself, to myself, myself (Luke 7:7; John 5:31; 8:14, 18, 54; 1 Cor 4:3; 2 Cor 2:1). With the prep. apó (575, III, A, 3), from or of myself (John 5:30; 7:17; 14:10), meaning by my own authority. The same with ek (ex) (1537, III, D), of, of myself (John 12:49). Sometimes used simply as *emoú* (Matt 8:9; Luke 7:8; John 12:32; Phile 1:13).

1684. ἐμβαίνω embaínō; fut. *embḗsomai*, from *en* (1722), into, and *baínō* (n.f., see *apobaínō* [576]), to go, come. In the NT only in the aor. *anébēn*; the inf. *embḗnai*; the part. *embás*. To go in, enter, used intrans. (John 5:4, within the water implied); to go on board, embark, when followed by "into the boat" (Matt 8:23; 9:1; 13:2; 14:22, 32; 15:39; Mark 4:1; 5:18; 6:45; 8:10, 13; Luke 5:3; 8:22, 37; John 6:17, 22, 24).
 Syn.: *eisérchomai* (1525), to enter; *eisporeúomai* (1531) or *eíseimi* (1524), to go into; *eisphérō* (1533), to carry in; *eispēdáō* (1530), to jump or rush in; *epérchomai* (1904), to arrive or come in.
 Ant.: *exérchomai* (1831), to get out; *apobállō* (577), to throw off; *ekpheúgō* (1628), to flee out.

1685. ἐμβάλλω embállō; fut. *embalṓ*, from *en* (1722), in, into, and *bállō* (906), to cast. To cast in (Luke 12:5; Sept.: Gen 37:22; Jon 1:12, 15).
 Syn.: *eisphérō* (1533), to bring in.
 Ant.: *apobállō* (577), to cast away; *ekbállō* (1544), to eject; *aphairéō* (851), to remove; *ekkomízō* (1580), to carry out.

1686. ἐμβάπτω embáptō; fut. *embápsō*, from *en* (1722), into, and *báptō* (911), to dip. To dip in or into anything. Trans. in Matt 26:23; mid. in Mark 14:20; John 13:26. The longer form *baptízō* (907) is a frequent form meaning to baptize or to immerse.
 Syn.: *buthízō* (1036), to plunge, begin to sink; *katapontízō* (2670), to submerge.
 Ant.: *pléō* (4126), to sail, floating.

1687. ἐμβατεύω embateúō; fut. *embateúsō*, from *en* (1722), in, and *bateúō* (n.f.), to step. To enter or intrude into, the word seemingly implying conceit and arrogance. Hence it is used in a hostile

sense. In the NT, used metaphorically meaning to go into a matter, to investigate with the idea of impertinence, to pry or intrude into, followed by the acc. with *eis* (1519), into, implied (Col 2:18).
 Syn.: *kataskopéō* (2684), to spy out.
 Ant.: *aphístemi* (868), to desist, refrain.

1688. ἐμβιβάζω embibázō; fut. *embibásō*, from *en* (1722), in, and *bibázō* (n.f., see below), to cause to go or come. To cause to enter, usually spoken of a ship, to embark, put on shipboard. Used trans. in Acts 27:6.
 Deriv. of *bibázō* (n.f.), to make to go up: *anabibázō* (307), to draw up; *epibibázō* (1913), to set on, mount; *katabibázō* (2601), to bring down; *probibázō* (4264), to push forward, promote; *sumbibázō* (4822), to bring together.
 Syn.: *epibaínō* (1910), to embark; *embaínō* (1684), to go in; *anabaínō* (305), to go or come up.
 Ant.: *katabaínō* (2597), to descend; *katabibázō* (2601), to bring down; *katérchomai* (2718), to descend; *apobaínō* (576), to disembark.

1689. ἐμβλέπω emblépō; fut. *emblépsō*, from *en* (1722), in or on, and *blépō* (991), to look. To look in the face, fix the eyes upon, stare at. Followed by the dat. (Mark 10:21, 27; 14:67; Luke 20:17; 22:61; John 1:36, 42; Acts 1:10, 11 where it is *atenízontes* [816], gazing, followed by *eis* [1519], unto). In the sense of to look at or upon, meaning to contemplate, consider (Matt 6:26; Sept.: Isa 51:1, 2, 6). By implication, to look at distinctly, see clearly, discern, used trans. (Mark 8:24, 25; Acts 22:11).
 Syn.: *horáō* (3708), to look, implying perception; *theōréō* (2334), to look with emphasis on details, interest and astonishment; *theáomai* (2300), to behold, with contemplation implied as well as wonderment; *diakrínō* (1252), to scrutinize, discern; *exetázō* (1833), to search; *skopéō* (4648), to look at, implying mental consideration; *episkopéō* (1983), to

look upon carefully; *paratēréō* (3906), to observe, watch.

Ant.: *tuphlóō* (5186), to make blind; *paratheōréō* (3865), to overlook, disregard.

1690. ἐμβριμάομαι *embrimáomai*; contracted *embrimômai*, fut. *embrimḗsomai*, from *en* (1722), in or on account of, and *brimáomai* (n.f.), to roar, storm with anger. In the mid., used as a deponent verb, to be enraged, indignant, to express indignation against someone. Followed by the dat., to murmur against, blame (Mark 14:5), and by implication to admonish sternly, charge strictly, threaten indignantly for disobedience (Matt 9:30; Mark 1:43; Isa 17:13). Also spoken of any agitation of the mind as grief, to be greatly moved or agitated, followed by the dat. of manner (John 11:33, 38, syn. with *tarássō* or *taráttō* [5015], to trouble).

Syn.: *epitimáō* (2008), to admonish, adjudge, find fault with, rebuke; *stenázō* (4727), to groan, grieve; *goggúzō* (1111), to mutter, murmur, grumble; *aganaktéō* (23), to become indignant.

Ant.: *eudokéō* (2106), to approve; *suneudokéō* (4909), to consent in full approval; *homologéō* (3670), to assent; *exomologéō* (1843), to agree openly; *epineúō* (1962), to nod assent; *sugkatatíthēmi* (4784), to agree with, assent to; *déchomai* (1209), to accept; *apodéchomai* (588), to welcome heartily; *prosdéchomai* (4327), to accept favorably.

1691. ἐμέ *emé*; the emphatic form of *mé* (3165), I, me, myself. See *hēmás* (2248), acc. pl. of *emé*, ours, us, we.

1692. ἐμέω *eméō*; contracted *emô*, fut. *emésō*. To spit out, vomit. With the acc. meaning with contempt (Rev 3:16; Sept.: Isa 19:14). See also *exérama* (1829), vomit.

Syn.: *ptúō* (4429), to spit.

Ant.: *eisdéchomai* (1523), to receive, take into one's favor; *katapínō* (2666), to devour.

1693. ἐμμαίνομαι *emmaínomai*; fut. *emmanoúmai*, from *en* (1722), in, and *maínomai* (3105), to act as a maniac. To be mad or furious with or against any person or thing, followed by the dat. (Acts 26:11).

Syn.: *paraphronéō* (3912), to be insane, a fool; *exístēmi* (1839), to be beside oneself, mad; *áphrōn* (878), stupid, mindless, ignorant.

Ant.: *ananḗphō* (366), to come to one's senses; *exupnízō* (1852), metaphorically to awake out of sleep, to be aware of one's actions; *sōphronéō* (4993), to be of sound mind; *hēsucházō* (2270), to be quiet, hold one's peace; *eirēnéúō* (1514), to be peaceful.

1694. Ἐμμανουήλ *Emmanouḗl*; masc. proper noun transliterated from the Hebr. *'Immānu'ēl* (6005, OT), God with us. Emmanuel, a name of the Savior (Matt 1:23 [cf. Isa 7:14; 8:8, 10]).

1695. Ἐμμαούς *Emmaoús*; fem. proper noun. Emmaus, meaning hot springs, a village about seven and one half miles from Jerusalem probably in a northern direction (Luke 24:13). Another Emmaus lay in the plain of Judah, toward Joppa, which the Romans called Nicopolis; not mentioned in the NT and not to be confused with the Nicopolis in Greece (Titus 3:12).

1696. ἐμμένω *emménō*; fut. *emmenô*, from *en* (1722), in, and *ménō* (3306), to remain. To remain, persevere in, followed by the dat. (Acts 14:22), followed by *en* with the dat. (Gal 3:10; Heb 8:9; Sept.: Deut 27:26).

Syn.: *epiménō* (1961), to continue in, metaphorically to persevere; *kartaréō* (2594), to endure; *diaménō* (1265), to stay through, remain; *paraménō* (3887), to persevere; *diateléō* (1300), to persist, continue.

Ant.: *arnéomai* (720), to deny, renounce; *paraitéomai* (3868), to give up, avoid, reject; *aparnéomai* (533), to renounce.

1697. Ἐμμόρ *Emmór*; masc. proper noun transliterated from the Hebr. *Chamōr* (2544, OT), donkey. Hamor, the father of Shechem (Acts 7:16) who ravished Dinah (Gen 33:19). He and Shechem were killed by Jacob's sons (Gen 34:26; Josh 24:32).

1698. ἐμοί *emoí*; the emphatic form of *moí* (3427), I, me, mine, my.

1699. ἐμός *emós*; fem. *emḗ*, neut. *emón*, a poss. pron. of the 1st person sing. from *emoú* (1700). I, mine, my own.
(I) Marking possession, property (Matt 18:20; John 3:29; 4:34; Rom 10:1). With the def. art. in the sing. acc. *tó emón*; neut. pl. *tá emá*, my own, my property (Matt 20:15; 25:27; Luke 15:31). Emphatic in the dat., *tḗ emḗ cheirí* (*cheirí* [5495], hand), with my own hand (1 Cor 16:21; Gal 6:11; Col 4:18). Implying power or office, it "is not mine to give" (Matt 20:23; Mark 10:40).
(II) Spoken of things which proceed from someone as the source, author, agent (Mark 8:38; Luke 9:26; John 6:38; 7:16; 8:16; 14:27; Rom 3:7). With the neut. art. and the sing. acc., my doctrine (John 16:14, 15).
(III) Obj. or pass., spoken of that which is appointed or destined for a person, as "my own time" (a.t. [John 7:6, 8]); "my day" or "the day the mine" (a.t. [John 8:56]); "the time of my departure" (2 Tim 4:6). Of that which is done to or in respect to a person, as "in my memory," meaning "in memory of me" (author's translations [Luke 22:19; 1 Cor 11:24, 25]); "my love" or "the love of me" (a.t. [John 15:9]).

1700. ἐμοῦ *emoú*; the emphatic form of *moú* (3450), of me, mine, my.

1701. ἐμπαιγμός *empaigmós*; gen. *empaigmoú*, masc. noun from *empaízō*

(1702), to mock. Derision, scoffing, mocking (Heb 11:36).
Syn.: *loidoría* (3059) and *oneidismós* (3680), reproach.
Ant.: *ékstasis* (1611), amazement; *thámbos* (2285), astonishment; *sébasma* (4574), devotion; *thaúma* (2295), admiration; *megaleíon* (3167), a great thing.

1702. ἐμπαίζω *empaízō*; fut. *empaíxō*, aor. *enépaixa*, from *en* (1722), in, and *paízō* (3815), to play, to sport with or against someone. To deride, mock, scoff at (Matt 27:29, 31; Mark 10:34; 15:20; Luke 14:29; 22:63; 23:36). Used in an absolute sense (Matt 20:19; 27:41; Mark 15:31; Luke 18:32; 23:11; Sept.: Gen 39:14, 17; Ex 10:2). In the sense of to delude, deceive, only in the pass. (Matt 2:16; Sept.: Jer 10:15).
The noun from which the verb is derived is *país* (3816), child, and therefore *paízō* is to act like a child, to sport or jest. *Empaízō* is used in the Synoptic Gospels of the mockery of Christ, except in Matt 2:16 (where it is used in the sense of deluding or deceiving Herod by the wise men) and in Luke 14:29 (of ridicule cast upon the one who, after laying the foundation of a tower, was unable to finish it). The word is used prophetically by the Lord of His impending sufferings (Matt 20:19; Mark 10:34; Luke 18:32) and of the insults actually inflicted upon Him by the men who were taking Him from Gethsemane (Luke 22:63); by Herod and his soldiers (Luke 23:11); by the soldiers of the governor (Matt 27:29, 31; Mark 15:20; Luke 23:36); by the chief priests, scribes, and elders (Matt 27:41; Mark 15:31).
Deriv.: *empaigmós* (1701), scoffing; *empaigmonḗ*, an abstract noun meaning mockery used in 2 Pet 3:3 in some MSS, but not in the TR; *empaíktēs* (1703), a mocker, scoffer.
Syn.: *muktērízō* (3456), to turn up the nose or sneer at; *ekmuktērízō* (1592), to deride, scoff; *chleuázō* (5512), to jest, mock, jeer.

Ant.: *ainéō* (134), to speak in praise of; *epainéō* (1867), to commend; *humnéō* (5214), to sing, laud; *exomologéō* (1843), to give praise (Rom 15:9); *eulogéō* (2127), to bless or speak well of.

1703. ἐμπαίκτης *empaíktēs*; gen. *empaíktou*, masc. noun from *empaízō* (1702), to deride, mock. A mocker, scoffer, spoken of impostors, false prophets (2 Pet 3:3; Jude 1:18).

Syn.: *loídoros* (3060), railer, reviler.
Ant.: *thaumastós* (2298), wonderful, marvelous; *zēlōtḗ* (2207), a zealot.

1704. ἐμπεριπατέω *emperipatéō*; contracted *emperipatṓ*, fut. *emperipatḗsō*, from *en* (1722), in, among, and *peripatéō* (4043), to walk about. To walk about in a place, e.g., the earth (Sept.: Job 1:7; 2:2). Used metaphorically, meaning to walk or live among a people, be habitually conversant with (2 Cor 6:16; Sept.: Lev 26:12; Deut 23:14).

1705. ἐμπίπλημι *empíplēmi* and ἐμπιπλάω *empipláō*; fut. *emplḗsō*, aor. *enéplēsa*, aor. pass. *eneplḗsthēn*, from *en* (1722), in, and *pímplēmi* (4130), to fill. To fill, to fill in or up, to make full (Sept.: Gen 42:25; Prov 24:4). In the NT spoken only of food, to fill with food, satisfy, satiate (John 6:12; Sept.: Lev 26:26; Ps 78:29, metaphorically), to fill in regard to one's desire with good (Luke 6:25); followed by the acc. and gen. (Luke 1:53; Acts 14:17; Sept.: Isa 27:6; Ps 107:9; Jer 31:14). Metaphorically in the pass., to be filled with any person or thing, meaning to enjoy the society or communion of someone (Rom 15:24). The verb is never used in relation to the filling of or by the Holy Spirit. The basic verb *pímplēmi* or *plḗthō* (4130), to fill, is used in relation to the Holy Spirit (Luke 1:15, 41, 67; Acts 2:4; 4:8, 31; 9:17; 13:9).

Syn.: *chortázō* (5526), to fill or satisfy with food; *gemízō* (1072), to fill or load full; *korénnumi* (2880), to satisfy; *mestóō* (3325), to fill full; *plērṓ* (4137), to fill.

1706. ἐμπίπτω *empíptō*; fut. *empesoúmai*, 2d aor. *enépeson*, from *en* (1722), in, into, and *píptō* (4098), to fall. To fall in. Followed by *eis* (1519), into, with the acc. of place, to fall into (Matt 12:11; Luke 14:5; Sept.: Ex 21:33; Prov 26:27). Of persons, to fall in with or among, to meet with (Luke 10:36). Metaphorically, to fall into any state or condition, to come into, followed by *eis*, into (1 Tim 3:6, 7; 6:9; Sept.: Prov 17:20; 28:10). In Heb 10:31, "to fall into the hands of the living God" means into His power for punishment. See Sept.: 2 Sam 24:14; 1 Chr 21:13.

Syn.: *emplékomai* (1707), to become entangled.
Ant.: *apéchomai* (567), to refrain; *apopheúgō* (668), to escape; *paraitéomai* (3868), to decline, avoid.

1707. ἐμπλέκω *emplékō*; fut. *empléxō*, from *en* (1722), in, and *plékō* (4120), to connect, tie. To braid in, interweave, entangle, implicate. In the NT used metaphorically, to involve in, entangle. In the mid., meaning to entangle oneself in (2 Tim 2:4; 2 Pet 2:20 [pass. cf. Sept.: Prov 28:18]).

Deriv.: *emplokḗ* (1708), intertwining.
Syn.: *pagideúō* (3802), to ensnare; *enéchō* (1758), to hold in a yoke or bondage; *planáō* (4105), to seduce; *exapatáō* (1818), to beguile, deceive; *empíptō* (1706), to fall into or among.
Ant.: *eleutheróō* (1659), to liberate; *apallássō* (525), to release.

1708. ἐμπλοκή *emplokḗ*; gen. *emplokḗs*, fem. noun from *emplékō* (1707), to interweave, braid in, entangle. A braiding, intertwining, plaiting as of the hair in ornamentation (1 Pet 3:3 [cf. 1 Tim 2:9]).
Syn.: *plégma* (4117), a braid of hair.

1709. ἐμπνέω *empnéō*; contracted *empnṓ*, fut. *empneúsō*, from *en* (1722), in, and *pnéō* (4154), to breathe. To blow in or upon, to breathe in. In the NT used intrans. meaning to breathe, respire, followed by the gen., to breathe of any-thing, to be full of, ready to burst with (Acts 9:1).

Syn.: *emphusáō* (1720), to breathe upon.

Ant.: *ekpnéō* (1606), to expire, give up the spirit; *kopázō* (2869), to stop, relax.

1710. ἐμπορεύομαι *emporeúomai*; fut. *emporeúsomai*, mid. deponent from *en* (1722), in, and *poreúomai* (4198), to go, to trade. To go or enter in, travel about in, journey. In the NT, to travel about as a merchant or trader on a large scale, meaning to trade, to traffic (James 4:13; Sept.: Gen 34:10; 42:34; 2 Chr 9:14). Followed by the acc., to traffic in, make gain of (2 Pet 2:3, meaning they will de-ceive you for their own gain).

Syn.: *agorázō* (59), to do business, buy or sell; *ōnéomai* (5608), to buy; *pōléō* (4453), to change or barter, sell; *pipráskō* (4097), to export; *pragmateúomai* (4231), to trade; *diapragmateúomai* (1281), to gain by trading.

Ant.: *achreióō* (889), to spoil, become unprofitable.

1711. ἐμπορία *emporía*; gen. *emporías*, fem. noun from *émporos* (1713), a mer-chant. A journey for trafficking or trad-ing. In the NT, trade, business, traffic, commerce (Matt 22:5; Sept.: Ezek 27:15; 28:5). Contrasted to *empórion* (1712), which denotes a trading place, exchange, a house of merchandise (John 2:16).

Syn.: *gómos* (1117), merchandise, car-go, freight.

1712. ἐμπόριον *empórion*; gen. *empo-ríou*, neut. noun from *émporos* (1713), merchant. Emporium, market, a place where commerce occurs (John 2:16). Contrasted to *emporía* (1711), which means trade, commerce.

1713. ἔμπορος *émporos*; gen. *empórou*, masc. noun from *en* (1722), in, and *póros* (n.f.), a way, passage. Original-ly it designated a passenger in a ship go-ing from one place to another, a traveler.

Later *émporos* was substituted by the word *epibátēs*, one who boards, from *epibaínō* (1910), to go aboard. In the NT, *émporos* means a merchant, trader, one who trades with foreign countries by sea or land on a large scale, a wholesale deal-er; distinguished from the *kápelos*, the verb *kapēleúō* (2585) or *agoraíos* (60), a retailer, one who purchased his wares from the *émporos*, the wholesaler, and dealt them out at retail (Matt 13:45; Rev 18:3, 11, 15, 23; Sept.: Gen 37:28; 1 Kgs 10:28; Ezek 27:12, 15, 20). Also from *póros* (n.f.): *poreúomai* (4198), to trans-port oneself.

Deriv.: *emporía* (1711), commerce, business, trade; *empórion* (1712), mer-chandise, trading place.

1714. ἐμπρήθω *emprḗthō*; fut. *emprḗsō*, from *en* (1722), in, and *prḗthō* (n.f.), to set on fire, burn. To inflame, set on fire, destroy by fire (Matt 22:7; Sept.: Deut 13:16; Judg 18:27).

Syn.: *kaíō* (2545), to set fire to, to light; *katakaíō* (2618), to burn up; *ekkaíō* (1572), to burn out; *puróomai* (4448), to glow with heat.

Ant.: *sbénnumi* (4570), to quench, put out, extinguish; *psúchō* (5594), to chill, cool.

1715. ἔμπροσθεν *émprosthen*; adv. governing a gen. from *en* (1722), in, and *prósthen* (n.f.), in front of, before, which is from *prós* (4314), toward, and the syl-labic suffix *-then* denoting direction, a place. Before, in front of.

(I) As an adv. of place after verbs of motion, meaning forward (Luke 19:4, 28, "he went before," someone else, implied). In the pl. with the art., *tá émprosthen*, things before (Phil 3:13). Of the body, "before," "in front" (Rev 4:6; Sept.: Ezek 2:10). In Sept. and Gr. writers, spoken also of time (Judg 1:11; Ruth 4:7).

(II) As a prep. followed by the gen., spoken of:

(A) A place, meaning before, with the gen. of person, after verbs of motion (Matt 11:10; Mark 1:2; Luke 7:27; John

3:28; 10:4; Sept.: Gen 24:7; 32:3, 16; 1 Chr 15:24). Generally it means before, in the presence of (Matt 5:16; 6:1; 7:6, casting one's pearls before swine; 10:32, 33; 17:2; 23:13, shutting up the kingdom of heaven before men with the meaning of against them, so as to prevent them from entering; 25:32; 26:70; 27:11, 29; Mark 9:2; Luke 5:19; 12:8; 14:2; 19:27; 21:36; John 12:37; Gal 2:14; 1 Thess 2:19; Sept.: Isa 45:1). The expression "before God" means in the sight of God, i.e., God being witness, God knowing and approving (Matt 11:26; Luke 10:21, "it seemed good in thy sight"; 1 Thess 1:3; 3:9, 13; 1 John 3:19). "It is not the will of your Father which is in heaven" (Matt 18:14 [cf. Ex 28:38; Ps 19:14]). Followed by the gen. of thing, "before," "at" (Matt 5:24; Acts 18:17; 2 Cor 5:10; Rev 19:10; 22:8 [cf. Sept.: 2 Chr 5:6; Neh 8:3]).

(B) Time, meaning before, followed by the gen. of person (John 1:15, 27, 30; Sept.: 2 Kgs 17:2; 23:25).

Syn.: *próton* (4412), before, first; *próteron* (4386), before, always used of time; *prín* (4250), formerly; *katenópion* (2714), *enantíon* (1726), or *énanti* (1725), before, in the sight of; *katénanti* (2713) and *enópion* (1799), in the sight of.

Ant.: *opísō* (3694) and *hexés* (1836), after, and the strengthened comp. *kathexés* (2517), afterwards or in order; *metépeita* (3347), afterwards, without necessarily indicating an order of events; *hústeron* (5305), afterwards, with the suggestion of at length, at last; *épeita* (1899), afterwards, thereupon; *eíta* (1534), afterwards, then; *ópisthen* (3693), behind; *metá* (3326), after.

1716. ἐμπτύω emptúō; fut. *emptúsō*, from *en* (1722), in, upon, and *ptúō* (4429), to spit. To spit in or on (followed by *eis* [1519], to spit in one's face, Matt 26:67; Matt 27:30; Sept.: Num 12:14; followed by the dat., Mark 10:34; 14:65; 15:19; pass., Luke 18:32; Sept.: Deut 25:9).

1717. ἐμφανής emphanḗs; gen. *emphanoús*, masc.-fem., neut. *emphanés*, adj.

from *emphaínō* (n.f.), to appear, which is from *en* (1722), in, into, and *phaínō* (5316), to show. Metaphorically meaning apparent, manifest, known (Rom 10:20 quoted from Isa 65:1; Sept.: Ex 2:14).

Deriv.: *emphanízō* (1718), to make apparent.

Syn.: *délos* (1212), evident; *ékdēlos* (1552), quite evident; *pródēlos* (4271), evident beforehand.

Ant.: *kruptós* (2927), secret, hidden; *apókruphos* (614), made or kept secret; *ésō* (2080), inward, inner; *ésōthen* (2081), from within, inner; *aphanḗs* (852), not manifest; *ádēlos* (82), indistinct.

1718. ἐμφανίζω emphanízō; fut. *emphanísō*, from *emphanḗs* (1717), manifest, known. To make apparent, cause to be seen, to show; in the pass., to appear, be seen openly (Matt 27:53; Heb 9:24, "in our behalf" [a.t.]). With the meaning to manifest, make known, declare, show (Heb 11:14), followed by the dat. (Acts 23:15; Sept.: Esth 2:22), followed by the acc. (Acts 23:22). In a judicial sense with the dat., to inform against, accuse (Acts 24:1; 25:2, 15); of a person, to manifest oneself meaning to let oneself be intimately known and understood (John 14:21, 22; Sept.: Ex 33:13).

Syn.: *phaneróō* (5319), to make visible; *óptomai* (3700) or *optánō*, to see and to allow oneself to be seen; *apokalúptō* (601), to uncover, unveil; *anakalúptō* (343), to conceal; *epikalúptō* (1943), to conceal.

Ant.: *krúptō* (2928), to cover, conceal, keep secret; *kalúptō* (2572), to cover; *parakalúptō* (3871), to cover with a veil; *lanthánō* (2990), to escape notice.

1719. ἔμφοβος émphobos; gen. *emphóbou*, masc.-fem., neut. *émphobon*, adj. from *en* (1722), in, and *phóbos* (5401), fear. In fear, terrified (Luke 24:5, 37; Acts 10:4; 22:9; 24:25; Rev 11:13).

Syn.: *deilós* (1169), timid, fearful; *éntromos* (1790), terrified; *phoberós*

(5398), painful, terrible; *ékphobos* (1630), frightened outright.

Ant.: *tolmētēs* (5113), a daring man.

1720. ἐμφυσάω emphusáō; contracted *emphusō*, fut. *emphusēsō*, from *en* (1722), in, upon, and *phusáō* (n.f.), to breathe on, blow. To blow in or on, breathe on (John 20:22; Sept.: Ezek 21:31; 22:21; 37:9). Also from *phusáō* (n.f.): *phusióō* (5448), to inflate.

Syn.: *empnéō* (1709), to breathe in or on.

Ant.: *ekpnéō* (1606), to expire.

1721. ἔμφυτος émphutos; gen. *emphútou*, masc.-fem., neut. *émphuton*, adj. from *emphúō* (n.f.), to implant, which is from *en* (1722), in, and *phúō* (5453), to germinate, to grow or spring up, produce. Inborn, implanted, engrafted from another source (James 1:21, the gospel being here represented under the figure of a seed or shoot implanted or engrafted, as elsewhere by seed sown [cf. Mark 4:14ff.]).

Ant.: *xénos* (3581), alien, strange.

1722. ἐν en; prep. governing the dat. In, on, at, by any place or thing, with the primary idea of rest. As compared with *eis* (1519), into or unto, and *ek* (1537), out of or from, it stands between the two; *eis* implies motion into, and *ek* motion out of, while *en*, in, means remaining in place.

(I) Of place, which is the primary and most frequent use and spoken of everything which is conceived as being, remaining, taking place, meaning within some definite space or limits, in, on, at, by.

(A) Particularly with the meaning of in or within (Matt 4:21) as in a ship; in the synagogues (Matt 4:23); in the corners of the streets (Matt 6:5); at home (Matt 8:67); in the prison (Matt 11:2); in the market (Matt 11:16; Luke 7:32); in his field (Matt 13:24, 27); in the tomb (Mark 5:3; John 5:28; 11:17; 19:41); in a certain place (Luke 11:1); in their midst (Luke 22:5); in the temple (Acts 2:46); in the praetorium (Phil 1:13). With the names of cities, countries, places (Matt 2:1, 5, 19; 3:1, 3; 4:13; 9:31; Acts 7:36; 9:36; 10:1; Rom 1:7; 1 Thess 1:7, 8). In hell (*Hádēs* [86]) (Luke 16:23 [cf. Matt 10:28; Rev 21:8]); in earth, in heaven (Matt 5:12; 6:10, 20; 16:19; Luke 15:7); your Father which is in heaven (Matt 5:45; 7:11 [cf. 18:35]); in the kingdom of heaven (Matt 5:19; 8:11); in the earth (Matt 25:18, 25; John 13:1; Rom 9:17; Col 1:6); in the sea (Mark 5:13; Mark 6:47; 2 Cor 11:25). Of a book, writing (Mark 12:26; Luke 2:23; 20:42; John 6:45; Acts 13:33; Rom 11:2 in the section respecting Elijah; Heb 4:5, 7; 5:6). Of the body and its parts (Matt 1:18, 23; 3:12; 7:3, 4; Luke 1:44; Rom 6:12; 2 Cor 12:2; 1 Pet 2:22; Rev 6:5). Spoken of persons, particularly in one's body (Matt 1:20; Acts 19:16; 20:10; figuratively, Matt 6:23; Rom 7:17, 18, 20; 1 Pet 2:22).

(B) Spoken of elevated objects, a surface, meaning in, i.e., on, upon, as a fig tree (Mark 11:13); a mountain (Luke 8:32; John 4:20; Heb 8:5; Sept.: Ex 31:18); engraven in stone (2 Cor 3:7); in my throne (Rev 3:21); See Luke 12:51; John 20:25; Acts 7:33. Rev 13:12; 18:19. Figuratively, Jude 1:12.

(C) In a somewhat wider sense, simply implying contact, close proximity, meaning in, at, on, by, near, with, equivalent to *pará* (3844), near (Matt 6:5; 7:6, at or under the feet; Luke 13:4; 16:23; John 11:10; 15:4, remains on, attached to the vine; 19:41; Acts 2:19; Rom 8:34; Heb 1:3; 8:1; 10:12; Rev 9:10). **(1)** Of those with whom someone is in near connection, intimate union, oneness of heart, mind, purpose, especially of Christians, in union with Christ by faith and who are become as branches in the true vine (John 15:2, 4, 5; see John 6:56; 14:20; Rom 16:7, 11; 1 Cor 1:30; 9:1, 2; 2 Cor 5:17; Eph 2:13; 1 Thess 4:16, those who died in union with Christ by faith, as Christians [cf. 1 Cor 15:18; Rev 14:13]). Hence, those "in Christ" means Christians (2 Cor 12:2; Gal 1:22; 1 Pet

5:14). Generally those in connection with Christ, in the Christian faith (Rom 12:5; Gal 3:28; 5:6; 6:15; Phil 4:1; 1 Thess 3:8; 1 John 2:24). Christ is in the believer and vice versa, in consequence of faith in Him (John 6:56; 14:20; 15:4, 5; 17:23, 26; Rom 8:9; Gal 2:20); of the believer's union with God (1 Thess 1:1; 1 John 2:24; 3:6, 24; 4:13, 15, 16); of the mutual union of God and Christ (John 10:38; 14:10, 11, 20); of the Holy Spirit in Christians (John 14:17; Rom 8:9, 11; 1 Cor 3:16; 6:19). (2) Of those in, with, on whom, i.e., in whose person or character anything exists, is done (cf. *pará* [3844], near), e.g., in one's external life and conduct (John 18:38; 19:4, 6; Acts 24:20; 25:5; 1 Cor 4:2; 1 John 2:10). Generally of any power, influence, efficiency, e.g., from God, the Spirit (Matt 14:2; John 1:4; 14:13, 30; 17:26; 1 Cor 12:6; 2 Cor 4:4, 12; 6:12; Gal 4:19; Phil 2:5, 13; Col 1:19; Heb 13:21; 1 John 3:9, 15); also *en heautō* ([1438], himself, in the dat.), meaning in, with, or of oneself (Matt 13:21; John 5:26; 6:53; 2 Cor 1:9). (3) Of those in or with whom, i.e., in whose mind, heart, soul, anything exists or takes place (cf. *pará* [3844], near) as virtues, vices, faculties (John 1:47; 4:14, meaning in his soul; 17:13; Rom 7:8; 1 Cor 2:11; 8:7; 2 Cor 11:10; Eph 4:18). "Your life is hid with Christ in God" (Col 3:3) means in the mind and counsels of God. See Eph 3:9. The expression *en heautō*, *en heautoís*, in or with oneself or themselves, means in one's heart (Matt 3:9; Luke 7:39, 49; Rom 8:23; James 2:4).

(D) Of a number or multitude, as indicating place, meaning in, among, with, equivalent to *en mésō* (3319), in the midst (Matt 2:6). With the same meaning of among (Matt 11:11, 21; 20:27; Mark 10:43; Luke 1:1; John 1:14; 11:54; Acts 2:29; 20:32; Rom 1:5, 6; 1 Cor 11:18; Eph 5:3; 1 Pet 5:1, 2; 2 Pet 2:8). Also in the dat. pl. *en heautoís* (1438), in themselves, meaning among themselves (Matt 9:3; 21:38; Acts 28:29); *en allélois* (240), one another, meaning with one another

(Mark 9:50; John 13:35; Rom 15:5). With the dat. sing. of a coll. noun (Luke 1:61; 2:44; 4:25, 27, "in Israel"; John 7:43; Acts 10:35; Eph 3:21; 2 Pet 2:1; Sept.: Gen 23:6; Lev 16:29; 2 Kgs 18:5). Hence with dat. pl. of person by whom one is accompanied, escorted (Luke 14:31; Jude 1:14; Sept.: Num 20:19). With the dat. pl. of thing (1 Cor 15:3, adv., "first of all," among the first).

(E) Of persons, by implication meaning before, in the presence of (Mark 8:38; Luke 1:25; Acts 6:8; 24:21, as before judges; 1 Cor 2:6; 2 Cor 10:1). Figuratively (Luke 4:21 [cf. Sept.: Deut 5:1]), hence metaphorically, meaning in the sight of someone, he being judge (Luke 16:15, "in the sight of," or judgment of men; 1 Cor 14:11; Col 3:20). Also, by Hebraism, *en ophthalmoís humōn* (*ophthalmoís*, dat. pl. of *ophthalmós* [3788], eye; *humōn* [5216], of you) meaning before your eyes, in your judgment (Matt 21:42; Mark 12:11; Sept.: Ps 118:23).

(F) Spoken of that by which one is surrounded or enveloped, meaning in, with (Matt 16:27; 25:31; Mark 13:26; Luke 21:27; Acts 7:30); of clothing (Matt 7:15; 11:8; Mark 12:38; Heb 11:37; James 2:2); ornaments (1 Tim 2:9); bonds (Eph 6:20). Also *en sarkí* (4561), flesh, meaning in the flesh, clothed in flesh, in the body (1 John 4:2; 2 John 1:7); to live in the flesh (Gal 2:20; Phil 1:22; Sept.: Deut 22:12; Ps 147:8). Hence of that with which one is furnished, which he carries with him (1 Cor 4:21; Heb 9:25). Metaphorically (Luke 1:17; Rom 15:29; Eph 6:2; Sept.: Josh 22:8; 1 Sam 1:24; Ps 66:13).

(II) Of time:
(A) Of time meaning when, i.e., a definite point or period in, during, on, at which anything takes place (Matt 2:1; 3:1; 8:13; 12:1, 2; Acts 20:7; 1 Cor 11:23; John 11:9, 10, by day, by night). With a neut. adj. (Acts 7:13; 2 Cor 11:6; Phil 4:6). In Acts 26:28, "partly" (Acts 26:29, in part or in whole). With a pron. used in an absolute sense, *en hō* (3739), in which, in the dat. sing. implying *chrónō*, the dat.

sing. of *chrónos* (5550), time (Mark 2:19;
John 5:7). With the art. and adv. (Luke
7:11; 8:1; John 4:31). Spoken of an action or event which serves to mark a definite time (Matt 22:28; Luke 11:31, 32;
John 21:20; 1 Cor 15:52; 2 Thess 1:7; 1
John 2:28). With *en hoís* (the dat. pl. of
hós [3739], which) implying *prágmasi*
(the dat. pl. of *prágma* [4229], affair,
matter, thing) meaning during which
things, meanwhile (Luke 12:1). Especially with the dat. art. and inf., *en* is used to
mean on or at an action or event, while it
is taking place (Luke 1:8; 2:6; 5:1; 9:36;
24:51; Acts 8:6; Sept.: 1 Sam 1:7).

(**B**) Of time meaning how long a space
or period which anything takes place
in or within, such as within or in three
days (Matt 27:40; Mark 15:29; Sept.: Isa
16:14).

(**III**) Figuratively of the state, condition or manner in which one is, moves,
acts; of the ground, occasion, means, on,
in, by, or through which one is affected,
moved, acted upon.

(**A**) Of the state, condition, or circumstances in which a person or thing is:
(**1**) Generally, of an external state (Luke
2:29; 8:43; 11:21 [cf. Luke 16:23; 23:12,
40; Rom 1:4; 8:37; 1 Cor 7:18, 20, 24;
15:42, 43; 2 Cor 6:4, 5; Gal 1:14; Phil
2:7]; 2 Thess 3:16, in every state, at every turn; 1 Tim 2:2); of an internal state
of the mind or feelings (Acts 11:5; Rom
15:32; 1 Cor 1:10; 2:3; 14:6, in the state
or condition of one who receives and utters a revelation; 2 Cor 11:17, 21; Eph
3:12; 5:21; 1 Thess 2:17; 1 Tim 1:13;
2:11; Heb 3:11; James 1:21; 2:1; Jude
1:24). In this usage *en* with its dat. is often equivalent to an adj. (Rom 4:10; 2
Cor 3:7, 8; Phil 4:19; 1 Tim 2:7, 12, 14;
Titus 1:6; 3:5); an adv. (Acts 5:23; Rom
2:28, 29; Eph 6:24). (**2**) Of the business,
employment or actions in which one is
engaged (Matt 20:15, in my own affairs;
21:22; 22:15, "in his talk"; 23:30, in slaying the prophets; Mark 4:2; 8:27; Luke
16:10; 24:35; John 8:3; Acts 6:1; 24:16;
Rom 1:9, "laboring in the gospel" [a.t.];
14:18; 1 Cor 15:58; 2 Cor 7:11; Col 1:10;

4:2; 1 Tim 4:15; 5:17; Heb 6:18; 11:34;
James 1:8; 4:3). Also with the dat. of person, meaning in the work, business, cause
of someone (Rom 16:12; 1 Cor 4:17;
Eph 6:21). (**3**) Implying in the power of
someone (Acts 4:12; 5:4 [cf. 1:7; John
3:35]); in the power or under the influence of the Spirit (*en pneúmati*, the dat.
sing. of *pneúma* [4151], spirit) in Matt
12:28; 22:43; Mark 12:36; Luke 2:27;
4:1; 1 Cor 12:3; Rev 1:10; 4:2; 17:3; of
demoniacs, *en pneúmati akathártō* (dat.
sing. of *akáthartos* [169], unclean), in the
power of or possessed by an unclean spirit (Mark 1:23; 5:2); of one's sound mind,
genómenos en heautō (*gínomai* [1096],
to become; *heautō* [1438] in the dat.
sing., himself), having come to himself
(Acts 12:11).

(**B**) Of manner or mode, i.e., the external or internal state or circumstances by which any action is accompanied,
in, with or in reference to which it is performed: (**1**) Generally of manner (cf. *ek*
[1537, III, E]; Matt 22:37 quoted from
Deut 6:5; Mark 4:2; Luke 2:36; 21:25;
John 16:25; Acts 2:46; 10:48 [cf. *baptízō*
{907, III}; Rom 1:9; 9:22; 15:6; 1 Cor
2:4, 7; 14:21; 2 Cor 3:7; Col 3:22; 1 Pet
2:24; 2 Pet 2:3; 1 John 5:6]). In an adv.
sense (Matt 22:16, truly, in reality; Mark
9:1; Acts 12:7; 22:18; Eph 6:19, boldly;
Col 4:5; Rev 18:2; 19:11, righteously).
(**2**) Of a rule, law, standard, in, by, according to, conformable to (Matt 7:2; Luke
1:8; 1 Cor 15:23; Phil 1:8; 1 Thess 4:15;
1 Tim 1:18; Heb 4:11). Of a rule of life
(Luke 1:6) With the dat. of person (2 Cor
10:12). In conformity with the will, law
or precept of someone (John 3:21; 1 Cor
7:39; Eph 6:1). (**3**) In the sense meaning in respect to, as to (Luke 1:7, 18;
Eph 2:11; Titus 1:13; James 2:10; 3:2).
Also *en pantí* (dat. sing. of *pás* [3956],
all), in every respect (2 Cor 8:7; 9:8, 11);
en mēdení (dat. sing. of *mēdén*, the neut.
of *mēdeís* [3367], no one) meaning in no
respect (2 Cor 7:9; James 1:4); and *en
oudení* (dat. sing. of *oudén*, the neut. of
oudeís [3762], no one), in a more absolute way, meaning in no way or respect

(Phil 1:20). After words meaning plenty or want (Rom 15:13; 1 Cor 1:5, 7; 2 Cor 3:9; 8:7; Eph 2:4; Col 2:7; 1 Tim 6:18).

(**C**) Of the ground, basis, occasion, in, on or upon which anything rests, exists, takes place. (**1**) Of a person or thing with a dat. of thing (1 Cor 2:5; 2 Cor 4:10; Gal 4:14; Eph 2:11); with the dat. of person, i.e., in the person or case of someone, in or by his example (Luke 22:37; John 9:3; Acts 4:2; Rom 9:17; 1 Cor 4:6; 2 Cor 4:3; Eph 1:20; Phil 1:30). After verbs implying to do anything in one's case, i.e., to or for one where the acc. or dat. might stand (Matt 17:12; Luke 23:31; 1 Cor 9:15; 1 Thess 5:12, for your benefit). With the verb *homologéō* (3670), to confess, followed by *en* and the dat. means to confess in one's case or cause, to acknowledge (Matt 10:32; Luke 12:8). With the verb *skandalízomai* (4624), to be offended, followed by *en* and the dat. sing. meaning to take offense in someone, in his case or cause (Matt 11:6; 13:57; 26:31, 33). Spoken of that in which anything consists, is comprised, fulfilled, manifested (John 9:30; Rom 13:9; Gal 5:14; Eph 2:7; 5:9; Heb 3:12; 1 Pet 3:4; 1 John 3:10; 4:9, 10, 17). Also from looseness of expression (Acts 7:14, consisting in 75 souls [cf. Deut 10:22]). After verbs of swearing, to mark the ground, basis, or object on which the oath rests, expressed in Eng. as "by," or "upon" (Matt 5:34–36; 23:16, 18, 20; Rev 10:6; Sept.: 1 Sam 24:22; 2 Sam 19:7; 1 Kgs 2:8). (**2**) Of the ground, motive or exciting cause in consequence of which any action is performed, in, on, at, by, i.e., because of, on account of (Matt 6:7; Acts 7:29; 1 Cor 11:22; 2 Cor 6:12; 1 Pet 4:14, 16 [cf. Mark 9:41; Sept.: 2 Chr 16:7]). *En toútō*, sing. dat. of *toúto* (5124), this, meaning herein, hereby, on this account, therefore (John 15:8; 16:30; Acts 24:16; 1 Cor 4:4, to know herein, hereby, by this. See John 13:35; 1 John 2:3, 5). When the relative pron. *en hṓ* is used, it is equivalent to *en toútō* followed by *hóti* (3754), that, meaning herein that, in that, because

(Rom 8:3; Heb 2:18; 6:17, wherefore; 1 Pet 2:12). In this sense, *en* does not occur with the dat. of person. Spoken also of the authority in consequence of which anything is done, in, by, under, i.e., by virtue of (Matt 21:9; Luke 20:2; John 5:43; 10:25; 12:13; 14:26; Acts 4:7; 1 Cor 5:4; 2 Thess 3:6). The word *aitéō* (154), to ask as a beggar in the name of Jesus, means to come to Him, dependent on His authority and sanction (John 14:13, 14; 15:16; 16:23, 24, 26). (**3**) Of the ground or occasion of an emotion of mind, after words expressing joy, wonder, hope, confidence, and the reverse. With the dat. of thing (Matt 12:21; Mark 1:15; Luke 10:20; Acts 7:41; Rom 2:23; Eph 3:13; Phil 3:3, 4; Sept.: Ps 33:21; Jer 48:7); of person (Rom 5:11; 1 Cor 15:19; 2 Cor 7:16; Eph 1:12; 1 Tim 6:17; Sept.: 2 Kgs 18:5; Hos 10:13).

(**D**) Of the means, by the aid or intervention of which anything takes place, is done, meaning in, by means of. (**1**) With the dat. of person, by whose aid or intervention, in, by, with, through whom, anything is done (Matt 9:34; Acts 4:9; 17:28, 31; 1 Cor 15:22; Gal 3:8, "in and through you" [a.t. {cf. Acts 3:25; Heb 1:1; 1 John 5:11}]). (**2**) With the dat. of thing, but used strictly only of such means as imply that the obj. affected is actually in, among, surrounded by them, particularly in and through (Matt 8:32, "in [and by] the waters"; 1 Cor 3:13; Rev 14:10; 16:8; Sept.: Lev 8:32). Hence generally where the obj. is conceived as being in or in contact or connection with the means (Matt 3:11, "baptize you in water" [a.t.]; 5:13; 17:21; 25:16; Luke 21:34; Acts 7:35, in or "by the hand" of someone; 11:14; 20:19; Rom 10:5, 9; 12:21; 1 Cor 6:20; Gal 3:19; Heb 10:29; 13:20; Rev 1:5; Sept.: Num 36:2; Judg 16:7; Job 18:8). Hence in the NT and later writers, simply of the instrument, where Class. Gr. writers usually use the dat. alone (Luke 22:49; Rom 16:16; James 3:9; Rev 6:8; 12:5; 13:10; Sept.: Gen 48:22; Deut 15:19; Jer 14:12; Hos 1:7). (**3**) Spoken of price or exchange, of that by means of which or with which anything is purchased or exchanged (Rom 1:23, "for an image" [a.t.], 25; Rev 5:9; Sept.: 1 Sam 24:20; Eccl 4:9; Lam 5:4).

(IV) Sometimes *en* with the dat. is where the natural construction would seem to require *eis* (1519), unto, into, with the acc. as after verbs which imply, not rest in a place or state, but motion or direction into or toward an object. In such cases, the idea of arrival and subsequent rest in that place or state is either actually expressed or is implied in the context. See the converse of this in *eis* (1519, V). After verbs of motion (Matt 10:16, "in the midst of wolves," by whom you are already surrounded; 14:3, to put in prison or into prison; Mark 1:16; 15:46 [cf. Luke 23:53, they placed him in the tomb]; Luke 5:16, He withdrew and abode in deserts; 7:17, went out, spread abroad, in the whole land; John 3:35; 5:4; Rev 11:12; Sept.: Judg 6:35; Ezra 7:10). Metaphorically, after words expressing an affection of mind toward someone (2 Cor 8:7; 1 John 4:9, 16); wrath upon the people (Luke 21:23 [{TR} cf. Sept.: 2 Sam 24:17]).

(V) In composition *en* implies:

(A) A being or resting in, as *éneimi* (1751), to be within; *emménō* (1696), to stay in the same place, persevere.

(B) Into, when compounded with verbs of motion, as *embaínō* (1684), to walk on, embark, come into, step in.

(C) Conformity, as *éndikos* (1738), equitable, just; *énnomos* (1772), lawful.

(D) Participation, as *énochos* (1777), guilty of.

1723. ἐναγκαλίζομαι *enagkalízomai*; fut. *enagkalísomai*, from *en* (1722), in, into, and *agkalízomai* (n.f.), to take in arms, which is from *agkálē* (43), arm. To take in one's arms, to embrace (Mark 9:36; 10:16; Sept.: Prov 6:10).

Syn.: *aspázomai* (782), to embrace.

Ant.: *apóthéomai* (683), to cast away, push off.

1724. ἐνάλιος *enálios*; gen. *enalíou*, masc.-fem., neut. *enálion*, adj. from *en* (1722), in, and *háls* (n.f., see *aigialós* [123]), sea. Belonging in the sea, marine (James 3:7).

Syn.: *thálassa* (2281), sea; *pélagos* (3989), the deep sea or vast expanse of open water.

Ant.: *epígeios* (1919), earthly, terrestrial.

1725. ἔναντι *énanti*; adv. from *en* (1722), in, into, and *antí* (473), against, opposite. Over against, in the presence of, before (Luke 1:8).

Deriv.: *apénanti* (561), opposite; *katénanti* (2713), down over against.

Syn.: *émprosthen* (1715), in front of; *enṓpion* (1799), before or opposite; *katenṓpion* (2714), over against, opposite.

Ant.: *ópisthen* (3693), at the back.

1726. ἐναντίον *enantíon*; the neut. of *enantíos* (1727). Over against, opposite, used as an adv. joined with a gen. and applied in the same sense as *énanti* (1725), before. In front of, before (Mark 2:12; Luke 20:26; Acts 7:10, he won his favor, 8:32 [cf. Sept.: Gen 20:15; 41:46; Ex 7:20; 11:3; 12:36; Num 20:8]). In Luke 24:19, "in the sight of God" (a.t.), i.e., God being judge (cf. Sept.: Gen 10:9; 21:11, 12).

Deriv.: *tounantíon* (5121), contrariwise.

Syn.: *émprosthen* (1715), in front of; *katenṓpion* (2714), before the presence of; *antikrú* (481), over against.

Ant.: *ópisthen* (3693), from the rear; *opísō* (3694), behind.

1727. ἐναντίος *enantíos*; fem. *enantía*, neut. *enantíon* (1726), adj. from *en* (1722), in, and *antíos* (n.f.), set against. Over against, opposite. Spoken of a wind as contrary, adverse (Matt 14:24; Acts 27:4); followed by the dat. (Mark 6:48). As an adv. followed by a gen., over against (Mark 15:39). Metaphorically, meaning contrary, adverse, hostile, followed by a dat. (Acts 28:17; 1 Thess 2:15); followed by *prós* (4314), toward, with an acc. (Acts 26:9; Sept.: Ezek 18:18). The expression *ho ex enantías*, the equivalent of *ho enantíos*, an adversary, enemy (Titus 2:8).

Deriv.: *hupenantíos* (5227), opposite to, adversary.

Syn.: *antídikos* (476), a plaintiff, an opponent in a law suit; *antíkeimai* (480), to stand against, be an adversary; *asúmphōnos* (800), disagreeable.

Ant.: *súmphōnos* (4859), agreeable.

1728. ἐνάρχομαι *enárchomai*; fut. *enárxomai*, from *en* (1722), in, and *árchomai* (756), to begin. To make a beginning, to begin, commence (Gal 3:3; Phil 1:6; Sept.: Deut 2:24, 25, 31).

Deriv.: *proenárchomai* (4278), to begin before.

Syn.: *egkainízō* (1457), to inaugurate.

Ant.: *teléō* (5055), to complete, finish; *suntéléō* (4931), to bring to an end, finish completely; *plēróō* (4137), to fulfill, complete; *gínomai* (1096), to bring to completion; *ekpnéō* (1606), to expire; *katantáō* (2658), to arrive at; *apobaínō* (576), to eventuate; *kleíō* (2808), to close; *paúō* (3973), to cease; *teleutáō* (5053), to expire.

1729. ἐνδεής *endeḗs*; gen. *endeoús*, masc.-fem., neut. *endeés*, adj. from *endéō* (n.f.), to be in want of, which is from *en* (1722), in, and *déō* (1210), to lack, want. In want, needy, destitute, indigent, poor (Acts 4:34; Sept.: Deut 15:4, 7; Isa 41:17).

Syn.: *hustérēma* (5303), a deficiency, lack; *elattonéō* (1641), to be less, short; *leípō* (3007), to be left behind, to lack; *ptōchós* (4434), poor, helpless, beggar; *pénēs* (3993), poor but capable of taking care of oneself; *penichrós* (3998), one who has scanty means of livelihood; *chreía* (5532), need, lack; *hysteréō* (5302), to come behind, lack.

Ant.: *ploúsios* (4145), rich; *perissós* (4053), superabundant; *pleonázōn* (the pres. part. of *pleonázō* [4121]), superabundant, increasing; *plḗrēs* (4134), full; *mestós* (3324), replete.

1730. ἔνδειγμα *éndeigma*; gen. *endeígmatos*, neut. noun from *endeíknumi* (1731), to show. Indication, token, proof (2 Thess 1:5). The act of proving is *éndeixis* (1732), evidence.

Syn.: *sēmeíon* (4592), a sign, token, indication; *sússēmon* (4953), a fixed sign or signal agreed upon with others; *apódeixis* (585), manifestation, demonstration; *bebaíōsis* (951), confirmation; *martúrion* (3142), evidence; *deígma* (1164), specimen, example; *tekmḗrion* (5039), token, proof.

1731. ἐνδείκνυμι *endeíknumi*; fut. *endeíxō*, from *en* (1722), in, to, and *deíknumi* (1166), to show. To point out or show in anything, trans. (Sept.: Josh 7:14ff.). In the NT used in the mid. *endeíknumai*, to show forth, to manifest in connection with anything relating to or depending on oneself, followed by the acc. (Rom 2:15; 9:17, 22; 2 Cor 8:24; Eph 2:7; 1 Tim 1:16; Titus 2:10; 3:2; Heb 6:10, 11; Sept.: Ex 9:16). By implication, to manifest towards someone, to do to someone, with the acc. and dat. (2 Tim 4:14; Sept.: Gen 50:15, 17).

Deriv.: *éndeigma* (1730), manifest token; *éndeixis* (1732), the act of proving.

Syn.: *dēlóō* (1213), to declare; *emphanízō* (1718), to exhibit, manifest; *marturéō* (3140), to witness; *probállō* (4261), to put forward; *apokalúptō* (601), to reveal.

Ant.: *krúptō* (2928), to hide; *kalúptō* (2572), to cover; *parakalúptō* (3871), to conceal; *lanthánō* (2990), to escape notice.

1732. ἔνδειξις *éndeixis*; gen. *endeíxeōs*, from *endeíknumi* (1731), to show forth. The act of pointing out, particularly with the finger. Manifestation, declaration (Rom 3:25, 26), indication, token, proof, similar to *éndeigma* (1730), with the difference being that *éndeigma* is the actual demonstration, while *éndeixis* is the act of proving (2 Cor 8:24; Phil 1:28).

Syn.: *dokimḗ* (1382), proof, trial; *dokímion* (1383), test, proof; *tekmḗrion* (5039), a positive proof; *anádeixis* (323), a showing forth; *sēmeíon* (4592), a sign, indication; *sússēmon* (4953), a fixed sign or signal; *apódeixis* (585), demonstration, manifestation; *martúrion* (3142), evidence, testimony; *deígma* (1164), example.

Ant.: *anaíresis* (336), the act of killing, cancellation; *athétēsis* (115), annulment; *apistía* (570), faithlessness.

1733. ἔνδεκα *héndeka*; indeclinable, cardinal number from *hén* (the neut. of *heís* [1520]), one, and *déka* (1176), ten. Eleven. In the NT, used only of the eleven disciples after Judas forsook Jesus (Matt 28:16; Mark 16:14; Luke 24:9, 33; Acts 1:26; 2:14).

Deriv.: *hendékatos* (1734), eleventh.

1734. ἐνδέκατος *hendékatos*; fem. *hendekátē*, neut. *hendékaton*, ordinal number from *héndeka* (1733), eleven. Eleventh (Matt 20:6, 9; Rev 21:20).

1735. ἐνδέχομαι *endéchomai*; fut. *endéxomai*, from the prep. *en* (1722), in, upon, and *déchomai* (1209), to receive. As an impersonal verb *endéchetai*, used with the neg., it is not possible, it may not be (Luke 13:33).

Deriv.: *anéndektos* (418), impossible.

Syn.: *dúnamai* (1410), to be able; *ischúō* (2480), to be strong.

Ant.: *adunatéō* (101), to be unable.

1736. ἐνδημέω *endēméō*; contracted *endēmṓ*, fut. *endēmḗso*, from *éndemos* (n.f.), one who is at home, in his own country, or among his own people, which is from *en* (1722), in, and *dḗmos* (1218), an organized body of people. To be at home, to be present in any place or with any person (2 Cor 5:6, 8, 9 [cf. Phil 1:23]).

Syn.: *páreimi* (3918), to be at hand or present; *enístēmi* (1764), to be

present; *ephístēmi* (2186), to stand over with the meaning to be present; *paragínomai* (3854), to be beside, present; *parákeimai* (3873), to lie beside, be present; *sumpáreimi* (4840), to be present with; *ménō* (3306), to abide; *parístēmi* (3936), to place oneself beside, be present; *hḗkō* (2240), to be present; *oikéō* (3611), to dwell; *enoikéō* (1774), to inhabit; *sunoikéō* (4924), to dwell with.

Ant.: *ekdēméō* (1553), to vacate, be absent; *ápeimi* (548), to be absent.

1737. ἐνδιδύσκω *endidúskō*; mid. *endidúskomai*, the same as *endúnō* (1744) and *endúō* (1746), to clothe in a garment. To clothe oneself in, wear, followed by the acc. (Luke 8:27; 16:19; Sept.: 2 Sam 1:24; 13:18).

Syn.: *amphiénnumi* (294), to enwrap with clothes; *himatízō* (2439), to put on clothes; *peribállō* (4016), to wrap around; *egkombóomai* (1463), to gird oneself with something; *phoréō* (5409), to wear and also bear; *peritíthēmi* (4060), to put around or on.

Ant.: *ekdúō* (1562), to undress; *apekdúō* (554) or *apotíthēmi* (659), to put off; *apōthéomai* (683), to put away.

1738. ἔνδικος *éndikos*; gen. *endíkou*, masc.-fem., neut. *éndikon*, adj. from *en* (1722), in, and *díkē* (1349), justice. Fair, just. A just or fair recompense (Heb 2:2). In Rom 3:8, *éndikon* presupposes that which has been decided justly.

Syn.: *díkaios* (1342), just. *Díkaios* characterizes the subject so far as he is one with *díkē* (1349), justice, while *éndikos* characterizes the subject so far as he occupies the proper relation to *díkē*, justice, or is within the confines of the law. *Dikaíōs* (1346), justly, is that which leads to the just sentence.

Ant.: *ékdikos* (1558), one bringing out justice.

1739. ἐνδόμησις *endómēsis*; gen. *endomēseōs*, from *endoméō* (n.f.), to build in. The act of building a structure, something built on, a structure (Rev 21:18).

Syn.: *oikodomḗ* (3619), a building under construction; *ktísis* (2937), creation, building, the process of building.
Ant.: *katalúō* (2647), to destroy.

1740. ἐνδοξάζω *endoxázō*; fut. *endoxásō*, from *éndoxos* (1741), glorious. To glorify. Used only in 2 Thess 1:10, 12 in the mid. voice, *endoxázomai*. In the aor. pass., to appear glorious; with reference to God, to appear and be recognized for all that He is (Sept.: Ex 14:4; Ezek 28:22).
Syn.: *megalúnō* (3170), to make great; *peripoiéomai* (4046), to make something of oneself.
Ant.: *katadikázō* (2613), to condemn; *krínō* (2919), to judge, punish; *katakrínō* (2632), to judge against.

1741. ἔνδοξος *éndoxos*; gen. *endóxou*, masc.-fem., neut. *éndoxon*, adj. from *en* (1722), in, and *dóxa* (1391), glory. Glorious, splendid.
(I) Of persons, honored, respected, noble (1 Cor 4:10; Sept.: 1 Sam 9:6; Isa 23:8). Of deeds, in the neut. pl. *tá éndoxa*, glorious, memorable (Luke 13:17; Sept.: Ex 34:10; Job 5:9; Isa 12:4).
(II) Of external appearance, splendid, glorious, as of raiment (Luke 7:25; Sept.: 2 Chr 2:9; Isa 22:17; 23:9). Metaphorically, a glorious Church, signifying the Church adorned in pure and splendid raiment as a bride (Eph 5:27 [cf. Eph 5:25, as well as Rev 19:7, 8; 21:9]).
Deriv.: *endoxázō* (1740), to glorify.
Syn.: *tá éndoxa* implying glorious things, miracles, unusual acts; *sēmeía* (4592), signs; *dunámeis* (1411), mighty works; *megaleía* (3167), great works; *parádoxa* (3861), strange works; *thaumásia* (2297), admirable works; *tímios* (5093), precious, valuable, honorable; *éntimos* (1784), honorable; *euschḗmōn* (2158), comely, honorable; *kalós* (2570), good; *semnós* (4586), honorable, grave, modest.
Ant.: *átimos* (820), without honor; *aischrós* (150), shameful.

1742. ἔνδυμα *énduma*; gen. *endúmatos*, neut. noun from *endúō* (1746), to clothe. A garment, raiment, clothing (Matt 6:25, 28; 28:3; Luke 12:23; Sept.: 2 Sam 1:24; Prov 31:22; Zeph 1:8). Spoken of the outer garment (Matt 3:4) made of camel hair, the usual garment of the ancient prophets (cf. 2 Sam 20:8; 2 Kgs 1:8; Zech 13:4); a wedding garment (Matt 22:11, 12) presented to guests as a token of honor according to oriental custom (cf. Gen 45:22; Judg 14:12ff.; 2 Kgs 5:5, 22ff.). Metaphorically, "in sheep's clothing" (Matt 7:15) means externally showing the meekness and gentleness of lambs in contrast to the spirit of wolves.
Syn.: *phelónēs* (5341), a cape, coat (sometimes *phailónēs*); *himátion* (2440), an outer garment, a cape; *chitṓn* (5509), an inner vest or undergarment distinguished from *himátion*; *himatismós* (2441), clothing as collectively spoken of; *ependútēs* (1903), an upper garment, a kind of linen frock which fishermen wore at their work; *esthḗs* (2066), clothing; *stolḗ* (4749), a stately robe, a long garment reaching to the feet or with a train behind; *peribólaion* (4018), a wraparound; *ésthēsis* (2067), robe, garment; *chlamús* (5511), a short cloak or robe worn over the *chitṓn* the inner vest, especially by emperors, kings, and other officials; *podḗrēs* (4158), an outer garment reaching to the feet (*pódes*, the pl. of *poús* [4228], foot); *katastolḗ*, costume, apparel, similar to the coll. noun *himatismós* (2441); *othónion* (3608), linen clothes; *porphúra* (4209), a garment dyed with purple.
Ant.: *gumnótēs* (1132), nakedness.

1743. ἐνδυναμόω *endunamóō*; contracted *endunamṓ*, fut. *endunamṓsō*, from *en* (1722), in, and *dunamóō* (1412), to strengthen. Found only in biblical and ecclesiastical Gr. meaning to make strong, vigorous, to strengthen. Used in the pass., to be strengthened, become strong. In connection with Heb 11:34 (TR), reference is appropriately made to

Samson and Hezekiah. Elsewhere only metaphorically or spiritually and in the moral sphere (1 Tim 1:12; 2 Tim 4:17, where it is used of the equipping with the power necessary to the office of an apostle). Used also in Acts 9:22; Rom 4:20; Eph 6:10; Phil 4:13; 2 Tim 2:1.

Syn.: *ischúō* (2480), to strengthen, enable; *enischúō* (1765), to strengthen fully; *epischúō* (2001), to make strong; *krataióō* (2901), to strengthen with the implied meaning of to establish; *sthenóō* (4599), to strengthen; *stērízō* (4741), to establish; *epistērízō* (1991), to confirm, establish; *stereóō* (4732), to make stable.

Ant.: *asthenéō* (770), to lack strength; *échō kakós* (*échō* [2192], to have; *kakós* [2560], badly), to have it badly, to be ill.

1744. ἐνδύνω *endúnō*; fut. *endúsō*, aor. *enédusa*, aor. pass. *enedúthēn*, 2d aor. *enédun*, perf. pass. *endédumai*, from *en* (1722), in, into, and *dúnō* (1416), to sink, go in. To go in, enter in, such as a house (2 Tim 3:6). Equivalent to *eisérchomai* (1525), to enter in.

1745. ἔνδυσις *éndusis*; gen. *endúseōs*, fem. noun from *endúō* (1746), to put on. The putting on or wearing of clothes (1 Pet 3:3).

Syn.: *epíthesis* (1936), putting on.

Ant.: *apóthesis* (595), a putting off; *apékdusis* (555), a stripping off; with its metaphorical meaning *athétēsis* (115), putting away or setting aside.

1746. ἐνδύω *endúō*; fut. *endúsō*, from *en* (1722), in, and *dúō* (1416), to sink, go in or under, to put on. To enter, put on.

(I) To put on as a garment, to cause to get into a garment, to clothe, dress; in the pass., to be clothed; in the mid., to clothe oneself. With the acc. of thing, in or with which (Matt 6:25; 22:11; 27:31; Mark 1:6; 6:9; 15:17, 20; Luke 12:22; 15:22; Acts 12:21; Rev 1:13; 15:6; 19:14; Sept.: Gen 41:42; Ex 29:5, 8; Lev 6:10, 11). Spoken of armor (Rom 13:12; Eph 6:11, 14; 1 Thess 5:8; Sept. 1 Sam 17:5; Jer 46:4).

(II) Metaphorically used of the soul as clothed with the body (2 Cor 5:3; see Job 10:11); of a person as clothed, i.e., endued, furnished with any power, quality (Luke 24:49; 1 Cor 15:53, 54 referring to incorruptibility and immortality; Col 3:12 referring to the bowels of compassion; Sept.: 2 Chr 6:41; Job 29:14; Ps 93:1; Ezek 7:27). Of one who puts on or assumes a new character, the new man (Eph 4:24; Col 3:10) We are to "put on Christ" (a.t.), which means to be filled, endued with Christ's spirit, be like Him (Rom 13:14; Gal 3:27).

Deriv.: *énduma* (1742), anything put on, a garment of any kind; *éndusis* (1745), the act of putting on apparel; *ependúō* (1902), to put on.

Syn.: *amphiénnumi* (294), to put clothes on; *endidúskō* (1737), to wear (the suffix *-skō* suggests the beginning or progress of the action); *ependúō* (1902), to put on; *himatízō* (2439), to put on raiment; *peribállō* (4016), to enwrap oneself with clothing as used in the mid. voice; *egkombóomai* (1463), to gird oneself with something; *peridéomai* (4019), to bind around oneself.

Ant.: *gumnēteúō* (1130), to be naked or scantily clothed; *apobállō* (577), to throw off from; *apotíthēmi* (659), to put off, lay aside; *ekdúomai* (1562), to take off, undress; *apekdúomai* (554), to undress.

1747. ἐνέδρα *enédra*; gen. *enédras*, neut. *énendron* (1749), fem. noun from *en* (1722), in, and *hédra* (n.f., see *aphedrón* [856]), a seat or sitting. A lying in wait as in war, an ambush in order to kill someone (Acts 25:3; 23:16).

Deriv.: *enedreúō* (1748), to lie in wait.

Syn.: *epiboulé* (1917), a plot; *methodeía* (3180), a wile, a method for doing evil, cunning device; *apátē* (539), deceivableness; *pagís* (3803), a trap, snare; *dólos* (1388), guile, deceit; *rhadiourgía* (4468), malignity, mischief; *empaigmós* (1701), derision, mocking; *sunōmosía* (4945), plot, conspiracy.

Ant.: *eilikríneia* (1505), sincerity; *euthútēs* (2118), rectitude, straightforwardness; *tímios* (5093), honorable.

1748. ἐνεδρεύω *enedreúō*; fut. *enedreúsō*, from *enédra* (1747), an ambush. To lie in wait as in war or in ambush in order to kill someone (Acts 23:21; Sept.: Deut 19:11; Lam 4:19). By implication, to lie in wait as for prey in order to ensnare or seize, to watch narrowly (Luke 11:54; Sept.: Lam 3:10).
Syn.: *agreúō* (64), to entrap, catch; *thēreúō* (2340), to hunt an animal, catch; *zōgréō* (2221), to catch alive, capture or ensnare; *deleázō* (1185), metaphorically to beguile, entice.
Ant.: *amúnomai* (292), to defend.

1749. ἔνεδρον *énedron*; gen. *enédrou*, fem. *enéndra* (1747), neut. noun. An ambush, a lying in wait (Acts 23:16; Sept.: Judg 9:35).

1750. ἐνειλέω *eneiléō* contracted *eneilṓ*; fut. *eneilḗsō*, from *en* (1722), in, and *heiléō* (1507), to roll. To roll or wrap up in, used trans. followed by the dat. of the thing (Mark 15:46; Sept.: 1 Sam 21:9).
Syn.: *entulíssō* (1794), to roll in; *sustéllō* (4958), to wrap or wind up; *sustréphō* (4962), to twist together, collect, gather.
Ant.: *anaptússō* (380), to unroll a scroll or volume; *apokulíō* or *apokulízō* (617), to roll away, such as a sepulcher stone.

1751. ἔνειμι *éneimi*; from *en* (1722), in, and *eimí* (1510), to be. To be in any place or with any person. In the NT used impersonally, *énesti*, but only in the form *éni* (1762) which is the Ionic form of the prep. *en*, the verb *eimí* being dropped. The pres. part. *tá enónta*, things within (Luke 11:41 [cf. Matt 23:25f.]), means those things which are within the human heart, paralleled to the contents of the cup and platter, should be given as alms. This being compared with Luke 11:39, where the Lord speaks of the inner man (i.e., the heart) from which one should give alms and not merely externally. Another possible interpretation of *tá enónta* is that it means those things which one possesses. However, if this were to be the preferred meaning, it would have said, *ek* (1537), from, *tốn enóntōn*, those things which one possesses.
Syn.: *hupárchō* (5225) which would make *tá hupárchonta* syn. with *tá enónta*, those things which one possesses.
Ant.: *éxeimi* (1826), to leave, depart; *éxesti* (1832), it is permissible, lawful, as the opposite of *énesti*.

1752. ἕνεκα *héneka*, ἕνεκεν *héneken*; adv. governing a gen. (Luke 6:22; Acts 26:21; Rom 8:36), the Attic *heíneken* (2 Cor 7:12). As a prep. governing the gen. meaning on account of, because of, for the sake of (Matt 5:10, 11; 10:18, 39; 16:25; 19:29; Mark 8:35; 10:29; 13:9; Luke 6:22; 9:24; 18:29; 21:12; Acts 28:20; Rom 8:36; 14:20; 2 Cor 3:10); by reason of (2 Cor 7:12; Sept.: Gen 20:11, 18; Deut 18:12). *Héneken toútou*, for this cause, therefore (Matt 19:5; Mark 10:7; Acts 26:21); *hoú héneken*, for which cause, wherefore (Luke 4:18); *tínos héneka*, for what cause, wherefore (Acts 19:32); *heíneken toú*, followed by the inf. (2 Cor 7:12), in order that. In such constructions, *héneka* is often omitted.
The expression *héneken emoú* (Matt 5:11) is not as strong as the expression *diá* (1223), for, followed by an acc. as *tó ónomá mou*, my name, meaning for my name. The latter indicates more aggressive participation in the purpose of Christ for one's life and the resultant suffering (Rev 2:3).
Syn.: *antí toútou* (*antí* [473], for or instead), for this cause; *diá toúto* (*diá* [1223], for), on account of this, for this cause; *chárin toútou* or *toútou chárin* (*chárin* [5484], for the sake of, in favor of), for this cause; *eis toúto* (*eis* [1519], unto), unto this or unto this end, for this cause; *dió* (1352), for which cause, there-

fore; *aitía* (156), a cause; *aítion* (158), a fault, cause; *lógos* (3056), reason, cause.

Ant.: *eikḗ* (1500), in vain; *mátēn* (3155), to no purpose; *dōreán* (1432), in vain, without a cause.

1753. ἐνέργεια *enérgeia*; gen. *energeías*, fem. noun from *energḗs* (1756), at work, operative, active. Energy, the being at work, operation, efficiency, active power. In Eph 1:19, according to the efficiency, active exhibition of His power in raising up Jesus. See Eph 3:7; 4:16; Col 1:29. Especially power as exhibited in mighty works, miracles, e.g., of God (Phil 3:21; Col 2:12); of Satan (2 Thess 2:9). By metonymy, the works or miracles themselves (2 Thess 2:11, *enérgeian plánēs* [4106], fraudulence, deceit, i.e., false miracles, delusive signs, meaning those mentioned in 2 Thess 2:9, 10).

Syn.: *dúnamis* (1411), power; *ischús* (2479), ability, strength; *exousía* (1849), authority; *krátos* (2904), power, dominion; *ergasía* (2039), work.

Ant.: *scholḗ* (4981), leisure; *katápausis* (2663), cessation of work.

1754. ἐνεργέω *energéō*; contracted *energṓ*, fut. *energḗsō*, from *energḗs* (1756), in work, operative, active. To be at work, to be effective, operative.

(I) To work, be active, produce an effect, spoken of things (Matt 14:2; Mark 6:14, the power of miracles, works, "miracles are wrought by him" [a.t.]; see Eph 1:20; 2:2; Phil 2:13). With the dat. of person (Gal 2:8, *ho energḗsas Pétrō eis*, "he that wrought effectually in Peter" means He who effected in the case of Peter that he should be the apostle of the Jews, effected also in my case that I should go to the Gentiles [cf. Gal 2:7; Sept.: followed by the dat. Prov 31:12]).

(II) Trans., to work, to effect, produce, followed by the acc. spoken of persons (1 Cor 12:6, *ho energṓn tá pánta*, "which worketh all"; see 1 Cor 12:11; Gal 3:5; Eph 1:11; Phil 2:13; Sept.: Prov 21:6; Isa 41:4).

(III) Mid., to show activity, i.e., to work, be active, operate, spoken only of things (Rom 7:5; 2 Cor 1:6; 4:12; Gal 5:6; Eph 3:20; Col 1:29; 1 Thess 2:13; 2 Thess 2:7). In the part. *energouménē* as adj., working, effective (James 5:16, "an effective supplication" [a.t.]).

Deriv.: *enérgēma* (1755), operation, working, an effect.

Syn.: *ergázomai* (2038), work; *katergázomai* (2716), to achieve, effect by toil; *douleúō* (1398), work; *poiéō* (4160), to do; *dunatéō* (1414), to be powerful, be able; *ischúō* (2480), to prevail, able to do; *epiteléō* (2005), accomplish, perform; *prássō* (4238), to execute, accomplish; *kámnō* (2577), to toil.

Ant.: *eukairéō* (2119), to have leisure; *scholázō* (4980), to be at leisure; *katargéō* (2673), to abolish, cease; *kenóō* (2758), to empty, make of no effect; *athetéō* (114), to annul; *akuróō* (208), to make void.

1755. ἐνέργημα *enérgēma*; gen. *energḗmatos*, neut. noun from *energéō* (1754), to effect. Effect, working. The suffix *-ma* makes it the result or effect of *enérgeia* (1753), energy. In the NT, used only in 1 Cor 12:6, 10 of the results of the energy of God in the believer. Though *enérgēma* is translated "operations," it is actually the results energized by God's grace.

1756. ἐνεργής *energḗs*; gen. *energoús*, masc.-fem., neut. *energés*, adj. from *en* (1722), in, and *érgon* (2041), work. Referring to energy, i.e., engaged in work, capable of doing, active, powerful, effective (1 Cor 16:9; Phile 1:6; Heb 4:12). In Class. Gr., *energḗs*, *enérgeia* (energy), and the verb *energéō* (1754), to be at work, seem to have been used almost exclusively as medical terms referring to medical treatment and the influence of medicine.

Deriv.: *enérgeia* (1753), operation, working; *energéō* (1754), to be active, efficient.

1757. ἐνευλογέω *eneulogéō*; contracted *eneulogṓ*, fut. *eneulogḗsō*, from *en* (1722), in, and *eulogéō* (2127), to bless. To bless in or through someone. In the NT, only in the pass. (Acts 3:25; Gal 3:8; Sept.: Gen 12:3; 18:18; 26:4; 28:14).

Syn.: *eúchomai* (2172), to wish; *makarízō* (3106), to be blessed.

Ant.: *kataráomai* (2672), to curse; *blasphēméō* (987), to blaspheme; *anathematízō* (332), to disavow.

1758. ἐνέχω *enéchō*; fut. *enéxō*, from *en* (1722), in or upon, and *échō* (2192), to have. To hold on, endure. With the dat.: to urge, press upon one (Luke 11:53), to have a quarrel, to spite or have resentment against one, very close to hatred (Mark 6:19; Sept.: Gen 49:23). In the pass. *enéchomai*, to be held in or by anything, metaphorically meaning to be entangled in, subject to, followed by the dat. (Gal 5:1).

Deriv.: *énochos* (1777), to be held fast, bound, obliged.

Syn.: *pagideúō* (3802), to ensnare; *emplékō* (1707), to entangle.

Ant.: *apallássō* (525), to release, deliver; *eleutheróō* (1659), to set free; *rhúomai* (4506), to rescue from; *sṓzō* (4982), to save, rescue; *charízomai* (5483), to forgive; *lúō* (3089), to loose.

1759. ἐνθάδε *entháde*; adv., strengthened form for *éntha* (n.f.), here, there. Hither, to this place (John 4:15, 16; Acts 17:6; 25:17); here, in this place (Luke 24:41; Acts 16:28; 25:24 [cf. Acts 10:18]).

Syn.: *hṓde* (5602), and *autoú* (847), here.

Ant.: *ekeí* (1563), there; *ekeíse* (1566), thither; *ekeíthen* (1564), thence.

1760. ἐνθυμέομαι *enthuméomai*; contracted *enthumoúmai*, fut. *enthumḗsomai*, mid. deponent from *en* (1722), in, and *thumós* (2372), the mind, thought, but also anger, wrath, indignation, a spirit that is aroused. Used in the pres. and aor. mid., to have or resolve in mind, to think upon, used trans. (Matt 1:20; 9:4; followed by *perí* [4012], concerning, followed by the gen. in Acts 10:19 [TR], in later editions *dienthumouménou*). The element of wrath is implied in the use of *thumós* both as a verb in Matt 1:20; 9:4; Acts 10:19, and also as the subst. *enthúmēsis* (1761) in Matt 9:4; 12:25; Acts 17:29; Heb 4:12. It means remembrance, bringing into the mind, but with agitation of spirit.

Deriv.: *enthúmēsis* (1761), thought, cognition.

Syn.: *mimnḗskō* (3403) and the older form *mnáomai* (3415) and *mnēmoneúō* (3421), to remember; *anamimnḗskō* (363), to bring to remembrance; *hupomimnḗskō* (5279), to put in remembrance; *epanamimnḗskō* (1878), to remind again.

Ant.: *lanthánō* (2990), to escape notice; *epilanthánomai* (1950), to forget or neglect; *eklanthánomai* (1585), to forget completely.

1761. ἐνθύμησις *enthúmēsis*; gen. *enthuméseōs*, fem. noun from *enthuméomai* (1760), to think. Thought, device, contrivance (Matt 9:4; 12:25; Acts 17:29; Heb 4:12).

Syn.: *nóēma* (3540) and *dianóēma* (1270), thought; with the simple meaning of remembrance: *anámnēsis* (364), a remembrance; *hupómnēsis* (5280), a reminding, reminder; *mneía* (3417), mention; *mnḗmē* (3420), memory.

Ant.: *lḗthē* (3024), forgetfulness.

1762. ἔνι *éni*; a contraction of *énesti*, there is, the pres. indic. 3d person sing. of *éneimi* (1751), to be in. There is in, there is (Gal 3:28; Col 3:11; James 1:17).

Ant.: *éxesti* (1832), it is right, lawful.

1763. ἐνιαυτός *eniautós*; gen. *eniautoú*, masc. noun. A year (John 11:49, 51; 18:13; Acts 11:26; 18:11; Gal 4:10; Heb 9:7, 25; 10:1, 3; James 4:13; 5:17; Rev 9:15; Sept.: Gen 17:21; Ex 12:2). Any definite time, era (Luke 4:19 from Isa 61:2).

1764. ἐνίστημι *enístēmi*; fut. *enstḗsomai*, perf. *enéstēka*, part. *enestēkṓs*, from *en* (1722), in, with, and *hístēmi* (2476), to stand. To be present, instant or at hand (Rom 8:38, "nor . . . present" [*enestṓta*], "nor . . . future" [a.t. {*méllonta* (3195)}]; 1 Cor 3:22; 7:26; Gal 1:4; 2 Thess 2:2, "be at hand" [a.t.], impending; 2 Tim 3:1; Heb 9:9).

Syn.: *hḗkō* (2240), to come, be present; *ephístēmi* (2186), to arrive; *parístēmi* (3936), to be near at hand; *proseggízō* (4331), to come near; *páreimi* (3918), to be near.

1765. ἐνισχύω *enischúō*; fut. *enischúsō*, from *en* (1722), in, and *ischúō* (2480), to strengthen. To be strong in anything. In the NT, used intrans. meaning to be invigorated, become strong (Acts 9:19; Sept.: Gen 48:2; 2 Sam 16:21; Dan 10:19); trans. meaning to invigorate, strengthen or to cause to be strong, followed by the acc. (Luke 22:43; Sept.: Judg 3:12; 2 Sam 22:40; Isa 41:10; Dan 10:18).

Syn.: *krataióō* (2901) and *sthenóō* (4599), to strengthen; *stērízō* (4741), to establish; *stereóō* (4732), to make firm; *epistērízō* (1991), to confirm. For contrast, see *dunamóō* (1412) and *endunamóō* (1743), to make strong, which words are not as forceful in meaning as *ischúō* and *enischúō*, as well as the other compounds as *exischúō* (1840), to be thoroughly strong, and *katischúō* (2729), to prevail against.

Ant.: *asthenéō* (770), to lack strength, be weak.

1766. ἔννατος *énnatos*; fem. *ennátē*, neut. *énnaton*, ordinal number from *ennéa* (1767), nine. Ninth (Rev 21:20). Elsewhere used with *hē hṓra* (5610), the hour, i.e., the hour the ninth (Matt 20:5; 27:45, 46; Mark 15:33, 34; Luke 23:44; Acts 3:1; 10:3, 30). According to the Jewish reckoning of time, the ninth hour is 3:00 p.m., the hour of evening sacrifice and prayer (Acts 3:1).

1767. ἐννέα *ennéa*; indeclinable, cardinal number. Nine (Luke 17:17).

Deriv.: *énnatos* (1766), ninth; *ennenēkontaennéa* (1768), ninety-nine.

1768. ἐννενηκονταεννέα *ennenēkontaennéa*; indeclinable, from *ennenēkonta* (n.f.), ninety, and *ennéa* (1767), nine. Ninety-nine (Matt 18:12, 13; Luke 15:4, 7).

1769. ἐννεός *enneós*; better *eneós*, fem. *enneá*, neut. *enneón*, adj. Speechless, dumb with amazement (Acts 9:7; 22:9; Sept.: Isa 56:10); speechless by nature, also a deaf-mute.

Syn.: *kōphós* (2974), deaf or speechless.

1770. ἐννεύω *enneúō*; fut. *enneúsō*, from *en* (1722), in or to, and *neúō* (3506), to nod, beckon. To make signs with the head or eyes (Luke 1:62; Sept.: Prov 6:13; 10:10).

Syn.: *sēmaínō* (4591), to indicate, signify.

1771. ἔννοια *énnoia*; gen. *ennoías*, fem. noun from *en* (1722), in, and *noús* (3563), mind. What is in the mind, idea, notion, intention, purpose (Heb 4:12; 1 Pet 4:1; Sept.: Prov 3:21 [cf. Prov 23:19]).

Syn.: *lógos* (3056), reason, cause, intent; *aitía* (156), cause; *aítion* (158), fault; *enthúmēsis* (1761), device, thought; *epínoia* (1963), a thought by way of design; *nóēma* (3540), a purpose, a device of the mind; *dianóēma* (1270), a thought, machination; *logismós* (3053), imagination; *dialogismós* (1261), reasoning.

Ant.: *ánoia* (454), folly, stupidity; *mōría* (3472) or *aphrosúnē* (877), foolishness.

1772. ἔννομος *énnomos*; gen. *ennómou*, masc.-fem., neut. *énnomon*, adj. from *en* (1722), in, and *nómos* (3551), law. What is within range of law and governed or determined by law. *Énnomos* refers to an assembly (Acts 19:39, legal, legitimate);

the church (1 Cor 9:21, "subject to law" [a.t. {cf. Gal 6:2}]).

Syn.: *éndikos* (1738), equitable, just.

Ant.: *paranomía* (3892), wrongdoing; *ádikos* (94), unjust; *ékthetos* (1570), cast out; *athémitos* (111), unlawful; *ánomos* (459), without law, lawless (1 Cor 9:21); *parabátēs* (3848), a transgressor; *hamartōlós* (268), a sinner, one who misses the mark.

1773.　ἔννυχον *énnuchon*; gen. *ennúchou*, adj., neut. of *énnuchos*, from *en* (1722), in, and *núx* (3571), night. Night, nocturnal. As an adv., in the night or by night (Mark 1:35), very early, yet in the night, the same as *órthrou bathéos* (*órthrou* [3722], dawn; *bathéos* [901], deep) (Luke 24:1, "very early in the morning," while it was still dark).

1774.　ἐνοικέω *enoikéō*; contracted *enoikṓ*, fut. *enoikḗsō*, from *en* (1722), in, and *oikéō* (3611), to dwell. To dwell in, inhabit. Used metaphorically, meaning to dwell in or with someone, to be in or with, spoken of the indwelling of the Holy Spirit in Christians (Rom 8:11; 2 Tim 1:14); of the divine presence and blessing (2 Cor 6:16 [cf. 1 Cor 3:16]); of the faith (2 Tim 1:5); of the word of Christ (Col 3:16).

Syn.: *ménō* (3306), to abide, remain; *skēnóō* (4637), to pitch a tent; *kataskēnóō* (2681), to pitch one's tent.

Ant.: *astatéō* (790), to wander about.

1775.　ἑνότης *henótēs*; gen. *henótētos*, fem. noun from *heís* (1520), one, and the gen. *henós*, of one. Oneness, unity (Eph 4:3, 13).

Syn.: *súndesmos* (4886), that which unites, a bond; *desmós* (1199), bond; *harmós* (719), joint.

Ant.: *diastolḗ* (1293), a variation, difference; *diamerismós* (1267), disunion, division; *schísma* (4978), schism, division; *diaíresis* (1243), diversity, division.

1776.　ἐνοχλέω *enochléō*; contracted *enochlṓ*, fut. *enochlḗsō*, from *en* (1722), in, and *ochléō* (3791), to disturb. To excite, disturb, trouble, annoy a group or person (Heb 12:15).

Deriv.: *parenochléō* (3926), to create additional disturbance.

Syn.: *tarássō* (5015), to trouble, disturb; *diatarássō* (1298), to agitate greatly; *ektarássō* (1613), to throw into great trouble; *skúllō* (4660), to vex; *anastatóō* (387), to stir up; *thorubéō* (2350), to cause an uproar; *throéō* (2360), to make an outcry; *thorubázō* and *thorubéō* (2350) and *turbázō* (5182), to disturb; *adēmonéō* (85), to cause trouble with distress; *diaponéō* (1278), to grieve; *kópous paréchō* (*kópous* [2873], fatigue [pl.], pains; *paréchō* [3930], to furnish, give), to disturb, cause pains; *basanízō* (928), to torture, vex.

Ant.: *euthuméō* (2114), to cheer up; *eupsuchéō* (2174), to be of good comfort, encourage; *euphraínō* (2165), to rejoice.

1777.　ἔνοχος *énochos*; gen. *enóchou*, masc.-fem., neut. *énochon*, adj. from *enéchō* (1758), to hold in or to be ensnared. Held in, contained in. With a gen. following, meaning bound, subject or liable to (Heb 2:15, "subject to bondage"), guilty, deserving of and subject to punishment, guilty of death (Matt 26:66; Mark 3:29; 14:64). Followed by a dat., obnoxious, liable to the punishment inflicted by a tribunal (Matt 5:21, 22 [cf. Sept.: Gen 26:11; Num 35:31, guilty of death]). Bound by sin or guilt, guilty of sin and consequently obliged to punishment on that account (1 Cor 11:27; James 2:10).

Syn.: *episphalḗs* (2000), prone to fall, dangerous; *hupódikos* (5267), under judgment, guilty; *parabátes* (3848), transgressor; *ánomos* (459), lawless.

Ant.: *áxios* (514), worthy; *hikanós* (2425), able; *athṓos* (121), innocent; *ákakos* (172), not bad, harmless, guileless; *kalós* (2570), good; *agathós* (18), benevolent; *díkaios* (1342), just; *énnomos* (1772), lawful.

1778. ἔνταλμα *éntalma*; gen. *entálmatos*, neut. noun from *entéllomai* (1781), to charge, command. A commandment but emphasizing the thing commanded, a commission (Matt 15:9; Mark 7:7; Col 2:22; Sept.: Job 23:11, 12; Isa 29:13), mandate, precept.

Syn.: *diátagma* (1297), that which is imposed by decree or law in contrast to *diatagé* (1296), a decree which emphasizes the authority of the one who issues it; *epitagé* (2003), command with stress on the authoritativeness of it; *paraggelía* (3852), a proclamation, charge; *nómos* (3851), law.

Ant.: *paráklēsis* (3874), request, entreaty.

1779. ἐνταφιάζω *entaphiázō*; fut. *entaphiásō*, from *entáphios* (n.f.), a shroud, which is from *en* (1722), in, and *táphos* (5028), sepulcher, tomb. To entomb. *Tá entáphia* were the grave clothes and the accompanying ornaments. To prepare for burial, lay out, to decorate, to embalm in the Jewish manner. To prepare a corpse for burial as by washing, anointing, swathing (Matt 26:12; John 19:40; Sept.: Gen 50:2).

Deriv.: *entaphiasmós* (1780), preparation for burial.

Syn.: *tháptō* (2290), to inter.

Ant.: *exorússō* (1846), to dig out.

1780. ἐνταφιασμός *entaphiasmós*; gen. *entaphiasmoú*, masc. noun from *entaphiázō* (1779), to prepare a corpse for burial and to bury. The process of preparing a corpse for burial, a laying out, embalming (Mark 14:8; John 12:7).

Syn.: *taphé* (5027), a burial.

Ant.: *skápto* (4626), to dig; *anástasis* (386), resurrection; *égersis* (1454), a rising up.

1781. ἐντέλλομαι *entéllomai*; fut. *enteloúmai*, perf. pass. *entétalmai*, with act. or mid. meaning (Acts 13:47), mid.

deponent from *en* (1722), in, upon, and *téllō* (5056), to accomplish, charge, command. To order, command, enjoin upon. With the acc. of thing and dat. of person, one or both of which are often implied (Matt 4:6; 15:4; 17:9; 28:20; Mark 10:3; 11:6; 13:34; John 14:31; 15:14, 17; Acts 1:2; Heb 9:20); followed by the inf. (Matt 19:7; Luke 4:10; John 8:5, see *diathḗkē* [1242], testament, "which God enjoined upon [or toward] you" [a.t.], Heb 9:20 quoted from Ex 24:8, see Sept.: Gen 2:16; 21:4; Ex 7:2; Deut 4:13; Josh 23:16; Judg 2:20).

Deriv.: *éntalma* (1778), commandment, precept; *entolḗ* (1785), commandment.

Syn.: *diatássō* (1299), appoint; *embrimáomai* (1690), to charge strictly; *paraggéllō* (3853), to request with a command or charge implied, but not as strong as *entéllomai*; *keleúō* (2753), to urge; *prostássō* (4367), to order, command, probably the closest syn. to *entéllomai*.

Ant.: *aphíēmi* (863), to let alone; *epitrépō* (2010), to allow; *dikaióō* (1344), to free, justify, give right to; *anéchomai* (430), to put up with; *sugkatatíthemai* (4784), to consent.

1782. ἐντεῦθεν *enteúthen*; adv., a strengthened form of *énthen*. Hence, thence, the syllabic suffix -*then* denoting from a place. From this or that place (Matt 17:20; Luke 4:9; 13:31; 16:26 [TR]; John 2:16; 7:3; 14:31; 18:36). The expression in John 19:18; Rev 22:2, *enteúthen* and *enteúthen*, hence and hence, means on this side and that side, on each side (Sept.: Num 22:24; Dan 12:5). Of the cause or source, hence (James 4:1). In some MSS *énthen* (Matt 17:20; Luke 16:26).

Ant.: *ekeíthen* (1564), thence, on that side.

1783. ἔντευξις *énteuxis*; gen. *enteúxeōs*, fem. noun from *entugchánō* (1793), to chance upon, to entreat. A falling in with, meeting with, coming together, intercession, prayer, address to God for oneself or others (1 Tim 2:1; 4:5, prayer according to God's will). The verb *entugchánō* means to interpolate with familiarity and freedom of access, to interrupt another in speaking, to come to God with boldness.

1784. ἔντιμος *éntimos*; gen. *entímou*, masc.-fem., neut. *éntimon*, adj. from *en* (1722), in, and *timḗ* (5092), honor, esteem, price. Honored, estimable, dear (Luke 7:2; 14:8; Phil 2:29; Sept.: Num 22:15; Neh 2:16; 4:14); precious, costly, spoken of Christ as a stone (1 Pet 2:4, 6 [cf. Isa 28:16]).

Syn.: *polútimos* (4186), extremely valuable; *agapētós* (27), beloved and therefore esteemed; *éndoxos* (1741), held in honor; *euschḗmōn* (2158), of honorable position; *kalós* (2570), good, honest, honorable; *polutelḗs* (4185), very precious or costly.

Ant.: *átimos* (820), without honor; *anáxios* (370), unworthy.

1785. ἐντολή *entolḗ*; gen. *entolḗs*, fem. noun from *entéllomai* (1781), to charge, command. Commandment, whether of God or man.

(I) Charge, commission, direction (John 10:18; 12:49, 50; Acts 17:15; Col 4:10; Heb 7:5; Sept.: 2 Kgs 18:36; 2 Chr 8:15). With the meaning of a public charge or edict from magistrates (John 11:57; Sept.: 2 Chr 35:16).

(II) In the sense of precept, commandment, law as spoken of:

(A) The traditions of the rabbis (Titus 1:14).

(B) The precepts and teachings of Jesus (John 13:34; 15:12; 1 Cor 14:37; 1 John 2:8).

(C) The precepts and commandments of God in general (1 Cor 7:19; 1 John 3:22, 23; Sept.: Deut 4:2, 40).

(D) The precepts of the Mosaic Law, in whole or in part (Matt 5:19; 19:17; 22:36, 38, 40; Mark 10:5, 19; Rom 7:8–13).

(E) Generally and collectively, *hē entolḗ* or *hē entolḗ Theoú*, the commandment of God, used either for the Mosaic Law (Matt 15:3, 6; Mark 7:8, 9; Luke

23:56; Sept.: 2 Kgs 21:8; 2 Chr 12:1) or for the precepts given to Christians, Christian doctrines and duties (1 Tim 6:14; 2 Pet 2:21; 3:2).

Syn.: *prostássō* (4367), to charge. *Entolḗ* is the most common of the words meaning commandment, stressing the authority of the one commanding, while *éntalma* (1778), a religious commandment, stresses the thing commanded. Other syn.: *diátagma*, (1297), edict, decree; *diatagḗ* (1296), ordinance, disposition; *epitagḗ* (2003), commanding authority, order, command; *paraggelía* (3852), charge.

1786. ἐντόπιος *entópios*; gen. *entopíou*, masc.-fem., neut. *entópion*, adj. from *en* (1722), in, and *tópos* (5117), a place. An inhabitant of a place, a resident (Acts 21:12).

Syn.: *sumpolítēs* (4847), a fellow citizen; *polítēs* (4177), citizen.

Ant.: *xénos* (3581) a stranger; *apódēmos* (590), a foreign traveler; *allóphulos* (246); of another tribe; *allótrios* (245), alien.

1787. ἐντός *entós*; adv. from *en* (1722), in. Within. Used also as a prep. with the gen. (Luke 17:21, "the kingdom of God is within you," meaning it is located in your heart and affections, not external). With the neut. def. art., *tó entós*, the inside (Matt 23:26; Sept.: Ps 39:4; 109:22).

Syn.: *ésōthen* (2081), from within, within; *ésō* (2080), within.

Ant.: *ektós* (1622), outside; *éxōthen* (1855), from without; *éxō* (1854), without.

1788. ἐντρέπω *entrépō*; fut. *entrépsō*, from *en* (1722), in, upon, and *trépō* (n.f., see *anatrépō* [396]), to turn. To withdraw, invert, turn about or back, to bring to reflection and, therefore, to affect, to act. In the NT, to shame, put to shame, used trans. (1 Cor 4:14); in the pass. (2 Thess 3:14; Titus 2:8; Sept.: Ps 35:26; 40:15; 83:18; Isa 41:11; Ezek 36:32); in the mid., *entrépomai*, to shame oneself before someone, to turn inside, withdraw, to feel respect or deference toward, reverence (Matt 21:37; Mark 12:6).

Deriv.: *entropḗ* (1791), shame.

Syn.: *aischúnō* (152), to be ashamed due to consequences of one's actions or attitudes; *epaischúnomai* (1870), to be ashamed of; *kataischúnō* (2617), to bring shame down upon. Another related word occurring only as a noun is *aidṓs* (127), modesty resulting from a sense of what is right and proper, reverence.

Ant.: *epaíromai* (1869), to exalt oneself, be proud; *kaucháomai* (2744), to boast, vaunt.

1789. ἐντρέφω *entréphō*; fut. *enthrḗpsō*, from *en* (1722), in or with, and *tréphō* (5142), to nourish. To nourish up in anything, to bring or train up in. In the pass., to be skilled in, imbued with; with the dat. of thing (1 Tim 4:6).

Syn.: *ektréphō* (1625), to nourish or train; *anatrépho* (397), to bring up, nourish up; *diatéréō* (1301), to maintain; *suntēréō* (4933), to preserve.

Ant.: *nēsteúō* (3522), to abstain from food; *peináō* (3983), to go hungry.

1790. ἔντρομος *éntromos*; gen. *entrómou*, masc.-fem., neut. *éntromon*, adj. from *en* (1722), in, and *trómos* (5156), a tremor, terror. To be in terror or trembling with fear, terrified (Acts 7:32; 16:29; Heb 12:21; Sept.: Dan 10:11).

Syn.: *phoberós* (5398), causing fear, fearful, terrible, formidable; *ékphobos* (1630), frightened; *émphobos* (1719), terrified; *deilós* (1169), cowardly.

Ant.: *tolmētḗs* (5113), a daring man.

1791. ἐντροπή *entropḗ*; gen. *entropḗs*, fem. noun from *entrépō* (1788), to withdraw. Shame (1 Cor 6:5; 15:34; Sept.: Ps 35:26; 69:8, 20). Implies something found in neither *aidṓs* (127), modesty from a sense of what is right and becoming, nor *aischúnē* (152), shame from a sense of one's wrong action or motive having been made manifest. *Entropḗ* is the withdrawal which is the result of

exposure of wrongdoing. *Entropḗ* becomes *aidṓs* when the change becomes part of one's character.

Syn.: *óneidos* (3681), reproach; *atimía* (819), dishonor, shame; *spílos* (4696), disgrace, spot; *stígma* (4742), scar; *skándalon* (4625), scandal, offence; *aischúnē* (152), shame. The difference between *aischúnē* and *entropḗ* is that the first is shame resulting from having been found doing or saying something wrong. That shame may be expressed variably. *Entropḗ* is the shame which is expressed by withdrawing oneself, introversion.

Ant.: *kaúchēma* (2745), boasting; *kaúchēsis* (2746), the act of boasting; *phḗmē* (5345), fame; *timḗ* (5092), honor; *dóxa* (1392), glory.

1792. ἐντρυφάω *entrupháō*; contracted *entruphō̂*, fut. *entruphḗsō*, from *en* (1722), in, and *trupháō* (5171), to indulge in luxury. To live luxuriously in, to revel (2 Pet 2:13, to revel in their fraud or by means of them; Sept.: Isa 55:2).

Syn.: *euphraínomai* (2165), to make merry; *euarestéō* (2100), to gratify; *kō̂mos* (2970), a revel, carousal.

Ant.: *stenochōréō* (4729), to distress; *pikraínō* (4087), to embitter; *choláō* (5520), to be irritable; *lupéō* (3076); to grieve; *thlíbō* (2346), to afflict.

1793. ἐντυγχάνω *entugchánō*; fut. *enteúxomai*, from *en* (1722), in, and *tugchánō* (5177), to get, obtain. To fall in with, light upon, to meet and talk with. In the NT, to come to, to address, apply to, followed by the dat. (Acts 25:24). In the sense of to intercede, make intercession for or against someone, followed by the dat. expressed or implied and *hupér* (5228), for (Rom 8:27, 34; Heb 7:25), versus *katá* (2596), against, with the gen. (Rom 11:2).

Deriv.: *énteuxis* (1783), a petition on behalf of others; *huperentugchánō* (5241), to intercede on behalf of another.

1794. ἐντυλίσσω *entulíssō*, ἐντυλίττω *entulíttō* fut. *entulíxō*, from *en* (1722), in, and *tulíssō* (n.f.), to twist, roll up or wrap around. To roll up in, wrap in, to fold or wrap together (John 20:7). Used trans. with the dat. of thing (Matt 27:59; Luke 23:53).

Syn.: *sustréphō* (4962), to twist together; *heilíssō* (1507), to coil or wrap, roll together.

Ant.: *anaptússō* (380), to unroll.

1795. ἐντυπόω *entupóō*; contracted *entupó*, fut. *entupṓsō*, from *en* (1722), in, and *túpos* (5179), form, stamp. To stamp or impress in or on, to engrave. Used in the pass. (2 Cor 3:7).

Ant.: *exaleíphō* (1813), to wipe away, obliterate, remove.

1796. ἐνυβρίζω *enubrízō*; fut. *enubrísō*, from *en* (1722), in, and *hubrízō* (5195), to use reproachfully. To treat with despite or reproach. Used with the acc. (Heb 10:29).

Syn.: *epēreázō* (1908), to despitefully use, revile; *loidoréō* (3058), to revile; *oneidízō* (3679), to reproach; *blasphēméō* (987), to speak profanely, to rail at.

Ant.: *epainéō* (1867), to praise and its syn.

1797. ἐνυπνιάζω *enupniázō*; fut. *enupniásō*, from *enúpnion* (1798), something seen in the sleep, a dream. Used intrans. and spoken of visions in dreams (Acts 2:17 [cf. Sept.: Gen 28:12; Joel 2:28]). Pres. mid. part. nom. *enupniazómenoi*, dreamers, meaning ones holding vain and empty opinions, deceivers (Jude 1:8).

1798. ἐνύπνιον *enúpnion*; gen. *enupníou*, neut. noun from *en* (1722), in, and *húpnos* (5258), sleep. A vision in sleep, a dream, spoken in the NT of visions in dreams (Acts 2:17).

Deriv.: *enupniázō* (1797), to dream.

Syn.: *ónar* (3677), a vision while sleeping.

Ant.: *hórasis* (3706), sight, vision; *optasía* (3701), an apparition, vision; *hórama* (3705), a spectacle, sight; *théatron* (2302), theater, spectacle, a show.

1799. ἐνώπιον *enṓpion*; adv. from *en* (1722), in, and *ṓps* (n.f., see *skuthrōpós* [4659]), face, eye, countenance. In the face of, in the presence of, before, found only in the later Gr. In the NT used mostly by Luke, Paul and in the Book of the Revelation.

(I) Used of things meaning before, in front of (Rev 1:4; 4:5, 6, 10; 7:9, 11, 15; Sept.: Gen 30:38; 1 Sam 5:3). Elsewhere of persons, before, in the presence of, in the sight of (Luke 1:17; 5:18, 25; 13:26; Acts 6:6; 10:4, 31; Rev 7:9; Sept.: Lev 4:4; Num 17:10; Jer 7:10; Ezek 16:41); as a herald equivalent to "before His face" (a.t. [Luke 1:19 referring to Gabriel who stood before God being an archangel]). Used in the expression of worshiping and falling before someone meaning to prostrate oneself before another (Luke 4:7; Acts 9:15; Rev 3:9; 4:10; 5:8; 15:4; Sept.: Ps 22:30, "before nations" [a.t.]).

(II) As marking the manner, and especially the sincerity with which anything is done before God or in the sight of God, meaning God being present and witness (Rom 14:22; 2 Cor 4:2; 7:12 [cf. Sept.: 1 Sam 12:7; 23:18]). In Gal 1:20; 1 Tim 5:21; 6:13; 2 Tim 2:14; 4:1, "before God" means God being witness.

(III) Metaphorically, meaning in the sight of or in the mind, will, purpose or judgment of someone (Luke 1:6, 15, 75; 15:18, 21; Acts 8:21; Rom 12:17; 2 Cor 8:21; Sept.: Deut 4:25; 1 Sam 20:1; 2 Sam 16:19; 1 Kgs 11:33, 38; Neh 9:28; Ps 5:9; 19:15). With the gen. as in Luke 15:10, "joy before the angels" (a.t.) meaning joy to the angels in that they rejoice. In Luke 24:11 used as "seemed to them" and in Acts 6:5 "the word was pleasing to all" (a.t. [Sept.: Num 13:34; Deut 1:42; 2 Sam 3:36]). In Acts 7:46, the phrase "to find grace before" (a.t.) someone means to find favor in the sight of someone (cf. Luke 1:30, when *pará* [3844] followed by the dat. is used).

Deriv.: *katanópion* (2714), in the presence of.

Syn.: *émprosthen* (1715), in the sight of a person, before; *métōpon* (3359), forehead; *ópsis* (3799), appearance; *enantíon* (1726), in the presence of; *énanti* (1725), before; *apénanti* (561), in the sight of, before; *katénanti* (2713), down over against, in the sight of; *katenṓpion* (2714), right over against, opposite; *antikrú* (481), opposite, over against.

Ant.: *ópisthen* (3693), behind; *opísō* (3694), to the back.

1800. Ἐνώς *Enós*; masc. proper noun transliterated from the Hebr. *'Enōsh* (583, OT), man. Enos (Luke 3:38 [cf. Gen 4:26]).

1801. ἐνωτίζομαι *enōtízomai*; fut. *enōtísomai*, mid. deponent from *en* (1722), in or into, and *oús* (3775), ear. To receive in the ear, to give ear to, listen to, with the acc. (Acts 2:14; Sept.: Gen 4:23; Job 37:14; Jer 8:6).

Syn.: *akoúō* (191), to hear; *hupakoúō* (5219), to hearken with the idea of obeying; *epakoúō* (1873), to hear attentively.

1802. Ἐνώχ *Enóch*; masc. proper noun transliterated from the Hebr. *Chanōch* (2585, OT), dedicated. Enoch.

(I) A son of Cain after whom he named the first city mentioned in the Bible (Luke 3:37; Heb 11:5; Sept.: Gen 4:17 [cf. 5:18ff.]).

(II) The son of Jared and father of Methuselah. He is called "the seventh from Adam" (Jude 1:14) to distinguish him from Enoch, the son of Cain, who was only third from Adam. We are told that he "walked with God," an expressive figure denoting the closest communion with the divine Being and entire conformity to His will. Concerning Enoch's departure from the world, we are told that, "He was not, for God took him"—a phrase which represents a mere change of residence without suffering the ordinary dissolution of the body. In this case, as well as in Elijah's, the body was clothed with immortality by the immediate power of God (1 Cor 15:50).

1803. ἕξ *héx*; indeclinable, used for all genders, cardinal number. Six (Matt 17:1; Mark 9:2; Luke 4:25; 13:14; John 2:6, 20; 12:1; Acts 11:12; 18:11; 27:37; James 5:17; Rev 4:8; 13:18).

Deriv.: *héktos* (1622), sixth; *hexakósioi* (1812), six hundred; *hexḗkonta* (1835), sixty.

1804. ἐξαγγέλλω *exaggéllō*; fut. *exaggelō*, from *ek* (1537), out, and *aggéllō* (n.f., see *anaggéllō* [312]), to tell, declare. To declare abroad, make widely known (1 Pet 2:9; Sept.: Ps 9:14; 79:13).

Syn.: *phaneróō* (5319), to manifest; *dēlóō* (1213), to make plain; *diēgéomai* (1334), to declare; *légō* (3004), to tell; *apaggéllō* (518), to declare, tell; *kērússō* (2784), to proclaim, preach; *kataggéllō* (2605), to proclaim; *marturéō* (3140), to witness.

Ant.: *sigáō* (4601), to be silent; *phimóō* (5392), to put to silence; *siōpáō* (4623), to keep quiet.

1805. ἐξαγοράζω *exagorázō*; fut. *exagorásō*, from *ek* (1537), out or from, and *agorázō* (59), to buy. To buy out of, redeem from. Used of our redemption by Christ from the curse and yoke of the Law (Gal 3:13; 4:5). To redeem as spoken of time (Eph 5:16; Col 4:5). The same phrase is used in the Gr. version of Dan 2:8, meaning that you are gaining or protracting time. Similarly to be understood in Eph 5:16, "because the days are evil," or afflicting and abounding in troubles and persecutions. This sense of the expression is still more evident in Col 4:5 as "redeeming the time" by prudent and blameless conduct, gaining as much time and opportunity as possible in view of persecution and death. The word generally means to buy up, to buy all that is anywhere to be bought, and not to allow the suitable moment to pass by unheeded but to make it one's own.

Syn.: *lutróō* (3084), to release on receipt of ransom, redeem.

Ant.: *doulóō* (1402), to become or make a servant; *katadoulóō* (2615), to enslave utterly.

1806. ἐξάγω *exágō*; fut. *exáxō*, from *ek* (1537), out, and *ágō* (71), to bring, lead. To lead or conduct out, referring to a place with the acc. of person, e.g., out of prison (Mark 15:20; Acts 5:19; 7:36; 16:37, 39; 21:38). Followed by *ek* (1537), out of (Acts 7:40; 12:17; 13:17; Heb 8:9; Sept.: Ex 6:7; Lev 25:38; Ps 142:7; Isa 42:7); by *éxō* (1854), out, away (Mark 8:23; Luke 24:50; Sept.: Gen 15:7; 19:17). As a shepherd leads his flock (John 10:3).

Syn.: *apophérō* (667), to carry forth; *ekphérō* (1627), to bring forth; *ekbállō* (1544), to cast out; *apokuéō* (616), to bring forth, usually referring to childbirth; *apágō* (520), to take away.

Ant.: *eiságō* (1521), to bring in; *eisphérō* (1533), to carry in; *proságō* (4217), to lead to.

1807. ἐξαιρέω *exairéō*; contracted *exairṓ*, fut. *exairḗsō*, mid. *exairéomai*, from *ek* (1537), out, and *hairéō* (138), to take. It borrows most of its tenses from the obsolete verb *exeílō*, to take out. 2d aor. *exeílon*, 2d aor. mid. irregular *exeíleto* (Acts 7:10; 12:11). To take or pluck out.

(I) To take or pluck out, as an eye (Matt 5:29; 18:9).

(II) To take out of affliction or danger, to deliver, followed by the acc. and *ek* (1537), out of (Acts 7:10; 12:11; Gal 1:4; Sept.: Gen 32:11; 37:21).

(III) To take out from a number, select, in the mid., to select for oneself, to choose, with the acc. (Acts 26:17; Sept.: Deut 25:11; Job 36:21).

Syn.: *aphairéō* (851), to remove; *apallássō* (525), to free from, release; *eleutheróō* (1659), to set free, deliver; *rhúomai* (4506), to rescue from; *charízomai* (5483), to let go free, deliver; *harpázō* (726), to snatch or pluck; *apochōrízō* (673), to separate; *dicházō* (1369), to divide; *exorússō* (1846), to dig out or up; *ekrizóō* (1610), to pluck up by

the roots; *diaspáō* (1288), to rend asunder; *ekbállō* (1544), to cast out.

Ant.: *proskolláō* (4347), to glue to, adhere; *déō* (1210), to bind; *sundéō* (4887), to bind together; *sumbállō* (4820), to combine, attach; *sunéchō* (4912), to hold together; *prostíthēmi* (4369), to add.

1808. ἐξαίρω *exaírō*; fut. *exarṓ*, from *ek* (1537), out of, and *aírō* (142), to take, remove. To take up out of any place, to lift up from, remove; used trans. and followed by *ek* (1537), out of or from, with the gen. (1 Cor 5:2 [TR], 13, to expel or excommunicate). See Sept.: Deut 19:19; Josh 7:13; Ezek 14:8.

Syn.: *aphairéō* (851), to take away; *apospáō* (645), to draw away; *kóptō* (2875), to cut; *ekbállō* (1544), to put or cast out; *chōrízō* (5563), to separate, put away; *apolúō* (630), to let go.

Ant.: *paréchō* (3930), to furnish, give; *paradídōmi* (3860), to deliver; *ekdídōmi* (1554), to give forth; *metadídōmi* (3330), to give over, impart; *apodídōmi* (591), to give away, recompense; *prosphérō* (4374), to offer, tender; *charízomai* (5483), to deliver, to freely give; *dōréomai* (1433), to give.

1809. ἐξαιτέω *exaitéō*; contracted *exaitṓ*, fut. *exaitḗsō*, from *ek* (1537), out, and *aitéō* (154), to ask, require or demand. To claim back, require something to be delivered up. In the mid. voice as a deponent verb, *exaitéomai*, to claim back for oneself (Luke 22:31).

Syn.: *epithuméō* (1937), to covet, desire; *zētéō* (2212), to require; *epizētéō* (1934), to crave; *diṓkō* (1377), to seek; *axióō* (515), to deem entitled; *apaitéō* (523), to demand back.

1810. ἐξαίφνης *exaíphnēs*; adv. from *ek* (1537), of, and *aíphnēs* (n.f.), suddenly. Suddenly, unexpectedly, at once (Mark 13:36; Luke 2:13; 9:39; Acts 9:3; 22:6; Sept.: Prov 24:22; Isa 47:9; Jer 6:26). The same as *aíphnēs* or *áphnō* (869) and *exápina* (1819). Also from *aíphnēs* (n.f.): *aiphnídios* (160), sudden, unawares.

Syn.: *apotómōs* (664), abruptly; *tachú* (5035), suddenly; *en táchei* (*en* [1722], in; *táchei* [5034], quickly), quickly, suddenly; *exápina* (1819), suddenly, unexpectedly.

1811. ἐξακολουθέω *exakolouthéō*; contracted *exakolouthó*, fut. *exakolouthḗsō*, from *ek* (1537), out, or an intens., and *akolouthéō* (190), to follow. To follow; metaphorically, to copy after, conform to, followed by the dat. pl. (2 Pet 1:16; 2:2); with the dat. sing. (2 Pet 2:15; Sept.: Isa 56:11).
Syn.: *summorphóō* (4833), to become conformed to or with; *suschēmatízō* (4964), to take the same shape as someone else, to imitate outwardly.
Ant.: *egkataleípō* (1459), to forsake, leave, desert; *kataleípō* (2641), to leave behind; *paúō* (3973), to cease; *leípō* (3007), to leave; *paraitéomai* (3868), to give up; *apochōréō* (672), to give up; *apostréphomai* (654), to turn away.

1812. ἑξακόσιοι *hexakósioi*; fem. *hexakósiai*, neut. *hexakósia*, cardinal number from *héx* (1803), six, and *hekatón* (1540), a hundred. Six hundred (Rev 13:18; 14:20).

1813. ἐξαλείφω *exaleíphō*; fut. *exaleípsō*, from *ek* (1537), out of or off, and *aleíphō* (218), to smear or rub. To smear out, blot out, expunge, wipe off ointment.
(I) Used in reference to blotting a name out of the book of life (Rev 3:5; Sept.: Ex 32:32, 33; Ps 69:28). The assurance that the Lord will not blot the name of the victor from the book of life is an assurance that once God writes in a believer's name, there is no way that anyone else will be able to blot it out. This is proof that the Lord cannot make a mistake. He is the only one who could blot it out since He is the one who wrote it in. If anyone else would have the power to blot it out, then he would be more powerful than the Lord Jesus. The only ones who, during the Tribulation period, will worship the Antichrist will be those whose names were never written in the book of life, nor were they written during the Tribulation period (Rev 13:8; 17:8). Other references to the book of life containing the believers' names are Phil 4:3; Rev 20:12, 15. The theory that God writes in His book of life the name of everyone born into the world and then erases those who do not believe is unfounded. The word *exaleíphō* is also used to mean abrogating a law (Col 2:14), pardoning (Acts 3:19; Sept.: Ps 51:2; Isa 43:25; Jer 18:23).
(II) By implication, it also means to wipe off or away as "all tears from their eyes" (Rev 7:17 referring to the alleviation of the pain of the tribulation saints from the sufferings of the period; while 21:4 refers to the alleviation of the pain which now accompanies our mortal bodies).
Syn.: *aphanízō* (853), to cause to disappear; *sbénnumi* (4570), to extinguish; *aphairéō* (851), to take away; *exaírō* (1808), to remove; *ekmássō* (1591), to wipe away.
Ant.: *entupóō* (1795), to imprint, engrave; *gráphō* (1125), to write; *eggráphō* (1449), to write in; *apográphō* (583), to enroll; *prostíthēmi* (4369), to add.

1814. ἐξάλλομαι *exállomai*; fut. *exaloúmai*, from *ek* (1537), out, forth, and *állomai* (242), to leap. To leap out as from a house. To leap up or forth as from the place where one sat or was (Acts 3:8; Sept.: Joel 2:5).
Syn.: *eupsuchéō* (2174), to be in good spirit; *ephállomai* (2177), to leap upon; *skirtáō* (4640), to leap; *paraphéromai* (3911), to be carried off.
Ant.: *chalinagōgéō* (5468), to curb.

1815. ἐξανάστασις *exanástasis*; gen. *exanastáseōs*, fem. noun from *exanístēmi* (1817), to rise up. The resurrection from among the dead (Phil 3:11). This resurrection may very well refer to the one experienced by those resurrected first from among all the dead (1 Cor 15:23; 1 Thess 4:16; Rev 20:5).

1816. ἐξανατέλλω *exanatéllō*; fut. *exanatelō*, from *ek* (1537), out, and *anatéllō* (393), to rise, spring. To spring up out of a place as the ground. Spoken of plants, to shoot forth, sprout up. Intrans. (Matt 13:5; Mark 4:5); of light (Sept.: Ps 112:4); trans. of plants (Gen 2:9; Ps 104:14).

Syn.: *phúō* (5453), to bring forth, produce; *blastánō* (985), to sprout, spring up; *exágō* (1806), to lead out; *anabaínō* (305), to go up, spring up; *hállomai* (242), to leap, spring up; *ekpēdáō* in some MSS, to spring forth.

1817. ἐξανίστημι *exanístēmi*; fut. *exanastēsō*, from *ek* (1537), out of or from, and *anístēmi* (450), to rise up. To rise up from among others (Acts 15:5; Sept.: Gen 18:16; 19:1; Judg 3:20); trans., to raise up seed from a woman (Mark 12:19; Luke 20:28; Sept.: Gen 4:25; 19:32, 34).

Deriv.: *exanástasis* (1815), resurrection.

Syn.: *exegeírō* (1825), to arouse fully, awaken; *anorthóō* (461), to straighten up; *stēkō* (4739), to stand; *exanatéllō* (1816), to spring from.

1818. ἐξαπατάω *exapatáō*; contracted *exapatō*, fut. *exapatēsō*, from *ek* (1537), an intens., and *apatáō* (538), to seduce, deceive. To deceive completely, beguile, seduce, meaning to lead out of the right way into error. Used trans. (Rom 7:11; 16:18; 1 Cor 3:18; 2 Cor 11:3; 2 Thess 2:3).

Syn.: *dolióō* (1387), to lure as by bait; *dolóō* (1389), to corrupt; *kapēleúō* (2585), to corrupt by way of huckstering; *planáō* (4105), to lead astray; *paralogízomai* (3884), to beguile.

Ant.: *sōphronéō* (4993), to be of a sober mind; *sōphronízō* (4994), to make of a sound mind.

1819. ἐξάπινα *exápina*; a later form for *exapínēs* (n.f.), which is the Ionian for *exaíphnēs* (1810), suddenly,

unexpectedly (Mark 9:8; Sept.: Num 6:9; Josh 11:7; Ps 64:4).

Syn.: *áphnō* (869), suddenly; *en táchei* (*en* [1722], in; *táchei* [5034], haste), quickly or speedily, with suddenness; *apotómōs* (664), abruptly; *tachú* (5035), suddenly; *tachéōs* (5030), hastily, rapidly, suddenly.

1820. ἐξαπορέομαι *exaporéomai*; contracted *exaporoúmai*, fut. *exaporēsomai*, a mid. deponent from *ek* (1537), an intens., and *aporéō* (639), to be at a loss. To be wholly without resource, to despair utterly (2 Cor 1:8; 4:8; Sept.: Ps 88:15).

Syn.: *ekplēssomai* (1605), to be surprised; *apelpízō* (560), to give up hope in despair.

Ant.: *katalambánō* (2638), to comprehend; *noéō* (3539), to understand; *katanoéō* (2657), to fully comprehend; *hupoménō* (5278), to abide under, endure, be patient toward things and circumstances; *makrothuméō* (3114), to be patient or longsuffering toward persons; *elpízō* (1679), to hope; *proelpízō* (4276), to hope before; *tharréō* (2292), to be confident; *tharséō* (2293), to have courage; *euthuméō* (2114), to keep up one's courage.

1821. ἐξαποστέλλω *exapostéllō*; fut. *exapostelō*, from *ek* (1537), out, forth, and *apostéllō* (649), to send away or forth. To send away or forth out of the place where one is (Acts 7:12; 9:30; 11:22; 12:11; 22:21; Gal 4:4, 6; Sept.: Gen 24:40; Ex 3:12); to send away, dismiss (Luke 1:53; 20:10, 11; Sept.: Gen 31:42; 45:24; Deut 15:13; 1 Sam 9:19, 26; Job 22:9).

Syn.: *pémpō* (3992), to send; *apostéllō* (649), to send, commission; *ekpémpō* (1599), to send out or away.

Ant.: *apodéchomai* (588), to accept, receive heartily, and the plain verb *déchomai* (1209), to accept; *prosdéchomai* (4327), to accept favorably, to receive to oneself; *lambánō* (2983), to receive; *paralambánō* (3880), to receive from another; *proslambánō* (4355), to welcome; *eisdéchomai* (1523), to receive into;

hupodéchomai (5264), to receive under one's roof.

1822. ἐξαρτίζω *exartízō*; fut. *exartísō*, from *ek* (1537), an intens., and *artízō* (n.f.), to put in appropriate condition. To complete entirely, spoken of time (Acts 21:5); to furnish or fit completely (2 Tim 3:17). In this last text, the use of *exartízō* and its root, *ártios*, appears redundant but actually conveys a subtle nuance. Paul states that inspired Scripture can make the man of God *ártios*, competent, proficient, adept or capable. This is followed by a subordinate clause containing the perf. pass. part. of *exartízō* which is not simply an intens. form of *ártios*, as though Paul were saying, "that the man of God may be competent having been made very competent" (a.t.). Rather, *exartízō* means to equip, outfit, furnish. The part. is causal and the sentence therefore reads periphrastically, "that the man of God may be competent because he has been equipped [outfitted, furnished]" (a.t.). God's word is that which gives one the necessary skills and tools to be capable in performing every good work. Also from *artízō* (n.f.): *katartízō* (2675), to fit, restore.

Syn.: *kataskeuázō* (2680), to make, fit, prepare; *katartízō* (2675), to fit, frame, prepare; *sunistéō* (4921), to set together; *sunarmologéō* (4883), to fit together; *plēróō* (4137), to bring to completion; *teléō* (5055), to accomplish, complete.

Ant.: *lúō* (3089), to loose; *dialúō* (1262), to dissolve.

1823. ἐξαστράπτω *exastráptō*; fut. *exastrápsō*, from *ek* (1537), out, and *astráptō* (797), to lighten forth. To flash out as lightning (Sept.: Ezek 1:4). Used of raiment, intrans., meaning to shine out, glitter (Luke 9:29 [cf. Matt 17:2]; Sept.: of armor in Ezek 1:7; Nah 3:3).

Syn.: *augázō* (826), to shine forth with the light of dawn coming on; *phaínō* (5316), to shine; *epiphaínō* (2014), to shine upon; *lámpō* (2989), to shine as a torch; *stílbō* (4744), to glisten; *eklámpō*

(1584), to shine forth; *perilámpō* (4034), to shine around; *epiphaúō* (2017), to shine forth.

Ant.: *skotízō* (4654), to darken; *skotóō* (4656), to obscure, blind; *tuphlóō* (5186), obscure, make blind.

1824. ἐξαυτῆς *exautḗs*; adv. from *ek* (1537), from, and *autḗs*, fem. gen. of *autós* (846), it, this. From this time, forthwith, presently, immediately (Mark 6:25; Acts 10:33; 11:11; 21:32; 23:30; Phil 2:23).

Syn.: *háma* (260), immediately; *euthéōs* (2112) and *euthús* (2117), immediately, forthwith; *parautíka* (3910), at the very instant; *parachrḗma* (3916), instantly; *suntómōs* (4935), shortly.

Ant.: *en kairō̄* (*en* [1722], in; *kairō̄*, the dat. of *kairós* [2540], time, season, opportunity), at the proper time, season.

1825. ἐξεγείρω *exegeírō*; fut. *exegerō̄*, from *ek* (1537), out, and *egeírō* (1453), to raise. To raise up, wake out of sleep (Rom 9:17, to come to arise or exist, as spoken of Pharaoh quoted from Ex 9:16 [cf. Sept.: *dietēréthēs*, the aor. of *diatēréō* {1301}, to observe strictly]; 1 Cor 6:14, to raise up out of death; Sept.: Dan 12:2).

Syn.: *anorthóō* (461), to raise up; *exanístēmi* (1817), to rise up.

Ant.: *anaklínō* (347), to lay down; *píptō* (4098), to fall; *katákeimai* (2621), to lie down; *keímai* (2749), to lie.

1826. ἔξειμι *éxeimi*; from *ek* (1537), out, and *eími* (n.f., see *ápeimi* [549]), to go. To go out of a place, used intrans. with *ek* ([1537] Acts 13:42), *epí* ([1909] Acts 27:43). In the sense of to go away, depart out of a place (Acts 17:15; 20:7).

Syn.: *apérchomai* (565), to go away; *exérchomai* (1831), to go out of; *poreúomai* (4198), to go away; *anachōréō* (402), to retire; *apochōréō* (672), to depart from; *ekchōréō* (1633), to depart out; *analúō* (360), to depart; *metaírō* (3332), to lift away; *aphístēmi* (868), to cause to depart; *metabaínō* (3327), to depart;

apodēméō (589), to go to another country.

Ant.: *eisérchomai* (1525), to come into; *eisporeúomai* (1531), to go into; *embaínō* (1684), to go in; *eíseimi* (1524), to go into.

1827. ἐξελέγχω *exelégchō*; fut. *exelégxō*, from *ek* (1537) an intens., and *elégchō* (1651), to rebuke, reprove. To convict fully, to show to be wholly wrong, to rebuke sternly, condemn, punish (Jude 1:15; Sept.: Isa 2:4; Mic 4:3).

Syn.: *epitimáō* (2008), to rebuke.

Ant.: *epainéō* (1867), to praise; *eulogéō* (2127), to speak well of, bless.

1828. ἐξέλκω *exélkō*; fut. *exelkúsō*, from *ek* (1537), out or away, and *hélkō* (1670), to draw. To draw or drag out, as from the right way, to draw away, hurry away (James 1:14).

1829. ἐξέραμα *exérama*; gen. *exerámatos*, neut. noun from *exeráō* (n.f.), to vomit out, eject. Vomit, that which is thrown up (2 Pet 2:22).

Syn.: *eméō* (1692), to vomit.

1830. ἐξερευνάω *exereunáō*; contracted *exereunō*, fut. *exereunḗsō*, from *ek* (1537) an intens., and *ereunáō* (2045), to search. To search out, explore, to search very diligently or carefully (1 Pet 1:10; Sept.: 1 Sam 23:23; 1 Chr 19:3; Prov 2:4; Zeph 1:12).

Deriv.: *anexereúnētos* (419), unsearchable.

Syn.: *exetázō* (1833), to examine closely; *anakrínō* (350), to examine.

Ant.: *agnoéō* (50), to ignore.

1831. ἐξέρχομαι *exérchomai*; fut. *exeleúsomai*, 2d aor. *exḗlthon*, from *ek* (1537), out, and *érchomai* (2064), to go or come. To go or come out of a place.

(I) Of persons, to go or come forth.

(A) With adjuncts implying the place, followed by the gen. (Matt 10:14, "coming out of the house" [a.t.]; Acts 16:39); by *ek* (1537), from, with the gen. of place

(Matt 8:28, "from the tombs" [a.t.]; John 4:30; Acts 16:40; 1 Cor 5:10; Sept.: Gen 8:16, 19); by *éxō* (1854), out (Matt 26:75; John 19:4; Rev 3:12); by *éxō* with the gen. (Matt 21:17, "out of the city"; Heb 13:13); by *apó* (575), from, with the gen. of place, to depart from (Matt 13:1, "Jesus went out of the house"; 24:1; Mark 11:12); by an adv. (Matt 5:26, *ekeíthen* [1564], from that place, thence; 12:44, *hóthen* [3606], "from whence").

(B) With an adjunct of person, "out of" or "from" whom, as of those out of whose bodies demons depart; followed by *ek* (1537), from, with a gen. (Mark 1:25, 26; Luke 4:35); by *apó* (575), from (Matt 12:43; Luke 4:35). Used in an absolute sense as in Acts 16:18. Of those from whom or from whose presence one goes forth with authority, i.e., to be sent out by someone, followed by *apó* (575) with a gen. (John 13:3, "from God he came out" [a.t.]. See John 16:30; Sept.: Gen 4:16; Ex 8:12); by *pará* (3844), from, with a gen. (John 16:27; 17:8 [cf. Sept.: Num 16:35]). Generally, to depart from someone, i.e., from his presence, intimacy (Luke 5:8; 2 Cor 6:17).

(C) The place not being expressed but implied, to go out, i.e., to go away, depart (Matt 9:31; Mark 2:12; Luke 4:42; Acts 7:7; Rev 6:2). Of demons departing from the body (Matt 8:32; Acts 8:7).

(D) With an adjunct of the place from which someone departs, followed by *eis* (1519), into (Matt 11:7; Mark 8:27; Luke 10:10; John 1:43; Acts 11:25); with *eis*, final (Matt 8:34, unto meeting, "to meet Jesus"; Mark 1:38, *eis toúto* [5124], this, unto this). Followed by *epí* (1909), upon, with the acc. (Luke 8:27, from a vessel to the land; Acts 1:21); by *pará* (3844), near, with the acc. (Mark 2:13; Acts 16:13); by *prós* (4314), toward, with the acc. of person (John 18:29; 2 Cor 8:17).

(II) Metaphorically of person:

(A) To go forth or proceed from (Matt 2:6; Acts 15:24; Heb 7:5, to descend from; Sept.: Gen 35:11; 1 Kgs 8:19 [cf. Gen 15:4]).

(B) John 10:39, "he escaped out of their hand," escaped from their power.

(C) 1 John 4:1, "have gone forth [gone abroad] into the world" (a.t.).

(III) Of things, to go or come forth, proceed from.

(A) Of a voice, doctrine, rumor (Rev 16:17; 19:5). Of doctrine or rumor meaning to go forth, spread abroad (1 Cor 14:36). With place whither or where, followed by *eis* (1519), into, with the acc. (Matt 9:26; John 21:23; Rom 10:18); by *en* (1722), in, with the dat. (Luke 7:17; 1 Thess 1:8); by *katá* (2596), in, with the gen. (Luke 4:14, "in all the region").

(B) Of thoughts, words, *ek tḗs kardías* (*tḗs* [3588], the; *kardías* [2588], heart), out of or from the heart (Matt 15:18); "Out of the same mouth" (James 3:10). Of healing power or virtue, to emanate, *ex autoú* (846), of himself, out of himself (Mark 5:30); *par' autoú* (*pará* [3844], from; *autoú* [846], him), from him (Luke 6:19). Of an edict, to be published, *pará* (3844), by, by Caesar (Luke 2:1). Of lightning, *apó anatolṓn* (*apó* [575], from; *anatolṓn* [395], east), to come out of or appear from the east (Matt 24:27; Sept.: Zech 9:14).

(C) Of liquids, to flow out (John 19:34, blood and water came out or flowed out; Rev 14:20, "came out of the winepress").

(D) Of a hope, to depart, i.e., to be at an end, to vanish (Acts 16:19); of time, the year went out or passed (Sept.: Gen 47:18).

(IV) The expression *eisérchomai* (1525), enter in, and *exérchomai* (1831), go out (Acts 1:21, to go in and out, meaning to perform one's daily duties, as spoken of one's daily walk and life; John 10:9).

Syn.: *ekbaínō*, akin to *ékbasis* (1545), to go out; *ekporeúomai* (1607), to depart; *hupágō* (5217), to go, depart; *apérchomai* (565), to go away from; *poreúomai* (4198), to depart from one place to another; *anachōréō* (402), to retire, recede; *apochōréō* (672), to depart from; *ekchōréō* (1633), to depart out of;

apochōrízomai (673), to remove myself; *analúō* (360), to depart; *apolúomai* (630), to let myself go; *éxeimi* (1826), to go out; *metaírō* (3332), to remove; *metaíromai*, to remove myself; *aphístēmi* (868), to stand off or aloof; *metabaínō* (3327), to depart; *apobaínō* (576), to go away or from; *apodēméō* (589), to go on a journey abroad; *ekpetánnumi* (1600), to spread out or stretch forth.

Ant.: *eisérchomai* (1525), to enter in.

1832. ἔξεστι *éxesti*; impersonal verb. from *éxeimi* (n.f.), which is from *ek* (1537), and *eimí* (1510), to be. It is possible, referring to moral possibility or propriety meaning it is lawful, right, permitted, can, may. With the dat. of person and inf. expressed or implied, specifically with the pres. inf., it marks prolonged or customary action (Matt 14:4; Mark 6:18; Acts 16:21; 22:25); with the dat. implied (Matt 12:2, 10, 12; Luke 6:2); followed by the aor. inf. marking transient action (Matt 19:3; 20:15; Mark 2:26; 10:2; Luke 20:22; John 5:10; 18:31; Acts 21:37). *Exón én* (instead of *éxesti*) with the imperf. of *eimí*, *én*, followed by the aor. inf. (Matt 12:4); *exón* followed by *lalḗsai* (aor. inf. of *laléō* [2980], to speak), with the neg. meaning "not permissible to speak" (2 Cor 12:4); with the dat. implied (Matt 22:17; 27:6; Mark 3:4; 12:14; Luke 6:4; 14:3); with *exón* and *éstō* (2077), let it be, implied meaning "let me" (Acts 2:29); with the inf. implied (Mark 2:24, "which is not permitted unto them to do" [a.t.]; Acts 8:37; 1 Cor 6:12; 10:23).

Deriv.: *exousía* (1849), power, authority.

Syn.: *eáō* (1439), to let, permit (Acts 27:32); *epitrépō* (2010), to allow.

Ant.: *adunatéō* (101), to be unable, impossible.

1833. ἐξετάζω *exetázō*; fut. *exetásō*, from *ek* (1537), out, or an intens., and *etázō* (n.f.), to test, examine, inquire. To verify, examine, explore with the idea of determining whether or not something is true. Also from *etázō* (n.f.): *anetázō* (426), to examine, thoroughly.

(I) Generally to inquire or seek out the truth by inquiry, followed by the prep. *perí* (4012), in regard to (Matt 2:8); by *tís* (5101), who, interrogatively (Matt 10:11; Sept.: Deut 19:18).

(II) By implication, to question, ask, followed by the acc. of person (John 21:12).

Syn.: *erōtáō* (2065), to ask, inquire; *eperōtáō* (1905) with the strengthened meaning of questioning; *punthánomai* (4441), to ask by way of inquiry; *anakrínō* (350), to question in a legal setting; *dierōtáō* (1331), to find by inquiry; *epizētéō* (1934), to seek after, inquire; *diaginóskō* (1231), to ascertain or determine exactly; *ereunáō* (2045), to search, examine, and the comp. *exereunáō* (1830), a strengthened form of the basic verb; *dokimázō* (1381), to accept as proved; *peirázō* (3985), to examine (e.g., 2 Cor 13:5).

1834. ἐξηγέομαι *exēgéomai*; contracted *exēgoúmai*, fut. *exēgésomai*, mid. deponent from *ek* (1537), out, or an intens., and *hēgéomai* (2233), to tell, lead forward. To bring or lead out, declare thoroughly and particularly.

(I) To unfold, reveal, make known, as a teacher (John 1:18 [cf. Matt 11:27; Sept.: Lev 14:57]).

(II) To tell, narrate, account (Luke 24:35; Acts 10:8; 15:12, 14; 21:19; Sept.: Judg 7:13). From this verb comes the Eng. word "exegesis," the unfolding interpretation through teaching of Scripture.

Syn.: *diasaphéō* (1285), to make clear; *phaneróō* (5319), to manifest.

Ant.: *krúptō* (2928), to hide.

1835. ἐξήκοντα *hexḗkonta*; indeclinable, used for all genders, cardinal number from *héx* (1803), six. Sixty (Matt 13:8, 23; Mark 4:8, 20; Luke 24:13; 1 Tim 5:9; Rev 11:3; 12:6; 13:18).

1836. ἑξῆς *hexēs*; adv. from *échō* (2192), to be joined to. In order, successively, follow next in time or order. With the fem. art. used as an adj., followed by *hēméra* (2250), day (Luke 9:37); implied (Luke 7:11; Acts 21:1; 25:17; 27:18).

Deriv.: *kathexēs* (2517), successively.

Syn.: *épeita* (1899), thereafter; *eíta* (1534), then, moreover; *hústeron* (5305), afterward, finally; *katōtérō* (2736), following, below; *metá* (3326), after; *metépeita* (3347), afterwards; *opísō* (3694), behind.

Ant.: *prōton* (4412), firstly; *prín* (4250), before; *próteron* (4386), previously, former; *palaiós* (3820), old; *ēdē* (2235), already.

1837. ἐξηχέω *exēchéō*; contracted *exēchō*, fut. *exēchéso*, from *ek* (1537), out or forth, and *ēchéō* (2278), to sound. To sound out, sound abroad (Sept.: Joel 3:14 [act. voice]). Used only in the pass. in regard to the gospel, to be sounded abroad, proclaimed (1 Thess 1:8).

Syn.: *salpizō* (4537), to sound a trumpet; *krázō* (2896), to cry out; *phōnéō* (5455), to call, cry, sound; *boáō* (994), to shout; *thorubéō* (2350), to make noise; *kraugázō* (2905), to cry loudly.

Ant.: *sigáō* (4601), to keep silent.

1838. ἕξις *héxis*; gen. *héxeōs*, fem. noun from *échō* (2192), to have. Habit. Used usually of life or body, therefore, practice or exercise (Heb 5:14).

Syn.: *chrēsis* (5540), use; *éthos* (1485), custom, manner; *sunétheia* (4914), habit; *páthos* (3806), passion.

Ant.: *parádoxon* (3861), an extraordinary thing.

1839. ἐξίστημι *exístēmi*; imperf. *existámēn*, fut. *ekstēsō*, aor. *exéstēsa*, 2d aor. *exéstēn*, from *ek* (1537), out, and *hístēmi* (2476), to stand. To remove out of a place or state. In the NT applied only to the mind, meaning to be out of one's mind, beside oneself (2 Cor 5:13; Sept.: Job 12:17); in a neut. or pass. sense, to be transported beyond oneself with astonishment, to be amazed, astounded (Matt 12:23; Mark 2:12; 5:42; Sept.: Gen 27:33); in an act. or trans. sense, to astonish (Luke 24:22; Acts 8:9, 11); "they were sore amazed in themselves [*en* {1722}, in; *heautoís* {1438}, themselves, dat. pl.]" (Mark 6:51). See Luke 8:56; Acts 2:7, 12; 8:13; 9:21; 10:45; 12:16; Sept.: Gen 43:33; Ex 19:18; Ruth 3:8; Job 26:11.

Deriv.: *ékstasis* (1611), bewilderment, wonder.

Syn.: *ekpléssomai* (1605), to be astonished; *thambéomaī* (2284), to be amazed; *ekthambéomai* (1568), to be utterly amazed; *maínomai* (3105), to rave; *paraphronéō* (3912), to act as a fool; *thaumázō* (2296), to marvel.

Ant.: *sōphronéō* (4993), to think soberly; *sōphronízō* (4994), to make soberminded.

1840. ἐξισχύω *exischúō*; fut. *exischúsō*, from *ek* (1537), an intens., and *ischúō* (2480), to be strong, able. To be in full strength, fully able, followed by the inf. (Eph 3:18). It is the strongest word available to indicate strength or ability, a comp., and stronger than *ischúō*, which in turn is stronger than *dúnamai* (1410), to be able, have power, or *dunamóō* (1412) used trans. meaning to make strong, or *hikanóō* (2427), to be competent, able, qualified.

Ant.: *asthenéō* (770), to lack strength, *noséō* (3552), to be sick; *échō kakôs* (*échō* [2192], to have; *kakôs* [2560], badly), to have it badly, to be ill; *páschō* (3958), to suffer; *hupophérō* (5297), to endure, to bear from underneath; *basanízō* (928), to suffer pain; *phtheírō* (5351), to pine or waste away, to corrupt in the sense of degeneration; *sunéchō* (4912), to be sick, confined.

1841. ἔξοδος *éxodos*; gen. *exódou*, fem. noun from *ek* (1537), out, and *hodós* (3598), a way. A going out, departure (Heb 11:22, where it is applied to the children of Israel's departure out of

Egypt from which event the Sept. entitled the second book of Moses as *Exodus*. See Ex 19:1; Num 33:38). Decease, meaning exit or departure from life (Luke 9:31; 2 Pet 1:15).

Deriv.: *diéxodos* (1327), a highway.

Syn.: *análusis* (359), an unloosing, metaphorically departure from life; *thánatos* (2288), death; *anaíresis* (336), a taking up or off, death; *teleutḗ* (5054), an end of life; *ékbasis* (1545), exit, end, result.

Ant.: *áphixis* (867), arrival; *eísodos* (1529), entrance.

1842. ἐξολοθρεύω *exolothreúō*; fut. *exolothreúsō*, from *ek* (1537), an intens., and *olothreúō* (3645), to destroy. To destroy utterly (Acts 3:23; Sept.: Ex 30:33; 31:14; Deut 7:10). The word and its syn. never mean extinction, but a change of one's state involving retribution or punishment.

Syn.: *katastréphō* (2690), to destroy; *aphanízō* (853), to cause to disappear; *lumaínomai* (3075), to make havoc of; *phtheírō* (5351), to ruin, corrupt, destroy; *kaíō* (2545), to burn, consume; *nekróō* (3499), to deaden; *thúō* (2380), to sacrifice, kill; *apóllumi* (622), to destroy, perish; *suntríbō* (4937), to crush, shatter, break to pieces; *patássō* (3960), to strike, smite; *pléssō* (4141), to smite; *katakrēmnízō* (2630), to cast down headlong; *erēmóō* (2049), to render desolate, waste.

Ant.: *sózō* (4982), to save, rescue; *lutróō* (3084), to redeem.

1843. ἐξομολογέω *exomologéō*; contracted *exomologô*, fut. *exomologḗsō*, from *ek* (1537), out, and *homologéō* (3670), to assent. To confess, admit, profess or express agreement with. Confession to God involves concurring with Him in His verdict.

(I) To promise, assent fully, agree (Luke 22:6). In the mid. voice, *exomologéomai*, to confess one's own sin (Matt 3:6; Mark 1:5; Acts 19:18; James 5:16; Sept.: Dan 9:4).

(II) To profess, confess, as the truth (Phil 2:11); to confess, acknowledge as belonging to one (Rev 3:5). With a dat. following, to give praise or glory to, glorify (Matt 11:25; Luke 10:21; Rom 14:11; 15:9 quoted from Ps 18:49, 50; Sept.: 1 Chr 16:4; 2 Chr 30:22; Ps 57:9, 10).

Syn.: *homologéō* (3670), to speak the same thing, confess, declare, admit; *epineúō* (1962), to nod to, express approval; *sumphōnéō* (4856), to agree; *egkrínō* (1469), judge in; *apodéchomai* (588), to accept; *anagnōrízō* (319), to recognize.

Ant.: *arnéomai* (720), to refuse; *aparnéomai* (533), to deny completely; *antitássō* (498), to set oneself against; *aporríptō* (641), to reject; *periphronéō* (4065), to despise; *apōthéō* (683), to put away; *apotrépō* (665), to turn away from; *apophérō* (667), to bear off.

1844. ἐξορκίζω *exorkízō*; fut. *exorkísō*, from *ek* (1537), an intens., and *horkízō* (3726), to adjure. To exact an oath, put under an oath, adjure (Matt 26:63; Sept.: Gen 24:3).

Deriv.: *exorkistḗs* (1845), exorcist.

1845. ἐξορκιστής *exorkistḗs*; gen. *exorkistoú*, masc. noun from *exorkízō* (1844), to adjure. An exorcist, one who binds by an oath; generally one who by adjuration and incantation professes to expel demons (Acts 19:13).

Syn.: *mágos* (3097), a magician, sorcerer; *góēs* (1114), an impostor, a seducer.

1846. ἐξορύσσω *exorússō*, ἐξορύττω *exorúttō*; fut. *exorúxō*, from *ek* (1537), out, and *orússō* (3736), to dig. To dig out, used trans. (Mark 2:4 meaning digging out or removing the tiles, equivalent to *apostegázō* [648], to unroof). Used metaphorically (Gal 4:15) in regard to digging out one's eyes, meaning total devotion. See Sept.: Judg 16:21 (*ekkóptō* [1581], to cut down); 1 Sam 11:2.

Syn.: *exairéō* (1807), to take out; *ekrizóō* (1610), to pluck up by the roots; *ekbállō* (1544), to cast out, pluck out; *exágō* (1806), to pull out; *aphairéō* (851), to take away; *apobállō* (577), to cast away.

1847. ἐξουδενόω *exoudenóō*; contracted *exoudenó*, fut. *exoudenṓsō*, from *ek* (1537), an intens., and *oudenóō* (n.f.), to bring to naught. To set at naught, despise, treat with scorn and, by implication, to reject with contempt (Mark 9:12; Sept.: 1 Sam 15:23, 26; 16:1; 2 Kgs 19:21; Eccl 9:16).

Syn.: *katargéō* (2673), to abolish; *exouthenéō* (1848), to set at naught; *athetéō* (114), to reject; *katalúō* (2647), to overthrow; *erēmóō* (2049), to make desolate; *hupōpiázō* (5299), to buffet, keep under, hit under the eye.

Ant.: *kataxióō* (2661), to deem entirely worthy; *hupsóō* (5312), to lift up; *timáō* (5091), to honor; *doxázō* (1392), to glorify, praise; *epainéō* (1867), to applaud; *eulogéō* (2127), to praise, speak well of.

1848. ἐξουθενέω *exouthenéō*; contracted *exouthenó*, fut. *exouthenḗsō*, from *ek* (1537), an intens., and *outhenéō* (n.f.), to bring to naught. To despise, treat with scorn (Luke 18:9; 23:11; Rom 14:3, 10; 1 Cor 1:28; 6:4; 16:11; 2 Cor 10:10, where *exouthenēménos* means contemptible, abject; Gal 4:14; 1 Thess 5:20). By implication, to reject with scorn (Acts 4:11 [cf. Matt 21:42]; Sept.: 1 Sam 8:7).

Syn.: *exoudenóō* (1847), to set at naught.

Ant.: *timáō* (5091), to honor; *hēgéomai* (2233), to lead, to esteem; *doxázō* (1392), to glorify, honor.

1849. ἐξουσία *exousía*; gen. *exousías*, fem. noun from *éxesti* (1832), it is permissible, allowed. Permission, authority, right, liberty, power to do something (Acts 26:12). As *éxesti* denies the presence of a hindrance, it may be used either of the capability or the right to do a certain action. The words *éxesti* and *exousía* combine the two ideas of right and might. As far as right, authority, or capability is concerned, it involves ability, power, strength (*dúnamis* [1411]) as in Matt 9:8; 28:18.

(I) The power of doing something, ability, faculty (Matt 9:8; John 19:11; Acts 8:19; Rev 13:12). Followed by the gen. art. and the pres. inf. (Luke 10:19); by the pres. inf. (Matt 9:6, i.e., He is able to forgive; Mark 2:10; Luke 5:24; John 5:27); by the aor. inf. (Luke 12:5; John 10:18; 19:10; Rev 9:10). With the meaning of strength, force, efficiency (Matt 7:29; Mark 1:22; Rev 9:3, 19), with the prep. *en* (1722), in, and the dat., *en exousía* as adjunct, powerful (Luke 4:32); with the prep. *katá* (2596), according to, *kat' exousían* being equivalent to *en exousía*, as adv., i.e., with intensive strength, with point and effect (Mark 1:27 [cf. Luke 4:36]).

(II) Power of doing or not doing, i.e., license, liberty, free choice (Acts 1:7; 5:4; Rom 9:21; 1 Cor 7:37, "if it stands in his own free will" [a.t.]; 8:9; 9:4–6, 12, 18; 2 Thess 3:9; Rev 22:14).

(III) Power as entrusted, i.e., commission, authority, right, full power (Matt 8:9; 21:23, 24, 27; Mark 3:15; 11:28, 29, 33; Luke 20:2, 8; John 1:12; Acts 9:14; 26:10, 12; 2 Cor 10:8; 13:10; Heb 13:10; Rev 13:5).

(IV) Power over persons and things, dominion, authority, rule.

(A) Particularly and generally (Matt 28:18, "Unto me was given all authority in heaven and on earth" [a.t.]; Mark 13:34; Luke 7:8, i.e., subject to authority, rule; Jude 1:25; Rev 13:2, 4; 17:12, 13; 18:1; Sept.: Ps 136:8, 9; Dan 3:33; 4:31). Before the gen. of person to whom the power belongs (Luke 20:20; 22:53, "of darkness"; Acts 26:18, "the power of Satan"; Col 1:13; Rev 12:10, "the authority of Christ" [a.t.]). Followed by the gen. of the object subjected to the power (Matt 10:1; Mark 6:7, "power over unclean spirits"; John 17:2). Followed by *epí* (1901), upon, with the gen. (Rev 2:26,

"power over"; 11:6; 14:18; 20:6); by *epí*, with the acc. in the same sense (Luke 9:1; Rev 6:8; 13:7; 16:9); by the inf. with *hóste* (5620), so that, implied (Rev 11:6 [cf. Matt 10:1]); by *epánō* (1883), on, with the gen. (Luke 19:17).

(B) As a metonym used for: **(1)** What is subject to one's rule, dominion, domain, jurisdiction (Luke 4:6; 23:7; Sept.: 2 Kgs 20:13; Ps 114:2). **(2)** In pl. or coll., those invested with power as the powers of rulers, magistrates (Luke 12:11; Rom 13:1–3; Titus 3:1). For the celestial and infernal powers, princes, potentates, e.g., angels, archangels (Eph 1:21; 3:10; Col 1:16; 2:10; 1 Pet 3:22); demons (Eph 6:12; Col 2:15). See *aḗr* (109), air, in Eph 2:2. Generally of the powerful adversaries of the gospel (1 Cor 15:24 [cf. *archḗ* {746}, principality]). **(3)** In 1 Cor 11:10, where *exousía* is used as an emblem of power, i.e., a veil or covering (cf. 1 Cor 11:13, 16) as an emblem of subjection to the power of a husband, a token of modest adherence to duties and usages established by law or custom lest spies or evil-minded persons should take advantage of any impropriety in the meetings of the Christians (cf. *timḗ* [5092], honor).

Syn.: *krátos* (2904), dominion; *dúnamis* (1411), power. *Exousía* denotes the executive power while *archḗ* (746), rule, represents the authority granting the power.

Deriv.: *exousiázō* (1850), to exercise authority.

Ant.: *asthéneia* (769), weakness.

1850. ἐξουσιάζω *exousiázō*; fut. *exousiásō*, from *exousía* (1849), authority, right and power. To have or exercise power in the sense of permitting (1 Cor 7:4), meaning that one has no separate power or liberty over his own body to use it as he will (Sept.: Eccl 5:18; 6:2). To exercise authority, rule, reign (Luke 22:25; Sept.: Neh 5:15; 9:37; Eccl 10:4). In the pass., to be ruled by or be under the power of, to be in bondage to, metaphorically (1 Cor 6:12).

Deriv.: *katexousiázō* (2715), to exercise full authority upon.

Syn.: *authentéō* (831), to exercise authority or domineer over; *hupotássō* (5293), to put in subjection or in one's proper order; *basileúō* (936), to reign; *hēgemoneúō* (2230), to act as a ruler.

Ant.: *hupakoúō* (5219), to submit, obey; *peíthomai* (3982), to be persuaded, agree; *peitharchéō* (3980), to be obedient.

1851. ἐξοχή exochḗ; gen. *exochḗs*, fem. noun from *exéchō* (n.f.), to be prominent, which is from *ek* (1537), out, and *échō* (2192), to have, be. Prominence, projection, a point, corner (Sept.: Job 39:28). Metaphorically, eminence, distinction (Acts 25:23).

Syn.: *megaleiótēs* (3168), splendor, magnificence; *megalōsúnē* (3172), majesty; *dúnamis* (1411), power; *exousía* (1849), authority, the right to exercise power; *krátos* (2904), dominion; *kuriótēs* (2963), lordship.

Ant.: *tapeínōsis* (5014), humiliation.

1852. ἐξυπνίζω exupnízō; fut. *exupnísō*, from *éxupnos* (1853), awake. To wake out of sleep. Used also in regard to the dead (John 11:11; Sept.: 1 Kgs 3:15; Job 14:12). This is a word of the later Gr. instead of the earlier *aphupnízō*, to bring out of sleep.

Syn.: *egeírō* (1453), to awake, to raise; *diegeírō* (1326), to arouse, stir up; *eknḗphō* (1594), to become sober; *diagrēgoréō* (1235), to be watchful.

Ant.: *aphupnóō* (879), to fall asleep, although literally it means to become awake; *katheúdō* (2518), to go to sleep; *koimáomai* (2837), to sleep.

1853. ἔξυπνος éxupnos; gen. *exúpnou*, masc.-fem., neut. *éxupnon*, adj. from *ek* (1537), out, and *húpnos* (5258), sleep. Out of sleep, awakened, awake (Acts 16:27).

Deriv.: *exupnízō* (1852), to wake up.
Syn.: *grēgoréō* (1127), to wake, watch.

Ant.: *katheúdō* (2518), to go to sleep; *koimáomai* (2837), to sleep.

1854. ἔξω éxō; adv. of place, from *ek* (1537), out. Also a prep. with a gen., out, without. Out, without, as opposed to within.

(I) Of place where, without, out of doors, after verbs not implying motion, as to stand (Matt 12:46, 47; 26:69; Mark 3:31, 32; John 18:16, "Peter stood near the door outside" [a.t.]). Generally, outside a place or city, abroad (Mark 1:45; Luke 1:10; Rev 22:15; Sept.: Gen 24:31; Ezra 10:13). With the def. art., *hoi éxō* used as an adj., external, those without (Acts 26:11, "even to foreign cities" [a.t.]; Sept.: 2 Kgs 16:18). Metaphorically, of those not belonging to one's society, church, i.e., not Christians (1 Cor 5:12, 13; Col 4:5; 1 Thess 4:12). Of those not belonging to the number of the apostles (Mark 4:11). In 2 Cor 4:16, "our outward man," meaning the body. As a prep. followed by the gen., out of, outside of (Luke 13:33, "outside of Jerusalem" [a.t.]; Heb 13:11–13).

(II) Of place, whither, out, forth, out of doors, from a place, after verbs implying motion or direction (Matt 5:13, "but to be cast out"; 13:48; Luke 14:35; John 11:43 "come forth"; 19:4, "I bring him forth to you"; Acts 5:34, "to put the apostles out" [a.t.]; Acts 16:30, "brought them out"; 1 John 4:18). Also after verbs of motion, compounded with *ek* (1537), out of as *exágō* (1806), to bring forth (Luke 24:50); *exérchomai* (1831), to come out (Matt 26:75; John 19:5); *ekbállō* (1544), to cast out, send forth (Luke 8:54; Acts 9:40). As a prep. followed by the gen. (Matt 21:17, 39; Mark 5:10; 8:23; Acts 4:15; 14:19).

Deriv.: *éxōthen* (1855), from without; *exóteros* (1857), outer.

Syn.: *ektós* (1622), outside.

Ant.: *entós* (1787), inside, within; *ésō* (2080), within, inside; *ésōthen* (2081), from within.

1855. ἔξωθεν éxōthen; adv. from *éxō* (1854), out, with the syllabic suffix *-then*, denoting from or at a place. From without (Mark 7:18); without, outwardly, used in an absolute sense (Matt 23:27, 28; 2 Cor 7:5; Sept.: Gen 6:15; Ex 25:11) or construed with a gen. (Mark 7:15). With the art. prefixed, it assumes the nature of a noun, *tó éxōthen*, the outside (Matt 23:25; Mark 7:18; Luke 11:39, 40); *ho éxōthen kósmos* (as an adj.), the "outward [or external] adorning" (1 Pet 3:3); *apó* (575) *tón éxōthen*, from those that are without, or the strangers to the Christian community (1 Tim 3:7); "the outside" (Rev 11:2); "outside the city" (a.t. [Rev 14:20; Sept.: Ex 40:22; Lev 24:3; Jer 11:6]).

Ant.: *ésōthen* (2081), from within.

1856. ἐξωθέω exōthéō; contracted *exōthṓ*, fut. *exōthéso*, from *ek* (1537), out, and *ōthéō* (n.f.), to thrust. To drive out, expel (Acts 7:45; Sept.: Deut 13:5; Jer 8:3; Joel 3:6); to drive or thrust a ship out of the sea into a creek or onto the shore (Acts 27:39). Also from *ōthéō* (n.f.): *apōthéō* (683), to thrust away, cast off.

Syn.: *ekbállō* (1544), to cast forth; *elaúnō* (1643), to drive; *apelaúnō* (556), to drive from; *apōthéō* (683), to thrust away.

Ant.: *helkúō* (1670), to draw; *hélkō* (1670), to attract.

1857. ἐξώτερος exōteros; the comparative of *éxō* (1854), out. Outer, exterior. Matt 8:12; 22:13 refer to a place for unbelievers, while Matt 25:30 may refer to a place of less reward for servants who did not use their God-given talents.

Ant.: *esōteros* (2082), inner.

1858. ἑορτάζω heortázō; fut. *heortásō*, from *heortḗ* (1859), feast. To keep a festival, celebrate a holiday. Used intrans. (1 Cor 5:8; Sept.: Ex 5:1; Ps 42:4).

Syn.: *suneuōchéō* (4910), to entertain sumptuously in company with, feast with.

Ant.: *penthéō* (3996), to mourn; *thrēnéō* (2354), to lament; *lupéomai* (3076), to be sorrowful; *sunéchomai* (4912), to be perplexed; *thlíbomai* (2346), to be afflicted; *klaíō* (2799), to weep.

1859. ἑορτή heortḗ; gen. *heortḗs*, fem. noun. A feast, festival, holy day (John 5:1; Acts 18:21; Col 2:16; Sept.: Ex 10:9; Lev 23:2; Num 10:10; Hos 2:11; Amos 8:10) as spoken of the Passover and the Festival of Unleavened Bread connected with it or the Paschal Festival. See *ázumos* (106), unleavened, and *deuteróprōtos* (1207), the Sabbath immediately after the Paschal week. Thus the Feast of Passover, *páscha* ([3957] Luke 2:41; John 2:23; 13:1); the Feast of the Unleavened Bread (Luke 22:1); the feast (Matt 26:5; 27:15; Mark 14:2; 15:6; Luke 2:42; 23:17; John 4:45; 6:4; 11:56; 12:12, 20; 13:29; Sept.: Ex 12:14; 23:15; 34:18, 25); the Feast of Tabernacles (John 7:2, 8, 10, 11, 14, 37; Sept.: Deut 16:16; 31:10).

Deriv.: *heortázō* (1858), to keep a feast.

Syn.: *panḗguris* (3831), festive gathering.

Ant.: *pénthos* (3997), mourning; *thrénos* (2355), lamentation; *thlípsis* (2347), tribulation; *stenochōría* (4730), anguish, distress.

1860. ἐπαγγελία epaggelía; gen. *epaggelías*, fem. noun from *epaggéllō* (1861), to announce. Primarily a legal term denoting a summons or promise to do or give something. Used only of the promises of God except in Acts 23:21 where it means order or mandate. The thing promised, a gift graciously given, not a pledge secured by negotiation (Luke 24:49; Acts 2:33; Gal 3:14; Eph 1:13; Heb 9:15).

(I) Particularly in 1 John 1:5 (TR), where later editions have *aggelía* (31), message (Sept.: Ezek 7:26).

(II) By implication, a promise.

(A) Particularly a promise given (2 Cor 1:20; Eph 1:13; 6:2; 1 Tim 4:8; 2 Pet 3:4, 9; Sept.: Esth 4:7). Of special promises, e.g., made to Abraham (Acts 7:6, 17; Rom 4:16, 20; Heb 6:12, 15; 7:6; 11:9, promised land); in respect to Isaac (Rom 9:9; Gal 4:23); of a spiritual seed (Rom 9:8; Gal 4:28); as made to Abraham and the Jewish patriarchs and prophets in general, e.g., of a future Savior (Acts 13:23, 32; 26:6); of future blessings and the enjoyment of God's favor (Acts 2:39; Rom 4:13, 14, 16; 9:4; 15:8; 2 Cor 7:1; Gal 3:16–18, 21, 22, 29; Eph 2:12; 3:6; Heb 6:12, 17; 11:17); of salvation in Christ (2 Tim 1:1); an apostle in respect to the promise of eternal life in Christ, that is, appointed to announce it (Heb 4:1; 8:6; 9:15; 1 John 2:25).

(B) Metonymically used for the thing promised (Heb 11:13, 33, 39); of salvation in Christ (Heb 10:36); of the Holy Spirit (Luke 24:49; Acts 1:4). In Acts 2:33; Gal 3:14, "having received the promise of the Spirit" (a.t.) means having received the promised effusions of the Spirit.

Ant.: *agnóēma* (51), a thing ignored.

1861. ἐπαγγέλλω *epaggéllō*; fut. *epaggelṓ*, from *epí* (1909), an intens., and *aggéllō* (n.f., see *anaggéllō* [312]), to tell, declare. To proclaim as public announcements or decrees; hence to announce a message, summons, or a promise. In the Class. Gr., used more in the sense of announcing a summons, issuing a command. In the NT, used only in the mid. voice, *epaggéllomai*, as a deponent verb meaning basically to announce oneself, offer oneself for a responsibility or service. Used primarily as "to promise" in Mark 14:11; Acts 7:5; Rom 4:21, *apéggelmai*, with mid. meaning; 2 Pet 2:19, and "to profess" in 1 Tim 2:10; 6:21 with the meaning of pretending. When used with this special meaning, the word and its deriv. refer to God's divine promise of spontaneous salvation. To render a service. (See Acts 1:4, *epaggelían* [1860] "the promise"; 7:5;

Rom 4:21; Titus 1:2; Heb 12:26; James 1:12; 2:5; 1 John 2:25.) Used in an absolute sense, meaning to give a promise (Gal 3:19 with pass. meaning; Heb 6:13; 10:23; 11:11; Sept.: Esth 4:7).

Deriv.: *epaggelía* (1860), an announcement, message; *epággelma* (1862), promise; *proepaggéllō* (4279), to promise before.

1862. ἐπάγγελμα *epággelma*; gen. *epaggélmatos*, neut. noun from *epaggéllō* (1861), to proclaim. Promise, assurance. The suffix *-ma* makes it the result of *epaggéllō*. Found only in 2 Pet 1:4; 3:13.

1863. ἐπάγω *epágō*; fut. *epáxō*, 2d aor. *epḗgagon*, from *epí* (1909), upon, and *ágō* (71), to lead away. To lead up to, to bring upon, introduce, particularly to a place (Sept.: Ezek 14:15). In the NT, upon persons, with the acc. and dat. (2 Pet 2:1, 5; Sept. followed by *epí*, Gen 6:18; Ex 11:1; Lev 26:25). Followed by *epí* (Acts 5:28, "to bring . . . upon us," i.e., to impute to us, make us answerable for; Sept.: Gen 20:9; Ex 34:7).

Syn.: *komízō* (2865), to bring in; *eisphérō* (1533), to bring to, into; *epiphérō* (2018), to bring upon.

Ant.: *apágō* (520), to lead away; *exágō* (1806), to lead out.

1864. ἐπαγωνίζομαι *epagōnízomai*; fut *epagōnísomai*, from *epí* (1909), for, and *agōnízomai* (75), to strive, contend earnestly. To fight for or in reference to something, with the dat. of that which gives the occasion (Jude 1:3).

Syn.: *máchomai* (3164), to fight; *diamáchomai* (1264), to struggle against; *erízō* (2051), to strive; *athléō* (118), to contend in games; *poleméō* (4170), to fight in war.

Ant.: *eirēneúō* (1514), to keep peace or be at peace, reconcile; *eirēnopoiéō* (1517), to make peace; *anéchomai* (430), to tolerate; *hēsucházō* (2270), to be quiet.

1865. ἐπαθροίζω *epathroízō*; fut. *epathroísō*, from *epí* (1909), upon, and *athroízō* (n.f.), to collect, add up. Used trans., to collect together to or upon any place. In the mid. intrans. *epathroízomai*, to collect together to or upon, to crowd together upon (Luke 11:29). Also from *athroízō* (n.f.): *sunathroízō* (4867), to gather together.

Syn.: *episunágō* (1996), to gather together; *sullégō* (4816), to collect, gather up.

Ant.: *skorpízō* (4650), to disperse; *diaskorpízō* (1287), to scatter abroad; *diaspeírō* (1289), to scatter abroad as seed; *likmáō* (3039), to winnow; *dialúō* (1262), to dissolve, scatter.

1866. Ἐπαίνετος *Epaínetos*; gen. *Epainétou*, masc. proper noun. Epenetus, meaning praised, one whom Paul called his "well-beloved" and "the firstfruits of Achaia unto Christ" (Rom 16:5).

1867. ἐπαινέω *epainéō*; contracted *epainṓ*, fut. *epainésō*, from *epí* (1909), upon, and *ainéō* (134), to praise. To bestow praise upon, applaud, commend, used trans. (Luke 16:8; Rom 15:11; 1 Cor 11:2, 17, 22; Sept.: Gen 12:15; Ps 10:3; Eccl 8:15).

Syn.: *doxázō* (1392), to glory, honor; *hupsóō* (5312), to exalt; *timáō* (5092), to honor.

Ant.: *tapeinóō* (5013), to humble; *kataphronéō* (2706), to disesteem, despise; *periphronéō* (4065), to depreciate.

1868. ἔπαινος *épainos*; gen. *epaínou*, masc. noun from *epí* (1909), upon, and *aínos* (136), praise. Applause, commendation, praise, approbation (Rom 2:29; 13:3; 2 Cor 8:18; Eph 1:6, 12, 14; Phil 1:11; 1 Pet 1:7). The object of praise, something praiseworthy (Phil 4:8; Sept.: 1 Chr 16:27); reward (1 Cor 4:5; 1 Pet 2:14).

Syn.: *euphēmía* (2162), good reputation; *aínos* (136), praise, only in reference to God; *húmnos* (5215), a hymn,

praise; *dóxa* (1391), glory, praise; *kaúchēma* (2745), a boast, something to boast about.

Ant.: *epitimía* (2009), rebuke, punishment; *momphḗ* (3437), a blame, fault; *kólasis* (2851) and *timōría* (5098), punishment.

1869. ἐπαίρω *epaírō*; fut. *eparṓ*, from *epí* (1909), upon, and *aírō* (142), to lift up. To raise up. Trans., to hoist up as a sail (Acts 27:40); in the pass., to be taken up, be borne upward (Acts 1:9); spoken of the hands, to lift up in regard to prayer and benediction (Luke 24:50; 1 Tim 2:8; Sept.: Ex 17:11; Ps 134:2). To lift up the eyes, meaning to look upon (Matt 17:8; Luke 6:20; 16:23; 18:13; John 4:35; 6:5; 17:1; Sept.: Gen 13:10; Ezek 18:6); the voice, meaning to cry out with a loud voice (Luke 11:27; Acts 2:14; 14:11; 22:22; Sept.: Judg 2:4; 9:7); the head, meaning to take courage (Luke 21:28); the heel in order to attack and injure (John 13:18 quoted from Ps 41:9; Sept.: 1 Sam 20:33). In the mid. *epaíromai*, to lift up oneself, to rise up against something, followed by *katá* (2596), against (2 Cor 10:5; Sept.: Ezra 4:19; Dan 11:14). Metaphorically, to lift up or exalt oneself (2 Cor 11:20; Sept.: Prov 19:18; Jer 13:15).

Syn.: *huperupsóō* (5251), to highly exalt; *huperphronéō* (5252), to esteem oneself above what is proper; *phusióō* (5448), to puff up; *hupsóō* (5312), to lift.

Ant.: *tapeinóō* (5013), to humble.

1870. ἐπαισχύνομαι *epaischúnomai*; fut. pass. *epaischunthḗsomai*, aor. pass. *epēschúnthēn*, pass. deponent, from *epí* (1909), upon or on account of, and *aischúnō* (153), to be ashamed. To bring shame upon oneself, to be ashamed of, with the acc. (Mark 8:38; Luke 9:26; Rom 1:16; 2 Tim 1:8, 16; Heb 11:16); used in an absolute sense (2 Tim 1:12; Sept.: Job 34:19); followed by *epí* (1909), upon, and the dat. (Rom 6:21; Sept.: Isa 1:29); the pres. inf. (Heb 2:11; 11:16).

Deriv.: *anepaíschuntos* (422), not to be ashamed.

Syn.: *lupéomai* (3076), to be sorry; *entrépomai* (1788), to invert, withdraw; *aidṓs* (127), shame, a modesty that springs from a sense of proper discernment and behavior.

Ant.: *euphraínomai* (2165), to rejoice; *euthuméō* (2114), to be merry.

1871. ἐπαιτέω *epaitéō*; contracted *epaitṓ*, fut. *epaitḗsō*, from *epí* (1909), an intens., and *aitéō* (154), to ask, implore, claim. To beg, ask for alms (Luke 16:3; Sept.: Ps 109:10). The literal word for "beg" from which *epaítēs*, beggar, is derived, is not found in the NT. The word *ptōchós* (4434), helplessly poor and depending on others for one's survival, is sometimes translated "beggar" (Luke 16:20; Gal 4:9). This is only a consequential translation because *ptōchós* is a helplessly poor person who can survive only by begging. See *ptōchós* for its contrast with *pénēs* (3993), indigent person. *Epaítēs* is one who realizes his inferior position and need and asks as a beggar.

Syn.: *zētéō* (2212), to ask; *epithuméō* (1937), to desire; *exaitéomai* (1809), to desire, demand; *axióō* (515), to consider oneself entitled to; *apaitéō* (523), to demand back, ask again, require; *epizētéō* (1934), to inquire for.

Ant.: *euergetéō* (2109), to do good; *eulogéō* (2127), to bless, speak well of, act benevolently; *lusiteléō* (3081), to be advantageous; *ōpheléō* (5623), to benefit; *therapeúō* (2323), to heal by ministering; *hupēretéō* (5256), to minister to; *dōréomai* (1433), to bestow.

1872. ἐπακολουθέω *epakolouthéō*; contracted *epakolouthṓ*, fut. *epakolouthḗsō*, from *epí* (1909), upon, or an intens., and *akolouthéō* (190), to follow. To follow the steps of another, but in a figurative sense (1 Pet 2:21, "to follow upon his footsteps" [a.t.], i.e., to follow his example; Sept.: Deut 12:30); to be subsequent, ensue (Mark 16:20, "the accompanying signs" [a.t.]; 1 Tim 5:24, "and some . . .

they follow after," i.e., are manifest subsequently; Sept.: Job 31:7; Prov 7:22); to follow diligently, prosecute, pursue a work (1 Tim 5:10, "diligently followed every good work," i.e., been studious of, devoted to; Sept.: Josh 14:8, 9).

Syn.: *diṓkō* (1377), to pursue without hostility; *katadiṓkō* (2614), to follow after with hostility; *hexḗs* (1836), next; *eimí metá* (*eimí* [1510], to be; *metá* [3326], after), to be after; *katatréchō* (2701), to run after in a hostile manner.

Ant.: *kataleípō* (2641), to forsake; *aphíēmi* (863), to let go; *paraitéomai* (3868), to decline, shun.

1873. ἐπακούω *epakoúō*; fut. *epakoúsō*, from *epí* (1909), upon, and *akoúō* (191), to hear. To hear, listen to, to hear something firsthand, to hearken to in answer to prayer, followed by the gen. (2 Cor 6:2; Sept.: Gen 17:20; 35:3; 1 Sam 7:9; 2 Kgs 13:4).

Syn.: *enōtízomai* (1801), to give ear to; *eisakoúō* (1522), to listen to, hear; *hupakoúō* (5219), to listen, obey; *peíthomai* (3982), to be persuaded; *pisteúō* (4100), to trust; *peitharchéō* (3980), to obey one in authority; *hupotássomai* (5293), to be in subjection; *hupakoúō* (5219), to obey, listen.

Ant.: *parakoúō* (3878), to hear amiss, neglect, disobey; *apeithéō* (544), to disobey; *apistéō* (569), to disbelieve.

1874. ἐπακροάομαι *epakroáomai*; contracted *epakroṓmai*, fut. *epakroásomai*, mid. deponent from *epí* (1909), upon, and *akroáomai* (n.f.), to hear. To hear, listen to (Acts 16:25).

Syn.: *epakoúō* (1873), to hearken; *enōtízomai* (1801), to give an ear to, to listen.

Ant.: *parakoúō* (3878), to mishear, neglect to hear, disobey; *apeithéō* (544), to disobey, to be undisciplined or perverse; *apopheúgō* (668), to avoid.

1875. ἐπάν *epán*; conj. from *epeí* (1893), because, since, and *án* (302), if. Whenever, as soon as (Matt 2:8; Luke 11:22, 34).

1876. ἐπάναγκες *epánagkes*; adv. from *epí* (1909), upon, on account of, and *anágkē* (318), necessity. Necessarily. With the art. it assumes the meaning of a noun, *tó epánagkes*, necessities or things of necessity (Acts 15:28).

Syn.: *anagkaíos* (316), necessary; *deí* (1163), that which must be; *prépon* (4241), that which is proper; *chreía* (5532), need, necessity.

Ant.: *truphḗ* (5172), indulgence, debauchery.

1877. ἐπανάγω *epanágō*; fut. *epanáxō*, from *epí* (1909), upon, to, and *anágō* (321), to bring back or forth. To lead up or upon. Used as a nautical term meaning to lead a ship to or out upon the sea, to put out to sea (Luke 5:3, 4); to lead back upon or to a place, to cause to return or to return to, such as the city (Matt 21:18).

Syn.: *ekbállō* (1544), to cast out; *exaírō* (1808), to put away from the midst of; *epistréphō* (1994), to turn towards; *analúō* (360), to depart; *anakámptō* (344), to turn back.

Ant.: *aírō* (142), to take away; *ekphérō* (1627), to bring out.

1878. ἐπαναμιμνήσκω *epanamimnḗskō*; fut. *epanamimnḗsō*, from *epí* (1909), upon, or an intens., and *anamimnḗskō* (363), to remind. To remind of, to put in mind of, with the acc. of person (Rom 15:15).

1879. ἐπαναπαύω *epanapaúō*; fut. *epanapaúsō*, from *epí* (1909), upon, and *anapaúomai* (373), to rest. In the NT, only in the mid. *epanapaúomai*. To rely, rest, repose oneself upon (Rom 2:17; Sept.: Mic 3:11); to rest with the sense of remaining upon (Luke 10:6; Sept.: Num 11:25, 26; 2 Kgs 2:15).

1880. ἐπανέρχομαι *epanérchomai*; fut. *epaneleúsomai*, 2d aor. *epanélthon*, from *epí* (1909), unto, and *anérchomai* (424), to go up. To come back, to return hither or thither, used in an absolute sense (Luke 10:35; 19:15; Sept.: Gen 33:18; 50:5).

Syn.: *epistréphō* (1994), to return towards; *anakámptō* (344), to turn back; *epanágō* (1877), to return.

Ant.: *hupágō* (5217), *metabaínō* (3327) and *poreúomai* (4198), to depart; *apérchomai* (565), to go away; *exérchomai* (1831) and *éxeimi* (1826), to go out; *ekporeúomai* (1607), to proceed; *anachōréō* (402), to retire, go away; *apochōréō* (672), to depart from; *ekchōréō* (1633), to depart out; *apochōrízomai* (673), to separate oneself; *analúō* (360), to unloose, depart; *aphístēmi* (868), to withdraw.

1881. ἐπανίστημι *epanístēmi*; fut. mid. *epanistḗsomai*, from *epí* (1909), upon or against, and *anístēmi* (450), to arise. To rise up against someone, revolt (Matt 10:21; Mark 13:12; Sept.: 1 Sam 17:35; Dan 11:14; Mic 7:6). In the NT, only in the mid. *epanístamai*.

Syn.: *egeírō* (1453), to rouse; *diegeírō* (1326), to stir up.

Ant.: *miméomai* (3401), to imitate; *ménō* (3306), abide.

1882. ἐπανόρθωσις *epanórthōsis*; gen. *epanorthōseōs*, fem. noun from *epanorthóō* (n.f.), to set right again, correct, which is from *epí* (1909), upon, and *anorthóō* (461), to make straight. Correction, setting up straight again. Used only in 2 Tim 3:16 where it is cited as one of four benefits of the word of God. These effects are not isolated but are interdependent and set forth an entire process of sanctification. First of all, the word of God is presented as doctrine (*didaskalía* [1319]), instruction, authoritative teaching, i.e., truth. Secondly, as truth it is ethically persuasive (*élegchos* [1650], proof, conviction) convincing us of our error. Thirdly, it then places us in a correct moral posture. Fourthly, the word of God continues to provide discipline (*paideía* [3809], training, discipline, chastisement) in righteousness.

Syn.: *nouthesía* (3559), admonition; *paideía* (3809), instruction; *apokatástasis* (605), restitution.

Ant.: *ptôsis* (4431), downfall.

1883. ἐπάνω *epánō*; adv. from *epí* (1909), upon, and *áno* (507), above, up. Up, up above, above; also a prep. with the gen. meaning over, upon. As an adv. of place, above, over (Matt 2:9; Luke 11:44). Of number, above, more than (Mark 14:5 where the gen. depends on the verb; 1 Cor 15:6; Sept.: Ex 30:14; Lev 27:7). As prep. with a gen. of place, above, over (Matt 27:37; Luke 4:39; Rev 20:3; Sept.: Gen 22:9; Isa 14:13, 14); upon (Matt 5:14; 21:7; 23:18, 20, 22; 28:2; Luke 10:19; Rev 6:8; Sept.: Gen 1:29; 7:18; 40:17). Spoken of authority and dignity, over (Luke 19:17, 19; John 3:31).

Ant.: *kátō* (2736), down, under; *katóteros* (2737), inferior, lower; *hupokátō* (5270) and *hupó* (5259), under; *elásson* (1640), less, under.

1884. ἐπαρκέω *eparkéō*; contracted *eparkô*, fut. *eparkésō*, from *epí* (1909), to, unto, and *arkéō* (714), to suffice, satisfy. To hold up or in, to hold back from going further, restrain, ward off. In the NT by implication, to aid or relieve, with the dat. (1 Tim 5:10, 16).

Syn.: *ánesis* (425), a loosening, relaxation, breathing space; *hikanóō* (2427), to make sufficient.

Ant.: *leípō* (3007), to lack; *epileípō* (1952), to be insufficient, fail; *hupoleípomai* (5275), to be left under.

1885.ἐπαρχία *eparchía*; gen. *eparchías*, fem. noun from *éparchos* (n.f.), a governor of a province, which is from *epí* (1909), over, and *archê* (746), beginning, rule. A province, such as of the Roman Empire (Acts 23:34; 25:1).

1886. ἔπαυλις *épaulis*; gen. *epaúleōs*, from *epí* (1909), in, and *aúlis* (n.f.), a stall, which is from *aulízomai* (835), to lodge. A fold, stall (Sept.: Num 32:16,

24); country dwelling, cottage, tent (Sept.: Josh 15:45, 47). In the NT, generally, a house, dwelling, abode (Acts 1:20 quoted from Ps 69:25).

Syn.: *oikētérion* (3613), habitation; *katoikētérion* (2732), a more permanent place than that implied by *oikētérion*; *katoikía* (2733), dwelling, settlement; *skēnē* (4633), tent, tabernacle; *skēnōma* (4638), a booth, pitched tent, tabernacle.

1887. ἐπαύριον *epaúrion*; adv. of time, from *epí* (1909), upon, and *aúrion* (839), tomorrow. Upon the morrow, tomorrow, the next day (Matt 27:62; Mark 11:12; John 1:29, 35, 43; 6:22; 12:12; Acts 10:9, 23, 24; 14:20; 20:7; 21:8; 22:30; 23:32; 25:6, 23; Sept.: Gen 19:34; Lev 23:11, 16).

Syn.: *hexês* (1836), next, following.

Ant.: *sēmeron* (4594), today; *chthés* (5504) or *echthés*, yesterday.

1888. ἐπαυτοφώρῳ *epautophórō*; dat. of *epautóphoros* (n.f.), which is from *epí* (1909), in, and *autóphoros* (n.f.), taken in the very act of any crime, e.g., adultery (John 8:4 [TR]). Equivalent to the expression found in the UBS of John 8:4 *ep' autô phórō* (*epí* [1909], upon; *autó* [846], himself; *phórō*, the dat. of *phórá* [n.f.], theft), in the very act of theft.

1889. Ἐπαφρᾶς *Epaphrás*; gen. *Epaphrá*, masc. proper noun. Epaphras, meaning lovely, possibly a contraction of *Epaphróditos* (1891). A distinguished disciple of Colossae and a faithful minister of the gospel (Col 1:7). His character is described by the Apostle Paul (Col 1:7, 8; 4:12), who was imprisoned with him at Rome (Phile 1:23).

1890. ἐπαφρίζω *epaphrízō*; fut. *epaphrísō*, from *epí* (1909), upon, or an intens., and *aphrízō* (875), to foam. To foam upon or out, meaning to pour out like foam. Used trans. in Jude 1:13 (cf. Isa 57:20).

1891. Ἐπαφρόδιτος *Epaphróditos*; gen. *Epaphrodítou*, masc. proper noun. Epaphroditus, meaning one devoted to Aphrodite, the goddess of love and beauty. An eminent disciple who resided at Philippi. He was commissioned by the church in that city to visit the Apostle Paul during his imprisonment at Rome. The apostle alludes to Epaphroditus with strong commendation (Phil 2:25; 4:18). See *Epaphrás* (1889), a possible contraction of *Epaphróditos*.

1892. ἐπεγείρω *epegeírō*; fut. *epegerṓ*, from *epí* (1909), upon, and *egeírō* (1453), to raise. To wake up, rouse up out of sleep, excite against (Acts 13:50; 14:2; Sept.: 1 Sam 22:8; 2 Chr 21:16).
Syn.: *exegeírō* (1825), to rouse fully, raise up; *exanístēmi* (1817), to arise; *anístēmi* (450), to rise, raise; *diegeírō* (1326), to stir up; *paroxúnō* (3947), to provoke, stir; *erethízō* (2042), to stimulate.

1893. ἐπεί *epeí*; conj. from *epí* (1909), upon. Used of time and motive.
(I) Of time, meaning as, when, after that, followed by the aor. indic. (Luke 7:1; Sept.: Gen 46:30; Josh 7:8).
(II) Of ground or motive meaning inasmuch as, always in the apodosis (the conclusion of a supposition) which, however, may stand first, followed by the indic. (Matt 18:32; 27:6; Mark 15:42; Luke 1:34; John 13:29; 19:31; 1 Cor 14:12; 2 Cor 11:18; 13:3; Heb 2:14; 5:2, 11; 6:13; 11:11); followed by *mḗpote* (3379), not at all, meaning never (Heb 9:17); followed by *oún* (3767), therefore, meaning since therefore (Heb 4:6); followed by *ára* (686), therefore, truly, meaning since then, since in that case (1 Cor 5:10; 7:14). Before questions implying a neg. answer and before similar hypothetical clauses, it stands in the sense of "for," by implication meaning for then, for else, for otherwise (Rom 3:6; 11:6, 22; 1 Cor 14:16; 15:29; Heb 9:26; 10:2).

Syn.: *epeidḗ* (1894) and *héneka* (1752), because; *diá* (1223), for, due to; *kathó* (2526) and *kathóti* (2530), inasmuch; *hóti* (3754), that; *kathṓs* (2531), as; *dió* (1352), therefore; *dióper* (1355), wherefore.
Ant.: *eikḗ* (1500), without reason; *dōreán* (1432), without a cause; *mátēn* (3155), to no purpose, in vain; *anōphelḗs* (512), unprofitable; *alusitelḗs* (255), gainless; *áchrēstos* (890), useless; *perissós* (4053), superfluous.

1894. ἐπειδή *epeidḗ*; conj. from *epeí* (1893), as, because, and *dḗ* (1211), indeed, a particle of affirmation or emphasis. As indeed, as now, spoken in the NT only of a ground or motive, meaning since indeed, since now, because now, inasmuch as, and always in the apodosis (the conclusion of a hypothesis) which, however, may stand first, followed by the indic. (Matt 21:46, Luke 11:6; Acts 13:46; 14:12; 15:24; 1 Cor 1:21, 22; 14:16; 15:21; Phil 2:26; Sept.: Job 9:29).

1895. ἐπειδήπερ *epeidḗper*; conj. from *epeidḗ* (1894), since, and *per* (4007), truly, a particle of abundance. Since now, inasmuch as now (Luke 1:1). Stronger than *epeidḗ*.

1896. ἐπεῖδον *epeídon*; 2d aor. 1st person of *ephoráō* ([n.f.], to look upon favorably), from *epí* (1909), upon, and or *eídō* (1492), to look. "He looked on me" with favor, for good, with kindness (Luke 1:25; Sept.: Ex 2:25; Ps 31:7); or unfavorably for evil, followed by *epí* with the acc. (Acts 4:29).
Ant.: *kataphronéō* (2706), to disesteem, despise; *periphronéō* (4065), to depreciate, despise; *apostréphō* (654), to turn away from; *ektrépō* (1624), to avoid; *apopheúgō* (668), to escape.

1897. ἐπείπερ *epeíper*; conj. from *epeí* (1893), upon, if, and *per* (4007), truly, a particle of abundance or emphasis. Since indeed, since now (Rom 3:30). Stronger than *epeí*.

1898. ἐπεισαγωγή *epeisagōgḗ*; gen. *epeisagōgḗs*, fem. noun from *epí* (1909), upon, and *eisagōgḗ* (n.f.), introduction, which is from *eiságō* (1521), to introduce. Literally, a leading in upon, the bringing in or introduction of something additional (Heb 7:19).

Syn.: *eísodos* (1529), entrance; *parembolḗ* (3925), a throwing in beside, a juxtaposition.

Ant.: *apobolḗ* (580), a casting away; *ekbolḗ* (1546), a casting out.

1899. ἔπειτα *épeita*; adv. of time and order, from *epí* (1909), upon or at, and *eíta* (1534), then, moreover then, a particle of succession. Thereupon, then, afterwards, next (Luke 16:7; Gal 1:21; James 4:14). For the sake of emphasis when placed between a verb and preceding part. (Mark 7:5). With a more definite notation of time (John 11:7; Gal 1:18; 2:1). Also in enumerations when the preceding clause contains likewise a notation of time (1 Cor 12:28; 15:6, 7, 23; Heb 7:27). Preceded by *prṓton* (4412), first, followed by *épeita*, first—then, next (1 Cor 15:46; 1 Thess 4:17; Heb 7:2; James 3:17).

Deriv.: *metépeita* (3347), after that, then.

Syn.: *hústeron* (5305), afterward, finally; *hexḗs* (1836), after, following.

Ant.: *prín* (4250), before and its syn.

1900. ἐπέκεινα *epékeina*; adv. from *epí* (1909), upon, and *ekeínos* (1565), that one, those. Beyond, with the gen., "the [place, region] beyond [of] Babylon" (a.t.) referring to either Babylon itself (appositional gen.) or regions lying beyond Babylon (obj. or comparative gen. [Acts 7:43]).

Syn.: *péran* (4008), beyond; *hupér* (5228), beyond, above; *ekeí* (1563), there, thither.

Ant.: *hupó* (5259), under, below; *kátō* and *katōtérō* (2736), under; *entháde* (1759), hither, until now; *émprosthen* (1715), before.

1901. ἐπεκτείνω *epekteínō*; fut. *epektenṓ*, from *epí* (1909), to, unto, and *ekteínō* (1614), to extend. To reach towards. In the NT, only as a mid. part. *epekteinómenos* followed by a dat. (Phil 3:13).

Syn.: *ekpetánnumi* (1600), to spread; *auxánō* (837), to grow, increase; *prokóptō* (4298), to advance.

Ant.: *elattóō* (1642), to decrease; *elattonéō* (1641), to fall short, lack.

1902. ἐπενδύω *ependúō*; fut. *ependúsō*, from *epí* (1909), upon, and *endúō* (1746), to clothe. In the NT, only in the mid., to put on over one's outer garments, to clothe upon with the new spiritual body (2 Cor 5:2, 4).

Deriv.: *ependútēs* (1903), outer garment.

Syn.: *amphiénnumi* (294), to put clothes around; *endidúskō* (1737), to clothe; *himatízō* (2439), to put on raiment; *peribállō* (4016), to cast around or about; *egkombóomai* (1463), to gird oneself with something; *epitíthēmi* (2007), to put on; *bállō* (906), to put; *epibállō* (1911), to put on, throw upon.

Ant.: *apotíthēmi* (659), to put away; *ekbállō* (1544), to cast out; *apekdúomai* (554), to strip off clothes or arms; *apōthéomai* (683), to thrust away, put from; *gumnēteúō* (1130), to be poorly clad, naked; *ekdúō* (1562), to undress.

1903. ἐπενδύτης *ependútēs*; gen. *ependútou*, masc. noun from *ependúō* (1902), to clothe. Upper garment, tunic (John 21:7; Sept.: 2 Sam 13:18), the same as the Attic *chitṓn* (5509), coat, outer garment, in distinction from the inner garment next to the body which was called *hupodútes* (n.f.). For a full discussion of all Gr. words referring to clothing, see *énduma* (1742), garment.

Ant.: *gumnótēs* (1132), nudity, nakedness.

1904. ἐπέρχομαι *epérchomai*; fut. *epeleúsomai*, from *epí* (1909), upon, to, and *érchomai* (2064), to come. To go or come upon or over a person or place.

(I) Of person, to come to, upon, come thither, arrive (Acts 14:19); to come upon in a hostile sense, invade, attack (Luke 11:22; Sept.: 1 Sam 30:23; 2 Chr 22:1); of evils, calamities, to come upon, befall, followed by *epí* (1909), upon, with the acc. (Luke 21:35; Acts 8:24; 13:40; Sept.: Judg 9:57; 2 Chr 20:9; Mic 3:11).

(II) Spoken of the Holy Spirit as resting upon and operating in a person, followed by *epí* (1909), upon, with the acc. (Luke 1:35; Acts 1:8; Sept.: 1 Sam 11:7).

(III) As a part., *eperchómenos* (1904), spoken of time, season, destiny, coming on, impending, future (Luke 21:26; Eph 2:7; James 5:1; Sept.: Isa 41:22; 44:7; 45:11).

(IV) Of place, to come to or thither, to arrive, used in an absolute sense (Acts 14:19; Sept.: Judg 18:17).

Syn.: *eisérchomai* (1525), to enter; *episképtomai* (1980), to visit, come upon; *epipíptō* (1968), to fall upon; *prolambánō* (4301), to overtake; *prophthánō* (4399), to get there before, precede.

Ant.: *exérchomai* (1831), to come out; *apobaínō* (576), to go away; *ekporeúomai* (1607), to depart; *rhúomai* (4506), to rescue; *sṓzō* (4982), save, rescue; *diasṓzō* (1295), to rescue completely; *lutróō* (3084), to redeem; *phuláttō* (5442), to keep; *diaphuláttō* (1314), to keep completely.

1905. ἐπερωτάω *eperōtáō*; contracted *eperōtṓ*, fut. *eperōtḗso*, from *epí* (1909), an intens., and *erōtáō* (2065), to ask, inquire of, beg of. In the NT, to interrogate, inquire.

(I) Generally and with the duplicate acc. (Mark 11:29; Luke 20:40; Sept.: 2 Sam 14:18). Followed by the acc. and *perí* (4012), about, with the gen. of thing (Mark 7:17); by the acc. of person and *légōn*, the pres. part. of *légō* (3004), to speak, say, saying, or the question itself (Matt 12:10; Mark 5:9; Luke 3:10, 14; Acts 1:6; 1 Cor 14:35). Used in an absolute sense (Matt 22:35; Acts 23:34; Sept.: Gen 38:21; 43:7). In the sense of to require, demand, followed by the acc. of person and inf. (Matt 16:1; Sept.: Ps 137:3).

(II) In a judicial sense, to question, interrogate, with the duplicate acc. (John 18:21). Followed by the acc. of person and *légōn*, saying (Matt 27:11; Acts 5:27). Used in an absolute sense (Luke 23:6).

(III) To ask or inquire after God, i.e., to seek God, the same as *ekzētéō* (1567), to seek after (Rom 10:20 quoted from Isa 65:1).

Deriv.: *eperṓtēma* (1906), inquiry.

Syn.: *ereunáō* (2045), to investigate.

Ant.: *apokrínomai* (611), to answer; *apantáō* (528), to meet, answer.

1906. ἐπερώτημα *eperṓtēma*; gen. *eperōtḗmatos*, neut. noun from *eperōtáō* (1905), to question, inquire. A question, inquiry. In the NT, spoken of a question put to a convert at baptism, the whole process of question and answer, an examination, or the response to the inquiry, a pledge, profession (1 Pet 3:21) as marking the spiritual character of the baptismal rite in contrast to mere external purification. Some render the phrase *eperṓtēma eis* (1519), unto God, as inquiry or longing after God, while others make it mean desire, petition to God in regard to salvation.

Syn.: *anákrisis* (351), preliminary judicial investigation; *dokimḗ* (1382), proof, trial; *dokímion* (1383), a test, proof; *éndeixis* (1732), demonstration; *éndeigma* (1730), a token for the purpose of proving something; *tekmḗrion* (5039), a positive proof.

Ant.: *apókrisis* (612), answer; *apókrima* (610), a judicial answer or sentence; *chrēmatismós* (5538), a divine response or oracle; *apología* (627), a verbal defense; *plērophoría* (4136), confidence, full assurance.

1907. ἐπέχω *epéchō*; fut. *ephéxō*, 2d aor. *epéschon*, from *epí* (1909), upon, and *échō* (2192), to have, hold. To have or hold upon, to hold out towards, to direct upon.

(I) In the NT, used of the mind, to fix the mind upon, give heed to, pay attention, followed by a dat. and with *nous* (3563), mind, implied (Luke 14:7 followed by *pôs* [4459], how; Acts 3:5; 1 Tim 4:16).

(II) In common with Eng., to hold up or on, meaning to hold back in the sense of to retain, not to lose (Phil 2:16), persevering in the acknowledgement and practice of the Christian doctrine.

(III) More often, to keep back or detain a person, used in the NT intrans. or with *heautón* implied (acc. of *heautós* [1438], himself), to hold oneself back, remain, stay (Acts 19:22; Sept.: Gen 8:10; 2 Chr 18:5).

Syn.: *proséchō* (4337), to heed; *skopéō* (4648), to take heed; *phulássō* (5442), to guard; *kratéō* (2902), to prevail; *epilambánomai* (1949), to appropriate; *tēréō* (5083), to watch over, keep an eye on, give heed.

Ant.: *apoloúō* (628), to wash away; *apodídōmi* (591), to give away; *apallássō* (525), to release; *eleutheróō* (1659), to set free; *exaírō* (1807), to deliver, set free.

1908. ἐπηρεάζω *epēreázō*; fut. *epereásō*, from *epí* (1909), against, and *epéreia* (n.f.), threat, insult. To misuse, treat despitefully, insult (Matt 5:44; Luke 6:28). In the sense of to accuse falsely, followed by the acc. (1 Pet 3:16), syn. with *diabállō* (1225), to accuse falsely.

Syn.: *egkaléō* (1458), to bring legal charge against; *katēgoréō* (2723), to speak against, accuse; *sukophantéō* (4811), to accuse wrongfully; *enubrízō* (1796), to treat insultingly; *hubrízō* (5195), to insult; *loidoréō* (3058), to revile; *oneidízō* (3679), to upbraid; *blasphēméō* (987), to speak profanely; *antiloidoréō* (486), to revile back.

Ant.: *eulogéō* (2127), to speak well of, bless; *makarízō* (3106), to declare blessed.

1909. ἐπί *epí*; prep. governing the gen., dat., and acc. On, upon.

(I) With the gen.:

(A) Of place, in a great variety of relations which may, however, be understood under the two leading ideas of rest upon, on, in, and of motion upon, to, towards. **(1)** Of place where, after words implying rest, upon, on, in **(a)** Generally and followed by the gen. of place (Matt 4:6; 9:2, 6; 16:19; 18:19; 21:19, "upon the way" [a.t.], i.e., by the wayside; 24:30; 27:19; Mark 8:4, 6 "on [or in] the desert" [a.t.]; 14:51; Luke 4:29; 5:18; 12:3; 22:21, "on the table," 30, "of the things upon my table" [a.t.] or "at my table"; John 6:19, "walking on the lake" [a.t.]; 19:31; 20:7; 21:1, "on the shore of the lake" [a.t.]; Acts 8:28; 20:9, "in a window"; 21:40; James 5:5; Rev 1:17, 20, "on [or in] the hollow of my hand" [a.t.]; 4:9; 5:10, 13, "on the bottom of the sea" [a.t.], "in the deep" [a.t.]; 7:3; 10:1; 19:19; 20:11; Sept.: 2 Kgs 2:7; Dan 8:2). Metaphorically (Matt 18:16; Mark 12:26; Luke 20:37, "on [or in] the passage [section] of the bush" [a.t. {cf. Rom 11:2}]). (See *en* [1722, I, A]) Followed by the gen. of person (Acts 21:23, "have a vow on them"). **(b)** In the sense of before, in the presence of, chiefly judges, witnesses, as to stand before a court (Matt 28:14; Mark 13:9; Acts 23:30; 24:19, 20; 25:9, 10, 26; 26:2; 1 Cor 6:1, 6; 1 Tim 6:13). Generally (2 Cor 7:14, "our boasting . . . before Titus"). **(2)** Of place, whither, after words implying motion or direction, upon, to, toward, with subsequent rest upon (Matt 26:12; Mark 4:26; 9:20; 14:35; Luke 8:16; John 6:2, "which he did upon" [a.t.], to or on the sick, in the case of the sick; 6:21, "at the land," i.e., on the shore; 19:19; 21:11; Acts 5:30; Sept.: Gen 40:19; Acts 10:11; Heb 6:7; James 5:17; Rev 10:2; 13:16). Figuratively, upon the hearts (Heb 8:10; 10:16; Sept.: Job 17:16).

(B) Of time, when at a time, meaning on, at, in, during (Heb 1:2; 2 Pet 3:3); as marked by contemporary persons or events (Matt 1:11; Mark 2:26; Luke 3:2; 4:27; Acts 11:28, "in the days of," i.e., under; Sept.: Zech 1:1). Of actions as specifying time, e.g., in my prayers, i.e., when I pray (Rom 1:9; Eph 1:16; Phile 1:4).

(C) Metaphorically spoken of: (1) Dignity, authority, upon, over (Matt 2:22, "over Judea" [a.t.]; Acts 8:27; 12:20; Rom 9:5; Eph 4:6; Rev 2:26, "I shall give authority upon [or over] the nations" [a.t.]; 9:11; 17:18; 20:6; Sept: Gen 44:1, 4). With the verb *kathístēmi* (2525), to appoint, followed by *epí* (Matt 24:45; Luke 12:14; Acts 6:3; Sept.: Gen 39:5). (2) A subject of discourse, on, of, concerning, only after verbs of speech, writing (Gal 3:16). (3) Manner, where *epí* with a gen. is used periphrastically for an adv., e.g., *ep' alētheías* (the gen. of *alētheia* [225]), truth (literally, upon the truth), i.e., of a truth, truly, equal to *alēthōs* (230), truly, verily (Mark 12:14, 32; Luke 4:25; Acts 4:27; 10:34; Sept.: Job 9:2; 19:4; Dan 2:47).

(II) With a dat.:

(A) Place in the same sense and circumstances as *epí* with the gen. so that the Greek poets often used the gen. and dat. interchangeably, while in prose the dat. is more usual. (1) After words implying rest, upon, on, in (Matt 14:8, 11, "upon a plate" [a.t.]; Mark 2:4; 4:38; 6:39, 55; 11:7; Luke 12:44; 21:6; John 11:38; Acts 27:44; Rev 19:14); implying close proximity, contact, upon, at, close by (Matt 24:33; John 4:6, "by the fountain" [a.t.], i.e., on the side of the well; 5:2; Acts 3:10, 11; 5:9; Rev 21:12). Followed by the dat. pl. of person, i.e., with, among (Acts 28:14; 2 Cor 7:7). (2) After words implying motion or direction whither or where, upon, to, toward, and including the idea of subsequent rest upon. (a) Generally (Matt 9:16; 16:18; Mark 2:21; 5:33; John 8:7; Acts 5:35; 8:16; Eph 2:10). Metaphorically (Sept.: Job 29:9). (b) Metaphorically, of a direction of mind meaning toward someone, e.g., in a friendly sense (Luke 18:7; 2 Cor 9:14; Sept.: 2 Sam 14:1); a hostile sense, against (Luke 12:52, 53; Rev 12:17).

(B) Of time, meaning when, chiefly as marking a definite period of time, upon, at, in. (1) Generally (2 Cor 3:14, "in the reading," or whenever it is read; Phil 1:3, "as often as I think of you" [a.t.], or at every mention; Heb 9:15, during the first covenant or while it was in force; 9:26, at the consummation or completion of the ages, of time as we know it, of the dispensation of grace); as implying merely coexistence in time (2 Cor 7:4, "in [during, under] all our tribulation"; Eph 4:26, "during your wrath" [a.t.], i.e., while it continues). (2) In the sense of "after," immediately following upon (John 4:27, "upon this," thereupon; Acts 11:19, immediately after the persecution . . . about Stephen).

(C) Metaphorically spoken of: (1) Power, authority, care over (Matt 24:47; Luke 12:44). (2) Accession or addition, upon or unto something already mentioned or implied, besides (Matt 25:20, 22; Luke 3:20; 16:26, "besides all this" [a.t.]; Eph 6:16; Phil 2:27; Col 3:14; Heb 8:1). (3) That upon which something rests as a basis, foundation, support. (a) Generally (Matt 4:4; Luke 4:4, "to live upon" [a.t.], i.e., to sustain or support life upon, quoted from Deut 8:3). After words implying hope, trust, confidence upon or in any person or thing (Mark 10:24; Luke 11:22; 24:25; Acts 2:26, "shall rest in [or upon] hope"; 14:3, "speaking boldly in [trusting upon] the Lord"; Rom 4:18; 8:20; 15:12; 1 Tim 6:17; Titus 1:2; 1 Pet 2:6). *Epí* used with the dat. of *ónoma* (3686), name, in the phrase *epí tō onómati*, in or upon the name, followed by a gen. noun denoting attribution, i.e., to do anything based upon trust in someone's name and power, causing the enhancement of that person's character (Matt 18:5, "as resting upon [or professing] my name" [a.t.], as a Christian; 24:5; Mark 9:37; Luke 9:48, 49, "casting out devils in [or upon] thy name," i.e., resting the efficacy of their exorcism upon "thy name"; 24:47; Acts 2:38, "be baptized upon the name of Christ" [a.t.], i.e., the baptism being grounded upon the profession of His name; 4:17, 18, "to teach in [upon] the name of Jesus" means resting upon His name, upon Him as the ultimate Teacher and Author; 5:28, 40; Sept.: Deut 18:20). **(b)** Of the subject of an action in reference to (Mark 6:52, wrought upon the loaves). Of discourse on, about, concerning (Luke 23:38; John 12:16; Heb 11:4; Rev 10:11; 22:16). **(c)** Of a condition, law, sanction upon or under which something takes place (1 Cor 9:10; Heb 7:11; 8:6, "under the sanction of" [a.t.]; 9:17, "a testament is only valid the testator being dead" [a.t.]; 10:28, "was put to death under two or three witnesses" [a.t. {cf. Deut 17:6; 19:15}]). **(d)** Of the ground, motive or cause of some action upon or at, i.e., on account of, because of (Matt 19:9; Luke 2:20; 5:5; Acts 3:16; 4:21; 26:6; 1 Cor 1:4; 8:11; 2 Cor 9:15). Followed by the dat. of person *ep' autoís*, upon them (Acts 21:24). With the relative pron. *eph' hṓ* for *epí toútō hóti*, on this account that, because (Rom 5:12; 2 Cor 5:4; Phil 4:10). **(e)** Of the occasion upon, at, in connection with which something takes place; upon, at, over, after words of emotion such as joy, sorrow, compassion, astonishment (Matt 7:28, "they were astonished at his teaching" [a.t.]; 14:14; 18:13; 22:33; Mark 3:5; 6:34; 10:22, 24; Luke 1:14, 29, 47; 5:9; 9:43; 15:7; 19:41; Acts 3:12; 8:2; James 5:1; Rev 11:10; 18:9, 11). Of the occasion of penitence and shame (Rom 6:21; 2 Cor 12:21). **(f)** Of the object, purpose, end of any action, upon, unto, for (Gal 5:13; Phil 3:12; 1 Thess 4:7; 2 Tim 2:14). Also Acts 15:14 [TR], where later editions omit *epí* hence, *eph' hṓ* (*hṓ*, the dat. neut. sing. of the relative pron. *hós* [3739], which) for what, wherefore (Matt 26:50 [TR], for which others have *eph' hó*). **(g)** Of the norm or model upon or to which anything is adjusted or conformed, upon, after, according to (Luke 1:59; Sept.: Ezra 2:61; Neh 7:63). In 2 Cor 9:6; *ep' eulogías* used as an adv. meaning bountifully or according to God's blessing or intervention (see *eulogía* [2129], blessing).

(III) With the acc.:

(A) Of place, and generally combining the ideas of rest and motion upon. Sometimes, however, the idea of motion upon is more prominent, and rarely, rest upon. **(1)** As implying rest and motion combined, where it marks an extension or spreading out upon or over something, a stretching or spreading out in various directions, distribution upon, over, among; hence, particularly throughout, or else simply upon, over, at, among, the direction of the implied motion being determined by the adjuncts. **(a)** Generally (Matt 10:34; 13:2, "stood [or had stationed themselves] on the shore"; 14:19, 26, 28, 29; 15:35; 18:12, about or "upon the mountains" [a.t.]; 19:28; 22:9; 24:16; 27:45; Mark 4:38, "stretched upon" [a.t.]; Luke 5:36; John 9:6; Acts 7:11; 21:5; Rev 2:17; 4:4, "along upon the row [or circle] of thrones" [a.t.]; 7:1; 15:2; 20:4, 9; 21:5). With the acc. pl. of person, upon, over, toward all of whom (Matt 5:45; 12:49; Acts 19:12; Rev 14:6 in some editions). **(b)** Where the motion is directed to a higher place, implying elevation or placing upon, i.e., up upon, up over, up to, out upon, or simply upon, over (Matt 4:5; 5:23; 9:18; 13:48; 21:5; 27:29; Mark 8:25; 10:16; 11:2; 15:22; Luke 5:11, 19; 8:27; Acts 17:19; 20:13; 27:43, 44; Rom 12:20); of a yoke or burden taken up and placed upon someone (Matt 11:29; Acts 15:10). Metaphorically, of burdens (Matt 23:4); of a covenant (Heb 8:8); of fear, evil, guilt or punishment which come upon someone as a burden, as something laid upon one; so also after *gínomai* (1096), to be; *epérchomai* (1904), to come upon; *érchomai* (2064), to come; *epipíptō* (1968), to fall into, lie on, press upon (Matt 23:35, 36; Luke 1:12, 65; 21:34, 35; John 3:36; 18:4; Acts 5:28; 8:1; 13:11; 18:6; Rom 1:18; 15:3; 1 Pet 5:7). Similarly of good, prosperity (Matt 10:13; Luke 10:6; Acts 4:33; Rom 3:22; Gal 6:16). Of a lot, i.e., anything imposed by lot (Acts 1:26; Sept.: Lev 16:9; Jon 1:9). **(c)** Where the motion is directed to a lower place (Matt 10:29, "upon the earth" [a.t.]; 13:5, 7; 21:44;

26:7; Luke 22:44; Acts 2:3; Rev 8:10; 16:2). Metaphorically, of the divine Spirit or power descending and abiding upon someone (Matt 3:16; 12:18; Luke 1:35; 2:25; 24:49; 2 Cor 12:9; Rev 7:15). **(2)** Of place meaning whither, implying motion upon, to or toward a place or object as a limit, aim, end, with subsequent rest thereupon. **(a)** Particularly and generally, e.g., after *píptō* (4098), to fall; *epipíptō* (1968), to fall into or upon, as to fall upon the face, meaning forward (Matt 26:39; Luke 5:12; 9:62; 15:20, "fell on his neck"; John 21:20; Acts 10:25, "at his feet"; Phil 3:14; Rev 7:11). After verbs of going, coming, conducting, collecting, equivalent to *prós* (4314), toward, with the acc. (Matt 3:13, "upon the Jordan" [a.t.], i.e., to the region of Jordan; 5:23; 12:28; 27:27; Mark 11:13: Luke 24:24; John 6:16; Acts 1:21; 21:32, 35; 2 Thess 2:1; 2 Tim 4:4; Heb 6:1; Rev 7:17). To gather together or upon or at the same place (Matt 22:34; Acts 4:26; 1 Cor 7:5; 11:20). Of judges, tribunals, upon, unto, i.e., up before (Matt 10:18; Luke 12:11, 58; Acts 16:19). Of an oracle, miracle, testimony, upon, unto (Luke 3:2; Acts 4:22; 2 Thess 1:10; Sept.: 1 Chr 22:8). As implying accession, addition (Matt 6:27; Rev 22:18). **(b)** Where the motion or direction expressed by *epí*, upon, implies an affection of the mind for, i.e., favorable, kindly (Luke 1:48; 9:38; 1 Pet 3:12, "are directed upon" [a.t.], quoted from Ps 34:16 [cf. 31:8]), or against as disfavor upon or against (Acts 4:29; 1 Pet 3:12, "as directed against" [a.t.], quoted from Ps 34:17); in a hostile sense (Matt 10:21; Luke 14:31; 22:52, 53; John 13:18; Acts 7:57; 13:50, 51; 19:16; 2 Cor 10:2; 2 Thess 2:4; Sept.: Gen 16:12). Metaphorically, of conduct or testimony against someone (Mark 10:11; Luke 9:5); in an imprecation (2 Cor 1:23). **(c)** Figuratively, of measure or extent, upon or unto, i.e., up to, about. *Eph' hóson* ([3745], the acc. of *hósos*), soever, meaning insofar as, inasmuch as (Matt 25:40; Rom 11:13); *epí pleíon* (4119), more, further on, further, the more (Acts 4:17; 2 Tim

2:16; 3:9). **(d)** Rarely of place, where, after words signifying rest, upon, on, in or at, where the idea of previous motion, upon, is implied (Rev 5:1, "in [upon] his right hand"; 20:1). After verbs of sitting or standing, upon, at, by (Matt 9:9; Acts 10:17; 11:11; 14:10; 26:16, "stand upon thy feet"; Rev 3:20; 8:3; 11:11). *Epí tó autó*, literally upon the same place, as an adv., together (Luke 17:35; Acts 1:15).

(B) Of time meaning how long, during, for (Luke 4:25; Acts 13:31; 18:20; 19:8, 10; Heb 11:30). *Epí chrónon* (the acc. of *chrónos* [5550]), time, for a time (Luke 18:4). *Eph' hóson chrónon*, so long as (Rom 7:1; Gal 4:1). Without *chrónos* (Matt 9:15); *eph' hikanón* ([2425] the acc. of *hikanós*, sufficient, with *chrónon*, time implied), meaning a long while, long (Acts 20:11). As an adv., *epí polú* (4183), much, meaning long (Acts 28:6); *epí pleíon* (4119), more, meaning longer, further (Acts 20:9; 24:4). Implying a term or limit of time upon the coming of which anything is done or assigned, upon, at, about (Mark 15:1; Luke 10:35; Acts 3:1); joined with an adv. in later usage, e.g., *epí trís* (5151), three times, up to thrice (Acts 10:16; 11:10).

(C) Metaphorically spoken of: **(1)** Power, authority, care over, over, upon (Luke 1:33; 2:8, "over their flock"; 9:1; 10:19; Acts 7:10; Rom 5:14; Heb 2:7; 3:6; Rev 13:7; Sept.: Gen 39:5). **(2)** Accession or addition, upon, over (Phil 2:27 [TR], has *epí* with a dat.). **(3)** An object or substratum, upon, over, in respect to which anything is done, felt, directed. **(a)** Of the subject of an action or discourse, upon, over, in respect to (Mark 15:24; 1 Cor 7:36; James 5:14, "let them pray over him," i.e., in his behalf, perhaps in allusion to posture). Of a subject of discourse or writing, upon, of, concerning (Mark 9:12, 13; Rom 4:9; 1 Tim 1:18; Heb 7:13; Sept.: Jer 25:13). **(b)** Of that on which the mind, heart or feelings are directed in kindness, upon, over, toward (Matt 14:14; 15:32; Luke 6:35; Rom 9:23; 11:22; Eph 2:7; Sept.: Gen 47:29); in hostility, against (Matt 12:26; Mark 3:26;

Luke 11:17; Acts 7:54). Of the object of trust, confidence, hope (Matt 27:43; Acts 9:42; 11:17; Rom 4:5; 2 Cor 2:3; 1 Tim 5:5; Heb 6:1; 1 Pet 1:13; 3:5). Of the occasion or object upon or over which joy or sorrow is felt (Luke 23:28; Rev 1:7; 18:20 [TR]; Sept.: Ps 32:11; Isa 61:10; Zech 12:10). (c) Of that on which the will or intention is directed, the end, purpose or aim of an action, upon, for, for the sake of, after (Matt 3:7, "in order to be baptized" [a.t.]; 26:55; Luke 7:44, "water for my feet"; 15:4; 23:48). Of a result (2 Tim 3:13; Heb 12:10). (d) Spoken of persons, upon or over whom a name is called, who are called by that name, implying property, relationship (Acts 15:17, quoted from Amos 9:12; James 2:7; Sept.: 2 Sam 12:28; Jer 14:9).

(IV) In composition *epí* implies:

(A) Motion upon, toward, against, as *epágō* (1863), to bring upon; *epérchomai* (1904), to come upon, to attack, influence.

(B) Rest upon, over, at, as *epéchō* (1907), to hold upon; *epanapaúomai* (1879), to rest upon.

(C) Accession, addition, as *episunágō* (1996), to gather together in one place; *epaitéō* (1871), to ask for.

(D) Succession, as *epitássō* (2004), to arrange upon or to charge, command.

(E) Repetition or renewal as *epanórthōsis* (1882), rectification, a straightening up again. Very often the prep. *epí* in composition cannot be expressed in Eng. and should be taken simply as an intens. such as *epideíknumi* (1925), to exhibit; *epilanthánomai* (1950), to neglect, forget.

1910. ἐπιβαίνω epibaínō; fut. *epibḗsomai*, from *epí* (1909), upon, to, and *baínō* (n.f., see *apobaínō* [576]), to go. To go upon, mount, as upon a donkey (Matt 21:5); aboard ship (Acts 21:2, 6 [TR]; 27:2); to set foot upon, to come upon or, enter into (Acts 20:18; 25:1).

Syn.: *epérchomai* (1904), to come or go upon; *ephístēmi* (2186), to come up; *eíseimi* (1524) and *eisporeúomai* (1531),

to go into; *eisérchomai* (1525), to come into; *embaínō* (1684), to go into, step in; *embibázō* (1688), to place on, transfer, put on board ship.

Ant.: *exérchomai* (1831), to come out as; *ekporeúomai* (1607), to depart; *apobaínō* (576), *hupágō* (5217), *ápeimi* (548), and *apérchomai* (565), to go away; *éxeimi* (1826), to go out; *paragínomai* (3854), to go.

1911. ἐπιβάλλω epibállō; fut. *epibaló̄*, from *epí* (1909), upon or unto, and *bállō* (906), to cast, put. To throw upon, to think on.

(I) Followed by the dat. (Mark 11:7; 1 Cor 7:35); followed by *epí* (1909), upon, with the acc. (Sept. Num 4:6, 7; 19:2; Hos 7:12). In the sense of to put upon, i.e., to sew on a patch (Matt 9:16; Luke 5:36). In the phrase "to lay the hand (or the hands) upon" someone means to seize, to do violence to a person. Followed by *epí* and the acc., upon someone (Matt 26:50; Mark 14:46; Luke 20:19; 21:12; John 7:30, 44; Acts 5:18; 21:27); followed by the dat. (Sept.: Gen 22:12; Esth 6:2). In the sense of to lay hold of, undertake (Luke 9:62; Sept.: Deut 12:7, 18).

(II) Intrans. with *heautón* implied (the acc. of *heautoú* [1438], of himself), to cast oneself upon, i.e., to rush upon, fall upon. Followed by *eis* (1519), in or into with the acc. (Mark 4:37); used in an absolute sense (Mark 14:72, "rushing forward" [a.t.], i.e., out of the hall [cf. Matt 26:75; Luke 22:62]; Sept.: 2 Sam 15:30; 19:4; Jer 14:3, 4). Impersonally, to fall upon, to fall to, i.e., to pertain or belong to someone (Luke 15:12, "the portion . . . which falls to me" [a.t.]).

Deriv.: *epíblēma* (1915), patch.

Syn.: *epirríptō* (1977), to cast upon; *rhíptō* (4496), to fling, throw; *ekteínō* (1614), to stretch out or forth, to lay; *epekteínō* (1901), to stretch forth; *ekpetánnumi* (1600), to spread, put.

Ant.: *apokóptō* (609), to cut off or away; *aphairéō* (851), to remove; *aírō* (142), to lift, take up or away; *apaírō*

(522), to lift off; *ekbállō* (1544), to take out; *apágō* (520), to take away.

1912. ἐπιβαρέω *epibaréō*; contracted *epibarố*, fut. *epibarésō*, from *epí* (1909), upon, or an intens., and *baréō* (916), to burden. In the NT, used only metaphorically, meaning to be burdensome upon, followed by the acc. (2 Cor 2:5, "that I may not burden you" [a.t.], i.e., bear too hard upon you in my censure, or that I may not be too severe; 1 Thess 2:9; 2 Thess 3:8).
Syn.: *phortízō* (5412), to burden; *katanarkáō* (2655), to be a burden or burdensome; *thlíbō* (2346), to distress, trouble; *apothlíbō* (598), to crush; *sunéchō* (4912), to constrain; *enéchō* (1758), to press upon; *piézō* (4085), to press down together; *diṓkō* (1377), to pursue; *phérō* (5342), to bear.
Ant.: *kouphízō* (2893), to unload.

1913. ἐπιβιβάζω *epibibázō*; fut. *epibibásō*, from *epí* (1909), upon, and *bibázō* (n.f., see *embibázō* [1688]), to lift up. To cause to mount, to mount. Used trans., meaning to mount an animal for riding (Luke 10:34); with *epí* (1909), on, implied (Luke 19:35; Acts 23:24; Sept.: 1 Kgs 1:33; 2 Kgs 9:28).
Syn.: *epikathízō* (1940), to sit upon; *anérchomai* (424), to go up.
Ant.: *apobaínō* (576), to disembark, get off, go out; *katabaínō* (2597), to descend.

1914. ἐπιβλέπω *epiblépō*; fut. *epiblépsō*, from *epí* (1909), upon, and *blépō* (991), to look. To look upon, fix the eyes upon, followed by *epí* (1909), upon, with the acc. (Sept.: Num 21:9). In the NT, metaphorically, to look upon, to have respect to, followed by *epí* with the acc., with reference to kindness and favor (Luke 1:48; 9:38), with reference to partiality (James 2:3; Sept.: Lev 26:9; 1 Sam 1:11; 9:16; 1 Kgs 8:28; Ps 25:16).
Syn.: *diablépō* (1227), to see clearly; *proséchō* (4337), to take or give heed, attend; *phrontízō* (5431), to care for;

merimnáō (3309), to care; *epimeléomai* (1959), to take care of.
Ant.: *ameléō* (272), to neglect; *epilanthánomai* (1950), to neglect, forget; *oligōréō* (3643), to have little regard for, disesteem, despise; *periphronéō* (4065), to despise; *kataphronéō* (2706), to disesteem, to think against someone.

1915. ἐπίβλημα *epíblēma*; gen. *epiblḗmatos*, neut. noun from *epibéblēmai*, perf. pass. of *epibállō* (1911), to lay upon, cast up on, put on. Something put on, an addition, a patch (Matt 9:16; Mark 2:21; Luke 5:36; Sept.: Isa 3:22).
Syn.: *kálumma* (2571), a cover; *sképasma* (4629), a covering; *epikálumma* (1942), a covering over.
Ant.: *schísma* (4978), schism, gap; *rhēgma* (4485), something torn; *opḗ* (3692), a hole.

1916. ἐπιβοάω *epiboáō*; contracted *epiboố*, fut. *epiboésō*, from *epí* (1909), an intens., and *boáō* (994), to cry out. To cry out against, to exclaim vehemently (Acts 25:24).
Syn.: *thorubéō* (2350), to make a noise.
Ant.: *hēscházō* (2270), to be quiet; *sigáō* (4601), to keep silence; *phimóō* (5392), to muzzle.

1917. ἐπιβουλή *epiboulḗ*; gen. *epiboulḗs*, fem. noun from *epí* (1909), against, and *boulḗ* (1012), design, purpose. A scheme, a plot, conspiracy (Acts 9:24; 20:3, 19; 23:30; Sept.: Esth 2:22).
Syn.: *sunōmosía* (4945), conspiracy.

1918. ἐπιγαμβρεύω *epigambreúō*; fut. *epigambreúsō*, from *epí* (1909), to or after, and *gambreúō* (n.f.), to marry. To intermarry (Sept.: Gen 34:9). In the NT, to marry by right of affinity, used trans. (Matt 22:24 [cf. Mark 12:19; Luke 20:28]), spoken of the marriage of a brother's widow according to the Jewish law (Gen 38:8 [cf. Deut 25:5, 6; Ruth chap. 4]).

1919. ἐπίγειος *epígeios*; gen. *epigeíou*, masc.-fem., neut. *epígeion*, adj. from *epí* (1909), upon, and *gē* (1093), the earth. Earthly, being upon the earth (Phil 2:10; 3:19). Earthly, belonging to the earth or wrought in men upon the earth (John 3:12). Earthly, terrestrial, made of earth (1 Cor 15:40; 2 Cor 5:1 [cf. Job 4:19]). Earthly, arising from the earth and attached to it (James 3:15). In the NT, opposed to *epouránios* (2032), that which pertains to heaven (1 Cor 15:40); contrasted as an earthly house to the one not made by hands, eternal in the heavens (2 Cor 5:1; see John 3:12; Phil 2:10). Occurs with a moral contrast between earth and heaven (Phil 3:19 [cf. Phil 3:14]; Col 3:2; James 3:15 [cf. James 3:14, 16, 17]).

Ant.: *ouránios* (3770), heavenly; *epouránios* (2032), heavenly.

1920. ἐπιγίνομαι *epigínomai*; fut. *epigenḗsomai*, from *epí* (1909), upon, and *gínomai* (1096), to be, come. To arise upon, come on, used intrans. of wind, meaning to spring up (Acts 28:13).

Syn.: *epérchomai* (1904), to occur, come upon; *sumbaínō* (4819), to take place; *sunteléomai* (4931), to execute.

Ant.: *katastéllō* (2687), to put down; *katargéō* (2673), to destroy; *exoudenóō* (1847), to make utterly nothing of.

1921. ἐπιγινώσκω *epiginṓskō*; fut. *epignṓsomai*, from *epí* (1909), upon, and *ginṓskō* (1097), to know.

(I) To know fully, as an inceptive verb, to come to know, to gain or receive full knowledge of, become fully acquainted with.

(A) Generally, followed by the acc. of a thing expressed or implied (Luke 1:4; Acts 22:24; 1 Cor 14:37; 2 Pet 2:21); by *perí* (4012), concerning, with a gen. (Acts 24:8; Sept.: Jer 5:5; Jon 1:7); by the acc. of person (Matt 11:27). With *apó* (575), from, and the gen., to know from or by anything (Matt 7:16, 20).

(B) In the sense of to learn well from others, to ascertain, find out, learn, followed by *hóti* (3754), that (Luke 7:37;

23:7; Acts 19:34; 22:29; 28:1). Used in an absolute sense (Acts 9:30).

(C) In the sense of to perceive, be fully aware of, followed by the acc. (Mark 5:30; Luke 5:22); by *hóti* (3754), that (Mark 2:8; Luke 1:22).

(D) In the sense of to recognize, know by sight or person, followed by the acc. of person (Matt 14:35; Mark 6:33, 54; Luke 24:16, 31; Acts 3:10; 4:13). Also of things (Acts 12:14; 27:39, "did not know it from any other" [a.t.]; Sept.: Gen 42:7, 8; Judg 18:3; 1 Sam 26:17).

(II) To know fully in a completed sense, have a full knowledge of.

(A) Generally and followed by the acc. of a thing (Rom 1:32; Col 1:6; 1 Tim 4:3); by the acc. of a person (2 Cor 13:5). Used in an absolute sense (Acts 25:10). In the pass. (1 Cor 13:12 [*epegnṓsthēn*]; Sept.: Job 34:27; Ezek 6:7).

(B) In the sense of to acknowledge as being what one is or professes to be, a prophet, apostle, teacher (Matt 17:12; 2 Cor 1:14; 6:9). Of doctrines, an epistle (2 Cor 1:13; Sept.: Jer 28:9, "of a prophet" [a.t.]).

(C) With the idea of goodwill, to know and approve, acknowledge and care for, cherish, followed by the acc. (1 Cor 16:18; Sept.: Ruth 2:10, 19; Ps 142:4).

Deriv.: *epígnōsis* (1922), full or thorough knowledge.

Syn.: *epístamai* (1987), to comprehend; *eídō* (1492), to know intuitively.

Ant.: *agnoéō* (50), not to know, to be ignorant.

1922. ἐπίγνωσις *epígnōsis*; gen. *epignṓseōs*, fem. noun from *epiginṓskō* (1921), to recognize. It is more intens. than *gnṓsis* (1108), knowledge, because it expresses a more thorough participation in the acquiring of knowledge on the part of the learner. In the NT, it often refers to knowledge which very powerfully influences the form of religious life, a knowledge laying claim to personal involvement. When used as an obj. (Eph 1:17; 4:13; Col 1:9, 10; 2:2; 1 Tim 2:4; 2 Tim 2:25; 3:7; Titus 1:1; Heb 10:26; 2

Pet 1:2, 3), it shows the relationship of the learner to the object of his knowledge (2 Pet 1:8). It increases spiritual blessings upon the believer (Eph 1:17; 2 Pet 1:2, 3) and determines the manifestations of the religious life (2 Pet 2:20). When used without an obj. in a formal sense (Rom 1:28; Col 3:10), it gives a more precise definition as a knowledge which is self-determined or self-regulated, so that the difference mentioned in Col 3:10 disappears. In Col 2:2, meaning the discernment which comes in connection with possessing salvation which helps in determining the moral conduct (see Phil 1:9 which refers to the knowledge which enables one to avoid error [cf. Rom 10:2; 11:33; 2 Pet 1:5]).

Syn.: *pístis* (4102), faith, since it is the means of the acceptance of divine revelation as *epígnōsis* can be said to be the comprehension of divine revelation to man; *gnōsis* (1108), knowledge. See the contrasting use of *ginōskō* in Rom 1:21 and *epígnōsis* in Rom 1:28.

Ant.: *agnōsía* (56), lack of knowledge as the ant. of *gnōsis* (1108), knowledge, while *apistía* (570) could be regarded as the theological opposite of *epígnōsis* when the subject is man and the object is God.

1923. **ἐπιγραφή** *epigraphē*; gen. *epigraphḗs*, fem. noun from *epigráphō* (1924), to write upon, inscribe. Inscription, superscription, as on a coin (Matt 22:20; Mark 12:16; Luke 20:24); on the breast or over the head of one crucified, stating his name and crime (Mark 15:26; Luke 23:38).

Syn.: *ónoma* (3686), name; *títlos* (5102), title, placard.

1924. **ἐπιγράφω** *epigráphō*; fut. *epigrápsō*, from *epí* (1909), on, upon, or over, and *gráphō* (1125), to write. To make a mark upon. In the NT, to inscribe with a stylus, used of a public inscription (Mark 15:26; Acts 17:23; Rev 21:12; Sept.: Num 17:2, 3). Figuratively, to impress deeply as the laws upon their hearts

(Heb 8:10), their minds (Heb 10:16 quoted from Jer 31:33; Sept.: Prov 7:3).

Deriv.: *epigraphḗ* (1923), inscription.

Ant.: *exaleíphō* (1813), to erase; *aphanízō* (853), to cause to disappear.

1925. **ἐπιδείκνυμι** *epideíknumi*; fut. *epideíxō*, from *epí* (1909) and *deíknumi* (1166), to show. To show off before someone, to exhibit. Trans., having the idea of motion up to, toward, with someone being implied (Matt 22:19; Luke 20:24; 24:40). In the mid. (Luke 17:14, "show yourselves [or present yourselves] unto the priests"; Acts 9:39). Spoken of deeds or miracles, meaning to display, exhibit (Matt 16:1). In the sense of to point out to someone (Matt 24:1). To show by arguments, to demonstrate, prove (Acts 18:28; Heb 6:17).

Syn.: *sēmeióō* (4593), to mark, distinguish; *sēmaínō* (4591), to indicate; *dialaléō* (1255), to spread by word of mouth; *dēlóō* (1213), to declare; *emphanízō* (1718), to make manifest; *probállō* (4261), to put forth; *apokalúptō* (601), to reveal.

Ant.: *krúptō* (2928), to hide; *apokrúptō* (613), to keep secret from; *sugkalúptō* (4780), to conceal together; *kalúptō* (2572), to cover up; *egkrúptō* (1470), to conceal in.

1926. **ἐπιδέχομαι** *epidéchomai*; fut. *epidéxomai*, mid. deponent from *epí* (1909), an intens., and *déchomai* (1209), to receive. To receive to oneself, to receive, admit. In the NT used in connection with kindness, hospitality, trans. (Acts 28:30 in some MSS; 3 John 1:10). Metaphorically, to accept, assent to (3 John 1:9).

Syn.: *anéchomai* (430), to tolerate; *dokimázō* (1381), to approve; *hupophérō* (5297), to bear, endure.

Ant.: *aporríptō* (641), to reject; *periphronéō* (4065), to despise; *apobállō* (577), to cast away; *kataphronéō* (2706), to disesteem.

1927. ἐπιδημέω *epidēméō*; contracted *epidēmṓ*, fut. *epidēméso*, from *epídēmos* (n.f.), a sojourner, one who lives among another people, which is from *epí* (1909), in, among, and *dēmos* (1218), people. To be or reside among a people as a stranger, used intrans. (Acts 2:10; 17:21, "resident foreigners" [a.t.]). See *parepídēmos* (3927), pilgrim, stranger. Also from *epídēmos* (n.f.): *parepídēmos* (3927), a stranger, sojourner.

Syn.: *xénos* (3581), a stranger; *allótrios* (245), literally another or a stranger; *allogenḗs* (241) and *allóphulos* (246), a foreigner; *pároikos* (3941), sojourner; *parepí dēmos* (3927), pilgrim.

Ant.: *enoikéō* (1774), to inhabit; *polítēs* (4177), citizen; *katoikéō* (2730), to reside as an inhabitant.

1928. ἐπιδιατάσσομαι *epidiatássomai*, **ἐπιδιατάττομαι** *epidiatáttomai*; fut. *epidiatáxomai*, mid. deponent from *epí* (1909), upon, besides, and *diatássō* (1299), to order, appoint. To arrange in order, appoint in addition, supplement (Gal 3:15), to ordain something in addition.

Syn.: *epitíthēmi* (2007), to add on; *prostíthēmi* (4369), to give more, to add; *prosanatíthēmi* (4323), to lay up in addition.

Ant.: *aphairéō* (851), to remove; *methístēmi* (3179), to cause to remove; *metatíthēmi* (3346), to remove a person or thing from one place to another; *paraphérō* (3911), to take or carry away; *apochōrízō* (673), to separate.

1929. ἐπιδίδωμι *epidídōmi*; fut. *epidṓsō*, from *epí* (1909), to, into, or an intens., and *dídōmi* (1325), to give. To give forth as from oneself upon or to another, to give over, deliver over as to put into one's hands, used trans. (Matt 7:9, 10; Luke 4:17 referring to Isa 61:1, 2; Luke 11:11, 12; 24:30, 42; John 13:26; Acts 15:30). To put a ship into the wind (Acts 27:15).

Syn.: *charízomai* (5483), to give freely.

1930. ἐπιδιορθόω *epidiorthóō*; contracted *epidiorthṓ*, fut. *epidiorthṓsō*, from *epí* (1909), besides, above, and *diorthóō* (n.f.), to correct. Only in Titus 1:5, meaning to proceed in correcting or setting in order. See *diórthōsis* (1357), an amendment, restoration.

Syn.: *paideúō* (3811), to train up, correct; *morphóō* (3445), to fashion.

1931. ἐπιδύω *epidúō*; fut. *epidúsō*, from *epí* (1909), upon, and *dúō* (1416), to sink. To set fully or go down; spoken of the sun (Eph 4:26; Sept.: Deut 24:17).

Syn.: *buthízō* (1036), to sink.

Ant.: *anatéllō* (393) or *anabaínō* (305), to rise; *anístēmi* (450), to arise; *exanístēmi* (1817), to raise up or out of; *egeírō* (1453) to raise; *epanístamai* (1881), to rise up against.

1932. ἐπιείκεια *epieíkeia*; gen. *epieikeías*, fem. noun from *epieikḗs* (1933), fitting, appropriate. Clemency or gentleness (Acts 24:4; 2 Cor 10:1). Consideration springing from a recognition of the danger that ever lurks upon the assertion of legal rights lest they be pushed to immoral limits. The virtue that rectifies and redresses the severity of a sentence.

Syn.: contrast *ḗpios* (2261), mild; *anochḗ* (463), forbearance; *makrothumía* (3115), longsuffering; *hupomonḗ* (5281), patience; *praótēs* (4236), meekness.

Ant.: *sklērótēs* (4643), hardness; *bía* (970), force, violence; *trómos* (5156), fear, trembling.

1933. ἐπιεικής *epieikḗs*; gen. *epieikoús*, masc.-fem., neut. *epieikés*, adj. from *epí* (1909), upon, on, an intens., and *eikós* (n.f.), fair, equitable. Fitting, appropriate, suitable, proper, to be lenient, yielding, unassertive (1 Tim 3:3; Titus 3:2; James 3:17; 1 Pet 2:18; Sept.: Ps 86:5). Used in the neut. as a noun *tó epieikés*, your tolerance, clemency (Phil 4:5).

Deriv.: *epieíkeia* (1932), clemency or gentleness.

Syn.: *hḗpios* (2261), gentle, mild; *práos* (4235), meek.

Ant.: *austērós* (840), austere; *bíaios* (972), violent.

1934. ἐπιζητέω *epizētéō*; contracted *epizētṓ*, fut. *epizētḗso*, from *epí* (1909), an intens., and *zētéō* (2212), to seek. To seek for, inquire after, used trans. (Acts 12:19; also Luke 4:42 in later editions; Sept.: Eccl 7:29). In the sense of to seek at the hands of someone, to require, demand (Matt 12:39; 16:4; Mark 8:12; Luke 11:29; Acts 19:39; Phil 4:17). To seek to acquire, strive after, long for, used trans. (Matt 6:32; Luke 12:30; Rom 11:7; Phil 4:17; Heb 11:14; 13:14). Followed by the inf., to desire earnestly (Acts 13:7).

Syn.: *anazētéō* (327), to search out.

1935. ἐπιθανάτιος *epithanátios*; gen. *epithanatíou*, masc.-fem., neut. *epithanátion*, adj. from *epí* (1909), to, and *thánatos* (2288), death. Appointed to death, condemned (1 Cor 4:9).

1936. ἐπίθεσις *epíthesis*; gen. *epithéseōs*, fem. noun from *epitíthēmi* (2007), to put, to lay on. A placing or laying upon, imposition of hands. Used of that action marking the impartation of the Holy Spirit (Acts 8:18; 1 Tim 4:14; 2 Tim 1:6; Heb 6:2 [the verb in Num 27:18, 23; Deut 34:9]).

Syn.: *éndusis* (1745), a putting on.

Ant.: *apóthesis* (595), putting away, off; *apékdusis* (555), a putting off; *athétēsis* (115), a putting away.

1937. ἐπιθυμέω *epithuméō*; contracted *epithumṓ*, fut. *epithumḗso*, from *epí* (1909), in, and *thumós* (2372), the mind. To have the affections directed toward something, to lust, desire, long after. Generally (Luke 17:22; Gal 5:17; Rev 9:6). To desire in a good sense (Matt 13:17; Luke 22:15; 1 Tim 3:1; Heb 6:11; 1 Pet 1:12); as a result of physical needs (Luke 15:16; 16:21); in a bad sense of coveting and lusting after (Matt 5:28; Rom 7:7; 13:9; 1 Cor 10:6 [cf. James 4:2;

Sept.: Ex 20:17; Deut 5:21; 14:26; 2 Sam 3:21; Prov 21:26]).

Deriv.: *epithumētḗs* (1938), one who desires; *epithumía* (1939), desire.

Syn.: *sumpathéō* (4834), to like, sympathize; *agapáō* (25), to love; *homeíromai* or *himeíromai* (2442), to have a strong affection for, yearn after; *orégomai* (3713) or *epipothéō* (1971), to long after; *thélō* (2309), to wish, implying volition and purpose; *boúlomai* (1014), to will deliberately, design; *thélō*; *zēlóō* (2206), to have a zeal for; *aitéō* (154), to ask, desire; *epizētéō* (1934), to seek earnestly; *exaitéomai* (1809), to desire earnestly.

Ant.: *apostréphomai* (654), to turn away from; *pheúgō* (5343), to shun; *miséō* (3404), to hate.

1938. ἐπιθυμητής *epithumētḗs*; gen. *epithumētoú*, masc. noun from *epithuméō* (1937), to desire, lust. One who desires, longs, or craves for something (1 Cor 10:6).

Syn.: *authaíretos* (830), voluntary.

Ant.: *stugnētós* (4767), odious, hateful.

1939. ἐπιθυμία *epithumía*; gen. *epithumías*, fem. noun from *epithuméō* (1937), to desire greatly. Strong desire, longing, lust.

(I) Generally longing (Luke 22:15; Phil 1:23; 1 Thess 2:17; Rev 18:14; Sept.: Prov 10:24; 11:23; Dan 9:23; 10:3, 11).

(II) More frequently in a bad sense, irregular and inordinate desire, appetite, lust.

(A) Generally (Mark 4:19; Rom 6:12; 7:7, 8; 13:14, "for its lusts" [a.t.], i.e., to satisfy the carnal appetites; Col 3:5; 1 Tim 6:9; 2 Tim 3:6; 4:3; Titus 3:3; James 1:14, 15; 1 Pet 1:14; 4:2, 3; 2 Pet 1:4; 3:3; Jude 1:16, 18). The lust of the flesh means carnal desires, appetites (Gal 5:16, 24; Eph 2:3; 2 Pet 2:18; 1 John 2:16). Also *epithumíai sarkikaí* (4559), carnal, fleshly (1 Pet 2:11) referring to worldly desires; desires of the eyes (1 John 2:16); polluted desires (2 Pet 2:10); "lusts of deceit" (a.t.) means "deceitful lusts" (Eph

4:22); "youthful lusts" (2 Tim 2:22); see Sept.: Prov 21:25, 26. All these refer to the desires which are fixed on sensual objects as pleasures, profits, honors.

(B) Spoken of impure desire, lewdness (Rom 1:24; 1 Thess 4:5).

(C) By metonymy, lust, i.e., an object of impure desire, that which is lusted after (John 8:44; 1 John 2:17; Sept.: Dan 11:37).

Syn.: *eudokía* (2107), good pleasure or will; *epipóthēsis* (1972), an earnest desire; *epipothía* (1974), a great desire; *thélēma* (2307), a will; *boúlēma* (1013), desire, purpose; *órexis* (3715), desire of any kind with an evil connotation; *hēdonḗ* (2237), lust, pleasure; *páthēma* (3804), passion.

1940. ἐπικαθίζω *epikathízō*; fut. *epikathísō*, from *epí* (1909), upon, and *kathízō* (2523), to set. To cause to sit upon, to sit upon, used trans. (Matt 21:7; Sept.: 1 Kgs 1:38, 44). Intrans., to sit upon (Sept.: Gen 31:34; Lev 15:20).

Ant.: *egeírō* (1453), to raise up.

1941. ἐπικαλέω *epikaléō*; contracted *epikalṓ*; fut. *epikalésō*, from *epí* (1909), upon, and *kaléō* (2564), to call, to surname. To call upon.

(I) To call upon for aid. In the NT, only in the mid., to call upon for aid in one's own behalf, to invoke, trans.

(A) Particularly of invocation addressed to Christ for aid (Acts 7:59; see Sept.: 1 Sam 12:17, 18; 2 Sam 22:7). Generally, to invoke, pray to, worship, spoken of God (Rom 10:12, 14; 2 Tim 2:22); followed by "the name" (Acts 2:21; 9:14; Rom 10:13; Sept.: Gen 4:26; 26:25; Deut 33:19; Joel 2:32); of Christ, followed by "the name," implying the Lord Jesus Christ (Acts 9:21; 22:16; 1 Cor 1:2).

(B) In adjurations, imprecations, to call upon, invoke, as a witness (2 Cor 1:23).

(C) In a judicial sense, to call upon, invoke a higher tribunal or judge, i.e., to appeal to, e.g., Caesar (Acts 25:11, 12, 25; 26:32; 28:19). Followed by an inf.

(Acts 25:21, "demanding by appeal that" [a.t.]).

(II) To call a name upon, i.e., to name in addition, to surname with a duplicate acc. (Matt 10:25, UBS; Sept.: Num 21:3; Judg 6:32, the simple verb *ekálesen*). In the mid., in 1 Pet 1:17, "if ye call him your Father" (a.t. [cf. Jer 3:19]).

(A) Particularly in Matt 10:3; Luke 22:3; Acts 1:23; 4:36; 10:5, 18, 32; 11:13; 12:12, 25; 15:22; Heb 11:16; Sept.: Dan 10:1; Mal 1:4.

(B) "Upon whom my name is called" (Acts 15:17, i.e., who are called or surnamed by my name, implying property, relation, quoted from Amos 9:12; James 2:7; see 2 Sam 12:28, the simple verb *klēthḗ*, Jer 14:9).

Syn.: *aitéō* (154), to ask, call for; *phōnéō* (5455), to cry out; *krázō* (2896), to call aloud, cry; *kraugázō* (2905), to shout; *onomázō* (3687), to name; *eponomázō* (2028), to surname; *prosagoreúō* (4316), to salute or call upon by name; *prosphōnéō* (4377), to call unto.

1942. ἐπικάλυμμα *epikálumma*; gen. *epikalúmmatos*, neut. noun from *epikalúptō* (1943), to conceal. A covering (Sept.: 2 Sam 17:19). In the NT, metaphorically, a cloak, pretext (1 Pet 2:16).

Syn.: *epíblēma* (1915), a patch; *peribólaion* (4018), something thrown around such as a veil; *sképasma* (4629), a covering in the sense of roofing, something that goes on top; *stégē* (4721), a roof. For the different words meaning garment, see *énduma* (1742), clothing.

Ant.: *apokálupsis* (602), revelation, uncovering.

1943. ἐπικαλύπτω *epikalúptō*; fut. *epikalúpsō*, from *epí* (1909), over, and *kalúptō* (2572), to cover. To cover over (Sept.: Num 4:11). In the NT, metaphorically, to cover over sins, i.e., to forgive, pardon (Rom 4:7 quoted from Ps 32:1).

Deriv.: *epikálumma* (1942), a covering.

1944. ἐπικατάρατος *epikatáratos*; gen. *epikatarátou*, masc.-fem., neut. *epikatáraton*, adj. from *epí* (1909), upon, and *katáratos* (n.f.), cursed. Accursed, under a curse, doomed to punishment (John 7:49; Gal 3:10 quoted from Deut 27:26; Sept.: Gen 9:25; Deut 27:15). Used as a verbal adj. from *epikataráomai*, to lay a curse on with something, one on whom the curse rests or in whom it is realized. See Gal 3:10, 13, which corresponds with being under the curse.

Syn.: *epáratos*, accursed.

Ant.: *makários* (3107), blessed in one's inner self as a result of Christ's action in his life; *eulogētós* (2128), blessed, inherently worthy of praise.

1945. ἐπίκειμαι *epíkeimai*; fut. *epikeísomai*, from *epí* (1909), upon, and *keímai* (2749), to lie on. To rest upon, to be laid upon. Used intrans. (John 11:38; 21:9); metaphorically meaning to be laid upon, imposed upon, e.g., necessity (1 Cor 9:16); by law (Heb 9:10). By implication, to lie heavy upon, press upon with a dat. (Luke 5:1). Of a tempest, used in an absolute sense (Acts 27:20); metaphorically to press upon, be urgent with entreaties, used in an absolute sense (Luke 23:23).

Syn.: *ephístēmi* (2186), to stand by, be present, be at hand; *proskarteréō* (4342), to be prepared; *bállō* (906), to cast; *epipíptō* (1968), to fall upon; *anapíptō* (377), to fall back; *enedreúō* (1748), to lie in wait for; *anákeimai* (345), to recline.

Ant.: *anístēmi* (450), to stand up; *egeírō* (1453), to rise; *aphístēmi* (868), to depart.

1946. Ἐπικούρειος *Epikoúreios*; gen. *Epikoureíou*, masc. noun. An Epicurean, a follower of Epicurus, the Athenian philosopher (Acts 17:18). The Epicureans were a sect of Gentile philosophers founded by Epicurus, 342–271 B.C., who was born on the island of Samos. They were in high repute in Athens during Paul's time (Acts 17:18). Their doctrines held that the world came into being and will be dissolved by chance or by the effect of mechanical causes moved by chance; all events happen by chance or are occasioned by mechanical causes; the soul dies with the body; there is no future retribution; man's chief happiness lies in pleasure or bodily ease. This philosophy obtained a wide popularity in Asia Minor and Rome as well as in the city and land of its originator. It derided the mythology of the ancients but proposed nothing better. It created a frame of mind hostile to all religion, particularly to the serious doctrines of the gospel.

1947. ἐπικουρία *epikouría*; gen. *epikourías*, fem. noun from *epíkouros* (n.f.), one who assists, a helper, especially in war, a military ally. Help (Acts 26:22). *Epíkouroi* were mercenaries helping troops, in contrast to the citizen soldiers who were known as *polítai* (4177).

Syn.: *boḗtheia* (996), help, succor.

1948. ἐπικρίνω *epikrínō*; fut. *epikrinō̄*, from *epí* (1909), besides, moreover, and *krínō* (2919), to judge, decree. To judge, to confirm by a like judgment, adjudicate, with the inf. (Luke 23:24).

1949. ἐπιλαμβάνω *epilambánō*; fut. *epilḗpsō*, from *epí* (1909), upon, and *lambánō* (2983), to take. To take hold upon, lay hold of in order to hold or detain oneself. With a gen. of the part, but also of person where, however, only a part is implied. Sometimes apparently with the acc. which, however, depends more on the force of the subsequent verb (Acts 9:27; 16:19; 18:17). In the NT, only in the mid. *epilambánomai*.

(I) Generally to take hold of, e.g., to take the hand or take by the hand (Mark 8:23; Acts 23:19). Metaphorically (Heb 8:9; Sept.: Jer 31:32; Zech 14:13). Followed by the gen. of person expressed or implied, denoting that some part is laid hold on, e.g., in order to lead, conduct (Luke 9:47; Acts 17:19); with the acc. (Acts 9:27). In order to succor, heal (Matt

14:31; Luke 14:4). With the idea of violence, to lay hold on, to seize by force as a prisoner (Luke 23:26; Acts 21:30, 33); followed by the acc. (Acts 16:19; 18:17; Sept.: Judg 12:6; 16:21, *ekrátēsan* [the aor. of *kratéō* {2902}, to hold]). Figuratively spoken of language, to lay hold on another's words, i.e., to censure (Luke 20:20, 26).

(II) Metaphorically, with a gen., to assume, take upon oneself (Heb 2:16. The Apostle begins the book speaking of angels [Heb 1; 2]. He tells us that when Christ came to redeem us, He did not assume a glorious, awful, and angelic appearance in fire and light, or in clouds of thick darkness, as He did at Sinai [Ex 19:18], but that He took upon Himself human nature as the seed of Abraham [Gal 3:16]. "For even though He was in the form of God, He thought it not robbery to be equal with God, yet He emptied [or stripped] Himself [of His glory], taking upon Himself the form of a servant, being made in the likeness of man" [a.t. {Phil 2:6, 7}]; Sept.: Judg 19:25; Isa 4:1).

(III) Metaphorically, to lay hold of in order to obtain and possess (1 Tim 6:12, 19).

Deriv.: *anepíleptos* (423), blameless.

Syn.: *sullambánō* (4815), to seize; *harpázō* (726), to snatch or catch away; *sunarpázō* (4884), to snatch, seize, keep a firm grip on; *katéchō* (2722), to hold firmly, fast; *kratéō* (2902), to prevail; *tēréō* (5083), to keep; *bastázō* (941), to bear; *epiphérō* (2018), to bring against.

Ant.: *kataleípō* (2641) and *egkataleípō* (1459), to leave behind; *aphíēmi* (863), forsake, leave.

1950. ἐπιλανθάνω *epilanthánō*; fut. *epilḗsō*, 2d aor. *epelathómēn*, from *epí* (1909), in, and *lanthánō* (2990), to lie hidden. To forget, not to remember (Matt 16:5; Mark 8:14; Phil 3:13; James 1:24; Sept.: Gen 40:23); to forget and therefore to neglect (Heb 6:10; 13:2, 16; Sept.: Deut 4:23; 6:12; 2 Kgs 17:38; Ps 119:83); in the perf. pass. part., *epilelēsménos*, meaning forgotten or neglected before

God (Luke 12:6; Sept.: Isa 23:16). It is construed with a gen. and more rarely with an acc. or inf.

Deriv.: *epilēsmoné* (1953), forgetfulness.

Ant.: *mimnḗskō* (3403), to remember.

1951. ἐπιλέγω *epilégō*; fut. *epiléxō*, from *epí* (1909), upon, moreover, and *légō* (3004), to say. To speak or say upon, i.e., moreover, besides, in addition to, hence, to choose either in addition or in succession to another (Acts 15:40, to choose for oneself, with the acc.; Sept.: 2 Sam 10:9, *epeléxato* [the aor. of *epilégomai* {1951}, to select]). To say or speak upon, i.e., by implication, to name, call (John 5:2).

Syn.: *eklégomai* (1586), to select out of; *hairéomai* (138), to choose in preference; *hairetízō* (140), to elect in preference; *kaléō* (2564), to call.

Ant.: *aporríptō* (641), to reject; *periphronéō* (4065), to despise; *kataphronéō* (2706), to disesteem; *apobállō* (577), to throw off; *apōthéō* (683), to push away.

1952. ἐπιλείπω *epileípō*; fut. *epileípsō*, from *epí* (1909), an intens., and *leípō* (3007), to fail. To fail or fail utterly, not to suffice, with the acc. of person (Heb 11:32).

Syn.: *píptō* (4098), to fall; *ekpíptō* (1601), to fall off; *hysteréō* (5302), to fall short; *apopsúchō* (674), to faint.

Ant.: *perisseúō* (4052), to be in excess, abound; *pleonázō* (4121), to have more than enough; *plēthúnō* (4129), to multiply; *huperbállō* (5235), to exceed.

1953. ἐπιλησμονή *epilēsmoné*; gen. *epilēsmonḗs*, fem. noun from *epilanthánō* (1950), to forget. Forgetfulness (James 1:25, "a forgetful hearer").

Syn.: *léthē* (3024), forgetfulness.

Ant.: *anámnēsis* (364), a remembrance; *hupómnēsis* (5280), a reminding; *mneía* (3417), a remembrance, mention, acknowledgement; *mnḗmē* (3420), memory.

1954. ἐπίλοιπος *epíloipos*; gen. *epiloípou*, masc.-fem., neut. *epíloipon*, adj. from *epí* (1909), upon, and *loipós* (3062), remaining. Remaining over as spoken of time (1 Pet 4:2; Sept.: Lev 27:18; Isa 38:10).

1955. ἐπίλυσις *epílusis*; gen. *epilúseōs*, fem. noun from *epilúō* (1956), to solve. Exposition, interpretation. In 2 Pet 1:20, 21, it indicates that no prophecy comes from any private source, referring to the exposition of the will and purposes of God by the prophets themselves. Others refer to this as meaning that no prophecy is capable of private interpretation by the prophets themselves, that they cannot explain their own predictions.
Syn.: *hermēneía* (2058), interpretation.
Ant.: *aporía* (640), perplexity.

1956. ἐπιλύω *epilúō*; fut. *epilúsō*, from *epí* (1909), an intens., and *lúō* (3089), to loose. Literally, to let loose upon. In the NT, to solve, in the sense of to explain, interpret (Mark 4:34), and in the sense of to determine upon a doubtful question (Acts 19:39).
Deriv.: *epílusis* (1955), exposition, interpretation.
Syn.: *krínō* (2919), to resolve; *horízō* (3724), to determine; *ektíthēmi* (1620), to bring out, expound; *diermēneúō* (1329), to interpret fully; *hermēneúō* (2059), to interpret; *katalambánō* (2638), to understand.

1957. ἐπιμαρτυρέω *epimarturéō*; contracted *epimarturṓ*, fut. *epimarturḗsō*, from *epí* (1909), an intens., and *marturéō* (3140), to witness. To testify emphatically, appear as a witness decidedly for something (1 Pet 5:12); also with the conj. *sún* (4862), together, as *sunepimarturéō* (4901), to give additional testimony (Heb 2:4).
Deriv.: *sunepimarturéō* (4901), to bear further witness with someone.

Syn.: *bebaióō* (950), to assure; *kuróō* (2964), to ratify, confirm.
Ant.: *pseudomarturéō* (5577), to give false witness.

1958. ἐπιμέλεια *epiméleia*; gen. *epimeleías*, fem. noun from *epimeléomai* (1959), to attend to, take care of. Care for, attention (Acts 27:3).
Syn.: *mérimna* (3308), care; *spoudḗ* (4710), diligence; *prónoia* (4307), providence, care.

1959. ἐπιμελέομαι *epimeléomai*; contracted *epimeloúmai*, fut. *epimelḗsomai*, mid. deponent from *epí* (1909), upon, and *mélō* (n.f., see *mélei* [3199]), to concern oneself. To have concern for, to take care of or care for, followed by the gen. (Luke 10:34, 35, of the incapacitated; 1 Tim 3:5, of the church; Sept.: Gen 44:21).
Deriv.: *epiméleia* (1958), care.
Syn.: *merimnáō* (3309) and *phrontízō* (5431), to take care of; *episkopéō* (1983), to oversee; *proséchō* (4337), to give heed to.
Ant.: *ameléō* (272), to neglect; *epilanthánomai* (1950), to be forgetful, neglectful; *oligōréō* (3643), to have little regard for, despise.

1960. ἐπιμελῶς *epimelṓs*; adv. from *epimelḗs* (n.f.), careful, which is from *epí* (1909), upon or for, and *mélō* (n.f.), to concern oneself. Carefully, sedulously (Luke 15:8; Sept.: Ezra 6:8, 12, 13), diligently.

1961. ἐπιμένω *epiménō*; fut. *epimenṓ*, aor. *epémeina*, from *epí* (1909), upon, in, or at, and *ménō* (3306), to stay or remain. To remain in addition, longer, to continue, abide in or at a place.
(I) Particularly in a place, followed by *autoú* (847), this, meaning this place or here (Acts 15:34; 21:4); by *en* (1722), in, with the dat. of place or condition (1 Cor 16:8; Phil 1:24); by *epí* (1909), with the dat. of person (Acts 28:14); by *prós* (4314), toward, with the acc. of person (1 Cor 16:7; Gal 1:18). With an acc. of time,

meaning how long (Acts 10:48; 21:10; 28:12, 14; Sept.: Ex 12:39).

(II) Metaphorically, to continue in any state or course, to be constant or persevere in. With the dat., as in the faith (Col 1:23); in grace (Acts 13:43); in sin (Rom 6:1; 11:22, 23); in one's duties (1 Tim 4:16). Followed by a part. (John 8:7; Acts 12:16, "Peter continued knocking").

Syn.: *proskarteréō* (4342), to endure or persevere in; *chronízō* (5549), to delay; *bradúnō* (1019), to stay on; *proskolláō* (4347), to adhere, cleave, join oneself.

Ant.: *metabállō* (3328), to change one's mind or opinion; *metallássō* (3337) or *allássō* (236), to change; *metaméllomai* (3338), to change one's mind, to regret; *metanoéō* (3340), to repent; *methístēmi* (3179), to change one's position; *aparnéomai* (533), to deny.

1962. ἐπινεύω *epineúō*; fut. *epineúsō*, from *epí* (1909), upon or to, and *neúō* (3506), to nod, beckon. To nod or wink upon with assent, to consent. Intrans. (Acts 18:20).

Syn.: *sugkatatíthēmi* (4784), to consent; *súmphēmi* (4852), to speak with or in agreement; *suneudokéō* (4909), to agree with.

Ant.: *arnéomai* (720), to reject; *antitássomai* (498), to oppose, resist; *aporríptō* (641), to cast, reject; *apōthéomai* (683), to reject, cast away; *periphronéō* (4065), to depreciate, despise; *apotrépō* (665), to deflect, avoid; *apophérō* (667), to bear off, carry away; *aparnéomai* (533), to deny, disown; *apotássomai* (657), to renounce, put away from oneself in its proper order.

1963. ἐπίνοια *epínoia*; gen. *epinoías*, fem. noun from *epinoéō* (n.f.), to think upon, from *epí* (1909), upon, and *noús* (3563), mind. A thought, purpose, cogitation (Acts 8:22).

Syn.: *nóēma* (3540), a purpose, device of the mind; *dianóēma* (1270), a plan, machination; *enthúmēsis* (1761), thought, device; *logismós* (3053), thought, imagination; *dialogismós* (1261), reasoning.

1964. ἐπιορκέω *epiorkéō*; contracted *epiorkô̄*, fut. *epiorkḗsō*, from *epíorkos* (1965), a perjured person. To swear falsely, not to fulfill one's oath (Matt 5:33).

Syn.: *athetéō* (114), to disannul, violate; *anairéō* (337), to abolish; *parabiázō* (3849), to go contrary; *pseudomarturéō* (5576), to be a false witness.

Ant.: *alētheúō* (226), to speak the truth.

1965. ἐπίορκος *epíorkos*; gen. *epiórkou*, masc.-fem., neut. *epíorkon*, adj. from *epí* (1909), against, and *hórkos* (3727), an oath. Perjured. Used subst. meaning a perjurer (1 Tim 1:10).

Deriv.: *epiorkéō* (1964), to swear falsely.

Syn.: *pseústēs* (5583), a liar; *pseudḗs* (5571), false; *pseudológos* (5573), one who speaks lies; *pseudomártur* (5575), a false witness.

Ant.: *alēthḗs* (227), true; *apseudḗs* (893), veracious; *eilikrinḗs* (1506), sincere.

1966. ἐπιοῦσα *epioúsa*; fem. sing. part. of *épeimi* (n.f.), which is from *epí* (1909), on, and *eími* (n.f.), to go, with the word day or night understood, referring to the following, the next. The approaching day, the next day. Masc. *epioúsios* (1967), for the coming day, daily. The ensuing day or night (Acts 7:26; 16:11; 20:15; 21:18; 23:11).

Syn.: *kathēmerinós* (2522), daily; *ephḗmeros* (2184), ephemeral, for a day.

Ant.: *katá kairón* (*katá* [2596], a particle of distribution; *kairós* [2540], time, season), at times.

1967. ἐπιούσιος *epioúsios*; gen. *epiousíou*, masc.-fem., neut. *epioúsion*, adj. from *epí* (1909), for or into, and *ousía* (3776), being, substance. Daily, used as an adj. Occurs only in the Lord's Prayer (Matt 6:11; Luke 11:3). The Greek Church Father, Chrysostom, explains the *epioúsion árton* (740) as that bread which is needed for our daily support of life. It is that bread which is needful to the *ousía*, substance, of our being, that will sustain us. Other interpreters derive it from *epioúsa* (1966), the next, fem. referring to *hēméra* (2250), day, but in the masc. for *ártos* (740), bread, bread for the coming day.

Syn.: *ephḗmeros* (2184), for the day; *kathēmerinós* (2522), daily; *kath' hēméran*, according to or for the day; *hēméra kaí hēméra*, literally day and day, day by day; *hēméran ex hēméras*, literally day from day, from day to day; *sémeron* (4594), today, this day; *tēs sémeron hēméras*, unto this very day; *tás hēméras*, every day, in the daytime; *pásan hēméran*, every day; *kath' hekástēn hēméran*, literally according to each day, day by day.

Ant.: *aiṓnios* (166), eternal, forever.

1968. ἐπιπίπτω *epipíptō*; fut. *epipesoúmai*, 2d aor. *epépeson*, perf. *epipéptōka*, from *epí* (1909), upon, and *píptō* (4098), to fall. To fall upon.

(I) To fall upon. In the NT, used only in respect to persons. To throw oneself upon, followed by a dat. (Acts 20:10 [cf. 1 Kgs 7:21; 2 Kgs 4:34ff.]); by the prep. *epí* (1909) with the acc. (Luke 15:20, meaning he embraced him; Acts 20:37; Sept.: Gen 46:29; 50:1). In John 13:25, "throwing himself back on Jesus' breast as he reclined at the table" (a.t.); followed by a dat. in the same sense as to rush or to press upon (Mark 3:10).

(II) Metaphorically, to fall upon, to come upon or over someone followed by *epí* with the acc. of person referring to fear (Luke 1:12; Acts 19:17; Sept.: Ex 15:16); ecstasy (Acts 10:10; Sept.: Dan 10:7); a mist (Acts 13:11); reproaches (Rom 15:3 [cf. Ps 69:10]). Spoken of the Spirit, meaning to descend upon someone (Acts 8:16; 10:44; 11:15).

1969. ἐπιπλήσσω *epiplḗssō*, **ἐπιπλήττω** *epiplḗttō*; fut. *epiplēxō*, from *epí* (1909), upon, and *plḗssō* (4141), to strike. To strike or give blows upon, to beat. In the NT, used only metaphorically,

followed by the dat., meaning to chide, rebuke (1 Tim 5:1).

Syn.: *epitimáō* (2008), to rebuke; *elégchō* (1651), to convict.

Ant.: *ainéō* (134), to speak in praise of.

1970. ἐπιπνίγω *epipnígō*; fut. *epipníxō*, from *epí* (1909), upon, and *pnígō* (4155), to choke. To choke upon, strangle, in some MSS of Luke 8:7.

1971. ἐπιποθέω *epipothéō*; contracted *epipothṓ*, fut. *epipothḗsō*, from *epí* (1909), an intens., and *pothéō* (n.f.), to yearn. To desire earnestly, long for, followed by the inf. (Rom 1:11; 2 Cor 5:2; 1 Thess 3:6; 2 Tim 1:4); by the acc. of thing (1 Pet 2:2; Sept.: Ps 119:174; Mic 7:1); by the acc. of person meaning to long after, regard with longing, love (2 Cor 9:14; Phil 1:8; 2:26); by *prós*, to incline towards, tend to (James 4:5).

Deriv.: *epipóthēsis* (1972), earnest desire; *epipóthetos* (1973), greatly desired or loved; *epipothía* (1974), great desire.

Syn.: *epithuméō* (1937), to desire greatly.

Ant.: *ameléō* (272), to neglect.

1972. ἐπιπόθησις *epipóthēsis*; gen. *epipothḗseōs*, fem. noun from *epipothéō* (1971), to desire earnestly. Earnest desire, strong affection (2 Cor 7:7, 11).

Syn.: *epithumía* (1939), a desire, craving, longing; *eudokía* (2107), goodwill; *thélēma* (2307), will, pleasure; *boúlēma* (1013), desire, will; *órexis* (3715), longing after; *euchḗ* (2171), vow, wish.

Ant.: *epilēsmonḗ* (1953), negligence, forgetfulness; *léthē* (3024), forgetfulness.

1973. ἐπιπόθητος *epipóthetos*; gen. *epipothḗtou*, masc.-fem., neut. *epipóthēton*, adj. from *epipothéō* (1971), to desire earnestly. Much desired, longed for (Phil 4:1).

1974. ἐπιποθία *epipothía*; gen. *epipothías*, fem. noun from *epipothéō*

(1971), to desire earnestly. Earnest desire (Rom 15:23), the same as *epipóthēsis* (1972), an earnest desire.

1975. ἐπιπορεύομαι *epiporeúomai*; fut. *epiporeúsomai*, mid. deponent from *epí* (1909), upon or to, and *poreúomai* (4198), to go, come. To go or come upon a place or person (Luke 8:4; Sept.: Ezek 39:14).

1976. ἐπιρράπτω *epirráptō*; fut. *epirrápsō*, from *epí* (1909), upon, and *rháptō* (n.f.), to sew. To sew upon (Mark 2:21). Also from *rháptō* (n.f.): *árraphos* (729), without seam.

1977. ἐπιρρίπτω *epirríptō*; fut. *epirrípsō*, from *epí* (1909), upon, and *rhíptō* (4496), to cast. To throw or cast upon, used trans., followed by *epí* with the acc. (Luke 19:35 [cf. Matt 21:7; Mark 11:7]; Sept.: Num 35:20; Ezek 43:24). Figuratively, in regard to concern or care, to cast off upon in filial confidence (1 Pet 5:7 quoted from Ps 55:22).

1978. ἐπίσημος *epísēmos*; gen. *episḗmou*, masc.-fem., neut. *epísēmon*, adj. from *epí* (1909), upon, for, and *sḗma* (n.f., see *ásēmos* [767]), a mark or sign. Having a mark upon, as spoken of money meaning stamped, coined. In the NT, figuratively, it signifies, in a good sense, being well-thought-of, distinguished, eminent (Rom 16:7); in a bad sense, notorious (Matt 27:16).

Syn.: *gnōstós* (1110), known, notable; *epiphanḗs* (2016), illustrious, renowned; *ischurós* (2478), powerful, mighty.

Ant.: *idiótēs* (2399), a private person in contrast to a state official; *agrámmatos* (62), unlettered; *amathḗs* (261), ignorant; *apaídeutos* (521), uninstructed.

1979. ἐπισιτισμός *episitismós*; gen. *episitismoú*, masc. noun from *episitízō* (n.f.), to give food, to feed. Food supply, provisions, victuals (Luke 9:12).

1980. ἐπισκέπτομαι *episképtomai*; fut. *episképsomai*, mid. deponent from *epí* (1909), upon, and *sképtomai* (n.f.), to look. To look at something, examine closely, inspect, observe.

(**I**) To look upon with mercy, favor, regard (Luke 1:68, 78; 7:16; Acts 15:14; Heb 2:6 quoted from Ps 8:5; see Gen 50:24, 25; Ps 106:4).

(**II**) To visit in order to punish (Sept.: Ps 89:32).

(**III**) To look after, with the acc., take care of, tend (Acts 7:23; 15:36; Sept.: Judg 15:1). Frequently used in the Class. Gr. for taking care of or nursing the sick (Matt 25: 36, 43; James 1:27)

(**IV**) To look at accurately or diligently with the meaning to look for, seek out, as persons for office, trans. (Acts 6:3; Sept.: Lev 13:36; Ezra 6:1; Ezek 20:40).

Syn.: *historéō* (2477), to visit, in order to be acquainted with; *epiphérō* (2018), to bear upon, add, bring against.

Ant.: *lanthánō* (2990), to forget willfully; *epilanthánomai* (1950), to forget, neglect; *eklanthánomai* (1585), to forget completely; *ameléō* (272), to neglect; *kataphronéō* (2706), to despise; *periphronéō* (4065), to depreciate.

1981. ἐπισκηνόω *episkēnóō*; contracted *episkēnṓ*, fut. *episkēnṓso*, from *epí* (1909), in, and *skēnóō* (4637), to pitch a tent, to dwell. To descend and abide upon, rest upon, or live in, abide, dwell (2 Cor 12:9). For additional syn. and ant., see *episképtomai* (1980), to visit favorably; *stégō* (4722), to provide a roof over; *episkiázō* (1982), to overshadow.

1982. ἐπισκιάζω *episkiázō*; fut. *episkiásō*, from *epí* (1909), upon or over, and *skiázō* (n.f., see *aposkíasma* [644]), to shade. To cast a shadow upon, to overshadow, with the acc. (Matt 17:5; Luke 9:34); with the dat. (Mark 9:7; Acts 5:15; Sept.: Ps 91:4; see Ex 40:35). Spoken of a divine power and influence, to overshadow, rest upon (Luke 1:35).

Syn.: *kataskiázō* (2683), to shadow or overshadow; *skotízō* (4654), to darken.

1983. ἐπισκοπέω *episkopéō*; contracted *episkopṓ*, fut. *episkopḗsō*, from *epí* (1909), upon, and *skopéō* (4648), to regard, give attention to. To look upon, observe, examine the state of affairs of something, look after, oversee. In the NT, used in Heb 12:15; 1 Pet 5:2 of the work of shepherding the flock (Sept.: Deut 11:12).
Deriv.: *episkopḗ* (1984), the office of a bishop.
Syn.: *poimaínō* (4165), to shepherd, tend a flock; *bóskō* (1006), to lead to pasture, fodder; *epimeléomai* (1959), to show concern over; *merimnáō* (3309) to be concerned.
Ant.: *ameléō* (272), to neglect.

1984. ἐπισκοπή *episkopḗ*; gen. *episkopḗs*, fem. noun from *episkopéō* (1983), to look after. Visitation, or the public office of an overseer (*epískopos* [1985]). The act of visiting or being visited, inspected. In the NT, metaphorically, of God, who is said to visit men for good, equal to *episképtomai* (1980), to visit upon, consider, examine, and provide covering for (Luke 19:44, "the time when God visited thee" [a.t.], i.e., was present to favor thee; 1 Pet 2:12; Sept.: Job 10:12; 34:9). To visit for evil in order to punish (Sept.: Ex 13:19; Isa 10:3; Jer 10:15). Also used of the office, charge or duty of an overseer in Christ's church (Acts 1:20 quoted from Ps 109:8; 1 Tim 3:1, "the office of a bishop," i.e., the care and oversight of a Christian church; Sept.: Num 4:16; Neh 11:9, *epískopos*).

1985. ἐπίσκοπος *epískopos*; gen. *episkópou*, masc. noun from *epí* (1909), upon, and *skopós* (4649), a watchman. Superintendent, overseer. The overseer of public works (Sept.: 2 Chr 34:12, 17); of cities, e.g., a prefect (Isa 60:17). In Athens *epískopoi* (pl.) were magistrates sent to outlying cities to organize and govern them. In the NT, used of officers in the local churches, overseers, superintendents. The *epískopoi* (Acts 20:28), are charged with exercising watchful care over God's church (cf. 1 Pet 5:2). In Phil 1:1 the title "elders" (*presbúteroi* [4245]), is used in place of *epískopoi* and are mentioned along with the deacons (*diákonoi* [1249]). In 1 Tim 3:2 and Titus 1:5, 7, an elder denotes the dignity of the office, and *epískopos*, bishop or overseer, denotes its authority and duties (cf. 1 Pet 2:25; 5:1, 2, 4).

In the NT, bishop (*epískopos*) and elder (*presbúteros*) are two names for the same official, which implies that the official function of episcopacy or eldership existed from NT times (see Acts 20:17, 28). Bishops and elders are never joined together in contrast to bishops and deacons, which are separate classes of officials. In Phil 1:1, the translation uses the def. art. before bishops and deacons, but in Gr. there is no art.: "To all the saints in Christ Jesus which are at Philippi, with bishops and deacons." Reference is made here to those saints who were functioning as overseers (bishops) and those who were functioning as servants (deacons). If elders were a separate order of individuals governing the local church, why would they be left out? 1 Timothy refers to bishops and deacons (1 Tim 3:2, 8), giving the qualifications of both. It makes no mention of elders, even though 1 Tim 5:17 expressly refers to them, indicating that there certainly were elders at Ephesus (who had been there according to Acts 20:17 for some time). In Titus 1:5, we have elders, but Paul continues to describe the characteristics of an elder by referring to a bishop (v. 7). The bishops described to Timothy (1 Tim 3:2), the elders of 1 Tim 5:17, and those of 1 Pet 5:2, have the same pastoral functions as the elders of Acts 20:17 (cf. v. 28, where they are called bishops). Similarly, in Titus 1:5, the elders are used syn. with the bishops as being engaged in the pastoral duty of teaching (v. 9). It is evident that same persons are called bishops and elders (Acts 20:17, 28; Titus 1:5, 7). As we have already pointed out, an elder denotes the dignity of the office, and a bishop (or overseer) denotes the duties and authority of the office.

The Apostles did not introduce distinct officials to be their successors, such as bishops. Churches were governed by a council of elders. In Titus 1:5, it is apparent that the Apostle Paul left Titus in Crete as a nonresident apostolic delegate to set in order things that were amiss. For the prominent and local administration of the church on the island of Crete, Paul asks Titus to appoint elders in every city. In this verse, the word translated "ordain" is *katastésēs*, the aor. subjunctive of *kathístēmi* (2525), to constitute, designate, appoint. He was not acting as a bishop but as an apostolic delegate appointing elders who in verse seven are called bishops. These bishops were elders of local churches who together comprised presbyteries (*presbutérion* [4244], council of elders) each superintending area churches.

The term bishop denotes a superior or inspector, but tells us nothing of what he supervises or inspects. It may be buildings, or business, or men. In the NT, it means an overseer of men in reference to their spiritual life, and is closely connected with the idea of shepherding. 1 Pet 2:25 refers to Jesus Christ as "the Shepherd and Bishop of your souls." This indicates that He who is the shepherd is also the overseer of the entire flock. To the elders of the church of Ephesus (Acts 20:17), Paul commands "Take heed therefore unto yourselves, and to all the flock [*poímnion* {4168}], over the which the Holy Ghost hath made you overseers [*episkópous*] to feed [*poimaínei*, aor. act. inf. of *poimaínō* {4165}, to shepherd] the church of God, which he hath purchased with his own blood" (v. 28).

Only once in the NT is shepherd or pastor [*poimḗn* {4166}] used of Christian ministers (Eph 4:11), and it is in conjunction with teachers. (The expression "pastors and teachers" is governed by one article and probably represents a single class of people, teachers, of which pastors are a sub-class.) The word "pastor," however, is used of Christ (Heb 13:20; 1 Pet 2:25; 5:4 [cf. John 10:11, 14]). The term *epískopos*, overseer or bishop, having been used of Christ as "the overseer of souls," would be naturally used of those of His ministers who in a special way continued in this work; and it is more probable that the Christian use of the title arose in this way rather than being adopted in imitation of the secular *epískopos* in a city.

Neither bishops, elders, nor deacons appear in the lists of ministers and ministerial gifts in Rom 12:6–8; Eph 4:11, or 1 Cor 12:28–30. This, however, does not prove that Paul did not know or care about such officials. Where such officials existed, they were as yet only local ministers, and there was no need to mention them in speaking of gifts to the church as a whole.

Timothy and Titus were not appointed monarchical bishops. They were temporary delegates or representatives of Paul in Ephesus or in Crete. They were forerunners of the monarchical bishops, not the first examples of them.

Neither is it probable that the "angels" of the Seven Churches (Rev 1—3) be regarded as the bishops of those churches.

That James was the monarchical bishop of the church in Jerusalem is mere conjecture, as is also true of the elder in the epistle of 3 John. There is no instance of the monarchical episcopate in the NT. It was established in Asia Minor before A.D. 100 and had become widespread in Christendom by A.D. 150. Furthermore, it has no basis in the teaching or the practice of the early church.

Since bishops and elders have the same referent, the ordination of one applies to the other. In Acts 14:23 we find that it was the Apostles themselves who ordained (*cheirotonéō* [5500], laying on or stretching hands over) elders in each church. The elders in Crete were appointed by Titus (Titus 1:5), and, apparently, the bishops at Ephesus by Timothy in like manner, though 1 Tim 5:22 does not seem to be especially concerned with the matter. They were formally instituted at the designation of the apostolic delegates without necessarily excluding popular confirmation. The elders were already attached to the Apostle, even in the conveyance of special gifts. Paul thus writes to Timothy, "Neglect not the gift that is in thee, which was given thee by [diá {1223}, through] prophecy [i.e., authoritative declaration], with [metá {3326}, accompanied by] the laying on of the hands of the presbytery" (1 Tim 4:14). 2 Tim 1:6 refers to the gift of God in Timothy and speaks of it as being in him "by the putting on of my hands." Here the prep. is diá, through, as in 1 Tim 4:14. This was the primary ordination of Timothy by the Apostle Paul. When, however, the nonlocal ministry of such men as Timothy and Titus died out, the local council of elders, the presbytery, would act alone in the institution of local elders or bishops and also deacons. The biblical evidence is that in the institution of local officers of a church, there was first designation and then institution by prayer with its symbolic accompaniments of laying on of hands and fasting. Thus, the local function was by popular election while the nonlocal function, such as that held by Barnabas and Paul, was purely by the will of the Holy Spirit as indicated by Acts 13:2, "As they ministered to the Lord, and fasted, the Holy Ghost said, Separate me Barnabas and Saul for the work whereunto I have called them."

The duties of elders and bishops:

(I) General superintendents. In Acts 20:28, referring to the elders of verse seventeen and to the bishops of verse twenty-eight, Paul says, "Take heed therefore unto yourselves, and to all the flock." This indicates a mutual superintendence among the elders and an overseeing of the entire flock. The word here is poímnion (4168), the entire group of believers. What follows in this verse indicates the supremacy of the call of the Holy

Spirit to such an office, "over the which the Holy Ghost hath made you overseers, to feed the church of God, which he hath purchased with his own blood." The verb translated "hath made you" is étheto, 2d aor. mid. indic. 3d person of títhēmi (5087), to place, set. Above everything, it was the Holy Spirit, not the church, placing these men into office. Their duty was the general care of the flock, especially, though not exclusively, teaching the word of God. While elders must be apt to teach, not all will do this as their primary ministry. There seems to be a distinction made in favor of those elders who labor in word and teaching as expressed in 1 Tim 5:17, "Let the elders that rule well be counted worthy of double honor, especially they who labor in the word and doctrine." That which is translated "that rule well" is proestótes, perf. part. of proḯstēmi (4291), to stand before. These have earned this position of standing over others because of their teaching. The part. indicates that these are not new elders, but those who have been in good standing for some time and have distinguished themselves by their example and teaching. Such deserve double honor. This has reference to any elder who exercises any duty, even other than that of the teaching and the ministry of the word, of which ample evidence is given to us by the word málista (3122), especially. There may be elders who have excelled among other elders in services other than the ministry of the word, but those who labor in the word especially deserve or are counted worthy of double honor. Undoubtedly, reference is here to the teaching elders with the expression "they who labor in the word and doctrine." The exact translation is, "Those who are laboring in word [perhaps gospel preaching, evangelism] and teaching [catechizing, expositing]." (a.t.) In Titus 1:9, the work of the bishop is designated as holding fast the faithful or trustworthy word according to the accepted doctrine. The bishop is described as a man who can refute false doctrine and exhort or comfort (*parakaléō* [3870]) through the teaching of sound doctrine even those who are opposed to that doctrine. He is a man who must reprove those who speak in contradiction to sound doctrine. In 1 Pet 5:2, the command is "feed the flock." The word is *poimánate*, aor. imper. of *poimaínō* (4165), to shepherd, pastor. It takes in all the activities of shepherding and especially feeding (*bóskō* [1006]) the flock. The elders are to give all-around care for the flock as well as to teach them. In 1 Tim 3:5, we read, "For if a man know not how to rule his own house, how shall he take care of the church of God?" The verb translated "rule" in this verse, as well as in 1 Tim 3:4, is *proḯstēmi* (4291), to lead, rule. In 1 Tim 3:3, the bishop is said to rule over his family well, and that manner of rulership is understood in verse five. The word which is translated "take care of" is *epimelḗsetai*, fut. of *epimeléomai* (1959), to show concern over. This word indicates a general care of the church of God and not simply preaching.

1 Cor 12:28 uses two words which indicate two of the gifts which are necessary in a local church, namely *kubernḗseis* (pl. of *kubérnēsis* [2941]), governments, and *antilḗmpseis* (pl. of *antílēmpsis* [484]), helps, which must refer to the functions of local elders. In Eph 4:11, we find that the Lord Jesus also gave the gifts of pastors and teachers which means pastors whose ability and special function is to preach. These can do the best job of preaching and teaching only if there are other elders in the local congregation who fill the other functions which meet the variety of needs of the flock. In 1 Thess 5:12, Paul asks that those who labor and rule in the Lord must be loved especially for their work. In Rom 12:6–8, Paul gives the different ministries for which the gifts are given and one of them is that of teaching. In Heb 13:7, 17, 24, they are called *hēgoúmenoi* (pres. part. of *hēgéomai* [2233], to lead), leaders. Thus the elders or bishops must have leadership gifts. In Acts 15:6, we find that the Apostles (the nonlocal leaders) and the elders gathered

together to discuss the teaching of those who taught the heresy of the Pharisees, demanding that believers be circumcised. When Paul and others were received in Jerusalem, it was not only by James but also by all the elders (Acts 21:18). The cooperation of the elders with the apostles is also indicated in 1 Tim 4:14.

(II) A distinct function of bishops or elders is teaching: "apt to teach" or capable of teaching (1 Tim 3:2); "they who labor in the word and doctrine" (1 Tim 5:17). Titus 1:9 refers to both teaching and counseling as well as exhortation.

(III) Pastoral care. This includes visiting the sick (James 5:14) and offering hospitality and caring for the poor (1 Tim 3:2; Titus 1:8).

Deriv.: *allotrioepískopos* (244), a busybody.

Syn.: *presbúteros* (4245), elder; *poimḗn* (4166), shepherd; *diákonos* (1249), minister.

1986. ἐπισπάω *epispáō*; contracted *epispṓ*, fut. *epispásō*, from *epí* (1909), over, and *spáō* (4685), to draw. In the NT, only in the mid., *epispáomai*, to draw upon or over oneself, to draw the foreskin over again (1 Cor 7:18, meaning let him not become as if uncircumcised). The allusion is to a mode of removing the mark of circumcision, apparently practiced by Jews who abandoned their religion and national customs.

Ant.: *peritémnō* (4061), to circumcise.

1987. ἐπίσταμαι *epístamai*; fut. *epistḗsomai*, from *epí* (1909), over, and *hístēmi* (2476), to stand. To fix one's mind upon, to understand, know how.

(I) To know well, followed by the acc. of thing (Acts 18:25); of person (Acts 19:15; Sept.: Deut 28:36); followed by the acc. and part. (Acts 24:10); followed by *hós* (5613) (Acts 10:28), *hóti* (3754) (Acts 15:7; 19:25; 22:19; Sept.: Josh 2:9), *pós* (4459) (Acts 20:18).

(II) In the sense of to understand, comprehend, with the acc. (Mark 14:68; 1 Tim 6:4; James 4:14; Jude 1:10).

Deriv.: *epistḗmōn* (1990), intelligent, scientist.

Syn.: *epiginṓskō* (1921), to fully perceive, discern, recognize; *suníēmi* (4920), to perceive; *noéō* (3539), to understand; *ginṓskō* (1097), to know; *gnōrízō* (1107), to make known.

Ant.: *agnoéō* (50), to be ignorant.

1988. ἐπιστάτης *epistátēs*; masc. noun from *ephístamai*, mid. of *ephístēmi* (2186), to stand over. One set over, a prefect, master, as a king, a commander of a ship, military officer (Sept.: 2 Kgs 25:19), a director in gymnastics or of public works. In the NT, only in Luke and addressed in the vocative to Jesus, "Master," as having the authority of a teacher or rabbi among His disciples.

Syn.: *Kúrios* (2962), Lord; *didáskalos* (1320), teacher; *despótēs* (1203), despot or absolute ruler; *rhabbí* (4461), an Aramaic word meaning master, a title of respectful address to Jewish teachers; *kathēgētḗ* (2519), a teacher or one who guides or leads; *kubernḗtēs* (2942), pilot, helmsman or governor of a ship.

1989. ἐπιστέλλω *epistéllō*; fut. *epistelṓ*, from *epí* (1909), to, and *stéllō* (4724), to send. To send upon, send to, meaning to send word to someone verbally or by letter. In the NT, to send word by letter, give direction by letter (Acts 21:25); with the dat. (Acts 15:20); in later usage, simply to send a letter or write to, followed by the dat. (Heb 13:22).

Deriv.: *epistolḗ* (1992), epistle, letter.

1990. ἐπιστήμων *epistḗmōn*; gen. *epistḗmonos*, masc.-fem., neut. *epístēmon*, adj. from *epístamai* (1987), to know thoroughly, understand. Endued with knowledge, understanding, expertise (James 3:13; Sept.: Deut 1:13; 4:6), the equivalent to the Eng. "scientist."

Syn.: *gnṓstēs* (1109), one who knows, an expert.

Ant.: *idiṓtēs* (2399), a person without professional knowledge, an unskilled, unlearned person; *agrámmatos* (62) or *amathḗs* (261), unlearned; *apaídeutos* (521), uninstructed.

1991. ἐπιστηρίζω *epistērízō*; fut. *epistēríxō*, from *epí* (1909), an intens., and *stērízō* (4741), to strengthen, support. Literally, to place firmly upon. In the mid. / pass., to rest or lean upon, be supported on (Sept.: 2 Sam 1:6; Isa 36:6). In the NT, to confirm, establish, trans. (Acts 14:22; 15:32, 41; 18:23).

1992. ἐπιστολή *epistolḗ*; gen. *epistolḗs*, fem. noun from *epistéllō* (1989), to send a letter or to enjoin by writing. An epistle or letter (Acts 15:30; 23:25, 33; Rom 16:22; 1 Cor 5:9; 16:3; 2 Cor 3:1; 7:8; 10:9–11; Col 4:16; 1 Thess 5:27; 2 Thess 2:2, 15; 3:14, 17; 2 Pet 3:1, 16). Used metaphorically (2 Cor 3:2, 3; Sept.: Ezra 4:8, 11; Neh 6:5, 17). By implication, meaning letter of authority, dispatch (Acts 9:2; 22:5; Sept.: Neh 2:7, 8).

1993. ἐπιστομίζω *epistomízō*; fut. *epistomísō*, from *epí* (1909), upon, and *stóma* (4750), mouth. To muzzle, stop the mouth, check, curb, put to silence, with the acc. (Titus 1:11).

Syn.: *phrássō* (5420), to fence, close, stop; *sunéchō* (4912), to hold together, stop which implies the ears; *phimóō* (5392), to close the mouth with a muzzle; *sigáō* (4601), to silence.

1994. ἐπιστρέφω *epistréphō*; fut. *epistrépsō*, 2d aor. pass. *epestráphēn*, with mid. meaning, from *epí* (1909), to, and *stréphō* (4762), to turn. To turn upon, toward.

(I) Trans., in a moral sense, to turn upon or convert unto (Luke 1:16, 17; Sept.: Ezra 6:22 [cf. Mal 4:5 where is found the verb *apokatastései* {the fut. of *apokathístēmi* (600), to restore}]). In the sense of to turn back again upon, to cause to return from error, with *epí* (1909) and the acc. implied (James 5:19, 20; Sept.: 1 Kgs 13:18–20).

(II) Intrans., and also in the mid., to turn oneself upon or toward, i.e., to turn toward or unto.

(A) Act. intrans. (Acts 9:40) (1) Figuratively, to turn to the service and worship of the true God (Acts 9:35; 11:21; 14:15; 15:19; 26:18, 20); to the Lord (2 Cor 3:16; 1 Thess 1:9); to the shepherd (1 Pet 2:25; Sept.: Gen 24:49; Deut 31:18, where is found the verb *apostréphō* [654], to turn away; Josh 19:34; 1 Chr 12:19; Hos 5:4; Amos 4:6, 8). (2) By implication, to turn about, upon or toward (Rev 1:12). Used in an absolute sense (Acts 16:18; Sept.: Judg 18:21). (3) To turn back upon, return unto, and followed by *opísō* (3694), back (Matt 24:18); *eis tá opísō*, backward (Mark 13:16; Luke 17:31); by *eis* (1519), unto, with the acc. (Matt 12:44); by *epí* (1909), upon, with the acc. (Luke 17:4; 2 Pet 2:22). Used in an absolute sense (Luke 2:20 [TR]; Acts 15:36). Of the breath or spirit returning to a dead body (Luke 8:55; Sept.: Ruth 1:7, 10; 2 Sam 6:20; 1 Kgs 2:30). Metaphorically spoken of a return to good, to return, be converted, used in an absolute sense (Luke 22:32; Acts 3:19; also Matt 13:15; Mark 4:12; Acts 28:27, all quoted from Isa 6:10); also to turn back unto evil (Gal 4:9; 2 Pet 2:21).

(B) Mid., intrans., with 2d aor. pass., *epestráphēn*. (1) By implication, to turn about, upon or toward (Matt 9:22; Mark 8:33; John 21:20); by *en* (1722), in (Mark 5:30; Sept.: Num 23:5). (2) To turn back upon, return unto (Matt 10:13; Sept.: Ruth 1:11, 12, 15). Metaphorically, to return to good, be converted (John 12:40 [cf. Isa 6:10]).

(III) The word commonly translated "convert" and "conversion" in the NT occurs as follows: the noun *epistrophé* only occurs once (Acts 15:3), but the verb is comparatively frequent as in Acts 3:19; 9:35; 26:18; 2 Cor 3:16; 1 Thess 1:9; 1 Pet 2:25. The aor. tense is used most often characterizing the action as definite and punctiliar (though in no way denying the continuity of the action Acts 14:15; 15:19; Gal 4:9 in contrast to Acts 3:19; 26:18; 2 Cor 3:16; James 5:19). The verb is used once in Gal 4:9 and twice in single passages (2 Pet 2:21, 22 quoting Prov 26:11) of perversion. The question that arises is whether man turns to God or God turns man to Himself. Where the verb is not trans., the subj. is a man (James 5:19, 20, and perhaps Acts 26:18). But it is impossible to deny the action of God in the process (Rom 11:30; Eph 2:5; Col 2:13; Titus 3:5; Heb 10:32; 1 Pet 1:3) or the connection between conversion and salvation (Rom 10:13; 1 Cor 1:21). The relationship of the action of God and of man in conversion is not a case of "either/or." Regeneration is wholly an act of God whereby the principle of spiritual life is imparted to man bringing him under the dominion of righteousness. Conversion is the human response of faith and repentance issuing forth from this new condition. Thus, conversion is both an act of God and man. Man cooperates because he has been made willing and able by divine grace. Exhorting the sinner, the preacher will say, "Turn to God"; looking back on the act, the sinner will say, "God turned me to Himself." Conversion and repentance are mentioned together twice (Acts 3:19; 26:20). Repentance comes first in both cases.

Deriv.: *epistrophé* (1995), conversion.

Syn.: *epanérchomai* (1880), to come back again; *anakámptō* (344), to return; *metastréphō* (3344), to change into something different.

Ant.: *apérchomai* (565) or *ápeimi* (548), to go away; *éxeimi* (1826) or *exérchomai* (1831), to go out; *ekklínō* (1578), to turn away; *apolúō* (630), to dismiss; *analúō* (360), to depart; *apostréphō* (654) or *apotrépō* (665), to cause to turn away; *ektrépō* (1624), to cause to turn aside.

1995. ἐπιστροφή *epistrophé*; gen. *epistrophḗs*, fem. noun from *epistréphō* (1994), to turn about. A turning around, conversion. Occurs only in Acts 15:3. It is the human side of God's redemption of sinful man.

1996. ἐπισυνάγω *episunágō*; fut. *episunáxō*, from *epí* (1909), upon, and *sunágō* (4863), to gather. To lead or bring together upon a place, to gather together, assemble. Trans. (Matt 23:37; 24:31; Mark 1:33; 13:27; Luke 12:1; 13:34; Sept.: 1 Kgs 18:20; 2 Chr 20:26; Isa 52:12; Zech 14:2).

Deriv.: *episunagōgḗ* (1997), assembling.

1997. ἐπισυναγωγή *episunagōgḗ*; gen. *episunagōgḗs*, fem. noun from *episunágō* (1996), to gather together. The act of gathering or assembling together (2 Thess 2:1 [cf. 1 Thess 4:17]). Heb 10:25 does not merely denote the assembling for corporate worship as a solitary or occasional act, but as customary conduct. The prep. *epí* (1909), to, must refer to Christ Himself as the one to whom this assembly was attached. Thus it would have the meaning of not betraying one's attachment to Jesus Christ and other believers, not avoiding one's own personal responsibility as part of the body of Christ.

Syn.: *sunagōgḗ* (4864), a gathering of Jews for worship, a synagogue; *ekklēsía* (1577), an assembly, church; *sunédrion* (4892), a council; *panḗguris* (3831), a festive assembly; *sunodía* (4923), synod, companionship on a journey.

Ant.: *egkataleípō* (1459), to desert or leave stranded, to abandon. It refers rather to the separating of oneself from the local Christian community (often because of the dread of persecution).

1998. ἐπισυντρέχω *episuntréchō*; fut. *episunthréchomai*, from *epí* (1909), upon or to, and *suntréchō* (4936), to run together. To run together to the scene of any action (Mark 9:25).

Syn.: *boēthéō* (997), to help; *sumpáreimi* (4840), to make oneself available; *enischúō* (1765), to strengthen; *suntugchánō* (4940), to chance togeth-

er, come at; *tugchánō* (5177), to chance upon.

Ant.: *anakóptō* (348), to hinder; *phrássō* (5420), to block up; *anastréphō* (390), to overthrow; *mataióō* (3154), to cancel out; *kōlúō* (2967), to forbid, hinder; *kolobóō* (2856), to abridge, shorten.

1999. ἐπισύστασις *episústasis*; gen. *episustáseōs*, fem. noun from *episunístēmi* (n.f.), to come together upon, which is from *epí* (1909), an intens., and *sunístēmi* (4921), to approve. Uprising, disturbance; occurs only in a hostile sense in Acts 24:12 (TR) and 2 Cor 11:28, referring to all the opposition that the Apostle Paul had to encounter. See Sept.: Num 16:40.

Syn.: *próskomma* (4348), stumbling; *proskopḗ* (4349), offense; *phragmós* (5418), a barrier.

Ant.: *boḗtheia* (996), a help; *epikouría* (1947), assistance.

2000. ἐπισφαλής *episphalḗs*; gen. *episphaloús*, masc.-fem., neut. *episphalés*, adj. from *epí* (1909), for, and *sphállō* (n.f.), to supplant, throw down. Literally, near to falling, ready to fall, not firm, insecure, dangerous (Acts 27:9). Also from *sphállō* (n.f.): *asphalḗs* (804), firm, sure.

Ant.: *asphalḗs* (804), without falling, safe, sure; *bébaios* (949), stable; *hedraíos* (1476), steadfast.

2001. ἐπισχύω *epischúō*; fut. *epischúsō*, from *epí* (1909), an intens., and *ischúō* (2480), to be strong. To give additional strength, used intrans. meaning to be stronger, grow stronger; figuratively, to be more violent, grow more fierce (Luke 23:5).

Syn.: *enischúō* (1765), to strengthen more.

Ant.: *asthenéō* (770), to be weak.

2002. ἐπισωρεύω *episōreúō*; fut. *episōreúsō*, from *epí* (1909), upon, and *sōreúō* (4987), to heap. To heap up, accumulate. Used metaphorically in 2 Tim 4:3.

2003. ἐπιταγή *epitagḗ*; gen. *epitagḗs*, fem. noun from *epitássō* (2004), to command, arrange upon. Authority, command imposed upon someone. Command of Christ (1 Cor 7:6, 25; 2 Cor 8:8); of God, will, decree (Rom 16:26 [TR]; 1 Tim 1:1; Titus 1:3); generally (Titus 2:15, "with all injunction" [a.t.], i.e., strongly, severely). Stresses the authoritativeness of the command.

Syn.: *diátagma* (1297), commandment, that which is imposed by decree or law stressing the concrete character of the commandment more than *epitagḗ*; *diatagḗ* (1296), an order, ordinance, disposition; *entolḗ* (1785), a general injunction, charge, precept of moral and religious nature; *éntalma* (1778), the thing commanded, a commission, precept; *paraggelía* (3852), a proclamation, charge.

2004. ἐπιτάσσω *epitássō*, **ἐπιτάττω** *epitáttō*; fut. *epitáxō*, from *epí* (1909), upon, over, and *tássō* (5021), to arrange, appoint or place appropriately. To appoint over, put in charge; put upon one as a duty, enjoin (Mark 1:27; 6:27, 39; 9:25; Luke 4:36; 8:25, 31; 14:22; Acts 23:2; Phile 1:8; Sept.: Gen 49:32; Esth 3:12; Dan 6:9).

Deriv.: *epitagḗ* (2003), injunction, command.

Syn.: *entéllomai* (1781), to order, command, enjoin; *diatássō* (1299), to set in order, command; *épō* (2036), command, bid; *keleúō* (2753), to order, bid; *paraggéllō* (3853), to order, give a charge; *prostássō* (4367), to prescribe, give command; *diastéllomai* (1291), to charge, enjoin.

2005. ἐπιτελέω *epiteléō*; contracted *epitelṓ*, fut. *epitelésō*, from *epí* (1909), an intens., and *teléō* (5055), to complete. To finish, complete, perfect (Rom 15:28; 2 Cor 7:1, "to practice" [a.t.], in KJV "perfecting"; 8:6, 11; Gal 3:3, "having begun in the Spirit, do ye now end in the flesh?" [a.t.] i.e., in attachment to carnal ordinances; Phil 1:6; Heb 8:5; Sept.: Num 23:23; 1 Sam 3:12; Zech 4:9); to perform, accomplish (Luke 13:32 [TR]; Heb 9:6, "performing the sacred rites" [a.t.]; 1 Pet 5:9, speaking of suffering, to accomplish, undergo, endure).

Syn.: *exartízō* (1822), to fit out, furnish completely, complete; *plēróō* (4137), to complete, fulfill, carry out; *ekplēróō* (1603), to fulfill, accomplish entirely; *teleióō* (5048), to make perfect, complete, accomplish; *plḗthō* (4130), to fulfill, accomplish; *ekteléō* (1615), to finish out or complete; *sunteléō* (4931), to bring to fulfillment, effect in concord with; *apoteléō* (658), to perfect, finish.

Ant.: *dialeípō* (1257), to cease, leave an interval.

2006. ἐπιτήδειος *epitḗdeios*; fem. *epitēdeía*, neut. *epitḗdeion*, adj. from *epítēdes* (n.f.), serviceable. Proper, apt. In the NT, by implication, needful, necessary (James 2:16, "things needful for the body" [a.t.], i.e., the necessities of life).

Syn.: *anagkaíos* (316), needful, necessary; *epánagkes* (1876), necessary (Acts 15:28); *chrēstós* (5543), serviceable; *eúchrēstos* (2173), profitable.

Ant.: *achreíos* (888), useless; *áchrēstos* (890), unprofitable, unserviceable; *alusitelḗs* (255), not advantageous; *anōphelḗs* (512), unprofitable.

2007. ἐπιτίθημι *epitíthēmi*; fut. *epithḗsō*, from *epí* (1909), upon or besides, and *títhēmi* (5087), to put. To put or lay on. Pres. act. indic. pl., *epitithéasi*, they place on (Matt 23:4). Pres. imper., *epitíthei* (1 Tim 5:22). 2d aor. imper. *epíthes* (Matt 9:18). Generally it means to place or put upon, to lay upon, impose. Used trans.:

(I) With *epí* and the acc. (Matt 23:4; 27:29; Mark 4:21; Luke 15:5; John 9:15; Acts 15:10; 28:3; Sept.: Gen 21:14; Ex 25:21, 30; Josh 10:24). Followed by the acc. and dat. (Luke 23:26; Acts 15:28). Figuratively spoken of a name (Mark 3:16, 17; Sept.: Dan 1:7; 5:12). Followed by *epí* and the gen. (Luke 8:16); by *epánō* (1883), above, over, with the gen. (Matt 21:7; 27:37). In the phrase, "to lay the hand [or hands] upon" as a symbol of healing power, followed by *epí* and the acc., meaning stretching out healing power (Matt 9:18; Mark 8:25; 16:18; Acts 9:17); followed by a dat. (Matt 19:13, 15; Mark 5:23; 6:5; 7:32; 8:23; Luke 4:40; 13:13; Acts 9:12; 28:8); for benediction or inauguration, followed by *epí* with the acc. (Acts 8:17); followed by a dat. (Acts 6:6; 8:19; 13:3; 19:6; 1 Tim 5:22 [cf. the noun *epíthesis* {1936}, laying on or putting on]). In Rev 1:17, "he laid his right hand on me" (TR). Sept. with *epí* (Lev 1:4; 3:2, 13). Spoken of stripes, meaning to lay on or to inflict (Luke 10:30); with a dat. (Acts 16:23); put on someone (Rev 22:18). Of gifts, to supply with, with a dat. (Acts 28:10).

(II) The mid. voice, *epitíthemai*, means to set oneself upon or against anyone, to assail, followed by the dat. (Acts 18:10; Sept.: Gen 43:18; 2 Chr 24:21, 25).

(III) By implication, to add upon, to superadd, with *prós* (4314), forward, toward, and the acc. (Rev 22:18).

Deriv.: *epíthesis* (1936), an imposition, laying on.

Syn.: *prostíthēmi* (4369), to add to; *prosanatíthēmi* (4323), to lay upon in addition; *epichorēgéō* (2023), to supply in addition; *epibállō* (1911), to lay upon; *epikathízō* (1940), to set on.

Ant.: *aírō* (142), to take away.

2008. ἐπιτιμάω *epitimáō*; contracted *epitimṓ*, fut. *epitimḗsō*, from *epí* (1909), upon, and *timáō* (5091), to evaluate. In the NT, to punish, rebuke, charge.

(I) One may rebuke another without bringing that one to a conviction of any fault, perhaps because there may have not been any fault or because there was fault but the rebuke was insufficient and ineffectual to bring the offender to acknowledge it. Therefore, *epitimáō* is merely the rebuke without any result in the person who is being rebuked. For instance, Peter or the other disciples were prone

to rebuke (*epitimáō*) the Lord or others (Matt 16:22; 19:13; Mark 8:32; 10:13; Luke 18:15; 19:39), but without any effect upon the Lord or the other people rebuked. The same is true when the penitent robber rebuked (*epitimṓn*) his fellow malefactor (Luke 23:40). With the idea of punishment (Jude 1:9 quoted from Zech 3:2). Followed by the dat. of thing and implying a desire to restrain, e.g., spoken of winds and waves (Matt 8:26; Mark 4:39; Luke 8:24; Sept.: Ps 106:9); of a fever (Luke 4:39).

(II) By implication, to admonish strongly, with urgency, authority, i.e., to enjoin upon, charge strictly, the idea of censure being implied, e.g., demons, followed by the dat. (Matt 17:18; Mark 1:25; 9:25; Luke 4:35, 41; 9:42); of persons (Luke 9:21). Followed by a dat. and *hína* (2443), so that (Matt 20:31; Mark 10:48; Luke 18:39). Followed by the dat. and *hína mḗ* (3363) so that not, equivalent to forbid strictly (Matt 12:16; Mark 3:12; 8:30).

Deriv.: *epitimía* (2009), punishment.

Syn.: *elégchō* (1651), to reprove with conviction; *apeiléō* (546), to threaten; *diamartúromai* (1263), to bear a solemn witness; *embrimáomai* (1690), to snort with anger, to charge strictly, rebuke sternly; *egkaléō* (1458), to accuse; *epiplḗssō* (1969), to strike at, rebuke.

Ant.: *ainéō* (134), to praise.

2009. ἐπιτιμία *epitimía*; gen. *epitimías*, fem. noun from *epitimáō* (2008), to censure or admonish. Penalty, punishment. In the NT, spoken of the estimate fixed by a judge upon a wrong, a judicial infliction (2 Cor 2:6).

Syn.: *kólasis* (2851), punishment; *díkē* (1349), execution of a sentence; *timōría* (5098), sentence or punishment.

2010. ἐπιτρέπω *epitrépō*; fut. *epitrépsō*, from *epí* (1909), to, and *trépō* (n.f., see *anatrépō* [396]), to turn. To turn upon, direct upon, give over to, commit to. In the NT, it means to permit, allow, suffer, entrust to (Matt 8:21, 31; 19:8; Mark

5:13; 10:4; Luke 8:32; 9:59, 61; Acts 21:39; 26:1; 27:3; 28:16; 1 Cor 14:34; 1 Tim 2:12; Sept.: Esth 9:14; Job 32:14). Used in an absolute sense (John 19:38; Acts 21:40; 1 Cor 16:7, "if the Lord permit"; Heb 6:3).

Deriv.: *epitropḗ* (2011), commission; *epítropos* (2012), steward, manager, agent.

Syn.: *éxesti* (1832), it is permitted; *anéchomai* (430), to tolerate; *eáō* (1439), to let.

Ant.: *kōlúō* (2967), to hinder.

2011. ἐπιτροπή *epitropḗ*; gen. *epitropḗs*, fem. noun from *epitrépō* (2010), to permit. A commission, an office granted or entrusted with full power (Acts 26:12).

Syn.: *presbeía* (4242), a committee sent to give a message.

2012. ἐπίτροπος *epítropos*; gen. *epitrópou*, masc. noun from *epitrépō* (2010), to permit. Steward, manager, agent. A person entrusted to act in another's name or to whose care anything is committed by another (Matt 20:8); a steward or treasurer to a prince, or a deputy governor, or a Roman procurator; a guardian to whom the care of orphans is committed, the same as *paidagōgós* (3807), a guardian (Gal 4:2). In Luke 8:3, a manager of private affairs.

Syn.: *oikonómos* (3623), steward.

2013. ἐπιτυγχάνω *epitugchánō*; fut. *epiteúxomai*, 2d aor. *epétuchon*, from *epí* (1909), an intens., and *tugchánō* (5177), to obtain. To light upon, chance to meet, to obtain, attain one's aim, acquire. It is either construed with a gen. or used in an absolute sense (Rom 11:7; Heb 6:15; 11:33; James 4:2; Sept.: Prov 12:27).

Syn.: *lagchánō* (2975), to obtain by lot; *ktáomai* (2932), to procure for oneself; *kratéō* (2902), to get possession of; *lambánō* (2983), to receive; *heurískō* (2147), to find; *katalambánō* (2638), to obtain securely.

2014. ἐπιφαίνω *epiphaínō*; fut. *epiphanō̃*, aor. *epéphēna*, 2d aor. pass. *epephánēn*, from *epí* (1909), over, upon or to, and *phaínō* (5316), to shine. Trans., to show forth, exhibit, shine light upon, e.g., upon the surface. Usually used in the pass. meaning to show oneself openly or before the people, to come forward, appear, with the idea of sudden or unexpected appearing. Often used in Greek literature of the gods and hence the significance of the NT *epipháneia* (2015), appearing, the noun from *epiphaínō* (Titus 2:11; 3:4). The word is often used in Patristic Gr. of the incarnation of Christ. Intrans., to appear, e.g., of the sun (Acts 27:20); to appear, shine (Luke 1:79).

Deriv.: *epipháneia* (2015), appearing; *epiphanḗ* (2016), memorable, notable.

Syn.: *phaneróō* (5319), to manifest; *emphanízō* (1718), to cause to appear; *óptomai* (3700), to appear; *optánomai* (3700), to allow oneself to be seen.

Ant.: *krúptō* (2928), to hide, conceal.

2015. ἐπιφάνεια *epipháneia*; gen. *epiphaneías*, fem. noun from *epiphaínō* (2014), to appear. An appearing, appearance. *Epipháneia* is spoken of the first advent of the Lord Jesus (2 Tim 1:10). *Epiphaínō* (2014) in the mid. pass. form, *epiphaínomai*, to appear, to manifest oneself. *Epipháneia* is used only by Paul for the second and future appearance of the Lord (2 Thess 2:8; 1 Tim 6:14; 2 Tim 4:1, 8; Titus 2:13 [cf. Luke 1:78, 79]).

Syn.: *apokálupsis* (602), revelation, unveiling; *parousía* (3952), appearance, appearing, presence; *phanérōsis* (5321), manifestation.

Ant.: *apousía* (666), absence.

2016. ἐπιφανής *epiphanḗs*; gen. *epiphanoús*, masc.-fem., neut. *epiphanés*, adj. from *epiphaínō* (2014), to cause to appear upon. Visible, clear, manifest. In the NT, splendid, illustrious, memorable (Acts 2:20 quoting Joel 2:31 [see Joel 2:11]).

Syn.: *gnōstós* (1110), known, notable; *epísēmos* (1978), official, notable.
Ant.: *ásēmos* (767), insignificant.

2017. ἐπιφαύσκω *epiphaúskō*; fut. *epiphaúsō*, from *epí* (1909), upon, to, and *phaúō* (n.f.), to shine. To shine upon, give light to (Eph 5:14 [cf. Isa 60:1]). The same as *epiphaínō* (2014), to appear, give light, and *epiphṓskō* (2020), to dawn upon.

2018. ἐπιφέρω *epiphérō*; fut. *epoísō*, 2d aor. *epénegkon*, from *epí* (1909), upon, to, and *phérō* (5342), to bring. To bring, carry to (Acts 19:12); to bring upon, to inflict wrath or vengeance (Rom 3:5); to add unto (Phil 1:16); to bring against as an accusation, judicial sentence (Acts 25:18; Jude 1:9).
Syn.: *epágō* (1863), to bring upon; *komízō* (2865), to bring in.
Ant.: *aphairéō* (851), to remove.

2019. ἐπιφωνέω *epiphōnéō*; contracted *epiphōnṓ*, fut. *epiphōnéso*, from *epí* (1909), against, or an intens., and *phōnéō* (5455), to cry. To cry aloud, clamor, shout (Luke 23:21; Acts 12:22, "in acclamation" [a.t.]); followed by a dat. meaning to cry out against (Acts 22:24).
Syn.: *boáō* (994), to cry out; *anaboáō* (310), to cry out greatly; *epiboáō* (1916), to cry out; *krázō* (2896), to cry, cry out; *anakrázō* (349), to cry out greatly; *kraugázō* (2905), to make an outcry.
Ant.: *sigáō* (4601), to keep silence.

2020. ἐπιφώσκω *epiphṓskō*; fut. *epiphaúsō*, from *epí* (1909), upon or besides, denoting accession, coming or drawing toward, and *phṓskō* (n.f.), to shine. In Luke 23:54 the verb has the meaning to draw near, as the Jewish Sabbath which began in the evening (Lev 23:32 [cf. John 19:31 with Deut 21:22, 23]). To dawn as the daylight, to grow toward daylight (Matt 28:1). In the evening of the Sabbath when the Jewish day was drawing on towards the first day of the week, Mary Magdalene and the other

Mary went (or better, set out). It does not appear that they actually came at this time to visit the sepulcher, perhaps being delayed by the great earthquake (Matt 28:2) which preceded our Lord's resurrection.
Syn.: *augázō* (826), to dawn; *diaugázō* (1306), to dawn, metaphorically to shine with spiritual light.
Ant.: *skotízō* (4654), to darken; *skotóō* (4656), to obscure; *episkiázō* (1982), to envelop in a haze, throw a shadow over.

2021. ἐπιχειρέω *epicheiréō*; contracted *epicheirṓ*, fut. *epicheirḗsō*, from *epí* (1909), upon or in, and *cheír* (5495), hand. To take in hand, undertake, attempt, whether effective or not (Luke 1:1; Acts 9:29; 19:13).
Syn.: *analambánō* (353), to take up; *epilambánomai* (1949), to take hold of; *drássomai* (1405), to grasp with the hand, take hold of; *piázō* (4084), to take hold of forcefully.
Ant.: *paraitéomai* (3868), to avoid.

2022. ἐπιχέω *epichéō*; fut. *epicheúsō*, aor. *epéchea*, from *epí* (1909), upon or in, and *chéō* (n.f., see below), to pour. To pour upon or in, infuse (Luke 10:34).
Deriv. of *chéō* (n.f.), to pour: *ekchéō* (1632), to pour out; *katachéō* (2708), to pour down; *sugchéō* (4797), to pour together, confuse; *cholḗ* (5521), bile; *chóos* (5522), dust.

2023. ἐπιχορηγέω *epichorēgéō*; fut. *epichorēgéso*, from *epí* (1909), upon, and *chorēgéō* (5524), to furnish, give. To furnish upon, i.e., besides, in addition, to supply further, to add more unto. With the acc., to supply, furnish, or furnish abundantly (2 Cor 9:10; Gal 3:5 [cf. Isa 55:10]). In the pass., *epichorēgéomai*, to be supplied, vigor or nourishment ministered (Col 2:19); also to be supplied with or ministered to (2 Pet 1:11). With the prep. *en* (1722), in, and a dat., to supply, add to (2 Pet 1:5).
Deriv.: *epichorēgía* (2024), supply.

Syn.: *dídōmi* (1325), to give; *paréchō* (3930), to present, give; *eparkéō* (1884), to supply.

Ant.: *aposteréō* (650), to deprive; *aphairéō* (851), to remove.

2024. ἐπιχορηγία *epichorēgía*; gen. *epichorēgías*, fem. noun from *epichorēgéō* (2023), to supply. A supply, aid, help (Eph 4:16; Phil 1:19).

Syn.: *dósis* (1394), a gift; *apodochḗ* (594), acceptance.

Ant.: *harpagḗ* (724), extortion; *hustérēma* (5303), deficit, want; *hustérēsis* (5304), a falling short; *apṓleia* (684), loss.

2025. ἐπιχρίω *epichríō*; fut. *epichrísō*, from *epí* (1909), upon, and *chríō* (5548), to anoint. To anoint, smear over. *Epichríō* occurs only in John 9:6, 11, in the case of the blind man at the temple for whom the Lord spit on the ground, made mud, and placed it or smeared (*aleíphō* [218]) it on his eyes. But in reality, it was not the mud that brought healing to this blind man. It was God's miraculous grace and power. In order to qualify this nonmedicinal healing element of the mud, the word *epichríō* is used. If *aleíphō* were used, meaning just to smear on without the element of divine power, it would have led both the blind man and others to believe that there was miraculous healing power in the mud. This impression the Lord wanted to avoid giving.

2026. ἐποικοδομέω *epoikodoméō*; contracted *epoikodomṓ*, fut. *epoikdomḗsō*, from *epí* (1909), upon, and *oikodoméō* (3618), to build. To build upon, to erect a superstructure (1 Cor 3:10, 12, 14; Eph 2:20); to build up, edify (Acts 20:32 [TR]; Col 2:7; Jude 1:20).

Syn.: *ktízō* (2936), to build; *egeírō* (1453), to erect; *anoikodoméō* (456), to rebuild; *epoikodoméō* (2026), to build upon, edify; *kataskeuázō* (2680), to construct, build.

Ant.: *kathairéō* (2507), to demolish; *katakrēmnízō* (2630), to demolish completely; *katabibázō* (2601), to bring down; *anatrépō* (396), to overturn.

2027. ἐποκέλλω *epokéllō*; fut. *epokeló*, from *epí* (1909), an intens., and *okéllō* (n.f.), to bring a ship to land or to run it aground. To run aground; used trans. in Acts 27:41.

Syn.: *katapléō* (2668), to sail down upon a place, land at.

Ant.: *apopléō* (636), to sail away; *ekpléō* (1602), to depart by ship.

2028. ἐπονομάζω *eponomázō*; fut. *eponomásō*, from *epí* (1909), upon, and *onomázō* (3687), to name. To call, used in the pass. with the meaning to be named in addition to some other name, to be surnamed (Rom 2:17; Sept.: Gen 4:17, 25, 26).

Syn.: *epikaléō* (1941), to surname; *kaléō* (2564), to call.

2029. ἐποπτεύω *epopteúō*; fut. *epopteúsō*, from *epóptēs* (2030), a supervisor, beholder. To look upon or to oversee, inspect. In the NT, generally to behold, contemplate, trans. (1 Pet 2:12; 3:2).

Syn.: *epiblépō* (1914), to look upon; *episkopéō* (1983), to oversee; *epopteúō* (2029), to inspect.

Ant.: *ameléō* (272), to neglect; *epilanthánomai* (1950), to be forgetful of; *oligōréō* (3643), to despise.

2030. ἐπόπτης *epóptēs*; gen. *epóptou*, masc. noun from *epópsomai*, the fut. of *ephoráō* (n.f.), to observe. Inspector, onlooker, an eyewitness (2 Pet 1:16).

Deriv.: *epopteúō* (2029), to inspect.

Syn.: *autóptēs* (845), an eyewitness; *epistátēs* (1988), a supervisor; *oikonómos* (3623), an overseer; *epískopos* (1985), overseer.

2031. ἔπος *épos*; gen. *épous*, neut. noun from *épō* (2036), to speak. A word. As used in Heb 7:9, "so to speak" (a.t.).

Deriv.: *nḗpios* (3516), one who cannot speak, infant.

Syn.: *lógos* (3056), word, expression of thought; *rhḗma* (4487), that which is spoken, word; *laliá* (2981), saying, speech; *lógion* (3051), utterance of God, oracle.

Ant.: *sigḗ* (4602), silence.

2032. ἐπουράνιος *epouránios*; gen. *epouraníou*, masc.-fem., neut. *epouránion*, adj. from *epí* (1909), upon, in, and *ouranós* (3772), heaven. Heavenly, celestial, what pertains to or is in heaven. In Matt 18:35, "the Father, the heavenly One [*epouránios*]" (a.t.). The meaning of this word is determined according to the various meanings of heaven. In Phil 2:10, "the heavenly ones" (a.t.), i.e., angels. Of those who come from heaven (1 Cor 15:48, 49 [see 1 Cor 15:47 *ex* {*ek* (1537), of; *ouranoú* (3772), heaven}]; Phil 3:21). Of heavenly or celestial bodies, the sun, moon (1 Cor 15:40 [see 1 Cor 15:44]). The neut. pl. with the def. art. *tá epouránia* means the heavens, heaven (Eph 1:20); *en toís epouraníois*, in the heavenlies (Eph 2:6; 3:10), in heaven. Of the lower heavens, the sky or air as the seat of evil spirits (Eph 6:12; see *ouranós* [3772], heaven, sky, and *aḗr* [109], air). Spoken of the kingdom of heaven and whatever pertains to it, see *basileía* (932), kingdom. In 2 Tim 4:18, unto the kingdom, the heavenly one. Also Heb 3:1; 6:4; 8:5; 9:23; 11:16; 12:22 (cf. Rev 21:2, "out of heaven"). In Eph 1:3, *tá epouránia*, "things pertaining to the kingdom of God" (a.t.), or generally things spiritual (John 3:12).

Ant.: *epígeios* (1919), earthly, terrestrial; *katachthónios* (2709), subterranean.

2033. ἑπτά *heptá*; indeclinable, used for all genders, cardinal number. Seven (Matt 15:34, 36, 37; Acts 20:6). It is the number denoting sufficiency (Matt 12:45; 22:25; Luke 11:26; Rev 1:4; Sept.: Ruth 4:15; 1 Sam 2:5; Isa 4:1; Prov 26:25; Jer 15:9) and its meaning is from the Hebr. word meaning sufficiency or fullness. It was on the seventh day that the Lord completed or finished all His work of creation, or made it sufficient for the purposes for which it was designed (Gen 2:2). The seventh day was also sanctified, or set apart, from the beginning as a religious Sabbath, or rest, to remind believers of that rest which God then entered into and of that sufficiency or fullness of joy which is in His presence forevermore (Ps 16:11). Hence the very early and general division of time into weeks or periods of seven days, and the sacredness of the seventh day, not only among believers before the giving of the law, but also among the heathen for which they give the very same reason as Moses does (Gen 2:2); namely, that on it all things were ended or completed (cf. Gen 7:4, 10; 8:10, 12; 29:27; Ex 16:22, 31; Heb 4:1–11). Seven, therefore, was both among believers and nonbelievers the number of sufficiency or completion. Note also the seventy weeks of the prophecy of Daniel (Dan 9:20–27) of which the last week, the seventieth week, represented the Great Tribulation which would come on earth (Rev 6—19), indicating the sufficiency of God's dispensation of grace. See Acts 6:3; Rev 1:4, 12, 16; 2:1 (cf. Gen 21:28; Ex 37:23; Lev 4:6, 17).

Deriv.: *hebdomḗkonta* (1440), seventy; *hébdomos* (1442), seventh; *heptákis* (2034), seven times; *heptakischílioi* (2035), seven thousand.

2034. ἑπτάκις *heptákis*; adv. from *heptá* (2033), seven. Seven times or an indefinite, unlimited number (Matt 18:21, 22; Luke 17:4; Sept.: Ps 119:164; 2 Kgs 5:10, 14) bearing the meaning of sufficient, complete.

2035. ἑπτακισχίλιοι *heptakischílioi*; fem. *heptakischíliai*, neut. *heptakischília*, cardinal number from *heptákis* (2034), seven times, and *chílioi* (5507), a thousand. Seven thousand or seven times a thousand (Rom 11:4 quoted from 1 Kgs 19:18).

2036. ἔπω *épō*; obsolete verb, fut. *eró*, with 1st aor. ending, *eípas*, ([aor. act. indic. 2d person sing.] Matt 26:25), *eípate*, ([aor. act. imper. 2d person pl.] Mark 11:3), 2d aor. *eípon*, pluperf. *eirḗkein*, opt. *eípoimi*, subjunctive *eípō*, inf. *eipeín*, part. *eipṓn*, imper. *eipátōsan* (Acts 24:20), perf. pass. *eírēmai*, aor. pass. *erréthēn* or the less usual *errḗthēn*, fut. pass *rhēthḗsomai* and *eirḗsomai*. In the NT:

(I) Generally to say, speak, with an acc. of the thing said (Matt 26:44; Luke 12:3; John 2:22; Acts 1:9; Rom 3:5; 6:1; Heb 7:9, so to speak). The acc. is often supplied by the words or clause spoken (Matt 2:8; 4:3, Luke 5:13; John 4:27; 6:59). Hence, *eípe* is inserted like *éphē* in the mid. of a clause (Luke 7:42). With an acc. of person, used once in John 1:15, of whom I said, "of whom I spake," the same as in John 1:30, *perí oú* (*perí* [4012], about; *oú* [3739], of whom), concerning whom. Other constructions:

(A) Followed by the dat. of person (Matt 16:8; Mark 2:9; Luke 4:3; 7:40; John 14:26; 16:4; Rev 17:7).

(B) Followed by *katá* (2956), against, with the gen. of person, to speak against (Matt 5:11; 12:32).

(C) Followed by *perí* (4012), about, with the gen. of person or thing, to speak of or concerning (John 7:39; 10:41; 18:34); with the dat. of person (Matt 17:13).

(D) Followed by *prós* (4314), to, with the acc. of person, to speak or say to anyone (Luke 11:1; 12:16; John 6:28; Acts 2:37; Heb 1:13). In the sense of for, with reference to (Mark 12:12).

(E) With an adv. or a prep. and its noun, implying manner, such as *homoíōs* (3668), similarly (Matt 26:35) and *hōsaútōs* (5615), likewise (Matt 21:30); *kathṓs* (2531), as (Matt 28:6); *kalṓs eípas* (*kalós* [2573], well; *eípas*, "Thou hast well said," i.e., rightly, correctly [Luke 20:39]); used in an absolute sense with *kalós*, well, implied (Matt 26:25, 64); *sú eípas* (*sú* [4771], you), you said;

hence with an acc. of person *kalós eípen* (*kalós*, well; *eípen*, he said), he spoke well of (Luke 6:26); of speaking in parables, using the dat. (Matt 22:1); with *diá* (1223), through a parable (Luke 8:4); *eípon prós heautoús* (*prós* [4314], to; *heautoús* [1438], them or to each other), they said among themselves or to one another (Mark 12:7; Luke 2:15; John 7:35; 16:17; 19:24); *en heautoís* (*en* [1722], in, *heautoís*, the dat. pl. of *heautós* [1438], himself, meaning themselves), meaning they said among themselves (Matt 21:38). Metaphorically followed by *en tḗ kardía autoú* (*kardía* [2588], heart; *autoú* [847], his), he said in his heart, meaning he thought (Matt 24:48; Luke 12:45; Rom 10:6). See Sept.: Ps 10:6, 11; 14:1; Isa 49:21. In the same sense also, to say in oneself (Matt 9:3; Luke 7:39; 16:3; 18:4; Sept.: Esth 6:6).

(F) Followed by the inf. with the acc. implied (Matt 16:12); with *eínai*, inf. of *eimí* (1510), to be, implied, where *eípe* may be rendered he called, he named (John 10:34, "I said, Ye are gods" [a.t.]; 1 Cor 12:3).

(G) Followed by *hóti* (3754), that (John 8:55; 1 Cor 1:15). With the dat. (Mark 16:7).

(II) As modified by the context where the sense often lies not so much in *eípen* as in the adjuncts; e.g., spoken:

(A) Before interrogations, to ask, inquire (Matt 9:4; 11:3; 13:10; John 8:10; Acts 8:30; 19:2, 3).

(B) Before replies, to answer or reply, to a direct question (Matt 15:34; Mark 8:5; Luke 8:10) and so preceded by *apokritheís*, the aor. part. or *apekríthē*, the aor. of *apokrínomai* (611), to answer, and *kaí* (2532), and (Matt 11:4; 15:13; John 7:20; Acts 5:29). Without a preceding question (Matt 14:18; Acts 5:9; 11:8). With *apokritheís*, aor. pass. part. of *apokrínomai* (611), I answer (Matt 4:4; 12:39).

(C) Of narration or teaching, to tell, make known, declare (Matt 8:4; 16:20; 18:17; 16:7, 8; John 3:12; 12:49; Rev

17:7; Sept.: 2 Kgs 22:10; Job 12:7; Isa 41:22).

(D) Of predictions, to foretell, prophesy (Matt 28:6; Mark 14:16; John 2:22).

(E) Of what is spoken authoritatively, to direct, bid, command (Matt 8:8; Mark 5:43; 10:49; Luke 7:7; 19:15; 2 Cor 4:6; James 2:11). Followed by *hína* (2443), so that (Matt 4:3; Mark 3:9; Sept. Ex 35:1; Lev 9:6).

Deriv.: *anteípon* (471), to say against, gainsay; *apeipómēn* (550), to renounce; *épos* (2031), the articulated expression of a thought; *proeípon* (4277), to say before, forewarn.

Syn.: *légō* (3004), to say, speak; *laléō* (2980), to speak, to break silence; *phthéggomai* (5350), to utter a sound; *apophthéggomai* (669), to speak forth; *phēmí* (5346), to declare; *pháskō* (5335), to affirm, say.

Ant.: *sigáō* (4601), to be silent; *phimóō* (5392), to muzzle, put to silence; *siōpáō* (4623), to keep silence.

2037. Ἔραστος *Érastos*; gen. *Erástou*, masc. proper noun. Erastus, meaning beloved.

(I) One of Paul's attendants whom he sent with Timothy into Macedonia (Acts 19:22) and whom he salutes in 2 Tim 4:20.

(II) The chamberlain or treasurer of Corinth and one of Paul's converts (Rom 16:23). Some identify him with the preceding, but upon insufficient grounds, for if such were the case, we should expect mention of his office in the books of Acts, Romans, and Timothy (unless, indeed, he received the office after his conversion which is very unlikely).

2038. ἐργάζομαι *ergázomai*; imperf. *eirgazómēn*, fut. *ergásomai*, aor. *eirgasámēn*, perf. pass. part. *eírgasmai*, mid. deponent (2 John 1:8); with pass. significance (John 3:21), mid. deponent from *érgon* (2041), work. To work, labor.

(I) Intrans., to work, labor, that is:

(A) Particularly in a field (Matt 21:28); at a trade (Acts 18:3; 1 Cor 4:12; 1 Thess 2:9; 2 Thess 3:8); generally (Luke 13:14; John 9:4; 1 Cor 9:6; 1 Thess 4:11; 2 Thess 3:10–12; Sept.: Ex 5:18; Deut 5:13).

(B) In the sense of being active, i.e., to exert one's powers and faculties (John 5:17; Rom 4:5).

(C) Also to do business, i.e., to trade, to deal (Matt 25:16).

(II) Trans., to work, perform by labor, to do, produce.

(A) Of things wrought, done, performed, e.g., miracles (John 6:30; Acts 13:41 [cf. Hab 1:5]); of sacred rites (1 Cor 9:13); generally (Eph 4:28; Col 3:23). To work the works of God (John 6:28; 9:4); the work of the Lord (1 Cor 16:10); works wrought in God, i.e., in conformity to His will (John 3:21; Sept.: Num 3:7; 8:11; Job 33:29; Ps 7:15); to work a good work upon or for someone (Matt 26:10; Mark 14:6; 3 John 1:5). In Gal 6:10, "let us do good unto all men"; in Rom 13:10, "worketh no ill" (cf. Prov 3:30). Figuratively, to work good or evil, to do, commit, practice, with the acc. (Matt 7:23; Acts 10:35; Rom 2:10; Heb 11:33; James 2:9; Sept.: Ps 5:5; 6:8; Job 34:32).

(B) In the sense of to till, cultivate, e.g., the earth (Sept.: Gen 2:5, 15). In the NT, metaphorically spoken only of the sea, to cultivate the sea, i.e., to ply or follow the sea as an occupation as sailors, mariners (Rev 18:17).

(C) In the sense of to work for, labor for, earn, e.g., one's food (John 6:27; 2 John 1:8; Sept.: Prov 31:18).

Deriv.: *ergasía* (2039), craft, diligence, gain; *ergátēs* (2040), laborer; *katergázomai* (2716), to work fully, accomplish; *periergázomai* (4020), to be a busybody; *prosergázomai* (4333), to gain, acquire besides.

Syn.: *poiéō* (4160), to do; *prássō* (4238), to do work; *katergázomai* (2716), to work; *epiteléō* (2005), to perform; *prosergázomai* (4333), to work out in addition; *kopiáō* (2872), to toil; *kámnō* (2577), to toil; *pragmateúomai* (4231), to trade; *energéō* (1754), to work in; *hupēretéō* (5256), to minister, serve.

Ant.: *argéō* (691), to delay, linger, be idle; *scholázō* (4980), to be at leisure.

2039. ἐργασία *ergasía*; gen. *ergasías* fem. noun from *ergázomai* (2038), to toil, work. Work.

(I) Work or labor accompanied with pain; effort with diligence, pain, and elaborate handling (Luke 12:58).

(II) A practice or practicing, performance of evil (Eph 4:19, "so as to work all uncleanness" [a.t. {cf. 1 Chr 6:49; 28:20}]).

(III) Work, business, trade, craft, manufacture (Acts 19:25; Sept.: Jon 1:8 [cf. Ps 107:23]).

(IV) Gain (Acts 16:16, 19; 19:24).

Syn.: *téchnē* (5078), trade, craft; *spoudḗ* (4710), diligence; *porismós* (4200), means of gain; *kérdos* (2771), gain; *enérgeia* (1753), energy, working.

Ant.: *scholḗ* (4981), leisure.

2040. ἐργάτης *ergátēs*; gen. *ergátou*, masc. noun from *ergázomai* (2038), to toil, work. Laborer, worker.

(I) A worker or laborer, primarily in farming (Matt 20:1, 2, 8; Luke 10:2, 7; 1 Tim 5:18; James 5:4 [cf. Matt 9:37, 38]).

(II) A workman, an artisan (Acts 19:25).

(III) A spiritual workman or laborer, either good (2 Tim 2:15 [cf. Matt 9:37, 38; 10:10]) or evil (Luke 13:27; 2 Cor 11:13; Phil 3:2).

Ant.: *argós* (692), idle, inactive, unemployed.

2041. ἔργον *érgon*; gen. *érgou*, neut. noun from *érgō* (n.f.), to work. Work, performance, the result or object of employment, making or working.

(I) Labor, business, employment, something to be done.

(A) Generally (Mark 13:34; Eph 4:12; 1 Tim 3:1; Sept.: Gen 2:2; 39:11; Ex 35:2); of the work which Jesus was sent to fulfill on earth (*tó érgon* [John 17:4], pl. *tá érga*, the works [John 5:20, 36; 10:38]).

The work of the Father which He gave Christ to do (John 4:34; 9:4 [cf. 17:4]). *Tó érgon toú Kuríou*, the work of the Lord, i.e., which He began and left to be continued by His disciples, e.g., the cause of Christ, the gospel-work (1 Cor 15:58; 16:10; Phil 2:30); the work as committed to apostles and teachers (2 Tim 4:5; see Acts 13:2; 14:26; 15:38; Phil 1:22); the work of God, i.e., the work which God requires, duty toward Him (John 6:28, 29; Rev 2:26).

(B) In the sense of undertaking, attempt (Acts 5:38; 2 Tim 4:18; Sept.: Deut 15:10; Job 34:21).

(II) Work, i.e., deed, act, action, something done.

(A) Generally, to work a work, do a deed (Acts 13:41 quoted from Hab 1:5). Of the works of Jesus, miracles, mighty deeds (Matt 11:2; John 7:3, 21; 14:10–12; 15:24); of God (Heb 3:9 from Ps 95:9).

(B) Where *lógos* (3056), word, and *érgon*, work, stand in contrast, word and work (Luke 24:19; Acts 7:22; Rom 15:18; 2 Cor 10:11; Col 3:17; Titus 1:16). By implication in James 1:25, not a hearer, "but a doer of the work" or the deed.

(C) Of the works of men in reference to right and wrong as judged by the moral law, the precepts of the gospel **(1)** Generally (Matt 23:3, 5; John 3:20, 21; Acts 26:20; Rom 3:27; Gal 6:4). The expression *katá tá érga* (2596), according to, according to one's works (Rom 2:6; 2 Cor 11:15; 1 Pet 1:17; Rev 20:12; Sept.: Prov 24:12; Jer 50:29). **(2)** Of good works, with an adj., e.g., benevolent work (*érgon agathón* [18]) or in the pl. good deeds (*érga agathá*), i.e., either benefit or kindness (Acts 9:36), well-doing, virtue, piety (Rom 2:7; 13:3; Eph 2:10; 2 Thess 2:17; Heb 13:21); *érgon kalón* (2570), constitutionally good, but not necessarily *agathón*, beneficent, doing somebody else good, and in the pl. *érga kalá*, a good deed or good deeds, i.e., a pious act, well-doing, virtue (Matt 5:16; Mark 14:6; 1 Tim 6:18; Titus 2:7; Heb 10:24; 1 Pet 2:12). *Tá érga en dikaiosúnē* (righteousness or justice) meaning just works

(Titus 3:5); *érgon téleion* (5046), perfect or reaching its goal, perfect work, meaning full, complete in well-doing (James 1:4). Without an adj., as in John 8:39, "the works of Abraham"; also James 3:13. **(3)** Of evil works, with an adj., e.g., *érga ponērá* (4190), evil, wicked works, evil deeds (John 3:19; Col 1:21; 1 John 3:12); *érga nekrá* (3498), dead, dead works, i.e., sinful (Heb 6:1); *érga ánoma* (459), lawless, lawless works (2 Pet 2:8); *érga asebeías* (763), wickedness, ungodliness, meaning works that do not please God (Jude 1:15); *érga toú skótous* (4655), of darkness, meaning of moral darkness, sin (Rom 13:12); *érga tḗs sarkós* (4561), of the flesh, carnal works, works that demonstrate the resurgence of the old man (Gal 5:19). Without an adj., by implication as in Rev 2:6, the sins of the Nicolaitans; see also John 8:41, 44; 1 Cor 5:2; Rev 2:13, 22; 3:1; 18:6. **(4)** Of works of the law (*érga toú nómou* [3551], of the law), meaning works required or conformable to the Mosaic moral law and required by this law (Rom 2:15, "the work of the law" or conformable to this law; 3:20; Gal 2:16). With *toú nómou*, of the law implied in Paul's writings (Rom 4:2, 6; 9:11; 11:6; Eph 2:9; 2 Tim 1:9). **(5)** Of works of faith (*érga písteōs* [4102], of faith), meaning springing from faith, combined with faith (1 Thess 1:3; 2 Thess 1:11). With *tḗs pístseōs*, of the faith, implied (Heb 6:10; James 2:14, 17–26 [cf. especially vv. 22, 26]).

(III) Work, i.e., the thing wrought, something made or created generally by men (Acts 7:41) such as an idol (Sept.: Deut 27:15; 2 Kgs 19:18; Ps 9:16). Of the works of God, generally (Acts 15:18; Rom 14:20; Phil 1:6; Heb 1:10 quoted from Ps 102:25, see Ps 103:22; 104:31 [cf. Isa 45:11; 64:8; 2 Pet 3:10; Rev 15:3]). Also of works implying power, and used for power or might, e.g., of God (John 9:3); of Satan (1 John 3:8).

Sometimes it means work as a single act (Matt 26:10; Mark 14:6; John 7:21; 10:32, 33; 1 Cor 5:2). Denotes any matter or thing, any object which one may have to do or attain (1 Tim 3:1; 2 Tim 4:18); the general object or result of doing and working, an object or result whose attainment or realization is not accomplished by a single act but by accumulated labor and continued work (Rom 14:20; 1 Cor 3:15; 9:1 [cf. Phile 1:10]); calling or occupation (Acts 14:26; Eph 4:12; 1 Thess 5:13; 2 Tim 4:5); labor enjoined by and done for Christ as the spreading of His gospel and the furthering of His Church; moral conduct (Rom 2:6; 1 Cor 3:13; 1 Pet 1:17).

It is especially used in the pl., *tá érga* (Matt 11:2) of Christ's miracles (John 5:20, 36; 7:3). In John 6:28, "the works of God" must be understood to be works such as God does. On the other hand, in verse twenty-nine, "the work of God" must be understood as that which God requires to be done. The question in verse twenty-eight implies misapprehension of Christ's words, which He corrects in verse twenty-nine.

In the Pauline Epistles, those works to which Christians are called are designated not simply as *érga*, but *érga agathá* (18), benevolent works. In James, however, *érga* generally denotes acts in which the man proves his genuineness and his faith (James 2:14). Faith is proven by its works (James 2:22, 25). Elsewhere in the NT, *tá érga*, the works, usually denotes comprehensively what a man is and how he acts (Rom 2:6; 2 Cor 11:15; 2 Tim 4:14; 3 John 1:10; Rev 2:2, 5, 6, 22, 23; 3:1, 2, 8, 15; 14:13; 16:11; 18:6; 20:12, 13).

Good works acceptable unto God are only possible through God's grace active in one's heart (Matt 5:16; John 6:28; 14:12). They are always the result of salvation and not the means of salvation. The person who has no faith demonstrates by his evil works his separation from God (John 3:19; Eph 5:11; Col 1:21; 2 Pet 2:8).

Good works are the evidence of living faith, as James emphasizes in opposition to those who, while claiming to be saved by faith, lack good works. The Jews relied upon their confessional adherence to monotheism believing that such religion was sufficient for salvation. James asserts that faith that does not change one's life is dead faith, and faith that results in conversion and, therefore, unto good works, is living faith (James 2:14–26). Therefore, the word "works" as used by Paul are the dead works which are not wrought by faith, but "works" as used by James are those which definitively involve faith as their initiator. James, therefore, is in harmony with Paul, who also repeatedly declared the necessity for works, i.e., for behavior appropriate to the new life in Christ following our entry into it by faith alone (Eph 2:8–10; 1 Cor 6:9–11; Gal 5:16–26).

Man cannot do any work to earn God's favor unto salvation (Rom 4:1–5; Eph 2:8, 9; Titus 3:5). Salvation is given by God in grace, and there is no way that it can be earned.

God is a just God and distinguishes between the benevolent and malevolent works of an unbeliever, and although his good works are dead insofar as the procurement of salvation is concerned, yet they are remembered by God in mitigation of the final punishment of the unbelievers (Acts 10:31). This is made amply clear in the teaching of our Lord concerning the last judgment in Matt 25:31–46 (and especially in His pronouncements in vv. 41–46 upon the unbelievers who did not engage in any deeds of human benevolence). In Rev 20:11–15, where the Great White Throne Judgment is spoken of, we find books kept wherein the works of unbelievers are written, as well as the works of believers. These works are recorded for corresponding retribution for the unbelievers and the corresponding rewards for believers. There is ample evidence from the Scriptures that hell is not going to be equal for all unbelievers and heaven is not going to be equal for all believers. Each is going to be judged according to his works, which for unbelievers could never lead unto salvation and which for believers come from living faith.

Deriv.: *ampelourgós* (289), vinedresser; *argós* (692), idle, barren; *geōrgós* (1092), husbandman; *dēmiourgós* (1217), one who works for the public; *energḗs* (1756), active; *ergázomai* (2038), to work; *euergétēs* (2110), benefactor; *leitourgós* (3011), public servant, minister; *panoúrgos* (3835), crafty; *períergos* (4021), busybody; *sunergós* (4904), workfellow.

Syn.: *ergasía* (2039), a working, indicative of a process in contrast to the concrete *érgon* (Eph 4:19 [see also v. 12]), business, craft, diligence, gain; *téchnē* (5078) craft, occupation; *práxis* (4234), transaction, a deed, the action of which is looked upon as incomplete but in progress; *poíēsis* (4162), a doing, deed; *prágma* (4229), an accomplished act, deed; *dúnamis* (1411), miracle, a powerful deed or act; *ktísma* (2938), product, creature; *ktísis* (2937), creature, creation; *plásma* (4110), thing formed; *karpós* (2590), fruit; *katórthōma* (2735), very worthy deed, achievement.

Ant.: *scholḗ* (4981), loitering, leisure, school; *katápausis* (2663), cessation of work, hence rest.

2042. ἐρεθίζω *erethízō*; fut. *erethísō*, from *eréthō* (n.f.), to stir to anger. To excite, anger, provoke, irritate. Used trans. (Col 3:21). Also to incite or stimulate to action (2 Cor 9:2).

Syn.: *orgízō* (3710), to provoke, arouse to anger; *parorgízō* (3949), to arouse to wrath; *choláō* (5520), to enrage; *thumóō* (2373), to provoke to anger; *parapikraínō* (3893), to embitter; *paroxúnō* (3947), to sharpen or to rouse to anger; *parazēlóō* (3863), to provoke to jealousy; *apostomatízō* (653), to provoke one to speak; *prokaléō* (4292), to challenge; *epegeírō* (1892), to stir up; *anastatóō* (387), to unsettle.

Ant.: *hēsucházō* (2270), to be quiet, keep still; *eirēnopoiéō* (1517), to make peace; *sumbibázō* (4822), to unite, knit together; *diallássō* (1259), to reconcile when two may be at fault; *katallássō* (2644), to reconcile when one is at fault.

2043. ἐρείδω *ereídō*; fut. *ereísō*. To fix firmly. In the NT, used intrans. implying to become fixed, to stick fast as a ship upon a sandbank (Acts 27:41).

2044. ἐρεύγομαι *ereúgomai*; fut. *ereúxomai*, mid. deponent. To eject through the mouth, vomit. To belch out, to bellow. To speak out, utter, used trans. (Matt 13:35; Sept.: Ps 19:2; 119:171; 145:7).

2045. ἐρευνάω *ereunáō*; contracted *ereunṓ*, fut. *ereunḗsō*. To search into, investigate, explore. Used trans. (John 5:39; 7:52; Rom 8:27; 1 Cor 2:10; 1 Pet 1:11; Rev 2:23; Sept.: Gen 44:12; 2 Sam 10:3; 1 Kgs 20:6; Prov 20:27).
Deriv.: *exereunáō* (1830), to search diligently.
Syn.: *exetázō* (1833), to examine closely; *anakrínō* (350), to search; *zētéō* (242), to seek; *anazētéō* (327), to search out; *thēreúō* (2340), to hunt.
Ant.: *apokrúptō* (613), to hide, keep secret.

2046. ἐρέω *eréō*; some tenses use *rhéō* (4483) or *épō* (2036). To say, declare (Matt 26:75; Luke 2:24; 22:13; John 4:18). To promise (Heb 13:5); to call (John 15:15). The verbal adj. *rhētós*, spoken, expressly named, and the adv. *rhētṓs* (4490), expressly, occur especially in later writers, denoting the exactness of the quotation (as in 1 Tim 4:1, in which Paul may be stressing verbal inspiration).
Deriv.: *anantírrētos* (368), indisputable; *proeréō* (4280), to say before, foretell.
Syn.: *légō* (3004), to speak; *épō* (2036), to speak or say; *laléō* (2980), to talk; *phēmí* (5346), to speak, affirm; *apophthéggomai* (669), to enunciate plainly.
Ant.: *siōpáō* (4623), to keep silence.

2047. ἐρημία *erēmía*; gen. *erēmías*, fem. noun from *érēmos* (2048), desert, wilderness. Wilderness, primarily an uninhabited and uncultivated land, a solitude, desert (Matt 15:33; Mark 8:4; 2 Cor 11:26; Heb 11:38; Sept.: Ezek 35:4). It does not always denote a barren region, void of vegetation; it is often used of a place uncultivated but fit for pasture.

2048. ἔρημος *érēmos*; gen. *erēmou*, masc.-fem., neut. *érēmon*, adj. Desolate, deserted, lonely. Used as a noun and translated "wilderness" thirty-two times in the KJV. Also with the meanings desert, desolate, waste (Matt 14:13, 15; 23:38; Mark 1:35, 45; 6:31, 32, 35; Luke 4:42; 9:10, 12; 13:35; Acts 1:20; 8:26; Sept.: Lev 26:31, 33; Neh 2:17; Jer 33:10, 12 [cf. Ps 69:25]). As a subst. with *chóra* (5561), country, land or region implied, a desert, wilderness (Matt 4:1; John 3:14; 6:31; Acts 7:30, 36). Sometimes it denotes no more than an uncultivated piece of ground used for pasture in distinction from arable or enfenced land (Luke 15:4). Used of a woman meaning solitary, destitute of a husband, unmarried (Gal 4:27 quoted from Isa 54:1). As a subst., *hē érēmos*, referring to *chóra* (5561), region, a solitary desert, equivalent to *erēmía* (2047), i.e., an uninhabited and uncultivated tract of country (Matt 3:3; Mark 1:3; Luke 3:4; John 1:23, all quoted from Isa 40:3. See also Matt 11:7; 24:26; Luke 5:16; 7:24; 8:29; Rev 12:6, 14; 17:3). Spoken of the desert of Judea, i.e., the southeastern part of Judea from the Jordan along the Dead Sea which was mostly uninhabited (Matt 3:1; Mark 1:4; Luke 1:80; 3:2 [cf. Judg 1:16]); of the desert or mountainous region where Jesus was tempted, probably near Jericho (Matt 4:1; Mark 1:12, 13; Luke 4:1); of a desert probably between the Mount of Olives and Jericho (Acts 21:38). As to John 11:54 see *Ephraím* (2187). Of the Arabian Desert between Mount Sinai and Palestine (John 3:14; 6:31, 49; Acts 7:30, 36, 38, 42, 44; 13:18; 1 Cor 10:5; Heb 3:8, 17; Sept.: Ps 78:15, 19; 136:16).
Deriv.: *erēmía* (2047), solitude; *erēmóō* (2049), to desolate.

Syn.: *mónos* (3441), alone; *steíros* (4723), barren.

Ant.: *chlōrós* (5515), verdant; *kḗpos* (2779), garden.

2049. ἐρημόω *erēmóō*; contracted *erēmó*, fut. *erēmóso*, from *éremos* (2048), desert, wilderness. To desolate, lay waste (Sept.: Isa 37:18). In the NT found only in the pass., to be made desolate, be laid waste, such as the kingdom (Matt 12:25; Luke 11:17); the city (Rev 18:19); wealth, meaning to be destroyed, come to nothing (Rev 18:17). Of a person (Rev 17:16), meaning shall make her desolate, despoil her (Sept.: Isa 54:3; Jer 26:9; Ezek 26:19; 32:15).

Deriv.: *erémōsis* (2050), the act of rendering desolate, desolation.

Syn.: *kathairéō* (2507), to demolish; *monóō* (3443), to leave alone.

Ant.: *anoikodoméō* (456), to rebuild; *blastánō* (985), to bud, spring up.

2050. ἐρήμωσις *erḗmōsis*; gen. *erēmóseōs*, fem. noun from *erēmóō* (2049), to desolate. The act or the process of making desolate (Matt 24:15; Mark 13:14) in the phrase "the abomination of desolation" meaning the abomination that makes desolate, stressing the effect of the process (Luke 21:20), and referring to the desolation or depopulation of Jerusalem and the temple as a result of their abomination or desecration. See Dan 8:13 referring to "transgression of desolation"; 9:25, 27; 11:31; 12:11.

The original reference is clearly to the desecration of the temple by the soldiers of Antiochus IV (Epiphanes), the ceasing of the daily burnt offering, and the erection of an idol altar upon the Great Altar of Sacrifice in 168 B.C. Thus it is plain that Christ, in quoting the words of Daniel, intended to foretell a desecration of the temple (or perhaps of the Holy City) resembling that of Antiochus and resulting in the destruction of the national life and religion. Josephus draws a similar parallel between the Jewish misfortunes under Antiochus and the desolation caused by the Romans. There was also the desecration of the temple by the Zealots just before the attack on Jerusalem by Titus. Having seized the temple, they made it a stronghold and "entered the sanctuary with polluted feet." In opposition to Ananus, they set up as high priest Phannias, described by Josephus as "a man not only unworthy of the high priesthood, but ignorant of what the high priesthood was." The temple areas were defiled with blood, and Ananus was murdered. His murder, says Josephus, was the beginning of the capture of the city. Between the first appearance of the Roman armies before Jerusalem (A.D. 66) and the final appearance by Titus (just before Passover A.D. 70), there was ample time for flight "into the mountains" (Matt 24:15–20).

This, however, is also an event that will characterize the coming of the Lord Jesus following the Great Tribulation predicted in Matt 24:21–28. Therefore, what we have in the Olivet Discourse (Matt 24—25; Mark 13; Luke 21) is a double reference as far as the future is concerned, i.e., the desolation of the temple at Jerusalem which culminated in a final attack by Titus in A.D. 70 and the one that is eschatological and related to the Great Tribulation and the Second Coming of the Lord Jesus. This eschatological abomination of desolation must be related to the Great Tribulation which comes immediately afterwards, to be followed by heavenly disturbances such as the world has never seen before (Matt 24:21, 29).

Syn.: *katastrophḗ* (2692), destruction; *kathaíresis* (2506), demolition.

2051. ἐρίζω *erízō*; fut. *erísō*, from *éris* (2054), a quarrel. To contend, dispute. In the NT, by implication, to cry out (Matt 12:19 quoted from Isa 42:2).

Syn.: *agōnízomai* (75), to strive; *máchomai* (3164), to fight, quarrel; *diamáchomai* (1264), to struggle against; *logomachéō* (3054), to strive about words; *antagōnízomai* (464), to strive against, antagonize.

Ant.: *eirēneúō* (1514), to reconcile, keep peace or be at peace; *eirēnopoiéō* (1517), to make peace.

2052. ἐριθεία eritheía; gen. *eritheías*, fem. noun from *eritheúō* (n.f.), to work for hire, usually in the mid. voice, used in a bad sense of those who seek only their own. Contention, strife, rivalry. It represents a motive of self-interest, mercenary interest (Phil 1:16; 2:3). It also meant canvassing for public office, scheming. (Rom 2:8; 2 Cor 12:20; Gal 5:20; James 3:14, 16.)
   Syn.: *philoneikía* (5379), dispute, quarrelsomeness; *éris* (2054), strife, quarrel, rivalry; *paroxusmós* (3948), paroxysm, a sharpening of the feeling or action, irritation; *antilogía* (485), strife, answering back; *máchē* (3163), fighting; *logomachía* (3055), strife of words.

2053. ἔριον érion; gen. *eríou*, neut. noun from *éros* (n.f.), wool. Wool (Heb 9:19; Rev 1:14; Sept.: Lev 13:47, 48; Prov 31:13; Isa 1:18).

2054. ἔρις éris; gen. *éridos*, fem. noun. Strife, contention, wrangling (Rom 13:13; 1 Cor 1:11; 3:3; 2 Cor 12:20; Gal 5:20; 1 Tim 6:4; Titus 3:9); acc. *érin* (Phil 1:15), pl. *érides* (1 Cor 1:11) / *éreis* (2 Cor 12:20). Metaphorically, it means love of strife (Rom 1:29; Phil 1:15).
   Deriv.: *erízō* (2051), to strive.
   Syn.: *eritheía* (2052), contention, rivalry; *antilogía* (485), verbal dispute; *máchē* (3163), fighting; *philoneikía* (5379), love of quarreling or contention; *logomachía* (3055), strife of words; *paroxusmós* (3948), paroxysm, incitement.
   Ant.: *eirénē* (1515), peace.

2055. ἐρίφιον eríphion; gen. *eriphíou*, neut. noun, a diminutive of *ériphos* (2056), a goat. A kid, young goat (Matt 25:33). The words *ériphos*, a young goat, and the diminutive *eríphion*, appear in the picture of the last judgment where they are contrasted with sheep (*próbata* [4263]). The point of contrast lies in the color rather than the character of the animals, the sheep being pure white while the goats are mostly covered with long black hair. In Song 4:1, the locks of the beloved are compared to "a flock of goats, that appear from Mount Gilead." The Son of Man shall separate all the nations "as a shepherd divideth his sheep from the goats" (Matt 25:32), which simile is quite true to pastoral life. Sheep and goats pasture together, but never trespass on each other's domains; they are kept together but they do not mix; they may be seen to enter the fold in company, but once inside they are kept separate.

2056. ἔριφος ériphos; gen. *eríphou*, masc. noun. A kid, young goat (Luke 15:29; Sept.: Gen 27:9; 37:31; 38:17; Ex 12:5). Used as the emblem of wicked men because of their inferior value (Matt 25:32 [cf. Lev 16:5–26]). The kid formed the ordinary dish at an eastern feast, since lambs were preserved for the sake of wool and were, as a rule, slain only in sacrifice. The fatted calf (*móschos* [3448], calf; *siteutós* [4618], grain fed) appears only in the Parable of the Prodigal Son (Luke 15:23, 27, 30) and indicates a unique feast made to celebrate an unusual joy. The fatted calf is contrasted with a kid, the customary meal or meat, which oriental hospitality provides even to this day. There is no other direct mention of the goat in the gospels, though wine bottles (*askoí* [779], skin bags used as bottles) referred to in Matt 9:17; Mark 2:22; Luke 5:37f. were doubtless made of goat skin. These bottles were made by cutting off the head and legs and drawing the carcass out through the neck, and then tying the neck and legs and tanning the skin with the hairy side out.
   Deriv.: *eríphion* (2055), a young kid.
   Syn.: *aígeios* (122), belonging to a goat; *trágos* (5131), a he-goat.

2057. 'Ερμᾶς Hermás; gen. *Hermã*, masc. proper noun. Hermas. A Roman Christian whom Paul greets in Rom 16:14.

2058. ἑρμηνεία *hermēneía*; gen. *hermēneías*, fem. noun from *hermēneúo* (2059), to interpret. Interpretation, explanation (1 Cor 14:26), metonym for the ability to interpret, as a charisma (1 Cor 12:10), gift.

 Syn.: *epílusis* (1955), solution, explanation.

 Ant.: *súgchusis* (4799), a mixing together, confusion.

2059. ἑρμηνεύω *hermēneúō*; fut. *hermēneúsō*. To interpret, explain. In the NT, it means to translate from one language to another (John 1:38, 42; 9:7; Heb 7:2; Sept.: Ezra 4:7).

 Deriv.: *diermēneúō* (1329), to interpret; *hermēneía* (2058), interpretation; *methermēneúō* (3177), to change or translate from one language to another.

 Syn.: *epilúō* (1956), to explain, expound; *exēgéomai* (1834), to unfold, declare, bring out.

 Ant.: *sugchéō* (4797), to confuse.

2060. Ἑρμῆς *Hermḗs*; gen. *Hermoú*, masc. proper noun. Hermes, Mercury. The name means Mercury who in heathen mythology was the son of Jupiter and Maia, and who was the messenger and interpreter of the messages of the gods, the patron of eloquence, learning, and traffic (Acts 14:12).

2061. Ἑρμογένης *Hermogénēs*; gen. *Hermogénous*, masc. proper noun. Hermogenes, meaning begotten of Hermes (*Hermḗs* [2060]). One who forsook Paul (2 Tim 1:15).

2062. ἑρπετόν *herpetón*; gen. *herpetoú*, neut. noun from *hérpō* (n.f.), to creep. A creeping thing, animal, reptile (Acts 10:12; 11:6; Rom 1:23; James 3:7; Sept.: Gen 1:20, 24; 6:7; Lev 11:41).

 Syn.: *óphis* (3789), a serpent; *échidna* (2191), a viper; *skṓlēx* (4663), worm. Contrasted to those animals which creep are *zōon* (2226), animal; *tetrápous* (5074), a four-footed beast; *ktḗnos*

(2934), a domestic animal; *hupozúgion* (5268), an animal under the yoke such as a donkey; *thēríon* (2342), a wild beast; *kḗtos* (2785), a huge fish; *ichthús* (2486), fish; *ichthúdion* (2485), little fish; *ptēnón* (4421), bird; *órneon* (3732), a birdling; *órnis* (3733), a bird, hen; *neossós* (3502), a youngling, nestling bird.

2063. Ἐρυθρά *Eruthrá*; masc. *eruthrós*, neut. *eruthrón*. Red. Combined with *Thálassa* (*thálassa* [2281], sea), meaning the Red Sea (Acts 7:36; Heb 11:29; Sept.: Ex 10:19; 13:18).

 Syn.: *purrós* (4450), red, from *púr* (4442), fire; *kókkinos* (2847), crimson, scarlet.

2064. ἔρχομαι *érchomai*; fut. *eleúsomai*, 2d aor. *ḗlthon*; perf. *elḗlutha*, pluperf. *elēlúthein*, mid. deponent. In the common Gr., the forms of the Attic verb *eími*, to go, were used more frequently for the fut., imper., and imperf., but in the NT the imper. *érchou*, pl. *érchesthe* (Matt 8:9; John 1:39) was used instead of *íthi* and *íte*, the imperf. *ērchómēn* (Mark 1:45), was used instead of *ḗein* or *ḗa*; and the fut. *eleúsomai* (Matt 9:15; 1 Cor 4:19). To come, to go, move or pass along, intrans. in any direction, as marked by the adjuncts or often simply by the context. The forms from *ḗlthon*, the 2d aor., however, more frequently signify "to come," so that *ḗlthen*, for example, is rarely used of one who goes from or away (Luke 2:44) while the forms derived from *érchomai* are used indifferently of travel in both directions.

 (I) To go, with adjuncts implying motion from a place or person to another.

 (A) Pres. and imperf. followed by *eis* (1519) with the acc., of place (John 6:17); followed by the acc., to go one's way (Acts 9:17; Heb 11:8).

 (B) 2d aor. *ḗlthon*, in an absolute sense (Mark 11:13); followed by *prós* (4314), toward, and the acc. as in Luke 15:20; followed by the acc. of distance, *hodón hēméras* (*hodón* [3598], the journey, road; *hēméras* [2250], of a day), a day's distance (Luke 2:44).

(II) To come, with adjuncts implying motion to or toward any person or place.

(A) As spoken of persons: **(1)** In an absolute sense (Matt 8:9; Mark 4:4; 6:31; John 1:39; Acts 5:15). In the pres. in a historical sense, that is, instead of the aor. (Matt 25:11, 19; Mark 2:18; John 20:18; 3 John 1:3); in a fut. sense, apparently, but only of what is certain to take place (John 4:25; 14:3, 30; Rev 1:7). Especially in the phrase *ho erchómenos*, the coming One, i.e., the future One, He who shall come, the Messiah (Matt 11:3; 21:9; Luke 7:19, 20; John 6:14; 11:27; 12:13). In the expression *ho ón kaí ho én kaí ho erchómenos* (*ho* [3588], the; *ón* [5607], being; *kaí* [2532], and; *én* [2258], was), the One being, the One who was (or had been) and the coming One (Rev 1:4, 8; 4:8). See *eimí* (1510, I, D). By a species of pleonasm, the aor. part. *elthón*, the one who came, is prefixed to other verbs in which the idea of coming is already presupposed in order to render the idea more full and complete (Matt 2:23, "he came and dwelt"; 8:2; Mark 5:23; 12:14; Luke 7:3; Eph 2:17). **(2)** With adjuncts marking object or purpose, e.g., followed by the inf. (Matt 2:2; Mark 2:17; Luke 4:34); followed by the fut. part. (Matt 27:49; Acts 8:27); with the pres. part., implying purpose and manner (Luke 13:7). **(3)** With the dat. of person, either pleonastic (as a redundancy) or meaning in respect to, for (Matt 21:5; Rev 2:5, 16); with the dat. of thing, as manner or instrument (John 21:8). **(4)** With an adv. of place (Matt 8:29; Mark 5:27; John 4:16; 8:14); with an adv. and inf. of purpose (John 4:15). In Acts 9:21, *érchomai hôde eis toúto* (*hôde* [5602], here; *eis* [1519], unto; *toúto* [5124], this one), "come hither for that intent" (a.t.). **(5)** Construed with a prep.: **(a)** *Apó* (575), from, with the gen. of place (Mark 1:9; 7:1; Acts 18:2); with the gen. of person, from a person (Mark 5:35; John 3:2; Gal 2:12). **(b)** *Eis* (1519), unto, with the acc. of place, to come into, e.g., into the house, to enter (Matt 2:11;

Luke 14:1); of a country, city, to come to or into (Mark 5:1; 8:10; John 11:38; Acts 8:40; Gal 2:11; 1 Tim 1:15); With the acc. of purpose, i.e., *eis*, unto, as final (John 1:7, "unto the testimony" [a.t.]; 4:45, "unto the feast," i.e., to attend the feast; 11:56); with *eis* repeated, both of place and final (John 9:39; 2 Cor 2:12). **(c)** *Ek* (1537), from or out of, with a gen. of place, whence (Luke 5:17; John 7:41); *ek* and *eis* (John 4:54). **(d)** *En* (1722), in, with the dat. of manner (Luke 23:42). **(e)** *Epí* (1909), upon, with the gen. of thing, implying rest upon (Matt 24:30, "upon the clouds" [a.t.]); with the acc. of place, upon or to which one comes (Mark 6:53; Luke 19:5; 24:1; Acts 12:10); with the acc. of obj. or purpose (Matt 3:7, "come to his baptism," i.e., to participate in his baptism); with the acc. of person, to come to or before anyone (Acts 24:8); to come upon anyone, e.g., the Spirit (Matt 3:16; Acts 19:6). Also to come against (Luke 14:31). **(f)** *Héōs autoú* (*héōs* [2193], until; *autoú* [846], him), "up to him" (a.t. [Luke 4:42]). **(g)** *Katá* (2596), toward, with the acc., to move to, toward, along by (Acts 16:7; Luke 10:33). **(h)** *Metá* (3326), after, with the acc. of person, to come after in time, to follow, appear later (Acts 13:25; 19:4). **(i)** *Opísō* (3694), after, with gen. of person, to come after, i.e., to follow, figuratively to become the follower or disciple of anyone (Matt 16:24; Luke 19:23). Of time, to come after, appear later (Matt 3:11; John 1:27). **(j)** *Pará* (3844), from, with gen. of person, to come from anyone, i.e., as sent (Luke 8:49). With the acc. of place, at, near, along (Matt 15:29). **(k)** *Prós* (4314), with the acc. of person, to whom one comes (This is the more usual construction. See Matt 7:15; Luke 7:7; John 3:2; 11:19; 14:6, 23.); with the acc. of thing (John 3:20, 21).

(B) In the sense of to come forth before the public, to appear, make one's appearance (Matt 11:14, 19; Mark 9:11, 12; Gal 3:19; 2 Pet 3:3). Pres. in the fut. sense (Matt 17:11; 1 Cor 15:35). Followed by the pres. part. of manner (Matt 11:19; John 1:31). To come in the flesh, *en sarkí* (*en* [1722], in; *sarkí* [4561], flesh), meaning come or appear in the flesh as spoken of Christ (1 John 4:2; 2 John 1:7); *epí tō onómati* (*epí* [1909], upon; *tō* [3588], the; *onómati* [3686], name) followed by the gen., meaning in the name of someone (Matt 24:5), depending upon His name as the ultimate Teacher and Author to give their own teachings authority. See *epí* (1909, II, B, 3, a), upon.

(**C**) In the sense of to come again, back, to return, in an absolute sense (Luke 15:30, of the prodigal son; Rom 9:9; Heb 13:23). *Héōs érchomai* (*héōs* [2193], until; *érchomai*, I come) (Luke 19:13; John 21:22). *Elthōn*, used pleonastically (Matt 5:24; Luke 18:8); followed by the inf. of purpose (2 Thess 1:10); followed by the pres. part. of manner (John 9:7, "he came back seeing" [a.t.]); followed by *eis* (1519), to, with the acc. of place (Matt 2:21); followed by *prós* (4314), toward, with the acc. of person (John 7:45; 14:18, 28).

(**D**) Metaphorically of persons, for example, followed by *diá* (1223), through, as in 1 John 5:6, "He that came through water and blood" (a.t.); see *diá* (1223, I, D), through; followed by *eis* (1519), unto, as *eis heautón elthōn* (*heautón*, [1438], himself, *elthōn*, coming), i.e., coming to himself, recovering his right mind (Luke 15:17); *eis cheíron elthoúsa* (*eis* [1519], unto; *cheíron* [5501], worse; *elthoúsa* [aor. part. of *érchomai*], came), growing worse (Mark 5:26). In John 12:27, "unto this hour"; followed by *ek* (1537), from or out of the Tribulation (Rev 7:14, "having escaped from" [a.t.]).

(**E**) Metaphorically spoken of things, for example: (**1**) Of time (Matt 9:15; John 16:4, 32; Acts 2:20; 3:19). Pres. tense with a fut. meaning, of a time near and certain, to be coming, be near (Luke 23:29; John 4:35; 9:4; Heb 8:8). The part. *erchómenos*, coming in the future (Mark 10:30; Luke 18:30; John 16:13; Sept.: Isa 44:7; Acts 18:21). (**2**) Of the kingdom of God, to come, i.e., to be established (Matt 6:10; Mark 11:10). (**3**) Of good or evil, e.g., of a good result (Rom 3:8); followed by *eis* and the acc., unto something (Phil 1:12); followed by *epí* (1909), upon, and the acc., to come upon, e.g., peace (Matt 10:13); of evil, guilt, followed by *epí* and the acc., to come upon, i.e., to happen to, to be laid upon (John 18:4; Eph 5:6). See also 1 Thess 1:10, "from the wrath to come." Of guilt, *haíma* (129), blood (Matt 23:35); of offenses, to come, to arise (Matt 18:7). (**4**) Generally of a voice, with *ek* (1537), out of (Mark 9:7); of a star (Matt 2:9); of floods (Matt 7:25, 27); of rain (Luke 12:54; Heb 6:7); of wind (John 3:8); of utensils, to be brought (Mark 4:21); of a law, faith, to come, i.e., to be announced, made known (Rom 7:9; Gal 3:23). To come into the open, to come abroad, i.e., be manifested (Mark 4:22). "When that which is perfect is come," i.e., is established (1 Cor 13:10).

Deriv.: *anérchomai* (424), to go up; *apérchomai* (565), to come away or from; *diérchomai* (1330), to come or go through; *eisérchomai* (1525), to come into; *éleusis* (1660), advent, coming; *exérchomai* (1831), to come out; *epérchomai* (1904), to come or go upon; *katérchomai* (2718), to come down; *parérchomai* (3928), to pass by; *periérchomai* (4022), to come or go all around; *proérchomai* (4281), to go before, precede; *prosérchomai* (4334), to come or go near; *sunérchomai* (4905), to come together.

Syn.: *paragínomai* (3854), to arrive, be present; *hḗkō* (2240), to come, with the emphasis of being present; *aphiknéomai* (864), to arrive at a place; *enístēmi* (1764), to be present, be imminent; *ephístēmi* (2186), to come up or arrive; *katantáō* (2658), to come to; *parístēmi* (3936), to stand by or near, to come; *phthánō* (5348), to anticipate, to come sooner than expected; *proseggízō* (4331), to come near; *gínomai* (1096), to come to pass.

Ant.: *poreúomai* (4198), to go on one's way; *ápeimi* (548), to go away; *metabaínō* (3327), to go over from one place to another, depart; *apérchomai* (565), to go away; *anachōréō* (402), to depart, retire, recede; *apobaínō* (576), to go away or from; *éxeimi* (1826), to go out; *apodēméō* (589), to go to another country; *paragínomai* (3854), to go; *apochōréō* (672), to depart from; *ekchōréō* (1633), to depart out of; *apochōrízomai* (673), to separate oneself from; *analúō* (360), to unloose, depart; *aphístēmi* (868), to depart.

2065. ἐρωτάω erōtáō; contracted *erōtṓ*, fut. *erōtḗso*, from *éromai* (n.f.), to ask, inquire. To ask, with an acc. of person and also acc. of thing, or other adjunct.

(I) To ask, i.e., to interrogate, inquire of, with the acc. of person (Matt 16:13; John 1:19; 16:5; Sept.: Gen 24:47; 32:17); followed by the acc. of person and thing (Matt 21:24; Mark 4:10; Luke 20:3; Sept.: Jer 38:14); followed by the acc. of person and *perí* (4012), concerning, with the gen. of thing (Luke 9:45). In an absolute sense (Luke 22:68; Sept.: Deut 13:14).

(II) To request, entreat, beseech, with the acc. of person (Matt 15:23; Luke 14:18, 19; John 12:21; Phil 4:3); followed by the acc. of thing (Luke 14:32; Sept.: Ps 122:6); followed by the acc. of person and a prep., e.g., *perí* (4012), concerning, followed by the gen. (Luke 4:38; John 16:26); *hupér* (5228), for, with the gen., for someone (2 Thess 2:1 [cf. Sept.: 1 Kgs 2:22]); with the meaning of *aitéō* (154), to ask, followed by the acc. of person and *hína* (2443), so that (Mark 7:26; Luke 7:36; John 4:47; 1 Thess 4:1); with *hópōs* (3704), that (Luke 7:3; Acts 23:20); followed by the acc. of person and aor. inf. (Luke 5:3; John 4:40; Acts 3:3); perf. inf. (1 Thess 5:12).

(III) A very distinct meaning of the verb *erōtáō* is "to pray," but it is in contrast to the verb *aitéō* (154). *Erōtáō* provides the most delicate and tender expression for prayer or request with the one asking and the one being asked being on an equal level, such as the Lord Jesus asking of the Father. The contrast is made clear in John 14:13, 14, where the word *aitéō* is used in the case of our asking

God as an inferior to a superior, leaving it up to Him to do that which pleases Him. However, in John 14:16, when the Lord Jesus is praying to the Father or asking the Father, the verb *erōtáō* is used, as also in John 17:9, 15, 20.

Deriv.: *dierōtáō* (1331), to inquire; *eperōtáō* (1905), to interrogate, inquire of.

Syn.: *punthánomai* (4441), to ask by way of inquiry; *exetázō* (1833), to search out; *zētéō* (2212), to seek; *ekzētéō* (1567), to seek out; *diaginóskō* (1231), to inquire; *akribóō* (198), to learn by diligent or exact inquiry; *anakrínō* (350), to examine judicially; *déomai* (1189), to beseech; *parakaléō* (3870), to beseech; *exaitéomai* (1809), to demand, desire; *epikaléomai* (1941), to invoke; *epaitéō* (1871), to ask for, beg.

Ant.: *apokrínomai* (611), to answer.

2066. ἐσθής esthḗs; gen. *esthḗtos*, fem. noun from *énnumi* (n.f.), to clothe, dress. A garment, clothing, raiment (Luke 23:11; Acts 1:10; 10:30; 12:21; James 2:2, 3).

Syn.: *himátion* (2440), an outer cloak or cape; *himatismós* (2441), clothing, apparel; *chlamús* (5511), a military cloak worn over the *chitón* by emperors, kings, magistrates, military officers; *stolḗ* (4749), a stately robe or uniform, a long gown worn as mark of dignity; *katastolḗ* (2689), long robe of dignity; *ésthēsis* (2067), clothing; *énduma* (1742), a garment of any kind; *ependútēs* (1903), an upper or outer garment which sometimes fishermen wore when at work; *phelónēs* (5341), a mantle, traveling robe for protection against stormy weather, overcoat; *peribólaion* (4018), a wrap or cape, a garment thrown around one; *podḗrēs* (4158), an outer garment reaching to the feet; *sképasma* (4629), a covering, raiment; *phelónēs* (5341), a traveling cloak.

Ant.: *gumnótēs* (1132), nudity.

2067. ἔσθησις ésthēsis; gen. *esthḗseōs*, fem. noun from *esthéō* (n.f.), to be dressed, which is from *esthḗs* (2066), apparel. A garment, raiment (Luke 24:4).

Syn.: *esthḗs* (2066), a garment.
Ant.: *gumnótēs* (1132), nudity.

2068. ἐσθίω *esthíō*; fut. *phágomai*, 2d aor. *éphagon*, (*phágō* [5315], to eat, is used in the aor. and fut.), strengthened form of the obsolete *édō* (n.f.), to eat. To eat, consume food, spoken both of men and animals.

(I) Generally and in an absolute sense of persons (Matt 12:1; 14:21; 26:21, 26; Mark 7:3; Luke 6:1; Acts 27:35; 1 Cor 10:28; Sept.: 1 Sam 1:7, 8).

(II) With an adjunct of the obj. or thing eaten:

(A) Followed by *ek* (1537), of, with the gen., to eat of something, i.e., a part of it; to eat of the bread (1 Cor 11:28; Sept.: 2 Sam 12:3; 2 Kgs 4:40) In the sense of to live from (1 Cor 9:7, 13).

(B) Followed by *apó* (575) with the gen., to eat from, i.e., of anything, a part of it, spoken of dogs (Matt 15:27; Mark 7:28).

(C) Followed by the acc. of the thing eaten: **(1)** In 1 Cor 11:26, "to eat the bread and drink the cup" means to celebrate the Lord's Supper. **(2)** To eat bread means to take food or a meal (Matt 15:2; Mark 7:5). In 2 Thess 3:12, "to eat their own bread" means to support themselves. **(3)** By implication, to eat in order to support life, to use as food, to live upon (Mark 1:6; Rom 14:2, 3, 6; 1 Cor 10:25, 27). **(4)** In a partitive sense, to eat of, partake of (1 Cor 8:7, 10; 11:26, 27).

(III) To eat and drink, used in an absolute sense or with the acc.

(A) To live in the usual manner (Matt 11:18, "not living as other mèn" [a.t. {cf. Matt 3:4; 11:19, "The Son of man came eating and drinking" means like other men}]; Luke 7:33, 34). Used as an opposite of *nēsteúō* (3522), to fast, it means not to fast (Luke 5:33).

(B) By implication, to feast, banquet, with the idea of luxury, reveling (Matt 24:49; Luke 12:45; 17:27, 28; 1 Cor

11:21, 22; Sept.: 1 Sam 30:16; Job 1:4, 18).

(C) Followed by *enópion* (1799), before someone, to eat and drink in the presence of someone, i.e., to live in acquaintance and communion with him (Sept.: 1 Kgs 1:25). Metaphorically in Luke 22:30, "that you may feast at my table" (a.t.), i.e., live in familiar companionship with me.

(IV) Metaphorically, to devour, consume, trans. of fire (Heb 10:27). In the OT, to eat is often applied to the action of fire, for which in this sense the Sept. uses other words expressive of eating such as *édomai* or *kataphágomai*, but never *esthíō*.

Deriv.: *katesthíō* (2719), to devour; *nḗstis* (3523), fasting; *sunesthíō* (4906), to eat with or together.

Syn.: *trṓgō* (5176), primarily to gnaw, chew, eat; *geúomai* (1089), to taste; *bibrṓskō* (977), to eat, voraciously devour; *korénnumi* (2880), to satiate, satisfy with food; *nomḗn échō* (*nomḗn* [3542], pasture; *échō* [2192], to have), to have pasture; *metalambánō* (3335), to take part or share.

Ant.: *nēsteúō* (3522), to fast.

2069. Ἐσλί *Eslí*; masc. proper noun transliterated from the Hebr. Esli, meaning reserved by Jehovah. A person in Christ's genealogy (Luke 3:25).

2070. ἐσμέν *esmén*; pres. act. indic. 1st person pl. of *eimí* (1510), to be. We are.

2071. ἔσομαι *ésomai*; fut. act. indic. 1st person sing. of *eimí* (1510), to be. I shall be.

2072. ἔσοπτρον *ésoptron*; gen. *esóptrou*, neut. noun, a variant of *eísoptron* (n.f.), which is from *eisópsomai* (n.f.), to look into. A looking glass, mirror (James 1:23). In 1 Cor 13:12, it means that we now see only a refracted image, obscurely, and not face to face as we shall hereafter. Mirrors in Bible times were usually made of polished metal (Ex 38:8; Job 37:18).

Syn.: *húalos* (5194), glass.

2073. ἑσπέρα hespéra; gen. *hespéras*, noun, fem. of *hésperos* (n.f.), evening. Evening (Luke 24:29; Acts 4:3; 28:23). The Jews did not divide the days into hours until later times. The custom long persisted of counting by portions of the day. Earlier than the division of the day into hours was a division of the night into three watches (Ex 14:24; Judg 7:19; 1 Sam 11:11; Lam 2:19). The three-fold division continued into post-Roman times, first century, but the Roman division into four watches was also known. In Mark 13:35, all four watches are referred to. *Opsé* (3796), was the close of the day when the evening began; *mesonúktion* (3317), midnight; *alektorophōnía* (219), the third night watch from midnight to 3 a.m., literally meaning cock-crowing; and *prōí* (4404), early in the morning which would be from 3 to 6 a.m. There were four equal watches in a day.

Syn.: *opsía*, fem. of *ópsios* (3798), evening; *prōía* (4405), morning.

2074. Ἐσρώμ Esrṓm; indeclinable masc. proper noun transliterated from the Hebr. *Chetsrōn* (2696, OT). Hezron, meaning walled in. The grandson of Judah (Matt 1:3; Luke 3:33 [cf. Gen 46:12; 1 Chr 2:5]).

2075. ἐστέ esté; pres. act. indic. 2d person pl. of *eimí* (1510), to be. You are.

2076. ἐστί estí; pres. act. indic. 3d person sing. of *eimí* (1510), to be. He (she, it) is.

2077. ἔστω éstō; pres. act. imper. 2d person sing. of *eimí* (1510), to be. Be thou; 3d person pl. *éstōsan*, let them be.

2078. ἔσχατος éschatos; fem. *eschátē*, neut. *éschaton*, noun from *ek* (1537), from, primarily with reference to place.

The extreme, most remote, spoken of place and time.

(I) Of place:

(A) Particularly extreme, most remote, the neut. as subst. *tó éschaton*, the extremity (Acts 1:8; 13:47; Sept.: Deut 28:49; Isa 48:20; Jer 16:19).

(B) Metaphorically implying rank or dignity, the last, lowest, least (Luke 14:9, 10). Generally (Matt 19:30; Mark 9:35; 10:31; Luke 13:30; John 8:9; 1 Cor 4:9).

(C) Of order or number, the last, utmost (Matt 5:26; Luke 12:59).

(II) Of time, the last or latest.

(A) Generally of persons (Matt 20:8, 12, 14, 16 means the laborers last hired; 1 Cor 15:26, 45, where *ho éschatos Adám*, the last Adam, means the final Adam since the second was the last). In an adv. sense (Mark 12:6, 22, "the last to die being the woman" [a.t.]). Of things, the last, or the latter, the latter state or condition of anyone or anything (Matt 12:45; Luke 11:26; 2 Pet 2:20; Sept.: Job 8:7; 42:12); the last error, (Matt 27:64); the last works, (Rev 2:19); the last plagues, (Rev 15:1; 21:9); the trumpet of the last day (1 Cor 15:52, "In the last trumpet" [a.t.]). In the neut. *éschaton* as an adv. (1 Cor 15:8, "last of all").

(B) With a noun of time, as the last day, e.g., of a festival (John 7:37); of the world, the day of judgment (John 6:39, 40, 44, 54; 11:24; 12:48); in the phrase "the last days" (Acts 2:17; 2 Tim 3:1; James 5:3). The expression *ep' eschátou tōn hēmerō* (*epí* [1909], upon; *tōn* [3588], the; *hēmerōn* [2250], days), literally means "upon the last of the days" (a.t. [Heb 1:2; 2 Pet 3:3]) or *en kairō eschátō* (*en* [1722], in; *kairō* [2540], time) (1 Pet 1:5) means "in the last time." *Kairós* involves opportunity, whereas *chrónos* (5550) involves only the chronology of time. In 1 Pet 1:20 and Jude 1:18, it is *chrónos* that is used in the pl. and sing. In 1 John 2:18, reference is made to the last chronological hour. All the above refer to the last times of this age (*aiṓn* [165]). These are the times since the coming of Christ in which the power of this world (*kósmos* [2889]) is in part broken, and will be wholly destroyed only at Christ's Second Advent, designated in 1 Cor 10:11 as *tá télē tōn aiōnōn* (*tá* [3588], the; *télē* [5056], end; *tōn* [3588], the; *aiōnōn* [165], ages), the ends of the ages or the end of the age. See *aiōn* (165, II), age, and *basileía* (932, III), kingdom. These expressions cover the whole interval between the first and the final advent of Christ. The present and final period of the history of unredeemed humanity prior to the new heavens and earth is the *eschaton*. Some do not believe that Acts 2:17–21 refers to the advent of Pentecost since the signs detailed in verses nineteen and twenty relating to the heavenly bodies were never realized. (However, such language may be apocalyptic imagery designed simply to signify the dramatic visitation by God in time and space.) These are the events detailed by the Lord Jesus as future occurrences immediately after the Great Tribulation (Matt 24:29; Mark 13:24, 25; Luke 21:25–27). The expression, however, sometimes refers to the times adjacent to the period in which the writers were writing as in Heb 1:2; 1 Pet 1:20; Jude 1:18. In 1 John 2:18, the expression *eschátē hōra* (*hōra* [5610], hour), last hour, refers to the prolonged period of time just before the Second Coming as also 2 Tim 3:1; James 5:3; 1 Pet 1:5; 2 Pet 3:3.

(C) The phrase *ho prōtos kaí ho éschatos* (*ho* [3588], the; *prōtos* [4413], first; *kaí* [2532], and), the first and the last, is spoken of the Messiah in glory (Rev 1:11, 17; 2:8; 22:13) in the sense of eternal, the beginning and the end, equivalent to the expressions *tó Álpha kaí tó Ōméga* (*tó* [3588], the; *Álpha* [1], the first letter of the Gr. alphabet; *Ōméga* [5598], the last letter of the Gr. alphabet), and *hē archē* (746) (the active causal beginning) *kaí tó télos* (*télos* [5056]), the causal end), the One to bring the termination of the present state of affairs or age (Rev 21:6; 22:13 [cf. Isa 41:4; 44:6; 48:12]). In 2 Chr 9:29, the words "first and last," meaning all. See also 2 Chr 12:15.

Deriv.: *eschátōs* (2079), extremely.

Syn.: *télos* (5056), end; *péras* (4009), extremity, end; *teleutē* (5054), the end, decease, death; *ōméga* (5598), the termination, the last letter of the Gr. alphabet.

Ant.: *archē* (746), beginning; *álpha* (1), the first letter of the Gr. alphabet; *prōtos* (4413), first; *themélios* (2310), foundational; *aparchē* (536), beginning, as the start of more to come; *anatolē* (395), dawn, dayspring, the beginning of something.

2079. ἐσχάτως *eschátōs*; adv. from *éschatos* (2078), last. Extremely, i.e., in extremity, to be at the last gasp, at the point of death (Mark 5:23).

Syn.: *hústeron* (5305), used as an adv. meaning afterward; *metépeita* (3347), afterward; *épeita* (1899), after that, afterward, then; *opsé* (3796), in the end, late, after; *nún* (3568), of late, now with the idea of finally; *prosphátōs* (4373), recently, lately.

Ant.: *prōton* (4412), firstly, of time; *en archē* (*en* [1722]; *archē* [746]), at the beginning; *ap' archēs* (*apó* [575]), from the beginning; *próteron* (4386), first, before; *prōton* (4412), an adv. from *prōtos* (4413), first, firstly (Acts 11:26).

2080. ἔσω *ésō*; adv. from *eis* (1519), in, into, with a gen. Into, in, within.

(I) Used in an absolute sense meaning in, within, implying motion (Matt 26:58; Mark 14:54; 15:16; Sept.: 2 Chr 29:16, 18).

(II) Of place meaning within (John 20:26; Acts 5:23; Sept.: Gen 39:11). With the art. prefixed it assumes the role of an adj., *ho ésō ánthrōpos* (*ho* [3588], the; *ánthrōpos* [444], man), i.e., the inner man, mind, soul or spirit of man (Rom 7:22; Eph 3:16). As used by Paul, the inner man means the mind or soul considered as being renewed and strengthened by the Holy Spirit (cf. 2 Cor 4:16). With the noun implied, *hoi ésō*, those within, the Church, i.e., the Christians (see 1 Cor 5:12); the opposite of *hoi éxō* (1854), those that are without.

Deriv.: *ésōthen* (2081), from within; *esōteros* (2082), inner.

Syn.: *entós* (1787), within; *ésōthen* (2081), from within; *en* (1722), in; the expression *en tṓ kruptṓ* (*kruptṓ* [2927], secret), secretly, in a hidden manner.

Ant.: *éxō* (1854), without; *éxōthen* (1855), outward; the expression *en tṓ phanerṓ* (*phanerṓ* [5318], open), manifest, outwardly; *ektós* (1622), outside, out of.

2081. ἔσωθεν *ésōthen*; adv. of place, from *ésō* (2080), within, and the suffix *-then*, denoting "from a place." From within (Mark 7:21, 23; Luke 11:7); within, internally. Spoken of persons (Matt 7:15; 23:25, 27, 28; 2 Cor 7:5; Rev 4:8; 5:1; Sept.: Gen 6:14; Ex 25:11; 39:19). With the art. prefixed, it assumes the nature of an adj., *to ésōthen*, the inner part, the inside (Luke 11:39, 40). *Ho ésōthen*, implying *ánthrōpos* (444), the inner man (2 Cor 4:16), which is opposite of *éxōthen* (1855), outwardly, from without.

2082. ἐσώτερος *esōteros*; fem. *esōtéra*, neut. *esōteron*, the comparative of *ésō* (2080), inside. Inner, interior (Acts 16:24). With the neut. def. art., *tó esōteron*, the part within, within the veil (Heb 6:19 [cf. Sept.: Lev 16:15]).

Ant.: *exōteros* (1857), outer.

2083. ἑταῖρος *hetaíros*; gen. *hetaírou*, masc. noun. Some lexicographers suggest that it is derived from *éthos* (1485), custom, manner, and possibly what would have been *hétairos*, a customary companion. Others theorize that it is derived from *étēs*, used always in the pl. *étai*, meaning kinsmen and dependents of a great house. Exact derivation not certain. The fem. *hetaíra* was a woman having a status between that of a legal wife and of a prostitute and who, in our culture, would be called a mistress, or "kept woman." Aphrodite was known as the goddess of the *hetaírai*, and her temple was on Acrocorinth. It is from the known meaning of the fem. word that we can get an idea of the masc. word as a male companion who is neither one's very own by legally accepted ties nor one who is a prostitute and belongs to anybody and everybody.

The Class. Gr. occurrences of the masc. *hetaíros* refer to comrades or companions who were mostly followers of a chief. They were not necessarily companions for the sake of helping the chief, but for getting whatever advantage they could. They were partners at meals or messmates. The pupils or disciples were usually called the *hetaíroi* of their masters, such as those of Socrates. Political partisans were also called *hetaíroi*. It was rarely used of lovers.

The verb *hetairéō* (n.f.) basically means to keep company with or to establish and maintain a meretricious, pretentious, ostentatious, deceptive, and misleading friendship. True friendship is expressed by the verb *philéō* (5368), to befriend which means to appropriate another person's interests unselfishly. The noun is *phílos* (5384), friend, and the quality that brings two people together to share common interests is *philía* (5373), friendship.

The corresponding word to *hetaíros* is *hetaireía* which has come down from Class. Gr. to Mod. Gr. Today it means a company or corporation which involves people who associate together for the primary purpose of making money or for personal interest through corporate design. The study of the word *hetaíros* causes us to conclude that it could not be used as syn. with *phílos*, a true friend who seeks the other's good. *Hetaíros* is one who only projects his own interest. The inference, therefore, is that *hetaíros* means a selfish acquaintance, one who seeks his own interests above the interests of others. He is a partner in a company, not necessarily for the good of others but primarily for his own advantage. The good of others is acceptable only when it promotes his own well-being.

To discover the NT meaning, it is necessary for us to remember the fact that the Lord Jesus called His true disciples *phílous* (Luke 12:4; John 11:11; 15:14, 15). Abraham was not called an *hetaíros* of God, but a *phílos* of God (James 2:23). When Jesus was accused of being a friend (*phílos* [5384]) of publicans and sinners, they had in mind more the meaning of *hetaíros*, one who had adopted their philosophy of life instead of one who wanted to be a true friend by helping them (Matt 11:19; Luke 7:34; John 11:11).

A definite distinction between these two Gr. words must be made in Eng., but unfortunately the Eng. language has only one word, and that is "friend," which the translators have used in three of the four instances of the occurrence of the word *hetaíros* (Matt 20:13; 22:12; 26:50). All the occurrences are in Matthew and each one is attributed to the Lord Jesus Christ.

In the first instance, in Matt 11:16, our Lord said, "But whereunto shall I liken this generation? It is like unto children sitting in the markets, and calling unto their fellows." (*Hetaírois* [TR], the UBS and the Majority Text having *hetérois* [2087], which is an entirely different word meaning others of a different kind. The TR is to be preferred.) Why did the Lord call these fellows *hetaírous* and not *phílous* (5384)? Because if they were *phíloi*, friends, they would have acted in agreement with the others and rejoiced with them as they played their musical instruments for them. Even if we take the word to be *hetérois*, others of a different kind, the ultimate meaning of the two words *hetaíroi* and *héteroi* would coincide. These contrary ones, in spite of hearing the notes of joy, would not rejoice with them. They were obstinate. Nor would they sorrow with the singing of their lamentations as we have in the second part of Matt 11:17. What the Lord Jesus was saying is that we, as believers, are like children, and no matter what we do, in our rejoicing or in our lamentation, this contrary generation will not agree with us. Why? Because they are *hetaíroi*, companions who seek their own interests and benefit, not caring whether others

rejoice or sorrow. The sons of the kingdom are, as the Apostle Paul designates them, those who rejoice with them that rejoice, and those who weep with them that weep (Rom 12:15). It is interesting to note that while those of the world who do not respond properly to the children of the kingdom are called *hetaíroi* or *héteroi* in Matt 11:16, the description of our Savior in Matt 11:19 is not *hetaíros*, but *phílos* (friend).

The next occurrence of *hetaíros* is in Matt 20:13 and in this, as well as in the other two occurrences (Matt 22:12; 26:50), it is a direct appellation that our Lord gives to certain types of people. The character of these people is adequately clarified by the context. Whom does the Lord call *hetaíre* in Matt 20:13? It is the contracted, hired worker who signed an agreement with the householder or the owner of the vineyard, the latter person in this Parable of the Laborers representing God. He agreed to work a twelve-hour day starting at 6 a.m. This laborer represents those who will not go out to work for the Lord in His vineyard unless they have a signed contract bearing a designated obligation on the part of the Lord. When, however, the contracted laborer found that the householder generously rewarded the others who had not gone out on a contractual basis, but trusted the Master to give whatever he would consider a just reward to them, he was angry. The Master had given as much for one hour's work to the trusting servants as the contractual laborer received for twelve hour's work, and he implied that the Master was totally unjust. It is on the expression of grumbling, complaint, and the accusation that the Master was unjust that He turned to this contracted laborer and called him *hetaíre*. Did the Lord make a mistake in calling him that instead of *phíle* (5384), or was the meaning of *hetaíre* descriptive of his character? In contrast, note that *phíle* is used in Luke 14:10 to designate a humble person who, in being entertained at a feast, does not take the higher place of honor but the lowly place of humility. How then should the word *hetaíre* in Matt 20:13 be translated? A qualified "comrade" would have been better than "friend." This was a *philía hetaírousa*, a meretricious, parasitic or deceitful friendship. This man was not a true friend, but he was a friend for what he could get out of the relationship, a leech, a parasite. Therefore, he could be called a selfish companion, which would have been a more accurate translation of the Gr. word *hetaíre*. Would not our Savior have been counted as a hypocrite to call someone what he really was not?

The next occurrence in Matt 22:12 is in connection with our Lord's Parable of the Marriage Supper (Luke 14:15–24). The person who entered the banquet hall without the accepted dress was called *hetaíre*, and the comment following that appellation was, "How camest thou in hither not having a wedding garment?" That was a rebuke for having pretended to have the right to be there when he did not. The derogatory implication of the word cannot be doubted. The punishment that was imposed upon this impostor as described in Matt 22:13 certainly cannot be that of a true friend: "Bind him hand and foot, and take him away, and cast him into outer darkness; there shall be weeping and gnashing of teeth." This represents the fate of religious hypocrites who appear to be God's elect when in fact they are not.

The fourth and last occurrence of the word is in Matt 26:50, and the character of the one addressed as *hetaíre* is none other than Judas at the time that he betrayed his Master with a kiss as if he were a true friend (*phílos*). Quite the contrary, the Lord called him *hetaíre*, indicating that while Judas was giving Him a kiss pretending that he was a friend, all he was interested in was the thirty pieces of silver. Therefore, the meaning of the word is a person who attaches himself to another for what he can get out of him, a leech or a phony friend as we would say in our culture today, a selfish comrade. It would be far better not to use

the word "friend" at all, but rather "selfish colleague" or "friendly opportunist" or "impostor."

2084. ἑτερόγλωσσος *heteróglōssos*; gen. *heteroglōssou*; masc.-fem., neut. *heteróglōsson*, adj. from *héteros* (2087), another but different, and *glōssa* (1100), a tongue, language. One of another tongue or language (1 Cor 14:21, equal to *glōssais hetérais* [pl. of *héteros* {2087}], with other languages, an allusion to Isa 28:11).

2085. ἑτεροδιδασκαλέω *heterodidaskaléō*; contracted *heterodidaskalō*, fut. *heterodidaskalēsō*, from *héteros* (2087), other but different, and *didáskalos* (1320), teacher. To teach a doctrine different from one's own (1 Tim 1:3; 6:3). Equal to the phrase *hétera didáskō* ([1321], to teach), to teach differently.

2086. ἑτεροζυγέω *heterozugéō*; contracted *heterozugō*, fut. *heterozugēsō*, from *heterozugéō* (n.f.), unequally yoked, which is from *héteros* (2087), another, different, and *zugós* (2218), a yoke. To be yoke unequally, as with pagan idolaters and by extension, particularly in marriage (2 Cor 6:14; Sept.: Lev 19:19).

2087. ἕτερος *héteros*; fem. *hetéra*, neut. *héteron*, correlative pronoun. Other but different, another.

(I) Particularly and definitely with the art. *ho héteros*, the other of two where one has been already mentioned (Matt 6:24; Luke 5:7; 7:41; 23:40; 1 Cor 14:17). In Luke 4:43, in those "other [*hetérais*] cities" where the gospel has not yet been preached. In distinction from oneself, another person (Rom 2:1; 1 Cor 4:6; 14:17; Gal 6:4; James 4:12). In Acts 20:15, "on the other" (a.t.), implies day meaning the next day, the day after; also Acts 27:3.

(II) Indef. and without the art., other, another, some other, equivalent to *állos* (243), another, but with a stronger expression of difference.

(A) In Matt 8:21, "another of his disciples"; Luke 8:3; John 19:37; Acts 1:20; Eph 3:5, "in other ages" means former generations (Sept.: Gen 4:25; 8:10). Joined with *tis* (5100), someone indefinitely; *héterós tis*, some other one, any other (Acts 8:34; 27:1; Rom 8:39; 1 Tim 1:10). Distributively, either repeated as 1 Cor 15:40, *hétera mén . . . hétera dé*, some [pl.] . . . and others, or with other pron. (Matt 16:14; Luke 11:16; 14:19, 20; 1 Cor 12:9, 10; Sept.: Gen 31:49; Ex 26:3).

(B) Of another kind, another, different, in another form (Mark 16:12; Acts 7:18; Rom 7:23; Gal 1:6; James 2:25); of a priest from a different line or family (Heb 7:11, 15). In the sense of foreign, strange (Jude 1:7; Sept.: Ex 30:9); of other languages (Acts 2:4; 1 Cor 14:21). See *glṓssa* (1100, II, C), tongue. Contrast *állos* (243), another numerically or coming after. *Héteros* and *héteros* repeated, one and another different from each other (1 Cor 15:40). Different, altered (Luke 9:29).

Deriv.: *heteróglōssos* (2084), one of a different tongue; *heterodidaskaléō* (2085), to teach a doctrine different than one's own; *hetérōs* (2088), otherwise, differently; *póteron* (4220), which of two?

2088. ἑτέρως *hetérōs*; adv. from *héteros* (2087), a different one, another of a different quality. Otherwise, differently (Phil 3:15). Contrast *állos* (243), another numerically but not qualitatively different. The adv. from the adj. *állos* is *állōs* (247), otherwise, in 1 Tim 5:25, where the contrast is not with works that are not good, but with good works which are not evident.

2089. ἔτι *éti*; adv. Yet, still.
(I) Implying duration, for example:
(A) Spoken of the present time, yet, still, hitherto (Matt 12:46, "While he yet spoke" [a.t.]; 27:63, "while he was yet alive"; Luke 9:42; 24:6; John 20:1; Rom 5:6). Of the present in allusion to the past, yet, still, even now, as before

(Mark 8:17; Luke 24:41; Acts 9:1; Rom 3:7; Gal 1:10). Followed by *nún* (3568), now, *éti nún*, yet now, even now (1 Cor 3:2). In the sense of even, already (Luke 1:15; Heb 7:10).

(B) Of the future, yet still, still further, longer (Mark 5:35; Luke 16:2, "for you shall not be able to further manage" [a.t.]; John 4:35; 7:33; 14:19; Rom 6:2; 2 Cor 1:10). Especially with a neg., not further, no more, no longer (Matt 5:13; Luke 20:40; John 14:30; Gal 4:7; Heb 8:12; Rev 3:12; 7:16).

(II) Implying accession or addition meaning yet, more, further, besides.
(A) Generally (Matt 18:16; 26:65; Heb 11:32, 36); *éti dé kaí* (*dé* [1161], and; *kaí* [2532], and), and further also, moreover also (Luke 14:26; Acts 2:26; 21:28).

(B) With a comparative, intensively, yet, much, far (Phil 1:9; Heb 7:15).

Deriv.: *oukéti* (3765), no more, no longer, usually referring to what had been a matter of fact but is no longer, in contrast to *mēkéti* (3371) which suggests that something is a matter of thought or supposition but not a matter of fact, no more, no longer.

Syn.: *kaí* (2532), also, even; *dé* (1161), even; *hōs* (5613), as, but sometimes translated "even as" (Matt 15:28); *hoútōs* (3779), thus, even so; *kathṓs* (2531), even as; *hṓsper* (5618), even as; *katháper* (2509), even as; *naí* (3483), even so; *hómōs* (3676), yet, even; *mállon* (3123), the more; *apárti* (534), from now, henceforth; *loipón* (3063), the rest, from now; *pleíon* (4119), more; *perissós* (4053), over and above; *állos* (243), more, other; *akmḗn* (188), even to this point and time; *oudépō* (3764), never yet; *mḗpō* (3380), not yet; *ḗdē* (2235), yet.

Ant.: *ektós* (1622), unless, except; *parektós* (3924), except, without; *plḗn* (4133), except, nevertheless; *chōrís* (5565), without; *tóte* (5119), then, at that time.

2090. ἑτοιμάζω *hetoimázō*; fut. *hetoimásō*, from *hétoimos* (2092), ready. To prepare, make ready.

(I) Particularly the way of a king as was customary for oriental kings in their journeys (Rev 16:12); metaphorically of the Messiah (Matt 3:3; Mark 1:3; Luke 1:76; 3:4, all quoted from Isa 40:3); of a meal, banquet (Matt 22:4; Luke 17:8); of the Passover meal (Matt 26:17, 19; Mark 14:12, 15, 16; Luke 22:8, 9, 12, 13; Sept.: Gen 43:16); of a place, dwelling (John 14:2, 3; Rev 12:6); city (Heb 11:16); of hospitality or lodging (Luke 9:52; Phile 1:22; Sept.: 1 Chr 15:3); of a people unto the Lord (Luke 1:17 [cf. Sept.: 2 Chr 27:6]); of persons, to prepare, put in readiness, e.g., soldiers (Acts 23:23); of a bride (Rev 19:7; 21:2); of a servant or minister (Luke 12:47; Rev 8:6; 9:15). Pass. part. *hētoimasménos*, prepared, metaphorically meaning apt, ready (2 Tim 2:21). Particularly of horses ready for war (Rev 9:7). In the sense of to provide, e.g., spices (Luke 23:56; 24:1); goods (Luke 12:19, 20; Sept.: 2 Chr 26:14).

(II) Of God as having in His counsels prepared good or evil for men, i.e., to destine, appoint (Matt 20:23; 25:34, 41; Mark 10:40; Luke 2:31; 1 Cor 2:9; Sept.: Gen 24:14, 44; Ex 23:20; Isa 14:21).

Deriv.: *proetoimázō* (4282), to prepare beforehand.

Syn.: *katartízō* (2675), to furnish completely; *kataskeuázō* (2680), to make ready; *paraskeuázō* (3903), to make ready a meal.

Ant.: *ameléō* (272), to neglect; *paratheōréō* (3865), to overlook.

2091. ἑτοιμασία hetoimasía; gen. *hetoimasías*, fem. noun from *hétoimos* (2092), ready. Preparation or a basis, foundation, firm footing as the noun is applied by the Sept. (Ezra 2:68; 3:3; Ps 89:14; Zech 5:11 [cf. Dan 11:7, 21]). This meaning best agrees with the scope of Eph 6:15, the only passage in the NT where the word occurs in relation to the use of the military shoe. Paul advises Christian converts to "put on the whole armor of God, that ye may be able to stand against the wiles of the devil" (Eph 6:11); to "take . . . the whole armor of God that ye may be able to withstand in the evil day, and having done all, to stand. Stand therefore having . . . your feet shod with the preparation [*hetoimasía*, or firm footing for the foundation] of the gospel of peace" (Eph 6:13–15). This intimates the firm and solid knowledge of the gospel in which the believer may stand firm and unmoved like soldiers in their military duty. The Roman soldiers were furnished with shoes that had cleats on the soles for this purpose.

Syn.: *paraskeuḗ* (3904), preparation, which also means a day of preparation for the Sabbath.

2092. ἕτοιμος hétoimos; fem. *hetoímē*, neut. *hétoimon*, adj. Ready, prepared (Matt 22:4, 8; 24:44; Mark 14:15; John 7:6; 2 Cor 10:16). Preceding an inf. meaning ready to be done (1 Pet 1:5); of persons (Matt 25:10); with *prós* (4314), unto, with the acc., ready for anything (Titus 3:1; 1 Pet 3:15); followed by the inf. meaning ready to do (Luke 22:33; Acts 23:15); with the inf. implied (Acts 23:21). To become ready, be prepared (Matt 24:44; Luke 12:40; Sept.: Ex 19:15; 34:2). The expression *en hetoímō échō* (*en* [1722], in; *hetoímō* [the dat. of *hetoímos*] *échō* [2192], to have) means to have in readiness, be prepared (2 Cor 10:6).

Deriv.: *hetoimázō* (2090), to prepare; *hetoimasía* (2091), preparation; *hetoímōs* (2093), ready.

Syn.: *próthumos* (4289), predisposed, willing; *katērtisménos* (the perf. pass. part. of *katartízō* [2675], to prepare), prepared; *kateskeuasménos* (the perf. pass. part. of *kataskeuázō* [2680], to prepare), prepared, made ready, equipped; *pareskeuasménos* (the perf. pass. part. of *paraskeuázō* [3903], to prepare), make ready, prepared, ready.

Ant.: *aparaskeúastos* (532), unprepared.

2093. ἑτοίμως hetoímōs; adv. from *hétoimos* (2092), ready. Ready, in readiness

(Acts 21:13; 2 Cor 12:14; 1 Pet 4:5; Sept.: Dan 3:15).

2094. ἔτος *étos*; gen. *étous*, neut. noun. A year (Luke 3:1; Acts 7:30; Sept.: 1 Kgs 15:1; Jer 1:2, 3). In the dat. pl., marking a period in or during which (John 2:20; Acts 13:20). In the acc. pl. of time, how long (Matt 9:20; Luke 2:36; John 5:5). To be of such and such an age (Mark 5:42; Luke 2:37, 42; Acts 4:22). "Thou hast not yet fifty years" (a.t. [John 8:57]), meaning you are not yet fifty years old. With the prep. *katá* (2596), at, used distributively, *kat' étos*, year by year, every year (Luke 2:41).

    Deriv.: *dietḗs* (1332), lasting two years; *hekatontaetḗs* (1541), one hundred years old; *tessarakontaetḗs* (5063), of forty years; *trietía* (5148), three years.

    Syn.: *eniautós* (1763), a cycle of time.

2095. εὖ *eú*; adv., neut. of *eús* (n.f.), good, brave, noble. Well, good.

    (I) Particularly with verbs, "that it may be well with thee," that you may be prosperous (Eph 6:3; Sept.: Gen 12:13; Deut 4:40). In Mark 14:7, to do good to someone; Sept.: Gen 32:9, 12; Deut 8:16. In Acts 15:29, to do well, i.e., to do right, to act well (cf. 1 Kgs 8:18; 2 Kgs 10:30).

    (II) In commendations as "Well done!" (Matt 25:21); followed by a noun and an adj. (Matt 25:23), "Well done, servant, a good one" (a.t.). See Luke 19:17.

    (III) Used extensively as a prefix to comp. verbs with the meaning of well, good, and hence often used as an intens., e.g., *eulogéō* (2127), to eulogize, bless; *eukairía* (2120), good or appropriate opportunity.

    Syn.: *kalṓs* (2573), well.

2096. Εὖα *Eúa*; gen. *Eúas*, fem. proper noun transliterated from the Hebr. *Chawāh* (2332, OT). Eve, meaning life. The name was applied by Adam to his wife because "she was the mother of all living" (Gen 3:20). She was formed out of Adam's rib, taken while he slept—a fact which teaches the identity or nature

and the oneness of the origin of man and woman, stamping divine disapproval upon any degradation of women. For her prominent part in the fall, God said to her, "I will greatly multiply thy sorrow and thy conception; in sorrow thou shalt bring forth children; and thy desire shall be to thy husband, and he shall rule over thee" (Gen 3:16). But it was the seed of Eve which was to bruise the serpent's head. She is twice mentioned by Paul, once as the subject of the serpent's guile (2 Cor 11:3), and once as the second person created (1 Tim 2:13). The latter reference is in an argument for women to be silent in public, in the context of a local church, if their speaking would cause a diminuation of the role of the husband as the head in the one-body relationship in marriage.

2097. εὐαγγελίζω *euaggelízō*; fut. *euaggelísō*, aor. *euēggélisa*, from *euággelos* (n.f.), bringing good news, which is from *eu* (2095), good, well, and *aggéllō* (n.f.), to proclaim, tell. To evangelize, proclaim the good news, preach the gospel. It was at the time that the first Christians were "scattered abroad, and went about preaching the Word" after the martyrdom of Stephen (he being one of the seven), that the verb *euaggelízō* (2097), to publish the good tidings or good news, was used by Luke in Acts 8:4, 12, 25, 35, 40. Used in the act. voice meaning to declare, proclaim (Rev 10:7; 14:6); in the pass. voice, *euaggelízomai*, of matters to be proclaimed as glad tidings (Luke 16:16; Gal 1:11; 1 Pet 1:25); of persons to whom the proclamation is made (Matt 11:5; Luke 7:22; Heb 4:2, 6; 1 Pet 4:6); in the mid. voice especially of the message of salvation with a personal obj., either of the person preached (Acts 5:42; 11:20; Gal 1:16), or with a prep., of persons evangelized (Acts 8:12; 13:32; Eph 3:8). Not found in Gospel of Mark, or the epistles and Gospel of John, only once in the Gospel of Matthew, and twice in the Book of the Revelation. Related to *euaggélion* (2098), a good message.

Also from *euággelos* (n.f.): *euaggélion* (2098), good news.

(I) Act. with the acc. of person with an acc. of thing implied, to announce unto, to publish unto, as glad tidings (Rev 10:7; 14:6; Sept., with the dat.: 1 Sam 31:9; 2 Sam 18:19, 20). The act. form is not found in earlier writers.

(II) Mid., in earlier writers and in the NT, to announce, publish, as glad tidings.

(A) Generally and with the acc. of thing (Acts 10:36; Rom 10:15 quoted from Isa 52:7; Sept.: 1 Kgs 1:42). Followed by the acc. of thing and dat. of person, which was the more usual construction (Luke 1:19; 2:10; Eph 2:17; 1 Thess 3:6; Sept.: 2 Sam 1:20; 1 Chr 10:9; Ps 40:9). With an acc. of thing implied (Luke 4:18 [cf. Isa 61:1]). By attraction for *hóti* (3754), that (Acts 13:32).

(B) Spoken of the annunciation of the gospel of Christ and all that pertains to it, to preach, proclaim, the idea of glad tidings being implied. **(1)** To preach the kingdom of God meaning the things concerning the kingdom of God (Luke 8:1; Acts 8:12). With the dat. of person (Luke 4:43). With the kingdom implied, in an absolute sense (Luke 9:6; 20:1). With the acc. of person, as in Luke 3:18. **(2)** To preach Jesus Christ or the Lord Jesus (Acts 5:42; 11:20; 17:18). With the dat. of person (Acts 8:35). Followed by "among the nations" (a.t. [Gal 1:16]). In Eph 3:8, "the riches of Christ among the nations" (a.t.). **(3)** Generally to preach the gospel, the Word, the faith (Acts 8:4; 15:35; Gal 1:23); followed by the dat. of person (1 Cor 15:1, 2, "the gospel . . . unto you [*humín*]"; also 2 Cor 11:7; Gal 1:8); with the gospel, the Word implied, i.e., to preach the gospel, with the dat. of person (Rom 1:15; Gal 4:13); with the acc. of person (Acts 14:15; 16:10; Gal 1:9; 1 Pet 1:12); with the acc. of place or person (Acts 8:25, 40; 14:21). Followed by *eis* (1519), with the acc., marking extent (2 Cor 10:16). In an absolute sense (Acts 14:7; Rom 15:20; 1 Cor 1:17; 9:16, 18).

(III) Pass., to be announced, be published, as glad tidings.

(A) Particularly with a nom. of the thing announced (Luke 16:16; Gal 1:11; 1 Pet 1:25); with the dat. of person (1 Pet 4:6).

(B) With a nom. of person (Heb 4:2, "to us good tidings have been proclaimed, as well as unto them" [a.t. {see also v. 6; Sept.: 2 Sam 18:31}]). In respect to the gospel, to have the gospel preached, to hear the gospel tidings (Matt 11:5; Luke 7:22).

Deriv.: *euaggelistḗs* (2099), evangelist; *proeuaggelízomai* (4283), announce good news beforehand.

2098. εὐαγγέλιον *euaggélion*; gen. *euaggelíou*, neut. noun from *euággelos* (n.f.), bringing good news, which is from *eú* (2095), good, well, and *aggéllō* (n.f.), to proclaim, tell. Originally a reward for good news, later becoming good news. In the Sept.: 2 Sam 18:22, 25. In the NT, spoken only of the glad tidings of Christ and His salvation, the gospel. Found twice in Acts, once in Peter's epistles, once in the Book of the Revelation, but not found in Luke, nor in the epistles or Gospel of John Related to *euaggelízō* (2097), to announce good news. Also from *euággelos* (n.f.): *euaggelízō* (2097), to evangelize, proclaim the good news.

(I) In the books of the NT, particularly in the sense of glad tidings, except in the writings of Paul.

(A) The gospel of the kingdom of God (Matt 4:23; 9:35; 24:14; Mark 1:14). By implication (Matt 26:13; Mark 1:15; 13:10; 14:9; Rev 14:6, "eternal gospel" [a.t. {cf. Luke 2:10}]). See *basileía* (932), kingdom. "Kingdom" must be interpreted in this context as the rule which God establishes in the hearts of men when Jesus Christ is received by faith. The gospel of the kingdom of heaven and the kingdom of God are one and the same thing (Matt 19:23, 24). It means first and primarily the rule of God in the human heart because of Christ (Luke 17:20, 21). It also refers to the kingdom in its future state during which the believers will reign with Christ forever (Rev 22:1–5). In the above references, however, when it is the gospel of the kingdom of God or the eternal gospel, reference is to the invisible rule of Christ in the hearts of believers. By metonymy, it means annunciation of the gospel through Christ (Mark 1:1), also the gospel of the grace of God as manifested in Christ (Acts 20:24).

(B) In respect to the coming and life of Jesus as the Messiah, gospel, glad tidings (Mark 8:35; 10:29; 16:15; Acts 15:7; 1 Pet 4:17). Later, *euaggélion* came to mean a history of Jesus' life such as we have in the Gospels of Matthew, Mark, Luke and John.

(II) In the writings of Paul, the gospel, that is:

(A) Generally the gospel plan of salvation, its doctrines, declarations, precepts, promises (Rom 2:16, "according to the gospel which I preach" [a.t.]; 11:28; 16:25; 1 Cor 9:14, 18; 15:1; 2 Cor 4:3, 4; 9:13; 10:14; Gal 1:11, "the gospel which was preached by me" [a.t.]; 2:2, 5, 14; Eph 1:13; 3:6; 6:19; Phil 1:5, 7, 17, 27; 2:22; Col 1:5, 23; 1 Thess 1:5; 2:4; 2 Tim 1:10; 2:8). The gospel of Christ made known by Him as its founder and chief cornerstone (Rom 15:19, 29; 1 Cor 9:12, 18; Gal 1:7; 1 Thess 3:2; 2 Thess 1:8). The gospel of God, of which God is the Author through Christ (Rom 15:16; 2 Cor 11:7; 1 Thess 2:2, 8, 9; 1 Tim 1:11). By antithesis, *héteron* (2087), another but different gospel, including other precepts (2 Cor 11:4; Gal 1:6).

(B) By metonymy, the gospel work, i.e., the preaching of the gospel, labor in the gospel (Rom 1:1, 9, 16; 1 Cor 4:15; 9:14, 23; 2 Cor 2:12; 8:18; Gal 2:2, 7, "I was entrusted to preach the gospel to the Gentiles" [a.t.]; Eph 6:15; Phil 1:12; 4:3, 15; 2 Thess 2:14; 2 Tim 1:8; Phile 1:13, "in bonds on account of labors in the gospel" [a.t.]). In Rom 10:16, "all have not obeyed the preaching of the gospel" (a.t.), i.e., the gospel as preached.

2099. εὐαγγελιστής *euaggelistḗs*; gen. *euaggelistoú*, masc. noun from *eauggelízō* (2097), to evangelize. Evangelist, one who declares the good news (Rom 10:15). An evangelist, a preacher of the gospel. He was often not located in any particular place but traveled as a missionary to preach the gospel and establish churches (Acts 21:8; Eph 4:11; 2 Tim 4:5).

The only evangelist named is Philip (Acts 21:8). He was one of the seven who were appointed to serve the physical needs of the church in Jerusalem. These were men of a good testimony filled with the Holy Spirit and wisdom. It is evident that Philip was a renowned preacher among them. His name and work are mentioned in one of the "we" passages of Acts (Acts 21:7), which may mean that he was the spokesman for the seven or the best spokesman. He was called the evangelist because of his good work in preaching to the heathen.

In Eph 4:11, Paul lists the five kinds of ministers which have been given by Christ to His Church with evangelists being third: apostles, prophets, evangelists, pastors, and teachers. The first three of these were itinerant ministers, apostles, prophets and evangelists, who were preaching wherever they found an opportunity, while pastors and teachers were attached to some congregation or location. Philip was a traveling missionary. He went from Jerusalem to preach in Samaria and was on the road to Gaza when he met the eunuch whom he baptized (Acts 8:5f., 26f.). He afterwards came to Azotus (known as Ashdod today), and passing through, he preached the gospel to all the cities until he came to Caesarea (Acts 8:40). Perhaps prophets preached to believers and evangelists to unbelievers, while apostles addressed either. An apostle is a prophet and an evangelist, but a prophet or an evangelist is not an apostle if we take the word "apostle" with the narrow sense of the apostles who had seen Jesus Christ in His resurrection (1

Cor 9:1). Apparently those who acted as missionaries to the Gentiles and to those who never heard the gospel were called evangelists.

An evangelist knew the gospel narrative thoroughly and was capable of explaining it, as Philip the evangelist did to the eunuch. We need not suppose that Eph 4:11 gives us five orders of ministers appointed to discharge five different kinds of duties. No such organization existed. The distinctions of ministry lay in the work that was done by individual workers, and that depended on their personal gifts, which often overlapped.

The third passage is 2 Tim 4:5, where Timothy is charged to "do the work of an evangelist" in addition to his other duties as an apostolic delegate at the church at Ephesus. Although he was ministering for a while at the church of Ephesus, he was not to forget the work of an evangelist, preaching the gospel to unbelievers. A local ministry should never in any way neglect evangelism.

The term was later used to indicate the writers of the life of Christ, such as Matthew, Mark, Luke, and John. The list of gifted persons in Eph 4:11 is short as compared with the 3 lists in 1 Cor 12:8–10, 28–30. Why is it that the gifts, especially the sign gifts which were extraordinary, are not also mentioned in the list of gifts in Ephesians? It is to be remembered that 1 Cor was written in the spring of A.D. 57 (or, according to some, as early as A.D. 54), while the Epistle to the Ephesians was written between A.D. 60–61, corresponding to the time of Paul's Roman imprisonment. It is quite possible that the regular exercise of extraordinary gifts was already dying out. However, in the short list in Eph 4:11, there are two items which are not found in any of the other lists, evangelists and pastors. Of Timothy we read, "do the work of an evangelist" (2 Tim 4:5); that he had served with Paul in the gospel (Phil 2:22); that he was "a minister (*diákonos* [1249], deacon) of God" and Paul's fellow laborer (*sunergós* [4904]) in the gospel (1 Thess 3:2).

The number of evangelists must have been greater than the number suggested by NT references (2 Cor 8:18; Phil 4:3; Col 1:7; 4:12).

Originally, *euaggelistḗs* denoted a function rather than an office. There could have been little difference between an apostle and an evangelist, all the apostles being evangelists, but not all evangelists being apostles. Evangelists were subordinate to the apostles. In Eph 4:11, the evangelists are mentioned only after the apostles. They were not just missionaries. A distinction must be made between the office of an evangelist and the work of one.

Syn.: *kḗrux* (2783), preacher; *ággelos* (32), messenger.

2100. εὐαρεστέω *euarestéō*; contracted *euarestṓ*, fut. *euarestḗsō*, from *euárestos* (2101), well pleasing. To gratify entirely, to please. With the dat. (Heb 11:5, 6; Sept.: Gen 5:22, 24). In the mid., to take pleasure in, to be pleased with, with the dat. (Heb 13:16).

Syn.: *suneudokéō* (4909), to consent.

Ant.: *apeithéō* (544), to be disobedient; *atimázō* (818), to dishonor; *kataischúnō* (2617), to bring shame to; *parakoúō* (3878), to neglect to hear, disobey.

2101. εὐάρεστος *euárestos*; gen. *euaréstou*, masc.-fem., neut. *euáreston*, adj. from *eu* (2095), well, and *aréskō* (700), to please. Well-pleasing, acceptable. Used with reference to God, that which God wills and recognizes (Rom 12:1, 2; Eph 5:10; Phil 4:18; Col 3:20; Heb 13:21); to persons (Rom 14:18; 2 Cor 5:9); concerning slaves (Titus 2:9).

Deriv.: *euarestéō* (2100), to please well; *euaréstōs* (2102), acceptably.

Syn.: *kalós* (2570), good; *euprósdektos* (2144), welcome; *glukús* (1099), sweet.

Ant.: *dusbástaktos* (1419), hard to bear, oppressive; *kakós* (2556), bad; *pikrós* (4089), bitter; *barús* (926), heavy, grievous; *chalepós* (5467), difficult, perilous.

2102. εὐαρέστως euaréstōs; adv. from *euárestos* (2101), pleasing, well-pleasing. Pleasingly, acceptably (Heb 12:28).

Syn.: *hḗdista* (2236), with great pleasure; *hēdéōs* (2234), with pleasure.

2103. Εὔβουλος Eúboulos; gen. *Euboúlou*, masc. proper noun. Eubulus, meaning prudent, well-intentioned. A Roman Christian who greeted Timothy (2 Tim 4:21).

2104. εὐγενής eugenḗs; gen. *eugenoús*, masc.-fem., neut. *eugenés*, adj. from *eu* (2095), good, well, and *génos* (1085), race, family. Noble, descended from a good family, of high rank (Luke 19:12; 1 Cor 1:26; Sept.: Job 1:3). Metaphorically, meaning noble-minded, generous (Acts 17:11).

Syn.: *krátistos* (2903), most noble or excellent; *basilikós* (937), belonging to a king, royal, and hence noble; *árchōn* (758), prince, ruler.

2105. εὐδία eudía; gen. *eudías*, fem. noun from *eúdios* (n.f.), fair weather, which is from *eu* (2095), good or well, and *Diós*, the gen. of *Zeús* (2203), Jupiter, the supreme deity of the Greeks. Serene sky, fair weather (Matt 16:2).

Ant.: *cheimṓn* (5494), winter storm, bad weather; *laílaps* (2978), storm, hurricane; *thúella* (2366), whirlwind, hurricane, cyclone; *seismós* (4578), a shaking, earthquake.

2106. εὐδοκέω eudokéō; contracted *eudokṓ*, fut. *eudokḗsō*, from *eú* (2095), well, good, and *dokéō* (1380), to think. To be well-pleased, to think it good. It means to think well of something by understanding not only what is right and good, as in *dokéō*, but stressing the willingness and freedom of an intention or resolve regarding what is good (Luke 12:32; Rom 15:26, 27; 1 Cor 1:21; Gal 1:15; Col 1:19; 1 Thess 2:8). To take pleasure in (Matt 3:17; 12:18; 17:5; Mark 1:11; Luke 3:22; 1 Cor 10:5; 2 Cor

12:10; 2 Thess 2:12; Heb 10:6, 8, 38; 2 Pet 1:17). In the NT, to approve, please, like, take pleasure in.

(I) Generally to view with approbation. Followed by *en* (1722), in, with the dat. of person (Matt 3:17, "in whom I am well pleased"; 17:5; Mark 1:11; Luke 3:22; 1 Cor 10:5; Heb 10:38); followed by *en* with the dat. of thing (2 Cor 12:10; 2 Thess 2:12; Sept.: 2 Sam 22:20; Isa 62:4; see also 1 Chr 29:3; Ps 44:3); followed by *eis* (1519), in or into, with the acc. of person implying direction of mind (Matt 12:18, "in whom my soul is well pleased"; 2 Pet 1:17); followed by the acc. of thing (Heb 10:6, 8; Sept.: Ps 51:16, 19).

(II) In the sense of to will, desire, followed by the inf. expressed or implied.

(A) Generally, to be willing, ready (2 Cor 5:8; 1 Thess 2:8).

(B) By implication to determine, resolve, with the idea of benevolence being implied (Rom 15:26, 27; 1 Thess 3:1). Spoken of God (Luke 12:32; 1 Cor 1:21; Gal 1:15; Col 1:19). The noun *eudokía* (2107), good pleasure, implies a gracious purpose, a good object with the idea of a resolution showing the willingness with which it is made.

Deriv.: *eudokía* (2107), good will, pleasure; *suneudokéō* (4909), to think well of with others.

Syn.: *euarestéō* (2100), gratify, please.

2107. εὐδοκία eudokía; gen. *eudokías*, fem. noun from *eudokéō* (2106), to please, favor. Good will, good pleasure, good intent, benevolence, a gracious purpose (Matt 11:26; Luke 10:21). In this sense it is parallel to *eulogía* (2129), blessing. *Eudokía* must be an outcome of *agathōsúnē* (19), goodness, the virtue of beneficence even as works are the product of faith. Therefore, the *eudokía*, the good will of *agathōsúnē*, denotes that which pleases, goodness, the tendency to the good.

(I) Particular delight in any person or thing and hence good will, favor (Luke 2:14, "good will toward men" on the part of God; Sept.: Ps 5:12; 19:14; Prov 11:1, 20). See *eudokéō* (2106, I). See *dektós* (1184), approved, accepted. Of men, good will, kind intention (Phil 1:15). By implication, desire, longing (Rom 10:1).

(II) In the sense of good pleasure, will, purpose, the idea of benevolence being included, spoken of God (Eph 1:5, 9; Phil 2:13; 2 Thess 1:11, "fulfill in you the virtue which his good pleasure has purposed" [a.t.]; also Matt 11:26; Luke 10:21, "such was your good pleasure" [a.t.]).

Syn.: *hēdonḗ* (2237), pleasure, but only in respect to lust; *apólausis* (619), enjoyment in regard to pleasures; *thélēma* (2307), will, pleasure, favor; *epipóthēsis* (1972), an earnest desire, and with the same meaning *epipothía* (1974); *boúlēma* (1013), deliberate design, purpose; *eúnoia* (2133), good will; *apodochḗ* (594), acceptance; *homología* (3671), acknowledgement.

2108. εὐεργεσία euergesía; gen. *euergesías*, fem. noun from *euergétēs* (2110), benefactor. A good deed, benefit (Acts 4:9). Generally meaning well-doing, duties in connection with the requirements of the gospel (1 Tim 6:2).

Syn.: *cháris* (5485), grace, benefit; *apodochḗ* (594), acceptance, appreciation; *haplótēs* (572), generosity; *agathón* (18), good, benefit; *eúnoia* (2133), good will; *philanthrōpía* (5363), benevolence; *agathopoiía* (16), the virtue of well-doing; *boḗtheia* (996), help; *eleēmosúnē* (1654), benefaction, alms; *dósis* (1394), gift, giving; *dóma* (1390), a present, gift; *dōreá* (1431), a gratuity, gift.

Ant.: *katákrisis* (2633), condemnation; *krísis* (2920), judgment; *élegchos* (1650), reproof; *momphḗ* (3437), fault, blame; *kakía* (2549), wickedness; *adíkēma* (92), an injustice; *panourgía* (3834), alertness, unscrupulous conduct, craftiness; *katára* (2671), curse.

2109. εὐεργετέω euergetéō; contracted *euergetṓ*, fut. *euergetḗsō*, from *euergétēs*

(2110), benefactor. To do good, confer benefits (Acts 10:38; Sept.: Ps 13:6).

Syn.: *agathopoiéō* (15), to do good, be beneficent; *agathoergéō* (14), to do good; *sumphérō* (4851), to be of common advantage, profit; *eupoiéō*, to do good, from *eupoiía* (2140), beneficence.

Ant.: *kakopoiéō* (2554), to injure; *kakologéō* (2551), to speak evil; *kakóō* (2559), to ill-treat; *adikéō* (91), to be unjust, do wrong.

2110. εὐεργέτης euergétēs; gen. *euergétou*, masc. noun from *eú* (2095), good, well, and *érgon* (2041), work. One that does good, a benefactor. In the NT, used as a title of honor (Luke 22:25), even as Ptolemy was called *euergétēs*, king and benefactor of Egypt.

Deriv.: *euergesía* (2108), beneficence; *euergetéō* (2109), to do good.

Syn.: *agathopoiós* (17), one who does well, virtuous; *eleḗmōn* (1655), merciful; *eúsplagchnos* (2155), tenderhearted.

Ant.: *aneleḗmōn* (415), unmerciful.

2111. εὔθετος eúthetos; gen. *euthétou*, masc.-fem., neut. *eútheton*, adj. from *eú* (2095), good, well, and *títhēmi* (5087), to place, set. Well-situated, convenient. In the NT, fit, meet, proper (Luke 9:62; 14:35). By implication, it means useful (Heb 6:7).

Deriv.: *aneúthetos* (428), unfit.

Syn.: *arestós* (702), pleasing; *áxios* (514), worthy, of value; *hikanós* (2425), sufficient, confident; *kalós* (2570), good; *díkaios* (1342), just, meet, right; *agathós* (18), benevolent.

Ant.: *akatástatos* (182), unstable.

2112. εὐθέως euthéōs; adv. from *euthús* (2117), straight, immediate. Immediately, instantly, straightway, forthwith (Matt 8:3; 13:5; Mark 1:31; Acts 12:10). By implication, meaning shortly (3 John 1:14).

Syn.: *parautíka* (3910), at the very instant; *parachrēma* (3916), immediately; *suntómōs* (4935), concisely; *háma* (260), at the same time; *orthós* (3723), rightly; *exautēs* (1824), at once; *tachéōs* (5030), quickly; the expression *en táchei* (*en* [1722], in; *táchei* [5036], swiftly, quickly), suddenly, quickly; *tachinós* (5031), shortly, impending.

 Ant.: *eschátōs* (2079), finally, lastly.

2113. εὐθυδρομέω *euthudroméō*; contracted *euthudromṓ*, fut. *euthudromḗsō*, from *euthúdromos* (n.f.), running a straight course, which is from *euthús* (2117), immediate, straight, and *drómos* (1408), road, career, course. To run straight, to sail a straight course (Acts 16:11; 21:1).

2114. εὐθυμέω *euthuméō*; contracted *euthumṓ*, fut. *euthumḗsō*, from *eúthumos* (2115), of a good mind, attitude. To be of good cheer, of a cheerful mind (Acts 27:22, 25; James 5:13 [see Prov 15:15]).

 Syn.: *chaírō* (5463), to rejoice, be glad; *hēsucházō* (2270), to be peaceful, quiet, restful; *tharséō* (2293), to be of good courage; *euphraínō* (2165), to be happy, cheery, merry.

 Ant.: *lupéō* (3076), to sorrow; *athuméō* (120), to be spiritless, dismayed; *barúnō* (925), to be heavy; *baréō* (916), to weigh down; *basanízō* (928), to vex; *skúllō* (4660), to trouble, annoy; *stenochōréō* (4729), to be pressed; *sunéchō* (4912), to constrain; *odunáō* (3600), to suffer pain; *kataponéō* (2669), to exhaust; *katadunasteúō* (2616), to oppress.

2115. εὔθυμος *eúthumos*, **εὐθυμότερον** *euthumóteron*; gen. *euthúmou*, masc.-fem., neut. *eúthumon*, adj. from *eú* (2095), good, well, and *thumós* (2372), mindset, temperament. Well-minded, well-disposed, benign. In the NT, meaning of good cheer, cheerful or having the proper positive and hopeful attitude (Acts 24:10 [TR], *euthumóteron*, a comparative degree meaning more cheerfully. In other MSS, as an adv. *euthúmōs*, cheerfully; Acts 27:36).

 Deriv.: *euthuméō* (2114), to be of good cheer or have the proper mindset.

 Syn.: *alupóteros* (253), less sorrowful; *hilarós* (2431), cheerful.

 Ant.: *skuthrōpós* (4659), gloomy; *stugnētós* (4767), odious, hateful.

2116. εὐθύνω *euthúnō*; fut. *euthunṓ*, from *euthús* (2117), immediate, straight. To make straight. Trans. spoken of a way: to make straight and level the way (John 1:23 [cf. Matt 3:3]), with the same significance as carried by the verb *hetoimázō* (2090), prepare. To guide straight, i.e., to direct, steer in regard to a ship, and hence *ho euthúnōn*, pres. part., a steersman, pilot (James 3:4).

 Deriv.: *kateuthúnō* (2720), to guide.

 Syn.: *anorthóō* (461), to make straight.

 Ant.: *kámptō* (2578), to bend; *diastréphō* (1294), to corrupt, pervert.

2117. εὐθύς *euthús*; fem. *eutheía*, neut. *euthú*, adj. Straight. As an adj.: Make the way straight and level before the king (Matt 3:3; Mark 1:3; Luke 3:4, 5 from Isa 40:3). In Acts 9:11, "a street called straight" (a.t.). Metaphorically, of the heart and life, right, true (Acts 8:21; 13:10; 2 Pet 2:15; Sept.: 1 Sam 12:23; 1 Kgs 11:33; Hos 14:10).

 Deriv.: *euthéōs* (2112) immediately; *euthúnō* (2116), to make straight or to govern; *euthútēs* (2118), rectitude.

 Syn.: *aklinḗs* (186), firm, unwavering; *hétoimos* (2092), ready, prepared; *orthós* (3717), straight, upright; *díkaios* (1342), righteous, just, right; *agathós* (18), good; *tímios* (5093), honorable; *éntimos* (1784), valued; *tachinós* (5031), swift; *chrēstós* (5543), gracious, kind; *akéraios* (185), harmless, honest; *áxios* (514), worthy; *eilikrinḗs* (1506), sincere.

 Ant.: *kakós* (2556), bad; *phaúlos* (5337), foul; *ponērós* (4190), evil; *aischrós* (150), shameful; *achreíos* (888), useless; *skoliós* (4646), curved, crooked; *átimos* (820), without honor; *dólios* (1386), deceitful; *anáxios* (370), unworthy; *hupokritḗs* (5273), a hypocrite.

2118. εὐθύτης *euthútēs*; gen. *euthútētos*, fem. noun from *euthús* (2117), straight, immediate, immediately. Straightness, rectitude (Heb 1:8;

Sept.: Ps 45:6); referring to a just attitude, it means devoid of hypocrisy.

Syn.: *dikaiosúnē* (1343), righteousness; *eilikríneia* (1505), sincerity; *chrēstótēs* (5544), kindness, usefulness, gentleness; *éthos* (2239), moral custom, manner of life; *agathōsúnē* (19), goodness; *timiótēs* (5094), honesty.

Ant.: *adikía* (93), injustice, unrighteousness; *anomía* (458), lawlessness; *ponēría* (4189), wickedness; *kakía* (2549), malice; *atimía* (819), dishonor, reproach; *kakoétheia* (2550), mischievousness; *hupókrisis* (5272), hypocrisy; *pseúdos* (5579), falsehood; *apátē* (539), deceit; *panourgía* (3834), trickery, craftiness; *dólos* (1388), deceit.

2119. εὐκαιρέω *eukairéō*; contracted *eukairṓ*, fut. *eukairḗsō*, from *eúkairos* (2121), convenient. It is related to *eukairía* (2120), opportunity, favorable occasion. To take advantage of the element of time as providing an opportunity, to have opportunity (Mark 6:31; 1 Cor 16:12); to have leisure for or to spend one's time in anything (Acts 17:21).

Ant.: *akairéomai* (170), to lack opportunity; *argéō* (691), to delay, be idle; *chronotribéō* (5551), to procrastinate; *anabállō* (306), to defer.

2120. εὐκαιρία *eukairía*; gen. *eukairías*, fem. noun from *eúkairos* (2121), convenient. The right and suitable time or convenient opportunity (Matt 26:16; Luke 22:6). The root is *kairós* (2540), a suitable or convenient time.

Syn.: *apokaradokía* (603), earnest expectation; *aphormḗ* (874), opportunity, occasion.

2121. εὔκαιρος *eúkairos*; gen. *eukaírou*, masc.-fem., neut. *eúkairon*, adj. from *eú* (2095), well, good, and *kairós* (2540), opportune time. Well-timed, opportune (Mark 6:21; Heb 4:16).

Deriv.: *eukairéō* (2119), to have convenient time or opportunity; *eukairía* (2120), opportunity; *eukaírōs* (2122), conveniently.

2122. εὐκαίρως *eukaírōs*; adv. from *eúkairos* (2121), opportune, convenient. Opportunely, conveniently, in season (Mark 14:11; 2 Tim 4:2).

Ant.: *akaírōs* (171), inopportunely, out of season; *duskólōs* (1423), impracticably, with difficulty.

2123. εὔκοπος *eúkopos*; gen. *eukópou*, masc.-fem., neut. *eúkopon*, adj. from *eú* (2095), well, good (in this instance, denoting lightness), and *kópos* (2873), fatigue resulting from labor. Easier, lighter (Matt 9:5; 19:24; Mark 2:9; 10:25; Luke 5:23; 16:17; 18:25).

Ant.: *sklērós* (4642), exacting, austere; *sklerotráchēlos* (4644), obstinate; *dúskolos* (1422), difficult.

2124. εὐλάβεια *eulábeia*; gen. *eulabeías*, fem. noun from *eulabḗs* (2126), devout. The internal attitude of reverence toward a person, thing or event. The syn. *eusébeia* (2150) includes *eulábeia* as an attitude of the inner being, but also externalizes that attitude in worship or other demonstrations.

Eulábeia occurs in Heb 5:7 referring to Jesus' prayer in view of His crucifixion "and was heard in that he feared" (KJV); "because of his piety" (NASB); "because of his reverent submission" (NIV). What is translated "fear," "piety" or "reverent submission" is *eulábeia*. Of the three, the last is the closest to the Gr., which is because of or on account of His good acceptance of what He was accomplishing as the High Priest (Heb 4:14; 5:1, 7). That was His role in His crucifixion. As a human being, He had an aversion to physical death which He expressed, showing that He was truly man and the Son of man. However, as God in the flesh He had full and immediate acceptance of His role in the work of man's redemption. Observe in Heb 5:7 the use of the prep. *apó* (575), from, on account of, preceding *tēs eulabeías*, meaning on account of His direct consciousness or acceptance of His deity. As God in the flesh, Jesus received the cross and death well (*eulábeia*) from God the Father (Matt 26:39, 42; Mark 14:36; John 12:28). Jesus' prayer was indeed answered, not by sparing Him from physical death, but by giving Him *eulábeia*, good, joyful acceptance of what He would accomplish through death (Matt 26:42).

The second instance is in Heb 12:28 where *eulábeia* is translated in the KJV "godly fear," in the NASB and the NIV "awe." The whole verse in the KJV reads, "Wherefore we receiving a kingdom which cannot be moved, let us have grace [*chárin* {5485}], whereby we may serve God acceptably with reverence and godly fear [*eulabeías*]." In Heb 12:25–29, we have the admonition to give earnest heed to what has been spoken from heaven. That word shook the earth at Mount Sinai (Judg 5:4, 5; Ps 68:8, 9; 77:18; 114:7). An even greater shaking of earth and heaven is predicted, and that prediction ought to be taken as surely as if it were history (Hag 2:6 [cf. Hag 2:26, 27]). All this means our receiving of the kingdom. "We receive" is *paralambánontes* (pres. act. part. of *paralambánō* [3880], to receive). It has a causal force and means "since we are receiving." This word *eulábeia* (in the gen.) should rather be translated "with a welcome" or "good acceptance." In the midst of the shaking of everything on earth and in heaven we receive "an unshakable kingdom." For this "let us have grace." This kingdom must be received as an undeserved benefit. What God does must always be considered as part of His work of grace—even the coming kingdom, and it is this grace (*di' hḗs*) through which we serve with reverence (*aidṓ* [127]) and awe (*eulabeías*). For a discussion of the meaning of the verb *eulabéomai* (2125) and the adj. *eulabḗs* (2126) in their contexts and meanings, see respective words. *Eulábeia*, translated "feared" and "godly fear" (Heb 5:7; 12:28), although used predominantly in a good sense, yet like *phóbos* (5401), fear, it has not altogether escaped being employed in an evil sense. Verb *eulabéomai* (2125), fearing (Acts 23:10 [TR]; Heb

11:7); adj. *eulabḗs* (2126), devout (Luke 2:25; Acts 2:5; 8:2). *Eulábeia* relates to the good, and *deilía* (1167), cowardice, to the bad, with *phóbos*, fear or reverence, as the mid. term.

2125. εὐλαβέομαι *eulabéomai*; contracted *eulaboúmai*, fut. *eulabḗsomai*, from *eulabḗs* (2126), one who receives well, pious. To be cautious, thoughtful, circumspect, to receive well. To be afraid, to be moved or impressed with a natural or religious fear (Acts 23:10 [TR]; Heb 11:7; Sept.: 1 Sam 18:29; Nah 1:7; Zech 2:13).

The first occurrence of the word is Acts 23:10 where *eulabētheís* (aor. pass. part. of *eulabéomai*) is translated "fearing." Literally, it means "having well received," indicating that the Roman centurion rightly perceived the situation that if Paul were left to the Pharisees and the scribes they would kill him. The meaning, therefore, is to perceive or receive a situation rightly.

The only other instance is in Heb 11:7, "By faith Noah, being warned of God [*chrēmatízomai* {5537}, to be warned by a divine oracle] of things not seen as yet, moved with fear [*eulabētheís*, aor. pass. part.], prepared an ark." Noah's action was not out of cowering, servile fear. Rather, he took what God uniquely revealed to him as if it were an oracle that He was going to flood the earth and that he should build an ark. Noah took God at His word, that what He was telling him was *eu*, good, right, and he received (*élaben*) it as such. He did not build the ark out of fear but from having received God's oracle as truth to be believed.

Syn.: *sebázomai* (4573), to venerate; *sébomai* (4576), to revere.

2126. εὐλαβής *eulabḗs*; gen. *eulaboús*, masc.-fem., neut. *eulabés*, adj. from *eú* (2095), good, well, right, rightly, and *lambánō* (2983), to take. One who properly receives someone or something. In the Eng. versions it is related to fear, but as demonstrated in the discussion

of the subst. *eulábeia* (2124), right attitude, reverence, and the verb *eulabéomai*
(2125), to receive with discernment, this
group of words really has nothing to do
with fear, but with the proper and rightful estimation of something. Likewise,
the NT contexts of *eulabés* also reflect
this meaning, as the following discussion
shows.

The first occurrence is Luke 2:25 and
it concerns Simeon who is called just
(*díkaios* [1342]) and devout (*eulabés*).
Simeon was waiting for the consolation
of Israel, the promise of the coming Messiah. He was one who had well and rightly received the promises of God and that
is the fundamental meaning of *eulabés*,
one who had taken seriously God's promises and God's Word.

The second occurrence is in Acts 2:5,
and it refers to the Jews who were assembled in Jerusalem for the feast of Pentecost. They are called devout men or
God-fearing (*eulabeís*). They were people who had accepted God's command
that this feast should be kept with every
male Israelite required to appear at the
sanctuary (Lev 23:21) fifty days from the
offering of the barley sheaf at the beginning of the Passover (Ex 23:16; 34:22;
Lev 23:10f.; Num 28:26; Deut 16:10;
16:9). They were people who rightly
and seriously received God's commandments, which is what the word *eulabeís*
means in this context.

The third instance is Acts 8:2 referring
to those who took the body of the martyred Stephen to bury. These could have
been Christians and Jews who had perceived rightly that Stephen had suffered
for a righteous cause.

The fourth instance is Acts 22:12 (in
MSS other than the TR, where *eusebés*
[2152], well-reverent, showing external
reverence, is used) referring to Ananias.
The difference between the two words is
that *eulabés* is an internal attitude of the
heart taking the word of God as true and
right, while *eusebés* is one who externalizes that feeling in acts of worship and
veneration. Both could perfectly apply

in the case of Ananias, who was a Christian.

The word *eulabés*, however, may refer
to a pious person who may or may not be
a Christian. On the three occasions where
eulabés occurs, it expresses Jewish piety
(Luke 2:25 of Simeon; Acts 2:5 of Jews
who came from distant places to keep the
commanded feasts at Jerusalem; Acts 8:2
of those who carried Stephen to his burial, i.e., devout Jews who had separated themselves in spirit from those who
murdered Stephen, perhaps joining with
Christians). *Eulabés* describes the scrupulous worshiper who may not demonstrate his internal attitude by performing
external acts of worship.

Deriv.: *eulábeia* (2124), right attitude,
reverence; *eulabéomai* (2125), to receive
with discernment.

Syn.: *sebastós* (4575), venerable.

Ant.: *asebés* (765), impious.

2127. εὐλογέω *eulogéō*; contracted
eulogṓ, imperf. *ēulógoun*, fut. *eulogḗsō*,
aor. *ēulóges*, from *eú* (2095), good,
well, and *lógos* (3056), word. To bless,
speak well of. This word should be distinguished from *makarízō* (3106), to acknowledge or pronounce as blessed.

(**I**) Of men toward God, to bless, i.e.,
to praise, speak well of with ascriptions
of praise and thanksgiving (Luke 1:64;
2:28; 24:53; 1 Cor 14:16; James 3:9;
Sept.: 1 Chr 29:10, 20).

(**II**) Of men toward men and things,
to bless, speak well of with praise and
thanksgiving, to invoke God's blessing
upon, which is God's action in their lives
or God's intervention to accomplish His
will.

(**A**) With the acc. of person expressed
or implied, to pray for one's welfare as
God perceives it for His actions in their
lives. Matt 5:44 [TR], Luke 6:28, and
Rom 12:14 do not mean that we should
say good things about those who curse us,
but rather that we should invoke God's
blessing upon them by praying that they
may be turned from their ways through
God's intervention in their lives. The

same applies in 1 Cor 4:12 and 1 Pet 3:9. It is the assurance that Jesus gave His disciples prior to His ascension that He was going to be acting in their lives and that He was not going to forsake them (Luke 24:50, 51). Mark 10:16 refers to Christ's goodwill and action toward children. See Luke 2:34 regarding Simeon's blessing upon Joseph and Mary, the mother of Jesus, in that he praised and spoke well of them. Of infants (Mark 10:16 [TR]), we consecrate them to divine use. Melchizedek blesses Abraham in Heb 7:1, 6 in that he praises him and speaks well of him, and in Heb 7:7, the lesser is blessed or well-spoken of by the better. In Heb 11:20, 21, we see Isaac blessing Jacob and Esau, speaking of the good things that were going to take place. See Sept.: Gen 14:19; 27:23, 27; 48:9, 15, 20.

(B) With acc. of thing expressed or implied, in the NT of food, to bless, i.e., to ask God to use that which is consumed so that those who consume it may praise God (Mark 6:41; 8:7; Luke 9:16, of bread). Implied in Matt 14:19. Of the Lord's Supper where we may render by implication the meaning of to consecrate, to use it for God's glory and the believer's edification (Matt 26:26; Mark 14:22; Luke 24:30; 1 Cor 10:16, "the cup . . . which we bless," meaning which we attribute as belonging to God and of which we speak well). Used of a sacrifice and feast (Sept.: 1 Sam 9:13); the Jewish formulas of benediction and at the Paschal Supper (Matt 26:26).

(III) Of God toward men, to bless, i.e., to distinguish with favor, to act in man's life and accomplish His purposes instead of allowing men to have their own way. When the subject is God, His speaking is action, for God's speech is energy released. When God is said to bless us (eulogize or speak well of us), He acts for our good as He sees our need and not necessarily our desire. Therefore, He blesses by intervening. In Acts 3:26, God sent His Son to bless us, to intervene in our lives with what He planned to do for us. Eph 1:3, referring to God who blessed us with all spiritual blessings, means the one who intervened and acted so that our spirits might be made conformable to His Spirit. In Heb 6:14, quoted from Gen 22:17, "blessing I will bless thee," i.e., since it is My nature to bless or to act in people's lives, I will act in yours as well (the pres. part. *eulogṓn* indicates the nature of God and the fut. indic. *eulogḗsō* indicates God's definitive action in the future). This means that God cannot act in individual cases contrary to His nature. Pass., to be blessed of God. In Gal 3:8, we have the comp. with the prep. *en* (1722), in, and the verb in the fut. pass. *eneulogēthḗsontai* (1757), they shall be blessed in; and in Gal 3:9 *eulogoúntai*, are blessed (Sept.: Gen 24:1, 35; Ps 45:3; 67:2, 7; pass. Isa 61:9).

(IV) *Eulogēménos*, the perf. pass. part. of *eulogéō*, refers to one upon whom God has acted or who has experienced His blessing (*eulogía* [2129]) of God (Matt 21:9; 23:39; 25:34; Mark 11:9, 10; Luke 1:28, 42; 13:35; 19:38; John 12:13). The *eulogía* of God is His action or intervention in men's lives to bring them into the desired relationship with Himself. *Eulogēménos* is used in joyful salutations to indicate that the blessing of the individual is due to God's intervention in his or her life.

In the case of the Messiah and His reign, "Blessed [or well favored] is the One coming in the name of the Lord" (a.t.), as having the concurrence of God the Father (Matt 21:9; 23:39; Mark 11:9, 10; Luke 13:35; 19:38; John 12:13). In Matt 25:34, "the blessed ones of the Father" (a.t.) means those who have been acted upon by the Father and have been saved. Luke 1:28, speaking of the virgin Mary, "You are blessed above all women" (a.t.), means uniquely favored or acted upon favorably from among all women (Sept.: Deut 28:3; Ruth 3:10; 1 Sam 26:25). Blessed, but more accurately one well-spoken of and the recipient of God's action.

Eulogēménos is distinguished from *eulogētós* (2128), well-spoken of, inherently praiseworthy (which is spoken only of the personalities of the Triune God), and from *makários* [3107], blessed (which is used in the Beatitudes and means to be indwelt by God permanently because of Jesus Christ [Matt 5:11] and thereby to be fully satisfied [Luke 6:20–22]). *Makários* refers to a permanent state of being and not a temporary effect such as *eulogēménos* would imply. *Eulogēménos* is syn. with *makários* when referring to man, while *eulogēménos* refers to the action of God in man's life and *makários* to the blessed state of being indwelt by God and thereby being fully satisfied.

Deriv.: *eneulogéō* (1757), to bless, blessed; *eulogētós* (2128), blessed; *eulogía* (2129), blessing.

Syn.: *makarízō* (3106), to pronounce as blessed. The verb is found in Luke 1:48 referring to the virgin Mary who was going to be acclaimed as having been indwelt by God in that she was to bear the Lord Jesus within her as the God-Man, and in James 5:11, improperly translated "happy," which in its Gr. equivalence is not found in the NT. Happy means to rejoice because of outward favorable circumstances and good luck (*eutuchés*, successful, lucky, fortunate, prosperous; or *eudaímōn*, equipped with a good genius, fortunate, happy). The verse speaks of those who endure suffering. "Behold, we bless [*makarízomen*] them" (a.t.), means we recognize in them the presence of God Who fully satisfies them in spite of their suffering. With the meaning to praise or speak well of, used always of praise (*ainéō* [134]) to God by angels (Luke 2:13) or by men (Luke 2:20; 19:37); *epainéō* (1867), to commend; *humnéō* (5214), to sing, laud, praise.

Ant.: *kataráomai* (2672), to curse; *epikatáratos* (1944), cursed; *anáthema* (331), something cursed because it is to be sacrificed.

2128. ευλογητóς *eulogētós*, gen. *eulogētoú*, masc.-fem., neut. *eulogētón*, adj. from *eulogéō* (2127), to bless. Inherently blessed, well-spoken of, worthy of praise

(Mark 14:61; Luke 1:68; Rom 1:25; 9:5; 2 Cor 1:3; 11:31; Eph 1:3; 1 Pet 1:3; Sept.: Gen 9:26; Ex 18:10; Deut 33:24; Ruth 2:20). This adj. ending in -*tos* makes the word to mean "inherently worthy to be praised," and is in all instances ascribed to God the Father and also to Christ (Rom 9:5), for no one else is inherently worthy of such praise. On the other hand, the part. adj. *eulogēménos* ([2127], fem. *eulogēménē*) refers to humans who have been well-spoken of and acted upon by God. *Eulogētós* is syn. with *makários* (3107) when the latter refers to God (1 Tim 1:11; 6:15). In Mod. and ancient Gr., a happy person is called *eutuchḗs* (n.f.), one who has good luck, from *eu* (2095), good or well, and *túchē* (n.f.), luck. The verb *tugchánō* (5177), to happen, to come upon or to be found in a certain state, related to *eutuchía* (n.f.), happiness, occurs in Luke 10:30 (TR); 20:35; Acts 19:11; 24:2; 26:22; 27:3; 28:2; 1 Cor 14:10; 15:37; 2 Tim 2:10; Heb 8:6; 11:35.

2129. ευλογια *eulogía*; gen. *eulogías*, fem. noun from *eulogéō* (2127), to bless. Commendation, blessing.

(I) In Rom 16:18, translated "fair speeches," and refers to false teachers who for personal gain flatter people.

(II) Blessing God or ascribing praise, implying also thanksgiving (Rev 5:12, 13; 7:12), speaking well of and glorifying our God.

(III) From men toward men, i.e., blessing, benediction, petition for good from God upon persons, e.g., Esau in Heb 12:17 who, having rejected the blessing of his birthright, could not regain it; upon things (1 Cor 10:16, "the cup of blessing which God has instituted" [a.t.]; see Matt 26:27).

(IV) By metonymy, blessing, favor conferred, gift, benefit, bounty.

(A) From God to men (Rom 15:29, "in the full, abundant blessings of the gospel" [a.t.]; Gal 3:14, the promised blessing of God to Abraham and his seed; Eph 1:3; Heb 6:7, "receiveth blessing from God"

in that God causes the growth of vegetation [cf. Ezek 34:26; 1 Pet 3:9; Sept.: Gen 49:25; Isa 65:8]).

(B) From men to men, a gift, bounty, present (2 Cor 9:5, a gift, contribution; Sept.: Gen 33:11; 1 Sam 25:27; 2 Kgs 5:15). Hence, by implication, for liberality, generosity (2 Cor 9:5, 6; in v. 6, *ep' eulogías* as an adv., liberally, generously). See *epí* (1909, II, C, 3, g).

Syn.: *makarismós* (3108), blessedness or the action of becoming blessed; *makários* (3107), indwelt by God; *chrēstología* (5542), good words (Rom 16:18); *euphēmía* (2162), good report.

Ant.: *katára* (2671), curse; *anáthema* (331), curse.

2130. εὐμετάδοτος *eumetádotos*; gen. *eumetadótou*, masc.-fem., neut. *eumetádoton*, adj. from *eu* (2095), well, good, denoting readiness, and *metadídōmi* (3330), to impart. Ready to impart, liberal, bountiful (1 Tim 6:18).

Syn.: *apodektós* (587), acceptable, agreeable.

Ant.: *pheidoménōs* (5340), stingily, sparingly.

2131. Εὐνίκη *Euníkē*; fem. proper noun. Eunice, meaning happily victorious. The mother of Timothy; by birth a Jewess, but married to a Gentile (2 Tim 1:5, see Acts 16:1).

2132. εὐνοέω *eunoéō*; contracted *eunoṓ*, fut. *eunoḗsō*, from *eúnoos* (n.f.), benevolent, kindly, which is from *eú* (2095), well, and *noús* (3563), mind. To be well-disposed or well-intentioned toward another, to be friends (Matt 5:25).

Deriv.: *eúnoia* (2133), benevolence.

Syn.: *eudokéō* (2106), to think well of; *eulogéō* (2127), to bless, speak well of; *charízomai* (5483), to forgive, show kindness.

Ant.: *anathematízō* (332), to curse; *katanathematízō* (2653), to utter curses against; *kataráomai* (2672), to wish evil against a person or thing; *kakologéō* (2551), to speak evil.

2133. εὔνοια *eúnoia*; gen. *eunoías*, fem. noun from *eunoéō* (2132), to favor. Benevolence, goodwill (1 Cor 7:3 [TR]; Eph 6:7).

Syn.: *eudokía* (2107), pleasure, good thought; *eulogía* (2129), blessing; *cháris* (5485), grace, acceptance, pleasure.

Ant.: *ará* (685), a malediction, cursing; *katára* (2671), curse.

2134. εὐνουχίζω *eunouchízō*; fut. *eunouchísō*, from *eunoúchos* (2135), eunuch. To make a eunuch. Reflexively, to make oneself a eunuch, meaning to live like a eunuch in voluntary sexual abstinence (Matt 19:12).

2135. εὐνοῦχος *eunoúchos*; gen. *eunoúchou*, from *eunḗ* (n.f.), a bed, and *échō* (2192), to have, keep. It indicates that one is alone in bed. A keeper of the bed or bed chamber, a chamberlain, one who has been emasculated, such persons being employed as the keepers of oriental harems or dwellings of females. A eunuch (Matt 19:12), those impotent from birth and those who live like eunuchs in voluntary abstinence (Sept.: Esth 2:14, 15; Isa 56:3, 4). By implication, a minister of court (Acts 8:27, 34, 36, 38, 39). Eunuchs often rose to stations of great power and trust in eastern courts so that the term apparently came to be applied to any high officer of court even though not emasculated (see Sept.: Gen 37:36; 39:1).

Deriv.: *eunouchízō* (2134), to make a eunuch.

2136. Εὐοδία *Euodía*; gen. *Euodías*, fem. proper noun. Euodia, meaning fragrant, a Christian woman of Philippi (Phil 4:2).

2137. εὐοδόω *euodóō*; contracted *euodṓ*, fut. *euodṓsō*, from *eúodos* (n.f.), easy to travel through, *eú* (2095), good, well, and *hodós* (3598), a way, journey. To lead in a good way, to prosper one's journey (Sept.: Gen 24:27, 48). Figuratively, to make prosperous, give success to. In the

NT, only in the pass., meaning to be led in a good way, to have a prosperous journey (Rom 1:10, "if I shall be prospered [permitted] to come to you" [a.t.]); figuratively to be prospered (1 Cor 16:2; 3 John 1:2, which is not a promise of God that Gaius, to whom this letter was written, would have a prosperous and healthy life. It was rather the wish of the writer in the same manner in which we write a letter saying, "I hope you are well and prosperous, having all your needs met."

Syn.: *epitugchánō* (2013), to chance upon, attain, succeed; *prokóptō* (4298), to advance, do well; *kerdaínō* (2770), to gain; *karpophoréō* (2592), to bear fruit; *telesphoréō* (5052), to come to completion.

Ant.: *nauagéō* (3489), to suffer shipwreck, fail.

2138. εὐπειθής *eupeithḗs*; gen. *eupeithoús*, masc.-fem., neut. *eupeithés*, adj. from *eú* (2095), denoting easiness, and *peíthō* (3982), to persuade. Easily persuaded, compliant (James 3:17).

Ant.: *átaktos* (813), insubordinate, unruly; *apeithḗs* (545), disobedient.

2139. εὐπερίστατος *euperístatos*; gen. *euperistátou*, masc.-fem., neut. *euperístatos*, adj. from *eú* (2095), well, easily, and *periḯstēmi* (n.f.), to surround, which is from *perí* (4012), around, and *hístēmi* (2476), to stand. Easily surrounding or encompassing, easily besetting, as sin (Heb 12:1). Others translate this adj. relating to sin as "the sin so full of peril which so easily subjects one to calamity" (a.t.), since the noun *perístasis* (n.f.) sometimes means impediment, calamity.

Ant.: *aprósitos* (676), inaccessible.

2140. εὐποιΐα *eupoiḯa*; gen. *eupoiḯas*, fem. noun from *eupoiéō* (n.f.), to do good, which is from *eú* (2095), well, and *poiéō* (4160), to do. Well-doing, beneficence (Heb 13:16).

Syn.: *chrēstótēs* (5544), goodness that manifests itself in actions; *éleos* (1656), mercy; *oiktirmós* (3628), compassion;

agathōsúnē (19), goodness indicating a moral quality; *agathopoiḯa* (16), virtue or well-doing; *philanthrōpía* (5363), philanthropy, kindness, love of people; *boḗtheia* (996), help; *eleēmosúnē* (1654), benefaction, alms; *dósis* (1394), giving.

Ant.: *zēmía* (2209), damage, loss; *epiboulḗ* (1917), a plan against someone, a plot.

2141. εὐπορέω *euporéō*; contracted *euporṓ*, imperf. *ēuporoúmēn*, fut. *euporḗsō*, from *eúporos* (n.f.), prosperous. To prosper (Acts 11:29 Sept.: Lev 25:26, 49).

Deriv.: *euporía* (2142), pecuniary resources, abundance, wealth.

Syn.: *perisseúō* (4052), to abound; *pleonázō* (4121), to have more, increase; *plēthúnō* (4129), to multiply; *huperbállō* (5235), to exceed.

Ant.: *gumnēteúō* (1130), to be poorly clad or naked as an indication of utter poverty.

2142. εὐπορία *euporía*; gen. *euporías*, fem. noun from *euporéō* (2141), to have plenty of anything. Prosperity, abundance, wealth (Acts 19:25).

Syn.: *porismós* (4200), procuring wealth, gain; *ploútos* (4149), material riches, wealth.

Ant.: *ptōcheía* (4432), poverty.

2143. εὐπρέπεια *euprépeia*; gen. *euprepeías*, fem. noun from *euprepḗs* (n.f.), beautiful, decent. Beauty, gracefulness (James 1:11; Sept.: Ps 50:2; Lam 1:6).

Syn.: *cháris* (5485), grace; *egkráteia* (1466), self-control; *semnótēs* (4587), decency, decorum, modesty.

Ant.: *akrasía* (192), lack of self-restraint, incontinency; *aischrótēs* (151), shamefulness, filthiness, obscenity; *aschēmosúnē* (808), indecency, shame, unseemliness.

2144. εὐπρόσδεκτος *euprósdektos*; gen. *euprosdéktou*, masc.-fem., neut. *euprósdektos*, adj. from *eú* (2095), well, and *prosdéchomai* (4327), to receive, accept. Well-accepted, acceptable (Rom 15:16, 31; 2 Cor 6:2; 8:12; 1 Pet 2:5). A strong affirmation of acceptability, favorably received, predicated as *dektós* (1184) of the time of grace (Rom 15:31; 2 Cor 8:12).

Syn.: *dektós* (1184), acceptable, favorable; *apodektós* (587), acceptable in the sense of what is pleasing and welcome; *euárestos* (2101), well-pleasing, acceptable, and the basic *arestós* (701), agreeable.

Ant.: *adókimos* (96), disapproved, rejected.

2145. εὐπρόσεδρος *euprósedros*; gen. *euprosédrou*, masc.-fem., neut. *euprósedron*, adj. from *eu* (2095) an intens., and *prósedros* (n.f.), an assessor, a constant attendant. Constantly attending, from which we have the neut. noun *euprósedron*, a constant or continual attendance, devotion (1 Cor 7:35 [TR]), and in other MSS *eupáredros*, devoted. See *prosedreúō* (4332), to attend as a servant.

Syn.: *bébaios* (949), steadfast, sure; *asphalḗs* (804), safe, sure.

Ant.: *astḗriktos* (793), vacillating, unstable; *ádēlos* (82), uncertain.

2146. εὐπροσωπέω *euprosōpéō*; contracted *euprosōpó*, fut. *euprosōpéso*, from *euprósōpos* (n.f.), good-looking, pleasant in appearance, which is from *eú* (2095), well, and *prósōpon* (4383), a face, appearance. Only in Gal 6:12, meaning to make a fair appearance or show (Sept.: Gen 12:11). It concerns the difference between appearance and reality.

Syn.: *deigmatízō* (1165), to exhibit, make a show; *aréskō* (700), to please, be agreeable.

2147. εὑρίσκω *heurískō*; fut. *heurḗso*, aor. *heúrēsa* (rarely used [Rev 18:14]), 2d aor. *heúron*, 2d aor. pass. *heurḗthēn*, perf. *heúrēka*. To find, either by a previous search (Matt 7:7, 8) or without (Matt 27:32). In the pass. voice, used of

Enoch's disappearance (Heb 11:5); of mountains (Rev 16:20); of Babylon and its occupants (Rev 18:21, 22). Metaphorically, to find out by inquiry, to learn, discover (Luke 19:48; John 18:38; 19:4, 6; Acts 4:21; 13:28; Rom 7:10; Gal 2:17; 1 Pet 1:7; Rev 5:4). In the mid. voice, to find for oneself, gain, procure, obtain (Matt 10:39; 11:29; Luke 1:30; Acts 7:46; 2 Tim 1:18).

(I) Generally to find without seeking, meet with, light upon.

(A) Particularly and followed by the acc. of person (Matt 18:28; John 1:41, 43, 45; 2:14; Acts 9:33; 28:14; Sept.: Gen 4:14; 1 Sam 10:2, 3); of thing (Matt 13:44; Luke 4:17; 18:8; John 12:14; Acts 21:2; Sept.: Gen 44:8; Jon 1:3).

(B) Metaphorically, to find, i.e., to perceive or learn by experience that a person or thing is or does a particular thing, the acc. usually having with it a part. or adj. **(1)** With the acc. and part. (Matt 12:44; Mark 7:30; Luke 8:35; 24:2; John 11:17; Acts 9:2). In the pass. construction (Matt 1:18; Luke 17:18). **(2)** With the acc. and adj. or other adjunct, the acc. of *ón* (pres. part. of *eimí* [1510], to be) being implied (Acts 5:10; 24:5; Rom 7:18; 2 Cor 9:4; Rev 2:2). In the pass. construction (Luke 9:36; Acts 5:39; Rom 7:10; 1 Cor 4:2; 2 Cor 5:3; 1 Pet 1:7; Rev 5:4).

(II) To find by search, inquiry, to find out, discover, trans.

(A) Particularly and in an absolute sense (Matt 7:7, 8). Followed by the acc. of person expressed or implied (Mark 1:37; Luke 2:45; John 7:34, 35; Acts 5:22; 2 Tim 1:17); of thing expressed or implied (Matt 7:14; 12:43; 13:46; Mark 11:13; Luke 15:4; John 10:9; Acts 7:11). Of a judge, after examination (John 18:38; 19:4, 6; Acts 13:28; 23:9; Sept.: Josh 2:22; 1 Sam 9:13; 10:21); of things (Sept.: 1 Sam 9:4; 2 Kgs 12:10, 18 [cf. 1 Sam 29:3, 6, 8]).

(B) To find God, be accepted by Him when humbly and sincerely turning to Him (cf. in *ekzētéō* [1567], to diligently inquire, investigate [Acts 17:27]). Pass. (Rom 10:20 quoted from Isa 65:1; Sept.:

1 Chr 28:9). **(1)** Spoken of computation, measurement, to find, figure out (Acts 19:19; 27:28). **(2)** To find out mentally, i.e., to invent, contrive, before an indirect clause with the neut. art. *to* expressed or implied (Luke 5:19; 19:48; Acts 4:21).

(III) Mid., to find for oneself, i.e., to acquire, obtain, used once with the acc. (Heb 9:12); with the act., to acquire, obtain, get for oneself or another (Matt 10:39; Luke 9:12; John 21:6; Rom 4:1; Heb 12:17; Rev 9:6; 18:14); with a dat. (Matt 11:29; Acts 7:46 [cf. Sept.: Ps 132:5; Prov 3:13]). To find grace, meaning to obtain favor with God (Luke 1:30); used in an absolute sense (Heb 4:16); to find mercy with the Lord (2 Tim 1:18; Sept.: Gen 6:8; 32:5; 47:25).

Deriv.: *aneurískō* (429), to find out by search, discover.

Syn.: *ktáomai* (2932), to acquire; *kerdaínō* (2770), to gain.

Ant.: *apóllumi* (622), to lose.

2148. Εὐροκλύδων *Euroklúdōn*; gen. *Euroklúdōnos*, from *eúros* (n.f.), east wind, and *klúdōn* (2830), a wave. Euroclydon, a tempestuous wind occurring on the Mediterranean (Acts 27:14). It blows from all points and its danger results from the violence and uncertainty of its course.

2149. εὐρύχωρος *eurúchōros*; gen. *euruchórou*, masc.-fem., neut. adj. from *eurús* (n.f.), wide, broad, and *chóros* (5561), a place. Broad or wide-spaced, spacious (Matt 7:13; Sept.: Isa 30:23).

Syn.: *platús* (4116), broad, wide.

Ant.: *stenós* (4728), narrow, strait.

2150. εὐσέβεια *eusébeia*; gen. *eusebeías*, fem. noun from *eusebḗs* (2152), devout, godly. Devotion, piety toward God (Acts 3:12; 1 Tim 2:2; 2 Pet 1:6, 7). Godliness or the whole of true religion, so named because piety toward God is the foundation and principal part of it (1 Tim 4:7, 8; 6:6, see Matt 22:37, 38; Heb 11:6). Although *eusébeia* in the NT is translated "godliness" (1 Tim 2:2;

3:16; 4:7, 8; 6:3, 5, 6, 11; 2 Tim 3:5; Titus 1:1; 2 Pet 1:3, 6, 7; 3:11), the word "God" is not in it. Only in 1 Tim 2:10 is it *theosébeia* (2317), where the word *Theós* (2316), God, occurs as a prefix instead of *eú*, good or well.

The word *eusébeia* literally means well-directed reverence, but does not imply an inward, inherent holiness. It is actually an externalized piety. Paul uses it only in the pastoral epistles.

In Acts 3:12, Peter denies that he healed the lame man in his own power and *eusébeia*, i.e., his good standing with God apart from his faith in Jesus Christ.

In Acts 10:2, Cornelius is called *eusebḗs* (2152), devout and fearing God. A soldier who attended to Cornelius is also called *eusebḗs* (Acts 10:7).

When Paul came to Athens and spoke to the Athenians who certainly were not believers, but worshiped idols, he used the verb *eusebeíte* (2151), to show piety, respect (Acts 17:23). An unbeliever in the NT may be *eusebḗs*, pious, or may be *asebḗs* (765), impious. However, neither condition is *díkaios* (1342), righteous, just, nor *dikaiōthḗs* (1344), one justified or having God's righteousness imputed to him by Jesus Christ, nor *pistós* (4103), a believer who is characterized by the exercise of *pístis* (4102), saving faith in the person of the Lord Jesus Christ. On the other hand, the opposite of *eusébeia* is *asébeia* (763), ungodliness, or, better still, impiety. *Asébeia* is a characteristic of unbelievers who have absolutely no fear of God and do not bow their knee even to idols or anything that is imagined to be beyond themselves. Therefore, while *eusébeia* can be a characteristic of both an unbeliever (with qualification) and a believer, *asébeia* can be a characteristic only of an unbeliever. The same is true with the adj. *eusebḗs* in that there can be a pious unbeliever and a pious believer, but not so with *asebḗs* which applies only to an unbeliever. Therefore, *eusébeia*, the demonstration of a good and worshipful attitude toward God when spoken of the Christian, is the proper attitude of reverence toward God akin to *hagiótēs* (41), holiness, sanctity.

In 1 Tim 2:2, the word *eusébeia* is coupled with *semnótēs* (4587), decorum, proper standard accepted by God and His people, propriety, orderliness, seemliness. *Eusébeia* here refers to the simple worship of the believer, and *semnótēs* refers to the proper attire of the believer. Neither should be flashy for the purpose of making an impression upon others.

When *eusébeia* is applied to the Christian life, it denotes a life that is acceptable to Christ, indicating the proper attitude of the believer toward Christ who has saved him. It is both an attitude and a manner of life. It is in this manner that 1 Tim 4:7 says, "Exercise thyself rather unto godliness." It does not come automatically, but is something into which we must put effort. In 1 Tim 6:11, we are urged to "follow after righteousness, godliness [*eusébeia*]." In 2 Tim 3:5, we are told that it is possible to fake *eusébeia*, "having a form [*mórphōsis* {3446}] of godliness," an appearance and not the real thing. 1 Tim 6:5 tells us that fake *eusébeia* may be used for personal profit by false teachers. In 1 Tim 6:3, we are told that there can be false teaching that does not lead to a holy life. The holiness of life is an indicator of sound doctrine and teaching.

In Titus 1:1, we are encouraged to have *epígnōsin* (1922), acknowledgment or knowledge of the truth, equivalent to revelation, which, however, does not make us proud, but "according to godliness" (a.t.). This means that it should lead us to a holy life of submission with proper respect and reverence to God. In 1 Tim 3:16, we are told that *eusébeia* is a mystery. This refers to a holy life resulting from God's incarnation in the person of Jesus Christ when that incarnation and all that it entails is truly believed. This is *eusébeia*, a holiness initiated in the life of the believer by Christ Himself through the Holy Spirit. In 1 Tim 4:8, *eusébeia* is contrasted to physical exercise with *eusébeia* having a far greater and wider usefulness, while the latter has limited usefulness.

In 2 Pet 1:3, we are instructed that our spiritual life and reverence toward God (*eusébeia*) are gifts of God. It is definitively designated as a Christian virtue in line with continence, patience, brotherly kindness and love (vv. 6, 7), and as part of a developmental process based upon an increased knowledge of God and how to please Him (2 Pet 1:5). The fact that *eusébeia* is man's attitude toward God is indicated in that it precedes *philadelphía* (5360), love of the brethren, man's attitude to man. This is the reason why the translators have usually translated it "godliness." This differentiation between *eusébeia* (our attitude toward God) and our attitude toward man, as indicated by other words, is shown in 2 Pet 3:11, "Seeing then that all these things shall be dissolved [speaking of the termination of this world and the ushering in of the new earth and heaven {Rev 21:1}], what manner of persons ought ye to be in all holy conversation and godliness?" What is translated "holy conversation" in Gr. is *hagíais* (40), holy, and *anastrophaís* (391), behavior in the pl. In view of the passing of the present age, we must behave in a holy manner and worship God acceptably.

2151. εὐσεβέω *eusebéō*; contracted *eusebô*, fut. *eusebḗsō*, from *eusebḗs* (2152), devout, godly. To be reverent, pious. In Acts 17:23, the Apostle Paul in speaking to the heathen of Athens uses the verb *eusebeíte* to indicate their idolatrous worship. The word translated "devotions" in this verse is *sebásmata* (4574), the idols who served as objects of worship. In 1 Tim 5:4, *eusebéō* refers to the respect and honor children were to learn in their home.

Syn.: *proskunéō* (4352), to make obeisance, do reverence to; *sebázomai* (4573), to honor religiously; *latreúō* (3000), to serve religiously, worship.

Ant.: *asebéō* (764), to be impious, disrespectful.

2152. εὐσεβής *eusebḗs*; gen. *euseboús*, masc.-fem., neut. *eusebés*, adj. from *eú* (2095), well, and *sébomai* (4576), to revere. Reverent, pious, devout (Acts 10:2, 7; 22:12 [TR], *eulabḗs* [2126] in some MSS; 2 Pet 2:9). The first two references concern pious people: Cornelius and a soldier who had not yet exercised faith in Jesus Christ. In 2 Pet 2:9, it refers to believers, in opposition to *adíkous* (94), unrighteous. Therefore, *eusebeís* can refer either to unbelievers or to Christian believers, the first characterized by piety but not spiritual enlightenment, and the second characterized by a holy life commitment within the Christian life.
 Deriv.: *eusébeia* (2150), piety, reverence; *eusebéō* (2151), to be pious; *eusebṓs* (2153), in a godly manner.
 Ant.: *asebḗs* (765), impious, applicable only to unbelievers; *átheos* (112), godless.

2153. εὐσεβῶς *eusebṓs*; adv. from *eusebḗs* (2152), devout, godly. Piously, religiously (2 Tim 3:12, in a holy manner; Titus 2:12 coupled with *dikaíōs* [1346], righteously, attributing to God those things which rightfully belong to Him), rendering to God the reverence and worship emanating from a holy life. Noun: *eusébeia* (2150), godliness; *theosébeia* (2317) in which the adv. *eú* (2095), well, or as an adj., good, is replaced by *Theós* (2316), God, meaning God-piety (1 Tim 3:16). In this connection see the verb *sébomai* (4576), to worship either God or other objects of respect, and the verb *sebázomai* (4573), to worship religiously; also the subst. *sébasma* (4574), an object of worship or veneration, but not necessarily the true object of worship, God Himself.
 Syn.: *eulabéomai* (2125), to show religious reverence; *eulabḗs* (2126), devout; *eulábeia* (2124), piety or reverential awe.

2154. εὔσημος *eúsēmos*; gen. *eusḗmou*, masc.-fem., neut. *eúsēmon*, adj. from *eu* (2095), well, and *sḗma* (n.f., see *ásēmos*

[767]), a sign. Well-expressed, significant, of good omen, distinguishable by certain marks such as speech in which case it means easily understood, distinct (1 Cor 14:9).
 Syn.: *éndeixis* (1732), proof, token; *éndeigma* (1730), an indication, manifest token; *deígma* (1164), a specimen; *haploús* (573), plain, simple; *dḗlos* (1212), evident.
 Ant.: *dusnóētos* (1425), difficult to understand.

2155. εὔσπλαγχνος *eúsplagchnos*; gen. *eusplágchnou*, masc.-fem., neut. *eúsplagchnon*, adj. from *eú* (2095), well, and *splágchnon* (4698), bowel. Tenderhearted, full of compassion, pity (Eph 4:32; 1 Pet 3:8).
 Syn.: *eleḗmōn* (1655), merciful, actively compassionate; *oiktírmōn* (3629), full of pity and compassion for the ills of others; *híleōs* (2436), propitious, a quality of compassion residing only in God.
 Ant.: *aneleḗmōn* (415), unmerciful; *aníleōs* (448), inexorable, without mercy; *sklērós* (4642), hard, tough; *ástorgos* (794), without natural affection or family love.

2156. εὐσχημόνως *euschēmónōs*; adv. from *euschḗmōn* (2158), honorable. Decorously, decently, honestly (Rom 13:13; 1 Cor 14:40; 1 Thess 4:12).
 Syn.: *kalṓs* (2573), honorably, honestly, well.

2157. εὐσχημοσύνη *euschēmosúne*; gen. *euschēmosúnēs*, fem. noun from *euschḗmōn* (2158), comely, honorable. Decorum, comeliness (1 Cor 12:23).
 Syn.: *semnótēs* (4587), decency, dignity; *euprépeia* (2143), good conduct, gracefulness, propriety; *egkráteia* (1466), continence.
 Ant.: *aschēmosúnē* (808), shame, indecency; *aischrótēs* (151), shamefulness, obscenity; *akrasía* (192), lack of self-restraint, incontinency.

2158. εὐσχήμων euschḗmōn; gen.
euschḗmonos, masc.-fem., neut.
euschḗmon, adj. from eú (2095), well,
good, and schḗma (4976), external condition, fashion. Well-fashioned, well-
formed, comely. Qualifying certain
members (1 Cor 12:24); used with the
neut. def. art. tó euschḗmon as a subst.
meaning decorum, propriety (1 Cor
7:35); metaphorically, of high standing, honorable, noble (Mark 15:43; Acts
13:50; 17:12).
  Deriv.: euschēmónōs (2156), decorously, decently; euschēmosúnē (2157),
decorousness, comeliness.
  Syn.: éntimos (1784), honorable;
eugenḗs (2104), noble; semnós (4586),
venerable, decorous.
  Ant.: aschḗmōn (809), literally shapeless, not elegant, uncomely; agenḗs (36),
ignoble, not decent, base; átopos (824),
improper, injurious.

2159. εὐτόνως eutónōs; adv. from
eútonos (n.f.), intense, which is from eú
(2095) well, or an intens., and teínō (n.f.),
to stretch, strain. Intensely, powerfully,
vehemently (Luke 23:10; Acts 18:28).
  Syn.: deinós (1171), vehemently.

2160. εὐτραπελία eutrapelía; gen.
eutrapelías, fem. noun from eutrápelos
(n.f.), courteous, sportive, which is from
eú (2095), easily, and trépō (n.f.), to turn.
Facetiousness, coarse wittiness, ribaldry.
The turning of one's speech for the purpose of exciting mirth or laughter. Since,
however, such persons can easily manip-
ulate circumstances, they are apt to deteriorate into mischief-makers and clowns.
Therefore, eutrápelos (n.f.), a witty person, is sometimes used in a bad sense
meaning a scoffer, a sneerer, or a coarse
joker to which Paul probably refers in
Eph 5:4.

2161. Εὔτυχος Eútuchos; gen. Eutú-
chou, masc. proper noun. Eutychus,
meaning fortunate. A young man who
fell from the third floor of a house where

Paul was preaching in Troas and was restored to life by Paul (Acts 20:9).

2162. εὐφημία euphēmía; gen. euphē-
mías, fem. noun from eúphēmos (2163),
reputable. Words of good import or
omen, acclamation. Of good report, famous, praiseworthy (2 Cor 6:8).
  Syn.: épainos (1868), commendation,
praise; aínos (136), praise; aínesis (133),
praise, metaphorically representing a
sacrificial offering; kolakeía (2850), flattery.
  Ant.: dusphēmía (1426), evil speaking,
defamation; epitimía (2009), censure, admonition; momphḗ (3437), a fault, blame;
mástix (3148), whipping, scourging.

2163. εὔφημος eúphēmos; gen. euphḗ-
mou, masc.-fem., neut. eúphēmon, adj.
from eú (2095), well, good, and phḗmē
(5345), rumor, fame. Well-spoken of, of
good report, praiseworthy, laudable (Phil
4:8).
  Deriv.: euphēmía (2162), acclamation.

2164. εὐφορέω euphoréō; contracted
euphorṓ, fut. euphorḗsō, from eúphoros
(n.f.), will or patiently borne, which is
from eú (2095), well, and phérō (5342),
to bear. To bear well, yield abundantly,
intrans. spoken of the earth (Luke 12:16).
  Syn.: apodídōmi (591), yield;
karpophoréō (2592), to be fruitful.
  Ant.: husteréō (5302), to fall short, be
wanting.

2165. εὐφραίνω euphraínō; fut. eu-
phranṓ, from eúphrōn (n.f.), gladsome,
cheerful, which is from eú (2095), well,
and phrḗn (5424), mind. To rejoice,
make joyful in mind. In a good and
spiritual sense, to rejoice, make joyful
(2 Cor 2:2; Sept.: Ps 19:9); in the mid.,
euphraínomai, to be glad, joyful (Acts
2:26; Rom 15:10; Gal 4:27). To be joyful
or merry, in a natural sense (Luke 15:23,
24, 29, 32; Sept.: Deut 14:26; 27:7) or in
a bad sense (Luke 12:19; Acts 7:41). In
Luke 16:19, it refers to the rich man's
luxurious and sumptuous living. See

euphrosúnē (2167), gladness, which is also from *eúphrōn* (n.f.).

Syn.: *chaírō* (5463), to rejoice; *agalliáō* (21), to exult, rejoice greatly; *euthuméō* (2114), to make cheerful.

Ant.: *klaíō* (2799), to weep; *dakrúō* (1145), to shed tears; *thrēnéō* (2354), to mourn; *stenázō* (4727), to groan; *alalázō* (214), to wail; *lupéō* (3076), to make sorry, and in the mid. to be sorry.

2166. Εὐφράτης *Euphrátēs*; gen. *Euphrátou*, masc. proper noun. Euphrates, meaning the abounding. The largest river in western Asia, which originates in Armenia on the northern side of Mount Ararat, runs in a southeasterly direction, and receives many tributaries in its winding course along the borders of Syria. Skirting the Arabian desert it passes through the middle of Babylon to Basra where it joins the Tigris, becoming the Shatt al Arab for about seventy-five miles before emptying into the Persian Gulf. Its whole length is 1,780 miles. The Tigris flows in a narrower channel with deeper banks and a less rapid current. The country between the two rivers slopes toward the Tigris and thus greatly favors the draining off of the superfluous waters of the Euphrates. The Euphrates is named as one of the rivers of Eden (Gen 2:14), called "the great river" (Gen 15:18; Deut 1:7). It is noted as the eastern boundary of the promised land (Deut 11:24; Josh 1:4; 1 Chr 5:9), and was one of David's conquests (2 Sam 8:3; 1 Chr 18:3); taken by the king of Babylon from Egypt (2 Kgs 24:7); referred to in prophecy (Rev 9:14; 16:12; see Jer 13:4–7; 46:2–10; 51:63). In more than twenty-six other passages, it is spoken of as "the river." By this stream, the captive Jews wept (Ps 137:1).

2167. εὐφροσύνη *euphrosúnē*; gen. *euphrosúnēs*, fem. noun from *eúphron* (n.f.), gladsome, cheerful, which is from *eu* (2095), well, and *phrén* (5424), mind. Joy, joyfulness, gladness (Acts 2:28; 14:17; Sept.: Esth 9:18, 19; Ps 4:8). See

euphraínō (2165), to rejoice, which is also from *eúphrōn* (n.f.).

Syn.: *chará* (5479), joy, delight; *agallíasis* (20), exultation, exuberant joy.

Ant.: *lúpē* (3077), grief, sorrow; *odúnē* (3601), pain, consuming grief; *ōdín* (5604), birth-pang, travail; *pénthos* (3997), mourning, sorrow; *thlípsis* (2347), affliction.

2168. εὐχαριστέω *eucharistéō*; contracted *eucharistṓ*, fut. *eucharistḗsō*, aor. *ēucharístēsa* or *eucharístēsa* (Rom 1:21), from *eucháristos* (2170), thankful, grateful, well-pleasing. To show oneself grateful, to be thankful, to give thanks. It does not occur in the Sept., where instead we find *eulogéō* (2127), to speak well of (which, in some respects, embraces a more narrow concept, and in others a wider concept than *eucharistéō*). In the NT, except in Rom 16:4, used in a religious sense with or without reference to God. In Luke's and Paul's writings, it is followed by *Theós* ([2316], God) in the dat., *tṓ Theṓ*. With the dat., it refers to thanks for any good experience (Luke 17:16; Acts 27:35; 28:15; Rom 14:6; 1 Cor 14:18; Col 1:12; 3:17). The reason for thanks is designated by *hupér* (5228), for the sake of or on the part of (Rom 1:8; 1 Cor 10:30; Eph 1:16; 5:20); by *perí* (4012), with respect to, with the gen. (1 Cor 1:4; 1 Thess 1:2; 2 Thess 1:3; 2:13); by *epí* (1909), upon, with the dat. (1 Cor 1:4; Phil 1:3). Sometimes it is added on with *hóti* (3754), that (Luke 18:11; John 11:41; Rom 1:8; 1 Cor 1:14; 1 Thess 2:13; Rev 11:17); also used with the acc., referring to a person or thing, meaning to praise God for something or someone (Rom 1:21; 2 Cor 1:11). This construction, unknown in Class. Gr., has its origin from the absolute use of *eucharistéō*.

In the NT, to give thanks, to thank, express one's gratitude. With the dat. of person (Luke 17:16; Rom 16:4).

Elsewhere in the NT, used only in reference to God, to give thanks to God, usually followed by *tṓ Theṓ*, to God

(Acts 28:15; Rom 7:25; 1 Cor 14:18; Col 1:12; 3:17; Phile 1:4; Rev 11:17), and other adjuncts as with *perí* (4012), concerning (Col 1:3), *hupér* (5228), on behalf of (Eph 5:20), *hóti* (3754), that (Luke 18:11; John 11:41; 1 Cor 1:14; 1 Thess 2:13). Used in an absolute sense (Eph 1:16; 1 Thess 5:18). Pass., with the acc. (2 Cor 1:11). Spoken of giving thanks before meals, followed by *tō̂ Theō̂*, to God (Acts 27:35; Rom 14:6); used in an absolute sense (Matt 15:36; 26:27; Mark 8:6; 14:23; Luke 22:17, 19; John 6:11, 23; 1 Cor 10:30; 11:24).

By implication, to praise, bless, worship (Rom 1:21; 1 Cor 14:17) corresponding to *eulogéō* (2127), to bless, praise, eulogize.

Syn.: *homologéō* (3670), to acknowledge, give thanks; *opheílō* (3784), to be under obligation; *eulogéō* (2127), to bless, praise.

Ant.: *krínō* (2919), to condemn, judge; *katakrínō* (2632), to condemn, damn; *elégchō* (1651), to rebuke, reprove, find fault; *apodokimázō* (593), to disallow, reject; *katadikázō* (2613), to pronounce guilty, condemn; *mémphomai* (3201), to blame, find fault; *diabállō* (1225), to accuse falsely; *kakologéō* (2551), to revile, speak evil of; *katalaléō* (2635), to slander; *katēgoréō* (2723), to accuse, object; *epikrínō* (1948), to adjudge.

2169. εὐχαριστία *eucharistía*; gen. *eucharistías*, fem. noun from *eucháristos* (2170), thankful, grateful, well-pleasing. Gratitude, thankfulness, thanksgiving (Acts 24:3). In Paul's writings and in the Book of the Revelation, it means thanksgiving, thanks, i.e., the expression of gratitude to God. Followed by the dat. *tō̂ Theō̂*, to God (2 Cor 9:11, 12; Rev 7:12). Generally (1 Cor 14:16; 2 Cor 4:15; Phil 4:6; Col 2:7; 4:2; 1 Thess 3:9; 1 Tim 2:1; 4:3, 4). In Eph 5:4, grateful speech or discourse. See Amos 4:5. Eucharist is used in modern language for Holy Communion, embodying the highest act of thanksgiving for the greatest gift received from God, the sacrifice of

Jesus. It is the grateful acknowledgement of past mercies.

Syn.: *eulogía* (2129), praise; *makarismós* (3108), the ascription of the blessed state and recognition of it.

Ant.: *katára* (2671), curse.

2170. εὐχάριστος *eucháristos*; gen. *eucharístou*, masc.-fem., neut. *eucháriston*, adj. from *eú* (2095), well, and *charízomai* (5483), to grant, give. Thankful, grateful, well-pleasing (Col 3:15; Sept.: Prov 11:16). Some attribute to it, by implication, the meaning of well-pleasing, acceptable to God, and others the meaning of liberal.

Deriv.: *eucharistéō* (2168), to be thankful; *eucharistía* (2169), thankfulness, giving of thanks.

Syn.: *arestós* (701), pleasing, agreeable; *euárestos* (2101), well-pleasing.

Ant.: *acháristos* (884), ungrateful.

2171. εὐχή *euchē̂*; gen. *euchē̂s*, fem. noun from *eúchomai* (2172), to wish, pray, vow. Prayer, wish. In James 5:15, it is translated "prayer" because, in verse fourteen, the comp. verb *proseúchomai* (4336), to pray, is used. If, however, prayer was meant by the *euchē̂* (v. 15), the more common word *proseuchē̂* (4335) would have been used. The basic meaning of the word *euchē̂* is wish or vow. When it is addressed to God, it becomes *proseuchē̂*, from *prós* (4314), toward, and *euchē̂*, wish. When we pray to God, we wish that He would intervene to permit something in our lives that we feel is proper and right. For the Christian, every prayer ought to be the result of his faith in God through Christ. In the NT, faith is the acceptance of God's revelation for man and the means whereby that revelation for each individual is appropriated. A Christian's wish is for God's will to take place in his life, even in the case of sickness. It is of such a wish coming from faith that James is speaking about in regard to a sick brother. In praying for the sick, we must exercise faith that God is able to heal, and we are free to express our wish for the healing of the sick. However, once we have expressed our wish, we must allow God to do as He pleases and in that find the satisfaction in faith.

In the other two instances (Acts 18:18; 21:23), it means a vow. In the case of Acts 18:18, it refers to Paul shaving his head in fulfillment of a vow that he had made. Among the Jews as well as the Gentiles, it was usual for persons in distress, danger, or any necessity to vow that, in case of deliverance, they would cut off their hair and offer sacrifices in honor to God.

In the case of Acts 21:23, reference is made to four members of the church at Jerusalem who had a vow on them. Paul had just returned from his third missionary journey. It was reported that he was teaching all the Jews of the Dispersion "to forsake Moses, telling them not to circumcise their children, neither to walk after the customs" (a.t. [Acts 21:21]). Grave offence was thereby being given to the Jewish Christians who were all "zealous of the law" (Acts 21:20). James and the elders, therefore, urged the apostle to seize the opportunity of vindicating his character which circumstances offered. By purifying himself with the men who had the vow and by bearing the expenses incidental to its completion, he would be able to prove that he had not abandoned the ancient custom of his nation. The vow was a unique Jewish custom which would be completed in the temple by a purely Jewish rite. Such vows are not uncommon in the OT. See the vow of the Nazarite in the Sept. (Num 6:1–22), where the word is euché, vow. These vows consisted of an obligation, commonly self-imposed, to observe some special form of ceremonial purity for a specified time. The duration of the vow was marked by allowing the hair of the head to grow freely, and its expiration by trimming the hair in the normal manner and the offering of certain special sacrifices. The vow of a Nazarite might be for life, as in the case of Samson (Judg 13:7), or might even include an entire clan for several generations, as in the case of the Rechabites (Jer 35:6–11).

We do not know what the vow of the Apostle Paul mentioned in Acts 18:18 was, but it is noteworthy that it was terminated at a distance from Jerusalem, and therefore, was without sacrifices. As his departure from Cenchreae was virtually the end of the evangelistic work pertaining to his second missionary journey, he may have considered that his vow expired at that point. Perhaps he may have terminated it in view of the impossibility of maintaining on shipboard the conditions which it imposed. Since, in both instances, the word euché definitely refers to a vow, the idea of a vow may even be present in James 5:14, but if such is the case, the vow is purely voluntary.

In Acts 23:13f., a vow of a rather different kind is referred to as anáthema (331) a curse, or anáthēma (334), a votive offering, in which case more than forty of the Jews bound themselves with an evil vow not to eat or drink until they had killed Paul. For a Jew, therefore, a vow was an obligation of a religious or semireligious character incurred for some definite, specified time. The expiration of the vow was, as a rule, marked by special sacrifices in the temple.

2172. εὔχομαι *eúchomai*; imperf. *euchómēn* or *ēuchómēn*, fut. *eúxomai*, mid. deponent. To pray or vow. The verb originally and literally means to speak out, utter aloud, and thus to express a wish. To pray or to vow to God (Acts 26:29; 2 Cor 13:7); in an absolute sense or on behalf of someone (James 5:16; Sept.: Ex 8:29, 30; Num 11:2; 21:7); by implication, to pray or wish for, to desire earnestly (Acts 27:29; Rom 9:3; 3 John 1:2). Used with the acc. and *toúto* (5124), this, in 2 Cor 13:9.

Deriv.: *euché* (2171), vow, wish, and by implication, prayer; *proseúchomai* (4336), to pray to God.

Syn.: *erōtáō* (2065), to ask on an equal basis; *aitéō* (154), to ask, pray for as from an inferior to a superior; *déomai* (1189), to desire, to pray with a specific end in mind; *epikaléomai* (1941), to invoke, call upon; *parakaléō* (3870), to pray, beseech; *eucharistéō* (2168), to thank, to wish well.

2173. εὔχρηστος *eúchrēstos*; gen. *euchrḗstou*, masc.-fem., neut. *eúchrēston*, adj. from *eú* (2095), well, and *chráomai* (5530), to furnish what is needful. Useful or very useful (2 Tim 2:21; 4:11; Phile 1:11).

Syn.: *chrḗsimos* (5539), serviceable, profitable, useful.

Ant.: *áchrēstos* (890), unprofitable, useless; *achreíos* (888), worthless; *alusitelḗs* (255), unprofitable; *anōphelḗs* (512), useless.

2174. εὐψυχέω *eupsuchéō*; contracted *eupsuchṓ*, fut. *eupsuchḗsō*, from *eúpsuchos* (n.f.), of good courage, which is from *eú* (2095), well, and *psuchḗ* (5590), soul, mind. To be animated, be in good spirits (Phil 2:19).

Syn.: *euthuméō* (2114), to cheer up; *protrépō* (4389), to urge forward; *parakaléō* (3870), to encourage, comfort; *paramuthéomai* (3888), to encourage; *empnéō* (1709), to inspire; *zōogonéō* (2225), to revive; *anazōpuréō* (329), to revive, stir up, rekindle; *enischúō* (1765), to invigorate, strengthen.

Ant.: *phobéomai* (5399), to fear; *trémō* (5141), to tremble; *sunéchō* (4912), to perplex, to constrain; *phríssō* (5425), to bristle, shudder; *athuméō* (120), to dishearten.

2175. εὐωδία *euōdía*; gen. *euōdías*, fem. noun from *euṓdēs* (n.f.), sweet-smelling; which is from *eú* (2095), well, good, and *ózō* (3605), to smell. A good smell, odor, fragrance. Used metaphorically of persons or things well-pleasing to God (2 Cor 2:15; Eph 5:2; Phil 4:18).

Syn.: *osmḗ* (3744), odor, smell; *thumíama* (2368), incense; *árōma* (759), aroma; *líbanos* (3030), incense, frankincense.

2176. εὐώνυμος *euṓnumos*; gen. *euōnúmou*, masc.-fem., neut. *euṓnumos*, adj. from *eú* (2095), well, good, and *ónoma* (3686), name. Of good name, honored, of good omen, used by way of euphemism instead of *aristerós* (710), the left, which was a word of ill omen, since all omens on the left were regarded as unfortunate by the Greeks and, in part, by the Romans. In the NT, the left, spoken chiefly of the left hand in opposition to the right (Matt 20:21, 23; 25:33, 41; 27:38; Mark 10:37, 40; 15:27); of the left foot (Rev 10:2); as on the left hand in passing, referring to Cyprus (Acts 21:3). See Sept.: Josh 23:6; Neh 8:4.

Ant.: *dexiós* (1188), right hand or side.

2177. ἐφάλλομαι *ephállomai*; fut. *ephaloúmai*, from *epí* (1909), upon, and *hállomai* (242), to leap. To leap or spring upon, assault (Acts 19:16; Sept.: 1 Sam 10:6; 11:6; 16:13).

2178. ἐφάπαξ *ephápax*; adv. from *epí* (1909), upon, at, and *hápax* (530), once. Once and for all (Rom 6:10; 1 Cor 15:6; Heb 7:27; 9:12; 10:10).

Ant.: *oudépote* (3763), never; *mēdépote* (3368), never; *oudépō* (3764), never yet; *oúpō* (3768), not yet; *pópote* (4455), not at any time; *pollákis* (4178) or *pollá* (4183), many times; *posákis* (4212) or *puknós* or *pukná* (4437), often, how many times.

2179. Ἐφεσῖνος *Ephesínos*; fem. *Ephesínē*, neut. *Ephésinon*, proper adj. Of Ephesus or an Ephesian (Rev 2:1 [TR]).

2180. Ἐφέσιος *Ephésios*; fem. *Ephesía*, neut. *Ephésion*, proper adj. Ephesian (Acts 19:28, 34, 35; 21:29).

2181. Ἔφεσος *Éphesos*; gen. *Ephésou*, masc. proper noun. Ephesus, the most important commercial city of Asia Minor, the capital of Ionia on the western coast of Asia Minor between Smyrna and Miletus. The city was surrounded on three sides by mountains and on the west by the Icarian Sea. The river Cayster ran across the plain. Apostle Paul visited Ephesus on his second missionary journey (Acts 18:19–21); Apollos was instructed there by Aquila and Priscilla (Acts 18:24–29); Paul dwelt there three years (Acts 19) and spoke to the elders of that church at Miletus (Acts 20:17–25); the angel of the church of Ephesus is named in Rev 2:1–7. The city is in complete desolation. Many ruins remain, including the stadium and theater. On the same plain is a little Turkish village called Ayasalouk, a corrupted form of "Ayios Theologos": "Saint [holy] Theologue," i.e., Saint John. Saint John is supposed to have ended his days at Ephesus. The ancient city often changed its name and its site. In apostolic times, Ephesus contained three remarkable buildings:

(I) The temple of Diana, one of the seven wonders of the world, was erected at the joint cost of all Asia and was 220 years in building. In the center of the court was an image of the goddess Diana, which superstitious people believed fell down from heaven (Acts 19:35). Ephesus fell prey to the Goths in A.D. 262, and the remains of its magnificent temple were hidden from the world until they were brought to light in 1869 by J. T. Wood who spent eleven years (1863–1874) in exploration of the ancient city.

(II) The theater (Acts 19:29) was the largest structure of its kind built by the Greeks and was claimed to be capable of seating 50,000 spectators. J.T. Wood, however, estimated its seating capacity at 24,500 persons.

(III) The stadium or circus, an arena in which the Ephesian people witnessed foot races, wrestling matches, and fights with wild beasts. The competitors were usually condemned criminals who were sent naked into the arena to be torn to pieces by wild beasts (1 Cor 15:32). The remains of the victims were sometimes exposed at the end of the combat which gives great vividness to the apostle's reference in 1 Cor 4:9. Some of these games were held in honor of Diana, and the silver shrines of the goddess made by Demetrius (1216) and his fellow craftsmen were eagerly purchased for household idols by visitors (Acts 19:24).

2182. ἐφευρετής *epheurétēs*; gen. *epheurétou*, masc. noun from *epheurískō* (n.f.), to invent, which is from *epí* (1909), an intens., and *heurískō* (2147), to find. An inventor (Rom 1:30).

2183. ἐφημερία *ephēmería*; gen. *ephēmerías*, fem. noun from *ephēmeros* (2184), temporary, daily, lasting one day (Eng. deriv.: "ephemeral"). Daily, as the service of the priests in the temple (2 Chr 13:10, 11). In the NT, used metonymically, a course or class into which the priests were divided for the daily temple service, each class continuing for a week at a time (Luke 1:5, 8). See Sept.: 1 Chr 23:6; 28:13; 2 Chr 8:13; 23:8; Neh 12:9, 24.

Syn.: *kathēmerinós* (2522), according to the day, day by day; *kath' hekástēn hēméran* (*kathí* [2596], every, in a distributive sense; *hekástēn* [1538], each one; *hēméran* [2250], day), according to each day, day by day; *epioúsios* (1967), that which suffices for this day (Matt 6:11; Luke 11:3).

2184. ἐφήμερος *ephḗmeros*; gen. *ephēmérou*, masc.-fem., neut. *ephḗmeron*, adj. from *epí* (1909), upon, and *hēméra* (2250), day. For the day, ephemeral, daily (James 2:15, "that which is necessary for the day" [a.t.]).

Deriv.: *ephēmería* (2183), course, daily.

Syn.: *próskairos* (4340), temporal.

Ant.: *aiốnios* (166), eternal, without end with reference to either space or time; *aídios* (126), everlasting in the sense of without interruption, permanent and unchangeable; *diēnekḗs* (1336), unbroken, continuous, perpetual.

2185. ἐφικνέομαι *ephiknéomai*; contracted *ephiknoúmai*, 2d aor. *ephiknómēn*, mid. deponent from *epí* (1909), unto, and *hiknéomai* (n.f., see *diïknéomai* [1338]), to come. To come upon or to someone, to arrive at (2 Cor 10:13, 14).

Syn.: *katantáō* (2658), to come to a place, arrive; *paragínomai* (3854), to come near or on the scene; *phthánō* (5348), to arrive at; *katapléō* (2668), to sail to, arrive at the shore.

Ant.: *apérchomai* (565), to go away.

2186. ἐφίστημι *ephístēmi*; fut. *epistḗsō*, from *epí* (1909), by, near, upon, and *hístēmi* (2476), to stand. Trans., to set over, place upon or over. In the NT, only in the intrans. forms: 2d aor. act. *epéstēn*; the perf. act. part. *ephestṓs* (mid. *ephístamai*), to place oneself upon or near, to stand upon, by, near.

(I) Of persons, to stand by, near (Luke 2:38; Acts 22:13, 20); with the dat. of person (Acts 23:11); followed by the prep. *epí* (1909) and the acc. of thing (Acts 10:17; 11:11); by *epánō* (1883), upon, with the gen. (Luke 4:39; Sept.: 1 Sam 17:51; 2 Sam 1:9; Zech 1:10, 11). See Sept.: Gen 24:43; Amos 9:1.

(II) Implying also approach, to come and stand by, to come to or upon a person or place (Luke 10:40; 20:1); sudden appearance (Luke 2:9; 24:4; Acts 12:7); approach in a hostile sense, to come upon, assail (Acts 6:12; 23:27), with a dat. (Acts 4:1; 17:5; Sept.: Jer 21:2).

(III) In regard to people, to stand by, to be at hand, pressing, earnest (2 Tim 4:2); of things evil, to come or fall upon, befall (Luke 21:34; 1 Thess 5:3); of a tempest (Acts 28:2); to impend, be at hand (2 Tim 4:6).

Deriv.: *epistátēs* (1988), a master; *katephístēmi* (2721), to assault; *sunephístēmi* (4911), to stand up together.

Syn.: *epérchomai* (1904), to come or go upon; *prosérchomai* (4334), to come or go near to; *paragínomai* (3854), to arrive, be present; *hḗkō* (2240), to come, be present; *phthánō* (5348), to arrive; *proseggízō* (4331), to come near; *eggízō* (1448), to approach; *epíkeimai* (1945), to lie or press upon or near; *páreimi* (3918),

to be near; *enístēmi* (1764), to be present, to stand by; *parákeimai* (3873), to lie beside, be present.

Ant.: *ápeimi* (548), to go or be away; *pheúgō* (5343), to flee.

2187. Ἐφραΐμ *Ephraím*; masc. proper noun that is transliterated from the Hebr. *'Ephrayim* (669, OT), double fruitfulness. Ephraim. In the NT, it is a town or city (John 11:54), located about eight miles north of Jerusalem, according to the church historian Eusebius. Jerome maintains that it was a town about twenty miles away. Josephus mentions Ephraim and Bethel as being small towns apparently near each other. Ephraim was the city to which Jesus resorted. See Sept.: 2 Sam 13:23; 2 Chr 13:19.

2188. ἐφφαθά *ephphathá*; an Aramaic imper. equivalent to the Gr. word *dianoíchthēti*, the aor. imper. pass. of *dianoígō* (1272). Be open or opened (Mark 7:34).

2189. ἔχθρα *échthra*; gen. *échthras*, fem. noun from *echthrós* (2190), enemy, Enmity, hatred, hostility (Luke 23:12; Rom 8:7; Gal 5:20; James 4:4; Sept.: Num 35:20; Prov 26:26). Metaphorically, as in Eph 2:15, 16, cause of enmity.

Syn.: *dusphēmía* (1426), defamation, evil report; *kakía* (2549), wickedness, malice; *ponēría* (4189), active malice, wickedness; *sunōmosía* (4945), plot, conspiracy; *phthónos* (5355), ill-will, envy.

Ant.: *agápē* (26), love; *philadelphía* (5360), brotherly love; *philanthrōpía* (5363), benevolence, philanthropy; *philía* (5373), friendship; *eúnoia* (2133), kindness, good-will, benevolence.

2190. ἐχθρός *echthrós*; fem. *echthrá*, neut. *echthrón*, adj. from *échthos* (n.f.), hatred, enmity. Hostile, inimical.

(I) In Rom 11:28, enemies, in contrast to *agapētós* (27), beloved.

(II) In an act. sense, as a subst., *ho echthrós*, an enemy, adversary (Matt 5:43; 10:36; 13:25; Luke 1:71; 19:43;

Phil 3:18, "enemies of the cross"); in a pass. sense, a person hated or rejected as an enemy (Matt 5:44; 13:28, 39, the adversary, Satan; 22:44, the adversaries of the Messiah; Mark 12:36; Luke 1:74; 6:27, 35; 10:19, Satan; 19:27; 20:43; Acts 13:10; Rom 5:10; 11:28; 12:20; 1 Cor 15:25; Gal 4:16; Col 1:21; 2 Thess 3:15; Heb 1:13; 10:13; James 4:4, of God; Rev 11:5, 12). Metaphorically (1 Cor 15:26).

Deriv.: *échthra* (2189), enmity, hatred.

Syn.: *enantíos* (1727), opposite, contrary, antagonistic; *anósios* (462), wicked, unholy; *stugnētós* (4767), hated, odious, hateful; *bdeluktós* (947), detestable, abominable; *misoúmenos*, the pres. pass. part. of *miséō* (3404), to hate, hated.

Ant.: *phílos* (5384), friend; *hetaíros* (2083), companion; *oikeíos* (3609), relative, adherent; *súntrophos* (4939), one who has been brought up together with someone, comrade; *adelphós* (80), brother.

2191. ἔχιδνα **échidna**; gen. *echídnēs*, fem. noun. A viper (Acts 28:3). Used metaphorically of wicked men, described as a generation of vipers (Matt 3:7; 12:34; 23:33; Luke 3:7).

Syn.: *óphis* (3789), a snake; *herpetón* (2062), a creeping thing.

2192. ἔχω **échō**; imperf. *eíchon*, fut. *héxō*, 2d aor. *éschon*, perf. *éscheka*. To have, to hold, i.e., to have and hold, implying continued possession, trans.

(I) Particularly and primarily to have in one's hands, to hold in the hand (Rev 1:16; 6:5; 10:2; 17:4). By implication (Matt 26:7; Heb 8:3; Rev 5:8; 6:2; 8:3, 6; 9:14).

(II) Generally and most frequently, to have, to possess externally.

(A) With the acc. of things in one's possession, power, charge, control. **(1)** Generally and simply, e.g., property (Matt 13:12; 19:21, 22; Mark 10:22, 23; Luke 18:24; 21:4; 2 Cor 6:10, to have nothing, to be poor; Rev 18:19). Hence in later usage, simply to have with a direct obj., i.e.,

to have something such as wealth, thus to be rich; or not to have money meaning to be poor (Matt 13:12; 25:29; 1 Cor 11:22; 2 Cor 8:11, 12; James 4:2). Of flocks, to have sheep (Matt 12:11). Of produce, estates (Luke 12:19; 13:6). Metaphorically meaning inheritance (Eph 5:5) and a part with someone (John 13:8 [cf. Gen 31:14; Num 18:20; Deut 12:12]). Of arms, utensils (Luke 22:36); garments (Luke 3:11; 9:3); provisions (Matt 14:17; Mark 8:1, 2, 5, 7; John 2:3; 1 Tim 6:8); a home, place (Matt 8:20; Mark 5:3; Luke 12:17). Members or parts of the body such as ears and eyes (Matt 11:15; Mark 8:18); flesh and bones (Luke 24:39); uncircumcision, i.e., Gentiles (Acts 11:3); tails (Rev 9:10); metaphorically the heart (Mark 8:17; 2 Pet 2:14). Power, faculty, dignity (John 4:44; 17:5; Heb 2:14; 7:24; Rev 9:11; 16:9; 17:18). Of any good, advantage, benefit, such as pay or reward (Matt 5:46); favor with someone (Acts 2:47; Sept.: Ex 33:12); faith as a gift (Rom 14:22; 1 Cor 13:2; James 2:1, 14, 18); eternal life (John 3:36; 6:40, 47, 53, 54). Of a law (John 19:7; 1 Cor 7:25; 1 John 4:21); of age, years (John 8:57; 9:21, 23); of a ground for complaint, followed by *katá* (2596), against, and the gen. or by *prós* (4314), toward, and the acc. (Matt 5:23; Acts 19:38; 24:19; 25:19; 1 Cor 6:1; Rev 2:4, 20); of a ground for reply (2 Cor 5:12); of a definite beginning and ending (Heb 7:3). **(2)** With an adjunct qualifying the acc., e.g., an adj. or part. in the acc. (Luke 19:20; Acts 2:44; 20:24, "nor do I hold my life dear" [a.t.]); with a noun in apposition (1 Pet 2:16). **(3)** By implication with the notion of charge, trust (Rev 1:18; 12:12; 15:1, 6). **(4)** In the sense of to have at hand, have ready (1 Cor 14:26).

(B) With the acc. of person implying some special relation or connection. **(1)** Generally and simply, e.g., of a husband or wife (Matt 14:4, "to have her as a wife" [a.t.]; Mark 12:23; John 4:17, 18); brothers (Luke 16:28); a high priest (Heb 4:14, 15); masters (1 Tim 6:2); steward (Luke 16:1); children (Matt 22:28; Gal

4:22; Titus 1:6); friend (Luke 11:5); widows (1 Tim 5:16). See Matt 9:36; 27:16, 65; Luke 4:40; John 5:7; Rev 2:14, 15. **(2)** With an adjunct qualifying the acc., e.g., a noun in apposition (Matt 3:9, "We have a father, Abraham" [a.t.]; John 8:41; Acts 13:5; Phil 3:17; Phile 1:17). With an adjunct or part. in the acc. (Luke 14:18, 19; 17:7; 1 Cor 7:12, 13; Phil 2:20, 29); with a prep. and its case (Acts 25:16). See Matt 26:11; John 12:8, "the poor always ye have with you." Also to have unto oneself (Matt 8:9; Luke 7:8; Rev 9:11). **(3)** Where the subj. is a thing, to have, implying the existence of something in or in close connection with the subj.; with the acc. of a thing (Matt 13:5, 6, 27; Luke 11:36; 20:24; Acts 27:39). See Acts 1:12, "having a sabbath day's journey" (a.t.), i.e., being that far from the city; 1 Cor 12:23; 1 Tim 4:8; 2 Tim 2:17, "shall eat around" (a.t.), spread; Heb 9:8, "having yet a standing" (a.t.); James 1:4; Rev 4:7, 8.

(III) Spoken of what one is said to have in, on, by, or with himself, i.e., of any condition, circumstance, state either external or internal in which one is.

(A) Generally of any obligation, duty, course (Luke 12:50; Acts 18:18; 21:23; Rom 12:4; 2 Cor 4:1; Phil 1:30; Col 2:1); of sin, guilt (John 9:41; 15:22; Acts 23:29; 1 Tim 5:12); lawsuits (1 Cor 6:4, 7; see Acts 28:29). To come to an end, be destroyed (Mark 3:26, "Satan . . . hath an end"). Metaphorically, to have an accomplishment, be fulfilled, as prophecy (Luke 22:37). Of effects or results depending on the subj. as a cause or antecedent (Heb 10:35, "which has [or brings with it] great reward" [a.t.]; 1 John 4:18, "fear has torment" [a.t.]).

(B) Of any condition or affection of body or mind **(1)** Of the body, to have disease, infirmity (Mark 3:10; Acts 28:9; Heb 7:28; Rev 13:14, wounds); a demon, a devil, to be possessed (Matt 11:18; Mark 3:22, 30; 9:17; Luke 13:11; Acts 16:16; 19:13). **(2)** Of the mind, as to have love (John 5:42; 13:35); need (Luke 14:18; 23:17); rest or peace (John 16:33; Acts 9:31; Rev 4:8); hope (Acts 24:15); desire (Phil 1:23; Col 4:13); affliction (1 Cor 7:28); wrath (Rev 12:12); fear (1 Tim 5:20); joy (3 John 1:4); favor toward anyone, i.e., to thank (Luke 17:9; 1 Tim 1:12); to have need, be in want, followed by the gen. (Matt 6:8; Luke 5:31; 1 Cor 12:21; Heb 5:12); the mind of Christ (1 Cor 2:16); courage (Eph 3:12); faith as an attitude of the mind (Matt 17:20); the spirit of Christ (Rom 8:9); the Holy Spirit (1 Cor 6:19; Jude 1:19). Generally (Mark 2:25; Acts 2:45; 4:35). Followed by an inf. (Matt 3:14; 1 Thess 1:8); by *hína* (2443), so that (John 2:25; 16:30; 1 John 2:27). An affection or emotion in Gr. writings is often said to have or to possess a person. In NT, only in Mark 16:8, possessed of fear and ecstasy.

(C) Particularly of things which one has in, on, or about himself, including the idea of to bear, carry, e.g., in oneself, as in the womb, to be pregnant (Matt 1:18; Rev 12:2). Metaphorically (2 Cor 1:9; 4:7; Phil 1:7). Speaking of garments, arms, ornaments upon oneself, i.e., to bear, to wear (Matt 3:4; John 12:6; Rev 9:17). Followed by *epí* (1909), upon, expressed or implied (1 Cor 11:10; Rev 9:4; 13:17; 14:1, 14; 16:2; 19:16). In 1 Cor 11:4, "to have upon the head" (a.t.) means so as to hang down from it, like a veil. Metaphorically of persons giving an appearance (Col 2:23; 2 Tim 3:5; Rev 3:1). Of a tree having leaves (Mark 11:13).

(D) In the sense of to contain, i.e., to have within oneself (Heb 9:4; Rev 21:11). Metaphorically used neg., to have root in themselves (Matt 13:21; Mark 4:17).

(IV) Metaphorically and intensively, to have firmly in mind, to hold to, hold fast.

(A) Generally of things (John 14:21; 1 Cor 11:16; Phil 3:9; 1 Tim 3:9; 2 Tim 1:13; Heb 6:19; 1 Pet 2:12; 1 John 5:10; Rev 2:24, 25). To have God and Christ, to hold fast to Them, i.e., to acknowledge with love and devotion (1 John 2:23; 5:12; 2 John 1:9).

(B) By implication, to hold for or as, to regard, to count, with the acc. of person with a noun in apposition (Matt 14:5, "they counted him as a prophet"; 21:26, 46; Mark 11:32).

(V) Followed by the inf., strictly with an acc., *échō ti eipeín* (*ti* [5100], something; *eipeín*, aor. inf. of *épō* [2036], to speak), to utter definite words; or *échō ti poiḗsai* (*poiḗsai*, aor. inf. of *poiéō* [4160], to do), to have something to say or do, i.e., by implication, to be able to say or do something. I can, implying only an objective or external ability, and thus differing from *dúnamai* (1410), I can, I have the ability to. Usually with the aor. inf. (Luke 7:40, "I have something to say to you" [a.t.]; 12:4; Acts 23:17, 18; 25:26; 28:19). With the pres. inf. (2 John 1:12). More direct is the meaning to be able, capable, when the acc. is suppressed, e.g., followed by the aor. inf. (Matt 18:25, literally, "not having to pay" [a.t.], i.e., not being able to pay; Heb 6:13). With the pres. inf. (John 8:6, "so that they could accuse him" [a.t.]; 2 Pet 1:15; Sept.: Prov 3:27). Where the inf. is suppressed (Mark 14:8; Acts 3:6).

(VI) Intrans. or with *heautón* (1438), himself, implied, always with an adv. or adv. phrase, to be in certain or specific circumstances. Equivalent of the phrase *hetoímōs échō*, to be ready (Acts 21:13; 2 Cor 12:14 [cf. *hetoímōs* [2093], in readiness]). With *eschátōs* (2079), finally, and *échei*, to be at extremity (Mark 5:23). To have it badly (*kakṓs* [2560]), to be sick (Matt 4:24; Luke 7:2). The opposite, to have it well (*kalṓs* [2573]), means to be well, i.e., to recover from sickness (Mark 16:18); *hoútōs* (3779), thus, to be so (Acts 7:1; 12:15); with the adv. *pṓs* (4459), how (Acts 15:36); with *állōs* (247), differently, otherwise (1 Tim 5:25). In Acts 24:25, "as it now is" (a.t.), "as the matter now stands" (a.t.), i.e., adv., for the present. Followed by *en* (1722), in, with a dat. noun or adj., used as an adv. (John 5:5, to be sick; 2 Cor 10:6); of place, to be in a place (John 11:17).

(VII) The mid. *échomai*, to hold oneself upon or to, to adhere to. Followed by the gen. of person (Sept.: Deut 30:20). To be near to, adjacent, contiguous. In the NT, only part., masc. *echómenos*, fem. *echoménē*, neut. *echómenon*, meaning near, next, e.g., of place (Mark 1:38, adjacent to, next); of time, *tḗ echoménē*, followed by *hēméra* (2250), day, the next day (Acts 21:26); in an absolute sense (Luke 13:33; Acts 20:15); followed by *Sábbaton* (4521), Sabbath, the next Sabbath (Acts 13:44; Sept.: 1 Chr 10:8). Figuratively (Heb 6:9, "things pertaining to salvation" [a.t.], conjoined with it).

Deriv.: *anéchō* (430), to tolerate, put up with, bear with, endure; *antéchō* (472), to hold firmly, cleave to, support; *apéchō* (568), to have in full; *enéchō* (1758), to hold fast, entangle; *hexḗs* (1836), successfully; *héxis* (1838), habit, practice; *epéchō* (1907), to hold fast, heed; *eunoúchos* (2135), a eunuch; *kakouchéō* (2558), to mistreat; *katéchō* (2722), to hold firmly, hold down, hold fast; *metéchō* (3348), to be partaker of, share, participate; *paréchō* (3930), to give from one to another; *periéchō* (4023), to include, contain; *pleonektéō* (4122), to take advantage, defraud; *pleonexía* (4124), covetousness, greediness; *proéchō* (4284), to excel, be better; *proséchō* (4337), to take heed; *rhabdoúchos* (4465), a rod-holder, officer; *sunéchō* (4912), to hold together, compress, arrest, afflict, be in a strait; *schedón* (4975), nigh, almost; *schḗma* (4976), shape, fashion, figure; *huperéchō* (5242), to be superior; *hupéchō* (5254), to suffer, endure.

Syn.: *ktáomai* (2932), to acquire; *diatēréō* (1301), to keep; *apolambánō* (618), to receive, take.

Ant.: *apóllumi* (622), to lose completely; *husteréō* (5302), to come or be behind, not to have; *leípō* (3007), to lack.

2193. ἑως *héōs*; adv. of time and place. In the NT, used as:

(I) An adv.:

(A) Until, used as a prep. meaning unto, as long as, marking the continuance of an action up to the time of another action and followed by the indic., subjunctive, or opt. according to whether the latter action is certain or uncertain.

(1) Followed by the indic. of a past action (Matt 2:9; 24:39); of a fut. action where the earlier Gr. preferred the subjunctive but later writers use the fut. So also with *érchomai* (2064, II, A), to come, in a fut. sense (Luke 19:13; John 21:22, 23; 1 Tim 4:13). **(2)** Followed by the aor. subjunctive with *án* (302), if, where the latter action is only probable (Matt 2:13; 5:18, 26; 10:11; 12:20; Mark 9:1; 12:36; Luke 9:27; 13:35; 21:32; 1 Cor 4:5; James 5:7; Sept.: Job 27:5). With *án* suppressed (Mark 6:45; 14:32; Luke 15:4; 17:8; 2 Thess 2:7; Heb 10:13; Rev 6:11; 20:5).

(B) By implication, meaning as long as, while, during the continuance of another action until it ends (John 9:4; 12:35, 36).

(II) As a prep. governing the gen. in later writers, until or unto, marking a terminus and spoken both of time and place:

(A) Of time: **(1)** Followed by the gen. of a noun of time (Matt 26:29, until that day; Mark 15:33; Luke 1:80; Acts 28:23; 1 Cor 16:8; Sept.: 2 Sam 6:23; Ezra 9:4); by the gen. of person or event (Matt 1:17; 28:20; Luke 11:51; 16:16). **(2)** Followed by the gen. of a pron. such as **(a)** *Héōs hoú* (*hoú* meaning of which, the gen. sing. of *hós* [3739], implying *chrónou* [5550], of time), until what time, until when, meaning simply "until," with the indic. or subjunctive. Followed by the indic. (Matt 1:25; 13:33; Acts 21:26); by the subjunctive aor. without *an*, if (Matt 14:22; 17:9; 18:30; 26:36; Luke 12:50, 59; 24:49; John 13:38; Acts 23:12, 14, 21; Sept.: Eccl 2:3). **(b)** Followed by *hótou* (3755), *héōs hótou*, the *hótou* referring to *chrónou*, time, meaning until when, until (Matt 5:25; John 9:18); by the subjunctive, without *án* (Luke 13:8; 15:8; 22:16, 18). **(3)** Followed by an adv. of time, with

or without the gen. art. *toú*, as *héōs toú nún* (*nún* [3568], now), until now (Matt 24:21; Mark 13:19; Sept.: Gen 46:34); *héōs tḗs sḗ*, until today (Matt 27:8; Rom 11:8); *héōs sḗmeron* without the def. art. (2 Cor 3:15); *héōs árti* (*árti* [737], now), until now (Matt 11:12; John 2:10); *héōs póte* (*póte* [4219], when), until when or how long (Matt 17:17; Mark 9:19; John 10:24; Sept.: 2 Sam 2:26; Ps 13:2).

(B) As a prep. it is also spoken of place, as far as, unto. **(1)** In various constructions: **(a)** Followed by the gen. of place (Matt 11:23, "unto heaven"; 24:31; 26:58; Luke 2:15; 4:29; Acts 1:8; 11:22; 23:23; 26:11, to and even into foreign cities with the meaning of *eis* [1519], unto). So also with the gen. of person as marking a place (Luke 4:42). **(b)** Followed by an adv. of place, *héōs ánō* (*ánō* [507], up), "up to the brim" (John 2:7); with *kátō* (2736), down, *héōs kátō*, to the bottom (Matt 27:51); with *ésō* (2080), inside, *héōs ésō* (Mark 14:54), even into; with *hṓde* (5602), here, *héōs hṓde* (Luke 23:5), to this place. **(c)** Followed by a prep. associated with a noun in the acc. case such as *héōs eis* (*eis* [1519], into) *Bēthanían*, as far as into Bethany (Luke 24:50). Also with *éxō* (1854), outside, as far as going outside the city or beyond the border of the city, completely out of the city (Acts 21:5). **(2)** Figuratively, followed by the gen. of a term or limit marking extent (Matt 26:38, "until death" [a.t.]; Mark 6:23; Luke 22:51; Sept.: Jon 4:9). Also followed by the gen. of person (Matt 20:8, "until the first ones" [a.t.]). See John 8:9; Acts 8:10; Rom 3:12, "not so much as one" (a.t.).

Syn.: *méchri* (3360), up to a certain point; *áchri* (891), until.

Z

2194. Ζαβουλών Zaboulṓn; masc. proper noun transliterated from the Hebr. Zᵉbūlūn (2074, OT), dwelling. Zabulon (Zebulun), the name of the tenth son of Jacob, born of Leah (Gen 30:20). In the NT, it is the name of the tribe of Zebulun (Matt 4:13, 15; Rev 7:8).

2195. Ζακχαῖος Zakchaíos; gen. Zakchaíou, masc. proper noun. Zacchaeus, meaning pure. The story of his conversion is related only in Luke 19:2–10. He was a rich Jew, a resident of Jericho and chief officer of the tax or tribute collectors. The Jews regarded all publicans or tax gatherers as sinners. Apparently the amount of taxes gathered from the people in Jericho was high. Zacchaeus' desire to see Christ was so great that he took pains to climb up a tree by the roadside that he might have a good view of Him as the crowd passed. Jesus, knowing his character and motives, proposed to spend the day with him to which Zacchaeus gladly consented. That encounter led to his salvation. He gave the best evidence of his conversion by declaring his intention to give half his goods to the poor and to restore fourfold for every illegal exaction he had made.

2196. Ζαρά Zará; masc. proper noun transliterated from the Hebr. Zerach (2226, OT), rising of light, dawn. Zara, a son of Judah by Tamar (Matt 1:3; Sept.: Gen 38:30; 46:12); called Zerah in Num 26:20; Josh 7:1, 18; 22:20; 1 Chr 2:4, 6; 9:6; see Neh 11:24.

2197. Ζαχαρίας Zacharías; gen. Zacharíou, masc. proper noun. Zechariah, meaning Jehovah remembers.

(I) The father of John the Baptist, a priest of the class of Abijah (Abiá [7])

(Luke 1:5, 12, 13, 18, 21, 40, 59, 67; 3:2).

(II) A person killed in the temple (Matt 23:35; Luke 11:51), where the allusion is probably to Zechariah the son of Jehoida, probably also called Barachías (914), who was stoned by order of Joash (2 Chr 24:21). Others refer it to the prophet Zechariah, son of Berachiah (Zech 1:1), but history gives no account of his death. Others again make the reference to Zacharias, the son of Baruch, who was slain by the Zealots in the temple just before the destruction of Jerusalem. It is doubtful whether this last application can be justified.

2198. ζάω záō, contracted zṓ, fut. zḗsō or zḗsomai (Matt 4:4), aor. ézēsa, pres. inf. zḗn. To live, intrans. The Attics rarely used this verb except in the pres. and imperf., supplying the other tenses from bióō (980), to spend one's existence, simply to pass one's life, from which is derived our word "biography," the narrative of how one spent his life.

(I) To live, have life, spoken of physical life and existence as opposed to death or nonexistence, and implying always some duration.

(A) Generally of human life (Acts 17:28; 22:22; Rom 7:1–3; 1 Cor 15:45; Heb 9:17); "while still alive" (a.t. [Matt 27:63]); "the living [zṓntes] and the dead [nekroí {3498}]" (a.t. [Acts 10:42; Rom 14:9; 1 Pet 4:5]). The pres. inf. is used as a subst. with the art. tó zḗn, life (2 Cor 1:8; Phil 1:21, 22; Sept.: Gen 2:7, 9; 42:2; 43:7; Ex 19:13). Of persons raised from the dead (Matt 9:18; Mark 16:11; Luke 24:23; John 5:25; Acts 1:3; 9:41; Rev 20:4; Sept.: 2 Kgs 13:21); of those restored from sickness, not to die, by implication to be well (John 4:50, "your son lives" [a.t.], or is well; 4:51, 53; Sept.: 2 Kgs 8:8, 9).

(B) In the sense of to exist, in an absolute sense and without end, now and hereafter, to live forever, of human beings (Matt 22:32, "God is not a God of the dead, but of the living ones" [a.t.]; Mark 12:27; Luke 20:38; John 11:25; 1 Thess 5:10; 1 Pet 4:6); by implication (Heb 7:8); of Jesus (John 6:57; 14:19; Rom 6:10; 2 Cor 13:4; Heb 7:25; Rev 1:18; 2:8); of God (John 6:57, "the living Father," meaning the one who has life in Himself; Rom 14:11, "As I live"; Sept.: Num 14:21, 28). The part. *zṓn*, ever living, eternal, the God the living One, means the Eternal One (Matt 16:16; Rom 9:26; 1 Tim 6:17; Heb 3:12; 12:22; Rev 4:9, 10; 10:6). As opposed to idols which are dead, nonexistent (Acts 14:15; 2 Cor 6:16; 1 Thess 1:9; Sept.: Deut 5:26; 2 Kgs 19:16).

(C) Metaphorically, of things, only in the part. *zṓn*, living, lively, active, also enduring, opposed to what is dead, inactive, and also transient (1 Pet 1:3, "living, enduring hope" [a.t.]). In Rom 12:1, "living and constant sacrifice" (a.t.), as opposed to the intermittent sacrifices of slaughtered victims; Heb 4:12, "the word of God," the divine threatenings are living, sure, never in vain; 1 Pet 1:23, "the living, efficient, enduring word" (a.t.); 1 Pet 2:4, "a living stone", i.e., Christ as the cornerstone of the church, not inactive and dead, but living and efficient; in 1 Pet 2:5, of Christians. "Living water" means the water of running streams and fountains, as opposed to that of stagnant cisterns, pools or marshes (John 4:10, 11; 7:38; Rev 7:17; Sept.: Gen 26:19; Lev 14:5, 50; Zech 14:8). By implication as a part. *zṓn*, life giving (John 6:51, "the life-giving bread" [a.t.] which imparts eternal life [cf. the following clauses; Acts 7:38, "living words"{a.t.}; Heb 10:20, "living way"; see Sept.: Ps 119:25, 37, 40, 50; Ezek 13:22]).

(II) To live, i.e., to sustain life, to live on or by anything (Matt 4:4; 1 Cor 9:14).

(III) To live in any way, to pass one's life in any manner (Luke 2:36; 15:13; Acts 26:5; Rom 7:9; Gal 2:14; 2 Tim 3:12; Titus 2:12). To live unto God (*tṓ Theṓ* [2316]) (Luke 20:38; Rom 6:10, 11; Gal 2:19) means to be devoted to Him, to live conformably to the will, purpose, precepts, and example of God; *tṓ Kuríō* (2962), unto the Lord or Christ (Rom 14:8; 2 Cor 5:15); *tṓ Pneúmati* (4151), unto the Spirit (Gal 5:25); *heautṓ* (1438), oneself, with the neg., not unto oneself (Rom 14:7; 2 Cor 5:15); *tḗ dikaiosúnē* (1343), unto righteousness (1 Pet 2:24); "to sin" means under the power of sin (Rom 6:2); "by faith" (a.t.) means full of faith, unto the power of faith (Gal 2:20); "in the world" means in conformity to the world (Col 2:20); *en autoís* (*en* [1722], in; *autoís* [846], them), "in themselves" (a.t. [Col 3:7]), being conformable to them; to live according to the flesh or "after the flesh" (Rom 8:12, 13).

(IV) By implication, to live and prosper, be blessed (used generally in Rom 10:5; Gal 3:12 [cf. Lev 18:5]). In 1 Thess 3:8, "we live," feel satisfied (Sept.: Deut 8:1; 1 Sam 10:24; Ps 22:26). In the sense of to have eternal life, to be admitted to the bliss and privileges of the Redeemer's kingdom (Luke 10:28; John 6:51, 58; Rom 1:17; Gal 3:11; Heb 12:9; 1 John 4:9).

Deriv.: *anazáō* (326), to revive; *zōḗ* (2222), life; *suzáō* (4800), to live with.

Syn.: *hupárchō* (5225), to be in existence; *bióō* (980), to live; *diágō* (1236), to spend one's life; *eimí* (1510), to be.

Ant.: *thnḗskō* (2348), to die; *apothnḗskō* (599), to die off or out; *teleutáō* (5053), to end one's life; *koimáomai* (2837), metaphorically to die, literally to sleep; *apogínomai* (581), to be absent, not to be anymore; *apóllumi* (622), to perish, die.

2199. Ζεβεδαῖος *Zebedaíos*; gen. *Zebedaíou*, masc. proper noun. Zebedee, meaning Jehovah's gift. A fisherman in or near Bethsaida, the husband of *Salṓmē* (4539) (Matt 27:56) and father of the apostles James the Great and John (Matt 4:21; 10:2; 20:20; 26:37; Mark 3:17; 10:35; Luke 5:10; John 21:2). When his two sons left him to follow Jesus, he made no objections (Mark 1:19, 20). His wife was one of the women who were in constant attendance on our Savior, but he himself is not mentioned as being among the disciples, although, no doubt, he was friendly to Christ.

2200. ζεστός zestós; fem. *zesté*, neut. *zestón*, adj. from *zéō* (2204), to be hot. Hot, used figuratively, meaning fervent in Rev 3:15, 16.

Syn.: *ektenés* (1618), strained, stretched, fervent; *purrós* (4450), red hot; *thérmē* (2329), heat.

Ant.: *psuchrós* (5593) chilly, cold.

2201. ζεῦγος zeúgos; gen. *zeúgous*, neut. noun from *zeúgnumi* (n.f.), to join, yoke. A yoke, two or more animals yoked and working together (Luke 14:19; Sept.: 1 Kgs 19:19; Isa 5:10); hence generally a pair, couple, such as doves (Luke 2:24; Sept.: Lev 5:11). Also from *zeúgnumi* (n.f.): *zugós* (2218), a yoke.

Deriv.: *suzeúgnumi* (4801), to yoke together as animals.

Syn.: *dúo* (1417), two.

Ant.: *mónos* (3441), single, alone; *haploús* (573), single.

2202. ζευκτηρία zeuktēría; gen. *zeuk-tērías*, fem. noun from *zeuktér* (n.f.), one who joins, which is from *zeúgnumi* (n.f.), to join. A band, fastening (Acts 27:40).

Syn.: *speíra* (4686), anything which might be woven together, such as a twisted rope or a group of men as an infantry; *desmós* (1199), something which binds; *súndesmos* (4886), that which binds firmly together, a bond; *zugós* (2218), yoke.

2203. Ζεύς Zeús; gen. *Diós*, masc. proper noun. Zeus, also called Jupiter. The supreme god of Greek mythology (Acts 14:12, 13).

2204. ζέω zéō; fut. *zésō*. To seethe, bubble, boil, from the sound of boiling water. In the NT, only applied spiritually, meaning to be fervent (Acts 18:25; Rom 12:11).

Deriv.: *zestós* (2200), fervent, hot; *zélos* (2205), zeal.

Syn.: *kaíō* (2545), to burn.

2205. ζῆλος zélos; gen. *zélou*, masc. noun from *zéō* (2204), to be hot, fervent. Zeal, used in a good sense (John 2:17; Rom 10:2; 2 Cor 7:7, 11; 11:2; Col 4:13; Sept.: Ps 69:9; 119:139) and more often in an evil sense, meaning envy, jealousy, anger (Acts 5:17; 13:45; Rom 13:13; 1 Cor 3:3; Gal 5:20; Phil 3:6; Heb 10:27, "fiery wrath" [a.t.]; James 3:14, 16; Sept.: Zeph 1:18; 3:8). Unlike *phthónos* (5355), envy, when used in a good sense, *zélos* signifies the honorable emulation with the consequent imitation of that which presents itself to the mind's eye as excellent. According to Aristotle, *zélos* grieves, not because another has the good, but that he himself does not have it and seeks to supply the deficiency in himself. However, *zélos* may degenerate into a jealousy which makes war upon the good it sees in another, thus troubling that good and diminishing it. This is why we find *zélos* joined together with *éris* (2054), contention (Rom 13:13; 2 Cor 12:20; Gal 5:20).

Deriv.: *zēlóō* (2206), to be zealous or jealous.

Syn.: *spoudé* (4710), diligence, forwardness; *prothumía* (4288), alacrity, readiness of mind; *órexis* (3715), excitement of the mind, a longing after;.

Ant.: *pórōsis* (4457), hardness, callousness; *psúchos* (5592), cold.

2206. ζηλόω zēlóō; contracted *zēló*, fut. *zēlósō*, from *zélos* (2205), zeal. To be zealous, filled with zeal, zealously affected whether in a good or bad sense (Acts 17:5; Gal 4:17, 18, to make a show of zeal, to profess affection in order to gain someone as a follower; Rev 3:19 [TR]); to desire zealously (1 Cor 12:31; 14:1, 39; Sept.: Prov 3:31); to be jealous over someone in a good sense, to love (2 Cor 11:2; Sept.: 2 Sam 21:2; Prov 24:1); to envy, be moved with envy (Acts 7:9; 1 Cor 13:4; James 4:2).

Deriv.: *zēlōtēs* (2207), a zealous person; *parazēlóō* (3863), to provoke to jealousy.

Syn.: *epithuméō* (1937), to desire, lust after, covet; *orégomai* (3713), to desire, covet; *phthonéō* (5354), to envy; *himeíromai* (2442), to have a strong affection for, a yearning after; *zētéō* (2212), to seek; *spoudázō* (4704), to be diligent.

Ant.: *ameléō* (272), to be negligent, to neglect.

2207. ζηλωτής *zēlōtēs*; gen. *zēlōtoú*, masc. noun from *zēlóō* (2206), to be zealous. A zealot, one zealous for or eagerly desirous of something. Used generally in that meaning in 1 Cor 14:12; Titus 2:14. The earnest supporters of ancient Jewish law and institutions were described as zealots (Acts 21:20; 22:3; Gal 1:14 [cf. Num 25:13]). At the time of Christ, the name "Zealots" was applied to a party among the Jews, half religious and half political, founded by Judas the Galilean (Acts 5:37). These undertook to punish without trial those guilty of violating Jewish practices, under which pretext they themselves committed the greatest excesses of crime.

2208. Ζηλωτής *Zēlōtēs*; masc. proper noun. Zealot. A surname of Simon, one of the apostles, probably so-called from his having been one of the party of Zealots (Luke 6:15; Acts 1:13). He is also called the Canaanite (*Kananítēs* [2581]), which see for further information.

2209. ζημία *zēmía*; gen. *zēmías*, fem. noun. Damage, loss, detriment (Acts 27:10, 21; Phil 3:7, 8).

Deriv.: *zēmióō* (2210), to bring or suffer loss.

Syn.: *apobolḗ* (580), a casting away; *héttēma* (2275), a defect, loss; *apóleia* (684), ruin, loss.

Ant.: *kérdos* (2771), gain, profit; *ōphéleia* (5622), profit, gain, advantage; *óphelos* (3786), benefit, profit, advantage; *porismós* (4200), money-getting, acquisition, gain, procuring; *ploútos* (4149), richness, wealth.

2210. ζημιόω *zēmióō*; contracted *zēmiṓ*, fut. *zēmiṓsō*, from *zēmía* (2209), loss, damage. To bring loss upon anyone. In the NT, only in the pass. or mid., meaning to suffer loss, receive detriment (1 Cor 3:15; 2 Cor 7:9; Phil 3:8, "I have suffered the loss of all things"). In the aor. pass. *ezēmiṓthēn*, with a mid. meaning, to bring loss upon oneself, to lose one's soul (Matt 16:26; Mark 8:36), oneself (Luke 9:25).

Syn.: *apóllumi* (622), to lose.

Ant.: *kerdaínō* (2770), to gain; *diapragmateúomai* (1281), to gain by trading; *apolambánō* (618), to receive in full; *ōpheloúmai* (5623), to derive profit, benefit; *sumphérō* (4851), to profit.

2211. Ζηνᾶς *Zēnás*; gen. *Zēná*, masc. proper noun. Zenas. A Christian lawyer whom Paul wished Titus to bring along with him (Titus 3:13).

2212. ζητέω *zētéō*; contracted *zētṓ*, fut. *zētḗsō*. To seek, trans.

(I) Particularly, to seek after, look for, strive to find.

(A) Generally without any direct obj. as in Matt 7:7, 8, "seek, and ye shall find." Followed by the acc. of person (Matt 2:13; Mark 3:32; Luke 2:45; John 7:11; Acts 9:11; 2 Tim 1:17; Sept.: Gen 37:15). To seek God means to turn to Him, to strive humbly and sincerely to follow and obey Him (Acts 17:27; Rom 10:20 [cf. Isa 65:1]; Sept.: Ex 33:7; Ps 24:6). See the comp. *ekzētéō* (1567), to search or seek out. Followed by the acc. of thing, something lost (Matt 18:12; Luke 19:10); with the acc. implied (Luke 15:8; Sept.: 1 Sam 10:2, 14); generally (Matt 12:43; 26:59; Mark 14:55; Luke 13:6, 7; 22:6; Rev 9:6); of what one seeks to buy, e.g., pearls (Matt 13:45). To seek the life of someone means seeking to kill him (Matt 2:20; Rom 11:3 [cf. 1 Kgs 19:10, 14]; Sept.: Ex 4:19; 2 Sam 16:11; Jer 44:30).

To seek how means to seek opportunity (Mark 11:18; 14:1, 11).

(B) To seek, in the sense of to endeavor, to try, e.g., followed by the acc. of thing, to try to gain, to strive after, with the idea of earnestness and anxiety (Matt 6:33; Luke 12:29; John 5:44; 7:18; 8:50; 1 Cor 10:24, 33; Phil 2:21; Col 3:1; Sept.: Ps 4:2; 34:14). Generally, to endeavor, strive, followed by *hína* (2443), so that (1 Cor 14:12); by the aor. inf. (Matt 21:46; Luke 5:18; 17:33; John 10:39; 19:12; Acts 13:8; 16:10; Rom 10:3); with the pres. inf. (Luke 6:19; Gal 1:10); with the inf. implied (John 5:30; Sept.: Deut 13:10; 1 Sam 19:10).

(C) By implication, to desire or wish, followed by the aor. inf. (Matt 12:46, 47 [cf. Luke 6:19; 9:9; 11:54; John 7:4; Acts 27:30]); by the acc. (John 1:38; 4:27; 1 Cor 7:27; 2 Cor 12:14; Sept.: Gen 37:15).

(II) To seek, require, demand, expect, with the acc. of thing (1 Cor 1:22; 2 Cor 13:3; Heb 8:7). Followed by *pará* and the gen., meaning from someone (Mark 8:11; Luke 11:16; 12:48). In 1 Cor 4:2, "it is required in the steward that one be found faithful" (a.t.). See John 4:23; Sept.: Neh 5:12, 18.

(III) By implication, to inquire, ask, with *perí* (4012), concerning (John 16:19).

Deriv.: *anazētéō* (327), to seek carefully; *epizētéō* (1934), to seek after; *ekzētéō* (1567), to seek out; *zḗtēma* (2213), debate, question; *zḗtēsis* (2214), a dispute; *suzētéō* (4802), to examine together.

Syn.: *punthánomai* (4441) and *eperōtáō* (1905), to inquire; *akribóō* (198), to learn by diligent inquiry; *axióō* (515), to demand, desire; *epithuméō* (1937), to desire earnestly; *erōtáō* (2065), to desire, ask; *himeíromai* or *homeíromai* (2442), to have a strong yearning after; *orégomai* (3713), to seek, desire, have an appetite for; *thélō* (2309), to wish, desire; *boúlomai* (1014), to strongly desire; *zēlóō* (2206), to have a zeal for; *aitéō* (154), to ask, an inferior of a superior; *epipothéō* (1971), to long for; *parakaléō* (3870), to

request; *spoudázō* (4704), to be diligent, to endeavor; *exetázō* (1833), to examine thoroughly, seek out; *diaginṓskō* (1231), to ascertain exactly; *apaitéō* (523), to demand back; *erōtáō* (2067), to ask; *diṓkō* (1377), to pursue; *exaitéomai* (1809), to seek after; *dierōtáō* (1331), to find by inquiry; *ereunáō* (2045), to search; *exereunáō* (1830), to search diligently; *agreúō* (64), to hunt; *thēreúō* (2340), to carp at, to find fault.

Ant.: *ameléō* (272), to neglect.

2213. **ζήτημα** *zḗtēma*; gen. *zētḗmatos*, neut. noun from *zētéō* (2212), to seek. Something sought, inquired about, or questioned; the topic of inquiry or dispute (Acts 15:2; 18:15; 23:29; 25:19; 26:3). To be distinguished from *zḗtēsis* (2214), which is the act of seeking.

Syn.: *lógos* (3056), a word, question; *eperṓtēma* (1906), inquiry.

2214. **ζήτησις** *zḗtēsis*; gen. *zētḗseōs*, fem. noun from *zētéō* (2212), to seek. A word used by the Greeks to indicate philosophical inquiry. In the NT, it indicates an exchange of words rather than a true search. Such was the strife between the disciples of John and the Jews (John 3:25); debates and arguments (2 Tim 2:23); general disputing (*logomachía* [3055]; 1 Tim 6:4f.; Titus 3:9). An evil connotation is attributed to these, indicative of the lack of faith. Used in the legal sense as "inquiry" in Acts 25:20. It is never found in the Sept.

Syn.: *dialogismós* (1261), reasoning, opinion, disputation; *antilogía* (485), contradiction, gainsaying; *lógos* (3056), question; *zḗtēma* (2213), the subject of an inquiry, whereas *zḗtēsis* is the act of inquiry; *eperṓtēma* (1906), an inquiry.

Ant.: *apodochḗ* (594), reception with approbation, acceptation.

2215. **ζιζάνιον** *zizánion*; gen. *zizaníou*, pl. *zizánia*, neut. noun. Darnel, tares. A plant, in appearance not unlike corn or wheat, having at first the same sort of stalk and the same greenness, but not bringing forth any worthwhile fruit (Matt 13:25–27, 29, 30, 36, 38, 40).

2216. Ζοροβάβελ *Zorobábel*; masc. proper noun, transliterated from the Hebr. *Zerubābal* (2216, OT). Zorobabel or Zerubbabel, meaning begotten in Babylon. The name of the leader of the first body of Jewish exiles returning to Jerusalem from Babylon (Matt 1:12, 13; Luke 3:27 [cf. 1 Chr 3:19; Ezra 2:2; 3:2, 8]).

2217. ζόφος *zóphos*; gen. *zóphou*, masc. noun. Darkness, foggy weather, smoke (Heb 12:18 [TR], *skótos* [4655], darkness). Elsewhere spoken of the darkness of Tartarus or Gehenna (2 Pet 2:4; Jude 1:6); of the darkness or thick darkness associated with the region of those who are lost (2 Pet 2:4, 17; Jude 1:6, 13).

Syn.: *gnóphos* (1105), blackness, gloom, associated with a tempest; *achlús* (887), a mist, especially as a dimness of the eyes; *homíchlē*, occurs only in certain MSS in 2 Pet 2:17 where the TR has *nephélai* (3507), cloud.

Ant.: *phõs* (5457), light; *phéggos* (5338), brightness, light, such as the light of the moon which reflects the light of the sun and not possessing its own source of light; *órthros* (3722), dawn; *apaúgasma* (541), effulgence, brightness.

2218. ζυγός *zugós*; gen. *zugoú*, masc. noun from *zeúgnuni* (n.f.), to yoke, bind. A yoke serving to couple any two things together, e.g., cattle (Sept.: 1 Sam 6:7). Also from *zeúgnumi* (n.f.): *zeúgos* (2201), a yoke. In the NT:

(I) A coupling, a beam of a balance which unites two scales, hence a balance, pair of scales (Rev 6:5; Sept.: Lev 19:36; Hos 12:7).

(II) Figuratively, a yoke.

(A) As an emblem of servitude (1 Tim 6:1; Sept.: Lev 26:13).

(B) As denoting severe precepts, moral bondage, e.g., the Mosaic Law (Acts 15:10; Gal 5:1); hence, by antithesis, the precepts of Christ (Matt 11:29, 30; Sept.: Jer 5:5).

Deriv.: *hupozúgion* (5268), a beast of burden.

Syn.: *ponēría* (4189), evil, wickedness, malevolence; *kakía* (2549), malice, naughtiness.

Ant.: *chrēstótēs* (5544), goodness, uprightness; *agathōsúnē* (19), benevolence; *dikaiosúnē* (1343), righteousness; *eupoiΐa* (2140), beneficence.

2219. ζύμη *zúmē*; gen. *zúmēs*, fem. noun. Leaven, fermenting matter, probably from *zéō* (2204), to heat, so-called from heating or fermentation of the mass of dough (*phúrama* [5445]) with which it is mixed (Matt 13:33; 1 Cor 5:6–8). Most often (though not always) in Scripture, the word *zúmē* represents evil, including Matt 13:33; Luke 13:21, if properly understood. The real significance of leaven is shown in 1 Cor 5:7 as being destructive and typifying what does not belong originally and essentially to life, namely, sin. It is sin disturbing and penetrating daily life. It first appears in the institution of the Passover (Sept.: Ex 12:15, 19, 20, 34, 39; 13:3, 7) and in the ritual of sacrifices (Sept.: Ex 23:18; 34:25; Lev 2:11; 6:17; 7:3; Deut 16:3, 4). All that disgraces the Christian and detracts from his holy newness of life is an example of the leaven of sin (1 Cor 5:6; Gal 5:9). It represents false doctrine as opposed to that which has been received (Gal 5:9). In Luke 12:1, hypocrisy is identified with leaven.

Deriv.: *ázumos* (106), unleavened; *zumóō* (2220), to leaven, mix with leaven.

2220. ζυμόω *zumóō*; contracted *zumõ*, fut. *zumōsō*, from *zúmē* (2219), leaven. To leaven, mix with leaven. In the act. voice, to permeate with leaven, cause to ferment, metaphorically to corrupt (1 Cor 5:6; Gal 5:9; Sept.: Ex 12:34, 39; Hos 7:4). In the pass. voice, used intrans., to be leavened or mixed with leaven and thus to ferment (Matt 13:33; Luke 13:21).

Syn.: *diaphtheírō* (1311), to corrupt utterly or through and through;

kataphtheírō (2704), to corrupt in mind; *sḗpō* (4595), to putrefy.

Ant.: *kathaírō* (2508), to purge, cleanse; *ekkathaírō* (1571), to cleanse thoroughly; *diakathaírō* (1245) and *diakatharízō*, to cleanse thoroughly; *katharízō* (2511), to cleanse, make clean; *hagnízō* (48), to purify from defilement ceremonially and morally.

2221. ζωγρέω *zōgréō*; contracted *zōgrṓ*, fut. *zogrḗsō*, from *zōós* (n.f., see below), alive, and *agreúō* (64), to catch or entrap. To take alive, to catch, as hunters or fishermen do their game, hence applied spiritually to taking or catching men by the preaching of the gospel (Luke 5:10). To take captive, used only spiritually for the captives of the devil in a moral sense, to ensnare, seduce (2 Tim 2:26).

Deriv. of *zōós* (n.f.), alive: *zōon* (2226), an animal, living creature; *zōopoiéō* (2227), to make alive.

Syn.: *aichmalōteúō* (162), to make a prisoner of war; *aichmalōtízō* (163), to lead away captive; *harpázō* (726), to snatch or catch away; *thēreúō* (2340), to hunt or catch wild beasts; *piázō* (4084), to capture; *sullambánō* (4815), to seize; *epilambánomai* (1949), to lay hold upon.

Ant.: *apóllumi* (622), to lose.

2222. ζωή *zōḗ*; gen. *zōḗs*, fem. noun from *záō* (2198), to live. Life.

(I) Generally, physical life and existence as opposed to death and nonexistence.

(A) Particularly and generally of human life (Luke 16:25; Acts 17:25; 1 Cor 3:22; 15:19; Heb 7:3; James 4:14; Rev 11:11). In Rev 16:3 (TR), *psuchḗ zōsa* (*psuchḗ* [5590], soul, life; *zōsa* [2198], living), living soul; in other MSS *psuchḗ zōḗs*, soul of life, means every living soul (Sept.: Gen 2:7; 25:7). Of life or existence after rising from the dead, only of Christ (Rom 5:10; 2 Cor 4:10–12). Metaphorically of the Jewish people (Rom 11:15).

(B) In the sense of existence, life, in an absolute sense and without end (Heb 7:16).

(C) The expression *xúlon zōḗs* (*xúlon* [3586], wood, tree) wood of life, is usually translated "tree of life" (Rev 2:7; 22:2, 14). This is a Hebraism. The Hebr. word *ets* (6086, OT) means both tree and wood. Although the word for "tree" is *déndron* (1186), *xúlon* may be taken as a metonym of "tree." Thus in each case that *xúlon* refers to the cross, the translators have rendered it "tree" instead of "wood" (Acts 5:30; 10:39; 13:29; Gal 3:13; 1 Pet 2:24). It was not on a tree (*déndron*) that Christ was crucified, but on pieces of wood (*xúlon*) in the form of a cross. There is a difference between the wood of a tree which is wet and living and wood that is cut off from the tree and is dry. The expression *xúlon zōḗs* occurring in Rev 2:7; 22:2, 14 is used of a living tree in Paradise and represents the rewards of the believer. It is called *xúlon*, wood, in symbolic connection with the cross of Christ, for Christ, through His death, brings yielding and fruitful life to the believer. A believer fitly identifies himself with Christ's death on the cross (Gal 2:20). Such a life of crucifixion with Jesus Christ is going to be rewarded by being given an opportunity to eat from the tree of life. The teaching is that believers are going to enjoy the fruits of the tree of life in Paradise (Rev 2:7). See Sept.: Gen 2:9; 3:21. Also water of life (*húdōr* [5204], water; *zōḗ*) in Rev 21:6; 22:1, 17. In Rev 7:17, which literally is "upon fountains of water of life" (a.t. [TR], "upon living fountains of waters"], the meaning is ever-flowing or fresh fountains of water. Metonymically, of God and Christ or the *Lógos* (3056), Word, *zōḗ* is used in an absolute sense for the source of all life (John 1:4; 5:26; 1 John 1:1, 2).

(II) Of life, i.e., manner of life, conduct, in a moral respect (Rom 6:4; Eph 4:18, "the life of God" meaning that which God requires, a godly life; 2 Pet 1:3).

(III) Life, i.e., blessed life, life that satisfies, being indwelt by God but not necessarily favored by circumstances.

(A) Generally (Luke 12:15; John 6:51; 2 Cor 2:16, "savor of life," i.e., fragrance); "the ways of life" (Acts 2:28 [cf. Ps 16:11]); to love or appreciate the life that God gives (1 Pet 3:10 from Ps 34:12).

(B) In the Christian sense of eternal life, i.e., that life of bliss and glory in the kingdom of God which awaits the true disciples of Christ after the resurrection (Matt 19:16, 17; John 3:15, 16; 5:24), or the life that is to come (*hē méllousa* [3195] in 1 Tim 4:8). In 1 Tim 6:19, *hē óntōs zōḗ* (UBS) (*hē* [3588], the; *óntōs* [3689], indeed, of a truth), the real life, while in TR *zōḗ aiōnios* (*aiōnios* [166], eternal), eternal life. In an absolute sense, *hē zōḗ*, the life (Matt 7:14; 18:8, 9; Acts 5:20), meaning the doctrine of eternal life. In Rom 5:17, "they shall reign in life" (a.t. [cf. Rom 5:18; 7:10; 8:2, 6, 10; Phil 2:16; 2 Tim 1:1; 1 John 3:14; 5:12, 13, 16. For the Book of Life, see *bíblos* (976), book. The crown of life refers to the Christian's final reward in heaven (James 1:12; Rev 2:10). The grace of life means the gift of eternal life (1 Pet 3:7). Metonymically, for the author and giver of eternal life (John 11:25; 14:6; Col 3:4; 1 John 1:2; 5:20). For the cause, source, or means of eternal life (John 5:39; 12:50; 17:3).

Syn.: *bíos* (979), the period or duration of life; *psuché* (5590), literally soul, the breath of life, natural life, the seat of personality; *bíōsis* (981), manner of life; *agōgḗ* (72), conduct of life as also *anastrophḗ* (391), behavior.

Ant.: *thánatos* (2288), death.

2223. ζώνη zōnē; gen. *zónēs*, fem. noun from *zónnumi* (2224), to wrap around. A belt, girdle (Matt 3:4; 10:9; Mark 1:6; 6:8; Acts 21:11; Rev 1:13; 15:6; Sept.: 1 Kgs 2:5; 2 Kgs 1:8). Jews of both sexes wore girdles or wide sashes because of their long flowing garments. These belts often had pockets and served as purses for money (Matt 10:9; Mark 6:8).

Syn.: *glōssókomon* (1101), a purse to keep money in, bag; *balántion* (905), money purse.

2224. ζώννυμι zónnumi, ζωννύω zōnnúō; fut. *zósō*. To gird, put on a belt (John 21:18; Sept.: Ex 29:9; 2 Kgs 4:29; Job 38:3; 40:2).

Deriv.: *anazónnumi* (328), to gird up; *diazónnumi* (1241), to gird tightly; *zónē* (2230), belt; *perizónnumi* (4024), to gird around or about; *hupozónnumi* (5269), to undergird.

2225. ζωογονέω zōogonéō; contracted *zōogonó*; fut. *zōogonḗsō*, from *zōogónos* (n.f.), life-giving. To give birth to living creatures, to vivify, make alive. In the NT, in Luke 17:33, to retain, preserve life; Acts 7:19; 1 Tim 6:13 UBS.

Syn.: *zōopoiéō* (2227), to cause to live; *suzōopoiéō* (4806), to quicken together or make alive with; *anazáō* (326), to recover life; *anazōpuréō* (329), to revive.

Ant.: *thanatóō* (2289), to put to death; *apokteínō* (615), to kill; *thúō* (2380), to kill for sacrifice; *phoneúō* (5407), to murder.

2226. ζῷον zōon; gen. *zóou*, neut. noun from *zōós* (n.f., see *zōgréō* [2221]), life. A living creature, an animal (Heb 13:11; 2 Pet 2:12; Jude 1:10; Rev 4:6–9; 5:6, 8, 11, 14; 6:1, 3, 5–7; 7:11; 14:3; 15:7; 19:4 [cf. Ezek 1:5; Dan 7:3]; Sept.: Ezek chap. 1).

There is a distinction between this and *thēríon* (2342). Although in Class. Gr., *zōon* is designated as a thinking animal to indicate that man also is such, this is not done in the NT. The fact that man lives does not make him a *zōon*, an animal. He is a living creature but not an animal in the sense of non-thinking animals. Similarly, in spite of the fact that God is living, He is never called a *zōon*. He is called life itself, as is Jesus Christ (John 1:4; 14:6; 1 John 1:2—*zōḗ* [2222], the source of life). *Thēríon* is predominately used of lower animal life and, in the Book of Revelation, is used of wicked beasts (11:7; 13:1).

Syn.: *thēríon* (2342), a wild beast; *kténos* (2934), a pack animal or beast of any kind except *thēríon* (1 Cor 15:39; Rev 18:13), and animals for slaughter; *tetrápous* (5074), a four-footed beast (Acts 10:12; 11:6; Rom 1:23).

Ant.: *ptōma* (4430), a corpse, carcass; *sphágion* (4968), a slain beast, a victim slaughtered for sacrifice; it sometimes refers to the sacrificial animal before it is slaughtered, and in this way it would be a syn. of *zōon*.

2227. ζωοποιέω *zōopoiéō*; contracted *zōopoió*, fut. *zōopoiēsō*, from *zōós* (n.f., see *zōgréō* [2221]), alive, and *poiéō* (4160), to make. To make alive, vivify (John 6:63; 1 Cor 15:45; 2 Cor 3:6). Used primarily in the NT of raising the dead to life (John 5:21; Rom 4:17; 8:11; 1 Cor 15:22, 36, to germinate; 1 Pet 3:18). Generally used in reference to salvation, answering to the Pauline connection between righteousness and life (Gal 3:21, to give eternal life, make alive).

Deriv.: *suzōopoiéō* (4806), to quicken together or make alive with.

Syn.: *zōogonéō* (2225), to give life, produce or preserve alive; *anazáō* (326), to live again; *anazōpuréō* (329), to revive.

Ant.: *thanatóō* (2289), to put to death; *apokteínō* (615), to kill; *thúō* (2380), to kill for sacrifice; *phoneúō* (5407), to murder; *anairéō* (337), to put to death.

H

2228. ἤ *é*; particle, disjunctive, interrogative, or comparative.

(I) Disjunctive: or, as used generally (Matt 5:17, 36; Mark 4:30; Luke 9:25; John 6:19; Acts 3:12; Heb 2:6); when repeated (*é . . . é*) it means either . . . or (Matt 6:24; Luke 16:13; 1 Cor 14:6; 2 Cor 1:13).

(II) Interrogative, with the primary force of "or" being strictly retained: or whether?, or if perhaps?:

(A) Indirect, in the latter clause of a double interrogation after *póteron* (4220), whether / or (John 7:17); also in cases where *póteron*, whether, or something equivalent is implied (Matt 9:5; 22:17; Luke 7:19, 20; Acts 8:34; Rom 2:4).

(B) Generally, and in a direct question where the interrogation implies a negation of something preceding (Matt 7:9; 20:15; Rom 3:29; 1 Cor 1:13; 9:6, 8, 10; 2 Cor 1:17).

(III) As a comparative, meaning than:

(A) After comparatives and words implying comparison (Matt 10:15; Mark 10:25; Luke 16:17; John 4:1; Rom 13:11); *mállon é* (*mállon* [3123], rather; *é*, than), rather than (Matt 18:13; John 3:19; Acts 4:19); *prín é* (*prín* [4250], before), sooner than, before (Matt 1:18; Mark 14:30; Luke 2:26; Acts 2:20). After *thélō* (2309), I wish (1 Cor 14:19), *thélō é*, I wish . . . rather.

(B) After *héteros* (2087), other of a different kind (Acts 17:21). So also with *állos* (243), other, or *héteros* implied (John 13:10; Acts 24:21).

(C) After the positive, where it may be rendered rather than, more than, equivalent to *mállon é*, so that the positive with *é* is equivalent to the comparative (Matt 18:8, 9; Mark 9:43, 45, 47; Luke 17:2; 18:14; Sept.: Gen 38:26; 49:12; Ps 118:8; Jon 4:3).

(IV) With other particles:

(A) *all' é* (235), unless, except (see *allá* [235, IV]).

(B) *é kaí* (*kaí* [2532], and), meaning or also, or even (Luke 18:11; 1 Cor 16:6; 2 Cor 1:13). Interrogatively (Luke 11:12; 12:41; Rom 4:9; 14:10).

2229. ἦ *é*; with circumflex (ˆ) instead of acute (´) accent as in *é* (2228), or. A particle of affirmation meaning truly, assuredly, certainly. In the NT, only in the connection *é mén* (3303), another particle of affirmation, the usual intens. form of oaths meaning most certainly, most surely (Heb 6:14 quoted from Gen 22:17; Sept.: Gen 42:16; Num 14:23; Judg 15:7).

2230. ἡγεμονεύω *hēgemoneúō*; fut. *hēgemoneúsō*, from *hēgemón* (2232), governor, prince, ruler. To go before or first, be a leader, chief. In the NT, to be governor, especially of a Roman province (Luke 2:2), or procurator (Luke 3:1).

Syn.: *kurieúō* (2961), to have dominion over, lord it over; *árchō* (757), to rule over; *prōteúō* (4409), to have the preeminence; *proéchō* (4284), to excel, lead the way for others; *huperéchō* (5242), to hold oneself above, be superior; *basileúō* (936), to reign.

Ant.: *hupēretō* (5256), to be a subordinate, to serve; *douleúō* (1398), to serve as a slave; *diakonéō* (1247), to minister, serve voluntarily.

2231. ἡγεμονία *hēgemonía*; gen. *hēgemonías*, fem. noun from *hēgemón* (2232), governor, ruler. Government, reign (Luke 3:1).

Syn.: *exousía* (1849), authority; *archē* (746), rule; *krátos* (2904), dominion; *basileía* (932), rule, dominion.

2232. ἡγεμών *hēgemón*; gen. *hēgemónos*, masc. noun from *hēgéomai* (2233), to lead, rule. Leader, commander of an army; equivalent to *stratēgós* (4755), a general. In the NT:

(I) A leader, chief, head (Matt 2:6 quoted from Mic 5:2).

(II) Used generally as a term for a prefect, proconsul, legate or procurator (Matt 10:18; Mark 13:9; Luke 21:12; 1 Pet 2:14). The fem. noun *hēgemonía* (2231), the term of office or reign. In the Roman Empire, there were two types of provinces, senatorial and imperial. Senatorial provinces, which did not require military occupation to keep them under control, were controlled directly by the senate. This was accomplished through the appointment of proconsuls (*anthúpatoi* [446], deputies). The power of the proconsul, who served a one-year term, varied from province to province; very often his authority was absolute, though he could be held accountable to the senate after his term expired. Imperial provinces, which did require military intervention to maintain control, were under the direct control of the emperor. Syria, which included the subprovinces of Phoenicia and Judea, was an imperial province. The emperor appointed legates, military governors, to govern these provinces. The legates, usually chosen from among the senators, had greater powers than even the proconsuls. Cyrenius, in Lat. *Quirinus*, was a legate (Luke 2:2). Augustus was the first to use separate officials, procurators, to manage the public finances of the provinces. The procurators, usually free men of good standing, did not have judicial power to enforce the collection of revenues until A.D. 50. Augustus also used prefects, or military officers who were placed in charge of small provinces or of small portions of the larger provinces. One such portion was Judea. Claudius later appointed prefects under the title of procurators (who were often subordinate to legates or more extensive political regions). Hence, the title of procurator (in Gr. *epítropos* [2012], one in charge) was often used anachronistically for prefects (*éparchos*, not used in the NT [cf. *eparchía* {1885}, prefecture, province]).

Hegemṓn is used in the NT of prefects, procurators, of Judea: Pilate (Matt 27:2, 11, 14, 15, 21, 23, 27; 28:14; Luke 20:20); Felix (Acts 23:24, 26, 33, 34; 24:1, 10); Festus (Acts 26:30).

Deriv.: *hēgemoneúō* (2230), to act as ruler; *hēgemonía* (2231), government, reign.

Syn.: *ethnárchēs* (1481), an ethnarch, ruler of a nation; *oikonómos* (3623), steward; *architríklinos* (755), ruler of a feast; *archēgós* (747), leader; *árchōn* (758), ruler; *megistán* (3175), usually used in the pl. *megistánes*, great men, lords; *archḗ* (746), a ruling person or persons; *kosmokrátōr* (2888), world ruler; *pantokrátōr* (3841), Ruler of all, Almighty; *politárchēs* (4173), a ruler of a city.

2233. ἡγέομαι *hēgéomai*; contracted *hēgoúmai*, fut. *hēgésomai*, mid. deponent of *ágō* (71), to lead. To lead or go before, go first, lead the way. The perf. *hḗgēmai* (Acts 26:2; Phil 3:7 with pres. meaning). In the NT:

(I) To be a leader, chief, generally only in the part. *hēgoúmenos* with the art. *ho*, a leader, chief, equivalent to *hēgemṓn* (2232), leader, chief (Acts 14:12, "chief speaker"). Spoken generally of those who have influence and authority (Luke 22:26; Acts 15:22); of officers and teachers in the churches (Heb 13:7, 17, 24); a chief magistrate such as Joseph in Egypt (Acts 7:10); the Messiah, a ruler, prince (Matt 2:6 quoted from Mic 5:2, where the Sept. has *árchōn* [758], ruler); *hēgoúmenos* (Sept.: Deut 1:13; 5:23; 2 Sam 3:38; 2 Chr 7:18; 9:26; Jer 51:28; Ezek 43:7, 9).

(II) Metaphorically, to lead out before the mind, i.e., to view, regard, esteem, count, reckon, spoken of things with the acc. (2 Pet 3:9); with the acc. and inf. (Phil 3:8); with the acc. and *eínai* (1511), to be, implied (2 Cor 9:5). To think to be such and such, to esteem as something (Phil 2:6, 25; 3:7; Heb 10:29; 11:26; James 1:2; 2 Pet 1:13; 2:13; 3:15; Sept.: Job 41:19); of persons, to hold or

esteem an individual in a particular light
(Acts 26:2; Phil 2:3; 1 Tim 1:12; 6:1; Heb
11:11). In 2 Thess 3:15, "not as an enemy." See Sept.: Job 19:11; 33:10. With
an acc. and adv. (1 Thess 5:13, "to regard
them as very highly deserving of love"
[a.t.]).

Deriv.: diēgéomai (1334), to declare,
show; exēgéomai (1834), to bring forth,
thoroughly explain; hēgemṓn (2232),
to lead, command; proēgéomai (4285),
to prefer or go before another; hodēgós
(3595), a guide.

Syn.: dokéō (1380), to be of an opinion,
think; logízomai (3049), to reckon; krínō
(2919), to judge, esteem; hēgemoneúō
(2230), to be a ruler; árchō (757), to rule;
oikodespotéō (3616), to be ruler of the
house; proḯstēmi (4291), to stand over or
before, to rule; poimaínō (4165), to shepherd; nomízō (3543), to suppose, think;
phronéō (5426), to think.

Ant.: akolouthéō (190), to follow.

2234. ἠδέως hēdéōs; adv. from hēdús
(n.f.), sweet. Sweetly. As used figuratively in the NT, with pleasure, gladly (Mark
6:20; 12:37; 2 Cor 11:19).

Ant.: pikrṓs (4090), bitterly.

2235. ἤδη édē; adv. of time. Now, even
now, already.

(I) In reference to time past and pres.,
marking an action as completed. Now,
already, by this time (Matt 3:10; 5:28;
14:15; 24:32; Mark 15:42, 44; Luke 7:6;
John 3:18; 4:35; 11:39). In 1 John 4:3,
"now even already"; Phil 4:10, "now at
length" (author's translations).

(II) By implication, of the immediate
future, now, presently, soon (Rom 1:10,
"if perhaps I may shortly [or at length]
be prospered to come" [a.t.]); already,
i.e., without mentioning or insisting upon
anything further (1 Cor 6:7).

Syn.: nún (3568), now; nuní (3570),
now in logical conclusion; árti (737), just
now, this moment in contrast to the past;
apárti (534) and loipón (3063), from
now, henceforth.

Ant.: oudépote (3763), never.

2236. ἥδιστα hḗdista; adv., the acc.
neut. pl. of hḗdistos which is the superlative of hēdús (n.f.), sweet. Most sweetly,
with great relish, when spoken of eating
and drinking. In the NT, used figuratively
in 2 Cor 12:9, 15, meaning most gladly.

Syn.: asménōs (780), with delight,
gladly; hēdéōs (2234), sweetly.

Ant.: pikrṓs (4090), bitterly.

2237. ἡδονή hēdonḗ; gen. hēdonḗs, fem.
noun from hḗdos (n.f.), delight, enjoyment, which is from hḗdomai (n.f.), to
have sensual pleasure. Pleasure, gratification, enjoyment. In the NT, used only
of physical pleasure (Luke 8:14; Titus
3:3; James 4:3; 2 Pet 2:13). Figuratively
used as desire, appetite, lust (James 4:1).

Deriv.: philḗdonos (5369), a lover of
pleasure.

Syn.: epithumía (1939), strong desire
of any kind; órexis (3715), desire; páthos
(3806), passion; euphrosúnē (2167),
joyfulness, gladness; aréskeia (699),
pleasing, pleasure; apólausis (619), enjoyment.

Ant.: pónos (4192), pain; odúnē
(3601), dejection; lúpē (3077), grief;
ōdín (5604), pain of childbirth; brugmós
(1030), gnashing; pikría (4088), bitterness; stenochōría (4730), straightness,
depression.

2238. ἡδύοσμον hēdúosmon; gen.
hēdúosmou, neut. of hēdúosmos, sweet-
scented, which is from hēdús (n.f.),
sweet, and osmḗ (3744), odor, smell.
Mint, an herb with a sweet smell (Matt
23:23; Luke 11:42). It was strewn by the
Jews on the floors of their houses and
synagogues.

2239. ἦθος éthos; gen. éthous, neut.
noun from éthos (1485), a habit, custom.
Accustomed seat, haunt, dwelling of animals and men. In the NT, manner, custom, morals, character (1 Cor 15:33).
From this word the Eng. ethics is derived.

Syn.: trópos (5158), manner, fashion; túpos (5179), a mark or impression,

manner; *agōgḗ* (72) and *anastrophḗ* (391), manner of life, especially in relation to one's conduct with others; *hagnótēs* (54), pureness; *aretḗ* (703), virtue.

Ant.: *pṓrōsis* (4457), callousness, hardness; *rhúpos* (4509), depravity, filth; *hamartía* (266), sin.

2240. ἥκω *hḗkō*; fut. *hḗxō*, aor. *hḗxa* (Rev 2:25; 3:9). To come or to have come, to be here. Generally of persons (Mark 8:3; Luke 15:27; John 4:47; Rev 3:9; 15:4); followed by *apó* (575), from, with the gen. of place, whence (Matt 8:11; Luke 13:29). In the sense of to come forth, arise (Rom 11:26; Sept.: Ex 20:24). Followed by *prós* (4314), to, and the acc., to come to one in a friendly sense (John 6:37; Acts 28:23) or to come upon one in a hostile sense (Rev 3:3; Sept.: 2 Sam 17:12). Used in an absolute sense (Matt 24:50; Luke 12:46; 15:27). To come, as from God (John 8:42; Heb 10:7, 9, 37; 1 John 5:20; Rev 3:3; see Sept.: 1 Kgs 8:42; Ps 40:7; Zech 8:20, 22). Figuratively, of things in relation to time (Luke 13:35; John 2:4; 2 Pet 3:10); of the end or consummation of anything (Matt 24:14); of evils, calamities (Rev 18:8). Followed by *epí* (1909), upon, and the acc., meaning to come upon anyone, as spoken of evil times (Luke 19:43); of guilt and its punishment, to be laid upon someone (Matt 23:36).

Deriv.: *anḗkō* (433), to come up; *kathḗkō* (2520), to be convenient, fit.

Syn.: *érchomai* (2064), to come or go, the emphasis on the act of coming rather than arriving and abiding; *epérchomai* (1904), to come or go upon; *aphiknéomai* (864), to arrive at a place; *enístēmi* (1764), to be present; *ephístēmi* (2186) and *phthánō* (5348), to come, arrive; *parístēmi* (3936), to be at hand, to come; *proseggízō* (4331), to approach near.

2241. ἠλί *ēlí*; transliterated from the Hebr. *'Ēl* (410, OT), God, and the 1st person pronominal suffix *ī*, my. Eli, meaning my God (Matt 27:46 from Ps 22:2).

2242. Ἠλί *Hēlí*. Heli or Eli, a name of the father of Joseph (Luke 3:23).

2243. Ἠλίας *Ēlías*; gen. *Ēlíou*, proper noun transliterated from the Hebr. *'Ēlīah* (452, OT). Elijah, meaning my God is Jehovah. The name of the prophet Elijah of the OT who was expected to be the forerunner of the Messiah (Matt 17:12; Mark 9:13; Luke 1:17; 4:25, 26). See 1 Kgs 17 with Mal 3:1; 4:5.

2244. ἡλικία *hēlikía*; gen. *hēlikías*, fem. noun from *hḗlix* (n.f.), adult, full-aged. Adulthood, maturity of life, mind or person. In the NT, age, full-age, vigor (Luke 2:52; John 9:21, 23; Heb 11:11); stature, size (Matt 6:27; Luke 12:25; 19:3). Metaphorically used in Eph 4:13; Sept.: Ezek 13:18. Also from *hḗlix* (n.f.): *hēlíkos* (2245), how great.

Ant.: *neótēs* (3503), youth.

2245. ἡλίκος *hēlíkos*; gen. *hēlíkē*, neut. *helíkon*, correlative pron. from *hḗlix* (n.f.), adult. How great (Col 2:1; James 3:5), used interrogatively with the emphasis of exclamation. Also from *hḗlix* (n.f.): *hēlikía* (2244), adulthood.

Syn.: *mégas* (3173), great; *polús* (4183), much, great; *hikanós* (2425), sufficient, great; *pēlíkos* (4080) as an interrogative, how large?; *pósos* (4214), how great?; *hósos* (3745), as much; *tosoútos* (5118) and *tēlikoútos* (5082), so great.

Ant.: *mikrós* (3398), little, small.

2246. ἥλιος *hḗlios*; gen. *helíou*, masc. noun from *hélē* (n.f.), shining, the splendor of the sun. The sun (Matt 13:43; Mark 1:32; Sept.: Gen 15:12, 17). Used figuratively for light, daylight (Acts 13:11 [cf. Ps 58:8]). Also from *heílē* (n.f.): *eilikrinḗs* (1506), sincere, pure.

2247. ἧλος *hḗlos*; gen. *hḗlou*, masc. noun. A nail (John 20:25; Sept.: 1 Chr 22:3).

2248. ἡμάς *hēmás*; personal pron., acc. pl. of *emé* (1691), me. Our, us, we. To be distinguished from *humás* (5209), your, you.

2249. ἡμεῖς *hēmeís*; personal pron., nom. pl. of *egṓ* (1473), I. We. To be distinguished from *humeís* (5210), you.

Deriv.: *hēméteros* (2251), our.

2250. ἡμέρα *hēméra*; gen. *hēméras*, fem. noun. Day, daytime, occasion, time.

(I) Day.

(A) Particularly the time from one sunrise or sunset to another, equal to *nuchthḗmeron* (3574), a day and a night, a full twenty-four hour day or only a part of it. **(1)** Generally (Matt 6:34; Mark 6:21; 8:2; Luke 1:23; 9:28; 24:21; John 11:9; Acts 2:15; 21:26; Rom 14:5, 6; 1 Cor 15:31; James 5:5, "as for the day of slaughter" [a.t.]; 2 Pet 2:13, daily riot; Rev 2:10, affliction for 10 days). With the gen., of a festival, the Sabbath day (Luke 4:16; John 19:31; Sept.: Jer 17:24, 27); day or days of unleavened bread, the Passover (Luke 22:7; Acts 12:3; 20:6); Day of Pentecost (Acts 2:1; 20:16). Often in specifications of time: in the gen., of time meaning when, i.e., indefinite and continued, e.g., "in a day," every day (Luke 17:4); in the dat., of time when, i.e., definite (Matt 16:21; Mark 9:31; Luke 9:22; 13:14; John 2:1; Acts 7:8; 2 Cor 4:16, "day by day," every day, daily; Sept.: Esth 3:4; Ps 68:19); in the acc., of time meaning how long, implying duration (Matt 20:2, for a dinar per day's work; 6, "idle all day long" [a.t.]; 28:20, "always"; Mark 1:13; John 1:39; Acts 5:42, every day, i.e., the whole time; 9:9; Gal 1:18; 2 Pet 2:8, literally day out of day or day after day; Rev 11:9). See *ek* (1537).

In these and similar specifications of time, *hēméra* is very often construed with a prep. In the gen., after *apó* (575), from; *áchri* (891), until; *diá* (1223), through; *héōs* (2193), until; *pró* (4253), before. In the dat., after *en* (1722), in. In the acc., after *eis* (1519), unto; *epí* (1909), upon; *katá* (2596), down; *metá* (3326), with; *prós* (4314), toward. For above constructions, see respective prep.

(2) Emphatically, a certain or set day (Acts 17:31; 1 Cor 4:3, human day of trial, meaning a court day; Heb 4:7).

(3) Specifically *hēméra toú kuríou* (*toú* [3588], the; *kuríou* [2962], Lord), Day of the Lord when Christ will return to judge the world and fully establish His kingdom (Luke 17:24, "the Son of man in his own day" [a.t.], 30, "in which the Son of man shall be revealed" [a.t.]; 1 Cor 1:8; 5:5; 2 Cor 1:14; 1 Thess 5:2, 4; 2 Pet 3:10). Used in an absolute sense (1 Cor 3:13); the great day of judgment (Matt 7:22; Mark 13:32; 2 Thess 1:10); with a gen., of what is then to take place, e.g., the day of judgment (Matt 10:15; 11:22, 24; 12:36 [cf. Rom 2:16; Jude 1:6]); *hēméra orgḗs* (3709), wrath, meaning the day of wrath (Rom 2:5; Rev 6:17); "the day of redemption" (Eph 4:30); "the last day" (John 6:39, 40); "the day of God" meaning the day by whose authority Christ sits as judge (2 Pet 3:12); "day of the Lord" meaning of Jehovah (Acts 2:20 quoted from Joel 2:31; in the Sept., the day of God's retribution, in general Isa 2:12; 13:6; Ezek 13:5; 30:3; Joel 1:15; 2:31; Zeph 1:7, 14); the day, the great one of God (Rev 16:14). See Heb 10:25 (cf. Heb 10:27, 31).

(B) Day, daylight, from sunrise to sunset, e.g., in antithesis with *núx* (3571), night. In the gen., by day and by night (Mark 5:5; Luke 18:7; Acts 9:24; 1 Thess 2:9); in the acc. meaning how long (Matt 4:2, "forty days and forty nights"). *Núkta kaí hēméran*, night and day, meaning continually (Mark 4:27; Luke 2:37; Acts 20:31; 26:7). Generally (Rev 8:12). Simply, for example, *tás hēméras*, in the acc., the days, i.e., during the daytime, every day (Luke 21:37); *hēméras mésēs* (3319), midst, between, "at midday" (Acts 26:13); *hēméras genoménēs* ([1096], to become), day being come, when it was day (Luke 4:42; Acts 12:18; 16:35; *hē hēméra klínei* (*klínei* [2827], to close), the day ends (Luke 24:29); "so long as it is day" (John 9:4); to "walk in the day," while it is day (John 11:9). Metaphorically for the light of true and higher knowledge, moral light (Rom 13:12; 1 Thess 5:5, 8; 2 Pet 1:19).

(II) Time in general, nearly equivalent to *chrónos* (5550), time.

(A) In the sing., of a point or period of time (Matt 13:1; John 14:20; Eph 6:13). Followed by the gen. of person (Luke 19:42, "in this thy time" [a.t.], meaning while you yet are living); by the poss. pron. and the art. (John 8:56, "so that he may see my day" [a.t.], meaning my time, the time of my manifestation). Followed by the gen. of thing (Luke 1:80); "day of salvation" (2 Cor 6:2); "day of temptation" (Heb 3:8); "day of visitation" (1 Pet 2:12). See *episkopḗ* (1984), visitation, equal to eternal time, forever.

(B) In the pl., *hēmérai*, days, i.e., time.

(1) Generally (Matt 9:15; Mark 2:20; 13:20; Luke 17:22). With adjuncts *aph' hēmerṓn archaíōn*, from ancient days (Acts 15:7); "in the last days" (Acts 2:17; James 5:3); "these days" (Acts 3:24; 11:27); "in those days" (Matt 3:1; Mark 13:24; Rev 9:6); "the former days" (Heb 10:32); "for a few days" (Heb 12:10). Followed by the gen. of person (Matt 11:12; Luke 4:25; Acts 7:45, "unto the days of David"). Followed by the gen. of an event (Matt 24:38; Luke 2:6, the days of her giving birth; Acts 5:37; Heb 5:7; Sept.: Gen 25:24; Ex 2:11; Judg 18:1; 2 Sam 21:1; 1 Kgs 10:21; Jer 1:2).

(2) Specifically the time of one's life, i.e., one's days, years, age, life, e.g., fully (Luke 1:75 [cf. Gen 47:8, 9]). Used in an absolute sense (Luke 1:7, 18, advanced in years or age; 2:36). Generally (Heb 7:3; Sept.: Gen 6:4; 24:1; Josh 13:1).

(III) A day in the Eastern way of thinking may be all or any part of a twenty-four-hour period (*nuchthēmerón* [3574], a unit consisting of a night and a day). Therefore, the three days and three nights of Matt 12:40 in which Jesus was in the grave should be considered as either the part or the whole of a twenty-four-hour period, i.e., Friday (being part of the first day / night), all of Saturday (being the second day / night), and part of Sunday (being the third day / night).

(IV) Figuratively, time for work or labor (John 9:4 [cf. Matt 20:6, 12]). The day of eternal life, as opposed to the spiritual darkness of our present state (Rom 13:12).

Deriv.: *ephḗmeros* (2184), for a day, daily; *kathēmerinós* (2522), daily; *mesēmbría* (3314), midday, noon; *nuchthḗmeron* (3574), a day and night; *oktaḗmeros* (3637), eighth day.

Syn.: *augḗ* (827), break of day, dawn; *órthros* (3722), sunrise; *chrónos* (5550), time; *kairós* (2540), season; *hṓra* (5610), hour; *diástēma* (1292), space.

Ant.: *núx* (3571), night; *stigmḗ* (4743), instant; *rhipḗ* (4493), twinkling; *aiṓn* (165), age, eternity.

2251. ἡμέτερος hēméteros; fem. *hēmetéra*, neut. *hēméteron*, 1st person sing. poss. pron. from *hēmeís* (2249), we; pl. masc. *hēméteroi*, fem. *hēméterai*, neut. *hēmétera*, our own. My own (Acts 2:11; 24:6; 26:5; Rom 15:4; 1 Cor 15:31; 2 Tim 4:15; Titus 3:14; 1 John 1:3; 2:2).

Ant.: *huméteros* (5212) and *sós* (4674), yours.

2252. ἤμην ḗmēn; lengthened form of *ḗn* (2258), was, the imperf. of *eimí* (1510), I am. I was.

2253. ἡμιθανής hēmithanḗs; gen. *hēmithanoús*, masc.-fem., neut. *hēmithanés*, adj. from *hēmi-* (n.f.), half, and *thnḗskō* (2348), to die. Half dead (Luke 10:30). Also from *hḗmi-* (n.f.): *hēmiṓrion* (2256), half hour.

2254. ἡμῖν hēmín; personal pron. dat. pl. of *egṓ* (1473), I. To us.

Ant.: *humín* (5213), to you.

2255. ἥμισυ hḗmisu; adj., neut. of the masc. *hḗmisus*, half. As a subst., *tó hḗmisu*, a half; in the gen., *hēmísous* (Mark 6:23); in the pl. with the def. art., *tá hēmíse* (Luke 19:8). See Rev 11:9, 11; 12:14; Sept.: Ex 24:6; Zech 14:2.

Ant.: *hólos* (3650), all; *pás* (3956), every, pl. all; *hápas* (537), whole, pl. all.

2256. ἡμιώριον hēmiṓrion; gen. *hēmiōríou*, neut. noun from *hḗmi-* (n.f.), half, and *hṓra* (5610), hour. A half hour (Rev 8:1). Also from *hḗmi-* (n.f.): *hēmithanḗs* (2253), half dead

2257. ἡμῶν hēmṓn; personal pron. gen. pl. of *egṓ* (1473), I. Us.
    Syn.: *hēmetérōn*, pl. gen. of *hēméteros* (2251), our.
    Ant.: *humṓn* (5216) and *humetérōn*, the gen. pl. of *huméteros* (5212), your.

2258. ἦν ḗn; imperf. 3d person sing. of *eimí* (1510), I am. Was, and in certain instances with the acc. pl., were.

2259. ἡνίκα hēníka; adv. of time. When, whenever (2 Cor 3:15, 16; Sept.: Gen 31:10).
    Syn.: *hóte* (3753), *hótan* (3752), *hopóte* (3698), and *hopótan*, when.

2260. ἤπερ ḗper; adv., from *ḗ* (2228), or, and *per* (4007), truly, an intens. Than indeed, more than (John 12:43). See *ḗ* (2228, IV, C).
    Syn.: *mén* (3375), assuredly.
    Ant.: *oudépote* (3763), never; *oudépō* (3764), never yet; *hoúpō* (3768), not yet; *mēdépote* (3368), not ever.

2261. ἤπιος ḗpios, gen. *ēpíou*, masc.-fem., neut. *ḗpion*, adj. Placid, gentle, mild, easy, compliant (1 Thess 2:7; 2 Tim 2:24).
    Syn.: *práos* (4235), meek; *praús* (4239), meek; *epieikḗs* (1933), gentle, tolerant; *hēsúchios* (2272), peaceable, quiet; *hḗremos* (2263), composed, peaceful.
    Ant.: *sklērós* (4642), hard; *austērós* (840), austere; *bíaios* (972), violent, quick; *anémeros* (434), fierce; *akatástatos* (182), unstable; *ágrios* (66), wild, raging.

2262. Ἤρ Ḗr; masc. proper noun transliterated from the Hebr. *'Ēr* (6147, OT). Er, meaning awake or watchful. A name

in the genealogical list of Christ (Luke 3:28).

2263. ἤρεμος éremos; gen. *ērémou*, masc.-fem., neut. *éremon*, adj. Placid, quiet, composed, tranquil (1 Tim 2:2).
    Syn.: *hēsúchios* (2272), quiet; *hḗpios* (2261), placid mild; *práos* (4235), meek; *epieikḗs* (1933), gentle, tolerant; *éremos* (2263), composed; *eirēnikós* (1516), peaceful.
    Ant.: *ágrios* (66), wild, raging.

2264. Ἡρώδης Hērṓdēs; gen. *Hērṓdou*, masc. proper noun. Herod. The name of four persons in the NT, all Idumeans by descent, who were successively vested by the Romans with authority over the Jewish nation in whole or in part. Their history is related chiefly by Josephus. They are as follows:
    (I) Herod, surnamed the Great (Matt 2:1, 3, 7, 12, 13, 15, 16, 19, 22; Luke 1:5), the son of Antipater, an Idumean in high favor with Julius Caesar. At the age of fifteen, Herod was made procurator of Galilee in which he was confirmed by Antony with the title of tetrarch, about 41 B.C. An opposite faction caused him to flee to Rome where, through the help of Antony, he was declared king of Judea. He collected an army, recovered Jerusalem, and extirpated the Maccabean family in 37 B.C. After the battle of Actium, he joined the party of Octavius, who confirmed him in his possessions. He then rebuilt and decorated the temple of Jerusalem, built and enlarged many cities, especially Caesarea, and erected theaters and gymnasiums in both of these places. He was notorious for his jealousy and cruelty, even putting to death his own wife, Mariamne, and her two sons, Alexander and Aristobulus. He died in A.D. 2 at seventy years of age after a reign of about forty years. It was near the close of his life that Jesus was born and the massacre of infants took place in Bethlehem (Matt 2:16). At Herod's death, half of his kingdom (Idumea, Judea, and Samaria) was given by Augustus to Herod's

son Archelaus with the title of ethnarch. See *Archélaos* (745). Augustus divided the remaining half between two of Herod's other sons, Herod Antipas and Philip, with the title of tetrarchs, the former having Galilee and Perea, and the latter Batanea, Trachonitis, and Auranitis (Luke 3:1).

(II) Herod Antipas, often called Herod the tetrarch (Matt 14:1, 3, 6; Mark 6:14, 16–18, 20–22; 8:15; Luke 3:1, 19; 8:3; 9:7, 9; 13:31; 23:7, 8, 11, 12, 15; Acts 4:27; 13:1), the son of Herod the Great by Malthace, and brother to Archelaus. After his father's death, Augustus gave him Galilee and Perea with the title of tetrarch (Luke 3:1) for which he is called by the general title of king (Matt 14:9; Mark 6:14). He first married a daughter of Aretas whom he dismissed on becoming enamored with Herodias. See *Arétas* (702). He induced Herodias, who was his own niece and the wife of his brother, Philip Herod, to leave her husband and live with him. It was for the bold remonstrance of this evil that John the Baptist was put to death through the contrivance of Herodias (Mark 6:17ff.). Herod went to Rome at the instigation of Herodias to ask for the title and rank of king. However, there he was accused before Caligula at the insistence of Herod Agrippa the elder, Herodias' own brother, and banished with her to Lugdumun (Lyons) in Gaul, France, about A.D. 41. His territories were given to Herod Agrippa. In Mark 8:15, the name Herod is used collectively for Herodians.

(III) Herod Agrippa the elder (Acts 12:1, 6, 11, 19–21; 23:35), mentioned by Josephus as Agrippa. He was the grandson of Herod the Great and Mariamne, the son of Aristobulus. On the accession of Caligula, he received, along with the title of king, the provinces which had belonged to his uncle Philip and Lysanias, to which were added those of Herod Antipas. In A.D. 43, Claudius gave him all those parts of Judea and Samaria which had belonged to Herod the Great. He died suddenly and miserably at Caesarea in A.D. 44 (Acts 12:21–23).

(IV) Herod Agrippa the younger, called by Josephus and in the NT as Agrippa (Acts 25:13, 22–24, 26; 26:1, 2, 7, 19, 27, 28, 32). He was the son of the elder Herod Agrippa and at his father's death received from Claudius the kingdom of Chalcis which had belonged to his uncle Herod, he being then seventeen years old. In A.D. 53, he was transferred with the title of king to the provinces which his father at first possessed (Batanea, Trachonitis, Auranitis, and Abilene), to which other cities were afterwards added. Paul was brought before him by Festus.

2265. Ἡρωδιανοί *Hērōdianoí*; gen. *Hērōdianṓn*, masc. pl. proper noun. Herodians. A Jewish political party originating probably in devotion to the Roman emperor and Herod his deputy (Matt 22:16; Mark 12:13). They were the court party and submitted willingly to the government of Rome, thus being at the opposite pole from the Pharisees. It may be that some of them were among those who regarded Herod as the Messiah. They combined with the Pharisees in the attempt to destroy Christ (Matt 22:16; Mark 3:6) and are probably referred to in the expression "leaven of Herod" (Mark 8:15).

2266. Ἡρωδιάς *Hērōdiás*; gen. *Hērōdiádos*, fem. proper noun. Herodias. The granddaughter of Herod the Great and mother of Salome (Matt 14:3; Mark 6:17, 19, 22; Luke 3:19). She first married her uncle Herod Philip; she afterward married Herod Antipas, another uncle, during her first husband's lifetime. For this unlawful and scandalous connection, John the Baptist faithfully reproved both parties, which cost him his life (Matt 14:3–10). When her husband Antipas was banished to Lyons, France, she shared his banishment with him.

2267. Ἡρωδίων Hērōdíōn; gen. *Hērōdíōnos*, masc. proper noun. Herodion. The name of a Christian whom Paul calls his kinsman (Rom 16:11).

2268. Ἡσαΐας Ēsaías, gen. *Ēsaíou*, proper noun, transliterated from the Hebr. *Yesh'yah* (3470, OT), Jehovah's salvation. Isaiah. The celebrated Hebrew prophet of whose personal history we know very little. He was the son of Amoz (2 Kgs 20:1; Isa 1:1). He began his prophetic career under Uzziah, probably in the last year of his reign (Isa 6:1), and continued it during the succeeding reigns of Jotham, Ahaz, and Hezekiah (Isa 7:1). His prophetic activity was between the years 760 B.C. and 713 or 698 B.C., the year of Hezekiah's death. He was married and had two sons (Isa 7:3; 8:3). His wife is called "the prophetess" and his children, like himself, had prophetical names emblematic of Israel's future. Isaiah is the evangelist among the prophets of the OT and is quoted more frequently than any other. In the Messianic prophecies that he recorded is drawn the most complete picture of the suffering, triumphant Savior of Israel and the world. The Messiah stands before us in unmistakable clarity and fullness. Isaiah gave us prophecies concerning the Messiah in regard to His birth (Isa 7:14; 9:6), His Davidic descent (Isa 11:1, 2), His suffering and death (chap. 53). The authenticity of Isa 40—66 has been assailed by critics who regard it as a later production by some "great unknown" prophet at the end of the Babylonian exile. But it is characteristic of prophetic visions to look into the far future as if it were present, and it makes no difference in the divine character of the prophecy whether it was uttered 500 or 700 years before its fulfillment. The description of the servant of God who suffers and dies for the sins of the people in Isa 53 applies to no other person in history with any degree of certainty or propriety except Jesus Christ. The book of Isa is mentioned in the NT in Matt 3:3; 4:14; 8:17; 12:17; 13:14, 35; 15:7; Mark 1:2; 7:6; Luke 3:4; 4:17; John 1:23; 12:38, 39, 41; Acts 8:28, 30; 28:25; Rom 9:27, 29; 10:16, 20; 15:12.

2269. Ἡσαῦ Ēsaú; masc. proper noun transliterated from the Hebr. *'Ēsaw* (6215, OT), hairy. Esau, the elder son of Isaac and Rebecca, and twin brother of Jacob (Gen 25:25f.; 27:6f.; 36:1). His family settled on Mount Seir, east of Jordan, which was hence called Edom, and his descendants were the Edomites, one of the most powerful and formidable nations of that age. See Rom 9:13; Heb 11:20; 12:16.

2270. ἡσυχάζω hēsucházō; fut. *hēsucháō*, from *hésuchos* (n.f.), quiet, still. To rest from labor (Luke 23:56); to be quiet, live quietly (1 Thess 4:11; Sept.: Judg 3:11, 30); to be silent, not speaking (Luke 14:4); to acquiesce (Acts 11:18; 21:14; Sept.: Neh 5:8).
Syn.: *paúō* (3973), to stop; *katapaúō* (2664), to rest, restrain; *kopázō* (2869), to cease raging; *eirēneúō* (1514), to bring peace, reconcile; *sigáō* (4601), to be silent; *siōpáō* (4623), to keep silence; *phimóō* (5392), to muzzle; *tarássō* (5015), to disturb; *katastéllō* (2687), to quiet, appease; *anapaúō* (373), to give rest; *epanapaúō* (1879), to cause to rest.
Ant.: *tarássō* (5015), to agitate.

2271. ἡσυχία hēsuchía; gen. *hēsuchías*, fem. noun from *hésuchos* (n.f.), quiet, still. Quietness, tranquility, stillness, referring to a quiet life (2 Thess 3:12). In the sense of stillness, it means silence (Acts 22:2; 1 Tim 2:11, 12; Sept.: Job 34:29).
Syn.: *galḗnē* (1055), tranquility; *eirḗnē* (1515), peace, quietness; *sigḗ* (4602), silence.
Ant.: *thórubos* (2351), noise; *homilía* (3657), talk; *tarachḗ* (5016), disturbance; *lógos* (3056), speech resulting from thought; *laliá* (2981), talk, saying, speech as the opposite of silence, repetition with-

out necessarily invoking thought; *kínēsis* (2796), moving.

2272. ἡσύχιος *hēsúchios*; gen. *hēsuchíou*, masc.-fem., neut. *hēsúchion*, adj., the same as *hḗsuchos* (n.f.), quiet, still. Quiet, tranquil, undisturbed from without (1 Tim 2:2; 1 Pet 3:4; Sept.: Isa 66:2).

Syn.: *ḗremos* (2263), tranquil; *eirēnikós* (1516), peaceful; *ḗpios* (2261), mild; *epieikḗs* (1933), gentle, tolerant; *práos* (4235), meek.

Ant.: *ágrios* (66), fierce; *anḗmeros* (434), fierce; *bíaios* (972), violent.

2273. ἤτοι *ḗtoi*; conj., from *ḗ* (2228), whether, or, and *toi* (5104), truly, or an intens. Whether truly, whether indeed, whether (Rom 6:16).

2274. ἡττάομαι *hēttáomai*; contracted *hēttṓmai*, fut. *hēttḗsomai*, mid. / pass. of *hēttáō*, from *hḗttōn* (found in the NT only in the neut. *hḗtton* [2276]), less, inferior. To overcome or be overcome as in battle or in a lawsuit (2 Pet 2:19, 20); to be inferior (2 Cor 12:13).

Deriv.: *hḗttēma* (2275), failure, fault.

Syn.: *nikáō* (3528), to overcome; *katakurieúō* (2634), to master; *kurieúō* (2961), to have dominion over; *kerdaínō* (2770), to gain; *kratéō* (2902), to seize.

2275. ἥττημα *hḗttēma*; gen. *hēttḗmatos*, neut. noun from *hēttáomai*, to be overcome, pass. of *hēttáomai* (2274), to overcome. Being inferior, a state worse than another or former state, defeat (Rom 11:12), meaning to be brought into a worse state, diminution, degradation, hence failure, fault (1 Cor 6:7).

Syn.: *paráptōma* (3900), a trespass, fault; *zēmía* (2209), loss.

Ant.: *plḗrōma* (4138), fullness; *níkē* (3529), victory.

2276. ἧσσον *hḗsson*, ἧττον *hḗtton*; gen. *hḗttonos* / *hḗssonos*, neut. of *hḗttōn*, used as an irregular comparative of *kakós* (2556), bad, evil. Worse, inferior,

weaker (1 Cor 11:17, "for the worse"). Used as an adv. (2 Cor 12:15, "the less I be loved").

Deriv. of *hḗttōn*: *hēttáomai* (2274), to overcome.

Syn.: *elássōn* (1640), less; *mikróteros* (3398), smaller, less.

Ant.: *meízōn* (3187), greater; *meizóteros* (3186), yet greater; *pleíōn* (4119), greater, more; *polús* (4183), great, much; *perissóteros* (4055), more abundant.

2277. ἤτω *ḗtō*; pres. imper. 3d person sing. of *eimí* (1510), I am. Let him or it be, let be (1 Cor 16:22; James 5:12).

Syn.: *génoito* (opt. 3d person sing. of *gínomai* [1096], to be), let it be.

Ant.: *mḗ génoito* (*mḗ* [3361], not; *génoito*, the opt. 3d person of *gínomai* [1096], to be) let it not be; *ou mḗ* (3364), not at all.

2278. ἠχέω *ēchéō*; contracted *ēchṓ*, fut. *ēchḗsō*, from *ḗchos* (2279), sound. To sound, resound, used intrans. of the roaring sea (Luke 21:25; 1 Cor 13:1; Sept.: Ex 19:16; Jer 50:42; 51:51).

Deriv.: *exēchéō* (1837), to sound forth as a trumpet; *katēchéō* (2727), to inform, teach.

Syn.: *ōrúomai* (5612), to howl, the roar of animals, of Satan; *salpízō* (4537), to sound a trumpet.

Ant.: *hēsucházō* (2270), to be quiet, silent.

2279. ἦχος *ḗchos*; gen. *ḗchou*, masc. noun. Sound, noise (Acts 2:2; Heb 12:19; Sept.: Ps 150:3). Used metaphorically for fame, rumor (Luke 4:37 [cf. Mark 1:28 with *akoḗ* {189}, report, rumor]), something which is heard.

Deriv.: *ēchéō* (2278), to sound or roar.

Syn.: *phḗmē* (5345), fame, rumor; *lógos* (3056), word, report; *phōnḗ* (5456), voice, sound; *phthóggos* (5353), voice, utterance.

Ant.: *sigḗ* (4602), silence; *hēsuchía* (2271), quietness.

2280. Θαδδαῖος *Thaddaíos*; gen. *Thaddaíou*, masc. proper noun. Thaddaeus, a surname of the Apostle Jude, also called Lebbeus (Matt 10:3; Mark 3:18).

2281. θάλασσα *thálassa*; gen. *thalássēs*, fem. noun from *háls* (n.f., see *aigialós* [123]), sea. Sea, as contrasted with the *gḗ* (1093), land (Matt 23:15; Acts 4:24; Sept.: Gen 1:10) or perhaps more strictly as contrasted with the shore. Another Gr. word, *pélagos* (3989), is also translated "sea," but there is a difference. The latter word occurring in Matt 18:6 and Acts 27:5 represents the vast uninterrupted expanse of open water.

(**I**) Generally, and as implying the vicinity of land (Matt 13:47; 18:6, "expanse of the sea" [a.t.]; Mark 9:42; Luke 21:25; Rom 9:27; 2 Cor 11:26; Rev 18:17; Sept.: Gen 22:17; Isa 5:30); the ocean (Rev 20:13; 21:1); the land and sea standing for the whole earth (Rev 7:1–3; 12:12). The heaven, the earth, and the sea standing for the universe (Acts 4:24; 14:15; Rev 5:13; Sept.: Ex 20:11; Hag 2:7). Poetically, of the waters above the firmament on which the throne of God is said to be founded, crystal sea (Rev 4:6; 15:2 [cf. Gen 1:7; Ps 29:10; 148:4]). See 1 Kgs 7:23; 2 Kgs 25:13.

(**II**) Of particular seas and lakes:

(**A**) By implication the Mediterranean (Acts 10:6, 32; 17:14; Sept.: Gen 13:14; Jon 1:4).

(**B**) The Red Sea (Acts 7:36). Used in an absolute sense (1 Cor 10:1, 2; Sept.: Ex 13:18; 14:2).

(**C**) The Sea of Galilee or Tiberias (Matt 4:18; Mark 1:16; John 21:1). Used in an absolute sense (Matt 4:15; John 6:16–19; Sept.: Num 34:11).

Deriv.: *dithálassos* (1337), between two seas; *parathalássios* (3864), along the sea.

Syn.: *límnē* (3041), lake; *kólpos* (2859), a bay; *aigialós* (123), shore; *parálios* (3882), beside the sea.

Ant.: *xērós* (3584), dry earth; *gḗ* (1093), land.

2282. θάλπω *thálpō*; fut. *thálpsō*. To make warm, heat. In the NT, used figuratively meaning to cherish, nourish (Eph 5:29; 1 Thess 2:7; Sept.: Deut 22:6; 1 Kgs 1:2, 4).

Syn.: *phrontízō* (5431), to care for; *peripoiéomai* (4046), to make around oneself or to care for; *proséchō* (4337), to give heed to, pay attention to; *diakonéō* (1247), to minister; *thermaínō* (2328), to warm.

Ant.: *ameléō* (272), to neglect.

2283. Θάμαρ *Thámar*; fem. proper noun transliterated from the Hebr. *Tāmār* (8559, OT), palm tree. Thamar, the widow of Er (2262) (Matt 1:3; see Gen 38).

2284. θαμβέω *thambéō*; contracted *thambṓ*, fut. *thambḗsō*, from *thámbos* (2285), astonishment, amazement, admiration. To be astonished, amazed (Acts 9:6; Sept.: 1 Sam 14:15; 2 Sam 22:5). In the pass.: *thambéomai*, to be astonished, amazed (Mark 1:27; 10:24, 32).

Syn.: *exístēmi* (1839), to be amazed, wonder; *ekplḗssō* (1605), to be astonished; *thaumázō* (2296), to marvel.

2285. θάμβος *thámbos*; gen. *thámbous*, neut. noun. Astonishment, amazement from admiration (Luke 4:36; 5:9; Acts 3:10).

Deriv.: *ékthambos* (1569), greatly amazed; *thambéō* (2284), to astonish.

Syn.: *ékstasis* (1611), ecstasy, a trance; *thaúma* (2295), a wonder, admiration, marvel; *téras* (5059), a marvel, astonishment.

2286. θανάσιμος *thanásimos*; gen. *thanasímou*, masc.-fem., neut. *thanásimon*, adj. from *thánatos* (2288), death. Deadly, poisonous (Mark 16:18).

Syn.: *thanatēphóros* (2287), death-bearing, deadly; *epithanátios* (1935), doomed to death.

2287. θανατηφόρος *thanatēphóros*; gen. *thanatēphórou*, masc.-fem., neut. *thanatēphóron*, adj. from *thánatos* (2288), death, and *phérō* (5342), to bring. Deadly death-bringing (James 3:8; Sept.: Num 18:22).

Syn.: *thanásimos* (2286), deadly, poisonous.

2288. θάνατος *thánatos*; gen. *thanátou*, masc. noun from *thnḗskō* (2348), to die. Death.

(I) Generally and of natural death (John 11:4, 13; Rom 8:38; Phil 1:20; Heb 7:23). To taste or to experience death (Matt 26:38; Mark 14:34, "sorrowful, even unto death," to grieve oneself to death; John 12:33, "by what death he should die" [a.t.]; 18:32; 21:19; Rev 13:3, "unto death" [a.t.] meaning deadly wound). In the pl., deaths means exposures to death (2 Cor 11:23). Metonymically for plague, pestilence (Rev 6:8; 18:8; Sept.: Ex 10:17; 1 Kgs 8:37; Jer 18:21; 21:7).

(II) Spoken of a violent death, e.g., as a punishment, guilty of death (Matt 26:66; Mark 14:64); worthy of death (Luke 23:15; Acts 23:29); to sentence someone to death (Matt 20:18; Mark 10:33); death on the cross (Phil 2:8). Generally (Matt 10:21; Mark 13:12; Luke 23:22; 24:20; Acts 22:4; 2 Cor 1:9, 10; Rev 2:10); the death of Jesus (Rom 5:10; 1 Cor 11:26; Phil 2:8; Col 1:22; Heb 2:9, 14; 5:7; 9:15). In Matt 15:4; Mark 7:10 quoted from Ex 21:17, "let him die [or end] in death" (a.t.); Rev 2:23, "I shall kill her children in death" (a.t.). See Sept.: Ex 22:19.

(III) Often in the Sept., *thánatos* has the sense of destruction, perdition, misery, implying both physical death and exclusion from the presence and favor of God in consequence of sin and disobedience, but never as extinction. Opposed to *zōḗ* (2222), life and blessedness (Sept.: Deut 30:19; Ps 16:11 [cf. Acts 2:28]; Prov 11:19; 12:28; see Isa 25:8). In the NT, this sense is applied with more definitiveness to the gospel plan of salvation, and as *zōḗ* is used to denote the bliss and glory of the kingdom of God including the idea of a joyful resurrection, so *thánatos* is used for the opposite, i.e., rejection from the kingdom of God. This includes the idea of physical death as aggravated by eternal condemnation; the idea of physical death being sometimes more prominent, and sometimes that of subsequent perdition (John 8:51; Rom 6:16, 21, 23; 7:5, 10; 8:2, 6; 2 Cor 2:16; 3:7; 2 Tim 1:10; Heb 2:15; James 5:20; 1 John 3:14; 5:16, 17). Called also the second death (Rev 2:11; 20:6, 14; 21:8), referring to eternal spiritual separation from God. In this sense *ho thánatos* is used as a kind of personification, the idea of physical death being prominent (Rom 5:12, 14, 17, 21; 1 Cor 15:26, 54–56; Sept.: Isa 25:8; Hos 13:14).

(IV) Poetically *ho thánatos* personified, death as the king of Hades (86) (Rev 6:8; 20:13, 14; 21:4. See Acts 2:24; Rev 1:18; Sept.: Ps 49:15 [cf. Job 18:13]). Metonymically for Hades itself (Matt 4:16; Luke 1:79, "the shadow of death," meaning thickest darkness, quoted from Isa 9:2 [cf. Prov 7:27]).

(V) In 1 John 5:16, 17, "a sin unto death" is a sin which, should a believer continue to engage in, may lead him to premature physical death (see Eccl 7:17; Jer 14:11, 12; 34:18–20; Acts 5:1–11; 1 Cor 11:30).

(VI) Spiritual death (John 5:24; 1 John 3:14). As spiritual life consists in constant communication with the divine Life, so spiritual death is the separation from that Life.

(VII) Eternal death (Rom 6:21, 23; James 5:20; 1 John 5:16, 17) which, in respect to the natural and temporal, is called the second death (Rev 2:11; 20:6, 14) and implies everlasting punishment (Rev 21:8).

(VIII) Plague or pestilence (Sept.: Ex 5:3; 9:3, 15; see Matt 24:7). *Thánatos* is joined with *limós* (3042), famine (Rev 6:8 [cf. Ezek 14:21]).

Deriv.: *epithanátios* (1935), about to die; *thanásimos* (2286), mortal; *thanatēphóros* (2287), death-bearing, deadly; *thanatóō* (2289), to put to death.

Syn.: *nékrōsis* (3500), a deadening; *apóleia* (684), loss; *phónos* (5408), murder; *sphagḗ* (4967), slaughter; *thusía* (2378), sacrifice; *anaíresis* (336), literally the taking up or off, symbolic of death; *teleutḗ* (5054), an end, death.

Ant.: *bíos* (979), life, its manner and length; *zōḗ* (2222), life, the essence of life; *psuchḗ* (5590), soul.

2289. θανατόω thanatóō; contracted *thanatṓ*, fut. *thanatṓsō*, from *thánatos* (2288), death. To put to death. In the NT by the intervention of others meaning to cause to be put to death, to deliver over to death. Used trans.

(I) Particularly, to kill, put to death (Matt 10:21; 26:59; 27:1; Mark 13:12; 14:55; Luke 21:16; 2 Cor 6:9; 1 Pet 3:18). In Rom 8:36, used hyperbolically as quoted from Ps 44:22; Sept.: 1 Kgs 11:40; Jer 38:15.

(II) In a figurative sense, it means to mortify, subdue evil desires (Rom 8:13); in the pass., to become dead to anything, to be freed from its power. With the dat. in Rom 7:4.

Syn.: *anairéō* (337), to put to death; *apokteínō* (615), to kill; *phoneúō* (5407), to slay, murder; *spháttō* or *spházō* (4969), to slaughter; *thúō* (2380), to sacrifice or kill and offer in sacrifice; *diacheirízomai* (1315), to kill, slay; *nekróō* (3499), to make dead, mortify; *apóllumi* (622), to destroy.

Ant.: *zōopoiéō* (2227), to make alive.

2290. θάπτω tháptō; fut. *thápsō*, 2d aor. *etáphēn*. To perform funeral rites. In the NT, used generally meaning to inter, bury. Used trans. in Matt 8:21, 22; 14:12; Luke 9:59, 60; 16:22; Acts 2:29; 5:6, 9, 10; 1 Cor 15:4; Sept.: Gen 23:4.

Deriv.: *suntháptō* (4916), to bury with; *taphḗ* (5027), burial; *táphos* (5028), a burial place, sepulcher.

Ant.: *exorússō* (1846), to dig out.

2291. Θάρα Thára; masc. proper noun transliterated from the Hebr. *Terach* (8646, OT), loiterer. Terach. Thara, or Terah, the father of Abraham, who accompanied him to Haran in Mesopotamia where he died at the age of 205, Abraham being then seventy-five years of age (Luke 3:34; Sept.: Gen 11:24ff., 31, 32; see Josh 24:2).

2292. θαρρέω tharréō; contracted *tharrṓ*, fut. *tharrḗsō*, from *thársos* (2294), boldness. To be of good cheer, have courage, be full of hope and confidence. Used intrans. in 2 Cor 5:6, 8; Heb 13:6; Sept.: Prov 1:21. Followed by *en* (1722), in, and the dat., to have hope and confidence in someone (2 Cor 7:16; Sept.: Prov 31:11); by the prep. *eis* (1519), in, and the acc., to be bold toward anyone (2 Cor 10:1).

Syn.: *anathállō* (330), to revive; *andrízomai* (407), to act as a man; *tolmáō* (5111), to be bold, dare; *parrēsiázomai* (3955), to speak boldly; *apotolmáō* (662), to speak out very boldly; *euthuméō* (2114), to make cheerful.

Ant.: *apopsúchō* (674), literally to breathe out one's life, faint; *eklúō* (1590), to enfeeble; *ekkakéō* (1573), to lack courage; *kámnō* (2577), to be weary; *sunéchomai* (4912), to constrain oneself; *phríssō* (5425), to shudder; *trémō* (5141), to tremble; *deiliáō* (1168), to show cowardice; *phobéomai* (5399) and *ptoéomai* (4422), to be afraid; *tarássomai* (5015), to be disturbed.

2293. θαρσέω tharséō; contracted *tharsṓ*, fut. *tharsḗsō*, from *thársos* (2294), boldness, courage. In the NT, only in the imper., *thársei*, and in the pl. *tharseíte*, be of good cheer, have courage, spoken by way of encouragement (Matt 9:2, 22;

14:27; Mark 6:50; 10:49; Luke 8:48; John 16:33; Acts 23:11; Sept.: Gen 35:17; Joel 2:21, 22). Equivalent to *tharréō* (2292), to be confident.

2294. θάρσος *thársos*; gen. *thársous*, neut. noun. Cheer, cheerful mind, courage (Acts 28:15).

Deriv.: *tharréō* (2292) and *tharséō* (2293), to have confidence, be of good cheer.

Syn.: *parrēsía* (3954), boldness, particularly in speech; *hilarótēs* (2432), cheerfulness in connection with showing mercy; *pepoíthēsis* (4006), assurance, confidence, trust.

Ant.: *phóbos* (5401), fear; *deilía* (1167), fearfulness; *trómos* (5156), trembling; *ptóēsis* (4423), alarm; *apeilé* (547), threatening; *taraché* (5016), disturbance, trouble.

2295. θαῦμα *thaúma*; gen. *thaúmatos*, neut. noun from *tháomai* (n.f.), to wonder. Wonder, admiration (Rev 17:6; Sept.: Job 17:8). Also from *tháomai* (n.f.): *theáomai* (2300), to behold, view.

Deriv.: *thaumázō* (2296), to admire.

Syn.: *téras* (5059), a strange thing, wonder; *sēmeíon* (4592), sign; *thámbos* (2285), astonishment, amazement, wonder; *dúnamis* (1411), power, miracle; *megaleíon* (3167), a great thing; *sébasma* (4574), an object of worship.

Ant.: *empaigmós* (1701), a ridicule, laughing stock; *loidoría* (3059), railing, reproach; *oneidismós* (3680), reproach; *óneidos* (3681), notoriety, disgrace.

2296. θαυμάζω *thaumázō*; fut. *thaumásomai*, from *thaúma* (2295), a wonder.

(I) Intrans., to wonder, marvel, be struck with admiration or astonishment (Matt 8:10, 27; 9:8, 33; 15:31; 21:20; 22:22; 27:14; Mark 5:20; 6:51; 15:5; Luke 1:63; 8:25; 11:14; 24:41; John 7:15, 21; Acts 2:7; 4:13; 13:41; Rev 17:6–8; Sept.: Isa 41:23). With adjuncts, to wonder at anything, e.g., followed by the acc. of pron. as a remote obj. (Luke 24:12; John 5:28). Wonder (Rev 17:6).

Followed by *diá* (1223), for, and the acc. (Mark 6:6); *en* (1722), in, followed by the dat. (Luke 1:21); *epí* (1909), upon, and the dat. (Mark 12:17, the intens. comp. *ekthaumázō* in some MSS; Luke 2:33; 4:22; 9:43; 20:26; Acts 3:12); *perí* (4012), concerning, and the gen. (Luke 2:18); *hóti* (3754), that, as to wonder that, because (Luke 11:38; John 3:7; 4:27; Gal 1:6). Followed by *ei* (1487), if, as to wonder if or whether (Mark 15:44; 1 John 3:13).

(II) By implication, trans., to wonder at, i.e., to admire with the acc. (Luke 7:9; Acts 7:31); pass. (2 Thess 1:10). In Rev 13:3, "to wonder after the beast" (a.t.), i.e., to admire and follow him, to become his worshiper.

(II) In the mid. *thaumázomai*, the same as the act. in meaning (Rev 17:8); in the inf. *thaumasthênai*, to be admired (2 Thess 1:10). Followed by *prósōpon* (4383), person or persons (Jude 1:16), it means to admire, reverence, respect a man's person, to respect him with special esteem on account of his outward appearance and thus give him undue favor (see Sept.: Lev 19:15; Job 13:10; 22:8; Isa 9:15).

Deriv.: *thaumásios* (2297), wonderful; *thaumastós* (2298), one deserving to be admired.

Syn.: *thambéō* (2284), to astound; *theōréō* (2334), to behold with amazement; *exístēmi* (1839), to be amazed; *ekpléssō* (1605), to astonish.

Ant.: *exouthenéō* (1848), to despise; *muktērízō* (3456), to mock; *chleuázō* (5512), to jeer at; *empaízō* (1702), to deride; *oneidízō* (3679), to upbraid.

2297. θαυμάσιος *thaumásios*; gen. *thaumasíou*, masc.-fem., neut. *thaumásion*, adj. from *thaumázō* (2296), to admire. Wonderful, admirable. In the pl. neut., wonderful things, miracles provoking admiration and astonishment (Matt 21:15; Sept.: Josh 3:5; Ps 9:1; 77:12, 14). To the Greek Church Fathers and in Mod. Gr., miracles are known as *thaúmata* (pl.), a word not used with such meaning in the NT, although it occurs as *thaúma* (2295), astonishment (sing.) in Rev 17:6. This word was used prior to this period by magicians and impostors of various kinds. See *sēmeíon* (4592), sign; *dúnamis* (1411), power, mighty work; *megaleíos* (3167), great work; *éndoxos* (1741), glorious, glorious work; *parádoxos* (3861), strange, astonishing work; *téras* (5059), frightful, terrifying work.

Syn.: *thaumastós* (2298), wonderful, marvelous, worthy of admiration.

2298. θαυμαστός *thaumastós*; fem. *thaumastḗ*, neut. *thaumastón*, adj. from *thaumázō* (2296), to marvel. Wonderful, admirable, wondrous (1 Pet 2:9; Rev 15:1, 3); worthy to be admired (Matt 21:42; Mark 12:11 quoted from Ps 118:23; Sept.: Ex 15:11; 34:10; Ps 8:1). In the sense of strange, unusual (John 9:30; 2 Cor 11:14).

2299. θεά *theá*; gen. *theás*. A goddess, referring to Diana (Acts 19:27, 35, 37 [TR]).

2300. θεάομαι *theáomai*; fut. *theásomai*, aor. pass. *etheáthēn*, mid. deponent from *tháomai* (n.f.) to wonder. To behold, view attentively, contemplate, indicating the sense of a wondering consideration involving a careful and deliberate vision which interprets its object. Also from *tháomai* (n.f.): *thaúma* (2295), wonder, admiration.

(I) Simply to see, perceive with the eyes, equivalent to *blépō* (991), to see indicating great vividness, and *horáō* (3708), to see, physically and mentally (John 8:10; Acts 21:27; 22:9; 1 John 4:12, 14); pass. *etheáthē*, was seen (Mark 16:11); followed by the acc. and part. (Mark 16:14; Luke 5:27; John 1:32, 38; Acts 1:11); by *hóti* (3754), that (John 6:5; Acts 8:18).

(II) Involving more than merely seeing and including the idea of desire, pleasure (Matt 6:1, "in order to be seen by them" [a.t.]; 11:7; 22:11; 23:5; Luke 7:24; 23:55; John 1:14; 4:35).

(III) In the sense of to visit (Rom 15:24; Sept.: 2 Chr 22:6).

Deriv.: *théatron* (2302), theater.

Syn.: *blépō* (991) to see; *emblépō* (1689), to look earnestly upon and learn from; *theōréō* (2334), to look at a thing with interest and attention to details, to consider; *epopteúō* (2029), to oversee; *atenízō* (816), to gaze intently; *katanoéō* (2657), to comprehend with the mind.

2301. θεατρίζω *theatrízō*; fut. *theatrísō*, from *théatron* (2302), theater. To be an actor in the theater, make a public spectacle. In the NT, to make a public spectacle of, to expose to public scorn, as used in the pass. (Heb 10:33). Criminals were sometimes exposed and punished in the theater.

2302. θέατρον *théatron*; gen. *theátrou*, neut. noun from *theáomai* (2300), to behold. Theater, a place where drama and other public spectacles were exhibited and where the people convened to hear debates or hold public consultations (Acts 19:29, 31). Figuratively, a spectacle, public show (1 Cor 4:9 [cf. Heb 10:33]).

Deriv.: *theatrízō* (2301), to make a public spectacle.

2303. θεῖον *theíon*; gen. *theíou*, neut. noun. Sulfur, brimstone (Rev 19:20). Joined with fire, fire and brimstone, sulfurous flames (Luke 17:29; Rev 14:10; 20:10; 21:8); including smoke, meaning sulfurous flames and smoke (Rev 9:17, 18; Sept.: Gen 19:24; Ezek 38:22).

Deriv.: *theiṓdēs* (2306), sulfurous.

2304. θεῖος *theíos*; fem. *theía*, neut. *theíon*, adj. from *Theós* (2316), God. Divine, what is uniquely God's and proceeds from Him. Distinguished from *Theós* (2316), God, as indeed *theiótēs* (2305), divinity, is distinguished from *Theótēs* (2320), Godhead. *Theíos* denotes an attribute of God such as His power and not His character in its essence and totality. See Acts 17:29; 2 Pet 1:3, 4; Sept.: Ex

31:3; 35:31. In Class. Gr. the adj. denoted the power of God, as the noun *theiótēs* does explicitly in Rom 1:20.

2305. θειότης *theiótēs*; gen. *theiótētos*, fem. noun from *Theós* (2316), God. Divinity, only in Rom 1:20.

2306. θειώδης *theiṓdēs*; gen. *theiṓdous*, masc.-fem., neut. *theiōdón*, adj. from *theíon* (2303), sulfur. Sulfurous, made of sulfur (Rev 9:17).

2307. θέλημα *thélēma*; gen. *thelḗmatos*, neut. noun from *thélō* (2309), to will. The suffix *-ma* indicates that it is the result of the will. Will, not to be conceived as a demand, but as an expression or inclination of pleasure towards that which is liked, that which pleases and creates joy. When it denotes God's will, it signifies His gracious disposition toward something. Used to designate what God Himself does of His own good pleasure.

(I) Will, active volition, wish, good pleasure (Matt 26:42; Acts 21:14; 1 Cor 16:12; Eph 5:17; 1 Pet 2:15; 4:2, 3, 19; 1 John 5:14); the will of the flesh, carnal desire (John 1:13; Sept.: Ps 1:2; Dan 8:4; 11:3).

(II) By metonymy, will, what one wills to do or have done (Matt 7:21; 12:50; 21:31; Mark 3:35; John 5:30; 6:38; Acts 13:22; Rom 12:2; Eph 6:6; Heb 13:21); the desires of the flesh (Eph 2:3; Sept.: 1 Kgs 5:8, 9; Ps 103:21; 143:10). By implication, will, i.e., purpose, counsel, decree, law (Matt 18:14; John 6:39, 40; Acts 22:14; Heb 10:7, 9, 10, 36). The will of God means the counsels or eternal purposes of God (Matt 6:10; Luke 11:2).

(III) By metonymy, will, the faculty of willing, free will (Luke 23:25; 1 Cor 7:37; 2 Pet 1:21); of God (Eph 1:5, 11; 1 Pet 3:17).

(IV) In the NT there are two principal verbs indicative of will: *thélō* (2309), to will, wish, implying volition and purpose, frequently a determination or execution of that which is desired; and *boúlomai* (1014), to wish or will deliberately which

expresses more strongly than *thélō* the deliberate exercise of the will but not necessarily the execution of it. Among the nouns derived from *thélō*, *thélēma* refers almost entirely to God, with exceptions in Eph 2:3 (cf. 1:11); 2 Pet 1:21. The word is generally sing., but the pl. occurs in Acts 13:22; Eph 2:3. In Heb 2:4, *thélēsis* (2308) is the act of the will or the process used. The *thélēma* is that which results from the process of determination. What God determines to do is the result of His *thélēsis* and it is His *thélēma*.

There are two corresponding nouns derived from *boúlomai* (1014) which means to will deliberately but not necessarily to execute that will. They are *boúlēma* (1013), a resolve or purpose, and *boulḗ* (1012), a counsel, determination. In both, there is the initiation of one's purpose. In *thélēma*, however, there is the finalization and the execution of that purpose. The differentiation in the meaning of the two nouns *thélēma* and *boúlēma* indicates why the first is used primarily of God and the second is always used of man. When God purposes something, He always has the power to bring it to execution, but man, not necessarily. There is a finality about God's *thélēma*, but there is not finality in regard to man's *boúlēma*. Man may determine to do what he may never fulfill.

(V) The only exceptions to the above are in Eph 2:3 where it is in the pl., *thelḗmata*, referring to the desires of the flesh and of the mind which clearly indicates the sinful desires from which Christ liberates a believer. An unbeliever, on the other hand, is free to consider and accomplish sin.

The same phrase, *thélēma sarkós* (*sárx* [4561], flesh) "the will of the flesh" (a.t.) that we find in Eph 2:3 relating *thélēma* to the flesh is found in John 1:13, which should also be taken as referring to the physical desire of the flesh for the reproductive act. The meaning of this expression induces us to believe that John 1:13 should not be linked directly to John 1:12

which refers to those who receive Jesus Christ and to whom He gives the right to become the children of God. Observe there is no *kaí* (2532), "and," as a connective between verses twelve and thirteen. John 1:13 should rather be connected to the *Lógos* (3056), the Word of verse one, which is the basic and general subject of this passage, the Word becoming flesh. The main subject of this entire passage is that the "Word [*Lógos* {3056}] . . . became flesh [*sárx* {4561}]" (John 1:1, 14) The flesh of Jesus, however, was different from any other flesh in that it was sinless (Heb 4:15). It was *hósios* (3741), sacred, pure, without the inherited sin of Adam (Rom 5:12; Heb 4:15), subject to natural growth (Luke 2:40, 52), but not to decomposition and corruption at death (Ps 16:8–11; Acts 2:27, 31; 13:35). Jesus therefore took upon Himself a body, fully human (Phil 2:6–8), capable of dying and yet incorruptible.

The manner in which this *Lógos* became flesh must be different than the ordinary manner in which all of us were conceived. Jesus Christ as the God-Man was not conceived out of an ordinary human desire of the flesh (*ek* [1537] of, *thelḗmatos sarkós* [4561], flesh) but of God. Tertullian was the first to propose that the *hós* (3739) who, the relative pron. in the sing. referring to the *Lógos*, Word (which is also in the sing.), was changed to *hoi* in the pl. to correspond to *hósoi* ([3745], pl.), "as many as" of verse twelve. Because of the proximity of the two verses, it seems quite possible that the scribes who were copying the text changed the *hós*, who, (referring to *ho Lógos*, the Word of John 1:1) to *hoi*, which, in the pl. referring to "as many" (*hósoi*). Therefore they had to change *egennḗthē* (aor. pass. of *gennáō* [1080]) "was born," from the 3d person sing. to *egennḗthēsan*, the 3d person pl. "were born" to refer to *hósoi* rather than to the *Lógos*. If verse thirteen is taken with *hós* referring to the Word and the verb is *egennḗthē*, "who [in the sing. referring to the *Lógos*] was born" (a.t.), then what it

states in the body of the verse fully applies to the virgin birth of Jesus Christ who was born not as a result of the interaction of a man with a woman (Matt 1:20, 23, 25; Luke 1:30, 34, 35). Jesus was not conceived out of the fleshly desire of a man, resulting in corruption. In John 1:13, the expression *oudé ek thelḗmatos andrós* (*oudé* [3761], nor; *ek* [1537], of; *thélēma*, desire; *andrós*, gen. sing. of *anḗr* [435], husband, man) should be translated, "nor of the desire of a husband" (a.t.). The declaration is that the *Lógos*, Jesus Christ in His preexistence as the Son (John 1:12, 14, 18), became flesh, not because of the desire of the flesh, nor the desire of a husband (since it is usually the husband who initiates the act of reproduction), but of God. Here the word "husband" is used to impress the legitimacy of marriage and human reproduction. The meaning of the previous expression *thélēma sarkós*, "the will of the flesh," is exactly the same in Eph 2:3, this being one of the exceptions of the use of *thélēma*, referring not to the will of God but the desire of the flesh of man.

(VI) Another exception to the word *thélēma* referring especially to man is found in 2 Pet 1:21, "For the prophecy came not in old time by the will of man: but holy men of God spake as they were moved by the Holy Ghost." This verse declares that the true and trustworthy prophecy of 2 Pet 1:19 was neither initiated nor brought forth by man. Any such prophecy initiated in the mind of and expounded by man must be considered false prophecy. True prophecy, conceived in the mind of God, was brought forth or executed, not by man, but by the Holy Spirit who prompted holy men of God to speak. It is interesting indeed to realize that the word for "spoke" in Gr. is *elálēsan*, the aor. of the verb *laléō* (2980), to speak. They faithfully reiterated that which was declared to them. See *laléō* (2980) as it contrasts with *légō* (3004), to speak or express one's thought.

(VII) The word *thélēma*, with the meaning of fatherly desire for the good of his daughter, is used in 1 Cor 7:37, "Nevertheless he that standeth steadfast in his heart, having no necessity, but hath power over his own will (*thélēma*), and hath so decreed in his heart that he will keep his virgin, doeth well." This verse speaks of the determination of a virgin's father for her to stay at home without marrying because it is his will to protect her against an undesirable marriage.

(**VIII**) In Acts 13:22, the word *thélēma* is used in the pl., *thelḗmata*, as in Eph 2:3, but in this instance it is used in regard to God and His precepts.

(**IX**) The corresponding noun *boúlēma* (1013), resolve, purpose, is used only in three instances.

(**A**) First it is used in Acts 27:43, where both the verb *boúlomai* and the subst. *boúlēma* are found: "But the centurion, willing (*boulómenos*) to save Paul, kept them from their purpose (*boulḗmatos*); and commanded that they which could swim should cast themselves first into the sea, and get to land." This concerned Paul in regard to the shipwrecked boat in which he and others were sailing. The verb expresses the centurion's desire to rescue Paul, and the subst. relates to the determination of the soldiers to kill the prisoners on board. Both the verb and the noun refer to the will or purpose of human beings.

(**B**) The second instance of the use of *boúlēma* is in regard to God in Rom 9:19, "Thou wilt say then unto me, Why doth he yet find fault? For who hath resisted his will? [*boulḗmati* in the dat. sing.]." In this entire passage of Rom 9:16–24, one of the most difficult in the NT, whenever the verb "will" is used (namely in vv. 16, 18, 22), it is the Gr. *thélō*. But in verse nineteen, in the phrase, "For who hath resisted his will?" it is not *thélēma* that is used but *boúlēma*. In verse sixteen, "So then it is not of him that willeth [*thélontos*], nor of him that runneth, but of God that showeth mercy." Evidently the reference here is made to the one who endeavors to save himself. He cannot do it by his own will, even though he

so desires (*thélō*). He could not possibly either conceive the plan of salvation nor execute it, both concepts existing in the verb *thélō*. Paul is saying here that man on his own does not have either the understanding or the power to save himself, being by nature ungodly and an enemy of God (Rom 5:6, 9). Man's salvation depends entirely on God's mercy. In Rom 9:17, the example of Pharaoh is given, stressing the power of God. Pharaoh did not will to be saved. He could not be saved on his own and he would not accept the mercy of God provided through Moses. Then in verse eighteen follows the statement that indicates the very character of God, "Therefore hath he mercy on whom he will have mercy, and whom he will he hardeneth." Observe that the relative pron. *hón* is in the sing. to indicate to us that God deals with individuals. As individuals we experience either the mercy of God or the consequence of our own choice to remain hardened because of original sin.

The verb used is *thélei*, the pres. 3d person sing. which indicates God's character without particular reference to historic instances. The two verbs following *thélei*, he wills, are also in the pres. tense (*eleeí* [1653], shows mercy on, and *sklērúnei* [4645], to harden). In this entire passage of Rom 9:16–24, the power of God to effectively apply His mercy and the inability of man on his own to obtain that mercy is stressed: "It is not of him that willeth, nor of him that runneth, but of God that showeth mercy" (v. 16). This definitely declares that man cannot by his own effort appropriate God's mercy. Observe that verse seventeen declares the purpose of God in dealing with Pharaoh was to demonstrate His power (*dúnamis* [1411], meaning manifest ability and not necessarily inherent power, which would be conveyed by *ischús* [2479]). Paul tells us here that what God purposes He is able to accomplish. The statement in verse eighteen is a general conclusion: "There-fore [and this is expressed by a double word in Gr., *ára* {686}, therefore, and *oún* {3767}, which in this instance could be translated "then and together," "so then," or "wherefore"] hath he mercy on whom he will have mercy, and whom he will he hardeneth." This whole passage declares that man does not have the power to save himself. He can only cast himself on the mercy of the Lord Jesus Christ for salvation. It also declares that God's mercy is available to all, but only appropriated by those whom God sovereignly regenerates.

The difficulty in understanding this passage is due to the translation of the word *boúlēma* in verse nineteen as "will." It is not the word *thélēma* used here, referring to God's executive will, but *boúlēma* which means God's purpose, His expressed desire. God's salvation is not a stamp He places upon unbelieving man. He purposes (*boúletai*) for all to be saved; nevertheless, there are some who resist, as declared in Rom 9:19, "Thou wilt say then unto me, Why doth he yet find fault? For who hath resisted his will?" The answer to that question is that any person who does not believe resists the will of God to save him. However, what he resists is not God's *thélēma*, His executive decision that one is going to be saved (Rom 8:29, 30), but it is God's *boúlēma*, His desire which he resists.

2 Pet 3:9 helps a great deal in understanding Rom 9:16–24, if we realize the word translated "not willing" is the verb *boúlomai* and not *thélō*. "The Lord is not slack concerning his promise, as some men count slackness; but is long-suffering to us-ward, not willing [*mē* {3361}, not; *boulómenos*, pres. part. of *boúlomai*, which would have been better translated "not desiring"] that any should perish, but that all should come to repentance." The general principle enunciated both in Rom 9:19 and 2 Pet 3:9 is that God does desire that anyone should perish. On the other hand, He has not actually willed or decreed the salvation of all men. Rom 9:20 makes it clear that no man can turn to God who is sovereign and say to Him, "You made me

the way I am and this is the reason I cannot believe." Refusal to believe can never be blamed on God. Rom 9:21 does not speak of God's executive will that someone should perish, but of His active desire to accept whoever believes and to work out His will in his life, even as the potter takes clay and shapes something out of that clay. The potter uses clay that is malleable. The lump not used represents people who do not believe and are condemned as is clearly stated in John 3:18. God's condemnation is simultaneous with man's decision to persist in his unbelief. Again, observe in Rom 9:21 the word *exousía* (1849), authority, jurisdiction or strength, is used. In verse seventeen the word *dúnamis* (1411), the factual power, is used; and in verse twenty-one it is *exousía*, authority; and in twenty-two we have the neut. expression *tó dunatón*, akin to *dúnamis*, used again. The whole concept is that God is able and free to save anyone.

One more important consideration is necessary. Who is the person who fits the vessels of wrath to destruction? The verb translated "fitted" is the Gr. *katērtisména*, perf. mid. / pass. part. of *katartízō* (2675), to fit perfectly or properly. The mid. tense would indicate that these vessels of wrath fitted themselves unto destruction. If it is taken as pass., it might be interpreted to mean that God actually fitted or created them for the purpose of placing them in hell. This is inconceivable as one views the total teaching of the Scriptures, particularly 1 Tim 2:4 and 2 Pet 3:9. It might be best taken as the mid. voice, considering the word "prepared" is in the act. voice in Rom 9:23, referring to God's effectively preparing the application of His mercy upon those who believe: "And that he might make known the riches of his glory on the vessels of mercy, which he had afore *prepared* unto glory." Also, an argument for taking the word *katērtisména* ("fitted to destruction" [v. 22]) as being in the mid. voice is what immediately precedes it: "God . . . endured with much long-suffering the vessels of wrath." The word *makrothumía* (3115), long-suffering, is God's patience toward men. How can one show patience and long-suffering toward someone He had predetermined to eternal condemnation? Rom 9:22 declares that God's executive will (*thélōn*) is shown toward those who have prepared themselves (*katērtisména*) unto destruction and toward those whom He has afore prepared unto glory (v. 23). The verb translated "he had afore prepared" is in the act. voice *proētoímasen* (aor. of *proetoimázō* [4282], to prepare beforehand) which means that when it comes to salvation He is the One who activates it. Men, however, prepare themselves unto destruction.

(C) The third instance of the occurrence of *boúlēma* is in 1 Pet 4:3 UBS, versus *thélēma* in the TR. The UBS reading is to be preferred because reference here is made to the purposes and desires of the nations to cause the believers to engage in sinful practices. They cannot force the believers to do so, in which case it would have been *thélēma*.

(X) In Eph 1:11, we find the expression *tēn boulēn toú thelēmatos*. The verse reads as follows: "In whom also we have obtained an inheritance, being predestinated according to the purpose of him who worketh all things after the counsel [*boulē*] of his own will [*thelēmatos*]." Here *boulē* is well translated "counsel" or purpose. Before God does (*thélēma*) something, He conceives of it as a purpose (*boulē*). The meaning of *boulē* is clearly indicated in Heb 6:17: "Wherein God, willing [*boulómenos*] more abundantly to show unto the heirs of promise the immutability [*ametátheton* {276}, unchangeableness] of his counsel [*boulēs*], confirmed it by an oath." This declares that what God purposes He does not change. *Boulē* seems to correspond somewhat closely to the Aristotelian *proaíresis* (n.f.), a choice made ahead of time (related verb *proairéomai* [4255], to choose for oneself before another thing, to prefer, to intend, which is used in the NT). *Eudokía* (2107), good purpose or desire, could be taken as a syn. of *boulē* or *boúlēma* (1013), purpose, rather than a syn. for *thélēma*. *Epithumía* (1939), longing or desire, however, is more of a syn. of *thélēma* when that expresses the desire of the flesh, a craving which may pass out of control and become *páthos* (3806), passion that is overpowering. While *páthos* suggests an ungovernable passion in the three places it occurs (Rom 1:26; Col 3:5; 1 Thess 4:5), a deep and overpowering longing for a good object is expressed by *epipóthēsis* (1972), earnest desire, and the verb *epipothéō* (1971), to intensely crave, greatly desire, long for (Rom 1:11; 2 Cor 9:14; Phil 1:8; James 4:5; 1 Pet 2:2). Man's will is affected by outside influences. Peter, for instance, said to Ananias in Acts 5:3, "Why hath Satan filled thine heart?" In Acts 5:9, however, we find that there was consent of the will: "How is it that ye have agreed together to tempt the Spirit of the Lord?" Paul's admonition in 2 Cor 2:11 is "that no advantage may be gained over us by Satan" (a.t.). See 2 Cor 4:4. In James 1:14, we find our will is also influenced by our lusts: "But every man is tempted, when he is drawn away of his own lust, and enticed." See Acts 8:23; 13:10; Rom 7:11, 20; Gal 3:1. In these passages, sin itself is spoken of as the agent of deception and death (Rom 8:20). These inducements, however, do not nullify the responsibility of the sinner (Acts 28:25ff. quoted from Isa 6:9, 10; Rom 1:24, 26; 2:1, 5, 6). These passages imply a state of being, the evil not being primarily a matter of actions but of habits (*héxis* [1838], habitual practice). Such a condition of the will is called death, the absence of power to do good (2 Cor 4:3; Eph 2:1). This state of death does not involve inability to exercise the will, but rather the inability to exercise the will for righteousness. A spiritually dead person is one who has refused to believe and is thus under condemnation (John 3:18). He continues to live in a state of spiritual estrangement from God. How could he be under condemnation without the option to believe or disbelieve? Very similar language is used by Paul about the race as a whole—"death passed upon all men, for that all have sinned" (Rom 5:12). On the other hand, a man dead in sin can be made alive (Eph 2:5; Col 2:13 [cf. 1 John 3:14, "We know that we have passed from death unto life, because we love the brethren"]). However, life means death to sin and to the Law which enslaved to sin (Rom 7:6; Col 2:20; 3:3, 4: "ye died, and your life is hid with Christ in God . . . Christ, who is our life" [a.t.]). In this state, the term "death" refers to one's ability to say no to evil impulses and yes to good ones. The activity of the will is still necessary: "Let not sin therefore reign in your mortal body" (Rom 6:11, 12, 16); and this activity is shown very clearly by the appeals to moral conduct which occur regularly at the close of Paul's epistles and elsewhere in the NT. With the unbeliever, there is first the active will to evil; then, evil becomes inevitable; the agent is practically powerless, "sold under sin" (Rom 7:14). After the sinner's rescue from this state, the will is again called for, but this time it points habitually in the opposite direction. Man's will appears to be clearly called for in such passages as 2 Cor 5:20, "Be ye reconciled to God." In Acts 2:21 we very clearly read, "That whosoever shall call on the name of the Lord shall be saved." Calling upon the Lord is necessary. Paul regards both grace and faith as vital to the changed life of the believer. "God . . . hath quickened us together with Christ (by grace ye are saved)" (Eph 2:4, 5). "For by grace are ye saved through faith; and that not of yourselves: it is the gift of God" (Eph 2:8 [cf. Rom 4:5; Gal 1:15]). By itself, the reference to grace might imply that man was merely passive, but the call for faith is an act of the will. Indeed, faith in general is emphasized considerably more than grace as the agent in conversion. A still more fundamental connection between the activities of God and man is expressed in what appears to be contradictory terms in Phil 2:12, 13: "Work out your own salvation. . . . For it is God which worketh in you both to will and to do of his good pleasure"; and

Gal 2:20: "I live; and yet no longer I, but Christ liveth in me" (a.t.). In Gal 3:25, we read of faith as "coming" (a.t.) with the result that we are "no longer under a tutor" (a.t.), but "sons of God through faith" (a.t. [cf. 1 Pet 1:13, "The grace that is being brought unto you" {a.t.}]). Even in this new sphere of life through faith, the will reappears as a persistent endeavor after progress (Phil 3:12; 2 Pet 1:10). The new life of grace is marked by the exercise of the gifts of grace (charísmata [5486]), but they must be diligently cultivated (Rom 12; 1 Cor 12). Acts 15:28 indicates a certain cooperation between the indwelling Holy Spirit and the will of the human personality: "For it seemed good to the Holy Ghost, and to us, to lay upon you no greater burden than these necessary things." The new life of the believer may be rightly called one of freedom (cf. Gal 5:13), characterized by the confidence of open speech with boldness (parrēsía [3954], Eph 3:12; Heb 3:6; 1 John 3:21). The Christian is conscious of a new power (Gal 2:20) infusing him (Phil 3:12). The result is to produce in him for the first time a true activity of a changed life, the boldness of the abundant life (John 10:10). Thélēma, as controlled desire, is found only in Luke 23:25; John 1:13; 1 Cor 7:37; Eph 2:3; 2 Tim 2:26; 2 Pet 1:21.

See discussion under epistréphō (1994), to convert, regarding the relationship between the divine will and the human will involved in conversion.

Syn.: boúlēma (1013), resolve, purpose, will; boulé (1012), volition, purpose, will; thélēsis (2308), determination, act of will; epithumía (1939), longing, desire, passion; entolé (1785), command with emphasis on the authority of the one commanding; éntalma (1778), injunction, commandment implying authority in itself; paraggelía (3852), a mandate, charge, request; diatagé (1296), arrangement, instrumentality; diátagma (1297), commandment, authoritative edict; epipóthēsis (1972), earnest desire.

2308. θέλησις thélēsis; gen. *theléseōs*, fem. noun from *thélō* (2309), to will. The act of willing as contrasted to *thélēma* (2307) which objectively is that which is willed (which see for full discussion and its contrast with *boulēma* [1013], resolve). Will, good pleasure of God. In Heb 2:4, *thélēsis* means that God conceived and purposed all the miracles and brought them about even in their distribution (*merismós* [3311]) through the Holy Spirit. Gifts of miracles are not man's but His from beginning to end in both their conception and execution, which is represented by *thélēsis*. It is entirely His action through the Holy Spirit.

Syn.: *boulḗ* (1012), purpose, counsel.

2309. θέλω thélō; fut. *thelḗsō*. To will, wish, desire, implying active volition and purpose.

(I) To will, i.e., to have in mind, purpose, intend, please.

(A) Of God and Christ, followed by the aor. inf. (Rom 9:22; Col 1:27); by the inf. and its subject (1 Tim 2:4). Used in an absolute sense with the inf. implied (John 5:21; Acts 18:21; 1 Cor 4:19; James 4:15).

(B) Of men, followed by the aor. inf. (Matt 2:18; 5:40; Mark 6:19, 26; Luke 7:24; 8:20; 15:28; John 1:43; Acts 7:28; 10:10; 1 Cor 7:7; 11:3; 14:5). With the pres. inf. (Matt 19:21; John 6:67; 7:1; 16:19; Acts 14:13; 24:6; Gal 4:20; 2 Thess 3:10). Followed by the inf. and acc. (Luke 1:62). Used in an absolute with the inf. implied (Matt 8:2; 15:28; Mark 3:13; 9:13; 18:30; 21:29; John 15:7; Rom 7:15; 1 Cor 4:21; 7:36; Rev 11:6). With the neg. *ou* (3756), not, meaning not to will, not to have in mind, and (by implication) to will not, to determine not to do this or that, to refuse. Followed by the aor. inf. (Matt 2:18; Mark 6:26; Luke 8:20; 15:28; 23:8). In antithesis of to will and to do (Rom 7:18; 2 Cor 8:10, 11; Phil 2:13). With a neg., the idea of *thélō* sometimes approaches that of *dúnamai* (1410), I am able, I can (Matt 1:19, "being unwilling" [a.t.], unable, i.e., not being able to bring

himself to do so and so; Luke 18:13, "would not [could not, dared not] lift up . . . his eyes").

(C) *Thélō* means to will as the equivalent of to purpose, to be decided upon, seeing one's desire to its execution. It may stand side by side with *poiéō* (4160), to do, to make (John 8:44; Rom 7:21; 2 Cor 8:11), and with *energéō* (1754), to effect (Matt 8:2; Phil 2:13).

(D) Metaphorically of the wind (John 3:8).

(II) Generally, to wish, desire, choose. Used in the sense of to endeavor, desire, rarely by itself as in Matt 5:42; 12:38; 15:28; 19:17; 20:26, 27. With the pres. inf. (John 16:19; Gal 4:20). Followed by the inf. and acc. (Mark 7:24; 1 Cor 7:7; 11:3; 14:5). Also with a neg. *ou* (3756), not, meaning to will not, be unwilling, choose not, followed by the aor. inf. (Luke 19:14; 1 Cor 10:20). With the pres. inf. (Rom 1:13; 1 Cor 10:1; 2 Cor 1:8). Followed by *ei* (1487), if, since (Luke 12:49). Sometimes simply with an acc. where, however, an inf. is strictly implied, e.g., in Luke 5:39; 2 Cor 11:12. Followed by *hína* (2443), so that, with the subjunctive (Matt 7:12; Mark 6:25; John 17:24). In interrogations, followed by the fut. indic. or more properly aor. subjunctive with *hína* ([2443], so that) implied, e.g., Matt 20:32, "What will ye that I shall do unto you?"; 26:17; Mark 14:12; 15:9, 12; Luke 9:54. Once with *ḗ* (2228), "or," to choose rather, prefer (1 Cor 14:19). Sometimes *thélō*, when followed by an inf., is to be rendered as an adv. before a finite verb, "willingly," "gladly," (John 6:21, "they gladly received him into the vessel" [a.t.]).

(III) By implication, it means to be disposed or inclined toward anything, delight in, love, in which case it is a syn. of *philéō* (5368), to love. *Thélō* means to be inclined toward something (Acts 26:5), to have a mind to, wish or desire (John 3:8); and with the neg. *ou*, not to be inclined, often not to intend (Matt 1:19). Used with the inf. of the subj. matter following (Matt 9:13; 12:7; 14:5; 26:15; 27:43; Heb

10:5, 8). Also followed by the inf. (Luke 20:46 [cf. Mark 12:38 where it seems to take the acc. as being syn. with *philéō*]). With the acc. (Matt 9:13 quoted from Hos 6:6; Matt 27:43 quoted from Ps 22:8; Heb 10:5, 8 quoted from Ps 40:6; Sept.: Ezek 18:23). Followed by *en* (1722), in, with the dat. sing. to delight in anything (Col 2:18).

(IV) By implication it means to be of a particular mind or opinion, to affirm (2 Pet 3:5, "for they want to be ignorant" [a.t. {cf. 2 Pet 3:4}]).

(V) *Thélō* differs from *boúlomai* (1014), to be disposed, to intend, purpose, design, decree, but not pressing on to execute that decision. *Thelō* indicates not only willing something, but also pressing on to action. When the subst. *boúlēma* (1013) is used, unlike *thélēma* (2307), it denotes the substance of the law and also the intention underlying the law, but not the execution thereof. Thus *boulē* (1012) is counsel, decision, conclusion. In Mod. Gr., this is the name given to a parliament which makes the laws and provides the intent of the law but not the execution of it. On the other hand, *thélēma* is resolve and denotes the will of God which must be done. However, *boulē Theoú*, the will of God, refers only to God's self-affirmation in His own action. *Boúlomai*, therefore, is not in agreement with the meaning *eudokéō* (2106), to be possessed of good will. *Boúlomai* and *thélō* differ as to degree and resolve, and *thélō* in the NT denotes elective inclination, love, occurring frequently in biblical Gr. with the acc. of the obj., which is rare with *boúlomai*. The neg. *ou*, not, and *thelō* means not to will, refuse, oppose (Matt 18:30; 21:29; 23:37). The refusal is usually rendered by *ou thélō* and rarely by *ou boúlomai*. *Thélō* may mean to be about to, but never *boúlomai*. Nevertheless, *boúlomai* may be used for *thélō*, and *thélō*, though far more rarely, for *boúlomai*.

Deriv.: *ethelothrēskeía* (1479), voluntary; *thélēma* (2307), will; *thélēsis* (2308), the act of the will, pleasure, desire.

Syn.: *epithuméō* (1937), to desire earnestly; *aitéō* (154), to ask, beg; *zētéō* (2212), to seek; *epizētéō* (1934), to crave, desire, seek after; *diṓkō* (1377), pursue, follow; *exaitéomai* (1809), to demand, desire; *axióō* (515), to desire, deem worthy; *epipothéō* (1971), to long after; *parakaléō* (3870), to beseech; *himeíromai* (2442), to have a strong desire for; *erōtáō* (2065), to desire, ask; *orégō* (3713), to desire; *zēlóō* (2206), to have a zeal for, desire earnestly.

2310. θεμέλιος *themélios*; gen. *themelíou*, masc.-fem., neut. *themélion*, adj. from *théma* (n.f.), that which is laid down, which is from *títhemi* (5087), to place, set. Placed or laid as a foundation, fundamental, hence in the NT:

(I) Used as a subst. with the masc. def. art., *ho themélios*, meaning foundation; with stone, foundation stone (Heb 11:10; Rev 21:19; Sept.: 1 Kgs 6:1; Job 22:16). Metaphorically used of elementary doctrine and instruction, the foundation (1 Cor 3:10; Eph 2:20); of a fundamental doctrine or principle, e.g., Christ (1 Cor 3:11, 12); a good foundation, on which hope and salvation may rest (1 Tim 6:19). Figuratively in 2 Tim 2:19, meaning that which God has founded, God's building, the gospel plan.

(II) In the neut. with the def. art., used as a subst., *tó themélion*, the foundation (Acts 16:26; Sept.: Prov 8:29; Isa 58:12; Lam 4:11; Mic 1:6).

Deriv.: *themelióō* (2311), to lay a basis or foundation.

Syn.: *katabolē* (2602), foundation as speaking metaphorically of the creation of the world; *archē* (746), beginning; *prṓton* (4412), at the first; *básis* (939), basis, footing.

2311. θεμελιόω *themelióō*; fut. *themelióō*, from the adj. *themélios* (2310), foundational, fundamental. To found, to lay the foundation of anything. Used trans. (Matt 7:25; Luke 6:48; Heb 1:10 quoted from Ps 102:25; Sept.: Josh 6:26). Metaphorically, to ground, establish, confirm (Eph 3:17; Col 1:23; 1 Pet 5:10).

Syn.: *edaphízō* (1474), to lay even with the ground.

2312. θεοδίδακτος *theodídaktos*; gen. *theodidáktou*, masc.-fem., neut. *theodídaktos*, adj. from *Theós* (2316), God, and *didáskō* (1321), to teach. Taught by God (1 Thess 4:9). Equivalent to *didaktoí toú Theoú*, taught of God (John 6:45). This is in fulfillment of Isa 54:13 and Mic 4:2.

2313. θεομαχέω *theomachéō*; contracted *theomachṓ*, fut. *theomachḗsō*, from *theomáchos* (2314), one who fights against God. To fight or contend against God (Acts 23:9 [TR]).
Syn.: *asebéō* (764), to be impious, irreverent; *hierosuléō* (2416), to commit sacrilege; *blasphēméō* (987), to blaspheme, speak impiously.
Ant.: *pisteúō* (4100), to believe; *latreúō* (3000), to minister to God, render religious homage; *eusebéō* (2151), to be pious; *eulabéomai* (2125), to be circumspect, reverent; *hagiázō* (37), to hallow, sanctify; *eulogéō* (2127), to bless, speak well of.

2314. θεομάχος *theomáchos*; gen. *theomáchou*, masc.-fem., neut. *themáchos*, adj. from *Theós* (2316), God, and *máchomai* (3164), to fight. One who fights against God or contends with God (Acts 5:39).
Deriv.: *theomachéō* (2313), to fight against God.
Syn.: *ápistos* (571), an unbeliever; *asebḗs* (765), impious, irreverent, ungodly; *anósios* (462), unholy, wicked; *bébēlos* (952), profane; *theostugḗs* (2319), hater of God.
Ant.: *pistós* (4103), a believer; *eusebḗs* (2152), pious; *eulabḗs* (2126), devout; *theosebḗs* (2318), pious, reverent of God; *philótheos* (5377), fond of God, pious, lover of God; *theóphilos* (2321), friend of God, as a proper name *Theophilus*; *hierós* (2413), sacred; *hágios* (40), holy; *theíos* (2304), divine; *hósios* (3741), sacred, one performing religious statutes.

2315. θεόπνευστος *theópneustos*; gen. *theopneústou*, masc.-fem., neut. *theópneuston*, adj. from *Theós* (2316), God, and *pnéō* (4154), to breathe or blow. Prompted by God, divinely inspired, occurs only in 2 Tim 3:16 in the NT. In Class. Gr., opposed to *phusikós* (5446), natural in contrast to divine. In reality, the formation of the word should be traced to *empnéō* (1709), inspire (Acts 9:1), urged by the *pneúma* (4151), spirit, whether one's own or God's or the spirit world, instead of *pnéō*. The simple verb *pnéō* is never used of divine action. Neither *empnéō* nor *pnéō* is used in 2 Pet 1:21, but the expression "by the Spirit, the Holy one, being driven or carried [*pherómenoi*, pres. pass. part. of *phérō* {5342}, to carry]" (a.t.) referring to those who wrote God's utterances or prophecies.

2316. Θεός *Theós*; gen. *Theoú*, masc. noun. God. Originally used by the heathen, but in the NT as the name of the true God. The heathen thought the gods were makers and disposers (*thetḗres*, placers) of all things. The ancient Greeks used the word both in the sing. and the pl. When they used the pl., they intimated their belief that elements had their own "disposer" or "placer," e.g., the god of money called mammon (Matt 6:24; Luke 16:9, 13). The heavens were the grand objects of divine worship throughout the heathen world as is apparent from the names attributed to the gods by the ancient Greeks. The Scriptures also attest to this (Acts 7:42, 43; Deut 4:19; 17:3; 2 Kgs 17:16; 23:4, 5; Job 31:26, 27; Jer 8:2; 19:13; Zeph 1:5).

The Sept. constantly translated the Hebr. pl. name *Elohim*, when used for the true God, by the sing. *Theós*, God, never by the pl. *theoi*, gods. The reason for this was that at the time the Sept. translation was made, Greek idolatry was the prevailing superstition, especially in Egypt under the Ptolemies. Their gods were regarded as demons, i.e., intelligent beings totally separate and distinct from each other. If the translators rendered the name of the true God by the pl. *theoi*, they would have given the heathen under Greek culture an idea of God inconsistent with the unity of the divine essence and conformable to their own polytheistic notions. However, by translating the Hebr. *Elohim* as "God," they inculcated the unity of God and at the same time did not deny a plurality of persons in the divine nature.

In the NT and the Sept., *Theós*, God, generally answers to the OT pl. name *Elohim* and so denotes God, the Trinity. See Matt 4:7 (cf. Deut 6:16 in the Hebr. and the Sept.); Matt 4:10 (cf. Deut 6:3); Matt 22:32 (cf. Ex 3:6); Matt 22:37 (cf. Deut 6:5); Mark 1:14, 15 (cf. Dan 2:44); Mark 12:29 (cf. Deut 6:4, 5); John 1:12 (cf. Gen 6:2); Acts 4:24 (cf. Gen 1:1 in the Hebr.); Acts 10:34 (cf. Deut 10:17). It is applied personally, but very rarely, to the Father (John 5:18; 13:3; 16:27, 30 [cf. John 16:28, 29]; 2 Cor 13:14; Phil 2:6); to the Son (Matt 1:23; John 1:1; 20:28; Rom 9:5; 1 Tim 3:16 [TR]; Titus 2:13; 2 Pet 1:1; 1 John 5:20); to the Holy Spirit (Acts 5:4 [cf. Acts 4:24, 25 with Acts 1:16; 1 Cor 3:16, 17; 6:19; 2 Cor 6:16; 2 Pet 1:21]). It also denotes the heathen gods or idols (Acts 14:11); magistrates (John 10:34, 35); by false application to Satan (2 Cor 4:4); to the belly which some people make their god or in which they place their supreme happiness (Phil 3:19).

In two passages, *Theós* is used to distinguish the one true God from all other beings. In 1 Cor 8:5, 6, it is put forth that even if all the gods of the heathen really did exist, yet to us there is but one true God. In Gal 4:8, Paul reminds the Galatians that the gods whom they served in the past as slaves, are not, in their essential character, in their very nature, gods at all.

Many times, *Theós* occurs with the def. art. *ho*, but it is not so rendered in translation because, in Eng., we never refer to God as *the God*, except if He is designated as belonging to someone specifically, such as the God of Abraham (Matt 22:32). In many instances when the def. art. *ho* occurs before *Theós*, God, particular reference is made to God the Father, making the distinction in the persons of the Trinity evident, e.g., in John 1:1b, "And the Word had been [*én*, imperf. act. of *eimí* {1510}] toward [*prós* {4314}] the God [*tón Theón*]" (a.t.). The def. art. here designates "the Father." The absence of the def. art. may refer to the Triune God in His infinity, eternity and totality (John 1:18).

Deriv.: *átheos* (112), without God; *theá* (2298), goddess; *theíos* (2304), divine; *theiótēs* (2305), divinity, referring to the power of God but not to His essential character and nature; *theodídaktos* (2312), taught of God; *theomáchos* (2314), one who fights against God; *theópneustos* (2315), inspired of God; *theosebḗs* (2318), reverent of God; *theostugḗs* (2319), hater of God; *theótēs* (2320), divinity, referring to the essence and nature of God; *philótheos* (5377), fond of God, lover or friend of God.

Syn.: *ho ṓn* (*ho* [3588], the; *ṓn* [5607], to be), the One being, One eternal in His existence, One who has always been, self-existent; *ho ṓn, ho én, kaí ho erchómenos* (*én* [2258], to be; *kaí* [2532], and; *erchómenos*, pres. part. of *érchomai* [2064], to come), the One being, who was, and who is coming, the One spanning time, the timeless One; *húpsistos* (5310), the Highest, the supreme One; *kúrios* (2962), lord, master, supreme in authority; *epouránios* (2032), one above the sky, celestial; *ouránios* (3770), heavenly, followed by *patḗr* (3962), father; *dēmiourgós* (1217), literally a worker for the people, creator, maker; *ktístēs* (2939), God, the author of all things, creator; *poiētḗs* (4163), doer, creator; *pantokrátōr* (3841), omnipotent, almighty.

2317. θεοσέβεια *theosébeia*; gen. *theosebeías*, fem. noun from *theosebḗs* (2318), God-fearing. Reverence toward

God, godliness (1 Tim 2:10; Sept.: Gen 20:11).

Syn.: *eusébeia* (2150), good reverence, godliness; *eulábeia* (2124), Godly fear, referring more to a passive acceptance of God than to an active demonstration of one's reverence; *pístis* (4102), faith; *hagiótēs* (41), holiness; *hagiōsúnē* (42), sanctification; *hosiótēs* (3742), piety.

Ant.: *apistía* (570), unbelief, unfaithfulness; *blasphēmía* (988), blasphemy, evil-speaking against God; *asébeia* (763), ungodliness, impiety, lack of a worshipful spirit.

2318. θεοσεβής *theosebḗs*; gen. *theoseboús*, masc.-fem., neut. *theosebés*, adj. from *Theós* (2316), God, and *sébomai* (4576), to reverence. Godly, devout, translated "worshiper of God" (John 9:31; Sept.: Ex 18:21; Job 1:1, 8).

Deriv.: *theosébeia* (2317), godliness.

Syn.: *eusebḗs* (2152), pious, reverent, devout, showing one's reverence in a worshipful attitude; *eulabḗs* (2126), one who receives something well, devout but in a more passive way than *eusebḗs*; *philótheos* (5377), fond or a friend of God; *theóphilos* (2321), a friend of God, also used as the proper noun Theophilus; *hierós* (2413), sacred, performing one's religious duties; *hágios* (40), holy; *theíos* (2304), Godlike.

Ant.: *ápistos* (571), an unbeliever, unfaithful; *asebḗs* (765), not worshipful, impious; *theostugḗs* (2319), hater of God; *hubristḗs* (5197), an insulter, irreverent; *blásphēmos* (989), scurrilous, impious or speaking against God, blasphemer; *hierósulos* (2417), temple despoiler, robber of churches; *anósios* (462), unholy, not respectful of religious matters and ordinances; *bébēlos* (952), profane.

2319. θεοστυγής *theostugḗs*; gen. *theostugoús*, masc.-fem., neut. *theostugés*, adj. from *Theós* (2316), God, and *stugéō* (n.f., see *apostugéō* [655]), to hate, abhor. Occurs only in Rom 1:30, translated "haters of God," and could

be held syn. with *átheos* (112), destitute of God. The ancient Greeks used to call *theostugḗs* someone who turned against God. When any heavy calamity befell such a person, He would accuse God and His providence.

2320. θεότης *theótēs*; gen. *theótētos*, fem. noun from *Theós* (2316), God. Deity, Godhead as directly revealed, God's personality (Col 2:9), as distinguished from *theiótēs* (2305) in Rom 1:20, divinity or divine power and majesty, a concept arrived at by observing God's mighty works.

2321. Θεόφιλος *Theóphilos*; gen. *Theophílou*, masc. proper noun. Theophilus, meaning lover of God. A distinguished individual probably of Greece or Rome to whom, as his particular friend or patron, Luke addressed both his gospel and his history of the Acts of the Apostles (Luke 1:3; Acts 1:1). The title "most excellent" probably denotes official dignity (Acts 23:26; 24:3; 26:25).

2322. θεραπεία *therapeía*; gen. *therapeías*, fem. noun from *therapeúō* (2323), to heal, serve. Voluntary service, attendance, ministry, and in the care of the sick by implication relief, healing (Luke 9:11; Rev 22:2); metaphorically and collectively meaning attendants, domestics, retinue (Matt 24:45; Luke 12:42; Sept.: Gen 45:16).

Syn.: *íama* (2386), a means of healing; *íasis* (2392), the process of healing; *oiketeía*, household of servants; *diakonía* (1248), service, ministry, rendering what is necessary to meet a need; *ōphéleia* (5622), usefulness, benefit, profit; *sumphéron* (4851), profit, collective advantage; *euergesía* (2108), beneficence, benefit; *chrēstótēs* (5544), usefulness, kindness.

2323. θεραπεύω *therapeúō*; fut. *therapeúsō*, from *therápōn* (2324), attendant, servant. To wait upon, minister to, render voluntary service, heal, but primarily signifies to serve as *therápōn*.

(I) In the pass., in Acts 17:25, "Neither is worshiped [*therapeúetai*, served, ministered to] with men's hands, as though he needed anything."

(II) To take care of the sick, to tend with the more general meaning of to relieve, heal, cure (Matt 4:24; 12:10; Mark 1:34; Luke 6:7; 10:9); with the gen. and *apó* (575), from (Luke 7:21; 8:2) followed by the acc. of disease (Matt 4:23). In Rev 13:3 of the healing of the wound. *Therapeúō* means to heal miraculously in Matt 4:23, 24; 10:1, 8; Acts 4:14.

Deriv.: *therapeía* (2322), service.

Syn.: *iáomai* (2390), to heal; *sṓzō* (4982), to save, rescue; *diasṓzō* (1295), to bring safely through, preserve, maintain.

Ant.: *asthenéō* (770), to be diseased, without strength; *páschō* (3958), to suffer; *hupophérō* (5297), to undergo hardship, endure; *basanízomai* (928), to suffer pain, torture, to be vexed.

2324. θεράπων *therápōn*; gen. *therápontos*, masc. noun. Servant, attendant, minister. It denotes a faithful friend to a superior, who solicitously regards the superior's interest or looks after his affairs, not a common or domestic servant (*oikétēs* [3610]). One who serves willingly regardless of whether he is a free man (*eleútheros* [1658]) impelled by love or a slave (*doúlos* [1401]) bound by duty. Thus the services of a *therápōn* (Heb 3:5; Sept.: of Moses in Ex 14:31; Num 12:7, 8; of Job in Job 2:3) are voluntary and higher than those of an ordinary *doúlos*, slave. *Therapeúō* (2323) may be used of the physician's watchful attendance of the sick and man's service to God. *Therápōn* approaches more closely the position of *oikonómos* (3623), manager, in God's house.

Deriv.: *therapeúō* (2323), to voluntarily serve.

2325. θερίζω *therízō*; fut. *therísō*, from *théros* (2330), summer, harvest time. To harvest, reap.

(I) Generally and in an absolute sense (Matt 6:26; Luke 12:24; James 5:4; Sept.: Ruth 2:3). In proverbial expressions as "reaping where thou hast not sown," it means turning the labors of others to one's own profit (Matt 25:24, 26; Luke 19:21, 22; similarly John 4:37). "That which man sows, that will he also reap" (a.t. [Gal 6:7]), means he will be rewarded according to his works (see 2 Cor 9:6; Jer 12:13).

(II) Metaphorically, it means to reap the fruits of one's labors, to receive in recompense (1 Cor 9:11; Gal 6:8, 9; Sept.: Prov 22:8). Spoken of a Christian teacher gathering converts into the kingdom of God (John 4:36, 38 [cf. Matt 9:37; Luke 10:2]).

(III) By implication, to cut down, destroy (Rev 14:15, 16, meaning the iniquity of men is fully ripe and is cut off [cf. Isa 17:5; Joel 3:13]).

Deriv.: *therismós* (2326), harvest; *theristḗs* (2327), reaper.

Syn.: *sugkomízō* (4792), to convey or bear away together; *trugáō* (5166), to collect the vintage, gather.

Ant.: *speírō* (4687), to sow; *skorpízō* (4650), to scatter; *diaskorpízō* (1287), to equally disperse, scatter.

2326. θερισμός *therismós*; gen. *therismoú*, masc. noun from *therízō* (2325), to harvest, reap. Harvest, harvesting (Matt 13:30, 39; Mark 4:29; John 4:35; Sept.: Gen 8:22; Jer 27:16); metonymically, the produce of the harvest. In the NT, used metaphorically, meaning the converts to be gathered into Christ's kingdom (Matt 9:37, 38; Luke 10:2); those whose iniquity is fully ripe for punishment (Rev 14:15).

Ant.: *sporá* (4701), a sowing; *diasporá* (1290), dispersion; *phuteía* (5451), planting.

2327. θεριστής theristḗs; gen. *theristoú*, masc. noun from *therízō* (2325), to reap. A reaper (Matt 13:30, 39).

2328. θερμαίνω thermaínō; fut. *thermanō̂*, from *thermós* (n.f.), warm, which is from *thérō* (n.f.), to heat. To warm. In the NT, only in the mid. *thermaínomai*, to warm oneself as by a fire (Mark 14:54) or near the light (Mark 14:67; John 18:18, 25); with clothing (James 2:16; Sept.: 1 Kgs 1:1, 2; Isa 44:15, 16). Also from *thermós* (n.f.): *thérmē* (2329), warmth, heat.

Syn.: *puróō* (4448), to burn, be on fire; *zéō* (2204), to boil, be hot; *kaíō* (2545), to burn.

Ant.: *psúchō* (5594), to chill, render cold; *katapsúchō* (2711), to cool down, refresh; *anapsúchō* (404), to cool off, refresh.

2329. θέρμη thérmē; gen. *thérmēs*, fem. noun from *thermós* (n.f.), warm, which is from *thérō* (n.f.), to heat. Warmth, heat (Acts 28:3; Sept.: Job 6:17; Ps 18:7). Also from *thermós* (n.f.): *thermaínō* (2328), to heat, warm.

Syn.: *kaúsōn* (2742), burning heat; *púr* (4442), fire; *purá* (4443), a fire; *púrōsis* (4451), a conflagration, burning; *kaúma* (2738), the result of burning or heat produced; *kaúsis* (2740), the process of burning.

Ant.: *psúchos* (5592), cold.

2330. θέρος théros; gen. *thérous*, neut. noun from *thérō* (n.f.), to heat. Summer, a warm season (Matt 24:32; Mark 13:28; Luke 21:30; Sept: Prov 6:8; 30:25), and, by implication, harvest time (Sept.: Prov 26:1).

Deriv.: *therízo* (2325), to harvest.

Ant.: *cheimṓn* (5494), winter, tempest.

2331. Θεσσαλονικεύς Thessalonikeús; gen. *Thessalonikéōs*, masc. proper noun. A Thessalonian, an inhabitant of Thessalonica (Acts 20:4; 27:2; 1 Thess 1:1; 2 Thess 1:1).

2332. Θεσσαλονίκη Thessaloníkē; gen. *Thessalonikēs*, fem. proper noun. Thessalonica, a city of Macedonia, known in ancient times by the name Thermae (Hot Baths). Cassander, one of the generals of Alexander the Great, rebuilt the city and called it after his wife, Alexander's sister, Thessaloniki. It is situated at the northeast corner of the Thermaic Gulf. In Paul's day, it was a free city of the Romans, the most populous city in Macedonia and the capital of one of the four Roman divisions of Macedonia which extended from the river Strymon on the east to the Axius on the west. The rulers of the city (Acts 17:6, 8) were called "politarchs." Paul and Silas, in A.D. 58, came from Philippi to Thessalonica, which was one hundred miles northeast on the Via Egnatia where there was a synagogue of the Jews. For at least three Sabbaths, the apostles preached to their countrymen. The Church which gathered there was primarily composed of Gentiles. At length the persecution became so violent as to drive the apostle away. He desired to revisit the Church there and sent Timothy to minister to them. Among his converts were Gaius, Aristarchus, Secundus, and perhaps Jason (Acts 17:1, 11, 13; 20:4; 27:2 [cf. Phil 4:16; 2 Tim 4:10]). Paul wrote two epistles to the Thessalonian Church from Corinth (1 Thess 1:1; 2 Thess 1:1).

2333. Θευδᾶς Theudás; gen. *Theudá*, masc. proper noun. Theudas, meaning thanksgiving. An insurrectionary chieftain mentioned by Gamaliel (Acts 5:36).

2334. θεωρέω theōréō; contracted *theōrō̂*, fut. *theōrḗsō*, from *theōrós* (n.f.), a spectator, from *theáomai* (2300), to look closely at. To gaze, to look with interest and for a purpose, usually indicating the careful observation of details. Distinguished from *blépō* (991), to look, see, take care, beware (Mark 15:47; Luke 10:18; 23:35; John 20:6, 12, 14; Heb 7:4).

(I) Simply to see, perceive with the eyes, behold, nearly equivalent to *blépō* (991), to look.

(A) Generally followed by the acc. of person (Mark 3:11; Luke 24:37; John 9:8; 14:19; 16:10, 16, 17, 19; Acts 3:16; 9:7; 25:24); with the part. added (Mark 5:15; Luke 10:18; 24:39; John 6:19, 62; 20:12, 14). Followed by the acc. of thing (Luke 21:6; John 7:3; Acts 20:38); with a part. added (John 10:12; 20:6; Acts 7:56; 10:11; Sept.: Ps 21:8; 30:12).

(B) To perceive, mark, note, followed by *hóti* (3754), that (Mark 16:4; John 4:19; 12:19; Acts 27:10); by *pósos* (4214), how much, how great (Acts 21:20); by the acc. of thing (Mark 5:38; Acts 4:13); with the part. added (Acts 17:16; 28:6); with the acc. of person (1 John 3:17); with the part. implied (Acts 17:22).

(C) To experience death (John 8:51). Used of experience in the sense of partaking of something (John 17:24).

(II) Including the notion of attention, wonder.

(A) Used in an absolute sense (Matt 27:55; Mark 15:40; Luke 14:29; 23:35; Acts 19:26; Sept.: Ps 27:4). Generally with the acc. of thing (Luke 23:48; John 2:23; 17:24; Acts 8:13); with the acc. of person (Rev 11:11, 12). Followed by *pós* (4459), how (Mark 12:41), *poú* (4226), where (Mark 15:47).

(B) To look at, view with attention (Matt 28:1). Metaphorically, to consider (Heb 7:4).

(C) To look at; by implication, to comprehend, recognize, acknowledge, with the acc. of person (John 6:40; 12:45; 14:17).

Deriv.: *anatheōréō* (333), to look again; *theōría* (2335), sight; *paratheōréō* (3865), to compare.

Syn.: *emblépō* (1689), to look earnestly; *blépō* (991), to look; *epopteúō* (2029), to oversee; *atenízō* (816), to gaze upon; *katanoéō* (2657), to perceive; *eídō* (1492), to know, consider, perceive; *epiginốskō* (1921), to know fully; *katalambánō* (2638), to comprehend, per-

ceive; *kathoráō* (2529), to discern clearly; *diablépō* (1227), to see through clearly.

Ant.: *tuphlóō* (5186), to make blind, obscure.

**2335. θεωρία *theōría*; gen. *theōrías*, fem. noun from *theōréō* (2334), to behold. A beholding, viewing, sight, spectacle (Luke 23:48).

Syn.: *hórasis* (3706) and *eídos* (1491), sight (2 Cor 5:7); *hórama* (3705), that which is seen, vision; *anáblepsis* (309), recovering of sight; *paratérēsis* (3907), inspection, ocular evidence, observation.

Ant.: *skótos* (4655), darkness, inability to see; *skotía* (4653), obscurity, metaphorically the result of darkness.

**2336. θήκη *thḗkē*; gen. *thḗkēs*, fem. noun from *títhēmi* (5087), to place, put. A place in which to put or set anything. A receptacle, chest, case, as for a sword, a sheath (John 18:11).

**2337. θηλάζω *thēlázō*; fut. *thēlásō*, from *thēlḗ* (n.f.), breast.

(I) To give suck (Matt 24:19; Mark 13:17; Luke 21:23; 23:29; in some texts *tréphō* [5142], to feed; Sept.: Gen 21:7; Ex 2:7).

(II) To suck or receive suck (Matt 21:16 quoted from Ps 8:2; Luke 11:27; Sept.: Job 3:12).

**2338. θῆλυς *thḗlus*; fem. *thḗleia*; neut. *thḗlu*, adj. Female.

(I) The adj. *thḗlus*, female or woman, is used as a pl. subst. in Rom 1:26, *haí thḗleiai*, the women, the females. In Rom 1:27, *tḗs thēleías*, womanhood, woman's nature, also as a subst. (Sept.: Lev 27:4).

(II) In the neut. in Matt 19:4; Mark 10:6; Gal 3:28, *tó thḗlu*, the female in the phrase *ársen kaí thḗlu* (*ársen*, from *árrēn* [730], male; *kaí* [2532], and), male and female as contrasting genders. See Sept.: Gen 1:27; 6:19. The generic word referring either to man or woman is *ánthrōpos* (444), human being. The masc. human being is *anḗr* (435) which, depending on the context, can also mean husband. The gender of man is *árrēn* or *ársēn* (730), male.

Syn.: *gunḗ* (1135), woman or wife.

2339. θήρα *thḗra*; gen. *thḗras*, fem. noun from *thḗr* (n.f.), wild beast. A hunt, a chase, prey, game, trap. Used metonymically meaning destruction, cause of destruction (Rom 11:9 quoted from Ps 69:22; Sept.: Ps 34:8).

Deriv.: *thēreúō* (2340), to hunt, take in hunting.

2340. θηρεύω *thēreúō*; fut. *thēreúsō*, from *thḗra* (2339), prey. To hunt wild beasts. To take or catch wild beasts in hunting. Used figuratively, meaning to catch or lay hold of (Luke 11:54).

Syn.: *harpázō* (726), to snatch or catch away; *agreúō* (64), to take by hunting, ensnare; *zōgréō* (2221), to take alive; *piázō* (4084), to capture, apprehend; *sullambánō* (4815), to seize.

2341. θηριομαχέω *thēriomachéō*; contracted *thēriomachṓ*, fut. *thēriomachḗsō*, from *thēríon* (2342), a wild beast, and *máchomai* (3164), to fight. To fight with wild beasts (1 Cor 15:32). Used figuratively as an allusion to Acts 19:29.

2342. θηρίον *thēríon*; gen. *thēríou*, neut. noun. A wild beast (Mark 1:13; Acts 10:12 [TR]; 11:6; Rev 6:8 [cf. 15:1, 2]; Sept.: Gen 1:24; Deut 7:22; 28:26; Jer 7:33). Denotes particularly a venomous creature and is applied to a viper (Acts 28:4, 5). May also refer to any kind of beast including the tame species (Heb 12:20), the same as *zṓon* (2226), animal. Paul applies to the Cretans the character of *kaká* (2556), evil, *thēría*, wild beasts (Titus 1:12). In the Sept., where sacrifices of beasts are mentioned, they are never mentioned as *thēría*, but as *zṓa*, because the wild and bestial element is brought out in *thēríon*. Throughout the NT, however, both *zṓon* and *thēríon* are rendered by the word "beast." Yet the animals represented by these two words are far removed from one another. The *zṓa*

or "living creatures" stand before the throne and in them dwells the fullness of all creaturely life as it gives praise and glory to God (Rev 4:6–9; 5:6; 6:1). They constitute a part of the heavenly symbolism. The *thēría*, the first and second beasts which rise up, one from the bottomless pit (Rev 11:7) and the other from the sea (Rev 13:1) with one making war upon the two witnesses and the other opening his mouth in blasphemies, form part of the hellish symbolism. Therefore, *thēríon* is predominately used of lower animal life and can never be the name applied to glorious creatures in the very court and presence of heaven. Consequently, in Scripture, *zṓa* should always be rendered as "living creatures" and *thēría* as "beasts."

Deriv.: *thēriomachéō* (2341), to fight with wild beasts.

2343. θησαυρίζω *thēsaurízō*; fut. *thēsaurísō*, from *thēsaurós* (2344), treasure. To lay, store or treasure up goods for future use (Matt 6:19, 20; Luke 12:21; 1 Cor 16:2; 2 Cor 12:14; Sept.: 2 Kgs 20:17; Amos 3:10; Zech 9:3). Metaphorically, to treasure up wrath or future punishment (Rom 2:5; James 5:3 [cf. James 5:5]; Sept.: Prov 1:18). By implication, to keep in store, reserve, in the pass. with a dat. noun (2 Pet 3:7).

Deriv.: *apothēsaurízō* (597), to treasure away or lay up in store.

Syn.: *títhēmi* (5087), to put, place, lay; *bállō* (906), to put; *sunathroízō* (4867), to gather together; *sullégō* (4816), to gather together or up, collect; *sunágō* (4863), to lead or collect together; *kerdaínō* (2770), to gain; *ploutízō* (4148), to make wealthy; *ploutéō* (4147), to become wealthy; *phulássō* (5442), to keep; *tēréō* (5083), to reserve.

Ant.: *ptōcheúō* (4433), to become poor.

2344. θησαυρός *thēsaurós*; gen. *thēsauroú*, masc. noun from *títhēmi* (5087), to put, set. Treasure, riches.

(I) Treasure, anything laid up in store, wealth (Matt 6:19, 21; 13:44; Luke 12:34; Heb 11:26; Sept.: 1 Kgs 14:26; Prov 15:16. See Gen 43:23; Prov 2:4). Metaphorically, of spiritual treasures pertaining to the mind or to eternal life (Matt 6:20; 19:21; Mark 10:21; Luke 12:33; 18:22; 2 Cor 4:7; Col 2:3).

(II) Treasury, place where treasures or stores are kept, storehouse (Matt 13:52). Metaphorically, the storehouse of the mind, where the thoughts, feelings or counsels are laid up (Matt 12:35; Luke 6:45; Sept.: 1 Kgs 7:37), hence a chest or box in which precious things are kept (Matt 2:11).

Deriv.: *thēsaurízō* (2343), to store treasure.

Syn.: *gáza* (1047), royal treasure; *gazophulákion* (1049), a special room in the women's court in the temple in which gold and silver bullion were kept; *korbanás* (2878), the temple treasury; *perisseía* (4050), abundance, surplus; *ploútos* (4149), wealth, abundance; *hadrótēs* (100), liberality, abundance; *tameíon* (5009), storage house or room.

Ant.: *ptōcheía* (4432), poverty, helplessness.

2345. θιγγάνω *thiggánō*; fut. *thíxomai*, 2d aor. *éthigon*, the lengthened form of *thígō* (n.f.), to touch. To touch so that one can exert a modifying influence on it (Col 2:21; Heb 11:28; 12:20; see Gen 32:25, 32; Ex 19:12).

Syn.: *háptomai* (680), to hurt; *psēlapháō* (5584), to touch lightly; *prospsaúō* (4379), to touch upon, touch slightly; *kolláō* (2853), to cleave, glue, join, stick; *proseggízō* (4331), to approach.

Ant.: *apochōrízō* (673), to separate, part asunder; *diachōrízō* (1316), to separate completely; *aphístēmi* (868), to stand aloof; *apōthéomai* (683), to push off.

2346. θλίβω *thlíbō*; fut. *thlípsō*. To press together, compress, afflict.

(I) To press as a person in a crowd (Mark 3:9); in the sense of to press together, compress, in the pass. part.

tethlimménos, pressed together, made narrow (Matt 7:14 concerning the narrow way).

(II) Figuratively, to oppress with evil, afflict, distress (2 Thess 1:6); pass. (2 Cor 1:6; 4:8; 7:5; 1 Thess 3:4; 2 Thess 1:7; 1 Tim 5:10; Heb 11:37; Sept.: Ex 22:20; Deut 28:53, 55; 1 Kgs 8:37; Ps 22:5).

Deriv.: *apothlíbō* (598), to crush; *thlípsis* (2347), tribulation, trouble; *sunthlíbō* (4918), to press together.

Syn.: *kakóō* (2559), to afflict; *kakouchéō* (2558), to torment; *talaipōréō* (5003), to make someone miserable; *sunéchō* (4912), to constrain; *baréō* (916), to weigh down, burden; *epibaréō* (1912), to overburden; *piézō* (4085), to press down together; *diṓkō* (1377), to persecute, pursue; *tarássō* (5015), to disturb; *diatarássō* (1298), to agitate greatly; *ektarássō* (1613), to throw into great trouble, agitate; *enochléō* (1776), to vex; *parenochléō* (3926), to annoy; *skúllō* (4660), to annoy; *anastatóō* (387), to upset; *thorubéō* (2350), to make an uproar; *throéō* (2360), to make an outcry; *adēmonéō* (85), to distress; *thorubázō* and *turbázō* (5182), to disturb, trouble.

Ant.: *anapsúchō* (404), to relieve; *anapaúō* (373), to give rest.

2347. θλίψις *thlípsis*; gen. *thlípseōs*, fem. noun from *thlíbō* (2346), to crush, press, compress, squeeze, which is from *thláō* (n.f.), to break. Tribulation, trouble, affliction.

(I) In a figurative manner, pressure from evils, affliction, distress (2 Cor 2:4; Phil 1:16); of a woman in travail (John 16:21). Often as a metonym for evils by which one is pressed, i.e., affliction, distress, calamity (Matt 13:21; Acts 7:10, 11; Rom 5:3; 2 Cor 1:4; Heb 10:33). In apposition in Mark 13:19. With the syn. *stenochōría* (4730), literally narrowness of room, anguish, distress (Rom 2:9); with *anágkē* (318), constraint, necessity (2 Cor 6:4; 1 Thess 3:7). See Sept.: 1 Sam 10:19; Ps 119:143; Isa 8:22.

(II) Related to *stenochōría* (4730), distress, narrowness, occurring only

four times with the connotation of narrowness, from *stenós* (4728), narrow of
room, confined space. In three of the four
occurrences in the NT, *stenochōría* is associated with *thlípsis* (Rom 2:9; 8:35; 2
Cor 6:4). *Thlípsis* refers more to being
crushed while *stenōchoría* refers more to
narrowness of room or discomfort. Tribulation may affect either body or mind or
both. Those who marry heedless of "the
present distress," which means the realization of the difficulties of married life,
"shall have tribulation in the flesh" (a.t.
[1 Cor 7:28]). Paul writes to the Corinthians, "Out of much tribulation and anguish of the heart" (a.t. [2 Cor 2:4]).
Paul's tribulation (expressed by the
pres. part. *thlibómenoi*, being afflicted)
in Macedonia consists of fears within,
while his flesh had no relief (2 Cor 7:5).
To Paul anxiety about the faithfulness of
his converts and the progress of the gospel is the source of tribulation (Phil 1:16;
1 Thess 3:7).

(III) Tribulation may be produced by
various causes. The famine caused the inhabitants of Egypt and Canaan great tribulation (Acts 7:11). The captured Joseph
suffered tribulation in Egypt (Acts 7:10).
At least part of the tribulation of the Corinthians was poverty (2 Cor 8:13). By
ministering to Paul's need, the Philippians had fellowship with his tribulation (Phil 4:14). The lot of the fatherless
and widows is tribulation (James 1:27).
Such tribulation may be relieved (1 Tim
5:10, where is found *thliboménois*, the pl.
dat. pres. part., to those afflicted). Sometimes tribulation is the punishment of
sin. To those who troubled the Thessalonian Christians, God would recompense
tribulation (2 Thess 1:6). There shall be
"tribulation and anguish upon every soul
of man that doeth evil" (Rom 2:9). God
will cast the woman, Jezebel, out of the
church of Thyatira and those who "commit adultery with her into great tribulation" (Rev 2:22).

(IV) Christians are not exempt from
tribulation, but rather they are especially subject to it. Their tribulation consists

largely of persecution and the opposition
their testimony meets in an unfriendly
world. "The persecution that arose about
Stephen" (Acts 11:19), was, of course,
thlípsis. Paul speaks of all the "persecutions and tribulations" which the Thessalonians endured (2 Thess 1:4). They
received the word "with much tribulation" (a.t.), and Paul entreats them not
to "be moved by these tribulations" (a.t.
[1 Thess 1:6; 3:3]). In 2 Cor 8:2, we are
told that the churches of Macedonia experienced much tribulation. Paul exhorts
other converts to be "patient in tribulation" (a.t.), and to bless them that persecute them (Rom 12:12, 14). In his work
of evangelization, the apostle met with
much tribulation. He told the elders of
Ephesus that "tribulations"awaited him
(Acts 20:23). He gloried in tribulations
(Rom 5:3), feeling that neither tribulation, nor anguish, nor persecution could
separate him from the love of Christ
(Rom 8:35). In this passage he is referring to the difficulties and the dangers
which he met with in his proclamation of
the gospel. Tribulations are mentioned in
the list he gives of his trials in 2 Cor 6:4,
5. Bad experiences and news caused him
tribulation (2 Cor 1:8; 2:4; 4:8).

(V) Tribulation, then, to the early
Christians meant not so much ill health,
poverty or loss of friends, but the sacrifices they had to make and the perils
they had to meet from their proclamation or profession of Christ. In Hebrews,
the writer says that after his readers were
converted, they "endured a great conflict of sufferings; partly, being made a
gazing stock, both by reproaches and afflictions; and partly, becoming partakers
with them that were so used" (a.t. [Heb
10:33 {cf. 11:37}]). Tribulation is the appointed destiny of Christians. Paul reminds the Thessalonians that both he and
they were appointed unto tribulation, and
that he had told them before that they
were to suffer tribulation (1 Thess 3:3f.).
John is also a partaker in the "tribulation
and kingdom and patience which are in
Jesus" (a.t. [Rev 1:9]); and he tells the

church of Smyrna that they shall suffer tribulation 10 days (Rev 2:10). "Through many tribulations we must enter into the kingdom of God" (a.t. [Acts 14:22]). The Christian is presented in the Scriptures as being joyful in tribulation since there is a deeper experience of the presence of Christ and of the kingdom of God when tribulations come. In the face of much affliction the churches of Macedonia had an abundance of joy (2 Cor 8:2). The Thessalonians received the word with much tribulation, with joy of the Holy Ghost (1 Thess 1:6).

(VI) In the case of the Christian, tribulation results in increased energy and blessedness of the spiritual life. "Our light tribulation, which is for the moment, worketh for us more and more exceedingly an eternal weight of glory" (a.t. [2 Cor 4:17]). "Tribulation worketh patience" (Rom 5:3 [cf. Rev 1:9]). God comforts the faithful in tribulation (2 Cor 1:4; 7:6), and the comfort thus given enables them to comfort others (2 Cor 1:4). His judgment will put an end to their tribulation, and they will be rewarded with rest (2 Thess 1:5ff. [cf. Rev 2:10]).

(VII) The word *thlípsis* is used also in a technical sense in the NT to refer to the period of time in the history of the world occasioned by God's direct interference. The word is found in the prophetic Olivet Discourse of our Lord in Matt 24:21, 29; Mark 13:19, 24. The events of this period are detailed in Rev 6—19; see particularly 7:14. The duration of this period of tribulation is symbolized by the expression "seven years," presented as one week (Dan 9:27). The whole period is called "the tribulation" (*hē thlípsis*). It is referred to by other expressions such as "the time of Jacob's trouble" (Jer 30:7) and "the day of the LORD" (Zech 14:1), although this expression does not limit itself to the time of the tribulation; similarly "the great and dreadful day of the LORD" (Mal 4:5); "that day" (Isa 11:10, 11); "the day" (Mal 4:1). This period stands in contrast to, and occurs at the end of, the present era of God's grace

(after the rapture of the Church according to some theologians). It is also called "the indignation" (Isa 26:20); "a time of trouble" (Dan 12:1). In Rev 6:17 it is called "the day, the great one, of God's wrath [*orgē* {3709}]" (a.t.). The word *orgē* is used as a syn. of *thlípsis*, although it, too, has its more general usage besides having a specialized technical meaning referring to the time of the expression of God's wrath during this period of tribulation. See Rev 14:10, 19 where *thumós* (2372), wrath, a syn. is used here as well as in 15:7; 16:1, 19. Another word that is used to indicate what God will do during this period is *krísis* (2920), judgment (see Rev 14:7; 16:7). As to the intensity of the suffering that shall be experienced during this period, see Rev 6:15–17. Paul in 1 Thess 1:10 calls this period "the wrath to come." Other expressions used in the Bible to indicate this seven-year period of the tribulation are, "the latter years" (Ezek 38:8); "the time of the end" (Dan 11:40); "the end of the world" which in Gr. is *suntéleia* (4930), consummation of the *aiṓn* (165), age, period of time (Matt 13:39); "the latter times" (2 Tim 4:1); and "the last days" (2 Tim 3:1).

The more severe portion of this period of tribulation is called "the great tribulation" of which, according to Matt 24:21, there can be only one in the history of the world. This period of the tribulation is described in Zeph 1:12–18, (beginning with the rapture of the Church [1 Thess 4:15–17] and ending with the millennial age). "The Day of the Lord" includes the millennial age and the judgment that follows as well as the bliss that God brings upon His own. This period, being part of the Day of the Lord, is described by the prophet as a day of wrath, a day of trouble, distress and death.

In Matt 24:4–14, Christ gives us a description of the initial events of this period. Then, in Matt 24:21, He summarizes this period telling us that it ought not to be mistaken by the general tribulation that Christians may have suffered on earth. Rather, it is a tribulation the kind

of which was never known from the beginning of the world and will never be repeated once it has been experienced.

According to Dan 9:24–27, the seven-
year period of tribulation is to be identified with the seventieth week of Daniel's
prophecy, which parallels the future of
Israel in the tribulation. There is the appearance of a prince who will have a definite relation to Israel (Dan 11:36–38; Rev
6:1, 2). Israel will receive another leader as her own and will make a firm covenant with him (John 5:43). He will then
break this covenant and turn upon Israel in great persecution (Rev 11:7; 12:6–
17; 13:7). Then there follows total war
against Israel and the supplanting of worship with abomination, the antichrist having rebuilt the temple for Israel (Matt
24:15, 21). This will then be brought to
a sudden end by the return of the Lord
Jesus in glory and the ushering in of the
kingdom (Matt 24:29, 30; 25:31).

During this period of the seven-years
of tribulation, or the seventieth week of
Daniel, the Church is in heaven (Rev 4:4;
13:6; 19:7, 8, 14). The mention of the
word *eklektoí* (1588), the elect, in Matt
24:22, 24, 31 should not be mistaken as
the saints of the church age but those who
will be saved during the tribulation as a
result of the testimony of the two Jewish
witnesses which the Lord is going to raise
during the tribulation (Rev 11:3). There
will also be the ministry of the 144,000
who will be saved during the tribulation
(Rev 7:4–8), and as a result there will be
great multitudes of Gentiles saved (Rev
7:9). These are the elect of that period
who will pay with their lives for embracing Christ (Rev 6:9–11). There will be
many, however, who will escape death.

It is a time of the judgment of human
conduct (Rom 2:6, 8, 9; Rev 20:11–15),
and it is going to be God's retribution
upon those who brought about suffering
in the lives of believers (2 Thess 1:6). It is
connected with the rapture of the Church
indicated in 2 Thess 1:7 by the word
ánesis (425), which is translated "rest"
but in reality is derived from *ánō* (507),

up or upward, and the verb *híemi* (n.f.),
to send, hasten. The relief which Christians are going to have is by being tak-
en or hastened upward which act of God
is expressed by the verb *harpázō* (726),
to catch up, rapture (1 Thess 4:17). The
thlípsis or tribulation is also called the hour
of temptation (*peirasmós* [3986]), which
in this instance is used as a metonym for
adversity or tribulation. Believers are not
going to be overtaken as if by the attack
of a thief (1 Thess 5:4). For believers, the
coming of the Lord is a blessed hope (Titus 2:13) and therefore they are not shak-
en in mind or troubled (2 Thess 2:2). The
parousía (3952), the coming of the Lord
to be present with the believers, is their
episunagōgḗ (1997), their assembling together unto Him (2 Thess 2:1) which is
consequent to the tribulation when the
Lord Jesus comes in power and glory
(Matt 24:21, 29, 30; 25:31).

Syn.: *kakopátheia* (2552), suffering affliction; *kákōsis* (2561), ill treatment; *páthēma* (3804), affliction, that
which one suffers; *sunochḗ* (4928), a
holding together, compressing, distress;
báros (922), heavy, burdensome weight;
phortíon (5413), a weight which one may
bear without it becoming a burden or
causing distress; *diōgmós* (1375), persecution; *tarachḗ* (5016), agitation, disturbance, trouble; *anágkē* (318), distress.

Ant.: *paráklēsis* (3874), consolation,
comfort; *paramuthía* (3889), consolation with the expression of tenderness;
paramúthion (3890) comfort; *parēgoría*
(3931), a soothing, solace; *anápausis*
(372), rest.

2348. θνήσκω *thnḗskō*; fut. *thanoúmai*,
2d aor. *éthanon*, perf. *téthnēka*, inf.
tethnánai. To die; naturally (Matt 2:20;
Mark 15:44; Luke 7:12; 8:49; John
11:21, 39, 41, 44; 12:1; 19:33; Acts
14:19; 25:19; Sept.: 2 Sam 12:18); spiritually (1 Tim 5:6).

Deriv.: *apothnḗskō* (599), to die off or
out, used of a separation of the soul from
the body and of the separation of man
from God; *hēmithanḗs* (2253), entirely

exhausted, half dead; *thánatos* (2288), death; *thnētós* (2349), mortal, mortality.

Syn.: *teleutáō* (5053), to end one's life; *koimáō* (2837), to sleep, metaphorically used with the meaning of to die; *apogenómenos* (581), to no longer be in one's present existence; *apóllumi* (622), to destroy, and in the mid. and pass., to die; *anairéō* (337), to take or lift up or away, hence to put to death; *apágō* (520), to lead away, put to death; *apokteínō* (615), to kill, slay; *thúō* (2380), to sacrifice.

Ant.: *záō* (2198), to live; *anazáō* (326), to live again; *bióō* (980), to spend one's life; *zōogonéō* (2225), to preserve alive; *zōopoiéō* (2227), to make alive, quicken; *hupárchō* (5225), to be, exist.

2349. θνητός *thnētós*; fem. *thnētḗ*, neut. *thnētón*, adj. from *thnḗskō* (2348), to die. Mortal, subject to death. In Class. Gr., contrasted to *athánatos* (n.f.), immortal, denoting that essential distinction between men and gods which lies at the foundation of all other differences. However, the subst. *athanasía* (110), immortality, occurs in the NT in 1 Cor 15:53, 54; 1 Tim 6:16 referring always to the immortality of the body.

Thnētós, according to the NT, is a condition of changeability or mortality of the body which is indirect punitive suffering as a result of man's sin. There is no indication whatsoever in the NT that this condition of the mortality of the body does not also belong to the Christian who receives Jesus Christ. Matt 8:17, speaking of Isa 53:5, refers to the fact that the Lord Jesus bore on His body both our spiritual iniquities and our physical sicknesses which resulted from our sin in Adam. When we exercise repentant faith, we are instantly redeemed from our spiritual iniquities and continue to be so until we meet the Lord face to face. Our redeemed soul remains in an unredeemed body. It is unredeemed because, as presently constituted, it is incapable of avoiding suffering, sickness and death. Whenever the body is referred to, even if it is a body that belongs to a Christian (Rom 6:12; 8:11; 1 Cor 15:53, 54; 2 Cor 4:11; 5:4; Sept.: Isa 51:12), it is referred to as a mortal body. Our present body, though now mortal, will be redeemed at our resurrection as indicated by Paul in Rom 8:23. This redemption of our mortal body was accomplished by Christ on the cross, but its effective realization takes place at our resurrection. An equivalent term of *thnētós* is *phthartós* (5349), corruptible (Rom 1:23; 1 Cor 15:53; 1 Pet 1:23).

2350. θορυβέω *thorubéō*; contracted *thorubṓ*, fut. *thorubḗsō*, from *thórubos* (2351), the noise of a tumult.

(I) To disturb, throw into a tumult, set in an uproar (Acts 17:5).

(II) In the mid. *thorubéomai*, to make a noise or disturbance, especially the noise made in lamenting the dead (Matt 9:23; Mark 5:39; Acts 20:10).

Syn.: *throéō* (2360), to make an outcry; *turbázō* (5182), to bustle about; *tarássō* (5015), to agitate; *diatarássō* (1298), to agitate greatly; *ektarássō* (1613), to throw into great agitation; *thlíbō* (2346), to afflict; *enochléō* (1776), to disturb; *parenochléō* (3926), to annoy; *skúllō* (4660), to vex, annoy; *anastatóō* (387), to trouble, agitate; *adēmonéō* (85), to trouble, distress; *diaponéō* (1278), to grieve, cause trouble; the expression *kópon paréchō* (*kópon* [2873], fatigue or toil; *paréchō* [3930], to give) to give trouble to.

Ant.: *hēsucházō* (2270), to be still, quiet; *katastéllō* (2687), to quiet, appease; *eirēneúō* (1514), to live in peace.

2351. θόρυβος *thórubos*; gen. *thorúbou*, masc. noun. Noise, uproar.

(I) Noise, uproar, clamor of a multitude (Matt 27:24; Acts 21:34; 24:18; Sept.: Jer 30:18); of loud lamentation, wailing (Mark 5:38).

(II) Popular commotion, tumult (Matt 26:5; Mark 14:2; Acts 20:1) similar to *stásis* (4714), uproar (Acts 19:40).

Deriv.: *thorubéō* (2350), to make noise.

Syn.: *akatastasía* (181), confusion, disorder; *rhoizēdón* (4500), similar to the noise produced by a rushing wind or a roaring flame; *thlípsis* (2347), affliction, tribulation, and its syn.

Ant.: *galḗnē* (1055), tranquility, calm; *sigḗ* (4602), silence; *hēsuchía* (2271), quietness.

2352. θραύω *thraúō*; fut. *thraúsō*, perf. pass. *téthrausmai*. To break in pieces, crush. In the NT, crushing the strength of anyone. In the perf. pass. part. *tethrausménos*, crushed, bruised, oppressed (Luke 4:18 quoted from Isa 61:1, 2; see Isa 58:6).

Syn.: *suntríbō* (4937), to break into pieces; *diarrḗssō* (1284), to tear asunder, break.

Ant.: *kolláō* (2853), to join fast together, glue; *proskolláō* (4347), to cleave unto.

2353. θρέμμα *thrémma*; gen. *thrémmatos*, neut. noun, from *tréphō* (5142), to nourish. Cattle which are kept and nourished by their owners, flocks, herds (John 4:12).

Syn.: *ktḗnos* (2934), cattle as property.

2354. θρηνέω *thrēnéō*; contracted *thrēnō̂*, fut. *thēnḗsō*, from *thrḗnos* (2355), lamentation. To lament in an audible manner, wail, mourn.

(I) Intrans. (Matt 11:17; Luke 7:32; John 16:20; Sept.: Jer 9:17; Joel 1:5, where we find *thrḗnos* [2355], wailing; Mic 2:4 [cf. 2 Sam 3:33]; Zeph 1:11).

(II) Trans., to bewail (Luke 23:27; Sept. Jer 28:8; Ezek 32:16).

Syn.: *lupéomai* (3076), to be grieved, sorrowful; *klaíō* (2799), to weep; *dakrúō* (1145), to shed tears; *stenázō* (4727), to groan; *diaponéō* (1278), to work out with labor, be grieved; *prosochthízo* (4360), to grieve, be displeased; *goggúzō* (1111), to murmur, grumble; *diagoggúzō* (1234), to complain indignantly; *embrimáomai* (1690), to show indignant displeasure; *anastenázō* (389), to sigh deeply;

thumomachéō (2371), to fight with great animosity, be very angry.

Ant.: *chaírō* (5463), to rejoice; *agalliáō* (21), to rejoice greatly, exult; *euphraínō* (2165), to cheer, make glad; *kaucháomai* (2744), to boast, glory, rejoice; *katakaucháomai* (2620), to boast or glory against; *euthuméō* (2114), to make cheerful, be of good cheer; *tharséō* (2293), to be of good courage; *doxázō* (1392), to extol, praise, glorify.

2355. θρῆνος *thrḗnos*; gen. *thrḗnou*, masc. noun from *thréō* (n.f.), to cry aloud. Loud weeping, wailing (Matt 2:18; Sept.: 2 Sam 1:17; Jer 9:17; Amos 8:10). *Thrḗnos* occurs together with *klauthmós* (2805), weeping, in Matt 2:18 (TR). This demonstration of grief may take the form of a poem such as the beautiful lamentation which David composed over Saul and Jonathan (2 Sam 1:17). The dirge over Tyre is called a *thrḗnos* (Sept.: Ezek 26:17 [cf. 2 Chr 35:25; Amos 8:10]). *Thrḗnos* is an outward demonstration of an inner grief or *lúpē* (3077), which is a stronger and more expressive outward demonstration of grief than that which is involved in *penthéō* (3996), to mourn, but not as strong as *kóptō* (2875), to strike one's breast in demonstration of grief.

Deriv.: *thrēnéō* (2354), to lament.

Syn.: *odurmós* (3602), mourning; *pénthos* (3997), mourning, sorrow; *klauthmós* (2805), wailing; *lúpē* (3077), grief, sorrow; *odúnē* (3601), pain, consuming grief, distress; *ōdín* (5604), birth pang, travail, pain; *pónos* (4192), pain; *basanismós* (929), torment; *básanos* (931), torment; *kólasis* (2851), punishment, torment.

Ant.: *chará* (5479), joy, delight; *agallíasis* (20), exultation; *euphrosúnē* (2167), gladness; *dóxa* (1391), glory; *kaúchēma* (2745), the ground of glorying or boasting; *kaúchēsis* (2746), the act of boasting or rejoicing.

2356. θρησκεία *thrēskeía*; gen. *thrēskeías*, fem. noun from *thrēskeúō* (n.f.), to worship God, which is from *thrḗskos*

(2357), religious, pious. Worshiping or worship. In Col 2:18, mentions the worship of angels. This is probably a gen. of association and alludes to the false, gnostic doctrine of celestial exaltation in which human worshipers were permitted to share in the worship activities of various grades of angelic beings. It also refers to the true worship of God (Acts 26:5; James 1:26, 27). *Thrēskeía* is contrasted with *theosébeia* (2317), external worship, meaning reverential worship, and *eusébeia* (2150), piety or godliness, and *eulábeia* (2124), devotion arising from godly fear or acceptance of what God directs or permits. *Thrēskeía* may thus refer only to ceremonial service or worship as Paul refers to the religion of the Jews (Acts 26:5). James refers to pure religion (James 1:26, 27), indicating there is also an impure religion which would be external worship but not the practice of that which God demands of man. Related words: *deisidaimonía* (1175), fear of the gods other than the true God, superstition; *sébasma* (4574), an object of worship.

Deriv.: *ethelothrēskeía* (1479), religion that is adopted in worship by the will of a person instead of being bidden by another source, what one chooses to worship on his own.

Ant.: *asébeia* (763), impiety, ungodliness; *anomía* (458), defiance of God's laws; *apistía* (570), unbelief; *blasphēmía* (988), vilification against God, blasphemy; *húbris* (5196), insolence, reproach.

2357. θρῆσκος *thrēskos*; gen. *thrēskou*, masc.-fem., neut. *thrēskon*, adj. Religious, devout; only in James 1:26, the diligent performer of divinely ascribed duties of outward service to God. The subst. *thrēskeía* (2356) (Acts 26:5; Col 2:18; James 1:26, 27) is predominantly the ceremonial service of religion. It is the external framework while as *eusébeia* (2150), godliness, is the inward piety of soul. According to James, true *thrēskeía* or religion is not merely cere-

monial formality, but acts of mercy, love, and holiness.

Syn.: *eusebḗs* (2152), pious, devout; *eulabḗs* (2126), reverent, one who accepts God's will; *theosebḗs* (2318), reverent toward God, pious, worshipful; *díkaios* (1342), just, righteous; *philótheos* (5377) and *theóphilos* (2321), a friend of God; *hierós* (2413), sacred.

Ant.: *ápistos* (571), an unbeliever; *asebḗs* (765), impious; *hubristḗs* (5197), despiteful, injurious; *blásphēmos* (989), impious, blasphemer; *hierósulos* (2417), temple despoiler, robber of churches.

2358. θριαμβεύω *thriambeúō*; fut. *thriambeúsō*, from *thríambos* (n.f.), a triumph. To triumph, hold triumphantly. To lead in triumph, triumph over, with the acc. (Col 2:15); in a causative sense, to cause to triumph (2 Cor 2:14).

Syn.: *nikáō* (3528), to have victory, prevail indicating victory in a lesser sense; *euodóō* (2137), to succeed, prosper; *hupernikáō* (5245), to be more than conqueror.

Ant.: *hēttáomai* (2274), to be defeated, overcome; *astochéō* (795), to miss the mark; *nauagéō* (3489), to be shipwrecked, stranded.

2359. θρίξ *thríx*; gen. *trichós*, pl. *tríches*, dat. pl. *thrixí*, fem. noun. A hair (also in the pl., the hairs of the head, but rendered in the sing. as "the hair") (Matt 5:36; Luke 21:18; Acts 27:34 [cf. 1 Sam 14:45; 1 Kgs 1:52]); in the pl. (Matt 10:30; Luke 7:38, 44; 12:7; John 11:2; 12:3; 1 Pet 3:3; Rev 1:14; 9:8; Sept.: Num 6:5, 18; Judg 16:22); the hair of animals (Matt 3:4; Mark 1:6; Sept.: Ex 25:4; 35:6, 26).

Deriv.: *tríchinos* (5155), made of hair.

Syn.: *kómē* (2864), human hair.

2360. θροέω *throéō*; contracted *throṓ*, fut. *throḗsō*, from *thróos* (n.f.), the cry or noise of a tumultuous multitude. To make a clamor, tumult. Used trans., meaning to disturb, trouble, terrify. In the pass. (Matt 24:6; Mark 13:7; 2 Thess 2:2).

Syn.: *thorubéō* (2350), to make an uproar; *turbázō* (5182), to disturb; *tarássō* (5015), to disturb, trouble; *diatarássō* (1298), to agitate greatly; *ektarássō* (1613), to throw into great trouble, agitate; *thlíbō* (2346) and *ochléō* (3791), to afflict, trouble; *parenochléō* (3926), to annoy concerning anything; *enochléō* (1776), to vex; *skúllō* (4660), to annoy, flay; *anastatóō* (387), to disturb, stir up.

Ant.: *sigáō* (4601), to silence or keep silent; *siōpáō* (4623), to be silent or still, keep silence; *hēsucházō* (2270), to be still, quiet; *phimóō* (5392), to muzzle; *katastéllō* (2687), to quiet, appease; *eirēneúō* (1514), to live in peace; *eirēnopoiéō* (1517), to make peace.

2361. θρόμβος *thrómbos*; gen. *thrómbou*, masc. noun. A large drop or clot, from which our word "thrombosis" is derived. Speaking of Christ's sweat being like clots of blood, i.e., thick (Luke 22:44).

2362. θρόνος *thrónos*; gen. *thrónou*, masc. noun from *thráō* (n.f.), to scat. A seat, usually high and having a footstool, a throne as the emblem of royal authority.

(I) A seat attributed to kings (Luke 1:52; Acts 2:30; Sept.: 1 Kgs 10:18; Job 36:7); also to God as the Sovereign of the universe (Matt 5:34; 23:22; Acts 7:49 [cf. Isa 66:1]; Heb 4:16; 12:2; Sept.: Ps 47:8; 103:19); to Jesus as the Messiah (Matt 19:28; 25:31; Rev 3:21; 20:11); to the apostles in the kingdom of God (Matt 19:28; Luke 22:30; Rev 20:4); also symbolically to the elders around God's throne (Rev 4:4; 11:16); to Satan (Rev 2:13; 13:2); to the beast (Rev 16:10).

(II) Metaphorically used for dominion (Luke 1:32; Heb 1:8 from Ps 45:6; Sept.: 2 Sam 3:10; 7:13, 16); to a potentate or higher power (Col 1:16, where *thrónoi*, thrones, generally refers to earthly or celestial potentates, archangels).

Syn.: *kathédra* (2515), a seat; *prōtokathedría* (4410), the first or chief seat; *bêma* (968), a judgment seat or a seat

from which someone makes a pronouncement; *exousía* (1849), authority; *krátos* (2904), dominion; *kuriótēs* (2963), mastery; *archế* (746), principality; *kubérnēsis* (2941), government.

2363. Θυάτειρα *Thuáteira*; gen. *Theiateírōn*, pl. proper noun. Thyatira, a city of Asia Minor on the northern border of Lydia near the road from Pergamos to Sardis and approximately twenty-seven miles from the latter city. It is known today as Ashisar, meaning white castle. It lies near the river Lycus and was a Macedonian colony bearing successively the names of Pelopia, Semiramis, and Euhippia. Dyeing was an important branch of its business from Homer's time, and the first NT mention of Thyatira (Acts 16:14) connects it with the purple seller named Lydia. It is probable that Lydia came to her own city and established a Christian witness there after being converted to Christ through Paul's ministry at Philippi (Acts 16:14, 15). The scarlet cloth dyed there had a reputation for being unsurpassed for brilliancy and permanence of color. Thyatira was the seat of one of the seven churches of Asia Minor (Rev 2:18–29).

2364. θυγάτηρ *thugátēr*; gen. *thugatéros* or *thugatrós*, fem. noun. A daughter.

(I) Generally and particularly (Matt 9:18; 10:35, 37; 14:6; 15:22, 28; Mark 5:35; 6:22; 7:26, 29, 30; Luke 2:36; 8:42, 49; 12:53; Acts 2:17; 7:21; 21:9; Heb 11:24; Sept.: Gen 5:4, 7; Ex 2:5). Metaphorically as expressing a relation of kindness and tenderness (2 Cor 6:18 [cf. Jer 31:1, 9]); used in the voc. in a direct address (Matt 9:22; Mark 5:34; Luke 8:48; Sept.: Ruth 2:8; 3:10, 11).

(II) A female descendant (Luke 1:5; 13:16; Sept.: Gen 36:2; Ex 2:1).

(III) Put before names of places as the daughters of Jerusalem (Luke 23:28; Sept.: Isa 3:16, 17; 4:4) meaning the female inhabitants born and living there; also in the sing. collectively, daughter of Sion or Zion (Matt 21:5 quoted from

Zech 9:9), meaning the inhabitants of Zion or Jerusalem.

Deriv.: *thugátrion* (2365), a little daughter.

Syn.: *korásion* (2877), a little girl; *parthénos* (3933), a virgin, maiden; *númphē* (3565), a bride; *téknon* (5043), a child which can also mean a son or a daughter.

Ant.: *huiós* (5207), son.

2365. θυγάτριον *thugátrion*; gen. *thugatríou*, neut. noun, a diminutive of *thugátēr* (2364), daughter. A little daughter, female child (Mark 5:23; 7:25).

Syn.: *korásion* (2877), a little girl; *tekníon* (5040), a little child, male or female.

2366. θύελλα *thúella*; gen. *thuéllēs*, fem. noun from *thúō* (n.f.), to rush on or along, speaking of wind or a storm. Tempest (Heb 12:18; Sept.: Deut 4:11; 5:22). Also from *thúō* (n.f.): *thumós* (2372), anger, wrath.

Syn.: *pnoḗ* (4157), wind; *seismós* (4578), earthquake; *cheimṓn* (5494), winter, tempest; *laílaps* (2978), storm, tempest; *chálaza* (5464), hail.

Ant.: *galḗnē* (1055), calm; *eudía* (2105), good weather.

2367. θύϊνος *thúinos*; fem. *thuínē*, neut. *thúinon*, adj. Thyine, thyine wood (Rev 18:12). The *thuía* or *thúia* was an African evergreen tree with aromatic wood from which statues and costly vessels were made. Derived from *thúō* (2380), to make aromatic, used as incense on account of the sweet smell of its burning wood.

2368. θυμίαμα *thumíama*; gen. *thumíamatos*, neut. noun from *thumiáō* (2370), to offer incense. Incense used in religious worship (Rev 5:8; 8:3, 4; 18:13; Sept.: Ex 30:7, 8). Metonymically (Luke 1:10, 11, the "time" or hour and the "altar of incense," meaning for burning incense. See Sept.: Ex 30:1, 27).

2369. θυμιαστήριον *thumiastḗrion*; gen. *thumiastēríou*, neut. noun from *thumiáō* (2370), to offer incense. A censer for burning incense (Heb 9:4; Sept.: 2 Chr 26:19) or altar of incense.

2370. θυμιάω *thumiáō*; fut. *thumiasō*, from *thúō* (2380), to sacrifice. To burn incense (Luke 1:9; Sept.: Ex 30:7, 8).

Deriv.: *thumíama* (2368), incense; *thumiastḗrion* (2369), altar of incense, censer.

2371. θυμομαχέω *thumomachéō*; contracted *thumomachṓ*, fut. *thumomachḗsō*, from *thumós* (2372), wrath, indignation, and *máchomai* (3164), to fight. To fight fiercely, to be greatly offended, enraged against (Acts 12:20).

Syn.: *aganaktéō* (23), to be irritated, indignant; *prosochthízō* (4360), to be angry or displeased with; *poleméō* (4170), to battle, make war; *agōnízomai* (75), to struggle; *antagōnízomai* (464), to strive against, antagonize; *pukteúō* (4438), to box, contend, fight.

Ant.: *boēthéō* (997), to help; *ōpheléō* (5623), to benefit; *eparkéō* (1884), to avail for, relieve; *antilambánomai* (482), to help support.

2372. θυμός *thumós*; gen. *thumoú*, masc. noun from *thúō* (n.f.), to move impetuously, particularly as the air or wind, a violent motion or passion of the mind. Anger, wrath, indignation (Heb 11:27; Rev 12:12; Sept.: Gen 49:6, 7; 2 Sam 11:20; 2 Chr 34:21.). Also from *thúō* (n.f.): *thúella* (2366), tempest.

(I) Mind or soul as the principle of life, the will, desire, emotion, passion, indignation, anger, wrath. As ascribed to man (Luke 4:28; Acts 19:28); to the devil (Rev 12:12); to God and including the idea of punishment or punitive judgment (Rev 15:1). In Rom 2:8 followed by *orgḗ* (3709), wrath, meaning the direct judgment (cf. Sept.: Gen 27:45; Ezek 5:13). In the OT, the prophets presented Jehovah as giving to the nations, in His wrath, an intoxicating cup so that they reeled and staggered to destruction; hence also in the NT "the wine of the wrath of God" as in Rev 14:10 (cf. 14:8; 16:19; 18:3). With *oínos* (3631), wine, implied (Rev 15:7; 16:1). See Job 21:20; Ezek 23:31–33. In Rev 14:19 and 19:15, "the great winepress of the wrath of God," in allusion to Isa 63:3 (cf. Joel 3:18).

(II) Found together with *orgḗ* (3709), wrath, anger (Rom 2:8; Eph 4:31; Col 3:8; Rev 19:15, fierceness; Sept.: Deut 6:15) which indicates a more enduring state of mind, whereas the more passionate and, at the same time, more temporary character of anger and wrath is *thumós*. *Thumós* is an outburst of *orgḗ*, anger.

(III) In the pl., bursts of anger (2 Cor 12:20; Gal 5:20).

Deriv.: *enthuméomai* (1760), to think upon; *epithuméō* (1937), to desire; *eúthumos* (2115), cheerful; *thumomachéō* (2371), to fight fiercely; *thumóō* (2373), to provoke to anger; *próthumos* (4289), predisposed, ready, willing; *prothúmōs* (4290), readily, willingly.

Syn.: *parorgismós* (3950), provocation; *aganáktēsis* (24), irritation, indignation; *zḗlos* (2205), zeal, fierceness; *cholḗ* (5521), bile, gall; *paroxusmós* (3948), provocation.

Ant.: *eirḗnē* (1515), peace; *hēsuchía* (2271), quietness; *galḗnē* (1055), calm.

2373. θυμόω *thumóō*; contracted *thumṓ*, fut. *thumṓsō*, from *thumós* (2372), wrath, indignation. To provoke to anger. In the pass., to be angry (Matt 2:16; Sept.: Judg 14:19; 1 Sam 20:30; Esth 3:5; 5:9).

Syn.: *orgízomai* (3710), to be angry; *parorgízomai* (3949), to be enraged; *choláomai* (5520), to be irritable, choleric, bitter; *thumomachéō* (2371), to fight with great animosity; *aganaktéō* (23), to be indignant; *erethízō* (2042), to irritate.

Ant.: *eupsuchéō* (2174), to be of good comfort or in good spirits; *chalinagōgéō* (5468), to curb, bridle; *paramuthéomai* (3888), to encourage; *hēsucházō* (2270), to be quiet, rest; *eirēneúō* (1514), to pacify; *anapaúō* (373), to cause to rest.

2374. θύρα *thúra*; gen. *thúras*, fem. noun. A door.

(I) Particularly and generally (Matt 6:6; 25:10; Mark 1:33; Luke 11:7; 13:25; John 18:16; 20:19, 26; Acts 5:9). A small door or wicket within a larger one (Acts 12:13); door of a prison (Acts 5:19, 23; 12:6; 16:26, 27); of the temple (Acts 3:2; 21:30); of a fold or an enclosure (Mark 11:4; John 10:1, 2). Symbolically (Rev 3:20; 4:1; Sept.: Gen 18:1, 2, 10; 19:6, 9, 10). The expression *tá prós tḗn thúran* (*tá* [the pl. of the def. art., neut. *tó*], implying the things; *prós* [4314], toward; *tḗn* [fem. acc. of the sing. def. art.]; *thúran*, vestibule, porch) the same as *próthuron*, meaning that which lies before the door (Mark 2:2). The expression *epí thúrais* (*epí* [1909], upon; *thúrais*, doors), to be "at the doors" (Matt 24:33; Mark 13:29) means near at hand; James 5:9, *pró tṓn thurṓn* (*pró* [4253], before) before the door.

(II) By implication it means the entrance of a cave or sepulcher, the mouth (Matt 27:60; 28:2; Mark 15:46; 16:3). Metaphorically meaning access or opportunity as in the expression "to set open a door" (*anoígō* [455], to open; *tḗn thúran*, to give access or present opportunity as in Acts 14:27; 1 Cor 16:9; 2 Cor 2:12; Col 4:3). In Rev 3:8 "an open door" means free access for oneself. In John 10:7, "I am the door of the sheep" means, I am the way of access or entrance.

Deriv.: *thureós* (2375), a door; *thurís* (2376), a window; *thurōrós* (2377), a person who attends the door, a gatekeeper or warden.

Syn.: *púlē* (4439), a larger gate such as leads into the city; *pulṓn* (4440), a porch or vestibule.

Ant.: *teíchos* (5038), the wall of a city; *toíchos* (5109), wall.

2375. θυρεός *thureós*; gen. *thureoú*, masc. noun from *thúra* (2374), door, gate. A door referring to a stone for closing the entrance of a cave. In later Gr., it came to refer to a shield in the form of a large, oblong-shaped door that acted as a cover for the entrance of a cave. In Eph 6:16, used symbolically of shielding like a door. See Sept.: 2 Sam 1:21; 2 Chr 9:15.

2376. θυρίς thurís; gen. *thurídos*, fem. noun, a diminutive of *thúra* (2374), door, gate. A little door, aperture. In the NT, it means a window (Acts 20:9; 2 Cor 11:33; Sept.: Josh 2:15, 18, 19; Judg 5:28).

2377. θυρωρός thurōrós; gen. *thurōroú*, masc.-fem., neut. *thurōrón*, noun from *thúra* (2374), a door and *oúros* (n.f.), a keeper. A doorkeeper, porter, whether male or female (Mark 13:34; John 18:16, 17). Spoken of a shepherd keeping watch at the door of a fold (John 10:3; Sept.: 2 Sam 4:6; 2 Kgs 7:11).

    Syn.: *phúlax* (5441), guard; *koustōdía* (2892), guard, watch; *spekoulátōr* (4688), a lookout officer, guard, member of the bodyguard.

2378. θυσία thusía; gen. *thusías*, fem. noun from *thúō* (2380), to sacrifice. The act of sacrificing or offering.

    (I) The act and rite of sacrificing (Matt 9:13; 12:7; Heb 9:26; 10:5, 8 quoted from Ps 40:6, 7; 11:4); of an expiatory sacrifice for sin (Eph 5:2; Heb 5:1; 7:27; 8:3; 9:9, 23; 10:1, 11, 12, 26).

    (II) By metonymy, the thing sacrificed, victim, the flesh of victims, part of which was burned on the altar and part given to the priests (Mark 9:49 [cf. Lev 2:13]; Mark 12:33; Luke 13:1; Acts 7:41, 42; see Lev chaps. 2; 3). In 1 Cor 10:18, "those who eat of the victims (or animals) sacrificed" (a.t.), as was done by the priests and persons offering the sacrifices (Sept.: Ex 34:15; Deut 12:27 [cf. Lev 8:31; Deut 12:6, 7]). Of birds as a sin offering (Luke 2:24 [cf. Lev 12:6]). Metaphorically (1 Pet 2:5, "spiritual sacrifices" [cf. Ps 51:19; Rom 12:1]).

    (III) Metaphorically, of service, obedience, praise offered to God, an offering, oblation (Phil 2:17; 4:18). In Heb 13:15, 16, "sacrifice of praise" means

offering of praise. See Sept.: Ps 107:22; 116:17 (cf. Ps 50:23).

    (IV) The Levitical system of sacrifices was the typological analogy of redemption by Christ. In the Jewish sacrifices we see an illustration for apostolic forms of teaching regarding redemption. We see the Jewish sacrificial system fulfilled in Jesus Christ's being sacrificed as the Lamb of God for the purpose of taking away the sin of the world (John 1:29). The sin offering became the ultimate sacrifice. Eventually this type of sacrifice appears to have overshadowed the other great type represented by the peace offerings which assumed that the covenant relationship with Jehovah was undisturbed. The expiatory type constituted the daily sacrifice—the continual burnt offering—up to apostolic times. Although most perfectly embodying the sacrificial idea through its vicarious character, it was not connected with any particular transgression but was maintained as the appropriate means of a sinful people's approach to a holy God. Essential features were the shedding and sprinkling of blood and the offering up of the entire sacrifice to God and His ministers. It was also accompanied by the laying on of hands. In this type of sacrifice, the utmost importance was attached to the disposition of the victim's blood: the blood belonged to God by right; the life was in it (cf. Lev 17:11); and safety for the individual and the nation lay in such sacrifices of blood.

    In view of apostolic concepts, it is of great importance to note that such sacrifices—the highest in value of the Levitical system—availed only for sins of ignorance, unwitting transgression of holy things, and the removal of physical uncleanness which implied moral as well as ceremonial disability in drawing near to God.

    For willful sins, however, no reconciling sacrifice was provided for Israel (Num 15:30). The penalty of such sins was death in the form of separation of the individual from Israel. Nevertheless, willful sins were not beyond the reach of forgiveness. That such sinners might approach God through confession and true penitence and meet with His mercy through His grace apart from sacrifice was the evangelical proclamation of the prophets. It was held by later Jewish interpreters that the scapegoat, on the great day of atonement, expiated the sins of all Israelites who had not deliberately put themselves outside its effects by forsaking the religion of their people. This expiation included sins for which the penalty was a cutting off from God's people or death.

(V) A number of controversies arose in the apostolic church during the transition from the sacrificial system to Christianity. The Lord Jesus recognized the authority of the sacrificial law as practiced in His time by observing it, keeping the Passover and other feasts, worshiping in the temple where sacrifice was the central act, and by commending its observance to others, e.g., the law of the leper in the day of his cleansing (Matt 8:4 [cf. Mark 1:44]). The Lord constantly favored the prophetic moral view of sacrifice rather than the priestly Levitical view. He quoted Hos 6:6, "I desired mercy, and not sacrifice" in Matt 9:13 and 12:7, and commended the judgment that love is more than all burnt offerings (Mark 12:33). He declared that sacrifice is futile in dealing with unrepented sin (Matt 5:23). He referred to His own death as sacrificial, comparing it especially with the covenant sacrifice with which the Mosaic system was instituted, "My blood of the new covenant, which is shed for many unto remission of sins" (a.t. [Matt 26:28; Luke 22:20 {cf. 1 Cor 11:25}]). In speaking of the new covenant (kainé [2537], qualitatively new), the inference is that the old covenant was abrogated, and with it the sacrifices that it had initiated and given historical continuity in Israel.

(VI) We cannot easily determine how long it was before the apostolic church appreciated all the implications of the new covenant with a complete cessation of the sacrifices of the old. The full inferences of the abrogation of the ancient sacrifices are first drawn by the writer of the Epistle to the Hebrews. The records of the apostolic preaching in Acts reveal the primary fact that "Christ died for our sins according to the Scriptures" (1 Cor 15:3). The death of Christ was regarded at the inception of the apostolic church as expiatory. It was looked upon as a sacrifice and spoken of in sacrificial terms.

(VII) No direct mention of the sacrifice of Christ is made by James or Jude in view of the fact that such a sacrifice was not within the subject of their treatises.

In the epistles of Peter, the sacrificial references are clear and interesting: "sprinkling of the blood of Jesus Christ" (1 Pet 1:2 [cf. Ex 24:8]); "Ye were not redeemed . . . , but with the precious blood of Christ, as of a lamb without blemish and without spot" (1 Pet 1:18, 19 [cf. Isa 53:7ff. with its clear echo in 1 Pet 2:21–25 where the sacrificial idea of vicarious suffering is too obvious to need comment]).

(VIII) In the Pauline references, the contrast between the Jewish and the Christian aspects of the sacrifice is more pronounced. Paul was intimately acquainted with the minute details of the Levitical system. He even definitely associated himself with its observance (Acts 21:26; 24:11, 17f.) despite the difficulty we may have in reconciling his action in the temple to the contrary precept he expressed so clearly (cf. Gal 4:9). Paul speaks definitely of the death as a sacrifice in Eph 5:2, "He gave himself up for us, an offering and a sacrifice to God for an odor of a sweet smell" (a.t.). In 1 Cor 5:7, he says, "Our passover also has been sacrificed, even Christ" (a.t.). The death of Christ as which brought about the reconciliation of man to God (man being an enemy of God due to Adam's fall), is the same as the blood (haíma [129], blood) of Christ which satisfied the justice of God. Paul presents the blood of Christ as the basis for the benefits conferred upon the believer (Rom 3:25; 5:9; 1 Cor 10:16; Eph 2:13). By the phrase "blood of Christ,"

Paul meant Christ's sacrificial death (cf. Rom 8:32; Gal 2:20; Eph 1:7; Col 1:20).

(IX) In the Epistle to the Hebrews we have:

(A) The doctrine of salvation wholly in terms of sacrifice. In this epistle, we find the running comparison between the sacrifices of the Levitical ritual and the perfect offering presented by Christ in the sacrifice of Himself. The sacrificial institutions associated with the old covenant are set forth as types and shadows of the heavenly and eternal reality in which the new covenant is established in the blood of Christ. The key word of the epistle and the comparison it elaborates is "better." The Son whose humanity is perfect, the Mediator of the new and better covenant, is the true High Priest (cf. 8:6–13; 9:15ff.). His constitutive function is to offer sacrifice (8:3). Christ offers Himself, the nature and effect of this perfect sacrifice being contrasted with the sacrifices of the law (8:10–13). The culmination of the contrast is the parallel between the action of the high priest in the Holy of Holies on the Day of Atonement (Ex 24:4–8) and Christ entering the heavenly places "through [the occasion of] his own blood [sacrificial death]" (a.t. [Heb 9:12ff.]). The superiority of Christ's sacrifice is impressively manifested everywhere. It was also an offering in close dependence upon the love of God, for by the grace of God, Christ tasted death for every man (2:9). It was never spoken of as "reconciling" God to man. What emerges from a careful study of the Epistle to the Hebrews is that the Levitical sacrifices could not permanently take away sin; they were rather temporary in their expiatory power (10:3). Christ's sacrifice is final and complete because it is related to the heavenly and eternal realm of reality (8:1f.; 9:1, 24; 10:1). Christ has entered into heaven itself with His sacrifice (9:24) and obtained eternal salvation for us (7:27; 9:12, 15; 10:10), having "through the eternal Spirit offered himself without blemish unto God" (a.t. [9:14]). It was an offering of a pure and spotless life on our behalf and as our representative. The solidarity of Christ with mankind is confidently stated: "Both he that sanctifieth and they who are sanctified are all of one: for which cause he is not ashamed to call them brethren" (2:11). The Levitical sacrifices were perpetually repeated because they had no permanent efficacy (9:6; 10:3f.). Christ's sacrifice is made once for all, perfecting forever them that are sanctified (7:27; 9:12, 25f., 28; 10:12, 14). Christ's sacrifice purged His people's conscience that they might serve the living God (9:14; 10:22), thus dealing with sin efficaciously and in its deepest seat instead of with its accidental expressions as in the limited efficacy of ceremonial sacrifices (9:9; 10:3). The sacrifices of the Law opened no way of spiritual access to the holy presence of God (9:8); by the blood of Jesus a new and living way was dedicated by which men could draw near to Him with spiritual confidence (10:19f.). The basic purpose of the writer of the Epistle to the Hebrews is to mark the radical difference between the Christian and the Levitical concepts of sacrifice.

(B) The importance of the blood is stressed in the sacrifice of Christ. In the Levitical system the use of the blood was of supreme importance. Nothing was cleansed without its use (9:21f.). The vital moment culminating the sacrifices of the Day of Atonement was when the high priest entered the Holy of Holies bearing the sacrificial blood (9:7). To explain that Christ fulfilled the great atoning work signified by this procedure, Hebrews describes Christ's work in the language of the type saying that Christ's sacrificial act was accomplished when He entered into the heavenly place "through his own blood" (a.t. [9:12ff.]) "to make propitiation for the sins of the people" (a.t. [2:17]). Such statements are not intended to teach that Jesus reenacted or copied this procedure in a one-for-one corresponding manner. The altar on which Jesus offered Himself was the cross of Calvary and not a sanctuary in heaven. However, what He accomplished was equivalent to that which was typified in the OT ritual sacrifice made on the Day of Atonement. Therefore the author portrays Christ's work in the language of OT type. Once for all He offered a sacrifice for sins "when he offered up himself" (7:27 [cf. 9:26, 28]). It is clear that the author makes distinct use of the concept of substitution. His blood refers to His death which in turn denotes the laying down of His life. It is the life yielded in death which is the essence of all true sacrifice. Even in the Levitical system the blood constitutes the sacrifice, because the life is in the blood (Lev 17:11). Christ's offering of Himself includes more than His dying; it is the willing offering of His life and the perfect ceaseless filial obedience to the will of God (see Heb 10:8ff.). This offering with which God was well pleased brought humanity into a new relationship with God. It was a positive, ethical, and religious evaluation of Christ's sacrifice that went beyond its value as merely legal substitution.

(C) The doctrine of the new covenant. The first covenant was not dedicated without blood (Heb 9:18 [cf. Ex 24:6, 8]). Sacrificial blood was, for Israel, essentially "the blood of the covenant" (a.t. [Heb 9:20 {cf. Matt 26:28}]). The sacrifices of the Mosaic covenant were the sign of the establishment of the Law; the new covenant in Christ's blood was the sign of its fulfillment, therefore, "unto the remission of sins" (a.t. [Matt 26:28; John 6:53–7:1; 1 John 1:7]). Jeremiah's prophecy of the new covenant (Jer 31:31) is the principal link between the sacrifice of the Law and Christ's fulfillment which consequently abolished it. This is a covenant under which God lays His laws upon the hearts of men and inscribes them upon their minds, no longer remembering their sins and iniquities (Heb 10:16ff.; 8:8ff.). "Now where remission of these is, there is no more offering for sin" (10:18). A real remission makes all other sacrifices useless. The sacrifice of Christ, "the mediator of a new covenant" (a.t. [9:15]), which established the new covenant is the "one offering by which he hath perfected forever them that are sanctified" (a.t. [10:14]). The prophetic idea of the value of the sacrificial sufferings of the Righteous Servant is thus restored in close association with the sacrificial ideas which were the current trend of Jewish thought. Henceforth there was no longer room for the sacrifices of the Law (10:18). The only sacrifice that retained its permanence for the future was a "sacrifice of praise to God continually, i.e., the fruit of lips which make confession to his name" (a.t. [13:15]). See discussion under diathḗkē (1242), covenant or testament.

In John's gospel, there are definite references to the sacrifice of Christ as the Lamb of God which takes away the sin of the world (John 1:29). See in Rev "stood a Lamb as it had been slain" (Rev 5:6, 12); those who have "washed their robes, and made them white in the blood of the Lamb" (Rev 7:14); "They overcame him by the blood of the Lamb" (Rev 12:11); salvation is ascribed unto "our God which sitteth upon the throne, and unto the Lamb" (Rev 7:10).

Syn.: sphagḗ (4967), slaughter.

Ant.: lútrōsis (3085), ransoming, redemption; apolútrōsis (629), deliverance from, redemption; lúsis (3080), a loosening, letting go free.

2379. θυσιαστήριον thusiastḗrion; gen. thusiastēríou, neut. noun from thusiázō (n.f.), to sacrifice. An altar of the true God (Matt 5:23, 24; 23:18–20; Rom 11:3; Heb 7:13; James 2:21; Sept.: Gen 8:20; 12:7). Used specifically of the altar for burnt offerings in the temple (Matt 23:35; Luke 11:51; 1 Cor 9:13; 10:18; Heb 13:10). Symbolically, in heaven (Rev 6:9; 8:3, 5; 9:13; 11:1; 14:18; 16:7, a voice from the altar; Sept.: Ex 30:27; 35:17); of the altar of incense in the temple, made of gold (Luke 1:11 [cf. 1 Chr 28:18]).

Syn.: *bōmós* (1041), an idol altar.

2380. θύω *thúō*; fut. *thúsō*, aor. pass. *etúthēn*, perf. pass. *téthumai*. To sacrifice, to kill and offer in sacrifice (Acts 14:13, 18; 1 Cor 10:20; Sept.: Gen 46:1; Ex 3:18; 8:26). Generally (John 10:10; Sept.: Deut 12:15; 1 Sam 28:24; 1 Kgs 19:21). "To sacrifice the passover" means to kill the paschal lamb as a species of sacrifice (Mark 14:12; Luke 22:7; 1 Cor 5:7; Sept.: Ex 12:21; Deut 16:2, 4–6). Of sacrifices connected with feasting (Sept.: Gen 31:54 [cf. 1 Sam 9:12, 13]). Generally, to offer bloody and nonbloody offerings, and only in a derived sense, to slay (Matt 22:4; Luke 15:23, 27, 30; Acts 10:13; 11:7).

Deriv.: *eidōlóthuton* (1494), sacrifice; *thusía* (2378), sacrifice.

Syn.: *apokteínō* (615), to kill; *anairéō* (337), to kill, used physically only; *phoneúō* (5407), to murder; *thanatóō* (2289), to put to death; *diacheirízō* (1315), literally to lay hands on for the purpose of killing, to slay; *spházō* (4969), to slay, slaughter.

Ant.: *anazáō* (326), to live again; *anathállō* (330), to flourish again, revive; *zōopoiéō* (2227), to make alive; *zōogonéō* (2225), to preserve alive.

2381. Θωμᾶς *Thōmás*; gen. *Thōmá*, masc. proper noun. Thomas, meaning twin. One of the Twelve Apostles who was also called *Didymus* (1324), twin. We know little of his history. He seems to have been of a cautious, skeptical, thoughtful, and gloomy temperament, yet holding tenaciously to that which he believed (Matt 10:3; Mark 3:18; Luke 6:15; John 11:16; 14:5; 20:24–29; 21:2; Acts 1:13).

2382. θώραξ *thốrax*; gen. *thốrakos*, masc. noun. A breastplate or armor covering the body from the neck to the thighs. It consisted of two parts, one covering the front and the other the back (Rev 9:9, 17; Sept.: 1 Sam 17:5; Neh 4:16; Isa 59:17). Used metaphorically (Eph 6:14; 1 Thess 5:8). In later Gr. writers, the word also means breast or chest.

Syn.: *stếthos* (4738), chest.

I

2383. Ἰάειρος *Iáeiros*; gen. *Iaeírou*, masc. proper noun. Jairus, meaning whom Jehovah enlightens. An officer of the Jewish community who appealed to Christ to restore to life his daughter who had been at the point of death when he left home. He demonstrated strong faith. Christ and His disciples went to the ruler's house and his daughter was restored (Mark 5:22; Luke 8:41).

2384. Ἰακώβ *Iakṓb*; masc. proper noun, transliterated from the Hebr. *Ya‘aqōv* (3290, OT), heel-catcher, supplanter. Jacob (Gen 25:26; 27:36).
 (I) The patriarch of the Jewish nation (Matt 1:2; Luke 13:28; Acts 7:8, 12, 14, 15, 32, 46; Rom 9:13).
 (II) The posterity of Jacob, the Jewish people (Rom 11:26).
 (III) The father of Joseph, the husband of Mary (Matt 1:15, 16).

2385. Ἰάκωβος *Iákōbos* or *Iakṓb*; gen. *Iakṓbou*, masc. proper noun. James
 (I) James the father of Judas (Luke 6:16), i.e., Judas "not Iscariot" (John 14:22), the Thaddaeus of Matt 10:3; Mark 3:18. The KJV translation "And Judas the brother of James" in Gr. is *Ioúdan Iakṓbou*, which the NKJV, NASB, and NIV correctly translate "son" instead of "brother." The relationship word "son" or "brother" is supplied by the translators. The word "son" is preferred because Luke inserts *adelphós* (80), brother, when he means brother (Luke 3:1; 6:14; Acts 12:2). Thus James is the father of Judas, not his brother. Nothing more is known of this James.
 (II) James the brother of John and one of the Twelve Apostles (Matt 10:2; Mark 3:17; Luke 6:14; Acts 1:13). He was the elder son of Zebedee, a well-to-do Galilean fisherman, most probably a native of Capernaum. The two sons of Zebedee were partners with Peter in the fishing industry from which they were called to follow Christ (Matt 4:21, 22; Mark 1:19, 20; Luke 5:10). The usual order is "James and John" and Luke sometimes inverts it (Luke 8:51; 9:28; Acts 1:13), probably because of the early death of James and the subsequent prominence of John. It is possible that their mother was Salome (Matt 27:56 [cf. Mark 15:40]).
 The Lord gave the two brothers the name Boanerges, "sons of thunder," perhaps because of their impetuous zeal for their Master's honor, shown by incidents like the wish to call down fire to consume certain Samaritans who refused Him passage through their country (Luke 9:54 [cf. Mark 9:38; Luke 9:49, 50]).
 James was part of the Inner Circle, which also included his brother John and Peter, thus he is specially mentioned as present at the healing of Peter's wife's mother (Mark 1:29), at the raising of Jairus' daughter (Mark 5:37), at the Transfiguration (Mark 9:2), at the Mt. of Olives during the great eschatological discourse (Mark 13:3), and at the agony in the Garden of Gethsemane (Mark 14:33). On two of these occasions, the first and the fourth, Andrew is associated with the three. The special favor accorded to the two brothers probably prompted the ambitious request of their mother that they might sit as assessors to Christ in His kingdom (Matt 20:20–23; Mark 10:35–40).
 James was the first of the apostolic band to be called upon to "drink the cup" of suffering (Mark 10:38, 39), being beheaded by Herod Agrippa I in A.D. 44 (Acts 12:2).
 (III) James the son of Alphaeus, one of the Twelve Apostles (Matt 10:3; Mark 3:18; Luke 6:15; Acts 1:13), referred to as James the lesser (*ho mikrós* [3398], the little), the son of Mary (Mark 15:40 [cf.

Matt 27:56]; John 19:25, probably Mary the wife of Cleophas making Cleophas and Alphaeus the same). It is possible that he was a brother of Matthew, who is also called a "son of Alphaeus" (Matt 9:9 [cf. Mark 2:14]).

(IV) James the Lord's brother (Matt 13:55; Mark 6:3), distinguished from the Twelve and particularly from James the son of Alphaeus (Matt 10:3; John 2:12; Acts 1:14 [cf. Matt 12:47–50]). Other references to the Lord's brothers are Matt 12:46–50; Mark 3:31–35; Luke 8:19–21. During Christ's ministry His brothers did not believe on Him (John 7:3–5), but later they were present with Mary and the apostles in an upper room (Acts 1:14). The following references outside the gospels have to do with James: Acts 1:13, 14; 12:17; 21:18–25; 1 Cor 15:7; Gal 1:18, 19; 2:1–10. From these passages we learn that he was converted to a full acknowledgement of Christ (probably by the Resurrection), that the Lord appeared to him specially, that he became head of the Church of Jerusalem, and that he was put to death by the Jews either just before the siege (Hegesippus) or some 10 years earlier (Josephus). He was surnamed the Just by his fellow countrymen, and was greatly respected by all classes in Jerusalem.

The Epistle of James is almost universally attributed to the brother of the Lord. This book is of greatest interest to students of the gospels. There is no epistle which contains in a small compass so many allusions to Christ's teachings. Note the following striking parallels: Matt 5:3 with James 2:5; Matt 5:7 with James 2:13; Matt 5:9 with James 3:18; Matt 5:11, 12 with James 1:2, 9; Matt 5:34–37 with James 5:12; Matt 6:19 with James 5:2; Matt 6:24 with James 4:4; Matt 7:1 with James 4:11, 12; Matt 7:7, 8 with James 1:5; Matt 7:12 with James 2:8; Matt 7:16 with James 3:11, 12; Matt 7:24 with James 1:22; Matt 12:36 with James 3:1, 2; Matt 18:4 with James 4:6; Luke 6:24 with James 5:1; Luke 8:15; 21:19 (*hupomonḗ* [5281], patience, used

by Luke only in his gospel) with James 1:3, 4; 5:11; Luke 12:16–21 with James 4:14; John 8:31 with James 1:25; John 13:17 with James 4:17. The Epistle of James is clearly the work of one trained in the strict observance of the Law, yet divorced from blind Pharisaic formalism denounced by our Lord (James 1:22–27; 2:8–12; 4:5–7; 5:10, 11).

2386. ἴαμα *íama*; gen. *iámatos*, neut. noun from *iáomai* (2390), to cure. Healing.

(I) A healing or cure, the result of the process of healing, which process is *íasis* (2392). Healings worked upon man: the curing of the demoniacs (Matt 8:28; 15:21; 17:14; Mark 1:23); the impotent man at the pool of Bethesda (John 5:9); the man with the withered hand (Matt 12:10); the woman with the spirit of infirmity (Luke 13:11); the dumb man with a devil (Matt 9:32); the man "possessed with a devil, blind, and dumb" (Matt 12:22); the paralytics (Matt 8:5; 9:2); the deaf man (Mark 7:32); the blind (Matt 9:27; 20:30; Mark 8:22; John 9:1); the man with dropsy (Luke 14:2); the patient suffering from fever healed with a touch (Matt 8:14); the woman with the issue of blood (Matt 9:20); the lepers (Matt 8:2; Luke 17:14, the healing in the former case being brought about by a touch, in the latter case by a mere word of power); Malchus' servant (Luke 22:50).

(II) Used in the phrase *charísmata iamátōn* (*charísmata* the pl. of *chárisma* [5486], gift; *iamátōn*, gen., of healings), gifts of healings. It is always in the pl. (1 Cor 12:9, 28, 30). The Lord did not give *iámata*, which would be certain drugs for healing, but only gifts or abilities to provide the means of various healings in His divine providence, whether they be with or without medicine.

Syn.: *therapeía* (2322), care, attention, medical service resulting in healing.

Ant.: *asthéneia* (769), feebleness, infirmity, sickness; *nósos* (3554), disease; *asthénēma* (771), infirmity; *nósēma* (3553), ailment.

2387. Ἰαμβρῆς Iambrḗs; gen. *Iambroú*, masc. proper noun. Jambres, with *Iannḗs* (2389), two famous magicians of Egypt who were supposed to have used their art to deceive Pharaoh (2 Tim 3:8 [cf. Ex 7:9–13]).

2388. Ἰαννά Ianná; masc. proper noun, transliterated from the Hebr. Janna, meaning whom Jehovah bestows, one of our Lord's ancestors (Luke 3:24).

2389. Ἰαννῆς Iannḗs; gen. *Iannoú*, masc. proper noun. Jannes, with *Iambrḗs* (2387), two famous magicians of Egypt who, according to extra-biblical tradition, used their art to deceive Pharaoh (2 Tim 3:8 [cf. Ex 7:9–13]).

2390. ἰάομαι iáomai; contracted *iṓmai*, imperf. *iṓmēn*, fut. *iásomai*, aor. mid. *iasámēn*, perf. pass. *íamai*, aor. pass. *iáthēn*, fut. pass. *iathḗsomai*, mid. deponent. To heal, cure, restore to bodily health. With the acc. (Luke 5:17; 6:19; 9:2, 11, 42; 14:4; 22:51; John 4:47; Acts 10:38; 28:8). Pass. (Matt 8:8, 13; 15:28; Luke 7:7; 8:47; 17:15; John 5:13; Acts 3:11; 9:34). Pass., followed by *apó* (575), from, meaning to be healed from or of anything (Mark 5:29; Luke 6:17; Sept.: Gen 20:17; Lev 14:3; 2 Kgs 20:8). Metaphorically, of moral diseases, to heal or save from the consequences of sin (Matt 13:15; John 12:40; Acts 28:27 quoted from Isa 6:10; Luke 4:18 [cf. Isa 61:1]; Heb 12:13; James 5:16; 1 Pet 2:24; Sept.: Isa 53:5; 61:1, equivalent to *sṓzō* [4982], used with the meaning to heal. See Matt 9:21, 22; Mark 5:23, 28, 34; Luke 7:50; 8:36; John 11:12; Acts 4:9; James 5:15; Jer 17:14).

Deriv.: *íama* (2386), the result or means of healing; *íasis* (2392), the act or process of healing; *iatrós* (2395), physician.

Syn.: *therapeúō* (2323), to heal with the additional meaning of caring for; *sṓzō* (4982), to save, with the additional meaning of rescuing from the effects of disease; *diasṓzō* (1295), to bring safely through.

Ant.: *asthenéō* (770), to be weak, without strength; *kámnō* (2577), to be weary, sick; *sunéchomai* (4912), to be seized or afflicted by illness; *noséō* (3552), to be sick; the expression *kakṓs échō* (*kakṓs* [2560], badly; *échō* [2192], I have), to have it badly, meaning to be ill.

2391. Ἰάρεδ Iáred; masc. proper noun, transliterated from the Hebr. *Yered* (3382, OT), descent. Jared, the father of Enoch (Luke 3:37; Sept.: Gen 5:15, 16, 18–20). In 1 Chr 1:2 he is called Jered.

2392. ἴασις íasis; gen. *iáseōs*, fem. noun from *iáomai* (2390), to cure. The process or act of healing or curing (Luke 13:32; Acts 4:22, 30; Sept.: Prov 3:8; 4:22; Mal 4:2). To be distinguished from the neut. noun *íama* (2386), the result or the means of healing.

Syn.: *therapeía* (2322) which stresses the care and attention or medical service given resulting in healing.

Ant.: *asthéneia* (769), weakness, sickness, lack of strength, infirmity; *asthénēma* (771), the infirmity itself, the result of being sick in that one has no strength; *nósos* (3554), disease with particular reference to the disease itself; *nósēma* (3553), ailment.

2393. ἴασπις íaspis; gen. *iáspidos*, fem. noun. Jasper, a precious stone of various colors such as purple or green (Rev 4:3; 21:11, 18, 19; Sept.: Ezek 28:13).

2394. Ἰάσων Iásōn; gen. *Iásonos*, masc. proper noun. Jason, meaning one who will heal. A Thessalonian and probably a relative of Paul whom he entertained and in consequence received rough treatment at the hands of the unbelieving Jews (Acts 17:5–7, 9; Rom 16:21).

2395. ἰατρός iatrós; gen. *iatroú*, masc. noun from *iáomai* (2390), to cure. A physician (Matt 9:12; Mark 2:17; 5:26; Luke 4:23; 5:31; 8:43; Col 4:14; Sept.: 2 Chr

16:12; Jer 8:22). Priests were examiners of leprosy (Matt 8:4; Luke 17:14), but they were not physicians. The physicians whom the woman with the issue of blood had consulted before she was healed by Christ are alluded to in one case (Mark 5:26; Luke 8:43). Elsewhere, physicians are mentioned in proverbial sayings (Matt 9:12; Mark 2:17; Luke 4:23; 5:31). There is no censure of them in Christ's words. On the contrary, He implies that the sick should resort to a physician, but Mark 5:26 probably gives a fair impression of their general value.

(I) References to remedies are few: a lotion (Luke 10:34); an anodyne (Mark 15:23). We can assume both of these were customary among the Jews, but in neither of these cases were they administered by physicians as also the oil in James 5:14 was administered by the elders of the church.

(II) References to surgical procedures: circumcision (Luke 1:59); castration (Matt 19:12).

(III) The language of Matt 18:8f. speaks of mutilation rather than of amputation.

(IV) Christ was the great physician (Luke 4:23; 5:31; 13:32).

(V) The verb *iáomai* (2390), to heal, is used with this particular meaning twenty times in the NT, and always directly of Christ, except in Acts 28:8 where it refers to Paul. The verb *sṓzō* (4982), save, implies healing (Matt 9:21f.; Mark 5:23, 28, 34; Luke 7:50; 8:36: John 11:12; Acts 4:9; James 5:15).

(VI) In Christ's healings, we find He healed a variety of sicknesses: blindness (Matt 9:27ff.; 20:29ff.; Mark 8:22ff.; John 9); deafness (Mark 7:31ff.); palsy (Matt 9:1ff.); withered hand (Matt 12:9ff.); issue of blood (Matt 9:20); dropsy (Luke 14:1f.); fever (Matt 8:14ff.); leprosy (Matt 8:1ff.; Luke 17:11ff.); restoration of a cut ear (Luke 22:49ff.); demon possession (Matt 8:28ff.; Mark 1:23ff.).

(A) His purpose in healing: not merely as works of mercy (Mark 3:4; John 10:32) but also as "signs" (John 4:54) and parables of spiritual healing (Luke 5:24, 31f.; John 9:25, 39).

(B) The universality of His healings: by the apostles without Christ (Matt 10:8); the daughter of Jairus (Mark 5:26); without exception (Matt 11:5; Mark 1:27; 7:37; John 9:32); without fail (Mark 5:4, 26; 9:18).

(C) The conditions of His healings: on Christ's part it was the expression of His divine will (Matt 8:3). In some cases it was in answer to human prayer (Mark 9:29; John 11:41). On the part of the sick one or his petitioner the condition was faith (Matt 8:13; 9:2, 22, 28; 15:28) and, though seldom mentioned, desire or will (Luke 22:50f.; John 5:6).

(D) Preliminaries were usually an application which was either personal (Luke 5:12; 17:13; 18:38) or intercessory, with the sufferer present (Mark 2:3; 7:32; 9:17) or without the presence of the sufferer (Matt 8:6; Mark 7:29f.; John 4:47ff.). Often, no application preceded the healing (Mark 5:28; Luke 13:12; 22:51; John 5:6; 9:2ff.; 11:11).

(E) Performance was usually immediate (Matt 8:3f.; Mark 5:29); sometimes delayed (Mark 9:21ff.); rarely a gradual process (Mark 8:23ff.).

(F) Accompaniments: a word (Matt 8:8, 13; 12:13); always used in the case of demon possession (Matt 8:16, 32); a touch (Matt 8:3; 9:18, 25, 29; Mark 5:28; 6:56); a symbolic action (Mark 7:33; John 9:6f.).

(G) Sequel: an assurance (Mark 5:34; Luke 17:19; 18:42); a command (Matt 8:4; 9:6; Mark 5:19, 43); a warning (John 5:14).

2396. ἴδε *íde*; the later form for *idé*, 2d aor. of imper. of *eídō* (1492), to see, calling attention to what may be seen or heard or mentally apprehended in any way. Lo, behold, observe. A particle of exclamation and calling attention to something present (Matt 25:20, 22, 25; Mark 11:21; John 1:47; 19:5, "Behold the man," 19:14). Addressed apparently to several, but directed to one (Mark

3:34; John 1:29; 7:26; 11:36; 19:4). With the meaning of behold, observe, consider (Mark 15:4; John 5:14; Rom 2:17; Gal 5:2).

Syn.: *blépō* (991), to see; *emblépō* (1689), to earnestly look; *theōréō* (2334), to look with careful observation to details; *theáomai* (2300), to view attentively, contemplate; *epopteúō* (2029), to be an eyewitness; *atenízō* (816), to gaze upon; *katanoéō* (2657), to perceive; *paratēréō* (3906), to note, observe.

Ant.: *paríēmi* (3935), to let by, disregard; *epilanthánomai* (1950), to neglect, forget; *ameléō* (272), to neglect, disregard; *aphíēmi* (863), to let go; *oligōréō* (3643), to despise.

2397. ἰδέα idéa; gen. *idéas*, fem. noun from *eídō* (1492), to see. Appearance (only in Matt 28:3). Idea, aspect, countenance. Something conceived in the mind without an objective reality, in contrast to *morphḗ* (3444), form, essence, and *schḗma* (4976), shape, which have objective reality. *Idéa* implies someone in whose mind an appearance is formed; there must be one forming the idea before the object may become visible. The Eng. word "idea" is derived from this word.

Syn.: *énnoia* (1771), intent in the mind, thought; *diánoia* (1271), mind as a faculty, imagination; *nóēma* (3540), intellect, mental disposition.

Ant.: *ousía* (3776), substance; *hupóstasis* (5287), essence.

2398. ἴδιος ídios; fem. *idía*, neut. *ídion*, adj. Properly one's own. As pertaining to a private person and not to the public, private, particular, individual, as opposed to *dēmósios* (1219), public, open, and *koinós* (2839), common. In John 5:18 the expression "God was his Father" has the word *ídion*, His own (NASB, NIV).

(I) Used adv.:

(A) *Idía*, individually, severally, to each one. In 1 Cor 12:11, "dividing to each one [*hekástō* {1538}] individually

[*idía*] as he pleases [*boúletai* {1011}, as He desires or wills]" (a.t.).

(B) *Kat' idían* with the prep. *katá* (2596), according to, meaning privately, by oneself, apart from others, e.g., one individual alone (Matt 14:13, 23; 17:1; Mark 6:31). Of several as apart from all others (Matt 17:19; Mark 4:34; 9:2, 28; Acts 23:19; Gal 2:2).

(II) As belonging to oneself and not to another, one's own, peculiar.

(A) Denoting ownership, that of which one is himself the owner, possessor, producer, as my own, your own, his own. Of things (Matt 22:5; 25:15; Mark 15:20; Luke 6:41, 44; John 5:43; 7:18; 10:3, 4; Acts 20:28; 28:30; Rom 10:3; 14:5; 1 Tim 3:4, 5; 2 Pet 1:20; 3:17). In Matt 9:1, "his own city," where he resides; "the seat of one's family" (a.t. [Luke 2:3]); "in one's own country" (a.t. [John 4:44]). Pleonastically, with a gen. of person in addition (John 10:12, "whose sheep are not his own" [a.t.]). See 2 Pet 3:3, 16; Sept.: Job 2:11; Ezek 21:30. Hence with the pl. neut. art. *tá ídia*, generally possessions, property (Luke 18:28 in some MSS), specifically one's own house or home (John 16:32; 19:27; Acts 21:6; Sept.: Esth 5:10; 6:12); own nation, people (John 1:11 which also includes the world, the total humanity that Christ made). With the verb *prássō* (4238), to do or perform, *tá ídia* means to do one's own business or duties (1 Thess 4:11). With the verb *laléō* (2980), to speak, *ek* (1537) *tōn idíōn*, out of his own, to speak out of one's own heart, disposition, or character (John 8:44). Spoken of persons, e.g., *ídios adelphós*, "his own brother" (John 1:41); "his own bond slave" (a.t.) or servant (Matt 25:14); father (John 5:18); "Son" (Rom 8:32); "to his own master" or lord (*kuríō* [2962]) (Rom 14:4); "her own husband" (1 Cor 7:2); "countrymen" (1 Thess 2:14); "their own prophets," meaning of their own country (1 Thess 2:15); "their own masters" (1 Tim 6:1); with a noun in the gen. added (Titus 1:12). Hence, with a def. art. in the nom. pl. *hoi ídioi* means own household, family

(1 Tim 5:8); one's own friends, companions (John 13:1; Acts 4:23; 24:23); one's own people, countrymen (John 1:11, spoken as individuals in contrast to the neut. pl. *tá ídia*, referring to the whole of humanity or to Israel collectively). *Tó ídion*, its own, that which by character belongs to it (John 15:19).

(B) In the sense of peculiar, particular, as distinguishing one person from others, e.g., *idía diálektos* (1258), dialect, language with its local peculiarities and pronunciations (Acts 1:19; 2:6, 8). In Acts 25:19, *deisidaimonía* (1175), superstition, their own superstition. In 1 Cor 7:7, *chárisma* (5486), gift, his own gift.

(C) As denoting that which in its nature or by appointment pertains in any way to a person or thing, e.g., in Acts 1:25, "to his own place," i.e., proper and appointed for him; "his own generation" in which he lived (Acts 13:36); "his own reward" (1 Cor 3:8); see 1 Cor 15:23; Jude 1:6. Also *kairós* ([2540], occasion, opportunity, appropriate time) *ídios*, or in the pl. *kairoí ídioi*, own times or opportunities, i.e., due or proper time as determined by God (Gal 6:9; 1 Tim 2:6; 6:15; Titus 1:3).

(D) Sometimes *ídios* is used instead of a poss. pron. without any emphasis, e.g., Matt 22:5; 25:14; 1 Pet 3:1, 5. Equivalent to *heautoú* (1438), of his own (John 1:41; 1 Cor 7:2).

Deriv.: *idiótēs* (2399), a common or private man.

Ant.: *xénos* (3581), strange; *allótrios* (245), belonging to another; *allogenḗs* (241), belonging to another race; *állos* (243), another numerically; *héteros* (2087), another qualitatively; *allḗlōn* (240), of one another.

2399. ἰδιώτης *idiótēs*; gen. *idiótou*, masc. noun from *ídios* (2398), one's own. A common man as opposed either to a man of rank or education (1 Cor 14:16); a person in the private sector or a common man (Acts 4:13); uninstructed, unskilled (1 Cor 14:23, 24); plain in speech (2 Cor 11:6, in this text referring both to speech

and knowledge). Our Eng. word "idiot" is derived from *idiótēs*, but has a very different meaning. The Gr. word never signifies, either in the sacred or secular writers, a person deficient in natural capacity for understanding.

2400. ἰδού *idoú*; demonstrative particle. "Lo and behold!", serving to call attention to something external or exterior to oneself; usually used at the beginning of a clause or only with *kaí* ([2532], and), before it, but sometimes in the mid. of a clause before words which are to be particularly noted (Matt 23:34; Luke 13:16; Acts 2:7).

(I) With the nom. and finite verb (Matt 1:20; 2:1, 13; Mark 3:32; Luke 2:10; John 4:35; Acts 9:11). Also in quotations from the OT (Matt 1:23; 21:5; Mark 1:2; Rom 9:33 [cf. Isa 7:14; 28:16; Zech 9:9; Mal 3:1]).

(II) With a nom. where the verb of existence is implied (Matt 3:17; Luke 5:12; John 19:26, 27; Acts 8:27, 36; 2 Cor 6:2; Rev 6:2; Sept.: Gen 47:1; Num 23:11; Josh 9:25). Followed by *egṓ* (1473), I, or an equivalent word, expressing resignation, obedience (Luke 1:38; Heb 2:13 quoted from Isa 8:18). Also in answers, *idoú egṓ*, behold I, (Acts 9:10; Sept.: Gen 22:11; 1 Sam 3:8; Isa 6:8).

2401. Ἰδουμαία *Idoumaía*; gen. *Idoumaías*, fem. proper noun transliterated from the Hebr. *'Edōm* (123, OT). Edom, Idumea (Mark 3:8; Sept.: Isa 34:5, 6). This was Mount Seir. Edom was the country extending from the Dead Sea southward to the Gulf of Aqabah and from the Valley of the Arabah eastward to the desert of Arabia, being about 125 miles long and thirty miles wide. Here dwelt the descendants of Esau who were usually hostile to the Jews. They were conquered by David (2 Sam 8:14) but were first completely subdued by John Hyrcanus about 125 B.C. During the Jewish exile, they had taken possession of the southern parts of Palestine as far as

Hebron so that the later name of Idumea includes this region also (see Ezek 36:5).

2402. ἱδρώς hidrṓs; gen. hidrṓtos, masc. noun from ídos (n.f.), sweat. Sweat (Luke 22:44; Sept.: Gen 3:19). See thrómbos (2361), thick sweat that looks like a blood clot.

2403. Ἰεζαβήλ Iezabél; fem. proper noun transliterated from the Hebr. Ízevel (348, OT), chaste. Jezebel or Jezabel, the wife of Ahab, king of Israel. She was the daughter of a Zidonian king (1 Kgs 16:31) and educated in the idolatrous practices of her native country. She was the virtual ruler of Israel. She introduced the worship of Baal and other idols, maintaining four hundred priests of Astarte at her own expense while Ahab maintained 450 priests of Baal (1 Kgs 18:19). She resolved to exterminate all the prophets of God. Obadiah, who was a pious man and principal officer of Ahab's household, rescued one hundred of the prophets at one time from Jezebel's grasp and supplied them with bread and water while they were concealed in a cave (1 Kgs 18:3, 4, 13). Soon after this, Elijah caused the 450 priests of Baal supported by Ahab to be put to death. As a result, Jezebel threatened to take the life of Elijah, but her purpose was frustrated. Soon afterward she planned and perpetrated the murder of Naboth, and by using the king's name and authority, she secured the cooperation of the leading men of Jezreel in her flagrant crime (1 Kgs 21:1–3). Her doom was predicted by Elijah and was in due time visited upon her exactly as prophesied (2 Kgs 9:30–37). In Rev 2:20, the name Jezebel is used symbolically and has become a name of infamy.

2404. Ἰεράπολις Hierápolis; gen. Hierapóleōs, fem. proper noun. Hierapolis, meaning sacred city. A city in Proconsular Asia (Col 4:13), now Turkey, near the river Lycus and in sight of Laodicea, which was about five miles to the south. It stood on a high bluff with a tall mountain behind it. In the city was the famous temple of Pluto, the remains of which are still to be seen. The ruins of the city are extensive and contain the remains of temples, churches, a triumphal arch, a theater, gymnasium, baths, and high ornamental sarcophagi. Hierapolis was celebrated for its warm springs which contained a solution of carbonate of lime, depositing incrustations on anything with which the waters came in contact. It is now called Pammukali, and the hot springs are still there.

2405. ἱερατεία hierateía; gen. hierateías, fem. noun from hierateúō (2407), to officiate as a priest. A priesthood, a priest's office (Luke 1:9 refers to the temple ministry [burning incense]; Heb 7:5 to the priestly office received by the descendants of Levi; Sept.: Ex 29:9; 40:15; Num 3:10; Josh 18:7).

2406. ἱεράτευμα hieráteuma; gen. hierateúmatos, neut. noun from hierateúō (2407), to officiate as a priest. A priesthood as a fraternity, a body of priests. Referring to all Christians, who are said to offer spiritual sacrifices (1 Pet 2:5) and are called a royal priesthood (1 Pet 2:9; Sept.: Ex 19:6 [cf. Rev 1:6; 5:10; 20:6]; Isa 61:6).

2407. ἱερατεύω hierateúō; fut. hierateúsō, from hiereús (2409), priest. To officiate as priest (Luke 1:8, of Zechariah; Sept.: Ex 28:1, 3, 4).

Deriv.: hierateía (2405), a priest's office; hieráteuma (2406), a priesthood.

2408. Ἰερεμίας Hieremías; gen. Hieremíou, masc. proper noun transliterated from the Hebr. Yirmᵉyāh (3414, OT), appointed of Jehovah. Jeremiah, a famous prophet of the OT (Matt 2:17; 16:14). In Matt 27:9 [TR] is find a quotation ascribed to Jeremiah, or "through Jeremiah the prophet" (a.t.), which is not found in his writings but in Zech 11:12, 13. Some

MSS read "Zachariou" here; others simply "through the prophet."

2409. ἱερεύς hiereús; gen. *hieréōs*, masc. noun from *hierós* (2413), sacred. A priest or sacred person serving at God's altar but not necessarily implying that he is also holy (*hágios* [40], holy).

(I) In the heathen religions there were also priests carrying on their religious rites. Such were the priests of Zeus or Jupiter (Acts 14:13; Sept.: 2 Kgs 11:18; 2 Chr 23:17 for the priests of Baal).

(II) It is used also to denote the Jewish priests, the descendants of Aaron generally (Matt 8:4; 12:4, 5; Mark 1:44; 2:26; Luke 1:5; 5:14; 6:4; 10:31; 17:14; John 1:19; Acts 6:7; Heb 9:6). They were divided into twenty-four classes for the service of the temple (1 Chr 24), and the heads of these classes were sometimes called *archiereís* (749), chief priests. These seem to be referred to in Acts 4:1. See Lev 1:5. Spoken of the high priest (Acts 5:24; Heb 7:21, 23; 8:4; 10:11, 21; Sept.: Ex 35:19; Lev 21:10; Num 35:25, 28).

(III) Of Melchizedek as a high priest of God (Heb 7:1, 3; see Gen 14:18; Ps 110:4); of Jesus as the spiritual High Priest (Heb 5:6, who in v. 5 is called "high priest"; 7:11, 15, 17, 21; 10:21).

(IV) Figuratively, Christians are also called priests unto God as offering Him spiritual sacrifices (Rev 1:6; 5:10; 20:6 [cf. 1 Pet 2:5]).

(V) The few passages in the gospels where the word "priest" occurs apply only to the Jewish priesthood, but of its position and functions, very little is recorded either in the gospels or in the NT generally. These Jewish priests in the NT appear in the following connections:

(A) The work of Zechariah (Luke 1:5–9) where we read of the priestly courses with the duties assigned to them by lot. The priesthood was divided into twenty-four courses (*ephēmeríai* [2183]) and each course was on duty twice during the year.

(B) The priests and Levites who interviewed John the Baptist (John 1:19).

(C) The lepers cleansed by our Lord were to show themselves to priests (Matt 8:4; Mark 1:44; Luke 5:14; 17:14) in proof of their healing and of the obedience of Jesus to the Law.

(D) The reference to the shewbread as eaten by the priests only (Mark 2:26).

(E) The priest who passed by the wounded traveler (Luke 10:31).

(F) The gospels are much more concerned with the chief or high priests (*archiereís* [749]) than with priests, which word is found frequently in all four gospels.

(VI) Christ in the NT is called a priest or high priest in the sense of a sacrificing priest. This application of the term to our Lord is found only in Hebrews while the priestly functions connected with sacrifice and intercession are found frequently in the NT (Matt 20:28; John 1:29; 14:6; Rom 8:34; Eph 2:18; 1 Pet 1:19–21; 3:18; Rev 1:5, 13). Elsewhere, they simply form part of His general work as Redeemer.

The pastoral task of writing the Epistle to the Hebrews was to promote advancement of the believers in spiritual maturity (Heb 6:1). These Hebrew believers knew the Lord Jesus as Savior, but had only an elementary knowledge of the truths of redemption. They did not realize what it meant to have Jesus Christ as priest also. The distinction between the two may be seen by consideration of the time and circumstances under which the priesthood appeared in connection with Israel. Apart from foreign priesthoods like those of Egypt and Midian (Gen 47; Ex 3), the first mention of the priesthood in Israel is at Sinai. There was no official, formal priesthood for the Hebrews in Egypt, only redemption. There was none at the Red Sea where deliverance was the one thing needful. At Sinai they were to realize for the first time their true relationship to God and His relationship to them in dwelling among them (Ex 19:4–6). The priesthood was appointed to provide the means of access to God and prevent fear in approaching Him. The essence of priesthood, therefore, is access to God based on an already existing redemption. The Hebrew Christians knew Christ as their Redeemer. They were now to be taught the possibility, power, and joy of constant free access to God through Him, and in this, the removal of all fear and dissatisfaction. Jesus Christ was to be their High Priest, giving them free access to God. There is thus a whole world of difference between knowing Christ as Savior and as Priest. The former may involve only spiritual childhood, while the latter must necessarily include spiritual maturity (Heb 5:12–14). This is one of the great distinctions between the teaching of the epistles of Romans and Hebrews. The former is concerned with the redemption which makes access possible (Rom 5:2), the latter with access made possible by redemption. Notice the admonitions found in the Epistle to the Hebrews: "draw near" (10:22); "draw not back" (a.t. [10:39]); "let us go on" (6:1).

The basic function of a priest was to represent man before God (Heb 5:1). It was the exact opposite of what a prophet did, speaking for God to man. The two ideas of prophet and priest are merged in the person of Jesus Christ. The other duties of the priests, such as teaching, receiving tithes, and blessing the people, were auxiliary functions and not most central to the priestcraft. The Levites could teach and kings could bless, but by no possibility could either do the essential duties of the priesthood in representing man before God. The Godward aspect of the priesthood is always stated and emphasized (Heb 6:20; 7:25; 9:24; see Ex 28:1; Num 16:39, 40; 2 Chr 26:18; Ezek 44:15). The priesthood's essential idea of representing man before God carries with it the right of access to God and abiding in His presence. Priesthood was thus the admission at once of the sinfulness of the race, the holiness of God, and the need for conditions permitting approach to God. Drawing near to

God was by means of an offering; dwelling near God was for the purpose of intercession (Ex 29:30; 30:7, 8; Lev 16:17; Ezek 44:16; Luke 1:9, 10).

For the comparison of the Lord Jesus with Melchizedek as a priest in His person and not in His function, see Melchisedék (3198). The main purpose of the comparison was to present Jesus Christ not only as a priest, but as a royal, abiding, and unique person, which Aaron was not. It is the personal superiority in these respects over the priesthood of Aaron that is dwelt upon in connection with Melchizedek. In reality, however, it must be remembered that there is no comparison drawn between Melchizedek and Christ, but use is made of Melchizedek to symbolize the personal superiority of Christ's priesthood over all others—a priesthood that is older, wider, and more lasting than that of Aaron. In contrasting Christ's priesthood with the Aaronic priesthood, it is constantly called a better priesthood (Heb 7:22; 8:6). Our Lord never was a priest of the Aaronic line (7:13, 14; 8:4). However, it was necessary to use the illustration of the Aaronic priesthood to denote Christ's priestly functions and not His descent, because no characteristic priestly functions are recorded about Melchizedek.

(VII) Comparisons between Aaron's and Christ's priesthoods:

(A) With reference to personal qualifications (Heb 2:17, 18; 3:1; 4:14–16; 5:1–10) where we have the first definite comparison as follows: in Heb 5:1–5, the requirements of the Aaronic priesthood are stated in regard to office (v. 1), character (vv. 2, 3), and divine appointment (vv. 4, 5); in Heb 5:5–10 the fulfillment of these requirements in Christ are stated in reverse order, i.e., divine appointment (vv. 5, 6), character (vv. 7, 8), and office (vv. 9, 10). In Heb 7, we have the comparison and contrast between Melchizedek and Aaron with the superiority of the former on these grounds: Aaron was not royal; he did not abide by reason of death; he had many successors. The superiority of the person gives superiority to the functions. In Heb 8—10 the superiority of the work of Christ is compared with that of Aaron under three aspects: a better covenant (chap. 8) because spiritual, not temporal; a better sanctuary (chap. 9) because heavenly, not earthly; a better sacrifice (chap. 10) because real, not symbolic.

(B) Christ's elements of superiority as a high priest: a superior order (Heb 7:1–17); a superior tribe (Heb 7:14); a superior calling (Heb 7:21); a superior tenure (Heb 7:23, 24); a superior character (Heb 7:26); a superior sanctuary and covenant (Heb 9); a superior sacrifice (Heb 10).

(C) After Heb 10 there is nothing priestly in the terms used, though Heb 13 refers to functions connected with the priesthood. The functions of priesthood may thus be summed up as approaching God for man, offering to God for man, and interceding with God for man.

(D) The superiority of our Lord's priesthood is shown in the following particulars: it is royal in character, heavenly in sphere, spiritual in nature, continuous in efficacy, perpetual in duration, universal in scope, and effectual in results.

(VIII) Christ is presented both as priest and high priest. There is no real distinction between these offices when it comes to the Lord Jesus. Christ is both (Heb 5:6, 10; 6:20; 7:1, 3, 15, 17, 21). The difference is one of rank only, the high priesthood being, as it were, a specialized form. The term "high priest" occurs only nine times in the OT, of which only two are in the Pentateuch. It is noteworthy that the term is never once applied to Aaron. This clearly shows that there is no real distinction between the two offices, for if there had been an essential difference from the first, Aaron would have been called a high priest. Christ is never termed high priest in connection with Melchizedek, but only when Aaron is under consideration. As, however, the distinction was current in NT times, it was necessary to show that Christ fulfilled both offices. See discussion of *haíma* (129), blood.

(IX) The spiritual work of Christ as priest is shown in various aspects in Hebrews: His propitiation (Heb 2:17); His ability to suffer (Heb 2:18); His ability to sympathize (Heb 4:15); His ability to save (Heb 7:25); His present appearance in heaven for us (Heb 9:24); His kingly position on the throne (Heb 8:1); and His coming again (Heb 9:28).

(X) The work of Christ as priest is both perpetual and permanent. He offered Himself through the eternal Spirit (Heb 9:14); He has made an eternal covenant (9:13–15, see *diathḗkē* [1242], testament, covenant); He is the source of eternal salvation (5:9); He obtained eternal redemption (9:12) which culminates in eternal inheritance (9:15).

(XI) What the Lord Jesus provided for us as our high priest is immediate, permanent, and direct access to God (Heb 4:14–16; 10:19). He secured for us what the NT calls *parrēsía* (3954), boldness of access (Heb 4:16; 10:19, 35). It is this privilege of access to God which belongs to all believers (Rom 5:2; Eph 2:18; Heb 4:16; 10:19; 1 Pet 3:18). All alike are called upon to offer spiritual sacrifices of praise and prayer of body and soul (Rom 12:1; Heb 13:15), with such actual gifts in charity and helpfulness as are prompted by love for God (2 Cor 9:7; Phil 4:18; Heb 13:16). None of these can be an offering for sin since the virtue of Christ's offering is inexhaustible. No longer does any distinct priestly class or caste mediate between God and man. The priestly functions and status, in a strict sense reserved entirely to the Savior, are transferred, as much as is possible, to the whole body of believers, each having the right of access to God through Christ alone. The individual has to give an account of himself and no artificial system of mediation prevents him from standing in personal responsibility before God.

(XII) Officials and ministers of local Christian churches are never referred to as priests but as elders (*presbúteroi* [4245]). For the use of the word *hierourgéō* (2418), to perform the duties of a priest or officiate as a priest, in Rom 15:16, see that entry. It is used with the metaphorical meaning of sacrificing in the ministry of the gospel. See *thusía* (2378), sacrifice.

Deriv.: *archiereús* (749), high priest; *hierateúō* (2407), to officiate as a priest.

Syn.: *Levítēs* (3019), Levite, a servant of the priests.

2410. Ἰεριχώ *Ierichṓ*; fem. proper noun transliterated from the Hebr. *Yerīchō* (3405, OT). Jericho, an ancient and celebrated city in OT and NT history. The name is generally thought to mean fragrance. It is situated in the Jordan Valley, about five miles west of the River Jordan and 6 or 7 miles north of the Dead Sea, and is a fertile area receiving its water from a large spring known as the Fountain of Elisha. The city has occupied at least two different sites:

(I) Ancient Jericho near the fountain Es-Sultan, or Elisha's Fountain at the foot of the Quarantania Mountain, and about one and one-half miles above the opening of the Valley of Achor.

(II) The Jericho of the gospels, southeast of the ancient one, near the opening to the valley, inhabited by Arab Muslims today and called Er-Riha. Jericho is first mentioned as the city against which the Israelites were encamped before entering the Promised Land. Moses looked down upon the plain of Jericho from the summit of Mount Nebo (Deut 34:3; Num 22:1; 26:3). The town was of considerable size, strongly fortified (Josh 2:15) and very rich (Heb 11:30; Josh 2). The wall fell after being compassed seven days, and the city and its inhabitants were destroyed (Josh 6:20, 21; 24:11). A curse was pronounced upon anyone who should thereafter rebuild it (Josh 6:26). This curse was fulfilled upon Hiel, 533 years later (1 Kgs 16:34), but the curse seems to have been for fortifying the city rather than for dwelling in its neighborhood since the site was assigned to Benjamin (Josh 18:21), was a boundary of Ephraim (Josh 16:7), and afterward belonged to Judah. In spite of many conquests, Jericho continued to flourish. Eglon, king of Moab, possessed it eighteen years (Judg 3:13). David's messengers tarried there in accordance with his advice, "until your beards be grown" (2 Sam 10:5). A school of the prophets, often visited by Elijah, flourished at Jericho (2 Kgs 2) and Elisha miraculously healed its water (2 Kgs 2:19–22). King Zedekiah and his men, fleeing from Jerusalem, were captured in the plains of Jericho (2 Kgs 25:5; Jer 39:5). After the return from the Babylonian captivity, Jericho was reoccupied (Ezra 2:34; Neh 7:36) and its people helped to rebuild the walls of Jerusalem (Neh 3:2). Jericho is mentioned 63 times in the Scriptures—56 times in the OT and 7 times in the NT (Matt 20:29; Mark 10:46 twice; Luke 10:30; 18:35; 19:1; Heb 11:30). The Roman Antony presented the district to Cleopatra who sold it to Herod. He embellished the city with palaces and made it his winter residence since it was the most beautiful spot for the purpose in his dominions. He died there. It was at Jericho that the Jewish pilgrims going up to Jerusalem (who had taken the route east of the Jordan) used to assemble on their way to the temple. Hence, Christ passed through it in His journeys. There He made the acquaintance of Zacchaeus who was the chief revenue officer for the wealthy district of Jericho (Luke 19:1–9). Near this city, He also healed a blind man (Matt 20:29–34; Mark 10:46–52; Luke 18:35–43). The rocky road from Jericho to Jerusalem, even as it is today, was used as the setting for Christ's parable of the Good Samaritan (Luke 10:25–37).

2411. ἱερόν *hierón*; gen. *hieroú*, neut. noun from *hierós* (2413), sacred. Temple.

(I) A temple, whether of the true God (Matt 12:5, 6) or an idol (Acts 19:27). It often includes not only the building but the courts and all the sacred ground or enclosure.

(II) When referred to as the temple in Jerusalem it is equivalent to the house (*oíkos* [3624]) of the Lord (1 Kgs 6:1, 37; 7:12; Isa 66:1) or the house of God (Ezra 3:8).

(III) In the NT, it always refers to the temple as rebuilt by Herod the Great, and minutely described by Josephus (Ant. 15.11.3). According to him, the temple consisted of three parts or enclosures with the temple proper or *naós* (3485) in the center and two circular courts or areas around it, one exterior to the other. The first enclosure or outer court surrounding the whole temple was the lowest and was open to all. It contained the porches where the people gathered, money was exchanged, and the animals and items pertaining to the sacrifices were bought and sold. It is sometimes referred to as the court of the Gentiles. From this to the second enclosure or inner court was an ascent of fourteen steps. This was divided into the court (or separate place) of the women and the court of Israel or of the priests. It is called by Josephus *hágion* (39), the holy one, and only those who were clean were permitted to enter it. Here the sacrifices were prepared and offered on the altar of burnt offerings which stood before the entrance of the *naós* (cf. Matt 23:35). The third and highest enclosure (*períbolos*) was the temple (*naós*) itself, called the third *hierón* into which only the priests might enter (cf. Luke 1:9, 10) and which was divided into two parts (*tó hágion* [39], the sanctuary, and *tó Hágion Hagíōn*, the Holy of Holies). The whole temple, therefore, consisted strictly of two parts: the physical structure (*ho naós*) and the courts leading into it. Hence, *tó hierón* is used for the whole and also for the courts, but not exclusively for the *naós*.

(A) Generally, and for the whole (Mark 13:1, 3; Luke 21:5; 22:52). In Matt 24:1, *tás oikodomás toú hieroú* (*tás oikodomás* [3619], structures, buildings; *tou hieroú*, of the temple), the buildings of the temple.

(B) Of the courts (Matt 12:5; Mark 11:11; Luke 2:27, 37; 18:10; Acts 2:46; 3:1; 21:26).

(C) Of the outer court where things were bought and sold (Matt 21:12, 14, 15; Mark 11:15, 16). It was here that Jesus disputed and taught (Matt 21:23; 26:55; Mark 11:27; Luke 2:46; John 5:14; 7:14, 28); also the apostles (Acts 5:20, 21, 25, 42).

(IV) The pinnacle of the temple (Matt 4:5; Luke 4:9), i.e., probably the apex or summit of Solomon's porch which Josephus describes as being exterior to the temple itself on the east side and built up to the height of 400 cubits from the foundation in the Valley of Kidron below.

Deriv.: *hierósulos* (2417), one who robs churches or temples.

Syn.: *naós* (3485), temple.

2412. ἱεροπρεπής *hieroprepés*; gen. *hieroprepoús*, masc.-fem., neut. *hieroprepés*, adj. from *hierós* (2413), sacred, and *prépō* (4241), to suit, become. Such as becomes sacred persons, venerable. Only in Titus 2:3, meaning to act like a sacred person (cf. 1 Tim 2:2).

Syn.: *áxios* (514), worthy, suitable; *kósmios* (2887), modest; *semnós* (4586), honorable, venerable; *sebastós* (4575), venerable, august; *eulabés* (2126), pious, devout; *hierós* (2413) and *hósios* (3741), sacred; *hágios* (40), holy; *theíos* (2304), divine; *tímios* (5093), esteemed, reputable, honorable.

Ant.: *asebés* (765), impious, ungodly; *hierósulos* (2417), temple-despoiler, robber of churches; *anósios* (462), unholy; *bébēlos* (952), profane; *theostugés* (2319), impious, hater of God.

2413. ἱερός *hierós*; gen. *hieroú*, fem. *hierá*, neut. *hierón*. Sacred.

(I) Not used of persons but of things (1 Cor 9:13) and of the Scriptures (2 Tim 3:15).

(II) That which may not be violated, externally related to God but not necessarily having a holy (*hágios* [40]) character.

(III) Thus, *hiereús* (2409), priest, is a sacred person serving at God's altar. The word does not have reference to priest's character but to his position. The true antithesis of *hierós* is *bébēlos* (952), profane (1 Tim 1:9; 4:7; 6:20; 2 Tim 2:16; Heb 12:16); verb: *bebēlóō* (953), to profane (Matt 12:5; Acts 24:6).

(IV) In the pl. neut. *tá hierá*, sacred things, sacred rites (1 Cor 9:13, "those performing the sacred rites" [a.t.], "ministering in holy things" [a.t.]).

Deriv.: *hiereús* (2409), priest; *hierón* (2411), the temple; *hieroprepés* (2412), that which is appropriate to a priest or a religious profession; *hierōsúnē* (2420), the office, quality, or rank and ministry of a priest; *hieróthutos*, something offered in sacrifice, spoken of the flesh of animals, in some MSS in 1 Cor 10:19, 28 instead of *eidōlóthutos* (1494), an offering or sacrifice to idols.

Syn.: *semnós* (4586), modest, venerable, honorable, worthy; *hagnós* (53), clean, pure, free from defilement; *hósios* (3741), sacred; *sebastós* (4575), venerable; *eusebés* (2152), pious; *eulabés* (2126), devout, one who acquiesces to that which God permits; *theosebés* (2318), reverent of God; *philótheos* (5377) and *theóphilos* (2321), a friend of God.

Ant.: *bébēlos* (952), profane; *asebés* (765), impious; *ápistos* (571), unbelieving; *hubristés* (5197), an insulter; *blásphēmos* (989), evil speaking; *hierósulos* (2417), a temple-despoiler, robber of churches.

2414. Ἱεροσόλυμα *Hierosóluma*; gen. pl. *Hierosolúmōn*, neut. pl. proper noun transliterated from the Hebr. *Yᵉrū-shāla-yim* (3389, OT). Jerusalem. The pl. is possibly an allusion to the two parts of the city, upper and lower. This holy city is thus designated in Matt 2:1, 3; 3:5; 4:25; 5:35; 15:1; 16:21; 20:17, 18; 21:1, 10; Mark 3:8, 22; 7:1; 10:32, 33; 11:11, 15, 27; 15:41; Luke 2:22; 19:28; 23:7; John 1:19; 2:13, 23; 4:20, 21, 45; 5:1, 2; 10:22; 11:18, 55; 12:12; Acts 1:4; 8:1, 14; 11:27; 13:13; 18:21; 20:16; 21:17;

25:1, 7, 9, 15, 24; 26:4, 10, 20; 28:17; Gal 1:17, 18; 2:1. In Matt 2:3 and 3:5, *hē Hierosóluma* is used in the fem. to indicate the inhabitants of Jerusalem (cf. Matt 23:37; Luke 13:34). It was the capital of Palestine, the seat of Jewish theocracy, and the center of Christ's ministry. The Arabs today call it El Kods, The Holy. It lies forty miles from the Mediterranean and twenty-five miles from the Jordan River and the Dead Sea. It lay on the confines of Judah and Benjamin, mostly within the limits of the latter, but was reckoned to the former. Its ancient name was Salem, meaning peace (Gen 14:18; Ps 76:2). Later it was known as Jebus and belonged to the Jebusites (Judg 19:10, 11). David made it the capital of his kingdom (2 Sam 5:6, 9), and this is why it is also called the City of David. Jerusalem was destroyed by the Chaldeans (2 Kgs 24 and 25), but rebuilt by the Jews on their return from exile. At a later period Herod the Great expended large sums in its reestablishment. At the time of Christ, the city was set chiefly on three hills.

After the destruction of Jerusalem by the Romans, about A.D. 70, they endeavored to eradicate its very name and nature as a sacred place from the heart and memory of the Jewish nation. In A.D. 136, the Emperor Hadrian caused all the remaining buildings to be demolished and then erected a new city which he called Aelia Capitolina. It was only in the beginning of the fourth century, after Constantine had embraced Christianity, that the name Jerusalem was restored.

2415. Ἱεροσολυμίτης *Hierosolumítēs*; gen. *Hierosolumítou*, masc. proper noun. An inhabitant of Jerusalem or one from Jerusalem (Mark 1:5; John 7:25).

2416. ἱεροσυλέω *hierosuléō*, contracted *hierosulṓ*, fut. *hierosulḗsō*, from *hierósulos* (2417), a sacrilegious person. To commit sacrilege, take to one's own private use what is consecrated to God, as in Rom 2:22.

Syn.: *kléptō* (2813), steal; *asebéō* (764), to commit ungodly deeds.

Ant.: *eusebéō* (2151), to show piety; *eulabéomai* (2125), to be reverent, religious.

2417. ἱερόσυλος *hierósulos*; gen. *hierosúlou*, masc.-fem., neut. *hierósulon*, adj. from *hierón* (2411), temple, and *suláō* (4813), to rob, spoil. A robber of a temple, a sacrilegious person. Used subst. (Acts 19:37).

Deriv.: *hierosuléō* (2416), to commit sacrilege.

2418. ἱερουργέω *hierourgéō*; contracted *hierourgṓ*, fut. *hierourgḗsō*, from *hierourgós* (n.f.), sacrificing, which is from *hierón* (2411), temple, and *érgon* (2041), work. To perform or be employed in a sacred office. Only in Rom 15:16, referring to the sacred business of preaching or administering the gospel. Those who believe that the office of the OT priest continued in the NT endeavor to base their argument of the priestly function of the minister or elder in a local church on the use of this verb by the Apostle Paul, "That I should be the minister [*leitourgós* {3011}, a public servant] of Jesus Christ to the Gentiles, ministering [*hierourgoúnta*, pres. act. part.] the gospel of God, that the offering up of the Gentiles might be acceptable, being sanctified by the Holy Ghost" (Rom 15:16). The verb here means that Paul was willing to make sacrifices as did the priests of the OT. However, the servant (*doúlos* [1401]) of Christ, as Paul so often called himself (not using the term "priest"), should imitate the priest of the OT only in that he must sacrifice for the cause of Christ (Rom 1:1; 2 Cor 4:5; Phil 1:1).

The sacrifice Paul refers to has nothing to do with animals, but that which is precious to self. Paul could in no way contradict the clear statements of Heb 10:12, 26, "But this man [Christ], after he had offered one sacrifice for sins for ever, sat down on the right hand of God. . . . there remaineth no more sacrifice for sins." The use, therefore, of *hierourgéō*, to act or work like a priest, must be taken as a figurative allusion.

By calling himself a *leitourgós* (3011), a public servant, Paul conceives of himself as one who performs functions that are sacred inasmuch as they serve the needs of the community, whether viewed as an ecclesiastical (1 Chr 16:4; Heb 8:2; 10:11) or a social unit (Num 18:2; 2 Cor 9:10). The word *leitourgéō* (3008) may be used of the work of prophets and teachers (Acts 13:2) and even of the ministry of the rich to the poor (Rom 15:27), and its technical use in nonsacrificial connections is well-authenticated. Paul, therefore, applies the term to himself as a minister of Christ to the Gentiles. By using a familiar metaphor, he compares his functions with those of the sacrificing priest, with converted men being the offering which Paul presents to God, notwithstanding that each convert figuratively presents himself as a personal sacrifice (Rom 12:1). The ministry of the church, however, is in no sense priestly and propitiatory, though it should be sacrificial in service. It is in the same sense that Paul says in Phil 2:17, "Yea, and if I be offered upon the sacrifice and service of your faith, I joy, and rejoice with you all." This metaphor does not make Paul the priest, but the Philippians themselves. Their faith, with the accompanying works, is the sacrifice. So great is Paul's eagerness to help them that he is ready to die for Christ's sake on their behalf or, as he metaphorically puts it, to have his blood poured out as a libation, comparable to the practice in the heathen rites with which they were familiar (Phil 2:30; 3:7, 10). There is no reference at all in the NT in regard to the priestly character of the ministry. The priesthood runs directly to Jesus Christ and terminates in Him, while the circle of analogy encompasses all the faithful, investing them with common privileges and the same obligations, recognizing no distinction between clergy or laity. All alike are priests of God and each is required to present himself a living sacrifice (Rom 12:1). The priestly work of Christ is complete and perfect. Even to suggest that any human official should repair or supplement it is not only superfluous in regard to man, but a deprecating reflection upon the Savior.

The ministers of congregations, whether engaged in teaching or administration (1 Tim 5:17), were called elders or presbyters (*presbúteroi* [4245]), probably after the practice of the synagogue (Acts 11:30; 14:23; 15:2). The term "bishops [*epískopoi* {1985}, overseers]" was sometimes substituted for "elders" in churches where Hellenistic influences were strong (Acts 20:28; Phil 1:1; 1 Tim 3:2; Titus 1:7; 1 Pet 5:1, 2). The new term was familiar to the people as the title of the presiding official in their local guilds. In NT times and afterwards, the terms were used interchangeably and substitutes could be used for either. The holders of the office were responsible rulers (Rom 12:8; 1 Thess 5:12; Heb 13:24), stewards of God (Titus 1:7), messengers of the churches (2 Cor 8:23), ministers (1 Tim 4:6), and servants (Phil 1:1) of Christ Jesus. They had no sacrificial duties, and in sacerdotal rank they ranged with the laity whose worship they shared and conducted and over whose fate they watched.

Since Christ died, there is no need for an earthly altar or blood-sacrifice. Even the altar of Heb 13:10 is that of Christ on which each Christian must offer for himself the sacrifice of praise (Heb 13:15f.) and good works. In all such things the minister should be an example (1 Tim 4:12; Titus 2:7; 1 Pet 5:3), but with the passing away of the sacrificial ritual the need and the possibility of any sacerdotal or vicarious activities also ceased.

For the sake of order, the minister still leads and represents the people and speaks with authority when he proclaims the Word of God. However, he is himself one of them, separated from them by no personal quality or privilege whatever. He has no offering to make on anybody's behalf, except his own, and has no immunity against sin except such as arises from his own relationship to God.

The apostles themselves never claimed either to be or to appoint priestly officers. Their specific work was to bear witness to the historical Christ (Acts 1:22; 1 John 1:1–3). While they were wise enough to take steps to effectively organize the little groups of disciples they attracted, they never pretended to encumber the new church with any fragments of a sacrificial system that was, in their opinion, outworn and obsolete.

Every disciple in the first Christian church had access through Christ to God and was charged with the work of evangelism, or the establishment of personal contact between man and God. When the communities became organized, suitable disciples were appointed to the various offices. The appointment of at least the presbytery (*presbutérion* [4244]) involved three concurrent actions: the commission of God (Rom 10:5; 1 Cor 9:16 [cf. John 17:18]); selection by the church leaders of "men of repute"; and the consent of the church (Acts 14:23; 15:27; Titus 1:5). But while such appointments carried the right to preside at church meetings, it added no priestly quality or prerogative to those which the minister, as a disciple, already possessed (R. W. Moss under "Priest" in *The Dictionary of the Apostolic Church* by J. Hastings, vol. 2).

Syn.: *diakonéō* (1247), to minister; *leitourgéō* (3008), to render public service; *latreúō* (3000), to serve for hire; *hupēretéō* (5256), to serve as rower on a ship, to do lower service; *ergázomai* (2038), to work, minister.

2419. Ἱερουσαλήμ *Hierousalém*; fem. noun transliterated from the Hebr. *Yᵉrū-shālēm* (3389, OT), dwelling of peace. Jerusalem (Matt 23:37; Luke 2:25, 38, 41, 45; 4:9; 5:17; 6:17; 9:31, 51, 53; 10:30; 13:4, 33, 34; 17:11; 19:11; 21:20, 24; 23:28; 24:13, 18, 33, 47, 52; Acts 1:8, 12, 19; 2:5, 14; 4:16; 5:16, 28; 6:7;

8:26, 27; 9:2, 13, 21, 26, 28; 10:39;
12:25; 13:27, 31; 15:2, 4; 20:22; 21:11–
13, 31; 22:5, 17, 18; 23:11; 24:11; 25:3;
Rom 15:19, 25, 26, 31; 1 Cor 16:3; Gal
4:25, 26; Heb 12:22; Rev 3:12; 21:2, 10).
Metaphorically, for the Jewish state as
spoken of the former or Mosaic dispensation in Gal 4:25 as the "now" or present
Jerusalem, and of the later Christian dispensation, the Redeemer's kingdom of
which the spiritual Jerusalem is the seat.
In Gal 4:26, it is called the upper Jerusalem; in Heb 12:22 the heavenly Jerusalem; in Rev 3:12; 21:2 the *kainē* (2537),
new Jerusalem. See *Hierosóluma* (2414),
Jerusalem.

2420. ἱερωσύνη hierōsúnē; from *hierós*
(2413), sacred. A priesthood signifying
the office, quality, rank, and ministry of
a priest (Heb 7:11, 12, 14, 24). The contrast between the Levitical priesthood
and that of Christ are set forth in the foregoing verses. See Sept.: 1 Chr 29:22.

2421. Ἰεσσαί Iessai; masc. proper noun
transliterated from the Hebr. *Yishay*
(3448, OT), strong. Jesse, the father of
David and grandson of Ruth. His genealogy is given in the OT (Ruth 4:18–21; 1
Chr 2:5–12) and in the N. T. (Matt 1:5, 6;
Luke 3:32–34; Acts 13:22; Rom 15:12).
He is usually called "Jesse the Bethle-
hemite" (1 Sam 16:1, 18; 17:58), but his
full and proper designation is Jesse "that
Ephrathite of Bethlehem-judah" (1 Sam
17:12). This latter verse calls him "an old
man" at the time of David's fight with
Goliath. He was a man of wealth and position and the affectionate father of eight
sons (1 Sam 17:17, 18). It is remarkable
that David is called "the son of Jesse" after his own fame was established (1 Chr
29:26; Ps 72:20). Jesse was, through David, the ancestor of the Judaic kings and
thus of Christ. The prophets announced
this (Isa 11:1, 10).

2422. Ἰεφθάε Iephtháe; masc. proper noun transliterated from the Hebr.
Yiphᵉtāh (3316, OT), he delivered.

Jephthah, a leader of Israel, the consequences of whose rash vow fell upon his
daughter (Heb 11:32; Judg 11:29–40).

2423. Ἰεχονίας Iechonías; gen. *Iecho-
níou*, masc. proper noun transliterated
from the Hebr. *Yᵉchōyākhīn* (3204, OT),
Jehovah appointed or Jehovah has established. Jechonias, King of Judah (609–
598 B.C.), a son of Josiah and elder
brother of Jehoahaz whose place he took
at the command of Necho II of Egypt.
His name was changed from Eliakim as
a mark of vassalage. The reign is recorded in 2 Kgs 23:34—24:6 and 2 Chr 36:4–
8, and is the last named entry in "the
book of the chronicles of kings of Judah"
(2 Kgs 24:5). Mentioned in Matt 1:11, 12
(cf. 1 Chr 3:15, 16; 2 Kgs 24:8ff.; 25:27;
2 Chr 36:8ff.). In Matt 1:11, he is said to
be the son of Josiah. The name of Jehoiakim is omitted in the genealogy in the
TR, though found in other MSS.

2424. Ἰησοῦς Iēsoús; gen. *Iēsoú*, masc.
proper noun transliterated from the Hebr.
Yēshū'a (3091, OT), Jehovah his help.
Jesus, Jehoshua, contracted to Joshua
(Neh 8:17).
  (I) Jesus means Savior (Matt 1:1, 16,
21). In the gospels, our Savior is designated by the name of Christ alone in
nearly 300 passages; by the name of Jesus Christ or Christ Jesus less than 100
times, and by the name of the Lord Jesus Christ less than 50 times. Prior to His
resurrection, He was designated as Jesus
Christ; after His resurrection, He is often referred to as Christ Jesus (Acts 19:4;
Rom 8:1, 2, 39; 1 Cor 1:2, 30; Gal 3:26,
28; Eph 2:6, 7, 10, 13; Phil 3:3, 8, 12, 14;
Col 1:4, 28; 1 Tim 1:12, 14, 15; 2 Tim
1:1, 2, 13; 1 Pet 5:10, 14).
  (II) In Acts 7:45 and Heb 4:8, *Iēsoús*
refers to Joshua, the successor of Moses.
  (III) In Col 4:11, Jesus, surnamed Justus, was a fellow-laborer with Paul.

2425. ἱκανός hikanós; fem. *hikanē*,
neut. *hikanón*, adj. from *hiknéomai*

(n.f., see *diïknéomai* [1338]), to come. Sufficient.

(I) Of things meaning enough (Luke 22:38, "It is enough, desist" [a.t.]; 2 Cor 2:6; Sept.: Gen 30:15, "Is it a small matter?" [a.t.]; Ex 36:7; Isa 40:16). Hence *tó hikanón*, satisfaction, e.g., to make satisfaction, to satisfy (Mark 15:15). In Acts 17:9, "had taken security of," i.e., satisfaction.

(II) Of persons meaning sufficient, adequate, competent; followed by *prós* (4314), unto, and *tis* (5100), who, "And who is sufficient for these things" (2 Cor 2:16); followed by the aor. inf. (2 Cor 3:5; 2 Tim 2:2). With the meaning of competent, worthy, followed by the inf. aor. (Matt 3:11; Mark 1:7; Luke 3:16); by the pres. inf. (1 Cor 15:9); by *hína* (2443), so that (Matt 8:8; Luke 7:6).

(III) Referring to number as magnitude, abundant, great, much, pl. much people (Luke 7:11; 8:32; 23:9; Acts 5:37; 12:12; 14:21; 19:19; 20:8; 22:6; 1 Cor 11:30); many (Matt 28:12; Mark 10:46; Luke 7:12; Acts 11:24, 26; 19:26); of time, meaning many days (Acts 9:23, 43; 18:18; 27:7); a long time, with the gen. (Luke 8:27; 23:8; Acts 27:9), with the dat. (Acts 8:11), with the acc. (Luke 20:9; Acts 14:3; 20:11).

Deriv.: *hikanótēs* (2426), sufficiency, ability, fitness; *hikanóō* (2427), to make sufficient or fit, qualify.

Syn.: *arketós* (713), enough; *perissós* (4053), abundant; *korénnumi* (2880), to satisfy.

Ant.: *olígos* (3641), little; *métron* (3358), a measure, limited portion.

2426. ἱκανότης *hikanótēs*; gen. *hikanótetos*, fem. noun from *hikanós* (2425), able, sufficient. Sufficiency, competency, ability (2 Cor 3:5).

Syn.: *autárkeia* (841), sufficiency; *dúnamis* (1411), power; *ischús* (2479), ability, force, strength; *krátos* (2904), dominion, power; *exousía* (1849), authority; *plérōma* (4138), fullness.

Ant.: *asthéneia* (769), weakness, lack of strength; *hustérēma* (5303), a deficit,

penury, want; *hustérēsis* (5304), a falling short; *ptōcheía* (4432), poverty, helpless.

2427. ἱκανόω *hikanóō*; contracted *hikanó*, fut. *hikanósō*, from *hikanós* (2425), able, sufficient. To make sufficient, render competent or worthy (2 Cor 3:6; Col 1:12).

Syn.: *arkéō* (714), to suffice; *eparkéō* (1884), to avail for, help; *dúnamai* (1410), to be able; *dunamóō* (1412), to make strong; *dunatéō* (1414), to show oneself powerful; *ischúō* (2480), to prevail; *endunamóō* (1743), to render strong, enable.

Ant.: *leípō* (3007), to be destitute, lack; *epileípō* (1952), to be insufficient; *hupoleípō* (5275), to leave under, be left; *asthenéō* (770), to lack strength; *husteréō* (5302), to lack.

2428. ἱκετηρία *hiketēría*; gen. *hiketērías*, fem. noun from *hikétēs* (n.f.), a suppliant. Supplication. Equivalent to a supplication or humble and earnest prayer (Heb 5:7).

Syn.: *euchḗ* (2171), wish; *proseuchḗ* (4335), prayer to God; *déēsis* (1162), supplication for a particular need; *énteuxis* (1783), intercession; *eucharistía* (2169), thanksgiving; *aítēma* (155), petition; *paráklēsis* (3874), entreaty.

Ant.: *diátagma* (1297), commandment; *entolé* (1785), commandment, precept; *éntalma* (1778), a thing commanded; *epitagé* (2003), an authoritative command; *paraggelía* (3852), a request, charge.

2429. ἱκμάς *ikmás*; gen. *ikmádos*, masc. noun. Moisture, dampness (Luke 8:6; Sept.: Jer 17:8).

2430. Ἰκόνιον *Ikónion*; gen. *Ikoníou*, neut. proper noun. Iconium meaning place of images. A large and rich city of Asia Minor in the province of Lycaonia, today known as Konieh. It was situated on the great Roman highway from Ephesus to Tarsus, Antioch, and the Euphrates. It was near the confines of Phrygia and Pisidia, at the foot of Mount Taurus, in a beautiful and fertile country about two hundred miles southeast of Istanbul (formerly known as Constantinople), and was about 120 miles inland from the Mediterranean. It was an important center for the spread of the gospel. Paul visited it on his first and second missionary journeys (Acts 13:51; 14:1, 19, 21; 16:2; 2 Tim 3:11).

2431. ἱλαρός hilarós; fem. *hilará*, neut. *hilarón*, adj. from *hílaos* (n.f., see *híleōs* [2436]), propitious. Cheerful, joyous (2 Cor 9:7; Sept.: Prov 22:8). Although the Eng. word "hilarious" is derived from *hilarós*, it does not at all convey its correct meaning. The word denotes a happy, glad or cheerful state of mind and not one overcome with laughter or mirth, or one humorously affected.

Deriv.: *hilarótēs* (2432), cheerfulness.

Syn.: *eúthumos* (2115), a cheerful person; *philóphrōn* (5391), courteous.

Ant.: *skuthrōpós* (4659), gloomy; *stugētós* (4767), odious, hateful; *pikrós* (4089), bitter, sharp.

2432. ἱλαρότης hilarótēs; gen. *hilarótētos*, fem. noun from *hilarós* (2431), cheerful. Cheerfulness, gladness (only in Rom 12:8; Sept.: Prov 18:22).

Ant.: *katépheia* (2726), with a long face, sadness; *pikría* (4088), bitterness; *lúpē* (3077), sorrow.

2433. ἱλάσκομαι hiláskomai; fut. *hilásomai*, from *hílaos* (n.f., see *híleōs* [2436]), propitious To be propitious, gracious, as of gods; of men, to be kind, gentle, gracious. A mid. deponent without an act. form in the NT. In Heb 2:17 Christ is spoken of as the High Priest who in the fashion of the OT sacrifices gave Himself to *hiláskesthai* (pres. inf. of *hiláskomai* [in the KJV it is translated "to make reconciliation for the sins of the people"], to cause God to be propitious or merciful toward sinful man). What Christ did in sacrificing Himself for our sins showed Him to be merciful (*eleḗmōn* [1655]) and faithful (*pistós* [4103]). His sacrifice as the God-Man satisfied God's justice so that, instead of God rightly demonstrating His wrath toward sinful man (Rom 1:18; 5:8–10), He demonstrated His mercy. Christ is the High Priest who offers Himself, becoming at once both victim and priest, thus satisfying the justice of God and at the same time procuring forgiveness of sins whereby reconciled man is offered access to and communion with God. Therefore, the Lord Jesus as the High Priest is said not to appease God in any way, but to make possible the taking away of the sins of the people without violating God's holiness. Observe that the sins of the people are the direct object of the verb *hiláskesthai*. Therefore, it is not the nature of God that is changed from one of hatred to one of love toward man, but it is the nature of man that is changed. In Rom 5:9, man is presented as having been justified by means of the blood (i.e., the sacrificial death) of Christ, and through Him escaping God's wrath. Man is then proclaimed as not guilty and is portrayed as reconciled to God through the death of His Son.

The word "reconciliation [*katallagḗ* {2643}]" involves a change which is brought about through the death of Christ. The blood of Christ satisfied God's justice and, through faith, this death of Christ changes man making him a friend with whom God can now have fellowship without any compromise of God's holiness.

The corresponding Hebr. verb is *kaphar* (3722, OT), which refers to reconciliation to God. It was closely connected with the three Levitical offerings mentioned in Ezek 45:15 which offerings were intended to reconcile God and a sinning people. These offerings were closely connected to propitiation: the burnt offering, the sin offering, and the trespass offering, each of which was geared toward reconciliation (Ezek 45:15). The burnt offering required the offerer to put his hand upon the offering's head (Lev 1:4). This indicated the identification between the offerer and the offering. The latter died as a substitute for the guilty offerer and accomplished an atonement (Lev 1:4). The sin offering applied to those who sinned inadvertently (Lev 4:2). As with the burnt offering, the offerer placed his hand upon the head of the sacrifice (Lev 4:4, 15, 24, 29). The blood of the sacrifice played an important part in the offering (Lev 4:6, 17, 25, 30). The trespass offering differed from the sin offering in that it stressed the harm done by the offerer (Lev 5:15, 16; 6:4, 5). It required restitution plus an additional 20% to be given (Lev 5:16; 6:3). It differed from the other two offerings in that no mention is made of the offerer placing his hand upon the head of the offering.

The propitiation offered by Christ is capable of dealing with every kind of sin barrier between God and man, not with sins of ignorance and infirmity alone. The key to the discussion is that Christ is a "better sacrifice" (Heb 9:23) which perfects the imperfect, abolishes the typical, and lifts the whole significance of propitiation from the circle of legal and ceremonial ideas into the realm of abiding ethical and spiritual realities. Therefore, Jesus, "who through the eternal Spirit offered Himself without blemish unto God" (a.t. [v. 14]), thus becomes the author of eternal salvation—a salvation whose characteristic is finality, i.e., through "His own blood [i.e., on the basis of His sacrificial death], [He] entered, once for all, into the holy place, having obtained eternal redemption for us" (a.t. [v. 12]).

The other instance of the verb is in Luke 18:13 in the aor. imper. pass. hilásthēti, in the plea of the publican crying to God and saying, "God be merciful [hilásthēti] to me a sinner." Here it is the sinner who is dealt with in mercy, not taking into account the consequences of his sin, while in Heb 2:17 the def. art. indicates the sins of the people which are removed from sinners because of Christ's sacrifice. That being accomplished, Christ liberates the sinner from the power of sin.

See Sept.: Ps 25:11; 65:3; 79:9; Dan 9:19. The verb hiláskomai is equivalent to the periphrasis híleōs moi gínomai (híleōs [2436], appeased, merciful; moi [3427], to me; gínomai [1096], to be), to become merciful to me (see Heb 8:12). The noun hilasmós (2434), propitiation, the act of expiation or removal of sin, also propitiator or the means of the removal of sin and reconciliation (1 John 2:2; 4:10), may have a personal object, i.e., the sinner, or an impersonal object, i.e., our sins. It provides the satisfaction demanded by God's justice whereby the removal of sins is attained. Katallássō (2644), however, signifies not only the removal of the demands of justice, but God taking upon Himself the expiation (hilasmós [2434]) and establishing a relationship of peace between God and man. While God katallássei, reconciles particularly, Christ hilásketai, expiates.

Deriv.: hilasmós (2434), propitiation; hilastḗrion (2435), propitiator, mercy seat.

Syn.: eleéō (1653), to show mercy; oikteírō (3627), to have compassion on.

Ant.: kataráomai (2672), to doom, curse.

2434. ἱλασμός hilasmós; gen. hilasmoú, masc. noun from hiláskomai (2433), to propitiate, expiate. Propitiation. The benefit of Christ's blood for the sinner in the acceptance by the Father. Hilasmós refers to Christ as the one who not only propitiates but offers Himself as the propitiatory sacrifice. He is both the sacrifice and the officiating High Priest (John 1:29, 36; 1 Cor 5:7; Eph 5:2; Heb 10:14; 1 Pet 1:19; Rev 5:6, 8). The sacrifice of Jesus Christ in shedding His blood, both as the victim and the high priest, is indicated by the use of the basic verb hiláskomai (2433) in Heb 2:17: "To make reconciliation for the sins of the people," which means to pay the necessary price for the expiation and removal of the sins of the people. This was parallel to that which the high priest did, but it was perfect and a far better sacrifice in that it was permanent and unrestricted. *Tó hilastérion*, the mercy seat (Heb 9:5), was the lid or cover of the ark of the covenant on which the high priest sprinkled the blood of an expiatory victim (Ex 25:17–22; Lev 16:11, 13–15). The use of all these words must, therefore, be connected with the blood of Christ shed on the cross. The cross was the place of expiation (the mercy seat) and Christ was the sacrifice whose blood (His sacrificial death) was sprinkled on it.

The periphrastic use of the verb is found also in Heb 8:12, "For I will be merciful to their unrighteousness, and their sins and their iniquities will I remember no more." The expression here is *híleōs ésomai* (*híleōs* [2436], merciful; *ésomai*, [fut. act. indic. of *eimí* {1510}, to be], I shall be), "I shall be merciful" (a.t.). The Lord Jesus is declaring here that He, through the sacrifice of Himself, will become the means of the removal of the sins of His people and of their status of unrighteousness or enmity with God.

Hilasmós, found only in 1 John 2:2 and 4:10, is equivalent to *hilastérion* (2435) as used by Paul in Rom 3:25. It is the means of putting away sin and establishing righteousness. God is never presented as changing His mind toward the sinner or the sin that estranged the sinner from Him. Man is never said to be able to appease God with any of his offerings, as in the heathen religions where man offered gifts in an attempt to accomplish this.

In the NT, we find man incapable of offering anything to placate God because He is a righteous God. For Him to accept sinful man, it was necessary for God, not man, to do something to deliver man from his sin. This is the reason why, in 1 John 2:1, we find Jesus Christ presented as the righteous One. God demands that the payment for sin be made once and for all. It is Christ Himself, therefore, who becomes *hilasmós*, the means which is acceptable to God to satisfy His righteousness or His justice. This does not merely appease God but provides

the means for the redemption of man. Christ is the propitiation which supplies the method of deliverance from our sin and, being reconciled to God, we are acceptable for fellowship with God. Christ became the vicarious and expiatory sacrifice for our sins. John adds that this sacrifice of Christ was a historical event. Jesus Christ does not need to shed his blood and die again for any new believers because it is all-encompassing. Nobody's sins have ever been permanently removed in any other way except by means of the Lord Jesus Christ and His death on Calvary's cross. OT sacrifices pointed toward Christ's sacrifice, which is an objective accomplishment, a finished work for the whole world as a basis from which individual forgiveness and cleansing from sin proceeds.

The virtue of the propitiation extends beyond the subjective experience of those who actually are made partakers of grace. 1 John 2:2 presents the propitiation of Christ as vividly personal: "He is our propitiation" (a.t.). The life of Christ as well as His death is involved, His person as well as His work. The use of the word *hilasmós* by John refers not only to the process of the atonement, but also to its final achievement as a fact: "He is the propitiation"; "His blood is cleansing us from all sin" (a.t. [1 John 1:7]). It is more than a completed act. The propitiation abides as a living, present energy residing in the personality of Christ Himself. According to John, therefore, the propitiation is the cleansing from sin rather than merely the work of justification before God or the acceptance of the sinner as if he had never sinned.

Paul associates Christ's propitiation as more closely connected with the righteousness of the Law. In John, love and propitiation become interchangeable realities necessary to one another, with one explaining the other, even lost in one another. John defines love by propitiation, and propitiation by love: "In this have we come to know what love is, that He for us laid down His life" (a.t. [1 John 3:16];

"Herein is love, not that we loved God, but that he loved us, and sent his Son to be the propitiation for our sins" (1 John 4:10). When John speaks of God as love, he refers to Him as the means of reconciliation of man to God. See *hiláskomai* (2433), to propitiate, to reconcile to oneself; *hilastḗrion* (2435), propitiator, mercy seat; *híleōs* (2436), mercy, merciful, propitious.

Syn.: *katallagē*; (2643), reconciliation.

Ant.: *katára* (2671), curse; *ará* (685), imprecation, curse; *anáthema* (331), accursed.

2435. ἱλαστήριος *hilastḗrios*; gen. *hilastēríou*, adj. from *hiláskomai* (2433), to propitiate, expiate. Propitiatory, expiatory, merciful. Mercy seat, viewed as a subst. Used in the NT as a neut. noun. The lid or covering of the ark of the covenant made of pure gold, on and before which the high priest was to sprinkle the blood of the expiatory sacrifices on the Day of Atonement, and where the Lord promised to meet His people (Ex 25:17, 22; Lev 16:2, 14, 15). Paul, by applying this name to Christ in Rom 3:25, assures us that Christ was the true mercy seat, the reality typified by the cover on the ark of the covenant (Heb 9:5). Therefore, it means a place of conciliation, of expiation, what the ancients called *thusiastḗrion* (2379), altar or place of sacrifice. It does not refer to the expiatory sacrifices themselves. Jesus Christ is designated as *hilastḗrion* in Rom 3:25 and Heb 9:5 because He is designated not only as the place where the sinner deposits his sin, but He Himself is the means of expiation. He is not like the high priest of the OT whose expiation of the people was accomplished through the blood of something other than himself (Heb 9:25).

What the Jews called the *Kapporeth* (3727, OT; Gr., the *hilastḗrion*) was the principal part of the Holy of Holies. Later it was even termed as "the house of the Capporeth" (a.t. [1 Chr 28:11]). Philo calls the Capporeth "the symbol of the mercy of the power of God." The *hilastḗrion* of the OT referred to in Heb 9:5 was actually the cover of the ark of the covenant in the Holy of Holies, in Eng. called the mercy seat. It was sprinkled with the blood of the victim slain on the annual Day of Atonement. We must point out, however, that the translation "mercy seat," symbolically referring to Jesus Christ, is an inadequate translation of the Gr. word which is rather equivalent to the Throne of Grace. The *hilastḗrion* means the propitiating thing or the propitiatory gift, that which causes God to deal with us mercifully. This is the connotation given by Paul to the word in Rom 3:25. Here Paul depicts Christ as the lamb slain whose blood cleanses us from sin (1 John 1:7). In heathen religions the people who sacrificed or did anything to appease their god appeared to be or believed that they were manipulating him. In Christianity, however, it is never people who take the initiative or make the sacrifice, but God Himself who, out of His great love for sinners, provided the way by which His wrath against sin might be averted. Jesus shed His blood and became the way to the Father for sinners.

The effect of Christ's work on the cross is the salvation of the sinner, who then becomes capable of fellowship with a holy God. In the OT, through the system of sacrifices, God taught the way by which a sinful man or woman might approach Him. Sin means death, which basically is separation from God. The sacrificial system was a way whereby God provided the means of approaching Him through escaping sin and its basic consequences. Through it another died in the sinner's place. This was never another man, but an animal. The individual Israelite was instructed to bring an animal for sacrifice whenever he approached God; the family was to kill and consume an animal at the yearly observance of the Passover; the nation was to be thus represented by the high priest annually on the Day of Atonement when the blood of the offering was sprinkled upon the mercy seat (*hilastḗrion*) on the ark of the covenant within the Holy of Holies of the Jewish temple. At the end of the Old dispensation, Jesus appeared as the offering that was to take away "the sin of the world" (John 1:29). In God's plan there was a progression: one sacrifice for one nation, one sacrifice for the world—Jesus Christ.

The way to God's presence is now open to anyone who will come, a fact symbolized by the rending of the veil of the temple (which separated the Holy of Holies from the rest of the temple) at Christ's death.

When we come to the Apostle Paul's use of the word *hilastḗrion* in Rom 3:25 (where the word may be the adj. *hilastḗrios* instead of the neut. noun *tó hilastḗrion*), it is scarcely possible that he conceives of the Messiah as a "mercy seat" or "covering of the ark," sprinkled with blood—His own blood. What the Apostle Paul refers to with the word *hilastḗrion* is the means of gaining the favor of God through Jesus Christ.

There is a fundamental difference, however, between the illustration that he brings by referring to the Levitical sacrificial system of the OT and the person of the Lord Jesus Christ. In the OT, it was the people who selected the animal to be sacrificed. However, in the NT, it is God the Father who provided ahead of time (*proétheto*, 2d aor. mid. indic. of *protíthēmi* [4388], to place before or ahead of time) for the whole world what the sacrifice of the individual was for himself in contrast to that of the high priest for Israel. God foreordained the Lord Jesus to become the Lamb whose slaying was predetermined before the world began (Rev 13:8). That Paul does not refer to the actual physical covering by the use of the word *hilastḗrion* is indicated by the fact that he does not use the def. art. What he means, however, is that like the covering of the ark, the mercy seat in the OT having been sprinkled with the blood of the victim became the proof of sacrifice

offered. Likewise, in the person of the Lord Jesus Christ and the shedding of His blood on the cross, we have the proof of the better sacrifice that God chose to make on behalf of all humanity.

Furthermore, the sinner could benefit from that sacrifice, not through repeating it himself, but through faith. Believing and accepting the actual bodily sacrifice of Jesus Christ in shedding His blood is a spiritual exercise of man which is sufficient to satisfy the justice of God. In this passage it is called "constant righteousness" (*dikaiosúnē* [1343]) (a.t.), which is what God requires. Since the punishment of sin is death, God permitted the sacrifice of Jesus, which removes the believer's sin. This is in adherence to His own principle. The word *dikaiosúnē*, justice or righteousness, is used by Paul in Rom 3:21, 22, 25, 26. In Rom 3:24 the verb *dikaióō* (1344), to justify, is used. What is stressed when speaking of Christ's being the means of our propitiation or the demonstration of God's mercy toward us is that this is done by means of Christ's sacrificial death, the shedding of His blood in contradistinction to the blood of animals. No priest had ever before sacrificed his own blood for the sins of his people. Jesus Christ is not only the Lamb of God which takes away the sin of the world, but He is also our High Priest whose sacrifice applies not only to Israel, but to the whole world.

As the blood of the animals sprinkled upon the mercy seat of the ark of the covenant is simply an illustration of what the sacrifice (blood) of Christ does when applied to believing sinners, so is also the phrase in Rom 3:25, "for the remission of sins." However, the word here is not the word that is usually translated "remission" (*áphesis* [859]), but the word *páresis* (3929), forbearance or passing by, winking at. Some theologians believe that this indicates that the work of the OT sacrifices did not result in the removal of the sins of the people, but in causing God to be merciful enough to overlook or not take into account their sins. That is why the sacrifices needed to be repeated. These sacrifices provided *páresin*, forbearance or toleration by God, but the blood of Jesus Christ provides *áphesin*, forgiveness or actual deliverance from sin and the nature of sin. However, the word may have been used because of the relative inefficacy of the OT sacrifices. Their efficacy was only temporary and in comparison to the eternal efficaciousness of Christ's sacrifice, they seemed as ineffectual.

On the other hand, God's passing over the sins of Israel did not involve the sin nature of man, but simply the concrete sins of the individual indicated by the word *hamartḗmata* (265). The acceptance of the OT sacrifices in connection with the mercy seat demonstrated the forbearance of God as indicated by the word *anochḗ* (463), forbearance, tolerance, with which this verse closes. To put it succinctly, through the sacrifices of the OT we have the demonstration of God's toleration of sin; however, through the blood of Christ we have the demonstration of the love and justice of God in that He took the initiative to send His Son into the world to shed His blood. Thus God's justice demands that sin must be paid for by death involving the shedding of blood and the radical change of the individual in turning him from that sin, delivering him from it and thereby bringing him into fellowship with Himself (Rom 5:1, 2).

Syn.: *híleōs* (2436), propitious; *éleos* (1656), mercy.

Ant.: *ará* (685) and *katára* (2671), curse; *anáthema* (331), accursed.

2436. ἵλεως *híleōs*; masc.-fem., neut. *híleon*, adj., the Attic for *hílaos* (n.f.). Appeased, merciful, as of gods; cheerful, propitious, favorable, merciful, as of men. In Matt 16:22, what is translated "Be it far from thee, Lord" in Gr. is *híleṓs soi* (unto you) *Kúrie* (Lord) and it is elliptical for *híleṓs soi hḗ* (be) *Kúrie* (Lord). Literally, it is "Be merciful to thyself, Lord" (a.t.). In these and such phrases the word *híleōs* implies an invocation of mercy for the overturning of evil, that is to say for the cancellation of the consequence of the evil that others are contemplating. See *éleos* (1656), mercy. In modern vernacular we would say, "God forbid!" as an exclamation of aversion. See 2 Sam 20:20; 23:17; 1 Chr 11:19. In Heb 8:12, the meaning is "I will be merciful to their iniquities" (a.t.) or "I will alleviate the results of their iniquities; I will pardon them." (a.t.) See Sept.: 2 Chr 6:25, 27.

Deriv. of *híleōs*: *aníleōs* (448), unmerciful.

of *hílaos* (n.f.): *hilarós* (2431), cheerful, joyous; *hiláskomai* (2433), to be propitious, gracious.

Syn.: *pheídomai* (5339), to spare.

Ant.: *aníleōs* (448), without mercy; *kataráomai* (2672), to curse.

2437. Ἰλλυρικόν *Illurikón*; gen. *Illurikoú*, neut. proper noun. Illyricum, a Roman province of southeastern Europe lying along the eastern coast of the Adriatic Sea and west of Macedonia. On account of the insurrection of the Dalmatians (11 B.C.), the province was divided and the northern portion called Dalmatia; the southern portion remained one of the Senate's provinces. Paul preached around the area as far as Illyricum (Rom 15:19).

2438. ἱμάς *himás*; gen. *imántos*, masc. noun. Generally a string or strap.

(I) The thong or string of leather with which sandals were tied to the foot (Matt 1:7; Luke 3:16; John 1:27; Sept.: Isa 5:27).

(II) Thongs or straps of leather used to bind and scourge criminals, and especially slaves (Acts 22:25).

2439. ἱματίζω *himatízō*; fut. *himatísō*, from *himátion* (2440), apparel, garment. To clothe. In the mid. *himatízomai*, to be clothed (Mark 5:15; Luke 8:35).

Deriv.: *himatismós* (2441), clothing, raiment.

Syn.: *endúō* (1746), to clothe.

Ant.: *gumnēteúō* (1130), to strip, be naked.

2440. ἱμάτιον *himátion*; gen. *himatíou*, neut. noun. Garment.

(I) Generally any garment (Matt 9:16; 11:8; Mark 2:21; Luke 5:36; 7:25; Heb 1:11). Pl.: *tá himátia*, garments, clothing, raiment including the outer and inner garment, cape and shirt or coat (Matt 17:2; 24:18; 27:31, 35; Mark 15:24; John 13:4, 12; James 5:2; Rev 4:4); "to rend the clothes" (a.t. [Matt 26:65; Acts 14:14; 16:22; 22:23; Sept. sing.: Ps 102:26; Isa 50:9; pl.: Gen 27:27; 38:19; 2 Sam 1:2; 3:31; 1 Kgs 1:1]).

(II) The outer garment, mantle, cape different from the tunic or *chitón* (5509), a shirt over which the *himátion* is worn (cf. Acts 9:39). The *himátion* seems to have been a large piece of woolen cloth nearly square, which was wrapped around the body or fastened about the shoulders, and served also to wrap oneself in at night (Ex 22:26, 27); hence it might not be taken by a creditor, though the tunic could be (cf. Matt 5:40; Luke 6:29 [see Matt 9:20, 21; 14:36; John 19:2; Acts 12:8]). Pl., *tá himátia*, outer garments which were often laid aside (Matt 21:7, 8; Acts 7:58; 22:20; Sept.: Ex 22:26, 27; 1 Sam 21:9; Isa 3:6, 7).

Deriv.: *himatízō* (2439), to clothe.

Syn.: *himatismós* (2441), clothing, apparel; *chlamús* (5511), a military cloak worn over the *chitón* by emperors, kings, magistrates, military officers; *stolḗ* (4749), a stately robe or uniform, a long gown worn as mark of dignity; *katastolḗ* (2689), long robe of dignity; *esthḗs* (2066) and *ésthēsis* (2067), clothing; *énduma* (1742), a garment of any kind; *ependútēs* (1903), an upper or outer garment which sometimes fishermen wore when at work; *phelónēs* (5341), a mantle, traveling robe for protection against stormy weather, overcoat; *peribólaion* (4018), a wrap or cape, a garment thrown around one; *podḗrēs* (4158), an outer garment reaching to the feet; *sképasma* (4629), a cover-

ing, raiment; *phelónēs* (5341), a traveling cloak.

Ant.: *gumnótēs* (1132), nakedness.

2441. ἱματισμός *himastismós*; gen. *himatismoú*, masc. noun from *himatízō* (2439), to clothe. Clothing, raiment. Garments stately and costly (Matt 27:35; Luke 7:25; 9:29; John 19:24 quoted from Ps 22:18; Acts 20:33; 1 Tim 2:9; Sept.: 1 Kgs 22:30; 2 Kgs 7:8).

Syn.: *himátion* (2440), an outer cloak or cape; *esthḗs* (2066), dress, robe; *stolḗ* (4749), uniform, distinctive garment indicative of dignity.

Ant.: *gumnótēs* (1132), nakedness.

2442. ἱμείρομαι *himeíromai*; aor. mid. *himeirámēn*, mid. deponent from *hímeros* (n.f.), a longing or yearning after. To desire, to be affectionately desirous of (only in 1 Thess 2:8 [TR]).

Syn.: *epithuméō* (1937), to desire earnestly; *epipothéō* (1971), to long for or after.

Ant.: *apōthéomai* (683), to push off, and its syn.

2443. ἵνα *hína*; conj. That, so that, for the purpose of, construed usually with a subjunctive, seldom with the opt., often with the indic. marking the end, purpose. Also used to indicate the cause for, or on account of which anything is done. Can be translated, "to the end that," "in order that it might [or may] be." It may also be used simply to indicate a happening, event or result of anything, or that in which the action terminates. *Hína* can be translated "so that it was [is, or will be]."

(I) Indicating purpose, end (*télos* [5056], end) in which case we call it a telic conj. It marks the final end, purpose, or cause and can be translated "to the end that," "in order that," and with the neg. *mḗ* (3361), not, *hína mḗ*, it means "in order that not," "lest."

(A) With the subjunctive: **(1)** Preceded by the pres. or an aor. of any mood except the indic., or by the perf. in a pres. sense (John 6:38). Here the subjunctive marks that which is supposed will really take place. "I have come from heaven and I am here to do" (a.t.), with the meaning I am now doing not My will but the will of the One who sent Me. In Matt 9:6, "To the end that ye may know" (a.t. [cf. Mark 2:10; Luke 5:24]). See Matt 18:16; 19:16; Luke 8:10; 12:36; John 1:7; 5:34; 6:38; 11:4; 17:21; Acts 16:30; Rom 1:11; 1 Cor 9:12; 2 Cor 4:7, 10, 11; Gal 6:13; James 4:3. With the neg. *mḗ* in Luke 8:12; John 7:23; Rom 11:25, meaning lest. (2) Preceded by the imper., the subjunctive (cf. A, 1 above), e.g., after the pres. imper., Luke 21:36, "watch . . . and pray . . . that ye may be accounted worthy." Also John 7:3; 1 Cor 7:5; Eph 4:28; 6:3; 1 Tim 5:7; with the neg. *mḗ* (Matt 7:1, "Judge not, that ye be not judged"; 17:27; John 4:15; 5:14; Heb 12:13); after an imper. aor. (Matt 14:15, "dismiss the crowds that they may go into the village and buy"; Mark 15:32; Luke 16:9; 1 Cor 3:18; Eph 6:13); after an exhortation, e.g., *ágōmen* (71), "Let us go" (Mark 1:38; Luke 20:14; Rom 3:8); after an imper. implied (Matt 26:5; John 1:22; 1 Pet 4:11; Sept.: Josh 4:6). (3) Preceded by the fut., the subjunctive (cf. A, 1 above): Luke 16:4, "I am resolved what to do, that . . . they may receive me"; 1 Cor 16:6; 2 Cor 12:9; Eph 6:21; 2 Thess 2:12. Interrogative (Matt 19:16; John 6:5); with the neg. *mḗ* (Luke 18:5). (4) Preceded by a past tense, the subjunctive strictly stands instead of the opt. and marks an action which, in itself or in its consequences, is still continued or which the speaker regards as certain. (a) Generally as in Mark 3:14, "and he ordained twelve, that [*hína*] they should be with him," meaning that He knew for sure, not simply hoped or wished, that they were going to be with Him; Luke 1:3, 4, "It seemed good to me also . . . to write unto thee in order. . . . That [*hína*] thou mightest know [*epignōs*, the subjunctive aor. of *epiginōskō* {1921}, to know fully]." See Matt 12:10; John 1:31; 3:16, 17; 8:6; Acts 27:42; Rom 1:13; 1 Cor 1:27, 28; 2 Cor 2:4; Gal 1:16; 2:4, 5; Heb 2:14, 17.

With the neg. *mḗ* (1 Cor 12:25; Eph 2:9; Heb 11:28); elliptically (John 1:8, with the verb "was sent" [a.t.] implied; John 9:3 where the phrase "this was done" [a.t.] is understood before *hína*). (b) In simple narrations where the subjunctive is used (Matt 27:26, "He delivered him [Jesus] to be crucified [*hína staurōthḗ*]"; Mark 6:41; 9:18, 22; 10:13; Luke 19:4, 15; John 1:19); with the neg. *mḗ* (John 18:28; 19:31).

(B) With the opt. preceded by the pres., where the opt. marks what may possibly take place as in Eph 1:17 where *hína* is translated "may," expressing a wish. See Eph 3:16.

(C) With the indic., but only the indic. fut. or pres., and not with a past tense as often in Class. Gr. writers. (1) With the fut. indic., in the same sense as the subjunctive (cf. A, 1 above [Acts 21:24 UBS]). Also fut. and subjunctive together (Rev 22:14). In Eph 6:3, "That it may be well with thee, and thou mayest live long on the earth," *ésē*, the fut. indic. of *eimí* (1510), to be, may be taken independently of *hína*, i.e., "and thou shalt live long" (a.t.). (2) With the pres. indic., in the same sense (1 Cor 4:6; Gal 4:17; 1 Pet 3:1).

(II) As marking simply the event, result or outcome of an action, so that, so as that. In the NT, only with the subjunctive, implying something which really takes place; in Class. Gr. writers more often with the indic. of a past tense.

(A) Preceded by the pres. tense (Luke 22:30; John 6:7; Rom 3:19; 6:1; 7:13; 15:6, 16; Rev 14:13).

(B) Preceded by the imper. (Acts 8:19; James 1:4; 1 Pet 4:13; 5:6; 1 John 2:28). With the neg. *mḗ* (Titus 3:14).

(C) Preceded by the fut. (Luke 11:50; John 5:20; 16:24; 2 Cor 1:11; Phil 1:26).

(D) Preceded by a past tense (cf. I, A, 3 above [Luke 9:45; John 9:2; Rom 5:20; 6:4, 6; 11:11]). Here belongs the frequent phrase *hína plērōthḗ hē graphḗ* (*plērōthḗ* [4137], be fulfilled; *graphḗ* [1124], the Scripture) or *tó rhēthén* (*rhēthén* [4483], that which was spoken), that the Scripture might be fulfilled, or that which was said might be fulfilled, used as a formula of quotation and implying that something took place, not *in order that* (purpose) a prophecy might be fulfilled, but *so that* (result) it was fulfilled; not in order to make the event correspond to the prophecy, but the fact that the event did correspond to it. See Matt 1:22; 2:15; 21:4; 26:56; John 15:25. With a past tense implied (Mark 14:49; John 13:18). See *plēróō* (4137), to fulfill.

(III) In later Gr., *hína* in various constructions lost the power of marking either purpose or event and became simply a demonstrative conj. like our Eng. "that," i.e., merely pointing out that to which the preceding words refer or introducing something already implied in the preceding words. In this way *hína* with the subjunctive often came to be used where earlier writers used the inf. or other particles, e.g.:

(A) Used instead of the construction with the inf., originally perhaps because the inf. also often implies purpose. (1) After words and phrases implying command and the like, as in Eng. "I command that you do it," or "I command you to do it." See Mark 13:34; John 11:57; 13:34; Acts 17:15. Similarly, *hína* after the verbs *aggareúō* (29), to force or press into public service (Matt 27:32); *apaggéllō* (518), to announce, declare (Matt 28:10); *apostéllō* (649), to send (Acts 16:36); *gráphō* (1125), to write (Mark 12:19); *diastéllomai* (1291), to enjoin (Mark 13:34); *eípon* (2046), I said (Matt 4:3; Mark 3:2, 9; Rev 6:11); *exorkízō* (1844), to adjure (Matt 26:63); *epitimáō* (2008), to rebuke (Matt 12:16; Mark 3:12); *légō* (3004), to speak (John 13:29; Acts 19:4; 1 John 5:16); *paraggéllō* (3853), to enjoin, charge (Mark 6:8), with the inf. (Mark 8:6); *suntíthemai* (4934), to consent (John 9:22). See Mark 11:16; Rev 9:5. With some word of command implied (Eph 5:33). (2) After verbs of entreating, persuading, and the like as with *déomai* (1189), to beseech (Luke 9:40; 22:32); *diamartúromai* (1263), to protest

(1 Tim 5:21); *erōtáō* (2065), to entreat (Mark 7:26; Luke 7:36; John 17:15); *parakaléō* (3870), to entreat (Matt 14:36; Mark 5:10; Luke 8:31, 32); *proseúchomai* (4336), to pray (Matt 24:20); *eúchomai* (2172), to wish, with the inf. (2 Cor 13:7); *peíthō* (3982), to persuade (Matt 27:20). (3) After verbs of desire and the like (cf. as above, e.g., *thélō* [2309], wish Matt 7:12; Mark 6:25; Luke 6:31; 18:41; John 17:24). Also with the subst. *thélēma* (2307), wish or desire in the expression *thélēmá esti* (is) *hína* (Matt 18:14; John 6:39, 40; 1 Cor 16:12); preceded by *zēteítai* (2212), is demanded or asked (1 Cor 4:2); with *thélō* (2309), desire or wish, implied (Gal 2:10). (4) After *poiéō* (4160), to make or do in the sense of to cause, to effect, where in earlier Gr. the inf. is used. See John 11:37; Col 4:16; Rev 3:9; 13:12, 15, 16. In Rev 3:9 the fut. also is joined with the subjunctive after *hína*. (5) After words implying fitness, sufficiency, need, and the like, e.g., *áxios* (514), worthy (John 1:27); after *hikanós* (2425), fit, able (Matt 8:8; Luke 7:6); *arketós* (713), enough (Matt 10:25). With the expression *chreían échō* (*chreían* [5532], need; *échō* [2192], to have), to have need (John 2:25; 16:30; 1 John 2:27; Rev 21:23). Also after the impersonal *sumphérei* (4851), it is profitable (Matt 5:29, 30; 18:6; John 11:50; 16:7). (6) After a word or phrase followed by a defining or explanatory clause, the latter is sometimes introduced by *hína*, where the Class. Gr. construction would be with the inf., e.g., John 4:34; 18:39; 1 Cor 4:3. Also especially after *hoútos* (3778), this one, used emphatically or demonstratively in reference to a following clause. See Luke 1:43; John 6:29, 39; 17:3; 1 John 3:11, 23; 4:21; 2 John 1:6. Also with the expression *en toútō hína*, translated "Herein . . . that" (John 15:8; 1 John 4:17). See John 15:13; 3 John 1:4. Also with *hoútos*, this one, or *en toútō*, in this, which is implied (1 Cor 9:18).

(B) Instead of *hópōs* (3704), so that, after verbs of taking care, endeavoring, and the like, e.g., *blépō* (991), to see, to heed (1 Cor 16:10; Col 4:17; 2 John 1:8); *zēlóō* (2206), to desire, be zealous for (1 Cor 14:1); *zētéō* (2212), to seek (1 Cor 14:12); *merimnáō* (3309), to be anxious for (1 Cor 7:34); *phulássomai* (5442), to watch oneself (2 Pet 3:17). See 2 Cor 8:7.

(**C**) Instead of *hóti* (3754), that, e.g., after *gráphō* (1125), to write (Mark 9:12). In Rom 4:23 with *hóti*. See 1 Cor 9:10 (for Rev 14:13 see II, A). After *agalliáō* (21), to rejoice greatly (John 11:15); *hóti* used with *chaírō* (5463), to rejoice (Luke 10:20).

(**D**) Of time, but only in John after *hṓra* (5610), hour, instead of the more usual *hóte* (3753), when, or the expression *en hḗ*, in which. See John 12:23; 13:1; 16:2, 32, in Eng., "The hour is come, *that* the Son of man should be glorified," i.e., for, when, or in which. Here we may take *hína* as "*so that* he shall be glorified" (a.t., italics added).

Syn.: *hṓste* (5620), that, thus; *hoútō* or *hoútōs* (3779), so that.

2444. ἰνατίχ ἵνα τί *hinatí*, *hína tí* interrogative expression from *hína* (2443) and *ti* (5101), what, to what end, sometimes used as two words. Wherefore, why (Matt 9:4; 27:46; Luke 13:7; Acts 4:25; 7:26; 1 Cor 10:29; Sept.: Ps 2:1).

Syn.: *diatí* (1302), why, wherefore; *pṓs* (4459), how, in what way.

2445. Ἰόππη *Ióppē*; gen. *Ióppēs*, fem. noun transliterated from the Hebr. *Yāphō'* (3305, OT), beauty. Joppa, an ancient walled town on the coast of Palestine, about thirty-five miles from Jerusalem. It was allotted to Dan, but there is no evidence that the Israelites ever possessed it in pre-exilic times. It was the seaport for Jerusalem. Timber from the forests of Lebanon were floated from Tyre to Joppa for the building of the temple of Solomon (2 Chr 2:16), and again when the temple was being rebuilt after the return from the Babylonian captivity (Ezra 3:7). At that time it was under Phoenician control. Jonah there boarded a ship bound for Tarshish when he fled from the presence of the Lord (Jon 1:3). It was here that Peter raised Dorcas to life (Acts 9:36f.), and on the roof of Simon the Tanner's house he received the famous vision which taught him that the gospel was intended for Jew and Gentile alike (Acts 10:5ff.; 11:5ff.). The city today is joined to Tel Aviv.

2446. Ἰορδάνης *Iordánēs*; gen. *Iordánou*, masc. proper noun transliterated from the Hebr. *Yardhēn* (3383, OT), the descender. Jordan, the great river of Palestine. The river was known to Abraham (Gen 13:10). It begins at the mountains of Anti-Lebanon not far from the village Paneas or Banias near Caesarea Philippi and is joined by other streams. After a course of about fifteen miles, it passes through the lake or marsh of Merom or Samochon, and after a similar distance further flows into the Sea of Galilee. It flows through the lake into a fertile valley and continues down to the Dead Sea. The average breadth of the Jordan is from 60 to 85 feet and its depth about 10 or 12 feet. Mentioned in Matt 3:5, 6, 13; 4:15, 25; 19:1; Mark 1:5, 9; 3:8; 10:1; Luke 3:3; 4:1; John 1:28; 3:26; 10:40.

2447. ἰός *iós*; gen. *ioú*, masc. noun from *híēmi* (n.f., see below), to send. Something sent out, emitted, hence venom that serpents eject from their fangs (Rom 3:13 quoted from Ps 140:3; James 3:8); rust as being emitted or formed on metals (James 5:3; Sept.: Ezek 24:6).

Deriv. of *híēmi* (n.f.): *aníēmi* (447), to send up, to loosen; *aphíēmi* (863), to send, dismiss; *kathíēmi* (2524), to let down; *paríēmi* (3935), to neglect; *suníēmi* (4920), to put together.

2448. Ἰούδα *Ioúda*; masc. proper noun transliterated from the Hebr. *Yᵉhūdāh* (3063, OT), confessor of Jehovah, praise. Judah, the fourth son of Jacob and Leah, born in Mesopotamia (Gen 29:35). The name was given as an expression of the mother's gratitude. We know more of him than of the other patriarchs except Joseph. Judah advised his brothers to sell rather than kill Joseph (Gen 37:26–28). Judah became surety for the safety of Benjamin on the second journey to Egypt (Gen 43:3–10). The tribe of Judah was always large and prominent, vying with Ephraim for supremacy. The prophetic blessing which his father pronounced on Judah (Gen 49:8–12) is remarkable. It describes the warlike character and steadily increasing strength of the tribe (Rev 5:5; Sept.: Num 2:3; Josh 15:1; Judg 1:2, 3; Isa 29:1 [where its capital is called Ariel, "Lion of God"]; the duration of its power until the coming of Christ when Judea became a province of Rome (cf. Luke 2:1–7; Acts 5:37); and the destruction of their city (A.D. 70), when the Christian dispensation had become established (cf. Matt 24:14; Acts 2:8; Rom 10:18) in the glory and triumph of the Messiah. Judah's descendants took the southern section of Canaan from the Jordan to the Mediterranean Sea and northward to the territory of Benjamin and Dan (Josh 15:1–63). The kingdom of Judah embraced not only the territory of the tribe of Judah, but also included the larger part of Benjamin on the northeast, Dan on the northwest, and Simeon on the south. After the division of the kingdom (975 B.C.), Judah maintained its separate existence for 389 years, until 586 B.C. During this period there were nineteen rulers, all of the lineage of David, excepting Athaliah. During the first three reigns, Israel and Judah were in an attitude of hostility. Israel under Jeroboam was decidedly defeated (2 Chr 13). Later, an alliance was formed by the marriage of Jehoshaphat's son with Ahab's daughter, Athaliah (2 Kgs 11; 2 Chr 22), who usurped the crown. The two great foes of Judah were Egypt on the southwest and Assyria on the northeast. The children of Ammon, Moab, and Mount Seir also invaded Judah during Jehoshaphat's reign, but they only destroyed one another (2 Chr 20:22–25). The district, with its cities, assigned to the tribe of Judah in the promised land, is described in Josh 15.

2449. Ἰουδαία *Ioudaía*; gen. *Ioudaías*, fem. proper noun. Judea. The province of Judea, a name applied to that part of Canaan occupied by those who returned after the Assyrian and Babylonian captivities. The word first occurs in Dan 5:13 ("Jewry" in the KJV) and the first mention of the province of Judea is in Ezra 5:8; it is alluded to in Neh 11:3 ("Judah" in the KJV). In the NT, the expressions are "the land of Judea" and simply "Judea." In a wider and improper sense, Judea was sometimes applied to the whole country of the Canaanites, its ancient inhabitants, and even in the gospels we read of the coasts of Judea, "beyond Jordan" (a.t. [Matt 19:1 implied; Mark 10:1]). Judea was strictly the third district west of the Jordan and south of Samaria. It was made a portion of the Roman province of Syria after Archelaus was deposed in A.D. 6 and was governed by a procurator who was subject to the governor of Syria. Judea is also called the hill country, as the center ridge of mountains stretches from north to south and forms, as it were, the backbone of the land of Palestine (Luke 1:65). The wilderness of Judea is a wild and desolate region extending from the hill country near Jerusalem southeast of the Dead Sea and averaging about fifteen miles in breadth (Matt 3:1). It is a limestone country, rough and barren, with only patches of grass. It seems never to have had many inhabitants and no cities. The traditional scene of the temptation of Christ is in this district on a high, frightfully desolate mountain behind Jericho (Matt 4:1; Mark 1:13).

2450. ἰουδαΐζω *Ioudaḯzō*; fut. *Ioudaḯsō*, from *Ioudaíos* (2453), a Jew. To Judaize or conform to or live according to Jewish customs or manners (Gal 2:14).

2451. Ἰουδαϊκός *Ioudaïkós*; fem. *Ioudaïkḗ*, neut. *Ioudaikón*, adj. Jewish (Titus 1:14).
Ant.: *ethnikós* (1482), Gentile.

2452. Ἰουδαϊκῶς *Ioudaïkṓs*; adv. After the manner and customs of the Jewish people.
Ant.: *ethnikṓs* (1483), in the manner of Gentiles.

2453. Ἰουδαῖος *Ioudaíos*; fem. *Ioudaía*, neut. *Ioudaíon*, adj. Jewish, subst., a Jew or a Judean, from Judea. All the posterity of Jacob were called "Israel" or "children of Israel" from the surname of the patriarch, until the time of King Rehoboam. Ten tribes, revolting from this prince and adhering to Jeroboam, became known from then on as the House of Israel. The two tribes of Judah and Benjamin, remaining faithful to the family of David, were called the House of Judah. Therefore, after the defection of the ten tribes, *Ioudaíoi*, Jews, signified subjects of the kingdom of Judah (2 Kgs 16:6; 25:25; Jer 38:19; 40:11). After the Babylonian captivity, the name "Jews" was extended to all the descendants of Israel who retained the Jewish religion, whether they belonged to the two or the ten tribes and whether or not they returned to Judah as no doubt some of them did. It is in this extensive sense that the word is applied in the NT (Acts 2:5, 10 [cf. 26:7; James 1:1]). The Apostle Paul distinguishes between the one who is a Jew outwardly and the one who is a Jew inwardly (Rom 2:29; 3:1). By the former he means a person descended from Abraham, Isaac, and Jacob according to the flesh and observing the outward ordinances of the Mosaic Law, but destitute of the faith of Abraham, not believing in the seed which is Christ. By one who is a Jew inwardly Paul means one who, whether Jew or Gentile by natural descent, is a child of Abraham through faith in Christ, the promised seed (cf. Rom 4:16; Gal 3:7,

29), and consequently is a true confessor of Jehovah.
Christ also speaks of the apostate unbelieving Jews of Asia Minor, i.e., those which say they are Jews, but are not (Rev 2:9; 3:9).
Luke also makes a similar allusion to the importance of Judas who betrayed Jesus in Luke 22:47. He was called Judas which means a confessor of Jehovah, but was far from deserving the glorious name.
Ant.: *ethnikós* (1482), Gentile.

2454. ἰουδαϊσμός *Ioudaïsmós*; gen. *Ioudaïsmoú*, masc. proper noun. Judaism (Gal 1:13, 14), the religious system held by the Jews. Its teachings emanate from the OT, especially from the Law of Moses as found from Ex 20 through Deuteronomy, and also from the traditions of the elders (Mark 7:3–13), some of which the Lord Jesus condemned. The main emphases of Judaism are circumcision and Sabbath keeping.

2455. Ἰούδας *Ioúdas*; masc. proper noun transliterated from the Hebr. *Yᵉhū-dāh* (3063, OT), confessor of Jehovah, praise. Judah or Judas. The name of eight persons mentioned:
(I) Judah, the fourth son of Jacob and head of the tribe of Judah (Matt 1:2, 3; Luke 3:33). Used metonymically for the tribe and posterity of Judah (Matt 2:6; Heb 7:14; Rev 5:5; 7:5). House (*oíkos* [3624]) of Judah means the kingdom of Judah, as opposed to that of Israel (Heb 8:8).
(II) Judas or Judah, two of the ancestors of Jesus, elsewhere unknown (Luke 3:26, 30).
(III) The eleventh name of two lists of the apostles (Luke 6:16; Acts 1:13). He is called *Ioúdas Iakṓbou* which the KJV translates "Judas the brother of James," while the NASB and NIV translate it "the son of James" These two passages need to be carefully examined to see how they would be correctly translated. The gen. is used in regard to James, *Iákōbon tón toú*

Alphaíou, "James the son of Alphaeus" (Luke 6:15) and also in regard to Judas in the next verse, *Ioúdan Iakóbou*, "Judas the brother of James" It is inconceivable that in the one case the gen. *Alphaíou* makes James his son and the gen. *Iakóbou* makes Judas his brother. Likewise, in Acts 1:13, *Ioúdas Iakóbou* is translated in the KJV "the brother of James" while it should be "the son of James" as in the NASB and the NIV.

This same apostle in the other two lists does not appear as "Judas the son of James," but he is called by his alternate name of Lebbaeus (Matt 10:3) and Thaddaeus (Mark 3:18).

On the only occasion when this obscure apostle is referred to in the gospels, he is distinguished from his notorious namesake as "Judas . . . , not Iscariot" (John 14:22). All that we know of Judas Lebbaeus or Thaddaeus is that he asked the question, "Lord, how is it that thou wilt manifest thyself unto us, and not unto the world?" (John 14:22). He could not understand how the kingdom was to come unless the Messiah would make a public disclosure (*emphanízo* [1718], to exhibit) of His glory. The answer of the Lord Jesus explains that, in the very nature of the case, it is not possible for Him to reveal His glory to unloving and unrepentant, disobedient hearts. See 1 Cor 2:13ff.

(IV) Judas the brother of James. In two gospels (Matt 13:55; Mark 6:3) James, Joseph, Simon, and Judas are named conjointly with the mother of Jesus as brothers of Jesus.

In Jude 1:1, the author of that epistle is described as "Judas . . . the brother of James" (a.t.). The KJV has "Jude," and in Mark 6:3, he is called "Judas." These designations distinguish this Judas from the Jude (cf. III) who is described as "Judas the son of James" (a.t.), one of the Twelve Apostles. The confusion in not distinguishing between (III) and (IV) is the mistranslation of *Iakóbou* (Judas) in Luke 6:16 and Acts 1:13 as the brother of James (in the KJV) instead of his son

(as in the NASB and the NIV). He who is a brother cannot also be a son. In Matt 13:55, it is clearly stated that the two brothers, Judas and James, were also the (note the def. art. *hoi*) brothers of Jesus.

Of "Judas . . . the brother of James" (a.t.) as an individual we know nothing, but account should be taken of what is said collectively of our Lord's brothers. He was probably a son of Joseph and Mary, and thus a younger half-brother of Jesus. Judas misunderstood the popularity of Jesus (Matt 12:46ff.). In his estimation, Jesus was a foolish enthusiast (Mark 3:21). Before the resurrection of Jesus, he did not acknowledge his Brother as the Messiah (John 7:3ff.), but after the resurrection he is found "in prayer" in the upper room (Acts 1:14); his doubts, like those of his brother James (1 Cor 15:7), may have vanished in the presence of the risen Lord. The distinct mention of the brothers of Jesus (Acts 1:13, 14) after the eleven have been named, is another reason for rejecting the KJV translation of Luke 6:16 which identifies Judas the apostle as the brother of James As we pointed out in (III), he was the son of James and was also called Lebbaeus and Thaddaeus in Matt 10:3 and Mark 3:18 respectively. It also is further proof for the correctness of translating *Ioúdas Iakóbou* in Luke 6:16 and Acts 1:13 as "Judas the son of James" (as in the NASB and NIV) instead of "Judas the brother of James" (as the KJV has it).

(V) Judas, surnamed Iscariot, meaning man of Kerioth, an apostle and the traitor who betrayed the Lord Jesus. He seems to have been dishonest previously, though he enjoyed the confidence of the other apostles (cf. John 12:6). See Matt 10:4; 26:14, 25, 47; 27:3–6; Mark 3:19; 14:10, 43; Luke 22:3, 47, 48; John 6:71; 12:4; 13:2, 26, 29; 18:2, 3, 5; Acts 1:16, 25.

(VI) Judas surnamed Barsabas, a Christian teacher sent from Jerusalem to Antioch with Paul and Barnabas (Acts 15:22, 27, 32).

(VII) Judas, a Jew living in Damascus with whom Paul lodged at his conversion (Acts 9:11).

(VIII) Judas, surnamed the Galilean (Acts 5:37), so-called also by Josephus. In company with one Sadoc or Saddacus, he attempted to raise a sedition among the Jews but was destroyed by Cyrenius, then proconsul of Syria and Judea.

2456. 'Ιουλία *Ioulía*; gen. *Ioulías*, fem. proper noun. Julia, probably the wife of Philologus whom Paul salutes in Rom 16:15.

2457. 'Ιούλιος *Ioúlios*; gen. *Ioulíou*, masc. proper noun. Julius, a Roman centurion of the Augustian band in whose care Paul was placed for the journey to Rome (Acts 27:1, 3). He trusted Paul to go to his friends at Sidon and, along with his soldiers, saved the lives of all aboard the ship by frustrating the sailors' plot near Malta.

2458. 'Ιουνίας *Iounías*; gen. *Iounía*, fem. proper noun. Junias, a kinsman and fellow prisoner of Paul (Rom 16:7).

2459. 'Ιοῦστος *Ioústos*; gen. *Ioústou*, masc. proper noun. Justus. Three distinct people:

(I) The surname of Joseph Barsabas, one of the two whom the brethren appointed as candidates for Judas' place among the Twelve Apostles (Acts 1:23).

(II) The surname of a Christian in Corinth with whom Paul lodged for a time (Acts 18:7).

(III) The surname of Jesus, an early Hebrew Christian at Rome, evidently known to the Christians at Colossae (Col 4:11).

2460. ἱππεύς *hippeús*; gen. *hippéōs*, masc. noun from *híppos* (2462), horse. A horse soldier, cavalryman (Acts 23:23, 32; Sept.: Gen 50:9; Ex 14:9).

2461. ἱππικόν *hippikón*; adj., neut. of *hippikós*, which is from *híppos* (2462),

horse. Equestrian. In the NT, used subst. meaning cavalry, the horsemen (Rev 9:16 translated "horsemen").

2462. ἵππος *híppos*; gen. *híppou*, masc. noun. A horse (James 3:3; Rev 6:2, 4, 5, 8; 9:7, 9, 17; 14:20; 18:13; 19:11, 14, 18, 19, 21; Sept.: Gen 47:17.

Deriv.: *hippeús* (2460), horse soldier; *hippikón* (2461), cavalry; *phílippos* (5376), Philip, a lover of horses.

2463. ἶρις *íris*; gen. *íridos*, fem. noun. An iris or rainbow (Rev 4:3; 10:1). After the flood, the rainbow was appointed by God as a sign to Noah and his descendants that God would never again cut off all flesh nor destroy the earth by the waters of a flood (Gen 9:11–17).

2464. 'Ισαάκ *Isaák*; masc. proper noun transliterated from the Hebr. *Yitschāq* (3327, OT), derider, one who laughs. Isaac, the only son of Abraham by Sarah, and the second of the three Hebrew patriarchs who were the ancestors of the Jewish race. He was probably born in Beersheba (Gen 21:14, 31) when Abraham was one hundred and Sarah ninety years old (Gen 17:17; 21:5). He was named Isaac because both Abraham and Sarah had laughed incredulously at the thought of having a child at their age (Gen 17:17–19; 18:9–15; 21:6). God's promise was fulfilled twenty-five years after He made it. God commanded Abraham to sacrifice Isaac on Mount Moriah (Gen 22). Sarah died at Hebron when Isaac was thirty-six years old (Gen 23:1). At the age of forty, he married Rebekah, a kinswoman from Mesopotamia (Gen 24) to whom twin sons, Esau and Jacob, were born when Isaac was sixty (Gen 25:20, 26). In the NT, Abraham's willingness to sacrifice Isaac is mentioned twice (Heb 11:17–19; James 2:21). He is contrasted with Ishmael as the child of promise and the progenitor of the children of promise (Rom 9:7, 10; Gal 4:28; Heb 11:18). Our Lord represents Isaac as still living, although he was gathered to his people (Luke 20:37).

2465. ἰσάγγελος *isággelos*; gen. *isaggélou*, masc.-fem., neut. *isággelon*, adj. from *ísos* (2470), similar or equal, and *ággelos* (32) angel. Angel-like (Luke 20:36, which, if taken in connection with Mark 12:25, would be better translated "like" instead of "equal" [see Matt 22:30]. According to these passages, neither mortality nor sexual union pertains to either the sons of the resurrection or to the angels.)

2466. Ἰσαχάρ *Isachár*; masc. proper noun transliterated from the Hebr. *Yissāshkhār* (3485, OT), God has given me my hire. Issachar.

(I) The ninth son of Jacob and the fifth son of Leah (Gen 30:17, 18; 35:23). We do not know much of the personal history of this man except that he had four sons, and with them he went down with Jacob into Egypt (Gen 46:13; Ex 1:3). There he died and was buried. His descendants formed a tribe consisting of four great tribal families (Num 26:23). The tribe's possession lay south of Zebulun and Naphtali, north of Manasseh, and was bounded on the east by the Jordan. It occupied the greater part of the very fertile plain of Esdraelon which, however, was mostly held by the Canaanites. The princes of Issachar abandoned allegiance to Saul's family and accepted David as king of all Israel (1 Chr 12:32). In the NT, the tribe is mentioned in Rev 7:7, where we are told that 12,000 from Issachar were sealed.

(II) A Korhite doorkeeper during the reign of David (1 Chr 26:5).

2467. ἴσημι *ísēmi*; from *eísō*, the fut. of *eídō* (1492), to know. To confirm, know (Acts 26:4; Heb 12:17).
     Syn.: *epístamai* (1987), to understand, know; *epiginṓskō* (1921), to know fully.
     Ant.: *agnoéō* (50), to be ignorant.

2468. ἴσθι *ísthi*; pres. imper. 2d person sing. of *eimí* (1510), to be. Be thou (Matt 2:13; 5:25; Mark 5:34; Luke 19:17; 1 Tim 4:15).

2469. Ἰσκαριώτης *Iskariṓtēs*; gen. *Iskariṓtou*, masc. noun. Iscariot, the surname of Judas who betrayed Jesus. His name was probably derived from Kerioth, a town in the country of Judah (Josh 15:25). He was called Judas Iscariot to distinguish him from the other Judas, the son of James (Matt 10:4; 26:14; Mark 3:19; 14:10; Luke 6:16; 22:3; John 6:71; 12:4; 13:2, 26; 14:22). See *Ioúdas* (2455, V), Judas.

2470. ἴσος *ísos*; fem. *ísē*, neut. *íson*, adj. Equal, alike in quantity, quality, dignity (Matt 20:12; Luke 6:34; John 5:18 of nature and conditions; Acts 11:17; Rev 21:16; Sept.: Ezek 40:5, 6). Spoken of testimonies, it means equal, sufficient, coming up to the purpose (Mark 14:56, 59). In the neut. pl., *ísa* is used as an adv. as in Phil 2:6 where it modifies the articular inf. *tó eínai* (1511), "to be equal with God." Jesus did not consider the action of being equal to God, i.e., maintaining a state of being equal to God, as an act of robbery. Here *ísa Theó* (*ísa*, pl.; *Theó*, dat. sing. of *Theós* [2316], God) is similar to John 5:18 where *íson*, the acc. sing., is used. *Ísa* in the neut. pl. as in Phil 2:6 better corresponds to "as" than to "equal to."
     Deriv.: *isággelos* (2465), like or equal to an angel; *isótēs* (2471), equality, likeness; *isótimos* (2472), of equal value or honor; *isópsuchos* (2473), of like or similar soul or spirit, like-minded; *ísōs* (2481), equally.
     Syn.: *hómoios* (3664), similar, like.
     Ant.: *diáphoros* (1313), different, diverse; *héteros* (2087), different, another but of varying quality.

2471. ἰσότης *isótēs*; gen. *isótetos*, fem. noun from *ísos* (2470), equal, like. Likeness, equality, i.e., equal state or proportion (2 Cor 8:14); equity, what is equitable (Col 4:1).

Syn.: *homoíōsis* (3669), likeness, the act of making one like another; *homoiótēs* (3665), likeness, the result of making one like another.

Ant.: *diastolḗ* (1293), difference, distinction; *diaíresis* (1243), diversity, difference.

2472. ἰσότιμος *isótimos*; gen. *isotímou*, masc.-fem., neut. *isótimon*, adj. from *ísos* (2470), equal, and *timḗ* (5092), price. Equally precious or valuable (2 Pet 1:1).

Syn.: *áxios* (514), worthy.

Ant.: *átimos* (820), without honor or value; *anáxios* (370), unworthy.

2473. ἰσόψυχος *isópsuchos*; gen. *isopsúchou*, masc.-fem., neut. *isópsuchon*, adj. from *ísos* (2470), equal, and *psuchḗ* (5590), soul, mind. To be activated by the same motives, of like character, like-minded (Phil 2:20).

Syn.: *homóphrōn* (3675), like-minded.

Ant.: *echthrós* (2190), enemy; *antídikos* (476), opponent in a law suit, plaintiff; *hupenantíos* (5227), one opposed; *enantíos* (1727), antagonist.

2474. Ἰσραήλ *Israḗl*; masc. proper noun, transliterated from the Hebr. *Yisrāēl* (3478, OT), wrestler with God. Israel, a name given to Jacob after wrestling with the angel (Gen 32:24ff.). In the NT, spoken only in reference to his posterity, as the House of Israel (Matt 10:6; Acts 7:42); the people of Israel (Acts 4:10; 13:17); the sons (*huioí* [5207]) of Israel (Acts 7:23, 37; 9:15).

(I) Generally the word "Israel" is used for the Israelites or the children of Israel. In the OT, it is spoken of the kingdom of Israel in opposition to that of Judah, but in the NT, it is applied to all the descendants of Israel then remaining, and after the exile syn. with *hoi Ioudaíoi* (2453), the Jews, i.e., Israel, the nation to which God's promises had been given.

(II) The idea of privilege is usually associated with the use of the word just as "Israel" was originally the name of special privilege given by God to Jacob, the great ancestor of the race (Gen 32:28; 35:10). It differs from both "Hebrew" which stood, in NT times at least, for Jews of purely national sympathies who spoke the Hebr. or Aramaic dialect (Acts 6:1), and "Jew," a term originally applied to all who belonged to the province of Judah and, after the Babylonian captivity, to all of the ancient race wherever located. "Israel," on the other hand, is preeminently the people of privilege, the people who had been chosen by God and received His covenant. Thus a Jewish orator frequently addressed the people as "men of Israel" (Acts 2:22; 3:12; 4:8, 10; 5:35; 13:16).

(III) In the Acts of the Apostles, we find the word used historically with reference to the ancestors of the Jews of apostolic times and the Jews generally. The past history of Israel as God's chosen people is referred to in the speeches contained in the book of Acts, e.g., by Stephen (7:23, 37, 42) and by Paul (13:17; 28:20). It is usually assumed or suggested in Acts that the Jews to whom the gospel was being preached are the Israelites of that day, the people for whom God had special favor and who might expect special blessings (5:31; 13:23).

(IV) Later the term "Israel" acquired a spiritual significance and was used metaphorically. This was due to the rejection of the gospel by the nation of Israel as such. Thus we find Paul differentiating between the natural descendants of Israel and the spiritual descendants whom he calls the true Israel of God. In this manner, he speaks on the one hand of "Israel after the flesh" (1 Cor 10:18), or of those who belong to the "stock of Israel" (Phil 3:5). On the other hand, he speaks of a "commonwealth of Israel" (Eph 2:12) or "Israel of God" (Gal 6:16) from which many, even Jews by birth, are aliens, and into which the Ephesians had been admitted (Eph 2:13). By this "commonwealth of Israel" or "Israel of God" the apostle means a true spiritual Israel, practically equivalent to all the faithful. It might be defined as the whole number of the elect, who have been, are, or shall be gathered into one under Christ. In other words, all the believers of all time constituting the Church universal.

This true Israel does necessarily coincide with the nation or the stock of Abraham. "They are not all Israel, which are of Israel" (Rom 9:6), i.e., by racial descent. Branches may be broken off the olive tree of God's privileged people and wild olive branches may be grafted into the tree (Rom 11:17–21).

Sometimes it is difficult to determine the exact application of the term in different passages of the Pauline Epistles. Thus the sentence, "All Israel shall be saved" (Rom 11:26), refers to the true or spiritual Israel in the sense of an elect people. The apostle is speaking of the actual nation of Israel as a whole, and contrasting it with the fullness of the Gentiles. Paul teaches that when the fullness of the Gentiles is complete, Israel as a nation will also turn to God by confessing Christ. The phrase "all Israel" does not necessarily apply to every member of the race, nor does the passage teach anything as to the fate of the individuals who in the apostle's day or since have composed the nation. Just as the ancient historical Israel was the recipient of special privileges and stood in a particular relationship to God, so the spiritual Israel in apostolic times is the bearer of special privileges and also stands in a unique relationship to God. Ancient Israel had "the oracles of God" (Rom 3:2). They had the sign of circumcision. To them, Paul declares, "pertaineth the adoption, and the glory, and the covenants, and the giving of the law, and the service of God, and the promises; whose are the fathers, and of whom as concerning the flesh Christ came" (Rom 9:4, 5). The great essential features of these privileges are transferred to the spiritual Israel, the believing Church which has been grafted into the true olive tree. They have the adoption, they are sons of God (Rom 8:15–17). They have the glory both present and future (Rom 8:18). They are partakers of the new covenant which has been ratified by the death and resurrection of Jesus Christ (1 Cor 11:25).

The analogy between the first and the second covenant is fully worked out by the writer of the Epistle to the Hebrews who dwells upon the ritual and ceremonial aspect of ancient Israel's relationship to God. He shows the higher fulfillment of that relationship under the new covenant where there is direct personal access to God. Here the human priesthood of the sons of Aaron and the sacrifices of bulls and goats are superseded by the Divine Mediator who offered Himself a sacrifice once and for all (Heb 7:27; 10:10). The Mediator of the new covenant has entered, not into an earthly temple, but, as it were, into heaven itself, there to make continual intercession for His people (Heb 7:25). The writer further emphasizes the superiority of the new covenant relationship of the spiritual Israel as being a fulfillment of the prophecy of Jer 31:31–34 presupposing that the old covenant has proved ineffective (Heb 8:7). The Law is no longer to be written on tables of stone, but in the mind and in the heart (Heb 8:10).

(V) In the book of Revelation, ancient Israel is referred to historically in connection with Balaam, "who taught Balak to cast a stumblingblock before the children of Israel" (Rev 2:14). On the other hand, the symbolical or metaphorical use of the term applied to the spiritual Israel is found in connection with the sealing of the servants of God which takes place according to the tribes of the children of Israel (Rev 7:4); also in the description of the new Jerusalem, where the names of the twelve tribes are engraved on the twelve gates (Rev 21:12). The author of the Revelation, following the usage of Paul and the example of Peter (1 Pet 1:1) and James (James 1:1), applies the passage of Rev 7:1–8 regarding the sealing of the tribes taken from the Jewish source to the true spiritual Israel who are to be kept secure in the day of the world's overthrow. It is the same body of believers referred to in Rev 7:9–17 which appears in heaven clothed in white robes and with palms in their hands (see J. Hastings *Dictionary of the Apostolic Church* under "Israel").

2475. Ἰσραηλίτης *Israēlítēs*; gen. *Israēlítou*, masc. proper noun, from *Israēl* (2474), Israel. An Israelite, one descended from Israel or Jacob (Acts 2:22; 3:12; 5:35; 13:16; 21:28; Rom 9:4; 11:1; 2 Cor 11:22); "an Israelite indeed" (John 1:47); one who is not only a natural descendant from Israel but is also a believer (cf. Gen 32:28 with John 1:48; 8:39; Rom 9:6; Gal 6:16). "Israelite" is a name of honor. It is to be distinguished from both "Hebrew [*Hebraíos* {1445}]" being, at least in NT times, a Jew with purely national sympathies who spoke the native Hebr. or Aramaic dialect of Palestine, and "Jew [*Ioudaíos* {2453}]", one who belonged to the ancient race wherever he might be settled and whatever his views. However, every Jew regarded himself as a true Israelite and prided himself on the privileges which he as a member of the favored nation had received when other nations had been passed by. Paul refers to these privileges when he describes his "kinsmen according to the flesh" as Israelites to whom "the adoption, and the glory, and the covenants, and the giving of the law, and the service of God, and the promises" apply (Rom 9:4). He knows the way in which the Jew boasts of them and claims that he can share in that boasting as well as any of his detractors. "Are they Israelites? So am I. Are they the seed of Abraham? So am I" (2 Cor 11:22). This feeling of exclusive national privilege led, in many cases, to the rejection of the gospel by the Jews who did not wish their privileges to be extended to the heathen world. Those who were Israelites by birth and rejected his message caused the apostle to realize that a

believer in Jesus Christ is equivalent to a true or spiritual Israelite— one after the type of Nathanael in John 1:47, "an Israelite indeed, in whom is no guile." Paul applies the term in its natural sense to himself in Rom 11:1, "I also am an Israelite," in order to show that not all the members of the race have been rejected by God. There is a remnant according to the election of grace—Israelites who are Israelites indeed, not merely by outward physical connection, but also by moral and spiritual characteristics (W. F. Boyd in J. Hastings *Dictionary of the Apostolic Church*).

2476. ἵστημι *hístēmi*; fut. *stēsō*, aor. *éstēsa*, 2d aor. *éstēn*, perf. *éstēka* and *hestḗkasin* (Luke 8:20), pluperf. *heistḗkeisan*, perf. inf. *hestēkénai* contracted to *hestánai*, perf. part. *hestēkós* contracted to *hestós*, fem. *hestōsa*, neut. *hestós*, aor. pass. *estáthēn*, fut. pass. *stathḗsomai*. A less usual form is *histómen* (Rom 3:31 [TR]). Pluperf. 3d person pl. *hestḗkesan*, Attic for *hestḗkeisan* (Rev 7:11). When used trans., the verb means to cause to stand, to place. When used intrans., it means to stand.

(I) Trans., in the pres., imperf., fut. and aor. of the act., to cause to stand, to set or place.

(A) With the acc. and with an adjunct implying the place where, e.g., "before them" (Acts 22:30); "on his right hand" (Matt 25:33); "in their midst" (a.t. [Matt 18:2; see John 8:3; Acts 4:7]); "before the council" (Acts 5:27; see Acts 6:6; Jude 1:24 [cf. Lev 27:11]). *Epí* (1909), upon, with the acc. (Matt 4:5; see Luke 4:9). *Pará* (3844), near, with the dat. (Luke 9:47). Generally, to cause to stand forth (Acts 1:23; 6:13), the opposite of falling (Rom 14:4; Sept.: Gen 47:7; Ex 40:2, 17; Lev 14:11; Josh 4:9).

(B) To establish, confirm (Rom 3:31; 10:3; Heb 10:9; Sept.: Ex 6:4). Of time, meaning to fix, appoint (Acts 17:31).

(C) To place in a balance, i.e., to weigh, with the acc. and dat. (Matt 26:15, "they weighed out to him" [a.t.]; Sept.:

Ezra 8:25, 26, 33; Isa 46:6). Metaphorically, to impute, e.g., sin unto someone (Acts 7:60).

(II) Intrans. in the perf., pluperf., and 2d aor. of the act. and mid., and by implication in aor. and fut. of the pass., to stand, and so perf. act. *héstēka*, used as pres.; pluperf. *hestḗkein*, used as imperf.

(A) As opposed to falling (1 Cor 10:12); also standing in prayer or sacrifice (Matt 6:5; Heb 10:11); with an adjunct implying the place where, e.g., an adv. (Matt 12:46, *éxō* [1854], out; Mark 11:5, *ekeí* [1563], there; 13:14; Luke 9:27; 17:12; 18:13). Followed by *eis* (1519), into, with the acc. (John 20:19); *ek* (1537), out of, on, with *dexiṓn* (1188), right side (Luke 1:11); *en* (1722), in, with the dat. of place (Matt 20:3, see Matt 20:6; John 7:37; 11:56; Acts 5:20; 7:33 implied); among them, meaning before them (Acts 24:21); *enṓpion* (1799), in the presence of someone (Acts 10:30; Rev 7:9); *epí* (1909), upon, with the gen. of place (Luke 6:17; Rev 10:5); *epí* in the sense of before (Acts 25:10 [cf. Mark 13:9; Acts 24:20]); with the acc. of place (Matt 13:2; Rev 7:1); to stand upon one's feet (Acts 26:16 [cf. 3:8]; Sept.: 2 Chr 3:13); *metá* (3326) followed by the gen., with someone (John 18:5); *pará* (3844) with the acc. (Luke 5:1; 7:38); *péran* (4008), beyond (John 6:22); *pró* (4253), in front of (Acts 5:23); *prós* (4314), toward, near (John 18:16). With the acc. and *prós* (4314), toward, near (John 20:11); *sún* (4862), with (Acts 4:14). In John 1:26, "there stands one among you" (a.t.); Rev 7:11, *kúklō* (2945), round about, "round about the throne." Without an adjunct of place expressed, but in the sense of to stand by, near, there, according to the context, i.e., to be present (Matt 26:73; Luke 19:8; 23:35; John 1:35; 3:29; 18:18; Acts 2:14). Joined with an adj. or part. (Acts 9:7; Eph 6:14). Of persons standing before a judge, either as accusers (Luke 23:10) or as accused (Acts 26:6). In Matt 27:11, "stood before the governor," *émprosthen* (1715), before, instead of *epí* (1909), upon. Also before

Christ as Judge, where it is (by implication) to stand erect or firm in the consciousness of acquittal and final approval (Luke 21:36). Spoken of fishing boats, to stand or be stationed, lie (Luke 5:2).

(B) Figuratively to stand fast, i.e., to continue, endure, persist, e.g., of things (Matt 12:25; Luke 11:18; 2 Tim 2:19); of persons (Acts 26:22; 1 Cor 7:37; Col 4:12). See John 8:44; Rom 5:2; 1 Pet 5:12. In 2 Cor 1:24, simply with the dat. Also Sept.: Josh 2:11; 2 Kgs 23:3; Eccl 8:3; Isa 46:10; 66:22. To stand fast against an enemy, as opposed to *pheúgō* (5343), to run away (Eph 6:11, 13; Sept.: Ex 9:11; Nah 2:8); also against evils, i.e., to endure, sustain (Rev 6:17). In the sense of to be established, confirmed (Matt 18:16; 2 Cor 13:1 in allusion to Deut 19:15; see Num 30:5, 12).

(C) *Éstēn* and *estáthēn*, to stand still, stop, e.g., of persons (Matt 20:32; Mark 10:49; Luke 7:14; 18:40), of things (Matt 2:9; Acts 8:38); to cease (Luke 8:44; Sept.: Josh 3:13; Jon 1:15; Hab 3:11); to remain, abide, continue (John 8:44); to make to stand, establish, confirm (Rom 14:4); to appoint (Acts 17:31); to agree, covenant (Matt 26:15 [cf. *epēggeílanto* {1861} in Mark 14:11]); impute, lay to one's charge (Acts 7:60). In the pass., to be established, stand firm, stand (Matt 12:25, 26; Mark 3:25, 26); to be confirmed (Matt 18:16; 2 Cor 13:1).

Deriv.: *anthístēmi* (436), to oppose; *anístēmi* (450), to raise (trans.), and to rise, (intrans.); *aphístēmi* (868), to withdraw from or stand away from; *diḯstēmi* (1339), to remove; *enístēmi* (1764), to set in; *exístēmi* (1839), to be in ecstasy; *epístamai* (1987), to understand; *ephístēmi* (2186), to set or stand over, be present; *kathístēmi* (2525), to appoint a person to a position; *methístēmi* or *methistánō* (3179), to remove; *parístēmi* or *paristánō* (3936), to stand by or beside; *periḯstēmi* (4026), to stand around; *proḯstēmi* (4291), to preside, rule; *prōtostátēs* (4414), a leader or captain; *stádios* (4712), furlong, race; *stámnos* (4713), a jar, earthen pot; *stásis* (4714), a standing; *statḗr* (4715), piece of money; *staurós* (4716), stake, cross; *stḗthos* (4738), the breast; *stḗkō* (4739), to stand firm; *stērízō* (4741), to set fast, to fix firmly; *stoá* (4745), a pillar, column; *sunistánō* (4921), to set together, introduce, consist.

Syn.: *ménō* (3306), abide, continue, stand; *diatríbō* (1304), to stay, tarry; *títhēmi* (5087), to put, set; *tássō* (5021), to place in order; *keímai* (2749), to lie, set; *phérō* (5342), to carry, bring; *stērízō* (4741), to fix, make fast, set; *stereóō* (4732), to make firm; *bebaióō* (950), to confirm, establish; *kratéō* (2902), to be strong, prevail; *páreimi* (3918), to be at hand, present; *paragínomai* (3854), to be beside, present; *anorthóō* (461), to set straight or up; *egeírō* (1453), to raise.

Ant.: *píptō* (4098), to fall; *hysteréō* (5302), to come behind, fall short; *ekleípō* (1587), to leave off, cease, fail; *katargéō* (2673), to reduce to inactivity; *apopsúchō* (674), to faint, fail; *metatíthēmi* (3346), to remove, transfer; *metakinéō* (3334), to remove, move away; *methístēmi* (3179), to transfer, remove, figuratively to pass on into the next world; *astatéō* (790), to be wandering, homeless; *ekchōréō* (1633), to depart.

2477. ἱστορέω *historéō*; contracted *historṓ*, fut. *historḗsō*, from *hístōr* (n.f.), knowing. To ascertain by inquiry and personal examination. This is the verb from which the Eng. word "history" (*historía*) is derived. In the NT, to know or to visit, so as to consider and observe attentively and gain knowledge. Only in Gal 1:18 ("to see," and hence become acquainted with). In Class. Gr., to narrate.

Syn.: *horáō* (3708), to see with the idea of becoming acquainted and obtaining mutual understanding.

2478. ἰσχυρός *ischurós*; fem. *ischurá*, neut. *ischurón*, adj. from *ischúō* (2480), to be able. Strong, mighty, powerful.

(I) Of persons, spoken of the powers both of body and mind, physical and moral (Matt 3:11; Mark 1:7; Luke 3:16). In

Heb 11:34, "valiant in war" (a.t.), meaning able to overcome; also Matt 12:29; Mark 3:27; Luke 11:21, 22; 1 Cor 1:25; 10:22. In 1 John 2:14, "strong" means firm in faith. Of angels (Rev 5:2; 10:1; 18:21); of God (Rev 18:8; Sept.: Num 13:19; Deut 10:17; Josh 10:2; Judg 5:13; Neh 1:5; 9:32). Figuratively, meaning strong in influence and authority, mighty, honorable (1 Cor 1:27, *tá ischurá* in the neut. pl. for the masc. pl. *hoi ischuroí* 4:10, "the strong ones of the earth" [a.t.]; Rev 19:18; Sept.: 2 Kgs 24:15; 1 Chr 7:7, 40).

(II) Of things, meaning strong, i.e., vehement, great, as *ánemos* (417), wind (Matt 14:30); *limós* (3042), famine (Luke 15:14); *kraugḗ* (2906), cry (Heb 5:7); *phōnḗ* (5456), voice (Rev 18:2 [TR]); *brontaí* (1027), thunders (Rev 19:6). See Sept.: Gen 41:31; Ex 19:19; Dan 6:20. Also firm, sure, strong consolation (Heb 6:18). In 2 Cor 10:10, "strong letters" (a.t.) meaning severe letters. Of a city, strong, fortified (Rev 18:10).

Syn.: *dunatós* (1415), powerful, mighty; *bíaios* (972), violent, strong, spoken of a wind; *krataiós* (2900), strong, mighty, used in a relative sense as possessing delegated and manifested power which prevails; *megaleíos* (3167), wonderful, great, that which produces wonder; *mégas* (3173), great, mighty; *tēlikoútos* (5082), such a one, so great, so mighty; *energḗs* (1756), active, operative.

Ant.: *asthenḗs* (772), weak; *árrōstos* (732), feeble, sickly; *adúnatos* (102), one without power or strength, powerless; *oligópsuchos* (3642), fainthearted.

2479. ἰσχύς *ischús*; gen. *ischúos*, fem. noun from *is* (n.f.), strength, and *échō* (2192), to have. Physical strength, mental or moral power as an endowment. Thus *ischúō* may mean to have health, syn. with *hugiaínō* (5198), to be healthy, as opposed to *asthenéō* (770), to be weak, sickly. Verb: *ischúō* (2480), syn. with *dúnamai* (1410), but in the case of the basic *ischús*, there is more emphasis on the actual inherent power. In *dúnamis* (1411) there is implied ability or capacity to perform. Adj.: *ischurós* (2478), strong, powerful.

(I) Of physical strength, in Rev 18:2, *en ischúi*, meaning mightily, vehemently (cf. Sept.: Isa 58:1; Dan 3:4; 4:11).

(II) Of mental and moral power, meaning might, ability, facility (Mark 12:30, "with all thy might" [a.t.], 33; Luke 10:27; 1 Pet 4:11; Sept.: Gen 31:6; 2 Kgs 23:25).

(III) Generally meaning power, potency, preeminence, e.g., with *dúnamis* (1411), strength (2 Pet 2:11 where the two words *ischús* and *dúnamis* occur together, the first meaning inherent power and the latter the ability to perform what one desires with that power). In Eph 1:19 and 6:10, *krátos* ([2904], dominion, might) *tḗs ischúos* (of the strength), meaning the strength that has prevailed manifestly and demonstratively, translated "mighty power" and "power of his might." See 2 Thess 1:9.

(IV) Also in ascriptions to God (Rev 5:12; 7:12; Sept.: Isa 11:2).

Deriv.: *ischúō* (2480), to be strong.

Syn.: *dúnamis* (1411), power in action, while *ischús* denotes power which may remain inactive; *exousía* (1849), authority or the right to exercise power; *krátos* (2904), dominion, the outward manifestation of power; *megaleiótēs* (3168), greatness, mighty power; *archḗ* (746), a rule, power; *enérgeia* (1753), energy, efficiency, effectual working.

Ant.: *asthéneia* (769), infirmity, weakness.

2480. ἰσχύω *ischúō*; fut. *ischúsō*, from *ischús* (2479), strength. To be strong, i.e., to have strength, ability, power, both physical and moral.

(I) Physically, to be strong, robust (Matt 9:12; Mark 2:17, *hoi ischúontes*, "the strong" [a.t.], i.e., the well, not the weak and sickly; Sept.: Josh 14:11; Ezek 34:16).

(II) Generally, to be able, i.e., I can, followed by the inf. (Matt 8:28; 26:40;

Mark 5:4; 14:37; Luke 6:48; 8:43; 14:6, 29, 30; 16:3; 20:26; John 21:6; Acts 6:10; 15:10; 25:7; 27:16). With the inf. implied (Mark 9:18; Luke 13:24; Phil 4:13, "I can do [or endure] all things"; Sept.: 2 Chr 2:6).

(III) The equivalent of to have efficacy, to avail, have force and value (Gal 5:6; 6:15; Heb 9:17; James 5:16, "it has value" [a.t.], is worthy; see Matt 5:13).

(IV) The equivalent of to prevail, followed by *katá* (2596), against or over anyone (Acts 19:16; see Rev 12:8; Sept.: Ps 13:4; Dan 7:21). Figuratively equivalent to spread abroad, to acquire strength and be effective (Acts 19:20).

Deriv.: *enischúō* (1765), to be strong; *exischúō* (1840), to be able; *epischúō* (2001), to be stronger; *ischurós* (2478), strong, powerful; *katischúō* (2729), to overpower, prevail against.

Syn.: *dúnamai* (1410), to be able, have power, however, not as strong as *ischúō*, but more with the implication of exercising one's will in the demonstration of power; *dunamóō* (1412), to make strong; *endunamóō* (1743), to enable, strengthen; *dunatéō* (1414), to show oneself powerful; *hikanóō* (2427), to enable; *energéō* (1754), to work, operate, effect, energize; *nikáō* (3528), to conquer, prevail; *krataióō* (2901), to establish, strengthen; *sthenóō* (4599), to fix firmly, set fast, make strong; *stērízō* (4741), to establish; *stereóō* (4732), to confirm, make firm; *epistērízō* (1991), to support further, confirm; *hugiaínō* (5198), to be in good health; *sṓzō* (4982), to save, heal.

Ant.: *asthenéō* (770), to render weak or to lack strength; *échō kakṓs* (*échō* [2192], to have; *kakṓs* [2560], badly), to be sick; *kámnō* (2577), to be weary; *sunéchomai* (4912), to be sick, afflicted; *noséō* (3552), to be sick.

2481. ἴσως *ísōs*; an adv. from *ísos* (2470), equal. Equally, equitably, but not used in this manner in the NT. Perhaps, peradventure, it may be, the chances being equal on both sides (only in Luke 20:13; Sept.: Gen 32:20; Dan 4:24).

2482. 'Ιταλία *Italía*; gen. *Italías*, fem. proper noun. Italy. Originally it applied only to the extreme south of what is presently Italy, the region now called Calabria. Later the name included the area that we know as Italy today (Acts 18:2; 27:1, 6; Heb 13:24).

2483. 'Ιταλικός *Italikós*; fem. *Italikḗ*, neut. *Italikón*, adj. Italian. Belonging to Italy (Acts 10:1).

2484. 'Ιτουραῖος *Itouraía*; gen. *Itouraías*, fem. proper noun. Iturea (Luke 3:1), indicating the region northeast of Palestine, beyond the Jordan. The Itureans were descended from Ishmael (Gen 25:15), who had a son named Jetur from whom the name Iturea is derived. The Itureans were seminomadic people. Until the fourth century A.D., there was no defined territory called Iturea; only the ethnic name Iturean was used.

2485. ἰχθύδιον *ichthúdion*; gen. *ichthudíou*, neut. noun, a diminutive of *ichthús* (2486), fish. A little or small fish (Matt 15:34; Mark 8:7).

2486. ἰχθύς *ichthús*; gen. *ichthúos*, masc. noun. A fish (Matt 7:10; 14:17, 19; 15:36; 17:27; Mark 6:38, 41, 43; Luke 5:6, 9; 9:13, 16; 11:11; 24:42; John 21:6, 8, 11; 1 Cor 15:39; Sept.: Gen 9:2).
Deriv.: *echthúdion* (2485), a little fish.

2487. ἴχνος *íchnos*; gen. *íchnous*, neut. noun from *hiknéomai* (n.f., see *diïknéomai* [1338]), to go, come. The sole of the foot on which men and animals go, hence a footstep, the impression left by the sole of the foot in walking. Used only figuratively, meaning to imitate one's example (Rom 4:12; 2 Cor 12:18; 1 Pet 2:21).

2488. 'Ιωάθαμ *Iōátham*; masc. proper noun transliterated from the Hebr. *Yōthām* (3147, OT), Jehovah is perfect. Joatham (Matt 1:9). A king of Judah, the son and successor of Uzziah who reigned 759–743 B.C. (2 Kgs 15:7, 32 ff; 2 Chr 27).

2489. 'Ιωάννα *Iōánna*; gen. *Iōánnas*, fem. proper noun. Joanna, the wife of Chuza, Herod Antipas' steward, one of the women healed of evil spirits and infirmities, and who ministered to the Lord Jesus and His disciples during His Galilean ministry (Luke 8:3; 24:10). She, with other women, accompanied Jesus from Galilee to Jerusalem. They prepared spices and ointments for His burial and went to the tomb with the intention of embalming the body of Jesus. There they received from the angels the message of the resurrection (cf. Luke 23:55, 56).

2490. 'Ιωαννᾶς *Iōannás*; gen. *Iōannâ*, masc. proper noun. Joannas, an ancestor of Jesus (Luke 3:27). He lived about 500 B.C.

2491. 'Ιωάννης *Iōánnēs*; gen. *Iōánnou*, masc. proper noun transliterated from the Hebr. *Yōchānān* (3110, OT), Jehovah-given or Jehovah has been gracious. John. This name is given to five different persons in the NT:
    (I) John the Baptist (Matt 3:1), the son of Zechariah and forerunner of Christ, beheaded by order of Herod Antipas (Matt 3:4, 13, 14; 14:2–4, 8, 10; Luke 1:13, 60, 63).
    (II) The apostle, the son of Zebedee and brother of James (Matt 4:21; 10:2; 17:1; Mark 1:19, 29; Luke 5:10).
    (III) John Mark, the companion of Paul and Barnabas and writer of the second gospel (Acts 12:25; 13:5, 13; 15:37).
    (IV) A relative of Annas the high priest and a member of the Sanhedrin who took part with Annas, Caiaphas, Alexander, and other relatives of Annas in calling Peter and John to account for their preaching about Jesus (Acts 4:6).

2492. 'Ιώβ *Iōb*; masc. proper noun transliterated from the Hebr. *Īōv* (347, OT), poorly treated. Job, the principle character in the OT book which bears his name. In the NT, only in James 5:11, as an example of perseverance (hupomoné [5281]).

2493. Ἰωήλ Iōél; masc. proper noun transliterated from the Hebr. Yōēl (3100, OT), Jehovah is God. Joel, an OT prophet, son of Pethuel, is the author of the second of the books of the minor prophets. We know nothing of his life and times. In the NT, only in Acts 2:16 (cf. Joel 1:1).

2494. Ἰωνάν Iōnán; masc. proper noun transliterated from the Hebr. Jonan, meaning Jehovah is gracious. An ancestor of Jesus (Luke 3:30) who lived about 200 years after David.

2495. Ἰωνᾶς Iōnás; gen. Iōnā́, masc. proper noun transliterated from the Hebr. Yōnāh (3124, OT), dove. Jonas.
(I) The name given in Matt 12:39–41; 16:4; Luke 11:29, 30, 32 KJV to the OT prophet Jonah.
(II) The name given in John 21:15–17 KJV to the father of the Apostle Peter. In John 1:42 KJV, he is called Jona.

2496. Ἰωράμ Iōrám; masc. proper noun transliterated from the Hebr. Yᵉhōrām (3141, OT), Jehovah is exalted. Joram, same as Jehoram, king of Judah, 884–871 B.C. (2 Kgs 8:21–24; 11:2; 1 Chr 3:11. See Matt 1:8), the son and successor of Jehoshaphat.

2497. Ἰωρείμ Iōreím; masc. proper noun. Jorim. An ancestor of Jesus (Luke 3:29).

2498. Ἰωσαφάτ Iōsaphát; masc. proper noun transliterated from the Hebr. Yōshāphāt (3146, OT), Jehovah is judge, a form of Yᵉhōshāphāt (3092, OT). Josaphat or Jehoshaphat. A pious king of Judah, 914–889 B.C. He was the son and successor of Asa, and an ancestor of Jesus (Matt 1:8). See 1 Kgs 15:24; 22:41ff.

2499. Ἰωσή Iōsḗ; masc. proper noun. A form for Iosés, Joses, one of the ancestors of Jesus (Luke 3:29).

2500. Ἰωσῆς Iōsḗs; masc. proper noun. Joses, Joseph.
(I) One of the half-brothers of Jesus (Matt 13:55; 27:56; Mark 6:3; 15:40, 47).
(II) A name of Barnabas, for a time a co-worker of Paul (Acts 4:36, the Gr. having "Joseph" [a.t.] in this passage).

2501. Ἰωσήφ Iōsḗph; masc. proper noun transliterated from the Hebr. Yōsēph (3130, OT), may God add. Joseph, the name of seven persons in the NT:
(I) The eleventh of Jacob's twelve sons and the firstborn son of Rachel. He became the ancestor of the two northern tribes, Manasseh and Ephraim. The story of his birth is in Gen 30:22–24; the rest of his life in Gen 37—50. See John 4:5; Acts 7:9, 13, 14, 18; Heb 11:21, 22; Rev 7:8.
(II) The name of three ancestors of Jesus (Luke 3:24, 26, 30).
(III) Husband of Mary, the mother of Jesus (Matt 1:16, 18, 20, 24; Luke 1:27; 2:4, 33, 43; John 1:45; 6:42). He was a carpenter (Matt 13:55) living in Nazareth (Luke 2:4), of Davidic descent (Matt 1:20; Luke 2:4), the son of Heli (Luke 3:23) or Jacob (Matt 1:16), and the wrongly supposed father of Jesus (Matt 13:55; Luke 3:23; 4:22; John 1:45; 6:42). He was assured by an angel that the child his wife was going to bear was of the Holy Spirit (Matt 1:18–25). He went with Mary to Bethlehem where the baby Jesus was born and was with her when the shepherds came to greet the Lord (Luke 2:8–20), as well as when Jesus was presented in the temple forty days after His birth. Warned by the Lord in a dream that Herod was plotting the murder of the child, he fled to Egypt with Mary and Jesus (Matt 2:13–19), returning to Nazareth after the death of Herod. Every year, at the Passover, he attended the feast in

Jerusalem (Luke 2:41) and when Jesus was twelve, He too went with Joseph and Mary. Joseph undoubtedly taught Jesus the carpentry trade (Mark 6:3). He was probably alive after the ministry of Jesus had begun (Matt 13:55). There is, however, no record of him in connection with the crucifixion, and since Jesus commended his mother to John the disciple, it is presumed that Joseph must have died before that time (John 19:26, 27).

(IV) A Jew of Arimathaea, a place probably to the northwest of Jerusalem, described as a rich man and a member of the Sanhedrin (Matt 27:57, 59; Mark 15:43, 45), a righteous man looking for the kingdom of God (Mark 15:43; Luke 23:50). He was a secret disciple of Jesus because of his fear of the Jews (John 19:38). After the crucifixion, he secured permission from Pilate to remove the body of Jesus from the cross and lay it in his own newly-hewn tomb (Matt 27:57–60; Luke 23:50–53; John 19:38).

(V) A Christian also called Barsabas (son of Sabas), surnamed Justus (Acts 1:23), who had accompanied Jesus and the apostles from the time of Jesus' baptism. He was one of the two candidates considered by the apostles as a replacement of Judas Iscariot. The lot fell upon Matthias (Acts 1:21, 26).

2502. Ἰωσίας *Iōsías*; gen. *Iōsíou*, masc. proper noun. Josias, meaning whom Jehovah heals. A pious king of Judah, the son and successor of Amon. He reigned 642–611 B.C. (2 Kgs 22:1ff.; 2 Chr 34:1; 35:1). An ancestor of Jesus (Matt 1:10, 11).

2503. ἰῶτα *iōta*; indeclinable neut. noun. The ninth letter of the Gr. alphabet. Used to express smallness or the minutest part of something, being the smallest letter in the Gr. alphabet (Matt 5:18). It is translated "jot" and refers to the Hebr. *yodh*, the smallest letter of the Hebr. alphabet.

K

2504. κἀγώ *kagṓ*; crasis from *kaí* (2532), and, and *egṓ* (1473), I. And I, I also (Matt 2:8; 10:32; 11:28; Luke 2:48; John 1:34; 2 Cor 11:22). In the dat. (Luke 1:3; Acts 8:19; 1 Cor 15:8); in the acc. (John 7:28; 1 Cor 16:4).

2505. καθά *kathá*; adv. from *katá* (2596), according to, and *ha* (neut. pl. acc. of *hós* [3739], which, who), which things. According as, according to those things which (Matt 27:10; Sept.: Gen 19:8).

2506. καθαίρεσις *kathaíresis*; gen. *kathairéseōs*, fem. noun from *kathairéō* (2507), to cast down. Demolition, destruction of a fortress (2 Cor 10:4). Figuratively of religious knowledge and experience, demolition, destruction, opposite of *oikodomḗ* (3619), building, edifying (2 Cor 10:8; 13:10).
   Syn.: *apóleia* (684), loss, ruin, perdition; *ólethros* (3639), ruin, destruction; *phthorá* (5356), corruption, destruction through corruption; *súntrimma* (4938), shattering.
   Ant.: *égersis* (1454) and *anástasis* (386), a raising up, resurrection; *oikodomḗ* (3619), a building up, edifying.

2507. καθαιρέω *kathairéō*; contracted *kathairṓ*, 2d fut. *kathelṓ*, 2d aor. *katheílon*, from *katá* (2596), down, and *hairéō* (138), to take for oneself. To take down or away (Mark 15:36, 46; Luke 23:53; Acts 13:29; Sept.: Josh 8:29; 10:27); to cast or pull down as princes or potentates (Luke 1:52); to take, pull down, demolish buildings (Luke 12:18), reasonings (2 Cor 10:5; Sept.: Zech 9:6); to destroy nations (Acts 13:19; Sept.: Jer 24:6; 49:10) or grandeur, magnificence (Acts 19:27).
   Deriv.: *kathaíresis* (2506), a casting down.

Syn.: *katargéō* (2673), to abolish; *lúō* (3089), to dissolve, destroy, demolish; *katalúō* (2647) and *apóllumi* (622), to destroy utterly; *olothreúō* (2645), to destroy, especially in the sense of slaying; *exolothreúō* (1842), to destroy utterly; *phtheírō* (5351), to corrupt; *porthéō* (4199), to ruin; *apotíthēmi* (659), to put away; *ekbállō* (1544), to put out; *rhíptō* (4496), to cast forth, throw; *ekpíptō* (1601), to fall out; *katabállō* (2598), to cast down; *aporríptō* (641), to cast off; *apōthéō* (683), to thrust away.
   Ant.: *oikodoméō* (3618), to build.

2508. καθαίρω *kathaírō*; fut. *katharṓ*, from *katharós* (2513), pure, clean, without stain or spot. To cleanse from filth, purify. Occurs in John 15:2, referring to the vine in that the vinedresser cleanses a branch in order that it may bear more fruit. See Sept.: 2 Sam 4:6; Isa 28:27. In Heb 10:2, to expiate or redeem referring to the once-and-for-all redemption by Jesus Christ, cleansing the sinner and positioning him in Christ.
   Deriv.: *akáthartos* (169), unclean; *ekkathaírō* (1571), to purge out, cleanse thoroughly.
   Syn.: *katharízō* (2511), to cleanse, make free from admixture; *hagnízō* (48), to cleanse from defilement, to purify ceremonially or morally.
   Ant.: *koinóō* (2840), to make common, defile; *miaínō* (3392), to stain, tinge; *molúnō* (3435), to besmear as with mud or filth, befoul; *spilóō* (4695), to make a stain or spot, defile; *phtheírō* (5351), to corrupt.

2509. καθάπερ *katháper*; adv. from *kathá* (2505), as, and *per* (4007), very. As, even as, as well as (Rom 4:6; 12:4; 1 Cor 12:12; 2 Cor 1:14; 3:13, 18; 8:11; 1 Thess 2:11; 3:6, 12; 4:5; Heb 4:2; 5:4; Sept.: Gen 12:4; Ex 7:6, 10).

Syn.: *hōs* (5613), as; *hoútōs* (3779), even so; *kathṓs* (2531), according as; *hṓsper* (5618), even as; *naí* (3483), verily, even so; *hōsaútōs* (5615), in like manner as.

2510. καθάπτω *katháptō*; fut. *kathápsō*, from *katá* (2596), an intens., and *háptō* (681), to adjoin, bind. To bind, wind, fasten, twist (Acts 28:3).
Ant.: *apotinássō* (660), to shake off; *ektinássō* (1621), to shake out.

2511. καθαρίζω *katharízō*; fut. *katharísō*, in the Attic *kathariṓ* (Heb 9:14), from *katharós* (2513), pure. To cleanse, free from filth (Matt 8:2, 3; 23:25; Luke 4:27; 5:12, 13; 7:22; 11:39; 17:14, 17 [cf. Mark 7:19]; Sept.: Ps 12:6). To cleanse or make clean from leprosy (Matt 8:2, 3; 10:8; 11:5; Mark 1:40–42), often used in the Sept. for legal cleansing from leprosy (Lev 14:7, 8, 11; 15:28). To cleanse in the sense of purification, legal or ceremonial (Heb 9:22, 23 [cf. Acts 10:15; 11:9]; Sept.: Lev 13:6, 23, 28, 34), frequently so used in the Sept. In a spiritual sense, to purify from the pollution and guilt of sin (Acts 15:9; 2 Cor 7:1; Eph 5:26; Titus 2:14; Heb 9:14; James 4:8; 1 John 1:7, 9; Sept.: Ex 29:37; Ps 51:7).

In the OT, there were four main types of uncleanness. These were connected with the functions of reproduction (Gen 31:35; Ex 19:15; Lev 15:18, 19; 20:18; Deut 24:5; 1 Sam 21:4; 2 Sam 11:4, 8–13); food (Gen 1:29; 9:3, 4; Lev 11:3; Deut 14:4–20); death (Num 19:11–22; 2 Kgs 23:16, 20 [cf. Matt 23:27; Luke 11:44]); leprosy (Lev 13—14).

In the NT, the removal of leprosy is called cleansing (Matt 8:3; 10:8; 11:5; Mark 1:42; Luke 4:27; 7:22; 17:17) while the removal of other diseases is spoken of as healing (*therapeúō* [2323] and *iáomai* [2390], to heal). The words in the NT related to the state of ceremonial or moral uncleanness are the adj. *akáthartos* (169) and noun *akatharsía* (167), unclean, impure.

The idea of ceremonial or ethical cleansing is expressed by the deriv. of the word *katharízō* as indicated above, but the idea of cleansing and purifying is also expressed by other Gr. words which are cognates of the verb *hagnízō* (48) such as *hagneía* (47), purity in the sense of chastity (1 Tim 4:12; 5:2); *hagnótēs* (54), purity (2 Cor 6:6; 11:3); *hagnismós* (49), lustration, religious abstinence consequent to a vow; adv.: *hagnós* (55), with pure intention, sincerely. All the words in this group, except for *hagnízō* and *hagnismós* (Acts 21:26 only), are used exclusively in an ethical sense. However, *katharós* and its cognates are used mostly in a moral sense in the NT.

Related to both *katharízō* and *hagnízō* (48) is *hagiázō* (37), to sanctify, make clean, render pure, especially in its use in 1 Cor 7:14 in relation to 1 Thess 4:3, where *hagiasmós* (38), sanctification, refers to the abstaining from fornication. The intrinsic meaning of *hágios* (40), holy, is one who, as related to God, is absolutely separate from all evil. Therefore, *hágios* indicates one's position as consecrated to and by God, and thus summoned to be separate in godlikeness from all the defilements of heathenism (Lev 11:44; 19:2). When *hágios* or the verb *hagiázō* refer to material things, it is in the sense of being separate for the service of God.

Hagnós (53) and its cognates may assume a wider sweep of meaning covering purity of motive (James 4:8; 1 Pet 1:22) and of character generally (1 Cor 11:3; James 3:17; 1 John 3:3). *Hagnós* and *katharós* (2513), may perhaps be distinguished, according to Westcott (B. F. Westcott, *The Epistles of St. John*, 1966), in 1 John 3:3 as predominantly connoting feeling and state respectively. *Hagnós* may be derived from the verb *házomai* (n.f.), meaning to stand in awe of, dread, and implies a shrinking from pollution while *katharós* expresses simply the fact of cleanness. Hence, in 1 John 3:3, "And every man that hath this hope in him purifieth [*hagnízei*, pres. act indic. of *hagnízō*] himself, even as he is pure [*hagnós*]," and

James 4:8 where both verbs are used, "cleanse [*katharísate*] your hands, ye sinners; and purify [*hagnísate*] your hearts, ye double-minded," *hagnízō* penetrates more deeply towards the root of the matter than the verb *katharízo*. Whereas one can *katharízei* his hands, the heart must be *hagnízo*. In 1 John 1:7 we have the statement that "The blood of Jesus Christ his Son cleanseth us [*katharízei*, pres. act indic., keeps cleansing or is able to cleanse] from all sin," and in the 1 John 1:9 He cleanses (*katharísē* [aor. act. subjunctive], will cleanse) us from all unrighteousness. In Titus 2:14, the statement that God will "purify [*katharísē*] unto Himself a people" refers to God's people and their external acts as a manifestation of the work of God or Christ, while *hágios* (holy) is one's position in Christ. The state of *katharós* (pure) and *hagnós* (chaste) indicates the work of Christ in one's life individually on earth whereby discipline is administered.

Another word that could be counted as a syn. of the adj. *katharós* is *eilikrinḗs* (1506), pure, sincere (Phil 1:10; 2 Pet 3:1). *Eilikrinḗs* denotes freedom from the falsehood of life, life without adulteration, while *katharós* denotes freedom from the pollutions of life. Yet another word, *hósios* (3741), sacred, has the connotation of piety along with purity (Heb 7:26).

Deriv.: *diakatharízō* (1245), to cleanse thoroughly; *katharismós* (2512), the action or the result of cleansing, purification.

Ant.: *koinóō* (2840), to make common, hence unclean, to defile; *miaínō* (3392), to stain, tinge or dye with another color, to pollute, contaminate, used of ceremonial defilement and of moral defilement; *molúnō* (3435), to besmear as with mud or filth, befoul; *spilóō* (4695), to make a stain or spot, defile; *phtheírō* (5351), to corrupt.

2512. καθαρισμός *katharismós*; gen. *katharismoú*, masc. noun from *katharízo* (2511), to make clean. Purification. In

Class. Gr., *katharmós*. It actually refers to the process of purification, the sacrifice of purification. The purification of women (Luke 2:22; Sept.: Lev 14:32; 15:13; see Lev 12); ritual purification (Mark 1:44; Luke 5:14; John 2:6). The baptism both of John and the Lord Jesus is designated as *katharismós* in John 3:25, not that the ritual of physical baptism brought about spiritual results or spiritual purification, but only as a parallel in its results. As water cleanses the body in baptism, the grace it symbolizes cleanses the soul. Its designation as a "baptism of repentance for the remission of sins" (Mark 1:4; Luke 3:3; Acts 2:38) means an identification with the forgiveness of sins. In Heb 1:3, the word denotes the objective removal of our sins by Jesus Christ (see Heb 9:22, 23; Sept.: Ex 30:10; Job 7:21). In 2 Pet 1:9, it refers to the actual purification accomplished in man, while in Heb 1:3 to the propitiation provided by the Lord Jesus.

The concept of purity in the NT and in the prophetic teachings of the OT is entirely ethical. *Hagnós* (53) and *katharós* (2513) can be distinguished in that *hagnós* connotes the feeling and *katharós* the state (see *katharízō* [2511]). *Hagnós* implies a certain inward shrinking from pollution and is applied to the Lord Jesus, while *katharós* expresses simply the condition of cleanness. In the Sept., *hagnós* and *katharós* are used indiscriminately to translate the Hebr. word *tāhor* (2889, OT), brightness. *Katharós* occasionally is used for the Hebr. *bōr* (1252, OT), separate. *Hagnós* as well as the noun *hagnótēs* (54), pureness, is always ethical in meaning. *Hagnízō* (48), sanctify or purify, has a ceremonial meaning in John 11:55; Acts 21:24, 26; 24:18. In 1 Tim 4:12 and 5:2, *hagneía* (47) has the meaning of chastity.

Katharós and its cognates vary in meaning between the ceremonial and the moral. In John 15:3, we see the word in process of passing from the ceremonial to the ethical meaning.

Eilikrinḗs (1506), sincere, pure (Phil 1:10; 2 Pet 3:1), and its noun *eilikríneia*

(1505), purity, sincerity (1 Cor 5:8; 2 Cor 1:12; 2:17), refer to a quality that is made clear in Phil 1:10: "That ye may approve things that are excellent; that ye may be sincere [*elikrineís*] and without offense till the day of Christ." It is having the quality of discerning not only what is good, but what is excellent (Rom 2:18). It indicates a moral purity which is expressed in a mind uncontaminated and unwarped by sensual or sordid passion as is clearly demonstrated by Paul in 2 Cor 1:12; 2:17. His motives are unmixed as indicated by the phrase, "the unleavened bread of sincerity [*eilikrineías*]" in 1 Cor 5:8.

Rhantismós (4473), sprinkling, and the verb *rhantízō* (4472), to sprinkle, is applied to the cleansing influence of the sacrifice of Jesus on the human conscience (Heb 9:13, 21; 10:22; 1 Pet 1:2). It is frequently used in conjunction with blood. Its use can be understood only if we remember that in the consciousness of the pious Israelite, sin, guilt, and punishment are ideas so directly connected that the words for them are interchangeable. Guilt is a state of impurity which manifests itself in a consciousness of alienation from God and antagonism to the divine Law. It is from this sense of guilt that the blood of Jesus is said to "sprinkle" or "cleanse" men. Heb 12:24 speaks of the "blood of sprinkling, that speaketh better things than that of Abel" in that the blood of Abel cried for vengeance (Gen 4:10) while the life-blood of Jesus has a much more powerful appeal than a mere martyr's blood.

Syn.: *hagnismós* (49), cleansing, purification, which involves careful ceremonial cleansing in order to approach God. *Katharismós*, however, implies that we are unable to do so without the help of a mediator who cleanses (Acts 21:26; see Lev 16:4, 23, 24; Num 6). In addition to the above syn. we also have *baptismós* (909), ablution. This is used in the sense of cleansing (Mark 7:4; Heb 6:2; 9:10) and should be differentiated from *báptisma* (908), baptism, and *rhantismós* (4473), sprinkling.

Ant.: *miasmós* (3394), the act of defiling, the process in contrast to the defiling thing, *míasma* (3393), pollution; *molusmós* (3436), defilement in the sense of an action by which anything is defiled as *spílos* (4696), a spot, a moral blemish.

2513. καθαρός *katharós*; fem. *kathará*, neut. *katharón*, adj. Clean, pure, clear, in a natural sense unsoiled, unalloyed. A primary root, not related to *aírō* (142), to take up or away.

(I) Particularly (Matt 27:59; John 13:10; Heb 10:22; Rev 15:6; 19:8, 14; 21:18, 21; 22:1).

(II) Clean in the sense that something is lawful to be eaten or used (Luke 11:41; Rom 14:20, lawful, not forbidden; Titus 1:15; Sept.: Ex 25:29, 36; Ezek 36:25; Dan 7:9). In all these passages there is clear reference to legal or ceremonial cleanness.

(III) Clean or pure in a spiritual sense from the pollution and guilt of sin (Matt 5:8, sincere, upright, void of evil; John 13:10, 11, metaphorically in the Levitical sense; 15:3, cleansed, pruned, see *kathaírō* [2508], to cleanse, to purify, 1 Tim 1:5; 3:9; 2 Tim 1:3; 2:22; Titus 1:15; James 1:27; 1 Pet 1:22; Sept.: Gen 20:5, 6; Ps 24:4; 51:10).

(IV) Sometimes applied to purity or cleanness from blood or blood guiltiness (Acts 18:6, innocent; 20:26; Sept.: Gen 24:8; 44:10; Job 4:7).

(V) In the physical or nonethical sense, opposite of *rhuparós* (4508), dirty (Matt 27:59; Heb 10:22; Rev 15:6).

(VI) Sometimes the meaning of *katharós* is very close to the meaning of *eilikrinḗs* (1506), sincere, or something that has been cleansed by shaking to and fro as in a sieve or in winnowing. *Katharós* describes the purity contemplated under the aspect of that which is free from soil or stain (James 1:27). Sometimes seen as the opposite of *koinós* (2839), common, as well as *akáthartos* (169), unpurified (Rom 14:14, 20; Heb 9:13). For a full discussion of the difference in the syn. see *hágios* (40), holy, indicating position; *hagnós*

(53), chaste, clean, indicating also motive; *hósios* (3741), pure, associated somewhat with piety; *eilikrinḗs* (1506), sincere, pure with the connotation of one who differentiates between that which is good and that which is excellent.

Deriv.: *kathaírō* (2508), to cleanse; *katharízō* (2511) to make clean; *katharótēs* (2514), purity.

Ant.: *koinós* (2839), common in the sense of coming into contact with everything, defiled.

2514. καθαρότης *katharótēs*; gen. *katharótētos*, fem. noun from *katharós* (2513), pure. Purity, referring to the result of cleansing or purification. In Heb 9:13, *katharótēs* is freedom from the guilt of filthiness.

Deriv.: *akathártēs* (168), uncleanness.

2515. καθέδρα *kathédra*; gen. *kathédras*, fem. noun from *kathézomai* (2516), to sit. A seat (Matt 21:12; Mark 11:15). In Matt 23:2, to "sit in Moses' seat," or figuratively speaking, to occupy his place as an expounder of the Law; Sept.: 1 Sam 20:18, 25; 1 Kgs 10:19.

Deriv.: *prōtokathedría* (4410), the chief seat.

Syn.: *tópos* (5117), place, room; *thrónos* (2362), throne, seat.

2516. καθέζομαι *kathézomai*; imperf. *ekathezómēn*, fut. *kathedoúmai* and later *kathedḗsomai* or *kathesthḗsomai*, from *katá* (2596), down, and *ézomai* (n.f.), to sit. To sit down, sit (Matt 26:55; Luke 2:46; John 4:6; 11:20; 20:12; Acts 6:15). In John 11:20, *ekathézeto*, continued sitting (Sept.: Ezek 26:16).

Deriv.: *kathédra* (2515), a seat.

Syn.: *káthēmai* (2521), to sit; *anákeimai* (345), to recline at the table; *kathízō* (2523), to make to sit down or to sit down.

Ant.: *hístēmi* (2476), to stand; *stḗkō* (4739), to stand, to stand fast or uprightly; *egeírō* (1453), to raise or to rise.

2517. καθεξῆς *kathexḗs*; adv. from *katá* (2596), according to, and *hexḗs* (1836),

following. In order, according to the order or succession, successively, consecutively in connected order (Luke 1:3; Acts 11:4; 18:23). With the art. prefixed, it assumes the meaning of a noun and denotes following, succeeding (Luke 8:1), or afterwards. Those prophets which were or came after (Acts 3:24).

Syn.: *metépeita* (3347), afterwards; *hústeron* (5305), afterwards implying at length; *eíta* (1534), then, afterwards; *épeita* (1899), then, afterwards, thereupon; *epí* (1909), in the sense of after, immediately following upon.

Ant.: *prṓton* (4412), before; *próteron* (4386), before, former time; *prín* (4250), before, formerly; *émprosthen* (1715), in front.

2518. καθεύδω *katheúdō*; imperf. *ekátheudon*, fut. *katheudḗsō*, from *katá* (2596), an intens., and *heúdō* (n.f.), to sleep. To sleep, fall asleep, be fast asleep (Matt 8:24; 13:25; 25:5; 26:40, 43, 45; Mark 13:36; 14:37, 40, 41; Luke 22:46; 1 Thess 5:7; Sept.: Gen 28:13; 1 Sam 3:2, 3, 5; 2 Sam 12:3); to sleep the sleep of death (Matt 9:24; Mark 5:39; Luke 8:52 [cf. John 11:11–14; 1 Thess 5:10; Sept.: Dan 12:2]). To be spiritually asleep, i.e., secure and unconcerned in sin, or indolent and careless in the performance of duty (Eph 5:14; 1 Thess 5:6 [cf. Rom 13:11–13; 1 Cor 15:34]).

In Mark 4:27, it is used with the meaning of sleep in disregard of the duty of the sower of the seed in contrast to *grēgoréō* (1127), to stay awake and do what is necessary for utmost fruitfulness (Mark 4:26–29). See how *katheúdō* is used in Matt 26:43, 45 as an ant. of *grēgoréō* in Mark 4:38, 41.

Syn.: *koimáō* or *koimáomai* (2837), to sleep; *koimáomai* (2837), to fall asleep. Both of these words refer to ordinary sleep, and in a symbolic manner, they are used with reference to death. Christ uses *katheúdō* in describing the condition of Jairus' daughter (Matt 9:24; Mark 5:39; Luke 8:52), and *koimáomai* in the case of Lazarus (John 11:11). In both of these cases, natural death is spoken of by Christ as sleep indicating that through the exercise of His miraculous power, this sleep would be followed by an awakening in the present world. As in the OT, sleep is used in the apostolic church as a euphemistic term for death. Stephen is said to have fallen asleep when he died as the result of stoning (Acts 7:60). According to Paul, true believers live and die unto the Lord under the symbolism of waking and sleeping respectively (1 Thess 5:10), hence the beautiful phrases "fallen asleep in Christ" (1 Cor 15:18) and "them also which sleep [or are fallen asleep] in Jesus" (1 Thess 4:14). Sleep is also used as a symbol of spiritual lethargy and death, especially in several of our Lord's parables; hence the duty of watchfulness (Matt 25:1–13) occurs. Paul is emphatic in warning men against that suspension of spiritual activity which is implied by the word "sleep" inasmuch as Christians are the children of the day (1 Thess 5:6, 7) and not of the night, and he calls upon them to awake out of sleep (Rom 13:11; Eph 5:14). The metaphorical use of death as sleep implies that as the sleeper does not cease to exist while his body sleeps, so the person who dies does not cease to exist, but simply is not naturally aware of his environment. As only the body sleeps, so at death only the body ceases to function. It is to be noted that the early Christians called a cemetery *koimētērion*, a sleeping place, from the verb *koimáomai* (2837), to sleep, and *koímēsis* (2838), a sleeping or taking of rest.

Ant.: *egeíro* (1453), to raise, or *egeíromai*, to rise; *anístēmi* (450), to rise, stand upright; *exupnízō* (1852), to awake out of sleep; *grēgoréō* (1127), to keep awake, watch.

2519. καθηγητής *kathēgētēs*; gen. *kathēgētoú*, masc. noun from *kathēgéomai* (n.f.), to lead or guide in the way, which is from *katá* (2596), an intens., and *hēgéomai* (2233), to lead. A guide in the way, a teacher, leader (Matt 23:8, 10). Equivalent to *rhabbí* (4461), rabbi,

master, a title of respectful address to Jewish teachers.

Syn.: *didáskalos* (1320), a teacher, indicating a relationship between a teacher and a pupil; *kúrios* (2962), a lord, one who exercises power; *despótēs* (1203), despot, one who has absolute power and exercises it; *epistátēs* (1988), overseer, one who stands over and superintends the work of others; *kubernētēs* (2942), governor, one who has the authority and the responsibility of steering or piloting a ship.

Ant.: *mathētēs* (3101), disciple.

2520. καθήκω *kathēkō*; fut. *kathēxō*, from *katá* (2596), according or together with, and *hēkō* (2240), to come. To be convenient, fit. In the NT, used impersonally, *kathēkei*, it is becoming or fit, and *kathēkon* with the def. art. *tó* (neut.), what is right, fit, fitting, convenient (Acts 22:22 [TR]; Rom 1:28, things not necessary or becoming, hence abominable [cf. *anēkō* {433}, to be proper, convenient]).

Syn.: *prépō* (4241), to be fit, to do that which is right; *katartízō* (2675), to make fit, to prepare for fulfilling one's purpose in a general plan; *sunarmologéō* (4883), to fit or frame together; *exartízō* (1822), to furnish completely, equip fully; *hetoimázō* (2090), to prepare, make ready; *kataskeuázō* (2680), to shape properly, make ready; *paraskeuázō* (3903), to make ready, prepare; *proetoimázō* (4282), to prepare beforehand.

Ant.: *lúō* (3089), to loose, unbind; *kláō* or *klázō* (2806), to break or break off pieces; *ekkláō* (1575), to break off; *katakláō* (2622), to break into pieces; *suntríbō* (4937), to shatter, break in pieces by crushing; *rhēgnumi* (4486), to tear, rend; *diarrēgnumi* or *diarrēssō* (1284), to burst asunder, rend, cleave, and *prosrēgnumi* (4366), to beat; *katágnumi* (2608), to break; *sunthláō* (4917), to break or crush, shatter; *sunthrúptō* (4919), to break small; *schízō* (4977), to split, rend open; *diorússō* (1358), to dig through in order to break into; *exorússō* (1846), to dig out, to break up a part of a roof.

2521. κάθημαι *káthēmai*; fut. *kathḗsomai*, 2d person *káthē* (Acts 23:3), imper. *káthou* (Heb 1:13), from *katá* (2596), down, and *hḗmai* (n.f.), to sit. To sit down, sit, intrans.

(I) To sit down (Matt 15:29; 27:36; John 6:3; Sept.: Gen 21:16).

(A) Generally meaning to sit, used in an absolute sense, i.e., to sit there, to sit by (Matt 13:2; Luke 5:17; 1 Cor 14:30). With an adjunct of place, e.g., *ekeí* (1563), there (Mark 2:6); *hoú* (3757), where (Acts 2:2); *hṓde* (5602), in this same spot, here or hither (James 2:3). Also with a prep., e.g., *apénanti* (561), in front, opposite, before (Matt 27:61; Sept.: Gen 21:16); *eis* (1519), to, with the acc. of place (Mark 13:3); *ek dexiṓn* (*ek* [1537], on, out of; *dexiṓn* [1188], right hand), on the right hand (Matt 22:44; Acts 2:34); *en* (1722), in, with the dat. of place (Matt 11:16; Mark 4:1; Luke 10:13; Sept.: 2 Kgs 6:32); *en dexiá* or *en toís dexioís* (*en* [1722], in; *dexiá* [1188], right hand), on the right hand (Mark 16:5; Col 3:1); *epánō* (1883), upon followed by the gen. (Matt 28:2; Rev 6:8); *epí* (1909), upon, with the gen. (Matt 24:3; Acts 8:28; Rev 4:2; 9:17; Sept.: 1 Sam 1:9, where the verb is implied; Esth 5:13), with the dat. of place (Acts 3:10; Sept.: Isa 36:12), with the acc. (Matt 9:9; Mark 2:14; John 12:15; Rev 6:2); *metá* (3326), with, after, with the gen. of person (Matt 26:58); *pará* (3844), near, with the acc. of place (Matt 13:1; Mark 10:46); *perí* (4012), around, with the acc. of person meaning around whom, in whose circle one sits (Mark 3:32, 34); *prós* (4314), toward (Luke 22:56); *hupó* (5259), under with the acc. (James 2:3; Sept.: Judg 4:5; 1 Kgs 13:14).

(B) Spoken of any dignitary who sits in public, e.g., as a judge (Matt 27:19; Acts 23:3); a queen (Rev 18:7; Sept.: Ex 18:14).

(II) In the sense of to abide, dwell, to be, followed by *en* (1722), in, with the dat. of place (Matt 4:16 quoted from Isa 9:2; Luke 1:79; Acts 14:8; Sept.: Neh 11:6); by *epí* (1909), upon, with the gen. of place (Rev 14:16 [TR] *katoikoúntas* [2730], dwelling). With the acc. (Luke 21:35).

Deriv.: *sugkáthēmai* (4775), to sit with.

Syn.: *kathízō* (2523), to sit down, dwell; *anákeimai* (345), to recline at a meal; *anaklínō* (347), to cause to recline, sit down.

Ant.: *hístēmi* (2476), to cause to stand; *anístēmi* (450), to raise, arise; *egeírō* (1453), to raise; *stḗkō* (4739), to stand upright.

2522. καθημερινός *kathēmerinós*; fem. *kathēmerinḗ*, neut. *kathēmerinón*, adj. from *katá* (2596), each, and *hēméra* (2250), day. Daily (Acts 6:1, "in the daily ministration" of alms).

Syn.: *epioúsios* (1967), daily, that which is sufficient for one's sustenance; *ephḗmeros* (2184), for the day.

Ant.: *hápax* (530), once; *ephápax* (2178), once for all.

2523. καθίζω *kathízō*; fut. *kathísō*, from *katá* (2596), down, and *hízō* (n.f.), to sit, to cause to sit. To cause to sit down.

(I) Trans. to cause to sit down, to seat, for example, with *en* (1722), in, speaking of place (Eph 1:20; Sept.: 2 Chr 23:20). To cause to sit, to set, as judges (1 Cor 6:4).

(II) Intrans. to sit down, to sit, or with *heautón* (1438), himself implied, and also mid., to seat oneself, i.e., to sit down, to sit.

(A) Particularly and generally (Matt 5:1; 13:48; Mark 9:35; Luke 4:20; 5:3; 14:28, 31; 16:6; John 8:2; Acts 13:14; 16:13; 1 Cor 10:7; Sept.: Gen 37:25; Neh 1:4). With an adjunct of place, e.g., *autoú* (847), here (Matt 26:36); *hṓde* (5602), here or hither (Mark 14:32). Also with prep.: *eis* (1519), into, in (2 Thess 2:4); *ek dexiṓn* (*ek* [1537], from; *dexiṓn* [1188], right hand), on the right hand (Matt 20:21, 23; Mark 10:37, 40; 16:19); *en* (1722), in, with the dat. (Heb 1:3; 8:1; 10:12; 12:2; Rev 3:21); *epí* (1909), upon, with the gen., upon a throne (Matt 19:28; 25:31; Luke 22:30; Acts 2:30; Sept.: 1 Kgs 2:12;

8:20); upon the platform or tribunal of a judge (John 19:13; Acts 12:21; 25:6, 17); upon the seat of Moses (Matt 23:2). With the dat. (Mark 11:7). With the acc. (Mark 11:2; Luke 19:30; John 12:14; Rev 20:4). Metaphorically (Acts 2:3; Sept.: Gen 48:2). *Katénanti* (2713), directly opposite of something (Mark 12:41). *Metá* (3326), with, followed by the gen., with someone (Rev 3:21); *sún* (4862), together, followed by the dat., with someone (Acts 8:31).

(B) By implication to abide, continue, e.g., in the city (Luke 24:49). Used in an absolute sense (Acts 18:11; Sept.: Ex 16:29).

Deriv.: *anakathízō* (339), to set up, and intrans., to sit up; *epikathízō* (1940), to set upon; *parakathízō* (3869), to sit down beside; *sugkathízō* (4776), to make to sit together, and intrans., to sit down together; trans.

Syn.: *káthēmai* (2521), to sit down; *stērízō* (4741), to establish; *anaklínō* (347), to cause to recline, to make to sit down; *kataklínō* (2625), to set down or to sit down to eat.

Ant.: *egeírō* (1453), to raise or rise; *anístēmi* (450), to stand up.

2524. καθίημι *kathíēmi*; fut. *kathḗsō*, aor. *kathḗka*, from *katá* (2596), down, and *híēmi* (n.f., see *iós* [2447]), to send, let go. To let down, trans. (Luke 5:19; Acts 9:25; 10:11; 11:5; Sept.: 1 Chr 21:27).

Syn.: *katágō* (2609), to lead down; *katabibázō* (2601), to bring down; *hupostéllō* (5288), to withhold under, shrink; *chaláō* (5465), to lower; *kataphérō* (2702), to bring down.

Ant.: *aníēmi* (447), to send upwards or to let up; *anabibázō* (307), to cause to go up; *aírō* (142), to take up or away; *apaírō* (522), to take away; *anágō* (321), to lead up; *egeírō* (1453), to raise; *hupsóō* (5312), to lift up; *epaírō* (1869), to raise up; *exaírō* (1808), to take away.

2525. καθίστημι *kathístēmi* or *kathistáō*; fut. *katastḗsō*, aor. *katéstēsa*, from *katá* (2596), down, and *hístēmi* (2476), to stand. To set, set down, place.

(I) To set, place. Trans., to set down, bring to pass, cause to stand (Acts 17:15). Mid. or pass. to stand, metaphorically, to stand, be set, to be (James 3:6; 4:4). Act. to cause to be, make (2 Pet 1:8); pass. to be made, to become, Rom 5:19).

(II) Of persons, to set, constitute, to place anywhere in an office, in a condition (Matt 24:45, 47; 25:21, 23; Luke 12:42, 44; Acts 6:3); with double acc., to make somebody something, to put in a situation or position, to constitute (Luke 12:14; Acts 7:10, 27, 35; Heb 7:28). For example, in Rom 5:19: "For as by one man's disobedience many were made [*katestáthēsan*, aor. pass. indic.] sinners, so by the obedience of one shall many be made [*katastathésontai*, fut. pass. indic.] righteous." Another syn. which was not used is *gínomai* (1096), to become, or, in this case, to make. To have used this latter word would have actually meant that God is responsible for making transgressors. As a judge does not make lawbreakers or bear moral responsibility for what they do, so it is with the Lord. God does not make sinners or cause them to sin, but He declares them to be such. He set the consequence of the disobedience of man, but He was not responsible for that disobedience. The verb *kathístēmi* used in this regard means that God has set or placed man in a definite place or position, that of the transgressor, but He did not *make* him a transgressor. The responsibility is entirely man's.

(III) Intrans., existing as inactive and unfruitful (2 Pet 1:8). In the pres. mid. voice, to take a position, come forward, appear (James 3:6; 4:4).

To constitute, to make (Luke 12:14). See Acts 7:10, 27, 35; Heb 7:28. Also with acc. of person omitted (Titus 1:5). In the pass. with the acc. of manner (Heb 5:1; 8:3; Sept.: Gen 47:5; Ex 2:14).

Deriv.: *akatástatos* (182), unstable; *antikathístēmi* (478), to resist; *apokathístēmi* (600), to restore; *katástēma* (2688), behavior.

Syn.: *títhēmi* (5087), to put; *tássō* (5021), to place in order; *diatássō* (1299), to appoint, prescribe; *cheirotonéō* (5500), to appoint by placing hands on as in the appointment of elders; *horízō* (3724), to mark by a limit, to determine, ordain; *anadeíknumi* (322), to show up, appoint to a position or a service; *poiéō* (4160), to make; *kataskeuázō* (2680), to prepare; *gínomai* (1096), to become; *anorthóō* (461), to set straight up.

Ant.: *katargéō* (2673), to reduce to inactivity, abolish; *paúō* (3973), to stop; *kopázō* (2869), to cease raging; *aphíēmi* (863), to let go; *katapaúō* (2664), to put at rest.

2526. καθό *kathó*; adv. from *katá* (2596), according to, and *hó* (neut. sing. of *hós* [3739], which), that which. According, to that which, according to what (2 Cor 8:12); according to, inasmuch as (Rom 8:26; 1 Pet 4:13; Sept.: Lev 9:5).

Syn.: *kathóti* (2530), because that, inasmuch as; *kathōs* (2531), according as; *hōs* (5613), according as, seeing that; *kath' hóson* (*katá* [2596], according to; *hóson* [3745], as much as), inasmuch as, and *eph' hóson* (*epí* [1909], upon), inasmuch as; *hōste* (5620), insomuch that; *eis tó* (*eis* [1519], unto, followed by the neut. art. *tó* [3588], the), followed by the inf. meaning insomuch that.

2527. καθόλου *kathólou*; adv. from *katá* (2596), of, concerning, and *hólou* (gen. sing. of *hólos* [3650], all), of all. Whole, wholly, entirely; followed by *mē* (3361), not, meaning not at all (Acts 4:18; Sept.: Ezek 13:3, 22; 17:14).

Syn.: *hólōs* (3654) and *holotelēs* (3651), complete to the end, wholly; *pántōs* (3843), wholly, entirely, by all means; *holóklēros* (3648), entire.

2528. καθοπλίζω *kathoplízō*; fut. *kathoplísō*, from *katá* (2596), an intens., and *hoplízō* (3695), to arm or be armed. To arm well, fully, or all over. To be fully armed (Luke 11:21).

2529. καθοράω *kathoráō*; contracted *kathorō*, fut. *katópsomai*, from *katá*

(2596), an intens., and *horáō* (3708), to see. To look down upon from a higher place, to behold (Sept.: Num 24:2). In the NT, generally and figuratively to perceive, to see or know clearly (Rom 1:20).

Syn.: *blépō* (991), to perceive, behold; *emblépō* (1689), to look earnestly; *diablépō* (1227), to see clearly or through; *theōréō* (2334), to look with interest, inspect; *theáomai* (2300), to behold with the sense of a wondering regard, to investigate; *epopteúō* (2029), to oversee, supervise; *atenízō* (816), to gaze upon with steadfastness; *katanoéō* (2657), to perceive by looking.

Ant.: *muōpázō* (3467), to be shortsighted, myopic.

2530. καθότι *kathóti*; adv. from *katá* (2596), according to, and *hóti* (3754), that.

(I) According as, as (Acts 2:45; 4:35; Sept.: Ex 1:12, 17; Lev 27:12).

(II) For that, because that, forasmuch (Luke 1:7; 19:9; Acts 2:24; Sept.: Dan 2:8).

Syn.: *kathó* (2526), according to.

2531. καθώς *kathōs*; adv. from *katá* (2596), according to, and *hōs* (5613), as. According as, equivalent to the simple *hōs* (5613), as.

(I) Implying manner.

(A) Generally (Matt 21:6; Mark 11:6; Luke 11:1; John 1:23; Acts 10:47; 1 Cor 4:17; Gal 2:7). In Mark 15:8, "began to demand [that he should do] according as he had ever done to them" (a.t.). See John 6:58. With *eimí* (1510), to be, equivalent to such as (1 Thess 2:13; 1 John 3:2); with *hoútos* (3779), thus, meaning correspondingly (John 3:14; 2 Cor 1:5; 1 Thess 2:4); with *homoíōs* (3668), likewise (Luke 6:31 [cf. 1 Chr 24:31]).

(B) After verbs of speaking, "such as," "how" (Acts 15:14; 3 John 1:3).

(C) In the sense of proportion, comparison (Mark 4:33; John 5:30; Acts 11:29; 1 Pet 4:10; Sept.: Num 26:54).

(II) In a causal sense, "as," i.e., even as, inasmuch as (John 17:2; Rom 1:28; 1 Cor 1:6; 5:7; Eph 1:4; Phil 1:7).

(III) Of time meaning "as," "when" (Acts 7:17).

Syn.: *kathóti* (2530), according as, inasmuch as; *hōs* (5613), according as, seeing that; *kathó* (2526), inasmuch as; *hoútōs* (3779), even so; *hósper* (5618), even as; *katháper* (2509), just as, even as; *naí* (3483), yes, verily, even so; *hōsaútōs* (5615), likewise, even so; *katá* (2596), according.

Ant.: *hómōs* (3676), nevertheless, yet, even; *állōs* (247), otherwise; *hetérōs* (2088), otherwise, differently minded; *epeí* (1893), otherwise; *ei dé mē̄* (*ge*) (1490), but if not, indeed, otherwise; *eíge* (1489), unless, otherwise, if it so be that, yet.

2532. καί *kaí*; copulative conj. And, also.

(I) And, used as a copulative.

(A) As simply joining single words and clauses, e.g., nouns (Matt 2:11; 13:55; 23:6, 7; Luke 6:38). When the latter noun is in place of a gen. (Acts 23:6; Rom 2:20; Sept.: Gen 1:14; 3:16). When joining pronouns (Matt 8:29); adj. (Rom 7:12); verbs (Mark 4:27; Acts 1:21; 7:17; 9:28); where one verb is taken adverbially (Luke 6:48; Rom 10:20); adv. (Heb 1:1). When joining clauses (Matt 1:17; 7:25; John 1:1; Rom 14:7). Hence *kaí* is mostly a simple continuative, marking the progress of a continued discourse, e.g., Matt 1:23; Mark 4:32; Luke 2:34; 11:44; 1 Cor 12:5, 6. As connecting neg. clauses, where the neg. particle may be omitted in the latter, which is then rendered neg. by the continuative power of *kaí*, e.g., Mark 4:12; John 12:40; Acts 28:27; 2 Cor 12:21 (cf. Matt 13:15; James 3:14). In two examples after *oúte* (3777), nor, the *kaí* does not thus carry forward the neg. (John 4:11; 3 John 1:10). The use of *kaí* in this continuative sense takes a strong coloring in the NT. Hence, the simple *kaí* is used frequently in the NT, particularly in the narrative style where Class. Gr. writers either

used nothing or used some other particle as *dé* (1161), but, and; *allá* (235), but; *tóte* (5119), then, and the like. This is especially true in Matthew, Mark, Luke, and Revelation, e.g., Matt 14:9ff.; 27:28ff.; Mark 1:31ff.; 3:13ff.; Luke 2:25ff.; 4:14ff.; Rev 11:7ff. (cf. Sept.: 1 Sam 15:3ff.; Isa 11:12ff.; Ezek 5:1ff.).

(B) As a continuative in respect to time, i.e., connecting clauses and sentences in the order of time. **(1)** At the beginning of a sentence where anything is narrated as being done immediately or soon after that which the preceding context narrates. Here *kaí* is equivalent to the more usual *tóte* (5119), then, after that (Matt 3:16; 4:3, 21; 10:1; 14:12, 14; Mark 1:29; 4:21, 24, 26 [cf. *tóte* in Matt 15:12]). Here belongs the form *kaí egéneto* (the 2d aor. 3d person of *gínomai* [1096], to take place), then it came to pass. Usually with a notation of time, e.g., by *hóte* (3753), then (Matt 7:28; 19:1); *hōs* (5613), as (Luke 2:15); *en* (1722), in, with the dat. (Mark 1:9; 4:4; Luke 1:59; 9:18; 14:1); *metá* (3326), with (Luke 2:46). Followed by the gen. absolute (Matt 9:10); by the acc. and inf. (Mark 2:23). Elsewhere *egéneto dé* (Luke 3:21; 5:1; 6:1). **(2)** In the apodosis (conclusion), e.g., where anything is said to follow at once upon that which is contained in the protasis (proposition), i.e., and immediately (Matt 8:15; 26:53; Mark 1:27; 2:14; Luke 4:36; 8:25). Also where the time is less definite, i.e., and then, and afterwards, without any notation of time (Mark 12:1; Luke 1:56; John 4:40; 6:58; Acts 5:7; 7:7). With a notation of time (Matt 28:9). After *kaí egéneto* or *egéneto dé* with a note of time (see 1 above). In Matt 9:10, *kaí idoú* (*idoú* [2400], behold), and behold (Mark 2:15; Luke 2:15, 21; 5:1; 9:28, 51). Specifically in the construction *éggiken* (perf. indic. 3d person sing. of *eggízō* [1448], to come near, approach), "the hour is near" (a.t.), or has come (Matt 26:45); "and the hour was the third" (a.t. [Mark 15:25; Luke 23:44]).

(C) As continuative in respect to sense, i.e., before the apodosis and connecting it as a consequent with the protasis as its antecedent. (**1**) Where the apodosis affirms what will take place provided that what is contained in the protasis is done, i.e., and so, and thus, and then, usually followed by the fut. or pres. in a fut. sense. So also with the imper. in the protasis (Matt 4:19; 5:15; 7:7; 9:18; 11:29; Mark 6:22; 11:29; Luke 6:35; John 2:19; 4:35; 7:33; Acts 9:6; 2 Cor 13:11; James 1:5; Sept.: 1 Sam 15:16). Also generally (Matt 27:64; Luke 12:19; Heb 3:19; 12:9; Sept.: Gen 24:40). After *ei* (1487) or *eán* (1437), if, in the protasis, meaning "then" (James 4:15, "If God will and we live, *then* we shall do this or that" [a.t., italics added]; Rev 3:20 *eán* . . . *kaí* Sept.: Lev 26:3, 4; Deut 11:13, 14). Once followed by the imper. (John 7:52, "Search and thou shalt see" [a.t.], where the second imper. is equivalent to a fut., "and so thou shalt see" [a.t.]). (**2**) Where the apodosis affirms what is or will be done in consequence of or because of that which is contained in the protasis, i.e., and so, and therefore, so that, wherefore. Followed by the fut. (Acts 7:43 quoted from Amos 5:26; Rom 11:35); by the pres. (Matt 11:18, 19, "and they say"). See John 7:22; Acts 10:28; Rom 4:3; Gal 2:16; 3:6; James 2:23; Sept.: 1 Sam 15:23.

(**D**) As an explicative copula meaning, i.e., namely, to wit, even, between words and clauses. (**1**) Between nouns which are strictly in apposition (Matt 21:5; 1 Cor 15:24; James 1:27; 3:9). In the phrase, "the God and Father of the Lord Jesus Christ" (a.t.), it is merely a copulative (2 Cor 1:3; 11:31; see Matt 13:41; Rom 1:5 [cf. 1 Sam 17:40; 28:3]). (**2**) Before a clause added by way of explanation or a further explanation (Matt 1:25; Luke 5:35; John 2:16; 1 Cor 3:5).

(**E**) As having an intens. force (**1**) Where two or more words are connected by *kaí*, and *kaí* is then also inserted emphatically before the first word *kaí—kaí*, as in Eng. both—and (Matt 10:28; Mark 9:22; Acts 26:29; Rom 14:9; Phil 4:12, 16). (**2**) Before comparatives, for example, and even (Matt 11:9; Luke 7:26; John 10:10). (**3**) Before interrogations where

in strictness it is simply copulative, and, but serves to add strength and vivacity to the question, and, and then, then. Before a pron. or adv. (Mark 10:26), "and who" or "who then [in that case] can be saved?" (author's translations [Luke 3:14; 10:29; 2 Cor 2:2]); *kaí póthen* (*póthen* [4159], whence), and whence (Mark 12:37); *kaí pṓs* (*pṓs* [4459], how), and how (Luke 20:44; John 14:9). Generally (Acts 23:3; 1 Cor 5:2). (**4**) Before an imper., *kaí* is often intensive in the Class. Gr. writers. Some apply this also to several passages in the NT, as Matt 23:32; Mark 9:5; 11:29; Luke 12:29; 20:3; Eph 4:26. But in all these, *kaí* is simply copulative, without any intens. force, and may be referred to some of the meanings given above. (**5**) Where a part is subjoined to a whole by way of emphasis, *kaí* may be rendered "and especially" (Matt 8:33; Mark 1:5; 16:7, "and especially to Peter" [a.t.]; 1 Cor 9:5). Vice versa, where a whole is subjoined to a part, as in the summing up of particulars, i.e., and in a word, or yea (Matt 26:59, "the chief priests and the elders and [in a word, yea] the whole Sanhedrin" [a.t.]; Mark 15:1).

(**F**) Apparently adversative, but only where the opposition or antithesis of the thought is sufficiently strong in itself without the aid of an adversative particle. (**1**) And yet, and nevertheless (Matt 6:26; 10:29; 12:5; John 1:10; 6:70; 7:19; 9:30; 17:25, "and yet the world hath not known thee" [a.t.], i.e., notwithstanding all thy love [cf. John 17:23, 24]). See Gal 4:14; Heb 3:9, "they proved me, and yet [i.e., although] they saw my works" (a.t.), quoted from Ps 95:9; 1 John 2:4; Rev 3:1; Sept.: 2 Sam 3:8; Mal 2:14. (**2**) Where it connects a neg. antithetic clause with a preceding positive one where we often use but, though not necessarily, e.g., Matt 12:39; 13:14, 17; 17:16; 26:60; Mark 9:18; 14:55, 56; John 10:25. In all these passages, the rendering "but" is admissible but not necessary; in others it would destroy the true sense, e.g., "I will have mercy and not [merely] sacrifice" (Matt 9:13; 12:7, quoted from Hos 6:6, "I want mercy rather than sacrifice" [a.t.]).

(3) Rarely in a strong antithesis without a neg., *kaí* may be translated by "but," though not necessarily, e.g., Acts 10:28 (see C, 2 above). In Mark 12:12 we may also render "and yet," "and nevertheless" (author's translations [1 Cor 12:5, 6]).

(II) "Also" or "too," used not merely as a copulative but likewise emph., implying increase, addition, something more, e.g., always so in the connection *dé* (1161), but, followed by *kaí* (*dé kaí*), or preceded *kaí dé*, and also, i.e., and in addition, and likewise (see *dé* [1161, II, D]).

(A) Generally (Matt 5:39; 6:12; Mark 2:16, 28; Luke 1:35; 6:16; John 8:19; Rom 1:15; 1 Cor 14:12).

(B) In comparisons, e.g., *hoútō kaí* (*hoúdō* [3779], thus), so also (1 Cor 15:22); with *hoútō* implied (Matt 6:10; John 13:15; Acts 7:51; Gal 1:9); with *kathṓs* (2531), even as, *kathṓs kaí*, as also, even as also (1 Cor 13:12; 14:34); with *hōs* (5613), as, followed by *kaí hōs kaí*, as also (Acts 11:17; 1 Cor 7:7).

(C) In interrogations, e.g., *ti* (5101) in the neut., *tí kaí*, why also? why too? (1 Cor 15:29, 30); *hínati kaí*, (*hínati* [2444], why), why moreover? (Luke 13:7).

(D) Before a part., *kaí* implies an emph. antithesis with that which precedes and may be rendered even, although (Matt 26:60; Luke 18:7; 1 Cor 16:9).

(E) As an intens., even, even also, yea (Matt 10:30, "the very hairs"; Mark 1:27; 4:25; 9:13, "That Elias is even already come" [a.t.]; Luke 8:18; Rom 8:23; 1 Cor 2:10; 11:6, "let her be even also shorn" [a.t.]; 2 Cor 8:3, "yea, above their ability" [a.t.]).

(III) With other particles, meaning chiefly, e.g., *kaí dé*, and also, but also, likewise; also *dé kaí*, but also (Matt 3:10; John 15:24). See *dé* (1161, II, D). Others are: *allá* (235), but, followed by *kaí*, *allá kaí*, but also (see *allá* [235, I, A, 1]); *gár* (1063), because, for, followed by *kaí* (see *gár* [1063, 2]); *eán dé kaí* (see *eán* [1437. II, A]); *ei kaí*, *ei gár kaí*, *eí ge kaí*, *ei dé kaí*, (see *ei* [1487, III, C, D]; *ge* [1065, II, 3]); *ḗ kaí* (*ḗ* [2228], or), or also, or even (Luke 18:11) (see *ḗ* [2228, IV, B]); *kaí gár*, for also (see *gár* [1063, II]); *kaí* followed by *ge* (see *ge* [1065, II, 5]); *kaí ei*, even if, *kaí gár ei*, and even though, *kaí gár eíper*, and even though certainly (see *ei* [1487, III, D]).

2533. Καϊάφας *Kaïáphas*, gen. *Kaïápha*, masc. proper noun. Caiaphas, the high priest at the time of the crucifixion. He was appointed by Valerius Gratus, the predecessor of Pilate, around A.D. 26, and deposed by Vitellius in A.D. 35 (see Matt 26:3, 57; Luke 3:2; John 11:49; 18:13, 14, 24, 28; Acts 4:6). Annas, the father-in-law of Caiaphas (John 18:13), had been high priest (Luke 3:2), and several of his sons succeeded him for a short period. Though Caiaphas held the office of high priest, Annas was still a sort of "high priest emeritus." Caiaphas (John 11:41–53) declared that it would be better for Jesus to die than the nation to be destroyed. The Lord Jesus was brought first to the house of Annas where He underwent His initial trial (John 18:12–23). Then Annas sent Him bound to Caiaphas before whom the trial continued (John 18:24–27). After that, He was delivered to Pilate because the Jews could not legally execute Him.

2534. καίγε *kaíge*; conj. from *kaí* (2532), and, and the particle *ge* (1065) used for emphasis (Luke 19:42, "and at least" [a.t.]; Acts 2:18, "and even," "yea even" [author's translations]). And, at least, indeed. See *ge* (1065, II, 5).

2535. Κάϊν *Káïn*; masc. proper noun transliterated from the Hebr. *Qayin* (7014, OT). Cain, the first son of Adam and Eve and a farmer by occupation. He brought farm products to God as an offering, whereas his brother Abel brought an animal sacrifice which God accepted. Being angry that his offering was not received (Heb 11:4), Cain slew his brother. See 1 John 3:12; Jude 1:11.

2536. Καϊνάν *Kaïnán*; masc. proper noun transliterated from the Hebr. *Qēnān* (7018, OT), possession. Cainan.

(I) Kenan, the fourth from Adam in the Messianic line (Gen 5:9–14; 1 Chr 1:2; Luke 3:37).

(II) A son of Arphaxad (Luke 3:36, omitted in the Hebr. text of Gen 10:24, but found in the Sept. from which Luke quotes).

2537. καινός *kainós*; fem. *kainḗ*, neut. *kainón*, adj. New. Qualitatively new, as contrasted with *néos* (3501), temporally new. Contextual meanings:

(I) Newly made, not impaired by time or use, as *askoí* (779), skins used as containers (Matt 9:17; Mark 2:22; Luke 5:38; Sept.: Josh 9:13), *mnēmeíon* (3419), grave, sepulcher (Matt 27:60; John 19:41), *himátion* (2440), garment (Luke 5:36; Sept.: 1 Kgs 11:29ff.). Also Matt 13:52, in the pl., "treasures new and old" (a.t.). In Mark 2:21, the word "new" occurs twice, but it is two different words in Gr., the first being *ágnaphos* (46), one that has not been washed and properly shrunk. The second "new" is *kainós* in the neut., *tó kainón*, which means another patch but derived from a cloth that has been washed and shrunk. Therefore it will not shrink when used as a patch and thus tear the garment. It makes no difference from where this patch is taken as long as the patch itself can provide proper replacement for that part of the garment which has been worn or somehow needs replacement. A new patch is needed, but that patch must be of shrunken cloth. Thus it is qualitatively different from just any new (*néos*) piece of cloth that has not been shrunk. See Luke 5:36.

(II) New, i.e., current or not before known, newly introduced. Of doctrine: *didachḗ* (1322), the content of teaching (Mark 1:27; Acts 17:19); *entolḗ* (1785), commandment, precept (John 13:34; 1 John 2:7, 8; 2 John 1:5); *ónoma* (3686), name (Rev 2:17; 3:12; Sept.: Isa 62:2). In the comparative degree in Acts 17:21, "to tell or to hear some new thing," meaning something that was not introduced until that time and thus different. In the sense of other, i.e., foreign or different from their own mother tongues (Mark 16:17). Nevertheless, they were languages, equal to dialects, spoken by other groups of people (see Acts 2:6, 8).

(III) New as opposed to old or former and hence also implying better because different, as *kainḗ diathḗkē* ([1242] testament), meaning a new testament which is better than the old. See *diathḗkē* (1242) (Matt 26:28; Mark 14:24; Luke 22:20; 1 Cor 11:25; 2 Cor 3:6; Heb 8:8, 13; 9:15; Sept.: Jer 31:31). "A new song" means a nobler, loftier strain (Rev 5:9; 14:3; Sept.: Ps 33:3; 40:3; Isa 42:10). "New heavens and a new earth" (2 Pet 3:13; Rev 21:1; Sept.: Isa 65:17; 66:22) refers to heaven and earth which have been renewed, and, therefore, made superior, more splendid; as also the "new Jerusalem" (Rev 3:12; 21:2); "I make all things new" or nobler (Rev 21:5). Metaphorically speaking of Christians who are renewed and changed from evil to good by the Spirit of God (2 Cor 5:17; Gal 6:15; Eph 4:24); a new heart, a transformed, saved heart (Sept.: Ezek 18:31; 36:26).

Deriv.: *egkaínia* (1456), dedication; *kainótēs* (2538), newness.

Syn.: *prósphatos* (4372), occurring in the immediate past, recent; *ágnaphos* (46), new, unshrunken.

Ant.: *palaiós* (3820), old, that which has been around for a long time but not necessarily from the beginning as the word *archaíos* (744) would imply, as being original.

2538. καινότης *kainótēs*; gen. *kainótētos*, fem. noun from *kainós* (2537), new. Renewal, not simply an experience similar to the past, but a qualitatively different one. In the NT used in a moral sense, "in newness of life" (Rom 6:4), meaning in a qualitatively new life with the indwelling of Christ. See Rom 7:6. Contrast *néos* (3501), temporally new, and also the verb *ananeóō* (365), to renew, to have a new or another experience the same as in the past.

Syn.: *neótēs* (3503), newness, youthfulness; *anakaínōsis* (342), renewing.

Ant.: *palaiótēs* (3821), oldness; in the moral sense: the old man, *ho palaiós ánthrōpos* (*palaiós* [3820]; *ánthrōpos* [444]).

2539. καίπερ kaíper; conj. from *kaí* (2532), and, though, and *per* (4007), very. Though indeed, though, although (Phil 3:4; Heb 5:8; 7:5; 12:17; 2 Pet 1:12; Rev 17:8).

Ant.: *oudépō* (3764), never yet; *oúpō* (3768), not yet; *pṓpote* (4455), never yet, at no time.

2540. καιρός kairós; gen. *kairoú*, masc. noun. Season, opportune time. It is not merely as a succession of minutes, which is *chrónos* (5550), but a period of opportunity (though not necessity). There is really no Eng. equivalent to the word *kairós*, appropriate or opportune time, which when used in the pl. with *chrónoi* (times), is translated as "seasons," times at which certain foreordained events take place.

(**I**) Fit time, proper season.

(**A**) Generally equivalent to opportunity, occasion (Acts 24:25; Rom 13:11; 2 Cor 6:2; Gal 6:10; Eph 5:16; Col 4:5; Heb 11:15; see John 7:6).

(**B**) Appointed time, set time, certain season, equivalent to a fixed and definite time or season. Followed by the gen. (Matt 13:30, "in the time of harvest," i.e., the usual season; 21:34, 41; Mark 11:13; Luke 1:20; 8:13; 19:44; Acts 3:19, "times of refreshing" or appointed of God; 2 Tim 4:6; Heb 9:10; 11:11; Sept.: Eccl 3:1ff.); by the gen. of person or a pron. as "my time," as appointed of God, e.g., in which I am to suffer (Matt 26:18) or accomplish any duty (Luke 21:24, "the times [or seasons] of the Gentiles"; John 7:6, 8; 2 Thess 2:6; Rev 11:18). In Gal 6:9, "one's own due time" (a.t.); see 1 Tim 2:6; 6:15; Titus 1:3. With a demonstrative art. or pron. as *ho nún*, the present

season or opportunity; *hoútos* (3778), this; *ekeínos* (1565), that time, i.e., definitely marked out and expressed (Matt 11:25; 12:1; 14:1; Mark 10:30; Luke 13:1; 18:30; Acts 12:1; Rom 3:26; 8:18; 11:5; 2 Cor 8:14; Eph 2:12). *Kairós éschatos* (*éschatos* [2078], last), last time, season, opportunity (1 Pet 1:5); *kairoí hústeroi* (*hústeroi* [5306], later, final), latter or final times (1 Tim 4:1); *kairós enestēkṓs*, perf. part. of *enístēmi* (1764), to be present, the present time (Heb 9:9). Generally (Mark 12:2, at the proper season; Acts 17:26; Gal 4:10; 2 Tim 4:3, time appointed of God; Rev 12:12, a short time to use). With a prep., e.g., *áchri* (891), until, *áchri kairoú*, for or during a certain season (Luke 4:13; Acts 13:11); *en* (1722), in, *en kairṓ*, in due time (Matt 24:45; Luke 20:10; 1 Pet 5:6; see Acts 7:20); *katá* (2596), according as, *katá kairón*, at the set time (John 5:4; Rom 5:6; see Acts 19:23; Rom 9:9); *pró* (4253), before, *pró kairoú*, before the proper time (1 Cor 4:5); *prós* (4314), toward, *prós kairón*, for a season (Luke 8:13; 1 Cor 7:5); *prós kairón hṓras* (5610), hour, meaning for a short time (1 Thess 2:17). In allusion to the set time for the coming of the Messiah in His kingdom or for judgment (Matt 8:29; 16:3; Mark 1:15; 13:33; Luke 12:56; 21:8; Acts 1:7; Rom 13:11; 1 Cor 7:29; Eph 1:10; 1 Thess 5:1; 1 Pet 1:11; 4:17; Rev 1:3; 22:10). In the pl., *kairoí* is used in an absolute sense of times and circumstances appointed of God (2 Tim 3:1).

(**II**) Generally meaning time, season, equivalent to *chrónos*.

(**A**) In Luke 21:36 and Eph 6:18, although chronological time is involved, a judgment of the propriety of the time is implied. That one should pray at any time is discerned as being the proper time.

(**B**) A season of the year as *kairoí karpophóroi* (2593), fruitful, fruitful seasons (Acts 14:17).

(**C**) In a prophetic style as used for a year (Rev 12:14, three and one-half years [cf. Rev 12:6 in allusion to Dan 7:25, where *kairoí*, times, also stands for two years]).

Deriv.: *akairéomai* (170), to lack opportunity; *akaírōs* (171), inopportunely, out of season; *eúkairos* (2121), well-timed; *próskairos* (4340), recent, temporary, temporal, for a season.

Syn.: *chrónos* (5550), time, duration of a period; *hṓra* (5610), hour, used sometimes with the meaning of season, opportunity; *hēméra* (2250), day as a point in time, era.

2541. Καῖσαρ *Kaísar*; gen. *Kaísaros*, masc. proper noun. Caesar.

(I) The name of a prominent Roman family from the third century B.C., of whom Julius Caesar was by far the most renowned.

(II) The title taken by each of the Roman emperors, e.g., Augustus Caesar who reigned when the Lord Jesus was born (Luke 2:1); his successor Tiberius Caesar, who reigned from A.D. 14–37 (Luke 3:1); Claudius Caesar, from A.D. 41–54 (Acts 11:28; 18:2); Nero, under whom Peter and Paul were martyred, A.D. 54–68 (Phil 4:22); Domitian was Caesar from A.D. 81–96, and under him John was exiled to Patmos. Caesar is mentioned by the Lord Jesus in Luke 20:22–25, both literally as referring to Tiberius Caesar and figuratively as meaning any earthly ruler. The name Caesar came to be used as a symbol of the state in general and is often used in this sense in the NT (Matt 22:17, 21; Mark 12:14, 16, 17; Luke 20:22, 24, 25).

2542. Καισάρεια *Kaisáreia*; gen. *Kaisareías*, fem. proper noun. Caesarea.

(I) Caesarea Philippi. A city built in upper Galilee near the sources of the Jordan River, at the foot of Mount Hermon, called Paneas because it was the center of the worship of the heathen god Pan. Augustus Caesar presented it, with the surrounding country, to Herod the Great who built a temple there in honor of the emperor. Herod's son, Philip the Tetrarch, enlarged the town and named it Caesarea Philippi to distinguish it from the other Caesarea and in honor of himself and

Tiberius. Thereafter, for a time, it bore the name of Neronias, in honor of Nero. It is generally believed to have occupied the site of the ancient city called Laisch or Leshen (Josh 19:47; Judg 18:29) and Dan (Judg 18:2). It was in this area that Peter made his confession in regard to Jesus Christ (Matt 16:13–17; Mark 8:27). Now the village is called Banias.

(II) Caesarea of Palestine or Maritime, on the coast of the Mediterranean, south of Mount Carmel. Herod the Great rebuilt it with great splendor and strength, created an artificial harbor, and named it Caesarea in honor of Augustus. Josephus calls it one of the largest cities in Palestine and says the inhabitants were mostly Greeks. It was the seat of the Roman procurator and, after the destruction of Jerusalem, became the capital of Palestine (Acts 8:40; 9:30; 10:1, 24; 11:11; 12:19; 18:22; 21:8, 16; 23:23, 33; 25:1, 4, 6, 13). It was the hometown of the Gentile Cornelius in whose house Peter first preached to the Gentiles (Acts 10—11). It was the place of residence of Philip the evangelist with his four unmarried prophesying daughters (Acts 8:40; 21:8, 9) who entertained Paul and Luke and their party on their return from their third missionary journey. While Paul was kept prisoner there for two years, he preached before King Agrippa (Acts 26:12–23, 32).

2543. καίτοι *kaítoi*; particle from *kaí* (2532), though, and *toi* (5104), denoting contrast. Though, and indeed, and yet, nevertheless (Heb 4:3).

Syn.: *alēthṓs* (230), truly; *óntōs* (3689), indeed, truly.

Ant.: *ou mḗ* (3364), in no wise; *oudamōs* (3760), by no means, in no wise; *ou pántos* (*ou* [3756], not; *pántos* [3843], at all), not under any circumstances, not at all, in no way.

2544. καίτοιγε *kaítoige*; particle from *kaítoi* (2543) and the particle *ge* (1065), indeed. The same as *kaítoi* (2543) the only difference being that *kaítoige* is stronger

than *kaítoi*. Though truly, though indeed (John 4:2; Acts 14:17; 17:27).

2545. καίω *kaíō*; fut. *kaúsō*, aor. pass. *ekaúthēn*. To burn, and the mid. *kaíomai*, to be burned.

(I) Causative: to make to burn, to kindle, light, e.g., a fire, lamp. Pass. part. *kaiómenos*, burning, flaming. In Matt 5:15, "men light a candle"; Luke 12:35. See Mark 4:21. In Heb 12:18, *kekauménō* (perf. pass. part. neut.), fire that was lit and is still burning, flaming fire. See Rev 4:5; 8:8, 10; 19:20; 21:8; Sept.: Lev 24:3, 4; Deut 4:11; 5:23 (cf. Dan 3:6ff.). Figuratively, in John 5:35, of John the Baptist as a distinguished teacher spoken of as "a burning and a shining light." Metaphorically, *kaíomai*, to burn, i.e., to be greatly moved in the heart (Luke 24:32).

(II) Trans.: to burn, i.e., to consume with fire (John 15:6 [cf. Matt 13:40]). In 1 Cor 13:3, *hína* (2443), so that, for the purpose of, *kauthésomai*, to be burned, in the fut. subjunctive pass., 1st person sing., providing an unusual form in that the verb is not in the 3d person sing. to correspond to the body being subject (Sept.: Lev 4:12; 1 Kgs 13:2; Isa 5:24).

Deriv.: *ekkaíō* (1572), to burn, kindle; *katakaíō* (2618), to burn up utterly; *kaúma* (2738), heat, the result of burning or heat produced; *kaúsis* (2740), a burning; *kaúsōn* (2742), a burning heat.

Syn.: *puróō* (4448), to burn, glow with heat; *empíprēmi* or *empréthō* (1714), to burn up; *phlogízō* (5394), to set on fire, burn up, used figuratively.

Ant.: *sbénnumi* (4570), to quench.

2546. κακεῖ *kakeí*; crasis from *kaí* (2532), and, and *ekeí* (1563), there. And there (Matt 5:23; 10:11; 28:10; Mark 1:35, 38; John 11:54; Acts 14:7; 17:13; 22:10; 25:20; 27:6; Sept.: Ruth 1:17).

2547. κακεῖθεν *kakeíthen*; crasis from *kaí* (2532), and, and *ekeíthen* (1564), from there. Referring to place, it means and from there (Mark 10:1; Acts 7:4; 14:26; 20:15; 21:1; 27:4, 12; 28:15; Sept.:

2 Kgs 2:25); referring to time, it means and from that time (Acts 13:21).

2548. κακεῖνος *kakeínos*; fem. *kakeínē*, neut. *kakeíno*, crasis from *kaí* (2532), and, and *ekeínos* (1565), that one. And he, she, or it. In the pl., and they, those (Matt 15:18; 20:4; 23:23; Mark 12:4; Luke 20:11; 22:12; John 7:29; 14:12).

2549. κακία *kakía*; gen. *kakías*, fem. noun from *kakós* (2556), bad. Wickedness as an evil habit of the mind, while *ponēría* (4189) is the active outcome of the same. *Ponēría* is malevolence, not only doing evil, but being evil.

(I) Evil in a moral sense meaning wickedness of heart, life, and character (Acts 8:22; 1 Cor 14:20 [cf. Matt 18:3; James 1:21; 1 Pet 2:16; Sept.: Ex 32:12; Isa 29:20]).

(II) In an act. sense, especially where joined with *ponēría* (4189), malevolence, malice, (1 Cor 5:8), as if *ponēría*, the endeavor to do evil to others, emanates from being inherently evil (*kakía*). See Eph 4:31; Col 3:8; Titus 3:3; 1 Pet 2:1; Sept.: Prov 1:16; Nah 3:19.

(III) Evil, i.e., trouble, affliction (Matt 6:34; Sept.: Eccl 7:4).

Syn.: *anomía* (458), lawlessness; *hamartía* (266), sin; *adikía* (93), unrighteousness; *paranomía* (3892), transgression; *húbris* (5196), insult, harm, reproach; *phaúlon*, the neut. of *phaúlos* (5337) used as a noun, that which is trivial; *adíkēma* (92), injustice, iniquity.

2550. κακοήθεια *kakoḗtheia*; gen. *kakoētheías*, fem. noun from *kakoḗthēs* (n.f.), mischievous, which is from *kakós* (2556), bad, evil, and *éthos* (2239), disposition, custom. Mischief, malignity, evil habit. Occurs only in Rom 1:29, translated "malignity." It actually means ill-nature, taking everything with an evil connotation and giving a malicious interpretation to the actions of others, a nature which is evil and makes one suspect evil in others. On the other hand, *kakía* (2549), wickedness, is not the name of one vice, but of the viciousness out of which all vices spring, as the ancients saw it. In the NT, however, *kakía* is not so much viciousness as a special form of vice. It is more the evil habit of the mind. Contrast *ponēría* (4189), malevolence, the acting out or externalization of an evil habit of mind, attributing to others and their actions the worst imaginable motives.

Syn.: *aischrótēs* (151), shamefulness, obscenity, filthiness; *atimía* (819), dishonor, indignity; *rhuparía* (4507), filthiness; *diaphthorá* (1312), corruption.

Ant.: *éthos* (2239), moral habits; *suneídēsis* (4893), conscience; *euprépeia* (2143), gracefulness, what one ought to do; *aretē* (703), virtue; *chrēstótēs* (5544), goodness, kindness; *agathōsúnē* (19), benevolence; *dikaiosúnē* (1343), righteousness, ideal character; *eupoiḯa* (2140), beneficence, the desire to do good.

2551. κακολογέω *kakologéō*; contracted *kakologṓ*, fut. *kakologḗsō*, from *kakológos* (n.f.), evil-speaking, which is from *kakós* (2556), evil, and *légō* (3004), to speak. To curse, speak evil of. In Matt 15:4 and Mark 7:10, it is translated as "cursing" parents in contrast to honoring them (*timáō* [5091]). The translation "cursing" in this verse is too strong. We must remember that the word *kakós* stands in contrast to *ponērós* (4190). *Kakós* is constitutionally but not viciously evil, and *ponērós* is actively malevolent or trying to harm. In that relationship, therefore, it is wrong to translate the word either "curse" or "speak evil of." Rather it means to attribute evil to the motive of parental interference in the lives of their children and involves failure on the part of the children to see that behind what seems to be evil are good intentions of concern. Used in Mark 9:39 in regard to someone who was casting out demons but was not of the disciples' entourage. The Lord, in answer to the disciple's objections, said, "Forbid him not: for there is no man which shall do a miracle in my name, that can lightly speak evil of me." What Jesus was saying was that this man's miracle working was

not going to bring dishonor to the name of Christ since His name was being implored in the performance of the miracle. We can say as in the two previous cases that the word stands in contrast to honor. See also Acts 19:9, in which case speaking evil about the way something was done was speaking as if there were actually nothing good in it.

Syn.: *anathematízō* (332), to declare anathema, i.e., destined to destruction or accursed; *katanathematízō* (2653), to curse against; *kataráomai* (2672), to wish evil against a person or thing; *blasphēméō* (987), to speak impiously, blaspheme, generally to speak evil of; *katalaléō* (2635), to speak against, slander; *sukophantéō* (4811) and *diabállō* (1225), to falsely accuse; *egkaléō* (1458), to bring an accusation against a person before a court or in a legal manner; *katēgoréō* (2723), to accuse; *loidoréō* (3058), to revile; *oneidízō* (3679), to reproach.

Ant.: *eulogéō* (2127), to speak well of, bless.

2552. κακοπάθεια *kakopátheia*; gen. *kakopatheías*, fem. noun from *kakopathéō* (2553), to suffer misfortune, hardship. A suffering of evil; suffering, affliction (James 5:10 [cf. 2 Tim 1:8]; Sept.: Mal 1:13).

Syn.: *kákōsis* (2561), affliction, ill-treatment; *páthēma* (3804), suffering, affliction; *thlípsis* (2347), pressure and hence affliction, being squeezed from the outside, constriction; *stenochōría* (4730), anguish which results from narrowness of space; *anágkē* (318), constraint, distress, need; *diōgmós* (1375), persecution; *sunochē* (4928), being in straits, distress; *tarachḗ* (5016), agitation, disturbance, trouble.

Ant.: *eulogía* (2129), blessing; *makarismós* (3108), the pronouncement that a person is blessed *eudokía* (2107), approval, good pleasure, delight.

2553. κακοπαθέω *kakopathéō*; contracted *kakopathṓ*, fut. *kakopathḗsō*, from *kakopathḗs* (n.f.), suffering ill, which is from *kakós* (2556), evil, and *páthos* (3806), passion. To suffer evil or afflictions, to be afflicted (2 Tim 2:9; James 5:13 [cf. 2 Tim 1:8]). To endure, sustain afflictions (2 Tim 2:3; 4:5), endure hardships (Sept.: Jon 4:10).

Deriv.: *kakopátheia* (2552), suffering, affliction; *sugkakopathéō* (4777), to suffer hardship with someone.

Syn.: *kakóō* (2559), to treat badly, hurt; *thlíbō* (2346), to suffer affliction; *talaipōréō* (5003), to be afflicted, suffer hardship, be miserable; *basanízō* (928), to toil, be tormented; *odunáō* (3600) to be tormented.

Ant.: *eulogéō* (2127) and the mid. / pass. *eulogéomai*, to be blessed, well-spoken of; *euthuméō* (2114), to make cheerful, and in the mid. / pass. voice *euthuméomai*, to be cheerful.

2554. κακοποιέω kakopoiéō; contracted *kakopoiṓ*, fut. *kakopoiḗsō*, from *kakopoiós* (2555), evildoer. To do evil in the moral sense (1 Pet 3:17; 3 John 1:11 [cf. 1 John 2:16]). Equivalent to doing that which appears to be mischievous or evil as perceived by another (Mark 3:4; Luke 6:9; Sept.: Gen 31:7; 1 Sam 25:34; Ezra 4:13, 15).

Syn.: *kakóō* (2559), to ill-treat, exasperate, vex, afflict; *basanízo* (928), to torment, pain; *bláptō* (984), to injure, hurt; *atimázō* (818), to dishonor; *diaphtheírō* (1311), to corrupt, ruin.

Ant.: *agathopoiéō* (15) and *euergetéō* (2109), to do good.

2555. κακοποιός kakopoiós; gen. *kakopoioú*, masc.-fem., neut. *kakopoión*, adj. from *kakós* (2556), evil, and *poiéō* (4160), to do or make. Pernicious, injurious, evil, behaving in a bad way. As a subst., an evildoer, malefactor. Used in John 18:30; 1 Pet 2:12, 14; 3:16 in a moral sense, corresponding to behaving in an evil way or doing evil. Only in 1 Pet 4:15 does it appear in the sense of being generally harmful, denoting one who is injurious to the community.

Deriv.: *kakopoiéō* (2554), to do evil.

Syn.: *ponērós* (4190), one of the names attributed to Satan, malevolent; *kakoúrgos* (2557), evil worker, malefactor; *blaberós* (983), injurious, hurtful.

Ant.: *agathós* (18), benevolent; *kalós* (2570), good; *chrēstós* (5543), kind; *ákakos* (172), unsuspecting, innocent; *philágathos* (5358), fond of good, one who loves to do good.

2556. κακὸς kakós; fem. *kakḗ*, neut. *kakón*, adj. Bad, worthless externally. Of a soldier, cowardly. In the NT evil, wicked, from the verb *cházō* or *cházomai* (n.f.), to give back, recede, retire, retreat in battle. One who is evil in himself and, as such, gets others in trouble.

(I) In a moral sense meaning wicked, vicious, bad in heart, conduct, and character (Matt 21:41; 24:48; Phil 3:2; Rev 2:2, impostors). Of things (Mark 7:21, evil thoughts; Rom 13:3, evil works; 1 Cor 15:33, evil conversations; Col 3:5; Sept.: Prov 6:18; 15:3). In the neut. *tó kakón*, and pl., *tá kaká*, evil, evil things, wickedness, fault, crime (Matt 27:23; Mark 15:14; Luke 23:22; John 18:23; Acts 23:9; Rom 1:30; 2:9; 3:8; 7:19, 21; 9:11; 13:4; 16:19; 1 Cor 10:6; 2 Cor 5:10; 13:7; 1 Tim 6:10; Heb 5:14; James 1:13; 1 Pet 3:12; 3 John 1:11; Sept.: Prov 3:7).

(II) Actively causing evil, i.e., hurtful, harmful (Rom 14:20; Titus 1:12, "ravenous beasts" [a.t.]; Rev 16:2; Sept.: Prov 16:4; Amos 6:3). In the neut., *to kakón*, evil, i.e., cause or source of evil (James 3:8); evil done to anyone, harm, injury (Acts 16:28; 28:5; Rom 12:17, 21; 13:10; 1 Cor 13:5; 1 Thess 5:15; 1 Pet 3:9, 11). In words, evil speaking (1 Pet 3:10; Sept.: Mic 7:3). Pl., *tá kaká*, evils, i.e., troubles, afflictions (Luke 16:25; Acts 9:13; 2 Tim 4:14; Sept.: Gen 44:34; 48:16; Isa 46:7; Jer 14:8).

Deriv.: *ákakos* (172), one without evil, upright; *anexíkakos* (420), without evil, longsuffering; *ekkakéō* or *egkakéō* (1573), to treat badly; *kakía* (2549), wickedness, trouble; *kakopoiós* (2555), evildoer; *kakoúrgos* (2557), one who works evil; *kakouchéō* (2558), to suffer adversity; *kakóō* (2559), to ill-treat; *kakós* (2560), badly.

Syn.: *ponērós* (4190), malicious which indicates willful harm to others, an element not necessarily found in *kakós*.; *kakía* (2549), wickedness, iniquity, evil, affliction.; *phaúlos* (5337), trivial, bad in the sense of being worthless; *saprós* (4550), corrupt, rotten, unfit for use, putrid; *phthartós* (5349), corruptible; *átopos*, amiss, out of place; *áthesmos* (113), contrary to custom; *ánomos* (459), lawless as a characterization of the person himself in regard to obedience to the law.

Ant.: *agathós* (18), beneficial in addition to being good; *kalós* (2570), that which is intrinsically good, beautiful; *chrēstós* (5543), good, gracious, kind, smooth; *asteíos* (791), urbane, fair.

2557. κακοῦργος *kakoúrgos*; gen. *kakoúrgou*, masc. noun from *kakós* (2556), bad, and *érgō* (n.f.), to work, which is the obsolete root of *érgon* (2041), work. An evildoer, malefactor (Luke 23:32, 33, 39 [cf. Matt 27:38, *lēstés* {3027}, robber]; 2 Tim 2:9; Sept.: Prov 21:15). In the Gr. writers, the word is joined with thieves as also in Luke 23:32. There are some who suggest the deriv. of the word from *kakós*, bad, and *orgḗ* (3709), anger, in which case the accent is placed on the ultima making it not *kakoúrgos* but *kakourgós*, the opposite of *agathoergós* (n.f.) or *euergós* (n.f.), doer of good. In this sense, of course, *kakourgós* would be evildoer, one who is malicious, cunning, treacherous.

Syn.: *kakopoiós* (2555), an evildoer; *lēstés* (3027), a robber, plunderer. Luke attributes the term *kakoúrgos* to the two malefactors crucified with Christ, while Matt 27:38–44 and Mark 15:27 use the term *lēstaí*, plunderers. The crime attributed to these two malefactors was severe enough to deserve death. *Kakourgós* has a lighter criminal connotation than *kakoúrgos*, the latter making crime his occupation (*érgon* [2041]).

Ant.: *euergétēs* (2110), benefactor; *agathós* (18), benevolent; *eleḗmōn* (1655),

merciful; *agathopoiós* (17), a benefactor; *eúsplagchnos* (2155), compassionate.

2558. κακουχέω *kakouchéō*; contracted *kakouchṓ*, fut. *kakouchḗsō*, from *kakós* (2556), badly, ill, and *échō* (2192), to have. To ill-treat, mistreat, afflict, harass. Used in the pres. part. of the heroes of faith who were constantly ill-treated (Heb 11:37) indicating that being faithful does not exempt one from mistreatment by others. In the same sense used also in Heb 13:3; Sept.: 1 Kgs 2:26; 11:39.

Deriv.: *sugkakouchéō* (4778), to be ill-treated together.

Syn.: *kakóō* (2559), to vex, affect for evil; *kakopathéō* (2553), to undergo hardship, suffer afflictions; *thlíbō* (2346), to afflict, in the mid. to suffer; *atimázō* (818), to dishonor; *talaipōréō* (5003), to afflict, and in the mid. voice *talaipōréōmai*, to be afflicted.

Ant.: *eulogéō* (2127), to speak well of, to bless; *eneulogéomai* (1757), to be blessed in; *makarízō* (3106), to declare blessed; *charitóō* (5487), to grace, favor.

2559. κακόω *kakóō*; contracted *kakṓ*, fut. *kakṓsō*, from *kakós* (2556), bad, evil. To harm or do evil to someone, ill-treat, plague, injure (Acts 7:6, 19; 12:1; 18:10; 1 Pet 3:13; Sept.: Gen 15:13; Ex 5:22; Num 24:24); to put one into a bad mood against another (Acts 14:2).

Deriv.: *kákōsis* (2561), distress.

Syn.: *kakopoiéō* (2554), to do evil; *kakologéō* (2551), to speak evil; *kakopathéō* (2553), to endure evil; *kakouchéō* (2558), to suffer adversity; *blasphēméō* (987), to blaspheme, revile; *loidoréō* (3058), to abuse, revile; *oneidízō* (3679), to reproach, upbraid; *epēreázō* (1908), to revile, accuse.

Ant.: *eulogéō* (2127), to bless, speak well of.

2560. κακῶς *kakós*; adv. from *kakós* (2556), bad, evil. Badly, and with *échō* (2192), to have, meaning to have it badly.

(I) Physically: to be ill (Matt 4:24; 8:16; 9:12; 14:35; Mark 1:32, 34; 2:17; 6:55; Luke 5:31; 7:2). With *páschō* (3958), to suffer badly, i.e., grievously (Matt 17:15). The phrase *kakoús kakōs apolésai* ([622], destroy) in Matt 21:41 means to destroy miserably, utterly, however not involving annihilation but punishment. In the sense of grievously in Matt 15:22 with *daimonízomai* (1139), to be tormented by a demon.

(II) Morally: with *eréō* (2046), to utter, call, to speak evil of anyone, revile (Acts 23:5 quoted from Ex 22:28; see Isa 8:21); with *laléō* (2980), to speak, utter words, speak evil (John 18:23); with *aitéomai* (154), to request, ask, meaning to ask amiss, badly, improperly (James 4:3).

Syn.: *árrōstos* (732), infirm, sick; *asthéneia* (769), sickness, weakness; *asthenḗs* (772), without strength, weak; *deinōs* (1171), grievously, severely; *ek perissoú* (*ek* [1537], of; *perissoú* [4053], abundant), exceedingly.

Ant.: *kalōs* (2573) and *eú* (2095), well.

2561. κάκωσις *kákōsis*; gen. *kakōseōs*, fem. noun from *kakóō* (2559), to hurt, vex. Ill-treatment, vexation, affliction (Acts 7:34 quoted from Ex 3:7, 17).

Syn.: *kakopátheia* (2552), suffering; *páthēma* (3804), affliction; *thlípsis* (2347), pressure; *stenochōría* (4730), straitness, anguish; *anágkē* (318), distress; *diōgmós* (1375), persecution; *sunochḗ* (4928), compression, distress; *básanos* (931), torment; *tarachḗ* (5016), agitation, trouble.

Ant.: *eulogía* (2129), blessing.

2562. καλάμη *kalámē*; gen. *kalámēs*, fem. noun. The stalk of corn, straw, or stubble (1 Cor 3:12; Sept.: Ex 15:7; Joel 2:5).

2563. κάλαμος *kálamos*; gen. *kalámou*, masc. noun. Flexible stalk or stem of a vegetable, hence the stalk of corn. The plant itself, a reed which is easily bent or shaken by the wind (Matt 11:7; 12:20; "a bruised [crushed] reed," quoted from Isa

42:3; Luke 7:24; Sept.: 1 Kgs 14:15; Job 40:21), the stalk as cut for use, a reed, i.e., as a mock scepter (Matt 27:29, 30; Mark 15:36). A stalk or stem of hyssop (Matt 27:48; Mark 15:19 [cf. John 19:29]). A measuring reed or stick (Rev 11:1; 21:15, 16; Sept.: Ezek 40:3, 5, 6). A reed for writing, a quill (3 John 1:13; Sept.: Ps 44:1).

Syn.: *rhábdos* (4464), rod, staff, stick; *kalámē* (2562), stubble, straw.

2564. καλέω *kaléō*; contracted *kalṓ*, fut. *kalésō*, aor. *ekálesa*, perf. *kéklēka*, aor. pass. *eklḗthēn*. To call, trans.

(I) To call to someone in order that he may come or go somewhere.

(A) Particularly with a voice as a shepherd calls his flock (Matt 4:21; 20:8; Mark 1:20, "he called them" means He called them to follow as His disciples; Luke 19:13, "calling them together" [a.t.]; John 10:3).

(B) Generally to call in some way, send for, direct to come (Matt 2:7); followed by *ek* (1537), out of with a gen. of place (Matt 2:15); with *ek* implied (Heb 11:18 [cf. Hos 11:1 in its comp. form: *metakaléō* {3333}, to call elsewhere]).

(C) To call authoritatively, to call forth, summon, e.g., before a judge (Acts 4:18; 24:2). Figuratively, of God calling forth and disposing of things that are not, even as though they were, i.e., calling them into existence (Rom 4:17; Sept.: Isa 41:4; 48:13).

(D) In the sense of to invite, particularly to a banquet as the wedding feast (Matt 22:3, 9; John 2:2). Used in an absolute sense in Matt 22:8; Luke 7:39; 14:8, 17; 1 Cor 10:27. Metaphorically, to call or invite to anything, e.g., of Jesus, to call to repentance, exhort (Matt 9:13; implied in Mark 2:17); of God (1 Cor 1:9; 2 Thess 2:14; 1 Tim 6:12; 1 Pet 2:9; 5:10; Rev 19:9). To call into the kingdom of God means to the duties, privileges, and bliss of the Christian life here and hereafter (1 Thess 2:12; by implication Rom 9:24; 1 Cor 7:15, 17 ff; Gal 5:8, 13; 2 Tim 1:9; Heb 9:15; 1 Pet 2:21).

(E) In the sense of to call to any station, i.e., to appoint, choose (Gal 1:15 [cf. Sept.: Isa 49:1; 51:2]; Heb 5:4).

(II) To call, i.e., to name, to give a name to any person or thing.

(A) Particularly as spoken of: (1) A proper name or surname, e.g., of persons, followed by *tó ónoma* (3686), the name in apposition (Matt 1:21, "thou shalt call his name JESUS"; also Matt 1:23, 25; Luke 1:13; 2:21; Rev 19:13; Sept.: Gen 27:1, 42; 29:35; 35:8, 10, 18; 38:3–5, 29, 30). In the pass. construction (Luke 1:60, 62; Acts 1:23; Rev 12:9). With *epí tố onómati* (*epí* [1909], upon; *tố onómati* [3686], the name), upon the name, meaning after the name of someone (Luke 1:59). Pass. with the dat. *onómati*, by name (Luke 1:61; 19:2). With *en* (1722), in (Rom 9:7; Heb 11:18, "in and through Isaac [in his line] shall thy seed bear name" [a.t.], quoted from Gen 21:12). Of places in Matt 27:8; Luke 2:4; Acts 3:11; 28:1; Rev 1:9; Sept.: Gen 31:48. (2) An epithet or a descriptive adj. or appellation, e.g., of persons (Matt 2:23, "He shall be called a Nazarene"; 22:43; 23:7, 8, 10; Luke 6:15; 15:19, 21; Acts 14:12; Rom 9:26; James 2:23; 1 John 3:1); of things (Acts 10:1).

(B) Pass., in the sense of to be regarded, accounted, i.e., to be (Matt 5:9, 19; 21:13; Mark 11:17 quoted from Isa 56:7; Luke 1:32, 35, 36, 76; 2:23; 15:19; 1 Cor 15:9; Heb 3:13; Sept.: Isa 35:8; 47:1, 5; 48:8; 56:7).

(III) Generally speaking, the word and its cognates involve: (1) Invitation (Matt 9:13; 22:3; 1 Cor 10:27; Rev 19:9, all using *kaléō*; and, in Acts 2:39, *proskaléō* [4341]). (2) Designation, with *kaléō* (Matt 1:21; 5:9; Acts 14:12; Heb 2:11; 11:18) and *epikaléō* (1941), to invoke, appeal (Matt 10:25; Luke 22:3; Acts 1:23; Heb 11:16). (3) Invocation, with *epikaléomai* (Acts 2:21; 7:59; 1 Cor 1:2; 2 Cor 1:23; 1 Pet 1:17). (4) Summons, with *metakaléō* (3333) (Acts 7:14; 10:32).

(IV) In the OT a call of God to His servants and His people is part of His gracious dealing with mankind. It was in response to a divine call that Abraham (Gen 12:1–3), Moses (Ex 3:10), Bezaleel (Ex 31:2), Isaiah (Isa 6:8, 9), Jeremiah (Jer 1:4, 5), Ezekiel (Ezek 2:3), and other eminent servants of God fulfilled the tasks committed to them. The word refers to Israel when thus called "the people of God," but complaint is made again and again by the prophets that they refused to hearken, stopping their ears so that they should not hear (Isa 6:9; Zech 7:11–13). The prophets, moreover, had visions of the day when the Gentiles would be called into the covenant and service of Jehovah (Isa 55:4, 5). Of this OT meaning, examples found in the NT are the Spirit's call of Barnabas and Saul (Acts 13:2) and the call of the High Priest of the old dispensation (Heb 5:4) where a divine call to special services is accepted.

In the epistles, particularly Paul's, there is found a more definite meaning of the word *kaléō* as the call of God to the blessings of salvation. It is here intimately associated with the eternal purpose of God in human redemption. This is in advance of what we find in the gospels, "the called [*hoi klētoí* {2822}]" distinguished from "the chosen [*hoi eklektoí*, from *eklégomai* {1586}, to choose; see also *eklektós* {1588}, chosen, elect]." The *klētoí* are those invited to the gospel feast and the *eklektoí* are the more select company who had heard and accepted (Matt 22:14). In the epistles, "the called" are frequently syn. with "the chosen" (Rom 8:28; 9:24; 2 Thess 2:13, 14; 1 Pet 2:9, where *génos* [1085], nation or offspring, *eklektón* are those who are "called . . . out of darkness into his marvelous light"). Thus the choosing is included in the calling. See also *klḗsis* (2821), calling, which includes *eklogḗ* (1589), choice, election. With Paul and also Peter, the calling is more than an invitation. It is an invitation responded to and accepted. In the epistles, *klētós* (sing.) or *klētoí* (pl.) refer to those who had an effectual call (Rom 1:1, 6, 7; 8:28; 1 Cor 1:2, 24) and also to the appointed ones (Rom 1:1; 1 Cor 1:1).

Deriv.: *antikaléō* (479), to invite in return; *egkaléō* (1458), to accuse; *eiskaléō*

(1528), to call in; *epikaléomai* (1941), to call upon, to appeal; *klḗsis* (2821), calling; *klētós* (2822), called; *metakaléō* (3333), to recall; *parakaléō* (3870), to call near, to comfort; *prokaléō* (4292), to provoke; *proskaléō* (4341), to invite; *sugkaléō* (4779), to call together.

Syn.: *keleúō* (2753), to bid, command; *prostássō* (4367), to command; *phōnéō* (5455), to call with a loud voice; *krázō* (2896), to shout or call aloud; *onomázō* (3687), to name, call, command; *eponomázō* (2028), to surname; *légō* (3004), to call; *prosagoreúō* (4316), to address, call; *prosphōnéō* (4377), to call unto.

Ant.: *pémpō* (3992), to send; *stéllō* (4724), to avoid, withdraw self.

2565. καλλιέλαιος *kalliélaios*; fem. *kallielaía*, neut. *kalliélaion*, adj. from *kálli-*, denoting beauty, and *elaía* (1636), an olive tree. A good olive tree as opposed to *agriélaios* (65), a wild one (Rom 11:24).

2566. κάλλιον *kállion*; neut. of *kallíōn*, the comparative of *kalós* (2570), good, beautiful. Better. Used adv. as the comparative of the adv. *kalṓs* (2573), well (Acts 25:10, "as you also better know" [a.t.], meaning better than I can explain).

Syn.: *béltion* (957), better; *kreísson* (2908), better with the connotation of more advantageous; *mállon* (3123), rather; *pollṓ* (4183), much, by far; *polú* (4183), much.

Ant.: *cheírōn* (5501), worse; *elássōn* (1640), less; *hḗssōn* (2276), less, inferior.

2567. καλοδιδάσκαλος *kalodidáskalos*; gen. *kalodidaskálou*, masc.-fem., neut. *kalodidáskalon*, adj. from *kalós* (2570), good, and *didáskalos* (1320), teacher. A teacher of what is good (Titus 2:3) and right (*orthós* [3717], right). Hence, the verb *orthotoméō* (3718), to handle correctly. Bad teaching is that which displays a lack of skill and competence in handling the Scriptures. This word is not found in the Classics.

Ant.: *pseudodidáskalos* (5572), a false teacher.

2568. Καλοὶ Λιμένες *Kaloí Liménes* sing. *Kalós Limḗn*, proper noun from *kalós* (2570), good, and *limḗn* (3040), harbor. Good Harbors or Fair Havens, a small bay on the southern coast of Crete. Paul stayed there on his way to Rome (Acts 27:8–12). The harbor was not a suitable place to spend the winter, so it was decided to sail from there to a more secure harbor.

2569. καλοποιέω *kalopoiéō*; contracted *kalopoiṓ*, fut. *kalopoiḗsō*, from *kalós* (2570), good, and *poiéō* (4160), to do. To do good (2 Thess 3:13. An alternative interpretation is to take *kalopoiéō* from *kalṓs* (2573), well. In which case the meaning is to live honestly, i.e., not idly but as a result of one's honest labor [see 2 Thess 3:6–15]), the opposite being *kakopoiéō* (2554), to harm someone or to do badly or commit sin. *Kalopoiéō* is different from *agathopoiéō* (15) in that the first is doing good because one is good and the other is being beneficent because one wants to help another.

Syn.: *sṓzō* (4982), to save, rescue, and hence to help someone; *antilambánō* (482), to help, support; *sullambánō* (4815), to assist, take part with; *sunantilambánō* (4878), to assist by taking hold of the opposite side, to help; *boēthéō* (997), to come to the aid of someone, succor; *sunergéō* (4903), to cooperate; *parístēmi* (3936), to stand by.

Ant.: *egkóptō* (1465), to interrupt, hinder; *kōlúō* (2967), to hinder, restrain; *diakōlúō* (1254), to hinder thoroughly; *bláptō* (984), to injure, damage, with stress on the injury done; *adikéō* (91), to be unjust to or to harm with emphasis on the unrighteousness of the act and not necessarily on the hurt done; *kakóō* (2559), to do evil to anyone.

2570. καλός *kalós*; fem. *kalḗ*, neut. *kalón*, adj. Good. Constitutionally good without necessarily being benevolent;

expresses beauty as a harmonious completeness, balance, proportion.

(I) Good as to quality and character.

(A) Generally the earth (Matt 13:8, 23; Mark 4:8, 20; Luke 8:15); a tree (Matt 12:33; Luke 6:43); seed (Matt 13:24, 27, 37, 38); a measure with a meaning of bountiful, proper measure (Luke 6:38).

(B) By implication, choice, excellent, e.g., fruit (Matt 3:10; 7:17–19; Luke 3:9; 6:43); wine (John 2:10); pearls (Matt 13:45); stones (Luke 21:5). See Matt 13:48; Rom 7:16; 1 Tim 3:1, 13; 4:6, "good doctrine"; 6:12, 13, 19, good profession; 2 Tim 1:14; Heb 6:5. In the neut., *tó kalón*, the good (1 Thess 5:21; Sept.: Gen 27:9; 30:20; Zech 1:13).

(C) With a meaning of honorable, distinguished (1 Tim 1:18; 3:7; James 2:7, "the good name" [a.t.]).

(II) Good as to effect or influence, useful, profitable, equivalent to *hálas* (217), salt, which metaphorically means preservation (Mark 9:50; Luke 14:34). Hence the expression *kalón ésti* (1510), meaning it is good, profitable, followed by the acc. and inf. (Matt 17:4; Mark 9:5; Luke 9:33). Followed by the dat. of person and inf. as the subj. (Matt 18:8, 9; Mark 9:43, 45, 47; 1 Cor 7:1; 9:15). Followed by *ei* (1487), if, whether (Matt 26:24; Mark 14:21). In Mark 9:42, "it were better for him" (a.t.), followed by *eán* (1437), if, in 1 Cor 7:8.

(III) Good in a moral sense, virtuous, spoken of:

(A) Thoughts, feelings, actions, e.g., a good conscience (Heb 13:18); good conduct (James 3:13; 1 Pet 2:12); "the good fight" (1 Tim 6:12; 2 Tim 4:7). In 1 Tim 2:3; 5:4, "it is good in the sight of [*enópion* {1799}, before] God" (a.t.); in Luke 8:15 of the heart being both *kalé* (2570), inherently good, and *agathé* (18), benevolent, able to externalize its qualities. Also used of work or works (*érgon* [2041]) as in *érgon kalón* or *érga kalá*, good work or good works; and with the article in the pl., *tá kalá érga* meaning a good deed, good works. **(1)** Generally meaning well-doing, virtue, as in Eng., a good or noble deed or deeds (Matt 5:16; 1 Tim 5:25; Titus 2:7,

14; Heb 10:24; 1 Pet 2:12); with *érga* implied (Rom 12:17; 2 Cor 8:21; Titus 3:8 in *tá kalá*). **(2)** In the sense of useful work, i.e., benefit (Matt 26:10; Mark 14:6; John 10:32, 33; 1 Tim 5:10; 6:18; Titus 3:8, 14). In the neut., *tó kalón*, that which is good, right (Rom 7:18). With the verb *poiéō* (4160), to do, in the phrase *tó kalón*, to do good, meaning to act well, virtuously (Rom 7:21; 2 Cor 13:7; Gal 6:9; James 4:17). Hence, *kalón esti*, it is good, meaning it is right, followed by the inf. (Matt 15:26; Mark 7:27; Rom 14:21; Gal 4:18; Heb 13:9).

(B) Persons in reference to the performance of duty, e.g., "the shepherd, the good one" (a.t. [John 10:11, 14]); "the good deacon" (a.t. [1 Tim 4:6]); "a good soldier" (2 Tim 2:3); "good stewards" (1 Pet 4:10).

The Lord Jesus said that God alone was good without limitation or qualification (Mark 10:18; Luke 18:19). The reason Christ questioned the rich, young ruler who came to Him was because he acknowledged Jesus to be only a teacher (Matt 19:16; Mark 10:17; Luke 18:18), and a mere teacher could not be what God is. Jesus wanted to stress that no teacher, no matter how good he is, can be what only God is, i.e., inherently benevolent.

However, a person can be made *kalós*, good, what God is, through faith in Jesus Christ, but only insofar as he is a partaker of God's nature (2 Pet 1:4). Hence, a man's works are divided into two categories: the dead works performed before his salvation (Heb 9:14), and the good works motivated by the grace of God after his salvation. For works to be good, Christ must first be in the heart. Jesus' works did not make Him good, for He is goodness personified; and pertaining to man, only if he believes in Christ as God can he, as a believer, do works which are accepted as good (Matt 11:4, 5; Acts 10:38). Such activity is consequent to His making man blessed (*makários* [3107]), indwelt by God, and capable of performing what pleases God. The Lord Jesus enjoins the practice of good works, but only on His believing disciples and those who would believe (Luke 6:27; 19:8). Paul echoes the teaching of Jesus when he bids the Romans to overcome evil with good (Rom 12:21) and assures them that such conduct will have its reward (Rom 2:10).

One should never lose sight of the fact that the Greeks believed that which is good is also beautiful. Thus, by accenting the same word differently, *kalós* meant beautiful, and the neut. *tó kállos*, although not in the NT, meant beauty. It is used even today in Mod. Gr. Generally speaking, the two basic words, *kalós* and *agathós*, may be used of any quality (physical as well as moral), thing, or person that may be approved as useful, fit, admirable, right. In the moral sense, *kalós* connotes righteousness, good in oneself, while *agathós* adds the quality of kindness, helpfulness, benevolence, love.

The distinction Paul makes between "a righteous man" and "the good [*agathós* {18}] man" (Rom 5:7) deserves special attention. Christ is inherently righteous. Therefore He is the only one who can reveal to man what God expects of him. But because man is incapable in himself of doing what God expects of him, Christ makes him righteous and justifies *dikaióō* (1344) him. His works are then truly *kalá* (2570), good in themselves, and *agathá* (18), benevolent and can truly benefit others and be acceptable to God. Observe how Paul handles the transition from *díkaios* (1342), righteous, to *agathós* (18), benevolent. "For scarcely for a righteous man will one die." *Díkaios* here is equivalent to *kalós*, inherently good. This is inherent goodness which is not easily manifest. But when this inherent righteousness or goodness is externalized and becomes benevolence, then one may indeed dare to die for such. "Yet peradventure for a good man [*agathós*] some would even dare to die" (Rom 5:7).

Deriv.: *kállion* (2566), very well; *kalopoiéō* (2569), to do well, excellently; *kalós* (2573), well.

Syn.: *agathós* (18), benevolent. *Kalós* means intrinsically good while *agathós*

carries with it the meaning of benevolence, doing something that is useful and beneficial for others; *chrēstós* (5543), smooth, easy, kindly; *áxios* (514), worthy; *arestós* (701), agreeable; *ákakos* (172), without evil or badness, unsuspicious; *philágathos* (5358), a lover of benevolence.

Ant.: *kakós* (2556) bad; *ponērós* (4190), malevolent; *phaúlos* (5337), bad, rotten.

2571. κάλυμμα *kálumma*; gen. *kalúmmatos*, neut. noun from *kalúptō* (2572), to cover. A covering, veil (2 Cor 3:13 [cf. Ex 34:33ff.]). Figuratively an impediment (2 Cor 3:14–16). To be distinguished from *peribólaion* (4018) which in 1 Cor 11:15 is translated "covering" but actually means that which is placed around.

Syn.: *sképasma* (4629), a covering, roofing, shelter; in the pl. clothing, raiment.

Ant.: *apokálupsis* (602), the act of uncovering, revelation.

2572. καλύπτω *kalúptō*; fut. *kalúpsō*. To envelop, wrap around as bark, skin, shell or plaster, to cover over. Used trans.:

(I) To cover (Matt 8:24; Luke 8:16; 23:30; Sept.: Gen 7:19; Ex 8:6).

(II) By implication, to hide, the same as *krúptō* (2928), to hide (Matt 10:26; 2 Cor 4:3; James 5:20; 1 Pet 4:8; in the two latter cases, it means to cause a multitude of sins to be overlooked and not punished [cf. Ps 32:1 where the comp. verb *epikalúptō* {1943}, to conceal is used]).

Deriv.: *anakalúptō* (343), to uncover in the sense of removing all impediments to knowledge, equal to discover; *apokalúptō* (601), to disclose, reveal; *epikalúptō* (1943), to cover up or over; *kálumma* (2571), covering, veil; *katakalúptō* (2619), to cover completely; *parakalúptō* (3871), to hide; *perikalúptō* (4028), to cover around, blindfold; *sugkalúptō* (4780), to cover together or up.

Syn.: *krúptō* (2928), to hide; *apokrúptō* (613), to conceal from; *egkrúptō* (1470), to hide in something; *parakalúptō* (3871), to cover with a veil, hide; *lanthánō* (2990), to escape notice.

Ant.: *apokalúptō* (601), to uncover, unveil, reveal; *chrēmatízō* (5537), to reveal as if by divine oracle; *emphanízō* (1718), to exhibit, disclose.

2573. καλῶς *kalōs*; adv. from *kalós* (2570), good. Well, good in various senses.

(I) As to manner and external character, well, i.e., right, suitably, properly (John 18:23; Acts 10:33; 1 Cor 7:37, 38; 14:17; Phil 4:14; Heb 13:18; James 2:8, 19; 2 Pet 1:19; 3 John 1:6). With the neg. *ou* (3756), not, meaning not well (Gal 4:17; Sept.: 1 Kgs 8:18). Spoken in regard to office or duty, well, faithfully (1 Tim 3:4, 12, 13; 5:17); with emphasis meaning very well, excellently (Mark 7:37; Gal 5:7); ironically (Mark 7:9; 2 Cor 11:4); honorably (James 2:3).

(II) As to effect or tendency, well, i.e., justly, aptly, as of declarations (Matt 15:7; Mark 7:6; 12:28, 32; Luke 20:39; John 4:17; 8:48; 13:13; Acts 28:25; Rom 11:20).

(III) In phrases, e.g.:

(A) To speak well of, praise, followed by the acc., as in Luke 6:26.

(B) With *échō* (2192), have, to have it well, meaning to be well, to recover from sickness (Mark 16:18).

(C) With *poiéō* (4160), to do, followed by the acc. or dat., to do well to anyone, to benefit (Matt 5:44; Luke 6:27). Used in an absolute sense in Matt 12:12.

Syn.: *eu* (2095), well, good; *béltion* (957), better.

Ant.: *kakós* (2560), badly.

2574. κάμηλος *kámēlos*; gen. *kamélou*, masc.-fem. noun. A camel. John the Baptist had a rough garment made of camel's hair, a kind of sackcloth (Matt 3:4; Mark 1:6). In Matt 19:24; Mark 10:25; Luke 18:25, the Lord says, proverbially, that it is easier for a camel to go through the eye of a needle than for a rich man to enter into the kingdom of heaven. If the word *kámēlos* is spelled as *kámilos*, it can mean a cable rope. There should be no difficulty, however, in taking the word as meaning a camel, since in the Jewish Talmud there is a familiar proverb about an elephant. In Matt 23:24, there is another proverbial expression, "strain at a gnat, and swallow a camel," applied to those who were superstitiously anxious to avoid small faults while at the same time committing great sins without scruples. This proverb plainly refers to the Mosaic Law, since both gnats and camels were unclean animals prohibited for food.

2575. κάμινος *káminos*; gen. *kamínou*, fem. noun. A furnace for smelting metals, burning pottery, and so forth (Matt 13:42, 50; Rev 1:15; 9:2; Sept.: Gen 19:28; Jer 11:4; Dan 3:6f.).

The furnace of fire is part of the natural imagery of the Parable of the Tares (Matt 13:30), which in the Parable of the Dragnet becomes a standing expression for the destiny of the wicked (Matt 13:50). The word furnace must be viewed as the equivalent of *púr* (4442), fire, in referring to punishment. Thus we have eternal fire (Matt 18:8; 25:41), unquenchable fire (Matt 3:12; Mark 9:43, 48; Luke 3:17), and the *géenna* (1067) of fire, translated as "the hell of fire" (a.t.) or "hell fire" (Matt 5:22; 18:9; Mark 9:43, 45, 47). The last of these expressions is found in the same context as the other two and gives the key to their meaning. From the OT associations, the Valley of Hinnom (the name Gehenna in Christ's time had been appropriated in Jewish thought for the place of the final punishment of the wicked) was a place of burning and corruption, in which body as well as spirit would be tortured. In order to convey His teaching of the final punishment, our Lord used a symbol of punishment of His day. Our Lord's sayings in Mark 9:43–48 should be considered in connection with Mark 9:49 in which fire is the emblem of the self-discipline in this world by which the destruction of Gehenna in the next world is to be avoided. The destructiveness of fire made the phrase "I will send fire" a common form of prophecy of divine judgment in the OT. This phrase is taken up by Christ (Luke 12:49) as expressing in one aspect the result of His earthly mission. The eyes of the glorified Christ are seen in the vision of the Revelation as a flame of fire (Rev 1:14; 2:18; 19:12).

Syn.: *kaúsis* (2740), burning; *phlóx* (5395), a blaze, flame; *púr* (4442), fire; *purá* (4443), bonfire; *holokaútōma* (3646), holocaust, a wholly consumed sacrifice; *anthrakiá* (439), burning coals, fire of coals; *kaúma* (2738), a burning, glow, heat.

Ant.: *psúchos* (5592), cold.

2576. καμμύω *kammúō*; fut. *kammúsō*, from *katá* (2596), down, an intens., and *múō* (n.f.), to shut, primarily used with reference to the eyes. To shut or close the eyes (Matt 13:15; Acts 28:27 quoted from Isa 6:10). See *muōpázō* (3467), to shut the eyes, blink, be myopic, unable to see far.

Syn.: *kleíō* (2808), to shut.

Ant.: *anoígō* (455), to open.

2577. κάμνω *kámnō*; fut. *kámō*, 2d aor. *ékamon*, perf. *kékmēka*. Primarily to work, be weary from constant work (Heb 12:3; Sept.: Job 10:1). When used in connection with *asthenéō* (770), to be sick, it suggests the common accompaniment of sickness, weariness of mind which may hinder physical recovery (James 5:15). In some MSS, it occurs also in Rev 2:3.

Syn.: *eklúō* (1590), to become feeble, grow weary; *ekkakéō* or *egkakéō* (1573), to be faint-hearted, weary; *apopsúchō* (674), to be faint at heart; *asthenéō* (770), to be weak, feeble; *sunéchō* (4912), to be afflicted; *noséō* (3552), to be sick; the expression *échō kakós* (*échō* [2192], to have; *kakós* [2560], bad) to have it badly or to be sick; *kopiáō* (2872), to grow weary, to toil.

Ant.: *anapaúō* (373), to give rest, and in the mid. *anapaúomai*, to rest; *katapaúō* (2664), to rest, cease from work; *hēsucházō* (2270), to rest from la-

bor; *epanapaúomai* (1879), to rest upon; *anapsúchō* (404) to refresh.

2578. κάμπτω *kámptō*; fut. *kámpsō*. To bend, such as the knees, to which it is applied in the NT (Rom 11:4, "bent the knee in homage" [a.t.] or worship; Rom 11:4 quoted from Isa 45:23; Eph 3:14, followed by *prós* [4314], toward with the acc.; Phil 2:10).

Deriv.: *anakámptō* (344), to return; *sugkámptō* (4781), to bend completely, to bend down by compulsory force.

Syn.: *kúptō* (2955), to stoop; *sugkúptō* (4794), to bow together; *klínō* (2827), to bow down; *gonupetéō* (1120), to bow at the knee; *proskunéō* (4352), to prostrate oneself in homage or worship.

Ant.: *egeírō* (1453) to arise; *anorthóō* (461), to set up, make upright; *hupsóō* (5312) and *epaírō* (1869), to lift or raise up; *aírō* (142), to raise, take up; *anakúptō* (352), to lift oneself up.

2579. κάν *kán*; crasis from *kaí* (2532), and, and *eán* (1437), if. And if, also if.

(I) And if, with the aor. or perf. subjunctive and, in the apodosis (conclusion), the fut. or *ou mē* (3364), double neg., with the subjunctive meaning "and if" (James 5:15). In Mark 16:18, and if, and also (Luke 13:9).

(II) Also if, even if, although with the subjunctive.

(A) Generally with the aor. subjunctive and the apodosis with the fut. (Matt 21:21; John 11:25; Heb 12:20). Also with the subjunctive and the apodosis with pres. or fut. or aor. subjunctive (Matt 26:35; John 8:14; 10:38).

(B) If even, if but, at least, where *kaí* (2532), and, is intens. by way of diminution. Followed by the aor. subjunctive and, in the apodosis, the fut. (Mark 5:28). Elliptically, without the apodosis (Mark 6:56; Acts 5:15; 2 Cor 11:16).

2580. Κανᾶ *Kaná*; fem. proper noun transliterated from the Hebr. *Qānāh* (7071, OT). Cana, a village in Galilee mentioned four times in the Gospel of John. It was located about five miles northeast of Nazareth where Jesus performed His first miracle (John 2:1, 11) and where He announced to the nobleman from Capernaum the healing of his dying son (John 4:46–53). Nathanael was from Cana (John 21:2).

2581. Κανανίτης *Kananítēs*; gen. *Kananítou*, masc. proper noun. Canaanite. One of the Twelve Apostles was known as Simon the Canaanite (Matt 10:4; Mark 3:18 [Cananean in the KJV, and is called Zealot in the margin to distinguish him from Simon Peter {cf. Luke 6:15; Acts 1:13}]). Perhaps the same as Simon the brother of James and Jude (Matt 13:55; Mark 6:3).

2582. Κανδάκη *Kandákē*; gen. *Kandákēs*, fem. proper noun. Candace, the Queen of Ethiopia (Acts 8:27). The name seems to have been a general designation for Ethiopian queens, much like the name Pharaoh was for Egyptian kings and Caesar for Roman emperors. Her chief treasurer, a eunuch, went to Jerusalem to worship and was led to faith in Christ by Philip the evangelist.

2583. κανών *kanṓn*; gen. *kanónos*, masc. noun from *kánē* (n.f.), reed or cane. Anything straight used in examining other things, as the tongue or needle of a balance, a plumb line in building. In the NT, a rule of conduct or behavior (Gal 6:16; Phil 3:16 [TR]). A measure or measuring rod or the like. Paul uses the word in a figurative sense to the thing or quantity measured or to the portion of the Lord's field which he had, as it were, measured out and allotted to be cultivated by himself (2 Cor 10:13, 15, 16). The word is given as a technical term to the accepted books of the Bible considered as inspired. The idea is clearly implied in the expression "the Scriptures," as employed by Jews in the NT (see Matt 21:42; John 5:39; Acts 18:24).

Syn.: *arché* (746), rule.

2584. Καπερναούμ *Kapernaoúm*; fem. proper noun transliterated from the Hebr. *kāpār* (3723, OT), village, and *Nachūm* (5151, OT), Nahum. Capernaum, meaning village of Nahum. A town on the northwest shore of the Sea of Galilee where the Lord Jesus made His headquarters during His ministry in Galilee (Matt 4:13; 9:1; Mark 2:1). It must have been a sizable town because a tax collector had his office there (Mark 2:14); a high officer of the king (Herod Antipas) had his residence there and built a synagogue for the people (Matt 8:5–13; Luke 7:1–10). The Lord performed many striking miracles there, among them the healing of the centurion's palsied servant (Matt 8:5–13), the man sick of the palsy borne to Jesus by four friends (Mark 2:3–12), and the nobleman's son (John 4:46–54). In Capernaum He called Matthew to the apostleship as he was sitting at the receipt of custom (Matt 9:9–13). Among many addresses given there was the discourse on the Bread of Life (which followed the feeding of the 5000 [Mark 6:32–59]). In spite of Jesus' miraculous works and teachings, the people did not repent and Jesus predicted the complete ruin of the town (Matt 11:23, 24; Luke 10:15). His prophecy was so completely fulfilled that the town has disappeared and its very site is a matter of debate. The two main claimants are about two and one half miles apart: Tell Hum, which is about two and one half miles southwest of the mouth of the Jordan, and Khan Minyeh, which is southwest of Tell Hum. The present trend of opinion is in favor of Tell Hum. Other references: Matt 17:24; Mark 1:21; 9:33; Luke 4:23, 31; John 2:12; 6:17, 24, 59.

2585. καπηλεύω *kapēleúō*; fut. *kapēleúsō*, from *kápēlos* (n.f.), a retailer, huckster. To treat as if for personal profit, a profiteer. Used only in 2 Cor 2:17 translated "corrupt," i.e., corrupting God's Word for personal gain. See Rom 16:17, 18; 2 Pet 2:3. It means to profiteer from

God's Word, to preach for money or to profess faith for personal gain.

The *kápēlos* may also be derived from *kápē* (n.f.), food, nutriment, from *káptō* (n.f.), to eat; a huckster or petty retail trader, contrasted with *émporos* (1713), merchant (Matt 13:45; Rev 18:3, 11, 15, 23), who sells his wares wholesale. *Kápēlos* refers especially to the retailer of wine who is exposed to the strong temptation to tamper with it or sell it in short measure in order to make additional profit. *Kapēleúō* includes *dolóō* (1389), falsify (2 Cor 4:2), to adulterate wine with water to make an unworthy personal gain.

Syn.: *phtheírō* (5351), to corrupt; *kataphtheírō* (2704), to corrupt unto destruction; *diaphtheírō* (1311), to corrupt utterly.

2586. καπνός *kapnós*; gen. *kapnoú*, masc. noun. Smoke (Acts 2:19; Rev 8:4; 9:2, 3, 17, 18; 14:11; 15:8; 18:9, 18; 19:3; Sept.: Ex 19:18; Josh 8:20).

2587. Καππαδοκία *Kappadokía*; gen. *Kappadokías*, fem. proper noun. Cappadocia, a large inland region of Asia Minor which apparently was given this name by the Persians though its people were called Syrians by the Greeks. Later the empire was divided into two, the northern part called Pontus and the southern called Cappadocia, by which name the region was known in NT times. It was bounded on the north by Pontus, on the east by Syria and Armenia, on the south by Cilicia, and on the west by Lycaonia. The Romans built roads through the Cilician gates in the Taurus range so that Cappadocia could readily be entered from the south. The Cappadocians were Aryans. Jews from Cappadocia (Acts 2:9) were among the hearers of the first Christian sermon, along with men from other Anatolian provinces. Peter also directed his first epistle (1 Pet 1:1) in part to "the elect of the dispersion [*diasporá* {1290}]" (a.t.) who lived in various provinces in the north. Many of these Cappa-

docian Jews were converted on the day of Pentecost.

2588. καρδία *kardía*; gen. *kardías*, fem. noun. Heart. The seat and center of human life. In the NT, used only figuratively.

(I) As the seat of the desires, feelings, affections, passions, impulses, i.e., the heart or mind.

(A) Generally (Matt 5:8), "the pure in heart" meaning those whose center of life has been made pure by Jesus Christ. See Matt 5:28; 6:21; Mark 4:15; Luke 1:17; John 14:1; Acts 11:23; Rom 2:5; 1 Cor 4:5 for the counsels or dispositions of the heart or inner man. See also 2 Tim 2:22; Heb 3:8, 12; 10:22; Sept.: Ps 51:12; Prov 31:11.

(B) In phrases as *ek* (1537), out of, or *apó* (575), from, *kardías*, out of or from the heart, meaning willingly (Matt 18:35; Rom 6:17). *Ex hólēs tēs kardías* and *en hólē kardía* meaning with the whole heart (Matt 22:37; Mark 12:30; Sept.: Deut 6:5; Ps 119:34). *Hē kardía kaí hē psuchē* (5590), soul, meaning one's heart and soul, and referring to entire unanimity (Acts 4:32). With *enthuméomai* (1760), to ponder, remember (Matt 9:4); with *dialogízomai* (1260), to think deliberately, when preceding *en taís kardíais*, meaning as they deliberately considered in their hearts (Luke 3:15); with *sumbállō* (4820), to consider or ponder in mind (Luke 2:19), with *anabaínō* (305), to arise, to come up in or into one's heart (Luke 24:38; Acts 7:23; Sept.: Isa 65:17; Jer 3:16); with *bállō* (906), to place or put into one's heart, to suggest (John 13:2); with *dídōmi* (1325), to give or place, and *epí* (1909), upon, meaning to put upon or into the hearts (Heb 10:16). To have in the heart, meaning to love, cherish (Phil 1:7). To be in one's heart meaning to be the object of his love (2 Cor 7:3). A man after one's own heart, meaning like-minded and therefore approved and beloved (Acts 13:22). The inner man (1 Pet 3:4).

(C) Used for the person himself in cases where values, affections or passions are attributed to the heart or mind in John 16:22, "your heart shall rejoice [*chaírō* {5463}]"; Acts 2:26 "my heart rejoiced {*euphraínō* {2165}]" (a.t.). See Acts 14:17; Col 2:2; 2 Thess 2:17; James 1:26; 5:5. To say in one's heart means to think (Matt 24:48; Rom 10:6; Rev 18:7).

(II) As the seat of the intellect meaning the mind, understanding (Matt 13:15; Mark 6:52; Luke 24:25; John 12:40; Rom 1:21; 2 Pet 1:19). In Eph 4:18 (TR) *dianoía* (1271), with the understanding; Sept.: Job 12:3; 34:10; Isa 6:10. To place (*títhēmi* [5087]) and to keep (*diatēréō* [1301]) in the heart means to lay up or keep in one's mind (Luke 1:66; 2:51). In the sense of conscience (Rom 2:15; 1 John 3:20, 21).

(III) In the NT the heart represents especially the sphere of God's influence in the human life. It is in the heart that the natural knowledge of God has its seat (Rom 1:21), and there also in the light of His knowledge, the glory of God shines in the face of Jesus Christ (2 Cor 4:6). In the heart faith springs up, dwells, and works (Acts 15:9; Rom 10:9), and unbelief in the heart draws men away from belief in God (Heb 3:12). It may become the haunt of unclean lusts that make men blind to the truth of God (Rom 1:24), but it is into the heart that God sends the Spirit of His Son (Gal 4:6) and in the heart that Christ Himself takes up His abode (Eph 3:17). This life of the heart is a hidden life (1 Cor 4:5; 1 Pet 3:4), but it lies clearly open to the eyes of God who searches in private (Rom 8:27; 1 Thess 2:4). The most important thing in anybody's life is the necessity of having a heart that is "right in the sight of God" (Acts 8:21). Such a heart can be obtained only through faith (Acts 15:9; Rom 10:10; Eph 3:17) and as a gift from God Himself (cf. Ezek 36:26, "A new heart also will I give you"). This is achievable by virtue of a new creation in Jesus Christ (2 Cor 5:17), whereby a heart that is hard and impenitent (Rom 2:5) is transformed into one in which the love of God has been shed through the Holy Spirit (Rom 5:5).

(IV) Figuratively the heart of something, the middle or central part, i.e., the heart of the earth (Matt 12:40; Sept.: Ezek 27:4; Jon 2:4).

Deriv.: *kardiognṓstēs* (2589), heart-knower, heart-searcher; *sklērokardía* (4641), hardening of the heart, stubbornness.

Syn.: *psuchḗ* (5590), soul, the very center; *noús* (3563), mind; *súnesis* (4907), understanding, prudence; *phrónēsis* (5428), prudence.

2589. καρδιογνώστης *kardiognṓstēs*; gen. *kardiognṓstou*, masc. noun from *kardía* (2588), heart, and *ginṓskō* (1097), to know. One who knows the heart, searcher of hearts (Acts 1:24; 15:8).

2590. καρπός *karpós*; gen. *karpoú*, masc. noun. Fruit or produce both of trees and plants and of the earth.

(I) Particularly in Matt 3:10, "a tree that does not bear good fruit" (a.t.); 13:8; Luke 12:17; 13:6, 7, 9; John 12:24; 2 Tim 2:6. Allegorically in John 15:2, 5, 8. To pay in produce as a share given for rent (Matt 21:41; Luke 20:10; Sept.: Ps 1:3; Jer 12:2). Of children or offspring as "the fruit of thy womb" (Luke 1:42); "fruit of his loins" (Acts 2:30; Sept.: Gen 30:2; Mic 6:7).

(II) Metaphorically, fruit, meaning:

(A) Of deeds, works, conduct (Matt 3:8; 7:16, 20; 21:43; Luke 3:8; Sept.: Prov 10:16).

(B) For effect, result (Rom 15:28; Gal 5:22, "the fruit of the Spirit"; Eph 5:9; Heb 12:11; James 3:17; Sept.: Jer 17:10; Mic 7:13).

(C) By implication, for profit, advantage, good (John 4:36; Rom 1:13; 6:21, 22; James 3:18; Sept.: Ps 58:11).

(D) "Fruit of our lips," meaning praise (Heb 13:15 in allusion to Sept.: Hos 14:3 [cf. Sept.: Prov 12:14]).

(E) In the NT, the redeemed human life is presented as a field with God being the owner, in expectation of fruit to be rendered and shared with Him. In 1 Cor 3:9, Paul reminds his readers that they

821 καρποφόρος (2593)

are God's husbandry (*geórgion* [1091], field, farm). This recalls the parable of the vineyard spoken by the Lord Jesus in Matt 21:33–44 and Luke 20:9–19. Christians, individually and collectively, are expected to produce good results, "fruit unto God" (Rom 7:4). Also those who are His overseers, those who plant and water, naturally look for produce and the reward of their toil. Thus Paul hopes, as he looks forward to his visit to Rome, that he may have some "fruit" among the people of that city as he had in Corinth and Ephesus (Rom 1:13).

The fruit of a tree is the evidence of its being attached to the true vine (John 15:1, 2). The fruit of the new life is regarded as sanctification (Rom 6:22). The fruit of the spirit (Gal 5:22) is equivalent to the good works that follow faith as indicated in James 2:14–19. The "fruit of righteousness" is an OT phrase and is found again in Phil 1:11 and Heb 12:11, where "righteousness" or conformity to the highest moral standards is described as the "peaceful fruit" or discipline patiently endured. We must never forget that the word "righteousness" refers to the rights of God clearly desired by the child of God in whose heart His righteousness dwells. One who does not produce fruit in his life is unfruitful (*ákarpos* [175]). Those who walk in darkness are spoken of as unfruitful (Eph 5:11; Rom 6:21). In Rom 7:5, Paul describes the unregenerate life as producing "fruit unto death" which fruit is given in detail in Gal 5:19–21 (cf. Col 3:5–9). For the final harvesting we have the picture of Rev 14.

It is evident from a study of John 15 that Christ expects much fruit from His branches. If there is no fruit on a branch, that branch is not truly attached to Christ. He is not satisfied with little, but demands that our fruit may be commensurate to His investment in us as indicated by the parable of the talents (Matt 25:14–30 [cf. Luke 12:48]). Our rewards or lack of rewards in heaven are commensurate with the fruits of our labor on earth.

Deriv.: *ákarpos* (175), unfruitful; *karpophóros* (2593), fruitful.

Syn.: *opóra* (3703), early autumn or late summer being the time of fruit-bearing; *aúxēsis* (838), increase; *prokopḗ* (4297), advancement, progress.

Ant.: *gumnótēs* (1132), nudity, nakedness, unyieldedness; *erḗmōsis* (2050), despoliation; *katastrophḗ* (2692), destruction; *steíros* (4723), barren, sterile.

2591. Κάρπος *Kárpos*; gen. *Kárpou*, masc. proper noun. Carpus, a Christian living at Troas, mentioned only in 2 Tim 4:13. He apparently had given hospitality to Paul while he was in Troas.

2592. καρποφορέω *karpophoréō*; contracted *karpophorṓ*, fut. *karpophorḗsō*, from *karpophóros* (2593), fruitful. To bring forth fruit, intrans.

(I) As the earth (Mark 4:28; Sept.: Hab 3:17).

(II) Metaphorically, to bring forth fruit, i.e., good works as believers (Matt 13:23; Mark 4:20; Luke 8:15; Rom 7:4; Col 1:10); Christian graces as faith, hope, love (Col 1:6 [cf. Col 1:4, 5]). To bring forth evil fruit, i.e., sin, as uncontrolled passions do (Rom 7:5).

Syn.: *teléō* (5055), to finish, perform; *teleióō* (5048) to fulfill, reach the goal; *epiteléō* (2005), to accomplish; *apoteléō* (658), to consummate; *poiéō* (4160), to perform, do; *gínomai* (1096), to come to pass, become; *apodídōmi* (591), to deliver; *apophérō* (667), to bear up, bring; *epitugchánō* (2013), succeed; *euodóō* (2137), to prosper; *prokóptō* (4298), to grow from within; *auxánō* (837), to grow, increase due to influences and processes outside oneself or the element of life received; *kerdaínō* (2770), to gain; *telesphoréō* (5052), to ripen fruit or to bring to perfection or its intended goal; *euphoréō* (2164), to bear well, to bring forth abundant fruit.

2593. καρποφόρος *karpophóros*; gen. *karpophórou*, masc.-fem., neut. *karpophóron*, adj. from *karpós* (2590), fruit, and *phérō* (5342), to bring. Bringing forth fruit, fruitful (Acts 14:17).

Deriv.: *karpophoréō* (2592), to bear fruit.

Ant.: *ákarpos* (175), unfruitful.

**2594. καρτερέω *karteréō*; contract-ed *karteró*, fut. *karterēsō*, from *karterós* (n.f.), strength. To be strong, steadfast, firm, to endure, hold out, bear the burden. In Heb 11:27, meaning that he endured severe yet voluntary exile with strength and courage.

Deriv.: *proskarteréō* (4342), to persist, hold fast.

Syn.: *ménō* (3306), to abide, endure; *hupoménō* (5278), to abide under, bear up courageously, endure circumstanc-es; *makrothuméō* (3114) to be longsuf-fering toward people; *phérō* (5342), to bear; *hupophérō* (5297), to bear by be-ing under, endure; *anéchō* (430), to hold up; *kakopathéō* (2553), to suffer evil; *sugkakopathéō* (4777), to suffer hard-ship together; *páschō* (3958), to suffer; *hupéchō* (5254), to hold under.

Ant.: *adēmonéō* (85), to be in distress.

**2595. κάρφος *kárphos*; gen. *kárphous*, from *kárphō* (n.f.), to dry. Anything that is dry and light, such as straw, stubble, chaff, a little splinter of wood, a mote (Matt 7:3–5; Luke 6:41, 42) as opposed to *dokós* (1385), beam (Sept.: Gen 8:11).

Syn.: *áchuron* (892), chaff; *chórtos* (5528), grass; *keraía* (2762), the apex of a piece of wood (*xúlon* [3586]).

**2596. κατά *katá*; prep. governing the gen. and acc. with the primary meaning of down. Down from, down upon, down in.

(I) With the gen.:

(A) Of place: **(1)** Indicating motion meaning down from a higher to a low-er place, down a precipice into the sea as in Matt 8:32; Mark 5:13; Luke 8:33. In 1 Cor 11:4, *katá kephalḗs* (*kephalḗs* [2776], head) and *échō* ([2192], have), where it means to hang down from the head like a veil. **(2)** Of motion meaning down upon a

lower place, upon (Mark 14:3). **(3)** Gen-erally of motion or direction upon, to-wards or through any place or object: **(a)** Particularly in the sense of upon, against (Acts 27:14). **(b)** In the sense of through, throughout, where *katá* with the acc. is more usual (Luke 4:14, "through the whole area" [a.t.]; 23:5, "through all Judea" [a.t.]; Acts 9:31, 42; 10:37). For adv., *kath' hólou*, see no. 2527. **(c)** Af-ter verbs of swearing, i.e., to swear upon or by anything, at the same time stretch-ing out the hand over, upon, or toward it (Matt 26:63; Heb 6:13, 16; Sept.: 2 Chr 36:13; Isa 45:23).

(B) Metaphorically, of the object to-ward or upon which something tends or aims. Upon, in respect to (1 Cor 15:15; Jude 1:15). More usually in a hostile sense: against; or after words of speak-ing, accusing, warring, and the like (Matt 5:11, 23; 10:35; 12:14, 30; 26:59; Mark 11:25; 14:55ff.; Luke 23:14; John 18:29; Acts 4:26; 16:22; 21:28; 2 Cor 13:8; Gal 5:17).

(II) With the acc., where the primary and general idea is down upon, out over:

(A) Of place, that is: **(1)** Of motion expressed or implied or of extension out over, through, or throughout a place (Luke 8:39, "out over the city preaching" [a.t.]; 15:14; Acts 5:15; 8:1; 11:1, "who were throughout Judea" [a.t.]; 15:23; 24:12). With *poreúomai* (4198), to travel through (Acts 8:36), and generally *katá tḗn hodón* ([3598], way), meaning along or by the way, while traveling upon it (Luke 10:4; Acts 25:3; 26:13). Hence, from the idea of motion throughout every part of the whole arises the distributive sense of *katá*, e.g., Matt 24:7, "throughout all places," "in various parts" (a.t.); Luke 8:1, "throughout every city and village," i.e., to every one generally (see also Luke 8:4; 9:6; 13:22; Acts 2:46, "from house to house"; 8:3; 14:23; 15:21, 36; 22:19). **(2)** Of motion referring to a situation upon, at, near to, or adjacent to (Luke 10:32, 33; Acts 2:10; 16:7; 27:2, places on or near the coast of Asia Minor, Acts 27:7). **(3)** Of motion or direction, upon, i.e., toward any place

(Acts 8:26; 27:12; Phil 3:14). Figuratively, to withstand one to his face (Gal 2:11). **(4)** Place where, i.e., being at, in, within a place (where sometimes as *en* [1722], in, might be employed though not strictly syn.), as the Eng. phrases "at a house" or "in a house" may be used interchangeably. **(a)** Followed by the acc. of place (Acts 13:1; Rom 16:5, "the church that is in [or at] their house," i.e., accustomed to meet there; 1 Cor 16:19; Phile 1:2). **(b)** Followed by the acc. of person implying place, i.e., in, with, or among (Acts 17:28, "your own poets"; 18:15; 21:21, "the Jews dispersed among [throughout] the Gentiles" [a.t.]. 26:3; Eph 1:15, "in regard to your faith" [a.t.]). *Kath' heautón*, in or with oneself, particularly in one's own house and hence generally by or for oneself, alone (Acts 28:16; Rom 14:22; James 2:17). **(c)** Followed by the acc. of thing implying place, e.g., *katá prósōpon* (4383), face, followed by the gen., meaning in the presence of anyone (Luke 2:31; Acts 3:13). With the gen. implied, e.g., *hautoú* (848), himself (Acts 25:16); *humōn* (5216), of you (2 Cor 10:1); *kat' ophthalmoús* ([3788], eye), "before . . . eyes" (Gal 3:1). Metaphorically of a state or condition in which anything is or is done, thus implying also manner, e.g., in or by a dream (Matt 1:20; 2:12, 13; 1 Cor 2:1, "I . . . came not with excellency of speech"). Adv., *kat' exousían* ([1849], authority) (Mark 1:27, "with authority"); *katá krátos* ([2904], strength), meaning strongly, vehemently (Acts 19:20); *kath' huperbolḗn* ([5236], excess), meaning exceedingly (Rom 7:13; Gal 1:13 [cf. 2 Cor 4:17]) or excellently (1 Cor 12:31); *hoi kat' exochḗn* ([1851], prominence), those in distinction, e.g., the distinguished ones (Acts 25:23).

(B) Of time, i.e., of a period or point of time, down upon, e.g., in, at, or during which anything takes place, as *katá tó autó*, the neut. of *autós* (846), the same, meaning at the same time, together; *katá kairón* ([2540], occasion, season, opportune time), meaning in due time (John 5:4; Rom 5:6); *kat' ekeínon* ([1565], that) *tón kairón*, during that time (Acts 12:1;

19:23), during this time (Rom 9:9), every Saturday (Acts 13:27), about midnight (Acts 16:25; 27:27); *kat' archás* (746) in the beginning (Heb 1:10), during the time (day) of temptation (Heb 3:8), for the time then present (*enestēkóta*, perf. part. of *enístēmi* [1764], to be at hand) Heb 9:9; see Sept.: Gen 18:10); *kath' hēméran* ([2250], day), meaning daily, every day (Matt 26:55; Mark 14:49), also with the def. art. *tó kath' hēméran* (Luke 11:3; 19:47, daily); *kat' étos* ([2094], year), or *kat' eniautón* ([1763], a designated year), meaning yearly, every year (Luke 2:41; Heb 9:25; 10:1, 3); *katá heortēn* ([1859], feast), meaning at each Passover (Matt 27:15; Luke 23:17); *katá mían* ([3391], one) *Sabbátōn* (pl. of *Sábbaton* [4521], Sabbath), meaning every first day of the week (1 Cor 16:2); *katá pásan* (the fem. of *pás* [3956], every) *hēméran* ([2250], day), every day (Acts 17:17); *katá pán* ([3956], all, every) *Sábbaton*, every Sabbath (Acts 18:4); *kath' hekástēn* ([1538], each one, every) *hēméran* (day), every single day (Heb 3:13); *katá mēna* ([3376], month), meaning during each month (Rev 22:2).

(C) In a distributive sense, derived strictly from the idea of pervading all the parts of the whole; as of place, see I, A above, and of time, see I, B. Also generally of any parts, number, e.g., *katá méros* ([3313], part), i.e., part for part, particularly (Heb 9:5). Of number, *kath' héna* ([1520], one), meaning one by one (1 Cor 14:31). See *heís* (1520, II, C), one, as also for *hoi kath' héna*, *kath' hén*, *heís kath' heís*. Also *katá dúo* ([1417], two), meaning two and two (1 Cor 14:27).

(D) Metaphorically, as expressing the relation in which one thing stands towards another, thus also everywhere implying manner. Spoken of: **(1)** Accordance, conformity, e.g., **(a)** Of a norm, rule, standard of comparison meaning according to, conformable to, after: "According to your faith be it unto you" (Matt 9:29); "do not do according to their works" (a.t. [Matt 23:3]); "according to the tradition of the elders" (Mark

7:5); "according to the law" (Luke 2:22, 39); "according to the commandment" (Luke 23:56); "Ye judge after [according to] the flesh," meaning from external circumstances (John 8:15); "according to our law" (a.t. [John 19:7]); "according to the law" (Acts 22:12); "according to what was commanded" (a.t. [Acts 23:31]); "according to the strictest sect" (a.t. [Acts 26:5]); *katá alḗtheian* ([225], truth), "according to truth," means true with reference to God's judgment (Rom 2:2, see Rom 2:6, 7); *katá sárka* ([4561], flesh), *katá pneúma* ([4151], spirit), "after the flesh . . . after the Spirit," meaning conformable to the will of the flesh or of the Spirit (Rom 8:4, 5); "not according to knowledge" (Rom 10:2); "according to the former behavior" (a.t. [Eph 4:22]); "according to the tradition of men" (a.t. [Col 2:8]). Also with the acc. of person, i.e., according to the will of anyone; "according to . . . God" (Rom 8:27; 2 Cor 7:9–11; 1 Pet 4:6); "according to Christ Jesus" (Rom 15:5); "according to the same Spirit" (a.t. [1 Cor 12:8]); "by command of the Lord" (a.t. [2 Cor 11:17]); "not according to man" (a.t.), meaning not human or of human origin (Gal 1:11). With the idea of proportion (Matt 2:16; 25:15; Rom 12:6; 1 Cor 3:8; 2 Cor 10:13). Used adv. meaning accidentally, by chance (Luke 10:31); by name (John 10:3); *katá lógon* ([3056], reason), meaning reasonably (Acts 18:14); *katá táxin* ([5010], order), according to order (1 Cor 14:40); *kat' ophthalmodouleían* ([3787], eyeservice), "according to eyeservice" (a.t. [Eph 6:6]); *katá zḗlon* ([2205], zeal), zealously, righteously, "according to zeal" (a.t. [Phil 3:6]); *katá gnṓsin* ([1108], knowledge), discreetly or "according to knowledge" (1 Pet 3:7). *Katá* followed by the interrogative *ti*, neut. of *tis* (5101), thing, meaning "How?" (Luke 1:18). **(b)** Of an occasion, by virtue of, because of, for, by, through (Matt 19:3, "to dismiss his wife for any cause" [a.t.]; Acts 3:17, "because of ignorance" [a.t.], ignorantly; Rom 2:5; 2 Cor 8:8; Gal 1:4; 2:2; Eph 1:5f.; 3:3; Phil 2:3; 4:11; 2 Thess

2:9; 2 Tim 1:1; Phile 1:14, "of necessity"; Heb 2:4). **(c)** Of any general reference or allusion, in respect to, as to (Rom 1:3, "as to the flesh" [a.t.]; 9:5; 11:28; Phil 3:6; Titus 1:4; Heb 9:9; 1 Pet 4:14). Followed by the acc. with a preceding art., it forms a periphrase for the cognate adj. of, e.g., *hoi katá phúsin* ([5449], nature) natural (Rom 11:21); "your masters according to the flesh" (Col 3:22); *tá katá tón Paúlon*, "Paul's cause," his affairs (Acts 25:14); *tá kat' emé*, "my affairs" (Eph 6:21; Col 4:7). In phrases such as *katá pánta* ([3956], all), "in all things" meaning in all respects (Acts 3:22; Heb 2:17); *katá pánta trópon* ([5158], manner), in every respect, "every way," (Rom 3:2); with the neg. (2 Thess 2:3); *kath' hóson* ([3745], how much), by how much, i.e., inasmuch (Heb 3:3; 7:20); *katá tosoúton* ([5118], such), meaning insomuch (Heb 7:22); *tó kat' emé*, literally, "as to what concerns me" (a.t.), so far as in me lies (Rom 1:15). **(2)** Of likeness, similitude, after the manner of; *katá sárka* ([4561], flesh), i.e., like a frail and feeble man (2 Cor 1:17; 10:2). "According to the order of Melchizedek" (a.t.), i.e., of an order like that of Melchizedek (Heb 5:6, 10); like my inclinations(Acts 13:22; Sept.: Deut 4:32; Lam 1:12). With the acc. of person, "as Isaac," like Isaac (Gal 4:28); "I speak as a man" (Rom 3:5; Gal 3:15) with the idea of a common man (1 Cor 3:3). Adv., *kath' hón trópon* (*hón* [3739], which; *trópon* [5158], manner), as, even as (Acts 15:11); *katá taúta* ([5024], these), in the same way, thus, so (Luke 6:23, 26; 17:30); *kath' homoiótēta* ([3665], likeness), like, similarly (Heb 4:15). **(3)** Of the end, aim, or purpose toward which anything is directed, for, by way of: "I say it by way of reproach" (a.t.) or disparagement (2 Cor 11:21); "the teaching that is directed toward godliness" (a.t.) or piety (1 Tim 6:3; 2 Tim 1:1; Titus 1:1). **(4)** Figuratively, in 2 Cor 8:2 meaning poverty down to the very depths, deepest poverty.

(III) *Katá* is used in many comp. verbs:

(A) Indicating motion downwards, as *katabaínō* (2597), to descend; *kathairéō* (2507), to demolish, put down, destroy; *katapíptō* (2667), to fall down.

(B) Indicating opposition against in a hostile sense as *kataginóskō* (2607), to blame; *katēgoréō* (2723), to accuse; *katalaléō* (2635), to slander.

(C) Indicating distribution as *kataklērodotéō* (2624), to apportion an estate by casting lots.

(D) In a general sense, down, down upon, and also throughout, where it cannot be expressed in Eng. and is then simply an intens.

(E) Sometimes it gives to an intrans. verb a trans. sense such as *katargéō* (2673), to make void.

(F) As an intensive as in *kataphtheírō* (2704), to corrupt or spoil entirely, completely.

2597. καταβαίνω *katabaínō*; fut. *katabésomai*, 2d aor. *katébēn*, aor. imper. *katábēthi* and *katába* (Mark 15:30), from *katá* (2596), down, and *baínō* (n.f., see *apobaínō* [576]), to go or come. To come or go down, descend from a higher to a lower place. Intrans.:

(I) Spoken of persons, followed by *apó* (575), from, with the gen. of place meaning from whence (Matt 8:1, "when he descended from the mountain" [a.t.]; 14:29, "from the boat" [a.t.]; 17:9; Mark 9:9; 15:30, "from the cross"; Sept.: Ex 34:29 followed by *ek*; Judg 4:14 followed by *katá*). Followed by *eis* (1519), into, with the acc. of place, meaning whither, to which (Mark 13:15, "let him . . . not go down into the house"; Acts 8:38; Eph 4:9; Sept.: Job 7:9; Jon 2:7). Followed by *epí* (1909), upon, meaning "down upon the seashore," namely from the mountain (John 6:16); by *prós* (4314), toward someone (Acts 10:21; 14:11; Sept.: Ex 19:14). Used in an absolute sense in Matt 24:17; Luke 6:17; John 5:7. Spoken of those who go from a higher to a lower region of a country, e.g., *apó Hierousalém*, from Jerusalem (Mark 3:22; Luke 10:30). Followed by *eis* (John

2:12, "unto Capernaum" [a.t.]; Acts 7:15, "unto Egypt" [a.t.]; 14:25; 16:8). Used in an absolute sense (Luke 2:51; John 4:47; Acts 8:15; 24:1; Sept.: Gen 12:10; 42:3). Spoken of those who descend or come down from heaven, e.g.: of God as affording aid to the oppressed (Acts 7:34 quoted from Ex 3:8); of the Son of Man and followed by *ek* (1537), out of (John 6:38, 42); followed by *apó* (575), from (1 Thess 4:16); of the Holy Spirit followed by *ek* (1537), out of (John 1:32), *epí* (1909), upon someone (Luke 3:22; John 1:33); of angels followed by *ex ouranoú* (3772), heaven, out of heaven (Matt 28:2); *en* (1722), in, with the dat. of place meaning into (John 5:4); *epí* (1909), upon someone (John 1:51; Sept.: Gen 28:12); of Satan as cast down from heaven (Rev 12:12 [cf. Rev 12:9, 10]).

(II) Spoken of things: a way leading down from a higher to a lower tract of country as the way coming down from Jerusalem unto Gaza (Acts 8:26); of things descending from heaven, i.e., let down or sent down from God as a vessel (Acts 10:11; 11:5); spiritual gifts, followed by *apó* (575), from, (James 1:17); the New Jerusalem, the one descending out of heaven from God (Rev 3:12). Also generally from the heavens or the clouds, to fall, e.g., the rain (Matt 7:25, 27); a storm (Luke 8:23); fire from heaven (Luke 9:54; see Rev 13:13; Sept.: 2 Kgs 1:10, 12). In the general sense of to fall or drop, e.g., sweat like drops of blood descending upon the earth (Luke 22:44).

Deriv.: *katábasis* (2600), descent; *sugkatabaínō* (4782), to go down with.

Syn.: *katérchomai* (2718), to come down; *katapíptō* (2667), to fall down.

Ant.: *anabaínō* (305), to go up; *anatéllō* (393), to arise; *anérchomai* (424), to go up.

2598. καταβάλλω *katabállō*; fut. *katabaló*, from *katá* (2596), down, and *bállō* (906), to throw, cast. To cast down, used trans., e.g., from heaven (Rev 12:10). In the sense of to prostrate (2 Cor

4:9; Sept.: Ps 73:18). In the mid., to lay down a foundation (Heb 6:1).

Deriv.: *katabolḗ* (2602), foundation, founding.

Syn.: *rhíptō* (4496), to throw with a sudden motion; *kathairéō* (2507), to cast down, demolish; *katatíthēmi* (2698), to lay down.

Ant.: *egeírō* (1453), to arise, raise up; *aírō* (142), to take up, lift; *epaírō* (1869), to lift up; *hupsóō* (5312), to lift or raise up; *anístēmi* (450), to raise up; *anorthóō* (461), to set upright; *anakúptō* (352), to lift oneself up.

2599. καταβαρέω katabaréō; contracted *katabarṓ*, fut. *katabaréso*, from *katá* (2596), down, and *baréō* (916), to burden. To burden, oppress, weigh down (2 Cor 12:16), to burden in a pecuniary sense (cf. 2 Sam 13:25).

Syn.: *epibaréō* (1912), to burden heavily; *katanarkáō* (2655), to be burdensome, be a dead weight.

Ant.: *kouphízō* (2893), to lighten; *húpsóō* (5312), to elevate.

2600. κατάβασις katábasis; gen. *katabáseōs*, fem. noun from *katabaínō* (2597), to descend. Descent, a going down, or the place of descent, lower part (Luke 19:37; Sept.: Josh 10:11; Mic 1:4).

2601. καταβιβάζω katabibázō; fut. *katabibásō*, from *katá* (2596), down, and *bibázō* (n.f., see *embibázō* [1688]), to cause or make to come. To cause to come down, to bring down (Matt 11:23; Luke 10:15; Sept.: Ezek 28:8; 31:16, 18).

Syn.: *katágō* (2609), to bring down; *kataphérō* (2702), to bring down; *tapeinóō* (5013), to humble.

Ant.: *anabibázō* (307), to cause to go up, to haul up as a net; *anaphérō* (399), to bring up; *aírō* (142), to lift; *anairéō* (337), to take up.

2602. καταβολή katabolḗ; gen. *katabolḗs*, fem. noun from *katabállō* (2598), to cast down. A casting or laying down.

(I) A laying down, founding, foundation. In the NT the absolute beginning only in the phrase, *katabolḗ toú kósmou* ([2889], world), the creation of the world (Matt 13:35; 25:34; Luke 11:50; John 17:24; Heb 4:3; 9:26; 1 Pet 1:20; Rev 13:8; 17:8). The whole expression, "the foundation of the world," is equivalent to the phrase found in Mark 10:6; 13:19, "from the beginning of the creation [*ap' archḗs* {746}, from the beginning; *ktíseōs* {2937}, creation]." In Hebr., there is no term which would quite correspond to the Gr. *ho kósmos*, the world as the universe. Matt 13:35 is a nonliteral rendering of Ps 78:2, which the Sept. translates as *ap' archḗs* "from the beginning." The foundation of the world stands for the definite time when this present universe was originated. It definitely intimates a Creator, not self-creation.

(II) Of seed, a casting in metaphorically; in Heb 11:11, literally strength for the casting in or implanting of seed, i.e., strength for conception, procreation. In general, the term *katabolḗ kósmou* denotes a time sense, implying a strong declaration of priority. It always occurs with the prep. *apó* (575), from (Matt 13:35; 25:34; Luke 11:50; Heb 4:3; 9:26; Rev 13:8); *pró* (4253), before (John 17:24; Eph 1:4; 1 Pet 1:20); *eis* (1519) unto (Heb 11:11).

(III) *Katabolḗ* is always in the act. except in Heb 11:11, when used of Sarah. A syn. is *themélios* (2310), something put down, a substructure or foundation with both a literal and a figurative meaning. *Themélios*, when used in an act. sense, represents *katabolḗ*, founding.

(IV) The pass. sense of *katabolḗ* in the NT is represented by *themélios*, both literal and metaphorical, which is used, for example, in our Lord's figure of the two buildings (Luke 6:48f.), as well as in Paul's figure of the building tested by fire (1 Cor 3:10ff.). In 1 Cor 3:11, the Church's foundation is Christ. In Eph 2:20, she is built upon the foundation of the apostles and NT prophets, Jesus Christ being the chief cornerstone. In Heb 11:11, *katabolḗ* is translated "to conceive," which in reality means Abraham's discharge or seed. It is used in the pass. because the seed was received by Sarah. Her conception was not only due to the natural process, but also to faith that the placement of Abraham's seed in her would, in spite of her advanced age, result in the birth of a child according to the promise given to Abraham.

Syn.: *sullambánō* (4815), to take together (a syn. for conception); *archḗ* (746), beginning (a syn. for foundation); *ktísis* (2937), creation; *génesis* (1078), generation, making.

Ant.: *katastrophḗ* (2692), destruction, demolition; *télos* (5056) and *suntéleia* (4930), consummation, as of an age.

2603. καταβραβεύω *katabrabeúō*; fut. *katabrabeúsō*, from *katá* (2596), against, and *brabeúō* (1018), to be a judge or umpire and thus award the prize in a public game. To judge against someone in a game, to defraud or deprive of the prize (Col 2:18 [cf. 1 Cor 9:24 and Phil 3:14, which refer to the prize {*brabeíon* (1017)} of the Christian calling]).

Syn.: *aposteréō* (650), to deprive; *husteréō* (5302), to lack, be behind, come short of.

Ant.: *brabeúō* (1018), to give the prize, to rule, govern, prevail; *apodídōmi* (591), to pay wages; *antapodídōmi* (467), to recompense.

2604. καταγγελεύς *kataggeleús*; gen. *kataggeléos*, masc. noun from *kataggéllō* (2605) to proclaim. A proclaimer, publisher (only in Acts 17:18).

Syn.: *kḗrux* (2783), a herald, preacher.

2605. καταγγέλλω *kataggéllō*; fut. *kataggelṓ*, from *katá* (2596), an intens., and *aggéllō* (n.f., see *anaggéllō* [312]), to tell, declare. To declare plainly, openly, or aloud.

(I) To announce, proclaim (Acts 13:38). In the sense of to laud, celebrate (Rom 1:8; 1 Cor 11:26).

(II) By implication meaning to preach, set forth, inculcate (Acts 4:2; 13:5; 15:36; 16:17, 21; 17:3, 13, 23; 26:23; 1 Cor 2:1; 9:14; Phil 1:16, 18; Col 1:28).

Deriv.: *kataggeleús* (2604), a proclaimer, publisher; *prokataggéllō* (4293), to foretell.

Syn.: *kērússō* (2784), to preach, proclaim.

Ant.: *apokrúptō* (613), to hide.

2606. καταγελάω *katageláō*; contracted *katagelṓ*, fut. *katagelásō*, from *katá* (2596), against, denoting opposition, and *geláō* (1070), to laugh. To laugh at, laugh to scorn, deride, ridicule (Matt 9:24; Mark 5:40; Luke 8:53; Sept.: Job 21:3; 30:1; Prov 17:5).

Syn.: *ekmuktērízō* (1592), to sneer at, deride; *chleuázō* (5512), to mock.

Ant.: *epainéō* (1867), to commend, praise; *eulogéō* (2127), to speak well of, bless, praise.

2607. καταγινώσκω *kataginṓskō*; fut. *katagnṓsomai*, from *katá* (2596), against, and *ginṓskō* (1097), to know. To perceive something concerning one, observe, usually to discern in a bad sense and therefore to detect something bad about another, to incriminate, condemn (1 John 3:20, 21; Sept.: Prov 28:11). The perf. pass. part. is *kategnōsménos*, to be blamed, worthy of blame, reprehensible (Gal 2:11).

Deriv.: *akatágnōstos* (176), unblamable.

Syn.: *mōmáomai* (3469), to find fault with, blame; *mémphomai* (3201), to find fault; *katadikázō* (2613), to pronounce judgment, condemn; *katakrínō* (2632), to condemn; *elégchō* (1651), to reprove, convict; *katamarturéō* (2649), to testify against; *kolázō* (2849), to chastise, punish; *timōréō* (5097), to avenge, protect one's honor.

Ant.: *apolúō* (630), to set free, let go; *aphíēmi* (863), to send away, to free from; *charízomai* (5483), to deliver, forgive.

2608. κατάγνυμι *katágnumi*; fut. *katáxō*, aor. *katéaxa*, 2d aor. pass. *kateágēn*,

Attic fut. *kateáxō* (Matt 12:20, probably to distinguish it from the fut. of *katágō* [2609], to lead down, to land), from *katá* (2596), an intens., and *ágnumi* (n.f.), to break. To break in two, break down (Matt 12:20; John 19:31–33; Sept.: Jer 31:25). Also from *ágnumi* (n.f.): *axínē* (513), an axe.

Syn.: *kláō* or *klázō* (2806), to break, to break in pieces; *katakláō* (2622), to break down into smaller pieces; *suntríbō* (4937), to break into pieces by crushing; *sunthláō* (4917), to crush in pieces, shatter; *sunthrúptō* (4919), to break small; *kóptō* (2875), to cut down; *katakóptō* (2629), to chop down, to cut; *dichotoméō* (1371), to cut asunder.

Ant.: *sugkomízō* (4792), to convey together; *sunistáō* or *sunístēmi* (4921), to put together, constitute; *katartízō* (2675), to complete thoroughly, mend, restore; *sundéō* (4887), to bind with; *sunarmologéō* (4883), to closely fit or join together.

2609. κατάγω *katágō*; fut. *katáxō*, from *katá* (2596), an intens., and *ágō* (71), to lead or to bring.

(I) To bring down (Acts 9:30; 22:30; 23:15, 20, 28; Rom 10:6; Sept.: Gen 44:21; 1 Kgs 1:33).

(II) As a term of navigation it means to bring a vessel to land (Luke 5:11). In the mid., *katágomai*, to be brought down, to make land or port, to touch, to land (Acts 21:3; 27:3; 28:12).

Syn.: *anabibázō* (307), to haul or draw to shore, meaning to make land; *katabibázō* (2601), to cause to go down; *phérō* (5342), to carry, bring, move; *kataphérō* (2702), to bear down; *katérchomai* (2718), to come down; *kathairéō* (2507), to put down.

Ant.: *anaphérō* (399), to bring up; *anágō* (321), to depart or launch out; *pléō* (4126), to sail; *apopléō* (636), to sail away; *ekpléō* (1602), to sail out of.

2610. καταγωνίζομαι *katagōnízomai*; fut. *katagōnísomai*, mid. deponent from *katá* (2596), against, and *agōnízomai* (75), to contend for victory in the public games. To throw down, contend against, subdue (only in Heb 11:33).

Syn.: *hupotássō* (5293), to subdue or bring into subjection; *nikáō* (3528), to be victorious; *hupernikáō* (5245), to be more than a conqueror; *katakurieúō* (2634), to conquer, master; *ischúō* (2480), to prevail; *katischúō* (2729), to be strong against, prevail against.

Ant.: *zēmióō* (2210), to inflict loss, suffer loss.

2611. καταδέω *katadéō*; fut. *katadésō*, from *katá* (2596), an intens., and *déō* (1210), to bind. To bind up, such as wounds (Luke 10:34; Sept.: Ezek 34:4, 16).

Syn.: *peridéō* (4019), to bind around, about.

Ant.: *lúō* (3089), to loose, unbind; *chaláō* (5465), to let down; *aphíēmi* (863), to let stand away from.

2612. κατάδηλος *katádēlos*; gen. *katadélou*, masc.-fem., neut. *katádēlon*, adj. from *katá* (2596), an intens., and *délos* (1212), manifest. Quite manifest, exceedingly evident (Heb 7:15).

Syn.: *pródēlos* (4271), manifest, clearly evident; *phanerós* (5318), apparent; *emphanés* (1717), openly manifest; *lamprós* (2986), bright, clear, luminous.

Ant.: *kruptós* (2927), hidden, secret, inward, not externally manifest; *apókruphos* (614), something which is made secret or which is hidden from oneself.

2613. καταδικάζω *katadikázō*; fut. *katadikáso*, from *katá* (2596), against, and *dikázō* (n.f.), to judge, pronounce sentence, which is from *díkē* (1349), judgment. To give judgment against a person, recognize the evidence against him, pass sentence, condemn (Matt 12:7, 37; Luke 6:37; James 5:6; Sept.: Ps 36:33).

Syn.: *kataginóskō* (2607), to know something against, to condemn; *krínō* (2919), to judge, distinguish, to condemn; *katakrínō* (2632), to give judgment against, pass sentence on, condemn.

Ant.: *apōlúō* (630), to dismiss as innocent; *dikaióō* (1344), to justify; *aníēmi* (447), to forbear, to let up, cease from; *eleutheróō* (1659), to liberate, deliver; *aphíēmi* (863), to forgive.

2614. καταδιώκω *katadiṓkō*; fut. *katadiṓxō*, from *katá* (2596), an intens., and *diṓkō* (1377), to follow, pursue. To follow earnestly (Mark 1:36; Sept.: Judg 7:25; Ps 22:6).

Syn.: *akolouthéō* (190), to follow; *epakolouthéō* (1872), to follow after, close upon; *katakolouthéō* (2628), to follow closely; *miméomai* (3401), to imitate.

Ant.: *apoleípō* (620) and *kataleípō* (2641), to leave behind; *egkataleípō* (1459), to leave behind, forsake; *aphíēmi* (863), to forsake; *apotássō* (657), to set apart, renounce; *hupoleípō* (5275), to leave behind; *perileípō* (4035), to remain; *hupolimpánō* (5277), to leave.

2615. καταδουλόω *katadoulóō*; contracted *katadoulṓ*, fut. *katadoulṓsō*, from *katá* (2596), an intens., and *doulóō* (1402), to enslave. To enslave utterly, reduce to absolute slavery (2 Cor 11:20); in the mid. to make a slave for oneself (Gal 2:4, "that they might make us their slaves" [a.t.]; Sept.: Ex 1:14; 6:5).

Syn.: *doulagōgéō* (1396), to lead into slavery, bondage, to subject.

Ant.: *eleutheróō* (1659), to make free; *lúō* (3089), to release, loose; *aníēmi* (447), to forbear, loose; *aphíēmi* (863), to release.

2616. καταδυναστεύω *katadunasteúō*; fut. *katadunasteúsō*, from *katá* (2596), denoting ill, and *dunasteúō* (n.f.), to rule, which is from *dunástēs* (1413), a potentate. To tyrannize, oppress harshly (Acts 10:38; James 2:6; Sept.: 2 Sam 8:11; Jer 22:3).

Syn.: *kataponéō* (2669), to cause hardship and pain; *basanízō* (928), to vex, torment; *skúllō* (4660), to annoy, trouble, bother; *stenochōréō* (4729), to cause anguish; *kakouchéō* (2558), to treat in an

evil way, torment; *odunáō* (3600), to cause anguish; *enochléō* (1776), to trouble; *kakóō* (2559) and *thlíbō* (2346), to afflict; *talaipōréō* (5003), to cause hardship.

Ant.: *hēgéomai* (2233), to govern, rule; *hēgemoneúō* (2230), to be a governor; *árchō* (757), to rule; *proḯstēmi* (4291), to stand before, hence to lead, superintend; *poimaínō* (4165), to act as a shepherd, pastor. In the sense of obey: *hupakoúō* (5219), to obey; *hupotássomai* (5293), to subject oneself to; *peitharchéō* (3980), to be persuaded, submit to authority; *summorphóōmai* (4833), to conform to; *sebázomai* (4573), to venerate; *eulabéomai* (2125), to receive with respect.

2617. καταισχύνω *kataischúnō*; fut. *kataischunṓ*, from *katá* (2596), denoting ill, and *aischúnō* (153), to shame. To shame, make ashamed, confound, dishonor, disgrace.

(I) To dishonor, disgrace, trans., referring to the head (1 Cor 11:4, 5, to offend against decorum).

(II) Equivalent to *aischúnō*, shame, but stronger.

(A) To shame, trans. (Luke 13:17; 1 Cor 1:27; 11:22; 2 Cor 7:14; 9:4; 1 Pet 3:16; Sept.: 2 Sam 19:6).

(B) By metonymy of cause or effect, to frustrate one's hope, disappoint (Rom 5:5; 9:33; 10:11; 1 Pet 2:6 quoted from Isa 28:16; Sept.: Ps 22:5; 44:7; 119:31, 116).

Syn.: *epaischúnomai* (1870), to be ashamed of, or bring shame upon a person, cause, or thing; *entrépō* (1788), to put to shame, and in the mid. or pass. *entrépomai*, to withdraw, put oneself to shame or be put to shame and look inward and withdraw; *atimázō* (818), to dishonor, insult; *atimóō* (821), to dishonor; *paradeigmatízō* (3856), to set forth as an example, put to open shame.

Ant.: *timáō* (5091), to honor; *doxázō* (1392), to glorify; *endoxázō* (1740), to glorify in; *kaucháomai* (2744), to boast or glory; *katakaucháomai* (2620), to boast against, exult.

2618. κατακαίω *katakaíō*; fut. *kata-kaúsō*, 2d aor. *katekáēn*, fut. pass. *kata-kauthḗsomai* (Rev 18:8) and later *katakaésomai* (1 Cor 3:15; 2 Pet 3:10), from *katá* (2596), an intens., and *kaíō* (2545), to burn. To burn, burn up, consume with fire (Matt 3:12; 13:30, 40; Luke 3:17; Acts 19:19; 1 Cor 3:15; Heb 13:11; 2 Pet 3:10; Rev 8:7; 17:16; 18:8; Sept.: Ex 32:20; Lev 6:30).
　Syn.: *ekkaíō* (1572), to burn out, and in the pass. to be kindled, burned up; *puróomai* (4448), to glow with heat; *emprḗthō* (1714), to burn up; *katanalískō* (2654), to consume.
　Ant.: *sbénnumi* (4570), to quench fire.

2619. κατακαλύπτω *katakalúptō*; fut. *katakalúpsō*, from *katá* (2596), an intens., and *kalúptō* (2572), to cover. To cover with a veil or something which hangs down, hence, to veil; in the pass., *katakalúptomai*, to be covered, veiled, to wear a veil (1 Cor 11:6, 7). The covering here involves either the hair of a woman hanging down or, in case that may not be possible, the veil. It must be remembered in this connection that women of loose morals, especially the prostitute priestesses of the temple of Aphrodite at Corinth, kept their hair very short in order to be distinguished for what they were. This was strictly forbidden for Christian women in order that no one would mistake them as women of loose morals. What happened, however, when one of these prostitute priestesses was saved in Corinth? Since she could not grow her hair immediately, she used a veil to cover her head to show that she no longer belonged to the prostitute caste. See also *akatakáluptos* (177), uncovered, which (in 1 Cor 11:5, 13) is equivalent to being shaven.
　Deriv.: *akatakáluptos* (177), unveiled, uncovered.
　Syn.: *stégō* (4722), to roof over, endure patiently, suffer silently; *epikalúptō* (1943), to conceal; *komáō* (2863), to wear long hair.
　Ant.: *apokalúptō* (601), to uncover, unveil; *anakalúptō* (343), to discover; *dēlóō* (1213), to declare, signify; *phaneróō* (5319), to manifest; *apodeíknumi* (584), to prove, set forth, show; *emphanízō* (1718), to show, manifest.

2620. κατακαυχάομαι *katakaucháomai*; contracted *katakauchṓmai*, fut. *katakauchḗsomai*, mid. deponent from *katá* (2596), against, and *kaucháomai* (2744), to boast. To boast or rejoice against.
　(I) In Rom 11:18, Gentile believers are contrasted with the Jews who rejected Christ. Paul presents an illustration in which the Jews are a cultivated olive tree with its natural branches while the Gentiles are branches from a wild olive tree which have been grafted into the Jewish olive tree. To the superciliously contemptuous Gentile believers Paul warns, "Boast not against [*mḗ katakauchṓ*, 2d person sing.] the branches [Jews who have not believed but should have]." He goes on to say, "But if thou boast [against them], thou bearest not the root, but the root thee." The root is God the Father who sent His Son to be born of a Jewish mother. Thus in spite of the fact that the Jews are not yet believing branches, we must remember salvation is of the Jews (John 4:22). Keep in mind that Christ Himself was a Jew just as the natural branches of the olive tree are Jews. The Gentiles (ingrafted branches) owe their salvation to Jesus Christ who as a Jewish Man came to save His own people first. It is on that Jewish foundation that the Gentile Church has been built (Eph 2:20).
　(II) In James 3:14, it has the same meaning, "Glory [boast] not, and lie not against the truth." In James 2:13, the word is used in a positive sense and not negatively as in the previous two occasions. In James 2:12, James speaks of the future judgment of God that is going to be in accordance with the law of liberty. In verse thirteen he explains what that law of liberty will be. A literal translation

of the first part of verse thirteen is "For the judgment shall be without mercy to him who did not do mercy" (a.t.). James here refers to the believer who did not show mercy to his fellow believers or to others when he should have. That same believer, when he appears before the merciful Judge, will not experience mercy, for he deserves to receive judgment as per his behavior on earth. This will not be so, however, for the believer who has demonstrated mercy to his fellow believers or fellow humans. He will want the liberal Judge to show him mercy for the many times he failed Christ on earth. That mercifulness he demonstrated on earth will be considered on the day of judgment, and thus James closes this most important verse by saying, "Mercy rejoiceth against judgment." What is translated "rejoiceth" is *katakauchátai*, which would have been better translated "boasteth against" judgment. The reservoir of mercifulness obtained by the believer on earth will stand against his deserved judgment when he must appear before the judgment seat of Christ to "receive the things done in his body, according to that he hath done, whether it be good or bad" (2 Cor 5:10).

2621. κατάκειμαι *katákeimai*; fut. *katakeísomai*, from *katá* (2596), down, and *keímai* (2749), to lie. To lie or be laid down upon a bed or couch, as a person who is sick (Mark 1:30; 2:4; Luke 5:25; John 5:3; Acts 9:33; 28:8). To lie down, recline in order to eat, the same as *anákeimai* (345), to lean at the table (Mark 2:15; 14:3; Luke 5:29; 1 Cor 8:10).

Syn.: *káthēmai* (2521), to sit; *kataklínomai* (2625), to recline, to sit down; *anaklínomai* (347), to sit down, lean back; *kathízō* (2523), to make to sit down, trans., and to sit down, intrans.; *parakathízō* (3869), to sit down, beside; *anapíptō* (377), to fall back, to recline for a meal; *kathézomai* (2516), to sit down.

Ant.: *anakathízō* (339), to set up, sit up, intrans., of two who are raised from the dead; *hístēmi* (2476), to stand; *anístēmi* (450), to arise; *stḗkō* (4739), to stand fast; *egeírō* (1453), to raise, arise.

2622. κατακλάω *katakláō*; contracted *kataklṓ*, fut. *kataklásō*, from *katá* (2596), an intens., and *kláō* (2806), to break. To break in pieces (Mark 6:41; Luke 9:16).

Syn.: *katágnumi* (2608), to break in pieces.

Ant.: *sullégō* (4816), to gather together; *sunágō* (4863), to collect.

2623. κατακλείω *katakleíō*; fut. *katakleísō*, from *katá* (2596), an intens., and *kleíō* (2808), to shut. To shut up as in prison, to confine (Luke 3:20; Acts 26:10; Sept.: Jer 39:3).

Syn.: *phrássō* (5420), to fence, enclose; *sugkleíō* (4788), to enclose; *apokleíō* (608), to enclose.

Ant.: *anoígō* (455), to open up; *eleutheróō* (1659), to deliver; *aphíēmi* (863), to let go; *apolúō* (630), to dismiss; *lúō* (3089), to loose.

2624. κατακληροδοτέω *kataklērodotéō*; contracted *kataklērodotṓ*, fut. *kataklērodotḗso*, from *katá* (2596), according to, a distributive, and *klērodotéō* (n.f.), to distribute by lot, which is from *klḗros* (2819), part, lot, and *dídōmi* (1325), to give. To distribute by, or according to lot or for an inheritance (Acts 13:19 [TR]). In some Sept. MSS, *kataklēronoméō* (Num 33:54; Josh 14:1; 18:2), to inherit down from an ancestor. The verb *kataklērṓ*, which in Class. Gr. is equivalent to *kataklērodotéō* or *kataklēronoméō*, embraces the two meanings, to distribute or to receive by lot. See Deut 21:16; Josh 19:51.

Syn.: *diairéō* (1244), to divide into parts, distribute; *diadídōmi* (1239), to distribute; *merízō* (3307), to divide into parts; *diamerízō* (1266), to divide completely; *dianémō* (1268), to disseminate.

Ant.: *sunágō* (4863), to gather or bring together; *episunágō* (1996), to gather together upon one place; *sullégō* (4816), to collect, gather up; *sunathroízō* (4867), to gather together.

2625. κατακλίνω *kataklínō*; fut. *kataklínō*, from *katá* (2596), down, and *klínō* (2827), to incline or recline, to bend, lie sloping towards, bow. To make to incline or to lie down. In the NT, only of the oriental posture at meals, to make to recline; trans. mid. *kataklínomai*, to recline at a meal (Luke 9:14; 14:8; 24:30). Same as *anákeimai* (345), to sit at the table.

Syn.: *káthēmai* (2521), to sit down; *katákeimai* (2621), to lie down or recline at a meal; *kathízō* (2523), trans. meaning to make to sit down, or intrans. meaning to sit down; *kathézomai* (2516), to sit.

Ant.: *anístēmi* (450), to arise.

2626. κατακλύζω *kataklúzō*; fut. *kataklúsō*, from *katá* (2596), an intens., and *klúzō* (n.f.), to dash, dash away, flood. To dash down upon, to overflow, flood (2 Pet 3:6; Sept.: Job 14:19; Jer 47:2). Also from *klúzō* (n.f.): *klúdōn* (2830), a tempest.

Deriv.: *kataklusmós* (2627), inundation, flood.

Ant.: *xēraínō* (3583), to dry up.

2627. κατακλυσμός *kataklusmós*; gen. *kataklusmoú*, masc. noun from *kataklúzō* (2626), to flood or overflow. A flood, deluge. Spoken of the flood of Noah's time (Matt 24:38, 39; Luke 17:27; 2 Pet 2:5; Sept.: Gen 6:17; 7:6ff.).

Syn.: *plēmmúra* (4132), a flood of a sea or river.

2628. κατακολουθέω *katakolouthéō*; contracted *katakolouthṓ*, fut. *katakolouthḗsō* from *katá* (2596), an intens., and *akolouthéō* (190), to follow. To follow closely (Acts 16:17), with the dat. (Luke 23:55).

Syn.: *parakolouthéō* (3877), to follow closely; *diṓkō* (1377), to follow, pursue; *katadiṓkō* (2614), to follow up or closely.

Ant.: *kataleípō* (2641), to leave behind; *egkataleípō* (1459), to forsake, abandon; *aphíēmi* (863), to forsake or leave; *apotássō* (657), to bid farewell or take one's leave; *hupoleípō* (5275), to leave behind; *perileípō* (4035), to remain;

aspázomai (782), to embrace, salute, take leave of someone.

2629. κατακόπτω *katakóptō*; fut. *katakópsō*, from *katá* (2596), an intens., and *kóptō* (2875), to cut. To hew or cut down, to cut in pieces. In the NT, to beat, cut, wound, trans. in Mark 5:5.

Syn.: *diapríō* (1282), to saw asunder; *dichotoméō* (1371), to cut into two parts.

Ant.: *kolláō* (2853), to glue, join; *proskolláō* (4347), to glue to, adhere; *sundéō* (4887), to bind with; *sunágō* (4863), to gather or bring together.

2630. κατακρημνίζω *katakrēmnízō*; fut. *katakrēmnísō*, from *katá* (2596), an intens., and *krēmnós* (2911), precipice, steep place. To cast down from a precipice, cast down headlong, trans. (Luke 4:29; Sept.: 2 Chr 25:12).

Syn.: *rhíptō* (4496), to throw off or down; *katalúō* (2647), to disintegrate or to throw down; *katabállō* (2598), to cast down; *kathairéō* (2507), to demolish, destroy; *katabibázō* (2601), to thrust or bring down.

Ant.: *hupsóō* (5312), to lift up; *egeírō* (1453), to raise up; *aírō* (142), to take up; *epaírō* (1869), to lift up; *anístēmi* (450), to raise up; *anorthóō* (461), to set upright; *anakúptō* (352), to lift oneself up.

2631. κατάκριμα *katákrima*; gen. *katakrímatos*, neut. noun from *katakrínō* (2632), to condemn. The suffix *-ma* makes it the result of judgment. A decision against someone, a condemnatory judgment. Only in Rom 5:16, 18; 8:1. In verse sixteen, contrast *dikaíōma* (1345), the right given to the believer as a result of his acknowledgment of the lordship of God in his life. In verse eighteen *katákrima* contrasted with a more definite *dikaíōsis* (1347), the act of making life righteous; therefore, a judgment of condemnation in the sense of the economy of redemption.

Syn.: *kríma* (2917), the verdict or sentence pronounced, condemnation; *krísis* (2920), the process of investigation in the execution of justice; *katákrisis* (2633), the process of judging which leads to condemnation.

Ant.: *dikaíōsis* (1347), acquittal, the process of pronouncing not guilty or justified; *dikaíōma* (1345), righteous deed; *dikaiosúnē* (1343), righteousness.

2632. κατακρίνω *katakrínō*; fut. *katakrinṓ*; from *katá* (2596), against, and *krínō* (2919), to judge. To pronounce sentence against, condemn, adjudge guilty.

(I) Followed by the acc. of person and the dat., of punishment (Matt 20:18, "they shall condemn him to death"; Mark 10:33; 2 Pet 2:6); by the acc. of person and inf. (Mark 14:64); by the acc. of person, the crime or punishment being implied (John 8:10, 11; Rom 2:1). Used in an absolute sense (Rom 8:34; pass. in Matt 27:3). Of the last judgment (Mark 16:16; 1 Cor 11:32). Figuratively (Rom 8:3, condemned or passed sentence upon all carnal lusts and passions, in antithesis to Rom 8:1 [cf. Rom 6:1ff.]).

(II) By implication, to condemn by contrast, i.e., to show by one's good conduct that others are guilty of misconduct and deserve condemnation, followed by the acc. (Matt 12:41, 42; Luke 11:31, 32; Heb 11:7). Pass. in Rom 14:23.

(III) Temporal punishment (Matt 20:18; 27:3; John 8:10, 11).

Deriv.: *akatákritos* (178), without trial, uncondemned; *autokatákritos* (843), self-condemned; *katákrima* (2631), condemnation; *katákrisis* (2633), the act of condemning

Syn.: *kataginṓskō* (2607), to know something against, to condemn; *katadikázō* (2613), to exercise the right of law against someone, to pronounce judgment, condemn.

Ant.: *dikaióō* (1344), to pronounce innocent or justified.

2633. κατάκρισις *katákrisis*; gen. *katakríseōs* fem. noun from *katakrínō* (2632), to condemn. Condemnation against someone. *Katákrisis*, the act of condemnation or the doing of it, must

be distinguished from *katákrima* (2631), which is the actual condemnation or the judgment itself (2 Cor 3:9; 7:3, censure, blame).

2634. κατακυριεύω *katakurieúō*; fut. *katakurieúsō*, from *katá* (2596), an intens., and *kurieúō* (2961), to have dominion over. To rule over, exercise authority, with the gen. (Matt 20:25; Mark 10:42; 1 Pet 5:3; Sept.: Ps 19:13; Jer 3:14). By implication, to get the mastery of, overpower, subdue (Acts 19:16; Sept.: Gen 1:28; Num 32:29).

Syn.: *authentéō* (831), to exercise absolute authority; *nikáō* (3528), to overcome; *kurieúō* (2961), to exercise lordship.

Ant.: *doulóō* (1403), to serve as a slave; *diakonéō* (1247), to serve, minister; *hupotássō* (5293), to submit.

2635. καταλαλέω *katalaléō*; contracted *katalalṓ*, fut. *katalalḗsō*, from *katá* (2596), against, and *laléō* (2980), to speak. To speak against, to speak evil of (James 4:11; 1 Pet 2:12; 3:16).

Deriv.: *katalalía* (2636), backbiting, defamation; *katálalos* (2637), a backbiter.

Syn.: *katēgoréō* (2723), to accuse; *egkaléō* (1458), to accuse in court; *elégchō* (1651), to rebuke; *sukophantéō* (4811), to accuse falsely; *kataginṓskō* (2607), to blame, condemn; *mémphomai* (3201), to find fault; *krínō* (2919), to judge; *diabállō* (1225), to falsely accuse; *kakologéō* (2551), to speak evil; *blasphēméō* (987), to blaspheme, revile.

Ant.: *ainéō* (134), to speak in praise of; *epainéō* (1867), to commend; *eulogéō* (2127), to speak well of, bless; *humnéō* (5214), to laud; *dikaióō* (1344), to justify.

2636. καταλαλία *katalalía*; gen. *katalalías*, fem. noun from *katalaléō* (2635), to speak evil of. Evil-speaking, slander (2 Cor 12:20; 1 Pet 2:1). The related noun used of persons is *katálalos* (2637), backbiter.

Syn.: *blasphēmía* (988), blasphemy, evil speaking, railing; *dusphēmía* (1426), defamation; *katákrisis* (2633), condemnation; *momphḗ* (3437), blame; *katēgoría* (2724), accusation; *égklēma* (1462), accusation, indictment; *élegchos* (1650), conviction, reproof.

Ant.: *euphēmía* (2162), euphemy, speaking well of; *eulogía* (2129), speaking well of; *aínos* (136), praise; *épainos* (1868), commendation, praise; *dikaíōsis* (1347), justification.

2637. κατάλαλος katálalos; gen. *katalálou*, masc.-fem., neut. *katálalon*, adj., from *katalaléō* (2635)to speak against. Slanderous. Used as a subst., a slanderer, backbiter (Rom 1:30).
Syn.: *kritikós* (2924), critical; *blásphēmos* (989), blasphemer; *katḗgoros* (2725), accuser; *hubristḗs* (5197), insulter; *diábolos* (1228), devil, slanderer.

2638. καταλαμβάνω katalambánō; fut. *katalḗpsomai*, from *katá* (2596), an intens., and *lambánō* (2983), to take. To apprehend, attain, obtain, find.
(I) To lay hold of, seize, with eagerness, suddenness (John 8:3, 4). Of an evil spirit which seizes, takes possession of a person (Mark 9:18). Figuratively of darkness or evil, to come suddenly upon someone (John 12:35; 1 Thess 5:4; Sept.: Gen 19:19; 31:23; 1 Kgs 18:44).
(II) In allusion to the public games, to obtain the prize with the idea of eager and strenuous exertion, to grasp, seize upon (Rom 9:30; 1 Cor 9:24; Phil 3:12, 13, "for which very end I also have been taken hold of by Christ" [a.t.], v. 12).
(III) Figuratively, to seize with the mind, to comprehend (John 1:5, the darkness did not admit or receive the light [cf. John 1:10–12; 3:19]). The darkness is here presented as being so thick that the light could not penetrate it. In the mid. to comprehend for oneself, perceive, find, followed by *hóti* (3754), that (Acts 4:13; 10:34); by the inf. and its subject (Acts 25:25); by *ti* (5101), what (Eph 3:18).

Syn.: *piázō* (4084), to seize; *phthánō* (5348), to attain; *ktáomai* (2932), to gain, acquire; *kratéō* (2902), to get possession of, to hold; *heurískō* (2147), to find; *ginṓskō* (1097), to know by experience and observation; *epiginṓskō* (1921), to gain full knowledge; *aisthánomai* (143) to understand, perceive through the senses; *noéō* (3539), to perceive with the mind; *katanoéō* (2657), to perceive fully; *aírō* (142), to take up or away; *harpázō* (726), to catch; *katéchō* (2722), to possess; *epéchō* (1907), to hold, retain.
Ant.: *kataleípō* (2641), to leave behind; *agnoéō* (50), to be ignorant of; *apōthéomai* (683), to cast away; *aporríptō* (641), to reject; *apostréphomai* (654), to turn away from; *apodokimázō* (593), to disapprove; *aphíēmi* (863), to leave alone, forsake.

2639. καταλέγω katalégō; fut. *kataléxō*, from *katá* (2596), to or with, and *légō* (3004), to choose, conclude as a result of exercising discernment, intellectual power. To lay down; in the mid. meaning to lay apart from others, to select. In the NT, to lay down to or among others, i.e., to include in a list or a number, to enroll. Pass. in 1 Tim 5:9.
Syn.: *apográphō* (583), to enroll, inscribe as in a register; *stratologéō* (4758), to enlist in the army, to choose to be a soldier.
Ant.: *aporríptō* (641), to reject.

2640. κατάλειμμα katáleimma; gen. *kataleímmatos*, neut. noun from *kataleípō* (2641), to leave down or behind, abandon. A remnant (Rom 9:27 quoted from Isa 10:22 referring to Israel).
Syn.: *leímma* (3005), a remnant; *loipós* (3063), the rest; *katáleimma* (2640), remnant; *perísseuma* (4051), that which remains over, a surplus, a superabundance; *katáloipos* (2645), remaining.

2641. καταλείπω kataleípō; fut. *kataleípsō*, from *katá* (2596), an intens., and *leípō* (3007), to leave behind. To forsake, leave, reserve.

(I) To leave behind at death (Mark 12:19; Luke 20:31; Sept.: Deut 28:54). Generally, in any place, trans. (Mark 14:52; John 8:9). Followed by *en* (1722), in, with the dat. of place (Luke 15:4; 1 Thess 3:1; Titus 1:5); by *autoú* (847), there (Acts 18:19); by *eis Hádou* (*eis* [1519], unto; *Hádou* [86], Hades [acc.]), in Hades (Acts 2:31); by the acc. and predicate of condition (Acts 24:27, "forsook Paul bound" [a.t.]; 25:14; Sept.: Gen 39:12, 13).

(II) In the sense of to leave, to abandon, forsake, equivalent to *leípō* (3007), to leave but stronger. Of place (Matt 4:13; Heb 11:27). By implication (Acts 21:3; Sept.: 1 Sam 31:7). Hence of person, to leave, forsake utterly (Matt 16:4; 19:5; 21:17; Mark 10:7; Eph 5:31); of things, to leave behind, abandon (Luke 5:28, all; Acts 6:2; 2 Pet 2:15; Sept.: Gen 2:24; 44:22; Deut 31:17). With the predicate *mónos* (3441), alone (Luke 10:40).

(III) To leave remaining, equivalent to have left, to reserve (Rom 11:4 quoted from 1 Kgs 19:18). In the pass. (Heb 4:1).

Deriv.: *egkataleípō* (1459), to leave behind; *katáleimma* (2640), a remnant, residue.

Syn.: *egkataleípō* (1459), to leave behind, forsake, abandon; *aphíēmi* (863), to separate from someone; *apotássō* (657), to send away; *apoleípō* (620), to leave behind; *hupoleípō* (5275), remain; *perileípō* (4035), to survive; *hupolimpánō* (5277), to leave.

Ant.: *kratéō* (2902), to seize or retain, keep; *katéchō* (2722), to hold fast.

2642. καταλιθάζω *katalitházō*; fut. *katalitháso*, from *katá* (2596), an intens., and *litházo* (3034), to stone. To stone to death. Used trans. in Luke 20:6 (cf. Ex 17:4; Num 14:10).

Syn.: *lithoboléō* (3036), to stone or cast stones.

2643. καταλλαγή *katallagé*; gen. *katallagés*, fem. noun from *katallássō* (2644), to reconcile. Reconciliation, restoration,

exchange. A change or reconciliation from a state of enmity between persons to one of friendship. Between God and man it is the result of the *apolútrōsis* (629), redemption, the divine act of salvation, the ceasing of God's wrath. In the NT, it means reconciliation, i.e., restoration to divine favor by bringing about a change in man, conversion (Rom 5:11; 11:15), the means or occasion of reconciling the world to God.

Syn.: *apokatástasis* (605), restoration.

2644. καταλλάσσω *katallássō*, **καταλλάττω** *katalláttō*; fut. *katalláxō*, from *katá* (2596), an intens., and *allássō* (236), to change. To reconcile. Used of the divine work of redemption denoting that act of redemption insofar as God Himself is concerned by taking upon Himself our sin and becoming an atonement. Thus a relationship of peace with mankind is established which was hitherto prevented by the demands of His justice. In *katallássō*, God is the subject, man the object. While *hilasmós* (2434), propitiation (1 John 2:2; 4:10) and *hiláskomai* (2433), to make reconciliation (Luke 18:13; Heb 2:17), aim at averting God's wrath; *katallássō* implies God has laid aside or withdrawn His wrath. In the NT, spoken of the change that God makes in man through conversion so that he may be reconciled to the holy God (2 Cor 5:18, 19; 2d aor. pass. imper. *katallágēte*, "be ye reconciled to God," 2 Cor 5:20). In 1 Cor 7:11, *katallássō* is used in the matter of marital relationships. If a wife decides to leave her husband for reasons other than his unfaithfulness, she should remain unmarried. But in case there is the necessary change in him, she should then be reconciled to him. The change here is in the one at fault just as man is at fault in the case of the God-Man relationship (2 Cor 5:18, 19).

Deriv.: *apokatallássō* (604), to reconcile fully; *katallagé* (2643), reconciliation.

Syn.: *diallássō* (1259), to reconcile when the fault may lie on the part of both parties concerned; *apokatallássō* (604), to reconcile completely and change from one condition to another; *apokathístēmi* (600) or *apokathistṓ*, to restore, reclaim.

Ant.: *apodokimázō* (593), to reject, disapprove; *paraitéomai* (3868), to refuse; *aporríptō* (641), to reject.

2645. κατάλοιπος *katáloipos*; gen. *kataloípou*, masc.-fem., neut. *katáloipon*, adj. from *katá* (2596) and *loipós* (3062), remnant. Left over or behind, remaining. In the pl., the rest, residue (Acts 15:17 quoted from Amos 9:12).

2646. κατάλυμα *katáluma*; gen. *katalúmatos*, neut. noun from *katalúō* (2647), to unloose. A lodging place or inn. It was so-called because of the ancient travelers who on arrival loosened their own belts or girdles, sandals, and the saddles or harnesses of their animals. In the ancient Greek writings, the place of entertainment is called *katáluma*, where animals and burdens are loosened. See Sept.: Ex 4:24. Guests were highly regarded in biblical times (Judg 19:9, 15). *Katáluma* was also a guest chamber (Mark 14:14; Luke 2:7; 22:11), a dining room where the guests loosened their sandals before they sat down to eat. In the East it is called *khan* or *caravanserai*.

Syn.: *pandocheíon* (3829), a place where all are received, comparable to an inn; in Luke 10:34, a place where beasts and cattle could also be sheltered as travelers usually used such places for that purpose.

2647. καταλύω *katalúō*; fut. *katalúsō*, from *katá* (2596), an intens., and *lúō* (3089), to loose. To loose or unloose what was before bound or fastened as used in Class. Gr. To refresh oneself, to lodge or be a guest (Luke 9:12; 19:7; Sept.: Gen 24:23, 25; 42:27; 43:21). It properly refers to travelers loosening their own burdens or those of their animals when they stayed at a house on a journey (Luke 9:12). To dissolve, demolish, destroy, or throw down as a building or its materials

(Matt 24:2; 26:61; 27:40; Mark 13:2; 14:58; 15:29; Luke 21:6; Acts 6:14); as the law and the prophets (Matt 5:17); as a work (Acts 5:38, 39; Rom 14:20; Gal 2:18). Figuratively, of the body (2 Cor 5:1).

Deriv.: *akatálutos* (179), indissoluble; *katáluma* (2646), lodging place.

Syn.: *katargéō* (2673), to abolish; *phtheírō* (5351), to corrupt, destroy; *diaphtheírō* (1311), to utterly destroy; *analískō* (355), to destroy, consume; *apóllumi* (622), to destroy; *aulízomai* (835), to lodge in a courtyard or in the open; *kataskēnóō* (2681), to pitch one's tent; *xenízō* (3579), to receive as a guest; *katastréphō* (2690), to overthrow, ruin; *anatrépō* (396), to turn over, upset; *kathairéō* (2507), to put down; *katastrṓnnumi* (2693), to spread out; *erēmóō* (2049), to make desolate; *katakrēmnízō* (2630), to throw over a precipice or down; *akuróō* (208), to invalidate, disannul; *dialúō* (1262), to dissolve utterly, scatter; *anairéō* (337), to abolish.

Ant.: *oikodoméō* (3618), to build; *anoikodoméō* (456), to build again; *epoikodoméō* (2026), to build upon; *apokathístēmi* (600), to restore; *katartízō* (2675), to mend, restore; *kuróō* (2964), to ratify, confirm.; *kathístēmi* (2525), to constitute, establish; *ktízō* (2936), to create; *kataskeuázō* (2680), to build, construct.

2648. καταμανθάνω *katamanthánō*; fut. *katamathḗsomai*, from *katá* (2596), an intens., and *manthánō* (3129), to learn, understand. To learn thoroughly, fully. In the NT, to note accurately, observe, consider, with the acc. (Matt 6:28; Sept.: Gen 34:1; Lev 14:36).

Syn.: *epiginṓskō* (1921), to know or perceive fully; *epístamai* (1987), to concentrate the mind upon, comprehend.

Ant.: *agnoéō* (50), not to know or understand.

2649. καταμαρτυρέω *katamarturéō*; contracted *katamarturṓ*, fut. *katamarturḗsō*, from *katá* (2596) against, and *marturéō* (3140), to bear witness. To witness or testify against someone (Matt

26:62; 27:13; Mark 14:60; 15:4; Sept.: 1 Kgs 20:10, 13; Job 15:6).

Syn.: *katēgoréō* (2723), to accuse; *epikrínō* (1948), to adjudge; *kakologéō* (2551), to speak evil of; *katalaléō* (2635), to speak against; *diabállō* (1225), to falsely accuse; *egkaléō* (1458), to indict; *elégchō* (1651), to rebuke; *sukophantéō* (4811), to speak false information; *kataginṓskō* (2607), to condemn; *mémphomai* (3201), to blame.

Ant.: *amúnō* (292), to defend; *apologéomai* (626), to answer, respond.

2650. καταμένω *kataménō*; fut. *katamenṓ*, from *katá* (2596), an intens., and *ménō* (3306), to remain. To remain fixed, abide, dwell, used intrans. (Acts 1:13; Sept.: Num 20:1; Josh 2:22).

Syn.: *diateléō* (1300), to continue; *paraménō* (3887), to continue to remain; *diaménō* (1265), to remain, continue; *epiménō* (1961), to tarry; *diatríbō* (1304), to abide, continue; *emménō* (1696), to continue, persevere; *hupoménō* (5278), to endure, bear up; *apókeimai* (606), to be laid up; *katoikéō* (2730), to settle down in a dwelling.

Ant.: *astatéō* (790), to wander about, to have no fixed place to live; *kataskēnóō* (2681), to pitch one's tent, and the basic verb *skēnóō* (4637), to pitch a tent; *paroikéō* (3939), to sojourn, remain temporarily in a place.

2651. καταμόνας *katamónas*; adv. from *katá* (2596), in, at, and *mónos* (3441), sole or single. Alone, by oneself (Mark 4:10; Luke 9:18).

Syn.: *kat' idían* (*katá* [2596], by; *ídios* [2398], one's own), by oneself; *aph' heautoú* (*apó* [575], from; *heautoú* (1438), oneself), by oneself.

Ant.: *homoú* (3674), in connection with, together; *homothumadón* (3661), gathered together; *pamplētheí* (3826), all together, simultaneously; *allélous* (240), together; *met' allélōn* (*metá* [3326], with), with one another.

2652. κατανάθεμα *katanáthema*; gen. *katanathématos*, neut. noun from *katá* (2596), an intens., and *anáthema* (331), a curse. A curse against someone, equivalent to *anáthema*, but stronger. By metonymy, accursed thing, one accursed (Rev 22:3 [UBS has *katáthema*]). Verb: *katanathematízō* (2653), to curse.

Syn.: *ará* (685), cursing; *katára* (2671), a great curse.

Ant.: *eulogía* (2129), blessing, a speaking well of; *chrēstología* (5542), smooth talk; *makarismós* (3108), an ascription of blessing or being blessed; *makários* (3107), inwardly satisfied because of God's presence.

2653. καταναθεματίζω *katanathematízō*; fut. *katanathematísō*, from *katá* (2596), an intens., and *anathematízō* (332), to bind with an oath. To utter curses against, to curse, equivalent to *anathematízō*, but stronger (Matt 26:74 [TR]). In other MSS, it is *katathematízō*.

Syn.: *kataráomai* (2672), to wish evil against someone or something; *kakologéō* (2551), to speak evil.

Ant.: *eulogéō* (2127), to bless, speak well of.

2654. καταναλίσκω *katanalískō*; fut. *katanalṓsō*, from *katá* (2596), an intens., and *analískō* (355), to consume. To consume wholly, as by fire (Heb 12:29; Sept.: Lev 6:3; Deut 4:24).

Syn.: *aphanízō* (853), to cause to disappear; *dapanáō* (1159), to waste; *katakaíō* (2618), to burn up.

Ant.: *diasṓzō* (1295), to bring safely through; *ekpheúgō* (1628), to flee out of a place; *phulássō* (5442), to keep, preserve.

2655. καταναρκάω *katanarkáō*; contracted *katanarkṓ*, fut. *katanarkḗsō*, from *katá* (2596), against, and *narkáō* (n.f.), to be numb. To become numb or apathetic toward someone, to be indifferent to another's damage, to be burdensome or a dead weight to someone in a pecuniary sense (2 Cor 11:9; 12:13, 14).

Syn.: *baréō* (916), to be heavy; *epibaréō* (1912), to burden heavily; *katabaréō* (2599), to weigh down.

Ant.: *boēthéō* (997), to come to the aid of someone; *antilambánomai* (482), to help, support; *antéchomai* (472), to support, hold.

2656. κατανεύω *kataneúō*; fut. *kataneúsō*, from *katá* (2596), downwards, and *neúō* (3506), to nod, beckon. To make signs to someone with the head or eyes, to beckon (Luke 5:7).
Syn.: *kataseiō* (2678), to shake the hand or wave in beckoning.

2657. κατανοέω *katanoéō*; contracted *katanoō̄*, fut. *katanoésō*, from *katá* (2596), an intens., and *noéō* (3539), to think. To observe, notice, consider, contemplate (Matt 7:3; Luke 6:41; 12:24, 27; 20:23; Acts 7:31, 32; 11:6; 27:39; Rom 4:19, to have respect to, regard; Heb 3:1; 10:24; James 1:23, 24; Sept.: Num 32:8, 9; Isa 5:12).
Syn.: *katamanthánō* (2648), to learn thoroughly or consider accurately; *epiginóskō* (1921), to perceive fully; *theōréō* (2334), discern; *katalambánō* (2638), to apprehend, comprehend, perceive.
Ant.: *parakoúō* (3878), to disobey.

2658. καταντάω *katantáō*; contracted *katantō̄*, fut. *katantḗsō*, from *katá* (2596), an intens., and *antáō* (n.f., see below), to meet. To arrive at a place (Acts 16:1; 18:19, 24; 20:15), to come to, attain (Acts 26:7; Eph 4:13; Phil 3:11). Of things to come or be brought to someone (1 Cor 14:36). To come upon, to occur in the time of someone (1 Cor 10:11).
Deriv. of *antáō* (n.f.), to meet: *apantáō* (528), to encounter; *sunantáō* (4876), to come together; *hupantáō* (5221), to encounter, chance upon.
Syn.: *paragínomai* (3854), to come near; *phthánō* (5348), to attain, reach to; *katalambánō* (2638), to seize, apprehend, attain; *tugchánō* (5177), to obtain, reach; *érchomai* (2064), to come; *epérchomai* (1904), to come upon; *hḗkō* (2240), to

come, be present; *aphiknéomai* (864), to arrive at a place; *enístēmi* (1764), to settle in; *proseggízō* (4331), to approach.
Ant.: *apérchomai* (565), to depart.

2659. κατάνυξις *katánuxis*; gen. *katanúxeōs*, fem. noun from *katanússō* (2660), to prick, pierce, stab. A piercing through, penetrating, especially of sleep or slumber, stupefying, hence the condition, stupor, slumber, dullness (Rom 11:8; Sept.: Ps 60:3; Isa 29:10). To be silent, dumb (Lev 10:3; Ps 4:4; Dan 10:9, 15).
Syn.: *lḗthē* (3024), forgetfulness; *húpnos* (5258), sleep.
Ant.: *égersis* (1454), a resurgence, arousal; *anástasis* (386), resurrection; *paroxusmós* (3948), excitement, provocation in a good or bad sense.

2660. κατανύσσω *katanússō*; **κατανύττω** *katanúttō*, fut. *katanúxō*, from *katá* (2596), an intens., and *nússō* (3572), to prick, pierce. To prick through, pierce. Used in the pass. metaphorically meaning to be greatly pained or deeply moved (Acts 2:37; Sept.: Ps 109:16).
Deriv.: *katánuxis* (2659), a piercing through, slumber.
Syn.: *diüknéomai* (1338), to penetrate or pierce, as the word of God.
Ant.: *diegeírō* (1326), to awaken someone from sleep; *eknéphō* (1594), to become sober, wake up.

2661. καταξιόω *kataxióō*; contracted *kataxiō̄*, fut. *kataxiṓsō* from *katá* (2596), an intens., and *axióō* (515), to think worthy, fit. To count worthy of something. In the NT, only in the pass. meaning to be counted worthy (Luke 20:35; 21:36; Acts 5:41; 2 Thess 1:5).
Syn.: *hikanóō* (2427), to enable; *endunamóō* (1743), to empower.
Ant.: *exouthenéō* (1848), to make of no account, despise.

2662. καταπατέω *katapatéō*; contracted *katapatō̄*, fut. *katapatḗsō*, from *katá* (2596), an intens., and *patéō* (3961), to tread. To tread or trample upon (Luke 12:1), to tread underfoot (Matt 5:13; 7:6; Luke 8:5; Sept.: 2 Chr 25:18; Ezek 34:18), to trample underfoot in a figurative sense, to treat with the utmost contempt and indignity (Heb 10:29).

Syn.: *laktízō* (2979), to kick.

Ant.: *epainéō* (1867), to praise.

2663. κατάπαυσις *katápausis*; gen. *katapaúseōs*, fem. noun from *katapaúō* (2664), to make to cease. The act of resting, ceasing from labor, or the place of rest, dwelling, fixed abode. Used as a dwelling in Acts 7:49 in allusion to a temple, quoted from Isa 66:1. See Ps 132:14 where God is represented as searching through the earth and selecting Zion as His dwelling place. Also of the rest and quiet abode of the Israelites in the promised land after their wanderings (Heb 3:11 quoted from Ps 95:11; Heb 3:18; 4:3, 5, the rest which God promised, see Deut 12:9, 10). Hence, figuratively, the quiet abode of those who will dwell with God in heaven, in allusion to the Sabbath rest. (Heb 4:1, 3, 10, 11).

Syn.: *hēsuchía* (2271), quietness; *scholḗ* (4981), loitering, leisure; *anápsuxis* (403), recovery of breath, revival; *anápausis* (372), not primarily the cessation of work with the resultant rest, but the restoration of lost strength and inner rest experienced simultaneously in the work.

Ant.: *tarachḗ* (5016), disturbance, trouble; *thórubos* (2351), a disturbance, uproar; *stásis* (4714), a popular uprising; *ergasía* (2039), work; *kópos* (2873), toil.

2664. καταπαύω *katapaúō*; fut. *katapaúsō*, from *katá* (2596), an intens., and *paúō* (3973), to make to cease. To make to cease.

(I) Trans., to cause to rest, give rest (Heb 4:8 [cf. Heb 4:1, 9]; Sept.: Josh 1:13, 15; 22:4).

(II) To restrain (Acts 14:18; Sept.: Job 26:12; Ps 85:3).

(III) Intrans., to rest entirely (Heb 4:4, 10; Sept.: Gen 2:2, 3; 49:33; Ex 31:17).

Deriv.: *akatápaustos* (180), incessant; *katápausis* (2663), cessation from work, rest.

Syn.: *anapaúō* (373), to rest inwardly, but not necessarily from a cessation of work as is expressed by *katapaúō*; *aníēmi* (447), to rest from endurance and suffering or persecution by intervention from above; *anapsúchō* (404), to cool, refresh; *kopázō* (2869), to relax from toil, to cease raging; *hēsucházō* (2270), to be quiet, still, at rest; *dialeípō* (1257), to pause awhile, intermit, desist, cease.

Ant.: *parateínō* (3905), to extend, stretch; *ochléō* (3791), to vex; *enochléō* (1776), to crowd in, trouble; *skúllō* (4660), to trouble, harass; *tarássō* (5015), to stir, agitate; *thorubéō* (2350), to disturb, make a noise, cause an uproar; *exegeírō* (1825), to rouse fully.

2665. καταπέτασμα *katapétasma*; gen. *katapetásmatos*, neut. noun from *katapetánnumi* (n.f.), to expand from. A veil. In the NT used for the veil of the tabernacle and temple which separated the holy place or sanctuary from the Holy of Holies (Matt 27:51; Mark 15:38; Luke 23:45; Heb 6:19; 9:3). This veil was a type of the flesh or body of Christ (Heb 10:19, 20), and accordingly, at the moment when He breathed His last, this veil was rent in the midst from the top to the bottom. Further, as the Holy of Holies was a type or figure of that heaven wherein God dwells (Heb 6:19; 9:12, 24), the expression "within the veil" means into heaven (Heb 6:19). In front of the doorway to the Hekhal, or Holy Place, of the temple built by Herod hung a beautifully colored Babylonian curtain or veil. The inner area of the Hekhal was forty cubits long, twenty cubits broad and sixty cubits high (a cubit is approximately 18 inches). It contained the altar of incense in the middle, the table of shewbread on the north, and the lampstand on the south. Only the officiating priest could enter this room to bring in the incense morning and evening, to trim the lamps daily, and to replace the shewbread every Sabbath. Between the Hekhal and the Devir, or Holiest Place, hung two curtains with a cubit's space between them. On the Day of Atonement, the high priest entered the Devir with his censer by going to the south side, passing between the curtains to the north side, and thus entering into the Holiest Place. The Gospels refer to these as one veil (*katapétasma* [2665]) which was rent at the time of Jesus' crucifixion (Luke 23:45), indicating that the intercessory priest and blood sacrifices were no longer necessary and that the believers could have direct access to God through the sacrifice of His Son. The Devir was empty and entered by the high priest only once a year upon the Day of Atonement.

Syn.: *kálumma* (2571), a covering such as the veil; *peribólaion* (4018), a veil worn over the head.

2666. καταπίνω *katapínō*; fut. *katapíomai*, from *katá* (2596), down, and *pínō* (4095), to drink. To swallow as in drinking, whether in a natural or figurative sense (Matt 23:24; 1 Cor 15:54; 2 Cor 2:7; 5:4; Heb 11:29; 1 Pet 5:8; Rev 12:16).

Syn.: *esthíō* (2068), to eat up, devour; *katesthíō* (2719) and *kataphágō*, to consume by eating, to devour, metaphorically to squander, waste.

Ant.: *ptúō* (4429), to spit; *ekptúō* (1609), to spit out; *eméō* (1692), vomit, spew.

2667. καταπίπτω *katapíptō*; fut. *katapesoúmai*, from *katá* (2596), down, and *píptō* (4098), to fall. To fall down, to prostrate oneself (Acts 26:14; 28:6; Sept.: Ps 145:14).

Syn.: *tapeinóō* (5013), to humble; *kámptō* (2578), to bend.

Ant.: *hupsóō* (5312), to exalt, lift up; *epaírō* (1869), to raise or lift up.

2668. καταπλέω *katapléō*; fut. *katapleúsō*, from *katá* (2596), down, and *pléō* (4126), to sail. To sail down as from the high sea to land, to sail to a place, to come by ship (Luke 8:26).

Syn.: *katágō* (2609), to moor a vessel; *paragínomai* (3854), to arrive; *parabállō* (3846), to come or arrive alongside; *phthánō* (5348), to arrive.

Ant.: *apopléō* (636), to sail away; *ekpléō* (1602), to sail from; *parapléō* (3896), to sail by; *diapléō* (1277), to sail across; *hupopléō* (5284), to sail under; *anágō* (321), to lead up; *paralégomai* (mid. of *paralégō* [3881]), to sail past, coast alongside; *diaperáō* (1276), to cross over by sailing; *braduploéō* (1020), to sail slowly.

2669. καταπονέω *kataponéō*; contracted *kataponṓ*, fut. *kataponésō*, from *katá* (2596), an intens., and *ponéō* (n.f.), to labor, which is from *pónos* (4192), pain, toil. To wear out or down by labor. In the pass. *kataponéomai*, to be vexed, weary, oppressed, afflicted (Acts 7:24; 2 Pet 2:7).

Syn.: *basanízō* (928), to torment; *skúllō* (4660), to trouble, annoy; *stenochōréō* (4729), to cause anguish; *katadunasteúō* (2616), to oppress; *ochléomai* (3791), to be troubled, especially by evil spirits; *enochléō* (1776), to trouble; *tarássō* (5015), to trouble; *adēmonéō* (85), to be in distress; *thorubéomai* (2350), to be disturbed, troubled; *anéchomai* (430), to put up with, suffer, endure.

Ant.: *anapaúō* (373), to rest, refresh; *katapaúō* (2664), to cease, rest; *hēsucházō* (2270), to be still, at rest; *epanapaúō* (1879), to cause to rest; *aníēmi* (447), to let up, rest, relieve.

2670. καταποντίζω *katapontízō*; fut. *katapontísō*, mid. *katapontízomai*, from *katá* (2596), down, and *pontízō* (n.f.), to sink. To sink in the sea. Used intrans. in Matt 14:30. In the pass. to be sunk, drowned in the depth of the sea, the allusion being to the punishment by drowning practiced by the Egyptians, Greeks, and Romans, though apparently not by the Jews (Matt 18:6).

Syn.: *buthízō* (1036), to plunge into the deep, to sink; *báptō* (911), to cover wholly with a fluid; *baptízō* (907), to immerse.

Ant.: *pléō* (4126), to sail.

2671. κατάρα katára; gen. katáras, fem. noun from katá (2596), against, and ará (685), a curse. A curse, imprecation, malediction. The opposite is eulogía (2129), blessing (James 3:10; Sept.: Gen 27:12, 13). The same antithesis occurs in Gal 3:10, 13; Heb 6:8; 2 Pet 2:14; Sept.: Deut 28:15–68; Judg 9:57; Prov 3:33; Dan 9:11; Mal 2:2, and means the rejection and curse proceeding from God, the destruction resulting from judgment. It is equivalent to judgment without mercy in James 2:13. The word involves both the sentence of the divine judgment and the ruin therein inflicted, the manifested curse. The expression, "Christ who became for us a curse [katára]" (a.t.), means that the Lord Himself and the curse He bore are not to be separated from each other (Gal 3:13).

Syn.: katáthema (2652), sometimes katanáthema, an accursed thing from which is derived katanathematízō (2653), to utter a curse against; anáthema (331) which translates the Hebr. cherem (2764, OT), a thing devoted to God such as sacrifices; a votive offering, gift, or for its destruction as an idol, a city. In the NT, it is used with this latter meaning as also anathematízō (332), to curse.

Ant.: eulogía (2129), blessing, benediction; chrēstología (5542), fair speech; makarismós (3108), the ascription of blessedness, internal relationship with God; euphēmía (2162), euphemy, good report, fame; cháris (5485), grace, favor; euergesía (2108), benefit, good deed.

2672. καταράομαι kataráomai; contracted katarṓmai, fut. katarásomai, mid. deponent from aráomai (n.f.), to wish something to happen. To wish anyone evil or ruin, to curse, to give one over to ruin (Matt 5:44 [TR]; Mark 11:21; Luke 6:28; Rom 12:14; James 3:9; Sept.: Gen 12:3; Num 24:9). In the perf. pass., to be cursed (Matt 25:41).

Syn.: anathematízō (332), to declare anáthema (331), accursed, devoted to destruction, to curse; katanathematízō (2653), to utter curses against; kakologéō

(2551), to speak evil; katalaléō (2635), to speak against.

Ant.: eulogéō (2127), to speak well of, bless; eneulogéomai (1757), to pronounce blessing upon; makarízō (3106), to pronounce blessed, indwelt by God.

2673. καταργέω katargéō; contracted katargṓ, fut. katargḗsō, from katá (2596), an intens., and argéō (691), to be idle. To render inactive, idle, useless, ineffective, trans.

(I) The katá gives to the intrans. argéō the trans. meaning of to make to cease (Heb 2:14). Paul often uses it to signify more than hindrance or cessation from outward activity, thus to rest, as in Luke 13:7 where the idle earth does not denote unused or untilled, but rather unfruitful land lying fallow, opposite of energḗs (1756), active. To abrogate, make void, do away with, put an end to (Rom 3:3, "make . . . without effect," 31; 4:14; 6:6)

(II) To destroy, cause to cease, do away with, put an end to (1 Cor 6:13; 13:11; 15:24; Gal 3:17; Eph 2:15; 2 Thess 2:8; 2 Tim 1:10). With Paul it always denotes a complete cessation, not a temporary or partial ceasing (1 Cor 1:28; 6:13).

(III) Pass. katargéomai, contracted katargoúmai, to cease, to be done away (1 Cor 2:6; 13:8, 10; 2 Cor 3:7, 11, 13, 14; Gal 5:11); katargéomai apó (575), from, meaning to cease from, i.e., to cease being under or connected with any person or thing such as the Law, meaning to be freed from a law (Rom 7:2, 6). In Gal 5:4, katērgḗthēte apó toú Christoú, "ye have withdrawn from Christ" (a.t.), you do not have any fellowship with Him. In this case, although katērgḗthēte is in the pass. voice, it has a mid. meaning.

Syn.: paúō (3973), to stop, make an end; perispáō (4049), to draw away, distract; kathairéō (2507), to pull down by force, destroy; lúō (3089), to loose, dissolve, sever; katalúō (2647), to destroy utterly; akuróō (208), to render void, deprive of force or authority; kenóō (2758), to make empty, of no effect; ekpíptō (1601), to fall off; exouthenéō (1848), to set at naught, treat with utter contempt, despise; *exoudenóō* (1847), to treat as nothing; *athetéō* (114), to set aside, reject; *erēmóō* (2049), to make desolate; *apotíthēmi* (659), to put away; *aphorízō* (873), to separate from; *aphanízō* (853), to cause to vanish.

Ant.: *stērízō* (4741), to fix, make fast; *epistērízō* (1991), to strengthen; *stereóō* (4732), to make firm; *kuróō* (2964), to make valid, ratify; *hístēmi* (2476), to cause to stand, establish; *sthenóō* (4599) and *dunamóō* (1412), to strengthen; *endunamóō* (1743), to make strong; *ischúō* (2480), to render strong; *enischúō* (1765), to strengthen; *bebaióō* (950) and *krataióō* (2901), to establish, render firm.

2674. **καταριθμέω** *katarithméō*; contracted *katarithmṓ*, fut. *katarithmḗsō*, from *katá* (2596), with or to, and *arithméō* (705), to number. To number with, or enroll among (Acts 1:17; Sept.: 2 Chr 31:19).

Syn.: *sumperilambánō* (4843), to include, take in together; *sugkatapsēphízō* (4785), to number with or enroll among; *logízomai* (3049), to reckon, to number among; *katalégō* (2639), to take into the number, to count in.

Ant.: *apaírō* (522), to remove, take away; *egkataleípō* (1459), to leave behind; *kataleípō* (2641), to leave behind; *apoleípō* (620), to leave behind; *apotássomai* (657), to send away; *diachōrízō* (1316), to remove wholly; *chōrízō* (5563), to separate.

2675. **καταρτίζω** *katartízō*; fut. *katartísō*, from *katá* (2596), with, and *artízō* (n.f.), to adjust, fit, finish, from *ártios* (739), fit, complete. The fundamental meaning is to put a thing in its appropriate condition, to establish, set up, equip, arrange, prepare, mend. Also from *artízō* (n.f.): *exartízō* (1822), to accomplish.

(I) To refit, repair, mend that which is broken such as the nets (Matt 4:21; Mark 1:19). Metaphorically, of a person in error, to restore, set right (Gal 6:1). By implication and in the proper force of *katá*

(2596), meaning to make a perfect fit, suitable, such as one should be, deficient in no part. Of persons (Luke 6:40; 1 Cor 1:10; 2 Cor 13:11; Heb 13:21; 1 Pet 5:10); of things, e.g., to fill out, supply (1 Thess 3:10).

(II) Generally to prepare, set in order, constitute, only in the pass. and mid. (Rom 9:22) where the perf. must be taken with the mid. sense in that the vessels of wrath, or the unsaved, fitted themselves unto destruction. They were not fitted for destruction by God. See Matt 21:16 from Ps 8:2. In Heb 10:5, "a body hast thou prepared me," as a sacrifice, see Ps 40:7. In Heb 11:3, the ages were created and set in order (cf. Sept.: Ps 74:16; 89:37).

Deriv.: *katártisis* (2676), the act of completion, making fit; *katartismós* (2677), complete furnishing, fitting; *prokatartízō* (4294), to perfect or make fit beforehand, make right, equip beforehand.

Syn.: *sunistáō* (4921), to constitute; *suníēmi* (4920), to put together; *suntássō* (4929), to arrange jointly; *sundéō* (4887), to bind with; *déō* (1210), to bind; *sunarmologéō* (4883), to fit or frame together; *harmózō* (718), to adapt, fit, join together; *exartízō* (1822), to accomplish, equip fully.

Ant.: *chōrízō* (5563), to put asunder, separate; *dialúō* (1262), to dissolve utterly; *lúō* (3089), to loose; *apotássō* (657), to renounce or disown; *aporríptō* (641), to reject.

2676. **κατάρτισις** *katártisis*; gen. *katartíseōs*, fem. noun from *katartízō* (2675), to make fully ready, put in order. The act of completing, perfecting (2 Cor 13:9).

Syn.: *teleíōsis* (5050), a fulfillment, completion, perfection, an end accomplished as the effect of a process.

Ant.: *apóleia* (684), loss, waste.

2677. **καταρτισμός** *katartismós*; gen. *katartismoú*, masc. noun from *katartízō* (2675), to make fully ready. Perfection or completion (Eph 4:12). Differs from *katártisis* (2676), the act of making perfect, fitting in that the latter denotes the process in progress while *katartismós* denotes the process as completed (Eph 4:12).

2678. κατασείω *kataseíō*; fut. *kataseísō*, from *katá* (2596), down, and *seíō* (4579), to move, shake. To shake violently to and fro, move backward and forward, wave the hand, beckon as a signal for silence and attention (Acts 19:33), which means waving the hand (Acts 13:16); with the dat. of person (Acts 12:17; 21:40).
Syn.: *neúō* (3506), to give a nod; *dianeúō* (1269), to express oneself by a sign; *kataneúō* (2656), to beckon.
Ant.: *apéchō* (568), to keep away, avoid; *entrépō* (1788), to be put to shame by causing introspection.

2679. κατασκάπτω *kataskáptō*; fut. *kataskápsō*, from *katá* (2596), down, and *skáptō* (4626), to dig. To dig down under a building, undermine and hence overthrow, destroy, raze such as cities, buildings. In Rom 11:3 quoted from Sept.: 1 Kgs 19:10. Pass. part. *tá kateskamména*, in Acts 15:16, referring to ruins mentioned in Amos 9:11.
Syn.: *orússō* (3736), to dig up soil; the more intens. *diorússō* (1358), to dig or break through; *exorússō* (1846), to dig out; *katastréphō* (2690), to destroy or ruin; *anatrépō* (396), to turn over; *katalúō* (2647), to destroy; *katastrónnumi* (2693), to overthrow.
Ant.: *oikodoméō* (3618), to build; *anoikodoméō* (456), to build again; *epoikodoméō* (2026), to build upon; *kataskeuázō* (2680), to establish; *ktízō* (2936), to make, create.

2680. κατασκευάζω *kataskeuázō*; fut. *kataskeuásō*, from *katá* (2596) an intens., and *skeuázō* (n.f., see *anaskeuázō* [384]), to prepare, which is from *skeúos* (4632), implement, vessel. To prepare fully, put in readiness. Trans. as preparing a way before an oriental monarch (Matt 11:10; Mark 1:2; Luke 7:27 quoted from Mal

3:1). In Luke 1:17, the TR and UBS texts have *hetoimázō* (2090), prepare, i.e., a people fully prepared to receive the Messiah. Spoken of buildings with the meaning of to build, construct (Heb 3:3; 9:2, 6; 11:7; 1 Pet 3:20); of God, to create (Heb 3:4; Sept.: Isa 40:28; 43:7).
Syn.: *oikodoméō* (3618), to build; *katartízō* (2675), to fit, prepare, make suitable, from *ártios* (739), suitable; *proetoimázō* (4282), to prepare beforehand; *paraskeuázō* (3903), to make ready; *prokatartízō* (4294), to make ready beforehand; *ktízō* (2936), to make, create, manufacture; *sunarmologéō* (4883), to fit or frame together.
Ant.: *apóllumi* (622), to perish, destroy; *katargéō* (2673), abolish; *kathairéō* (2507), to cast down, depose, destroy; *lúō* (3089), to loose, dissolve, demolish; *analískō* (355), to destroy, consume; *katalúō* and *exolothreúō* (1842), to destroy completely; *olothreúō* (3645), to destroy, especially in the sense of slaying; *phtheírō* (5351), to corrupt; *diaphtheírō* (1311), to corrupt throughout.

2681. κατασκηνόω *kataskēnóō*; contracted *kataskēnó*, fut. *kataskēnṓsō*, from *katá* (2596), an intens., and *skēnóō* (4637), to dwell, literally in a tent. To pitch a tent. In the NT generally to sojourn or to dwell, spoken of birds as nesting in the branches (Matt 13:32; Luke 13:19), or under the shadow (Mark 4:32; Sept.: Ps 104:12; Dan 4:12). With the meaning of to rest, remain (Acts 2:26 quoting Ps 16:9).
Deriv.: *kataskḗnōsis* (2682), a dwelling place, nest.
Syn.: *aulízomai* (835), to lodge in a courtyard; *katalúō* (2647), to lodge for the night; *xenízō* (3579), to receive as a guest.
Ant.: *hupágō* (5217) and *analúō* (360) and *metabaínō* (3327), to depart; *apérchomai* (565), to go away; *poreúomai* (4198), to go on; *apochōréō* (672), to depart from; *aphístēmi* (868), to cause to depart; *apodēméō* (589), to emigrate.

2682. κατασκήνωσις *kataskḗnōsis*; gen. *kataskēnṓseōs*, fem. noun from

kataskēnóō (2681), to lodge, rest, pitch a tent (Sept.: 1 Chr 28:2). The act of pitching a tent, building, hence a tent pitched. A dwelling place, abode, and as spoken of birds, a nesting place (Matt 8:20; Luke 9:58).
Syn.: *xenía* (3578), a lodging place; *paroikía* (3940), a sojourning; *katoíkēsis* (2731), a dwelling, habitation; *katoikía* (2733), habitation.
Ant.: *éxodos* (1841), departure.

2683. κατασκιάζω *kataskiázō*; fut. *kataskiásō*, from *katá* (2596), an intens., and *skiázō* (n.f., see *aposkíasma* [644]), to shade, shadow. To throw a shadow upon, overshadow. Used trans. in Heb 9:5.
Syn.: *episkiázō* (1982), to throw a shadow upon, overshadow.

2684. κατασκοπέω *kataskopéō*; contracted *kataskopó*, fut. *kataskopḗsō*, from *katá* (2596), down, and *skopéō* (4648), to take aim at, mark. To view accurately, contemplate. In the NT with sinister intent, to spy out, explore. Trans. in Gal 2:4; Sept.: 2 Sam 10:3; 1 Chr 19:3).
Deriv.: *katáskopos* (2685), a spy.

2685. κατάσκοπος *katáskopos*; gen. *kataskópou*, masc. noun from *kataskopéō* (2684), to spy. A scout, spy (Heb 11:31; Sept.: Gen 42:9, 11).
Syn.: *egkáthetos* (1455), one who lies in wait, a spy.
Ant.: *sustratiṓtēs* (4961), fellow soldier.

2686. κατασοφίζομαι *katasophízomai*; fut. *katasophísomai*, mid. deponent from *katá* (2596), against, and *sophízō* (4679), to deal with subtly. To play the sophist, to deal insidiously, deceitfully, to use one's intellectual powers for a ploy (Acts 7:19 in allusion to Ex 1:10). The word refers to the misuse of reason, an exercise of reason for the purpose of fooling others and gaining an advantage. See 2 Sam 13:3.
Syn.: *apatáō* (538), to cheat, delude, deceive; *dolóō* (1389), to ensnare, handle deceitfully; *planáō* (4105), to lead astray.

Ant.: *sōphronéō* (4993), to exercise soundness of mind.

2687. καταστέλλω *katastéllō*; fut. *katasteló*, from *katá* (2596), down, and *stéllō* (4724), to repress. Literally, to put or let down, lower. To quell, assuage, pacify, e.g., a crowd (Acts 19:35, 36).
Deriv.: *katastolḗ* (2689), a letting down, apparel.
Syn.: *hēsucházō* (2270), to quiet; *eirēneúō* (1514), to pacify.
Ant.: *diegeírō* (1326), to arouse, stir up; *erethízō* (2042), to stimulate, provoke.

2688. κατάστημα *katástēma*; gen. *katastḗmatos*, neut. noun from *kathístēmi* (2525), to make, ordain. Position or state, condition spoken of external circumstances and deportment (Titus 2:3).
Syn.: *anastrophḗ* (391), manner of life, behavior.

2689. καταστολή *katastolḗ*; gen. *katastolḗs*, fem. noun from *katastéllō* (2687), to put or let down, appease. A long garment or robe reaching down to the feet (see Sept.: Isa 61:3). Apparel, dress in general, a garment, a long robe of dignity (1 Tim 2:9).
Syn.: *himátion* (2440), an outer cloak or cape; *himatismós* (2441), clothing, apparel; *chlamús* (5511), a military cloak worn over the *chitṓn* by emperors, kings, magistrates, military officers; *stolḗ* (4749), a stately robe or uniform, a long gown worn as mark of dignity; *esthḗs* (2066) and *ésthēsis* (2067), clothing; *énduma* (1742), a garment of any kind; *ependútēs* (1903), an upper or outer garment which sometimes fishermen wore when at work; *phelónēs* (5341), a mantle, traveling robe for protection against stormy weather, overcoat; *peribólaion* (4018), a wrap or cape, a garment thrown around one; *podḗrēs* (4158), an outer garment reaching to the feet; *sképasma* (4629), a covering, raiment; *phelónēs* (5341), a traveling cloak.
Ant.: *gumnótēs* (1132), nakedness.

2690. καταστρέφω *katastréphō*; fut. *katastrépsō*, from *katá* (2596), down or denoting evil, and *stréphō* (4762), to turn. To overturn or overthrow; used trans. in Matt 21:12 and Mark 11:15.
Deriv.: *katastrophḗ* (2692), overthrow, destruction, subversion.
Syn.: *anatrépō* (396), to upset; *katalúō* (2647), to destroy, overthrow; *anastréphō* (390), to overthrow; *katabállō* (2598), to throw down; *katalúō* (2647), to destroy, dissolve; *apóllumi* (622), to destroy, lose; *phtheírō* (5351), to corrupt, ruin; *diaphtheírō* (1311), to corrupt, ruin completely; *kathairéō* (2507), to demolish; *analískō* (355), to consume.
Ant.: *oikodoméō* (3618), to build; *anoikodoméō* (456), to build again; *epoikodoméō* (2026), to build upon; *kataskeuázō* (2680), to establish; *ktízō* (2936), to fabricate, make; *anístēmi* (450), to stand up; *egeírō* (1453), to raise.

2691. καταστρηνιάω *katastrēniáō*; contracted *katastrēnió*, fut. *katastrēniásō*, from *katá* (2596), against, and *streniáō* (4763), to live a profligate, luxurious life. To revel or riot against someone, show insolence (1 Tim 5:11, meaning they lived a life of luxury and gaiety to the neglect of Christ and the detriment of His cause).
Syn.: *spatalǻō* (4684), to live in pleasure, waste; *entruphǻō* (1792), to revel in; *euphraínomai* (2165), to be in a good frame of mind, to have fun.
Ant.: *egkrateúomai* (1467), to exercise self-restraint; *néphō* (3525), to be discreet, sober; *sōphronéō* (4993), to be of sound mind.

2692. καταστροφή *katastrophḗ*; gen. *katastropḗs*, fem. noun from *katastréphō* (2690), to overthrow, overturn, ruin. A catastrophe, overthrow, destruction, as of cities (2 Pet 2:6). Metaphorically, subversion, the opposite of *tó chrḗsimon* (5539), profit, profitable (2 Tim 2:14).
Syn.: *kathaíresis* (2506), a pulling down; *apóleia* (684), ruin, perdition, destruction; *ólethros* (3639), ruin, destruction, (often the effect of divine judgment);

phthorá (5356), corruption; *diaphthorá* (1312), complete destruction; *súntrimma* (4938), a breaking in pieces, shattering.
Ant.: *oikodomḗ* (3619), building in process, edification; *endómēsis* (1739), a thing built, structure; *ktísis* (2937), a creation; *ktísma* (2938), that which is built, creature; *dóma* (1430), an edifice.

2693. καταστρώννυμι *katastrṓnnumi*; fut. *katastrṓsō*, from *katá* (2596), down, and *strṓnnumi* (4766), to strew or spread. To spread down, or overthrow. Used of persons in 1 Cor 10:5, meaning they were scattered as corpses in the desert, were destroyed (cf. Sept.: Num 14:16; see Heb 3:17; Jude 1:5).
Syn.: *katastréphō* (2690), to ruin; *katalúō* (2647), overthrow, destroy; *apóllumi* (622), to perish.
Ant.: *sullégō* (4816), to collect, gather together; *sunágō* (4863), lead or bring together; *episunágō* (1996), to gather together in one place.

2694. κατασύρω *katasúrō*; fut. *katasurṓ*, from *katá* (2596), an intens., and *súrō* (4951), to drag. To drag down, force along. Of a person, to drag or pull along to the judge (Luke 12:58).
Syn.: *anaspáō* (385), to extricate; *helkúō* (1670), to draw with affection and attraction as contrasted to *katasúrō* and *súrō* which involve compulsion.
Ant.: *leípō* (3007), to leave; *kataleípō* (2641), to abandon, forsake; *egkataleípō* (1459), to leave behind in some place; *aphíēmi* (863), to leave, forsake, lay aside; *eáō* (1439), to leave alone.

2695. κατασφάζω *kataspházō*, **κατασφάττω** *kataspháttō*; fut. *kataspháxō*, from *katá* (2596), an intens., and *spházō* (4969), to slay. To slaughter, butcher, or kill, as with a sword (Luke 19:27; Sept.: Zech 11:5).
Syn.: *apokteínō* (615), a more common word for to slay or kill; *anairéō* (337), to take away, destroy, kill, consume; *phoneúō* (5407), to murder; *thúō* (2380), to kill for sacrifice; *thanatóō* (2289), to

kill; *nekróō* (3499), to deaden; *apóllumi* (622), to perish.

Ant.: *zōogonéō* (2225), to rescue from death.

2696. κατασφραγίζω *katasphragízō*; fut. *katasphragísō*, from *katá* (2596), an intens., and *sphragízō* (4972), to seal. To seal up. Referring to a book or scroll (Rev 5:1; Sept.: Job 9:7).

Syn.: *kleíō* (2808), to shut up; *katakleíō* (2623), to shut down, incarcerate; *asphalízō* (805), to render secure.

Ant.: *anoígō* (455), to open; *dianoígō* (1272), to open up thoroughly; *apokalúptō* (601), to reveal.

2697. κατάσχεσις *katáschesis*; gen. *kataschéseōs*, fem. noun from *katéchō* (2722), to take possession. A possession or thing owned, a dwelling, land (Acts 7:5, 45; Sept.: Gen 17:8; Neh 11:3; Ps 2:8).

Syn.: *ktḗma* (2933), a possession, property; *peripoíēsis* (4047), an acquisition or purchased possession; *húparxis* (5223), subsistence, substance.

Ant.: *antapódosis* (469), requital, reward; *epistrophḗ* (1995), return.

2698. κατατίθημι *katatíthēmi*; fut. *katathḗsō*, from *katá* (2596), down, and *títhēmi* (5087), to put, lay, set. To put or lay down, deposit, trans.

(I) In a tomb (Mark 15:46).

(II) In the mid., to deposit for oneself, lay up for future use. With the dat., to lay up favor with anyone, to win his favor (Acts 24:27; 25:9).

Deriv.: *parakatathḗkē* (3872), that which is committed unto trust; *sugkatatíthemai* (4784), to consent.

Syn.: *kerdaínō* (2770), to gain; *peripoiéō* (4046), to save for oneself, gain; *katabállō* (2598), to lay down.

Ant.: *analambánō* (353) and *anairéō* (337), to take up; *aírō* (142), to take up or away; *apaírō* (522), to lift off; *aphairéō* (851), to take away; *harpázō* (726), to catch away.

2699. κατατομή *katatomḗ*; gen. *katatomḗs*, fem. noun from *katatémnō* (n.f.), to cut through or off. A cutting away, mangling. Used sarcastically in Phil 3:2. The words *katatomḗ* and *peritomḗ* (4061), circumcision, seem alike. However, *peritomḗ*, ordained by the Law of Moses, has a spiritual significance distinguishing God's people (Israel in the OT) from the heathen. When this spiritual meaning is forgotten, then *peritomḗ*, circumcision, becomes *katatomḗ*, a mutilation, a butchering up, a mere cutting away flesh which in itself is of no value. Paul thus calls the Jewish teachers "butchers," because after the coming of Christ they taught that the outward circumcision of the flesh was necessary to salvation while at the same time they were destitute of the circumcision of the heart. This word of the apostle not only depreciates the carnal circumcision, but seems also to allude to the superstitious cuttings and manglings of the flesh practiced among the heathen (Lev 21:5).

Syn.: *kopḗ* (2871), cutting.

Ant.: *akrobustía* (203), uncircumcision.

2700. κατατοξεύω *katatoxeúō*; fut. *katatoxeúsō*, from *katá* (2596), against or denoting evil, and *toxeúō* (n.f.), to shoot an arrow, which is from *tóxon* (5115), a bow. To shoot down with an arrow or dart, used in the pass. with the dat. in Heb 12:20, an allusion to Ex 19:13.

Syn.: *bállō* (906), to thrust or cast.

2701. κατατρέχω *katatréchō*; fut. *katadramoúmai*, from *katá* (2596), down, and *tréchō* (5143), to run. To run down from a higher to a lower place (Acts 21:32, *katédramen*, he ran down to them from the tower of Antonia). See Sept.: 1 Kgs 19:20. In a hostile sense, Sept.: Lev 26:37.

Syn.: *katadiṓkō* (2614), to hunt down.

Ant.: *prosdéchomai* (4327), to admit, accept.

For καταφάγω see 2719.

2702. καταφέρω *kataphérō*; fut. *katoísō*, aor. pass. *katēnéchthēn*, from *katá* (2596), down or against, and *phérō* (5342), to bring. To bear or carry down from a higher to a lower place, to bring down with violence, overthrow. In the NT, only in the pass., *kataphéromai*, to be borne or thrown down, fall (Acts 20:9 referring to Eutychus who fell down having been overcome by sleep). To cast one's vote for or to assent (Acts 26:10 [cf. 22:20]).

Syn.: *katapíptō* (2667), to fall down; *katágō* (2609), to bring down; *katabibázō* (2601), to bring or go down; *katabaínō* (2597), to come or fall down.

Ant.: *anaphérō* (399), to lead to a higher place; *anágō* (321), to lead or bring up to; *anabibázō* (307), to bring up.

2703. καταφεύγω *katapheúgō*; fut. *katapheúxomai*, from *katá* (2596), an intens., and *pheúgō* (5343), to flee. To flee away to some place for refuge (Acts 14:6; Heb 6:18; Sept.: Num 35:26; Deut 4:42).

Syn.: *prostréchō* (4370), to run toward; *epikaléomai* (1941), to invoke, implore.

Ant.: *ménō* (3306), to abide; *kataménō* (2650), to remain, wait.

2704. καταφθείρω *kataphtheírō*; fut. *kataphtherō̂*, from *katá* (2596), an intens., and *phtheírō* (5351), to corrupt, destroy. To spoil utterly, corrupt, lay waste. Referring to the mind in a moral sense, to deprave (2 Tim 3:8). To destroy, used in the pass. meaning to perish (2 Pet 2:12; Sept.: Gen 6:17; Ex 18:18; 2 Chr 24:23).

Syn.: *bláptō* (984) to harm; *analískō* (355), to consume; *katastrēniáō* (2691), to revel wantonly.

Ant.: *diasṓzō* (1295), to preserve; *sṓzō* (4982), to save, preserve; *tēréō* (5083), to preserve, keep; *phrontízō* (5431), to care for; *phulássō* (5442), to keep, guard.

2705. καταφιλέω *kataphiléō*; contracted *kataphilō̂*, fut. *kataphilḗsō*, from *katá* (2596), an intens., and *philéō* (5368), to love, kiss. To kiss eagerly, affectionately, or repeatedly (Matt 26:49; Mark 14:45;

Luke 7:38, 45; 15:20; Acts 20:37; Sept.: Gen 31:28, 55; Ruth 1:9, 14).

Syn.: *aspázomai* (782), to embrace; *enagkalízomai* (1723), to take in one's arms.

2706. καταφρονέω *kataphronéō*; contracted *kataphronō̂*, fut. *kataphronḗsō*, from *katá* (2596), against or denoting evil, and *phronéō* (5426), to think. To hold in contempt, to think lightly of, despise (Matt 18:10; Rom 2:4; 1 Cor 11:22; 1 Tim 4:12; Heb 12:2; 2 Pet 2:10), to neglect, not to care for (Matt 6:24; Luke 16:13, as the opposite of *antéchomai* [472], to care for, support; 1 Tim 6:2).

Deriv.: *kataphronētḗs* (2707), a despiser.

Syn.: *periphronéō* (4065), despise; *exouthenéō* (1848), to regard as nothing, despise completely; *athetéō* (114), to cast off, reject; *atimázō* (818), to dishonor, treat shamefully; *oligōréō* (3643), to disesteem, despise.

Ant.: *timáō* (5091), to honor; *doxázō* (1392), to glorify; *sébomai* (4576), to revere.

2707. καταφρονητής *kataphronētḗs*; gen. *kataphronētoú*, masc. noun from *kataphronéō* (2706), to despise. A despiser, disdainer, one who condemns others (Acts 13:41 quoted from Hab 1:5).

Syn.: *aphilágathos* (865), not loving the good, a despiser; *hubristḗs* (5197), despiteful.

Ant.: *sustatikós* (4956), commendatory.

2708. καταχέω *katachéō*; fut. *katacheúsō*, from *katá* (2596), down, and *chéō* (n.f., see *epichéō* [2708]), to pour down or out. To pour down upon (Matt 26:7; Mark 14:3; Sept.: Job 41:14).

Syn.: *spéndō* (4689), to pour out; *rhéō* (4483), to flow.

2709. καταχθόνιος *katachthónios*; gen. *katachthoníou*, masc.-fem., neut. *katachthónion*, adj. from *katá* (2596),

down, and *chthōn* (n.f.), ground, earth. Under-ground, subterranean (Phil 2:10).
Ant.: *ouránios* (3770), heavenly.

2710. καταχράομαι *katachráomai*; contracted *katachrōmai*, fut. *katachrēsomai*, mid. deponent from *katá* (2596), against, denoting wrong, or an intens., denoting excess, and *chráomai* (5530), to use. To use immoderately, abuse (1 Cor 7:31; 9:18).
Ant.: *ōpheléō* (5623), to be useful; *lusiteléō* (3081), to be advantageous; *sumphérō* (4851), to be expedient.

2711. καταψύχω *katapsúchō*; fut. *katapsúxō*, from *katá* (2596), an intens., and *psúchō* (5594), to cool. To cool, refresh (Luke 16:24).
Syn.: *anapsúchō* (404), to refresh.
Ant.: *katakaíō* (2618), to burn; *puróō* (4448), to be on fire; *zéō* (2204), to be hot; *thermaínō* (2328), to warm.

2712. κατείδωλος *kateídōlos*; gen. *kateidólou*, masc.-fem., neut. *kateídōlon*, adj. from *katá* (2596), an intens., and *eídōlon* (1497), idol. Full of idols (Acts 17:16). It is a peculiar word describing the *deisidaímones* (1174), superstitious, those wholly given up to the worship of false gods (Acts 17:22).

2713. κατέναντι *katénanti*; adv. from *katá* (2596), against, and *énanti* (1725), opposite, before. Literally it means down over against, at the point over against, opposite (Mark 11:2; 12:41; 13:3). With the def. art. used as an adj. meaning opposite (Luke 19:30; Sept.: Ex 19:2; 1 Chr 5:11; Zech 14:4). In the sense of "before" or "in the sight of" (Ex 32:5; 2 Chr 2:6; Rom 4:17).
Syn.: *émprosthen* (1715), in front of or in the sight of a person; *apénanti* (561), opposite or in the sight of; *enópion* (1799), before or opposite a person; *katenópion* (2714); *antikrú* (481), opposite, over against; *péran* (4008), across, over.
Ant.: *eggús* (1451), near; *plēsíon* (4139), close by; *pará* (3844), near, by.

2714. κατενώπιον *katenópion*; adv. from *katá* (2596), against, and *enópion* (1799), before. In the very presence of (2 Cor 2:17; 12:19; Eph 1:4; Col 1:22; Jude 24; Sept.: Lev 4:17; Josh 1:5).

2715. κατεξουσιάζω *katexousiázō*; fut. *katexousiásō*, from *katá* (2596), against, denoting hostility, and *exousiázō* (1850), to exercise authority. To exercise authority against or over someone (Matt 20:25; Mark 10:42).
Syn.: *authentéō* (831), to domineer over; *katakurieúō* (2634), to lord it over; *árchō* (757), to rule over; *basileúō* (936), to reign; *hēgéomai* (2233), to lead; *basileúō* (936), to reign.
Ant.: *hupotássō* (5293), to subordinate.

2716. κατεργάζομαι *katergázomai*; fut. *katergásomai*, aor. pass. *kateirgásthēn*, mid. deponent from *katá* (2596), an intens., and *ergázomai* (2038), to work. To work out; trans. to bring about, accomplish, to carry out a task until it is finished.
(I) To work out, to effect, produce, to be the cause or author of (Rom 4:15; 5:3; 7:8, 13; 15:18; 2 Cor 4:17; 7:10, 11; 9:11; Phil 2:12; James 1:3, 20).
(II) To work up, make an end of, vanquish (Eph 6:13).
(III) Generally to work, do, practice: of actions (Rom 1:27; 2:9; 7:15, 17, 18, 20; 1 Cor 5:3; 1 Pet 4:3); of miracles, pass. (2 Cor 12:12). In the sense of to make, to form (2 Cor 5:5).
Syn.: *poiéō* (4160), to do; *prássō* (4238), to practice; *energéō* (1754), to work effectually in, energize, operate; *teléō* (5055), to finish, to perform; *epiteléō* (2005), to accomplish completely.
Ant.: *ameléō* (272), to neglect; *paratheōréō* (3865), to overlook.

2717. Omitted in *Strong's Dictionary of the Greek Testament.*

2718. κατέρχομαι *katérchomai*; fut. *kateleúsomai*, 2d aor. *katēlthon*, from *katá* (2596), down, and *érchomai* (2064), to come or go. To go or come down, descend, used of persons going from a higher to a lower region of a country, as to the sea coast (Luke 4:31; Acts 8:5; 13:4). Followed by *apó* (575), from, and the gen. of place (Luke 9:37; Acts 15:1; 18:5; 21:10); followed by both *apó* and *eis* (1519), to or unto, and *apó* (575), from (Acts 11:27; 12:19); by *prós* (4314), toward, with the acc. of person (Acts 9:32). Of persons coming from the high sea down to land; followed by *eis* (1519), to or unto (Acts 18:22; 27:5). Spoken of divine gifts (James 3:15).

Syn.: *katabaínō* (2597), to go down; *katágō* (2609), to land.

Ant.: *anérchomai* (424), to ascend; *anabaínō* (305), to ascend; *anístēmi* (450), to arise; *anatéllō* (393), to arise, usually of the sun, moon and stars.

2719. κατεσθίω *katesthíō*; fut. *katédomai*, 2d aor. *katéphagon*, from *katá* (2596), an intens., and *esthíō* (2068), to eat.

(I) To eat, swallow, devour. Metaphorically, of things such as fire, to consume (Rev 11:5; Sept.: Isa 29:6); of persons (Gal 5:15, meaning to consume or destroy one another; Sept.: Isa 9:12); to plunder or obtain by extortion (2 Cor 11:20), of the houses of widows (Matt 23:14; Mark 12:40; Luke 20:47).

(II) The 2d aor. is supplied by *kataphágō*, from *katá* (2596), an intens., and *phágō* (5315), to eat.

(A) To consume, eat up, devour; used trans. of animals (Matt 13:4; Mark 4:4; Luke 8:5; Rev 12:4; Sept.: Gen 37:20; Ex 10:15); of persons, to devour a book, meaning to absorb its contents mentally (Rev 19:9, 10 [cf. Ezek 3:1]); to devour or consume as by fire (Rev 20:9; Sept.: Lev 10:2); to consume or spend in riotous or luxurious living (Luke 15:30, where it means to eat up one's paternal estate or substance).

(B) Metaphorically, of zeal (John 2:17, quoted from Ps 69:9).

Syn.: *katapínō* (2666), to drink down, devour; *trṓgō* (5176), to munch or gnaw, indicating slow eating; *bibrṓskō* (977), to eat, devour; *analískō* (2654), to consume.

Ant.: *nēsteúō* (3522), to fast.

2720. κατευθύνω *kateuthúnō*; fut. *kateuthunṓ*, from *katá* (2596), an intens., down, and *euthúnō* (2116), to direct. To guide straight towards or upon something. Generally, it means to guide or direct one's way or journey to a place (1 Thess 3:11). Symbolically in Luke 1:79, directing the feet in the way of peace; the hearts, in 2 Thess 3:5; Sept.: Ps 5:8; 2 Chr 12:14; 19:3.

Syn.: *hodēgéō* (3594), to guide; *hegéomai* (2233), to lead; *ágō* (71), to carry, lead away.

Ant.: *planáō* (4105), to cause to wander; *periérchomai* (4022), to go about or around; *apóllumi* (622), to perish.

2721. κατεφίστημι *katephístēmi*; fut. *katepistḗsō*, from *katá* (2596), an intens., and *ephístēmi* (2186), to come upon. In the NT, only in the 2d aor., *katepéstēn*, intrans. meaning to stand forth against, and by implication in a hostile sense, to rush upon, assault, followed by the dat. (Acts 18:12).

Syn.: *epitíthēmi* (2007), to set upon, attack; *anthístēmi* (436), to stand against, withstand; *prospíptō* (4363), to rush upon; *apeiléō* (546), to threaten; *epicheiréō* (2021), to lay a hand upon; *hubrízō* (5195), to abuse.

Ant.: *phulássō* (5442), to guard, watch, keep; *diaphulássō* (1314), to guard carefully, defend; *phrouréō* (5432), to keep by guarding militarily; *tēréō* (5083), to watch over, preserve.

2722. κατέχω *katéchō*; fut. *kathéxō*, 2d aor. *katéschon*, from *katá* (2596), an intens., and *échō* (2192), to have, hold. Hold fast, retain, or hold down, quash, suppress.

(I) In a spiritual sense (Luke 8:15; 1 Cor 11:2; 15:2; 1 Thess 5:21; Heb 3:6, 14; 10:23 [cf. Rom 7:6]).

(II) To possess (1 Cor 7:30; 2 Cor 6:10).

(III) To take possession, seize (Matt 21:38 [{TR} cf. John 5:4, a disease]).

(IV) To occupy a place (Luke 14:9).

(V) To detain, retain (Luke 4:42; Phile 1:13; Sept.: Gen 24:56; 42:19).

(VI) To suppress, restrain, hinder, withhold (2 Thess 2:6, 7 [cf. Rom 1:18]).

(VII) With the prep. *eis* (1519), to bring a ship toward the shore (Acts 27:40).

Deriv.: *akatáschetos* (183), not to be restrained; *katáschesis* (2697), possession.

Syn.: *kratéō* (2902), to hold fast; *sunéchō* (4912), to hold together, keep; *ktáomai* (2932), to procure for oneself; *sullambánō* (4815), to take hold of; *sunarpázō* (4884), to seize, catch; *lambánō* (2983), to lay hold of; *katalambánō* (2638), to apprehend; *piázō* (4084), to lay hold of forcefully; *harpázō* (726), to catch.

Ant.: *ekdídōmi* (1554), to give up, surrender; *apolúō* (630), to dismiss; *epitrépō* (2010), to allow, let, give liberty; *apotíthēmi* (659), to put away from oneself; *chōrízō* (5563), to separate; *exaírō* (1808), to put away from the midst; *methístēmi* (3179), to remove; *apostréphō* (654), to turn away; *apōthéomai* (683), to thrust away; *lúō* (3089), to loose; *exapostéllō* (1821), to send forth; *ekbállō* (1544), to cast out; *apotássomai* (657), to send away.

2723. κατηγορέω *katēgoréō*; contracted *katēgorō*, fut. *katēgorēsō*, from *katá* (2596), against, and *agoreúō* (n.f.), to speak. To speak openly against, to condemn or accuse mainly in a legal sense (Matt 12:10; Mark 3:2; 15:3; Luke 11:54; 23:2, 10, 14; John 5:45; 8:6; Acts 22:30; 24:2, 8, 19; 25:5, 11; 28:19; Rom 2:15; Rev 12:10). Also from *agoreúō* (n.f.): *prosagoreúō* (4316), to address, greet.

Deriv.: *katēgoría* (2724), accusation, incrimination; *katégoros* (2725), accuser.

Ant.: *ainéō* (134), to praise; *epainéō* (1867), to commend; *humnéō* (5214), to laud; *eulogéō* (2127), to speak well of, praise, bless.

2724. κατηγορία *katēgoría*; gen. *katēgorías*, fem. noun from *katēgoréō* (2723), to accuse. Accusation, incrimination of a person (Luke 6:7 [TR]; John 18:29; 1 Tim 5:19). With the gen. (Titus 1:6), it does not refer to judicial punishment, but public condemnation.

Syn.: *aitía* (156), cause, accusation; *aitíama* (157), a complaint or accusation; *aítion* (158), fault; *lógos* (3056), cause or reason; *égklēma* (1462), accusation; *héttēma* (2275), fault, defect; *paráptōma* (3900), trespass.

Ant.: *aínos* (136), praise; *épainos* (1868), approbation, commendation; *aínesis* (133), the actual praise; *eulogía* (2129), a pronounced blessing; *makarismós* (3108), declaration of blessedness.

2725. κατήγορος *katégoros*; gen. *katēgórou*, masc. noun from *katēgoréō* (2723), to accuse. Accuser (John 8:10 [TR]; Acts 23:30, 35; 24:8; 25:16, 18). *Katégōr* is used in Rev 12:10 (UBS) instead of *katégoros* (TR).

Syn.: *kritikós* (2924), critical; *diábolos* (1228), accuser, slanderer, the devil.

Ant.: *eulogōn*, the pres. part. of *eulogéō* (2127), to speak well of, the one speaking well of or blessing.

2726. κατήφεια *katépheia*; gen. *katēpheías*, fem. noun from *katēphḗs* (n.f.), dejected, with downcast eyes. A dejection of countenance, sorrow (James 4:9).

Syn.: *lúpē* (3077), grief, sorrow; *odúnē* (3601), consuming grief or pain; *ōdín* (5604), a birth pang; *pénthos* (3997), mourning, sorrow.

Ant.: *chará* (5479), joy; *agallíasis* (20), exultation; *euphrosúnē* (2167), gladness; *kaúchēsis* (2746), boasting, rejoicing; *hēdoné* (2237), delight, pleasure.

2727. κατηχέω *katēchéō*; contracted *katēchō*, fut. *katēchḗsō* from *katá* (2596), an intens., and *ēchéō* (2278), to sound. To teach, instruct orally. Spoken of the oral instruction or preaching of the Apostles and early Christian teachers (1 Cor 14:19; Gal 6:6). In the pass. with the acc. of thing (Luke 1:4; Acts 18:25; Rom 2:18). Generally, to inform, apprise of, and in the pass., to be informed of, hear by report (Acts 21:21, 24).

Syn.: *paideúō* (3811), to train children, teach with the added element of discipline; *mathēteúō* (3100), to make a disciple; *muéō* (3453), to instruct; *didáskō* (1321), to teach.

2728. κατιόω katióō; contracted *katiṓ*, fut. *katiṓsō*, from *katá* (2596), an intens., and *ióō* (n.f.), to rust, which is from *iós* (2447), rust. To cause to rust, corrode with rust. In the pass., to be rusted out, be corroded (James 5:3), used hyperbolically.

Syn.: *phtheírō* (5351), to corrupt; *diaphtheírō* (1311), to corrupt completely, and *kataphtheírō* (2704), to corrupt wholly; *sḗpō* (4595), to become rotten; *aphanízō* (853), to consume.

Ant.: *katharízō* (2511), to make clean; *diakatharízō* (1245), to cleanse thoroughly; *kathaírō* (2508), to purge.

2729. κατισχύω katischúō; fut. *katischúsō*, from *katá* (2596), against, and *ischúō* (2480), to prevail. To be strong against someone, prevail against or over. Used in a hostile sense, meaning to overcome, vanquish (Matt 16:18); to prevail, get the upper hand, used in an absolute sense (Luke 23:23).

Syn.: *nikáō* (3528), to conquer, prevail; *hupernikáō* (5245), to be more than conqueror.

Ant.: *hēttáomai* (2274), to be overcome; *asthenéō* (770), to lack strength; *kámnō* (2577), to be weary; *sunéchomai* (4912), to be sick, to constrain; *noséō* (3552), to be sick.

2730. κατοικέω katoikéō; contracted *katoikṓ*, fut. *katoikḗsō*, from *katá* (2596), an intens., and *oikéō* (3611), to dwell. Reside.

(I) A certain, fixed and durable dwelling, as distinguished from *paroikéō*

(3939), to sojourn, dwell in a place temporarily. To dwell in, inhabit a house or place (Matt 2:23; 4:13; Acts 7:4). Followed by *en* (1722), in, with the dat. (Luke 13:4; Acts 1:20; 2:5; 7:2, 4; 9:22; 11:29; 13:27; Heb 11:9; Rev 13:12); by *epí* (1909), upon, with the gen. (Rev 3:10; 6:10; 8:13; 11:10; 13:8, 14; 17:8; Sept.: Lev 20:22; 25:18, 19); with the acc. (Acts 17:26); by *poú* (4226), where, and *hópou* (3699), wherever (Rev 2:13); by *ekeí* (1563), there (Matt 12:45; Luke 11:26; Sept.: Gen 11:2); implied (Acts 22:12; Sept.: Gen 13:12; 19:29).

(II) Metaphorically of God, with *en* (1722), in (Acts 7:48; 17:24; Sept.: Ps 2:4; 9:11); of Christ as being permitted to take up full residence by His Spirit in the hearts of Christians (Eph 3:17); of the fullness of the Godhead which was in Jesus (Col 1:19; 2:9); of the Spirit dwelling in man (James 4:5); of the righteousness dwelling in the new heavens and the new earth (2 Pet 3:13 [cf. Sept.: Jer 32:17]).

Deriv.: *egkatoikéō* (1460), to dwell among; *katoíkēsis* (2731), the act of coming to dwell, a dwelling, habitation; *katoikētérion* (2732), a settling-down place, habitation; *katoikía* (2733), habitation, house.

Syn.: *enoikéō* (1774), to dwell in; *perioikéō* (4039), to dwell around; *sunoikéō* (4924), to dwell with; *ménō* (3306), to abide, remain; *skēnóō* (4637), to live in a tent; *kataskēnóō* (2681), to pitch one's tent and lodge in it.

Ant.: *astatéō* (790), to wander about not having a permanent dwelling place; *diérchomai* (1330), to travel, pass through; *apodēméō* (589), to go to a foreign country, to journey.

2731. κατοίκησις katoíkēsis; gen. *katoikḗseōs*, fem. noun from *katoikéō* (2730), to dwell, inhabit. The act of dwelling or inhabiting (Mark 5:3; Sept.: Gen 10:30). To be contrasted with *katoikētérion* (2732) as the place one inhabits.

Syn.: *paroikía* (3940), a temporary sojourn.

Ant.: *análusis* (359), a loosing or departure from life, loosing from mooring; *éxodos* (1841), exodus, departure, decease.

2732. κατοικητήριον *katoikētḗrion*; gen. *katoikētēríou*, neut. noun from *katá* (2596), an intens., and *oikētḗrion* (3613), a dwelling place (Eph 2:22; Rev 18:2). A dwelling place. It is distinct from *katoíkēsis* (2731), the act of dwelling, and *katoikía* (2733), a house, settlement, colony.

Syn.: *épaulis* (1886), farm, a country house, cottage or cabin; *skēnḗ* (4633), a tent or tabernacle indicating a temporary dwelling place; *skḗnōma* (4638), a pitched tent, used metaphorically for the body as the temporary dwelling place of the soul.

2733. κατοικία *katoikía*; gen. *katoikías*, fem. noun from *katoikéō* (2730), to dwell. Dwelling place. Used only in Acts 17:26 to indicate a settlement or colony where God appointed nations to dwell.

2734. κατοπτρίζω *katoptrízō*; fut. *katoptrísō*, from *kátoptron* (n.f.), a mirror, looking glass. In the NT, only in the mid. *katoptrizomai*, to look or behold in a mirror (2 Cor 3:18, meaning beholding the glory of the Lord as reflected and radiant in the gospel in contrast to 2 Cor 3:15).

2735. κατόρθωμα *katórthōma*; gen. *katorthṓmatos*, neut. noun from *katorthóō* (n.f.), to erect or order, to establish. Something happily achieved, a noble deed (Acts 24:2, in reference to the government and institutions, spoken in flattery to Felix).

Syn.: *diórthōsis* (1357), reformation; *érgon* (2041), a work, deed; *práxis* (4234), a transaction, a deed the action of which is looked upon as incomplete, still in progress; *prágma* (4229), deed; *poíēsis* (4162), a doing, deed; *poíēma* (4161), a work done; *euergesía* (2108), benefit; *enérgeia* (1753), operation, working; *enérgēma* (1755), an effect, accomplishment.

2736. κάτω *kátō*; adv. of place, from *katá* (2596), down. Downwards, below. The comparative is *katṓteros* (2737), lower (Eph 4:9).

(I) Of place implying motion meaning down (Matt 4:6; Luke 4:9; John 8:6, 8; Acts 20:9; Sept.: Eccl 3:21; Isa 37:31); below, underneath (Matt 27:51; Mark 14:66; 15:38; Acts 2:19; Sept.: Ezek 1:27). With the art., used as an adj., meaning that which is below, i.e., earthly (John 8:23).

(II) Of time, meaning comparatively *katṓtérō* (Matt 2:16, "under two years old" [a.t.]; Sept.: 1 Chr 27:23).

Deriv.: *hupokátō* (5270), under.

Syn.: *élasson* (1640), less, under, less than.

Ant.: *ánō* (507), above, in a higher place; *anṓteron* (511), higher; *epánō* (1883), above, used adv.; *ánōthen* (509), from above.

2737. κατώτερος *katṓteros*; fem. *katṓtéra*, neut. *katṓteron*, the comparative of *kátō* (2736), below. Lower. In Eph 4:9, referring to the lower parts of the earth. Some have believed this implies that Christ became subject to death (see Eph 1:20) and went to the dwelling place of the disembodied spirits which is called *Hádēs* (86) in the NT and *Shᵉol* (7585, OT) in the OT (Sept.: Ps 63:9). Others have understood this instead to be a gen. of apposition and that the reference is to the earth itself as the lower realms in contrast to the heavens as the upper realms from which Christ originally descended.

Ant.: *anṓteros* (511), higher.

2738. καῦμα *kaúma*; gen. *kaúmatos*, neut. noun from *kaíō* (2545), to burn, light. Burning, heat, scorching (Rev 7:16; 16:9; Sept.: Gen 8:22). With the suffix *-ma*, it means the result of burning or the heat produced.

Deriv.: *kaumatízō* (2739), to burn or scorch.

Syn.: *thérmē* (2329), warmth; *púr* (4442), fire; *purá* (4443), the actual fire.

Ant.: *psúchos* (5592), cold.

2739. καυματίζω *kaumatízō*; fut. *kaumatísō*, from *kaúma* (2738), heat or the result of burning. To burn, scorch, used trans. (Matt 13:6; Mark 4:6; Rev 16:8, 9).

Syn.: *zéō* (2204), to be hot; *puróō* (4448), to burn, be on fire.

Ant.: *psúchō* (5594), to cool by blowing.

2740. καῦσις *kaúsis*; gen. *kaúseōs*, fem. noun from *kaíō* (2545), to burn, light. The act of burning (Heb 6:8, "the end of which is to be burned" [a.t.]; Sept.: Isa 40:16; 44:15).

Deriv.: *kausóomai* (2741), to burn.

Ant.: *psúchos* (5592), cold.

2741. καυσόομαι *kausóomai*; contracted *kausoúmai*, from *kaúsis* (2740), the act of burning. Used only in the pass. in the NT. To be set on fire, burn (2 Pet 3:10, 12). Used also to indicate burning with fever.

Syn.: *kaumatízō* (2739), to burn, scorch; *kaíō* (2545), to burn.

Ant.: *psúchō* (5594), to cool; *katapsúchō* (2711), to cool down, refresh.

2742. καύσων *kaúsōn*; gen. *kaúsōnos*, masc. noun from *kaíō* (2545), to burn. Fervent or scorching heat as of the sun (Matt 20:12; Luke 12:55; James 1:11; Sept.: Job 27:21, scorching wind; Jer 18:17; Ezek 17:10).

Syn.: *thérmē* (2329), heat; *púr* (4442), fire; *purá* (4443), the actual fire.

Ant.: *psúchos* (5592), cold.

2743. καυτηριάζω *kautēriázō*; fut. *kautēriásō*, from *kautérion* (n.f.), a red-hot iron, which is from *kaíō* (2545), to burn. To cauterize, brand with a hot iron; used in the pass. in 1 Tim 4:2, meaning branded or having the marks of their guilt burnt in upon their own consciences, making them seared or hardened in their consciences.

Syn.: *katakaíō* (2618), to burn completely; *pímprēmi* (4092), to fire, burn, become inflamed with fever; *ekkaíō* (1572), to inflame deeply, burn.

Ant.: *anapsúchō* (404), to relieve, refresh.

2744. καυχάομαι *kaucháomai*; contracted *kauchṓmai*, fut. *kauchḗsomai*, pres. 2d person *kauchásai*, (Rom 2:17, 23). Some Greek lexicons deduce it from *auchén* (n.f.), the neck, which vain persons are apt to carry in a proud manner (Ps 75:5; Isa 3:16). To boast, glory, exult, both in a good and bad sense. Used in an absolute sense (1 Cor 1:29, 31; 4:7; 2 Cor 10:13, 17; 11:18, 30; 12:1, 6, 11; Gal 6:14; Eph 2:9). Followed by the acc. of thing of which one boasts (2 Cor 9:2; 11:16, 30, with the acc. of degree); by *en* (1722), in, with the dat. of that in which one glories, of things (Rom 2:23; 5:3; 2 Cor 5:12; 10:15, 16; 11:12; 12:9; Gal 6:13; James 1:9; 4:16); of persons (1 Cor 3:21; 2 Thess 1:4); in God (Rom 2:17; 5:11; 1 Cor 1:31; 2 Cor 10:17; Phil 3:3); by *epí* (1909), upon with the dat. (Rom 5:2); by *katá* (2596), according, with the acc. meaning as to anything (2 Cor 11:18); by *perí* (4012), about, with the gen. (2 Cor 10:8); by *hupér* (5228), on behalf of, with the gen. (2 Cor 7:14; 9:2; 12:5).

Deriv.: *katakaucháomai* (2620), to boast greatly; *kaúchēma* (2745), the result of bragging, a boast; *kaúchēsis* (2746), the act of boasting.

Syn.: *megalauchéō* (3166), to speak haughtily; *huperaíromai* (5229), to become haughty; *tuphóō* (5187), to envelop with smoke, inflate with self-conceit, be proud; *huperéchō* (5242), to hold oneself above; *huperupsóō* (5251), to elevate oneself above others; *huperphronéō* (5252), to think of oneself as above others; *doxázō* (1392), to glorify, magnify; *perpereúomai* (4068), to be vainglorious, vaunt oneself.

Ant.: *tapeinóō* (5013), to make low, humble, and in the mid. *tapeinóomai*, to be abased, to humble oneself; *elattonéō* (1641), to diminish; *elattóō* (1642), to decrease, make lower.

2745. καύχημα *kaúchēma*; gen. *kau-chḗmatos*, neut. noun from *kaucháomai* (2744), to boast.

(I) The result of boasting, a boast (Heb 3:6 referring to the boast of hope, meaning the hope in which we glory). A boast in regard to anything (2 Cor 5:12; 9:3). Used in an absolute sense (1 Cor 5:6).

(II) It also refers to the object of boasting, ground of glorying, exultation (Rom 4:2; 1 Cor 9:15, 16; 2 Cor 1:14; Gal 6:4; Phil 1:26; 2:16; Sept.: Deut 10:21; Prov 17:6; Jer 17:14). Contrasted to *kaúchēsis* (2746), the act of boasting.

Syn.: *alazoneía* (212), thinking of oneself higher than one really is, arrogant display, boasting, pride; *huperēphanía* (5243), pride, appearing above others; *huperochḗ* (5247), superiority; *mataiótēs* (3153), vanity; *kenodoxía* (2754), vainglory; *dóxa* (1391), glory, dignity, honor.

Ant.: *atimía* (819), shame, dishonor; *aischúnē* (152), shame; *entropḗ* (1791), introspection, withdrawal, shame; *aidṓs* (127), modesty, bashfulness arising from moral conviction; *aschēmosúnē* (808), unseemliness, shame.

2746. καύχησις *kaúchēsis*; gen. *kauchḗseōs*, fem. noun from *kaucháomai* (2744), to boast. Boasting.

(I) The act of boasting about something (2 Cor 7:14; 9:4; 11:17; 1 Thess 2:19 meaning the crown in which we glory; James 4:16); on behalf of someone (2 Cor 8:24; Sept.: Prov 16:31; Ezek 16:12; 23:42).

(II) Metonymically, the matter or cause for glorying or boasting (Rom 3:27; 15:17; 1 Cor 15:31; 2 Cor 1:12; 7:4; 11:10; Sept.: Jer 12:13).

Syn.: *kaúchēma* (2745), a boast; *kenodoxía* (2754), vainglory; *alazoneía* (212), boasting, appearing greater than what one is.

Ant.: *tapeinophrosúnē* (5012), lowliness of mind, humility of mind; *tapeínōsis* (5014), humiliation.

2747. Κεγχρεαί *Kegchreaí*; gen. pl. *Kegchreṓn*, fem. pl. proper noun.

Cenchrea, the eastern harbor of Corinth on the Saronic Gulf, about seven miles east of that city. The western harbor was Lechaeum. A church was formed at Cenchrea at which Phoebe served (Rom 16:1). Here Paul shaved his head in observance of a vow he had taken. From here he sailed to Ephesus (Acts 18:18). The town was full of idolatrous monuments and shrines. Today it is called Kichries.

2748. Κεδρών *Kedrṓn*, **κέδρος** *kédros*; masc. proper noun transliterated from the Hebr. *Qidrōn* (6939, OT), black brook. Kidron, Cedron, or Kedron. In the summer, it is a small, insignificant stream which grows into a torrent in the rainy season. Situated one and one-half miles northwest of Jerusalem, it runs in a southeast direction touching the corner of the northeast wall of the city. Then it sweeps through the Valley of Jehoshaphat in a deep gorge along the east side of the city where the wall rises one hundred feet above the river bottom. On the other side, the peak of Mount Olivet rises about five hundred feet. Breaking through a still narrower cleft between the Hill of Offense and Mount Moriah, Kidron continues its course through a wild and dismal channel in the wilderness of Judah, passing by the curious convent of Mar Saba until it reaches the northwest shore of the Dead Sea.

Its name perhaps refers to the gloom of the valley, or perhaps to the peculiar nature of impurity connected with it. Maachah's idols were burned nearby (1 Kgs 15:13; 2 Chr 15:16), and the impurities and abominations of idol worship were regularly carried and destroyed (2 Kgs 23:4, 6, 12; 2 Chr 29:16; 30:14). In the time of King Josiah, Kidron was near the common burial place of Jerusalem (2 Kgs 23:16). David crossed it on his flight from Jerusalem when Absalom rebelled (2 Sam 15:23, 30). Christ crossed it on His way to Gethsemane (John 18:1 [cf. Mark 14:26; Luke 22:39]).

2749. κεῖμαι *keímai*; fut. *keísomai*. To lie upon.

(I) To lie down, be laid down (Matt 28:6; Luke 2:12, 16; 23:53 [TR]; 24:12; John 11:41 [TR]; 20:5–7, 12; 21:9).

(II) To be placed or set (Matt 5:14; John 2:6; 19:29; 2 Cor 3:15; Rev 4:2); to be laid, applied (Matt 3:10; Luke 3:9); to be laid, as a foundation (1 Cor 3:11); to be stored up (Luke 12:19); to be set, appointed (Luke 2:34; Phil 1:17; 1 Thess 3:3); to be made or promulgated as a law (1 Tim 1:9).

(III) To be in the power of someone (1 John 5:19).

(IV) In Matt 3:10 and Luke 3:9, in regard to the ax that lies at the root of the trees, it does not simply mean that it is lying there, but also implies the necessity of its being taken up and used.

Deriv.: *anákeimai* (345), to rest on; *antíkeimai* (480), to lie over against or to oppose; *apókeimai* (606), to be laid, reserved, appointed; *epíkeimai* (1945), to rest upon, impose, be instant, press upon; *katákeimai* (2621), to lie down; *kṓmē* (2968), a village; *parákeimai* (3873), to lie ready; *períkeimai* (4029), to lie around; *prókeimai* (4295), to lie before, set forth, to lie in front of.

Syn.: *kataklínomai* (2625), to recline, sit down.

Ant.: *hístēmi* (2476), to stand; *anístēmi* (450), to stand up; *egeírō* (1453), to raise; *stḗkō* (4739), to stand.

2750. κειρία *keiría*; gen. *keirías*, fem. noun. Band or bandage for swathing infants or dead bodies. In the NT, used only in relation to dead bodies (John 11:44).

Syn.: *sindṓn* (4616), linen cloth, sheet; *línon* (3043), linen; *othónion* (3608), used in the pl. to indicate the strips of cloth with which the body of the Lord was bound; *bússos* (1040), linen cloth for wrapping the dead.

2751. κείρω *keírō*; fut. *kerṓ*. To shear, especially to shave the head. (Acts 18:18, "having shorn his head," indicates that possibly Paul had taken a Nazarite vow, which signifies the consecration of the body to God. The fact that his head was shorn would indicate that the period of his special vow was over. It was customary at the end of the vow period to have the head shaved at the door of the tabernacle. Acts 21:24 also associates the shorn head with the taking of a vow.) See 1 Cor 11:6, which indicates that cutting the hair very short was the custom of prostitutes so that they could be easily identified by potential customers (Sept.: 2 Sam 14:26; Job 1:20; Jer 7:29). Used trans. in regard to sheep (Acts 8:32 from Isa 53:7).

Deriv.: *kérma* (2772), small coin.

Syn.: *kóptō* (2875), to cut.

Ant.: *komáō* (2863), to let the hair grow long.

2752. κέλευσμα *kéleusma*, gen. *keleúsmatos*, neut. noun from *keleúō* (2753), to bid, exhort. A shout. In the Class. Gr. writers, used for the shout of soldiers charging their enemies, rowers encouraging each other in their work, charioteers inciting their horses. 1 Thess 4:16 refers to the shout of the Lord Jesus when He comes to call His own to meet Him in the air at His *parousía* (3952), appearance.

Syn.: *boḗ* (995), cry; *phōnḗ* (5456), voice.

Ant.: *sigḗ* (4602), silence; *hēsuchía* (2271), quietness.

2753. κελεύω *keleúō*; fut. *keleúsō*. To set in motion, urge on. In the NT, used generally with the meaning of to command, order something to be done (Matt 8:18; 14:9, 19, 28; 15:35; 18:25; 27:58, 64; Luke 18:40; Acts 4:15; 5:34; 8:38; 12:19; 16:22; 21:33, 34; 22:24, 30; 23:3, 10, 35; 24:8; 25:6, 17, 21, 23; 27:43).

Syn.: *kaléō* (2564), to call; *prostássō* (4367), to command; *diatássō* (1299), to set in order, command; *entéllomai* (1781), to enjoin upon; *paraggéllō* (3853), to command.

Ant.: *agnoéō* (50), to ignore; *ameléō* (272), to neglect; *epilanthánomai* (1950), to forget.

2754. κενοδοξία *kenodoxía*; gen. *kenodoxías*, fem. noun from *kenódoxos* (2755), self-conceited. Vainglory, empty pride, desire for praise (Phil 2:3).

Syn.: *alazoneía* (212), boasting, vaunting, appearing to be what one is not, compared to *kenodoxía* which is an empty pride having nothing about which to boast; *kaúchēsis* (2746), the act of boasting; *kaúchēma* (2745), a boast; *huperēphanía* (5243), haughtiness, pride, appearing above others.

Ant.: *tapeinophrosúnē* (5012), humility, lowliness of mind; *tapeínōsis* (5014), humiliation, the act of being humble.

2755. κενόδοξος *kenódoxos*; gen. *kenodóxou*, masc.-fem., neut. *kenódoxon*, adj. from *kenós* (2756), empty or vain, and *dóxa* (1391), glory or praise. It denotes a person who is void of real worth but who wants to be admired by others (Gal 5:26). Contrast with *alazón* (213) which means self-assuming, arrogant and boasting, one who wants to appear as something more than he is, i.e., higher, more important, but not necessarily characterized by worthlessness.

Deriv.: *kenodoxía* (2754), self-conceit.

Syn.: *huperḗphanos* (5244), haughty, proud.

Ant.: *tapeinós* (5011), humble; *semnós* (4586), modest.

2756. κενός *kenós*; fem. *kenḗ*, neut. *kenón*, adj. Empty, hollow. Contrast *mátaios* (3152), meaninglessness, aimlessness. In 1 Thess 2:1, it means unaccompanied with the demonstration of Spirit and of power. When used not of things but of persons, it predicates not merely an absence of good, but also, since a vacuum does not exist in man's moral nature, the presence of evil (James 2:20).

(I) With empty hands, having nothing (Mark 12:3; Luke 1:53; 20:10, 11; Sept.: Gen 31:42; Deut 15:13).

(II) Metaphorically, meaning empty, vain.

(A) Fruitless, without usefulness or success (Acts 4:25; 1 Cor 15:10, 14, 58; 2 Cor 6:1; Gal 2:2; Phil 2:16; 1 Thess 2:1; 3:5; Sept.: Job 7:6; Jer 6:29; 18:15).

(B) Of that in which there is nothing of truth or reality, false, fallacious, e.g., empty words meaning false words, deceitful (Eph 5:6; Col 2:8; Sept.: Ex 5:9; Hos 12:1); of persons, meaning empty, foolish (James 2:20).

Deriv.: *kenódoxos* (2755), self-conceited; *kenophōnía* (2757), empty speaking; *kenóō* (2758), to be in vain; *kenós* (2761), in vain.

Ant.: *alēthḗs* (227), actual, true to fact; *alēthinós* (228), real, genuine; *gnḗsios* (1103), genuine, sincere; *eilikrinḗs* (1506), pure, sincere; *ádolos* (97), without guile.

2757. κενοφωνία *kenophōnía*; gen. *kenophōnías*, fem. noun from *kenós* (2756), vain, and *phōnḗ* (5456), a voice. Empty or fruitless speaking. In 1 Tim 6:20 and 2 Tim 2:16, Paul designates the *bébēloi* (952), godless, as those who engage in *kenophōnía*, senseless or wicked discourses, speeches that are devoid of any divine or spiritual character, fruitless as far as the satisfaction of man's need of salvation and the molding of Christian life and character are concerned. It is equivalent to the "empty [*kenós* {2756}] words [*lógos* {3056}]" (a.t.) in Eph 5:6.

2758. κενόω *kenóō*; contracted *kenṓ*, fut. *kenṓsō*, from *kenós* (2756), empty, void. To make empty, to empty, falsify, be fallacious.

(I) The antithesis of *plēróō* (4137), to fill. *Kenóō* is used in Rom 4:14; 1 Cor 1:17; 9:15; 2 Cor 9:3; Phil 2:7 meaning to empty oneself, to divest oneself of rightful dignity by descending to an inferior condition, to abase oneself.

(II) The use in Phil 2:7 is of great theological importance. It refers to Jesus Christ as emptying Himself at the time of His incarnation, denoting the beginning of His self-humiliation in verse eight. In order to understand what is meant by Jesus' emptying Himself, the whole passage (Phil 2:6–8) must be examined.

The two states of the Lord Jesus are spoken about here. In verse seven, the state of His humiliation is referred to as having taken "the form [*morphḗn* {3444} {acc.}] of a servant [*doúlou* {1401} {acc.}]," and having become "in the likeness [*homoiṓmati* {3667}{dat.}] of men [*anthrṓpōn* {444}{gen. pl.}]." In contrast to this, we have His preincarnate, eternal state spoken of in verse six as "being in the form [*morphḗ*] of God," and "equal [*ísa* {2470}] with God." The truth expressed here concerning His preincarnate state is that He had to be equal with God in order to have the form of God. He could not be God the Son without being Deity. He who showed us the *morphḗ* of God, the form of God, the essence of God, had to be equal with God Himself.

The fact that Christ in His human form showed us God presupposes His being God at all times. He never claimed to be something without really being that in His essence. If He had, He would have been making a false claim.

As to the use of the subst. *harpagmós* (725), robbery or plunder, see the verb *harpázō* (726), to seize, catch, pluck or pull (2 Cor 12:2, 4; 1 Thess 4:17; Jude 23; Rev 12:5). As a subst., *harpagmós* is used only in Phil 2:6. It refers to Christ's not taking that which did not belong to Him by being in the form of God. His whole life was characterized by being (*hupárchōn* [5225]) that which He always was. Prior to His incarnation He was in the form, the essence of God, and after His incarnation He was still in the form of God in spite of His voluntary humiliation.

Notwithstanding His essence of deity, He took upon Himself the true essence of a servant (*morphḗn doúlou*). In order to be a servant, however, He had to become

a man and appear in the likeness of men (*en homoiṓmati anthrṓpōn*). By doing this He emptied Himself of the proper recognition that He had with the Father as God who is Spirit (*pneúma* [4151]; John 4:24) and entered into the world of men, most of whom did not at all recognize Him for who He was. The use of the aor. act. part. *labṓn* (*lambánō* [2983], to take), having taken (with reference to the form of a servant), indicates that humanity did not displace deity in His personality. Rather He took upon Himself voluntarily, in addition to His preincarnate condition, something which veiled His deity. Proper recognition is called *dóxa* (1391), glory, praise, from the verb *dokéō* (1380), to recognize. In the form of man and servant, He lacked the recognition among men that He had with the Father (John 17:5). This voluntary humiliation of Christ began with the incarnation and was carried through to His crucifixion. In His resurrection, He laid aside His form of a servant.

(III) The word *kenóō*, to make empty, is used metaphorically as meaning to bring to nothing in the sense of not accomplishing what one set out to accomplish as in Rom 4:14, the faith not accomplishing its purpose. Used as an adj. in reference to the cross of Christ, meaning the cross not accomplishing its purpose, i.e., salvation for unbelieving man (1 Cor 1:17, 18). In the same manner, life can be vain or empty, not accomplishing its God-intended purpose (1 Cor 9:15; 2 Cor 9:3).

Syn.: *mataióō* (3154), to render vain, without meaning or fulfillment.

Ant.: *plēróō* (4137), to fill; *pímplēmi* and *plḗthō* (4130), to fill; *gemízō* (1072), to fill or load fully; *mestóō* (3325), to be full.

2759. κέντρον *kéntron*; gen. *kéntrou*, neut. noun from *kentéō* (n.f.), to prick, stimulate. Anything by which a puncture is made. Also from *kentéō* (n.f.): *ekkentéō* (1574), to dig out, pierce through.

(I) A goad, point, or prick (Acts 9:5; 26:14; "to kick against the pricks" or goads, meaning to offer vain and rash resistance which is a proverbial expression alluding to unruly oxen and applied to those who by unruly ráge hurt themselves).

(II) In 1 Cor 15:55, 56, it is translated "sting" or that which hurts, referring to death. See Rev 9:10. In these instances, the sting is equated with the sting of a scorpion or a serpent. See Sept.: Hos 5:12; 13:14.

2760. κεντυρίων kenturíōn; gen. *kenturíōnos*, masc. noun from the Lat. *centurio*. A centurion, originally the commander of one hundred foot soldiers, the same as the Gr. *hekatóntarchos* (1543), the one who rules over one hundred (Mark 15:39, 44, 45).

2761. κενῶς kenós; adv. from *kenós* (2756), empty, vain. Vainly, in vain, for no purpose (James 4:5; Sept.: Isa 49:4).

Syn.: *eis mátēn* (*eis* [1519], in; *mátēn* [3155], purposelessness), in vain, to no purpose; *dōreán* (1432), literally meaning freely or uselessly; *eikḗ* (1500), without cause; *dōreán* (1432), gratuitously, for nothing, freely.

Ant.: *alēthós* (230), truly; *óntōs* (3689), really, actually, actually indeed; *gnēsíōs* (1104), sincerely, honorably, truly.

2762. κεραία keraía; gen. *keraías*, fem. noun from *kéras* (2768), a horn. A point, extremity. In the NT, the apex, tittle, point of a letter as in the Hebr. alphabet; referred to in Matt 5:18 and Luke 16:17 by the Lord, meaning that not the least part should pass from the Law.

Syn.: *ióta* (2503), the ninth letter of the Gr. alphabet used as an equivalent for *yōd*, the tenth letter of the Hebr. alphabet, a jot; figuratively, a very small part of anything.

2763. κεραμεύς kerameús; gen. *keraméōs*, masc. noun from *kéramos* (2766), potter's clay. A potter (Matt 27:7, 10; Rom 9:21; Sept.: Isa 29:16).

Deriv.: *keramikós* (2764), made of clay.

2764. κεραμικός keramikós; fem. *keramikḗ*, neut. *keramikón*, adj. from *kerameús* (2763), a potter. Of clay or made by a potter, earthen (Rev 2:27 quoted from Ps 2:9).

2765. κεράμιον kerámion; gen. *keramíou*, adj., neut. of *kerámios* (n.f.), earthen or made of potter's clay. An earthen vessel, a pot, pitcher (Mark 14:13; Luke 22:10; Sept.: Jer 35:5).

2766. κέραμος kéramos; gen. *kerámou*, masc. noun from *keránnumi* (2767), to mix or mingle, and by implication to pour out for drinking. Potter's clay or any earthen vessel. A tile of burnt clay for covering roofs (Luke 5:19).

Deriv.: *kerameús* (2763), a potter.

2767. κεράννυμι keránnumi; fut. *kerásō*, perf. pass. *kekérasmai*. To mix, mingle, such as wine with water or spices. In the NT, by implication, to prepare a drink, to pour out for drinking, to fill one's cup (Rev 14:10; 18:6; Sept.: Prov 9:2, 5; Isa 19:14).

Deriv.: *akéraios* (185), without mixture; *ákratos* (194), pure wine; *sugkeránnumi* (4786), to mix together.

Syn.: *plēróō* (4137), to make full; *pímplēmi* or *plḗthō* (4130), to fill; *empíplēmi* or *emplḗthō* (1705), to fill, satisfy; *gemízō* (1072), to fill or load fully, e.g., a boat; *korénnumi* (2880), to satisfy, used metaphorically of spiritual things; *mestóō* (3325), to fill full; *mígnumi* (3396), to mix, mingle.

2768. κέρας kéras; gen. *kératos*, neut. noun. A horn. Horns are well-known emblems of strength, power, or glory, both in the sacred and Class. Gr. writers. This comes from the strength or force exhibited in the horns of animals, whether for offense or defense (Deut 33:17; Ps 22:21; Dan 8). The symbol is applied to Christ who is called a "horn of salvation," meaning a mighty and glorious Savior (Luke 1:69). Used of a beast (Rev 5:6; 12:3; 13:1, 11; 17:3, 7, 12, 16; Sept.: Gen 22:13; Dan 7:7, 8). Its significance as a symbol of strength or power is derived from its use in the OT (Sept.: 2 Sam 22:3; Ps 75:10; Jer 48:25). It also refers to any extremity or projecting point resembling a horn, as upon the four corners of the Jewish altars (Rev 9:13 [cf. Ex 27:2]).

Deriv.: *keraía* (2762), point, tittle; *kerátion* (2769), little horn.

2769. κεράτιον *kerátion*; gen. *keratíou*, neut. noun, a diminutive of *kéras* (2768), horn. Little horn. A pod such as the carob pod (Luke 15:16), the fruit of the carob tree (which in Gr. is called *kerateía* [n.f.], horn tree). This tree is common in Syria and the southern parts of Europe. It produces long slender pods shaped like a horn or sickle containing a sweet pulp and several brown shining seeds like beans. These pods are sometimes used as food by the poorer classes in the East, and swine are commonly fed with them.

2770. κερδαίνω *kerdaínō*; fut. *kerdanō*, later fut. *kerdḗsomai*, aor. *ekérdēsa*, fut. pass. 3d person pl. *kerdēthḗsontai* (1 Pet 3:1), from *kérdos* (2771), gain, profit. To gain, acquire as gain, to win. Used trans.

(I) Of things such as the whole world, meaning the wealth of the whole world (Matt 16:26; Mark 8:36; Luke 9:25). In trade, with the acc. (Matt 25:17, 20, 22). Used in an absolute sense in James 4:13. Spoken of gaining any loss or evil in Acts 27:21, and implying that they could have been saved from or avoided this loss.

(II) Metaphorically used of persons meaning to gain or win someone, i.e., as a friend or patron, referring to Christ (Phil 3:8); a brother (Matt 18:15). To gain over to one's side, meaning to win over to Christ and thus bring to salvation (1 Cor 9:19–22, where it is equivalent to *sṓzō* [4982], to save or to deliver in v. 22; see 1 Cor 7:16, where *sṓzō* is used; 1 Pet 3:1).

Syn.: *diapragmateúomai* (1281), to gain by trading; *peripoiéomai* (mid. of *peripoiéō* [4046]) to save for oneself, gain; *ktáomai* (2932), to acquire, procure for oneself, gain; *ploutéō* (4147), to become rich; *ploutízō* (4148), to make rich.

Ant.: *zēmióō* (2210), to suffer loss, forfeit, lose.

2771. κέρδος *kérdos*; gen. *kérdous*, neut. noun. Gain, profit (Phil 1:21; 3:7; Titus 1:11).

Deriv.: *aischrokerdḗs* (146), a greedy person, one who endeavors to gain by unbecoming means; *kerdaínō* (2770), to gain.

Syn.: *porismós* (4200), a means of gain.

Ant.: *zēmía* (2209), loss; *héttēma* (2275), defect, loss.

2772. κέρμα *kérma*; gen. *kérmatos*, neut. noun from *keírō* (2751), to shear or cut off. A small piece of money, so-called because, in the ancient world, coins were frequently clipped off larger metal pieces to transact business (John 2:15).

Syn.: *argúrion* (694), a piece of silver; *chalkós* (5475), a copper coin; *nómisma* (3546), currency or the current coin of a state; *statḗr* (4715), a coin equivalent to four *drachmaí* (1406), the name of the currency used even today among the Greeks.

2773. κερματιστής *kermatistḗs*; gen. *kermatistoú*, masc. noun from *kermatízō* (n.f.), to divide into smaller money, which is from *kérma* (2772), coin. A dealer in small money, a money changer (John 2:14), the same as *kollubistḗs* (2855), a coin dealer or money changer (Matt 21:12). The annual tribute of each Jew to the temple was a Jewish half-shekel (Ex 30:13). It is this that the money changers who sat in the outer court of the temple furnished to the people as they came in exchange for Greek and Roman coins called *drachmḗ* (1406), drachma, and *statḗr* (4715), a coin equivalent to four drachma.

2774. κεφάλαιον *kephálaion*; gen. *kephalaíou*, noun, neut. of *kephálaios* (n.f.), the head, which is from *kephalē* (2776), a head. A principal thing, a sum.

(I) The chief thing, main point (Heb 8:1) meaning the great and essential point in what has been said, amount in computing, summing up in regard to money, a sum.

(II) Capital, amount (Acts 22:28; Sept.: Lev 6:4).

Deriv.: *proskephálaion* (4344), pillow.

Syn.: *pterúgion* (4419), pinnacle, winglet; *ákron* (206), tip.

2775. κεφαλαιόω *kephalaióō*; contracted *kephalaiō*, fut. *kephalaiṓsō*, from *kephálaios* (n.f.), the head, which is from *kephalē* (2776), a head. To strike or wound the head; the same as *kephalízō* (Mark 12:4). In Luke 20:12, the word *traumatízō* (5135), to inflict a wound, is used. The word also can be used as a syn. of *anakephalaióō* (346), to sum up, gather up.

Deriv.: *anakephalaióō* (346), to sum up.

2776. κεφαλή *kephalē*; gen. *kephalēs*, fem. noun. The head, top, that which is uppermost in relation to something.

(I) Particularly of man (Matt 6:17; 8:20; 27:30; Luke 7:38); as cut off (Matt 14:11; Mark 6:27); of animals (Rev 9:17, 19; 12:3; Sept.: Gen 3:15; 40:19); as the principal part, but emphatically for the whole person (Acts 18:6, "Your blood be upon your own heads," meaning the guilt for your destruction rests upon yourselves; Rom 12:20 quoted from Prov 25:22; Sept.: 2 Sam 1:16; 1 Kgs 2:33, 37). Metaphorically of things, the head, top, summit, e.g., the head of the corner, meaning the chief stone of the corner, the cornerstone (Matt 21:42; Mark 12:10; Luke 20:17; Acts 4:11; 1 Pet 2:7, all quoted from Ps 118:22), the same as *akrogōniaíos* (204), belonging to the ex-

treme corner, chief corner (Sept.: Gen 8:5; 11:4).

(II) Metaphorically of persons, i.e., the head, chief, one to whom others are subordinate, e.g., the husband in relation to his wife (1 Cor 11:3; Eph 5:23) insofar as they are one body (Matt 19:6; Mark 10:8), and one body can have only one head to direct it; of Christ in relation to His Church which is His body, and its members are His members (cf. 1 Cor 12:27; Eph 1:22; 4:15; 5:23; Col 1:18; 2:10, 19); of God in relation to Christ (1 Cor 11:3). In Col 2:10 and Eph 1:22, God the Father is designated as the head of Christ. Generally, of a leader or ruler (Sept.: Judg 11:11).

Deriv.: *apokephalízō* (607), to decapitate, behead; *kephalís* (2777), a knob, roll, volume; *perikephalaía* (4030), helmet.

Syn.: *hēgemṓn* (2232), a leader.

Ant.: *poús* (4228), foot; *hupopódion* (5286), footstool, something under the feet.

2777. κεφαλίς *kephalís*; gen. *kephalídos*, fem. noun from *kephalē* (2776), a head. A little head such as a bulb of garlic; head, knob of a column. In the NT, probably the head or knob of the wooden rod on which Hebrew manuscripts were rolled, and hence used to designate a roll, volume (Heb 10:7 quoted from Ps 40:7).

2778. κῆνσος *kḗnsos*; gen. *kḗnsou*, masc. noun. Lat. *census*, meaning a counting of the people and valuation of property; equivalent to the Gr. *apographḗ* (582), literally a write-up, an assessment. In the NT, tribute or poll-tax paid by each person whose name was taken in the census which the Greeks called *epikephálaion*, head tax (Matt 17:25; 22:17, 19; Mark 12:14). In Matt 22:19 called the tribute money; in Mark 12:15 called dinar (*dēnárion* [1220]).

Syn.: *phóros* (5411), the tribute paid by a subjugated nation; *dídrachmon* (1323), half-shekel, tribute or temple tax which was a half *statḗr* (4715), the Roman currency.

2779. κῆπος *kḗpos*; gen. *kḗpou*, masc. noun. A garden, any place planted with herbs and trees (Luke 13:19; John 18:1, 26; 19:41; Sept.: Deut 11:10; Amos 4:9).
Deriv.: *kēpourós* (2780), gardener.
Ant.: *erēmía* (2047), wilderness; *érēmos* (2048), a desert.

2780. κηπουρός *kēpourós*; gen. *kēpouroú*, masc. noun from *kḗpos* (2779), garden, and *oúros* (n.f.), a keeper, inspector. A garden caretaker, gardener (John 20:15).

2781. κηρίον *kēríon*; gen. *kēríou*, neut. noun from *kērós* (n.f.), wax. A honeycomb (Luke 24:42; Sept.: Ps 19:10; Prov 24:13).

2782. κήρυγμα *kḗrugma*; gen. *kḗrugmatos*, neut. noun from *kērússō* (2784), to preach, discharge a herald's office, cry out, proclaim. Sermon, message, proclamation. With the suffix -*ma*, it means the result of preaching, that which is cried by the herald, the command, communication, proclamation of the redeeming purpose of God in Christ (Rom 16:25); the proclamation of Jesus Christ (1 Cor 1:21; 2:4; 15:14; 2 Tim 4:17; Titus 1:3); the message of denunciation from God to the Ninevites through Jonah (Matt 12:41; Luke 11:32; Sept.: Jon 3:2).
Syn.: *aggelía* (31), a message, proclamation, news; *epaggelía* (1860), a promise, message; *lógos* (3056), a word, message.

2783. κῆρυξ *kḗrux*; gen. *kḗrukos*, masc. noun from *kērússō* (2784), to preach. Herald, crier, proclaimer, preacher. In Class. Gr., a public servant of supreme power both in peace and in war, one who summoned the *ekklēsía* (1577), the town gathering. This word, *ekklēsía*, later was used for the Church. A *kḗrux*, messenger, was the public crier and reader of state messages such as the conveyor of a declaration of war. In the NT, except in 2 Pet 2:5 (where it speaks of Noah as the herald of righteousness), the word denotes one who

is employed by God in the work of proclaiming salvation (1 Tim 2:7 [cf. 1 Tim 2:5, 6; 2 Tim 1:11, where it is conjoined with *apóstolos* {652}, apostle]). When both designations are used, *kḗrux* designates the herald according to his commission and work as a proclaimer, while *apóstolos*, apostle, indicates more his relationship to the one who sent him. The authority of the herald or preacher lies in the message he has to bring (2 Pet 2:5), while the apostle is protected by the authority of his Lord who sends him. In 1 Tim 2:7 and 2 Tim 1:11, *kḗrux* is also conjoined with *didáskalos* (1320), teacher.
Ant.: *akroatḗs* (202), a hearer.

2784. κηρύσσω *kērússō*, **κηρύττω** *kērúttō*; fut. *kērúxō*. To preach, to herald, proclaim.
(I) Generally, to proclaim, announce publicly (Matt 10:27; Luke 12:3; Acts 10:42; Rev 5:2; Sept.: Ex 32:5; Esth 6:9, 11; Joel 2:1). In the sense of to publish abroad, announce publicly (Mark 1:45; 5:20; 7:36; Luke 8:39).
(II) Especially to preach, publish, or announce religious truth, the gospel with its attendant privileges and obligations, the gospel dispensation.
(A) Generally of John the Baptist (Matt 3:1; Mark 1:4, 7; Luke 3:3; Acts 10:37); of Jesus (Matt 4:17, 23; 9:35; 11:1; Mark 1:14, 38, 39; Luke 4:44; 8:1; 1 Pet 3:19); of apostles and teachers (Matt 10:7; 24:14; 26:13; Mark 3:14; 6:12; 13:10; 14:9; 16:15, 20; Luke 9:2; 24:47; Acts 20:25; 28:31; Rom 10:8, 14, 15; 1 Cor 9:27; 15:11; Gal 2:2; Col 1:23; 1 Thess 2:9; 2 Tim 4:2). "To preach Christ" means to announce Him as the Messiah and urge the reception of His gospel (Acts 8:5; 9:20; 19:13; 1 Cor 1:23; 15:12; 2 Cor 1:19; 4:5; 11:4; Phil 1:15; 1 Tim 3:16).
(B) In allusion to the Mosaic and prophetic institutions, to preach, teach (Luke 4:18, 19 quoted from Isa 61:1; Acts 15:21; Rom 2:21; Gal 5:11). See Prov 8:1.
Deriv.: *kḗrugma* (2782), the message of a herald, denotes preaching, the

substance of which is distinct from the act; *kḗrux* (2783), a herald, a preacher; *prokērússō* (4296), to proclaim before or ahead.

Syn.: *euaggelízō* (2097), to proclaim the good news, evangelize; *kataggéllō* (2605), to proclaim, promulgate, declare; *diamartúromai* (1263), to testify thoroughly; *laléō* (2980), to speak; *parrēsiázomai* (3955), to speak or preach boldly; *diaggéllō* (1229), to herald thoroughly, declare, preach, signify.

Ant.: *phimóō* (5392), to muzzle, put to silence; *sigáō* (4601), to be silent; *hēsucházō* (2270), to be still.

2785. κῆτος *kḗtos*; gen. *kḗtous*, neut. noun. Any large fish or sea creature. In Matt 12:40, used for the fish which swallowed Jonah. In the book of Jonah, it is called *dāg gādōl* (*dāg* [1709, OT], fish; *gādōl* [1419, OT], large, great}, a great fish, or *haddag* (1709, OT), the fish, without determining anything as to its species. Jon 1:17 tells us that God prepared a great fish. He, who can do anything, could have made the fish capable of swallowing Jonah, preserving him in its belly and then casting him out again alive. God does not need to be assisted by natural possibilities to perform a miracle. This term was in that day, as it is today, common parlance for any kind of aquatic creature. Its nontechnical usage would allow for a mammal such as a whale and would therefore contain no error.

2786. Κηφᾶς *Kēphás*; gen. *Kēphá*, masc. proper noun. Cephas, meaning rock. A Syriac surname given to Simon which in the Gr. is rendered *Pétros* (4074), Peter, also meaning a rock (John 1:42; 1 Cor 1:12; 3:22; 9:5; 15:5; Gal 2:9).

2787. κιβωτός *kibōtós*; gen. *kibotoú*, fem. noun. An ark or a wooden chest, coffer, a hollow vessel. In the NT, spoken of the ark of the covenant (Heb 9:4; Rev 11:19; Sept.: Ex 25:10; Lev 16:2). Used of Noah's ark (Matt 24:38; Luke 17:27;

Heb 11:7; 1 Pet 3:20; Sept.: Gen 6:14; 7:1).

2788. κιθάρα *kithára*; gen. *kitháras*, fem. noun from *kítharis* (n.f.), harp. A lyre, harp. The Eng. "guitar" is derived from this word, although the modern instrument is different. The ancient *kithára* (or lyre) was without a neck and the strings were open like the modern harp (1 Cor 14:7; Rev 5:8; 14:2; 15:2; see Sept.: Gen 31:27; 2 Chr 9:11). Josephus describes the Hebrew harp as having ten strings and being struck with a key.

Deriv.: *kitharōdós* (2790), a harp player.

2789. κιθαρίζω *kitharízō*; fut. *kitharísō*, from *kítharis* (n.f.), harp. To play upon a harp or lyre (1 Cor 14:7; Rev 14:2; see Sept.: Isa 23:16).

2790. κιθαρῳδός *kitharōdós*; gen. *kitharōdoú*, masc. noun from *kithára* (2788), harp, lyre, and *aoidós* (n.f.), a singer. A harpist, lyrist, one who plays on the harp or lyre and accompanies it with song (Rev 14:2; 18:22).

2791. Κιλικία *Kilikía*; gen. *Kilikías*, fem. proper noun. Cilicia, the southeastern province of Asia Minor having Cappadocia on the north, Syria on the east, the Mediterranean Sea on the south with Pamphylia and Pisidia on the west. Eastern Cilicia was a rich plain; western Cilicia was rough and mountainous, lying on the Taurus range. Its capital was Tarsus, and many of its people were Jews. Frequently mentioned in Acts 6:9; 15:23, 41; 21:39; 22:3; 23:34; 27:5; Gal 1:21.

2792. κινάμωμον *kinámōmon*; gen. *kinamómou*, neut. noun. Cinnamon (Rev 18:13; see Sept.: Ex 30:23; Jer 6:20).

2793. κινδυνεύω *kinduneúō*; fut. *kinduneúsō*, from *kíndunos* (2794), danger. To be in danger, used intrans. in Luke 8:23; 1 Cor 15:30; followed by the inf. (Acts 19:27, 40).

Ant.: *bebaióō* (950), to confirm, establish; *asphalízō* (805), to secure, make safe.

2794. κίνδυνος *kíndunos*; gen. *kindúnou*, masc. noun from *kinéō* (2795), to move. Danger, peril (Rom 8:35; 2 Cor 11:26; Sept.: Ps 114:3).
Deriv.: *kinduneúō* (2793), to be in danger.
Ant.: *aspháleia* (803), safety; *sōtēría* (4991), salvation, safety; *bebaíōsis* (951), confirmation.

2795. κινέω *kinéō*; contracted *kinṓ*, fut. *kinḗsō*, from *kió* (n.f.), to go. To move, put in motion, used trans. in Matt 23:4. See Sept.: Job 13:25; Isa 41:7. In the mid. pass., *kinéomai* or *kinoúmai*, to move oneself or be moved (Acts 17:28; Sept.: Gen 7:21). To move, agitate, wag as the head (Matt 27:39; Mark 15:29; Sept.: 2 Kgs 19:21; Job 16:4). To move, remove, used trans. (Rev 2:5). Metaphorically meaning to move, excite to sedition (Acts 24:5). In the aor. pass. *ekinéthē*, to be moved, put into commotion or tumult (Acts 21:30).
Deriv.: *kínēsis* (2796), the act of moving; *metakinéō* (3334), to move something away; *sugkinéō* (4787), to stir, rouse, incite.
Syn.: *seíō* (4579), to shake, stir; *saleúō* (4531), to stir up, shake; *saínō* (4525), to move, metaphorically meaning to disturb, disquiet; *phérō* (5342), to bear, carry, move; *anaseíō* (383), to shake to and fro, stir up.
Ant.: *aphíēmi* (863), to leave alone; *kataleípō* (2641), *apoleípō* (620), and *egkataleípō* (1459), to leave behind; *hupoleípō* (5275), to leave remaining; *perileípō* (4035), to leave over; *stērízō* (4741), to confirm, establish; *stḗkō* (4739), to stand.

2796. κίνησις *kínēsis*; gen. *kinḗseōs*, fem. noun from *kinéō* (2795), to move, stir. The act of moving (John 5:3).
Ant.: *stērigmós* (4740), stability; *stásis* (4714), a standing.

2797. Κίς *Kís*; masc. proper noun, transliterated from the Hebr. *Qīs* (7027, OT). Cis or Kish, a Benjamite, father of King Saul (1 Sam 9:1, 2) and an ancestor of Mordecai (Esth 2:5). In Acts 13:21, he is called Kis. See 1 Sam 9:1.

2798. κλάδος *kládos*; gen. *kládou*, masc. noun from *kláō* (2806) to break or prune. A small branch or twig which is easily broken. It is usually called *kládos*, the shoot which springs from the larger branches (Matt 13:32; 21:8; 24:32; Mark 4:32; 13:28; Luke 13:19; Rom 11:16–19, 21; Sept.: Jer 11:16; Ezek 31:7). In Rom 11:16–19, 21, used metaphorically to refer to the descendants of Israel.
Syn.: *rhábdos* (4464), rod, stick; *klḗma* (2814) from *kláō* (2806), to break, denoting a tender, flexible shoot of a vine or a sprout; *stoibás* or *stibás* (4746), a layer of leaves, reeds or twigs serving for a bed, hence a branch full of leaves which may be used in making a bed or for walking on; *báion* (902), a branch of the palm tree used for papyri writings.
Ant.: *rhíza* (4491), root.

2799. κλαίω *klaíō*; fut. *klaúsō*. To weep, wail, lament, implying not only the shedding of tears, but also every external expression of grief.
(I) Used intrans. and in an absolute sense (Matt 26:75; Mark 14:72; Luke 6:21; 7:13; 8:52; John 11:31, 33; 1 Cor 7:30). Followed by *epí* (1909), upon with a dat., to weep for or over someone (Luke 19:41); *epí* with acc. (Luke 23:28, "Do not cry over me" [a.t.]). Joined with *alalázō* (214), to wail (Mark 5:38); with *thorubéō* (2350), to clamor or make noise (Mark 5:39); with *thrēnéō* (2354), to lament, mourn (John 16:20); with *kóptomai* (2875), to bewail (Rev 18:9); with *ololúzō* (3649), to howl (James 5:1); with *penthéō* (3996), to mourn (Mark 16:10; Luke 6:25; Rev 18:11, "upon her," 15, 19; Sept.: Gen 33:4; 2 Sam 19:1).
(II) Followed by the acc. meaning to bewail, lament, especially for the dead

(Matt 2:18; see Sept.: Gen 37:34; Deut 34:8).

Deriv.: *klauthmós* (2805), weeping.

Syn.: *kóptō* (2875), to beat the breast, smite, as an expression of sorrow; *penthéō* (3996), to mourn, especially for the dead; *thrēnéō* (2354), to lament, wail; *lupéomai*, the mid. of *lupéō* (3076), to grieve; *dakrúō* (1145), to shed tears; *alalázō* (214), to wail; *stenázō* (4727), to groan.

Ant.: *geláō* (1070), to laugh; *katageláō* (2606), to laugh scornfully; *chaírō* (5463), to rejoice; *agalliáomai* (21), to rejoice greatly, exult; *euphraínomai* (2165), to rejoice, make merry; *kaucháomai* (2744), to boast, glory, rejoice; *katakaucháomai* (2620), to boast against.

2800. κλάσις *klásis*; gen. *kláseōs*, fem. noun from *kláō* (2806), to break. The act of breaking, particularly with reference to the bread in the Lord's Supper (Luke 24:35; Acts 2:42).

Ant.: *súndesmos* (4886), a tie that joins, uniting bond.

2801. κλάσμα *klásma*; gen. *klásmatos*, neut. noun from *kláō* (2806), to break. That which is broken off, indicated by the suffix *-ma*, a fragment, crumb, used only of pieces of bread (Matt 14:20; 15:37; Mark 6:43; 8:8, 19, 20; Luke 9:17; John 6:12, 13; Sept.: Lev 2:6; 1 Sam 30:12). The act of breaking is *klásis* (2800).

Ant.: *hólos* (3650), the whole; *pás* (3956) or *hápas* (537), the whole; *holóklēros* (3648), entire.

2802. Κλαύδη *Klaúdē*; gen. *Klaúdēs*, fem. proper noun. Clauda, a small island seven miles long by three miles wide in the Mediterranean Sea, south of Crete (Acts 27:16), now called Gozzo.

2803. Κλαυδία *Klaudía*; gen. *Klaudías*, fem. proper noun. Claudia, a Christian woman in Rome who joined Paul in greeting Timothy (2 Tim 4:21).

2804. Κλαύδιος *Klaúdios*; gen. *Klaudíou*, masc. proper noun. Claudius, meaning lame.

(I) The fifth Roman Emperor, successor of Caius Caligula, A.D. 41–54 (Acts 11:28). Herod Agrippa I was mainly instrumental in securing the throne for him. Several different famines took place during his reign, one of which, predicted by Agabus, was very severe and lasted three years. In the ninth or twelfth year of his reign he banished the Jews, probably including the Christian converts, from Rome (Acts 18:2).

(II) Claudius Lysias, a Roman officer (*chiliarchos* [5506], commander of a thousand soldiers) commanding in Jerusalem (Acts 23:26).

2805. κλαυθμός *klauthmós*; gen. *klauthmoú*, masc. noun from *klaíō* (2799), to weep, bewail. Weeping, wailing (Matt 2:18; 8:12; 13:42, 50; 22:13; 24:51; 25:30; Luke 13:28; Acts 20:37; see Sept.: Gen 45:2; Ezra 3:13).

Syn.: *dákru* (1144), tear; *kopetós* (2870), lamentation by beating the breast in expression of sorrow; *pénthos* (3997), mourning, sorrow; *thrḗnos* (2355), lamentation; *odurmós* (3602), wailing as a part of mourning; *lúpē* (3077), grief, sorrow; *thlípsis* (2347), affliction, tribulation.

Ant.: *gélōs* (1071), laughter; *chará* (5479), joy, delight; *agallíasis* (20), exultation, exuberant joy; *euphrosúnē* (2167), joy, gladness.

2806. κλάω *kláō*; fut. *klásō*. To break. In later Gr. it especially came to mean the breaking off of leaves, sprouts, tendrils. In the NT, used only of the breaking of bread which was made in thin cakes, not in loaves (Matt 14:19; 15:36; Mark 8:6, 19; Luke 24:30; Acts 27:35; Sept.: Jer 16:7); in the Lord's Supper and *agápē* (26), love feast (Matt 26:26; Mark 14:22; Luke 22:19; Acts 2:46; 20:7, 11; 1 Cor 10:16). The fellowship of the Lord with His people is described as a table fellowship (Luke 24:30 [cf. John 13:18]).

Applied to Christ's body broken on the cross (1 Cor 11:24).

Deriv.: *ekkláō* (1575), to break off; *katakláō* (2622), to break loaves and put them down; *kládos* (2798), branch; *klásis* (2800), the breaking; *klásma* (2801), that which is broken off, fragment, crumb; *klḗma* (2814), twig.

Syn.: *lúō* (3089), to loosen, break down, destroy; *suntríbō* (4937), to shatter, break in pieces by crushing; *rhḗgnumi* (4486), to rend or rip as garments, burst; *diarrḗgnumi / diarrḗssō* (1284), to burst asunder, rip; *katágnumi* (2608), to break, crack apart; *sunthláō* (4917), to break or crush in pieces, shatter; *schízō* (4977), to split, rip open as a piece of cloth.

Ant.: *kolláō* (2853), to glue or cement together; *proskolláō* (4347), to stick to, join oneself to.

2807. κλείς *kleís*; gen. *kleidós*, fem. noun. A key. In the NT, used only figuratively (Matt 16:19, where the Lord said to Peter, "I will give to thee the keys of the kingdom of heaven" [a.t.]). In ancient times, the steward of a wealthy family, especially of the royal household, was given a key, probably a golden one in recognition of his office. Therefore, the phrase referring to giving a person the key naturally grew into an expression of raising him to great power (cf. Isa 22:22; Rev 3:7). The Lord designated Peter as the one who at Pentecost was going to open the kingdom of heaven to a great crowd which was of the Jewish stock (Acts 2) and later at Caesarea Maritime, which was of the Gentiles (Acts 10).

In addition, we may take this to refer to the power that the Lord Jesus later gave to all believers in binding and loosing the sins of those who repent. This is not to be taken to mean that believers themselves have the actual power to forgive sins (Mark 2:1–12), but to declare the forgiveness granted by God Himself on the basis of personal confession, repentance from sin, and the seeking of Christ (John 20:21–23).

The "key of knowledge" referred to in Luke 11:52 is the means of attaining true knowledge in respect to the kingdom of God. It is said that authority to explain the Law and the Prophets was given among the Jews by the delivery of a key. The "keys of hell and of death" (Rev 1:18) denote power to call men out of this life into the state of departed souls, and finally to raise them from death to reunite their souls and bodies at the resurrection. The "key of David" (Rev 3:7) alludes to the promise made to Eliakim (Isa 22:22 [cf. 2 Kgs 18:18]) and signifies the unlimited power of Christ in His household, the Church. The "key of the pit of the abyss" (a.t. [Rev 9:1]) is power or permission to open it, as the "key of the abyss" (a.t. [Rev 20:1]) is power to shut it.

2808. κλείω *kleíō*; fut. *kleísō*, aor. pass. *ekleísthēn*, perf. pass. *kékleismai*. To shut, close. Used trans. in Matt 6:6; 25:10; Luke 11:7; John 20:19, 26; Acts 5:23; 21:30; Rev 20:3; 21:25. See Sept.: Gen 7:16; Josh 2:7. Spoken of the windows of the heavens, meaning that no rain could fall (Luke 4:25; Rev 11:6). Metaphorically used in Matt 23:13 in regard to shutting up the kingdom of heaven, meaning willfully preventing men from entering. Used also concerning authority to exclude or omit (Rev 3:7, 8). In 1 John 3:17, to "shut up one's bowels" (a.t.) from someone means not to let one's compassion flow out, to be hard-hearted [cf. *splágchnon* {4698}, bowel].

Deriv.: *apokleíō* (608), to exclude; *ekkleíō* (1576), to shut out, exclude; *katakleíō* (2623), to shut down or to enclose and confine; *sugkleíō* (4788), to enclose.

Syn.: *kammúō* (2576), to shut, particularly the eyes; *ptússō* (4428), to fold, used of a scroll of parchment.

Ant.: *anoígō* (455), to open; *dianoígō* (1272), to open up completely; *anaptússō* (380), to unroll; *anakalúptō* (343), to unveil, open.

2809. κλέμμα klémma; gen. *klémmatos*, neut. noun from *kléptō* (2813), to steal. A theft (Rev 9:21; Sept. Ex 22:2, 3).

2810. Κλεόπας Kleópas; gen. *Kleópa*, masc. proper noun. Cleopas, meaning very renowned, one of the two disciples who were met by Christ on the way to Emmaus (Luke 24:18). Some regard him as the same as Cleophas.

2811. κλέος kléos; gen. *kléous*, neut. noun from *kléō* (n.f.), to tell. Report, rumor. In the NT, generally fame, renown, glory (1 Pet 2:20; Sept.: Job 28:22).
   Syn.: *dóxa* (1391), glory, estimate, opinion; *phḗmē* (5345), fame; *timḗ* (5092), honor.
   Ant.: *dusphēmía* (1426), defamation.

2812. κλέπτης kléptēs; gen. *kléptou*, from *kléptō* (2813), to steal. Thief (Matt 6:19, 20; Luke 12:33, 39; 1 Cor 6:10; 1 Thess 5:2, 4; 1 Pet 4:15; 2 Pet 3:10; Rev 3:3; 16:15; Sept.: Ex 22:1; Joel 2:9) Occurring along with *lēstḗs* (3027), robber (John 10:1, 8).The *kléptēs* steals by fraud and in secret (Matt 24:43; John 12:6) while the *lēstḗs* by violence and openly. Metaphorically, of false teachers or deceivers who steal men away from the truth (John 10:8, 10; Sept.: Hos 7:1).
   Syn.: *hierósulos* (2417), one who robs temples; *hárpax* (727), extortioner.
   Ant.: *euergétēs* (2110), a worker of good; *dótēs* (1395), a giver.

2813. κλέπτω kléptō; fut. *klépsō*. To steal. Used in an absolute sense (Matt 6:19, 20; Mark 10:19; Luke 18:20; John 10:10; Rom 2:21; Eph 4:28). The fut. with the neg. *ou klépseis*, used as an imper. (Matt 19:18; Rom 13:9; Sept.: Ex 20:14; Deut 5:19). In the sense of to steal furtively, to take by stealth, with the acc., as a dead body (Matt 27:64; 28:13; Sept.: 2 Sam 21:12).
   Deriv.: *klémma* (2809), that which is stolen; *kléptēs* (2812), thief; *klopḗ* (2829), theft.

Syn.: *diarpázō* (1283), to plunder; *harpázō* (726), to seize; *apágō* (520), to take away; *nosphízomai* (3557), to embezzle; *apatáō* (538), to cheat, deceive.
   Ant.: *euergetéō* (2109), to do good; *antilambánomai* (482), to help; *eleéō* (1653), to have mercy on.

2814. κλῆμα klḗma; gen. *klḗmatos*, neut. noun from *kláō* (2806), to break. That which is broken off from a plant, a shoot, young twig, like the shoots of the vine or the branches (John 15:2, 4–6; Sept.: Ezek 15:2; 17:6, 7).
   Syn.: *kládos* (2798), young tender shoot, branch; *stoibás* (4746), a branch full of leaves or a layer of leaves; *báïon* (902), a branch of the palm tree.

2815. Κλήμης Klḗmēs; gen. *Klḗmentos*. Clement, a fellow laborer of Paul (Phil 4:3), probably the same person who was afterward bishop of Rome and wrote two Corinthian epistles, which are still extant and were once read in some churches.

2816. κληρονομέω klēronoméō; contracted *klēronomṓ*, fut. *klēronomḗsō*, from *klēronómos* (2818), an heir. To be an heir, to inherit, obtain for an inheritance by casting lots as the children of Israel did for the promised land (Num 26:55; 33:54; Josh 14:1, 2; 16:4). To inherit, to be heir to any person or thing.
   (I) To inherit, to be heir, in an absolute sense (Gal 4:30 quoted from Gen 21:10; see Sept.: Gen 15:4; Num 27:11).
   (II) In later usage followed by the acc., simply to obtain, acquire, possess. Spoken only of the friends of God as receiving admission to the kingdom of heaven and its attendant privileges (Matt 5:5; "they shall possess the land" [a.t.], referring to the Messiah's kingdom [cf. Sept.: Ps 25:13; 37:11, 22, 29]). To inherit the kingdom of God (Matt 25:34; 1 Cor 6:9, 10; 15:50; Gal 5:21); eternal life (Matt 19:29; Mark 10:17; Luke 10:25; 18:18); incorruptibility (1 Cor 15:50). See Heb 1:4, 14; 6:12; 12:17; 1 Pet 3:9; Rev 21:7; Sept.: Gen 15:7; Deut 1:21.

Syn.: *klēróō* (2820), to determine by lot.

2817. κληρονομία *klēronomía*; gen. *klēronomías*, fem. noun from *klēronómos* (2818), an heir. Inheritance, that which constitutes one as an heir. An inheritance by lot (Matt 21:38; Mark 12:7; Luke 12:13; 20:14; Sept.: Num 27:7–11). As the inheritance of the earthly Canaan typified that of the heavenly, so the latter is often called *klēronomía*, inheritance (Acts 20:32; Gal 3:18; Eph 1:14, 18; 5:5; Col 3:24; Heb 9:15; 11:8; 1 Pet 1:4). Heritage (Acts 7:5). Divine salvation, considered both promised and already bestowed, is designated an inheritance in the NT so far as man, the heir, obtains possession of it (1 Pet 1:4).

2818. κληρονόμος *klēronómos*; gen. *klēronómou*, masc. noun from *klēros* (2819), lot, and *némō* (n.f., see *aponémō* [632]), to hold, have in one's power, to distribute. An heir, or an inheritance divided by lot (Matt 21:38; Mark 12:7; Luke 20:14; Sept.: 2 Sam 14:7; Jer 8:10). Applies to the heirs of the heavenly Canaan (Rom 4:13, 14; 8:17; Gal 3:29; 4:1, 7; Titus 3:7; Heb 1:2; 6:17; James 2:5) and to Christ who is appointed heir and possessor, the Lord of all things (Matt 21:38; Heb 1:2).
    Deriv.: *klēronoméō* (2816), to be an heir; *klēronomía* (2817), that which constitutes one as heir, inheritance; *sugklēronómos* (4789), he who participates in the same inheritance or lot, joint-heir.

2819. κλῆρος *klēros*; gen. *klērou*, masc. noun probably from *kláō* (2806), to break. A lot.
    (I) A lot, the stone or mark itself which was cast into the urn or lap (Matt 27:35; Mark 15:24; Luke 23:34; John 19:24; Acts 1:26; Sept.: Ps 22:18; Jon 1:7). It seems that the Greek method of casting lots was also followed by the Romans. The lots of several parties were properly marked or distinguished and put into a vessel which was violently shaken by one who turned his face away. The lot which first fell upon the ground indicated the man chosen or preferred for the occasion. The Romans attributed divine choice to this method.
    (II) A lot, allotment, part, or share (Acts 1:17 [TR], 26; 8:21; Sept.: Deut 10:9; 12:12).
    (III) An inheritance (Acts 26:18 [cf. 20:32]; Col 1:12 [cf. the noun *klēronomía* {2817}, inheritance]).
    (IV) *Klēroi*, in the pl. (1 Pet 5:3), seems to denote those distinct congregations of Christians (cf. Deut 4:20; 9:29) which fell to the lot, as it were, of different pastors.
    Deriv.: *klēronómos* (2818), one who has an inheritance, a lot; *klēróō* (2820), to cast lots, determine by lot; *naúklēros* (3490), an owner of a ship; *holóklēros* (3648), an entire portion, intact.
    Syn.: *méros* (3313), a part, portion of the whole; *merís* (3310), part, share.

2820. κληρόω *klēróō*; contracted *klēró*, fut. *klērósō*, from *klēros* (2819), a lot. To cast lots, determine by lot, i.e., to determine something, choose someone. In Eph 1:11, it means, "in whom the lot has fallen upon us also, as foreordained thereto . . . to be" (a.t.). The idea expressed here is that Christians have become heirs of God due to the fact that God predestined them according to His purpose. In a manner of speaking, the "lot" fell to believers not by chance but solely because of the gracious and sovereign decision of God-Almighty to select them to be His heirs.
    Deriv.: *prosklēróō* (4345), to give or assign by lot.

2821. κλῆσις *klēsis*; gen. *klēseōs*, fem. noun from *kaléō* (2564), to call. A call, invitation to a banquet.
    In the NT, metaphorically, a call, invitation to the kingdom of God and its privileges, i.e., the divine call by which Christians are introduced into the privileges of the gospel (Rom 11:29, "calling of God"; Eph 1:18; Phil 3:14; 2 Thess

1:11; 2 Tim 1:9; Heb 3:1; 2 Pet 1:10). In Eph 1:18 and 4:4, the "hope of . . . calling" means the hope which the Christian's call permits him to cherish. In 1 Cor 1:26, "For ye see your calling" means to consider the circumstances of your call, the factors involved in your call. In 1 Cor 7:20, "Let every man abide in the same calling wherein he was called" means as he was called, so let him remain.

God's invitation (klḗsis) to man to accept the benefits of His salvation is what this calling is all about, particularly in the gospels. It is God's first act in the application of redemption according to His eternal purpose (Rom 8:28). A distinction is made between God's calling and men's acceptance of it (Matt 20:16), the unrestricted offer and the appropriation resulting from a hearty appreciation of its implications. On God's part it is sure and without repentance (Rom 11:29), repentance here being not the ordinary word translated as repentance, metánoia (3341), but ametamélētos (278), which means something irrevocable. God's call is heard by all so that none may one day have the excuse that they did not hear the call and that is why they did not repent. Those who believe on Him and accept His call are truly saved (John 3:15, 16; Phil 3:14). For those who truly believe this is a holy calling (2 Tim 1:9 [cf. Rom 1:7; 1 Cor 1:2]) and a heavenly calling (Heb 3:1).

The calling is "not of works" but of the sovereign grace of God (Rom 9:11), "who saved us and called us with a holy [hagía {40}, holy in the effect of that calling] calling, not according to our works, but according to His own purpose and grace, which was given in Christ Jesus before times eternal" (a.t. [2 Tim 1:9]). The call which thus comes from God is "in Christ" (a.t. [1 Pet 5:10]) and "through the gospel" (a.t. [2 Thess 2:14]), to "the fellowship of his Son" (1 Cor 1:9), to "freedom" (a.t. [Gal 5:13]), not "for uncleanness but in sanctification" (a.t. [1 Thess 4:7]), to "eternal life" (1 Tim 6:12), to holiness "as he which hath called you is holy"

(1 Pet 1:15). It is therefore well designated "the high calling of God in Christ Jesus" (Phil 3:14), a "heavenly calling" (Heb 3:1), and those who are partakers of it are exhorted to make their "calling and election sure" (2 Pet 1:10). For the goal, though predestined and prepared aforetime (Rom 8:28f.; 9:24), is not attained without labor and conflict, as Paul exhorts Timothy "Fight the good fight of faith, lay hold on eternal life, whereunto thou art also called, and hast professed a good profession before many witnesses" (1 Tim 6:12).

The calling is accompanied with a great hope—"ye are called in one hope of your calling" (Eph 4:4). Those that experience the call not only partake of justification, adoption, and sanctification in this life, but when Christ who is their life shall appear, they shall also appear with Him in glory (Col 3:4 [cf. 1 Thess 2:12]). For this the called are kept (Jude 1:1), and though the adversaries and difficulties are many, "Faithful is he that calleth you, who also will do it" (1 Thess 5:24). A grace and power from the Holy Spirit is exercised upon those who are subjects of the call which Paul and the apostolic writers generally have in view.

Klḗsis can also refer to a call unto Christian service or ministry. That the calling is to more than a Christian profession is clear from the experiences which Paul associates with it. If he is a "called . . . apostle" (Rom 1:1), the particulars of his call, pertinent to his conversion, are given when he tells how it pleased God to separate him from his mother's womb and to call him by His grace to reveal His Son in him (Gal 1:15, 16).

2822. κλητός klētós; fem. klētḗ, neut. klētón, verbal adj. from kaléō (2564), to call. Called, invited, welcomed, appointed. Originally it was used to designate those invited to a banquet (Sept.: 1 Kgs 1:41, 49). In the gospels, it is found only in Matt 20:16 and 22:14.

(I) In the gospels, there is a distinction between the klētoí, the called ones, and the *eklektoí*, the chosen ones, relative to both service (Matt 20:16) and salvation (Matt 22:14).

The first instance in which we find both words is Matt 20:16, at the end of the parable of the workers in the vineyard (Matt 20:1–15). This parable has nothing to do with entrance into the kingdom of God but with the call to service that those who belong to the kingdom receive from the householder or the ruler of the house (*oikodespótēs* [3617], the despot of the house). There were two categories of workers. Those who were called at 6 a.m. labored with a contractual agreement calling for one dinar for a twelve-hour work day beginning at 6 a.m. and ending at 6 p.m. All the other workers were called simply to meet the need for workers in the vineyard and were promised a reward, though not a specific amount of pay. There were those who were thus called at 9 a.m., 12 noon, 3 p.m., and 5 p.m. They went without contractual agreement. They could be called the *éschatoi* (2078), the last ones. The first ones (*hoi prótoi* [4413]) went to work under contractual agreement. For believers, the reward varies in accordance with the motivation to work for the Lord and the believer's demand for such reward. Those who labor for the Lord and obey His call to perform a needed task without the promise of a specific reward are chosen for special consideration. Indeed, as in the days of Christ, many were called (*klētoí*) to labor for the Lord, but few were choice servants (*eklektoí*) who did not demand of God that they be rewarded for their service.

The second time these words are found together is in Matt 22:14. This follows the parable of the marriage supper. Here the *klētoí*, the called, are those who have received the invitation to enter Christ's kingdom, and the *eklektoí* (1588), the chosen ones, are those who have obeyed the call. "Many are called, but few are chosen."

The interesting thing about these two parables is that the same word, *hetaíros*

(2083), is used both in Matt 20:13 for the first workers who went to the field on a contractual agreement and remonstrated against the householder on account of the unequal pay, and in Matt 22:12 for the person who entered the marriage feast without a marriage garment. Unfortunately the translators have rendered *hetaíros* as "friend." In reality, the word *phílos* (5384) means friend, one who adopts the interest of another as his own, while *hetaíros* refers to a selfish comrade who chooses his friends or comrades for his own advantage. Therefore, *klētoí*, the called, are those whom the Lord calls for service or for the enjoyment of His salvation on His own terms, but who prefer either to serve in the vineyard or enter the banquet hall of salvation on their own terms. The *eklektoí* are those who accept the Lord's terms for both salvation and service, and only they are truly obedient.

The only other reference where *klētoí* and *eklektoí* are used together is Rev 17:14. These triumphant ones were first called and then chosen and they are also called the faithful ones (*pistoí* [4103]).

(II) This distinction, however, vanishes in the epistles, the writers having in mind the divine greatness and force of the call and not the human acceptance or rejection of it (Rom 1:1 [cf. Col 3:12]). One who is called means one who is saved (Rom 1:1; 1 Cor 1:1). The called ones (*klētoí*) are those who have received the divine call (*klēsis* [2821]), having conformed to God's saving purpose (Rom 1:6, 7; 8:28; 1 Cor 1:2, 24); although they did not necessarily give immediate obedience to the call (Matt 20:16; 22:14; Jude 1:1 [cf. Rev 17:14]). See *eklektós* (1588), elect.

Generally, in the epistles, *hoi klētoí*, "the called," are the *eklektoí*, "chosen" (Rom 9:24; 2 Thess 2:13, 14; 1 Pet 2:9, *génos eklektón*, a chosen generation [*génos* {1085}, generation, offspring, stock]), those whom God "called out of darkness into His marvelous light." *Klēsis*, with Paul and Peter, is more than an invitation; it is an invitation responded to and accepted, and it is so because "the called [*hoi klētoí*]" are already "the chosen [the *eklektoí*]". See Rom 8:28; 2 Thess 2:13, 14. "The called [*hoi klētoí*]" to whom Paul addresses the Epistle to the Romans, are "called to be Jesus Christ's" (a.t. [Rom 1:6]) and they are "called to be saints" (Rom 1:7), the meaning of the word "called" being identical with "converted." They are "called according to His purpose" (Rom 8:28), i.e., God's elective purpose for all eternity, "for whom He foreknew, He also foreordained to be conformed to the image of His Son, that he might be the firstborn among many brethren; and whom He foreordained, them He also called; and whom He called, them He also justified; and whom He justified, them He also glorified" (a.t. [Rom 8:29, 30]).

The "called" in Paul's thinking are the elect from all eternity, and their calling (*klēsis*) through the gospel and the means of grace is the realization of God's eternal purpose for them: "that he might make known the riches of his glory on the vessels of mercy, which he had afore prepared unto glory, even us whom he hath called, not of the Jews only, but also of the Gentiles" (Rom 9:23, 24).

We find this same thinking in John's writings. In Rev 17:14, he designates the victorious followers of the Lamb as "called, and chosen, and faithful [*klētoí kaí eklektoí kaí pistoí*]", a description entirely in keeping with John's record of the words of Christ: "All that the Father giveth me shall come to me" (John 6:37, 38), and the record of Jesus' promise concerning the sheep to whom He gives eternal life and whom no man can pluck out of His Father's hand (John 10:28).

2823. κλίβανος *klíbanos*; gen. *klibánou*, masc. noun, Attic *kríbanos*. An oven for baking bread (Matt 6:30; Luke 12:28; Sept.: Ex 8:3; Lev 26:26). It was a large round dome of earthen or other materials, two or three feet high, narrowing toward the top. This being first heated by a fire made within, the dough or paste was spread upon the side of the pot to bake, thus forming thin cakes. This method of baking is still used in the Middle East and was common, as it is still, around the island of Cyprus.

2824. κλίμα *klíma*; gen. *klímatos*, neut. noun from *klínō* (2827), to incline, recline. It means the inclination of the heavens toward the poles in ancient geography, whence the northern hemisphere was divided into seven *klímata*, climates, by lines parallel to the equator. In the NT, it generally means climate, region (Rom 15:23; 2 Cor 11:10; Gal 1:21).

Syn.: *méros* (3313), part, portion; *tópos* (5117), a place; *chṓra* (5561), country, land, region; *períchōros* (4066), a region round about.

2825. κλίνη *klínē*; gen. *klínēs*, fem. noun from *klínō* (2827), to recline, lie. Specifically it means a bed, couch, sofa, divan for sitting or reclining (Luke 17:34, where it refers to two persons sitting or reclining together [cf. the expression in Matt 24:40; Mark 4:21; 7:4; Luke 8:16; Sept.: Amos 6:4]). In all these passages, *klínē* may be taken in the sense of triclinium, the couch or sofa on which the ancients reclined at meals. The diminutive is *klinídion* (2826), a little couch or bed. In the NT, *klínē* is generally used only when referring to the sick (Mark 7:30; Rev 2:22; Sept.: Gen 48:2; 49:33; 2 Sam 4:7; 1 Kgs 17:19); also of a bed on which the sick are borne (Matt 9:2, 6; Luke 5:18; Acts 5:15).

Syn.: *koítē* (2845), a place for lying down; *krábbatos* (2895), a bed, pallet, or mattress for the poor.

2826. κλινίδιον *klinídion*; gen. *klinidíou*, neut. noun, a diminutive of *klínē* (2825), bed. A little bed, couch (Luke 5:19, 24 [cf. Luke 5:18 where it is *klínē*]).

2827. κλίνω *klínō*; fut. *klinṓ*, the perf. *kéklika*. To incline, trans. to bend something from a straight position, whether downwards or horizontally. To recline, lie down (Matt 8:20; Luke 9:58; Sept.: Ps 144:5; 2 Kgs 19:16), to bow down (Luke 24:5; John 19:30); spoken of the day, to decline, giving way or yielding of the day to the evening or night (Luke 9:12; 24:29; Sept.: Judg 19:8, 11; Jer 6:4); spoken of an army, to cause to give way, put to flight, rout (Heb 11:34).

Deriv.: *aklinḗs* (186), steady; *anaklínō* (347), to recline, in the act., to lay down; *ekklínō* (1578), to avoid; *kataklínō* (2625), to recline down; *klíma* (2824), region, climate; *klínē* (2825), a bed; *klinídion* (2826), a little bed; *klisía* (2828) a company reclining at a meal.

Syn.: *kámptō* (2578), to bend; *sugkámptō* (4781), to bow down, bend together; *sugkúptō* (4794), to bow together.

Ant.: *euthúnō* (2116), to straighten; *anorthóō* (461), to make straight.

2828. κλισία klisía; gen. *klisías*, fem. noun from *klínō* (2827), to incline or recline. A place where one may recline or rest, hence a hut, tent. It also meant couches for reclining at a meal or a table party, company reclining around a table. In the NT, used adv. in the acc. pl. *klisías* meaning by tables, in companies (Luke 9:14).

Deriv.: *prōtoklisía* (4411), the chief place at a banquet.

2829. κλοπή klopḗ; gen. *klopḗs*, the fem. noun from *kléptō* (2813), to steal. The act of stealing, theft (Matt 15:19; Mark 7:22). The thing stolen is *klémma* (2809).

Syn.: *apátē* (539), deceit; *harpagḗ* (724), snatching away, rapture; *harpagmós* (725), plunder, robbery.

Ant.: *eleēmosúnē* (1654), alms; *euergesía* (2108), beneficence; *dóma* (1390), a gift; *dôron* (1435), a gift.

2830. κλύδων klúdōn; gen. *klúdōnos*, from *klúzō* (n.f.), to dash, dash away, dash over. The raging of the sea, a tempest (Luke 8:24; James 1:6; Sept.: Jon 1:4, 11, 12). See the comp. *kataklúzō* (2626), to overflow, deluge. Also from *klúzō* (n.f.): *kataklúzō* (2626), to overflow.

Deriv.: *kludōnízomai* (2831), to toss to and fro.

Syn.: *kúma* (2949), the wave; *sálos* (4535), the rolling swell of the sea.

Ant.: *galḗnē* (1055), calmness; *eudía* (2105), fine weather.

2831. κλυδωνίζομαι kludōnízomai; fut. *kludōnísomai*, deponent from *klúdōn* (2830), a surge of the sea, wave. To surge, be tossed in billows; metaphorically, to fluctuate (Eph 4:14; Sept.: Isa 57:20).

Syn.: *kinéō* (2795), to move; *metakinéō* (3334), to move something away; *seíō* (4579), to shake, move to and fro; *saleúō* (4531), to shake.

Ant.: *stērízō* (4741), to steady; *asphalízō* (805), to make secure; *stereóō* (4732), to establish, make strong.

2832. Κλωπᾶς Klōpás; gen. *Klōpá*, masc. proper noun. Cleophas (John 19:25). This name is to be distinguished from Cleopas (Luke 24:18) and is perhaps identical with Alpheus or Alphaios (Matt 10:3; Luke 6:15).

2833. κνήθω knḗthō; fut. *knḗsō*, a later form of *knáō* (n.f.), to cut, scrape, scratch, tickle. In the NT, only in the pass. meaning to be tickled, to feel an itching. Metaphorically in 2 Tim 4:3 meaning being tickled, itching referring to the ears, having an itch to hear something pleasing.

2834. Κνίδος Knídos; gen. *Knidou*, fem. proper noun. Cnidus, a Greek city at the extreme southwestern corner of Asia Minor, between the islands of Rhodes and Cos, known for the worship of Venus (Acts 27:7).

2835. κοδράντης kodrántēs; gen. *kodrántou*, masc. noun, Lat. *quadrans*, the fourth part of an *as*, the same as *assárion* (787), a Roman coin, farthing. A small brass coin equal to two *leptá* (3016), mite, a small coin (Matt 5:26; Mark 12:42).

2836. κοιλία koilía; gen. *koilías*, fem. noun from *koílos* (n.f.), hollow. The belly of man, the bowels, as the receptacle of food, meaning the stomach, either in man or animals (Matt 12:40; 15:17; Mark 7:19; Luke 15:16; Rom 16:18; 1 Cor 6:13; Phil 3:19; Rev 10:9, 10; Sept.: Num 5:22; Ps 22:14; Jon 2:2); the womb (Matt 19:12; Luke 1:15, 41, 42, 44; 2:21; John 3:4; Acts 3:2; 14:8; Gal 1:15). As personification of a woman (Luke 11:27; 23:29; Sept.: Gen 25:23, 24; Ruth 1:11; Isa 44:2). It also means the inward part, the inner man, similar to the breast, the heart as we speak of it in Eng. (John 7:38; Sept.: Job 15:35; Ps 40:8; Prov 20:27).

Syn.: *gastḗr* (1064), womb; *mḗtra* (3388), womb of a mother; *mḗtēr* (3384), mother.

2837. κοιμάω koimáō; contracted *koimṓ*, fut. *koimḗsō*, related to *keímai* (2749), to lie outstretched, to lie down. To cause to lie down to sleep. In the NT, generally in the mid. *koimáomai* or *koimṓmai*, with the fut. mid. *koimḗsomai*, to fall asleep, to sleep. Used intrans. (Matt 28:13; Luke 22:45; John 11:12; Acts 12:6; Sept.: Ruth 3:8; 1 Sam 3:15; Isa 5:27). Spoken of the sleep of death, to die, be dead (Matt 27:52; John 11:11; Acts 7:60; 13:36; 1 Cor 7:39; 11:30; 15:6, 18, 20, 51; 1 Thess 4:13–15; 2 Pet 3:4; Sept.: 1 Kgs 2:10; 11:43; Isa 43:17).

Deriv.: *koímēsis* (2838), the act of sleeping.

Syn.: *katheúdō* (2518), to go to sleep; *aphupnóō* (879), to fall asleep.

Ant.: *anístēmi* (450), to rise; *exanístēmi* (1817), to raise up out of; *egeírō* (1453), to raise.

2838. κοίμησις koímēsis; gen. *koimḗseōs*, fem. noun from *koimáō* (2837), to slumber, to die. The act of sleeping or dying, symbolically meaning rest, repose (John 11:13).

Syn.: *húpnos* (5258), sleep; *thánatos* (2288), death.

Ant.: *anástasis* (386), resurrection; *exanástasis* (1815), resurrection from among the dead; *égersis* (1454), a rousing.

2839. κοινός koinós; fem. *koinḗ*, neut. *koinón*, adj. Defiled, common, unclean, to lie common or open to all, common or belonging to several or of which several are partakers (Acts 2:44; 4:32; Titus 1:4; Jude 1:3); unclean hands (Mark 7:2) or meats (Acts 10:14, 28; 11:8; Rom 14:14; Heb 10:29, unconsecrated and therefore having no atoning efficacy) such as were common to other nations but were avoided by the Jews as polluted and unclean (Mark 7:2).

Deriv.: *koinóō* (2840), to make common, unclean; *koinōnós* (2844), an associate, companion, partner, participant.

Syn.: *akáthartos* (169), unclean; *anósios* (462), unholy, profane.

Ant.: *katharós* (2513), clean; *hagnós* (53), pure from defilement; *eilikrinḗs* (1506), unalloyed, pure, sincere; *amíantos* (283), undefiled; *ídios* (2398), private.

2840. κοινόω koinóō; contracted *koinṓ*, fut. *koinṓsō*, from *koinós* (2839), common. To make common, unclean, pollute or defile (Matt 15:11, 18, 20; Mark 7:15, 18, 20, 23; Acts 21:28; Heb 9:13; Rev 21:27 [TR]); to pronounce or call common or unclean (Acts 10:15; 11:9).

Syn.: *miaínō* (3392), to stain, defile; *molúnō* (3435), to besmear; *spilóō* (4695), to defile, spot.

Ant.: *katharízō* (2511), to cleanse; *diakatharízō* (1245), to cleanse thoroughly; *kathaírō* (2508), to purge; *ekkathaírō* (1571), to cleanse; *hagnízō* (48), to purify.

2841. κοινωνέω koinōnéō; contracted *koinōnṓ*, fut. *koinōnḗsō*, from *koinōnós* (2844), an associate, partaker. With a dat. of thing: to communicate, participate in, be a partaker of (Rom 15:27; 1 Tim 5:22; 1 Pet 4:13; 2 John 1:11), as it is also with the gen. in Heb 2:14. With a dat. of person: to communicate, distribute, impart (Rom 12:13; Gal 6:6; Phil 4:15).

Deriv.: *koinōnía* (2842), fellowship; *sugkoinōnéō* (4790), to share with.

Syn.: *metéchō* (3348), to partake of, share; *metalambánō* (3335), to have a share of; *summerízomai* (4829), to have a share in, be a partaker with.

2842. κοινωνία *koinōnía*; gen. *koinōnías*, fem. noun from *koinōnéō* (2841), to share in. Fellowship with, participation.

(I) Participation, communion, fellowship (Acts 2:42; 1 Cor 1:9; 10:16; 2 Cor 6:14; 8:4; 13:14; Gal 2:9, "right hands of fellowship," the pledge of communion; Eph 3:9 [TR]; Phil 1:5, "your fellowship in the gospel," accession to it; 2:1; 3:10; Phile 1:6; 1 John 1:3, 6, 7).

(II) Communication, distribution, a metonym for contribution, collection of money in behalf of poorer churches (Rom 15:26; 2 Cor 9:13; Heb 13:16).

Syn.: *eleēmosúnē* (1654), compassion, beneficence, alms; *metochḗ* (3352), partnership.

2843. κοινωνικός *koinōnikós*; fem. *koinōnikḗ*, neut. *koinōnikón*, adj. from *koinōnós* (2844), an associate, partaker. Communicative, social. In the NT, ready to give, liberal (1 Tim 6:18).

Syn.: *philóphrōn* (5391), friendly, courteous.

Ant.: *phílautos* (5367), selfish.

2844. κοινωνός *koinōnós*; gen. *koinōnoú*, masc.-fem., neut. *koinōnón*, adj. from *koinós* (2839), common. A partaker, partner, companion, used in an absolute sense in 2 Cor 8:23; Phile 1:17. Followed by the gen. of person of whom one is the companion, with whom he partakes in something (Matt 23:30; 1 Cor 10:20; Heb 10:33; Sept.: Isa 1:23); by the dat. of person to or with whom one is partner (Luke 5:10); by the gen. of thing (1 Cor 10:18, "partakers of the altar" may mean of the victims sacrificed; 2 Cor 1:7; 1 Pet 5:1; 2 Pet 1:4).

Deriv.: *koinōnéō* (2841), to share in; *koinōnikós* (2843), communicative, generous; *sugkoinōnós* (4791), joint participator, companion.

Syn.: *sunékdēmos* (4898), a fellow traveler; *métochos* (3353), partner.

2845. κοίτη *koítē*; gen. *koítēs*, fem. noun from *keímai* (2749), to lay, lie. A lying down for rest or sleep. In the NT, a place of repose, a bed (Luke 11:7). Spoken of the marriage bed, metaphorically for marriage itself (Heb 13:4). Cohabitation, whether lawful or unlawful (Rom 13:13; Sept.: Lev 18:22; Num 31:17, 18, 35). Also it means seed, semen as necessary for conception (Rom 9:10, "had conceived by one"; Sept.: Lev 15:16, 32; 18:20, 23; 22:4; Num 5:20).

Deriv.: *arsenokoítēs* (733), a sodomite, homosexual; *koitṓn* (2846), a bedroom, chamberlain.

Syn.: *klínē* (2825), couch; *krábbatos* (2895), a mattress, bed for the poor; *gámos* (1062), marriage.

2846. κοιτών *koitṓn*; gen. *koitṓnos*, masc. noun from *koítē* (2845), bed. Marriage bed, a bedroom (Acts 12:20; Sept.: Ex 8:3; 2 Sam 4:7).

2847. κόκκινος *kókkinos*; fem. *kokkínē*, neut. *kókkinon*, adj. from *kókkos* (2848), seed, a grain. Scarlet, of a scarlet color, so named because this color was produced by dyeing with what was called *kókkos baphikḗ*, the dyeing grain, the grains which adhere to a small dry twig of a little bush. These grains were full of little worms or maggots whose fluids were remarkable for dyeing scarlet and making the famous color which the ancients adored. Both the insect and the color were called by the Arabs "alkermes," from which our Eng. word "crimson" is derived (Matt 27:28; Heb 9:19; Rev 17:3, 4; 18:12, 16; Sept.: Ex 25:4; 28:5; Josh 2:18).

Syn.: *eruthrós* (2063), red; *purrós* (4450), fiery red.

2848. κόκκος *kókkos*; gen. *kókkou*, masc. noun. Grain, a kernel, seed (Matt 13:31; 17:20; Mark 4:31; Luke 13:19; 17:6; John

12:24; 1 Cor 15:37). See *kókkinos* (2847), scarlet.

Deriv.: *kókkinos* (2847), scarlet.

Syn.: *sítos* (4621), wheat, corn; *stáchus* (4719), a head of grain.

2849. κολάζω *kolázō*; fut. *kolásomai*, from *kólos* (n.f.), abridged, shortened. To mutilate, prune, such as trees. Metaphorically, to correct, moderate. In the NT, and generally, to discipline, punish, with the acc. (Acts 4:21; 2 Pet 2:9, meaning to reserve as subject to punishment). Also from *kólos* (n.f.): *kōlúō* (2967), to cut off, weaken, hinder.

Deriv.: *kólasis* (2851), torment, punishment.

Syn.: *timōréō* (5097), to punish.

Ant.: *aphíēmi* (863), to forgive; *charízomai* (5483), to show grace to, bestow a favor unconditionally; *apolúō* (630), to release.

2850. κολακεία *kolakeía*; gen. *kolakeías*, fem. noun from *kolakeúō* (n.f.), to flatter. Flattery, adulation (1 Thess 2:5).

2851. κόλασις *kólasis*; gen. *koláseōs*, fem. noun from *kolázō* (2849), to punish. Punishment (Matt 25:46), torment (1 John 4:18), distinguished from *timōría* (5098), punishment, which in Class. Gr. has the predominating thought of the vindictive character of the punishment which satisfies the inflicter's sense of outraged justice in defending his own honor or that of the violated law. *Kólasis*, on the other hand, conveys the notion of punishment for the correction and bettering of the offender. It does not always, however, have this strict meaning in the NT. In Matt 25:46, *kólasis aiốnios* (166), eternal, does not refer to temporary corrective punishment and discipline, but has rather the meaning of *timōría*, punishment because of the violation of the eternal law of God. It is equivalent to *géenna* (1067), hell, a final punishment about which offenders are warned by our Lord (Mark 9:43–48). In this sense it does not have the implication of bettering one who endures such punishment. In *kólasis*, we have the relationship of the punishment to the one being punished while in *timōría* the relationship is to the punisher himself.

Syn.: *ekdíkēsis* (1557), vengeance; *epitimía* (2009), penalty; *díkē* (1349), the execution of a sentence.

Ant.: *áphesis* (859), forgiveness, dismissal, release; *apolútrōsis* (629), redemption, deliverance; *páresis* (3929), a passing by of death or sin.

2852. κολαφίζω *kolaphízō*; fut. *kolaphísō*, from *kólaphos* (n.f.), a blow. To strike with the fist, to buffet, with the acc. (Matt 26:67; Mark 14:65); to mistreat (1 Cor 4:11; 2 Cor 12:7; 1 Pet 2:20).

Syn.: *hupōpiázō* (5299), to strike under the eyes; *túptō* (5180), to beat; *paíō* (3817) and *patássō* (3960), to hit, strike; *rhapízō* (4474), to strike a blow, hit; *bállō* (906), to strike.

2853. κολλάω *kolláō*; contracted *kollṓ*, fut. *kollḗsō*, from *kólla* (n.f.), glue. To glue together, to make cohere. In the NT, in the mid. *kolláomai* or *kollṓmai*, the aor. pass. *ekollḗthēn*, with mid. meaning, to adhere, cleave to, be glued to, of things followed by the dat. (Luke 10:11; Sept.: Job 29:10; Ps 102:5); of persons, metaphorically meaning to join oneself unto, to follow, accompany (Acts 8:29); cleave to (Rom 12:9; Sept.: 2 Kgs 3:3). Followed by the dat. of person, to become a servant to someone (Luke 15:15). To follow, to cleave to, e.g., a prostitute (1 Cor 6:16); the Lord (1 Cor 6:17; Sept.: 2 Kgs 18:6). To follow the side or party of someone, to associate with (Acts 5:13; 9:26; 10:28; 17:34; Sept.: 2 Sam 20:2).

Deriv.: *proskolláō* (4347), to stick to, cleave.

Syn.: *suzeúgnumi* (4801), to yoke together.

2854. κολλούριον *kolloúrion*, κολλύριον *kollúrion*; gen. *kollouríou*, neut. noun, a diminutive of *kollúra* (n.f.), a coarse bread or cake. In the NT, collyrium, a topical remedy applied to the eyes (Rev 3:18).

2855. κολλυβιστής *kollubistḗs*; gen. *kollubistoú*, masc. noun from *kóllubos* (n.f.), a small coin, change. A money changer, broker (Matt 21:12; Mark 11:15; John 2:15), equal to *kermatistḗs* (2773). Money changers sat in the outer court of the temple.

2856. κολοβόω *kolobóō*; contracted *kolobṓ*, fut. *kolobṓsō*, from *kolobós* (n.f.), maimed, cut off. To cut off, mutilate (Sept.: 2 Sam 4:12). In the NT, used of time in the pass., meaning to cut off, shorten (Matt 24:22; Mark 13:20).
   Syn.: *sustéllō* (4958), to draw together, contract, shorten; *suntémnō* (4932), to cut down or shorten; *kóptō* (2875), to cut down; *anakóptō* (348), to check, hinder; *sunéchō* (4912), to arrest, hold together, stop.
   Ant.: *teleióō* (5048), to fulfill; *sumplēróō* (4845), to complete; *sunteléō* (4931), to execute; *apoteléō* (658), to complete entirely.

2857. Κολοσσαί *Kolossaí*, **Κολασσαί** *Kolassaí* gen. *Kolossṓn* / *Kolassṓn*, pl. fem. proper noun. Colosse / Colossae, a city of Phrygia on the Lycus, a branch of the Maeander, and twelve miles above Laodicea. With Laodicea and Hierapolis (Col 4:13), it forms a triangle. Paul wrote to the Church there (Col 1:2) and possibly visited it on his third missionary journey (Acts 18:23; 19:10). The town is now in ruins, but there is a little village called Chonus.

2858. Κολοσσαεύς *Kolossaeús*; gen. *Kolossaéōs*, masc. proper noun. Colossian, an inhabitant of Colossae. Found only in the inscription to the Book of Colossians.

2859. κόλπος *kólpos*; gen. *kólpou*, masc. noun. Bosom, the front of the body between the arms. In John 13:23, "reclining on Jesus' bosom" (a.t.), meaning next to Him on the couch at supper, so that his head was opposite to Jesus' bosom. To be in or on the bosom of someone means to be in his embrace, to be cherished by him as the object of intimate care and dearest affection, or as we say in Eng., to be a bosom friend. John 1:18 speaks of the eternal close fellowship of the Son with the Father as the unique Son being in the bosom of the Father. This indicates the eternal coexistence of the Son with the Father. In Luke 16:22, "into Abraham's bosom" means in intimate communion with Abraham as the father of faith. See Luke 16:23; Sept.: Deut 13:6; 28:54, 56 (cf. 2 Sam 12:3, 8). The bosom of an oriental garment, the loose cavity or hollow formed by the doubling of a robe, a fold for carrying things as a pocket (Luke 6:38; Sept.: Isa 65:6; Jer 39:18). A bay, creek (Acts 27:39).

2860. κολυμβάω *kolumbáō*; contracted *kolumbṓ*, fut. *kolumbḗsō*. To swim (Acts 27:43).
   Deriv.: *ekkolumbáō* (1579), to swim out of; *kolumbḗthra* (2861), a pool.

2861. κολυμβήθρα *kolumbḗthra*; gen. *kolumbḗthras*, fem. noun from *kolumbáō* (2860), to swim. A swimming place, pool, pond (John 5:2, 4, 7 refers to Bethesda as a healing pool; 9:7, 11, the "pool of Siloam"; Sept.: 2 Kgs 18:17; Isa 7:3).

2862. κολωνία *kolōnía*; gen. *kolōnías*, fem. noun. Lat. *colonia*. A Roman colony. In Acts 16:12 referring to Philippi which had been conquered by Augustus and colonized with many Romans who mingled with the natives.

2863. κομάω *komáō*; contracted *komṓ*, fut. *komḗsō*, from *kómē* (2864), hair. To have long hair (1 Cor 11:14, 15). Paul teaches that a woman's hair ought to be different from a man's, and that a woman's hair is equivalent to a *peribólaion* (4018), something that is wrapped around, a veil or mantle. From the context, it seems that the woman's hair ought to be distinct from a man's hair, not only in length, but also in ornamentation.

2864. κόμη *kómē*; gen. *kómēs*, fem. noun. Hair. In the NT, used only of human hair. However, it does not always refer to hair per se, but to the way that it is styled (1 Cor 11:15; Sept.: Num 6:5) as distinguishing a woman from a man in which case it takes the place of a mantle or veil wrapped around (*peribólaion* [4018]).
Deriv.: *komáō* (2863), to have long hair.
Syn.: *thríx* (2359), hair, but not necessarily of humans as is *kómē* (2864). It can be the hair of an animal such as a camel.

2865. κομίζω *komízō*; fut. *komísō*, from *koméō* (n.f.), to take care of. To bring, bear. In the mid. *komízomai*, the Attic fut. *komioúmai*, to take for oneself, to bear or bring to oneself, acquire, obtain, receive. Used trans. (Matt 25:27; Luke 7:37; 2 Cor 5:10; Col 3:25; Heb 10:36; 11:39; 1 Pet 1:9; 5:4; 2 Pet 2:13). Followed by *pará* (3844), near, with the gen. (Eph 6:8). In the sense of to receive again, recover, used trans. (Heb 11:19; Sept.: Gen 38:20). Also from *koméō* (n.f.): *glōssókomon* (1101), bag, case, purse.
Deriv.: *ekkomízō* (1580), to bear or carry out; *sugkomízō* (4792), to gather crops together.
Syn.: *phérō* (5342), to bear, carry; *aírō* (142), to bring; *ágō* (71), to bring; *lambánō* (2983), to receive.
Ant.: *aphíēmi* (863), to leave alone, forsake; *aníēmi* (447), to let go; *kataleípō* (2641) and *hupolimpánō* (5277), to leave behind, bequeath; *apoleípō* (620), to leave behind, forsake; *egkataleípō* (1459), to leave behind in; *hupoleípō* (5275), to leave under; *perileípō* (4035), to leave over; *eáō* (1439), to leave.

2866. κομψότερον *kompsóteron*; adv., the comparative of *kompsós* (n.f.), elegantly, well. Better, used with *échō* (2192), to have, meaning improved in health (John 4:52).

2867. κονιάω *koniáō*; contracted *konió*, fut. *koniásō*, from *konía* (n.f.), dust, lime. To whitewash with lime, used trans. (Matt 23:27). The Jews, on the twenty-fifth day of the month Adar, whitewashed their sepulchers in accordance with an annual custom. See Deut 27:2, 4. In Acts 23:3, "thou whited wall" means thou hypocrite, fair without and foul within. Also from *konía* (n.f.): *koniortós* (2868), dust.

2868. κονιορτός *koniortós*; gen. *koniortoú*, masc. noun from *konía* (n.f.), dust, and *órnumi* (n.f.), to excite, raise. Dust. Dust which becomes airborne when disturbed (Matt 10:14; Luke 9:5; 10:11; Acts 13:51; 22:23; Sept.: Ex 9:9; Deut 9:21; Nah 1:3). Also from *konía* (n.f.): *koniáō* (2867), to whitewash with lime. Also from *órnumi* (n.f.): *hormḗ* (3730), violent impulse, assault.

2869. κοπάζω *kopázō*; fut. *kopásō*, from *kópos* (2873), labor, fatigue. To cease because of extreme fatigue or being worn out with labor; to cease as the wind (Matt 14:32; Mark 4:39; 6:51; Sept.: Gen 8:1; Jon 1:11, 12).
Syn.: *paúō* (3973), to stop; *dialeípō* (1257), to leave between; *hēsucházō* (2270), to be at rest; *eirēneúō* (1514), to pacify; *katapaúō* (2664), to cease or rest completely.
Ant.: *árchomai* (756), to begin; *anastatóō* (387), to disturb; *tarássō* (5015), to stir, agitate; *diegeírō* (1326), to arouse; *maínomai* (3105), to rave.

2870. κοπετός *kopetós*; gen. *kopetoú*, from *kóptomai*, the mid. of *kóptō* (2875), to lament. Lamentation, wailing as accompanied with beating the breast (Acts 8:2; Sept.: Gen 50:10; Zech 12:10, 11).
Syn.: *thrḗnos* (2355), wailing, lamentation; *klauthmós* (2805), weeping but not necessarily wailing.
Ant.: *eirḗnē* (1515), peace; *galḗnē* (1055), tranquility, calmness.

2871. κοπή *kopḗ*; gen. *kopḗs*, fem. noun from *kóptō* (2875), to cut down, lament, mourn. Slaughter, carnage (Heb 7:1 in allusion to Gen 14:17; Sept.: Josh 10:20).

Syn.: *sphagḗ* (4967), slaughter; *phónos* (5408), a killing, murder.

2872. κοπιάω *kopiáō*; contracted *kopiṓ*, fut. *kopiásō*, from *kópos* (2873), labor, fatigue. To be worn out, weary, faint, used intrans. (Matt 11:28; John 4:6; Rev 2:3). To weary oneself with labor, to toil, used in an absolute sense (Luke 5:5; Acts 20:35; 1 Cor 4:12; Eph 4:28; 2 Tim 2:6); of the lilies (Matt 6:28; Luke 12:27); of a teacher who labors in the gospel (John 4:38; 1 Cor 15:10; 16:16 [cf. Sept.: Josh 24:13; Ps 127:1]). Followed by *en* (1722), in, to labor in, such as the Word (1 Tim 5:17); in the Lord, meaning in the work of the Lord (Rom 16:12); among you (1 Thess 5:12); by *eis* (1519), upon, with the acc. of person, upon or for whom (Rom 16:6; Gal 4:11; Phil 2:16; Col 1:29; 1 Tim 4:10; Sept.: Isa 65:23).

Syn.: *athléō* (118), to strive; *ergázomai* (2038), to work; *spoudázō* (4704), to be diligent; *agōnízomai* (75), to strive or wrestle; *cheimázō* (5492), to labor in a storm or tempest.

Ant.: *anapaúō* (373), to give rest, refresh; *katapaúō* (2664), to cause to cease, restrain; *hēsucházō* (2270), to be still; *epanapaúō* (1879), to cause to rest, refresh; *aniēmi* (447), to let up.

2873. κόπος *kópos*; gen. *kópou*, from *kóptō* (2875), to strike. Beating, wailing, grief with beating the breast, equal to *kopetós* (2870), lamentation, wailing (Sept.: Jer 51:3). In the NT, toil, labor, i.e., wearisome effort, generally (John 4:38; 1 Cor 3:8; 15:58; 2 Cor 6:5; 10:15; 11:23, 27; 1 Thess 1:3, "labor of love," meaning work of beneficence; 2:9; 3:5; 2 Thess 3:8; Heb 6:10; Rev 2:2; 14:13; Sept.: Gen 31:42). In the sense of trouble, vexation (Matt 26:10; Mark 14:6; Luke 11:7; 18:5; Gal 6:17; Sept.: Job 5:6; Jer 20:18). Used to denote not so much the actual exertion which a man makes, but the weariness which he experiences from that exertion. Designates that which we as

Christians ought to render to the Lord as labor in the Christian ministry.

Deriv.: *eúkopos* (2123), easier, lighter; *kopázō* (2869), to tire, cease; *kopiáō* (2872), to feel fatigue from labor.

Syn.: *móchthos* (3449), the everyday word for human labor; *pónos* (4192), the labor which demands the whole strength of a man exerted to the utmost to accomplish the task before him.

Ant.: *anápausis* (372), inner rest; *anápsuxis* (403), recovery of breath, revival; *ánesis* (425), relief, rest; *katápausis* (2663), cessation of work; *sabbatismós* (4520), Sabbath rest, repose; *scholḗ* (4981), leisure.

2874. κοπρία *kopría*; gen. *koprías*, fem. noun from *kópros* (n.f.), dung, filth. Dung hill (Sept.: 1 Sam 2:8). In the NT, dung, manure (Luke 13:8 [TR]; 14:35; Sept.: 2 Kgs 9:37; Jer 25:33).

Syn.: *skúbalon* (4657), refuse of whatever kind.

2875. κόπτω *kóptō*; fut. *kópsō*. To cut off or down, trans. (Matt 21:8; Mark 11:8; Sept.: Num 13:24; Judg 9:48); in the mid. voice *kóptomai*, to strike or beat one's body, particularly the breast, with the hands in lamentation, to lament, wail, equivalent to *túptō* (5180), to beat (Luke 18:13; 23:48). Used intrans., to beat the breast or cut oneself in loud expressions of grief, to lament, wail (Matt 11:17; 24:30; Luke 23:27); with the intens. prep. *epí* (1909), upon (Rev 1:7; 18:9; Sept.: 2 Sam 1:12); with the acc. (Sept.: Gen 23:2; 50:10); followed by *epí* (1909), upon, (Sept.: 2 Sam 11:26; Zech 12:10).

Deriv.: *anakóptō* (348), to hinder, beat back; *apokóptō* (609), to cut off; *argurokópos* (695), silversmith; *egkóptō* (1465), to cut off, hinder; *ekkóptō* (1581), to cut or strike out; *katakóptō* (2629), to cut down; *kopetós* (2870), beating, mourning; *kopḗ* (2871), slaughter; *kópos* (2873), labor, weariness; *kōphós* (2974), blunted, deaf, dumb; *prokóptō* (4298), to advance, increase; *próskomma* (4348), offense, stumbling block; *proskóptō* (4350), to strike at, trip.

Syn.: *lupéō* (3076), inner grief without necessarily an outward expression.; *penthéō* (3996), to mourn, and *thrēnéō* (2354), to wail; *klaíō* (2799), to weep; *stenázō* (4727), to groan.

2876. κόραξ *kórax*; gen. *kórakos*, masc. noun. A raven or crow (Luke 12:24; Sept.: Gen 8:7; Lev 11:15).

2877. κοράσιον *korásion*; gen. *korasíou*, neut. noun, a diminutive of *kórē* (n.f.), a maiden. A little girl, damsel (Matt 9:24, 25; 14:11; Mark 5:41, 42; 6:22, 28; Sept.: Ruth 2:8, 22; 1 Sam 25:42).

Syn.: *paidíon* (3813), a young child, male or female; *paidískē* (3814), a young girl or a female slave; *país* (3816), a child, denoting a maid or maiden.

2878. Κορβᾶν *Korbán*, **κορβανᾶς** *korbanás*; masc. noun transliterated from the Hebr. *qārbān* (7133, OT). A gift or an offering dedicated to God (Lev 2:1, 4, 12, 13). This gift was used to excuse a person from doing his or her filial duty toward one's parents (Mark 7:9–13). Something devoted to God (Mark 7:11). *Korbanás* is spoken of money offered in the temple, the sacred treasure, and therefore representing the treasury, equivalent to *gazophulákion* (1049), a court in the temple for the collection boxes, treasury (Matt 27:6).

Syn.: *dōron* (1435), gift, offering.

2879. Κορέ *Koré*; masc. proper noun transliterated from the Hebr. *Qōrach* (7141, OT). Core, the Gr. form of Korah (Jude 1:11; see Num 16).

2880. κορέννυμι *korénnumi*; fut. *korésō*, aor. pass. *ekorésthēn*, perf. pass. *kekóresmai*. To have enough, abundance, to satisfy (Acts 27:38; 1 Cor 4:8).

Syn.: *plēróō* (4137), to make full, to fill; *gemízō* (1072) and *pímplēmi* (4130), to fill; *empíplēmi* (1705), to fill full, satisfy, fill the hungry; *chortázō* (5526), to fill

or satisfy with food; *mestóō* (3325), to fill to the brim.

Ant.: *peináō* (3983), to hunger; *hasteréō* (5302), to come short, lack.

2881. Κορίνθιος *Korínthios*; fem. *Korinthía*, neut. *Korínthion*. A Corinthian, an inhabitant of Corinth (Acts 18:8; 2 Cor 6:11).

2882. Κόρινθος *Kórinthos*; gen. *Korínthou*, fem. proper noun. Corinth, the capital of Achaia and a renowned and sinful city of Greece, about forty miles west of Athens on an isthmus between the Peloponnesus and the mainland (Acts 18:1; 19:1; 1 Cor 1:2; 2 Cor 1:1, 23; 2 Tim 4:20). Athens had two seaports, Cenchrea on the east, about nine miles distant, and Lechaeum on the west, only about two miles away. Corinth was about five miles in circumference, and on the south an immense rocky mountain called Acrocorinth rises abruptly to the height of two thousand feet, upon the summit of which was a temple of Venus or Aphrodite. It had an extensive commerce, like all the large towns on the Mediterranean Sea, and became celebrated for its wealth, magnificence, and learning. It was esteemed as the light and ornament of all Greece; it was, however, no less remarkable for its corruption and licentiousness. "To live as at Corinth" was a proverb meaning profligate indulgence, and the name "Corinthian" applied to women who were infamous. The city is now desolate with just a little village near the ancient Corinth. There is, however, a modern city of Corinth, a few miles away, with about twenty thousand inhabitants.

Paul preached at Corinth about A.D. 53 for eighteen months (Acts 18:11). He paid it a short second visit during the period A.D. 54–57, not mentioned specifically in Acts but implied in 1 Cor 16:7; 2 Cor 12:14; 13:1, where he speaks of an intended third journey to Corinth which coincides with that in Acts 20:2. He spent three winter months there (A.D. 57 and 58), during which he wrote the Epistle to the Romans (Acts 20:2, 3 [cf. 1 Cor 16:6]; Rom 16:1). He wrote two letters to the Corinthians rebuking their sins, and he alluding to the Isthmian games celebrated at Corinth.

2883. Κορνήλιος _Kornélios_; gen. _Kornélíou_, masc. proper noun. Cornelius, a Roman centurion of the Italian cohort stationed at Caesarea Maritime. He was the first heathen convert to Christianity. He was a Gentile by birth but a God-fearing man, a half-proselyte leaning toward the Jewish religion, yet uncircumcised and hence considered unclean (Acts 10:1). His prayers, being offered in the faith of a promised Messiah, were heard, and God sent Peter to make known to him the plan of salvation through a crucified and risen Redeemer; thus the door of faith was opened to the Gentiles. Cornelius and his family were baptized in the name of the Lord Jesus (Acts 10:1, 3, 7, 17, 21, 22, 24, 25, 30, 31).

2884. κόρος _kóros_; gen. _kórou_, masc. noun, Hebr. _kor_. The largest Hebrew measure of volume, equal to ten ephahs (Ezek 45:14), which was used exclusively for measuring grain and other dry substances. It was also equal to ten baths, which measurement was used exclusively for liquids. The one hundred measures (_bátoi_, the pl. of _bátos_ [943], baths) of oil in Luke 16:6 were close to nine hundred gallons. The _kóros_, equivalent to the _homer_ (Ezek 45:14), was used as a measure of barley (Lev 27:16), wheat (Ezek 45:13), and cereals generally. The identity of the _kor_ and the _homer_ as each containing ten ephah or baths, with the information that the _kor_ was also used for liquids, is given by Ezek 45:11ff. This was used for both wet and dry measure and passed to the Greeks as the _kóros_. The "hundred measures of wheat" of Luke 16:7 are one hundred kors or _kóroi_, equal to more than 1110 bushels (depending on the estimated content of _bátos_), in Gr. _bátoi_, translated "bushels." Sometimes the _kóros_ was also a liquid

measure equal to about eleven gallons. See 1 Kgs 4:22; 5:11; 2 Chr 2:10; 27:5; Ezek 45:13, 14; Luke 16:7.

Syn.: _métron_ (3358), measure; _méros_ (3313), a part, portion; _sáton_ (4568), a Hebrew dry measure of about a peck and a half, the ephah being equal to three _sáta_; _bátos_ (943), a bath, being a Jewish liquid measure the equivalent of an ephah, containing between eight and thirteen and one half gallons; _choínix_ (5518), a dry measure of less than a quart and sufficient for a day's consumption.

2885. κοσμέω _kosméō_; contracted _kosmố_, fut. _kosmésō_, from _kósmos_ (2889), world, adorning, order. To order, set in order (Matt 12:44; Luke 11:25; Sept.: Ezek 23:41). To adorn, garnish, decorate the sepulchers with garlands and flowers or by adding columns or other ornaments (Matt 23:29). It was a custom among the Greeks as well as the Jews not only to erect, but also to repair and adorn the monuments of those who had merited them or who had suffered an undeserved death. To trim, as a lamp (Matt 25:7). Metaphorically to honor, dignify (1 Tim 2:9, "In like manner also, that women adorn themselves"; Titus 2:10; 1 Pet 3:5; Rev 21:2, 19; Sept.: Jer 4:30; Ezek 16:11). This may refer to the internal adorning of the soul, but the external appearance is also implied.

2886. κοσμικός _kosmikós_; fem. _kosmikế_, neut. _kosmikón_, adj. from _kósmos_ (2889), world. Worldly, what belongs to the world. In the NT, it corresponds to the idea of _kósmos_ (2889), world (Heb 9:1), the opposite of heavenly and spiritual (Heb 9:11). In Titus 2:12 "worldly lusts" pertain to those desires of the world which estrange a person from God (Eph 2:1, 2).

Syn.: _sarkikós_ (4559), fleshly, carnal; _sōmatikós_ (4984), bodily; _phusikós_ (5446), physical.

Ant.: _hágios_ (40), saintly; _euschếmōn_ (2158), decorous, honorable, noble; _pneumatikós_ (4152), spiritual.

2887. κόσμιος *kósmios*; gen. *kosmíou*, masc.-fem., neut. *kósmion*, adj. from *kósmos* (2889), order, arrangement. Orderly, decent (1 Tim 2:9; 3:2). Plato presents someone who is *kósmios* as the citizen who quietly fulfills the duties which are incumbent on him and is not disorderly. He associates such a person, even as Paul does, with the *sṓphrōn* (4998), sensible, self-controlled, one who voluntarily places limitations on his own freedom. The virtue of the *kósmios*, however, is not only the propriety of his dress and demeanor, but of his inner life, uttering and expressing itself outwardly. Contrasted with *semnós* (4586), venerable, this latter person has a grace and dignity not obtained from earth only. While a *kósmios* person behaves himself well in his earthly citizenship and is an asset, the person who is *semnós* owes his quality to a higher citizenship. *Semnós* inspires not only respect but reverence and worship.

Syn.: *hieroprepḗs* (2412), one who acts in a way befitting holiness; *euschḗmōn* (2158), decorous, honorable; *eulabḗs* (2126), circumspect.

Ant.: *aschḗmōn* (809), shapeless, not elegant, uncomely; *átopos* (824), out of place, improper.

2888. κοσμοκράτωρ *kosmokrátōr*; gen. *kosmokrátoros*, masc. noun from *kósmos* (2889), world, and *kratéō* (2902), to hold. Lord of the world. Used in the NT of Satan as the prince of this world, i.e., of worldly men (Eph 6:12, in the pl., referring to Satan and his angels [cf. John 12:31; 2 Cor 4:4]).

Syn.: *pantokrátōr* (3841), the ruler of everything; *árchōn* (758), ruler; *despótēs* (1203), a despot, absolute ruler; *kúrios* (2962), lord; *hēgemṓn* (2232), chief person, leader; *basileús* (935), king.

Ant.: *hupērétēs* (5257), servant.

2889. κόσμος *kósmos*; gen. *kósmou*, masc. noun probably from *koméō* (n.f.), to take care of. World, with its primary meaning being order, regular disposition and arrangement.

(I) A decoration, ornament (1 Pet 3:3; Sept.: Ex 33:4–6; Jer 4:30).

(II) Order of the universe, the world.

(A) The universe, heavens and earth (Matt 13:35; 24:21; Luke 11:50; John 17:5, 24; Acts 17:24; Rom 1:20; Heb 4:3). Metonym for the inhabitants of the universe (1 Cor 4:9). Figuratively and symbolically, a world of something, as an aggregate such as in James 3:6, "a world of iniquity" (cf. Sept.: Prov 17:6).

(B) The earth, this lower world as the abode of man. **(1)** The then-known world and particularly the people who lived in it (Mark 16:15; John 16:21, 28; 21:25; 1 Tim 3:16; 1 Pet 5:9; 2 Pet 3:6). To come or be sent into the world means to be born, as in John 1:9. To go forth into the world means to appear before men as in John 3:17, 19; 6:14; 1 Tim 1:15; Heb 10:5; 1 John 4:1, 9; 2 John 1:7. Hyperbolically (Matt 4:8, "all the kingdoms of the world"; see Rom 1:8). **(2)** Metonymically, the world meaning the inhabitants of the earth, men, mankind (Matt 5:14; 13:38; John 1:29; 3:16; Rom 3:6, 19; 1 Cor 4:13; 2 Cor 5:19; Heb 11:7; 2 Pet 2:5; 1 John 2:2). Hyperbolically, the world for the multitude, everybody (John 7:4 "show thyself to the world" means manifest thyself, do not remain in secret; 12:19); metaphorically, that is openly (John 14:22; 18:20; 2 Cor 1:12). It also stands for the heathen world, the same as *tá éthnē* (1484), "the nations" (a.t. [Rom 11:12, 15 {cf. Luke 12:30}]).

(C) The present world, the present order of things, as opposed to the kingdom of Christ; and hence, always with the idea of transience, worthlessness, and evil both physical and moral, the seat of cares, temptations, irregular desires. It is thus nearly equivalent to *ho aiṓn hoútos* (*aiṓn* [165], age; *hoútos* [3778], this), this age. **(1)** Generally with *hoútos* (3778), this (John 12:25, "in this world," during this life; 18:36, "of this world," meaning this earth; 1 Cor 5:10; Eph 2:2; 1 John 4:17). Specifically the wealth and enjoyments of this world, this life's goods (Matt 16:26; Mark 8:36; Luke 9:25; 1 Cor 3:22; 7:31, 33, 34; Gal 6:14; James 4:4; 1 John 2:17). **(2)** Metonymically for the men of this world as opposed to those who seek the kingdom of God, e.g., with *hoútos*, this (1 Cor 1:20; 3:19); as subject to Satan, the ruler of this world (John 12:31; 14:30; 16:11); without *hoútos* (John 7:7; 14:17; 16:8; 17:6, 9; 1 Cor 1:21; 2 Cor 7:10; Phil 2:15; James 1:27).

(III) Idiomatic expressions with *kósmos*:

(A) A rhetorical expression for the great majority of people in a particular place (John 12:19).

(B) Almost equivalent to the modern phrase "the public" (John 7:4 [cf. 18:20]).

(C) Means of sustenance for the body is called *bíos* (979), i.e., means of livelihood. *Bíon toú kósmou* (1 John 3:17), the material things provided in the world.

(D) "The tongue . . . a world of iniquity" (James 3:6), the sum total.

(E) The world before the flood (Heb 11:7; 2 Pet 2:5; 3:6). The population of the world then and its accumulations of wealth and the products of its labor are no doubt chiefly in view; yet the comparison in 2 Pet 3:6, 7 with "the heavens and the earth, which are now," suggests a sweeping away at that time of the whole order of nature.

(IV) *Kósmos* used with ethical meaning:

(A) As material and transitory, the world presents a contrast with that which is spiritual and eternal. So Paul regards it in Gal 4:3; 6:14; Col 2:8, 20. His general teaching is that the Law and its ordinances belong to an external sphere, the things that are seen (2 Cor 4:18) which lose their value through Christ's death, in comparison with the things spiritual. So it should be with all Christians. Here he is not considering the world to be evil as indeed the Law is not evil, but only of temporary value (see 1 Cor 7:31, 34 [cf. Luke 12:30]).

(B) Devotion to the things of the world produces a certain attitude of mind which under the sense of laws is manifested in "the sorrow of the world" which is not "godly sorrow" (2 Cor 7:10). The things of this world are thus spoken of as altogether incomplete (1 Cor 1:27, 28; 4:13; James 2:5). The world has its own wisdom which does not have concern for God (John 1:10; 1 Cor 1:20, 21; 3:19) and which cannot receive the Spirit of truth (John 14:17). There is a spirit of this world (1 Cor 2:12). Those who have this spirit are described as being "of the world" or "of this world" (John 8:23; 1 John 4:4, 5). In contrast, Christ's disciples are described as being "not of the world" (John 15:19; 17:14 [cf. 1 Cor 5:10]). The state of the world arising from the influence of this worldly spirit is one of dire moral corruption (Eph 2:2; James 1:27; 4:4; 2 Pet 1:4; 2:20; 1 John 2:15–17).

(C) The word "world" denotes the mass of people who are hostile or at least indifferent to the truth and the followers of Christ (John 7:7; 16:20, 33; 1 John 3:1, 13; 4:4, 5).

(D) The world is dominated by the evil one (John 12:31; 1 John 4:4, 5).

(E) The world is the object of judgment and saving mercy (John 1:29; 3:16–19; 4:42; 6:33, 51; 8:12, 26; 9:5; 12:46, 47; Rom 3:19; 11:12, 15; 1 Cor 6:2; 2 Cor 5:19). Men are the objects of judgment individually but they will also be objects of a collective judgment or a collective restoration (cf. Rom 8:19f.).

(F) The Holy Spirit has a special office in regard to the world, distinct from that which He exercises toward believers (John 16:8–11).

(G) Through faith, the Christian can overcome the world, i.e., no doubt, the worldly spirit in himself and the opposition of worldly men and the world's ruler (1 John 4:4; 5:4, 5).

(V) *Kósmos*, at times, bears a distinction to *aiōn* (165), age, a period of time, but a much longer one than we usually think of, probably indeed the whole period during which the present order of nature has continued and shall continue. *Aiōn* is used in many places with much the same connotation as "world." It is often rendered by this word in our translations though *aiōn* should often be distinguished from *kósmos*, even where the two seem to express the same idea as in 1 Cor 1:20 and Eph 2:2, 3. This *aiōn* is contrasted to that which is to come (Matt 12:32; Mark 10:30; Luke 18:30; Heb 6:5). We read of its cares (Matt 13:22; Mark 4:19); its sons (Luke 16:8; 20:34, 35); its rulers, i.e., the kings and great ones of the earth (1 Cor 2:6, 8); its wisdom (1 Cor 1:20; 2:6; 3:18, 19); its fashion, to which the Christian must not be conformed (Rom 12:2). It is evil (Gal 1:4) and under the dominion of the evil one (2 Cor 4:4). This use of *aiōn* with an ethical meaning is not difficult to understand, easier indeed than the corresponding and more common one of *kósmos*. It is otherwise with the expression in Heb 1:2, "He made the worlds [*aiōnas*, ages]." Here, *hoi aiōnes*, the ages, seems to mean the sum of the periods of time including all that is manifested in and through them.

Deriv.: *kosméō* (2885), to order, put in order, decorate, adorn; *kosmikós* (2886), worldly, earthly; *kósmios* (2887), well-ordered, well-mannered, decorous; *kosmokrátor* (2888), a world ruler.

Syn.: *aiōn* (165), age; *oikouménē* (3625), the inhabited earth, civilization; *gḗ* (1093), earth as arable land, but also the earth as a whole, the world in contrast to the heavens.

2890. Κούαρτος *Koúartos*; gen. *kouártou*, masc. noun. Quartus, meaning fourth, a Christian who lived at Corinth and sent his greetings by Paul to the Christians in Rome (Rom 16:23).

2891. κοῦμι *koúmi*; transliterated from the imper. of the Aramaic *qūm* (6966, OT). Arise (Mark 5:41).

Syn.: *anístēmi* (450), to stand up; *egeírō* (1453), to arise.

Ant.: *keímai* (2749), to lie; *katákeimai* (2621), to lie down; *píptō* (4098), to fall; *katapíptō* (2667), to fall down.

2892. κουστωδία *koustōdía*; gen. *koustōdías*, fem. noun. Lat. *custodia*, custody. A watch, guard, keeper, sentinel, used of the Roman soldiers at the sepulcher of the Lord Jesus (Matt 27:65, 66; 28:11).

Syn.: *spekoulátōr* (4688), the Lat. for speculator or a lookout officer, bodyguard; *phúlax* (5441), a guard, keeper.

2893. κουφίζω *kouphízō*; fut. *kouphiso*, from *koúphos* (n.f.), hollow, light in weight. To lighten, make light or less heavy, as a ship by throwing things overboard (Acts 27:38; Sept.: Jon 1:5).

Syn.: *kenóō* (2758), to empty.

Ant.: *phortízō* (5412), to load up; *gémō* (1073), to fill; *gemízō* (1072), to fill; *barúnō* (925), to burden, make heavy.

2894. κόφινος *kóphinos*; gen. *kophínou*, masc. noun. A wicker basket (Matt 14:20; 16:9; Mark 6:43; 8:19; Luke 9:17; John 6:13; Sept.: Ps 81:6). The *kóphinos* was proverbially the Jewish traveling basket. The word is used in the accounts of the miracles of feeding the five thousand and the four thousand for the baskets in which the fragments were gathered (Matt 14:20; Mark 6:43; Luke 9:17; John 6:13). The Jews carried their food in these wicker baskets while traveling in Gentile countries to avoid defilement. *Kóphinoi* were used to carry agricultural produce. They were probably large provision baskets, possibly of ropework, such as those which the lake-dwelling Paeonians used for fishing. Their sizes were variable, but they were probably not as large as *spurídes* (the pl. of *spurís* [4711], a long reed basket). The *spurís* and *kóphinos* are contrasted in Matt 16:9, 10; Mark 8:19, 20. In the early church, *kóphinoi*, wicker baskets, were used for carrying the communion bread and wine to those not present at the Lord's table.

Syn.: *spurís* (4711), a braided reed basket large enough to hold a man; *sargánē* (4553), a braided rope or band making a large basket; *pḗra* (4082), a wallet or leather pouch for food; *glōssókomon* (1101), a case for keeping the mouthpieces of wind instruments and money; *balántion* (905), a pouch for money, a purse made of leather; *pínax* (4094) a platter.

2895. κράββατος *krábbatos*; gen. *krabbátou*, masc. noun. A small couch used by the poor. It denotes a simple kind of bed such as the ancients used to rest on at noon (Mark 2:4, 9, 11, 12; 6:55; John 5:8–12; Acts 5:15; 9:33 [cf. Luke 5:18, 24]).

Among the ancient Jews, like other oriental and middle east people in the day of Christ, the bed usually consisted of a padded quilt or thin mattress to be used according to the season or the condition of the owner with or without covering (cf. Ex 22:27). The outer garment worn in the daytime served as a covering for the night also. The very poor often made their bed of the skins of animals, old cloaks, rugs, or slept in their ordinary clothing on the bare ground floor as they do today in the East.

Various allusions are made in the gospels to beds that could be carried: "Arise, take up thy bed [*klínē*], and go unto thine house" (Matt 9:6); "Rise, take up thy bed [*krábbatos*], and walk" and "immediately the man . . . took up his bed [*krábbatos*], and walked" (John 5:8, 9); "Behold, men brought in a bed [*klínē*] a man which was taken with a palsy" (Luke 5:18). In Luke 5:19, the diminutive *klinídion* is used; Mark 2:4 uses the word *krábbatos*.

For ordinary use at night, the bed was laid on the floor, generally on a mat or a light, portable wooden frame which served to keep it off the ground. Sometimes a more elevated bedstead was used ("under a bed" [Mark 4:21]); the beds were on a raised platform on the side of the room (cf. Prov 7:16, 17; 1 Sam 28:23). In the morning the bedding, after being aired and sunned, was rolled up and put aside

on the raised platform or packed away for the day in a chest or closet. A bedstead was ordinarily considered a luxury.

Usually a room was set apart as a bedroom where the whole family slept: "My children are with me in bed; I cannot rise and give thee" (Luke 11:5–8). Among the poorest, a portion of the single room occupied by the family was set apart for sleeping and was generally raised above the level of the floor. When the house was of two stories, beds were laid in one of the rooms in the upper story or, preferably during the summer, on the flat roof.

Syn.: *koítē* (2845), a bed, the marriage bed.

2896. κράζω *krázō*; fut. *kekráxomai*, aor. *ékraxa*, the perf. *kékraga*, with the meaning of the present. This is an onomatopoeia imitating the hoarse cry of the raven. To cry out, entreat.

(I) Used intrans. of inarticulate cries, clamor, or exclamation derived from fear (Matt 14:26); from pain (Matt 27:50; Mark 15:39; Rev 12:2); from abhorrence (Acts 7:57). Spoken of demoniacs (Mark 1:26; 5:5; 9:26; Luke 9:39; Sept.: 2 Sam 13:19; Jer 25:34). Expressing joy (Luke 19:40; Sept.: Josh 6:16; Ps 65:13).

(II) It is used of words uttered with a loud voice: to cry, exclaim, call aloud (Mark 10:48; 15:13, 14; Luke 18:39; John 12:13; Acts 19:32, 34; 23:6); "with a loud voice" (Acts 7:57; Rev 14:15); by a tense or part. of *légō* (3004), to speak, "he cried, saying" (a.t. [Matt 14:30; Mark 3:11; John 1:15]); "they cried out, saying" (a.t. [Matt 8:29; 27:23]); "cried . . . and said" (a.t. [Mark 5:7; Luke 4:41]); pl. *krázontes kaí légontes*, they "crying and saying" (a.t. [Matt 9:27; 21:15]); *kráxas kaí eípe*, "when he cried, he said" (a.t. [Mark 9:24]). With the dat. *phōnḗ megálē* (*phōnḗ* [5456], voice; *megálē* [3173], great), "with a loud voice" (Rev 6:10; 7:2, 10; 19:17).

(III) Also used of urgent prayer, supplication (Rom 8:15; Gal 4:6); metaphorically (James 5:4; Sept.: Ps 28:1; 30:8; 2 Sam 19:28; Jer 11:11, 12).

Deriv.: *anakrázō* (349), to cry out loudly; *kraugḗ* (2906), an outcry, clamor.

Syn.: *boáō* (994), to raise a cry or the voice; *anaboáō* (310), to cry out or to lift up the voice; *epiboáō* (1916), to exclaim vehemently; *phōnéō* (5455), to utter a loud sound or cry; *epiphōnéō* (2019) to shout.

Ant.: *sigáō* (4601), to be silent; *siōpáō* (4623), to keep silent; *hēsucházō* (2270), to be quiet.

2897. κραιπάλη *kraipálē*; gen. *kraipálēs*, fem. noun. A headache, a hangover, a shooting pain or a confusion in the head arising from intemperance in wine or strong liquors. Translated in Luke 21:34 as "surfeiting," the sense of disgust and loathing from an overindulgence in wine and carousing.

Syn.: *méthē* (3178), drunkenness in the abstract; *pótos* (4224), a drinking bout leading possibly to excess; *oinophlugía* (3632), excess of wine; *kṓmoi*, the pl. of *kṓmos* (2970), revelings and riotings.

Ant.: *sōphrosúnē* (4997), sobriety.

2898. κρανίον *kraníon*; gen. *kraníou*, neut. noun from *kára* (n.f.), head, top. A skull, in Lat. *cranium* (Matt 27:33; Mark 15:22; Luke 23:33; John 19:17). The corresponding Aramaic word is *golgotha* (Judg 9:53; 2 Kgs 9:35). The place where Jesus was crucified may have looked like a skull and was thus called Golgotha. However, the traditional cite of Jesus' crucifixion which bears this unusual feature is widely rejected by scholars today. It may have been that the place of Jesus' crucifixion was a common location for executions and that the skeletal remains, especially the skulls, of those put to death laid visibly scattered in the area.

2899. κράσπεδον *kráspedon*; gen. *kraspédou*, neut. noun. A border of the garment which the Jews in general and particularly our Lord wore in obedience to the Mosaic Law (Matt 9:20; 14:36; 23:5; Mark 6:56; Luke 8:44; see Num 15:38; Deut 22:12). The scribes and

Pharisees wore the borders of these flowing garments unusually large to call attention to their extraordinary piety and uncommon obedience to the divine commandment (Matt 23:5).

In the Sept., the word answers not only to the Hebr. word for border or extremity (Deut 22:12; Zech 8:23), but also to the fringes which the Jews were commanded to wear on the borders of their garments (Num 15:38, 39). These fringes were a very proper and striking emblem of the radiation or emission of light. The Israelites were commanded to put a "ribbon" of blue or sky-color on the fringes (Num 15:38), representative of the blue appearance at the extremity of the sky. Wearing such "ribbons" of blue on the borders of their garments was meant to remind them of all the commandments of the Lord.

For Christians, the figure in the NT is the putting on of Christ, the divine light (Rom 13:14; Gal 3:27). Having this in mind, they should walk as children of light, putting on the new man, which after God is created in righteousness and true holiness (Eph 4:24). This figure was to have reminded believers that they should walk in the Spirit (Gal 5:16, 26), being adorned with the accompanying graces (Gal 5:22, 23 [cf. Num 15:39, 40]).

2900. κραταιός *krataiós*; fem. *krataiá*, neut. *krataión*, adj. from *krátos* (2904), power, dominion, strength. Strong, mighty, referring to the hand of God (1 Pet 5:6). Strength which is established and manifested.

Deriv.: *krataióō* (2901), to strengthen.

Syn.: *dunatós* (1415), powerful, mighty in expressing power; *ischurós* (2478), strong, usually referring to inherent physical strength; *mégas* (3173), great.

Ant.: *asthenḗs* (772), weak; *adúnatos* (102), not powerful, not able to demonstrate strength.

2901. κραταιόω *krataióō*; fut. *krataiṓsō*, from *krataiós* (2900), strong. To make strong, to establish. In the NT, only in the pass., to be strong, grow strong (Luke

1:80; 2:40; 1 Cor 16:13; Eph 3:16; Sept.:
2 Sam 10:12; 2 Chr 21:4; Ps 31:24).

Syn.: *dunamóō* (1412), to strength-
en; *endunamóō* (1743), to make strong;
ischúō (2480), to have strength; *enischúō*
(1765), to make strong; *sthenóō* (4599),
to strengthen; *stereóō* (4732), to establish;
epistērízō (1991), to confirm, establish.

Ant.: *asthenéō* (770), to lack strength;
the expression *échō kakṓs* (*échō* [2192],
I have; *kakṓs* [2560], badly), to be sick;
kámnō (2577), to be weary; *sunéchō*
(4912), to be afflicted; *noséō* (3552), to
be sick.

2902. κρατέω *kratéō*; contracted *kratṓ*,
fut. *kratḗsō*, from *krátos* (2904), strength.
To take hold of, grasp, hold fast, followed
by the gen. of person meaning to have
power over, rule over. In the NT, followed by the gen. of thing or acc. of person or thing.
  (I) Followed by the gen. of thing
meaning to have power over, to be dominant, or become master of, i.e., to gain,
attain to (Acts 27:13; Heb 4:14, "let us attain to the full benefit of our profession in
Him" [a.t.], equivalent to Heb 6:18; Sept.:
Prov 14:18). To take the hand of someone
(Matt 9:25; Mark 1:31; 5:41; Luke 8:54;
Sept.: Gen 19:16; 2 Sam 1:11).
  (II) Followed by the acc.:
  (A) To have power over, to be or become the master of, which always implies a certain degree of force with which
one brings a person or thing wholly under his power, even when resistance is encountered. Generally to bring under one's
power, lay hold of, seize, or take a person (Matt 14:3; 18:28; 21:46; 22:6; 26:4,
48, 50, 55, 57; Mark 3:21; 6:17; 12:12;
14:1, 44, 46, 49, 51; Acts 24:6; Rev 20:2);
an animal (Matt 12:11). To take one by
the hand (Mark 9:27; Sept.: Judg 16:26).
"They . . . held him by the feet" (Matt
28:9).
  (B) To have in one's power, be master of, i.e., to hold, hold fast, not to let
go, e.g., of things (Rev 2:1 [cf. 1:16];
7:1; pass., Luke 24:16); of persons, to
hold in subjection (pass., Acts 2:24). To

hold one fast, i.e., to hold fast to someone, cleave to him, for example, in person (Acts 3:11), or in faith hold on to the
head, i.e., Christ (Col 2:19). Metaphorically spoken of sins, to retain, not to remit
(John 20:23). To keep to oneself, e.g., the
word (Mark 9:10). Generally to hold fast
in mind, observe (Mark 7:3, 4, 8; 2 Thess
2:15; Rev 2:13–15, 25; 3:11).

Deriv.: *kosmokrátōr* (2888), a world
ruler; *perikratḗs* (4031), strong enough
for something.

Syn.: *piázō* (4084), to take hold, apprehend; *katéchō* (2722), to hold firmly; *antéchomai* (472), to hold firmly
to; *sunéchō* (4912), to hold a prisoner; *epilambánō* (1949), to lay hold of;
tēréō (5083), to keep, hold fast; *diatēréō*
(1301), to keep carefully; *suntēréō*
(4933), to keep safe; *phulássō* (5442),
to guard; *diaphulássō* (1314), to guard
thoroughly; *phrouréō* (5432), to guard;
nosphízomai (3557), to keep for oneself;
ktáomai (2932), to gain, acquire; *échō*
(2192), to have; *bastázō* (941), to bear,
hold; *harpázō* (726), to take by force suddenly.

Ant.: *lúō* (3089), to loose, let go;
apolúō (630), to set free, release.

2903. κράτιστος *krátistos*; fem. *kratístē*,
neut. *krátiston*, adj., the superlative of
kratús (n.f.), strong, mighty, powerful,
from *krátos* (2904), power, strength. Most
excellent, most noble, used in addressing
persons of rank and authority (Luke 1:3;
Acts 23:26; 24:3; 26:25).

Syn.: *megaloprepḗs* (3169), magnificent, majestic; *diaphorṓteros* (1313),
more excellent, or literally more different; *eugenḗs* (2104), noble.

2904. κράτος *krátos*; gen. *krátous*, neut.
noun. Strength or might, more especially
manifested power, dominion. More closely related to *ischús* (2479), strength, than
dúnamis (1411), power. Denotes the presence and significance of force or strength
rather than its exercise.
  (I) Generally meaning might or power (Acts 19:20), with *katá* ([2596],

according), mightily, vehemently. "According to the working of his mighty power" (Eph 1:19) means the prevalence of His power, the word for "power" being *ischús* (2479), inherent power (Eph 6:10; Col 1:11; Sept.: Isa 40:26 [cf. Sept.: Ps 89:10]). Metonymically meaning might, for mighty deeds (Luke 1:51).

(II) Power, dominion (1 Tim 6:16; Heb 2:14; 1 Pet 4:11; 5:11; Jude 1:25; Rev 1:6; 5:13).

Deriv.: *akratḗs* (193), incontinent; *egkratḗs* (1468), temperate; *kratéō* (2902), to be strong, to seize; *krátistos* (2903), most excellent; *pantokrátōr* (3841), ruler over all, almighty.

Syn.: *dúnamis* (1411), strength, power and its execution; *ischús* (2479), strength possessed; *exousía* (1849), authority.

Ant.: *asthéneia* (769), weakness, infirmity.

2905. κραυγάζω kraugázō; fut. *kraugásō*, from *kraugḗ* (2906), clamor, cry. To cry aloud, clamor (Matt 12:19; 15:22; John 11:43; 18:40; 19:6, 15; Acts 22:23).

Syn.: *krázō* (2896) to cry; *anakrázō* (349) to cry out; *epiboáō* (1916), to cry; *boáō* (994), to raise a cry; *anaboáō* (310), to lift up the voice, cry out; *phōnéō* (5455), to utter a loud sound or cry; *epiphōnéō* (2019), to shout against.

Ant.: *sigáō* (4601), to be silent; *siōpáō* (4623), to be silent or still; *hēsucházō* (2270), to hold one's peace, be silent.

2906. κραυγή kraugḗ; gen. *kraugḗs*, fem. noun from *krázō* (2896), to clamor or cry. An outcry, usually for public information (Matt 25:6; Rev 14:18); of tumult or controversy, clamor (Acts 23:9; Eph 4:31); of sorrow, wailing (Rev 21:4; Sept.: Ex 12:30); of supplication (Heb 5:7; Sept.: Job 34:28).

Syn.: *boḗ* (995), a cry for help.

Ant.: *sigḗ* (4602), silence.

2907. κρέας kréas; gen. *kréatos*, neut. noun. Meat, nonliving flesh (Rom 14:21; 1 Cor 8:13; Sept.: Ex 12:8; Deut 12:15).

Syn.: *sárx* (4561), flesh.

Ant.: *ostéon* (3747), bone.

2908. κρεῖσσον kreísson; the neut. of *kreíssōn* (2909) used as an adv. Better (1 Cor 7:38).

2909. κρείσσων kreissōn, κρείττων kreíttōn gen. *kreíssonos*, masc.-fem., neut. *kreísson*, adj., the comparative of *kratús* (n.f.), strong, also of *agathós* (18), benevolently good. Better.

(I) Better, i.e., more useful, more profitable (1 Cor 7:9; Phil 1:23; Heb 11:40; 2 Pet 2:21); used with the art. *tó kreítton* (1 Cor 11:17; 12:31 [pl.]; Sept.: Ex 14:12; Prov 25:25). Used as an adv. in Heb 12:24.

(II) Better in value or dignity, nobler, more excellent (Heb 1:4; 6:9; 7:7, 19, 22; 8:6; 9:23; 10:34; 11:16, 35; 1 Pet 3:17; 2 Pet 2:21).

Syn.: *meízōn* (3187), greater.

Ant.: *cheírōn* (5501), bad, worse; *elássōn* (1640), less; *hḗssōn* or *hḗttōn* (2276), less, inferior.

2910. κρεμάννυμι kremánnumi and κρεμάω kremáō; fut. *kremásō*, aor. pass. *ekremásthēn*. To hang, suspend. As trans. mid. *krémamai* after the form *hístamai* (2476), to stand, meaning to hang, be suspended, intrans. The pres. *kremáō* is found only in very late writers.

(I) Act. followed by *epí* (1909), upon, with the gen. (Acts 5:30; 10:39, *kremásantes* [*autón*] *epí xúlou*, when "they . . . hanged Him on wood" [a.t.]). Pass. followed by *epí* (1909), upon (Matt 18:6); in an absolute sense (Luke 23:39). See Sept.: Gen 40:19, 22; pass., Esth 5:14; 7:10.

(II) Mid., in Acts 28:4, "hanging from his hand" (a.t.); followed by *epí*, upon with the gen., *epí xúlou* (3586), wood (Gal 3:13). Figuratively, followed by *en* (1722), in. In Matt 22:40, the expression possibly being a metaphor taken from the custom mentioned by Tertullian of hanging up the laws in a public place to be seen of all men. This would imply that all of the Law and the prophets are succinctly contained in the precepts here mentioned, setting forth our duty to God and man. Others believe that the interpretation of this verse is that the Law and the prophets depend upon these two basic commandments.

Deriv.: *ekkremánnumi* (1582), to hang from or upon; *krēmnós* (2911), a steep place, an overhanging precipice.

Syn.: *paríēmi* (3935), to leave hanging or undone; *períkeimai* (4029), to lie or hang around; *apágchō* (519), to strangle.

2911. κρημνός *krēmnós*; gen. *krēmnoú*, masc. noun from *kremánnumi* (2910), to hang. A steep place, a precipice overhanging the ground below (Matt 8:32; Mark 5:13; Luke 8:33; Sept.: 2 Chr 25:12).

Deriv.: *katakrēmnízō* (2630), to cast down from a precipice.

2912. Κρής *Krḗs*; gen. *Krētós*, masc. proper noun. An inhabitant of Crete, a Cretan. See *Krḗtē* (2914), Crete. Cretans were at Jerusalem on the day of Pentecost (Acts 2:11).

2913. Κρήσκης *Krḗskēs*; gen. *Krḗskentos*, masc. proper noun. Crescens, meaning growing, a Christian at Rome of whom Paul speaks (2 Tim 4:10).

2914. Κρήτη *Krḗtē*; gen. *Krḗtēs*, fem. proper noun. Crete, a large Greek island in the Mediterranean Sea, midway between Syria and Italy. It is about 140 miles long by thirty-five miles wide. The people were proverbially said to be liars (Titus 1:12). Paul was shipwrecked near the island. He left Titus there as the first pastor and superintendent who was to "ordain elders in every city" of the island (Titus 1:5; see Acts 27:7, 12, 13, 21). It was said to have one hundred cities, from which it was known as *hekatópolis*.

2915. κριθή *krithḗ*; gen. *krithḗs*, fem. noun. Barley (Rev 6:6; Sept.: Deut 8:8). Barley was cultivated everywhere in Palestine, principally as food for horses (1

Kgs 4:28) and donkeys. It is mentioned by Ezekiel as the fee paid to false prophetesses by people who consulted them (Ezek 13:19).

Deriv.: *kríthinos* (2916), consisting of barley.

2916. κρίθινος *kríthinos*; fem. *krithínē*, neut. *kríthinon*, adj. from *krithḗ* (2915), barley. Made of barley, barley loaves (John 6:9, 13; Sept.: 2 Kgs 4:42). It was used to make bread (Judg 7:13; 2 Kgs 4:42; John 6:9, 13) and cakes (Ezek 4:12). It was mixed with other cheap grains for the same purpose (Ezek 4:9). When someone wished to express the extremity of his poverty, he would say, "I have no barley bread to eat." This illustrates several allusions to barley in Scripture, one being that barley meal was the jealousy offering (Num 5:15).

2917. κρίμα *kríma*; gen. *krímatos*, neut. noun from *krínō* (2919), to judge. The suffix *-ma* indicates the result of judging. Judgment, sentence, the reason for judgment.

(I) The act of judging, giving judgment, equivalent to *krísis* (2920), judgment spoken only in reference to future reward and punishment as in John 9:39, "for judgment I came into the world" (a.t.), meaning in order that the righteous may be approved and the wicked condemned, as is figuratively said in the next clause (see 1 Pet 4:17). Of the judgment of the last day (Acts 24:25; Heb 6:2). Metonymically for the power of judgment (Rev 20:4; Sept.: *krísis*, Lev 19:15; Deut 1:17; Ezek 21:32).

(II) Judgment given, decision, award, sentence.

(A) Generally (Matt 7:1; Rom 5:16; 11:33 (pl.), the judgments of God, meaning His decrees; Sept.: Ps 17:2; 119:7; Zech 8:16).

(B) More often a sentence of punishment or condemnation, implying also the punishment itself as a certain consequence (Matt 23:14; Mark 12:40; Luke 20:47; 23:40; 24:20; Rom 2:2, 3; 3:8; 13:2; 1

Cor 11:29, 34; Gal 5:10; 1 Tim 3:6; 5:12; James 3:1; 2 Pet 2:3; Jude 1:4; Rev 17:1; 18:20; Sept.: Deut 21:22; Jer 4:12).

(C) Lawsuit, cause, something to be judged (1 Cor 6:7, to go to law means to have lawsuits; Sept.: Job 23:4; 31:13).

Syn.: *díkē* (1349), judgment, a decision or its execution; *apókrima* (610), sentence, answer.

Ant.: *áphesis* (859), a dismissal, release; *páresis* (3929), a passing by of death or sin.

2918. κρίνον krínon; gen. *krínou*, neut. noun. A lily (Matt 6:28; Luke 12:27). Mentioned by various OT writers (Song 4:5; 2:16; 1 Kgs 7:19; 2 Chr 4:5; Hos 14:5). From the expression "lilies of the field," we gather that they were wild flowers, while the comparison of them with the royal robes of Solomon (Matt 6:29) implies that they were not white, but multi-colored.

2919. κρίνω krínō; fut. *krinō̄*, aor. *ékrina*, aor. pass. *ekríthēn*, perf. *kékrika*. To separate, distinguish, discriminate between good and evil, select, choose out the good. In the NT, it means to judge, to form or give an opinion after separating and considering the particulars of a case.

(I) To judge in one's own mind as to what is right, proper, expedient; to deem, decide, determine, followed by the inf. (Acts 3:13; 15:19, meaning my decision is; 20:16; 25:25; 1 Cor 2:2; Titus 3:12). Followed by the gen. art. *toú* with the inf. (Acts 27:1, "when we decided to sail" [a.t.]); by the acc. and the inf. (Acts 21:25); with the inf. *eínai* (1511), to be (Acts 16:15), implied (Acts 13:46, "and judge [or deem] yourselves unworthy of everlasting life"; 26:8; Rom 14:5, "One man esteems [judges] one day to be above another, another judges every day to be alike" [a.t.], as we must supply from the force of the antithesis). Followed by the acc. of thing, to determine, decree (Rev 16:5). In Acts 16:4, "the decrees . . . that were ordained [*tá kekriména*]." Followed by the acc. (*toúto* [5124]), this one,

as introducing the inf. with the art. *tó*, "but judge this rather, that no man put a stumblingblock" (Rom 14:13 [see 1 Cor 7:37; 2 Cor 2:1]). With *toúto hóti* (3754), that as (2 Cor 5:14).

(II) To judge, to form and express a judgment or opinion as to any person or thing, more commonly unfavorable. Followed by the acc. of person (John 8:15; Rom 2:1, 3; 3:7; 14:3, 4, 10, 13; Col 2:16); by the acc. of thing (1 Cor 10:15). In an absolute sense (Matt 7:1, 2; Luke 6:37; John 8:16, 26; Rom 2:1; 1 Cor 4:5; 10:29). Followed by the interrogative with *ei* (1487), if (Acts 4:19). Also with an adjunct of manner, equivalent to *krínō krísin*, to make a judgment according to appearance (John 7:24); to judge that which is right (Luke 12:57); to judge rightly (Luke 7:43); to judge according to the flesh (John 8:15). By implication to condemn, followed by the acc. (Rom 2:27; 14:22; James 4:11, 12; Sept.: Job 10:2).

(III) To judge in a judicial sense.

(A) To sit in judgment on any person, to try. Followed by the acc. (John 18:31; Acts 23:3; 24:6; 1 Cor 5:12). In the pass. *krínomai*, to be judged, tried, be on trial (Acts 25:10; Rom 3:4; Sept.: Ps 51:6). Followed by *perí* (4012), concerning, with the gen., to judge for something (Acts 23:6; 24:21); by *epí* (1909), upon, with the dat., for (Acts 26:6 "to be judged for the hope" [a.t.]); by *epí* with the gen., meaning before someone (Acts 25:9). Spoken in reference to the gospel dispensation, to the judgment of the great day of God as judging the world through Christ (John 5:22; 8:50; Acts 17:31; Rom 3:6); the secret things (Rom 2:16. See 1 Cor 5:13; James 2:12; 1 Pet 1:17; 2:23; Rev 11:18; 20:12, 13); of Jesus as the Messiah and Judge (John 5:30; 2 Tim 4:1); of Jesus Christ who will judge the living and the dead (1 Pet 4:5; Rev 19:11); figuratively of the Apostles and saints (Matt 19:28; Luke 22:30; 1 Cor 6:2, "And if the world shall be judged by you").

(B) In the sense of to pass judgment upon, condemn, with the acc. (Luke 19:22; John 7:51; Acts 13:27). As also implying punishment (1 Cor 11:31, 32; 1 Pet 4:6). Of the condemnation of the wicked and including the idea of punishment as a certain consequence, meaning to punish, take vengeance on. Spoken of God as judge (Acts 7:7 quoted from Gen 15:14; Rom 2:12; 2 Thess 2:12; Heb 13:4; Rev 6:10; 18:8, 20; 19:2); of Jesus (John 3:17, 18; 12:47, 48; James 5:9; Sept.: Isa 66:16; Ezek 38:22).

(C) To vindicate, avenge (Heb 10:30, "The Lord will avenge His people" [a.t.], i.e., by punishing their enemies).

(IV) Mid. *krínomai*, particularly to let oneself be judged, i.e., to have a lawsuit, go to law, with the dat., meaning with someone (Matt 5:40; 1 Cor 6:6); with the gen., to be judged before, followed by *epí* (1909), upon or before someone (1 Cor 6:1, 6). With *metá* (3326), with, and the gen., with someone (Sept.: Eccl 6:10); with *prós* (4314), before or toward and the acc., toward someone (Sept.: Job 31:13).

Deriv.: *anakrínō* (350), to judicially investigate, examine; *apokrínomai* (611), to respond; *diakrínō* (1252), to separate thoroughly, discriminate, make to differ, judge thoroughly; *egkrínō* (1469), to class with, count along, approve; *eilikrinḗs* (1506), pure, sincere; *epikrínō* (1948), to give sentence; *katakrínō* (2632), to judge against, condemn; *kríma* (2917), judicial decision; *krísis* (2920), judgment; *kritḗs* (2923), judge; *sugkrínō* (4793), to judge one thing comparing it with another, to interpret; *hupokrínomai* (5271), to speak or act under false identity.

Syn.: *egkaléō* (1458), to accuse before a court of justice; *kataginṓskō* (2607), to know something against, think ill of, condemn as a result of an enlightened conscience; *katadikázō* (2613), to pronounce judgment, condemn; *diaginṓskō* (1231), to ascertain exactly; *diakrínō* (1252), to discern; *logízomai* (3049), to reckon, esteem; *exouthenéō* (1848), to set at naught; *dokéō* (1380), to form an opinion.

Ant.: *apologéomai* (626), to answer back in making a defense, to excuse oneself; *dikaióō* (1344), to regard as just or innocent; *aphíēmi* (863), to dismiss, forgive, remit, let go; *apolúō* (630), to release; *timáō* (5091), to judge well, render honor;

2920. κρίσις *krísis*; gen. *kríseōs*, fem. noun from *krínō* (2919), to judge. Separation, figuratively division, dissension, decision, crisis, turn of affairs, judgment.

(I) Generally an opinion formed and expressed (John 7:24; 8:16).

(II) An official judgment.

(A) The act of judging in reference to the final judgment, the day of judgment (Matt 10:15; 11:22, 24; 12:36; Mark 6:11; 2 Pet 2:9; 3:7; 1 John 4:17); the hour of judgment (Rev 14:7); the judgment of the great day (Jude 1:6). Simply *krísis* standing for the judgment of the great day (Matt 12:41, 42; Luke 10:14; 11:31, 32; Heb 9:27). For the present judgment, the pronouncement of the punishment that was necessary and which Christ took on Himself on the cross (John 12:31, "now is the world judged" [a.t.]. See John 16:8, 11). In John 5:27; Jude 1:15, "to execute judgment" simply means to judge and enforce that judgment (cf. John 5:30). Used metonymically for the power of judgment (John 5:22; Sept.: Lev 19:15; Deut 1:17; Isa 28:6).

(B) Generally meaning judgment given, sentence pronounced (John 5:30; 2 Pet 2:11; Jude 1:9). Specific sentence of punishment or condemnation, e.g., to death (Acts 8:33; Sept.: Jer 39:5). Usually implying also punishment as a certain consequence from God (Rev 16:7; 18:10 [see Rom 8:8]; 19:2; Sept.: Jer 1:16). Of Christ as judge of the world condemning the wicked, judgment, condemnation (Matt 23:33; Mark 3:29; John 5:29, resurrection for judgment. See John 3:19; 5:24; Heb 10:27; James 2:13; 2 Pet 2:4). In 1 Tim 5:24, "some men's sins lead on to condemnation" (a.t.), i.e., accuse them, cry for condemnation; in others, their sins follow after, i.e., they persevere in them, though conscious of present guilt and future condemnation.

(C) Metonymically for a court of justice, a tribunal, judges, i.e., the smaller tribunals established in the cities of Palestine and subordinate to the Sanhedrin (cf. Deut 16:18; 2 Chr 19:5). These courts consisted of twenty-three judges, though Josephus expressly says the number was seven (Matt 5:21, 22; Sept.: Job 9:32; 22:4).

(III) Right, justice, equity (Matt 23:23; Luke 11:42; Sept.: Gen 18:25; Deut 32:4). Also for law, statutes, i.e., the divine law, the religion of Jehovah as developed in the gospels (Matt 12:18, 20 quoted from Isa 42:1–3).

(IV) The object of the Lord Jesus coming again is expressed as the final judgment. It is a judgment of individuals (Matt 22:1–14), a judgment of universal scope (Matt 13:36–42, 47–50; 16:27; 25:31), and a judgment in which Christ, the Son of Man, is Himself to be the Judge (Matt 25:31).

Because the resurrection will be universal, the judgment will be also (Matt 22:30; 24:31; Mark 13:27; Luke 14:14; 20:36, 37). See *anástasis* (386), resurrection. The judgment will be a transformation of all that exists in accordance with the advent of a new heaven and a new earth (Rom 8:18–30; Rev 21:1). On the day of judgment, the people of Christ will be called to an everlasting participation in the glories of His heavenly kingdom, and His enemies will be sentenced to eternal condemnation (Matt 13:36ff., 47ff.; 25; Mark 13; Luke 21).

In the last judgment Christ will be the judge as before, i.e., here and now (Matt 25:31ff.; Acts 10:42; 17:31; 2 Cor 5:10; 2 Tim 4:1). All mankind will appear before His judgment seat (see *béma* [968]). The righteous will thus have in His presence a perfect vision and possession of the goodness they have chosen in Him (2 Tim 4:8; 1 John 3:2). The wicked will see with regret what an abyss of sin and suffering they have fallen into (Rev 1:7). In such an aspect, it may be said men will hereafter

judge themselves. Those who are unlike Christ will find themselves as such to be separate from Him. The two classes of people are parted because they have acquired distinct natures like the sheep and the goats (Matt 25:31ff.).

The future judgment will thus be determined only by what people made of themselves when they were in the body (2 Cor 5:10). At the judgment, the books will be opened and every man will be judged according to his works (Rev 20:12). Each man's character will be manifested as the light of Christ falls upon it. The people of Christ will receive various awards at the last according to what their life has been (Luke 19:11ff.; 1 Cor 3:12ff.). A test like fire will try every believer's work. Some have acquired a close likeness to Christ by their lives of true holiness and love. The greater the likeness, the more He will be known, loved, and enjoyed, and the richer they themselves will be.

(V) *Krísis*, on the part of God, is an absolute necessity because He is a just God, rewarding those who obey Him and His laws and punishing the disobedient.

The moral aspect of judgment was dealt with under *kríno* (2919). There is, however, an eschatological judgment which is going to be executed in the Day of the Lord involving the judgment of the faithless when the divine kingdom will be consummated.

The Day of the Lord, or the final judgment, is always connected with the promise of the return of Christ to this earth. Christ connects the completion of the kingdom with a decisive occurrence, the great event of His own *parousía* (3952), coming and presence (Matt 24:3, 37, 39). The time of this occurrence is unknown (Matt 24:36; Mark 13:32). There are tokens of it, however, expressed in Matt 24—25.

In the Gospel of John, this judgment is treated proleptically, fulfilling itself in a probation of character and a self-verdict which takes place in the present (John 3:17, 18; 12:47, 48). The phrase "the last day" (John 12:48) points to the future judgment (1 John 2:28; 4:17) and is connected with the coming of Christ (for the teaching concerning this final judgment in the OT, see Isa 9; 11; Jer 23; 33; 34; 36; Ezek 34; 37; Mic 5; Zech 9—11).

The resurrection of the body is definitely connected with the coming judgment (Dan 12:2; Matt 22:23–33; Mark 12:18–27; Luke 20:27–40). It is alluded to in Matt 8:11; Luke 13:28, 29. The Lord Jesus personally affirmed the resurrection in John 11:23, 26 and connected it with the judgment to come in John 5:25, 27.

(VI) The judgment to come is not the only one spoken about in the Scripture. There is a judgment here and now for which Christ has come to the world (John 12:31). This means that an actual separation of men is in progress, and to a great extent, they themselves can see that nothing is arbitrary in God's judgment upon them. The spiritual blessings bestowed on the one hand, and the mental sufferings or want endured on the other, commend themselves to the enlightened conscience as just and inevitable. Christ is as a present light in the world, discerning between the souls of men, attracting and gladdening those who know and love Him, and repelling those who do evil and multiplying for them the pains of darkness, hatred, and sin (John 3:18ff.; 12:31). The former are called even now to everlasting life (John 3:36; 6:47; 1 John 3:14) and should know that they have it (1 John 5:13). The latter do not know life but abide in death and experience the wrath of God (John 3:36; 1 John 3:14f.; 5:12).

(VII) From the ethical point of view, we are told in Scripture that we should not judge others according to appearance (John 7:24) or according to the flesh (John 8:15). The reason why we should not judge others is because our judgment, at best, can only be based on partial knowledge. We are not entirely aware of the inner lives, motives, and principles of other people. We are not acquainted either with the antecedent conditions of their actions, or the possibilities of justification, progress, or amendment that their future may contain. Both Christ and Paul clearly expressed caution in one man judging another even if the outward evidence seems convincing (John 8:11; 1 Cor 4:5). This is the reason why we are enjoined to exercise patience and forbearance in the interest of an individual and also of the church. This teaching is incorporated in the parable of the tares (Matt 13:24–30, 36–43) and in Paul's teaching in Rom 14. It does not, however, mean that we should not properly exercise the grace of discernment and proper evaluation of people. How would we know not to give that which is holy to those who are like dogs if we do not evaluate them properly (Matt 7:6)? Or how would we guard ourselves against false prophets (Matt 7:15–20) or false disciples (Matt 7:21–23)? Our judgment of others must never be for the purpose of self-elevation or entertainment of a Pharisaic attitude of self-praise.

Syn.: with the meaning of accusation: *aitía* (156), cause, charge; *aítion* (158), a fault; *aitíama* (157), an accusation, complaint; *égklēma* (1462), an accusation made in public before a tribunal; *katēgoría* (2724), accusation; *hēméra* (2250), a day when reference is made to the judgment that will occur. With the meaning of opinion expressed: *gnómē* (1106), thought, expression of one's judgment, mind; *aísthēsis* (144), discernment, judgment as through the senses.

Ant.: *dikaíōsis* (1347), acquittal, justification; *áphesis* (859), release; *apolútrōsis* (629), redemption, deliverance; *eleuthería* (1657), freedom; *páresis* (3929), a passing by of death or sin.

2921. Κρίσπος Kríspos; gen. *Kríspou*, masc. proper noun. Crispus (Acts 18:8). An officer of the Jewish synagogue at Corinth. He and his family were converted under Paul's preaching, and he was one of the few who were baptized by Paul himself (1 Cor 1:14).

2922. κριτήριον *kritḗrion*; gen. *kritēríou*, neut. noun from *kritḗs* (2923), a judge. Judgment, the art, act, or authority of judging or determining (1 Cor 6:2); judicial contest or controversy, a lawsuit (1 Cor 6:4); judgment seat, tribunal, court of justice (James 2:6). See Sept.: Judg 5:10; Dan 7:10, 26.

Syn.: *bḗma* (968), judgment seat, tribunal; *gnṓmē* (1106), opinion, counsel; *boulḗ* (1012), advice as the result of determination; *nómos* (3551), law; *díkē* (1349), justice.

2923. κριτής *kritḗs*; gen. *kritoú*, masc. noun from *krínō* (2919), to judge. He who decides, a judge.

(I) Generally, in James 2:4, those who make a judgment or render an opinion concerning the thoughts of others. See Matt 12:27; Luke 11:19. In an unfavorable sense (James 4:11; Sept.: 1 Sam 24:16).

(II) In a judicial sense, one who sits to render justice (Matt 5:25; Luke 12:58; 18:2, 6; Acts 18:15; 24:10). Of Christ the final judge (Acts 10:42; 2 Tim 4:8; James 5:9); of God (Heb 12:23; Sept.: Ps 50:6).

(III) A leader, ruler, chief, spoken of the Hebrew judges from Joshua to Samuel (Acts 13:20 [cf. Judg 2:16ff.]).

Dikastḗs (1348) is used in Acts 7:35 and, in some MSS, in Luke 12:14. *Dikastḗs* refers to a judge appointed by society to solve the differences between individuals according to established custom of what is proper, and to give direction as to what is to be done. It is a judge who applies accepted law for the regulation of the relationships between individuals. *Kritḗs*, as used of God (Heb 10:30; 12:23; James 4:12), involves the inherent power to discern the character of a person. Similarly it is an attribute of Christ in the same manner as it is an attribute of God (Acts 10:42; 2 Tim 4:8; James 5:9). On the human level, a *kritḗs* is one who makes a judgment as to the character and actions of others without receiving such appointment from someone whereas *dikastḗs* implies a responsibility attributed by society and others. Therefore *dikastḗs* is more of a forensic term, a judicial judge, while *kritḗs* is one who uses his subjective criteria to evaluate others.

During the nomadic period of Israel, family disputes were settled by the head of the family; but Moses was the supreme judge to whom appeals were brought (Ex 18:13), and he is represented as bringing the matters himself to God for decision (Ex 18:19). Moses appealed to those who agreed with him to carry out his punishments by force (Ex 32:26). With the judgment becoming too burdensome, at the advice of his father-in-law, he selected a number of the heads of families who were already accustomed to judging in matters pertaining to their own families. These he set as judges over intertribal disputes, reserving for himself the right of settling the more difficult questions that arose (Ex 18:20ff. [cf. Num 11:16, 24ff.]).

The settlement of Canaan, and consequent change from a nomadic to a settled life, led to the emphasizing of local rather than family and tribal authority. The ancient customs were continued, but the elders of the city took the place of the elders of the tribe (Deut 16:18). During this period, the term "judges [*kritaí*]" was applied to the local heroes who delivered and ruled the tribes of Israel. During the time of monarchy, the administration of justice naturally remained in the hands of city elders and men who had gained a reputation for wisdom. The settlement of disputes was by arbitration rather than royal justice, but where a royal officer was stationed, there he would often be appealed to.

The king was always the supreme judge. The men of Israel brought their troubles regularly to David (2 Sam 15:2ff.). The power of the king enabled him, when present, to override the local courts.

The destruction of the monarchies and the exile of both kingdoms limited the power of the judges of the people. In their captivity, they were entirely subject to their conquerors. Under the Persians, the Jews were allowed to follow their own laws in purely internal matters (the elders of the city are mentioned in Ezra 7:25; 10:14), but quarrels were submitted to the Persian court (Ezra 4; 5). It was probably during the time of the Greek domination that further organization led to the establishment in Jerusalem of the Sanhedrin as the supreme court of the Jewish community. In the small towns and villages, justice was administered by a council of seven, and in larger places by one of twenty-three members. Christ refers to one of these councils in Matt 5:22, and to their members in verse twenty-five.

Throughout the Gospel of Matthew, Jesus appears as the judge of men and is always discriminating in separating the good from the bad, the sheep from the goats, the wheat from the tares, the grain from the chaff, the sincere man from the hypocrite (Matt 3:12; 6:5, 6; 13:25–30; 25:33). The Lord Jesus as *kritēs* (judge) constantly separates men into two classes (Matt 5:3–10; 25:34, 46). All the gospels present Jesus as the judge. The Father gives all judgment to the Son (John 5:22–27). Jesus came into the world for judgment (John 9:39). He separates men under moral tests (Matt 25:31–46 [cf. 7:23]). He pronounces judgment on the Pharisees (Matt 22:15–46). He judges Satan (Matt 16:23). He imparts the authority of judgment unto men (Matt 16:19 [cf. Acts 10:42; Rom 14:10; 2 Cor 5:10; 2 Tim 4:1]). His judgment seat is at the same time the throne of His glory (Matt 25:31). He associates Himself as judge with the twelve disciples who are to judge the twelve tribes of Israel (Matt 19:28; Luke 22:30 [cf. 1 Cor 6:3]).

The Lord Jesus does not leave us ignorant as to the tests that He is going to apply as our judge and He urges us to judge ourselves ahead of time for the purpose of self-correction. Therefore, every one of us is called upon to evaluate his own life in looking at his works and deeds (Matt 16:27; 25:31 [cf. Rom 2:6; Rev 20:12]), in showing kindness toward others (Matt 10:42; Mark 9:41), and in taking care lest we be a cause of stumbling to one of His little ones, whether they be little in age or little in faith (Luke 17:2).

The Lord Jesus places Himself as the supreme and personal judge of our attitude toward Him and presents Himself as a standard whereby we must judge ourselves. These are some areas to test when judging ourselves: devotion to Him (Matt 10:38; 19:28; Mark 8:34); confession of Him (Matt 10:32; Luke 12:8); appreciation of His presence and work (Matt 11:21); accountability to Him (John 5:40); belief in Him (John 3:18, 36; 5:24; 6:40); honor of Him (John 5:23); willingness to stand with Him (Matt 12:30; Mark 8:38); right fruitage (Matt 21:31–42; 7:16; Luke 6:44); outward conduct (Matt 22:11–13); willingness to help men (Matt 25:31–46); use of God's gifts (Matt 25:14–30); attitude toward His personal invitations (Matt 22:1–7); willingness to hear His words (Matt 10:14, 15; 12:41–42); willingness to forgive an injury (Matt 6:15; 18:28–30); obedience to the commandments (Matt 5:19); spirit of judgment on others (Matt 7:2); faith (Matt 8:10; 9:22, 29; 15:28; Mark 5:34); love of God (Matt 10:37); love of Christ (Luke 7:47; John 21:16); love of enemies (Luke 6:27); generosity to a disciple (Matt 10:42); mercifulness (Luke 6:36); humility as a child (Matt 18:4); endurance in well-doing (Matt 24:13); obedience to God (Matt 12:50); hypocrisy (Matt 23:13–36); idle words (Matt 12:36); lip service without the heart (Matt 15:8); selfish conceit (Matt 6:2); wicked pride (Mark 12:38); love of darkness (John 3:19); rejection of His disciples (Luke 10:10); adultery (Matt 19:9); commercialism in worship (Matt 21:13); blasphemy against the Spirit (Matt 12:31, 32); deeds in general (Matt 16:27); inward thoughts and motives (Mark 7:21; Luke 5:22, 23).

The Lord Jesus will be the final judge (Matt 8:29; 13:40–42; 16:27; Heb 9:27). He will appear as the final judge when He comes in His glory with His angels after the resurrection from the dead (John 5:29). All nations (Matt 25:32) and individuals are to be judged (Matt 12:36; John 5:29 [cf. Rom 14:10; 2 Cor 5:10; Rev 20:12–15]). It is implied in Matt 8:29 that evil spirits are also to stand in the judgment, but it is clear that the holy angels do not come into judgment, for they accompany and serve the Holy Judge (Matt 16:27; 25:31).

Deriv.: *kritḗrion* (2922), judgment, tribunal; *kritikós* (2924), decisive, discerner.

Syn.: *dikastḗs* (1348), a judicial judge.

2924. κριτικός *kritikós*; fem. *kritikḗ*, neut. *kritikón*, adj. from *kritḗs* (2923), a judge. Able to discern or decide, critical, skilled in judging. Used only in Heb 4:12 of Scripture.

2925. κρούω *kroúō*; fut. *kroúsō*. To knock, rap at a door for entrance (Luke 13:25; Acts 12:13). Used in an absolute sense (Matt 7:7, 8; Luke 11:9, 10; 12:36; Acts 12:16; Rev 3:20; Sept.: Judg 19:22).

Syn.: *túptō* (5180), to thump, strike; *plḗssō* (4141), to pound, smite; *rhapízō* (4474), to rap, slap.

Ant.: *siōpáō* (4623), to keep quiet; *sigáō* (4601), to keep silent.

2926. κρύπτη *krúptē*; gen. *krúptēs*, fem. noun from *kruptós* (2927), secret. A crypt, secret cell or vault (Luke 11:33 [TR]).

2927. κρυπτός *kruptós*; fem. *kruptḗ*, neut. *kruptón*, adj. from *krúptō* (2928), to keep secret. Hidden, concealed, and thus secret (Matt 10:26; Mark 4:22; Luke 8:17; 12:2). In secret where one cannot be seen by others (Matt 6:4, 6, 18). In secret (*en* [{1722}, in] *kruptṓ*), privately (John 7:4, 10; 18:20 [cf. Luke 11:33 {*krupton* (TR)}, *eis krúptēn*, {*eis* (1519), in, and *krúptē* (2926), a hiding place}, in a secret place where it cannot be seen, a cellar {1 Cor 4:5, "secret things of darkness" (a.t.)}]). "The hidden things of shame" (a.t. [2 Cor 4:2]) refers to clandestine conduct of which one would be ashamed (see Sept.: Jer 49:9). Figuratively, the secrets

of one's heart, secret thoughts (Rom 2:16; 1 Cor 14:25). "The secret man of the heart" (a.t. [1 Pet 3:4]) means the internal man. The Jew in secret (Rom 2:29) means a Jew at heart. *Kruphaíos* occurs in some MSS in Matt 6:18 for *kruptós*.

Apókruphos (614), hidden away from, and *kruptós* occur together in Mark 4:22; Luke 8:17. *Kruptós* is translated "hid" in Mark and "secret" in Luke, while *apókruphos* is translated "kept secret" in Mark and "hid" in Luke. *Kruptós* refers to something that is kept hidden either to protect it or for self-serving reasons. Consider a candle as an example. The nature of a lit candle is to give light and whatever one does with it, it cannot help but give light. To hide a candle is not to allow it to do its natural work of giving light, whether to others or only to oneself. No matter what one does, light is light and it cannot but illuminate. This is what a Christian ought to be. Therefore *krúptō* (2928), to hide, in this instance means to cover. One cannot annul the nature of something such as light.

Apókruphos, however, means to hide away from somebody. It is usually used with a good sense meaning to keep something secret or hidden from someone for benevolent reasons for a calculated time. God keeps certain things secret from us for a certain time, but this is for our good, exactly as we withhold certain knowledge from our children until the appropriate time. The distinction is clearly indicated in the third occurrence of *apókruphos* in Col 2:3, "In whom [Christ] are hid [*apókruphoi*] all the treasures of wisdom and knowledge." One can never know certain truths which are treasures unless one knows Jesus Christ Himself. Our knowledge of what Christ knows comes only as we become intimately related to Him and in the growth of that relationship. The treasures of wisdom are hidden from people as long as they do not know Christ Himself. *Apokrúptō* may be used in what God keeps secret from man because either man is not mature enough for certain knowledge or because man is inherently incapable of understanding such knowledge.

Deriv.: *krúptē* (2926), a secret cell or vault.

Syn.: *ésō* (2080), within, inward; *ésōthen* (2081), within; *aphanḗs* (852), unseen, hidden; *ágnōstos* (57), unknown.

Ant.: *emphanḗs* (1717), manifest; *phanerós* (5318), open to sight, visible; *dḗlos* (1212), evident, manifest; *ékdēlos* (1552), completely evident or manifest; *pródēlos* (4271), evident beforehand, clearly evident; *gnōstós* (1110), known.

2928. κρύπτω *krúptō*; fut. *krúpsō*. To hide, conceal. In the mid. / pass. to hide oneself, to be hidden; 2d aor. pass. *ekrúbēn*, was hidden (Matt 5:14; Luke 19:42); with the mid. meaning to hide oneself (John 8:59; 1 Tim 5:25; Rev 2:17 where "the hidden manna" symbolizes the enjoyments of the kingdom of heaven in allusion, perhaps, to the Jewish tradition that the ark with the pot of manna was hidden by order of King Josiah and will again be brought to light in the reign of the Messiah). To be hidden in something, with *en* (1722), in, followed by the dat. (Matt 13:44; 25:25; Col 3:3); with *eis* (1519), in, and the acc. (Rev 6:15); followed by *apó* (575), from, and the gen. meaning to hide from (Luke 18:34; 19:42, Christ's word made hidden, i.e., the people did not understand that Christ came to give them peace; John 12:36, He hid Himself from them by miraculously causing others not to recognize Him; Rev 6:16). Perf. mid. part. *kekrumménos*, hiding Himself or hidden as an adv., secretly (John 19:38).

Deriv.: *apokrúptō* (613), to hide from, to hide with a benevolent purpose; *egkrúptō* (1470), to hide in something; *kruptós* (2927), hidden, secret; *kruphḗ* (2931), privately; *perikrúptō* (4032), to hide by placing something around or to conceal entirely.

Syn.: *kalúptō* (2572), to cover in order to hide; *parakalúptō* (3871), to cover with a veil; *lanthánō* (2990), to escape notice, be hidden from; *sigáō* (4601), to keep silent, and therefore, secret.

Ant.: *apokalúptō* (601), to uncover, unveil; *chrēmatízō* (5537), to reveal through some divine intervention; *phaneróō* (5319), to make visible, manifest; *phaínō* (5316), to shine, appear; *epiphaínō* (2014), to cause light to fall upon; *anaphaínō* (398), to appear suddenly; *emphanízō* (1718), to bring out into visibility from a hidden state, manifest; *deíknumi* (1166), to show, exhibit; *anadeíknumi* (322), to lift up and show; *endeíknumi* (1731), to show forth, to prove; *epideíknumi* (1925), to display, exhibit, point out, demonstrate; *hupodeíknumi* (5263), to show secretly, make known; *mēnúō* (3377), to disclose, reveal before a court, tell; *exēgéomai* (1834), to declare, bring out the meaning, give an exegesis; *diasaphéō* (1285), to make clear; *prolégō* (4302), to foretell; *exaggéllō* (1804), to tell out, proclaim abroad; *anaggéllō* (312), to declare; *kataggéllō* (2605), to proclaim, show forth; *diēgéomai* (1334), to recount; *euaggelízō* (2097), to bring glad tidings; *katatíthēmi* (2698), to state; *légō* (3004), to tell; *apaggéllō* (518), to declare; *dēlóō* (1213), to make plain; *diaggéllō* (1229), to declare, announce thoroughly.

2929. κρυσταλλίζω *krustallízō*; fut. *krustallísō*, from *krústallos* (2930), crystal. To shine like crystal, clear and sparkling (Rev 21:11).

Syn.: *lámpō* (2989), to shine as a torch; *stílbō* (4744), to glisten; *eklámpō* (1584), to shine forth; *perilámpō* (4034), to shine around; *astráptō* (797), to flash as lightning, flare; *periastráptō* (4015), to flash around; *epiphaúskō* or *epiphaúō* (2017), to shine forth.

Ant.: *skotízō* (4654), to deprive of light, make dark; *skotóō* (4656), to darken.

2930. κρύσταλλος *krústallos*; gen. *krustállou*, masc. noun from *krúos* (n.f.), cold. Ice, water solidified by cold (Sept.: Job 6:16; Ps 148:8). Crystal, so-called from its resemblance to ice (Rev 4:6; 22:1).

2931. κρυφῇ *kruphḗ*; adv. from *krúptō* (2928), to hide or keep secret. Secretly, not openly (Eph 5:12; Sept.: Deut 28:57).
Syn.: *láthra* (2977), secretly or privately.
Ant.: *phanerōs* (5320), manifestly, evidently; *parrēsía* (3954), with boldness, publicly.

2932. κτάομαι *ktáomai*; contracted *ktōmai*, fut. *ktēsomai*, perf. *kéktēmai*, used with the pres. meaning (Luke 18:12 [TR]), mid. deponent. To get for oneself, acquire, procure, by purchase or otherwise. To acquire, prepare, provide (Matt 10:9). To acquire or purchase for a price (Acts 1:18; 8:20; 22:28). To possess (Luke 21:19, meaning keep in possession of your souls, have them under your control [cf. 1 Thess 4:4]).
Deriv.: *ktēma* (2933), that which one possesses; *ktēnos* (2934), a beast possessed; *ktētōr* (2935), possessor.
Syn.: *heurískō* (2147), to find; *kerdaínō* (2770), to gain; *katéchō* (2722), to hold fast, possess.

2933. κτῆμα *ktēma*; gen. *ktēmatos*, neut. noun from *ktáomai* (2932), to possess. That which is possessed, in possession (Matt 19:22; Mark 10:22). Also an immovable possession, an estate, land (Acts 2:45; 5:1 [cf. Acts 5:8]; Sept.: Job 20:29; Prov 23:10; 31:16).
Syn.: *katáschesis* (2697), taking over of a possession; *peripoíēsis* (4047), an acquisition; *húparxis* (5223), property, something which one has been possessing; *ktēnos* (2934), cattle or animals representing what one possesses.
Ant.: *zēmía* (2209), loss; *apobolē* (580), a casting away; *hēttēma* (2275), a defect, loss.

2934. κτῆνος *ktēnos*; gen. *ktēnous*, neut. noun from *ktáomai* (2932), to possess. Equal to *ktēma* (2933), possession, property, but applicable particularly to flocks and herds of every kind. In the NT, a beast or domestic animal as bought or

sold (Rev 18:13); as yielding meat (1 Cor 15:39); as used for riding, carrying burdens (Luke 10:34; Acts 23:24; Sept.: Ex 9:20; Num 20:8; Josh 8:27; see Gen 13:2, 7; 30:43).
Syn.: *zōon* (2226), a living creature, usually an animal; *tetrápous* (5074), a four-footed beast.
Ant.: *ánthrōpos* (444), man.

2935. κτήτωρ *ktḗtōr*; gen. *ktḗtoros*, masc. noun from *ktáomai* (2932), to possess. A possessor, owner (Acts 4:34).

2936. κτίζω *ktízō*; fut. *ktísō*. In Homer the word meant to found a city or a habitable place. In the NT, to create, produce from nothing (Mark 13:19; Rom 1:25; Eph 3:9; Col 1:16; 3:10; 1 Tim 4:3; Rev 4:11; 10:6; Sept.: Deut 4:32; Ps 89:13); to form out of preexistent matter (1 Cor 11:9); to make, compose (Eph 2:15); to create and form in a spiritual sense, regeneration or renewal (Eph 2:10; 4:24; Sept.: Ps 51:12).
Deriv.: *ktísis* (2937), creation; *ktísma* (2938), a place founded, built or colonized; *ktístēs* (2939), creator, founder, inventor.
Syn.: *poiéō* (4160), to make; *kataskeuázō* (2680), to prepare, make ready, build; *oikodoméō* (3618), to build a house; *katartízō* (2675), to furnish completely, to prepare for fitting together with others.
Ant.: *apóllumi* (622), to destroy utterly; *katargéō* (2673), to abolish; *kathairéō* (2507), to cast down; *lúō* (3089), to loose, dissolve; *katalúō* (2647), to destroy utterly; *katastréphō* (2690), to ruin.

2937. κτίσις *ktísis*; gen. *ktíseōs*, fem. noun from *ktízō* (2936), to create, form or found. Something founded, i.e., of a city, colonization of a habitable place. Creation, in a pass. sense, what has been created, the sum total of what has been created (Mark 10:6; 13:19; Rom 1:20; 8:19–22; Heb 9:11; 1 Pet 2:13; 2 Pet 3:4; Rev 3:14). Denotes a particular created thing (Rom 1:25; 8:39; Col 1:15; Heb 4:13). Refers specifically to mankind as

God's creation (Mark 16:15; Col 1:23 [cf. *kainé* {2537}, qualitatively new, with *ktísis*, creation or creature {2 Cor 5:17; Gal 6:15}]).

Syn.: *oikodomé* (3619), a building in the process of being erected; *endómēsis* (1739), a thing built, structure; *égersis* (1454), a raising up.

Ant.: *kathaíresis* (2506), demolition.

2938. κτίσμα *ktísma*; gen. *ktísmatos*, neut. noun from *ktízō* (2936), to create, form or found. That which is created. With the suffix *-ma*, the result of building. In the NT, creature, created thing (1 Tim 4:4; James 1:18; Rev 5:13; 8:9). It is slightly different in meaning than *ktísis* (2937), creation. *Ktísis* stresses the *work* of the original formation of an object and represents something which has undergone a *process* of creation. *Ktísma* stresses the *result* of this work and represents something which is the *product* of creation.

Syn.: *plásma* (4110), something molded or formed; *poíēma* (4161), a product.

2939. κτίστης *ktístēs*; gen. *ktístou*, masc. noun from *ktízō* (2936), to create, form or found. Creator, founder, inventor. Only in 1 Pet 4:19, a creator.

Syn.: *dēmiourgós* (1217), builder, maker; *technítēs* (5079), architect, designer; *poiētés* (4163), a maker, performer.

2940. κυβεία *kubeía*; gen. *kubeías*, fem. noun from *kúbos* (n.f.), dice. A playing at dice (Eph 4:14) implying trickery, fraud.

Syn.: *apátē* (539), deceit or deceitfulness; *dólos* (1388), craftiness; *pseúdos* (5579), a lie; *panourgía* (3834), craftiness; *plánē* (4106), deceit, wandering.

Ant.: *alétheia* (225), truth; *eilikríneia* (1505), sincerity, purity.

2941. κυβέρνησις *kubérnēsis*; gen. *kubernéseōs*, fem. noun from *kubernáō* (n.f.), to govern. Government, a governing in relation to the churches (1 Cor 12:28). Perhaps since this occurs in the pl., it represented the elders appointed to examine those professing faith in Christ as candidates for baptism. Also from *kubernáō* (n.f.): *kubernétēs* (2942), pilot, captain.

Syn.: *hēgemonía* (2231), government; *exousía* (1849), authority; *krátos* (2904), dominion; *kuriótēs* (2963), mastery, rule, government; *arché* (746), power, rule.

2942. κυβερνήτης *kubernétēs*; gen. *kubernétou*, masc. noun from *kubernáō* (n.f.), to govern. Governor of a ship, the captain or pilot responsible for the direction of the ship (Acts 27:11; Rev 18:17; Sept.: Ezek 27:8, 27, 28). Also from *kubernáō* (n.f.): *kubérnēsis* (2941), governor, government.

Syn.: *archēgós* (747), leader, author; *chiliarchos* (5506), a commander of a thousand soldiers; *stratēgós* (4755), commander of an army; *hēgemón* (2232), governor, ruler; *ethnárchēs* (1481), an ethnarch, governor of a nation; *oikonómos* (3623), steward; *architríklinos* (755), the ruler of a feast; *árchōn* (758), a ruler, chief; *arché* (746), a ruler; *kosmokrátōr* (2888), ruler of the world; *politárchēs* (4173), ruler of a city.

2943. κυκλόθεν *kuklóthen*; adv. from *kúklos* (n.f., see below), a circle, with the suffix *-then*, denoting from or at a place. From around, round about (Rev 4:3, 4, 8; 5:11). Used in an absolute sense in Rev 4:8; Sept.: Judg 8:34; 1 Kgs 2:46; 6:5.

Deriv. of *kúklos* (n.f.): *kuklóō* (2944), to encircle, surround; *kúklō* (2945), around.

Syn.: *périx* (4038), round about; *pántothen* (3840), on all sides.

2944. κυκλόω *kuklóō*; contracted *kuklô*, fut. *kuklósō*, from *kúklos* (n.f., see *kuklóthen* [2943]), circle. To encircle, surround (Luke 21:20; John 10:24; Acts 14:20; Heb 11:30; Rev 20:9; Sept.: 1 Sam 7:16; 1 Kgs 7:3; Isa 29:3).

Deriv.: *perikuklóō* (4033), to encompass.

2945. κύκλῳ kúklō; the dat. sing. of *kúklos* (n.f., see *kuklóthen* [2943]), a circle. Used adv. meaning all around, round about (Mark 3:34; 6:6, 36; Luke 9:12; Rom 15:19; Rev 4:6; 7:11; Sept.: Gen 23:17; Ex 30:3; Josh 6:3).

    Syn.: *kuklóthen* (2943), all around; *périx* (4038), all around.

2946. κύλισμα kúlisma; gen. *kulísmatos*, neut. noun from *kulíō* (2947), to roll about. Something rolled, a wheel. Wallowing place (2 Pet 2:22).

2947. κυλίω kulíō; fut. *kulísō*, later form of *kulíndō*. To roll, trans. for rolling stones (Sept.: Josh 10:18). Used intrans. in the mid. meaning to roll, wallow, roll about (Mark 9:20).

    Deriv.: *apokulíō* (617), to roll away; *anakulíō*, to roll up or back; *kúlisma* (2946), wallowing; *proskulíō* (4351), to roll up or to.

    Syn.: *eneiléō* (1750), to roll in; *sustéllō* (4958), to enwrap or enfold; *helíssō* (1667), to roll or fold up a mantle, a scroll, and figuratively of heaven; *entulíssō* (1794), to wrap up, entwine.

    Ant.: *anaptússō* (380), to unroll, open; *anakalúptō* (343), to unveil, to cause to understand.

2948. κυλλός kullós; fem. *kullḗ*, neut. *kullón*, adj. Bent, crooked, as for instance the hand as held out in begging; used with reference to the limbs in the NT generally meaning crippled, lame, especially of the hands (Matt 15:30, 31; 18:8; Mark 9:43).

    Syn.: *anápēros* (376), crippled, maimed.

2949. κῦμα kúma; gen. *kúmatos*, neut. noun from *kúō* (n.f.), to be pregnant, stretched, expanded. A wave, billow (Matt 8:24; 14:24; Mark 4:37; Acts 27:41; Jude 1:13; Sept.: Job 38:11; Isa 48:18).

    Syn.: *sálos* (4535), the rolling swell of the sea; *klúdōn* (2830), a billow, wave, raging water; *kínēsis* (2796), moving; *hormḗ* (3730), rush, onset.

    Ant.: *hēsuchía* (2271), stillness; *nékrōsis* (3500), deadness; *stásis* (4714), standing.

2950. κύμβαλον kúmbalon; gen. *kumbálou*, neut. noun from *kúmbos* (n.f.), hollow, a cup. A cymbal which was a convex plate of brass or other metal that, when struck against another of the same kind, produced a clanging unharmonious sound (1 Cor 13:1; Sept.: 1 Chr 13:8).

2951. κύμινον kúminon; gen. *kumínou*, neut. noun. Cumin, an herb, a plant with aromatic seeds of a warm and bitter taste similar to caraway seeds, used as a condiment (Matt 23:23; Sept.: Isa 28:25, 27).

2952. κυνάριον kunárion; gen. *kunaríou*, neut. noun, a diminutive of *kúōn* (2965), a dog. A little dog, puppy (Matt 15:26, 27; Mark 7:27, 28). The Lord, speaking as a Jew, applies the word *kunárion* to the heathen who might justly be so-called on account of their many impurities and abominations.

2953. Κύπριος Kúprios; gen. *Kupríou*, masc. proper noun. An inhabitant of Cyprus, a Cypriot (Acts 4:36; 11:20; 21:16).

2954. Κύπρος Kúpros; gen. *Kúprou*, fem. proper noun. Cyprus, a large fertile island in the eastern Mediterranean about 150 miles long and from 50 to 60 miles broad. Venus (or Aphrodite) was its chief goddess, hence her name Cypria. In ancient times, it contained two prominent cities, Salamis and Paphos, and seventeen towns. Salamis was at the east and Paphos at the west end of the island (Acts 13:4). Barnabas was a native of Cyprus and its people are mentioned in biblical history (Acts 4:36; 13:4; 15:39). Sergius Paulus, proconsul of Cyprus, was converted through Paul on his first missionary journey (Acts 13:7ff.) and thus became the first Christian ruler on record. Cyprus was colonized by the Phoenicians at a very early date. Known as Chittim or Kittim in the OT (Num 24:24). Through

Greek colonists it received the name of *Kúpros*, perhaps from the cypress tree. Thothmes III of Egypt conquered the island. In 294 B.C., the island was a dependency of Egypt. Cato took possession of it for the Romans. Cicero was proconsul there in 52 B.C.

2955. κύπτω *kúptō*; fut. *kúpsō*. To bow the head, stoop down (Mark 1:7; John 8:6, 8; Sept.: 1 Sam 24:9; 1 Kgs 1:16, 31).
   Deriv.: *anakúptō* (352), to lift up; *parakúptō* (3879), to stoop to look into; *sugkúptō* (4794), to bend or bow down over.
   Syn.: *klínō* (2827), to bow down.
   Ant.: *egeírō* (1453), to rise; *anístēmi* (450), to stand up; *stékō* (4739), to stand; *anorthóō* (461), to straighten up; *exanístēmi* (1817), to raise or rise up.

2956. Κυρηναῖος *Kurēnaíos*; gen. *Kurēnaíou*, masc. proper noun. An inhabitant of Cyrene, a Cyrenian. In the NT, spoken of Jews born or residing there (Matt 27:32; Mark 15:21; Luke 23:26; Acts 6:9; 11:20; 13:1).

2957. Κυρήνη *Kurénē*; gen. *Kurénēs*, fem. proper noun. Cyrene, the capital of a small province and the chief city of Libya in northern Africa, a Greek city founded about 639 B.C. It was the center of a wide district between Carthage and Egypt, corresponding to modern Tripoli. Under Alexander the Great, the Jews made up about one-fourth of the population and were granted citizenship on the same terms as Greeks. At Alexander's death, it was attached to Egypt, and became a Roman province in 75 B.C. Simon, who bore our Lord's cross, was from that city (Matt 27:32). Many of its people were at Jerusalem during Pentecost and had a synagogue there (Acts 2:10; 6:9), and some of them became preachers of the gospel (11:20; 13:1). Cyrene was destroyed by the Saracens in the fourth century.

2958. Κυρήνιος *Kurénios*; gen. *Kuréniou*, masc. proper noun. Cyrenius, in Lat.

Quirinus (Luke 2:2) which refers to Publius Sulpitius Quirinus, a Roman Senator of an obscure family raised to the highest honors by Augustus. He was sent as governor or proconsul to Syria, first from 4 B.C. (the year of Jesus Christ's birth) to 1 B.C., and again in A.D. 6–11. During his first governorship the first taxing or enrollment occurred, which necessitated the visit of Joseph and Mary to Bethlehem. The second census took place A.D. 6 and is mentioned by Luke in Acts 5:37 and by Josephus.

2959. κυρία *kuría*; gen. *kurías*, the fem. of *kúrios* (2962), lord, mister. Mistress, lady, Mrs. It is used in 2 John 1:1, 5 in reference to either a local church itself or a well-respected lady within the church. Some have even speculated that the lady may have been Mary, the mother of Jesus.

2960. κυριακός *kuriakós*; fem. *kuriakē*, neut. *kuriakón*, adj. from *kúrios* (2962), lord, master. Belonging to a lord or ruler. Only in 1 Cor 11:20; Rev 1:10 as belonging to Christ, to the Lord, having special reference to Him. Hence, *Kuriakē*, which came to mean *Kuriakē Hēméra*, the "Day of the Lord," what we call Sunday. It was the day kept in commemoration of Christ's resurrection (John 20:19–23; Acts 20:7; 1 Cor 16:2 [see Rev 1:10]).

2961. κυριεύω *kurieúō*; fut. *kurieúsō*, from *kúrios* (2962), lord, master. To have or exercise rule or authority over, lord over (Luke 22:25; Rom 14:9; 2 Cor 1:24; 1 Tim 6:15). Spoken of things as exercising mastery over us (Rom 6:9, 14; 7:1; Sept.: Judg 9:2; Isa 19:4).
   Deriv.: *katakurieúō* (2634), to completely dominate over.
   Syn.: *authentéō* (831), to exercise authority over, have dominion; *epitássō* (2004), to commandeer; *katalambánō* (2638), to seize; *hupotássō* (5293), to place in one's proper category, put in subjection under; *doulagōgéō* (1396), to bring into

subjection, bondage; *katadoulóō* (2615), to bring into complete bondage.

2962. κύριος *kúrios*; gen. *kuríou*, masc. noun from *kúros* (n.f.), might, power. Lord, master, owner. Also the NT Gr. equivalent for the OT Hebr. Jehovah. See *kuróō* (2964), to give authority, confirm, which is also from *kúros* (n.f.).

(I) Generally:

(A) As the possessor, owner, master, e.g., of property (Matt 20:8; 21:40; Gal 4:1; Sept.: Ex 21:28, 29, 34); master or head of a house (Matt 15:27; Mark 13:35; Sept.: Ex 22:8); of persons, servants, slaves (Matt 10:24; 24:45, 46, 48, 50; Acts 16:16, 19; Rom 14:4; Eph 6:5, 9; Col 3:22; 4:1; Sept.: Gen 24:9f.; Judg 19:11). Spoken of a husband (1 Pet 3:6; Sept.: Gen 18:12). Followed by the gen. of thing and without the art., lord, master of something and having absolute authority over it, e.g., master of the harvest (Matt 9:38; Luke 10:2); master of the Sabbath (Matt 12:8; Mark 2:28).

(B) Of a supreme lord, sovereign, e.g., the Roman emperor (Acts 25:26); the heathen gods (1 Cor 8:5).

(C) As an honorary title of address, especially to superiors, equivalent to mister, sir, as a servant to his master (Matt 13:27; Luke 13:8); a son to his father (Matt 21:30); to a teacher, master (Matt 8:25; Luke 9:54, equal to *epistátēs* [1988], superintendent, commander. See Matt 7:21, 22; Luke 6:46); to a person of dignity and authority (Mark 7:28; John 4:11, 15, 19, 49); to a Roman procurator (Matt 27:63). When addressing someone respectfully (John 12:21; 20:15; Acts 16:30; Sept.: Gen 19:2; 23:6, 11, 15).

(II) Spoken of God and Christ:

(A) Of God as the supreme Lord and Sovereign of the universe, usually corresponding in the Sept. to the Hebr. Jehovah. With the art. *ho Kúrios* (Matt 1:22; 5:33; Mark 5:19; Luke 1:6, 28; Acts 7:33; Heb 8:2; James 4:15). Without the art. *Kúrios* (Matt 27:10; Mark 13:20; Luke 1:58; Acts 7:49; Rom 4:8; Heb 7:21; 1 Pet 1:25). With adjuncts,

without the art., e.g., *Kúrios ho Theós* (2316), God, the Lord God, followed by the gen. (Matt 4:7, 10; 22:37; Luke 1:16; Sept.: Ezek 4:14); *Kúrios Sabaōth* (4519), Lord Sabaoth, meaning Lord of hosts, armies, a military appellation of God (Rom 9:29; James 5:4; Sept.: 1 Sam 15:2; Isa 1:9); *Kúrios Pantokrátōr* (3841), Lord Almighty or ruler of all (2 Cor 6:18; Sept.: 2 Sam 7:8; Nah 2:13); *Kúrios ho Theós ho Pantokrátōr*, Lord, the God, the Almighty (Rev 4:8; 11:17); *Kúrios tōn kurieuóntōn* (2961), Lord of lords referring to those who are ruling (1 Tim 6:15); Lord of heaven and earth (Acts 17:24). In a similar manner applied also to God as the Father of our Lord Jesus Christ (Matt 11:25, "Father, Lord of heaven and earth"; Luke 10:21 [cf. Sept.: 2 Chr 36:23; Ezra 1:2; Neh 1:5]).

(B) Of the Lord Jesus Christ: **(1)** In reference to His abode on earth as a master and teacher, where it is equivalent to *rhabbí* (4461), rabbi, and *epistátēs* (1988), master, superintendent (Matt 17:4 [cf. Mark 9:5; Luke 9:33]. See John 13:13, 14). Chiefly in the gospels before the resurrection of Christ and with the art. *ho Kúrios*, the Lord, used emphatically (Matt 21:3; 28:6; Luke 7:13; 10:1; John 4:1; 20:2, 13; Acts 9:5; 1 Cor 9:5). With adjuncts, e.g., *ho Kúrios kaí ho didáskalos* (1320), teacher, the Lord and the teacher (John 13:13, 14); *ho Kúrios Iēsoús* (2424), the Lord Jesus (Luke 24:3; Acts 1:21; 4:33; 1 Cor 11:23). **(2)** As the supreme Lord of the gospel dispensation, "head over all things to the church" (Rom 10:12; Rev 17:14); with the art. *ho Kúrios* (Mark 16:19, 20; Acts 8:25; 19:10; 2 Cor 3:17; Eph 5:10; Col 3:23; 2 Thess 3:1, 5; 2 Tim 4:8; James 5:7); with the gen. of person, *ho Kúriós mou*, my Lord (Matt 22:44; Heb 7:14; Rev 11:8); without the art., *Kúrios* (Luke 1:76; 2 Cor 3:16, 17; Col 4:1; 2 Pet 3:10). With adjuncts, e.g., with the art., *ho Kúrios Iēsoús* or *Iēsoús ho Kúrios* (Rom 4:24); *ho Kúrios hēmṓn Iēsoús*, "our Lord Jesus" (1 Cor 5:5; Heb 13:20); *ho Kúrios Iēsoús Christós*, the Lord Jesus Christ, or

Iēsoús Christós ho Kúrios, Jesus Christ the Lord (Acts 16:31: Rom 1:4; 13:14; 1 Cor 1:9); *ho Kúrios hēmṓn Iēsoús Christós*, our Lord Jesus Christ (Rom 16:18; 1 Cor 1:2, 10; Gal 6:18); *Iēsoús Christós ho Kúrios hēmṓn*, Jesus Christ our Lord (Eph 3:11; 1 Tim 1:2). Without the art., *Kúrios Iēsoús* (Rom 10:9; 1 Cor 12:3; Phil 2:19); *Christós Kúrios*, meaning the Messiah (Luke 2:11); *Kúrios Iēsoús Christós* or *Iēsoús Christós Kúrios*, Jesus Christ Lord (Rom 1:7; 2 Cor 1:2; 4:5; Phil 1:2); *Kúrios hēmṓn Iēsoús Christós*, our Lord Jesus Christ (Gal 1:3). In the phrase *en Kuríō*, (*en* [1722], in) in the Lord, without the art., used only by Paul and once in Rev 14:13 referring to the fact that believers are represented as one with Christ, as members of His body (Eph 5:30 [cf. 1 Cor 12:27, one spiritual body of which He is the Head] Eph 2:20). Hence *en Kuríō*, means: **(a)** In the Lord, after verbs of rejoicing, trusting (1 Cor 1:31; Phil 2:19; 3:1). **(b)** In or by the Lord, meaning by His authority (Eph 4:17; 1 Thess 4:1). **(c)** In or through the Lord, meaning through His aid and influence, by His help (1 Cor 15:58; 2 Cor 2:12; Gal 5:10; Eph 2:21; Col 4:17). **(d)** In the work of the Lord, in the gospel work (Rom 16:8, 13; 1 Cor 4:17; 9:2; Eph 6:21; 1 Thess 5:12). **(e)** As indicating condition meaning one in the Lord, united with Him, His follower, a Christian (Rom 16:11; Phil 4:1; Phile 1:16). **(f)** As denoting manner, meaning in the Lord, as becomes those who are in the Lord, Christians (Rom 16:2, 22; 1 Cor 7:39; Eph 6:1; Phil 2:29; Col 3:18).

Deriv.: *kuría* (2959), lady; *kuriakós* (2960), the Lord's; *kurieúō* (2961), to be lord; *kuriótēs* (2963), lordship, dominion.

Syn.: *árchōn* (758), ruler; *despótēs* (1203), despot; *pantokrátōr* (3841), almighty; *hēgemṓn* (2232), governor, ruler; *Kaísar* (2541), Caesar; *ethnárchēs* (1481), leader of a nation; *archēgós* (747), leader; *kosmokrátōr* (2888), world ruler.

Ant.: *hupērétēs* (5257), lower servant; *doúlos* (1401), slave; *therápōn* (2324), attendant; *diákonos* (1249), minister.

2963. κυριότης kuriótēs; gen. *kuriótetos*, fem. noun from *kúrios* (2962), lord, mighty one. Dominion, civil power, authority or magistracy (2 Pet 2:10; Jude 1:8); a certain order of angels, an abstract term being used for a concrete position (Eph 1:21; Col 1:16). Reference is made to evil angelic powers as indicated in 2 Pet 2:11, although not in Jude 1:9. The word is peculiar to NT and Patristic Gr. and denotes the kingly glory of Christ.

Syn.: *krátos* (2904), dominion; *exousía* (1849), authority; *dúnamis* (1411), power; *hēgemonía* (2231), government; *archḗ* (746), rule; *kubérnēsis* (2941), government.

Ant.: *douleía* (1397), slavery; *zugós* (2218), yoke; *hupotagḗ* (5292), subjection; *hupakoḗ* (5218), obedience.

2964. κυρόω kuróō; contracted *kurṓ*, fut. *kurṓsō*, from *kúros* (n.f.), authority, confirmation. To give authority, establish as valid, confirm (2 Cor 2:8; Gal 3:15; Sept.: Gen 23:20). Also from *kúros* (n.f.): *kúrios* (2962), lord, master.

Deriv.: *akuróō* (208), to cancel; *prokuróō* (4300), to confirm before.

Syn.: *bebaióō* (950), to make sure.

Ant.: *akuróō* (208), to invalidate, disannul.

2965. κύων kúōn; gen. *kunós*, masc., fem. noun. A dog (Luke 16:21; 2 Pet 2:22; Sept.: Ex 22:31; Judg 7:5); diminutive *kunárion* (2952), little dog. In the East, dogs were not usually pets and were without masters, wandering at large in the streets and fields and feeding upon whatever they could find (1 Kgs 14:11; 16:4; 21:19; Ps 59:6, 14). They were looked upon as unclean, and to call one a "dog" was a stronger expression of contempt than even today (1 Sam 17:43; 2 Kgs 8:13). The Jews called the Gentiles "dogs." It is used metaphorically for an impudent, shameless person in Phil

3:2 where it is spoken of Judaizing teachers (cf. Isa 56:11). In Matt 7:6, "Give not that which is holy unto the dogs" generally means to not offer good and holy things to those who will spurn and pervert them. It refers in the pl. to Sodomites (Rev 22:15; Sept.: Deut 23:18).

2966. κῶλον *kṓlon*; gen. *kṓlou*, neut. noun. A limb, member of the human body or of an animal. In the pl. *ta kṓla*, the carcasses, corpses (Heb 3:17; Sept.: Num 14:29, 32; Isa 66:24).

    Syn.: *ptṓma* (4430), a dead body.

2967. κωλύω *kōlúō*; fut. *kōlúsō*, from *kólos* (n.f.), dwarf. To cut off, weaken, and hence generally to hinder, prevent, restrain. Followed by the acc. of person and generally of thing (Acts 27:43; Sept.: 1 Sam 25:26); the acc. of person and inf. (Acts 8:36; 16:6; 24:23; 1 Thess 2:16; Heb 7:23); with the acc. (Matt 19:14; Luke 23:2); with the inf. (1 Tim 4:3); with the inf. implied (Mark 9:38, 39; 10:14; Luke 9:50; 11:52; 18:16; Acts 11:17; 3 John 1:10). Followed by the acc. of thing (1 Cor 14:39; 2 Pet 2:16); with *toú* and inf. (Acts 10:47); by the acc. of thing and *apó* (575), from, with the gen. of person (Luke 6:29; Sept.: Gen 23:6; 2 Sam 13:13). Also from *kólos* (n.f.): *kolázō* (2849), to mutilate, prune.

    Deriv.: *akōlútōs* (209), without hindrance; *diakōlúō* (1254), to hinder.

    Syn.: *egkóptō* (1465), to impede, detain; *anakóptō* (348), to break up; *ekkóptō* (1581), to cut out, repulse.

    Ant.: *boēthéō* (997), to help; *sumbállō* (4820), to help, succor; *sunupourgéō* (4943), to help together; *sunergéō* (4903), to help in work, cooperate; *parístēmi* (3936), to place beside, stand by, help.

2968. κώμη *kṓmē*; gen. *kṓmēs*, fem. noun from *keímai* (2749), to lie outstretched. A village or hamlet in the country and without walls (Matt 9:35; 10:11; 14:15; 21:2; Mark 6:6, 36, fields and villages, 56; 11:2; Luke 5:17; 8:1; 9:6, 12, 52, 56; 10:38; 13:22; 17:12; 19:30; 24:13, 28; John

11:1, 30). In John 7:42, of Bethlehem before the time of Rehoboam, who fortified it (see 2 Chr 11:6). With the meaning of the inhabitants of villages (Acts 8:25). The villages of Caesarea, meaning those villages around and dependent upon it (Mark 8:27; Sept.: Josh 15:31, 45; 17:11; 19:6). Also it apparently means a large town or city, perhaps without walls or partly in ruin as Bethsaida, probably of Galilee (Mark 8:23, 26 [cf. Mark 8:22]; Sept.: Josh 10:37).

    Deriv.: *kōmópolis* (2969), a country town or large village, usually without walls.

    Syn.: *pólis* (4172), a town enclosed with a wall or fortification, distinguished from *kṓmē* not because of its size, but because of its structure and land.

2969. κωμόπολις *kōmópolis*; gen. *kōmopóleōs*, fem. noun from *kṓmē* (2968), village, and *pólis* (4172), a town. Literally a village city, meaning a large village or town like a city but without walls (Mark 1:38).

2970. κῶμος *kṓmos*; gen. *kṓmou*, masc. noun. A feasting, used in the pl. only in the NT meaning riotous conduct (Rom 13:13); revelings (Gal 5:21; 1 Pet 4:3); festivities in honor of several gods, especially Bacchus, the god of wine, hence feastings and drunkenness with impurity and obscenity of the grossest kind. Therefore, it always presupposes a festive company and drunken revellers.

    Syn.: *méthē* (3178), drunkenness; *pótos* (4224), a drinking bout or banquet giving opportunity for excessive drinking but not necessarily realizing it; *oinophlugía* (3632), excess of wine; *kraipálē* (2897), the sense of overindulgence in wine.

    Ant.: *egkráteia* (1466), temperance; *sōphrosúnē* (4997), sound mind, self-critical.

2971. κώνωψ *kṓnōps*; gen. *kṓnōpos*, masc., fem. noun. A gnat, mosquito (Matt 23:24).

2972. Κῶς *Kṓs*; gen. *Kṓ*, fem. proper noun. Cos, a small Greek island northwest of Rhodes (Acts 21:1) in the Aegean Sea.

2973. Κωσάμ *Kōsám*; masc. proper noun transliterated from the Hebr. *qōsem* (not found in the OT), a diviner. Cosam, one of Christ's ancestors (Luke 3:28).

2974. κωφός *kōphós*; fem. *kōphḗ*, neut. *kōphón*, adj. from *kóptō* (2875), to cut down. Blunted, dull. In the NT, used of the senses and faculties. As pertaining to the tongue, meaning speechless or dumb (Matt 9:32, 33; 12:22; 15:30, 31; Luke 1:22; 11:14; Sept.: Hab 2:18); to hearing, meaning blunted, dull, deaf (Matt 11:5; Mark 7:32, 37; 9:25; Luke 7:22; Sept.: Ps 38:14; Isa 35:5; 43:8).

Syn.: *álalos* (216), speechless; *áphōnos* (880), voiceless.

Λ

2975. λαγχάνω lagchánō; fut. *léxomai*, 2d aor. *élachon*. To obtain by lot (Luke 1:9), to have fallen to oneself. To obtain (Acts 1:17; 2 Pet 1:1). To cast lots (John 19:24). The Mishna informs us that the various offices of priests and Levites in the daily service were determined by lot.

Syn.: *tugchánō* (5177), to obtain, gain, receive, attain; *epitugchánō* (2013), to light upon; *ktáomai* (2932), to procure for oneself; *lambánō* (2983), to take, receive; *heurískō* (2147), to find.

2976. Λάζαρος Lázaros; gen. *Lazárou*, masc. proper noun. Lazarus, meaning helped of God.

(I) A citizen of Bethany residing with his two sisters, Mary and Martha, where Christ frequently visited. He was raised from the grave by Christ in the presence of the family and a number of Jews after he had been dead four days. The Jews were so incensed about this that they sought to kill not only Christ, but even Lazarus (John 11:1, 2, 5, 11, 14, 43; 12:1, 2, 9, 10, 17).

(II) A beggar, probably a leprosy victim, to whose great suffering the rich man showed marked indifference (Luke 16:19–31).

2977. λάθρα láthra; adv. from *lanthánō* (2990), to be hidden. Secretly, privately (Matt 1:19; 2:7; John 11:28; Acts 16:37; Sept.: Deut 13:7; 1 Sam 18:22; Job 31:27).

Syn.: *kruphḗ* (2931), secretly.

Ant.: *parrēsía* (3954), openly; *phanerṓs* (5320), manifestly, evidently.

2978. λαῖλαψ laílaps; gen. *laílapos*, fem. noun. Whirlwind, hurricane, tempest (Mark 4:37; Luke 8:23; 2 Pet 2:17; Sept.: Job 21:18; 38:1; Jer 25:32).

Syn.: *thúella* (2366), hurricane, cyclone; *cheimṓn* (5494), winter, storm.

Ant.: *hēsuchía* (2271), stillness; *galḗnē* (1055), calm; *eudía* (2105), fair weather.

2979. λακτίζω laktízō; fut. *laktísō*, from *láx* (n.f.), with the foot. To kick, strike with the heel (Acts 9:5; 26:14).

2980. λαλέω laléō; contracted *laló*, fut. *lalḗsō*. To talk at random, as contrasted with *légō* (3004) which involves the intellectual part of man, his reason. It is used especially of children with the meaning of to talk much. The dumb man is *álalos* (216), mute (Mark 7:37; 9:17, 25); when restored to speech, he is said to *elálēse*, the aor. of *laléō* (Matt 9:33; Luke 11:14), emphasizing the fact of speech versus speechlessness. When reference is made to those who spoke in tongues, whether foreign languages or the Corinthian unknown tongue, it is always referred to as *laléō glṓssais* (*glṓssa* [1100], tongue), to speak in tongues (Mark 16:17; Acts 2:4; 1 Cor 12:30). This emphasized not the content of the speech, but merely that they uttered sounds as far as the hearers were concerned. *Laléō* is ascribed to God (Heb 1:1, 2), indicating not that the content of His speech was meaningless, but simply that He spoke. Contrast *légō* (3004), to speak expressing thoughts, or *apophthéggomai* (669), to speak forth, made up from *apó* (575), from, and *phthóggos*, any clear and distinct sound which makes sense or, if it is a musical sound, conveying harmony (Acts 2:14 in which case when Peter spoke he was understood). The same word *apophthéggomai* is used in Acts 2:4, certifying that the other languages which the Holy Spirit enabled the Jews gathered at Pentecost to speak were other ethnic languages, not the unknown tongue of the Corinthians. The verse reads, "And all were filled with the Holy Spirit and they began speaking [*lalein* {2980}, to speak] other languages [*hetérais* {2083}, qualitatively different] that the Spirit was giving to them [*apophthéggesthai*] to sound out" (a.t.). The idea here is that the Holy Spirit gave the ability to these Jews at Pentecost to say certain things in languages other than their own with sounds that were not gibberish but were well formulated syllabic utterances which could be understood by others. The basic verb *phthéggomai* (5350), to utter a sound or voice as we do when we ordinarily speak, also occurs in Acts 4:18, "And they called them, and commanded them not to speak [*phthéggesthai*] at all nor teach in the name of Jesus." When one teaches, he pronounces words clearly in order that others may understand him. This verb occurs also in 2 Pet 2:16 and indicates that the donkey which spoke to Balaam actually pronounced syllabic human words: "The dumb ass speaking [*phthegxámenon*, pronounced words in the language which Balaam could understand] with man's voice." When God spoke to Balaam, He did not use an unknown tongue, but spoke through a donkey in human speech, using the very language which Balaam could understand. *Phthéggomai* is also used in 2 Pet 2:18 and the comp. *apophthéggomai* is used in Acts 26:25. The verb *phēmí* (5346), to speak but in a revealing manner making known one's thoughts, from which verb *prophḗtēs* (4396), a prophet, is derived, is never used for speaking in the manner that *laléō* is used in connection with other languages or language or the unknown tongue of the Corinthians. The verb *laléō* being the only verb used in the expression "speaking in tongues" or "in a tongue," indicates that the speaking in these languages other than their own was not something that was of a permanent acquisition or learning which could be done at will. It was

a temporary supernatural enablement of the Holy Spirit in actually putting utterances in the mouths of these people. What they were saying was not a product of their own intelligence, but a direct product of the Holy Spirit. The Eng. word "glossolalia" is derived from the noun *glóssa* and *laliá* ([2981], the subst. of *laléō*). In Gr. *glōssolaliá* as a comp. word does not occur in the NT.

(I) Particularly of persons, used in an absolute sense (Matt 9:33; 12:22; 15:31; Mark 5:35; Luke 7:15; Acts 18:9; James 1:19; Sept.: 1 Sam 3:9, 10; Isa 1:2); followed by adv. (Mark 7:35; John 18:23; Acts 7:6; Heb 6:9). In 2 John 1:12, "face to face" is synonymous with mouth to mouth (see Sept.: Num 12:8). With adjuncts of manner, e.g., dat. as *parrēsía* (3954), boldly, openly (John 7:26). *Idía dialéktō* (*idía* [2398], own; *dialéktō* [1258], dialect), in their own dialect (Acts 2:6; see Acts 6:10; 1 Cor 13:1). With a prep., e.g., *eis* (1519), unto, *aéra* (109), air (1 Cor 14:9), i.e., aimlessly; *ek* (1537), out of, with gen. of manner or source (Matt 12:34; John 8:44, "he speaketh of his own," out of himself, externalizing what he actually is); with *en* (1722), in or by means of, followed by dat. is that no man speaking in (or by means of) the "Spirit of God calls [*légei* {3004}] Jesus accursed" (a.t. [1 Cor 12:3]). Here the part. *lalōn* is used along with *légei*, thus the two words are being contrasted in their meaning. No one pretending to speak in the Spirit of God (*lalōn*) can actually use his mental faculties (*légei*) to call Jesus accursed. When the Holy Spirit puts words in one's mouth, they are words that extol the Lord Jesus Christ knowingly. Followed by the part. of manner as in Luke 1:64, "and he spoke [*elálei*], praising God" (a.t.). What the Holy Spirit put in his mouth was praise to the Lord. The part. *eulogōn* (2127), praising, is from *eú* (2095), well, and *légō* (3004), to speak intelligently, speak well of. See 2 Cor 11:23.

In various constructions designating the person or thing to or of whom one speaks:

(A) Following the dat. of person meaning to speak to or with someone (Matt 12:47; Luke 1:22; John 9:29; 19:10; Acts 7:38; Rom 7:1; Sept.: Gen 18:33). With an adjunct of manner added, e.g., the dat. *parrēsía* (3954), boldly (John 7:13; Eph 5:19, singing psalms together). Followed by *en* (1722), in, with the dat. (1 Cor 14:6, 21); *perí* (4012), about, and the gen. (Luke 2:38); a part. such as *légōn* (3004), speaking with understanding, thus giving definiteness to the idea of *laléō* (Matt 14:27; 23:1; 28:18; Luke 24:6; Sept.: Gen 17:3; 34:8; 42:22).

(B) Followed by *metá* (3326) and the gen., with someone, meaning to speak with (John 4:27; 9:37; Sept.: Gen 35:13; Num 11:17). With *légō* (Mark 6:50).

(C) Followed by *prós* (4314), toward someone, with the acc. meaning to speak to, found only three times except in Luke's writings (1 Thess 2:2; Heb 5:5; 11:18); speaking to the people (Acts 4:1; 21:39; Sept.: Gen 18:27, 29); by *euaggelízomai* (2097), to evangelize (Luke 1:19; Acts 11:20); with *légō* implied (Heb 5:5; 11:18).

(D) Followed by *perí* (4012), about someone, with the gen., to speak about or of someone (John 8:26; 12:41; Sept.: Ezek 33:30).

(E) With the acc. of a kindred noun or a pron., in a general or adv. sense, and thus differing from *légō*, with the acc. which implies a def. obj. or is followed by the express words spoken. In Mark 2:7; Acts 6:13, to speak blasphemies; in John 8:44, to speak falsehood, a lie (see Jude 1:15, 16; Sept.: Ex 4:12). With other adjuncts, e.g., acc. and dat. of thing (Matt 9:18; John 14:25; 15:11; Sept.: Gen 28:15). With the dat. of manner (Mark 8:32; 1 Cor 14:2); *en Christō̂*, in Christ, meaning by His authority (2 Cor 12:19); *katá* (2596), according to, followed by the acc. (2 Cor 11:17); *perí* (4012), concerning, followed by the gen., to say something concerning someone (Luke 2:33).

(II) As modified by the context where the meaning lies not so much in the verb itself, *laléō*, as in the adjuncts.

(A) Of one teaching, meaning to teach, preach, used in an absolute sense (Luke 5:4; 1 Cor 14:34, 35; 1 Pet 4:11). Followed by an adv. (John 12:50; Acts 14:1; Eph 6:20); *apó* (575), from, versus *ek* (1537), out of, with the gen. of source or occasion (John 7:17, 18); *ek* with the gen. of manner (John 3:31); the dat. of manner (Mark 16:17, "they shall speak with new tongues"; Acts 2:4). With adjunct of person, to whom, e.g., dat. (John 15:22; 1 Cor 3:1); *en* (1722), in, with the dat. of manner (Matt 13:10, "Why do you speak to them in parables?" [a.t.]; 13:34, "without a parable"); with *epí* (1909), upon, *tō̂ onómati* (3686), name, followed by the gen., to speak the name with the def. art., to speak in or upon or about this name to someone (Acts 5:40); *perí* (4012), about, to speak about something (Luke 9:11); with the acc. of the thing taught, in an absolute sense (John 3:11; 8:30, 40; 18:20; Acts 20:30; Titus 2:1). Also in reference to the doctrines of Jesus (John 8:28, 38; 12:50; Acts 5:20; 17:19; 1 Cor 2:6, 7) with *didáskō* (1321), to teach (Acts 18:25); with person to whom, e.g., dat. (Mark 2:2, "he was speaking to them the word" (a.t.); 4:33; John 6:63; Acts 8:25). Followed by *en* (1722), in, with dat. of manner (John 16:25); with *légōn*, saying (Matt 13:3). To speak something to someone (Acts 3:22; 1 Thess 2:2, "to speak unto you the gospel" [a.t.]).

(B) Of those who tell, relate, declare, announce something (John 1:37); with *prós* (4314), to, followed by the acc. and preceded by an adv. (Luke 2:20, "as it was spoken [or announced] to them" [a.t.]). Following the acc. of thing (Matt 26:13; Acts 4:20, "which we saw and heard, not to speak [*mē laleín*]" [a.t.]); the acc. and dat. of person (Matt 13:33); *kath' hón trópon* (5158), manner, in which manner (Acts 27:25); *pará* (3844), by, with the gen. (Luke 1:45, "the things spoken to her by the Lord" [a.t.]).

(C) Of prophecy or predictions meaning to foretell, declare (Acts 3:24; 26:22; James 5:10; 2 Pet 1:21). With *prós* (4314), to, with the acc. meaning to speak, foretell, declare to someone (Acts 28:25, "the Holy Spirit spoke [or prophesied] . . . to our fathers" [a.t.]); followed by the acc. of thing (see I, A, 5 above). In Luke 24:25, the dat. *hoís* is used by attraction for the antecedent noun, *hoís elálēsan*, instead of *há elálēsan*. See Acts 3:21, where the gen. *hôn* is used instead of the acc. *há*. Followed by the dat. of person (John 16:1, 4); by the acc. (Luke 1:55, 70).

(D) Of what is said with authority, meaning to direct, charge, prescribe, followed by the dat. (Mark 16:19). With the acc. and dat., *taúta* ([acc.] these things) *lelálēka* (I have spoken) *humín* ([dat.] unto you; John 15:11). The acc. and *eis* (1519), unto, and *perí* (4012), about (Heb 7:14). With the meaning to publish or promulgate authoritatively (Heb 3:5; 9:19).

(E) Figuratively to speak by writing or letter (2 Cor 11:17; Heb 2:5; 2 Pet 3:16); of one dead who speaks or exhorts by his example (Heb 11:4).

(III) Metonymically of things, e.g.:

(A) Of a law, meaning to prescribe (Rom 3:19).

(B) Of the expiatory blood of Jesus (Heb 12:24) meaning speaking better than (the blood of) Abel, since the latter cried only for vengeance (Gen 4:10).

(C) In the vision of the Revelation, spoken of a voice (Rev 1:12; 4:1; 10:4); thunders which are said to utter their own voices (Rev 10:3, 4); a beast (Rev 13:5, 11, 15).

Deriv.: *alálētos* (215), unspeakable; *álalos* (216), unable to speak; *dialaléō* (1255), to converse; *eklaléō* (1583), to speak out; *katalaléō* (2635), to speak against, backbite; *laliá* (2981), saying, speech; *mogilálos* (3424), speaking with difficulty, a stutterer; *proslaléō* (4354), to speak to or with; *sullaléō* (4814), to speak with.

Syn.: *apaggéllō* (518), to announce, declare, report; *anaggéllō* (312), to announce, declare; *apophthéggomai* (669), to speak forth; *diēgéomai* (1334), to declare, report, narrate; *eréō* (2046), to speak; *hēsucházō* (2270), to be still, silent *légō* (3004), to speak thoughtfully; *homiléō* (3656), to talk, converse; *phēmí* (5346), to declare; *phthéggomai* (5350), to utter a sound or voice, to proclaim.

Ant.: *phimóō* (5392), to muzzle; *sigáō* (4601), to be silent; *siōpáō* (4623), to hush, be speechless.

2981. λαλιά laliá; gen. *laliás*, fem. noun from *laléō* (2980), to utter words, speak. Speech, utterance meaning what is uttered, words, talk (John 8:43; Sept.: Job 33:1; Isa 11:3). To be contrasted with *rhēma* (4487), the utterance itself or that which is spoken. Talk where it seems to imply contempt (John 4:42). Speech, manner of speech, idiom, dialect (Matt 26:73; Mark 14:70; Sept.: Song 4:3).

Syn.: *lógos* (3056), a word resulting from reason and thought; *rhēma* (4487), that which is said, while *laliá* is the sound itself, the utterance; *eulogía* (2129), blessing, praise, but also fair speech, flattery; *chrēstología* (5542), smooth talk; *épos* (2031), a word.

Ant.: *sigē* (4602), silence; *hēsuchía* (2271), quietness.

2982. λαμά lamá, λαμμά lammá; transliterated from the Hebr. *lāmāh* (4100, OT). For what? why? (Matt 27:46; Mark 15:34, from Ps 22:2, in the Sept.: translated *hinatí*, for what purpose).

2983. λαμβάνω lambánō; fut. *lēmpsomai*, 2d aor. *élabon*, perf. *eílēpha*. To take in whatever manner. Almost syn. with *déchomai* (1209), to accept or receive, and yet distinct from it in that *lambánō* sometimes means to receive as merely a self-prompted action without necessarily signifying a favorable reception (Gal 2:6). In the NT, to actively take, and, partially in the pass. sense, to receive, trans.

(I) To take:

(A) Particularly with the hand, followed by the acc. expressed or implied. **(1)** Generally (Matt 14:19; 25:1; 26:26, 52; 27:6, 30, 48; Mark 9:36; Luke 22:17; John 12:3, 13; 13:4, 12, 30; 1 Cor 11:23; Rev 5:8; 22:17). With *ek* (1537), out of, followed by the gen. (John 16:14; Rev 5:7). Figuratively followed by the acc., to receive honor unto oneself (Heb 5:4); power (Rev 11:17). The part. *labṓn* is often used before other verbs by a species of pleonasm, i.e., using two words meaning almost the same thing in order to express the idea more completely and graphically (Matt 13:31, 33; Luke 24:43; Acts 16:3; Sept.: Josh 2:4). **(2)** Of taking food or drink, with the acc. (Mark 15:23; John 19:30; Acts 9:19); used in an absolute sense (1 Tim 4:4). **(3)** With the meaning of to make provision for or take with (Matt 16:5, 7; 25:4; John 18:3). To take a wife (Mark 12:19–22; Luke 20:28; Sept.: Gen 16:21; 11:29). **(4)** Figuratively, to take upon oneself, to bear, e.g., the cross (Matt 10:38); our sicknesses (Matt 8:17 quoted from Isa 53:4 where *phérō* [5342], bring or bear, is used). **(5)** To take up, gather up (Matt 16:9, 10 [cf. Mark 8:19, 20]). Figuratively, to take the soul, as opposed to *títhēmi* (5087), to place (John 10:17, 18).

(B) To take out from a number, to choose, to take a people out of the nations (Acts 15:14).

(C) To take, i.e., to seize, lay hold of, with the idea of force or violence. **(1)** Particularly (Matt 21:35, "and when they took his servants" [a.t.]; 21:39; Mark 12:3, 8; John 19:1). Used in an absolute sense (2 Cor 11:20). In hunting or fishing, to take, catch (Matt 4:19; Luke 5:5); metaphorically (2 Cor 12:16, "I caught you with guile"). **(2)** Figuratively, of any strong affection or emotion, to seize, to come or to fall upon someone, e.g., ecstasy fell upon all (Luke 5:26); fear (Luke 7:16); temptation (1 Cor 10:13; Sept.: Ex 15:15); an evil spirit, demon (Luke 9:39).

(D) To take away, e.g., from someone by force (Matt 5:40); "take away thy crown" (a.t. [Rev 3:11; 6:4; Sept.: Gen 27:35; 31:1]).

(E) To take up with a person, i.e., to receive him as a friend or guest into one's house or society, equivalent to *déchomai* (1209), to accept. **(1)** Generally (John 6:21, "into the boat" [a.t.]; 19:27, "that disciple took her unto his own home"; 2 John 1:10, "receive him not into your house"). Metaphorically of a teacher, to receive, acknowledge, embrace and follow his instructions (John 1:12; 5:43; 13:20; 14:17); of doctrine, to embrace, admit, e.g., the word (Matt 13:20; Mark 4:16); the witness (John 3:11, 32, 33); the words (John 12:48; 17:8; 1 John 5:9). **(2)** To receive the person of someone, spoken of a king or judge who receives or admits the visits of those who bring him greetings and presents and thus favors their cause (see especially Job 13:10). Therefore, to favor someone, both in a good and bad sense. In the NT, however, used only in a bad sense, to accept one's person, meaning to be partial toward him, with the gen. (Gal 2:6, "God accepts no man's person" [a.t.]). Used in an absolute sense (Luke 20:21; Sept.: Lev 19:15; Ps 82:2).

(F) Figuratively in places where *lambánō* with its acc. is often equivalent to the verb corresponding to the acc. such as *archḗn* (746), beginning, meaning to begin (Heb 2:3); *aphormḗn* (874), opportunity, occasion, to take occasion (Rom 7:8, 11); to take courage (Acts 28:15); to take security (Acts 17:9); to take *lḗthēn* (3024), forgetfulness, meaning to forget (2 Pet 1:9). In Phil 2:7, *morphḗn* (3444), form, nature, meaning to take the likeness of someone. In Heb 11:29, 36, *peíran* (3984), experience, to make trial of, meaning to attempt; *sumboúlion* (4824), to take counsel, meaning to consult (Matt 12:14; 27:1, 7; 28:12); *hupódeigma* (5262), specimen, example, pattern, meaning to take someone as an example (James 5:10); *hupómnēsin* (5280), recollection, remembrance, meaning to recollect, remember (2 Tim 1:5); *cháragma*

(5480), an engraving, meaning to take or adopt the mark of someone (Rev 14:11).

(II) To receive what is given or imparted, imposed, to obtain, partake of.

(A) Generally used in an absolute sense (Matt 7:8, "for everyone that asketh receiveth"; 10:8; John 16:24; 1 Cor 4:7). With *ek* (1537), out of, indicating source (John 1:16; Rev 18:4, "that you may not receive of her plagues" [a.t.]). Followed by the acc. (Matt 20:9, 10; 25:16; Mark 10:30; 11:24; John 4:36; Acts 3:3 UBS; Rom 4:11; 1 Cor 9:24; Gal 3:14; Heb 11:35; James 1:12; 1 Pet 4:10; Rev 4:11); by *ek* (1537), out of. With an adjunct of the source, as *apó* (575), from, with the gen. (1 John 2:27); with *pará* (3844) with the gen. meaning from someone (John 5:41, 44, "I receive not honor from men"; Acts 2:33; James 1:7; Rev 2:27); *hupó* (5259), by, with the gen. (2 Cor 11:24, "by the Jews" [a.t.]).

(B) Of those who receive an office, station, dignity, either as committed or transmitted, such as an *episkopḗn* (1984), bishopric (Acts 1:20); *klḗron* (2819), inheritance, lot (Acts 1:25); *hierateían* (2405), priesthood (Heb 7:5); *basileían* (932), royalty, rule (Luke 19:12, 15); with *pará* (3844), from someone and the gen. (Acts 20:24); *diádochon* (1240), a successor in office (Acts 24:27).

(C) Of persons appointed to receive tribute, rent, to collect, exact (Matt 17:24, "they that received tribute money" means collectors; 21:34; Heb 7:8). With *apó* (575), from someone (Matt 17:25; 3 John 1:7).

(D) Figuratively to receive instruction, equal to be instructed, to learn (Rev 3:3).

(E) Figuratively in phrases such as to receive a commandment from someone (*entolḗn* [1785], commandment; John 10:18; 2 John 1:4). With *perí* (4012), concerning someone (Col 4:10); *prós* (4314), to, and the acc., to someone (Acts 17:15). To receive *katallagḗn* (2643), reconciliation (Rom 5:11); *kríma* (2917), condemnation (Matt 23:14; James 3:1); with the dat. reflexive, receive condemnation to oneself (Rom 13:2); *oikodomḗn* (3619),

edification (1 Cor 14:5); *paraggelían* (3852), mandate, charge (Acts 16:24); *peritomḗn* (4061), circumcision (John 7:23).

Deriv.: *analambánō* (353), to take up; *antilambánō* (482), to take instead of or in turn; *apolambánō* (618), to receive, take apart, take aside; *dexiolábos* (1187), a guardsman; *epilambánomai* (1949), to grasp; *eulabḗs* (2126), devout; *katalambánō* (2638), to seize, apprehend, attain; *lḗpsis* (3028), a receiving; *metalambánō* (3335), to take part, share; *paralambánō* (3880), to take over, receive from another; *prolambánō* (4301), to anticipate, overtake; *proslambánō* (4355), to receive or take to oneself; *prosōpolḗptēs* (4381), a respector of persons; *sullambánō*, (4815), to seize, catch; *hupolambánō* (5274), to take or bear up, support.

Syn.: *déchomai* (1209), to receive deliberately and readily what is offered; *anadéchomai* (324), to receive gladly; *apodéchomai* (588), to accept gladly from; *eisdéchomai* (1523), to receive into favor; *epidéchomai* (1926), to accept besides; *paradéchomai* (3858), to receive or admit with approval; *prosdéchomai* (4327), to receive to oneself; *hupodéchomai* (5264), to receive as a guest; *komízō* (2865), to bear, carry; *apéchō* (568), to have in full; *lagchánō* (2975), to obtain by lot; *harpázō* (726), to snatch or catch away; *agreúō* (64), to take by hunting; *thēreúō* (2340), to catch wild beasts; *zōgréō* (2221), to take alive; *piázō* (4084), to capture; *tugchánō* (5177), to obtain, attain to, get; *epitugchánō* (2013), to obtain; *ktáomai* (2932), to procure for oneself; *aírō* (142), to carry, take up or away, and the comp. *apaírō* (522), to lift off; *exaírō* (1808), to take away; *epaírō* (1869), to lift, raise; *anairéō* (337), to take up; *aphairéō* (851), to take away; *kathairéō* (2507), to take down; *periairéō* (4014), to take away that which surrounds; *apágō* (520), to take away.

Ant.: *dídōmi* (1325), to give; *charízomai* (5483), to give freely; *paréchō*

(3930), to furnish, provide, supply; *dōréō* (1433), to make a gift of; *aponémō* (632), to apportion; *chorēgéō* (5524), to supply, render; *merízō* (3307), to divide into parts.

2984. Λάμεχ *Lámech*; masc. proper noun transliterated from the Hebr. *Lemek* (3929, OT). Lamech, a patriarch, the father of Noah (Luke 3:36; Sept.: Gen 5:25ff.).

2985. λαμπάς *lampás*; gen. *lampádos*, fem. noun from *lámpō* (2989), to light, shine. A torch, lamp, lantern (John 18:3; Acts 20:8; Rev 4:5; 8:10; Sept.: Gen 15:17; Ex 20:18; Judg 15:4, 5). A lamp fed with oil (Matt 25:1, 3, 4, 7, 8; Sept.: Judg 7:16, 20). There are two Gr. words in the gospels translated "lamp": *lampás* and *lúchnos* (3088) which sometimes is translated "candle." See Matt 5:15; Mark 4:21; Luke 8:16. These were the usual means of lighting a house. In Matt 6:22, the eye, as the source of light or the organ by which light is received, is called the "lamp [*lúchnos*] of the body" (a.t.). In John 5:35, the same word is applied to John the Baptist who is not the eternal Light (*phōs* [5457], ascribed to Christ [John 1:4]) as we have in John 1:8, but the burning and shining lamp, kindled by the eternal Light and bearing witness to it. The word *lampás* occurs in John 18:3 where it is rendered "torch." It is also used in the parable of the ten virgins (Matt 25:1–13), where it would be better translated "torch." In eastern countries, the torch, like the lamp, is fed with oil which is carried in small vessels constructed for the purpose and called *aggeía* (30) as in Matt 25:4.

2986. λαμπρός *lamprós*; fem. *lamprá*, neut. *lamprón*, adj. from *lámpō* (2989), to shine. Shining, bright, radiant, resplendent, clear (Rev 22:1, 16 [cf. Acts 10:30]). White, bright, dazzling raiment (Luke 23:11; Acts 10:30; Rev 15:6; 19:8 [cf. Matt 17:2; Mark 16:5; Luke 9:29]). The meaning of white is derived from the fact that whiteness arises from the composition of the luminous rays of all other colors. Splendid, gorgeous (Mark 15:17; James 2:2, 3 [cf. Rev 18:14]).

Deriv.: *lamprótēs* (2987), brightness; *lamprōs* (2988), brilliantly.

Syn.: *leukós* (3022), white; *phōteinós* (5460), bright; *epiphanēs* (2016), conspicuous.

Ant.: *skoteinós* (4652), dark; *auchmērós* (850), dry, murky, dark as a result of covering; *mélas* (3189), black.

2987. λαμπρότης *lamprótēs*; gen. *lamprótetos*, fem. noun from *lamprós* (2986), bright. Brightness, splendor such as of the sun (Acts 26:13; Sept.: Isa 60:3; Dan 12:3).

Syn.: *apaúgasma* (541), a shining forth from a luminous body as spoken of Christ; *epipháneia* (2015), a shining forth or upon, a manifestation.

Ant.: *skótos* (4655), darkness; *skotía* (4653), physical darkness, secrecy, metaphorically the result of sin; *zóphos* (2217), a darkness of the underworld, blackness; *gnóphos* (1105), blackness, gloom as associated with the idea of a tempest.

2988. λαμπρῶς *lamprōs*; adv. from *lamprós* (2986), bright. Splendidly, sumptuously, for show (Luke 16:19).

2989. λάμπω *lámpō*; fut. *lámpsō*. To shine, give light. Used intrans. with the dat. (Matt 5:15); in an absolute sense (Matt 17:2; Luke 17:24; Acts 12:7; 2 Cor 4:6); metaphorically (Matt 5:16; 2 Cor 4:6; Sept.: Prov 4:18).

Deriv.: *eklámpō* (1584), to shine out; *lampás* (2985), a light; *lamprós* (2986), bright, shining; *perilámpō* (4034), to shine around.

Syn.: *phaínō* (5316), to cause to appear, give light; *epiphaínō* (2014), to shine upon, appear; *phaneróō* (5319), to make manifest; *emphanízō* (1718), to make physically manifest; *optánomai* (3700), to allow oneself to be seen; *stílbō* (4744), to glisten; *exastráptō* (1823), to dazzle; *periastráptō* (4015), to flash around, shine round about; *epiphaúō* (2017), to shine, to shine forth; *astráptō* (797), to flash as lightning; *augázō* (826), to shine forth as the dawn.

Ant.: *skotízō* (4654), to deprive of light, make dark; *skotóō* (4656), to darken.

2990. λανθάνω *lanthánō*; 2d aor. *élathon*. To lie hidden, concealed, to be unknown, used in an absolute sense in Mark 7:24 and Luke 8:47. Followed by the acc. of person, to be hidden from someone, to escape his knowledge or notice (Acts 26:26; 2 Pet 3:5, 8). Joined with the part. of another verb, it has the force of an adv. meaning secretly, unawares (Heb 13:2).

Deriv.: *alēthḗs* (227), true, one who cannot lie; *eklanthánomai* (1585), to forget utterly; *epilanthánomai* (1950), to forget or neglect; *láthra* (2977), secretly; *léthē* (3024), forgetfulness.

Syn.: *krúptō* (2928), to cover, conceal; *apokrúptō* (613), to conceal from; *egkrúptō* (1470), to hide in something; *perikrúptō* (4032), to hide by placing something around; *kalúptō* (2572), to cover, conceal; *parakalúptō* (3871), to cover with a veil; *agnoéō* (50), to be ignorant; *pareisdúnō* (3921), to slip in secretly.

Ant.: *apokalúptō* (601), to uncover, unveil, reveal; *chrēmatízō* (5537), to reveal by divine admonition or instruction; *anoígō* (455), to open; *dianoígō* (1272), to open up completely; *anaptússō* (380), to unroll; *anakalúptō* (343), to unveil, open, discover inductively; *anaphaínō* (398), appear; *katanoéō* (2657), to perceive, discover.

2991. λαξευτός *laxeutós*; fem. *laxeutḗ*, neut. *laxeutón*, adj. from *laxeúō* (n.f.), to cut in stone. Something hewn in rock, such as a sepulcher (Luke 23:53).

2992. λαός *laós*; gen. *laoú*, masc. noun. A people, nation, a number of people joined together by the common bonds of society (Luke 2:10, 31, 32; Acts 4:25 quoted from Ps 2:1; Rev 5:9; Sept.: Job

36:31; Ezek 20:41). The common people, the multitude (Matt 26:5; 27:64; Luke 1:10; 7:29; 8:47; 9:13; 18:43; 23:27; Acts 2:47; 3:9, 11, 12; 5:37; 18:10; 21:30, 36); of Galilee (Matt 4:23; 9:35). The common people as distinguished from magistrates (Matt 26:5; 27:25, 64; Mark 11:32; Luke 19:48; 20:6; 23:13; Acts 6:12; Sept.: Ex 18:22; Josh 6:8, 9). The society of Christians or of the Christian church (Titus 2:14; Heb 4:9; 13:12; 1 Pet 2:9, 10). In the Sept., it is a title almost totally reserved for the elect people, the Israel of God (Sept.: Ex 1:20; 8:1; Deut 2:4; see Matt 1:21; 2:4, 6; Mark 7:6; Luke 2:32; John 11:50; Heb 7:5;).

Syn.: *éthnos* (1484), nation, signifying the heathen or Gentiles as distinguished from the Jews or believers; *dēmos* (1218) a community of free citizens, a people commonly bound together; *óchlos* (3793), a disorganized crowd or multitude.

2993. Λαοδίκεια *Laodíkeia*, gen. *Laodikeías*, fem. proper noun. Laodicea, a city in Asia Minor on the banks of the Lycus, a few miles away from Colossae and Hierapolis, known today in Turkish as Eski-hissar. It was formerly known as Diospolis. The Syrian King Seleucus II changed its name to that of his wife, Laodice. It was a rich, commercial city. After a great earthquake had destroyed Colossae, Hierapolis, and Laodicea, the latter was rebuilt by its own inhabitants without any aid from the Roman Senate. A Christian church was established here early, probably by the Ephesian believers, and to this church Paul sent a salutation when writing to the Colossians (Col 4:15). It is also mentioned in Rev 1:11; 3:14. From Col 4:16, it appears that Paul wrote a letter to the Laodiceans, but of this letter no certain account can be made. Some think that it was the same as the Epistle to the Ephesians since it was a letter circulated among the churches. There is what is known as the "Epistle to the Laodiceans" which exists only in Latin. It is a literary forgery of late date and compiled from the books of Galatians and Ephesians. The church of Laodicea flourished for several centuries. In the fourth century, an important council gathered here. The Muslims destroyed the city, and today it is a heap of ruins.

2994. Λαοδικεύς *Laodikeús*; gen. *Laodikéōs*, masc. noun. A Laodicean (Col 4:16; Rev 3:14), an inhabitant of Laodicea.

2995. λάρυγξ *lárugx*; gen. *láruggos*, masc. noun. Larynx, the throat as an organ of the voice (Rom 3:13 from Ps 5:9).

2996. Λασαία *Lasaía*; gen. *Lasaías*, fem. proper noun. Lasea, a maritime city of Crete (2914) on the southern coast (Acts 27:8) not mentioned by the Class. Gr. writers.

2997. λάσχω *láschō* or *láskō*; fut. *lakḗsō*. To crack, snap, burst, open (Acts 1:18).
    Syn.: *schízō* (4977), to split, rend.

2998. λατομέω *latoméō*; contracted *latomṓ*, fut. *latomḗsō*, from *latómos* (n.f.), to cut stones. To cut stone, to hew in stone, such as a sepulcher (Matt 27:60; Mark 15:46; Sept.: Deut 6:11; Isa 22:16).
    Syn.: *kóptō* (2875), to cut; *apokóptō* (609), to cut off or away; *katakóptō* (2629), to cut down; *ekkóptō* (1581), to cut out or down, hew down; *diapríō* (1282), to saw asunder, divide by means of a saw.
    Ant.: *kolláō* (2853), to glue together; *proskolláō* (4347), to join to, attach.

2999. λατρεία *latreía*; gen. *latreías*, fem. noun from *latreúō* (3000), to worship. Service for hire or as a slave, divine service (only in John 16:2; Rom 9:4; 12:1; Heb 9:1, 6; Sept.: Ex 12:25, 26; Josh 22:27). That sacrifice seems especially to be the service denoted is clear from Rom 9:4; 12:1; Heb 9:1, 6. In Rom 12:1, with *logikḗ* (3050), logical, *latreía*

is service which conforms to human reason.
    Deriv.: *eidōlolatreía* (1495), idolatry.
    Syn.: *thrēskeía* (2356), religion, worship; *ethelothrēskeía* (1479), voluntarily adopted worship; *eusébeia* (2150), piety; *theosébeia* (2317), godliness; *diakonía* (1248), service, ministry; *leitourgía* (3009), public ministry.

3000. λατρεύω *latreúō*; fut. *latreúsō*, from *latrís* (n.f.), one hired. To serve, in a religious sense to worship God (Matt 4:10; Luke 1:74; 2:37; 4:8; Acts 7:7; 24:14; 27:23; Rom 1:9; Phil 3:3; 2 Tim 1:3; Heb 9:14; 12:28; Rev 22:3); used in an absolute sense (Acts 26:7; Sept.: Deut 6:13; 10:12; Josh 24:15); creatures (Rom 1:25; Sept.: Deut 4:28; Judg 2:11, 13). It refers particularly to the performing of the Levitical service (Heb 8:5; 9:9; 10:2; 13:10); of the celestial temple (Rev 7:15). Generally to offer sacrifice, to worship (Heb 9:9; 10:2 [cf. Sept.: Ex 3:12; 7:16]). Allied to *látris*, a hired servant as opposed to *doúlos* (1401), a bond slave. Therefore, to serve or worship but not out of compulsion. *Latreúō* originally meant to work for reward, to serve. The meanings of service and worship are intertwined. It occurs some 90 times in the Sept. and 21 times in the NT, 8 of which are in Luke and Acts with its syn. *douleúō* (1398), to work, serve.
    Deriv.: *latreía* (2999), service, worship.
    Syn.: *proskunéō* (4352), to make obeisance, do reverence to, worship, do homage; *sébomai* (4576), to revere, render devotion; *sebázomai* (4573), to honor religiously, render reverence; *eusebéō* (2151), to act piously toward, worship. With the meaning of rendering service: *therapeúō* (2323), to heal, to serve with tenderness; *diakonéō* (1247), to minister; *douleúō* (1398), to serve as a slave, and therefore of necessity; *hupēretéō* (5256), to serve as an underling, as an under rower; *leitourgéō* (3008), to render public service, such as the priesthood.

3001. λάχανον *láchanon*; gen. *lachánou*, neut. noun from *lachaínō* (n.f.), to dig, till. Literally a plant in tilled ground, hence a garden plant, herb (Matt 13:32; Mark 4:32; Luke 11:42; Rom 14:2; Sept.: Gen 9:3; 1 Kgs 21:2).

Syn.: *botánē* (1008), grass, fodder; *phuteía* (5451), plant.

3002. Λεββαῖος *Lebbaíos*; gen. *Lebbaíou*, masc. proper noun. Lebbaeus, a name of the Apostle Jude, also called Thaddaeus (Matt 10:3).

3003. λεγεών *legeōn*; gen. *legeōnos*, Lat. *legio*, masc. noun. A legion, which is the largest division of troops in the Roman army, varying greatly in number at different periods as 3,000; 4,200; 5,000; 6,600. Used for an indefinitely great number of angels (Matt 26:53); of demons (Mark 5:9, 15; Luke 8:30).

3004. λέγω *légō*; fut. *léxō*. Originally to lay or let lie down for sleep, to lay together, i.e., to collect. Finally to lay before, i.e., to relate, recount; and hence the prevailing Attic and later meaning of to say, speak, i.e., to utter definite words, connected and significant speech equal to discourse. It thus differs in some instances from *laléō* (2980), to utter sounds, which may refer only to words spoken and not to their connected sense. In the NT:

(**I**) To lay before, i.e., to relate such as a parable, to put forth, propound, with the dat. of person (Luke 18:1. See also Luke 13:6). With the prep. *prós* (4314), to someone (Luke 12:41; 14:7). Of events, to narrate, tell, with the dat. (Luke 9:21). With *prós* (4314), to, and the acc. (Luke 24:10).

(**II**) To say, speak, discourse.

(**A**) Generally and construed (**1**) With an adjunct of the object, i.e., the words spoken, the thing or person spoken of. (**a**) Followed by the words uttered (Matt 1:20; Mark 6:2; Luke 2:13; 12:54; John 1:29, 36; Acts 4:16; Rom 9:25; Heb 1:6; 8:13; James 3:23); followed by *hóti* (3754), that, before the words quoted (Matt 9:18; Mark 2:12; 3:21; Luke 4:41; 23:5; John 8:33; Acts 2:13; 6:11; Rom 3:8). In the part. *légōn* and the pl. *légontes*, saying, it is often put after other verbs or nouns implying speech and introducing the exact words, equivalent to "in these words" (Matt 5:2; 6:31; 9:30; 12:38; 16:7; Mark 1:7, 24; 11:31; Luke 4:35, 36; 7:39; 20:5; John 4:31, 51; Acts 2:13, 40; 24:2; Heb 12:26; Rev 6:10). This is not found in the epistles of Paul. (**b**) Followed by the acc. of thing or person, e.g., the thing spoken (Matt 21:16; Mark 11:23; Luke 8:8; John 5:34; Rom 10:8; Eph 5:12); hence, *tá legómena*, the things said (Luke 18:34; Acts 8:6); followed by the acc. of person spoken of, but only in attraction with *hóti* (3754), that (John 8:54; 9:19). (**c**) Followed by the acc. and inf. (Matt 16:13; Luke 11:18; John 12:29; Acts 4:32; 5:36; Rom 15:8; 2 Tim 2:18), with *eínai* (1511), to be implied (Rev 2:20). (**d**) Followed by *hóti* (3754), that, instead of the acc. and inf. (Mark 9:11; Luke 9:7; John 4:20; 1 Tim 4:1). Also with *hóti* and the apodosis implied in the phrase *sú légeis*, thou sayest (Matt 27:11; John 18:37 [cf. Luke 22:70]). (**e**) Followed by an adv. or adv. phrase (John 13:13; Rom 3:5; Gal 3:15). Metaphorically (Rev 18:7. Also Matt 3:9, to say in one's heart, in or among themselves, i.e., to think). (**2**) With a further adjunct of the person to whom one speaks, e.g., with the dat. *metá* (3326), with; *prós* (4314), to; and also of whom, e.g., with *eis* (1519), in; *perí* (4012), about; *hupér* (5228), for, on behalf. The adjunct of the obj. is then always present or implied in one of the preceding constructions. (**a**) Followed by the dat. of person, e.g., with the words uttered (Matt 8:26; 14:4; Mark 2:5, 14; 2 John 1:10, 11). With the dat. of thing personified (Matt 21:19; Rev 6:16). Also followed by *hóti* (3754), that, before the words quoted (cf. II, A, 1, a) (Luke 8:49; John 4:42). So also *kaí* (2532), and; *élegen*, was saying; *autō*, to him, is put after other verbs of speaking, like *légōn* (cf. II, A, 1, a) (Mark 9:31; 14:61). With an acc. of thing (John 16:7; 2 Thess 2:5; Rev 2:7), acc. of person, of whom, as an object (John 8:27; Phil 3:18). With *hóti* (3754), that, instead of acc. and inf. (Matt 16:18; John 16:26). With an adv. construction of manner, as Mark 3:23, "in parables he was saying to them" (a.t.); 4:2; 12:38. With *perí* (4012), about with the gen. (Matt 11:7). (**b**) Followed by the phrase *met' allḗlōn*, with one another (*metá* [3326], with; *allḗlon* [240], one another), with the words spoken (John 11:56). (**c**) Followed by *prós* (4314), to, with the acc. of person, to whom, e.g., with the words uttered (Mark 10:26; Luke 14:7; John 4:17; Heb 7:21). With *hóti* (3754), that, indicating citation (Luke 4:21). With an acc. of thing (Luke 11:53). With *perí* (4012), about followed by the gen., about someone (Luke 7:24). Further with an adjunct of person of whom one speaks. (**d**) Followed by *eis* (1519), to, with the acc. meaning of or concerning someone generally (Eph 5:32). With the words uttered (Acts 2:25). With an acc. of thing (Luke 22:65). (**e**) Followed by *perí* (4012), concerning, with the gen. of person with the words uttered (Matt 11:7). With the acc. of thing (John 1:22; Acts 8:34; Titus 2:8). With *hóti* (3754), that (Luke 21:5). (**f**) Followed by *hupér* (5228), on behalf of, to speak for oneself (Acts 26:1).

(**B**) As modified by the context, where the meaning lies not so much in *légō*, as in the adjuncts, e.g.: (**1**) Before questions, meaning to ask, inquire, followed by the words spoken (Matt 9:14; Mark 5:30; 14:14; Luke 7:20; John 7:11; Rom 10:19). With the dat. of person (Mark 6:37; Luke 16:5; 22:11). Followed by *ei* (1487), if, whether (Acts 25:20). With the dat. of person (Acts 21:37). (**2**) Before replies meaning to answer, reply, followed by the words spoken, e.g., after a direct question (Matt 17:25; John 18:17). With the dat. of person (Matt 18:22; 20:7, 21). Also with *hóti* (3754), that, indicating citation (Matt 19:8;

John 20:13). Preceded by *apokritheís* (611), having answered (Mark 8:29; Luke 3:11). Without a preceding question, with dat. of person and the words spoken (Matt 4:10; 26:35; Luke 16:29; John 2:4). With *apokritheís*, and so forth (Mark 9:19; Luke 11:45). (**3**) In affirmations meaning to affirm, maintain, e.g., with the words or proposition uttered (Mark 14:31; Gal 4:1; 1 John 2:4). Followed by the acc. and inf. (Matt 22:23; Luke 24:23). With the acc. implied (James 2:14; 1 John 2:6, 9). Followed by *hóti* (3754), that, instead of acc. and inf. (Matt 17:10; Rom 4:9). With a dat. of person in the formulas *légō soi* versus *humín*, I say unto thee (or unto you), in solemn affirmations, generally (Matt 11:22; Mark 11:24; Luke 4:25). With *amḗn* (281), verily (Matt 5:18; 25:12; John 1:51; 3:3; 8:51). In the middle of a clause (Matt 11:9; Luke 7:14; 11:51; 15:10). Followed by *hóti* (3754), that, for acc. with inf. (Matt 3:9; Mark 9:13; Luke 4:24; John 3:11). (**4**) Of teaching, meaning to teach, inculcate, e.g., with the proposition taught (Matt 15:5); with the acc. (Acts 1:3); with the acc. and inf. (Acts 21:21); with the acc. implied (Acts 15:24); with the acc. and dat. of person (Matt 10:27; John 16:12). (**5**) Of predictions, to foretell, prophesy, with the acc. and dat. (Mark 10:32); with the acc. (Luke 9:31); with the dat. (John 13:19). (**6**) Of what is spoken with authority, to command, direct, charge, and used in an absolute sense (Matt 23:3); with the acc. (Luke 6:46); with the acc. and dat. (Mark 13:37; John 2:5); with the dat. of person and imper. (Matt 5:44; 8:4; 20:8; Mark 5:41; 6:10; Luke 5:24; John 2:7, 8); with the dat. and inf. (Rev 13:14); with the inf. (Rom 2:22); followed by *hína* (2443), so that (Acts 19:4). In the sense of to charge, exhort, with the dat. (Acts 5:38); with the dat. and inf. (Acts 21:4); with *toúto* (5124), this, followed by the inf. (Eph 4:17). (**7**) Of calling out, with the meaning of to call, exclaim (Matt 25:11; Luke 13:25; Acts 14:11). (**8**) Figuratively, to say or speak by writing, by letter, e.g., with the words written (Luke 1:63; 20:42); with the acc. (1 Cor 7:6); implied (Phile 1:21); with the acc. and dat. (1 Cor 15:51); with the dat. (1 Cor 6:5; 10:15; 2 Cor 6:13); with *hóti* (3754), that, for acc. and inf. (Gal 5:2); *toúto hóti* (1 Thess 4:15). Followed by an adv. (2 Cor 7:3; 11:16; Phil 4:11; also Sept.: 2 Kgs 10:6).

(C) Metonymically, of things, e.g., **(1)** "a voice . . . saying" (Matt 3:17; Rev 6:6); with the dat. (Acts 9:4; Rev 16:1); with the dat. of manner (Acts 26:14). **(2)** A writing, Scripture, with the words quoted (John 19:37; James 4:5, 6); with *tí* (5101), what (Rom 4:3; Gal 4:30); with *hē graphḗ* (1124), the Scripture, implied (Gal 3:16; Eph 4:8). **(3)** A law, with the acc. (1 Cor 9:8). In an absolute sense (1 Cor 9:10; 14:34). **(4)** Generally, *ho chrēmatismós* (5538), a divine answer from God (Rom 11:4); the righteousness of faith as personified (Rom 10:6).

(D) Metaphorically, meaning to have in mind, to mean. Followed by an imper. (Gal 5:16). With the acc. of thing (1 Cor 10:29, "Conscience, I say"; see also 1 Cor 1:12; Gal 3:17). With the acc. of person (Mark 14:71; John 6:71, he meant Judas).

(III) To call, to name, equal to *kaléō* (2564), to call, particularly to speak of as being something or being called something (Matt 19:17; Mark 15:12; Luke 20:37; John 5:18; 15:15; Acts 10:28). Pass. (Matt 13:55; Heb 11:24). Part. *ho legómenos*, called, named (Matt 2:23; 9:9; 26:3, 14; Mark 15:7; John 4:5; 9:11; 21:2; Acts 3:2; Eph 2:11). Also surnamed (Matt 4:18; 10:2; Col 4:11). With the idea of translation into another language, e.g., fully (John 1:38; 19:17; Acts 9:36). Simply (John 4:25, "Messiah . . . who is called Christ," [a.t.], i.e., in Gr.; John 11:16; 20:16 [cf. 1:38]).

Deriv.: *antilégō* (483), to contradict, speak against; *genealogéō* (1075), to reckon by generation; *dialégomai* (1256), to discuss, reason; *dílogos* (1351), double-tongued; *eklégomai* (1586), to choose, elect; *epilégō* (1951),

to call, select; *katalégō* (2639), to reckon among, to count in; *logía* (3048), collection, gathering; *lógos* (3056), word, reason, expression; *mataiológos* (3151), one talking lightly; *paralégō* (3881), to pass, sail by; *prolégō* (4302), to tell before, foretell; *spermológos* (4691), babbler; *stratologéō* (4758), to enlist; *sullégō* (4816), to collect; *Philólogos* (5378), Philologus; *pseudológos* (5573), one speaking lies.

Syn.: *laléō* (2980), to babble, say something, (sometimes in contrast with *légō*, the former indicating a mere repetition of sounds, breaking silence, or speaking); *parrēsiázomai* (3955), to be bold in speech; *prophēteúō* (4395), to prophesy; *homiléō* (3656), to converse with; *eréō* (2046), to tell, say; *diasaphéō* (1285), to make clear; *phēmí* (5346), to say by way of enlightening, explaining, affirming; *pháskō* (5335), to affirm by repetition; *epaggéllō* (1861), to announce, proclaim; *exaggéllō* (1804), to publish, proclaim; *apokrínomai* (611), to give an answer to a question; *antapokrínomai* (470), to reply against; *anaggéllō* (312), to announce, report; *apaggéllō* (518), to announce, report; *diaggéllō* (1229), to announce, declare; *kataggéllō* (2605), to declare, proclaim; *paraggéllō* (3853), to charge, command; *diēgéomai* (1334), to narrate; *ekdiēgéomai* (1555), to narrate in full; *exēgéomai* (1834), to declare, bring out the meaning; *dēlóō* (1213), to make plain; *phrázō* (5419), to declare; *suzētéō* (4802), to discuss; *euaggelízō* (2097), to evangelize; *kērússō* (2784), to preach, herald; *plērophoréō* (4135), to inform fully.

Ant.: *phimóō* (5392), to muzzle, put to silence; *sigáō* (4601), to be silent; *siōpáō* (4623), to be silent or still; *hēsucházō* (2270), to be silent, hushed.

3005. λεῖμμα *leímma*; gen. *leímmatos*, neut. noun from *leípō* (3007), to lack. A remnant, what is left, used of persons, meaning some remaining (Rom 11:5; Sept.: 2 Kgs 19:4; see Josh 10:30).

Syn.: *loipós* (3062), the rest.

Ant.: *períseuma* (4051), a surplus.

3006. λεῖος leíos; fem. *leía*, neut. *leíon*, adj. Smooth, level, plain (Luke 3:5 quoted from Isa 40:4).

Syn.: *chrēstós* (5543), smooth.
Ant.: *trachús* (5138), rough

3007. λείπω leípō; fut. *leípsō*. To leave, forsake, fail, be wanting or deficient. Intrans. to fail, lack, be wanting (Luke 18:22; Titus 1:5; 3:13). In the pass., *leípomai*, to be deficient in or destitute of, forsaken of, to lack (James 1:5; 2:15). In the NT, it either governs a gen. of thing or is followed by the prep. *en* (1722), in (James 1:4, to be wanting in nothing).

Deriv.: *apoleípō* (620), to leave behind; *dialeípō* (1257), to leave off in the middle; *ekleípō* (1587), to omit, fail; *epileípō* (1952), to fail, be insufficient; *kataleípō* (2641), to leave behind; *leímma* (3005), a remnant; *loipós* (3062), remnant, remaining one; *perileípō* (4035), to leave all around; *hupoleípō* (5275), to leave remaining.

Syn.: *aposteréō* (650), to defraud; *husteréō* (5302), to lack, be destitute; *elattonéō* (1641), to be less.

Ant.: *perisseúō* (4052), to abound; *huperperisseúō* (5248), to abound exceedingly; *pleonázō* (4121), to superabound; *huperpleonázō* (5250), to abound exceedingly; *plēthúnō* (4129), to multiply; *huperbállō* (5235), to exceed; *huperéchō* (5242), to hold oneself above; *auxánō* (837), to grow; *prokóptō* (4298), to increase.

3008. λειτουργέω leitourgéō; contracted *leitourgó*, fut. *leitourgḗsō*, from *leitourgós* (3011), public servant. To minister publicly in sacred office (Acts 13:2); in works of charity (Rom 15:27); to lead in public worship (*latreía* [2999], public worship implying service) (Heb 10:11). It came to mean performing priestly or ministerial functions. To serve God (*latreúō* [3000]) is the duty of all, but to serve Him in special offices and ministries can be the duty and privilege of only a few who are set apart for such functions.

Syn.: *diakonéō* (1247), to minister voluntarily; *douleúō* (1398), to serve as a slave, and therefore to serve by compulsion; *latreúō* (3000), primarily to work for hire, but when it involves service to God, it is also part of worship; *hupēretéō* (5256), to serve in a low capacity as an under rower.

Ant.: *argéō* (691), to be idle.

3009. λειτουργία leitourgía; gen. *leitourgías*, fem. noun from *leitourgós* (3011), public servant. A public service or office, such as in Athens and elsewhere, administered by the citizens at their own expense as a part of the system of finance. In the NT, service or ministry as of the public ministrations of the Jewish priesthood (Luke 1:23; Heb 8:6; 9:21). Used of the ministry of the Christian teacher in bringing men to the faith (Phil 2:17 [cf. Sept.: Num 8:22]). By implication it means friendly service, kind office (Phil 2:30). Spoken of alms, i.e., public collections in the churches (2 Cor 9:12).

Syn.: *diakonía* (1248), ministry but not necessarily public; *latreía* (2999), worship, service without compulsion.

3010. λειτουργικός leitourgikós; fem. *leitourgikḗ*, neut. *leitourgikón*, adj. from *leitourgós* (3011), public servant, minister. In the Sept. referring to the implements used in worship (Num 4:12, 26). In the NT, used of the activity of ministering, rendering service to others (Heb 1:14, referring to spirits who are rendering service [cf. Ps 34:7; 91:11; 104:4; Matt 13:49; 16:27 in regard to the ministry of angels]).

Syn.: *eúchrēstos* (2173), profitable, useful; *chrḗsimos* (5539), serviceable; *ōphélimos* (5624), helpful, profitable.

Ant.: *achreíos* (888), useless, unprofitable; *áchrēstos* (890), unprofitable, useless; *anōphelḗs* (512), not beneficial or serviceable.

3011. λειτουργός leitourgós; gen. *leitourgoú*, masc. noun from *léïtos* (n.f.), of the people, and *érgon* (2041), work. A public servant, minister, such as those in Athens who performed or administered the *leitourgíai* (3009), the public functions. In the NT a minister, servant, generally of God (Rom 13:6). In Heb 1:7, "Who makes . . . his servants a flame of fire," (a.t.) quoted from Ps 104:4 (cf. Sept.: 1 Kgs 10:5). Spoken of a priest in the Jewish sense (Heb 8:2; Sept.: Neh 10:39); of Paul as a minister of Christ and the gospel (Rom 15:16). By implication, one who ministers to someone's wants (Phil 2:25).

Deriv.: *leitourgéō* (3008), to be a public servant; *leitourgía* (3009), public function, ministry; *leitourgikós* (3010), ministering.

Syn.: *diákonos* (1249), a servant, minister; *hupērétēs* (5257), an attendant, one who is not an officer; *místhios* (3407), and *misthōtós* (3411), a hired servant; *país* (3816), a boy, a household servant; *doúlos* (1401), a bondslave; *hiereús* (2409), priest; *ergátēs* (2040), a worker; *sunergós* (4904), a fellow worker; *boēthós* (998), a helper; *oikétēs* (3610), domestic servant.

Ant.: *argós* (692), an idle person, one doing nothing.

3012. λέντιον *léntion*; gen. *lentíou*, neut. noun, Lat. *lenteum*. A linen cloth, towel, or apron worn by servants and persons-in-waiting (John 13:4, 5).

3013. λεπίς *lepís*; gen. *lepídos*, fem. noun from *lépō* (n.f.), to peel, flake. A scale or crust over the eyes (Acts 9:18). In the Sept., used of fish (Lev 11:9, 10).

Deriv.: *lépra* (3014), leprosy.

3014. λέπρα *lépra*; gen. *lépras*, fem. noun from *lepís* (3013), a scale. Leprosy, so-called because the skin becomes scaly or scabby (Matt 8:3; Mark 1:42; Luke 5:12, 13; Sept.: Lev 13:2, 3ff.). Whereas the cure of disease in general is known as healing (*íasis* [2392], cure, from *iáomai* [2390], to heal), that of leprosy is called *katharismós* (2512), cleansing,

from *katharízō* (2511), to clean. This is, no doubt, appropriate on account of the very evident restoration of cleanliness to the skin, but primarily because the miracle enabled the leper to become ceremonially clean. Lepers were shut out from the temple and synagogues and were deprived of the social life of their fellow beings, a very pitiable lot indeed. Their cleansing meant much more than getting rid of a disagreeable disease, repulsive to all their fellowmen. It also meant restoration to the worship and service of God. Of the lepers mentioned in the NT, we have but one named, Simon of Bethany (Matt 26:6; Mark 14:3), probably a grateful recipient of the Lord's mercy. Lazarus, in the account of the rich man in Luke 16, was most probably leprous, as the open visible sores would indicate (Luke 16:20). In the story of the nine thankless lepers and the grateful tenth who was a Samaritan (Luke 17:11ff.), it is noticeable that he turned back because he was healed (*iáomai* [2390]), but he was not yet finally cleansed (*katharízō* [2511]) since he had not yet been to the priest. See Num 12:10, 12; Lev 13:47; 14:34; 2 Kgs 5:7. The various symptoms of this disease, which was a striking emblem of sin both original and actual, may be seen in Lev 13—14. See *leprós* (3015), a leper.

3015. λεπρός *leprós*; fem. *leprá*, neut. *leprón*, adj. from *lépos* (n.f.), a scale. Leprous; subst. a leper (Matt 8:2; 10:8; 11:5; Mark 1:40; Luke 4:27; 7:22; 17:12). In Matt 26:6; Mark 14:3, "Simon the leper" means Simon who had been a leper. See Sept.: Lev 13:44, 45; 2 Sam 3:29; 2 Kgs 7:3.

3016. λεπτόν *leptón*; gen. *leptoú*, neut. noun from *leptós* (n.f.), thin. Something scaled down or light, a small coin, mite, the smallest coin in use among the Jews, equal to half a *kodrántēs* (2835), a farthing which was the eighth part of an *assárion* (787), a Roman coin (Mark 12:42; Luke 12:59; 21:2). The value of the widow's gift (Mark 12:42) was little more than a farthing. The fact that it consisted of two tiny coins—a fact which is obscured by our careless referral to "the widow's mite"—is full of significance. She might have kept back one, but in spite of her penury she cast in all that she had.

3017. Λευΐ *Leuí*; masc. proper noun transliterated from the Hebr. *Lēwī* (3878, OT), joining. Levi, the name of three Israelites.

(**I**) The third son of Jacob and Leah, whom Leah so named because "Now . . . will my husband be joined unto me, because I have born him three sons" (Heb 7:5, 9; Rev 7:7; Gen 29:34). Together with Simeon, he avenged the wrongs done to their sister Dinah by slaying the Shechemites (Gen 34:25–31), but thereby he incurred a curse from Jacob (Gen 49:5–7). By the zeal of his descendants, however, on the occasion of the golden calf (Ex 32:26–29), the curse was transformed into a blessing. He had three sons.

(**II**) Son of Melchi, an ancestor of our Lord (Luke 3:24).

(**III**) Son of Simeon, an ancestor of our Lord (Luke 3:29).

3018. Λευΐς *Leuís*; gen. *Leuí*, acc. *Leuín*, masc. proper noun transliterated from the Hebr. *Lēwī* (3878, OT), joining. Levi. The original name of Matthew, the publican, who became an Apostle (Mark 2:14; Luke 5:27, 29 [cf. Matt 9:9]). See *Matthaíos* (3156), Matthew.

3019. Λευΐτης *Leuítēs*; gen. *Leuítou*, masc. proper noun. Levite. A Levite was one of the posterity of Levi (3017). These were appointed by the Mosaic law to be the ministers and servants of the priests and to perform the menial offices of the temple and temple service (Luke 10:32; John 1:19; Acts 4:36; see also Num 1:50ff.; 3:17; 4; 8:5ff.).

3020. Λευϊτικός *Leuïtikós*; fem. *Leü-tikḗ*, neut. *Leuïtikón*, adj. Levitical, pertaining to the Levites (Heb 7:11).

3021. λευκαίνω *leukaínō*; fut. *leukanṓ*, from *leukós* (3022), white. To whiten, make white (Mark 9:3; Rev 7:14; Sept.: Ps 51:7; Isa 1:18).

   Syn.: *koniáō* (2867), to whitewash as tombs.

   Ant.: *skotízō* (4654), to make dark; *skotóō* (4656), to darken, of the heavenly bodies, and metaphorically the mind.

3022. λευκός *leukós*; fem. *leukḗ*, neut. *leukón*, adj. White, also shining, glittering. Used of clothing sometimes in the sense of bright (Matt 17:2; 28:3; Mark 9:3; 16:5; Luke 9:29; John 20:12; Acts 1:10); of hair (Matt 5:36; Rev 1:14); of harvest meaning ripe (John 4:35); of stone (Rev 2:17); symbolically (Rev 3:4, 5, 18; 4:4; 6:11; 7:9, 13; 19:14); of a horse (Rev 6:2; 19:11, 14); of a cloud (Rev 14:14); of the throne of God (Rev 20:11).

   Deriv.: *leukaínō* (3021), to make white.

   Syn.: *phōteinós* (5460), bright, light; *lamprós* (2986), bright, clear, white.

   Ant.: *mélas* (3189), black, dirty; *skoteinós* (4652), dark; *auchmērós* (850), murky, dark.

3023. λέων *léōn*; gen. *léontos*, masc. noun. A lion (Heb 11:33; 1 Pet 5:8; Rev 4:7; 9:8, 17; 10:3; 13:2; Sept.: Judg 14:5, 8, 9; 1 Sam 17:34, 36, 37). A lion. Used to indicate a cruel adversary, persecutor (2 Tim 4:17, some thinking it to refer to Nero and others to Satan [cf. Ps 7:2; Prov 28:15; Ezek 22:25]). It also refers to a hero, a powerful deliverer (Rev 5:5, "the lion of the tribe of Judah" [cf. Jer 49:19; Nah 2:13]).

3024. λήθη *lḗthē*; gen. *lḗthēs*, fem. noun from *lanthánō* (2990), to forget. Forgetfulness, oblivion (2 Pet 1:9). This is the word from which "lethal" and "lethargy" are derived. The mythical river *Lēthē* was supposed to cause forgetfulness of the past to those who drank of it.

Syn.: *epilēsmonḗ* (1953), forgetfulness.

Ant.: *anámnēsis* (364), a remembrance, recalling in one's mind without an outward prompting; *hupómnēsis* (5280), a reminder, a remembrance prompted by another; *mneía* (3417), a mention; *mnḗmē* (3420), memory.

3025. ληνός *lēnós*; gen. *lēnoú*, masc. noun. A trough for drinking or watering. In the Sept.: Gen 30:38, 41. In the NT, used to mean wine trough, wine vat, as for instance the upper vat or press into which the grapes were cast and trodden by men (Rev 14:19, 20; 19:15; Sept.: Neh 13:15; Isa 63:2). It was sometimes hewn in a rock and had a grated opening near the bottom through which the liquid flowed off into a lower vat dug in the rock or earth (Matt 21:33; Mark 12:1; Prov 3:10; Isa 5:2; Joel 2:24).

Deriv.: *hupolḗnion* (5276), a vessel placed beneath the wine press for receiving the juice.

3026. λῆρος *lēros*; gen. *lērou*, masc. noun. An idle tale, tattle, idle talk (Luke 24:11).

Syn.: *mōrología* (3473), foolish talk; *mataiología* (3150), vain talk.

Ant.: *lógos* (3056), a word.

3027. ληστής *lēstḗs*; gen. *lēstoú*, masc. noun from *leízomai* (n.f.), to plunder. A robber, one depriving another of his property openly and by violence (Matt 21:13; 26:55; 27:38, 44; Mark 11:17; 14:48; 15:27; Luke 10:30, 36; 19:46; 22:52; John 10:1; 18:40; 2 Cor 11:26; Sept.: Jer 7:11); metaphorically (John 10:8). The *lēstḗs*, as in the case of the penitent one on a cross near Jesus, may have been a person who turned insurgent for some presumed righteous cause, thus seeking by the wrath of man to work out what he presumes to be God's righteousness.

The difference between a *lēstḗs*, commonly translated "robber" and *kléptēs* is that the latter does his work in a secret manner so that he may not be discovered. Violence is the characteristic of a *lēstḗs* while stealth is the characteristic of the *kléptēs*. Judas was a thief (*kléptēs* [John 12:6]) doing no violence to anyone. He stole secretly. Barabbas was a robber (*lēstḗs* [John 18:40 {cf. Mark 15:7}]). Palestine was infested by robbers to whom its walks and caves afforded a great deal of cover and shelter (cf. Judg 9:25; Hos 6:9; 7:1), hence, the expression "den of robbers" (Jer 7:11; Matt 21:13). The temple became a haunt of robbers. The dealers in the temple market were notorious for their extortion, but it gave them fancied security in their evildoing. It is probable that some of these robbers were really zealots in rebellion against the authority of Rome, so that there was an element of misplaced patriotism and even religion in their proceedings. Josephus identified robbers with zealots.

Syn.: *kakoúrgos* (2557), an evil worker, malefactor; *kakopoiós* (2555), an evil doer; *hierósulos* (2417), a robber of temples; *kléptēs* (2812), thief.

Ant.: *agathopoiós* (17), a benefactor; *euergétēs* (2110), one who does a good work.

3028. λῆψις *lēpsis*; gen. *lēpseōs*, fem. noun from *lambánō* (2983), to receive. Receipt or the act of receiving (Phil 4:15).

Syn.: *apodochḗ* (594), acceptance.

Ant.: *dósis* (1394), a gift or the act of giving; *parádosis* (3862), transmission, delivery; *prosphorá* (4376), offer.

3029. λίαν *lían*; adv. Much, very, exceedingly. Used with a verb (Matt 2:16; 27:14; Luke 23:8; 2 Tim 4:15; 2 John 1:4; 3 John 1:3; Sept.: Gen 4:5; 1 Sam 11:15); with an adj. (Matt 4:8; 8:28; Mark 9:3; Sept.: Gen 1:31); with other adv. (Mark 1:35; 16:2); with the prep. *hupér* (5228), above, occurs as *huperlían* (2 Cor 11:5;

12:11), meaning to pretend to be much above the apostles, "super" apostles.

Syn.: *sphódra* (4970), very much, exceedingly; *sphodrós* (4971), exceedingly; *perissós* (4057), out of measure, exceedingly, more; *perissotéros* (4056), abundantly; *hyperekperissoú* (*húper* [5228], above; *ek* [1537], of; *persissoú* [4053], abundantly), superabundantly; *polús* (4183), much; *megálōs* (3171), greatly; *huperbolḗ* (5236), exceeding greatness; *hikanós* (2425), much.

Ant.: *elássōn* (1640), less; *hḗssōn* (2276), inferior, less; *cheírōn* (5501), worse.

3030. λίβανος líbanos; gen. *libánou*, masc. noun. The tree which produces frankincense, growing in Arabia and around Mount Lebanon. A transparent and fragrant gum which distills from incisions in the tree. It was used for incense (cf. Ex 30:34; Matt 2:11; Rev 18:13; Sept.: Lev 2:1; 5:11). The ritual use of frankincense in the OT, as among the heathen, denotes direct adoration (Lev 2:2). The frankincense offered by the Magi signified the divinity of the Holy Child, the gold representing His royalty, the myrrh either His healing powers or the prospect of His suffering.

Deriv.: *libanōtós* (3031), a vessel to hold incense.

3031. λιβανωτός libanōtós; gen. *libanōtoú*, masc. noun from *líbanos* (3030), frankincense. An incense vessel or censer (Rev 8:3, 5).

Syn.: *thumiatḗrion* (2369), a vessel for burning incense.

3032. Λιβερτῖνος Libertínos; gen. *Libertínou*, masc. proper noun. Libertine, meaning freed-man. The Libertines, mentioned only in Acts 6:9, were Jews who, having been taken prisoner in the Syrian wars, were carried to Rome and reduced to slavery but afterward freed. In Jerusalem, they had a synagogue, where they came in collision with Stephen.

3033. Λιβύη Libúē; gen. *Libúēs*, fem. proper noun. Libya, a country in northern Africa, west of Egypt. Inhabited by a Hamitic race under the name of Lehabim or Lubim (Acts 2:10; Sept.: Ezek 30:5).

3034. λιθάζω litházō; fut. *lithásō*, from *líthos* (3037), a stone. To stone or pelt with stones in order to wound or kill (John 10:31–33; 11:8; Acts 5:26; 14:19; 2 Cor 11:25; Heb 11:37; Sept.: 2 Sam 16:6, 13).

Deriv.: *katalitházō* (2642), to cast stones at.

3035. λίθινος líthinos; fem. *lithínē*, neut. *líthinon*, adj. from *líthos* (3037), a stone. Made of stone (John 2:6; 2 Cor 3:3; Rev 9:20; Sept.: Gen 35:14; Ex 31:18).

Syn.: *petrṓdēs* (4075), rocky, stony ground; *pṓrōsis* (4457), callousness; *sklērós* (4642), hard.

3036. λιθοβολέω lithoboléō; contracted *lithobolṓ*, fut. *lithobolḗsō*, from *líthos* (3037), a stone, and *bállō* (906), to throw, cast. To pelt with stones or stone to death (Matt 21:35; 23:37; Mark 12:4; Luke 13:34; Acts 7:58, 59; 14:5); as a Mosaic punishment (John 8:5 [cf. Lev 20:10; Deut 22:22]). See also Heb 12:20 (cf. Ex 19:13; Lev 20:27; 24:14, 16).

3037. λίθος líthos; gen. *líthou*, masc. noun. A stone. Used of small stones (Matt 4:3, 6; 7:9; Mark 5:5; Sept.: 1 Chr 12:2; 2 Chr 1:15); of building stones (Luke 19:44); of the size and beauty of the stones with which the temple was built (Matt 24:1, 2; Mark 13:1, 2; Luke 21:5, 6; Sept.: Ezra 5:8); of a millstone, *líthos mulikós* (3457) (Mark 9:42; Rev 18:21); of a stone for covering the door or entrance to a tomb (Matt 27:60, 66; 28:2; Mark 15:46; Luke 24:2; John 11:38; Sept.: Gen 29:2, 3, 8, 10); of stone tablets (2 Cor 3:7 [cf. Ex 31:5]); of idols carved in stone, statues of marble (Acts 17:29; see also Deut 4:28; 28:36); of precious stones (Rev 17:4; 18:12, 16; 21:11, 19). Figuratively (1 Cor 3:12;

Rev 4:3; 21:11; see Sept.: 2 Sam 12:30; 1 Kgs 10:2, 11; Ezek 10:1); of Christ as the chief cornerstone (Eph 2:20; 1 Pet 2:6). See *akrogōniaíos* (204), chief corner; as a living stone (1 Pet 2:4; see the verb *záō* [2198], to live); as a stumbling-stone (Rom 9:32, 33; 1 Pet 2:7), meaning the occasion or cause of fall, destruction to the Jews since they took offense at Christ's person and character and thus rejected their spiritual deliverer (cf. Isa 8:14). Used of Christians as living stones (1 Pet 2:5).

Deriv.: *litházō* (3034), to stone; *líthinos* (3035), of stone; *lithoboléō* (3036), to stone to death; *lithóstrōtos* (3038), stone pavement; *chrusólithos* (5555), a chrysolite.

Syn.: *pétros* (4074), a piece of a rock, a detached stone or boulder; *pétra* (4073), a mass of rock; *psêphos* (5586), a smooth stone, a pebble worn smooth as by water or polished indicating a pebble cast for a vote.

3038. Λιθόστρωτος *Lithóstrōtos*; gen. *lithostrṓtou*, masc.-fem., neut. *lithóstrōton*, adj. from *líthos* (3037), a stone, and *strṓnnumi* (4766), to strew or spread. Stone-strewed or paved. In the NT, the neut. is used subst., *tó Lithóstrōton*, the pavement, a road paved with stones or mosaics, common not only in Rome but imitated also in the provinces. Julius Caesar in his military expeditions took with him pieces of marble ready cut and fitted in order that, wherever he encamped, they might be laid down in the praetorium. In John 19:13, it means that Pilate led Jesus out of the praetorium (where the Jews could not enter) and set Him upon the public tribunal which stood upon a stone-paved area. In Hebr., it is called *Gabbathá* (1042).

3039. λικμάω *likmáō*; contracted *likmô*, fut. *likmḗsō*, from *likmós* (n.f.), a winnowing fork. To winnow grain. In the East it is done by throwing it with a fork against the wind which scatters the straw and chaff. The figurative meaning is to scatter, disperse (Sept.: Isa 17:13; Amos 9:9). In the NT used symbolically (Matt 21:44; Luke 20:18, where it means it shall scatter him to the winds, crush him in pieces, make chaff of him). See Sept.: Dan 2:44; Job 27:21.

Syn.: *skorpízō* (4650), to disperse; *diaskorpízo* (1287), to scatter abroad; *diaspeírō* (1289), to scatter the seed; *dialúō* (1262), to dissolve.

Ant.: *sullégō* (4816), to collect, gather up.

3040. λιμήν *limḗn*; gen. *liménos*, masc. noun. A haven, harbor, port (Acts 27:12; Sept.: Ps 107:30; see also Gen 49:13; Acts 27: 8 in the pl. "fair havens").

3041. λίμνη *límnē*; gen. *límnēs*, fem. noun from *leíbō* (n.f.), to pour. Any standing water, pool, lake. Used of the Lake of Gennesareth (Luke 5:1). Used in an absolute sense (Luke 5:2; 8:22, 33); of a lake of burning sulfur, meaning *Géenna* (1067), Gehenna (Rev 19:20; 20:10, 14, 15; 21:8; Sept.: Ps 107:35; 114:8).

3042. λιμός *limós*; gen. *limoú*, masc. noun. It refers to hunger, famine, want of food. It is spoken of single persons suffering hunger (Luke 15:17; Rom 8:35; 2 Cor 11:27; Sept.: Lam 5:10); of cities or countries experiencing famine, scarcity of grain (Matt 24:7) where the difference between *limoí*, famines, and *loimoí* (3061), pestilences, is that the first is spelled with only *i* and the second with *oi*. See also Mark 13:8; Luke 4:25; 15:14; 21:11; Acts 7:11; 11:28; Rev 6:8; 18:8; Sept.: Gen 12:10; Ruth 1:1.

Ant.: *plēsmonḗ* (4140), a filling up, satiety; *chórtasma* (5527), food, sustenance.

3043. λίνον *línon*; gen. *linoú*, neut. noun. Flax. In the NT it generally means what is made of flax, i.e., linen for clothing (Rev 15:6 [cf. Sept.: Isa 19:9]). A strip of linen used for the wick of a candle or lamp (Matt 12:20, meaning that Christ will not extinguish the faint and almost expiring light, quoted from Isa 42:3. The Messiah will speak peace and comfort to the oppressed and will not add to their sorrows.).

Syn.: *sindṓn* (4616), cloth made of fine linen; *othónion* (3608), fine linen usually used in the pl. referring to the strips of cloth with which the body of the Lord was bound after being wrapped in the *sindṓn*, a wrapping sheet; *bússos* (1040), fine linen.

3044. Λîνος *Línos*; gen. *Línou*, masc. proper noun. Linus, a Christian of Rome, a friend of Paul and Timothy (2 Tim 4:21).

3045. λιπαρός *liparós*; fem. *lipará*, neut. *liparón*, adj. from *lípos* (n.f.), grease, fat. In the Sept.: Neh 9:35, the "fat land" means full, fresh. In the NT, used of things, especially as belonging to ornament and luxury, shining, freshness, sumptuous (Rev 18:14).

3046. λίτρα *lítra*; gen. *lítras*, fem. noun. A measurement of weight, a pound (John 12:3; 19:39). This measurement varied in different countries. The Roman *litra* or *libra* was divided into twelve ounces and was equivalent to about a pound.

Syn.: *mná* (3414), a Semitic word, both a weight and a sum of money. In the Hebr., one hundred shekels; in Attic Gr., one hundred *drachmaí* (1406). In weight it is about fifteen ounces.

3047. λίψ *líps*; gen. *libós*; masc. noun. The south or southwest wind (Acts 27:12; Sept.: Gen 13:14; Num 2:10; Ps 78:26).

3048. λογία *logía*; gen. *logías*, fem. noun from *légō* (3004), to gather, collect. A collection, usually of money (1 Cor 16:1, 2).

3049. λογίζομαι *logízomai*; fut. *logísomai*, fut. pass. *logisthḗsomai*, aor. *elogisámēn*; aor. pass. *elogísthēn*, mid. deponent from *lógos* (3056), reason, word, account. To reckon, impute, number.

(I) Actually, the verb *logízomai* means to put together with one's mind, to count, to occupy oneself with reckonings or calculations.

(II) In the NT, the pres. used in a pass. sense, as in Rom 4:4, 5, 24; 9:8, also means to reckon, count (1 Cor 13:5); to reason (Mark 11:31); to think (Rom 2:3; 8:18; 1 Cor 13:11; 2 Cor 3:5; 10:7, 11; Phil 4:8; 1 Pet 5:12). To count something to somebody means to reckon something to a person, to put to his account, either in his favor or for what he must be answerable (Rom 4:3, 4, 6, 8, 9, 11, 22; 2 Cor 5:19; Gal 3:6; 2 Tim 4:16; James 2:23).

In Rom 4:11, the expression is used as a technical term applied to God's act of justification which is more fully explained in verse six. It is that imputation of righteousness whose correlative is freedom from guilt, and the emphasis clearly rests upon "it is counted" (Rom 4:10, 23, 24).

In Acts 19:27, it means esteeming or reckoning as of no account. Such a usage is common with Paul (Rom 2:26; 9:8). When something is counted to somebody for something, it denotes that it is imputed to the person in a substitutionary manner. The expression, "to count someone with somebody," means to number someone with (Mark 15:28; Luke 22:37).

Logízomai also means to reckon, to value or esteem (Rom 8:36; 1 Cor 4:1; 2 Cor 10:2; 12:6); followed by the acc. with the inf. (Rom 14:14; 2 Cor 11:5; Phil 3:13); followed by *hóti* (3754), that (Heb 11:19); followed by two acc. (Rom 6:11). To account, to conclude or infer, to believe (Rom 3:28).

Deriv.: *analogízomai* (357), to estimate, consider; *dialogízomai* (1260), to reckon distributively, to settle with one, to consider, deliberate; *logismós* (3053), reckoning; *paralogízomai* (3884), to beguile, deceive; *sullogízomai* (4817), to reason with.

Syn.: *dokéō* (1380), to think, suppose; *ellogéō* (1677), to put to a person's account, to reckon, impute; *kataxióō* (2661), to count worthy; *noéō* (3539), to perceive, understand; *huponoéō* (5282), to suppose, surmise, think; *nomízō* (3543), to suppose; *phronéō* (5426), to think; *oíomai* (3633) I suppose, think; *krínō* (2919), to judge, reckon; *arithméō* (705), to count; *katarithméō* (2674), to count along; *egkrínō* (1469), to reckon along; *sugkatapsēphízō* (4785), to reckon together with; *katalégō* (2639), to count in; *dialégomai* (1256), to ponder; *sullogízomai* (4817), to compute, reason; *sugkleíō* (4788), to include; *ginōskō* (1097), to know, recognize.

Ant.: *exouthenéō* (1848), to make of no account, despise; *agnoéō* (50), not to know, to ignore; *apodokimázō* (593), to reject as the result of examination and disapproval, disallow, despise; *athetéō* (114), to set aside, modify, disannul, reject; *kataphronéō* (2706), to despise; *periphronéō* (4065), to despise; *akuróō* (208), to make of no effect, disannul; *kenóō* (2758), to make of no effect, to empty; *katargéō* (2673), to make void, of no effect, to abolish.

3050. λογικός *logikós*; fem. *logikē*, neut. *logikón*, adj. from *lógos* (3056), reason, word. Pertaining to reason and therefore reasonable, or pertaining to speech as reasonable expression. In Rom 12:1, the "reasonable service" or worship is to be understood as that service to God which implies intelligent meditation or reflection without the kind of heathen practices intimated in 1 Cor 12:2 and without the obsolete system of OT worship (Isa 1:12–15).

In 1 Pet 2:2, the phrase *logikón gála*, literally "logical milk," refers to the spiritual nourishment found in the Word of God. *Lógos*, from which *logikós* is derived, means reason, and is often used to describe God's intelligence expressed in human speech or form (John 1:1, 14). Some reach this interpretation merely from the context of the passage, as a spiritual explanation of the words. Others reach this interpretation by recognizing that it is not only true but that it is reasonable that the Word of God is our nourishment (cf. Deut 8:3; Matt 4:4). The second adj. *ádolon* (97), unadulterated, agrees with this, meaning that the Word of God, when not mixed with human error, is nourishing.

3051. λόγιον *lógion*; gen. *logíou*, neut. noun of *lógios* (3052) an orator. Sentence, declaration, especially the utterance of the oracles of the gods, equivalent to *chrēsmós*. In Acts 7:38; Rom 3:2; Heb 5:12; 1 Pet 4:11, the expression, *tá lógia*, in the neut. pl., means the declarations of God, and differs from *ho lógos*, the Word of God, i.e., that which God has to say. The neut. pl. *tá lógia* denotes rather the historical manifestations of this Word of God. In 1 Pet 4:11, it does not say the Word (*lógon*) of God, but *lógia Theoú*, the object being to give prominence to the contrast between the word and the mere subjectivity of the speaker.

3052. λόγιος *lógios*; fem. *logía*, gen. *logíou*, masc.-fem., neut. *lógion*, adj. from *lógos* (3056), reason, thought, expression, word. Learned, eloquent (Acts 18:24). As a subst., a learned person, an orator, the neut. of which is *lógion* (3051), an oracle.

3053. λογισμός *logismós*; gen. *logismoú*, masc. noun from *logízomai* (3049), to reckon. A reckoning, calculation, consideration, reflection (Rom 2:15). In the Class. Gr. writers, used of the consideration and reflection preceding and determining conduct, the same meaning as in John 11:50, *dialogízomai* (1260), to deliberate. In the sense of device, counsel (2 Cor 10:5; Sept.: Prov 6:18; Jer 11:19).

Syn.: *boulé* (1012), purpose or thought still in the mind; *nóema* (3540), thought.

Ant.: *aphrosúnē* (877), senselessness, folly.

3054. λογομαχέω *logomachéō*; contracted *logomachō̂*, fut. *logomachēsō*, from *logomáchos* (n.f.), warring about words. To contend or debate about words, dispute about trifles (2 Tim 2:14).

Deriv.: *logomachía* (3055), word battle or dispute about trifles.

Syn.: *dialégomai* (1256), to argue, dispute; *dialogízomai* (1260) and *suzētéō* (4802), to discuss.

3055. λογομαχία *logomachía*; gen. *logomachías*, fem. noun from *logomachéō* (3054), to strive about words. Strife of words or dispute about trifles (1 Tim 6:4).

Syn.: *paradiatribḗ* (3859), incessant wrangling; *antilogía* (485), contradiction, dispute; *suzḗtēsis* (4803), a discussion, disputation.

Ant.: *sumphonía* (4858), agreement.

3056. λόγος *lógos*; gen. *lógou*, masc. noun from *légō* (3004), to speak intelligently. Intelligence, word as the expression of that intelligence, discourse, saying, thing.

(I) Word, both the act of speaking and the thing spoken.

(A) Word, as uttered by the living voice, a speaking, speech, utterance (Matt 8:8; Luke 7:7; 23:9; 1 Cor 14:9; Heb 12:19); a saying, discourse, conversation (Matt 12:37; 15:12; 19:22; 22:15; 26:1; John 4:29; Acts 5:24). Metonymically, the power of speech, delivery, oratory, eloquence (1 Cor 12:8; 2 Cor 11:6; Eph 6:19). To speak a word against someone (Matt 12:32); to someone (Luke 12:10). The Word of God, meaning His omnipotent voice, decree (2 Pet 3:5, 7; Sept.: Ps 32:6 [cf. Gen 1:3; Ps 148:5]).

(B) An emphatic word, meaning a saying, declaration, sentiment uttered. **(1)** Generally (Matt 10:14; Luke 4:22; 20:20; John 6:60; Sept.: Prov 4:4, 20). In reference to words or declarations, e.g., which precede (Matt 7:24, 26; 15:12; 19:22; Mark 7:29; John 2:22; 4:50; 6:60; 7:40; 10:19; Acts 5:24; Titus 3:8; Rev 19:9); which follow (John 12:38; Acts 20:35; Rom 9:9; 13:9; 1 Cor 15:54; 1 Tim 3:1; Sept.: 1 Kgs 2:4). Followed by the gen. of thing (Heb 7:28); the word, declaration of a prophet, meaning prediction, prophecy (Luke 3:4; John 12:38;

Acts 15:15; 2 Pet 1:19; Rev 1:3). With the meaning of a proverb, maxim (John 4:37). **(2)** In reference to religion, religious duties, with the meaning of doctrine, precept (Acts 15:24; 18:15; Titus 1:9; Heb 2:2); words of faith (1 Tim 4:6); word of men (1 Thess 2:13; 2 Tim 2:17); of a teacher (John 15:20); especially of God, the Word of God, meaning divine revelation and declaration, oracle (John 5:38; 10:35); as announcing good, divine promise (John 5:24; Rom 9:6; Heb 4:2; Sept.: Ps 50:6), or evil (Rom 3:4 from Ps 51:4; Rom 9:28 from Isa 10:22, 23; Heb 4:12). In relation to duties, precept (Mark 7:13; 8:55; Sept.: Ex 35:1). Of the divine declarations, precepts, oracles, relating to the instructions of men in religion, the Word of God, i.e., the divine doctrines and precepts of the gospel, the gospel itself (Luke 5:1; John 17:6; Acts 4:29, 31; 8:14; 1 Cor 14:36; 2 Cor 4:2; Col 1:25; 1 Thess 2:13; Titus 1:3; Heb 13:7). With "of God" implied (Mark 16:20; Luke 1:2; Acts 10:44; Phil 1:14; 2 Tim 4:2; James 1:21; 1 Pet 2:8; Rev 12:11); the word of truth (2 Cor 6:7; Eph 1:13; 2 Tim 2:15; James 1:18); the word of life (Phil 2:16); the word of salvation (Acts 13:26); the word of the kingdom (Matt 13:19); with the kingdom implied (Matt 13:20; Mark 4:14); the word of the gospel (Acts 15:7); the word of the cross (1 Cor 1:18); the word of His grace (Acts 14:3; 20:32). In the same sense of Christ, the word of Christ (John 5:24; 14:23, 24; Col 3:16); the word of the Lord (Acts 8:25).

(C) Word or words, meaning talk, discourse, speech, the act of holding forth. **(1)** Particularly: **(a)** Matt 22:15, "that they may entrap him in word" (a.t.); Luke 9:28; Acts 14:12, the one leading in the word; 2 Cor 10:10; with *en* (1722), in, meaning in word or discourse (1 Tim 4:12; James 3:2); in flattering words (1 Thess 2:5); with *diá* (1223), through, by, meaning by discourse or orally (Acts 15:27; 2 Thess 2:2, 15). In agreement *lógos* and *érgon* (2041), work, meaning word and deed (2 Cor 10:11; Col 3:17). *Lógos* and *dúnamis*

(1411), power (1 Cor 4:19, 20; 1 Thess 1:5). In Heb 5:11, "of whom we have much to say" (a.t.). With the gen. in 1 Tim 4:5, "through the word of God and supplication" (a.t.). **(b)** Of teachers, meaning discourse, teaching, preaching, instruction (Matt 7:28; 26:1; Luke 4:32, 36; John 4:41; Acts 2:41; 13:15; 20:7; 1 Cor 1:17; 2:1, 4; 1 Tim 5:17; 1 Pet 3:1). **(c)** Of those who relate something as a narration, story (John 4:39; Acts 2:22). Metonymically for history, treatise, meaning a book of narration (Acts 1:1). **(d)** In the sense of conversation (Luke 24:17); answer, reply (Matt 5:37). **(2)** Metonymically for the subject of discourse, meaning topic, matter, thing. **(a)** Generally (Matt 19:11; Luke 1:4; Acts 8:21; Sept.: 2 Sam 3:13; 11:18). **(b)** Specifically a matter of dispute, discussion, question, e.g., judicial (Acts 19:38); moral (Matt 21:24).

(D) Word, meaning talk, rumor, report (Matt 28:15; Mark 1:45; John 21:23). Followed by *perí* (4012), about, with the gen. (Luke 5:15; 7:17; Acts 11:22; Sept.: 1 Kgs 10:6). Mere talk, pretense, show (Col 2:23).

(II) Reason, the reasoning faculty as that power of the soul which is the basis of speech, rationality.

(A) A reason, ground, cause (Matt 5:32; Acts 10:29; Sept.: 2 Sam 13:22). With *katá* (2596) meaning with reason, reasonable, for good cause (Acts 18:14). In the sense of argument (Acts 2:40).

(B) Reason as demanded or assigned, meaning reckoning, account. **(1)** Used in an absolute sense (Heb 13:17; 1 Pet 4:5). **(2)** With *sunaírō* (4868), to reckon, compute together, meaning to take up account with someone, reckon with (Matt 18:23; 25:19); with *apodídōmi* (591), to give over, meaning to render an account of a business management (Luke 16:2). **(3)** Metaphorically with *dídōmi* (1325), to give, or *apodídōmi*, meaning to give an account, the relation and reasons of any transaction, explanation (Acts 19:40). With *aitéō* (154), to ask, beg, meaning to ask for a reason from someone (1 Pet 3:15). In Heb 4:13, "with whom we have

to do" or we have to render an account. **(4)** With *poiéō* (4160), to make, do, to make account of, i.e., to regard, care for (Acts 20:24), meaning I take into account none of these things, I am not moved by them. **(5)** Followed by *perí* (4012), concerning someone or something (Matt 12:36; Rom 14:12).

(III) The word *Lógos* in John 1:1, 14; 1 John 1:1; and Rev 9:13 stands for the preincarnate Christ, the spiritual, divine nature spoken of in the Jewish writings before and about the time of Christ, under various names, e.g., Son of Man (Dan 7:13).

(IV) As to the distinction between *lógos* and *laliá* (2981), speech:

John 8:43 is a problematic passage in which we have both words, *laliá* and *lógos*, used by our Lord. He was debating with the Pharisees. They were listening to what He had to say, but they were not capable of understanding because they did not want to understand. The Lord said to them, "Why do ye not understand my speech [*lalián*]?" In other words, What I am saying to you seems to have no meaning whatsoever. And why did it have no meaning? The reason is explained in the balance of the paragraph, "Even because ye cannot hear my word [*lógon*]," or better still, "Because you cannot understand and obey [*akoúō* {191}] my *lógon*," (a.t.) or speech, with its intended meaning. What the Lord really meant is that those who will not give room in their hearts to His truth will not understand His speech or utterance, the outward form of His language which His Word (*lógos*) assumes. Those who are of God hear God's words (*rhḗmata*, pl. of *rhḗma* [4487], John 3:34; 8:47). The word *rhḗma* here is equivalent to *lógos*. John 3:34 says that Jesus Christ, being sent of God, speaks exactly God's utterances which those who are of God understand and which those who are not of God do not understand because they do not accept them as the utterance of God.

In John 1:1, Jesus Christ in His preincarnate state is called *ho Lógos*, the Word, presenting Him as the Second Person of the Godhead who is the eternal expression of the divine intelligence and the disclosure of the divine essence. This self-revealing characteristic of God was directed toward, and utterly achieved for mankind in the incarnation (John 1:14, 18).

Deriv.: *álogos* (249), irrational, without intelligence; *analogía* (356), analogy; *analogízomai* (357), to contemplate, consider; *apologéomai* (626), to answer back, respond; *battologéō* (945), to use vain repetitions; *ellogéō* (1677), to account, reckon in; *eulogéō* (2127), to speak well of, bless; *logízomai* (3049), to reckon, impute; *logikós* (3050), reasonable; *lógios* (3052), fluent, orator, intelligent person; *polulogía* (4180), much speaking.

Syn.: *phēmí* (5346), to speak in a prophetic sense; *propheteía* (4394), prophecy, something spoken ahead of its occurrence or spoken forth; *homilía* (3657), homily, communication, speech; *laliá* (2981), speech, not necessarily the result of reasoning, but speaking as contrasted with silence or communication of a message received; *rhéma* (4487), utterance, sayings in particular as contrasted with sayings in their totality; *stóma* (4750), mouth, that which is uttered by the mouth; *eperótēma* (1906), an inquiry, answer; *suzétēsis* (4803), mutual questioning, *phthóggos* (5353), sound of the mouth revealing one's identity; *phémē* (5345), fame, report, that which is being said about someone; *phōné* (5456), voice; *aggelía* (31), message, announcement. With the meaning of reason, excuse: *aitía* (156), reason, cause; *aphormē* (874), occasion. With the meaning of reason, intelligence: *súnesis* (4907), understanding; *sōphrosúnē* (4997), soundness of mind.

3057. λόγχη *lógchē*; gen. *lógchēs*, fem. noun. The point of a weapon. A lance or spear, specifically the iron tip which reaches an enemy (John 19:34).

Syn.: *bélos* (956), arrow, dart; *kéntron* (2759), point, goad, prick.

3058. λοιδορέω *loidoréō*; contracted *loidorṓ*, fut. *loidorḗsō*, from *loídoros* (3060), a reviler. To revile, reproach (John 9:28; Acts 23:4; 1 Cor 4:12; 1 Pet 2:23; Sept.: Deut 33:8).

Deriv.: *antiloidoréō* (486), to revile again.

Syn.: *blasphēméō* (987), to revile, blaspheme; *oneidízō* (3679), to reproach; *chleuázō* (5512), to mock; *muktērízō* (3456), to ridicule; *empaízō* (1702), to jeer; *katageláō* (2606), to deride, laugh to scorn; *theatrízō* (2301), to expose as a spectacle; *hubrízō* (5195), to insult, to use despitefully or shamefully; *atimázō* (818), to dishonor.

Ant.: *ainéō* (134), to speak in praise of.

3059. λοιδορία *loidoría*; gen. *loidorías*, fem. noun from *loidoréō* (3058), to revile. A railing, reproach (1 Tim 5:14; 1 Pet 3:9; Sept.: Prov 20:3).

Syn.: *blasphēmía* (988), blasphemy, evil speaking; *oneidismós* (3680), a reproach, defamation; *óneidos* (3681), a reproach, disgrace; *atimía* (819), a dishonor; *empaigmós* (1701), derision, mocking; *mômos* (3470), blame, blemish; *húbris* (5196), insult, hurt; *anaídeia* (335), insolence.

Ant.: *aínos* (136), praise.

3060. λοίδορος *loídoros*; gen. *loidórou*, masc.-fem., neut. *loídoron*, adj. Railing, reviling. Used also as a subst., meaning a railer, reviler (1 Cor 5:11; 6:10).

Deriv.: *loidoréō* (3058), to revile.

Syn.: *blásphēmos* (989), a blasphemer; *hubristḗs* (5197), an insulter.

3061. λοιμός *loimós*; gen. *loimoú*, masc. noun. Pestilence, plague (Matt 24:7; Luke 21:11). Metaphorically used of a malignant and mischievous person, a pest (Acts 24:5; Sept.: 1 Sam 2:12; 25:25; Ps 1:1; Ezek 7:21). To be distinguished from *limós* (3042), destitution, famine.

Ant.: *eulogía* (2129), blessing.

3062. λοιπός *loipós*; fem. *loipé*, neut. *loipón* (3063), adj. from *leípō* (3007), to leave, lack. Something remaining, in the pl., the remaining ones (Matt 25:11; Acts 2:37; Rom 1:13; 2 Cor 12:13; 2 Pet 3:16). Used in an absolute sense with the def. art., *hoi loipoí*, the rest, the others (Matt 22:6; Mark 16:13; Luke 18:9; Rom 11:7; Rev 2:24; Sept.: Josh 13:27; 17:2). In the neut. pl. acc. with the art., *tá loipá* (Mark 4:19; 1 Cor 11:34; Sept.: 2 Kgs 1:18).

Deriv.: *epíloipos* (1954), remaining; *katáloipos* (2645), remnant.

Syn.: *perísseuma* (4051), that which remains over.

Ant.: *hustérēma* (5303), deficiency, shortcoming; *chreía* (5532), lack; *hustérēsis* (5304), the act of causing deficiency.

3063. λοιπόν *loipón*; adj., neut. sing. of *loipós* (3062), remaining. With the neut. def. art. *tó*, used of time meaning henceforth, hence forward (Matt 26:45; Mark 14:41 meaning "Sleep ye ever still" [a.t.]; 1 Cor 7:29; Heb 10:13); as to the rest, finally (Eph 6:10; Phil 3:1; 4:8; 2 Thess 3:1). With the acc. *loipón*, also, *ho dé loipón* (1 Cor 4:2), as to the rest, finally, but now (Acts 27:20; 1 Cor 1:16; 2 Cor 13:11; 1 Thess 4:1; 2 Tim 4:8).

3064. λοιποῦ *loipoú*; adj., gen. sing. of *loipós* (3062), remaining. Used adv. with the gen. neut. def. art. *toú loipoú*, referring to time meaning in the fut., henceforth (Gal 6:17).

Syn.: *eíta* (1534), furthermore, afterward, then; *leímma* (3005), that which is left, remnant; *katáleimma* (2640), a remnant; *katáloipos* (2645), residue; *apó toú nún* (*apó* [575], from; *ho* [3588], the; *nún* [3568], now), from now on, henceforth.

3065. Λουκᾶς *Loukás*; gen. *Louká*, masc. proper noun. Lucas or Luke (Col 4:14; 2 Tim 4:11; Phile 1:24), possibly an abbreviation of Lucanus or Lucilius, but not of Lucius (Acts 13:1; Rom 16:21). The writer of the Gospel of Luke

and the Acts. The evangelist was not a Jew, as is evident from Col 4:11, 14 where the "beloved physician" is distinguished from those "of the circumcision." The opinion that he was a native of Antioch may have arisen from confusing him with Lucius. That Luke was one of the seventy or of the two who were walking to Emmaus is unlikely, as he was not himself an eyewitness of the gospel facts (Luke 1:2). The way Luke describes diseases in his writings proves him to be an educated physician. He became prominent as the companion of Paul in his later journeys. He joined the apostle at Troas (Acts 16:8–10) and accompanied him to Philippi on his second journey, rejoining him some years later at the same place (Acts 20:5). He remained with Paul until the close of his second Roman captivity (2 Tim 4:11). The Gospel which bears Luke's name and the Acts were written primarily for the use of one called Theophilus (Luke 1:3; Acts 1:1).

A large number of words are peculiar to Luke's Gospel, and to him we are indebted for nearly all the chronological notices which link the gospel facts with ancient history in general. The narrative is more complete than the others and contains several portions peculiar to it, e.g., the account of the Nativity, the presentation in the temple, the miraculous draught of fishes, the sending out of the seventy, the parables of the good Samaritan, the barren fig tree, the lost sheep, the prodigal son, the unjust employer, and the account of the rich man and Lazarus. The Gospel was written before the destruction of Jerusalem and also before the Acts (Acts 1:1). It was probably written at Caesarea Maritime on the Mediterranean coast at the same time Paul was a prisoner there between A.D. 58–60. Some, however, date it still earlier.

3066. Λούκιος *Loúkios*; gen. *Loukíou* masc. proper noun. Lucius, a kinsman of the Apostle Paul (Rom 16:21) and according to tradition, bishop of Cenchraea, the place from where the Epistle to the Romans was written. His name is identical with that of Lucius of Cyrene, a Christian teacher in Antioch (Acts 13:1).

3067. λουτρόν *loutrón*; gen. *loutroú*, neut. noun from *loúō* (3068), to bathe. A basin or laver for washing, the washing itself. For its possible relativity to baptism in Eph 5:26, see *báptisma* (908), baptism. It is used metaphorically of the Word of God as the instrument of spiritual cleansing. In Titus 3:5, "the washing [bath] of regeneration" brings to mind the close connection between cleansing from sin and regeneration (cf. John 3:8; Rom 6:4; 2 Cor 5:17). Although these two passages are often, and with valid exegetical support, classified as relating to baptism, the language of the texts is not so unequivocal that such a claim can be made with dogmatic certitude. The weakest case is Titus 3:5. The washing mentioned can easily be understood metaphorically. Regeneration itself is an operation portrayed in Scripture as effecting a spiritual cleansing (Ezek 36:25, 26; John 3:5; 1 Cor 6:11). In addition, since the expression "washing of regeneration" stands parallel to "renewal of the Holy Ghost", it is more natural to assume the force of the gen. is also parallel. The gen. of latter phrase is certainly subjective. Hence, the words "washing of regeneration" refer to the washing produced by regeneration. Any other gen. classification would not suit both constructions and to treat them differently would destroy the literary symmetry of the passage. The possible exception to this would be a descriptive gen., but this would seem to be an awkward way to treat the personal reference to the Holy Spirit. Not so easily disputed is its meaning in Eph 5:26 where it is said that the purpose of Christ's sacrifice is to sanctify the church "and cleanse it with the washing of water by the word." Here *tó loutró* (dat. sing.) is modified by *toú húdatos* (*húdōr* [5204], water), of the water. The def. art. points to a particular occasion or use of water, one with which the readers would have been readily familiar. It has been suggested that this is a reference to the custom practiced by Jews and Gentiles alike of brides taking preparatory baths prior to the marriage ceremony. While this may be the source of Paul's analogy, it does not settle the question of where and when such a cleansing is accomplished. What is the corresponding reality to such a figure? Proponents of the baptismal interpretation say that either the washing is at once the figure and the reality, or that no figure is present. In this latter argument, it is contended that the washing is a direct reference to baptism itself. This indeed may be the case. However, Paul is careful to finish his statement with the phrase *en rhḗmati* (*en* [1722], in; *rhḗma* [4487], word), by (the) word. Whatever cleansing is signified by the washing of water, it is accomplished by the word. The anarthrous construction makes the expression adv. indicating the manner (or means) of the cleansing action, that it is in word form, through teaching or preaching, that the cleansing is effected. The regenerative and cleansing powers of God's Word are attested to throughout Scripture (John 15:3; James 1:18; 1 Pet 1:23). Therefore, it is plausible to understand Paul to be saying that the word of God is the cleansing agent in sanctification and it is the reality for which washing stands as a figure. In Class. Gr., the pl. *loutrá* denotes propitiatory offerings and offerings for purification.

Syn.: *katharismós* (2512), cleansing.

Ant.: *akatharsía* (167), uncleanness.

3068. λούω *loúō*; fut. *loúsō*. To bathe oneself, used of washing the whole body and not part of it as indicated by *níptō* (3538). Both of these verbs refer to the washing of living persons while *plúnō* (4150) refers to the washing of inanimate things. Trans. spoken only of persons, followed by the acc. (Acts 9:37). With the acc. implied and followed by *apó* (575), from (Acts 16:33). Pass. (John

13:10; Heb 10:22; 2 Pet 2:22; Sept.: Lev 8:6; Ruth 3:3). Figuratively to cleanse, purify, with the acc. and *apó* (575), from (Rev 1:5 [{TR} cf. Sept.: Isa 1:16]). For the relationship of the verb *loúō* and *loutrón* (3067), bath, see *báptisma* (908), baptism.

Deriv.: *apoloúō* (628), to wash fully; *loutrón* (3067), bath.

Syn.: *katharízō* (2511), to cleanse.

3069. Λύδδα Lúdda; gen. *Lúddēs*, fem. proper noun. Lydda, the Gr. name for the Hebr. Lod, a flourishing town situated in the plain of Sharon a few miles east of Joppa on the road to Jerusalem, today the site of the Tel Aviv Airport. It was burned several times by the Romans, but again rebuilt. Vespasian gave it the name of Diospolis (City of Jupiter), but the old name prevailed. Here Peter healed the paralytic, Aeneas (Acts 9:33–35, 38; see 1 Chr 8:12).

3070. Λυδία Ludía; gen. *Ludías*, fem. proper noun. Lydia.

(I) A coastal region of Asia Minor extending along the Mediterranean from the promontory of Mycale to the mouth of the Hermas. It formed the center of a great empire under Croesus. Later it belonged to Syria, Pergamus, and the Romans. Its principal cities were Sardis, Thyatira, and Philadelphia.

(II) The name of a woman of Thyatira residing at Philippi, a dealer in purple (Acts 16:14, 40).

3071. Λυκαονία Lukaonía; gen. *Lukaonías*, fem. proper noun. Lycaonia. A province of Asia Minor which the Apostle Paul visited twice (Acts 14:6). It was separated from Phrygia and bounded on the north by Galatia, east by Cappadocia, south by Cilicia, and west by Pisidia and Phrygia. Its principal industry was wool. Its chief towns were Iconium, Derbe, and Lystra. Their language (Acts 14:11) is thought to have been either Syrian or a corrupted Gr. dialect. Their civilization apparently was not very highly developed.

3072. Λυκαονιστί Lukaonistí; adv. In the Lycaonian speech (Acts 14:11). See *Lukaonía* (3071), Lycaonia.

3073. Λυκία Lukía; gen. *Lukías*, fem. proper noun. Lycia, a region of Asia Minor extending along the Mediterranean just opposite the island of Rhodes. Its two cities, Patara and Myra, were very rich. In the reign of Claudius it became a Roman province. Paul visited both Patara (Acts 21:1) and Myra (Acts 27:5).

3074. λύκος lúkos; gen. *lúkou*, masc. noun. A wolf (Matt 10:16; Luke 10:3; John 10:12; Sept.: Isa 11:6). Metaphorically used of a rapacious and violent person, wolf-like (Matt 7:15; Acts 20:29; Sept.: Zeph 3:3).

3075. λυμαίνομαι lumaínomai; fut. *lumainoúmai*, mid. deponent from *lúmē* (n.f.), destruction. To ravage, waste, make havoc of. Metaphorically, it means to disgrace as by insult, treat with indignity, injure, destroy (Acts 8:3; Sept.: Jer 31:18; Amos 1:11).

Syn.: *diaskorpízō* (1287), to scatter abroad; *porthéō* (4199), to ravage.

Ant.: *euodóō* (2137), to help prosper; *boēthéō* (997), to help.

3076. λυπέω lupéō; contracted *lupó*, fut. *lupésō*, from *lúpē* (3077), sorrow. Trans. to grieve, afflict with sorrow; mid. or pass., to be grieved, sad, sorrowful (Matt 14:9; 17:23; 18:31; 19:22; 26:22, 37; Mark 10:22; 14:19; John 16:20; 21:17; 2 Cor 2:2, 4, 5; 6:10; 7:8, 9, 11; 1 Thess 4:13; 1 Pet 1:6; Sept.: Deut 15:10; 2 Sam 19:3; Jon 4:1). With the meaning of to cause grief, offend (Rom 14:15; Eph 4:30).

Deriv.: *sullupéō* (4818), to sorrow together.

Syn.: *penthéō* (3996), mourn; *thrēnéō* (2354), bewail; *kóptō* (2875), to beat the breast, an outward sign of an inward grief; *odunáō* (3600), to cause pain, anguish; *stenochōréō* (4729), to crowd into a narrow space, to be straitened, in distress; *sunéchō* (4912), in the pass., to be pressed, thronged; *basanízō* (928), to torture; *skúllō* (4660), to trouble, vex, annoy; *tarássō* (5015), to trouble; *thlíbō* (2346), to afflict; *enochléō* (1776), to vex; *anastatóō* (387), to stir up; *thorubéō* (2350), to be in an uproar; *adēmonéō* (85), to be in distress; *turbázō* (5182), to disturb, trouble; *diaponéō* (1278), in the pass., to be troubled as the result of pain and toil.

Ant.: *chaírō* (5463), to rejoice; *agalliáō* (21), to rejoice greatly, exult; *euphraínō* (2165), to cheer, gladden; *kaucháomai* (2744), boast, glory, rejoice; *katakaucháomai* (2620), to glory, boast against.

3077. λύπη lúpē; gen. *lúpēs*, fem. noun. Grief, sorrow (Luke 22:45; John 16:6, 20–22; Rom 9:2; 2 Cor 2:1, 3, 7; 7:10; 9:7; Phil 2:27; Heb 12:11; Sept.: Gen 42:38; Jon 4:1). Metonymically for cause of grief, grievance, trouble (1 Pet 2:19; Sept.: Prov 31:6).

Deriv.: *alupóteros* (253), less sorrowful; *lupéō* (3076), to make sorry; *perílupos* (4036), surround with grief.

Syn.: *katépheia* (2726), a downcast look expressive of sorrow; *odúnē* (3601), pain, distress, sorrow; *ōdín* (5604), a birth pang, travail; *pénthos* (3997), mourning; *stenochōría* (4730), anguish, distress; *thrēnos* (2355), wailing, lamentation; *kópos* (2873), weariness; *sunochḗ* (4928), anxiety, distress; *básanos* (931), torture, torment; *pónos* (4192), pain; *tarachḗ* (5016), disturbance, trouble; *thlípsis* (2347), tribulation, affliction; *thórubos* (2351), disturbance.

Ant.: *chará* (5479), joy; *agallíasis* (20), exultation, exuberant joy; *euphrosúnē* (2167), gladness.

3078. Λυσανίας Lusanías; gen. *Lusaníou*, masc. proper noun. Lysanias, governor of Abilene, which was a small district of Palestine on the eastern slopes

of Anti-Libanus, of which Abila on the river Darada was the capital. It was governed by Lysanias in the time of John the Baptist (Luke 3:1).

3079. Λυσίας Lusías; gen. *Lusíou*, masc. proper noun. Lysias, the same as Claudius Lysias, the chief captain or commander of a band of soldiers stationed as a public guard over the temple. He interposed his authority and saved Paul from violence at the hands of a temple mob. Afterwards he sent Paul with a strong guard to the procurator, Felix, at Caesarea Maritime (Acts 23:26; 24:7, 22).

3080. λύσις lúsis; gen. *lúseōs*, fem. noun from *lúō* (3089), to loose, dissolve. A loosening of or from any tie or constraint. Spoken of the conjugal tie, it means separation, divorce (1 Cor 7:27).

Syn.: *diastolé* (1293), difference, setting apart; *schísma* (4978), schism, division; *dichostasía* (1370), dissension, division; *diamerismós* (1267), division, disunion.

Ant.: *súndesmos* (4886), bond, uniting principle; *desmós* (1199), a bond; *zugós* (2218), a yoke, something which joins; *zeuktēría* (2202), a bond.

3081. λυσιτελέω lusiteléō, contracted *lusitelō*, fut. *lusitelēsō*, from *lusitelḗs* (n.f.), paying dues, profitable, which is from *lúō* (3089), to loose, and *télos* (5056), expense, tool, cost. To pay or make good an expense incurred, to make oneself useful or to be useful, profitable (Luke 17:2).

Syn.: *sumphérei*, 3d person sing. of *sumphérō* (4851), it is profitable; *ōpheléō* (5623), to benefit.

Ant.: *achreóō* or *achreióō* (889), to make useless.

3082. Λύστρα Lústra; gen. *Lústras*, fem. proper noun. Lystra, a city of Lycaonia (3071). Paul visited there twice, the first time with Barnabas (Acts 14:6–21) when he was saluted as the god Mercury, but afterward was stoned; the second time with Silas (Acts 16:1, 2 used in the neut. with art. *tá*). Timothy was probably born there (2 Tim 3:11).

3083. λύτρον *lútron*; gen. *lútrou*, neut. noun from *lúō* (3089), to loose. Ransom or price paid for redeeming captives, loosing them from their bonds and setting them at liberty. In Matt 20:28 and Mark 10:45, it applies spiritually to the ransom paid by Christ for the delivering of men from the bondage of sin and death. See Sept.: Ex 30:12; Lev 25:24, 51; Num 35:31, 32.
Deriv.: *antílutron* (487), ransom; *lutróō* (3084), to ransom.
Syn.: *timḗ* (5092), price.

3084. λυτρόω *lutróō*; contracted *lutró*, fut. *lutrósō*, from *lútron* (3083), a ransom. To bring forward a ransom. The act. verb is not used of him who gives, but of him who receives it; hence to release on receipt of a ransom. In the mid. voice, to release by payment of a ransom, to redeem; in the pass., to be redeemed or ransomed. Thus *lutróō* means to receive a ransom. In the NT, used in the mid. voice in Luke 24:21; Titus 2:14; it denotes that aspect of the Savior's work wherein He appears as the Redeemer of mankind from bondage (1 Pet 1:18). This bondage was still regarded quite generally as oppression in Luke 24:21 because of the deficient understanding of Christ's death by the Emmaus disciples.
Deriv.: *lútrōsis* (3085), the act of redemption or deliverance; *lutrōtḗs* (3086), redeemer.
Syn.: *sṓzō* (4982), to save, deliver; *diasṓzō* (1295), to rescue completely; *charízomai* (5483), to grant as a favor, show grace; *eleutheróō* (1659), to free; *apallássō* (525), to release, deliver.
Ant.: *doulóō* (1402), to enslave; *aichmalōteúō* (162), to capture; *aichmalōtízō* (163), to make captive.

3085. λύτρωσις *lútrōsis*; gen. *lutróseōs*, fem. noun from *lutróō* (3084), to release on receipt of a ransom. The act of freeing

or releasing, deliverance. In biblical Gr., redemption, deliverance, not with reference to the person delivering, but to the person delivered, and, therefore, in a pass. sense like most subst. ending in -*sis* (Luke 1:68; 2:38). Used of redemption from guilt and punishment of sin brought about by expiation (Heb 9:12; Sept.: Lev 25:48; Ps 111:9; 130:7).
Syn.: *sōtēría* (4991), salvation, rescuing; *sōtḗrion* (4992), the means of salvation; *eleuthería* (1657), freedom, *dikaíōsis* (1347), justification; *áphesis* (859), release.
Ant.: *douleía* (1397), bondage; *aichmalōsía* (161), captivity; *phulakḗ* (5438), prison; *desmōtḗrion* (1201), a dungeon, prison.

3086. λυτρωτής *lutrōtḗs*; gen. *lutrōtoú*, masc. noun from *lutróō* (3084), to release on receipt of a ransom. Redeemer, liberator. In the NT, used only in Acts 7:35 of Moses (Sept.: Ps 19:14; 78:35).
Syn.: *sōtḗr* (4990), savior.
Ant.: *kritḗs* (2923), judge; *olothreutḗs* (3644), destroyer; *desmophúlax* (1200), jailor, keeper of the prison.

3087. λυχνία *luchnía*; gen. *luchnías*, fem. noun from *lúchnos* (3088), a lamp, lantern. A lampstand, candlestick (Matt 5:15; Mark 4:21; Luke 8:16; 11:33; Heb 9:2; Sept.: Ex 25:31; Lev 24:4). In Rev 1:12, 13, 20; 2:1, 5, it symbolizes a Christian church, and in Rev 11:4, a Christian teacher or prophet (in allusion to Zech 4:2).
Syn.: *lampás* (2985), lamp, torch; *phanós* (5322), lantern.

3088. λύχνος *lúchnos*; gen. *lúchnou*, masc. noun. A portable lamp fed with oil, not a candle as commonly translated (Matt 5:15; Mark 4:21; Luke 8:16; 11:33, 36; 12:35, "let your lamps stand burning" [a.t.], i.e., be ready, watch [cf. Matt 25:7; Luke 15:8; 2 Pet 1:19; Rev 18:23; 22:5]). "The lamp of the body" (a.t.) represents the eye (Matt 6:22; Luke 11:34; Sept.: Ex 25:37; Zech 4:2). Metaphorically, of

John the Baptist as a distinguished teacher (John 5:35); of the Messiah, the lamb (Rev 21:23 [cf. Sept.: Ps 119:105; Prov 6:23]).

Deriv.: *luchnía* (3087), lampstand

Syn.: *lampás* (2985), a torch, but frequently fed like a lamp with oil from a little vessel used for the purpose; *phanós* (5322), a lantern or torch,

3089. λύω *lúō*; fut. *lúsō*. To loose, loosen what is fast, bound, meaning to unbind, untie. Trans.

(I) Particularly of loosing something fastened (Mark 1:7; Luke 3:16; John 1:27; Acts 7:33; 13:25; Sept.: Ex 3:5); figuratively, the impediment of the tongue (Mark 7:35); the pains of death (Acts 2:24); "whatsoever you shall loose on earth," (a.t.) or declare as not a part of the individual anymore such as his sins, having been forgiven, as the opposite of *déō* (1210), to bind (Matt 16:19; 18:18); of animals tied, e.g., a colt (Matt 21:2; Mark 11:2, 4; Luke 19:30, 31, 33). Followed by *apó* (575), from (Luke 13:15); of a person swathed in bandages or grave clothes (John 11:44).

(II) Spoken of persons bound, to let go, loose, set free, e.g., prisoners (Acts 22:30; 24:26; Rev 20:3, 7); figuratively (Luke 13:16; 1 Cor 7:27, "Art thou free from a wife?" [a.t.] in antithesis with *dédesai*, bound, from *déō* [1210], to bind; Sept.: Ps 105:20; 146:7).

(III) To loosen, dissolve, i.e., to sever, break (Acts 27:41, "but the stern went to pieces from the violence of the waves" [a.t.]; Rev 5:2, 5, the seals); figuratively of an assembly, to dissolve or break up (Acts 13:43).

(IV) By implication, to destroy, e.g., buildings, to demolish (John 2:19; Eph 2:14); figuratively (1 John 3:8); of the world to be destroyed by fire, to dissolve, melt (2 Pet 3:10–12); figuratively of a law or institution, to loosen its obligation, i.e., either to make void, to do away (Matt 5:19; John 10:35), or to break, to violate (John 7:23 [cf. Matt 5:18]).

Deriv.: *analúō* (360), to return; *apolúō* (630), to dismiss; *dialúō* (1262), to dissolve; *eklúō* (1590), to set free from; *epilúō* (1956), to loose, dissolve; *katalúō* (2647), to loose, unloose; *lúsis* (3080), a loosening, divorce; *lútron* (3083), ransom; *paralúō* (3886), to loosen at or from the side.

Syn.: *chōrízō* (5563), to separate; *apochōrízō* (673), to separate off; *diachōrízō* (1316), to separate throughout, completely; *metaírō* (3332), to remove, lift away; *apallássō* (525), to change from, release, deliver; *metabaínō* (3327), to depart; *aphíēmi* (863), to send forth, dismiss, take away from; *epitrépō* (2010), to allow, let go; *eáō* (1439), to let, permit; *apekdúō* (554), to strip off clothes, put off; *methístēmi* (3179), to remove.

Ant.: *déō* (1210), to bind; *desmeúō* (1195) or *desméō* (1196), to put in bonds; *doulóō* (1402), to make a slave, bring into bondage; *doulagōgéō* (1396), to lead into bondage; *katadoulóō* (2615), to bring into complete bondage; *sumbibázō* (4822), to coalesce, join, knit together; *kolláō* (2853), to glue; *proskolláō* (4347), to stick to; *suzeúgnumi* (4801), to yoke together; *háptomai* (680), to attach oneself, touch; *sunarmologéō* (4883), to fit or frame together.

3090. Λωΐς *Lōΐs*; gen. *Lōΐdos*, fem. proper noun. Lois, the grandmother of Timothy (2 Tim 1:5).

3091. Λώτ *Lṓt*; masc. proper noun transliterated from the Hebr. *Lōṭ* (3876, OT), covering, veil. Lot, the son of Haran and nephew of Abraham. He was born in Ur, a city of Chaldea. Here his father died, and he went with Abraham and Terah to Mesopotamia where the latter died at Haran (Gen 11:31, 32). Thence he traveled to Canaan (Gen 12:4, 5) and probably also to Egypt. After the return from Egypt, the herds of Abraham and Lot had so greatly increased that the tract of land they occupied was inconveniently small. Strife arose between their herdsmen, and

Abraham proposed they should separate, leaving the choice to Lot whether he would go eastward or westward. Lot chose the more fertile region of the valley of the Jordan in which Sodom and Gomorrah were situated. He thereby became involved in the warfare waged by Chedorlaomer and his allies against the two cities and was carried away as a prisoner of war. He was rescued by the valor of Abraham who attacked and defeated Chedorlaomer. Lot returned to Sodom and, though he loathed the life of immorality which was led in that city, he remained there and chose his sons-in-law from among the Sodomites. When at last the measure of iniquity was full and doom was passed upon the city, Lot and his family were saved only by the aid of special messengers from the Lord who accompanied them from Sodom to Zoar. However, Lot's "wife looked back from behind him, and she became a pillar of salt" (Gen 19:26). Lot removed from Zoar and dwelt in the mountains. During this time his two daughters made him drunk and became pregnant by him, after which he disappears from history. The nations of the Ammonites and Moabites descended from Lot. In the NT, his name occurs in Luke 17:28, 29, 32; 2 Pet 2:7 (cf. Gen 11:31; 13:5ff.; 14:12ff.; 19).

M

3092. Μαάθ *Maáth*; masc. proper noun transliterated from the Hebr. Maath, meaning small, an ancestor of Jesus (Luke 3:26).

3093. Μαγδαλά *Magdalá*; fem. proper noun transliterated from the Hebr. Magdala (Matt 15:39), the town on the Sea of Galilee from which Mary Magdalene came.

3094. Μαγδαληνή *Magdalēnē*; gen. *Magdalēnēs*, fem. proper noun. Magdalene, of Magdala, referring to the Mary of Magdala (Matt 27:56, 61; 28:1; Mark 15:40, 47; 16:1, 9; Luke 8:2; 24:10; John 19:25; 20:1, 18).

3095. μαγεία *mageía*; gen. *mageías*, fem. noun from *mágos* (3097), sorcerer. Magic, and in the pl. *mageíai*, magical arts, sorceries (Acts 8:11).
 Syn.: *pharmakeía* (5331), the use of medicine, drugs, or spells.

3096. μαγεύω *mageúō*; fut. *mageúsō*, from *mágos* (3097), a sorcerer. To practice magic, sorcery, used intrans. (Acts 8:9).

3097. μάγος *mágos*; gen. *mágou*, pl. *mágoi*, masc. noun. Magi, the name for priests and wise men among the Medes, Persians and Babylonians. Great, powerful men (see also *mégas* [3173], great, derived from the same stem). Magi specialized in the study of astrology and enchantment and thus were known as enchanters, magicians (Dan 1:20; 2:2, 27; 5:7). The Chaldeans called them wise (*sophós* [4680]) (Dan 2:12, 18, 24, 27; 5:7, 8 [cf. 5:11, 12]). In the NT they represent the name of the Magi, wise men from the East, most probably from Persia or Arabia, who came to salute the newborn Messiah (Matt 2:1, 7, 16). Also spoken of a magician, sorcerer, diviner (Acts 13:6, 8).
 Deriv.: *mageía* (3095), sorcery; *mageúō* (3096), to practice magic.

3098. Μαγώγ *Magōg*; masc. proper noun transliterated from the Hebr. *Māgōg* (4031, OT). Magog, a region of Gog, and Gog, the second son of Japheth (Gen 10:2; 1 Chr 1:5) and the name of a people descending from him or the country inhabited by that people and of which Gog was the king (Ezek 38:2; 39:1, 6). In the Middle Ages, the Syrians applied the name of Magog to Asiatic Tartary, and the Arabians to the region between the Caspian and the Black Seas. Generally, the people of Magog are identified with the Scythians who, in the time when Ezekiel wrote, were well-known in western Asia. Descending from the Caucasian Mountain regions in the beginning of 700 B.C., they conquered Sardis, the capital of Lydia, in 629 B.C. and defeated Cyaxares, King of Media, in 624 B.C. They penetrated even into Egypt, but were bought off by Psammetichus. They were not expelled, however, from western Asia until the beginning of the next century. They are described as excellent horsemen, skilled in the use of the bow (Ezek 38:14, 15; 39:1–3), and by exactly the same traits prominent in the descriptions of the Scythians by the Class. Gr. historians. In Rev 20:7, 8, we are told that Satan, after being bound for one thousand years, "shall be loosed" and "go out to deceive the nations which are in the four quarters of the earth, Gog and Magog, to gather them together to battle." This is referred to as the last great battle between the powers of evil and the armies of God and as the occasion of the final overthrow of the wicked when fire comes forth from heaven to devour them. In this passage, Gog and Magog are represented as nations dwelling in the four quarters of the earth and are symbolic of the enemies of the Lord. The names are taken from the prophecy of Ezek 38—39, where Gog is represented as a person, "the chief prince of Meshech and Tubal," and "Magog" as the name of his land (Ezek 38:2). The prophet depicts this prince as leading a great host against the people of God, and being utterly defeated and overthrown. This final and abortive attack on the part of the powers of evil is referred to in Rev 19:17ff., while in Rev 20:8 the names of Gog and Magog appear as a description of hostile nations.

3099. Μαδιάν *Madián*, **Μαδιάμ** *Madiám*; masc. proper noun transliterated from the Hebr. *Midhyān* (4080, OT), strife. Madian, or Midian (Acts 7:29). The territory of Midian extended, according to some scholars, from the Elanitic Gulf to Moab and Mount Sinai, or, according to others, from the Sinaitic Peninsula to the desert and the banks of the Euphrates. The people traded with Palestine, Lebanon, and Egypt (Gen 37:28). Joseph was probably bought by them, perhaps in company with the Ishmaelites (Gen 25:2, 4, 12, 16; 37:25, 27, 28, 36). Moses dwelled in Midian (Ex 2:15–21; Num 10:29). Midian joined Moab against Israel and enticed that nation into sin, for which it was destroyed (Num 22, 24, and 25). Midian recovered and became a powerful nation. The nation oppressed the Jews but was miraculously defeated by Gideon (Judg 6:1–40; 7:1–25; 8:1–28; Ps 83:9, 11; Isa 9:4; Hab 3:7). Later the Midianites gradually were incorporated into the Moabites and Arabs.

3100. μαθητεύω *mathēteúō*; fut. *mathēteúsō*, from *mathētés* (3101), disciple. As governing a dat., to be a disciple or follower of another's doctrine (Matt 27:57); governing an acc., to make a disciple (Matt 28:19; Acts 14:21); to instruct (Matt 13:52) with the purpose of making a disciple. *Mathēteúō* must be distinguished from the verb *mathéō* (n.f.) or *manthánō* (3129) which simply mean to learn without any attachment to the teacher who teaches. *Mathēteúō* means not only to learn, but to become attached to one's teacher and to become his follower in doctrine and conduct of life. It is really not sufficient to translate this verb as "learn" but as "making a disciple," in the NT sense of *mathētés*.

Syn.: *katēchéō* (2727), to teach orally, instruct, catechize; *didáskō* (1321), to give instruction, teach; *paideúō* (3811), to instruct and train; *heterodidaskaléō* (2085), to teach a different doctrine; *muéō* (3453), to learn.

3101. μαθητής *mathētés*; gen. *mathētoú*, masc. noun from *manthánō* (3129), to learn, to understand. A learner, pupil.

(I) *Mathētés* means more in the NT than a mere pupil or learner. It is an adherent who accepts the instruction given to him and makes it his rule of conduct, e.g., the disciples of John (Matt 11:2; Mark 2:18; Luke 5:33; 7:18; John 3:25); the disciples of the Pharisees (Mark 2:18). In John 9:28, the Pharisees told the healed blind man, "Thou art his disciple; but we are Moses' disciples." Jesus had disciples in the sense that they believed and made His teaching the basis of their conduct. (Matt 5:1; 9:19; 14:22; Luke 14:26, 27, 33; John 9:27; 15:8).

(II) Besides these believers, however, there was a smaller select group of twelve apostles whom Jesus chose out of the general group of His followers (Matt 8:21; Luke 6:13, 17; 7:11; John 6:60, 66). They were to teach and exercise power in performing miracles in substantiation of His authority transferred to them. Thus, "the twelve" are so designated in Matt 26:14 and called "the eleven" after Judas betrayed Jesus (Mark 16:14). These were not ordinary disciples, but those who remained with Him and followed Him (Matt 5:1; 8:23, 25 [TR]; 9:10; 11:1; 14:22).

(III) The general designation of *mathētēs* was given to those who believed on Christ (John 8:31). They were disciples but not *the* disciples (Matt 10:42; John 8:31; Acts 6:2; 19:9). The name *mathētaí* (pl. of *mathētēs*) was applied to John's disciples at Ephesus due to the relationship of John the Baptist to the Messiah (Acts 19:1). These disciples were ignorant of the fact that Jesus was the Messiah (Acts 19:4). Generally speaking, however, the term *mathētaí*, disciples, denoted just the followers of Christ, the Messiah.

Deriv.: *mathēteúō* (3100), to disciple; *summathētēs* (4827), a fellow disciple.

Ant.: *didáskalos* (1320), an instructor, a teacher; *paideutēs* (3810), a trainer, instructor; *paidagōgós* (3807), a schoolmaster; *kathēgētēs* (2519), a teacher, master.

3102. μαθήτρια *mathḗtria*; gen. *mathētrías*, fem. noun from *manthánō* (3129), to learn, to understand. A pupil, a female disciple (Acts 9:36).

Ant.: see ant. of *mathētēs* (3101), male pupil.

3103. Μαθουσάλα *Mathousála*; masc. proper noun transliterated from the Hebr. *Mᵉthúshelach* (4968, OT), man of the dart, or he dies and it [the flood] is sent. Methuselah (Luke 3:37). He was the son of Enoch and, according to Hebrew chronology, was 969 years old when he died. He died in the year of the flood and was the oldest man who ever lived (Gen 5:27; 1 Chr 1:3).

3104. Μαϊνάν *Maïnán*; masc. proper noun transliterated from the Hebr. Mainan or Menan, as mentioned in Luke 3:31.

3105. μαίνομαι *maínomai*; fut. *manoúmai*, mid. deponent. To be mad, to rave, used intrans. of persons who speak and act in such a way that they appear to others as being out of their mind or senses (John 10:20; Acts 12:15; 26:24, 25; 1 Cor 14:23; Sept.: Jer 36:26). This is the word from which the Eng. "maniac" is derived.

Deriv.: *emmaínomai* (1693), fierce rage or excessive anger, fury; *manía* (3130), frenzy, madness.

Syn.: *paraphronéō* (3912), to be out of one's mind; *paroxúnomai* (3947), to be provoked; *daimonízomai* (1139) to be possessed by a demon; *selēniázomai* (4583), to be moon-struck, lunatic; *paralogízomai* (3884), to act or talk irrationally; *aphrízō* (875), to foam at the mouth from epilepsy.

Ant.: *sōphronéō* (4993), to be of sound mind.

3106. μακαρίζω *makarízō*; fut. *makarísō*, from *mákar* (n.f.), the poetic form of *makários* (3107), blessed. To pronounce as blessed, fully satisfied. Used of the virgin Mary (Luke 1:48), as well as of the persecuted prophets and all who endure (James 5:11).

Deriv.: *makarismós* (3108), a state of blessedness.

Syn.: *eulogéō* (2127), to speak well of, bless.

Ant.: *kataráomai* (2672), to curse.

3107. μακάριος *makários*; fem. *makaría*, neut. *makárion*, adj. A prose form of the poetic *mákar* (n.f.), blessed one. Blessed, possessing the favor of God, that state of being marked by fullness from God. It indicates the state of the believer in Christ (Matt 5:3–11, "Blessed . . . for my sake"; Luke 6:20–22, "Blessed . . . for the Son of man's sake"), said of one who becomes a partaker of God's nature through faith in Christ (2 Pet 1:4). The believer is indwelt by the Holy Spirit because of Christ and as a result should be fully satisfied no matter the circumstances. *Makários* differs from the word "happy" in that the person is happy who has good luck (from the root *hap* meaning luck as a favorable circumstance). To be *makários*, blessed, is equivalent to having God's kingdom within one's heart (Matt 5:3, 10). Aristotle contrasts *makários* to *endeés* (1729), the needy one. *Makários* is the one who is in the world yet independent of the world. His satisfaction comes from God and not from favorable circumstances.

Deriv.: *makarízō* (3106), to declare blessed.

Syn.: *eulogētós* (2128), blessed, well-spoken of; *eulogēménos*, blessed; *eulogéō* (2127), to eulogize, bless, thank.

Ant.: *talaípōros* (5005), miserable, wretched; *eleeinós* (1652), pitiable, miserable.

3108. μακαρισμός *makarismós*; gen. *makarismoú*, masc. noun from *makarízō* (3106), to consider or count blessed. Blessedness.

In the NT, *makarismós* is the blessedness of a person who is indwelt by the Holy Spirit because of faith in Jesus Christ. See the word *makários* (3107), blessed, and note how the phrase, "for my sake" at the end of Matt 5:11 applies to each of the preceding of the Beatitudes. The disciples were called by the Lord *makárioi*, blessed (Matt 5:3, 10, in which instances the promise of the kingdom of heaven is in the pres. tense in distinction to all the other promises in the Beatitudes being in the fut. tense).

Makarismós, the blessed state (Rom 4:6), is imputed to the man whom God counts righteous apart from works. In Rom 4:9, this state of blessedness is given to Abraham as a result of his faith.

In Gal 4:15, *makarismós* is used in the form of a question: "Where is then the blessedness ye spake of?" Here Paul is speaking about how in the infirmity of the flesh (probably referring to his poor eyesight) he preached the gospel to the Galatians. That they joyfully received him in that physically weak state is what Paul meant with the word *makarismós*. Neither their joy nor his was the result of perfect health but in spite of physical weakness and sickness. *Makários* means to be indwelt by God through the Holy Spirit and, therefore, because of His in-

dwelling to be fully satisfied in spite of the afflictions of life.

Syn.: *eulogía* (2129), blessing; *eudokía* (2107), satisfaction, goodwill; *euphēmía* (2162), commendation, good report; *cháris* (5485), grace; *euergesía* (2108), beneficence.

Ant.: *katára* (2671), curse.

3109. Μακεδονία *Makedonía*; gen. *Makedonías*, fem. proper noun. Macedonia, meaning extended land. A noted country and kingdom lying north of Greece in ancient times. Today, however, it is the northern part of Greece, having been captured from the Turks who had occupied it previously. The kingdom was founded about 814 B.C. and became famous as the third great world kingdom associated with King Philip of Macedon and Alexander the Great (Dan 8:5–8, 21). Its capital was Thessalonica, where the proconsul resided. It was important in NT history because of the labors of the Apostles. Paul was called there by the vision of the "man of Macedonia" and made a most successful missionary tour (Acts 16:9, 11; 17:1–12). He visited it once again (Acts 20:1–6), and probably for the third time (cf. Phil 2:24; 1 Tim 1:3). Philippi was in Macedonia. Paul's epistles to the Thessalonians and the Philippians show that the Macedonian Christians exhibited many excellent traits. These details of Paul's work can be studied in connection with the cities of Macedonia visited by him: Neapolis, Philippi, Apollonia, Thessalonica, Berea.

3110. Μακεδών *Makedṓn*; gen. *Makedónos*, masc. noun. A Macedonian, an inhabitant of Macedonia (3109) (Acts 16:9; 19:29; 27:2; 2 Cor 9:2, 4).

3111. μάκελλον *mákellon*; gen. *makéllou*, Lat. *macellum*, neut. noun. A market place for meat, fish, and all manner of provisions. A butcher's row where all kinds of provisions were displayed for sale, even as one sees today in the Middle East (1 Cor 10:25).

3112. μακράν makrán; adv. from makrós (3117), far, long, far off. Used in the acc. with hodón (3598), way, meaning a long way or a great way, far (Matt 8:30; Mark 12:34; Luke 7:6; John 21:8; Acts 17:27; Sept.: Josh 9:22; Judg 18:7). With the def. art. in the pl., hoi makrán, those far off from God, meaning the Gentiles as opposed to those who are near, hoi eggús (1451), those near, meaning the Jews (Eph 2:13, 17; see Acts 2:39, "to all that are afar off"; Sept.: Isa 57:19).

Syn.: pórrō (4206), a great way off; péran (4008), across, beyond, farther; epékeina (1900), on the further side of, beyond; aprósitos (676), inaccessible, unreachable.

Ant.: plēsíon (4139), near; eggús (1451), near at hand; pará (3844), by, near; perí (4012), around.

3113. μακρόθεν makróthen; adv. from makrós (3117), far, long. From afar (Mark 8:3; 11:13; Luke 18:13; 22:54; 23:49; Sept.: Gen 22:4; 37:17; 2 Kgs 2:7). With the prep. apó (575), from (Matt 26:58, "afar off" [cf. Matt 27:55; Mark 5:6; 14:54; 15:40; Luke 16:23; Rev 18:10, 15, 17; Sept.: Ps 138:6]).

Syn.: pórrōthen (4207), afar off.

3114. μακροθυμέω makrothuméō; contracted makrothumṓ, fut. makrothumḗsō, from makróthumos (n.f.), long-suffering, which is from makrós (3117), long, and thumós (2372), wrath, anger. To suffer long, be long-suffering, as opposed to hasty anger or punishment (1 Cor 13:4; 1 Thess 5:14; 2 Pet 3:9), to forbear (Matt 18:26, 29), to endure patiently as opposed to losing faith or giving up (Heb 6:15; James 5:7, 8), to tarry, delay (Luke 18:7). Makrothuméō involves exercising understanding and patience toward persons while hupoménō (5278) involves putting up with things or circumstances.

Deriv.: makrothumía (3115), long-suffering.

Syn.: hupoménō (5278), to endure; anéchomai (430), to tolerate, endure; karteréō (2594), to endure; pheídomai (5339), to spare.

Ant.: adēmonéō (85), to be in distress.

3115. μακροθυμία makrothumía; gen. makrothumías, fem. noun from makrothuméō (3114), to be long-suffering. Forbearance, long-suffering, self-restraint before proceeding to action. The quality of a person who is able to avenge himself yet refrains from doing so (Rom 2:4; 9:22; Gal 5:22; Eph 4:2; Col 1:11; 3:12; 1 Tim 1:16; 2 Tim 4:2; Heb 6:12; James 5:10; 2 Pet 3:15; Sept.: Prov 25:15; Isa 57:15; Jer 15:15). In Heb 6:15, makrothuméō (3114) is used of Abraham's patient faith in God under the pressure of trying circumstances (James 5:7, 8). Makrothumía is patience in respect to persons while hupomoné (5281), endurance, is putting up with things or circumstances. Both words are often found together (2 Cor 6:4, 6; 2 Tim 3:10). Makrothumía is associated with mercy (éleos [1656]) and is used of God.

Syn.: anochḗ (463), tolerance; epieíkeia (1932), clemency.

Ant.: aganáktēsis (24), indignation; orgḗ (3709), wrath; thumós (2372), fierceness, indignation.

3116. μακροθύμως makrothúmōs; adv. from makróthumos (n.f.), long-suffering, which is from makrós (3117), long, and thumós (2372), wrath, anger. This adv. occurs only in Acts 26:3, where Paul asks Agrippa, "hear me patiently." Hupomoné (5281) is exercised toward things and circumstances, while makrothumía is exercised toward people. When makrothumía is exercised toward another, one reaches out to that person in the hope of winning him to Christ. The basic words makrothumía and makrothuméō (3114) stand in contrast to hupomoné and hupoménō (5278), patience or ability to stand under pressure of circumstances and things.

3117. μακρός makrós; fem. *makrá*, neut. *makrón*, adj. Long, as used of space, meaning from one point to another and hence far, far distant (Luke 15:13; 19:12); as used of time, only in the neut. pl. *makrá* as an adv., meaning long, e.g., praying long or making long prayers (Matt 23:14; Mark 12:40; Luke 20:47).
Deriv.: *makrán* (3112), far away; *makróthen* (3113), from a distance; *makrochrónios* (3118), long-lived.
Syn.: *ektenḗs* (1618), protracted, long; *diēnekés* (1336), perpetual; *adiáleiptos* (88), unceasing.
Ant.: *brachús* (1024), short of; *ephḗmeros* (2184), ephemeral, daily; *mikrós* (3398), small, less; *suntómōs* (4935), concisely.

3118. μακροχρόνιος makrochrónios; gen. *makrochroníou*, masc.-fem., neut. *makrochrónion*, adj. from *makrós* (3117), long, and *chrónos* (5550), time. Enduring a long time, long-lived (Eph 6:3 quoted from Ex 20:12; Deut 5:16).
Syn.: *diēnekés* (1336), perpetual; *adiáleiptos* (88), without interruption; *ektenḗs* (1618), long-lasting; *makrós* (3117), long.
Ant.: *brachús* (1024), short.

3119. μαλακία malakía; gen. *malakías*, fem. noun from *malakós* (3120), soft. Softness, disease, a debility, infirmity (Matt 4:23; 9:35; 10:1). As referring to men, it means characterized by delicacy, effeminacy. In Aristotelian ethics it is the opposite of *kartería* (n.f.), patient endurance, meekness.
Syn.: *asthéneia* (769), disease, weakness; *nósos* (3554), malady, infirmity; *nósēma* (3553), ailment, disease.
Ant.: *ischús* (2479), strength; *dúnamis* (1411), power, might; *sklērótēs* (4643), hardness.

3120. μαλακός malakós; fem. *malakḗ*, neut. *malakón*, adj. Soft to the touch,

spoken of clothing made of soft materials, fine texture (Matt 11:8; Luke 7:25). Figuratively it means effeminate or a person who allows himself to be sexually abused contrary to nature. Paul, in 1 Cor 6:9, joins the *malakoí*, the effeminate, with *arsenokoítai* (733), homosexuals, Sodomites.
Deriv.: *malakía* (3119), softness.
Syn.: *hapalós* (527), soft, tender.
Ant.: *sklērós* (4642), hard; *trachús* (5138), rough.

3121. Μαλελεήλ Maleleḗl; masc proper noun transliterated from the Hebr. *Machalal'ēl* (4111, OT), praise of God. Maleleel, Mahalaleel, the son of Cainan (Luke 3:37 [cf. Gen 5:12]).

3122. μάλιστα málista; adv., the superlative of *mála* (n.f.), very. Mostly, especially (Acts 20:38; 25:26; 26:3; Gal 6:10; Phil 4:22; 1 Tim 4:10; 5:8, 17; 2 Tim 4:13; Titus 1:10; Phile 1:16; 2 Pet 2:10).
Syn.: *pleíōn* (4119), more; *pleístos* (4118), the maximum part of, chiefly, primarily.
Ant.: *eláchistos* (1646), least.

3123. μᾶλλον mállon; adv., the comparative of *mála* (n.f.), very. More, rather.
(I) In its general use (1 Cor 14:1, 5; 2 Cor 5:8); with the gen. (1 Cor 14:18); with *pollṓ*, the dat. of *polús* (4183), much more (Matt 6:30; Mark 10:48; Luke 18:39; Rom 5:9, 10, 15, 17; 1 Cor 12:22; 2 Cor 3:9, 11; Phil 2:12; Heb 12:9, 25); with the dat. of *pósos* (4214), how great, meaning how much more (Matt 7:11; 10:25; Luke 11:13; 12:24, 28; Rom 11:12, 24; Phile 1:16; Heb 9:14); with the dat. of *tosoútos* (5118), so great, meaning so much the more (Heb 10:25). *Mállon kaí mállon*, more and more (Phil 1:9); with *ḗ* (2228), than, and, but, meaning more than, rather than (Matt 18:13; John 3:19; Acts 4:19; 5:29; 27:11; 1 Tim 1:4; 2 Tim 3:4); with *éper* (2260), than (John 12:43). Used elliptically where *ḗ* (2228), than, and its verb

are to be supplied in thought as in Phile 1:9, "I rather beseech," instead of command (2 Cor 2:7; 12:9, in connection with v. 7, meaning "Most gladly therefore will I rather glory in my infirmities" rather than in the abundance of the revelations). It is used also as an intens., the more, the rather, still more (Matt 27:24 [cf. Matt 27:23, meaning that there was still more of a tumult]; Mark 14:31 in conjunction with Mark 14:29; Luke 5:15; John 5:18 [cf. John 5:16; 19:8]; Acts 5:14; 9:22; 22:2; 2 Cor 7:7; Phil 1:12; 3:4; 1 Thess 4:1, 10; 2 Pet 1:10). With the neg. *ou* (3756) in interrogative sentences (1 Cor 9:12).

(II) Joined with the positive *mállon*, followed by *ḗ* (2228), than (Acts 20:35, "It is more blessed to give than to receive"; 1 Cor 9:15; Gal 4:27). With *ei* (1487), if (Mark 9:42).

(III) Joined emphatically with a comparative, either in form or sense (Mark 7:36; 2 Cor 7:13; Phil 1:23); with verbs of comparison (Matt 6:26; Heb 11:25).

(IV) After a neg. clause or prohibition expressed or implied, meaning rather; with the particle *dé* (1161), and, but, meaning but rather (Matt 10:6, 28; 25:9; Luke 10:20; Eph 4:28; Heb 12:13); with *hína* (2443), so that, meaning so that rather (Mark 15:11); with *allá* (235), but, meaning "but rather" (Rom 14:13; 1 Cor 7:21; Eph 5:4; 1 Tim 6:2).

(V) Used as an intens., *mállon dé* before an antithetic clause, or rather, yea more (Rom 8:34; Gal 4:9; Eph 5:11).

(VI) With *ouchí* (3780), not, in interrogative sentences (1 Cor 5:2; 6:7).

Syn.: *megálōs* (3171), much, greatly; *lían* (3029), greatly, exceedingly, much; *polús* (4183), much; *sphódra* (4970), greatly, vehemently; *sphodrṓs* (4971), very much, exceedingly; *pleíōn* (4119), more.

Ant.: *kathólou* (2527), at all; *eláchistos* (1646), least; *olígos* (3641), little.

3124. Μάλχος *Málchos*; gen. *Málchou*, masc. proper noun. Malchus, meaning reigning, or with the Aramaic

significance, counselor. A servant of the high priest (John 18:10).

3125. μάμμη *mámmē*; gen. *mámmēs*, fem. noun. A grandmother (2 Tim 1:5).

3126. μαμμωνᾶς *mammōnás*, **μαμωνᾶς** *mamōnás*; gen. *mammōná*, masc. noun. Wealth, the personification of riches. Mammon, the comprehensive word for all kinds of possessions, earnings, and gains, a designation of material value, the god of materialism. In Luke 16:9, 11, it denotes riches, equivalent to *ploútos* (4149), wealth. In Matt 6:24 and Luke 16:13, the Lord personifies mammon, the god of materialism.

3127. Μαναήν *Manaḗn*; masc. proper noun transliterated from the Hebr. Manaen, meaning comforter, consoler. One of the teachers of the church of Antioch and foster brother of Herod Antipas, the Tetrarch (Acts 13:1).

3128. Μανασσῆς *Manassḗs*; gen. *Manassḗ*, masc. proper noun transliterated from the Hebr. *Mᵉnashshī* (4519, OT), making to forget. Manasses or Manasseh.

(I) The firstborn of Joseph. When he and his younger brother Ephraim were boys and Jacob their grandfather was about to die, Joseph took them into the patriarch's presence to receive a blessing. On this occasion, Jacob predicted the ascendancy of Ephraim over Manasseh (Gen 48:5–20). Nothing further is known of the personal history of Manasseh except that his only son was Machir whose children were embraced by Joseph. On their way to Canaan, the Israelites conquered a large territory east of the Jordan. Some of the Manassites who had possessions chiefly in cattle desired to have their portion assigned to them among the rich pastures and fruitful hills of Bashan and the surrounding country. This request was granted, and half of the tribe of Manasseh received the territory stretching from near Caesarea-Philippi along the Jordan almost down to Mahanaim. The other half had its portion on the west side of the Jordan, between the lands allotted to Ephraim and those given to Issachar, across the country from the Jordan to the Mediterranean. Several great men, such as Gideon and (probably) Jephthah, issued from Manasseh. The eastern part of the tribe prospered much and spread to Mt. Hermon, but they eventually mixed with the Canaanites, adopted their idolatry, became scattered as Bedouins in the desert, and were the first to be carried away to captivity by the kings of Assyria (1 Chr 5:25, 26). The western part of Manasseh, of which only a few glimpses are visible in the later history of Israel, always showed itself on the right side; as for instance, in the cases of Asa (2 Chr 15:9), Hezekiah (2 Chr 30:1, 11, 18), and Josiah (2 Chr 34:6, 9).

(II) Son and successor of Hezekiah, king of Judah, who ascended to the throne at the age of twelve years, in 696 B.C. The first part of his reign was distinguished for acts of impiety and cruelty (2 Kgs 21:16). He succeeded in drawing his subjects away from the Lord (2 Kgs 21:2–9). Having supported the Babylonians in his revolt against Assyria, he was at last taken captive by the Assyrian kings and ignominiously transported to Babylon. Upon his repentance, however, he was liberated and returned to his capital, where he died in 641 B.C. after having done much to repair the evils of his past life (2 Chr 33:1–20). He is referred to in Matt 1:10.

3129. μανθάνω manthánō; fut. *mathḗsomai*, 2d aor. *émathon*. To learn (Matt 9:13; 11:29; 24:32; Mark 13:28; Acts 23:27; Gal 3:2; 1 Tim 5:4, 13; 2 Tim 3:14; Titus 3:14; Heb 5:8). The aor., to have learned something, to understand it (Phil 4:11), answers to *didáskō* (1321), to teach (John 7:15; Rom 16:17; 1 Cor 4:6; 14:31, 35; 1 Tim 2:11; Rev 14:3) which denotes instruction concerning the facts and plan of salvation. In this sense

it means to learn with a moral bearing and responsibility (John 6:45; Phil 4:9). In Col 1:6, 7, *manthánō* is equivalent to *epiginōskō* (1921), to know more fully. The syn. use is also indicated in 2 Tim 3:7 where the two words, *manthánō* and *epígnōsis* (1922), a full knowledge, are used. In Eph 4:20, *manthánō* has Christ as the direct obj. He is presented as the sum and substance of the gospel. To become related to Him is to know Him, and knowing Him is to know His teaching and abide by it.

Deriv.: *amathḗs* (261), unlearned; *katamanthánō* (2648), to learn, to understand thoroughly; *mathētḗs* (3101), disciple.

Syn.: *eídō* (1492), to consider, know; *noéō* (3539), to perceive with the mind; *katanoéō* (2657), to perceive clearly; *logízomai* (3049), to take account of; *theōréō* (2334), to behold; *anatheōréō* (333), to consider carefully; *analogízomai* (357), to consider; *suníēmi* (4920), to put it together, understand; *epiginōskō* (1921), to know fully; *epístamai* (1987), to comprehend.

Ant.: *agnoéō* (50), to be ignorant, ignore.

3130. μανία manía; gen. *manías*, fem. noun from *maínomai* (3105), to rave as a maniac. Mania, madness, insanity (Acts 26:24).

Syn.: *ánoia* (454), without understanding; *paraphronía* (3913), the state of being out of one's mind; *hormḗ* (3730), violent impulse, assault; *tarachḗ* (5016), disturbance.

3131. μάννα mánna; neut. noun transliterated from the Hebr. *mān* (4478, OT), "what is it?" Manna, that miraculous food the Israelites ate in the desert (John 6:31, 49, 58; Heb 9:4; Sept.: Num 11:6). Symbolically, in Rev 2:17 (cf. Ex 16:15, 31).

3132. μαντεύομαι manteúomai; fut. *manteúsomai*, mid. deponent from *mántis* (n.f.), a soothsayer, diviner, which is

from *maínomai* (3105), to be mad, beside oneself. To divine or utter spells.
Such soothsayers raged, foamed and
screamed, making strange and terrible noises, sometimes gnashing with
their teeth, shaking and trembling, with
many strange motions. Plato calls people
caught up in such ecstasy possessed of
madness *mánteis*, from Muses which excited and inspired the mind into enthusi-
astic songs and poems. In many instances
there was a real possession by the devil, e.g., in the case of the prophetic slave
girl (Acts 16:16, 18). The *mánteis* (pl.)
were possessed of a maniacal fury which
displayed itself by rolling eyes, foaming
mouth, and flying hair. It is quite possible that these symptoms were sometimes
produced by the inhalation of vapors or
other drugs, as they were often aggravated in the seers, the Pythonesses, Sib-
yls, and the like. No doubt such belonged
to a spiritual world not related to the
true God, a relationship not with heaven
above but with hell below.

The Word of God condemns this maniacal fury. Paul says in 1 Cor 14:32:
"The spirits of the prophets are subject
to the prophets" and not to any devilish
powers. A prophet of God speaks not in
an unknown tongue as the soothsayers,
but in an understandable language. He
indeed speaks not of himself but is possessed by the Spirit of God (Rev 1:10);
his ecstasy is of God (Acts 11:5), being
"moved by the Holy Ghost" (2 Pet 1:21).
Man is not "beside himself" when he is
moved or led by the Spirit and filled with
the presence of God, but is wise and discreet. However, in the *mántis* or the sorcerer, as Plato testifies, we have one in
whom all sense of reason is suspended.
Thus the line is drawn sharply between a
mántis and a *prophḗtēs* (4396), prophet.

Syn.: *proginṓskō* (4267), to foreknow;
apokalúptō (601), to disclose; *prolégō*
(4302), to foretell; *prophēteúō* (4395),
to prophesy; *pronoéō* (4306), to consider in advance; *prooráō* (4308), to behold
in advance.

Ant.: *agnoéō* (50), to be ignorant.

3133. μαραίνω *maraínō*; fut. *maranṓ*.
To put out, to extinguish as fire; in the
pass., to go out, expire, hence to dry up,
cause to wither, to fade away as flowers,
spoken of the body and the person. Used
symbolically of the rich in James 1:11.
Deriv.: *amárantos* (263), unfading.
Syn.: *xēraínomai* (3583), to dry out.
Ant.: *akmázō* (187), to mature;
anathállō (330), to flourish again.

3134. μαράν ἀθά *marán athá*. Maranatha, two Aramaic words meaning "our
Lord has come." (1 Cor 16:22), an exclamation uttered in connection with the
approaching judgment when the Lord returns (cf. Jude 1:14, 15).

3135. μαργαρίτης *margarítēs*; gen.
margarítou, masc. noun. Pearl (Matt
13:45, 46; 1 Tim 2:9; Rev 17:4; 18:12,
16; 21:21). Used metaphorically in Matt
7:6 indicating something precious, not to
be given to dogs.

3136. Μάρθα *Mártha*; gen. *Márthas*,
fem. proper noun. Martha, the sister of
Lazarus and Mary. She seems to have
been the eldest of the family, as she is
always mentioned before Mary and generally portrayed as the mistress of the
house. She was more active in practical
life than the younger sister, but was deficient in her concentration on the one
thing needful. However, she was sincere,
devoted, and beloved by Christ (John
11:5). Although she was somewhat overwhelmed by the distractions of daily life,
she at last concentrated her faith in the
Savior. See Luke 10:38, 40, 41; John
11:1, 5, 19, 21, 24, 30, 39; 12:2.

**3137. Μαρία *María*, Μαριάμ *Mar-
iám***; gen. *Marías*, fem. proper noun.
Sometimes Mariam, Mary or Miriam,
the proper names of several females:
(I) The mother of our Lord, and hence,
"blessed among women." See Matt 1:16,
18, 20; 2:11; 13:55; Mark 6:3; Luke 1:27,
30, 34, 38, 39, 46, 56; 2:5, 16, 19, 34;
Acts 1:14. She was of the tribe of Judah,

of the lineage of David. By marriage, she was related to Elizabeth, the mother of John the Baptist, who was of the tribe of Levi (3017), of the lineage of Aaron. After the period belonging to the childhood of Jesus (the visit of the shepherds, the circumcision, the adoration of the wise men, the presentation in the temple, and the flight into Egypt), Mary (the mother of our Lord) is mentioned only four times in the records of sacred history. She was present at the marriage in Cana which took place in the three months between the baptism of Christ and the Passover of the year A.D. 27, and at which Jesus wrought His first miracle after she had called attention to the lack of wine at the feast (John 2:3); she sought to speak with Him in company with others of the family when He was preaching to a crowd in a country place (Matt 12:46; Mark 3:31; Luke 8:19); she was present at the crucifixion and was there commended by the dying Christ to the kindness and attention of the beloved John (John 19:26); she is also mentioned as one among the praying company in the upper room at Jerusalem after the ascension of the Lord Jesus (Acts 1:14).

(II) The mother of James the Less and Joses (Matt 27:56; Mark 15:40; Luke 24:10). She was present at the crucifixion and burial of our Lord (Matt 27:56, 61; John 19:25); she was among those who went to anoint His body (Mark 16:1–10); she was among the earliest to whom the news of His resurrection was announced (Luke 24:6, 10), and on her way to the disciples, she met her risen Lord and worshiped Him (Mark 15:40, 47; Luke 24:10). She may be "the other Mary" of Matt 27:61; 28:1 (cf. Mark 15:47; 16:1). From John 19:25, it appears that she was the sister of Jesus' mother and wife of Clopas. This name is distinct from Cleopas (Luke 24:18), and is perhaps identical with Alphaeus (Matt 10:3; Luke 6:15). The claim that John 19:25 refers to four women **(1)** Jesus' mother, **(2)** the sister of His mother who here is unnamed, **(3)** Mary (the wife) of Klopas,

and **(4)** Mary Magdalene, may be untenable if the *kai* (2532), "and," (a connective conj.) is taken as connecting the different women. *Kaí* is used only three times, necessitating the phrase "and his mother's sister, Mary the wife of Cleophas" to be taken as one person.

(III) The mother of John Mark (Acts 12:12) and sister to Barnabas (Col 4:10). She was a godly woman residing in Jerusalem, at whose house the disciples were convened the night Peter was miraculously delivered from prison (Acts 12:12).

(IV) The sister of Lazarus and Martha and a devoted friend and disciple of our Savior from whom she received the testimony that she had chosen the good part which should not be taken from her (Luke 10:39–42). Compared with her sister, she appears of a more contemplative mind and more occupied with the "one thing" needful (John 11:1, 2, 19, 20, 28, 31, 32, 45; 12:3).

(V) Mary Magdalene or Mary of Magdala (Luke 8:2). The general impression that she was an unchaste woman is entirely without foundation. There is nothing to warrant the opinion that she is identical with the woman who was a prostitute. On the contrary, she seems to have been a woman in good circumstances and of unblemished character. Having been relieved of a demoniac possession by the divine power of the Lord Jesus, she became His follower (Luke 8:2, 3) and proved faithful to Him and His cause to the very end. She was at His crucifixion (Matt 27:56; John 19:25) and burial (Matt 27:61; Mark 15:40, 47) and was among those who had prepared the materials to embalm Him (Mark 16:1) and who first went to the sepulcher after the resurrection (Matt 28:1; Luke 24:10). What is particularly interesting is that she was the first to whom the risen Lord appeared (Mark 16:9), and His conversation with her never ceases to attract great attention (John 20:11–18).

(VI) A Christian woman in Rome to whom Paul sends his greeting (Rom 16:6).

3138. Μάρκος *Márkos*; gen. *Márkou*, masc. proper noun. Marcus or Mark, the writer of one of the four gospels and properly known as John Mark (Acts 12:12, 25; 15:37). He was a Jew, probably a native of Jerusalem where his mother Mary resided (Acts 12:12). She was a person of some repute among the early Christians, as Peter, when released from prison, immediately went to her house.

Mark was probably converted through Peter who calls him "his son" (1 Pet 5:13). The inclusion in the Gospel of Mark of the minute account of the young man who followed Jesus on the night of the betrayal (Mark 14:51, 52), together with the omission of the name, points to the evangelist as the person concerned. He went as a servant with Paul and Barnabas, who was his uncle (Col 4:10), on their first missionary journey. He left them at Perga (Acts 13:13), and in consequence became the occasion of "sharp contention" between them (Acts 15:36–40). Later he appears as a companion of Paul in Rome (Col 4:10; Phile 1:24). He was with Peter when that apostle wrote his first epistle (1 Pet 5:13), but was at Ephesus with Timothy at a date probably later (2 Tim 4:11).

Trustworthy details are missing concerning his later life, but ancient writers agree in speaking of him as the "interpreter" of Peter. This may mean that he translated for the apostle, but more likely means that he wrote his gospel in close conformity to Peter's preaching.

The second gospel was written by him with evidence of his close association with Peter. The style shows the influence of Peter. Peter's address to Cornelius (Acts 10) has been called the Gospel of Mark in a nutshell. Mark alone mentions the two cock crowings (Mark 14:72), thus increasing the guilt of Peter's denial.

Although the Gospel was written in Gr., it was designed for Roman readers and is especially adapted to their minds. It exhibits Christ as the spiritual conqueror and wonder-worker, the Lion of the tribe of Judah filling the people with amazement and fear. Mark introduces several Lat. terms; he even substitutes Roman money for Greek (Mark 12:42), which Luke does not do. He notes that Simon of Cyrene was the father of Alexander and Rufus (Mark 15:21) who probably were Christians in Rome (Rom 16:13). It is, therefore, quite likely that the Gospel was written in that city. The great similarity between the Gospels of Mark and Matthew has led some to consider the former a mere abridgment of the latter, but without sufficient reason. It occupies an independent position as a connecting link between Matthew and Luke, Peter and Paul, the Jewish and the Gentile Christianity.

The last part of the closing chapter (Mark 16:9–20) is not found in the two oldest and best MSS of the Bible, thus giving occasion to some writers to declare it a later addition. However, it has been recognized as part of the Gospel and quoted by the Fathers of the Second Century—for instance, Irenaeus, whose testimony is older than the oldest MSS Possibly, it was a later postscript of Mark, added to a second copy; hence its omission in some MSS.

3139. μάρμαρος *mármaros*; gen. *marmárou*, masc. noun from *marmaírō* (n.f.), to glitter, shine, referring to stone or rock. Marble (Rev 18:12).

3140. μαρτυρέω *marturéō*; contracted *marturō̂*, fut. *marturḗsō*, from *mártus* (3144), witness. To be a witness, bear witness.

(I) To be a witness, to be able or ready to testify. With the dat. (John 3:28; Acts 22:5); used in an absolute sense (2 Cor 8:3); followed by the dat. of person or thing, meaning in favor of whom or what one bears testimony (John 3:26; 5:33; 18:37).

(II) To bear witness, to testify to the truth of what one has seen, heard, or knows.

(A) Particularly and generally, followed by *perí* (4012), concerning, with the gen. meaning to bear witness concerning a person or thing (John 1:7, 8, 15; 2:25; 5:31, 32; 8:13, 14, 18; 15:26; 21:24); followed by *hóti* (3754), that, as equivalent to the acc. and inf. (John 1:34; 4:44; 1 John 4:14); by *hóte* (John 12:17); with *katá* (2596), against, with the gen. (1 Cor 15:15). Followed by the words testified, after *légon* (3004), saying, *eípe* (2036), he said, and *hóti*, that, of a quotation (John 1:32; 4:39; 13:21). Preceded by the acc. expressed or implied, e.g., of cognate or syn. nouns as in John 5:32: *hē marturía* (3141), the testimony; *hēn* (3739), which; *martureí perí emoú*, he testifies about me, i.e., "the testimony which he testifies about me" (a.t. [cf. 1 John 5:9, 10]). In 1 Tim 6:13, "who . . . testifies the good confession" (a.t. [*homologían* {3671}]). With the acc. of something, generally, to testify something (John 3:11, "that which we have seen, we testify" [a.t.]; also John 3:32; 1 John 1:2; Rev 1:2; 22:20, *ho marturón taúta*, "He who witnesses these things" [a.t.], with a causative meaning as [cf. with Rev 22:16]). Followed by the acc. and dat. (Rev 22:16). With an acc. implied from the context, e.g., *tá perí emoú*, "those things concerning me" (a.t. [Acts 23:11]); whatever follows (John 19:35; Acts 26:5; Heb 10:15; 1 John 5:6–8). Rom 3:21, pass. with *hupó* [5259], by. With the meaning of to prove by testimony (John 18:23).

(B) Figuratively, of God as testifying by His Spirit, by signs and miracles. Followed by *perí* (4012), concerning (John 5:37; 8:18; 1 John 5:9, 10); *hóti* (3754), that, of quotation (Heb 7:17). Of the Scriptures or prophets, with *perí*, concerning (John 5:39); with the dat. and followed by inf. with the acc. (Acts 10:43).

Of one's deeds, works with *perí* (John 5:36; 10:25). See Sept.: Gen 31:48.

(III) Emphatically, to testify strongly, bear honorable testimony; and pass., to be well-testified about, to have good witness, with *hóti*, that (Heb 7:8); with the inf. (Heb 11:4, 5). Generally, to speak well of, applaud, followed by the dat. (Luke 4:22; Acts 15:8); used in an absolute sense (3 John 1:12); with *epí* (1909), upon with the dat. (Heb 11:4). In the pass., meaning to be lauded, to be of good report (Acts 6:3); with *hupó* (5259), by (Acts 10:22; 16:2; 22:12; 3 John 1:12); with *en* (1722), in (1 Tim 5:10; Heb 11:2); with *diá* (1223), through (Heb 11:39).

Deriv.: *epimarturéo* (1957), to bear witness to; *katamarturéo* (2649), to bear witness against; *marturía* (3141), a testimony; *martúrion* (3142), a declaration of facts, proof, a testimony; *summarturéo* (4828), to bear witness with; *pseudomarturéo* (5576), to bear false witness.

Syn.: *bebaióō* (950), to assure; *katēgoréō* (2723), to accuse; *deiknúō* (1166), to show; *dēlóō* (1213), to declare; *emphanízō* (1718), to manifest; *pháneróō* (5319), to manifestly declare; *probállo* (4261), to put forward; *apokalúptō* (601), to reveal; *plērophoréō* (4135), to inform fully; *diasaphéō* (1285), to make plain.

Ant.: *krúptō* (2928), to keep secret; *apokrúptō* (613), to keep secret from someone; *kalúptō* (2572), to cover; *sugkalúptō* (4780), to completely conceal; *egkrúptō* (1470), to conceal inside something.

3141. μαρτυρία marturía; gen. *marturías*, fem. noun from *marturéō* (3140), to witness. A witness, certification (John 1:7), testimony (Mark 14:55, 56, 59; Luke 22:71), that which someone witnesses or states concerning a person or thing (Acts 22:18; 1 Tim 3:7; Titus 1:13). Used of the testimony of John the Baptist concerning Jesus (John 1:19; 5:36); of the declarations of Jesus concerning Himself (John 5:31; 8:13, 14). It is a declaration by a witness who speaks with the authority of one who knows (John 5:34; 3 John 1:12). In 1 John 5:9–11, John refers to the record of witness as being the fact that God in His Son has given eternal life to believers. In John 3:11, 32, 33, the testimony of Jesus is that which He declares with the authority of a witness, of one who knows (v. 11). However, in Rev 1:2, 9, "the testimony of Jesus" is the announcement of the gospel, the apostolic preaching of Christ as determined by the Apostle's testimony (v. 2, "all things that he saw"). This testimony especially concerns Christ and is based upon a personal knowledge of Him (Rev 12:17; 19:10; 20:4). That *marturía* is used in the NT to denote martyrdom is an untenable inference from Rev 11:7; 12:11.

Deriv.: *pseudomarturía* (5577), a false witness.

Syn.: *bebaíōsis* (951), confirmation; *plērophoría* (4136), complete information, full assurance; *phanérōsis* (5321), manifestation; *éndeixis* (1732), evident token; *apódeixis* (585), demonstration, proof; *apokálupsis* (602), revelation.

Ant.: *kálumma* (2571), cover, veil.

3142. μαρτύριον *martúrion*; gen. *marturíou*, neut. noun from *marturéō* (3140), to witness. Testimony, witness, proof, the declaration which confirms or makes something known (Matt 8:4; 10:18; 24:14; Mark 1:44; 6:11; 13:9; Luke 5:14). Condemnatory testimony (Luke 9:5; 21:13; 2 Cor 1:12; 2 Thess 1:10; 1 Tim 2:6; James 5:3). In the Class. Gr., used also for proof. In the NT usage, it is the witness or the testimony of Christ (1 Cor 1:6 [cf. 2 Tim 1:8]). The meaning is that the preacher bases what he says on his own intimate or personal knowledge, and the gospel is preached as a narrative of truth, a declaration of facts. This form of expression distinguishes *martúrion* from the teaching of Christian doctrine (Acts 4:33; Heb 3:5; Sept.: Deut 31:26; Josh 22:27). The preaching of the gospel in 1 Cor 2:1 is

called *martúrion*, the witness of God (Acts 7:44; Rev 15:5).

Syn.: *apódeixis* (585), proof, demonstration; *bebaíōsis* (951), confirmation; *tekmḗrion* (5039), a token, infallible proof.

Ant.: *sigḗ* (4602), silence; *dikaíōsis* (1347), acquittal.

3143. μαρτύρομαι *martúromai*; fut. *marturḗsomai*, mid. deponent from *mártus* (3144), witness. To witness for oneself, to call to witness, attest, ratify, affirm (Acts 20:26; 26:22; Gal 5:3; Eph 4:17; 1 Thess 2:10, to exhort solemnly; Sept.: Gen 43:3).

Deriv.: *diamartúromai* (1263), to bear witness, to charge, protest; *promartúromai* (4303), to witness beforehand.

Syn.: *bebaióō* (950), to confirm; *dēlóō* (1213), to declare; *plērophoréō* (4135), to assure completely.

Ant.: *anairéō* (337), to repudiate, retract.

3144. μάρτυς *mártus*; gen. *márturos*, masc.-fem. noun. A witness. One who has information or knowledge of something, and hence, one who can give information, bring to light, or confirm something (Matt 18:16; 26:65; Mark 14:63; Luke 24:48; Acts 1:22; 5:32; 7:58; 2 Cor 13:1; 1 Tim 5:19; Heb 10:28). It denotes that the witness confirms something, though that witness may have been bribed or otherwise persuaded to make a false statement (Acts 6:13). In the sense of a simple confirmation (2 Cor 1:23); of the Apostle's faithfulness and spiritual integrity (Rom 1:9; Phil 1:8; 1 Thess 2:5, 10; 1 Tim 6:12; 2 Tim 2:2). In Heb 12:1, a "cloud of witnesses" is mentioned. This may refer to them as spectators at a race, but seems to imply that they also testify, whether by word or deed, regarding the race they themselves have run.

Peculiar to the NT is the designation as *mártures* (pl., witnesses) of those who announce the facts of the gospel and tell its tidings (Acts 2:32; 3:15; 10:39, 41;

13:31; Rev 11:3). Also *mártus* is used as a designation of those who have suffered death in consequence of confessing Christ (of Stephen, Acts 22:20; of Antipas, Rev 2:13; see Rev 17:6. These verses, however, should not be understood as if their witness consisted in their suffering death, but rather that their witnessing of Jesus became the cause of their death). The Lord Jesus in Rev 1:5 is called "the faithful witness," the faithful one (see Rev 3:14).

Deriv.: *amárturos* (267), without a witness; *martureó* (3140), to witness; *martúromai* (3143), to summon as a witness, adjure; *pseudomártur* (5575), a person who bears false witness.

Syn.: *autóptēs* (845), eyewitness; *katḗgoros* (2725), an accuser.

3145. μασσάομαι *massáomai*; contracted *massṓmai*, fut. *massḗsomai*, mid. deponent from *másso* (n.f., see *ekmássō* [1591]), to handle, squeeze. To chew, gnaw, referring to chewing tongues in pain (Rev 16:10; Sept.: Job 30:4).

3146. μαστιγόω *mastigóō*; contracted *mastigó*, fut. *mastigṓsō* from *mástix* (3148), plague, whip, scourge. To scourge, used trans. (Matt 10:17; 20:19; 23:34; Mark 10:34; Luke 18:33; John 19:1; Sept.: Ex 5:14; Deut 25:3). Used figuratively of God, meaning to chastise, correct (Heb 12:6 quoted from Prov 3:12; Sept.: Prov 17:10). Divine chastisement, (as denoted by *mastigóō*) though inclusive of it, is not strictly action taken for sins in particular (as denoted by *mastízō* [3147]). Rather, it entails all and any suffering which God ordains for His children which is always designed for their good (Rom 5:3, 4; 8:28). God's chastisement of us includes not only His "whipping" us, as it were, for specific transgressions (with remedial not retributive intent), but also the entire range of trials and tribulations which He providentially ordains and which work to mortify sin and nurture faith.

Syn.: *phragellóō* (5417), to scourge with a whip; *dérō* (1194), to smite.

Ant.: *thálpō* (2282), to brood, cherish; *peripoiéomai* (4046), to acquire, take care of; *proséchō* (4337), to attend to; *diakonéō* (1247), to minister to; *phrontízō* (5431), to take care of.

3147. μαστίζω *mastízō*; fut. *mastíxō*, from *mástix* (3148), plague, whip, scourging. To scourge, used trans. in regard to a person as a criminal (Acts 22:25; Sept.: Num 22:25).

3148. μάστιξ *mástix*; gen. *mástigos*, fem. noun. A whip, a scourge (Acts 22:24; Heb 11:36; Sept.: 1 Kgs 12:11, 14; Prov 26:3). Figuratively, a scourge from God meaning a disease, plague (Mark 3:10; 5:29, 34; Luke 7:21; Sept.: Ps 32:10; 39:10; 89:32).

Deriv.: *mastigóō* (3146), to flog, scourge; *mastízō* (3147), to scourge.

Syn.: *phragéllion* (5416), a whip made of small cords which the Lord employed in the temple (John 2:15).

Ant.: *aspasmós* (783), greeting, embracing; *phílēma* (5370), a kiss.

3149. μαστός *mastós*; gen. *mastoú*, masc. noun. The breast (Luke 11:27; 23:29; Rev 1:13; Sept.: Job 3:13; Song 1:12).

Syn.: *stéthos*, connected with *hístēmi* (2476), to stand, that which stands out, or the breast.

3150. ματαιολογία *mataiología*; gen. *mataiologías*, fem. noun from *mataiológos* (3151), a vain talker. Vain talk, empty conversation or babbling (1 Tim 1:6).

Syn.: *mōrología* (3473), foolish talk; *kenophōnía* (2759), empty sounds, fruitless discussions.

Ant.: *sigḗ* (4602), silence; *eulogía* (2129), good speaking, benediction.

3151. ματαιολόγος *mataiológos*; gen. *mataiológou*, masc.-fem., neut. *mataiológon*, adj. from *mátaios* (3152), vain,

and *légō* (3004), to speak. Idly talking.
Used as a subst. a vain talker, one idly
speaking trivialities (Titus 1:10).
   Deriv.: *mataiología* (3150), vain talk.
   Syn.: *phlúaros* (5397), tattler.
   Ant.: *sṓphrōn* (4998), discreet.

3152. μάταιος *mátaios*; fem. *mataía*,
neut. *mátaion*, adj. from *mátēn* (3155), to
no purpose, in vain. Vain, empty, fruitless, aimless. It is building houses on
sand, chasing the wind, shooting at stars,
pursuing one's own shadow (1 Cor 3:20
quoted from Ps 94:11; see 1 Cor 15:17;
Titus 3:9; James 1:26; Sept.: Isa 31:2;
Zech 10:2). In the pl., with the ant., *tá
mátaia*, "vanities," meaning idols, idolatry (Acts 14:15; Sept.: 1 Kgs 16:13; 2
Kgs 17:15; Jer 2:5; 8:19). In 1 Pet 1:18,
idolatrous walk, practice of idolatry.
   Deriv.: *mataiológos* (3151), one who
talks vainly; *mataiótēs* (3153), vanity;
mataióō (3154), to become vain.
   Syn.: *kenós* (2756), empty, vacant,
inane; *kenódoxos* (2755), self-centered,
conceited, vain; *alazṓn* (213), braggart, boastful; *ákarpos* (175), unfruitful;
alusitelḗs (255) and *anōphelḗs* (512), unprofitable.
   Ant.: *karpophóros* (2593), fruitful;
ōphélimos (5624), profitable.

3153. ματαιότης *mataiótēs*; gen.
mataiótetos, fem. noun from *mátaios*
(3152), vain. Vanity, futility, worthlessness, used in Rom 8:20 (see Sept.:
Ps 39:6; 62:9; Eccl 1:2, 14) to show the
emptiness of the present in contrast with
the living fullness of the future (Eph
4:17; 2 Pet 2:18; Sept.: Ps 4:2; 26:4;
119:37; 144:8, 11).
   Ant.: *ōphéleia* (5622), usefulness;
chrḗsis (5540), use; *euergesía* (2108),
beneficence; *chrēstótēs* (5544), goodness; *sumphéron* (4851), mutual benefit.

3154. ματαιόω *mataióō*; contracted *mataiṓ*, fut. *mataiṓsō*, from *mátaios*
(3152), vain. To make vain or worthless,
to cancel out. In the pass. *mataióomai*,
to become vain, destitute of real wisdom

(Rom 1:21), to be or act perversely, foolish. In reality, to get off the right path,
to follow foolish or bad courses (Sept.:
1 Sam 13:13; 26:21; 2 Kgs 17:15; Jer
2:5).
   Syn.: *astochéō* (795), to miss the
mark, fail; *lanthánō* (2990), to escape
notice, be ignorant of; *hamartánō* (264),
to sin; *paraphronéō* (3912), to act foolishly, thoughtlessly.
   Ant.: *epitugchánō* (2013), to chance
upon, succeed, attain, obtain; *euodóō*
(2137), to be successful; *auxánō* (837),
to grow up, increase; *prokóptō* (4298), to
drive forward; *kerdaínō* (2770), to gain.

3155. μάτην *mátēn*; adv. In a causal
sense, meaning groundless, invalid; and
in a final sense, purposeless, useless, futile; and according to circumstances it
may be both idle and vain. Falsely, fruit-
lessly (Matt 15:9; Mark 7:7; Sept.: Jer
2:30).
   Deriv.: *mátaios* (3152), vain.
   Syn.: *dōreán* (1432), gratuitously, in
vain; *adíkōs* (95), wrongfully.
   Ant.: *ōphéleia* (5622), advantage,
usefulness; *chrḗsis* (5540), use.

3156. Ματθαῖος *Matthaíos*; gen. *Mat-
thaíou*, masc. proper noun. Matthew,
meaning gift of God (Acts 1:23, 26), an
apostle (Matt 9:9; 10:3; Mark 3:18; Luke
6:15) and author of the first of the four
Gospels. His original name was Levi
([3018] Mark 2:14; Luke 5:29, 27). His
name, as that of Simon and Saul, was
changed on his being called to the apostleship.
   Matthew was a publican or tax collector near the Sea of Galilee on route
between Damascus and the Phoenician
seaports, and he was called by our Lord
from his tollbooth (Matt 9:9; Mark 2:14;
Luke 5:27, 28). He was one among those
who met in the upper room at Jerusalem after the ascension of our Lord (Acts
1:13).
   His Gospel was written in Palestine and specifically for Jewish Christians, with frequent references to OT

prophecies. It presents Christ as the last and greatest lawgiver and prophet, and as the fulfillment of the OT prophecies of the Messiah and King of the true people of Israel. Its arrangement is not strictly chronological, grouping together the works and sayings of Christ according to their topics. Although it is not certain that this was the first Gospel to be written, Matthew deserves the first place in the NT, forming the best link between the OT and NT and between the Law and the Gospels. It seeks to prove not the abolition of the OT, but the fulfillment of the old dispensation in the new. Where citations from the OT occur in the discourses of our Lord, they are usually from the Sept., while those in the narrative appear to be independent translations from the Hebr.

There is no absolute certainty as to the time of its writing. Evidently, Jerusalem had not yet been destroyed because its destruction is foretold (Matt 24) in a manner that is only explicable on the assumption of its being still a future event to the writer. On the other hand, some time had elapsed since the events recorded in it had occurred (27:7, 8; 28:15). Some give the eighth year after the ascension as the date of its writing and others the fifteenth. If there had been an original Hebr. Gospel, as claimed by some (the drift of scholarly opinion is toward the acceptance of a Gr. original), the earlier date would belong to it; but we would place our present gospel between A.D. 60 and 66, a period during which both Mark and Luke probably wrote their Gospels.

3157. Ματθάν *Matthán*; masc. proper noun, transliterated from the Hebr. *Matān* (4977, OT), gift. Matthan, a person in the genealogy of Joseph, the husband of Mary, the mother of Jesus Christ (Matt 1:15).

3158. Ματθάτ *Matthát*; masc. proper noun, transliterated from the Hebr. Mat-

that, meaning gift of God, two persons in the genealogy of Jesus (Luke 3:24, 29).

3159. Ματθίας *Matthías*, gen. *Matthía*, masc. proper noun transliterated from the Hebr. Matthias, meaning gift of Jehovah. A disciple of Christ appointed by lot to fill the vacancy in the company of the Twelve Apostles created by the departure of Judas (Acts 1:23, 26).

3160. Ματταθά *Mattathá*; masc. proper noun, transliterated from the Hebr. Mattatha, meaning gift of Jehovah, a son of Nathan and grandson of David in the genealogy of Jesus (Luke 3:31).

3161. Ματταθίας *Mattathías*; gen. *Mattathíou*, masc. proper noun. Mattathias. Two persons in the genealogy of Jesus (Luke 3:25, 26).

3162. μάχαιρα *máchaira*; gen. *machaíras*, fem. noun. A knife, slaughter-knife, a sword for cutting (Matt 26:47, 51, 52, 55; Mark 14:43, 47, 48; Luke 21:24; 22:36, 38, 49, 52; John 18:10, 11; Acts 16:27; Heb 4:12; Rev 6:4; 13:10, 14; Sept.: Gen 34:25; Judg 3:16). Metaphorically in Eph 6:17. The sword of justice in relation to the executioner (Acts 12:2; Rom 8:35; Heb 11:34, 37). To bear the sword, meaning to have the power of life and death (Rom 13:4). The sword as standing for war, as opposed to peace (Matt 10:34; see Lev 26:6; Jer 14:13).

Syn.: *rhomphaía* (4501), a sword, usually longer than *máchaira*, figuratively used of judgment.

Ant.: *eirḗnē* (1515), peace.

3163. μάχη *máchē*; gen. *máchēs*, fem. noun from *máchomai* (3164), to fight. Fighting, battle (2 Cor 7:5; 2 Tim 2:23, controversies respecting the Mosaic laws; James 4:1; Sept.: Gen 13:7; Prov 15:18).

The NT includes many kinds of battles such as legal battles as in Titus 3:9, and battles of words (*logomachíai* [3055]) in 1 Tim 6:4.

Deriv.: *ámachos* (269), not contentious.

Syn.: *agōn* (73), strife, fight; *pálē* (3823), wrestling; *pólemos* (4171), war which embraces the whole course of hostilities, not a mere battle; *máchē* (3164), battle, strife; *stásis* (4714), insurrection or sedition as a civil war; *pólemos*, a battle between nations.

Ant.: *anápausis* (372), inner rest; *anápsuxis* (403), revival; *ánesis* (425), liberty, relief; *katápausis* (2663), rest from, cessation of work; *eirḗnē* (1515), peace; *hēsuchía* (2271), quietness.

3164. μάχομαι *máchomai*; fut. *machḗsomai*, mid. deponent. To fight as in war or battle. In the NT, more generally, it means to strive, to contend physically in a private quarrel (Acts 7:26; Sept.: Ex 21:22; 2 Sam 14:6), also to strive or dispute with words (John 6:52; 2 Tim 2:24; James 4:2; Sept.: Gen 31:36).

Deriv.: *diamáchomai* (1264), to fight fiercely; *theomáchos* (2314), one who fights against God; *thēriomachéō* (2341), to fight with wild beasts; *thumomachéō* (2371), to fight fiercely; *máchē* (3163), battle, fighting.

Syn.: *agōnízomai* (75), to contend; *antagōnízomai* (464), to strive against; *puktéō* (4438), to box, fight, as in the Olympic games; *poleméō* (4170), to wage war.

Ant.: *anapaúomai* (373), to rest inwardly; *katapaúomai* (2664), to cease, rest; *anapsúchomai* (404), to refresh oneself; *hēsucházō* (2270), to be quiet; *eirēneúō* (1514), to be at peace; *diallássomai* (1259), to reconcile oneself when the strife may be due to both parties; *katallássomai* (2644), to be reconciled when one is partly to blame, mostly toward God.

3165. μέ *mé*; personal pronoun, 1st person acc. sing., an abbreviated form of the emphatic *emé* (1691), me, I, my.

3166. μεγαλαυχέω *megalauchéō*; contracted *megalauchṓ*, fut. *megalauchḗsō*, from *mégas* (3173), big, and *auchéō* (n.f.), to boast. To brag exceedingly, boast greatly, be a braggart (James 3:5).

Syn.: *hupsóomai* (5312), to exalt; *huperupsóō* (5251), to elevate above others; *huperphronéō* (5252), to think more highly of oneself than is proper; *huperaíromai* (5229), to become haughty, exalt oneself; *huperéchō* (5242), to hold oneself above, to excel; *hupsēlophronéō* (5309), to be arrogant, high-minded; *kaucháomai* (2744), to boast; *doxázō* (1392), to glory.

Ant.: *elattoúmai* (1642), to diminish, lessen; *elattonéomai* (1641), to diminish, fall short; *tapeinoúmai* (5013), to humble oneself, to be humiliated.

3167. μεγαλεῖος *megaleíos*; fem. *megaleía*, neut. *megaleíon*, adj. from *mégas* (3173), great, indicating great works or miracles. Great, glorious, wonderful. As a subst. with the pl. art. *tá megaleía*, great things, wonderful works, contemplated as the outworking of the greatness (*megaleíon*) of God's power and glory (Luke 1:49 [TR]; Acts 2:11; Sept.: Ps 71:19).

Deriv.: *megaleiótēs* (3168), majesty.

Syn.: in the pl. as great things, miracles: *sēmeía* (4592), signs; *dunámeis* (1411), mighty works; *éndoxa* (1741), glorious things; *parádoxa* (3861), strange or extraordinary things; *thaumásia* (2297), astonishing things; *térata* (5059), wonders.

Ant.: *mikrós* (3398), small; *eláchistos* (1646), least; *elachistóteros* (1647), less then the least; *olígos* (3641), little.

3168. μεγαλειότης *megaleiótēs*; gen. *megaleiótētos*, fem. noun from *megaleíos* (3167), great, glorious. Greatness, majesty, glory in connection with God (Luke 9:43); the Lord (2 Pet 1:16); Artemis (Acts 19:27; Sept.: Jer 40:9).

Syn.: *lamprótēs* (2987), brightness; *húpsos* (5311), height; *megalōsúnē* (3172), majesty, a quality recognized by others, while *megaleiótēs* is inherent greatness, not merely attributed. In the case of the goddess Diana (Artemis) of the Ephesians, she was regarded as deity, *megaleiótēs* being attributed to her by her adherents. In the papyri, *megaleiótēs* is used as a ceremonial title. See the distinction between *hagiótēs* (41), holiness per se, and *hagiōsúnē* (42), sanctity which is recognizable by others.

Ant.: *tapeínōsis* (5014), humiliation; *douleía* (1397), bondage; *aischúnē* (152), shame; *entropḗ* (1791), withdrawal; *aidṓs* (127), modesty, reverence; *semnótēs* (4587), modesty, venerableness.

3169. μεγαλοπρεπής *megaloprepḗs*; gen. *megaloprepoús*, masc.-fem., neut. *megaloprepés*, adj. from *mégas* (3173), strong, mighty, great, and *prépō* (4241), it is right or proper. Resplendent, glorious, magnanimous, magnificent, suitably splendid (2 Pet 1:17).

Syn.: *megaleíos* (3167), magnificent; *lamprós* (2986), bright; *áxios* (514), worthy; *megistán* (3175), a great man; *hupsēlós* (5308), lofty; *diaphorṓteros* (1313), differing, surpassing; *pleíōn* (4119), superior; *krátistos* (2903), most honorable or excellent.

Ant.: *eleeinós* (1652), miserable, needing mercy; *talaípōros* (5005), wretched; *tapeinós* (5011), humble; *anáxios* (370), unworthy.

3170. μεγαλύνω *megalúnō*; fut. *megalunṓ*, from *mégas* (3173), great, strong. To make great, enlarge. With the acc., in relation to the borders of garments (Matt 23:5); to show great mercy to someone or to do him great kindness (Luke 1:58); magnify or praise (Luke 1:46; Acts 5:13; 10:46; 19:17; 2 Cor 10:15; Phil 1:20; Sept.: 2 Sam 7:26; Ps 34:3; 69:31).

Syn.: *doxázō* (1392), to glorify; *hupsóō* (5312), to, elevate; *sébomai* (4576), to revere; *hairéomai* (138), to prefer; *aírō* (142), to lift up; *phusióō* (5448), to inflate; *auxánō* (837), to grow, increase; *prokóptō* (4298), to cut one's way forward, advance.

Ant.: *tapeinóō* (5013), to humble; *kataischúnō* (2617), to put to shame; *elattonéō* (1641), to have less; *elattóō* (1642), to decrease, make lower.

3171. μεγάλως *megálōs*; adv. from *mégas* (3173), great, big. Greatly, very (Phil 4:10).

Syn.: *lían* (3029), very, exceedingly, greatly; *sphódra* (4970), greatly; *sphodrōs* (4971), vehemently; *huperbolḗ* (5236), exceeding greatness; *meízon* (3185), the more.

3172. μεγαλωσύνη *megalōsúnē*; gen. *megalōsúnēs*, fem. noun from *mégas* (3173), great, strong. Majesty, usually the divine majesty of God Himself (Heb 1:3; 8:1). In Jude 1:25, used as an ascription. See Sept.: Deut 32:3; 1 Chr 29:11; Ps 145:6.

Syn.: *megaleiótēs* (3168), magnificence, splendor, majesty (which see for distinction from *megalōsúnē*); *mégethos* (3174), greatness as used by the Greek writers; *lamprótēs* (2987), brightness.

Ant.: *tapeínōsis* (5014), humiliation; *douleía* (1397), servitude, slavery.

3173. μέγας *mégas*; fem. *megálē*, neut. *méga*, adj. Great, large, particularly of physical magnitude.

(I) Of men or creatures, great in size, stature (John 21:11, fish; Rev 12:3, dragon); of persons, meaning full-grown (Heb 11:24); see Acts 8:10; 26:22; Heb 8:11; Rev 11:18; Sept.: Gen 19:11; Ezek 17:3; 29:3.

(II) Of things, meaning great:

(A) In size, extent (Matt 27:60, stone; Mark 13:2; Luke 16:26, chasm, gulf; 22:12; Acts 10:11; 1 Cor 16:9, door; Rev 8:10; 11:8; 14:19; 18:21); tall, large (Mark 4:32; Luke 13:19, tree); long (Rev 6:4, sword; 9:14, broad, large river; 20:1, chain).

(B) Of number or amount (Mark 5:11, herd; Heb 10:35); metaphorically (Acts 4:33, grace; Sept.: 1 Kgs 8:65; 2 Chr 7:8).

(C) In price or cost, great, costly, splendid (Luke 5:29, great feast; 14:16, a great supper; 2 Tim 2:20; Sept.: Gen 21:8). Of a day, meaning celebration, great, solemn (John 7:37; 19:31); of the day of judgment (Acts 2:20; Jude 1:6; Rev 6:17; 16:14).

(D) Metaphorically, great in estimation, weight, importance (Matt 22:36, 38, commandment; 1 Cor 9:11; Eph 5:32; 1 Tim 3:16, mystery; Sept.: 1 Sam 22:15). In 1 Tim 6:6 "godliness with contentment" is said to be "great gain." The meaning is that such a virtue represents what is truly significant and genuinely important. *Meízōn* (3187), greater, more important (Matt 23:19; 1 Cor 13:13; Heb 11:26). *Mégistos* (3176), greatest (2 Pet 1:4).

(III) Figuratively, great in force, intensity, effect, e.g.:

(A) As affecting the external senses, great, vehement, violent. Used of a fall (Matt 7:27); earthquake (Luke 21:11); voice (Matt 24:31); storm of wind (Mark 4:37); calm (Mark 4:39); ruin (Luke 6:49); wind (John 6:18); cry (Acts 23:9; Rev 14:18); hail (Rev 11:19; 16:21); fever (Luke 4:38); lamentation (Acts 8:2; Sept.: Gen 50:10).

(B) As affecting the mind and causing emotion, used of joy (Matt 2:10); ecstasy (Mark 5:42); fear (Luke 2:9); sorrow (Rom 9:2); wrath (Rev 12:12). Of events: tribulation (Matt 24:21); famine (Luke 4:25); distress (Luke 21:23); persecution (Acts 8:1); plague (Rev 16:21); see Sept.: Job 2:13. Of things exciting admiration, meaning great, mighty, wonderful, e.g., *sēmeía* (4592), signs, great signs, mighty wonderful miracles (Matt 24:24; Luke 21:11; Acts 6:8); *dúnamis*, power (Acts 8:10). Joined with *thaumastós* (2298), wonderful (Rev 15:1, 3); with *oún* (3767), therefore, what wonder then (2 Cor 11:15). Sept.: Deut 6:22; 10:21; 29:2.

(IV) Figuratively, great in power, dignity, authority, e.g., *hoi megáloi*, the great, meaning nobles, princes (Matt 20:25; Mark 10:42); king (Matt 5:35);

high priest (Heb 4:14; 10:21); God (Titus 2:13; Rev 19:17); Diana (Acts 19:27, 28, 34, 35). Generally with the meaning of great, distinguished (Matt 5:19; Mark 10:43); prophet (Luke 7:16; Acts 8:9). In a bad sense, meaning great, noted, *hē pórnē* (4204), harlot (Rev 17:1; 19:2).

(V) Implying censure, too great, i.e., lofty, boastful, arrogant (Rev 13:5; Sept.: Dan 7:8, 20).

Deriv.: *megalauchéō* (3166), to boast or to talk big; *megaleíos* (3167), magnificent; *megaloprepés* (3169), excellent; *megalúnō* (3170), to magnify; *megálōs* (3171), greatly; *megalōsúnē* (3172), greatness, majesty; *mégethos* (3174), magnitude; *mégistos* (3176), greatest.

Syn.: *dunatós* (1415), powerful, mighty; *ischurós* (2478), valiant, strong; *krataiós* (2900), mighty, powerful; *dunástēs* (1413), potentate, despot; *hikanós* (2425), sufficient, competent; *pēlíkos* (4080), how large; *hupsēlós* (5308), high, lofty; *húpsistos* (5310), the highest; *meízōn* (3187), greater; *meizóteros* (3186), greater; *polús* (4183), much, great; *pósos* (4214), how much; *hósos* (3745), as much as; *tosoútos* (5118), so much; *tēlikoútos* (5082), so mighty.

Ant.: *mikrós* (3398), small; *olígos* (3641), little; *eláchistos* (1646), least; *elachistóteros* (1647), less than the least; *ásēmos* (767), not distinguished; *elásson* (1640), less; *brachús* (1024), short, little.

3174. μέγεθος *mégethos*; gen. *megéthous*, neut. noun from *mégas* (3173), strong, great. Greatness, used metaphorically (Eph 1:19; Sept.: Ex 15:16).

Syn.: *huperbolé* (5236), immeasurable greatness; *megalōsúnē* (3172), majesty; *megaleiótēs* (3168), splendor, magnificence.

3175. μεγιστᾶνες *megistánes*; gen. *megistánōn*, pl. masc. noun from *mégistos* (3176), the greatest. Persons of the highest ranks, great men, lords, magnates (Mark 6:21; Rev 6:15; 18:23;

Sept.: 2 Chr 36:18; Jer 14:3; Jon 3:7; Nah 2:5).

Syn.: *despótēs* (1203), despot; *archēgós* (747), a founder or leader; *árchōn* (758), a ruler or prince; *hēgemṓn* (2232), a leader or governor; *ethnárchēs* (1481), ethnarch, national leader; *kúrios* (2962), lord; *kubernḗtēs* (2942), captain, master.

Ant.: *doúlos* (1401), servant, slave; *hupērétēs* (5257), a subordinate; *therápōn* (2324), a menial attendant; *diákonos* (1249), minister, deacon.

3176. μέγιστος *mégistos*; fem. *megístē*, neut. *mégiston*, adj., the superlative of *mégas* (3173), great, strong. Preeminent, great, strong (2 Pet 1:4).

Deriv.: *megistánes* (3175), great men, lords.

3177. μεθερμηνεύω *methermēneúō*, fut. *methermēneúsō*, from *metá* (3326), after, with, and *hermēneúō* (2059), to interpret. To translate from one language into another, interpret. Used only in the pass. (Matt 1:23; Mark 5:41; 15:22, 34; John 1:41; Acts 4:36; 13:8).

Syn.: *diermēneúō* (1329), to translate, interpret; *exēgéomai* (1834), to lead out, explain, declare; *phōtízō* (5461), to illuminate, enlighten; *orthotoméō* (3718), to rightly divide, expound correctly.

Ant.: *sugchéō* (4797), to throw into confusion; *skotízō* (4654), to obscure.

3178. μέθη *méthē*; gen. *méthēs*, fem. noun from *méthu* (n.f., see below), mulled wine. Drunkenness (Luke 21:34; Rom 13:13; Gal 5:21; Sept.: Ezek 23:32; 39:19).

Deriv. of *méthu* (n.f.): *methúskō* (3182), to make or become drunk; *méthusos* (3183), a drunkard; *methúō* (3184), to be drunk.

Syn.: *pótos* (4224), banqueting or a drinking party, not necessarily ending in *méthē*, actual drunkenness; *pósis* (4213), the act of drinking; *kraipálē* (2897), dissipation, excess, a headache from drunkenness; *oinophlugía* (3632), excess of

wine. *Méthē* is stronger and expresses a greater excess than *oínōsis*, the influence of wine.

Ant.: *egkráteia* (1466), continence, temperance; *sōphrosúnē* (4997), sobriety, self-control.

3179. μεθιστάνω *methistánō*, **μεθίστημι** *methístēmi* fut. *metastḗsō*, from *metá* (3326), denoting change of place or condition, and *hístēmi* (2476), to place, stand. To remove from an office, trans. (Luke 16:4; Acts 13:22); to move someone into the kingdom of the Son of God (Col 1:13; Sept.: Isa 54:10); to turn away, pervert (Acts 19:26; Sept.: Isa 59:15). Spelled *methistánō*, to remove from its place, transfer (1 Cor 13:2).

The verb *methístēmi* in Acts 13:22 refers to the death of Saul and not to the mere removal from being king since he was king until his death (1 Sam 31; 2 Sam 2 and 5) when David became king.

Syn.: *metatíthēmi* (3346), to transport, change, remove; *metakinéō* (3334), to move away; *astatéō* (790), to have no permanent dwelling place; *ekchōréō* (1633), to depart.

Ant.: *ménō* (3306), remain, abide; *paraménō* (3887), to remain permanently; *hístēmi* (2476), to stand, stay; *stḗkō* (4739), to stand fast; *períkeimai* (4029), to lie all around; *parákeimai* (3873) to lie near, to be present; *periménō* (4037), to wait; *perileípō* (4035), to remain; *anaménō* (362), to await; *apókeimai* (606), to await, be laid up; *títhēmi* (5087), to place; *paratíthēmi* (3908), to place alongside, deposit; *apokathístēmi* (600), to restore.

3180. μεθοδεία *methodeía*; gen. *methodeías*, fem. noun from *methodeúō* (n.f.), to work by method. Method, the following or pursuing of an orderly and technical procedure in the handling of a subject. In the NT, connected with evil doing, a device, artifice, art, artificial method, craft or wile (Eph 4:14; 6:11; Sept.: 2 Sam 19:27, the verb *methodeúō*).

Syn.: *dólos* (1388), wile, craft; *apátē* (539), deceit; *panourgía* (3834), trickery, craftiness.

Ant.: *ōphéleia* (5622), benefit; *boétheia* (996), help; *óphelos* (3786), benefit, advantage; *epikouría* (1947), assistance.

3181. μεθόριος *methórios*; gen. *methoríou*, masc.-fem., neut. *methórion*, adj. from *metá* (3326), with, and *hóros* (n.f., see below), boundary, limit. Bordering upon, frontier, used only in the pl. with the def. art. as a subst., *tá methória*, in relation to the *chōría* (5564), lands or fields, meaning borders, confines (Mark 7:24).

Deriv. of *hóros* (n.f.): *horízō* (3724), to mark out definitely, determine; *horothesía* (3734), a setting of bounds or a limit.

3182. μεθύσκω *methúskō*; fut. *methúsō*, aor. pass. *emethústhēn* (with mid. meaning), from *méthu* (n.f., see *méthē* [3178]), wine. To make drunk. In the mid., to become drunk, be drunken, get drunk. Used in an absolute sense (Luke 12:45, drinking and getting drunk; 1 Thess 5:7). With the dat. noun *oínō* (3631), wine (Eph 5:18, which would prove that *oínos*, wine, cannot be taken as referring to unfermented grape juice).

Syn.: *methúō* (2184), to be drunk.

Ant.: *néphō* (3525), to be sober; *sōphronéō* (4993), to act soberly, restrict one's freedom, exercise sound mind; *ananéphō* (366), to become sober again; *sunérchomai* (4905), to come to oneself; *egkrateúomai* (1467), to exercise self-restraint.

3183. μέθυσος *méthusos*; gen. *methúsou*, masc.-fem., neut. *méthuson*, adj. from *méthu* (n.f., see *méthē* [3178]), wine. Drunken; used as a subst., a drunkard (1 Cor 5:11; 6:10; Sept.: Prov 23:21; 26:9). Earlier Greek writers used *méthusos* only of females, but later it was used also of men.

Syn.: *pároinos* (3943), given to wine; *akratés* (193), incontinent; *ékdotos* (1560), given over to.

Ant.: *nēphálios* (3524), sober; *sóphrōn* (4998), of sound mind, self-controlled; *egkratés* (1468), continent, self-controlled.

3184. μεθύω *methúō*; fut. *methúō*, from *méthu* (n.f., see *méthē* [3178]), wine. Generally to drink wine or strong drink more freely than usual without any reference to whether one gets drunk or not. To be drunk, get drunk, and by implication to carouse. Used in an absolute sense in Matt 24:49 as a pl. subst., *tón methuóntōn*, "with the drunken." See Acts 2:15; 1 Cor 11:21; 1 Thess 5:7. Used metaphorically in Rev 17:2 (meaning to become drunk with fornication, i.e., never having enough of it); 17:6 (equating the blood shed with the means of drunkenness. See Sept.: 1 Sam 1:13; Job 12:25; Isa 28:21 [cf. Deut 32:42]).

Deriv.: *améthustos* (271), amethyst.

Syn.: *methúskō* (3182), to intoxicate.

Ant.: *néphō* (3525), to be sober; *ananéphō* (366), to become sober again; *sunérchomai* (4905), to come to oneself; *sōphronéō* (4993), to act soberly, restrict one's freedom, exercise sound mind; *egkrateúomai* (1467), to exercise self-restraint.

3185. μεῖζον *meízon*; adv., the neut. of *meízōn* (3187). In a greater degree, the more. Used as an adv. only in Matt 20:31 meaning the more.

Syn.: *polús* (4183), much, great; *pleíōn* (4119), more; *tosoútos* (5118), so great; *tēlikoútos* (5082), so vast, great; *hósos* (3745), as great; *pósos* (4214), how much, large; *hēlíkos* (2245), how great, how large; *perissós* (4053), superabundant.

3186. μειζότερος *meizóteros*; adj., the comparative of *meízōn* (3187). Larger, greater, stronger. Only in 3 John 1:4, meaning greater.

Syn.: *mégistos* (3176), greatest; *pleíōn* (4119), greater; *perissóteros* (4055), more abundant; *perissóteron* (4054), more abundantly.

Ant.: *mikróteros* (3398), smaller; *elássōn* (1640), smaller in quantity, quality, or age; *ḗttōn* (2276), less, worse; *eláchistos* (1646), least, smallest; *elachistóteros* (1647), less than the least.

3187. μείζων *meízōn*; adj., the comparative of *mégas* (3173), great, strong, large. Greater, more, older (Matt 12:6; 13:32; 18:4; 23:11, 17, 19; Mark 4:32; 9:34; 12:31; Luke 9:46; 12:18; 22:26, 27; John 1:50; 4:12; 5:36; 8:53; 10:29; 14:12, 28; 15:13, 20; 1 Cor 13:13; Heb 6:13, 16; 9:11; 11:26; James 3:1; 4:6; 1 John 3:20; 4:4; 5:9). Of age, *ho meízōn*, meaning the elder (Rom 9:12 quoted from Gen 25:23). Followed by the gen. (Matt 11:11; Luke 7:28; John 13:16; 1 Cor 14:5). Used simply without any qualification (Matt 18:1; Luke 22:24; 2 Pet 2:11). Metaphorically, of guilt (John 19:11). *Meízona érga* (*érga* [2041], works) greater works (John 5:20) As an adv., with *krázō* (2896), to cry more vehemently (Matt 20:31). The comparative *meizóteros* (3186), in the greater degree, the more.

Syn.: *prṓtos* (4413), first, the best; *pleíōn* (4119), greater; *perissóteros* (4055), more abundant; *mállon* (3123), much more; *perissóteron* (4054), more abundantly; *hupér* (5228), over, above, more; *hóson* (3745), the more; *perissós* (4053), abundant.

Ant.: *hḗssōn* (2276), less, worse.

3188. μέλαν *mélan*; gen. *mélanos*, neut. noun from *mélas* (3189), black. Something black, such as ink (2 Cor 3:3; 2 John 1:12; 3 John 1:13).

Ant.: *leukós* (3022), white.

3189. μέλας *mélas*; fem. *mélaina*, neut. *mélan* ([3188], something black), adj. Black (Matt 5:36, referring to hair; Rev 6:5, 12; Sept.: Lev 13:37; Song 1:5).

Syn.: as a subst.: *gnóphos* (1105), blackness, gloom, associated with the idea of a tempest; *skótos* (4655), darkness; *zóphos* (2217), the gloom of the regions of the lost, darkness, blackness.

Ant.: *leukós* (3022), white.

3190. Μελεᾶς *Meleás*; gen. *Meleá*, masc. proper noun. Meleas (Luke 3:31), an ancestor of the Lord Jesus.

3191. μελετάω *meletáō*; contracted *meletṓ*, fut. *meletḗsō*, from *melétē* (n.f.), care, meditation, which is from *mélō* (n.f.), to be of interest, to concern oneself. To consider, weigh or ponder over something so as to be able to perform well; equal to meditate, with the acc. of thing (Mark 13:11; Acts 4:25 quoted from Ps 2:1; 1 Tim 4:15).

Deriv.: *promeletáō* (4304), to premeditate.

Syn.: *spoudázō* (4704), to study or show diligence; *phrontízō* (5431), to exercise thought; *suntēréō* (4933), to observe, keep, preserve; *gumnázō* (1128), to exercise.

3192. μέλι *méli*; gen. *mélitos*, neut. noun. Honey (Matt 3:4; Mark 1:6; Rev 10:9, 10; Sept.: Gen 43:11; Judg 14:8, 18).

3193. μελίσσιος *melíssios*; gen. *melissíou*, masc.-fem., neut. *melíssion*, adj. from *mélissa* (n.f.), bee. Of bees, made by bees (Luke 24:42).

3194. Μελίτη *Melítē*; gen. *Melítēs*, fem. proper noun. Melita, an island in the Mediterranean lying to the south of Sicily (Acts 28:1). Here Paul was shipwrecked after being driven by a storm for fourteen days in the Adriatic Sea, between Sicily and Greece. From there he sailed again on a direct course by Syracuse and Rhegium to Puteoli (Acts 28:11ff.).

3195. μέλλω *méllō*; imperf. *émellon* or *émellon*, fut. *mellḗsō*. To be about to do or suffer something, to be at the point of, to be impending, followed by the inf. (mostly the fut. inf., although infrequently in the NT the pres. inf.). When followed by the pres. and aor. inf., it implies duration or transientness.

(I) Particularly and generally followed by the pres. inf. *émelle teleután* (5053), to die, meaning "about to die" or "at the point of death" (a.t. [Luke 7:2; John 4:47; Acts 21:27; 27:33]); followed by the aor. inf., *há méllei apothaneín* (*apothaneín* [599], to die), that are ready to die (Rev 3:2 [TR], see Rev 12:4).

(II) Also as implying purpose, meaning to have in mind, to intend, will, followed by the pres. inf. as in Matt 2:13, *méllei . . . zēteín* ([2212], seek), will seek. See Luke 10:1; John 6:6; Acts 3:3; 12:6; Rev 10:4. Followed by the aor. inf. (Rev 2:10; 3:16).

(III) Meaning ought, should, must, as implying necessity in accordance with the nature of things or with the divine appointment and therefore certain, destined to take place. Followed by the pres. inf. (Matt 11:14; 20:22; Mark 10:32; Luke 9:31, 44; John 11:51; Acts 28:6; Rom 4:24; 8:13; Heb 1:14; James 2:12); followed by the aor. inf. (Rom 8:18; Gal 3:23; Rev 2:10); by the fut. inf. (Acts 11:28; 24:15). As a part., *méllōn*, masc.; *méllousa*, fem.; *méllon*, neut.; meaning to be impending or future. With the inf. implied as *ésesthai* (2071), shall be, *érchesthai* (2064), to come (Matt 3:7; 12:32; Rom 5:14; 1 Tim 4:8; Heb 9:11; 13:14). *Méllonta*, things to come (Rom 8:38; 1 Cor 3:22). *Eis tó méllon* (*eis* [1519], in); in the future, hereafter (Luke 13:9; 1 Tim 6:19).

(IV) With the meaning of may, can, implying possibility, probability, what one hopes or fears, followed by the pres. inf. (Matt 24:6; Luke 22:23, *ho toúto méllōn prássein* [*toúto* {5124}, this; *prássō* {4238}, do, perform], who might or could do this). See Acts 20:38; 1 Tim 1:16. Followed by the fut. inf. (Acts 27:10).

(V) Always about to do a thing, i.e., to linger, delay (Acts 22:16).

3196. μέλος *mélos*; gen. *mélous*, neut. noun. A limb or member of the body (Matt 5:29, 30; Rom 12:4; 1 Cor 12:12, 14, 18–20, 22, 25, 26; James 3:5, 6). In the pl. *tá mélē*, the members of the body as the seat of the desires and passions (Rom 6:13, 19; 7:5, 23; 1 Cor 6:15; Col 3:5; James 4:1). Used metaphorically, meaning a member of the Church of which Christ is the head (1 Cor 12:27; Eph 5:30). In Rom 12:5, "members one of another" means intimately united in Christian fellowship (Eph 4:25).

Syn.: *kôlon* (2966), a severed limb of the body; *polítēs* (4177), a citizen, member of a state.

3197. Μελχί *Melchí*; masc. proper noun transliterated from the Hebr. Melchi, meaning my king. Two of Jesus' ancestors (Luke 3:24, 28).

3198. Μελχισεδέκ *Melchisedék*; masc. proper noun transliterated from the Hebr. *Malkī-Tsedek* (4442, OT), king of righteousness. Melchizedek, a king of Salem (or Jerusalem) and a patriarchal priest of Jehovah, contemporary with Abraham (see Gen 14:17–20).

The meaning of the name is interpreted in Heb 7:2 as "King of righteousness." Melchizedek reigned as king of Salem (which means peace), or king of Jerusalem He is presented as being a prototype of Jesus Christ, who is the King of righteousness and peace. Further, Melchizedek combined in himself both kingly and priestly offices.

In Heb 5:6, 10; 6:20 and all of Heb 7, Melchizedek marks the character of the permanent priesthood of Jesus Christ. The order of this priesthood was above that of Aaron, having no defects inherent to human priesthood. Being the possessor of righteousness and peace, he was able to impart them with royal bounty. He was beyond ancestral limitations, without beginning or end ascribed to his priesthood. He represented what Christ as the incarnate *Lógos* (3056), Word, came to be.

Some have ventured the interpretation of Melchizedek as a theophany, an appearance of Jesus Christ in human form before His incarnation. Other possibilities suggested regarding Melchizedek's identity are that he was actually the patriarch Shem or that he was a Canaanite king-priest.

3199. μέλει *mélei*; imperf. *émele*; fut. *melései*, the impers. form of *mélō* (n.f., see below), to care, be concerned. To be of interest to, to concern oneself (Matt 22:16; Mark 4:38; 12:14; Luke 10:40; John 10:13; 12:6; Acts 18:17; 1 Cor 7:21; 9:9; 1 Pet 5:7).

Deriv. of *mélei*: *ameléō* (272), to neglect.

of *mélō* (n.f.): *epimeléomai* (1959), to take care of; *metamélomai* (3338), to regret.

Syn.: *merimnáō* (3309), to be concerned or anxious about; *epimeléomai* (1959), to take care of with forethought and provision; *phrontízō* (5431), to exercise care and make provision; *phronéō* (5426), to think, mind; *episkopéō* (1983), to show oversight; *proséchō* (4337), to pay attention.

Ant.: *ameléō* (272), to neglect; *epilanthánomai* (1950), to put out of one's mind, be forgetful; *oligōréō* (3643), to have little time or regard for, despise; *amérimnos* (275), an adj. meaning without anxiety or care.

3200. μεμβράνα *membrána*; gen. *membránēs*, Lat. *membrana*, fem. noun. Membrane, skin, parchment (2 Tim 4:13). The Eng. "parchment" is a form of *pergaménē*, an adj. meaning from Pergamum, the city in Asia Minor mentioned in Rev 2:12, where parchment was invented and named after the city. When Paul wrote to Timothy (2 Tim 4:13) to "bring . . . the parchments," he may have been asking for blank parchments in order to write letters. These parchments were prepared from the skin of a sheep or goat. They were first soaked in lime for the purpose of removing the hair. Then they were shaved, washed, dried, stretched, and kneaded or smoothed with fine chalk or lime and pumice stone. The best kind was called vellum, and was made from the skins of calves or kids.

3201. μέμφομαι *mémphomai*; fut. *mémpsomai*, mid. deponent. To find fault with, blame, censure, used with a dat. (Heb 8:8); used in an absolute sense (Mark 7:2 [TR]; Rom 9:19).

Deriv.: *ámempos* (273), unblamed; *mempsímoiros* (3202), complaining, finding fault; *momphḗ* (3437), blame, quarrel with.

Syn.: *mōmáomai* (3469), to find fault with; *kataginṓskō* (2607), to condemn; *elégchō* (1651), to convict; *hamartánō* (264), to censure, fault; *katadikázō* (2613), to condemn; *krínō* (2919), to judge; *katakrínō* (2632), to pronounce sentence upon; *epitimáō* (2008), to rebuke.

Ant.: *ainéō* (134), to praise; *epainéō* (1867), to commend; *eulogéō* (2127), to speak well of, praise.

3202. μεμψίμοιρος *mempsímoiros*; gen. *mempsimoírou*, masc.-fem., neut. *mempsímoiron*, adj. from *mémphomai* (3201), to blame, and *moíra* (n.f.), a portion, allotment. A discontented, complaining person, one who finds fault with his lot (Jude 1:16).

Ant.: *makários* (3107), blessed, satisfied.

3203–3302. These numbers skipped over in *Strong's Dictionary of the Greek Testament*.

3303. μέν *mén*; conj., implying affirmation or concession. Indeed, truly, and at the same time pointing forward to something other than the one affirmed which is opposite to it or at least different. It is commonly subjoined with *dé* (1161), and used as a particle although contrast or another equivalent particle may be used. Thus the two words *mén* and *dé* correspond to each other and mark the protasis (proposition or condition) and apodosis (conclusion or promise of fulfillment). Where the antithesis is strong, *mén* / *dé* may be rendered indeed / but. In many instances, however, they merely mark a transition or are continuative, and cannot be rendered well in Eng. *Mén* is regularly placed after the word to which it belongs in sense, usually after one, two, three, or even four words in a clause as in John 16:22, but never at the beginning.

(I) Where there is a distinct and definite antithesis and *mén* retains its concessive power, it means indeed.

(A) With some other particle in the apodosis so that *mén* / *dé* is equivalent to "indeed / but" (a.t. [Matt 3:11; 9:37; 17:11; Mark 1:8; 10:39, 40; John 16:22; Acts 1:5; 22:9; Rom 2:7, 8; 1 Cor 11:14; 12:20; Phil 3:1; Heb 3:5, 6; 1 Pet 1:20]). Placed irregularly, i.e., before the word to which it refers (Acts 22:3; Titus 1:15; Sept.: Job 42:5); with *gár* (1063) or *oún* (3767), therefore, where each particle retains its own proper force, e.g., *mén gár* / *dé* meaning "for indeed / but" (a.t. [Acts 13:36, 37, "for David / but"; 23:8; 25:11; 28:22; Rom 2:25; 1 Cor 11:7; 2 Cor 9:1, 3; Heb 7:18]; *mén oún* / *dé*, where *oún* is inferential (illative) and *mén* refers to *dé*, indeed, therefore or then / but (Acts 18:14f.; 19:38f.; 1 Cor 9:25; Phil 2:23).

(B) With some other particle in the apodosis, such as *allá* (235), but (Acts 4:16; 1 Cor 14:17); *mén* / *épeita* (1899), after that (John 11:7; James 3:17); *mén* / *kaí* (2532), and (Acts 27:21; 1 Thess 2:18); *mén* / *plḗn* (4133), except (Luke 22:22); *mén oún* / *tanún* (3569), but now (Acts 17:30).

(C) The adversative particle *dé* or the like is sometimes missing after *mén*, either because the antithesis is expressed in some other way, as Heb 12:9, or because the apodosis itself is omitted. (1) Where the apodosis is obviously implied (Acts 19:4; Rom 7:12; Col 2:23;

Heb 6:16). (2) Where through a change of construction the writer neglects the apodosis and turns to something else (Rom 1:8; 10:1; 2 Cor 12:12) and also with *mén gár* in 2 Cor 11:4. (3) Sometimes the apodosis is, as it were, obliterated, in which case *mén* serves to isolate some person or thing and thus to exclude everything else which might otherwise be expected or implied. This is especially true with a personal pron. as *egṓ mén* (*egṓ* [1473, I]), meaning I indeed, I at least (Acts 26:9; Rom 11:13; 1 Cor 3:4; 11:18; 1 Thess 2:18). In opposition, the adversative *dé* sometimes stands in the apodosis without *mén* in the protasis (Luke 11:47; 23:56; 24:1).

(II) Where the antithesis is less definite, so that *mén* / *dé* serve to mark transition or are merely continuative. Here the force of *mén* cannot be given exactly in Eng., while *dé* is rendered as "but" or "and."

(A) Simply *mén* / *dé* as in Matt 25:33, in which the translation is, "He shall set the sheep on his right hand, but (and) the goats on the left." See Luke 13:9; Acts 14:12; Rom 8:17; 1 Cor 1:23; 2 Tim 4:4; Jude 1:8.

(B) With *oún* (3767), therefore, in the expression *mén* / *oún*, meaning only therefore, then. (1) Followed by *dé* (Mark 16:19, 20; John 19:24, 25; Acts 1:6, 7; 2:41, 42; 8:4, 5; 9:31, 32; 12:5; 13:4, 6; 14:3f.; 15:3f.; 23:18f.; 28:5f.). (2) Without *dé* where *mén* / *oún* then serves as a continuative with a certain degree of illative (inferential) force, meaning therefore (Acts 23:22; 1 Cor 6:4; Heb 7:11); followed by *kaí* (2532), and (Acts 1:18; 26:4, 6). Also with an affirmative power, yea, indeed, certainly, verily (Acts 26:9; 1 Cor 6:7; Phil 3:8; Heb 9:1).

(III) In partition or distribution, joined with the art. *ho*, *hē*, *tó* (masc., fem., neut.) or the relative pron. *hós*, *hḗ*, *hó*, meaning "the one / the other" (a.t.), "this / that" (a.t. [Phil 1:16, 17; Heb 7:5, 6, 21]); "one / another" (a.t.), and in the pl. "some / others" (a.t. [Matt 22:5, 6; Acts 14:4; 17:32]); *hoi mén* / *álloi dé*, "one /

another" (a.t. [Matt 16:14; John 7:12]); *mén / dé*, "the one / the other" (a.t. [Luke 23:33; 2 Cor 2:16]). See Matt 13:4, 8; Mark 4:4, 5; Luke 8:5, 6; Acts 27:44; Rom 9:21; Jude 1:22. Joined with other pron. (1 Cor 1:12; 15:39; Heb 10:33). Joined with an adv. (Heb 7:8).

3304. μενοῦνγε *menoúnge*; compound particle of affirmation or concession, from *mén* (3303), indeed, and *oún* (3767), but now, verily, therefore, and *ge* (1065), an emphatic. Yes indeed, yes verily, found in composition (Luke 11:28; Rom 9:20; 10:18; Phil 3:8).

3305. μέντοι *méntoi*; conj. from *mén* (3303), indeed, and the enclitic *toí* (5104), yet. Indeed, truly, certainly, especially in neg. clauses and answers. With the meaning of though, yet, nevertheless (John 4:27; 7:13; 12:42; 20:5; 21:4; 2 Tim 2:19; Jude 1:8). With the meaning of indeed therefore, therefore then (James 2:8).

Syn.: *ára* (686), therefore; *hóthen* (3606), wherefore; *hóste* (5620), therefore; *loipón* (3063), henceforth.

3306. μένω *ménō*; fut. *menō̃*, aor. *émeina*, perf. *meménēka*, pluperf. 3d person pl. *memenḗkeisan* (1 John 2:19). To remain, abide, dwell, live.
(I) Intrans., to remain, dwell.
(A) Of place, i.e., of a person remaining or dwelling in a place (Matt 10:11; 26:38; John 2:12). Followed by *en* (1722), in, with the dat. of place (Luke 8:27; 19:5; John 7:9; 8:35; Acts 20:15; 27:31; 2 Tim 4:20); by *pará* (3844), with, with the dat. of person (John 4:40; 14:25; Acts 9:43; 18:3, 20); with *tḗ oikía* (*oikía* [3614], house) or *tō̃ oíkō* implied (John 8:35; Acts 16:15); by *metá* (3326), with, with the gen. of person (Luke 24:29); with the notion of help (John 14:16, 17); *katá heautón* (*katá* [2596], by; *heautón* [1438], himself), by himself (Acts 28:16); by *sún* (4862), with, and the dat. of person (Luke 1:56). With the meaning of to lodge, preceded by *pou* (4226),

where (John 1:38, 39). Of things, followed by *epí* (1909), upon with the gen. (John 19:31). Figuratively, followed by *epí* with the dat. (2 Cor 3:14).
(B) Of a state or condition. Followed by an adv. (1 Cor 7:8, 40); by *en* (1722), in, with the dat. (John 12:46; 1 Cor 7:20, 24; 1 John 3:14); with *en* implied (Phil 1:25); by the dat. of person meaning to remain one's own, i.e., in his power (Acts 5:4). With a subst. or adj. implying condition, character (1 Cor 7:11; 2 Tim 2:13; Heb 7:3, "remains a priest" [a.t.]). Also with things (John 12:24 with *mónos* [3441], alone, meaning remains sterile; Acts 27:41). With the adj. implied, e.g., *asáleutos* (761), firm, steadfast (Rom 9:11 opposed to *katakaíomai* [2618], to burn down; 1 Cor 3:14, 15). With the part., remaining unsold (Acts 5:4). With the adjunct of time during or to which a person or thing remains, continues, endures (1 Cor 15:6, "until this day" [a.t.]; see Matt 11:23). "If I wish him to remain until I come" (a.t. [John 21:22, 23]); retain his power (Rev 17:10); to remain forever (John 12:34; 2 Cor 9:9; 1 Pet 1:25; Sept.: Ps 9:7; 111:5, 9); "unto everlasting life" (John 6:27). Used in an absolute sense, with the idea of perpetuity, i.e., to remain or endure forever, to be perpetual, e.g., Christian graces, rewards, institutes. "Now there remains faith, hope, love" (a.t. [1 Cor 13:13]). See John 15:16; 2 Cor 3:11; Heb 10:34; 12:27; 13:1.
(C) Of the relation in which one person or thing stands with another, chiefly in John's writings; thus to remain in or with someone, i.e., to be and remain united with him, one with him in heart, mind, and will; e.g., with *en* and the dat. of person (John 6:56; 14:10; 15:4–7; 1 John 2:6; 3:24; 4:15, 16); by *metá* (3326), with, and the gen. (1 John 2:19). Also to remain in something which is equivalent to remaining steadfast, persevering in it, e.g., with *en* and the dat. (John 8:31; 15:9; 1 John 4:16); in the light (1 John 2:10); in the doctrine (1 Tim 2:15, "if they continue in the faith" [a.t.]; 2 John

1:9). Conversely and in a like general sense, the same things are said to remain in a person, e.g., with *en* and the dat. of person (John 5:38; 15:11; 1 John 2:14; 3:17; 2 John 1:2). In a similar sense, spoken of divine gifts or privileges, followed by *epí*, upon, and the acc., or by *en* and the dat. (John 1:32, 33); *en autô*, "in him" (1 John 3:15). Also of evils (John 3:36; 9:41, "your sin remains upon you" [a.t.] means you remain in your sin).

(II) Trans., to remain for someone, wait for, await, with the acc. (Acts 20:5, 23; Sept.: Isa 8:17).

Deriv.: *anaménō* (362), to await; *diaménō* (1265), to continue abiding throughout; *emménō* (1696), to persevere; *epiménō* (1960), to continue in, tarry; *kataménō* (2650), to remain or abide constantly or frequently; *moné* (3438), an abode, place to stay; *paraménō* (3887), to remain beside, endure; *periménō* (4037), to stay around, wait for; *prosménō* (4357), to abide still longer, continue with; *hupoménō* (5278), to hold out, wait on, remain or abide under, be patient.

Syn.: *diatríbō* (1304), to spend or pass time, stay; *diateléō* (1300), to continue right through; *proskarteréō* (4342), to continue steadfast; *dianuktereúō* (1273), to pass the night; *kathízō* (2523), to sit down; *apoleípō* (620), to remain; *chronízō* (5549), to tarry; *anastréphō* (390), to abide; *aulízomai* (835), to pass the night in the open air; *agrauléō* (63), to lodge in a fold or in a field; *hístēmi* (2476), to abide, continue.

Ant.: *apérchomai* (565), pass away.

3307. μερίζω merízō; fut. *merísō*, from *merís* (3310), a part. To divide, part, share (Mark 6:41; Luke 12:13 [cf. Heb 7:2]; Sept.: Ex 15:9; Josh 14:5). To divide, separate into parts (1 Cor 1:13). To distribute (Rom 12:3; 1 Cor 7:17; 2 Cor 10:13). In the pass., to be divided, disunited by discord (Matt 12:25, 26; Mark 3:24–26). To be different, to differ (1 Cor 7:34).

Deriv.: *diamerízō* (1266), to divide among, distribute; *merismós* (3311), a

division, partition, distribution; *meristḗs* (3312), divider, distributor; *summerízō* (4829), to have a share in, be a partaker of, distribute in shares.

Syn.: *diaphérō* (1308), to be different from; *diakrínō* (1252), to discriminate, make a distinction; *aphorízō* (873), to mark off boundaries; *diairéō* (1244), to divide into parts, distribute; *diadídōmi* (1239) and *aponémō* (632), to distribute; *kataklērodotéō* (2624), to distribute as an inheritance; *dídōmi* (1325), to give; *apodídōmi* (591), to restore; *epidídōmi* (1929), to hand over; *metadídōmi* (3330), to share; *paradídōmi* (3860), to give or hand over; *charízomai* (5483), to show favor or kindness; *paréchō* (3930), to furnish, provide; *dōréomai* (1433), to bestow; *diḯstēmi* (1339), to set apart, separate; *apospáō* (645), to drag off or draw away; *chōrízō* (5563), to part; *apochōrízō* (673), to part from; *klēróō* (2820), to assign, obtain an inheritance; *skorpízō* (4650) and *diaskorpízō* (1287), to dissipate, disperse, scatter; *diaspeírō* (1289), to distribute in foreign lands, scatter abroad; *speírō* (4687), to scatter, sow; *dialúō* (1262), to dissolve utterly, scatter; *suntríbō* (4937), to break, crush completely; *diaspáō* (1288), pluck asunder, draw apart, pull in pieces.

Ant.: *sunágō* (4863), to gather together, assemble; *episunágō* (1996), to gather together into one place; *sullégō* (4816), to collect, gather up; *sōreúō* (4987), to pile up, heap; *sunathroízō* (4867), to call, convene, gather together.

3308. μέριμνα mérimna; gen. *merímnēs*, fem. noun from *merís* (3310), a part. Anxiety, care that brings disruption to the personality and the mind (Matt 13:22; Mark 4:19; Luke 8:14; 21:34; 2 Cor 11:28; 1 Pet 5:7).

Deriv.: *amérimnos* (275), free from care or anxiety; *merimnáō* (3309), to care or be anxious about.

Syn.: *spoudé* (4710), diligence; *epiméleia* (1958), carefulness, diligence; *prónoia* (4307), provident care, providence, provision; *episkopḗ* (1984), inspection or superintendence.

3309. μεριμνάω *merimnáō*; contracted *merimnṓ*, fut. *merimnḗsō*, from *mérimna* (3308), anxious care. To care, be anxious, troubled, to take thought, used in an absolute sense (Matt 6:27, 31; Luke 12:25; Phil 4:6), followed by the dat. (Matt 6:25; Luke 12:22); by "unto tomorrow" (a.t. [Matt 6:34]); by *perí* (4012), concerning, with a gen. (Matt 6:28; Luke 12:26), with the acc. (Luke 10:41); by *hupér* (5228), regarding, with the gen. (1 Cor 12:25); by *pōs* (4459), how (Matt 10:19; Luke 12:11). By implication it means to care for or take care of (Matt 6:34; 1 Cor 7:32–34; Phil 2:20).
Deriv.: *promerimnáo* (4305), to be anxious ahead of time.
Syn.: *mélō* (3199), to be concerned; *epimeléomai* (1959), and *phrontízō* (5431), to take care of; *phronéō* (5426), to take thought; *episkopéō* (1983), to oversee; *pronoéō* (4306), to provide for or exercise providence.
Ant.: *ameléō* (272), to neglect; *paratheōréō* (3865), to overlook; *oligōréō* (3643), to have little regard for, despise.

3310. μερίς *merís*; gen. *merídos*, fem. noun from *méros* (3313), a part, a share. A part.
(I) A part of a country, a division, province (Acts 16:12; Sept.: Josh 18:6).
(II) A part assigned, portion, share, used metaphorically (Acts 8:21; see Sept.: Gen 31:14; Deut 12:12.) Also portion, lot, destiny as assigned of God (Luke 10:42; see Sept.: Eccl 3:22; 9:9).
(III) As implying participation, fellowship (2 Cor 6:15; Col 1:12; see Sept.: Deut 10:9).
Deriv.: *merízō* (3307), to divide into parts; *merimna* (3308), anxiety.
Syn.: *tópos* (5117), a place; *klēros* (2819), a lot, portion; *klásma* (2801), fragment, piece; *méros* (3313), part.
Ant.: *hólos* (3650), the whole; *pás* (3956), each in its totality; *hápas* (537),

entire; *holóklēros* (3648), entire, the whole.

3311. μερισμός *merismós*; gen. *merismoú*, masc. noun from *merízō* (3307), to divide into parts. The act of distribution, separation, or that which is distributed. Translated "gifts" in Heb 2:4 and "dividing asunder" in Heb 4:12 (see Sept.: Josh 11:23; Ezra 6:18).
Syn.: *diamerismós* (1267), disunion, division; *diaíresis* (1243), division, distribution; *analogía* (356), analogy, proportion; *klēronomía* (2817), inheritance, heirship; *klásis* (2800), breaking, fracture; *súntrimma* (4938), utter fracture, complete ruin.
Ant.: *súndesmos* (4886), uniting principle, bond; *sunagōgḗ* (4864), a gathering together, synagogue.

3312. μεριστής *meristḗs*; gen. *meristoú*, masc. noun from *merízō* (3307), to apportion. A divider, distributor (Luke 12:14).

3313. μέρος *méros*; gen. *mérous*, neut. noun. A part, side (John 21:6). Coast (Matt 15:21; 16:13; Acts 19:1).
Deriv.: *merís* (3310) a part, a share; *polumerōs* (4181), by or in many parts.
Syn.: *hórion* (3725), a boundary, limit; *métron* (3358), a measure; *sáton* (4568), a Hebrew dry measure; *kóros* (2884), the largest Hebrew dry measure containing about eleven bushels; *bátos* (943), a Jewish liquid measure; *choínix* (5518), a dry measure, a little less than a quart; *tópos* (5117), place; *klēros* (2819), a lot; *klásma* (2801), a broken piece.
Ant.: *hólos* (3650), the whole; *pás* (3956), each in its totality; *hápas* (537), entire; *holóklēros* (3648), entire, the whole.

3314. μεσημβρία *mesēmbría*; gen. *mesēmbrías*, fem. noun from *mésos* (3319), middle, and *hēméra* (2250), day. Midday, noon (Acts 22:6; Sept.: Gen 43:16, 25). Metonymically, the south

(Acts 8:26), the part of the heavens where the sun is at midday.

Syn.: *nótos* (3558), south or south wind.

Ant.: *mesonúktion* (3317), midnight; *borrás* (1005), north, north wind.

3315. μεσιτεύω *mesiteúō*; fut. *mesiteúsō*, from *mesítēs* (3316), mediator. To be a mediator between two contending parties (Heb 6:17).

3316. μεσίτης *mesítēs*; gen. *mesítou*, masc. noun from *mésos* (3319), middle, in the midst. A mediator, one who mediates between two parties (Gal 3:20). Ascribed to Christ (1 Tim 2:5; Heb 8:6; 9:15; 12:24; Sept.: Job 9:33); to Moses (Gal 3:19). In Paul's language, *mesítēs* is one who unites parties or who mediates for peace (1 Tim 2:5). Christ is thus called the "mediator" because in man's behalf He satisfies the claims of God upon man (Heb 8:6; 9:15; 12:24). It is he who, with reference to mankind, mediates or guarantees for them a new and better covenant, and with reference to God, appears as High Priest (Heb 7:20–22). What the Epistle to the Hebrews divides into two elements, the high priesthood and the mediatorship of Christ, Paul represents as blended in the mediatorship (1 Tim 2:5).

Deriv.: *mesiteúō* (3315), to mediate, intercede.

Syn.: *práktōr* (4233), agent, officer.

3317. μεσονύκτιον *mesonúktion*; gen. *mesonuktíou*, neut. of *mesonúktios*, from *mésos* (3319), middle, and *núx* (3571), night. Midnight (Luke 11:5; Acts 16:25; 20:7). Used for the midnight watch (Mark 13:35). See Sept.: Judg 16:3; Ruth 3:8.

Ant.: *mesēmbría* (3314), midday, noon.

3318. Μεσοποταμία *Mesopotamía*; gen. *Mesopotamías*, fem. proper noun. Mesopotamia, meaning the region between the rivers. The name given by the Greeks and Romans to the tract of fertile country lying between the rivers Euphrates and Tigris from near their sources to the vicinity of Babylon (Acts 2:9; 7:2); called by the Jews Aramnaharaim or Aram [or Syria] of the two rivers (Sept.: Gen 24:10; Deut 23:4; 1 Chr 19:6). It was also called Padan-Aram or Plain of Syria (Sept.: Gen 25:20; 28:2–7; 46:15); Aram or Syria (Sept.: Gen 31:18).

Mesopotamia is first mentioned in Scripture as the country of Nahor (Sept.: Gen 24:10). Bethuel and Laban lived there. Abraham sent his servants there to fetch Isaac a wife (Gen 24:38). A century later Jacob came on the same errand and returned with his wives after an absence of twenty-one years. No mention of Mesopotamia occurs again until the close of the wanderings in the wilderness (Sept.: Deut 23:4). About a half century later, Mesopotamia appears as the seat of a powerful monarchy (Sept.: Judg 3) The children of Ammon, having provoked a war with David, "sent a thousand talents of silver to hire them chariots and horsemen out of Mesopotamia, and out of Syria-maachah, and out of Zobah" (Sept.: 1 Chr 19:6).

Assyrian inscriptions and Scripture records show that Mesopotamia was inhabited in the early times of the Assyrian empire, 1200–1100 B.C., by a vast number of petty tribes. Each one was under its own prince with every tribe quite independent of the others (Sept.: Judg 3:8–10; 2 Kgs 19:12, 13; Isa 37:12). This continued until Mesopotamia was subjugated by the king of Assyria. However, even after Mesopotamia became a province of Assyria, it formed part of the great monarchies which successively arose in upper Asia: the Babylonian, Persian, and Macedonian. The conquest of Cyrus brought it wholly under the Persian yoke, and thus it continued to the time of Alexander the Great. The whole region is studded with mounds and ruins of Assyrian and Babylonian greatness. See Acts 2:9; 7:2.

3319. μέσος *mésos*; fem. *mésē*, neut. *méson*, adj. Middle, in the midst. Used of time or place (Matt 10:16; 14:24; 18:2; 25:6; Mark 6:47; Luke 10:3; 21:21; 23:45; John 1:26; 19:18; Acts 1:18; 26:13; Phil 2:15; Rev 1:13). With the neut. art. *to*, the middle part, the midst (Matt 14:6; Mark 3:3; John 20:19, 26). Used with different prep. as follows: *ek* (1537), from, meaning from the midst, from among, away (Matt 13:49; Acts 17:33; 23:10; 1 Cor 5:2; 2 Cor 6:17; Col 2:14; 2 Thess 2:7); *aná* (303), up, meaning in or through the midst, between (Matt 13:25; Mark 7:31; 1 Cor 6:5; Rev 7:17); *diá* (1223), through, meaning through the midst (Luke 4:30; 17:11; John 8:59); *eis* (1519), into, and the art. meaning in or into the midst (Mark 14:60; Luke 4:35; 5:19; 6:8); *en* (1722), in, meaning in the midst, among (Matt 10:16; 14:6; 18:2, 20; Mark 9:36; Luke 2:46; 8:7; 10:3; 22:27, 55; 24:36; John 8:3; Acts 1:15; 2:22; 4:7; 17:22; 27:21; 1 Thess 2:7; Heb 2:12; Rev 1:13; 2:1; 4:6; 5:6; 6:6).

Deriv.: *mesēmbría* (3314), midday; *mesítēs* (3316), mediator, one standing in the middle, a go-between; *mesonúktion* (3317), midnight; *mesótoichon* (3320), a partition, middle wall; *mesouránēma* (3321), mid-sky, midst of heaven; *mesóō* (3322), to be in the middle; *metaxú* (3342), in the midst of.

Ant.: *ákron* (206), the extremity; *éschatos* (2078), farthest, final; *télos* (5056), the end; *kráspedon* (2899), a fringe or tassel, border, hem.

3320. μεσότοιχον *mesótoichon*; gen. *mesotoíchou*, neut. noun from *mésos* (3319), middle, and *toíchos* (5109), wall. Middle-wall, partition, used metaphorically of the Mosaic Law as separating the Jews and Gentiles (Eph 2:14). This is probably an allusion to the wall between the inner and outer courts of the temple. See Rev 11:1, 2.

3321. μεσουράνημα *mesouránēma*; gen. *mesouranēmatos*, neut. noun from

mésos (3319), middle, and *ouranós* (3772), heaven. Mid-heaven, the midst of the heavens (Rev 8:13; 14:6; 19:17).

3322. μεσόω *mesóō*; contracted *mesó*, fut. *mesósō*, from *mésos* (3319), middle. To be in or at the middle, in the midst, midway. Used intrans. (John 7:14) meaning at the middle of the festival. See Sept.: Ex 12:29.

3323. Μεσσίας *Messías*; gen. *Messíou*, masc. proper noun transliterated from the Hebr. *Māshīach* (4899, OT), a consecrated or anointed person. Messiah, corresponding to the Gr. *Christós* (5547), Christ. In ancient times not only the king, but also the priest and the prophet were consecrated to their calling by being anointed. In the OT, the word is used in its literal sense, meaning one who has been anointed (Sept.: 1 Sam 24:7; Lam 4:20). Usually it has a more specific application, meaning the Anointed One who was the supreme Deliverer promised from the beginning (Sept.: Gen 3:15). A long series of prophecies about Christ runs through the whole history of Israel from Abraham (Sept.: Gen 12:3; 22:18), Jacob (Sept.: Gen 49:10), Balaam (Sept.: Num 24:17), Moses (Sept.: Deut 18:15, 18), and Nathan (Sept.: 2 Sam 7:16); through the psalmists and the prophets (Sept.: Ps 2; 16; 22; 40; 45; 110; Isa 7:10–16; 9:1–7; 11; 13; 53; 61; Jer 23:5, 6; Mic 5:2; Mal 3:1–4); to His immediate precursor, John the Baptist. The character of these prophecies is very definite. The lineage from which Messiah should descend was foretold (Sept.: Gen 49:10; Isa 11:1) as well as the place in which He should be born (Sept.: Mic 5:2) and the time of His appearance (Sept.: Dan 9:20, 25; Hag 2:7; Mal 3:1). The Jews, however, mistook the true meaning of these prophecies. They expected a mere physical deliverer who would take revenge on their enemies and oppressors and give into their hands the empire, the glory and wealth of the world. Hence they failed to recognize the Messiah in Jesus of Nazareth. When He and His disciples demonstrated the spiritual meaning of these prophecies and their glorious fulfillment (Matt 26:54; Mark 9:12; Luke 18:31; 22:37; John 5:39; Acts 2:16–31; 26:22, 23; Eph 4:8; 1 Pet 1:11), the Jews felt scandalized. They expected one who would triumph according to Ps 2; Jer 23:5, 6; Zech 9:9. They could not understand how His triumph was to be accomplished by sufferings and death. The word *Messías* appears in Gr. form in John 1:41 and 4:25.

3324. μεστός *mestós*; fem. *mestḗ*, neut. *mestón*, adj. Full, filled, stuffed. Used generally in reference to that of or with which a person or thing is full (John 19:29; 21:11; Sept.: Nah 1:10). Metaphorically (Matt 23:28, "full of hypocrisy"; Rom 1:29; 15:14; James 3:8, 17; 2 Pet 2:14).

Deriv.: *mestóō* (3325), to fill.
Syn.: *plḗrēs* (4134), full.
Ant.: *kenós* (2756), empty.

3325. μεστόω *mestóō*; contracted *mestṓ*, fut. *mestṓsō*, from *mestós* (3324), full, filled. To fill. In the pass., to be filled, full, followed by the gen. (Acts 2:13, in this instance meaning to be intoxicated).

Syn.: *plēróō* (4137), to make full; *pímplēmi* (4130) and also *plḗthō*, to fill, and the compounds *empíplēmi, emplḗthō, empipláō* (1705), to fill, satisfy; *gemízō* (1072), to fill or be full; *korénnumi* (2880), to satisfy, satiate.
Ant.: *kenóō* (2758), to empty.

3326. μετά *metá*; prep. governing the gen. and acc. Its primary meaning is mid, amid, in the midst, with, among, implying accompaniment and thus differing from *sún* (4862), together with, a conj. expressing union.

(I) With the gen. implying companionship, fellowship.

(A) With, i.e., amid, among, in the midst of, as where one is said to be, sit, stand. Meaning with or in the midst of others, followed by the gen. pl. of person or thing (Matt 26:58; Mark 1:13; 14:54, 62, "coming in the clouds of heaven," in the midst of the clouds of heaven; Luke 24:5; John 18:5; Acts 20:18; Rev 21:3).

(B) With, i.e., together with. **(1)** Particularly and followed by a gen. of person. **(a)** Where one is said to be, go, remain, sit, or stand with someone, in his company; so also with the notation of place added (Matt 5:25; 9:15; Mark 5:18; Luke 11:7; 15:31; 22:21; John 3:26; 7:33; 11:31; 2 Tim 4:11; Rev 3:21); also with *gínomai* (1096), to become, meaning to be with someone (Acts 7:38; 9:19). Often without notation of place, e.g., to abide, walk, dwell with someone (Luke 22:28; 24:29; John 6:66; 1 Cor 7:13). Figuratively, to be or continue on the side of someone, of his party (Matt 12:30; 1 John 2:19). With *eínai* (1511), to be, implied (Mark 9:8; John 18:26); figuratively (2 John 1:2). Figuratively, the hand of the Lord (Luke 1:66; Acts 11:21), so also of Jesus (Matt 28:20), and the Holy Spirit (John 14:16). Also with *eínai* implied meaning to be ever with someone, i.e., to be ever bestowed, given, e.g., the divine favor, blessing, as in the closing benedictions of the epistles (Rom 16:20, 24; 1 Cor 16:23, 24; Heb 13:25; Rev 22:21). Hence *hoi óntes* and *genómenoi metá* with the gen., or simply *hoi metá* followed by the gen., meaning those with someone, his companions (Matt 12:3, 4; Mark 16:10; Luke 6:3, 4; Titus 3:15). To be present with someone for aid, e.g., God (John 3:2, "if God be not with him" [a.t.]; 8:29; Acts 7:9; 2 Cor 13:11). **(b)** Where one is said to do or suffer something with another, implying joint or mutual action, influence, suffering (Matt 2:3; 12:30, 41; 18:23; Mark 3:6, 7; Luke 5:29, 30; John 11:16; 19:18; Acts 24:1; Rom 12:15; 1 Thess 3:13; Heb 13:23; Rev 3:20). As an equivalent to "and" (Matt 2:11; 22:16, "their disciples with [*metá*] the Herodians"; 1 Cor 16:11) **(c)** Followed by the gen. of a personal or reflexive pron. after verbs of having or taking with oneself

(Matt 15:30; 25:3; Mark 14:33; 2 Tim 4:11). (d) Where the accompaniment implies only nearness or proximity (Matt 21:2; Rev 14:1). "In thy presence" (a.t.) or near thy person, as in Acts 2:28 (cf. Psalm 16:11). (e) After the verb *akolouthéō* (190), to follow (Luke 9:49; Rev 6:8; 14:13). (f) Together with the verbs compounded with *sún* (4862), together, instead of the more usual dat. (Matt 17:3; 20:2; Acts 1:26; 2 Cor 8:18; Gal 2:12). (2) Metaphorically following the gen. of thing, e.g.: (a) As designating the state or emotion of the mind which accompanies the doing of something or with which one acts (Matt 28:8; Mark 3:5; Luke 14:9; Acts 20:19; 24:3; Eph 4:2; 2 Thess 3:12; 1 Tim 2:9; Heb 10:22). (b) As designating an external action, circumstance, or condition with which another action or event is accompanied (Matt 14:7; 24:31; 27:66; Mark 6:25; 10:30; Luke 9:39; 17:20; Acts 5:26; 13:17; 14:23; 24:18; 2 Cor 8:4; 1 Tim 4:14; Heb 5:7; 7:21). Also often where it is equivalent to *kai* (2532), and (Eph 6:23; Col 1:11; 1 Tim 1:14; 2:15; 3:4; 2 Tim 2:10; Heb 9:19). (c) Followed by a gen. of thing which one has or takes along with him or with which he is supplied (Matt 24:30; Mark 14:43; John 18:3; Acts 26:12 [cf. 9:2; 22:5]). (d) With the verb *mígnumi* (3396), to mingle (Matt 27:34; Luke 13:1). (3) After act. verbs and nouns implying joint or mutual action, influence, suffering. (a) After words implying accord or discord (Luke 23:12; Rom 12:18; Sept.: 1 Kgs 22:45). (b) After *moicheúō* (3431), to commit adultery (Rev 2:22); *molúnō* (3435), to defile (Rev 14:4); *porneúō* (4203), to commit fornication (Rev 18:3, 9; Sept.: Ezek 16:17). (c) After words signifying participation, fellowship (John 13:8; 2 Cor 6:15, 16; 1 John 1:3, 6, 7). With *logízomai* (3049), to reckon, meaning to be reckoned, counted with someone (Mark 15:28; Luke 22:37 quoted from Isa 53:12). (d) After the verbs implying to speak or talk with someone (Mark 6:50; John 6:43; 16:19; Sept.: Gen 31:29). (e) To do something with someone, i.e., to or towards him (Luke 1:72;

10:37; Acts 14:27; 15:4; Sept.: Gen 24:12). With *megalúnō* (3170), to magnify something or someone (Luke 1:58).

(II) With the acc., *metá* strictly implies motion toward the middle or into the midst of something, and also motion after a person or thing, i.e., either so as to follow and be with a person or to fetch a person or thing. Hence also spoken of succession either in place or time meaning after.

(A) Of succession in place meaning after, behind (Heb 9:3).

(B) Of succession in time, e.g., with a noun of time (Matt 17:1, "after six days"; 25:19, "after a long time"; Mark 8:31; Luke 15:13, "not many days after"; Acts 12:4; 28:11; Gal 1:18). With a noun of person (Acts 5:37, "after him Judas rose" [a.t.]; 19:4); with a noun marking an event or point of time (Matt 1:12; Mark 13:24; Luke 9:28; John 13:27; 2 Pet 1:15). Also "after these things" (a.t.), after this (Mark 16:12; Luke 5:27; John 3:22). Followed by an adj. (Luke 22:58; Acts 27:14); by an inf. with the art. (Matt 26:32, "after I am risen again"; Mark 1:14; Luke 12:5; Acts 1:3; 1 Cor 11:25).

(III) In composition *metá* implies:

(A) Fellowship, partnership, as *metadídōmi* (3330), to impart; *metéchō* (3348), to partake; *metalambánō* (3335), to participate.

(B) Proximity, contiguity, as *methórios* (3181), contiguous.

(C) Motion or direction after, as *metapémpō* (3343), to summon or invite.

(D) Transition, transposition, change, meaning over as in *metabaínō* (3327), to go over, depart; *metatíthēmi* (3346), to remove; *methístēmi* (3179), to carry away, transfer, remove.

(IV) In its relation with *sún* (4862), together, the former expressing intimate personal union (Col 3:4) whereas *metá* denotes close association (1 Thess 3:13).

3327. μεταβαίνω *metabaínō*; fut. *metabésomai*, from *metá* (3326), denoting change of place or condition, and *baínō* (n.f., see *apobaínō* [576]), to go or come. To pass or go from one place or state to another (Matt 17:20; Luke 10:7; John 5:24; 1 John 3:14); to go away, depart (Matt 8:34; 11:1; 12:9; 15:29; John 7:3; 13:1; Acts 18:7).

Syn.: *hupágō* (5217), to depart, go; *apérchomai* (565), to go away; *poreúomai* (4198), to go one's way; *anachōréō* (402), to depart, retire; *chōrízō* (5563), to separate, put apart; *analúō* (360), to depart; *metaírō* (3332), to remove; *aphístēmi* (868), to stand off, depart from someone.

Ant.: *érchomai* (2064), to come; *gínomai* (1096), to change one's condition, come; *paragínomai* (3854), to arrive, be present; *hḗkō* (2240), to come with the emphasis of being present; *aphiknéomai* (864), to go forth, spread abroad; *enístēmi* (1764), to stand in, be present or about to come; *ephístēmi* (2186), to come up, be at hand, present; *katantáō* (2658), to come to, arrive; *parístēmi* (3936), to stand by or near, be at hand, come; *phthánō* (5348), to arrive; *proseggízō* (4331), to come near; *eisporeúomai* (1531), to enter.

3328. μεταβάλλω *metabállō*; fut. *metabalṓ*, from *metá* (3326), denoting change of place or condition, and *bállō* (906), to cast, put. To throw or turn over as with a plow, to change. In the NT, in the mid., to change oneself, change one's mind (Acts 28:6).

Syn.: *allássō* (236), to change; *metallássō* (3337), to exchange one thing for another; *metaschēmatízō* (3345), to change outwardly; *metamorphóō* (3339), to change inwardly; *metastréphō* (3344), to turn.

Ant.: *ménō* (3306), abide, stay; *tropophoréō* (5159), to endure one's habits; *hupoménō* (5278), to abide under, endure; *hupophérō* (5297), to bear, endure; *anéchomai* (430), to endure, tolerate; *karteréō* (2594), to be steadfast; *emménō* (1696), to persevere, stay in the same place.

3329. μετάγω *metágō*; fut. *metáxō*, from *metá* (3326), denoting change of place or condition, and *ágō* (71), to lead. To lead over, transfer (James 3:3, 4).

Syn.: *metabaínō* (3327), to depart, pass over; *stréphō* (4762), to turn; *apobaínō* (576), to go from; *metatíthēmi* (3346), to remove oneself, to turn; *methístēmi* (3179), to remove, turn away; *ekklínō* (1578), to turn aside; *komízō* (2865), to carry off; *phérō* (5342), to carry, bring; *analúō* (360), to depart.

Ant.: *epanágō* (1877), to bring back; *epanérchomai* (1880), to come back again; *anakámptō* (344); to turn back; *hupostréphō* (5290), to turn back or behind; *epistréphō* (1994), to turn back to the same place; *anastréphō* (390), to return; *apokathístēmi* (600), to restore.

3330. μεταδίδωμι *metadídōmi*; fut. *metadṓsō*, from *metá* (3326), with, denoting association, and *dídōmi* (1325), to give. To share with someone, to impart, communicate, followed by the dat. (Luke 3:11; Eph 4:28). Used in an absolute sense meaning one who distributes alms, an officer of the church (Rom 12:8). With the acc. and the dat. (Rom 1:11; 1 Thess 2:8).

Deriv.: *eumetádotos* (2130), ready to impart.

Syn.: *prosanatíthēmi* (4323), to confer, impart; *paréchō* (3930), to give, offer; *prosphérō* (4374), to bring to, offer; *koinōnéō* (2841), to communicate, distribute; *charízomai* (5483), to give, grant, deliver; *dōréomai* (1433), to bestow gratuitously, give.

Ant.: *paralambánō* (3880), to receive from; *proslambánō* (4355), to receive, take to oneself; *apospáō* (645), to withdraw; *aphairéō* (851) and *exaírō* (1808), to remove, take away.

3331. μετάθεσις *metáthesis*; gen. *metathéseōs*, fem. noun from *metatíthēmi* (3346), to transfer. Transposition, a moving to another place.

(I) Translation, with the meaning of removal from one place to another (Heb 11:5).

(II) Mutation, change (Heb 7:12; 12:27).

Syn.: *metoikesía* (3350), expatriation, change of dwelling place.

Ant.: *epistrophḗ* (1995), return, conversion.

3332. μεταίρω *metaírō*; fut. *metarṓ*, from *metá* (3326), denoting change of place or condition, and *aírō* (142), to take up, raise, lift. To lift away, remove from one place to another (Sept.: 2 Kgs 25:11). In the NT, intrans. or with *heautón* (1438), oneself, implied, to take oneself away, i.e., to go away, depart (Matt 13:53; 19:1).

Syn.: *hupágō* (5217), to go; *apérchomai* (565) and *poreúomai* (4198), to go away; *apochōréō* (672), to depart from; *chōrízomai* (5563), to separate oneself, and the comp. *apochōrízomai* (673), to separate; *analúō* (360), *anachōréō* (402), and *metabaínō* (3327), to depart; *éxeimi* (1826), to go out; *aphístēmi* (868), to depart, stand away from.

Ant.: *epistréphō* (1994), to return.

3333. μετακαλέω *metakaléō*; contracted *metakalṓ*, fut. *metakalésō*, from *metá* (3326), denoting change of place or condition, and *kaléō* (2564), to call from one place to another, summon. As used in the mid. voice, to call to oneself, send for, beckon (Acts 7:14; 10:32; 20:17; 24:25).

Syn.: *metapémpō* (3343), to send after or for.

Ant.: *anapémpō* (375), to send back.

3334. μετακινέω *metakinéō*; contracted *metakinṓ*, fut. *metakinḗsō*, from *metá* (3326), denoting change of place or condition, and *kinéō* (2795), to move. To move from one place to another, move away, remove. Metaphorically in Col 1:23, "not moved away from the hope," i.e., not fallen away, wavering.

Deriv.: *ametakínētos* (277), immovable.

Syn.: *saleúō* (4531), to move; *aphístēmi* (868), to depart.

Ant.: *katéchō* (2722), to hold down firmly; *kratéō* (2902), to hold; *tēréō* (5083), to keep.

3335. μεταλαμβάνω *metalambánō*; fut. *metalḗpsomai*, from *metá* (3326), with, denoting association, and *lambánō* (2983), to take, receive. To take a part or share of something, particularly with others, i.e., to partake of, share, followed by the gen. (2 Tim 2:6; Heb 6:7; 12:10). To partake of food, meaning generally to eat (Acts 2:46; 27:33). Generally to take, have, followed by the acc. (Acts 24:25).

Deriv.: *metálēpsis* (3336), participation, a partaking of something.

Syn.: *esthíō* (2068), to eat; *phágō* (5315), eat, devour; *trṓgō* (5176), to eat stressing the slow process of gnawing or chewing; *geúomai* (1089), to taste; *bibrṓskō* (977), to devour; *koinōnéō* (2841), to have a share of, take part in; *metéchō* (3348), to partake of; *koinōnéō* (2841), to participate, share.

Ant.: *aporríptō* (641), to reject; *apobállō* (577), to cast out; *periphronéō* (4065), to despise; *apophérō* (667), to bear away; *eméō* (1692), to vomit; *oligōréō* (3643), to have little regard for, despise.

3336. μετάληψις *metálēpsis*; gen. *metalḗpseōs*, fem. noun from *metalambánō* (3335), to take a portion or share. The act of partaking of something (1 Tim 4:3).

Syn.: *koinōnía* (2842), communion, fellowship, sharing in common; *metochḗ* (3352), partnership, participation; *apóchrēsis* (671), to act of using up, consumption.

3337. μεταλλάσσω *metallássō*, μεταλλάττω *metaláttō*; fut. *metalláxō*, from *metá* (3326), denoting change of place or condition, and *allássō* (236), to change. To exchange, to convert from one state to another (Rom 1:25, 26).

Syn.: *metatíthēmi* (3346), to place differently, change; *metabállō* (3328), to change; *metaschēmatízō* (3345), to change one's outward shape; *metamorphóō* (3339), to transform, change one inwardly; *metanoéō* (3340), to change one's mind; *metamélomai* (3338), to regret, bring about a change.

Ant.: *diaménō* (1265), to remain unchanged.

3338. μεταμέλομαι *metamélomai*; fut. *metamelḗsomai*, from *metá* (3326), denoting change of place or condition, and *mélomai*, mid. of *mélō* (n.f. see *mélei* [3199], to concern), to be concerned. To regret (Matt 21:29, 32; 27:3; 2 Cor 7:8; Heb 7:21 quoted from Ps 110:4). The aor. pass. *metemelḗthēn* has the meaning of changing one's mind or purpose after having done something regrettable. Contrasted with *metanoéō* (3340), to repent, it expresses the mere desire that what is done may be undone, accompanied with regrets or even remorse, but with no effective change of heart. *Metaméleia* (which does not occur in the NT) is an ineffective repentance for which the forgiveness of sins is not promised (as it is for *metánoia* [3341], repentance, see Mark 1:4; Luke 3:3; Acts 2:38). *Metamélomai*, on the part of man, means little or nothing more than a selfish dread of the consequence of what one has done, whereas *metanoéō* means regret and forsaking the evil by a change of heart brought about by God's Spirit. On the part of God in Heb 7:21, *metamélomai* means His plan of salvation for man can have no improvement; He made no mistake.

Deriv.: *ametamélētos* (278), not regretted.

Syn.: *epimeléomai* (1959), to take care of, be concerned.

3339. μεταμορφόω *metamorphóō*; contracted *metamorphó̄*, fut. *metamorphṓsō*, from *metá* (3326), denoting change of place or condition, and *morphóō* (3445), to form. To transform, transfigure, change one's form. In the NT, only in the mid., *metamorphóomai*, to be transfigured. Used of the Lord's transfiguration on the mount (Matt 17:2; Mark 9:2) involving the miracle of transformation from an earthly form into a supernatural form which was externally denoted by the radiance of His garments and countenance. This suggests what the bodies of the righteous may be like as a result of the resurrection of our bodies (1 Cor 15:51f.). In Rom 12:2 and 2 Cor 3:18, the idea of transformation refers to an invisible process in Christians which takes place or begins to take place during their life in this age.

Syn.: *metaschēmatízō* (3345), to change one's outward form; *metastréphō* (3344), to turn from; *schḗma* (4976), external condition, fashion; *metallássō* (3337), to change one thing for another, exchange; *metabállō* (3328) and *allássō* (236), to change.

3340. μετανοέω *metanoéō*; contracted *metanoó̄*, fut. *metanoḗsō*, from *metá* (3326), denoting change of place or condition, and *noéō* (3539), to exercise the mind, think, comprehend. To repent, change the mind, relent. Theologically, it involves regret or sorrow, accompanied by a true change of heart toward God. It is distinguished from *metamélomai* (3338), to regret. Intrans.:

(I) Generally (Luke 17:3, 4). After *epí* (1909), upon, with the dat. (2 Cor 12:21).

(II) In a religious sense implying pious sorrow for unbelief and sin and a turning from them unto God and the gospel of Christ. Used in an absolute sense (Matt 3:2; 4:17; 11:20; Mark 1:15; 6:12; Luke 13:3, 5; 15:7, 10; 16:30; Acts 2:38; 3:19; 17:30; 26:20, meaning to repent and turn to God from idolatry; Rev 2:5, 16, 21; 3:3, 19; 16:9); followed by *apó* (575), from (Acts 8:22; Sept.: Jer 8:6); *ek* (1537), from or out of (Rev 2:21, 22; 9:20, 21; 16:11). As attended with external acts of sorrow (Matt 11:21; Luke 10:13 [cf. John 3:5–10]). Followed by *eis* (1519), unto (Matt 12:41; Luke 11:32).

(III) Although the Lord Jesus insisted on repentance by all others, He Himself never expresses any feeling of penitence or regret for something He ever did or left undone, for something He ever said or left unsaid. He never prayed for forgiveness. He never knew of a time when He was not in peace and harmony with the Father, nor spoke of coming into such a relationship. Of Him, John wrote, "Ye know that he was manifested to take away our sins; and in him is no sin" (1 John 3:5). Peter, on the day of Pentecost, referred to the Lord Jesus as the "Holy and Righteous One" (a.t. [Acts 3:14]). Paul says "He who knew no sin was made to be sin on our behalf, that we might become the righteousness of God in him" (a.t. [2 Cor 5:21]). The Apostle, in Heb 7:26, calls Him "Holy, guileless, undefiled, separated from sinners" (a.t.). The sinlessness of Jesus and, therefore, the needlessness of repentance is clearly stated in Heb 4:15, "We have not an high priest who cannot be touched with the feelings of our infirmities, but one who has been in all points tempted like as we are, yet without sin" (a.t.). The testimony of the Lord Jesus Himself about His sinlessness is noteworthy: "Which of you convinceth me of sin?" (John 8:46). In John 8:29 He said, "He that sent Me is with Me: He hath not left Me alone; for I do always the things that are pleasing to Him" (a.t.).

(IV) There are two words in the NT which convey the idea of repentance, *metanoéō* and *epistréphō* (1994), to come back, convert, turn about. These words derive their moral content not from Greek, but from Jewish and Christian thought, since nothing analogous to the biblical concept of repentance and conversion was known to the Greeks. *Metanoéō* presents repentance in its negative aspect as a change of mind or turning from sin while *epistréphō* presents it

in its positive aspect as turning to God. Both, however, have much the same content of meaning. Christ's call to repentance (Matt 4:17) has as its motive the nearness of the kingdom, participation in which is conditioned upon the new disposition (Matt 18:3). It is addressed, not as in the OT to the nation, but to the individual; and not merely to flagrant sin, but to all sin (Luke 13:3), both great and small. The inner and radical character of the change required is illustrated by the figure of the tree and its fruits. The first four Beatitudes may be taken as descriptive of elements of true repentance. Poverty of spirit (the confession of one's spiritual helplessness—see *ptōchós* [4434], poor), sorrow for sin, meekness, and hunger and thirst for righteousness are all characteristics of the soul that is turning to God from sin. In the parable of the prodigal son, Jesus draws a picture of the true penitent person. Such is assured of the forgiveness of the Father whose love has anticipated his return and gone out to seek and save (Luke 15:4). Of fastings and other external accompaniments Christ says little, as indicated in the parable of the publican and the Pharisee (Luke 18:10–14). No external acts can take the place of an internal sorrow for one's sins.

Deriv.: *ametanóētos* (279), impenitent *metánoia* (3341), a change of mind, repentance.

Ant.: *emménō* (1696), to continue in; *sunédomai* (4913), to delight; *euphraínomai* (2165), to be in a good frame of mind.

3341. μετάνοια *metánoia*; gen. *metanoías*, fem. noun from *metanoéō* (3340), to repent. A change of mind, repentance (Heb 12:17).

Repentance, change of mind from evil to good or from good to better (Matt 3:8, 11; 9:13 [TR]; Mark 2:17; Luke 3:8; 5:32; 15:7; Acts 5:31; 20:21; 26:20; Rom 2:4; Heb 6:6; 12:17; 2 Pet 3:9). In the NT, used with reference to *noús* (3563), mind, as the faculty of moral reflection

(Acts 11:18; 20:21; 2 Cor 7:9, 10; 2 Tim 2:25; Heb 6:1).

It is combined with *áphesis* (859), remission of sins (Luke 24:47 [cf. baptism of repentance Matt 3:11; Mark 1:4; Luke 3:3; Acts 13:24; 19:4]) which identifies one as having repented.

In the Sept., *metánoia* occurs only in Prov 14:15. In the NT, we find John the Baptist preaching repentance (Matt 3:2, 8, 11; Mark 1:4; Luke 3:3, 8). Jesus began His ministry by preaching repentance (Matt 4:17; Mark 1:15; Luke 5:32; 13:3, 5; 15:7). The noun occurs six times in Acts (5:31; 11:18; 13:24; 19:4; 20:21; 26:20), and *metanoéō* occurs five times in Acts (2:38; 3:19; 8:22; 17:30; 26:20). This early Christian preaching involved the announcement of Jesus as the Messiah and the simple call for repentance. This is equally true of the sermons of the original apostles and of Paul. Paul tells the Athenians that God is summoning all to repentance, using the same phrase (Acts 17:30) as he expresses his own action in Acts 26:20 with the use of *apaggéllō* (518), command. Essentially, this is identical with the preaching of John the Baptist (Acts 13:24; 19:4 [cf. Matt 3:2]). However, John the Baptist spoke of Jesus as coming and of the kingdom of the Messiah as at hand, while the Apostles referred to Jesus as having already come.

How repentance is to be brought about is not stated. The imper. mood implies an act of human will possible for all to whom the call comes. On the other hand, the apostles speak of Jesus as having been exalted by God as Captain and Savior to give repentance unto Israel and remission of sins (Acts 5:31); and the Christians in Jerusalem, hearing of the conversion of Cornelius, exclaim "Why, God has given repentance to the Gentiles!" (a.t. [Acts 11:18]). Man could not be thought of as forced into repentance independently of his own will, although repentance is made possible only through a dispensation of God's grace. 2 Pet 3:9 states that the Lord wills

(*boúlomai* [1014], will, which is expressive of His desire) that all men should come to repentance.

As in the preaching of John the Baptist (Matt 3:8), repentance is expected to manifest itself in conduct (Acts 26:20). From the references to repentance in Acts, it is demonstrated that repentance was an integral part of Paul's preaching, yet references to repentance in the Pauline Epistles are rare. (The verb occurs only in 2 Cor 12:21 and the noun in Rom 2:4; 2 Cor 7:9, 10; 2 Tim 2:25). The kindness of God leading to repentance stated in Rom 2:4 provides a striking similarity to Ezek 36:29ff. In Ezek 6:9, the impulse to repentance is attributed to a different cause. The forbearance and mildness of the servant of God may lead to God's giving repentance to those who experience such treatment (2 Tim 2:25). In each case, the simple concept of Acts 5:31; 11:18 (that repentance is an attitude induced or made possible by God) is at once elaborated upon and modified. There is no explicit reference here to the work of Christ; but, as in Ezekiel, the experience of blessings felt to be unmerited or the surprise of unmerited forbearance from Christian people brings about a change of mind toward sin and God.

Is it possible for God to deny a man's repentance? There are two statements in Hebrews which may falsely give that impression. The first is in Heb 6:4–6: "For it is impossible for those who were once enlightened, and have tasted of the heavenly gift, and who were made partakers of the Holy Ghost, and have tasted the good word of God, and the powers of the world to come, if they shall fall away, to renew them again unto repentance; seeing they crucify to themselves the Son of God afresh, and put him to an open shame." The key for the understanding of this passage is the verb *anakainízō* (340), to make new again, referring to the repentance experience. Here repentance is intimately related to the sacrifice of Christ on the cross once and for all (Heb 9:26, 28). Peter states it very clearly in 1 Pet 3:18: "For Christ also hath once suffered for sins, the just for the unjust, that he might bring us to God, being put to death in the flesh, but quickened by the Spirit." The supposition in Heb 6:4–6 is that if an individual has repented and his repentance is based on the death of Christ, if that repentance fails in any way, then it must be concluded that it is Christ who failed. However He cannot suffer again; it is impossible that He be recrucified to provide a new kind of repentance that would be effective. Therefore, true repentance based on the once-and-for-all death of Christ on the cross must avail the sinner to the very end. The other passage is Heb 12:17: "For ye know how that afterward, when he would have inherited the blessing, he [Esau] was rejected: for he found no place of repentance, though he sought it carefully with tears." "Repentance" here is spoken of Esau's changing his mind for what he had done in selling his birthright as the firstborn "for one morsel of meat." Although he repented, it was impossible for him to recover the privilege of being the firstborn anymore. This proves that repentance does not necessarily guarantee the restoration of the loss caused by a wrong decision even as was the case with Lot who selfishly chose the green pastures of the plain of the Jordan in the area of Sodom (Gen 13:8–13; 2 Pet 2:7). Repentance brings eternal salvation to us, but it does not necessarily bring deliverance from the consequences of our wrong choices whether as unbelievers or believers.

While in the Synoptic Gospels, repentance as a rule covers the whole process of turning from sin to God (as in Luke 24:47), it also includes faith which is a part of the process, the last step of it. This application is also used in the discourses of the early chapters of Acts. In these, the comprehensive condition of admission to the brotherhood of believers and of participation in the life of the Spirit is repentance (Acts 2:38; 3:19; 5:31). Faith

is not mentioned, though, in the nature of the case, it is included. In the Gospel of John, the reverse is the case. There faith is the condition of salvation (John 3:15, 16, 36), and while repentance is not specifically mentioned, it is included in the notion of faith. Faith is the trustful commitment of oneself to God for forgiveness of sins, deliverance from sin, and victory over sin; but it is impossible to commit oneself thus to God without renouncing and turning away from all that is contrary to God. This impossibility is expressed or implied in the discourses of the Gospel of John. They clearly set forth the moral conditionality of faith. A man cannot exercise faith whose heart is not right (John 5:44). Faith is the condition of entrance into the experience of salvation, the enjoyment of eternal life; but repentance is the psychological and moral condition of faith. As eternal life is unattainable without faith, faith is unattainable without repentance. If repentance means to change from the self-centered life to the God-centered life, then Jesus is the Author and Inspiration of repentance. No other was ever able to reach down deep enough into human nature to effect this change.

Syn.: *epistrophḗ* (1995), conversion, the positive side of the process of salvation (*sōtēría* [4991]), the negative being *metánoia*, repentance; *metaméleia*, regret, from *metamélomai* (3338), to change one's mind because of the consequences of one's sin.

Ant.: *pṓrōsis* (4457), hardness, callousness; *sklērokardía* (4641), hardness of heart.

3342. μεταξύ *metaxú*; adv. from *metá* (3326), with or after, and *mésos* (3319), middle, midst, between. In the midst of.

(I) Used in an absolute sense only of time, meantime, meanwhile, e.g., in the phrase *en tṓ metaxú* (*en* [1722], in; *tṓ metaxú* implying *chrónō* [5550], time), in the meantime (John 4:31). With the def. art. *ho*, *metaxú* means intervening, intermediate; used for next following, next, as in Acts 13:42, *tó metaxú Sábbaton* (4521), Sabbath, meaning the next Sabbath.

(II) Followed by the gen. of place or person (Luke 11:51; 16:26; Acts 12:6). Figuratively of persons (Matt 18:15, "between thee and him alone"; Acts 15:9; Rom 2:15; "between one another" [a.t.], i.e., in turn, alternately).

Syn.: *aná méson* (*aná* [303], in; *méson* [3319], middle), in the middle or up to the middle or between.

Ant.: *metépeita* (3347), afterwards; *hústeron* (5305), after.

3343. μεταπέμπω *metapémpō*; fut. *metapémpsō*, from *metá* (3326), denoting change of place or condition, and *pémpō* (3992), to send, dispatch. To send after or for. In the NT, only in the mid. *metapémpomai*, fut. mid. *metapémpsomai*, to send for, to invite to come (Acts 10:5, 22; 11:13; 24:24, 26; 25:3; Sept.: Num 23:7); pass. (Acts 10:29).

Syn.: *apostéllō* (649), to send forth.

Ant.: *kaléō* (2564) and *metakaléō* (3333), to summon; *proskaléō* (4341), to call, mid. *proskaléomai*, to call to oneself, bid to come.

3344. μεταστρέφω *metastréphō*; fut. *metastrépsō*, from *metá* (3326), denoting change of place or condition, and *stréphō* (4762), to turn. To turn about from one direction to another. In the NT, to turn into something else, to change. Trans. and followed by *eis* (1519), into (James 4:9). "The sun shall be turned into darkness" (Acts 2:20 quoted from Joel 2:31). In a bad sense, to change for the worse, to pervert (Gal 1:7).

Syn.: *apostréphō* (654), to turn away, pervert; *diastréphō* (1294), to distort, twist, pervert; *ekstréphō* (1612), to turn inside out, pervert; *metágō* (3329), to move from one side to another; *metatíthēmi* (3346), to turn.

Ant.: *sózō* (4982), to save; *diasózō* (1295), to bring safely through; *phulássō* (5442), to guard, keep, preserve; *tēréō*

(5083), to keep; *peripoiéomai* (4046), to preserve.

3345. μετασχηματίζω *metaschēmatízō*; fut. *metaschēmatísō*, from *metá* (3326), denoting change of place or condition, and *schēmatízō* (n.f.), to form, which is from *schéma* (4976), shape, outward form. To transform, change the outward form or appearance of something. Occurs only in 1 Cor 4:6; 2 Cor 11:13–15; Phil 3:21.

This outward change is best illustrated by contrasting *metaschēmatízō* with *metamorphóō* (3339), to transform. If one were to change a Japanese garden into an Italian one, this would be *metaschēmatízō*. But if one were to transform a garden into something wholly different, as a ball-field, it is *metamorphó*. It is possible for Satan to *metaschēmatízō*, transform himself into an angel of light (2 Cor 11:14), i.e., he can change his whole outward semblance. But it would be impossible to apply *metamorphóō* to any such change for this would imply an internal change, a change not of appearance but of essence, which lies beyond his power.

In the *metaschēmatismós*, a transformation of the bodies (Phil 3:21; 1 Cor 15:53), there is to be seen a transition but no absolute dissolution of continuity. The outer physical transformation of believers at the end of the days (1 Cor 15:44ff., 51f.) is called by Paul in Phil 3:21 *metaschēmatízō*, but such transformation has already begun in this life from within. Paul speaks of the final *metaschēmatismós*, outer transformation, shaping.

3346. μετατίθημι *metatíthēmi*; fut. *metathésō*, from *metá* (3326), denoting change of place or condition, and *títhēmi* (5087), to place. To transpose, put in another place and hence to transport, transfer, translate. Trans. (Acts 7:16; Heb 7:12, the priesthood being transferred to Christ or to the tribe of Judah [cf. Heb 7:11, 14]; 11:5 of Enoch who was translated to heaven [cf. 2 Kgs 2:11]; Sept.: Gen 5:24). In the mid., *metatíthēmi*, to transfer oneself, change sides or parties, turn away from someone (Gal 1:6). Metaphorically, to transfer to another use or purpose, pervert, abuse (Jude 1:4, "perverting the grace of God into licentiousness" [a.t.]).

Deriv.: *ametáthetos* (276), unchangeable; *metáthesis* (3331), a change of position.

Syn.: *apágō* (520), to lead or carry away; *metágō* (3329), to transfer; *apophérō* (667) and *aírō* (142), to carry away; *methístēmi* (3179), to cause to remove; *metoikízō* (3351), to remove to a new place or abode; *kinéō* (2795), to move; *metastréphō* (3344), to change.

Ant.: *ménō* (3306), to remain, abide.

3347. μετέπειτα *metépeita*; adv. of time, from *metá* (3326), after, and *épeita* (1899), then, thereupon. After that, then, thereafter, afterwards (Heb 12:17).

Syn.: *metá* (3326), afterward; *hexés* (1836), after, with the meaning of a succession of events; *kathexés* (2517), afterward; *hústeron* (5305), afterwards, with finality implied; *eíta* (1534), after, afterwards.

Ant.: *próton* (4412) first, at first; *próteron* (4386), before; *prín* (4250), formerly.

3348. μετέχω *metéchō*; fut. *methéxō*, from *metá* (3326), with, denoting association, and *échō* (2192), have. To have together with others, to partake of, share in (1 Cor 10:21, 30; Heb 5:13; 7:13).

Deriv.: *metoché* (3352), a partaking, participation, fellowship; *métochos* (3353), a partaker, an associate.

Syn.: *koinōnéō* (2841), to participate, share.

Ant.: *apéchō* (568), to hold oneself from, abstain; *arnéomai* (720), to deny, reject; *paraitéomai* (3868), to refuse, avoid, reject; *apodokimázō* (593), to reject after examining, disapprove; *exouthenéō* (1848), to despise.

3349. μετεωρίζω *meteōrízō*; fut. *meteōrísō*, from *metéōros* (n.f.), high, which is from *metá* (3326), denoting change of place or condition, and *aeírō*, another form of *aírō* (142), to raise, lift up high, raise in the air. To lift up on high. Used figuratively of the mind, to animate, incite, also to cause to be hesitant, to fluctuate, make one's faith waver as if blown about by wind. In the NT, used in the pass. or mid., meaning to be in suspense or of a doubtful mind, anxious, fluctuating between hope and fear (Luke 12:29).

Syn.: *aporéō* (639), to be without a way, direction, or resource, to be in perplexity and doubt; also the comp. *diaporéō* (1280), to be thoroughly perplexed; *diakrínomai* (1252), to be wavering; *distázō* (1365), to stand at the crossroads or be in uncertainty, to hesitate.

Ant.: *stereóō* (4732), to make strong, establish; *stērízō* (4741), to make fast, set; *bebaióō* (950), to confirm, establish; *epistērízō* (1991), to strengthen; *kuróō* (2964), to make valid, ratify; adj. *hedraíos* (1476), settled, steadfast.

3350. μετοικεσία *metoikesía*; gen. *metoikesías*, fem. noun from *metoikéō* (n.f.), to move from one dwelling place to another. A moving from one habitation or country to another, a transportation or transplantation (Matt 1:11, 12, 17; Sept.: 2 Kgs 24:16; 1 Chr 5:22).

Ant.: *monḗ* (3438), an abode, abiding place; *katoíkēsis* (2731), a habitation; *katoikía* (2733), a dwelling place; *paroikía* (3940), a sojourning.

3351. μετοικίζω *metoikízō*; fut. *metoikísō*, from *metá* (3326), denoting change of place or condition, and *oikízō* (n.f.), to cause to dwell, which is from *oíkos* (3624), a house. To cause to change one's habitation, move from one habitation to another, migrate. Used trans. (Acts 7:4, 43; Sept.: 1 Chr 5:6; Amos 5:27).

Syn.: *metabaínō* (3327), to pass over from one place to another; *methístēmi* (3179), to cause to move; *metatíthēmi* (3346), to move a person or thing from one place to another; *paraphérō* (3911), to take or carry away, bring to or before; *apochōrízō* (673), to separate, remove; *aírō* (142), to lift, take up; *kinéō* (2795), to move; *astatéō* (790), to wander about, to lack a fixed dwelling place.

Ant.: *ménō* (3306), to abide; *kataménō* (2650), to stay in one place; *paraménō* (3887), to stay continuously; *diatríbō* (1304), to stay; *oikéō* (3611), to dwell; *katoikéō* (2730), to dwell continuously in one place; *paroikéō* (3939), to reside as an alien; *skēnóō* (4637), to pitch a tent; *kataskēnóō* (2681), to lodge in a tent.

3352. μετοχή *metochḗ*; gen. *metochḗs*, fem. noun from *metéchō* (3348), to partake of, from *metá* (3326), with, denoting association, and *échō* (2192), to have. Partnership, fellowship (2 Cor 6:14).

Syn.: *koinōnía* (2842), fellowship, partnership; *merís* (3310), a part.

Ant.: *hustérēma* (5303), a deficit; *hustérēsis* (5304), doing without; *aporía* (640), without means, quandary, perplexity; *chreía* (5532), necessity, need.

3353. μέτοχος *métochos*; gen. *metóchou*, masc.-fem., neut. *métochon*, adj. from *metéchō* (3348), to partake. Partaking, participating. As a noun, a partaker (Heb 3:1, 14; 6:4; 12:8), partner, companion, fellow worker (Luke 5:7; Heb 1:9 quoted from Sept.: Ps 45:7).

Deriv.: *summétochos* (4830), a coparticipant.

Syn.: *koinōnós* (2844), one having communion, being a partner; *sunékdēmos* (4898), a fellow traveler; *sunergós* (4904), a fellow worker.

Ant.: *endeḗs* (1729), lacking.

3354. μετρέω *metréō*; contracted *metrṓ*, fut. *metrḗsō*, from *métron* (3358), measure. To measure, mete out (Matt 7:2; Mark 4:24; Luke 6:38; 2 Cor 10:12;

Rev 11:1, 2; 21:15–17; Sept.: Ex 16:18; Num 35:5).

Deriv.: *antimetréō* (488), to measure in return; *metrētḗs* (3355), a measurer.

Syn.: *arithméō* (705), to number; *katarithméō* (2674), to number with.

3355. μετρητής *metrētḗs*; gen. *metrētoú*, masc. noun from *metréō* (3354), to measure. A measure of capacity (John 2:6), meaning the Attic amphora, a measure for liquids equivalent to about thirty-three and one-half quarts or eight and three-eighths gallons. The Roman amphora was smaller, being equal to two-thirds of the *metrētḗs*. It is translated "firkin" in John 2:6. See *métron* (3358) for the various measurements in the NT.

3356. μετριοπαθέω *metriopathéō*; contracted *metriopathṓ*, fut. *metriopathḗsō*, from *metriopathḗs* (n.f.), moderate in passions, which is from *métrios* (n.f.), moderate, and *páthos* (3806), passion. To act with moderation. In Plutarch, *metriopátheia*, moderation, is the same as *praótēs* (4236) or *prautēs* (4240), meekness. With a dat. following, to moderate one's anger towards, to pardon, treat with mildness or meekness (Heb 5:2).

Syn.: *sōphronéō* (4993), to be sober minded, to place voluntary limitations on one's freedom; *anéchomai* (430), to bear with tolerance; *makrothuméō* (3114), to be long-suffering; *oikteírō* (3627), to have pity; *splagchnízomai* (4697), to be moved with compassion; *sumpathéō* (4834), to suffer with another, commiserate; *eleéō* (1653), to have mercy.

Ant.: *maínomai* (3105), to rage, be mad, and its comp. *emmaínomai* (1693), to be furious against, show much anger; *paraphéromai* (3911), to be carried away in one's mind and disposition; *paraphronéō* (3912), to be carried away in one's mind.

3357. μετρίως *metríōs*; adv. from *métrios* (n.f.), moderate, which is from *métron* (3358), measure. Moderately, with moderation. Used neg. in Acts 20:12, meaning not a little, but much, greatly.

Syn.: the phrase *ek métrou* (*ek* [1537], from; *métrou*, the gen. of *métron* [3358], measure), moderately, sparingly; *mikrón* (3397), the neut. of *mikrós* (3398), a little, small, a while; *olígon* (3641), the neut. of *olígos*, used adv., awhile, a little, briefly.

Ant.: *huperballóntōs* (5234), beyond measure; *perissōs* (4057), exceedingly, and the comp. *huperperissōs* (5249), exceedingly abundantly; the phrase *kath' huperbolēn* (*katá* [2596], according to), exceedingly great; *sphódra* (4970), excessively, violently; *sphodrōs* (4971), exceedingly; *perissōs* (4057), abundantly; *perissotérōs* (4056), more abundantly, exceedingly.

3358. μέτρον *métron*; gen. *métrou*, neut. noun. Measure.

(I) A measure of capacity (Matt 7:2; Mark 4:24; Luke 6:38; Sept.: Deut 25:14).

(II) Of length or surface, meaning a measuring rod (Rev 21:15, 17 referring to man's measure as common, ordinary; Sept.: Ex 26:2, 8; 2 Kgs 21:13; Ezek 42:16). See *kálamos* (2563), a reed.

(III) Metaphorically used of sins (Matt 23:32).

(IV) Generally and adv., *ek métrou* (*ek* [1537], from; gen. *métrou*), by measure, equivalent to *metríos* (3357), moderately, sparingly (John 3:34). It also means a portion measured off or allotted (Rom 12:3; 2 Cor 10:13; Eph 4:7, 13, 16).

Deriv.: *ámetros* (280), without measure; *metréō* (3354), to measure, mete out; *sitométrion* (4634), a portion, grain measured out.

Syn.: the measures or measurements in the NT are: *méros* (3313), a part, a portion without specifying any definitive quantity; *sáton* (4568), a Hebr. word for a dry measure equivalent to about one and one-half pecks (Matt 13:33; Luke 13:21); *kóros* (2884), the largest Hebrew dry measure containing about

eight to thirteen bushels (Luke 16:7); *bátos* (943), a bath, a Jewish liquid measure the equivalent of an ephah containing between five and three-fourths and seven and one-half gallons (Luke 16:6); *choínix* (5518), a dry measure equal to about a quart.

Ant.: *hadrótēs* (100), abundance, bountifulness; *perisseía* (4050), a generous measure, abundance, superfluity; *perísseuma* (4051), that which remains over after satisfaction has been experienced; *huperbolē* (5236), hyperbole, excellence, exceeding greatness, abundance; *huperochē* (5247), superiority, preeminence.

3359. μέτωπον *métōpon*; gen. *metōpou*, neut. noun from *metá* (3326), after, above, and *óps* (n.f.), the eye. The forehead (Rev 7:3; 9:4; 13:16; 14:1, 9; 17:5; 20:4; 22:4; Sept.: Ex 28:38; 1 Sam 17:49).

3360. μέχρι *méchri*, μέχρις *méchris*; adv. marking a terminus both of place and time. The latter spelling occurs before a vowel. It differs, therefore, from *áchri* (891) ln that *áchri* fixes the attention upon the whole duration up to the limit, leaving the further continuance suspect, while *méchri* refers solely to the limit implying that the action terminates there.

(I) Used in the NT as a prep. with the gen. meaning unto, until.

(A) Of place meaning unto, as far as (Rom 15:19).

(B) Of time meaning until. **(1)** With a gen. of a noun (Matt 13:30; Acts 10:30; 20:7; Rom 5:14, "to [until] Moses," meaning that death reigned from Adam until Moses without there being any written law, but not so afterwards [cf. 1 Tim 6:14; Heb 3:6, 14; 9:10; Sept.: Ps 105:19]). **(2)** Followed by the relative pron. *hoú*, gen. of *hós* (3739), relating to time, until what time, until, as a conj.; with the subjunctive where the thing is uncertain (Mark 13:30). **(3)** "Until this day" (Matt 11:23; 28:15) where *áchri* might properly have been used; however, the writer employs *méchri*, probably as not looking beyond the present time because the present moment is all he is concerned with.

(C) Used metaphorically of degree or extent (Phil 2:8, 30; 2 Tim 2:9; Heb 12:4).

(II) Used as a conj. meaning "until," before a verb in the subjunctive where the thing is either pres. or fut., and, therefore, uncertain (Eph 4:13).

Syn.: *héōs* (2193), until, so long as, marking the continuance of an action up to the time of another action; *eis* (1519), to, used of time implying a term or limit, up to, until. It also marks duration, in which case it means for, as long as.

3361. μή *mḗ*; neg. particle. Not. This word implies a dependent and conditional neg., i.e., depending on the idea, concept or thought of some subject, and, thus, subjective. However the other neg. particle, *ou* (3756), not, expresses the direct and full negation independently and in an absolute sense and is therefore obj. Thus *mḗ* is the neg. of will, wish, doubt, while *ou* denies the fact. *Mḗ* implies that one conceives or supposes a thing not to exist, while *ou* expresses that it actually does not exist. The same distinction holds true in all the comp. of *mḗ* and *ou*.

(I) As a neg. particle, meaning "not," and where the following special uses all flow from the general principles stated above. Cases in which *mḗ* and not *ou* is used:

(A) In all neg. conditions and suppositions: In the NT after *eán* (1437), if, and *ei* (1487), if: *eán mḗ* (Matt 5:20; Mark 3:27; Luke 13:3, 5); *ei mḗ* (Matt 24:22; Mark 2:7; John 3:13; Acts 21:25); with *eán* or *ei* implied (Mark 12:19; Luke 10:10; John 12:47; 1 Cor 13:1–3; James 2:14). Sometimes *ei* is followed by *ou*, but then *ou* refers not to the condition, but to the verb alone, which it renders neg. (Matt 26:24, "not being born would have been better for him" [a.t.], if *mḗ* were used here, it would have implied

doubt whether he had actually been born; Mark 11:26; Luke 14:26; 18:4, *ei kaí Theón ou phoboúmai* means not to fear or to reject God; John 10:37, *ei ou poiṓ* [4160] *tá érga* [2041] *toú Patrós* [3962] *mou*, "If I do not the works of my Father" means to not do or to leave undone the works of the Father; see James 2:11).

(B) After particles implying purpose, also result anticipated or supposed. In the NT, after *hína* (2443), so that; *hópōs* (3704), that, for; *hṓste* (5620), so that, therefore; *hína mḗ* (Matt 26:5, "so that no noise may be created" [a.t.]; see Matt 5:29, 30; Mark 4:12; Luke 8:10; John 3:16; 11:50; Acts 5:26; Heb 13:17); *hṓste* (5620), so that, which marks a result anticipated or supposed on the part of the speaker or writer (Matt 8:28; Mark 3:20; 1 Cor 1:7; 2 Cor 3:7; 1 Thess 1:8); *hópōs mḗ* (Matt 6:18; Luke 16:26; Acts 20:16; 1 Cor 1:29). Also before an inf. expressing purpose, either with or without *hṓste* (5620), so that; *eis* (1519), unto; *prós* (4314), toward, unto; *diá* (1223), through. See D below.

(C) After a relative pron. as *hós* (3739), who; *hóstis* (3748), who, whosoever; *hósos* (3745), whosoever, where they do not refer to def. antecedents but to such as are indef. and general or implied (Matt 10:14 "whosoever shall not receive you"; 11:6; Mark 6:11 "whosoever shall not receive you"; Luke 8:18; 9:5; Acts 3:23; Rev 13:15). However, *ou* is put after *hós* or *hóstis* where these refer to a def. antecedent (Luke 14:33) or where something is said actually not to be or to be done (Matt 10:38; 13:12; Mark 9:40; Luke 14:27).

(D) With the inf. as being dependent upon another finite verb or word expressed or implied. Here the inf. may usually either itself be resolved into a supposition or the verb on which it depends expresses supposition, condition, thought, purpose. **(1)** With a simple inf. (Matt 22:23, "which say that there is no resurrection" meaning as they suppose and believe that there is no [*mḗ* *eínai*] resurrection). See Luke 2:26; 20:7; 21:14; Acts 15:19, 38; 23:8; 25:24, 27; Rom 13:3; 1 Cor 7:1; 1 Tim 1:20; 2 Pet 2:21). After *opheílō* (3784), bound to (Rom 15:1); *deí* (1163), must (Matt 23:23; Luke 18:1; Acts 27:21; see Titus 2:3, 9, 10). After *omnúō* (3660), to swear, which implies future purpose (Heb 3:18). After verbs of commanding, entreating, with the pres. inf. as continued (Acts 1:4; 21:4; Rom 2:21, 22; Eph 3:13; 2 Tim 2:14), with the aor. inf., transient action (Matt 2:12; 5:34; Luke 22:40; Heb 12:19). After verbs implying a neg., e.g., of denying (Luke 20:27; 22:34), and vice versa after *ou dúnamai* (1410), cannot, which constitutes a neg., and *mē̄*, which has the power of an emphatic affirmative (Acts 4:20, "we cannot but speak"). (**2**) Inf. with *toú*, as dependent on a subst. (Rom 11:8; 1 Cor 9:6, "Do we not have authority not to work" (a.t.) which implies the possibility of not working, but does not refer to the will. After verbs of hindering or being hindered (Luke 4:42; 24:16; Acts 10:47; 14:18; 20:27; Rom 11:10; 1 Pet 3:10). By implication (Luke 17:1; Heb 11:5; James 5:17). As marking purpose or result, where *hóste* might stand instead of *toú* (cf. 4 below [Rom 7:3]). (**3**) Inf. with *to* (2 Cor 2:13), marking a cause as existing in the mind of someone. (**4**) Inf. with *to* where the inf. is then equivalent to a subst. (Rom 14:13 preceded by *toúto* [5124], this; Rom 14:21 meaning "if one would eat no meat" [a.t.]; 1 Cor 4:6; 2 Cor 2:1; 1 Thess 4:6); with the prep. *eis* (1519), unto, and *prós* (4314), toward, as marking purpose, supposed result, e.g., *eis tó mē̄* (Acts 7:19; 1 Cor 9:18; 10:6; Heb 11:3; 1 Pet 3:7); *prós tó mē̄* (2 Cor 3:13; 1 Thess 2:9; 2 Thess 3:8); with *diá* (1223), for, as marking the probable or supposed cause of something (Matt 13:5, 6; Mark 4:5; James 4:2).

(**E**) With part. when they stand elliptically for any of the above constructions or refer to an indef. subj., or in general where they imply supposition, condition, purpose, something subj. (**1**) When the part. may be resolved into the construction with *ei* (1487) or *eán* (1437), if (Luke 11:36; Rom 5:13; Gal 6:9; Col 1:23; 1 Pet 3:6 [cf. A above]). (**2**) Where the part., either with or without the art., is equivalent to a relative pron. referring to a general or indef. antecedent (cf. B above). *Ho mē̄* with the part. (Matt 12:30, "whosoever" (a.t.) or "he that" meaning if someone, where *ou* would only have referred to some particular and def. individual (Luke 11:23; John 3:18; 10:1; 1 Thess 4:13). *Apó* (575) *toú mē̄ échontos* (2192), "from the one who does not have" (a.t. [Matt 25:29]). See Matt 3:10; 13:19; Luke 3:11; 19:26, 27; John 15:2; Rom 4:19; 1 Cor 7:37; James 4:17; 1 John 3:10. Generally (Matt 9:36; 10:28; Luke 12:47; Acts 20:22 where the subj. or antecedent is indeed specific, but the part. expresses a subj. doubt or uncertainty; Rom 2:14; 1 Cor 7:29; 9:21; 1 John 2:4). Here also belong such phrases as *tá mē̄ déonta* (1210), "those things that ought not to be" (a.t. [1 Tim 5:13]); *tá mē̄ kathḗkonta* (2520), "those things that are not becoming" or that ought not to be; (a.t. [Rom 1:28]); *tá mē̄ ónta* (the pres. neut. pl. part. of *eimí* [1510], to be), meaning "those things which be not" (Rom 4:17). Metaphorically (1 Cor 1:28). (**3**) Where the part. with *mē̄* expresses the supposed or apparent cause for occasion of something (Matt 1:19; 18:25; Mark 2:4; 12:24; Luke 5:19; 9:33; Acts 9:26; 12:19; 2 Cor 3:14; Heb 4:2). (**4**) Where the part. with *mē̄* expresses a supposed or apparent result, like *hóste mē̄* (*hóste* [5620], so that), so that not, followed by the inf. (cf. D, 1 above [Luke 7:30; Acts 20:29; 2 Cor 4:2; Phil 1:28; see Acts 9:9, "He was for three days apparently blind, so as not to see" [a.t.], i.e., he was as a blind man]). Also with *kaí* (2532), and, as equivalent to *hóste* (Luke 1:20; 13:11; Acts 27:15).

(**F**) In all neg. expressions of wish, entreaty, command, where *mē̄* then often stands at the beginning of a short independent clause, the idea of wishing, not being expressed, but retained in the mind. Thus to express a neg. wish, *mé* is construed with the opt. in a neg. entreaty and command, with the imper. and subjunctive, as follows: (1) With the opt. implying a neg. wish in the frequent exclamation *mé génoito* (1096), may it not be! let it not happen! (Luke 20:16; Rom 3:4, 6, 31; 1 Cor 6:15; Gal 2:17; 6:14). (2) With the imper. (which never takes *ou*), usually with the pres. imper. implying continued action and forbidding what one is already doing (Matt 6:16, 19, 25; 17:7; 24:6, "beware, be not troubled" [a.t.]; Mark 9:39; Luke 23:28; John 2:16; Acts 10:15; 1 Pet 4:12). Pres. imper. 3d person (Rom 6:12; 14:6; 1 Cor 7:12, 13; Col 2:16; 1 Tim 6:2; James 1:7). With the imper. implied (Luke 13:14; John 18:40; Rom 14:15; Gal 5:13). In antithetic clauses (2 Cor 9:7; Col 3:2, "things above, not on things on the earth"; James 1:22; 1 Pet 3:9). *Mé allá* (235), "not / but" (a.t. [Luke 22:42; John 6:27; Phil 2:12]). Very rarely *mé* is found with the aor. imper. (in the NT only in the 3d person) implying transient action and forbidding that which one may be about to do, e.g., *mé gnótō* (1097), "let your left hand not know" (a.t. [Matt 6:3]); "let him not come down into the house" (Matt 24:17 [UBS]; Mark 13:15, 16 [UBS]; Luke 17:31). (3) With the subjunctive in neg. entreaties, commands or exhortations where the action is to be expressed as transient and momentary. In pres. subjunctive 1st person pl., where it stands in place of the imper. 1st person (Gal 5:26; 6:9; 1 Thess 5:6; 1 John 3:18); aor. subjunctive (John 19:24). In aor. subjunctive 2d and 3d person (Matt 1:20; 3:9; 5:17; 6:13; 10:5, 9; Mark 5:7; Rom 10:6; 1 Cor 16:11; Col 2:21; Heb 3:8; 10:35; James 2:11). With *genēthé* of the verb *gínomai* (1096), to become, or the like implied (Matt 26:5; Mark 14:2).

(G) Generally in any construction where the negation is from the nature of the case subj., conditional, or a matter of supposition and where *mé* either depends upon the preceding relative pron. *hós* or it expresses condition (Matt 19:9, "if not for fornication" [a.t.]; Mark 12:15, implying subj. uncertainty; John 3:18 because by the very supposition, "he hath not believed"; Rom 3:8, hypothetically, "and not rather?" i.e., and why should it not rather be the case?; Col 2:18, meaning into what he cannot possibly have seen or was supposed to have seen. Here *ou* would have expressed that he had not seen them though he had the power). In 1 Thess 4:5, *mé* refers to the preceding inf. *ktásthai* from *ktáomai* (2932), to possess. See Rom 14:1.

(II) As a conj., that not, lest. In the NT only after verbs expressing fear, anxiety or foresight, with which the Greeks connect a neg., implying a wish that the thing feared may not be or happen.

(A) With the subjunctive where the preceding or governing verb is in the pres., as after verbs of fear (Acts 27:17; 2 Cor 12:21); with *phoboúmenos*, the pres. mid. part. of *phobéō* (5399), to frighten or to be afraid, implied (2 Cor 12:6). The preceding verb may be expressing a past time except in the indic. (Acts 23:10). After verbs of foresight or caution, the verb being in the pres. (Matt 18:10; Mark 13:5, 36; 2 Cor 8:20; Gal 6:1; Heb 12:15, 16; Rev 19:10; 22:9).

(B) With the opt. where the preceding verb is in a past tense of the indic. as after a verb of foresight (Acts 27:42).

(C) With the indic. less often, and implying that the thing feared already exists or is about to happen. With the pres. indic. (Luke 11:35). With the fut. indic. (Col 2:8).

(D) With the inf. in neg. wishes or admonitions, implying a fear of the contrary, i.e., with the acc. and inf. (2 Cor 6:1; 13:7).

(III) As an emphatic interrogative particle which has lost its own neg. power, but expressing a degree of fear or anxiety and implying the expectation of a neg. answer, while *ou* interrogative demands an affirmative answer. Simply, with the pres. indic. (Matt 9:15; John 3:4; Acts 7:28; 1 Cor 12:29, 30; James 2:14). With *estí*, pres. 3d person sing. of *eimí* (1510), to be, implied (Rom 3:5; 9:14; 1 Cor 12:29); fut. (Matt 7:9, 10; Rom 3:3); with the aor. (Luke 22:35; John 7:48; Rom 11:1); perf. (John 7:47).

Deriv.: *mēdé* (3366) and not, neither, not even; *mēkéti* (3371), no further, not any longer, not henceforth; *mḗ ouk* (3378), used as an interrogative and neg., "Is it not that?" never, not; *mḗpō* (3380), not yet; *mḗpōs* (3381), lest somehow; *mḗte* (3383), but not, not even, neither, nor; *mḗti* (3385), whether at all; *mḗtis* (3387), whether any.

Syn.: *ou* (3756), not; *oudamōs* (3760), by no means, not; *oudé* (3761), not however, neither, nor, not even; *oudeís* (3762), not a single one (fem. *oudemía* neut. *oudén*); *oudépote* (3763), never at all, neither at any time, never; *oudépō* (3764), not even yet, never before yet, not yet; *oukéti* (3765), not yet, no longer, not any more or henceforth; *oukoún* (3766), is it not therefore that, hence, so, then; *oúpō* (3768), hitherto not, as yet, not yet; *oúte* (3777), not even, neither, none, not, nothing; *ouchí* (3780), not indeed.

Ant.: *naí* (3483), yes; *málista* (3122), most of all, especially; *mén* (3303), indeed; *mḗn* (3375), indeed; *méntoi* (3305), indeed; *asphalōs* (806), assuredly; *alēthōs* (230), truly; *óntōs* (3689), really; *amḗn* (281), truly.

3362. ἐάν μή *eán mḗ*; neg. conditional expression consisting of *eán* (1437), if, and *mē* (3361), not. If not, unless, in all neg. conditions and suppositions (Matt 5:20; 6:15; Mark 3:27; 7:4; Luke 13:3, 5; John 3:2, 5; 15:6; Gal 2:16; Sept.: Ex 3:19; 4:1, 8, 9). In the sense of except, that, but that (Matt 26:42, "so but that I drink" [a.t.]; Mark 4:22, "but that it shall be revealed" [a.t.]; 10:30, "but that he shall receive" [a.t.], i.e., who shall not receive). Also *ei* (1487) *mē* with the same meaning as *eán mḗ* (Matt 24:22; Mark 2:7; John 3:13). With *eán* or *ei* implied

(Mark 12:19; Luke 10:10; 1 Cor 13:1–3; James 2:14). Sometimes *ei* is followed by *ou*, but *ou* then refers not to the condition, but to the verb alone which is rendered neg. (Matt 26:24, meaning that not being born would have been better for him [*mē* in this instance would have implied doubt whether he had been born]; Mark 11:26; Luke 14:26; 18:4).

3363. ἵνα μή *hína mḗ* expression consisting of *hína* (2443), in order that, and *mē* (3361), not. In order not, so that not, lest. See *hína* (2443, I, A, 1). In the expression *hína mḗ*, the *hína* (2443) implies purpose or either anticipated or supposed result, in which case it is syn. with *hópōs* (3704) or *hōste* (5620). See Matt 26:5; Mark 4:12; Acts 5:26.

3364. οὐ μή *ou mḗ*; negative expression consisting of *ou* (3756), not, and *mē* (3361), not. A double neg. strengthening the denial, meaning not at all, no never. See *mē* (3361, I, H). In the NT, *mē* is used only interrogatively (expressing a degree of fear or anxiety and implying the expectation of a neg. answer) while *ou*, when used interrogatively, demands an affirmative answer. When these two neg. are coupled together they refer to emphatic negations as to the fut., meaning not at all, by no means, construed particularly with the fut. indic. or more commonly with the aor. subjunctive (Matt 16:22; 26:35; Luke 22:34; John 8:12; 20:25; Rev 3:5). In an emphatic interrogation (Luke 18:7; John 18:11); followed by the aor. subjunctive (Matt 24:2; Luke 22:16, 18; Heb 8:12; 1 Pet 2:6); 2d aor. act. and mid. (Matt 5:18, 20; 18:3; Mark 13:19; Luke 1:15; John 6:37; Rev 3:3, 12). Strengthened by *oukéti* (3765), not now, no more (Mark 14:25; Luke 22:16), and by *oudé* (3761), neither (Matt 24:21). In an emphatic interrogative (John 11:56); followed by aor. act. (Matt 10:23; Mark 9:41; John 4:14, 48; Acts 13:41; Heb 8:11; 2 Pet 1:10); in the mid. (Matt 16:28; Rom 4:8); with *oukéti* (3765), not as yet (Rev 18:14).

3365. μηδαμῶς *mēdamôs*, adv. from *mēdamós* (n.f.), not even one, which is from *mēdé* (3366), not even, and *amós* (n.f.), one, someone. By no means (Acts 10:14; 11:8).

Syn.: *oudamôs* (3760), by no means. The differences between *mḗ* (3361), not, being subj. and relative, while *ou* (3756), not, is obj. and absolute, apply here in the comp. adv. *mēdamôs* and *oudamôs*.

Ant.: *asphalôs* (806), assuredly; *óntōs* (3689), certainly; *alēthôs* (230), surely; *pántōs* (3843), surely, doubtless; *hólōs* (3654), actually, assuredly.

3366. μηδέ *mēdé*; neg. conj. from *mḗ* (3361), not, and *dé* (1161), but, and. Neither, nor, not even. A conj. differing from *oudé* (3761) as *mḗ* differs from *ou* (3756) and having the same general meaning as *mḗ*, and not, also not, neither, not even, acting as connecting whole clauses or propositions.

(I) In continued negation at the beginning of a subsequent clause, meaning neither, nor, mostly preceded by *mḗ* (Matt 10:14; Mark 6:11; Luke 16:26; John 4:15; Rom 14:21; 1 Tim 1:4); preceded by *mḗpō* (3380), not yet (Rom 9:11). Also in continued prohibition, usually after *mḗ*, when it takes the same construction as *mḗ* with the imper. or subjunctive. See *mḗ* (3361, I, F, 2 and 3). Followed by the pres. imper. expressed or implied (Matt 6:25; Mark 13:11; Rom 6:13; Heb 12:5). Preceded by *mēdeís* (3367), no one (Luke 3:14; 1 Tim 5:22). Followed by a verb in the aor. pass. (1 Pet 3:14); by the pres. subjunctive 1st person pl. in exhortations (1 Cor 10:8, 9; 1 John 3:18); 2d aor. 2d person (Matt 7:6; Col 2:21; 2 Tim 1:8). *Mēdé / mēdé* (Mark 8:26). Followed by the inf. depending on a verb of prohibition (Acts 4:18). It is used once in antithetic apodosis followed by the imper. (2 Thess 3:10).

(II) It may be used also in the middle of a clause meaning not even (Mark 2:2; 1 Cor 5:11; Eph 5:3).

Deriv.: *mēdamôs* (3365), by no means; *mēdeís* (3367), not even one.

Ant.: *kaí* (2532), and, also, indeed; *alēthôs* (230), truly; *óntōs* (3689), really, verily; *gnēsíōs* (1104), sincerely, genuinely, truly; *mén* (3303), a conj. particle placed in opposition to the adversative particle *dé* (1161), but, meaning indeed; the phrase *kaí gár* (*kaí*, and; *gár* [1063], a particle meaning therefore), and in fact, for also; the phrase *allá kai* (*allá* [235], but; *kaí*), but even, and indeed.

3367. μηδείς *mēdeís*; fem. *mēdemía*, neut. *mēdén*, adj. from *mēdé* (3366), and not, also not, and *heís* (1520), one. Not even one, no one, i.e., no one whoever he may be, from the indef. and hypothetical power of *mḗ*, differing from *oudeís* (3762), not even one, as *mḗ* differs from *ou*. For the difference, see *mḗ* (3361).

(I) Generally (Matt 16:20; Mark 6:8; John 8:10; Acts 4:21; 1 Cor 1:7; Heb 10:2). With *mḗ* (3361), not, *mēkéti* (3371), no further, or *mēdeís* (3367), not a single one, repeated in a strengthened negation (1 Pet 3:6). See Mark 11:14; Acts 4:17; 2 Cor 6:3.

(II) In prohibitions, e.g., after the pres. imper. (Luke 3:13; 1 Cor 3:18, 21; Titus 2:15; James 1:13); with the imper. implied (Matt 27:19; Phil 2:3); with duplicate neg. (Mark 1:44; Rom 13:8). Followed by the aor. subjunctive (Matt 8:4; 17:9; Acts 16:28).

(III) Neut. *mēdén*, nothing.

(A) As an adv., not at all, in no respect, e.g., without gainsaying (Acts 10:20; 11:12; James 1:6). After verbs of profit or loss, deficiency (Mark 5:26; Luke 4:35; 2 Cor 11:5; Phil 4:6); with *en* (1722), in, meaning in nothing, in no respect (2 Cor 7:9; Phil 1:28; James 1:4).

(B) Metaphorically, *mēdén ón* (*ón* [5607], the pres. part. of *eimí* [1510], to be), meaning being nothing, i.e., of no account, no weight of character (Gal 6:3).

Syn.: *oudeís* (3762), no one, more absolute and obj. than *mēdeís métis* (3387), no man, not anyone.

Ant.: *hékastos* (1538), each one; *pás* (3956), every; *hápas* (537), the whole, all.

3368. μηδέποτε *mēdépote*; adv. from *mēdé* (3366), not even, and *poté* (4218), at any time, ever. Not even ever (2 Tim 3:7).

Syn.: *oudépote* (3763), not even at any time, more obj. and absolute than *mēdépote*; *oudépō* (3764), and; *oúpō* (3768), not yet; *pópote* (4455), never; the phrase *eis tón aiṓna* (*eis* [1519], unto; *tón* [3588], the; *aiṓna* [165], age), meaning "never" (when used negatively) and "forever" (if used positively). In all the comp. from *mē̃* (3361), not, and *ou* (3756), not, the difference is that the first is subj. and relative while the second is obj. and absolute. The first represents conceptual thought and the second reality. See *mē̃* (3361).

Ant.: *aeí* (104), perpetually, forever; *hekástote* (1539), each time; *diapantós* (1275), through all time, forever; *pántē* (3839) and *pántote* (3842), always; the phrase *en pantí kairṓ* (*en* [1722] in; *pantí*, the dat. sing. of *pás* [3956], every; *kairṓ*, the dat. of *kairós* [2540], season, occasion), on every occasion or season; the phrase *pásas tás hēméras* (*pásas* the fem. of *pás* [3956], each, all; *tás hēméras* [2250], days), all the days, always; the phrase *eis tó diēnekés* (*eis* [1519], unto; *tó diēnekés* [1336], in continuity), continually, forever.

3369. μηδέπω *mēdépō*; adv. from *mēdé* (3366), not even, and *pō* (n.f.), yet. Not yet (Heb 11:7).

Syn.: *oudépō* (3764), not yet; *oúpō* (3768), not yet.

Ant.: *nún* (3568), now; *nuní* (3570), now, but more emphatic than *nún*; *ḗdē* (2235), now, already; *árti* (737), just now; *apárti* (534), from now, henceforth; *loipón* (3063), from now.

3370. Μῆδος *Mḗdos*; gen. *Mḗdou*, masc. proper noun. A Mede (Acts 2:9), one who comes from Media, the country

which lay between the Caspian Sea on the north and Persia on the south, and extended on the north and west to Armenia. It was incorporated into the kingdom of Persia.

3371. μηκέτι *mēkéti*; adv. from *mē̃* (3361), not, and *éti* (2089), anymore, yet, with the *k* (kappa) being inserted for the sake of sound. No more, no further, no longer, in the general sense of *mē̃* and constructed in the same manner. After *hína* (2443), so that (2 Cor 5:15; Eph 4:14, "so that we no more be babies" [a.t.]). With the inf. (Acts 4:17; 25:24; Eph 4:17). With the inf. after *hóste* (5620), so that (Mark 1:45; 2:2). With the inf. and *toú*, (Rom 6:6). With part., as expressing a cause (Rom 15:23; 1 Thess 3:1, 5); a result (Acts 13:34). In neg. expressions of wish, entreaty, command, followed by an opt. implying a neg. wish (Mark 11:14); by the pres. imper. (John 5:14; 8:11; Eph 4:28; 1 Tim 5:23); by the pres. subjunctive 1st person pl. (Rom 14:13); 2d aor. 3d person (Matt 21:19).

Syn.: *oukéti* (3765), no more, more objective and absolute than *mēkéti*; *mḗpō* (3380) and *oúpō* (3768), not yet; *oudépō* (3764), not ever yet; *mḗpote* (3379), not ever.

Ant.: *pántote* (3842), always; *aeí* (104), ever, perpetually; *hekástote* (1539), each time; *diapantós* (1275), through all time, forever; *pántē* (3839) and *pántote* (3842), always; the phrase *en pantí kairṓ* (*en* [1722], in; *pantí*, the dat. sing. of *pás* [3956], each; *kairṓ* the dat. sing. of *kairós* [2540], season, occasion), in every season, at every occasion; the phrase *pásas tás hēméras* (*pásas*, the acc. pl. fem. of *pás* [3956], all, every; *tás hēméras* [2250], the days), all the days or always; the phrase *eis tó diēnekés* (*eis* [1559], unto; *tó diēnekés* [1336], perpetuity, unbroken, continuous), perpetually, forever.

3372. μῆκος *mḗkos*; gen. *mḗkous*, neut. noun. Length (Rev 21:16). Metaphorically used in Eph 3:18; Sept.: Gen

6:16. Other dimensions: *plátos* (4114), breadth; *báthos* (899), depth; *húpsos* (5311), height.

Deriv.: *mēkúnō* (3373), to lengthen.

3373. μηκύνω *mēkúnō*; fut. *mekunṓ*, from *mḗkos* (3372), length. To make long, lengthen. In the NT, only in the mid., *mēkúnomai*, to lengthen oneself, spoken of plants and meaning to grow up (Mark 4:27; Sept.: Isa 44:14).

Syn.: *auxánō* (837), to grow or increase; *epekteínomai* (1901), to stretch; *ekteínō* (1614), to stretch forth; *prokóptō* (4298), to cut forward, advance.

Ant.: *kolobóō* (2856), to curtail, shorten; *sustéllō* (4958), to contract, shorten, bring together; *suntémnō* (4932), to cut short; *kóptō* (2875), to cut; *elattóō* (1642), to decrease; *elattonéō* (1641), to diminish, fall short.

3374. μηλωτή *mēlōtḗ*; gen. *mēlōtḗs*, fem. noun from *mḗlon* (n.f.), a sheep. A sheepskin. The word may come either from *mélei* (3199), 3d person sing. of *méllō* (3195), to care or to show concern, derived from the care which the sheep require in tending, or from *málos*, soft, tender, a term applicable to sheep either from the gentleness of their disposition, the tenderness of their bodies, or the softness of their wool, which in Gr. is sometimes called *mállos* and in the demotic Gr. *mallí*. A sheepskin used for clothing (Heb 11:37; Sept.: 1 Kgs 19:13, 19; 2 Kgs 2:8, 13, 14 spoken of Elijah's mantle).

Syn.: *himátion* (2440), an outer garment, a mantle, cape.

3375. μήν *mḗn*; particle of strong affirmation. Yes, assuredly; in connection with the adv. *ē* (2229), assuredly (Heb 6:14).

Syn.: *naí* (3483), a particle of affirmation meaning yes; *kaí* (2532), and, yes; *menoúnge* (3304), yes, rather, doubtless; *mén* (3303), a conj. particle meaning indeed.

Ant.: *mḗ* (3361), a particle of qualified negation; *ou* (3756), no or not, a more absolute neg. particle.

3376. μήν *mḗn*; gen. *mēnós*, masc. noun. A month (Luke 1:24, 26, 36, 56; 4:25; Acts 7:20; 18:11; 19:8; 20:3; 28:11; James 5:17; Rev 9:5, 10, 15; 11:2; 13:5; 22:2; Sept.: Gen 7:11; 8:4, 5). It also stands for the new moon which was the first day of the month and a festival (Gal 4:10). In the Sept. *neomēnía* (Ps 81:3).

Deriv.: *noumēnía* (3561), new moon; *trímēnon* (5150), a space of three months; *tetrámēnos* (5072), a space of four months.

3377. μηνύω *mēnúō*; fut. *mēnúsō*, aor. *emḗnusa*, perf. *memḗnuka*. To make known, show, disclose something previously unknown. Used trans. (Luke 20:37; John 11:57; 1 Cor 10:28); with the dat. (Acts 23:30). It also meant in Class. Gr., as even today in Mod. Gr., to report to the authorities or to sue.

Syn.: *exaggéllō* (1804), to tell out, tell abroad; *kataggéllō* (2605), to proclaim; *phaneróō* (5319), to manifest; *dēlóō* (1213), to state; *egkaléō* (1458), to accuse.

Ant.: *ainéō* (134), to speak in praise of, and its comp. *epainéō* (1867), to commend; *sunístēmi* or *sunistánō* (4921), to represent someone as worthy; *eulogéō* (2127), to speak well of, bless.

3378. μὴ ου *mḗ ou*; interrogative expression consisting of *mḗ* (3361), not, and *ou* (3756), not. In this combination *mḗ* is interrogative and *ou* belongs solely to the verb following (Rom 10:18, "Have they not heard?" where the answer must still be neg. as in Rom 10:19, meaning "Hath then Israel not known?" or "Is he then ignorant?" [author's translations]; 1 Cor 9:4, 5; 11:22).

3379. μήποτε *mḗpote*, **μή ποτε** *mḗ poté*; neg. particle from *mē* (3361) and *poté* (4218), at any time. Lest at any time.

(I) As a neg. particle, not even, never, in no supposable case (Heb 9:17).

(II) As a conj., that not ever, that never, lest ever, i.e., lest at some time or other, indef. meaning lest perhaps. After verbs implying purpose, followed by the subjunctive and preceded by a pres., fut., or aor., or something that has gone before. In the indic. as with *hína* (2443), so that (see I, A, 1, 3 and 4). With a fut. preceding (Matt 4:6; Luke 4:11). With the pres. versus the aor. preceding (Matt 5:25; 7:6; 13:29; 27:64; Mark 4:12; Luke 12:58; 14:8, 12, 29); *hína mḗpote* (Luke 14:29). With a past occurrence (Matt 13:15; Acts 28:27). Followed by the fut. indic. (Mark 14:2; Heb 3:12). See *mḗ*, II, C. After verbs implying fear or caution, followed by the subjunctive (Matt 15:32; Luke 21:34; Heb 2:1; 4:1); with the preceding verb implied (Matt 25:9; Acts 5:39).

(III) As an interrogative particle equal to *poté* (4218), sometime, in a direct inquiry implying a neg. answer (John 7:26, "Do the rulers then certainly know?" [a.t.], Do they perhaps know?). Indirectly, meaning whether perhaps, if perhaps, followed by the opt. (Luke 3:15); by the subjunctive (2 Tim 2:25).

Syn.: *mḗpō* (3380), lest at any time, not yet; *houpō* (3768), not yet; *mēkéti* (3371), not any more, no longer; *oukéti* (3765), no longer (used in a more absolute sense); *oudépō* (3764), never; *eis tón aiōna* (*eis* [1519], unto; *tón*, the; *aiōn* [165], age), unto the age, forever, never.

Ant.: *ḗdē* (2235), already; *dḗ* (1211) and *nún* (3568), now; *árti* (737), this day, present; *sḗmeron* (4594), today; *chthés* (5504), yesterday; *aúrion* (839), tomorrow.

3380. μήπω *mḗpō*; adv. from *mḗ* (3361), not, and *pō*, (4452), yet. Not yet (Rom 9:11; Heb 9:8). For syn. and ant., see *mēkéti* (3371) and *mḗpote* (3379), never.

3381. μήπως *mḗpōs*, μή πως *mḗ pōs*; conj. from *mḗ* (3361), not, lest, and *pōs* (4458), by any means. Lest by any means,

that in no way, that by no means, lest perhaps. With the aor. preceding (Gal 2:2); after verbs implying fear or caution, followed by the indic. (Gal 4:11); followed by the aor. subjunctive (Acts 27:29; Rom 11:21; 1 Cor 8:9; 9:27; 2 Cor 2:7; 9:4; 11:3; 12:20, where the verb *heurethṓsi*, be found, from *heurískō* [2147], to find, is implied). Once construed with both indic. and subjunctive (1 Thess 3:5, "fearing lest perhaps the tempter" [a.t.]).

Syn.: *ára* (687), then, therefore, an interrogative particle necessitating a negative answer; *tácha* (5029), peradventure, perhaps; *pṓs* (4459), how, in what way.

Ant.: *asphalṓs* (806), assuredly; *akribṓs* (199), exactly.

3382. μηρός *mērós*; gen. *mēroú*, masc. noun. The thigh (Rev 19:16 where Christ appears in the manifestation of His judicial capacity and action because the sword is worn on the thigh; Sept.: Gen 24:2, 9; Ps 45:3).

3383. μήτε *mḗte*; continuative conj. from *mḗ* (3361), not, and *te* (5037), and. And not, also not, neither, not even, referring usually to a part of a proposition or clause. It is used in continued negation, at the beginning of a subsequent clause, after *mḗ*, "neither / nor" (a.t. [Eph 4:27; 2 Thess 2:2]). When it is repeated *mḗte / mḗte*, it means "neither / nor" before different parts of the same clause (a.t. [Matt 5:34; Acts 23:8 {UBS}, 12, 21; 1 Tim 1:7; James 5:12]). When alone in the mid. of a clause, it means not even (Mark 3:20).

Syn.: *oúte* (3777), nor, but more obj. and absolute than *mḗte*.

Ant.: *naí* (3483), yes; *málista* (3122), yes.

3384. μήτηρ *mḗtēr*; gen. *mētrós*, fem. noun. A mother.

(I) Particularly (Matt 1:18; 2:11, 13, 20; Sept.: Gen 2:24; 44:20). Figuratively of one in the place of a mother (Matt 12:49, 50; Mark 10:30; John 19:27; Rom 16:13).

(II) Generally for a parent, ancestor, progenitor (Gal 4:26 representing Sarah our common mother; Sept.: Gen 3:21; 2 Sam 20:19).

(III) Figuratively of a city as the parent or source of wickedness and abominations (Rev 17:5).

Deriv.: *amḗtōr* (282), without the record of a mother, spoken of Melchizedek; *métra* (3388), the womb, matrix; *mētrópolis* (3390), the city of birth, mother city.

Ant.: *patḗr* (3962), a father.

3385. μήτι *mḗti*; neg. particle from *mḗ* (3361), not, and *tí*, which is from *tís* (5101), anything. Not at all, not perhaps.

(I) As a neg. only in the connection of supposition with *ei* (1487), if, *ei mḗti* (1509), if not perhaps, unless perhaps (Luke 9:13; 1 Cor 7:5; 2 Cor 13:5).

(II) As an interrogative meaning "whether at all?" "whether perhaps?" i.e., "is or has then perhaps?" (Matt 7:16; 12:23; 26:22, 25; Mark 4:21; 14:19; Luke 6:39; John 4:29; 7:31; 8:22; 18:35; 21:5; Acts 10:47; 2 Cor 12:18; James 3:11). In the expression *mḗti ára* (686) which is a particle denoting an inference more or less decisive as used in 2 Cor 1:17, it could be translated "whether at all for sure" (a.t.); see Sept.: Gen 20:9; Mal 3:8. For syn. and ant., see *mḗpote* (3379), lest at any time, never, lest ever.

3386. μήτι γε *mḗti ge*; neg. expression consisting of *mḗti* (3385), not at all, and *ge* (1065), yet, an intens. Not at all then, not to say then, much more than (1 Cor 6:3).

3387. μήτις *mḗtis*, **μή τις** *mḗ tis*; masc. interrogative pron. from *mḗ* (3361), denoting a question, and *tis* (5101), anyone. Whether anyone is, or has anyone (John 4:33; 7:48 [cf. *mḗ* {3361, III}]).

3388. μήτρα *métra*; gen. *métras*, fem. noun from *mḗtēr* (3384), a mother. The womb, matrix (Luke 2:23; Rom 4:19; Sept.: Num 3:12; 1 Sam 1:5, 6; Jer 1:5).

Syn.: *koilía* (2836), womb, belly, referring generally to man's inner being; *gastḗr* (1064), womb, belly.

3389. μητραλῴας *mētralṓas*; gen. *mē-tralṓou*, masc. noun from *mḗtēr* (3384), a mother, and *aloiáō* (n.f.), to strike, smite, beat. One who physically abuses his own mother (1 Tim 1:9 [cf. Rom 1:30]).

3390. μητρόπολις *mētrópolis*; gen. *mētropóleōs*, fem. noun from *mḗtēr* (3384), a mother, and *pólis* (4172), a city. Metropolis, the mother city or principal city, found only in the spurious subscription following 1 Tim 6:21.

3391. μία *mía*; gen., *miás*, cardinal number, the fem. of *heís* (1520), one. One.

3392. μιαίνω *miaínō*; fut. *mianṓ*, aor. pass. *emiánthēn*, perf. pass. *memíasmé-nos*, perf. pass. 3d person pl. *memíantai*. To stain with color as the staining of glass, to tinge, pollute, defile. Trans.:

(I) In the Levitical sense (John 18:28; Sept.: Lev 5:3; 22:5, 8).

(II) In a moral sense (Jude 1:8). Pass., to be polluted, corrupt (Titus 1:15; Heb 12:15).

Deriv.: *amíantos* (283), undefiled; *míasma* (3393), defilement, referring to the vices of the ungodly which contaminate one in his contact with the world; *miasmós* (3394), the act of defiling.

Syn.: *koinóō* (2840), to make common, render unholy or unclean in a ceremonial sense; *molúnō* (3435), to besmear or soil in a figurative moral sense, while *miaínō* is used to indicate ceremonial defilement; *spilóō* (4696), to defile, which in James 3:6 expresses the defiling effects of the evil use of the tongue and in Jude 1:23 is used of moral defilement; *phtheírō* (5351), to corrupt; *diaphtheírō* (1311), to corrupt completely; *kataphtheírō* (2704), to corrupt utterly; *sḗpō* (4595), to render rotten;

aphanízō (853), to cause to disappear, e.g., the destructive work of rust (Matt 6:19, 20) which causes a metal to lose its proper function, to corrupt, disfigure.

Ant.: *katharízō* (2511), to make clean; *diakatharízō* (1245), to cleanse thoroughly; *kathaírō* (2508), to purge; *ekkathaírō* (1571), to cleanse out thoroughly; *hagnízō* (48) to purify, cleanse from defilement. The difference between *hagnós* (53) and *katharós* (2513), pure and clean (see 1 John 3:3), is that the first implies shrinking from pollution while the second expresses simply the fact of cleanliness.

3393. μίασμα *míasma*; gen. *miásmatos*, neut. noun from *miaínō* (3392), to defile. Pollution (2 Pet 2:20). The contamination of the world upon the godly as a result of living in it; the result of *miasmós* (3394), the act of polluting.

Syn.: *molusmós* (3436), defilement in the sense of an action by which something is defiled; *spílos* (4695), a spot, moral blemish; *phthorá* (5356), corruption; *alísgēma* (234), pollution, contamination, especially the pollution resulting from contact with idolatry including meats from sacrifices offered to idols.

Ant.: *katharismós* (2512), the act of cleansing which results in cleanliness which is expressed by *katharótēs* (2514), cleansing; *hagnismós* (49), a ceremonial purification; *hagnótēs* (54), pureness, purity; *hagneía* (47), chastity, excluding all impurity of spirit and conduct.

3394. μιασμός *miasmós*; gen. *miasmoú*, masc. noun from *miaínō* (3392), to pollute, defile. The act of defiling resulting in *míasma* (3393), polluted desire or unclean lust (2 Pet 2:10).

Syn.: *molusmós* (3436), defilement in the sense of an action by which something is defiled; *spílos* (4695), a moral blemish; *phthorá* (5356), corruption; *diaphthorá* (1312), thorough corruption; *alísgēma* (234), contamination resulting from contact with idolatry.

Ant.: *katharismós* (2512), cleansing, the act of cleansing resulting in *katharótēs* (2514), the state of being clean, purity; *hagnismós* (49), ceremonial purification.

3395. μίγμα *mígma*; gen. *mígmatos*, neut. noun from *mígnumi* (3396), to mingle. Mixture (John 19:39).

Syn.: *keránnumi* (2767), to mix, mingle. (Chiefly used of diluting wine from which comes the adj. *ákratos* [194], without mixture, undiluted.)

3396. μίγνυμι *mígnumi*; fut. *míxō*. To mix, mingle (Matt 27:34; Luke 13:1; Rev 8:7; 15:2).

Deriv.: *migma* (3395), mixture.

Syn.: *keránnumi* (2767), to mix, used chiefly of the diluting of wine, implying a mixing of two things so that they are blended and form a compound as in wine and water, whereas *mígnumi* implies a mixing without such composition as in two sorts of grain.

Ant.: *ákratos* (194), undiluted, without mixture.

3397. μικρόν *mikrón*; neut. of *mikrós* (3398), small. A small space of time or degree. Used adv., of space (Matt 26:39; Mark 14:35). Used in an absolute sense referring to time, a little while, particularly the acc. of time, meaning "how long?" (John 13:33; 14:19; 16:16–19). With *metá* (3326), after, meaning after a while, a little after (Matt 26:73; Mark 14:70).

Syn.: *olígon* (3641), little, small; *brachú* (1024), short.

Ant.: *mégas* (3173), great; *meízōn* (3187), greater; *meizóteros* (3186), greater; *polús* (4183), much, great, many; *pleíōn* (4119), greater; *hikanós* (2425), sufficient, great; *hēlíkos* (2245), as big as; *pēlíkos* (4080), how large! how great!; *lían* (3029), exceeding; *perissós* (4053), abundant, over; *perissóteros* (4055), more abundant.

3398. μικρός *mikrós*; fem. *mikrá*, neut. *mikrón*, adj. Small, little. Comparative degree *mikróteros* (n.f.) smaller, less, the opposite of *mégas* (3173), large.

(I) Of magnitude (Matt 13:32; Mark 4:31; James 3:5); of stature (Luke 19:3; Sept.: Ezek 17:6); of age meaning small, young, not grown up (Acts 8:10; 26:22; Heb 8:11; Rev 11:18; 13:16; 19:5, 18; 20:12); in the comparative degree meaning less, younger (Mark 15:40); of quantity meaning a little (1 Cor 5:6; Gal 5:9); figuratively (Rev 3:8); of number meaning little, few (Luke 12:32; Sept.: Gen 30:30; 47:9). As an adv. (2 Cor 11:1, 16; Sept.: Job 10:20; Prov 6:10).

(II) Of time (John 7:33; 12:35; Rev 6:11; 20:3).

(III) Figuratively, of dignity, authority, meaning low, humble (Matt 10:42; 18:6, 10, 14; Mark 9:42; Luke 17:2). The comparative degree is *mikróteros*, smaller, humbler (Matt 11:11; Luke 7:28; 9:48) or *elássōn* or *eláttōn* (1640), smaller. The superlative degree is *eláchistos* (1646), least; *elachistóteros* (1647), less than the least.

Deriv.: *mikrón* (3397), a small space of time or degree.

Syn.: *néos* (3501), young.

Ant.: *mégas* (3173), large; *beltíon* (957), better.

3399. Μίλητος *Mílētos*; gen. *Milḗtou*, fem. proper noun. Miletus, a city and seaport of Ionia in Asia Minor. Situated thirty-six miles south of Ephesus, it stood on the southwestern side of the Latmian Gulf, directly opposite the mouth of the river Meander. The sediment from the river gradually filled up the gulf and the site is now about ten miles inland. However, in Paul's time it had four docks and much commerce. Paul stopped here on his voyage from Greece to Jerusalem returning from his third missionary journey and met the elders from Ephesus (Acts 20:15–38). 2 Tim 4:20 states that Paul left Trophimus sick in Miletus (cf. Acts 21:29).

3400. μίλιον *mílion*; gen. *milíou*, neut. noun. A mile (Matt 5:41), formed from the Lat. *mille*, a thousand. A Roman mile consisted of 1,000 paces, *passuum*, each of which was equal to nearly five feet. It is estimated to be 1,611 yards, while the English mile is 1,760 yards.

3401. μιμέομαι *miméomai*; contracted *mimoúmai*, fut. *mimḗsomai*, mid. deponent from *mímos* (n.f.), an imitator. To mimic, but in a good sense, to imitate, follow as an example, with the acc. (2 Thess 3:7, 9; Heb 13:7; 3 John 1:11).

Deriv.: *mimētḗs* (3402), an imitator.

Syn.: *akolouthéō* (190), to follow; *deúte opísō* (*deúte* [1205], come; *opísō* [3694], after), follow after.

Ant.: *apodokimázō* (593), to reject as the result of examination and disapproval; *paraitéomai* (3868), to reject, refuse; *exouthenéō* (1848), to despise; *periphronéō* (4065), to despise; *kataphronéō* (2706), to think lightly of, despise.

3402. μιμητής *mimētḗs*; gen. *mimētoú*, pl. *mimētaí*, masc. noun from *miméomai* (3401), to imitate. An imitator, follower (1 Cor 4:16; 11:1; Eph 5:1; 1 Thess 1:6; 2:14; Heb 6:12; 1 Pet 3:13).

Deriv.: *summimētḗs* (4831), a fellow imitator.

Syn.: *mathetḗs* (3101), disciple.

3403. μιμνήσκω *mimnḗskō*; fut. *mnḗsō*. To recall to one's mind, to remind (Heb 2:6; 13:3). In the NT, only in the mid. *mimnḗskomai*, to remember.

Deriv.: *anamimnḗskō* (363), to recall or bring back into remembrance; *hupomimnḗskō* (5279), to cause one to remember.

Syn.: *mnēmoneúō* (3421), to remember; *mnáomai* (3415), to remind, remind oneself of, remember.

Ant.: *lanthánō* (2990), to willfully forget; *epilanthánomai* (1950), to forget or neglect completely; *eklanthánomai* (1585), to forget utterly; *ameléō* (272), to be careless about, neglect; *paratheōréō* (3865), to overlook.

3404. μισέω miséō; contracted *misó*, fut. *misēsō*. To hate.

(I) With the acc. of person, usually implying active ill will in words and conduct, a persecuting spirit (Matt 5:43 where it stands as opposite to *agapáō* [25], to love, in Matt 5:44; 10:22; 24:9, 10; Mark 13:13; Luke 1:71; 6:22, 27; 19:14; 21:17; John 7:7; 15:18, 19, 23–25; 17:14; Titus 3:3; 1 John 2:9, 11; 3:13, 15; 4:20; Sept.: Gen 37:4; Lev 26:17). By implication, meaning to persecute (Rev 17:16; Sept.: 2 Sam 5:8; 22:18).

(II) With the acc. of thing meaning to detest, abhor (John 3:20; Rom 7:15; Eph 5:29; Heb 1:9; Jude 1:23; Rev 2:6, 15; 18:2).

(III) Specifically as the opposite of *agapáō* (25), to love, or *philéō* (5368), to be a friend to, it is equivalent to not loving, loveless, to slight, with the acc. of person (Matt 6:24; Luke 16:13; John 12:25; Rom 9:13; Sept.: Gen 29:31; Deut 21:16; Mal 1:3).

(IV) To love less. In Luke 14:26 Jesus contrasts love to family with love to Himself "If any come to me, and hate [*miseí*, pres. act. indic. 3d person sing.] not his father, and mother, and wife, and sisters, yea, and his own life also, he cannot be my disciple." Here Jesus asserts His deity. Every member of man's family is a human being, and the love shown to humans compared to the love shown to Jesus Christ, God in the flesh, must be so different that the former seems like hatred. The meaning of *miséō* as loving less is made clear in Matt 10:37, "He that loveth father or mother more than me is not worthy of me: and he that loveth son or daughter more than me is not worthy of me." In His commands for loving other human beings, the Lord never said, "Love other human beings as you love Me," but "Thou shalt love thy neighbor as thyself" (Matt 19:19). When it comes to loving God, however, He is placed in a unique position (Matt 22:37, 38).

Syn.: *apéchomai* (567), to refrain.

Ant.: *agapáō* (25), to love; *philéō* (5368), to befriend.

3405. μισθαποδοσία misthapodosía; gen. *misthapodosías*, fem. noun from *misthapodótēs* (3406), rewarder. A recompense, whether a reward (Heb 10:35; 11:26) or a punishment (Heb 2:2).

Syn.: *antapódosis* (469), the act of rewarding, recompensing or punishing accordingly; *antapódoma* (468), the reward or punishment itself; *antimisthía* (489), a reward, requital; *amoibé* (287), recompense; *opsónion* (3800), a soldier's pay. With the meaning of punishment: *ekdíkēsis* (1557), vengeance or the bringing out of justice; *epitimía* (2009), penalty, the curtailment of rights due to a sense of honor; *kólasis* (2851), punishment, the negation of the enjoyment of life; *díkē* (1349), justice, a sentence; *timōría* (5098), vengeance, punishment, the vindication of honor.

3406. μισθαποδότης misthapodótēs; gen. *misthapodótou*, masc. noun from *misthós* (3408), a reward, and *apodídōmi* (591), to render. A recompenser, rewarder (Heb 11:6). The reward for good or evil is *misthapodosía* (3405).

Deriv.: *misthapodosía* (3405), a punishment, recompense.

3407. μίσθιος místhios; fem. *misthía*, neut. *místhion*, adj. from *misthós* (3408), hire, pay, reward. Hired servant, an adj. related to *misthōtós* (3411), a hireling (Luke 15:17, 19; Sept.: Lev 25:50; Job 7:1).

Syn.: *ergátēs* (2040), a worker.

Ant.: *doúlos* (1401), slave; *andrapodistḗs* (405), an enslaver.

3408. μισθός misthós; gen. *misthoú*, masc. noun. Wages, hire, reward.

(I) Particularly and generally (Matt 20:8; Luke 10:7, "worthy is the worker of his hire" [a.t.]; Acts 1:18, "the wages of his crime" [a.t.]; Rom 4:4; 1 Cor 3:8; 1 Tim 5:18; James 5:4; 2 Pet 2:15, "the wages of unrighteousness" [a.t.], hence wages gotten through iniquity; Jude 1:11, "for hire" or gain; Sept.: Gen 30:28; 31:7; Mal 3:5).

(II) In the sense of reward to be received hereafter (Matt 5:12, 46; 6:1, 2, 5, 16; 10:41, 42; Mark 9:41; Luke 6:23, 35; John 4:36; 1 Cor 3:14; 9:17, 18; 2 John 1:8; Rev 11:18; 22:12; Sept.: Gen 15:1).

(III) In the sense of retribution, punishment (2 Pet 2:13); see *misthapodosía* (3405), reward, punishment.

Deriv.: *antimisthía* (489), reward, penalty; *misthapodótēs* (3406), rewarder; *místhios* (3407), a day laborer, one paid by the day; *misthóō* (3409), to hire; *misthōtós* (3411), a hired worker.

Syn.: *amoibḗ* (287), recompense; *antapódoma* (468), recompense, what one receives in reward or punishment; *antapódosis* (469), the act of recompensing; *opsṓnion* (3800), rations for soldiers, wages.

Ant.: *ekdíkēsis* (1557), vengeance, punishment, the bringing out of justice, what is due; *epitimía* (2009), a privation of honor or rights; *kólasis* (2851), punishment as the negation of the enjoyment of love; *díkē* (1349), the execution of a sentence; *timōría* (5098), disciplinary punishment, the vindication of honor.

3409. μισθόω *misthóō*; contracted *misthṓ*, fut. *misthṓsō*, from *misthós* (3408), pay, reward. To let for hire. In the NT only in the aor. mid., *emisthṓsato*, and the fut. *misthṓsomai*, to hire, used trans. (Matt 20:1, 7; Sept.: Judg 9:4; 2 Chr 24:12).

Deriv.: *místhōma* (3410), a hired house; *misthotós* (3411), hired one.

Ant.: *apolúō* (630), to dismiss.

3410. μίσθωμα *místhōma*; gen. *misthṓmatos*, neut, noun from *misthóō* (3409), to hire. A hired house (Acts 28:30; Sept.: Deut 23:18). It can also indicate something hired or rented.

3411. μισθωτός *misthōtós*; gen. *misthōtoú*, masc. noun from *misthóō* (3409),

to hire. Hired one. Sometimes indicating one who is not showing real interest in his duty and who is unfaithful, a hireling (Mark 1:20; John 10:12, 13; Sept.: Ex 12:45; Lev 19:13).

Syn.: *místhios* (3407), hired servant; *ergátēs* (2040), worker.

Ant.: *despótēs* (1203), a despot, one who has absolute ownership and uncontrolled power, master; *kúrios* (2962), lord, master, owner.

3412. Μιτυλήνη *Mitulḗnē*; gen. *Mitulḗnēs*, fem. proper noun. Mitylene, meaning hornless. The chief town and capital of the isle of Lesbos, situated on the east coast of the Aegean Sea. Mitylene is the intermediate place where Paul stopped for the night between Assos and Chios (Acts 20:14).

3413. Μιχαήλ *Michaḗl*; masc. proper noun transliterated from the Hebr. *Mīkhāēl* (4317, OT), "who is like God?" Michael. In the NT used principally as the prince among the angels, the archangel (Jude 1:9) described in Dan 10:13, 21; 12:1 as standing in a special relationship to the Jewish nation, and in Rev 12:7–9 as leading the hosts of the angels.

3414. μνᾶ *mná*; gen. *mnás*, fem. noun from the Lat. *mina* representing a Greek weight containing one hundred *drachmaí* (1406). It is larger than the Roman *libra* or pound in the proportion of four to three. It is equivalent to twelve ounces. In the NT, *mná* is a silver coin, estimated by weight, containing one hundred *drachmaí*, and being itself the sixtieth part of a talent. Its value varied in different countries (Luke 19:13, 16, 18, 20, 24, 25).

Syn.: *lítra* (3046), a Sicilian coin, the equivalent of the Lat. *libra*, a measure of weight, a pound.

3415. μνάομαι *mnáomai*; fut. *mnḗsomai*, aor. pass. *emnḗsthēn*, both as mid. and pass.; perf. part. *memnēménos* used as a pres. tense (2 Tim 1:4), mid. deponent from *mimnéskō* (3403), to recall to one's mind. To remember, be mindful, recollect.

(I) In the aor. and perf., used as mid. in Matt 26:75; Luke 1:54, 72; 23:42; 24:8; Acts 11:16; 1 Cor 11:2; 2 Tim 1:4; 2 Pet 3:2; Jude 1:17. Followed by *hóti* (3754), that (Matt 5:23; 27:63; Luke 16:25; John 2:17, 22; 12:16); by *hōs* (5613), as, like (Luke 24:6).

(II) In the aor., *emnésthēn*, used as pass. in regard to Cornelius' prayer and almsgivings having been remembered (Acts 10:31, see Acts 10:4). Used in regard to punishment (Rev 16:19).

(III) In Heb 8:12 and 10:17, the apostle brings forth Jer 31:34, in which God says in relation to His new covenant with Israel, "For I will forgive their iniquity, and I will remember their sin no more." This does not mean that God does not exercise memory with which He has so beneficially endowed His creatures; nor does it mean that when we appear before Him to have our lives reviewed and judged that God will forget all that we have ever done (Rom 14:10; 1 Cor 3:11–15; 2 Cor 5:10; Rev 20:11–15). The apportionment of rewards to the believers necessitates God's and their remembrance of their works (James 2:12, 13). The Heb 8:12 and 10:17 passages specifically speak of the new covenant of the Lord with Israel which, being accepted, brings an end to His remembrance by Him regarding whether or not they kept the old covenant. This is equivalent to God forgetting all the sins of the individual before he was saved and ushered into the kingdom of God. However, there is certainly a remembrance of all one's works, whether good or bad (2 Cor 5:10), performed during his entire life of faith from the moment he has been attached to the body of Jesus Christ (1 Cor 12:13).

Deriv.: *mneía* (3417), remembrance; *mnéma* (3418), a monument, memorial; *mnēmeíon* (3419), a memorial, grave; *mnémē* (3420), memory, remembrance;

mnēmoneúō (3421), to remember, make mention; *mnēsteúō* (3423), to give a souvenir or engagement present as a reminder that one is spoken for or espoused.

Syn.: *enthuméomai* (1760), to bring to one's mind; *historéō* (2477), to narrate history; *analogízomai* (357), to bring to mind, consider; *mimnéskomai* (3403), to remember.

Ant.: *lanthánomai* (2990), to escape notice, forget; *epilanthánomai* (1950), to forget, neglect; *eklanthánomai* (1585), to forget completely.

3416. Μνάσων Mnásōn; gen. *Mnásōnos*, masc. noun. Mnason, meaning remembering. A native of Cyprus but a resident of Jerusalem, an early convert to Christianity mentioned in Acts 21:16 as the host of the Apostle Paul.

3417. μνεία mneía; gen. *mneías*, fem. noun from *mnáomai* (3415), to recollect. Recollection, remembrance (Phil 1:3; 1 Thess 3:6; 2 Tim 1:3). To have remembrance, meaning to bear in mind, make mention of (Rom 1:9; Eph 1:16; 1 Thess 1:2; Phile 1:4; Sept.: Job 14:13; Ps 111:4; Isa 26:8).

Syn.: *enthúmēsis* (1761), deliberation, thoughtful remembering; *mnémē* (3420), remembrance.

Ant.: *léthē* (3024), forgetfulness; *epilēsmonḗ* (1953), forgetfulness characterized by moral irresponsibility.

3418. μνῆμα mnéma; gen. *mnématos*, neut. noun from *mnáomai* (3415), to remember. A memorial or monument intended to preserve the memory of some person or thing, hence sepulcher. In the NT used to indicate a tomb (Mark 5:5; Luke 8:27; 23:53; 24:1; Acts 2:29; 7:16; Rev 11:9; Sept.: Ex 14:11; Ezek 32:23; 37:12). It is never used in relation to the soul.

Syn.: *táphos* (5028), burial place or tomb; *mnēmeíon* (3419), grave, sepulcher.

3419. μνημεῖον *mnēmeíon*; gen. *mnēmeíou*, neut. noun from *mnáomai* (3415), to remember. A memorial or monument in contrast to *mnêma* (3418), which is more of a tomb, grave, sepulcher. In the NT used for a tomb, sepulcher (Matt 8:28; 27:52, 53; 28:8; Mark 5:2). In Matt 23:29, "you adorn the sepulchers" and Luke 11:47, "you build the sepulchers" (a.t.), means you adorn, build up, or repair the sepulchers of the prophets. One must remember that the sepulchers of the Jews were often caverns (Gen 23:9ff.; 35:20; 49:30), or were hewn artistically out of rocks or in the sides of hills in various forms and sizes, sometimes with several compartments. They were closed by a door or layer of stone, and the entrance was often decorated with ornaments and whitewashed.

Syn.: *táphos* (5028), grave, tomb, sepulcher; *hádēs* (86), Hades, the dwelling place of departed spirits.

3420. μνήμη *mnḗmē*; gen. *mnḗmēs*, fem. noun from *mnáomai* (3415), to remember. Remembrance, recollection (2 Pet 1:15; Sept.: Ps 30:4).

Syn.: *enthúmēsis* (1761), deliberation, remembrance; *mneía* (3417), remembrance.

Ant.: *lḗthē* (3024), forgetfulness; *epilēsmonḗ* (1953), forgetfulness characterized by moral responsibility.

3421. μνημονεύω *mnēmoneúō*; fut. *mnēmoneúsō*, from *mnáomai* (3415), to remember, call to mind, bear in mind. To exercise memory, be mindful of, remember. Followed by *hóti* (3754), that (Acts 20:31; Eph 2:11; 2 Thess 2:5); by *póthen* (4159), whence (Rev 2:5); by *pṓs* (4459), how (Rev 3:3). By implication it means to mention, to speak of, with *perí* (4012), about, around (Heb 11:22). *Mnēmoneúō* is used in an absolute sense in Mark 8:18 where it means to exercise the God-given gift of memory. Elsewhere it has an obj. of person (Luke 17:32; Gal 2:10; Heb 13:7). In 2 Tim 2:8, the Apostle

Paul wrote that he need not remind Timothy that the Lord Jesus was raised from the dead, but to remind him to have that in his mind constantly. The object of remembrance may also be things (Matt 16:9; John 15:20; 16:21; Acts 20:35; Col 4:18; 1 Thess 1:3; 2:9; Heb 11:15; Rev 18:5) or some circumstance that ought to be kept in mind (John 16:4; Acts 20:31; Eph 2:11; 2 Thess 2:5; Rev 2:5; 3:3). In Heb 11:22, it means to make mention of. *Mnēmoneúō* therefore means to use the faculty of memory given by God and to keep in one's mind people, things, and circumstances, because memory is the basis of learning and prevention of the dangers of life. However, *mimnḗskō* (3403) means to bring to the surface of one's memory.

Ant.: *lanthánomai* (2990), to forget, sometimes unwittingly; *epilanthánomai* (1950), to willfully forget, implying moral culpability.

3422. μνημόσυνον *mnēmósunon*; gen. *mnēmosúnou*, neut. noun from *mnēmósunos* (n.f.), commemorative. A memorial, monument, equivalent to *mnēmeíon* (3419). In the NT, generally, it means a memorial, something causing or preserving the remembrance of a person or thing (Matt 26:13; Mark 14:9, meaning her honorable remembrance or fame).

In Acts 10:4, reference is made to the prayers of Cornelius prior to his coming into the circle of Christian believers as having ascended as a memorial before God. (See Sept.: Ex 12:14; 17:14; Ps 102:13; Mal 3:16.) In Acts 10:2, we read that Cornelius was "a devout man, and one that feared God with all his house, which gave much alms to the people, and prayed to God always." Although devout, he was ignorant of the way of salvation brought through the Lord Jesus Christ. It is evident that both his prayers and his alms to others were heard and noticed by God. They became a memorial (*mnēmósunon*) before God. Thus the prayers and almsgivings of Cornelius were indications before God that he was a man who was indeed yearning for God and His more perfect way in Christ although ignorant of it. God looks at the hearts of such people and gives them the opportunity of a fuller knowledge of Himself.

But what happens to those who, unlike Cornelius, do not accept Christ's more perfect way of salvation, although during their lives they exhibited a certain degree of moral or religious consciousness? The ultimate end of these is described in Rev 20:11–15 at "the judgment of the great white throne" which is the last judgment. We are told that God keeps books in which He registers the works of both good and evil whereby He judges individuals. The bringing forth of these works constitutes the basis of God's final judgment. In addition to these books there is also the Book of Life in which only the names of those who believed on the Lord Jesus Christ, God's Lamb, are written (Phil 4:3; Rev 3:5; 13:8; 17:8; 20:12; 21:27). But the other books are those in which the works of both believers and unbelievers are written and according to which the rewards for believers are distributed and the punishments to the unbelievers. The unbelievers are going to be ushered into a resurrection of damnation (John 5:29), but they are not all going to suffer equally. God is going to remember all that they did in their lives. The fact that they did not believe on the Lord Jesus Christ leaves them out of the Book of Life. However, they will be judged according to the works of their own lives, which are written in the books kept by God.

Ant.: *aphanismós* (854), disappearance.

3423. μνηστεύω *mnēsteúomai*; fut. *mnēsteuthḗsomai*, from *mnáomai* (3415), to remember. To ask in marriage, to woo. In the NT used only in the pass. meaning to be asked in marriage, to be betrothed (Matt 1:18; Luke 1:27; 2:5).

It is related to the verb used for "remember" because it was a ceremony which was to be remembered when a person was espoused or committed to another for marriage (Sept.: Deut 22:23, 25, 27, 28). The betrothal ceremony perpetuated in a conventional fashion the recollection of the time when a woman was purchased from her family (Deut 20:7). When a woman was designated (Ex 21:8, 9) by the head of her family as the future wife of another man, the prospective bridegroom paid a certain sum of money (or service as in the case of Jacob). A contract, which was inviolable, was then entered into (Gen 34:12; Ex 22:17). Until the time of the actual marriage, the bride-to-be remained in her own family. It was not permissible to betroth her to any other man except by action amounting to divorce, and any violation of the rights established by the betrothal was as serious as if the two persons had been ceremonially married (Deut 22:23, 24). In the OT, it is impossible to say with precision just how soon the wedding followed betrothal. In later times, in the case of a virgin, it was after the lapse of a year, and at least thirty days in the case of a widow. So, too, it is impossible to describe with any great precision the betrothal ceremony, but it certainly included the payment of a particular sum (1 Sam 18:25) and the making of a betrothal contract (Ezek 16:8) by the prospective bridegroom. The money payment belonged originally to the family of the woman, but gradually came to belong in part or wholly to the woman herself. The first advances might come from the family of either party. There is no clear evidence that the young woman had any right of appeal as to her family's choice. The bridegroom himself did not conduct the negotiations, but the matter was in the hands of a third party such as his parents or some trusted servant or friend.

After the exile, the custom of the earlier period seems to have continued, although with certain modifications. The payment to the bride's father on the part of the prospective groom had been increasingly regarded as the property, at least in part, of the bride. Such a payment during this period was often supplemented by a dowry in the true sense. No consent of the girl was demanded, nor do we know of the recognition of any legal age of consent, unless, as in somewhat later times, it was not expected that boys would marry before the age of eighteen or girls before twelve. In Talmudic times, there was a distinct tendency to combine the betrothal with the wedding. Today the Jews seem to combine the two ceremonies.

Probably the ceremony of betrothal in NT times involved the following acts: First, a contract drawn up by the parents or by the friend of the bridegroom. Second, the meeting of the two families concerned, with other witnesses, at which time the groom gave the bride jewelry (Gen 24:53) and declared his intention to observe the terms of the contract already arranged. Third, the payment of the *mōhar* (4119, OT) by the prospective bridegroom. This occurred during a ceremony at which a priest may have been present. The status of the man and woman was now, as in Hebrew times, practically the same as that of married persons, although it was generally customary for the wedding ceremony proper to be celebrated at a later date. As in the older times, separation of betrothed persons demanded a divorce, and there seems to have been no taboo in their living together as man and wife previous to the wedding ceremony. The children of such a union would be regarded as legitimate. Insofar as the virgin Mary and Joseph are concerned, the use of the verb *mnēsteúomai*, to betroth (Matt 1:18; Luke 1:27; 2:5), indicates a betrothal ceremony. There is no mention, however, of a subsequent wedding ceremony. It was during this period of betrothal that the angel appeared to Mary (Matt 1:18). It is clearly stated, however, that the angel appeared to announce to Mary her conception by the Holy Spirit before she had sexual relations with Joseph. The same angel also appeared to Joseph to tell him of the supernatural conception of his betrothed, Mary (Matt 1:24; see Luke 1:26ff.).

Syn.: *ekdídōmi* (1554), to give forth.

Ant.: *aphíēmi* (863), to let go; *ekpémpō* (1599), to send away; *apolúō* (630), to dismiss.

3424. μογιλάλος *mogilálos*; gen. *mogilálou*, masc.-fem., neut. *mogilálon*, adj. from *mógis* (3425), with difficulty, hardly, and *laléō* (2980), to speak. Speaking with difficulty, a stutterer or stammerer (Mark 7:32; Sept.: Isa 35:6).

3425. μόγις *mógis*, adv. from *mógos* (n.f.), labor, pain. With difficulty, hardly (Luke 9:39).

Deriv.: *mogilálos* (3424), a stammerer.

Syn.: *duskólōs* (1423), with difficulty; *mólis* (3433), scarcely.

Ant.: *eukopōteros* (2123), easier.

3426. μόδιος *módios*; gen. *modíou*, masc. noun from the Lat. *modius*. A Roman measuring basket of various sizes to measure dry things (Matt 5:15; Mark 4:21; Luke 11:33). For words indicating measurement, see *métron* (3358), measure.

3427. μοι *moi*; personal pron., 1st person dat. sing., the abbreviated form of the emphatic *emoí* (1698), to me. Me, mine, my.

3428. μοιχαλίς *moichalís*; gen. *moichalídos*, fem. noun. An adulteress (Rom 7:3; 2 Pet 2:14, "eyes full of adultery," meaning gazing with desire after such persons. See Sept.: Ezek 16:38; 23:45). Used figuratively to indicate one who is unfaithful toward God as an adulteress is unfaithful toward her husband. In the Greek OT spoken mainly of those who forsook God for idols (Isa 57:3, 7; Ezek 16, 23; Hos 3:1). In the NT, the word is generally used of those who neglect God and their duty toward Him and yield themselves to their own lusts and passions (Matt 12:39; 16:4; Mark 8:38; James 4:4 where the word *moichalís* stands as a characteristic of infidelity, adulterous or faithless, idolatrous).

Syn.: *pórnē* (4204), a harlot, one engaging in illicit sex of any kind, whether married or not, while *moichalís* refers to an unfaithful married woman.

3429. μοιχάω *moicháō*; contracted *moichó*, fut. *moichésō* from *moichós* (3432), an adulterer. To commit adultery. In the NT used only in the mid., *moicháomai*, equal in meaning to *moicheúō* (3431), to commit adultery.

The inf. of *moicháomai* is used in Matt 5:32 in the phrase, *poieí autén moichásthai* (*poieí* pres. act. indic. of *poiéō* [4160], makes; *autén*, the fem. of *autós* [846], her; *moichásthai*, to be considered or counted as an adulteress, and not "to commit adultery," as some translations have it). The subj. of this sentence is the licentious person described in Matt 5:27–30 who constantly looks upon and touches a woman other than his wife. If he consequently dismisses his own wife and does not give her the bill of divorcement spoken of in Matt 5:31 and Deut 24:1–4, which amounted to a certificate of innocence for his unjustifiably dismissed wife, he causes her dismissal to be looked upon as adultery on her part. An innocently dismissed wife cannot possibly be conceived of as having committed adultery herself. It is her licentious husband who has dismissed her for a reason other than sexual infidelity who commits adultery against her and, therefore, causes her to be thought of as an adulteress. In addition, the person who would marry such a dismissed woman also assumes her undeserved "adultery." The TR has the pres. mid. / pass. inf. *moichásthai* which is derived from *moicháomai*, whereas the UBS has the aor. pass. *moicheuthénai* derived from the syn. *moicheúō* (3431), to commit adultery.

The verb occurs for the second time in Matt 5:32 in the pres. indic., *moichátai*, not in the act. voice, but in the mid. / pass. form. *Moichátai*, therefore, should be translated "has adultery committed against him" (a.t.). Since the form of the verb is the same whether it is mid. or pass., the exegetical context of the verb is used to determine its meaning. In this verse, the meaning can be both mid. and pass. The phrase, "whosoever marries a dismissed woman" (a.t.), refers to an innocent woman unjustifiably dismissed by her licentious husband and not having been given a bill of divorcement clearing her of extramarital sexual sin (see Matt 5:31 and Deut 24:1–4). She must bear upon herself the presumed and assumed guilt of an adulteress because of the action of her husband.

The same is true in Matt 19:9 where the verb in the mid. / pass. form, *moichátai*, appears twice in the TR and once in the UBS text. In this verse, the licentious person not only dismisses his own wife, but also marries another woman. The verb *moichátai* means to commit adultery against himself (mid. voice), because he dismissed his innocent wife and married another one. It can also be understood in the pass. voice indicating that the woman he marries becomes an adulteress, i.e., she becomes an adulteress because of his action.

The second statement in Matt 19:9 is "and whoso marrieth her which is put away doth commit adultery." This phrase, which is missing from the UBS, is found in the TR. The phrase "which is put away" is the pass. part. *apoleluménēn* from *apolúō* (630), referring to the one unjustifiably dismissed by her husband in order that he might marry another. This woman is not really an adulteress, but has been caused by her husband to be counted as an adulteress since she was dismissed without having been given a bill of divorcement certifying her innocence. Therefore, the person who marries such a presumed adulteress (*moichátai*, the pres. indic. of *moicháomai*, which in this instance may be taken with a mid. meaning) assumes adultery against himself. If taken as a pass., it means that he allows presumed adultery to be committed against himself. We find the parallel passage in Mark 10:11, 12: "Whosoever shall put away his wife, and marry another, committeth adultery against her." The verb here is *moichátai* and should be translated "causes adultery upon her" (a.t. [*ep' autēn*; *epí* {1909}, upon; *autēn*, the fem. of *autós* {846}, her]). The verb is used in the pass. form meaning that adultery is caused to be committed against his new wife. The verb is used again in the pass. voice, *moichátai*, in verse twelve: "And if a woman shall put away her husband, and be married to another, she committeth adultery." In this instance, the verb is understood as having a mid. meaning. Here we are told about a woman who dismisses her husband unjustifiably and marries another. First of all, this woman brings the guilt of adultery upon her own self (*moichátai*) since she becomes married to a man other than her husband. Secondly, the verb can have a pass. meaning in that she causes her new husband to commit adultery in marrying her since she made herself an adulteress in dismissing her previous husband. These are the only places that the verb is used in the mid. and pass. voice.

Syn.: *moicheúō* (3431), to commit adultery; *porneúō* (4203), to commit fornication or any sexual sin, while *moicháō* refers to a married person committing sexual acts with someone other than his or her own spouse.

3430. μοιχεία *moicheía*; gen. *moicheías*, fem. noun from *moicheúō* (3431), to commit adultery. The act of adultery (Matt 15:19; Mark 7:21; John 8:3; Gal 5:19; Sept.: Jer 13:27 [cf. Hos 2:4]). *Moicheía* is included in the more general word *porneía* (4202), fornication, which encompasses all kinds of

sexual sins. *Moicheía* involves at least one person who is married.

Ant.: *hagnótēs* (54), pureness.

3431. μοιχεύω *moicheúō*; fut. *moicheúsō*, mid. / pass. *moicheúomai*, from *moichós* (3432), an adulterer. To commit adultery. Used in the act. voice (Matt 5:27, 28; 19:18; Mark 10:19; Luke 16:18; 18:20; Rom 2:22; 13:9; James 2:11; Rev 2:22). In the mid. / pass. voice as a part. *moicheuoménē* (John 8:4), "being considered an adulteress" (a.t.).

Deriv.: *moicheía* (3430), adultery.

Syn.: *moicháō* (3429), to commit adultery; *porneúō* (4203), to commit sexual infidelity of any kind, whether involving a married person or not; *ekporneúō* (1608), to give oneself up to fornication, implying excessive sexual indulgence.

3432. μοιχός *moichós*; gen. *moichoú*, masc. noun. An adulterer (Luke 18:11; 1 Cor 6:9; Heb 13:4; Sept.: Job 24:15; Prov 6:32). Figuratively, as the fem. *moichalís* (3428), of one who is faithless toward God (James 4:4; Sept.: Isa 57:3).

Deriv.: *moicháō* (3429), to commit adultery; *moicheúō* (3431), commit adultery.

Syn.: *pórnos* (4205), male prostitute, fornicator, which can refer to any type of sexual immorality and unfaithfulness.

3433. μόλις *mólis*; adv. from *mólos* or *mólos* (n.f.), labor pains. With difficulty, hardly, scarcely (Acts 14:18; 27:7, 8, 16; Rom 5:7; 1 Pet 4:18).

Syn.: *duskólōs* (1423), with difficulty; *mógis* (3425), painfully or with toil.

3434. Μολόχ *Molóch*; masc. proper noun transliterated from the Hebr. *Mōlek* (4432, OT), king. Moloch (Acts 7:43), an idol-god worshiped by the Ammonites with human sacrifices, especially children. The rabbis tell us that the idol, having the head of a calf with a crown upon it, was made of brass and placed on a brazen throne. The throne and image were hollow, and a raging fire was kindled within it. The flames penetrated into the body and limbs of the idol, and when the arms were red-hot, the victim was thrown into them and almost immediately burned to death while its cries were drowned by the beat of drums. Although warned against this idolatry common to all the Canaanite tribes, though probably not of Canaanite origin, the Jews were repeatedly enticed to adopt it (Sept.: 2 Kgs 23:10). In the Valley of Hinnom, they set up a tabernacle to Moloch and there they sacrificed their children to the idol.

3435. μολύνω *molúnō*; fut. *molunṓ*. To defile, besmear or soil as with mud or filth (1 Cor 8:7; Rev 3:4; 14:4).
Deriv.: *molusmós* (3436), defilement, the act of defiling.
Syn.: *miaínō* (3392), to stain; *spilóō* (4695), to spot, pollute; *phtheírō* (5351), to corrupt.
Ant.: *katharízō* (2511), to cleanse.

3436. μολυσμός *molusmós*; gen. *molusmoú*, masc. noun from *molúnō* (3435), to defile. Filthiness (2 Cor 7:1); the act of defilement produced by the body (Sept.: Jer 23:15).
Syn.: *miasmós* (3394), the act of defiling; *míasma* (3393), defilement, the result of defilement; *phthorá* (5356), corruption; *diaphthorá* (1312), complete corruption.
Ant.: *hagnismós* (49), cleansing, a ceremonial cleansing; *katharismós* (2512), the act of cleansing; *katharótēs* (2514), the state of being clean, purity; *hagiasmós* (38), sanctification.

3437. μομφή *momphḗ*; gen. *momphḗs*, fem. noun from *mémphomai* (3201), to find fault or blame. Fault-finding, blame, censure, an occasion of complaint (Col 3:13).
Syn.: *aitíama* (157), a charge; *aitía* (156), accusation, charge; *hamártēma* (265), a sin; *epitimía* (2009), penalty; *katēgoría* (2724), accusation.

Ant.: *aínos* (136), praise; *épainos* (1868), commendation, praise; *eulogía* (2129), blessing, speaking well of; *euphēmía* (2162), good report.

3438. μονή *monḗ*; gen. *monḗs*, fem. noun from *ménō* (3306), to remain, dwell. A mansion, habitation, abode (John 14:2, 23 [cf. Rev 21:3]). Also related to *mónos* (3441), alone, only, single.
Syn.: *oikētḗrion* (3613), a habitation; *katoikētḗrion* (2732), a place where one dwells permanently; *katoikía* (2733), dwelling place; *épaulis* (1886), a country house, cottage, cabin; *skēnḗ* (4633), a tent or tabernacle; *skḗnōma* (4638), a pitched tent, metaphorically refers to the body.

3439. μονογενής *monogenḗs*; gen. *monogenoús*, masc.-fem., neut. *monogenón*, from *mónos* (3441), only, and *génos* (1085), stock. Unique, one of a kind, one and only. The only one of the family (Luke 7:12 referring to the only son of his mother; 8:42, the daughter of Jairus; Luke 9:38, the demoniac boy).
John alone uses *monogenḗs* to describe the relation of Jesus to God the Father, presenting Him as the unique one, the only one (*mónos*) of a class or kind (*génos*), in the discussion of the relationship of the Son to the Father (John 1:14, 18; 3:16, 18; 1 John 4:9). *Génos*, from which *genḗs* in *monogenḗs* is derived, means race, stock, family, class or kind, and *génō* comes from *gínomai* (1096), become, as in John 1:14, "and the Word became [*egéneto*] flesh." This is in distinction from *gennáō* (1080), to beget, engender or create. The noun from *gennáō* is *génnēma* (1081), the result of birth. So then, the word means one of a kind or unique. There are two schools of thought regarding the meaning of this term. The first view, which began with Origen, teaches that Christ's unique Sonship and His generation by the Father are eternal being predicated of Him in respect to His participation in the Godhead.

Although *monogenḗs* was traditionally cited in proof of this explanation, modern proponents, recognizing the mistaken identification of *genḗs* as a derivative of *gennáō* instead of *génos*, understand the word to be descriptive of the kind of Sonship Christ possesses and not of the process establishing such a relationship. This would serve to distinguish the Sonship of Christ to God from that spoken of other beings, e.g., Adam (Luke 3:28), angels (Job 1:6), or believers (John 1:12). The last view teaches that Christ's unique Sonship and generation by the Father are predicated of Him in respect to the incarnation. The proponents of this interpretation unequivocally affirm the triune nature of the Godhead and Christ's deity teaching that it is the word *lógos* (3056), Word, which designates His personage within the Godhead. Christ's Sonship expresses an economical relationship between the Word and the Father assumed via the incarnation. This stands in fulfillment of OT prophecies which identify Christ as both human, descending from David, and divine, originating from God. Like David and the other kings descending from him, Christ is the Son of God by position (2 Sam 7:14), but unlike them and because of His divine nature, He is par excellence the Son of God by nature (Psalm 2:7; Heb 1:5). Thus the appellation refers to the incarnate Word, God made flesh, not simply the preincarnate Word. Therefore, *monogenḗs* can be held as syn. with the God-Man. Jesus was the only such one ever, in distinction with the Holy Spirit, the third Person of the Triune God.

He is never called *téknon Theoú* (*téknon* [5043], child; *Theoú* [2316], of God) as the believers are (John 1:12; 11:52; 1 John 3:1, 2, 10; 5:2). In John 5:18, Jesus called God His very own (*ídion* [2398]) Father. To Jesus, God was not a Father as He is to us. See John 20:17. He never spoke of God as the common Father of Him and believers. The term *monogenḗs* also occurs in Heb 11:17.

3440. μόνον *mónon*; adv., neut. of *mónos* (3441), alone. Only, alone (Matt 5:47; 9:21; Mark 5:36; Acts 18:25; 1 Cor 7:39; Gal 1:23; Heb 9:10). After *ei mḗ* (1508), if not (Matt 21:19; Mark 6:8; Acts 11:19). With a neg. such as *mḗ* (3361), not, meaning not only, simply (Gal 4:18; James 1:22). In antithesis or gradation followed by *allá* (235), but (Acts 19:26; Phil 2:12); with *allá kaí* (2532), but also (Matt 21:21; John 5:18; 11:52; 13:9; Acts 21:13; Rom 1:32; Heb 12:26). With the neg. *ou* (3756), not, meaning not only, simply this or that (James 2:24).

Syn.: *plḗn* (4133), howbeit, except that.

3441. μόνος *mónos*; fem. *mónē*, neut. *mónon*, adj. Only, alone, without others, without companions speaking of persons (Matt 14:23; Mark 6:47; 9:2, 8; Luke 10:40; John 8:9; Rom 11:3; 16:4; Heb 9:7; 2 John 1:1; Sept.: Gen 2:18; 32:24). Figuratively used of one acting on his own authority, alone (John 8:16); devoid of help from another (John 8:29; 16:32). Used of things (Luke 24:12; John 12:24, meaning the seed remains sterile or barren). Spoken in an adv. sense of persons and things (Matt 4:4; John 5:44; Jude 1:4; Rev 15:4). After *ei mḗ* (1508), if not (Matt 12:4; 17:8; 24:36; Luke 5:21; Phil 4:15; Rev 9:4). It also means one out of many (Luke 24:18; 1 Cor 9:6; 2 Tim 4:11).

Deriv.: *katamónas* (2651), alone; *monogenḗs* (3439), only child or one of its kind, unique; *monóphthalmos* (3442), with one eye; *monóō* (3443), to isolate.

Syn.: *autós* (846), himself, expressing exclusion meaning he himself.

Ant.: *pás* (3956), every; *hápas* (537), the whole.

3442. μονόφθαλμος *monóphthalmos*; gen. *monophthálmou*, masc.-fem., neut. *monóphthalmon*, adj. from *mónos* (3441), alone, only, and *ophthalmós* (3788), eye. With one eye, one-eyed (Matt 18:9; Mark 9:47).

3443. μονόω *monóō*; contracted *monó*, fut. *monósō*, from *mónos* (3441), only, alone. To leave alone, isolate. In the pass., to be left alone as a widow, to be solitary, probably childless (1 Tim 5:5).

Syn.: *erēmóō* (2049), to make desolate, lay waste.

Ant.: *suzeúgnumi* (4801), to yoke together.

✓ **3444. μορφή** *morphḗ*; gen. *morphḗs*, fem. noun. Form, shape.

Morphḗ appears with *schḗma* (4976), fashion, the whole outward appearance, in Phil 2:6–8. These two words stand for the form and fashion of a person or thing. A form would exist were it alone in the universe even if there were none to behold it. There may be a concept (*tó nooúmenon*, pres. act. part. of *noéō* [3539], to conceive, exercise the mind) without becoming apparent or externally visible. The *nooúmenon*, conceptual, may remain such or may become *phainómenon* (pres. act. part. of *phaínō* [5316], to appear), visible, with a shape, which can be observed. The use of *morphḗ* and *schḗma* implies that an appearance is made in a visible form and fashion.

Morphḗ in Phil 2:6–8 presumes an obj. reality. No one could be in the form (*morphḗ*) of God who was not God. However, *morphḗ* is not the shaping of pure thought. It is the utterance of the inner life, a life that bespeaks the existence of God. He who had been in *morphḗ Theoú*, in the form of God, from eternity (John 17:5) took at His incarnation the *morphḗn doúlou* (*doúlos* [1401], servant), a form of a servant. The fact that Jesus continued to be God during His state of humiliation is demonstrated by the pres. part. *hupárchōn*, "being" in the form of God. *Hupárchō* (5225) involves continuing to be that which one was before. Nothing appeared that was not an obj. reality from the beginning. In His incarnation, Jesus took upon Himself the form (*morphḗ*) of a servant by taking upon Himself the shape (*schḗma*) of man. The *schḗma*, shape or fashion, is the ✓ outward form having to do not only with His essential being, but also with His appearance. The eternal, infinite form of God took upon Himself flesh (John 1:1a, 14a). See Sept.: Dan 4:36; 5:6, 9, 10.

In Mark 16:12, the expression *en hetéra morphḗ* (*en* [1722], in; *hetéra* [2087], qualitatively another; *morphḗ*, the same as *metemorphóthē*, aor. pass. of *metamorphóō* [3339]), in another form, means that Christ was transformed (Matt 17:2; Mark 9:2; Sept.: Isa 44:13). The transfiguration upon the mount was a prophetic anticipation of that which we shall all experience at Christ's return (1 Thess 4:17; 1 Cor 15:52). This form in which the risen Lord appeared to two disciples on the road to Emmaus (Luke 24:13ff.) was a human form but different from that which Jesus had during His life on earth, yet He was readily recognized by His disciples.

Another word, *idéa* (2397), idea or concept of the mind, is subjective (Matt 28:3). *Idéa* is from *idéō* or *eídō* (1492), to see, which, in turn, is from *eídos* (1491), appearance, visible form (Luke 3:22; 9:29; John 5:37; 2 Cor 5:7; 1 Thess 5:22).

Deriv.: *morphóō* (3445), to form, fashion; *súmmorphos* (4832), conformed to.

3445. μορφόω *morphóō*; contracted *morphó*, fut. *morphósō*. from *morphḗ* (3444), form, shape. To form, fashion, originally used of artists who shaped their material into an image. Found only in Gal 4:19 where the Christian is described as a little child who needs to mature until the very image of Christ be impressed upon his heart.

Deriv.: *metamorphóō* (3339), to transform, transfigure; *mórphōsis* (3446), formulation, impression.

Syn.: *plássō* (4111), to shape, form

3446. μόρφωσις *mórphōsis*; gen. *morphóseōs*, fem. noun from *morphóō* (3445), to form. Formulation, impression, embodiment. As a verbal noun, signified by the -sis ending, it denotes primarily the process or activity of forming or shaping. Secondarily, it can denote the thing formed or shaped and is equivalent to the Classical term *mórphōma* (n.f.). In Rom 2:20 this latter meaning in view. The expression "a form of knowledge [*gnṓsis* {1108}] and of the truth [*alḗtheia* {225}] in the law" characterizes the Law as the exhibition or impression (revelation) of divine knowledge and truth. The Law stands as the proper verbal form which the ideals of knowledge and truth (or "true knowledge" if a hendiadys) assume when so communicated. In 2 Tim 3:5, *mórphōsis* is used ironically referring to that godliness (*eusébeia* [2150]) which is merely a form and simply an external appearance. Such godliness is a sham and devoid of any real power (*dúnamis* [1411]) to break the power of sin. Those who practice such religion find the external forms and expressions of evangelical worship to be amenable to their lifestyles but they are violently at odds with the gospel's internal effects of subduing sin and nurturing holiness.

Syn.: *hupókrisis* (5272), hypocrisy; *charaktḗr* (5481), exact image.

Ant.: *hupóstasis* (5287), substance, essence.

3447. μοσχοποιέω *moschopoiéō*; contracted *moschopoiṓ*, fut. *moschopoiḗsō*, from *móschos* (3448), calf, and *poiéō* (4160), to make. To make a calf, i.e., the image of a calf or bullock (Acts 7:41, spoken of the golden calf made by Aaron in imitation of the Egyptian god Apis; see Ex 32:4).

3448. μόσχος *móschos*; gen. *móschou*, masc. noun. Homer uses this word as an adj. with the meaning of tender. This seems to be its primary meaning. Later it came to denote young, tender animals, calves. Therefore, in the NT, it means a young animal, especially a calf or a young bullock (Luke 15:23, 27, 30; Heb 9:12, 19; Rev 4:7; Sept.: Gen 12:16; 24:35; Ex 29:10; 32:4, 8, 19; Lev 4:3ff.).

Deriv.: *moschopoiéō* (3447), to make a calf.

3449. μόχθος *móchthos*; gen. *móchthou*, masc. noun from *mógos* (n.f.), labor, toil. Toil, travail, afflicting and wearisome labor. It is the everyday word for that labor which, in one shape or another, is the lot of all the sinful children of Adam. It is more than *kópos* (2873), labor, and it therefore follows *kópos* in all the three passages wherein it occurs, namely 2 Cor 11:27; 1 Thess 2:9; 2 Thess 3:8; see Sept.: Deut 26:7; Eccl 2:18ff.

Syn.: *agṓn* (73), conflict; *pónos* (4192), pain; *lúpē* (3077), sorrow.

Ant.: *anápausis* (372), rest which comes from inner tranquility; *ánesis* (425), rest which comes from on high; *katápausis* (2663), rest which comes from cessation of work; *sabbatismós* (4520), Sabbath rest.

3450. μου *mou*; personal pron., 1st person gen. sing., an abbreviated form of the emphatic *emoú* (1700), of me, mine.

3451. μουσικός *mousikós*; fem. *mousikḗ*, neut. *mousikón*, adj. from *moúsa* (n.f.), a muse. Devoted to the muses, i.e., to the liberal arts and sciences, learned. In the NT, it means skilled in music, a musician (Rev 18:22).

3452. μυελός *muelós*; gen. *mueloú*, masc. noun. Marrow (Heb 4:12; Sept.: Gen 45:18).

3453. μυέω *muéō*; contracted *muṓ*, fut. *muḗsō*, from *múō* (n.f.), to shut the mouth. To initiate into the mysteries, introduce to things not known before, to learn a secret. Used only in Phil 4:12 where the verb is parallel to *manthánō* (3129), to learn or understand, in Phil 4:11.

3454. μῦθος múthos; gen. *múthou*, masc. noun. Commonly rendered as a tale or a fable or that which is fabricated by the mind in contrast to reality. It is the word from which "mythology" is derived. There may be much *lógos* (3056), logic and reasoning, in a myth. In the NT, however, the word "myth" does not have the meaning of being a vehicle of some lofty truth as in the early use of the word. Mostly used in the NT denoting a fable full of falsehoods and pretenses. Thus, in 1 Tim 4:7, fables are described as *bébēloi* (952), profane, and *graṓdēs* (1126), belonging to old women; in Titus 1:14 as Jewish fables; in 2 Pet 1:16 as *múthoi sesophisménoi* (perf. pass. part. of *sophízō* [4679], to make or appear wise), the result of sophistry, cunning fables for the purpose of deceiving others. In 1 Tim 1:4 and 2 Tim 4:4, the use of the word is equally contemptuous. Although *lógos* and *múthos* begin together with the thought, intelligence, or mind, they part ranks since the first ends in the kingdom of light and truth and the second in the kingdom of darkness and lies.

3455. μυκάομαι mukáomai; contracted *mukṓmai*, fut. *mukḗsomai*. To moo or low as the cow or ox. It also came to mean the sound produced by other animals. Used to indicate the roar of a lion (Rev 10:3).
    Syn.: *ōrúomai* (5612), to roar.
    Ant.: *siōpáō* (4623), to keep silent; *sigáō* (4601), to hold one's peace; *phimóō* (5392), to muzzle.

3456. μυκτηρίζω muktērízō; fut. *muktērísō*, from *muktḗr* (n.f.), the nose, nostril, which is from *mússō* (n.f.), to clear away mucus (*múxa* [n.f.]) by blowing. To turn up one's nose in scorn and hence to mock, deride (Gal 6:7, meaning God will not let Himself be mocked; see Sept.: Job 22:19; Ps 80:6).
    Deriv.: *ekmuktērízō* (1592) to scoff severely.

Syn.: *empaízō* (1702), to play like a child, jest; *chleuázō* (5512), to mock, ridicule; *katageláō* (2606), to laugh at, deride; *diachleuázō*, to mock severely (the word found in some MSS in Acts 2:13).
    Ant.: *ainéō* (134), to speak in praise of; *epainéō* (1867), to commend; *eulogéō* (2127), to speak well of, bless.

3457. μυλικός mulikós; fem. *mulikḗ*, neut. *mulikón*, adj. from *múlē* (n.f.), a mill. Belonging to a mill, a millstone (Mark 9:42).

3458. μύλος múlos; gen. *múlou*, masc. noun from *múlē* (n.f.), a mill. A mill, a grinder. The mills used by the Jews are still common in the East. They were composed of two stones of which the lower was fixed and had a hole in the middle to receive the grain while the upper was turned around upon it. The grinding was mostly done by hand by female slaves. Though exceedingly laborious, it was usually accompanied by song. Larger mills were turned by a donkey, the upper millstone being called *onikós* (3684), from *ónos* (3688), ass (Matt 18:6; Luke 17:2). A mill (Rev 18:22 [cf. Sept.: Ex 11:5; Isa 47:2]).

3459. μύλων múlōn; gen. *múlōnos*, masc. noun. A building housing a mill (Matt 24:41).

3460. Μύρα Múra; gen. *Múrōn*, neut. proper noun. Myra, meaning flowing, weeping. An ancient port of Lycia on the southwest coast of Asia Minor (Acts 27:5).

3461. μυριάς muriás; gen. *muriádos*, fem. noun from *muríos* (3463), very many, innumerable. A myriad or ten thousand (Acts 19:19; Sept.: Lev 26:8; Deut 33:17; Ezra 2:64; Neh 7:66). It also denotes an indefinite, large number (Luke 12:1; Acts 21:20; Heb 12:22; Jude 1:14; Rev 5:11; 9:16; Sept.: Gen 24:60; 1 Sam 21:11).

Syn.: *óchlos* (3793), a crowd; *pléthos* (4128), a multitude; *anaríthmētos* (382), innumerable.

Ant.: *mónos* (3441), alone, single.

3462. μυρίζω *murízō*; fut. *murísō*, from *múron* (3464), ointment. To anoint for burial, embalm. Trans. (Mark 14:8).

Syn.: *aleíphō* (218), to rub, usually with a non-religious meaning; *chríō* (5548), to anoint, used with a religious meaning; *egchríō* (1472), to rub in, besmear; *epichríō* (2025), to rub on.

3463. μυρίος *muríos*; fem. *muría*, neut. *muríon*, adj. Ten thousand. In the NT, only in the masc. pl. *muríoi* (Matt 18:24; Sept.: 1 Chr 29:7; Esth 3:9). Used to denote an indefinite, large number (1 Cor 4:15; 14:19).

Deriv.: *muriás* (3461), a myriad or ten thousand.

3464. μύρον *múron*; gen. *múrou*, neut. noun. Ointment, the base of which is *élaion* (1637), oil. It is mixed, however, with aromatic substances and thus is fit for finer uses as by women, men preferring plain oil (Matt 26:7, 9, 12; Mark 14:3, 4; Luke 7:37, 38; 23:56; John 11:2; 12:3, 5; Rev 18:13). For syn. and the distinction between the two and the explanation of Luke 7:46, see *élaion*.

Deriv.: *murízō* (3462), to anoint for burial, embalm.

3465. Μυσία *Musía*; gen. *Musías*, fem. proper noun. Mysia, meaning beach or region. A province in the northwestern angle of Asia Minor separated from Europe by the Propontis and the Hellespont, having Lydia on the south, Bithynia on the east, and including the Troad. Mysian cities were Assos, Pergamus, and Troas. Mysia was famous for its fertility and is to this day a beautiful and fertile area (Acts 16:7, 8).

3466. μυστήριον *mustérion*; gen. *mustēríou*, neut. noun from *mústēs* (n.f.), a person initiated into sacred mysteries, which is from *muéō* (3453), to initiate, learn a secret. A secret, or esoteric knowledge.

(I) Denotes in general something hidden or not fully manifest. 2 Thess 2:7 speaks of "the mystery of iniquity" which began to work in secret and was not then completely disclosed or manifested.

(II) Some sacred thing hidden or secret which is naturally unknown to human reason and is only known by the revelation of God (Rom 11:25; 1 Cor 4:1; 14:2; 15:51; Col 2:2; 1 Tim 3:16; see 1 Cor 2:7).

(III) Paul speaks of the mystery of the relationship between Christ and His Church as being great (cf. Eph 5:32). The Apostle speaks in 1 Cor 13:2 of a man understanding all mysteries, i.e., all the revealed truths of the Christian religion which is elsewhere called "the mystery of the faith" (1 Tim 3:9). In Matt 13:11, "to them it is not given" means the mysteries of the kingdom of heaven are not revealed to them since they are not related to King Jesus. *Mustérion* denotes a spiritual truth couched under an external representation or similitude and concealed or hidden thereby unless some explanation is given (Mark 4:11; Luke 8:10; Rev 1:20; 10:7; 17:5, 7, in their respective contexts).

(IV) In the writings of Paul, the word *mustérion* is sometimes applied in a peculiar sense to the calling of the Gentiles. In Eph 3:3–6, the fact that Gentiles could be fellow-heirs and of the same body and partakers of Christ by the gospel is called "the mystery" and "the mystery of Christ." In other generations, such a thing was not made known to the sons of man as it has been revealed to His Apostles and prophets by the Spirit (cf. Rom 16:25; Eph 1:9; 3:9; 6:19; Col 1:26, 27; 4:3).

3467. μυωπάζω *muōpázō*; fut. *muōpásō*, from *múōps* (n.f.), shortsighted, which is derived from *múō* (n.f.), to shut, and *ōps* (n.f.), the eyes. To shut the eyes, blink, to squint like one who cannot see clearly; hence by implication to be near-sighted. Used metaphorically in 2 Pet 1:9.

Ant.: *kathoráō* (2529), to see clearly.

3468. μώλωψ mólōps; gen. *mólōpos*, masc. noun from *mōlos* (n.f.), a battle, fighting, and *ōps* (n.f.), eye, face. A welt, a mark of fighting, a blow or wound made in war, also a scar, wheal, or the mark left on the body by the stripe of the whip. Used figuratively in 1 Pet 2:24 referring to stripes, quoted from Isa 53:5.

Syn.: *plēgḗ* (4127), wound.

3469. μωμάομαι mōmáomai; contracted *mōmômai*, fut. *mōmḗsomai*, from *mômos* (3470), blemish. To find fault with, blame (2 Cor 8:20). Used as aor. pass., *mōmēthḗ*, in 2 Cor 6:3.

Deriv.: *amômētos* (298), blameless.

Syn.: *mémphomai* (3201), to find fault; *kataginōskō* (2607), to condemn; *epitimáō* (2008), to admonish; *kolázō* (2849), to chastise; *katakrínō* (2632), to condemn.

Ant.: *ainéō* (134), to speak in praise of; *epainéō* (1867), to commend; *eulogéō* (2127), to bless, speak well of.

3470. μῶμος mômos; gen. *mômou*, masc. noun. Blame, fault, blemish, disgrace, used only in 2 Pet 2:13; see Sept.: Lev 21:17; Deut 15:21.

Deriv.: *ámōmos* (299), without spot; *momáomai* (3469), to find fault with, blame.

Syn.: *aítion* (158), fault; *aitía* (156), ground for punishment, accusation; *hḗttēma* (2275), defect; *paráptōma* (3900), a trespass; *hamártēma* (265), a sin; *parábasis* (3847), transgression.

Ant.: *ámemptos* (273), blameless, faultless; *hosiótēs* (3742), sacredness; *hagiótēs* (41), the state of holiness; *hagiōsúnē* (42), the quality of holiness.

3471. μωραίνω moraínō; fut. *mōranô*, from *mōrós* (3474), foolish. To make dull, not acute, to cause something to lose its taste or the purpose for which it exists, e.g., salt not being able to make things salty (Matt 5:13; Luke 14:34). Used of the mind meaning to make foolish or to show to be foolish (1 Cor 1:20); in the pass. (Rom 1:22, meaning they became foolish or acted like fools; see Sept.: 2 Sam 24:10; Isa 19:11).

Syn.: *paraphronéō* (3912), to be beside oneself.

Ant.: *sōphronéō* (4993), to be of a sound mind; *sōphronízō* (4994), to act with a sound mind; *sophízō* (4679), to make wise.

3472. μωρία mōría; gen. *mōrías*, fem. noun from *mōrós* (3474), foolish. Folly, foolishness, absurdity (1 Cor 1:18, 21, 23; 2:14; 3:19).

Syn.: *aphrosúnē* (877), senselessness, foolishness; *paraphronía* (3913), foolhardiness, insanity; *agnōsía* (56), ignorance.

Ant.: *phrónēsis* (5428), insight, prudence; *sōphrosúnē* (4997), soundness of mind; *sophía* (4678) wisdom; *súnesis* (4907), comprehension, ability to rightly relate concepts; *gnōsis* (1108), knowledge; *nóēma* (3540), thought; *epígnōsis* (1922), discernment.

3473. μωρολογία mōrología; gen. *mōrologías*, fem. noun from *mōrológos* (n.f.), speaking foolishly, which is from *mōrós* (3474), foolish, and *légō* (3004), to speak. Foolish talking (Eph 5:4). It is that type of speech which betrays a person as foolish. Besides this word, there are two others that show the sins of the tongue; namely *aischrología* (148), foul speech, and *eutrapelía* (2160), the ability to extricate oneself from difficult situations with witty or clever words.

Ant.: *chrēstología* (5542), pleasant speech; *eulogía* (2129), blessing, speaking well of; *makarismós* (3108), ascription of blessedness.

3474. μωρός mōrós; fem. *mōrá*, neut. *mōrón*, adj. Silly, stupid, foolish, from which the Eng. word "moron" is derived. Used of persons meaning morally

worthless (Matt 5:22). It is a more serious reproach than *raká* (4469), raca,
which scorns a man by calling him stupid, whereas *mōrós* scorns him concerning his heart and character. Used of
things (2 Tim 2:23 "foolish and ignorant
questionings" [a.t.]; Titus 3:9). In Matt
5:13 and Luke 14:34, it refers to salt
that has lost its flavor, become tasteless
(*mōraínō* [3471]).

Deriv.: *mōraínō* (3471), to make dull;
mōría (3472), foolishness as a personal quality; *mōraínō* (3471) in the causal
sense, to make foolish, in the pass. sense,
to become foolish.

Syn.: *áphrōn* (878), foolish, a fool;
anóētos (453), senseless, one lacking understanding; *asúnetos* (801), without discernment; *ásophos* (781), unwise.

Ant.: *sōphrōn* (4998), of sound mind;
sunetós (4908), sagacious, understanding; *phrónimos* (5429), thoughtful, prudent; *sophós* (4680), wise.

3475. Μωσεύς *Mōseús*, **Μωσῆς** *Mōsḗs*,
Μωϋσεύς *Mōüseús*, and **Μωϋσῆς**
Mōüsḗs; gen. *Mōüséōs*, masc. proper noun transliterated from the Hebr.
Mōsheh (4872, OT). Moses, the name
of the great Hebrew prophet and legislator. In the NT, his name occurs in Matt
8:4; 17:3, 4; 19:7, 8; 22:24; 23:2; Mark
1:44; 7:10; 9:4, 5; 10:3, 4; 12:19; Luke
2:22; 5:14; 9:30, 33; 16:29, 31; 20:28,
37; 24:27, 44; John 1:17, 45; 3:14; 5:45,
46; 6:32; 7:19, 22, 23; 8:5; 9:28, 29; Acts
3:22; 6:11; 7:20, 22, 29, 31, 32, 35, 40,
44; 13:39; 15:21; 21:21; 26:22; 28:23;
Rom 5:14; 9:15; 10:5, 19; 1 Cor 9:9;
10:2; 2 Cor 3:7, 13, 15; Heb 3:2, 3, 5, 16;
7:14; 8:5; 10:28; 11:23, 24; 12:21; Jude
1:9; Rev 15:3. In the form *Mōüseús* it occurs in Acts 15:1, 5; 2 Tim 3:8; Heb 9:19.
In the form of *Mōüsḗs* it occurs in Acts
6:14; 7:35, 37. The name means something drawn out, particularly from the water. Of all the prophets of the OT, Moses
occupies a unique place. He was a political leader, a mediator, a worker of miracles (Ex 4:16; 7:1; 32:31–34; 33:11; Num
12:1–8; Deut 5:24–28). God communicated His commandments to him. These
commandments remain valid (Matt 23:1,
2; Acts 7:38); however, the Lord Jesus
emphasizes the new significance (Matt
5:1–48; Mark 10:1–12).

There is a prophetic significance to
Moses in connection with the person of
Jesus Christ. He announced the coming
of Christ (Luke 24:27, 44; John 1:45;
5:46; Acts 3:22), the resurrection of the
dead (Luke 20:37), the preaching of the
gospel to the Gentiles (Rom 10:19), and
the sovereignty of God's grace (Rom
9:15). In the person of Moses we see a
prototype of Christ. As Moses was the
mediator between God and Israel, so is
Christ between God and all men (John
6:32; Heb 3:1–6).

N

3476. Ναασσών Naassốn; masc. proper noun transliterated from the Hebr. *Nachshōn* (5177, OT), diviner. Naasson, Nahshon (Matt 1:4; Luke 3:32). He was a chief of Judah whose sister was the wife of Aaron (Ex 6:23; Num 2:3).

3477. Ναγγαί Naggaí; masc. proper noun. Nagge, meaning shining. An ancestor of the Lord Jesus (Luke 3:25).

3478. Ναζαρέτ Nazarét, Ναζαρέθ Nazaréth; masc. proper noun, transliterated from the Hebr. Nazareth, a city of Galilee famous as the home of the Lord Jesus during His childhood and even until He began His public ministry. It was about fourteen miles from the Sea of Galilee, six miles west of Mount Tabor and sixty-six miles due north of Jerusalem. Nazareth is mentioned twenty-nine times in the NT, but it is not mentioned in the OT nor by any Class. Gr. author or writer before the time of Christ. For some unknown reason, it was held in disrepute among the Jews of Judea (John 1:46). It was situated on a mountain (Luke 4:29) within the province of Galilee (Mark 1:9) and near Cana (John 2:1, 2, 11). There was a precipice near the town from which the people proposed to cast Jesus (Luke 4:29). The angel appeared to Mary at Nazareth, which was also the home of Joseph (Luke 1:26; 2:39). Joseph and Mary returned to Nazareth after their flight into Egypt (Matt 2:23). Jesus preached in its synagogue, but was rejected by the people. He was known as "Jesus of Nazareth" (see Acts 2:22; 3:6; 4:10; 6:14) and His disciples were called Nazarenes. When the Turks conquered Palestine in A.D. 1517, the Christians were driven from the town. In A.D. 1620 the Franciscan monks gained a foothold there and began to rebuild the village. At the Battle of Mount Tabor in A.D. 1799, Napoleon and his army encamped near Nazareth.

3479. Ναζαρηνός Nazarēnós; gen. *Nazarēnoú*, masc. proper noun. An inhabitant of Nazareth, a Nazarene, used of the Lord Jesus (Mark 1:24; 14:67; 16:6; Luke 4:34).

3480. Ναζωραῖος Nazōraíos; gen. *Nazōraíou*, masc. proper noun. A Nazarene, an inhabitant of Nazareth. Spoken of Jesus (Matt 26:71; Mark 10:47; Luke 18:37; 24:19; John 18:5, 7; Acts 3:6; 4:10; 6:14); in the inscription on the cross (John 19:19); by Peter (Acts 2:22); by Paul (Acts 26:9); by our Lord Himself (Acts 22:8). In Matt 2:23, we find the expression "He shall be called a Nazarene," i.e., according to the meaning of the Hebr. word *netser* (5342, OT), "he shall be called a shoot" or branch. This is in allusion to such passages as Isa 11:1; 53:2; Zech 3:8; 6:12, but here also it implies reproach from the contempt in which Nazareth was held. Used once of Christians held in contempt as the followers of Jesus of Nazareth (Acts 24:5).

3481. Νάθαν Náthan; masc. proper noun transliterated from the Hebr. *Nāthān* (5416, OT), given by God. Nathan.

(I) A distinguished prophet of Judea who lived during the reigns of David and Solomon and enjoyed a large share of their confidence (2 Sam 7:2). David first intimated his desire to build the temple to Nathan, but the prophet was divinely instructed to inform the king that this honor was not for him but for his posterity. Nathan was also charged with the divine message to David upon the occasion of his sin against Uriah. He conveyed this message under the significant allegory of the rich man and the young lamb. Nathan was one of David's biographers (1 Chr 29:29) and also Solomon's (2 Chr 9:29).

(II) In Luke 3:31, given as the proper name of one of the sons of David by Bathsheba (cf. 2 Sam 5:14).

(III) Father of one of David's warriors (2 Sam 23:36).

(IV) Names of two of the chief men who returned to Jerusalem with Ezra (Ezra 8:16; 10:39).

(V) A descendant of Caleb (1 Chr 2:36).

3482. Ναθαναήλ *Nathanaél*; masc. proper noun transliterated from the Hebr. *N^ethan'ēl* (5417, OT), gift of God. Nathanael, a native of Cana of Galilee (John 21:2) and an Israelite without guile, as stated by our Lord in John 1:47. He was led into the presence of Christ by Philip immediately after his call. Nathanael confessed Jesus to be the Son of God and the King of Israel. Because the name Nathanael occurs only in John 1:45–49 and 21:2, combined with the fact that John never mentions the name of Bartholomew, it is generally supposed that the two are identical.

3483. ναί *naí*; adv. of affirmation. Yea, yes, certainly.

(I) In answer to a question (Matt 9:28; 13:51; 17:25; John 11:27; 21:15, 16; Acts 5:8; 22:27; Rom 3:29).

(II) As expressing assent to the words or deeds of another (Matt 11:26; Luke 10:21; Rev 16:7). Followed by *kaí* (2532), and, introducing a subsequent limitation or modification (Matt 15:27; Mark 7:28).

(III) Used as an intens. in strong affirmation (Luke 11:51; 12:5; Phile 1:20; Rev 1:7; 14:13). Also followed by *kaí* (2532), and, meaning yes and more also (Matt 11:9; Luke 7:26). With the art. *to*, the, meaning the word yea, yes (2 Cor 1:17, meaning when I say the word "yes" and when I say the word "no," also 2 Cor 1:20; James 5:12); with the art. implied (Matt 5:37; 2 Cor 1:18, 19).

Syn.: *alēthós* (230), truly; *pántōs* (3843), at all events, altogether; *óntōs* (3689), indeed.

Ant.: *ou* (3756), no; *mḗ* (3361), no; *ou mḗ* (3364), by no means, in no wise.

3484. Ναΐν *Naḯn*; fem. proper noun transliterated from the Hebr. Nain, meaning beauty. A town in Galilee where Christ raised the widow's dead son to life (Luke 7:11). Located six miles southeast of Nazareth and twenty-five miles southwest of Capernaum, it is in full view of Mount Tabor.

3485. ναός *naós*; gen. *naoú*, masc. noun from *naíō* (n.f.), to dwell. A dwelling, temple. In Class. Gr., mostly equivalent to the syn. word *hierón* (2411), the entire area of a temple which included the inner temple (though sometimes *naós* referred only to the interior and most sacred part of a temple where the image of a god was set up).

(I) Generally, of any temple (Acts 7:48; 17:24; 19:24 referring to the miniature copies of the temple of Diana at Ephesus containing a small image of the goddess. Such shrines of other gods were also common, made of gold, silver, or wood, and were purchased by pilgrims and travelers, probably as souvenirs or to be used in their devotions).

(II) Of the temple in Jerusalem or in allusion to it, but in distinction from *hierón*, the entire area (Matt 23:16, 17, 35).

(A) The building itself (John 2:19, 20).

(B) The inner sanctuary. This is to be distinguished from *thusiastḗrion* (2379), altar, referring to the altar of burnt offerings. This stood in the court of the priests before the entrance of the *naós* (Matt 27:5) where Judas threw the silver coins since he could not enter (Matt 26:61; 27:40; Mark 14:58; 15:29; Luke 1:9, 21, 22; 2 Thess 2:4). In the expression "the veil of the temple" (a.t. [Matt 27:51; Mark 15:38; Luke 23:45; Sept.: 1 Kgs 6:5, 17; Ps 5:7; 11:5]).

(III) Symbolically, of the temple of God in heaven to which that of Jerusalem was to correspond (cf. Rev 3:12; 7:15; 11:1, 2, 19; 14:15, 17; 15:5, 6, 8; 16:1, 17; 21:22).

(IV) Metaphorically, of persons in whom God or His Spirit is said to dwell or act, e.g., the body of Jesus (John 2:19, 21); of Christians (1 Cor 3:16, 17; 6:19; 2 Cor 6:16; Eph 2:21).

Deriv.: *neōkóros* (3511), a temple servant, worshiper.

Syn.: *tó hágion* (39) a sacred thing, holy place, sanctuary, spoken of the temple, in the pl., *tá hágia hagíōn*, the Holy of Holies, the inner sanctuary.

3486. Ναούμ *Naoúm*; masc. proper noun, transliterated from the Hebr. *Nachūm* (5151, OT), comfort. Naum, Nahum, an ancestor of the Lord Jesus, not the prophet (Luke 3:25).

3487. νάρδος *nárdos*; gen. *nárdou*, fem. noun. Nard, spikenard, a plant that grows in India, the root of which is very small and slender and which puts forth a long thin stalk with several ears or spikes at ground level, thus giving it the name of spikenard. A highly prized, very aromatic oil or ointment was extracted from it. In the NT, we have the ointment of pure spikenard, indicating that it is most precious (Mark 14:3; John 12:3; Sept.: Song 1:12; 4:13, 14).

3488. Νάρκισσος *Nárkissos*; gen. *Narkíssou*, masc. proper noun. Narcissus, meaning the daffodil flower. Also the name of a Christian at Rome to whom Paul sends greetings (Rom 16:11). He is supposed to have been the freedman and favorite of the emperor Claudius.

3489. ναυαγέω *nauagéō*; contracted *nauagṓ*, fut. *nauagḗsō*, from *nauagós* (n.f.), one shipwrecked, which is from *naús* (3491), a ship, and *ágnumi* (n.f.), to break. To make shipwreck or to be shipwrecked (2 Cor 11:25). Metaphorical-

ly in 1 Tim 1:19 in regard to the faith of some professing Christ.

Ant.: *diasṓzō* (1295), to rescue.

3490. ναύκληρος *naúklēros*; gen. *nauklḗrou*, masc. noun. from *naús* (3491), a ship, and *klḗros* (2819), lot. An owner of a ship or one who took passengers and freight for hire (Acts 27:11).

Syn.: *kubernḗtēs* (2942), captain of a ship; *kúrios* (2962), master.

3491. ναύς *naús*; gen. *nēós*, acc. *naún*, fem. noun from *náō* or *nauṓ* (n.f.), to move, agitate. A ship, vessel (Acts 27:41; Sept.: 1 Kgs 9:26; Job 9:26).

Deriv.: *naúklēros* (3490), owner of a ship; *naútēs* (3492), sailor.

Syn.: *ploiárion* (4142), a small ship; *ploíon* (4143), a boat.

3492. ναύτης *naútēs*; gen. *naútou*, masc. noun from *naús* (3491), a ship. A sailor, seaman (Acts 27:27, 30; Rev 18:17).

3493. Ναχώρ *Nachṓr*; masc. proper noun transliterated from the Hebr. *Nāchōr* (5152, OT), snorting. Nahor, the name of the grandfather of Abraham (Luke 3:34 [cf. Gen 11:22ff.]).

3494. νεανίας *neanías*; gen. *neaníou*, masc. noun from *néos* (3501), new, young. A youth, a young man (Acts 20:9; 23:17, 18, 22). Spoken of Saul or Paul (Acts 7:58), although it does not give us any definite information concerning his age. However *neanías*, like *neanískos* (3495), young man, was applied to men in the prime of manhood up to the age of forty years. Spoken also of soldiers (Sept.: 2 Sam 6:1; 1 Chr 19:10).

Ant.: *presbútēs* (4246), an old man; *presbúteros* (4245), elder; *patḗr* (3962), father.

3495. νεανίσκος *neanískos*; gen. *neanískou*, masc. noun from *néos* (3501), new, young. A youth, a young man (Mark 14:51; 16:5; Luke 7:14; Acts 2:17; 1 John 2:13, 14). Spoken of young men in the prime and vigor of manhood up to the age of forty years or more (Matt 19:20, 22 [cf. Luke 18:18 where the word used is *árchōn* {758}, ruler]). Referring to the younger members of the community (Acts 5:10), equivalent to *neóteroi*, the comparative of *néos* (3501) in Acts 5:6. See Sept.: Gen 41:12; Josh 2:1, 23; 6:23.

Syn.: *neanías* (3494), a youth.

Ant.: *presbútēs* (4246), an old man; *presbúteros* (4245), elder; *patḗr* (3962), father.

3496. Νεάπολις *Neápolis*; gen. *Neapóleōs*, fem. proper noun from *néa* (n.f.), new, and *pólis* (4172), city. Neapolis, meaning new city. A place in northern Greece where Paul first landed in Europe and where he probably landed on his second visit (Acts 16:11; 20:1). From there, he embarked on his last journey to Jerusalem (Acts 20:6). Neapolis was located on a rocky projection into the sea. Its most conspicuous object was a temple of Diana which crowned the top of the hill. Neapolis was eight to ten miles from Philippi, and the great Roman road, Via Egnatia, from Macedonia to Thrace, passed through the city. Today it is the Greek town called Kaballa.

3497. Νεεμάν *Neemán*; masc. proper noun, transliterated from the Hebr. *Na'amān* (5283, OT), pleasantness. Naaman, the name of a Syrian warrior and captain (2 Kgs 5) who was afflicted with leprosy. Hearing through a captive Jewish girl who waited on his wife of the fame of the prophet Elisha, he set out on a journey to Israel with letters of recommendation from his sovereign to the king of Israel. When the king of Israel read the letter requesting that he heal Naaman, he was filled with apprehension, fearing that perhaps the king of Syria intended to find a pretext for a quarrel in his incapability to cure Naaman's leprosy. Elisha, on receiving the news of Naaman's arrival and the king's predicament, dispatched word to the king to forget his fears and send the distinguished stranger

to him. Naaman went and received from Elisha's messenger the prescription to bathe seven times in the Jordan. The leper disdained the remedy at first. It was too simple, and he would not attribute to the Jordan a virtue which he knew the Abana and the Pharpar rivers of his own land did not possess. Nevertheless, under the advice of his counselors, he washed himself seven times in the Jordan and his "flesh came again like unto the flesh of a little child" (2 Kgs 5:14). The Lord Jesus refers to Naaman's cure in His sermon to the Nazarenes (Luke 4:27).

3498. νεκρός *nekrós*; fem. *nekrá*, neut. *nekrón*, adj. from *nékus* (n.f.), a corpse. Dead.

(I) Subst.: a dead person, dead body, corpse (Matt 23:27; Rev 20:13; Sept.: Deut 28:26; Jer 7:33).

(A) As yet unburied (Matt 8:22; Luke 7:15; Heb 9:17); one slain (Rev 16:3; Sept.: Gen 23:4).

(B) As buried, laid in a sepulcher, and therefore the spirit being in Hades (Luke 16:30; John 5:25; Acts 10:42; Rom 14:9; Heb 11:35; Rev 1:18). The dead in Christ (1 Thess 4:16) means those in the Christian faith who have died.

(C) In reference to being raised again from the dead, the resurrection (Rom 6:13, "alive from out of the dead" [a.t.]; figuratively 11:15); "quickened" or gave life to the dead (Rom 4:17); to raise the dead (Matt 10:8; John 5:21; Acts 26:8; 2 Cor 1:9); to raise someone from the dead (Matt 14:2; 27:64; Acts 3:15; Gal 1:1; 1 Thess 1:10); to rise from the dead (Matt 17:9; Luke 16:31; John 20:9). Metaphorically to rise from the dead (Eph 5:14). Concerning the resurrection of the dead (Matt 22:31; Acts 17:32; Rom 1:4; 1 Cor 15:13, 21, 42). The resurrection from among the dead (Acts 4:2). The resurrection from out of the dead (*exanástasis* [1815]) in Phil 3:11 refers to a selective resurrection.

(D) Emphatically, with a def. art. pl., *hoi nekroí*, the dead, meaning those completely dead. Christ affirmed that death is not extinction when He affirmed that God is the God of the patriarchs who were dead and yet alive (Matt 22:32). He implied that even those who are dead are still alive in their spirits (see Mark 12:27; Luke 20:38).

(E) Figuratively in the pl., those dead to Christ and His gospel, meaning spiritually dead (Matt 8:22, "Let the spiritually dead bury their dead" [a.t.], meaning let no lesser duty keep you from the one great duty of following Me; Luke 9:60; Rom 6:13; 11:15; Eph 5:14).

(II) As an adj:

(A) Particularly (Matt 28:4, "they became as if dead" [a.t.]; Acts 20:9, "was taken up dead" [a.t.], meaning considered dead; 28:6; Rev 1:17; Sept.: 2 Sam 19:6; Isa 8:19). Figuratively for lost, perished, given up as dead, e.g., the prodigal son (Luke 15:24, 32). Equal to *apolōlós* from *apóllumi* (622), to perish, lose.

(B) Metaphorically, in opposition to the life of the gospel, e.g.: (1) Of persons, dead to Christ and His gospel and thus exposed to punishment, spiritually dead (Rev 3:1); with the dat. of cause or manner (Eph 2:1, 5; Col 2:13). Followed by *diá* (1223), for (Rom 8:10, i.e., as to the body you still remain subjected to sinful passions); followed by dat. (Rom 6:11, "to be dead indeed unto sin" [a.t.], i.e., no longer willingly subject to it). (2) Of things, dead, i.e., inactive, inoperative (Rom 7:8; James 2:17, 20, 26). The phrase dead works (Heb 6:1; 9:14) refers to either acts (especially religious) not borne from faith and spiritual life, hence fruitless and sinful, or it refers to the external ceremonies and rituals of the OT which, standing in contrast to their NT realities and antitypes, are impotent and transitory.

Deriv.: *nekróō* (3499), to put to death.

3499. νεκρόω *nekróō*; contracted *nekrṓ*, fut. *nekrṓsō*, aor. *enékrōsa*, from *nekrós* (3498), dead. To put to death; pass., to be put to death, to die. Used metaphorically meaning to deaden, to deprive of force

and vigor, e.g., the members, in which case the meaning is to mortify (Col 3:5). In the perf. pass. part., *nenekrōménos*, deadened, means dead, powerless, impotent, referring to the body (Rom 4:19; Heb 11:12).

Deriv.: *nékrōsis* (3500), the act of putting to death or making spiritually impotent.

Syn.: *thanatóō* (2289), to put to death; *apokteínō* (615), to kill; *phoneúō* (5407), to murder.

Ant.: *zōogonéō* (2225), to rescue from death; *zōopoiéō* (2227), to make alive.

3500. νέκρωσις *nékrōsis*; gen. *nekrṓseōs*, fem. noun from *nekrós* (3498), dead, and *nekróō* (3499), to mortify. The act of killing, putting to death (2 Cor 4:10, "always carrying about in the body the putting to death of the Lord Jesus" (a.t.), i.e., being exposed to cruelties resembling those which He sustained in His last sufferings. It also means deadness (Rom 4:19).

Ant.: *anástasis* (386), resurrection; *égersis* (1454), a rising up from death; *exanástasis* (1815), the resurrection from among the dead; *zōḗ* (2222), life as a principle.

3501. νέος *néos*; fem. *néa*, neut. *néon*, adj. New, recent. New in relation to time, that which has recently come into existence or become present. New in the aspect of quality is *kainós* (2537) which also means novel or strange. The *kainón* is the *héteron* (2087), another of a different kind, the qualitatively new. The *néon* is the *állon* (243), another of the same kind, the numerically distinct. *Néos* may be derived from *néō* (n.f.), to move or agitate, hence one who moves briskly, a young man, so-named either because of the activity and vigor exhibited in youth, or of the unsettled attitude of that age of life (Luke 15:12, 13; 22:26; John 21:18; Acts 5:6; 1 Tim 5:1, 2, 11, 14; Titus 2:6; 1 Pet 5:5; Sept.: Gen 9:24; 27:15; 42:13); young women (Titus 2:4); new referring to recently made fermenting wine (Matt 9:17; Mark 2:22; Luke 5:37–39); new man (Col 3:10). In this last reference, both *néos* and a comp. verb with the stem *kainóō* (n.f.), to make new, *anakainoúmenos* (part. of *anakainóō* [341]), to renew, make new again, restore, are used. Paul refers to the new nature the believer puts on, but this new nature becomes qualitatively new by the activity of God Himself through His renewing power (*anakainoúmenon*). Man on his own can only reform (become *néos*), but by God's activity, he becomes *kainós*, qualitatively new. This is the impartation by God of His divine nature to man spoken of in 2 Cor 5:17 and 2 Pet 1:4.

Deriv.: *neanías* (3494), a youth; *neanískos* (3495), a youth under forty; *neossós* (3502), a young bird; *neótēs* (3503), newness; *neóphutos* (3504), newly planted; *neōterikós* (3512), youthful; *noumēnía* (3561), new moon.

Syn.: *prósphatos* (4372), recent, new in the sense of time; *kainós* (2537), new.

Ant.: *archaíos* (744), ancient, old; *palaiós* (3820), old.

3502. νεοσσός neossós; gen. *neossoú*, masc. noun from *néos* (3501), young. A young animal, or often specifically a young bird (Luke 2:24).

Deriv.: *nossiá* (3555), a nest of young birds; *nossíon* (3556), a young bird.

3503. νεότης neótēs; gen. *neótetos*, fem. noun from *néos* (3501), young. Youth, age or time of youth (Matt 19:20 [TR]; Mark 10:20; Luke 18:21; Acts 26:4; 1 Tim 4:12, "Let no man despise [*kataphronéō* {2706}] thy youth," meant that Timothy was not to tolerate any disparagement of himself due to his more youthful age; Sept.: Gen 8:21; Num 30:17; Eccl 11:9, 10).

Syn.: *kainótēs* (2538), newness but qualitatively different.

Ant.: *palaiótēs* (3821), oldness; *géras* (1094), old age; *presbeía* (4242), seniority.

3504. νεόφυτος neóphutos; gen. *neophútou*, masc.-fem., neut. *neóphuton*, adj. from *néos* (3501), new, and *phúō* (5453), to germinate. Newly sprung up or, figuratively, one who is but lately converted to Christianity and newly implanted in the Church, newly instructed or a novice (1 Tim 3:6; Sept.: Job 14:9; Ps 144:12).

Syn.: *ápeiros* (552), inexperienced.

Ant.: *epistḗmōn* (1990), one possessing knowledge.

3505. Νέρων Nérōn; gen. *Nérōnos*, masc. proper noun. Nero, the Roman emperor to whom Paul appealed against the vacillations of the deputy Festus (Acts 25:10, 11). In A.D. 64, Nero set fire to the city of Rome and then accused Christians of having perpetrated the crime. This he used as an excuse to conduct mass arrests and then torture and burn his victims alive in public. Rom 13 was written by Paul in the context of Nero's reign. The Book of 1 Peter also reflects such persecution against Christians.

3506. νεύω neúō; fut. *neúsō*. To nod or beckon as signaling to someone, followed by the dat. (John 13:24; Acts 24:10; Sept.: Prov 4:25).

Deriv.: *dianeúō* (1269), to make oneself understood through signs; *ekneúō* (1593), to shake off; *enneúō* (1770), to nod or beckon; *epineúō* (1961), to consent; *kataneúō* (2656), to beckon towards; *nustázō* (3573), to fall asleep.

Syn.: *kataseíō* (2678), to beckon, make a signal.

Ant.: *agnoéō* (50), ignore; *epilanthánomai* (1950), to neglect, forget.

3507. νεφέλη nephélē; gen. *nephélēs*, fem. noun, a diminutive of *néphos* (3509), a cloud. A small cloud (Luke 12:54 [cf. 1 Kgs 18:44]); used generally (2 Pet 2:17; Jude 1:12; Sept.: Gen 9:13, 14; Judg 5:4; Ps 36:6; Eccl 11:4); the pillar of cloud in the desert which accompanied supernatural appearances and events (1 Cor 10:1, 2 [cf. Sept.: Ex 13:21, 22]);

in connection with Christ (Luke 9:35, "a voice out of the cloud"); at His transfiguration, a luminous cloud (Matt 17:5; Mark 9:7; Luke 9:34); as receiving Christ up at His ascension (Acts 1:9); as surrounding Him at His Second Coming (Matt 24:30; 26:64; Mark 13:26; 14:62; Luke 21:27; Rev 1:7; 14:14–16); as surrounding ascending or descending saints or angels (1 Thess 4:17; Rev 10:1; 11:12 [cf. in regard to God in Sept.: Ps 18:12; 97:2; Isa 19:1]).

Ant.: *eudía* (2105), fair weather (Matt 16:2).

3508. Νεφθαλείμ *Nephthaleím*; masc. proper noun, transliterated from the Hebr. *Naphtālī* (5321, OT), my wrestling. Naphtali or Nephthalim, the name of the sixth son of Jacob, born of Bilhah (see Gen 30:8). In the NT, used only for the tribe of Naphtali (Matt 4:13, 15; Rev 7:6).

3509. νέφος *néphos*; gen. *néphous*, neut. noun. A cloudy, shapeless mass covering the sky. Used metaphorically for a crowd, throng (Heb 12:1).

Deriv.: *gnóphos* (1105), dark cloud, blackness; *nephélē* (3507), a small cloud.

3510. νεφρός *nephrós*; gen. *nephroú*, masc. noun. Kidney, usually used in the pl., *hoi nephroí*, the kidneys, loins (Sept. Ex 29:13, 22; Job 16:13). Used metaphorically for the innermost mind, the seat of the desires and passions, such as we refer to the heart today (Rev 2:23 [cf. Sept.: Ps 7:10; Jer 11:20; 17:10; 20:12]).

3511. νεωκόρος *neōkóros*; gen. *neōkórou*, masc. noun from *neós*, the Attic of *naós* (3485), temple or shrine, and *koréō* (n.f.), to sweep clean. A temple sweeper, hence temple-keeper, an official of a temple who also had charge of the decorations. It also came to mean a worshiper who frequents the temple of God, and particularly the Israelites in the desert. Used as an honorary title assumed by

cities distinguished for the worship of a particular deity as Ephesus being a worshiper or devotee of Diana (Acts 19:35). It occurs in inscriptions and on the coins of several cities.

Syn.: *proskunētḗs* (4353), he who makes obeisance; *theosebḗs* (2318), one who reverences God.

Ant.: *asebḗs* (765), ungodly, not respectful, not worshipful.

3512. νεωτερικός *neōterikós*; fem. *neōterikḗ*, neut. *neōterikón*, adj. from *néos* (3501), young. Youthful, pertaining to youth (2 Tim 2:22).

Ant.: *graṓdēs* (1126), old-womanish.

3513. νή *nḗ*; particle. Used in swearing or affirming an oath, always affirmative and taking the acc. of that by which one swears (1 Cor 15:31, meaning "by all my ground of glorying in you, I protest" [a.t.]; Sept.: Gen 42:15, 16).

Syn.: *mḗn* (3375), indeed.

Ant.: *ou* (5756), no, not; *oudé* (3761), never, not at all; *oudépō* (3764), never yet.

3514. νήθω *nḗthō*; fut. *nḗsō*. To spin (Matt 6:28; Luke 12:27; Sept.: Ex 35:25 [cf. 26:31]).

3515. νηπιάζω *nēpiázō*; fut. *nēpiásō*, from *nḗpios* (3516), babe, child. To be as a child, child-like (1 Cor 14:20, where it means to be ignorant of evil [cf. Matt 18:3]).

3516. νήπιος *nḗpios*; fem. *nēpía*, neut. *nḗpion*, adj. from *nḗ-*, not, and *épos* (2031), word. One who cannot speak, hence, an infant, child, baby without any definite limitation of age. *Nḗpios* is used for either masc. or fem.

(I) Particularly (Matt 21:16, "out of the mouth of babes and sucklings" [a.t.], quoted from Ps 8:3; see 1 Cor 13:11). By implication, a minor, one not yet of age (Gal 4:1). Generally in the Sept., used of a child playing in the streets (Jer 6:11; 9:21); asking for bread (Lam 4:4); borne in the arms (Lam 2:20); a fetus (Job 3:16).

(II) Metaphorically a babe, one unlearned, unenlightened, simple, innocent (Matt 11:25; Luke 10:21; Rom 2:20). Implying censure (1 Cor 3:1; Gal 4:3; Eph 4:14; Heb 5:13; Sept.: Ps 19:8; 119:130; Prov 1:32).

Deriv.: *nēpiázō* (3515), to be as a child.

Syn.: *bréphos* (1025), an unborn or a newborn child, infant; *téknon* (5043), child; *tekníon* (5040), little child.

Ant.: *anḗr* (435), a mature man; *gérōn* (1088), an old man; *presbútēs* (4246), an elder.

3517. Νηρεύς *Nēreús*; gen. *Nēréōs*, masc. proper noun. Nereus, a Christian at Rome (Rom 16:15).

3518. Νηρί *Nērí*; masc. proper noun, transliterated from the Hebr. Neri, meaning lamp of Jehovah. One of the ancestors of the Lord Jesus (Luke 3:27).

3519. νησίον *nēsíon*; gen. *nēsíou*, neut. noun, a diminutive of *nḗsos* (3520), island. A small island, islet (Acts 27:16).

3520. νῆσος *nḗsos*; gen. *nḗsou*, fem. noun. An island (Acts 13:6; 27:26; 28:1, 7, 9, 11; Rev 1:9; 6:14; 16:20; Sept.: Ps 72:10; Ezek 26:15, 18).

Deriv.: *nēsíon* (3519), a small island.

3521. νηστεία *nēsteía*; gen. *nēsteías*, fem. noun from *nēsteúō* (3522), to fast. A fasting, fast, abstinence from eating, generally for want of food (2 Cor 6:5; 11:27). In a religious sense of the private fastings of the Jews (Matt 17:21; Mark 9:29 [TR]; Luke 2:37) to which great merit was attributed, the Pharisees practiced often, sometimes twice a week (cf. Luke 18:12; Sept.: Isa 58:3ff.; Dan 9:3). In their longer fastings they abstained only from better kinds of food. The Jews used to call such a fast "The great annual public fast of the great Day of Atonement" which occurred in the month Tisri,

corresponding to the new moon of October. It thus served to indicate the season of the year after which the navigation of the Mediterranean became dangerous (Acts 27:9 [cf. Lev 16:29ff.; 23:27ff.]).

Syn.: *asitía* (776), without food.

Ant.: *diatrophḗ* (1305), sustenance, food; *brōsis* (1035), eating, the act of eating; *trophḗ* (5160), food; *brōma* (1033), foodstuff.

3522. νηστεύω *nēsteúō*; fut. *nēsteúsō*, from *nēstis* (3523), fasting. To fast or abstain from eating. In the NT, only of private fasting (Matt 6:16–18; 9:14; Mark 2:18, 19; Luke 5:33; 18:12; Acts 10:30; 13:2, 3; Sept.: Judg 20:26; 1 Sam 7:6). With the notion of grief or mourning with which fasting was often connected (Matt 9:15; Mark 2:20; Luke 5:34, 35 [cf. 2 Sam 12:16]). Of the Savior's supernatural fast of 40 days (Matt 4:2).

On two occasions our Lord spoke of fasting as a voluntary exercise. In Mark 6:16–18 the disciples are warned against making it an occasion for a parade of piety. And in Matt 9:14–17; Mark 2:18–22; Luke 5:33–39, in replying to the question of the disciples of John and of the Pharisees, the Lord deliberately refused to enjoin fasting on His followers. The allusions to fasting in connection with prayer in Matt 17:21 and Mark 9:29 are considered by some to be corruptions of the text. Taken as genuine, they mean that fasting gives concentration to prayer. See 1 Sam 31:13; Dan 10:2, 3.

Deriv.: *nēsteía* (3521), fasting.

Ant.: *esthíō* (2068) and *bibrōskō* (977), to eat; *phágō* (5315), to eat, devour, consume; *trōgō* (5176), to chew, gnaw, eat; *korénnumi* (2880), to satiate, satisfy with food.

3523. νῆστις *nēstis*; gen. *nēstios*, masc.-fem., neut. *nēston*, adj. from *nē-*, not, and *esthíō* (2068), to eat. Not having eaten, fasting, as an adj.; pl. *nēsteis* (Matt 15:32; Mark 8:3).

Deriv.: *nēsteúō* (3522), to abstain from food, fast.

Syn.: *ásitos* (777), without food.

Ant.: *gastér* (1064), glutton, literally belly; *phágos* (5314), a glutton.

3524. νηφάλιος *nēphálios*, **νηφάλεος** *nēpháleos*; fem. *nēphalía*, neut. *nēphálion*, adj. from *nēphō* (3525), to be sober. Sober, temperate, self-controlled, especially in respect to wine. Used metaphorically, meaning sober-minded, watchful, circumspect (1 Tim 3:2, 11; Titus 2:2 [cf. 1 Thess 5:6]). In some MSS of the TR, in 1 Tim 3:2, 11 we find the later syn. form *nēpháleos*. It is that state of mind which is free from the excessive influence of passion, lust or emotion.

Syn.: *sōphrōn* (4998), of sound mind, sober-minded, one who voluntarily places limitations on his own freedom; *egkratēs* (1468), self-controlled, temperate.

Ant.: *pároinos* (3943), wine-bibber, drunkard; *oinopótēs* (3630), wine-drinker; *méthusos* (3183), a drunkard.

3525. νήφω *nēphō*; fut. *nēpsō*. To be sober-minded, watchful, circumspect (1 Thess 5:6, 8; 2 Tim 4:5; 1 Pet 1:13; 4:7; 5:8). The word does not mean to abstain from the use of alcohol but rather to refrain from the abuse of it which leads to intoxication.

Deriv.: *ananēphō* (366), to become sober; *eknēphō* (1594), to return to one's sense from drunkenness, become sober; *nēphálios* (3524), sober.

Syn.: *egkrateúomai* (1467), to exercise self-restraint; *sōphronéō* (4993), to act and think soberly; *sōphronízō* (4994), to cause someone to be of a sound mind or sober.

Ant.: *methúō* (3184), to be drunk with wine; *methúskō* (3182), to make drunk.

3526. Νίγερ *Níger*; masc. proper noun. Niger, meaning black. A surname of Simeon, a teacher at Antioch (Acts 13:1).

3527. Νικάνωρ *Nikánōr*; gen. *Nikánoros*, masc. proper noun. Nicanor, meaning conqueror. One of the first sev-

en servants appointed by the early church to wait on tables (Acts 6:5).

3528. νικάω *nikáō*; contracted *nikō*, fut. *nikēsō*, from *níkē* (3529), victory. To be victorious, prevail (Rom 3:4 quoted from Sept.: Ps 51:4 where the Hebr. word means to be pure; Rev 5:5). Used trans., meaning to overcome, conquer, subdue (Luke 11:22; Rom 12:21). Spoken of Jesus or His followers as victorious over the world, evil, and all the adversaries of His kingdom with the acc. expressed or implied (1 John 5:4, 5; Rev 3:21; 12:11; 17:14). In the perf., for pres. or fut. (John 16:33; 1 John 2:13, 14; 4:4). As a part., without any qualification, he that overcometh (Rev 2:7, 11, 17; 3:5; 21:7). Used in an absolute sense in the nom. (Rev 2:26; 3:12, 21; 15:2). Of the adversaries of Christ's kingdom as temporarily victorious (Rev 11:7; 13:7).

Deriv.: *hupernikáō* (5245), to be more than conquerors.

Syn.: *thriambeúō* (2358), to triumph; *kurieúō* (2961), to have dominion over; *katakurieúō* (2634), to completely overcome; *hēttáō* (2274), to overcome or to cause somebody to be defeated; *ischúō* (2480), to be powerful; *katischúō* (2729), to be strong against; *kratéō* (2902), to control.

Ant.: *hēttáomai* (2274), to be defeated.

3529. νίκη *níkē*; gen. *níkēs*, fem. noun. Victory.

Deriv.: *nikáō* (3528), to overcome; *níkos* (3534), a later form of *níkē*, victory.

Syn.: *exousía* (1849), authority.

Ant.: *hēttēma* (2275), defeat, spiritual loss.

3530. Νικόδημος *Nikódēmos*; gen. *Nikodēmou*, masc. proper noun. Nicodemus, meaning victor among the people, one who has won distinction among the people. A ruler of the Jews and a distinguished member of the sect of the Pharisees. His conversation with the Lord

Jesus (John 3:1, 4, 9) reveals one of the great doctrines of Christianity, the birth from above or regeneration by the Spirit of God. Later he defended Christ against the bitter injustice of the Pharisees (John 7:50), and finally he appeared as a professed follower, helping in the burial of the crucified Lord (John 19:39).

3531. Νικολαΐτης *Nikolaïtēs*, gen. *Nikolaïtou*, masc. proper noun. An adherent of Nikolaos, or a Nicolaitan. An ancient sect whose deeds were expressly and strongly reprobate (Rev 2:6, 15). Some have supposed that they were the followers of Nicolas (Acts 6:5), one of the first deacons of the church, whom they regard as having apostatized from the true faith. For this view, however, there is no authority. Others regard the term "Nicolaitans" as a symbolic expression. Since Nicolaos means victor of the people and Balaam means devourer of the people, the two in symbolic unity signify religious seducers of the people. It is more probable that the Nicolaitans were identical with those who held the doctrine of Balaam, mentioned in Rev 2:14 (cf. 2 Pet 2:15), so that likely the Nicolaitans practiced fornication and the eating of things sacrificed to idols while outwardly professing Christianity.

3532. Νικόλαος *Nikólaos*; gen. *Nikoláou*, masc. proper noun. Nicolaos or Nicolas, meaning victor over the people. He was one of the servants of the church at Jerusalem in the days of the apostles (Acts 6:5), a native of Antioch converted to Judaism and thence to Christianity.

3533. Νικόπολις *Nikópolis*; gen. *Nikopóleōs*, fem. proper noun. Nicopolis, meaning city of victory. A city Paul determined to enter (Titus 3:12). There has been some uncertainty about which city he had in mind as there were four cities by this name in Asia, five in Europe and one in Africa. Most probably it was the Nicopolis, now called Paleoprevesa or

Old Prevesa, on the boundary between Thrace and Macedonia in Greece.

3534. νῖκος *níkos*; gen. *níkous*, neut. noun, a later form of *níkē* (3529), victory. Victory (1 Cor 15:55, 57). With the prep. *eis* (1519), unto, *eis níkos*, used adv., meaning victoriously, triumphantly (Matt 12:20; 1 Cor 15:54, 55, 57 [cf. Sept.: 2 Sam 2:26; Job 36:7]).
Ant.: *hḗttēma* (2275), defeat, loss.

3535. Νινευΐ *Nineuḯ*; fem. proper noun transliterated from the Hebr. *Nīnᵉwēh* (5210, OT), dwelling of Nin. Ninev or Nineveh, the capital and greatest city of Assyria. Founded by Asshur (Gen 10:11), it was situated on the eastern bank of the river Tigris opposite the modern town of Mosul. It was about 250 miles in a direct line north of the rival city of Babylon and 550 miles northwest of the Persian Gulf. Nineveh most probably became the capital of Assyria during the reign of Sennacherib. The prophecies of the books of Jonah and Nahum are chiefly directed against this city. The latter prophet indicates the mode of its capture (Nah 1:8; 2:6, 8; 3:18). It was besieged for two years and captured by the combined forces of the Medes and Babylonians, and finally destroyed in 606 B.C.

3536. Νινευΐτης *Nineuḯtēs*, gen. *Nineuḯtou*, masc. proper noun. Ninevite, an inhabitant of Nineveh (3535). Used in the pl. in Matt 12:41 and Luke 11:30.

3537. νιπτήρ *niptḗr*; gen. *niptḗros*, masc. noun from *níptō* (3538), to wash. A washbasin (John 13:5).

3538. νίπτω *níptō*; fut. *nípsō*. To wash some part of the body, as the face, hands or feet. Ablutions of the hands and feet were very common with the Jews. *Níptō* stands in contrast with *loúō* (3068), to bathe, and *plúnō* (4150), to wash things. *Níptō* usually expresses the washing of a part of the body as the hands (Matt 15:2; Mark 7:3), the feet (John 13:5, 6,

8, 10, 12, 14; 1 Tim 5:10; Sept.: Gen 18:4; 43:30; Ex 30:20; Deut 21:6; 1 Sam 25:41), the face (Matt 6:17), the eyes (John 9:7, 11, 15). On the other hand, *loúō*, to bathe oneself, always implies not the washing of a part of the body, but the whole (Acts 9:37; Heb 10:22; 2 Pet 2:22; Rev 1:5). The lesson in John 13:9, 10 symbolizes justification as the bathing of the whole body (*loúō*), while sanctification is the constant need of *níptō*, washing individual parts of the body.

Deriv.: *ániptos* (449), unwashed; *aponíptō* (633), to wash off; *niptḗr* (3537), a washbasin.

Syn.: *loúō* (3068), to wash, bathe; *rhantízō* (4472), to sprinkle; *bréchō* (1026), to wet; *baptízō* (907), baptize, dip, wash ceremonially; *plúnō* (4150), to wash things.

3539. νοέω noéō; contracted *noṓ*, fut. *noḗsō*, from *noús* (3563), the mind. To perceive, observe. To perceive with thought coming into consciousness as distinct from the perception of senses. To mark, understand, apprehend, discern.

(I) To perceive, understand, comprehend, used in an absolute sense (Matt 16:9; Mark 8:17); with the heart (John 12:40); with the acc. expressed or implied (Rom 1:20; Eph 3:4, 20; 1 Tim 1:7); followed by the inf. (Heb 11:3); *hóti* (3754), that (Matt 15:17; 16:11; Mark 7:18; Sept.: Prov 1:2, 6).

(II) With the meaning to have in mind, think about, consider, used in an absolute sense (Matt 24:15; Mark 13:14); with the acc. (2 Tim 2:7).

Deriv.: *agnoéō* (50), not to understand, not know; *anóētos* (453), foolish, unintelligent; *katanoéō* (2657), to ponder, study; *metanoéō* (3340), to repent, change one's mind; *nóēma* (3540), perception, meaning, thought; *pronoéō* (4306), to provide for; *huponoéō* (5282), to conjecture, think, suppose.

Syn.: *phronéō* (5426) to think; *epístamai* (1987) and *diaginṓskō* (1231), to know well; *punthánomai* (4441), to inquire, understand; *gnōrízō* (1107), to make known; *manthánō* (3129), to learn; *diaginṓskō* (1231), to determine, ascertain exactly, enquire; *akribóō* (198), to learn by diligent inquiry; *oída* (1492), to know intuitively or instinctively; *ginṓskō* (1097) to know experientially; *gnōrízō* (1107), to make known; *plērophoréō* (4135), to know fully; *anagnōrízō* (319), to recognize, make known; *diagnōrízō* (1232), to make known; *dokéō* (1380), to suppose, think; *logízomai* (3049), to reckon, take into account; *nomízō* (3543), to suppose; *oíomai* (3633), to imagine, suppose; *krínō* (2919), to judge, reckon; *suníēmi* (4920), to understand.

Ant.: *agnoéō* (50), to be ignorant, not to know; *aisthánomai* (143), to perceive through the senses.

3540. νόημα nóēma; gen. *noḗmatos*, neut. noun from *noéō* (3539), to perceive. A thought, concept of the mind (2 Cor 10:5); a device, contrivance (2 Cor 2:11); the understanding, the mind (2 Cor 3:14; 4:4; 11:3; Phil 4:7).

Syn.: *enthúmēsis* (1761), an inward reasoning, device, thought; *énnoia* (1771), an inward thought; *epínoia* (1963), a purposeful thought; *diánoia* (1271), deep thought; *dianóēma* (1270), a discerning thought, machination; *logismós* (3053), thought, reason, imagination; *dialogismós* (1261), reasoning through; *suzḗtēsis* (4803), disputation, reasoning; *phrónēma* (5427), mental inclination; *phrónēsis* (5428), prudence.

Ant.: *agnóēma* (51), shortcoming, error; *plánē* (4106), error, fraud, deceit; *dólos* (1388), guile; *apátē* (539), delusion; *aísthēsis* (144), a perception of the senses.

3541. νόθος nóthos; gen. *nóthou*, masc.-fem., neut. *nóthon*, adj. An illegitimate or misbegotten child, one who is spurious (Heb 12:8).

Syn.: *pseudḗs* (5571), false, untrue; *hupokritḗs* (5273), hypocrite

Ant.: *alēthḗs* (227), telling the truth, unconcealed, true; *alēthinós* (228), real, true, genuine; *gnḗsios* (1103), lawfully begotten, genuine.

3542. νομή nomḗ; gen. *nomḗs*, fem. noun from *némō* (n.f.), to pasture, feed. Pasture, the act of feeding. Used metaphorically for a feeding, eating, the spreading as gangrene (2 Tim 2:17). Pasturage, metaphorically in John 10:9, meaning shall have enjoyment, find happiness. See Sept.: Gen 47:4; 1 Chr 4:39, 40; Ps 74:1; Prov 24:15.

Syn.: *brṓsis* (1035), the act of eating; *brṓma* (1033), meat, food; *trophḗ* (5160), food; *sítos* (4621), corn, wheat.

Ant.: *hustérēsis* (5304), lack, going without; *hustérēma* (5303), that which is lacking, *chreía* (5532), want; *asitía* (776), without wheat, abstinence; *nēsteía* (3521), abstinence, fast.

3543. νομίζω nomízō; fut. *nomísō*, from *nómos* (3551), law, custom. To suppose, assume, to regard or acknowledge as custom, to have and hold as customary. In Acts 16:13, it means "where according to custom was the prayer by the river" (a.t.). This refers to the Jews who were permitted to offer their prayers by the river close to the sea. Generally the word means to regard or acknowledge something in its customary character or manner, as in Luke 3:23, meaning "as he was regarded" (a.t.) or reckoned according to Jewish custom. It thus came to mean to regard, think, suppose (Luke 2:44; Acts 7:25; 8:20; 14:19; 16:27; 17:29; 1 Cor 7:26; 1 Tim 6:5). Followed by the inf. (1 Cor 7:36). With *hóti* (3754), that (Matt 5:17; 10:34; 20:10; Acts 21:29).

Deriv.: *nómisma* (3546), anything acknowledged by law, currency.

Syn.: *dokéō* (1380), to be of an opinion; *oíomai* (3633), to suppose; *logízomai* (3049), to reckon; *hēgéomai* (2233) and *phronéō* (5426), to think; *noéō* (3539), to perceive; *huponoéō* (5282), to deem; *krínō* (2919), to reckon; *hupolambánō* (5274), to assume, suppose; *doxázō* (1392), to esteem; *phrázomai* (5419), to indicate, declare.

Ant.: *agnoéō* (50), to be ignorant, not to know; *epilanthánomai* (1950), to forget.

3544. νομικός nomikós; fem. *nomikḗ*, neut. *nomikón*, adj. from *nómos* (3551), law. Pertaining to the law, a matter of law; subst. one skilled in the law, a lawyer. Lawyers appear together with the Pharisees in Luke 7:30 and 14:3. Apparently they were from among the Pharisees (Matt 22:35) and with the scribes (Mark 12:28; Luke 10:25; 11:45, 46, 52) and were experts in the Mosaic law. In all places where the word is employed and legal questions come into consideration, the scribes appear as authorities in questions concerning prophecy (Matt 2:4; 13:52). It may be inferred that "scribes" is a generic name, and the *nomikoí*, lawyers, are the specialized ones skilled in law and jurisprudence of the Law of Moses. *Nomodidáskalos* (3547), teacher of the law (Luke 5:17; Acts 5:34), is apparently another name. Probably the members of the Sanhedrin and the Council were learned in the law. The lawyer Zenas, whom Paul mentions in Titus 3:13, was probably an attorney of Roman law and not Mosaic law.

Syn.: *nomothétēs* (3550), a lawyer, legislator.

3545. νομίμως nomímōs; adv. from *nómimos* (n.f.), lawful, which is from *nómos* (3551), law. Lawfully, according to law and custom (1 Tim 1:8; 2 Tim 2:5).

Syn.: *éxesti* (1832), it is permitted, it is lawful.

Ant.: *anómōs* (460), unlawfully, lawlessly.

3546. νόμισμα nómisma; gen., *nomísmatos*, neut. noun from *nomízō* (3543), to acknowledge, assume. Anything acknowledged and sanctioned by custom or law; hence currency, money, coins (Matt 22:19). The Lat. is *numisma*.

Syn.: *argúrion* (694), a piece of silver or a silver coin; *chrḗma* (5536), a thing that one uses, money, riches; *chalkós* (5475), copper or a copper coin; *kérma* (2772), literally a slice, thus a small coin, change; *statḗr* (4715), a coin; *drachmḗ* (1406), drachma, a piece of money used by the Greeks, smaller in value than *statḗr*.

3547. νομοδιδάσκαλος *nomodidáskalos*; gen. *nomodidaskálou*, masc noun from *nómos* (3551), law, and *didáskalos* (1320), a teacher. A teacher and expounder of Jewish law, equal to *nomikós* (3544), a lawyer, and *grammateús* (1122), a scribe (Luke 5:17; Acts 5:34). *Nomodidáskaloi* (pl.) were those whom Paul identified as teachers who were disturbing the peace and corrupting the doctrine of the church by illegitimately using the Law of Moses (1 Tim 1:7). Related words: *kalodidáskalos* (2567), a teacher of what is good; *pseudodidáskalos* (5572), a false teacher.

3548. νομοθεσία *nomothesía*; gen. *nomothesías*, fem. noun from *nomothetéō* (3549), to legislate. The act of law giving, legislation, the giving of a code of laws. In the NT, metonymically, the laws given, code of laws, the Mosaic Code of Law (Rom 9:4).

   Ant.: *athétēsis* (115), cancellation; *anomía* (458), illegality; *paranomía* (3892), transgression of the law.

3549. νομοθετέω *nomothetéō*; contracted *nomothetṓ*, fut. *nomothetḗsō*, from *nomothétēs* (3550), a legislator. To legislate, to make or give laws, establish as law. In the NT, in the pass., to be legislated, to receive laws (Heb 7:11, meaning for the people received the Mosaic Law upon condition of being under the Levitical priesthood). To establish, to sanction as law or bylaw (pass. in Heb 8:6).

   Deriv.: *nomothesía* (3548), giving of the law.

   Ant.: *athetéō* (114), to violate what is commonly accepted; *paranoméō* (3891), to transgress.

3550. νομοθέτης *nomothétēs*; gen. *nomothétou*, masc noun from *nómos* (3551), a law, and *títhēmi* (5087), to put, set. A lawgiver, legislator (James 4:12).

   Deriv.: *nomothetéō* (3549), to establish or receive the law.

   Syn.: *nomikós* (3544), a lawyer.

   Ant.: *ánomos* (459), lawless; *áthesmos* (113), one without custom or law.

3551. νόμος *nómos*; gen. *nómou*, masc noun from *némō* (n.f., see *aponémō* [632]), to divide among, parcel out, allot. Etymologically something parceled out, allotted, what one has in use and possession; hence, usage, custom (Sept.: 2 Sam 7:19). In the NT, law.

   (I) Generally, without reference to a particular people or state (Rom 4:15; 5:13; 7:8; 1 Tim 1:9).

   (II) Specifically of particular laws, statutes, ordinances, spoken in the NT mostly of the Mosaic statutes:

   (A) Of laws relating to civil rights and duties (John 7:51; 8:5 [cf. Lev 20:10]; John 19:7 [cf. Lev 24:16 and Deut 13:5]; Acts 23:3; 24:6); the law of marriage (Rom 7:2, 3; 1 Cor 7:39); the Levitical priesthood (Heb 7:16); according to the ordinance or command respecting the promulgation of the Law (Heb 9:19 [cf. Ex 20:18, 19; 24:2ff.]; Sept.: Num 19:14).

   (B) Of laws relating to external religious rites, e.g., purification (Luke 2:22; Heb 9:22); circumcision (John 7:23; Acts 15:5 [cf. 21:20, 24]); sacrifices (Heb 10:8; see Sept.: Lev 6:9, 14).

   (C) Of laws relating to the hearts and conduct of men (Rom 7:7; Heb 8:10; 10:16 quoted from Jer 38:31–34; James 2:8).

   (D) By implication, for a written law, a law expressly given, i.e., in writing (Rom 2:14).

   (III) The Law, i.e., a code or body of laws. In the NT used only of the Mosaic code.

   (A) Specifically in Matt 5:18; 22:36; Luke 16:17; John 1:17; 7:19; Acts 7:53;

Rom 2:13ff.; 5:13; 1 Cor 15:56; Gal 3:10ff.; 1 Tim 1:8; James 2:9, 11. Works of the Law (Rom 2:15; Gal 2:16; 3:10) meaning those of the Law, in the Law, or under the Law, i.e., the Mosaic law (Rom 2:12; 3:19; 4:16; 1 Cor 9:20; Sept.: Deut 1:5; 4:44).

(B) Metaphorically for the Mosaic dispensation (Rom 10:4; Heb 7:12; 10:1).

(C) As a metonymy for the Book of the Law, i.e., particularly the books of Moses, the Pentateuch (Matt 12:5; Luke 2:23 [cf. Ex 13:2]; Luke 10:26; 1 Cor 9:8, 9 [cf. Deut 25:4]; 1 Cor 14:34 [cf. Gen 3:16]). As forming part of the OT, the Law and the prophets (Matt 5:17; Luke 16:16; John 1:45; Acts 13:15; 28:23; Rom 3:21); the Law, the prophets, and the Psalms (Luke 24:44); also simply the Law for the OT (John 10:34; 12:34; 15:25 from Ps 35:19; 1 Cor 14:21 from Isa 28:11, 12).

(IV) Metaphorically, the perfect law, meaning the more perfect law for the Christian dispensation, in contrast with that of Moses (James 1:25); without *téleios* (5046), perfect (James 2:12; 4:11); of the laws and precepts established by the gospel, e.g., the law of Christ (Rom 13:8, 10; Gal 5:23; 6:2).

(V) Metaphorically, the law, i.e., rule, norm and/or standard of judging or acting (Rom 3:27; 7:23, 25; 8:2, 7; 9:31). In the sense of a rule of life, discipline (Phil 3:5).

Deriv.: *ánomos* (459), without law; *énnomos* (1772), lawful; *nomízō* (3543), to acknowledge as custom; *nomikós* (3544), one learned in the law; *nomodidáskalos* (3547), teacher of the law; *nomothétēs* (3550), a lawgiver.

Syn.: *archḗ* (746), principle, rule; *exousía* (1849), authority; *krátos* (2904), dominion, power, government; *kanṓn* (2583), rule; *dógma* (1378), decree, a law.

Ant.: *anomía* (458), lawlessness; *paranomía* (3892), transgression; *adikía* (93), injustice; *parábasis* (3847), transgression.

3552. νοσέω *noséō*; contracted *nosṓ*, fut. *nosḗsō*, from *nósos* (3554), sickness. To be sick, delirious. Used metaphorically meaning to have a sickly longing for something, to pine after, dote on (1 Tim 6:4).

Deriv.: *nósēma* (3553), disease.

Syn.: *asthenéō* (770), to be weak, sick; *kámnō* (2577), primarily to overwork and hence to be weary and sick; *sunéchomai* (4912), to be afflicted, to be held in or seized by ills; *échō kakṓs* (*échō* [2192], have; *kakṓs* [2560], badly), to have it badly.

Ant.: *hugiaínō* (5198), to be healthy; *therapeúō* (2323), to heal, cure; *iáomai* (2390), to heal; *sṓzō* (4982), to heal, literally to save.

3553. νόσημα *nósēma*; gen. *nosḗmatos*, neut. noun from *noséō* (3552), to be sick. A particular sickness, disease (John 5:4 [TR]), equal to *nósos* (3554), sickness.

Syn.: *asthéneia* (769), infirmity, disease, weakness; *asthénēma* (771), infirmity.

Ant.: *therapeía* (2322), cure, health; *íama* (2386), healing; *íasis* (2392), the process of healing; *hugiḗs* (5199), to be healthy.

3554. νόσος *nósos*; gen. *nósou*, masc. noun. Disease, sickness (Matt 4:23, 24; 9:35; 10:1; Mark 1:34; 3:15; Luke 4:40; 6:17; 7:21; 9:1; Acts 19:12; Sept.: Ex 15:26; 2 Chr 21:19). Metaphorically, pain, sorrow, evil (Matt 8:17 from Isa 53:4).

Deriv.: *noséō* (3552), to be sick.

Syn.: *asthéneia* (769), sickness, weakness; *malakía* (3119), ailment, softness; *árrōstos* (732), sick or ill, a disease of a more grievous kind; *malakía* (3119) a slighter infirmity.

3555. νοσσιά *nossiá*; gen. *nossiás*, fem. noun from *neossós* (3502), young. A nest with the young (Sept.: Ps 84:4). In the NT, a nest of young birds, brood (Luke 13:34; Sept.: Deut 32:11).

3556. νοσσίον *nossíon*; gen. *nossíou*, neut. noun contracted for the Attic *neossíon*, a diminutive of *neossós* (3502), young. A young bird. In the pl., *tá nossía*, a brood of young birds (Matt 23:37; Sept.: Ps 84:4).

3557. νοσφίζω *nosphízō*; fut. *nosphísō*, from *nósphi* (n.f.), apart, separated. In the NT, only in the mid. *nosphízomai*, to embezzle, keep back something which belongs to another (Acts 5:2, 3; Titus 2:10; Sept.: Josh 7:1). Applied by Greek writers to embezzlement of public treasures.

Syn.: *kléptō* (2813), to steal; *aposteréō* (650), to deprive by fraud.

Ant.: *euergetéō* (2109), to do good.

3558. νότος *nótos*; gen. *nótou*, masc. noun. The south wind or specifically the southwest wind; the Lat. is *notus* (Luke 12:55; Acts 27:13; 28:13; Sept.: Song 4:16). By metonymy, the south, the southern part (Matt 12:42; Luke 11:31 [cf. 1 Kgs 10]; Luke 13:29; Rev 21:13; Sept.: Ex 26:35; Eccl 1:5; Ezek 40:24).

Syn.: *mesēmbría* (3314), south, noon.

Ant.: *borrás* (1005), north wind, north; *anatolḗ* (395), east; *dusmḗ* (1424), west.

3559. νουθεσία *nouthesía*; gen. *nouthesías*, fem. noun from *nouthetéō* (3560), to admonish. Admonition, warning, exhortation (1 Cor 10:11; Eph 6:4; Titus 3:10). *Nouthesía* is any word of encouragement or reproof which leads to correct behavior. *Paideía* (3809) is instruction and training by act and discipline. *Nouthesía* is the milder term without which *paideía* would be incomplete. In both words there is the appeal to the conscience, will, and reasoning faculties.

Syn.: *epanórthōsis* (1882), correction; *epitimía* (2009), rebuke; *paráklēsis* (3874), encouragement.

Ant.: *ánoia* (454), folly, stupidity.

3560. νουθετέω *nouthetéō*; contracted *nouthetṓ*, fut. *nouthetḗsō*, from *noús* (3563), mind, and *títhēmi* (5087), to place. To warn, admonish, exhort. Trans. (Acts 20:31; Rom 15:14; 1 Cor 4:14; Col 1:28; 3:16; 1 Thess 5:12, 14; 2 Thess 3:15; Sept.: Job 4:3).

Syn.: *parainéō* (3867), to admonish, exhort; *protrépō* (4389), to exhort; *parakaléō* (3870), to admonish, comfort; *paideúō* (3811), to correct by discipline; *hupodeíknumi* (5263), to show secretly, forewarn; *chrēmatízō* (5537), to be divinely warned, be admonished; *sumbouleúō* (4823), to consult jointly, to counsel; *sunistáō / sunístēmi* (4921), to stand with, commend; *epitimáō* (2008), to rebuke.

Ant.: *planáō* (4105), to lead astray; *exapatáō* (1818), to deceive; *dolóō* (1389), to handle deceitfully; *apatáō* (538), to delude.

3561. νουμηνία *noumēnía*; gen. *noumēnías*, fem. noun from *néos* (3501), new, and *mḗn* (3376), month, moon. The new moon. As a festival (Col 2:16; see Sept.: Ex 40:2, 15; Num 10:10; 28:11; 2 Chr 2:4; 29:17).

3562. νουνεχῶς *nounechṓs*; adv. from *nounechés* (n.f.), wise, discreet, which is from *noús* (3563), mind, and *échō* (2192), have. Wisely, discreetly, sensibly, as possessing discernment (Mark 12:34).

Syn.: *phronímōs* (5430), prudently; *sōphrónōs* (4996), with sound mind.

3563. νοῦς *noús*; gen. *noós*, acc. *noún*, masc. noun. Mind, the organ of mental perception and apprehension, of conscious life, of the consciousness preceding actions or recognizing and judging them, intelligent understanding.

(I) As the seat of emotions and affections, mode of thinking and feeling, disposition, moral inclination, equivalent to the heart (Rom 1:28; 12:2; 1 Cor 1:10; Eph 4:17, 23; Col 2:18; 1 Tim 6:5; 2 Tim 3:8; Titus 1:15); firmness or presence of mind (2 Thess 2:2); implying heart, reason, conscience, in opposition to fleshly appetites (Rom 7:23, 25; Sept.: Isa 10:7, 12).

(II) Understanding, intellect (Luke 24:45; 1 Cor 14:14, 15, 19; Phil 4:7; Rev 13:18, "... him that hath understanding"; Sept.: Josh 14:7).

(III) Metonymically for mind, what is in the mind, thought, counsel, purpose, opinion, of God or Christ (Rom 11:34 quoted from Isa 40:13; 1 Cor 2:16); of men (Rom 14:5).

(IV) Metaphorically of things, sense (Rev 17:9, the deep or hidden sense).

(V) While, in the OT, the heart (*kardía* [2588]) is used to represent man's whole mental and moral activity (Gen 6:5), the word "mind [*noús*]" in the NT is used to denote the faculty of thinking, especially the organ of moral consciousness. The word *noús* must be associated with the derivatives *nóēma* (3540), thought, design, device; *diánoia* (1271), the faculty of knowing and understanding or moral reflection; and *énnoia* (1771), an idea, notion, intent. It is interesting indeed that outside of the epistles of the Apostle Paul, the word *noús* occurs only in Luke 24:45; Rev 13:18; 17:9. Though *diánoia* (1271) occurs in Matt 22:37; Mark 12:30; Luke 1:51; 10:27; Heb 8:10; 10:16; 1 Pet 1:13; 2 Pet 3:1; 1 John 5:20, *énnoia* occurs only in Heb 4:12 and 1 Pet 4:1. The word translated "mind" in Acts 14:2; Phil 1:27; Heb 12:3 represents not *noús* but *psuché* (5590), soul. In Phile 1:14 and Rev 17:13, the word "mind" stands for *gnómē* (1106), judgment, opinion, and in Rom 8:7, 27 it stands for *phrónēma* (5427) which denotes not the mental faculty itself, but its thoughts and purposes.

(VI) It will help us to understand the distinctive meaning which Paul attributes to *noús* when we notice the two contrasts in which he sets it, in the one case with flesh (*sárx* [4561]), and in the other with spirit (*pneúma* [4151]). In Rom 7:23, 25, he contrasts the flesh with the mind, i.e., the sinful principle of human nature in his members with the law of his mind which is also the law of God. Here the mind is clearly the conscience or organ of moral knowledge, man's highest faculty, by which he recognizes the will of God for his own life. When in Rom 8:6 the apostle speaks of "the mind of the flesh [*phrónēma* {5427}, frame of mind]," (a.t. [cf. Col 2:18, where it is translated "fleshly mind"], the suggestion is that man's highest faculty has been debased to serve the lowest part of his nature so that the mind has itself become fleshly and sinful. In 1 Cor 14:14, 15, 19, *noús* is again contrasted with *pneúma* (4151), spirit. Man's natural faculty of conscious knowledge and reflection are shown to be the antithesis of that divinely bestowed, higher principle of the Christian life which may manifest itself in ways that lie beyond the reach of consciousness. The mind, as man's highest natural faculty, thus stands between the flesh, being the lower, sinful principle of his nature, and the spirit which is the distinctive principle of the divinely given Christian life. Just as the mind may be dragged down by the flesh until it becomes a "mind of the flesh" (a.t.), so it may also be raised up and reformed by the Spirit until it becomes a "mind of the Spirit" (a.t. [Rom 8:6 {cf. 12:2; Eph 4:23}]).

Deriv.: *ánoia* (454), madness, folly; *énnoia* (1771), notion, intention; *epínoia* (1963), a thought; *noéō* (3539), to perceive, think; *nouthetéō* (3560), to admonish.

Syn.: *súnesis* (4907), understanding, the ability to rightly relate concepts; *nóēma* (3540), thought, intellect; *diánoia* (1271), the faculty of the mind, intelligence; *phónēsis* (5428), insight, prudence; *phrónēma* (5427), state of mind, manner of thinking.

3564. Νυμφᾶς *Numphás*; gen. *Numphá*, masc. proper noun. Nymphas, meaning bridegroom, a member of the church of Laodicea (Col 4:15).

3565. νύμφη *númphē*; gen. *númphēs*, fem. noun. A bride, spouse, newly married (John 3:29; Rev 18:23; 21:2, 9; 22:17; Sept.: Jer 2:32; 7:34; Joel 2:16).

Opposite of *hē penthérá* (3994), mother-in-law, where it is taken as daughter-in-law (Matt 10:35; Luke 12:53; Sept.: Gen 38:11; Ruth 1:6, 7; Mic 7:6).

Deriv.: *numphíos* (3566), a bridegroom; *numphṓn* (3567), bridal chamber.

3566. νυμφίος *numphíos*; gen. *numphíou*, masc. noun from *númphē* (3565), a bride. A bridegroom, spouse, newly married (Matt 9:15; 25:1, 5, 6, 10; Mark 2:19, 20; Luke 5:34, 35; John 2:9; 3:29; Rev 18:23; Sept.: Ps 19:6; Jer 7:32).

3567. νυμφών *numphṓn*; gen. *numphṓnos*, masc. noun from *númphē* (3565), a bride. The bridal chamber in which the marriage bed was prepared, usually in the house of the bridegroom where the bride was brought in procession. In the NT, only in the phrase, "children of the bridechamber" (Matt 9:15; Mark 2:19; Luke 5:34). The companions of the bridegroom were called bridesmen (*paránumphoi*) by the Greeks, just as the bride had her companions or bridesmaids (cf. Judg 14:11; Jer 7:34).

3568. νῦν *nún*; adv. Now, also *nuní* (3570) as strengthened by the demonstrative *i* (iota).

(I) Used as an adv. of time:

(A) Now, at the actual present time (Luke 6:21, 25; John 4:18; 12:27; 16:22; 17:5, 7; Acts 2:33; 10:33; 26:6; 1 Cor 16:12; Gal 2:20; 1 John 2:18; Sept.: Josh 14:11; Isa 48:7).

(B) Used as a direct antithesis to something done in time past with the particle *dé* (1161), but (Luke 16:25; Gal 4:9; Eph 5:8; Phil 3:18; Heb 9:26; James 4:16); *allá* (235), but (Luke 22:36), but now. Also in antithesis to something fut. for emphasis (Mark 10:30, "now," at this time, as opposed to the coming time). With the art. *ho* (3588), the, and *nún*, as an adj. meaning the now existing, the present (Rom 3:26; 8:18; 2 Cor 8:14; Gal 4:25; 1 Tim 4:8; 2 Tim 4:10; 2 Pet 3:7). In Luke 1:48 and 2 Cor 5:16, we have *apó toú nún* (*apó*

[575], from; *toú* the gen. of *tó* [neut. def. art.]) referring to time and meaning from now on, henceforth. In Rom 8:22 and Phil 1:5, *áchri toú nún* (*áchri* [891], till; *toú nún*, implying *chrónou* [5550], time), until now; with *héōs* (2193), till, instead, *héōs toú nún*, until now (Matt 24:21; Mark 13:19). *Tó nún échon* (neut. part. of *échō* [2192]), meaning as it now is, for the present (Acts 24:25).

(C) In reference to time just past, meaning now, just now, even now (Matt 26:65; John 11:8; 13:31; 14:29; 21:10; Acts 7:52; Rom 5:11).

(D) In reference to fut. time just at hand, now, even now, presently, immediately (John 12:31; Acts 13:11; Phil 1:20). As implying what is immediately to take place (John 16:5, 32; Acts 26:17).

(II) Used as a particle of transition or continuation meaning now.

(A) As marking a present condition, in the present state of things, as things are (Luke 2:29; 11:39; Acts 3:17; 20:25; Rom 5:9; 2 Cor 7:9; Col 1:24). Used also in antithesis, *nuní dé* (3570), (1 Cor 13:13); also preceded by *ei* (1487), if (Luke 19:42; John 8:40; 1 Cor 7:14).

(B) Used to imply that one thing follows now out of another, thus marking a conclusion, inference, equal to "now then," "now therefore," equivalent to "since these things are so" (Acts 12:11; 16:36; 22:16; 23:15). Used interrogatively (Acts 15:10); as a conclusion, *nún ára* (686), therefore, now therefore (Rom 8:1).

(C) Also for emphasis in commands and exhortations implying that what is to be done should be done now, at once, on the spot (Matt 27:42, 43; John 2:8; Acts 7:34; James 4:13; 5:1; 1 John 2:28).

Syn.: *ḗdē* (2235), already, now, with a suggested reference to some other time or to some expectation; *árti* (737), expressing coincidence and holding strictly to the present time, just now, this moment (in contrast to the past); *apárti* (534) and sometimes as two words *ap' árti*, from now on, henceforth; *loipón* (3063), from now.

Ant.: *oudépote* (3763), not at any time; *mēdépote* (3368), never, but not as strong as *oudépote*; *oudépō* (3764), never; *oúpō* (3768), not yet; *pópote* (4455), not at any time, never yet.

3569. ταvῦν *tanún*; adv. expression from the neut. pl. art. *tá*, the, and *nún* (3568), now, the things now, used adv. meaning at present. But now (Acts 4:29; 5:38; 17:30; 20:32; 27:22).

3570. νυνί *nuní*; adv., identical to *nún* (3568), now, strengthened by the demonstrative *i* (iota) for emphasis. Just now (Rom 6:22; 7:6, 17; 15:23, 25; 1 Cor 5:11; 12:18; 13:13; 14:6; 15:20; 2 Cor 8:11, 22; Eph 2:13; Col 1:21, 26; 3:8; Phile 1:9, 11; Heb 8:6; 11:16). With *dé* (1161), and, but (Rom 3:21; 6:21; 1 Cor 5:11; 2 Cor 8:11; Phile 1:11). *Nuní dé* after *ei* (1487), if (Rom 7:17; Heb 11:16). For syn. and ant. see *nún* (3568), now.

3571. νύξ *núx*; gen. *nuktós*, fem. noun. Night (Matt 14:25; Mark 6:48; Luke 2:8; John 9:4; Rev 8:12; 21:25; 22:5; Sept.: Gen 1:5; Job 3:6, 7). When used in the gen., *nuktós* means by night (Matt 2:14; 27:64; John 3:2). With day and night both in the gen., *hēméras kaí nuktós* (*hēméras* [2250], by day; *kaí* [2532], and; *nuktós*), it means by day and by night, continually (Luke 18:7; Acts 9:24; 2 Tim 1:3; Rev 4:8). *Mésēs dé nuktós* (*mésēs*, the fem. of *mésos* [3319], middle, midst), in the middle of the night (Matt 25:6); *katá méson tḗs nuktós* (*katá* [2596], at), in the middle of the night (Acts 27:27); *diá tḗs nuktós* (*diá* [1223], through), during the night, either the whole night (Luke 5:5) or by night (Acts 5:19; 16:9). In Luke 12:20, with the dat. *taútē tḗ nuktí* (*taútē* [5026], this), this very night; with *en* (1722), in or by night (Acts 18:9); with the def. art. *en tḗ nuktí*, by night (Matt 26:31; see John 11:10). "Forty nights" (Matt 4:2); "three nights" (Matt 12:40); the nights or during the nights (Luke 21:37); night and day (*núkta kaí hēméran*) in Mark 4:27 means continually. See Luke 2:37;

Acts 26:7; 2 Thess 3:8. Metaphorically, it means a time of moral and spiritual darkness, the opposite of gospel light and day (Rom 13:12; 1 Thess 5:5).

Deriv.: *énnuchon* (1773), night; *mesonúktion* (3317), midnight; *nuchthḗmeron* (3574), a night and day.

Ant.: *hēméra* (2250), day.

3572. νύσσω *nússō*, νύττω *núttō*; fut. *núxō*. To stab, pierce, prick, as the side of Jesus' body when He was crucified (John 19:34).

Deriv.: *katanússō* (2660), to pierce.

Syn.: *ekkentéō* (1574), to pierce.

3573. νυστάζω *nustázō*; fut. *nustáxō*, from *neúō* (3506), to nod. To slumber, doze, nod off (Matt 25:5). Metaphorically, in 2 Pet 2:3. Sept.: Ps 121:3; Nah 3:18.

Ant.: *grēgoréō* (1127), to keep awake, watch; *agrupnéō* (69), to be sleepless; metaphorically *néphō* (3525), to be sober.

3574. νυχθήμερον *nuchthḗmeron*; gen. *nuchthēmérou*, neut. noun from *núx* (3571), night, and *hēméra* (2250), day. A day and night, twenty-four hours or a part of the day or night thereof as per the inclusive counting of time by the Eastern people. As a combined word it occurs only in 2 Cor 11:25, not necessarily implying that the Apostle Paul spent exactly twenty-four hours in the depth of the sea, but it may have been only a portion of a twenty-four-hour period. In Matt 4:2; 12:40 the two words *hēmérai*, days, and *núktes*, nights, occur separately, but like *nuchthḗmeron* do not necessarily imply exact periods. Thus we can understand Matt 12:40 that as Jonah was three days and three nights in the fish's belly, so our Lord stayed in the heart of the earth three days and three nights, or parts of them. The first being part of Friday; the second being a twenty-four-hour period until Saturday at the setting of the sun, and the third day would be part of Sunday from the setting of the sun on Saturday until early Sunday morning.

This would make one full twenty-four-hour period and two parts of two different twenty-four-hour periods.

3575. Νῶε *Nóe*; masc proper noun transliterated from the Hebr. *Nōach* (5146, OT), rest. Noe or Noah, meaning, the name of the patriarch preserved from the flood (Matt 24:37, 38; Luke 3:36; 17:26, 27; Heb 11:7; 1 Pet 3:20; 2 Pet 2:5; Sept.: Gen 6:9). He was the ninth in descent from Adam (Gen 6:8); described as a "just and perfect" man who "pleased God" (Sept.: Gen 6:9), and as a "preacher of righteousness" (2 Pet 2:5); has a place in the catalog of those who are eminent for their faith (Heb 11:7). Noah is the second father of the human race, all the families of the earth being in a direct line of descent from him. Our Lord illustrates the suddenness of His Second Coming and the wickedness of the world by the circumstances prior to the flood (Matt 24:32, 38).

3576. νωθρός *nōthrós*; fem. *nōthrá*, neut. *nōthrón*, adj. Slothful, sluggish, dull (Heb 5:11; 6:12; Sept.: Prov 22:29).
    Syn.: *bradús* (1021), slow; *argós* (692), idle; *oknērós* (3636), lazy.
    Ant.: *tachús* (5036), quick, swift; *tachinós* (5031), swift.

3577. νῶτος *nótos*; gen. *nótou*, masc noun. The back of men or animals (Rom 11:10 quoted from Ps 69:24, where it is the translated in the Sept. "loins"; see Sept.: 1 Kgs 7:19; 2 Kgs 17:14).
    Syn.: *opísō* (3694), back, backward; *ópisthen* (3693), backside, behind.
    Ant.: *prósōpon* (4383), face, presence.

3578. ξενία xenía; gen. *xenías*, fem. noun from *xénos* (3581), a stranger, foreigner. Hospitality, entertainment. A place for a guest, a lodging for a foreigner (Acts 28:23; Phile 1:22).

Syn.: *katáluma* (2646), a lodging place, guest chamber, inn.

3579. ξενίζω xenízō; fut. *xenísō*, from *xénos* (3581), a stranger, foreigner. To receive as a guest, entertain; in the pass. to be entertained, to lodge with someone (Acts 10:6, 18, 23, 32; 21:16; 28:7; Heb 13:2). To appear strange to someone, to surprise. In the NT, used as a pl. part. with the neut. def. art. *tá xenízonta*, meaning strange things, novel or surprising (Acts 17:20). In the mid. *xenízomai*, to be surprised, to think something strange, with the dat. of cause or obj. (1 Pet 4:4, 12).

Syn.: *aulízomai* (835), to lodge in a courtyard; *kataskēnóō* (2681), to lodge in a tent, pitch a tent; *katalúō* (2647), to lodge.

3580. ξενοδοχέω xenodochéō; contracted *xenodochṓ*, fut. *xenodochḗsō*, from *xenodóchos* (n.f.), receptive to strangers, which is from *xénos* (3581), stranger, and *déchomai* (1209), to receive, reception. To entertain strangers, practice hospitality (1 Tim 5:10).

3581. ξένος xénos; fem. *xénē*, neut. *xénon*, adj. Strange, foreign, not of one's family; subst. *ho xénos*, a guest, stranger, meaning a friend although a stranger (Rom 16:23 refers to Gaius as a host of Paul and of the whole church, meaning that possibly the church met in his house). It generally means a stranger from another place (Matt 25:35, 38, 43, 44; 27:7; Acts 17:21; Heb 11:13; Sept.: Ruth 2:10; 2 Sam 15:19; Job 31:32). Used metaphorically with the meaning of

not belonging to a Christian community, an alien (Eph 2:12, 19, meaning a stranger, not a Christian; 3 John 1:5). As an adj., it means strange, foreign, unknown, as coming from another country (Acts 17:18). Metaphorically used to refer to strange doctrines, foreign to the Christian faith (Heb 13:9); strange, novel, unheard of, and thus causing surprise and wonder (1 Pet 4:12).

Deriv.: *xenía* (3578), hospitality; *xenízō* (3579), to appear as a stranger or to entertain a stranger.

Syn.: *allótrios* (245), one belonging to another country, an alien; *parádoxos* (3861), strange or something contrary to the accepted opinion; *éxō* (2192), literally outside, something different from one's own people or opinions, foreign; *héteros* (2087), another of a different kind, therefore strange; *allogenḗs* (241), one belonging to another race; *pároikos* (3941), one who remains temporarily in a place, sojourner; *parepídēmos* (3927), a pilgrim.

Ant.: *oikeíos* (3609), one who belongs to a household, kindred; *oikiakós* (3615), belonging to one's household; *suggenḗs* (4773), fellow countryman, cousin, kin.

3582. ξέστης xéstēs; gen. *xéstou*, masc noun, Lat. *sextus* or *sextarius*. A Roman measure, the sixteenth part of a modius, containing about one and a half pints, but varying in different countries (cf. with *bátos* [943], a bath or measure for liquids, a Jewish liquid measure equivalent to an ephah containing eight to nine gallons, Luke 16:6], and *kóros* [2884], a cor, the largest Hebrew dry measure equal to ten ephahs, containing about eleven bushels [Luke 16:7]). In the NT, *xéstēs* stands generally for any small measure or vessel such as a cup, pitcher (Mark 7:4, 8).

3583. **ξηραίνω** *xēraínō*; fut. *xēranṓ*, aor. *exḗrana* (James 1:11), perf. pass. *exḗrammai* (Mark 3:1), 3d person sing. *exḗrantai* (Mark 11:21), from *xērós* (3584), dry. To dry or make dry. Of plants, to dry up, wither (James 1:11). In the pass.: to be dried up, become dry, wither away (Matt 13:6; 21:19, 20; Mark 4:6; 11:20, 21; Luke 8:6; John 15:6; 1 Pet 1:24); of fluids, to be dried up (Mark 5:29; Rev 16:12; Sept.: Gen 8:7; 1 Kgs 17:7; Isa 19:5); of the body or its members, to wither, pine away (Mark 3:1, 3; 9:18; Sept.: 1 Kgs 13:4; Prov 17:22). In the sense of to be dry, ripe (Rev 14:15; Sept.: Jer 12:4; Hos 9:16).

Syn.: *maraínō* (3133), to fade away.
Ant.: *bréchō* (1026), to wet.

3584. **ξηρός** *xērós*; fem. *xērá*, neut. *xērón*, adj. Dry. Used of the body or its members (John 5:3); of the hand (Matt 12:10; Luke 6:6, 8); of a tree, withered (Luke 23:31). A green tree and a dry tree are used to symbolize the righteous and the wicked (Sept.: Isa 56:3; Ezek 17:24; 20:47 [cf. Ps 1:3]). The dry land as opposed to the sea (Matt 23:15; Heb 11:29; Sept.: Gen 1:9, 10; Jon 1:9).

Deriv.: *xēraínō* (3583), to dry.
Syn.: *ánudros* (504), waterless.
Ant.: *hugrós* (5200), wet, green, fresh; *chlōrós* (5515), greenish, verdant, moist.

3585. **ξύλινος** *xúlinos*; fem. *xulínē*, neut. *xúlinon*, adj. from *xúlon* (3586), wood. Wooden, made of wood (2 Tim 2:20; Rev 9:20; Sept.: Lev 11:32; Deut 10:1).

3586. **ξύλον** *xúlon*; gen. *xúlou*, neut. noun from *xúō* (n.f.), to scrape. Wood, generally for fuel, timber (1 Cor 3:12; Rev 18:12; see Gen 22:3, 6ff.). Anything made of wood: a staff, club (Matt 26:47, 55; Mark 14:43, 48; Luke 22:52); stocks or wooden blocks with holes in which the feet and sometimes the hands and neck of prisoners were confined (Acts 16:24; Sept.: Job 33:11); a stake, cross, equivalent to *staurós* (4716), stake, post (Acts 5:30; 10:39; 13:29; Gal 3:13; 1 Pet 2:24; see Sept.: Deut 21:22, 23; Esth 5:14 [cf. Josh 10:26, 27]). In Luke 23:31, *en tṓ hugrṓ xúlō* (*en* [1722], in; *tṓ*, the dat. sing. of *tó*, the neut. def. art. *ho* [3588], the; *hugrṓ*, the dat. neut. sing. of *hugrós* [5200], wet), in the wet wood, refers to a living tree in contrast to a dead one, *xērṓ* (the dat. sing. of *xērós* [3584], dry one). In Rev 2:7; 22:2, 14, it is conceivable that the "tree of life" may be an allusion to the cross and could be rendered "wood of life" (a.t.). Sept.: Gen 1:11, 12; 2:9.

Deriv.: *xúlinos* (3585), wooden.
Syn.: *rhábdos* (4464), rod; *déndron* (1186), a tree; *staurós* (4716), cross.

3587. **ξυράω** *xuráō*; contracted *xurṓ*, fut. *xurḗsō*, from *xurón* (n.f.), a razor. To shave or shear the locks or beard; in the mid. *xuráomai* (Acts 21:24, "that they may shave their heads," meaning let them be shorn); in the pass. part. fem. *exurēménē* (1 Cor 11:5, 6, "shorn" or shaven; Sept.: Gen 41:14; Num 6:9, 19).

Ant.: *komáō* (2863), to let the hair grow long.

O

3588. ὁ *ho*; fem. *hē*, neut. *tó*, def. art. Originally a demonstrative pron. meaning this, that, but in Attic and later usage it became mostly a prepositive art. The.

(I) As a def. art., the, that, this (Matt 21:7; John 6:10; 7:40; Gal 5:8; Col 4:16 [cf. Rom 16:22; 1 Thess 5:27]). Of this or that way (Acts 9:2; 19:9, 23; 24:22 [cf. 22:4]).

(II) The neut. art. *tó* is often applied in a similar sense in Luke 22:2 with *pós* (4459), how, *tó pós*, meaning "how [literally, the how] they might kill Him" (cf. Luke 22:4; 19:48; Acts 4:21). Also similarly with *tís* (5101) in Luke 9:46, meaning a dispute arose among them, namely, who should be the greatest of them (cf. Luke 22:24). Similarly in Mark 9:23, "And Jesus said unto him [this, or thus], If thou canst believe."

(III) Used as an emphatic, *hē parthénos*, "the virgin" (a.t., italics added [Matt 1:23]); *ho huiós* (5207), son, *ho hoiós mou*, my son; *ho agapētós* (27), the beloved one, my beloved Son (Matt 3:17).

(IV) It is prefixed to the noun when used for the voc. case as in Luke 8:54; Rom 8:15.

(V) Used in an explanatory or exegetical manner as "to wit," "that is to say" (Rom 8:23).

(VI) Often prefixed to proper nouns as *ho Iēsoús*, Jesus or *ho Iōánnēs*, John (Matt 3:13, 14). The art. of any gender are prefixed to adv. which are then to be construed as nouns, such as *ho ésō* (2080), inside, the inner one, as opposed to *ho éxō* (1854), the outside one, the outer; *ho plēsíon* (4139), the near, the near one or a neighbor; *tá ánō* (507), above, the things above.

(VII) Used as an indef. art. corresponding to the Eng. a or an; any sower (Matt 13:3).

(VIII) Before verbs it is frequently used in the nom. for *autós* (846), this one, meaning he (Matt 13:28, 29).

(IX) Repeated with the part. *mén* (3303) and *dé* (1161) subjoined, *ho mén / ho dé*, meaning the one and the other, also in the pl., *hoi mén / hoi dé*, some and the others (Phil 1:16, 17 [cf. Matt 13:23]). Some-times *hoi dé* is used in an absolute sense for some or by all concerned without being preceded by *hoi mén* (Matt 26:67; 28:17; John 19:29).

(X) With a part., it may be generally rendered by who, that, which, and the part., as if it were a noun preceded by the art. Thus 1 John 2:4, *ho légōn*, the one saying or the one who says, meaning the person saying. See John 1:18, *ho ōn*, "the one being [or who has always been] in the bosom of the Father" (a.t.). It is used elliptically often implying the part. *ōn* (5607), being, especially before a prep. or adv. as in Matt 6:9, *ho en toís ouranoís*, "the one [*ōn*, being] in heaven" (a.t.). See Matt 5:12, *toús pró humón*, implying *óntas*, "those being before you" (a.t.); Acts 13:9; Col 3:5.

(XI) With a proper noun in the gen. following, it often denotes affinity as in Matt 10:3, *ho toú Alphaiou* "James the son of Alpheus," but where "the son" is implied. See Mark 16:1, "Mary the mother of James" (cf. Mark 15:40); John 19:25, meaning Mary the wife of Cleophas; Acts 7:16.

(XII) The neut. art. *tó* in the sing. or pl. with a noun in the gen. implies possession, property, or relation as Matt 22:21, "the things of Caesar" (a.t. [see Rom 8:5 {cf. Matt 21:21; Luke 2:49; 1 Cor 7:32–34}]).

(XIII) The neut. art. sing. *tó* is used in several adv. phrases, the prep. *katá* (2596) and the noun *prágma* (4229), thing, or the like, being understood as in Acts 4:18, *tó kathólou*, meaning at all, for *katá tó prágma* or *chrḗma* (5536), need, *kathólou*. See Luke 11:3, *tó kath' hēméran*, for *katá tó kath' hēméran chrḗma*, meaning according to our daily need; in Rom 9:5, *tó katá sárka*, meaning in respect of the flesh.

(XIV) When the art. is omitted, the special qualities of a person or thing are spoken about, e.g., in John 1:18 *Theón* (2316), God, referring not to any theophany in any visible and limited appearance but God in His eternal, infinite and spiritual self-existence. When the def. art. is used as in John 1:1b, "and the Word had been toward the God [*tón Theón*]," (a.t.) reference is made to the Father as a distinct personality within the Trinity. See Rev 1:1, "The Revelation of Jesus Christ which God [*ho Theós* with the def. art.] gave unto him." Clearly the inclusion of the art. makes "God" refer to the Father.

3589. ὀγδοήκοντα *ogdoḗkonta*; indeclinable, used for all genders, cardinal number, from *oktṓ* (3638), eight. Eighty (Luke 2:37; 16:7).

3590. ὄγδοος *ógdoos*; fem. *ogdóē*, neut. *ógdoon*, ordinal number, from *oktṓ* (3638), eight. Eighth (Luke 1:59; Acts 7:8; Rev 17:11; 21:20). In 2 Pet 2:5, where it speaks of Noah, the eighth person, it means one of eight, i.e., Noah and seven others (cf. 1 Pet 3:20).

3591. ὄγκος *ógkos*; gen. *ógkou*, masc. noun. A tumor, mass, magnitude, weight, burden, impediment (Heb 12:1 where the apostle speaks of our Christian course under the similitude of a race).
Deriv.: *hupérogkos* (5246), oversized, much swollen.
Syn.: *báros* (922), weight, burden.

3592. ὅδε *hóde*; fem. *hḗde*; neut. *tóde*; demonstrative pron. from *ho* (3588), the, as a pron., and the enclitic particle *dé* (1161), this, that. This, that, such a one. It refers to the person or thing which was last mentioned (Luke 10:39; 16:25). It introduces what follows (Acts 15:23;

21:11; Rev 2:1, 8, 12, 18; 3:1, 7, 14). Used instead of an adv. for here, there (James 4:13).

3593. ὁδεύω *hodeúō*; fut. *hodeúsō*, from *hodós* (3598), way. To be on the way, to journey, travel (Luke 10:33).
Deriv.: *diodeúō* (1353), to travel or pass through; *sunodeúō* (4922), to journey with or accompany.
Syn.: *poreúomai* (4198), to proceed, go; *diaporeúomai* (1279), to travel through; *apodēméō* (589), to go on a journey to another country.
Ant.: *ménō* (3306), to abide; *kataménō* (2650), to reside; *paraménō* (3887), to remain around; *diatríbō* (1304), to stay; *aulízomai* (835), to lodge.

3594. ὁδηγέω *hodēgéō*; contracted *hodēgṓ*, fut. *hodēgḗsō*, from *hodēgós* (3595), guide, leader. To lead the way, guide (Matt 15:14; Luke 6:39; Rev 7:17; Sept.: Ex 13:17; Josh 24:3; Ps 80:2). Metaphorically, of teaching (John 16:13; Acts 8:31; Sept.: Ps 25:5; 86:11).
Syn.: *kateuthúnō* (2720), to direct; *hēgéomai* (2233), to lead; *ágō* (71), to lead, to bring; *exágō* (1806), to bring out; *proḯstēmi* (4291), to rule over.
Ant.: *akolouthéō* (190), to follow.

3595. ὁδηγός *hodēgós*; gen. *hodēgoú*, masc noun from *hodós* (3598), way, and *hēgéomai* (2233), to lead. A leader of the way, a guide (Acts 1:16). Metaphorically, of a teacher (Matt 15:14; 23:16, 24; Rom 2:19).
Deriv.: *odēgéō* (3594), to guide, lead.
Syn.: *pródromos* (4274), one who runs ahead, forerunner; *prógonos* (4269), an ancestor, forefather; *árchōn* (757), a ruler; *politárches* (4173), a ruler of a city.
Ant.: *diádochos* (1240), successor; *mathētḗs* (3101), a learner; *mathḗtria* (3102), a female disciple; *hetaíros* (2083), a comrade, fellow; *súntrophos* (4939), a comrade.

3596. ὁδοιπορέω *hodoiporéō*; contracted *hodoiporṓ*, fut. *hodēporḗsō*, from *hodoipóros* (n.f.), traveling, which is from *hodós* (3598), way, and *póros* (n.f.), passage. To be on the way, to travel (Acts 10:9).

Deriv.: *hodoiporía* (3597), journeying.

Syn.: *hodeúō* (3593), to be on a journey; *sunodeúō* (4922), to accompany, journey with; *apodēméō* (589), to go on a journey to another county, emigrate; *diérchomai* (1330), to go or pass through; *ágō* (71), to lead, go; *metabaínō* (3327), to go over; *apérchomai* (565), *hupágō* (5217), *apobaínō* (576), and *ápeimi* (549), to go away; *anachōréō* (402), to depart; *hupochōréō* (5298), to go back, retire; *proérchomai* (4281), to go before, precede; *probaínō* (4260), to go on forward; *éxeimi* (1826), to go out; *diodeúō* (1353), to travel throughout; *anérchomai* (424), to go up; *periérchomai* (4022), to go around; *katérchomai* (2718), to go down; *paragínomai* (3854), to go; *ekporeúomai* (1607), to go out of; *diaperáō* (1276), to pass through; *diodeúō* (1353), to go through; *peripatéō* (4043), to walk; *stoichéō* (4748), to walk in an orderly manner.

Ant.: *méno* (3306), to remain, abide; *kataménō* (2650), to reside; *paraménō* (3887), to remain around; *diatríbō* (1304), to stay; *aulízomai* (835), to lodge.

3597. όδοιπορία *hodoiporía*; gen. *hodoiporías*, fem. noun from *hodoiporéō* (3596), to go on a journey. A journey, travel (John 4:6; 2 Cor 11:26).

Ant.: *katápausis* (2663), stopping.

3598. όδός *hodós*; gen. *hodoú*, fem. noun. Way.

(I) In respect to place, a way, highway, road, street.

(A) Used generally (Matt 2:12; 8:28; 13:4, 19; Acts 8:26; James 2:25; Sept.: Num 21:4; Deut 28:7); of a street in a city (Matt 22:9, 10; Luke 14:23; Sept.: Jer 5:1; 7:17). The phrase *katá tḗn hodón* (*katá* [2596], along), along or on the way (Luke 10:4; Acts 8:36).

(B) Followed by the gen. of place meaning to which a way leads (Heb 9:8, a way or entrance into the sanctuary; Sept.: Gen 3:24). Metonymically for the whole region through which the way leads (Matt 4:15, "the way of the sea," meaning the region around the Sea of Galilee quoted from Isa 8:23; Matt 10:5, "into the way," meaning the country of the Gentiles).

(C) In the phrases *hetoimázō* (2090), to prepare, and *kataskeuázo* (2680), to fit, *tḗn hodón*, meaning to prepare the way for a king (Rev 16:12); metaphorically (Matt 3:3; 11:10; Mark 1:2, 3). With the verb *euthúnō* (2116), to straighten, *tḗn hodón* (John 1:23, to straighten or to make ready). These all allude to Isa 40:3.

(D) Metonymously of Jesus as the way, i.e., the author and medium of access to God and eternal life (John 14:6).

(II) In action, way, i.e., a being on the way, a going, journey, progress, course.

(A) Generally, *eis tḗn hodón* (*eis* [1519], unto) for the way or journey (Luke 9:3). With *ex* (1537), out of or from, followed by the gen. *ex hodoú* (Luke 11:6, from the way); *en tḗ hodṓ* (*en* [1722], in), in or by the way, on the journey (Matt 15:32; Mark 8:3, 27; Acts 9:17, 27); *katá* (2596) by, *katá tḗn hodón*, by or on the way (Acts 25:3; 26:13); *kateuthúnō* (2720), to direct, guide the way (1 Thess 3:11); *poreúomai* (4198), go, *poreúomai tḗn hodón*, to go on one's way, continue one's journey (Acts 8:39); with *poiéō* (4160), to make, "and his disciples began to go plucking the ears of corn" (a.t.) meaning they went along plucking the ears (Mark 2:23). The use of *hodón poiéō*, to make, is a Hebraism from Judg 17:8. Used generally (Sept.: Gen 24:21, 40; 42:25; 45:21).

(B) Following the gen. of time (Luke 2:44; Acts 1:12, "a Sabbath day's journey" [a.t.], 1,000 large paces, equal to about seven and one-half furlongs; Sept.: Gen 30:36; 31:23).

(III) Metaphorically meaning way, manner, means.

(A) Way or method of proceeding, of doing or affecting something (1 Cor 4:17; 12:31). *Hai hodoí* means the way of proceeding, administration, counsels (Acts 13:10; Rom 11:33; Rev 15:3; Sept.: Ps 18:31).

(B) Way or means of arriving at or obtaining something as a means of salvation (Luke 1:79); a way of life (Acts 2:28; 16:17; 2 Pet 2:21; Sept.: Prov 10:17).

(C) Way of thinking, feeling, acting, manner of life and conduct (Matt 21:32, living a just and holy life); way of peace or peaceful life (Rom 3:17, quoted from Isa 59:8; see James 5:20). Followed by the gen. of person, the way or ways of someone, meaning his way of life, conduct, actions (Acts 14:16; Rom 3:16; James 1:8; 2 Pet 2:15; Jude 1:11; Sept.: Job 23:10). The way of God or of the Lord is also the way, walk, or life which God approves and requires (Matt 22:16; Luke 20:21; Acts 18:25, 26; Heb 3:10; Sept.: Job 23:11; Ps 25:4). Hence used in an absolute sense for the Christian way, the Christian religion (Acts 9:2; 19:9, 23; 22:4; 24:14, 22). "The way of truth" (2 Pet 2:2) means the way of true faith.

Deriv.: *ámphodon* (296), when two roads meet; *eísodos* (1529), entrance, access; *éxodos* (1841), way out, exodus, an exit; *hodeúō* (3593), to travel, journey; *hodēgós* (3595), guide, leader; *párodos* (3938), a passing or passage; *sunodía* (4923), a caravan.

Syn.: *drómos* (1408), a race, running, career, course; *tríbos* (5147), a worn path; *trochiá* (5163), a track of a wheel; *trópos* (5158), manner.

3599. ὁδούς odoús; gen. *odóntos*, masc. noun. A tooth (Matt 5:38; 8:12; 13:42, 50; 22:13; 24:51; 25:30; Mark 9:18; Luke 13:28; Acts 7:54; Rev 9:8; Sept.: Lev 24:20; Job 16:9).

3600. ὁδυνάω odunáō; contracted *odunṓ*, fut. *odunḗsō*, from *odúnē* (3601), sorrow. To pain, distress in body or mind. In the NT, only pass. or mid., meaning to be pained, distressed, sorrowful (Luke

2:48; 16:24, 25; Acts 20:38; Sept.: Zech 9:5; 12:10).

Syn.: *stenochōréomai* (4729), to be crowded into a narrow space, be distressed; *sunéchomai* (4912), to be held together, be pressed, to be sick; *lupéomai* (3076), to grieve; *basanízomai* (928) and *kakouchéō* (2558), to be tormented.

Ant.: *paramuthéomai* (3888), to be soothed, consoled, encouraged; *parakaléomai* (3870), to be comforted; *eupsuchéō* (2174), to take heart; *tharséō* (2293), to have courage; *chaírō* (5463), to rejoice; *agalliáō* (21), to exult; *euphraínō* (2165), to make or be merry.

3601. ὁδύνη odúnē; gen. *odúnēs*, fem. noun. Sorrow, torment, grief, pain, distress of body or mind (Rom 9:2; 1 Tim 6:10; Sept.: Gen 35:18; Job 7:3; Jer 8:18).

Deriv.: *odunáō* (3600), to pain.

Syn.: *lúpē* (3077), sorrow; *ōdín* (5604), a birth pang; *pénthos* (3997), mourning; *kakopátheia* (2552), suffering, affliction; *kákōsis* (2561), ill-treatment; *páthēma* (3804), affliction; *thlípsis* (2347), pressure, tribulation; *stenochōría* (4730), anguish; *anágkē* (318), distress; *diōgmós* (1375), persecution; *sunochḗ* (4928), compression, narrowing of the way, distress; *tarachḗ* (5016), agitation, disturbance, trouble.

Ant.: *thársos* (2294), encouragement; *paráklēsis* (3874), consolation, *paramuthía* (3889), comfort with tenderness; *paramúthion* (3890), means of comforting; *parēgoría* (3931), soothing, comfort.

3602. ὁδυρμός odurmós; gen. *odurmoú*, masc. noun from *odúromai* (n.f.), to bewail. Wailing, lamentation, mourning (Matt 2:18, quoted from Jer 31:15; 2 Cor 7:7).

Syn.: *pénthos* (3997), mourning; *lúpē* (3077), sorrow; *odúnē* (3601), pain; *ōdín* (5604), a birth pang; *klauthmós* (2805), weeping.

3603. ὁ ἐστί ho estí epexegetical expression from the neut. of *hós* (3739), which, and *estí*, pres. act. indic. 3d person sing. of *eimí* (1510), to be. Used like our Eng., "that is to say" (Mark 3:17; 7:11, 34; 12:42; 15:16, 42; Eph 6:17; Col 1:24; Heb 7:2; Rev 21:8, 17).

3604. 'Οζίας *Ozías*; gen. *Ozíou*, masc. proper noun transliterated from the Hebr. 'Uzīāh (5818, OT), might of Jehovah. Uzziah, a godly king of Judah from 811 to 759 B.C. (Matt 1:8, 9). See 2 Chr 26 (cf. 2 Kgs 15, where he is called Azariah).

3605. ὄζω *ózō*; fut. *ozḗsō*. To smell, emit an odor. As a corpse, to stink (John 11:39; Sept.: Ex 8:14).
  Deriv.: *osmḗ* (3744), a smell, odor.
  Ant.: *murízō* (3462), to apply perfume, anoint.

3606. ὅθεν *hóthen*; relative adv. from *hós* (3739), who, which, and the syllabic ending -*then*, denoting from or at a place. Whence, used of place (Matt 12:44; Luke 11:24; Acts 14:26; Heb 11:19; Sept.: Ps 121:1). In the sense of *ekeíthen* (1564), thence, there, and *hópou* (3699), where, *ekeíthen hópou*, from the place where (see Matt 25:24, 26, "gather where I have not strewed"; Acts 28:13). Of a source (1 John 2:18). Used as an illative, as referring to a cause, ground, motive, equivalent to wherefore, whereupon (Matt 14:7; Acts 26:19; Heb 2:17; 3:1; 7:25; 8:3; 9:18).
  Ant.: *enteúthen* (1782), hence, from here.

3607. ὀθόνη *othónē*; gen. *othónēs*, fem. noun. Fine white linen. Generally linen cloth, e.g., a sheet, sail (Acts 10:11; 11:5).
  Deriv.: *othónion* (3608), a small linen cloth, bandage.
  Syn.: *línon* (3043), linen; *sindṓn* (4616), sheet; *bússos* (1040), fine, white linen.

3608. ὀθόνιον *othónion*; gen. *othoníou*, neut. noun, a diminutive of *othónē* (3607),

a linen cloth, sheet. A smaller linen cloth, bandage. In the NT, used only of material in which dead bodies were swathed for burial (Luke 24:12; John 19:40; 20:5–7; Sept.: Judg 14:13).
  Syn.: *sindṓn* (4616), bleached linen, sheet for wrapping; *bússos* (1040), fine, white linen.

3608a. οἶδα *oída*. See *eídō* (1492, II), generally meaning to know intuitively or instinctively.

3609. οἰκεῖος *oikeíos*; fem. *oikeía*, neut. *oikeíon*, adj. from *oíkos* (3624), a house or household. Belonging to a certain household (1 Tim 5:8); subst. one belonging to a certain house. Used of a believer, one belonging to the Church which is the household of God (Gal 6:10; Eph 2:19; Sept.: Lev 18:6; 21:2). See *oikétēs* (3610), a household servant.
  Syn.: *oikiakós* (3615), belonging to one's household; *suggenḗs* (4773), a relative.
  Ant.: *xénos* (3581), a stranger; *allótrios* (245), a stranger, one belonging to another race or group; *allogenḗs* (241), a foreigner; *pároikos* (3941), an alien, sojourner; *parepídēmos* (3927), a resident alien; *héteros* (2087), another of a different kind, a stranger.

3610. οἰκέτης *oikétēs*; gen. *oikétou*, masc. noun from *oíkos* (3624), house. A domestic servant (Luke 16:13; Acts 10:7; Rom 14:4; 1 Pet 2:18; Sept.: Gen 9:25; 27:37). One of the household, belonging to the family but not *oikogenḗs* (n.f.), one necessarily born in the house. *Oikétēs* does not bring out the servile relation as strongly as does *doúlos* (1401), slave.
  Deriv.: *oiketeía*, a household of servants (Matt 24:45 UBS).
  Syn.: *diákonos* (1249), a servant, minister, deacon; *país* (3816), an attendant, boy, one acting as a servant; *hupērétēs* (5257), an under-rower, a menial servant; *therápōn* (2324), attendant, healer; *místhios* (3407) and *misthōtós* (3411), hired servant; *doúlos* (1401), slave.

Ant.: *oikodespótēs* (3617), master of a house; *despótēs* (1203), absolute owner, master; *epistátēs* (1988), chief, commander, overseer; *kúrios* (1962), lord, owner, master.

3611. οἰκέω *oikéō*; contracted *oikṓ*, fut. *oikḗsō*, from *oíkos* (3624), a dwelling. To reside, dwell, abide.

(I) Intrans.: followed by *en* (1722), in, to dwell in, metaphorically of the Holy Spirit abiding in Christians (Rom 8:9, 11; 1 Cor 3:16). Of sin or a sinful propensity abiding in men (Rom 7:17, 18, 20; Sept.: Gen 19:30). Followed by *metá* (3326), with, with the gen., to dwell with someone, and as spoken of man and wife, to live together, cohabit (1 Cor 7:12, 13; Sept.: Prov 21:19 [cf. 1 Kgs 3:17]).

(II) Trans.: to dwell in, inhabit (1 Tim 6:16; Sept.: Gen 24:13).

Deriv.: *enoikéō* (1774), to dwell in; *katoikéō* (2730), to settle down in a dwelling; *oíkēma* (3612), a house; *oikḗterion* (3613), habitation; *oikouménē* (3625), the inhabited world; *paroikéō* (3939), to sojourn, dwell temporarily; *perioikéō* (4039), to dwell around, as a neighbor; *sunoikéō* (4924), to dwell with.

Syn.: *ménō* (3306), to abide, remain; *skēnóō* (4637), to pitch a tent; *kataskēnóō* (2681), to pitch one's tent; *embateúō* (1687), to dwell in, metaphorically to trespass unlawfully, invade.

Ant.: *astatéō* (790), to wander about without a permanent dwelling place.

3612. οἴκημα *oíkēma*; gen. *oikḗmatos*, neut. noun from *oikéō* (3611), to dwell. A house, dwelling, prison (Acts 12:7).

3613. οἰκητήριον *oikētḗrion*; gen. *oikētēríou*, neut. noun from *oikéō* (3611), to dwell. A dwelling, habitation, abode, e.g., of angels, who supposedly relinquished heaven out of love for the daughters of men (Jude 1:6; see Gen 6:2). Figuratively of the future spiritual body as the abode of the soul (2 Cor 5:2; Sept.: Jer 25:30).

Deriv.: *katoikētḗrion* (2732), a habitation, dwelling-place.

3614. οἰκία *oikía*; gen. *oikías*, fem. noun from *oíkos* (3624), a house. A building, house, dwelling. *Oíkos* had a broader range than *oikía*. *Oíkos* is the whole of person's possessions, his whole estate, whereas *oikía* is simply his residence and only occasionally includes its contents.

(I) In the NT *oikía* is used for an actual house (Matt 2:11; 5:15; 7:24–27; 8:6, 14; 9:10, 23, 28; 10:12, 14; 12:29; 13:1, 36, 57; 17:25; 19:29; 24:17; 26:6; Mark 1:29; 2:15; 3:25, 27; 6:10; 7:24; 9:33; 10:10, 30; 13:15, 34; 14:3; Luke 4:38; 5:29; 6:48, 49; 7:6, 37, 44; 8:27, 51; 9:4; 10:5, 7, 38; 15:8, 25; 17:31; 18:29; 22:10, 11, 54; John 11:31; 12:3; Acts 4:34; 9:11, 17; 10:6, 17, 32; 11:11; 12:12; 16:32; 17:5; 18:7; 1 Cor 11:22; 1 Tim 5:13; 2 Tim 2:20; 3:6; 2 John 1:10; Sept.: Gen 19:4; Ex 1:21).

(II) It came to figuratively mean family, household (Matt 10:13; 12:25; Mark 6:4; John 4:53; 1 Cor 16:15; Sept.: Gen 50:8). In Mark 10:29 *oikía* refers to the whole family.

(III) The word can also mean possessions, one's belongings (Matt 23:14; Mark 12:40, the expression "which devour widow's houses [*oikías*]," means widows' [a.t.] possessions which are precious and needed; Luke 20:47). In Mark 13:35 the expression "the master of the house [*oikías*]" is equivalent to *ho oikodespótēs* (3617) which is commonly translated "householder" (Matt 13:27, 52; 20:1; 21:33) or "goodman of the house" (Matt 24:43).

(IV) The word *oikía* can also be used figuratively, as in John 8:35, as a reference to the kingdom of God. The term *oikía* does not refer to a ruling house, but simply to a family. In John 14:2, which states that, "in my Father's house [*oikía*] are many mansions [*monaí*, pl. of *monḗ* {3438}, resting places]." This may have reference to individual places for families even as they lived on earth.

In 2 Cor 5:1 the metaphorical *oikía toú skḗnous*, "the house of this tabernacle," denotes the corruptible body which we have on earth. Its counterpart is *oikodomḗ* (3619), a building in process of preparation by God, incorruptible, eternal, a house "in the heavens".

In Phil 4:22, "those of the household of Caesar" (a.t.) might mean the ruling family with all its members, but more likely the staff of the imperial household, both slaves and freedmen. (See Sept.: Gen 24:2.)

Deriv.: *oikiakós* (3615), a relative, pertaining to one's family or household.

3615. οἰκιακός *oikiakós*; fem. *oikiakḗ*, neut. *oikiakón*; adj. from *oikía* (3614), house, sometimes including its contents. Belonging to the house, domestic. Equivalent to *oikeíos* (3609). In the NT used only in the pl., *hoi oikiakoí*, followed by the gen., those of one's house, household or family (Matt 10:25, 36).

Syn.: *patriá* (3965), ancestry, lineage, family or tribe.

Ant.: *xénos* (3581), stranger.

3616.οἰκοδεσποτέω*oikodespotéō*;contracted *oikodespotṓ*, fut. *oikodespotḗsō*, from *oikodespótēs* (3617), the master of the house To be master of a house exercising authority, with the emphasis on absolute rule, as of a despot (*despótēs* [1203]). To govern or manage a household or the domestic affairs of a family (1 Tim 5:14). As the ruler of the house is *oikodespótēs*, the one who serves is *oikétēs* (3610), a house servant.

Syn.: *hēgéomai* (2233), to lead, but not with the emphasis of despotic lordship; *árchō* (757), to be the head of, stronger than *hēgéomai*, but not as strong as *oikodespotéō*; *proḯstēmi* (4291), to stand before, preside over, meaning to lead; *brabeúō* (1018), to arbitrate, to decide as an umpire for the sake of awarding a prize.

Ant.: *diakonéō* (1247), to minister; *douleúō* (1398), to serve as a *doúlos* (1401), slave; *latreúō* (3000), to labor

but also to worship, implying that there is labor in worship and worship in labor; *hupēretéō* (5256), to serve as an underrower, i.e., in a subservient capacity.

3617. οἰκοδεσπότης *oikodespótēs*; gen. *oikodespótou*, masc. noun from *oíkos* (3624), a house and *despótēs* (1203), a lord, despot, master. The master of the house, head of a family (Matt 10:25; 13:27, 52; 20:1, 11; 21:33; 24:43; Mark 14:14; Luke 12:39; 13:25; 14:21; 22:11).

Deriv.: *oikodespotéō* (3616), to act as head of the house or family.

Syn.: *despótēs* (1203), absolute owner, master; *epistátēs* (1988), chief, commander, overseer; *kúrios* (1962), lord, owner, master.

Ant.: *oikétēs* (3610), a house servant.

3618. οἰκοδομέω *oikodoméō*; contracted *oikodomṓ*, fut. *oikodomḗsō*, from *oikodómos* (n.f.), building a house, builder. To build, construct, erect. Trans.:

(I) Particularly *oikían* (3614), a house (Luke 6:48), a tower (Matt 21:33; Mark 12:1; Luke 14:28); a temple (Mark 14:58; Luke 12:18). Followed by a dat. (Luke 7:5; Acts 7:47, 49); with *epí* (1909), upon, with the acc. (Matt 7:24, 26; Luke 6:49). Used in an absolute sense (Luke 14:30; 17:28; John 2:20). Particularly *hoi oikodomoúntes*, the building ones, meaning the builders (Matt 21:42; Mark 12:10; Luke 20:17; Acts 4:11; 1 Pet 2:7). With *epí* (1909), upon (Sept.: Ezek 16:31). Metaphorically of a system of instruction or doctrine (Rom 15:20; Gal 2:18).

(II) By implication, to rebuild or renew a building decayed or destroyed (Matt 23:29, such as the sepulchers of the prophets; Luke 11:47, 48; see also Matt 26:61; 27:40; Mark 15:29; Sept.: Josh 6:26; Job 12:14; Amos 9:14).

(III) Metaphorically, to build up, establish, confirm. Spoken of the Christian Church and its members who are thus compared to a building, a temple of God, erected upon the one and only foundation, Jesus Christ (1 Cor 3:9, *oikodomḗ* [3619], building; 1 Cor 3:10, *epoikodomeí*, pres. act. indic. 3d person sing. of *epoikodoméō* [2026], to build upon) and ever built up progressively and unceasingly more and more from the foundation.

(**A**) Externally (Matt 16:18, "On this stone I shall build my church" [a.t.]; Acts 9:31; 1 Pet 2:5).

(**B**) Internally, in a good sense, to build up in the faith, to edify, to cause to advance in the divine light (1 Cor 8:1; 10:23; 14:4, 17; 1 Thess 5:11). In a bad sense, to embolden (1 Cor 8:10).

Deriv.: *anoikodoméō* (456), to build again; *epoikodoméō* (2026), to build upon; *sunoikodoméō* (4925), to build together.

Syn.: *kataskeuázō* (2680), to prepare, establish, build; *ktízō* (2936), to create, make; *plássō* (1411), to shape; *morphóō* (3445), to form; *suntássō* (4929), to arrange together.

Ant.: *katargéō* (2673), to abolish; *kathairéō* (2507), to cast down; *lúō* (3089), to demolish; *katalúō* (2647), to destroy completely; *phtheírō* (5351), to corrupt; *diaphtheírō* (1311), to completely corrupt.

3619. οἰκοδομή *oikodomḗ*; gen. *oikodomḗs*, fem. noun, a later word used for *oikodómēsis* (n.f.), a building up. The act of building, building as a process, also that which is built, the building. NT meanings: a building, edifice (Matt 24:1; Mark 13:1, 2 [cf. 1 Cor 3:9; 2 Cor 5:1; Eph 2:21]); edification, spiritual profit or advancement (Rom 14:19; 15:2; 1 Cor 14:3, 5, 12, 26; 2 Cor 10:8; 12:19; 13:10; Eph 4:12, 16, 29).

In 1 Cor 14:26–31 the outstanding admonition to the brethren who lead in the public worship is that only one at a time should speak. "How is it then, brethren? when ye come together, every one of you hath a psalm, hath a doctrine . . . hath a revelation. Let all things be done unto edifying." It is unfortunate that the Gr. word *hékastos* (1538), each or every one, meaning each individual, is translated "every one." It should be each one as an individual. It derives from *hekás* which means separate. The injunction is that each one should speak separately, and not while others are speaking. It should be done for public edification.

The word for "edification" is *oikodomḗ* (3619), building up the house (*oíkos* [3624]). A house is a building to shelter people. When one is in public worship, the paramount concern must be how all the believers should be built up and not how someone or a small group may selfishly benefit by the public experience. In Christian worship individuals ought to be concerned how they can spiritually benefit others by what they do or say.

Syn.: *endómēsis* (1739), a thing built, structure; *ktísis* (2937), a creation.

Ant.: *katastrophḗ* (2692), destruction.

3620. οἰκοδομία *oikodomía*; gen. *oikodomías*, fem. noun from *oikodoméō* (3618), to build. A building up, the act of building. Used metaphorically for edification, spiritual advancement (1 Tim 1:4 [TR]). The same as *oikodomḗ* (3619), a building in process of construction.

Syn.: *endómēsis* (1739), a thing built, structure; *ktísis* (2937), a creation, creature, building.

Ant.: *kathaíresis* (2506), demolition.

3621. οἰκονομέω *oikonoméō*; contracted *oikonomṓ*, fut. *oikonomḗsō*, from *oikonómos* (3623), a house manager. To be a manager of a household, a steward (Luke 16:2).

Deriv.: *oikonomía* (3622), administration, stewardship.

Syn.: *oikodespotéō* (3616), to rule a household.

3622. οἰκονομία *oikonomía*; gen. *oikonomías*, fem. noun from *oikonoméō* (3621), to be a manager of a household. The position, work, responsibility or arrangement of an administration, as of a house or of property, either one's own or another's (Luke 16:2; Sept.: Isa 22:19); a spiritual dispensation, management, or economy (1 Cor 9:17; Eph 1:10; 3:2; Col

1:25). The "dispensation of God" means the administration of divine grace.

Act., the administrative activity of the owner or of the steward; pass., that which is administered, the administration or dispensation of the fullness of times (Eph 1:10). The object of *oikonomía*, dispensation, is the relative phrase *hến proétheto* of Eph 1:9, translated "which he hath purposed." It is the divine purpose which is said to be administered. The meaning is the administration of God's saving purpose pertaining to the fullness of the times. Therefore, *oikonomía* here is to be taken as pass. See Eph 3:2, 9 (UBS); 1 Tim 1:4 (UBS).

3623.　οἰκονόμος *oikonómos*; gen. *oikonómou*, masc. noun from *oíkos* (3624), house, and *némō* (n.f., see *aponémō* [632]), to deal out, distribute, apportion. An administrator, a person who manages the domestic affairs of a family, business, or minor, a treasurer, a chamberlain of a city, a house manager, overseer, steward.

(I) Particularly, one who has authority over the servants or slaves of a family to assign their tasks and portions. Along with this was the general management of affairs and accounts. Such persons were themselves usually slaves (Luke 12:42 [cf. Eliezer {Gen 15:2} and Joseph {Gen 39:4}]). Free persons appear also to have been thus employed (Luke 16:1, 3, 4, 8). The *oikonómoi* also had some charge over the sons of a family, probably in respect to monetary matters, thus differing from the *epítropoi* (2012), guardians or tutors (Gal 4:2 [cf. Gen 24:3]).

(II) In a wider sense, one who administers a public charge or office, a steward, minister, agent, generally (1 Cor 4:2); of the fiscal officer of a city or state, treasurer (Rom 16:23). Metaphorically of the Apostles and other teachers as stewards or ministers of the gospel (1 Cor 4:1; Titus 1:7; 1 Pet 4:10).

Deriv.: *oikonoméō* (3621), to be a manager of a household.

Syn.: *epítropos* (2012), guardian; *epistátēs* (1988), an overseer, master, one who stands over; *archēgós* (747), leader, captain; *árchōn* (758), ruler; *hēgemṓn* (2232), leader; *megistán* (3175), great man; *oikodespótēs* (3617), ruler of a household.

Ant.: *oikétēs* (3610), a house servant; *doúlos* (1401), slave, servant.

3624.　οἶκος *oíkos*; gen. *oíkou*, masc. noun. A house, dwelling, home.

(I) Generally (Matt 9:6, 7; Mark 5:19; Luke 1:40; John 7:53; Acts 10:22). With the preposition *en* (1722) in, *en oíkō*, at home (1 Cor 11:34; 14:35; Sept.: Gen 39:2, 16); with the prep. *katá* (2596) with the acc., possessing a distributive meaning, *kat' oíkon*, from house to house, in private houses (Acts 2:46; 5:42; 8:3; 20:20; Rom 16:5, the church at a private home). Spoken of various kinds of houses or edifices, such as the house of the king or the chief priest, a palace (Matt 11:8; Luke 22:54; Sept.: Gen 12:15; 2 Kgs 20:18; Dan 1:4). A house of commerce, meaning a bazaar (John 2:16). Specifically, house of God, meaning the tabernacle or temple where the presence of God was manifested and where God was said to dwell, e.g., the tabernacle (Matt 12:4; Mark 2:26; Luke 6:4); the temple at Jerusalem (Matt 21:13; John 2:16, 17; Acts 7:47, 49); for *ho naós*, with a def. art. (Luke 11:51 [cf. Matt 23:35]); the house of prayer (Matt 21:13; Mark 11:17; Luke 19:46). A room or part of a house, e.g., the dining room (Luke 14:23), the upper room as a place of prayer (Acts 2:2; 10:30; 11:13). Figuratively of persons, Christians as the spiritual house or temple of God (1 Pet 2:5). Of those in whom evil spirits dwell (Matt 12:44; Luke 11:24).

(II) In a wider sense, a dwelling place, habitation, abode, as a city or country (Matt 23:38; Luke 13:35).

(III) Metonymically, a household, family, those who live together in a house (Luke 10:5; Acts 10:2; 11:14; 16:15; 1 Cor 1:16; 2 Tim 1:16; Titus

1:11). Including the idea of household affairs (Acts 7:10; 1 Tim 3:4, 5, 12; Sept.: Gen 7:1; 12:17). Metaphorically, *oíkos tou Theoú*, the household of God, i.e., the Christian Church, Christians (1 Tim 3:15; Heb 3:6; 10:21; 1 Pet 4:17); the Jewish assembly (Heb 3:2, 5; Sept.: Num 12:7).

(IV) Metonymically, family, lineage, posterity, descended from one head or ancestor (Luke 1:27, 69; 2:4; Sept.: Ex 6:14; 1 Kgs 12:16, 19). A whole people or nation as descended from one ancestor such as the house or people of Israel (Matt 10:6; 15:24); the house of Jacob (Luke 1:33); the house of Judah (Heb 8:8; Sept.: Ex 19:3; Lev 10:6; Judg 1:23; 1 Kgs 12:23; Jer 31:31).

Deriv.: *oikeíos* (3609), of one's own household; *oiketeía*, a household of servants, in Matt 24:45 in some MSS; *oikétēs* (3610), a fellow resident, a domestic servant; *oikéō* (3611), to reside; *oikía* (3614), a house including its contents, family; *oikodespótēs* (3617), the master of the house; *oikodómos*, builder of the house, only in Acts 4:11 in some MSS; *oikonómos* (3623), steward, manager; *oikourós* (3626), one who stays at home, a housekeeper; *panoikí* (3832), with all the house; *pároikos* (3941), a sojourning; *períoikos* (4040), someone living near a neighbor.

Syn.: *skēnē* (4633), a tabernacle, tent, temporary dwelling place; *skénos* (4636), used of the body as a tabernacle of the soul; *skénōma* (4638), a temporary habitation.

3625. οἰκουμένη *oikouménē*; gen. *oikouménēs*, fem. noun from *oikéō* (3611), to dwell, abide.

(I) The inhabited earth, the world.

(A) The Roman Empire (Acts 17:6); the Jews in the world (Acts 24:5).

(B) Of Palestine and the adjacent countries (Luke 2:1; Acts 11:28).

(II) Generally, and in later usage, the habitable globe, the earth, the world as known to the people of ancient times

(Matt 24:14; Luke 21:26; Rom 10:18; Heb 1:6; Rev 16:14).

(A) Hyperbolically (Luke 4:5; Sept.: Ps 19:4; 24:1; Isa 23:17).

(B) Metonymically, the world or the inhabitants of the earth, mankind (Acts 17:31; 19:27; Rev 3:10; 12:9; Sept.: Ps 98:9).

(C) Metaphorically, the future age (Heb 2:5).

Syn.: *gē* (1093), the earth; *kósmos* (2889), world.

3626. οἰκουρός *oikourós*; gen. *oikouroú*, masc.-fem., neut. *oikourón*, adj. from *oíkos* (3624), house, and *ourós* (n.f.), a keeper. A keeper at home, one who looks after domestic affairs with prudence and care (Titus 2:5 [TR]; *oikourgós* in the UBS text [cf. 1 Tim 5:13]).

3627. οἰκτείρω *oikteírō*; contracted *oiktírō*, fut. *oikterō* or *oiktērésō*, from *oíktos* (n.f.), compassion, pity. To pity, have compassion on; predicated of God (Rom 9:15, quoted from Ex 33:19; see Sept.: 2 Kgs 13:23; Mic 7:19). *Oikteírō* is closer to *splagchnízomai* (4697), to pity, both words being connected with sympathetic feelings which seek expression in tears and lamentation while *eleéō* (1653) and *éleos* (1656), mercy, involve the intent to help. *Éleos* and *eleéō* are connected with *híleōs* (2436), merciful, gracious, and *hiláskomai* (2433), to conciliate, atone, propitiate, which involve the provision of relief. A criminal begs *éleos*, mercy, of his judge, whereas hopeless suffering can be the object of *oiktirmós* (3628), a feeling of pity, mercy or compassion. Such a distinction between *oikteírō* and *eleéō* can be applied in Class. Gr., but in biblical Gr. *oikteírō* does carry, although not as strongly, the implication of the intent to help. In the Sept. it is often equivalent to *eleéō* (Ps 102:13, 14). The adj. *oiktírmōn* (3629), compassionate, occurs of men in Luke 6:36 and of God in James 5:11. *Eleéō*, however, stands for lovingkindness, not merely for pity aroused by the sight of misery. It has a background of love and affection (Eph 2:4).

Deriv.: *oiktirmós* (3628), mercy or compassion; *oiktírmōn* (3629), compassionate.

Syn.: *splagchnízomai* (4697), to be moved to sympathy or compassion; *sumpathéō* (4834), to suffer with another, show sympathy; *metriopathéō* (3356), to be moderate in one's passions, gentle, compassionate; *hiláskomai* (2433), to be propitious, merciful.

Ant.: *pōróō* (4456), to harden, desensitize; *sklērúnō* (4645), to harden the heart.

3628. οἰκτιρμός *oiktirmós*; gen. *oiktirmoú*, masc. noun from *oikteírō* (3627), to have compassion on. Pity, compassion, mercy, but referring to a feeling that is not as strong as *éleos* (1656), mercy. *Oiktirmós* is the pity or compassion which one shows for the sufferings of others. It is used in reference to God as the Father of mercies (2 Cor 1:3) showing His character and that upon which believers can depend as they make their bodies a living offering to Him (Rom 12:1; see Heb 10:28); of believers who are to show compassion one for another (Phil 2:1; Col 3:12). Used with *splágchna*, the pl. of *splágchnon* (4698), bowel (Col 3:12 UBS), as *splágchna oiktirmoú*; in the TR in the pl. *splágchna oiktirmṓn* (Rom 12:1; 2 Cor 1:3; Phil 2:1; Heb 10:28; Sept.: 2 Sam 24:14; Dan 9:9; Zech 1:16; 7:9).

Syn.: *eleēmosúnē* (1654), compassion, mercy; *philanthrōpía* (5363), philanthropy, benevolence; *éleos* (1656), sympathy accompanied by a real endeavor to bring relief.

Ant.: *sklērótēs* (4643), hardness; *pṓrōsis* (4457), hardening of the heart; *sklērokardía* (4641), hardness of heart.

3629. οἰκτίρμων *oiktírmōn*; gen. *oiktírmonos*, masc.-fem., neut. *oiktírmon*, adj. from *oikteírō* (3627), to pity, have compassion upon. Compassionate, merciful

(Luke 6:36; James 5:11; Sept.: Ex 34:6; Neh 9:17).

Syn.: *eleḗmōn* (1655), merciful, actively compassionate *híleōs* (2436), propitious, merciful.

Ant.: *sklērós* (4642), hard; *austērós* (840), harsh, severe.

3630. οἰνοπότης *oinopótēs*; gen. *oinopótou*, masc. noun, from *oínos* (3631), wine, and *pótēs* (n.f.), a drinker, which is from *pínō* (4095), to drink. A drinker of wine, wine-bibber (Matt 11:19; Luke 7:34; Sept.: Prov 23:20).

Syn.: *méthusos* (3183), a drunkard.

Ant.: *nēphálios* (3524), temperate; *sṓphrōn* (4998), sober-minded.

3631. οἶνος *oínos*; gen. *oínou*, masc. noun. Wine derived from grapes. The mention of the bursting of the wine skins in Matt 9:17; Mark 2:22; Luke 5:37, 38 implies fermentation. See Luke 1:15; 7:33; 10:34; Rom 14:21; Eph 5:18 [cf. John 2:3, 9, 10; 4:46]; 1 Tim 3:8; 5:23; Titus 2:3; Rev 6:6; 18:13; Sept.: Gen 9:21, 24; 14:18; 27:28; Judg 9:13. From the intoxicating effects of wine and the idolatrous use of it among the heathen, wine signifies communion in the intoxicating idolatries of the mystic Babylon (Rev 14:8 [cf. Jer 51:7]). It denotes metaphorically the dreadful judgments of God upon sinners (Rev 14:10; 16:19; 19:15 [cf. Isa 51:17; Jer 25:15; Ezek 23:31]). The drinking of wine, though not forbidden by Scripture (as is drunkenness [Eph 5:18]), is to be avoided in the presence of weaker brothers who might be influenced to partake against their consciences (Rom 14:21). In 1 Tim 5:23 *oínos* is recommended for medicinal purposes.

Deriv.: *oinopótēs* (3630), a drinker of wine; *pároinos* (3943), a heavy drinker.

Syn.: *gleúkos* (1098), sweet new wine; *síkera* (4608), strong drink.

3632. οἰνοφλυγία *oinophlugía*; gen. *oinophlugías*, fem. noun from *oinophlugéō* (n.f.), to be drunken, which is from *oínos* (3631), wine, and *phlúō* (n.f.), to overflow. Drunkenness, indulging in wine to excess with its consequent results (1 Pet 4:3). The verb *oinophlugéō* is used in the Sept. in Deut 21:20. In strict definition *oinophlugía* is an insatiate desire for wine, alcoholism and was commonly used for debauchery. No single word renders it better than debauchery since it is an extravagant indulgence in long, drawn-out drinking bouts which may induce permanent damage to the body. The death of Alexander the Great was ascribed to *oinophlugía*.

Syn.: *akrasía* (192), lack of strength or self-control, incontinence; *anáchusis* (401), an outpouring or overflowing, excess; *asōtía* (810), prodigality; *asélgeia* (766), lasciviousness, outrageous conduct; *kraipálē* (2897), intoxication.

Ant.: *sōphrosúnē* (4997), soberness; *egkráteia* (1466), self-control.

3633. οἴομαι *oíomai*; contracted *oímai*, fut. *oiḗsomai*. To suppose, think, be of an opinion, followed by the inf. and acc. as in John 21:25. In Phil 1:16 the subject of *oiómenoi*, pres. part., and the inf., *epiphérein*, is the same. In James 1:7, instead of an inf. *oíomai* is used with *hóti* (3754), that.

Syn.: *dokéō* (1380), to suppose, think; *logízomai* (3049), to reckon, think; *nomízō* (3543), suppose; *phronéō* (5426), to think; *krínō* (2919), to reckon, judge.

3634. οἷος *hoíos*; fem. *hoía*, neut. *hoíon*, correlative relative pron. corresponding to *poíos* (4169), which, and *toíos* (used only as a comp. in *toiósde* [5107], so great), sort. Of what kind or sort, what manner of, such as.

(I) In a dependent clause as a comparative with *tón autón* (*tón*, acc. of *hó* [3588] and *autón*, acc. of *autós* [846]), the same (1 Cor 15:48; 2 Cor 10:11; Phil 1:30); with *toioútos* implied (Matt 24:21; Mark 9:3; 13:19; 2 Cor 12:20; 2 Tim 3:11; Rev 16:18).

(II) In an independent clause it has the nature of an exclamation implying something great or unusual, what, what manner of, how great (Luke 9:55; 1 Thess 1:5; 2 Tim 3:11).

(III) In the neut., with the neg. *ouk* becoming *ouch* in front of *hoíon* because of the latter's rough breathing, e.g., *ouch hoíon*, used as an adv. meaning not so as, not so, usually followed by an antithesis as *allá* (235), but, with the meaning of not so—but (Rom 9:6).

3634a. οἴω *oíō* fut. *oísō*, an obsolete form of *phérō* (5342) to bring. To bring, carry (John 21:18; Rev 21:26). To think, with the connotation of to keep or bear in mind. In the NT, only in the mid. *oíomai*, to think, suppose, as in Phil 1:16; James 1:7.

Syn.: *nomízō* (3543), to suppose, think, have an opinion; *dokéō* (1380), to be of an opinion; *hupolambánō* (5274), to suppose, surmise; *huponoéō* (5282), to conjecture; *logízomai* (3049), to reckon; *hēgéomai* (2233) and *phronéō* (5426), to think; *krínō* (2919), to judge, reckon.

3635. ὀκνέω *oknéō*; contracted *oknṓ*, fut. *oknḗsō*, from *óknos* (n.f.), slowness, tardiness. To be slow, tardy, to delay. Used intrans. with the inf. (Acts 9:38; Sept.: Num 22:16; Judg 18:9).

Deriv.: *oknērós* (3636), lazy, indolent, slothful.

Syn.: *chronízō* (5549), time, to take one's time; *anabállomai* (306), to defer, put off.

Ant.: *speúdō* (4692), to hasten.

3636. ὀκνηρός *oknērós*; fem. *oknērá*, neut. *oknērón*, adj. from *oknéō* (3635), to be slow, to delay. Slow, tardy, slothful, lazy. Of persons (Matt 25:26; Rom 12:11; see Sept.: Prov 6:6, 9); of things in the neut. meaning tedious, tiresome (Phil 3:1).

Syn.: *barús* (926), heavy, burdensome; *chalepós* (5467), grievous, hard to deal with; *bradús* (1021), slow; *argós* (692), inactive; *nōthrós* (3576), sluggish.

Ant.: *tachús* (5036), swift.

3637. ὀκταήμερος *oktaḗmeros*; gen. *oktaēmérou*, masc.-fem., neut. *oktāmeron*, adj. from *oktṓ* (3638), eight, and *hēméra* (2250), day. Eighth-day, describing a person or thing (Phil 3:5); as to circumcision, an "eighth-day man" (a.t.) means one who was circumcised on the eighth day (as was Paul).

3638. ὀκτώ *oktṓ*; indeclinable, used for all genders, cardinal number. Eight (Luke 2:21; 9:28; 13:4, 11, 16; John 5:5; 20:26; Acts 9:33; 1 Pet 3:20).
    Deriv.: *ogdoḗkonta* (3589), eighty; *ógdoos* (3590), eighth; *oktaḗmeros* (3637), an eight-day old person or thing.

3639. ὄλεθρος *ólethros*; gen. *oléthrou*, masc. noun, from *óllumi* (n.f.), to destroy, kill. Ruin, destruction. Used of divine punishment (1 Cor 5:5; 1 Thess 5:3; 2 Thess 1:9; 1 Tim 6:9; Sept.: Prov 21:7). The verb *óllumi* (n.f.) does not occur, but its derivative, *apóllumi* (622), to destroy, does. The fundamental thought is not annihilation by any means, but unavoidable distress and torment.
    Deriv.: *olothreúō* (3645), to destroy.
    Syn.: *phthorá* (5356), corruption; *diaphthorá* (1312), complete destruction; *apṓleia* (684), perdition.

3640. ὀλιγόπιστος *oligópistos*; gen. *oligopístou*, masc.-fem., neut. *oligópistos*, adj. from *olígos* (3641), little, and *pístis* (4102), faith. Having but little faith (Matt 6:30; 8:26; 14:31; 16:8; Luke 12:28).

3641. ὀλίγος *olígos*; fem. *olígē*, neut. *olígon*. Small or little, the opposite of *polús* (4183), much.
    (I) Of number, meaning small. In the NT only in the pl. *olígoi* (masc.), *olígai* (fem.), *olíga* (neut.), meaning few (Matt 7:14; 9:37; 15:34; 20:16; 22:14; 25:21, 23; Mark 6:5; 8:7; Luke 10:2; 12:48; 13:23; Acts 17:4, 12; Heb 12:10; 1 Pet 3:20; Rev 2:14, 20; 3:4; Sept.: Num 13:19; Isa 10:7). The expression *di' olígon* in 1 Pet 5:12 means in few words, briefly.

    (II) Of quantity or amount, it means little, small. In the NT, only in the sing. (Luke 7:47; Acts 12:18; 15:2; 19:23, 24; 27:20; 2 Cor 8:15; 1 Tim 4:8, "profitable for little" [a.t.]; 5:23; James 3:5; Sept.: 1 Kgs 17:10, 12). In Eph 3:3 *en olígō* means in brief, briefly.
    (III) Of time, meaning little, short, brief (Acts 14:28; James 4:14; Rev 12:12). So *en olígō*, implying *chrónō* (the dat. of *chrónos* [5550], time), means in a little time (Acts 26:28, 29).
    (IV) In the neut. *olígon*, as an adv., spoken of space, amount, time (Mark 1:19; 6:31; Luke 5:3; 7:47; 1 Pet 1:6; 5:10; Rev 17:10; Sept.: Ps 37:10).
    Deriv.: *oligópistos* (3640), of little faith; *oligópsuchos* (3642), of little soul or spirit, faint-hearted.
    Syn.: *brachús* (1024), short, in regard to time or quantity; *mikrós* (3398), little or small, used of persons, rank, influence, things, quantity, or time; *mikrón* (3397) used of distance, quantity, or time being small or a little.
    Ant.: *mégas* (3173), great; *polús* (4183), much; *hikanós* (2425), sufficient; *hēlíkos* (2245), as big as; *pēlíkos* (4080), how large, great; *pósos* (4214), how great; *hósos* (3745), how much; *tosoútos* (5118), so great, pl. *tosoútoi*, so many; *tēlikoútos* (5082), so great; *lían* (3029), exceeding, great; *pás* (3956), all.

3642. ὀλιγόψυχος *oligópsuchos*; gen. *oligopsúchou*, masc.-fem., neut. *oligópsuchos*, adj. from *olígos* (3641), small or little, and *psuchḗ* (5590), soul, mind. Fainthearted, fretful, worried. Only in 1 Thess 5:14; Sept.: Prov 14:29; Isa 54:6.
    Syn.: *deilós* (1169), cowardly; *ékphobos* (1630), terrified; *éntromos* (1790), terror-stricken.
    Ant.: *tolmētḗs* (5113), daring.

3643. ὀλιγωρέω *oligōréō*; contracted *oligōrṓ*, fut. *oligōrḗsō*, from *olígōros* (n.f.), careless, caring little, which is from *olígos* (3641), little, and *ṓra* (n.f.), care. To disesteem or care little for, to consider of small worth, to despise something (Heb 12:5, quoted from Prov 3:11).

Syn.: *exouthenō* (1848), to regard as nothing, despise utterly, hold in contempt; *kataphronéō* (2706), to think little of someone; *periphronéō* (4065), to think in circles (i.e., ponder) about a thing or think oneself above, to despise; *athetéō* (114), to disannul, reject; *atimázō* (818), to dishonor; *logízomai eis oudén* (*logízomai* [3049], to think; *eis* [1519], unto; *oudén*, the neut. of *oudeís* ([3762], no one, nothing), to reckon as nothing.

Ant.: *timáō* (5091), to value; *hēgéomai* (2233), to esteem.

3644. ὀλοθρευτής *olothreutḗs*; gen. *olothreutoú*, masc. noun from *olothreúō* (3645), to destroy. A destroyer (1 Cor 10:10).

Syn.: *apollúōn* (623), destroyer.

Ant.: *sōtḗr* (4990), a savior, deliverer, preserver.

3645. ὀλοθρεύω *olothreúō*; fut. *olothreúsō*, from *ólethros* (3639), destruction. To destroy, especially in the sense of slaying (Heb 11:28), in the pres. part. (*ho holothreúōn*). Also in Sept.: Ex 12:23; Josh 3:10. The more intens. verb is *exolothreúō* (1842) from *ek* (1537), out, completely, and *olothreúō* (3645).

Deriv.: *exolothreúō* (1842), to destroy; *olothreutḗs* (3644), destroyer.

Syn.: *apóllumi* (622), to utterly destroy; *katargéō* (2673), to abolish; *kathairéō* (2507), to cast or pull down by force; *lúō* (3089), to loose, dissolve; *katalúō* (2647), to destroy utterly or overthrow completely; *phtheírō* (5351), to corrupt; *diaphtheírō* (1311), to corrupt utterly; *porthéō* (4199), to make havoc of.

Ant.: *sṓzō* (4982), to save, preserve; *diasṓzō* (1295), to bring safely through; *rhúomai* (4506), to rescue.

3646. ὁλοκαύτωμα *holokaútōma*; gen. *holokautṓmatos*, neut. noun from *olokautóō* (n.f.), to burn whole. A holocaust, a whole burnt offering indicating that the whole victim was burned.

Generally in the NT it means a burnt offering (Mark 12:33; Heb 10:6, 8; Sept.: Ex 18:12; 24:5; 30:20; Lev 4:35; see Ex 29:38–42; Lev 1; 6:8ff.; Num 28:3ff.).

The burnt offering was the most general of all the offerings. The victims were of preeminent value because they most perfectly embodied the sacrificial idea (Lev 1:3). They could be oxen, sheep, goats, turtle-doves, or young pigeons. These victims were to be males without blemish (Lev 1:3). The offerer placed his hands upon the victim (Lev 1:4) and slaughtered it at the door of the tabernacle, north of the altar (Lev 1:3, 11). The priest sprinkled the blood about the altar (Lev 1:5) and cut up the carcass (Lev 1:6). The entrails and legs were washed (Lev 1:9) and the pieces burned on the wood of the altar (Lev 1:8, 9). When a dove was killed by the priest, its crop and feathers were flung aside as unsuitable (Lev 1:14ff.). This ritual was occasioned because of a vow or spontaneous choice of an individual (Lev 22:18). However, the occasions of this sacrifice were primarily connected with collective worship, since the sacrifice constituted the chief element.

The daily services of the temple consisted of burnt offerings wherein male lambs were offered every morning and evening, accompanied by cereal oblations and libations (Ex 29:38ff.; Num 28:1–8). On holy days it was celebrated on a magnified scale. On the Sabbath two pairs of lambs were offered (Num 28:9, 10). At the new moon, the Passover, and the Feast of Weeks, it consisted of two bullocks, a ram, and seven male lambs, with a corresponding increase of the concomitant offerings (Num 1:11ff.).

The purpose of the burnt offering may be understood from its use as the constant element in the organized worship of the community. It was not connected with any particular form of transgression but was appropriate as the means of approach to God by the people, collectively or individually, who were sensitive to God's majesty and holiness and their standing in His sight. The effects are described from three points of view—that it is a "savor" or acceptable to God (Lev 1:9), that it surrounds the worshiper with a "covering" (Lev 1:4), and that it cleanses from ceremonial impurity (Lev 14:20).

Syn.: *prosphorá* (4376), a bringing to, hence an offering accentuating the act instead of the thing offered; *anáthēma* (334), a gift set up in a temple, an offering as a result of a vow; *anáthema* (331), a curse, or the object to be sacrificed on which the curse is laid; *dóron* (1435), a gift with the emphasis on the fact that it is a free-will offering; *thusía* (2378), sacrifice.

3647. ὁλοκληρία *holoklēría*; gen. *holoklērías*, fem. noun from *holóklēros* (3648), whole in every part, entire, perfect. Perfect soundness, wholeness, integrity.
Syn.: *teleiótēs* (5047), completeness, perfection; *sōtēría* (4991), health, salvation.
Ant.: *asthéneia* (769) and *asthénēma* (771), weakness, infirmity.

3648. ὁλόκληρος *holóklēros*; gen. *holoklḗrou*, masc.-fem., neut. *holóklēron*, adj. from *hólos* (3650), all, the whole, and *klḗros* (2819), a part, share. Whole, having all its parts, sound, perfect. That which retains all that was initially allotted to it and wanting nothing for its wholeness. It expresses the perfection of man before the fall (1 Thess 5:23; James 1:4; see Sept.: Deut 27:6; Ezek 15:5). The *holóklēros* is one who has persevered or, having once suffered loss, has now regained completeness. In the *holóklēros* no grace which a Christian man should possess is deficient.
Deriv.: *holoklēría* (3647), soundness.
Syn.: *téleios* (5046), perfect; *ártios* (739), with all its needed parts; *pantelḗs* (3838), entire, complete; *hólos* (3650), whole, complete; *holotelḗs* (3651), complete, utter.
Ant.: *asthenḗs* (772), weak; *adúnatos* (102), without strength; *árrōstos* (732), feeble, sickly.

3649. ὀλολύζω *ololúzō*; fut. *ololúxō*. Formed by onomatopoeia from the sound produced when one is crying aloud to the gods, either in supplication or thanksgiving. Used especially of prayers and hymns of joy accompanied with shouts and shrieks uttered on festival days. Later it came to mean generally to cry aloud in joy or to shout. Also used in complaints meaning to shriek, howl (James 5:1; Sept.: Isa 13:6; 15:3; 16:7).
Syn.: *thrēnéō* (2354), to lament; *klaíō* (2799), to weep; *ōdínō* (5605), to travail, have birth pains; *kóptomai* (2875), to cut down, lament, mourn.
Ant.: *geláō* (1070), to laugh; *agalliáō* (21), to rejoice exceedingly.

3650. ὅλος *hólos*; fem. *hólē*, neut. *hólon*, adj. Whole, used as a demonstrative pron. To say *tó hólon*, the whole, the noun must have the art. and *hólos* must be placed in the position of predicate. *Hólos* is declined as a masc. noun such as *ánthrōpos* (444), man; e.g., *hólon tón kósmon* (*kósmon* [2889], world), the whole world (Mark 14:9). It can also be expressed with *hólon* at the end, as *tón kósmon hólon*, the world, all of it (Mark 8:36). Of space, extent, amount (Matt 4:23; 5:29; 16:26; 21:4; 22:40; Mark 1:33; Luke 1:65; John 4:53; 1 Cor 5:6; Rev 6:12 UBS). Neut. *hólon*, the whole, referring to mass (Matt 13:33; Luke 13:21; John 19:23; Sept.: Gen 25:25; Ex 28:27; Zech 4:2), time (Matt 20:6; Luke 5:5; Acts 11:26; 28:30; Sept.: Ex 10:13; Lev 25:30), an affection, emotion, condition (Matt 22:37, quoted from Deut 6:5; Luke 10:27; John 9:34; 13:10).
Deriv.: *kathólou* (2527), wholly, entirely; *holóklēros* (3648), entire; *holotelḗs* (3651), wholly, through and through; *hólōs* (3654), at all.
Syn.: *pás* (3956), all; *hápas* (537), the whole; *plḗrōma* (4138), fullness.
Ant.: *hékastos* (1538), each; *méros* (3313), part, piece; *merís* (3310), share, part; *diaíresis* (1243), division; *klásma* (2801), piece, fragment.

3651. ὁλοτελής *holotelḗs*; gen. *holoteloús*, pl. *holoteleís*, masc.-fem., neut. *holotelés*, adj. from *hólos* (3650), all, the whole, and *télos* (5056), completion. All or the whole, completely or entirely (1 Thess 5:23).

Syn.: *holóklēros* (3648), whole; *téleios* (5046), perfect; *pantelḗs* (3838), entire; *akéraios* (185), complete; *ártios* (739), complete, perfect; *plḗrēs* (4134), full of moral meaning; *ámemptos* (273), unblamable; *áptaistos* (679), faultless.

Ant.: *mónos* (3441), alone.

3652. Ὀλυμπᾶς *Olumpás*; gen. *Olumpá*, masc. proper noun. Olympas, a Christian at Rome (Rom 16:15).

3653. ὄλυνθος *ólunthos*, gen. *olúnthou*, masc. noun. An unripe fig or a winter fig. These grow under the leaves and do not ripen at the normal season but hang upon the trees during winter (Rev 6:13; Sept.: Song 2:13).

Syn.: *súkon* (4810), a ripe fig.

3654. ὅλως *hólōs*; adv. from *hólos* (3650), whole. Wholly, altogether, in every part or sense (1 Cor 6:7). In the sense of "everywhere" (a.t. [1 Cor 5:1]). Neg., with *ou* (3756), not, or *mḗ* (3361), not, meaning "not at all" (Matt 5:34; 1 Cor 15:29).

Syn.: *teleíōs* (5049), fully, completely; *pántē* (3839), wholly, always; *pántōs* (3843), entirely.

Ant.: *mēdamṓs* (3365), by no means; *mólis* (3433), scarcely; *duskólōs* (1423), with difficulty; *mógis* (3425), with difficulty, hardly; *metríōs* (3357), moderately, slightly, a little; *schedón* (4975), almost, nearly.

3655. ὄμβρος *ómbros*; gen. *ómbrou*, masc. noun. A heavy shower, violent rain with thunder, a tempest (Luke 12:54; Sept.: Deut 32:2).

Syn.: *huetós* (5205), rain, used especially but not entirely of showers; *brochḗ*

(1028), rain; *laílaps* (2978), whirlwind, hurricane.

Ant.: *eudía* (2105), fine, fair weather, a clear sky.

3656. ὁμιλέω *homiléō*; contracted *homilṓ*, fut. *homilḗsō*, from *hómilos* (3658), a multitude, a crowd or company. To converse, talk with (Luke 24:15; Acts 20:11; 24:26). Followed by *prós allḗlous* (*prós* [4314], unto, toward; *allḗlous* [240], one another), to speak with one another (Luke 24:14).

Deriv.: *homilía* (3657), homily, communication; *sunomiléō* (4926), to converse or talk with.

Syn.: *dialégomai* (1256), to discourse; *dialaléō* (1255), to proclaim abroad; *laléō* (2980), to speak; *légō* (3004), to say; *phēmí* (5346), to make known one's thoughts; *eréō* or *rhéō* (4483), to pour forth, utter; *suzētéō* (4802), to investigate jointly, discuss, reason together.

Ant.: *siōpáō* (4623) and *sigáō* (4601), to be silent; *phimóō* (5392), to muzzle, put to silence.

3657. ὁμιλία *homilía*; gen. *homilías* fem. noun from *homiléō* (3656), to converse, talk. Originally the word meant being together in company, companionship, but in the NT it means conversation (1 Cor 15:33). Some Eng. words derived from this are "homiletic" (pertaining to the art of preaching), "homily" (a discourse), and "homilist," (one who writes or delivers homilies).

Syn.: *lógos* (3056), speech; *laliá* (2981), talk, speech; *rhḗma* (4487), utterance; *stóma* (4750), mouth, or what is spoken; *suzḗtēsis* (4803), discussion.

Ant.: *sigḗ* (4602), silence.

3658. ὅμιλος *hómilos*; gen. *homílou*, masc. noun from *homoú* (3674), together, and *ílē* (n.f.), crowd. A throng, crowd, multitude (Rev 18:17 [TR]).

Deriv.: *homiléō* (3656), to converse, talk.

Syn.: *dḗmos* (1218), political body of people; *óchlos* (3793), a throng of people, an irregular crowd; *sunodía* (4923), a caravan, company of travelers; *sumpósion* (4849), a drinking party, a roomful of guests; *klisía* (2828), a company that relaxes together; *plḗthos* (4128), a multitude, denoting fullness; *sunagōgḗ* (4864), synagogue, congregation; *chorós* (5525), choir; *speíra* (4686), a mass of men, a military cohort, squad, band; *akroatḗrion* (201), audience, group of hearers; *ekklēsía* (1577), a popular gathering, religious congregation, church; *panḗguris* (3831), a mass meeting, a festive group.

Ant.: *heís* (1520), one; *mónos* (3441), single, alone.

3659. ὄμμα *ómma*; gen. *ómmatos*, neut. noun from *óptomai* (3700), to see. Eye. The pl., *tá ómmata*, the eyes (Mark 8:23; Sept.: Prov 6:4).

Syn.: *hórasis* (3706), sight; *ophthalmós* (3788), the physical eye; *trumaliá* (5168), used for the eye of a needle, some texts have *trúpēma* (5169), a hole; *opḗ* (3692), a hole.

Ant.: *skótos* (4655), darkness.

3660. ὀμνύω *omnúō* and ὄμνυμι *ómnumi*; fut. *omoúmai*, aor. *ómosa*. To take or make an oath (Matt 5:34; 26:74; Mark 14:71). The person or thing by which one swears is variously construed as with the acc., e.g., *tón ouranón*, the heaven (James 5:12); with *katá* (2596), against, and the gen. (Heb 6:13, 16; Sept.: Isa 45:23; Amos 4:2); with *eis* (1519), unto (Jerusalem as in Matt 5:35); with *en* (1722), in, and the dat. (Matt 5:34, 36; 23:16, 18, 20, 22; Rev 10:6; Sept.: Ps 63:11; Jer 5:7). It also means to declare with an oath or swear, followed by the words of the oath (Heb 3:11; 4:3; 7:21; with the inf., Heb 3:18). Hence, to promise with an oath, followed by the dat. and *hóti* (3754), that (Mark 6:23; followed by the dat., Acts 2:30); the nom. and dat. (Acts 7:17). With *prós* (4314), toward, and the acc. (Luke 1:73 [cf. Gen 26:3]; followed by the dat., Sept.: Deut 7:8).

Syn.: *bebaióō* (950), to confirm; *horkízō* (3726), to adjure; *epimarturéō* (1957), to corroborate; *plērophoréō* (4135), to completely assure; *dēlóō* (1213), to declare; *marturéō* (3140), to witness.

Ant.: *epiorkéō* (1964), to swear falsely; *arnéomai* (720), to deny; *aparnéomai* (533), to deny utterly.

3661. ὁμοθυμαδόν *homothumadón*; adv. from *homóthumos* (n.f.), unanimous, of one mind, which is from *homós* (n.f.), one and the same, and *thumós* (2372), temperament, mind. With one mind, with unanimous consent, in one accord, all together (Acts 1:14; 2:1, 46; 4:24; 5:12; 7:57; 8:6; 12:20; 15:25; 18:12; 19:29; Rom 15:6; Sept.: Ex 19:8; Jer 26:21).

Syn.: *sún* (4862), with, together.

Ant.: *aná heís* (*aná* [303], separately; *heís* [1520], one), each one; *kat' idían* (*katá* [2596], apart from; *idían* from *ídios* [2398], oneself), privately, apart from others.

3662. ὁμοιάζω *homoiázō*; fut. *homoiásō*, from *hómoios* (3664), similar. To resemble, be like something. Used intrans. in Mark 14:70.

Deriv.: *paromoiázō* (3945), to resemble.

Syn.: *eíkō* (1503), to resemble, to be like.

Ant.: *diaphérō* (1308), to be different; *diakrínō* (1252), to distinguish; *diastéllomai* (1291), to set oneself apart, distinguish oneself.

3663. ὁμοιοπαθής *homoiopathḗs*; gen. *homoiopathoús*, masc.-fem., neut. *homoiopathés*, adj. from *hómoios* (3664), similar, and *páthos* (3806), passion. Liable to be affected in a similar manner, of like infirmities and passions or subject to such (Acts 14:15; James 5:17).

3664. ὅμοιος *hómoios*; fem. *homoía*, neut. *hómoion*, adj. from *homós* (n.f., see *homótechnos* [3673]), one and the same. Like, similar. It denotes a correspondence in feature, property or nature, while *ísos* (2470), equal, denotes a correspondence in measure, capacity or position. In biblical Gr. it means of the same kind, like, e.g., the two commandments which form the sum of the Law, as on a par with each other (Matt 22:38, 39; Mark 12:31). It denotes the rest that are of the same kind in Gal 5:21 after a list of the works of the flesh.

(I) Generally, similarity in external form and appearance (John 9:9; Rev 1:13, 15; 2:18; 4:3, 6, 7; 9:7, 10, 19; 11:1; 13:2, 11; 14:14; 16:13; 21:11, 18); in kind or nature (Acts 17:29; Gal 5:21); in conduct, character (Matt 11:16; 13:52; Luke 7:31, 32; 12:36); in conditions, circumstances (Matt 13:31, 33, 44, 45, 47; 20:1; Luke 6:47–49; 13:18, 19, 21; 1 John 3:2; Rev 18:18).

(II) Just like, equal, the same with, in kind or nature (Jude 1:7). In conduct, character, once followed by the gen. (John 8:55); in authority, dignity, power (Matt 22:39; Mark 12:31; Rev 13:4).

Deriv.: *homoiázō* (3662), to resemble; *homoiopathḗs* (3663), similarly affected, affected in a like fashion; *homoiótēs* (3665), similarity; *homoióō* (3666), to make like; *homoíōs* (3668), in a similar way, likewise; *parómoios* (3946), similar, much like.

Syn.: *eíkō* (1503), to be like, resemble; *hoíos* (3634), such as; *toiósde* (5107), such, like; *toioútos* (5108), such, of this kind; *hopoíos* (3697), what manner; *ísos* (2470), equal.

Ant.: *diáphoros* (1313), different; *héteros* (2087), another of a different kind; *állos* (243), numerically another; *allótrios* (245), foreign, alien.

3665. ὁμοιότης *homoiótēs*; gen. *homoítētos*, fem. noun from *hómoios* (3664), similar. Likeness, similitude (Sept.: Gen 1:11, 12). Of Christ it is written that He was tempted in a manner similar to our temptation (Heb 4:15). In Heb 7:15 Christ is called a priest in the likeness of Melchizedek. Christ was a priest, not on the basis of descent and law, but

by virtue of the power within Him which was that of inherent and indestructible life (John 1:4). *Homoiótēs*, therefore, means correspondence, not identity.

The word *homoíōsis* (3669) refers to likeness or similarity to another.

Homoíōma (3667) is what is made similar, the copy. In Rev 9:7 the word translated "shapes" (a.t.) is *homoiṓmata*, the pl. of *homoíōma*, which means that the locusts had the forms or shapes of horses.

Syn.: *analogía* (356), analogy, proportion; *antítupon* (499), antitype, after a true likeness, not the thing itself but a figure of the true thing.

Ant.: *diákrisis* (1253), difference; *parallagḗ* (3883), variableness; *diastolḗ* (1293), difference, distinction.

3666. ὁμοιόω *homoióō*; contracted *homoiṓ*, fut. *homoiṓsō*, from *hómoios* (3664), similar. To make like; with the acc. and dat. Aor. pass. *homoiṓthēn*, to be or become like, with the dat. Generally used only in the pass. with the meaning of having an external form (Acts 14:11; Sept.: Isa 40:18); in conduct, character (Matt 6:8); in condition, circumstances (Heb 2:17). Once followed by *hōs* (5613), as, in a manner similar to (Rom 9:29 quoted from Isa 1:9). Used in comparison meaning to liken, compare. In the pass., to be likened, to be like (Matt 7:24, 26; 11:16; 13:24; 18:23; 22:2; 25:1; Mark 4:30; Luke 7:31; 13:18, 20; Sept.: Ps 102:6; Song 2:17; 7:7).

Deriv.: *aphomoióō* (871), to make like; *homoíōma* (3667), that which resembles, similitude, copy; *homoíōsis* (3669), the act of making alike, likeness.

Syn.: *eíkō* (1503), to resemble, be like.

Ant.: *diaphérō* (1308), to be different; *diakrínō* (1252), to make a distinction, differ; *diastéllomai* (1291), to distinguish.

3667. ὁμοίωμα *homoíōma*; gen. *homoiṓmatos*, neut. noun from *homoióō* (3666), to make like. Likeness, shape, similitude, resemblance. It is important to realize that the resemblance signified by *homoíōma* in no way implies that one of the objects in question has been derived from the other. In the same way two men may resemble one another even though they are in no way related to one another. This word is so important to the proper understanding of the incarnation of Christ that it is necessary to consider the context of the more important passages where it occurs.

(I) Abstractly, in the sense of a noun meaning likeness, resemblance (Rom 1:23; 5:14; 6:5; 8:3).

(A) In Rom 1:23 Paul speaks about fallen man exchanging the glory or essence of the immaterial, incorruptible God for a likeness of an image (*en homoiṓmati eikónos* [gen. sing. of *eikṓn* {1504}, image]) "made like to corruptible man, and to birds, and four-footed beasts, and creeping things." The Scripture does not distinguish between the various types of idols, the visible representation which Paul calls an image. The Romans were deeply involved in idolatry. In fact the loss of revenue to the idol makers was one of the chief causes of Rome's displeasure with Christianity. Some of Paul's chief persecutors were those who made their living by the carving of idols (Acts 19:23–41).

The construction of the Gr. is very similar to the Sept. rendering of Ps 105:20, "Thus they changed their glory, for the likeness of [*homoiṓmati*, dat. sing.] an ox that eateth grass." This passage in Psalm 105 describes the time when Aaron made a golden calf while Moses was receiving the Ten Commandments on Mount Sinai. The Israelites then bowed down and worshiped the image (*eikṓn*). Some of the most important gods and goddesses of the Egyptian religion had been represented by cattle (Hathor, the mother goddess; Mnevis, the sacred bull of Heliopolis; and Apis, the symbol of fertility). Aaron wanted to present this golden calf to Israel as the *eikṓn*, image, of the gods they left behind (cf. Ps 106:19; Acts 7:39, 40).

It is foolish for man to think of God as being mortal man, much less an animal (whether in the form of a flying bird, a four-legged creature, or a creeping thing). And still more foolish is the thought that God can be represented by a mere hand-held trinket. Can God be a *homoíōma*, a representation, of an *eikṓn*, image? Paul is endeavoring to make the heathen Romans realize that even the concept of God as a creature, a corruptible being, is wrong. Fallen man, apart from the gracious work of the Holy Spirit, can only conceive of God as a corruptible being. Hence, it is by corruptible things that he seeks to represent Him. Christ, however, was the Word (*Lógos* [3056]) who became flesh. His body was never subject to decay or corruption (*diapthorá* [1312]). It was *hósios* (3741), sacred (Acts 2:27–31).

(B) In Rom 5:14 Paul says that even those who lived from the time of Adam to the time of Moses were subject to eternal death, "even over them that had not sinned after the similitude of Adam's transgression." Before there was even a written law, they were disobedient to the law which God wrote on the heart of man. Though they might not have broken a direct command, written or verbal, yet death reigned over them because of Adam's transgression.

(C) In Rom 6:5, "For if we have been planted together in the likeness of his death, we shall be also in the likeness of His resurrection." Paul in this passage is speaking about baptism as a symbol of our voluntary death and burial even as in the case of the Lord Jesus Christ who died and was buried. If we are baptized unto the death of Christ, then we shall participate also, both here and hereafter, in the likeness of His life.

(D) In Rom 8:3, "For what the law could not do, in that it was weak through the flesh, God sending his own Son in the likeness [*homoiṓmati*] of sinful flesh, and for sin, condemned sin in the flesh." Paul indicates not that the body of Christ was merely human, but that in spite of His having a real body and a truly human nature, yet these were only similar to ours, without sin or the propensity to sin.

(II) In the literal sense, meaning shape, form, figure (Phil 2:7; Rev 9:7; Sept.: Ex 20:4; Deut 4:16; 1 Sam 6:5; 2 Kgs 16:10; 2 Chr 4:3). In Phil 2:6–8, three synonymous words occur:

(A) The first word is *morphḗ* (3444), form or inward identifiable existence. Christ's identification as God in heaven is clear, "Who being in the form of God thought it not robbery to be equal with God [He was not made equal to God but that He always was of the same essence as God and of the same rank {cf. John 1:18}]" (Phil 2:6). No person could be in the form of God and not be God. In Phil 2:7, the Gr. text simply says, "But He emptied Himself." When the Lord Jesus Christ spoke to the Samaritan woman in John 4:24, He revealed that the nature of God is Spirit. This is the eternal form of God which Jesus Christ always had and never gave up.

In His incarnation, however, He voluntarily took on the form of a man and His humanity was fully recognized by men on earth. While He lived on earth as the God-Man, He was simultaneously the Son of God in heaven. In other words, He did not empty Himself of His divine perfections nor of the essence of His being, but He emptied Himself into a life of humiliation that was itself emptied into death.

Although He was always spiritually rich, He became materially poor. The word "poor" in 2 Cor 8:9 is *eptṓcheuse* (aor. act. of *ptōcheúō* [4433], to be poor). The act. voice indicates that He voluntarily gave up something which He always had. The form of slavery and poverty the Lord took upon Himself was a necessary condition. Only in this manner could He yield His body unto death, for without the shedding of blood there could be no remission of sin (Heb 9:22). Jesus Christ did not have His life taken from Him. He died because He chose to die (John 10:17, 18).

This is the reason why in Phil 2:7 for the statement that Jesus "was made in the likeness of men [*en homoiṓmati anthrṓpōn*]"; and in verse eight that He was "found in fashion as a man [*hōs ánthrōpos*]." In shape (*schḗma* [4976]), He was exactly as man. In this instance the words *homoíōma*, likeness, and *schḗma*, shape, are parallel. In His essence (*morphḗ*) He was God, but took upon Himself, in addition to His deity, the likeness of men (with a true human nature in a real body), yet without sin (Heb 4:15). For this reason we are told that he was made *en homoiṓmati anthrṓpōn*, "in the likeness of men," not merely that He became man.

(B) The second word that is used in Phil 2:7 is *homoíōma*, "But made himself of no reputation, and took upon him the form of a servant, and was made in the likeness [*homoíōma*] of men." Paul declares here that Jesus Christ, whose essential preincarnate form was spirit (*pneúma* [4151]), emptied Himself and took upon Himself the form of man. But His was, as Rom 8:3 says, not the flesh of sin, but sinless flesh. He became man so that He could die for the sin of man. It was as the Son of God that Christ become the Son of Man, He never ceasing to be the Son of God. This is made clear by what the Lord Jesus said to the Father in John 17:5 just before His crucifixion: "And now, O Father, glorify thou me with thine own self with the glory [*dóxa* {1391}] which I had with thee before the world was." This glory of His proper recognition as the Son which he had before His incarnation was not attributed to Him by sinful man while He lived on earth.

(C) The third word that occurs in the Philippian passage (v. 8) is *schḗma* (4976), form, fashion. It refers here to the physical form that Jesus took. *Schḗma* is more closely related to *homoíōma*, likeness, than to *morphḗ*, form or substance, essence. "And being found in fashion [*schḗmati*, sing. dat. of *schḗma*] as a man, he humbled himself, and became obedient unto death, even the death of the cross." The Lord Jesus did not deliver His divine nature to man to kill; His spirit could not be killed. His enemies, failing to recognize His deity, found "a man." This one they killed, not knowing that He was indeed the God-Man. Even so, the Apostle Paul tells us that the only reason they could kill Him was that "He humbled Himself, and became obedient unto [until] death, even the death of the cross."

Homoiótēs occurs only in Heb 4:15; 7:15. In Heb 4:15 *homoiótēs* is translated "like." "For we have not a high priest which cannot be touched with the feeling of our infirmities; but was in all points tempted like as we are [*kath' homoiótēta*], yet without sin." Similarity does not necessarily involve identity of nature. The temptations that came to Jesus in His humanity were similar to ours, but they could not entice Him to sin because His human nature was perfectly holy. (Were it not so, His human nature could never have joined with His divine nature, nor could He have been an acceptable sacrifice for the sins of mankind.) There was nothing in Christ's perfect human nature to make Him even desire to sin (James 1:14).

In Heb 7:15 the word *homoiótēs* is translated "similitude": "And it is yet far more evident: for that after the similitude of Melchizedek there ariseth another priest." Here Melchizedek and Christ were not declared to be one and the same person, but similarities were said to exist between them. Melchizedek was, as Heb 7:3 states, "without father, without mother, without descent, having neither beginning of days, nor end of life; but made like unto the Son of God; abideth a priest continually." Just as his ancestry is not known, Jesus Christ, being God, did not have an ancestry. Yet Melchizedek was a human being and as such did indeed have a father and mother. He performed the duties of a high priest, but his sacrifices had to be repeated. Jesus also possessed a human nature, yet without sin.

In addition, Christ also, being God Almighty, possessed a divine nature. He thereby offered Himself as the perfect sacrifice, once for all.

(III) The distinction in meaning between this word and related terms is essential in understanding certain passages in the NT.

(A) *Eikốn* (1504), image, is derived from *eíkō* (1503), to resemble, be like. It refers to an artistic representation of an historical personality, a mental image, a likeness, a manifestation of someone or something visible or invisible. For instance, the Lord Jesus pointed to the emperor's image on a coin and referred to it as an *eikốn* (Matt 22:20; Mark 12:16; Luke 20:24). This was a representation of an historic person who symbolized rule and governing power. These are the only references in the gospels where *eikốn* is used.

In Rom 1:23, both *homoíōma* and *eikốn* occur together. Paul refers to fallen men and their endeavor to represent the immaterial God (called here *áphthartos* [862], incorruptible). The word *áphthartos* refers to material substances which cannot decay. Paul is declaring that when God became man, even the material substance of that Man was not *phthartós* (5349), corruptible. We have no reference whatsoever to the body of Jesus Christ being corruptible despite the fact that it was in the likeness (*homoiốmati*) of men and adhered to the laws of physical nutrition, growth, and maturity (Luke 2:52). Although it was a real body, subject to aging and growth, there was no sin in it to cause decay. Peter declared this fact clearly in his Pentecostal address in Acts 2:27, "Because thou wilt not leave my soul in hell, neither wilt thou suffer thine Holy One to see corruption [*diaphthorán* {1312}, decay]."

In 2 Cor 4:4, Paul calls Christ "the image [*eikốn*] of God," the physical representation of the Godhead. As John says in John 1:18, "He, being in the bosom of the Father, He Himself brought Him out to the open [*exēgésato*, aor. of *exēgéomai*

{1834}, to bring out of]" (a.t.). From His eternal, infinite, spiritual self-existence, He came out into the open for humans to see with their physical eyes. He came in human flesh, a bodily representation of the fullness of the Godhead. This is made even clearer by the declaration in Col 1:15, "Who is the image [*eikón*] of the invisible God."

(B) *Charaktḗr* (5481) denotes an engraving. In Heb 1:3 we read, "who being the brightness of his glory, and the express image [*charaktḗr*] of his person [*hupostáseōs* {gen.} {5287}, substance]." *Charaktḗr* is the Gr. word from which the Eng. "character" is derived. However, both the modern Gr. meaning and the Eng. meaning of this word are different from the original meaning. In Eng. the primary meaning is a person's traits or characteristics which distinguish him.

In NT times the word meant an engraving, in particular an engraving of the likeness of someone or something on a coin. It might also be used of a seal. When one sees a coin, one has a general idea of what the stamp looked like that produced it. When one sees the impression of a seal in wax, one has a good representation of the seal that made the impression. In the same way, Jesus was the physical engraving of God's spiritual nature. The fact that God is Spirit does not preclude His having substance (*hupóstasis*). That spiritual reality or substance was inherently impressed in the person of Jesus Christ, the God-Man. See John 14:9.

Syn.: *schḗma* (4976), form, fashion; *morphḗ* (3444), form or inward identifiable existence; *homoíōsis* (3669), the action of making alike, similitude, likeness; *homoiótēs* (3665), similarity but not identical substance, or (in Jesus' case) similar human nature but without participation in man's sinfulness.

3668. ὁμοίως *homoíōs*; adv. from *hómoios* (3664), like, resembling. Like, of equal degree or manner and denoting perfect agreement, similarly, in like

manner. To do likewise (Matt 22:26; 26:35; 27:41; Mark 4:16; 15:31; Luke 3:11; 5:10, 33; 6:31; 10:32, 37; 13:5; 16:25; 17:28, 31; 22:36; John 5:19; 6:11; 21:13; Rom 1:27; 1 Cor 7:3, 4, 22; Heb 9:21; James 2:25; 1 Pet 3:1, 7; 5:5; Jude 1:8; Rev 8:12; Sept.: Esth 1:18).

Syn.: *hōsaútōs* (5615), thus, in the same way; *hōs* (5613), in like manner, likewise; *kaí* (2532), and, even; *paraplēsíōs* (3898), similarly; *hoútōs* (3779), thus, likewise; *pōs* (4459), after what manner; *katá* (2596), according, in accordance with.

Ant.: *polutrópōs* (4187), in different ways; *állōs* (247), otherwise; *hetérōs* (2088), otherwise, differently.

3669. ὁμοίωσις *homoíōsis*; gen. *homoiōseōs*, fem. noun from *homoióō* (3666), to make like. Likeness, resemblance. The only instance in the NT of this is James 3:9 (in allusion to Gen 1:26; Sept.: Ezek 1:10; Dan 10:16) where man is said to bear God's likeness. Although theologians continue to debate about the precise nature of the *imago Dei* in man, variously defining it as ontological, sociological, functional or moral, one thing is certain from this passage, namely, that even fallen man retains some semblance (however badly marred by sin) of the divine impress given him at the original creation.

Syn.: *homoíōma* (3667), the likeness of something, a resemblance, while *homoíōsis*, in its literal sense, is the act of making something like something else, likening; *homoiótēs* (3665), likeness, similitude; *antítupon* (499), an antitype, something that is stamped out of a true likeness; *eikṓn* (1504), a physical representation, image.

Ant.: *diastolḗ* (1293), difference, distinction; *diákrisis* (1253), difference.

3670. ὁμολογέω *homologéō*; contracted *homologṓ*, fut. *homologḗsō*, from *homólogos* (n.f.), assenting, which is from *homoú* (3674), together with, and *légō* (3004), to say. To assent, consent, admit, as used commonly in Class. Gr.; to promise, i.e., to agree with or consent to the desire of another.

(I) To concede, admit, confess (Acts 24:14); of sins (1 John 1:9). Hence, to confess publicly, acknowledge openly, profess (1 Tim 6:12). Followed by the acc. generally (Acts 23:8); by the inf. (Titus 1:16); by a part. (1 John 4:2, 3; 2 John 1:7). With the part. *ónta*, being, implied (John 9:22; Rom 10:9, "the Lord, being Jesus" [a.t.]). In an absolute sense, but with part. implied (John 12:42; Rom 10:10). Followed by *hóti* (3754), that, instead of the inf. (Heb 11:13; 1 John 4:15); or as citing the express words (Matt 7:23; John 1:20). Followed by *en* (1722), in, to confess Christ personally, meaning to profess or acknowledge Him (Matt 10:32; Luke 12:8). Followed by the dat. of person, to acknowledge in honor of someone, meaning to give thanks, to praise (Heb 13:15).

(II) To be in accord with someone, to promise, followed by the dat. and inf. (Matt 14:7).

Deriv.: *anthomologéomai* (437), to confess in return, respond in praise; *exomologéō* (1843), to confess verbally, to profess or acknowledge, promise, praise; *homología* (3671), confession; *homologouménōs* (3672), confessedly, surely, without controversy.

Syn.: *epaggéllō* (1861), to announce, promise, profess; *pháskō* (5335), to assert, affirm, profess; *eucharistéō* (2168), to give thanks; *eulogéō* (2127), to speak well of.

Ant.: *arnéomai* (720), to deny, refuse; *aparnéomai* (533), to deny utterly; *paraitéomai* (3868), to avoid, reject; *apodokimázō* (593), to reject, disapprove; *exouthenéō* (1848), to despise.

3671. ὁμολογία *homología*; gen. *homologías*, fem. noun from *homologéō* (3670), to agree, confess, say the same. A confession, profession, or recognition. In Heb 3:1 Christ is called "the High Priest of our profession," i.e., our common faith. *Homología* is also used in

2 Cor 9:13; Heb 10:23. Used in an absolute sense, meaning confession of Christ and to Christ (1 Tim 6:12, 13; Heb 4:14 [cf. Rom 10:10]), and as a vow, especially in the Sept.

Syn.: *pístis* (4102), faith, the body of confession; *eulogía* (2129), blessing, commendation; *eucharistía* (2169), expressing gratitude, thanksgiving; *épainos* (1868), commendation, praise; *euphēmía* (2162), speaking well of, good report.

3672. ὁμολογουμένως *homologouménōs*; adv. from *homologéō* (3670), to confess. Confessedly (1 Tim 3:16).

Syn.: *asphalós* (806), assuredly; *anantirrḗtōs* (369), without objection; *óntōs* (3689), verily, certainly; *pántōs* (3843), surely, altogether; *alēthós* (230), truly.

Ant.: *oudamós* (3760), by no means, in no wise.

3673. ὁμότεχνος *homótechnos*; gen. *homotéchnou*, masc.-fem., neut. *homótechnon*, adj. from *homós* (n.f., see below), one and the same, like, and *téchnē* (5078), trade, skill. Of the same trade (Acts 18:3).

Deriv. of *homós* (n.f.), one and the same thing: *hómoios* (3664), like similar; *homóphrōn* (3675), like-minded, of the same mind; *hómōs* (3676), at the same time, yet, nevertheless.

3674. ὁμοῦ *homoú*; adv., the neut. gen. of *homós* (n.f.), one and the same, like, similar. At the same place or time, together. Used of place (John 21:2); of time (John 4:36; 20:4; Sept.: Job 34:29).

Deriv.: *hómilos* (3658), crowd.

Syn.: *homothumadón* (3661), of one accord, simultaneously as one; *háma* (260), as one, together; *pamplētheí* (3826), with the whole multitude; *epí tó autó* (*epí* [1909], upon; *to autó* [846], this), at the same place; *met' allḗlōn* (*metá* [3326], with; *allḗlōn* [240], one another), with one another; *prós allḗlous* (*prós* [4314], toward; *allḗlous* [240], one another), to one another or together; *allélōn* (240), one another or together; *sún* (4862), together; *metá* (3326), with, together, in association with.

Ant.: *chōrís* (5565), separately; *kat' idían* (katá [2596], by; *ídios* (2398), one's own, private), alone, by oneself; *katá mónas* (katá [2596], by, according; *mónos* [3441], alone), privately, by oneself.

3675. ὁμόφρων homóphrōn; gen. *homóphronos*, masc.-fem., neut. *homóphronon*, adj. from *homós* (n.f., see *homótechnos* [3673]), one and the same, and *phrén* (5424), mind, understanding. Of the same mind, like-minded (1 Pet 3:8 [cf. Rom 12:16]). The verb *homophronéō* does not occur in the NT, although *phronéō* (5426), to think, does occur with the expression *tó autó* (the neut. of *autós* [846], the same thing), meaning to think the same thing (Rom 15:5; Phil 2:2)

Syn.: *isópsuchos* (2473), of a kindred spirit, like-minded; *súmphōnos* (4859), agreeing.

Ant.: *asúmphōnos* (800), not agreeing.

3675a. ὁμόω omóō; the obsolete form of *ómnumi* / *omnúō* (3660), to swear, to take an oath.

3676. ὅμως hómōs; adversative particle from *homós* (n.f., see *homótechnos* [3673]), like, similar. Nevertheless, notwithstanding, yet. As strengthened by *méntoi* (3305), however, as in John 12:42, meaning yet, nevertheless; 1 Cor 14:7, yet even, how much more then? Also in Gal 3:15 meaning "yet even a man's covenant, duly confirmed, no one annuls" (a.t.).

Syn.: *plén* (4133), yet, howbeit; *kaítoi* (2543), and yet, nevertheless, although; *kaíper* (2539), and yet, notwithstanding; *dé* (1161), but, an adversative particle.

Ant.: *amén* (281), certain, as an adv.: certainly, surely; *akribōs* (199), exactly; *mén* (3303), a particle of affirmation; *méntoi* (3305), indeed; *mén* (3375),

assuredly; *dé* (1211), doubtless; *ge* (1065), indeed.

3677. ὄναρ ónar; neut. noun found only in the nom. and acc. A dream. When used with *katá* ([2596], in, according to), it means in a dream (Matt 1:20; 2:12, 13, 19, 22; 27:19). In the Sept., *kath' húpnon* (5258), sleep (Gen 20:6; 31:11).

Syn.: *enúpnion* (1798), what appears in ordinary sleep; *hórama* (3705), a spectacle, appearance, vision; *hórasis* (3706), sense of sight, in the pl. visions; *optasía* (3701), that which comes into view, vision; *phantasía* (5325), fantasy; *phántasma* (5326), phantasm, specter, spirit; *skiá* (4639), shadow.

3678. ὀνάριον onárion; gen. *onaríou*, neut. noun, a diminutive of *ónos* (3688), a donkey, ass. A little donkey, young ass (John 12:14).

3679. ὀνειδίζω oneidízō; fut. *oneidísō*, from *óneidos* (3681), reproach. To defame, disparage, reproach. Generally it means to rail at, revile, assail with abusive words, with the dat. or acc. of person (Matt 5:11; 27:44 [TR]; Mark 15:32; Luke 6:22; Rom 15:3 quoted from Ps 69:9; 1 Tim 4:10; 1 Pet 4:14). It also, at times, means to reproach someone for something, i.e., to upbraid, chide (Matt 11:20; Mark 16:14). Used in an absolute sense with a neg., to not upbraid with benefits conferred (James 1:5).

Deriv.: *oneidismós* (3680), reproach.

Syn.: *hubrízō* (5195), to insult, treat insolently; *loidoréō* (3058), to revile; *diabállō* (1225), to accuse falsely; *atimázō* (318), to dishonor; *blasphēméō* (987), to blaspheme, defame, revile, speak evil of; *katēgoréō* (2723), to accuse, to charge against.

Ant.: *ainéō* (134), praise; *epainéō* (1867), to commend; *eulogéō* (2127), to speak well of, praise, bless.

3680. ὀνειδισμός oneidismós; gen. *oneidismoú*, masc. noun from *oneidízō* (3679), to revile. Reviling, upbraiding

(Rom 15:3; 1 Tim 3:7; Heb 10:33; 11:26; 13:13; Sept.: Ps 68:8, 10; Joel 2:19).

Syn.: *atimía* (819), dishonor; *loidoría* (3059), reviling; *húbris* (5196), insult.

Ant.: *aínos* (136), praise; *épainos* (1868), commendation; *aínesis* (133), the act of praise; *eulogía* (2129), blessing, praise.

3681. ὄνειδος *óneidos*; gen. *oneídous*, neut. noun. In the NT, ill-fame, reproach, disgrace (Luke 1:25) referring to sterility, in allusion to Gen 30:23. See Sept. 2 Sam 13:13; Prov 6:33.

Deriv.: *oneidízō* (3679), to revile, upbraid.

3682. Ὀνήσιμος *Onēsimos*; gen. *Onēsímou*, masc. proper noun. Onesimus, meaning useful. A slave of Philemon in whose behalf Paul wrote the epistle to Philemon (Col 4:9). It seems that he fled from his master (Phile 1:15), but when he returned, he was a Christian. His conversion was brought about through Paul at Rome (Phile 1:10).

3683. Ὀνησίφορος *Onēsíphoros*; gen. *Onēsiphórou*, masc. proper noun. Onesiphorus, meaning profit bringing. A Christian who ministered to the wants of Paul at Ephesus and afterward sought him out at Rome and openly sympathized with him (2 Tim 1:16–18; 4:19).

3684. ὀνικός *onikós*; fem. *oniké*, neut. *onikón*, adj. from *ónos* (3688), a donkey, ass. Pertaining to a donkey, used with *múlos* (3458), a millstone or grinder, meaning a donkey millstone or a millstone turned by a donkey (Matt 18:6; Luke 17:2).

3685. ὀνίνημι *onínēmi*; fut. *onḗsō*. To be of use, to profit, gratify. In the NT, only in the mid. *onínamai* 2d aor. opt. *onaímēn*, to profit by or obtain profit from someone (Phile 1:20).

Syn.: *ōpheléō* (5623), to be useful; *lusiteléō* (3081), to be advantageous; *euergetéō* (2109), to do good.

Ant.: *achreióō* (889), to become unprofitable.

3686. ὄνομα *ónoma*; gen. *onómatos*, neut. noun. Name, title, character, reputation, person.

(I) Particularly and generally (Luke 1:63; 10:20; Acts 13:8; 1 Cor 1:13, 15; Phil 4:3; Rev 13:1, a blasphemous name; 17:3; 21:14); of the Twelve Apostles (Matt 10:2); "His name had become known abroad" (a.t. [Mark 6:14]). The verb *kaléō* (2564), to call, sometimes takes *ónoma*, with the name in apposition (Matt 1:21, 23, 25; Mark 3:16, 17); also to call someone by a particular name (Luke 1:61). Preceded by *kaléō* and *epí* (1909) (Luke 1:59). "Whose name is" (a.t. [Mark 14:32; Luke 1:5; see Mark 5:9; Luke 2:25; John 1:6; 3:1]). In the acc. (Matt 27:57; Mark 14:32); the dat. (Matt 27:32; Luke 1:5), followed or preceded by the dat. (Luke 2:25; John 1:6; 3:1; Acts 5:1). Adv., with *katá* ([2596], according to or by), *kat' ónoma*, by name, individually (John 10:3; 3 John 1:14). Metonymically, "name" is put for the person or persons bearing that name (Luke 6:22; Acts 1:15; Rev 3:4; 11:13).

(II) Implying authority, e.g., to come or to do something in or by the name of someone, meaning using his name; as his messenger, envoy, representative; by his authority, with his sanction (Matt 21:9; 23:39; Mark 16:17; Luke 10:17; 24:47; John 5:43; 10:25; 14:26; Acts 3:6; 4:7; 9:27, 29; 1 Cor 5:4; 2 Thess 3:6; James 5:14). With the prep. *epí* (1909), upon (Mark 9:39; Luke 9:49). To ask (*aitéō* [154], ask, as an inferior from a superior) (John 14:13, 14). With the verb *laléō* (2980), to speak, and *didáskō* (1321), to teach (Acts 4:17, 18; 5:28, 40). Of impostors (Matt 7:22; Mark 9:38 [presumed]; 13:6; Luke 21:8).

(III) As implying character, dignity, referring to an honorable appellation, title (Matt 10:41, in the character of a prophet, as a prophet; see Matt 10:42; 18:5, in the character of being mine, as my disciple; Mark 9:37 [cf. the fuller expression in Mark 9:41]); "above . . . every name" (Eph 1:21); "a name which is above every name" (Phil 2:9). See Acts 4:12; Heb 1:4; Rev 19:16. A mere name, as opposed to reality (Rev 3:1, you have a name as though you lived, but you are dead).

(IV) Emphatic, the name of God, of the Lord, of Christ, as the metonymic expression for God Himself, Christ Himself, in all their being, attributes, relations, manifestations (Matt 6:9; 18:20; 28:19).

(A) Specifically of God where His name is said to be hallowed, revealed, invoked, honored (Matt 6:9; Luke 1:49; 11:2; John 12:28; 17:6; Rom 9:17; Heb 2:12). After *epikaléō* (1941), to invoke (Acts 2:21; 9:14; Rom 10:13; Sept.: Gen 4:26; Ps 9:2, 10; Isa 26:8). Of praise, homage (Rom 15:9; Heb 6:10; 13:15; Rev 11:18); of the knowledge, observance, and enjoyment of God's name (Matt 28:19; John 17:11, 12): in this sense also, after *epikaléō* (1941), to invoke (Acts 9:21; 22:16; 1 Cor 1:2); *baptízō* (907), to baptize in the name of the Lord (Matt 28:19; Acts 8:16; 19:5), and with the prep. *epí* (1909), upon (Acts 2:38); with the prep. *en* (1722), in (Acts 10:48 [cf. being baptized into {*eis* (1519)} Christ [Rom 6:3]); by antithesis, to baptize in the name of Paul (1 Cor 1:13, 15). In honor of His name, of Himself (Acts 15:14 [cf. Acts 15:17]); the blaspheming of His name (Rom 2:24; 1 Tim 6:1).

(B) Of Christ as the Messiah where His name is said to be honored, revered, believed on, invoked (Matt 12:21; John 1:12; 2:23; Acts 19:17; Rom 1:5; Phil 2:10; 2 Thess 1:12; Rev 2:13; 3:8). Where benefits are said to be received in or through the name of Christ (John 20:31; Acts 4:10, 30; 10:43; 1 Cor 6:11; 1 John 2:12). Where something is done in His name meaning in and through Him, through faith in Him (Eph 5:20; Col 3:17). Especially where the name of Christ stands for Christ as the head of the gospel dispensation (Matt 18:20; Acts 8:12). Where evils and sufferings are endured for the name of Christ (Matt 10:22; Mark 13:13; John 15:21; Rev 2:3). In the name of Christ (1 Pet 4:14). For the sake of the name of Christ (Matt 19:29; Luke 21:12, where *héneken* [1752], for the sake of, is used). With the prep. *hupér* (5228), for the name of Christ (Acts 5:41; 9:16; 21:13; 3 John 1:7). Where one opposes and blasphemes the name of Christ (Acts 26:9; James 2:7).

(C) Of the Holy Spirit (Matt 28:19).

Deriv.: *euốnumos* (2176), of good name; *onomázō* (3687), to name; *pseudố-numos* (5581), bearing a false name.

Syn.; *phḗmē* (5345), fame, good repute; *timḗ* (5092), honor; *dóxa* (1391), glory, recognition.

3687. ὀνομάζω *onomázō*; fut. *onomásō*; from *ónoma* (3686), name. To name, call by name. To name or mention (1 Cor 5:1; Eph 1:21; 5:3 [cf. Acts 19:13; Rom 15:20]; 2 Tim 2:19 where "to name the name of Christ" [a.t.] means to practice what He professes [cf. Sept.: Lev 24:16; Josh 23:7; Isa 26:13; Jer 20:9]). To name, give a name, denominate (Luke 6:13, 14 [cf. Eph 3:15]; Sept.: Gen 26:18 *eponomázō* [2028], to name further; Jer 25:29). To call (1 Cor 5:11 [cf. Sept.: Esth 9:4]).

Deriv.: *eponomázō* (2028), to call by name, nickname.

Syn.: *kaléō* (2564), to call; *epikaléō* (1941), to call upon; *prosagoreúō* (4316), to salute by name.

Ant.: *agnoéō* (50), to ignore.

3688. ὄνος *ónos*; gen. *ónou*, masc.-fem., neut. *ónon*, noun. A beast of burden, a donkey, colt, an ass (Matt 21:2, 5, 7; Luke 13:15; 14:5; John 12:15; Sept.: Gen 12:16; Judg 5:10). The diminutive: *onárion* (3678), a little donkey.

Deriv.: *onikós* (3684), pertaining to a donkey.

Syn.: *hupozúgion* (5268), under a yoke; *pốlos* (4454), a foal, whether colt or filly with emphasis on its being young.

3689. ὄντως *óntōs*; adv. from *ón*, pres. part. of *eimí* ([1510], to be), being. Really, truly (Mark 11:32; Luke 23:47; 24:34;

John 8:36; 1 Cor 14:25; Gal 3:21; 2 Pet 2:18 [TR]). With the art. *ho, hē óntōs* is used as an adj., meaning real, true (1 Tim 5:3, 5, 16; Sept.: Num 22:37).

Syn.: *mén* (3375), surely; *ge* (1065), doubtless; *alēthōs* (230), truly, indeed; *kaí gár* (*kaí* [2532], and; *gár* [1063], a particle of intensification), and in fact; *allá kaí* (*allá* [235], but; *kaí* [2532], and), but even, and indeed; *ei mḗ ti* (1509), unless indeed, except; *gnēsíōs* (1104), truly; *amḗn* (281), verily, a word with which our Lord introduces solemn pronouncements by repeating it twice.

Ant.: *tácha* (5029), possibly, perhaps; *ísōs* (2481), perhaps; *oudamōs* (3760), by no means; *oudé* (3761), not, neither, no more; *oudépote* (3763), not even at any time; *oudépō* (3764), not even yet; *oukéti* (3765), no longer; *oukoún* (3766), is it not therefore that, hence; *oúpō* (3768), not yet; *ou mḗ* (3364), not at all; *mēdamōs* (3365), by no means; *mēdé* (3366), but not, not even; *mēdépote* (3368), not even ever, never; *mēdépō* (3369), not even yet; *mēkéti* (3371), no further; *mḗ ouk* (3378), neither; *mḗpote* (3379), not ever; *mḗpōs* (3381), lest somehow; *mḗpō* (3380), not yet.

3690. ὄξος *óxos*; gen. *óxous*, neut. noun from *oxús* (3691), sharp. Sharp wine, vinegar. It used to be cheap, poor wine which was mixed with water, common drink especially for the poorer classes and soldiers (Sept.: Num 6:3; Ruth 2:14). Mingled with myrrh or bitter herbs, it was given to persons about to be executed in order to stupefy them. Alluded to in Sept.: Prov 31:6 *oínos* (3631), wine. In the NT: Matt 27:34, 48; Mark 15:36; Luke 23:36; John 19:29, 30.

3691. ὀξύς *oxús*; fem. *oxeía*, neut. *oxú*, adj. Sharp, having a piercing point or keen edge (Rev 1:16; 2:12; 14:14, 17, 18; 19:15; Sept.: Isa 49:2; Ezek 5:1). Swift, nimble, since the idea of sharpness or keenness implies also eagerness, vehemence (Rom 3:15 [cf. Isa 59:7]; Sept.: Prov 22:29; Amos 2:15).

Deriv.: *óxos* (3690), sharp wine, vinegar; *paroxúnō* (3947), to sharpen or whet.

Syn.: *tachús* (5036), speedy; *tachinós* (5031) a poetical form of *tachús*, meaning a swift approach or swiftly; *spoudáios* (4705), prompt, earnest, diligent.

3692. ὀπή *opḗ*; gen. *opḗs*, fem. noun. A hole, referring to a hole or cavern because of the light which shines in; therefore, a hole or cavern in the earth (Heb 11:38). A hole or opening from which a spring of water issues (James 3:11; Sept.: Ex 33:22).

Syn.: With the meaning of hole or opening: *spḗlaion* (4693), a grotto, cavern, den; *phōleós* (5454), den or hole; *ánoixis* (457), an opening, metaphorically the mouth; *tópos* (5117), place; *chásma* (5490), chasm, gulf; *ábussos* (12), abyss; *trúpēma* (5169), an aperture, the eye of a needle.

Ant.: *phragmós* (5418), a fence; *kálumma* (2571), a cover; *epíblēma* (1915), a patch; *epikálumma* (1942), a covering.

3693. ὄπισθεν *ópisthen*; adv. from *ópis* (n.f.), a looking back, and the syllabic suffix -*then* denoting from or at a place. Behind, after, at the back of any person or thing (Matt 9:20; 15:23; Mark 5:27, "from behind" [a.t.]; Luke 8:44; 23:26; Rev 4:6; 5:1, "a book" [a.t.] "written within and on the back side" [a.t.]; Sept.: Gen 18:10; Ruth 2:7). In Class. Gr. also used of time. Also from *ópis* (n.f.): *opísō* (3694), back, behind.

Syn.: *hústeron* (5305), eventually as terminal, last.

Ant.: *prín* (4250), before; *émprosthen* (1715), in front, before; *métōpon* (3359), forehead; *ópsis* (3799), visage, sight, face to face; *énanti* (1725), in front; *katenópion* (2714), directly in front of; *antikrú* (481), over against, opposite.

3694. ὀπίσω *opísō*; adv. from *ópis* (n.f.), a looking back. Shows the extremity or end of a thing, used with a gen. Behind, back, backwards, speaking of place and time. In the NT used in an absolute sense only of place (Luke 7:38). With the art., in the pl., *tá opísō*, implying "things behind" and with the prep. *eis* (1519), unto or toward the back, backward, back, to go back, fall back (John 18:6); looking backward (Luke 9:62); to turn back (Matt 24:18; Mark 13:16; Luke 17:31; John 6:66; 20:14; Sept.: Gen 19:17, 26; 2 Sam 1:22; 1 Kgs 18:37 without the art.). Metaphorically used in Phil 3:13, referring to former pursuits and accomplishments. It is used often in the NT and Sept. with the gen. as a prep., but in Class. Gr. it is normally not used when spoken of place or time. Also from *ópis* (n.f.): *ópisthen* (3693), behind, after.

(I) Of place, behind, after, meaning a place where (Rev 1:10, "behind me"; Sept.: Song 2:9; Isa 57:8). With verbs implying motion, as after someone, meaning a following as a disciple or otherwise "followeth after me" (Matt 10:38; see Matt 4:19; 16:24; Mark 1:17, 20; 8:34; Luke 9:23; 14:27; 19:14; 21:8; John 12:19; Acts 5:37; 20:30). Metaphorically (1 Tim 5:15; 2 Pet 2:10; Jude 1:7; Rev 12:15; Sept.: Deut 4:3; 2 Kgs 13:2). See Sept.: 1 Sam 13:7; 2 Kgs 6:19. Also implying motion meaning behind someone, to his rear, in expressions of aversion, "get thee behind me," meaning go away (Matt 4:10 in some MSS; 16:23; Mark 8:33; Luke 4:8; Sept.: Isa 38:17).

(II) Of time, after, as "he who comes after me" (a.t. [Matt 3:11; Mark 1:7; John 1:15, 27, 30; Sept.: 1 Kgs 1:24]).

3695. ὁπλίζω *hoplízō*; fut. *hoplísō*, from *hóplon* (3696), weapon. To furnish, prepare, referring to food or drink; to equip with arms, as a chariot or ship. In the NT, only in the mid., *hoplízomai*, to prepare oneself for a work, to arm oneself, take up arms; used metaphorically in a moral sense with the acc. (1 Pet 4:1).
Deriv.: *kathoplízō* (2528), to furnish or be armed fully.

3696. ὅπλον *hóplon*; gen. *hóplou*, neut. noun. An instrument, implement for preparing a thing, and in the pl. standing for weapons of warfare. In the NT only pl., *tá hópla*, instruments, implements.

(I) Of war as weapons, arms, armor (John 18:3; metaphorically Rom 13:12; 2 Cor 6:7; 10:4; Sept.: 2 Chr 23:10; Jer 21:4; 26:3).

(II) Metaphorically meaning instruments with which something is effected or done (Rom 6:13; Sept.: Prov 14:7).
Deriv.: *hoplízo* (3695), to arm.
Syn.: *hárma* (716), a chariot; *lógchē* (3057), a spear; *máchaira* (3162), sword, knife; *tóxon* (5115), a bow; *rhomphaía* (4501), sword; *thureós* (2375), a large shield; *perikephalaía* (4030), helmet.

3697. ὁποῖος *hopoíos*; fem. *hopoía*, neut. *hopoíon*, relative pron. Of what kind or sort (Acts 26:29; 1 Cor 3:13; Gal 2:6; 1 Thess 1:9; James 1:24). In some of the above expressed also as *hopoíos kaí*, such as (Acts 26:29).
Syn.: *potapós* (4217), from what country, of what sort; *poíos* (4169), of what kind; *hoíos* (3634), of what sort; *mégas* (3173), great.
Ant.: *olígos* (3641), little; *mikrós* (3398), small; *eláchistos* (1646), least; *ásēmos* (767), insignificant.

3698. ὁπότε *hopóte*; comp. relative particle of time, from *hóte* (3753), when. When, at what time, of what actually took place at a certain time (Luke 6:3).
Syn.: *hótan* (3752), when, while; *hóte* (3753), when; *háma* (260), at the same time; *tóte* (5119), then.
Ant.: *poté* (4218), never; *oudépō* (3764), not even yet; *oudépote* (3763), not even at any time; *mēdépote* (3368), never; *mēdépō* (3369), not yet; *mēkéti* (3371), not any more.

3699. ὅπου *hópou*; comp. relative adv. from *poú* (4226), where. Of place, meaning where, in which or what place. Used after the express mention of a place (Matt 6:19, 20; Mark 9:44; Luke 12:33; John 1:28; Rev 12:6, 14; 17:9; Sept.: Judg 18:10 *hou . . . ekeí*). Followed by the subjunctive of that which is indef. (Mark 14:14; see Matt 6:21; Luke 12:34; 17:37; John 12:26). Including the idea of a demonstrative meaning, there, where (Matt 25:24, 26; Mark 5:40; John 3:8; 7:34; Rom 15:20). With *án* (302), meaning wheresoever, followed by a subjunctive (Mark 9:18; 14:9); followed by *eán* (1437), if (Matt 24:28; Mark 6:10, 56 followed by *án* [302], a suppositional particle suggesting an uncertainty, a wish, a possibility, followed by the indic.). Metaphorically it is used in a wider sense including time, manner, circumstances (Col 3:11; 2 Pet 2:11). With *ekeí* (1563), there, as an emph. (James 3:16). With the meaning of there where (Heb 9:16; 10:18; Sept.: Prov 26:20). In reasoning meaning where, whereas, since (1 Cor 3:3). After verbs of motion, whither (John 8:21, 22; 14:4; Heb 6:20). Followed by *án* (302), if, with the subjunctive (Luke 9:57; James 3:4; Rev 14:4) or by *eán* (1437), if, soever (Matt 8:19).

Syn.: *hoú* (3757), where.

3700. ὀπτάνομαι *optánomai* and ὄπτομαι *óptomai*; fut. *ópsomai*, aor. pass. *óphthēn*, aor. subjunctive *ópsesthe* (Luke 13:28), pass. in Acts 1:3 (1 Kgs 8:8), used to supply the aor. mid. and pass. and the future tenses for *horáō* (3708), to see. To see, perceive with the eyes, to look at, trans. implying not only the mere act of seeing but also the actual perception of what one sees, thus differing from *blépō* (991), to see, behold (Matt 24:30; 26:64; 28:7; Mark 16:7; John 16:17 [cf. Matt 5:8; Mark 13:26; 14:62; 16:7; Luke 3:6; 17:22; 21:27; John 1:50, 51; 16:16, 19, 22; 19:37]; Acts 20:25; Rom 15:21; Heb 12:14; 13:23; 1 John 3:2; Rev 22:4).

(I) To look upon, behold, contemplate, followed by *eis* (1519), unto (John 19:37 from Zech 12:10; see Ps 8:4; Isa 17:8).

(A) In the form of an aor. pass., *óphthē* is used in a pass. sense meaning to be seen, appear (Matt 17:3; Mark 9:4; Luke 1:11; 9:31; 22:43; 24:34; Acts 2:3; 7:2, 26, 30, 35; 9:17; 13:31; 16:9; 26:16; 1 Cor 15:5–8; 1 Tim 3:16; Heb 9:28; Rev

11:19; 12:1, 3). Particularly and spoken of things, followed by *en* (1722), in, of place (Rev 11:19; 12:1, 3); with the dat. of person (Acts 2:3; 16:9). Spoken of angels followed by the dat. of person, such as Zechariah (Luke 1:11, "there appeared unto him an angel"; 22:43; Acts 7:30, 35; see Sept.: Ex 3:2; Judg 6:12); of God (Acts 7:2; see Gen 12:7; 17:1); of dead persons (Matt 17:3, "appeared unto them Moses"; Mark 9:4); with *en*, in, of manner (Luke 9:31, "who appeared in glory"); of Jesus after His resurrection (Luke 24:34; Acts 9:17; 13:31; 26:16; 1 Cor 15:5–8; 1 Tim 3:16). In the fut., *ópsomai* (Matt 28:7, 10 "there shall ye see him"; Luke 3:6 "All flesh shall see the salvation of God" [cf. Isa 40:5; Luke 13:28; John 11:40; Acts 2:17, cf. Joel 2:28; 3:1; Rev 1:7]). Parallel with the meaning of *suníēmi* (4920), to comprehend, understand (Rom 15:21). Fut. pass. *ophthḗsomai* (Heb 9:28).

(II) In the sense of to visit (John 16:22; Heb 13:23). See Sept.: 2 Sam 13:5; 2 Kgs 8:29. As mid., meaning to show oneself, present one's self to or before someone (Acts 7:26; Sept.: 2 Kgs 14:8).

(III) With the meaning to see take place, witness (Luke 17:22, "to see one of the days"). Fut. pass. *ophthḗsomai*, as causative (Acts 26:16, "a witness both of these things which thou hast seen and of those things in the which I will appear unto thee").

(IV) In the fut., *sú ópsei* or in the pl. *humeís ópsesthe*, see thou to it, look ye to it, a milder form for the imper. (Matt 27:4, 24; Acts 18:15).

(V) To experience, attain to, enjoy (John 3:36, "shall not see life" or enjoy life; Sept.: Ps 48:20. In a wider sense, to see God, to be admitted to His presence, enjoy His fellowship and special favor, the figure being drawn from the customs of oriental courts (Matt 5:8; Heb 12:14; Rev 22:4).

Deriv.: *ómma* (3659), the eye; *optasía* (3701), vision.

Syn.: *horáō* (3708), to behold, perceive, beware, heed; *emblépō* (1689), to look earnestly; *eídō* (1492) to know; *theōréō* (2334), to look at a thing with interest and for a purpose, usually with amazement; *anatheōréō* (333), to consider contemplatively; *theáomai* (2300), to look carefully and deliberately; *epopteúō* (2029), to oversee; *atenízō* (816), to gaze; *katanoéō* (2657), to comprehend or perceive fully; *phaínō* (5316), to shine, appear; *epiphaínō* (2014) in the act. voice, to give light, and in the pass., to appear; *anaphaínō* (398), to appear suddenly; *phaneróō* (5319) in the act. to manifest, and in the pass. to be manifested; *emphanízō* (1718), to shine or to make known, signify, inform; *blépō* (991), to see or perceive, to beware, heed; *noéō* (3539), to perceive with the mind; *katanoéō* (2657), to perceive clearly, consider carefully; *proséchō* (4337), to turn one's attention to; *epéchō* (1907), to give attention to; *skopéō* (4648), to take heed; *phulássō* (5442), to guard; *ginōskō* (1097), to know by experience and observation; *epiginōskō* (1921), to become fully acquainted with; *aisthánomai* (143), to perceive.

3701. ὀπτασία *optasía*; gen. *optasías*, fem. noun from *optánomai* (3700), to appear. A sight, appearance, especially a vision or apparition (Luke 1:22; 24:23; Acts 26:19; 2 Cor 12:1; Sept.: Dan 9:23; 10:1, 7, 8).
    Syn.: *hórama* (3705), a spectacle, an appearance, vision; *hórasis* (3706), a sense of sight, the ability to see; *phantasía* (5325), fantasy; *phántasma* (5326), phantasm, specter, spirit which has no material reality; *enúpnion* (1798), dream; *ónar* (3677), dream.
    Ant.: *alḗtheia* (225), truth, reality; *hupóstasis* (5287), substance.

3702. ὀπτός *optós*; fem. *optḗ*, neut. *optón*, adj. from *optáō* (n.f.), to roast. Roasted, broiled, cooked by fire (Luke 24:42, of the fish; Sept.: Ex 12:8, 9).

3703. ὀπώρα *opṓra*; gen. *opóras*, fem. noun. Fruit of late summer or autumn

(Rev 18:14; Sept.: Jer 47:10, 12). Most probably derived from *opós* (n.f.), juice, and *hṓra* (5610), hour, time, season. Fruit, literally time of juice. Since autumn is the season when fruits in general are full of juice and when the juices of grapes, apples, and so forth, are pressed out.
    Deriv.: *phthinoporinós* (5352), pertaining to the autumn.
    Syn.: *karpós* (2590), fruit; *génnēma* (1081), produce.

3704. ὅπως *hópōs*; adv. of manner, also used as a conj.
    (I) As a relative adv. meaning in what manner, how (Luke 24:20).
    (II) As a conj., meaning in such manner that, so that, that, similar in use to *hína* (2443), so that, which indicates purpose, to the end that, in order that, but also as marking the event, result or upshot of an action. In the NT, *hópōs* is found only with the subjunctive indicating the final purpose, to the end that, in order that, or in a neg. sense meaning in order not to, lest.
    (A) When it is used without *án* (302), if (a particle denoting supposition or wish), and preceded **(1)** By a pres. or by an aor. of any mood except the indic. and then the subjunctive, it marks that what is supposed will really take place; the aor. (Matt 6:2, 16; Mark 5:23; Acts 9:12; 2 Cor 8:14; 2 Thess 1:12; Heb 9:15; 1 Pet 2:9); with the neg. *mḗ* (3361), *hópōs mḗ* (Acts 20:16; 1 Cor 1:29). **(2)** By an aor. imper. (Matt 2:8; 6:4; Acts 23:15, 23; 2 Cor 8:11); with the neg. *mḗ* (Matt 6:18). **(3)** By a fut. (Acts 24:26). **(4)** By a past tense (Matt 26:59; Acts 9:17, 24; 25:26; Rom 9:17).
    (B) With *án*, "for the purpose that" (Matt 6:5; Rom 3:4); preceded by the imper. (Acts 3:19, "that at length the times . . . may come" [a.t.]); by the fut. (Acts 15:17).
    (C) Expressing mere result or consequence, so that, so as that, with the subjunctive. Preceded by: **(1)** A pres. (Matt 5:45, "That ye may be the children of

your Father"); by a perf. as pres. (Luke 16:26). **(2)** A fut. (Matt 23:34, 35). **(3)** A perf. (Heb 2:9, "we see Jesus . . . for the suffering of death, crowned with glory and honor; that he by the grace of God should taste death for every man"). Here belongs the phrase *hópōs plērōthḗ tó rhēthén* (*plērōthḗ*, from *plēróō* [4137], to fulfill; *rhēthén*, from *rhéō* [4483] or *eréō*, to utter, speak), so that which has been said may be fulfilled (Matt 2:23); preceded by a past tense or by *toúto gégonen*, implied (*toúto* [5124], this; *gégonen*, from *gínomai* [1096], to become) as in Matt 2:23; 8:17; 12:17; 13:35. This is equivalent to *hína plērōthḗ* (*hína* [2443], so that) so that it be fulfilled. **(4)** In Luke 2:35, it is used with *án* (302), if, a particle of possibility, *hópōs án*, so that.

(D) Used after verbs of asking, entreating, exhorting, and also of deciding, commanding, which in themselves imply a purpose, *hópōs* became equivalent to a demonstrative conj. like the Eng. word that, simply pointing out or introducing that to which the preceding words refer. The same verbs often take after them the inf. or *hína* (Matt 8:34; 9:38; Luke 7:3; 10:2; 11:37; Acts 8:15, 24; 9:2; 23:20; 25:3; James 5:16); after verbs of decision (Matt 12:14; 22:15; Mark 3:6 [cf. Matt 27:1, *hṓste* {5620}, so that]); so also after verbs or phrases implying decision, authority, command.

Syn.: *hína* (2443), so that.

3705. ὅραμα *hórama*; gen. *horámatos*, neut. noun from *horáō* (3708), to see, behold. A sight, spectacle, that which is seen (Matt 17:9; Acts 7:31; Sept.: Ex 3:3; Deut 28:34). Used of a supernatural appearance, a vision (Acts 9:10, 12; 10:3, 17, 19; 11:5; 12:9; 16:9, 10; 18:9; Sept.: Gen 15:1; 46:2; Dan 8:1).

Syn.: *blémma* (990), vision; *eídos* (1491), sight, appearance; *theōría* (2335), a spectacle, a sight; *optasía* (3701), apparition, vision; *ópsis* (3799), appearance, face; *prósōpon* (4383), face, countenance.

3706. ὅρασις *hórasis*; gen. *horáseōs*, fem. noun from *horáō* (3708), to see, perceive, heed. Sight, sense of seeing. With the meaning of *hórama* (3705), what one sees, a sight or vision presented to the mind, that which is appearing (Acts 2:17 quoted from Joel 2:28; Rev 4:3; 9:17; Sept.: Isa 1:1; Jer 14:14).

Syn.: *optasía* (3701), vision; *hórama* (3705), a vision. *Hórama* differs from *hórasis* in that it contemplates the vision objectively and focuses upon its content presenting the vision as that which results from the act of appearing, namely, that which is manifested, what is seen. *Hórasis*, contemplates the vision subjectively and focuses upon its character presenting the vision as that which performs the act of appearing, that which appears, that which makes itself visible.

Ant.: *skótos* (4655), darkness; *tuphlós* (5185), blind.

3707. ὁρατός *horatós*; fem. *horatḗ*, neut. *horatón*, adj. from *horáō* (3708), to see. Visible (Col 1:16; Sept.: Job 34:26; 37:21).

Syn.: *emphanḗs* (1717), manifest; *phanerós* (5318), open, apparent; *dḗlos* (1212), evident, manifest; *diaphanḗs* (1307), transparent; *katádēlos* (2612), completely manifest.

Ant.: *aóratos* (517), not seen, invisible; *aphanḗs* (852), nonapparent; *apókruphos* (614), secret; *kruptós* (2927), concealed, hidden; *ádēlos* (82), not evident.

3708. ὁράω *horáō*; contracted *horṓ*; fut. *ópsomai*, perf. *heóraka*, pluperf. *heōrákein*, which takes a double augment; perf. 3d person pl. *heórakan* instead of *heōrákasi* (Luke 9:36[TR]; Col 2:1); the 2d aor. is made throughout by *eídon*, from *eídō* (1492), to see, perceive; the aor. mid. and pass. and the future tenses are supplied by *óptomai* (3700), to see. To see, perceive with the eyes, look at, trans. implying not the mere act of seeing, but also the actual perception of some object, thus differing from *blépō* (991), to see.

(I) Particularly with the acc. of person or thing (Luke 1:22, "he had seen a vision"; 9:36; 16:23, "seeth Abraham afar off"; 24:23; John 4:45; 5:37; 6:2; 9:37; 20:18, 25, 29; Acts 7:44; 22:15; 1 John 1:1); with the acc. (John 1:34; 1 Pet 1:8; Sept.: Gen 13:15; Ex 2:12); with the gen. (Acts 22:15). Followed by the acc. and part. (Heb 2:8).

In various modified senses. To see face to face, meaning to see and converse with, have personal acquaintance and fellowship with (John 6:36; 8:57; 14:9; 15:24); followed by *tó prósōpon* (4383), face, to see one's face (Acts 20:25; Col 2:1). To see God, figuratively meaning to know Him, be acquainted with Him, know His character, only in John's writings (John 1:18; 6:46; 14:7, 9; 15:24; 1 John 3:6; 4:20; 3 John 1:11). In these cases, it is equivalent to *blépō* (991), to see (cf. 1 Kgs 10:8).

(II) Figuratively of the mind, meaning to see, perceive with the mind or senses.

(A) Generally to be aware of, observe, with the acc. and part. (Acts 8:23); followed by *hóti* (3754), that (James 2:24; Sept.: Gen 26:28).

(B) Of things, meaning to see and know, to come to know, learn (John 3:11, 32; 8:38). In the sense of to understand (Col 2:18).

(III) In an absolute sense, meaning to see to it, take care, take heed, only in imper. phrases. *Hóra* (Heb 8:5 quoted from Ex 25:40); followed by *mḗ* (3361), not, meaning take heed lest, beware; followed by the subj. (Matt 8:4; Mark 1:44; 1 Thess 5:15); followed by the imper. (Matt 9:30; 24:6). Before another similar imper., followed by *apó* (575), of, from, meaning beware of (Matt 16:6; Mark 8:15; Luke 12:15).

Deriv.: *aóratos* (517), invisible; *aphoráō* (872), to look away from one thing so as to see another; *kathoráō* (2529), to see clearly; *hórama* (3705), a spectacle, appearance, vision; *hórasis* (3706), vision,

sight; *horatós* (3707), visible; *prooráō* (4308), to foresee.

Syn.: *blépō* (991), to see; *theōréō* (2334), to view, contemplate; *eídō* (1492), to see, perceive; *diakrínō* (1252), to distinguish, discern; *blépō* (991), to see; *paratēréō* (3906), to observe; *theáomai* (2300), to look closely; *theōréō* (2334), to discern, perceive; *exetázō* (1833), to ascertain.

Ant.: *apokrúptō* (613), to keep secret; *krúptō* (2928), to hide; *egkrúptō* (1470), to hide in; *tuphlóō* (5186), to blind; *skotízō* (4654), to darken; *episkiázō* (1982), to overshadow.

3709. ὀργή *orgḗ*; gen. *orgḗs*, fem. noun from *orégō* (3713), covet after, desire. Wrath, anger as a state of mind. Contrast *thumós* (2372), indignation, wrath as the outburst of a vengeful mind. Aristotle says that *orgḗ*, anger, is desire with grief (cf. Mark 3:5; Rom 12:19; Eph 4:31; Col 3:8). Fretfulness (1 Tim 2:8; James 1:19, 20; Sept.: Deut 32:19; Josh 9:20; 2 Sam 12:5; Job 16:10; Prov 21:14). The Stoics sought to let go of all passion, but were insensitive to others, often punishing any who had hurt them. The anger or wrath of man (Eph 4:31; Col 3:8; James 1:19, 20); of God as utter abhorrence to sin but longing mixed with grief for those who live in it (Heb 3:11; 4:3; Sept.: Ex 4:14; 32:11; Deut 29:20; Isa 10:5); the effect of anger or wrath, i.e., punishment (Rom 4:15) from man (Rom 13:4, 5) or from God, referring to divine judgment to be inflicted upon the wicked (Matt 3:7; Luke 3:7; 21:23, John 3:36; Rom 1:18; 2:5, 8; 3:5; 5:9; 9:22; Eph 2:3; 5:6; Col 3:6; 1 Thess 1:10; 2:16; 5:9; Rev 6:16, 17; 11:18; 14:10; 16:19; 19:15).

Deriv.: *orgízō* (3710), to make angry, provoke; *orgílos* (3711), angry, quick-tempered.

Syn.: *pikría* (4088), bitterness; *cholḗ* (5521), gall; *eritheía* (2052), partisan strife; *aganáktēsis* (24), indignation.

Ant.: *egkráteia* (1466), self-control; *praótēs* (4236), meekness; *praǘtēs* (4240), mildness; *hēsuchía* (2271), quietness;

eirḗnē (1515), peace; *galḗnē* (1055), calm; *hupomonḗ* (5281), patience.

3710. ὀργίζω *orgízō*; fut. *orgísō*, from *orgḗ* (3709), wrath. To make angry, provoke. In the NT, only in the mid. / pass. *orgízomai*, aor. *orgísthēn*, to. be or become angry, provoked (Matt 18:34; 22:7; Luke 14:21; 15:28; Eph 4:26; Rev 11:18). Followed by the dat. (Matt 5:22); with *epí* (1909), upon (Rev 12:17; Sept.: Num 25:3; 1 Kgs 11:9; Isa 12:1).

　　Deriv.: *parorgízō* (3949), to arouse to wrath, provoke.

　　Syn.: *puróō* (4448), to burn up with anger or passion; *phruássō* (5433), to rage; *aphrízō* (875), to foam with anger; *ōrúomai* (5612), to roar; *thumóō* (2373), to be very angry; *exegeírō* (1825), to arouse, instigate; *choláō* (5520), to be melancholy, irritable; *aganaktéō* (23), to be indignant; *erethízō* (2042), to provoke; *diegeírō* (1326), to stir up; *paroxúnō* (3947), to exasperate, provoke.

　　Ant.: *egkrateúomai* (1467), to exercise self-restraint, be temperate; *eupsuchéō* (2174), to be in good spirits; *katastéllō* (2687), to appease; *hēsucházō* (2270), to hold one's peace, be quiet; *eirēnopoiéō* (1517), to be a peacemaker; *sunéchomai* (4912), to control oneself.

3711. ὀργίλος *orgílos*; fem. *orgílē*, neut. *orgílon* adj. from *orgḗ* (3709), anger, wrath. Prone to anger (Titus 1:7; Sept.: Prov 22:24).

　　Ant.: *práos* (4235), meek; *hēsúchios* (2272), quiet; *eirēnikós* (1516), peaceable; *éremos* (2263), tranquil.

3712. ὀργυιά *orguiá*; gen. *orguiás*, fem. noun from *orégō* (3713), to desire, to stretch oneself. A fathom, the space which one can measure by extending the arms laterally to clasp as much as possible. It includes the breadth of the chest (Acts 27:28).

　　Syn.: *métron* (3358), a measure; *péchus* (4083), a cubit.

3713. ὀρέγω *orégō*; fut. *oréxō*. Literally, to stretch out especially with the hands, to snatch. In the NT, only in the mid. *orégomai*, to stretch oneself, reach after something, and hence metaphorically meaning to covet, long after, desire, try to gain, be ambitious (in a benign manner) (1 Tim 3:1; Heb 11:16). By implication, to indulge in, to love (1 Tim 6:10).

　　Deriv.: *orgé* (3709), wrath, anger as a state of mind; *orguiá* (3712) a fathom; *órexis* (3715), appetite, lust or concupiscence.

　　Syn.: *epithuméō* (1937), to fix the desire upon; *zēlóō* (2206), to covet earnestly; *pleonektéō* (4122), to be covetous, to defraud; *epipothéō* (1971), to long for; *axióō* (515), to desire; *himeíromai* (2442), to yearn after; *thélō* (2309), to wish, implying volition and purpose as well as the ability to execute that which one wishes; *boúlomai* (1014), to intend or be inclined to do something; *zētéō* (2212), to seek; *epizētéō* (1934), to seek earnestly; *anazētéō* (327), to seek carefully; *ekzētéō* (1567), to seek out; *epizētéō* (1934), to seek after.

　　Ant.: *arkéō* (714), to suffice, satisfy; *eparkéō* (1884), literally to ward off, relieve, in the mid. to find satisfaction in what one is and has.

3714. ὀρεινός *oreinós*; fem. *oreinḗ*, neut. *oreinón*, adj. from *óros* (3735), mountain. Mountainous, found on mountains, wild, such as grass (Sept.: Prov 27:25). In the NT, used of the hill-country (Luke 1:39, 65; Sept.: Gen 14:10; Deut 11:11).

　　Syn.: *anōterikós* (510), upper, referring to the coast or country, also the high central plateau.

　　Ant.: *pedinós* (3977), level, such as ground, a plain.

3715. ὄρεξις *órexis*; gen. *oréxeōs*, fem. noun from *orégō* (3713), to desire. Appetite, lust or concupiscence (Rom 1:27). It is always the reaching out after an object with the purpose of drawing it to oneself and appropriating it. The opposite is *hormé* (3730), the hostile motion of springing toward an object with the purpose of assaulting it.

Syn.: *epithumía* (1939), desire, longing; *euché* (2171), wish; *thélēma* (2307), desire.

Ant.: *kóros* (2884), measure, satiety; *chórtasma* (5527), sustenance, repletion.

3716. ὀρθοποδέω *orthopodéō*; contracted *orthopodó*, fut. *orthopodḗsō*, from *orthópous* (n.f.), standing upright, which is from *orthós* (3717), right, level, and *poús* (4228), foot. To walk uprightly, correctly, carefully. Used figuratively in Gal 2:14.

Syn.: *stoichéō* (4748), to walk in an orderly manner; *euthudroméō* (2113), to proceed on a straight course.

Ant.: *metatíthēmi* (3346), to pervert, change positions; *metakinéō* (3334), to place elsewhere, move away; *parabaínō* (3845), to transgress; *ekklínō* (1578), to deviate, turn from.

3717. ὀρθός *orthós*; fem. *orthḗ*, neut. *orthón*, adj. Straight, erect, upright. Used with *anístēmi* (450), to stand, to stand straight up from a prostrate position (Acts 14:10). In a moral sense, straight as opposed to crooked, meaning upright, true, right, good (Heb 12:13).

Deriv.: *anorthóō* (461), to make straight or upright again; *orthotoméō* (3718), to rightly divide; *orthós* (3723), rightly.

Syn.: *alēthinós* (228), truthful; *díkaios* (1342), just; *eúthetos* (2111), appropriate; *euthús* (2117), straight.

Ant.: *ádikos* (94), unrighteous; *pseudḗs* (5571), false; *átopos* (824), out of place; *aneúthetos* (428), not well set; *skoliós* (4646), crooked

3718. ὀρθοτομέω *orthotoméō*; contracted *orthotomó*, fut. *orthotomḗsō*, from *orthós* (3717), right and *témnō* (n.f., see below), to cut or divide. To handle correctly, skillfully; to correctly teach the

word of truth (2 Tim 2:15; Sept.: Prov 3:6; 11:5).

Deriv. of *témnō* (n.f.): *peritémnō* (4059), to circumcise; *suntémnō* (4932), to cut short; *tomóteros* (5114), finer edged, sharper.

Syn.: *alētheúō* (226), to be true.

Ant.: *streblóō* (4761), to pervert, twist, wrest; *planáō* (4105), to lead astray; *pseúdomai* (5574), to deceive by falsehood; *diastréphō* (1294), to distort; *apatáō* (538), to deceive; *exapatáō* (1818), to greatly deceive.

3719. ὀρθρίζω *orthrízō*; fut. *orthrísō*, from *órthros* (3722), dawn. To rise early, to work early in the morning (Luke 21:38; Sept.: Gen 19:27; Judg 19:9; Job 7:21). The Attic form was *orthreúō*.

3720. ὀρθρινός *orthrinós*; fem. *orthrinḗ*, neut. *orthrinón*; adj. from *órthros* (3722), dawn. Pertaining to morning, early (Rev 22:16 [TR]; Sept.: Hos 6:4; 13:3). Same as *órthrios* (3721), early in the morning.

Syn.: *prōía* (4405), morning, early; *prṓimos* (4406), early, autumnal; *prōïnós* (4407), pertaining to the morning; *háma prōí* (*háma* [260], at the same time; *prōï* [4404], morning, early), early in the morning; *anatolḗ* (395), sunrise; *augḗ* (827), dawn.

Ant.: *hespéra* (2073), evening; *opsé* (3796), late in the day, after the close of the day; *ópsimos* (3797), later, latter; *ópsios* (3798), afternoon, nightfall, evening.

3721. ὄρθριος *órthrios*; fem. *orthría*, neut. *órthrion*; adj. Early, as a subst. morning. Used as an adv. in Luke 24:22. Same as *orthrinós* (3720).

3722. ὄρθρος *órthros*; gen. *órthrou*, masc. noun. The daybreak or dawning of the day, the early morning (Luke 24:1; John 8:2; Acts 5:21; Sept.: Josh 6:15; Joel 2:2).

Deriv.: *orthrízō* (3719), to use the dawn; *orthrinós* (3720), relating to the dawn; *órthrios* (3721), in the dawn, early.

Syn.: *prōïa* (4405), morning; *prōï* (4404), at dawn, daybreak; *prōïmos* (4406), dawning, early; *prōïnós* (4407), pertaining to the dawn; *anatolē* (395), sunrise; *augē* (827), dawn.

Ant.: *hespéra* (2073), evening; *opsé* (3796), evening, the close of the day; *núx* (3571), night; *skótos* (4655), darkness.

3723. ὀρθῶς *orthōs*; adv. from *orthós* (3717), right. Rightly, plainly (Mark 7:35). With a figurative moral sense (Luke 7:43; 10:28; 20:21; Sept.: Gen 40:16; Deut 5:28).

Syn.: *akribōs* (199), circumspectly, exactly, accurately; *asphalōs* (806), securely, assuredly, safely; *kalōs* (2573), well; *eu* (2095), well, good; *dikaíōs* (1346), righteously, rightly; *axíōs* (516), worthily.

Ant.: *adíkōs* (95), wrongfully; *kakōs* (2560) badly, amiss, grievously.

3724. ὀρίζω *horízō*; fut. *horísō*, from *hóros* (n.f., see *methórios* [3181]), boundary, limit. To mark out definitely, determine, appoint, constitute. Of persons, to constitute, appoint (Rom 1:4 [cf. Eph 1:20; Phil 2:8]; Acts 10:42; 17:31); in respect to time it means to determine the time (Acts 17:26; Heb 4:7). To determine, resolve, decree (Luke 22:22; Acts 2:23; 11:29).

Deriv.: *aphorízō* (873), to set off by boundary, exclude, separate; *prooorízō* (4309), foreordain.

Syn.: *tássō* (5021), ordain, appoint; *diatássō* (1299), to arrange thoroughly; *diachōrízō* (1316), to apportion, separate; *aphorízō* (873), to set off by boundary, exclude.

Ant.: *katargéō* (2673), to abolish.

3725. ὅριον *hórion*; gen. *horíou*, neut. noun, the diminutive of *hóros* (n.f.), boundary, limit. A boundary, limit, border. In the NT, only in the pl., *tá hória*, the borders of a land, frontiers (Matt 4:13; 19:1; Mark 10:1; Sept.: Gen 10:19; Num 21:13). Figuratively, it stands for a space within certain boundaries, region,

territory, district (Matt 2:16; 8:34; 15:22, 39; Mark 5:17; 7:31; Acts 13:50; Sept.: Gen 23:17; Ex 7:27; Judg 20:6).

3726. ὀρκίζω *horkízō*; fut. *horkísō*, from *hórkos* (3727), an oath. To put to an oath, make to swear. In the NT, to adjure a person (Mark 5:7; Acts 19:13; 1 Thess 5:27; Sept.: Gen 50:25). In Matt 26:63, *exorkízō* (1844), to adjure.

Deriv.: *exorkízō* (1844), to adjure.

Syn.: *ómnumi* (3660), to make an oath, to declare or promise with an oath; *epimarturéō* (1957), to corroborate; *marturéō* (3140), to testify; *bebaióō* (950), to confirm.

Ant.: *pseudomarturéō* (5576), to give false witness; *pseúdomai* (5574), to lie.

3727. ὅρκος *hórkos*; gen. *hórkou*, masc. noun. An oath (Matt 14:7, 9; 26:72; Mark 6:26; Luke 1:73; Acts 2:30; Heb 6:16, 17; James 5:12; Sept.: Gen 24:8; 26:3). Metonymically for what is promised with an oath (Matt 5:33 [cf. Sept.: Num 30:3]).

Deriv.: *horkízō* (3726), to put to an oath, make to swear.

3728. ὀρκωμοσία *horkōmosía*; gen. *horkōmosías*, fem. noun from *horkōmotéō* (n.f.), to take an oath, swear, which is from *hórkos* (3727), an oath, and *omnúō* (3660), to swear, take an oath. The swearing or taking of an oath, and by implication an oath (Heb 7:20, 21, 28; Sept.: Ezek 17:18, 19).

3729. ὀρμάω *hormáō*; contracted *hormō*, fut. *hormēsō*, from *hormē* (3730), onset, assault. To rush violently or impetuously, to impel, incite. In the NT, used mostly intrans., meaning to rush on, move forward impetuously (Matt 8:32; Mark 5:13; Luke 8:33; Acts 7:57; 19:29).

Deriv.: *hórmēma* (3731), an attack, violence.

Syn.: *katatréchō* (2701), to run down; *biázō* (971), to force; *tréchō* (5143), to run; *prostréchō* (4370), to run to.

Ant.: *hupochōréō* (5298), to withdraw.

3730. ὁρμή hormḗ; gen. *hormḗs*, fem. noun from *órnumi* (n.f.), to excite, arouse. Violent impulse, assault, attempt. Used metaphorically of the mind, impulse, will (Acts 14:5; James 3:4). *Hormḗ* often times has in view motion toward an object with the purpose of propelling and repelling it still further from oneself. Contrast *órexis* (3715), translated as "lust" or "concupiscence," from *orégomai* (3713), to covet, desire, which is always the reaching out after an object with the purpose of appropriation. Also from *órnumi* (n.f.): *koniortós* (2868), dust.
    Deriv.: *aphormḗ* (874), an occasion; *hormáō* (3729), to rush violently, incite.
    Syn.: *epithumía* (1939), a desire, craving; *hēdonḗ* (2237), pleasure, lust; *páthos* (3806), passion, lust; *bía* (970), force, violence.
    Ant.: *egkráteia* (1466), self-control; *sōphrosúnē* (4997), self-control.

3731. ὅρμημα hórmēma; gen. *hormḗmatos*, neut. noun from *hormáō* (3729), to run violently. Impetuousness, violence (Rev 18:21; Sept.: Deut 28:49).
    Syn.: *bía* (970), force, violence.
    Ant.: *praûtēs* (4240), mildness; *praótēs* (4236), gentleness, meekness; *chrēstótēs* (5544), mellowness; *euprépeia* (2143), gracefulness; *epieíkeia* (1932), mildness, clemency.

3732. ὄρνεον órneon; gen. *ornéou*, neut. noun, the diminutive of *órnis* (3733), a hen. A bird, fowl (Rev 18:2; 19:17, 21; Sept.: Gen 6:21; 15:11; Ezek 39:4).
    Syn.: *peteinón* (4071), a winged creature, bird; *ptēnón* (4421), feathered, winged bird.

3733. ὄρνις órnis; gen. *órnithos*, masc.-fem. noun, the diminutive *órneon* (3732), a bird, fowl. In the NT, only of poultry, the hen (Matt 23:37; Luke 13:34).

3734. ὁροθεσία horothesía; gen. *horothesías*, fem. noun from *hóros* (n.f., see *methórios* [3181]), boundary, and *títhēmi* (5087), to set. A setting of bounds or a limit (Acts 17:26).

3735. ὄρος óros; gen. *órous*, neut. noun. A mountain, hill (Matt 5:1, 14; 8:1; Luke 19:29; 21:37; Acts 1:12; 7:30; Rev 6:15). In the pl., *tá órē* (Matt 18:12; 24:16; Mark 5:5, 11; 13:14; Luke 21:21; 23:30; Rev 6:15, 16; Sept.: Isa 13:4) The proverbial expression "to remove mountains" means to accomplish great and difficult things (Matt 17:20; 21:21; 1 Cor 13:2;).
    Deriv.: *oreinós* (3714), mountainous, hilly.
    Syn.: *bounós* (1015), a mound, heap, hill.
    Ant.: *pedinós* (3977), level, such as ground, a plain.

3736. ὀρύσσω orússō, ὀρύττω orúttō; fut. *orúxō*. To dig, dig out or through (Matt 21:33; 25:18; Mark 12:1; Sept.: Gen 21:30; 26:25; Isa 5:2).
    Deriv.: *diorússō* (1358), to break through; *exorússō* (1846), to pluck or dig out.
    Syn.: *skáptō* (4626), to dig, hollow out; *kataskáptō* (2679), to dig down, undermine.
    Ant.: *kalúptō* (2572), to cover up.

3737. ὀρφανός orphanós; fem. *orphanḗ*, neut. *orphanón*, adj. from *orphnós* (n.f.), obscure, dark, because the orphan is often little esteemed and neglected and thus forced, as it were, to wander in obscurity and darkness. Orphaned, bereaved, spoken particularly of children bereaved of parents (James 1:27). Metaphorically, of disciples without a master (John 14:18; Sept.: Ps 68:5; Jer 7:6).
    Deriv.: *aporphanízō* (642), to bereave of parents.
    Syn.: *érēmos* (2048), desolate, left alone.

3738. ὀρχέομαι orchéomai; fut. *orchḗsomai*. In the act. sense, it means to take or lift up, raise aloft. More usual is its use in the mid. *orchéomai*, to dance

(Matt 11:17; 14:6; Mark 6:22; Luke 7:32; Sept.: 1 Chr 15:29; Eccl 3:4).

3739. ὅς *hós*; fem. *hḗ*, neut. *hó*; relative pron. Who, which, what, that.

(I) As a demonstrative pron. it means this, that, only in distinctions and distributions with *mén* (3303), a particle of affirmation, *dé* (1161), an adversative particle in the expressions *hós mén* / *hós dé*, meaning that one / this one, the one / the other, equal to *hó mén* / *hó dé* (Matt 13:4, 8; 21:35, "one . . . another"; 25:15; Luke 23:33; Rom 9:21; 2 Cor 2:16, "to the one . . . to the other").

(II) As a relative pron., meaning who, which, what, that, strictly implying two clauses, in the first of which there should stand with the verb a noun (the antecedent), and in the second clause the corresponding relative pron., each in the case which the verb of its own clause demands, the relative pron. also agreeing with the antecedent in gender and number. But the form and power of the relative pron. is varied much, both in construction and meaning and by the connection with its other particles.

(A) In construction: (1) As to gender, the relative pron. agrees regularly with its antecedent (Matt 2:9; Luke 5:3; John 6:51). Thus *hós* relates to a more remote antecedent in 1 Cor 1:8, referring to *tō Theō* (*ho Theós*, God of 1:4 [cf. *ho Theós* of 1:9]). From this rule there are two departures: (a) Where the relative pron. with the verb "to be" conforms in gender to the following noun (Gal 3:16, *spérmatí sou*, *hós esti Christós*, "And to thy seed, which is Christ"; Eph 1:14; 6:17, *máchairan*, *hó esti rhḗma Theoú*, "and the sword of the Spirit, which is the word of God"). (b) Where it takes the gender implied in the antecedent, and not that of its own external form (Rom 9:23, *skeúē eléous*, *há proētoímasen . . . hoús kaí ekálesen*, "vessels of mercy, which he had afore prepared"; Gal 4:19; Phil 2:15; 2 Pet 3:16, *en pásais taís epistolaís* [fem.] . . . *en hoís*, referring to the implied *grámmasi* [1121], letters [masc.];

2 John 1:1). So the neut. *hó* often refers to a masc. or fem. antecedent taken in the general sense of "thing" (Matt 1:23, *Emmanouēl*, *hó esti methermēneuómenon* [*Emmanouēl*, masc.; *hó*, neut.]; 27:33; Mark 3:17; 12:42, *leptá dúo*, *hó esti kodrántēs* [*leptá*, pl.; *hó*, sing.]; 15:16, 42; Heb 7:2). Also where the neut. *hó* refers to a whole preceding clause (Mark 15:34; 1 John 2:8) (2) As to number, the relative pron. agrees regularly with its antecedent as in the examples above. The departures from this rule are rare, e.g., (a) A relative sing. pron. after a pl. antecedent (Phil 3:20, "in heavens [literal] . . . from which [sing.]" [a.t.], where *hoú* may be taken as an adv.). See below B, 7. (b) Relative pl. masc. *hós* after a sing. fem. antecedent (Phil 2:15, *en mésō geneás skoliás . . . en hoís phaínesthe*) where the antecedent includes the idea of plurality (cf. Acts 15:36, *katá pásan pólin*, *en haís* [*pólin*, fem. sing; *haís*, fem. pl.]; 2 Pet 3:1, *deutéran epistolḗn*, *en haís* [*epistolḗn*, fem. sing.; *haís*, fem. pl.]). (3) As to case, the general rule is that the relative pron. stands in that case required by the verb of its own clause (John 1:9, *tó phōs . . . hó phōtízei pánta ánthrōpon* [*phōs*, sing. neut.; *hó*, sing. neut.]). Since "light" is neut., the relative pron. (*hó*) is neut., both being the nom. case. In John 1:30, however, since *anḗr* (435), man, is masc., the relative pron. (*hós*) is also masc., and both are in the nom. case. See Matt 10:26; Acts 8:27. As obj. acc. (Matt 2:9, *ho astḗr*, *hón eidón*, "the star [nom.] which [acc.]"; Acts 6:3, 6). In the dat. (Acts 8:10, *anḗr . . . hó proseíchon pántes* [*anḗr*, man, nom. sing.; *hó proseíchon*, to whom, dat. sing.]; Col 1:27; 1 Pet 1:12; 5:9). The departures from this rule are frequent: (a) By attraction, i.e., where the relative pron. in respect to its own verb would stand in the acc. but the antecedent stands in the gen. or dat. In this case the relative pron. is attracted by the antecedent into the same case with itself (Matt 18:19). In John 4:14, *húdatos* (5204), "of the water" (gen.), and then

the relative pron. is drawn into the gen. (*hoú*) although the proper construction should have been *hó* (nom. neut.), because it constitutes the subj. of *dṓsō*, "I shall give." See John 7:31, 39; Acts 1:1; 24:21; Eph 4:1; Jude 1:15; Rev 1:20. In Heb 8:2, *skēnḗs* is in the gen. while *hḗn* is in the acc. All of the above except Heb 8:2 have nouns in the gen. and they also have the relative pron. in the gen. The following have a dat. noun and in each instance the relative pron. is in the dat. case, e.g., Mark 7:13; Luke 2:20, *epi pásin hoís ḗkousan* (*pásin*, dat. pl.; *hoís*, dat. pl.), "for all the things that they had heard"; 5:9; John 4:50, *tṓ lógō hṓ eípen Iēsoús* (*lógō*, dat. neut.; *hṓ*, dat. neut.), "the word that Jesus had spoken"; Acts 20:38; 2 Cor 12:21; 2 Thess 1:4; Sept.: Jer 15:14. Here the antecedent is often omitted, especially the demonstrative pron. *hoútos* (3778), this one, *ekeínos* (1565), that one (compare below 4); and then the relative pron. stands alone in a case not properly belonging to it. The relative pron. itself, then, is like the Eng. "what," standing for "that which," and so forth, as in Luke 9:36 in which *oudén hṓn heōrákasin* stands for *oudén toútōn hṓn* (*há*) *heōrákasin* (see Luke 23:41; Acts 22:15; 26:16; Rom 15:18; 2 Cor 12:17). **(b)** By inverted attraction, i.e., where the antecedent is attracted by the relative pron. into the same case with itself, as e.g.: **(i)** Where the antecedent remains connected with its own clause and before the relative pron. (Matt 21:42, *líthon hṓn apedokímasan hoi oikodomoúntes*, *hoútos*; "the stone [should have been *líthos*, nom.] which [acc.] the builders rejected, the same [*hoútos*, masc. nom.]"; Luke 1:73, *hórkon* [for *hórkou*, gen.] *hṓn* [acc.] *ōmose*; 20:17; 1 Cor 10:16, *tón árton hṓn klṓmen*, *ouchí koinōnía*). **(ii)** Where the antecedent itself is attracted over into the clause of the relative pron. and stands after it in the proper case of the relative pron. (Mark 6:16, *Hērṓdēs eípen*, *hóti hṓn egṓ apekephálisa Iōánnēn*, *hoútos estín* stands for *hoútos estín Iōánnēs hṓn egṓ*

apekephálisa). See Luke 1:4; Acts 21:16; Rom 6:17; 1 John 2:25. **(iii)** This transposition may also take place when the antecedent would already stand in the same case with the relative pron., e.g., in John 11:6, *émeinen en hṓ ḗn tópō* for *en tópō en hṓ ḗn*. See Matt 7:2; 24:44; Mark 15:22. Here belongs the adv. phrase *hón trópon*, *kath' hón trópon*, for *katá tón trópon hón*, meaning in the manner in which, in the same manner as, and hence equal with "as" (Matt 23:37; Luke 13:34; Acts 15:11; Sept.: Isa 14:19, 24). **(c)** Often the case of the relative pron. depends on a prep. with which the verb is construed. **(i)** Generally as in Matt 3:17, *ho huiós mou*, *en* (i.e., the prep. *en* [1722], in, must take the dat., hence *hṓ*) *eudókēsa*. See Matt 11:10, with the prep. *perí*, which takes a gen.; Luke 1:4; Rom 10:14; 1 Cor 8:6, with *ex* (1537), of, which takes the gen. **(ii)** Sometimes the prep. which stands with the antecedent is repeated before the relative pron. as in John 4:53, *en ekeínē tḗ hṓra*, *en hḗ eípen* Acts 7:4; 20:18. More commonly, when the prep. stands before the antecedent, it is omitted before the relative pron., as in Matt 24:50, *en hēméra* (*en*) *hḗ ou prosdoká*. See Luke 1:25; 12:46; Acts 13:2, 39. **(iii)** By attraction the relative pron. is joined with the prep. belonging to the omitted antecedent (cf. above II, A, 3, a), e.g., John 6:29, *hína pisteúsēte eis hón apésteilen ekeínos* for *eis* (*toúton*) *hón*. See John 19:37; Rom 14:22; 1 Cor 7:1; Gal 1:8, 9; Heb 5:8; 2 Pet 2:12. **(d)** Sometimes the relative pron. is not dependent on the verb, but on some noun connected with the verb, and then the relative pron. is put in the gen. (Matt 3:11, *hoú ouk eimí hikanós tá hupodémata bastásai* where ordinarily *hoú* should have been *há*, referring to *hupodémata*; also 3:12; Mark 14:32; Luke 13:1; John 1:27; 4:46; 11:2; Acts 16:14; Rom 2:29; Col 1:25; Rev 13:12; Sept.: Dan 2:11). **(4)** As to position, here the relative pron. with its clause regularly follows the antecedent, as in most of the preceding examples. But for the sake of emphasis the relative clause may precede the antecedent, especially where a personal pron. follows such as *autós* (846), *hoútos* (3778), this one (Matt 26:48, *hón án philḗsō, autós esti*; John 3:26; Heb 13:11; 2 Pet 2:19). In both of these positions, the antecedent, especially the personal pron. *autós, hoútos, ekeínos* (1565), this one, that one, is frequently omitted so that the relative pron. is like the Eng. "what," which can mean that which, whatsoever, and so forth. See Matt 13:17, *akoúsai há akoúete*, for *taúta há*; Matt 14:7; Mark 2:24; Luke 8:17; John 14:22. Note also the inverted position as in Matt 7:2; 10:38; 19:6; 25:29; Mark 9:40; Luke 4:6; 12:40; John 8:38; 13:27; Rom 2:1; Heb 2:18; 1 John 1:1, 3. Here belongs the elliptic use of the neut. *hó* with its clause before another proposition, in the sense of "as to that," "in that," the corresponding *tout' ésti, tout' estín hóti* (*toúto* [5124], this one; *estín* [1510], is; *hóti* [3754], that), or the like, being omitted before the latter clause as in Rom 6:10; Gal 2:20.

(B) Meaning: Strictly speaking, the relative pron. serves simply to introduce a dependent clause and mark its close relation to the leading proposition (Matt 2:9, *ho astḗr, hón eídon en tḗ, anatolḗ, proḗgen autoús*, "the star, which they saw in the east [the dependent clause], went before them"). However, in common use the relative pron. had a wide range of functions, both as a general connective particle and sometimes as implying purpose, result, or cause which would properly be expressed by a conj. These would be equivalent to what, that which, he who. See above II, A, 4. (1) As a general connective: (a) Generally as in John 4:46; 11:2, "whose brother Lazarus was sick." In this way it is not uncommon for both Paul and Peter to connect two, three, or more clauses by relative pronouns, referring to the same or different subjects (see Acts 26:7; Eph 3:11, 12; Col 1:13ff., 24–29; 1 Pet 1:8, 10, 12; 2:22ff.; 3:19ff.; 4:4, 5; 2 Pet 2:2, 3; 3:16). (b) Where it is equivalent to a demonstrative, "and this

/ these"; "and he / they" (Luke 12:1, 24; Acts 6:6; 7:45; 11:30; Gal 1:7; Phil 3:12; Col 1:29; 1 Pet 1:12; 2:4). (c) In the formula *hón trópon* (5158), manner, means; see above II, A, 3, b, ii. (2) As implying purpose, equivalent to *hína* (2443), so that (Matt 11:10, *Egṓ apostéllō tón ággelón mou . . . hós kataskeuásei tḗn hodón sou*, "I send my messenger . . . which [*hós* for *hína*] shall prepare thy way"; Mark 1:2; Luke 7:27). (3) As marking a result or event, equivalent to *hṓste* (5620), wherefore, when used after *tís* (5100), who (Luke 5:21, *Tís estin hoútos hós* [who as a result] *laleí blasphēmías*, "Who is this which speaketh blasphemies?"; 7:49, *hós* [who as a result] *kaí hamartías aphíēsi*, "Who is this that forgiveth sins also?"). In Luke 11:6, *ouk échō hó parathḗsō autṓ* which, however, is equivalent to purpose, *hína*, not result (cf. John 5:7). (4) As implying cause, ground, or reason, equivalent to *hóti* (3754), because (Luke 8:13), equal to since (Luke 4:18). (5) Once, *eph' hṓ* (*eph'* [1909], upon) in direct interrogative for *epí*, followed by the dat. (Matt 26:50, "Wherefore [for what purpose] art thou come?"). (6) Including the notion of a particle of time, as *hóte* (3753), when, *hótan* (3752), when. So *aph' hḗs hēméras* is equivalent to *apó tḗs hēméras hóte* in Col 1:6, 9; see Luke 7:45; 2 Pet 3:4. (7) Neut. gen. *hoú*, as an adv. of place, meaning where. See Luke 4:16; 23:53; Acts 1:13; Col 3:1; Heb 3:9; Rev 17:15; figuratively in Rom 4:15; 5:20. So also with *ekeí* (1563), there, an emphatic corresponding (Matt 18:20; 2 Cor 3:17; Sept.: Gen 13:4) with a prep., as *epánō* (1883), above (Matt 2:9), *ex, ek* (1537), meaning whence (Phil 3:20). In attraction with verbs of motion, for "whither" as in Eng. often "where," "whither" (Matt 28:16; Luke 10:1; 22:10; 24:28); *hoú eán* (1437), if, meaning whithersoever (1 Cor 16:6). (c) In its connection with other particles: *hós án* (302), *hós eán* (1437), meaning whosoever; *hós ge* (Rom 8:32); *hō dḗpote* (John 5:4); *hósper*, masc.; *hḗper*, fem.; *hóper*, neut., meaning who indeed, who namely, equivalent to *hós* but stronger and more definite, as in Mark 15:6.

Deriv.: *hós* (5613), as, so as, how.

3740. ὁσάκις *hosákis*; adv. from *hósos* (3745), how great, how many, and the suffix *-kis*, the numeral termination meaning times. How many times, how often. In the NT, "as many times as you do," followed by *án* (302), a particle denoting supposition, wish, possibility, or uncertainty. The two words together, *hosákis án*, mean however often, as often as (1 Cor 11:25, 26), "each time that you do so" (a.t.). There is no implication of urgency or frequency. It rather means that each and every time you do so, no matter whether frequently or otherwise, the Lord's table must be a reminder of Christ's death until He comes back. With *eán* (1437), a conditional particle, *hosákis eán* (Rev 11:6, "every time they will" [a.t.]).

Syn.: *posákis* (4212), how many times, how often; *pukná* (4437), often; *hekástote* (1539), every time; *háma* (260), at the same time; *hótan* (3752) or *hóte* (3753), when; *hópote* (3698), whenever; *tóte* (5119), then; *póte* (4219), when; *pollákis* (4178), often; *polús* (4183), much, many, often.

Ant.: *hápax* (530), once; *pléon* (4119), anymore; *poté* (4218), never; *mēdépote* (3368) and *mēdépō* (3369), never, subjectively and conditionally; *oudépote* (3763) and *oudépō* (3764), never.

3741. ὅσιος *hósios*; fem. *hosía*, neut. *hósion*, adj. Holy, righteous, unpolluted with wickedness, right as conformed to God and His laws, thus distinguished from *díkaios* (1342), righteous, which refers to human laws and duties. Corresponds to the Hebr. *hasid* (2623, OT), denoting the person who readily accepts the obligations which arise from the covenant people's relationship to God. Such a person was known as "the loyal, the pious one" (a.t.). Used in the NT:

(I) Of God, as the personification of holiness and purity (Rev 15:4; 16:5;

Sept.: Deut 32:4; Ps 145:17); of men meaning pious, godly, careful of all duties toward God (Titus 1:8); of Christ (Heb 7:26). Acts 2:27 and 13:35 refer to the incorruptibility of His body although subject to natural growth. At death, Christ's body did not decompose as dead bodies do. These verses are quoted from Ps 16:10. See Deut 33:8).

(II) Of things meaning holy, sacred (1 Tim 2:8 implying pure hands, spotless; Sept.: Prov 22:11, *hosía kardía* [2588], heart). In Acts 13:34, "I will give you the sure mercies [promises] of David," i.e., those inviolably promised by God to David, an allusion to Isa 55:3, mercies, favors. Often grouped with *díkaios* (1342), righteous, just (Titus 1:8) or its corresponding deriv.

(III) It cannot be ascertained that *hósios* (Acts 2:27; Heb 7:26) refers to the one who is holy unto God and *díkaios* (Luke 1:6; Rom 1:17; 1 John 2:1) to the one who is righteous toward his fellow men. The Scriptures recognize that all righteousness has one root, i.e., one's relationship to God. Our righteousness toward men is rooted in our relationship to God. *Hierós* (2413), holy, is related to *hósios*, both of which refer to the ordinances of righteousness which no law or custom of men has constituted. They rest on the divine constitution of the moral universe and man's relation to this. *Hósios* is one who reverences these everlasting sanctities and recognizes the duty for such reverencing. Thus *hósios* may be one who is a performer of the ordinances but not necessarily *hágios* (40), holy in character.

Deriv.: *anósios* (462), unholy, ungodly; *hosiótēs* (3742), sacredness, holiness; *hosíōs* (3743), piously.

Syn.: *hieroprepḗs* (2412), reverent, as is becoming to sacredness; *hágios* (40), holy with the implication of purity; *áspilos* (784), unblemished.

Ant.: *bébēlos* (952), profane; *theostugḗs* (2319), impious, hater of God; *anósios* (462), one who violates the ordinances.

3742. ὁσιότης hosiótēs; gen. *hosiótētos*, fem. noun from *hósios* (3741), sacred, holy. Holiness manifesting itself in the discharge of pious duties in religious and social life. Twice in the NT joined with *dikaiosúnē* (1343), righteousness (Luke 1:75; Eph 4:24). *Hosiótēs* is related more to the keeping of the ordinances than the character of life (*hagiótēs* [41] which denotes the spirit and conduct of one who is joined in fellowship with God). Later *hosiótes* was used as an ecclesiastical title or term of respect.

Syn.: *hagiótēs* (41), inherent holiness implying pure moral character which *hosiótēs* does not necessarily possess; *hagiōsúne* (42), acquired holiness; *theiótēs* (2305), divinity, divine power.

Ant.: *miasmós* (3394), contamination, uncleanness; *míasma* (3393), that which contaminates, pollution; *molusmós* (3436), filthiness; *momphḗ* (3437), blame, fault; *apistía* (570), unbelief; *asébeia* (763), irreverence, ungodliness; *anósios* (462), sacrilege.

3743. ὁσίως hosiōs; adv. from *hósios* (3741), sacred, holy. Sacredly. As an adv., used only in 1 Thess 2:10, usually coupled with *dikaíōs* (1346). In Luke 1:75 the subst. *hosiótēs* (3742) clearly refers to Jewish piety in the exercise of the traditional ordinances. In 1 Tim 1:9 we see that the Law is made for the impious (*anósios* [{462} cf. 2 Tim 3:2]). Eph 4:24 mentions *hosiótēs* as one of the qualities of the new man. Thus the word is used adv. and refers to the conduct of Paul among the Thessalonians and has the connotation of piety, his actions being pure and morally clean. The distinction in the meaning of *hósios*, faithful in the performance of the ordinances, versus *hágios* (40), referring to the holiness of character, ought to be remembered.

3744. ὁσμή osmḗ; gen. *osmḗs*, fem. noun from *ózō* (3605), to send, emit an odor whether good or bad. A smell, odor of any kind. In the NT, used only of fragrant odor (John 12:3; see Sept.: Song 1:3; 2:13). In Eph 5:2, *osmḗ euōdías* (2175), odor of fragrance, means sweet odor as accompanying an acceptable sacrifice. See 2 Cor 2:14, "odor of knowledge" (a.t.); 2 Cor 2:16, "odor of death" (a.t.); Phil 4:18; Sept.: Lev 1:9, 13, 17; 2:2, 9.

Syn.: *euōdía* (2175), fragrance; *thumíama* (2368), incense, odor, aroma from the burning of incense; *árōma* (759), aroma, sweet smell.

3745. ὅσος hósos; fem. *hósē*, neut. *hóson*; correlative relative pron. How great, how much, how many, as great as, as much as. Akin to *tósos* or *tosoútos* (5118). It may refer to:

(I) Magnitude, meaning how great, as great as (Rev 21:16).

(II) Time, meaning how long, as long as (Mark 2:19). With the prep. *epí* (1909), upon, abbreviated as *eph' hóson*, as long as (Matt 9:15; Rom 7:1; 1 Cor 7:39; Gal 4:1). When repeated as in Heb 10:37, *éti mikrón hóson hóson* (*éti* [2089], yet; *mikrón* [3397], a little while), it is intensive meaning yet a very, very little while.

(III) Quantity, number, multitude, meaning how much, how many.

(A) In the sing. meaning as much as (John 6:11).

(B) In the pl. *hósoi* or *hósai* (fem.), meaning as many as, all who, and in the neut. *hósa*, as many as, all that or which or what (Matt 14:36; Mark 3:10; Acts 4:6, 34; Rom 2:12; 2 Cor 1:20; Gal 3:10; Rev 2:24). In the neut. (Luke 12:3; John 15:14; Acts 9:39; Jude 1:10). Preceded by *pántes*, masc. pl. of *pás* (3956), all, it is equivalent to *hósoi* but stronger, as all those who (Matt 13:46; 22:10; Mark 12:44; Luke 4:40). With *hoútos* (3778) or *autós* (846), this one, corresponding (Rom 8:14; Gal 6:12). With *án* (302), a suppositional particle as *hósos án* or *hósos eán* (1437), meaning whosoever, whatsoever (Matt 18:18; Mark 6:11; Luke 9:5; John 11:22; Rev 3:19, every). Strengthened by *pántes*, masc. pl. of *pás* (3956), every, all (Matt 7:12; Acts 3:22).

(C) The neut. *hósa* by implication also expresses admiration, e.g., how many and great things, as in the Eng. "what things" meaning "what great things" (Acts 9:13, 16; 15:12). Generally of great or unusual deeds (Mark 6:30; Luke 4:23; 9:10; John 21:25); of benefits conferred (Mark 3:8; 5:19, 20; Luke 8:39; Acts 14:27; 15:4; 2 Tim 1:18).

(IV) Measure, degree, extent:

(A) Before a comparative, as *kath' hóson*, *kath'* being an abbreviation of *katá* (2596), a particle meaning in the measure of or according to; *katá tosoúton, kath' hóson / katá tosoúton*, meaning by how much / by so much (Heb 7:20, 22); *hósō / tosoútō* (Heb 1:4). Thus *hósō* in the dat. means "by how much," with *tosoútō* (in the dat.) implied as in Heb 8:6. With *mállon* (3123), rather, omitted after *hósō* (in the dat.) as in Heb 10:25, and *tosoútō* (dat.) *mállon hósō* (dat.) *blépete*, "so much the more, as ye see the day approaching."

(B) Used in an absolute sense in the neut., *hóson* as an adv. meaning, how much, by how much, as in Mark 7:36; in the pl. *hósa*, used idiomatically with *tosoúton, hósa / tosoúton*, "How much . . . so much" (Rev 18:7); *eph' hóson*, inasmuch as (Matt 25:40, 45; Rom 11:13); *kath' hóson*, by how much, as, followed by *hoútō* (3779), as, thus, *kath' hóson . . . hoútō*, so; "as it is . . . so" or thus (Heb 9:27, 28).

Deriv.: *hosákis* (3740), how many times, how often.

Syn.: *pósos* (4214), how much, how great, what; *pēlíkos* (4080), how great; *toioútos* (5108), such as.

Ant.: *mēdeís* (3367), none; *mēdén* (3367), nothing (more subjective and relative); *oudeís* and *oudén* (3762), none, nothing (more objective and absolute); *eláchistos* (1646), least.

3746. ὅσπερ *hósper*; fem. *héper*, neut. *hóper*, emphatic relative pronoun from *hós* (3739), he who, and the enclitic particle *per*, very, an intens. Who indeed, who namely, the same as *hós* (3739) but stronger and more definite (Mark 15:6), meaning the very one whom they demanded.

3747. ὀστέον *ostéon*; contracted *ostoún*, gen. *ostoú*, neut. noun. A bone or bones. In Matt 23:27, "full of dead men's bones"; Luke 24:39, *sárka kaí ostéa* (the acc. of *sárx* [4561], flesh; *kaí* (2532), and; *ostéa*, bones), "flesh and bones"; John 19:36, "A bone of him shall not be broken." See Eph 5:30; Heb 11:22; Sept.: Gen 2:23; Num 9:12; Lam 3:4; 4:8. Usually *ostá* (Sept.: Gen 50:25; Ex 13:19); *ostéōn*, uncontracted gen. pl. (Sept.: Gen 2:23).

3748. ὅστις *hóstis*; pl. *hoítines* fem. *hétis*, pl. *haítines* neut. *hóti*, pl. *hátina* (1 Tim 3:15), indefinite relative pronoun from *hós* (3739), he who, and *tís* (5101), anyone, someone. Anyone who, someone who, whoever, whatever, differing from *hós* in referring to a subject only generally as one of a class and not definitely, thus serving to render a proposition as general. It has mostly the regular relative construction for instances where it conforms in gender and number to the following noun:

(I) The meaning of *hóstis* is virtually the same as the basic relative pron. *hós*, he who, strengthened by *tís* (5100), an enclitic meaning, a, someone. The neut. *hó, tí*, that which, is written with the comma in order to distinguish it from the conj. *hóti* (3754), that.

(II) In the proper relative sense:

(A) Particularly and generally meaning who, i.e., one who, someone who, whoever (Matt 2:6, "one who" [a.t.]; 7:24, 26; 13:52; Luke 2:10; 7:37; 12:1; Acts 16:16; 24:1; Rom 16:6, 12; 1 Cor 7:13; Phil 2:20); pl. (Matt 16:28; 25:1; 1 Cor 6:20; Col 2:23). In 1 Cor 3:17, *hoítines* agrees with the subsequent *humeís*, you, instead of *naós* (3485), temple.

(B) By implication, it means everyone who, all who, whosoever, whatsoever, where the relative clause often stands first. **(1)** Generally with the indic. (Matt

5:39, 41; 13:12; 23:12; Mark 8:34; Luke 14:27). With the subjunctive in Matt 18:4, perhaps because of *án* (302), if, implied from 18:3. Pl. (Mark 4:20; Luke 8:15; Rev 1:7). **(2)** Strengthened by *pás* (3956), every, but only in the sing., the pl. form being always *pántes hósoi* (3745), those who, and not *pántes hoítines*. Thus *pás . . . hóstis* (Matt 7:24; 10:32; Col 3:17); *pása psuchḗ, hḗtis án* (Acts 3:23 [cf. Deut 1:39]). **(3)** With *án* which strengthens the indefiniteness, whosoever, whatsoever, in the NT only with the sing. and subjunctive (Matt 10:33; Luke 10:35; John 2:5; 1 Cor 16:2; Gal 5:10). *Hó, tí eán* (Col 3:23), *hó eán tí* for *hó, tí eán* (Eph 6:8).

(C) Sometimes *hóstis* refers to a def. subj. and is then apparently equal to *hós* (Luke 2:4; John 8:53; Acts 11:28; 16:12; Rev 1:12; 11:8). However, in all these instances the ultimate reference may perhaps be to a general idea, as in Luke 2:4, "to the city of David, one which is called Bethlehem" (a.t.); and so also of the rest; John 8:53, "Abraham, who is dead" (a.t.).

(III) Like *hós*, so also *hóstis* is employed in a wider extent, both as a connective and as implying result, cause, or the like, where a conj. might also stand.

(A) As a general connective (Luke 1:20; 23:19; John 21:25; Rom 9:4; Gal 4:24; Heb 2:3; 8:5; 10:11).

(B) As marking a result or event, equivalent to *hṓste* (5620), so that. After *toiaútē*, the fem. of *toioútos* (5108), such an one (1 Cor 5:1).

(C) Implying cause, ground, or reason equivalent to *hóti* (3754), because (Matt 7:15, as those who, because such, for such come to you; 25:3, because they were foolish; Acts 10:41, 47; 17:11; Rom 6:2). Fem. *hḗtis* (Col 3:5, 14; Heb 10:35). Sometimes it takes the number and gender of the following noun (Gal 5:19; Eph 3:13; Phil 1:28; 1 Tim 1:4).

(D) Including the notion of a particle of time, as *hóte* (3753), when; *hótan* (3752), when, only in the phrase *héōs*

hótou (*héōs* [2193], until), until, until when (Matt 5:25; Luke 13:8; John 9:18).

3749. ὀστράκινος *ostrákinos*; fem. *ostrakínē*, neut. *ostrákinon*, adj. from *óstrakon* (n.f.), shell, burnt clay. Earthen (2 Tim 2:20); metaphorically used as an emblem of frailty (2 Cor 4:7; Sept.: Lev 6:21; 15:12).

Syn.: *epígeios* (1919), terrestrial; *choikós* (5517), earthy; *sárkinos* (4560), fleshly.

Ant.: *ouránios* (3770), heavenly; *epouránios* (2032), celestial, above the sky; *pneumatikós* (4152), noncorporeal, spiritual, ethereal.

3750. ὄσφρησις *ósphrēsis*; gen. *osphrḗseōs*, fem. noun from *osphraínomai* (n.f.), to smell. The sense of smell, used as a metonym for the nose (1 Cor 12:17).

Syn.: *osmḗ* (3744), smell.

3751. ὀσφύς *osphús*; gen. *osphúos*, pl. *haí osphúes*, fem. noun. Loin, the lower region of the back, the lumbar region, the hips as opposed to the shoulders and thighs, the organs of reproduction.

(I) The loins of the human body comprising the five lower vertebrae of the back, so-called perhaps from the labor they can do and sustain when a man exerts his strength (Matt 3:4; Mark 1:6). The expression, "to have the loins girded," means to be in readiness for anything (Luke 12:35; Eph 6:14; 1 Pet 1:13. See *anazṓnnumi* [328], to gird). The garments of the Orientals being loose and flowing, it was necessary to wrap them about their hips when they wanted to exert or display their strength. Spiritually, as in Luke 12:35; Eph 6:14; metaphorically in 1 Pet 1:13 (cf. *anazṓnnumi* [328], to gird or wrap up anew). See Sept.: Ex 12:11; 2 Kgs 4:29; 9:1; Job 38:3; 40:2, and also *perizṓnnumi* (4024), to fasten on one's belt, wrap about.

(II) Internally, the Scriptures refer to children as being in and proceeding from the loins of their father or progenitor (Heb 7:5, 10 [cf. Gen 35:11]). Hence "the fruit of the loins" is used for offspring in Acts 2:30; Sept.: 2 Chr 6:9).

3752. ὅταν hótan; conj. from *hóte* (3753), when, and *án* (302), a prep. denoting a supposition, wish, possibility, or uncertainty. When, with the accessory idea of uncertainty or possibility, meaning whensoever, if ever, in case that, so often as. Construed regularly with the subjunctive, referring to an often repeated or possible action in the pres. or fut. time.

(**I**) With the subjunctive:

(**A**) In general propositions, with the pres. subjunctive (Matt 15:2; Luke 11:21; John 16:21; 2 Cor 13:9). With the aor. (Matt 5:11; Mark 4:15, 16; John 2:10; 1 Tim 5:11; Rev 9:5), so also in general exhortations with the pres. (Matt 6:5, 6; Mark 11:25; Luke 14:12). With the aor., indicating the fut. with exactness (Luke 14:8; 17:10). In a general comparison with the pres. (Luke 11:36).

(**B**) In reference to a fut. action or time: with the pres. subjunctive (Matt 26:29; Mark 13:4; John 7:27; Rev 10:7; 18:9); with *tóte* (5119), then, at that time, corresponding (1 Thess 5:3). With the aor. subjunctive, indicating the fut. with exactness (Matt 19:28; Mark 8:38; Luke 13:28; John 5:7; 15:26; Acts 23:35; 1 Cor 16:2, 3, 5; Rev 12:4); with *tóte* corresponding (Matt 9:15; 24:15; John 8:28). Once with the fut. indic. (Rev 4:9).

(**II**) With the imperf. indic., in narrating an actual event (Mark 3:11, meaning whenever, as often as; Rev 4:9, fut. action).

(**III**) By implication *hótan* is used like the Eng. since, while, in assigning a cause, reason. It is equivalent to because, in that, with the subjunctive (John 9:5; Rom 2:14; 1 Cor 15:27).

Syn.: *hóte* (3753), when; *háma* (260), at the same time; *hopóte* (3698), when; *euthéōs* (2112), immediately; *hosákis* (3740), whenever; *tóte* (5119), then; *poté* (4218), when; *póte* (4219), when?, at what time?

Ant.: *oudépō* (3764), never before; *oudépote* (3763), never at any time; *mēdépō* (3369), not yet; *mēdépote* (3368), never, not even ever.

3753. ὅτε hóte; adv. of time, correlated with *póte* (4218), at what time, *tóte* (5119), then. When. Construed regularly with the indic. as relating to an actual event, something actually taking place. Rarely with the subjunctive.

(**I**) With the pres. indic. in general propositions meaning while (John 9:4; Heb 9:17).

(**II**) Usually of time past, with the aor. or pres. indic. in the historical sense (Matt 21:1; Mark 11:1). With the imperf. (Mark 14:12; 15:41; John 17:12; 21:18; Rom 6:20; 1 Cor 13:11; Jude 1:9) and *poté* corresponding (1 Pet 3:20). With the aor. (Matt 7:28; 12:3; Mark 1:32; Luke 2:21f.; 22:14; John 1:19; 6:24; Acts 1:13; Gal 2:11f.; Rev 1:17; 6:3). So with *tóte* (5119), then, corresponding (Matt 21:1; John 12:16). With the perf. (1 Cor 13:11).

(**III**) Of fut. time, so with the fut. indic. (Luke 17:22; John 4:21, 23; 5:25; 16:25; Rom 2:16; 2 Tim 4:3). Used once with the aor. subjunctive instead of the fut. indic. (Luke 13:35).

Syn. and **Ant**.: see *hótan* (3752), when.

For a discussion of ὅ, τε hó, *te* see *te* (5037, IV, C).

3754. ὅτι hóti; conj. That (demonstrative), because (causal). Originally it was the neut. of *hóstis*. As a demonstrative it stands particularly for *toúto hó, ti* (*toúto* [5124], this; *hó ti*, that which), this which, introducing the object, contents, or argument to which the preceding words refer. As a causal, it is particularly equivalent to *diá* ([1223], for) *toúto*, for this reason, assigning the cause, motive, ground of something, "that, because." Construed in the NT with the indic. before the inf. (Acts 27:10).

(**I**) As a demonstrative conj.:

(A) Particularly after a demonstrative pron. as *toúto* or a similar or implied expression (John 3:19; Rom 2:3; 2 Cor 5:14; Rev 2:4, 6, implied). *En toútō . . . hóti* (1 John 3:16; 4:9, 10, 13), in this . . . that; *perí toútou . . . hóti* (*perí* [4012], concerning), concerning this . . . that (Matt 16:7, 17, implied; John 16:19).

(B) After an interrogative pron. *tís, tí* (5101), who, what (John 14:22); *tí hóti* for *tí estí hóti* (*estí*, the 3d person sing. of *eimí* [1510]), what cause is there that (Mark 2:16; Luke 2:49; Acts 5:4, 9); with a pron. or subst. (Mark 4:41; Luke 8:25; Heb 2:6, "what cause is there in man that" [a.t.] quoted from Sept.: Ps 8:4; 144:3 [cf. Ex 16:7; Num 16:11; Job 15:14]); after *potapós* (4217), what manner of (Matt 8:27; Luke 7:39).

(C) Most frequently *hóti* with the indic. is put after certain classes of verbs to express the obj. or reference of the verb. It is then equivalent to an acc. with inf. or to the corresponding part. construction, and often alternates with these in one and the same verb. (1) After verbs meaning to say, speak, and those including the idea of "I say that it is so" or "I say it to be so." After *légō* (3004), to say (Matt 3:9; 12:6; Mark 3:28; Luke 10:24; 2 Cor 11:21; 1 Tim 4:1); *eípon* (2036) (the aor. of *eréō* [2046]), said (Matt 28:7, 13; John 7:42; 1 Cor 1:15); *gráphō* (1125), to write (Mark 12:19; 1 John 2:12, 13); *didáskō* (1321), to teach (1 Cor 11:14); *marturéō* (3140), to witness (Matt 23:31; John 4:44); *mártura . . . epikaloúmai* (*mártus* [3144], witness; *epikaloúmai* [1941], to call upon), I call upon as a witness (2 Cor 1:23); *ómnumi* (3660), to swear (Rev 10:6); *homologéō* (3670), to confess (Heb 11:13); *sphragízō* (4972), to seal (John 3:33). Sometimes *légō* (3004), to say, or the like, is implied in the preceding verb or words, e.g., *parakaléō* (3870), to exhort (Acts 14:22). After a Hebr. formula of swearing, like *zō̂ egṓ* (*záō* [2198], I live; *egṓ* [1473], I), I live (Rom 14:11 in allusion to Isa 45:23 [cf. Isa 49:18]). Here also belongs *ouch hóti* (*ouch* [3756], not), not

that, at the beginning of a clause, equivalent to *ou légō hóti*, I do not say that, used by way of explanation or limitation of something previously said, meaning although (John 6:46; 7:22; 2 Cor 1:24; Phil 3:12; 4:11, 17); *ouch hoíon dé hóti* (Rom 9:6), not as though. (2) After verbs signifying to show, make known, with part. or inf. equivalent to "I show that it is so," or "I show it to be so." After *deiknúō* (1166), to show (Matt 16:21; John 2:18); *apodeíknumi* (584), to demonstrate, prove (2 Thess 2:4); *dēlóō* (1213), to make plain, declare (1 Cor 1:11); *dêlon hóti* (*dêlon* [1212], evident), it is evident that (1 Cor 15:27; Gal 3:11; 1 Tim 6:7); after *apokalúptō* (601), to reveal (1 Pet 1:12); *emphanízō* (1718), to exhibit (Heb 11:14); *phaneróō* (5319), to manifest (2 Cor 3:3; 1 John 2:19). (3) After verbs signifying to hear, see, and (figuratively) to perceive, know, with a part. or the inf.: *akoúō* (191), to hear (Matt 20:30; Mark 2:1; 10:47; John 14:28); *blépō* (991), to see (2 Cor 7:8; James 2:22; Rev 17:8); *horáō* (3708), to see, perceive (James 2:24); *eídon* (the aor. ind. of *horáō*), I saw, perceived (Mark 9:25; John 6:22); *idṓn* (the aor. part. of *horáō*), when he saw (Matt 2:16) *theáomai* (2300), to look closely at, perceive (John 6:5); *theōréō* (2334), behold, perceive (John 9:8; Acts 27:10); *ginṓskō* (1097), to know (Matt 21:45; Luke 10:11); *gnōstón ésti* (*gnōstón* [1110], known; *ésti*, the 3d person sing. of *eimí* [1510], to be), let it be known (Acts 28:28); *anaginṓskō* (314), to read (Matt 12:5; 19:4); *epiginṓskō* (1921), to recognize, acknowledge (Mark 2:8; Luke 1:22); *oída* (the perf. of *eídō* [1492], to know, used as pres.), to know (Matt 6:32; Mark 2:10; 2 Cor 11:31); *agnoéō* (50), to be ignorant of (Rom 6:3; 7:1); *epístamai* (1987), to comprehend (Acts 15:7); *katalambánō* (2638), to comprehend (Acts 4:13; 10:34); *noéō* (3539), to think, perceive (Matt 15:17); *suníēmi* (4920), to understand, comprehend (Matt 16:12). (4) After verbs signifying to remember, care for: *mimnḗskō* (3403), to remind, remember (Matt 5:23; John 2:22); *hupomimnḗskō* (5279), to remind quietly, suggest (Jude 1:5); *mnēmoneúō* (3421), to recollect (John 16:4); *mélei moi* (*mélō* [3199], to concern; *moi*, the simpler form of *emoí* [1698], me), it concerns me (Mark 4:38; Luke 10:40). **(5)** After verbs signifying to hope, believe, think, consider: *elpízō* (1679), to hope (Luke 24:21; Acts 24:26); *pisteúō* (4100), believe (Matt 9:28; Mark 11:23; Luke 1:45); *pépoitha, pépeismai* (perf. pass. of *peíthō* [3982], to persuade), I am persuaded (Rom 8:38; 15:14; Phil 2:24); *dokéō* (1380), to think (Matt 6:7; 26:53); *logízomai* (3049), to reason, estimate, conclude (Heb 11:19); *dialogízomai* (1260), to deliberate (John 11:50); *nomízō* (3543), to regard, suppose (Matt 5:17); *oímai* from *oíomai* (3633), to suppose (James 1:7); *hupolambánō* (5274), to take up (Luke 7:43). **(6)** *Hóti* serves also to introduce words quoted without change chiefly after verbs implying to say, and is then merely a mark of quotation, not to be translated (Matt 2:23; 5:31; 7:23; 26:74; Mark 3:21, 22; 9:28 [cf. Matt 17:19]; Luke 1:25, 61; John 1:20, 32; Acts 11:3; 15:1; Heb 10:8; Rev 3:17; Sept.; Gen 29:33; Josh 2:24).

(II) As a causal conj., used particularly:

(A) After a demonstrative pron. as *toúto* (5124), this (neut.) or the like, meaning that, because, *diá toúto hóti* (Matt 13:13; John 8:47; 10:17; 12:39; 1 John 3:1); *en toúto hóti* (Luke 10:20), in this . . . that; *hoútōs hóti* (Rev 3:16), because that.

(B) After an interrogative pron. as *tís*, (*tí* [5101], when, what), *diatí* (1302), why (Rom 9:32; 2 Cor 11:11), *chárin tínos* (*chárin* [5485], grace; *tínos*, of which, gen. sing. of the interrogative pron. *tís* [5101], who, which), for whose sake (1 John 3:12).

(C) Used in an absolute sense, *hóti* is put after certain classes of verbs and also generally to express the cause, reason, motive, occasion of the action or event mentioned. It means, "that", equivalent to because, seeing that, for. **(1)** After verbs

or words signifying an emotion of the mind such as wonder, joy, pity, sorrow; *thaumázō* (2296), to admire (Luke 11:38; John 3:7; Gal 1:6); *exístamai* (1839), to wonder (Acts 10:45); *chaírō* (5463), to rejoice (Luke 10:20; John 14:28; 2 Cor 7:9); *sugchaírō* (4796), to rejoice with (Luke 15:6, 9); *splagchnízomai* (4697), to have compassion on (Matt 9:36; Mark 6:34); *klaíō* (2799), to weep (Rev 5:4; 18:11); *penthéō* (3996), to mourn (Rev 18:11). **(2)** After verbs or words expressing praise, thanks, and the like: *epainéō* (1867), to applaud, praise (Luke 16:8; 1 Cor 11:2); *ouk epainéō* (1 Cor 11:17), not to praise; *exomologéō* (1843), to confess (Matt 11:25); *eucharistéō* (2168), to thank (Luke 18:11); *cháris hóti* (5485), thanks (grace) be to God . . . that (Rom 6:17; 1 Tim 1:12). **(3)** Generally (Matt 2:18; Mark 1:27; 5:9; Luke 4:36; 11:42, 43; 16:3; 23:40, seeing that; John 1:30, 50; Acts 1:17; Rom 6:15; 1 Cor 3:13; 1 John 3:20; 2 John 1:7; Rev 3:4, 8).

Deriv.: *dióti* (1360), because, for.

3755. ὅτου *hótou*; relative pron., the gen. of *hóstis* (3748), he who. Used as an adv. meaning during which same time, while. With *héōs* (2193), until, implying *chrónou*, the gen. of *chrónos* (5550), time, meaning until when, until, with the indic. as in John 9:18. With the indic. without *án* (302), a particle denoting supposition, wish, possibility or uncertainty (Matt 5:25). See also Luke 13:8; 15:8; 22:16, 18.

3756. οὐ *ou* and *ouk / ouch* (before a vowel i.e., aspirated), neg. particle. Usually without an accent, but written *ou* when standing alone or at the end of a sentence. Not, no, expressing direct and full negation, independently and absolutely, and hence, objectively. This differs from *mḗ* (3361) which implies a conditional and hypothetical neg., and is, thus, subjective.

(I) Before a verb where it renders the verb and proposition neg. in respect to the subject.

(A) Generally (Matt 1:25; Mark 3:26; 14:68; Luke 6:43, 44; John 1:10, 11; 8:50; Acts 2:15, 34; Rom 3:11; Rev 2:2, 3).

(B) With the fut. 2d person in prohibitions, where the neg. fut. thus stands for a neg. imper., precisely as in the Eng. "thou shalt not," which is stronger than the direct imper., "do it not" (a.t. [Matt 6:5]). Elsewhere only in citations from the Sept. and Hebr. (Luke 4:12 [cf. Deut 6:16]; Acts 23:5 [cf. Ex 22:28]; 1 Cor 9:9 [cf. Deut 25:4]). So also from the law (Matt 5:21, 27; Rom 7:7; 13:9).

(C) Where the subj. is *pás* (3956), every, whosoever, or *heis* (1520), one, and *ou* is joined with the verb. Thus *pás . . . ou* or *ou . . . pás* is equivalent to *oudeís* (3762), not one, none. So Matt 24:22 means all flesh would not be saved, i.e., no flesh would be saved (Mark 13:20; Luke 1:37; Rom 3:20; 1 Cor 15:51; Gal 2:16; Eph 5:5; 2 Pet 1:20; 1 John 2:21; Rev 22:3). Also *heís . . . ou*, not one, none (Matt 10:29), *hén . . . ou* (Luke 12:6).

(D) Where *ou* with its verb is followed by *allá* (235), but, i.e., *ou . . . allá* (Matt 9:12; 15:11; John 7:16; 1 Cor 7:10). In other passages some think that *ou* is to be taken in a modified or comparative sense, meaning not so much as, but this is unnecessary, e.g., Matt 10:20 means "it is not you at all who speaks, but the Spirit" (a.t.). This is far more specific than "it is not so much you as the Spirit" (a.t. [see John 12:44]). Also *ouch hóti . . . all' hóti* (John 6:26; 12:6; 1 John 4:10).

(E) Sometimes *ou* stands in a conditional sentence after *ei* (1487), if, a particle of conditionality, where the usual neg. is *mḗ* (3361), not, subj. and conditional.

(F) As strengthened by other neg. particles, e.g., *mḗ ou* only in interrogatives. *Ou mḗ* as an intens. neg. Strengthened also by comparison of *ou*, e.g., *ouk oudé*, not even (Luke 18:13). *Ouk oudeís, ouk oudén* means no one whatsoever, nothing at all (see Mark 5:37; Luke 4:2; 23:53; John 6:63; 8:15; Rom 3:10; 2 Cor 11:9).

(II) Before the obj. of a verb, where it then renders the proposition neg. in respect to the obj., e.g., generally as in Matt 9:13; 1 Cor 4:15; Heb 2:16. More frequently as followed by *allá* (235), but (Mark 9:37; Acts 5:4; 10:41; 1 Cor 1:17; 14:22; Eph 6:12; 1 Thess 4:8). *Ouch hóti . . . all' hóti* (2 Cor 7:9). Also *ouch hína* as marking the object, purpose (John 6:38; 2 Cor 2:4; 8:13).

(III) Before the adjunct of a verb, adv., or the like, where it then renders the proposition neg. in respect to the adjunct, e.g., before a noun implying manner (John 3:34; Acts 5:26; 1 Cor 1:17; 2 Cor 3:3; 5:7; Gal 2:16; James 2:25; 2 Pet 1:21). Before an adj. used as an adv. (Rom 8:20). So also before an adv. (1 Cor 5:10), meaning not altogether, not generally. See also John 7:10; 2 Cor 8:5, 12. *Ou mónon allá* (*mónon* [3440]), only, versus *allá kaí*, meaning not only, but also, expressing a gradation of meaning, as referring to place, time, manner (Acts 19:26; Rom 9:24; 2 Cor 7:7; Eph 1:21; 1 Thess 1:8; 1 John 5:6). Also as referring to the subj. (Acts 19:27; Rom 1:32; 1 Tim 5:13); or to the obj. (Acts 21:13; Rom 4:12; 2 Cor 8:10).

(IV) Before a part., where a direct and absolute neg. is to be expressed; otherwise *mḗ* ([3361] 2 Cor 4:8; Gal 4:27; Eph 5:4; Phil 3:3; Heb 11:35; 1 Pet 1:8; 2:10).

(V) As affecting single words, *ou* not only renders them neg., but often gives them the directly contrary sense, sometimes as a sort of comp., like the Eng. prefix non- or un-.

(A) With verbs, as *ouk agapáō*, to not love, meaning to be careless of (Rev 12:11). In 2 Pet 1:12, *ouk ameléō* (272), not to neglect, means to be careful. See Matt 3:11; 23:37; Acts 13:25; 1 Cor 10:1.

(B) With nouns, as *ouk éthnos, ou laós*, meaning a non-people in 1 Pet 2:10. See Rom 9:26; 10:19; Sept.: Deut 32:21; Hos 2:23.

(C) With an adj., e.g., with *pás* (3956), whosoever, where in the form *ou pás, ou pántes* (pl.), it merely takes away the positive force, meaning not everyone, not all (Matt 7:21; 19:11; Rom 9:6; 10:16; 1 Cor 15:39). In 1 Cor 15:51 *pántes . . . ou* is equivalent to *ou pántes*, not all. With other adj., it expresses the contrary, *ouk ásēmos* (767), not ignoble, renowned (Acts 21:39); *ouk olíga*, not few, many (Luke 15:13; John 2:12).

(D) With an adv., *ou metríōs* (3357), moderately (Acts 20:12); *ouk euthéōs* (2112), not immediately (Luke 21:9).

(VI) In neg. answers, no, nay, not, meaning, not at all (Matt 13:29; John 1:21). Repeated twice, as an inténs. in Matt 5:37. With the art. *tó, tó ou* refers to the word *ou* (2 Cor 1:17; James 5:12). *Ou gár* (1063), a particle assigning a reason for, then (Acts 16:37). *Ou pántōs* (3843), entirely, in Rom 3:9, means not at all.

(VII) In neg. questions such as "None?" "Is not?" "Are not?" where an affirmative answer is always presupposed, so that the neg. question stands instead of a direct affirmation. See Matt 6:26; 12:3, 5; Mark 4:13, 21; John 6:42; 1 Cor 6:2, 3. *Ouk apokrínē oudén?* (*apokrínō* [611], to answer), meaning "Do not you answer anything?" (a.t. [Mark 14:60; 15:4]). With other particles as *ouk ára* (686), therefore (Acts 21:38).

Syn.: *mḗ* (3361), not; *ouchí* (3780), indeed not.

Ant.: *naí* (3483), yes.

3757. οὖ *hoú*; adv. of place. Where (Luke 4:16; 23:53; Acts 1:13; Col 3:1; Heb 3:9; Rev 17:15). Figuratively in Rom 4:15; 5:20. So also with *ekei* (1563), there, as an emphatic corresponding (Matt 18:20, "where there are two or three . . . there" [a.t.]; 2 Cor 3:17). With a prep., as *epánō* (1883), on, over, followed by *hoú* (Matt 2:9), *ex* ([1537], from, indicating origin), whence, from which (Phil 3:20).

3758. οὐά *ouá*; interjection similar to ah! aha! uttered in derision (Mark 15:29).

3759. οὐαί *ouaí*; interjection of grief or indignation, joined with a dat. Of denouncing misery and pitying it. Woe, alas! (Matt 11:21; 23:13f.; Mark 13:17;

Luke 6:24f.; Jude 1:11; Rev 12:12); with the dat. implied (Luke 17:1). It is repeated intensively three times in Rev 8:13. See also Rev 18:10, 16, 19; Sept.: Num 21:29; Eccl 10:16; Isa 10:1, 5. As an onomatopoeia (an imitation of the sound), a subst., indeclinable, a woe, disaster (1 Cor 9:16; Sept.: Hos 9:12 [cf. Prov 23:29]). Hence with the fem. art. *hḗ ouaí*, a woe, calamity (Rev 9:12; 11:14).

Syn.: *anáthema* (331) accursed; *kataráomai* (2672), to curse.

Ant.: *hōsanná* (5614), Hosanna.

3760. οὐδαμῶς *oudamṓs*; adv. from *oudamós* (n.f.), not even one, which is from *oudé* (3761), not even, and *amós* (n.f.), one. In no wise, by no means (Matt 2:6).

Syn.: *mēdamṓs* (3365), by no means, not so, not as absolute as *oudamós*.

Ant.: *asphalṓs* (806), assuredly.

3761. οὐδέ *oudé*; conj. from *ou* (3756), not, and *dé* (1161), but. *Oudé* is continuative, meaning and not, also not, and hence, not, neither, not even, usually as connecting whole clauses or propositions. Differing from *mēdé* (3366), a denial more subj. and conditional. The distinction of *ou* (3756) as an obj. absolute neg. as distinguished from *mḗ* (3361), a subj. conditional neg., holds throughout in all the deriv.

(I) In continued negation, at the beginning of a subsequent clause.

(A) And not, nor, neither, generally preceded by *ou* (Matt 5:15; 6:20, 26, 28; Mark 4:22; Luke 12:33; John 1:13; 6:24; Acts 8:21; Gal 1:1; Rev 21:23). *Ou . . . oudé oúte* (3777), nor (1 Thess 2:3); *oúpō . . . oudé* (*oúpō* [3768], not yet), not yet . . . neither (Matt 16:9f.; Mark 8:17). Preceded by *oudeís* (3762), none (Matt 9:17; Rev 5:3); in apposition with *oudeís*, e.g., *oudé . . . oudé*, neither . . . nor (Mark 13:32); *hina mḗ . . . oudé* (*hína* [2443], in order), neither . . . nor (Rev 9:4); *oudé mḗ*, preceded by *ou, oudé* (Rev 7:16).

(B) *Oudé* also means not, neither, in a stronger transition or antithesis, e.g., preceded by *ou* (Matt 21:27; Mark 12:10, 21; Luke 16:31). See also John 15:4; Rom 4:15; 1 Cor 15:13, 16. *Oudeís . . . oudé* (*oudeís* [3762], none), no man . . . neither (John 8:11; 1 Tim 6:16); *oudeís . . . oudé oukéti* (*oukéti* [3765], no longer), no man . . . neither . . . any more (Matt 22:46); *eán mḗ . . . oudé* (*eán* [1437], if; *mḗ* [3361], not), if ye not . . . neither (Matt 6:15); with the preceding neg. implied in *apistéō* (569), to disbelieve (Mark 16:13). With *gár* (1063), a particle assigning a reason, and *allá* (235), but, after a preceding neg. expressed or implied in the context; e.g., *oudé gár*, for not also, for neither, where *ou* denies, *dé* connects, and *gár* assigns a reason (John 7:5, "nor did his brothers believe" [a.t.]). See also Acts 4:34; Rom 8:7; strengthened by *oudeís* (John 5:22, "nor does the father judge anyone" [a.t.]; Gal 1:12, *oudé gár . . . oúte* (*oúte* [3777], neither, nor, neither . . . neither). In *all' oudé*, meaning, yea neither, *allá* merely strengthens the negation (Luke 23:15; Gal 2:3).

(II) Not even, not so much as.

(A) In the middle of a clause (Matt 6:29; Mark 6:31; Luke 7:9; John 21:25; 1 Cor 5:1). As strengthening *ou*, i.e., *ouk oudé* (Luke 18:13). Preceded by *allá* (235), but, *all' oudé*, yea not even (Acts 19:2; 1 Cor 4:3).

(B) In interrogatives (Mark 12:10; Luke 6:3; 23:40).

Syn.: *oúte* (3777), neither, nor; *mēdé* (3366), neither, nor, not as absolute as *oudé*; *mḗte* (3383), not even; *ou* (3756), not.

Ant.: *málista* (3122), specially; *alēthṓs* (230), truly; *asphalṓs* (806), assuredly.

3762. οὐδείς *oudeís*; fem. *oudemía*, neut. *oudén*, adj. from *ou* (3756), not, and *heís* (1520), one. Not even one, not the least. When it is used in the neut., *oudén*, it means nothing or not a thing (1 Cor 13:2 [TR]; Sept.: Gen 41:44; Isa 41:28). Neg. adj. denying absolutely and obj., and differing from *mēdeís* (3367), no one, as *ou* (3756), not, absolutely and obj., from *mḗ* (3361), not, subj. and conditionally. Generally it means no one, nothing, none at all; particularly placing emphasis as not even one, not the least. However, when it is used so emphatically, it is commonly written separately, *oudé heís*, *oudé hén*.

(I) As an adj. with a subst., it means no one, no (Luke 4:24, "No prophet"; John 16:29; 18:38; 1 Cor 8:4; neut. Luke 23:4; John 10:41; Acts 17:21). Partitively, followed by a gen. of a whole (Luke 4:26, 27; Acts 5:13; 18:17; 1 Cor 1:14; 9:15); *oudeís ex autṓn* (*ek* or *ex* [1537], of; *autṓn*, them, gen. pl. of *autós* [846], he, himself), none of them (John 17:12; 18:9).

(II) Used in an absolute sense, as a subst., *oudeís* means no one, no man, no person (Matt 6:24; Mark 5:4; Luke 5:36, 37, 39; John 5:22; Acts 9:8; Eph 5:29; Rev 2:17). With other neg. for strength after *ou* (Matt 22:16; John 8:15; Acts 4:12; 2 Cor 11:9); *oudépō oudeís* (*oudépō* [3764], as yet not, never before), never before anyone (Luke 23:53); *oudeís oukéti* (*oukéti* [3765], not yet), anymore, no one, any more (Mark 12:34).

(III) Neut. *oudén*, used in an absolute sense, generally means "nothing" (Matt 10:26; 27:24; Luke 22:35; John 8:28; Acts 15:9; Gal 2:6; Heb 2:8). With other neg. for strength, after *ou* (Mark 14:60; Luke 4:2; John 3:27; Acts 26:26); *oukéti . . . oudén*, not yet . . . nothing (Mark 7:12); *oudépō oudén*, never yet nothing (1 Cor 8:2); *oudén . . . ou mḗ*, nothing . . . not at all (Luke 10:19). The acc. *oudén* as an adv. means in no way, in no respect (John 6:63; Acts 25:10; 1 Cor 13:3; 2 Cor 12:11; Gal 4:12). Metaphorically, it means of no account, weight, value, authority (Matt 23:16, 18; John 8:54; 1 Cor 7:19; 13:2). *Gínomai eis oudén*, to come to naught (*eis* [1519], unto; *gínomai* [1096], to become) (Acts 5:36). See also Acts 19:27; Sept.: Isa 14:23).

Syn.: *mēdeís* (3367), none.

Ant.: *pás* (3956), every; *hápas* (537), absolutely everybody, all; *hékastos* (1538), each one.

3763. οὐδέποτε *oudépote*; adv. from *oudé* (3761), not even, and *poté* (4218), ever. Not ever, never (Matt 7:23; 9:33; 21:16, 42 in an interrogation [also Matt 26:33; Mark 2:12, 25]; Luke 15:29; John 7:46; Acts 10:14; 11:8; 14:8; 1 Cor 13:8; Heb 10:1, 11).

Syn.: *oudépō* (3764), never yet; *oúpō* (3768), not yet; *mēdépote* (3368), not yet ever; *pṓpote* (4455), not at any time; *ou mḗ poté* (*ou* [3756], not; *mḗ* [3361], not; *poté* [4218], ever) by no means ever.

Ant.: *pántote* (3842), always.

3764. οὐδέπω *oudépō*; adv. from *oudé* (3761), not even, and *pō* (4452), yet. Not yet, never yet, never (Luke 23:53; John 7:39; 19:41; 20:9; 1 Cor 8:2; Sept.: Ex 9:30).

Syn.: *oudépote* (3763), not ever, never; *mēdépote* (3368), not yet ever; *oúpō* (3768), not yet.

Ant.: *nún* (3568), now; *pántote* (3842), always.

3765. οὐκέτι *oukéti*; adv. from *ouk* (3756), not, and *éti* (2089), yet, still. An adv. meaning no more, no further, no longer, in the general sense of *ou* (3756), not (Matt 19:6; Mark 10:8; Luke 15:19; John 4:42; Rom 7:17, 20; 2 Cor 1:23; Rev 10:6 UBS). With other neg. for strength: *ouk* . . . *oukéti* (Acts 8:39); *oudé* . . . *oukéti* (Matt 22:46); *oudeís* . . . *oukéti* (Rev 18:11); *oukéti* . . . *oudeís* (Mark 7:12; 15:5; Luke 20:40). *Ouketi ou mḗ* as an intens. (Mark 14:25; Luke 22:16; Rev 18:14). It may also appear as two separate words, *oúk éti* (Rev 10:6 TR).

Ant.: *ap' árti* (*apó* [575], from, and *árti* [737], present) from now on; *tó loipón* (3063), the remainder, the remaining time; *apó toú nún* (*toú* [3588], gen. art.; *nún* [3568], now), from henceforth; *mēkéti* (3371), no longer; *metá taúta* (*metá* [3326], after; *taúta*, the pl. of *toúto* [5124], these things), after these things; *eis tón aiṓna* (*eis* [1519], unto; *tón aiṓna* [165], the age), forever; *pántote* (3842), always; *nún* (3568), now; *ḗdē* (2235), already; *dḗ* (1211), now; *pálai* (3819),

formerly; *en archḗ* (*en* [1722], in; *archḗ*, the dat. sing. of *archḗ* [746], beginning), in the beginning, originally.

3766. οὐκοῦν *oukoún*; adv. from *ou* / *ouk* (3756), no, not and *oún* (3767), certainly, accordingly. Used interrogatively meaning "not so then?" (implying an affirmative answer) and meaning "Not so then? Thou art a king" (a.t. [John 18:37]); with or without the interrogative, "Thou art then a king" (a.t.).

Syn.: *oudépote* (3763), never; *oukéti* (3765), no longer.

Ant.: *málista* (3122), specially, certainly; *alēthṓs* (230), truly; *asphalṓs* (806), assuredly; *amḗn* (281), verily, truly.

3767. οὖν *oún*; conj. Accordingly, thereupon, then, now, certainly. Put after one or more words in a clause, and expressing either the merely external connection of two sentences, that the one follows upon the other, or also the internal relation of cause and effect, that the one follows from the other.

(I) As marking mere external connection and thus denoting transition or continuation from what precedes to what follows with the meaning of thereupon, now then.

(A) Generally (Luke 6:9; John 12:1, 9; 18:11, 16; 19:29; 21:5; Rom 11:1, 11; 15:17). Where there is introductory matter, the transition is made to the thing itself (Matt 13:18; Luke 20:29 [cf. 20:28]; John 4:5; 19:40; Acts 2:33; 1 Cor 7:26); also *mén oún* (*mén* [3303], even), so then, with *dé* (1161) following (Mark 16:19, "so then . . . he was received up"; Acts 1:6; 8:4; 19:38; 23:18, 31). Without *dé* (Acts 23:22; 26:4, 9; 1 Cor 6:4; Heb 7:11).

(B) Joined with a particle of time or words implying time (Matt 6:2; 21:40; Luke 11:34); *hóte oún* / *hótan oún* (*hóte* [3753], when; *hótan* [3752], when), when therefore (John 2:22; 19:6, 8, 30); *hōs oún* (*hōs* [5613], as), when therefore) (John 4:1, 40; 20:11); *exautḗs oún* (*exautḗs* [1824], from that hour), from that hour then (Acts 10:33); *nún oún* (*nún* [3568], now), now therefore (Acts 10:33); *palin oún*, or *oún pálin* (*pálin* [3825], again), again therefore (John 8:12, 21; 10:7, 19, 31, 39); *tóte oún* (*tóte* [5119], then), then therefore (John 11:14; 20:8). So also with a particle which may be resolved by a particle of time, as *hótan* (3752), *hóte* (3753), when, *hōs* (5613), as soon as, with a finite verb (John 6:14), "Then those men, when they had seen" (see John 6:15; 11:17; 19:13; Acts 15:2; Rom 15:28).

(II) As expressing the internal connection of two sentences that the one follows from the other as effect or consequence, i.e., therefore, then, consequently, with the meaning for this cause, for this reason, from these premises.

(A) Generally where something is said to be done in consequence of what has happened previously: **(1)** Generally (Luke 15:28; John 9:7; 19:24; Acts 17:20; Rom 9:19; Eph 4:1; 1 Tim 5:14; 1 Pet 2:7). Frequently, especially in John, in the phrases *eípon oún* (*eípon*, the aor. of *eréō* [2046], to say); therefore (John 8:13; 11:12). **(2)** In exhortations founded on what precedes (Matt 5:48; Mark 13:35; Luke 6:36; Acts 3:19; 13:38; Rom 11:22; 1 Cor 16:11; Col 3:5; Heb 4:1; James 5:7). **(3)** Where the consequence is connected with a conditional or causal clause, e.g., *eán* (1437), if, followed by *oún* and meaning if therefore (Matt 5:23; Luke 4:7; John 6:62; Rom 2:26); *ei* (1487), if, followed by *oún* (Matt 6:23; Luke 16:11; John 18:8); *eíte* (1535), whether, followed by *oún* (1 Cor 10:31); *epeí* (1893), since, followed by *oún* (Heb 2:14; 4:6). Like-wise with a part. equivalent to *epeí* with a finite verb (Acts 17:29; Rom 5:1; 2 Cor 7:1; Heb 4:14; 1 Pet 4:1).

(B) Illative, expressing an inference or conclusion from what precedes: **(1)** Generally (Matt 3:10; Mark 10:9; Luke 20:44; John 3:29; 8:38; Rom 6:4; Heb 9:23; James 4:17; 3 John 1:8). So also in *ára* (686), therefore, followed by *oún*, consequently therefore. **(2)** After an enumeration of particulars expressing the

general result or conclusion (Matt 1:17; John 7:43; 12:17 [cf. 12:9f.]; see also Luke 3:18; John 20:30). **(3)** Where the conclusion is connected with a conditional or causal clause such as *ei* (1487), if, followed by *oún* in the sense of *epeí* (1893), whereupon, followed by *oún* (Matt 7:11; John 13:14; Acts 11:17).

(C) Where a sentence has been interrupted by a parenthesis or intervening clauses and is again taken up; equivalent to "I say," "as before said" (Matt 7:24 [cf. 7:21]; Matt 10:32 [cf. 10:22]; Mark 3:31 [cf. 3:21]; John 6:24 [cf. 6:22]; John 18:12 [cf. 18:3]; 1 Cor 8:4 [cf. 8:1]; Gal 3:5 [cf. 3:2]; Heb 4:11).

(D) In interrogative sentences referring back to a previous assertion, supposition or circumstance (Matt 13:28; 17:10; 19:7; Mark 12:9; Luke 3:10; John 1:21; Rom 3:1; 4:1; 1 Cor 14:15, 26); *póthen oún* (*póthen* [4159], whence), whence therefore (Matt 13:27, 56); *pṓs oún* (*pṓs* [4459], how), how therefore (Matt 12:26; 26:54; John 6:42; 9:19; Rom 10:14).

Syn.: *dé* (1161), such as but, and, now; *dḗ* (1211), now; *kaí* (2532), used with the meaning of now; *ára* (686), therefore, then; *houtōs* or *houtō* (3779), so; *épos* (2031), so to say; *hōsaútōs* (5615) and *homoíōs* (3668), likewise; *hōs* (5613), so; *tóte* (5119), at that time, then; *eíta* (1534), after, furthermore; *épeita* (1899), after; *loipón* (3063), finally, then; *oukoún* (3766), so then; *toínun* (5106), therefore; *te* (5037), and or then; *alēthṓs* (230), truly; *amḗn* (281), verily, amen.

3768. οὔπω *oúpō*; adv. from *ou* (3756), not, and *pō* (n.f.), yet. Not even yet, not yet (Matt 24:6; John 2:4; 3:24; 7:39; 8:57; 11:30; Acts 8:16; Heb 2:8; 12:4). In interrogatives (Matt 15:17; 16:9; Mark 8:17).

Syn.: *héōs árti* (*héōs* [2193], until; *árti* [737], now), until now; *áchri toú deúro* (*áchri* [891], until; *toú deúro* (1204), come), until the hither or the present, hitherto; *oudépō* (3764), never yet, as yet not; *mḗpō* (3380), not yet, not as absolute as *oudépō*.

Ant.: *nún* (3568), now; *pántote* (3842), always.

3769. οὐρά *ourá*; gen. *ourás*, fem. noun. Tail of an animal (Rev 9:10, 19; 12:4; Sept.: Deut 28:13; Job 40:17).

3770. οὐράνιος *ouránios*; fem. *ouranía*, neut. *ouránion*, adj. from *ouranós* (3772), heaven. Celestial, heavenly. In the NT, a heavenly host of angels (Luke 2:13); a heavenly vision (Acts 26:19). "Heavenly Father" occurs only in Matthew (Matt 6:14, 26, 32; 15:13).

Syn.: *epouránios* (2032), heavenly.
Ant.: *katachthónios* (2709), subterranean, underground; *epigeíos* (1919), earthly.

3771. οὐρανόθεν *ouranóthen*; adv. from *ouranós* (3772), heaven, and the adj. suffix *-then* meaning from a place. From heaven (Acts 14:17; 26:13).

Syn.: *ánōthen* (509), from above.

3772. οὐρανός *ouranós*; gen. *ouranoú*, masc. noun. Heaven, sky, air. The sing. and pl. are used similarly and interchangeably. There is no difference in meaning between them.

(I) In the NT, in a physical sense, it means the over-arching, all-embracing heaven beneath which is the earth and all that is therein. In this not only do the fowl of the air fly (Matt 6:26; 8:20; 13:32), but the clouds are suspended (Matt 24:30; 26:64; Luke 12:56) and the rain is formed (James 5:18); also the sun, moon and stars are placed in the same celestial expanse (Mark 13:25; Heb 11:12).

(II) It is also used for that heaven where the residence of God is, called by the Psalmist "the holy heavens" (a.t.), or "heavens of holiness" (a.t.), of separation (Sept.: Ps 20:6). It is God's dwelling or resting place (Matt 5:34, 45, 48); where the blessed angels are (Mark 13:27); from whence Christ descended (John 3:13, 31; 6:32, 33, 38); where after His resurrection and ascension "He sitteth at the right hand of the Majesty on high" (a.t. [Heb

8:1]) and appears in the presence of God on our behalf (Heb 9:24); and where a reward is reserved for the righteous (Matt 5:12; 1 Pet 1:4).

(III) The heavens are used metonymically of God in the OT (2 Chr 32:20 [cf. 2 Kgs 19:25; Isa 37:15, 16; Dan 4:23, 28]). *Ouranós*, heaven, is used with the same sense in the NT (Matt 21:25; Mark 11:30, 31; Luke 15:18, 21; 20:4, 5; John 3:27). Thus, the kingdom of the heavens, or heaven, is syn. with the kingdom of God (Matt 19:23, 24).

(IV) In 2 Cor 12:2, Paul was raptured to the third heaven and returned. This is called Paradise (12:4) which is applied to the state of the faithful souls between death and the resurrection where they are admitted to immediate communion with God in Christ, and to a partaking of the true Tree of Life which is in the midst of the paradise of God (Luke 22:43; Rev 2:7).

(V) There is a final heaven which in Heb 11:16 is referred to as a better or a heavenly country; in 13:14 as a continuing city; and in Rev 21:2 the holy city, new Jerusalem. It is the place where the believers are going to receive their inheritance which is incorruptible (1 Pet 1:3–5). See also Matt 6:19, 20; 1 Cor 2:9; Col 3:2; Rev 21:1–5. Consult a Gr. concordance for the rest of the references.

Deriv.: *epouránios* (2032), heavenly, what pertains to or is in heaven; *ouránios* (3770), heavenly; *ouranóthen* (3771), from heaven; *messouránēma* (3321), mid-heaven, the midst of the heavens.

Syn.: *parádeisos* (3857), paradise.
Ant.: *gḗ* (1093), earth; *geénna* (1067), hell, everlasting punishment; *hádēs* (86), the state or place of departed spirits.

3773. Οὐρβανός *Ourbanós*; gen. *Ourbanoú*, masc. proper noun. Urbanus, also Urbane, meaning refined or polite. One of the Christians in Rome to whom Paul sent greetings (Rom 16:9).

3774. Οὐρίας *Ourías*; gen. *Ouríou*, masc. proper noun transliterated from the Hebr. *'Urīāh* (223, OT), flame of Jehovah. Urias or Uriah, a Hittite (2 Sam 11:3f.), but probably converted to Judaism, commander of one of the bands of David's army and the husband of Bathsheba. His death was purposely brought about by an understanding between Joab and David in order that David's guilt in the case of Bath-sheba might be concealed and that he might obtain her for his wife. Bath-sheba is referred to in Matt 1:6.

3775. οὖς *oús*; gen. *ōtós*, neut. noun. An ear, pl. *tá ōta*, the ears (Mark 7:33; 8:18; Luke 22:50; Acts 7:57; 1 Cor 12:16; Sept.: Ex 29:20; Deut 15:17). In phrases such as *ho échōn ōta* (*échōn*, pres. part. of *échō* [2192], I have), "he who has ears," or *eí tis échei oús akoúein, akouétō* (*eí* [1487], if; *tis* [5100], anyone; *échei*, has; *oús*, ear; *akoúein*, the pres. inf. of *akoúō* [191], hear, also implying understanding; *akouétō*, the indirect imper. of *akoúō*, let him hear and understand), whosoever can hear and understand, "let him hear and attend" (Matt 11:15; 13:9, 43; Mark 4:9, 23; 7:16; Luke 8:8; 14:35; Rev 2:7, 11, 17, 29; 3:6, 13, 22; 13:9). The expression *thésthe humeís eis tá ōta* (*thésthe*, 2d aor. imper. mid. of *títhēmi* [5087], to place; *eis* [1519], into; *tá ōta*, the ears), *humōn*, put in your ears, means to let sink into the ears, to fix deep in the mind (Luke 9:44; see also Ex 17:14). In Luke 1:44 the expression "to come to" or "into the ears" (a.t.) means to be heard. See also Acts 11:22; James 5:4; Sept.: Isa 5:9. The expression *laléō* or *akoúō eis tó oús* (*laléō* [2980], to speak; *akoúō* [191], to hear; *eis* [1519], into, or *prós* [4314], toward), to speak or hear in the ear, means to speak or hear privately (Matt 10:27; Luke 12:3; Sept.: Ex 11:2). The expression to do something "in the ears" of someone means in his hearing or presence (Luke 4:21; Sept.: Judg 17:2). In 1 Pet 3:12, the expression that the ears of the Lord "are open unto their prayers" (quoted from Ps 34:15) means that God listens to prayer. See also 2 Chr

6:40; 7:15. In Matt 13:15 and Acts 28:27, what is translated "their ears are dull of hearing" in Gr. is *toís ōsí*, as to their ears, *baréōs* (917), heavily, *ékousan*, the aor. or *akoúō* (191), hear, they heard heavily, they did not heed or pay attention to what they heard. In Rom 11:8 the expression *kaí ōta toú mḗ akoúein* (*kaí* [2532], and; *hōta*, ears; *toú mḗ* [3361], not; *akoúein*, the pres. inf. of *akoúō* [191], to hear), they have ears with the capability but not the will to hear. In Acts 7:51, the expression "uncircumcised in ears" means that the ears are covered and that they neither listen to nor obey the divine precepts. They are stubborn and perverse. The ear is designated as the organ for hearing and thus obeying (Matt 13:16; 1 Cor 2:9).

Deriv.: *entōtízomai* (1801), to hearken; *ōtíon* (5621), ear.

Syn.: *akoḗ* (189), hearing, audience.

Ant.: *kōphós* (2974), deaf.

3776. οὐσία *ousía*; gen. *ousías*, fem. noun from *oúsa* (n.f.), being, which is the pres. part. fem. of *eimí* (1510), to be. Entity, essence, substance, nature. In the NT, it usually refers to that which belongs to someone, or what he has, his substance, property (Luke 15:13).

Deriv.: *epioúsios* (1967), daily.

Syn.: *hupárchonta* (5224), property, possessions; *húparxis* (5223), existence, possession; *hupóstasis* (5287), substance; *ploútos* (4149), wealth; *euporía* (2142), pecuniary resources; *agathá* (18), benefits, goods; *bíos* (979), the livelihood; *thēsaurós* (2344), treasure.

Ant.: *ptōcheía* (4432), poverty, helplessness; *gumnótēs* (1132), nakedness.

3777. οὔτε *oúte*; conj. from *ou* (3756), not, and the enclitic *te* (5037). Neither, nor, not even, and not, also not; referring usually to a part of a proposition or clause.

(I) As introducing a neg. clause, with or without a preceding negation, meaning neither, nor, e.g., *oúte gár* (1063) then, therefore (Luke 20:36; Acts 4:12). *Oúte . . . kaí* (2532), nor . . . and (John

4:11). See also 3 John 1:10. More frequently repeated, *oúte . . . oúte*, neither . . . nor, before different parts of a clause (Matt 6:20; Luke 20:35; John 5:37; Acts 15:10; Gal 5:6). Also three times or more, *oúte, oúte, oúte* (Acts 25:8; Rom 8:38, 39; 1 Cor 6:9, 10; Rev 9:20, 21). After another neg., as *ou* (3756), not, *ou . . . oúte*, neither . . . nor (John 1:25; Rev 20:4; 21:4). *Oudé . . . oúte*, neither . . . neither (*oudé* [3761], neither, nor (Gal 1:12; 1 Thess 2:3).

(II) In the sense of "not even" (Mark 5:3; Luke 12:26; 1 Cor 3:2 TR).

Syn.: *oudé* (3761), neither, nor; *mēdé* (3366), neither, nor, not even; *mēte* (3383), neither, not even.

Ant.: *málista* (3122), certainly, indeed; *mēn* (3375), assuredly; *ḗ* (2228), either; *amphóteros* (297), both.

3778. οὗτος *hoútos*; fem. *haútē*, neut. *toúto*, demonstrative pron. This, that.

(I) As referring to a person or thing before mentioned, i.e., to something preceding:

(A) To that next preceding (Luke 1:32; 2:25; John 1:2; 3:2; 6:71; Acts 10:36; Rom 14:18, *en toútois*, pl. dat., "in these"; 2 Pet 2:20; 1 John 5:6, 20). The neut. pl. *taúta* (5023) sometimes refers only to one thing (Luke 12:4; see also John 15:17). The expression *katá taúta* (*katá* [2596], according to; *taúta*, these things) means *oútō* (3779), thus (Luke 6:23, 26). The expression also appears as *katá tautá* (*katá* [2596], according; *tautá* (5024), in the same way), accordingly in the same way.

(B) Sometimes *hoútos* refers not to the nearest, but to a person or thing, the chief topic of discourse (Matt 3:3 [cf. 3:1]; John 1:41; 11:37, *kaí hoútos*, "even this man," i.e., Lazarus; 21:24; Acts 4:11, "This is the stone," referring to Christ; Acts 7:19; 2 John 1:7). As referring generally to the preceding discourse (Matt 7:28; Luke 1:29; 24:21; John 2:11; Acts 19:17; Rom 11:27; 1 John 2:1, 26).

(II) As referring to or introducing what follows, with emphasis as in the

Eng. "this," meaning the following (Gal 3:17; 1 John 4:2), or with the subst. (Matt 10:2; Luke 2:12; Acts 8:32; 1 Cor 9:3). With a noun as the predicate (2 Cor 13:9; 1 John 5:4). With an inf., e.g., without the art. (Acts 24:16; 26:16; James 1:27) and with the art. (Rom 14:13; 2 Cor 2:1). With *diá* (1223), for, *diá toúto*, before a part. of cause (Mark 12:24); *en toútō* (*en* [1722], in) (2 Cor 5:2). Also before *hóti* (3754) (John 21:23; Acts 20:29; Rom 6:6; 1 Cor 1:12; 1 John 1:5). Followed by *hína* (2443), so that, e.g., of purpose, *eis toúto hína* (*eis* [1519], unto; John 6:29, 39, 40; 17:3; Rom 14:9; 1 Pet 3:9; 4:6; 1 John 4:17; 5:3).

(III) Used as pointing to a person or thing present, either to the eyes or to the mind:

(A) Generally (Matt 3:17; 8:9; 17:5, 20; 26:26, 28, 34; Mark 9:7; 12:43; 14:22, 24, 69; Luke 9:35; 12:26; 21:6; John 1:15; 7:46; Acts 1:5; 2:7; 1 Cor 11:24, 25). With a numeral referring to time (Luke 24:21; 2 Cor 13:1).

(B) In admiration (Matt 8:27; 12:23; Luke 4:22; John 6:14).

(C) More usually in contempt or aversion, equivalent to the Eng. "this fellow" (Matt 9:3; 12:24; 13:54; Mark 6:2, 3; Luke 5:21; John 6:42; Acts 7:40; 1 Cor 5:2, 3).

(IV) Inserted for emphasis:

(A) Between the subj. or obj. of a verb and the verb. After a noun (Matt 13:38; Luke 8:21; Acts 4:10; 1 Cor 6:4; 1 Pet 2:7). After a relative pron. (Matt 5:19 where in the preceding clause *hoútos* is omitted; Mark 3:35; Luke 9:24; John 1:33; Rom 8:30; Phil 4:8). After a part. (Matt 13:20; Mark 12:40; Luke 9:48; John 6:46; Acts 17:6).

(B) In an apodosis, a concluding clause of a conditional sentence, after *ei* (1487), if (Rom 8:9; 1 Cor 3:17; Phile 1:18; James 3:2; 1 Pet 2:20).

(C) After a parenthesis or intervening sentence when the writer again returns to the leading subject (Acts 7:35 [cf. 7:31, 37, 38]).

(**V**) Where *hoútos* is followed by a relative pron., *hoútos . . . hós* (3739), meaning this who, he who, that which (Luke 9:9; 1 John 5:9). Both before and after a relative pron. *hoútos* is frequently omitted and the relative then implies it and stands for he who or that which, equivalent to the Eng. "what."

(**VI**) As strengthened by *autós* (846), i.e., *autoí hoútoi*, these themselves, or they themselves (Acts 24:15, 20). More often in the neut. *autó toúto, toúto autó*, this very thing, as referring to what precedes (2 Cor 2:3; Eph 6:18), or with the relative *hó . . . autó toutó* (Gal 2:10). As referring to and introducing what follows, followed by *tó*, the neut. art. with the inf. (2 Cor 7:11); *hóti* (3754), that (Phil 1:6); *hína* (2443), so that (Eph 6:22; Col 4:8); *hópōs* (3704), so that (Rom 9:17).

(**VII**) After *kaí* (2532), and, as *kaí hoútos*, and this man, and he (Luke 16:1); he also (Luke 20:30); demonstratively (Luke 22:56, 59). Especially in *kaí hoútos, kaí toúto, kaí taúta*, and he too, and this too, and that indeed, i.e., where a particular stress is to be laid upon the connection of two circumstances, *hoútos* is thus joined to *kaí*, and then always refers back to the former. So also in 1 Cor 2:2, "and him crucified." More often in the neut. *kaí toúto* (Rom 13:11, *kaí toúto eidótes* [1492], knowing, meaning and knowing this, refers to Rom 8; 1 Cor 6:6; Eph 2:8).

(**VIII**) In distribution, *toúto mén* (3303), on the one hand . . . *toúto dé* (1161), that on the other hand, meaning as to this . . . as to that, i.e., "partly . . . partly" (Heb 10:33).

(**IX**) Neut. *taúta*, acc. used as an adv. meaning thus, so, equivalent to *hoútōs*. Also after *kathós* (2531), according to (John 8:28, *taúta laló* [2980], such I speak); with *hoútōs* (Mark 2:8), *hoútōs . . . tí taúta*, thus . . . why so, making *hoútōs* and *tí taúta* syn. with *taúta eínai*, to be thus, such (1 Cor 6:11). As referring to what follows (Luke 18:11, *taúta* refers to the manner of prayer).

(**X**) In gender, the use of *hoútos* exhibits some anomalies of syntax, e.g., where *hoútos* refers in sense to a preceding noun or pron., it still sometimes takes the gender and number of a noun following (Matt 7:12, *hoútos* refers not to *pánta*, but to the Law and the Prophets which is taken as sing.; 13:38; Luke 8:14, 15; Gal 4:24). In Matt 21:42 and Mark 12:11 (quoted from Ps 118:23), *haútē*, the fem., stands twice for the neut. *toúto*.

Deriv.: *hoútō, hoútōs* (3779), in this manner, thus.

Syn.: *hós* (3739), who; *hóstis* (3748), which.

Ant.: *ékeinos* (1565), that one.

3779. οὕτω *hoútō*, οὕτως *hoútōs*; demonstrative adv. from *hoútos* (3778), this one. In this manner, on this wise, thus, to which corresponds the relative *hōs* (5613), as.

(**I**) As referring to what precedes and in complete sentences preceded by a relative adv. or adv. word:

(**A**) With a preceding relative adv. as . . . so, e.g., *katháper . . . hoútōs* (*katháper* [2509], exactly as . . . *hoútō*, thus as . . . so; Rom 12:4, 5; 1 Cor 12:12; 2 Cor 8:11); *kathōs . . . hoútōs* (*kathōs* [2531], as . . . *hoútōs*), as . . . so (Luke 11:30; John 3:14; 2 Cor 1:5; 1 Thess 2:4); *hōs . . . hoútōs* (*hōs* [5613], as . . . *hoútōs*), as . . . so (Acts 8:32; Rom 5:15; 2 Cor 7:14; 1 Thess 2:7, 8); *hósper . . . hoútōs* (*hósper* [5618], exactly like . . . *hoútōs*), as . . . so (Matt 12:40; John 5:21; Rom 6:4; 1 Cor 11:12); *kath' hóson . . . hoútōs* (*kath'* [2596]), according to; *hóson* [3745], as much, or inasmuch . . . *hoútōs*), as . . . so (Heb 9:27, 28); *hón trópon . . . hoútōs* (*hón* [3739], that; *trópon* [5158], in which manner . . . *hoútōs*), in which manner . . . so (2 Tim 3:8); *katá tḗn hodón . . . hoútōs* (*katá* [2596], according to; *tḗn hodón* [3598], the way; *hoútōs*), as per the way . . . so (Acts 24:14); *há . . . hoútōs*, according to those things which . . . so, with *hōs* (5613), as, implied (*há*, the which, [pl.]) (Acts 3:18).

(B) Alone and as referring general-ly to the preceding discourse (Matt 3:15 [cf. 3:13]; Matt 5:12; 6:30 [cf. 6:29, 30]; Matt 9:33; 17:12; 18:14; Luke 1:25; John 11:48; 1 Cor 2:11; 7:26, 40 [cf. 7:24]; Rev 2:15). Interrogative (John 18:22). So, *ei taúta hoútōs échei* (*ei* [1487], if; *taúta*, these things; *hoútōs échei* [2192], thus have), so as they appear, are report-ed (Acts 7:1; 17:11). In an emphatic af-firmation or prohibition, *hoútōs éstai*, so shall it be (Matt 12:45; 13:49; 20:26; 24:39; Mark 10:43; Luke 22:26).

(II) As referring to and introducing what follows; in complete sentences fol-lowed by a relative adv. or adv. word.

(A) With a following relative adv., so . . . as, equivalent to *hoútōs* . . . *kathṓs* (2531), just as (Luke 24:24; Rom 11:26); *hoútōs* . . . *hōs* (5613), just as (John 7:46; see 1 Cor 4:1; James 2:12); *hoútōs* . . . *hōste*, followed by an inf., in a way or manner resulting in (Acts 14:1); *hoútōs* . . . *hón trópon*, thus . . . in the way that (Acts 1:11); *hoútōs* . . . *kath' hón trópon*, thus . . . according to the way that (Acts 27:25).

(B) Alone, e.g., as followed by direct narration or quotation (Matt 1:18; 2:5; John 21:1; Heb 4:4; Rev 9:17); or fol-lowed by an inf. (1 Pet 2:15). Also fol-lowed by *hóti* (3754), that, of quotation (Luke 19:31; Acts 7:6; 13:34). Followed by *hína* (2443), so that (1 Cor 9:24).

(III) Used demonstratively meaning in this manner (Acts 21:11; Rom 9:20). With the idea of aversion (1 Cor 5:3, the one who did thus).

(IV) Inserted for emphasis:

(A) After part. and before the fol-lowing verb, like *hoútōs* (Acts 20:11; 27:17).

(B) In a concluding clause of a con-ditional sentence after *ei* (1487), if; *hóti* (3754), that (1 Thess 4:14; Rev 3:15, 16; 11:5).

(V) Spoken of degree, extent, so, so much, to such a degree, in such a man-ner; so with adj. and adv. (Gal 1:6; Heb 12:21; Rev 16:18). Interrogative (Matt 26:40; Mark 4:40; 7:18; Gal 3:3; 1 Cor

6:5). With a verb (1 John 4:11). Followed with *hōste* (5620), therefore, with the in-dic. (John 3:16).

Syn.: *hōs* (5613), as; *homoíōs* (3668), similarly.

Ant.: *állōs* (247), otherwise; *hetérōs* (2088), in a different way.

3780. οὐχί *ouchí*; adv. from *ou* (3756), not.

(I) Generally stronger than *ou* for em-phasis (John 13:10, meaning but not all, or by no means all [cf. 13:11]; 1 Cor 6:1). *Ouchí* . . . *allá* (235), but (1 Cor 10:29; 2 Cor 10:13).

(II) In neg. answers it means no, nay, by no means; followed by *allá* (Luke 1:60; 12:51; 13:3; Rom 3:27; Sept.: Gen 18:15; 19:2).

(III) Often in neg. questions, meaning "Is not?" or "Are not?" implying an af-firmative answer (Matt 5:46; 20:13; Luke 12:6; 17:8, 17; John 11:9; Rom 3:29; Sept.: Gen 40:8; Judg 4:6).

Syn.: *ou, ouk, ouch* (3756), no, not; *hoúpō* (3768), not yet; *mḗ* (3361), not.

Ant.: *naí* (3483), yes; *málista* (3122), yes indeed.

3781. ὀφειλέτης *opheilétēs*; gen. *opheilétou*, masc. noun from *opheílō* (3784), to owe. A debtor.

(I) One owing money (Matt 18:24). One indebted for favors (Rom 15:27).

(II) One morally bound to the perfor-mance of any duty, followed by the inf. (Gal 5:3, he is bound to keep the whole law).

(III) Delinquent, one who fails in the performance of duty (Matt 6:12, meaning those who fail in their duty toward us). Forgiving our debtors does not imply that man has the ability to forgive another hu-man being in the same way that God for-gives a sinner. Generally a transgressor, sinner (*hamartōlós* [268], sinner) (Luke 13:4 [cf. 13:2]; see also Gen 18:23; Ps 1:1).

Deriv.: *chreōpheilétēs* (5533), one who owes a debt.

Ant.: *daneistḗs* (1157), a lender, creditor.

3782. ὀφειλή *opheilḗ*; gen. *opheilḗs*, fem. noun from *opheílō* (3784), to owe. A debt which must be paid (Matt 18:32), obligation, a service which one owes someone (Rom 13:7).

Syn.: *opheílēma* (3783), an amount due while *opheilḗ* is a duty owed.

Ant.: *pístis* (4102), trust, credit; *dáneion* (1156), a loan, debt.

3783. ὀφείλημα *opheílēma*; gen. *opheilḗmatos*, neut. noun from *opheílō* (3784), to owe. Debt, that which is owed, which is strictly due (Rom 4:4). Also an offense, a trespass which requires reparation (Matt 6:12, equivalent to *paraptṓmata* [3900], transgressions of 6:14 and *hamartías* [266], sins of Luke 11:4). The suffix makes it that which is owed and makes it syn. with *opheilḗ* (3782), a debt or obligation (Matt 18:32; Rom 13:7 [cf. Matt 18:30, 34]).

Ant.: *dáneion* (1156), a loan debt.

3784. ὀφείλω *opheílō*; fut. *opheilḗsō*. To owe, to be indebted.

(I) Particularly in a pecuniary sense, with the acc. and dat. expressed or implied (Matt 18:28; Luke 7:41; 16:5, 7; Phile 1:18; Sept.: Deut 15:2; Isa 24:2, every creditor shall remit what he has lent to his neighbor, meaning what his neighbor owes him). Pass. part. neut. *tó opheilómenon*, what is owed, debt, due (Matt 18:30, 34; 1 Cor 7:3 [TR]).

(II) Metaphorically, to be bound or obligated to perform a duty, meaning I ought, must, followed by the inf. Of what is required by law or duty in general, with the inf. implied (Matt 23:16, 18). Elsewhere with the inf. (Luke 17:10; John 13:14; 19:7, he ought to die; Rom 15:1, 27; 2 Cor 12:14; Eph 5:28; 2 Thess 1:3; 2:13; 1 John 2:6; 3:16; 4:11; 3 John 1:8). Also of what the circumstances of time, place, or person render proper, to be fit and proper (Acts 17:29; 1 Cor 7:36; 11:7, 10; 2 Cor 12:11; Heb 2:17; 5:3, 12); what

is from the nature of the case necessary (1 Cor 5:10; 9:10).

(III) By implication, to fail in duty, be delinquent, be at fault with someone, with the dat. (Luke 11:4).

Deriv.: *opheilétēs* (3781), debtor; *opheilḗ* (3782), debt, obligation; *opheílēma* (3783), that which is owed, obligation; *óphelon* (3785), to owe; *prosopheílō* (4359), to owe in addition to.

Syn.: *anagkázomai* (315), to be compelled, to have to; *deí* (1163), it is necessary, an obligation out of intrinsic necessity or inevitability, contrasted to *opheílō*, which implies moral or personal obligation; *chrḗzō* (5535), to need; *chrḗ* (5534), it needs be, ought; *prépō* (4241), it is proper or right.

Ant.: *apotínō* (661), to repay, to pay in full; *apokatástasis* (605), retribution; *apodídōmi* (591) give again, repay.

3785. ὄφελον *óphelon*; 2d aor. of *opheílō* (3784), to owe. I ought, but used only in the implied sense of wishing. (The Attic form is *óphelon*.) In earlier Gr. writers, it is still a verb, followed by the inf. and often preceded by *hōs* (5613), as, *ei* (1487), if, *eíthe*, expressing a wish. In later writers and the NT, *óphelon* is an indeclinable particle of wishing or interjection. It means Oh that! Would that! (1 Cor 4:8; 2 Cor 11:1; Gal 5:12; Rev 3:15; Sept.: Ex 16:3; Num 14:3; 20:3; 2 Kgs 5:3).

Syn.: *eúchomai* (2172), I wish, I would, I make a vow; *epithuméō* (1937), to desire, lust; *boúlomai* (1014), I purpose; *thélō* (2309), I wish with the power to execute the wish; *epipothéō* (1971), to crave; *orégomai* (3713), to desire, have an appetite for.

Ant.: *ameléō* (272), to neglect; *parérchomai* (3928), to bypass.

3786. ὄφελος *óphelos*; gen. *ophélous*, neut. noun from *ophéllō* (n.f.), to heap up. Increase, profit, meaning furtherance, advantage (1 Cor 15:32; James 2:14, 16; Sept.: Job 15:3).

Deriv.: *ōpheléō* (5623), to be profitable.

Syn.: *kérdos* (2771), gain; *perissós* (4053), what is superior and advantageous; *ōphéleia* (5622), profit, advantage; *sumphéron*, neut. form of the pres. part. of *sumphérō* (4851), the common profit; *prokopḗ* (4297), progress, furtherance; *euergesía* (2108), beneficence; *aúxēsis* (838), increase.

Ant.: *mataiótēs* (3153), vanity; *kópos* (2873), toil, weariness; *zēmía* (2209), loss, damage; *apobolḗ* (580), loss; *opheílēma* (3783), that which is owed, obligation.

3787. ὀφθαλμοδουλεία *ophthalmodouleía*; gen. *ophthalmodouleías*, fem. noun from *ophthalmós* (3788), eye, and *douleía* (1397), service. Eyeservice, implying either service rendered only when one is being scrutinized or service rendered only for appearance sake (Eph 6:6; Col 3:22).

Syn.: *hupókrisis* (5272), hypocrisy.
Ant.: *eilikríneia* (1505), sincerity.

3788. ὀφθαλμός *ophthalmós*; gen. *ophthalmoú*, masc. noun from *óptomai* or *optánomai* (3700), to gaze. Eye.

(I) An eye; pl. *ophthalmoí*, eyes.

(A) Generally (Matt 5:29, 38; Mark 8:25; Luke 24:16; Acts 9:18; 1 Cor 12:16; 15:52; Rev 3:18; Sept.: Gen 29:17; 48:10).

(B) In phrases, *ophthalmós haploús* (*haploús* [573], single, without folds), meaning a sound eye, as contrasted to *ophthalmós ponērós* (*ponērós* [4190], evil), an unsound, evil or diseased eye (Matt 6:22, 23). With *anoígō* (455), to open, to open the eyes (Acts 9:8, 40), means either one's own eyes or those of another, i.e., to cause to see, to restore sight (Matt 9:30; 20:33; John 9:10, 14, 17, 21, 26, 30, 32; 10:21; 11:37; Sept.: Isa 35:5; 37:23; 42:7); metaphorically, it means to open the eyes of the mind, i.e., cause to perceive and understand (Acts 26:18). With *dianoígō* (1272), to open wide the eyes, means to cause to see what was not seen before (Luke 24:31; Sept.: 2 Kgs 6:17); with *exorússō* (1846), to dig out, denotes entire devotedness

(Gal 4:15; Sept.: 1 Sam 11:2); with *epaírō* (1869), to raise up, to lift up the eyes, means to look upon (Matt 17:8; Luke 6:20; 16:23; 18:13; John 4:35; 6:5; 17:1; Sept.: Gen 13:10; Ezek 18:6); with *kamnúō* (2576), to shut down, to close the eyes so as not to see (Matt 13:15; Acts 28:27, quoted from Isa 6:10). In 1 Pet 3:12, "The eyes of the Lord are over the righteous" means the eyes of the Lord are directed upon the righteous implying affection, quoted from Ps 34:15. In 2 Pet 2:14 "eyes full of adultery" indicates one who looks at others with adulterous desire. Heb 4:13, "naked and open in his eyes" (a.t.), means uncovered, manifest. See also Sept.: Job 27:19.

(C) The eye as the organ of seeing is used for the person who sees (Matt 13:16; Luke 2:30; 10:23; Rev 1:7; Sept.: Deut 3:21; Isa 30:20). Further, as affections of mind are manifested through the eyes, hence that which strictly belongs only to the person (e.g., affection) is attributed to the eyes, e.g., envy (Matt 20:15; Mark 7:22, "an evil eye" refers to an envious one).

(II) Metaphorically the eye of the mind or the eye of the heart is the power of perceiving and understanding (Eph 1:18 [TR]) Elsewhere it is used in an absolute sense (Luke 19:42; John 12:40; Acts 26:18; Rom 11:8, 10). The expression "in your eyes" means in your judgment (Matt 21:42; Mark 12:11; Sept.: Ps 118:23). In Rom 3:18, *apénanti* (561), before their eyes (quoted from Ps 36:1), means in the mind.

Deriv.: *antophthalméō* (503), to face, bear up; *monóphthalmos* (3442), one-eyed; *ophthalmodouleía* (3787), eyeservice

Syn.: *ómma* (3659), sight.

3789. ὄφις *óphis*; gen. *ópheōs*, masc. noun. A snake, serpent. The Gr. word *drákōn* (1404), dragon, was a huge serpent (Sept.: Job 26:13). In the NT, standing symbolically for Satan (2 Cor 11:3 in allusion to Gen 3:1; Rev 12:9, 14, 15). It refers to the serpent because it eyes its objects attentively (Matt 7:10; Mark 16:18; Luke 10:19; 11:11; 1 Cor 10:9; Rev 9:19). Used for the brazen serpent (John 3:14). Used as the emblem of wisdom or cunning, e.g., in a good sense (Matt 10:16); in a bad sense of maliciousness (Matt 23:33).

Syn.: *échidna* (2191), an adder, viper or other poisonous snake, metaphorically used for evil character; *herpetón* (2062), a creeping thing, a reptile, serpent.

3790. ὀφρύς *ophrús*; gen. of *ophrúos*, fem. noun. The brow of the human forehead. In the NT, a brow of a mountain, edge of a precipice (Luke 4:29). See Sept.: Lev 14:9.

3791. ὀχλέω *ochléō*; contracted *ochlô*, fut. *ochlḗsō*, from *óchlos* (3793), multitude. To harass with crowds, tumults, to mob. In the NT, only in the pass. *ochléomai*, generally to harass, vex (Luke 6:18; Acts 5:16).

Deriv.: *enochléō* (1776), more intens. than *ochléō*.

Syn.: *basanízō* (928), to torment; *kataponéō* (2669), to wear down with toil; *kakóō* (2559), to afflict; *tarássō* (5015), to disturb; *thorubéō* (2350), to set on an uproar; *turbázō* (5182), to trouble; *talaipōréō* (5003), to make miserable; *lumaínomai* (3075), to insult; *mástizō* (3147), to scourge.

3792. ὀχλοποιέω *ochlopoiéō*; contracted *ochlopoió*, fut. *ochlopoiḗsō*, from *óchlos* (3793), a multitude, and *poiéō* (4160), to make. To gather a crowd, raise a mob, used intrans. in Acts 17:5.

Syn.: *epanístamai* (1881), to revolt.

Ant.: *hēsucházō* (2270), to be quiet.

3793. ὄχλος *óchlos*; gen. *óchlou*, masc. noun.

(I) A crowd, throng, confused multitude.

(A) Particularly in the sing. (Matt 9:23, 25; Mark 2:4; Luke 5:1; John 5:13; Acts 14:14). With *polús* (4183), much, great (Matt 14:14; 20:29; Mark

4:1; 6:34; 12:37); with *pleístos* (4118), the greater part, the superlative of *polús* (Matt 21:8); with *pámpolus* (3827), immense, very great (Mark 8:1); with *pás* (3956), all (Matt 13:2; Mark 4:1); with *tosoútos* (5118), as large, so great (Matt 15:33); with *hikanós* (2425), much, sufficient (Mark 10:46); with *muriádes*, the pl. of *muriás* (3461), myriad, ten thousand (Luke 12:1); see Sept.: Num 20:20; 1 Kgs 20:13; Dan 10:6.

(B) In the pl., with the def. art., *hoi óchloi*, used intens. with the same sense as the sing., crowds, multitude (Matt 5:1; 7:28; 21:46; Luke 4:42; 5:3; John 7:12; Acts 8:6; 17:13). With *polloí*, the masc. pl. of *polús* (4183), much, great, many crowds (Matt 4:25; Luke 5:15; with *pántes*, the masc. pl. of *pás* (3956), every, all the crowds (Matt 12:23).

(II) Specifically used for the common people, the rabble (Matt 14:5; 21:26; Mark 12:12; John 7:12, 49; Acts 16:22; 24:12). In the pl. with the def. art., *hoi óchloi* (Matt 21:46; Acts 17:13).

(III) Generally a multitude, a great number. With the gen. of class (Luke 5:29, a great multitude of publicans; 6:17; Acts 1:15; 6:7); with *ek* (1537), of, and the gen. (John 12:9); with *hikanós*, great, sufficient (Acts 11:24, 26; 19:26).

Deriv.: *ochléō* (3791), to harass with crowds; *ochlopoiéō* (3792), to raise a public disturbance.

Syn.: *laós* (2992), people; *pléthos* (4128), a multitude of people, populace; *dēmos* (1218), an organized group of people governing themselves.

Ant.: *mónos* (3441), sole, single, alone; *idiốtēs* (2399), a private person; *polítēs* (4177), a citizen.

3794. ὀχύρωμα *ochúrōma*; gen. *ochurṓmatos*, neut. noun from *ochuróō* (n.f.), to fortify, which is from *échō* (2192), to hold fast. A stronghold, fortification, fortress (Sept.: Isa 34:13). Used metaphorically of any strong points or arguments in which one trusts (2 Cor 10:4, Sept.: Prov 10:29; 21:22).

Syn.: *teíchos* (5038), wall of a city; *púrgos* (4444), a tower, castle.

3795. ὀψάριον opsárion; gen. *opsaríou*, neut. noun, the diminutive of *ópson* (n.f.), which meant whatever in general is eaten with bread, but later came to be applied particularly to fish. In the NT, a fish (John 6:9, 11; 21:9, 10, 13).

Syn.: *ichthús* (2486), fish; *ichthúdion* (2485), a little fish.

3796. ὀψέ opsé; adv. Late, after a long time. Used to mean late evening (Mark 11:19); the evening watch (Mark 13:35; Sept.: Gen 24:11). Followed by the gen. it means at the end of, at the close of, after (Matt 28:1).

Deriv.: *ópsimos* (3797), late; *ópsios* (3798), late.

Syn.: *hespéra* (2073), evening; *télos* (5056), the end; *suntéleia* (4930), consummation; *péras* (4009), an end; *ékbasis* (1545), issue; *nún* (3568), now.

Ant.: *prōí* (4404), daybreak; *prōía* (4405), dawn of the day; *prōïnós* (4407), pertaining to the dawn; *órthrios* (3721), in the dawn; *órthros* (3722), dawn; *orthrízō* (3719), to come early in the morning.

3797. ὄψιμος ópsimos; gen. *opsímou*, masc.-fem., neut. *ópsimon*, adj. from *opsé* (3796), late. Late, latter (James 5:7), referring to the early and latter rain, the early rain falling over Palestine in October, and the latter rain during March and April.

Syn.: *ópsios* (3798), late, evening; *hústeros* (5306), latter.

Ant.: *prōïnós* (4407), pertaining to the dawn; *prōïmos* (4406), autumnal, early; *orthrinós* (3720), relating to the dawn; *órthrios* (3721), at daybreak.

3798. ὄψιος opsíos; fem. *opsía*, neut. *opsíon*, adj. from *opsé* (3796), after the close of the day. Late (Mark 11:11, meaning it being now late evening). Used with the fem. def. art. *hē* (3588), *hē opsía*, implying *hōra* (5610), hour, as a subst. it means late evening. The Jews reckoned two evenings, the first from the ninth hour or about 3:00 p.m. until sunset, the other from sunset onward (cf. Matt 14:15, 23).The Passover lamb was to be killed and the evening sacrifice offered, denoted strictly the time of sunset, as is expressly said in Deut 16:6 (cf. Ex 12:6; 29:39, 41; Lev 23:5). But in the practice of the Jews, this was reckoned the early evening from the ninth hour or 3:00 p.m. onward (cf. Acts 3:1). In the NT, *hē opsía*, as a noun, appears to denote the early evening (Matt 8:16; 14:15; 27:57; Mark 4:35; 15:42; and the latter in Matt 14:23 [cf. 14:15]; 16:2; 20:8; 26:20; Mark 1:32; 6:47; 14:17; John 6:16; 20:19).

3799. ὄψις ópsis; gen. *ópseōs*, fem. noun from *óptomai* (3700), to gaze. Sight, faculty of seeing, a sight, appearance, thing seen. In the NT aspect, looks, face, countenance (John 11:44; Rev 1:16; Sept.: Gen 24:16; 29:17). External appearance, show (John 7:24).

Syn.: *epipháneia* (2015), surface; *phantasía* (5325), show; *phántasma* (5326), specter, phantasm; *eídos* (1491), that which strikes the eye, appearance; *idéa* (2397), countenance; *prósōpon* (4383), countenance, face.

Ant.: *tuphlós* (5185), blindness; by implication, *ousía* (3776), substance; *hupóstasis* (5287), essence.

3800. ὀψώνιον opsṓnion; gen. *opsōníou*, neut. noun from *ópson* (n.f.), meat, and *ōnéomai* (n.f.), to buy. It primarily signifies whatever is bought to be eaten with bread, provisions, supplies for a soldier's pay (Luke 3:14; 1 Cor 9:7). Metaphorically, it means general wages, recompense (Rom 6:23; 2 Cor 11:8). Also from *ópson* (n.f.): *paropsís* (3953), a side dish.

Syn.: *misthós* (3408), pay, wages.

3801. ὁ ὢν καὶ ὁ ἦν καὶ ὁ ἐρχόμενος *ho ṓn kaí ho ḗn kaí ho erchómenos*. This phrase is made up of the pres. part. of *eimí* (1510), to be (*ho ṓn*, the one being), the imperf. of the same verb (*ho ḗn*), and the pres. part. of *érchomai* (2064), to come, with the def. art. *ho* (3588), the, and the connective *kaí* (2532), and. It means the One being and the One who had been, and the One coming (Rev 1:4, 8; 4:8; 11:17; 16:5). This is used to indicate that God is timeless.

(I) The first expression (*ho ṓn*) declares that there has never been a time when God was not existent, hence He is self-existent. If we translate *ho ṓn* "who is," then we acknowledge His present existence only. See how the same pres. part. is used in John 1:18 to express the eternal and unbroken relationship of the Son to the Father as two coequal and coeternal personalities of the Triune God. "God [anarthrous meaning divine essence] no one has ever seen, the one and only Son who has always been [*ho ṓn*] in the bosom of the Father, He Himself explained Him." (a.t.) The first part. *ho ṓn* affirmatively answers the question, "Has God always been around?"

(II) The second expression (*ho ḗn*) answers the question, "since when has God been around?" (a.t.). The imperf expression *ho ḗn*, the One who had been, takes us back all the way before the beginning of creation, to which He gave existence, He Himself having been self-existent. This is the same verb used three times in John 1:1 and translated "was." "In the beginning was the Word, and the Word was with God, and the Word was God." The imperf. tense of the first declaration takes us back to a time before the passive beginning or the creation. A more adequate translation of *ḗn* in this context would be "before there was any beginning, the Word [Christ in His eternal spiritual essence] had been" (a.t.). This is a declaration of the coeternity of the Son with the Father. The Son's relationship with the Father must not be taken as dormant but active as indicated by the prep. *prós* in the phrase *prós tón Theón* (*prós* [4314], toward; *tón*, acc. art., the; *Theón* [2316], God). Here the word *Theós* with the def. art. must be taken as referring

to the Father to agree with the declaration of John 1:18, "*ho ṓn eis tón kólpon toú Patrós*," (*eis* [1519], in, but indicating individuality and active relationship, in contrast to *en* [1722], in, which would have indicated passivity and control of the Son by the Father; *tón*, acc. art., the; *kólpon* [2859], bosom; *toú*, gen. art., the; *Patrós*, the gen. of *patḗr* [3962], Father), "the One being in the bosom of the Father" (a.t.). In John 1:1a, the Father is called "the God" (a.t.) and the prep. *prós* agrees with the *eis* of John 1:18.

(III) *Ho erchómenos* is the pres. part. of the mid. deponent *érchomai* (2064), to come. A literal translation is "the coming One" (a.t.). This does not exclude the fact that He came at different times and in different ways speaking to His creation (Heb 1:1, 2). He came, He is here, and He will yet keep coming in ways peculiar and necessary for the execution of His eternal plan until He creates a qualitatively new (*kainós* [2537]) heaven and new earth (Rev 21:1). The Bible does not teach Deism. (This is the teaching that there is a God but that He has nothing to do with His creation.) It rather teaches Theism, which is that God who keeps in touch with and sovereignly controls all things (Col 1:17). God will finally intervene through His Son, the Lord Jesus, to ultimately realize His eternal purposes. At Christ's return all men will stand before God in judgment and receive their due reward (Matt 16:27; Rom 2:5–10; 2 Tim 4:1; Rev 20:11–15). Maybe the reason why this designation of God as "the existing One, the One who was, and the coming One" (a.t.) is given only in the Book of the Revelation is because it is only there that God's plan of sending Jesus Christ for the final bringing out of justice on earth is described more fully. See the word *ekdíkēsis* (1557), commonly translated "vengeance" or "punishment," but which in reality means "bringing out of justice [*ek* {1537}, out; *díkē* {1349}, justice]."

(IV) This declaration of the timelessness of God must be taken as applying to all three personalities of the Triune God, to God the Father, God the Son, and God the Holy Spirit.

(A) On the surface, in its occurrences in Rev, it would appear as applying only to God the Father. Not so, if the references are carefully studied. It applies to both the Father and the Son. (1) In Rev 1:4, the TR has "grace unto you and peace from God" (a.t.), and then gives the designation of God's timelessness, "the existing One, the One who was, and the coming One" (a.t.). The UBS leaves out the phrase *apó Theoú* (*apó* [575], from; *Theoú* [2316], God), which the Majority Text has, and should be translated "from God [without the def. art., which refers to deity]" (a.t.), the Triune God (which includes God the Father but not exclusively). Observe how clearly the other two personalities of the Godhead are mentioned: "and from the seven Spirits which are before his throne; and from Jesus Christ . . . " (Rev 1:4, 5). The seven Spirits here are equivalent to the Holy Spirit. Observe that the same prep. (*apó* [575], from) is used for both, for God (who is designated as the existing One, the One who was, and the coming One) and for the seven Spirits, and again (in v. 5) referring to Jesus Christ. Grace and peace derive from the Triune God. (2) Who is the particular personality of the Trinity described in the Book of the Revelation as "the coming One" (a.t.)? It is Jesus Christ. The Revelation closes like this: "He which testifieth these things saith, Surely I come quickly [*tachú* {5035}, suddenly]." And what is John's reply? "Amen. Even so come, Lord Jesus" (Rev 22:20). In Rev 1:7, John says, "Behold he cometh with clouds; and every eye shall see him, and they also which pierced him. . . . " There is no doubt that this refers to the Lord Jesus. In 1:8 it is the Lord Jesus who asserts His divine titles, "the Alpha and the Omega, the beginning and the ending [TR], saith the Lord [*kuriós ho Theós*, the Lord God, UBS), which is, and which was, and which is to come, the Almighty."

Here Jesus Christ is speaking, assuming all the glory which belongs to God the Father as if confirming what He had stated when on earth: "I and my Father are one [*hén*, the neut. of *heís* {1520}, one, making it to mean one in substance, power, glory, but not one personality]" (John 10:30). The same Christ speaking as the God-man said, " . . . my Father is greater than I" (John 14:28). In Rev 1:8, he calls Himself the *pantokrátōr* (3841), ruler of all, for that is how He is presented throughout Revelation in regard to His Second Advent.

Of these two instances (Rev 1:4, 8), the claim of deity being beyond time must apply both to God the Father and to the eternal Son who has always been in the bosom of the Father. It is in His glory that He will return (Matt 25:31).

(B) The third occurrence of the phrase (although slightly different) is in Rev 4:8. The scene of Rev 4:5, is located in heaven (1 Thess 4:15–17). Jesus is surrounded by His saints and the ascription of praise found in Rev 4:8 is to Him: "Holy, holy, holy, Lord God Almighty." And then follows: *ho én kaí ho ón kaí ho erchómenos*, the One who had been, and the One being, and the coming One. In the previous two occurrences, the phrase started with the pres. part *ho ón*, the One being, while here it starts with the imperf. *ho én*, the One who had been. Why? Possibly because of the desire of the now heavenly worshipers wanting to identify the One on the throne as the One who had been on earth, the same Lord Jesus whom they believed on while on earth.

(C) The fourth occurrence is in Rev 11:17 (TR), which presents us with the return of Jesus, the resurrection and worship of the saints in heaven, and their prayer of thanksgiving: " . . . We give thee thanks, O Lord God Almighty, which art, and wast, and art to come; because thou hast taken to thee thy great power, and hast reigned." The same majestic sovereign characteristics are ascribed to the Lord Jesus here too. The phrase in the TR is exactly the same as in Rev 1:4, 8 and so the ascription "Lord God ... the Almighty" is almost the same as in Rev 1:8. The UBS omits the expression "[which] art to come" evidently because at this point Christ has already come and such a designation would no longer apply.

(D) In Rev 16:5, in the execution of the judgment of the third bowl, we have the angel of the waters saying, " . . . Thou art righteous, O Lord, which art, and wast, and shalt be, because thou hast judged thus." Here the phrase in the TR is *ho ón kaí ho én kaí ho esómenos*. The only difference is that it has *esómenos* (which is the fut. part. of *eimí* [1510],

to be), instead of *erchómenos* (as in Rev 1:4, 8; 4:8; 11:17). The events described under the figure of bowls in Rev 16 occur at the end of the Great Tribulation and take a very short time, maybe only a few days. Therefore, the Lord Jesus is no more described as *ho erchómenos* (the coming One) as before, but as the One about to be here. The UBS and Majority Text have *ho hósios* (*hósios* [3741], sacred), the sacred One. If we take this text, it must be remembered that Jesus' body was called *hósios*, incapable of experiencing corruption at death as ours does (see Acts 2:27, 31; 13:35, 37 [cf. Ps 16:8–11]).

Π

3802. παγιδεύω *pagideúō*; fut. *pagideúsō*, from *pagís* (3803), a trap. To lay snares for, snare, trap (see Sept.: Eccl 9:12). In the NT, used metaphorically meaning to ensnare, to entangle, e.g., by difficult questions, with the acc. (Matt 22:15).

Syn.: *emplékō* (1707), to weave in, metaphorically, to involve, to entangle.

Ant.: *eleutheróō* (1659), to make free; *lúō* (3089), to loose.

3803. παγίς *pagís*; gen. *pagídos*, fem. noun from *pégnumi* (4078), to set up, to fix. Whatever makes fast or holds fast; hence a snare, trap (Luke 21:35), meaning as a snare shall it come upon them, i.e., suddenly, unexpectedly (see Sept.: Eccl 9:12; Amos 3:5). Metaphorically, the trap of the devil means snare of the devil, i.e, his wile, stratagem (1 Tim 3:7; 2 Tim 2:26). Used in an absolute sense (1 Tim 6:9). Also by implication for "cause of destruction" (Rom 11:9 quoted from Ps 69:22; see Sept.: Josh 23:13; Prov 18:7; Isa 24:18).

Deriv.: *pagideúō* (3802), to lay snare for, trap.

Syn.: *bróchos* (1029), a noose, a slip-knot, metaphorically snare.

Ant.: *eleuthería* (1657), freedom.

3804. πάθημα *páthēma*; gen. *pathḗmatos*, neut. noun from *páschō* (3958), to suffer. The suffix -*ma* makes it mean that which is suffered. Suffering, affliction (Rom 8:18; 2 Cor 1:5; Col 1:24; 2 Tim 3:11; Heb 2:9, 10; 10:32; 1 Pet 1:11; 5:1, 9). The sufferings of a Christian are so called because they are endured for the sake of Christ and in conformity to His suffering (cf. 2 Cor 4:10; Phil 3:10; 1 Pet 4:13). A passion, an affection (Rom 7:5; Gal 5:24). In this latter passage, *pathḗmata* (pl.), passions or affections, denotes those passions that are bad, as an equivalent to *epithumíai* (1939), desires.

Syn.: *páthos* (3806), suffering, passion, lust; *plēgḗ* (4127), wound; *mástix* (3148), whip, suffering; *gággraina* (1044), gangrene, canker; *asthéneia* (769), weakness, sickness; *nósos* (3554), sickness; *nósēma* (3553), illness; *talaipōría* (5004), wretched-ness, misery; *kakopátheia* (2552), affliction.

Ant.: *euergesía* (2108), beneficence; *eupoiḯa* (2140), well-doing.

3805. παθητός *pathētós*; gen. *pathētoú*, masc.-fem., neut. *pathētón*, adj. from *páschō* (3958), to suffer, to undergo pain, inconvenience, or punishment. Subject to suffer; one who suffers, as in Acts 26:23, where it must be understood in this sense (cf. Luke 24:26, 27). See *páthēma* (3804), suffering.

3806. πάθος *páthos*; gen. *páthous*, neut. noun from *páschō* (3958), to suffer. Passion, lust. *Páthos* occurs three times in the NT; once coordinated with *epithumía* (1939), desire (Col 3:5), and once subordinated to it, *páthos epithumías*, the lust of desire (1 Thess 4:5), and in the third reference modified by *atimía* ([819], dishonorable), vile affections (Rom 1:26). These are lusts that dishonor those who indulge in them. *Páthos* is the soul's diseased condition out of which the various lusts spring. *Epithumía* is the active lust or desire springing from the diseased soul.

Deriv.: *sumpathḗs* (4835), compassionate, sympathizing; *homoiopathḗs* (3663), of like passions.

Syn.: *órexis* (3715), a longing after; *hormḗ* (3730), violent impulse; *asélgeia* (766), licentiousness; *epithumía* (1939), desire.

3807. παιδαγωγός *paidagōgós*; gen. *paidagōgoú*, masc. noun from *país* (3816), a child, and *agōgós* (n.f.), a leader, which is from *ágō* (71), to lead. An instructor or teacher of children, a schoolmaster, a pedagogue (1 Cor 4:15; Gal 3:24, 25). Originally referred to the slave who conducted the boys from home to the school. Then it became a teacher or an educator. The ancient Greeks regarded a philosopher as a teacher, but not necessarily as *paidagōgós*.

Syn.: *paideutḗs* (3810), a trainer, instructor; *didáskalos* (1320), teacher; *epítropos* (2012), guardian; *kathēgētḗs* (2519), a guide, teacher, master.

Ant.: *plános* (4108), an impostor, seducer.

3808. παιδάριον *paidárion*; gen. *paidaríou*, neut. noun, a diminutive of *país* (3816), a boy. A little boy, lad (Matt 11:16 [TR]; John 6:9; Sept.: Gen 22:5, 12; 42:22; 2 Sam 12:18). Perhaps a boy under twelve years of age.

Syn.: *paidíon* (3813), a young child; *tekníon* (5040), a little child; *korásion* (2877), a little girl; *paidískē* (3814), bondmaid.

Ant.: *gérōn* (1088), old person; *presbútēs* (4246), an elder; *goneús* (1118), a parent.

3809. παιδεία *paideía*; gen. *paideías*, fem. noun from *paideúō* (3811), to instruct. Originally instruction of children. It evolved to mean chastening because all effectual instruction for the sinful children of men includes and implies chastening, correction. *Paideía* occurs with *epanórthōsis* (1882), rectification, in 2 Tim 3:16. In *paideía* there is discipline. In Eph 6:4, *en paideía . . . kuríou* (*en* [1722], in; *kuríou*, the gen. of *kúrios* [2962], Lord) means such training as the Lord approves. By synecdoche, taking a part for the whole, it means correction, chastisement (Heb 12:5, 7, 8, 11; Sept.: Prov 3:11; 22:15). See *nouthesía* (3559), which means instruction mainly by word, while *paideía* is by deed. To be distinguished from *kólasis* (2851), penal infliction, punishment and *timōría* (5098), penalty, punishment which denote penal retribution while *paideía* speaks of correction, educative discipline.

Syn.: *epanórthōsis* (1882), rectification; *nouthesía* (3559), instruction.

3810. παιδευτής *paideutḗs*; gen. *paideutoú*, masc. noun from *paideúō* (3811), to instruct, correct, chastise. An instructor (Rom 2:20); a corrector, a chastiser (Heb 12:9; Sept.: Hos 5:2).

Syn.: *paidagōgós* (3807), instructor; *didáskalos* (1320), an instructor, teacher; *kathēgētḗs* (2519), a guide, master, teacher; *cheiragōgós* (5497), a personal conductor, one who leads by the hand.

Ant.: *plános* (4108), a misleader, deceiver.

3811. παιδεύω *paideúō*; fut. *paideúsō*, from *país* (3816), child. Originally to bring up a child, to educate, used of activity directed toward the moral and spiritual nurture and training of the child, to influence conscious will and action. To instruct, particularly a child or youth (Acts 7:22; 22:3; 2 Tim 2:25 [cf. Titus 2:12]); to instruct by chastisement (1 Tim 1:20; Sept.: Ps 2:10); to correct, chastise (Luke 23:16, 22; 1 Cor 11:32; 2 Cor 6:9; Heb 12:6; Rev 3:19 [cf. Prov 3:12]). In a religious sense, to chastise for the purpose of educating someone to conform to divine truth (Heb 12:7, 10; Sept.: Prov 19:18; 29:17).

Deriv.: *apaídeutos* (521), unlearned; *ektréphō* (1625), to bring up a child; *paideía* (3809), training, chastening; *paideutḗs* (3810), instructor, trainer; *tréphō* (5142), to bring up a child.

Syn.: *didáskō* (1321), to teach; *hodēgéō* (3594), to show the way, lead, guide; *mastigóō* (3146), to scourge, whip; *gumnázō* (1128), to train.

Ant.: *ameléō* (272), to neglect; *kolázō* (2849), to punish; *timōréō* (5097), to avenge.

3812. παιδιόθεν *paidióthen*; adv. from *paidíon* (3813), a little child, and the suffix *-then*, denoting from a place or time. From a child, from childhood (Mark 9:21).

3813. παιδίον *paidíon*; gen. *paidíou*, neut. noun, a diminutive of *país* (3816), child. A little child, either male or female; pl. *tá paidía*, the little children.

(I) A child or children recently born, a baby, infant (Matt 19:13, 14; Mark 10:13–15; Luke 18:16, 17 [cf. 18:15 where it is *tá bréphē* {1025}, the infants]; John 16:21). Also of those more advanced (Matt 11:16 [*paidaríois* {TR}]; 14:21; 15:38; 18:2–5; Mark 7:28; Luke 7:32; 9:47, 48; 11:7; Sept.: Gen 30:26; 45:19; 1 Sam 1:2). Especially of a male child, a boy (Matt 2:8, 9, 11, 13, 14, 20, 21; Luke 1:59, 66, 76, 80; 2:17, 21, 27, 40; Heb 11:23; Sept.: Ex 2:8, 9). Also more advanced (Mark 9:24, 36, 37; John 4:49 [cf. 4:47]; Sept.: Gen 21:14, 15; 22:19). Of a female child, girl, maiden, partly grown (Mark 5:39–41).

(II) Metaphorically in 1 Cor 14:20, "be not children in understanding," meaning weak, ignorant, childish. As an endearing appellation for the followers of Christ (Heb 2:13, 14 [cf. Isa 8:18]). In direct address (John 21:5; 1 John 2:13, 18).

Deriv.: *paidióthen* (3812), of a child.

Syn.: *téknon* (5043), a child; *tekníon* (5040), a little child; *paidárion* (3808), a little boy or girl; *népios* (3516), a baby; *korásion* (2877), a little girl; *paidískē* (3814), a young girl, a female slave; *bréphos* (1025), infant.

Ant.: *gérōn* (1088), old person; *presbútēs* (4246), an elder; *goneús* (1118), a parent.

3814. παιδίσκη *paidískē*; gen. *paidískēs*, fem. noun, a diminutive of *país* (3816), a girl. A young girl, maiden, free-born (Sept.: Ruth 4:12). In the NT, a bond-maid, female slave or servant (Matt 26:69; Mark 14:66, 69; Luke 12:45; 22:56; John 18:17; Acts 12:13; 16:16; Gal 4:22 [see also 4:23, 30, 31]; Sept.:

Gen 16:1, 2; 21:10; 25:12; 30:3; especially 1 Sam 25:41).

Syn.: *korásion* (2877), a little girl; *paidíon* (3813), a little child, either male or female; *país* (3816), a child, male or female.

Ant.: *presbútis* (4247), an aged woman; *gunḗ* (1135), a woman.

3815. παίζω *paízō*; fut. *paíxomai*, aor. *épaixa*, from *país* (3816), child. To play or sport as a child. To play by singing, leaping, dancing, as connected with worship (1 Cor 10:7 quoted from Ex 32:6.; see also Sept.: Judg 16:25; 2 Sam 6:5; 1 Chr 13:8; 15:29).

Deriv.: *empaízō* (1702), to deride.

Ant.: *kámnō* (2577), to toil.

3816. παῖς *país*; gen. *paidós*, masc.-fem. noun. A child in relation to descent; a boy or girl in relation to age; a manservant, attendant, maid in relation to cultural condition. Spoken of all ages from infancy up to full-grown youth (Matt 2:16; Acts 20:12 [cf. 20:9]).

(I) Particularly and generally (Matt 2:16; 21:15); sing. *ho país* (Matt 17:18; Luke 2:43; 9:42; John 4:51; Acts 20:12 [cf. 20:9 *neanías* {3494}, a young man]); sing. fem *hē país* (Luke 8:51, 54 [cf. 8:42 *thugátēr* {2364}, daughter]); Sept.: Gen 24:28, 57; 34:12; Ruth 2:6).

(II) Boy, servant.

(A) Particularly and generally, equivalent to *doúlos* (1401), a servant, slave (Matt 8:6, 8, 13 [cf. 8:9, *doúlos*]; Luke 7:7 [cf. 7:3]; Luke 12:45; 15:26; Sept.: Gen 9:26, 27; 24:2; 26:15).

(B) An attendant, minister, as of a king (Matt 14:2; Sept.: Gen 41:38; Jer 36:24).

(C) The servant of God, spoken of a minister or ambassador of God, called and beloved of God, and sent by Him to perform any service, e.g., of David (Luke 1:69; Acts 4:25); of Israel (Luke 1:54 [cf. Sept.: Isa 41:8, 9; 44:1, 2; 45:4]); of Jesus the Messiah (Matt 12:18 in allusion to Isa 42:1; Acts 3:13, 26; 4:27, 30; Sept.: Isa 49:6; 50:10; 52:13).

Deriv.: *paidagōgós* (3807), school-master; *paideúō* (3811), to train, chasten; *paízō* (3815), to play.

Syn.: *paidískē* (3814), a maidservant; *téknon* (5043), child; *tekníon* (5040), small child; *bréphos* (1025), infant; *hupērétēs* (5257), a subordinate servant; *therápōn* (2324), a menial servant; *oikétēs* (3610), a domestic servant.

Ant.: *goneús* (1118), parent; *patḗr* (3962), father; *mḗtēr* (3384), mother; *despótēs* (1203), despot, master; *kúrios* (2962), master, lord, owner.

3817. παίω *paíō*; fut. *paísō*. To strike or smite, with the acc., e.g., with the fist, a rod, sword (Matt 26:68; Mark 14:47; Luke 22:64; John 18:10; Sept.: Num 22:28; 2 Sam 20:10). By a scorpion, to strike or sting (Rev 9:5).

Syn.: *patássō* (3960), to strike, smite, give a blow with the hand; *túptō* (5180), to beat; *dérō* (1194), to flay, skin, beat; *plḗssō* (4141), to wound; *rhapízō* (4474), to strike with a rod; *katabállō* (2598), to smite down; *proskóptō* (4350), to beat upon.

3818. Πακατιανή *Pakatianḗ*; gen. *Pakatianḗs*, fem. proper noun. Pacatiana or Phrygia Pacatiana, the western part of *Phrugía* (5435), as divided by the Romans mentioned in the superscription of the Book of 2 Timothy.

3819. πάλαι *pálai*; adv. of time. In the past, long ago, of olden times, formerly, long before now. *Pálai* in reality means old, what lies behind (Heb 1:1). In 2 Pet 1:9, that which is designated "old sins" (*pálai*) does not have a temporal significance referring to what has taken place in the past but a qualitative significance referring to that which belongs to the past, that which is characteristic of the former way of life. Such sins, in consequence of the cleansing, have passed away. This differs from Rom 3:25, where the sins are called previous, *progegonótōn* (the perf. part. neut. pl. of *progínomai* [4266], previously transpired), and refer to what is

past, not necessarily long ago, but nevertheless already past for sometime (Mark 15:44). *Pálai* may also mean "a great while ago" (Matt 11:21; Luke 10:13).

Deriv.: *ékpalai* (1597), of old; *palaiós* (3820), old.

Syn.: *poté* (4218), in time past; *ékpalai* (1597), of old; *ap' archḗs* (*apó* [575], from; *archḗ* [746], beginning, start), from the start.

Ant.: *tachéōs* (5030), shortly; *pántote* (3842), always, from the past also; *prosphátōs* (4373), recently; *eschátōs* (2079), recently; *árti* (737), just now; *nún* (3568), now; *ḗdē* (2235), already, by this time; *dḗ* (1211), now.

3820. παλαιός *palaiós*; fem. *palaiá*; neut. *palaión*, adj. from *pálai* (3819), in the past, long ago. Old, not new, what is of long standing.

(I) In age or time, old, former, not recent, such as *oínos* (3631), wine (Luke 5:39); *zúmē* (2219), leaven (1 Cor 5:7, 8); *diathḗkē* (1242), testament (2 Cor 3:14); *entolḗ* (1785), commandment (1 John 2:7); *ánthrōpos* (444), man (Rom 6:6; Eph 4:22; Col 3:9) means the sinful and unregenerate self previous to salvation, standing in contrast to the *kainós* (2537), qualitatively new, regenerate man. See also Sept.: Lev 25:22.

(II) From use meaning old, worn-out, as *himátion* (2440), garment, a worn-out garment (Matt 9:16; Mark 2:21; Luke 5:36); *askós* (779), bottles (made of goatskins), bags (Matt 9:17; Mark 2:22; Luke 5:37). See Matt 13:52; Sept.: Josh 9:4, 5; Jer 38:11 for usages of *palaiós*.

Deriv.: *palaiótēs* (3821), aged, obsolete; *palaióō* (3822), to make old.

Syn.: *archaíos* (744), old, ancient, original, what has exited from the beginning. *Palaiós* is not necessarily from the beginning but just old.

Ant.: *néos* (3501), new in time or order, recent; *kainós* (2537), new qualitatively; *prósphatos* (4372), recent, just available.

3821. παλαιότης *palaiótēs*; gen. *palaiótētos*, fem. noun from *palaiós* (3820), old. Age, antiquity, lengthy existence. Used only in Rom 7:6, referring to the oldness of the letter of the Law as compared to the newness of the Spirit. The Spirit comes in the place of the letter (though not the Law). The letter is something belonging to the past and no longer has force since it belongs to an age and economy now past and gone (cf. Heb 8:13).

Ant.: *neótēs* (3503), newness; *kainótēs* (2538), renewal, qualitative, newness.

3822. παλαιόω *palaióō*; contracted *palaiṓ*, fut. *palaiṓsō*, from *palaiós* (3820), old. In the act., to make old, render obsolete, abrogate (Heb 8:13; Sept.: Deut 29:5; Josh 9:13; Ps 102:27; Isa 50:9; Lam 3:4). In the pass., to grow old, *palaióomai*, contracted *palaioúmai* (Luke 12:33; Heb 1:11 quoted from Ps 102:27).

Ant.: *ananeóō* (365), to renovate, renew; *anakainóō* (341), to renew; *anakainízō* (340), to restore, make new.

3823. πάλη *pálē*; gen. *pálēs*, fem. noun from *pállō*, (n.f.) to shake, vibrate. A wrestling, struggle or hand-to-hand combat. It was used of the wrestling of athletes and the of the hand-to-hand combat of soldiers both of which required deftness and speed. It denoted the struggle between individual combatants in distinction from an entire military campaign (*strateía* [4752]). Used figuratively in Eph 6:12, meaning struggle, combat.

Syn.: *agṓn* (73), struggle; *kópos* (2873), toil; *móchthos* (3449), painfulness, travail; *talaipōría* (5004), wretchedness; *kopetós* (2870), lamentation.

Ant.: *anápausis* (372), inner rest; *katápausis* (2663), rest or cessation of work; *anápsuxis* (403), a recovery of breath; *ánesis* (425), relief; *anápsuxis* (403), revival.

3824. παλιγγενεσία *paliggenesía*; gen. *paliggenesías*, fem. noun from *pálin* (3825), again, and *génesis* (1078), generation, nation. Regeneration, restoration, renovation, rebirth. Occurs in Matt 19:28, which refers to the coming state of the whole creation, equivalent to the restoration of all things of Acts 3:21 which will occur when the Son of Man shall come in His glory. In this sense, it is equivalent to *apokatástasis* (605), restitution. The washing of regeneration (*paliggenesía*, Titus 3:5) refers to the spiritual rebirth of the individual soul.

Syn.: *anakaínōsis* (342), renewing.

Ant.: *nékrōsis* (3500), deadening; *anaíresis* (336), a killing.

3825. πάλιν *pálin*; adv. Back, back again, again, as simply implying to return back to a former place, state or act.

(I) Of place, especially after verbs of motion (Mark 2:1; 5:21; John 6:15; 11:7; 14:3, "I will come again," meaning I will return; Acts 18:21; 2 Cor 1:16; 13:2; Gal 1:17; 4:9; Phil 1:26). To take again (*lambánō* [2983], to receive; *pálin*), to take back again (John 10:17, 18).

(II) Of time, meaning again, another time, once more.

(A) Generally (Matt 4:8; 20:5; Luke 23:20; John 4:13; 16:16; Acts 27:28; Rom 8:15; Heb 5:12; 6:6; James 5:18). Pleonastically, *pálin ek deutérou* (*ek* [1537], of, for; *deúteron* [1208], second time), again the second time (Matt 26:42; Acts 10:15). In the sense of another time (John 1:35; 8:12, 21; Acts 17:32). Including also perhaps the idea of reference, i.e., again in another Scripture (Matt 4:7; John 12:39; Rom 15:10–12; Heb 2:13).

(B) Hence as a continuative particle, connecting circumstances which refer to the same subj., again, once more, further (Matt 5:33; 13:44; 18:19; Luke 13:20; John 12:22; 1 Cor 12:21; Heb 1:5, 6; 2:13); also where there is an implied opposite or antithesis, again, on the other hand, on the contrary (Matt 4:7; 2 Cor 10:7; Gal 5:3; 1 John 2:8).

Deriv.: *paliggenesía* (3824), a rebirth, restoration.

Ant.: *poté* (4218), never; *mēdépote* (3368), not ever, never; *mēdépō* (3369), not yet; *oudépō* (3764), not yet.

3826. παμπληθεί *pamplētheí*; adv. from *pás* (3956), all, every, and *plḗthos* (4128), throng. The whole multitude together, all at once (Luke 23:18).

Syn.: *homoú* (3674), together; *homothumadón* (3661), all together, with one accord.

Ant.: *mónos* (3441), alone.

3827. πάμπολυς *pámpolus*; fem. *pampóllē*, neut. *pámpollu*, adj. from *pás* (3956), all, every, and *polús* (4183), much, many. Very much, very great, vast (Mark 8:1).

Syn.: *sphódra* (4970), exceeding; *lían* (3029), very; *mégas* (3173), great; *pleístos* (4118), the most; *ámetros* (280), uncountable, immeasurable; *pleíōn* (4119), greater; *pollaplasíōn* (4179), manifold.

Ant.: *olígos* (3641), little; *eláchistos* (1646), the least; *elássōn* (1640), the smaller; *mikrós* (3398), small.

3828. Παμφυλία *Pamphulía*; gen. *Pamphulías*, fem. proper noun. Pamphylia, meaning of every tribe. A Roman province in Asia Minor (Acts 27:5). It was bounded on the east by Cilicia, on the north by Pisidia from which it was separated by the Taurus Mountains, on the west by Lycia, and on the south by the sea. Claudius made Pamphylia an imperial province, including in it the regions of Pisidia and Lycia which are distinguished from Pamphylia proper (Acts 13:13, 14; 14:24; 27:5). Its capital, Perga, was the first place in Asia Minor visited by Paul on his first missionary journey, and there Mark left him (Acts 13:13). On his return to Pisidia he preached at Perga and from Attalia sailed to Antioch (Acts 14:24–26). Men from Pamphylia were at Jerusalem on the day of Pentecost (Acts 2:10).

3829. πανδοχεῖον *pandocheíon*; gen. *panodocheíou*, neut. noun from *pandocheús* (3830), an innkeeper. A place where all are received, an inn or khan so-called in the East, or caravansary (Luke 10:34).

Syn.: *katáluma* (2646), guest chamber.

3830. πανδοχεύς *pandocheús*, gen. *pandacheíou*, masc. noun from *pás* (3956), all, every, and *déchomai* (1209), to receive. An innkeeper, a host (Luke 10:35).

Deriv.: *pandocheíon* (3829), an inn.

3831. πανήγυρις *panḗguris*; gen. *panēgúreōs*, fem. noun from *pás* (3956), all, and *águris* (n.f.), an assembly, which is from *agorá* (58), public square, marketplace. A solemn assembly convened for purposes of festal rejoicing. Occurs only in Heb 12:23 (cf. Rev 5:11; Ps 148:2; Dan 7:10); Sept.: Ezek 46:11; Hos 2:11; Amos 5:21.

Syn.: *ekklēsía* (1577), church; *sunagōgḗ* (4864), synagogue. These words do not inherently imply gatherings for festivities as *panḗguris* does.

Ant.: *klauthmós* (2805), lamentation; *odurmós* (3602), mourning; *thrḗnos* (2355), wailing; *pénthos* (3997), mourning, sorrow; *stenagmós* (4726), groaning.

3832. πανοικί *panoikí*; adv. from *pás* (3956), all, every, and *oíkos* (3624), house. With all one's household or family (Acts 16:34).

Ant.: *mónos* (3441), alone; *kath' heautoú* (*katá* [2596], by; *heautón*, the acc. of *heautón* [1438], himself), by himself, alone.

3833. πανοπλία *panoplía*, gen. *panoplías* fem. noun from *pánoplos* (n.f.), which is from *pás* (3956), all, every, and *hóplon* (3696), weapon. Panoply, complete armor, offensive and defensive

(Luke 11:22), metaphorically of spiritual armor (Eph 6:11, 13; Sept.: 2 Sam 2:21).

3834. πανουργία panourgía; gen. *panourgías*, fem. noun from *panourgéō* (n.f.), to be crafty, which is from *panoúrgos* (3835), shrewd, crafty. Shrewdness, cunning, craftiness, unscrupulousness; the word signified the employment of any or all means necessary to realize an end (Luke 20:23; 1 Cor 3:19; 2 Cor 4:2; 11:3; Eph 4:14; Sept.: Josh 9:4). In a good sense in Sept.: Prov 1:4; 8:5.
Syn.: *dólos* (1388), fraud; *ponēría* (4189), malice; *methodeía* (3180), trickery, deceptive tactics; *epínoia* (1963), a purpose, thought; *dialogismós* (1261), mental reflection, thought; *apátē* (539), deceit; *enédra* (1747), ambush; *rhadiourgía* (4468), mischief; *plánē* (4106), deceit; *dianóēma* (1270), thought, meditation, machination.
Ant.: *euprépeia* (2143), good behavior; *aretḗ* (703), virtue; *chrēstótēs* (5544), gentleness, goodness; *agathōsúnē* (19), beneficence; *eúnoia* (2133), kindness; *euergesía* (2108), a benefit, good deed; *alḗtheia* (225), truthfulness.

3835. πανοῦργος panoúrgos; gen. *panoúrgou*, masc.-fem., neut. *panoúrgon*, adj. from *pás* (3956), all, every, and *érgon* (2041), deed, work. Able to do anything, hence shrewd, cunning, crafty, unscrupulous (2 Cor 12:16; Sept.: Job 5:12). In late writers, also in a good sense, wise (Sept.: Prov 13:1; 14:8, 15).
Syn.: *dólios* (1386), deceitful; *ponērós* (4190), evil; *plános* (4108), deceiver; *katachthónios* (2709), infernal.
Ant.: *eilikrinḗs* (1506), sincere; *anupókritos* (505), not hypocritical; *euthús* (2117), straight; *ádolos* (97), without deceit; *alēthḗs* (227), true; *chrēstós* (5543), gracious, kind; *agathós* (18), benevolent; *kalós* (2570), good.

3836. πανταχόθεν pantachóthen; adv. from *pás* (3956), all, and the suffix *-then*,

meaning from a place. From every place or quarter, from all sides (Mark 1:45).
Syn.: *pántothen* (3840), from all sides.

3837. πανταχοῦ pantachoú; adv. from *pás* (3956), all, and the suffix *-chou*, meaning in a place. An adv. meaning in all places, everywhere (Mark 16:20; Luke 9:6; Acts 17:30; 21:28 [TR]; 24:3; 28:22; 1 Cor 4:17).
Syn.: *pántothen* (3840) or *pantachóthen* (3836), from all sides, from every quarter; *en pantí tópō* (*en* [1722], in; *pantí*, neut. dat. of *pás* [3956], all, every; *tópō* ([5117] place), in every place, everywhere.

3838. παντελής pantelḗs; gen. *panteloús*, masc.-fem., neut. *pantelés*, adj. from *pás* (3956), any, all, and *télos* (5056), end. Complete, whole, entire. In the NT expression *eis tó pantelés* (*eis* [1519], unto; *tó pantelés* [neut.]), unto the completion of all, means completely, wholly, entirely, as referring to time, always, forever (Heb 7:25); with the neg. *mḗ* (3361), not, not at all (Luke 13:11).
Syn.: *eis tón aiōna* (165), unto the age, forever; *téleios* (5046), complete; *aiōnios* (166), forever, eternal.
Ant.: *próskairos* (4340), temporary.

3839. πάντη pántē; adv. from *pás* (3956), all, every. Used of manner meaning in every way, in all things (Acts 24:3).
Syn.: *hólōs* (3654), altogether, utterly; *teleíōs* (5049), completely; *pantachoú* (3837), everywhere.
Ant.: *mólis* (3433), scarcely; *metríōs* (3357), moderately; *schedón* (4975), hardly; *mēdamōs* (3365), not at all; *oudamōs* (3760), by no means, in an absolute sense.

3840. πάντοθεν pántothen; adv. of place, from *pás* (3956), every, all, and the suffix *-then*, denoting from or at a place. From every side or quarter and hence on every side, round about (Luke 19:43; Heb

9:4). The same as *pantachóthen* (3836), from all sides (Mark 1:45).

Syn.: *pantachoú* (3837), everywhere (*pantachoú* [Acts 21:28 {TR}]); the phrase *en pantí* (*en* [1722], in; *pantí*, the neut. dat. of *pás* [3956], all, every), everywhere; *en pantí tópō* ([5117], place), in every place.

3841. παντοκράτωρ *pantokrátōr*; gen. *pantokrátoros*, masc. noun from *pás* (3956), all, every, and *krátos* (2904), power, strength, dominion. Ruler over all, omnipotent, almighty, spoken only of God (2 Cor 6:18; Rev 1:8; 4:8; 11:17; 15:3; 16:7, 14; 19:6, 15; 21:22; Sept.: 2 Sam 5:10; 7:25, 27; Job 5:17; 8:5).

Syn.: *árchōn* (758), ruler; *despótēs* (1203), despot, absolute master; *kúrios* (2962), lord; *hēgemṓn* (2232), a leader.

Ant.: *hupērétēs* (5257), servant; *doúlos* (1401), slave; *therápōn* (2324), attendant; *diákonos* (1249), servant, deacon.

3842. πάντοτε *pántote*; adv. of time, from *pás* (3956), all, and *tóte* (5119), then. Always, at all times, ever (Matt 26:11; Mark 14:7; Luke 15:31; 18:1; John 6:34; 2 Cor 2:14).

Syn.: *aeí* (104), perpetually, ever; *hekástote* (1539), always, each time; *diapantós* (1275), through all time; *pántē* (3839), evermore; *diēnekés* (1336), continuous, forever; *eis tó diēnekés*, forever; *eis aiṓna* (*eis* [1519], unto; *aiṓna* [165], age), unto an age, forever; *eis tón aiṓna*, unto the age; *eis toús aiṓnas*, unto the ages; *eis aiṓnas aiṓnōn*, unto ages of ages; *eis tón aiṓna toú aiṓnos*, unto the age of the age; *toú aiṓnos tṓn aiṓnōn*, of the age of the ages; *eis pántas toús aiṓnas*, unto all the ages; *eis hēméran aiṓnos* (*eis*, unto; *hēméran* [2250], day; *aiṓnos*, of an age), unto a day of an age.

Ant.: *poté* (4218), never; *oudépote* (3763), never; *mēdépote* (3368), never.

3843. πάντως *pántōs*; adv. from *pás* (3956), all. Wholly, all together, entirely (1 Cor 5:10; 9:10; 16:12). With the meaning of by all means, at all events,

assuredly (Luke 4:23; Acts 18:21; 21:22; 28:4; 1 Cor 9:22). So also in a neg. reply, emphatic (Rom 3:9), meaning not at all, not in the least.

Syn.: *málista* (3122), especially, chiefly; *teleíōs* (5049), completely; *pántē* (3839), wholly; *hólōs* (3654), altogether, actually; *óntōs* (3689), really, actually; *pṓs* (4459), in any way; the expression *eis tó pantelés* (*eis* [1519], unto; *tó* [3588], the [neut. acc.]; *pantelés* [3838], uttermost], unto the uttermost.

Ant.: *oudamṓs* (3760), by no means; *ouchí* (3780), not; *ou* (3756), not; *mḗ* (3361), not; *ou mḗ* (3364), not at all; *mḗ ouk* (3378), never, not; *mḗte* (3383), neither, not even; *oúte* (3777), neither, nor; *oudé* (3761), not however; *kathólou* (2527), at all; *mēkéti* (3371), not any more; *mḗpō* (3380), not yet; *mḗpote* (3379), if peradventure, not at all; *oukéti* (3765), no longer.

3844. παρά *pará*; prep. governing the gen., dat., and acc. It means primarily, near, nearby, expressing the notion of immediate vicinity or proximity which is differently modified according to the force of each case.

(I) With the gen., expressing the meaning from near, from with. In the NT, only with a gen. of person, implying a going forth or proceeding from the near vicinity of someone, from the presence or side of someone.

(A) Particularly after verbs of motion, as of coming, sending (Mark 14:43; Luke 8:49; John 15:26; 17:8). After *eínai* (1511), to be, meaning to be from or come from (John 6:46; 7:29); in John 1:14, implied. Of things (Luke 6:19, virtue went out from Him, was diffused around Him).

(B) Figuratively, after verbs of asking, receiving, or those which imply these ideas. After verbs of asking, seeking (Matt 2:4, 7; 20:20; Mark 8:11; Luke 12:48; John 4:9; Acts 3:2; 9:2; James 1:5); verbs of hearing, learning (John 1:40; Acts 24:8; 28:22; Gal 1:12; 1 Thess 2:13; 2 Tim 1:13; 2:2; 3:14; 2 John 1:4);

verbs of receiving, obtaining, buying, being promised (Matt 18:19; Mark 12:2; Luke 6:34; John 5:34; Acts 7:16; 9:14; 26:12; Rom 11:27; Eph 6:8; 2 Pet 1:17; Rev 3:18); after *eínai* (1511), to be, expressed or implied, meaning to be from anyone, to come, to be given, bestowed, from or by anyone (John 17:7; Acts 26:22; 2 John 1:3). Of hospitality or gifts (Luke 10:7; Phil 4:18). Generally, to come from someone, to be derived from or possessed by someone (Mark 5:26). Of persons, *hoi pará* followed by the gen., particularly of those close to someone, meaning his kindred, relatives (Mark 3:21).

(C) Figuratively, with the gen. of person as the source, author, director, meaning from whom something proceeds or is derived. **(1)** Generally (Matt 21:42, quoted from Ps 118:22; Luke 1:45; 2:1; John 1:6). **(2)** Hence after passive verbs instead of *hupó* (5259), by (Acts 22:30).

(II) With the dat. both of person and thing, expressing rest or position, near, hard by, with; and with the dat. pl., meaning among.

(A) Particularly of place, after verbs implying rest or remaining in a place. **(1)** Generally and with the dat. of thing (John 19:25); with the dat. of person (Matt 6:1; 22:25; 28:15; John 1:39; 8:38; 14:17, 23; 17:5; Acts 10:6; 1 Cor 16:2, with himself, meaning at home; Col 4:16; 2 Tim 4:13; Rev 2:13). **(2)** Rarely after verbs of motion, and only when subsequent rest is also implied (Luke 9:47; 19:7).

(B) With the dat. of person, the reference being to the person himself without regard to place. **(1)** Particularly and generally meaning with, among (Matt 21:25; Luke 1:30; 2:52; 2 Cor 1:17; 1 Pet 2:20). **(2)** Metaphorically, meaning with or before anyone, in his sight, presence, judgment, that person being judge (Acts 26:8; Rom 2:13; 11:25; 1 Cor 3:19; Gal 3:11; James 1:27; 1 Pet 2:4; 2 Pet 2:11; 3:8). Of what is in the power of anyone (Matt 19:26); of the moral qualities of someone, i.e., belong to his character (Rom 2:11; 9:14; Eph 6:9; James 1:17; Sept.: Job 12:13). **(3)** Figuratively (1 Cor 7:24,

with God, i.e., in union and fellowship by faith with Him, devoted to Him as Christians, equivalent to being in the Lord [cf. 7:22]).

(III) With the acc., particularly expressing motion near a place.

(A) Particularly implying motion along the side of something, meaning nearby, by, along, after verbs of motion with the acc. of thing (Matt 4:18, by the sea, along the seashore; 13:4; Mark 2:13; 4:15, by the wayside; Luke 8:5).

(B) As expressing motion to a place, near to, to, at, after verbs of motion, and so equivalent to *prós* (4314), toward, or *eis* (1519), unto, with the acc. (Matt 15:29, He came near to the sea, approached the sea [cf. Matt 15:30, at His feet]; Luke 8:41; Acts 4:35; 7:58).

(C) Sometimes also expressing the idea of rest or remaining near a place, near, by, at, equivalent to its use with the dat. Here, however, the idea of previous motion, or coming to the place, is strictly implied (cf. in *eis*, unto, IV). **(1)** Particularly after verbs of rest or remaining (Matt 13:1, He went and sat by the seaside; Mark 5:21; Luke 5:1; 7:38; 10:39). Elliptically, with a verb implied (Mark 4:1; Acts 22:3; Heb 11:12). **(2)** Metaphorically, of the ground or reason by or along with which a conclusion follows by reason of, because of, meaning thereby, therefore, on this account (1 Cor 12:15, 16).

(D) As denoting motion by or past a place. In the NT, only figuratively, as implying a failure to reach the exact point of aim, a want of coincidence with something else, either from passing beside it, or falling short, or going beyond, with the general meaning of "other than." **(1)** Aside from, not coincident with, not conformable to, i.e. contrary to, against (Acts 18:13, aside from the law, i.e., contrary to law; Rom 1:26; 4:18; 11:24; 16:17; Gal 1:8, 9). **(2)** Beside, with the meaning of except, save, particularly failing, falling short (2 Cor 11:24, forty stripes save one, i.e., falling short by one). **(3)** Past, in the sense of beyond, besides, more than (Heb 11:11, past the proper age, failing the usual age). More commonly, more than, above, beyond; used generally (Luke 13:2 [cf. 13:4]; Rom 1:25; 12:3; 14:5; Heb 1:9). The same after comparatives, where *pará* with the acc. is equivalent to *ḗ katá* (*ḗ* [2228], than; *katá* [2596], according to), than according to, what is ordained (Luke 3:13; Heb 1:4; 2:7, 9; 3:3; 9:23; 11:4; 12:24). After *állos* (243), other (1 Cor 3:11, another foundation).

(**IV**) In composition, *pará* implies:

(**A**) Nearness, proximity, near, by, as in *parakathízō* (3869), to sit down near; *parístēmi* (3936), to stand beside, to aid; *parathalássios* (3864), along the sea.

(**B**) Motion or direction, near to, by, as in *parabállō* (3846), to throw alongside, compare; *paradídōmi* (3860), to surrender, betray; *paréchō* (3930), to hold near, bring, offer; *parateínō* (3905), to extend along.

(**C**) Motion, by or past any place, going beyond, as *parágō* (3855), to go beyond; *parérchomai* (3928), to go by, pass by; *parapléō* (3896), to sail by.

(**D**) Metaphorically, of whatever swerves from the true point, comes short of it, goes beyond it, as the prefix *mis-* in Eng., wrongly, falsely, as *parakoúō* (3878), to mishear, disobey; *paratheōréō* (3865), to overlook, disregard.

(**E**) It implies violation, as *parabaínō* (3845), to disobey a command; *paranoméō* (3891), to transgress. Also by stealth, *pareiságō* (3919), to secretly bring in.

Syn.: *hupó* (5259), by; *prós* (4314), toward, near; *eggús* (1451), near; *plēsíon* (4139), nearby; *schedón* (4975), nigh, almost; *katá* (2596), against; *paraplḗsion* (3897), close by; *paraplēsíōs* (3898), similarly; *geítōn* (1069), neighbor.

Ant.: *makrán* (3112), far; *pórrō* (4206), at a distance.

3845. παραβαίνω *parabaínō*; fut. *parabḗsomai*, 2d aor. *parébēn*, from *pará* (3844), beyond or contrary to, and *baínō* (n.f., see *apobaínō* [576]), to go. To transgress, violate. In the NT, it always has a moral sense (Matt 15:2, 3; 2 John 1:9). To fall from or lose one's station or office by transgression (Acts 1:25; Sept.: Ex 32:8; Num 14:41; Josh 7:11, 15).

Deriv.: *aparábatos* (531), unchangeable; *parábasis* (3847), transgression; *parabátēs* (3848), transgressor.

Syn.: *hamartánō* (264), to sin; *parakoúō* (3878), to disobey; *paranoméō* (3891), to transgress the law; *apistéō* (569), to disobey; *parapíptō* (3895), to fall or stumble. *Parabaínō* has more of the guilt of willful stepping out of line than *parapíptō* (3895), which is not stepping out of line but falling off.

Ant.: *summorphóō* (4833), to conform; *hupakoúō* (5219), to obey; *hupotássomai* (5293), to submit.

3846. παραβάλλω *parabállō*; fut. *parabaló*, from *pará* (3844), near, and *bállō* (906), to cast, put. To cast or put near. As a term of navigation it means to arrive or touch at; properly, to bring a ship near (Acts 20:15). To compare (Mark 4:30).

Deriv.: *parabolḗ* (3850), comparison.

Syn.: *sugkrínō* (4793), to compare; *paromoiázō* (3945), to resemble; *homoióō* (3666), to resemble, make similar.

Ant.: *diaphérō* (1308), to differ; *diakrínō* (1252), to distinguish.

3847. παράβασις *parábasis*; gen. *parabáseōs*, fem. noun from *parabaínō* (3845), to transgress. Transgression, wrongdoing, lawbreaking (Rom 2:23; 4:15; 5:14; Gal 3:19; 1 Tim 2:14; Heb 2:2; 9:15; Sept.: Ps 101:3).

Syn.: *hamartía* (266), sin; *paráptōma* (3900), a fault, mistake, error, sin; *hamártēma* (265), act of sin; *paranomía* (3892), lawbreaking; *athétēsis* (115), cancellation, disannulling.

Ant.: *pístis* (4102), faith, faithfulness.

3848. παραβάτης *parabátēs*; gen. *parabátou*, masc. noun from *parabaínō* (3835), to transgress. Transgressor, violator of the law; used with reference to the imputation of those who transgress the law and deviate from the truth (Rom 2:25, 27; Gal 2:18; James 2:9, 11).

Syn.: *hamartōlós* (268), a sinner; *ánomos* (459), lawless person, transgressor; *ádikos* (94), an unjust person.

Ant.: *pistós* (4103), faithful, dependable; *énnomos* (1772), lawful; *díkaios* (1342), righteous, just; *euthús* (2117), straight, true; *orthós* (3717), upright; *alēthḗs* (227), true; *alēthinós* (228), truthful; *apseudḗs* (893), veracious; *éntimos* (1784), honorable.

3849. παραβιάζομαι *parabiázomai*; fut. *parabiásomai*, mid. deponent from *pará* (3844), to the point of, unto, implying movement toward a certain point, and *biázō* (971), to force. To press, compel, coerce, persuade (Luke 24:29; Acts 16:15; Sept.: 1 Sam 28:23; 2 Kgs 2:17; 5:16).

Syn.: *anagkázō* (315), to force, constrain; *sunéchō* (4912), to constrain, press.

3850. παραβολή *parabolḗ*; gen. *parabolḗs*, fem. noun from *parabállō* (3846), to compare. A parable, placing side by side. In the NT, a comparison, similitude.

(I) Generally (Mark 4:30; Heb 11:19). In the sense of image, figure, symbol, equivalent to *túpos* (5179), type (Heb 9:9, a symbol or type of spiritual things in Christ [cf. 9:11]).

(II) Specifically, a parable, i.e., a short story under which something else is figured or in which the fictitious is used to represent and illustrate the real. This common oriental method of teaching was much used by Christ in the first three Gospels, but not elsewhere in the NT (Matt 13:24, 31, 33; 15:15; 21:33; 22:1; Mark 4:10, 11, 13; 7:17; 12:12; Luke 5:36; 6:39; 8:9–11; 12:16, 41; 13:6; 15:3; 18:1, 9; 19:11; 20:9, 19; 21:29, through or by means of parables). To speak in parables (Matt 13:3, 10, 13, 34; 22:1; Mark 3:23; 12:1); with *en* (1722), in, implied (Mark 4:33); with *didáskō* (1321), to teach (Mark 4:2); *eípe* (the aor. of *eréō* [2046], to say), said, through a parable

(Luke 8:4); with *chōrís* (5565), without, without a parable (Matt 13:34; Mark 4:34); with *manthánō* (3129), to learn (Matt 24:32; Mark 13:28, learn the parable drawn from the fig tree); with the gen. of the object from whence the parable is drawn (Matt 13:18, 36); of a series of comparisons, including also a parable (Luke 14:7 [cf. 14:7–11, 12–14, 16–24]; Sept.: Ezek 17:2; 24:3).

(III) In a wider sense, a figurative discourse, a dark saying, i.e., obscure and full of hidden meaning (Matt 13:35, quoted from Ps 78:2 [cf. Prov 1:6; Eccl 12:9]). Hence also a proverb, adage (Luke 4:23; Sept.: 1 Sam 10:12; Ezek 18:2).

(IV) Long and short parables. The evangelists call both the longer stories and the short figurative sayings parables of Jesus (Matt 15:15; Mark 3:23; 7:17; Luke 6:39), and so also does Christ Himself (Matt 24:32; Luke 4:23). In both parables and proverbs, there is a comparison, and the hearer has to catch the analogy in order to be instructed. Thus Christ's sayings about the salt of the earth, the lilies of the field, building on the sand, whited sepulchers (Matt 5:13; 6:26; 7:26; 23:27), fishers of men, light under the bushel (Mark 1:17; 4:21), a reed shaken with the wind, the green and the dry trees (Luke 7:24; 23:31), living water, fields white unto harvest, a woman in travail (John 4:10, 35; 16:21), and so forth, can be classified as parables. A number of these could be expanded into a narrative.

(V) Parables may be considered illustrations of truths already set forth rather than as a means of conveying truths. His miracles may be considered as parables in action.

(VI) The dual purposes of Christ's parables:

(A) To reveal truth to His disciples. **(1)** The meanings of some of these parables were obvious and He did not explain them. Most of His parables fall into this category. **(2)** He explained only two of His parables: that of the Sower (Matt 13:1–9, 18–23; Mark 4:1–9, 13–20; Luke

8:4–8, 11–15) and that of the Wheat and the Tares (Matt 13:24–30, 36–43).

(B) To veil truth from those whom He knew would not believe even if they understood the meaning of the parables. This veiling of the truth was merciful because, for the unbeliever, understanding and refusing to believe increases his responsibility and the consequent execution of God's justice at the end. The apologetic of the parables and their dual purpose (to help the believer understand God's truth for them and to hinder unbelievers from understanding so as not to increase their responsibility for unbelief) is given by Christ in Matt 13:10–17; Mark 4:10–12; Luke 8:9, 10. Note that, in Matt 13:11, the conj. *hóti* (3754), that, is used to indicate the fact of Christ's operation, while in Mark 4:12 and Luke 8:10, the telic conj. *hína* (2443), for the purpose of, is used to indicate that Christ designed the parabolic teaching to have this dual purpose. As A. Plummer says in *Hasting's Dictionary of the Bible*, "This withholding is therefore a judgment; but a judgment which is merciful in its operation." This confirms the general theology of the NT that judgment is according to opportunity of understanding. "It saves unworthy hearers from the responsibility of knowing the truth and rejecting it, for they are not allowed to recognize it. It saves them also from the guilt of profaning it, for herein Christ observes His own maxim (Matt 7:6)."

(VII) Parables introduce the unfamiliar through the familiar in nature and life experience. Although Jesus was familiar with the mountains and forests, cedars and palm trees, yet He chose things which are common, not only in the narrow region of Palestine, but almost universally: the bread, water, light, lamps, doors, sheep, and so forth. He concentrated on the commonly familiar and the practical that is forever part and parcel of human life in the realm of the natural to project man's life in the realm beyond this life.

(VIII) The parables were provided in pairs for purposes of contrast: the Treasure in the Field and the Pearl of Great Price (Matt 13:44–46); the Ten Virgins and the Talents (Matt 25:1–30); the Garment and Wineskins (Luke 5:36–39); the Mustard Seed and the Leaven (Luke 13:18–21); the Builder and the King (Luke 14:28–32); the Lost Sheep and the Lost Coin (Luke 15:3–10). Observe how Jesus drew the contrasts between: obedient and disobedient sons (Matt 21:28); wise and foolish virgins (Matt 25:1); profitable and unprofitable servants (Matt 25:14); heartless clergy and a charitable Samaritan (Luke 10:30); the rich man and Lazarus (Luke 16:19); the Pharisee and the publican (Luke 18:9), and so forth.

(IX) The distribution of parables.

(A) Luke's Gospel has the greatest number of parables: **(1)** The Garment and Wineskins (5:36–39); **(2)** Children at Play (7:31–35); **(3)** The Two Debtors (7:41–43); **(4)** The Sower (and the explanation) (8:4–8, 11–15); **(5)** The Lamp (8:16–18); **(6)** Following Jesus and the privations involved therein (9:57–62); **(7)** The Good Samaritan (10:25–37); **(8)** The Friend at Midnight (11:5–13); **(9)** A House Divided (11:14–26); **(10)** The Lamp and the Body (11:33–36); **(11)** The Inside and Outside of the Glass (11:39, 40); **(12)** Tithing (11:42); **(13)** Birds and The Divine Providence (12:4–7); **(14)** The Rich Foolish Farmer (12:13–21); **(15)** Nature and Providence (12:22–31); **(16)** The Faithful and the Bad Servants (12:41–48); **(17)** Fire on the Earth (12:49–53); **(18)** Weather Prediction (12:54–56); **(19)** Reconciliation (12:57–59); **(20)** Accidents and Destruction (13:1–5); **(21)** The Barren Fig Tree (13:6–9); **(22)** The Mustard Seed (13:18, 19); **(23)** The Leaven (13:21); **(24)** The Narrow Way (13:22–30); **(25)** Hospitality (14:7–14); **(26)** The Marriage Supper (14:15–24); **(27)** Building a Tower (14:28–30); **(28)** The Warring King (14:31–33); **(29)** Tasteless Salt (14:34, 35); **(30)** The Lost Sheep (15:1–7); **(31)** The Lost Coin (15:8–10); **(32)**

The Lost Son (15:11–32); (33) The Unrighteous Servant (16:1–9); (34) The Rich Man and Lazarus (16:19–31); (35) The Millstone Around One's Neck (17:1–4); (36) Faith and the Sycamore Tree (17:5, 6); (37) The Unprofitable Servant (17:7–10); (38) The Persistent Widow (18:1–8); (39) The Pharisee and the Publican (18:9–14); (40) The Rich and the Eye of a Needle (18:24–29); (41) The Pounds (19:11–27); (42) The Wicked Vinedressers (20:9–19); (43) The Dinar and Taxes (20:20–26); (44) The Fig Tree and the Coming of the Son of Man (21:29–33).

The parables in Luke deal more with ethical matters and stress mercy.

Parables found only in Luke: (1) Contrast of Forgiveness and Gratitude (7:41–43); (2) The Good Samaritan (10:25–37); (3) The Friend at Midnight (11:5–13); (4) The Faithful and the Bad Servants (12:41–48); (5) The Barren Fig Tree (13:6–9); (6) Hospitality (14:7–14); (7) Building a Tower (14:28–30); (8) The Warring King (14:31–33); (9) The Lost Coin (15:8–10); (10) The Lost Son (15:11–32); (11) The Unrighteous Servant (16:1–9); (12) The Rich Man and Lazarus (16:19–31); (13) The Unprofitable Servant (17:7–10); (14) The Persistent Widow (18:1–8); (15) The Pharisee and the Publican (18:9–14); (16) The Pounds (19:11–27).

(B) Mark, who records events more than discourses (which are often a follow-up on parables), gives us the fewest parables. Only one parable is peculiar to the Gospel of Mark, that of the Planted and not the Scattered Seed (4:26–29). Note the verb *bálē* (aor. of *bállō* [906]) in v. 26 translated "cast" (KJV, NASB; "scatters," NIV), which should not be taken as uncontrolled scattering, as is denoted by the word *speírō* (4687), to sow, used in Matt 13:3, 4, 18–20, 22–24, 27, 31, 37, 39; Mark 4:3, 4, 14, 15, 18, 20, 31, 32; Luke 8:5).

The parables in Mark's Gospel are: (1) The Garment and Wineskins (2:21, 22); (2) The Divided House (3:23–27); (3) The Sower (4:1–9, 13–20); (4) Light Under a Bushel (4:21–23); (5) The Growing Seed (4:26–29), unique to Mark; (6) The Mustard Seed (4:30–32); (7) The Millstone, Mutilation of the Body, and Gehenna (9:42–47); (8) Fire and Salt (9:49, 50); (9) The Barren Fig Tree (11:12–14); (10) The Wicked Vinedressers (12:1–12); (11) The Coin and Taxes (12:13–17); (12) The Fig Tree (13:28–31); (13) Guarding the House During the Owner's Absence (13:32–37).

(C) Parables in Matthew's Gospel are: (1) Salt (5:13); (2) Light (5:14–16); (3) The Eye (6:22, 23); (4) The Birds and the Flowers (6:25–34); (5) The Beam and the Sliver in the Eye (7:1–6); (6) Asking, Bread, Stone, Fish, Snake (7:7–12); (7) The Narrow Way (7:13, 14); (8) Trees and Fruits (7:15–20); (9) The Rock and the Sand (7:24–27); (10) Discipleship, Foxes and Birds (8:18–22); (11) Fasting, Bridegroom (9:14, 15); (12) The Garment and Wineskins (9:16, 17); (13) Sheep Without a Shepherd (9:36–38); (14) Children Performing in the Squares (11:16–19); (15) A Kingdom Divided (12:25–30); (16) A Good Tree Is Known by Its Fruits (12:33); (17) The Sign of Jonah (12:39–42); (18) The Exorcised Evil Spirit Returns Home (12:43–45); (19) The Sower (and the explanation) (13:1–9, 18–23); (20) The Wheat and the Tares (13:24–30, 36–43); (21) The Mustard Seed (13:31, 32); (22) The Leaven (13:33); (23) The Hidden Treasure (13:44); (24) The Pearl of Great Price (13:45, 46); (25) The Fish in the Net (13:47–50); (26) The Old and the New Out of the Treasury (13:51, 52); (27) Plants Not Planted by God (15:13–20); (28) Discerning the Signs of the Times Through the Weather (16:1–4); (29) The Leaven of the Pharisees (16:5–12); (30) The Coin and Taxes (17:24–27); (31) The Greatest in the Kingdom (18:1–5); (32) The Millstone Around One's Neck (18:6–9); (33) The Lost Sheep (18:10–14); (34) The Unforgiving Servant (18:21–35); (35) The Rich and the Eye of a Needle (19:23–30); (36) The Workers in the Vineyard (20:1–16); (37) The Barren Fig Tree (21:18–22);

(38) The Two Sons (21:28–32); (39) The Wicked Vinedressers (21:33–46); (40) The Marriage Supper (22:1–14); (41) The Dinar and Taxes (22:15–22); (42) Marriage and Heaven (22:23–33); (43) The Fig Tree (24:32–35); (44) The Absent Lord (24:45–51); (45) The Wise and Foolish Virgins (25:1–13); (46) Talents (25:14–30); (47) The Sheep and the Goats Separated (25:31–46).

Parables found only in Matt: (1) The Wheat and the Tares (13:24–30, 36–43); (2) The Hidden Treasure (13:44); (3) The Pearl of Great Price (13:45, 46); (4) The Fish in the Net (13:47–50); (5) The Old and the New Out of the Treasury (13:51, 52); (6) The Unforgiving Servant (18:21–35); (7) The Workers in the Vineyard (20:1–16); (8) The Two Sons (21:28–32); (9) The Marriage Supper (22:1–14); (10) The Wise and Foolish Virgins (25:1–13); (11) Talents (25:14–30).

The parables in Matt are more theocratic and stress God's judgment.

(X) The Classification of the Parables. Various attempts have been made:

(A) By Goebel, who classifies them into three categories: (1) Those connected with Christ's ministry in and around Capernaum, mostly in Matt 13; (2) Those belonging from Galilee to Jerusalem, recorded mostly in Luke 10–18; (3) Those belonging to the last days in Jerusalem.

(B) By others, two main divisions: (1) Parables drawn from man's relations to hell; (2) Those drawn from man's relations to his fellows.

(XI) The Interpretation of the Parables:

(A) There is usually one basic lesson. This is usually discernible by the question or circumstances which prompted the parable, as for instance the parable of the Workers in the Vineyard (Matt 20:1–16) resulted from Peter's question in Matt 19:27.

(B) No major doctrine can be derived from the details pertaining to the description of the physical circumstances in attributing parallel realities to the spiritual.

In the teaching, the physical invariably falls short of adequate representation of the spiritual.

(C) Except for the two parables explained by the Lord (The Sower [Matt 13:1–90, 18–23], and the Wheat and the Tares [Matt 13:24–30, 36–43]), the meaning is to be sought in the application given to the parable by our Lord. For instance, in the parable of the dismissed steward (Luke 16:1–13), the basic lesson is revealed in v. 9, where our Lord instructs His disciples to use money (which is commonly used for unrighteous purposes) to gain friends for oneself who will provide a welcome in heaven.

While a parable uses earthly things to convey a spiritual or heavenly meaning, a myth distorts the earthly things in using them as a vehicle of instruction. Myths are used by men for their own ends. They are never used by God's prophets in conveying His message nor by Christ in explaining His kingdom. While the noun "allegory [*allegoría*]" does not occur in the NT, the verb *allēgoréō* (238), to allegorize, does. In an allegory, figure and fact (or interpretation) are not mixed, but are parallel and move simultaneously, as in the allegory of the True Vine or of the Good Shepherd.

Syn.: *paroimía* (3942), a proverb; *analogía* (356), analogy.

3851. παραβουλεύομαι *parabouleúomai*; fut. *parabouleúsomai*, from *pará* (3844), aside, implying error, hence, wrongly, and *bouleúō* (1011), to consult. To disregard (Phil 2:30 [TR], where other editions and MSS read *paraboleúomai*, to hazard, bring into danger, expose).

3852. παραγγελία *paraggelía*; gen. *paraggelías*, fem. noun from *paraggéllō* (3853), to command. A proclamation, command (Acts 16:24); a charge by the Apostles (1 Thess 4:2; 1 Tim 1:5, 18). Strictly used of commands received from a superior and transmitted to others.

Syn.: *éntalma* (1778), an injunction; *entolḗ* (1785), command, precept; *diatagḗ*

(1296), arrangement, order; *diátagma* (1297), edict; *kéleusma* (2752), a cry of incitement, a shout.

3853. παραγγέλλω *paraggéllō*; fut. *paraggelṓ*, from *pará* (3844), to the side of, and *aggéllō* (n.f., see *anaggéllō* [312]), to tell, declare. To pass on an announcement, hence, to give the word to someone nearby, to advance an order, charge or command. With *mḗ* (3361), not, followed by the dat. of person expressed or implied, the thing commanded being put in the acc., or as an inf., or with *hína* (2443), so that.
(I) With the dat. and acc. (2 Thess 3:4 [cf. 3:10]); followed by *hóti* (3754), that, with the dat. implied (1 Cor 11:17); followed by *hína* (2443), so that (1 Tim 5:7).
(II) With the dat. and aor. inf. (Luke 5:14; 8:29, 56; Acts 10:42; 16:18; 23:22); dat. and pres. inf. (Acts 1:4; 4:18; 5:28 [cf. 5:40]; Acts 16:23; 17:30; 23:30; 2 Thess 3:6; 1 Tim 1:3; 6:17); with the acc. and pres. inf. (1 Tim 6:13, 14); with the dat. implied (Acts 15:5).
(II) Followed by the dat. and *hína*, so that (Mark 6:8; 2 Thess 3:12); with the dat. and *kathṓs* (2531), as (1 Thess 4:11, 12); with *légōn* (the pres. part. of *légō* [3004], to say), saying, before the expressed words (Matt 10:5).
Deriv.: *paraggelía* (3852), a proclamation.
Syn.: *keleúō* (2753), to summon, bid; *entéllomai* (1781), to command; *mēnúō* (3377), to declare.

3854. παραγίνομαι *paragínomai*; fut. *paragenḗsomai*, from *pará* (3844), to, at, and *gínomai* (1096), to be, come. To come to be or present, i.e., to come, approach, arrive (Matt 3:1, 13; Mark 14:43). Elsewhere only in the 2d aor. *paregenómēn*, to be near, present, i.e., to have come or arrived (Luke 19:16; Acts 11:23; 25:7; 1 Cor 16:3; Sept.: Gen 26:32; Ex 2:16, 17). With an adjunct of place, it means whither, e.g., followed by *eis* (1519), to, at, with the acc. of place (Matt 2:1; John

8:2; Acts 13:14; 15:4; Sept.: Josh 24:11). Followed by *epí* (1909), upon, with the acc. of place (Matt 3:13); with the acc. of person meaning to come upon someone (Luke 22:52; Sept.: Josh 10:9); followed by *prós* (4314), toward, with the acc. of person (Luke 7:4; 11:6; Acts 20:18; Sept.: Ex 2:17; 18:6). With an adjunct of place, meaning whence, such as *apó* (575), from, with the gen. (Matt 3:13); with *ex* [1537], from, and the gen. (Luke 11:6); *pará* (3844), from beside, with the gen. of person (Mark 14:43). With the sense of to come or appear publicly, e.g., John the Baptist (Matt 3:1); Jesus (Luke 12:51; Heb 9:11). With the meaning to come back, return (Luke 14:21; Sept.: Num 14:36; Josh 18:8).
Deriv.: *sumparagínomai* (4836), to come together, stand with.
Syn.: *katantáō* (2658), to come to, arrive at; *katapléō* (2668), to sail into harbor; *parabállō* (3846), a nautical word meaning to touch at or arrive at a place; *phthánō* (5348), to arrive at, attain; *érchomai* (2064), to come, go; *anabaínō* (305), to ascend, enter, go; *hḗkō* (2240), to come; *aphiknéomai* (864), to arrive at a place; *enístēmi* (1764), to set in; *ephístēmi* (2186), to come up; *parístēmi* (3936), to stand by or near; *prosporeúomai* (4365), to go towards; *proseggízō* (4331), to approach; *páreimi* (3918), to be at hand or present; *parákeimai* (3873), to lie beside, be near; *ménō* (3306), to abide.
Ant.: *poreúomai* (4198), to go on one's way; *paraporeúomai* (3899), to pass by; *hupágō* (5217), to go away; *ágō* (71), to go; *ápeimi* (548), to go away; *anachōréō* (402), to depart; *epidúō* (1931), to go down; *éxeimi* (1826), to go out.

3855. παράγω *parágō*; fut. *paráxō*, from *pará* (3844), by or past, denoting transitoriness, and *ágō* (71), to lead. To lead along, near, to lead by or past. In the mid. *parágomai*, to pass along, to pass away (1 John 2:8). Figuratively, with the meaning of to disappear, perish (1 John 2:17). To pass along, pass by (Matt 20:30; Mark 2:14; 15:21; John 9:1; Sept.:

2 Sam 15:18; Ps 129:8). In the sense of to pass on further (Matt 9:9, 27; John 8:59). Metaphorically with the meaning of to disappear, perish (1 Cor 7:31; Sept.: Ps 144:4).

Syn.: *aphanízō* (853), to render unapparent, destroy, obliterate, mid. to disappear; *parérchomai* (3928), to pass by, elapse; *metabaínō* (3327), to change places; *paraporeúomai* (3899), to go beside; *diaperáō* (1276), to cross over.

Ant.: *paragínomai* (3854), to approach.

3856. παραδειγματίζω *paradeig-matízō*; fut. *paradeigmatíso*, from *pará* (3844), near, i.e., to those in view, visibly, openly, publicly, and *deigmatízō* (1165), to make a show. To make a public example of, expose to public shame (Matt 1:19); implying punishment as an example to others (Deut 22:23, 24). In Heb 6:6, it means to bring shame upon the sacrificial death of Christ or to declare it ineffective because it did not result in eternal salvation for those who grounded their repentance and faith upon it. The teaching of Heb 6:4–6 is that if those who were once enlightened, having tasted of the heavenly gift, the good word of God, and the powers of the world to come, and after having become partakers of the Holy Spirit, should fall away, it would be impossible for them to have a qualitatively new kind (*anakainízō*, [340]) of repentance. Such a new repentance would necessitate a new crucifixion of Christ, rendering His once-for-all crucifixion for sin as a public example of unworthiness and ridicule.

Syn.: *atimázō* (818), to dishonor; *atimóō* (821), to handle shamefully; *entrépō* (1788), to put to shame; *kataischúnō* (2617), to put utterly to shame.

3857. παράδεισος *parádeisos*; gen. *paradeísou*, masc. noun. Paradise. This is an oriental word which the Greeks borrowed from the Persians, among whom it meant a garden, park, or enclosure full of all the vegetable products of the earth. In Xenophon's economics, Socrates said

that the king of Persia took particular care, wherever he was, to have gardens or enclosures full of every beautiful and good thing the earth could produce. These were called *paradises*. The original Eastern word *pardes* occurs in Neh 2:8; Eccl 2:5; Song 4:13. In Sanskrit, *paradésha* and *paradisha* meant a land elevated and cultivated. In Armenian, *pardes* means a garden around the house planted with grass, herbs, and trees for food and ornament. The Sept. uses it to refer to the Garden of Eden (Gen 2:8). In later Jewish usage and in the NT, *parádeisos* is used for the abode of the blessed after death. Paradise, before Christ's resurrection, has been thought to be the region of the blessed in Hades although it was not specifically called by that name (Luke 16:23). Jesus said He would take the repentant thief with Him to paradise (Luke 23:43).

Hades (86) in the NT was the world or abode of the dead in general. According to the notions of the Jews, Hades was a vast subterranean area where the souls or the spirits of the dead existed in separate states until the resurrection of their bodies. The region of the blessed during this interval, or the inferior paradise, was thought to be in the upper part of this receptacle. Beneath this was the abyss, Gehenna (1067) or Tartarus (5020), in which the souls of the wicked were subjected to punishment.

The expression "the paradise of God" means the celestial paradise where the spirits of the just dwell with God. By comparing 2 Cor 12:4 to 12:2, we see that it is also called the third heaven. This is an allusion to the three heavens: the lower heaven or hemisphere; the middle heaven or firmament; and the superior heaven, i.e., the highest heaven, the abode of God, the angels, and glorified spirits, the spiritual paradise (cf. Eph 4:10; Heb 4:14; 7:26; Sept.: Deut 10:14; 1 Kgs 8:27; see Rev 2:7 in relation to Gen 2:8).

Syn.: *ouranós* (3772), heaven.

Ant.: *hadḗs* (86), abode of the dead; *géenna* (1067), the place of eternal punishment.

3858. παραδέχομαι *paradéchomai*; fut. *paradéxomai*, from *pará* (3844), from, and *déchomai* (1209), to receive. In the NT, to receive, admit (Acts 16:21; 1 Tim 5:19; Sept.: Ex 23:1); to receive, embrace with assent and obedience (Mark 4:20; Acts 22:18); to receive or embrace with special favor (Heb 12:6 from Sept.: Prov 3:12).

 Syn.: *hupolambánō* (5274), to take from below, receive; *apodéchomai* (588), to approve, welcome; *anagnōrízō* (319), to recognize; *homologéō* (3670), to acknowledge.

 Ant.: *apōthéō* (683), to put away from; *periphronéō* (4065), to despise; *apotrépō* (665), to turn away; *apophérō* (667), to bear off; *aparnéomai* (533), to deny; *apotássomai* (657), to put away from oneself in the proper place.

3859. παραδιατριβή *paradiatribḗ*; gen. *paradiatribḗs*, fem. noun from *pará* (3844), aside, implying error, hence, wrongly, and *diatribḗ* (n.f.), waste, passing time, which is from *diatríbō* (1304), to abide. Pastime, misuse of time, idle occupation. The meetings, discourses, and disputations of the philosophers were called *diatribaí*. The Apostle Paul must have had this in mind in 1 Tim 6:5 (TR), meaning misuse, idle occupation, unprofitable dispute or debate.

 Syn.: *chronotribéō* (5551), to pass time, linger, procrastinate; *asōtía* (810), profligacy of life.

3860. παραδίδωμι *paradídōmi*; fut. *paradṓsō*, from *pará* (3844), to the side of, over to, and *dídōmi* (1325), to give. To deliver over or up to the power of someone.

 (I) Spoken of persons delivered over with evil intent to the power or authority of others as to magistrates for trial or condemnation, followed by the acc. and dat. (Matt 5:25; Mark 15:1; Luke 20:20; John 19:11); with the dat. implied (Matt 27:18; Acts 3:13). To soldiers for punishment or keeping (Matt 18:34; Luke 18:32; Acts 12:4). Followed by the acc. with *eis* (1519), unto (Matt 20:19; Luke 24:20, to be punished with death). With *hína* (2443), so that (Matt 27:26; Mark 15:15). To the power and pleasure of one's enemies with acc. and dat. (Matt 26:15; Luke 23:25; 1 Tim 1:20). With the acc. (Matt 10:4; 24:10; Mark 3:19; 14:11; Luke 22:21). In the pass. (Matt 4:12; Mark 1:14). In Matt 10:17, *eis sunédria* (*sunédria* [4892], councils), into councils, means before councils. To deliver someone into the hands means into the power of someone (Matt 17:22; Mark 14:41; Luke 24:7; Acts 21:11). With *eis*, unto or for the purpose of (Matt 24:9; 26:2; Mark 13:12; Acts 8:3, "unto prison" [a.t.]; 2 Cor 4:11, "unto death" [a.t.]), and so also with "unto death" (*eis thánaton* [2288]) implied when referring to the death of Jesus (Rom 4:25; 8:32; 1 Cor 11:23); also where Jesus is said to deliver Himself (Gal 2:20; Eph 5:2, 25). See 1 Cor 5:5.

 (II) Spoken of persons or things delivered over to do or suffer something, in the general sense of to give up or over, to surrender, to permit, with the acc. (Acts 15:26, "men who have given up [risked] their lives" [a.t.]). With the acc. and *hína* (2443), so that (1 Cor 13:3). Used of persons given over to follow their passions, with the acc. and dat. of thing (Eph 4:19); with the acc. and inf. (Acts 7:42). Followed by the acc. and *eis* (1519), unto, i.e., unto the power or practice of someone or something (Rom 1:24, 26, 28).

 (III) Spoken of persons and things delivered over to the charge, care, or kindness of someone, in the general sense of giving up, committing, entrusting, generally with the acc. and dat. (Matt 11:27; 25:14; Luke 4:6; 10:22; Acts 27:1; 1 Pet 2:23; 2 Pet 2:4). To commit or commend someone to the favor of God (Acts 14:26; 15:40). To give up the ghost (John 19:30). Also in the sense of to give back, deliver up or render to (1 Cor 15:24).

(IV) Spoken of things delivered orally or by writing, i.e., to deliver, declare, teach; trans. (Mark 7:13; Luke 1:2; Acts 6:14; 16:4; 1 Cor 11:2, 23; 15:3; 2 Pet 2:21; Jude 1:3). In the pass. (Rom 6:17).

(V) Spoken intrans. or with *heautón* (1438), himself, implied, meaning to deliver up oneself, yield oneself, e.g., as the harvest yields itself to the sickle (Mark 4:29).

Deriv.: *parádosis* (3862), ordinance, tradition; *patroparádotos* (3970), traditional.

Syn.: *prosphérō* (4374), to offer; *paréchō* (3930), to offer, furnish, present, provide; *ekdídōmi* (1554), to give forth.

Ant.: *lambánō* (2983), to receive; *paralambánō* (3880), to receive unto; *proslambánō* (4355), to welcome; *apospáō* (645), to draw away; *aphairéō* (851), to remove; *exairéō* (1807), to pluck out; *exaírō* (1808), to remove.

3861. παράδοξος *parádoxos*; gen. *paradóxou*, masc.-fem., neut. *parádoxon*, adj. from *pará* (3844), beyond, and *dóxa* (1391), opinion, expectation, glory. Paradoxical, strange, other than accepted opinion. When used as a noun, something beyond one's expectation, a miracle. In Luke 5:26, used to express new things, miracles not yet seen as of that time (cf. Mark 2:12) and thus surpassing all the opinions and expectations of men.

Syn.: *sēmeíon* (4592), sign; *dúnamis* (1411), power, miracle; *megaleíon* (3167), magnificent thing; *éndoxos* (1741), something glorious; *thaumásios* (2297), wonderful thing; *téras* (5059), terrifying thing.

3862. παράδοσις *parádosis*; gen. *paradóseōs*, fem. noun from *paradídōmi* (3860), to deliver in teaching. A tradition, doctrine or injunction delivered or communicated from one to another, whether divine (1 Cor 11:2; 2 Thess 2:15; 3:6) or human (Matt 15:2, 3, 6; Gal 1:14; Col 2:8). In Mark 7:3, 5, the expression "the tradition of the elders" occurs. The Pharisees delivered to the people by tradition their ancestors' many injunctions which were not written in the Law of Moses. For this reason the sect of the Sadducees rejected them, saying that what was written should be esteemed obligatory, but that which came from oral tradition need not be observed. Thus, Josephus explains the expression "the traditions of the elders" or of the Pharisees. The words of the elders were considered more desirable than the words of the prophets.

Syn.: *dógma* (1378), ordinance, decree; *diatagé* (1296), ordinance, disposition; *éthos* (1484), custom.

3863. παραζηλόω *parazēlóō*; contracted *parazēló*, fut. *parazēlṓsō*; from *pará* (3844), to the point of, unto, implying movement toward a certain point, and *zēlóō* (2206), to desire, be zealous. To make jealous, provoke to jealousy or emulation. Figuratively spoken of Israel whom God would make by bestowing her covenant privileges on other nations. Trans. (Rom 10:19 quoted from Deut 32:21; Rom 11:11, 14). Also to provoke God to jealousy or anger by rendering to idols the homage due to Him alone (1 Cor 10:22; Sept.: 1 Kgs 14:22; Ps 37:1, 7, 8).

Syn.: *paroxúnō* (3947), to sharpen or to provoke; *erethízō* (2042), to excite, stir up; *prokaléō* (4292), to stir up.

3864. παραθαλάσσιος *parathalássios*; fem. *parathalássia*, neut. *parathalássion*, adj. from *pará* (3844), near, and *thálassa* (2281), sea. Near the sea, by the seaside, maritime (Matt 4:13; Sept.: 2 Chr 8:17).

Syn.: *parálios* (3882), by the sea.

3865. παραθεωρέω *paratheōréō*; contracted *paratheōró*, fut. *paratheōrḗsō*, from *pará* (3844), aside or beyond, implying error, hence, wrongly, and *theōréō* (2334), to behold, contemplate. To look at a thing by the side of another, to compare. In the NT, to look past something, i.e., to overlook, neglect, slight, in the pass. (Acts 6:1).

Syn.: *ameléō* (272), to neglect; *epilanthánomai* (1950), to neglect, forget; *paríēmi* (3935), to let by, relax.

Ant.: *phrontízō* (5431), to exercise care; *merimnáō* (3309), to be anxious; *proséchō* (4337), to pay attention; *epimeléomai* (1959), to take care of.

3866. παραθήκη *parathḗkē*; gen. *parathḗkēs*, fem. noun from *paratíthēmi* (3908) to deposit. A deposit, trust, something committed to one's charge (2 Tim 1:12). Used also in 1 Tim 6:20 and 2 Tim 1:14, in later editions of the TR, for *parakatathḗkē* (3872). See Sept.: Lev 6:2, 4.

Syn.: *apothḗkē* (596), a repository; *apóthesis* (595), a laying aside.

Ant.: *análēpsis* (354), a taking up, withdrawal; *lḗpsis* (3028), a receiving.

3867. παραινέω *parainéō*; contracted *parainō*, fut. *parainésō*, from *pará* (3844), to the point of, unto, implying movement toward a certain point, and *ainéō* (134), to praise. To exhort, admonish, with the inf. and acc. of person (Acts 27:22 [see 27:9]).

Syn.: *noutheteō* (3560), to put in mind, admonish; *chrēmatízō* (5537), to warn; *parakaléō* (3870), to entreat, exhort; *protrépō* (4389), to impel morally, encourage, exhort; *sumbouleúō* (4823), to advise, counsel; *sunistáō* (4921), to commend; *kateuthúnō* (2720), to guide, direct.

Ant.: *planáō* (4105), to seduce; *apatáō* (538), to delude; *exapatáō* (1818), to beguile.

3868. παραιτέομαι *paraitéomai*; contracted *paraitoúmai*, fut. *paraitésomai*, mid. deponent from *pará* (3844) aside, implying something more then is proper, hence, wrongly, and *aitéō* (154), to ask, beg. Never used in the act. sense, but only in the mid. voice. To try to obtain by asking, to beg a person's release, the person addressed being regarded as reluctant, or the thing asked for as difficult to obtain. Later it came to mean begging to be

excused, to decline or refuse the request. In the NT, to decline, refuse, avoid, with the acc. following (Acts 25:11; 1 Tim 4:7; 5:11; 2 Tim 2:23; Titus 3:10; Heb 12:25). Followed by *mḗ* (3361), not, with the inf. (Heb 12:19), to excuse oneself (see Luke 14:18, 19, where it is used as an inf. and followed by a part. adj.).

Syn.: *egkataleípō* (1459), to forsake, give up.

Ant.: *déchomai* (1209), to accept; *anadéchomai* (324), to receive as a guest.

3869. παρακαθίζω *parakathízō*; fut. *parakathísó*, from *pará* (3844) by, near, and *kathízō* (2523), to sit down, appoint, settle. To sit down near, to seat oneself near, followed by *pará* with the acc. (Luke 10:39; Sept.: Job 2:13).

Syn.: *káthēmai* (2521), to sit; *anákeimai* (345), to recline at a table; *katákeimai* (2621), to lie down; *kathézomai* (2516), to sit down.

Ant.: *anístēmi* (450), to stand up; *egeírō* (1453), to raise, mid., to rise.

3870. παρακαλέω *parakaléō*; contracted *parakalō*, fut. *parakalésō*, from *pará* (3844), to the side of, and *kaléō* (2564), to call. To aid, help, comfort, encourage. Translated: to comfort, exhort, desire, call for, beseech with a stronger force than *aitéō* (154).

(I) To invite to come (Acts 28:20).

(II) To call for or upon someone as for aid, to invoke God, to beseech, entreat, with the acc. (Matt 18:32; Acts 16:39; 2 Cor 12:18). With the acc. expressed or implied with other adjuncts, e.g., *légō* (3004) or similar adjuncts (Matt 8:5, 31; Mark 1:40; 5:23; Acts 16:15; 25:2). With the aor. inf. (Mark 5:17; Acts 8:31; 9:38; 19:31). With the aor. inf. and the acc. (Acts 24:4). With *toú* and the inf. (Acts 21:12). With *hína* (2443), in order to (Mark 5:18; Luke 8:31; 1 Cor 16:12; 2 Cor 12:8). With *hópōs* (3704), so that (Matt 8:34). With *perí* (4012), concerning (Phile 1:10).

(III) To call upon someone to do something, to exhort, admonish, with the acc. of person (Acts 15:32; 1 Cor 14:31; 2 Cor 10:1; 1 Thess 2:11; 1 Tim 5:1; Heb 3:13). With the acc. and with further adjuncts, meaning with the express words (1 Cor 4:16; 1 Pet 5:1). With the pres. inf. (Acts 11:23; Phil 4:2; 1 Tim 2:1; 1 Pet 2:11). With the aor. inf. (Acts 27:33; Rom 12:1; 2 Cor 2:8; Eph 4:1; Heb 13:19). With *hína* (2443), so that (1 Cor 1:10; 2 Cor 8:6; 1 Thess 4:1). Used in an absolute sense with the acc. of person implied (Luke 3:18; Rom 12:8; 2 Cor 5:20; 13:11; Titus 1:9; Heb 10:25); with *légōn* (3004), saying (Acts 2:40); with the inf. and acc. (2 Cor 6:1); in the pres. imper. *parakálei* (1 Tim 6:2; Titus 2:15).

(IV) To exhort in the way of consolation, encouragement, to console, comfort, with the acc. of person (Matt 2:18; 5:4; 2 Cor 1:4; 2:7; 7:6; 1 Thess 3:7; 4:18). Followed by "your hearts" (Eph 6:22; Col 4:8; 2 Thess 2:17; Sept.: Gen 24:67; 37:34; Deut 32:36). In the sense of to make glad, in the pass., to be glad, rejoice (Luke 16:25; Acts 20:12).

Deriv.: *paráklēsis* (3874), an appeal, an encouragement, exhortation, consolation, comfort; *paráklētos* (3875), a counselor, an advocate, a comforter; *sumparakaléō* (4837), to comfort together.

Syn.: *paramuthéomai* (3888), to console, comfort; *nouthetéō* (3560), to admonish.

3871. παρακαλύπτω *parakalúptō*; fut. *parakalúpsō*, from *pará* (3844), to the side of or from, and *kalúptō* (2572), to cover, hide. To cover over or hide, especially by putting something out of sight, or near or before an object, e.g., the eyes (Sept.: Ezek 22:26). Metaphorically in Luke 9:45, referring to the saying of Jesus.

Syn.: *sugkalúptō* (4780), to cover up completely; *krúptō* (2928), to cover, conceal, keep secret; *apokrúptō* (613), to conceal from; *egkrúptō* (1470), to hide something; *perikrúptō* (4032), to hide by placing something around or to conceal

entirely; *lanthánō* (2990), to escape notice.

Ant.: *apokalúptō* (601), to uncover, unveil; *anakalúptō* (343), to discover.

3872. παρακαταθήκη *parakatathḗkē*; gen. *parakatathḗkēs*, fem. noun from *pará* (3844), with, and *katatíthēmi* (2698), to place down. A deposit left with or entrusted to one's charge (1 Tim 6:20; 2 Tim 1:14 [TR], where in later editions it appears in the later form *parathḗkē* [3866]).

3873. παράκειμαι *parákeimai*; fut. *parakeísomai*, from *pará* (3844), near, with, and *keímai* (2749), to lie. To lie near, be adjacent to. In the NT used metaphorically, meaning to be at hand, present, immediate (Rom 7:18, 21).

Syn.: *páreimi* (3918), to be close by, at hand or present; *enístēmi* (1764), to set in, mid. to be present; *ephístēmi* (2186), to set over, stand over; *paragínomai* (3854), to be beside; *sumpáreimi* (4840), to be present with; *parístēmi* (3936), to place beside, become present.

Ant.: *aphístēmi* (868), to stand away from, remove, withdraw.

3874. παράκλησις *paráklēsis*; gen. *paraklḗseōs*, fem. noun from *parakaléō* (3870), to beseech. The act of exhortation, encouragement, comfort. All of Scripture is actually a *paráklēsis*, an exhortation, admonition or encouragement for the purpose of strengthening and establishing the believer in the faith (see Rom 15:4; Phil 2:1; Heb 12:5; 13:22). Paul speaks of his preaching of the gospel as *paráklēsis* in 1 Thess 2:3 (see Acts 13:15; 2 Cor 8:4, 17). The contents of the letter addressed to the church at Antioch from the Apostolic Council are *paráklēsis* in Acts 15:31. Comforting words, consolation (Acts 9:31; 2 Thess 2:16; Phile 1:7; Heb 6:18), the opposite of tribulation and suffering in 2 Cor 7:4 and joined with joy in 2 Cor 7:7, 13 (see 2 Cor 1:3–7). In Luke 6:24, used to designate the comfort in heaven which will be denied the wicked who enjoy the riches and comforts of this world. See the Beatitudes and woes in Luke 6:20–26. In Luke 2:25, the title of Messiah, "the consolation of Israel," is eschatological pointing to Him as the one who brings the predicted and long-awaited comfort to Israel. In Acts 4:36, Barnabas is called "the son of consolation," referring to his prophetic gift manifested especially in the exercise of comforting others. In connection with Acts 13:15; 1 Tim 4:13, *paráklēsis* was regarded as based on the reading of a portion of Scripture (Luke 4:20, 21, an expository application of the prophetic word), although this was by no means the whole.

Syn.: *paramuthía* (3889), consolation, comfort; *nouthesía* (3559), admonition.

3875. παράκλητος *paráklētos*; gen. *paraklḗtou*, masc. noun from *parakaléō* (3870), to comfort, encourage or exhort. It is properly a verbal adj. referring to an aid of any kind. In the Greek writers, used of a legal advisor, pleader, proxy, or advocate, one who comes forward in behalf of and as the representative of another. Thus, in 1 John 2:1, Christ is termed our substitutionary, intercessory advocate. Christ designates the Holy Spirit as Paraclete (John 14:16), and calls Him *állos* (243), another, which means another of equal quality and not *héteros* (2087), another of a different quality. Therefore, the Holy Spirit is designated by Jesus Christ as equal with Himself, i.e., God (1 John 2:1). This new Paraclete, the Holy Spirit, was to witness concerning Jesus Christ (John 14:26; 16:7, 14) and to glorify Him. The Holy Spirit is called a Paraclete because He undertakes Christ's office in the world while Christ is not in the world as the God-Man in bodily form. In addition, the Holy Spirit is also called the Paraclete because He acts as Christ's substitute on earth. When Christ in John 14:16 designates Himself as a Paraclete, the same as the Holy Spirit, the word must not be understood as applying to Christ in the same sense as in

1 John 2:1 where it refers to our substitutionary Advocate who pleads our cause with the Father. It should rather be taken as He who pleads God's cause with us (see John 14:7–9). The words *parakaléō* (3870) and *paráklēsis* (3874), the act or process of comforting or advocating, do not occur at all in the writings of John.

3876. παρακοή *parakoē̇*; gen. *parakoḗs*, fem. noun from *parakoúō* (3878), to disobey. In its strictest sense, it means a failing to hear or hearing amiss, with the notion of active disobedience which follows this inattentive or careless hearing (cf. Rom 5:19; 2 Cor 10:6; Heb 2:2).

Syn.: *apeítheia* (543), disobedience; *parábasis* (3847), transgression; *apostasía* (646), apostasy.

Ant.: *hupakoē̇* (5218), obedience; *hupotagē̇* (5292), submission

3877. παρακολουθέω *parakolouthéō*; contracted *parakolouthṓ*, fut. *parakoluthḗsō*, from *pará* (3844), near, and *akolouthéō* (190), to follow. To accompany side by side, follow closely, attend to carefully. In the NT:

(I) Of things meaning to accompany, to be done by someone, with the dat. (Mark 16:17, where it should be observed that *pisteúsasi* is an aor. part. referring to those who did believe in the past).

(II) Metaphorically, to follow closely in mind, to investigate, search out or trace so as to attain knowledge of (Luke 1:3).

(III) To conform to, compare, with the dat. referring to teaching (1 Tim 4:6; 2 Tim 3:10).

Syn.: *suníēmi* (4920), to perceive, understand; *ginṓskō* (1097), to come to know; *epístamai* (1987), to understand; *punthánomai* (4441), to inquire; *gnōrízō* (1107), to make known; *manthánō* (3129), to understand, learn.

3878. παρακούω *parakoúō*; fut. *parakoúsō*, from *pará* (3844), aside, implying error, hence, wrongly, and *akoúō* (191), to hear. To hear amiss, slightly, inattentively. In the NT, to neglect to hear, disregard, be disobedient (Matt 18:17; Sept.: Esth 3:8).

Deriv.: *parakoḗ* (3876), disobedience.

Syn.: *apeithéō* (544), to disobey; *parabaínō* (3845), to transgress; *anthístēmi* (436), to resist; *epanístamai* (1881), to revolt; *ataktéō* (812), to act disorderly; *antidiatíthemai* (475), to set oneself opposite; *antíkeimai* (480), to set oneself against; *antistrateúomai* (497), to war against.

Ant.: *akoúō* (191), to hear or obey; *hupakoúō* (5219), to obey; *epakoúō* (1873), to pay attention; *peitharchéō* (3980), to be persuaded or to obey; *enōtízomai* (1801), to give ear to; *peíthomai* (3982), to be persuaded.

3879. παρακύπτω *parakúptō*; fut. *parakúpsō*, from *pará* (3844), to, beside, and *kúptō* (2955), to bend, stoop. To stoop down near or by something, bend forward or near in order to look at something more closely. Metaphorically, meaning to look into, find out, know. Used in the account of the early morning arrival of Mary Magdalene and the disciples at the sepulcher (John 20:5, 11) indicating a bending forward at the door of the tomb of Christ (Luke 24:12; Sept.: 1 Chr 15:29; Prov 7:6). With *eis* (1519), unto (James 1:25; 1 Pet 1:12).

Syn.: of the literal meaning: *klínō* (2827), to bow down; *kámptō* (2578), to bend; of the metaphorical meaning: *blépō* (991), to take heed; *horáō* (3708), to look to it, heed.

Ant.: *egeírō* (1453), to raise; *anorthóō* (461), to straighten up; *stḗkō* (4739), to stand; *exanístēmi* (1817), to stand out from; *exegeírō* (1825), to raise up.

3880. παραλαμβάνω *paralambánō*; fut. *paralḗpsomai*, from *pará* (3844), from, and *lambánō* (2983), to take, receive. To take near, with, or to oneself, to receive to oneself.

(I) To take to oneself, seize or take into one's possession. In the NT used only of persons, to take unto or with oneself, as an associate or companion, with the acc. (Matt 1:20, 24; 17:1; 20:17; 26:37; Mark 4:36; 5:40; 9:2; 10:32; Luke 9:10, 28; 11:26; 18:31; Acts 15:39; 16:33; 21:24, 26, 32; 23:18). Also with *eis* (1519), to, followed by the acc. of place (Matt 4:5, 8; 27:27); by *metá* (3326), with, with the gen. of person (Matt 12:45; 18:16; Mark 14:33); by *prós* (4314), toward, with the acc. of person (John 14:3). In the Sept. with *eis* (1519), unto (Num 23:14); with *metá* (3326), with (Gen 22:3). Used pleonastically and synonymously with the basic verb *lambánō* (2983) with the acc. expressed or implied, before other verbs, in order to express the idea more fully and graphically, e.g., having taken or taken to oneself as in *lambánō* (Matt 14:19; 25:1; 26:26, 52; 27:6, 30, 48; Mark 9:36; Luke 22:17; John 12:3, 13; 13:4, 12, 30; 1 Cor 11:23; Rev 5:8; 22:17). So also the verb itself with *kaí* (2532), and, before another verb (Matt 2:13, 14, 20, 21; John 19:16).

In Matt 24:40, 41; Luke 17:34, 35, *paralambánō* in the pass. form is used as the opposite of *aphíēmi* (863), to let be. In these verses, those who are taken are not to be misconstrued as those whom the Lord favors, as if they were the same saints spoken of in 1 Thess 4:17 who will be raptured (*harpázō* [726], to seize, catch away, as if by force) to meet the Lord in the clouds. The verb *paralambánō* in most cases indicates a demonstration in favor of the one taken, but not always. In Matt 4:5, 8, it is used of Satan taking Jesus up to tempt Him. In John 19:16 it is used of taking Jesus to lead Him to the cross. The verb *paralambánō* is to be contrasted in Matt 24:40, 41 to *aírō* (142), to take up and away. It is used to refer to those in the days of Noah who were taken away, not being favored but being punished, while Noah and his family were left intact. Therefore, in this passage in Matt and the parallel passage in Luke, *paralambánō* must not be equated to the believers who are to be raptured at the coming of the Lord for His saints. It refers rather to those who, as in the days of Noah, are taken to destruction. The others are left alone (*aphíemi*) for the purpose of entering into the blessings of Christ's kingdom (identified by some as the Millennium) and the righteous rule of Christ upon earth.

The word *paralambánō* is also used in relation to a teacher, to receive, acknowledge, embrace and follow his instructions (John 1:11), as also can be the meaning of *lambánō* (2983), to take up a person or receive him as a friend or guest into one's house or society. Equivalent to *déchomai* (1209), to receive, accept.

(II) To receive with or to oneself what is given, imparted, delivered over, equal to take from another into one's own hands such as an office, dignity, ministry (Col 4:17); a kingdom (Heb 12:28; Sept.: Dan 5:31). Metaphorically to receive into the mind, be taught, learn with the acc. of thing (Mark 7:4; 1 Cor 15:1, 3; Gal 1:9; Phil 4:9; Col 2:6, where Christ stands for the gospel of Christ). With the acc., meaning from someone (1 Cor 11:23; Gal 1:12; 1 Thess 2:13; 4:1; 2 Thess 3:6).

Deriv.: *sumparalambánō* (4838), to take with.

Syn.: *lambánō* (2983), to receive; *analambánō* (353), to take up; *apolambánō* (618), to receive from another as one's due; *proslambánō* (4355), to take to oneself; *metalambánō* (3335), to partake of; *hupolambánō* (5274), to take or bear up; *epilambánomai* (1949), to take hold of; *katalambánō* (2638), to lay hold of; *sumparalambánō* (4838), to take along with oneself; *prolambánō* (4301), to overtake; *sullambánō* (4815), to seize; *déchomai* (1209), to receive by deliberate and ready reception that which is offered; *komízō* (2865), to carry; *apéchō* (568), to have received in full; *chōréō* (5562), to give space or make room for; *lagchánō* (2975), to obtain by lot; *kratéō* (2902), to take hold of; *drássomai* (1405), to grasp with the hand; *katéchō* (2722), to hold; *piázō* (4084), to take hold of forcefully; *paraphérō* (3911), to bear away; *sunágō* (4863), to bring together.

Ant.: *paréchō* (3930), to give; *paradídōmi* (3860), to deliver; *ekdídōmi* (1554), to give forth; *apodídōmi* (591), to recompense, requite; *prosphérō* (4374), to offer; *charízomai* (5483), to give freely; *dōréomai* (1433), to bestow; *apọthéomai* (683), to put away; *aporríptō* (641), to reject; *apobállō* (577), to cast away from oneself; *periphronéō* (4065), to reject.

3881. παραλέγω *paralégō*; fut. *paraléxō*, from *pará* (3844), near, and *légō* (3004), in this instance meaning to lie. In the NT, only in the mid. *paralégomai*, to lie near or with someone. As a nautical term, meaning to lay one's course near, sail nearby or along a place or coast. With the acc., to sail near (Acts 27:8, 13).

Syn.: *parapléō* (3896), to sail near; *pléō* (4126), to sail; *diapléō* (1277), to sail across; *hupopléō* (5284), to sail under; *anágō* (321), to lead up or to put to sea; *diaperáō* (1276), to cross or sail over; *braduploéō* (1020), to sail slowly.

Ant.: *apopléō* (636), to sail away; *ekpléō* (1602), to sail from or thence.

3882. παράλιος *parálios*; gen. *paralíou* masc.-fem., neut. *parálion*, adj. from *pará* (3844), near, and *háls* (251), salt or the sea. Near the sea, maritime. Used also as a subst. meaning the sea coast (Luke 6:17), with *chóra* (5561), country or region being understood, the sea coast (Sept.: Gen 49:13; Josh 11:3).

Syn.: *thálassa* (2281), the sea; *pélagos* (3989), the deep sea; *enálios* (1724), belonging to the sea; *parathalássios* (3864), by the sea coast; *dithálassos* (1337), a reef or rocky projection protruding out into the sea and dividing it.

3883. παραλλαγή *parallagḗ*; gen. *parallagḗs*, fem. noun from *parallátto* (n.f.), to change alternately or in succession from one to another, which is from *pará* (3844), denoting transition, and *alláttō* or *allássō* (236), to change. Change, alteration, variableness, vicissitude (James 1:17; Sept.: 2 Kgs 9:20).

Syn.: *diákrisis* (1253), discrimination; *diastolé* (1293), difference, distinction.

Ant.: *bébaios* (949), firm.

3884. παραλογίζομαι *paralogízomai*; fut. *paralogísomai*, from *pará* (3844), aside, implying error, hence, wrongly, and *logízomai* (3049), to exercise one's reason. To reason falsely or incorrectly. In the NT, to deceive, to mislead, with the acc. of person (Col 2:4; James 1:22; Sept.: Josh 9:22; 1 Sam 19:17).

Syn.: *apatáō* (538), to deceive; *exapatáō* (1818), to deceive thoroughly; *phrenapatáō* (5422), to deceive; *dolióō* (1387), to lure; *dolóō* (1389), to ensnare; *planáō* (4105), to lead astray or wander; *kapēleúō* (2585), to gain by dealing in something for sordid personal advantage; *deleázō* (1185), to catch by bait; *katabrabeúō* (2603), beguile.

Ant.: *alētheúō* (226), to deal honestly, to be truthful or speak truthfully.

3885. παραλυτικός *paralutikós*; fem. *paralutikḗ*, neut. *paralutikón*, adj. from *paralúō* (3886), to paralyze. Paralytic, palsied; used as a subst. (Matt 4:24; 8:6; 9:2, 6; Mark 2:3–5, 9, 10). The paralytic is also called *paraleluménos* (Luke 5:17–26), the perf. pass. part. of *paralúō* (3886), to paralyze. Both of these are used to designate the nervous affliction variously known as paralysis or palsy, the latter denoting loss of motor power in a muscle or set of muscles and being equivalent to motor paralysis.

Syn.: *asthenés* (772), one lacking strength; *anápēros* (376), a handicapped person.

Ant.: *hugiḗs* (5199), whole, healthy.

3886. παραλύω *paralúō*; fut. *paralúsō*, from *pará* (3844) from, and *lúō* (3089), to loose. To loosen at or from the side, disjoin, relax (Sept.: Lev 13:45). In the NT, to dissolve, meaning to enfeeble, only in the perf. pass. part., *paraleluménos*, relaxed, enfeebled. The "feeble knees" referred to in Heb 12:12 is an allusion to Isa 35:3. See Sept.: Gen 19:11. It is also

used in the sense of paralytic (*paralutikós* [3885]; Luke 5:18, 24; Acts 8:7; 9:33).

Deriv.: *paralutikós* (3885), a paralytic.

Syn.: *asthenéō* (770), to make sick, enfeeble.

Ant.: *rhónnumi* (4517), to strengthen; *epischúō* (2001), to make strong; *sthenóō* (4599), to invigorate.

3887. παραμένω *paraménō*; fut. *paramenṓ*, from *pará* (3844), with, and *ménō* (3306), to remain. To stay, remain nearby with someone, abide (1 Cor 16:6; James 1:25, to persevere); remain in the priest's office (Heb 7:23).

Deriv.: *sumparaménō* (4839), to remain together.

Syn.: *diateléō* (1300), to continue; *apókeimai* (606), to be appointed, stay; *parákeimai* (3873), to be at hand, be present; *diaménō* (1265), to remain throughout or constant.

Ant.: *metakinéō* (3334), to move away; *metatíthēmi* (3346), to remove; *methístēmi* (3179), to transfer; *astatéō* (790), to be unsettled; *ekchōréō* (1633), to depart.

3888. παραμυθέομαι *paramuthéomai*; contracted *paramuthoúmai*, fut. *paramuthḗsomai*, mid. deponent from *pará* (3844), to, and *muthéomai* (n.f.), to speak, which is from *múthos* (3454), a tale, myth, speech. To speak kindly, soothingly, to comfort or pacify. In the NT, to encourage with the acc. of person expressed or implied (1 Thess 2:11; 5:14). To console, comfort, with the acc. of person stated (John 11:19, 31).

Deriv.: *paramuthía* (3889), consolation, comfort; *paramúthion* (3890), the agent of comfort.

Syn.: *parakaléō* (3870), to comfort; *sumparakaléō* (4837), to comfort together; *eupsuchéō* (2174), to make the soul feel good; *tharséō* (2293), to be of good comfort, to cheer.

Ant.: *lupéomai* (3076), to be sad; *thlíbō* (2346), to afflict; *turbázō* (5182), to disturb, trouble; *ochléō* (3791), to harass, vex; *enochléō* (1776), to disturb.

3889. παραμυθία *paramuthía*; gen. *paramuthías*, fem. noun from *paramuthéomai* (3888), to console. Exhortation, encouragement. In the NT, consolation, comfort (1 Cor 14:3). *Paramuthía* expresses a greater degree of tenderness, at least by word of mouth, than *paráklēsis* ([3874], comfort, encouragement) which carries a more general sense of helpfulness and comfort. It should also be distinguished from the neut. noun *paramúthion* (3890), the instrument or manner of comfort. A closer distinctive syn. of *paramuthía* is *parēgoría* (3931), to comfort through speech, from which is derived the Eng. word "paregoric," a soothing medication.

   Syn.: *parēgoría* (3931), comfort; *paráklēsis* (3876), encouragement.

   Ant.: *lúpē* (3077), sadness, sorrow; *thlípsis* (2347), affliction, trouble; *stenochōría* (4730), anguish, distress; *odúnē* (3601), dejection, grief; *pónos* (4192), pain.

3890. παραμύθιον *paramúthion*; gen. *paramuthíou*, neut. noun from *paramuthéomai* (3888), to comfort verbally. Consolation, comfort (Phil 2:1). This neut. noun has nearly the same meaning as the fem. *paramuthía* (3889). They differ in that the neut. noun indicates the instrument used by the one who is comforting, and the fem. noun stresses the process or progress of the act. The same distinction between the fem. noun and the neut. noun (the fem. being the result of comfort and the neut. the means for producing that result) holds true for *sōtēría* (4991), salvation, and *sōtḗrion* (4992); *marturía* (3141), testimony, and *martúrion* (3142), evidence, proof.

3891. παρανομέω *paranoméō*; fut. *paranomḗsō*, from *paránomos* (n.f.), contrary to the law, which is from *pará* (3844), beyond or contrary to, and *nómos* (3551), the law. To act aside from the law, violate law, transgress. Used in an absolute sense (Acts 23:3; Sept.: Ps 119:51). The high priest who had Paul struck on the mouth during interrogation was accused by Paul of violating the law (*paranoméō*, referring to an established ordinance, see Lev 19:15a [cf. John 18:22f.]) while pretending to administer the law. *Paranoméō* involved the law which was specific in not permitting the beating or striking of a person who was under judgment, as Paul mentioned in Acts 23:3, "And commandest me to be smitten contrary to the law?" Therefore, the word has the specific sense of transgressing a particular ordinance or regulation and is not just a general term for wrongdoing. The Roman authorities tended to reject the Jewish claims that Christian preaching was "contrary to the law," attributing them rather to internal controversies among the Jews. See the claims of Gallio (Acts 18:15); Claudius Lysias (Acts 23:29 [cf. Pilate in John 18:31]). The Christians did not believe that preaching the gospel was contrary to the Jewish law, but it was rather the fulfillment of the law (Matt 5:17–20).

   Deriv.: *paranomía* (3891), a transgression of the law.

   Syn.: *adikéō* (91), to act wrongly; *bláptō* (984), to injure, hurt; *parabaínō* (3845), to transgress; *athetéō* (114), to violate a law or custom.

   Ant.: *hupakoúō* (5219), to obey; *hupotássō* (2293), to submit; *peitharchéō* (3980), to obey authority.

3892. παρανομία *paranomía*; gen. *paranomías*, fem. noun from *paranoméō* (3891), to transgress the law. A transgression or an offense of the law (only in 2 Pet 2:16; see Sept.: Ps 37:7). The verb *paranoméō* (3891) occurs in Acts 23:3.

   Syn.: *anomía* (458), lawlessness; *hamartía* (266), sin; *adikía* (93), unrighteousness, injustice, wrong; *parábasis* (3847), the act of transgression; *parakoḗ* (3876), disobedience; *paráptōma* (3900), error; *kríma* (2917), judgment; *katákrima* (2631), condemnation; *opheílēma* (3783), fault, debt; *égklēma* (1462), crime; *sunōmosía* (4945), conspiracy.

Ant.: *hupakoḗ* (5218), obedience; *hupotagḗ* (5292), submission.

3893. παραπικραίνω *parapikraínō*; fut. *parapikranṓ*, from *pará* (3844), to the point of, unto, implying movement toward a certain point, and *pikraínō* (4087), to embitter. To provoke unto bitterness or anger, to exasperate, make bitter with or towards anyone, treat with bitterness. In the NT, only in Heb 3:16, meaning to provoke God by disobedience See Sept.: Ps 5:10; 78:17, 40, 56; Lam 1:20; Ezek 20:21.

Deriv.: *parapikrasmós* (3894), irritation, provocation.

Syn.: *paroxúnō* (3947), literally to sharpen, metaphorically to rouse to anger, provoke; *erethízō* (2042), to excite, stir up; *parorgízō* (3949), to provoke to wrath; *parazēlóō* (3863), to provoke to jealousy; *apostomatízō* (653), to cause someone to speak out; *prokaléō* (4292), to call forth to a contest.

Ant.: *paramuthéomai* (3888), to soothe.

3894. παραπικρασμός *parapikrasmós*; gen. *parapikrasmoú*, masc. noun from *parapikraínō* (3893), to provoke to bitterness. A bitter provocation, exasperation (Heb 3:8, 15; Sept.: Ps 95:8).

Syn.: *paroxusmós* (3948) stimulation.

Ant.: *chrēstótēs* (5544), gentleness.

3895. παραπίπτω *parapíptō*; fut. *parapesoúmai*, 2d aor. *parépeson*, from *pará* (3844), to the side of or from, implying error, and *píptō* (4098), to fall. To fall aside or away, err, stray, lapse. Used only in Heb 6:6, denoting a falling away, an abandonment. Some have suggested that this word and its noun *paráptōma* ([3900], a lapse, error, wrongdoing) indicate errors of weakness, faults or accidents and do not represent deliberate, blameworthy or willful sin, contending that this would be expressed by *parabaínō* (3845), to willfully transgress.

However, the *usus loquendi* of the words (verb and noun) yield no such meaning but in every case signify deliberate acts of sin. See Sept.: Ezek 18:24; 20:27.

Deriv.: *paráptōma* (3900), transgression.

Syn.: *rhíptomai* (4496), to fling oneself; *katapíptō* (2667), to fall down.

Ant.: *orthopodéō* (3716), to walk straight; *ananēphō* (366), to recover self, regain one's senses; *anorthóō* (461), to straighten up.

3896. παραπλέω *parapléō*; fut. *parapleúsomai*, from *pará* (3844), by, past, beyond, and *pléō* (4126), to sail. To sail near, by, or past a place (Acts 20:16).

Syn.: *paralégomai* (3881), to sail along; *diaperáō* (1276), to cross over; *braduploéō* (1020), to sail slowly.

3897. παραπλήσιον *paraplḗsion*; adv., the neut. of *paraplḗsios*, nearby, from *pará* (3844), close to, and *plēsíos* (4139), near. Nearby, close to, similarly (Phil 2:27, meaning he was sick near to death).

Deriv.: *paraplēsíōs* (3898), near to, nigh.

Syn.: *pará* (3844), near; *perí* (4012), around, nearby; *eggús* (1451), nigh or near; *paraplēsíōs* (3898), nearby; *homoíōs* (3668), in like manner; *hōsaútōs* (5615), as, likewise; *kaí* (2532), and, even, likewise; *hoútōs* (3779), thus, likewise; *oún* (3767), therefore, likewise.

Ant.: *makrán* (3112), far; *pórrō* (4206), at a distance; *péran* (4008), beyond, on the other side; *epékeina* (1900), beyond.

3898. παραπλησίως *paraplēsíōs*; adv. from *paraplḗsion* (3897), close to. Near to, nigh, and thus: like, in like manner though not altogether the same as (Heb 2:14).

Syn.: *homoíōs* (3668), likewise; *hōsaútōs* (3615), just so, likewise; *kaí* (2532), and, likewise; *hoútōs* (3779), thus, likewise; *kathṓs* (2531), as, likewise; *hópōs* (3704), in the manner that;

hósper (5618), exactly like; *hōseí* (5616), as if, as.

Ant.: *polutrópōs* (4187), in various ways; *állōs* (247), otherwise; *hetérōs* (2088), otherwise.

3899. παραπορεύομαι *paraporeúomai*; fut. *paraporeúsomai*, from *pará* (3844), near, by, or denoting transition, and *poreúomai* (4198), to go, pass. To go near or by the side of someone, accompany. Used intrans. meaning to pass by or along by (Mark 11:20). As a part., *hoi paraporeuómenoi*, the passers-by (Matt 27:39; Mark 15:29). Followed by *diá* (1223), through, with the gen. of place, through which (Mark 2:23; 9:30; Sept.: Deut 2:4; Josh 6:7).

Syn.: *parérchomai* (3928), to come or go by or past; *paragínomai* (3854), to go by; *chōréō* (5562), to pass by; *parágō* (3855), to pass by.

Ant.: *apochōréō* (672), to go away.

3900. παράπτωμα *paráptōma*; gen. *paraptṓmatos*, neut. noun from *parapíptō* (3895), to fall by the wayside. Fault, lapse, error, mistake, wrongdoing. Sometimes used in profane Gr. when it is intended to designate a sin not necessarily heinous in nature. Although it represents errors or faults of weakness, it does not necessarily fail to imply culpability. The related word, *parábasis* (3847), designates sin which is the willful transgression of a known rule of life and involves guilt (Rom 5:14, 15). *Parábasis* is the stronger of the two words being used once in connection with salvation (Heb 9:15), and elsewhere only with reference to imputation and punishment (Heb 2:2). *Paráptōma*, on the other hand, occurring only in Paul's writings and Matt 6:14, 15; 18:35; Mark 11:25, 26; James 5:16, is often used where pardon is spoken of (Gal 6:1). It is used of sin in general (Gal 6:1; Sept.: Ps 19:12). In Rom 5:16, it stands in antithesis to *dikaíōma* (1345), righteousness or justification, or an acquittal from past offenses and the ability to exercise the right of a child toward God as one's

legitimate Father (see Rom 5:18). It also occurs in Rom 4:25; 5:15–18, 20; 11:11, 12; 2 Cor 5:19; Eph 1:7; 2:1, 5; Col 2:13; James 5:16.

Syn.: *hamartía* (266), offense, sin; *parábasis* (3847), violation, transgression.

3901. παραρρέω *pararréō*; contracted *paararruō̂*, fut. *parareúsomai*, from *pará* (3844), by, past, beyond, and *rhéō* (4483), to flow. To float by or drift past as a ship, or to flow past as a river. Figuratively to slip away, suggesting a gradual and almost unnoticed movement past a certain point. Of a person, to move stealthily as a thief. It is used figuratively of persons meaning to glide away, to swerve or deviate from something, such as the truth, law, precepts; equivalent to *parapíptō* (3895), to fall aside. It occurs only in Heb 2:1 where it is used in an absolute sense "lest we drift away from that which we have heard" (a.t.), transgress. It is parallel with *parabaínō* (3845), to go contrary to, transgress, and *parakoúō* (3878), to disobey. See Sept.: Prov 3:21.

3902. παράσημος *parásēmos*; gen. *parasḗmou*, masc.-fem., neut. *parásēmon*, adj. from *pará* (3844), to the side of or at, and *sḗma* (n.f., see *ásēmos* [767]), a mark. The sign or ensign of a ship by which it is distinguished from others (Acts 28:11).

3903. παρασκευάζω *paraskeuázō*; fut. *paraskeuásō*, from *pará* (3844), for, and *skeuázō* (n.f., see *anaskeuázō* [384]), to prepare. To make ready, to prepare food or something else. Used in an absolute sense in Acts 10:10. In the mid. / pass. *paraskeuázomai* to prepare oneself, get ready (2 Cor 9:2, 3). Followed by *eis pólemon* (*eis* [1519], unto; *pólemon* [4171], war), to the battle (1 Cor 14:8; Sept.: Jer 50:42).

Deriv.: *aparaskeúastos* (532), unprepared; *paraskeué* (3904), readiness, preparation, used of the day of preparation for the Sabbath.

Syn.: *hetoimázō* (2090), to prepare; *katartízō* (2675), to make completely ready for a purpose; *kataskeuázō* (2680), to put together, establish, build; *proetoimázō* (4282), to prepare beforehand; *prokatartízō* (4294), to prepare in advance.

Ant.: *ameléō* (272), to neglect; *paratheōréō* (3865), to overlook.

**3904. παρασκευή *paraskeuḗ*; gen. *paraskeuḗs*, fem. noun from *paraskeuázō* (3903), to prepare. Making ready, preparation. In the NT, used in reference to the day or hours spent in preparation for the Jewish Sabbath or festivals; the eve of the Sabbath (Matt 27:62; Mark 15:42; Luke 23:54; John 19:14, 31, 42). The same is also called *prosábbaton* (4315), the day before the Sabbath (Mark 15:42).

Syn.: *hetoimasía* (2091), readiness, preparation; *katártisis* (2676), the process of making fit; *katartismós* (2677), fitting preparation.

**3905. παρατείνω *parateínō*; fut. *paratenṓ*, from *pará* (3844), to, and *teínō* (n.f., see below), to stretch out. To stretch out near, by, or to; to extend near (Sept.: Gen 49:13). In the NT, used metaphorically, meaning to extend, prolong, continue with reference to time (Acts 20:7).

Deriv. of *teínō* (n.f.): *ekteínō* (1614), to stretch out; *proteínō* (4285), to stretch forward.

Ant.: *suntémnō* (4932), to cut short.

**3906. παρατηρέω *paratēréō*; contracted *paratērṓ*, fut. *paratērḗsō*, from *pará* (3844), near or close, to and *tēréō* (5083), to keep, observe. To watch closely, observe, as the gates of a city (Acts 9:24; Sept.: Ps 37:12); to observe a person insidiously (Mark 3:2; Luke 6:7; 14:1; 20:20); to observe days scrupulously (Gal 4:10).

Deriv.: *paratērēsis* (3907), attentive watching.

Syn.: *parakolouthéō* (3877), to attend to, follow near, watch; *blépō* (991), look at; *theáomai* (2300), to look closely at, perceive; *theōréō* (2334), to behold intensely, consider, perceive, see; *horáō* (3708), to attend to.

Ant.: *ameléō* (272), to neglect; *paratheōréō* (3865), to overlook; *kōlúō* (2967), to hinder, stop.

**3907. παρατήρησις *paratḗrēsis*; gen. *paratērḗseōs*, fem. noun from *paratēréō* (3906), to watch closely. Attentive watching (Luke 17:20, as can be observed by the eyes).

**3908. παρατίθημι *paratíthēmi*; fut. *parathḗsō*, from *pará* (3844), near or unto, and *títhēmi* (5087), to put. To put or place near someone, used trans.

(I) In regard to food, to set or lay before someone, with the acc. of thing and dat. of person expressed or implied (Mark 6:41; 8:6, 7; Luke 9:16; 10:8; 11:6; Acts 16:34; 1 Cor 10:27; Sept.: Gen 18:8; 24:33; 2 Sam 12:20).

(II) Metaphorically, as a teacher, to set or lay before, to propound, deliver, with the acc. and dat. (Matt 13:24, 31); mid. voice followed by *hóti* (3754), that (Acts 17:3).

(III) The mid. *paratíthemai* 2d aor. *parethḗmēn*, 2d aor. imper. *paráthou* (2 Tim 2:2), all meaning to place with someone for one's own sake, to give in charge, to commit, entrust, with acc. and dat. (Luke 12:48; 1 Tim 1:18; 2 Tim 2:2; 1 Pet 4:19). "Into thy hands I shall commit [*parathḗsomai*] my spirit" (a.t. [Luke 23:46 {cf. Ps 31:5}]). In the sense of to commend, with acc. and dat., *paréthento autoús tṓ kuriṓ*, "they commended them to the Lord" (Acts 14:23); *paratíthemai humás . . . tṓ theṓ*, "I commend you . . . to God" (Acts 20:32).

Deriv.: *parathḗkē* (3866), deposit.

Syn.: *paradídōmi* (3860), to deliver over; *parístēmi* (3936), to place near or set before; *sunístēmi* or *sunistánō* (4921), to approve or represent as worthy; *tēréō* (5083), keep, watch, preserve;

bállō (906), to throw, put; *dídōmi* (1325), to give.

Ant.: *metatíthēmi* (3346), to remove; *metakinéō* (3334), to move away; *methístēmi* (3179), to transfer; *ekchōréō* (1633), to depart out; *lambánō* (2983), to take; *analambánō* (353) and *anairéō* (337), to take up; *apolambánō* (618), to receive; *epilambánō* (1949), to lay hold of; *katalambánō* (2638), to take; *paralambánō* (3880), to receive to oneself; *proslambánō* (4355), to take to oneself; *aírō* (142), to lift, take up or away; *apaírō* (522), to lift off; *exaírō* (1808) and *aphairéō* (851), to take away; *epaírō* (1869), to lift, raise; *piázō* (4084), to seize; *harpázō* (726), to take forcibly.

3909. **παρατυγχάνω** *paratugchánō*; fut. *parateúxomai*, 2d aor. *parétuchon*, from *pará* (3844), near, and *tugchánō* (5177), happen to be, chance upon. To fall in with someone, to happen near. Part. noun in the pl., *hoi paratugchánontes* (Acts 17:17, those who happen to be near).

3910. **παραυτίκα** *parautíka*; adv. from *pará* (3844), at, and *autíka* (n.f.), immediately or at this present time, which is from *autós* (846), this, as referring to time, and *híkō* (n.f.), to come. Immediately, at this very instant, instantly. In the NT, used once with the art. as an adj. meaning momentary, transient (2 Cor 4:17).

Syn.: *en atómō* (*en* [1722], in; *atómō*, the dat. of *átomos* [823], that which cannot be cut) as in 1 Cor 15:52, "in a moment" or in a fraction of time, i.e., not divisible; *en rhipé ophthalmoú* (*en*, in; *rhipé* [4493], instance, twinkling; *ophthalmoú* [3788], eye), meaning in the twinkling of an eye or in a very short time; *en stigmé* (*en*, in; *stigmé*, the dat. of *stigmé* [4743], a prick or point, a moment), used metaphorically in Luke 4:5 to mean in a moment; *tachú* (5035), suddenly, speedily; *euthéōs* (2112), at once, forthwith, immediately; *parachréma* (3916), instantly, immediately.

Ant.: *hústeros* (5306), later.

3911. **παραφέρω** *paraphérō*; 2d aor. *parénegkon*, from *pará* (3844), past, by, beyond, and *phérō* (5342), to bring, bear. To carry past, bring or bear along or by, bear away (as a stream bears away). In the NT:

(I) Used metaphorically in the act. voice, meaning to let pass away, to avert evil, with the acc. of thing (Mark 14:36; Luke 22:42).

(II) In the pass. voice meaning to be borne along by or carried away, as clouds (Jude 1:12, where it means driven rapidly along). Metaphorically, to be borne or carried away in mind (Heb 13:9). In both of these passages, the TR has *periphéromai* (4064), to bear or carry about.

Syn.: *metabaínō* (3327), to pass over from one place to another; *methístēmi* (3179), to cause to remove; *metatíthēmi* (3346), to remove a person or thing from one place to another; *metoikízō* (3351), to remove to a new dwelling place; *apochōrízō* (673), to separate; *kinéō* (2795), to move; *apaírō* (522), to take up or away; *aphairéō* (851), to take away; *ekbállō* (1544), to take out; *parágō* (3855), to go along or away, depart, pass by; *exérchomai* (1831), to come forth, proceed; *parérchomai* (3928), to pass away.

3912. **παραφρονέω** *paraphronéō*; contracted *paraphronó*, fut. *paraphronésō*, from *pará* (3844), aside or beyond, i.e., extending past a given limit, and *phronéō* (5426), to think. To be beside oneself or out of one's mind, to be silly, act foolishly. Used in an absolute sense in 2 Cor 11:23.

Deriv.: *paraphronía* (3913), madness.

Syn.: *maínomai* (3105), to rage, act like a maniac.

Ant.: *sōphronéō* (4993), to be of a sound mind; *phronéō* (5426), to think; *logízomai* (3049), to reason.

3913. παραφρονία *paraphronía*; gen. *paraphronías*, fem. noun from *paráphrōnéo* (3912), to be beside oneself. Out of one's mind. Insanity, folly, madness (2 Pet 2:16).

Syn.: *aphrosúnē* (877), folly; *mōría* (3472), foolishness; *ékstasis* (1611), frenzied amazement; *manía* (3130), frenzy, madness; *ánoia* (454), lack of understanding or mind.

Ant.: *sōphrosúnē* (4997), self-control; *súnesis* (4907), understanding; *phrónēsis* (5428), prudence; *sophía* (4678), wisdom.

3914. παραχειμάζω *paracheimázō*; fut. *paracheimásō*, from *pará* (3844), at, and *cheimázō* (5492), to be tossed with tempest. To winter or spend the winter, used intrans. (Acts 27:12; 28:11; 1 Cor 16:6; Titus 3:12).

Deriv.: *paracheimasía* (3915), the spending of the winter.

3915. παραχειμασία *paracheimasía*; gen. *paracheimasías*, fem. noun from *paracheimázō* (3914), to spend the winter. Spending the winter (Acts 27:12).

3916. παραχρῆμα *parachrēma*; adv. from *pará* (3844), at, and *chrēma* (5536), something useful or needed. At the very moment, on the spot, forthwith, immediately, directly after something else has taken place (Matt 21:19, 20; Luke 1:64; 4:39; 5:25; 8:44, 47, 55; 13:13; 18:43; 19:11; 22:60; Acts 3:7; 5:10; 9:18; 12:23; 13:11; 16:26, 33; Sept.: Num 6:9; 12:14; Isa 30:13).

Syn.: *exautēs* (1824), at once, immediately; *euthéōs* (2112), at once, straightway; *euthús* (2117), forthwith, *parautíka* (3910), immediately; *tachéōs* (5030), quickly, suddenly.

Ant.: *hústeron* (5305), afterward, later; *épeita* (1899), then, afterward.

3917. πάρδαλις *párdalis*, gen. *pardáleōs*, fem. noun. A panther, leopard (Rev 13:2; Sept.: Isa 11:6; Jer 5:6).

3918. πάρειμι *páreimi*; fut. *parésomai*, from *pará* (3844), near, with, and *eimí* (1510), to be. To be nearby, present, to have come. Used in an absolute sense (John 7:6; 11:28; Acts 10:21; 17:6; 1 Cor 5:3; 2 Cor 10:2, 11; 13:2, 10; 2 Pet 1:12, meaning the truth which is with you, which ye have received). Followed by *en* (1722), in, with the dat. of time (Luke 13:1); *eis* (1519), into, and the acc. of person (Col 1:6); *epí* (1909), upon, with the gen. of person meaning before whom (Acts 24:19); *epí* (1909), upon, and the relative pron. *hō* ([3739] *eph' hō* or *eph' hō*, of purpose) meaning for what purpose (Matt 26:50); *enópion* (1799), before someone, with the gen. (Acts 10:33); *prós* (4314), toward, with the acc. (Acts 12:20; 2 Cor 11:9; Gal 4:18, 20). The part. in the neut. with the art. *tó parón*, the present, in reference to time (Heb 12:11, for this present time). When speaking of things, followed by the dat. of person (2 Pet 1:9, meaning the person who has not these things). With the def. art. in the pl. and the part., *tá parónta*, things which one has, property, fortune, condition (Heb 13:5).

Deriv.: *parousía* (3952), presence, coming or arrival; *sumpáreimi* (4840), to be present with.

Syn.: *paragínomai* (3854) and *hēkō* (2240), to be present; *aphiknéomai* (864), to arrive at a place; *ephístēmi* (2186), to stand by or over; *katantáō* (2658), to come to a place, arrive; *parístēmi* (3936), to stand by or near; *proseggízō* (4331), to come near; *parákeimai* (3873), to lie beside.

Ant.: *ápeimi* (548), to be absent; *hupágō* (5217), *apérchomai* (565), *apobaínō* (576), and *parérchomai* (3928), to go away; *metabaínō* (3327), to pass over, depart; *anachōréō* (402), to withdraw, to part; *éxeimi* (1826) and *exérchomai* (1831), to go out; *apodēméō* (589), to go to another country; *paragínomai* (3854) and *ágō* (71), to go; *ekporeúomai* (1607), to go out of, emanate, proceed; *hodoiporéō* (3596), to go on a journey.

3919. παρεισάγω *pareiságō*, fut. *pareisáxō*, from *pará* (3844), unto or at the side of, and *eiságō* (1521), to bring in, introduce. To bring in by the side of, to introduce along with others. In the NT, to lead or bring in secretly or craftily, to smuggle in. Used trans. in regard to heresies brought into the church (2 Pet 2:1).

Deriv.: *pareísaktos* (3920), smuggled in.

Syn.: *pareisdúnō* (3921), to creep in unawares; *pareisérchomai* (3922), to enter in secretly.

3920. παρείσακτος *pareísaktos*; gen. *pareisáktou*, masc.-fem., neut. *pareísakton*, adj. from *pareiságō* (3919), to smuggle in. Smuggled in, brought in secretly. Used subst. of false brothers (Judaizers) who were allowed to join the fellowship of the church (Gal 2:4).

3921. παρεισδύω *pareisdúō*; fut. *pareisdúsō*, from *pará* (3844), unto or at the side of, and *eisdúō* (n.f.), to enter in, which is from *eis* (1519), into, and *dúō* (1416), to go down, sink. To enter in craftily, secretly, without notice, like a thief. Used of the action of false teachers entering into the church under false claims (Jude 1:4).

Syn.: *pareiságō* (3919), to bring in secretly; *pareisérchomai* (3922), to come in or enter secretly.

3922. παρεισέρχομαι *pareisérchomai*; 2d aor. *pareisēlthon*, from *pará* (3844), alongside, and *eisérchomai* (1525), to enter. To enter, to come in privily. Intrans.:

(I) To come in to, near, or with something so as to be present with or beside it. In Rom 5:20, "the law entered besides" (a.t.), indicating that the Law of Moses was added to something already in existence. Men were sinners long before the Law was given; God had begun to implement the plan of salvation before the Law was given. The purpose of the Law's entrance into the world was not to redeem men (this only Christ could do), nor was it to make men sinful. Paul had already explained that man is guilty of Adam's sin, i.e., those from the time of Adam to the time of Moses (Rom 5:12). The Law was given that sin might be made more evident.

(II) To go or come in by stealth, to enter unawares. Used intrans. (Gal 2:4).

Syn.: *pareisdúnō* (3921), to creep in without notice, like a thief.

3923. παρεισφέρω *pareisphérō*; 2d aor. *pareisénegka*, from *pará* (3844), alongside or beside, and *eisphérō* (n.f.), to bring into, which is from *eis* (1519), into, and *phérō* (5342), to bring. To bring forth something additional, to contribute in addition to, yield more, add to (2 Pet 1:5).

3924. παρεκτός *parektós*; adv. from *pará* (3844), at or near, and *ektós* (1622), aside from, except. Out near, out by. Metaphorically, "besides," with the art. in the pl., *tá parektós*, the things besides, over and above (2 Cor 11:28). With a gen., in the sense of "except" (Matt 5:32; Acts 26:29).

Syn.: *plén* (4133), except; *chōrís* (5565), apart from, without; *áneu* (427), without; *mónon* (3440), alone.

Ant.: *metá* (3326), with; *sún* (4862), with; *homoú* (3674), together.

3925. παρεμβολή *parembolḗ*; gen. *parembolḗs*, fem. noun from *parembébola*, the perf. mid. of *parembállō* (only in Luke 19:43 [UBS]), to set up alongside, which is from *pará* (3844), alongside, and *embállō* (1685), to throw. Something thrown up next to, or between, something else; an interjection or an interpolation. As a military term, it demonstrated a certain method of drawing up troops. Metonymically it means array, an army or host drawn up in battle array (Heb 11:34). In later usage, encampment, hence, a camp. Spoken of a standing camp, equivalent to quarters or barracks, such as the quarters of

the Roman soldiers in Antonia, the fortress ("castle" in the KJV) in Jerusalem
which was adjacent to the temple and
from which the Romans kept control of
the Jews (Acts 21:34, 37; 22:24; 23:10,
16, 32). Spoken also of the encampments
of the Israelites in the desert (Heb 13:11,
13 [cf. Lev 4:12, 21; 16:27]; Sept.: 1 Sam
4:5, 6; 2 Kgs 7:5, 7).

Syn.: *stráteuma* (4753), an army;
stratópedon (4760), an army encampment.

3926. παρενοχλέω *parenochléō*; contracted *parenochló*, fut. *parenochlḗsō*,
from *pará* (3844), in addition to or beside, and *enochléō* (1776), to disturb. To
create additional disturbance, add ex-
tra trouble, with the dat. of person (Acts
15:19; Sept.: Job 16:3; Mic 6:3).

Syn.: *tarássō* (5015), to trouble;
diatarássō (1298), to agitate greatly,
and *ektarássō* (1613), to trouble greatly; *thlíbō* (2346), to afflict; *skúllō* (4660),
to vex, annoy; *anastatóō* (387), to upset;
thorubázō or *thorubéō* (2350), to disturb;
turbázō (5182), to trouble; *diaponéō*
(1278), to experience pain throughout;
basanízō (928), to torment, vex.

Ant.: *euthuméō* (2114), to cheer up;
eupsuchéō (2174), to be in good spirits.

3927. παρεπίδημος *parepídēmos*; gen.
parepídēmou, masc.-fem., neut. *parepí-
dēmon*, adj. from *pará* (3844), near or
close to, and *epídēmos* (n.f.), stranger,
which is from *epí* (1909), in or among,
and *dēmos* (1218), a people. A stranger,
sojourner; not simply one who is passing
through, but a foreigner who has settled
down, however briefly, next to or among
the native people (Heb 11:13; 1 Pet 1:1;
2:11; Sept.: Gen 23:4; Ps 39:12). Also
from *epídēmos* (n.f.): *epidēméō* (1927),
to reside as a stranger.

Syn.: *pároikos* (3941), alien, sojourner; *apódēmos* (590), sojourner, living in
another country; *xénos* (3581), a stranger, foreigner; *allótrios* (245), stranger;
allogenḗs (241), one of a different race.

Ant.: *oikeíos* (3609), one of the
same household; *polítēs* (4177), citizen;
sumpolítēs (4847), fellow citizen.

3928. παρέρχομαι *parérchomai*; fut.
pareleúsomai, 2d aor. *parḗlthon*, from
pará (3844), near, denoting proximity,
and *érchomai* (2064), to come, go. To
pass near, away, by, or over. Intrans.:
(I) To come near to any person or
thing, to draw near, to come (Mark 6:48);
as to a table (Luke 12:37; 17:7); in a hostile manner (Acts 24:7).

(II) To pass near, to pass along by.
(A) Particularly and in an absolute
sense (Luke 18:37). Followed by the
acc. of person or place (Mark 6:48; Acts
16:8); *diá tḗs hodoú* (*diá* [1223], through,
by; *tḗs hodoú* [3598], the road) meaning
by the road (Matt 8:28). Spoken of time
in an absolute sense, meaning to pass by,
to be past (Matt 14:15; Acts 27:9; 1 Pet
4:3; Sept.: Job 17:11; Song 2:11).

(B) Metaphorically, to pass away, perish. **(1)** Used in an absolute sense in a
general way (Matt 5:18; 24:34, 35; Mark
13:30, 31; Luke 16:17; 21:32, 33; 2 Cor
5:17; James 1:10; 2 Pet 3:10; Rev 21:1;
Sept.: Ps 37:36). **(2)** Used also of words
or declarations meaning to pass away
without fulfillment, to be in vain (Matt
5:18; 24:35; Mark 13:31; Luke 21:33).

(C) Metaphorically of evils, to pass
away from someone, be removed, averted, followed by *apó* (575), from, with
the gen. of person (Matt 26:39, 42; Mark
14:35).

(D) Metaphorically meaning to pass
by or over, to neglect, transgress, with
the acc. (Luke 11:42; 15:29; Sept.: Deut
26:13; Jer 34:18).

Deriv.: *antiparérchomai* (492), to pass
by on the other side.

Syn.: *anachōréō* (402), to withdraw,
depart; *hupochōréō* (5298), to go back,
retire; *éxeimi* (1826), to go out; *ápeimi*
(549), to go away; *apodēméō* (589), to
go to another country; *parágō* (3855),
to pass by or away; *katargéō* (2673), to
abolish; *anastréphō* (390), to turn back.

Ant.: *paragínomai* (3854), to arrive; *hḗkō* (2240), to come, be present; *aphiknéomai* (864), to arrive; *katantáō* (2658), to come to; *parístēmi* (3936), to stand by or near.

3929. πάρεσις *páresis*; gen. *paréseōs*, fem. noun from *paríēmi* (3935), to let pass by. A passing over, an overlooking of faults. It refers to the putting aside of our sins, without punishment, as in Rom 3:25 (KJV) where it is translated "remission." This is more equivalent to *áphesis* (859), forgiveness, pardon. *Áphiesis* is the actual remission of sins, the canceling of moral indebtedness. This presupposes Christ's sacrifice as punishment for sin, which *páresis* does not. *Páresis* is only the passing over of transgression, i.e., the suspension of a penalty and not the removal of it.

3930. παρέχω *paréchō*; fut. *paréxō*, from *pará* (3844), unto, at, near, and *échō* (2192), to have, hold. To hold out toward someone, to present, offer.

(I) Particularly with the acc. (Luke 6:29).

(II) Figuratively, meaning to be the cause, source, occasion of something to a person, to make or do, give or bestow, show, occasion in one's behalf, with the acc. and dat. expressed or implied. With *kópon* (2873), trouble, to give one trouble, to vex (Matt 26:10; Mark 14:6; Luke 11:7; 18:5; Gal 6:17); *ergasía* (2039), work, to make or bring gain to someone (Acts 16:16); *pístis* (4102), faith, having made available to everyone the capacity to experience saving faith so that all who do not believe are responsible for their unbelief (Acts 17:31); *hēsuchía* (2271), quietness, silence (Acts 22:2; Sept.: Job 34:29); *philanthrōpía* (5363), benevolence (Acts 28:2). In the mid. *paréchomai*, to do or show for oneself, for one's own part (Luke 7:4, "for whom he should [on His part] do this"; Acts 19:24). With *tó díkaion* (1342), that which is just (Col 4:1, "bestow on your part that which is just to servants" [a.t.]); *seautón* (4572),

thyself (Titus 2:7, "showing thyself a pattern of good works").

Syn.: *prosphérō* (4374), to bring, present, offer; *gínomai* (1096), to become; *dídōmi* (1325), to give; *chorēgéō* (5524), supply.

Ant.: *déchomai* (1209), to receive, accept; *paradéchomai* (3858), to receive; *prosdéchomai* (4327), to receive to oneself; *apodéchomai* (588), to accept gladly.

3931. παρηγορία *parēgoría*; gen. *parēgorías*, fem. noun from *parēgoréō* (n.f.), to speak with, hence to exhort, console. Consolation, comfort, solace (using more than just words as *paramuthía* [{3889}, consolation] implies). Found only in Col 4:11. The Eng. "paregoric," a soothing medication, is derived from the word *parēgoría*.

Syn.: *paráklēsis* (3874), consolation; *paramúthion* (3890), the instrument of consolation; *paramuthía* (3889), the act of consoling.

3932. παρθενία *parthenía*; gen. *parthenías*, fem. noun from *parthénos* (3933), virgin. Virginity, virgin age (Luke 2:36, meaning she had married as a virgin; Sept.: Jer 3:4).

3933. παρθένος *parthénos*; gen. *parthénou*, masc.-fem., adj. In the NT:

(I) In the fem. as a subst., *hē parthénos* means a virgin, maiden.

(A) Particularly in the sense of one who has not known a man (Matt 1:23: "A virgin shall be with child," quoted from Isa 7:14; Luke 1:27 [cf. Luke 1:34]; Sept.: Gen 24:16; 1 Kgs 1:2). Used metaphorically (2 Cor 11:2).

(B) Generally it refers to a maiden or damsel of marriageable age (Matt 25:1, 7, 11; Acts 21:9; 1 Cor 7:25, 28, 34, where the "virgin" stands as equivalent to the unmarried; vv. 36, 37 referring to a virgin daughter, marriageable but unmarried; Sept.: Gen 24:14, 43, 55; 34:3).

(II) Used as a masc. adj. in Rev 14:4, referring either literally to chaste, pure men who have not known women or are unmarried for the sake of greater devotion to Christ (1 Cor 7:33), or figuratively to the spiritually pure, God's people who have not defiled themselves with the daughters of this world (i.e., the world-system, called Babylon in Rev).

Deriv.: *parthenía* (3932), virginity.

Syn.: *ágamos* (22), unmarried, (subst.) an unmarried person.

Ant.: *gunḗ* (1135), a woman or wife; *anḗr* (435), a man or husband.

3934. Πάρθος Párthos; gen. *Párthou*, masc. proper noun. A Parthian, an inhabitant of Parthia. Little is known of their origin, though there appears to be a definite connection to the Iranian tribes. Though they revolted against the Persians, it was the middle of the third century B.C. before King Arsaces led them to independence. They became a powerful enemy of the Roman Empire. In fact the Parthians and the Romans were almost constantly at war. It was the Parthian invasion of Syria in 40 B.C. that forced Herod to flee to Rome for military aid. When he arrived in Rome, Herod was recognized as a hero and named "king of the Jews." Parthians were at Jerusalem during Pentecost (Acts 2:9).

3935. παρίημι paríēmi; fut. *parḗsō*, from *pará* (3844), aside, and *híēmi* (n.f., see *iós* [2447]), to send. To neglect, leave unattended, figuratively to loosen, relax. Found in Luke 11:42 in the UBS; occurs in the TR only in Heb 12:12, *cheíres pareiménai* (*cheíres* [5495], hands; *pareiménai*, perf. pass. part., enfeebled), hands hanging down from weariness or despondency (Sept.: Zeph 3:16).

Deriv.: *páresis* (3929), a passing by.

Syn.: *paralúō* (3886), to paralyze, enfeeble.

Ant.: *dunamóō* (1412), to strengthen.

3936. παριστάνω paristánō and **παρίστημι parístēmi** fut. *parastḗsō*, 2d aor. *paréstēn*, from *pará* (3844), near, and *hístēmi* (2476), to place, stand. Trans., to cause to stand near or before; intrans., to stand near or before, to be present.

(I) Trans. in the pres. imperf., fut., and aor. in the act., to cause to stand near, to place nearby. In the NT, to place or set before someone, present, exhibit.

(A) Generally with the acc. and dat. expressed or implied (Luke 2:22; Acts 1:3; 9:41; 23:33; Rom 6:13, 16, 19; 12:1; 2 Cor 4:14; 11:2; Eph 5:27; Col 1:22, 28; 2 Tim 2:15).

(B) To place at hand, supply (Matt 26:53; Acts 23:24).

(C) In the sense of commend (1 Cor 8:8), the same as *epainéō* (1867), to applaud, praise.

(D) Metaphorically, to set forth by arguments, to show, prove (Acts 24:13).

(II) Intrans. in the 2d aor., perf., and pluperf. in the act. and in the mid., to stand near or by.

(A) Generally with the meaning of to be present, with the dat. expressed or implied (Mark 15:39, meaning who stood by him; John 18:22; 19:26; Acts 1:10; 9:39; 27:23; Sept.: Gen 18:8; 45:1; 1 Sam 22:6, 7). As a part. used as a subst., *hoi parestēkótes* or *hoi parestótes*, those standing by, the bystanders (Mark 14:47, 69, 70; 15:35; Acts 23:2, 4) With *enṓpion* (1799), before someone (Acts 4:10). Figuratively, in a friendly sense, to stand by, to aid, with a dat. (Rom 16:2; 2 Tim 4:17). By implication in a hostile sense, in an absolute sense (Acts 4:26 quoted from Ps 2:2). Spoken of time, a season, equivalent with to be present, to have come (Mark 4:29).

(B) To stand before someone, in his presence, e.g., in a rhetorical sense, before a judge (Acts 27:24). Spoken of attendants or ministers who wait in the presence of a superior (Luke 1:19). In the dat. (Luke 19:24). Followed by the dat. (Sept.: Gen 40:4; Ex 24:13; Deut 1:38; 1 Sam 16:21, 22).

Syn.: *phérō* (5342), to bring; *érchomai* (2064), to come, go; *prosérchomai* (4334), to come or go near to; *paragínomai* (3854), to come, to stand or be by, be present; *hḗkō* (2240), to come, to be present; *aphiknéomai* (864), to arrive; *katantáō* (2658), to come to, arrive; *phthánō* (5348), to arrive; *proseggízō* (4331), to come near; *prosphérō* (4374), to offer, present; *emphanízō* (1718), to appear, manifest; *anaphaínomai* (398), to appear; *epiphaínō* (2014), to shine upon, appear; *phaneróō* (5319), to appear, declare, manifest; *epideíknumi* (1925), to exhibit, show.

Ant.: *aphístēmi* (868), to depart or withdraw; *ápeimi* (549), to be absent; *ekdēméō* (1553), to be absent or away from.

3937. Παρμενᾶς *Parmenás*; gen. *Parmená*, masc. proper noun. Parmenas, meaning steadfast. One of the seven deacons ordained by the disciples to administer alms to the widows and the poor of the church (only in Acts 6:5).

3938. πάροδος *párodos*; gen. *paródou*, fem. noun from *pará* (3844), by or through, and *hodós* (3598), road, way, journey. A passing by or through. With the prep. *en* (1722), in, and the dat. *paródō*, meaning by the way or in passing (1 Cor 16:7).

Syn.: *poreía* (4197), a journey.

3939. παροικέω *paroikéō*; contracted *paroikṓ*, fut. *paroikḗsō*, from *pará* (3844), near or at, and *oikéō* (3611), to dwell. To be a stranger, dwell or sojourn as a stranger, to dwell at a place only for a short time (Luke 24:18; Heb 11:9; Sept.: Gen 20:1; 24:37; 26:3).

Syn.: *epidēméō* (1927), to reside in a foreign country.

Ant.: *katoikéō* (2730), to settle down.

3940. παροικία *paroikía*; gen. *paroikías*, fem. noun from *pároikos* (3941), a sojourner. A dwelling nearby, neighborhood. In the NT, a sojourning, residence in a foreign land without the right of a citizenship (Acts 13:17). Metaphorically of human life (1 Pet 1:17 [cf. Heb 11:13]; Sept.: Ps 119:54).

Ant.: *katoíkēsis* (2731), the settling down or dwelling of one.

3941. πάροικος *pároikos*; gen. *paroíkou*, masc.-fem., neut. *pároikon*, adj. from *pará* (3844), near or at, and *oíkos* (3624), to dwell. A sojourner, one who dwells in a foreign country, a temporary dweller not having a settled habitation in the place where he currently resides (Acts 7:6, 29; Sept.: Gen 15:13; Ex 2:22). Applied spiritually (Eph 2:19; 1 Pet 2:11 [cf. 1:17]).

Deriv.: *paroikía* (3940), a sojourning.

Syn.: *parepídēmos* (3927), one sojourning in a strange place; *xénos* (3581), a stranger, foreigner; *allótrios* (245), stranger; *allogenḗs* (241), one of a different race.

Ant.: *oikeíos* (3609), one of the same household; *polítēs* (4177), citizen; *sumpolítēs* (4847), fellow citizen.

3942. παροιμία *paroimía*; gen. *paroimías*, fem. noun, from *pará* (3844), by, and *oímos* (n.f.), a way, a highway. Something by the way, a byword, a proverb or adage (2 Pet 2:22). Used by John as synonymous with *parabolḗ* (3850), a parable, though a parable is a short discourse, usually a narrative, in which the fictitious is employed to represent and illustrate the real (John 10:6). A figurative discourse, a dark saying, obscure and full of hidden meaning (John 16:25, 29), a proverb, a short saying illustrating a general principle. In the Sept. it is used of short, one sentence maxims (Prov 1:1).

3943. πάροινος *pároinos*; gen. *paroínou*, masc.-fem., neut. *pároinon*, adj. from *pará* (3844), near or by, and *oínos* (3631), wine. Pertaining to wine, drunken. The word does not include the responsible and temperate usage of alcohol, rather, it has in view the abuse or incessant use of it. The word-picture is that of an individual who always has a bottle (or wineskin) on the table and so signifies addiction (1 Tim 3:3; Titus 1:7).

Syn.: *oinopótēs* (3630), a wine drinker; *méthusos* (3183), a drunkard; *oinophlugía* (3632), excess of wine, drunkenness.

Ant.: *egkratḗs* (1468), self-controlled, even-tempered; *sṓphrōn* (4998), sober, self-controlled; *nēpháleos* or *nēphálios* (3524), sober, circumspect.

3944. παροίχομαι *paroíchomai*; fut. *paroichḗsomai*, perf. *parṓchēmai*, from *pará* (3844), by or past, and *oíchomai* (n.f.), to go, go away. To go by, to pass along; intrans. In the NT, used of time, to pass away. (Acts 14:16, referring to generations).

Syn.: *parágō* (3855), to pass by or away; *parérchomai* (3928), to go or pass by.

Ant.: *ménō* (3306), to remain, abide; *paraménō* (3887), to remain near.

3945. παρομοιάζω *paromoiázō*; fut. *paromoiásō*, from *pará* (3844), near or close to, and *homoiázō* (3662) to be like. To be like, similar to, to resemble; used with the dat. (Matt 23:27).

Syn.: *eíkō* (1503), to be like, resemble; *aphomoióō* (871), to make like; *homoióō* (3666), to become similar.

Ant.: *diaphérō* (1308), to differ from.

3946. παρόμοιος *parómoios*; fem. *paromoía*, neut. *parómoion*, adj. from *pará* (3844), near or close to, and *hómoios* (3664), like. Resembling, similar, like (Mark 7:8, 13).

Syn.: *hoíos* (3634), such as, similar; *toiósde* (5107), like, such as; *toioútos* (5108), such, like; *hopoíos* (3697), such as.

Ant.: *diáphoros* (1313), different; *állos* (243), another; *héteros* (2087), another of a different quality; *monogenḗs* (3439), unique.

3947. παροξύνω *paroxúnō*; fut. *paroxunṓ*, from *pará* (3844), at the point of, unto, implying movement toward a certain point, and *oxúnō* (3691), to sharpen, incite, irritate. To sharpen or whet

(Sept.: Deut 32:41). Metaphorically, to sharpen the mind, temper, or courage of someone, to incite, to impel. In the NT, it means to provoke or rouse to anger or indignation; only in the mid. / pass. *paroxúnomai* (Acts 17:16; 1 Cor 13:5; Sept.: Deut 1:34; 9:18, 19).

Deriv.: *paroxusmós* (3948), incitement, provocation, paroxysm.

Syn.: *erethízō* (2042), to excite, stir up; *parorgízō* (3949), to provoke to wrath or anger; *parazēlóō* (3863), to provoke to jealousy.

3948. παροξυσμός *paroxusmós*; gen. *paroxusmoú*, masc. noun from *paroxúnō* (3947), to stir up, provoke. In a good sense, a sharpening; used figuratively meaning an encouragement to some action or feeling (Heb 10:24). In a bad sense, a paroxysm, the stirring up of anger, sharp contention, angry dispute (Acts 15:39; Sept.: Deut 29:28; Jer 32:37). The Eng. "paroxysm" is derived from it.

Syn.: *éris* (2054), strife, quarrel; *parapikrasmós* (3894), provocation or being aroused to bitterness; *tarachḗ* (5016), disturbance, stirring.

Ant.: *hēsuchía* (2271), stillness, quietness.

3949. παροργίζω *parorgízō*; fut. *parorgísō*, from *pará* (3844), at the point of, unto, implying movement toward a certain point, and *orgízō* (3710), to anger, irritate. To provoke to anger, irritation or resentment. With the acc. (Rom 10:19 quoted from Deut 32:21; Eph 6:4; Sept.: Judg 2:12; 1 Kgs 14:15).

Deriv.: *parorgismós* (3950), rage, wrath.

Syn.: *choláō* (5520), to enrage or be full of gall or bitterness; *thumóō* (2373), to provoke to anger; *parapikraínō* (3893), to embitter; *paroxúnō* (3947), to sharpen, provoke; *erethízō* (2042), to provoke, excite; *parazēlóō* (3863), to provoke to jealousy.

Ant.: *katapaúō* (2664), to settle down, cease; *katastéllō* (2687), to put down, quell, appease.

3950. παροργισμός *parorgismós*; gen. *parorgismoú*, masc. noun from *parorgízō* (3949), to make angry, provoke to violent or bitter anger. The irritation, exasperation or anger to which one is provoked. Found only in Eph 4:26.

Although both *parorgismós* and *orgḗ* are translated "wrath," they are not the same in meaning. On the one hand, *parorgismós* signifies the kind of severe or violent anger which arises from direct provocation, an aroused anger or seething exasperation. Such behavior is contrary to the Spirit and Word of God. On the other hand, *orgḗ* (3709) refers to anger in general and though it is used of sinful anger it is also used of righteous indignation (Mark 3:5; Eph 4:26).

Syn.: *cholḗ* (5521), gall, bitterness; *eritheía* (2052), strife, contention; *aganáktēsis* (24), indignation.

Ant.: *egkráteia* (1466), self-control, temperance; *sōphrosúnē* (4997), sobriety, self-control; *praótēs* (4236), meekness.

3951. παροτρύνω *parotrúnō*; fut. *parotrunṓ*, from *pará* (3844), at the point of, unto, implying movement toward a certain point, and *otrúnō* (n.f.), to spur, advise, exhort, urge, incite. To urge along, to stir up, incite; with the acc. (Acts 13:50).

Syn.: *epegeírō* (1892) and *diegeírō* (1326), to stir up; *peíthō* (3982), to persuade, urge; *enéchō* (1758), to urge; *protrépō* (4389), to encourage, to urge forward, exhort; *sumbouleúō* (4823), to consult together; *hupodeíknumi* (5263), to admonish, forewarn.

Ant.: *apotrépō* (665), to deflect, turn away, avoid.

3952. παρουσία *parousía*; gen. *parousías*, fem. noun from *parṓn* (part. of *páreimi* [3918], to be present) present, presence, a being present, a coming to a place. Presence, coming or arrival.

(I) A coming or visit (1 Cor 16:17; 2 Cor 7:6, 7; Phil 1:26, a return visit).

(II) A technical term used of the coming of Christ (Matt 24:3; 1 Cor 15:23; 1 Thess 2:19; 2 Thess 2:8; 2 Pet 3:4; 1 John 2:28); the Son of Man (Matt 24:27, 37, 39); the Lord (1 Thess 3:13; 4:15; 5:23; 2 Thess 2:1; James 5:7, 8; 2 Pet 1:16); the day of God (2 Pet 3:12). The term *parousía* refers to the Second Coming of the Lord, but the Second Coming is not just one event taking place at a particular time. Rather it is made up of a series of events. We can understand which event is referred to only by a careful examination of the context in which the terms *parousía* or *érchomai* ([2064], to come) occur.

The comings of the Lord spoken of prior to His death and resurrection may be distinguished as follows:

(A) His coming after His death to confirm the faith of His disciples. In this instance *proáxo*, the fut. tense of the verb *proágō* (4254), to lead or go before, is used (Matt 26:32; Mark 14:28). In John 16:16 *ópsesthe*, the fut. tense of the verb *horáō* (3708), to see, or *optánomai* (3700), to see with one's physical eyes, is used,

(B) His coming to enter into a closer spiritual fellowship with His disciples. As the Risen One, He was to return to them and to abide with them continually (John 14:16–22) manifesting His presence through the Paraclete, the Holy Spirit, and thereby guiding, teaching and sustaining them by His grace working in their hearts (John 14:16, 17; 15:26; 16:14). In this sense the Lord Jesus regarded His coming again as a vital experience to be shared by all believers in later generations. He thereby signified His abiding presence in the hearts of believers and corporately in the Christian church.

(C) His coming to remove His disciples from their toils and struggles on earth and to take them to the place He would prepare for them in His Father's house (John 14:2, 3, "that where I am, there ye may be also"). This is what is referred to as the *parousía* of the Lord in 1 Thess 4:15.

This coming is going to be startling and unexpected. The Lord will come to raise the dead in Christ, to transform the living who have believed, and to take them all to be with Him (1 Cor 15:50–54; 1 Thess 4:13–17). This will constitute the Day of Christ or the Day of the Lord Jesus (1 Cor 5:5; 2 Cor 1:14; Phil 1:6, 10; 2:16; 2 Thess 2:2). Simultaneously, however, there will begin a time of great suffering for those unbelievers who are alive at the time of the *parousía*. This is called the Day of the Lord (Isa 2:12; 13:6, 9; Ezek 13:5; 30:3; Joel 1:15; 2:1, 11, 31; 3:14; Amos 5:18, 20; Obad 1:15; Zeph 1:7, 14; Zech 14:1; Mal 4:5; Acts 2:20; 1 Thess 5:2; 2 Pet 3:10). The phrases "that day" or "the day" or "the great day" occur more than seventy-five times in the OT. All these passages speak of the period of the Tribulation and include judgments that extend over a period of time prior to the Second Coming of the Lord Jesus (which itself constitutes another time of His coming). Zech 14:1–4 makes it clear that the events of the Second Advent are included in the program of the "Day of the Lord." 2 Pet 3:10 appears to include the entire millennial age within this period.

(**D**) The coming of the Lord at the end of the seven-year tribulation period is what the Lord describes in Matt 24:15–22, 32–34; Mark 13:14–23, 29, 30 (cf. Luke 19:41–44; 21:20–23, 32, 33; 23:28–30). The judgment of the Lord is designated as a specific coming by the verb *élthē*, the aor. subjunctive of *érchomai* (2064) indicating that this specific coming is prior to the final judgment of the world. This coming is also called *apokálupsis* (602), revelation (Rom 2:5; 8:19; 1 Cor 1:7; 1 Pet 1:7, 13; 4:13) and *epipháneia* (2015), manifestation (2 Thess 2:8; 1 Tim 6:14; 2 Tim 1:10; 4:1, 8; Titus 2:13). This is going to be the Last Day and will bring about the termination of the existing order of things.

Thus the coming of the Lord or His *parousía* consists of several comings which are in reality stages of a continuous process.

(**III**) Of the coming or manifestation of the man of sin (2 Thess 2:9 [cf. 2 Thess 2:3]).

Syn.: *éleusis* (1660), coming.
Ant.: *apousía* (666), absence.

3953. παροψίς *paropsís*; gen. *paropsídos*, fem. noun from *pará* (3844), with, and *ópson* (n.f.), whatever is eaten with bread. A side dish consisting of delicacies used as a condiment or sauce. In the NT, a side plate in which some delicacies are served (Matt 23:25, 26). Also from *ópson* (n.f.): *opsónion* (3800), whatever is bought to be eaten with bread.

3954. παρρησία *parrēsía*; gen. *parrēsías*, fem. noun from *pás* (3956), all, and *rhésis* (n.f.), the act of speaking. Freedom or frankness in speaking. NT meanings: freedom in speaking all that one thinks or pleases (Mark 8:32; John 7:13, 26; Acts 4:13, 29, 31); confidence or boldness, particularly in speaking (Acts 2:29; 28:31; 2 Cor 7:4; Eph 3:12; 6:19; Phil 1:20; 1 Tim 3:13; Phile 1:8; Heb 3:6; 10:35 [cf. 1 John 2:28; 3:21; 4:17; 5:14]); plainness or exactness of speech (John 10:24; 11:14; 16:25, 29; 2 Cor 3:12; Sept.: Prov 13:5); openness, speaking publicly (John 18:20); freedom, liberty (Heb 10:19); being in the public eye rather than being concealed (John 7:4 [cf. John 7:10]; John 11:54; Col 2:15). Especially in Hebrews and 1 John the word denotes confidence which is experienced with such things as faith in communion with God, fulfilling the duties of the evangelist, holding fast our hope, and acts which entail a special exercise of faith. *Parrēsía* is possible as the result of guilt having been removed by the blood of Jesus (Heb 10:19 [cf. vv. 17, 18]; 1 John 3:21; 4:17) and manifests itself in confident praying and witnessing (Heb 4:16; 1 John 5:14).

Deriv.: *parrēsiázomai* (3955), to speak boldly or freely.

Syn.: *pepoíthēsis* (4006), persuasion, assurance, confidence; *phanerós* (5320), manifestly, openly; *orthós* (3723), in a straight manner; *alēthós* (230), truly, indeed, verily; *thársos* (2294), courage; *aphóbōs* (870), without fear.

Ant.: *phóbos* (5401), fear; *trómos* (5156), trembling; *deilía* (1167), cowardice; *ptóēsis* (4423), shaking, alarm.

3955. παρρησιάζομαι *parrēsiázomai*; fut. *parrēsiásomai*, mid. deponent from *parrēsía* (3954), freedom or frankness in speaking. To speak openly, boldly, and without constraint (Acts 9:27, 29; 13:46; 14:3; 18:26; 19:8; 26:26; Eph 6:20; 1 Thess 2:2; Sept.: Job 22:26).

Syn.: *tharréō* (2292), to be bold, courageous; *tolmáō* (5111), to dare; *apotolmáō* (662), to be very bold, to speak boldly.

Ant.: *trémō* (5141), to tremble; *deiliáō* (1168), to be timid, afraid.

3956. πάς *pás*; fem. *pása*, neut. *pán*, masc. gen. *pantós*, fem. gen. *pásēs*, neut. gen. *pantós*. All.

(I) Includes the idea of oneness, a totality or the whole, the same as *hólos* (3650), the whole. In this sense, the sing. is used with the noun having the art. The pl. also stands with the art. when a def. number is implied, or without the art. when the number is indef.

(A) Sing. before a subst. with the art. (Matt 6:29; 8:32; Mark 5:33; Luke 1:10; 4:25; John 8:2; Acts 1:8; Rom 3:19; 4:16) Also used metonymically with the names of cities or countries to speak of the inhabitants (Matt 3:5; Mark 1:5; Luke 2:1). With proper nouns, sometimes without the art. (Matt 2:3; Rom 11:26). After a subst. with the art. (John 5:22; Rev 13:12). On rare occasions between the art. and the subst. where *pás* is then emphatic (Gal 5:14; 1 Tim 1:16).

(B) Pl. (1) Before a subst. or other word. (a) A subst.: With the art. implying a def. number (Matt 1:17, "all the generations"; 4:8; Mark 3:28; Luke 1:6; Acts 5:20; Rom 1:5). Without the art., where the idea of number is then indef. as

pántes ánthrōpoi (*ánthrōpoi* [444], men, people) meaning all mankind indef. (Acts 22:15; Rom 5:12, 18), *pántes ággeloi* (*ággeloi* [32], angels; *Theoú* [2316], of God) meaning all angels of God (Heb 1:6); *pánta éthnē* (*éthnē* [1484], nations) meaning all nations (Rev 14:8). (b) A part. with the art. as subst. (Matt 4:24; 11:28; Luke 1:66, 71; John 18:4; Acts 2:44). (c) Before other words and periphrases with the art. in place of a subst., i.e, poss. pron. as *pánta tá emá* (*emá* [1700], mine), all things that are mine (Luke 15:31; John 17:10); with a prep. as *pási toís en tē̄ oikía* ([3614], house), to all those in the house (Matt 5:15); with an adv., *pánta . . . tá hóde* (*hóde*, [5602], in this spot), meaning all the things which are done on the spot or here (Col 4:9). (2) After a subst. or other word. (a) A subst. with the art. as def. *tás póleis pásas* (*tás póleis* [4172], the cities) meaning all the cities of that region (Matt 9:35). Without the art. with a proper noun as *Athēnaíoi dé pántes* (*Athēnaíoi* [117], Athenians) meaning all the Athenians (Acts 17:21). (b) After a part. with the art. of subst. as *en toís hēgiasménois pásin* (*en* [1722], in; *toís hēgiasménois* [37], the sanctified ones) meaning all the sanctified ones (Acts 20:32). (c) With a prep., *hoi ún emoí pántes* (*hoi*, they; *sún* [4862], with; *emoí* [1698], me), meaning all those with me (Gal 1:2). (3) Between the art. and subst. as emphatic (Acts 19:7; 27:37). (4) Before or after a personal or demonstrative pron., as *hēmeís pántes*, we all (John 1:16); *pántes hēmeís*, all we (Acts 2:32); *pántes humeís*, all you (Matt 23:8; Luke 9:48); *hoútoi pántes*, these all (Acts 1:14); *pántas autoús*, all of them (Acts 4:33); *autōn pántōn*, all of them (1 Cor 15:10); *taúta pánta*, all these things (Matt 4:9; Luke 12:30); *pánta taúta*, all these things (Mark 7:23). (5) Used in an absolute sense: (a) With the art., *hoi pántes*, they all, meaning all those definitely mentioned (Mark 14:64; Rom 11:32; 1 Cor 10:17; Eph 4:13; Phil 2:21. Neut. *tá pánta*, all things, meaning: (i) The universe or whole creation (Rom

11:36; 1 Cor 8:6; Eph 3:9; Col 1:16; Heb 1:3; Rev 4:11); metaphorically of the new spiritual creation in Christ (2 Cor 5:17, 18); metonymically for all created rational beings, all men, *hoi pántes* (Gal 3:22; Eph 1:10, 23, all the followers of Christ; Col 1:20; 1 Tim 6:13). **(ii)** Generally, all things before mentioned or implied, such as the sum of one's teaching (Mark 4:11); all the necessities and comforts of life (Acts 17:25; Rom 8:32; 1 Cor 9:22; 12:6; 2 Cor 4:15; Eph 5:13; Phil 3:8; Col 3:8). **(iii)** As a predicate of a proper noun, *ho Theós tá pánta en pásin* (*ho Theós* [2316], the God; *tá pánta en pásin*, all in all), meaning above all, supreme (1 Cor 15:28). **(b)** Without the art. *pántes*, all, meaning all men (Matt 10:22, "be hated of all"; Mark 2:12; 10:44; Luke 2:3, "all went," a hyperbole meaning many of the inhabitants of Judea; 3:15; John 2:15, 24). Neut., *pánta*, all things (Matt 8:33; Mark 4:34; Luke 3:20; John 4:25, 45; Acts 10:39; 1 Cor 16:14, *pánta humṓn*, meaning all your actions, whatever you do; Heb 2:8; James 5:12). Acc., *pánta*, as an adv. meaning as to or in all things, in all respects, wholly (Acts 20:35; 1 Cor 9:25; 10:33; 11:2); *katá pánta* (*katá* [2596], as, according) meaning as to all things, in all respects (Acts 3:22; Col 3:20; Heb 2:17); *eis pánta* (*eis* [1519], unto, in), in all things (2 Cor 2:9); *en pásin*, in all things, all respects (2 Cor 11:6; 1 Tim 3:11; 2 Tim 2:7; Titus 2:9; 1 Pet 4:11).

(II) Sing. *pás*, without the art. as including the idea of plurality meaning all or every, equivalent to *hékastos* (1538), each one.

(A) Without nouns (Mark 9:49).

(B) Before a relative pron. it is intens., *pás hós*, everyone who (Gal 3:10); *pán hó*, whatsoever (Rom 14:23); metonymically (John 6:37, 39; 17:2); *pás hóstis* (3748), meaning everyone who or whosoever, but stronger (Matt 7:24; Col 3:17, 23 [TR]); followed by the subjunctive, *pás hós án*, everyone who would call on or whosoever shall call (Acts 2:21; Rom 10:13).

(C) Before a part. with the art., where it becomes a subst. expressing a class (Matt 5:22, he who or everyone who is angry; Luke 6:47; John 6:45; Acts 10:43; Rom 2:10). Before or after a part. with the art., *tṓ échonti pantí* (Matt 25:29, "for unto everyone that hath"); without the art. where the part. sense then remains (Matt 13:19, *pantós akoúontos* [*akoúō* (191) to hear], everyone hearing; Luke 11:4, *pantí opheílonti* [*opheílō* (3784), owing], to everyone owing us).

(D) Used in an absolute sense (Mark 9:49, "every one shall be salted"; Heb 2:9); *diá pantós* (*diá* [1223] for; *pantós*, implying *chrónou* [5550], time), continually (Heb 13:15); *en pantí* (*en* [1722], in; *pantí*, everything), in every respect (1 Cor 1:5; 2 Cor 4:8; 6:4; 7:5, 11, 16; 11:9; Eph 5:24; Phil 4:6, 12).

(III) All, meaning of all kinds, of every kind and sort including every possible variety.

(A) Generally (Matt 4:23, "and healing all manner of sickness and all manner of disease" [*pásan*]; Acts 7:22, "all the wisdom" meaning all types of wisdom; Rom 1:18, 29; 2 Cor 1:4; Col 3:16; 1 Pet 2:1).

(B) In the sense of all possible, the greatest, utmost, supreme (Matt 28:18, "all possible authority in heaven and on earth" [a.t.], which means absolute authority; Acts 5:23; 17:11; 23:1; 2 Cor 12:12; Phil 1:20; 2:29; 1 Tim 2:2; 2 Tim 4:2; James 1:2; 1 Pet 2:18; Jude 1:3).

(IV) With a neg. meaning as *ou pás* (*ou* [3756], not), or in the pl. *ou pántes*, "not everyone," "not all," the neg. belonging to *pás* merely denies universality (Matt 7:21, "not every one that saith"; 19:11; Rom 9:6; 10:16; 1 Cor 15:39). (See *ou* [3756, V, C]). When, however, the neg. *ou* follows *pás* (*pás . . . ou*), then the *ou* belongs to the verb and is equivalent to *oudeís* (3762), not one, no one, nothing, none (2 Pet 1:20; 1 John 2:21). (See *ou* [3756, I, C]). *Oudépote éphagon pán koinón* (*oudépote* [3763], never at all; *éphagon* [5315], did eat; *pán*, anything; *koinón* [2839], common), "I never ate anything common" (a.t. [Acts 10:14]). *Pás* with *mḗ* (3361), not (1 Cor 1:29, "that no flesh should glory"; Eph 4:29); also *pás . . . ou mḗ*, "shall in no wise . . . any thing" (Rev 21:27).

Deriv.: *hápas* (537), whole, all; *diapantós* (1275), continually, always.

Syn.: *hólos* (3650), all, whole; *hápas* (537), absolutely all; *holóklēros* (3648), complete in every part, entire; *hékastos* (1538), each one.

Ant.: *oudeís* (3762), no one, none, or nothing; *mēdeís* (3367), no one, none, or nothing.

3957. πάσχα *páscha*; neut. noun transliterated from the Hebr. *pesach* (6453, OT), to pass over, spare. The Passover, an exemption, immunity (Sept.: Ex 12:11, 21). The great sacrifice and festival of the Jews which was instituted in commemoration of God's sparing the Jews when He destroyed the firstborn of the Egyptians. It was celebrated on the fourteenth day of the month Nisan. For the institution and particular laws of this festival see Ex 12; Lev 23:5; Num 9:2–6. The later Jews made some additions. In particular they drank four cups of wine at various intervals during the paschal supper. The third of these cups, called the cup of benediction, is referred to in 1 Cor 10:16 (cf. Matt 26:27). In the NT, *tó páscha*, the Passover, may refer to the festival or to the paschal lamb.

(I) The paschal lamb, a year-old lamb or kid, slain as a sacrifice (Sept.: Ex 12:27). According to Josephus, the number of lambs sacrificed at Jerusalem in his time was 256,500. They were slain between the ninth and eleventh hour, which is from 3:00 to 5:00 p.m. Metaphorically used of Christ (1 Cor 5:7).

(II) *Páscha* also referred to the paschal supper as the commencement of the seven day festival of unleavened bread called *tá ázuma* (106). See Ex 12:15ff.; Lev 23:5ff.

(A) It was used of the paschal supper alone (Matt 26:18 meaning to keep or celebrate the paschal supper). Heb 11:28

means that Moses instituted and kept the Passover (Sept.: Ex 12:48; Num 9:4ff.).

(B) In a wider sense it also included the seven days of unleavened bread, the paschal festival (Matt 26:2; Mark 14:1; Luke 2:41; 22:1; John 2:13, 23; 6:4; 11:55; 12:1; 13:1; 18:39; 19:14; Acts 12:4). The whole Passover is sometimes called the Feast of Unleavened Bread. See *ázumos* (106), unleavened; *arníon* (721), lamb; *amnós* (286), sacrificial lamb; *arḗn* (704), lamb.

(C) The expression "to eat the passover" means to keep the festival (Matt 26:17; Mark 14:12, 14; Luke 22:11, 15; John 18:28; Sept.: Ex 12:43 [cf. 2 Chr 30:18]); "to make ready the passover" (a.t.) means to prepare for eating (Matt 26:19; Mark 14:16; Luke 22:8, 13); to kill the passover (Mark 14:12; Luke 22:7; Sept.: Ex 12:21; Deut 16:2, 5, 6).

3958. πάσχω *páschō*; fut. *peísomai*, 2d aor. *épathon*; perf. *pépontha*. To suffer, to be affected by something from without, to be acted upon, to undergo an experience. Intrans. and also with the acc. of the thing or manner.

(I) Used of good, meaning to experience, to have happen to oneself, to receive (Gal 3:5, "have ye experienced such things [such blessings] in vain?" [a.t.]).

(II) Used of evil, meaning to suffer, be subjected to evil (Acts 28:5). Used in an absolute sense in the same sense (1 Cor 12:26; Heb 2:18; 1 Pet 2:20, 23; 3:17; 4:1, 19). Followed by the acc. of manner (Mark 9:12; Luke 13:2; 2 Tim 1:12; Heb 5:8; Rev 2:10). With a prep. marking source, manner, cause as *apó* (575), from, followed by the gen. (Matt 16:21); *hupó* (5259), by, followed by the gen. (Matt 17:12; Mark 5:26; 1 Thess 2:14); *diá* (1223), for or because of, followed by the acc. (Matt 27:19; 1 Pet 3:14); *hupér* (5228), for, on behalf of, followed by the gen. (Acts 9:16; Phil 1:29; 2 Thess 1:5); with an adv. (Matt 17:15; 1 Pet 2:19; 5:10). Spoken of the suffering and death of Christ (Luke 17:25; 22:15; 24:26, 46;

Acts 1:3; 3:18; 17:3; Heb 9:26; 13:12; 1 Pet 2:21; 3:18; 4:1).

Deriv.: a fellow-sufferer; *páthēma* (3804), suffering; *pathētós* (3805), subject to suffering; *páthos* (3806), suffering; *propáschō* (4310), to have suffered before; *sumpáschō* (4841), to suffer with.

Syn.: *hupophérō* (5297), to endure; *basanízomai* (the mid. of *basanízō* [928]), to be tormented; *kataponéomai* (the mid. of *kataponéō* [2669]), to be oppressed, be vexed; *talaipōréomai* (the mid. of *talaipōréō* [5003]), to be afflicted; *kakouchéomai* (the mid. of *kakouchéō* [2558]), to be inflicted with harm.

Ant.: *euphoréō* (2164), to fare well; *euthuméō* (2114), to be of good cheer; *euphraínō* (2165), to rejoice; *chaírō* (5463), to rejoice.

3959. Πάταρα *Pátara*; gen. *Patárōn*, neut. proper noun. Patara, a major seaport town on the southwest shore of Lycia, was located about seven miles southeast of the mouth of the Xanthus river (Acts 21:1). It had a good harbor and was a convenient stop for ships traveling east during the autumn winds. Paul stopped here on his way to Tyre during his third missionary journey.

3960. πατάσσω *patássō*; fut. *patáxō*. Intrans meaning to beat, strike, touch, or smite. In the NT, used trans. meaning to strike.

(I) To strike, smite gently with the sense of to touch, tap, with the acc. (Acts 12:7, "touching the side of Peter" [a.t.]).

(II) To strike with violence so as to wound, with the acc. (Matt 26:51; Luke 22:50; Sept.: Ex 21:12, 18). By implication, to strike with the meaning of to kill, slay, destroy (Matt 26:31; Mark 14:27 quoted from Zech 13:7; Acts 7:24; Rev 19:15; Sept.: Ex 12:12; 2 Chr 33:25).

(III) Figuratively, to smite, inflict evil, afflict with disease or calamity, spoken only of God or His emissaries (Acts 12:23; Rev 11:6; Sept.: Gen 19:11; Ex 12:23; Num 14:12; Mal 4:6).

Syn.: *paíō* (3817), to strike with the hand or fist; *pléssō* (4141), to smite, wound; *rhapízō* (4474), to strike with the palm of the hand; *túptō* (5180), to strike, smite.

3961. πατέω *patéō*; contracted *patô*, fut. *patḗsō*, from *pátos* (n.f.), a path, a beaten way. To tread, trample (Luke 10:19; Sept.: Isa 32:20; 42:5); to tread as a winepress (Rev 14:20; 19:15); to trample upon or have in subjection (Luke 21:24; Rev 11:2; Sept.: Isa 1:12). See *lēnós* (3025), winepress (Sept.: Isa 16:10; Lam 1:15).

Deriv.: *katapatéō* (2662), to trample; *peripatéō* (4043), to walk around.

3962. πατήρ *patḗr*; gen. *patéros* contracted *patrós*, masc. noun. Its etymology is uncertain. A father, spoken generally of men and in a special sense of God. Progenitor, ancestor, father, mentor, or model.

Related words: *mḗtēr* (3384), mother; *pentherá* (3994), mother-in-law; *pentherós* (3995), father-in-law; *adelphós* (80), brother; *adelphḗ* (79), sister; *anepsiós* (431), a cousin; *suggenḗs* (4773), a relative; *ékgonos* (1549), grandchild, literally a descendant; *mámmē* (3125), a grandmother; *génos* (1085), family, stock; *oíkos* (3624), family.

(I) Generally.

(A) Particularly father, genitor, by whom one is begotten (Matt 2:22; 19:5; Mark 5:40; Luke 2:48; John 4:53; Heb 7:10). Pl. *hoi patéres*, parents, both father and mother (Eph 6:4; Heb 11:23). Of one reputed to be a father or stepfather (Luke 2:48).

(B) Of a remote ancestor, forefather, progenitor, or founder of a tribe or people, patriarch. Sing. (Matt 3:9; Mark 11:10; Luke 1:32, 73; John 4:12; Rom 4:17, 18). Pl. *hoi patéres*, fathers, forefathers, ancestors (Matt 23:30, 32; Luke 6:23, 26; John 7:22; Acts 3:13; Rom 9:5; Heb 1:1; Sept.: Deut 1:11; 1 Kgs 8:21). Figuratively in a spiritual and moral sense (Rom 4:11, 12, 16, of Abraham; see Sept.: Gen 17:4, 5).

(C) Of Satan as the father of wicked and depraved men (John 8:38, 41, 44). He is the model whom sinners resemble, i.e., they have like evil character.

(D) As a title of respect and reverence, in direct address (Luke 16:24, 27, 30); of a teacher as exercising paternal care, authority and affection (Matt 23:9; 1 Cor 4:15 [cf. Phil 2:22; 1 Thess 2:11]; Sept.: of prophets, 2 Kgs 2:12; 6:21; 13:14). Pl. *hoi patéres*, nom. or voc., fathers, as an honorary title of address used toward older persons (1 John 2:13, 14); also toward magistrates, members of the Sanhedrin (Acts 7:2; 22:1).

(E) Metaphorically with the gen. of a thing; the author, source, beginner of something (John 8:44; Rom 4:12; Sept.: Job 38:28).

(II) Of God generally as the creator, preserver, governor of all men and things, watching over them with paternal love and care. Thus in the NT God is called Father.

(A) Of the Jews (2 Cor 6:18 [cf. John 11:52]; Sept.: Isa 63:16; 64:8; Jer 31:9).

(B) Of Christians and pious persons who are called children of God (Rom 8:15); thus Jesus in speaking with His disciples calls God *Patér humón*, "your Father" (a.t. [Matt 6:4, 6, 8, 15, 18; 10:20, 29; Luke 6:36; 12:30, 32; John 20:17]). With the adjunct, "your Father who is in heaven" (a.t. [Matt 5:16, 45, 48; 6:1; 7:11; Mark 11:25, 26; Luke 11:2]); *ho patér ho ouránios* (3770), "the heavenly Father" (a.t. [Matt 6:14, 26, 32]); *ho patér ho epouránios* (2032), "the Father, the One above the sky [or heaven]" (a.t. [Matt 18:35]); *ho ex ouranoú patér* (*ex* [1537], from, out of; *ouranoú* [3772], heaven), "the Father out of heaven" (a.t. [Luke 11:13]). The Apostles, speaking of themselves and other Christians, called God "our Father" (Rom 1:7; 1 Cor 1:3; 2 Cor 1:2; Gal 1:4; Eph 1:2; Phil 1:2; 4:20). Used in an absolute sense with the same meaning (Rom 8:15; Gal 4:6; Eph 2:18; Col 1:12; James 1:27; 3:9; 1 John

2:1, 15, 16; 3:1 [cf. Ps 89:26]). See Heb 12:9, "unto the Father of spirits," meaning our spiritual Father (in contrast to a human father).

(C) Specifically, God is called the Father of our Lord Jesus Christ in respect to that particular relation in which Christ is the Son of God. See *huiós* (5207) where the Father and Son are expressly distinguished (Matt 11:27; 28:19; Mark 13:32; Luke 9:26; 10:22; John 1:14, 18; 3:35; 5:26; 1 Cor 8:6; 1 Thess 1:1; Heb 1:5; 1 Pet 1:2; 1 John 1:3; 2:22; 4:14; 2 John 1:3, 9). Jesus calls God *patér mou*, "my Father" (a.t. [Matt 11:27; Mark 8:38; Luke 2:49; John 10:18, 25, 29; Rev 2:27; 3:5, 21]). Thus *ho patér mou ho en ouranoís*, "my Father in the heavens" (a.t. [Matt 7:21; 10:32, 33; 12:50]); *ho patér mou ho ouránios*, "my heavenly Father" (Matt 15:13). Used in an absolute sense with the same meaning (Matt 24:36; Mark 14:36; John 4:21, 23; 6:27, 37, 44ff.; 10:17; 13:1, 3; 14:6; Acts 1:4; Rom 6:4, cf. Luke 10:21; 22:42; 23:34). The Apostles also speak of God as "the Father of our Lord Jesus Christ" (Rom 15:6; 2 Cor 1:3; 11:31; Eph 1:3; 3:14; Col 1:3; 1 Pet 1:3). Used in an absolute sense (1 Cor 15:24; Gal 1:1; Eph 5:20; Col 3:17; 2 Pet 1:17; Jude 1:1). In Eph 1:17 "the God of our Lord Jesus Christ, the Father of glory," means "the God, the glorious Father of our Lord Jesus Christ" (a.t.).

(D) The Lord Jesus is designated *ho huiós* (5207), the Son, not only in His incarnation, but in His eternal, infinite, self-existence (John 1:18). The Lord Jesus in His incarnation is never called *téknon Theoú* (*téknon* [5043], child; *Theoú* [2316], of God), child of God, perhaps because *téknon* is derived from *tíktō* (5088), to give birth, which is used primarily of women giving birth. It would be preferable to say that the Son was *gennáō* ([1080], born, begotten, or conceived; used of the procreating act of men). However, this point is not to be pressed as it is only conjectural. Believers are called *tékna Theoú* (John 1:12;

11:52; Rom 8:16, 21; 9:8; Phil 2:15; 1 John 3:1, 2, 10; 5:2).

(E) Metaphorically followed by the gen. of thing (James 1:17, "from the Father of lights" meaning the author or creator of the heavenly luminaries, but not subject to change like them; Sept.: Job 38:28).

Deriv.: *apátōr* (540), literally without father; *patralṓas* (3964), a murderer of fathers; *patriá* (3965), paternal descent; *patriárches* (3966), patriarch, progenitor; *patrikós* (3967), paternal, ancestral; *patrís* (3968), a fatherland, native country, town, home; *patroparádotos* (3970), handed down from one's fathers.

Syn.: *goneús* (1118), a parent; *prógonos* (4269), an ancestor, forefather.

3963. Πάτμος *Pátmos*; gen. *Pátmou*, fem. proper noun. Patmos, a small island in the Aegean Sea located twenty-eight miles south of Samos. It is twenty-five square miles in area and very rocky and barren which made it one of the suitable spots for the banishment of Roman criminals. The coast is rock-bound, but indented with several deep bays. The Apostle John was banished to Patmos by the Emperor Domitian in A.D. 95 (Rev 1:9). A cave in the southern part of the island is held traditionally to be the place where John received the Revelation. On the top of the mountain is a monastery built in honor of Saint John with a library containing about 240 MSS.

3964. πατραλῴας *patralṓas*, or *patralías* gen. *patralíou*, masc. noun from *patér* (3962), father, and *aloiáō* (n.f.), to smite. One who murders his father (1 Tim 1:9 [cf. *mētralṓas* {3389}, one who murders his mother]).

Syn.: *phoneús* (5406), murderer; *anthrōpoktónos* (443), manslayer; *sika-ríos* (4607), assassin.

3965. πατριά *patriá*; gen. *patriás*, fem. noun from *patér* (3962), father. Lineage, family, descendants. Used thus in Luke 2:4, "Of the lineage [i.e., descendants] of David." Used in a wider sense as a people, nationality or race (Acts 3:25 in allusion to Gen 12:3; 1 Chr 16:28; Ps 22:27; 96:7). In Eph 3:14, 15 we have God presented as "the Father" who has only one *patriá* (family). This indicates the oneness of God's family, both Jews and Gentiles, both the saints of the OT as well as those of the NT who were all baptized into the body of Christ as is so clearly indicated in Acts chaps. 2; 10; 11; 19 and explained in 1 Cor 12:13. See Ex 6:15, 17, 19; 1 Sam 9:21.

Deriv.: *patriárchēs* (3966), patriarch.

Syn.: *phulḗ* (5443), tribe, race, clan; *oíkos* (3624), family; *geneá* (1074), age, generation; *génos* (1085), stock, race, kind.

3966. πατριάρχης *patriárchēs*; gen. *patriárchou*, masc. noun from *patriá* (3965), race, lineage, and *archḗ* (746), beginning or head. A patriarch, the father and founder of a family or tribe, e.g., Abraham (Heb 7:4); the sons of Jacob as heads of the twelve tribes (Acts 7:8, 9); David as the head of a family (Acts 2:29 [cf. Luke 2:4]; Sept.: 1 Chr 9:9; 24:31; 2 Chr 19:8 [cf. 1 Chr 27:22]).

3967. πατρικός *patrikós*; fem. *patrikḗ*, neut. *patrikón*, adj. from *patér* (3962), father, a father. Paternal, pertaining to one's father. In the NT, it means received from one's fathers, handed down from ancestors, hereditary, equivalent to *parádosis* (3862), tradition (Gal 1:14).

Syn.: *patrṓos* (3971), of one's fathers.

3968. πατρίς *patrís*; gen. *patrídos*, fem. noun of *pátrios* (n.f.), from *patér* (3962), father. One's own country, the place where one's father or ancestors lived, fatherland, native country. In the NT, one's own city, native place. Nazareth was the city of Jesus because He was brought up there (Matt 13:54, 57; Mark 6:1, 4; Luke 4:23, 24; John 4:44). Figuratively of our heavenly home (Heb 11:14 [cf. Heb 11:16]).

Ant.: *paroikía* (3940), a place where one dwells as a foreigner, sojourner.

3969. Πατρόβας *Patróbas*; gen. *Patróba*, masc. proper noun. Patrobas, meaning life of his father. A Christian in Rome to whom Paul sends greetings (Rom 16:14).

3970. πατροπαράδοτος *patroparádotos*, gen. *patroparádotou*, masc.-fem., neut. *patroparádoton*, adj. from *patér* (3962), father, ancestor, and *paradídōmi* (3860), to deliver. Delivered down from one's fathers, handed down from ancestors, hereditary (1 Pet 1:18, meaning a traditional way of life).
Syn.: *archaíos* (744), ancient, original; *palaiós* (3820), old; *patrốos* (3971), paternal, hereditary; *patrikós* (3967), ancestral, paternal, from one's forebearers.
Ant.: *néos* (3501), new, more recent; *kainós* (2537), new qualitatively.

3971. πατρῷος *patrốos*; fem. *patrốa*, neut. *patrốon*, adj. from *patér* (3962), father, and the suffix *-ios* (contracted *ốos* in certain compositions) denoting possession. Paternal, patrimonial, pertaining to one's father, transmitted from father to son. In the NT, received from one's fathers, handed down from ancestors, hereditary. With reference to the Law (Acts 22:3); custom (Acts 28:17); the God whom our fathers worshiped and made known to us (Acts 24:14).
Syn.: *patrikós* (3967), from one's fathers or ancestors; *patroparádotos* (3970), handed down from one's fathers.

3972. Παῦλος *Paúlos*; gen. *Paúlou*, masc. proper noun. Paul, meaning small, whereas Saul (his Hebr. name) means asked for.
(I) Paul was a Jew of the tribe of Benjamin, born in the Greek city of Tarsus in Cilicia, who inherited Roman citizenship (Acts 22:28, 29). Hence, He was well acquainted with the three great nationalities of the Roman Empire and was providentially prepared for his apostolic mission among the Jews, the Greeks, and the non-Greeks, who were then called barbarians. He was a student of language and literature, and he quotes from three poets who were well-known in that day: Aratus (Acts 17:28), Menander (1 Cor 15:33), and Epimenides (Titus 1:12).

Under the instruction of Gamaliel, a distinguished rabbi at Jerusalem (Acts 5:34), Paul became a master of the Jewish law (Acts 22:3; Gal 1:14). Paul was also a tentmaker, a trade that he performed so that he could support himself (Acts 18:3; 1 Cor 4:12; 9:18). It was Jewish custom for the father to train or provide training for his sons.

Paul's residence at Jerusalem commenced at an early period (Acts 26:4), and he was probably between twenty-two and twenty-five years old when Christ began His public ministry. Paul belonged to the strict sect of the Pharisees (Acts 23:6) and was among the spectators at the stoning of Stephen (Acts 7:58 [cf. 22:20]). On his way to Damascus to arrest and imprison Christians, he was restrained by a special appearance of the Lord, during which he was struck blind (Acts 9:3–9; 26:15 [cf. 1 Cor 15:8]). He received his commission as an apostle to the Gentiles directly from Christ (Acts 26:16, 17). After the restoration of his sight (Acts 9:17, 18), he began to preach the gospel (Acts 9:20, 21; Gal 1:16).

The Acts of the Apostles traces Paul's career until his first imprisonment at Rome. This imprisonment lasted two years (A.D. 61–63), and yet he was comparatively free to labor in the gospel. We have very little information on the remainder of his life. Some scholars maintain that he suffered martyrdom during the persecution under Nero in A.D. 64. Others say he was freed from the first Roman imprisonment, made new missionary tours in the East (and possibly also to the West as far as Spain), was taken prisoner to Rome a second time, and suffered martyrdom in A.D. 67 or 68.

Paul wrote thirteen or fourteen epistles (depending upon whether he is reckoned as the author of Hebrews). The time when the pastoral epistles were composed depends upon the question of whether there was a second Roman captivity. 2 Timothy, whether written during the first or second captivity, was most assuredly Paul's last epistle.

(II) A chronological summary of the chief events of Paul's life are as follows: **(A)** Paul's early Christian life: **(1)** A.D. 37, his conversion; **(2)** A.D. 37–40, sojourn in Arabia; **(3)** A.D. 40, first journey into Jerusalem after his conversion (Gal 1:18); **(4)** A.D. 40, sojourn to Tarsus and afterward to Antioch (Acts 11:26); **(5)** A.D. 44, second journey to Jerusalem in company with Barnabas with famine relief.

(B) Paul's first missionary journey: A.D. 45–49, with Barnabas and Mark (up to Perga) to Cyprus, Antioch in Pisidia, Iconium, Lystra, Derbe, and back to Antioch in Syria.

(C) Between the first and second missionary journeys: **(1)** Apostolic council at Jerusalem about whether Gentile Christians must keep the Mosaic Law; **(2)** Third journey to Jerusalem with Barnabas and Titus; **(3)** Settlement of a difficulty between the Jewish and Gentile apostles; his return to Antioch; **(4)** A.D. 50, disagreement with Barnabas at Antioch and temporary separation.

(D) Paul's second missionary journey: **(1)** With Silas, from Antioch to Asia Minor, Cilicia, Lycaonia, Galatia, Troas, and Greece (Philippi, Thessalonica, Berea, Athens, and Corinth); **(2)** Paul at Corinth (one and one-half years); A.D. 52–53, 1 and 2 Thessalonians written (with the possibility that 2 Thess was written first); **(3)** His fourth journey to Jerusalem in the spring with a short stay at Antioch.

(E) Paul's third missionary journey: **(1)** Initiated in the autumn of A.D. 54; **(2)** Paul at Ephesus (three years); A.D. 56 or 57, Epistle to the Galatians written; **(3)** Excursion to Macedonia, Corinth, and Crete (not mentioned in Acts); **(4)** A.D. 54–57 (spring), return to Ephesus; **(5)** A.D. 57 (summer), departure from Ephesus to Macedonia; 1 Corinthians and 2 Corinthians written, **(6)** A.D. 57; Paul's third sojourn at Corinth (three months); A.D. 57–58, Epistle to the Romans written.

(F) Paul's arrest and trial: **(1)** A.D. 58 (spring), his fifth and last journey to Jerusalem where he was arrested and sent to Caesarea; **(2)** A.D. 58–60, his captivity there; testimony before Felix, Festus, and Agrippa; **(3)** A.D. 60–61, Paul's voyage to Rome (autumn); shipwreck at Malta; arrival at Rome (spring); **(4)** A.D. 61–63, Paul's first captivity at Rome: epistles written to the Colossians, Ephesians, Philippians, and Philemon.

(G) Paul's final days: **(1)** A.D. 64 (July), conflagration at Rome; **(2)** A.D. 64, Nero's persecution of the Christians; **(3)** Hypo-thesis of missionary journeys by Paul to the east (and possibly to Spain) preceding a second Roman captivity; A.D. 63–67, the epistles of 1 Timothy, Titus, (possibly) Hebrews, and 2 Timothy are written.

3973. παύω *paúō*; fut. *paúsō*. To stop, pause, make an end. Used chiefly in the mid. *paúomai*, meaning to come to an end, take one's rest, a willing cessation (Luke 5:4). Contrast the pass. voice which denotes a forced cessation. Used in the act. voice in 1 Pet 3:10, to cause to cease, in allusion to Ps 34:13, 14. Intrans., to refrain, pause, leave off, followed by the gen. of the thing (1 Pet 4:1, "hath ceased from sin"; Sept.: Ex 32:12; Josh 7:26). With the neg. particle *ou* (3756), not (Acts 5:42, "they ceased not to teach"; 6:13; 13:10; 20:31; Eph 1:16; Col 1:9; Heb 10:2). Followed by a part. (Acts 21:32; Eph 1:16); with part. implied (Luke 11:1; Sept.: Gen 11:8; 18:33; 24:19, 22); used in an absolute sense, to cease, come to an end (Luke 8:24; Acts 20:1; 1 Cor 13:8; Sept.: Ex 9:33, 34).

Deriv.: *anapaúō* (373), to relax, rest inwardly but not necessarily as a result of the cessation of work; *katapaúō* (2664), to rest.

Syn.: *dialeípō* (1257), to leave an interval whether of space or time, to intermit, desist, cease; *kopázō* (2869), to stop as a result of being tired, relax, subside, calm down; *hēsucházō* (2270), to become quiet, still, at rest; *katargéō* (2673), to render inactive, abolish.

Ant.: *exakolouthéō* (1811), to follow out, continue; *epiménō* (1961), to persist, continue on; *epakolouthéō* (1872), to follow after; *diateléō* (1300), to continue.

3974. Πάφος *Páphos*; gen. *Páphou*, fem. proper noun. Paphos, meaning boiling or hot, was actually the name of two different towns on the western end of the island of Cyprus in the eastern Mediterranean.

Old Paphos, near the modern sight of Kouklia, was located on a hill about two miles from the sea. Although it may have been founded as early as 3000 B.C., it seems to have been most prosperous from about 1100 B.C. to A.D. 500. There was a famous temple in Old Paphos, the central place of the worship of Aphrodite, which was visited annually by great numbers of heathen pilgrims.

New Paphos was located on the seashore about eight miles to the northwest of the old town. Founded around 300 B.C., its marvelous harbor quickly made it the chief city of the region.

The fact that both cities are referred to in various places under the simple name Paphos has caused great confusion about them. Ancient historians relate the near destruction of one of the two cities by an earthquake. The city is elsewhere said to have been rebuilt by Augustus. In general, however, the name Paphos refers to Old Paphos only in poetical literature.

It was New Paphos that was the location of the Roman governorship, and most surely was the place Paul and Barnabas visited. The Roman proconsul, Sergius Paulus, was converted after the magician Elymas was miraculously blinded (Acts 13:6–11).

3975. παχύνω *pachúnō*; fut. *pachunṓ*, from *pachús* (n.f.), thick, gross. To make fat. In the NT, metaphorically and only in the pass. meaning to become gross, dull, callous as if from fat (Matt 13:15; Acts 28:27 quoted from Isa 6:10 [cf. Deut 32:15]).

Syn.: *pōróō* (4456), to blind, harden; *sklērúnō* (4645), to harden; *tuphlóō* (5186), to make blind.

Ant.: *aisthánomai* (143), to feel, perceive.

3976. πέδη *pédē*; gen. *pédēs*, fem. noun from *péza* (n.f., see below), the foot, which is from *pédon* (n.f.), the ground, earth, which is from *poús* (4228), foot. A fetter or shackle for the feet (Mark 5:4; Luke 8:29; Sept.: 2 Sam 3:34; 2 Kgs 25:7).

Deriv. of *péza* (n.f.): *pezeúō* (3978), to go or travel by foot; *trápeza* (5132), a table.

Syn.: *desmós* (1199), band, meaning shackle, chains of imprisonment; *hálusis* (254), chain; *seirá* (4577), band, chain.

3977. πεδινός *pedinós*; fem. *pedinḗ*, neut. *pedinón*, adj. from *pedíon* (n.f.) a field, a plain. Flat, plain, level land (Luke 6:17, Jesus stood upon a level place or upon the plain; Sept.: Deut 4:43; Josh 9:1; 2 Chr 1:15).

Ant.: *oreinós* (3714), hilly, mountainous.

3978. πεζεύω *pezeúō*; fut. *pezeúsō*, from *péza* (n.f., see *pédē* [3976]), the foot. To go or travel on foot or by land, as opposed to going by sea (Acts 20:13).

Syn.: *peripatéō* (4043), to walk about; *hodoiporéō* (3596), to travel by road.

Ant.: *pléō* (4126), to sail.

3979. πεζῇ *pezḗ*; adv., the dat. fem. of *pezós* (n.f.), on foot, pedestrian. On foot (Matt 14:13; Mark 6:33).

3980. πειθαρχέω *peitharchéō*; contracted *peitharchṓ*, fut. *peitharchḗsō*, from *peítharchos* (n.f.), submission to authority, which is from *peíthomai* (the mid. voice of *peíthō* [3982], to persuade), to obey, and *archḗ* (746), rule, beginning. To obey a person in authority; hence generally to obey; with a dat., as magistrates (Titus 3:1); God (Acts 5:29, 32). To obey or follow one's advice, with the dat. of person (Acts 27:21).

Syn.: *epakoúō* (1873), to hearken; *hupakoúō* (5219), to obey; *akoúō* (191), to hear with the meaning of obey; *hupotássomai* (the mid. of *hupotássō* [5293]), to be in subjection; *enōtízomai* (1801), to give ear, to hearken; *hupeíkō* (5226), to submit.

Ant.: *apeithéō* (544), to disobey; *apistéō* (569), to be unfaithful.

3981. πειθός *peithós*; fem. *peithḗ*, neut. *peithón*, adj. from *peíthō* (3982), to persuade. Persuasive, winning (1 Cor 2:4 [cf. 1 Cor 2:13]).

3982. πείθω *peíthō*; fut. *peísō*, aor. pass. *epeísthēn*, perf. pass. *pépeismai*, 2d perf. *pépoitha*. To persuade, particularly to move or affect by kind words or motives.

(I) Act. voice, to persuade.

(A) Generally, to persuade another to receive a belief, meaning to convince, and in this sense used mostly with the acc. of person (Acts 14:19; 18:4, "he . . . persuaded the Jews," meaning he sought to convince them; 2 Cor 5:11). With the duplicate acc. of person and thing (Acts 28:23, "persuading them concerning [the truth about] Jesus"). With the acc. of person being implied (Acts 19:8). Used in an absolute sense to persuade of alleged error (Acts 19:26). Followed by the acc. of person with the inf. meaning to persuade to do something, to induce (Acts 13:43; 26:28). With the acc. of person and *hina* (2443), so that, in the sense of to instigate (Matt 27:20).

(B) To bring over to kind feelings, to conciliate. **(1)** Generally, to pacify or quiet an accusing conscience, "our heart" (1 John 3:19; Sept.: 1 Sam 24:8). **(2)** To win over, gain the favor of, make a friend of, with the acc. of person (Gal 1:10); by presents, bribes (Matt 28:14; Acts 12:20).

(II) Mid. / pass., meaning to let oneself be persuaded, to be persuaded.

(A) Generally of any truth. Used in an absolute sense, to be convinced, believe (Luke 16:31; Acts 17:4; Heb 11:13 [TR]); used in an absolute sense, but with the inf. implied (Acts 21:14); followed by the dat. of thing (Acts 28:24); perf. pass. *pépeismai* with pres. meaning, I am persuaded, convinced (Heb 6:9), with the inf. and acc. (Luke 20:6); followed by *hóti* (3754), that (Rom 8:38; 14:14; 15:14; 2 Tim 1:5, 12).

(B) To assent to, obey, follow, followed by the dat. of person or thing (Acts 5:36, 37, 40; 23:21; 27:11; Rom 2:8; Gal 3:1; 5:7; Heb 13:17; James 3:3).

(III) 2d perf. *pépoitha*, intrans., to be persuaded, to trust.

(A) To be confident, assured, followed by the inf. and acc. (Rom 2:19); with *hóti* (3754), that (Phil 2:24; Heb 13:18); with *toúto* (5124), this thing, followed by *hóti* (Phil 1:6, 25); with *epí* (1909), upon, followed by acc. with *hóti* meaning in respect to (2 Cor 2:3; 2 Thess 3:4) with *eis* (1519), into, and the further adjunct *en* (1722), in, *en kuríō* (*kúrios* [2962], Lord) meaning in or through the Lord (Gal 5:10); with *en kuríō* alone (Phil 2:24; 2 Thess 3:4; Sept.: Deut 33:28 [cf. Job 12:5; Prov 10:9]).

(B) To confide in, rely upon, followed by the dat. (2 Cor 10:7; Phil 1:14; Phile 1:21; Sept.: Prov 14:16; Isa 28:17); by *en* (1722), in, with the dat., meaning to trust or have confidence in (Phil 3:3, 4); by *epí* (1909), upon (Mark 10:24; Luke 11:22; 18:9; 2 Cor 1:9; Heb 2:13; Sept.: Ps 2:12; 25:2; Prov 11:28); by *epí* with the acc. (Matt 27:43; Sept.: 2 Kgs 18:21, 22).

Deriv.: *anapeíthō* (374), to persuade or induce in an evil sense; *apeithḗs* (545), disobedient; *eupeithḗs* (2138), easy to be entreated; *peithós* (3981), persuasive, enticing; *peismonḗ* (3988), persuasion; *pepoíthēsis* (4006), trust, confidence;

pístis (4102), belief; *pistós* (4103), faithful.

Syn.: *pistóō* (4104), to trust or give assurance to; *plērophoréō* (4135), to be fully assured; *sumphōnéō* (4856), to agree; *suntíthēmi* (4934), to assent; *sugkatatíthēmi* (4784), to consent; *pisteúō* (4100), to believe, be persuaded of; *diabebaióomai* (1226), to affirm; *hupotássō* (5293), to subject; *parotrúnō* (3951), to urge; *metastréphō* (3344), to turn around; *protrépō* (4389), to exhort; *parotrúnō* (3951), to urge along, stimulate; *sumbouleúō* (4823), to give counsel; *hupodeíknumi* (5263), to indicate, show, admonish.

Ant.: *apeithéō* (544), to be disobedient; *apistéō* (569), to disbelieve; *apotrépō* (665), to turn away.

3983. πεινάω *peináō*; contracted *peinṓ*, fut. *peinásō*, aor. *epeínasa*, from *peína* (n.f.), hunger. To be hungry, famished, starved.

(I) Intrans. (Matt 4:2; 12:1, 3; 21:18; 25:35, 37, 42, 44; Mark 2:25; 11:12; Luke 4:2; 6:3; Rom 12:20 from Prov 25:21; 1 Cor 11:21, 34; Rev 7:16; Sept.: 2 Sam 17:29).

(II) Metonymically meaning to be famished, without food, poor, needy (Luke 1:53; 6:21, 25; 1 Cor 4:11; Phil 4:12; Sept.: Ps 107:9; Jer 31:12, 25).

(III) Metaphorically it means to hunger after something other than literal food, to long for; with the acc., *tḗn dikaiosúnēn* (1343), righteousness (Matt 5:6); spiritual nourishment (John 6:35).

Ant.: *korénnumi* (2880) and *chortázō* (5526), to satiate, satisfy with food; *esthíō* (2068), to eat; *phágō* (5315), to consume, eat; *trṓgō* (5176), to gnaw, chew; *bibrṓskō* (977), to eat a large meal; *kataphágō / katesthíō* (2719), to eat up.

3984. πεῖρα *peíra*; gen. *peíras*, fem. noun from *peírō* (n.f.), to perforate, pierce through to test the durability of things or simply to pass through. Experience, trial, attempt (Heb 11:29).

Deriv.: *ápeiros* (552), inexperienced, unskilled; *peirázō* (3985), tempt or test; *peiráō* (3987), to try, test, tempt.

Syn.: *dokimḗ* (1382), experience, trial; *dokímion* (1383), trial, proof.

Ant.: *ápeiros* (552), without experience; *ágnoia* (52), ignorance.

3985. πειράζω *peirázō*; fut. *peirásō*, from *peíra* (3984), experience, trial. To try, to prove in either a good or bad sense, tempt, test by soliciting to sin. Similar to *peiráō* (3987), to assay.

(I) Of actions, to attempt, assay, followed by the inf. (Acts 16:7; 24:6).

(II) Of persons, to tempt, prove, put to the test, followed by the acc.

(A) Generally and in a good sense in order to ascertain the character, views, or feelings of someone (Matt 22:35 [cf. Mark 12:28, 34; John 6:6; Rev 2:2]; Sept.: 1 Kgs 10:1; Ps 17:3).

(B) In a bad sense, with ill intent (Mark 8:11; 10:2; 12:15; Luke 11:16; 20:23; John 8:6). Hence by implication, to try one's virtue, tempt, solicit to sin (Gal 6:1, "lest thou also be tempted," yield to temptation; James 1:13, 14; Rev 2:10); especially by Satan (Matt 4:1, 3; Mark 1:13; Luke 4:2; 1 Cor 7:5; 1 Thess 3:5).

(C) God is said to try men by adversity, to test their faith and confidence in Him (1 Cor 10:13; Heb 2:18; 11:17, 37; Rev 3:10; Sept.: Gen 22:1; Ex 20:20; Deut 8:2). Men are said to prove or tempt God by doubting, distrusting His power and aid (Acts 5:9; 15:10; 1 Cor 10:9; Heb 3:9 quoted from Ps 95:9; Sept.: Ex 17:2, 7; Isa 7:12). *Peirázō* is connected with *peíra* (3984), experience (Heb 11:29, 36). To attempt (Acts 16:7; 24:6); to entangle a person in sin or to discover what good or evil, what weakness or strength, is in a person (Matt 16:1; 19:3; 22:18); to know what a person's weakness or strength is and to make it manifest to the one being tempted (2 Cor 13:5, "examine"). Satan tempts to show someone unapproved (Matt 4:1; Rev 2:10).

Satan is called *ho peirázōn*, the tempter (Matt 4:3).

Deriv.: *apeírastos* (551), not temptable (i.e., incapable of being tempted); *ekpeirázō* (1598), to try, put to the test; *peirasmós* (3986), testing, temptation.

Syn.: *anakrínō* (350), to examine; *exetázō* (1833), to search, question; *dokimázō* (1381), to prove, test, approve; *apodeíknumi* (584), to prove, approve; *ochléō* (3791), to harass, vex; *enochléō* (1776), trouble; *parenochléō* (3926), to annoy, trouble; *basanízō* (928), to torment.

3986. πειρασμός *peirasmós*; gen. *peirasmoú*, masc. noun from *peirázō* (3985), to make trial of, try, tempt. Trial, temptation, a putting to the test, spoken of persons only. When God is the agent, *peirasmós* is for the purpose of proving someone, never for the purpose of causing him to fall. If it is the devil who tempts, then it is for the purpose of causing one to fall.

(I) Generally, trial of one's character (1 Pet 4:12, "to try [or prove] you"). By implication, trial of one's virtue, temptation, solicitation to sin, especially from Satan (Luke 4:13; 1 Tim 6:9).

(II) Trial, temptation.

(A) A state of trial in which God brings His people through adversity and affliction in order to encourage and prove their faith and confidence in Him (Matt 6:13; 26:41; Mark 14:38; Luke 8:13; 11:4, "bring us not into a state of trial" [a.t.], lay not trials upon us; 22:40, 46; 1 Cor 10:13; James 1:2, 12; 1 Pet 1:6; 2 Pet 2:9; Sept.: Deut 7:19; 29:3). Hence used metonymically for adversity, affliction, sorrow (Luke 22:28; Acts 20:19; Gal 4:14; Rev 3:10).

(B) In the opposite way, man "tempts" God by distrusting Him and complaining to Him (Heb 3:8 quoted from Ps 95:8; Sept.: Ex 17:7; Deut 9:22).

Syn.: *dokimḗ* (1382), trial; *dokímion* (1383), proof.

3987. πειράω *peiráō*; contracted *peirō̄*, fut. *peirásō*, from *peíra* (3984), trial. In Class. Gr. when used with the gen. of the person it meant to try someone, put him to the test. In the NT, it means simply to attempt or try (Acts 9:26; 26:21).

3988. πεισμονή *peismonḗ*; gen. *peismonḗs*, fem. noun from *peíthō* (3982), to persuade. Persuasion, conviction (only in Gal 5:8).

The play on words in Gal 5:7–10 is quite interesting. In verse seven, Paul uses the word *peíthesthai* (pass. inf. of *peíthō*, translated "to obey" in the KJV), "to be persuaded," in order to chide the Galatians for having turned to the teachings of the Judaizers and for no longer being convinced of the truth. In verse eight, he uses *peismonḗ* to warn the Galatians that the persuasion brought about by the Judaizers is not the conviction that comes from God, but a stubborn reliance on the doctrine of men. Paul then emphasizes the turmoil that this false reliance has caused in the church, "A little yeast leavens the whole batch of dough" (a.t.). Finally, in verse ten, Paul uses *pépoitha* (2d perf. of *peíthō*) to inform the Galatians that it is the Lord that has convinced him of the truth, even with respect to the Galatians, "I, myself, am persuaded by the Lord with respect to you . . . " (a.t.). Paul was sure that the Galatians would be convinced of the truth and that those who had propounded the error would bear the burden of their sin.

Syn.: *elégchos* (1650), conviction; *plērophoría* (4136), full assurance; *pístis* (4102), faith; *pepoíthēsis* (4006), persuasion, assurance, confidence.

Ant.: *apistía* (570), unbelief.

3989. πέλαγος *pélagos*; gen. *pelágous*, neut. noun. A vast expanse of water or the open sea (Matt 18:6; Acts 27:5). In Class. Gr. *pélagos* also referred to the expanse of sand in the desert.

Pélagos denotes the open or high sea, that part of the water which is deep, in distinction from the its shoreline or other shallow portions. *Pélagos* must be distinguished from *thálassa* (2281), which means a sea or a body of salt water. The two words are used together in Matt 18:6, "It were better for him that a millstone were hanged about his neck, and that he were drowned in the depth of the sea." The picture is that of a person being drowned in the open sea far away from land where escape would be hopeless.

3990. πελεκίζω *pelekízō*; fut. *pelekísō*, from *pélekus* (n.f.), an axe. To chop off or behead with an axe. In the NT, in the pass. with the acc. of person (Rev 20:4).

Syn.: *apokephalízō* (607), to behead.

3991. πέμπτος *pémptos*; fem. *pémptē*, neut. *pémpton*, an ordinal number from *pénte* (4002), five. Fifth (Rev 6:9; 9:1; 16:10; 21:20; Sept.: Gen 1:23).

3992. πέμπω *pémpō*; fut. *pémpsō*. To dispatch, send, thrust out.

(I) Of persons, meaning to cause to go.

(A) Generally with the acc. (Matt 22:7; Acts 25:25; Phil 2:23); followed by the acc. and dat. of person to whom (1 Cor 4:17; Phil 2:19); with *eis* (1519), unto, and the acc. of place (Matt 2:8; Mark 5:12, "into them"; Eph 6:22; Col 4:8).

(B) Specifically of messengers, agents, ambassadors, with the acc. (Matt 11:2; Luke 16:24; John 1:22; 13:16; 1 Thess 3:2); *hoi pemphthéntes*, those sent, the messengers (Luke 7:10); *eis* (1519), unto, with the acc. of place (Luke 16:27; Acts 15:22); with the inf. of purpose (1 Cor 16:3; Rev 22:16); with the acc. of person implied followed by *eis* with the inf. of purpose (1 Thess 3:5, "I sent to know"); with the acc. of place (Acts 10:32; 20:17); *prós* (4314), toward, with the acc. (Luke 4:26; Acts 10:33; 15:25; 19:31; 23:30; 1 Pet 2:14); the aor. part. *pémpsas* before a finite verb, implying that one does a thing by an agent or messenger (Matt 14:10, "and having sent he beheaded John" [a.t. {cf. Mark 6:27}]). Spoken of teachers;

with the inf., "ambassadors sent from God" (a.t.) or in His name, e.g., John the Baptist (John 1:33, "he that sent me to baptize"); Jesus, as sent from God (John 4:34; 5:23, 24; 6:38ff.; 7:16, 28; Rom 8:3); the Spirit (John 14:26; 15:26; 16:7); the apostles, as sent out by Jesus (John 13:20; 20:21).

(II) Of things meaning to send, transmit.

(A) Particularly with the acc. of a thing and dat. of person (Rev 11:10). With the acc. of thing implied, followed by the dat. or acc. (Phil 4:16).

(B) Figuratively to send upon or among, with the acc. and dat. (2 Thess 2:11); with the acc., to send forth, thrust in (Rev 14:15, 18).

(III) *Pémpō* bears a significant relationship to *apostéllō* (649), to send. In secular Gr. there was usually a distinction between *pémpō* and *apostéllō*. The comp. verb *apostéllō* means to send away, referring to both persons and things. Delegation for a particular purpose is involved, and the cause for sending is often particularly stressed. This is the verb from which the word *apóstolos* (652), apostle, is derived. *Pémpō* was more common in secular Gr.; it merely stresses the fact of sending. In the NT, *apostéllō* occurs as a technical term denoting divine authorization.

Apostéllō is used 131 times in the NT, of which 119 occurrences are in the gospels and Acts. *Pémpō* occurs as a virtual syn., more often in John (32 times), but also in the Gospel of Luke and Acts (10 or 11 times). John uses the two words side by side in John 20:21 where *apostéllō* may be said to mean to send with delegated authority. *Pémpō*, however, means merely to send, the authority being retained by Jesus Christ and derived from the believer's attachment to Christ. This is clearly seen in Matt 28:18 where the Lord Jesus Christ sends forth His disciples to preach the gospel and disciple the nations. When speaking of the authority by which this was to be done, He said, "Unto me was given all authority in heaven and on earth" (a.t.). He did not say that unto *you* has been given this inherent authority. See the use of *pémpō* in John 5:23, 24, 30, 37; 6:38, 39, 44; 8:29; 16:5, 7.

Pémpō is not used in the Lord's high priestly prayer in John 17, while *apostéllō* is used six times (vv. 3, 8, 18, 21, 23, 25). Here He identifies Himself as the one whom God has sent, the sent one. The purpose and mission of His coming had been set prior to His incarnation (John 16:28). Therefore, *pémpō* is a general term, but *apostéllō* suggests official or authoritative sending.

Deriv.: *anapémpō* (375), to send up; *ekpémpō* (1599), to send forth; *metapémpō* (3343), to send after or for, to fetch; *propémpō* (4311), to send on before; *sumpémpō* (4842), to send along with.

Syn.: *apostéllō* (649), to send.

Ant.: *déchomai* (1209), to receive.

3993. πένης *pénēs*; gen. *pénētos*, masc.-fem., adj. from *pénomai* (n.f., see below), to work for a living. Poor, but able to help oneself through his own labor or toil, used subst. (2 Cor 9:9; Sept.: Ex 23:6; Deut 15:11; Prov 31:20; Ezek 18:12). Contrast *ptōchós* (4434), poor and helpless, dependent on alms such as a beggar (Luke 16:20).

Deriv. of *pénomai* (n.f.): *penichrós* (3998), miserably poor; *pónos* (4192), toil, pain.

Syn.: *endeḗs* (1729), deficient in, lacking; *ptōchós* (4434), utterly destitute.

Ant.: *ploúsios* (4145), rich; *polutelḗs* (4185), costly, very precious, of great price.

3994. πενθερά *pentherá*; gen. *pentherás*, the fem. of *pentherós* (3995), father-in-law. A mother-in-law, a wife's mother (Matt 8:14; Mark 1:30; Luke 4:38); a mother-in-law, in antithesis to her daughter-in-law (Matt 10:35; Luke 12:53; Sept.: Ruth 1:14; 2:11; 3:1). See *patḗr* (3962), father, for various relations.

3995. πενθερός *pentherós*; gen. *pentheroú*, masc. noun. Father-in-law (John 18:13; Sept.: Gen 38:13, 25). See *patḗr* (3962), father, for various relations.

3996. πενθέω *penthéō*; contracted *penthṓ*, fut. *penthḗsō*, from *pénthos* (3997), mourning. To mourn, lament.

(**I**) Trans. with the acc. of person to bewail someone, grieve for him (2 Cor 12:21); more commonly for one dead (Sept.: Gen 37:34; 50:3).

(**II**) Intrans., to mourn at the death of a friend, equivalent to *klaíō* (2799), to weep (Mark 16:10; Sept.: Gen 23:2); generally, to be sad, sorrowful (Matt 5:4; 9:15; 1 Cor 5:2), equivalent to *klaíō* (Luke 6:25; James 4:9; Rev 18:15, 19); with the prep. *epí* (1909), upon someone (Rev 18:11).

Syn.: *lupéō* (3076), to grieve, not signifying an outward expression of one's feelings; *thrēnéō* (2354), to bewail; *kóptō* (2875), to beat the breast as an outward sign of inward grief.

Ant.: *chaírō* (5463), to rejoice.

3997. πένθος *pénthos*; gen. *pénthous*, neut. noun related to *páthos* (3806), suffering. Mourning, grief, sadness (James 4:9; Rev 18:7, 8; 21:4; Sept.: Prov 14:13; Lam 5:15).

Deriv.: *penthéo* (3996), to mourn, lament.

Syn.: *odurmós* (3602), lamentation; *lúpē* (3077), inner grief, sorrow; *odúnē* (3601), pain, distress; *ōdín* (5604), birth pang, travail.

Ant.: *chará* (5479), joy, delight.

3998. πενιχρός *penichrós*; fem. *penichrá*, neut. *penichrón*, adj. from *pénomai* (n.f., see *pénēs* [3993]), to work for a living. Miserably poor, poor and needy (Luke 21:2; Sept.: Ex 22:25; Prov 28:15). Strong's *Dictionary of the Greek Testament* has it incorrectly spelled *penichrós*.

Syn.: *ptōchós* (4434), utterly destitute; *pénēs* (3993), one who is poor.

Ant.: *perissós* (4053), abundant; *ploúsios* (4145), wealthy, abounding; *plḗrēs* (4134), full, complete; *mestós* (3324), replete, full.

3999. πεντάκις *pentákis*; adv., from *pénte* (4002), five, and the suffix *-kis*, a numeral termination. Five times (2 Cor 11:24; Sept.: 2 Kgs 13:19).
Deriv.: *pentakischílioi* (4000), five thousand.

4000. πεντακισχίλιοι *pentakischílioi*; from *pentákis* (3999), five times, and *chílioi* (5507), thousands. Five thousand, literally five times one thousand (Matt 14:21; 16:9; Mark 6:44; 8:19; Luke 9:14; John 6:10; Sept.: 2 Chr 35:9).

4001. πεντακόσιοι *pentakósioi*; fem. *pentakósiai*, neut. *pentakósia*, cardinal number from *pénte* (4002), five, and *hekatón* (1540), a hundred. Five hundred (in the NT only in Luke 7:41; 1 Cor 15:6).

4002. πέντε *pénte*; indeclinable, used for all genders, cardinal numeral. Five (Matt 14:17, 19; 16:9; 25:2; Luke 1:24; Acts 4:4). As an indef., small number (1 Cor 14:19; Sept.: Gen 18:28; Ex 22:1).
Deriv.: *dekapénte* (1178), fifteen; *pémptos* (3991), fifth; *pentákis* (3999), five times; *pentakósioi* (4001), five hundred; *pentekaidékatos* (4003), fifteenth; *pentḗkonta* (4004), fifty; *pentēkostḗ* (4005), fiftieth, Pentecost.

4003. πεντεκαιδέκατος *pentekaidékatos*; fem. *pentekaidekátē*, neut. *pentekaedékaton*, ordinal number from *pentekaidéka* (n.f.), fifteen, which is from *pénte* (4002), five, *kaí* (2532), and, *dékatos* (1182), tenth. Fifteenth. In the NT, only in Luke 3:1 (Sept.: Num 28:17; 2 Kgs 14:23).

4004. πεντήκοντα *pentḗkonta*; indeclinable, used for all genders, cardinal number from *pénte* (4002), five. Fifty (Mark 6:40; Luke 7:41; 9:14, "by fifties";

16:6; John 8:57; 21:11; Acts 13:20; Sept.: Gen 6:15; Ex 26:5).

4005. πεντηκοστή *pentēkostḗ*; gen. *pentēkostḗs*, fem. of *pentēkostós* (n.f.), fiftieth, which is from *pénte* (4002), five. A fiftieth part. In the NT, Pentecost, the day of Pentecost (Acts 2:1; 20:16; 1 Cor 16:8), one of the three great Jewish festivals in which all the males were required to appear before God; so-called because it was celebrated on the fiftieth day, counting from the second day of the Festival of Unleavened Bread or Passover, i.e., seven weeks after the sixteenth day of Nisan (cf. Lev 23:15ff.; Deut 16:9ff.). In the Sept. it is called the Feast of Weeks or the Festival of Weeks (Deut 16:10). It was a festival of thanks for the harvest, which began directly after the Passover (Deut 16:9ff.) and was hence also called Day of the Firstfruits (Num 28:26). Josephus tells us that in his day great numbers of Jews came from every quarter to Jerusalem to keep this festival.

4006. πεποίθησις *pepoíthēsis*; gen. *pepoithḗseōs*, fem. noun from *peíthō* (3982), to persuade. Trust, confidence (2 Cor 1:15; 3:4; 8:22; 10:2; Eph 3:12; Phil 3:4).
Syn.: *elégchos* (1650), conviction; *plērophoría* (4136), full assurance; *pístis* (4102), faith; *peismonḗ* (3988), persuasion.
Ant.: *apistía* (570), unbelief.

4007. περ *per*; an enclitic emphatic particle from *perí* (4012), concerning, with respect, about. Very, wholly, ever. In the NT, it is always joined with a pron. or a particle for greater emphasis and strength; e.g., *eánper* (Heb 3:6, 14; 6:3) and *eíper* (1512), if perhaps; *epeíper* (1897), since indeed; *epeidḗper* (1895), since indeed, because of; *éper* (2260), than indeed; *katháper* (2509), exactly as, even as, as well; *kaíper* (2539), and yet, although; *hósper* (3746), whomsoever (Mark 15:6); *hṓsper* (5618), exactly like, even.

Deriv.: *dióper* (1355), wherefore, truly.

4008. πέραν *péran*; adv. of place, from *péra* (n.f.), beyond, over or across, further. Beyond, over, on the other side, as a prep. governing the gen. (Matt 4:15, 25; 19:1; Mark 3:8; John 1:28; 3:26; 10:40; Sept.: Gen 50:10, 11; Num 34:15); beyond the sea (John 6:1, 17, 22, 25); beyond the brook of Kedron (John 18:1); with neut. art. *tó péran*, meaning that beyond, the other side, the region beyond (Matt 8:18, 28; 14:22; 16:5; Mark 4:35; 5:1, 21; 6:45; 8:13; 10:1; Luke 8:22; Sept.: Num 21:13; 32:19; Deut 1:5). Also from *péra* (n.f.): *péras* (4009), end, extremity.

Deriv.: *antipéran* (495), over against.

Syn.: *epékeina* (1900), farther on, beyond; *makrán* (3112), way off, far; *pórrō* (4206), at a distance, far, a great way off; *huperékeina* (5238), beyond.

Ant.: *eggús* (1451), near; *pará* (3844), close by; *perí* (4012), around, near; *plēsíon* (4139), near.

4009. πέρας *péras*; gen. *pératos*, neut. noun from *péra* (n.f.), beyond, over or across, further. End or extremity of the earth, meaning the remotest region (Matt 12:42; Luke 11:31; Rom 10:18; Sept.: Ps 2:8; 19:4; 61:2). Figuratively, what comes to an end, conclusion, termination (Heb 6:16; Sept.: Nah 3:9). Also from *péra* (n.f.): *péran* (4008), beyond, over, on the other side.

Syn.: *suntéleia* (4930), the consummation or completion; *ékbasis* (1545), the outcome; *télos* (5056), the limit, end, goal.

Ant.: *archḗ* (746), the beginning.

4010. Πέργαμος *Pérgamos*; gen. *Pergámou*, fem. proper noun. Pergamos, meaning citadel. A celebrated city of Mysia, a province in northwest Asia Minor, located about three miles off the River Caicus and twenty miles from the sea. Though in existence by at least 500 B.C., Pergamos was not well known until

two centuries later when Lysimachus, a successor to Alexander the Great, chose to store his treasure in the city. He entrusted Philetaerus, his garrison commander, with his treasure of nine thousand talents. In 283 B.C. Philetaerus betrayed Lysimachus to Seleucus I when the latter was attacking Lysimachus. Philetaerus then appropriated the money and the city and became a vassal under the Seleucids.

Under the successors of Philetaerus, the small kingdom became independent. It retained this independence with the help of the Romans, until 133 B.C. when the last king of Pergamos bequeathed the vast treasure of the kingdom to the Romans. (The Romans claimed the entire kingdom, not just the treasure that had been bequeathed.) They vanquished the last of the kingly line and established the kingdom as the Province of Asia.

Pergamos was famous for its literary character and idolatry. Since the Egyptians, who controlled the production of papyrus, would not give Pergamos the paper to build a rival library, the people of Pergamos perfected the art of preparing animal skins for writing. Our word "parchment" is derived from the Lat. *pergamena*, Pergamos.

Pergamos had a vast library of 200,000 volumes (rolls), rivaling that at Alexandria. Unfortunately, Antony presented this library, which did not belong to him, to Cleopatra. After the library was moved to Egypt, it and the Alexandrian Library were destroyed by Caliph Omar.

The city had a cluster of famous temples dedicated to Zeus, Minerva, Apollo, Venus, Bacchus, and Aesculapius. One of the seven churches of Asia Minor was at Pergamos "where Satan's seat is" (see Rev 2:12–17). Some regard the term "Satan's seat" as referring to the worship of Aesculapius, the god of medicine, whose common emblem was the serpent. Others think it denotes the particular wickedness of the city with its various idolatries and the trials which had come upon the Church, one faithful member (Antipas) having already suffered martyrdom. The modern city is called Bergama. Ruins of fine churches and temples remain, indicating the former grandeur of the city.

4011. Πέργη Pérgē; gen. *Pérgēs*, fem. proper noun. Perga, meaning a tower, was a city of Pamphylia, a province of Asia Minor. Perga was situated on the river Cestrus, about seven miles from the sea. Originally it was the capital of the province. The inhabitants were Greeks and it had a temple, stadium, theaters, and a famous temple of Artemis, "queen of Perga," standing on a high elevation. Paul, Barnabas, and Mark landed at Perga in the spring when the road to Pisidia would be cleared of snow. It was here in Perga that Mark forsook Paul and returned to Jerusalem (Acts 13:13; 14:25).

4012. περί perí; a prep. which, in the NT, governs the gen. and acc. Around, about or of, in the sense of concerning or regarding.

(I) With a gen. where it expresses the central point from which an action proceeds or from which it is exerted. In John 19:24, it is used with this sense, "but cast lots for it," i.e., in regard to it. In Acts 25:18, *perí hoú stathéntes* can mean "standing about him" (a.t.), making it to agree with the verb *periéstēsan* (Acts 25:7), "stood round about," from *periístēmi* (4026). It is more natural, however, to take *perí hoú*, with which verse eighteen begins, as referring to what follows: "they brought none accusation," in which case *perí* means "concerning whom they could not bring an accusation" (a.t.). In the NT, *perí* can mean about, concerning, in respect to.

(A) Where the gen. denotes the obj. about which the action is exerted, as in Eng., to speak or hear about or of a thing. With a verb of speaking, asking, teaching, writing, e.g., *légō* (3004), to say (Matt 11:7; 21:45); *eípon*, said, the aor. of *épō* (2036) (Matt 17:13; John 1:30; 7:39); *laléō* (2980), to speak (Luke 2:17, 33, 38); *erōtáō* (2065), to ask (Luke

9:45; John 18:19); *didáskō* (1321), teach (1 John 2:27); *gráphō* (1125), write (Matt 11:10; John 5:46). See also Matt 12:36; John 1:7, 8; 6:41; Acts 1:1, 16; 7:52; 1 Cor 1:11; 1 Tim 1:7. After nouns of like meaning, where the simple gen. might usually stand (Luke 4:14, 37; Acts 11:22; 25:16; Rom 1:3; Heb 5:11). With verbs of hearing, learning, knowing: *akoúō* (191), to hear (Mark 5:27; Luke 7:3; 9:9); *katēchéō* (2727), to inform, instruct (Acts 21:21, 24); *epístamai* (1987), to understand (Acts 26:26); *gnōstón . . . éstin* (*gnōstós* [1110], known; *éstin*, from *eimí* [1510], is), it is known (Acts 28:22). With verbs of inquiring, deliberating, doubting, and the like: *zētéō* (2212), to seek (John 16:19); *exetázō* (1833), inquire, search (Matt 2:8); *punthánomai* (4441), to ascertain (Acts 23:20); *enthuméomai* (1760), to remember, ponder, think (Acts 10:19); *dialogízomai* (1260), to deliberate, think through (Luke 3:15); *diaporéō* (1280), to be perplexed (Luke 24:4; Acts 5:24); *dokéō* (1380) to think (Matt 22:42). With nouns such as *zétēsis* (2214), dispute, question (John 3:25; Acts 18:15).

(B) Where the gen. expresses the ground, motive or occasion of the action, meaning on account of, because of, for. **(1)** Generally with verbs of reproving, accusing, being tried, with the gen. of thing: *elégchō* (1651), to rebuke, reprove (Luke 3:19; John 8:46; 16:8); *egkaléō* (1458), to accuse legally (Acts 19:40; 26:2); *katēgoréō* (2723), to accuse (Acts 24:13); *krínomai* (2919), to be judged (Acts 23:6). After verbs expressing an attitude of the mind: *splagchnízomai* (4697), to have compassion for (Matt 9:36); *aganaktéō* (23) to be indignant (Matt 20:24; Mark 10:41); *thaumázō* (2296), to wonder (Luke 2:18); *kaucháomai* (2744), to boast (2 Cor 10:8). After words of thanksgiving: as *eucharistéō* (2168), to thank (1 Cor 1:4; 1 Thess 1:2; 2 Thess 2:13); *eucharistían . . . antapodoúnai* (*eucharistía* [2169], thanksgiving; *antapodídōmi* [467], to render), to render thanks (1 Thess 3:9). After *ou mélei soi* (*ou* [3756], not; *mélō* [3199], concern; *soi* [4671], thee), it does not concern thee (Matt 22:16; Mark 12:14). With *merimnáō* (3309), to be anxious about (Matt 6:28; Luke 12:26). Generally with various verbs and nouns (Matt 16:11; Mark 1:44; Luke 2:27; John 10:33, "concerning a good work" [author's translation]; Acts 19:24, "casts lots about it" [author's translation]; Acts 15:2; 19:23, "there arose no small stir about that way"; Col 2:1). (**2**) Where the action is exerted in favor of the person or thing denoted by the gen., meaning on account of, in behalf of, for (Matt 4:6; Luke 22:32; John 16:26; Eph 6:18; Phile 1:10; Heb 11:40; 1 Pet 5:7). After verbs of offering sacrifice, for example, one's life, meaning in behalf of (Matt 26:28; Mark 14:24; Heb 5:3). (**3**) Where the action is exerted "against" a person or thing, with the gen. of person after words of accusation (Acts 25:15 [cf. 25:2]; Acts 25:18 [cf. 25:27]). In the phrase *perí tḗs hamartías*, in the pl. *perí hamartiṓn* (*hamartía* [266], sin), meaning on account of sin, for sin, for the purpose of doing away with or expiating sin (Rom 8:3; 1 Pet 3:18). "Offering for sin" (Heb 10:18 [cf. 10:26]); "whose blood is brought . . . for sin" (Heb 13:11); "propitiation for our sins" (1 John 2:2; 4:10); "for sin," with a sacrifice being understood (Heb 10:6 quoted from Ps 40:6 [cf. Lev 5:8; 9:10; 2 Chr 29:24]).

(**C**) Where there is only a more general reference or allusion to the person or thing denoted by the gen., meaning as to, touching, in relation to. (**1**) Generally (Matt 18:19; Luke 11:53; John 9:18; 11:19; 15:22; Acts 28:21; Rom 15:14; 1 Cor 7:37; Col 4:10; Heb 11:20). (**2**) Used in an absolute sense, usually at the beginning of a sentence (Matt 22:31, "as touching [concerning] the resurrection of the dead, have ye not read"; Mark 12:26; Acts 28:22; 1 Cor 7:1, 25; 8:1, 4; 12:1; 1 Thess 4:9, 13; 5:1). (**3**) With the neut. pl. art. and the gen. of thing, meaning the things relating or pertaining to

something, as the things concerning the kingdom of God (Acts 1:3; 8:12; 19:8). Followed by the gen. of person meaning one's circumstances, state, cause (Luke 22:37; 24:19, 27; Acts 23:11, 15; Eph 6:22; Phil 1:27; Col 4:8).

(**D**) By implication from the primary idea of surrounding and including, in the phrase *perí pántōn* (*pántōn*, gen. pl. of *pás* [3956], all things), including all and hence above all. However, *perí* with such a literal meaning is not found in the NT or Sept. Thus in 3 John 1:2, due to the latter clause, "I wish that thou mayest prosper as to all things [external], even as thy soul prospers" (a.t.).

(**II**) With the acc., where the acc. then expresses the obj. around or about which something moves or comes, and also finally remains.

(**A**) Of place, around or about, meaning the place to which, after a verb of motion (Luke 13:8, "till I shall dig about [around] it"). More frequently of place where, implying the coming and remaining around, followed by the acc. of thing (Matt 3:4; Mark 9:42; Rev 15:6). Followed by the acc. of person (Matt 8:18, "around him" [a.t.]; Mark 3:32, 34; Acts 22:6). With the art. *hoi, hai, tá,* and the acc. of place (Mark 3:8, "they about Tyre and Sidon," i.e., those dwelling in and around these cities; Acts 28:7, in the parts around, environs [cf. Jude 1:7]). *Hoi perí* followed by the acc. of person, a person and his followers (Mark 4:10; Luke 22:49; John 11:19; Acts 13:13).

(**B**) Figuratively of that about which an action is exerted, meaning about, concerning, respecting, *perí* with the gen.: (**1**) Of a matter or business about which one is occupied (Luke 10:41, referring to Martha who was "preoccupied about much ministry" [a.t.]; Acts 19:25, meaning workmen engaged in the same occupation; 1 Tim 6:4). (**2**) Generally meaning as to, touching (1 Tim 1:19; 6:21; 2 Tim 2:18; 3:8; Titus 2:7). (**3**) With the neut. pl. art., *tá perí emé* (*emé* [1691], my), meaning my circumstances, affairs, state (Phil 2:23).

(C) Of time, i.e., of a point of time not entirely definite, i.e., "about" (Matt 20:3, "about the third hour"; Matt 20:5, 6, 9; 27:46; Mark 6:48; Acts 10:9; 22:6).

(III) In composition in the NT *perí* implies:

(A) A moving, being, spreading around on all sides, as *peribállō* (4016), to throw around; *periblépō* (4017), to look around; *periéchō* (4023), to include, contain.

(B) Generally used for emphasis denoting a completeness or strengthening of the simple idea meaning completely, very, exceedingly, as *perílupos* (4036), exceedingly grieved or very sorrowful; *peripeírō* (4044), to pierce through; *perí* (4012), about.

Deriv.: *per* (4007), very, wholly, ever.

Syn.: *hōseí* (5616), about; *périx* (4038), around; *héneka* (1752), on account of; *diá* (1223), for, because of; *hupér* (5228), on behalf of, over, above; *katá* (2596), against; *antí* (473), in opposition to; *prós* (4314), concerning.

Ant.: *epí* (1909), upon; *akribōs* (199), exactly; *en* (1722) on, in; *eis* (1519), in, unto.

4013. περιάγω periágō; fut. *periáxō*, from *perí* (4012), about, and *ágō* (71), to lead, carry, go. To lead about. Trans., of those whom one takes as companions (1 Cor 9:5; Sept.: Amos 2:10). Intrans. or with *heautón* (1438), "himself" implied, meaning to go about, to go up and down. Used in an absolute sense (Acts 13:11). Followed by the acc. of place (Matt 4:23, He "went about all Galilee"; 9:35; 23:15; Mark 6:6).

Syn.: *sumporeúomai* (4848), to go with; *periérchomai* (4022), to wander about, stroll.

4014. περιαιρέω periairéō; contracted *periairō̃*, fut. *periairḗsō*, 2d aor. *perieílon*, from *perí* (4012), around, suggesting completeness, and *hairéomai* (138), to lift up and take away. To take away, abandon.

(I) Used trans. (Acts 27:40, "taking up the anchors round about" [a.t. {cf. 27:29}]); of a veil, to remove (2 Cor 3:16, an allusion to Ex 34:34. Sept.: Gen 41:42; Esth 3:10; Jon 3:6).

(II) Metaphorically, to take away completely (Heb 10:11, "completely take away sins" [a.t.], to make complete expiation for sins [cf. Heb 10:4]).

Syn.: *periphérō* (4064), to bear about; *sunépomai* (4902), to accompany; *leípō* (3007), to leave; *kataleípō* (2641), to forsake; *apoleípō* (620), to leave behind; *egkataleípō* (1459), to abandon; *aphíēmi* (863), to leave; *eáō* (1439), to leave alone.

Ant.: *ménō* (3306), to remain, stay, abide; *epéchō* (1907), to retain.

4015. περιαστράπτω periastráptō; fut. *periastrápsō*; from *perí* (4012), about, around, and *astráptō* (797), to shine like lightning. To flash around, to shine around with the acc. of person (Acts 9:3). With *perí* followed by the acc. of person (Acts 22:6).

Syn.: *perilámpō* (4034), to shine around.

Ant.: *skotóō* (4656), to darken.

4016. περιβάλλω peribállō; fut. *peribalō̃*; from *perí* (4012), about, round about, and *bállō* (906), to cast, put. To cast or throw around, to put around a person or thing.

(I) Generally with the acc. and dat. (Luke 19:43; Sept.: Ezek 4:2).

(II) Specifically of clothing, i.e., to put on, clothe.

(A) Actively with the acc. of person expressed or implied (Matt 25:36, 38, 43; Sept.: Isa 58:7). Followed by a double acc., to put a garment around or upon someone, to clothe (Luke 23:11; John 19:2).

(B) In the mid. / pass., to put on one's own garments, to clothe oneself, to be clothed. Used in an absolute sense (Matt 6:29; Luke 12:27; Rev 3:18; 19:8). With the acc. of garment (Matt 6:31; Acts 12:8). The perf. part. (Mark 14:51, "clothed with a sheet of cloth" [author's translation]; 16:5; Rev 7:9, 13; 10:1; 11:3; 12:1; 17:4; 18:16; 19:13). Followed by *en* (1722), in, with the dat. of thing (Rev 3:5; 4:4; Sept.: Deut 22:12; Ps 147:8 [cf. Ps 45:14]). Once with the dat. of garment in the TR (Rev 17:4; Sept.: 1 Kgs 1:1).

Deriv.: *peribólaion* (4018), covering, vesture.

Syn.: *amphiénnumi* (294), to put clothes around; *endúō* (1746), to get into clothes or put on clothes; *endidúskō* (1737), to wear; *ependúō* (1902), to clothe; *himatízō* (2439), to put on clothes; *peritíthēmi* (4060), to put around or on; *peridéō* (4019), to bind around one; *periéchō* (4023), to hold all around; *perizónnumi* (4024), to gird all around; *peritíthēmi* (4060), to place around.

Ant.: *apobállō* (577), to throw off from.

4017. περιβλέπω *periblépō*; fut. *periblépsō*, from *perí* (4012), around, and *blépō* (991), to see. To look all around or upon, survey. In the NT, only in the mid. *periblépomai*, to look around.

(**I**) Intrans., meaning to look around. Used in an absolute sense (Mark 9:8; 10:23). Followed by the inf. of purpose (Mark 5:32).

(**II**) Trans., meaning to look around or upon, with the acc. (Mark 3:5, 34; 11:11; Luke 6:10; Sept.: Job 7:8).

Syn.: *emblépō* (1689), to look on, observe carefully; *atenízō* (816), to gaze intently.

4018. περιβόλαιον *peribólaion*; gen. *peribolaíou*, neut. noun from *peribállō* (4016), to cast around. A covering, cloak, wrap, cape, outer garment, or mantle (Heb 1:12 quoted from Ps 102:26; Ex 22:27). By implication, a covering for the head, a headdress or perhaps a veil (1 Cor 11:15).

Syn.: *sképasma* (4629), a roof, covering; *káluma* (2571), a covering; *kómē* (2864), the hair on the head; *himátion* (2440), an outer cloak or cape; *himatismós* (2441), clothing, apparel; *chlamús*

(5511), a military cloak worn over the *chitón* by emperors, kings, magistrates or military officers; *stolé* (4749), a stately robe or uniform, a long gown worn as mark of dignity; *katastolé* (2689), long robe of dignity; *esthḗs* (2066) and *ésthēsis* (2067), clothing; *énduma* (1742), a garment of any kind; *ependútēs* (1903), an upper or outer garment which sometimes fishermen wore when at work; *phelónēs* (5341), a mantle, traveling robe for protection against stormy weather, overcoat; *podérēs* (4158), an outer garment reaching to the feet; *phelónēs* (5341), a traveling cloak.

Ant.: *gumnótēs* (1132), nudity, nakedness.

4019. περιδέω *peridéō*; fut. *peridésō*; perf. pass. *peridédemai*, from *perí* (4012), about, and *déō*, (1210), to bind. To bind around. In the pass. (John 11:44).

Syn.: *desmeúō* (1195), to put together or to bind together; *peribállō* (4016), to throw around.

Ant.: *lúō* (3089), to loose; *apobállō* (577), to throw off from; *aníēmi* (447), loosen.

4020. περιεργάζομαι *periergázomai*; fut. *periergásomai*, from *perí* (4012), concerning, and *ergázomai* (2038), to work. To work all around, bustle about. In the NT, to be a busybody. In 2 Thess 3:11, there is a play on words: *ergazoménous allá periergazoménous* (*ergázomai* [2038], to work, *allá* [235], but), occupied but busybodies (i.e., everywhere doing everything but doing nothing).

Ant.: *pragmateúomai* (4231), to busy oneself with; *spoudázō* (4704), to make diligent effort.

4021. περίεργος *períergos*; gen. *periérgou*, masc.-fem., neut. *períergon*, adj. from *perí* (4012), an intens., and *érgon* (2041), work, business. Used of people who scurry about fussing over, and meddling in, other peoples' affairs being overwrought with unnecessary care (1 Tim 5:13). It was also a standard term for black arts or magic (Acts 19:19). It pointed to the lengthy and various rituals involved in incantation ceremonies and the fastidiousness with which they were performed.

4022. περιέρχομαι *periérchomai*; fut. *perieleúsomai*, 2d aor. *periélthon*, from *perí* (4012), about, and *érchomai* (2064), to come, go. To go about or wander around. Used in an absolute sense (Acts 19:13; Heb 11:37). Used of a ship sailing on an irregular course with unfavorable winds (Acts 28:13). With the acc. of place, dependent on *perí* in composition (1 Tim 5:13, going about to houses or "from house to house"; Sept.: Job 1:7).

Syn.: *periágō* (4013), to lead about; *diodeúō* (1353), to travel throughout or along; *peripatéō* (4043), to walk; *hodoiporéō* (3596), to go on a journey; *diaperáō* (1276), to pass over; *planáomai* (4105), to wander.

Ant.: *ménō* (3306), to abide, remain.

4023. περιέχω *periéchō*; fut. *periéxō*, 2d aor. *periéschon*, from *perí* (4012), about, and *échō* (2192), to have, hold. Trans., To surround, to encircle, as a mountain. In the NT, to enclose, embrace. Figuratively with the acc. of person, to clasp around, to seize (Luke 5:9). To contain, as a writing, with the acc. (Acts 23:25). Impersonal or with the subj. implied (1 Pet 2:6).

Deriv.: *periochē* (4042), a passage or portion.

4024. περιζώννυμι *perizṓnnumi*; fut. *perizṓsō*, from *perí* (4012), about or around, and *zṓnnumi* (2224), to gird. To gird or wrap around. In the NT, used only in the mid. or pass. meaning to wrap oneself around, to be wrapped around, spoken in reference to the long flowing garments of the Orientals which were pulled up and knotted at the waist for freedom of movement. Used in an absolute sense (Luke 12:35, perf. pass. part. used figuratively, "be ye ready" [author's translation]; Sept.: Ex 12:11). Used in an absolute sense in the mid. (Luke 12:37; 17:8; Acts 12:8). Used with the acc. in a figurative sense (Eph 6:14; Sept.: Ps 18:32, 39; 30:11). The thing with which one is wrapped may be shown by *en* (1722), in or with (Sept.: 1 Chr 15:27), or by the acc. of the thing, i.e., a girdle (Rev 1:13; 15:6).

Syn.: Of the literal meaning: *peribállō* (4016), to enwrap in clothing; *endúō* (1746), to clothe. Of the figurative meaning: *hetoimázō* (2090), make ready, prepare; *paraskeuázō* (3903), prepare self, be (make) ready; *katartízō* (2675), to fit or make fit; *kataskeuázō* (2680), to equip, make ready; *proetoimázō* (4282), to prepare beforehand; *phoréō* (5409), to wear.

Ant.: Of the literal meaning: *apekdúomai* (554), to put off; *ekdúō* (1562), to take off from; *apobállō* (577), to put off. Of the figurative meaning: *scholázō* (4980), to be at leisure; *paraitéomai* (3868), to beg off, quit; *egkataleípō* (1459), to desert, leave, forsake; *argéō* (691), to delay, linger, be idle.

4025. περίθεσις *períthesis*; gen. *panthéseōs*, fem. noun from *peritíthēmi* (4060), to set about, which is from *perí* (4012), around, and *títhēmi* (5087), to place. Wearing, adorning. In 1 Pet 3:3, *perithéseōs chrusṓn* (*chrusíon* [5553], gold, gold ornaments), "putting on of gold ornaments" (a.t.).

Syn.: *éndusis* (1745), a putting on; *epíthesis* (1936), a putting on; *peribólaion* (4018), something thrown around one, a veil.

Ant.: *apóthesis* (595), a putting off or away; *apékdusis* (555), a putting off, stripping off; *athétēsis* (115), a putting away, disannulling.

4026. περιΐστημι *periḯstēmi*; fut. *peristḗsō*, from *perí* (4012), about, and *hístēmi* (2476), to stand. To cause to stand around, to place around (used trans.). In the NT, only in the 2d aor., perf. and mid. intrans., to stand around.

(I) Used in an absolute sense (John 11:42; Acts 25:7, around the tribunal; Sept.: 2 Sam 13:31).

(II) The mid. *periístamai*, to place oneself at a distance from, to stand aloof from, avoid, with the acc. depending on *perí* in composition (2 Tim 2:16; Titus 3:9).

Syn.: *stékō* (4739), to stand; *ménō* (3306), to abide; *kuklóō* (2944), to stand around about.

Ant.: *ekklínō* (1578), to turn away from; *ektrépō* (1624), to turn or twist out; *paraitéomai* (3868), to resign, refuse.

4027. περικάθαρμα *perikátharma*; gen. *perikathármatos*, neut. noun from *perikathaírō* (n.f.), to purge or cleanse all around, which is from *perí* (4012), around, and *kathaírō* (2508), to cleanse. The filth or defilement washed away by cleansing; see *katharismós* (2512), the process of purification. It may be used to denote an expiatory victim or ransom, as cleansing from guilt and punishment (Sept.: Prov 21:18). It is used metonymically in the NT of wretches or outcasts. Paul, in 1 Cor 4:13, mentions that the disciples of Christ are considered to be the refuse or outcasts of the world.

Syn.: *rhúpos* (4509), dirt, filth; *rhuparía* (4507), filthiness.

Ant.: *thēsaurós* (2344), treasure.

4028. περικαλύπτω *perikalúptō*; fut. *perikalúpsō*, from *perí* (4012), around, and *kalúptō* (2572), to cover. To cover around. With reference to the face meaning to blindfold (Mark 14:65); with the acc. of person (Luke 22:64). In the pass., meaning to be overlaid with something, as gold (Heb 9:4).

Syn.: *epikalúptō* (1943), to cover up or over; *stégō* (4722), to provide a roof over.

Ant.: *apokalúptō* (601), to uncover; *apostegázō* (648), to unroof, uncover.

4029. περίκειμαι *períkeimai*; fut. *perikeísomai*, from *perí* (4012), about, and *keímai* (2749), to lie, to put. To lie around, to be circumspect. In the NT, to lie around, and also to be laid around. To surround, to encompass with the dat. of person (Heb 12:1). Used for the perf. pass. of *peritíthēmi* (4060), to place around, and so to be hung around, as around the neck (Mark 9:42; Luke 17:2). Following the acc. of thing in the manner of pass. verbs (Acts 28:20), meaning I have this chain hung around me and am bound with it.

Syn.: *kuklóō* (2944), to encircle, surround; *perikuklóō* (4033), to encircle or compass around; *periérchomai* (4022), to go about; *periéchō* (4023), to surround.

4030. περικεφαλαία *perikephalaía*; gen. *perikephalaías*, fem. noun from *perí* (4012), about, and *kephalé* (2776), head. A headpiece, helmet. Used metaphorically in the NT (Eph 6:17; 1 Thess 5:8 in allusion to Isa 59:17; Sept.: 1 Sam 17:5; 2 Chr 26:14).

4031. περικρατής *perikratḗs*; gen. *perikratoús*, masc.-fem., neut. *perikrarés*, adj. from *perí* (4012), around, hence, wholly or completely, and *kratéō* (2902), to hold. Strong enough for something, all-powerful, dominant. In the NT, having completely in one's power, being wholly master of. With a gen. in Acts 27:16, to become master of, to hoist into the ship and secure it (cf. vv. 17, 30).

Syn.: *dunatós* (1415), powerful, strong in accomplishing something; *ischurós* (2478), mighty, inherently strong.

Ant.: *asthenḗs* (772), powerless, weak; *adúnatos* (102), weak, unable; *árrōstos* (732), infirm.

4032. περικρύπτω *perikrúptō*; fut. *perikrúpsō*, from *perí* (4012), about, and *krúptō* (2928), to hide. To hide completely or carefully (Luke 1:24).

Syn.: *kalúptō* (2572), to conceal; *parakalúpto* (3871), to cover with a veil; *sugkalúpto* (4780), to conceal altogether, cover; *lanthánō* (2990), to escape notice, be hidden from; *aphanízō* (853), to cause to disappear.

Ant.: *apokalúptō* (601), uncover; *phaneróō* (5319), to appear.

4033. περικυκλόω *perikuklóō*; contracted *perikuklô*, fut. *perikuklôsō*, from *perí* (4012), about, and *kuklóō* (2944), to compass about. To encircle, to surround a city as besiegers (Luke 19:43; Sept.: 2 Kgs 6:14; Josh 7:9).

Syn.: *períkeimai* (4029), to be encompassed; *peribállō* (4016), to cast all around; *periéchō* (4023), to surround; *periḯstamai* (4026), to stand by; *sugkleíō* (4788), to enclose, surround.

4034. περιλάμπω *perilámpō*; fut. *perilámpsō*, from *perí* (4012), about, and *lámpō* (2989), to shine. To shine around, with the acc. (Luke 2:9; Acts 26:13). Another comp. of *lámpō* is *eklámpō* (1584), to shine forth.

Syn.: *phaínō* (5316), to shine; *epiphaúō* (2017) and *augázō* (826), to shine forth; *epiphaínō* (2014), to shine upon; *stílbō* (4744), to glisten; *astráptō* (797), to flash forth; *periastráptō* (4015), to flash around.

Ant.: *skotízō* (4654), to make dark; *skotóō* (4656), to darken.

4035. περιλείπω *perileípō*; fut. *perileípsō*, from *perí* (4012), an intens., and *leípō* (3007), to leave, lack. To leave over. In Class. Gr., the pass., *perileípomai*, meant those who survived and therefore remained or were left behind. In 1 Thess 4:15, 17, the pres. pass. part. occurs as a subst. with the def. art. in the pl., *hoi perileipómenoi*. Paul, in 1 Thess 4:13, contrasts the attitude of believers with "the rest" in regard to death and speaks of Christians as those who should not sorrow because of death (which he calls "sleep"). "The rest" are the unbelievers who have no hope. In 4:14 he speaks about those who slept or died, whom the Lord is going to bring with Him when He comes for His Church. Here he is referring exclusively to the believers who had already died or who will have died when the *parousía*

(3952), the coming of the Lord for His saints, is realized. In verse fifteen, the distinction is made between those believers who will have died and the believers who will still be alive, who, ironically, are referred to by the same part. phrase, *hoi perileipómenoi*, which was used previously of unbelievers. Here the meaning is exactly in accord with the Class. Gr. meaning of the word. In verse seventeen, this subst. part. again refers to the believers who will have escaped death and who will be caught up with the dead in Christ who will already have been raised from death. *Hoi perileipómenoi*, the surviving ones (v. 17), refers only to those who are in Christ and stands in contrast to "the dead in Christ" of 4:16.

Syn.: *aphíēmi* (863), to leave, to let go; *apéchō* (568), to keep away; *eáō* (1439), to permit, leave alone.

Ant.: *haírō* (142), to take up or away; *hairéomai* (138), to take for oneself; *lambánō* (2983), to take; *paralambánō* (3880), to receive near or unto oneself; *proslambánō* (4355), to take to oneself; *aphairéō* (851), to remove; *anairéō* (337), to take up; *harpázō* (726), to seize or snatch.

4036. περίλυπος *perílupos*; gen. *perilúpou*, masc.-fem., neut. *perílupon*, adj. from *perí* (4012), about, and *lúpē* (3077), sorrow as an adj. Surrounded with grief, severely grieved, very sorrowful (Matt 26:38; Mark 6:26; 14:34; Luke 18:23, 24; Sept.: Ps 42:6, 12; 43:5).

Ant.: *alupóteros* (253), less sorrowful; *hilarós* (2431), cheerful; *eúthumos* (2115), cheerful.

4037. περιμένω *periménō*; fut. *periménô*, from *perí* (4012), concerning, for, about, and *ménō* (3306), to remain, wait. To wait around. Trans. with an acc., to wait for (Acts 1:4, waiting for the fulfillment of the promise of the Holy Spirit). See Sept.: Gen 49:18.

Syn.: *ekdéchomai* (1551), expect; *apekdéchomai* (553), to await or expect eagerly; *prosdéchomai* (4327), to look for with patience; *prosdokáō* (4328), to anticipate, await; *anaménō* (362), to wait with expectancy; *epiménō* (1961), to persevere; *prosménō* (4357), to persevere in, stay further in, continue in; *epéchō* (1907), to give heed to; *diatríbō* (1304), to tarry; *proskarteréō* (4342), to continue steadfastly in, wait; *prosedreúō* ([4332] TR) or *paredreúō* (UBS), to sit constantly beside, wait upon, expect.

Ant.: *apelpízomai* (560), to give up hope; *dialeípō* (1257), to leave off in the middle of something; *lanthánomai* (2990), to forget; *epilanthánomai* (1950), to be forgetful, neglect; *ameléō* (272), to neglect; *kataleípō* (2641), to forsake.

4038. πέριξ *périx*; adv., a strengthened form of *perí* (4012), about, roundabout. Roundabout, with the art., the one surrounding, adjacent (Acts 5:16).

Syn.: *kuklóthen* (2943), roundabout; *pántothen* (3840), on all sides; *kúklō*, the dat. of the noun *kúklos* (2945), a ring or circle all around.

4039. περιοικέω *perioikéō*; contracted *perioikṓ*, fut. *perioikḗsō*, from *perí* (4012), about, and *oíkeo* (3611), dwell, abide. To dwell roundabout, with the acc. (Luke 1:65, meaning their neighbors).

4040. περίοικος *períoikos*; gen. *perioíkou*, masc.-fem., neut. *períoikon*, adj. from *perí* (4012), about, and *oíkos* (3624), house. Someone living near a neighbor (Luke 1:58; Sept.: Deut 1:7).

Syn.: *geítōn* (1069), neighbor; *plēsíon* (4139), the near one.

Ant.: *pároikos* (3941), foreigner, alien; *apódēmos* (590), sojourner; *parepídēmos* (3927), a resident foreigner; *allóphulos* (246), a foreigner; *allótrios* (245), alien, stranger; *xénos* (3581), stranger.

4041. περιούσιος *perioúsios*; gen. *periousíou*, masc.-fem., neut. *perioúsion*, adj. from *periousía* (n.f.), abundance, which is from *perí* (4012), beyond, and *ousía* (1511), substance, being. Abundant, costly, select. Used only in Titus

2:14 and translated "peculiar." It refers to God's chosen people in whom He has a special interest, one which exceeds His common concern for mankind in general. Thus the phrase should better be translated, "His treasured people" (a.t.), the same as the "purchased people" referred to in 1 Pet 2:9. (See Sept.: Ex 19:5; Deut 7:6; 14:2; 26:18).

Syn.: *eklektós* (1588), chosen, elect; *polútimos* (4186), extremely valuable; *áxios* (514), deserving, worthy.

Ant.: *anáxios* (370), unfit, unworthy; *koinós* (2839), common.

4042. περιοχή *periochḗ*; gen. *periochḗs*, fem. noun from *periéchō* (4023), to contain. A passage or portion, circumference, circuit, compass, contents of a writing, argument in general. The argument or contents within certain limits, a period, section, passage (Acts 8:32).

Syn.: *tópos* (5117), region; *chōríon* (5564), land, country, field; *chóra* (5561), a country, land, region; *períchōros* (4066), a country or region roundabout; *klíma* (2824), an inclination, slope, region.

4043. περιπατέω *peripatéō*; contracted *peripatṓ*, fut. *peripatḗsō*, from *perí* (4012), about, and *patéō* (3961), to walk. To tread or walk about, generally to walk. Intrans.:

(I) Particularly and generally (Matt 9:5; 11:5; Mark 2:9; 8:24; 16:12; Luke 24:17; John 1:36; Acts 3:8, 9; 1 Pet 5:8; Rev 9:20; Sept.: Prov 6:22). With an adjunct of place or manner: with an adv. (Luke 11:44; John 21:18); with the adj. *gumnós* (1131), naked, used as an adv. (Rev 16:15); so also with a prep. as *en* (1722), in, with the dat. of place (Mark 11:27; 12:38; John 10:23; Rev 2:1; Sept.: Gen 3:8). In John 7:1, *periepátei* in the imperf., meaning Jesus going about, remained in Galilee; and also, by implication, in John 11:54. *En* (1722), in, figuratively (John 8:12; 11:9, 10; 12:35; 1 John 1:6, 7; 2:11; Rev 21:24); *epí* (1909), upon, with the gen. (Matt 14:25, "upon the sea" [a.t.]; Mark 6:48, 49; John 6:19; Sept.: 2 Sam 11:2); with the acc. (Matt 14:26, 29); *metá* (3326) with the gen. of person to accompany, associate with (John 6:66; Rev 3:4 [cf. Job 34:8]); *pará* (3844), near, with the acc., "near the sea" (a.t. [Matt 4:18; Mark 1:16]).

(II) Figuratively, to live or pass one's life, always with an adjunct of manner or circumstances, i.e., with an adv. (Rom 13:13; 1 Cor 7:17; Eph 4:1, 17; 5:8, 15; Phil 3:17; Col 1:10; 2 Thess 3:6, 11; Sept.: 2 Kgs 20:3). Followed by the dat. of rule or manner (Acts 21:21; 2 Cor 12:18; Gal 5:16); with the prep. *diá* (1223), through, with the gen., "through faith" (a.t. [2 Cor 5:7]); *en* (1722), in, with the dat., of state or condition, "in the flesh" (a.t. [2 Cor 10:3]); also of rule or manner (Rom 6:4, "in newness of life"; 2 Cor 4:2; Eph 2:2; Col 2:6, i.e., in Christ; 3:7; Heb 13:9; 2 John 1:4; 3 John 1:3, 4; see Sept.: Prov 8:20; Eccl 11:9). *Katá* (2596), according, with the acc. implying manner or rule (Mark 7:5; Rom 8:1, 4; 14:15; 1 Cor 3:3; Eph 2:2; 2 John 1:6).

Deriv.: *emperipatéō* (1704), to walk about in or among.

Syn.: *poreúomai* (4198), to go, proceed on one's way; *ágō* (71), to lead; *hupágō* (5217), *ápeimi* (548), and *apérchomai* (565), to go away; *proágō* (4254), to lead forth; *metabaínō* (3327), to go from one place to another; *anachōréō* (402), to depart; *hupochōréō* (5298), to go back, retire; *proérchomai* (4281), to go before, precede; *apobaínō* (576), to go away or from; *éxeimi* (1826), to go out; *diodeúō* (1353), to travel throughout; *paragínomai* (3854), to come, arrive, be present; *hodoiporéō* (3596), to be on a journey; *epistréphō* (1994), to return; *stoichéō* (4748), to walk in line.

Ant.: *káthēmai* (2521) and *kathézomai* (2516), to sit; *anákeimai* (345), to recline at a table; *katákeimai* (2621), to lie down; *anaklínō* (347), to cause to recline; *kataklínō* (2625), to make to recline; *kathízō* (2523), to make to sit down; *epibaínō* (1910), to ride.

4044. περιπείρω *peripeírō*; fut. *peripérō*, from *perí* (4012), round about, and *peírō* (n.f.), to pierce through. To pierce through, to transfix. In the NT, metaphorically, to be pierced by many sorrows (1 Tim 6:10).

Syn.: *diïknéomai* (1338), to pierce, penetrate; *diérchomai* (1330), to go through; *ekkentéō* (1574), to pierce; *nússō* (3572), to pierce through, inflict severe wounds.

4045. περιπίπτω *peripíptō*; 2d aor. *periépeson*, from *perí* (4012), round, about, and *píptō* (4098), to fall. To fall around someone, to embrace someone. In the NT, to fall into the midst of something so as to be totally surrounded by it, to fall into or among, with the dat. (Luke 10:30; James 1:2). Followed by *eis* (1519), unto, and *tópos* (5117), place (Acts 27:41).

Syn.: *ptaíō* (4417), to err, fall, stumble; *proskóptō* (4350), to trip up, stumble.

Ant.: *ménō* (3306), abide, continue, stand; *stoichéō* (4748), to keep step, to conform to virtue and piety, walk orderly; *hístēmi* (2476), to stand; *stékō* (4739), to be stationary, stand.

4046. περιποιέω *peripoiéō*, contracted *peripoiṓ*, fut. *peripoiḗsō*, from *perí* (4012), denoting acquisition, and *poiéō* (4160), to make. To acquire, gain for oneself, trans. (Acts 20:28; 1 Tim 3:13; Sept.: Gen 31:18; Prov 6:32). Used in the NT in the mid. voice.

Deriv.: *peripoíēsis* (4047), preservation, possession.

Syn.: *kerdaínō* (2770), to gain; *diapragmateúomai* (1281), to gain by trading; *ktáomai* (2932), to obtain; *agorázō* (59), to buy.

Ant.: *zēmióō* (2210), to lose; *apóllumi* (622), to lose, perish; *ekpíptō* (1601), to drop away, become inefficient.

4047. περιποίησις *peripoíesis*; gen. *peripoiḗseōs*, fem. noun from *peripoiéō*

(4046), to acquire, purchase. An acquiring, obtaining, purchasing (Eph 1:14, where "until the redemption of the purchased possession" is equivalent to the redemption acquired for us by Christ; 1 Thess 5:9; 2 Thess 2:14; 1 Pet 2:9, "a people for an acquisition {or purchase}" a.t.] means a people acquired or purchased to Himself in a peculiar or unique manner; Sept.: Mal 3:17, "they shall be to me for an acquisition" [a.t.], i.e., a peculiar property). See the verbal use in Acts 20:28. Preservation, a saving of life (Heb 10:39). It stands as the opposite of *apóleia* (684), perdition, waste, loss.

Syn.: *ktḗma* (2933), possession, property; *hupóstasis* (5287), essence, substance; *stásis* (4714), position, existence; *katáschesis* (2697), a holding down or retaining a possession; *húparxis* (5223), substance. An adj. syn.: *perioúsios* (4041), one's own possession; *sōtēría* (4991), salvation, preservation.

Ant.: *zēmía* (2209), damage, loss; *apobolḗ* (580), a casting away, loss; *hḗttēma* (2275), defect, loss, diminishing.

4048. περιρρήγνυμι *perirrḗgnumi*; fut. *perirrḗxō*, from *perí* (4012), about, and *rhḗgnumi* (4486), to break, tear. To tear from around someone, i.e., to tear off fetters, strip off by tearing. In the NT, used only of garments (Acts 16:22, to tear off the clothes of persons about to be scourged. The Roman custom was to allow officers to tear off the clothes of criminals before being scourged). Another comp.: *diarrḗssō* (1284) a late form of *diarrḗgnumi*, to break asunder.

Syn.: *schízō* (4977), to split, rend open; *diaspáō* (1288), to tear asunder; *sparássō* (4682), to rend and cause convulsions.

Ant.: *amphiénnumi* (294), to put clothes around; *endúō* (1746) and *endidúskō* (1737) and *ependúō* (1902), and *himatízō* (2439), to put on or get into clothes; *peribállomai* (4016), to clothe oneself.

4049. περισπάω *perispáō*; contracted *perispō̂*, fut. *perispásō*, from *perí* (4012), around, and *spáō* (4685), to draw. To draw different ways at the same time, hence to distract with cares and responsibilities. In the NT, only in the pass., *perispáomai*, figuratively meaning to be drawn around in mind or to be distracted, preoccupied with cares or business (Luke 10:40).

Syn.: *merimnáō* (3309), to be anxious.

Ant.: *ameléō* (272), neglect; *proséchō* (4337), to take heed; *proskarteréō* (4342), to give unremitting care; *phrontízō* (5431), to exercise thought.

4050. περισσεία *perisseía*; gen. *perisseías*, fem. noun from *perissós* (4053), over and above. A superfluity, an overflowing, something above the ordinary (Rom 5:17; 2 Cor 8:2; 10:15; James 1:21; Sept.: Eccl 1:3; 5:8; 6:8).

Syn.: *perísseuma* (4051), abundance, that which remains over; *hadrótēs* (100), bounty, abundance; *huperbolḗ* (5236), excess, a great measure, more than necessary.

Ant.: *hustérēma* (5503), that which is lacking, deficiency; *chreía* (5532), need, lack; *anágkē* (318), necessity, need; *aporía* (640), a state of need, quandary.

4051. περίσσευμα *perísseuma*; gen. *perisseúmatos*, neut. noun from *perisseúō* (4052), to abound. Abundance, surplus (2 Cor 8:14, where it refers to the gifts supplied by the saints; see discussion under *pleonázō* [4121], to abound); of the abundance of the heart (Matt 12:34; Luke 6:45); of the pieces left over (Mark 8:8).

Ant.: *hustérēma* (5503), that which is lacking, need; *hustérēsis* (5304), the process of going without; *chreía* (5532), want; *aporía* (640), a state of need.

4052. περισσεύω *perisseúō*; fut. *perisseúsō*, from *perissós* (4053), abundant. To be in excess, exceed in number or measure. In the NT, to be or have more than enough.

(I) To be left over, remain, exceeding a number or measure which marks fullness, intrans. (John 6:12, 13). Part. noun with the art. *tó perisseúon*, that remaining, residue after the needs were met (Matt 14:20; 15:37). With the aor. part. *ó perisseúsan* with the dat. (Luke 9:17), "that which remained" (a.t.).

(II) To superabound, to abound richly, trans.:

(A) Of persons, to have more than enough, superabundance, used in an absolute sense (Phil 4:12, 18); followed by the gen. (Luke 15:17); by *eis* (1519), unto, to or for something (2 Cor 9:8, to superabound in every good work); by *en* (1722), in, with the dat. (Rom 15:13, meaning in respect to something; Phil 4:12; Col 2:7).

(B) Of things, to abound, intensively with *en* followed by the dat. as in Luke 12:15, meaning that life does not consist in an abundance of things. The adj. part. *tó perisseúon* followed by the dat., that which is surplus to someone, means one's abundance, what is not needed (Mark 12:44; Luke 21:4). Followed by *eis* (1519), unto, with the acc., to abound unto someone, to overflow for him (Rom 5:15; 2 Cor 1:5); to abound unto something, to redound, conduce (2 Cor 4:15; 8:2). Used in an absolute sense (2 Cor 1:5). With the idea of increment, to abound more and more, increase, be augmented, with the dat. (Acts 16:5, they increased in number). With *en* (1722), in, followed by the dat. (Phil 1:9); *diá* (1223), through, with the gen., through someone (2 Cor 9:12; Phil 1:26).

(C) Causatively, to cause to abound, to make overflow: in love (1 Thess 3:12); in grace (2 Cor 9:8; Eph 1:8). In the pass., to be made to abound: of persons, to have more abundantly (Matt 13:12; 25:29).

(III) By implication in a comparative sense, to be more abundant, conspicuous or distinguished than something else is; to excel, i.e., with *pleíon*, the neut. of *pleíōn* (4119), greater, and the gen.

(Matt 5:20, "if your righteousness does not exceed that of the Pharisees" [a.t.]). Followed by *en* (1722), in, with the dat. meaning in or in respect to something (1 Cor 15:58; 2 Cor 3:9; 8:7). In Rom 3:7, used in an absolute sense meaning that the truth of God has been made more glorious. See also 1 Cor 8:8; 14:12; 1 Thess 4:1, 10.

Deriv.: *perisseuma* (4051), a surplus; *huperperisseúō* (5248), to abound exceedingly.

Syn.: *pleonázō* (4121), to superabound, have too much; *plēthúnō* (4129), to increase, multiply; *huperéchō* (5242), to hold or have above; *proéchomai* (4284), to surpass; *huperbállō* (5235), to excel, surpass.

Ant.: *pheídomai* (5339), to spare; *husteréō* (5302), to lack; *elattonéō* (1641), to be less; *leípō* (3007), to lack; *déomai* (1189), to make a request because of need; *aporéō* (639), to be at a loss, perplexed, in need.

4053. περισσός *perissós*; fem. *perissḗ*, neut. *perissón*, adj. from *perí* (4012), around, over and above. Over and above, more than enough.

(I) Particularly as exceeding a certain measure, with the gen. meaning more than (Matt 5:37, "what is beyond" [author's translation] or more than these [cf. Sept.: Ex 10:5; 2 Kgs 25:11; 1 Sam 30:9]). In the sense of superfluous (2 Cor 9:1).

(II) Generally, superabundant, abundant, much, great.

(A) Positive, only as advantage used in the neut. *perissón* abundant, in superabundance (John 10:10, "that they might have it more abundantly"). With the prep. *ek* (1537), by means of, or expressing measure followed by the gen. *perissoú*, beyond measure, vehemently (Mark 6:51; 14:31). (See *ek* [1537, III, E].)

(B) By implication, in a comparative sense, more abundant, distinguished, excellent, better (Matt 5:47). The art. and the neut. *tó perrissón*, excellence, preeminence (Rom 3:1 [cf. Matt 11:9; Luke 7:26]; Sept. Dan 5:12; 6:4).

Deriv.: *perisseía* (4050), a superfluity, an overflowing; *perisseúō* (4052), to abound, be exceeding.

Syn.: *meízōn* (3187), greater; *hupér* (5228), over, above; *mállon* (3123), very much; *éti* (2089), more; *pleíōn* (4119), more than.

4054. περισσότερον *perissóteron*; neut. of *perissóteros* (4055), more abundant, greater Used adv., more abundantly, far more (Heb 6:17); followed by the gen. (1 Cor 15:10); with *mállon* (3123), greater (Mark 7:36; Heb 7:15).

Syn.: *meízōn* (3187), the more, greater; *pleíōn* (4119), much more; *mállon* (3123), more so, rather; *eti* (2089), yet; *hupér* (5228), more. Adv.: *perissotérōs* (4056), most abundantly.

Ant.: *elássōn* (1640), less in quality or age; *mikróteros* (3398), least, less; *hḗssōn* (2276), inferior; *olígos* (3641), little.

4055. περισσότερος *perissóteros*; fem. *perissotéra*, neut. *perissóteron* (4054), adj., the comparative of *perissós* (4053), abundant, more. More abundant, greater, more. Greater in number (Luke 12:4); in degree (Matt 23:14); greater condemnation (Mark 12:40; Luke 20:47; 1 Cor 12:23, 24; 2 Cor 2:7). More excellent, greater, more (Matt 11:9; Luke 7:26).

Syn.: *kreíssōn* (2908), better; *mállon* (3123), rather; *meízōn* (3187), greater; *meizóteros* (3186), greater still; *pleíōn* (4119), more; *éti* (2089), yet, still; *hósos* (3745), the more.

Ant.: *elásson* (1640), less; *hḗsson* (2276), less, worse; *olígos* (3641), little.

4056. περισσοτέρως *perissotérōs*; adv. of comparative degree instead of the more usual form *perissóteron* (4054), abundantly, more. Exceedingly, much more, more frequently, more superabundantly. The obj. compared is implied (Mark 15:14, "they cried out the more exceedingly" and the comparative is "than before" [TR]). In 2 Cor 1:12, it

is "more abundantly towards you" (a.t.) and the comparative is towards others; so also in 2 Cor 2:4; 7:15; 11:23; 12:15; Gal 1:14; Phil 1:14. Also the more abundantly, the more (1 Thess 2:17; Heb 2:1; 13:19). With *mállon* (3123), rather, more (2 Cor 7:13).

Syn.: *perissós* (4053), in a greater measure; *huperperissós* and *huperekperissoú* (5249), exceedingly, abundantly; *huperballóntōs* (5234), above measure; *plousíōs* (4146), richly.

Ant.: *elássōn* (1640), less in quality and age; *hḗtton* (2276), less, worse; *olígon*, the acc. of *olígos* (3641), a little; *en olígō* (dat.), in a little, implying time; *prós olígon* (*prós* [4314], for), for a while or a little time.

4057. περισσῶς *perissōs*; adv. of *perissós* (4053), over and above, more than enough. Abundantly, exceedingly, vehemently (Matt 27:23; Mark 10:26; Acts 26:11; Sept.: Dan 8:9). Equivalent to *perissotérōs* (4056), abundantly, more.

Deriv.: *huperperissōs* (5249), more than.

4058. περιστερά *peristerá*; gen. *peristerás*, fem. noun. A dove, pigeon (Matt 3:16; 10:16; 21:12; Mark 1:10; 11:15; Luke 3:22; John 1:32; 2:14, 16). In Luke 2:24, two young doves were the offering made by the poor (cf. Lev 5:7; 14:22. See Sept.: Nah 2:7; Isa 38:14).

Syn.: *trugṓn* (5167), a turtledove.

4059. περιτέμνω *peritémnō*; fut. *peritemṓ*, 2d aor. *periétemon*, from *perí* (4012), around, about, and *témnō* (n.f., see *orthotoméō* [3718]), to cut off. To cut off or around, to circumcise (Luke 1:59; 2:21; John 7:22; Acts 7:8; 15:5; 16:3; 21:21). In the mid. (Acts 15:1, 24; 1 Cor 7:18; Gal 2:3; 5:2, 3; 6:12, 13). In the pass. perf. part. *peritetmēménos*, circumcised (1 Cor 7:18); in the mid. (Sept.: Gen 34:15, 17). Metaphorically in a spiritual sense, meaning to put away impurity (Col 2:11; Sept.: Deut 10:16; Jer 4:4 [cf. Rom 2:29]).

Deriv.: *aperítmētos* (564), uncircum-cised; *peritomé* (4061), circumcision.

4060. περιτίθημι *peritíthēmi*; fut. *perithḗsō*, pres. 3d person pl. *peritithéasi* (Mark 15:17), from *perí* (4012), about, and *títhēmi* (5087), to put. To put or place around a person or thing, followed by the acc. and dat. expressed or implied (Matt 21:33; 27:28, 48; Mark 12:1; 15:17, 36; John 19:29; Sept.: Gen 27:16; Lev 8:13; Ruth 3:3). Figuratively, to bestow upon, give (1 Cor 12:23; Sept.: Esth 1:20; Job 39:19).

Deriv.: *períthesis* (4025), wearing.

Syn.: *dídōmi* (1325), to give; *charízomai* (5483), to grant, bestow; *peribállō* (4016), to throw around.

Ant.: *apotíthemi* (659), to put off or away; *aírō* (142), to take away; *anairéō* (337), to take away; *aphístēmi* (868), to remove; *kinéō* (2795), to move; *metakinéō* (3334), to move away.

4061. περιτομή *peritomḗ*; gen. *peritomḗs*, fem. noun from *peritémnō* (4059), to cut around, circumcise. Circumcision. It was practiced by the Jews as a distinguishing sign of the Jewish nation from Abraham (Gen 17:10f.; Lev 12:3; Luke 1:59) on, and also by several groups such as the Muslims.

(I) It refers to circumcision or cutting off the foreskin (John 7:22, 23; Acts 7:8; Rom 4:11; Gal 5:11; Phil 3:5; Sept.: Gen 17:13; Ex 4:25, 26; Jer 11:16).

(II) It is also used figuratively for persons practicing circumcision, the Jews, as opposed to the uncircumcised Gentiles (Rom 3:30; 4:9, 12; 15:8; Gal 2:7–9; Eph 2:11; Col 3:11).

(III) Denotes also spiritual circumcision of the heart and affections (see Deut 10:16; Jer 4:4) by putting off the body of the sins of the flesh (Rom 2:28, 29; Phil 3:3; Col 2:11, the true circumcision or true people of God, meaning persons who were spiritually circumcised).

Ant.: *akrobustía* (203), uncircumcision.

4062. περιτρέπω *peritrépō*; fut. *peritrépsō*, from *perí* (4012) about, and *trépō* (n.f., see *anatrépō* [396]). To turn about or upside down, to overturn. In the NT, used figuratively, to turn about into any state, to cause to become something, to make, followed by *eis* (1519), into, as in Acts 26:24, meaning turns one about into madness or makes one insane.

Syn.: *stréphō* (4762), to turn, change; *metabállō* (3328), to reverse one's opinion, change one's mind; *allássō* (236), to change, make other than something is; *metallássō* (3337), to exchange one thing for another; *metatíthēmi* (3346), to place differently, to change; *metaschēmatízō* (3345), to change shape; *metamorphóō* (3339), to change one's nature, transform; *metanoéō* (3340), to change one's mind, reconsider; *metaméllomai* (3338), to regret without a sense of true repentance.

Ant.: *emménō* (1696), to continue in the same place or attitude, persevere.

4063. περιτρέχω *peritréchō*; 2d aor. *periédramon*, from *perí* (4012), around, and *tréchō* (5143), to run. To run around. In the NT, to run about, with the acc. (Mark 6:55; Sept.: Jer 5:1; Amos 8:12).

Ant.: *diaménō* (1265), to remain throughout, to continue to stay in one place.

4064. περιφέρω *periphérō*; fut. *perioísō*, from *perí* (4012), around, and *phérō* (5342), to carry. To carry or bear around. In the NT:

(I) To bear about, with the acc. (Mark 6:55; 2 Cor 4:10).

(II) Pass., to be carried or driven about here and there as by the wind, i.e., like clouds (Jude 1:12 [TR], which in later editions reads *parapherómenai* [3911], being borne along). Figuratively in Eph 4:14; Heb 13:9 (TR).

Syn.: *bastázō* (941), to bear; *aírō* (142), to lift and to carry; *ágō* (71), to lead, to carry; *periágō* (4013), to take around.

4065. περιφρονέω *periphronéō*; contracted *periphronō̂*, fut. *periphronḗsō*, from *perí* (4012), around, and *phronéō* (5426), to think. To depreciate, despise. In the NT, to think above or beyond a thing, to ignore, despise, with the gen. (Titus 2:15).

Syn.: *kataphronéō* (2706), to think against; *exouthenéō* (1848), to make of no account; *athetéō* (114), to get rid of, disannul, reject; *atimázō* (818), to dishonor; *oligōréō* (3643), to care little for, regard lightly; the phrase *logízomai eis oudén* (*logízomai* [3049], to reckon; *eis* [1519], unto; *oudén*, the neut. of *oudeís* [3762], none at all), to reckon as nothing.

Ant.: *timáō* (5091), to honor; *doxázō* (1392), to glorify or to give glory to.

4066. περίχωρος *períchōros*; gen. *perichṓrou*, masc.-fem., neut. *períchōron*, adj. from *perí* (4012), around, and *chṓros* (5561), region, place. Around a place, i.e., surrounding, neighboring, hence, in the NT, *hē períchōros*, implying *gḗ* (1093), earth, ground, country roundabout, surrounding region (Matt 14:35; Mark 1:28; 6:55; Luke 3:3; 4:14, 37; 7:17; 8:37; Acts 14:6). Used metonymically of the inhabitants of a certain region (Matt 3:5; Sept.: Gen 13:10, 11; Deut 3:13, 14). Used in the pl. neut., *tá períchōra* (Sept.: 1 Chr 5:16).

Syn.: *chṓra* (5561), country, region, field; *agrós* (68), field, farm; *méros* (3313), a part, share; *tópos* (5117), place; *chōríon* (5564), a region; *periochḗ* (4042), an area around, environs.

Ant.: *péran* (4008), on the other side, beyond; *huperékeina* (5238), beyond.

4067. περίψημα *perípsēma*; gen. *peripsḗmatos*, neut. noun from *peripsáō* (n.f.), to scour or scrape off all around. Scrapings, offscouring, scum. Like *perikátharma* (4027), an expiatory victim, a ransom, spoken especially of human victims. A vile and worthless person, or more literally "the scum of all things" (a.t. [1 Cor 4:13]). Strong's *Dictionary*

of the Greek Testament has it incorrectly spelled *perípsōma*.

Ant.: *timḗ* (5092), value; *éntimos* (1784), honorable.

4068. περπερεύομαι *perpereúomai*; mid. deponent from *pérperos* (n.f.), braggart. To brag or boast (1 Cor 13:4).

Syn.: *huperphronéō* (5252), to think too highly; *huperupsóō* (5251), to elevate above others; *huperaíromai* (5229), to become haughty; *huperéchō* (5242), to surpass, excel; *hubrízō* (5195), to exercise violence, use despitefully; *tuphóō* (5187), to be lifted up with pride.

Ant.: *tapeinóō* (5013), to humble, bring low, and, in the mid., to humble oneself.

4069. Περσίς *Persís*; gen. *Persídos*, fem. proper noun. Persis, a Christian in Rome to whom Paul sends greetings (Rom 16:12).

4070. πέρυσι *pérusi*; adv. of time, from *péras* (4009), beyond, across. The past year, a year ago. In the NT, only with *apó* (575), from, meaning since last year (2 Cor 8:10; 9:2).

4071. πετεινόν *peteinón*; gen. *peteinoú*, adj., neut. of *peteinós* (n.f.), flying, winged. A bird or fowl. In the NT, only in the pl. *tá peteiná* (Matt 6:26; 8:20; 13:4, 32; Mark 4:4, 32; Luke 8:5; 9:58; 12:24; 13:19; Acts 10:12; 11:6; Rom 1:23; James 3:7; Sept.: pl., Gen 1:26; Deut 14:19, 20; sing., Ezek 39:4).

Syn.: *órneon* (3732), fowl; *órnis* (3733), a hen; *neossós* (3502), a nestling.

Ant.: *herpetón* (2062), a creeping thing.

4072. πέτομαι *pétomai* and **πετάομαι** *petáomai*; fut. *petḗsomai* / *ptḗsomai*, mid. deponent. To fly. Used intrans. in Rev 12:14. The part. is *petómenos*, flying, used in later editions (Rev 4:7; 8:13; 14:6; 19:17; Sept.: Gen 1:20; Isa 31:5). TR: *petómenos*.

Deriv.: *ptēnón* (4421), winged.

4073. πέτρα *pétra*; gen. *pétras*, fem. of *pétros* (4074), a rock. A projecting rock, cliff.

(I) In such cliffs, rock sepulchers were hewn (Matt 27:51, 60; Mark 15:46); houses and villages were built for security (Matt 7:24, 25; Luke 6:48). Also spoken of a rocky soil (Luke 8:6, 13; Rev 6:15, 16; Sept.: 1 Sam 13:6; Prov 30:19; Isa 2:10, 21).

(II) Figuratively of someone possessing firmness and stability, one like a rock (Sept.: 2 Sam 22:2); Christ, in allusion to the rock whence the waters flowed in the desert (1 Cor 10:4; see Ex 17:6; Num 20:8). Also the expression a "rock of offense" or "stumbling stone," referring to Christ as the occasion of destruction to those who reject Him (Rom 9:33; 1 Pet 2:8 quoted from Isa 8:14). Distinguished from the masc. *pétros* in that *pétra* is a mass of rock while *pétros* is a detached stone or boulder, a stone that might be thrown or easily moved. Therefore, when a type is sought to illustrate a sure foundation, the word *pétra*, an immovable rock, is used (Matt 7:24, 25; 27:51, 60; Mark 15:46; Luke 6:48. See also its illustrative use in Rev 6:15, 16 [cf. Isa 2:19ff.; Luke 8:6, 13]). Used metaphorically of Christ and the testimony concerning Him which is an unchangeable, immovable testimony (Matt 16:18). When reference is to Jesus Christ and His testimony, it is *pétra*, but when reference is made to the Apostle Peter, then it is *Pétros*.

Deriv.: *petródēs* (4075), rocky.

Syn.: *spilás* (4694), a rock or reef over which the sea dashes and thus a hidden rock; *líthos* (3037), stone used for buildings or tombs; *psēphos* (5586), a smooth pebble.

Ant.: *ámmos* (285), sand.

4074. Πέτρος *Pétros*, πέτρος *pétros*; gen. *Pétrou*, masc. proper noun. Peter, meaning stone. The masc. of the fem. *pétra* (4073), a massive rock or cliff. *Pétros* always means a stone, never a rock as referred to by Homer. It is a large stone, a piece or fragment of a rock such as a man might throw.

Peter, or *Pétros* (Syriac: Cephas), was the Gr. name of one of the principal apostles of Jesus Christ. His original name was Simon or Simeon. He was the son of Jonas or John and a brother of Andrew and was probably a native of Bethsaida in Galilee. He was a fisherman by trade and resided at Capernaum with his wife and mother-in-law who was healed by Christ of a fever (Matt 8:14, 15; 16:18; Mark 1:29–31; Luke 4:38; 5:3–10; John 1:42; 21:15).

He belonged to the inner circle of three disciples which included John and James and was the most prominent of the Twelve Apostles in action and word and deed. He sacrificed much to follow Jesus Christ and on his being called to be an apostle, he was renamed Peter or "stoneman" (John 1:42). This was confirmed on making his great confession about the Lord Jesus Christ (Matt 16:18). He laid the foundation of the church among the Jews on the Day of Pentecost (Acts chap. 2) and also among the Gentiles after a special revelation and in the conversion of the Gentile Cornelius (Acts chap. 10). He appears throughout the gospels and the first part of the Acts as the head and mouthpiece of the Twelve. He was the first to confess and the first to deny his Lord and Savior. Acts 1--12; 15 record the labors of Peter. He was the leading apostle from the day of Pentecost to the Council of Jerusalem in A.D. 50. We do not know his whereabouts after that. Paul mentions him being at Antioch about A.D. 52 and censures him for inconsistency of conduct which he exhibited at that time toward the Gentile converts through fear of offending the Judaizing party. Peter was indeed humble, alluding later to Paul as his "beloved brother" in 2 Pet 3:15. Paul mentions him again about A.D. 57 in 1 Cor 9:5 as engaged in missionary journeys and labors together with his wife, perhaps among the dispersed Jews in Asia Minor to whom he addressed his epistles (1 Pet 1:1). This allusion to Peter's wife is important in proving that he did not give up the family ties when he entered upon his spiritual calling. Clement of Alexandria expressly states that both Peter and Philip had children.

Peter suffered martyrdom in Rome under Nero, but the exact time is not known. When Paul arrived in Rome in A.D. 61 and during his imprisonment in A.D. 61–63, no mention is made of Peter. It is therefore improbable that Peter reached Rome before the close of A.D. 63. The report of a twenty or twenty-five year residence of Peter in Rome rests on a chronological miscalculation of Eusebius and Jerome who assumed that he went to Rome in A.D. 42 immediately after his deliverance from prison (Acts 12:17). All this verse says is that "he went into another place." Surely had he gone to Rome, Paul would have without a doubt mentioned him in his Epistle to the Romans written in A.D. 58, yet Paul does not say a single word of previous labors by Peter in that city. Peter's martyrdom may have taken place either in A.D. 64 during the terrible Neronian persecution after the great conflagration, or in A.D. 67. He is said to have been crucified, and thus he followed his Lord literally in the mode of his death (cf. John 21:18, 19). Origen adds, however, that Peter, deeming himself unworthy to die as his Master had died, was, at his own request, crucified with his head downward.

The Epistles of Peter belong to the last years of his life and are addressed to churches in Asia Minor, chiefly planted by Paul and his companions. They contain precious consolations and exhortations and confirm the harmony of his doctrine with that of the apostle of the Gentiles (1 Pet 5:12; 2 Pet 3:15).

The first epistle is dated from his mention of Babylon (1 Pet 5:13) which may be the Babylon in Asia or a Babylon in Egypt now called Old Cairo. Others believed that he wrote his epistle from Rome, it being referred to as "Babylon" in Rev 17:5; 18:2, 10, 21 (which is believed to be Rome). This last view is favored by 1 Pet 5:13 by the terms "co-elect" (elected together with you), which most probably refers not to Peter's wife but to the Christian church in Rome, and "Marcus, my son," or Mark the evangelist who was his spiritual son. In this case, the passage would be the first and only scriptural proof for Peter's presence in Rome. If the letter was written during or after the terrible persecution of A.D. 64 he might have had good reason to call Rome by the name of Babylon, the ancient enemy of the people of God. Mark was a companion and interpreter of Peter in his missionary labors. The epistle was transmitted by Silvanus (1 Pet 5:12), a disciple and fellow laborer of Paul and a connecting link between him and Peter, and was well qualified to assure the Jewish converts in the churches of Asia Minor of the harmony of the two great apostles, Peter and Paul, in all the essential doctrines of salvation.

The second Epistle of Peter is a valedictory of Peter written shortly before his martyrdom with warnings against antinomian heresies which began to disturb the harmony and purity of the church. The antinomians were those who denied the obligations of the moral law and maintained that Christians are freed from it by the dispensation of grace set forth in the gospel. Thus the heresy was called antinomianism (the term comes from the Gr. words *anti* [473], against, and *nómos* [3551], law). The external testimonies in favor of the Epistle of 2 Peter are not so numerous as those in favor of the first, nor was it used as much. However, the author expressly designates himself as an eyewitness of the transfiguration of Christ on the Mount (2 Pet 1:16–18) and bears ample evidence of apostolic depth and unction.

4075. πετρώδης *petrṓdēs*; gen. *petrṓdous*, masc.-fem., neut. *petrṓdes*, adj. from *pétra* (4073), a massive rock or cliff, and *eídos* (1491), shape or appearance. Rock-like, stone-like, having the form of a rock. In the NT, stony, rocky ground, stony soil (Mark 4:5). Used in the neut. pl., *tá petrṓdē* (Matt 13:5, 20; Mark 4:16).

Syn.: the phrase *tracheís tópoi* (*tracheís* [5138], rough; *tópoi* [5117], places), rough places, rocks or rocky ground.

4076. πήγανον *péganon*; gen. *pēgánou*, neut. noun. Rue, a fragrant plant found in the mountains, sometimes planted for borders in gardens (Luke 11:42).

4077. πηγή *pēgḗ*; gen. *pēgḗs*, fem. noun. A fountain or well. Fountains of waters (Rev 8:10; 14:7; 16:4; Sept.: Ex 15:27; Num 33:9; 1 Kgs 18:5; 2 Kgs 3:19, 25). Metaphorically of life-giving doctrine (John 4:14). An emblem of the highest enjoyment (Rev 7:17; 21:6; Sept.: Prov 13:14; 14:27 [cf. *phréar* {5421}, a well or a pit in which water is stored {John 4:6, 11}]). *Pēgḗ* also means an issue or flux of blood (Mark 5:29) which is equivalent to *rhúsis* (4511), a flow, flux or issue; of blood (Luke 8:44; Lev 12:7).

4078. πήγνυμι *pḗgnumi*; fut. *péxō*. To fix, fasten, make fast and firm, fasten together, construct, build. In the NT, used of a tent, to set up, pitch (Heb 8:2; Sept.: Gen 26:25; 1 Chr 16:1).
Deriv.: *pagís* (3803), a snare, trap; *prospḗgnumi* (4362), to fix or fasten something; *skēnopēgía* (4634), to pitch a tent.
Ant.: *lúō* (3089), to loose; *katalúō* (2647), to take apart.

4079. πηδάλιον *pēdálion*, gen. *pēdalíou*, neut. noun from *pédon* (n.f.), an oar. A rudder of a ship (Acts 27:40; James 3:4).

4080. πηλίκος *pēlíkos*; fem. *pēlíkē*, neut. *pēlíkon*, adj. How great. Corresponding to *hēlíkos* (2245), and *tēlikoútos* (5082). In Gal 6:11, meaning either large characters (implying a stiff and unpracticed hand which made the Gr. letters large like the Hebr.) or a large document. The first

meaning is given by Chrysostom, Theophylact, Jerome, and other church fathers. The latter by Erasmus and Bengel. Figuratively of dignity (Heb 7:4; Sept.: Zeph 2:6). Equivalent to the expression *hoútō gráphō* in 2 Thess 3:17 (*hoútō* [3779], thus; *gráphō* [1125], to write).
Syn.: *mégas* (3173), great; *polús* (4183), much; *tosoútos* (5118), so great; *pósos* (4214), how great, many; *perissós* (4053), abundant; *meízōn* (3187), greater.
Ant.: *mikrós* (3398), little, small.

4081. πηλός *pēlós*, gen. *pēloú*, masc. noun. Clay, mire, mortar (John 9:6, 11, 14, 15; Sept.: Job 30:19; 2 Sam 22:43). Potter's clay (Rom 9:21; Sept.: Isa 29:16; 41:25).
Syn.: *ámmos* (285), sand; *óstrakon* (3749), earthenware.
Ant.: *líthos* (3037), stone; *psḗphos* (5586), a smooth stone, a pebble; *pétros* (4074), a piece of a rock.

4082. πήρα *pḗra*; gen. *pḗras*, fem. noun. A bag, sack, wallet, usually of leather in which shepherds and travelers carried their provisions (Matt 10:10; Mark 6:8; Luke 9:3; 10:4; 22:35, 36).
Syn.: *balántion* (905), money box or purse; *zṓnē* (2223), a girdle or belt which served as a purse for money; *glōssókomon* (1101), a small box for any purpose, but especially a purse to keep money in.

4083. πῆχυς *pēchus*; gen. *pécheōs*, masc. noun. A cubit. In the NT, a cubit measure, equal to the length of a man's arm from the elbow to the end of his middle finger, i.e., about twenty-one inches (Matt 6:27; Luke 12:25; John 21:8; Rev 21:17; Sept.: Gen 6:15, 16).

4084. πιάζω *piázō*; fut. *piásō*, Doric form of *piézō* (4085), to press. To press, squeeze, compress, hold fast, and hence to lay hold of, take, seize. Trans.:
(I) Of persons, to take one by the hand, with the acc. and gen. of the part. (Acts 3:7). In a judicial sense, to take, arrest

(John 7:30, 32, 44; 8:20; 10:39; 11:57; Acts 12:4; 2 Cor 11:32).

(II) Of animals, to take in hunting or fishing, to catch, with the acc. (John 21:3, 10; Rev 19:20).

Syn.: *harpázō* (726), to snatch or catch away; *agreúō* (64), to take alive by hunting; *thēreúō* (2340), to hunt or catch wild beasts; *zōgréō* (4084), to take captive alive; *sullambánō* (4815), to seize; *kratéō* (2902), to hold; *lambánō* (2983), to take, lay hold of; *epilambánō* (1949) and *katalambánō* (2638), to lay hold of; *bastázō* (941), to lift, bear.

Ant.: *aphíēmi* (863), to leave, let go; *eáō* (1439), to let be.

4085. πιέζω *piézō*; fut. *piésō*, perhaps kindred to *biázō* (971), to force. To press down, make compact (Luke 6:38; Sept.: Mic 6:15).

Syn.: *thlíbō* (2346), to press; *sunéchō* (4912), to constrain; *anagkázō* (315), to compel.

Ant.: *aphíēmi* (863), to let, permit; *epitrépō* (2010), to permit; *apolúō* (630), to release; *eáō* (1439), to let.

4086. πιθανολογία *pithanología*; gen. *pithanologías*, fem. noun from *pithanológos* (n.f.), speaking persuasively, which is from *pithanós* (n.f.), persuasive, which is from *peíthō* (3982), to persuade; and *légō* (3004), to say. Persuasive speech, discourse, or enticing words (Col 2:4).

Syn.: *peithós* (3981), enticing.

4087. πικραίνω *pikraínō*; fut. *pikranō*, from *pikrós* (4089), bitter. To make bitter, embitter. Trans.:

(I) Of water, in the pass. (Rev 8:11). Metonymically of the pain caused by bitter and poisonous food or drink, to make painful, to cause bitter pain, with the acc. (Rev 10:9, 10; Sept.: Job 27:2).

(II) Figuratively of emotions: to embitter; pass., to be or become bitter, i.e., to be harsh, angry (Col 3:19; Sept.: Ex 16:20; Jer 2:19).

Deriv.: *parapikraínō* (3893), to exasperate, provoke.

Syn.: *stenochōréō* (4729), to distress; *choláō* (5520), to be full of gall, angry, bitter.

Ant.: *chaírō* (5463), to rejoice; *agalliáomai* (21), to rejoice greatly, exult; *euphraínō* (2165), to make merry, gladden; *euthuméō* (2114), to make cheerful, cheer; *tharséō* (2293), to give courage or be of good courage.

4088. πικρία *pikría*; gen. *pikrías*, fem. noun from *pikrós* (4089), bitter. Bitterness (Acts 8:23 where "gall of bitterness" denotes extreme wickedness, highly offensive to God and all good men, likely to be hurtful and destructive to others, for which much suffering is reserved in the world to come for unbelievers [cf. Deut 32:32]). A "root of bitterness" in Heb 12:15 means a wicked person whose life and behavior is now offensive to God and obnoxious to men (cf. Deut 29:17; 32:32; Rev 8:11). Bitterness in the sense of bitter anger (Eph 4:31; Sept.: Jer 15:17); of bitter and reproachful language (Rom 3:14, quoted from Ps 10:7, bitterness of speech; see Sept.: Job 7:11).

Ant.: *chará* (5479), joy, delight; *agallíasis* (20), exultation, exuberant joy; *euphrosúnē* (2167), good cheer, mirth, gladness of heart.

4089. πικρός *pikrós*; fem. *pikrá*, neut. *pikrón*, masc. adj. Bitter. In the Sept., it was used as a neut. or fem. pl. to indicate the fruits of the wild vine or bitter gourd which are so excessively bitter and acrid as to be a kind of poison (see 2 Kgs 4:39). In the NT, used of taste, meaning bitter, acrid, brackish (James 3:11). Metaphorically it means bitter, cruel, malignant (James 3:14, indicating bitter, harsh, cruel feelings).

Deriv.: *pikraínō* (4087), to make bitter, embitter; *pikría* (4088), bitterness; *pikrós* (4090), bitterly.

Ant.: *glukús* (1099), sweet.

4090. πικρῶς *pikrós*; adv. from *pikrós* (4089), bitter. Bitterly. Used of bitter weeping (Matt 26:75; Luke 22:62; Sept.: Isa 33:7).

4091. Πιλᾶτος *Pilátos*, gen. *Pilátou*, masc. proper noun. Pilate (John 19:1), known also as Pontius Pilate (Matt 27:2). He was appointed procurator of Judea in A.D. 29. The proper residence of the procurator was Caesarea Maritime, but it was customary for him to go to Jerusalem during Jewish festivals to secure order and safety in the city. Thus it happened that Pilate was present in Jerusalem during the Passover when the Lord Jesus suffered death. The chief duty of the procurator concerned the revenues, but in a minor territory such as Judea, which was dependent on a larger contiguous province (Syria), he was the head of the whole administration and held the highest military and judicial authority. Consequently Pilate became the judge in charge of the trial of the Lord Jesus. Pilate was greatly disliked by the Jews, and more than once he drove them to the verge of insurrection. Although convinced of the innocence of Jesus, he yielded to the demands of the Jews to avoid personal trouble. In A.D. 36 the governor of Syria raised some severe accusations against Pilate who went to Rome to defend himself before the Emperor. He did not succeed and was banished to France according to one tradition. Another tradition, however, says that he was banished to a mountain near Lake Lucerne which bears his name. He committed suicide shortly thereafter.

4092. πίμπρημι *pímprēmi*; fut. *prḗsō*. To set on fire. In the NT, used figuratively, only in the pass., to be inflamed, to swell, become swollen, e.g., from the bite of a serpent (Acts 28:6).

4093. πινακίδιον *pinakídion*; gen. *pinakidíou*, neut. noun, a diminutive of *pínax* (4094), a plate. A small tablet, writing tablet (Luke 1:63).
    Syn.: *paropsís* (3953), a side dish, platter.

4094. πίναξ *pínax*; gen. *pínakos*, masc. noun. A board, table, specifically a writing tablet covered with wax. In the NT, a plate, platter, dish on which food and the like was served (Matt 14:8, 11; Mark 6:25, 28; Luke 11:39).

4095. πίνω *pínō*; fut. *píomai*, 2d aor. *épion*, perf. *pépōka*. To drink.
    (I) Generally of persons, used in an absolute sense (Matt 27:34; Luke 12:19; Acts 9:9; 1 Cor 11:25); figuratively (John 7:37); as an inf., to give to drink (Matt 27:34; John 4:7, 10; Rev 16:6); to ask for a drink (John 4:9; Sept.: Gen 24:14, 18). With adjuncts:
    (A) Followed by *ek* (1537), of, with the gen., of the drink or metonymically of the vessel containing the drink, i.e., to drink of something, a part of it (Matt 26:27, 29; John 4:12; 1 Cor 10:4; Rev 14:10; 18:3; Sept.: Gen 9:21; 2 Sam 12:3).
    (B) Followed by *apó* (575), from, with the gen. of the drink (Luke 22:18; Sept.: Jer 28:7).
    (C) Followed by the acc. of the thing drunk, to drink something, to use as drink (Luke 1:15; Rom 14:21; 1 Cor 10:4); to drink of (Matt 26:29); figuratively (John 6:53, 54, 56; see also Sept.: Ex 7:18, 21; 1 Kgs 13:16–18f.; Isa 5:22). In 1 Cor 10:21 to "drink the cup." Figuratively of suffering, "to drink of the cup" (a.t.) which God presents means to submit to the allotments of His providence (Matt 20:22, 23; 26:42; Mark 10:38, 39; John 18:11). In Matt 24:38, eating and drinking means reveling.
    (II) Figuratively, of the earth, to drink in, imbibe, with the acc. (Heb 6:7; Sept.: Deut 11:11).
    Deriv.: *katapínō* (2666), to drink down, gulp; *póma* (4188), drink; *pósis* (4213), the act of drinking; *pótos* (4224), a drinking bout, banqueting; *sumpínō* (4844), to drink together with.

Syn.: *methúō* (3184) and *methúskō* (3182), to get drunk.

4096. πιότης *piótēs*; gen. *piótētos*, from *píon* (n.f.), fat. Fatness, figurative of blessing (Rom 11:17; Sept.: Judg 9:9; see Job 36:16; Zech 4:14).

4097. πιπράσκω *pipráskō*; aor. pass. *epráthēn*, perf. *pépraka*, perf. pass. *pépramai*, from *peráō* (n.f.), to traffic, traverse, which is from *péran* (4008), beyond, particularly beyond the sea in other lands. To sell, because people usually went to other lands for merchandise. With the acc. (Matt 13:46; Acts 2:45); pass. (Matt 18:25; Mark 14:5; Acts 4:34; 5:4). Followed by the gen. of price (Matt 26:9; John 12:5; Sept.: Gen 31:15). Figuratively, in the pass., to be sold to someone, thus becoming his slave, followed by *hupó* (5259), under, with the acc. (Rom 7:14 meaning to be the slave of sin, devoted to it.; Sept.: 1 Kgs 21:25; Isa 50:1).
 Syn.: *pōléō* (4453), to sell; *emporeúomai* (1710), to trade; *pragmateúomai* (4231), to engage in business, trade.
 Ant.: *agorázō* (59), to buy; *ōnéomai* (5608), to buy.

4098. πίπτω *píptō*; fut. *pesoúmai*, 2d aor. *épeson*, aor. *épesa* (Rev 1:17; 5:14). To fall.
 (I) Particularly, to fall from a higher to a lower place, spoken of persons and things. In the NT, always with an adjunct of place from where or to which one falls. Followed by *apó* (575), from (Matt 15:27; 24:29; Luke 16:21; Acts 20:9). Followed by *ek* (1537), out of, meaning to fall from (Luke 10:18; Acts 27:34; Rev 8:10; 9:1; See Sept.: Job 1:16); by *en* (1722), among or in the midst of, "among thorns" (Luke 8:7). By *epí* (1909), upon, with the acc., meaning upon any person or thing (Matt 10:29; 13:5, 7, 8; 21:44; Mark 4:5; Luke 8:6, 8; 20:18; 23:30; Rev 6:16; 7:16; 8:10). Followed by *eis* (1519), into, (Matt 15:14; 17:15; Mark 4:7, 8; Luke 6:39; 8:14; John 12:24; Rev 6:13);

by *pará* (3844), by, near, with the acc. of place, meaning to fall at, by, or near (Matt 13:4; Mark 4:4; Luke 8:5). Figuratively, to seize (Rev 11:11).
 (II) Of persons, meaning to fall down or prostrate, used in an absolute sense (Matt 18:29; Acts 5:5). Joined with *proskunéō* (4352), to prostrate, worship (Matt 2:11; 4:9; 18:26; Rev 5:14; 19:4; Sept.: 2 Sam 1:2; Dan 3:5, 6). More usually with an adjunct of place or manner, followed by *enópion* (1799), before, with the gen., in the presence of (Rev 5:8), with *proskunéō*, worship (Rev 4:10); by *eis* (1519), with the acc. (Matt 18:29 [TR]; John 11:32; Acts 22:7 [cf. 9:4]); by *epí* (1909), with the gen. of place (Mark 9:20; 14:35); with the acc. of place or manner (Acts 9:4; 10:25; Sept.: 1 Sam 25:23, 24); *epí prósōpon* (*epí* [1909], upon; *prósōpon* [4383], face), on one's face (Matt 17:6; 26:29; Luke 5:12); with *pará* (3844), near (Luke 17:16); with *proskunéō*, to worship (1 Cor 14:25; Rev 7:11; 11:16; Sept.: 1 Sam 25:23); followed by *pará* (3844), near the feet (Luke 8:41; Acts 5:10 [cf. Luke 17:16]); *prós* (4314), toward, with the acc., toward the feet (Mark 5:22; Rev 1:17); *émprosthen* (1715), before, with the gen., before the feet, with *proskunéō*, worship (Rev 19:10; 22:8); followed by *chamaí* (5476), ground, toward the ground (John 18:6; Sept.: Job 1:20). Spoken of those who fall dead (Luke 21:24; 1 Cor 10:8; Heb 3:17; Rev 17:10 [cf. Ex 32:28; Num 14:32; Acts 5:5, 10; Sept.: Num 14:43]).
 (III) Of edifices, meaning to fall, to fall in ruins (Matt 7:25, 27; Luke 6:49; 13:4; Heb 11:30). Figuratively (Luke 11:17; Acts 15:16); in prophetic imagery (Rev 11:13; 14:8; 16:19; 18:2; Sept.: Isa 21:9).
 (IV) Of a lot, meaning to fall to or upon someone. Followed by *epí* (1909), upon, with the acc. (Acts 1:26; Sept. Ezek 24:6; Jon 1:7).
 (V) Metaphorically of persons, meaning to fall into or under; with *hupó* (5259), under, meaning under condemnation

(James 5:12). Used in an absolute sense, to fall into sin, transgress, to sin (Rom 11:22; 14:4; 1 Cor 10:12). Hence, also to fall with the meaning of to be made miserable, to perish (Rom 11:11; Heb 4:11; Sept.: Prov 11:28; 24:16). Of things, meaning to fall to the ground, to fail, become void (Luke 16:17; Sept.: 1 Sam 3:19).

Deriv.: *anapíptō* (377), to fall back; *antipíptō* (496), to resist; *apopíptō* (634), to fall from; *gonupetéō* (1120), to bow down; *ekpíptō* (1601), to fall out of; *empíptō* (1706), to fall into or among; *epipíptō* (1968), to fall upon; *katapíptō* (2667), to fall down; *parapípto* (3895), to fall beside, to fall down; *peripíptō* (4045), to fall among; *prospíptō* (4363), to fall toward; *ptôma* (4430), a ruin, corpse, dead body; *ptôsis* (4431), the act of falling.

Syn.: *rhíptomai* (4496), to fling oneself, to deliberately fall or throw oneself; *katabállō* (2598), to cast down; *katapontízō* (2670), to sink.

Ant.: *egeírō* (1453), to raise; *aírō* (142), to lift; *anaírō* and *anairéō* (337), to take up; *epaírō* (1869), to raise, lift up; *anabibázō* (307), to cause to go up; *anágō* (321), to take up; *hupsóō* (5312), to exalt, lift up.

4099. Πισιδία *Pisidía*; gen. *Pisidías*, fem. proper noun. Pisidia, a district of Asia Minor, lying mostly on Mount Taurus, between Pamphylia, Phrygia, and Lycaonia. Its chief city was Antioch (Acts 13:14; 14:24).

4100. πιστεύω *pisteúō*; fut. *pisteúsō*, from *pístis* (4102), faith. To believe, have faith in, trust. NT meanings:

(I) Particularly, to be firmly persuaded as to something, to believe, followed by the inf. (Rom 14:2); by *hóti* (3754), that (Mark 11:23; Rom 6:8; 10:9). With the idea of hope and certain expectation (Acts 18:8).

(A) More commonly used of words spoken and things, followed by the dat. of the person whose words one believes and trusts in (Mark 16:13; John 5:46; Acts 8:12; 1 John 4:1); by *hóti* (John 4:21).

(B) With an adjunct of the words or thing spoken, followed by the dat. (Luke 1:20; John 4:50; Acts 24:14; 2 Thess 2:11; Acts 13:41); by *epí* (1909), upon, and the dat. (Luke 24:25); by *en* (1722), in, and the dat. (Mark 1:15, "in the glad tidings" [a.t.], meaning to believe and embrace the glad tidings announced; Sept.: Ps 78:22; Jer 12:6).

(C) With an adjunct of the thing believed, followed by the acc. of thing (1 Cor 13:7; 1 John 4:16). In the pass. (2 Thess 1:10). Followed by *eis* (1519), unto, with the acc. (John 11:26; 1 John 5:10); by *hóti*, that (John 14:10; Rom 10:9); by *perí* (4012), about, concerning, and the gen. (John 9:18).

(D) Used in an absolute sense where the case of person or thing is implied from the context (Matt 24:23; Mark 13:21; John 12:47; Acts 8:13 [cf. Acts 8:12; 15:7]).

(II) Of God, to believe in God, to trust in Him as able and willing to help and answer prayer. Followed by the dat. of person with *hóti*, that (Acts 27:25); by *eis*, in (John 14:1). Used in an absolute sense with the pres. part. *pisteúontes*, meaning if you believe (Rom 4:17, 18; Heb 4:3). Generally, to believe in the declarations and character of God as made known in the gospel, with the dat. (John 5:24; Acts 16:34; 1 John 5:10). Followed by *eis*, in, with the acc., meaning to believe and rest upon, to believe in and profess (1 Pet 1:21); by *epí*, on, with the acc. (Rom 4:24).

(III) Of a messenger from God, to believe on and trust in him (rather, when applied to a merely human messenger of God, to credit and trust him, as coming from God and acting under divine authority).

(A) Of John the Baptist, with the dat. (Matt 21:25, 32; Mark 11:31; Luke 20:5).

(B) Of Jesus as the Messiah, able and ready to help His followers, followed by *eis*, in (John 14:1); to heal the sick and comfort the afflicted, with *hóti*, that (Matt 9:28); used in an absolute sense (Matt 8:13; Mark 5:36; John 4:48). **(1)** Generally of Jesus as a teacher and the Messiah sent from God. Followed by the dat. of person (John 5:38; 8:31; 10:37, 38; Acts 5:14; 2 Tim 1:12); by *hóti*, that (John 8:24; 11:27; 13:19; 16:27, 30; 17:8, 21; 20:31); by *ginōskō* (1097), to know (John 6:69; 10:38); by *eis*, in, with the acc. of person meaning to believe and rest upon (Matt 18:6; Mark 9:42; John 2:11; 3:15, 16; 4:39; 6:35; 7:5, 38; 8:30; 17:20; Acts 10:43; 19:4; Rom 10:14; Gal 2:16; 1 Pet 1:8); figurative-ly, with *tó phōs* (*tó*, neut. def, art.; *phōs* [5457], light), the light (John 12:36); *tó ónoma* (*ónoma* [3686], name), the name, as to who Jesus is and what He has done (John 1:12; 2:23; 1 John 5:13); in the dat. (1 John 3:23). Followed by *epí*, upon, with the acc. of person (Acts 9:42; 11:17 [cf. 11:21]); with the dat. (Matt 27:42; 1 Tim 1:16); figuratively (Rom 9:33; 1 Pet 2:6, quoted from Isa 28:16); in the pass. (1 Tim 3:16). **(2)** Used in an absolute sense, to believe, meaning to become a Christian (Mark 15:32; Luke 22:67; John 1:7; 12:39; Acts 4:4; 14:1; 17:12, 34). In the pres. part. pl. (*hoi pisteúontes*) or aor. part. pl. (*hoi pisteúsantes*), those who have believed, believers, Christians (Acts 2:44; 4:32; 19:18; Rom 4:11; 1 Cor 1:21; Gal 3:22; 1 Thess 1:7; 1 Pet 2:7).

(IV) Trans., to entrust, commit in trust to someone (Luke 16:11; John 2:24). In the pass., *pisteúomai*, with the acc. of thing, to be entrusted with something, to have something committed to one's trust or charge (Rom 3:2; 1 Cor 9:17; Gal 2:7; 1 Thess 2:4; 1 Tim 1:11; Titus 1:3).

(V) Used in connection with the rela-tionship between believing and miracle working.

(A) "And Jesus said unto them, Be-cause of your unbelief: for verily I say unto you, If ye have faith as a grain of mustard seed, ye shall say unto this moun-tain, Remove hence to yonder place; and it shall remove: and nothing shall be im-possible unto you" (Matt 17:20). This

was what Jesus said to the disciples on His descent from the Mount of Transfigu-ration upon finding that they were unable to exorcise a boy's demon. This incident is given also in Mark 9:14–29 and Luke 9:37–43.

In Matthew 17:17, when He said, " . . . O faithless and perverse generation," He did not include the disciples as unbeliev-ers and perverse. The word for "faith-less" is *ápistos* (571), unbelieving, with the meaning of not trusting God to per-form this and other miracles as opportu-nity and need arose.

What the father of the child said to Je-sus explains how it is possible for him and the disciples to believe and, at the same time, to be beset by unbelief in ac-complishing the task at hand. The father said, "I believe, Lord, help me in my un-belief" (a.t.).

Belief creates complete dependence upon the Lord and not independence. "Howbeit this kind goeth not out but by prayer and fasting" (Matt 17:21; see also Mark 9:29). The end result of this whole incident was "And they were all amazed at the mighty power of God" (Luke 9:43).

(B) "And all things whatsoever ye shall ask in prayer, believing, ye shall receive" (Matt 21:22). "Therefore I say unto you, What things soever ye desire, when ye pray, believe that ye receive them, and ye shall have them" (Mark 11:24). This latter assurance of the Lord also express-es dependence on the Lord through two words: *proseuchómenoi* (the pres. part. of *proseúchomai* [4336], to pray to God) and *aiteísthe* (the subjunctive mid. of *aitéomai* [154], to request as an inferi-or from a superior). It is not a desire at all but a humble request. This speaks not of the omnipotence of the believer's faith but of its full dependence upon God. "Be-lieve that ye receive them, and ye shall have them," and, one could add, if the Lord consents to grant them.

(VI) The pres. part. *ho pisteúōn* (John 3:15, 16, 36; 5:24; 6:35, 40, 47; 7:38; 11:25, 26; 12:44, 46; 14:12) should not be taken as the one holding on to God constantly lest he would let loose and fall. It rather indicates that, once one believes, he continues to believe, for he has eternal life in him (John 3:15). The assurance Christ gave in John 10:28 is this: "And I give unto them eternal life; and they shall never perish, neither shall any man pluck them out of my hand." Once a believer places himself in Jesus, it is He who holds him firmly without someone being able to snatch him away, for if this could happen then there would be the acknowledgement that someone is mightier than Christ, which cannot be.

Syn.: *peíthomai* (3982), to be convinced; *hēgéomai* (2233), to deem, consider, think; *epiginōskō* (1921), to perceive, recognize.

Ant.: *aporéō* (639), to be at a loss; *diaporéō* (1280), to be much perplexed; *distázō* (1365), to doubt, hesitate; *apistéō* (569), to disbelieve; *diakrínomai* (1252), to doubt, hesitate.

4101. πιστικός *pistikós*; fem. *pistikḗ*, neut. *pistikón*, from *pístis* (4102), fidelity, faith. Causing belief, persuasive, faithful, trustworthy. Used metaphorically, meaning true, genuine, pure (Mark 14:3; John 12:3).

4102. πίστις *pístis*; gen. *písteōs*, fem. noun from *peíthō* (3982), to win over, persuade. Faith. Subjectively meaning firm persuasion, conviction, belief in the truth, veracity, reality or faithfulness (though rare). Objectively meaning that which is believed, doctrine, the received articles of faith.

(I) In the common Gr. usage:

(A) Particularly and generally (Acts 17:31, having given to all the ability to believe [cf. Rom 3:23ff.]).

(B) In Rom 14:22, "hast thou faith" means persuasion about what God wants you to do (see Rom 14:23).

(C) In Heb 11:1, "faith is the substance of things hoped for, the evidence of things not seen" means that persuasion is not the outcome of imagination but is based on fact, such as the reality

of the resurrection of Christ (1 Cor 15), and as such it becomes the basis of realistic hope.

(D) In 2 Cor 5:7, "for we walk by faith, not by sight" means that which appears before us may not be what it seems to be, while faith is something which stands on proof arrived at inductively. See also 1 Pet 1:5, which means that faith obtains the future entrance into salvation, safe existence which will be provided by God at the end of the present season (cf. 1 Peter 1:7, 9).

(E) Followed by the gen. of object (1 Thess 2:13, meaning the gospel truth).

(II) Good faith, faithfulness, sincerity (Matt 23:23; Rom 3:3; Gal 5:22; 1 Tim 1:19, being faithful, sincere; 2:7; 2 Tim 2:22; 3:10; Titus 2:10, all good fidelity; Rev 2:19; 13:10; Sept.: 1 Sam 26:23; Prov 12:22; Hab 2:4).

(III) Faith given as a pledge, promise (2 Tim 4:7, where the faith possessed by the Apostle Paul in Christ was considered by him as a deposit made by God in him [cf. 1 Tim 6:21; 2 Tim 1:12, 14]).

(IV) As a technical term indicative of the means of appropriating what God in Christ has for man, resulting in the transformation of man's character and way of life. Such can be termed gospel or Christian faith (Rom 3:22ff.).

(A) Of God, indicated as faith in, on, toward God, with adjuncts: *epí* (1909), on, with the acc. (Heb 6:1); *prós* (4314), toward, with the acc. preceded by the art. (1 Thess 1:8); *eis* (1519), in, with the acc. (1 Pet 1:21); with the gen. *Theoú* (*theós* [2316], God), of God, meaning the faith emanating from God (Mark 11:22; Col 2:12). Used in an absolute sense (Matt 17:20; 21:21; Luke 17:5, 6 [cf. Mark 11:22; Heb 4:2; 10:22, 38]); with *ek* (1537), from, and the gen., *ek písteōs* (Rom 1:17, in allusion to Hab 2:4 where the Sept. has "fidelity [rather, faith in Christ]"); *en pístei* (*en* [1722], in, and the dat.), in faith, meaning in filial confidence, nothing doubting (James 1:6); *hē euchḗ písteōs* (*hē*, def. art.; *euchḗ* [2171], vow), to wish, vow of faith, meaning expression of a wish but with trust in the Lord to accomplish His will (James 5:15). Spoken analogically of the faith of the patriarchs and pious men under the Jewish dispensation who looked forward in faith and hope to the blessings of the gospel (cf. Gal 3:7f.; Heb 11:13); of Abraham (Rom 4:5, 9, 11–14, 16, 19, 20; Heb 6:12).

(B) Of Christ, faith in Christ: (1) As able to work miracles, to heal the sick (Matt 8:10; 9:2, 22, 29; 15:28; Mark 2:5; 5:34; 10:52; Luke 5:20; 7:9, 50; 8:48; 17:19; 18:42; Acts 3:16). (2) Of faith in Christ's death, as the ground of justification before God, saving faith, found only in Paul's writings (Rom 3:22, 25–28, 30, 31; 1 Cor 15:14, 17). Generally (Rom 1:17; 5:1, 2; 9:30, 32; 10:6, 17; Gal 2:16, 20; 3:2, 5, 7–9, 11, 12, 14, 22, 24; 5:5, 6; Eph 2:8; 3:12; Phil 3:9. Of the faith of Abraham (see A above). Some interpreters take *eis pístin* of Rom 1:17 by metonymy as referring to those believing (*eis toús pisteúontas* [cf. Rom 3:22]). (3) Generally, as the Son of God, the incarnate Word, the Messiah and Savior, the Head of the true Church; with *eis*, unto (Acts 20:21; 26:18); with *en*, in, and the dat., *en Christṓ*, in Christ (Gal 3:26; Col 1:4; 1 Tim 1:14; 3:13; 2 Tim 1:13; 3:15); with the gen. (Eph 4:13; James 2:1; Rev 2:13, thy faith toward Me; 14:12). Used in an absolute sense (Mark 4:40; Luke 8:25; 22:32; Acts 6:5, 8; 11:24; Eph 3:17; 6:16; Col 2:7 [cf. 2:5]; 1 Thess 5:8).

(C) Generally, with the gen., *hē pístis toú euaggelíou* (*euaggelíou*, gen. of *euaggélion* [2098], gospel), the faith of or in the gospel, gospel faith (Phil 1:27); *en pístei alētheías* (*en* [1722], in; the dat. of *pístis* and the gen. of *alḗtheia* [225], truth), meaning faith in the truth, i.e., in the gospel (1 Thess 2:13). Used in an absolute sense with the same meaning, namely, Christian faith, a firm and confiding belief in Jesus and His gospel (1 Cor 2:5; 2 Cor 4:13; Phil 1:25; 2:17; 1 Thess 1:3; 1 Tim 1:5; 6:11, 12; 2 Tim 1:5; 2:18; Titus 1:1; Phile 1:6;

Heb 12:2; James 2:5; 1 Pet 5:9). Elsewhere also, *pístis* seems to mark various predominant traits of Christian character as arising from and combined with Christian faith, without implying, however, any sharp distinction; meaning Christian knowledge, especially in Paul and Peter (Rom 12:3, 6; 14:1; 1 Cor 12:9; 13:2, 13; Titus 1:13; 2 Pet 1:5). In James, *pístis* as opposed to *érga* (2041), works (James 2:14, 17, 18, 20, 22, 24, 26). Of the Christian profession, the faith professed (Acts 13:8; 14:22; 15:9; 16:5; 1 Cor 16:13; 2 Cor 1:24; Gal 6:10; 1 Tim 2:15; 2 Tim 4:7 [cf. above in Section I, C]). Of Christian zeal, ardor in the faith (Rom 1:8; 11:20; 2 Cor 8:7; 10:15; 13:5; Eph 6:23; 1 Thess 1:4, 11). Of Christian love, as springing from faith (Rom 1:12, mutual faith and love; 1 Thess 1:3; Phile 1:5). Of Christian life and morals, practical faith (1 Tim 4:12; 5:8, 12; 6:10; Titus 2:2). Of constancy in the faith (Col 1:23; 1 Thess 3:2, 5–7, 10; Heb 13:7; James 1:3).

(D) Metonymically of the object of Christian faith, meaning the doctrines received and believed, Christian doctrine, the gospel, all that Christianity stands for (Acts 6:7, "were obedient to the faith," meaning embraced the gospel; 14:27, a "door of faith," meaning access for the gospel; 24:24; Rom 1:5; 10:8; 2 Cor 1:24; Gal 1:23; 3:23, 25; Eph 4:5; 1 Tim 1:4, 19; 3:9; 6:21; 2 Pet 1:1; 1 John 5:4; Jude 1:3, 20). With *en*, in, and the dat., *en pístei*, meaning in the gospel as Christians (1 Tim 1:2; Titus 1:4).

(E) Especially, the object of justifying faith, that on which a sinner, believing the gospel, relies for acceptance with God, namely Christ, as having fulfilled all righteousness (Rom 4:5).

(V) In Rom 3:3, Paul asks rhetorically, "Their unfaithfulness will not nullify [*katargḗsei*, fut. act. indic. of *katargéō* {2673}, to nullify, destroy, render ineffective] the faithfulness [*pístis*] of God, will it?" (a.t.). Here *pístis* likely means faithfulness, although a few interpreters understand "the faith of God" to mean the principle of faith in God.

Deriv.: *oligópistos* (3640), having but little faith; *pisteúō* (4100), to believe, have faith in; *pistikós* (4101), persuasive, faithful.

Syn.: *bebaíōsis* (951), the act of assurance, confirmation; *pepoíthēsis* (4016), reliance, confidence; *dógma* (1378), dogma, ecclesiastical belief firmly held; *tḗrēsis* (5084), observance, keeping; *eusébeia* (2150), godliness; *theosébeia* (2317), piety, respect, reverence of God; *didachḗ* (1322), teaching; *didaskalía* (1319), teaching, doctrine; *eulábeia* (2124), inner piety; *alḗtheia* (225), truth.

Ant.: *súgchusis* (4799), confusion; *parakoḗ* (3876), disobedience; *parábasis* (3847), violation; *apistía* (570), unbelief, faithlessness; *asébeia* (763), ungodliness, lack of piety; *apostasía* (646), apostasy, departure from the truth; *haíresis* (139), heresy, discord in doctrine; *blasphēmía* (988), blasphemy, vilification against God; *hupókrisis* (5272), acting, hypocrisy; *pseúdos* (5579), falsehood; *dólos* (1388), guile, deceit.

4103. πιστός *pistós*; fem. *pistḗ*, neut. *pistón*, adj. from *peíthō* (3982), to win over, persuade. Worthy of belief, trust, or confidence.

(**I**) Trustworthy (1 Cor 7:25; 1 Tim 1:12; 2 Tim 2:2; 1 Pet 4:19; Rev 19:11; Sept.: 1 Sam 3:20; Prov 20:6). True, sure, trustworthy, believable, worthy of credit (Rev 1:5; 2:13; 3:14; Sept.: Ps 89:38; Prov 14:5; Isa 8:2). Of things, true, sure, such as *ho lógos* (*ho*, def. art.; *lógos* [3056], word), the word (1 Tim 1:15; 3:1; 4:3; 2 Tim 2:11; Titus 1:9; 3:8; Rev 21:5; 22:6). In Acts 13:34, *tá hósia Dabíd tá pistá* (*tá*, neut. def. art.; *hósia*, neut. pl. of *hósios* [3741], sacred; *Dabíd* [1138], of David), the sure, inviolable, sacred things (promises, blessings) of David, the sure ones.

(**II**) Faithful in duty to oneself and to others, of true fidelity (Col 4:9; 1 Pet 5:12, a faithful brother; Rev 2:10). Of God as faithful to His promises (1 Cor

1:9, "dependable the God" [a.t.]; 10:13; 1 Thess 5:24; 2 Thess 3:3; Heb 10:23; 11:11; 1 John 1:9; Sept.: Deut 32:4); of Christ (2 Tim 2:13). As an attestation or oath, God is faithful (2 Cor 1:18). Especially of servants, ministers, who are faithful in the performance of duty (Matt 24:45; 25:21, 23; Luke 12:42; 1 Cor 4:2; Eph 6:21; Col 1:7, 9; 4:7; Heb 2:17). With *epí* (1909), upon, with, followed by the dat. pl. of *olígos* (3641), a little, *ep' olíga*, with little things (Matt 25:21, 23); with *en* (1722), in, followed by the acc. (Luke 16:10–12; 19:17; Eph 1:1; Col 1:2; 1 Tim 3:11; Heb 3:5); by the dat. of person (Heb 3:2; Sept.: Num 12:7; 1 Sam 22:14).

(**III**) With an act. sense, firmness in faith, confiding, trusting, believing, equivalent to *ho pisteúōn*, the pres. part. of *pisteúō* (4100), to believe (John 20:27; Gal 3:9). Followed by the dat. (Acts 16:15; 1 Cor 4:17). Used in an absolute sense (Acts 10:45; 16:1; 2 Cor 6:15; 1 Tim 4:3, 10, 12; 5:16; 6:2; Titus 1:6; Rev 17:14). Used in the acc. as an adv., *pistón poiéō* (*poiéō* [4160], to do, perform), meaning to do faithfully, in a believing manner, as a Christian (3 John 1:5; Sept.: Ps 101:6).

Deriv.: *ápistos* (571), untrustworthy; *pistóō* (4104), to confirm, establish.

Syn.: *áxios* (514), worthy; *bébaios* (949), steadfast, sure; *alēthḗs* (227), true; *alēthinós* (228), truthful; *ámemptos* (273), blameless; *anepílēptos* (423), irreproachable; *eilikrinḗs* (1506), sincere; *apseudḗs* (893), veracious; *aklinḗs* (186), firm, without wavering; *ametamélētos* (278), irrevocable; *ametakínētos* (277), unmovable.

Ant.: *ádēlos* (82), uncertain; *astēriktos* (793), unstable; *ápistos* (571), unfaithful, untrustworthy; *oligópistos* (3640), little faith; *parabátēs* (3848), *pseudḗs* (5571), false; *dólios* (1386), deceitful; *plános* (4108), seducing.

4104. πιστόω *pistóō*; contracted *pistṓ*, fut. *pistṓsō*, from *pistós* (4103), faithful. To confirm, establish, ascertain, make sure or certain. In the pass.: *pistóomai*, spoken of a person's being confirmed in or assured of (2 Tim 3:14).

Syn.: *bebaióō* (950), to confirm, establish; *diabebaióō* (1236), to strongly confirm; *kuróō* (2964), to ratify.

Ant.: *seíō* (4579), to shake; *diaseíō* (1286), to shake thoroughly; *tarássō* (5015), to disturb; *enochléō* (1776), to trouble; *thorubéō* (2350), to set in an uproar; *turbázō* (5182), to trouble; *distázō* (1365), to waver, hesitate, doubt; *aporéō* (639), to be at a loss; *diaporéō* (1280), to be thoroughly perplexed.

4105. πλανάω *planáō*; contracted *planṓ*, fut. *planḗsō*, from *plánē* (4106), a wandering. To cause to wander, lead astray, with the acc. In the pass.: to wander, go astray.

(I) Particularly of persons (Heb 11:38); of flocks (Matt 18:12, 13; 1 Pet 2:25; Sept.: Gen 37:14; Ex 23:4).

(II) Figuratively, to mislead, cause to err.

(A) To deceive, cause to err. Act.: to err, mistake, form a wrong judgment (Matt 24:4, 5, 11, 24; Mark 13:5, 6; 1 John 1:8; 3:7; Rev 13:14; Sept.: Prov 12:27). Pass.: to be deceived, misled (Matt 22:29; Mark 12:24, 27; Luke 21:8; John 7:47; 1 Cor 6:9; 15:33; Gal 6:7; Heb 3:10; James 1:16).

(B) Act., to seduce a people into rebellion (John 7:12; Rev 20:8, 10); from the truth (2 Tim 3:13; 1 John 2:26 [cf. 2:21, 22]). Pass., to be seduced, go astray (James 5:19; 2 Pet 2:15). Part., *hoi planṓmenoi*, those seduced, gone astray (Titus 3:3; Heb 5:2). Specifically, to seduce to idolatry (Rev 2:20; 12:9; 18:23; 19:20; 20:3; Sept.: 2 Kgs 21:9; Ezek 44:10, 15).

Deriv.: *apoplanáō* (635), to mislead; *planḗtēs* (4107), a wanderer; *plános* (4108), a deceiver.

Syn.: *apatáō* (538) to seduce; *exapatáō* (1818), to seduce completely, and *phrenapatáō* (5422), to deceive mentally; *dolióō* (1387), to lure; *dolóō* (1389), to ensnare; *paralogízomai* (3884),

to beguile; *deleázō* (1185), to entrap; *skandalízō* (4624), to entice, entrap; *ptaíō* (4417), to err, offend; *peripíptō* (4045), to fall into or among; *astochéō* (795), to miss the mark, swerve; *hamartánō* (264), to sin.

Ant.: *orthopodéō* (3716), to walk uprightly; *orthotoméō* (3718), to handle correctly; *ananḗphō* (366), to come to one's senses; *anorthóō* (461), to straighten up.

4106. πλάνη *plánē*; gen. *plánēs*, fem. noun. A wandering out of the right way. In the NT, used only figuratively meaning error.

(I) Delusion, false judgment or opinion (1 Thess 2:3; 2 Thess 2:11; Sept.: Jer 23:17).

(II) In an active sense, deceit, fraud, seduction to error and sin (Matt 27:64; Eph 4:14; 2 Pet 3:17; 1 John 4:6 used of a spirit of error, a deceiving spirit, a teacher who seeks to seduce, deception, fraud; Sept.: Prov 14:8).

(III) Of conduct meaning perverseness, wickedness, sin (Rom 1:27; James 5:20; 2 Pet 2:18; Jude 1:11; Sept.: Ezek 33:10).

Deriv.: *planáō* (4105), to lead astray.

Syn.: *apátē* (539), deceit; *dólos* (1388), a bait, snare; *pseúdos* (5579), falsehood.

Ant.: *alḗtheia* (225), truth; *eilikríneia* (1505), sincerity; *epanórthōsis* (1882), correction.

4107. πλανήτης *planḗtēs*; gen. *planḗtou*, masc. noun from *planáō* (4105), lead astray. One who wanders about, a wanderer, from which is derived the Eng. "planet." In the NT, attributed to a star, a wandering star, planet; figuratively of a false teacher (Jude 1:13 as an explanation of 1:4).

Syn.: *pseudodidáskalos* (5572), false teacher; *phrenapátēs* (5423), a mind deceiver; *pseústēs* (5583), a liar; *góēs* (1114), charmer, seducer.

Ant.: *hodēgós* (3595), a leader of the way, guide.

4108. πλάνος plános; gen. *plánou*, masc.-fem., neut. *plánon*, adj. from *planáō* (4105), to deceive. Deceitful, deceiving, seducing (1 Tim 4:1); as a subst., a deceiver, impostor (Matt 27:63; 2 Cor 6:8; 2 John 1:7).

Syn.: *phrenapátēs* (5423), a mind-deceiver; *pseudodidáskalos* (5572), a false teacher; *pseudomártus* (5574), a false witness; *pseústēs* (5583), a liar; *dólios* (1386), guileful, deceitful; *panoúrgos* (3835), crafty; *agenḗs* (36), ignoble.

Ant.: *eugenḗs* (2104), noble; *euschḗmōn* (2158), decent; *semnós* (4586), honest, grave.

4109. πλάξ pláx; gen. *plakós*, fem. noun. Any broad and flat surface, as of the sea. In the NT, generally, a table, tablet of wood or stone for inscriptions as the two tables of the decalogue given to Moses (2 Cor 3:3; Heb 9:4; Sept.: Ex 31:17; 32:14; 34:1, 4); figuratively (2 Cor 3:3, the heart [cf. Rom 2:15; Heb 8:10]).

Syn.: *pínax* (4094), a board or plank, platter; *édaphos* (1475), ground; *chártēs* (5489), paper; *membrána* (3200), parchment; *pinakídion* (4093), a small tablet for writing; *bíblos* (976), book; *biblíon* (975), a small book, a scroll; *bibliarídion* (974), a booklet.

4110. πλάσμα plásma; gen. *plásmatos*, neut. noun from *plássō* (4111), to shape, form. A thing formed as by a potter (Rom 9:20 quoted from Isa 29:16).

Syn.: *ktísis* (2937), creation; *ktísma* (2938), a created thing, creature, product of a creative act; *poíēma* (4161), a thing that is made; *kósmos* (2889), the world; *phúsis* (5449), nature; *oikodomḗ* (3619), a building.

Ant.: *téktōn* (5045), a craftsman; *architéktōn* (753), architect; *ktístēs* (2939), creator; *dēmiourgós* (1217), a maker, creator; *technítēs* (5079), designer; *poiētḗs* (4163), maker, doer.

4111. πλάσσω plássō; or the Attic *pláttō*, fut. *plásō*. To form, fashion, mold,

with reference to any soft substance, as a potter does the clay (Rom 9:20). In the pass. (1 Tim 2:13; Sept.: Gen 2:7, 8; Isa 29:16).

Deriv.: *plásma* (4110), something molded; *plastós* (4112), molded.

Syn.: *morphóō* (3445), to form inwardly; *metaschēmatízō* (3345), to change in shape or appearance; *suschēmatízō* (4964), to give a shape or appearance that conforms to something; *metamorphóō* (3339), to change into another form, to transfigure; *metabállō* (3328), to change.

Ant.: *exaleíphō* (1813), to obliterate.

4112. πλαστός plastós; fem. *plastḗ*, neut. *plastón*, adj. from *plássō* (4111), to mold. Artificial, feigned, false, hypocritical, deceitful (2 Pet 2:3, "feigned words," or ones easily shaped as desired).

Syn.: *pseudḗs* (5571), false; *nóthos* (3541), spurious; *dólios* (1386), deceitful; *hupokritḗs* (5273), hypocrite.

Ant.: *bébaios* (949), firm, secure; *stereós* (4731), solid, firm; *hedraíos* (1476), fixed, steadfast; *pistós* (4103), trustworthy; *eilikrinḗs* (1506), sincere; *alēthḗs* (227), true; *alēthinós* (228), unfeigned, genuine, real; *gnḗsios* (1103), sincere, genuine, legitimate; *apseudḗs* (97), without deceit.

4113. πλατεῖα plateía; gen. *plateías*, fem. noun from *platús* (4116), broad. Broad street (Matt 6:5; 12:19; Luke 10:10; 13:26; 14:21; Acts 5:15; Rev 11:8; 21:21; 22:2; Sept.: Judg 19:15, 20; Isa 15:3; Zech 8:4, 5).

4114. πλάτος plátos; gen. *plátous*, neut. noun from *platús* (4116), broad. Breadth (Rev 21:16). Figuratively (Eph 3:18; Rev 20:9, meaning the great expanses of the earth, the width; Sept.: Gen 6:15; Hab 1:6).

Other distance measurements: *mēkos* (3372), length; *báthos* (899), depth; *húpsos* (5311), height.

4115. πλατύνω platúnō; fut. *platunṓ*; aor. pass. *eplatúnthēn*; perf. pass, *peplátumai*, 3d person pl., *peplátuntai* (2 Cor 6:11), from *platús* (4116), broad. To make broad, enlarge.

(I) Trans. (Matt 23:5; Sept.: Ex 34:24; Hab 2:5).

(II) Figuratively, to make broad or large to or for someone, i.e., to give him enlargement, deliverance from straits (see Ps 4:1 [cf. Ps 18:36]). In the pass., to be enlarged, i.e., to have enlargement, to rejoice; the opposite of *stenochōréō* (4729), to be in narrow places, straits (2 Cor 6:13 [cf. 6:12]; of the heart, 6:11).

Syn.: *megalúnō* (3170), to magnify, extol; *auxánō* (837), to grow, enlarge, increase; *anoígō* (455), to open up; *dianoígō* (1272), to open thoroughly.

Ant.: *elattonéō* (1641), to diminish; *stenochōréō* (4729), to hem in closely, straiten; *hupostéllō* (5288), to withdraw or lower (as a flag).

4116. πλατύς *platús*; fem. *plateía*, neut. *platú*, adj. Broad, wide (Matt 7:13).

Deriv.: *plateía* (4113), a broad street; *plátos* (4114), breadth; *platúnō* (4115), to broaden.

Syn.: *eurúchōros* (2149), spacious.

Ant.: *stenós* (4728), narrow.

4117. πλέγμα *plégma*; gen. *plégmatos*, dat. pl. *plégmasin*, neut. noun from *plékō* (4120), to plait. Anything plaited, braided, woven. A braid of hair, braided hair (1 Tim 2:9).

Deriv.: *emploké* (1708), braided.

4118. πλεῖστος *pleístos*; fem. *pleístē*, neut. *pleíston*, adj., the superlative of *polús* (4183), many, much. The greatest, very great, the most. In the NT, used only of number (Matt 11:20; 21:8, meaning a very great multitude). Used as an adv. with the neut. art., *tó pleíston*, at most (1 Cor 14:27). The comparative form is *pleíōn* (4119).

Syn.: *mégas* (3173), great; *mégistos* (3176), greatest; *meízōn* (3187), the greater; *málista* (3122), most of all; *ámetros* (280), without measure; *pollaplásios* (4179), multiple, manifold.

Ant.: *mikrós* (3398), little, small; *mikróteros* (3398), smaller; *olígos* (3641), little, few; *elássōn* (1640), smaller; *eláchistos* (1646), least; *brachús* (1024), of short duration; *ásēmos* (767), insignificant.

4119. πλείων *pleíōn*; πλεῖον *pleíon*, πλέον *pléon*, gen. *pleíonos*, masc.-fem., neut. *pleíon*, adj., the comparative of *polús* (4183), many, much. More (Matt 5:20; 6:25); usually in the neut., *pléon* (Luke 3:13; Acts 15:28). In the pl., *pleíous*, also *pleíones* (Heb 7:23). In the acc., *pleíous*, also *pleíonas* (Matt 21:36). Neut., *pleíona* (Matt 20:10). The superlative form is *pleístos* (4118), the utmost.

(I) Of number, magnitude, and in comparison expressed or implied, followed by the gen. (Matt 21:36, meaning more than the first time; Mark 12:43; Luke 21:3; John 7:31); followed by *é* (2228), more than (Matt 26:53; John 4:1). Before a numeral, *é* (2228), or, is regularly omitted (Acts 4:22; 23:13, 21). In Luke 9:13, *pléon é pénte*, (*pénte* [4002], five), "more than five" (a.t.); followed by *pará* (3844), than, as in Luke 3:13, "more than that appointed." In Acts 15:28, followed by *plén* (4133), except, with the' gen. When the obj. of comparison is implied (Matt 20:10; Luke 11:53; John 4:41 Acts 28:23); *tó pleíon*, meaning the more, the greater debt (Luke 7:43). Hence generally and emph., it is equivalent to many, very many (Acts 13:31; 21:10; 24:17; 25:14; 27:20). In Heb 7:23, it stands in opposition to "one" (a.t.).

(II) Pl. with the art., *hoi pleíones* or *hoi pleíous*, the more, the most, the many (Acts 19:32; 27:12; 1 Cor 9:19, meaning that I may gain, if not all, yet the greater part; 10:5; 15:6; 2 Cor 2:6; 4:15; 9:2; Phil 1:14).

(III) Figuratively of worth, importance, dignity, meaning more, greater, higher, with the gen. (Matt 6:25; 12:41, 42; Mark 12:33; Luke 11:31, 32; 12:23; Heb 3:3; Rev 2:19). Pleonastically with *perisseúō* (4052), to abound (Matt 5:20).

Followed by *pará* (3844), than (Heb 3:3; 11:4).

(IV) In the neut. *pleíon* as an adv. meaning more.

(A) With the gen. (Luke 7:42; John 21:15, "Do you love me more than these?" [a.t.] referring either to the fish caught or the other disciples).

(B) The expression *epí pleíon* (*epí* [1909], upon, moreover) means further, longer. Spoken of people (Acts 4:17; 2 Tim 3:9). In 2 Tim 2:16, with the gen. *asebeías* (763), ungodliness, it means "further as to" or "in ungodliness" (a.t.). Spoken of time (Acts 20:9; 24:4).

Deriv.: *pleonázō* (4121), to increase; *pleonektéō* (4122), to covet; *pleonexía* (4124), greed.

Syn.: *mállon* (3123), more; *éti* (2089), more, also; *perissóteron* (4056), more abundantly; *meízon* (3187), greater; *hupér* (5228), above, over, more; *perissós* (4053), over and above; *perissóteros* (4055), much more; *meizóteros* (3186) and *meízon* (3187), greater; *ánō* (507), above; *anóteron* (511), higher; *pleístos* (4110), most; *ámetros* (280), without measure; *pollaplasíōn* (4179), manifold, more.

Ant.: *olígos* (3641), little; *elássōn* (1640), little, less in quantity or age; *mikrós* (3398), small; *mikróteros* (3398), less, smaller; *eláchistos* (1646), least; *elachistóteros* (1647), less than the least; *hḗssōn* (2276), inferior, worse; *brachús* (1024), short (referring to time).

4120. πλέκω *plékō*; fut. *pléxō*. To plait, braid, weave, knit, used trans. (Matt 27:29; Mark 15:17; John 19:2; Sept.: Isa 28:5).

Deriv.: *emplékō* (1707), to entwine, entangle; *plégma* (4117), that which is woven.

4121. πλεονάζω *pleonázō*; fut. *pleonásō*, from *pleíōn* (4119), more. To have or cause to have much, or more than enough. Except in 2 Pet 1:8, the word occurs only in the Pauline epistles, as do the deriv. *pleonektéō* (4122), to be covetous,

and *pleonéktēs* (4123), one who holds or desires more, covetous. Used intrans.:

(I) Of persons, to have or do more than enough, to have a surplus (2 Cor 8:15, quoted from Ex 16:18). The commandment in Ex 16:16 was "Gather of it every man according to his eating, an omer." The phrase "according to his eating" is explained by 16:18 which makes it clear that God standardized each person's portion as an omer (a Hebrew measure, the tenth of an ephah [which was equal to a little more than a bushel]). Therefore the standard measurement was a tenth of a bushel of manna per person provided miraculously by God Himself. When each person took according to God's standard, there was neither surplus nor lack. God, in giving us the privilege of using His provisions, does not permit waste on our part. He knows what suffices for each one of us.

But there were people of smaller and larger appetites. Therefore the former found that a tenth of a bushel was too much, resulting in waste, and the latter found that an omer did not satisfy them. God expected each one to gather for himself and his dependents "according to his eating" so that there would be nothing left over for some and no lack for others. God wanted each one to have enough. Although the food was miraculously provided and God could have provided an over-abundance for the Israelites, He did not do it. He wanted His people to learn to consider the needs of others and to share. His measure of sufficiency takes into account the differences of appetite and need according to His non-uniform creation genius. God is never arbitrary.

To understand 2 Cor 8:15, we must study 8:8–14. In 2 Cor 8:8, Paul states that the Macedonians (see 8:1) were more diligent in giving than the Corinthians, not because they had an abundance (as the Corinthians) but out of their poverty they abounded (*perisseúō* [4052]) in their giving. In 8:8 Paul had two things to compare: the *spoudḗ* (4710), diligence, which was coupled with the speed of the Macedonians whom he calls *héteroi*

(2087), others (but different than the Corinthians), and the love of the Corinthians. Paul considered the motive very important (8:9–13). The equality (*isótēs* [2471]) he speaks about is equal to God's decision for the Israelites in the desert to measure their provision of the manna "according to their eating" and not the inflexible standard of the omer measurement, which for some was too little and for others too much.

God in Jesus Christ revealed that He gives the basic gifts of life and opportunity to all (see the parable of the pounds—one pound to each of ten [Luke 19:11–27]) and also differing talents to each according to that one's ability (see the parable of the talents [Matt 25:14–30]). Jesus does not present God as being unjust or unequal in His treatment of people, but as recognizing that He has made everybody as possessing natural life, but capable of accomplishing variably according to the strength (*dúnamis* [1411]) of each one (Matt 25:15).

Paul calls the possessions of the Corinthians *perísseuma* (4051), surplus, meaning that they had more than was necessary for their own needs. That was what they were able to earn, having been given greater ability to do so. They exercised their God-given talents to produce more than they needed. This is profit-making (*kerdaínō* [2770], to make profit, earn [cf. Matt 25:16, 17, 20, 22]). There was nothing wrong with this, but a responsibility did ensue in handling the surplus. It was to meet the lack (*hustérēma* [5303]) or the shortfall of the Macedonians so that there might be equality (*isótēs*), which meant the meeting of the needs of others through the Corinthians' giving according to their surplus.

And then comes 2 Cor 8:15, in the KJV translated, "As it is written, He that hath gathered much had nothing over; and he that had gathered little had no lack" (quoting Ex 16:18). The Gr. text says: *ho tó polú ouk epleónase* (*ho* [masc. art.], the; *tó* [neut. art.], the; *polú*, neut. sing of *polús* [4183], much), the one with much,

implying over-gathering either by miscalculation, a lessened appetite, or greed. The one who ended with much more than he needed was faced with a problem. He could not store it because it would spoil. He would not have to waste it by attempting to store it if he had shared it with the one who miscalculated in not gathering enough. He would not have the problem of having too much becoming waste while another did not have enough.

The ant. of *pleonázō* in 2 Cor 8:15 is *elattonéō* (1641), to make, have, or end with less or too little. He who *pleonázei* never has too little for himself, but his needs are fully met.

In this context then, the word *pleonázō*, to have much, is used in contradistinction to the word *perisseúō*, to have left over after needs have been met because of the utilization of the abilities God has given someone (2 Cor 8:2, 7; the subst. *perísseuma* in 8:14). Thus *pleonázō* here means to recognize that one has more than he needs as a result of God's direct gift, and not to allow it to go to waste but to share it with others so that they may not face a problem in their lack. The temptations faced in having too much can be alleviated by sharing with those who do not have enough. (See the parable of the rich farmer in Luke 12:15–21. The sin this parable was meant to counteract was *pleonexía* [4124], covetousness, a related word to *pleonázō*, both of which have the prefix *pléon*, more. *Pleonexía* is the sin of greed where one is never content with what he has. A *pleonéktēs* [4123], a covetous person, is one who increases his desires as he receives more, and therefore never has enough for himself and therefore to share.)

(II) The grace of God is presented as *pleonásasa* (the aor. part. fem.), having been given in greater measure than needed.

(A) Rom 5:20: "Moreover, the law entered that the offense might abound. But where sin abounded, grace did much more abound." The first occurrences of "abound" and "abounded" are the translations of *pleonázō*. The Law was given to make evident the transgression (*paráptōma* [3900], deviation, transgression, sin) of man. The Law revealed transgression to be sin (*hamartía* [266]), and sin *epleónasen* (aor. of *pleonázō*). Because of the efficacy of the Law, grace "did much more abound." This last phrase in Gr. is *hupereperísseusen* (aor. ind. of *huperperisseúō* [5248], to have a surplus). This last verb indicates an efficacious act of God in providing grace sufficiently to meet the need of the sinner for forgiveness (*áphesis* [859], which involves more than *páresis* [3929], toleration [Rom 3:25]). God's grace was more than enough, for it took away the desire of the sinner to sin (1 John 3:6). Of the grace of God, Paul says that it *eperísseuse* (aor. of *perisseúō* [4052]), abounded, in 1 John 3:15 without the superlative *hupér* (5228), more. The second statement with the superlative *hupereperísseuse* is for emphasis. Therefore, in the context of Rom 5:20, we have sin abounding but grace being more than sufficient to provide forgiveness, the obliteration of the guilt of sin, and the provision of the power against sinning.

(B) Rom 6:1 states: "What shall we say then? Shall we continue in sin, that grace may abound?" That word "abound" is *pleonáse*, the aor. subjunctive of *pleonázō*. God's grace in Christ does not merely *pleonázei*, happen to be there to cover sin automatically. God's provision in Christ is available for sinners, but it has to be sought, and one who continues in sin has never experienced it (1 John 3:6). Grace is made to be more than enough (*perisseúei*) for those who have experienced it in original repentance and to those who seek repentance for occasional sin in the exercise of their sainthood (1 John 2:1, 2). Rom 6:1 teaches that the abundance of grace is not automatically applied toward those who sin willfully. Its existence and sufficiency is no guarantee of its healing effect if one does not seek and desire it. Grace applied is preventive of sin, not merely therapeutic.

(C) 2 Cor 4:15: "For all things are for your sakes, that the abundant grace through the thanksgiving of many, might redound to the glory of God." Here we are told that: **(1)** God has provided full and complete benefits for our salvation. The raising of our mortal bodies (2 Cor 4:14 [cf. 4:11, 12]) is the ultimate fulfillment. But this applies to believers only, for this resurrection is the one unto life (4:12 [cf. John 5:24, 28, 29]) and not unto condemnation. **(2)** The purpose of this provision is expressed with the conj. *hína* (2443), so that. The verb is *perisseúsē*, the aor. subjunctive of *perisseúō*, to increase, excel. The subj. is *cháris* (5485), grace, with the def. art. *hē*. This grace of God in Christ is said to have abounded (*pleonásasa* aor. part. of *pleonázō*). This refers to the availability of grace for all. No one who ever wanted or wants to appropriate God's grace found it unavailable. But in spite of its availability, it is not automatically applied toward all. It must be appropriated by faith. The part. *pleonásasa* being in the aor. indicates that the provision of this grace was made available by Christ in its sufficiency for all who would believe. **(3)** The verb which goes with the opt. conj. *hína* is *perisseúsē* (pres. subj. of *perisseúō*), increase. It is a wish of Paul. "All things are for your benefit so that the grace which was made available in abundance may increase or excel . . . " (a.t.). **(4)** The obj. is "the thanksgiving" (a.t.), making the use of *perisseúsē* trans. It is the grace of God available in sufficient abundance which will increase the thanksgiving. The word for "thanksgiving" is *eucharistía* (2169). Thanksgiving is based in the acceptance of the grace of God in Christ. The more of His grace we possess, the more thankful we are. *Cháris*, grace, generates *eucharistía*, thanksgiving. **(5)** The increase of thanksgiving results "in the glory of God [*eis tēn dóxan toú Theoú*]" (a.t.). The appropriation of God's grace results in the increase of thanksgiving which glorifies or exalts God the Father. *Dóxa* (1391), glory, is what God receives from those who have experienced God's grace in Christ giving thanks for all that He is and has done for them. **(6)** There remains the phrase *diá tốn pleiónōn* "through as many as possible" or "through the many" (a.t.): *diá* (1223), through; *tốn*, gen. masc. pl. of *ho* [3588], the; *pleiónōn*, the gen. masc. pl. of *pleíōn* (4119), more (the usual comp. of *polús* [4183], much). It means "the most" (a.t.), as also in 1 Cor 9:19, "that I may gain," if not all, yet the greater part (see also 1 Cor 10:5; 15:6; 2 Cor 2:6; 9:2; Phil 1:14). The meaning of the phrase is "through the many" (a.t.). The contrast here is with the totality of humanity. Paul knew full well that the grace of God, which Christ provided in sufficient abundance (*pleonázō*), would not be appropriated by all (John 1:11). However, "the many" (a.t.) will, and their thanksgiving will increase to glorify God.

(III) Of the fruit (*karpós* [2590]) as Christian conduct: Phil 4:17, "Not because I desire a gift: but I desire fruit that may abound to your account." The gift concerns the monetary remittance to Paul when he left Macedonia (4:15). Apparently this was not the only gift the Philippians sent to him (4:16). Paul accepted these gifts. In 4:17, he explains his motive:

(A) "Not because I desire a gift." The word for "desire" is *epizētố* (1934), to crave. Paul did not crave or yearn to receive their gift.

(B) "But I desire fruit that may abound to your account." Here again "I desire" is *epizētố*, crave. "Fruit" is *karpós*, metaphorically meaning deeds, works, conduct (Matt 3:8; 7:16, 20; 21:43). The fruit or conduct is described in Phil 4:17 as *tón karpón tón pleonázonta*, abounding, thus "the fruit the abounding" (a.t.). What the Philippians sent to Paul was not really a deprivation for them, nor was it because they had so much money that they did not know what to do with it. Their lives were full of gracious conduct.

In Phil 4:11, he spoke of himself as having learned to be *autárkēs* (842), self-sufficient, content with whatever he had, whether much or little (4:12). Paul praised the Philippians, saying that their "poverty abounded [*eperísseusen*, aor. indic. of *perisseúō*] unto the riches of their liberality." This is the word used in Phil 4:12 and it means to abound, not as a result of having much from which to give, but to be generous even in poverty and need. But when it comes to the fruit or conduct of the Philippians, he called it *tón pleonázonta*, abundant, in that it was enough to meet their own needs and sufficient to send money to Paul. Because both the Philippians and Paul learned to abound (*perisseúō*) through adjusting their lifestyles in such a way as to have enough and to share, their conduct was pouring over (*pleonázonta*, pres. act. part. of *pleonázō*).

As Paul received the money, he did not feel his conscience bothering him because the Philippians were sacrificing to make him comfortable. Nevertheless, although what they gave him appeared as if it were surplus and not needed by them, he was assuring them that it would be counted in the plus column of the accounting ledger of their Christian works. *Lógos* (3056), account, here is that which is written in God's books by which the last judgment of works will occur (Rev 20:12).

The difference between *perisseúō*, to abound, and *pleonázō*, to have enough and left over or have too much, is this: *Perisseúō* is to make what one has be sufficient for oneself and, no matter how little it is, to have enough to share. *Pleonázō* is to have too much, enough for the satisfaction of one's needs and left over. The word *pleonázō* is related to *plếrēs* (4314), full, unable to contain more. Therefore, *pleonázō* is to have too much without the exercise of *autárkeia* (841), self-sufficiency, part of one's discipline. *Perisseía* (4050) is to make what one has, little enough though it may be, suffice for one's needs and have enough to share. The emphasis on *perisseúō* is self-discipline while on *pleonázō* it is actual abundance.

(IV) In regard to love:

(A) 1 Thess 3:12: "And the Lord make you to increase [*pleonásai*, the aor. inf. of *pleonázō*] and abound [*perisseúsai*, the aor. inf. or *perisseúō*] in love one toward another, and toward all men, even as we do toward you." The first verb is *pleonázō*, to have more than enough, denoting the attitude that a Christian adjusts his needs for himself so that he always has an abundance, which enables him to share. This refers to one's general attitude under any circumstances. *Perisseúsai* refers to the effort which must be exercised in a particular circumstance to have something left over to give.

A generous Christian heart loves those who are Christians (this is indicated by the word *allélous* [240], one toward another), and toward all people, even those who are not Christians. Thus our love should be both *pleonázousa* (pres. act. part.), naturally abounding (having not only enough for ourselves but also for others), and *perisseúousa* (pres. act. part.), spilling out to make whatever one has to be enough for himself by adjusting his needs accordingly. Thus the Christian will not only be *autárkēs*, self-sufficient, and hence content (Phil 4:11), but also have things left over for others. This applies to particular instances and circumstances (see Phil 4:11–13), but *pleonázō* is having more then enough and knowing what to do with the surplus. It is the attitude of readiness to share no matter how much or how little one has. The Christian attitude is one of being ever-ready to share no matter what the circumstances.

Because the Christian's attitude should always be that he has more than he deserves or needs, he can say with Paul, "But I have all and abound" (Phil 4:18). He *pleonázei*, abounds, without neglect for self. And when our love is such, we will have fulfillment for ourselves and we shall meet the need of others. Christian love is *pleonázousa* (pres. act. part.) always plentiful, and *perisseúousa* (pres. act. part.) reaching beyond self.

(B) 2 Thess 1:3: "We are bound to thank God always for you, brethren, as it is meet, because that your faith groweth exceedingly, and the charity [love] of every one of you all toward each other aboundeth [*pleonázei*, pres. act. indic.]." This is the attitude of love of the Christian which enables him to provide for himself and others (*allélous*, one another; see section IV, A).

(V) In regard to the accompaniments of faith: 2 Pet 1:8: "For if these things [virtue, knowledge, temperance {self-control}, patience, godliness, brotherly kindness, love—all in 1:6, 7] be in you, and abound [*pleonázonta*, pres. act. part.], they make [*kathístēmi* {2525}, constitute, establish] you that ye shall neither be barren nor unfruitful in the knowledge of our Lord Jesus Christ." This is the only time the verb *pleonázō* is used by Peter, although Paul uses it. The word translated "knowledge" is *epígnōsis* (1922), which, in this context, means the appropriation of God's revelation through faith. When one has partaken of God's nature (2 Pet 1:4), not only does he possess (*hupárchonta* [5224], having for oneself), but he always has a surplus (*pleonázonta*) left over which he can share with others. Contentment and sharing must not only be part of the nature of the Christian, but they should be part of his daily experience.

Deriv.: *huperpleonázō* (5250), to be exceedingly abundant.

Syn.: *perisseúō* (4052), to exceed, abound; *plēthúnō* (4129), to multiply; *huperbállō* (5235), to surpass, excel.

Ant.: *husteréō* (5302), to come behind, lack; *leípō* (3007), to be destitute; *chrézō* (5535), to need; *opheílō* (3784), to owe; *elattonéō* (1641), to be or have less.

4122. πλεονεκτέω *pleonektéō*; contracted *pleonektṓ*, fut. *pleonektḗsō*, from *pleíōn* (4119), more, and *échō* (2192), to have. Intrans., to have more than another, covet, take advantage, defraud. In the NT, trans., to take advantage of someone, defraud, with the acc. (2 Cor 7:2; 12:17, 18; 1 Thess 4:6); pass. (2 Cor 2:11).

Deriv.: *pleonéktēs* (4123), covetousness.

Syn.: *epithuméō* (1937), to long for, set the heart upon, lust after; *epipothéō* (1971), to dote upon, greatly desire; *himeíromai* (2442), to be affectionately desirous; *aposteréō* (650), to defraud.

Ant.: *husteréō* (5302), to come behind, lack; *leípō* (3007), to be destitute; *elattonéō* (1641), to be or have less; *chrḗzō* (5535), to need; *échō anágkēn* (*échō* [2192], have; *anágkēn* [318], need), to have need.

4123. πλεονέκτης *pleonéktēs*; gen. *pleonéktou*, masc. noun from *pleonektéō* (4122), to be covetous. One who wants more, a person covetous of something that others have, a defrauder for gain (1 Cor 5:10, 11; 6:10; Eph 5:5).

Syn.: *philárguros* (5366), a lover of silver or money, which has a more restricted sense than *pleonéktēs*; *aischrokerdḗs* (146), greedy for wrongful gain; profiteer.

Ant.: *autárkēs* (842), self-contented; *aphilárguros* (866), without covetousness or love of money; *sóphrōn* (4998), sober, self-controlled.

4124. πλεονεξία *pleonexía*; gen. *pleonexías*, fem. noun from *pleíōn* (4119), more, and *échō* (2192) to have. Covetousness, greediness (Luke 12:15; Rom 1:29 [cf. 1 Cor 5:10, 11]; 2 Cor 9:5, "as bounty or blessing on your part, and not as covetousness on ours, not as extorted by us from you" (a.t.); Eph 4:19; 1 Thess 2:5; 2 Pet 2:3, 14; Sept. Jer 22:17; Hab 2:9). *Pleonexía* is a larger term which includes *philarguría* (5365), love of money to hoard away, avarice. It is connected with extortioners (1 Cor 5:10); with thefts (Mark 7:22, covetous thoughts, plans of fraud and extortion); with sins of the flesh (Eph 5:3, 5; Col 3:5). *Pleonexía* may be said to be the root from which these sins grow, the longing of the creature which has forsaken God

to fill itself with the lower objects of nature.

Syn.: *epithumía* (1939), desire, lust; *órexis* (3715), appetite; *hormḗ* (3730), impulse.

Ant.: *autárkeia* (841), self-sufficiency, contentedness.

4125. πλευρά *pleurá*; gen. *pleurás*, fem. noun. A side, as the side of the body (John 19:34; 20:20, 25, 27; Acts 12:7; Sept.: Gen 2:21; Num 33:55; 2 Sam 2:16).

4126. πλέω *pléō*; fut. *pleúsō*. To sail (Luke 8:23; Acts 27:24). Followed by *eis* (1519), unto, with the acc. of place (Acts 21:3; 27:2 [UBS], to sail along or by the coast of Asia Minor; 27:6).

Deriv.: *apopléō* (636), to sail away; *braduploéō* (1020), to sail slowly; *diapléō* (1277), to sail across; *ekpléō* (1602), to sail from; *katapléō* (2668), to sail down; *parapléō* (3896), to sail by; *ploíon* (4143), ship; *plóos* (4144), sailing, navigation; *hupopléō* (5284), to sail under.

Syn.: *paralégomai* (3881), to sail by, coast along; *braduploéō* (1020), to sail slowly; *diaperáō* (1276), to cross over. Words relating to sailing: *naús* (3491), ship; *naúklēros* (3490), an owner or captain of a ship; *naútēs* (3492), a sailor; *skáphē* (4627), a small boat carried aboard a large vessel for landing or emergency.

Ant.: *katantáō* (2658) and *phthánō* (5348), to arrive at; *paragínomai* (3854), to come near; *epokéllō* (2027), to drive a ship aground; *prosormízō* (4358), to bring a ship to anchorage; *nauagéō* (3489), to be shipwrecked or stranded.

4127. πληγή *plēgḗ*; gen. *plēgḗs*, fem. noun from *plḗssō* (4141), to strike. A stroke, stripe, blow, wound or injury.

(I) In the pl. (Luke 12:48; Acts 16:23; 2 Cor 6:5; 11:23; Sept.: Deut 25:3; Prov 29:15).

(II) Metonymically a wound caused by a blow (Luke 10:30; Acts 16:33 in which "washed their stripes" denotes washing away the blood and filth of the wounds [cf. 16:23]; Rev 13:14); "deadly wound" (Rev 13:3, 12). See Sept.: 1 Kgs 22:35; Isa 1:5.

(III) A plague, meaning a stroke or blow inflicted by God, a calamity (Rev 9:20; 11:6; 15:1, 6, 8; 16:9, 21; 18:4, 8; 21:9; 22:18; Sept.: Lev 26:21; Deut 28:59, 61; 29:21).

Syn.: *traúma* (5134), wound; *hélkos* (1668), ulcer, open wound; *gággraina* (1044), gangrene; *mólōps* (3468), a bruise, a wound from a blow; *rhápisma* (4475), a slap with the palm of the hand.

Ant.: *eúnoia* (2133), benevolence; *eulogía* (2129), blessing; *cháris* (5485), grace; *aspasmós* (783), a greeting.

4128. πλῆθος *plḗthos*; gen. *plḗthous*, neut. noun from *plḗthō* (4130), to fill. Fullness, hence a great many, multitude, throng.

(I) Used generally (Luke 5:6; John 21:6; Acts 28:3; Heb 11:12; James 5:20; 1 Pet 4:8; Sept.: Gen 27:28; Isa 1:11).

(II) Of persons, a multitude, throng, followed by the gen. of class (Luke 21:36; Acts 4:32; 5:14, "multitudes of both men and women"; 6:2). With the gen. implied (Acts 2:6; 23:7). *Polú*, neut. of *polús* (4183), much, and *plḗthos* with the gen. (Mark 3:7, 8; Luke 1:10; 6:17; 8:37; 19:37; 23:1, 27; John 5:3; Acts 5:16; 6:2, 5; 14:1; 17:4; 25:24; Sept.: 2 Kgs 7:13; Isa 17:12).

(III) The multitude, meaning the people, populace (Acts 14:4; 19:9; 21:22, 36; Sept.: Ezek 30:15).

Deriv.: *plēthúnō* (4129), to multiply; *pamplētheí* (3826), the whole multitude together.

Syn.: *laós* (2992), people; *óchlos* (3793), crowd, mob, rabble, populace, people; *dēmos* (1218), a people bound together socially, a municipality; *klisía* (2828), a company of people reclining at a meal; *hómilos* (3658), company of passengers; *legeón* (3003), legion; *ekklēsía* (1996), assembly; *episunagōgē* (1997), a gathering.

Ant.: *heis* (1520), one; *hékastos* (1538), each one; *mónos* (3441), alone.

4129. πληθύνω *plēthúnō*; fut. *plēthunō*, from *pléthos* (4128), multitude. To make full; hence, to multiply, increase.

(I) Trans. (2 Cor 9:10; Heb 6:14 quoted from Gen 22:17 [cf. 3:16]). Pass. *plēthúnomai*, to be multiplied, increased in number (Acts 6:7; 7:17; 9:31); in magnitude, extent (Matt 24:12; Acts 12:24; Sept.: Gen 7:17, 18). Followed by the dat. of person (1 Pet 1:2, meaning to abound to someone; 2 Pet 1:2; Jude 1:2).

(II) Intrans., to multiply oneself, increase (Acts 6:1; Sept.: Ex 1:20; 1 Sam 14:19).

Syn.: *pleonázō* (4121), to have much or too much; *perisseúō* (4052), to abound, increase; *huperperisseúō* (5248) and *huperpleonázō* (5250), to abound exceedingly; *huperbállō* (5235), to exceed, excel; *auxánō* (838), to increase, grow; *prokóptō* (4298), to progress, to increase by one's own effort; *anathállō* (330), to flourish again; *akmázō* (187), to mature, thrive; *euporéō* (2141), to prosper; *ploutéō* (4147), to enrich oneself; *ploutízō* (4148), to make wealthy, enrich.

Ant.: *elattonéō* (1641), to diminish, fall short; *elattóō* (1642), to decrease; *husteréō* (5302), to come behind, lack; *leípō* (3007), to be destitute; *chrēzō* (5535), to need; the expression *échō anágkēn* (*échō* [2192], have; *anágkēn* [318], need), to have need.

4130. πίμπλημι *pímplēmi* and **πλήθω** *plḗthō*; fut. *plḗsō*, aor. *éplēsa*, aor. pass. *eplḗsthēn*, from the obsolete *pláō* (n.f.), to fill. To fill, make full. Trans.

(I) With the aor. *éplēsa* with the acc. (Luke 5:7); with the gen. of that with which one fills (Matt 27:48; John 19:29, "filled a sponge with vinegar"); pass., with the gen. (Matt 22:10; Sept.: Gen 21:19; 24:16).

(II) Metaphorically, aor. pass. *eplḗsthēn*, to be filled or to be full.

(A) Persons to be filled with something, i.e., to be wholly imbued, affected, influenced with or by something, with the gen. of thing as with the Holy

Spirit (Luke 1:15, 41, 67; Acts 2:4; 4:8, 31; 9:17; 13:9); with wrath (Luke 4:28); fear (Luke 5:26); madness (Luke 6:11). See Acts 3:10; 5:17; 13:45. Metonymically of a place (Acts 19:29; Sept.: Gen 6:11, 13; Prov 12:21).

(B) Of prophecy, to be fulfilled or accomplished (Luke 21:22 UBS; Sept.: 1 Kgs 21:27).

(C) Of time, to be fulfilled or completed, to be fully past (Luke 1:23, 57; 2:6, 21, 22).

Deriv.: *empímplēmi* (1705), to fill up, satisfy; *pléthos* (4128), multitude, throng; *plēsmonē* (4140), satiety, satisfaction, a filling up.

Syn.: *plēróō* (4137), to fulfill, complete; *anaplēróō* (378), to fill up adequately; *antanaplēróō* (466), to fill up in turn; *kataklúzō* (2626), to deluge, flood; *sumplēróō* (4845), to fill completely; *teléō* (5055), to finish; *epiteléō* (2005), to finish, bring to an end; *teleióō* (5048), to accomplish; *chortázō* (5526), to fill or satisfy with food; *gemízō* (1072), to load full; *korénnumi* (2880), to satisfy; *mestóō* (3325), to fill full.

Ant.: *kenóō* (2758), to empty; *elattóō* (1642), to decrease.

4131. πλήκτης *plḗktēs*; gen. *plḗktou*, masc. noun from *plḗssō* (4141), to strike. A striker, a violent person, figuratively a reviler, one who by reproachful and upbraiding language wounds the conscience of his brethren, a contentious person, a quarreler (1 Tim 3:3; Titus 1:7).

Syn.: *philóneikos* (5380), quarrelsome; *áspondos* (786), implacable, not wishing to be reconciled, trucebreaker; *asúmphōnos* (800), inharmonious; *asúnthetos* (802), not agreeing, covenant breaker.

Ant.: *eirēnikós* (1516), peaceable; *eirēnopoiós* (1518), peacemaker; *mesítēs* (3316), a reconciler, mediator.

4132. πλημμύρα *plēmmúra*; gen. *plēmmúras*, fem. noun from *plḗmme* (n.f.), fullness, which is from *plḗthō* (4130), to fill. Tide, floodtide, and hence by implication flood, inundation (Luke 6:48 [cf. Matt 7:27]).

Syn.: *kataklusmós* (2627), flood; *potamophórētos* (4216), carried away by a stream or river.

Ant.: *xērós* (3584), a dry land; *ánudros* (504), waterless.

4133. πλήν *plḗn*; prep. and adv. contracted from *pléon* or *pleíōn* (4119), more. More than, over and above; hence, besides, except, but, however, only that.

(I) In the middle of a clause with the gen. (Mark 12:32, "There is no other besides him" [a.t.]; John 8:10; Acts 8:1; 15:28; 27:22; Sept.: Lev 23:38; Deut 4:35; Isa 45:14; 46:9). Followed by *hóti* (3754), that (Acts 20:23, meaning except that, knowing nothing more than that).

(II) As an adv., at the beginning of a clause, meaning much more, rather, besides, passing over into an adversative particle, i.e., but rather, but yet, nevertheless (Matt 11:22, 24; 18:7; 26:39, 64; Luke 6:24, 35; 10:11, 14, 20; 11:41; 12:31; 13:33; 18:8; 19:27; 22:21, 42; 23:28; 1 Cor 11:11; Phil 1:18; 3:16; 4:14; Rev 2:25; Sept.: Num 22:35; Judg 4:9). Also where the writer returns after digression to a previous topic (Eph 5:33 [cf. 5:25, 28]). Once corresponding to *mén* (3303), a particle of contrast (Luke 22:22).

Syn.: *ektós* (1622), except; *parektós* (3924), without, except; *áneu* (427) and *chōrís* (5565), without; *allá* (235), but; *hómōs* (3676), but; *kaítoi* (2543), although; *kaíper* (2539), although, indeed.

Ant.: *éti* (2089), also, moreover; *epí* (1909), upon, also; *prós* (4314), in addition to.

4134. πλήρης *plḗrēs*; gen. *plḗrous*, masc.-fem., neut. *plḗres*, adj. from *pléos* (n.f.), full. Full, complete.

(I) Full, in a pass. sense, filled (Matt 14:20; 15:37; Sept.: Num 7:20; Deut 6:11).

(II) Of a surface, full, fully covered, with the gen. (Luke 5:12; Sept.: 2 Kgs 6:17; 7:15).

(III) Abounding or abundant (Luke 4:1; John 1:14; Acts 6:3, 5, 8; 7:55); abundant, ample (2 John 1:8; Acts 9:36); full, complete, perfect (Mark 4:28).

Deriv.: *plērophoréō* (4135), to fulfill, fully know; thoroughly accomplish; *plēróō* (4137), to make full, to fulfill or complete.

Syn.: *mestós* (3324), full; *perissós* (4053), more.

Ant.: *penichrós* (3998), poor, scanty, necessitous; *ptōchós* (4434), poor, helpless, dependent on others; *pénēs* (3993), indigent, making only little for one's sustenance; *olígos* (3641), little; *kenós* (2756), empty; *áneu* (427), without; *apó mérous* (*apó* [575], from; *mérous*, the gen. of *méros* [3313], part), in part, partly, in some degree; *ek mérous* (*ek* [1537], out of), in particular, in part, partly, imperfectly; *katá méros* (*katá* [2596], distributive particle meaning in, according to), particularly, in detail.

4135. πληροφορέω *plērophoréō*; contracted *plērophorṓ*, fut. *plērophorḗsō*, from *plḗrēs* (4134), full, and *phoréō* (5409), to fill. To fulfill, thoroughly accomplish, equivalent to persuade fully, give full assurance. Found for the most part only in biblical and Patristic Gr. Trans.

(I) Of persons, pass., to be fully assured, persuaded (Rom 4:21; 14:5; Sept.: Eccl 8:11).

(II) Of things, to make fully assured, give full proof of, confirm fully. With the acc. (2 Tim 4:5, "make full proof of thy ministry," i.e., by fulfilling to the utmost all its duties); pass., to be fully established as true (Luke 1:1; 2 Tim 4:17).

Deriv.: *plērophoría* (4136), perfect certitude, full conviction.

Syn.: *bebaióō* (950), to assure, establish; *kuróō* (2964), to ratify, confirm; *apodeíknumi* (584), to demonstrate, accredit; *pistóō* (4104), to assure; *marturéō* (3140), to witness.

Ant.: *aporéō* (639), to be uncertain; *diaporéō* (1280), to be thoroughly perplexed; *distázō* (1365), to doubt, hesitate.

4136. πληροφορία *plērophoría*; gen. *plērophorías*, fem. noun from *plērophoréō* (4135), to fulfill. Perfect certitude, full conviction (1 Thess 1:5), equivalent to *bebaíōsis* (951), confirmation. Full assurance (Col 2:2; Heb 6:11; 10:22), or complete understanding. Not found in Greek writers.

Syn.: *pepoíthēsis* (4006), reliance, confidence; *apódeixis* (585), demonstration, proof; *élegchos* (1650), proof, evidence; *pístis* (4102), faith, confidence, dependability; *marturía* (3141), witness.

Ant.: *apistía* (570), unbelief, faithlessness; *adēlótēs* (83), uncertainty.

4137. πληρόω *pleróō*; contracted *plērṓ*, fut. *plērṓsō*, from *plérēs* (4134), full. To make full, fill. Trans.

(I) Particularly, to fill a vessel or hollow place; pass. (Matt 13:48, the nets; Luke 3:5, a valley, quoted from Isa 40:4). Figuratively (Matt 23:32, the measure of their sins; Sept.: 2 Kgs 4:4; Jer 13:12). Generally of a place, to fill with something (John 12:3, the smell). (John 16:6, "sorrow has filled your heart" [a.t.]; figuratively, with the acc., Acts 5:3, "Satan filled your heart" [a.t.]; Acts 5:28, "you have filled Jerusalem with your teaching" [a.t. {cf. Sept.: 2 Chr 6:4}]).

(II) Figuratively, to fill, supply abundantly with something, impart richly, imbue with, followed by the acc., often also with an adjunct of that with which someone is filled or supplied.

(A) With the acc. or gen. (Luke 2:40 [TR]; Acts 2:28; 13:52; Rom 15:13, 14; Phil 1:11 [TR]; 2 Tim 1:4).

(B) Followed by the dat., in the pass. voice (Rom 1:29; 2 Cor 7:4).

(C) Followed by *en* (1722), in, with the dat. (Eph 5:18), instead of the simple dat. (Luke 2:40 [UBS]). In Eph 5:18, the case is either locative or instrumental in meaning.

(D) Followed by the acc., simply meaning to supply fully (Eph 1:23; 4:10, spoken of Christ as filling the universe with His influence, presence, and power; Phil 4:19). In the pass., used in an absolute sense, meaning to be filled, full, to be fully supplied, to abound (Eph 3:19, into or unto all the fullness of God [either that you may fully participate in all the rich gifts of God or that you may be received into full communion with the whole church of God]; Phil 4:18; Col 2:10, "complete in Him," i.e., in Christ, in His work). Also pass., with the acc. (Col 1:9).

(III) To fulfill, perform fully, with the acc.

(A) Spoken of duty or obligation (Matt 3:15; Acts 12:25; Col 4:17).

(B) Of a declaration or prophecy, to fulfill or accomplish (Acts 3:18; 13:27). More often in the pass., to be fulfilled, accomplished, to have been accomplished (Matt 2:17; 26:54; 27:9; Mark 15:28; Luke 1:20; 4:21; 21:22; 24:44; Acts 1:16; James 2:23). With *hína* (2443), so that, followed by the subjunctive (Matt 1:22; 2:15; 4:14; 21:4; 26:56; 27:35; Mark 14:49; John 12:38; 13:17; 15:25; 17:12; 18:9, 32; 19:24, 36); with *hópōs* (3704), so that, followed by the subjunctive (Matt 2:23; 8:17; 12:17; 13:35).

(IV) To fulfill, bring to a full end, accomplish, complete.

(A) In the pass., of time, to be fulfilled, completed, ended (Mark 1:15; Luke 21:24; John 7:8; Acts 7:23, 30; 9:23; 24:27).

(B) Of a business or work, to accomplish, finish, complete (Luke 7:1; 9:31; Acts 13:25; 14:26; 19:21; Rom 15:19, in the preaching of the gospel; Col 1:25; Rev 6:11 [TR], until their number is full or completed; Sept.: 1 Kgs 1:14).

(C) By implication, to fill out, complete, make perfect, accomplish an end (Matt 5:17; Phil 2:2; 2 Thess 1:11). In the pass., to be made full, complete (Luke 22:16; John 3:29; 15:11; 16:24; 17:13; 2 Cor 10:6; 1 John 1:4; 2 John 1:12; Rev 3:2). Of persons (Col 4:12).

Deriv.: *anaplēróō* (378), to fill up; *ekplēróō* (1603), to fill, fulfill; *plḗrōma* (4138), fullness; *sumplēróō* (4845), to fill completely.

Syn.: *pímplēmi* or *plḗthō* (4130), to fill, accomplish; *gémō* (1073), to be full; *mestóō* (3325), to fill, intoxicate; *korénnumi* (2880), to crave, glut, or satiate, to eat enough; *teleióō* (5048), to complete, fulfill, finish; *teléō* (5055), to complete, execute, conclude, finish; *epiteléō* (2005), to fulfill, complete, perform; *anaplēróō* (378), to complete, supply, fill up; *ekplēróō* (1603), to accomplish entirely, fulfill; *kuróō* (2964), to make authoritative, ratify.

Ant.: *kenóō* (2758), to empty; *antléō* (501), to dip out (usually water); *ekchéō* (632), to pour out; *akuróō* (208), to invalidate, disannul; *katargéō* (2673), to abolish; *lúō* (3089), to loose, dissolve, destroy; *katalúō* (2647), to demolish, abrogate; *dialúō* (1262), to dissolve entirely.

**4138.   πλήρωμα   plḗrōma;   gen.
plērṓmatos, neut. noun from *plēróō* (4137), to make full, fill, fill up. Fullness.

(I) Particularly meaning the contents of the earth (1 Cor 10:26, 28 quoted from Ps 24:1 [cf. Ps 50:12; 96:11]); of baskets (Mark 8:20, "how many baskets full of fragments"); supplement, that which fills up, such as a patch (*epíblēma* [1915]) (Matt 9:16; Mark 2:21).

(II) Figuratively meaning fullness, full measure, abundance.

(A) Generally (John 1:16; Eph 3:19; Col 2:9, the fullness, i.e., plenitude of the divine perfections); used in an absolute sense (Rom 11:12, of a state of fullness, abundance, opposite to *héttēma* [2275], failure, diminishing; 15:29, "in the full abundant blessings of the gospel" [a.t.]).

(B) Of persons, full number, complement, multitude (Rom 11:25, the full number, all the multitude of the Gentiles; Eph 1:23, of the church of Christ).

(III) Fulfillment, a fulfilling, full performance, equivalent to *plḗrōsis*, the act of fulfilling, which, however, does not occur in the NT (see *plḗroma*, Rom 13:10).

(IV) Fulfillment, full end, completion.

(A) Of time, full period (Gal 4:4; Eph 1:10).

(B) By implication, meaning completeness, reaching the intended goal (Eph 4:13, to the attainment of the state and stature of a man in Christ, to full maturity in Christian knowledge and love).

Syn.: *télos* (5056), end, goal; *teleiótēs* (5047), completeness; *ekplḗrōsis* (1604), completion, accomplishment; *holoklēría* (3647), wholeness.

Ant.: *lúsis* (3080), loosening, dissolution; *egkopḗ* (1464), hindrance, cutting short; *héttēma* (2275), failure, diminishing, fault.

4139. πλησίον *plēsíon*; adv. from *pélas* (n.f.), near, near to. Close by, near, neighbor.

(I) Particularly, followed by the gen. (John 4:5; Sept.: Deut 1:1; 11:30). Figuratively, to be near someone, a neighbor (Luke 10:29, 36).

(II) With the art., *ho plēsíon*, used as a subst. noun, one near, a neighbor, fellow, another person of the same nature, country, class.

(A) Generally, a fellow man, any other member of the human family, as in the precept "Thou shalt love thy neighbor as thyself" (Matt 19:19; 22:39; Mark 12:31, 33; Luke 10:27 quoted from Lev 19:18; Rom 13:9, 10; Gal 5:14; Eph 4:25; Heb 8:11 [TR]; James 2:8; Sept.: Ex 20:17; Deut 5:19).

(B) One of the same people or country, a fellow-countryman (Acts 7:27 [cf. 7:24, 26]).

(C) One of the same faith, a fellow Christian (Rom 15:2).

(D) A friend, associate, opposite of *echthrós* (2190), enemy (Matt 5:43), but the same as *phílos* (5384), friend.

Deriv.: *paraplḗsion* (3897), nearby, close to, similarly.

Syn.: *eggús* (1451), near; *pará* (3844), next to, beside; *geítōn* (1069), neighbor; *adelphós* (80), brother.

Ant.: *makrán* (3112), far; *pórrō* (4206), at a distance, a great way off; *echthrós* (2190), enemy.

4140. πλησμονή *plēsmonḗ*; gen. *plēsmonḗs*, fem. noun from *péplēsmai*, the perf. pass. of *plḗthō* (4130), to fill. A filling or satisfying as with food; also fullness, satiety, indulgence (Col 2:23; Sept.: Ex 16:3, 8).

Syn.: *ánesis* (425), relaxation, relief; *perisseía* (4050), abundance; *chórtasma* (5527), sustenance, fullness of food; *perisseía* (4050), abundance.

Ant.: *hustérēma* (5303), want; *chreía* (5532), need; *hustérēsis* (5304), self-denial, going without; *ptōcheía* (4432), destitution, poverty, helplessness; *limós* (3042), famine; *anágkē* (318), need, necessity; *aporía* (640), a state of need, quandary.

4141. πλήσσω *plḗssō*, or πλήττω *plḗttō*; fut. *plḗxō*. To strike. In the NT, equivalent to plague, to smite or to afflict with disease, calamity, evil; in the pass. (Rev 8:12; Sept.: Ex 9:32, 33; Ps 102:4).

Deriv.: *ekplḗssō* (1605), to astonish; *epiplḗssō* (1969), to beat, rebuke, *plēgḗ* (4127), a stroke, blow; *plḗktēs* (4131), a violent person, a reviler.

Syn.: *patássō* (3960), to strike, smite; *túptō* (5180), to beat; *paíō* (3817), to strike or smite with the hand or fist; *dérō* (1194), to slay, beat; *rhapízō* (4474), to strike with a rod; *traumatízō* (5135), to injure, traumatize.

Ant.: *eulogéō* (2127), to bless; *euthuméō* (2114), to cheer up; *eupsuchéō* (2174), to be of good comfort; *euphraínō* (2165), to make glad.

4142. πλοιάριον *ploiárion*; gen. *ploiaríou*, neut. noun from *pléō* (4126), to sail. A small vessel or boat, spoken of the fishing vessels on the Sea of Galilee (Mark 3:9; 4:36; John 6:22, 23; 21:8). A diminutive of *ploíon* (4143), ship.

Syn.: *skáphē* (4627), something dug or scooped out as a trough, used for a rowboat or a boat belonging to a larger vessel; *naús* (3491), a ship, from which comes our Eng. word "nautical," pertaining to the sea.

4143. πλοῖον *ploíon*; gen. *ploíou*, neut. noun from *pléō* (4126), to float, sail. A ship, vessel (Acts 20:13, 38; 21:2, 3; 27:2, 6, 10; James 3:4). Spoken in the Gospels of the small fishing vessels on the Sea of Galilee (Matt 4:21, 22; Mark 4:1, 36; Luke 5:2, 3; John 6:17, 19; Sept.: Gen 49:13; Deut 28:68; Jon 1:3–5).

4144. πλόος *plóos*; contracted *ploús*, masc. noun, from *pléō* (4126), to sail. Sailing, navigation, voyage (Acts 21:7; 27:9, 10).

4145. πλούσιος *ploúsios*; fem. *plousía*, neut. *ploúsion*; adj. from *ploútos* (4149), wealth, abundance, riches. Rich, wealthy. In the NT, only in the masc. (Matt 27:57; Luke 12:16; 16:1, 19); pl. (Luke 14:12). Figuratively meaning happy, prosperous, lacking nothing (2 Cor 8:9; Rev 2:9; 3:17; Sept.: 2 Sam 12:1, 2, 4; Prov 28:11). As a subst. with the def. art., *ho ploúsios* in the pl., *hoi ploúsioi*, a rich man, the rich (Matt 19:24; Mark 10:25; Luke 6:24; 16:21, 22; 18:25; 21:1; 1 Tim 6:17; James 1:10, 11; 2:6; 5:1; Rev 6:15; 13:16; Sept.: Prov 22:2, 7; Jer 9:22). Figuratively meaning rich in something, abounding, followed by *en* (1722), in, and the dat. (Eph 2:4, "rich in mercy"; James 2:5, "rich in faith").

Deriv.: *plousíōs* (4146), abundantly, richly.

Syn.: *plḗrēs* (4134) and *mestós* (3324), full; *polutelḗs* (4185), luxurious.

Ant.: *ptōchós* (4434), poor, helpless; *pénēs* (3993), pauper, destitute; *penichrós* (3998), needy, poor, skimpy; *olígos* (3641), little; *endeḗs* (1729), needy.

4146. πλουσίως *plousíōs*; adv. from *ploúsios* (4145), rich. Richly, abundantly, largely (Col 3:16; 1 Tim 6:17; Titus 3:6; 2 Pet 1:11).

Syn.: *perissós* (4053) abundantly; *perissotérōs* (4056), more abundantly, exceedingly; *lían* (3029), very, exceedingly; *sphodrós* (4971), excessively.

4147. πλουτέω *ploutéō*; contracted *ploutṓ*, fut. *ploutḗsō*, from *ploútos* (4149), wealth. To be rich, become rich. Intrans.:

(I) Particularly (Luke 1:53, the rich; 1 Tim 6:9, those desiring to be rich). Followed by *apó* (575), of, from, indicating source (Rev 18:15). Followed by *ek* (1537), from (Rev 18:3, 19; Sept.: Jer 5:27; Hos 12:9). Figuratively (Luke 12:21, "not rich toward God," meaning laying up no treasure in heaven. Equal to being happy (1 Cor 4:8, where it means to make oneself rich because of the belief that in riches there is happiness). See contrast in 2 Cor 8:9, where *ploutḗsēte* (aor. act. subj.) refers to personal enrichment by appropriating Christ's principle of sacrifice. Used in a similar sense in Rev 3:17, 18. In contrast to *ploutéō* in 1 Cor 4:8 stands 1 Cor 1:5, where the Corinthian believers are said to have been made wealthy in and through Christ. In the latter verse, *ploutízō* (4148), to make rich or enrich, is used in a trans. way.

(II) Figuratively, to be rich in something, abound. Followed by *en* (1722), in (1 Tim 6:18, "in good works" [a.t.]). Used in an absolute sense (Rom 10:12, rich in gifts and spiritual blessings toward all).

Syn.: *euporéō* (2141), to be well off.

Ant.: *ptōcheúō* (4433), to be or become poor.

4148. πλουτίζω *ploutízō*; fut. *ploutísō*, from *ploútos* (4149), wealth. To make rich, enrich, trans. In the NT, only figuratively, meaning to bestow richly, supply abundantly (2 Cor 6:10). In the pass., to be enriched, richly supply, followed by *en* (1722), in, and *pantí*, the dat. neut. of *pás* (3956), every, meaning in everything, in every way (1 Cor 1:5; 2 Cor 9:11; Sept.: Gen 14:23; Prov 13:7). For syn. and ant., see the *ploutéō* (4147), to be or to become rich.

4149. πλοῦτος *ploútos*; masc. noun, gen. *ploútou*. Riches, wealth, goods.

(I) Material goods (Matt 13:22, "the deceitfulness of riches"; Mark 4:19; Luke

8:14; 1 Tim 6:17; James 5:2; Rev 18:17). Metonymically as a source of power and influence in ascriptions (Rev 5:12; Sept.: 1 Kgs 3:11; Prov 8:18; 28:8; Isa 30:6). Metaphorically of the riches of God or Christ, the rich gifts and blessings imparted by God or Christ (Eph 3:8; Phil 4:19). In Rom 11:12 and Heb 11:26, it means good welfare, happiness.

(**II**) Figuratively, meaning riches, abundance, usually before the gen. of another noun, used as an adj. meaning rich, abundant, preeminent. In Rom 2:4, the figurative meaning is the abundance of His goodness or His rich goodness. See also 2 Cor 8:2; Eph 1:7; 2:7; Col 2:2. In Rom 9:23, "the riches of his glory" refers to the abundant, preeminent glory of God as displayed in His beneficence. See also Eph 1:18; 3:16; Col 1:27. In Rom 11:33, "the depth of the riches both of the wisdom and knowledge" means the unfathomableness of them.

Deriv.: *ploúsios* (4145), rich, abundant; *ploutéō* (4147), to be rich, become rich; *ploutízō* (4148), to make rich.

Syn.: *euporía* (2142), wealth, affluence; *hupárchonta* (5224), possessions; *autárkeia* (841), self-sufficiency; *bíos* (979), possessions; *truphḗ* (5172), luxury; *chrḗma* (5536), money, riches; *hadrótēs* (100), bounty; *perisseía* (4050), overflowing; *perísseuma* (4051), abundance; *thēsaurós* (2344), treasure.

Ant.: *ptōcheía* (4432), poverty; *hustérēma* (5303), lack; *limós* (3042), famine; *aporía* (640), state of need, quandary; *gumnótēs* (1132), nakedness, need; *chreía* (5532), need, lack; *anágkē* (318), need, distress.

4150. πλύνω *plúnō*; fut. *plunṓ*. To wash, as garments (Rev 7:14; 22:14 [UBS]; Sept.: Gen 49:11; Ex 19:10).

Deriv.: *apoplúnō* (637), to washing out.

Syn.: *níptō* (3538), to wash (part of the body); *loúō* (3068), bathe; *aponíptō* (634) to wash off; *apoloúō* (628), to bathe off; *rhantízō* (4472), to sprinkle; *bréchō* (1026), to wet, wash; *baptízō* (907), to

baptize, dip; *katharízō* (2511), to cleanse; *kathaírō* (2508), to cleanse, purge.

Ant.: *rhupóō* (4510), to become dirty; *spilóō* (4695), to soil; *molúnō* (3435), to defile, soil; *koinóō* (2840), to defile, make unclean.

4151. πνεῦμα *pneúma*; gen. *pneúmatos*, neut. noun from *pnéō* (4154), to breathe.

(**I**) Breath.

(**A**) Of the mouth or nostrils, a breathing, blast (2 Thess 2:8, "spirit [breath] of his mouth," spoken of the destroying power of God; Sept.: Isa 11:4). Of the vital breath (Rev 11:11, "breath of life" [a.t.]; Sept.: Gen 6:17; 7:15, 22 [cf. Ps 33:6]).

(**B**) Breath of air, air in motion, a breeze, blast, the wind (John 3:8; Sept.: Gen 8:1; Isa 7:2).

(**II**) Spirit.

(**A**) The vital spirit or life, the principle of life residing in man. The breath breathed by God into man and again returning to God, the spiritual entity in man (Sept.: Gen 2:7; Ps 104:29; Eccl 12:7). The spirit is that part that can live independently of the body (Christ [Matt 27:50, He gave up the spirit when He died; Luke 23:46 [cf. Ps 31:5]; John 19:30]; Stephen [Acts 7:59]). "Her spirit came again and she arose" (Luke 8:55 [cf. James 2:26]; Rev 13:15; Sept.: Gen 45:27; Judg 15:19). Metaphorically (John 6:63, "the spirit in man gives life to the body, so my words are spirit and life to the soul" [a.t.]; 1 Cor 15:45, "a quickening spirit," a spirit of life as raising the bodies of his followers from the dead into the immortal life [cf. Phil 3:21]).

(**B**) The rational spirit, mind, element of life. (**1**) Generally, spirit distinct from the body and soul. See also Luke 1:47; Heb 4:12. Soul and spirit are very closely related because they are both immaterial and they both contrast with body (*sṓma* [4983]) and flesh (*sarx* [4561]). Scripture, however, introduces a distinction between the two immaterial aspects of man's soul and spirit. That they cannot mean the same thing is evident from their mention together in 1 Thess 5:23, spirit, soul, body. The same distinction is brought out in Heb 4:12. The spirit is man's immaterial nature which enables him to communicate with God, who is also spirit. 1 Cor 2:14 states that "the natural man receiveth not the things of the Spirit of God . . . because they are spiritually discerned." What is translated "natural man" in Gr. is *psuchikós* (5591), psychic or soulish meaning the soul of man. The soul is the aspect of his immaterial nature that makes him aware of his body and his natural, physical environment. The difference between soul and spirit is not one of substance but of operation. Man's immaterial aspect is represented in Scripture by the single terms *pneúma*, spirit, or *psuché*, soul, or both of them together (Gen 35:18; 41:8; 1 Kgs 17:21; Ps 42:6; Eccl 12:7; Matt 10:28; 20:28; Mark 8:36, 37; 12:30; Luke 1:46; John 12:27; 1 Cor 15:44; 1 Thess 5:23; Heb 4:12; 6:18, 19; James 1:21; 3 John 1:2; Rev 6:9; 20:4). In 1 Cor 5:3 a distinction is made between the body and the spirit (see also 5:4, 5; 6:20; 7:34; 2 Cor 7:1; Phil 3:3; Col 2:5; Heb 12:9; 1 Pet 4:6; Sept.: Num 16:22; 27:16; Zech 12:1). Where soul and body are not expressed (Rom 8:16, "the divine Spirit itself testifies to our spirit" [a.t.], meaning to our mind; see Rom 1:9; Gal 6:18; 2 Tim 4:22; Phile 1:25). In John 4:23, 24, "in spirit and in truth" means with a sincere mind, with a true heart, not with mere external rites. See Phil 3:3, where the spirit stands in juxtaposition to the body. (2) As the seat of the affections, emotions, and passions of various kinds as humility (Matt 5:3, "poor in spirit," meaning those who recognize their spiritual helplessness; see *ptōchós* [4434], poor or helpless, and Sept.: Ps 34:18); enjoyment, quiet (1 Cor 16:18; 2 Cor 2:13; 7:13); joy (Luke 10:21). Of ardor, fervor (Acts 18:25; Rom 12:11). In Luke 1:17, in the powerful spirit of Elijah (see 1:12). Of perturbation from grief, indignation (John 11:33; 13:21; Acts 17:16; Sept.: Isa 65:14). (3) As referring to the disposition, feeling, temper of mind (Luke 9:55; Rom 8:15, a slavish spirit, as distinct from the spirit of adoption; 11:8; 1 Cor 4:21; Gal 6:1, a mild, gentle spirit). In 1 Cor 14:14, "my spirit prays" means "my own feelings find utterance in prayer, but I myself do not understand what I am praying" (a.t. [see 14:15, 16]; 2 Cor 4:13; 11:4; 12:18; Eph 2:2; 4:23; Phil 1:27; 2:1; 2 Tim 1:7; James 4:5 [cf. Prov 21:10, 26]; 1 Pet 3:4; Sept.: Eccl 4:4 [cf. Num 5:30]; Ezek 11:19; 18:31). (4) As implying will, counsel, purpose (Matt 26:41; Mark 14:38; Acts 18:5 [TR]; 19:21; 20:22; Sept.: 1 Chr 5:26). (5) As including the understanding, intellect (Mark 2:8; Luke 1:80; 2:40; 1 Cor 2:11, 12; Sept.: Ex 28:3; Job 20:3; Isa 29:24). (6) The mind or disposition as affected by the Holy Spirit. See below III, D, 2, e.

(III) A spirit; a simple, incorporeal, immaterial being (thought of as possessing higher capacities than man does in his present state).

(A) Spoken of created spirits: (1) Of the human soul or spirit, after its departure from the body and as existing in a separate state (Heb 12:23, "to the spirits of the just men," referring to those men advanced to perfect blessedness and glory; 1 Pet 3:19, "by which [spirit] also he once preached to those spirits now in prison" [a.t.], referring to the Spirit of Christ testifying through Noah, Christ testifying by His spirit between His death and resurrection, or Christ proclaiming victory in the triumphant procession of His ascension to the right hand of the Father [cf. 2 Pet 2:4, 5]). See Acts 23:8. Of the soul of a person reappearing after death, a spirit, ghost (Luke 24:37, 39; Acts 23:9). (2) Of an evil spirit, demon, mostly used with the adj. *akátharton* (169), unclean, as an unclean spirit (Matt 10:1; 12:43, 45; Mark 1:23, 26, 27; 3:11, 30; 5:2, 8, 13; 6:7; 7:25; 9:17, a spirit that could not speak; 9:25; Luke 4:33, unclean spirit of a demon; 4:36; 6:18; 7:21; 8:2, 29; 9:42; 11:24, 26; 13:11, "a spirit of infirmity," meaning causing infirmity; Acts 5:16; 8:7; 16:16, "a spirit of divination," a soothsaying demon; 19:12, 13, 15, 16; Rev 16:13, 14; 18:2). Used in an absolute sense (Matt

8:16; Mark 9:20; Luke 9:39; 10:20; Eph 2:2, meaning Satan). (**3**) Less often in the pl., of angels as God's ministering spirits (Heb 1:14; Rev 1:4, the seven archangels; 3:1; 4:5; 5:6).

(**B**) Of God in reference to His incorporeality (John 4:24, "God is spirit" [a.t.]).

(**C**) Of Christ in His exalted spiritual nature, His nature as true and proper God, in distinction from His human nature (1 Pet 3:18, referring to the spiritual exaltation of Christ after His resurrection to be Head over all things through the church [cf. Eph 1:20–22]); in which spiritual nature also He is said in 1 Peter 3:19 to have preached to "the spirits in prison." See above III, A, 1. See Rom 1:4; 1 Cor 15:45; 2 Cor 3:17; 1 Tim 3:16; Heb 9:14 (cf. 9:13).

(**D**) Of the Spirit of God. In the NT, referred to as "the Spirit of God," "the Holy Spirit," in an absolute sense as "the Spirit"; the Spirit of Christ as being communicated by Him after His resurrection and ascension. The same as the Spirit of Jesus (Acts 16:7 UBS); Christ (Rom 8:9; 1 Pet 1:11); the Spirit of Jesus Christ (Phil 1:19); the Spirit of the Lord (2 Cor 3:17); the Spirit of God's Son (Gal 4:6). The Holy Spirit is everywhere represented as being in intimate union with God the Father and God the Son. The passages with this meaning in the NT may be divided into two classes: those in which being, intelligence, and agency are predicated of the Spirit; and, metonymically, those in which the effects and consequences of this agency are spoken about. (**1**) The Holy Spirit as possessing being, intelligence, agency. (**a**) Joined with the Father and the Son, with the same or with different predicates (Matt 28:19, "baptizing them in the name of the Father, and of the Son and of the Holy Ghost," see *ónoma* [3686], name, IV; 1 Cor 12:4, 6, "but the same spirit . . . the same Lord . . . the same God"; 2 Cor 13:14; 1 Pet 1:2; Jude 1:20, 21; see 1 John 5:7). (**b**) Spoken in connection with or in reference to God, *ho Theós*, the God, *ho Patér* (3962), the Father, where intimate union or oneness

with the Father is predicated of *tó pneúma*, the Spirit (John 15:26, "the Spirit of truth" [a.t.]); see below d. Where the same omniscience is predicated of the Spirit as of *ho Theós*, the God (1 Cor 2:10, 11). Where the same things are predicated of the Spirit which in other places are predicated of *ho Theós*, the God, such as in the narrative of Ananias and Sapphira in Acts 5:3, 9 (where Peter refers to the Holy Spirit and then, in 5:4, where he alludes to God). As speaking through the prophets of the OT (Acts 1:16 [cf. 3:21; 4:24, 25]. In Acts 28:25, "well did the Holy Spirit speak through Isaiah" (a.t. [cf. Isa 6:8, 11; Heb 3:7 {cf. Ps 95:7}; Heb 9:8 {cf. 1:1}; Heb 10:15 {cf. Jer 31:31}]). Generally, as speaking and warning men through prophets and apostles (Acts 7:51 [cf. 7:52]). Where a person is said to be born of the Spirit, i.e., spiritual salvation, the new spiritual life imparted to those who believe in the gospel (John 3:5, 6, 8 [cf. John 1:13, if it is taken to refer to the believer instead of the Word]). Where the Spirit is said to dwell in or be with Christians (Rom 8:9, 11; 1 Cor 3:16; 6:19; Eph 2:22; 2 Tim 1:14 [cf. John 14:23; 2 Cor 6:16]). Where the Spirit and God are interchanged (1 Cor 12:11 [cf. 12:7]; Eph 6:17). (**c**) Spoken in connection with or in reference to Christ; joined with *Christós* (5547), Christ, in a form of an oath (Rom 9:1; 15:30 in a solemn calling upon as a witness "for the love of the Spirit"; 1 Cor 6:11, in the renewal and sanctification of Christians, "ye are sanctified . . . and by the Spirit of our God." See also 2 Cor 3:17, 18 (cf. 3:8); Heb 10:29. Thus we see that the Spirit and Christ are said to be or dwell with men (see above b and cf. with John 14:23; 15:4; 2 Cor 13:5; Eph 3:17). The Holy Spirit, having descended in a bodily form upon Jesus after His baptism (Matt 3:16; Mark 1:10; Luke 3:22; John 1:32, 33). (**d**) As coming to and acting upon Christians, illuminating and empowering them. As coming to Christians and remaining with them, imparting to them spiritual knowledge, aid, consolation, sanctification, and making intercession with and for them (John 14:17, 26; 15:26, the divine Spirit who will impart the knowledge of the divine truth; 16:13; Rom 8:14, 16, 26, 27; 14:17; 15:13, 16; 2 Cor 1:22; 5:5; Eph 3:16; 6:18; 1 Thess 1:6; 2 Thess 2:13; 1 Pet 1:22). Where someone is said to grieve the Holy Spirit (Eph 4:30 [cf. Isa 63:10]). Thus, the Holy Spirit is represented as the author of revelations to men through the prophets of the OT. Of that authority through which prophets and holy men were motivated when they are said to have spoken to or acted in the Spirit or through the Spirit, meaning by inspiration (Matt 22:43; Mark 12:36; 1 Pet 1:11; 2 Pet 1:21), or as communicating a knowledge of future events (Acts 10:19; 20:23; 21:11; 1 Tim 4:1; Rev 19:10); communicating instruction, admonitions, warnings, invitations through the Apostles (Rev 2:7, 11, 17, 29; 3:6, 13, 22; 14:13; 22:17), the Spirit and the whole Church. Of the Spirit teaching, enlightening, and guiding Christians in respect to faith and practice (Luke 11:13; John 7:39 [cf. 16:13, 14]; Rom 5:5; 1 Cor 12:3; 2 Cor 3:3; Gal 5:5; Titus 3:5; Heb 6:4; 1 Pet 4:14). Also 1 Cor 2:10 (cf. above b). As speaking through disciples when brought before rulers (Matt 10:20; Mark 13:11; Luke 12:12). As qualifying the Apostles to propagate the gospel powerfully (Acts 1:8); aiding in edifying and comforting the churches (Acts 9:31); directing in the appointment of church officers (Acts 20:28); assisting to speak and hear the gospel (1 Cor 2:13, in words taught, suggested by the Holy Spirit; 2:14). Emphatically, as the Spirit of the gospel (2 Cor 3:17, see above c [cf. 2, c below]). Used emphatically as the Spirit of the gospel, i.e., the gospel in contrast to the letter of Mosaic Law (2 Cor 3:6, 8 [cf. 3:17]). See above 1, d. (2) Used to indicate the work resulting from the immediate agency of the Holy Spirit, such as the power of the Holy Spirit (Acts 1:8). Spoken: (a) Of the role of the Holy Spirit in the miraculous conception of the Lord Jesus (Luke 1:35, equivalent to "the power of the Highest" in the next clause). See also Matt 1:18, 20.

(b) Of that special authority which rested upon and empowered the Lord Jesus after the descent of the Holy Spirit upon Him at His baptism (Luke 4:1 [cf. 3:22]; John 3:34); also Matt 12:18 quoted from Isaiah 42:1; Luke 4:18 quoted from Isaiah 61:1; Acts 1:2; 10:38; 1 John 5:6, 8 [cf. Heb 9:14]). As prompting Him to various actions (e.g., to go into the desert and be tempted [Matt 4:1; Mark 1:12; Luke 4:1], and afterwards to return into Galilee [Luke 4:14]). As authorizing Him to cast out demons (Matt 12:28 [cf. Luke 11:20]). In connection with this occasion, the Holy Spirit is said to be capable of being blasphemed against (Matt 12:31, 32; Mark 3:29; Luke 12:10 [cf. Matt 12:28]). (c) Of John in the Revelation as being in the Spirit, meaning rapt in prophetic vision (Rev 1:10; 4:2; 17:3; 21:10). Of the Spirit resting upon John the Baptist (Luke 1:15); Elizabeth (Luke 1:41); Zacharias (Luke 1:67); Simeon (Luke 2:25–27). The technical expression "to be baptized in [or with] the Holy Spirit" (a.t.) by Christ as the work which Christ was going to do as declared by John the Baptist, referring to the spiritual baptism into the body of Christ for all those who were truly saved (Matt 3:11; Mark 1:8; Luke 3:16; John 1:33; Acts 1:5; 11:16; 1 Cor 12:13). (d) Of that authority of the Holy Spirit by which the Apostles were qualified to act as directors of the church of Christ (John 20:22, 23). Specifically, of the empowerment imparted by the Holy Spirit on and after the Day of Pentecost, by which the apostles and early Christians were endowed with high supernatural qualifications for their work; knowledge equivalent to a full knowledge of gospel truth and the power of prophesying, working miracles, and speaking with languages previously unknown to them; all done in evidence of the baptism of the Holy Spirit. This baptism in the Holy Spirit as a historical event occurred on three distinct occasions: at Jerusalem, baptizing Jews into Christ's body; at Caesarea, baptizing Gentiles into His body; and, at Ephesus, similarly baptizing the disciples of John the Baptist

(Acts 2:1–21; 10:44–48; 19:1–7). The baptism with the Holy Spirit is not an experience to be sought by believers today. It is a historical event, even as the incarnation, the crucifixion, the resurrection, and the ascension of Christ, which, on the exercise of genuine faith by the individual seals that person as a member of the body of Christ. This is as a result of the miraculous application of what Christ did in history for all who would believe (1 Cor 12:13). The baptism of the Holy Spirit, which attached believers to the body of Christ, is to be distinguished from the continued and repeated experience of the inner filling by the Holy Spirit which is for service (Eph 5:18). The prophet Joel prophesied about the coming of the Holy Spirit (Joel 2:28, 29 [cf. Acts 2:4, 18, 33, 38; 5:32; 8:15, 17–19; 10:44, 45, 47; 11:15, 24; 13:9; 15:8; 19:2]). Joel, however, prophesied the outpouring of the Holy Spirit not only in connection with the first coming of the Lord Jesus, but also in connection with His Second Coming (Joel 2:10, 11) when the events described in Matt 24:29 concerning the sun, moon, and the stars will take place (Joel 2:30, 31). **(e)** The Holy Spirit prompts one to do or restrain from doing particular actions (Acts 6:3, 5, 10; 8:29, 39 [cf. Matt 4:1]; Acts 13:2, 4; 15:28; 16:6, 7); encourages holy boldness, energy, and zeal in speaking and acting (Acts 4:8, 31; 6:3, 5, 10 [cf. 6:8]); is the medium of divine communications and revelations (Acts 11:28; 21:4; Eph 3:5); is the source of support, comfort, Christian joy and triumph (Acts 7:55; 13:52; Eph 5:18; Phil 1:19). In the pl., *pneúmata* means spiritual gifts (1 Cor 14:12). **(f)** Spoken of that divine influence by which the temperament or disposition of mind in Christians is affected, i.e., correcting, elevating, and ennobling, filling the mind with peace and joy. The spirit in this case stands opposed to the flesh (John 3:6; Rom 8:1) because it does not indulge in the depraved affections and lusts of our physical natures and unrenewed hearts, but follows those holy and elevated actions and desires which the Spirit imparts

and cherishes (Rom 8:2, 4–6, 9, 13). Through the influence of the Spirit of God, Christians have the same disposition and the same frame of mind with Christ (Gal 5:16–18, 22, 25; 6:8). In Rom 8:9, having "the Spirit of Christ" means having the same mind as Christ possessed which is wrought in us by the Spirit (cf. Rom 7:6; 8:15, a spirit of sonship, a filial spirit, 8:23; 1 Cor 2:12; 2 Cor 6:6; Gal 4:6; Eph 1:17, "the spirit of wisdom and illumination" [a.t.] imparted by the Holy Spirit; 2:18, 22; 3:16, 17; 4:3, 4; 5:9; Col 1:8; 1 Tim 4:12; Jude 1:19). **(3)** Metonymically spoken of a person or teacher who acts or professes to act under the inspiration of the Holy Spirit by divine inspiration (1 Cor 12:10, "discerning of spirits" of teachers, a critical faculty of the mind quickened by the Holy Spirit, consisting not only of the power of discerning who was a prophet and who was not, but also of a distinguishing in the discourses of a teacher what proceeded from the Holy Spirit and what did not. Also 1 John 4:1–3, 6).

Deriv.: *pneumatikós* (4152), spiritual.

Syn.: *phántasma* (5326), a phantom, apparition, as spoken of a spirit, ghost; *psuchḗ* (5590), soul; *noús* (3563), mind; *phrónēma* (5427), state of mind.

Pnoḗ (4157), breath, wind, may be considered syn. only because of its common derivation with *pneúma* (from *pnéō* [4154], to breathe, blow) which, however, as a subst. should be translated "breath" (Acts 17:25) or "wind" (a.t. [Acts 2:2]). An attempt to substitute spirit for breath would indicate the definite difference between the two words (as evidenced in Acts 23:8, 9; Rom 2:29; 1 Cor 5:5; 2 Cor 7:1; Gal 6:18). The same logical conclusion would be arrived at if the substitution for the word *psuchḗ* is made with *pnoḗ*, breath (see Matt 10:28; Luke 12:19; 1 Thess 5:23; James 5:20; 2 Pet 2:8).

In the OT the word *nephesh* (5315, OT), soul, is translated *psuchḗ* in the Sept and *ruah* (7307, OT), spirit, is translated in the Sept *pneúma*. The soul stands for the natural life regarded from the point of view of its separate individuality (Gen 2:7; 17:14), while spirit is the principle of life considered as flowing from God Himself (Job 27:3; Ps 51:10; Eccl 12:7), who is thus called "the God of the spirits of all flesh" (Num 16:22; 27:16). The Apostle Paul follows this distinction of the OT words referring to the soulish (*psuchikós*) man as one who by nature is apart from divine grace, and to spiritual (*pneumatikós* [4152]), as applying to the new man in whom the Spirit of God has taken up His abode (Rom 8:9).

Ant.: *ousía* (3776), substance; *ógkos* (3591), a mass; *prágma* (4229), matter; *skēnōma* (4638), the body; *phúsis* (5449), nature, from which the Eng. "physics" is derived.

Sōma (4983), body, is the material part of man (in contrast to the spiritual which is represented by *pneúma* which gives man the ability to communicate with God, while *psuchē* gives man a consciousness of his environment). See *sárx* (4561), flesh (John 3:6–8). Only man is said to have a spirit (John 6:63). Because God is Spirit He can only be worshiped in spirit (John 4:24 [cf. Rom 8:15f.]; Eph 2:18). It is the spirit in man which responds to the Spirit of God. The Spirit of God in man guides him to and in all the truth (John 16:13; Rom 8:16).

Another ant. of spirit is *grámma* (1121), letter, referring to something that is visible or to a literal interpretation, as distinct from the spirit or spiritual interpretation (Rom 2:29; 2 Cor 3:6).

**4152. πνευματικός *pneumatikós*; fem. *pneumatikē*, neut. *pneumatikón*, adj. from *pneúma* (4151), spirit. Spiritual.

(I) Pertaining to the nature of spirits. "A spiritual body" (1 Cor 15:44) means a body dominated by the Spirit, in contrast to a natural or soulish body (*sōma psuchikón* [*sōma* {4983}, body; *psuchikón* {5591}, pertaining to soul]) which obeys one's natural instincts or soul. In Eph 6:12, *tá pneumatiká tēs ponērías* ([4189], iniquity) means the evil spirits.

(II) Pertaining to or proceeding from the Holy Spirit, *tó pneúma tó hágion* (see *pneúma* 3, D).

(A) Of persons who are spiritual, enlightened by the Holy Spirit, enjoying the influences, graces, gifts of the Holy Spirit (1 Cor 2:13, 15; 3:1; 14:37; Gal 6:1).

(B) Of things spiritual, communicated or imparted by the Holy Spirit: Rom 15:27; 1 Cor 2:13, meaning those things pertaining to the Spirit (*tá toú Pneúmatos* [as in 2:14]); 1 Cor 9:11; 12:1; 14:1, the things pertaining to the Spirit; Eph 1:3; 5:19; Col 1:9; 3:16, "spiritual songs," meaning those composed in the Spirit on spiritual and instructive subjects. In Rom 7:14 "the law is spiritual" means it is according to the mind and will of the Spirit. In Rom 1:11 *chárisma pneumatikón* (*chárisma* [5486], gift), "a spiritual gift," means a gift relating to the mind or spirit of Christians as enlightened and quickened by the Holy Spirit (cf. in 1:12, and see *pneúma*, III, D, 2, e). Also spoken of things in a higher and spiritual sense, not literal or corporeal, including also a reference to the Holy Spirit (1 Cor 10:3, 4, they ate spiritual food and drank spiritual drink; 1 Pet 2:5 "a spiritual house").

Deriv.: *pneumatikós* (4153), spiritually.

Ant.: *phusikós* (5446), natural, pertaining to or governed by natural instincts; *psuchikós* (5591), soulish, pertaining to or governed by the soul, the lower part of the immaterial natural in man. Both of these words, *phusikós* and *psuchikós*, stand in contrast to *pneumatikós*, spiritual (1 Cor 2:14; 15:44, 46; James 3:15); *sarkikós* (4559), pertaining to the flesh, carnal; *sárkinos* (4560), made of flesh.

**4153. πνευματικῶς *pneumatikōs*; adv. from *pneumatikós* (4152), spiritual. Spiritually, by the assistance of the Holy Spirit (1 Cor 2:14), prophetically, allegorically, mystically (Rev 11:8 [cf. Rev 17:5, 7]).

Ant.: *phusikós* (5447), physically, naturally; the expression *katá sárka* (*katá* [2596], according; *sárka* [4561], flesh), according to the flesh or obeying the flesh (Rom 8:4, 5).

4154. πνέω *pnéō*; fut. *pneúsomai*, aor. *épneusa*. To blow upon, as the wind or air (Matt 7:25, 27; Luke 12:55; John 3:8; 6:18; Acts 27:40; Rev 7:1; Sept.: Ps 147:18; Isa 40:24).

Deriv.: *ekpnéō* (1606), to die, expire; *empnéō* (1709), to inhale, breathe, to inspire; *theópneustos* (2315), God-breathed, inspired; *pneúma* (4151), wind, breath, life, spirit; *pnoḗ* (4157), wind, breath; *hupopnéō* (5285), to blow gently or softly.

Syn.: *anemízō* (416), to drive or toss with the wind; *rhipízō* (4494), to fan up, to agitate, toss.

Ant.: *kopázō* (2869), to subside or abate.

4155. πνίγω *pnígō*; fut. *pníxō*. To strangle or choke (Matt 18:28; Mark 5:13).

Deriv.: *apopnígō* (638), to stifle, choke severely; *epipnígō* (1970), to choke by overcrowding; *pniktós* (4156), an animal choked to death but not bled; *sumpnígō* (4846), to throttle.

Ant.: *boēthéō* (997), to help, succor, relieve; *sunantilambánomai* (4878), to cooperate, assist, help.

4156. πνικτός *pniktós*; fem. *pniktḗ*, neut. *pniktón*, from *pnígō* (4155), to strangle, choke. Strangled. In the NT, with a def. art., strangled meat, meaning the flesh of animals killed by strangling without shedding their blood (Acts 15:20, 29; 21:25). The Mosaic Law prohibited the eating of it (Lev 17:13, 14 [cf. 7:26, 27]; Deut 12:16, 23).

Ant.: *sphágion* (4968), a slain animal; *kréas* (2907), butchered meat.

4157. πνοή *pnoḗ*; gen. *pnoḗs*, fem. noun from *pnéō* (4154), to breathe, blow. Wind, breath. In Acts 2:2 translated wind, "a rushing mighty wind"; (See also Sept.: Job 37:10). The rushing wind in Acts 2:2 is a natural phenomenon symbolizing the supernatural phenomenon of the Holy Spirit's outpouring. Thus, *pneúma*

may mean either something material or something purely spiritual such as a spiritual gift or the spirit of man which enables him to communicate with the Spirit of God. Used only in John 3:8 with the meaning of wind. *Pnoḗ* conveys the impression of a lighter, gentler motion of the air than *pneúma*, spirit. In Acts 17:25 it is "breath," the air needed for breathing; Sept.: Gen 2:7; Isa 42:5.

Syn.: *ánemos* (417), violent wind; *aḗr* (109), air; *laílaps* (2978), storm, tempest; *thúella* (2366), a hurricane, cyclone; *seismós* (4578), earthquake, tempest in Matt 8:24.

4158. ποδήρης *podḗrēs*; gen. *podḗrous*, masc.-fem., neut. *podḗres*, adj. from *poús* (4228), foot, and *arṓ* (n.f., see below), to join, fasten, fit. A garment reaching down to the feet (Rev 1:13).

Deriv. of *árō* (n.f.), to adapt, adjust: *aréskō* (700), to please; *armós* (719), a joint.

Syn.: *stolḗ* (4749), a long robe worn by people of rank as a mark of distinction; *katastolḗ* (2689), costume.

4159. πόθεν *póthen*; an interrogative adv. From where, why, how?
(I) Of place, equivalent to "from what place" (Matt 15:33; Mark 8:4; John 4:11; 6:5; Rev 7:13; Sept.: Gen 29:4; Num 11:13; Judg 19:17). In indirect composition (Luke 13:25, 27; John 3:8; 8:14). Figuratively of state or condition indirectly (Rev 2:5).
(II) Of source, author, cause, or manner meaning Whence? How? (Matt 13:27, 54, 56; 21:25; Mark 6:2; John 1:48; 19:9; James 4:1). Indirect (Luke 20:7; John 2:9; 7:27, 28; 9:29, 30; Sept.: 2 Kgs 6:27). Spoken in surprise, admiration (Luke 1:43). Implying strong negation (Mark 12:37). As an answer to *póthen* there can be two possible responses; *enteúthen* (1782), from here, or *ekeíthen* (1564), from there.

4160. ποιέω *poiéō*; contracted *poiṓ*, fut. *poiḗsō*, aor. *epoíesa*, perf. *pepoíeka*, pluperf. 3d person pl. (without augment) *pepoiḗkeisan* (Mark 15:7). With variations from the regular forms being fut. Attic *poiṓ* (Matt 26:18); aor. opt. 3d person pl. *poiḗseian* (Luke 6:11). To make, do, expressing action either as completed or continued.

(I) To make, form, produce, bring about, cause, spoken of any external act as manifested in the production of something tangible, corporeal, obvious to the senses, completed action. The mid. also is often used with only a remote reference to the subject which not often wholly vanishes, so that the mid. does not apparently differ from the act.

(A) Generally: **(1)** Particularly and with the acc. (Matt 17:4; John 9:11; 18:18; 19:23; Acts 7:40, 43; 9:39; 19:24; Rom 9:20; Heb 12:13; Rev 13:14). Followed by *ek* (1537), of, with the gen. of material (John 2:15; 9:6; Rom 9:21; Sept.: Gen 6:14; Ex 25:10); by *katá* (2596), according to, indicating manner, model (Acts 7:44; Heb 8:5). **(2)** Spoken of God, to make, create, with the acc. (Acts 4:24; 7:50; 14:15; 17:24; Heb 1:2; Rev 14:7). In Luke 11:40 with duplicate in the acc. (see also Matt 19:4; Sept.: Isa 45:7).

(B) Figuratively spoken of a state or condition, or of things intangible and incorporeal, and generally of such things as are produced by an inward act of the mind or will; to make, cause, bring about, occasion. **(1)** Generally with the acc. (Luke 1:68; Acts 15:3; 24:12; Rom 16:17; 1 Cor 10:13; Eph 2:15; Heb 8:9; mid. Rom 15:26; Heb 1:3). Of mighty deeds, wonders, miracles, with the acc. pl. *dunámeis* (1411), powers (Matt 7:22; 13:58); with *krátos* (2904, dominion, strength (Luke 1:51); *érgon* (2041), works (John 5:36; 10:25); *sēmeía* (4592), miracles or signs (John 2:11, 23; 4:54; 6:30; 11:47); *térata* (5059), wonders, and *sēmeía* (4592), signs (Acts 6:8; 7:36; 15:12). **(2)** Spoken of a course of action or conduct, to do, execute, exercise, practice, *krísin poiéō* (*krísin* [2920], judgment), to do judgment, to act as judge, equivalent to *krínō* (2919), judge (John 5:27; Jude

1:15). Specifically of right, duty, virtue (John 3:21; Rom 2:14; 10:5; 1 John 1:6; 2:29; 3:7, "that doeth righteousness"; see also Matt 19:16, "what good thing shall I do"; John 5:29; 8:29; Rom 7:19; Eph 6:8; James 4:17; 3 John 1:5; Sept.: Gen 18:19). **(3)** Of evil deeds or conduct, to do, commit or practice *hamártēma* (265), a particular sin (1 Cor 6:18); *tḗn anomían* (458), the sin (Matt 13:41, the lawlessness; Luke 12:48, "worthy of stripes"; John 8:34; 2 Cor 11:7; 1 John 3:4); with *tá toiaúta* (5108), "these things" (a.t. [Rom 1:32; 2:3]); with *bdélugma* (946), "abomination" (Rev 21:27); *tó érgon toúto* (*tó érgon* [2041], the work; *toúto* [5124], this), "this work" (a.t. [1 Cor 5:2; 3 John 1:10]); *tá mḗ kathḗkonta* (*tá mḗ* [3361], the things not; *kathḗkonta* [2520], becoming, fitting), "those things not becoming" (a.t. [Rom 1:28]); *oudén enantíon poiḗsas tṓ laṓ* (*oudén* [3762], nothing; *enantíon* [1726], against; *tṓ laṓ* [2992], the people), "nothing against the people" (Acts 28:17); *kakón* (2556), "evil" (Matt 27:23; Luke 23:22); pl. *kaká*, "evil things, hurtful" (a.t. [Rom 3:8; 1 Pet 3:12]); *ponērá* (4190), "evil things" (a.t.), hurtful (Luke 3:19); *phónon* (5408), "murder" (Mark 15:7); *pseúdos* (5579), "falsehood" (a.t. [Rev 22:15]). Used with the acc. of various nouns as *ekdíkēsis* (1557), vindication or bringing out justice, meaning to defend one's cause (Luke 18:7, 8; Acts 7:24); with *enédra* (1747), murderous purpose, to wait around for the purpose of attacking, to ensnare (Acts 25:3); with *tó hikanón* (2425), sufficient ability, meaning to make satisfaction, to gratify (Mark 15:15); with *monḗ* (3438), abode, to make an abode, to abide, dwell (John 14:23); with *hodós* (3598), way, to make one's way, to go (Mark 2:23); with *pólemos* (4171), war, to make battle or war, to fight, followed by *metá* (3326), with someone, and the gen. instead of the dat. (Rev 11:7; 12:17; 13:7; 19:19); with *sumboúlion* (4824), counsel, to have a consultation, to consult together (Mark 3:6; 15:1). With *sunōmosía* (4945), plot, conspiracy (Acts 23:13); with *lútrōsis* (3085), redemption

(Luke 1:68); with *chará* (5479), joy (Acts 15:3); with *episústasis* (1999), conspiracy (Acts 24:12); with *dichostasía* (1370), dissension and *skándalon* (4625), scandal (Rom 16:17); with *ékbasis* (1545), way out (1 Cor 10:13); with *eirēnē* (1515), peace (Eph 2:15); with *aúxēsis* (838), increase (Eph 4:16); with *diathēkē* (1243), testament (Heb 8:9); with *koinōnía* (2842), partnership, benefaction (Rom 15:26); with *katharismós* (2612), expiation, cleansing (Heb 1:3); and the mid., often with only a remote reference to the subject; with *anabolē* (311), delay; *poiéomai*, meaning to make a delay (Acts 25:17); with *déēsis* (1162), supplication, to make supplications (Luke 5:33; Phil 1:4; 1 Tim 2:1); with *ekbolē* (1546), a throwing overboard, to casting out (Acts 27:18); with *kopetós* (2870), lamentation, to lament, make lamentation (Acts 8:2); in the Sept. with *pénthos* (3997), mourning, to mourn (Gen 50:10); with *lógos* (3056), account, to make account of (Acts 20:24); with *mneía* (3417), recollection, the same as *mimnēskomai* (3403), to remember, recall, to make remembrance of, to bear in mind, to make mention (Rom 1:9; Eph 1:16; 1 Thess 1:2; Phile 1:4); with *poreía* (4197), journey, way, meaning to make progress or a journey, which is equivalent to *poreúomai* (4198), to take a journey (Luke 13:22); with *prónoia* (4307), provision, care, thus to make provision for, the same as *pronoéomai* (4306), to consider in advance, provide (Rom 13:14); with *spoudē* (4710), earnest diligence, to give diligence, the same as *spoudázō* (4704), to be diligent, study (Jude 1:3). **(4)** Spoken of a feast or banquet, meaning to make, give, hold, to celebrate (Luke 5:29; 14:12, 13, 16). With the dat. of person to whom or in honor of whom (Matt 22:2; Mark 6:21; John 12:2). To celebrate, make, hold or keep a festival (Matt 26:18; Acts 18:21). In the sense of instituting (Heb 11:28).

(C) To cause to exist, as spoken of generative power, to beget, to bring forth, to bear. **(1)** Of trees and plants, to germinate, bring forth fruit, yield (Matt 3:10; 7:17;

13:23, 26; Luke 3:9; Rev 22:2). Metaphorically (Matt 3:8; 21:43; Luke 3:8). Of branches, to shoot forth (Mark 4:32); of a fountain (James 3:12); of plants (Sept.: Gen 1:11, 12; Isa 5:2, 4). **(2)** Figuratively of persons, to make for oneself, to get, acquire, gain (Luke 12:33; 16:9; John 4:1; Sept.: Gen 11:4). To profit, advantage, gain, generally (1 Cor 15:29); in a pecuniary sense, to make (Matt 25:16; Luke 19:18).

(D) Causative, to cause to do or be. **(1)** Followed by the inf. (Matt 5:32; Mark 1:17; 7:37; 8:25; Luke 5:34; John 6:10; Acts 17:26; Rev 13:13). In the inf. with *toú* (Acts 3:12). **(2)** Followed by *hína* (2443), so that, with the subjunctive, to make or cause that (John 11:37; Col 4:16). *Poiēsō autoús hína,* "to make them to" (Rev 3:9). **(3)** Followed by the duplicate acc. of obj. and a predicate of that obj., either subst. or adj. or adv., strictly with *eínai* (1511), to be, implied. **(a)** With subst. as predicate, of things (Matt 21:13; John 4:46; 1 Cor 6:15; Heb 1:7); of persons (Matt 4:19; 23:15; Luke 15:19; Sept.: Gen 27:37). To make, constitute, appoint (John 6:15; Acts 2:36; Rev 1:6; 3:12; 5:10). With a predicate implied (Heb 3:2 [cf. 3:1]). With *hína* (2443), so that, instead of the acc. (Mark 3:14). In the sense of to declare oneself to be something or somebody (John 8:53; 10:33; 19:7, 12; 1 John 1:10). **(b)** With adj. as predicate, of persons (Matt 20:12; 28:14; John 16:2; Rev 12:15). In the sense of declaring (John 5:18). Of things (Eph 2:14). To suppose, judge, assume (Matt 12:33, either assume the tree to be good and its fruit good, or the contrary. Also in this construction *poiéō* with the acc. of the adj. often forms a periphrasis for the cognate verb; with *dēlon* (1212), evident, meaning to make manifest or evident, betray (Matt 26:73); *éktheton* (1570), put or cast out, equivalent to *ektíthēmi* (1620), to expose, meaning to expose infants (Acts 7:19); *eutheías poiéō tás tríbous* (*eutheías* [2117], straight; *tás* [3588], the; *tríbous* [5147], ways), to make straight and level the ways (Mark 1:3; Luke 3:4 [cf. John

1:23]); *euthúnō* (2116), to straighten (Matt 3:3); with *hugiés* (5199), healthy, to make whole, to heal, equivalent to *hugiázō* (n.f.), to make healthy (John 5:11, 15; 7:23); *phanerón poiéō* (*phanerón* [5318], manifest), to make known, manifest, to betray, equivalent to *phaneróō* (5319), to manifest (Matt 12:16; Mark 3:12). In the mid. *bébaion poiéomai* (*bébaion* [949], firm, stable), to make firm, sure, equivalent to *bebaióomai* or *bebaioúmai* (2 Pet 1:10). **(c)** With the adv. as predicate, such as *éxō* (1854), out, to make one be or go out, cause one to go out, equivalent to "put forth" (a.t. [Acts 5:34]).

(II) To do, expressing an action as continued or not yet completed, what one does repeatedly, habitually, like *prássō* (4238), to practice.

(A) Followed by the acc. of thing, and without reference to a person as the remote object. See below D, e, 1. **(1)** Followed by the acc. pron., to do, generally (Matt 5:47; 8:9; 9:28; Mark 11:3; Luke 6:2; 7:8; 20:2; Acts 1:1; 14:11, 15; 1 Cor 7:36; Gal 2:10; Eph 6:9; Phil 2:14; Col 3:17; 1 Tim 5:21; James 4:15). With a part. following (Mark 11:5, "What do you do, loosing the colt?" [a.t.]; Acts 11:30). **(2)** Followed by the acc. of a subst. rarely implied and spoken of particular deeds, acts, works, done repeatedly, to do, equivalent to perform, execute (John 8:39, 41; 10:37, 38, the works which God requires; 2 Tim 4:5, the work of an evangelist; Rev 2:5, "the first works," meaning the works which were done at the beginning). To do mercy, show mercy (James 2:13); to bear or give alms (Matt 6:1–3; Acts 10:2; 24:17). Also of the will, precept, requirement of someone, to do, perform, fulfill (Matt 21:31; 23:3; Mark 6:20; Luke 17:9, 10; John 2:5; Acts 16:21; Eph 2:3; Rev 17:17); of the precepts of the Father or of the Son (Matt 5:19; 7:21, 24, 26; Luke 6:46; 8:21; John 7:19; Acts 13:22; Rev 22:14); of that which one asks, entreats, promises (John 14:13, 14; Rom 4:21; Eph 3:20; 1 Thess 5:24); with the dat. of person (Mark 10:35, 36); of a purpose, plan, decree (Acts 4:28; Rom 9:28, the Lord will execute His word, decree, i.e., His threatening; 2 Cor 8:10, 11; Gal 5:17; Eph 3:11); generally (John 7:51; 18:35; Acts 21:33; 1 Tim 1:13; Sept.: Gen 34:7; Ps 51:6).

(B) Intrans. to do, act. **(1)** Used in an absolute sense, meaning to be active, work (Matt 20:12; Rev 13:5; Sept.: Ruth 2:19). Both of these NT passages, however, may be referred to E below. **(2)** With *kalós*, an adv. of manner meaning to do well, to act in a good manner (Matt 12:12; 1 Cor 7:37); with *kreísson* (2908), better (1 Cor 7:38); *hoútō* (3779), thus, or so (John 14:31; 1 Cor 16:1); *phronímōs* (5430), prudently (Luke 16:8); *hōs* (5613), as (Matt 1:24; 28:15); with *katá* (2596), according to, followed by the acc. (Matt 23:3; Luke 2:27); *prós* (4314), according to, followed by the acc. (Luke 12:47).

(C) *Poiéō* is often used in the latter phrase of a sentence instead of repeating the verb of a preceding phrase. Followed by the acc. of thing (Matt 5:46; Luke 6:10; Rom 12:20; Heb 6:3). With an adv. as *hoútō* (3779), thus, or so (Matt 5:47; 24:45, 46; Luke 9:15; Acts 12:8); *hōsaútōs* (5615), likewise (Matt 20:5; 21:36); *kathós* (2531), as (1 Thess 5:11).

(D) Spoken in reference to a person's intentions regarding someone, for or against him, the person being the more remote object. **(1)** After the acc. of person, also with the acc. of thing (Matt 27:22; Mark 15:12); with an adv. such as *eu* (2095), well or good, meaning to do good to someone (Mark 14:7). **(2)** Followed by the dat. of person, meaning to do to or for someone, in his behalf, with the acc. of thing (Matt 20:32; Mark 5:19, 20; Luke 1:49; John 9:26; 12:16); with the acc. implied (Matt 25:40, 45); with an adv. (Matt 5:44; Mark 15:8; Luke 1:25; John 13:15; Sept.: Gen 21:1); against someone, to his detriment, with the acc. of thing (John 15:21; Acts 9:13; Heb 13:6); with an adv. (Luke 2:48). Generally in respect to someone, in his case, with the acc. of thing (Matt 7:12; 21:40; Mark 9:13; Acts 4:16); with an adv. (Matt 7:12; Luke 6:31). **(3)** Followed by *en* with the dat. of person meaning to do in respect to someone, in his case, with the acc. of thing (Matt 17:12; Luke 23:31; Sept.: Gen 40:14). **(4)** Followed by *metá* (3326), with, and by the gen. of person, meaning to do in respect to someone (Luke 1:72; 10:37; Acts 14:27; Sept.: Gen 24:12).

(E) Followed by the acc. of time, intrans. meaning to do or act for a certain time, up to a certain time, to spend, pass (Acts 15:33; 18:23; 20:3; 2 Cor 11:25; James 4:13; Sept.: Prov 13:23).

Deriv.: *eirēnopoiéō* (1517), to make peace; *zōopoiéō* (2227), to make alive; *kakopoiós* (2555), evildoer; *kalopoiéō* (2569), to live virtuously; *moschopoiéō* (3447), to make a calf; *ochlopoiéō* (3792), to make a crowd; *peripoiéō* (4046), to purchase, acquire, preserve, keep; *poíēma* (4161), creation, work, action; *poíēsis* (4162), performance, action; *poiētḗs* (4163), creator, maker, doer; *prospoiéomai* (4364), to pretend; *skēnopoiós* (4635), tentmaker; *cheiropoíētos* (5499), make by hands.

Syn.: *prássō* (4238), to practice, perform repeatedly or habitually, more often of evil deeds or conduct (unlike *poiéō* which refers to single acts of goodness); *ergázomai* (2038), to work; *katergázomai* (2716), to work fully, accomplish; *teléō* (5055), to complete, conclude; *ekteléō* (1615), to finish; *apoteléō* (658), to consummate; *epiteléō* (2005), to fulfill, perform completely; *diaponéomai* (1278), to toil through; *kámnō* (2577), to toil; *energéō* (1754), to be active, efficient; *douleúō* (1398), to labor as a slave.

Ant.: *argéō* (691), to be idle; *scholázō* (4980), to take a holiday, be at leisure; *katapaúō* (2664), to cease working.

4161. ποίημα *poíēma*; gen. *poiēmatos*, neut. noun from *poiéō* (4160), to make. Something made, a work, workpiece, workmanship (Rom 1:20). Figuratively in Eph 2:10; Sept.: Ps 143:5; Eccl 3:11; Isa 29:16. It denotes the result of work, what is produced as contrasted to *poíēsis* which is the act of making, the doing itself and not that which is made. He who

does the making is *poiētḗs* (4163), performer, doer, poet.

Syn.: *ktísis* (2937), creation; *ktísma* (2938), product of creation, creature, a word which emphasizes the thing created; *prágma* (4229), material thing, object; *plásma* (4110), something molded or formed; *phúsis* (5449), nature; *kósmos* (2889), world.

Ant.: *katastrophḗ* (2692), destruction, demolition.

4162. ποίησις *poíēsis*; gen. *poiēseōs*, fem. noun from *poiéō* (4160), to make. The act of making, doing or keeping as of the Law (James 1:25), whereas *poíēma* (4161) is the result of making, workmanship.

Syn.: *ergasía* (2039), a working; *práxis* (4234), a doing, transaction; *ktísis* (2937), creation.

Ant.: *kathaíresis* (2506), pulling down.

4163. ποιητής *poiētḗs*; gen. *poiētoú*, masc. noun from *poiéō* (4160), to make. One who makes something, a doer, performer, poet (Acts 17:28). A doer, keeper of a law or precept (Rom 2:13; James 1:22, 23, 25; 4:11).

Syn.: *dēmiourgós* (1217), creator, builder; *ktístēs* (2939), a maker, creator; *ergátēs* (2040), worker; *technítēs* (5079), craftsman, builder; *téktōn* (5045), carpenter.

Ant.: *olothreutḗs* (3644), a destroyer of physical existence; *apollúōn* (623), destroyer, Apollyon.

4164. ποικίλος *poikílos*; fem. *poikílē*, neut. *pokílon*, adj. Variegated, many-colored (Sept.: Gen 31:8, 10, 12). Used of sicknesses, meaning various, diverse, manifold (Matt 4:24; Mark 1:34; Luke 4:40); desires (2 Tim 3:6; Titus 3:3); of miracles (Heb 2:4); doctrines (Heb 13:9); temptations (James 1:2; 1 Pet 1:6); the grace of God, referring to the various gifts derived from that grace (1 Pet 4:10).

Deriv.: *polupoíkilos* (4182), much varied.

Syn.: *diáphoros* (1313), different, diverse.

Ant.: *hómoios* (3664), similar; *autós* (846), the same.

4165. ποιμαίνω *poimaínō*; fut. *poimanṓ*, from *poimḗn* (4166), shepherd. To shepherd, tend. Used particularly (Luke 17:7, shepherding; 1 Cor 9:7; Sept.: Gen 30:31, 36; Ex 3:1); figuratively, to care for, provide, referring to kings and princes in regard to their people (Matt 2:6; Rev 7:17); in regard to pastors and teachers in the church (John 21:16; Acts 20:28; 1 Pet 5:2; Sept.: 2 Sam 5:2; 1 Chr 11:2). From the context, to rule, to govern with severity (Rev 2:27; 12:5; 19:15; Sept.: Mic 5:3; 7:14). The realization of Christ's ruling activity is understood by some scholars to occur exclusively in the future (during an earthly Millennium). Others identify it with the present spiritual Lordship of Christ in which He shepherds His people and sovereignly controls all of human history. In a bad sense, with *heautón* (1438), himself, to feed or cherish oneself, to take care of oneself at the expense of others (Jude 1:12 [cf. Sept.: Ezek 34:8]).

Syn.: *bóskō* (1006), to feed, distinguished from *poimaínō* in that the latter implies the whole office of the shepherd as guiding, guarding, folding of the flock as well as leading it to nourishment; *árchō* (757), rule; *hēgéomai* (2233), to lead; *cheiragōgéō* (5496), to lead by the hand; *kateuthúnō* (2720), to guide, direct; *hēgemoneúō* (2230), to act as ruler; *basileúō* (936), to reign.

Ant.: *akolouthéō* (190), to follow.

4166. ποιμήν *poimḗn*; gen. *poiménos*, masc. noun. Shepherd, one who generally cares for flocks.

(I) Particularly (Matt 9:36, "sheep having no shepherd"; 25:32; Mark 6:34; Luke 2:8, 15, 18, 20; Sept.: Gen 4:2; Num 27:17).

(II) Metaphorically of Jesus as the Great Shepherd who watches over and provides for the welfare of the Church, His flock (Matt 26:31; Mark 14:27 quoted

from Zech 13:7; John 10:2, 11, 12, 14, 16; Heb 13:20; 1 Pet 2:25; Sept. of the Messiah: Ezek 34:23; 37:24). The spiritual guide of a particular church (Eph 4:11; Sept.: Jer 2:8; 3:15; Ezek 34:2, 5).

Deriv.: *archipoimḗn* (750), chief shepherd; *poimaínō* (4165), to tend, take general care of the flock; *poímnē* (4167) and *poímnion* (4168), flock.

Syn.: *hēgemṓn* (2232), a leader; *archēgós* (747), leader; *presbúteros* (4245), elder, spiritual leader; *didáskalos* (1320), teacher; *epískopos* (1985), overseer, superintendent.

Ant.: *próbaton* (4263), sheep, in its metaphorical sense; *mathētḗs* (3101), a learner, disciple.

4167. ποίμνη *poímnē*; gen. *poímnēs*, fem. noun from *poimḗn* (4166), shepherd. A flock of sheep (Luke 2:8; 1 Cor 9:7). A spiritual group of people (Matt 26:31; John 10:16, the flock of Christ, His disciples, the Church; Sept.: Gen 32:17); *ekklēsía* (1577), church, assembly.

Syn.: *poímnion* (4168), a flock.

4168. ποίμνιον *poímnion*; gen. *poimníou*, neut. noun from *poimḗn* (4166), shepherd. A flock. In the NT, it is applied only spiritually (Luke 12:32; Acts 20:28, 29; 1 Pet 5:2, 3; Sept.: Gen 29:2, 3; 31:4; 1 Sam 14:32; Jer 13:17; Zech 10:3). A diminutive of *poímnē* (4167).

Syn.: *mathētaí* (3101), disciples; *próbata* (4263), sheep; *hágioi* (40), saints; *pistoí* (4103), the faithful ones, believers; *ekklēsía* (1577), church.

4169. ποῖος *poíos*; fem. *poía*, neut. *poíon*, interrogative pron. corresponding to *hoíos* (3634), such as, of what sort, which kind, and *toíos*, such as. What, of what kind or sort.

(I) Particularly (Mark 4:30; Luke 6:33, 34; 24:19; John 12:33; 18:32; 21:19; Acts 7:49; Rom 3:27; 1 Cor 15:35; James 4:14; 1 Pet 1:11; 2:20). *En poía exousía* (*en* [1722], in; *exousía* [1849], authority), by what authority, meaning by whose authority (Matt 21:23, 24, 27; Mark 11:28,

29, 33; Luke 20:2, 8). "By what power or by what name" (Acts 4:7). In Luke 5:19 used adv., *diá poías* (*diá* [1223], through; *poías*, implying *hodoú* [3598], way), through what way, how. See also Luke 19:4; Sept.: 1 Kgs 22:24.

(II) With the meaning of what one? out of a number, what?, which? (Matt 19:18; 22:36, *poía entolḗ megálē en tṓ nómō* (*entolḗ* [1785], commandment; *megálē* [3173], great; *en* [1722], in; *tṓ* [3588], the; *nómō* [3551], law), "Which of the commandments in the Law is a great one?" (a.t.); Matt 24:42, 43, which hour of many; Mark 12:28; Luke 12:39; John 10:32; Acts 23:34; Rev 3:3; Sept.: 2 Sam 15:2; 1 Kgs 13:12; Jon 1:8).

Deriv.: *póteron* (4220), which of two? **Syn.**: *hopoíos* (3697), what manner of; *potapós* (4217), of what sort; *tís* (5101), who?, which?

Ant.: *oudeís* (3762), no one, in an absolute sense; *mēdeís* (3367), no one, relatively.

4170. πολεμέω *poleméō*; contracted *polemṓ*, fut. *polemḗsō*, from *pólemos* (4171), war. To war, make war, fight. Followed by *katá* (2596), against, with the gen. (Rev 12:7 [TR]), later editions with *metá* (3326), with. Followed by *metá* (3326), with or against, with the gen. (Rev 2:16; 12:7; 13:4; 17:14; Sept.: Judg 11:5, 20, 25; 2 Kgs 14:15). Joined with *kríno* (2919), to judge (Rev 19:11, meaning He makes war upon those whom He has condemned), equivalent to avenge, punish (cf. Jer 21:5). In James 4:2 it is used hyperbolically, meaning to contend, quarrel. See also Sept.: Ps 56:2, 3 (cf. 56:6).

Syn.: *agōnízomai* (75), to contend in public games, to fight; *pukteúō* (4438), to box; *máchomai* (3164), to fight; *thēriomachéō* (2341), to fight against wild beasts; *theomachéō* (2313), to fight against God; *strateúomai* (4754), to make war or to fight as a soldier; *antistrateúomai* (497), to fight as a soldier against something.

Ant.: *eirēneúō* (1514), to live peaceably; *eirēnopoiéō* (1517), to make peace;

sumphōnéō (4856), to be in accord, agree; *dialássō* (1259), to reconcile; *katallássō* (2644), to reconcile.

4171. πόλεμος *pólemos*; gen. *polémou*, masc. noun.

(I) Generally, war (Matt 24:6; Mark 13:7; Luke 14:31; 21:9; Sept.: Ex 1:10; 2 Kgs 3:7).

(II) Particularly, fight (1 Cor 14:8; Heb 11:34; Rev 9:7, 9; 11:7; 12:7, 17; 13:7; 16:14; 19:19; 20:8; Sept.: Ex 13:17; 2 Sam 19:11; Job 39:25). Hyperbolically referring to strife (James 4:1).

Deriv.: *poleméō* (4170), to make war, fight.

Syn.: while *pólemos* embraces the whole course of hostilities, *máchē* (3163), battle, includes the use of arms of hostile armies; *agṓn* (73), struggle; *pálē* (3823), wrestling.

Ant.: *eirḗnē* (1515), peace; *hēsuchía* (2271), quietness.

4172. πόλις *pólis*; gen. *póleōs*, fem. noun. Usually a city enclosed with a wall, a walled town.

(I) Particularly, a city in general (Matt 2:23; Mark 6:56; Luke 8:1; John 11:54; 2 Cor 11:26; Sept.: Gen 4:17; 11:4).

(A) With the art. *hē pólis*, the city, meaning the one mentioned before (Matt 21:10, 17, 18 referring to Jerusalem; Mark 11:19 referring to Jerusalem mentioned in 11:1; John 4:8, 28, 30 referring to 4:5; Acts 8:9 referring to 8:5). With *kat' exochḗn* (*katá* [2596], according to; *exochḗn* [1851], eminence), referring to the chief men of a city, such as Caesarea (Acts 25:23). Of Gadara (Matt 8:33 referring to 8:28; Mark 5:14; Luke 8:34).

(B) With an adj. or a similar adjunct (Matt 10:14, 15, "that city"; Acts 19:29, "the whole city"; 26:11, "strange cities"; Rev 16:19, "the great city," identifying Babylon; 18:10, 21). *Hē idía pólis* (*hē* [3588], the; *idía* [2398], one's own; *pólis* [4172], city), one's own city, meaning in which one lives (Matt 9:1 [cf. 4:13]); or the chief city of one's family (Luke 2:3). "The holy city," meaning Jerusalem as the public seat of God's worship (Matt 4:5; Rev 11:2; Sept.: Isa 52:1). Also called "the city, the loved one" (a.t. [Rev 20:9]).

(C) Followed by the gen. of person, the city of someone, meaning one's native city such as the city of David (Luke 2:4, 11; Sept.: 2 Chr 8:11), or the city in which one dwells (Luke 4:29); followed by *hē megálē* (the fem. of *mégas* [3173], great), the great city (Rev 16:19), "the city of the great King," meaning where God dwells (Matt 5:35 [cf. Ps 48:2]). Followed by the gen. of name (Matt 10:5, "any city of the Samaritans"; Luke 23:51; Acts 19:35; 2 Cor 11:32).

(D) With the proper noun of the city subjoined, e.g., in apposition in the same case (Luke 2:4, 39, the city of Nazareth; Acts 11:5; 27:8); or in the gen. (Acts 16:14; 2 Pet 2:6, "the cities of Sodom and Gomorrah").

(E) Followed by the gen. of region or province (Luke 1:26, "unto a city of Galilee"; John 4:5; Acts 21:39); with the region implied (Matt 14:13). In Luke 1:39, "into a city of Judah"; 5:12. See also Josh 21:16.

(II) Metonymically it refers to the inhabitants of a city (Matt 8:34; 21:10; Mark 1:33; Acts 13:44; 21:30).

(III) Symbolically of the celestial or spiritual Jerusalem, the seat of the Messiah's kingdom described as descending out of heaven (Heb 11:10, 16; 12:22; Rev 3:12; 21:2, 10, 14; 22:14, 19).

Deriv.: *politárchēs* (4173), ruler of the city; *polítēs* (4177), a citizen; *kōmópolis* (2969), a town, unwalled city; *mētrópolis* (3390), metropolis, chief city.

Syn.: *kṓmē* (2968), town, village; *políchōros* (4066), region; *chōríon* (5564), field, land, possession; *kṓmē* (2968), village, town.

Ant.: *kósmos* (2889), world; *oikouménē* (3625), inhabited world, earth; *gḗ* (1093), earth.

4173. πολιτάρχης *politárchēs*; gen. *politárchou*, masc. noun from *pólis* (4172), city, and *árchō* (757), to rule. A city ruler, prefect, magistrate (Acts

17:6, 8). In Class. Gr. *polítarchos* or *políarchos*.

Syn.: *árchōn* (758), ruler; *archḗ* (746), a ruler or the one who has power; *kúrios* (2962), lord; *despótēs* (1203), absolute ruler, despot; *hēgemṓn* (2232), leader, ruler; *kubernḗtēs* (2942), helmsman; *dunástēs* (1413), one who rules in an authoritarian manner, potentate.

Ant.: *polítēs* (4177), a citizen; *idiṓtēs* (2399), a private person, a layman.

4174. πολιτεία *politeía*; gen. *politeías*, fem. noun from *politeúō* (4176), to behave or act as a free citizen. The relation of a free citizen to the state.

(I) Citizenship, the right of citizenship, freedom of a city (Acts 22:28).

(II) The state itself, a community, commonwealth (Eph 2:12).

Syn.: *eleuthería* (1657), liberty; *anastrophḗ* (391), manner of life, conduct; *trópos* (5158), manner of life; *agōgḗ* (72), a way of life, conduct.

4175. πολίτευμα *políteuma*; gen. *politeúmatos*, neut. noun from *politeúō* (4176), to behave as a citizen. Any public measure, administration of the state, the condition or life of a citizen. In the NT, the state itself, community, commonwealth, used metaphorically of Christians in reference to their spiritual community and their status as citizens of heaven (Phil 3:20).

Syn.: *politeía* (4174), polity, citizenship, the relation in which a citizen stands to the state, the condition or right of a citizen; *anastrophḗ* (391), behavior; *agōgḗ* (72), a way of life, behavior.

4176. πολιτεύω *politeúō*; fut. *politeúsō*, from *polítēs* (4177), citizen. To live as a free citizen. In the NT, a pass. deponent *politeúomai*, to be a citizen of a state, to live as a good citizen, to conduct oneself according to the laws and customs of a state. It generally means to live or to order one's life and conduct in accordance with a certain rule. With an adv. in Phil 1:27, to behave worthily of the gospel.

With a dat. in Acts 23:1, to live worthily of or for God or according to His will.

Deriv.: *politeía* (4174), citizenship, a community; *políteuma* (4175), administration of the state.

Syn.: *anastréphomai* (390), to behave; *záō* (2198), to live; *bióō* (980), to pass one's life; *diágō* (1236), to live one's life; *hupárchō* (5225), to exist, to live; *échomai* (2192), to behave.

Ant.: *ataktéō* (812), to be disorderly; *aschēmonéō* (807), to act or live in an unseemly manner.

4177. πολίτης *polítēs*; gen. *polítou*, masc. noun from *pólis* (4172), city. A citizen, an inhabitant of a city, one who has the right of citizenship, a freeman (Acts 21:39). In Luke 15:15 it merely means an inhabitant of a city or town. Followed by the gen. *autoú* (846), of him, with the meaning fellow-citizen (Luke 19:14; Sept.: Gen 23:11; Prov 24:28; Jer 31:34).

Deriv.: *politeúō* (4176), to behave as a citizen, worthy citizen; *sumpolítēs* (4847), a fellow-citizen.

Syn.: *eleútheros* (1658), a free man.

Ant.: *doúlos* (1401), slave, one who does not have citizenship rights.

4178. πολλάκις *pollákis*; adv. from *pollá* (neut. pl. of *polús* [4183]), many, and the suffix *-kis*, a numerical term denoting frequency. Many times, often, frequently (Matt 17:15; Mark 5:4; 9:22; John 18:2; Acts 26:11; Rom 1:13; 2 Cor 8:22; 11:23, 26, 27; Phil 3:18; 2 Tim 1:16; Heb 6:7; 9:25, 26; 10:11).

Syn.: *posákis* (4212), how many times; *hosákis* (3740), as often as, each time; *pukná* (4437), thick, often.

Ant.: *oudépote* (3763), never, not at any time; *mēdépote* (3368), never; *oudépō* (3764), never before; *pópote* (4455), never yet; *mēpote* (3379), not at all.

4179. πολλαπλασίων *pollaplasíōn*; gen. *pollaplasíonos*, from *polús* (4183), many, much of. Manifold more, many times more (Luke 18:30).

Syn.: *pleístos* (4118), the largest number or very large, very great, most; *ámetros* (280), without measure; *pleíōn* (4119), more.

Ant.: *elássōn* (1640), less, worse; *mikrós* (3398), less or least; *mikróteros* (3398), smaller, lesser; *héssōn* (2276), inferior or less; *olígos* (3641), little or small, referring to amount, number, or time.

4180. πολυλογία *pololugía*; gen. *pololugías*, fem. noun from *polús* (4183), much, and *lógos* (3056), speech. Much speaking (Matt 6:7; Sept.: Prov 10:19).

4181. πολυμερῶς *polumerós*; adv. from *polús* (4183), much, many, and *méros* (3313), a part. By or in many parts. Josephus applies the word to various parts of Solomon's magnificent temple. The statement in Heb 1:1 that God gave OT revelation *polumerós* refers to the incremental and progressive manner in which God disclosed Himself up until the appearance of the Son. It was fragmentary, piece by piece.

Syn.: *polutrópos* (4187), many ways, in diverse manners.

Ant.: *hólōs* (3654), completely, wholly.

4182. πολυποίκιλος *polupoíkilos*; gen. *polupoikílou*, masc.-fem., neut. *polupoíkilon*, adj. from *polús* (4183), much, and *poikílos* (4164), diverse, various, multi-colored. Manifold, multifarious, greatly diversified, abounding in variety (Eph 3:10).

Ant.: *hómoios* (3664), similar, like.

4183. πολύς *polús*; fem. *pollé*, neut. *polú*, adj. Many, much of number, quantity, amount. The comparative *pleíōn* (4119); superlative *pleístos* (4118).

(I) Many, much; in the sing. and with nouns implying number or multitude, great, large.

(A) Without the art. with a subst. (Matt 13:5, "much earth," meaning much soil; Mark 5:24, "much people"; John 6:2, 10, "much grass"; 15:5, "much fruit"; Acts

11:21, "a great number", Acts 14:1, "a great multitude"; 15:32; 20:2, "with many words"; 16:16, "much gain"; 17:4; 18:10, "much people"; 22:28). Metaphorically (Matt 9:37, "much harvest" [a.t. {cf. 9:36}]). As used in an absolute sense, *polú* means much (Matt 26:9, "been sold for much"; Luke 12:48, "to whom much was given much will be asked for" [a.t.]; 16:10, "faithful also in much," "unjust also in much"; Acts 26:29).

(B) With the subst. and the art. (Mark 12:37, "the common people," the great multitude). Used in an absolute sense with the neut. art., *tó polú*, literally the much (2 Cor 8:15 quoted from Sept.: Ex 16:18 [cf. 16:17]).

(II) In the pl. masc. *polloí*, fem. *pollaí*, neut. *pollá*, meaning many. With nouns of multitude it means great, large.

(A) Without the art. with a subst. (Matt 8:16, many demoniacs; 24:11; Mark 2:15, "many publicans"; Luke 7:21; 12:7, 19, "much goods," 12:47; John 3:23, "many waters" [a.t.]; Acts 2:43; Heb 2:10). Used with a noun of multitude (Matt 4:25, "great crowds" [a.t.]; Luke 14:25). With another adj. such as *héteroi* (2087), others, *héteroi polloí* (Matt 15:30; fem. in Luke 8:3; neut. 22:65); Mark 15:41, *állai pollaí* (*állai* [243], others), many others; in the neut., *álla pollá* (Mark 7:4; John 21:25); in the masc. acc. pl., *polloús állous*, "many others" (Mark 12:5). Coupled by *kaí* (2532), and, *pollá kaí hétera*, ("many and different things" [a.t.], Luke 3:18). In John 20:30, *pollá kaí álla sēmeía* (*álla* [243], other; *sēmeía* [4592], signs [of the same kind]), many and other signs; *pollá kaí baréa aitiámata* (*baréa* [926], grave, heavy, *aitiámata* ([157], complaints), many and serious complaints (Acts 25:7). See also Titus 1:10. Used in an absolute sense, *polloí*, many (Matt 7:13, 22; Luke 4:41; John 8:30; Acts 10:27; 2 Pet 2:2). By implication, many, meaning a multitude; in Matt 20:28, *pollón* must be taken as "for all" in view of 1 Tim 2:6 which says "for all," (*hupér* [5228], for; *pántōn* [3843], all), each individual and all together. However, one may speak of all

without distinction as opposed to all without exception. Christ's death, though sufficient for every individual person, was efficient for His elect, who, according to Rev 7:9, 10, consist of every kind and class of humanity. See Mark 10:45; 14:24; Heb 9:28; Sept.: Isa 53:12. In the neut. pl., *pollá*, many things, much (Matt 13:3; Mark 5:26; Luke 10:41; John 8:26; 2 Cor 8:22, *en* [1722], in, *polloís*, meaning in many things or ways; 2 John 1:12). With the gen. partitive (Matt 3:7, "many of the Pharisees"; Luke 1:16; John 6:66; Acts 4:4). Followed by *ek* (1537), of, and the gen. (John 6:60, "many of his disciples," or from among the disciples). See John 10:20; Acts 17:12.

(B) With the art. as referring to something well-known; with a sub., *hai hamartíai autḗs hai pollaí* (*hai* [3588], the; *hamartíai* [266], sins; *autḗs*, fem. of *autós* [846], of her, *hai pollaí*, referring to her many sins), "her sins, the many" (a.t. [Luke 7:47 {cf. Luke 7:37, 39}; Rev 17:1 {cf. 17:15}]); *tá pollá grámmata* (*grámma* [1121], letter), means "the much learning which you have" (a.t.), or your extensive learning (Acts 26:24). Used in an absolute sense, *hoi polloí*, the many, meaning those before spoken of, including the idea of all (Rom 5:15, 19 referring to the many who had suffered through Adam). So also the many who receive Christ (Rom 5:15, 19; 12:5; 1 Cor 10:17). In 1 Cor 10:33, *tó tṓn pollṓn* means the many to whom I preach. Also the many, meaning the most, the greater number, but implying exceptions (Matt 24:12, "the love of the many" [a.t.], meaning the most; 2 Cor 2:17, *hōs hoi polloí* [*hōs* {5613}, as], meaning "as the most do" [a.t.], referring to the Judaizing teachers).

(III) Figuratively and intensively of amount or degree, meaning much, great, vehement (Matt 2:18; 5:12; 24:30, "great glory"; Mark 13:26; Luke 10:40; John 7:12, "much murmuring" or great groaning; Acts 15:7; 21:40, much or great silence; 24:2, 7; 25:23; 27:10, 21; Rom 9:22; 1 Cor 2:3, "in much trembling"; 2 Cor 8:4; Eph 2:4; Col 4:13, "much zeal" [a.t.]. See Sept.: Gen 41:29; Dan 11:44).

(IV) Of time, meaning much, long; pl., many (Matt 25:19, after much or a long time; Mark 6:35, after much time had passed; Luke 8:29; 12:19, "many years"; John 5:6; Acts 24:10; Rom 15:23). With *epí* (1909), upon, for, and the neut., *epí polú*, "for a long time" (a.t. [Acts 28:6]); *metá* (3326), after, followed by *ou polú* (*ou* [3756], not), not much, implying time, meaning after not much time, not long after (Luke 15:13; Acts 27:14) In Acts 1:5, "not many days hence" (see Hos 3:3, 4).

(V) Neut. *polú*, pl. *pollá*, used adv.

(A) In the sing. *polú*, much, greatly (Mark 12:27; Luke 7:47; Acts 18:27; Rom 3:2; James 5:16); with the comparative (2 Cor 8:22, "much more diligent" [a.t.]); with the dat. *pollō̂* and a comparative (John 4:41); *pollō̂ mállon* (*mállon* [3123], rather), much more rather (Matt 6:30; Mark 10:48; Sept.: Dan 6:14, 23).

(B) Pl. *pollá*, without the art., meaning many times, often (Matt 9:14; James 3:2). In Mark 1:45, "he started proclaiming much" (a.t.) or greatly. See also Mark 3:12; 5:10; 1 Cor 16:12; Rev 5:4; Sept.: 2 Kgs 10:18; Isa 23:16. With the art. *tá pollá* means oftentimes, for the most part, greatly (Rom 15:22).

Deriv.: *pámpolus* (3827), very much, very great; *pollákis* (4178), many times; *pollaplasíōn* (4179), manifold more; *polulogía* (4180), much speaking; *polumerō̂s* (4181), by or in many parts; *polupoíkilos* (4182), multicolored, in a variety of ways, manifold; *polúsplagchnos* (4184), extremely compassionate; *polutelés* (4185), extremely expensive; *polútimos* (4186), very costly; *polutrópōs* (4187), in different ways.

Syn.: *perissós* (4053), abundant; *perissō̂s* (4053), exceedingly, the more; *plousíōs* (4146), richly; *mégas* (3173), great; *hikanós* (2425), enough, much, sufficient; *hēlíkos* (2245), used in indirect interrogation meaning how great; *pēlíkos* (4080), used in direct interrogation meaning how large, how great; *pósos* (4214), an adj. of number meaning many,

much; *hósos* (3745), how much; *tosoútos* (5118) and *tēlikoútos* (5082), so great; *líαn* (3029) and *megálōs* (3171), greatly; *sphódra* (4970), exceedingly; *makrós* (3117), far, long; *pás* (3956), all; *pollákis* (4178), often, many times; *posákis* (4212), how many times, how often; the relative adv. *hosákis* (3740), as often, each time no matter how often; *pukná* (4437), often, frequently.

Ant.: *mikrós* (3398) and *olígos* (3641), little, small; *brachús* (1024), short; *mikrón* (3397), for a little referring to distance, quantity or time, meaning for a while; *olígon* (3641), a little, referring to time, space, duration; *metríōs* (3357), moderately, a little.

4184. πολύσπλαγχνος *polúsplagchnos*; gen. *polusplágchnou*, masc.-fem., neut. *polúsplagchnon*, adj. from *polús* (4183), much, and *splágchnon* (4698), a bowel. Very compassionate, of great mercy (James 5:11, literally "abounding in bowels [or in compassion]" [a.t.]). Some MSS have *polueúsplagchnos*, the difference being the prefix *eu* (2095), meaning good, well.

Syn.: *eúsplagchnos* (2155), compassionate, tender-hearted; *sumpathḗs* (4835), compassionate, sympathetic; *eleḗmōn* (1655), merciful; *oiktírmōn* (3629), compassionate, which is a stronger word than *eleḗmōn*.

Ant.: *aneleḗmōn* (415), devoid of mercifulness, unmerciful; *aníleōs* (448), without mercy; *sklērós* (4642), hard; *ástorgos* (794), without family love.

4185. πολυτελής *polutelḗs*; gen. *poluteloús*, masc.-fem., neut. *polutelés*, adj. from *polús* (4183), much, great, and *télos* (5056), expense, cost. Very expensive, costly, sumptuous (Mark 14:3; 1 Tim 2:9; Sept.: Prov 1:13). Figuratively, very precious, excellent (1 Pet 3:4).

Syn.: *tímios* (5093), costly; *éntimos* (1784), precious, dear; *polútimos* (4186), of great value; *barútimos* (927), of significant value.

Ant.: *ásēmos* (767), base, mean, unimportant; *koinós* (2839), common.

4186. πολύτιμος *polútimos*; gen. *polutímou*, masc.-fem., neut. *polútimon*, adj. from *polús* (4183), much, great, and *timḗ* (5092), price, honor. Of great price, very precious or valuable (Matt 13:46; John 12:3; 1 Pet 1:7 [TR], *polú timiṓteron* [*polú* {4183}, much; *timiṓteron*, the comparative of *tímios* {5093}, precious, valuable).
    Syn.: *tímios* (5093), costly; *polutelḗs* (4185), of great price; *barútimos* (927), of impressive value; *éntimos* (1784), precious.
    Ant.: *ásēmos* (767), base, mean, unimportant; *koinós* (2839), common.

4187. πολυτρόπως *polutrópōs*; adv. from *polús* (4183), many, and *trópos* (5158), a manner. In many ways, in diverse manners. The writer of Heb uses this word to qualify the manner in which divine revelation prior to the incarnation (i.e., the OT era) was given (Heb 1:1). As such it points to the diverse media and modes through which God disclosed His word, such as dreams, visions, angelic visitation, et al.

4188. πόμα *póma*; gen. *pómatos*, neut. noun from *pínō* (4095), to drink. A drink (1 Cor 10:4; Heb 9:10; Sept.: Ps 102:9; Dan 1:16). To be contrasted to *pósis* (4213) which means the act of drinking, and *pótos* (4224), a drinking bout, banqueting.
    Syn.: *húdōr* (5204), water; *potḗrion* (4221), a cup.

4189. πονηρία *ponēría*; gen. *ponērías*, fem. noun from *ponērós* (4190) evil, malicious. Evil nature, badness. In a physical sense (Sept.: Jer 24:2, 3, 8). In the NT, only in a moral sense, evil disposition, wickedness, malice (Matt 22:18; Luke 11:39; Rom 1:29; 1 Cor 5:8; Eph 6:12, "the spirits of malice" [a.t.] means the evil spirits). In the pl. *hai ponēríai*, wicked counsels (Mark 7:22; Acts 3:26,

"iniquities," wicked deeds; Sept.: Ex 32:12; Ps 28:5; pl. Jer 32:32; 33:5). *Ponēría* means maliciousness and it is to be distinguished from *kakía* (2549) which is simply the evil habit of mind, depravity, not necessarily being expressed and affecting others. Both words are contrasted, however, with *kakoḗtheia* (2550), a vicious ill will, active malevolence toward others.
    Syn.: *anomía* (458), lawlessness; *hamartía* (266), sin, missing the mark; *adikía* (93), unrighteousness; *adíkēma* (92), injustice, misdeed; *paranomía* (3892), law-breaking; *parábasis* (3847), an overstepping, transgression; *kakía* (2549), evil, badness.
    Ant.: *chrēstótēs* (5544), goodness, kindness, mellowness; *epieíkeia* (1932), gentleness, tolerance; *agathōsúnē* (19), goodness, benevolence; *dikaiosúnē* (1343), righteousness; *eupoiḯa* (2140), beneficence, doing good; *philanthrōpía* (5363), philanthropy, kindness; *haplótēs* (572), sincerity, simplicity, singleness, without duplicity.

4190. πονηρός *ponērós*; fem. *ponērá*, neut. *ponērón*, adj. from *pónos* (4192), labor, sorrow, pain. Evil in a moral or spiritual sense, wicked, malicious, mischievous.
    (I) In an act. sense, evil which corrupts others, evil-disposed, malevolent, malignant, wicked.
    (A) Of persons (Matt 5:45; 7:11; 12:34, 35; 13:49; 18:32; Luke 6:35, 45; 11:13; Acts 17:5; 2 Thess 3:2; Sept.: Esth 7:6; Job 21:30). *Pneúmata ponērá* (*pneúmata* [4151], spirits), evil spirits, malignant demons (Matt 12:45; Luke 7:21; 8:2; 11:26; Acts 19:12, 13, 15, 16; Sept.: 1 Sam 16:14f.). With the def. art. *ho ponērós*, the evil one, Satan (Matt 13:19, 38; Eph 6:16; 1 John 2:13, 14; 3:12; 5:18). See also Matt 5:37; 6:13; Luke 11:4; John 17:15; 1 John 5:19.
    (B) Of things, such as the eye, an evil eye referring to envy (Matt 20:15; Mark 7:22); evil thoughts (1 Tim 6:4; James 2:4). Particularly as causing pain or hurt,

hurtful, with injurious words (Matt 5:11; Acts 28:21; 3 John 1:10; Sept.: Ps 64:6). Also painful, grievous (Rev 16:2; Sept.: Deut 28:35, 59). The neut. with the def. art. *tó ponērón*, evil, evil intent, malice, wickedness (Matt 5:37, 39). Also evil as inflicted, calamity, affliction.

(II) In the pass., evil, made evil, evil in nature or quality, bad, ill, vicious.

(A) Morally, of persons, meaning wicked, corrupt, an evildoer (1 Cor 5:13; 2 Tim 3:13); an evil generation (Matt 12:39, 45; 16:4; Luke 11:29); evil age (Gal 1:4; Sept.: Deut 21:21; Isa 1:4; 9:16); of a servant, remiss, slothful (Matt 25:26; Luke 19:22); of things, wicked, corrupt, as of works (John 3:19; 7:7; Col 1:21; 2 Tim 4:18; 1 John 3:12; 2 John 1:11); criminality (*rhadioúrgēma* [4467]; Acts 18:14; 1 Thess 5:22, "from every form of evil" [a.t.]; Heb 3:12; 10:22; James 4:16; Sept.: Deut 17:7; 2 Kgs 17:13); of times, particularly as full of sorrow and affliction, evil, calamitous (Eph 5:16; 6:13; Sept.: Gen 47:9; Ps 94:13). In the neut. with the def. art., *tó ponērón*, evil, wickedness, guilt (Luke 6:45; Rom 12:9; 1 John 5:19). In the pl. *tá ponērá*, evil things, wicked deeds (Mark 7:23; Sept.: Deut 17:2; Judg 2:11; Eccl 8:12); without the art. (Sept.: Ps 97:10; Hos 7:15).

(B) In a physical sense, as of external quality and condition, evil, bad, bad fruit (Matt 7:17, 18). Of persons in reference to external state, dress (Matt 22:10, "bad and good," meaning high and low, rich and poor, a figure of speech indicating totality [merism]).

Deriv.: *ponēría* (4189), evil, wickedness, maliciousness.

Syn.: *kakós* (2556), bad character but not necessarily hurtful or malicious; *phaúlos* (5337), slight, trivial, mean, bad, in the sense of being worthless, contemptible; *kakoúrgos* (2557), an evil worker, malefactor; *áthesmos* (113), lawless, contrary to custom; *ánomos* (459), lawless; *parabátēs* (3848), a transgressor; *hamartōlós* (268), a sinner; *ádikos* (94), unrighteous; *kakopoiós* (2555), an evildo-

er; *aschēmōn* (809), uncomely; *anáxios* (370), unworthy.

Ant.: *agathós* (18), intrinsically good; *kalós* (2570), practically good, for appearance or use; *chrēstós* (5543), gentle, smooth, easy; *agathopoiós* (17), a doer of good; *aretḗ* (703), virtue; *euschḗmōn* (2158), comely; *áxios* (514), worthy.

4191. **πονηρότερος** *poneróteros*; adj., the comparative of *ponērós* (4190), wicked or malevolently evil. More wicked (Matt 12:45; Luke 11:26).

Syn.: *cheírōn* (5501), worse.

Ant.: *kallíon* (2566), better.

4192. **πόνος** *pónos*; gen. *pónou*, masc. noun from *pénomai* (n.f., see *pénēs* [3993]), to labor. Travail, toil, pain, (Col 4:13 [UBS]; Rev 16:10, 11; 21:4; Sept.: Gen 34:25; Job 4:5; Isa 65:14). It is labor which demands the whole strength of man.

Deriv.: *ponērós* (4190), evil, wicked.

Syn.: *móchthos* (3449), labor; *kópos* (2873), the weariness resulting from labor; *ōdín* (5604), pain, especially of childbirth; *lúpē* (3077), grief, sorrow; *odúnē* (3601), pain, distress; *pénthos* (3997), mourning, sorrow.

Ant.: *hēdonḗ* (2237), pleasure; *eudokía* (2107), satisfaction, delight; *apólausis* (619), enjoyment; *thélēma* (2307), pleasure, wish; *chará* (5479), joy, delight; *agallíasis* (20), exultation; *euphrosúnē* (2167), gladness.

4193. **Ποντικός** *Pontikós*; fem. *Pontikḗ*, neut. *Pontikón*, adj. Belonging to Pontus, one born in Pontus or a native of Pontus (4195). Only in Acts 18:2.

4194. **Πόντιος** *Póntios*; gen. *Pontíou*, masc. proper noun. Pontius, the name of Pontius Pilate (Matt 27:2; Luke 3:1; Acts 4:27; 1 Tim 6:13).

4195. **Πόντος** *Póntos*; gen. *Póntou*, masc. proper noun. Pontus, meaning the sea. The northeastern province of Asia Minor bordering on the Euxine Sea, originally considered a part of Cappadocia and called Cappodocia on the Sea. It was made a province under Nero before Paul's death after experiencing both independence and dependence upon other neighboring states. Polemon II who married Bernice, great granddaughter of Herod the Great and sister of Herod Agrippa (Acts 25:13), was its last king. This marriage of a Jewess with the king must have had an influence upon the Jewish population of Pontus from where some representatives were in Jerusalem on the day of Pentecost (Acts 2:9). Aquila, a Jew born in Pontus (Acts 18:2), was a very useful helper of Paul. Peter addressed his first epistle to the strangers scattered throughout Pontus (1 Pet 1:1). It formed part of the later Greek. empire because the seat of a new Christian empire founded by Alexius Comnenus in the thirteenth century was conquered by the Turks in A.D. 1461 and remained under their dominion.

4196. Πόπλιος *Póplios*; gen. *Poplíou*, masc. proper noun. Publius, the governor of Malta who received Paul when he was shipwrecked on that island (Acts 28:7, 8).

4197. πορεία *poreía*; gen. *poreías*, fem. noun from *poreúomai* (4198), to go. A going away, a journey, venture (Luke 13:22, meaning making his way or journeying; Sept.: Jon 3:3, 4). In James 1:11 it means a course or manner of life, also Sept.: Prov 2:7.

Syn.: *hodós* (3598), a way, road, journey; *hodoiporía* (3597), a wayfaring, journeying; *trópos* (5158), a manner, way; *drómos* (1408), course, race.

4198. πορεύομαι *poreúomai*; fut. *poreúsomai*, aor. pass. as mid. *eporeúthēn*, mid. deponent from *póros* (n.f.), a passing or passage, which is from *peírō* or *peráō* (n.f.), to pierce or run through. To transport oneself, to go from one place to another. Intrans. Also from *póros* (n.f.): *émporos* (1713), a merchant, trader.

(I) To pass, to go, implying motion from the place where one is, meaning to pass on, go away, depart (Matt 2:9; Mark 16:10; Luke 4:30; Acts 5:20; 1 Cor 10:27). Used once with the acc. (Acts 8:39, "he went on his way rejoicing" or he continued his journey with rejoicing). Followed by the inf. of obj. (Luke 2:3, "all went to be taxed"; John 14:2). Usually with an adjunct of place, whence or whither, i.e., with a prep. and its case as in *apó* (575), from, with the gen. (Matt 24:1, He was going away from the temple; Acts 5:41); *diá* (1223), through, with the gen. (Matt 12:1); *eis* (1519), to or into, with the acc. of place (Matt 2:20; Mark 16:15; Luke 4:42); with the acc. of state or condition (Luke 7:50, "unto peace" [a.t.]; 22:33, "unto death" [a.t.]); *émprosthen* (1715), before, with the gen. of person (John 10:4); *en* (1722), in, with the dat. of state or manner (Acts 16:36); *epí* (1909), upon, with the acc. of place (Matt 22:9; Acts 8:26; 9:11); with the acc. of person (Acts 25:12); also with the acc. of a thing sought, the object (Luke 15:4); *héōs* (2193), until, with the gen. of place (Acts 23:23); *katá* (2596), toward, with the acc. of place, meaning towards (Acts 8:26); of way, meaning along (Acts 8:36); *opísō* (3694), behind, with the gen. of person, to go after someone, follow (Luke 21:8; Sept.: Judg 2:12; 1 Sam 6:12); *prós* (4314), toward, with the acc. of person (Matt 10:6; Luke 11:5; Acts 27:3; Sept.: Gen 26:26); *sún* (4862), with, together, with a dat. of person (Luke 7:6). Also with an adv.: *ekeíthen* (1564), from there (Matt 19:15); *enteúthen* (1782), hence (Luke 13:31); *hoú* (3757), whither (Luke 24:28); *poú* (4226), where (John 7:35). Pleonastically for intensification of meaning, *poreúomai* is often prefixed to verbs which already imply the idea of going in order to render the expression more full and complete, e.g., in composition with *érchomai* (2064), I come (Matt 8:9). With the verb *anístēmi* (450), to stand up (Luke 1:39; 15:18; Acts 8:26, 27; 9:11). As a part., having gone astray (Matt 2:8; 9:13; 10:7; Luke 7:22; 14:10; 22:8; 1 Pet 3:19).

In the imper. (Luke 10:37). See also Sept.: Josh 23:16; 1 Kgs 9:6; 2 Kgs 5:10.

(II) By implication, to depart this life, to die (Luke 22:22). Syn. words used in the Sept. to denote the same meaning: *apolúō* (630), to let oneself loose; *apérchomai* (565), to depart.

(III) Generally, to go, walk. In the NT, used metaphorically with the meaning to walk, to live, to conduct oneself, joined with an adjunct of manner. With the dat. of rule or manner (Acts 9:31, meaning living in the fear of God; 14:16; Jude 1:11). Also with a prep. and the appropriate case: *en* (1722), in, with the dat. of rule or manner (Luke 1:6; 1 Pet 4:3; 2 Pet 2:10; Sept.: 1 Kgs 8:61; Prov 28:6); *katá* (2596), according to, with the acc. of rule or manner (2 Pet 3:3; Jude 1:16, 18; Sept.: Num 24:1); *opísō* (3694), after, with the gen. of rule or manner (2 Pet 2:10, "after the flesh"); *hupó* (5259), under, with the gen. meaning of under or among (Luke 8:14). In Luke 13:33 it is used in an absolute sense to mean to walk, act, fulfill one's duties.

Deriv.: *diaporeúomai* (1279), to travel or go through; *eisporeúomai* (1531), to enter in, go in; *ekporeúomai* (1607), to go out, proceed, emanate; *emporeúomai* (1710), to go in, to trade; *epiporeúomai* (1975), to come; *paraporeúomai* (3899), to go past; *poreía* (4197), a way, journey; *proporeúomai* (4313), to go before; *prosporeúomai* (4365), to go or come to someone; *sumporeúomai* (4848), to go together.

Syn.: *hupágō* (5217) and *metabaínō* (3327), to go, depart; *apérchomai* (565), to come or go away; *anachōréō* (402), to depart, withdraw; *apochōréō* (672), to depart from; *analúō* (360), to loose, untie, depart from this life, die; *éxeimi* (1826), to go out; *aphístēmi* (868), to abandon, depart; *ágō* (71), to go, to lead; *hupágō* (5217), to go away; *diodeúō* (1353), to travel throughout; *apodēméō* (589), to go to another country; *anabaínō* (305), to go up; *paragínomai* (3854), to go, to enter; *chōréō* (5562), to go find room in; *peripatéō* (4043), to walk about;

hodeúō (3593), to be on the way, to journey; *stoichéō* (4748), to walk orderly; *diérchomai* (1330), to go through.

Ant.: *ménō* (3306), to abide; *diatríbō* (1304), to stay; *anastréphomai* (390) and *apoleípō* (620), to remain; *aulízomai* (835), to lodge; *agrauléō* (63), to abide in a field; *hístēmi* (2476), to stand.

4199. πορθέω *porthéō*; contracted *porthō̂*, fut. *porthḗsō*. To ravage, destroy, such as the Church (Gal 1:13), the faith (Gal 1:23). See Acts 9:21.

Syn.: *apóllumi* (622) and *exolothreúō* (1842), to destroy utterly; *katargéō* (2673), to abolish; *kathairéō* (2507), to cast down; *lúō* (3089), to loose, dissolve; *katalúō* (2647), to destroy utterly; *olothreúō* (3645), to destroy physically; *phtheírō* (5351), to corrupt, ruin; *diaphtheírō* (1311), to corrupt completely; *lumaínomai* (3075), to make havoc.

Ant.: *tēréō* (5083), to preserve, keep; *diatēréō* (1301), to keep carefully; *suntēréō* (4933), to preserve, keep safe; *phulássō* (5442), to guard, keep watch, protect; *phrouréō* (5432), to keep with a military guard; *kratéō* (2902), to hold, keep.

4200. πορισμός *porismós*; gen. *porismoú*, masc. noun from *porízō* (n.f.), to get, gain, acquire. Acquisition, gain, used metaphorically to mean a source or means of gain (1 Tim 6:5, 6).

Syn.: *ergasía* (2039), work, business, gain; *kérdos* (2771), gain; *óphelos* (3786) and *ōphéleia* (5622), advantage, profit.

Ant.: *zēmía* (2209), loss; *apóleia* (684), loss, waste.

4201. Πόρκιος *Pórkios*; gen. *Porkíou*, masc. proper noun. Porcius, known also as Porcius Festus. He succeeded Felix in A.D. 60 as the procurator of Judea during the reign of Nero (Acts 24:27). He reinvestigated Paul's case and was satisfied as to his innocence. However, in an attempt to please the Jews, he suggested that Paul be tried in Jerusalem. It was against this injudicious proposal that Paul appealed to Caesar (Acts 25:12). Festus died at his post in A.D. 62.

4202. πορνεία porneía, gen. *porneías*, fem. noun from *porneúō* (4203), to commit fornication or any sexual sin. Fornication, lewdness, or any sexual sin.

(I) Any sexual sin; coupled with *moicheía* (3430), adultery (Mark 7:21), and other sins (Rom 1:29). Used generally to refer to any sexual sin (1 Cor 6:13, 18; 7:2; 2 Cor 12:21; Gal 5:19; Eph 5:3; Col 3:5; 1 Thess 4:3; Rev 9:21). In John 8:41, "We be not born of fornication" means, "We are not spurious children, born of a concubine, but are the true descendants of Abraham" (a.t. [Sept.: Gen 38:24; Hos 1:2]). Specifically of adultery (Matt 5:32; 19:9); of incest (1 Cor 5:1). *Porneía* may also refer to marriages within the degrees prohibited by the Law of Moses and generally to all such intercourse as prohibited in that Law (cf. Lev 18; 20:10ff.).

(II) Symbolically it stands for idolatry, the forsaking of the true God in order to worship idols. Since God is said to be married to His Church through Christ, then any idolatry is unfaithfulness toward God equal to sexual unfaithfulness to one's marriage partner (Rev 2:21; 14:8; 17:2, 4; 18:3; 19:2; Sept.: Jer 3:9; Ezek 16:15, 22; 23:27; Hos 2:2; 4:12).

(III) Fornication as a sexual vice was common before the time of Moses and was grossly prevalent in Egypt (Gen 39:7). Prostitution was not tolerated by the Sinaitical code, being an abomination in the sight of God (Lev 19:29; Deut 23:17, 18). Its price could not be accepted in the sanctuary (Mic 1:7), and death by stoning was the penalty for an unmarried woman who had concealed her crime (Deut 22:20, 21). The term "strange woman" in Prov 2:16 probably referred to a harlot procured from foreigners. See also Prov 2:16–19; 5:3–6; 7:5–27. God's displeasure was thus incited (Jer 5:7; Amos 2:7; 7:17). Such excesses were very common among the heathen in the times of the Apostles (1 Cor 5:1, 9, 10; 6:9). Israel is symbolically presented as a harlot (Isa 1:21; Jer 2:20; Ezek 16; Hos 1:2; 3:1).

Syn.: *akrasía* (192), lack of self-restraint; *asōtía* (810), profligacy; *hēdonḗ* (2237), pleasure, hedonism; *asélgeia* (766), intemperance, insatiable with regard to pleasure.

Ant.: *hagnótēs* (54), purity; *hagneía* (27), chastity; *katharótēs* (2514), the state of being cleansed, clean; *egkráteia* (1466), continence; *hagiótēs* (41), holiness; *hagiōsúnē* (42), sanctity.

4203. πορνεύω porneúō; fut. *porneúsō*, from *pórnos* (4205), a male prostitute. To commit fornication, to play the harlot. Intrans.:

(I) Particularly (1 Cor 6:18; 10:8; Sept.: Hos 3:3).

(II) From the Hebr. symbolism for idolatry, the relationship existing between God and His Church (being exemplified by the emblem of the conjugal union) which is broken by those who worship idols (Rev 2:14, 20); followed by *metá* (3326), with, and the gen. (Rev 17:2; 18:3, 9).

Deriv.: *ekporneúō* (1608), to practice fornication which implies excessive indulgence; *porneía* (4202), fornication, lewdness.

Syn.: *moicheúō* (3431) and *moicháō* (3429), to commit adultery.

4204. πόρνη pórnē; gen. *pórnēs*, fem. noun from *pernáō* (n.f.), to sell, which is from *peráō* (n.f.), to pass through, carry over (particularly as merchants) and thence to sell, which in the NT appears *pipráskō* (4097). A harlot or prostitute (Matt 21:31, 32; Luke 15:30; 1 Cor 6:15, 16; Heb 11:31; James 2:25; Sept.: Gen 38:15; Josh 2:1). Babylon is called *pórnē*, the great harlot, being the chief seat of idolatry since *porneía* is symbolic of idolatry (Rev 17:1, 5, 15, 16; 19:2; Sept.: Isa 1:21; Ezek 16:29ff.).

Syn.: *moichalís* (3428), an adulteress.

4205. πόρνος pórnos; gen. *pórnou*, masc. noun from *pernáō* (n.f.), to sell, which is from *peráō* (n.f.), to pass through, carry over (particularly as merchants) and thence to sell, which in the NT appears *pipráskō* (4097). A whoremonger or male prostitute. In the NT a fornicator (1 Cor 5:9–11; 6:9; Eph 5:5; 1 Tim 1:10; Heb 12:16; 13:4; Rev 21:8; 22:15). The Greeks considered one who prostituted himself for gain as a *pórnos*. In this sense it seems to be used in 1 Cor 6:9 where *malakoí* (pl.) (3120), the effeminate, are also mentioned. The distinction between them and *pórnoi*, fornicators, seems to consist in that the *pórnoi* prostitute themselves for gain, but the *malakoí*, effeminate ones, do it without charge. It is in this manner that the word is used in Eph 5:5; 1 Tim 1:10. The word also has the meaning of an impure or unclean person of whatever kind, and it is thus used in 1 Cor 5:9–11 (cf. 5:1, 13); Heb 12:16; 13:4; Rev 21:8; 22:15. *Pórnos* does not occur in the Sept.

Deriv.: *porneúō* (4203), to commit fornication.

4206. πόρρω *pórrō*; adv. from *pró* (4253), before. Forward, far ahead, hence far, far off, at a distance (Luke 14:32). Followed by *apó* (575), from (Matt 15:8; Mark 7:6 quoted from Isa 29:13; Sept.: Jer 12:2).

Deriv.: *pórrōthen* (4207), from afar, from a distance.

Syn.: *makrán* (3112), afar, a long way; *makróthen* (3113), from far.

Ant.: *eggús* (1451), near; *eggúteron* (1452), nearer; *plēsíon* (4139), near, close by, neighboring.

4207. πόρρωθεν *pórrōthen*; adv. from *pórrō* (4206), far off, and the suffix -*then*, denoting from or at a place. From afar, from a distance (Heb 11:13; Sept.: Job 2:12; Isa 49:12). Also far off, at a distance (Luke 17:12; Sept.: Isa 33:13; Jer 23:23).

Syn.: *makróthen* (3113), afar off, from afar.

Ant.: *paraplésion* (3897), near; *geítōn* (1069), one living nearby, neighbor; *períoikos* (4040), one living in the vicinity; *plēsíon* (4139), nearby; *eggús* (1451), near.

4208. πορρωτέρω *porrōtérō*; adv., the comparative of *pórrō* (4206), far off. Farther, a greater distance (Luke 24:28).

Syn.: *éti* (2089), yet, still further as to time or degree.

Ant.: *eggúteron* (1452), nearer.

4209. πορφύρα *porphúra*; gen. *porphúras*, fem. noun. The purple mussel, a type of shellfish found on the coasts of the Mediterranean yielding a reddish-purple dye of great value in biblical times. In the NT, used to refer to something dyed with purple, such as clothes or robes of purple worn by persons of rank and wealth (Luke 16:19; Rev 17:4 [TR]; 18:12; Sept.: Ex 25:4; 26:1, 31). Used specifically to denote a purple robe put upon Christ as a mock emblem of royalty (Mark 15:17, 20). In Matt 27:28 the same is called *chlamús kokkínē* (*chlamús* [5511], robe; *kokkínē* [2847], red), a crimson robe.

Deriv.: *porphuroús* (4210), purple; *porphurópōlis* (4211), a seller of purple cloth.

4210. πορφυροῦς *porphuroús*; fem. *porphurá*, neut. *porphuroún*, adj. from *porphúra* (4209), a purple dye or garment or cloth. Purple or reddish-purple (John 19:2, 5; Rev 17:4 [UBS]; 18:16; Sept.: Judg 8:26; Esth 1:6).

4211. πορφυρόπωλις *porphurópōlis*; gen. *porphuropóleōs*, fem. noun from *porphúra* (4209), a purple dye or garment or cloth, and *pōléō* (4453), to sell. A female seller of purple cloths, a purple dealer (Acts 16:14). See *Thuáteira* (2363), Thyatira (from where Lydia, who is called a seller of purple, originated).

4212. ποσάκις *posákis*; interrogative adv. from *pósos* (4214), how much, how many, and the suffix -*kis*, denoting a numerical termination referring to times.

How many times? How often? (Matt 18:21; 23:37; Luke 13:34).

Syn.: *pollákis* (4178), many times; *pollá* (4183), often, much; *hosákis* (3740), as often, each time.

4213. πόσις *pósis*; gen. *póseōs*, fem. noun from *pínō* (4095), to drink. The act of drinking. In the NT, drink (John 6:55; Rom 14:17). Coupled with *brósis* (1035), eating (John 6:55; Rom 14:17; Col 2:16; Sept.: Dan 1:10). To be distinguished from *póma* (4188), the liquid that is drunk, while *pósis* literally means the act of drinking.

Ant.: *dípsos* (1373), thirst.

4214. πόσος *pósos*; fem. *pósē*, neut. *póson*, interrogative pron. How great?

(I) Of magnitude, quantity, meaning how great, how much (Luke 16:5, 7). Used as an intens. (Matt 6:23; 2 Cor 7:11). In the dat. *pósō*, by how much, followed by the comparative *mállon* (3123), rather, much more, better, with the meaning of how much more (Matt 7:11; 10:25; Luke 11:13; 12:24, 28; Rom 11:12, 24; Phile 1:16; Heb 9:14). Coupled with *cheírōn* (5501), worse, more evil (Heb 10:29). With *diaphérei*, 3d person sing. of *diaphérō* (1308), to differ, meaning how much different (Matt 12:12). Used also of an amount of time, *póson chrónon* (5550), how long, how much time (Mark 9:21).

(II) In the pl., used of numbers, meaning how many (Matt 15:34; 16:9, 10; Mark 6:38; 8:5, 19, 20; Luke 15:17). Used intens. (Matt 27:13; Mark 15:4; Acts 21:20 meaning how many and great things, what things; Sept.: Gen 47:8; 2 Sam 19:35).

Deriv.: *posákis* (4212), how many times, how often.

Syn.: *mégas* (3173), great; *polús* (4183), great, much; *hikanós* (2425), worthy, sufficient; *hēlíkos* (2245), as big as, as old as; *pēlíkos* (4080), how large, how great; *hósos* (3745), how much, how many; *tosoútos* (5118), so great, so many, so much of quantity or quality; *tēlikoútos* (5082), so great; *makrós* (3117), far, long.

Ant.: *oudeís* (3762), no one; *mēdeís* (3367), no one; *mḗ tis* (3387), not anyone.

4215. ποταμός *potamós*; gen. *potamoú*, masc. noun from *potázō* (n.f.), to flow, which is from *pótos* (4224), a drinking match. A river, stream (Mark 1:5; Acts 16:13; Rev 8:10; 9:14; 16:4, 12; 22:1, 2; Sept.: Gen 2:10; 15:18; 41:1; Ex 1:22). Homer often uses *potamós* for the ocean. Spoken of a stream as swollen, overflowing, meaning a torrent, flood (Matt 7:25, 27; Luke 6:48, 49; 2 Cor 11:26; Rev 12:15, 16 [cf. Sept.: Isa 59:19]). Used allegorically (John 7:38).

Deriv.: *potamophórētos* (4216), river-borne.

Syn.: with the meaning of flood: *kataklusmós* (2627), a deluge; *plēmmúra* (4132), flood, from *pímplēmi* / *plḗthō* (4130), to fill; other words indicating the existence of water: *límnē* (3041), lake; *phréar* (5421), a well; *pēgḗ* (4077), fountain, well; *thálassa* (2281), sea; *pélagos* (3989), the deep sea in its great expanse.

Ant.: *xērós* (3584), dry land; *gḗ* (1093), land, as distinct from bodies of water.

4216. ποταμοφόρητος *potamophórētos*; gen. *potamophorḗtou*, masc.-fem., neut. *potamophórēton*, adj. from *potamós* (4215), river, and *phoréō* (5409), to carry constantly, to be tossed about. Carried away by a flood or stream (Rev 12:15).

4217. ποταπός *potapós*; fem. *potapḗ*, neut. *potapón*, interrogative adj. from the earlier form *podapós* (n.f.), which is from *poíos* (4169), what, and *dápedon* (n.f.), a soil. What, of what kind, sort, manner, spoken of disposition, character, quality, equivalent to *poíos*, what (Matt 8:27, "What manner of man is this?"; Mark 13:1, "What manner of stones and what buildings"; Luke 1:29; 7:39; 2 Pet 3:11; 1 John 3:1). The form *potapós* is a later corruption from *podapós*, which the earlier Greeks used only in the sense of "From what country?" "Whence" (as if from *poú* [4225], where, or *póthen* [4159], whence).

Syn.: *poíos* (4169), of what sort; *hoíos* (3634), what sort of or manner of; *hopoíos* (3697), what manner of.

4218. ποτέ *poté*; indef. and enclitic adv. When, whenever.

(**I**) At some time, one time or another, once, used both of time past and future. Of the past it means once, formerly (John 9:13, "one who was blind at one time" [a.t.]; Rom 7:9, "at one time without law" [a.t.]; see 11:30; Gal 1:13, 23; Eph 2:2, 3, 11, 13; 5:8; Phil 4:10, "that now at the last," meaning now at length; Col 1:21, "you who were at one time" [a.t.]; 3:7; Titus 3:3; Phile 1:11; 1 Pet 2:10; 3:5, 20; 2 Pet 1:21). Of the fut., meaning once, one day, at last (Luke 22:32; Rom 1:10).

(**II**) At any time, ever (Eph 5:29; 1 Thess 2:5; 2 Pet 1:10). Used intens. in an interrogation equivalent to the Eng. ever or now, expressing surprise (1 Cor 9:7; Heb 1:5, 13). Used indirectly (Gal 2:6).

Deriv.: *dépote* (1221), whatever; *mépote* (3379), lest ever; *pópote* (4455), by no means, not ever at any time.

Syn.: *próteron* (4386), formerly, before; *pálai* (3819), long ago, of old.

Ant.: *ḗdē* (2235), now, already; *nún* (3568), now; *aeí* (104), perpetually, forever; *diapantós* (1275), through all time; *pántē* (3839) and *pántote* (3842), always; *pantí kairṓ* (*pantí*, the neut. dat. sing. of *pás* [3956], all; *kairṓ*, the dat. sing. of *kairós* [2540], time, season, opportunity), at every opportunity; *pásas tás hēméras* (*pásas*, acc. fem. pl. of *pás* [3956], each or all; *tás hēméras*, days, the acc. pl. of *hēméra* [2250], day), all the days, always.

4219. ποτε *póte*; interrogative adv. "When?," "at what time?," used directly (Matt 24:3; 25:37–39, 44; Mark 13:4; Luke 17:20; 21:7; John 6:25; 10:24; Rev 6:10). So also *héōs póte* (*héōs* [2193], until), how long? (Matt 17:17; Mark 9:19;

Luke 9:41). Indirectly (Mark 13:33, 35, "when the time is"; Luke 12:36).

Syn.: *hopóte* (3698), when, at what time something actually took place.

4220. πότερος *póteros*; fem. *potéra*, neut. *póteron*, interrogative pron. from *poíos* (4169), which, and *héteros* (2087), another. "Which of two?" In the NT, only in the neut. *póteron*, as an adv., meaning "whether," used indirectly and followed by *ḗ* (2228), or (John 7:17, "whether it be"; Sept.: Job 7:12).

Syn.: *eíte* (1535) and *ei* (1487), if, whether.

4221. ποτήριον *potḗrion*; gen. *potēríou*, neut. noun from *póō* (n.f.), which later became *pínō* (4095), to drink. A drinking vessel, a cup.

(**I**) Particularly (Matt 10:42; 23:25, 26; 26:27; Mark 7:4, 8; 9:41; 14:23; Luke 11:39; 22:17, 20; 1 Cor 11:25; Rev 17:4; Sept.: Gen 40:11, 13, 21; 2 Chr 4:5).

(**II**) Metonymically cup as used for the contents of a cup, a cupful, cup of wine, spoken of the wine drunk at the Eucharist or communion (Luke 22:20; 1 Cor 10:16, "The cup of blessing"; 11:25, "this cup is the new testament"). To drink the cup (1 Cor 10:21, "the cup of the Lord, and the cup of devils," i.e., both the cups, whether consecrated to the Lord or devoted to idols; 11:26–28 [cf. John 4:14]).

(**III**) Metaphorically from the Hebr. meaning lot, portion, under the emblem of a cup which God presents to be drunk, either for good (Sept.: Ps 16:5; 23:5) or for evil (Sept.: Ps 11:6; 75:8; Ezek 23:31ff.). In the NT the cup of sorrow, meaning the bitter lot which awaited the Lord in His sufferings and death (Matt 20:22, 23; 26:39, 42; Mark 10:38, 39; 14:36; Luke 22:42; John 18:11). Spoken also of the cup from which God in His wrath causes the nations to drink so that they reel and stagger to destruction (Rev 14:10; 16:19; 18:6).

Syn.: *phiálē* (5357), a broad, shallow cup.

4222. ποτίζω *potízō*; fut. *potísō*, from *pótos* (4224), a drinking bout. To let drink, to give to drink.

(I) With the acc. of person (Matt 25:35, 42; 27:48; Mark 15:36; Rom 12:20; Sept.: Gen 19:32ff.; 21:19; 24:18; Judg 4:19; Job 22:7). With the acc. implied (Matt 25:37; Luke 13:15); figuratively (1 Cor 3:2; 12:13; Rev 14:8). With the acc. of *potérion* (4221), cup, and the acc. of person (Matt 10:42; Mark 9:41).

(II) As used of plants, to water, irrigate, and used only metaphorically of instruction, in an absolute sense (1 Cor 3:6–8; Sept.: Ezek 17:7).

Syn.: *antléō* (501), to dip water.

Ant.: *dipsáō* (1372), to thirst; *xēraínō* (3583), to dry.

4223. Ποτίολοι *Potíoloi*; gen. *Potiólōn*, masc. pl. proper noun. Puteoli, meaning sulfurous wells or springs, a seaport of Campania in Italy located on the northern shore on a small bay running northward from the Bay of Naples, now called Pozzuoli Bay. The town was originally confined to a rocky promontory, but afterward extended a considerable distance eastward and northward. Puteoli was the great port of Rome, and through it passed the immense exports and imports of the imperial city. Its ancient Greek name was *Dicaiárcheia*. Paul landed and tarried there with Christians for a week before setting out for Rome, 141 miles away (Acts 28:13).

4224. πότος *pótos*; gen. *pótou*, masc. noun from *pínō* (4095), to drink. A drinking match, a drunken bout (1 Pet 4:3).

Deriv.: *potízō* (4222), to let drink, to give to drink.

Syn.: *kṓmos* (2970), rioting or reveling; *kraipálē* (2897), debauchery, dissipation; *méthē* (3178), drunkenness; *oinophlugía* (3632), excess of wine.

Ant.: *egkráteia* (1466), temperance; *sōphrosúnē* (4997), soundness of mind.

4225. πού *poú*; with an acute accent, indef. particle, enclitic. Nearly, about (Rom 4:19, "being about one hundred years old" [a.t.]; Heb 2:6, meaning somewhere). In modern Gr. it may be preceded by the prep. *perí* (4012), coming around, or *perípou*, about.

Syn.: *hōs* (5613), about; *hōseí* (5616), as if, about, nearly.

4226. ποῦ *poú*; with a circumflex accent, interrogative adv. Where?, in what place?

(I) Generally:

(A) In a direct question with the indic., where?, in what place? (Matt 2:2; Mark 14:14; Luke 17:17, 37; 22:11; John 1:39; 7:11; 8:10, 19; 9:12; 11:34; 1 Pet 4:18). Followed by *thélō* (2309), to wish, and the subjunctive (Matt 26:17; Mark 14:12; Luke 22:9; Sept.: Gen 4:9; 18:9).

(B) Indirect question followed by the indic. (Matt 2:4; John 11:57; 20:15). Followed by the subjunctive (Matt 8:20; Luke 9:58; 12:17).

(C) In a direct question implying a neg., i.e., that a person or thing is not present, does not exist (Luke 8:25; Rom 3:27; 1 Cor 1:20; 12:17, 19; 15:55 referring to Hos 13:14; 2 Pet 3:4; Sept.: Judg 9:38; Job 17:15; Joel 2:17).

(D) In a simple statement (Mark 15:47; John 1:39; Rev 2:13).

(II) After verbs of motion, where?, with the meaning "whither?, to what place?" In a direct question (John 7:35; 13:36; 16:5; Sept.: Gen 16:8; Deut 1:28; Song 5:18); in a statement (John 3:8; 8:14; 12:35; 14:5; Heb 11:8; 1 John 2:11).

(III) Words that constitute an answer to the question "Where?": *pantachoú* (3837), everywhere; *pántothen* (3840) or *pantachóthen* (3834), from all sides; the expression *en pantí tópō* (*en* [1722], in; *pantí*, the sing. masc. dat. of *pás* [3956], all; *tópō* [5117], place), in every place, everywhere; *hṓde* (5603), here, hither; *autoú* (847) and *ekeí* (1563), there; *ekeíse* (1566), thither; *ekeíthen* (1564), thence; *entháde* (1759), here, hither, there; *hóthen*

(3606), from whence; *enteúthen* (1782), hence; *péran* (4008), beyond, farther, other side, over; *chamaí* (5476), prostrate, earthward.

Deriv.: *dḗpou* (1222), verily, indeed.

4227. Πούδης *Poúdēs*; gen. *Poúdentos*, masc. proper noun. Pudens, a Christian in Rome who sent a salutation to Timothy through Paul (2 Tim 4:21).

4228. πούς *poús*; gen. *podós*, masc. noun. The foot, of men (Matt 10:14; 18:8; 22:13; Luke 15:22; 24:39, 40; John 20:12; Acts 21:11; Rev 2:18); of animals (Matt 7:6; Sept.: Gen 8:9); anthropomorphically of God (Matt 5:35; Acts 7:49 [cf. Isa 66:1]).

(I) The expression "at the feet of someone" is spoken of that which is at one's feet, e.g., to cast or lay at one's feet, meaning to give over into one's care and charge, such as sick persons (Matt 15:30); money, property (Acts 4:35, 37; 5:2; 7:58). Also to sit at the feet of someone, as disciples were accustomed to sit on the ground before their master or teacher (Luke 8:35; 10:39; Acts 22:3). In Luke 7:38 a woman standing behind the recliner at the feet of Jesus.

(II) To put or subdue under one's feet means to make subject to someone, an allusion to the ancient manner of treading down or putting the foot on the necks of vanquished enemies (Rom 16:20; 1 Cor 15:25, 27; Eph 1:22; Heb 2:8 quoted from Ps 8:7; see Josh 10:24). In a similar sense after *hupopódion* (5286), footstool (Matt 22:44; Mark 12:36; Luke 20:43; Acts 2:35; Heb 1:13; 10:13, all quoted from Ps 110:1).

(III) Spoken of the oriental mode of making supplication or of doing reverence and homage to a superior by prostrating oneself before him (Sept.: Gen 44:14; Ruth 2:10; 2 Sam 1:2; Esth 8:3), "to fall at one's feet" means in supplication. The expression of reverence or homage; preceded by the prep. *eis* (1519) (John 11:32); the prep. *epí* (1909), upon (Acts 10:25); the prep. *pará* (3844), by (Luke 17:16);

the adv. prep. *enṓpion* (1799), before, in the presence of (Rev 3:9); the adv. prep. *émprosthen* (1715), before, in front of (Rev 19:10; 22:8); with the prep. *prós* (4314), before (Mark 5:22; 7:25; Sept.: Esth 8:3). In a similar manner, to hold one's feet (Matt 28:9).

(IV) Also in allusion to the custom of washing and anointing the feet of strangers and guests. Such washing was usually done by the lowest slaves (1 Sam 25:41 [cf. Gen 24:32; 43:24]), but sometimes by the master himself in token of respect (Gen 19:2; Luke 7:44; John 13:5, 6, 8–10, 12, 14). Thus also by Mary, who washed Jesus' feet with her tears and kissed and anointed them in token of affection and respect (Luke 7:38, 44–46; John 11:2 [cf. the verb *aleíphō* {218}, to rub]).

(V) Metonymically it refers to the feet as the instrument of moving. Therefore, the word "feet" is sometimes ascribed to that which strictly belongs to the person who moves about (Luke 1:79, "to guide our feet," means to direct us; Acts 5:9, "the feet of them which have buried thy husband"; Rom 3:15; 10:15 paraphrased from Isa 52:7; Heb 12:13 [cf. Ps 119:101; Prov 4:26]).

Deriv.: *tetrápous* (5074), four-footed.

4229. πρᾶγμα *prágma*; gen. *prágmatos*, neut. noun from *prássō* (4238), to do, perform. A thing done or to be done.

(I) Past: thing done, deed, act, fact, matter (Luke 1:1; Heb 6:18; 10:1; 11:1; James 3:16; Sept.: Judg 6:29).

(II) Pres. or fut.: thing being done or to be done, matter, business, affair (Matt 18:19; Acts 5:4; Rom 16:2; 2 Cor 7:11; 1 Thess 4:6; Sept.: Eccl 3:1). In a judicial sense it means to have a matter at law, a lawsuit (1 Cor 6:1).

Deriv.: *pragmateúomai* (4231), to trade.

Syn.: *érgon* (2041), work; *ergasía* (2039), a work or business; *ousía* (3776), goods; *hupóstasis* (5287), concrete essence.

Ant.: *nóēma* (3540), thought; *diánoia* (1271), mind, understanding; *dianóēma*

(1270), something thought through, sentiment; *énnoia* (1771), intent, mind; *phrónēma* (5427), mental inclination.

4230. πραγματεία *pragmateía*; gen. *pragmateías*, fem. noun from *pragmateúomai* (4231), to transact business. An affair, business, negotiation (2 Tim 2:4; Sept.: 1 Chr 28:21).

4231. πραγματεύομαι *pragmateúomai*; fut. *pragmateúsomai*, mid. deponent from *prágma* (4229), matter, business. To be doing, to be busy, occupied, to do business, to trade or traffic (Luke 19:13).

Deriv.: *diapragmateúomai* (1281), to gain by doing business, to bargain; *pragmateía* (4230), a transaction, affair.

Syn.: *ergázomai* (2038), to work; *katergázomai* (2716), to accomplish; *energéō* (1754), to effect, operate; *kámnō* (2577), to toil; *emporeúomai* (1710), to carry on business.

Ant.: *argéō* (691), to be idle.

4232. πραιτώριον *praitōrion*; gen. *praitōríou*, neut. proper noun from the Lat. *praetorium*. Originally the general's tent in a camp, the house or palace of a governor of a province. Any large house, palace. In the NT a governor's house, palace. Spoken of:

(I) The great and magnificent palace of Herod at Jerusalem built at the northern part of the upper city, westward of the temple and overlooking it, to which there was also access from the palace over the open place called Xystus, and a bridge across the Cheesemongers' Valley or Tyropoieion Valley. With the palace were connected the three towers Hippias, Phasael, and Mariamne. In this palace the Roman procurators, whose headquarters were probably at Caesarea Maritime (Acts 23:23; 25:1), took up their residence when they visited Jerusalem. This was their tribunal (*bēma* [968]) which was set up in the area of the open court before it (John 18:28, 33; 19:9). In Matt 27:27; Mark 15:16, it seems to refer to the court or part of the palace where the procurator's guards were stationed.

(II) The palace of Herod at Caesarea Maritime, perhaps in like manner the residence of the procurator (Acts 23:35).

(III) The praetorian camp at Rome, meaning the camp or quarters of the praetorian cohorts (Phil 1:13). These were a body of select troops instituted by Augustus to guard him and to have charge of the city.

Syn.: *koustōdía* (2892), a guard or a group of soldiers; *spekoulátōr* (4688), a soldier, an executioner; *phúlax* (5441), a guard, keeper; *aulé* (833), a court, palace.

4233. πράκτωρ *práktōr*; gen. *práktoros*, masc. noun from *prássō* (4238), to do, perform. A doer, agent. In the NT an exactor, collector, meaning a public officer who collected debts, fines, penalties, taxes (Luke 12:58 [cf. with *hupērétēs* {5257}, servant {Matt 5:25; Sept.: Isa 3:12}]).

4234. πρᾶξις *práxis*; gen. *práxeōs*, fem. noun from *prássō* (4238), to do, perform. Action.

(I) An act, deed, practice; in the pl., acts, works, meaning conduct (Matt 16:27; Luke 23:51; Acts 19:18; Rom 8:13; Col 3:9; Sept.: 2 Chr 13:22; 27:7). In the title the "Acts of the Apostles" the word used is *práxeis*.

(II) Business, office, function (Rom 12:4).

Syn.: *érgon* (2041), work; *ergasía* (2039), occupation, work; *pónos* (4192), toil; *téchnē* (5078), art, trade, occupation; *poíēsis* (4162), the act or process of doing something; *euergesía* (2108), a benefit; *enérgeia* (1753), energy, action.

4235. πρᾶος *práos*; fem. *praeía*, neut. *práon*, adj. Meek, mild, gentle (Matt 11:29). The subst. *praótēs* (4236), and *praǘtēs* (4240), meekness.

Deriv.: *praótēs* (4235), meekness, forbearance.

Syn.: *praǘs* (4239) meek, mild; *épios* (2261), affable, gentle.

Ant.: *orgílos* (3711), prone to anger, soon angry; *chalepós* (5467), fierce.

4236. πραότης *praótēs*; gen. *praótētos*, fem. noun from *práos* (4235), meek. Meekness, mildness, forbearance (1 Cor 4:21; 2 Cor 10:1; Gal 5:23; 6:1; Eph 4:2; Col 3:12; 1 Tim 6:11; 2 Tim 2:25; Titus 3:2; Sept.: Ps 45:6). Primarily it does not denote outward expression of feeling, but an inward grace of the soul, calmness toward God in particular. It is the acceptance of God's dealings with us considering them as good in that they enhance the closeness of our relationship with Him. However, *praótēs* encompasses expressing wrath toward the sin of man as demonstrated by the Lord Jesus (who indeed was called meek but expressed His anger toward those who were chiding Him because He had done good on the Sabbath day [Mark 3:5]). This meekness does not blame God for the persecutions and evil doings of men. It is not the result of weakness, and in the third Beatitude it expresses not the passivity of the second Beatitude, but the activity of the blessedness that exists in one's heart from being actively angry at evil. According to Aristotle, *praótēs* is that virtue that stands between two extremes, the *orgilótēs* (n.f.), uncontrolled and unjustified anger (see *orgílos* [3711], quickly angry), and *aorgisía* (n.f.), not becoming angry at all no matter what takes place around you. In the UBS text of 1 Tim 6:11 *praótēs* is *praüpatheía*, a disposition of meekness.

Syn.: *tapeinophrosúnē* (5012), humility; *tapeínōsis* (5014), the act of humiliation; *epieíkeia* (1932), mildness, clemency.

Ant.: *orgé* (3709), anger, mainly as a disposition; *thumós* (2372), wrath, outward anger; *parorgismós* (3950), anger, wrath; *aganáktēsis* (24), irritation, indignation.

4237. πρασιά *prasiá*; gen. *prasiás*, fem. noun. An ornamental garden with paths between the beds (Mark 6:40).

4238. πράσσω *prássō*, **πράττω** *práttō*; fut. *práxō*, aor. *épraxa*, perf. *pépracha*. To do, make, perform in general, expressing an action as continued or not yet completed, what one does repeatedly, continually, habitually, like *poiéō* (4160). Found in John 3:20 (TR); 5:29; elsewhere only in the writings of Luke and Paul.

(I) With the acc. of thing, without reference to a person as the remote obj.:

(A) Spoken of particular deeds, acts, or works done repeatedly or continually, to do, perform, execute (Acts 19:19, 36; 26:26; 1 Thess 4:11). Used once instead of repeating a preceding verb (1 Cor 9:17 [cf. 9:16]). See in *poiéō* (4160), II.

(B) Of a course of action or conduct, especially of right, duty, virtue, to do, meaning to exercise, practice (Acts 26:20; Rom 2:25; 7:15; 9:11; 2 Cor 5:10; Phil 4:9; Sept.: Prov 21:7).

(C) More often of evil deeds or conduct, to do, meaning to commit, practice (Luke 22:23; 23:15, 41; John 3:20 [TR]; 5:29; Acts 25:11, 25; 26:31; Rom 1:32; 2:1–3; 7:19; 13:4; 2 Cor 12:21; Gal 5:21; Sept.: Job 36:23; Prov 10:24; 30:20). See *phaúlos* (5337), evil, vile, foul.

(II) Intrans., to do.

(A) To do or act with an adjunct of manner (Acts 3:17; 17:7; Sept.: Gen 31:28; Prov 14:17).

(B) To do, fare, to be in any state of good or ill, with an adjunct of manner (Eph 6:21); with *eu* (2095), well (Acts 15:29).

(III) Spoken in reference to a person, to do to or in respect to someone. In the NT used only of harm or evil.

(A) Generally with the acc. of thing followed by the dat. of person (Acts 16:28); *epí* (1909) and the acc. meaning to do something with regard to someone (Acts 5:35); *prós* (4314), toward, and the acc., meaning against (Acts 26:9).

(B) In the sense of to exact or collect money from someone. In the NT used only with the acc. of thing (Luke 3:13; 19:23).

Deriv.: *prágma* (4229), deed, event, task; *práktōr* (4233), agent; *práxis* (4234), action, deed.

Syn.: *kámnō* (2577), to toil; *ergázomai* (2038), to work; *katergázomai* (2716), to accomplish; *energéō* (1754), to work energetically; *apoteléō* (658), to perform completely; *epitéléō* (2005), to perform fully; *poiéō* (4160), to do.

Ant.: *katapaúō* (2664), to settle down, cease working; *anapaúomai* (373), to rest, take one's ease; *améléō* (272), to neglect; *paratheōréō* (3865), to overlook, neglect; *argéō* (691), to be idle; *katheúdō* (2518), to sleep instead of watching; *hēsucházō* (2270), to be still.

4239. πραΰς *praΰs*; fem. *praeía*, neut. *praΰ*, adj. Meek, mild, gentle (Matt 5:5; 21:5; 1 Pet 3:4; Sept.: Job 24:4; Ps 37:11; Zech 9:9). See *praΰtēs* (4240), meekness, and *praótēs* (4236), meekness, mildness, forbearance, for full discussion of the meaning.

Deriv.: *praΰtēs* (4240), meekness.

Syn.: *ḗpios* (2261), gentle, of a soothing disposition; *epieikḗs* (1933), moderate, forbearing, fitting, lenient; *tapeinós* (5011), humble; *malakós* (3120), soft, tender.

Ant.: *orgílos* (3711), irascible, prone to anger; *anḗmeros* (434), savage, fierce; *chalepós* (5467), perilous, difficult, fierce.

4240. πραΰτης *praΰtēs*; gen. *praΰtetos*, fem. noun from *praΰs* (4239), meek. Meekness, but not in a man's outward behavior only, nor in his relations to his fellow man or his mere natural disposition. Rather, it is an inwrought grace of the soul, and the expressions of it are primarily toward God (James 1:21; 3:13; 1 Pet 3:15; Sept.: Ps 45:4). It is that attitude of spirit we accept God's dealings with us as good and do not dispute or resist. *Praΰtēs*, according to Aristotle, is the middle standing between two extremes, getting angry without reason (*orgilótēs* [n.f.]), and not getting angry at all (*aorgēsía* [n.f.]). Therefore, *praΰtēs* is

getting angry at the right time, in the right measure, and for the right reason. *Praΰtēs* is not readily expressed in Eng. (since the term "meekness" suggests weakness), but it is a condition of mind and heart which demonstrates gentleness, not in weakness, but in power. It is a balance born in strength of character.

Syn.: *epieíkeia* (1932), fairness, moderation, gentleness, expressing an active dealing with others; *chrēstótēs* (5544), kindness, mellowness; *tapeinophrosúnē* (5012), humility; *praΰpátheia* (found in some MSS in 1 Tim 6:11), a meek disposition, meekness.

Ant.: *orgḗ* (3709), a disposition to anger; *thumós* (2372), anger externalized; *parorgismós* (3950), exasperation; *aganáktēsis* (24), indignation.

4241. πρέπω *prépō*; fut. *prépsō*. To be eminent, distinguished, to excel. In the NT usually in the impersonal form *prépei*, it means becoming, proper. In the part. *prépon estí*, the 3d person sing. of *eimí* (1510), meaning it is becoming. Construed with the dat. of person and the inf. following as subj. (Matt 3:15). Followed by the simple dat. (Eph 5:3); the acc. and inf. (1 Cor 11:13). In the personal construction with a nom. (1 Tim 2:10; Titus 2:1; Heb 7:26; Sept.: Ps 33:1; 93:5).

Deriv.: *hieroprepḗs* (2412), as befitting a sacred person, reverent; *megaloprepḗs* (3169), magnificent.

Syn.: *chrḗ* (5534), it should be; *deí* (1163), it is necessary.

4242. πρεσβεία *presbeía*; gen. *presbeías*, fem. noun from *presbeúō* (4243), to perform the office of an ambassador. Age, seniority. In the NT, a delegation, used for persons sent as ambassadors (Luke 14:32; 19:14).

Syn.: *ággelos* (32), messenger, angel; *apóstolos* (652), apostle, messenger.

4243. πρεσβεύω *presbeúō*; fut. *presbeúsō*, from *présbus* (n.f.), an aged person, elder, also an ambassador. To be aged, elderly. In the NT, to be or act as an ambassador. Intrans. (2 Cor 5:20; Eph 6:20). Also from *présbus* (n.f.): *presbútēs* (4246), an old man.

Deriv.: *presbeía* (4242), delegation, message, ambassadors.

4244. πρεσβυτέριον *presbutérion*; gen. *presbuteríou*, neut. noun from *presbúteros* (4245), elder. Presbytery, referring to the council of elders in a given area (1 Tim 4:14) and also to the members of the Jewish Sanhedrin, otherwise called *sunédrion* (4892), a joint session, council. In the NT it is a governing ecclesiastical body comprised of *presbúteroi* (pl.) (4245), elders, (equivalent to *epískopoi* [1985], bishops). The first name shows veneration in age and the second the work and authority of the office (*episkopḗ* [1984]). From Acts 20:17, 28 it appears that the *presbutérion* was the collective body of elders from area churches. The church, although existing in separate fellowships with their respective ministers, was considered a single entity. The *presbutérion* represented this unity and together shepherded the church. Along with elders there were also *diákonoi* (pl.) (1249), deacons in the local church (Phil 1:1). Deacons are never presented as a governing council as are the elders; they exist to assist the elders. The churches collectively or locally is governed by a presbytery, a council of elders which is assisted by the deacons.

4245. πρεσβύτερος *presbúteros*; fem. *presbutéra*, neut. *presbúteron*, adj., the comparative of *présbus* (n.f.), an old man, an ambassador. Older, aged; as a subst. an elder, a senior.

(I) Particularly as a comparative adj. (Luke 15:25; Sept.: Job 1:13, 18; 32:4). As a subst. an older person, senior, in the pl. old men, seniors, the aged (Acts 2:17; 1 Tim 5:1, 2; 1 Pet 5:5; Sept.: Gen 18:11, 12; 24:1). In the pl. the ancients, the fathers, ancestors (Matt 15:2; Mark 7:3, 5; Heb 11:2).

(II) As a subst. in the Jewish and Christian usage, a title of dignity, an elder, pl. elders, meaning persons of ripe age and

experience who were called to take part in the management of public affairs. In the Sept.: Ex 18:12; 19:7; 24:1; Num 11:16 (cf. Gen 50:7). In the NT spoken of:

(A) The members of the Jewish Sanhedrin at Jerusalem, generally (Acts 24:1). One of the classes of members to which the chief priest and the scribes and the elders belonged (Matt 26:57). More often, however, the group is mentioned as the chief priests and the scribes and the elders (Matt 16:21; 26:3; 27:41; Mark 8:31; 11:27; 14:43, 53; 15:1; Luke 9:22; 20:1); also chief priests and elders, in the pl. (Matt 21:23; 26:47, 59; 27:1, 3, 12, 20; 28:11, 12; Luke 22:52; Acts 4:23; 23:14; 25:15); the elders and the scribes (Acts 6:12); the rulers (*árchontes* [758]) of the people and the elders of Israel (Acts 4:5, 8).

(B) The elders in other cities, such as Capernaum (Luke 7:3).

(C) The elders of Christian churches, presbyters, to whom was committed the direction and government of individual churches, equal to *epískopos* (1985), overseer, bishop (Acts 11:30; 14:23; 15:2, 4, 6, 22, 23; 16:4; 20:17 [cf. 20:28]; 21:18; 1 Tim 5:17; Titus 1:5; James 5:14; 1 Pet 5:1). In the sing., *presbúteros* (1 Tim 5:19; 2 John 1:1; 3 John 1:1).

That in the government of the local church there were only male bishops or elders, and deacons is supported by the fact that 1 Tim 3:2 states, "A bishop [*epískopos* {1985} refers only to a male as does *presbúteros* {4245}, a male elder. A female elder would have been *presbutéra*, which term is not used in the sense of a female elder in the NT] must be . . . the husband of one wife." This means totally dedicated to his wife, a "one-woman man." Only in 1 Tim 5:2 do we find the word *presbutéras*, the fem. pl. acc. of *presbúteros* (4245), elder, meaning female elders. However, there the reference is not to women elders of the church, but rather to older women which is the literal meaning of the word. When it comes to the discussion about deacons in 1 Tim 3:12, it states, "Let the deacons [*diákonoi*

{1249}] be the husbands of one wife," which indicates that the deacons in the NT church were always men and, if married, were to be totally dedicated to their wives as were the elders. We never find that a bishop or an elder or a deacon should be the wife of one husband.

(D) The twenty-four elders around the throne of God in heaven (Rev 4:4, 10; 5:5, 6, 8, 11, 14; 7:11, 13; 11:16; 14:3; 19:4).

Deriv.: *presbutérion* (4244), a council of elders, an assembly of aged men which acted as the governing body of the church; *sumpresbúteros* (4850), a fellow elder.

Syn.: *epískopos* (1985), overseer, bishop; *poimén* (4166), shepherd, pastor; *didáskolos* (1320), teacher.

Ant.: *neanískos* (3495), a youth; (3494), a young man.

4246. πρεσβύτης *presbútēs*; gen. *presbútou*, masc. noun, the comparative *presbúteros* (4245), an older person. An old man, one who is old (Luke 1:18; Titus 2:2; Phile 1:9; Sept.: 1 Sam 4:18; 1 Kgs 1:15). Also from *présbus* (n.f.): *presbeúō* (4243), to be aged, elderly.

Ant.: *néos* (3501) and *neanías* (3494), a young man; *neanískos* (3495), a young man.

4247. πρεσβύτις *presbútis*; gen. *presbútidos*, fem. noun. An aged woman (Titus 2:3). This cannot be taken to refer to the office of leading a local church as does *presbúteros* (4245), elder, which is equal to *epískopos* (Acts 20:17, 28). It refers to age, not office, as is clear from the consecutive use of the words *presbútas* in Titus 2:2 (the pl. of *presbútēs* [4246], aged men, not elders as leaders); *presbútidas* in 2:3 (the pl. of *presbútis* [4247], the fem. of *presbútēs*) meaning aged women and not female elders as leaders of local churches which are never mentioned in the NT; *neōtérous* (the pl. acc. comparative of *néos* [3501], young man) meaning the younger men, referring only to their age in contrast to the old men (*presbútas* in v. 2) and the old women (*presbútidas* in 2:3).

4248. πρηνής *prēnḗs*; gen. *prēnoús*, masc.-fem., neut. *prēnón*, adj. Bending forward, prostrate headlong (Acts 1:18, "falling headlong").

4249. πρίζω *prízō*, or **πρίω** *príō* fut. *prísō*. To saw, saw asunder. Pass. (Heb 11:37). This was spoken of a cruel punishment inflicted on captives in war (cf. 2 Sam 12:31; 1 Chr 20:3 [cf. *lithotoméō*, to cut a stone as if it were useless as a whole]).

Syn.: *kóptō* (2875), to cut; *katakóptō* (2629), to chop down; *dichotoméō* (1371), to cut asunder, bisect.

Ant.: *sundéō* (4887), to bind with; *stereóō* (4732), solidify, establish, make strong; *kolláō* (2853), to cleanse, join, glue; *harmózō* (718), to adapt, join together; *sunarmologéō* (4883), to fit together; *suzeúgnumi* (4801), to yoke together; *sumbállō* (4820), to put together; *katartízō* (2675), to join together.

4250. πρίν *prín*; adv. of time. Formerly, before, in independent clauses the opposite of *nún* (3568), now. Usually in the NT in a relative or conj. sense, connecting the clause before which it stands with a preceding one and having the force of a comparative, meaning before, sooner than.

(I) Simply followed by the aor. inf. with the acc. when something new is introduced, which was not mentioned before (Matt 26:34, 75, "before the cock crow"; Mark 14:72; Luke 22:61; John 4:49, "before my child dies" [a.t.]; 8:58; Sept.: Ezek 33:22).

(II) With *ḗ* (2228), a particle of distinction, or *prín ḗ*, sooner than, meaning before.

(A) Followed by the aor. inf. with the acc. where something new is introduced (Matt 1:18, "before they came together, she was found"; Mark 14:30; Acts 2:20; 7:2).

(B) Followed by the aor. subjunctive where the reference is to something future

(Luke 2:26, "not see death, before he had seen the Lord's Christ"; 22:34).

(C) Followed by the opt. where the preceding clause contains a neg. (Acts 25:16).

Syn.: *prŏton* (4412), first, at first; *próteron* (4386), aforetime, before; *émprosthen* (1715), before; *pálai* (3819), in time past.

Ant.: *metá* (3326), after; *ópisthen* (3693), after, behind; *eíta* (1534), afterwards; *hústeron* (5305), afterwards, with the idea of last; *épeita* (1899), afterwards, thereupon; *metépeita* (3347), afterwards, without necessarily indicating an order of events; *kathexēs* (2517), consecutively, following; *hexēs* (1836), after, with the meaning of a succession of events; *ekeíthen* (1564), afterwards, then.

4251. Πρίσκα *Príska*, gen. *Prískēs*, fem. proper noun. Prisca, meaning ancient (2 Tim 4:19). The same as *Prískilla* (4252).

4252. Πρίσκιλλα *Priskilla*; gen. *Priskíllēs*, fem. proper noun. Priscilla, the same as *Príska* (4251) (Acts 18:2, 18, 26; Rom 16:3; 1 Cor 16:19). She was the wife of Aquila (207), and partook with him not only in exercising hospitality but also in laboring for the Lord. See *Akúlas* (207).

4253. πρό *pró*; prep. governing the gen. Before, used both of place and time.

(I) Of place, before, in front of, in the presence of, in advance of; opposite of *metá* (3326), afterwards, with the acc. meaning behind. Followed by the gen. of place (Acts 5:23; 12:6, 14; 14:13; James 5:9). Of person from, particularly before the face of someone, but used pleonastically (Matt 11:10, "before your face" [a.t.], meaning ahead of you; Mark 1:2; Luke 1:76 [TR]; 7:27; 9:52; 10:1; Sept.: Ex 33:2; 34:6; Mal 3:1, 14).

(II) Of time, meaning before, earlier than, prior to.

(A) Followed by the gen. of a noun of time (Matt 8:29, "before the time appointed" [a.t.]; John 11:55, "before the passover"; 13:1; Acts 5:36; 21:38; 1 Cor 2:7;

4:5; 2 Cor 12:2, "before fourteen years" [a.t.]; 2 Tim 1:9; 4:21; Titus 1:2; Jude 1:25 in some MSS; Sept.: Zech 8:10). By inversion (John 12:1, "six days before the passover"); similar to "two years before the earthquake" (Sept.: Amos 1:1).

(B) Followed by the gen. of a noun implying an event marking a point of time (Matt 24:38; Luke 11:38; 21:12; John 17:24; Eph 1:4; Heb 11:5; 1 Pet 1:20; Sept.: Isa 18:5). In Acts 13:24, "before the face of his entrance" (a.t.) means before he entered.

(C) Followed by the gen. of person or thing, preceding one in time (Matt 5:12; John 5:7, "before me," meaning sooner than I; Rom 16:7; Gal 1:17; Col 1:17, before someone and consequently above all).

(D) Followed by *toú*, of, with the inf., indicating antecedent action (Matt 6:8; Luke 2:21; 22:15; John 1:48; 13:19; 17:5; Acts 23:15; Gal 2:12; 3:23; Sept.: Gen 13:10; 27:7, 10).

(III) Figuratively of precedence, preference, dignity, meaning before, above, as *pró pántōn*, the gen. neut. pl. of *pás* (3956), every, before all things (Matt 10:8, "all that ever came before me"; James 5:12; 1 Pet 4:8).

(IV) In composition *pró* implies:

(A) Place, meaning before, forward, forth, as *proágō* (4254), to lead forward, go before; *probaínō* (4260), to go forward, advance; *probállō* (4261), to put forward.

(B) Time, meaning before, beforehand, as *proeípon*, the aor. of *proeréō* (4280), to say beforehand; *prolégō* (4302), to foretell; *promerimnáō* (4305), to be anxious in advance, worry beforehand.

(C) Preference, as *proairéomai* (4255), to select, prefer.

Deriv.: *prōï* (4404), early in the morning.

Syn.: *prín* (4250), before, formerly; *prŏton* (4412), first, at the first; *próteron* (4386), aforetime, before; *émprosthen* (1715), in front; *pálai* (3819), in time past; *enantíon* (1726), in the presence of, in the sight of; *énanti* (1725), before; *apénanti*

(561), in the sight of, before; *katénanti* (2713), down over against, in the sight of; *enópion* (1799), before or in front of a person, in the sight of; *katenópion* (2714), right over against, opposite.

Ant.: *metá* (3326), after; *ekeíthen* (1564), afterwards, then; *eíta* (1534) and *épeita* (1899), then, afterwards; *hexḗs* (1836), after, involving succession; *kathexḗs* (2517), toward, also denoting succession; *metépeita* (3347), afterwards, but not necessarily indicating an order of events; *hústeron* (5305), afterwards, with the suggestion of an end involved.

4254. προάγω *proágō*; fut. *proáxō*, from *pró* (4253), before or forth, and *ágō* (71), to go. To go before, bring out.

(I) Trans., to lead or bring forth, as a prisoner out of prison, with the acc. (Acts 16:30); in a judicial sense (Acts 12:6; 25:26, "before you" as judges).

(II) Intrans., to go before, referring either to place or time.

(A) Of place, to go before, in front or in advance; used in an absolute sense (Matt 21:9; Mark 11:9; Luke 18:39); followed by the acc. of person, depending on the force of *pró*, before, in composition, although by itself it governs only the gen. (Matt 2:9; Mark 10:32).

(B) In time, to go first, precede; used in an absolute sense (Mark 6:45); figuratively (1 Tim 1:18; 5:24); followed by the acc. of person depending on *pró* (Matt 14:22; 21:31; 26:32; 28:7; Mark 14:28; 16:7). Part.: masc. *proágōn*, fem. *proágousa*, neut. *proágon*, meaning foregoing, former, previous (Heb 7:18).

Syn.: *protréchō* (4390), to run forward, precede; *progínomai* (4266), to have transpired already, be past; *propémpō* (4311), to conduct; *proporeúomai* (4313), to go before; *proérchomai* (4281), to go before, precede; *probaínō* (4260), to go on, proceed, advance.

Ant.: *akolouthéō* (190), to follow; *epakolouthéō* (1872), to follow after; *katakolouthéō* (2628), to follow behind; *diōkō* (1377), to pursue.

4255. προαιρέω *proairéō*; contracted *proairṓ*, fut. *proairḗsō*, from *pró* (4253), before, in preference, and *airéō* (138), to choose. In the NT, only in the mid. *proairéoami*, to take one thing before another, to prefer, choose, or intend for oneself, to purpose, resolve (2 Cor 9:7).

Syn.: *protíthēmi* (4388), to purpose; *bouleúomai* (1011), to resolve, purpose; *thélō* (2309), to will, wish, implying volition and purpose; *eudokéō* (2106), to approve, be willing.

Ant.: *apodokimázō* (593), to reject, disapprove; *athetéō* (114), to nullify, disannul, reject; *ekptúō* (1609), to spit out, metaphorically meaning to reject; *paraitéomai* (3868), to beg off, excuse oneself, refuse; *aporríptō* (641), to reject; *apōthéō* (683), to thrust away; *apostréphomai* (654), to turn away from.

4256. προαιτιάομαι *proaitiáomai*; contracted *proaitiṓmai*, fut. *proaitiásomai*, mid. deponent from *pró* (4253), before, and *aitiáomai* (n.f.), to blame, accuse, which is from *aitía* (156), an accusation or cause. To accuse beforehand. In the aor. it means to have already accused or already brought a charge, with the acc. and inf. (Rom 3:9).

4257. προακούω *proakoúō*; fut. *proakoúsomai* or *proakoúō*, aor. *proḗkousa*, from *pró* (4253), before, and *akoúō* (191), to hear. To hear beforehand. In the aor., to have heard of before, already, with the acc. (Col 1:5).

4258. προαμαρτάνω *proamartánō*; fut. *proamartḗsō*, perf. *proēmárteka*, from *pró* (4253), before, and *hamartánō* (264), to sin, and *hamartía* (266), sin. To have sinned already (2 Cor 12:21; 13:2).

4259. προαύλιον *proaúlion*; gen. *proaulíou*, neut. noun from *pró* (4253), before, and *aulḗ* (833), court or yard. A place before the interior court, the large gateway of an oriental house or palace, gateway, vestibule (Mark 14:68). The same as *pulón* (4440), vestibule, gate, porch (Matt 26:71).

Syn.: *stoá* (4745), a portico, porch, spoken of the covered colonnades in the temple.

4260. προβαίνω *probaínō*; fut. *probḗsomai*, from *pró* (4253), forward, and *baínō* (n.f., see *apobaínō* [576]), to go. To go forward, advance. Intrans. (Matt 4:21; Mark 1:19). Figuratively in the perf. part. masc. *probebēkós*, fem. *probebēkuía*, and neut. *probebēkós*, meaning advanced in life or years, followed by *en* (1722), in, with the dat. (Luke 1:7, "advanced in years," 1:18; 2:36; Sept.: with dat. Josh 23:1, 2; 1 Kgs 1:1).

Deriv.: *próbaton* (4263), whatever walks forward.

4261. προβάλλω *probállō*; fut. *probalṓ*, from *pró* (4253), before, forth, forward, and *bállō* (906), to cast, put. To cast or thrust forward. Trans.

(I) Generally (Acts 19:33, "the Jews putting him [Alexander] forward"; Sept.: Jer 46:4).

(II) Of plants and trees, to put forth leaves, blossoms, fruit (Luke 21:30 [cf. Matt 24:32]).

Syn.: *phúō* (5453), to spring up; *ekphúō* (1631), to cause to grow out, put forth; *poiéō* (4160), to shoot out or put forth fruit; *protíthēmi* (4388), to set forth; *prophérō* (4393), to bring forth; *phaneróō* (5319), to make manifest.

Ant.: *anastréphō* (390), to turn back, return; *epistréphō* (1994), to turn about, return; *hupostréphō* (5290), to turn around or back; *epanágō* (1877), to bring back; *epanérchomai* (1880), to come back again.

4262. προβατικός *probatikós*; fem. *probatikḗ*, neut. *probatikón*, adj. from *próbaton* (4263), sheep. Pertaining to sheep (John 5:2, "by the sheep market"). This was near the temple and was probably the place where sheep were sold for the sacrifices of the temple.

4263. πρόβατον *próbaton*; gen. *probátou*, neut. noun from *probaínō* (4260), to go before, walk ahead. Whatever walks forward. In the Ionic and Doric usages it was spoken of quadrupeds (in distinction from bipeds, and things flying, creeping, or swimming).

Generally, *tá próbata* were animals, but especially smaller animals such as sheep and goats (Matt 7:15, "in the dress of sheep" [a.t.]; 9:36; 10:16; 12:11, 12; 18:12; Mark 6:34; Luke 15:4, 6; John 2:14, 15; 10:1–4, 12, 13; Acts 8:32; Rom 8:36; 1 Pet 2:25; Rev 18:13; Sept.: Gen 12:16; 13:5; Ex 12:3ff.). In Attic and NT usage sheep are distinguished from goats (Matt 25:32, 33). Figuratively of those under the care and watch of someone as sheep under a shepherd (Matt 10:6; 15:24; 26:31; Mark 14:27; John 10:7, 8, 11, 15, 16; 21:16, 17; Heb 13:20).

In some texts as in John 21:16, 17 the word is found in its diminutive form, *probátion*, little sheep. This is to be distinguished from *arníon* (721), lamb. *Probátion* was used as a term of endearment. Sheep, on account of their simplicity, mildness, inoffensiveness, patience and obedience, are used as emblems of believers in Christ (John 10:15, 16, 26, 27 [cf. Matt 25:32, 33; Heb 13:20]). Lost or straying sheep represent unconverted persons wandering in sin and error (Matt 10:6; 15:24; John 10:26, 27; 1 Pet 2:25 [cf. Matt 9:36; Mark 6:34]).

Deriv.: *probatikós* (4262), pertaining to sheep.

Ant.: *ériphos* (2056), a goat; *eríphion* (2055), a kid, small goat; *trágos* (5131), he-goat.

4264. προβιβάζω *probibázō*; fut. *probibásō*, from *pró* (4253), before, forward, and *bibázō* (n.f., see *embibázō* [1688]), to cause to go up or be exalted. To cause to go forward or advance, trans. (Acts 19:33, "they caused Alexander to advance out of the crowd" [a.t.], to stand forth, probably in order to speak in behalf of the Jews). Figuratively it means to urge on, to instigate (Matt 14:8). In the Sept. to teach (Ex 35:34; Deut 6:7).

Ant.: *eáō* (1439), to leave alone; *hupostéllō* (5288), to hold under or back, shun, withdraw; *hupochōréō* (5298), to withdraw oneself, retire quietly.

4265. προβλέπω *problépō*; fut. *problépsō*, from *pró* (4253), before, and *blépō* (991), to see. To foresee (Sept.: Ps 37:13). In the NT, only in the mid. *problépomai*, to provide, with the acc. (Heb 11:40).

Syn.: *prooráō* (4308), to see before; *hetoimázō* (2090), to prepare; *pronoéō* (4306), to take thought for, provide; *parístēmi* (3936), to provide; *proginóskō* (4267), to know before.

Ant.: *ameléō* (272), to neglect; *paratheōréō* (3865), to overlook, neglect.

4266. προγίνομαι *proginomai*; fut. *progenēsomai*, 2d perf. *progégona*, from *pró* (4253), before, and *gínomai* (1096), to be or be done. To be done before, to have been before (Rom 3:25, "sins that are past," former sins).

Deriv.: *prógonos* (4269), Parent, ancestor, older.

Syn.: *proüpárchō* (4391), to exist before.

Ant.: *akolouthéō* (190), to follow; *epakolouthéō* (1872), to follow after; *katakolouthéō* (2628), to follow behind.

4267. προγινώσκω *proginōskō*; fut. *prognōsomai*, 2d aor. *proégnōn*, from *pró* (4253), before, and *ginōskō* (1097), to know. To perceive or recognize beforehand, know previously, take into account or specially consider beforehand, to grant prior acknowledgement or recognition to someone, to foreknow.

(I) Used of mere prescience, to know before (Acts 26:5; 2 Pet 3:17).

(II) Used of God's eternal counsel it includes all that He has considered and purposed to do prior to human history. In the language of Scripture, something foreknown is not simply that which God was aware of prior to a certain point. Rather, it

is presented as that which God gave prior consent to, that which received His favorable or special recognition. Hence, this term is reserved for those matters which God favorably, deliberately and freely chose and ordained.

(A) Used of persons, to foreknow with approbation, to foreapprove or make a previous choice of, as special people (Rom 8:29; 11:2).

(B) Used of events, to previously decide or plan, to foreknow for God is to foreordain 1 Pet 1:19, 20 presents Christ as the "Lamb of God foreknown from the foundation of the world" (a.t.). He is said to be foreknown because God had planned and determined in His eternal counsel to provide His Son as a sacrifice for His people. Certainly more is meant than that God knew ahead of time that Christ would so come and die. God's foreknowledge is given here as the cause for His Son's sacrifice—because He planned and decreed it.

(C) In Rom 8:29, in relation to believers, *proginóskō* occurs with the verb *proórise*, aor. act. indic. of *prooorízō* (4309), to predestinate. Foreknowledge and foreordination are logically coordinate. The former emphasizes the exercise of God's wisdom and intelligence in regard to His eternal purpose and the latter emphasizes the exercise of God's will in regard to it. What He has decreed is what He has decided. This foreknowledge and foreordination in the Scripture are always unto salvation and not unto perdition. Therefore, it should be said that the Lord never foreordains someone to be lost. Rather, He foreordains unto salvation those whom He specially considered and chose in eternity past (see Matt 7:23; John 10:14; Rom 11:2; 1 Cor 8:3; Gal 4:9; 2 Tim 2:19; Sept.: Hos 13:5; Amos 3:2). Any thought of the lost being appointed or ordained unto condemnation should be understood as an act of passing over in which the lost are permitted to suffer the consequences of their choice of sin (1 Pet 2:8). The salvation of every believer is known and determined in the mind of

God before its realization in time. Thus, *proginṓskō* corresponds with the idea of having been chosen (*eklégomai* [1586], to choose) before the foundation of the world mentioned in Eph 1:4 and logically precedes the action indicated by *proorízō*. *Proginṓskō* essentially entails a gracious self-determining on God's part from eternity to extend fellowship with Himself to undeserving sinners (Rom 8:29).

Deriv.: *prógnōsis* (4268), foreknowledge.

Syn.: *problépō* (4265), to look out beforehand, to supply in advance, foresee; *proeídō* (4275) and *prooráō* (4308), to foresee; *proetoimázō* (4282), to ordain or prepare before; *prokuróō* (4300), to confirm or ratify before; *prolégō* (4302), to tell or say beforehand; *promeletáō* (4304), to premeditate; *promerimnáō* (4305), to take thought or care beforehand; *pronoéō* (4306), to know or consider in advance; *proorízō* (4309), to set limits in advance, ordain beforehand, predestinate.

4268. πρόγνωσις *prógnōsis*; gen. *prognṓseōs*, fem. noun from *proginṓskō* (4267), to know beforehand. Foreknowledge, prior acknowledgement, favorable recognition or consideration beforehand (Acts 2:23; 1 Pet 1:2). It is used to denote the foreordained fellowship of God with the objects of His saving power.

Syn.: *prónoia* (4307), forethought, providence; *próthesis* (4286), a setting forth beforehand.

4269. πρόγονος *prógonos*; gen. *progónou*, masc.-fem., neut. *prógonon*, adj. from *progínomai* (4266), to become or be already. Born earlier; as a subst. parent, ancestor, older. In the NT, *prógonoi* means forefathers (2 Tim 1:3); parents (1 Tim 5:4).

Syn.: *goneús* (1118), a parent, a begetter; *patḗr* (3962), a father; *propátōr* (Rom 4:1 UBS), for *patḗr*; *mḗtēr* (3384), mother; *mámmē* (3125), grandmother.

Ant.: *ékgonos* (1549), a descendant; *spérma* (4690), offspring; *téknon* (5043), a child, one born; *tekníon* (5040), little child, infant; *país* (3816), a child; *sárx* (4561), flesh, descendant; *huiós* (5207), son; *karpós* (2590), fruit, meaning descendant; *thugátēr* (2364), daughter; *thugátrion* (2365), a little daughter; *korásion* (2877), a little girl.

4270. προγράφω *prográphō*; fut. *prográpsō*, from *pró* (4253), before, openly, plainly, and *gráphō* (1125), to write. To write before.

(I) In reference to time past, to have written before or at a former time (Rom 15:4; Eph 3:3).

(II) In reference to future time, to affix beforehand in writing, to announce by posting up a written tablet. Hence in the NT generally to announce, promulgate (Gal 3:1, "before whose eyes Jesus Christ has been announced among you crucified" [a.t.], or set forth as in a publicly-written notice).

In Jude 1:4 it means to proscribe, appoint, ordain, post up publicly in writing. Those who were summoned before courts of justice were said to be *progegramménoi*, posted up ahead of time, because they were cited by posting up their names in some public place. Even in our day the cases to be heard by a judge are written beforehand and appended in a public place in the courthouse. Thus what Jude is declaring is that judgment was published or declared in writing ahead of time. Those called *progegramménoi*, those whose names were posted up in writing in some public place, were proscribed as persons doomed to die with a reward offered to whoever would kill them. Thus Jude 1:4 may mean those who not only must give an account to God for their crimes and are liable to God's judgment, but who are destined to the punishment they deserve. As to where they are proscribed, we must look at Jude 1:5–7, 11.

Syn.: *proginṓskō* (4267), to foreknow.

4271. πρόδηλος *pródēlos*; gen. *prodḗlou*, masc.-fem., neut. *pródēlon*, adj. from *pró* (4253), before, and *dḗlos* (1212), manifest. Manifest openly. In the NT used emphatically meaning manifest before all, well-known, conspicuous (1 Tim 5:24, 25; Heb 7:14).

Syn.: *phanerós* (5318), visible, evident; *emphanḗs* (1717), openly apparent.

Ant.: *aphanḗs* (852), unseen, hidden, not manifest; *kruptós* (2927), secret, hidden; *apókruphos* (614), hidden, kept secret.

4272. προδίδωμι *prodídōmi*; fut. *prodṓsō*, from *pró* (4253), before or forth, and *dídōmi* (1325), to give. To give beforehand, to give first, with the dat. (Rom 11:35). Used by Greek writers meaning to give forth or over, betray.

Deriv.: *prodótēs* (4273), a betrayer, traitor.

4273. προδότης *prodótēs*; gen. *prodótou*, masc. noun from *prodídōmi* (4272), to give away, to betray. A betrayer, traitor (Luke 6:16; Acts 7:52; 2 Tim 3:4).

Syn.: *ápistos* (571), unfaithful.

Ant.: *pistós* (4103), faithful, dependable.

4274. πρόδρομος *pródromos*; gen. *prodrómou*, masc.-fem., neut. *pródromon*, adj. from *protréchō* (4390), to run ahead or before. The one running before. In the NT used as a masc. subst., a forerunner, precursor, spoken of Jesus as entering before His followers into the celestial sanctuary (Heb 6:20). John the Baptist could be also taken as *ho pródromos*, the forerunner of the Lord Jesus, although he is not called that.

Ant.: *ho opísō mou erchómenos* (*ho opísō* [3694], the one after; *mou*, me; *erchómenos*, the pres. part. of *érchomai* [2064], to come), the one coming after me.

4275. προεῖδον *proeídon*; 2d aor. of *proeídō* (n.f.), which is from *pró* (4253), before, and *eídō* (1492), to see, perceive, or know. To see ahead of oneself, see afar off (Sept.: Gen 37:18). In the NT, to foresee, used in an absolute sense (Acts 2:31; Gal 3:8).

Syn.: *prooráō* (4308), to see before; *problépō* (4265), to foresee, and metaphorically to provide; *pronoéō* (4306), to consider in advance.

Ant.: *agnoéō* (50), not to know, ignore; *ameléō* (272), to disregard, neglect.

4276. προελπίζω *proelpízō*; fut. *proelpísō*, from *pró* (4253), before, and *elpízō* (1679), to hope. To hope in advance or before. In the perf. *proēlpikótas* in Eph 1:12, referring to the Jews as having had of old the hope and promise of the Messiah in contrast to the Gentiles who had heard of Him just then (1:13 [cf. Rom 3:1ff.; 9:4ff.]).

4277. προεῖπον *proeípon*, 2d aor. of *proeípō* (n.f.), which is from *pró* (4253), before, and *épō* (2036), to tell. To say or tell before or formerly.

(I) In reference to time past, to have said before, to have already declared. In the aor. (Gal 5:21); with the dat. (1 Thess 4:6).

(II) In reference to fut. time, to say beforehand, foretell, predict. In the aor. with the acc. (Acts 1:16).

4278. προενάρχομαι *proenárchomai*; fut. *proenárxomai*, from *pró* (4253), before, and *enárchomai* (1728), to make a beginning in, to begin. To begin before. Aor., to have begun before, already started (2 Cor 8:6, 10).

4279. προεπαγγέλλω *proepaggéllō*; fut. *proepaggelō̂*, from *pró* (4253), before, and *epaggéllō* (1861), to bring word to, to announce, promise. In the NT, only in the mid. *proepaggéllomai*, to proclaim or promise beforehand (Rom 1:2; 2 Cor 9:5 [in some MSS], "promised afore," of old).

4280. προερέω *proeréō*; 2d aor. *proeípon*, perf. *proeírēka*, from *pró* (4253), before, and *eréō* (2046), to say, declare. To say before, foretell, speak of in advance.

(I) To say, speak, declare before or formerly. In the perf. (2 Cor 13:2, with *hóti*

[3754], that; Gal 1:9 [cf. 1:8]; Heb 10:15; 2 Pet 3:2; Jude 1:17 [cf. Rom 9:29]).

(II) To say or tell before an event, to foretell. In the perf. (Rom 9:29); with *humín*, to you (Matt 24:25); *humín pánta* (*humín* [5213], dat. pl. of *sú* [4771], you; *pánta*, the neut. pl. of *pás* [3956], all), "unto you all things" (a.t. [Mark 13:23]); with *hóti* (3754), that (2 Cor 13:2). In 2 Pet 3:2, *tón rhēmátōn* (*tón* [3588], the; *rhēmátōn* [4487], words), of these sayings, *proeirēménōn*, foretold. See Jude 1:17.

Syn.: *prolégō* (4302), to foretell; *prophēteúō* (4395), to foretell, prophesy.

4281. προέρχομαι *proérchomai*; fut. *proeleúsomai*, aor. *proélthon*, mid. deponent from *pró* (4253), before or forwards, and *érchomai* (2064), to go, come. To go before, pass on.

(I) To go forward, go further, pass on (Matt 26:39; Mark 14:35). Followed by the acc. of way (Acts 12:10).

(II) To go before someone, referring either to place or time.

(A) Of place, to go before in advance of someone, as a forerunner, messenger, with *enṓpion* (1799), before, followed by the gen. (Luke 1:17); or as a leader, guide, with the acc. (Luke 22:47). See *émprosthen* (1715), before, followed by the gen. (Sept.: Gen 33:3).

(B) Of time meaning to go first, precede, set off before another (Acts 20:5, 13; 2 Cor 9:5). In the sense of going out ahead, to arrive first (Mark 6:33 [TR]).

Syn.: *proporeúomai* (4313) and *proágō* (4254), to go before; *probaínō* (4260), to go forward; *apodēméō* (589), to go on a journey, to emigrate.

Ant.: *husteréō* (5302), to be behind.

4282. προετοιμάζω *proetoimázō*; fut. *proetoimásō*, from *pró* (4253), before, and *hetoimázō* (2090), to make ready. To prepare beforehand. In the NT equivalent to predestinate, to appoint before, trans. with *eis* (1519), into (Rom 9:23, "unto glory"). So also with a dat. (Eph 2:10). The only two times this verb is used in

the NT, it is used of God's foreordaining for good, referring to glory and to good works.

Syn.: *proorízō* (4309), to foreordain; *paraskeuázō* (3903), to prepare, make ready; *protíthēmi* (4388), to set before or forth, foreordain, purpose; *problépō* (4265), to foresee, look out beforehand, to furnish in advance, provide; *proginṓskō* (4267), to foreknow, know ahead; *prográphō* (4270), to write previously, to prescribe ahead, ordain before; *proeídō* (4275), to foresee; *promerimnáō* (4305), to take thought beforehand; *pronoéō* (4306), to consider in advance.

Ant.: *améléō* (272), to neglect; *paratheōréō* (3865), to overlook, neglect; *agnoéō* (50), to ignore.

4283. προευαγγελίζομαι *proeuaggelízomai*; fut. *proeuaggelísomai*, from *pró* (4253), before, and *euaggelízō* (2097), to preach the gospel or the good news. To proclaim the gospel beforehand. Only in Gal 3:8. See Gen 12:3; 18:18.

Syn.: *prokērússō* (4296), to preach, announce beforehand.

4284. προέχω *proéchō*; fut. *proéxō*, from *pró* (4253), forth, forward, and *échō* (2192), to have, be. To hold before oneself. Figuratively, to excel, to have preference or preeminence, be superior or better. In the NT, only in the mid. *proéchomai*, to excel, be superior (Rom 3:9, meaning "Can we Jews then claim ourselves to be better off than the Gentiles?" [a.t.] in respect to being sinners before God).

Syn.: *diaphérō* (1308), to be different, to excel; *perisseúō* (4052), to be over or above; *huperéchō* (5242), to consider better; *huperbállō* (5235), to surpass; *pleonektéō* (4122), to get an advantage.

Ant.: *leípomai* (3007), to lack.

4285. προηγέομαι *proēgéomai*; contracted *proēgoúmai*, fut. *proēgésomai*, from *pró* (4253), before, and *hēgéomai* (2233), to lead the way, to think. To lead forward or onward, to go before, take the lead. In the NT, figuratively it means to lead by example, with the acc. and dat. of that in which or as to which one excels (Rom 12:10, meaning in mutual respect taking the lead of each other).

Syn.: *proágō* (4254), to go before.
Ant.: *akolouthéō* (190), to follow.

4286. πρόθεσις *próthesis*; gen. *protheseōs*, fem. noun from *protíthēmi* (4388) to purpose or plan A setting forth, presentation, an exposition, determination, plan, or will. It involves purpose, resolve, and design. A placing in view or openly displaying something. A thought or purpose (Acts 11:23; 27:13). When used of the purpose of God, it exclusively refers to salvation (2 Tim 1:9). Therefore, in Rom 8:28, "those who are the called according to his purpose," *katá próthesin* must be taken as syn. with *eudokéō* (2107), indicating that those who are called are called because of God's good pleasure and not because they deserve it (Eph 1:8, 9).

(I) Of food, in an adj. sense, the bread set out before Jehovah on a table in the sanctuary, i.e., the shewbread. A setting before (Matt 12:4; Mark 2:26; Luke 6:4; Heb 9:2). The Sept. applies this word only to the shewbread (Ex 39:36; 2 Chr 13:11), referring to the loaves set before the Lord on the holy tables. See Ex 25:30; 40:23; 1 Sam 21:6; 1 Kgs 7:48; 1 Chr 9:32; 23:29; 2 Chr 4:19.

(II) Figuratively, a predetermination, purpose, intent, or design of God in calling men in general, Gentiles as well as Jews, to salvation (Rom 8:28); of gathering together all things in Christ (Eph 1:9–11); of making the Gentiles fellow heirs with the Jews of the same body and partakers of His promise in Christ by the gospel (Eph 3:11 [cf. 2 Tim 1:9]); in choosing one nation rather than another to certain privileges and blessings (Rom 9:11). All these passages are applied to the purpose of God in the NT.

(III) Predetermination, purpose, resolution of man (Acts 11:23; 2 Tim 3:10). Purpose, intent, design (Acts 27:13). Adj. *prothésmios* (4287), fixed beforehand, predesigned.

Syn.: *boúlēma* (1013), purpose, will; *thélēma* (2307), desire or will with the power to execute that will; *gnómē* (1106), opinion, purpose; *prógnōsis* (4268), forethought, foreknowledge; *prókrima* (4299), prejudgment; *prónoia* (4307), provision, providence, forethought.
Ant.: *metánoia* (3341), repentance, change of mind.

4287. προθεσμία *prothesmía*; gen. *prothesmías*, fem. noun from *pró* (4253), before, and *thesmós* (n.f.), custom, which is from *títhēmi* (5087), to set, place, lay. A pre-appointed day or time, the day or time being understood (Gal 4:2).

4288. προθυμία *prothumía*; gen. *prothumías*, fem. noun from *próthumos* (4289), ready. Eagerness, readiness, alacrity of mind (Acts 17:11; 2 Cor 8:11, 12, 19; 9:2).
Syn.: *spoudé* (4710), earnestness; *thélēsis* (2308), willingness.

4289. πρόθυμος *próthumos*; gen. *prothúmou*, masc.-fem., neut. *próthumon*, adj. from *pró* (4253), forward, and *thumós* (2372), mind, temperament, passion. Predisposed, ready, willing, prompt, referring to the spirit (Matt 26:41; Mark 14:38; Sept.: 1 Chr 28:21; 2 Chr 29:31). Neut. *tó próthumon*, readiness, alacrity (Rom 1:15, "I am ready," meaning there is readiness on my part).
Deriv.: *prothumía* (4288), eagerness, willingness; *prothúmōs* (4290), willingly.
Syn.: *hétoimos* (2092), prepared, ready; *hekoúsios* (1595), willing, voluntary; *spoudaíos* (4705), eager.
Ant.: *nōthrós* (3576), slothful; *asthenés* (772), weak, feeble (directly contrasted with *próthumos* in Matt 26:41 and Mark 14:38); *argós* (692), lazy.

4290. προθύμως *prothúmōs*; adv. from *próthumos* (4289), ready. Readily, willingly, with alacrity (1 Pet 5:2).
Syn.: *hetoímōs* (2093), readily; *hekousíōs* (1596), willingly; *hekón* (1635), willingly, of one's free will.

Ant.: *ákōn* (210), unwillingly; *anagkastôs* (317), by constraint or compulsion.

4291. προΐστημι *proïstēmi*; fut. *prostḗsō*, 2d aor. *proéstēn*, perf. part. *proestṓs*, from *pró* (4253), before, over, and *hístēmi* (2476), to place, to stand. Trans., to cause to stand before, to set over. In the NT only in the intrans., meaning to stand before.

(I) With the meaning to be over, to preside, rule (Rom 12:8; 1 Tim 5:17). Followed by the gen., like other verbs of ruling, through the force of *pró* (4253), before, in composition (1 Thess 5:12; 1 Tim 3:4, 5, 12).

(II) By implication meaning to care for something, to be diligent, to practice, with the gen. (Titus 3:8, 14).

Deriv.: *prostástis* (4368), leader, ruler, director.

Syn.: *árchō* (757), to rule; *oikodespotéō* (3616), to be master of a house; *hēgéomai* (2233), to lead; *poimaínō* (4165), to shepherd, guide.

Ant.: *akolouthéō* (190), to follow.

4292. προκαλέω *prokaléō*; contracted *prokalô*, fut. *prokalésō*, from *pró* (4253), forward, and *kaléō* (2564), to call. Used in the mid. to refer to calling before oneself, i.e., to challenge, provoke, irritate, with the acc. (Gal 5:26).

Syn.: *paroxúnō* (3947), to provoke, stir up; *erethízō* (2042), to excite, both in a good and bad sense; *parazēlóō* (3863), to provoke to jealousy.

Ant.: *paraitéomai* (3868), to beg off.

4293. προκαταγγέλλω *prokataggéllō*; fut. *prokataggelô*, from *pró* (4253), before, and *kataggéllō* (2605), declare, publish. To speak beforehand (Acts 3:18, 24; 7:52; 2 Cor 9:5).

Syn.: *prolégō* (4302), foretell; *proépō* (4277), to tell before; *prophēteúō* (4395), to prophesy.

Ant.: *exaírō* (1808), to remove, put away.

4294. προκαταρτίζω *prokatartízō*; fut. *prokatartísō*, from *pró* (4253), before, and *katartízō* (2675), to establish, set up. To perfect or equip beforehand, make right. Used in 2 Cor 9:5 of the offerings for the Jerusalem church which the Apostle wished to find already prepared.

Syn.: *hetoimázō* (2090), to prepare; *paraskeuázō* (3903), to prepare, make ready; *kataskeuázō* (2680), to prepare, make ready or fitting; *proetoimázō* (4282), to prepare beforehand.

Ant.: *ameléō* (272), neglect; *paratheōréō* (3865), to overlook, neglect; *agnoéō* (50), to ignore.

4295. πρόκειμαι *prókeimai*; fut. *prokeísomai*, pres. part. *prokeímenos*, from *pró* (4253), before or forth, and *keímai* (2749), to lie. To lie before, to be laid or set before someone. Intrans. (Sept.: Lev 24:7). In the NT used only figuratively:

(I) To lie or be before the mind of someone, to be present before him (2 Cor 8:12).

(II) In Heb 6:18 *prokeiménēs*, equivalent to the perf. pass. of *protíthēmi* (4388), to set forth, "the hope that is set forth" (a.t.). See Heb 12:1, 2; Jude 1:7, *prókeintai*, they lie before.

Syn.: *tēréō* (5083), to preserve; *phulássō* (5442), to keep; *apókeimai* (606), to await, to have in reserve, laid up; *diaphulássō* (1314) and *kratéō* (2902), to keep; *parístēmi* (3936), to stand beside.

Ant.: *kataleípō* (2641), to forsake; *egkataleípō* (1459), to leave behind; *paraitéomai* (3868), to shun; *aphíēmi* (863), to let go.

4296. προκηρύσσω *prokērússō*, **προκηρύττω** *prokērúttō*; fut. *prokērúxō*, from *pró* (4253), before, and *kērússō* (2784), to herald, preach. To proclaim beforehand. In the NT generally to announce or preach beforehand; in the past tenses, to have announced or preached before, trans. (Acts 3:20; 13:24).

Syn.: *proeuaggelízomai* (4283), to evangelize ahead of time.

4297. προκοπή *prokopḗ*; gen. *prokopḗs*, fem. noun from *prokóptō* (4298), to drive forward. A going forward, used only figuratively of progress, advancement, furtherance, either for good or evil (Phil 1:12, 25; 1 Tim 4:15).

Syn.: *ōphéleia* (5622), benefit, advantage; *óphelos* (3786), advantage, profit.

Ant.: *zēmía* (2209), loss; *apobolḗ* (580), a casting away; *héttēma* (2275), defect, diminishing; *apṓleia* (684), waste, loss; *hustérēma* (5303), a deficit, lack.

4298. προκόπτω *prokóptō*; fut. *prokópsō*; from *pró* (4253), before or forward, and *kóptō* (2875), to cut, strike, impel. To beat or drive forward as if with repeated strokes, hence to go forward or further, make progress, proceed. In the NT used only figuratively:

(I) To make progress in something, to advance, increase, with the dat. of that in or as to which (Luke 2:52). Followed by *en* (1722), in, with a dat. (Gal 1:14). With *epí* (1909), upon, with the acc. *cheíron* (5501), worse, meaning to grow worse and worse (2 Tim 3:13); *epí pleíon* (4119), more, meaning further (2 Tim 2:16; 3:9).

(II) Spoken of time, aor., to be advanced, far spent (Rom 13:12, in regard to the night).

Deriv.: *prokopḗ* (4297), furtherance, profit.

Syn.: *auxánō* (837), to grow as a result of life within or by external influence; *perisseúō* (4052), to abound; *pleonázō* (4121), to make to abound.

Ant.: *zēmióō* (2210), to lose.

4299. πρόκριμα *prókrima*; gen. *prokrímatos*, neut. noun from *prokrínō* (n.f.), to prefer, which is from *pró* (4253), before, and *krínō* (2919), to judge. With reference to place and time, to decide beforehand, prefer before, another being put aside (1 Tim 5:21). *Prókrima* includes an unfavorable prejudgment against one,

partiality being included in the attitude of this prejudgment.

4300. προκυρόω *prokuróō*; contracted *prokurṓ*, fut. *prokurṓsō*, from *pró* (4253), before, and *kuróō* (2964), to confirm. To establish or confirm before, previously. In the perf. pass. (Gal 3:17).

4301. προλαμβάνω *prolambánō*; fut. *prolḗpsomai*, 2d aor. *proélabon*, from *pró* (4253), before, and *lambánō* (2983), to take. To overtake.

(I) Used trans., to take before another, to anticipate and do before another. With the acc. (1 Cor 11:21, meaning the rich men ate the provisions they had brought without waiting for the poorer members to come). Intrans., to take up beforehand, to anticipate the time of doing something. With the inf. (Mark 14:8, "she hath anointed my body in anticipation of my burial" [a.t.]).

(II) Of persons: Gal 6:1, "Brothers, even if [or although] one has been overtaken [aor. pass. *proelḗphthēn*] by a fault. . . . " (a.t.). One of two interpretations are possible. If the prep. by (*en* [1722]) is taken as an instrumental then the idea is that the fault (*paráptoma* [3900]) catches the individual by surprise, suddenly, without notice, i.e., before he is aware of what has happened. The exhortation to restore a person in such a condition might be necessitated by the possible reluctance of spiritual leaders to do so, being annoyed at the irresponsibility of the offender and believing he should have known better or taken greater care. However, the concessive phrase "even if," *eán kaí* (*eán* [1437], if; *kaí* [2532], and), seems to introduce an exceptional case, implying a scandalous or flagrant sin. The prep. could therefore be taken as a locative and have reference to someone being caught in the act of a particular sin. The exhortation to restore the offender would then arise from the possible outrage which spiritual leaders might feel toward such a person because he was so brazen as to sin openly.

Syn.: *katalambánō* (2638), to overtake; *prophthánō* (4399), to get an earlier start; *proseggízō* (4331), to approach, come near.
Ant.: *argéō* (691), to delay, linger; *bradúnō* (1019), to delay, tarry.

4302. προλέγω *prolégō*; fut. *proléxō*, from *pró* (4253), before, and *légō* (3004), to say. To foretell, forewarn (2 Cor 13:2; Gal 5:21; 1 Thess 3:4; Sept.: Isa 41:26). For syn. and ant., see *proeréō* (4280) and *proépō* or *proeípon* (4277), to foretell.

4303. προμαρτύρομαι *promartúromai*; fut. *promarturoúmai*, from *pró* (4253), before, and *martúromai* (3143), to witness. To witness or testify or declare beforehand (1 Pet 1:11).

4304. προμελετάω *promeletáō*; contracted *promeletṓ*, fut. *promeletḗsō*, from *pró* (4253), before, and *meletáō* (3191), to meditate. To premeditate (Luke 21:14).
Syn.: *promerimnáō* (4305), to prepare beforehand; *pronoéō* (4306), to consider in advance.

4305. προμεριμνάω *promerimnáō*; contracted *promerimnṓ*, fut. *promerimnḗsō*, from *pró* (4253), before, and *merimnáō* (3309), to be anxious, worry, care for, take thought. To be anxious ahead of time (Mark 13:11).
Syn.: *promeletáō* (4304), to premeditate; *pronoéō* (4306), to consider in advance.

4306. προνοέω *pronoéō*; contracted *pronoṓ*, fut. *pronoḗsō*, from *pró* (4253), before, and *noéō* (3539), to think, comprehend. With a gen. of person following, to provide for (1 Tim 5:8). In the mid. voice, *pronoéomai*, with an acc. of the thing, to provide, take thought, care for beforehand (Rom 12:17; 2 Cor 8:21; Sept.: Prov 3:4).
Deriv.: *prónoia* (4307), providence.
Syn.: *problépō* (4265) or *prooráō* (4308) or *proeídō* (4275), to foresee.

4307. πρόνοια *prónoia*; gen. *pronoías*, fem. noun from *pronoéō* (4306), to know ahead. Providence, care, prudence (Acts 24:2), provision (Rom 13:14).
Syn.: *mérimna* (3308), care; *epiméleia* (1958), carefulness, attention.

4308. προοράω *prooráō*; contracted *proorṓ*, fut. *proópsomai*, perf. *proeṓraka*, from *pró* (4253), before, and *horáō* (3708), to see. To foresee or look ahead, fix one's eyes on something before them. In the NT:
(I) In the mid., to see before oneself, have before one's eyes. Figuratively of what one has vividly in mind, with the acc. (Acts 2:25 quoted from Ps 16:8).
(II) In the perf., to have seen before, in time (Acts 21:29).
Syn.: *proeídō* (4275), to foresee; *problépō* (4265), to foresee, make provision.
Ant.: *ameléō* (272), to neglect; *paratheōréō* (3865), to overlook, neglect.

4309. προορίζω *proorízō*; fut. *proorísō*, from *pró* (4253), before, and *horízō* (3724), to determine. To determine or decree beforehand (Acts 4:28; Rom 8:29, 30; 1 Cor 2:7; Eph 1:5, 11). The peace of the Christian Church has been disrupted due to the misunderstanding which surrounds this word. It behooves the Church to consider the divinely intended meaning of this word by carefully examining the critical passages where it is used.

In 1 Cor 2:7 it has a thing as its obj., namely, the wisdom of God. The purpose was our glory, i.e., our benefits of salvation.

In Acts 4:28 the verb is followed by the aor. inf. *genésthai* (*gínomai* [1096], to be, become), to be done. The action of Herod and Pontius Pilate in crucifying Jesus Christ is said to have been predetermined or foreordained by the hand and will of God. This indicates that Christ's mission, especially His death and resurrection, was not ultimately the result of human will but originated in the eternal counsel of God which decreed the event determining all its primary and secondary causes, instruments, agents, and contingencies.

In Rom 8:29, 30, predestination is used of God's actions in eternally decreeing both the objects and goal of His plan of salvation. *Proorízō* has a personal obj., the pl. relative pron. *hoús*, whom. This relative pron. refers to those previously mentioned as those whom God foreknew (*proégnō* [4267]). The translation is, "For whom he did foreknow, he also did predestinate." The objects of predestination are those whom He foreknew. Predestination does not involve a predetermined plan only but also includes the individuals for whom the plan is devised. The goal of predestination is expressed in the phrase, "to be conformed to the image of his Son."

In Eph 1:5, 11 this same purpose of foreordination is termed adoption. Adoption (*huiothesía* [5206]) is the placing into sonship or legal heirship of those who are born of God. According to 1:5 the basis of this prior decree is "the good pleasure of His will." The word rendered "good pleasure" is *eudokía* (2107) and means pleasure or satisfaction, that which seems good. Paul is careful to add that it is the good pleasure of God's will, it is what seems good to God—not man. Similarly, in 1:11 foreordination is based upon "the purpose (*próthesis* [4286]) of the One who is working all things ([neut. acc. pl.] *tá pánta* [3844], an idiom for the entire metaphysical and physical universe) according to the decision of His will" (a.t.). This same thinking is reflected in Rom 8:30 where foreordination is joined successively to foreknowledge. Here it is presented not as a capricious, arbitrary or whimsical exercise of raw will or unreasoned impulse, but as the expression of a deliberate and wise plan which purposes to redeem those undeserving sinners whom God freely favors as the objects of His mercy.

Because it is neither possible nor permissible for us to pry into God's secret counsel, it is not proper to be fixated with determining who the predestined are.

Instead, we should contemplate the glories of what they are predestined to, i.e., salvation, adoption, or glory.

Syn.: *protássō* (4384), to appoint before; *procheirízō* (4400), to appoint beforehand; *proetoimázō* (4282), to prepare before.

4310. προπάσχω *propáschō*; fut. *propeísomai*, 2d aor. *proépathon*, from *pró* (4253), before, and *páschō* (3958), to suffer. To be affected beforehand, to experience before. In the NT, to have suffered before, previously (1 Thess 2:2).

4311. προπέμπω *propémpō*; fut. *propémpsō*, from *pró* (4253), before, and *pémpō* (3992), to send. To send on before, send forward or forth. In the NT, to send forward on one's journey, bring someone on his way, especially to accompany for some distance in token of respect and honor. Trans. (Acts 20:38; 21:5). Hence, generally to help one forward on his journey (Acts 15:3; Rom 15:24; 1 Cor 16:6, 11; 2 Cor 1:16; Titus 3:13; 3 John 1:6).

Syn.: *proágō* (4254), to lead forth; *sunodeúō* (4922), to journey with; *apostéllō* (649), to send forth; *pémpō* (3992), to send.

Ant.: *metakaléō* (3333), to summon hither, recall; *prosphōnéō* (4377), to call unto; *proskaléō* (4341), to summon or bid.

4312. προπετής *propetḗs*; gen. *propetoús*, masc.-fem., neut. *propetés*, adj. from *propíptō* (n.f.), to fall forward, which is from *pró* (4253), forward, and *pípto* (4098), to fall. Rash, careless (Acts 19:36; 2 Tim 3:4). The word signifies the character of someone who rushes headlong or out of control into matters.

Syn.: *authádēs* (829), self-willed.

4313. προπορεύομαι *proporeúomai*; fut. *proporeúsomai*, mid. deponent from *pró* (4253), before, and *poreúomai* (4198), to go. To pass on before, go before someone as a leader or guide, with a gen. (Acts 7:40 quoted from Ex 32:1, 23);

as a forerunner, herald (Luke 1:76; Sept.: Ps 89:15; 97:3).

Syn.: *proágō* (4254), to lead forth, go before; *probaínō* (4260), to advance; *proēgéomai* (4285), to go on before, precede.

Ant.: *akolouthéō* (190), to follow.

4314. πρός *prós*; prep. governing the gen., dat., and acc. and corresponding in its basic meaning to the primary force of these cases themselves. Toward.

(I) With the gen., implying motion or direction from a place, hither. Also in the direction of a place meaning at or toward. Figuratively of the source, agent, or cause from which something comes or proceeds. Also expressing dependence or relation of any kind from or with someone, the pertaining or belonging in any way to a person or thing. In the NT, used once, figuratively meaning pertaining to, for, for the benefit of (Acts 27:34).

(II) With the dat., marking a place or object by the side of which a person or thing is, meaning rest or remaining by, at, near, as if in answer to the question "Where?" (Mark 5:11 [UBS], where TR has *tá órē* [pl.] [3735], the mountains, in the acc. pl.; Luke 19:37, "at the descent of the mount"; John 18:16, "at the door"; 20:12; Rev 1:13).

(III) With the acc., marking the object toward or to which something moves or is directed. See IV below.

(A) Of place, thing, or person meaning toward, to, unto, as if in answer to the question "Whither?" With the acc. of place, thing, person: **(1)** Particularly of motion or direction after verbs of going, coming, departing, returning, and also after similar nouns (Matt 2:12; 3:5, 14; 10:13; 11:28; 25:9; Mark 1:33; 6:25, 45; 10:1; Luke 8:4, 19; 24:12; John 3:20; 6:37; 7:33; Acts 3:11; 28:30; Rom 1:10; Gal 1:17). After or before *gínomai* (1096), to become (John 10:35; Acts 7:31; 13:32; 2 Cor 1:18). After verbs of sending, with the acc. of person (Matt 21:34; Luke 23:7; John 16:7; Acts 15:25; Eph 6:22; Titus 3:12), hence *epistolḗ*

prós (*epistolḗ* [1992], letter), letter for (Acts 9:2; 22:5; 2 Cor 3:1). After verbs of leading, bringing, or drawing by force or otherwise (Matt 26:57; Mark 9:17, 19; 11:7; Luke 12:58; John 12:32; 14:3; Acts 23:15; Rev 12:5). After verbs implying motion to a place and also a subsequent remaining there, meaning at, upon, but also to, unto. With verbs of falling such as *píptō* (4098), to fall, having the same meaning as *prospíptō* (4363), to fall toward (Mark 5:22; 7:25; Sept.: Ex 4:25). With verbs of laying, putting, casting (Matt 3:10; 4:6; Mark 10:7; Luke 3:9; 16:20; Acts 3:2; 5:10; 13:36). After verbs and words implying direction in a close proximity as turning, reaching, looking (Luke 7:44; Acts 9:40; Rom 10:21; 2 Cor 3:16; Eph 3:14; James 4:5). To see something face to face (1 Cor 13:12; Sept.: Gen 32:30). To speak mouth to mouth (2 John 1:12). **(2)** With all verbs and words which include the idea of speaking to someone, mostly with the acc. of person: **(a)** Generally after *épō* (2036), to say (Matt 3:15; Luke 1:13, 18, 34); *laléō* (2980), to speak (Luke 1:19, 55; 2:18, 20; Sept.: 2 Chr 10:16); *légō* (3004), to say (Luke 5:36; 7:24); *phēmí* (5346), to say (Luke 22:70; Acts 2:38). With verbs of answering, as *apokrínomai* (611), to answer (Acts 3:12; 25:16; Sept.: 1 Sam 14:19); accusing as *katēgoréō* (2723), to accuse (John 5:45); praying, entreating, as *boáō* (994), to cry (Luke 18:7; Sept.: 1 Sam 12:10); *déomai* (1189), to beseech (Acts 8:24); *déēsis* (1162), supplication (Rom 10:1); *eúchomai* (2172), wish (2 Cor 13:7); *proseuchḗ* (4335), prayer (Acts 12:5; Rom 15:30); *éran phōnḗn prós tón Theón* (*éran*, aor. of *aírō* [142], lift up; *phōnḗ* [5456], voice; *Theós* [2316], God), lift up the voice to God (Acts 4:24 [cf. Isa 24:14]). With words of declaring, making known, as *anádeixis* (323), exhibition, showing (Luke 1:80); *gnōrízō* (1107), to make known (Phil 4:6); *emphanízō* (1718), to exhibit, show (Acts 23:22); of command and the like, such as *entolḗ* (1785), precept, commandment (Acts 17:15); *apología* (627), defense (Acts 22:1); with the acc. of thing, as *laléō prós tó oús* (*laléō* [2980], to speak; *oús* [3775], ear), to speak to one in his ear meaning privately (Luke 12:3). **(b)** Of mutual words and sayings: *állos prós állon légontes* (*állos* [243], another [in this case, one to another]; *légontes* [3004], saying) "saying one to another" (Acts 2:12); *prós allélous* (240), themselves (Mark 8:16, to one another, one to another; 9:34; 15:31; John 6:52; 16:17; Acts 2:7; 4:15); *prós heautoús* (*heautoús* [pl.] [1438], themselves), among themselves (Mark 9:33; 14:4; 16:3; Luke 22:23). **(c)** After verbs of swearing to someone meaning to promise with an oath (Luke 1:73). **(3)** Figuratively after verbs and words implying direction of the mind or will, an affection or disposition meaning toward someone. **(a)** Favorable, implying good will, confidence (2 Cor 3:4; 7:4, 12; Gal 6:10; Eph 6:9; Phil 2:30; Col 4:5; 1 Thess 1:8; 4:12; 5:14; 2 Tim 2:24; Titus 3:2; Phile 1:5). **(b)** Unfavorable, meaning against (Acts 6:1; 24:19; 25:19; 1 Cor 6:1; Eph 6:11; Col 3:13, 19; Heb 12:4; Rev 13:6); after verbs of sending (Acts 23:30).

(B) Of time: **(1)** Particularly of a time when, meaning toward, near (Luke 24:29). **(2)** As forming with the acc. a periphrasis for an adv. of time, meaning at, for, *prós kairón* (*kairós* [2540], season), meaning for a season, a while, briefly (Luke 8:13; 1 Cor 7:5); *prós kairón hóras* (*hóra* [5610], hour), meaning for a short time (1 Thess 2:17); *prós hóran* (John 5:35, "for a season"; Gal 2:5); *prós olígas hēméras* (*olígos* [3641], a few; *hēméra* [2250], day.), for a few days (Heb 12:10); *prós tó parón* (*parón*, the pres. part. neut. of *páreimi* [3918], to be present), meaning for the present, at present (Heb 12:11); *prós olígon*, implying *chrónon* (5550), time (*olígos* [3641], a little; *chrónos*), "for a little time" (1 Tim 4:8; James 4:14).

(C) Figuratively denoting the direction, reference, or relation which one object has toward or to another. **(1)** Toward, in reference or respect to, as to, implying the direction or remote object of an action. **(a)** With the acc. of person (Mark 12:12; Acts 24:16; Rom 4:2; Heb 1:7, 8); *tí prós sé*, "What is that to thee?" or in the pl. *tí prós hēmás*, "What is that to us? [*se*, {4571}, thee; *hēmás*, {2248}, us]" (Matt 27:4; John 21:22, 23). **(b)** Followed by the acc. of thing (Luke 18:1; 2 Cor 4:2; Heb 9:13). After verbs of replying (Matt 27:14; Rom 8:31). The expression *tá prós* followed by the acc. sing. or pl. meaning things relating or pertaining to any person or thing or condition (Luke 14:32; 19:42; Acts 28:10; 2 Pet 1:3). *Tá prós* [*tón*] *Theón* means things pertaining to God, divine things (Rom 15:17; Heb 2:17; 5:1; Sept.: Ex 18:19). **(2)** Spoken of a rule, norm, or standard, meaning according to, in conformity with (Luke 12:47; 2 Cor 5:10; Gal 2:14; Eph 3:4). **(3)** Of the motive, ground, or occasion of an action, meaning on account of, because of, for (Matt 19:8; Mark 10:5). **(4)** As marking the end result, the aim or purpose of an action, followed by the acc. meaning for what, why, to what end, for what purpose (John 13:28). After verbs expressing the end, aim, tendency of an action or quality (Acts 3:10; Rom 3:26; 15:2; 1 Cor 6:5; 7:35; 10:11; 2 Cor 1:20; Eph 4:12; 1 Tim 1:16; 4:7; Heb 5:14; 6:11; 1 Pet 4:12). Especially followed by the inf. with the neut. def. art. *tó*, meaning in order that (Matt 5:28; 6:1; 13:30; 23:5; Mark 13:22; Eph 6:11; James 3:3). After nouns and adj. (John 4:35; 11:4; Acts 27:12; 2 Cor 10:4; Eph 4:14, 29; Col 2:23; 2 Tim 3:17; Titus 1:16; 1 Pet 3:15). Of a tendency and result (2 Pet 3:16; 1 John 5:16, 17). **(5)** The relation in which one person or thing stands toward or with another (Luke 23:12; Acts 2:47; 3:25; 28:25; Rom 5:1; 2 Cor 6:15; Heb 9:20; 10:16). In a comparison (Rom 8:18, "to be compared with").

(IV) Sometimes *prós* with the acc. is used after verbs which express simply rest, meaning at, by, in a place, the same as *prós* with the dat. However, in such instances, for the most part, the idea of a previous coming to or direction toward that place is either actually expressed or is implied in the context.

(A) Generally with the acc. of place (Mark 11:4; 14:54; Luke 22:56; John 20:11). With the acc. of person, meaning with, by, among (Matt 26:18, 55; Mark 14:49; Acts 12:20; 13:31; 1 Cor 16:7; 2 Cor 1:12; Gal 1:18; 2:5; 4:18; Phil 1:26; 2 Thess 2:5; Sept.: Isa 19:19). With the reflexive pron. *heautón* (1438), himself, meaning standing by himself or he prayed to or with himself (Luke 18:11).

(B) Rarely, and only in later usage, is the idea of previous motion or direction completely dropped, and *prós* with the acc. is then the same as *pará* (3844), near, with the dat. (Matt 13:56; Mark 2:2; 4:1; 6:3; John 1:1; Phile 1:13).

(V) In composition *prós* implies:

(A) Motion, direction, reference, meaning toward, to, at, as *proságō* (4317), to lead toward, to approach, bring near; *proseggízō* (4331), to approach near; *prosérchomai* (4334), to come near; *prosdokáō* (4328), to expect, wait for.

(B) Accession, addition, meaning thereto, over and above, moreover, further, as *prosaitéō* (4319), to ask repeatedly; *prosapeiléō* (4324), to threaten further. Used intensively as *próspeinos* (4361), intensely hungry; *prosphilḗs* (4375), friendly toward, acceptable, lovely, very dear.

(C) Nearness, a being or remaining near, at, by, as *prosedreúō* (4332), to attend as a servant, wait on; *prosménō* (4357), remain in a place, abide still.

Syn.: *epí* (1909), upon; *eis* (1519), to.

4315. προσάββατον *prosábbaton*; gen. *prosabbátou*, neut. noun from *pró* (4253), before, and *Sábbaton* (4521), the Sabbath. Foresabbath, eve of the Sabbath (Mark 15:42). Equivalent to *paraskeuḗ* (3904), preparation, day of preparation.

4316. προσαγορεύω *prosagoreúō*; fut. *prosagoreúsō*, from *prós* (4314), to, and *agoreúō* (n.f.), to speak, which is from *agorá* (58), the market place, also the town square which provided a public platform for speakers. To address, greet. In the NT, to designate, give a name to. Used once and only in the pass. voice

(Heb 5:10). Also from *agoreúō* (n.f.): *katēgoréō* (2723), to speak against.

Syn.: *onamázō* (3687), to name; *kaléō* (2564), to call, call a name; *katēgoréō* (2723), to speak against.

4317. προσάγω *proságō*; fut. *prosáxō*, 2d aor. *prosḗgagon*, from *prós* (4314), to or towards, and *ágō* (71), to bring, come. To lead or conduct to someone, to bring near.

(I) Trans. with the acc., to bring to (Luke 9:41; Acts 16:20 figuratively of God, to bring near, present before, with the acc. and dat.; 1 Pet 3:18; Sept.: Ex 29:4; 40:12; 1 Sam 1:25).

(II) Intrans., to come to or toward, to approach, with the dat. as above (Acts 27:27, "the sailors deemed that some country drew near to them" [a.t.], referring to the usual optical illusion on board a ship or land moving closer to the vessel; Sept.: Ex 14:10; Isa 34:1). Basically to make oneself inclined to another, to surrender oneself to another; to come to or hither, approach.

Deriv.: *prosagōgḗ* (4318), access, approach.

Syn.: *anágō* (321), to lead or bring up to; *epágō* (1863) and *epiphérō* (2018), to bring upon; *prosphérō* (4374), to bring to; *komízō* (2865), to provide, carry, bring; *eisphérō* (1533), to bring in; *eiságō* (1521), to introduce; *prosérchomai* (4334), to come near.

Ant.: *apágō* (520), to carry away; *ekphérō* (1627), to carry out; *apophérō* (667), to bear off; *exágō* (1806), to lead out; *hupostéllō* (5288), to draw under, withdraw; *anachōréō* (402), depart; *hupochōréō* (5298), to withdraw apart; *aphístēmi* (868), to withdraw, depart.

4318. προσαγωγή *prosagōgḗ*; gen. *prosagōgḗs*, fem. noun from *proságō* (4317), to bring near. Used intrans., meaning access, approach (Rom 5:2; Eph 2:18); used in an absolute sense (Eph 3:12). The term was commonly used for the audience or right of approach granted to someone by high officials and monarchs.

Syn.: *eísodos* (1529), entrance.

4319. προσαιτέω *prosaitéō*; contracted *prosaitṓ*, fut. *prosaitḗsō*, from *prós* (4314), for, adding intensity, and *aitéō* (154), to ask, beg. To ask earnestly, beg (Mark 10:46; Luke 18:35; John 9:8; Sept.: Job 27:14).

Syn.: *apaitéō* (523), to beg.

Ant.: *erōtáō* (2065), to ask, used of equals; *apaitéō* (523), to demand back.

4320. προσαναβαίνω *prosanabaínō*; fut. *prosanabḗsomai*, 2d aor. *prosébēn*, from *prós* (4314), to, and *anabaínō* (305), to ascend, go up. To go up further or higher; pleonastically with *anṓteron* (511), higher (Luke 14:10, meaning take a higher seat, a more honorable place; Sept.: Ex 19:23; Josh 11:17).

4321. προσαναλίσκω *prosanalískō*; fut. *prosanalṓsō*, from *prós* (4314), beside, meaning in addition to, and *analískō* (355), to consume. To consume besides, expend further (Luke 8:43).

Syn.: *prosdapanáō* (4325), to spend besides.

Ant.: *epichorēgéō* (2023), to supply fully, abundantly; *prosanaplēróō* (4322), to supply abundantly.

4322. προσαναπληρόω *prosanaplēróō*; contracted *prosanaplērṓ*, fut. *prosanaplērṓsō*, from *prós* (4314), beside, meaning in addition to, and *anaplēróō* (378), to supply. To supply abundantly (2 Cor 9:12; 11:9).

Syn.: *epichorēgéō* (2023), to supply fully, abundantly; *empíplēmi* (1705), to fill full.

Ant.: *kenóō* (2758), to empty.

4323. προσανατίθημι *prosanatíthēmi*; fut. *prosanathḗsō*, from *prós* (4314), beside, meaning in addition to, and *anatíthēmi* (394), to communicate. To lay up in addition. In the NT, only in the 2d aor. mid., *prosanethémēn*, figuratively

meaning to lay before in addition, to impart or communicate further, on one's own part.

(I) Generally with the acc. and dat. (Gal 2:6).

(II) By way of consultation, to confer with, consult, with the dat. (Gal 1:16).

Syn.: *prostíthēmi* (4369), to add; *epitíthēmi* (2007), to put upon; *epichorēgéō* (2023), to give in addition.

Ant.: *apaírō* (522), to lift from; *exaírō* (1808) and *aphairéō* (851) and *apágō* (520), to take away.

4324. προσαπειλέω *prosapeiléō*; contracted *prosapeilṓ*, fut. *prosapeilḗsō*, from *prós* (4314), beside, meaning in addition to, and *apeiléō* (546), to threaten. To threaten further (Acts 4:21).

4325. προσδαπανάω *prosdapanáō*; contracted *prosdapanṓ*, fut. *prosdapanḗsō*, from *prós* (4314), besides, and *dapanáō* (1159), to spend. To spend more, with the acc. (Luke 10:35).

Syn.: *prosanalískō* (4321), to spend besides.

4326. προσδέομαι *prosdéomai*; fut. *prosdḗsomai*, mid. deponent from *prós* (4314), beside, meaning in addition to, *déomai* (1189), to want, need, or make a request. To want or need something more, with a gen. (Acts 17:25; Sept.: Prov 12:9).

Syn.: *chrḗzō* (5535), to need.

Ant.: *euporéō* (2141), to be well off.

4327. προσδέχομαι *prosdéchomai*; fut. *prosdéxomai*, mid. deponent from *prós* (4314), unto or for, and *déchomai* (1209), to receive or accept. To receive or take, as the spoiling of one's goods with joy (Heb 10:34); receive, accept as deliverance (Heb 11:35); receive kindly as a friend (Luke 15:2); receive, entertain (Rom 16:2; Phil 2:29); receive, admit, as a hope (Acts 24:15); expect, look or wait for (Mark 15:43; Luke 2:25, 38; 12:36; 23:51; Acts 23:21; Titus 2:13).

Deriv.: *euprósdektos* (2144), acceptable.

Syn.: *lambánō* (2983), to receive; *paralambánō* (3880), to receive from; *proslambánō* (4355), to welcome; *apodéchomai* (588), to accept; *déchomai* (2983), to receive.

Ant.: *aporríptō* (641), to reject; *antitássō* (498), to oppose; *periphronéō* (4065), to despise.

4328. προσδοκάω *prosdokáō*; contracted *prosdokṓ*, fut. *prosdokḗsō*, from *prós* (4314), unto or for, and *dokáō* (n.f.), to look for. Expect, wait or look for (Matt 11:3; 24:50; Luke 1:21; 3:15; 7:19, 20; 8:40; 12:46; Acts 10:24; 28:6; 2 Pet 3:12–14; Sept.: Ps 119:166). In the sense of hope (Acts 27:33); with the inf. (Acts 3:5).

Deriv.: *prosdokía* (4329) looking for, expectation.

Syn.: *elpízō* (1679), to hope; *apekdéchomai* (553), to expect fully, look for; *anaménō* (362), to wait for.

Ant.: *apelpízomai* (560), to lose hope.

4329. προσδοκία *prosdokía*; gen. *prosdokías*, fem. noun from *prosdokáō* (4328), to wait, expect. A looking for, an expectation (Luke 21:26; Acts 12:11; Sept.: Gen 49:10).

Syn.: *apokaradokía* (603), strained expectancy, eager longing; *ekdochḗ* (1561), a receiving from, expectation; *elpís* (1680), hope.

4330. προσεάω *proseáō*; contracted *proseṓ*, fut. *proseásō*, from *prós* (4314), to, and *eáō* (1439), to permit. To permit or allow further, with a dat. (Acts 27:7 meaning the wind "was not permitting us" to proceed further on that course).

Syn.: *epitrépō* (2010), to permit; *aphíēmi* (863), to send away, to allow, suffer, permit.

Ant.: *kōlúō* (2967), to hinder; *diakōlúō* (1254), to forbid.

4331. προσεγγίζω *proseggízō*; fut. *proseggísō*, from *prós* (4314), to, and *eggízō* (1448), to approach. To approach or come near to (Mark 2:4; Sept.: Gen 33:6, 7; Josh 3:4).

Syn.: *prosérchomai* (4334), to draw near; *proságō* (4317), to draw near;.

Ant.: *aphístēmi* (868), to depart; *apérchomai* (565), to go away; *anachōréō* (402), to recede, retire; *apochōréō* (672), to depart from; *ekchōréō* (1633), to depart out; *metabaínō* (3327), to depart.

4332. προσεδρεύω *prosedreúō*; fut. *prosedreúsō*, from *prósedros* (n.f.), one sitting by, which is from *prós* (4314), to, and *hédra* (n.f.), a seat. To sit nearby. In the NT, to wait near, attend, serve, with the dat. (1 Cor 9:13, referring to those who were working in the sanctuary). In the UBS the word is *paredreúō* (with the prep. *pará* [3844], near, instead of *prós*).

4333. προσεργάζομαι *prosergázomai*; fut. *prosergásomai*, mid. deponent from *prós* (4314), besides, moreover, and *ergázomai* (2038), to work, gain, trade. To work out, to gain more by labor (Luke 19:16, meaning in addition they gained by working).

Syn.: *kerdaínō* (2770), to gain; *diapragmateúomai* (1281), to gain by trading.

Ant.: *argéō* (691), to do nothing, be unemployed; *katapaúō* (2664), to cease working.

4334. προσέρχομαι *prosérchomai*; fut. *proseleúsomai*, mid. deponent from *prós* (4314), to, and *érchomai* (2064), to come. To come to, approach as to location. Intrans.:

(I) Followed by the dat. of thing (Heb 12:18, "you did not come to the mountain which can be touched" [a.t.], see 12:22); the dat. of person (Matt 4:3, "and when the tempter came close to him, he said" [a.t.]; 8:5; Mark 14:45; Luke 23:52; John 12:21; Acts 9:1). Used in an absolute sense or with the dat. implied (Matt 4:11; Mark 1:31; Luke 8:24; 10:34; Acts 7:31; 28:9; Sept.: usually followed by *prós* or the simple dat., Gen 29:10; 43:19; Num

9:6; Deut 1:22). With the meaning of to visit, to have conversation with (Acts 10:28; 24:23).

(II) Figuratively:

(A) Of God or Christ, to come to God, draw near unto Him in prayer, sacrifice, worship, devotion of heart and life. Followed by the dat. or in an absolute sense (Heb 4:16; 7:25; 11:6; Sept.: Lev 21:17, 21; Deut 21:5); of Christ (1 Pet 2:4, "to whom coming" or whom embracing, becoming His disciples, followers).

(B) Followed by the dat. of thing, to assent to, embrace (1 Tim 6:3).

Deriv.: *prosélutos* (4339), a stranger, foreigner.

Syn.: *paragínomai* (3854), to arrive, to be present; *prosporeúomai* (4365), to come near to; *proseggízō* (4331), to approach, come near; *proságō* (4317), to draw or lead near; *emphanízomai* (1718) and *anaphaínomai* (398), to appear, show oneself; *epiphaínomai* (2014), to become visible; *epideíknumi* (1925), to show oneself.

Ant.: *kataleípō* (2641), to leave behind; *apérchomai* (565), to depart; *anachōréō* (402), to withdraw; *pheúgō* (5343), to escape, flee; *apochōréō* (672), to go away; *apochōrízō* (673), to separate from; *aphístēmi* (868), to depart.

4335. προσευχή *proseuchḗ*; gen. *proseuchḗs*, fem. noun from *proseúchomai* (4336), to offer prayer (James 5:17). Prayer, prayer to God.

(I) Particularly: *proseuchḗ prós tón Theón* (*prós* [4314], to; *Theós* [2316] God), prayer to God (Acts 12:5; Rom 15:30); *proseuchḗ toú Theoú*, literally, prayer of God, but since God does not pray, it is prayer to God (Luke 6:12). Generally and in an absolute sense (Matt 17:21; 21:13, *oíkos proseuchḗs* [*oíkos* {3624}, house], house of prayer, 21:22; Mark 9:29; 11:17; Luke 19:46; 22:45; Acts 1:14; 3:1; 6:4; 10:31; Rom 12:12; 1 Cor 7:5; Eph 6:18; Phil 4:6; Col 4:2; James 5:17). In the pl. (Acts 2:42; 10:4; Rom 1:9; Eph 1:16; Col 4:12; 1 Thess 1:2; 1 Tim 2:1; 5:5; Phile

1:4, 22; 1 Pet 3:7; 4:7; Rev 5:8; 8:3, 4; Sept.: 2 Chr 6:19, in the sing.; Ps 4:1).

(II) Metonymically for a house or a place of prayer (Acts 16:13, 16). Such places for social prayer and devotion were in the outskirts of those towns where the Jews were unable or not permitted to have a synagogue, and were usually near a river or the seashore for the convenience of ablution (to which the Jews were dedicated).

Syn.: *paráklēsis* (3874), entreaty; *déēsis* (1162), supplication.

4336. προσεύχομαι *proseúchomai*; imperf. *proseuchómēn*, fut. *proseúxomai*, aor. *proseuxámēn*, mid. deponent from the prep. *prós* (4314), to, and *eúchomai* (2172), to wish, pray. To pray to God, offer prayer. In the NT this comp. verb almost totally supplants the simple verb *eúchomai* in designating "to pray."

(I) The combination with a dat. as the indirect obj., although constant in Class. Gr., occurs in the NT only in Matt 6:6 (cf. Isa 44:17) and 1 Cor 11:13, referring to prayer to God, whether for the obtaining of good or the averting of evil (see Matt 6:9; 24:20; 26:36, 39, 44; Luke 1:10); with the acc. *prós Theón* (*Theós* [2316], God), to God (Sept.: Gen 20:17; 1 Sam 1:10). Used in an absolute sense or with *tō Theō̃* (dat.), to God, implied (Matt 6:5–7; 14:23; Mark 1:35; Luke 3:21; Acts 6:6; 1 Cor 11:4; 1 Thess 5:17; 1 Tim 2:8; James 5:13, 18).

(II) The manner in which one prays is expressed by the dat. (1 Cor 11:5; 14:14, 15; James 5:17); with *en* (1722), in (Eph 6:18; Jude 1:20).

(III) The matter of one's prayer or the words are used after *hoútōs* (3779), thus (Matt 6:9); with *légōn* (the pres. part. of *légō* [3004], to say; Matt 26:39, 42; Sept.: Isa 37:15); *eípon* (the 2d aor. of *épō* [2046], to say), said (Acts 1:24; Sept: 2 Kgs 6:17); followed by *kathó deí* (*kathó* [2526], in the manner; *deí* [1163], to be necessary), as we ought (Rom 8:26); with *makrá proseuchḗ* (*makrá*, fem. of *makrós* [3117], long), long prayer (Matt 23:14;

Mark 12:40; Luke 20:47); with *toúto hína* (*toúto* [5124], this; *hína* [2443], so that); with *taúta* (pl. of *toúto* [5124], this), these things (Luke 18:11).

(**IV**) The object or thing prayed for is put after *hína* (2443), so that (Matt 24:20, neg.; Mark 13:18; 14:35, 38; 1 Cor 14:13; Phil 1:9; Col 1:9; Sept.: Jer 14:11); *eis hó . . . hína* (*eis* [1519], unto; *hó*, neut. relative pron. meaning that which), for this purpose . . . that (2 Thess 1:11); followed by the inf. (Luke 22:40; James 5:17).

(**V**) The subject or person for whom one prays is used with the prep. *perí* (4012), about, with the gen. (Col 1:3; 4:3; 2 Thess 3:1; Sept.: Gen 20:7; Jer 42:20); with *perí* and *hópōs* (3704), so that (Acts 8:15); with *hupér* (5228), on behalf of, with the gen. (Matt 5:44); with *epí* (1909), over, with the acc. (James 5:14, "on his behalf" [a.t.]).

(**VI**) *Proseúchomai* embraces all that is included in the idea of prayer, i.e., thanks, requesting special things; however, the distinctive word for worshiping is not *proseúchomai*, but *proskunéō* (4352), meaning to prostrate before someone. *Proseúchomai* appears in combination with *aitéomai* (154), to ask (Mark 11:24; Col 1:9); with *eucharistéō* (2168), to thank (Col 1:3; 1 Thess 5:17).

Deriv.: *proseuché* (4335), prayer.

Syn.: *déomai* (1189), to make request for particular needs; *aitéomai* (154), to ask, as from an inferior to a superior; *erōtáō* (2065), to ask.

4337. προσέχω proséchō; fut. *proséxō*, from *prós* (4314), to, and *échō* (2192), to have. To have in addition, to hold the mind or the ear toward someone (Sept.: Jer 7:24), to pay attention. As a nautical term, it means to hold a ship in a direction, to sail towards. Intrans. it means to hold on one's course toward a place. In the NT used only figuratively.

(**I**) Used in an absolute sense (with *tón noún* [3563], the mind, implied), to apply one's mind to something, attend to, give heed to, and used as follows:

(**A**) Generally and with the dat. of person or thing spoken (Acts 8:6; Heb 2:1; 2 Pet 1:19; Sept.: Deut 1:45; Ps 141:1). In the sense of to yield assent, believe, embrace (Acts 16:14; 1 Tim 1:4; Titus 1:14). With the dat. of person, meaning to care for, watch over (Acts 20:28).

(**B**) Reflexive use with the dat. *heautō* (1438), unto oneself, meaning to take heed, beware, mostly in the imper. (Luke 17:3; Acts 5:35); with *heautoís* (pl. of *heautō*), to yourselves, followed by *apó* (575), from (Luke 12:1; Sept.: 2 Chr 35:21); by *mḗpote* (3379), lest (Luke 21:34; Sept.: Ex 34:12). Also elliptically with *heautoís* implied, unto yourselves, with a neg. *mḗ* (3361), not, and the inf. (Matt 6:1, "Be careful not to do" [a.t.]); with *apó* (575), of someone or something (Matt 7:15; 10:17; 16:6, 11, 12; Luke 20:46; Sept.: Gen 24:6, followed by *mḗ* and the subjunctive).

(**II**) Used intrans. or with *heautón*, himself, implied, meaning to hold to a person or thing, to apply oneself, give or devote oneself to something, e.g., with a dat. of thing (1 Tim 3:8, "to much wine"; 4:13, "to reading"; Heb 7:13, to give attendance to, to minister). With the dat. of person or thing, to adhere to, follow (Acts 8:10, 11; 1 Tim 4:1).

Syn.: *horáō* (3708), to take heed; *epéchō* (1907), to give attention to; *phulássō* (5442), to guard; *phrontízō* (5431), to be careful; *tēréō* (5083), to keep, guard; *grēgoréō* (1127), to be watchful.

Ant.: *ameléō* (272), to neglect.

4338. προσηλόω prosēlóō; contracted *prosēlṓ*, fut. *prosēlṓsō*, from *prós* (4314), to, and *hēlóō* (n.f.), to sharpen, become hard or fixed, which is from *hḗlos* (2247), nail, peg, stud or callous. To nail to something, affix with nails, with the acc. and dat. (Col 2:14).

Syn.: *prospḗgnumi* (4362), to fasten to; *stauróō* (4717), to crucify; *anastauróō* (388), to crucify again or afresh.

4339. προσήλυτος prosḗlutos; gen. *prosēlútou*, masc. noun from *prosérchomai*

(4334), to come near, come to. A stranger, foreigner, one who comes from his own people to another. See Sept.: Ex 22:21; 23:9. The Sept. also applies it to a stranger or foreigner who came to dwell among the Jews and embraced their religion (Ex 12:48, 49; 20:10; Lev 17:8, 10, 12, 15; Num 9:14). In the NT it is used for a proselyte, a convert from heathenism to Judaism (Matt 23:15; Acts 2:10; 6:5; 13:43). Elsewhere such are called *hoi sebómenoi tón Theón* (*hoi sebómenoi* [4576], the reverencing ones; *Theón* [2316], God), those reverencing God (Acts 13:43, 50; 16:14; 17:4, 17; 18:7), or *hoi phoboúmenoi tón Theón* (*hoi phoboúmenoi* [5399], the fearing ones), those fearing God (Acts 10:2; 13:16, 26); also *Ioudaḯzō* (2450), to Judaize, means to live like the Jews, to follow their manners, customs, rites (Gal 2:14). The words of Jesus in Matt 23:15 refer to the zeal of the Jews in making proselytes, even at Rome, such zeal being so remarkable at that time that it became proverbial among the Romans. Thus at Pentecost we have those who came from Rome who were both Jews and proselytes (Acts 2:10). There were also a number of Jewish proselytes at Antioch in Syria (Acts 6:5).

Some of the proselytes in Palestine in the day of Christ were the centurion (Matt 8:5–13; Luke 7:1–10), who was an officer in the army of Herod Antipas, the Greeks (John 12:20), and Pilate's wife (Matt 27:19).

4340. πρόσκαιρος *próskairos*; gen. *proskaírou*, masc.-fem., neut. *próskairon*, adj. from *prós* (4314), for, and *kairós* (2540), a time or season, opportunity. For a season, transient, temporary, enduring for a while (Matt 13:21; Mark 4:17; 2 Cor 4:18; Heb 11:25). It is to be noted that more comp. are formed with *kairós* then with *chrónos* (5550), measured time, time viewed as successive moments.

Syn.: *ephḗmeros* (2184), for a day, ephemeral.

Ant.: *aiṓnios* (166), eternal.

4341. προσκαλέω *proskaléō*; contracted *proskalṓ*, fut. mid./pass. *proskalésomai*, from *prós* (4314), to, and *kaléō* (2564), to call. To call to oneself, bid to come. Used only in the mid. voice (Matt 10:1; 15:10, 32; 18:2, 32; 20:25; Mark 3:13, 23; 6:7; 7:14; 8:1, 34; 10:42; 12:43; 15:44; Luke 7:19; 15:26; 16:5; 18:16; Acts 5:40; 6:2; 13:7; 20:1; 23:17, 18, 23; James 5:14; Sept.: Gen 28:1; Esth 4:5). God's call to Gentiles through the gospel (Acts 2:39); the Divine call in entrusting men with the preaching of the gospel (Acts 13:2; 16:10).

Syn.: *prosphōnéō* (4377), to call unto; *metakaléō* (3333), to summon hither, recall.

Ant.: *apostéllō* (649), to send forth; *pémpō* (3992), to send; *apolúō* (630) and *aphíēmi* (863), to let go; *prospémpō* (4311), to send forth.

4342. προσκαρτερέω *proskarteréō*; contracted *proskarterṓ*, fut. *proskarterḗsō*, from *prós* (4314), to, and *karteréō* (2594), to endure. To tarry, remain somewhere (Mark 3:9); to continue steadfastly with someone (Acts 8:13); to cleave faithfully to someone (Acts 10:7); referring to those who continually insist on something or stay close to someone (Acts 2:46; Rom 13:6); used metaphorically of steadfastness and faithfulness in the outgoings of the Christian life, especially in prayer (Acts 1:14; 2:42; 6:4; Rom 12:12; Col 4:2).

Deriv.: *proskartérēsis* (4343), perseverance.

Syn.: *diateléō* (1300), to bring through to an end, to continue; *ménō* (3306), to remain; *diaménō* (1265), to continue throughout; *emménō* (1696), to remain in; *epiménō* (1961), to insist; *paraménō* (3887), to remain by or near; *prosménō* (4357), to remain with.

4343. προσκαρτέρησις *proskartérēsis*; gen. *proskarterḗseōs*, fem. noun from *proskarteréō* (4342), to endure. Perseverance, continuance in something (Eph

6:18, which refers to perseverance in supplication).

Syn.: *hupomoné* (5281), patience; *anoché* (463), tolerance; *makrothumía* (3115), longsuffering; *spoudé* (4710), diligence.

4344. προσκεφάλαιον *proskephálaion*; gen. *proskephalaíou*, neut. noun from *prós* (4314), to, at, and *kephálaion* (2774), a principal thing, head. A pillow, cushion for the head (Mark 4:38; Sept.: Ezek 13:18, 20).

4345. προσκληρόω *prosklēróō*; contracted *prosklērô*, fut. *prosklērôsō*, from *prós* (4314), to, and *klēróō* (2820), to take by lot. To give or assign by lot, to allot to someone, such as fortune, destiny. In the NT, aor. pass. *proseklērôthēn*, meaning to join one's lot to another, consort with, adhere to, with the dat. (Acts 17:4).

4346. πρόσκλισις *prosklisis*; gen. *prosklíseōs*, fem. noun from *prosklínō* (n.f.), to incline to or toward, which is from *prós* (4314), to, and *klínō* (2827), to incline. Inclination towards, a leaning against. In the NT, figuratively meaning partiality (1 Tim 5:21).

4347. προσκολλάω *proskolláō*; contracted *proskollô*, fut. *proskollēsō*, from *prós* (4314), to, and *kolláō* (2853), to glue. To glue one thing to another. In the NT, aor. pass. *prosekollēthēn*, meaning to be joined to someone as a companion, follower, with the dat. (Acts 5:36 [TR]). Fut. pass. mid. *proskollēthēsomai*, to be joined with or to join oneself unto, equivalent to cleave to, such as a husband to his wife, with the dat. (Matt 19:5 quoted from Gen 2:24; Mark 10:7; Eph 5:31).

Syn.: *suzeúgnumi* (4801), to yoke together.

4348. πρόσκομμα *próskomma*; gen. *proskómmatos*, neut. noun from *proskóptō* (4350), to stumble. A stumbling. In the NT used figuratively, a stone of stumbling, spoken of Christ as the occasion to fall and the perdition of those who reject Him (Rom 9:32, 33; 1 Pet 2:8 [cf. Isa 8:14]). See *líthos* (3037), stone, where it is used with *próskomma* as a stumblingblock. Figuratively, a cause of falling, an occasion of sinning (Rom 14:13, 20; 1 Cor 8:9; Sept.: Ex 23:33; 34:12).

Syn.: *skándalon* (4625), an obstacle, that which causes someone to stumble.

Ant.: *boétheia* (996), help; *epikouría* (1947), assistance.

4349. προσκοπή *proskopé*; gen. *proskopés*, fem. noun from *proskóptō* (4350), to stumble. A stumbling, figuratively an offense, the act of offending versus *próskomma* (4348), the result of offending (2 Cor 6:3, giving no occasion for rejecting the gospel).

4350. προσκόπτω *proskóptō*; fut. *proskópsō*, from *prós* (4314), to, against, and *kóptō* (2875), to cut, strike. Trans., to strike or dash against as the foot against a stone (Matt 4:6; Luke 4:11 quoted from Ps 91:12). In these passages it is well worth noting that the devil frames his temptation not only by quoting a sentence of Scripture in isolation from its context, but by applying literally what was originally meant figuratively. With a dat. following, to dash or beat against, as winds and waters (Matt 7:27). With a dat., to stumble at or against but in a spiritual sense (Rom 9:32; 1 Pet 2:8). Used in an absolute sense, to stumble (John 11:9, 10; Rom 14:21).

Deriv.: *apróskopos* (677), faultless; *próskomma* (4348), the stumblingblock, offense, hindrance; *proskopé* (4349), stumblingblock, offense.

Syn.: *skandalízō* (4624), to put a snare or stumbling block in the way; *ptaíō* (4417), to stumble; *hamartánō* (264), to sin.

Ant.: *nikáō* (3528), to overcome; *katakurieúō* (2634), to overcome, master; *thriambeúō* (2358), to triumph.

4351. προσκυλίω *proskulíō*; fut. *proskulíso*, from *prós* (4314), to, and *kulíō*

(2947), to roll. To roll to or upon something, such as a stone upon the door (Matt 27:60; Mark 15:46).

Ant.: *anakulíō* (Mark 16:4 [UBS]), to roll from; *apokulíō* (617), to roll away.

4352. προσκυνέω *proskunéō*; contracted *proskunṓ*, fut. *proskunḗsō*, from *prós* (4314), to, and *kunéō* (n.f.), to kiss, adore. To worship, do obeisance, show respect, fall or prostrate before. Literally, to kiss toward someone, to throw a kiss in token of respect or homage. The ancient oriental (especially Persian) mode of salutation between persons of equal ranks was to kiss each other on the lips; when the difference of rank was slight, they kissed each other on the cheek; when one was much inferior, he fell upon his knees and touched his forehead to the ground or prostrated himself, throwing kisses at the same time toward the superior. It is this latter mode of salutation that Gr. writers express by *proskunéō*. In the NT, generally, to do reverence or homage to someone, usually by kneeling or prostrating oneself before him. In the Sept. it means to bow down, to prostrate oneself in reverence, homage (Gen 19:1; 48:12).

(I) Generally towards a person as superior to whom one owes reverence and homage or from whom one implores aid. Used in an absolute sense in Acts 10:25. In Matt 20:20 used with the word *aitéō* (154) which means to beg, to ask as from an inferior to a superior (Sept.: Gen 33:6, 7). Followed by the dat. of person and with words expressing prostration (Matt 2:11; 4:9; 18:26; 28:9; Mark 15:19). Used simply (Matt 2:2, "and came to worship Him" [a.t.]; 8:2; 9:18; 14:33; 15:25; 28:17; Mark 5:6; John 9:38; Sept.: Gen 27:29; 43:26, 28). Followed by the acc. (Luke 24:52; Sept.: Gen 37:7, 9); by *enópion* (1799), before, and the gen. of a person, in front of someone (Luke 4:7; Rev 3:9; Sept.: Ps 22:30; 86:9).

(II) Spoken of those who pay reverence and homage to deity, render divine honors, worship, adore, with the basic idea of prostration, which, however,

is often dropped (cf. Sept.: Gen 47:31; 1 Kgs 1:47).

(A) Of God, used in an absolute sense (John 4:20, 24; 12:20; Acts 8:27; 24:11; Heb 11:21, meaning he worshiped leaning upon the top of his staff, in allusion to Gen 47:31 [cf. 1 Kgs 1:47; Rev 11:1; Sept.: Ps 95:6; 138:2]). Followed by the dat. and with the words expressing prostration (1 Cor 14:25; Rev 4:10; 5:14 [TR]; 7:11; 11:16; 19:4). Used simply (John 4:21, 23; Rev 14:7; 19:10; 22:9; Sept.: Gen 24:26; 1 Sam 1:19; Isa 27:13). Followed by the acc. (Matt 4:10; Luke 4:8; John 4:22–24); by *enópion* (1799), before, and *sou*, you (Rev 15:4); by *autón* (acc. of *autós* [846], he), him.

(B) Of the Messiah with the dat. (Heb 1:6).

(C) Of angels with *épeson*, the aor. of *píptō* (4098), to fall, and *émprosthen* (1715), before, with the gen. (Rev 19:10; 22:8).

(D) Of false gods, idols, followed by the dat. (Acts 7:43; Rev 13:8; 16:2; 19:20; 20:4). Followed by the acc. (Rev 9:20; 13:4, 12, 15; 14:9, 11).

Deriv.: *proskunētḗs* (4353), worshiper.

Syn.: *sébomai* (4576), to revere, stressing the feeling of awe or devotion; *sebázomai* (4573), to honor religiously; *latreúō* (3000), to worship in the sense of serving; *eusebéō* (2151), to act piously toward; *eulabéomai* (2125), to reverence.

Ant.: *asebéō* (764), to be impious or wicked, ungodly; *blasphēméō* (987), to vilify, speak impiously or evil, blaspheme.

4353. προσκυνητής *proskunētḗs*; gen. *proskunētoú*, masc. noun from *proskunéō* (4352), to worship. A worshiper of God (John 4:23).

Syn.: *theosebḗs* (2318), one who reverences God.

Ant.: *theostugḗs* (2319), one who is impious, a hater of God.

4354. προσλαλέω *proslaléō*; contracted *proslalṓ*, fut. *proslalḗsō*, from *prós* (4314), to, and *laléō* (2980), to speak. To speak to or with someone, with the dat. (Acts 13:43); used in an absolute sense (Acts 28:20).

Syn.: *prosphōnéō* (4377), to address, call out to.

4355. προσλαμβάνω proslambánō; fut. *proslḗpsomai*, from *prós* (4314), to, and *lambánō* (2983), to take. To take in addition, receive besides, to take to or with oneself in one's company. In the NT, in the mid., *proslambánomai*, to take to oneself.

(I) To take to oneself food, with the gen. (Acts 27:36, see also 27:34 [TR]). With *mēdén*, nothing, the neut. acc. of *mēdeís* (3367), no one (Acts 27:33); the acc. of person, to take to oneself, meaning to take by the hand and draw aside (Matt 16:22; Mark 8:32); to take to one's company or house (Acts 17:5; 18:26).

(II) To receive to oneself, admit to one's society and fellowship, receive and treat with kindness, with the acc. of person (Acts 28:2; Rom 14:1, 3; 15:7; Phile 1:12, 17; Sept.: Ps 65:4).

Deriv.: *próslēpsis* (4356), a receiving, an admission.

Syn.: *déchomai* (1209), to deliberately and readily receive that which is offered; *anadéchomai* (324), to receive gladly; *apodéchomai* (588), to welcome; *prosdéchomai* (4327), to receive to oneself; *hupodéchomai* (5264), to receive under one's roof.

Ant.: *ekbállō* (1544), to cast or send out.

4356. πρόσληψις próslēpsis; gen. *proslḗpseōs*, fem. noun from *proslambánō* (4355), to receive unto oneself. A taking to oneself, acceptance. In the NT, a receiving, admission (Rom 11:15).

Syn.: *apodoché* (594), acceptance.

4357. προσμένω prosménō; fut. *prosmenṓ*, from *prós* (4314), to, with, and *ménō* (3306), to remain. To stay at a place (Acts 18:18; 1 Tim 1:3); with a dat. of person following, to remain or continue with (Matt 15:32; Mark 8:2). In a spiritual

sense, to adhere to (Acts 11:23). With a dat. of thing, to continue or persevere, with the dat. (1 Tim 5:5).

Syn.: *chronízō* (5549), to tarry; *periménō* (4037), to stay around, await, wait for; *proskarteréō* (4342), to continue in, remain constant.

4358. προσορμίζω prosormízō; fut. *prosormísō*, from *prós* (4314), to, and *hormízō* (n.f.), to anchor, make fast. To bring a ship to anchor, cast anchor, land at. In the NT, only in the mid., *prosormízomai*, meaning to come to anchor, draw into shore (Mark 6:53).

Ant.: *pléō* (4126), to sail; *parapléō* (3896), to sail past; *diaperáō* (1276), to cross over, sail over;.

4359. προσοφείλω prosopheílō; fut. *prosopheilēsō*, from *prós* (4314), besides, and *opheílō* (3784), to owe. To owe besides, in addition to (Phile 1:19).

4360. προσοχθίζω prosochthízō; fut. *prosochthísō*, from *prós* (4314), to, at, against, and *ochthízō* (n.f.), to be grieved, offended, take ill, which is from *áchthos* (n.f.), burden, load. To be burdened, grieved, indignant, to be grieved toward someone, angry, with the dat. (Heb 3:10, 17 in allusion to Ps 95:10; Sept.: Lev 26:15, 43).

Syn.: *aganaktéō* (23), to be indignant; *thumomachéō* (2371), to be very angry, highly displeased.

Ant.: *eudokéō* (2106), to be well-pleased, think well of.

4361. πρόσπεινος próspeinos; gen. *prospeínou*, masc.-fem., neut. *próspeinon*, adj. from *prós* (4314), an intens., and *peína* (n.f.), hunger. Very hungry (Acts 10:10).

4362. προσπήγνυμι prospḗgnumi; fut. *prospḗxō*, from *prós* (4314), to, and *pḗgnumi* (4078) to fix or pitch. To fix or fasten to something, affix, crucify trans. (Acts 2:23).

Syn.: *proséloō* (4338), to nail to; *stauróō* (4717), to crucify; *anastauróō* (388), to crucify again or afresh.

4363. προσπίπτω *prospíptō*; fut. *prospesoúmai*, from *prós* (4314), to, against, and *píptō* (4098), to fall. To fall towards or upon something, to strike against. In the NT with the idea of purpose.

(I) To fall or rush upon, dash against (as the wind), with the implication of to assault, with the dat. (Matt 7:25).

(II) Of persons, to fall down to or before someone, i.e., at his feet or knees as a suppliant or to reverence, followed by the dat. of person (Mark 3:11; 5:33; Luke 8:28, 47; Acts 16:29); by the dat. pl., to fall down at someone's knees (Luke 5:8; Sept.: with *autó* [846], him, Ps 95:6); by *prós toús pódas* (*prós* [4314], toward, against; *toús pódas* [4228], the feet), to fall down at someone's feet (Mark 7:25; Sept.: Ex 4:25).

Syn.: *katapíptō* (2667), to fall down; *proskunéō* (4352), to fall before, prostrate; *proségnumi* (4366), to break upon.

Ant.: *epaírō* (1869), to lift up, exalt; *huperaíromai* (5229), to become haughty.

4364. προσποιέομαι *prospoiéomai* or *prospoioúmai*; fut. *prospoiēsomai*, mid. form of *prospoiéō*, which is from *prós* (4314), to, besides, and *poiéō* (4160), to make. To make, acquire, claim or appropriate for oneself, to make pretension. In the NT, only in the mid. with the inf., meaning to make a show of being or doing something, to feign, pretend (Luke 24:28).

Syn.: *hupokrínomai* (5271), to pretend, feign, be a hypocrite.

Ant.: *alētheúō* (226), to be true, speak the truth.

4365. προσπορεύομαι *prosporeúomai*; fut. *prosporeúsomai*, pass. deponent from *prós* (4314), to, and *poreúomai* (4198), to go, come. To go or come to someone, with the dat. (Mark 10:35; Sept.: Ex 24:14).

Syn.: *prosérchomai* (4334), to come or go near to; *phthánō* (5348), to arrive, come; *proseggízō* (4331), to come near.

Ant.: *ekporeúomai* (1607), to depart; *aphístēmi* (868), to withdraw.

4366. προσρήγνυμι *prosrḗgnumi*; fut. *prosrḗxō*, from *prós* (4314), to, against, and *rhḗgnumi* (4486), to break. To break or burst towards or upon something, to dash against, as waves, intrans. with a dat. (Luke 6:48, 49).

Other comp.: *diarrḗgnumi* (1284), to rend, break through; *katágnumi* (2608), to break down, used of the breaking of the legs of those who were crucified; *diorússō* (1358), to dig through; *exorússō* (1846), to dig out.

Syn.: *prospíptō* (4363), to fall upon.

4367. προστάσσω *prostássō*, **προστάττω** *prostáttō*; fut. *prostáxō*, from *prós* (4314), to, and *tássō* (5021), to arrange. To set in order toward, in regard to a person or thing, to order towards or to someone, to command, prescribe to, followed by the dat. of person (Matt 1:24; 21:6; Sept.: Gen 50:2; Num 5:2); by the acc. and dat. in the pass. construction (Acts 10:33); with the dat. implied (Matt 8:4; Mark 1:44; Luke 5:14); by the inf. and acc. (Acts 10:48; Sept.: with the acc. and dat., Lev 10:1; Deut 17:3; with the inf., Esth 3:2). Spoken of times or seasons, to prescribe or appoint to someone, with the dat. implied (Acts 17:26, *prostetagménous* [UBS] and *protetagménous* [TR]).

Syn.: *keleúō* (2753) and *entéllomai* (1781), to command; *diatássō* (1299), to command with the implication of appointing or setting in order; *épō* (2036), to bid, command; *epitássō* (2004), to appoint over, put in charge; *paraggéllō* (3853), to order, give a charge, command; *diastéllomai* (1291), to charge, enjoin; *horízō* (3724), to mark out the bounds, ordain.

4368. προστάτις *prostátis*; gen. *prostátidos*, fem. noun from *proḯstēmi* (4291), to set before. It meant not only a leader, ruler, or director (Sept.: 1 Chr 27:31; 29:6; 2 Chr 8:10), but was also used by Plutarch for the Lat. *patronus*, a patron, a defender of a lower person. The word denoted those in Athens who were the patrons, i.e., took care of strangers. In Rom 16:2 it means a patroness, helper.

4369. προστίθημι *prostíthēmi*; fut. *prosthḗsō*; 3d person act. *prosetíthei*, from *prós* (4314), to or besides, and *títhēmi* (5087), to put. To set, add, put, lay unto or with something. Trans.:

(I) Particularly followed by *prós* (4314), toward, with the acc. (Acts 13:36, "and was added to his fathers" [a.t.], referring to David; Sept.: Judg 2:10).

(II) Generally to join, add, e.g., persons, with the acc. and dat. (Acts 2:47 referring to those who were saved being added to the church; 5:14; 11:24; "unto the Lord," implied Acts 2:41). Of things, with the acc. and dat. (Luke 17:5, "Add unto us faith" [a.t.]). Pass. with or without the dat. (Matt 6:33, "and all these things shall be added unto you"; Mark 4:24; Luke 12:31; Heb 12:19). Followed by the acc. and *epí* (1909), on, with the dat. (Luke 3:20); *epí* with the acc. (Matt 6:27; Luke 12:25). In the pass. used in the absolute sense (Gal 3:19 [TR]). In the mid. 2d aor., *prosethémēn*, followed by the inf. (Luke 20:11, 12, "again he sent"; Acts 12:3, "he further seized also Peter" [a.t.]). Also as a part. *prostheís*, before a finite verb (Luke 19:11, "he added and spake a parable"; Sept.: Gen 4:2; 18:29, followed by the inf.; 25:1).

Syn.: *epichorēgéō* (2023), to add, supply; *dídōmi* (1325), to give, add; *charízomai* (5483), to give or bestow freely and graciously; *paréchō* (3930) and *chorēgéō* (5524), to supply; *dōréō* (1433), to bestow as a gift; *aponémō* (632), to apportion, give.

Ant.: *aphairéō* (851), to lift off or remove away.

4370. προστρέχω *prostréchō*; fut. *prosdramoúmai*, 2d aor. *prosédramon*, from *prós* (4314), to, and *tréchō* (5143), to run. To run to or toward someone (Mark 9:15; 10:17; Acts 8:30; Sept.: Gen 18:2; 33:4).

4371. προσφάγιον *prosphágion*; gen. *prosphagíou*, neut. noun from *prós* (4314), besides, and *phágō* (5315), to eat. That which is eaten along with bread; hence, meat or fish (John 21:5).

4372. πρόσφατος *prósphatos*; gen. *prosphátou*, masc.-fem., neut. *prósphaton*, adj. from *prós* (4314) denoting nearness of time, and *phénō* (n.f.), to kill. Originally it was used to refer to the newly-killed animal or man; hence, of flesh just killed, fresh meat, or of fresh vegetables just picked. In the NT, generally it means recent, new, as a new way (Heb 10:20; Sept.: Eccl 1:9). Also from *phénō* (n.f.): *phónos* (5408), murder, slaughter.

Deriv.: *prosphátōs* (4373), lately.

Syn.: *kainós* (2537), new, but qualitatively so; *néos* (3501), new numerically, another; *éschatos* (2078), last, end; *hústeros* (5306), later with the idea of final.

Ant.: *archaíos* (744), original, ancient; *palaiós* (3820), old without reference to beginning or origin.

4373. προσφάτως *prosphátōs*; adv. from *prósphatos* (4372), recent. Recently, lately (Acts 18:2).

Syn.: *árti* (737), just now; *hústeron* (5305), lately with the idea of finality.

Ant.: *ékpalai* (1597), from of old, for a long time; *pálai* (3819), long ago, of old; *poté* (4218), once, formerly, ever, sometime in the past; *pántote* (3842), always, ever; *ap' archḗs* (apó [575], from; *archḗ* [746], beginning), from the beginning; *apó ktíseōs* (2937), original formation, creation, from the creation; *apó katabolḗs kósmou* (apó [575], from; *katabolḗ* [2602], deposition, founding; *kósmou* [2889], of the world), from the foundation of the world.

4374. προσφέρω *prosphérō*; fut. *prosoísō*, aor. *prosénegka*, 2d aor. imper. *prosénegke*, perf. *prosenénocha*, from *prós* (4314), to, and *phérō* (5342), to bring. To bear or bring to a place or person.

(I) Used of things with the acc. and dat. of place, meaning to bring near or put to (John 19:29, "and put it to his mouth"); with the dat. of person, to bring something to someone (Matt 22:19). Followed or proceeded by the acc. (Matt 25:20; Sept.: Gen 27:31; Ex 36:6). Of persons, in the pass. followed by the acc. and dat., e.g., the sick and afflicted as brought to Jesus (Matt 4:24; 8:16; 9:2, 32; 12:22; 14:35; 17:16); children (Matt 19:13; Mark 10:13); babies (Luke 18:15). To bring or conduct to or before someone, in the pass. with the acc. and dat. (Matt 18:24); in the act. aor, imper. (Luke 23:14); with *epí* (1909), upon, unto (Luke 12:11).

(II) To offer, present to someone, with the acc. and dat., e.g, *óxos* (3690), vinegar (Luke 23:36); money (Acts 8:18); gifts (Matt 2:11; Sept.: Gen 43:26; Judg 3:17). Of things offered to God, oblations, sacrifice, followed or preceded by the acc. and dat. (Luke 5:14; Acts 7:42; Heb 5:3; 11:4); service (John 16:2); Jesus Christ offering up Himself (Heb 9:14); offering up supplications to His Father (Heb 5:7). Elsewhere with "unto God" implied, followed by the acc. (Matt 5:23, 24; 8:4; Heb 8:3, 4; 9:25; 10:1, 11; 11:17). In the pass. (Heb 9:9, 28; 10:2, 8). The person or thing for or on account of which offering is made or is put, with *hupér* (5228), for, and the gen. (Heb 5:1; 9:7; 10:12); the same as with *perí* (4012), regarding (Mark 1:44); in the pass. (Acts 21:26).

(III) In the mid. with the dat., figuratively meaning to bear oneself towards someone, conduct towards, to deal with a person in a particular manner (Heb 12:7).

Deriv.: *prosphorá* (4376), an offering, oblation.

Syn.: *anágō* (321), to bring up; *proságō* (4317), to bring to or unto; *komízō* (2865), to bring in; *poiéō* (4160), to do; *paréchō* (3930), to present, bring and offer; *paradídōmi* (3860), to deliver, give over; *ekdídōmi* (1554), to give forth; *metadídōmi* (3330), to give over, impart; *apodídōmi* (591), to render, reward, give away; *charízomai* (5483), to grant as a favor, deliver, give; *dōréomai* (1433), to give gratuitously; *koinōnéō* (2841), to share with others, communicate.

Ant.: *lambánō* (2983), to receive; *piázō* (4084), to seize, take; *paralambánō* (3880), to receive near, take; *proslambánō* (4355), to receive, take unto; *aphairéō* (851), to remove, take away; *exaírō* (1808), to put or take away; *exairéō* (1807), to tear out, deliver, pluck out.

4375. προσφιλής *prosphilḗs*; gen. *prosphiloús*, masc.-fem., neut. *prosphilés*, adj. from *prós* (4314), to, and *philéō* (5368), friend, dear. Dear to someone, beloved. In the NT, used of things, acceptable, pleasing (Phil 4:8).

4376. προσφορά *prosphorá*, gen. *prosphorás*, fem. noun from *prosphérō* (4374), to offer. An offering, oblation.

(I) The act of offering to God (Heb 10:10). Figuratively (Rom 15:16).

(II) Metonymically for the thing offered, an offering, oblation, strictly without blood; opposite to *thusía* (2378), sacrifice, and *holokaútōma* (3646), a wholly consumed sacrifice, burnt offering (Eph 5:2; Heb 10:5, 8; Sept.: Ps 40:6). In Acts 21:26, however, it denotes a sacrifice with blood (*thusía*). See Num 6:13ff.; Acts 24:17, and *prosphorá perí hamartías* (*perí* [4012], for, concerning; *hamartías* [266], sin), "offering for sin" (Heb 10:18 [cf. Lev chaps. 4; 9]).

Syn.: *holokaútōma* (3646), a burnt offering; *anáthēma* (334), a gift set up in a temple, a votive offering; *dóron* (1435), a gift; *sphágion* (4968), a victim, slain beast; *dōreá* (1431), gift, gratuity; *dórēma* (1434), a bestowal or gift.

4377. προσφωνέω *prosphōnéō*; contracted *prosphōnó*, fut. *prosphōnḗsō*, from *prós* (4314), to, and *phōnéō* (5455), to call, speak. To utter sounds toward someone, to speak to or address someone.

(I) Generally with the dat. expressed or implied (Luke 13:12; 23:20; Acts 21:40; 22:2). In the sense of to call out to someone, exclaim, with the dat. (Matt 11:16; Luke 7:32).

(II) To call another to oneself, followed by the acc. (Luke 6:13).

Syn.: *proskaléō* (4341), to call for; *metakaléō* (3333), to summon hither, recall; *kaléō* (2564), to call; *proslaléō* (4354), to speak to or with; *epikaléomai* (1941), to invoke, call upon; *prosagoreúō* (4316), to address, call.

4378. πρόσχυσις *próschusis*; gen. *proschúseōs*, fem. noun from *proschéō* (n.f.), to pour upon, which is from *prós* (4314), to or upon, and *chúō* (n.f.), to pour. A pouring out upon, effusion (pouring) or more probably aspersion (sprinkling), such as blood (Heb 11:28 [cf. Ex 12:7, 22; 24:6]).

Syn.: *rhantismós* (4473), sprinkling; *baptismós* (909), ablution by dipping.

4379. προσψαύω *prospsaúō*; fut. *prospsaúsō*, from *prós* (4314), to, at, and *psaúō* (n.f.), to touch, touch lightly, which is from *psáō* (n.f., see *psēlapháō* [5584]), to touch. To touch instantly to or upon something. Trans. with a dat. (Luke 11:46).

Syn.: *háptō* (681), to touch; *thiggánō* (2345), to touch lightly; *psēlapháō* (5584), to feel, handle in an investigative manner. For the distinctions among these three words see *háptō*.

4380. προσωποληπτέω *prosōpolēptéō*; contracted *prosōpoleptṓ*, fut. *prosōpoleptḗsō*, from *prosōpolḗptēs* (4381), a respecter of persons. To accept or respect persons, to show partiality (James 2:9). Equivalent to the Hebraism *prósō pon lambánō* (*prósōpon* [4383], face, presence, person; *lambáno* [2983], to receive, take into account), to show favor or partiality (Luke 20:21). See Sept.: Lev 19:15; Mal 2:9.

Deriv.: *aprosōpolḗptōs* (678), impartially; *prosōpolēpsía* (4382), respect of persons, partiality.

Ant.: *krínō dikaíōs* (*krínō* [2919], judge; *dikaíōs* [1346], equitably), to judge righteously.

4381. προσωπολήπτης *prosōpolḗptēs*; gen. *prosōpolḗptou*, masc. noun from *prósōpon* (4383), face, and *lambánō* (2983), to receive. A respecter of persons (Acts 10:34). Only in the NT.

Deriv.: *prosōpolēptéō* (4380), to show partiality;.

Syn.: *ádikos* (94), as a subst., an unjust or unrighteous person.

Ant.: *díkaios* (1342), as a subst., a just or righteous person.

4382. προσωπολημψία *prosōpolēpsía*; gen. *prosōpolēpsías*, fem. noun which comes from *prosōpolēptéō* (4380), to show partiality. A respecting of persons, partiality, favoritism (Rom 2:11; Eph 6:9; Col 3:25; James 2:1).

Ant.: *dikaiokrisía* (1341), righteous judgment.

4383. πρόσωπον *prósōpon*; gen. *prosópou*, neut. noun from *prós* (4314), toward, and *ṓps* (n.f., see *skuthrōpós* [4659]), the eye or face. Literally the part toward, at, or around the eye. Hence, the face, countenance, presence, person.

(I) Particularly (Matt 6:16, 17; 17:2; 26:67; Mark 14:65; Luke 9:29; 22:64; 24:5; Acts 6:15; 2 Cor 3:7, 13, 18; 4:6; 11:20; Gal 1:22, "unknown by face," meaning by sight; James 1:23; Rev 4:7; 9:7; 10:1; Sept.: Gen 38:15; 40:7; 43:31). In phrases as *píptō epí prósōpon* (*píptō* [4098], fall; *epí* [1909], upon), to fall on one's face (Matt 17:6; 26:39; Luke 5:12; 17:16; 1 Cor 14:25; Rev 7:11; 11:16); *prósōpon prós prósōpon* ([4314], toward) "face to face," meaning with nothing intervening (1 Cor 13:12); Sept.: Gen 32:31); *katá prósōpon échō* (*katá* [2596], in view, against; *échō* [2192], to have), meaning before the face, face to face, present (Acts 25:16), the opposite of *apón*, absent; *tá katá prósopon* (*katá* [2596], against, in front) meaning things before the face, external things (2 Cor 10:7); *katá prósōpon autō̆ antéstēn* (*katá*, against; *prósōpon*, face; *autō̆* dat. of *autós* [846], his; *antéstēn*, the aor. of *anthístēmi* [436], to oppose, stand against), meaning I stood against him face to face (Gal 2:11). Figuratively (Luke 9:51, "he steadfastly set his face to go," he set forth with fixed purpose; Sept.: Jer 42:15, 17; 44:11; 2 Kgs 12:17). Elliptically, in the same sense (Luke 9:53, "his face was going {or set} toward Jerusalem" [a.t.]; 1 Pet 3:12, "the face of the Lord is against them that do evil," means the Lord is directed against those doing evil, quoted from Ps 34:17 [cf. Lev 26:17; Jer 21:10]). Figuratively, in antithesis with *kardía* (2588), heart, (2 Cor 5:12, "boasting in face and not in heart" [a.t.] means externally, in appearance, and not in reality; 1 Thess 2:17, "not in heart . . . your face," meaning in body not in spirit).

(II) Metonymically for face, meaning presence, person, chiefly in phrases borrowed from the Hebr.:

(A) With a prep. and followed by a gen. of person it forms a periphrasis for a simple prep., *apó* (575) from, followed by the gen. *prosópou*, from the face or presence of someone, from before, from (Acts 3:19; 5:41; 7:45; 2 Thess 1:9; Rev 6:16; 12:14; 20:11; Sept.: Gen 16:6; Deut 2:22; 1 Chr 19:18); *eis* (1519), into, followed by the acc. *prósōpon* (2 Cor 8:24, before or to the churches; *en* (1722), in, followed by the dat. *prosópō* (2 Cor 2:10, before him, as a formula of affirmation; Sept.: Prov 8:30); *katá prósōpon* (*katá* [2596], according to) followed by the acc., meaning in the presence of someone, before him (Luke 2:31; Acts 3:13; Sept.: Gen 25:18; 32:21); *metá toú prosópou sou* (*metá* [3326], with, followed by the gen. *prosópou*), with or in Thy presence, meaning with Thee (Acts 2:28 from Ps 16:11 with *pró* [4253], before, followed by the gen., meaning before the face of someone). Also of place (Matt 11:10,

"before thy face"; Mark 1:2; Luke 1:76; 7:27; 9:52; 10:1); of time (Acts 13:24).

(B) In construction with verbs, with or without an intervening prep. and with a gen. of person expressed or implied; here, too, it forms a periphrasis for the person designated by the gen. The phrase *horáō tó prósōpon* (*horáō* [3708], to see), followed by the gen., to see the face of someone means to see him face to face, to see and converse with him (Col 2:1; see Gen 32:20); *blépousi tó prósōpon toú Theoú* (*blépousi* [3d person pl. of *blépō* (991), to see], meaning to have access to God or being admitted into His presence, versus *horáō* [3708] meaning take heed), they behold the face of God, have access to God, and are admitted to His presence (Matt 18:10; Rev 22:4). *blépō* (991), see II, A, and *horáō* (3708), I, B. The meaning is similar in Heb 9:24, "to appear before the face of God" (a.t.) or before God in our behalf. See *emphanízō* (1718), to appear, I. Elsewhere it may include the idea of external condition and circumstances as *blépō eis prósōpon*, followed by the gen. meaning to regard the person or external appearance of someone (Matt 22:16; Mark 12:14). See *blépō*, II, B. With *thaumázō* (2296), to admire the face of someone (Jude 1:16), which see II. With *lambánō* (2983), to receive, accept or take into account the person of someone (Luke 20:21; Gal 2:6), which see I, E, 2.

(C) Once used in an absolute sense as in the later Gr., meaning a person (2 Cor 1:11, "the gift to us from many persons" [a.t.]).

(III) Of things meaning face, surface (Luke 21:35, "on the face of the whole earth"; Acts 17:26; Sept.: Gen 2:6; 11:4, 8), hence equal to the exterior or external appearance (Matt 16:3, "the face of the sky"; Luke 12:56; James 1:11; Sept.: Ps 104:30).

Deriv.: *prosōpolḗptēs* (4381), one who shows partiality.

Syn.: *eídos* (1491), that which strikes the eye, is exposed to view, external appearance, form, shape; sometimes *schéma* (4976), a figure, fashion, external appearance; *morphḗ* (3437), form, and *homoíōma* (3667), likeness, shape.

4384. προτάσσω *protássō*, προτάττω *protáttō*; fut. *protáxō*, from *pró* (4253), forth, and *tássō* (5021), to arrange, order. To arrange or set in order before or in front, to put a specific command forward for a specific purpose. In the NT, of time, to appoint before, as in the phrase *protetagménoi kairoí* (*protetagménoi*, perf. pass. part. of *protássō*, to prearrange; *kairoí* [2540], seasons, times), times before appointed (Acts 17:26 [TR]).

Syn.: *proginṓskō* (4267), to foreknow, to consider beforehand; *procheirízō* (4400), to appoint beforehand; *proetoimázō* (4282), to prepare before; *proorízō* (4309), to appoint or decree beforehand.

4385. προτείνω *proteínō*; fut. *protenō*, from *pró* (4253), forth, and *teínō* (n.f., see *parateínō* [3905]), to stretch out, extend, as the hand. To stretch forward, prolong. In the NT, to stretch out or extend before someone, a person bound with thongs in order to be scourged, with the acc. and dat. of instrument (Acts 22:25).

Syn.: *déō* (1210), to bind in any way; *peridéō* (4019), to bind around; *hupodéō* (5265), to bind underneath; *katadéō* (2611), to bind or tie down; *sundéō* (4887), to bind together; *desmeúō* (1195), to put in fetters or any other bond.

4386. πρότερον *próteron*; the neut. of *próteros* (4387), previous, which is from *pró* (4253), forth, before. In the NT, used as an adv. of time meaning before, former, prior. Used generally (John 7:51; 2 Cor 1:15; 1 Tim 1:13; Heb 4:6; 7:27; Sept.: Deut 9:18). With the masc. art., *ho* (or fem. art. *hē*) *proteron*, used together as an adj. meaning the former (Heb 10:32, "the former days"; 1 Pet 1:14, "the former lusts"; Sept.: Num 6:12). With the neut. art., *tó próteron* used as an adv. meaning before, formerly (John 6:62; 9:8; Gal 4:13; Sept.: Josh 11:10). Comparative of *próton* (4412), first.

Syn.: *émprosthen* (1715), before; *pálai* (3819), in time past; *poté* (4218), at one time.

Ant.: *nún* (3568), now; *nuní* (3570), just now; *tanún* (3569), at present.

4387. πρότερος *próteros*; adj. from *pró* (4253), forth, before. Prior, previous, former (Eph 4:22; Sept.: Lev 26:45; Deut 4:32; Jer 28:8). See *próteron* (4386). Comparative of *prōtos* (4413), first.

Syn.: *palaiós* (3820), not recent, old; *pálai* (3819), former.

Ant.: *hústeros* (5306), later or latter suggesting termination.

4388. προτίθημι *protíthēmi*; fut. *prothēsō*, from *pró* (4253), before, forth, and *títhēmi* (5087), to place. To set before someone. In the NT, only in the mid. *protíthemai*. To propose, set forth or before the eyes, publicly, with the acc. (Rom 3:25); to propose, purpose, design beforehand (Rom 1:13 with the inf.; Eph 1:9).

Deriv.: *próthesis* (4286), a setting forth, a purpose.

Syn.: *bouleúomai* (1011), to resolve, determine, purpose; *boúlomai* (1014), to will, be disposed, intend; *thélō* (2309), to desire with the power to execute that desire.

4389. προτρέπω *protrépō*; fut. *protrépsō*, from *pró* (4253), toward, and *trépō* (n.f., see *anatrépō* [396]), to turn. To turn forward, to propel, impel morally, to encourage. In the NT only in the mid. *protrépomai*, to cause one to turn himself, as it were, toward action (Acts 18:27).

Syn.: *paramuthéomai* (3888), to encourage, comfort; *parakaléō* (3870), to beseech, comfort; *parainéō* (3867), to exhort, warn; *nouthetéō* (3560), to admonish.

4390. προτρέχω *protréchō*; fut. *prodramoúmai*, 2d aor. *proédramon*, from *pró* (4253), before, and *tréchō* (5143), to run. To run before or in advance, with the gen. with a comparative (John 20:4, he went faster ahead of Peter; Sept.: 1 Sam

8:11). Pleonastically in Luke 19:4, "he ran before," i.e., ran ahead.

Deriv.: *pródromos* (4274), the one running before.

Syn.: *proporeúomai* (4313), to go ahead, precede.

Ant.: *diadéchomai* (1237), to succeed, come after; *akolouthéō* (190), to follow.

4391. προϋπάρχω *proüpárchō*; fut. *proüpárxō*, from *pró* (4253), before, and *hupárchō* (5225), to be. To be or exist before, to begin before, do first, precede in time. In the NT, only with a part. of another verb, thus forming a periphrasis for a finite tense of that verb (Luke 23:12, meaning who before were being in enmity; Acts 8:9, "who before . . . practiced sorcery" [a.t.]).

4392. πρόφασις *próphasis*; gen. *propháseōs*, fem. noun from *prophaínō* (n.f.), to appear before, be apparent, which is from *pró* (4253), before, and *phaínō* (5316), to appear, to shine before. An outward show or appearance, a pretense or pretext put forth in order to cover one's real intent, that which is put forth as a cause or reason, an apparent reason (Matt 23:14; Mark 12:40; Luke 20:47; Acts 27:30; Phil 1:18; 1 Thess 2:5, "a pretext for covetousness" [a.t.]; Sept.: Hos 10:4).

Syn.: *epikálumma* (1942), a covering, pretext.

4393. προφέρω *prophérō*; fut. *prooísō*, from *pró* (4253), forth, and *phérō* (5342), to bear, carry. To bear or bring forth out of any place or thing, with the acc. and *ek* (1537), out of, with the gen. (Luke 6:45).

4394. προφητεία *prophēteía*; gen. *prophēteías*, fem. noun from *prophēteúō* (4395), to prophesy. A prophesying or prophecy.

(I) Particularly prediction, the foretelling of future events, including the declarations, exhortations, and warnings uttered by the prophets while acting under divine influence; of the prophecies of the OT (Matt 13:14; 2 Pet 1:20, 21); the revelations and warnings of the Book of Revelation (Rev 1:3; 22:7, 10, 18, 19, equal to *marturía* [3141], witness, as in Rev 19:10. See also Sept.: 2 Chr 15:8). In 1 Tim 1:18; 4:14, *prophēteía* refers either to the prophetic revelations or directions of the Holy Spirit by which persons were designated as officers and teachers in the primitive church (cf. Acts 13:2; 20:28; 1 Cor 12:4–8ff.; 14:24, 30, 31), or to the authoritative declaration made by the presbytery of the fitness for ministry of one whom they are ordaining.

(II) Prophecy, meaning the prophetic office, the prophetic gift, spoken in the NT of the peculiar charisma or spiritual gift imparted to the primitive teachers of the church (Rom 12:6; 1 Cor 12:10; 13:2, 8; 14:22). See *prophḗtēs* (4396).

(III) Metonymically a prophesying, the exercise of the prophetic office, the acting as an ambassador of God and the interpreter of His mind and will (Rev 11:6). Specifically the exercise of the prophetic gift or charisma in the primitive church (1 Cor 14:6; 1 Thess 5:20).

(IV) *Prophēteía* is the prophetic rank or work, the office of a prophet or gift of prophecy. In Rom 12:6 it is classed with *diakonía* (1248), ministry or serving, and *didaskalía* (1319), teaching as a *chárisma* (5486), the result of God's grace or divine enablement to be exercised within the church (1 Cor 12:10; 13:2; 1 Thess 5:20; 1 Tim 4:14; Rev 11:6; 19:10). Elsewhere it means prophecy, that which is prophesied, foretold (Matt 13:14; 1 Cor 13:8; 14:6, 22; 1 Tim 1:18; 2 Pet 1:20, 21; Rev 1:3; 22:7, 10, 18, 19).

(V) A prophecy is something that any believer may exercise as telling forth God's Word. This, however, does not make him a prophet (*prophḗtēs* [4396]) which is used in the NT in a very restrictive sense. A prophet prophesies, but one who prophesies is not necessarily a prophet.

(VI) Prophecy was a distinctive *chárisma* (5486), gift, distinguishable from that of the apostle and the teacher.

While the apostle was a travelling missionary, the prophets and teachers were in general attached to a local church. For example, Silas and Judas, prophets of the church of Jerusalem, are described as *hēgoúmenoi*, leaders, from *hēgéomai* (2233) to lead (Acts 15:22). In Heb 13:7 such *hēgoúmenoi* or leaders are described as speaking "the word of God." Neither the prophet nor teacher was appointed by the apostles, as were bishops and elders; the gifts were an endowment of the Spirit, and both fulfilled the function of speaking in the Spirit.

(VII) That which is revealed constitutes a prophecy. The reception of such revelation and its communication did not entail states of rapture or ecstasy accompanied by unintelligible utterances. Prophecy is presented as a greater gift, a more noble function than *glōssolalía* or tongue-speaking which was severely abused in the church at Corinth. Prophecy was a gift exercised with a consciousness of the subject, and it issued in something logically intelligible.

(VIII) Prophecy is a larger term than revelation (*apokálupsis* [602]). It includes revelation among its various contents. In 1 Cor 14:6, the Apostle Paul presents four species of sacred utterance: revelation (*apokálupsis* [602]); knowledge (*gnōsis* [1108]); prophecy and teaching (*didachē* [1322]).

(IX) Prophecy is connected not only with revelation, but with vision (*optasía* [3701]) (2 Cor 12:1–3). What is revealed in the Book of the Revelation is called a prophecy seven times (Rev 1:3; 11:6; 19:10; 22:7, 10, 18, 19). It is a series of visions seen by a prophet and related to others by him.

(X) In 1 Tim 1:18, Paul expresses himself as guided by prophecy in relation to the separation of Timothy for the Christian ministry. These was possibly a specific revelation of God to Paul concerning the usefulness of Timothy. Others consider it to have been the formal declaration of Timothy as a minister and the sober charge of duty laid upon him by the presbytery. In 1 Tim 4:14, prophecy is presented as the vehicle through which the spiritual gift was formally imparted at Timothy's ordination. Certainly, Timothy's ministerial gift was present and developing in him before this time. However, the word of the church affords a formal and official recognition to Timothy as genuinely gifted and called to ministry. In 1 Cor 14:3 Paul mentions three functions of the prophet: "He that prophesieth speaketh unto men to edification, and exhortation, and comfort." In other words, he builds up the Christian's character, speaks moral precepts and warnings, and gives the encouragement arising from personal testimony, example and sympathy. "He . . . edifieth the church," while "He that speaketh in an unknown tongue edifieth himself."

(XI) In Rom 12:6 by the use of the phrase "according to the proportion [*analogía* {356}] of faith," the apostle declares that a prophecy is required to agree with the accepted doctrines of the faith; while in 1 Cor 12:10 "discernings of spirits [*diakríseis pneumátōn* {1253}]," shows that the gift of prophecy was a regular practice (1 Cor 14:29). The rule of edification is central in the rules laid down in 1 Cor 14:26ff. for prophetic and other utterances. Two or three prophets may speak, while the rest are to evaluate their addresses; but if a "revelation" be given to another sitting by, the first prophet must keep silent. "Ye may all prophesy one by one, that all may learn, and all may be comforted. And the spirits of the prophets are subject to the prophets" (14:31, 32), which means that although individual inspirations are legitimate and undoubted, they are subject to the control of the prophets collectively. Thus Paul did not limit freedom of speech, but in urging that only two or three prophets should address a given meeting, he aimed at securing not only spiritual edification, but reverence and order in the assembly.

Syn.: *apokálupsis* (602), revelation.

4395. προφητεύω *prophēteúō*; fut. *prophēteúsō*, from *prophḗtēs* (4396), prophet. To prophesy.

(I) To foretell things to come (Matt 11:13; 15:7; Mark 7:6; 1 Pet 1:10; Jude 1:14); to declare truths through the inspiration of God's Holy Spirit whether by prediction or otherwise (Luke 1:67; Acts 2:17, 18; 19:6; 21:9; 1 Cor 14:1, 3–5; Rev 10:11; 11:3; Sept.: 1 Kgs 22:12, 18; Ezra 5:1; Jer 11:21; Joel 2:28). The foretelling or foreannouncing may be, and often is, the responsibility of the prophet, but is not the essence of that office.

(II) To tell forth God's message, hence the noun *prophḗtēs* (4396), prophet, is the proclaimer, one who speaks out the counsel of God with the clearness, energy, and authority which spring from the consciousness of speaking in God's name and having received a direct message from Him to deliver. Thus one may prophesy without being a prophet in the strict sense of the word. A *prophḗtēs*, both in the OT and NT, is not primarily one who foretells things to come, but who (having been taught of God) speaks out His will (Deut 18:18; Isa chap. 1; Jer chap. 1; Ezek chap. 2; 1 Cor 14:3). The art of heathen divination, however, uses the word *manteúomai* (3132), to soothsay, divine.

(III) Used once of the high priest, with whose office the gift of prophecy was connected (John 11:51).

(IV) As including the idea of praise to God accompanied by prediction (Luke 1:67; Sept.: 1 Sam 10:5, 6, 11; 19:20, 21).

(V) Of false prophets (Matt 7:22; Sept.: Jer 14:14, 15).

(VI) Of mockery by the soldiers guarding Jesus, meaning to divine, guess, give a response, with the dat. (Matt 26:68; Mark 14:65; Luke 22:64).

(VII) Specifically of the prophetic gift or *chárisma* (5486), charisma, imparted by the Holy Spirit to the early Christians (Acts 19:6; 21:9; 1 Cor 11:4, 5; 13:9; 14:1, 3–5, 24, 31, 39).

Deriv.: *prophēteía* (4394), a prophecy.

Syn.: *apokalúptō* (601), to reveal; *prolégō* (4302), to foretell.

4396. προφήτης *prophḗtēs*; gen. *prophḗtou*, masc. noun from *próphēmi* (n.f.), to tell beforehand, which is from *pró* (4253), before or forth, and *phēmí* (5346), to tell. A prophet, a foreteller of future events, also an interpreter, what the Greeks called *ho mántis* (n.f.), the one who received the oracle. In the NT *prophḗtēs* corresponds to the person who in the OT spoke under divine influence and inspiration. This included the foretelling future events or the exhorting, reproving, and threatening of individuals or nations as the ambassador of God and the interpreter of His will to men (Ezek 2). Hence the prophet spoke not his own thoughts but what he received from God, retaining, however, his own consciousness and self-possession (Ex 7:1; 2 Pet 1:20, 21; especially 1 Cor 14:32). In a general sense, *prophḗtēs* is used for any friend of God to whom He makes known His will, such as Abraham (Sept.: Gen 20:7) and the patriarchs (Sept.: Ps 105:15).

(I) In the NT as spoken of the prophets of the OT:

(A) Particularly of Isaiah (Matt 1:22; 3:3; Luke 3:4; John 1:23); Jeremiah (Matt 2:17; 27:9); Joel (Acts 2:16); Micah (Matt 2:5); Jonah (Matt 12:39; Luke 11:29); Zechariah (Matt 21:4); Daniel (Matt 24:15; Mark 13:14); Samuel (Acts 13:20); David (Acts 2:30); Elisha (Luke 4:27); Asaph (Matt 13:35); Balaam (2 Pet 2:16 [cf. Num chap. 22]). In the pl. and generally (Matt 2:23; 5:12; 23:29ff.; Mark 8:28; Luke 1:70; Rom 1:2; Heb 1:1; James 5:10; 1 Pet 1:10; Sept.: 1 Kgs 16:7, 12; Isa 38:1; Jer 1:5).

(B) Metonymically of the prophetic books of the OT (Matt 26:56); generally (Matt 5:17; Mark 1:2; Luke 16:29, 31; 24:27, 44; Acts 8:28; 28:23; Rom 3:21); of the doctrines contained in the prophetic books (Matt 7:12; 22:40; Acts 26:27 where the expression *ho nómos kaí hoi prophḗtai* [*nómos* {3551}, law] comprises the whole OT and the term *prophḗtai* therefore includes the Psalms, which elsewhere are differentiated from the prophetic writings [Luke 24:44]).

(II) Generally of persons acting by divine influence as prophets and ambassadors of God under the new dispensation, equivalent to a teacher sent from God (Matt 10:41; 13:57; Mark 6:4; Luke 4:24; 13:33; John 7:52; Rev 11:10; 16:6; 18:20, 24); specifically of John the Baptist (Matt 11:9; 14:5; Mark 11:32; Luke 1:76; 20:6); of Jesus (Matt 21:11, 46; Luke 7:16; 24:19; John 9:17); the Messiah as a prophet coming into the world (John 1:21, 25; 6:14 in allusion to Deut 18:15; John 7:40; Acts 3:22, 23; 7:37).

(III) Specifically of those who possessed the prophetic gift or charisma imparted by the Holy Spirit to the primitive churches. Prophets were a class of instructors or preachers who were next in rank to the Apostles and before the teachers (1 Cor 12:28). Like the Apostles, however, they did not remain in one place as the teachers did. They seem to have differed from the teachers in that while the latter spoke in a calm, connected, didactic discourse, adapted to instruct and enlighten the hearers, the prophets spoke more from the impulse of sudden inspiration, from the light of a sudden revelation at the moment, as indicated in 1 Cor 14:30. It seems that this discourse was probably more adapted by means of powerful exhortations to awaken the feeling and consciousness of the hearers. The idea of speaking from an immediate revelation seems here to be fundamental, as relating either to future events or to the mind of the Spirit in general (cf. Acts 11:27; see 13:1; 1 Cor 12:28, 29; 14:29, 32, 37; Eph 2:20; 3:5; 4:11).

(IV) Perhaps it also referred to a Greek poet, as thought by Chrysostom, Theophylact, Epiphanius, and Jerome to be Epimenides (Titus 1:12). It is to be remembered that poets were held to be inspired. Epimenides may have been called *prophḗtēs* by Paul because he was reckoned among the seven wise men of Greece and was sent by the lawgiver Solon to aid in the preparation of his laws. Epimenides was especially considered a god-lover and wise concerning divine things (Plutarch, Solon 12). The term means a so-called prophet. It would be folly to infer from this that the early church recognized such persons as actual prophets of God. In fact, Paul is careful to call him "their own prophet" (a.t.). In this connection, Miriam is spoken of as a *prophḗtis* (4398), a prophetess (Ex 15:20).

(V) The word was used of soothsayers who announced beforehand the will of the gods with reference to the future. However, this is only a secondary and derived sense. The significance of *pró* must not be regarded as temporal, but as local, referring to position. It is one who speaks openly before others and is the technical name for an interpreter of an oracle or divine message. This meaning was never lost in Class. Gr. because the gods were considered to be knowledgeable of the future. This technical term came also to mean the interpreters of the future. In the OT, a prophet was one to whom and through whom God spoke (Gen 20:7, 8, 17, 18; Num 12:2 [cf. 12:6]); made known His mysteries (Amos 3:7, 8); and generally, revealed His purposes. That prediction of the future, while belonging to the subject matter of prophecy, did not form part of the true concept and is especially plain from the promise given in Deut 18:15, 18–20 (cf. Num 12:8). The earlier name of a prophet ("seer") indicated foretelling in Hebr. (1 Sam 9:9). It is clear that what really made one a prophet was immediate communion with God and a divine communication by the prophet of God's declaration. This is confirmed by the two terms, "reveal [*apokalúptomai* {601}] myself" (a.t.) and "prophesy" in 1 Cor 14:30, 31. See 1 Pet 1:12; Eph 3:5. That the special element of prophesying was not merely predictions but a showing forth of God's will, especially of His saving purpose, is confirmed by 1 Cor 14:37. Two things are combined to make the prophet: an insight granted by God into the divine secrets or mysteries, and a communication to others of these secrets. It includes the concept of divine grace, but with the warnings, announcements of judgment, and so forth, pertaining thereto. In the case of the OT, the prophets' preaching was a foretelling of the salvation yet to be accomplished. In the NT, prophecy was a publication of the salvation already accomplished, insofar as it did not concern itself with realities still future.

(VI) In Eph 2:20; 3:5, the prophets, named side by side with the Apostles (meaning the Eleven and those who were commissioned by Jesus directly) as the foundation of the NT church, are to be understood as exclusively NT prophets. They are listed in Eph 4:11 between apostles and evangelists (see 1 Cor 12:28). NT prophets were for the Christian church what OT prophets were for Israel. They maintained intact the immediate connection between the church and the God of their salvation. They were messengers or communicators. Such prophets were not ordained in local churches nor do they have successors.

(VII) The office of a prophet should not be confused with prophecy or the gift of prophecy which pertains to all believers (1 Cor 13:8; 14:3; 1 Tim 1:18; 4:14; Rev 11:6). Hence, the significant admonition in 1 Thess 5:20, "Despise not prophesyings." One thing must be remembered, namely, that he who prophesies is not necessarily a prophet in the OT or NT sense of a restricted office.

Deriv.: *prophēteúō* (4395), to prophesy; *prophētikós* (4397), prophetic; *pseudoprophḗtēs* (5578), a false prophet.

Ant.: *pseudoprophḗtēs* (5578), a false prophet.

4397. προφητικός *prophētikós*; fem. *prophētikḗ*, neut. *prophētikón*, adj. from *prophḗtēs* (4396), a prophet. Prophetic, uttered by prophets (Rom 16:26; 2 Pet 1:19).

4398. προφῆτις *prophḗtis*; gen. *prophḗtidos*, fem. noun from *próphēmi* (n.f.), to tell beforehand, which is from *pró* (4253),

before or forth, and *phēmí* (5346), to tell. A prophetess. In the Gr. sense, the interpreter or priestess of a god, oracle. In the Sept. and NT:

(I) Particularly, as speaking and acting (ostensibly) from a divine influence (Rev 2:20; Sept. Judg 4:4; 2 Kgs 22:14; 2 Chr 34:22).

(II) Spoken of a female friend of God, one who lives in communion with God and to whom God reveals Himself by His Spirit (Luke 2:36). In this manner Abraham is called *prophḗtēs*, a prophet. See Gen 20:7.

4399. προφθάνω *prophthánō*; fut. *prophthásō*, from *pró* (4253), before, and *phthánō* (5348), to come. To come or get before someone, to anticipate another in doing something or in speaking, with the acc. (Matt 17:25; Sept.: 2 Sam 22:19; Ps 17:13; 119:148).

4400. προχειρίζομαι *procheirízomai*; fut. *procheirísomai*, mid. deponent from *prócheiros* (n.f.), ready, at hand, which is from *pró* (4253), before, and *cheir* (5495), hand. To hand forth, to cause to be at hand, ready. In the NT figuratively to appoint, choose, destine, with the acc. and inf. (Acts 22:14); with the inf. implied (Acts 26:16). Perf. pass. *prokecheirisménos*, with the dat. (Sept.: Josh 3:12).

Syn.: *cheirotonéō* (5500), to ordain, select or appoint; *proginṓskō* (4267), to foreknow, to consider beforehand; *proorízō* (4309), to appoint or decree beforehand; *protássō* (4384), to appoint before; *proetoimázō* (4282), to prepare before.

4401. προχειροτονέω *procheirotonéō*; contracted *procheirotonō*, fut. *procheirotonḗsō*, from *pró* (4253), before, and *cheirotonéō* (5500), to choose, appoint. To choose beforehand or in advance (Acts 10:41, "forechosen" [a.t.]).

Syn.: *proorízō* (4309), to foreordain; *proginṓskō* (4267), to foreknow, to consider beforehand; *protássō* (4384), to appoint before; *proetoimázō* (4282), to prepare before.

4402. Πρόχορος *Próchoros*; gen. *Prochórou*, masc. proper noun. Prochorus, meaning leader of the chorus; one of the seven deacons (Acts 6:5).

4403. πρύμνα *prúmna*; gen. *prúmnēs*, fem. noun from *prumnós* (n.f.), extreme, last, hindermost, which is from *péras* (4009), extremity, end. The hindmost part of a ship, the stern (Mark 4:38; Acts 27:29, 41).
Ant.: *prṓra* (4408), bow, forward part of a vessel.

4404. πρωΐ *prōΐ*; adv. of time, from *pró* (4253), before. Early in the morning.
(I) Particularly and in an absolute sense (Matt 16:3; Mark 1:35; 11:20; 16:2, 9; John 20:1; Sept.: 1 Kgs 3:21; Isa 5:11). With the prep. *háma prōΐ* (*háma* [260], with, together with), very early, at dawn (Matt 20:1); *apó prōΐ* (*apó* [575], from), from morning (Acts 28:23); *epí tó prōΐ* (*epí* [1909], upon), in the morning (Mark 15:1).
(II) Metonymically the morning watch which ushers in the dawn (Mark 13:35).
Deriv.: *prōΐa* (4405), morning; *prṓïmos* (4406), pertaining to the morning; *prōïnós* (4407), early, at early morning.
Ant.: *opsé* (3796), late in the day, evening.

4405. πρωΐος *prṓïos*; fem. *prōΐa*, neut. *prṓïon*, adj. from *prōΐ* (4404), morning, early, daybreak. Early morning. In the NT, only subst. with the fem. def. art., *hē prōΐa*, with *hṓra* (5610), hour, the morning hour, morning (Matt 21:18; 27:1; John 18:28; 21:4; Sept.: 2 Sam 23:4).
Syn.: *augḗ* (827), the beginning of daylight, break of day; *anatolḗ* (395), dayspring; *órthros* (3722), daybreak, early in the morning.
Ant.: *hespéra* (2073), evening; *núx* (3571), night.

4406. πρώϊμος *prṓïmos*; fem. *prṓïme*, neut. *prṓïmon*, adj. from *prōΐ* (4404), daybreak, morning. Early, as spoken of the early rain (*huetós* [5205]; see James 5:7; Sept.: Deut 11:14; Jer 5:24).
Ant.: *ópsimos* (3797), later.

4407. πρωϊνός *prōïnós*; fem. *prōïnḗ*, neut. *prōïnón*, adj. from *prōΐ* (4404), early in the morning. Early morning (Rev 2:28, "the morning star"; 22:16 [UBS]; Sept.: Ex 29:41; 1 Sam 11:11; Hos 6:4).

4408. πρώρα *prṓra*; gen. *prṓras*, fem. noun from *pró* (4253), forward. The forward part of a ship, the bow (Acts 27:30, 41).
Ant.: *prúmna* (4403), the hindmost part of a ship, the stern.

4409. πρωτεύω *prōteúō*; fut. *prōteúsō*, from *prṓtos* (4413), first. To be first, chief, to hold the first rank, highest dignity (Col 1:18).
Deriv.: *philoprōteúō* (5383), to desire preeminence, to strive to be first.
Syn.: *hupsóō* (5312), to exalt; *huperupsóō* (5251), to highly exalt.

4410. πρωτοκαθεδρία *prōtokathedría*; gen. *prōtokathedrías*, fem. noun from *prṓtos* (4413), first, and *kathédra* (2515), seat. The first seat, chief seat (Matt 23:6; Mark 12:39; Luke 11:43; 20:46). Not found in Class. Gr.
Syn.: *prōtoklisía* (4411), the first reclining place, the head of the table; *huperochḗ* (5247), prominence.

4411. πρωτοκλισία *prōtoklisía*; gen. *prōtoklisías*, fem. noun from *prṓtos* (4413), first, and *klisía* (2828), a place to recline. The chief place at a banquet, usually the middle place on the middle triclinium where there is room for three (Matt 23:6; Mark 12:39; Luke 14:7, 8; 20:46).
Syn.: *prōtokathedría* (4410), a chief seat.

4412. πρῶτον *próton*; the neut. of *prótos* (4413), first. Used as an adv.

(I) Particularly of place, order, time, usually without the art.

(A) Generally (Matt 17:10, 11; Mark 7:27; Luke 9:59, 61; John 18:13; Acts 7:12, the first time; 15:14; 1 Cor 11:18; 1 Pet 4:17).

(B) Emphatically meaning first of all, before all (Matt 23:26; Acts 13:46; Rom 1:8; 1 Cor 11:18).

(C) In division or distribution, as referring to a series or succession of circumstances and followed by other adv. of order or time expressed or implied. Followed by *deúteron* (1208), second (1 Cor 12:28); *eíta* (1534), after that (Mark 4:28); *épeita* (1899), after that (1 Thess 4:16; James 3:17); *kaí tóte* (*kaí* [2532], and; *tóte* [5119], then), and then (Matt 5:24; 7:5; Mark 3:27; Luke 6:42). Similarly, *próton . . . kaí*, first and (Rom 1:16; 2:9, 10; 2 Cor 8:5).

(D) Rarely with the art. *tó próton*, the first, at first, formerly (John 10:40; 12:16; 19:39).

(II) Figuratively of dignity or importance, first, first of all, chiefly, especially (Matt 6:33; Rom 3:2; 1 Tim 2:1; 2 Pet 1:20; 3:3). See also the comp. *próteron* (4386), before, first.

Syn.: *en arché* (*en* [1722], in; *arché*, the dat. of *arché* [746], beginning), in the beginning; *émprosthen* (1715), in front of.

Ant.: *éschaton* (207), last, lowest; *hústeron* (5305), later, after, finally; *épeita* (1899), after that; *eíta* (1534), then in order of succession; *metá* (3326), with, expressing accompaniment; *sún* (4862), together with, expressing companionship or union; *deúteros* (1208), second.

4413. πρῶτος *prótos*; fem. *próte*, neut. *próton*, adj., the superlative of *pró* (4253), forward. Foremost, hence first, the first. The comparative is *próteros* (n.f.).

(I) Generally as an adj. spoken of place, order, time. Particularly and without the art. (Mark 16:9 implying *héméra* [2250],

day; Luke 2:2; 1 Cor 15:3, first of all; Eph 6:2; Phil 1:5). Followed by *deúteros* (1208), second (Acts 12:10; Sept.: Gen 33:2, with *en* [1722] in, among, and the pl., *en prótois*, among the first ones, foremost; Ex 12:15); with the art. (Matt 26:17, referring to *héméra*, day; Mark 14:12 [cf. Sept.: Lev 23:35, 40]; Acts 1:1; 1 Cor 15:45; Heb 9:2, 6, 8; Rev 1:17; 4:1, 7; 8:7). With the art. and the pl., *hoi prótoi*, the first (Matt 20:8, 10; 21:36); in the pl. neut. *tá próta*, the first things, meaning the former state or condition (Matt 12:45; 2 Pet 2:20; Rev 21:4). In 1 Tim 5:12 the first faith means the faith originally professed. In Rev 2:4 referring to love meaning the love first demonstrated (see 2:5). In this respect *prótos* stands in direct opposition to *kainós* (2537), qualitatively new (Heb 8:13; Rev 21:1; Sept.: 2 Chr 3:3; Dan 8:21; 2 Sam 18:27). In division or distribution, *ho prótos . . . ho deúteros* ([1208], second), the first . . . the second (Matt 22:25); *ho prótos . . . ho héteros* ([2087], the other, qualitatively different), the first . . . the other (Luke 14:18; 19:16). Where only two are spoken of (Matt 21:28; John 19:32; Heb 8:7).

(II) In an adv. sense (Matt 10:2; John 1:41; 8:7; Acts 26:23; Rom 10:19; 1 John 4:19). Used for the comparative *próteros*, adv. followed by the gen. (John 1:15, 30).

(III) Figuratively of rank, dignity, meaning first, chief, so without the art. (Matt 20:27; 22:38; Mark 12:30; Acts 16:12; Eph 6:2). Followed by the gen. partitive (Mark 10:44; 12:28–30; 1 Tim 1:15); with the art. (Luke 15:22; Acts 17:4). Thus *ho prótos*, pl. *hoi prótoi*, the first, the chief, followed by the gen., of a country or people (Mark 6:21; Luke 19:47; Acts 13:50; 25:2; 28:7, 17; Sept.: Neh 12:46). In the proverbial phrase: *polloí ésontai prótoi, éschatoi; kaí éschatoi, prótoi* (*polloí*, the masc. pl. of *polús* [4183], many; *ésontai*, fut. indic. of *eimí* [1510], to be, meaning will be; *prótoi*, first; *éschatoi* [2078], last), "the first shall be last, and the last first", meaning those who seem or claim to be first shall be last (Matt 19:30; 20:16; Mark 10:31; Luke 13:30).

Deriv.: *deuteróprōtos* (1207), the second-first; *prōteúō* (4409), to be first; *prōtokathedría* (4410), the first seat or the best seat; *prōtoklisía* (4411), the first place; *prṓton* (4412), first, at first; *prōtostátēs* (4414), a leader or captain; *prōtótokos* (4416), firstborn, chief in rank, heir.

Syn.: *archḗ* (746), beginning.

Ant.: *éschatos* (2078), last.

4414. πρωτοστάτης *prōtostátēs*; gen. *prōtostátou*, masc. noun from *prṓtos* (4413), first, and *hístēmi* (2476), to stand. One who stands first, a leader or captain (Sept.: Job 15:24). The word was used in secular Gr. to designate the highest ranking military officer. In the NT, a leader, ringleader (Acts 24:5).

Syn.: *hodēgós* (3595), a leader; *hēgemṓn* (2232), a leader, ruler.

Ant.: *idiṓtēs* (2399), a private person; *polítēs* (4177), a citizen.

4415. πρωτοτόκια *prōtotókia*; gen. *prōtotokíōn*, neut. pl. noun from *prōtótokos* (4416), firstborn. The rights of the firstborn, birthright (Heb 12:16; Sept.: Gen 25:32–34). Sometimes *prōtotókeia*. The birthright among the ancient patriarchal Hebrews conferred upon the eldest son the right of religious leadership (acting as the so-called priest of the family) and promised a double portion of the father's estate (Deut 21:17) which indicated his authority over the his younger siblings. Thus the firstborn was not only a type of Christ as the Firstborn and High Priest of God, but also a type of Christians as the firstborn who are written in heaven and are partakers of the eternal inheritance (cf. Heb 12:23). Slighting the birthright was both slighting the high honor of officiating in God's name, and despising that eternal inheritance which was typified by the double portion.

Syn.: *klēronomía* (2817), inheritance.

4416. πρωτότοκος *prōtótokos*; gen. *prōtotókou*, masc. noun from *prṓtos* (4413), first, and *tíktō* (5088), to bear, bring forth. Firstborn, preeminent.

(I) Particularly the firstborn of a mother (Matt 1:25; Luke 2:7). It also includes the firstborn of animals (Sept.: Gen 27:19, 32; Ex 12:12, 29).

(II) Of the saints in heaven, probably those formerly highly distinguished on earth by the favor and love of God, such as patriarchs, prophets, apostles (Heb 12:23; Sept.: of Israel, Ex 4:22).

(III) *Prōtótokos* is applied to Christ in Luke 2:7, "And she brought forth her firstborn son." Here the word carries none of the theological load which it bears elsewhere when used of Christ. Jesus is simply identified as the first child born to Mary. To be sure, this was no ordinary birth. As the Scripture records Mary's conception was wrought by the Holy Spirit and God Himself was the Father of this child (Luke 1:26–35). So in this text the word is quite ordinary and means simply firstborn.

(IV) *Prōtótokos* is a theologically significant title used of Christ in five NT passages.

(A) Rom 8:29, "For whom he did foreknow, he also did predestinate to be conformed to the image of his Son, that he might be the firstborn among many brethren." The predetermined goal of salvation for those whom God foreknew is stated to be conformity (*súmmorphos* [4832]) to the image (*eikṓn* [1504]) of God's Son. The stated purpose of this task is that the Son might be (*eis tó eínai* [*eis* {1519}, unto, for; *tó* {3588}, the; *eínai* {1511}, to be], in order to be) the firstborn among many brothers. *Prōtótokos* presents Christ as the preeminent or ranking member of the group. Interpreters have viewed the emphasis as falling upon either the phrase "among many brothers" or the word "firstborn." If the former, then the upshot of Paul's words is that God predestined the elect to glory so that they might share in the inheritance allotted to Christ as God's Son. That is, God desired to include with

Christ a host of other but lesser heirs, brothers among whom Christ would stand as preeminent. However, this misses the point of the passage which stresses not the number of the elect but the astonishing goal of their salvation—conformity to the very image of the Son Himself. The latter emphasis seems most fitting. The conformity of sinners into the glorious image of God's Son places Christ in a position of preeminence and glory among them. The ultimate goal of salvation, the glory of God, is thus achieved. Yet, some find it is difficult to understand how the conformity of God's elect would serve to bring about Christ's position as firstborn. How is it that the salvation of sinners makes Christ the firstborn? Is He not so upon His own merit and in consideration of His own character? It can be replied that the effect in view is not one that has reference to Christ Himself or the Father's estimation of Him. Rather, the effect has reference to Christ before man. God's design in original creation was to reflect His glory in man and the world. The fall of Adam defaced the *imago Dei* and consequently God's preeminence among humanity was lost. Salvation is the restoration of man to His original purpose. Therefore, since the salvation of sinners restores the divine image in man, Christ cannot but be exalted and made preeminent among them.

(B) The word *prōtótokos* is also used in relation to God's creation referring to Christ's supremacy over it. Jesus Christ cannot be both creator and creature. In Col 1:15 He is placed above His creation when He is called *prōtótokos pásēs ktíseōs* (*pásēs*, gen. fem. of *pás* [3956], every; *ktíseōs*, gen. of *ktísis* [2937], creation or creature), "the firstborn of every creature," or better still, "the one preeminent over all creation" (a.t.). The next verse makes it adequately clear, "For by him were all things created," meaning that He Himself is not part of creation (cf. John 1:3). The meaning approximates that of the noun *archē* (746), beginning, which means either objectively the first effect, the first created thing, or subjectively

the first cause, the source of creation. In Rev 3:14 the noun *archē* in the phrase *hē archē tēs ktíseōs toú Theoú* is intended to identify Jesus as the first cause or source of creation and not as the first object of creation. Jesus Christ is consequently the *archē*, the ruler over all.

(C) In Col 1:18 we have the use of both *archē* and *prōtótokos* together in regard to the resurrection. "And he [Christ] is the head of the body, the church: who is the beginning [*archē*], the firstborn [*prōtótokos*] from the dead; that in all things he might have the preeminence." As stated II, B above, *archē* means the first cause. Hence, *archē* in the clause "who is the beginning [i.e., principle cause or originator]," is parallel to *prōtótokos* in the clause "firstborn of all creation" in 1:15. Both of these expressions assert Christ's supremacy and preeminence over creation. Why then does Paul add that Christ is the "firstborn from among the dead?" Is this not redundant? Not at all. While it should suffice to say that Christ is the firstborn of the entire universe without qualification (heaven / earth, visible / invisible), a question may arise regarding the order of things in the new creation, that is, those things cleansed of sin and renewed by redemption. Recall that the Colossian church was being threatened by incipient gnosticism. In an effort to explain the presence of sin in the universe, this movement taught that the material universe was created by a kind of lesser god and not the highest essence of deity. God was a *plērōma* (4138), a fullness, from whom a succession of lesser beings, called aeons, emanated. The spiritual purity of these beings diminished with each lower order of their existence. Finally, an aeon far enough removed from the origin (*archē*) of deity created the material universe. The gnostics taught that Christ was only one of these aeons. If Paul then says that Christ is the creator of such a universe, some might therefore believe that surely He could not sustain any relation to the new creation. So Paul must say that Christ is supreme in redemption as well as in creation. All this is so that Christ might have "preeminence," the pres. part. *prōteúōn* from *prōteúō* (4409), to be first, to have the preeminence. *Prōteúōn* is used only in Col 1:18 and indicates not an acquired right to be ruler, preeminent, but an inherent right by virtue of His nature, He, being the creator, deserves to have the preeminence. "All things were made by him; and without him was not any thing made that was made" (John 1:3). The pres. tense indicates permanence and perpetuity. He is always preeminent.

(D) In Heb 1:6 we have another reference to Christ as *prōtótokos*, "And again, when he bringeth in the first begotten into the world, he saith, And let all the angels of God worship him." In this verse and Rev 1:5 (KJV) *prōtótokos* is translated "first begotten." Heb 1:6 refers to the Second Coming of the Lord Jesus into the inhabited world (*oikouménē* [3563]). As angels were present at His ascension so will they be at His return and must worship Him then. Christ's preeminence is cosmic. He is exalted over even the highest order of celestial creatures.

(E) The last verse where *prōtótokos* is used of Christ is Rev 1:5 and it follows the idea of Colossians 1:18 discussed IV, C.

Deriv.: *prōtotókia* (4415), the rights of the firstborn.

4417. πταίω *ptaíō*; fut. *ptaísō*. To stumble, fall (Sept.: 1 Sam 4:2; 2 Sam 18:7). In the NT, used figuratively, meaning to fall into sin.

(I) To err, offend, fail in duty, with *en* (1722), followed by a dat. (James 2:10; 3:2). Used in an absolute sense (Rom 11:11; James 3:2; Sept.: Deut 7:25).

(II) To fail, of success and happiness (2 Pet 1:10).

Deriv.: *áptaistos* (679), without stumbling.

Syn.: *husteréō* (5302), to fall short; *parabaínō* (3845), to transgress; *skandalízō* (4624), to offend; *hamartánō* (264), to sin; *proskóptō* (4350), to stumble against.

Ant.: *orthopodéō* (3716), to walk in a straight line, to act uprightly; *stoichéō* (4748), to walk orderly.

4418. πτέρνα *ptérna*; gen. *ptérnēs*, fem. noun. Heel. The expression *epeíren ep' emé tēn ptérnan* (*epeíren*, aor. of *epaírō* [1869], to lift up; *epí* [1909], against; *emé* [1691], me), he "lifted up his heel against me" (John 13:18 quoted from Ps 41:10; see Sept.: Gen 3:15; 25:26).

4419. πτερύγιον *pterúgion*; gen. *pterugíou*, neut. noun, the diminutive of *ptérux* (4420), a wing. A little wing (Sept.: 1 Kgs 6:22), and also the feather of an arrow. Anything shaped like a wing, running out to a point, a fin (Sept.: Lev 11:9, 10, 12); the corner or skirt of a garment (Sept.: Num 15:38; 1 Sam 24:5). In the NT, a pinnacle, spoken of the highest point of the temple, probably the apex of Solomon's porch (Matt 4:5; Luke 4:9).

4420. πτέρυξ *ptérux*; gen. *ptérugos*, fem. noun from *pterón* (n.f.), a feather. A wing (Matt 23:37; Luke 13:34; Rev 4:8; 9:9; 12:14; Sept.: Ex 19:4; Ps 55:7; Ezek 1:6). Diminutive, *pterúgion* (4419), a pinnacle.

4421. πτηνός *ptēnós*; fem. *ptēnḗ*, neut. *ptēnón*, adj. from *pétomai* (4072), to fly. Flying, winged. In the NT, as a subst. in the neut. pl. *tá ptēná*, birds, fowls (1 Cor 15:39).

Syn.: *órneon* (3732), fowl; *órnis* (3733), a hen; *peteinón* (4071), a bird.

4422. πτοέω *ptoéō*; contracted *ptoṓ*, fut. *ptoḗsō*. To terrify, frighten, scare. In the pass., to be terrified (Luke 21:9; 24:37; Sept.: Ex 19:16; Jer 1:17).

Deriv.: *ptóēsis* (4423), amazement.

Syn.: *ekphobéō* (1629), to frighten away; *ptúrō* (4426), to scare; *phríssō* (5425), to bristle, shudder, tremble; *trémō* (5141), to dread, be afraid, tremble; *phobéō* (5399), to fear.

Ant.: *tharséō* (2293), to have courage; *tharréō* (2292), to exercise courage, be bold; *tolmáō* (5111), to be daring, bold; *apotolmáō* (662), to venture, be very bold; *andrízomai* (407), to be manly.

4423. πτόησις *ptóēsis*; gen. *ptoéseōs*, fem. noun from *ptoéō* (4422), to frighten. Terror, trepidation, fear (1 Pet 3:6, "well, and are not afraid"; Sept.: Prov 3:25).
Syn.: *phóbos* (5401), fear; *trómos* (5156), trembling; *deilía* (1167), fearfulness, cowardice; *kíndunos* (2794), danger, peril; *phóbētron* (5400), a frightening thing, fearful sight; *apeilé* (547), menace.

4424. Πτολεμαΐς *Ptolemaΐs*; gen. *Ptolemaΐdos*, fem. proper noun. Ptolemais, a city named after one of the Ptolemies of Egypt; called Accho in Jewish annals, and Ptolemais under the rule of the Romans and Macedonians. It is often mentioned in the Apocrypha. Paul, on returning from his third missionary journey, visited Ptolemais and stayed there one day (Acts 21:7). The place is now called Akka or Accho.

4425. πτύον *ptúon*; gen. *ptúou*, neut. noun from *ptúō* (4429), to spit. A fan or winnowing shovel with which grain is thrown up against the wind in order to cleanse it and separate it from the chaff (Matt 3:12; Luke 3:17).

4426. πτύρω *ptúrō*; fut. *pturṓ*. To frighten, terrify. In the pass. (Phil 1:28).
Syn.: *ptoéō* (4422), to frighten; *ekphobéō* (1629), to frighten away; *ekthambéō* (1568), to throw into terror; *phríssō* (5425), to bristle, shudder, tremble; *trémō* (5141), to tremble; *phobéō* (5399), to fear.
Ant.: *tharséō* (2293), to have courage; *tharréō* (2292), to exercise courage, be bold; *tolmáō* (5111), to be daring, bold; *apotolmáō* (662), to venture, be very bold; *andrízomai* (407), to be manly.

4427. πτύσμα *ptúsma*; gen. *ptúsmatos*, neut. noun from *ptúō* (4429), to spit. Spittle (John 9:6).

4428. πτύσσω *ptússō*; fut. *ptúxō*. To fold or roll together, such as a book (Luke 4:20).
Deriv.: *anaptússō* (380), to unfold.
Syn.: *helíssō* (1667), to roll up a scroll or a mantle; *entulíssō* (1794), to wrap or roll up; *sustéllō* (4958), to wrap or wind up, shorten.
Ant.: *anaptússō* (380), to open up; *apokulíō* or *apokulízō* (617), to roll away; *anoígō* (455), to open.

4429. πτύω *ptúō*; fut. *ptúsō*. To spit, from the sound that is formed by the lips when one spits (Mark 7:33; 8:23; John 9:6; Sept.: Num 12:14).
Deriv.: *ekptúō* (1609), to spit out, reject; *emptúō* (1716), to spit upon; *ptúon* (4425), a fan or winnowing shovel; *ptúsma* (4427), spittle.

4430. πτῶμα *ptṓma*; gen. *ptṓmatos*, neut. noun from *píptō* (4098), to fall. A dead body fallen to the ground, a corpse, carcass (Sept.: Job 18:12). In the Class. Gr. it figuratively referred to anything fallen, as the ruins of a wall or building. In the NT, a body fallen, a dead body, corpse (Matt 24:28; Mark 6:29; Rev 11:8, 9).

4431. πτῶσις *ptṓsis*; gen. *ptṓseōs*, fem. noun from *píptō* (4098), to fall. A fall, downfall, crash as of a falling building (Matt 7:27). Figuratively a downfall, ruin (Luke 2:34, meaning a cause of fall and ruin).
Ant.: *anástasis* (386), resurrection; *égersis* (1454), resurgence, resurrection.

4432. πτωχεία *ptōcheía*; gen. *ptōcheías*, fem. noun from *ptōchós* (4434), poor and helpless. Poverty, want, helplessness (2 Cor 8:2, 9; Rev 2:9; Sept.: Deut 8:9; 1 Chr 22:14). The adj. *ptōchós* (4434), indicates complete helplessness (in contrast to *pénēs* [3993], which means poor but capable of providing for oneself). There-fore, *ptōchós* is sometimes translated "beggar" because of the helplessness of the individual, begging being the only means of survival.

Syn.: *aporía* (640), lack of means, state of quandary.

Ant.: *ploútos* (4149), material riches; *chrḗma* (5536), riches, money; *argúrion* (694), silver, a metaphor for wealth; *chalkós* (5475), copper, a metaphor for wealth; *mammōnás* (3126), wealth, the god of money, mammon; *euporía* (2142), having means, pecuniary resources, wealth; *hupárchonta* (5224), possessions; *bíos* (979), the means of livelihood; *thēsaurós* (2344), wealth, treasure; *chrusós* (5557), gold.

4433. πτωχεύω *ptōcheúō*; fut. *ptōcheúsō*, from *ptōchós* (4434), poor and helpless. To be or become poor, helpless, and therefore to beg. Used intrans. (2 Cor 8:9 [cf. Phil 2:7]; Sept.: Ps 34:11; 79:8).

Syn.: *aporéō* (639), to have no way out, no means; *epaitéō* (1871), to beg.

Ant.: *euporéō* (2141), to have pecuniary means, be well off; *ploutéō* (4147), to be rich.

4434. πτωχός *ptōchós*, fem. *ptōchḗ*, neut. *ptōchón*, adj. from *ptōssō* (n.f.), to crouch, cower like a beggar. Poor and helpless. As a subst., someone in abject poverty, utter helplessness, complete destitution.

(I) Particularly and often as subst:

(A) With the art. *ho ptōchós*, a poor, helpless man and therefore a beggar (Luke 14:13, 21; 16:20, 22; John 9:8, in some editions). Figuratively (Rev 3:17).

(B) In the pl. with the art., *hoi ptōchoí*, the poor, meaning the needy, those destitute of the necessities of life and subsisting on the alms from others (Matt 19:21; 26:9, 11; Mark 10:21; 14:5, 7; Luke 18:22; 19:8; John 12:5, 6, 8; 13:29; Sept.: Esth 9:22; Prov 28:27; 31:20). Of those who voluntarily become poor for the Son of man's sake (Luke 6:20 [cf. 6:22]).

(C) Generally, poor, needy, contrasted with *pénēs* (3993), one who may be poor but earns his bread by daily labor; also spoken of honest poverty without the idea of begging as opposed to the rich (Mark 12:42, 43; Luke 21:3; Rom 15:26;

2 Cor 6:10; Gal 2:10; James 2:2, 3, 5, 6; Rev 13:16; Sept.: Lev 19:15; Prov 22:7; 29:14).

(II) By implication, poor, low, humble, of low estate, including also the idea of being afflicted, distressed (Matt 11:5; Luke 4:18 quoted from Isa 61:1; Sept.: Ps 69:33; 109:16; Isa 29:19). Figuratively in Matt 5:3, "poor in spirit" means those who recognize their spiritual helplessness.

(III) Figuratively, of things beggarly, poor, imperfect (Gal 4:9).

Deriv.: *ptōcheía* (4432), poverty, want, helplessness; *ptōcheúō* (4433), to be or become poor.

Syn.: *endeḗs* (1729), lacking, deficient; *talaípōros* (5005), miserable; *eleeinós* (1652), pitiful, miserable.

Ant.: *ploúsios* (4145), rich; *poluteḗs* (4185), costly, very precious, of great price; *perissós* (4053), superabundant.

4435. πυγμή *pugmḗ*; gen. *pugmḗs*, fem. noun from *púx* (n.f.), the fist doubled and used as a weapon. The fist (Sept.: Ex 21:18; Isa 58:4). In the NT (Mark 7:3), meaning "unless they wash their hands" (i.e., rubbing them with the fist, carefully and diligently); equal to *epimelōs* (1960), carefully, diligently (Luke 15:8). Also from *púx* (n.f.): *puknós* (4437), dense, solid.

Deriv.: *pukteúō* (4438), to box.

4436. Πύθων *Púthōn*; gen. *Púthōnos*, masc. proper noun. Python, the Gr. name given to the mythological serpent or dragon which lived at Pytho beneath Mount Parnassus and guarded the Delphic Oracle. The name then became the surname of Apollo, the god of divination in Greek mythology, and hence applied to all oracular and divinatory spirits. Such persons generally spoke with their mouth closed, uttering words considered beyond their own control, and so were also known as ventriloquists. Acts 16:16 speaks of Paul meeting and subsequently exorcising such a spirit of divination from a young woman at Philippi. Luke uses the word *manteuoménē* (pres. part. of *manteúomai*

[3132], to divine, soothsay, never used of true inspiration or prophetic utterance, only here in NT) to describe her oracular speech, which was obviously inspired by a demonic power.

4437. πυκνός *puknós*; fem. *puknḗ*, neut. *puknón*, adj. from *púx* (n.f.), fist. Dense, firm, solid, closely-packed. In the NT, frequent (1 Tim 5:23). In the neut. pl., *pukná*, as adv., frequently, often (Luke 5:33). The comparative *puknóteron*, oftener, which Strong includes here, is likewise used as an adv. (Acts 24:26). Also from *púx* (n.f.): *pugmḗ* (4435), the fist.
Syn.: *pollákis* (4178), oftentimes; *polús* (4183), much.

4438. πυκτεύω *pukteúō*; fut. *pukteúsō*, from *pugmḗ* (4435), the fist. To box. Intrans. (1 Cor 9:26).
Syn.: *agōnízomai* (75), to fight; *máchomai* (3164), to strive; *poleméō* (4170), to make war.
Ant.: *hēsucházō* (2270), to be quiet; *eirēneúō* (1514), to be or act peaceful; *aspázomai* (782), to embrace.

4439. πύλη *púlē*; gen. *púlēs*, fem. noun. A door, gate, the large door or entrance of an edifice, city. To be distinguished from *thúra* (2374), a common door. Used of the gate to the temple (Acts 3:10); the gate of a prison (Acts 12:10); the gate of a city (Luke 7:12; Acts 9:24; Heb 13:12; Sept.: Gen 34:20, 24; Josh 6:26; 2 Chr 8:5); the gate of a building, (Jer 43:9). Symbolically in Matt 7:13, 14; Luke 13:24. Figuratively the gates of *hádēs* ([86], hell) refers to the powers of Satan and his hosts as commanding *hádēs*, the realm of death, including both the grave and the place of departed spirits. Death and hell are the effect of sin. Man is under the power of hell because he is under the power of sin. Satan is the father of sin and the lord of hell. Those whom he holds under sin, he holds under death. The redeeming work of Christ overcame the power of sin and hence the power of Satan and hell (1 Cor 15:52–57; Col 2:15; Heb 2:14; 1 John

3:8; Rev 1:18). The Church is the company of the redeemed and as such cannot be overcome by all the powers of hell. *Shᵉōl* (7585, OT) is the Hebr. equivalent of *Hádēs* (Sept.: Isa 38:10 [cf. Ps 9:14]).
Deriv.: *pulṓn* (4440), a large door or gate.

4440. πυλών *pulṓn*; gen. *pulṓnos*, masc. noun from *púlē* (4439), gate. A large door or gate as at the entrance of a building or city.
(I) Generally of a house (Acts 10:17; 12:13, 14); of a city (Acts 14:13; Rev 21:12, 13, 15, 21, 25; 22:14; Sept.: 1 Kgs 17:10; 1 Chr 19:9). Used for a building (Sept.: 1 Kgs 14:27; 2 Chr 12:10).
(II) A gateway, portal, vestibule, the deep arch under which a gate opens (Matt 26:71; Luke 16:20; Sept.: Judg 18:16, 17).

4441. πυνθάνομαι *punthánomai*; fut. *peúsomai*, 2d aor. *eputhómēn*, mid. deponent. To ask, inquire.
(I) Particularly followed by *pará* (3844), from or of, and the gen. or the acc., from or of someone (Matt 2:4; John 4:52; Sept.: Gen 25:22). Used in an absolute sense with a direct interrogative (Acts 4:7; 10:29; 23:19); also before an interrogative with the opt. (Luke 15:26; 18:36; John 13:24; Acts 21:33). In a judicial sense, meaning to inquire or examine someone, followed by the acc. and *perí* (4012), concerning, with the gen. (Acts 23:20).
(II) To find out by inquiry, to learn, hear, followed by *hóti* (3754), that (Acts 23:34).
Syn.: *erōtáō* (2065), to ask, beseech; *exetázō* (1833), to search out; *anakrínō* (350), to examine; *diakrínō* (1252), to discern.

4442. πῦρ *púr*; gen. *purós*, neut. noun. Fire.
(I) Literal fire (Matt 3:10, 12; 7:19; 13:40; 17:15; Mark 9:22; Luke 3:9, 17; 22:55; John 15:6; Acts 28:5; Heb 11:34; James 3:5; 5:3; 1 Pet 1:7; Rev 3:18; 8:5,

"upon the altar" (a.t.), Rev 8:8; 9:17, 18; 11:5; 14:18; 15:2; 16:8; 17:16; 18:8; Sept.: Gen 22:6, 7; Ex 32:20). The gen. *purós* often takes the place of an adj. (Acts 7:30, "fiery flame" [a.t.]; Heb 1:7; Rev 1:14; 2:18; 19:12; Sept.: Isa 29:6). The words are sometimes reversed, that is, the fire of the flame (*en purí phlogós* [5395]), (2 Thess 1:8; Sept.: Ps 104:4). In Rom 12:20, *ánthrakas* ([440], coals) *purós*, burning coals is used. See also Sept.: Lev 16:12. In Acts 2:3, "tongues like as of fire"; Rev 4:5, "pillars of fire"; 10:1, "fiery pillars" (a.t. [cf. Sept.: Ex 13:21, 22]). Spoken of fire from heaven (Luke 9:54; 17:29; Rev 13:13; 20:9). Used in an absolute sense (Acts 2:19 quoted from Joel 2:30; 3:3; Heb 12:18; Rev 8:7).

(II) Used symbolically:

(A) Of God, as inflicting punishment (Heb 12:29 [cf. Deut 4:24]).

(B) Of disunion (Luke 12:49); of the tongue, as kindling strife and discord (James 3:6).

(C) Of evils, calamities, trials which purify the faith in hearts of Christians, as fire tries and purifies the precious metals (cf. Mark 9:49; 1 Pet 1:7; Rev 3:18; Sept.: Isa 10:17). In 1 Cor 3:10–15, the works of men are represented as a building of which only the inflammable parts ("gold, silver, precious stones") can withstand fire; the worker (builder) "himself shall be saved; yet so as by fire," means that he will escape from the fire which destroys those of his works which are "wood, hay, [and] stubble." Fire is used in a proverbial expression, "out of the fire," implying "with difficulty," "scarcely" (Jude 1:23).

(D) Of the eternal fire, the place of punishment and abode of demons and the souls of wicked men in Hades, represented under various images, a fiery furnace (Matt 13:42, 50 [cf. Dan 3:6, 11, 15]); the Gehenna of fire (Matt 5:22; 18:9; Mark 9:47 [cf. Isa 66:24, the fire {which} is not quenched]); the fire, the eternal one (*tó púr tó aiōnion*) (Matt 18:8; 25:41; Jude 1:7); the lake of fire (Rev 19:20; 20:10, 14, 15; 21:8); simply, fire (Rev 14:10). Because fire is a frequent apocalyptic figure for divine judgment, one need not imagine that the flames spoken of in reference to hell are material. Undoubtedly fire signifies a horrible, painful and real judgment. Still, its symbolic usage in Scripture must be taken into account when interpreting these passages. Also, the fire associated with the baptism in the Holy Spirit is considered by many to be eschatological, alluding to the final judgment of the wicked in contrast to the baptism and gift of the Spirit given to the righteous (Matt 3:11; Luke 3:16).

(III) Figuratively, ardor, vehemence (Heb 10:27).

Deriv.: *purá* (4443), a fire; *puretós* (4446), fever; *púrinos* (4447), fiery; verb *puróō* (4448), to be on fire; *purrós* (4450), fiery-red.

Syn.: *phlóx* (5395), flame.

4443. πυρά *purá*; gen. *purás*, fem. noun from *púr* (4442), fire. A fire kindled and burning, burning fuel (Acts 28:2, 3).

Syn.: *anthrakiá* (439), burning coals.

4444. πύργος *púrgos*; gen. *púrgou*, masc. noun. A tower.

(I) Particularly for defense as in the wall of a city (Luke 13:4, meaning in the wall of the city near Siloam; Sept.: Judg 9:46). Spoken of the watchtower or turret of the vineyard (Matt 21:33; Mark 12:1; Sept.: Isa 5:2).

(II) Metonymically of any building with one or more towers, a castle, fortress, palace (Luke 14:28).

4445. πυρέσσω *puréssō*, πυρέττω *puréttō*; fut. *puréxō*, from *puretós* (4446), fire. To be feverish, sick of fever, intrans. (Matt 8:14; Mark 1:30).

4446. πυρετός *puretós*; gen. *puretoú*, masc. noun from *púr* (4442), fire. Fiery heat, fever (Matt 8:15; Mark 1:31; Luke 4:38, 39; John 4:52; Acts 28:8; Sept.: Deut 28:22).

Deriv.: *puréssō* (4445), to be feverish, sick.

4447. πύρινος *púrinos*; fem. *puríne*, neut. *púrinon*, adj. from *púr* (4442), adj. Fiery, burning (Sept.: Ezek 28:14, 16). In the NT by implication flaming, glittering (Rev 9:17).

4448. πυρόω *puróō*; contracted *puró*, fut. *purósō*, from *púr* (4442), fire. To ignite, set on fire. In the NT only in the pass. *puróomai* or *puroúmai*, to be ignited or set on fire, kindled, to burn, flame.
(I) Particularly in Eph 6:16, "the fiery darts"; 2 Pet 3:12, "the heavens being on fire"; Rev 1:15. Figuratively, to burn, be inflamed as with anger, to be incensed (2 Cor 11:29); with lust (1 Cor 7:9).
(II) By implication, to be tried with fire, purified as metals (Rev 3:18; Sept.: Ps 11:7; Prov 10:20).
Deriv.: *púrōsis* (4451), burning, fiery.
Syn.: *kaíō* (2545), to set on fire, to burn; *katakaíō* (2618), to burn completely; *ekkaíō* (1572), to burn out; *emprḗthō* (1714), to burn up; *phlogízō* (5394), to burn up.
Ant.: *sbénnumi* (4570), to put out, extinguish fire.

4449. πυρράζω *purrázō*; fut. *purrásō*, from *purrós* (4450), fiery-red. To be flame-colored, fiery red, used intrans. (Matt 16:2 of the sky (cf. 16:3]).

4450. πυρρός *purrós*; fem. *purrá*, neut. *purrón*, adj. from *púr* (4442), fire. Flame-colored, fiery red (Rev 6:4; 12:3; Sept.: Num 19:2; Zech 1:8).
Deriv.: *purrázō* (4449), to be fire-red.
Syn.: *eruthrós* (2063), red; *kókkinos* (2847), scarlet.

4451. πύρωσις *púrōsis*; gen. *purṓseōs*, fem. noun from *puróō* (4448), to burn, or *púr* (4442), fire. The act or condition of being on fire, burning, conflagration (Rev 18:9, 18). Figuratively meaning fiery trial, calamity, suffering (1 Pet 4:12; see Isa 48:10 where *káminos* [2575], a furnace, is used).
Syn.: *kaúsis* (2740), burning; *dokemé* (1382), test, trial; *peíra* (3984), test, trial.

4452. πω *pō*; enclitic particle. Yet, even; only in composition as *mḗpō* (3380), *mēdépō* (3369), or *oúpō* (3768), not yet; *oudépō* (3764), never before, and also *pṓpote* (4455), never.

4453. πωλέω *pōléō*; contracted *pōló*, fut. *pōlḗsō*. To trade merchandise, barter, sell, with the acc. (Matt 13:44; 19:21; 21:12; Mark 10:21; 11:15; Luke 12:33; 18:22; 22:36; John 2:14, 16; Acts 5:1). In the pass., followed by the gen. of price (Matt 10:29; Luke 12:6). Used in an absolute sense (Matt 21:12; 25:9; Mark 11:15; Luke 17:28; 19:45; Acts 4:34, 37; 1 Cor 10:25; Rev 13:17; Sept.: Ezek 7:13; Joel 3:3).
Deriv.: *porphurópōlis* (4211), a female seller of purple cloths.
Syn.: *pipráskō* (4097), to sell.
Ant.: *agorázō* (59), to buy; *ōnéomai* (5608), to purchase.

4454. πῶλος *pôlos*; gen. *pólou*, masc. noun. A foal. Generally a young animal (Sept.: Prov 5:19), especially of the horse, a colt. In the NT used of a donkey, foal, colt; joined with *ónos* (3688), a donkey (Matt 21:2, 5, 7; John 12:15). Used in an absolute sense (Mark 11:2, 4, 5, 7; Luke 19:30, 33, 35; Sept.: Gen 32:15; Judg 10:4; 12:14; Zech 9:9).

4455. πώποτε *pṓpote*; adv. from *pō* (4452), yet, even, and *poté* (4218), never. Yet ever, at any time. In the NT only after a neg. meaning not yet ever, never (Luke 19:30; John 1:18; 5:37; 6:35; 8:33; 1 John 4:12; Sept.: 1 Sam 25:28).
Syn.: *hótan* (3752), when, whenever; *hóte* (3753), when, after that, as soon as, while; *hopóte* (3698), as soon as, when, at which time; *hosákis* (3740), whenever; *póte* (4219), when, at what time.
Ant.: *oudépote* (3763), never, not at any time; *mēdépote* (3368), never; *oudépō* (3764), not yet, never yet.

4456. πωρόω *pōróō*; contracted *pōró*, fut. *pōrósō*, from *póros* (n.f.), a small piece of stone broken off from a larger one. The verb means to harden, make hard like a stone, or callous and insensible to the touch. In the NT applied only in a spiritual sense to the hearts or minds of men (Mark 6:52; 8:17; John 12:40; Rom 11:7, of persons; 2 Cor 3:14; Sept.: Job 17:7, of the eyes).

Deriv.: *pṓrōsis* (4457), hardening.
Syn.: *sklērúnō* (4645), to harden.

4457. πώρωσις *pṓrōsis*; gen. *pōrṓseōs*, fem. noun from *pōróō* (4456), to harden, petrify, render insensitive. Used figuratively meaning hardness, callousness, blindness, insensitivity (Mark 3:5; Rom 11:25; Eph 4:18).

Syn.: *sklērótēs* (4643), hardness; *sklērokardía* (4641), hardness of heart.

4458. πως *pōs*; enclitic particle of indefiniteness of manner. Somehow, anyhow, in any way, in some way or other. Only in the comps. *eípōs* (1513), if by any means; *mḗpōs* (3381), lest by any means. To be distinguished from the interrogative adv. *pṓs* (4459), with a circumflex accent, meaning how.

4459. πῶς *pṓs*; interrogative adv. How, in what way or manner, by what means.
(**I**) Particularly in a direct question.
(**A**) With the indic. (**1**) Generally and simply (Mark 9:12 [TR], "how it is written" [in other texts, *kathṓs* {2531}, as it is written]; Luke 10:26; John 7:15; 9:10; 1 Cor 15:35). (**2**) Implying surprise, wonder, admiration (Matt 22:12; John 3:9; 6:52). So also with the fut., expressing what may or can take place (Matt 7:4; Luke 1:34). With intens. particles *kaí pṓs* (*kaí* [2532], and), and how? (John 12:34;

14:9; Acts 2:8); *pṓs oún* (*oún* [3767]), how), how then (Matt 22:43; John 6:42; 9:19); *pṓs ou* (*ou* [3756], not), how not (Matt 16:11; Mark 4:40; Luke 12:56). (**3**) Often in questions which serve to affirm the contrary, e.g., a neg. (Matt 12:29, 34; Mark 3:23; John 3:4; 1 John 3:17; 4:20); *kaí pṓs* (with *pṓs* as an intens.), and how (Luke 20:44; John 14:5). So also with the fut. (Luke 11:18; Rom 3:6; 1 Cor 14:7, 9; Heb 2:3); *pṓs ouchí* (*ouchí* [3780], not), implying strong affirmation, how not (Rom 8:32; 2 Cor 3:8).
(**B**) With the subjunctive, in a question expressing doubt (Matt 23:33; 26:54).
(**C**) With the opt. and *án* (302), if, expressing a neg. subjectively (Acts 8:31, "for how can I?" [a.t.]).
(**II**) In an indirect question with the indic. expressing what is real and of actual occurrence (John 9:15). More often in oblique discourse after verbs of consideration, finding out, knowing, making known, and the like; here the interrogative force is dropped and *pṓs* is equivalent to its correlative *hópōs* (3704), as, meaning in what way, how.
(**A**) With the indic. (Matt 6:28; 12:4; Mark 5:16; 11:18; 12:41; Luke 8:18, 36; 12:27; 14:7; Acts 9:27; 11:13; 12:17; 15:36; 1 Cor 3:10; 7:32–34; 1 Thess 1:9; Rev 3:3).
(**B**) With the subjunctive where something is expressed as possible (Matt 10:19; Mark 14:1, 11; Luke 12:11; 22:2, 4; Acts 4:21).
(**III**) As an intens. exclamation meaning how! how very! how greatly! as before an adj. or adv. (Matt 21:20; Mark 10:23, 24; Luke 18:24); before a verb (Luke 12:50; John 11:36).

P

4460. Ῥαάβ *Rhaáb*, fem. proper noun transliterated from the Hebr. *Rāchāv* (7343, OT). Rahab, a woman of Jericho mentioned in Heb 11:31 as a prostitute (*pórnē* [4204]) and as a woman of faith. She had heard of the Israelites and of the favor of God toward them (Josh 2:8–11). When the two spies sent out by Joshua came to Jericho to explore the land of promise, she concealed them from the officers who were sent in search of them. At a convenient time she let them down by a cord upon the outside of the city wall to which her house joined. It was agreed between her and the spies that if she would take a scarlet thread and fasten it in the window or aperture through which they had escaped, when the city was destroyed, her house and all that were in it would be protected (Josh 2:17–23). When the city was taken and burned, Rahab and her family were preserved (Josh 6:17–25). While it is striking that a woman from her unseemly background is commended for her faith, it is even more fascinating to find that she stands in the line of Christ Himself (Matt 1:5). Surely the lesson of this woman's life is that God's grace alone can remove the stain of sin and that regardless of how deep the dye.

4461. ῥαββί *rhabbí*; indeclinable masc. noun transliterated from the Hebr. *rabbī* (not found in the OT), my master. A doctor, teacher, master; a title of honor in the Jewish schools which continues until modern times (Matt 23:7, 8; 26:25, 49; Mark 9:5; 11:21; 14:45; John 1:38, 49; 3:2, 26; 4:31; 6:25; 9:2; 11:8). In Matt 23:8 it is explained by *kathēgētés* (2519), a teacher, master; in John 1:39 by *didáskalos* (1320), an instructor in reference to usage rather than to meaning.

In Hebr. *rhabbí* means a great one, chief, master. This was introduced as a title into the Jewish schools under a threefold form, Rab, as the lowest degree of honor; Rab with the first person suffix *i*, Rabbi, my master, with higher dignity; and Rabboni, meaning my great master, the most honorable of all. This was publicly given to only seven persons, all of the school of Hillel and of great eminence.

In the days of Christ the title was misused by Jewish teachers in that they used it to require implicit obedience to their decisions and traditions and words rather than to those of the law and the prophets. Our Lord charged the Jewish scribes and Pharisees with being very fond of this presumptuous title, but commands His disciples not to be called Rabbi in the Jewish acceptance of the word (Matt 23:7, 8). Although the title Rabbi was often given to the Lord Jesus, we do not find that He ever rebuked those who gave it to Him because He was in truth the Teacher sent from God, even that great Prophet who should come into the world, and of whom the Lord had said by Moses in Deut 18:18, 19: "It shall come to pass that whosoever will not hearken unto my words which he shall speak in my name, I will require it of him."

Deriv.: *rhabboní* (4462), my great master.

Syn.: *didáskolos* (1320), teacher, instructor.

Ant.: *mathētés* (3101), a disciple.

4462. ῥαββονί *rhabboní*, ῥαββουνί *rhabbouní*; indeclinable masc. noun from *Rhabbí* (4461), master. The highest title of honors attributed, usually to the president of the Jewish Sanhedrin if he was a descendant of the school of Hillel. It means my great master and was addressed to Christ by blind Bartimaeus and Mary Magdalene (Mark 10:51; John 20:16).

4463. ῥαβδίζω rhabdízō; fut. *rhabdísō*, from *rhábdos* (4464), a rod. To beat with rods, scourge (Acts 16:22; 2 Cor 11:25, in 11:24 it is understood to refer to scourgings; see Deut 25:3; Sept.: Judg 6:11; Ruth 2:17).

   Syn.: *dérō* (1194), to flay, thrash, strike; *túptō* (5180), to strike or beat; *bállō* (906), to cast, beat; *mastízō* (3147), to scourge or flog.

4464. ῥάβδος rhábdos; gen. *rhábdou*, fem. noun. A rod, wand, staff.
   (I) General usage (Heb 9:4; Rev 11:1; Sept.: Ex 4:2); for chastising, scourging (1 Cor 4:21; Sept.: Ex 21:20; Prov 10:13; Isa 9:4); for leaning upon, walking (Matt 10:10; Mark 6:8; Luke 9:3; Heb 11:21 in allusion to Gen 47:31; Sept.: Gen 38:18; Ex 21:19; Zech 8:4).
   (II) Specifically a scepter, staff, or wand of office (Heb 1:8 quoted from Ps 45:7; Rev 2:27; 12:5; 19:15; Sept.: Ps 2:9; 110:2).
   Deriv.: *rhabdízō* (4463), to beat with rods; *rhabdoúchos* (4465), a rod-holder.
   Syn.: *xúlon* (3586), a club or staff.

4465. ῥαβδοῦχος rhabdoúchos; gen. *rhabdoúchou*, masc. noun from *rhábdos* (4464), a rod, and *échō* (2192), to have, hold, or use. A rod-holder, an officer or type of sergeant who attended to the magistrates of Roman cities and colonies and executed their decrees. It is said that they carried on their shoulders what they called the Roman *fasces* (i.e., bundles of rods with an axe in the middle of them) as the ensigns and instruments of their office (Acts 16:35, 38). They administered punishment by scourging or beheading. In Philippi they acted under the *stratēgoí* (4755), magistrates or governors (Acts 16:20, 22, 35, 36, 38).

4466. 'Ραγαῦ Rhagaú; masc. proper noun transliterated from the Hebr. *R°gū* (7466, OT). Ragau, the same person as

Reu, one of the ancestors of Jesus (Luke 3:35 [cf. Gen 11:18, 20, 21]).

4467. ῥαδιούργημα rhadioúrgēma; gen. *rhadiourgēmatos*, neut. noun from *rhadiourgéō* (n.f.), to be ready to commit wickedness. The suffix -*ma* indicates the result of the action. Literally that which is done easily, without consideration for ethics or propriety, hence a plot, scheme, act of intrigue and deceit (Acts 18:14). Also from *rhadiourgéō* (n.f.): *rhadiourgía* (4468), mischief, intrigue.
   Syn.: *methodeía* (3180), trickery.

4468. ῥαδιουργία rhadiourgía; gen. *rhadiourgías*, fem. noun from *rhadiourgéō* (n.f.), to be ready to commit wickedness. Mischief, intrigue, recklessness, unscrupulousness (Acts 13:10). In the papyri it is used of theft. The result of *rhadiourgía* is *rhadioúrgēma* (4467), wicked schemes or plots. Also from *rhadiourgéō* (n.f.): *rhadioúrgēma* (4467), a plot, scheme.

4469. ῥακά rhaká; indeclinable adj. transliterated from the Aramaic *rēqa'* (not found in OT). A word of contempt meaning empty, worthless, foolish. Transliterated into Eng. as "Raca" (Matt 5:22; see Judg 9:4; 2 Sam 6:20; 2 Chr 13:7; Prov 12:11; 28:19). Utter contempt, equivalent to the Gr. *kenós* (2756), empty, vain.

4470. ῥάκος rhákos; gen. *rhákous*, neut. noun from *rhḗgnumi* /*rhḗssō* (4486), to tear, break. In the NT, generally a piece or remnant of cloth (Matt 9:16; Mark 2:21); equivalent to *epíblēma* (1915), a patch (Luke 5:36).

4471. 'Ραμά Rhamá; fem. noun transliterated from the Hebr. *Rāmāh* (7414, OT), a high place. Rama, Ramah, the name of several towns in Palestine. In the NT it is mentioned in Matt 2:18 (quoted from Jer 31:15) and refers to a city of Benjamin a few miles north of Jerusalem between Gibeah and Bethel (cf. Josh 18:25; Judg 4:5; 19:13). It was once occupied by Saul

(Josh 18:25; Judg 19:13; 1 Sam 22:6) and was a naturally strong site. It was fortified by Baasha, but the king of Judah stopped the work through the cooperation of the Syrians (1 Kgs 15:17–22; 2 Chr 16:1–6). At the capture of Jerusalem by Nebuchadnezzar, the captives were placed under guard at Ramah; among them was the prophet Jeremiah (Jer 39:8–12; 40:1). It was here his prophecy was fulfilled, "A voice was heard in Ramah, lamentation and bitter weeping" (Jer 31:15). This prophecy was again illustrated and fulfilled by the slaughter of the innocents in Bethlehem when Jesus was born (Matt 2:17, 18). Ramah was reoccupied after the captivity (Ezra 2:26; Neh 7:30). The town has been identified with Er-Ram, five miles north of Jerusalem where broken columns, many large hewn stones of houses, and other ancient remains are to be found. It is also the birthplace, home, and burial place of the prophet Samuel, the word being a contraction of Ramathaim-zophim (1 Sam 1:1; 2:11; 7:17; 8:4; 15:34; 16:13; 19:18; 25:1; ch. 28).

4472. ῥαντίζω rhantízō; fut. *rhantísō*, from *rhaínō* (n.f.), to sprinkle. To sprinkle. Sprinkling was the method of application for the blood of the sacrifice in order to secure its atoning efficacy and the method of purifying connected with expiation. Sprinkling persons with blood took place upon the ratifying of the covenant (Ex 24:8; Heb 9:19, 20); upon the consecration of the family of Aaron to the priesthood (Ex 29:21); in cleansing from leprosy (Lev 14:2–7). The first two cases are dealing with the establishment of a covenant between God and His people and, accordingly, the application of the atoning blood by the mediator. The last case concerns the removal of that which has defiled those already within covenant. As leprosy was often seen as a judgment imposed for violating the covenant, its removal would indicate forgiveness and the sprinkling of blood would signify a renewal of the covenant and not its establishment. While the sprinkling with the

blood of Christ in Heb 12:24 is primarily connected with Ex 24:8, it is the antitype of all other OT ceremonial sprinklings. Some have imagined that the sprinkling of the holy place or altar find their fulfillment in another occasion, namely, when Christ ascended into heaven immediately following His resurrection. It is contended from Heb 9:21–24 that Christ entered heaven and, in some manner, applied His blood to a heavenly sanctuary. This idea undermines the completeness of Christ's work on the cross and requires something additional of Him. Furthermore, it over-literalizes the text of Heb 9 and fails to recognize that the writer explains in 9:26–28 that Christ's sacrifice, death, and offering of Himself accomplished these things. The purpose of the author in describing Christ's redemptive work in terms of Levitical ritualism is not to suggest that there are direct NT counterparts which bear a material correspondence or formal likeness to the various elements of that system. Instead, his aim is to explain how that Christ in His atoning death (and triumphant resurrection) accomplished what these things represented, their essential significance, and to say that they are therefore irrelevant and unnecessary. Calvary was both the altar and the mercy seat; Christ was both the priest and the sacrifice.

Deriv.: *rhantismós* (4473), sprinkling.

4473. ῥαντισμός rhantismós; gen. *rhantismoú*, masc. noun from *rhantízō* (4472), to sprinkle. Sprinkling. In the NT the blood of Christ corresponds to the OT blood of sprinkling (Heb 12:24 [cf. 9:13, 14]; 1 Pet 1:2; Sept.: Num 19:9, 13, 20, 21), which pointed forward to the expiation made by Christ.

4474. ῥαπίζω rhapízō; fut. *rhapísō*, from *rhapís* (n.f.), a rod or stick, which is from *rhábdos* (4464), a stick, wand. To beat with rods, scourge. Later, in the NT, to hit with the open hand, to cuff, slap, especially the cheeks or ears, with the acc.

(Matt 5:39, where it means to strike). To be distinguished from *kolaphízō* (2852), to punch, strike with a clenched fist; Matt 26:67; Sept.: Hos 11:4).

Deriv.: *rhápisma* (4475), a blow with the open hand.

Syn.: *patássō* (3960), to strike; *túptō* (5180), to beat; *paíō* (3817), to strike with the palm or fist; *dérō* (1194), to flay; *plḗssō* (4141), to smite, wound.

4475. ῥάπισμα *rhápisma*; gen. *rhapísmatos*, neut. noun from *rhapízō* (4474), to hit with the palm of the hand. A blow with the open hand, a cuff, slap, especially on the cheeks or ears (Mark 14:65; John 18:22; 19:3; Sept.: Isa 50:6).

4476. ῥαφίς *rhaphís*; gen. *rhaphídos*, fem. noun from *rháptō* (n.f.), to sew. A needle (Matt 19:24; Mark 10:25; Luke 18:25). The earlier word was *belónē* (n.f.), needle, from *bélos* (956), dart, arrow.

4477. Ῥαχάβ *Rhacháb*; fem. proper noun transliterated from the Hebr. *Rāchāv* (7343, OT). Rahab ([4460] Matt 1:5). See *Rhaáb* (4460).

4478. Ῥαχήλ *Rhachḗl*; fem. proper noun transliterated from the Hebr. *Rāchēl* (7354, OT), ewe. Rachel, the daughter of Laban, the wife of the patriarch Jacob and the mother of Joseph and Benjamin (Gen 29—35). She died after giving birth to Benjamin. On her grave, near the road from Bethlehem to Jerusalem, Jacob set up a pillar (Gen 35:19). At the time of Samuel and Saul the pillar was still standing (1 Sam 10:2). Jer 31:15–17 represents Rachel as weeping in her grave when her children pass by on their way to Babylon. Matt 2:17, 18 applies this to the massacre of the innocent.

4479. Ῥεβέκκα *Rhebékka*; gen. *Rhebékkēs*, fem. proper noun transliterated from the Hebr. *Rivᵉqāh* (7259, OT), fettering, enchaining. Rebecca, the daughter of Bethuel, sister of Laban, and wife of Isaac. The circumstances of her marriage with Isaac constitute one of the most charming and beautiful passages of sacred history (Gen chap. 24). She became the mother of Jacob and Esau. When they grew up, Jacob became his mother's favorite, and this undue partiality was the source of much trouble. She persuaded him to attain his father's blessings by practicing deceit, and he had to flee for fear of his brother's revenge. Rebecca died before Isaac and was buried in Abraham's tomb (Gen 49:31; see Rom 9:10).

4480. ῥέδα *rhéda*; gen. *rhédēs*, fem. noun from the Lat. *rheda*. A carriage with four wheels, used for traveling. A chariot (Rev 18:13).

Syn.: *hárma* (716), a war chariot with two wheels.

4481. Ῥεμφάν *Rhemphán*, **Ῥεφάν** *Rhephán*; masc. proper noun. Remphan, found only in Acts 7:43 which is a quotation from Amos 5:26 (where the corresponding word in Hebr. is *Chiun*). It is probable that these are interchangeable names for a god worshiped secretly by the Israelites in Egypt and in the wilderness, possibly answering to Saturn or Moloch (3434), the star-god. Some refer this worship to the time of Amos.

4482. ῥέω *rhéō*; fut. *rheúsō* or *rheúsomai*. To flow, used intrans. (John 7:38; Sept.: Lev 15:3; Jer 9:18).

Deriv.: *aimorréō* (131), to have a flow or issue of blood; *rhúsis* (4511), a flowing, flux; *cheímarros* (5493), a stream, brook.

4483. ῥέω *rhéō*; aor. pass. *errḗthēn*; perf. pass. *eírēmai* the obsolete theme of *eréō* (2046). To say, speak, utter definite words, and hence implying more than *laléō* (2980), to say or speak. Used especially in the pass. forms, e.g., *errḗthē*, it was said (Matt 5:21, 27, 31, 33, 38, 43; Rom 9:12, 26; Gal 3:16 [pl]; Rev 6:11; 9:4); *ho rhētheís*, the foretold (Matt 3:3);

with the neut. art. *tó rhēthén*, that which was foretold (Matt 1:22; 2:15, 17; 4:14; 8:17; 12:27; 13:35; 21:4; 22:31; 24:15; 27:9, 35); without the art. (Matt 24:15; Mark 13:14); the nom. sing. masc. aor. part. *rētheís*, that which was spoken of (Matt 3:3).

Deriv.: *pararruéō* (3901), to float by or drift apart; *rhḗma* (4487), statement, saying, an utterance; *rhḗtōr* (4489).

Syn.: *légō* (3004), to say, speak; *laléō* (2980), to speak, to break silence; *phthéggomai* (5350), to utter a sound; *apophthéggomai* (669), to speak forth; *phēmí* (5346), to declare; *pháskō* (5335), to affirm, say.

Ant.: *sigáō* (4601), to be silent; *siōpáō* (4623), to keep silence.

4484. 'Ρήγιον *Rhēgion*; gen. *Rhēgíou*, neut. proper noun. Rhegium, meaning breach. A city on the coast near the southwestern end of Italy and opposite Messina, on the northeastern part of Sicily, from which it is separated by a strait six miles wide. Paul was detained at this place for a day when on his journey to Rome (Acts 28:13). It is now called Rheggio and is a flourishing commercial town and the capital of Calabria.

4485. ῥῆγμα *rhḗgma*; gen. *rhḗgmatos*, neut. noun from *rhḗgnumi /rhḗssō* (4486), to break. A rending, breach, ruin (Luke 6:49; Sept.: Amos 6:11).

Syn.: *chásma* (5490), chasm, gulf; *ábussos* (12), bottomless pit, abyss; *schísma* (4978), gap, split, schism.

Ant.: *epíblēma* (1915), a patch.

4486. ῥήγνυμι *rhḗgnumi* and ῥήσσω *rhḗssō*; fut. *rhḗxō*. To rend, tear, break, break in pieces.

(I) Of things, to rend or burst, as leather bottles or skins, with the acc. (Mark 2:22; Luke 5:37). Pass. (Matt 9:17; Sept.: Num 16:31; Josh 9:19; Job 2:12).

(II) Of persons, to rend, tear, lacerate, as dogs would do (Matt 7:6); also to tear down, dash to the ground as a de-

mon does to one it possesses (Mark 9:18; Luke 9:42; Sept.: Isa 13:16).

(III) Used figuratively and in an absolute sense, to break forth into rejoicing and praise (Gal 4:27 quoted from Isa 54:1). Usually with the acc. of manner or instrument (Sept.: Isa 49:13; 52:9).

Deriv.: *diarrḗgnumi / diarrḗssō* (1284), to burst asunder; *perirrḗgnumi* (4048), to tear off all around; *prosrḗgnumi* (4366), to break upon; *rhákos* (4470), a piece of cloth; *rhḗgma* (4485), a breach, ruin.

Syn.: *láschō* (2997), to crack open, burst asunder; *schízō* (4977), to split, rend open; *sparássō* (4682), to tear, rend; *thrauō* (2352), crush, bruise.

Ant.: *kolláō* (2853), to glue or cement together.

4487. ῥῆμα *rhḗma*; gen. *rhḗmatos*, neut. noun from *rhéō* (4483), to speak. That which is spoken, a statement, word.

(I) Particularly a word as uttered by a living voice. Pl. *tá rhḗmata*, words (Matt 12:36; 26:75; Mark 9:32; 14:72; Luke 1:38; 2:17, 19, 50, 51; 7:1; 9:45; 18:34; 20:26; 24:8, 11; John 8:20; Acts 2:14; 6:11, 13; 10:44; 26:25; 11:16; 16:38; 28:25; Rom 10:18 quoted from Ps 19:5; 2 Cor 12:4; Heb 12:19; Sept.: Gen 27:34, 42; Job 15:3; 31:40; Ps 5:2).

(II) Collectively, word, pl. words, meaning saying, speech, discourse.

(III) In the NT usage, often it has a particular meaning depending on the adjuncts or context:

(A) Charge, accusation (Matt 5:11; 18:16; 27:14; 2 Cor 13:1 in allusion to Deut 19:15 [cf. Num 14:36]).

(B) Prediction, prophecy, equivalent to *rhḗmata proeirēména*, sayings foretold (2 Pet 3:2; Jude 1:17). *Rhḗmata toú Theoú* (2316), sayings of God (Rev 17:17 [TR]).

(C) Promise from God (Luke 2:29; Heb 6:5; Sept.: 1 Kgs 8:20; 12:15).

(D) Command (Matt 4:4; Luke 4:4, used metonymically meaning upon everything which God decrees, quoted from Deut 8:3, spoken in reference to the manna; 5:5, word of God, his omnipotent decree; Heb 1:3; Sept.: Josh 1:13; 1 Sam 17:29 [cf. Ex 34:28; Prov 3:1]).

(E) Spoken of a teacher, word, teaching, precept, doctrine, the same as *tá rhḗmata tḗs zōḗs* (2222), of life, that is, the words of life (John 6:68; Acts 5:20); with *pará* (3844), from, with the gen. (Acts 10:22); with *prós* (4314), to, with the acc. (Acts 11:14); with the gen. such as *rhḗma tḗs pistéōs* (gen. of *pístis* [4102], faith), word of the faith; *rhḗma Theoú* (2316), word of God (Luke 3:2), or *Kuríou* (2962), of the Lord, meaning the doctrines and promises of God revealed and taught in the Bible (John 3:34; 8:47; 17:8; Acts 10:37; Rom 10:17; Eph 5:26; 6:17; 1 Pet 1:25); of Jesus, *tá rhḗmata*, the words (John 5:47; 6:63; 10:21; 12:47, 48; 14:10; 15:7).

(F) A pronouncement from God. In the Sept., more often found as *lógos* (3056), word (Jer 1:4, 11; Ezek 3:16; 6:1).

(IV) Metonymically for things spoken of, a matter, affair, in the sing. (Luke 2:15; Sept.: Gen 21:11; 40:1); in the pl. (Luke 1:65; Acts 5:32; Sept.: Gen 20:8). The phrase *ou . . . pán rhḗma* (*ou* [3756], not; *pán*, the neut. of *pás* [3956], every), not every word meaning nothing at all, nothing whatever (Luke 1:37 [cf. Sept.: Gen 18:14; Deut 17:8]).

Syn.: *lógos* (3056), the expression of thought, while *rhḗma* stands for the subject matter of the word or the thing which is spoken about; *épos* (2031), a word or proverb; *laliá* (2981), saying, speech, talk.

Ant.: *sigḗ* (4602), silence.

4488. Ῥησά *Rhēsá*, masc. proper noun transliterated from the Hebr. Rhesa, meaning head. A name which occurs in the genealogy of Jesus in Luke 3:27.

4489. ῥήτωρ *rhḗtōr*; gen. *rhḗtoros*, masc. noun from *rhéō* (4483), to speak. A speaker, orator, an advocate (Acts 24:1).

4490. ῥητῶς *rhētós*; adv. from *rhētós* (n.f.), spoken, expressed in words, which

is from *rhéō* (4483), to speak. Distinctly, expressly (1 Tim 4:1).

Deriv.: *árrētos* (731), unspeakable.

4491. ῥίζα *rhíza*; gen. *rhízas*, fem. noun. A root (Matt 3:10; Luke 3:9); pl. (Mark 11:20, "from the roots" meaning wholly). In Matt 13:6; Mark 4:6; Sept.: Ezek 17:6, 7, 9; Job 28:9; 31:12, to have "no root" means not to have firm hold.

(I) Figuratively of being rooted and established in faith or doctrine (Matt 13:21; Mark 4:17; Luke 8:13). Figuratively the cause or source of something (1 Tim 6:10). Abraham and the Jewish people are the root from which the gospel dispensation with its blessings has sprung (Rom 11:16–18). In Heb 12:15 "the root of bitterness" means a person who has turned away from following the teachings of Christ, in allusion to Deut 29:18.

(II) Metonymically, a sprout or shoot from the root meaning offspring, descendant (Rom 15:12 in allusion to Isa 11:10 [cf. 11:1]; Rev 5:5; 22:16).

Deriv.: *rhizóō* (4492), to cause to take root.

4492. ῥιζόω *rhizóō*; contracted *rhizó*, fut. *rhizṓsō*, from *rhíza* (4491), root. To root, take root; mid./pass. to be or become rooted, take root. Later intrans., to take root (Sept.: Isa 40:24; Jer 12:2). In the NT, only pass. figuratively, to be rooted, strengthened with roots, firmly fixed, constant (Eph 3:17; Col 2:7).

Deriv.: *ekrizóō* (1610), to uproot.

4493. ῥιπή *rhipḗ*; gen. *rhipḗs* fem. noun from *rhíptō* (4496), to throw, cast. A quick motion, such as a fling or toss. In the NT, a blink of the eye, a wink, twinkling (1 Cor 15:52 referring to a moment of time [cf. Luke 4:5]).

4494. ῥιπίζω *rhipízō*; fut. *rhipísō*, from *rhipís* (n.f.), a fan, blower, which is from *rhíptō* (4496), to cast. To stir up a fire by fanning it. In the NT, generally it means to move to and fro, to toss, agitate as waves (James 1:6).

Syn.: *kludōnízomai* (2831), to be tossed by billows, figuratively to be in an unsettled condition; *anemízō* (416), to toss with the wind.

4495. ῥιπτέω *rhiptéō*; contracted *rhiptṓ*, only in the pres. act. and imper. as a frequentative from *rhíptō* (4496), to throw or cast repeatedly. Tossing outer garments and dust into the air as part of an uproar (only in Acts 22:23). This was customary in theaters and other assemblies.

4496. ῥίπτω *rhíptō*; fut. *rhípsō*, from *rhépō* (n.f.), to incline, fall. To throw or cast, to hurl, scatter, disperse. Akin to *rhiptéō* (4495), to throw or cast repeatedly. With the acc.:
   (I) Particularly followed by *eis* (1519), into (Luke 4:35; 17:2); by *en* (1722), in (Matt 27:5); *ek* (1537) with a gen., to cast out (Acts 27:19, 29, "from the ship" [a.t.] implied) In Acts 22:23 we have *rhiptéō* (4495), meaning tossing their outer garments into the air repeatedly in support of the uproar (Sept.: Gen 37:20, 24; Ex 1:22; Judg 9:53). In a gentler sense, meaning to deposit a load by laying down a sick person, with the acc. (Matt 15:30 [cf. Sept.: 2 Kgs 2:16]).
   (II) To cast forth, throw aside, scatter. In the perf. pass. part. *errimménos*, cast forth, scattered (Matt 9:36).
   Deriv.: *epirríptō* (1977), to cast upon; *rhipḗ* (4493), a quick motion; *rhiptéo* (4495), tossing outer garments and dust into the air.
   Syn.: *bállō* (906), to throw, hurl, cast; *apobállō* (577), to throw off from; *ekbállō* (1544), to cast out of; *embállō* (1685), to cast into; *epibállō* (1911), to cast on or upon; *apōthéomai* (683), to thrust away; *kathairéō* (2507), to cast down; *katakrēmnízō* (2630), to throw over a precipice.
   Ant.: *sunágō* (4863), to gather or bring together; *episunágō* (1996), to gather together in one place; *sullégō* (4816), to collect, gather up; *sustréphō* (4962), to twist together or assemble

in one; *trugáō* (5166), to gather in, as a harvest; *analambánō* (353), to take up; *katalambánō* (2638), to apprehend; *paralambánō* (3880), to receive; *proslambánō* (4355), to take to oneself; *aírō* (142), to lift, carry, take up or away; *apaírō* (522), to lift off; *exaírō* (1808), to take away; *epaírō* (1869), to lift; *anairéō* (337), to take up; *déchomai* (1209), to receive; *prosdéchomai* (4327), to receive favorably; *kratéō* (2902) and *katéchō* (2722), to hold; *drássomai* (1405), to grasp with the hand; *piázō* (4084), to lay hold of forcibly; *paraphérō* (3911), to bear away; *bastázō* (941), to lift, take up, bear; *sunéchō* (4912), to take with; *harpázō* (726), to snatch, take suddenly by force.

4497. Ῥοβοάμ *Rhoboám*; proper noun transliterated from the Hebr. *Rᵉchav'ām* (7346, OT), enlarger of the people. Rehoboam, a son of Solomon by the Ammonite princess Naamah (1 Kgs 12; 14:21) who, after the death of his father, ascended the throne at the age of forty-one and reigned approximately twenty years, 975–957 B.C.

4498. Ῥόδη *Rhódē*; gen. *Rhódēs*, fem. proper noun. Rhoda, meaning rose or rose bush. A maid in the house of Mary, the mother of John Mark (Acts 12:13).

4499. Ῥόδος *Rhódos*; gen. *Rhódou*, masc. proper noun. Rhodes, meaning a rose. A beautiful island in the Mediterranean, thirteen miles from the coast of Asia Minor. It is forty-six miles long, eighteen miles wide and has an area of about 420 square miles. The city of Rhodes at the western end of the island was founded about 400 B.C. by the Dorians and was very prosperous in the reign of Alexander. Jews were among its inhabitants during the Maccabaean period. Paul visited it on his return from his third missionary journey (Acts 21:1). He might have seen there the ruins of the Colossus of Rhodes, the greatest of the seven wonders of the world. This was made of brass and was 105 ft. high. It stood at the right of the port as vessels entered, and not astride the channel as is generally represented in pictures. It was erected 290 B.C. and toppled by an earthquake in 224 B.C. The city also had a beautiful temple of Apollo built by Herod the Great. In the Middle Ages the city was held by the Knights of Saint John. It was captured by the Turks in A.D. 1522 and is now part of Greece.

4500. ῥοιζηδόν *rhoizēdón*; adv. from *rhoizéō* (n.f.), to make a whizzing or whistling noise, which is from *rhoízos* (n.f.), used in Homer for the whizzing of an arrow in its flight and by Plutarch for the whistling of the wind in a storm. Rushing as of winds and waves with great noise or a crash (2 Pet 3:10). Most probably a word formed by an onomatopoeia from the sound.

4501. ῥομφαία *rhomphaía*; gen. *rhomphaías*, fem. noun. A broadsword used especially by the Thracians and carried on the right shoulder. In the NT, generally a sword (Rev 1:16; 2:12, 16; 6:8; 19:15, 21). Figuratively (Luke 2:35 meaning anguish of soul; Sept.: Ex 32:27; Ezek 5:1).
    Syn.: *máchaira* (3162), a short sword or dagger more like a knife.

4502. Ῥουβήν *Rhoubēn*; masc. proper noun transliterated from the Hebr. *Re'ūvēn* (7205, OT), behold a son. Reuben, the eldest son of Jacob and Leah (Gen 29:32). He lost the privilege of birthright in consequence of a grievous sin (Gen 35:22; 49:3, 4). In spite of his impulsiveness, he was kind of heart as is shown in his reaction to the conspiracy against Joseph (Gen 37:18–30; 42:37). The Reubenites became wealthy herdsmen, but they were averse to war (Judg 5:15, 16) and were the first who were carried away into captivity. In the NT found only in Rev 7:5 speaking of the tribe of Reuben.

4503. Ῥούθ *Rhoúth*; fem. proper noun transliterated from the Hebr. *Rūth* (7327, OT), a friend, or beauty. Ruth, a Moabitess woman (Ruth 1:4) who married a son of Naomi and showed her strong attachment to her mother-in-law by leaving her own country and following her into Judea. Her kindness was abundantly rewarded when she found favor in the eyes of a kinsman who afterward married her. Through this event she became the ancestor of the royal family of David. In the NT only in Matt 1:5.

4504. Ῥοῦφος *Rhoúphos*; gen. *Rhoúphou*, masc. proper noun. Rufus, meaning red. A Christian to whom Paul sent his salutation (Rom 16:13), probably identical with Rufus, the son of Simon the Cyrenian (Mark 15:21).

4505. ῥύμη *rhúmē*; gen. *rhúmēs*, fem. noun from *rhúō* (n.f.), to draw, drag along the ground. Impetus, impulse. In the NT, a street, lane, alley of a city, in distinction from *hē plateía* (4113), open square (Matt 6:2; Luke 14:21; Acts 9:11; 12:10; Sept.: Isa 15:3).
    Deriv. of *rhúō* (n.f.): *rhúomai* (4506), to deliver; *rhutís* (4512) a wrinkle.
    Syn.: *ámphodon* (296), a fork in the road; *hodós* (3598), a road; *párodos* (3938), a passing or passage.

4506. ῥύομαι *rhúomai*; fut. *rhúsomai*, aor. pass. *errústhēn* (Luke 1:74), mid. deponent from *rhúō* (n.f., see *rhúmē* [4505]), to draw, drag along the ground. To draw or snatch from danger, rescue, deliver. This is more with the meaning of drawing to oneself than merely rescuing from someone or something. Followed by the acc. (Matt 27:43; 2 Pet 2:7). Used in an absolute sense (Rom 11:26 "the Deliverer" quoted from Isa 59:20; Sept.: Ex 2:19; Isa 5:29; 48:20). With an adjunct followed by *apó* (575), from, with the gen. (Matt 6:13, "deliver us from the evil one" [a.t.]; Luke 11:4; Rom 15:31; 1 Thess 1:10; 2 Thess 3:2; 2 Tim 4:18;

Sept.: 2 Sam 19:9; Ezek 37:23); by *ek* (1537), out of, with the gen. (Rom 7:24; 2 Cor 1:10; Col 1:13; 2 Tim 3:11; 2 Pet 2:9; Sept.: Gen 48:16; Judg 8:34; 2 Sam 22:49). Pass. (Luke 1:74; 2 Tim 4:17).

Syn.: *apallássō* (525), to free from, release, deliver; *eleutheróō* (1659), to deliver, free; *exairéō* (1807), to take out, deliver; *sōzō* (4982), to save, deliver, rescue; *lutróō* (3084), to ransom, redeem; *lúō* (3089), to loose; *apolúō* (630), to dismiss.

Ant.: *apoleípō* (620), to leave behind, forsake; *apóllumi* (622), to destroy; *aphístēmi* (868), to desert; *tēréō* (5083), to detain; *pagideúō* (3802), to ensnare, entangle; *emplékō* (1707, to entangle; *katadunasteúō* (2616), to oppress.

4507. ῥυπαρία rhuparía; gen. *rhuparías*, fem. noun from *rhuparós* (4508), dirty, filthy. Filth, filthiness, figuratively in a moral sense (James 1:21).

Syn.: *aischrótēs* (151), shame, obscenity; *molusmós* (3436), defilement; *asélgeia* (766), lasciviousness, licentiousness; *aischrología* (148), filthy talk; *míasma* (3393), defilement; *miasmós* (3394), the act or process of defiling; *akatharsía* (167), uncleanness.

Ant.: *katharótēs* (2514), cleanness, purity; *katharismós* (2512), the act of cleansing, purification; *hagnótēs* (54), cleanness, blamelessness, pureness; *hagneía* (47), chastity, purity; *hagnismós* (49), cleansing, purification.

4508. ῥυπαρός rhuparós; fem. *rhupará*, neut. *rhuparón*, adj. from *rhúpos* (4509), filth. Filthy, foul (James 2:2). Figuratively in a moral sense (Rev 22:1 [UBS]; Sept.: Zech 3:3, 4).

Deriv.: *rhuparía* (4507), filthiness.

Syn.: *aischrós* (150), base, shameful, filthy; *aischrokerdḗs* (146), greedy of base gain or filthy lucre; *koinós* (2839), unclean; *akáthartos* (169), unclean, impure; *anósios* (462), unholy, profane; *auchmērós* (850), dirty, obscure, dark; *saprós* (4550), worthless, corrupt, bad, rotten; *spílos* (4696), spotted.

Ant.: *katharós* (2513), clean; *hagnós* (53), free from defilement, pure; *hósios* (3741), religiously right, sacred, undefiled; *hágios* (40), holy; *hierós* (2413), sacred, associated with God; *ákratos* (194), undiluted, without admixture; *akéraios* (185), innocent, pure; *amíantos* (283), undefiled; *áspilos* (784), unblemished; *amṓmētos* (298), unblamable; *ámemptos* (273), faultless.

4509. ῥύπος rhúpos; gen. *rhúpou*, masc. noun. Filth, filthiness (1 Pet 3:21; Sept. Job 14:4; Isa 4:4). Equivalent to *rhuparía* (4507), filthiness.

Deriv.: *rhuparós* (4508), dirty, filthy; *rhupóō* (4510), to soil, to be filthy.

Syn.: *akatharsía* (167), impurity, uncleanness.

Ant.: *katharótēs* (2514), cleanness; *katharismós* (2512), purification; *hagnótēs* (54), pureness; *hagneía* (47), chastity; *hagnismós* (49), the act of purifying.

4510. ῥυπόω rhupóō; contracted *rhupṓ*, fut. *rhupṓsō*, from *rhúpos* (4509), dirt. Trans., to defile, pollute (Rev 22:11 [TR]). Used in a moral sense, to make oneself filthy, the opposite of morally pure.

Syn.: *koinóō* (2840), to make common, filthy, to defile; *miaínō* (3392), to stain, pollute; *molúnō* (3435), to besmear as with mud or filth; *spilóō* (4695), to stain or spot, defile.

Ant.: *katharízō* (2511), to make clean; *diakatharízō* (1245), to cleanse thoroughly; *kathaírō* (2508), to purge; *ekkathaírō* (1571), to cleanse thoroughly; *hagnízō* (48), to purify, cleanse from defilement.

4511. ῥύσις rhúsis; gen. *rhúseōs*, fem. noun from *rhéō* (4482), to flow. A flowing. In the NT, of blood (Mark 5:25; Luke 8:43, 44).

Syn.: *haimatekchusía* (130), shedding of blood.

Ant.: *paúō* (3973), to cease, desist; *kopázō* (2869), to relax, cease; *dialeípō* (1257), to cease.

4512. ῥυτίς *rhutís*; gen. *rhutídos*, fem. noun from *rhúō* (n.f., see *rhúmē* [4505]), to draw, contract. A wrinkle, as drawn together, contracted. Used figuratively (Eph 5:27).

4513. Ῥωμαϊκός *Rhōmaïkós*; fem. *Rhō-maïkḗ*, neut. *Rhōmaïkón*, adj. Roman or Latin (Luke 23:38).

4514. Ῥωμαῖος *Rhōmaíos*; gen. *Rhō-maíou*, masc. noun. Roman, of Rome, meaning a Roman citizen (Acts 2:10; 16:21, 37, 38; 22:25–27, 29; 23:27). Generally the Romans (John 11:48; Acts 25:16; 28:17).

4515. Ῥωμαϊστί *Rhōmaïstí*; adv. In the Roman or Latin language (John 19:20).

4516. Ῥώμη *Rhṓmē*; gen. *Rhṓmēs*, fem. proper noun. Rome. Rome in the NT was the capital of the empire in its greatest prosperity and the residence of its emperors. Among the inhabitants were many Jews (Acts 28:17). They had received the liberty of worship and other privileges from Caesar and lived in the district across the Tiber near the Porta Portese. Paul was kept in Rome two whole years, dwelling in his own rented house with a soldier who had charge of him (Acts 28:16, 30). In accordance with the usual Roman custom of treating prisoners, he apparently was bound to the soldier with a chain (Acts 28:20; Eph 6:20; Phil 1:16). To those coming to visit him he preached the gospel, and no one forbade him (Acts 28:30, 31). Several of Paul's epistles were believed to have been written from Rome, such as Colossians, Ephesians, Philippians, Philemon, and 2 Timothy, the last shortly before his death on a second and final imprisonment (2 Tim 4:6). On Paul's approach to Rome he was met by brethren who came out on the Appian Way as far as the little town of Appii Forum (Acts 28:15). In his letter to the Philippians he also refers to the "palace" or Caesar's court (Phil 1:13). This probably does not refer to the imperial palace, but to the residence of the Praetorian guards or to a military barrack attached to the imperial house. There were Christians also belonging to the imperial household even during the reign of the cruel Nero (Phil 4:22). Rome is presented as a persecuting power referred to by the "seven heads" and "seven mountains" in Rev 17:9, and described under the name of "Babylon" elsewhere in the same book (Rev 14:8; 16:19; 17:5; 18:2, 21).

4517. ῥώννυμι *rhṓnnumi*; fut. *rhṓsō*. To strengthen, make firm. The perf. pass. *érrōmai* is used with the pres. meaning I am well or in good health. The imper. *érrōso* and the pl. *érrōsthe* are usually used in the conclusion of letters as a wish of health and happiness, equivalent to our good-bye (Acts 15:29; 23:30).

Deriv.: *árrōstos* (732), infirm, sick.

Syn.: *hugiaínō* (5198), to be sound; *euphraínō* (2165), to be merry; *chaírō* (5463), to rejoice; *aspázomai* (782), to bid farewell; *sthenóō* (4599), to strengthen, confirm.

Ant.: *anathematízō* (332), to curse; *katanathematízō* (2653), to curse blatantly; *kataráomai* (2672), to wish evil against a person or thing, curse; *kakologéō* (2551), to speak evil.

Σ

4518. σαβαχθανί *sabachthani*; A Chaldean word meaning, "Thou hast forsaken me," a 2d person sing. with the 1st. pers. suffix (Matt 27:46; Mark 15:34 quoted from Ps 22:2).

4519. σαβαώθ *sabaōth*; noun transliterated from the Hebr. *Tsᵉvā'āh* (6635, OT), hosts, armies, hence the Lord of Hosts, meaning of the angelic hosts (cf. 2 Chr 18:18; Ps 103:21; Luke 2:13). In the NT, the general meaning is Jehovah omnipotent (Rom 9:29 quoted from Isa 1:9; James 5:4; Sept.: Isa 2:12; 6:3); and the Sept. translation *pantokrátōr* (3841), all-ruling, almighty, omnipotent.

4520. σαββατισμός *sabbatismós*; gen. *sabbatismoú*, masc. noun from *sabbatízō* (n.f.), to keep the Sabbath (Sept.: Ex 16:30; Lev 26:35). A keeping of a Sabbath, a rest as on the Sabbath. In the NT used only of an eternal rest with God (Heb 4:9). Therefore, the intimation is that the Sabbath was instituted as a symbol of that eternal rest at the completion of God's work. This rest remains with the people of God and is also called *katápausis* (2663), a cessation from work or causing to cease work, putting to rest, repose. The teaching of the Apostles as to the rest in its relation to the believer's life is confined to two passages, Heb 4:1–11 and Rev 14:13. The basis of the idea is the Divine rest, the rest on which God entered at the completion of His work of creation. Participation in this rest is a divine gift to man. The natural tendency is to conceive rest as mere cessation of work. In Heb 4:9 we have the word *sabbatismós*, referring to the rest which is going to be enjoyed by the people of God when their earthly work is finished. However, the word *katápausis* is used in 4:1, 3 (twice), 4:5, 10, 11 and also Heb 3:11, 18. Since the Jews shared this

misapprehension, it was corrected by our Lord in the discourse of John 5:17ff., beginning with the words, "My Father worketh hitherto, and I work." This idea of rest as freedom from further work finds expression in Rev 14:13; "Blessed are the dead which die in the Lord from henceforth: Yea, saith the Spirit, that they may rest from their labors; and their works do follow them." The word for rest here is *anapaúsōntai* (TR), the aor. subjunctive of *anapaúō* (373), which means inner rest and refreshment, not due to the cessation of work but to the result of the right performance of work (Matt 11:28; 1 Pet 4:14). The earthly labors of the Christian's life are ended at death; its "works," i.e., habits, methods, and results abide and remain in the new life.

Heb 4:1–11 gives the most exhaustive treatment of this theme. The whole passage may possibly be called a discourse, having for its text the words of Ps 95:11: "Unto whom I sware in my wrath that they should not enter into my rest [*katápausin*]." The rest to which God refers, as quoted by the Psalmist, is the divine rest after creation of which Gen 2:2 speaks: "And on the seventh day God ended his work which he had made; and he rested on the seventh day from all his work which he had made." This passage links the idea of divine rest indissolubly with the Sabbath. The writer's argument is briefly as follows: The inspired message in Psalm 95 speaks of a "rest" of God. The Psalmist tells how in the days of Moses this rest lay open to God's people, but they did not enter in through disobedience. Neither then nor at the entry into Canaan under Joshua was the divine idea of rest realized. The Psalmist, in fact, implies that the divine idea still remains unrealized and still awaits fulfillment; and the author of Hebrews, taking the Psalmist's word as the last utterance of the OT on the subject of rest, applies it with confidence to his hearers of the NT epoch. He draws the inference that "there remaineth therefore a rest [*sabbatismós*] to the people of God" (Heb 4:9). The word *sabbatismós* is used here purposely in lieu of *katápausis*, the word employed throughout the remainder of the passage. It not only denotes the divine rest as a Sabbatic rest, but it links together, in a most suggestive way, the end with the beginning, the consummation with the creation. It implies that the rest which God gives is one which He also enjoys. Just as in the case of salvation, the Christian rest (*anápausis* [Matt 11:28]) may be viewed both as a present possession and as a future blessing. On the one hand, we who have believed do enter into that rest (*katápausin*). Our life of sin has ended and we are enjoying the cessation of sin with the *anápausin*, the inner joy that we can have while in this life and work till our true *katápausis*, or cessation of this life, is realized. Therefore we as Christian believers enjoy the *anápausin* (inner rest) which the Lord gives us while we are here on earth, working and waiting for our *katápausin*. This is similar to the *sabbatismós* which the Lord enjoyed and which He promises for his people.

There is yet a third word which means rest, *ánesis* (425), which is derived from *ánō* (508), up, and *híēmi* (n.f.), to send (Acts 24:23; 2 Cor 2:13; 7:5; 8:13; 2 Thess 1:7). The verb *aníēmi* (447) occurs in Acts 16:26; 27:40; Eph 6:9; Heb 13:5. The basic verb *híēmi* never occurs by itself in the NT. *Aníēmi* in Acts 16:26; 27:40 is translated "loose," the first in regard to chains and the second in regard to the rudder bands. The chain became loose as a result of the earthquake and the rudder bands as a result of the activity of the sailors. In both instances, it was a loosening that was effected by an outside force. In Eph 6:9 *aníēmi* is used figuratively and is translated "forbearing" referring to threatening that may be given to the slaves. In other words, if a master wants to correct a slave, he must refrain from threats. Heb 13:5 translates it "leave," which means

abandon, let go. In both of these instances where the verb is used in a figurative sense, it refers to the kindness of the master toward the slave and the faithfulness of God toward His own.

The use of the subst. *ánesis* in the Scriptures in which it is found is as follows: Acts 24:23: "And he commanded a centurion to keep Paul, and to let him have liberty [*ánesin*], and that he should forbid none of his acquaintances to minister or come unto him." This refers to the time that Paul was imprisoned in Caesarea. The command was that Paul was not to be restricted in his movements but was to enjoy the liberty to move around. 2 Cor 2:13: "I had no rest [*ánesin*] in my spirit." Paul is here referring to the fact that he did not feel free to stay at Troas because he did not find Titus there. 2 Cor 7:5: "For, when we were come into Macedonia, our flesh had no rest [*ánesin*], but we were troubled on every side; without were fightings, within were fears." The circumstances which enveloped them produced unrest or affliction (*thlípsis* [2347] which occurs in this verse and to which *ánesis* stands in opposition or antithesis). 2 Cor 8:13: "For I mean not that other men be eased [*ánesis*], and ye burdened [*thlípsis*]." Paul is saying here that one's giving should be in such a way that it relieves others but does not afflict the giver. Here also the word *ánesis* stands in contrast to *thlípsis*, tribulation or affliction. In 2 Thess 1:7 the meaning is eschatological. "And to you who are troubled [*thliboménois*, the pres. pass. part. of *thlíbō* {2346}, to afflict, trouble] rest [*ánesin*] with us, when the Lord Jesus shall be revealed from heaven with his mighty angels." Here the Apostle Paul is speaking of the taking up (*anōtēmi*) of the believers before those who are afflicting them are punished (1:5, 6). This word *ánesis* is used in the NT by Paul and always in contrast with *thlípsis* as expressed in 2 Thess 1:7 or implied in the other references. For the time of our earthly sojourn, we experience *ánesin*, the beginning of the loosening of our bonds, the bond of our spirit, the bonds of our flesh, the bonds of adverse circumstances. However, we are going to experience deliverance (1 Thess 4:13–18), so that we may not experience the coming *thlípsis*, or tribulation. Our present *ánesis* is but a foretaste of the coming *ánesis* of which the Lord Jesus speaks so clearly (cf. Matt 24:21, 29; Mark 13:19, 24).

The noun *sabbatismós*, a Sabbath keeping, is used in Heb 4:9 to indicate the perpetual Sabbath rest to be enjoyed uninterruptedly by believers in their fellowship with the Father and the Son in contrast to the weekly Sabbath under the Law. It is a divine rest into which the believers enter in their relationship with God here on earth and in eternity.

Ant.: *érgon* (2041), work; *ergasía* (2039), work or business, performance; *kópos* (2873), toil resulting from labor; *móchthos* (3449), toil, hardship, distress; *pónos* (4192), pain; *thlípsis* (2347), tribulation, affliction; *talaipōría* (5004), wretchedness, calamity, misery; *básanos* (931), torture, torment; *lúpē* (3077), sadness, grief, sorrow.

4521. σάββατον *sábbaton*; gen. *sabbátou*, neut. noun transliterated from the Hebr. *shabāth* (7676, OT). Rest, a cessation from labor, Sabbath, pl. *tá sábbata* (Matt 12:1, 5).

(I) The Jewish Sabbath, the seventh day of the week, kept originally by a total cessation from all labor as even the kindling of a fire, but apparently without any public solemnities except an addition to the daily sacrifice in the tabernacle and the changing of the shewbread (cf. Ex 20:8ff.; 31:13ff.; Lev 24:8; Num 15:32ff.; 28:9). The custom of reading the Scriptures in public assemblies and synagogues appears to have been introduced after the exile (cf. Neh 8; Luke 4:16).

(A) Sing. *tó sábbaton*, the Sabbath, used in the nom. (Mark 2:27; Luke 23:54; John 5:9, 10; 9:14); acc. (Matt 12:5; Mark 2:27; Luke 23:56; John 5:18; 9:16; Acts 13:27, 42; 15:21; 18:4); gen. *(toú)* *sabbátou* (Matt 12:8; Mark 2:28; 6:2; 16:1; Luke 6:5; Acts 1:12). In Acts 1:12,

"a sabbath day's journey" means, according to rabbinical limitation, one thousand larger paces, equal to about seven and one-half furlongs, about 1,650 yards. The day of the Sabbath (*hēméra* [2250], day; *toú sabbátou*) (Luke 13:14, 16; 14:5; John 19:31); in the dat. (Luke 13:14, 15; 14:1, 3; Acts 13:44); with *en* (1722), in, and the dat. (Matt 12:2; 24:20; Luke 6:1, 6, 7; John 5:16; 7:22, 23; 19:31). So also generally in the Sept.: Ex 31:13; 2 Kgs 4:23; Neh 10:31; 13:15.

(B) Pl. meaning more than one Sabbath (Acts 17:2; Col 2:16; Sept.: Isa 1:13; Hos 2:11). Elsewhere only in the pl. gen. (Matt 28:1, *opsé dé sabbátōn* [*opsé* {3796}, late], at the end of the Sabbaths, meaning at the end of the Sabbath or after the Sabbath, the Sabbath being now ended, toward the dawn as explained in Mark 16:2). The day of the Sabbaths (Luke 4:16; Acts 13:14; 16:13); dat., *toís sábbasi* (Matt 12:1, 5, 10–12; Mark 1:21; 3:2, 4; Luke 6:9); with the prep. *en* (1722), in, and the pl. dat. *toís sábbasi* (Mark 2:23, 24; Luke 4:31; 6:2; 13:10); *hēméra tōn sabbátōn* (Sept.: Ex 35:3; Deut 5:12); *toís sábbasi* or *sabbátois* (Sept.: Num 28:10; 2 Chr 2:4; 8:13).

(II) Metonymically it denotes a period of seven days, a week (Matt 28:1, "the first day of the week"; Mark 16:2, "the first day of a week"; see Luke 18:12, "twice in the week"; 24:1; John 20:1, 19; Acts 20:7; 1 Cor 16:2). Sept.: *hebdomádas*, weeks (Lev 23:15 [cf. Deut 16:9]).

The word "Sabbath" first occurs in Ex 16:23, but the institution of the day of rest is much older and is founded in nature and, like marriage, was instituted in Paradise (Gen 2:2, 3). The word usually indicates the seventh day of the week which by God's appointment was set apart for His service, but it is used also of other days or times separated and sanctified in a similar way (Lev 25:4).

Originally the Sabbath was devoted to simple rest from worldly toil. The fourth commandment in Ex 20:8–11; Deut 5:12–15 enjoins no specific religious service, except generally to keep it holy. But the opportunity thus given was improved. Subsequent legislation made it a day of holy convocation. The sacrifices of the temple were doubled; the shewbread was changed; the inner court of the temple was opened for solemn services; the prophets and the Levites took the occasion for imparting religious instruction to the people. It was a day of holy joy. There was freedom for social enjoyment. Indeed, the fear was that the day would be "wasted by idleness and degraded by sensuality and drunkenness" because it was so joyous (Neh 8:9–12; Hos 2:11).

But after the captivity arose the school of the Pharisees, and by them the attractive character of the Sabbatical observances was destroyed. In place of the joy, they imposed upon the people the yoke of a scrupulous, slavish sabbatarianism which made the Sabbath an end instead of a means, hampered the spirit of true worship, and laid greater stress upon a punctilious obedience to mere human regulations than upon the commands of the Law. Some of the ridiculous prohibitions were as follows: walking in the grass on the Sabbath because its bruising effect would constitute a kind of threshing; wearing nailed shoes because they would be viewed as carrying a burden; mounting a tree lest a twig should be broken. It was against this perversion of the commandment that the Lord protested. He refused to sanction Pharisaical legalism and vigorously defended His Sabbath miracles.

The example of Christ represents the Sabbath, not as a day of gloom, but as a pleasant and healthful day of rest, quiet religious service, and Christian benevolence. Jesus kept the Sabbath in the highest sense of the term. He observed every jot and tittle of the Mosaic Law in the freedom of the spirit. He taught us that acts of necessity and mercy are to be performed always, even on the Sabbath, and worldly occupations are to be put as far as possible out of our thoughts. In the Christian church the first day of the week has been substituted for the last day as a day of worship and rest. This, however, is in commemoration of the resurrection of Christ. By adopting the first day of the week instead of the last day of the week for rest and worship, the Christian church at the same time unloaded all the detailed rules and regulations that rendered the Sabbath day a day of legalistic bondage. The Christian church has full justification for this change. Upon the first day of the week Christ arose from the dead. The disciples before the Ascension assembled on Sunday when Jesus appeared to them (John 20:26). According to all authenticated tradition, Pentecost occurred on the first day of the week. Paul preached at Troas on the first day of the week which was, among those Christians, the day of religious service. Apparently they met at night because they may have had to work, being in a heathen environment (Acts 20:7). Paul tells the Corinthians that everyone is "to lay by him in store" upon the first day of the week as he is prospered (1 Cor 16:2). It was upon the Lord's day, and by this name he calls it, that John on Patmos saw through the open door into heaven (Rev 1:10). The following are additional passages of Scripture respecting the Sabbath and its proper observance: the divine institution of the Jewish Sabbath (Gen 2:2, 3; Ex 20:8–11; Deut 5:12, 15; Ezek 20:12; 44:24); servile labor forbidden (Ex 16:23, 29; 20:10, 11; 23:12; 34:21; 35:2, 3; Deut 5:14, 15; Jer 17:21, 22; Mark 15:43); the profanation of the Sabbath, the cause of national judgments (Neh 13:15–18; Ezek 20:15, 16; 23:38, 47); the Jewish Sabbath and the gospel dispensation (Matt 5:17; 12:12; Mark 2:27); the change of the Sabbath as a day of rest and worship from the seventh to the first day of the week (John 20:19; Acts 20:7; 1 Cor 16:2; Rev 1:10); the duties of the Sabbath enjoined (Lev 19:30; 26:2; Ezek 46:3; Mark 6:2; Luke 4:16, 31; Acts 13:14–16, 27, 42, 44; 17:2, 3); works of necessity and mercy to be done on this day (Matt 12:1, 3, 5, 7, 12, 13; Mark 2:23, 27; 3:2, 4; Luke 6:9; 13:15, 16; 14:3, 5; John 5:8–10, 18; 7:22; 9:14); blessings promised to those who keep the Sabbath

(Isa 56:2, 4, 5, 7; 58:13, 14); threatenings against Sabbath-breakers (Ex 31:14, 15; 35:2; Num 15:32–36; Jer 17:27; Ezek 20:13, 16, 21, 24; 22:8, 14, 26, 31; 23:38); Sabbath privileges taken away (Isa 1:13; Amos 8:10, 11).

Deriv.: *prosábbaton* (4315), the eve of the Sabbath.

4522. **σαγήνη** *sagḗnē*; gen. *sagḗnēs*, fem. noun. A seine, a long-drawn net or sweep-net, the ends of which were spread out by boats so as to cover a large portion of open sea, then drawn together, and all which they contain is taken (Matt 13:47; Sept.: Ezek 26:5, 14; 47:10); also a somewhat smaller net cast over the shoulder, spreading out in a circle and made to sink by weights.

Syn.: *díktuon* (1350), a net in a general sense; *amphíblēstron* (293), casting net.

4523. **Σαδδουκαῖος** *Saddoukaíos*; gen. *Saddoukaíou*, masc. proper noun. Sadducee, in the pl. *hoi Saddoukaíoi*, the Sadducees, who were a sect of the Jews in opposition to the Pharisees and Essenes (Matt 3:7; 16:1, 6, 11, 12; 22:23, 34; Mark 12:18; Luke 20:27; Acts 4:1; 5:17; 23:6–8). The origin of the name and its meaning are really unknown, but the most satisfactory theory is that the sect was derived from Sadok or Zadok and constituted a form of sacerdotal aristocracy. The Sadok is spoken of the famous high priest by that name whom Solomon appointed to succeed the deposed Abiathar (1 Kgs 2:35). The Sadducees were a small party with limited influence among the people and of a rationalistic turn of mind. From their connection with the priests, they were men of position and more or less of wealth. They were worldly-minded and had only a superficial interest in religion. Their theology was in direct contradiction to the Pharisees, and from its nature, could not be popular. It embraced four principal tenets:

(I) A denial of the divinity and consequent authority of the oral law, the body of commentary on the written Law which the Pharisees, without any historic evidence, maintained was handed down by tradition from the Law-giver Himself.

(II) The Sadducees accepted the teaching of Moses only and seemed to have rejected the later books of the OT.

(III) The denial of man's resurrection. They maintained that the soul dies with the body (Matt 22:23). Of course, the doctrine of future rewards and punishments fell with it, likewise the belief in angels or spirits (Acts 23:8).

(IV) The fourth principal tenet was that man had absolute moral freedom, for upon this freedom depended the moral quality of his actions. This tenet was, however, so excessive as to almost entirely exclude the divine government of the world. In the NT, however, the Sadducees are not spoken of with the same bitterness as the Pharisees, yet they were nonetheless determined foes of the Lord Jesus Christ and made common cause with the Pharisees in condemning Him to the cross. Annas and Caiaphas were Sadducees. The sect disappeared after the first Christian century. However, they have their counterparts in the reformed Jews and liberal Christians of the present day.

4524. **Σαδώκ** *Sadṓk*; masc. proper noun transliterated from the Hebr. *Tsādōq* (6659, OT), just. Sadoc, one of our Lord's ancestors (Matt 1:14).

4525. **σαίνω** *saínō*; fut. *sanṓ*. To wag, to move to and fro as dogs and other animals wag their tails in friendliness. Figuratively, to caress, flatter. In the NT figuratively to move in mind, disturb. In the pass. (1 Thess 3:3).

Syn.: *kinéō* (2795), to set in motion, to stir; *saleúō* (4531), to shake, agitate; *turbázō* (5182), to trouble, disturb.

Ant.: *eirēneúō* (1514), to be peaceful; *anapaúō* (373), to rest, give rest; *eirēnopoiéō* (1517), to make peace.

4526. **σάκκος** *sákkos*; gen. *sákkou*, masc. noun. Sackcloth, coarse black cloth commonly made of the long hair of goats

(Rev 6:12) and called mohair. Used for straining, for sacks, and for mourning garments. In the latter case it was worn instead of the ordinary garments or bound around the loins or spread under a person on the ground (Sept.: Gen 37:34; 1 Kgs 20:32; Isa 58:5; Joel 1:8; Jon 3:5ff.). Such garments were also worn by prophets and ascetics (Isa 20:2; Zech 13:4 [cf. 2 Kgs 1:8; Matt 3:4]). Hence in the NT generally (Rev 6:12, "the sun became black as sackcloth of hair" [cf. Isa 50:3]); of mourning garments (Matt 11:21; Luke 10:13); of a prophet's garment (Rev 11:3).

4527. Σαλά Salá; masc. proper noun transliterated from the Hebr. *Shelach* (7974, OT), sprout. Sala or Salah, a descendant of Shem (Gen 10:24; 11:12–15; Luke 3:35). In 1 Chr 1:18, 24 the name is given as Shelah.

4528. Σαλαθιήλ Salathiél; masc. proper noun transliterated from the Hebr. *Sheʾaltī'ēl* (7597, OT), I have asked God. Shealtiel, a descendant of David (1 Chr 3:17; Ezra 3:2), most often called Salathiel (Matt 1:12; Luke 3:27).

4529. Σαλαμίς Salamís; gen. *Salamínos*, fem. proper noun. Salamis, meaning salt. A seaport town with a good harbor on the eastern coast of Cyprus in the Mediterranean visited by Paul and Barnabas on their missionary journey (Acts 13:5). The city was once the capital of Cyprus and stood on the north side of the river Pediaeus. There was a Jewish population and synagogues there. In the time of Trajan and Hadrian there were great insurrections of the Jews, and Salamis was partially destroyed with its demolition being completed by an earthquake. It was, however, rebuilt by the Christian emperor Constantius and renamed Constantia. The ruins are known as old Famagusta.

4530. Σαλείμ Saleím; fem. proper noun transliterated from the Aramaic Salim, meaning completed A place named to mark the locality of Aenon where John

baptized (John 3:23). Eusebius and Jerome mentioned Salim as near the Jordan River, eight miles south of Scythopolis.

4531. σαλεύω saleúō; fut. *saleúsō*, from *sálos* (4535), wave. To move to and fro, shake. Trans., to put into a state of waving, rocking, vibratory motion.

(I) With the acc. (Luke 6:48; Heb 12:26). In the pass. (Matt 11:7; 24:29; Mark 13:25; Luke 7:24, "A reed shaken by the wind" [a.t.]; Luke 21:26; Acts 4:31; 16:26; Sept.: Ps 18:8; 82:5; 1 Chr 16:30). A measure, a quantity shaken down (Luke 6:38). Figuratively of things ready to fall and perish (Heb 12:27, "things that are shaken," perishable, indicating the Mosaic dispensation, while things that cannot be shaken represent the Christian dispensation).

(II) Metaphorically, to move in mind, agitate, disturb, with the acc. (Acts 17:13, to excite the people, cause a tumult). In the pass. (2 Thess 2:2). Acts 2:25 is a quotation from Ps 16:8.

Deriv.: *asáleutos* (761), immovable.

Syn.: *kinéō* (2795), to move, set in motion; *seíō* (4579), to shake, move to and fro; *saínō* (4525), to shake, disturb; *anaseíō* (383), to move or excite; *anastatóō* (387), figuratively to unsettle; *turbázō* (5182), to trouble, disturb.

Ant.: *eirēneúō* (1514), to be peaceful; *anapaúō* (373), to rest, give rest; *eirēnopoiéō* (1517), to make peace.

4532. Σαλήμ Salēm; fem. proper noun transliterated from the Hebr. *Shālēm* (8004, OT), peace. Salem, the place of which Melchizedek was king (Gen 14:18; Heb 7:1, 2). This word is used elsewhere in Ps 76:2. Some would interpret it in the first two passages as not referring to a place, but that Melchizedek was "king of peace." The majority of scholars, however, understand it to mean a place, and it is usually interpreted as referring to Jerusalem. Josephus also understands it this way. The name Jireh from Gen 22:14 was supposed to have been added to Salem, thus making Jerusalem, but this is uncertain. Jerome made the Salem of Gen 14:18 and the Shalem of Gen 33:18 identical and fixed it six miles from Scythopolis. There may be an identity between *Salḗm* and *Saleím* (4530).

4533. Σαλμών *Salmṓn*; masc. proper noun transliterated from the Hebr. *Salmōn* (8012, OT). Solomon (Judg 9:48), one of the high hills which were in the area of ancient Shechem and provided pasture for Jacob's flock. The word means clothing or investitures and is the name of the father of Boaz (Matt 1:4, 5; Luke 3:32; see Ps 68:14).

4534. Σαλμώνη *Salmṓnē*; fem. proper noun. Salmone, meaning clothing, a promontory forming the eastern extremity of the island of Crete (2914) and noticed in the account of Paul's journey to Rome (Acts 27:7).

4535. σάλος *sálos*; gen. *sálou*, masc. noun. Motion to and fro, agitation, tossing, any waving, rocking or vibratory motion. In the NT used only of the sea, and hence means the rolling billows (Luke 21:25; Sept.: Jon 1:15).

　　Deriv.: *saleúō* (4531), to move to and fro.

　　Syn.: *kúma* (2949), a wave; *klúdōn* (2830), a billow.

　　Ant.: *galḗnē* (1055), calmness.

4536. σάλπιγξ *sálpigx*; gen. *sálpiggos*, fem. noun. A trumpet (1 Cor 14:8; Rev 1:10; 4:1; 8:2, 6, 13; 9:14). As announcing the approach or presence of God (Heb 12:19 [cf. Ex 19:13, 16, 19; 1 Kgs 1:34, 39]), or the final advent of the Messiah (Matt 24:31). In 1 Cor 15:52 the last trumpet (1 Thess 4:16, "the trumpet of God" [a.t.], which means a trumpet which sounds by command of God; 1 Sam 13:3; 2 Kgs 12:13).

　　The trumpets in Scripture are of great significance in eschatology in determining when the rapture of the church takes place (1 Thess 4:13–18). This involves the question of whether the mention of the "last trumpet" in 1 Corinthians 15:52, simply referred to as "the trumpet" in 1 Thessalonians 4:16, is the same as the seventh trumpet in Revelation 11:11–15. Some assume that these trumpets are identical and thus presume that the rapture of the church will take place at the time of the occurrence of the seventh trumpet of Revelation 11:15. This seventh trumpet is in the middle or toward the latter part of the seven-year tribulation period, i.e., Daniel's prophetic seventieth week (Dan 9:25–27).

　　The contexts of the passages make it clear that not all references to trumpets in Scripture describe the same event nor are all the trumpets sounded for the same purpose. The trumpet of 1 Thessalonians 4:16 is mentioned in association with the resurrection of believers. Two events are described as taking place. The first is the resurrection of the believers who had died (v. 16). Immediately following this, the believers who are alive at that time will be raptured (1 Thess 4:17). According to 1 Corinthians 15:52, all believers, both the dead and living, will be changed at this time. This changing process will be simultaneous with the resurrection. The trumpet of 1 Thessalonians 4:16 and 1 Corinthians 15:52 deals entirely with believers and their resurrection and change. The seven trumpets of Revelation, however, deal with God's demonstration of wrath and judgment on unbelievers. It has nothing to do with the last trumpet for the church, for believers of the dispensation of grace. Believers are raptured from the earth because God did not appoint believers unto wrath (1 Thess 5:9).

　　The rapture is said to be at the last trumpet (1 Cor 15:52), but the last trumpet is not to be equated with the seventh trumpet of Revelation 11:15. The word for "last" in 1 Corinthians 15:52 is not *hústerē* (5305), hindermost, final or closing, but *eschátē* (2078), the latest, not in the process of time but pertaining to the events spoken of. This trumpet then is not necessarily the final trumpet. Also, the seventh trumpet of Revelation 11:15

is not designated as the last trumpet although numerically it is the last in a series of seven. The trumpet of Revelation 11:15 is only the last of seven trumpets spelling the judgments of God and is to be followed by the seven bowls of Revelation 15; 16.

In Matt 24:31 the Lord speaks of God sending His angels with a great sound of a trumpet. They shall gather together His elect from the four winds, from one end of heaven to the other. This is not called the last trumpet, yet it follows the Great Tribulation of Matthew 24:29. It concerns the elect of the Tribulation period who responded to God's heavenly witnesses of Revelation 7. This is actually the last trumpet although not called such.

Deriv.: *salpízō* (4537), to sound a trumpet.

4537. σαλπίζω *salpízō*; fut. *salpísō*, aor. *esálpisa*, from *sálpigx* (4536), a trumpet. To sound a trumpet, intrans. (Matt 6:2; Rev 8:6–8, 10, 12, 13; 9:1, 13; 10:7; 11:15). Of angels sounding the trumpet before the Messiah; *ho salpistḗs* (4538), the trumpeter being implied in 1 Cor 15:52. See Sept.: Num 10:3ff.; Isa 27:13; Joel 2:1.

Deriv.: *salpistḗs* (4538), a trumpeter.

Syn.: *ēchéō* (2278), to echo, sound; *exēchéō* (1831), to sound forth as a trumpet, to thunder; *bolízō* (1001), to sound.

Ant.: *sigáō* (4601), to keep silent.

4538. σαλπιστής *salpistḗs*; gen. *salpistoú*, masc. noun from *salpízō* (4537), to sound a trumpet. A trumpeter (Rev 18:22).

4539. Σαλώμη *Salṓmē*; gen. *Salṓmēs*, fem. proper noun. Salome, meaning peaceful.

(I) The wife of Zebedee and the mother of James the elder and John the evangelist. She was one of the followers of Christ (Matt 27:56; Mark 15:40; 16:1), though she seems, like many others, to have at first mistaken the true nature of His kingdom (Matt 20:21).

(II) The daughter of Herodias who danced before Herod (Matt 14:6; Mark 6:22). She is not named in the NT, but by Josephus. The graphic account of Herod's feast may be traced to Joanna, the wife of Chusa who was Herod's steward (Luke 8:3) and who was probably present. Salome married her uncle Philip, tetrarch of Trachonitis (5139), and next Aristobulus (711), king of Chalcis.

4540. Σαμάρεια *Samáreia*; gen. *Samareías*, fem. proper noun transliterated from the Hebr. *Shōmᵉrōn* (8111, OT), watchpost. Samaria, a famous city of central Palestine founded by Omri, king of Israel, situated thirty miles north of Jerusalem and six miles northwest of Shechem. It was built in 925 B.C. (1 Kgs 16:23, 24). After Omri made it the capital of Israel, it continued in that capacity for two hundred years until the fall of the northern kingdom in 721 B.C. It was the scene of many idolatrous practices. Ahab erected a great temple of Baal there; Jehu destroyed it and massacred the priest (1 Kgs 16:32, 33; 2 Kgs 10:18, 28). Twice the city was besieged by the Syrians, once in the reign of Ahab in 901 B.C., and once during the reign of Joram, 892 B.C. (1 Kgs 20:1). At the latter siege the people were reduced to the most terrible distress by famine but were wonderfully delivered in accordance with the prophecy of Elisha (2 Kgs 6:24–33; 7:1–20). About 170 years later, the city was captured by the king of Assyria after a siege of nearly three years. The northern kingdom was destroyed and the ten tribes carried into captivity (2 Kgs 18:9–12). Colonists from Assyria were sent to repopulate the country (2 Kgs 17:24; Ezra 4:9, 10). The city of Samaria continued to be a place of some importance. It was captured by Alexander the Great, who used the Syro-Macedonians to populate it. It was also taken by John Hyrcanus and after a year's siege was razed to the ground (109 B.C.). It was rebuilt again and adorned by Herod the Great who named it Sebaste in honor of Augustus. Herod gave it to him and settled a colony of six thousand persons there composed of veteran soldiers and peasants. He enlarged the city and surrounded it with a wall and colonnade. In NT times, Philip preached the gospel in Samaria (Acts 8:5, 9).

4541. Σαμαρείτης *Samareitēs*; gen. *Samareítou*, masc. proper noun. A Samaritan (Matt 10:5; Luke 9:52; 10:33; 17:16; John 4:9, 39, 40; 8:48; Acts 8:25). An inhabitant of Samaria (2 Kgs 17:29). In the NT, however, the term in the pl. is applied to the people who were settlers in Samaria in the place of the Israelites who had been exiled by the Assyrian king. Their defiled origin (Ezra 4:1ff.), their compromise with the Persian kings (Neh 4:1ff.) and their selection of Mt. Gerizim, the mountain of cursing (Deut 27:11–13), as a place of worship in separation from the Jews' place of worship (Luke 9:52, 53; John 4:20, 21) created severe animosity between the Samaritans and the Jews (Matt 10:5; John 4:9). Hence the name Samaritan was, to the Jew, a term of reproach and contempt (John 8:48). The Samaritans too expected a Messiah (John 4:25), and many of them followed Christ (Acts 8:1; 9:31; 15:3). The history of the country of Samaria up to 720 B.C. belongs to the kingdom of Israel. After Israel was carried into captivity, the history of the Samaritans as such begins.

A much-debated question has been whether the NT Samaritans were of purely foreign extraction or were of mixed blood. The latter opinion seems most reasonable. It is very likely that all the Jews were carried away out of the land. This opinion is supported by the fact that money was contributed from the cities of Manasseh and Ephraim to repair the temple in Josiah's time (2 Chr 34:9), and idols were destroyed in the same region (2 Chr 34:6, 7). The Assyrian colonists obtained a priest to teach them "the manner of the God of the land" and combined some forms of Jehovah-worship with their idolatry (2 Kgs 17:25–41). When the Jews returned from the captivity with a spirit more exclusive than ever, the contrast between Jew and Samaritan was very strong indeed. The Samaritans wished to have a share in rebuilding the temple, but the Jews refused to allow them to cooperate. The breach widened, and the Samaritans succeeded in hindering the work at Jerusalem by misrepresentations to the Persian kings (Ezra chap. 4; Neh chaps. 4; 6). At length the opposition culminated in the setting up of a rival temple by the Samaritans on Mount Gerizim. The occasion of this seems to have been the expulsion from Jerusalem by Nehemiah of the son of the high priest, who was a son-in-law of Sanballat (Neh 13:28). According to Josephus, the person expelled was Manasseh, whose father-in-law, Sanballat, obtained from Alexander the Great permission to erect the temple. But the temple was probably erected at an earlier date. After this time the city of Samaria declined, and Shechem increased in importance. This temple was destroyed by John Hyrcanus after standing for two hundred years.

Conflicts between the Jews and the Samaritans were frequent. The Samaritans defiled the temple at Jerusalem with bones of the dead. There was a general insurrection among them in the time of Pilate, whose severity resulted in his removal from office. A crowd arrayed themselves against Vespasian, and he slew 1,600 Samaritans. The bitter animosity between the two races must be understood in order to comprehend many facts in NT history. Thus the Galileans avoided going through Samaria in their journeys to Jerusalem since they were exposed to insult, assault, and even danger of death. The Twelve Apostles were not to go among the Samaritans (Matt 10:5), and the inhospitality of that people excited the blazing indignation of James and John (Luke 9:52–56). Yet the Lord Jesus showed Himself to be far superior to the narrow feeling of race by the parable of the Good Samaritan (Luke 10:30–37), His commendation of the healed Samaritan (Luke 17:11–19), and His conversation with the woman of Samaria (John 4:1–42). This interview throws light upon the Samaritan character and claims. The woman asserts Abrahamic descent for them—"Our father Jacob"—but this the Jews would not allow. It was probable the people had become more of a mixed blood, since according to Josephus, many renegade, apostate, and law-breaking Jews sought refuge among the Samaritans. The gospel gained some success there (Acts 1:8; 8:5–25). However, most of the Samaritans adhered to their old religion, and therefore, frequently came into collision with Christianity and with the Roman emperors, particularly in A.D. 529. Today there is a small community of Samaritans near Nablus (Shechem). They claim to possess and show the Pentateuch in the old Hebr. or Samaritan writing which has attracted great attention as a very ancient version. Three times a year, the Feast of Unleavened Bread, the Feast of Weeks, and the Feast of Tabernacles, they make a pilgrimage to the sacred Mount Gerizim. They celebrate all the Mosaic festivals, and on the Passover they offer sacrifices on Mount Gerizim.

4542. Σαμαρεῖτις Samareítis; gen. *Samareítidos*, fem. proper noun. A woman of Samaria (John 4:9).

4543. Σαμοθράκη Samothrákē; gen. *Samothrákēs*, fem. proper noun. Thracian Samos, or Samos of Thrace, an island in the northeastern part of the Aegean Sea eight miles long and six miles broad. Homer says that from its lofty ridges the battlefield of Troy might be seen, and one of its mountains has an elevation of 5,248 feet, affording a wide view. Paul visited it on his second missionary journey (Acts 16:11). It is today a Greek island called Samothraki.

4544. Σάμος Sámos; gen. *Sámou*, fem. proper noun. Samos, meaning a height. An island in the Aegean Sea, a few miles from the mainland and forty-two miles southwest of Smyrna (4667). The island

is twenty-seven miles long, ten miles wide, and has an area of 165 square miles. It was the seat of Juno worship, the birthplace of Pythagoras, and was noted for its valuable pottery. Paul visited the island on his third missionary journey (Acts 20:15).

4545. Σαμουήλ Samouḗl, masc. proper noun transliterated from the Hebr. *Sh^emūēl* (8050, OT), heard of God. Samuel, the son of Elkanah and Hannah. He was a celebrated Hebrew prophet and the last of their judges. As a child, he officiated in some form in the temple and was favored with revelations of the divine will respecting the family of Eli, the high priest, under whose care and training his mother had placed him (1 Sam 3:4–14). After Saul was rejected for his disobedience in the matter of Agag, Samuel was instructed to anoint David as king, after which he returned to Ramah where he died (1 Sam 25:1). The books of 1 and 2 Samuel in the Sept. are called also the 1 and 2 books of Kings. The books of 1 and 2 Samuel bear this name, perhaps because he wrote the history of his own times as given in the first book, and therefore, the entire work went under his name. But it is more probable that the name was in consequence of Samuel being the hero of the first part of the history, and that the author belonged to a later period. See Acts 3:24; 13:20; Heb 11:32.

4546. Σαμψών Sampsṓn. masc. proper noun transliterated from the Hebr. *Shimshōn* (8123, OT), sun-like. Sampson or Samson, son of Manoah of the tribe of Dan and for twenty years a judge of Israel, famous for his strength (Heb 11:32 [cf. Judg 13:1–16]). Samson is ranked with the heroes of the faithful (Heb 11:32, 33). He lived in the anarchical period of the judges and ironically was ultimately defeated because of his own rebellion against God's rule in his life.

4547. σανδάλιον sandálion; gen. *sandalíou*, neut. noun, a diminutive of *sándalon* (n.f.), a sole or sandal. A sandal, i.e., a sole of wood or hide covering the bottom of the foot and bound on with straps (Mark 6:9; Acts 12:8; Sept.: Josh 9:5; Isa 20:2).

Syn.: *hupódēma* (5266), shoe or a sole bound under the foot.

4548. σανίς *sanís*; gen. *sanídos*, fem. noun. A board, plank of a ship (Acts 27:44; Sept.: Song 8:9; Ezek 27:5).

4549. Σαούλ *Saoúl*; masc. proper noun transliterated from the Hebr. *Sha'ūl* (7586, OT). Saul, the Jewish name for Paul (3972). It means asked, desired. In Gr. his Jewish name is *Saúlos* (4569) (Acts 9:4, 17; 22:7, 13; 26:14). The first king of Israel (Acts 13:21 [cf. 1 Sam chap. 9]).

4550. σαπρός *saprós*; fem. *saprá*, neut. *saprón*, adj. from *sḗpō* (4595), to rot. Bad, rotten, putrid.

(I) Particularly of vegetable or animal substances as a tree and its fruit, fish (Matt 7:17, 18; 12:33; 13:48; Luke 6:43).

(II) Figuratively in a moral sense, corrupt, foul, referring to the spoken word (Eph 4:29).

Syn.: *kakós* (2556), bad; *ponērós* (4190), malevolent; *aischrós* (150), base, shameful, filthy; *átimos* (820), without honor; *dólios* (1386), deceitful; *phaúlos* (5337), foul, corrupt; *aschḗmōn* (809), uncomely; *koinós* (2839), unclean; *akáthartos* (169), unclean, impure; *anósios* (462), unholy, profane; *auchmērós* (850), dirty, obscure, dark; *spílos* (4696), spotted.

Ant.: *kalós* (2570), good; *agathós* (18), benevolent; *ákakos* (172), harmless; *eilikrinḗs* (1506), sincere, genuine; *euthús* (2117), upright; *tímios* (5093), honorable; *ádolos* (97), without deceit; *chrēstós* (5543), good, gracious, kind; *katharós* (2513), clean; *hagnós* (53), free from defilement, pure; *hósios* (3741), religiously right, sacred, undefiled; *hágios* (40), holy; *hierós* (2413), sacred, associated with God; *akéraios* (185), innocent, pure; *amíantos* (283), undefiled; *áspilos* (784), unblemished; *amṓmētos* (298),

unblamable; *ámemptos* (273), faultless; *áxios* (514), worthy; *euschḗmōn* (2158), comely, honorable.

4551. Σαπφείρη *Sappheírē*; gen. *Sappheírēs*, fem. proper noun. Sapphira, meaning beautiful. The wife of Ananias and partner in his guilt and punishment (Acts 5:1).

4552. σάπφειρος *sáppheiros*; gen. *sappheírou*, fem. noun. Sapphire, a precious stone, next in hardness and value to the diamond, mostly of a blue color in various shades (Rev 21:19; Sept.: Ex 24:10; 28:18).

4553. σαργάνη *sargánē*; gen. *sargánēs*, fem. noun. Something braided, twisted, interwoven, such as cords. In the NT, a rope basket, network of cords in which Paul was let down from a window in Damascus (2 Cor 11:33 [cf. Acts 9:25 where the word *spurís* {4711}, a round large basket, is used]).

Syn.: *kóphinos* (2894), a wicker basket, originally containing a particular measure or capacity.

4554. Σάρδεις *Sárdeis*; gen. *Sárdeōn*, fem. pl. proper noun. Sardis, a city in Asia Minor, the capital of Lydia. Sardis was situated at the foot of Mount Tmolus, about fifty miles northeast of Smyrna and thirty miles southeast of Thyatira. It was on the river Pactolus, celebrated for its golden sands, and some two miles from the river Hermes, a site of great beauty. Sardis was famous because of Croesus, whose name was syn. with wealth. When Cyrus conquered Croesus in 548 B.C., he took his treasure. The Persians kept a garrison in the citadel. Alexander gained possession of the city after the battle of Granicus and garrisoned it. Antiochus the Great sacked the city in 214 B.C.; afterward it was subject to the kings of Pergamos. An earthquake destroyed it in the reign of Tiberius, A.D. 17, but it was rebuilt, the emperor remitting tribute for five years and granting the money to assist in reconstructing the city. The prosperity of Sardis arose from its convenience as a commercial market and its prosperous manufacturers. The art of dyeing wool was discovered here. Sardis was the seat of one of the seven churches of Asia Minor, and the Christians were so corrupted by the prevailing worldliness that they received a severe rebuke (Rev 3:1–5).

4555. σάρδινος sárdinos; gen. *sardínou*, masc. noun. A sardius, a precious stone of red color, so-named either because it was first discovered by the inhabitants of Sardis in Asia Minor or from the island of Sardinia where the best quality was found (Rev 4:3 [TR]). The same as *sárdinos* (4555).

4556. σάρδιος sárdios; gen. *sardíou*, masc. noun. A sardius, a precious stone of a blood-red or sometimes flesh color, more commonly known by the name of carnelian (Rev 4:3 [UBS]; 21:20; Sept.: Ex 28:17; Ezek 28:13). The same as *sárdinos* (4555).

4557. σαρδόνυξ sardónux; gen. *sardónuchos*, fem. noun. Sardonyx. A precious stone exhibiting a milk-white variety of the onyx or chalcedony, intermingled with shades or stripes of sardian or carnelian (Rev 21:20).

4558. Σάρεπτα Sárepta; gen. *Saréptōn*, neut. pl. proper noun. Sarepta, meaning smelting house, the Zarephath of the OT. A Phoenician town on the Mediterranean Sea between Tyre and Sidon (Luke 4:26).

4559. σαρκικός sarkikós; fem. *sarkikḗ*, neut. *sarkikón*, adj. from *sárx* (4561), flesh. Fleshly, carnal, pertaining to the flesh or body. Found only in the epistles.

(I) Generally, of things, *tá sarkiká*, things corporeal, external, temporal (Rom 15:27; 1 Cor 9:11).

(II) As implying weakness, frailty, imperfection; e.g., of persons as being carnal, worldly (1 Cor 3:1, 3, 4); of things,

carnal, human, frail, transient, temporary (2 Cor 1:12; 10:4; Heb 7:16). Some MSS read *sárkinos* (4560) in 1 Cor 3:1; Heb 7:16 meaning made of flesh. *Sarkikós* means with tendency to satisfy the flesh, implying sinfulness, sinful propensity, carnal (Rom 7:14, under the influence of carnal desires); of things (1 Pet 2:11, carnal desires, having their seat in the carnal nature).

Syn.: *phusikós* (5446), physical; *sōmatikós* (4984), bodily; *psuchikós* (5591), soulish, with affinity to natural sinful propensities, the person in whom the *sárx*, the flesh, is more the ruling principle even as *psuchikós* and *psuchḗ* (5590) is for the animalistic instincts. Here *psuchḗ*, the nonphysical element which makes one alive, conscious of the environment, is to be distinguished from *pneúma* (4151), spirit, which is distinctive of man as the element of communication with God. *Sárx* covers that entire domain of our fallen nature made subject to vanity in which sin springs up and moves (Rom 7:18; 8:5).

Ant.: *pneumatikós* (4152), spiritual, pertaining to *pneúma* (4151), spirit with which man can know and communicate with God.

4560. σάρκινος sárkinos; fem. *sarkínē*, neut. *sárkinon*, adj. from *sárx* (4561), flesh, body. Fleshly, material, made or consisting of flesh (2 Cor 3:3; 1 Cor 3:1 [UBS]). Characterized by the suffix *-inos*, referring to being made of flesh, matter, versus *-ikós* which carries an ethical meaning as in *sarkikós* (4559), with propensities of the flesh unto sin.

4561. σάρξ sárx; gen. *sarkós*, fem. noun. Flesh of a living creature in distinction from that of a dead one, which is *kréas* (2907), meat.

(I) Specifically flesh. Sing. as one of the constituent parts of the body (Luke 24:39; 1 Cor 15:39; Sept.: Gen 2:21; 2 Kgs 5:10, 14). Pl. *kaí sárkas*, fleshy parts (Rev 19:18); figuratively and hyperbolically, with *phágō* (5315), to eat, consume, to destroy flesh (pl. *sárkas*, acc. [James 5:3; Rev 17:16]).

(II) Metonymically meaning flesh as used for the body, the corpus, the material nature as distinguished from the spiritual and intangible (*pneúma* [4151], the spirit). This usage of *sárx* is far more frequent in the NT than in classical writers.

(A) Generally and without any good or evil quality implied. **(1)** The opposite of *to pneúma*, the spirit expressed (1 Cor 5:5; 2 Cor 7:1; Col 2:5; 1 Pet 4:6 [cf. Sept.: Job 14:22; Isa 10:18]). Also *sárx* and *haíma* (129), blood, as a periphrasis for the whole animal nature of man consisting of flesh and blood (Heb 2:14). Simply, the physical part of the personality of man (John 6:52 [cf. 2 Cor 12:7, *skólops* {4647}, thorn in the flesh, meaning physical ailment]; Col 1:24; 2:1, 23; Heb 9:10, 13; 1 Pet 3:21; Jude 1:8, 23). In Acts 2:26, 31, *hē sárx mou*, my body meaning I, quoted from Ps 16:9. Metaphorically in John 6:51, "and the bread . . . is my flesh," meaning that Jesus Himself is the principle of life and nutrition to the regenerated soul; see vv. 53–56 (cf. Matt 26:26 where it is *sôma* [4983], body); Sept.: generally in Ezek 36:26. Specifically it means mortal body in distinction from a future and spiritual existence (2 Cor 4:11; Gal 2:20; Phil 1:22, 24; 1 Pet 4:2). **(2)** Used for that which is merely external or only apparent, in opposition to what is spiritual and real (John 6:63, "It is the spirit that quickeneth; the flesh profiteth nothing"; 8:15; 1 Cor 1:26; 2 Cor 5:16; Eph 6:5; Col 3:22; Phile 1:16); of outward affliction, trials (1 Cor 7:28; 2 Cor 7:5; Gal 4:13, 14; 1 Pet 4:1); specifically of circumcision in the flesh, the external rite (Rom 2:28; 4:1; 2 Cor 11:18; Gal 3:3, i.e., by Judaism [cf. v. 2]; Gal 6:12, 13; Eph 2:11; Phil 3:3, 4; Col 2:13). **(3)** As the medium of natural generation and descent, and consequently kindred (John 1:13). The children of the flesh, the natural descendants (Rom 9:8; Eph 5:29, 30 [in allusion to Gen 2:23; 29:14]; Heb 12:9). Of one's countrymen (Rom 11:14) with *katá* (2596), according to the flesh meaning by natural descent

(Acts 2:30; Rom 9:3; 1 Cor 10:18; Gal 4:23, 29; perhaps Rom 1:3; 9:5 [cf. Eph 2:11 with the prep. *en* {1722}, in, followed by the dat. *sarkí*, meaning Gentiles according to the flesh]; Sept.: Gen 37:27 [cf. Judg 9:2]; 2 Sam 5:1; 19:13, 14).

(B) As implying weakness, frailty, imperfection, both physical and moral; the opposite being *pneúma* (4151), the spirit (Matt 26:41; Mark 14:38, "the spirit truly is ready, but the flesh weak" [a.t.]). Also as opposed to *tó Pneúma Hágion* (39), holy, meaning the Holy Spirit (John 3:6). Simply (Rom 6:19; 2 Cor 1:17; 10:2, 3). In 1 Cor 15:50 "flesh and blood" means frail, feeble man (Gal 1:16; Eph 6:12). In opposition to *ho patér* (3962), the Father, the one in the heavens (Matt 16:17). Generally (Gen 6:3; Ps 78:39).

(C) As implying sinfulness, proneness to sin, the carnal nature, the seat of carnal appetites and desires, of sinful passions and affections whether physical or moral (the epistles of 2 Pet and 1 John [cf. Eccl 2:3; 5:5]). The Gr. ascribed a similar influence to the body (*sôma* [4983]). As opposed to *Pneúma* (4151), the Spirit, referring to the Holy Spirit or His influences (Rom 8:1, 4–6, 9, 13; Gal 5:16, 17, 19, 24; 6:8). Simply (Rom 7:5, 18, 25; 8:3, 7, 8, 12; 13:14; Gal 5:13; Eph 2:3; Col 2:1, 18; 2 Pet 2:10, 18; 1 John 2:16).

(III) Metonymically meaning flesh, human nature, man (Matt 19:5, 6; Mark 10:8; 1 Cor 6:16; Eph 5:31; Jude 1:7, "other flesh" [a.t.], meaning other than their own, committing adultery with other men's wives or with foreigners; Sept.: Gen 2:24). Preceded by *pása* (3956), *pása sárx*, all flesh, meaning all men, all mankind (Luke 3:6; John 17:2; Acts 2:17; 1 Pet 1:24; Sept.: Gen 6:12; Ps 65:3). Preceded by *ou* (3756), not, the neg. in its absolute sense, i.e., *ou pása sárx* meaning absolutely no flesh, no man, where *ou* qualifies the intervening verb; preceded by *mé* (3361), not, the neg. in its conditional sense (Matt 24:22; Mark 13:20; Rom 3:20; 1 Cor 1:29; Gal 2:16). Specifically of the incarnation of Christ, His incarnate human nature (John 1:14; Rom

1:3, "according to the flesh"; 9:5; Eph 2:15, "in his flesh"; Col 1:22, in His body incarnate; 1 Tim 3:16; Heb 5:7; 10:20; 1 Pet 3:18; 4:1; 1 John 4:2, 3; 2 John 1:7).

Deriv.: *sarkikós* (4559), fleshy, pertaining to the flesh, carnal, sensual, with proneness to satisfy the desires of the flesh; *sárkinos* (4560), of the flesh, made of flesh, flesh being the material from which it is made. Note the distinction that when an adj. ends in -*ikós* it refers to the willing proneness to do that which the noun stands for such as the flesh. However, when the suffix is -*inos* it refers to the material from which the noun is composed.

Syn.: *sṓma* (4983), body, standing either for the body as part of the composite nature of man or for the complete man, although sometimes the word *psuchḗ* (5590), soul, may also stand for the complete man which would include his spirit and body; *ptṓma* (4430), a corpse; *chrṓs* (5559), the body, but referring rather to the exterior of it, the surface; *kréas* (2907), flesh in the sense of meat; *húlē* (5208), matter.

Ant.: *pneúma* (4151), spirit; *psuchḗ* (5590), soul, that which enables man to know his environment; *phántasma* (5326), that which only appears, a specter or phantom as opposed to the reality of the flesh which can be touched.

4562. Σαρούχ *Saroúch*; masc. proper noun transliterated from the Hebr. *S*ᵉ*rūg* (8286, OT), branch. Saruch, Serug, the father of Nahor (Luke 3:35 [TR]), one of the post-diluvian patriarchs in the line of Shem (Gen 11:20, 23; 1 Chr 1:26).

4563. σαρόω *saróō*; contracted *sarṓ*, fut. *sarṓsō*, from *saírō* (n.f.), to sweep. To sweep, cleanse with a broom (Luke 15:8). Pass. (Matt 12:44; Luke 11:25).

Ant.: *likmáō* (3039), to winnow, scatter; *skorpízō* (4650), to scatter, dissipate.

4564. Σάρρα *Sárra*; gen. *Sárras*, fem. proper noun transliterated from the Hebr. *Sārāh* (8283, OT), Jehovah is prince.

Sarah, the name of the wife of Abraham (Rom. 4:19; 9:9; Heb 11:11; 1 Pet 3:6). She was known as Sarai until Gen 17:15 when God changed her name from "my princess," referring to Abraham, to "princess" for all the race. She lived to 127 years of age, or more than thirty-six years after the birth of Isaac, and was buried in a field of Machpelah in Hebron which Abraham bought for the purpose.

4565. Σάρων *Sárōn*; gen. *Sárōnos*, masc. proper noun transliterated from the Hebr. *Shārōn* (8289, OT), a palin. Saron, Sharon, a level tract along the Mediterranean between Caesarea and Joppa (Acts 9:35). It is twenty-five or thirty miles in length and from eight to fifteen miles in width. See 1 Chr 27:29; Isa 33:9; 65:10.

4566. Σατᾶν *Satán*; masc. noun transliterated the Hebr. *Sātān* (7854, OT), adversary. Satan. Found as *Satán* only in 2 Cor 12:7. The same as *Satanás* (4567), Satan.

Syn.: *diábolos* (1228), the slanderer; *ho peirázōn* (pres. act. part. of *peirázō* [3985], to tempt), the tempter; *drákōn* (1404), dragon; *óphis* (3789), serpent; *ho planṓn* (pres. act. part. of *planáō* [4105], to deceive), the deceiver; *Apollúōn* (623), the destroyer; *ponērós* (4190), the evil one; *antídikos* (476), the adversary; *ho katḗgoros* (2725), the accuser; *ho antikeímenos* (pres. act. part. of *antíkeimai* [480], to be contrary), the one who has set himself against all, the adversary. See *Satanás* (4567), Satan, for discussion.

4567. Σατανᾶς *Satanás*; masc. noun transliterated the Hebr. *Sātān* (7854, OT), adversary. Satan. The same as *Satán* (4566). *Satanás* occurs thirty-four times in the NT: in Matt 4:10; 12:26; 16:23; Mark 1:13; 3:23, 26; 4:15; 8:33; Luke 4:8; 10:18; 11:18; 13:16; John 13:27; Acts 5:3; 26:18; Rom 16:20; 1 Cor 5:5; 7:5; 2 Cor 2:11; 11:14; 1 Thess 2:18; 2 Thess 2:9; 1 Tim 1:20; 5:15; Rev 2:9, 13, 24; 3:9; 12:9; 20:2, 7. Satan is present in the world and tempts both believers and unbelievers (Matt 16:23; Mark 8:33; Luke 22:3; Acts 5:3; 1 Kgs 11:14, 23, 25 [cf. 2 Sam 19:23]). This is one name given to the prince of the devils. Another name is *diábolos* (1228), devil, slanderer, false accuser. In his name as Satan, he is the opposer, the adversary of both believers and unbelievers. *Satanás* is the prince of the fallen angels (Matt 4:10; Mark 1:13; Rev 12:9) and is also used as a general word for evil spirits or devils (Matt 12:26; Mark 3:23, 26; Luke 11:18). Applied by the Lord to Peter who was considered as opposing the divine plan of man's redemption through Christ's sufferings and death, and thus as joining with Satan (Matt 16:23; Mark 8:33). The name Satan had not been translated into Gr. until shortly before the Christian era, for we never find it so rendered in the Sept. but always as *ho diábolos*, the devil. This is used as a proper noun in the Sept.: Job 1:6–12; Zech 3:1.

In the NT, however, we find frequently as *ho diábolos*, the expression *ho Satanás*, Satan, almost always with an art. Yet in 2 Cor 12:7 we have Satan (4566) without the art. The transliteration Satan is found thirty-four times in the NT, of which at least thirteen cases are in the Gospels.

In the Apostolic writings we find some periphrases of the name Satan such as "the evil one [*ho ponērós* {4190}, the malevolent one]" (see Eph 6:16; 1 John 2:13f.; 3:12; 5:19f.). This designation is also used five times in the Gospels; in addition, in the last clause of the Lord's prayer (see Matt 5:39; 6:13; Luke 11:4).

In the Revelation, "the dragon [*drákōn* {1404}]" is frequently used as a syn. for Satan, probably meaning "the sharp-seeing one" from *dérkomai* (n.f.), to see clearly, sharply. It is used in Rev 12:3ff.; 13:2, 4, 11; 16:13; 20:2 as denoting a large serpent as in Class. Gr., explicitly identified with the "old serpent" of Gen 3. (See Rev 12:9; 20:2.) This identification is perhaps implied in Rom 16:20; 2 Cor 11:3.

Satan is also called *ho katḗgoros* (2725), the accuser (Rev 12:10); and *ho Apollúōn* (623), the destroyer (Rev 9:11).

He is also called the *antídikos* (476), the adversary (1 Pet 5:8); *ho antikeímenos*, the pres. part. of *antíkeimai* (480), to be contrary, the one who has set himself against all, the adversary (1 Tim 5:14); the prince of the power of the air (Eph 2:2); *Belíal* or *Belíar* (955), meaning worthlessness (2 Cor 6:15).

In 1 Cor 5:5f. and 1 Tim 1:20 the expression "to deliver someone unto Satan" (a.t.) is probably based on Job 1:12; 2:6, where the patriarch is delivered to Satan to be tried by suffering. When Paul uses it, it means excommunication, the excommunicated becoming a target of the evil one. This, however, is with a redemptive purpose to bring the sinner back to Christ and to relieve the church of the charge of tolerating flagrant evil. The "destruction of the flesh" in 1 Cor 5:5 means the infliction of physical death as in the case of Ananias and Sapphira (Acts 5:1–11). In 1 Tim 1:20, however, death cannot be intended, for the object of the discipline is that the offender may be taught not to blaspheme. In 1 Cor 5:5f. the discipline was intended to bring about repentance as indeed it may have (2 Cor 2:7; 7:12).

4568. σάτον *sáton*; gen. *sátou*, neut. noun. A measure for dry things in Hebr. called *seah* (Matt 13:33; Luke 13:21), equivalent to nearly one and one-half pecks according to some (cf. *módios* {3426}, bushel).

4569. Σαῦλος *Saúlos*; gen. *Saúlou*, masc. proper noun transliterated from the Hebr. *Sha'ūl* (7586, OT). The same as *Saoúl* (4549), the Jewish name of Paul (Acts 7:58; 8:1, 3; 9:1, 8, 11, 19, 22, 24, 26; 11:25, 30; 12:25; 13:1, 2, 7, 9).

4570. σβέννυμι *sbénnumi*; fut. *sbésō*. To quench, extinguish. Trans.:

(I) Of light or fire with the acc. (Matt 12:20; Eph 6:16; Heb 11:34). Pass., to be quenched, go out (Matt 25:8; Mark 9:44, 46, 48; Sept.: Lev 6:12, 13; Job 21:17; Isa 42:3).

(II) Figuratively to dampen, hinder, repress, as in preventing the Holy Spirit from exerting His full influence, with the acc. (1 Thess 5:19; Sept.: Song 8:7).

Deriv.: *ásbestos* (762), unquenchable.

Ant.: *anáptō* (381), to kindle; *puróō* (4448), to be fiery, on fire, burn; *kaíō* (2545), to burn, set on fire; *phlogízō* (5394), to cause a blaze, inflame, set on fire; *anazōpuréō* (329), rekindle, stir up, set on fire; *katakaíō* (2618), to burn down.

4571. σέ *sé*; personal pron., acc. sing. of the *sú* (4771), thou, you in the sing. Thee, thou.

4572. σεαυτοῦ *seautoú*; reflexive pron. gen. sing. from *sé* (4571), thee, and *autós* (846), self. Of thyself. Dat. *seautō̂*, to thyself, masc., fem. *seautē̂*. Gen. (John 1:22; Acts 26:1); dat. (Acts 9:34; 16:28); acc. *seautón*, to thyself (Matt 4:6; 8:4; Luke 10:27). Where special emphasis is to be laid on *autē̂s*, it is written separately (Luke 2:35, *kaí soú dé autē̂s*, "and of thy own" [a.t.]). No reflexives occur in the nom. case.

4573. σεβάζομαι *sebázomai*; fut. *sebásomai*, mid. deponent from *sébas* (n.f.), reverential awe, which is from *sébomai* (4576), to worship religiously. To stand in awe of someone, to reverence, venerate, worship (Rom 1:25). Occurs with *latreúō* (3000), to worship. *Sebázomai* denotes religious expressions of veneration in particular as well as reverential behavior in general.

Deriv.: *sébasma* (4574), object of worship; *sebastós* (4575), venerable, august.

Syn.: *proskunéō* (4352), to make obeisance, worship, reverence; *therapeúō* (2323), to serve; *latreúō* (3000), to perform (religious) service; *eulabéomai* (2125), to reverence inwardly.

Ant.: *asebéō* (764), to act impiously; *hierosuléō* (2416), to commit sacrilege.

4574. σέβασμα *sébasma*; gen. *sebásmatos*, neut. noun from *sebázomai*

(4573), to worship, venerate. The object of worship or veneration (Acts 17:23; 2 Thess 2:4).

Syn.: *thrēskeía* (2356), religion.

4575. σεβαστός *sebastós*; fem. *sebastē̂*, neut. *sebastón*, adj. from *sebázomai* (4573), to venerate. Venerated, august. In Lat. Augustus. In the NT used as an honorary title and then a proper noun, *ho Sebastós*, Augustus.

(I) A title first assumed by Caesar Octavianus and retained by his successors as a personal appellation. Spoken of Nero (Acts 25:21, 25).

(II) An adj., Augustan, pertaining to Augustus, as the Augustan cohort (Acts 27:1). Several of the Roman legions also bore this honorary title. Others suppose it to be a Samaritan cohort, so-called from *Sebastē̂*, Sebaste, the name given by Herod the Great to Samaria in honor of Augustus. Josephus mentions troops called *Sebastēnoí*, probably from Sebaste or Samaria.

4576. σέβομαι *sébomai*; fut. *sebésomai*, pass. deponent. to worship. To worship, to reverence. In the NT, only in the mid. (Matt 15:9; Mark 7:7 quoted from Isa 29:13; Acts 16:14; 18:7, 13; 19:27; Sept.: Josh 4:24; Job 1:9). The part. noun *sebómenos*, a worshiper of the true God (Acts 13:43, 50; 16:14; 17:4, 17). These were Gentile proselytes as expressed in Acts 13:43.

Deriv.: *asebḗs* (765), godless; *eusebḗs* (2152), devout, godly; *theosebḗs* (2318), godly; *semnós* (4586), worthy of respect.

Syn.: *proskunéō* (4352), to make obeisance, worship, reverence; *therapeúō* (2323), to serve; *latreúō* (3000), to perform (religious) service; *eulabéomai* (2125), to reverence inwardly.

Ant.: *asebéō* (764), to act impiously; *hierosuléō* (2416), to commit sacrilege.

4577. σειρά *seirá*; gen. *seirás*, fem. noun from *eírō* (n.f.), to fasten. A cord, band, chain. In 2 Pet 2:4, the chains mentioned are not to be understood as literal material shackles. The expression "of darkness" (*zóphou*, gen. of *zóphos* [2217], darkness) indicates that darkness itself somehow serves to restrain these fallen spirits. If taken as a parallel passage, Jude 1:6 states that these creatures have been bound by "eternal" (*aḯdios* [126]) chains and are being kept (*tetḗrēken*, perf. act. ind. of *tēréō* [5083], to keep) under (*hupó* [5259]) darkness. The phrase "under darkness" suggests that darkness exercises some kind of dominion over these immured angels, it is something under the control of which the angels remain imprisoned.

Syn.: *hálusis* (254), chain or bond for binding the body or any part of it; *desmós* (1199), usually in the pl. neut. *desmá*, bonds, chains.

4578. σεισμός *seismós*; gen. *seismoú*, masc. noun. from *seíō* (4579), to shake. Earthquake, a shaking.

(I) Generally, in the sea meaning a tempest, tornado (Matt 8:24).

(II) Specifically, an earthquake (Matt 24:7; 27:54; 28:2; Mark 13:8; Luke 21:11; Acts 16:26; Rev 6:12; 8:5; 11:13, 19; 16:18; Sept.: Isa 29:6; Jer 23:19; Amos 1:1; Zech 14:5).

Syn.: *thúella* (2366), storm, tempest; *cheimṓn* (5494), a winter storm; *laílaps* (2978), a tempest, hurricane.

Ant.: *galḗnē* (1055), calm; *eudía* (2105), calm weather.

4579. σείω *seíō*; fut. *seísō*. To agitate, to shake with the idea of shock, cause to tremble with fear, concussion. Trans.:

(I) Particularly (Rev 6:13). Of earthquakes (Matt 27:51). Act. with the acc. (Heb 12:26 in allusion to Hag 2:6; Joel 3:16).

(II) Figuratively, to disturb in mind, agitate, to put in commotion and perturbation (Matt 21:10; 28:4; Sept.: Isa 14:16; Ezek 31:16).

Deriv.: *anaseíō* (383), to excite, stir up; *diaseíō* (1286), to shake thoroughly; *kataseíō* (2678), to shake violently; *seismós* (4578), earthquake, tempest.

Syn.: *kinéō* (2795), to set in motion, move; *saleúō* (4531), to shake, specifically of the action of stormy wind; *turbázō* (5182), to trouble, disturb.

Ant.: *stērízō* (4741), to make fast; *stereóō* (4732), establish, make strong; *asphalízō* (805), to render secure, make fast; *eirēneúō* (1514), to be peaceful; *anapaúō* (373), to rest, give rest; *eirēnopoiéō* (1517), to make peace.

4580. Σεκοῦνδος *Sekoúndos*; gen. *Sekoúndou*, masc. proper noun. Secundus, meaning second or fortunate. A Christian of Thessalonica (Acts 20:4).

4581. Σελεύκεια *Seleúkeia*; gen. *Seleukeías*, fem. proper noun. Seleucia, the seaport of Antioch from where Paul and Barnabas embarked on their missionary journey. It was on the Mediterranean about five miles north of the river Orontes and sixteen miles west of Antioch. It was founded by Seleucus Nicator. There is still a gateway at the southeastern corner of the city through which Paul and Barnabas probably passed (Acts 13:4).

4582. σελήνη *selḗnē*; gen. *selḗnēs*, fem. noun from *sélas* (n.f.), light, brightness. The moon (Matt 24:29; Mark 13:24; Luke 21:25; Acts 2:20; 1 Cor 15:41; Rev 6:12; 8:12; 12:1; 21:23; Sept.: Gen 37:9; Jer 31:35; Joel 2:31). Related words: *neomēnía* or *noumēnía* (3561), a new moon (Col 2:16); *hḗlios* (2246), sun; *astḗr* (792) and *ástron* (798), a star.

Deriv.: *selēniázomai* (4583), to be moonstruck, a lunatic.

4583. σεληνιάζομαι *selēniázomai*; fut. *selēniásomai*, from *selḗnē* (4582), the moon. To be moonstruck, to be a lunatic. In Gr. usage equivalent to being epileptic, afflicted with epilepsy, the symptoms of which were supposed to have become more aggravated during certain lunar periods. This disease in the NT and elsewhere is ascribed to the influence of unclean spirits or demons. Therefore, *daimonízomai* (1139), to be possessed by a demon, is considered to be an equivalent term (Matt 4:24; 17:15).

Syn.: *maínomai* (3105), to rave as a maniac, be beside oneself; *paraphronéō* (3912), to be insane, act as a fool; *exístēmi* (1839), to be out of one's mind, astounded, amazed.

Ant.: *sōphronéō* (4993), to have a healthy mind, to be soberminded; *ananḗphō* (366), to come back to one's senses.

4584. Σεμεΐ *Semeï*; masc. proper noun transliterated from the Hebr. *Shimᵉʿī* (8096, OT), renowned. Semei or Shemei, mentioned in Jesus' genealogy (Luke 3:26).

4585. σεμίδαλις *semídalis*; gen. *semidáleōs*, fem. noun. Fine flour (Rev 18:13; Sept.: Ex 29:2, 40; Lev 2:1).

4586. σεμνός *semnós*; fem. *semnḗ*, neut. *semnón*, adj. from *sébomai* (4576), to worship, venerate. Venerable, reverend, reputable, dignified. *Semnós* represents not only earthly dignity (*kósmios* [2887]), but that which is derived from a higher citizenship, a heavenly one, which is the possession of all believers. There lies something of majestic and awe-inspiring qualities in *semnós* which does not repel but rather invites and attracts (Phil 4:8; 1 Tim 3:8, 11; Titus 2:2).

Deriv.: *semnótēs* (4587), gravity.

Syn.: *hieroprepḗs* (2412), reverent; *eugenḗs* (2104), noble; *euschḗmōn* (2158), honorable, decorous; *sophós* (4680), wise; *éntimos* (1784), honorable; *semnótēs* (4587), gravity.

Ant.: *agenḗs* (36), ignoble; *aschḗmōn* (809), uncomely; *átopos* (824), improper, injurious; *authádēs* (829), self-pleasing, arrogant; *propetḗs* (4312), headlong, rash; *asebḗs* (765), impious, ungodly.

4587. σεμνότης *semnótēs*; gen. *semnótetos*, fem. noun from *semnós* (4586), venerable. Decency, dignity, seriousness. Aristotle defined *semnótēs* as the average of virtue that lies between two extremes,

authádeia (n.f.), arrogance, (related to *authádēs* [829], arrogant), and *aréskeia* (699), pleasure, (the subst. of *aréskō* [700], to please, or an ignoble attempt to please everybody, the endeavoring at all costs of dignity and truth to stand well with all the world). Therefore, *semnótēs* stands between caring to please nobody and endeavoring at all costs to please everybody. It is the ability not only to perform well one's duties as a citizen, but also to adhere to the highest principles and ideals of earth and heaven, and thus drawing respect and approval. See 1 Tim 2:2; 3:4; Titus 2:7.

Syn.: *euprépeia* (2143), gracefulness; *aidṓs* (127), modesty, reverence toward God; *eusébeia* (2150), godliness, piety.

4588. Σέργιος *Sérgios*; gen. *Sergíou*, masc. proper noun. Sergius, otherwise known as Sergius Paulus, a Roman proconsul in command at Cyprus, converted under the preaching of Paul and Barnabas (Acts 13:7). See *anthúpatos* (446), deputy.

4589. Σήθ *Séth*; masc. proper noun transliterated from the Hebr. *Shēth* (8352, OT), compensation. Seth, son of Adam and Eve. He was born when Adam was 130 years old and lived 912 years (Luke 3:38f.; see Gen 5:3).

4590. Σήμ *Sḗm*; masc. proper noun transliterated from the Hebr. *Shēm* (8035, OT), name. Sem, or Shem (Luke 3:36). See Gen 5:32; 10:1ff.

4591. σημαίνω *sēmaínō*; fut. *sēmanō*, aor. *esḗmana*, from *sḗma* (n.f., see *ásēmos* [767]), a mark, sign. To give a public sign or signal (Sept.: Num 10:9). In the NT to signify, make known, declare (John 12:33; 18:32; 21:19; Acts 11:28; 25:27; Rev 1:1; Sept.: Judg 7:21; Esth 2:22).

Syn.: *dēlóō* (1213), to declare; *emphanízō* (1718), to manifest; *diaggéllō* (1229), to declare, announce; *gnōrízō* (1107), to make known.

4592. σημεῖον *sēmeíon*; gen. *sēmeíou*, neut. noun. Sign, mark, token, miracle with a spiritual end and purpose. In the pl., miracles which lead to something out of and beyond themselves; finger-marks of God, valuable not so much for what they are as for what they indicate of the grace and power of the Doer (Mark 16:20).

(**I**) Particularly a sign by which something is designated, distinguished, known (Matt 26:48; Rom 4:11, circumcision as a sign [cf. Gen 9:12, 13; 17:11]). Specifically a sign by which the character and truth of any person or thing is known, a token, proof (Luke 2:12; 2 Cor 12:12; 2 Thess 3:17; Sept.: 1 Sam 14:10; 2 Kgs 19:29; 20:8).

(**II**) A sign by which the divine power in majesty is made known, a supernatural event or act, a token, wonder, or miracle by which the power and presence of God is manifested, either directly or through the agency of those whom He sends (Sept.: Ex 4:8, 17, 28, 30).

(**A**) As wrought of God (1 Cor 14:22), a token to the unbelieving of God's presence and power (cf. v. 25); or perhaps a sign of divine displeasure (cf. v. 21). "The sign of the prophet Jonah" means the miracle which God wrought in the case of Jonah concerning the great fish that swallowed him and the three days therein that followed (Matt 12:39 [cf. v. 40]; Matt 16:4; Luke 11:29). Metonymically of persons sent from God, whose character and acts are a manifestation of the divine power (Luke 11:30). In Luke 2:34 for a sign which shall be spoken against. Of signs, wonders, miracles which God did through someone, joined with *térata* (5059), things out of the ordinary, wonders (Acts 2:22, 43; 4:30; 5:12; 14:3; 15:12). Specifically as revealing future events, a sign of future things, a portent, presage (Matt 16:3), the miraculous events and deeds which reveal the coming of the Messiah in His kingdom (Matt 24:3, 30; Mark 13:4; Luke 21:7, 11, 25; Acts 2:19; Rev 12:1, 3; 15:1; Sept.: Deut 13:1, 2).

(**B**) Of signs, wonders, miracles wrought by Jesus and His Apostles and the prophets in proof and furtherance of their divine mission (Matt 12:38, 39; 16:1, 4; Mark 8:11, 12; 16:17, 20; Luke 11:16, 29; 23:8; Acts 4:16, 22; 8:6; 1 Cor 1:22). In John the word is used only in this sense (John 2:11, 18, 23; 3:2; 4:54; 6:2, 14, 26, 30; 7:31; 9:16; 10:41; 11:47; 12:18, 37; 20:30). Joined with *térata*, wonders, and *dunámeis* (1411), mighty works (John 4:48; Acts 6:8; 7:36; 8:13; 14:3; Rom 15:19; 2 Cor 12:12; Heb 2:4).

(**C**) Spoken analogically of signs, wonders, wrought by false prophets claiming to act by divine authority (Rev 13:13, 14; 16:14; 19:20); with *térata* (Matt 24:24; Mark 13:22; 2 Thess 2:9).

Deriv.: *sēmeióō* (4593), to denote, signify.

Syn.: *megaleía* (3167), great work; *thaúma* (2295), wonder; *thaumásios* (2297), a miracle, wonderful things (pl.); *dúnamis* (1411), mighty work, miracle; *téras* (5059), wonder.

4593. σημειόω *sēmeióō*; contracted *sēmeió*, fut. *sēmeiốsō*, from *sēmeíon* (4592), sign. To sign, mark, note. In the NT, only in the mid. *sēmeíoumai*, to note, with the acc. (2 Thess 3:14, meaning note someone for the purpose of not associating with [*sunanamígnumi* {4874}] him).

Syn.: *skopéō* (4648), to mark; *epéchō* (1907), to pay attention, mark; *katanoéō* (2657), to perceive, consider.

Ant.: *parérchomai* (3928), to pass by, neglect; *agnoéō* (50), not to acknowledge, ignore; *hupereídō* (5237), to overlook, wink at; *paratheōréō* (3865), to overlook.

4594. σήμερον *sēmeron*; adv., in the Attic dialect *tḗmeron*, from *tḗ hēméra* (*tḗ* [dat. fem. of *ho* {3588}, the]; *hēméra* [2250], on the day, to-day). Today, this day.

(**I**) Particularly (Matt 6:11, 30; 16:3; 21:28; 27:19; Mark 14:30; Luke 2:11; 5:26; 12:28; 19:5, 9; 22:34; 23:43; 24:21; Acts 27:33; Heb 13:8; James 4:13). In

Luke 13:32, 33, "today and tomorrow," meaning now and in the future. See Sept.: Gen 4:14; 40:7; Ex 16:25. With the art. *hē* (3588) as adj. *tḗs sḗmeron* (*tḗs*, gen. of *hē* [3588]) implying *hēméra* (2250), day, meaning this very day (Acts 19:40); with *hēméra* (2250), day, meaning this very day (Matt 11:23; 27:8; 28:15; Rom 11:8, "unto this day," until the present time, until now; 2 Cor 3:14, "until this day").

(II) At this time, now (Luke 4:21; Acts 4:9; 13:33; 22:3; 24:21; 26:2, 29; Heb 1:5; 3:7, 13, 15; 4:7; 5:5; 2 Cor 3:15. See also Deut 1:39; 1 Sam 12:17).

Syn.: *nuní* (3570), just now, momentarily; *édē* (2235), already; *árti* (737), just now.

Ant.: *aúrion* (839), tomorrow; *chthés* (5504), yesterday; *pálai* (3819), formerly; *próteron* (4386), previously; *hústeron* (5305), afterward, last of all.

4595. σήπω *sḗpō*; fut. *sḗpsō*. To rot, corrupt, destroy (Sept. Job 40:12). Usually in the NT in the pass. *sḗpomai*, 2d perf. *sésēpa* intrans. meaning to rot, be corrupted, i.e., to perish (James 5:2, "your wealth has rotted" [a.t.], meaning your hoarded stores or goods).

Deriv.: *saprós* (4550), corrupt.

Syn.: *phtheírō* (5351), to bring into a worse state, to decay; *diaphtheírō* (1311), to corrupt utterly.

Ant.: *suntēréō* (4933), to preserve; *sṓzō* (4982), to save, preserve; *diasṓzō* (1295), to preserve completely; *phulássō* (5442), to protect, keep.

4596. σηρικός *sērikós*; fem. *sērikḗ*, neut. *sērikón*, adj. from *sēr* (n.f.), silkworm. Of silk. In the NT in the neut. *tó sērikón*. used as a subst. meaning silk or silken materials (Rev 18:12).

4597. σής *sḗs*; gen. *sētós*, masc. noun. A moth (Matt 6:19, 20; Luke 12:33; Sept.: Isa 50:9; 51:8).

Deriv.: *sētóbrōtos* (4598), moth-eaten.

4598. σητόβρωτος *sētóbrōtos*; gen. *sētobrótou*, masc.-fem., neut. *sētóbrōton*, adj. from *sḗs* (4597), moth, and *bibrṓskō* (977), to eat. Moth-eaten (James 5:2; Sept.: Job 13:28).

4599. σθενόω *sthenóō*; contracted *sthenô*, fut. *sthenṓsō*, from *sthénos* (n.f.), strength. To strengthen, used only in 1 Pet 5:10. Far more common with the neg. prefix *a*, not, without, as in *asthenéō* (770), to lack in strength or to be sick; *asthéneia* (769), disease, infirmity, sickness, weakness; *asthenḗs* (772), sick, without strength, weak. Also from *sthénos* (n.f.): *asthenḗs* (772), without strength.

Syn.: *endunamóō* (1743), to make strong; *zōogonéō* (2225), to engender alive, to make alive; *zōopoiéō* (2227), to vitalize, make alive; *anathállō* (330), to revive; *ischúō* (2480), to prevail, be of strength; *enischúō* (2001), to reinforce, to strengthen more.

Ant.: *katabállō* (2598), to exhaust, to make weak, tired; *katapíptō* (2667), to fall down, weaken; *asthenéō* (770), to be feeble; *adunatéō* (101), to be unable; *noséō* (3552), to be sick.

4600. σιαγών *siagṓn*; gen. *siagónos*, fem. noun. The jawbone, chin, generally in the NT, the cheek (Matt 5:39; Luke 6:29; Sept.: Judg 15:15; 1 Kgs 22:24; Song 5:13; Lam 3:30).

4601. σιγάω *sigáō*; contracted *sigô*, fut. *sigḗsō*, from *sigē* (4602), silence. To be silent, still, keep silence.

(I) Generally intrans. (Luke 9:36; 20:26; Acts 12:17; 15:12, 13; 1 Cor 14:28, 30, 34; Sept.: Ex 14:14; Eccl 3:7).

(II) Trans., to keep in silence, keep secret, pass. (Rom 16:25).

Syn.: *siōpáō* (4623), to be silent or mute; *hēsucházō* (2270), to be still; *phimóō* (5392), to forcibly muzzle.

Ant.: *homiléō* (3656), to converse; *légō* (3004), to speak.

4602. σιγή *sigḗ*; gen. *sigḗs*, fem. noun. Silence (Acts 21:40; Rev 8:1).

Deriv.: *sigáō* (4601), to keep silence.

Syn.: *hēsuchía* (2271), quietness, silence; *eirénē* (1515), peace.
Ant.: *lógos* (3056), word; *homilía* (3657), communication.

4603. σιδήρεος *sidéreos*; contracted *sideroús*, fem. *siderá*, neut. *sideroún*, adj. from *síderos* (4604), iron. Made of iron (Acts 12:10; Rev 2:27; 9:9; 12:5; 19:15; Sept.: Lev 26:19; Deut 3:11; 1 Kgs 6:7).

4604. σίδηρος *síderos*; gen. *sidérou*, masc. noun. Iron (Rev 18:12; Sept.: Gen 4:22).
Deriv.: *sidereos* (4603), made of iron.

4605. Σιδών *Sidón*; gen. *Sidónos*, fem. proper noun transliterated from the Hebr. *Tsīdōn* (6721, OT), fishery. Zidon, Sidon (Gen 10:15, 19). One of the most ancient cities of the world, it was a rich Phoenician city situated on the Mediterranean coast, on the northern slope of a small promontory, forty miles south of Beirut and twenty miles north of Tyre (Gr. *Túros* [5184]).
Sidon was named after the firstborn son of Canaan, the grandson of Noah (Gen 10:15; 1 Chr 1:13). In Joshua's time it was "great Zidon" (Josh 11:8; 19:28) and the city appears to have been the metropolis of Phoenicia. It was one of the limits of the tribe of Asher (Josh 19:28), but was never possessed by the Israelites (Judg 1:31; 3:3). In fact, the Sidonians considered themselves to be secure from all attacks and lived carelessly (Judg 18:7, 28).
In NT times the area was visited by the Lord Jesus (Matt 15:21; Mark 7:24, 31). The "coasts of Tyre and Sidon" denoted the adjacent region as well as the cities themselves, and some think that the Lord did not enter the cities. Hearers from among those people were drawn to His preaching (Luke 6:17 [cf. Matt 11:21, 22; Luke 10:13, 14]). Herod was displeased with this region (Acts 12:20). The Apostle Paul embarked at Sidon on his way to Rome and visited the Christians there (Acts 27:3).

4606. Σιδώνιος *Sidónios*; fem. *Sidónía*, neut. *Sidónion*, adj. Sidonian; as a subst. an inhabitant of Sidon, a Sidonian (Acts 12:20). In some MSS Luke 4:26 reads "Sarepta [Gr. *Sárepta* {4558}], a city of Sidonias," meaning the region of Zidon.

4607. σικάριος *sikários*; gen. *sikaríou*, masc. noun from the Lat. *sicarius*. An assassin, murderer (Acts 21:38). Contrasted with the general term *phoneús* (5406), murderer, and *anthrōpoktónos* (443), man-slayer.

4608. σίκερα *síkera*; indeclinable neut. noun transliterated from the Hebr. *shēkhār* (7941, OT). Strong drink, any intoxicating liquor, whether wine (Sept.: Num 28:7) or, more usually, that prepared from grain, fruit, honey, or dates, (Luke 1:15, where it occurs together with *oínos* [3631], wine; see Lev 10:9; Deut 29:6; Judg 13:4, 7, 14).

4609. Σίλας *Sílas*; masc. proper noun. Silas, the same as *Silouanós* (4610), Silvanus. A distinguished Christian teacher, the companion of Paul in his journeys in Asia Minor and Greece (Acts 15:22, 27, 32, 34, 40; 16:19, 25, 29; 17:4, 10, 14, 15; 18:5).

4610. Σιλουανός *Silouanós*; masc. proper noun. Silvanus (2 Cor 1:19; 1 Thess 1:1; 2 Thess 1:1; 1 Pet 5:12), the same as *Sílas* (4609), Silas.

4611. Σιλωάμ *Silōám*; masc. proper noun. Siloam, meaning sent. The name of the pool and tower near the temple in Jerusalem. Also known as the Pool of Shiloah by the king's garden (Neh 3:15; Isa 8:6); called the Pool (John 9:7, 11). According to Josephus, Siloam was a pool at the mouth of the Tyropoeon valley, about sixty yards west of the southern point of Ophel at Jerusalem. It is probable that this was the pool dug by King Hezekiah. It was to the Pool of Siloam that a Levite was sent with a golden pitcher on "the last day, that great day of the feast" of tabernacles. To this Jesus alluded when, standing in the temple, He cried, "If any man thirst, let him come unto me and drink" (John 7:37–39). To this pool the blind man was sent to wash and returned seeing (John 9:7–11). The tower of Siloam, which killed eighteen men in its fall (Luke 13:4), was nearby.

4612. σιμικίνθιον *simikínthion*; gen. *simikinthíou*, neut. noun. An apron, probably of linen, worn by artisans (Acts 19:12).

4613. Σίμων *Símōn*; gen. *Símōnos*, masc. proper noun. Simon, meaning hearing.

(**I**) Simon Peter (Matt 4:18). See *Pétros* (4074), Peter.

(**II**) Simon the Canaanite (Matt 10:4) or Simon Zelotes (i.e., the zealous one). One of the Twelve Apostles, he was of the party called Zealots, hence his name. The epithet Canaanite is properly "Kananite," Aramaic for "zeal," and has no reference to locality.

(**III**) A brother of our Lord (Matt 13:55; Mark 6:3), not to be confused with the preceding nor with the Symeon who succeeded James as bishop of the church in Jerusalem.

(**IV**) The father of Judas Iscariot (John 6:71).

(**V**) A Pharisee (Luke 7:40, 43, 44).

(**VI**) A leper (Matt 26:6).

(**VII**) A man of Cyrene who was compelled to bear our Lord's cross when He was no longer able to carry it (Matt 27:32; Mark 15:21; Luke 23:26).

(**VIII**) A native of Samaria and famous sorcerer. He professed to be a convert to the Christian faith and was baptized as such by Philip, but was severely rebuked by Peter as a hypocrite because he sought to purchase apostolic gifts (Acts 8:9, 13, 18, 24). Hence the buying and selling of ecclesiastical rights, benefits, or privileges is known as simony.

(**IX**) A tanner at Joppa with whom Peter lodged (Acts 9:43).

4614. Σινᾶ *Siná*; neut. proper noun transliterated from the Hebr. *Şīnay* (5514, OT) Sina (Sept.: Ex 19:1, 2), or Sinai, the site of the burning bush. The name of a peninsula and a mountain or group of mountains. See Acts 7:30, 38; Gal 4:24, 25.

The peninsula of Sinai is a triangular region of about 11,500 square miles lying between the two arms of the Red Sea. On the west, it extends along the Gulf of Akabah about 130 miles. The base of the triangle, on a line from Suez to the north end of Aqabah, is 150 miles long. It is a great cluster of granite mountains in a rugged, tumbled chaos, the highest peaks reaching to an elevation of between eight thousand and nine thousand feet. Between the mountains are deeply cut valleys through which a large company might march into the very heart of the mountain region. The area is rich in copper.

Sinai peninsula was known and settled almost as early as Egypt itself. When the Hyksos came, the region was subdued by Egypt. The Israelites wandered in this area for forty years after they left Egypt prior to their entrance into Canaan. Christianity was planted here very early, perhaps by Paul. The peninsula was annexed by the Roman Empire, A.D. 105. In the fourth century, it was populated by Anchorites and various brotherhoods of hermits and monks. They suffered terrible massacres from the Saracens, A.D. 373–411. In the reign of Justinian, the Church of the Virgin was founded on Mount Sinai. The church was later destroyed by the Muslims on their pilgrimages to Mecca.

The highest summits in the peninsula are Jebel (Arabic for "mount") Serbal, 6,734 feet; Jebel Musa, 7,363 feet; Jebel Umm Shomer, 8,449 feet; Jebel Katharina, 8,536 feet; and Jebel Zebir, 8,511 feet. Sinai is also used to designate the range of mountains from which the Israelites received the Law.

We do not know for sure from which of these mountains God delivered the Commandments to Moses. In determining its identity, however, with any existing peak, several conditions must be met. First, the mountain must have before it an open space within sight of the summit (Ex 19:11; 20:18) and be large enough to contain at least two million people. It must also rise sharply from the plain since the people "came near and stood under the mountain" (Deut 4:11). It "might be touched" (Heb 12:18; see Ex 19:12); and Moses was commanded to "set bounds . . . round about" (Ex 19:12). As the Israelites remained in the neighborhood for a year, they must have found a sufficient supply of water and pasture.

The actual mountain, therefore, is most probably Jebel Musa, including its peak Ras es-Sufsafeh, which is situated a little northwest of the center of the Sinaitic Sea and some twenty miles southeast of Jebel Serbal. At the northern end of the mountain, all the conditions are met in the peak of Ras es-Sufsafeh. This whole block is isolated from the surrounding mountains by deep valleys so that boundaries might have been set completely around it (Ex 19:12, 23). To the north of Ras es-Sufsafeh and extending to the very base is the plain of Er Rahah, two miles long and a half mile wide, embracing four hundred acres of available standing ground directly in front of the mountain. The plain with its branches contains 4,293,000 square yards (ca. 887 acres) in full view of the mountain, affording more than sufficient standing ground for the two million Israelites. Here they might stand "at the nether part of the mountain" (Ex 19:17), which rises so abruptly from the plain as to answer the description of "the mount that might be touched" (Heb 12:18). This fulfills all the conditions of the Scripture narrative, and the conclusion is that this stately, awful-looking, isolated mass of Ras es-Sufsafeh is the very mountain where "the Lord came down upon mount Sinai, on the top of the mount" (Ex 19:20), and where "God spake all these words" of the Ten Commandments (Ex 20:1–17).

The southern summit (Jebel Musa) is completely hidden from the plain. It is quite possible that Moses went to this secluded spot when the Lord called him up to the top of the mountain (Ex 19:20). There, too, perhaps he was "with the Lord forty days and forty nights" (Ex 34:28). On the eastern declivity is the Convent of St. Katharine founded by the Emperor Justinian in A.D. 527 where Tischendorf discovered the famous Codex Sinaiticus, one of the oldest and best MSS of the NT in existence.

4615. σίναπι sínapi; gen. *sinápeōs*; neut. noun. Mustard, a plant often growing to a very considerable size in the fertile soil of Palestine (Matt 13:31; Mark 4:31; Luke 13:19). The expression *kókkon sinápeōs* (*kókkon* [2848], grain), a grain of mustard seed, is a proverbial phrase meaning the least, the smallest particle (Matt 17:20; Luke 17:6).

4616. σινδών sindốn; gen. *sindónos*, fem. noun. Linen cloth, a sheet or wrapping of linen, probably square or oblong in form, worn by the Orientals at night (Mark 14:51, 52). Used also for wrapping dead bodies (Matt 27:59; Mark 15:46; Luke 23:53; Sept.: Judg 14:12, 13; Prov 31:24).

Syn.: *othónion* (3608), usually found in the pl., strips with which the body of the Lord was bound after the *sindốn* was removed.

4617. σινιάζω siniázō; fut. *siniásō*, from *siníon* (n.f.), sieve. To sift, to shake as grain in a sieve. Figuratively, with the acc. of person implied (Luke 22:31, meaning to agitate and prove by trials and afflictions).

4618. σιτευτός siteutós; fem. *siteutế*, neut. *siteutón*, adj. from *siteúō* (n.f.), to feed or fatten with grain, which is from *sítos* (4621), grain, as wheat or corn. Fattened with grain, as corn (Luke 15:23, 27, 30; Sept.: 1 Kgs 4:23; Jer 46:21).

4619. σιτιστός sitistós; fem. *sitistế*, neut. *sitistón*, adj. from *sitízō* (n.f.), to feed upon, eat, which is from *sítos*

(4621), corn, wheat, food. Fed with grain, fattened; pl. *tá sitistá*, the fatlings (Matt 22:4).

4620. σιτομέτριον *sitométrion*; gen. *sitometríou*, neut. noun from *sítos* (4621), grain, wheat, meal, and *métron* (3358), a measure. Grain measured out, an allowance, portion, ration (Luke 12:42).

4621. σῖτος *sítos*; gen. *sítou*, pl. *tá síta*, masc. noun. Wheat and generally grain, corn (Matt 3:12; 13:25, 29, 30; Mark 4:28; Luke 3:17; 16:7; 22:31; John 12:24; Acts 7:12; 27:38; 1 Cor 15:37; Rev 6:6; 18:13; Sept.: Gen 27:28, 37; 41:49; 42:3; Isa 36:17).
   Deriv.: *ásitos* (777), without food, fasting; *sitométrion* (4620), grain measured out, an allowance, portion, ration.
   Syn.: *stáchus* (4719), an ear of grain; *kókkos* (2848), a kernel of grain.

4622. Σιών *Siōn*; indeclinable masc., fem., or neut. proper noun transliterated from the Hebr. *Tsīōn* (6726, OT), sunny. Sion, the name of two mountains in Palestine, being one of the various names of Mount Hermon (Deut 4:48).
   Sometimes Zion is used to denote the whole of Jerusalem, but in its literal and restricted sense, it was the southwestern hill of Jerusalem. On every side but the north, this hill was surrounded with deep valleys having precipitous sides. To the east was the valley of the Tyropoeon, the cheese-making valley, separating Zion from Moriah, the temple mount, and from Ophel. On the south and west was the deep valley of Hinnom, called on the west the Valley of Gihon. The northern boundary of Zion is uncertain. Some authorities think it extended to the Tower of David near the Damascus Gate and suppose the Tyropoeon Valley to have ended here. Others would extend Zion farther northward toward the Jaffa Gate. Zion was the higher hill, being 105 feet above Moriah and 2,539 feet above the level of the Mediterranean Sea. The valleys were originally much deeper than at present, so that Zion was really encompassed on three sides by precipices. It was also guarded by a strong wall. At the northwest corner of Mount Zion stood the magnificent palace erected by Herod the Great and afterward called the Praetorium, the residence of the Roman procurator (Mark 15:16). On the south of this were three famous towers or fortresses of which one is now the Tower of David.
   Jerusalem is first mentioned as a stronghold of the Jebusites (Josh 15:63). It remained in their possession until captured by David who made it "the city of David," the capital of his kingdom. He built there a citadel, his own palace, houses for the people, and a place for the ark of God (2 Sam 5:7; 1 Kgs 8:1; 2 Kgs 19:21, 31; 1 Chr 11:5; 2 Chr 5:2).
   In the prophetical and poetical books of the OT, Zion occurs no less than 148 times and in the NT it occurs seven times as "Sion" (Matt 21:5; John 12:15; Rom 9:33; 11:26; Heb 12:22; 1 Pet 2:6; Rev 14:1). In later books, Zion was no longer confined to the southwestern hill, but sometimes denoted Jerusalem in general (Sept.: Ps 87:2; 149:2; Isa 33:14; Joel 2:1); sometimes it meant God's chosen people (Ps 51:18; 87:5); sometimes the Church (Heb 12:22); and sometimes the heavenly city (Rev 14:1). Thus Zion has come to symbolize the aspirations and hopes of God's children.

4623. σιωπάω *siōpáō*; contracted *siōpṓ*, fut. *siōpḗsō*, from *siōpḗ* (n.f.), silence, stillness. To be silent, mute. Intrans.:
   (I) Particularly of persons, to keep silence, hold one's peace (Matt 20:31; 26:63; Mark 3:4; 9:34; 10:48; 14:61; Luke 18:39; 19:40; Acts 18:9; Sept.: Job 29:21; Isa 36:21; 42:14); of one unable to speak, dumb (Luke 1:20).
   (II) Figuratively of a sea or lake, to be still, calm, hushed (Mark 4:39).
   Syn.: *sigáō* (4601), to be silent; *hēsucházō* (2270), to be quiet.
   Ant.: *légō* (3004), to speak; *homiléō* (3656), to converse, talk.

4624. σκανδαλίζω *skandalízō*; fut. *skandalísō*, from *skándalon* (4625), a trap, stumbling block. To cause to stumble and fall, not found in Gr. writers. In the NT, figuratively to be a stumbling block to someone, to cause to stumble at or in something, to give a cause of offense to someone. Trans.:

(I) Generally, to offend, vex, particularly to scandalize, with the acc. of person (Matt 17:27; John 6:61; 1 Cor 8:13); pass. (Matt 13:21; 15:12; 24:10; Mark 4:17; John 16:1; 2 Cor 11:29); pass., followed by *en* (1722), in, to be offended by someone, to take offense at his character, words, conduct, so as to reject him (Matt 11:6; 13:57; 26:31, 33; Mark 6:3; 14:27; Luke 7:23).

(II) Causative, to cause to offend, lead astray, lead into sin, be a stumbling block or the occasion of one's sinning. With the acc. of person (Matt 5:29, 30; 18:6, 8, 9; Mark 9:42, 43, 45, 47; Luke 17:2; Rom 14:21). Hence in the pass., to be offended, be led astray or into sin, fall away from the truth. In Rom 14, In the case of *adiáphora* (i.e., matters of liberty or conscience), the act of offending is indeed causative. To offend is not to upset, annoy, vex or irritate. Rather, to offend in this case is to cause one to offend himself, to stumble, by leading him to exercise a liberty against his conscience.

Syn.: *píptō* (4098), to fail or fall; *hysteréō* (5302), to come behind, fall short; *proskóptō* (4350), to stumble; *ptaíō* (4417), to offend, stumble, sin; *diabállō* (4624), to falsely accuse.

Ant.: *boēthéō* (997), to help.

4625. σκάνδαλον *skándalon*; gen. *skandálou*, neut. noun. The trigger of a trap on which the bait is placed, and which, when touched by the animal, springs and causes it to close causing entrapment. The word and its deriv. belong only to biblical and ecclesiastical Gr. In the Sept. it answers to the word for *pagís* (3803), trap. However, *pagís* always refers simply to a trap hidden in an ambush and not to the

results; whereas *skándalon* involves a reference also to the conduct of the person who is thus trapped. *Skándalon* always denotes an enticement to conduct which could ruin the person in question. See Sept.: Lev 19:14.; Josh 23:13; 1 Sam 18:21.

In the NT *skándalon* is used figuratively in a moral sense. It is concerned mainly with the fact that it produces certain behavior which can lead to ruin (Rom 9:33; 11:9; 14:13; 16:7; 1 Cor 1:23; Gal 5:11; 1 Pet 2:8; 1 John 2:10; Rev 2:14). Also in the pl. *tá skándala* (Matt 18:7; Luke 17:1).

(I) Generally as a cause of stumbling, falling, ruin, morally and spiritually. Of Christ, rock of stumbling (Rom 9:33; 11:9 quoted from Ps 69:22; 1 Pet 2:7, 8; see Sept.: Ps 119:165).

(II) As a cause of offense and indignation, a scandal (Matt 16:23).

(III) Metonymically of person (Matt 13:41).

Deriv.: *skandalízō* (4624), to cause to stumble.

Syn.: *próskomma* (4348), an obstacle; *proskopé* (4349), occasion of stumbling.

Ant.: *hupódeigma* (5262) and *hupogrammós* (5261), an example; *túpos* (5179), a type; *hupotúpōsis* (5296), a pattern to be followed.

4626. σκάπτω *skáptō*; fut. *skápsō*. To dig, intrans. (Luke 6:48; 13:8; 16:3; Sept.: Isa 5:6).

Deriv.: *kataskáptō* (2679), to dig; *skáphē* (4627), a drain, trench.

Syn.: *orússō* (3736), to dig a hole or burrow; *diorússō* (1358), to excavate; *exorússō* (1846), to dig out, to mine.

4627. σκάφη *skáphē*; gen. *skáphēs*, fem. noun from *skáptō* (4626), to dig. Something dug out, a channel, trench, a bowl. In the NT, a skiff, boat (Acts 27:16, 30, 32).

Syn.: *ploíon* (4143), ship; *ploiárion* (4142), a skiff or small boat.

4628. σκέλος *skélos*; gen. *skélous*, pl. *tá skélē*, neut. noun. The leg from the hip to the foot (John 19:31–33; Sept.: Lev 11:21; Amos 3:12). Related words: *brachíōn* (1023), the arm; *poús* (4228), foot; *cheír* (5495), hand.

4629. σκέπασμα *sképasma*; gen. *sképásmatos*, neut. noun from *skepázō* (n.f.), to cover. Covering, clothing, raiment (1 Tim 6:8).
Syn.: *peribólaion* (4018), a veil, covering; *himátion* (2440) and *esthḗs* (2066), raiment; *énduma* (1742), apparel; *himatismós* (2441), clothing; *stolḗ* (4749), garment or robe.

4630. Σκευᾶς *Skeuás*; gen. *Skeuá*, masc. proper noun. Sceva, meaning fitted. An Ephesian Jewish high priest whose seven sons attempted an exorcism (Acts 19:14).

4631. σκευή *skeuḗ*; gen. *skeuḗs*, fem. noun from *skeúos* (4632), a vessel, utensil. Apparatus, equipment for war, apparel, equipage. Used of a ship, apparatus, furniture, implements (Acts 27:19).

4632. σκεῦος *skeúos*; gen. *skeúous*, masc. noun. A vessel, utensil, implement.
(I) Generally of items or objects:
(A) Particularly of a hollow vessel for containing things (Luke 8:16; John 19:29; Acts 10:11, 16; 11:5; Sept.: 2 Kgs 4:3, 4, 6); a potter's vessel (Rom 9:21; Rev 2:27; Sept.: Lev 6:28; 14:50); any vessel or implement (Mark 11:16; 2 Tim 2:20; Heb 9:21; Rev 18:12; Sept.: Ex 3:22; Num 1:50; 1 Chr 9:28). In the pl., *tá skeúē*, household goods, furniture (Matt 12:29; Mark 3:27; Luke 17:31; Sept.: Gen 31:37).
(B) Figuratively of the human body as formed of clay and thus frail and feeble (2 Cor 4:7); of persons, in a moral respect (Rom 9:22, 23, referring to those on whom the divine wrath or mercy is to be exercised according to the purpose of the divine potter [cf., in an active sense, *skeúē orgḗs* {*orgḗs*, gen. of *orgḗ* (3709), wrath},

vessels of wrath, meaning instruments of wrath {Sept.: Jer 50:25 (see 2 Tim 2:21)}]). *Skeúos* is used to identify a wife as the vessel of her husband (1 Pet 3:7, the female as the weaker vessel). See also 1 Thess 4:4, where one possible meaning is to learn to live with his own wife or to acquire a wife (cf. 1 Cor 7:2).
(II) In respect to use, an implement, instrument.
(A) Specifically, the mast of a ship as the chief instrument of sailing (Acts 27:17, the sails having probably been furled before [cf. 27:15]). Ancient ships usually had but one mast which was raised or lowered as necessary, so *tá skeúē* (pl.) refers to the implements and tackle of a ship.
(B) Figuratively of a person as the instrument of someone (Acts 9:15, "a chosen vessel" or instrument).
Deriv.: *skeuḗ* (4631), equipment.
Syn.: *aggeíon* (30), a small vessel.

4633. σκηνή *skēnḗ*; gen. *skēnḗs*, fem. noun. A booth, hut, tabernacle, tent, any covered or shaded place. Equivalent to *skḗnos* (4636), tent, human body.
(I) As built of branches, a booth (Matt 17:4; Mark 9:5; Luke 9:33; Sept.: Gen 33:17; Isa 1:8; Jon 4:5); also of cloth, skins, as a tent (Heb 11:9; Sept.: Gen 4:20; 18:1ff.; Lev 23:42, 43; 2 Sam 11:11). Once used diminutively of a house in ruins (Acts 15:16 quoted from Amos 9:11 where metaphorically it stands for the family or royal line of David fallen into weakness and decay). Generally an abode, dwelling (Luke 16:9; Rev 13:6; Job 36:29; Ps 18:11). See Judg 8:11.
(II) Specifically, the tabernacle, the sacred tent of the Jews in which the ark was kept, the seat of Jewish worship prior to the building of the temple. The ark, however, was separated from the tabernacle long before that period and was kept in Jerusalem while the tabernacle itself remained in Gibeon (2 Chr 1:3, 4, 13 [cf. 2 Sam 6:17; 1 Chr 15:1]).
(A) Generally, as the tabernacle that stood for a witness, *hē skēnḗ toú marturíou* (*marturíou* [3142], witness) (Acts

7:44; Rev 15:5; Sept.: Ex 29:4, 10; 33:7; Num 1:50ff.). By connection, spoken of the outer sanctuary of the tabernacle (Heb 9:2, 6, 8); the inner sanctuary, the Holy of Holies (Heb 9:3).

(B) Symbolically, of the spiritual or celestial tabernacle from which the material one is said to have been copied (Heb 8:2; 9:11 [cf. 8:5; 9:23, 24]); the temple in the heavenly Jerusalem (Rev 15:5; 21:3).

(III) The tabernacle of Moloch (Acts 7:43 quoted from Amos 5:26), a tabernacle which the idolatrous Israelites constructed in the desert in honor of Moloch, like that in honor of Jehovah, possibly of a small size so as to elude the notice of Moses.

Deriv.: *skēnopēgía* (4634), pitching tents, feast of tabernacles; *skēnopoiós* (4635), tent maker.

Syn.: *oikētérion* (3613), a habitation; *katoikētérion* (2732), a more permanent dwelling place; *katoikía* (2733), a dwelling place, house; *épaulis* (1886), a country house, cottage; *Hádēs* (86), the dwelling place of disembodied spirits; *oíkos* (3624) and *oidía* (3614), house.

4634. σκηνοπηγία *skēnopēgía*; gen. *skēnopēgías*, fem. noun from *skēnē* (4633), tent, habitation, tabernacle, and *pḗgnumi* (4078), to set up, pitch. The pitching of a booth or tent, the festival of booths or tabernacles. It was the third great annual festival of the Jews in which all the males were required to appear before God at the tabernacle or temple (Lev 23:39–44; Deut 16:13; Zech 14:16, 18, 19), the other two being the Passover and Pentecost (John 7:2; Deut 16:16; 31:10). The festival of booths (or tents) was so-called from the booths of green branches and leaves in which the people dwelt during its continuance. They were built on the roofs of the houses and in the courts and streets.

The festival commenced on the fifteenth day of the seventh month, Tishri (also called Ethanim), which corresponds to the new moon of October. It was celebrated for eight days, partly as a memorial of the forty years wandering in the desert where the Israelites dwelt in booths (Lev 23:42, 43), and partly as a season of thanksgiving for the ingathering of the harvest, hence called feast of gathering (Ex 23:16; 34:22). The first and eighth days were Sabbaths to the Lord with holy convocations (Lev 23:35, 36, 39; Num 29:12, 35), and the eighth especially is called the great day of the festival (John 7:37 [cf. Neh 8:18]).

It was a season of rejoicing and feasting; particular sacrifices were offered and portions of the Law were read in public (Deut 31:10ff.; Neh 8:18). To these the later Jews added a libation of water brought from the fountain of Siloam. This was mixed with wine and poured upon the altar (Lev 23:34ff.; Neh 8:14).

4635. σκηνοποιός *skēnopoiós*; gen. *skēnopoioú*, masc. noun from *skēnē* (4633), tent, and *poiéō* (4160), to make. A tentmaker, spoken of Paul (Acts 18:3).

4636. σκῆνος *skḗnos*; gen. *skḗnous*, neut. noun. A booth, tent, tabernacle. In the NT, also used figuratively for the body as the frail and temporary abode of the soul (2 Cor 5:1, meaning this earthly house or tabernacle, the gen. here being appositional [see 5:4]). Equivalent to *skēnē* (4633), tent, tabernacle, habitation.

Deriv.: *skēnóō* (4637), to reside, dwell.

Syn.: *sṓma* (4983), body.

4637. σκηνόω *skēnóō*; contracted *skēnô*, fut. *skēnṓsō*, from *skḗnos* (4636), tent, abode. To encamp, pitch a tent (Sept.: Gen 13:12). In the NT, to dwell as in tents, to tabernacle. Intrans., followed by *en hēmín* (*en* [1722], in; *hēmín* [2254], us), among us (John 1:14); *en*, with a dat. of place (Rev 12:12; 13:6); *metá* (3326), with, with a gen. (Rev 21:3); *epi* (1909), upon, with the acc. (Rev 7:15).

Deriv.: *episkēnóō* (1981), to abide; *kataskēnóō* (2681), to dwell, to camp down, lodge, remain; *skḗnōma* (4638), literally an encampment, the temple as

God's residence, the body as the dwelling place of the soul, tabernacle, tent.

Syn.: *oikéō* (3611), to dwell; *ménō* (3306), to abide, remain.

Ant.: *apodēméō* (589), to go into a far country; *analúō* (360), *anachōréō* (402), and *poreúomai* (4198), to depart.

4638. σκήνωμα *skēnōma*; gen. *skē-nṓmatos*, neut. noun from *skēnóō* (4637), to pitch a tent. A booth or tent pitched, a tabernacle. Figuratively, temple or tabernacle for God (Acts 7:46; Sept.: 1 Kgs 2:28; 8:4; Ps 46:4; 132:5). The body as the frail tenement of the soul (2 Pet 1:13, 14).

Syn.: *oikētḗrion* (3613), a habitation; *katoikētḗrion* (2732), a more permanent habitation; *katoikía* (2733), a dwelling, residence; *épaulis* (1886), a country house, cottage; *monḗ* (3438), residence; *oîkos* (3624) and *oikía* (3614) and *oíkēma* (3612), house.

4639. σκιά *skiá*; gen. *skiás*, fem. noun. Shadow, shade.

(I) Particularly, an actual shadow or shade (Mark 4:32; Acts 5:15; Sept.: Judg 9:36; Ezek 17:23). In the sense of darkness, gloom, such as the foreboding "shadow of death," meaning the thickest darkness (Matt 4:16; Luke 1:79).

(II) Metaphorically, a foreshadowing, in distinction from *tó sṓma* (4983), the body (or reality), and *hē eikṓn* (1504), the full and perfect image; so also of the Jewish rites and dispensation as prefiguring things future and more perfect (Col 2:17; Heb 8:5; 10:1).

Ant.: *hupóstasis* (5287), essence, substance, reality; *phṓs* (5457), light.

4640. σκιρτάω *skirtáō*; contracted *skirtṓ*, fut. *skirtḗsō*. To leap, spring, especially of animals (Sept.: Mal 4:2). To leap for joy, to exult (Luke 6:23). Of the fetus in the womb (Luke 1:41, 44 [cf. Sept. Gen 25:22]).

Syn.: *hállomai* (242), to leap, used metaphorically as the springing up of water; *exállomai* (1814), to leap up; *ephállomai*

(2177), to leap upon, spring upon, as in mounting a horse; *eispēdáō* (1530), to leap in.

Ant.: *lupéomai* (3076), to be sorrowful.

4641. σκληροκαρδία *sklērokardía*; gen. *sklērokardías*, fem. noun from *sklērós* (4642), hard, and *kardía* (2588), heart. Hardness of heart, stubbornness, obstinacy, perverseness (Matt 19:8; Mark 10:5; 16:14; Sept.: Deut 10:16; Jer 4:4). It indicates man's attitude toward God and His grace when he ought to have a willing and receptive heart.

Syn.: *pṓrōsis* (4457), dullness of heart; *sklērótēs* (4643), callousness; *ástorgos* (794), without natural affection, hardhearted.

Ant.: *apalós* (527), tender, soft; *malakós* (3120), soft, mild (though it can also mean weak or effeminate); *oiktírmōn* (3629), merciful; *splágchnon* (4698), pity.

4642. σκληρός *sklērós*; fem. *sklērá*, neut. *sklērón*, adj. from *skéllō* (n.f.), to harden, dry up. Dried up, dry, hard, stiff; of the voice or sounds as hoarse or harsh; of things as hard, tough, not soft. In the pl., *tá sklērá*, the hard things, stands in contrast to *tá malaká* (3120), the soft things, or with a neg. connotation, the effeminate (1 Cor 6:9). Also from *skéllō* (n.f.): *skoliós* (4646), crooked, warped.

(I) Of winds as fierce, violent, (James 3:4; Sept.: Prov 27:16).

(II) Of things spoken as hard, harsh, offensive, such as words (John 6:60; Jude 1:15, "hard speeches"; Sept. Gen 42:7, 30; 1 Kgs 12:13). Of things done being hard, difficult, grievous (Acts 9:5; 26:14; Sept.: Ex 1:14; 6:9; Deut 26:6).

(III) Of persons as harsh, stern, severe (Matt 25:24; Sept.: 1 Sam 25:3; Isa 48:4).

Deriv.: *sklērokardía* (4641), hardness of heart; *sklērótēs* (4643), hardness; *sklērotráchēlos* (4644), stiff-necked; *sklērúnō* (4645), to make stubborn or hard.

Syn.: *dúskolos* (1422), difficult, finicky; *austērós* (840), rough, severe, austere (*Sklērós* always indicates a harsh, brutal character which is not the case with *austērós*); *ágrios* (66), wild, raging; *chalepós* (5467), perilous.

Ant.: *apalós* (527), soft, tender.

4643. σκληρότης *sklērótēs*; gen. *sklērótētos*, fem. noun from *sklērós* (4642), dry, hard. Hardness, obstinacy, stubbornness (Rom 2:5; Sept.: Deut 9:27).

Syn.: *pórōsis* (4457), a hardening, dullness of the heart.

Ant.: *hupotássomai* (the mid. of *hupotássō* [5293]), to submit oneself to, be subject to; *malakía* (3119), softness.

4644. σκληροτράχηλος *sklērotráchēlos*; gen. *sklērotrachélou*, masc.-fem., neut. *sklēpotráchēlon*, adj. from *sklērós* (4642), hard, and *tráchēlos* (5137), the neck. Hard or stiff-necked, obstinate, proud (Acts 7:51; Sept.: Ex 33:3, 5; Deut 9:6, 13).

Syn.: *authádēs* (829), self-pleasing, arrogant, self-willed.

Ant.: *eupeithés* (2138), compliant.

4645. σκληρύνω *sklērúnō*; fut. *sklērunō̂*, from *sklērós* (4642), hard. To make hard or stiff, make obdurate. In the NT applied only figuratively to the heart or mind (Acts 19:9; Rom 9:18; Heb 3:13; Sept.: Judg 4:24; 2 Chr 10:4); of words (2 Sam 19:43). Joined with the pl. *kardías* (2588), hearts (Heb 3:8, 15; 4:7 quoted from Ps 95:8; see Ex 9:12; 10:20).

Syn.: *pōróō* (4456), to make hard, callous.

4646. σκολιός *skoliós*; fem. *skoliá*, neut. *skolión*, adj. from *skéllō* (n.f.), to dry. Crooked, bent or warped from dryness, such as wood. Of a way or parts of it (Luke 3:5 quoted from Isa 40:4; Sept.: Prov 2:15; Isa 42:16). Figuratively, meaning crooked, perverse, wicked (Acts 2:40; Phil 2:15; Sept.: Ps 78:8; Prov 22:5). Of masters, perverse, unjust, in contrast to *epieikḗs* (1933), gentle, tolerant (1 Pet

2:18 [cf. Sept.: Prov 16:28]). Also from *skéllō* (n.f.): *sklērós* (4642), dried up, dry.

Syn.: *dólios* (1386), deceitful; *ádikos* (94), unjust; *diastréphō* (1294), to make crooked; *metastréphō* (3344), to pervert, corrupt; *kakós* (2556), bad; *paradiatribḗ* (3859), perverse disputing; *ponērós* (4190), evil, harmful; *phaúlos* (5337), evil.

Ant.: *orthós* (3717), straight, right; *agathós* (18), benevolent, good; *euthús* (2117), straight; *díkaios* (1342), just.

4647. σκόλοψ *skólops*; gen. *skólopos*, masc. noun. Something pointed, sharp, as a stake, the point of a hook, a thorn, prickle (Sept.: Hos 2:6). In 2 Cor 12:7, "a thorn in the flesh," something which causes severe pain or constant irritation, probably some bodily infirmity, equal to *asthéneia* (769), sickness, weakness.

Syn.: *ákantha* (173), a thorn, brier.

4648. σκοπέω *skopéō*; contracted *skopō̂*, fut. *skopḗsō*, from *skopós* (4649), mark, goal, spy. Used only in the pres. and imperf., meaning to spy out, look towards an object, to contemplate, give attention to (Luke 11:35; Rom 16:17; 2 Cor 4:18; Gal 6:1; Phil 2:4; 3:17).

Deriv.: *episkopéō* (1983), to look after; *kataskopéō* (2684), to spy out.

Syn.: *sēmeióō* (4593), to mark, note; *sēmaínō* (4591), to mark, indicate; *proséchō* (4337), take heed, beware; *epéchō* (1907), give attention to, mark; *phulássō* (5442), to guard; *blépō* (991), to watch; *horáō* (3708), to discern clearly.

Ant.: *agnoéō* (50), not to know, be ignorant of; *ameléō* (272), neglect, not regard; *lanthánō* (2990), forget; *hupereídō* (5237), wink at, overlook; *paratheōréō* (3865), to overlook.

4649. σκοπός *skopós*; gen. *skopoú*, masc. noun, from *sképtomai* (n.f.), to look about. Goal, the mark at the end of a race (Phil 3:14 [cf. 2 Cor 4:18]; Sept.: Job 16:12; Lam 3:12). Also from *sképtomai* (n.f.): *episképtomai* (1980), to look upon.

Deriv.: *epískopos* (1985), overseer, bishop; *skopéō* (4648), to look toward a goal, give heed.

Syn.: *télos* (5056), the point aimed at, end.

4650. σκορπίζω skorpízō; fut. *skorpísō*. To scatter, disperse, trans.:
(I) Generally (John 10:12; 16:32; Sept.: 2 Sam 22:15; Ps 18:14). In the proverbial expression, "He that gathereth not with me scattereth" (Matt 12:30; Luke 11:23), *skorpízō* means to waste.
(II) To scatter one's gifts, distribute liberally, bountifully (2 Cor 9:9 quoted from Ps 112:9).
Deriv.: *diaskorpízō* (1287), to scatter abroad.
Syn.: *diaspeírō* (1289), to disseminate; *dialúō* (1262), to cause to disperse and disappear; *speírō* (4687), to sow, scatter.
Ant.: *sunágō* (4863), to gather; *sullégō* (4816), to collect.

4651. σκορπίος skorpíos; gen. *skorpíou*, masc. noun. A scorpion, a large insect sometimes several inches long shaped somewhat like a small lobster and having a stinger at the extremity of its tail (Luke 10:19; 11:12; Rev 9:3, 5, 10; Sept.: Deut 8:15; 1 Kgs 12:11, 14). Scorpions are found in hot countries, where they lurk in decayed buildings and among the stones of old walls. Their sting is venomous, producing inflammation and swelling, but is seldom fatal unless treatment of the wound is neglected.

4652. σκοτεινός skoteinós; fem. *skoteinḗ*, neut. *skoteinón*, adj. from *skótos* (4655), darkness. Dark, without light (Matt 6:23; Luke 11:34, 36; Sept.: Job 10:21; 15:23; Ps 88:6).
Syn.: *auchmērós* (850), dismal, dark; *mélas* (3189), black; *dusnóētos* (1425), difficult to understand; *katachthónios* (2709), subterranean, infernal, belonging to the world of departed spirits.
Ant.: *phōteinós* (5460), full of light; *lamprós* (2986), bright; *eilikrinḗs* (1506),

judged by sunlight, tested as genuine, sincere.

4653. σκοτία skotía; gen. *skotías*, fem. noun from *skótos* (4655), darkness. Darkness (Matt 10:27; Luke 12:3; John 6:17; 20:1; Sept.: Job 28:3). Figuratively, with the associated idea of unhappiness or ruin (John 8:12; 12:35, 46). As light is not only the emblem of happiness but is also itself beneficial, darkness in like manner works unhappiness and death (John 12:35; 1 John 1:5; 2:8, 9, 11 [cf. Job 37:19]). Thus, *skotía* is not only a figurative term for sin itself, but also for the consequences of sin.

4654. σκοτίζω skotízō; fut. *skotísō* from *skótos* (4655), darkness. To darken, deprive of light. In NT, only in the pass., to be darkened.
(I) Particularly (Matt 24:29; Mark 13:24; Luke 23:45; Rev 8:12; 9:2; Sept.: Eccl 12:2.
(II) Figuratively of moral darkness, ignorance (Rom 1:21; 11:10 quoted from Ps 69:23; Eph 4:18). See *skotía* (4653), darkness as the consequence of sin.
Syn.: *skotóō* (4656), to darken; *en ainígmati* (*en* [1722], in; *ainígmati*, dat. of *aínigma* [135], enigma, obscureness), as if in a puzzle, darkly.
Ant.: *phōtízō* (5461), to lighten, give light, enlighten; *epiphaúō* (2017), illuminate; *lámpō* (2989), to give light, shine; *epiphaínō* (2014), to appear, shine upon; *háptō* (681), to kindle; *astráptō* (797), to illuminate, flash or shine; *apokalúptō* (601), to reveal, uncover; *epiphṓskō* (2020), to begin to dawn; *phaínō* (5316), to give light; *anaphaínō* (398), to appear suddenly; *eklámpō* (1584), to shine forth; *exastráptō* (1823), to glisten; *perilámpō* (4034) and *periastráptō* (4015), to shine around; *phaneróō* (5319), to manifest; *emphanízō* (1718), to make manifest.

4655. σκότος skótos; gen. *skótous*, neut. noun. Darkness.

(I) Physical darkness (Matt 27:45; Mark 15:33; Luke 23:44; 2 Cor 4:6 [cf. Acts 13:11]).

(II) Spiritual darkness, implying ignorance or error (John 3:19; Rom 2:19); eternal misery and damnation (Matt 8:12; 2 Pet 2:17; Jude 1:13); sin and misery (Matt 4:16; Luke 1:79; Acts 26:18; 1 Thess 5:4; 1 Pet 2:9), as well as persons in such a state (Eph 5:8); the works of darkness, such works as are usually practiced by men in darkness or secretly (Rom 13:12; Eph 5:11 [cf. 1 Cor 4:5; 1 John 1:6]).

(III) The infernal spirits as the opposite of Christ, the sun or light of righteousness (Luke 22:53).

Deriv.: *skoteinós* (4652), dark; *skotía* (4653), darkness; *skotízō* (4654), to darken, deprive of light; *skotóō* (4656), to darken.

Syn.: *gnóphos* (1105), a thick dark cloud; *zóphos* (2217), gloom, darkness; *achlús* (887), a thick mist, fog.

Ant.: *phṓs* (5457), light; *phōstḗr* (5458), a luminary, light, light-giver; *phōtismós* (5462), illumination; *phéggos* (5338), brightness, borrowed light such as that of the moon; *lúchnos* (3088), a portable lamp; *lampás* (2985), a torch, lamp.

4656. σκοτόω skotóō; contracted *skotṓ*, fut. *skotṓsō*, from *skótos* (4655), darkness. To darken, cover with darkness. In the pass. (Rev 16:10 used as emblematic of distress, calamity, destruction; Sept.: Ps 105:28). In Rev 9:2 UBS, it is used of the darkening of the sun and the heavenly bodies; the word used in Rev 9:2 TR is its syn *skotízō* (4654). In Eph 4:18, the TR has *eskotisménoi*, spiritually or mentally confused (from *skotízō* [4654]) while the UBS has *eskotōménoi* (from *skotóō*).

4657. σκύβαλον skúbalon; gen. *skubálou*, neut. noun equal to *kusíbalon* (n.f.), something thrown to the dogs, which is from *kusí*, dat. pl. of *kúōn* (2965), dog, and *bállō* (906), to cast. That which is thrown to the dogs, dregs, refuse, what is thrown away as worthless. Spoken of the refuse of grain, chaff, or of a table, of

slaughtered animals, of dung, and figuratively of the filth of the mind. In the NT, meaning refuse, things that are worthless (Phil 3:8).

Syn.: *kopría* (2874), refuse, manure, a dung hill.

Ant.: *gáza* (1047), treasure; *dóxa* (1391), glory, honor, recognition; *euporía* (2142), wealth; *thēsaurós* (2344), treasure; *margarítēs* (3135), pearl (of great price); *ploútos* (4149), wealth; *timḗ* (5092), honor, value; *chrḗma* (5536), riches.

4658. Σκύθης Skúthes; gen. *Skúthou*, masc. proper noun. A Scythian (Col 3:11). A name used indefinitely by ancient writers. Sometimes the term denotes all the nomadic tribes that roamed over the countries north of the Black and Caspian Seas.

Ant.: *bárbaros* (915), barbarian, a non-Greek.

4659. σκυθρωπός skuthrōpós; gen. *skuthrōpoú*, masc.-fem., neut. *skuthrōpón*, adj. from *skuthrós* (n.f.), grim, stern, and *óps* (n.f., see below), the countenance. Grim-faced, of a stern, gloomy, sad countenance; either affected (Matt 6:16) or real (Luke 24:17; Sept.: Gen 40:7).

Deriv. of *óps* (n.f.): *enṓpion* (1799), before, in the presence of; *prósōpon* (4383), face, presence, person.

Syn.: *athuméō* (120), to be discouraged; *perílupos* (4036), sorrowful; *stugnētós* (4767), odious, hateful.

Ant.: *chaírōn* (the pres. part. of *chaírō* [5463]), rejoicing; *agallómenos* (the pres. part. of *agalliáō* [21]), rejoicing greatly; *euphraínomai* (the pass. of *euphraínō* [2165]), to be merry.

4660. σκύλλω skúllō; fut. *skulṓ*. To skin, flay, lacerate. In the NT used metaphorically, meaning to harass, trouble, weary, with the acc. (Mark 5:35; Luke 8:49). In the mid. (Luke 7:6).

Deriv.: *skúlon* (4661), spoil, booty.

Syn.: *basanízō* (928), to vex, torment; *stenochōréō* (4729), to crowd in, to annoy, distress; *kataponéō* (2669), to afflict, oppress; *enochléō* (1776), to annoy; *ochléō* (3791), to harass.

Ant.: *aréskō* (700), to be pleasing to; *euarestéō* (2100), to be well-pleasing; *eudokéō* (2106), to think or wish well; *euphraínō* (2165), to make merry; *onínēmi* (3685), to gratify.

4661. σκῦλον *skúlon*; gen. *skúlou*, neut. noun from *skúllō* (4660), to flay, harass. Skin, hide, as stripped off. Spoil, booty, as stripped from an enemy (Luke 11:22; Sept:. Isa 53:12; Zech 14:1).

Syn.: *akrothínion* (205), the top of a heap, in the choicest spoils of war; *harpagḗ* (724), pillage, spoils, booty; *dérma* (1192), skin.

4662. σκωληκόβρωτος *skōlēkóbrōtos*; gen. *skōlēkobrótou*, masc.-fem., neut. *skōlēkóbrōtón*, adj. from *skṓlēx* (4663), a worm, and *bibrṓskō* (977), to eat. Eaten by worms (Acts 12:23).

4663. σκώληξ *skṓlēx*; gen. *skṓlēkos*, masc. noun. A worm, maggot or grub which sometimes feeds on dead bodies (Mark 9:44, 46, 48 in allusion to Isa 66:24 as the place of punishment of the wicked [cf. *géenna* {1067}, Gehenna]; Sept.: Deut 28:39; Isa 66:24; Jon 4:7).

Deriv.: *skōlēkóbrōtos* (4662), worm-eaten.

4664. σμαράγδινος *smarágdinos*; fem. *smaragdínē*, neut. *smarágdinon*, adj. from *smáragdos* (4665), emerald. Of emeralds (Rev 4:3).

4665. σμάραγδος *smáragdos*; gen. *smarágdou*, masc. noun. An emerald, a precious stone of a beautiful, pure green variety of the mineral beryl (Rev 21:19; Sept.: Ex 28:9, 17; 35:27).

Deriv.: *smarágdinos* (4664), of emeralds.

4666. σμύρνα *smúrna*; gen. *smúrnēs*, fem. noun. Myrrh, perfume which exudes spontaneously or is procured by incisions made on a small thorny tree growing in Arabia or (especially) in Ethiopia. These droplets soon hardened into a bitter aromatic gum which was highly prized by the ancient people for use in incense and perfumes (Matt 2:11; John 19:39; Sept.: Ps 45:8; Song 3:6; 5:5). It is still used medicinally and in perfumes.

Deriv.: *smurnízō* (4669), to mingle with myrrh.

4667. Σμύρνα *Smúrna*; gen. *Smúrnēs*, fem. proper noun. Smyrna, meaning myrrh. A city of Asia Minor named in Scripture as containing one of the seven churches of Asia (Rev 1:11; 2:8–11). It is situated on the Aegean Sea about forty miles north of Ephesus. The modern town is located two and one-half miles from the ancient city of the same name, encompassing both the slopes of Mount Pagus and the low ground at its foot. Christianity was planted there early and the church is commended in the Revelation of John. Polycarp, a pupil of John, suffered martyrdom in Smyrna in A.D. 155 in extreme old age.

4668. Σμυρναῖος *Smurnaíos*; fem. *Smurnaía*, neut. *Smurnaíon*, adj. Smyrnean; as a subst. someone hailing from Smyrna (Rev 2:8 [TR]).

4669. σμυρνίζω *smurnízō*; fut. *smurnísō*, from *smúrna* (4666), myrrh. To mingle with myrrh. In the pass. (Mark 15:23, wine mingled with myrrh and other herbs). See *óxos* (3690), vinegar.

4670. Σόδομα *Sódoma*; gen. *Sodómōn*, neut. pl. proper noun transliterated from the Hebr. S͎e͎dōm (5467, OT), burning. Sodom, one of a group of cities in the Valley of Siddim which was destroyed due to the great wickedness of their inhabitants (Gen 10:19; 13:10–13; 18:16; 19:1–29). It was chosen by Lot as his home, the country around it being fertile and well-watered everywhere, "even as the garden of the Lord." The history of its great wickedness and terrible punishment is given in Gen 18:16–33; 19:1–29. Sodom is often held up as a warning to sinners to escape the terrible vengeance of God (Matt 10:15; 11:23, 24; Mark 6:11; Luke 10:12; 17:29; Rom 9:29; 2 Pet 2:6–8; Jude 1:7; Rev 11:8; Sept.: Deut 29:23; Isa 1:9, 10; 3:9; 13:19; Jer 23:14; 49:18; Ezek 16:48, 49; Amos 4:11; Zeph 2:9).

4671. σοί *soí*; 2d person personal pron., dat. sing. of *sú* (4771), thou, you in the sing. To thee, thine own, thou, thy.

4672. Σολομών *Solomṓn*; gen. *Solomónos*, masc. proper noun transliterated from the Hebr. *Shᵉlōmōh* (8010, OT), peaceful. Solomon, the name of the son and successor of David, celebrated for his wisdom, wealth, and splendor (Matt 1:6, 7; 6:29; 12:42; Luke 11:31; 12:27; John 10:23; Acts 3:11; 5:12; 7:47; Sept.: 1 Kgs chap. 1ff.; 1 Chr chaps. 28; 29; 2 Chr chap. 1ff.).

4673. σορός *sorós*; gen. *soroú*, fem. noun. A coffin, urn, any receptacle for a dead body. In the Sept., it stands for a mummy chest (Gen 50:26). In the NT, an open coffin or bier on which the dead person was carried to burial (Luke 7:14 [cf. Sept.: 2 Sam 2:32]).

4674. σός *sós*; poss. adj. of the 2d person personal pron. *sú* (4771), thou, you. Thine, yours, your (in the sing.). See Matt 7:3, 22; 13:27; 25:25; Luke 6:30; Acts 5:4; 1 Cor 8:11, "thy knowledge"). Of society, companionship (Mark 2:18; Luke 5:33; John 17:6, 9, 10; 18:35). Of origin, as proceeding from someone (Matt 24:3, of thy appearing; Luke 22:42, thy will; John 4:42; 17:17, "thy word"; Acts 24:2, 4; 1 Cor 14:16; Phile 1:14).

4675. σοῦ *soú*; 2d person personal pron., gen. of *sú* (4771), thou. Of thee, thy, thine (Matt 7:3; 15:28; 25:25).

4676. σουδάριον *soudárion*; gen. *soudaríou*, neut. noun. A sweat-cloth, gener-

ally a handkerchief, napkin (Luke 19:20; John 11:44; 20:7; Acts 19:12).

4677. Σουσάννα *Sousánna*; gen. *Sousánnēs*, fem. proper noun. Susanna, meaning lily. One of the women who ministered to the Lord Jesus (Luke 8:3).

4678. σοφία *sophía*; gen. *sophías*, fem. noun from *sophós* (4680), wise. Wisdom, skill, tact, expertise in any art.

In the NT, it refers to wisdom:

(I) Skill in the affairs of life, practical wisdom, wise management as shown in forming the best plans and selecting the best means, including the idea of sound judgment and good sense (Acts 6:3; 7:10: Col 1:28; 3:16; 4:5). *Stóma* (4750), mouth, and *sophían* in Luke 21:15 means wise utterance. See Sept: 1 Kgs 2:6.

(II) In a higher sense, wisdom, deep knowledge, natural and moral insight, learning, science, implying cultivation of mind and enlightened understanding.

(A) Generally (Matt 12:42; Luke 11:31 [cf. 1 Kgs 4:30]; Acts 7:22). Implying learned research (Col 2:23); a knowledge of hidden things, of enigmatic and symbolic language (Rev 13:18; 17:9; Sept.: Job 11:6; Prov 1:2; Dan 1:17).

(B) Specifically of the learning and philosophy current among the Greeks and Romans in the apostolic age intended to draw away the minds of men from divine truth, and which stood in contrast with the simplicity of the gospel; called by Paul *sarkikḗ* (4559), fleshly, pertaining to the flesh (2 Cor 1:12); the wisdom of the world (1 Cor 1:20ff.; 3:19ff.); of men (1 Cor 2:5); of the wise (1 Cor 1:19); words of man's wisdom (1 Cor 2:4, 13); the world through wisdom (1 Cor 1:21); not in wisdom of words, meaning not with mere philosophy and rhetoric (1 Cor 1:17; 2:1).

(C) In respect to divine things, wisdom, knowledge, insight, deep understanding, represented everywhere as a divine gift, and including the idea of practical application. It is used metonymically for *gnṓsis* (1108), knowledge or theoretical knowledge (Matt 13:54; Mark 6:2; Acts 6:10); divine knowledge (Eph 1:8). *Sophía* stands for divine wisdom, the ability to regulate one's relationship with God, and is distinct from *phrónēsis* (5428), prudence, the ability to know and deal with people (1 Cor 12:8; Eph 1:17; Col 1:9: 2 Pet 3:15). Specifically of insight imparted from God in respect to the divine counsels (1 Cor 2:6, 7). Metonymically of the author and source of this wisdom (1 Cor 1:30). As conjoined with purity of heart and life (James 1:5; 3:13, 15, 17). See Luke 2:40, 52.

(III) The wisdom of God means the divine wisdom, including the ideas of infinite skill, insight, knowledge, purity (Rom 11:33; 1 Cor 1:21, 24; Eph 3:10; Col 2:3; Rev 5:12; 7:12). Of the divine wisdom as revealed and manifested in Christ and His gospel (Matt 11:19; Luke 7:35; 11:49).

(IV) Fear, wisdom, generally the knowledge of how to regulate one's relationship with God, wisdom which is related with goodness. When one is wise unto God, he is *phrónimos* (5429), prudent with others and knows how to regulate circumstances.

Deriv.: *philósophos* (5386), philosopher.

Syn.: *sōphrosúnē* (4997), soundness of mind; *súnesis* (4907), the capacity for reasoning, intelligence, understanding; *phrónēsis* (5428), prudence, moral insight; *epínoia* (1963), thought.

Ant.: *ánoia* (454), stupidity, folly, madness; *mōría* (3472), absurdity, foolishness; *aphrosúnē* (877), senselessness, folly, foolishness.

4679. σοφίζω *sophízō*; fut. *sophísō*, from *sophós* (4680), wise. To make wise, skillful, expert. Pass., to be skilled, expert. In the NT, in the act., to make wise, enlighten in regard to divine things, with the acc. of person (2 Tim 3:15; Sept.: Ps 19:7; 105:22); in the mid. *sophízomai*, as a deponent with acc. of thing, to make wisely, devise skillfully, artfully. As a perf. pass. part., *sesophisménoi múthoi* (*múthoi* [3454], fables), skillfully devised fables

(2 Pet 1:16). In the Class. Gr. writers also with the acc. of person, with the meaning of deceive or delude.

Deriv.: *katasophízomai* (2686), to deal subtly with.

Syn.: *suníēmi* (4920), to perceive, understand.

Ant.: *agnoéō* (50), not to know.

4680. σοφός *sophós*; fem. *sophḗ*, neut. *sophón*, adj. In Class. Gr. it not only described respected philosophers and other truly learned men but was also appropriated by vain quibblers and rhetoricians whom Aristophanes parodied and Plato and Aristotle censured. The meaning of *sophós* in the NT and its Hebr. equivalent, *chōkmah*, differs from the classical meaning in at least two ways. First of all, the biblical concept of wisdom is theocentric rather than anthropocentric. It denotes a fear of God and an understanding of His ways. Lastly, wisdom signifies the possession of a certain adeptness or practical ability. It does not necessarily imply brilliance or scholastic training; rather, *sophós* indicates adroitness, the ability to apply with skill what one knows (especially religious truth). In some instances, however, particularly in the Pauline writings, the word is used of one who has acquired special information, secret doctrine (*mustḗrion* [3466]). Here the noetic aspect of the word is prominent in its meaning. Hence, the following meanings:

(I) Skillful, expert (1 Cor 3:10; Sept.: 2 Chr 2:7; Isa 3:3).

(II) Skilled in the affairs of life, discreet, judicious, practically wise (1 Cor 6:5; Sept.: Deut 1:13; 2 Sam 13:3; Isa 19:11).

(III) Skilled in learning, learned, intelligent, enlightened, in respect to things human and divine.

(A) Generally as to human beings (Rom 16:19; 1 Cor 1:25; Sept.: Prov 1:6; Eccl 2:14, 16); coupled with *sunetón* (4908), prudent ones (Matt 11:25; Luke 10:21); coupled with *anoḗtois*, (453), foolish ones, unwise (Rom 1:14).

(B) Specifically as to the philosophy current among the Greeks and Romans (Rom 1:22; 1 Cor 1:19, 20, 26, 27; 3:18–20).

(C) In respect to divine things, wise, enlightened, as conjoined with purity of heart and life (Eph 5:15; James 3:13).

(IV) Spoken of God as surpassing all others in wisdom, being infinite in skill, insight, knowledge, purity (Rom 16:27; 1 Tim 1:17; Jude 1:25).

Deriv.: *ásophos* (781), unwise, foolish; *sophízō* (4679), to make wise, instruct.

Syn.: *logikós* (3050), logical; *sunetós* (4908), one who can reason, prudent; *orthós* (3717), correct; *sóphrōn* (4998), of sound mind; *phrónimos* (5429), prudent, ethical, well-behaved; *epistémōn* (1990), scientist, intelligent.

Ant.: *ásophos* (781), one devoid of wisdom; *mōrós* (3474), stupid, foolish; *asúnetos* (801), foolish, without understanding; *anóetos* (453), unintelligent, unwise; *áphrōn* (878), foolish; *mátaios* (3152), vain.

4681. Σπανία *Spanía*; gen. *Spanías*, fem. proper noun. Spain, the name of the Spanish peninsula, including modern Spain and Portugal, as constituting a province of the Roman Empire. Because Paul's missionary strategy often made Jewish communities primary evangelism targets (eliminating the necessity of pre-evangelism work and facilitating the establishment of sound churches), his mention of plans to visit Spain (Rom 15:24, 28) may suggest that a Jewish settlement existed in that country.

4682. σπαράσσω *sparássō*, σπαράττω *sparáttō*, fut. *sparáxō*. To tear, rend, lacerate. In the NT equivalent to convulse, throw into spasms as epilepsy, spoken of the effects of demoniac possessions, with the acc. (Mark 1:26; 9:20, 26; Luke 9:39).

Deriv.: *susparássō* (4952), to convulse violently.

Syn.: *kóptō* (2875), to cut down, bewail; *katakóptō* (2629), to wound; *thraúō*

(2352), crush, bruise; *suntríbō* (4937), to break in pieces, bruise; *diarrḗssō* (1284), to tear asunder; *diaspáō* (1288), to dismember; *túptō* (5180), to beat, wound.

Ant.: *hēsucházō* (2270), to rest; *iáomai* (2390), to cure, heal; *sōphronéō* (4993), to be of sound mind; *hugiaínō* (5198), to be well, in health.

4683. σπαργανόω *sparganóō*; contracted *sparganṓ*, fut. *sparganṓsō*, from *spárganon* (n.f.), a swathing or swaddling band. To swathe, wrap in swaddling clothes, trans. (Luke 2:7, 12; Sept.: Ezek 16:4).

4684. σπαταλάω *spataláō*; contracted *spataló*, fut. *spatalḗsō*, from *spatálē* (n.f.), luxury in eating and drinking. To live in luxury or pleasure, be self-indulgent. Paul counsels Timothy about the widows that "live in pleasure" or "in self-gratification" (a.t. [1 Tim 5:6]). In James 5:5 the rich men are warned against being "wanton" in their lifestyle.

Syn.: *strēniáō* (4763), to live luxuriously, sensuously; *trupháō* (5171), to live in pleasure, self-indulgence.

Ant.: *oikonoméō* (3621), to abstain, manage; *sōphronéō* (4993), to be of sound mind.

4685. σπάω *spáō*; contracted *spó*, fut. *spásō*. To draw, to pull, to breathe. In the NT, to draw out, such as a sword. In the mid. (Mark 14:47; Acts 16:27; Sept.: Num 22:31; Judg 9:54).

Deriv.: *anaspáō* (385), to draw up; *apospáō* (645), to draw away; *diaspáō* (1288), to pull in pieces; *epispáomai* (1986), to become uncircumcised; *perispáō* (4049), to drag around, distract.

Syn.: *hélkō* (1670), to drag; *súrō* (4951), to draw; *exélkō* (1828), to lure; *apochōrízō* (673), to separate; *aphairéō* (851), to remove; *exaírō* (1808), to remove, take away; *antléō* (501), to draw.

Ant.: *sundéō* (4887), to bind with; *déō* (1210), to bind; *proskolláō* (4347), to join, glue together.

4686. σπεῖρα speíra; gen. *speírēs*, fem. noun. A cord, rope, band. In the NT, a band, troop, company:

(I) Spoken of Roman foot soldiers, probably a cohort (numbering between four hundred and six hundred), of which there were ten in every legion (*legeón* [3003]). Each legion contained from 4,000 to 6,600 foot soldiers (Matt 27:27; Mark 15:16; Acts 10:1; 21:31; 27:1).

(II) Spoken of a band from the guards of the temple (John 18:3, 12). These were Levites who filled the menial offices of the temple and kept watch by night (Sept.: Ps 134:1 [cf. 2 Kgs 12:9; 25:18; see especially 1 Chr 9:17, 27ff.]). They were under the command of officers called *stratēgós* (4755), temple wardens (Luke 22:52), or *chilíarchos* (5506), colonels or chief captains, commanders of one thousand soldiers.

Deriv.: *spurís* (4711), a basket.

Syn.: *stratiá* (4756), an army.

4687. σπείρω speírō; fut. *sperṓ*. To sow, scatter seed.

(I) Used in an absolute sense (Matt 6:26; 13:3, 4; Mark 4:3, 4; Luke 8:5; 12:24). Part., *ho speírōn*, the sowing one, sower (Matt 13:3, 18; Mark 4:3, 14; Luke 8:5; 2 Cor 9:10). Followed by the acc. of the seed sown (Matt 13:24, 25, 27, 31, 37, 39; 1 Cor 15:36, 37). In the pass., figuratively of a single seed of grain (Mark 4:31, 32); also by analogy of the body as committed to the earth (1 Cor 15:42–44). With prep. of place, e.g., *eis* (1519), unto, with the acc. (Matt 13:22; Mark 4:18); *en* (1722), in, with a dat. (Matt 13:31; Sept.: Gen 26:12); *epí* (1909), upon, with a gen. (Mark 4:31), with the acc. (Matt 13:20, 23); *pará* (3844), near, with the acc. (Matt 13:19; Sept.: Eccl 11:4; Jer 12:13). In proverbial expressions (Matt 25:24, 26; Luke 19:21, 22, "reaping where you did not sow" [a.t.]; John 4:37, "another one is the reaper" [a.t.]; 2 Cor 9:6, "he who sows sparingly" [a.t.]; Gal 6:7, "whatsoever a man soweth"); figuratively (1 Cor 9:11, meaning to disseminate, to impart spiritual truths). See Gal 6:8 (cf. Prov 22:8).

(II) Figuratively of a teacher, to sow the "Word of Life," disseminate instruction (Mark 4:14; John 4:36). In the pass. (Matt 13:19, "that which was sown in his heart"; Mark 4:15, "where the word is sown," 16, 20; James 3:18).

Deriv.: *diaspeírō* (1289), to sow abroad, distribute in foreign lands; *spérma* (4690), seed, offspring, posterity; *sporá* (4701), a sowing; *spórimos* (4702), a planted field; *spóros* (4703), seed.

Syn.: *skorpízō* (4650), to scatter; *likmáō* (3039), to winnow; *diaskorpízō* (1287), dissipate, disperse, scatter.

Ant.: *therízō* (2325), to reap; *sugkomízō* (4792), to collect or bear, carry away; *trugáō* (5166), to collect the vintage, gather the fruit; *sullégō* (4816) and *sunágō* (4863), to gather.

4688. σπεκουλάτωρ spekoulátōr; gen. *spekoulátoros*, from the Lat. *speculator*, spy. A soldier, a sentinel. These were soldiers forming the bodyguard of kings and princes who also, according to oriental custom, acted as executioners (Mark 6:27).

Syn.: *koustōdía* (2892), a Roman sentry; *phúlax* (5441), a guard, keeper; *stratopedárchēs* (4759), a captain of the guard; *stratiṓtēs* (4757), soldier.

4689. σπένδω spéndō; fut. *speísō*. To pour out, to make a libation (Sept.: Gen 35:14). In the NT, figuratively, in the mid. *spéndomai*, to pour out oneself, as one's blood, to offer up one's strength and life (Phil 2:17; 2 Tim 4:6).

Syn.: *prosphérō* (4374), to offer; *dídōmi* (1325), to give; *paréchō* (3930), to furnish, offer up, present; *thúō* (2380), to sacrifice; *katachéō* (2708), to pour.

Ant.: *katéchō* (2722), hold fast, retain; *kratéō* (2902), keep, hold fast; *pheídomai* (5339), to spare.

4690. σπέρμα spérma; gen. *spérmatos*, neut. noun from *speírō* (4687), to sow. Seed, both what is sown as containing the germ of new fruit, and what is growing out of the seed sown, produce. Originally *spérma* was used of plants as seed (Matt 13:24, 27, 32, 37, 38; Mark 4:31; 1 Cor 15:38; 2 Cor 9:10; Sept.: Gen 1:11; 47:23). In 1 John 3:9 the *spérma* of God denotes the power of God operative through the Holy Spirit working in believers. Also figuratively used of living beings as the seed of man; i.e., of posterity or descendants. By implication, *spérma* means a remnant, a few survivors, such as those remaining from a former year (Rom 9:29 alluding to Isa 1:9).

In the Class. Gr. terminology, *spérma* rarely signifies descendants collectively, and even less, posterity as a whole, but primarily only the individual, the child, offspring, son or daughter. In the Sept. however, *spérma* has mostly a collective meaning. In the few places where it is used of an individual (Sept.: Gen 4:25; 21:13; 1 Sam 1:11; 2 Sam 7:12), it includes oneself or represents the progeny (Sept.: 1 Sam 2:20). In Isa 59:21 it signifies primarily the immediate descendants, the children (see Sept.: Gen 15:3; 21:13), and hence *spérma* denotes the descendants collectively traced back to one ancestor (Sept.: Gen 13:16; 15:13, 18; 22:17; 28:14; 32:12). Therefore, it passes into the meaning of family, stock (Sept.: 2 Kgs 11:1; 25:25), and of Israel collectively (Sept.: Ezra 9:2). In some instances such as Ps 37:28; 69:36; Prov 11:18; Isa 1:4; 57:4; 65:23, it has the meaning of *génnēma* (1081), offspring, and signifies an ethical spiritual fellowship without reference to relationship of race. *Spérma* is used especially of the people of Israel as descendants of Abraham or Jacob, with whom Ishmael or Esau and their descendants were not reckoned (Sept.: Gen 21:12, 13; 28:4, 13, 14; Ps 105:6; Isa 41:8). Besides these, we find it employed of individual families, such as the family of Aaron, David, and others. With these aforementioned exceptions, *spérma* is everywhere a collective concept for which the pl. is never used.

The word continues in its collective meaning in the NT (Rev 12;17). Thus, it denotes immediate descendants, children (Matt 22:24, 25; Mark 12:19–22; Luke 20:28). The expression "the seed of David" (John 7:42; Rom 1:3; 2 Tim 2:8) means progeny, posterity (see Acts 13:23). Similarly with "the seed of Abraham" (a.t. [Luke 1:55; John 8:33, 37; Acts 3:25; 7:5, 6; 13:23; Rom 4:13, 16, 18; 11:1; 2 Cor 11:22; Gal 3:19; Heb 2:16; 11:18]). Where Christ is designated as the progeny or offspring of Abraham, He is referred to as the Messiah. He is the offspring of Abraham as Isaac is the offspring of Abraham, including and exhibiting in himself that progeny (Rom 9:7). There are, indeed, *spérmata*, seeds, of Abraham, lines of descent, namely those of Ishmael or Esau besides Isaac or Israel. However, the promise does not apply to all the lines of descent, but to one line which alone is always meant by the seed of Abraham, i.e., the Messiah, which henceforward is brought into existence through Christ. To take *spérmata* (pl.) as a collective term, and *spérma* (sing.) as an individual person, is foreign to Pauline phraseology. In Gal 3:16 we must distinguish between one line of progeny and more than one (*spérma*, seed, coll. *spérmata*, seeds, lines of descendants) and bear in mind Gen 21:12, 13 (with which Gal 3:29 very well agrees). That Paul has in mind the several lines of descendants from Abraham is evident in Gal 4:22.

Deriv.: *spermológos* (4691), seed-gathering, chatterer, babbler.

Syn.: *spóros* (4703), seed; *sporá* (4701), seed, a sowing.

4691. σπερμολόγος *spermológos*; gen. *spermológou*, masc.-fem., *spermológon*, adj. from *spérma* (4690), a seed, and *légō* (3004), to collect, gather. Used as a subst., a trifler, babbler, chatterer who picks up and repeats trifling things (Acts 17:18). It is said that the Athenians applied this name to those who made their living by collecting and selling refuse they found in the market places. Therefore, they were men of no account, low and contemptible persons.

Syn.: *mataiológos* (3151), vain talker; *katálalos* (2637), slanderer.

4692. σπεύδω speúdō; fut. *speúsō*. Trans., to urge on, hasten. In the NT, intrans., to urge oneself on, hasten, make haste, in respect simply to time (Acts 22:18), and thus differing from *spoudázō*, which involves diligence, earnestness, zeal. With the inf. (Acts 20:16). In Luke 2:16, as a part. with a verb of motion, used adv. and meaning hastily, quickly. See Luke 19:5, 6; Sept.: Gen 45:9; Ex 34:8; Josh 8:19. With an acc., meaning to hasten after something, to await with eager desire (2 Pet 3:12; see Sept.: Isa 16:5).

Deriv.: *spoudé* (4710), haste, diligence with haste.

Syn.: *biázō* (971), to press; *grēgoréō* (1127), to be vigilant; *energéō* (1754), to be active, fervent; *epimeléomai* (1959), to take care with forethought and provision; *mélō* (3199), to show concern, interest; *merimnáō* (3309), to be anxious about; *phronéō* (5426), to take thought; *phrontízō* (5431), to care for with thought and consideration.

Ant.: *bradúnō* (1019), to delay; *chronízō* (5549), to linger, delay.

4693. σπήλαιον spélaion; gen. *spēlaíou*, neut. noun from *spéos* (n.f.), a cave. A cave, cavern, den (Matt 21:13; Mark 11:17; Luke 19:46; John 11:38; Heb 11:38; Rev 6:15; Sept.: Gen 19:30; Josh 10:16, 17).

Syn.: *opḗ* (3692), a hole, opening; *katáluma* (2646), a lodging place; *phréar* (5421), a well or pit, hole; *phōleós* (5454), lurking place, hole.

4694. σπιλάς spilás; gen. *spiládos*, fem. noun. A rock by or in the sea, a cliff or sandbank on which vessels are shipwrecked. Figuratively of false teachers who, as hidden reefs, cause others to make shipwreck of their faith (Jude 1:12 [cf. 1 Tim 1:19]).

Syn.: *pétra* (4073), a mass of rock; *líthos* (3037), stone.

4695. σπιλόω spilóō; contracted *spilṓ*, fut. *spilṓsō*, from *spílos* (4696), a spot, stain. To defile, spot, stain (James 3:6; Jude 1:23).

Syn.: *rhupóō* (4510), to soil, become dirty; *bebēlóō* (953), to desecrate; *hierosuléō* (2416), to commit sacrilege; *molúnō* (3435), to soil, defile; *miaínō* (3392), to defile.

Ant.: *kathaírō* (2508), to cleanse; *katharízō* (2511), to cleanse, purge; *hagnízō* (48), to purify.

4696. σπίλος spílos; gen. *spílou*, masc. noun. A spot, stain, figuratively in a moral sense (Eph 5:27; 2 Pet 2:13).

Deriv.: *áspilos* (784), without spot; *spilóō* (4695), to defile, spot.

Syn.: *rhúpos* (4509), depravity, filth; *rhupáría* (4507), dirtiness; *akatharsía* (167), impurity, uncleanness; *míasma* (3393), foulness, pollution; *stígma* (4742), mark, scar; *skúbalon* (4657), refuse; *molusmós* (3436), filthiness.

Ant.: *katharismós* (2512), the act of cleansing; *katharótēs* (2514), cleanness, purity; *hagnoía* (47), chastity; *hagnótēs* (54), pureness.

4697. σπλαγχνίζομαι splagchnízomai; fut., *splagchnisthḗsomai*, pass. deponent from *splágchnon* (4698), bowel. To feel deeply or viscerally, to yearn, have compassion, pity. Used in an absolute sense (Matt 20:34; Mark 1:41; Luke 10:33; 15:20). Followed by *epí* (1909), upon, with the dat. (Mark 6:34), with the acc. (Matt 14:14; Mark 8:2; 9:22); *perí* (4012), about, with the gen. (Matt 9:36); with only the gen. (Matt 18:27). *Splagchnízomai* indicates an inner feeling and is frequently recorded of Christ's attitude toward multitudes and individuals.

Syn.: *oikteírō* (3627), to have pity, a feeling of distress from the ills of others; *sumpathéō* (4834), to suffer with another; *eleéō* (1653), to have mercy, to alleviate the consequences of sin or suffering in the lives of others; *metriopathéō* (3356), to bear, to moderate one's anger, treat with mildness, moderation, gentleness; *sumpáschō* (4841), to suffer with.

Ant.: *sklērúnō* (4645), to render stubborn, harden; *pōróō* (4456), to petrify, harden; *oligōréō* (3643), to show little regard for.

4698. σπλάγχνον *splágchnon*; gen. *splágchnou*, neut. noun. An intestine, bowel. In the NT only pl. *tá splágchna*, the bowels, viscera. In Class. Gr. writers, it is chiefly spoken of the upper viscera of animals, as the heart, lungs, and liver which were eaten during or after the sacrifice. In the NT, of persons generally, the intestines, bowels:

(I) Used particularly (Acts 1:18).

(II) Figuratively, the inward parts indicating the breast or heart as the seat of emotions and passions. In the NT, of the gentler emotions as compassion, tender affection indicating the mind, soul, the inner man:

(A) Generally (2 Cor 6:12, parallel with *kardía* (2588), the heart, in 6:11). See Phile 1:7, 20; 1 John 3:17; Sept.: Prov 12:10 (cf. Gen 43:30; 1 Kgs 3:26).

(B) Metonymically, inward affection, compassion, pity, love (2 Cor 7:15; Phil 1:8, meaning in my ardent love to Christ; 2:1). Intens. (Luke 1:78; Col 3:12). In the Sept. it stands for *éleos* (1656), mercy (Deut 13:18; Isa 47:6).

(C) As the object of affection (Phile 1:12, "mine own bowels," equal to "my heart" [a.t.], spoken of a person and implying strong affection.

Deriv.: *eúsplagchnos* (2155), tenderhearted; *splagchnízomai* (2697), to have compassion; *polúsplagchnos* (4184), very compassionate.

Syn.: *páthos* (3806), affection of the mind; *oiktirmós* (3628), the feeling of pity and the external exhibition of it; *éleos* (1656), the outward manifestation of pity and participation in the sufferings of others; *sumpathḗs* (4835), one having compassion.

Ant.: *sklērokardía* (4641), hardness of heart; *sklērótēs* (4643), hardness; *pṓrōsis* (4457), callousness, hardness.

4699. σπόγγος *spóggos*; gen. *spóggou*, masc. noun. A sponge (Matt 27:48; Mark 15:36; John 19:29).

4700. σποδός *spodós*; gen. *spodoú*, fem. noun. Ashes, of a heifer (Heb 9:13). Metaphorically in Matt 11:21; Luke 10:13, "they would have repented in sackcloth and ashes" (a.t.) means to dress in a coarse cloth made of goat hair and to cast ashes or dust on one's head which was a rite of oriental mourning (cf. Sept.: Esth 4:1, 3; Isa 58:5; Jer 6:26; Jon 3:6).

Syn.: *koniortós* (2868), dust; *tapeínōsis* (5014), humiliation, low estate; *tapeinophrosúnē* (5012), humbleness of mind, humility.

Ant.: *huperēphanía* (5243), haughtiness, pride.

4701. σπορά *sporá*; gen. *sporás*, fem. noun from *speírō* (4687), to sow. The act of sowing, seedtime (2 Kgs 19:29). Figuratively for spiritual seed or the Word of God (1 Pet 1:23).

4702. σπόριμος *spórimos*; gen. *spórimou*, masc.-fem., neut. *spórimon*, adj. from *speírō* (4687), to sow. In the neut. pl., *tá spórima*. Sown fields, fields of growing grain (Matt 12:1; Mark 2:23; Luke 6:1 [see Gen 1:29; Lev 11:37]).

4703. σπόρος *spóros*; gen. *spórou*, masc. noun from *speírō* (4687), to sow. Seed, seed that is supplied for sowing (2 Cor 9:10; Sept.: Ex 34:21, green sprout or growing grain; Deut 11:10). Equivalent to *spérma* (4690), seed. Figuratively (Mark 4:26, 27; Luke 8:5, 11).

4704. σπουδάζω *spoudázō*; fut. *spoudásō*, from *spoudḗ* (4710), earnestness, diligence (2 Pet 1:5). To be diligent, earnest, or eager.

(I) Generally, with the inf. (2 Tim 4:9, 21; Titus 3:12).

(II) To make every effort to do one's best, to be eager, with the inf. (Gal 2:10; Eph 4:3; 1 Thess 2:17; 2 Tim 2:15; Heb 4:11; 2 Pet 1:10, 15; 3:14; Sept.: Isa 21:3).

Syn.: *philotiméomai* (5389), to strive or labor to be diligent; *zēlóō* (2206), to see or desire eagerly.

Ant.: *ameléō* (272), to neglect; *epilan-thánomai* (1950), to neglect, be forgetful; *aphíēmi* (863), to forsake, let go; *oknéō* (3635), to delay, be lazy.

4705. σπουδαῖος *spoudaíos*; fem. *spou-daía*, neut. *spoudaíon*, adj. from *spoudḗ* (4710), diligence, eagerness. Earnest, diligent (2 Cor 8:22). The comparative *spoudaióteros* (4707), more diligent.

Deriv.: *spoudaíōs* (4709), earnestly, diligently.

Syn.: *tachús* (5036), ready, swift; *ektenḗs* (1618), insistent, without ceasing, fervent.

4706. σπουδαιότερον *spoudaióteron*; neut. acc. of *spoudaióteros* (4707), more prompt or very diligent. Used adv., more diligently (2 Tim 1:17 [TR], *spoudaíōs* [4709], diligently [UBS]).

4707. σπουδαιότερος *spoudaióte-ros*; adj., the comparative of *spoudaíos* (4705), earnest, prompt. More diligent (2 Cor 8:17, 22). The neut. acc. is also used adv. *spoudaióteros* (4706), more promptly or diligently.

4708. σπουδαιοτέρως *spoudaiotérōs*; adv., the comparative of *spoudaíōs* (4709), more earnestly and diligently. More earnestly, diligently (Phil 2:28).

4709. σπουδαίως *spoudaíōs*; adv. from *spoudaíos* (4705), prompt, diligent. Earnestly, diligently, eagerly, promptly (Luke 7:4; 2 Tim 1:17 [UBS]; Titus 3:13).

Syn.: *epimelṓs* (1960), diligently; *akribṓs* (199), accurately, carefully; *tachú* (5035), without delay, suddenly, quickly.

4710. σπουδή *spoudḗ*; gen. *spoudḗs*, fem. noun from *speúdō* (4692), to speed, urge, hasten, press. Speed, haste, earnestness, diligence, zeal.

(I) Generally, with the prep. *metá* (3326) and the gen., meaning with haste, hastily, eagerly (Mark 6:25; Luke 1:39; Sept.: Ex 12:11).

(II) Diligence, earnest effort (Rom 12:8, 11; 2 Cor 7:11; 8:7, 8; 2 Pet 1:5; Jude 1:3). On behalf of someone (2 Cor 7:12; 8:16). With *prós* (4314), toward (Heb 6:11).

Deriv.: *spoudázō* (4704), endeavor; *spoudaíos* (4705), prompt.

Syn.: *epiméleia* (1958), attention, diligence; *prothumía* (4288), readiness; *táchos* (5034), speed, haste.

Ant.: *anabolḗ* (311), delay.

4711. σπυρίς *spurís*; gen. *spurídos*, fem. noun from *speíra* (4686), something that is coiled. A basket for storing grain or provisions (Matt 15:37; 16:10; Mark 8:8, 20; Acts 9:25).

Syn.: *kóphinos* (2894), a wicker basket; *sargánē* (4553), a large basket made of ropes or a wicker basket made of entwined twigs.

4712. στάδιον *stádion*, gen. *stadíou*, neut. noun from *hístēmi* (2476), to stand. A stadium, a measure of distance. The pl. occurs in both the masc. (*stádioi*) and neut. (*stádia*) forms.

(I) In the sing., a stadium or an arena in which public games were held, the track in the arena, or as a metonym the race run on the track (1 Cor 9:24). The arena was so-called because the Olympic course was a stadium in length.

(II) In the pl., a measure of length or distance containing 600 (Gr.) or 625 (Rom) feet (Luke 24:13; John 6:19; 11:18; Rev 14:20; 21:16). This is equivalent to about 604.5 feet or 201.5 yards (the proportion of the Gr. foot to the Eng. being about 1007 to 1000, and that of the Roman foot about 970 to 1,000, or about

11.6 inches). The Roman mile, *mílion* (3400), contained eight stadia.

4713. στάμνος *stámnos*; gen. *stámnou*, masc.-fem. noun from *hístēmi* (2476), to stand. An urn, pot, jar, an earthen jug usually for keeping wine. In the NT, a pot or vase in which the manna was placed in the ark (Heb 9:4 [see Ex 16:33]).

Syn.: *xéstēs* (3582), a pitcher of wood or stone holding about a pint; *kéramos* (2766), earthenware; *aggeíon* (30), vessel.

4714. στάσις *stásis*; gen. *stáseōs*, fem. noun from *hístēmi* (2476), to stand. A stance, a posture (Heb 9:8); an insurrection, sedition or uprising (Mark 15:7; Luke 23:19, 25; Acts 19:40; 24:5). A contention, dissension, dispute (Acts 15:2; 23:7, 10; Sept.: Prov 17:14). *Stásis* is applied to civil insurrection while *pólemos* (4171), war, refers to foreign strife.

Deriv.: *sustasiastēs* (4955), a fellow insurgent; *dichostasía* (1370), division, separation.

4715. στατήρ *statēr*; gen. *statēros*, masc. noun from *hístēmi* (2476), to stand. A weight or stater, an Attic silver coin equal to four Attic silver drachmae, which at that time was equivalent to the shekel among the Jews. There was also a *statēr* of gold. Generally it was a standard weight which then became a standard coin. In Athens it was at first applied to the *dídrachmon* (1323), two drachmae. The *statēr* (Matt 17:27) in the fish's mouth was to pay the temple tax of a *dídrachmon* for two persons, our Lord and Peter. For a full discussion of the monetary system, see *argúrion* (694), a silver piece, which was looked upon as a standard coin of the monetary system (though afterwards the *tetrádrachmon* [n.f.] [four drachmae] came to be such).

4716. σταυρός *staurós*; gen. *staurou*, masc. noun from *hístēmi* (2476), to stand. A cross, a stake, often with a crosspiece, on which criminals were nailed for execution. The cross was an instrument of most dreadful and agonizing torture. This mode of punishment was known to the Persians (Ezra 6:11; Esth 7:10); and the Carthaginians. However, it was most common among the Romans for slaves and criminals, and was introduced among the Jews by the Romans. It was not abolished until the time of Constantine who did so out of regard for Christianity.

Persons sentenced to be crucified were first scourged and then made to bear their own cross to the place of execution. A label or title was usually placed on the chest of or over the criminal. Crucifixion was at once an execution, a pillory, and an instrument of torture.

In biblical Gr., *staurós* occurs only in the NT and refers to:

(I) A Roman cross consisting of a straight piece of wood erected in the earth, often with a transverse beam fastened across its top and another piece nearer the bottom on which the crucified person's feet were nailed, as was the cross on which the Lord Jesus suffered (Matt 27:32, 40, 42; Mark 15:21, 30, 32; Luke 23:26; John 19:17, 25, 31; Phil 2:8; Col 1:20; 2:14).

(II) It denotes the whole passion of Christ and the merit of His sufferings and death (Eph 2:16) as well as the doctrine concerning this (1 Cor 1:17; Gal 6:12, 14; Phil 3:18). Used in an absolute sense (Gal 5:11); "the word of the cross" ([1 Cor 1:18] a.t.).

When we read of the antagonism to the cross of Christ, we must understand it as antagonism to a redemption which was accomplished by the deepest humiliation, not by the display of power and glory (Gal 6:14; Phil 2:5–8). Where other NT authors (and Paul elsewhere) employ the word blood (*haíma* [129]) as a symbol for Christ's sacrificial death, Paul often uses the word cross. Although both terms refer to Christ's death, each emphasizes a particular aspect regarding it. Christ's blood represents His death as sacrifice and connects it with the OT sacrifices. The cross of Christ represents His death as suffering and connects it with the curse of sin. The cross shows this peculiar manner of His death as that which entailed suffering, shame, rejection, and humiliation. In Col 1:20, Paul reaches a high point in his cross-theology by combining these two words and saying that God has "made peace through the blood of his cross" (a.t.).

(III) That portion of affliction which is endured by pious and good men as a trial of their faith and to conform them to the example of their crucified Master (Matt 10:38; 16:24; Mark 8:34; 10:21; Luke 9:23; 14:27). The expressions "taking up the cross" or "carrying the cross" (a.t.) allude to the Roman custom of making the criminal carry the cross on which he was to suffer (John 19:17).

Deriv.: *stauróō* (4717), to crucify.
Syn.: *xúlon* (3586), tree, cross.

4717. **σταυρόω** *stauróō*; contracted *staurô*, fut. *staurōsō*, from *staurós* (4716), cross. To crucify, spoken of the punishment by crucifixion.

(I) To crucify, affix, or nail to a cross (Matt 20:19; 23:34; 26:2; 27:22f.; Mark 15:13f.; Acts 2:36; Sept.: Esth 7:10).

(II) Metaphorically, to crucify the flesh with the affections and lusts is to mortify them through the faith and love of Christ crucified (Gal 5:24; 6:14). When Paul says, "The world is crucified unto me, and I unto the world," he means that his regard for his crucified Savior was so great that the world had no more charm for him than the corpse of a crucified malefactor would have had, nor did he take any more delight in worldly things than a person expiring on the cross would do in the objects around him.

Deriv.: *anastauróō* (388), to recrucify; *sustauróō* (4957), to crucify with.

4718. **σταφυλή** *staphulḗ*; gen. *staphulḗs*, fem. noun. A cluster of grapes (Matt 7:16; Luke 6:44; Rev 14:18; Sept.: Gen 40:11; Isa 5:2).

Syn.: *bótrus* (1009), a bunch of grapes, a cluster.

4719. **στάχυς** *stáchus*; gen. *stáchuos*, masc. noun. An ear of corn or a head of grain (Matt 12:1; Mark 2:23; 4:28; Luke 6:1; Sept.: Gen 41:6, 7; Ruth 2:2).

Syn.: *sítos* (4621), wheat, corn; *kókkos* (2848), a grain.

4720. **Στάχυς** *Stáchus*; gen. *Stáchuos*, masc. proper noun. Stachys, the name of a Christian mentioned in Rom 16:9.

4721. **στέγη** *stégē*; gen. *stéges*, fem. noun from *stégō* (4722), to cover or put a roof over. A covering, roof (Matt 8:8; Mark 2:4; Luke 7:6).

Deriv.: *trístegon* (5152), three-roofed, three-storied.

4722. **στέγω** *stégō*; fut. *stéxō*. To cover. In the NT, to cover over in silence.

(I) Generally meaning to conceal, with the acc. (1 Cor 13:7, love hides the faults of others or covers them up).

(II) To hold out, forbear, bear with, endure (1 Thess 3:1, 5); with the acc. (1 Cor 9:12; 13:7).

Deriv.: *stégē* (4721), a covering, roof.
Syn.: *anéchomai* (430), to forbear; *makrothuméō* (3114), to be long-suffering, usually toward people; *hupoménō* (5278), to suffer, endure, be patient, usually toward circumstances; *kalúptō* (2572), to cover up; *katakalúptō* (2619), to cover, hide; *epikalúptō* (1943), to conceal, cover; *krúptō* (2928), to hide.

4723. **στεῖρος** *steíros*; fem. *steíra*, neut. *steíron*, adj. from *stereós* (4731), firm, solid. Deprived of bearing children, sterile, barren, spoken only of females (Luke 1:7, 36; 23:29; Gal 4:27; Sept.: Gen 11:30; Judg 13:2, 3).

Syn.: *áteknos* (815), without children.

4724. **στέλλω** *stéllō*; fut. *stelō*. To set, place, appoint to a position (such as soldiers in battle array). As such, it does not occur in the NT, but it does occur in many deriv. with a prefix prep., especially *apostéllō* (649), send from, and *apóstolos*

(652), an apostle, emissary. In its pass. form, *stéllomai*, with the mid. voice meaning, with an acc. and the prep. *apó* (575) following, it means to avoid or withdraw oneself from, shrink back (2 Cor 8:20; 2 Thess 3:6; Sept.: Mal 2:5).

Deriv.: *apostéllō* (649), to commission, send; *diastéllō* (1291), to differentiate, set oneself apart, order; *epistéllō* (1989), to enjoin or communicate by letter; *katastéllō* (2687), repress, curb; *stolé* (4749), a robe, clothing of distinction; *sustéllō* (4958), to draw together, to contract, wind up, shorten; *hupostéllō* (5288), to hold out of sight, to lower, draw back.

Syn.: *anachōréō* (402), to withdraw; *apochōréō* (672), to depart, withdraw; *apochōrízō* (673), to separate.

4725. στέμμα *stémma*; gen. *stémmatos*, neut. noun from *stéphō* (n.f.), to crown or surround with a garland. A garland, wreath (Acts 14:13, the oxen being victims adorned with garlands, as was customary in heathen sacrifices).

Syn.: *stéphanos* (4735), crown; *diádēma* (1238), diadem, a symbol of a certain degree of dignity.

4726. στεναγμός *stenagmós*; gen. *stenagmoú*, masc. noun from *stenázō* (4727), to groan. A groaning, sighing, as of the oppressed (Acts 7:34 quoted from Ex 2:24; see Ex 6:5; Judg 2:18); referring to prayers to God expressed inarticulately (Rom 8:26; Sept.: Ps 38:10).

Ant.: *agallíasis* (20), exultation.

4727. στενάζω *stenázō*; fut. *stenáxō*, from *stenós* (4728), narrow, contracted (as when one is squeezed or pressed by circumstances). To groan, sigh, used intrans. of persons in distress, affliction (Rom 8:23; 2 Cor 5:2, 4; Heb 13:17); grumble from impatience, ill-humor (James 5:9); of those who offer silent prayer (Mark 7:34 [see Isa 24:7; Lam 1:21]).

Deriv.: *anastenázō* (389), to sigh or groan deeply; *stenagmós* (4726), groaning; *sustenázō* (4959), to groan together.

Syn.: *embrimáomai* (1690), to groan.

Ant.: *humnéō* (5214), to praise, sing hymns of praise; *agalliáomai* (21), to exult; *chaírō* (5463), to rejoice; *euphraínomai* (2165), to be glad.

4728. στενός *stenós*; fem. *stené*, neut. *stenón*, adj. Straight, narrow, with reference to the gate leading to life (Matt 7:13, 14; Luke 13:24; Sept. Isa 49:20).

Deriv.: *stenázō* (4727), to sigh; *stenochōréō* (4729), to crowd into a narrow space; *stenochōría* (4730), distress.

Ant.: *eurúchōros* (2149), broad, spacious, wide; *platús* (4116), broad, wide.

4729. στενοχωρέω *stenochōréō*; contracted *stenochōrṓ*, fut. *stenochōrḗsō*, from *stenós* (4728), narrow, and *chóra* (5561), space, territory. To crowd into a narrow space, straiten as to room (Sept.: Josh 17:15). In the NT, in the mid. / pass., figuratively, to be constrained, reserved, be unable to express oneself (2 Cor 4:8; 6:12).

Syn.: *sunéchō* (4912), to throng, press; *basanízō* (928), to vex; *thlíbō* (2346), to afflict; *apothlíbō* (598), to crowd from every side, press.

4730. στενοχωρία *stenochōría*; gen. *stenochōrías*, fem. noun, from *stenós* (4728), narrow, and *chóra* (5561), territory, a space. Symbolically, great distress, straits (Rom 2:9; 8:35; 2 Cor 6:4; 12:10). *Stenochōría* is different from *thlípsis* (2347), tribulation. In three of the four occurrences in the NT these two words are used together (Rom 2:9; 8:35; 2 Cor 6:4). *Thlípsis* refers to troubles pressing upon someone from without, such as persecution, affliction, or tribulation. *Stenochōría* has in view the distress which arises from within (usually caused by *thlípsis*), such as anguish or discomfort.

Syn.: *sunoché* (4928), a restraint, distress, anguish; *kakopátheia* (2552), hardship; *talaipōría* (5004), misery; *páthēma* (3804), misfortune, affliction; *báros* (922), burden.

Ant.: *chará* (5479), joy; *agallíasis* and *euphrosúnē* (2167), gladness; *ánesis*

(425), relief, liberty, rest; *hēdonḗ* (2237), pleasure.

4731. στερεός *stereós*; fem. *stereá*, neut. *stereón*, adj. Stable, firm, solid (as opposed to a liquid), e.g., *stereá trophḗ* (*trophḗ* [5160], food), solid food, in contrast to *gála* (1051), milk (Heb 5:12, 14). Figuratively meaning firm, strong, immovable (2 Tim 2:19; 1 Pet 5:9).
Deriv.: *steíros* (4723), sterile, barren; *stereóō* (4732), to establish.
Syn.: *bébaios* (949), firm, steadfast, secure; *hedraíos* (1476), sedentary, settled, morally stable; *ametakínetos* (277), immovable; *ametáthetos* (276), unchangeable, immovable.

4732. στερεόω *stereóō*; contracted *stereó*, fut. *stereōsō*, from *stereós* (4731), solid, stable. To make stable, firm, strong, strengthen, trans. (Acts 3:7, 16; Sept.: Ps 33:6; Isa 44:24). Figuratively, to confirm or establish in faith (Acts 16:5; Sept.: 1 Sam 2:1).
Deriv.: *aposteréō* (650), to deprive, wrong; *steréōma* (4733), the firmament, steadfastness.
Syn.: *stērízo* (4741), to fix, make fast, strengthen; *hístēmi* (2476), to cause to stand; *bebaióō* (950), to establish; *dunamóō* (1412), to strengthen; *endunamóō* (1743), to make strong; *ischúō* (2480), to be strong; *enischúō* (2001), to strengthen; *krataióō* (2901) and *sthenóō* (4599), to make strong; *epistērízo* (1991), to confirm, reestablish; *asphalízo* (805), to make secure or firm.
Ant.: *dialúō* (1262), to dissolve; *astatéō* (790), to be unsettled, transient, homeless; *kinéō* (2795), to stir, move.

4733. στερέωμα *steréōma*; gen. *steréōmatos*, neut. noun from *stereóō* (4732), to strengthen, confirm. Anything firm, solid, such as the firmament (Sept.: Gen 1:6; Ezek 1:22). In the NT, stability, firmness, steadfastness (Col 2:5).
Syn.: *stērigmós* (4740), stability, support, steadfastness; *hedraíōma* (1477), a support, basis; *ouranós* (3772), sky;

aspháleia (803), safety; *hupóstasis* (5287), essence, a substratum, firmness, confidence.

4734. Στεφανᾶς *Stephanás*; gen. *Stephaná*, masc. proper noun. Stephanas, meaning crown. A Christian at Corinth baptized by Paul (1 Cor 1:16; 16:15, 17).

4735. στέφανος *stéphanos*; gen. *stephánou*, masc. noun. Crown. In Class. Gr., not used of the kingly crown but of the crown of victory in games, of civic worth, military valor, nuptial joy, festival gladness. Woven of oak, ivy, myrtle, olive leaves or flowers. Used as a wreath or garland.
(I) As the emblem of royal dignity (Rev 6:2; 12:1; 14:14). Ascribed to saints in heaven, elsewhere called kings (Rev 4:4, 10). Of the crown of thorns set upon Christ in derision as King of the Jews (Matt 27:29; Mark 15:17; John 19:2, 5).
(II) As the prize conferred on victors in public games and elsewhere, a wreath (1 Cor 9:25). Figuratively as a symbol of the reward of eternal life (2 Tim 4:8; James 1:12; 1 Pet 5:4; Rev 2:10; 3:11).
(III) Figuratively, an ornament, honor, glory, that in which one may glory (Phil 4:1; 1 Thess 2:19; Sept.: Prov 12:4; 16:31; 17:6).
(IV) The popular doctrine that the five crowns mentioned in the NT (1 Cor 9:25, "incorruptible crown"; 1 Thess 2:19, "crown of joy"; 2 Tim 4:8, "crown of righteousness"; James 1:12, "crown of life"; 1 Pet 5:4, "crown of glory") refer to five separate rewards which believers may earn is a gross misinterpretation of Scripture and fraught with theological problems. First of all, the figure of the crown in 1 Thess 2:19 is quite different than that in view in the other passages. Here Paul has in mind the custom of cities preparing wreaths of various material (olive, ivy, oak, beaten gold) in anticipation of the arrival of high ranking dignitaries. These wreaths were either worn on the body and clothing or strewn about the streets. They were emblems of

joy and expressions of devotion given by the people to the visiting official. As such, the Thessalonian converts are analogous to these wreaths and represent not what Christ will give to Paul but what Paul will offer to Christ in joyous tribute to Him at His return. Secondly, the crowns of life and righteousness are promised respectively to those who love Christ and His appearing. Such persons are not a special class of believers, but represent all true Christians. The expression "those who love him" is just another and descriptive name for believers commonly used in Scripture (Rom 8:28; 1 Cor 2:9; 1 Pet 1:7–8; Sept.: Ex 20:6; Ps 97:10; 145:20). The expression "those who love His appearing" serves to distinguish the saved from the unsaved (Heb 9:28, "He shall appear a second time for salvation, apart from sin, for those who eagerly await Him" [a.t.]). Thirdly, the various designations of the crown as consisting of righteousness, life, and glory are simply intended to highlight different facets of the same thing. To make these separate items introduces an unnecessary complexity to the matter and creates confusion. This is not to deny the biblical teaching of rewards but only to say that these passages do not touch upon that issue.

Deriv.: *stephanóō* (4737), to crown.

Syn.: *diádēma* (1238), diadem, a white linen encircling the brow to indicate the assumption of royal dignity; *misthós* (3408), reward, wages; *timé* (5092), honor; *antapódosis* (469), reward.

4736. Στέφανος *Stéphanos*; gen. *Stephánou*, masc. proper noun. Stephen, meaning a crown. The first martyr of the Christian church; one of the seven men of honest report who were elected, at the suggestion of the Apostles, to relieve them of the duty of serving at the tables (Acts 6:5). He is described as a man full of faith and of the Holy Ghost (Acts 6:8–10). In Acts 7 we find Stephen giving a courageous message for which he was martyred. See Acts 7:59; 8:2; 11:19; 22:20. His death was soon followed by the conversion of his persecutor, Saul of Tarsus, who became the Apostle Paul.

4737. στεφανόω *stephanóō*; contracted *stephanō̂*, fut. *stephanṓsō*, from *stéphanos* (4735), crown. Trans., to crown as a victor in the public games (2 Tim 2:5). Figuratively it means to adorn, decorate (Heb 2:7, 9 in allusion to Ps 8:6).

4738. στῆθος *stē̂thos*; gen. *stḗthous*, neut. noun from *hístēmi* (2476), to stand. The breast; pl. *tá stḗthē* (Luke 18:13; 23:48; John 13:25; 21:20; Rev 15:6; Sept.: Dan 2:32).

Syn.: *mastós* (3149), as used in the pl., meaning a woman's breasts; *thṓrax* (2382), chest, breastplate.

4739. στήκω *stḗkō*; a late form found only in the pres., corrupted from *éstēka*, the perf. of the verb *hístēmi* (2476), to stand. To stand, intrans. (Mark 11:25). Elsewhere only figuratively meaning to stand firm in faith and duty, to be constant, to persevere. With the dat. (Rom 14:4, "to his own master he standeth or falleth," meaning it is for his own master, not someone else, to judge whether or not he is faithful). Followed by dat. of thing (Gal 5:1). With *en* (1722), in, with the dat. (1 Cor 16:13; Phil 1:27; 4:1, meaning steadfast in the faith and profession of Christ; 1 Thess 3:8). Used in an absolute sense (2 Thess 2:15).

Syn.: *ménō* (3306), to abide, remain; *hupoménō* (5278), to stand up under, endure; *paraménō* (3887), to persevere, abide.

Ant.: *píptō* (4098), to fall; *katapíptō* (2667), to fall down; *ekpíptō* (1601), to drop away, fail; *parapíptō* (3895), to fall away.

4740. στηριγμός *stērigmós*; gen. *stērigmoú*, masc. noun from *stērízō* (4741), to establish, fix. A setting firmly, stability, for instance of the stars. In the NT, figuratively meaning steadfastness in mind and faith (2 Pet 3:17).

Syn.: *steréōma* (4733), steadfastness; *bebaíōsis* (951), stability, confirmation.

Ant.: *akatastasía* (181), instability, disorder.

4741. στηρίζω *stērízō*; fut. *steríxō*, from *hístemi* (2476), to stand. To set fast, to fix firmly, trans.:

(I) In the perf. pass., *estériktai* (Luke 16:26, meaning is set fast, established permanently, stands fixed; Sept. Gen 28:12).

(II) Trans. (Luke 9:51, "he steadfastly set his face to go").

(III) Of persons, to make steadfast in mind, confirm, strengthen (Luke 22:32; Rom 1:11; 16:25; 1 Thess 3:2, 13; 2 Thess 2:17; 3:3; James 5:8; 1 Pet 5:10 ([TR] in the aor. opt., but in later editions *stēríxei* [fut. indic. 3d person sing]); 2 Pet 1:12; Rev 3:2).

Deriv.: *astériktos* (793), unsettled, unstable; *epistērízō* (1991), to strengthen; *stērigmós* (4740), stability.

Syn.: *stereóō* (4732), to make firm; *bebaióō* (950), to confirm; *krataióō* (2901) and *dunamóō* (1412), to strengthen; *endunamóō* (1743), to make strong; *exischúō* (1840), to have full strength; *sthenóō* (4599), to make strong.

4742. στίγμα *stígma*; gen. *stígmatos*, neut. noun from *stízō* (n.f.), to make a puncture or a mark (e.g., with a hot iron), to brand. A mark, brand, as pricked into or burnt upon the body, such as the marks with which slaves and sometimes prisoners were branded. Figuratively (Gal 6:17 [cf. 2 Cor 4:10; 11:23ff.; Rev 14:9, *cháragma* {5480}, imprint, something engraven]).

Syn.: *éndeigma* (1730), manifest token; *cháragma* (5480), imprint, something engraven; *charaktḗr* (5481), impression, exact image.

4743. στιγμή *stigmḗ*; gen. *stigmḗs*, fem. noun from *stígma* (4742), to make a puncture or a mark (e.g., with a hot iron), to brand. A point of time, figuratively referring to the briefest moment. In the NT, used as a point of time, a moment, an instant (Luke 4:5; Sept. Isa 29:5).

Syn.: *átomos* (823), atom, something which cannot be divided, the briefest conceivable moment of time; *rhipḗ* (4493), instant, twinkling.

Ant.: *aiṓn* (165), age, eternity.

4744. στίλβω *stílbō*; fut. *stílpsō*. To shine, be bright, glitter, used intrans. (Mark 9:3; Sept.: Ezra 8:27; Nah 3:3).

Syn.: *phaínō* (5316), to lighten, shine; *lámpō* (2989), to beam, radiate brilliantly; *eklámpō* (1584), to be resplendent, glisten; *exastráptō* (1823), to be radiant.

Ant.: *skotízō* (4654), to obscure, darken; *skotóō* (4656), to be full of darkness.

4745. στοά *stoá*; gen. *stoás*, fem. noun from *hístēmi* (2476), to stand. A pillar, column, portico, porch, an open space surrounded and supported by columns, e.g., Solomon's porch (John 5:2; 10:23; Acts 3:11; 5:12).

Syn.: *pulṓn* (4440), a porch or vestibule of a house or palace; *proaúlion* (4259), the exterior court or vestibule between the door and the street, usually part of a rich person's house.

4746. στοιβάς *stoibás*; gen. *stoibádos*, fem. noun from *steíbō* (n.f.), to tread, trample upon. Found only in the NT, meaning a green bough, branch (Mark 11:8). In Matt 21:8 the word *kládos* (2798), branch, is used.

Syn.: *kléma* (2814), the shoot or branch of a vine, a sprout; *báïon* (902), the branch of a palm tree.

4747. στοιχεῖον *stoicheíon*; gen. *stoicheíou*, neut. noun, a diminutive *stoíchos* (n.f.), row. Always in the pl., *tá stoicheía*, the basic parts, rudiments, elements, or components of something. Among the ancient Greek philosophers, it designated the four basic and essential elements of which the universe consisted, namely, earth, water, air, and fire. In 2 Pet 3:10, 12 the word carries this meaning. Figuratively it refers to the elements or first principles of the Christian doctrine (Heb 5:12). Paul calls the ceremonial ordinances of the Mosaic Law worldly elements (Gal 4:3; Col 2:8, 20). In Gal 4:9 he calls them weak and poor elements when contrasted with the great realities to which they were designed to lead. These elements contain the rudiments of the knowledge of Christ. The Law, as a school-master, was to bring the Jews to this knowledge (Gal 3:24).

4748. στοιχέω *stoichéō*; contracted *stoichṓ*, fut. *stoichḗsō*, from *stoíchos* (n.f.), row, line, rank. To stand or go in order, advance in rows or ranks. In the NT used figuratively, meaning to walk orderly, with the dat. of rule, to live according to any rule or duty, to follow (Rom 4:12; Gal 5:25; 6:16; Phil 3:16); used in an absolute sense (Acts 21:24).

Deriv.: *stoicheíon* (4747), the elements or first principles of matter; *sustoichéō* (4960), to walk together in file as soldiers in rank.

Syn.: *patéō* (3962), to trample, tread; *peripatéō* (4043), to walk; *hodoiporéō* (3596), to go on a journey.

Ant.: *astochéō* (795), to miss the mark, swerve, deviate; *parabaínō* (3845), to transgress.

4749. στολή *stolḗ*; gen. *stolḗs*, fem. noun from *stéllō* (4724), to send. A stately robe reaching to the feet or a train sweeping the ground. More often worn by women (Mark 12:38; 16:5; Luke 15:22; 20:46; Rev 6:11; 7:9, 13, 14; Sept.: Ex 28:2f.; 1 Chr 15:27; 2 Chr 18:9).

Deriv.: *katastolḗ* (2689), long robe of dignity.

Syn.: *himátion* (2440), an outer cloak or cape; *himatismós* (2441), clothing, apparel; *chlamús* (5511), a military cloak worn over the *chitón* by emperors, kings, magistrates, military officers; *katastolḗ* (2689), long robe of dignity; *esthḗs* (2066) and *ésthēsis* (2067), clothing; *énduma* (1742), a garment of any kind; *ependútēs* (1903), an upper or outer garment which sometimes fishermen wore when at work;

phelónēs (5341), a mantle, traveling robe for protection against stormy weather, overcoat; *peribólaion* (4018), a wrap or cape, a garment thrown around one; *podḗrēs* (4158), an outer garment reaching to the feet; *sképasma* (4629), a covering, raiment; *phelónēs* (5341), a traveling cloak.

4750. στόμα *stóma*; gen. *stómatos*, neut. noun. Mouth, opening, edge.

(I) Of animals (Matt 17:27; 2 Tim 4:17; Heb 11:33 [cf. Judg 14:8]; James 3:3; Rev 9:17f.; 12:15; Sept.: Gen 8:11; Ps 22:21). Of persons, as the opening through which breathing or blowing occurs (2 Thess 2:8 [cf. Ps 33:6]; Rev 1:16; 2:16; 11:5; Sept.: 2 Kgs 4:34); as receiving food and drink (Matt 15:11, 17; John 19:29; Acts 11:8; Rev 10:9, 10); chiefly as the instrument of speech (Matt 12:34; Rom 3:14, 19; 10:8; Col 3:8; James 3:10; Sept.: Ex 4:15; Isa 1:20). Used metonymically for words, sayings, discourse (Matt 15:8 quoted from Isa 29:13; Matt 18:16; Luke 11:54; 19:22, "out of thine own mouth will I judge thee"; 21:15, "I will give you a mouth and wisdom" means wise utterance; 2 Cor 13:1, "in the mouth of two or three witnesses").

(II) In phrases borrowed mostly from the Hebr.:

(A) To open one's mouth; figuratively of the earth as rent in chasms (Rev 12:16).

(B) That which comes out of the mouth means words uttered, sayings, discourse (Matt 15:11, 18 [cf. Num 30:3; 32:24]); that which comes through the mouth of God means word, precept (Matt 4:4 in allusion to Deut 8:3).

(C) For God to speak through the mouth of someone or by His intervention, as God by a prophet or messenger (Luke 1:70; Acts 1:16; 3:18, 21; 4:25; 15:7; Sept.: 2 Chr 36:21, 22).

(D) To speak face to face (2 John 1:12; 3 John 1:14; Sept. Num 12:8 [cf. Jer 32:4]).

(III) Figuratively meaning edge or point, as of a weapon, the figure being taken from the mouth as armed with teeth and biting, as in beasts, the front or foremost part, also of the front of an army. In the NT, a sword, the point of a knife (Luke 21:24; Heb 11:34; Sept.: Gen 34:26; Judg 20:37, 48).

Deriv.: *apostomatízō* (653), to provoke to speak; *dístomos* (1366), double-tongued, two-edged; *epistomízō* (1993), to cover the mouth or to put to silence; *stómachos* (4751), stomach.

Syn.: *laliá* (2981), speech; *lógos* (3056), word, discourse, expression.

4751. στόμαχος *stómachos*; gen. *stomáchou*, masc. noun from *stóma* (4750), mouth, and *échō* (2192), to have. Originally it meant a mouth, opening, hence the throat. In NT and today, the stomach (1 Tim 5:23).

Syn.: *gastér* (1064), belly; *koilía* (2836), belly, womb, cavity.

4752. στρατεία *strateía*; gen. *strateías*, fem. noun from *strateúomai* (4754), to lead an army. Military service, warfare, a military expedition or campaign. Metaphorically of the apostolic office as connected with hardships, dangers, trials, a warfare (2 Cor 10:4; 1 Tim 1:18).

4753. στράτευμα *stráteuma*; gen. *strateúmatos*, neut. noun from *strateúomai* (4754), to perform military duty, to be a soldier. An army, soldiers, men of war, forces, troops, host, generally (Matt 22:7; Rev 9:16; 19:14, 19). A band or detachment of troops, such as the garrison in the fortress of Antonia in Jerusalem (Acts 23:10, 27) or Herod's bodyguards (Luke 23:11).

Syn.: *stratiá* (4756), an army; *stratópedon* (4760), an army.

4754. στρατεύομαι *strateúomai*; fut. *strateúsomai*, mid. deponent from *stratós* (n.f., see *stratēgós* [4755]), camp, army. To lead an army, wage war, be a soldier. In the NT, to serve in war, to war, be a soldier, warrior. Intrans.:

(I) To wage war (1 Cor 9:7; 1 Tim 2:4); part. *ho strateuómenos*, a soldier (Luke 3:14).

(II) Figuratively, to war, as spoken of:

(A) The apostolic office as connected with hardships, trials, dangers (2 Cor 10:3); with the acc. of a cognate noun (1 Tim 1:18).

(B) Desires and lusts which war against right principles and moral precepts (James 4:1; 1 Pet 2:11).

Deriv.: *antistrateúomai* (497), to war against; *strateía* (4752), military service; *stráteuma* (4753), an army, soldiers.

Syn.: *poleméō* (4170), to make war; *máchomai* (3164), to fight, strive; *diamáchomai* (1264), to fight fiercely; *pukteúō* (4438), to box, fight with fists; *agōnízomai* (75), to struggle, fight; *antagōnízomai* (464), to strive against.

Ant.: *eirēnopoiéō* (1517), to make peace.

4755. στρατηγός *stratēgós*; gen. *stratēgoú*, masc. noun from *stratós* (n.f., see below), an army, and *ágō* (71), to lead. The leader of an army, commander, general.

The ten Athenian commanders chosen annually (with whom the *polémarchos* [n.f.], leader of the war, joined) were called generals. Afterwards only one or two were sent abroad with the army as circumstances required, and the others had charge of military affairs at home. They were the same as *polémarchos*, war minister or the leader of a war. In other Greek cities, they were the chief magistrates or prefects. *Stratēgós* was also the name given to Roman officers as consuls and also the leaders of cities. In Roman colonies and municipal towns, the chief magistrates were usually two in number, occasionally four or six who sometimes were called praetors, the Gr. equivalent of which was *stratēgós*.

(I) The magistrates of Philippi, where there was a Roman colony at the time (Acts 16:20, 22, 35, 36, 38). It may also refer to the magistrates of the Jewish people under Ezra and Nehemiah.

(II) A captain or governor or prefect of the temple, spoken generally of the chief officers of the priests and Levites who kept guard in and around the temple, one of whom perhaps held the chief command (Luke 22:4, 52; Acts 4:1; 5:24, 26).

Deriv. of *stratós* (n.f.): *strateúomai* (4754), to wage war, be a soldier; *stratía* (4756), a host of heaven; *stratópedon* (4760), an encampment.

Syn.: *chilíarchos* (5506), commander of one thousand soldiers, the chief captain; *archēgós* (747), the leader; *árchōn* (758), ruler, chief.

4756. στρατιά *stratiá*; gen. *stratiás*, fem. noun from *stratós* (n.f., see *stratēgós* [4755]), an army. An army, host (Sept.: 2 Sam 3:23; 1 Kgs 11:15). A host of heaven, as the angelic host (Luke 2:13; Sept.: 1 Kgs 22:19 [cf. 2 Chr 18:18; Ps 103:21; 148:2]); the sun, moon, stars, the whole host of the firmament (Acts 7:42; Sept.: 2 Chr 33:3, 5; Jer 19:13; Zeph 1:5).

Deriv.: *stratópedon* (4760), an army.

Syn.: *stráteuma* (4753), an army; *stratópedon* (4760), an army.

4757. στρατιώτης *stratiōtēs*; gen. *stratiōtou*, masc. noun from *stratiá* (4756), an army. A soldier, warrior, spoken of common soldiers (Matt 8:9; Mark 15:16; Luke 7:8; John 19:23; Acts 12:4). Figuratively of a Christian minister (2 Tim 2:3).

Deriv.: *sustratiōtēs* (4961), fellow soldier.

Syn.: *spekoulátōr* (4688), soldier or guardsman.

4758. στρατολογέω *stratologéō*; contracted *stratologṓ*, fut. *stratologḗsō*, from *stratós* (n.f.), warfare, and *légō* (3004), in this instance meaning to collect, to choose. To collect or enlist an army, to draft. The part. *ho stratologḗsas*, one who has recruited, means a commander or general (2 Tim 2:4). Figuratively, to enlist, sign up.

4759. στρατοπεδάρχης *stratopedárchēs*; gen. *stratopedárchou*, masc. noun from *stratópedon* (4760), an encampment of troops, and *árchō* (757), to rule over. The magistrate of a camp, an officer into whose charge Paul was committed at Rome (Acts 28:16). Some here understand that this refers to the commander of the emperor's bodyguards as having the general charge of all prisoners sent to Rome (cf. Phil 1:13). This is perhaps too broad an inference from the single-known instance where the elder Herod Agrippa was imprisoned by such an officer at the express command of the Emperor Tiberius.

4760. στρατόπεδον *stratópedon*; gen. *stratopédou*, neut. noun from *stratós* (n.f., see *stratēgós* [4755]), an army and *pédon* (n.f.), a ground, field. A camping ground of an army, an encampment; an army encamped, a host (Luke 21:20; Sept.: Jer 34:1).

Deriv.: *stratopedárchēs* (4759), the magistrate of a camp.

Syn.: *stratiá* (4756), an army; *stráteuma* (4753), an army.

4761. στρεβλόω *streblóō*; contracted *streblṓ*, fut. *streblṓsō*, from *stréblos* (n.f.), distorted, crooked, which is from *strépho* (4762), to twist, turn, distort. To wrench. A *stréblē* was a winch, an instrument of torture. In the NT, figuratively, to wrest, pervert. Trans. (2 Pet 3:16). In the pass., to show oneself perverse (2 Sam 22:27).

Syn.: *diastréphō* (1294), to pervert; *metastréphō* (3344), to corrupt, turn.

Ant.: *euthúnō* (2116), to straighten; *orthotoméō* (3718), to handle correctly; *epanórthōsis* (1882), a straightening up, correction.

4762. στρέφω *stréphō*; fut. *strépsō*. To turn, turn about.

(I) Trans., 2d aor. pass. *estráphē*, as mid., to turn oneself, turn about (John 20:14).

(II) Act. with acc. and dat. of person, toward whom (Matt 5:39; Sept.: Ps 114:3); mid., with *eis* (1519), to, and the acc. (Acts 13:46); with the acc. of place (Acts 7:39). Mid. part. *straph
eís* (sing.) or *straphéntes* (pl.), used in an absolute sense (Matt 7:6; 16:23; Luke 9:55; 14:25; 22:61; John 1:38; 20:16); with the dat. (Luke 7:9); with *prós* (4314), toward, and the acc. (Luke 7:44; 10:23; 23:28).

(III) Figuratively, to turn into something, meaning to convert or change, used trans. Act. or Pass., with *eis* (Rev 11:6, the waters into blood; Sept.: Ex 7:15; Ps 114:8; Jer 31:13); mid., of persons, to turn in mind, be converted or changed, become another kind of person (Matt 18:3; Sept.: 1 Sam 10:6). In Acts 7:42, intrans., to turn oneself, to change one's mind and conduct.

Deriv.: *anastréphō* (390), to overturn; *apostréphō* (654), to turn away or back; *diastréphō* (1294), to turn, twist throughout, pervert; *ekstréphō* (1612), to subvert, pervert; *epistréphō* (1994), to turn back again, turn about; *katastréphō* (2690), to ruin; *metastréphō* (3344), to pervert, turn; *sustréphō* (4962), to revolve or rotate together; *hupostréphō* (5290), to turn back, return.

Syn.: *metabállō* (3328), to turn about.

4763. στρηνιάω *strēniáō*; contracted *strēniō*, fut. *strēniásō*, from *strēnos* (4764), profligate luxury, voluptuousness (Rev 18:3). To live luxuriously, act with wantonness from abundance (Rev 18:7, 9).

Deriv.: *katastrēniáō* (2691), to become lascivious against.

Syn.: *spataláō* (4684), to live in pleasure, be wanton; *trupháō* (5171), to live in pleasure and luxury.

4764. στρῆνος *strēnos*; gen. *strēnous*, neut. noun from *strēnés* (n.f.), rough, harsh, grating. Profligate luxury, such as men abandon themselves to when they have shaken off the reins of religion and reason (Rev 18:3).

Deriv.: *strēniáō* (4763), to live luxuriously.

Syn.: *asélgeia* (766), lasciviousness, licentiousness, inability to have enough pleasure; *truphē* (5172), indulgence.

4765. στρουθίον *strouthíon*; gen. *strouthíou*, neut. noun, the diminutive of *strouthós* (n.f.), a sparrow. Any small bird, especially a sparrow (Matt 10:29, 31; Luke 12:6, 7; Sept.: Ps 11:1; Lam 3:52).

Syn.: *peteinón* (4071), bird.

4766. στρώννυμι *strónnumi* and **στρωννύω *strōnnúō*;** fut. *strōsō*. To strew, spread, trans. (Matt 21:8; Mark 11:8). For this custom, see Sept.: 2 Kgs 9:13; Esth 4:3; Isa 14:11. Specifically of a bed, couch (Acts 9:34 [cf. 9:33]; Sept.: Job 17:13; Ezek 28:7). Pass., of a supper chamber with couches around the table, meaning furnished, prepared (Mark 14:15; Luke 22:12; Sept.: Ezek 23:41).

Deriv.: *katastrónnumi* (2693), to overthrow; *Lithóstrōtos* (3038), the Pavement; *hupostrōnnúō* / *hupostrónnumi* (5291), to spread underneath, as a carpet.

4767. στυγητός *stugētós*; fem. *stugētē*, neut. *stugētón*, adj. from *stugéō* (n.f., see *apostugéō* [655]), to shudder with horror, to hate. Hateful, detestable (Titus 3:3).

Syn.: *bdeluktós* (947), abominable, detestable.

4768. στυγνάζω *stugnázō*; fut. *stugnásō*, from *stugnós* (n.f.), hateful, gloomy. To be or become somber, gloomy. Intrans., of the countenance (Mark 10:22). Figuratively of the sky, to be overcast, intrans. (Matt 16:3).

4769. στύλος *stúlos*; gen. *stúlou*, masc. noun. A pillar or column which stands by itself or supports a building. Something in shape resembling a pillar, as a column of fire (Rev 10:1; Sept.: Ex 13:21, 22; 14:24). Figuratively, any firm support, persons of authority and influence in the church (Gal 2:9; Rev 3:12); of the church as that which upholds the truth (1 Tim 3:15).

4770. Στωϊκός Stōïkós; fem. *Stoïkē̃*, neut. *Stoïkón*, adj. Stoic, stoical; as a subst. a Stoic, a person who belonged to a sect of heathen philosophers which was founded by Zeno, a Cypriot philosopher (336–264 B.C.). He taught that men should be free from passion, and submit without complaint to unavoidable situations. The name came from the *stoá* (4745), a porch on which Zeno taught in Athens (300 B.C.).

The Stoics generally taught that it is virtue alone that renders men happy, that the ills of life are but fancied evils, and that a wise man will not to be moved with either joy or grief. In their practice they displayed much patience and were very strict in their regard to moral virtue. They held justice in high regard, sometimes taking it upon themselves to enact it. They were very insensitive to others, expecting others to patiently endure their faults. The best known Stoics are Seneca, Epictetus, and the Roman emperor Marcus Aurelius. Some Stoics met Paul in Athens (Acts 17:18). The Stoics were pantheistic and believed that sometime after death the soul was reabsorbed into the cosmic whole.

4771. σύ sú; gen. sing. *soú* (4675), acc. sing. *sé* (4571), dat. sing. *soí* (4671), nom. pl. *humeís* (5210), you, 2d person personal pron. You, thou. The oblique cases of the sing. are all enclitic except after a prep.

(I) Nom. sing. *sú*, pl. *humeís* (5210), usually omitted except where a certain emphasis is required. In the NT, inserted:

(A) With emphasis, before a voc. (Matt 2:6; Matt 16:16; Mark 1:11; Luke 1:76; 3:22; 2 Tim 2:1); in distribution (James 2:3); with an adjunct between it and the verb (John 4:9); in interrogations (Matt 27:11; Mark 8:29; Luke 24:18; John 8:53); in a subordinate clause introduced by *hóti* (3754) (John 2:20; 8:48); in answers (Matt 26:25; Mark 15:2); in

antitheses (Matt 3:14; Luke 9:60; 11:48; 22:26; John 3:2; 1 Cor 3:23); with *kaí* (2532), and, that is, *kaí sú*, *kaí humeís* (Matt 7:12; Luke 10:37; 22:58).

(B) Without special emphasis, *sú* (Luke 4:7; John 4:10; 21:15–17); *humeís* (Matt 28:5).

(II) Gen. sing. *soú* and the pl. *humōn* (5216) are often used instead of the corresponding possessive pron. *sós* (4674) and *huméteros* (5212) (Matt 4:6; Mark 1:2; Rom 6:12); generally, *soú* (Matt 2:6; 3:14; 5:29); *humōn* (Matt 5:12; Luke 11:5). For Luke 2:35 (*kaí soú dé autḗs*), see in *seautoú* (4572), of thyself.

(III) Dat. sing. *soí* (4671), pl. *humín* (5213), generally (Matt 4:9; 7:7; 21:5; Mark 5:9; Luke 1:19; 10:13; 2 Cor 5:12, 13; 12:20; Rev 2:16). For the phrase *tí emoí kaí soí*, see *egṓ* (1473), I.

Deriv.: *sós* (4674), yours.

4772. συγγένεια suggéneia; gen. *suggeneías* fem. noun from *suggenḗs* (4773), relative, kin. Kin, kindred, relatives, relationship (Luke 1:61; Acts 7:3, 14; Sept.: Ex 12:21; Josh 6:23).

Ant.: *xénos* (3581), stranger; *allótrios* (245), alien.

4773. συγγενής suggenḗs; gen. *suggenoús*, masc.-fem., neut. *suggenés*, adj. from *sún* (4862), with, denoting fellowship, and *génos* (1085), offspring, stock, nation, family. A kinsman or kinswoman, a relative, one of the same family (Mark 6:4; Luke 1:36, 58; 2:44; 14:12; 21:16; John 18:26; Acts 10:24; Sept.: Lev 18:14; 25:45). In a wider sense one of the same nation, a fellow-countryman, spoken by Paul of the Jews as being all descended from a common ancestor (Rom 9:3; 16:7, 11, 21).

Deriv.: *suggéneia* (4772), relationship.

Syn.: *patriárchēs* (3966), patriarch, progenitor; *patrikós* (3967), paternal; *patrṓos* (3971), that which is hereditary from fathers; *patḗr* (3962), father; *mḗtēr* (3384), mother; *goneús* (1118), parent; *pentherós* (3995), father-in-law;

pentherá (3994), mother-in-law; *génnēma* (1081), offspring; *adelphós* (80), brother; *adelphḗ* (79), sister; *anepsiós* (431), cousin; *thugátēr* (2364), daughter; *thugátrion* (2365), little daughter; *téknon* (5043), child; *tekníon* (5040), little child; *huiós* (5207), son; *mámmē* (3125), grandmother.

Ant.: *xénos* (3581), stranger.

4774. συγγνώμη *suggnṓmē*; gen. *suggnṓmēs*, fem. noun from *suggnṓnai* (n.f.), to think alike, agree with. Concession, permission, leave (1 Cor 7:6).

4775. συγκάθημαι *sugkáthēmai*; fut. *sugkathḗsomai*, from *sún* (4862), with, together with, and *káthēmai* (2521), to sit down. To sit down with, to sit with. With *metá* (3326), with (Mark 14:54). With the dat., depending on *sún* (4862), with, in composition (Acts 26:30; Sept.: Ex 23:32).

Syn.: *sugkathízō* (4776), to make to sit together; *sunanákeimai* (4873), to recline at a table with or together.

4776. συγκαθίζω *sugkathízō*; fut. *sugkathísō*, from *sún* (4862), with, and *kathízō* (2523), to set or sit down. Trans., to cause to sit down with, to seat with, intrans. to sit down with, to sit with. Trans. followed by *en* (1722), in, with the dat. of place (Eph 2:6, "in the heavenlies" [a.t.]). Intrans. of several, to sit down together (Luke 22:55; Sept.: Ex 18:13; Jer 16:8).

Syn.: *sugkáthēmai* (4775), to sit with; *sunanákeimai* (4873), to recline at a table with or together.

4777. συγκακοπαθέω *sugkakopathéō*; contracted *sugkakopathṓ*, fut. *sugkakopathḗsō*, from *sún* (4862), together, or with, and *kakopathéō* (2553), to suffer evil or affliction. To suffer hardship, evil or affliction along with someone. Only in 2 Tim 1:8.

Syn.: *sumpáschō* (4841), to suffer with; *sunōdínō* (4944), to travail in pain together; *sustenázō* (4959), to groan together; *sullupéomai* (4818), to sorrow with; *sugkakouchéō* (4778), to suffer affliction with.

Ant.: *sugchaírō* (4796), to rejoice with.

4778. συγκακουχέω *sugkakouchéō*; contracted *sugkakouchṓ*, fut. *sugkakouchḗsō*, from *sún* (4862), together, or with, and *kakouchéō* (2558), to maltreat. Only in the pass., to be mistreated or tormented with others, to suffer affliction with someone, with the dat. of person (Heb 11:25).

Syn.: *sumpáschō* (4841), to suffer with; *sugkakopathéō* (4777), to be afflicted with; *sunōdínō* (4944), to travail in pain together; *sustenázō* (4959), to groan together; *sullupéomai* (4818), to sorrow with.

Ant.: *sugchaírō* (4796), to rejoice with.

4779. συγκαλέω *sugkaléō*; contracted *sugkalṓ*, fut. *sugkalésō*, from *sún* (4862), together, and *kaléō* (2564), to call. To call together (Mark 15:16; Luke 9:1; 15:6, 9; 23:13; Acts 5:21; 10:24; 28:17; Sept.: Ex 7:11; Josh 9:22; Zech 3:10); mid. / pass. (Luke 15:9; 23:13; Acts 10:24; 28:17).

Ant.: *exapostéllō* (1821), to dismiss, send away.

4780. συγκαλύπτω *sugkalúptō*; fut. *sugkalúpsō*, from *sún* (4862), an intens., and *kalúptō* (2572), to cover. To cover altogether, to conceal or hide, trans. (Luke 12:2; Sept.: Judg 4:18, 19; 1 Kgs 20:4).

Syn.: *epikalúptō* (1943), to cover up or over; *krúptō* (2928), to hide or keep secret; *apokrúptō* (613), to hide from.

Ant.: *apokalúptō* (601), to reveal; *anakalúptō* (343), to discover.

4781. συγκάμπτω *sugkámptō*; fut. *sugkámpsō*, from *sún* (4862), together, and *kámptō* (2578), to bend, bow. To bend together, to bow down low (Rom 11:10, i.e., figuratively to oppress, afflict, quoted from Sept.: Ps 69:24; see 2 Kgs 4:35).

Ant.: *anorthóō* (461), to make straight, to straighten; *orthós* (3717), erect, upright.

4782. συγκαταβαίνω *sugkatabaínō*; fut. *sugkatabésomai*, from *sún* (4862), together, or with, and *katabaínō* (2597), to go down. To go down with someone from a higher to a lower place, as from Jerusalem to Caesarea. Intrans. (Acts 25:5; Sept.: Ps 49:18).
Syn.: *katabaínō* (2597), to descend, to go or step down; *katéchomai* (2718), to descend, to come or go down.
Ant.: *anabaínō* (305), to ascend, to go or come up.

4783. συγκατάθεσις *sugkatáthesis*; gen. *sugkatathéseōs*, fem. noun from *sugkatatíthēmi* (4784), to consent. Assent, accord, agreement (2 Cor 6:16).
Syn.: *homología* (3671), acknowledgement, agreement; *sumphōnía* (4858), agreement.
Ant.: *stásis* (4714), dissension, controversy; *éris* (2054), contention, strife; *diákrisis* (1253), disputation; *antíthesis* (477), opposition.

4784. συγκατατίθεμαι *sugkatatíthemai*; fut. mid. *sugkatatithésomai*, mid. form of *sugkatatíthēmi*, which is from *sún* (4862), together with, and *katatíthēmi* (2698), to put down. To place or lay down with another, to deposit with. In the NT, only with the acc. *pséphon* (5586), vote, implied, meaning to deposit one's vote with others in the urn, to give one's vote with others. Figuratively, to assent to, agree with, to consent, with the dat. (Luke 23:51).
Deriv.: *sugkatáthesis* (4783), agreement.
Syn.: *sumphōnéō* (4856), to be in agreement; *suntíthemi* (4934), to consent; *homologéō* (3670), to acknowledge, agree.
Ant.: *anthístēmi* (436), to oppose; *antitássomai* (498), to resist; *antipíptō* (496), to range oneself against, oppose;

antilégō (483), to dispute, contradict; *antíkeimai* (480), to be opposed to.

4785. συγκαταψηφίζω *sugkatapsēphízō*; fut. *sugkatapsēphísō*, from *sún* (4862), together, or with, *katá* (2596), according to, and *psēphízō* (5585), to count or compute. To be reckoned or numbered with, to be received into the number of. In the pass (Acts 1:26).
Syn.: *arithméō* (705), to number; *katarithméō* (2674), to number with or count among; *logízomai* (3049), to reckon; *katalégō* (2639), to enroll or take into the number.
Ant.: *aporríptō* (641), to reject; *apodokimázō* (593), to disapprove, reject; *athetéō* (114), to cast off, reject.

4786. συγκεράννυμι *sugkeránnumi*, fut. *sugkerásō*, from *sún* (4862), together, or with, and *keránnumi* (2767), to mix. To mix together, intermingle with. In the NT figuratively to join together, temper together so that one part counterbalances another. With the acc. (1 Cor 12:24). Pass., with the dat. (Heb 4:2).

4787. συγκινέω *sugkinéō*; contracted *sugkinō*, fut. *sugkinésō*. from *sún* (4862), an intens., and *kinéō* (2795), to stir up or move. Trans., to stir or rouse; act. trans., to move oneself and others. To incite, rouse to similar exertion or to sympathy. Specifically of a popular commotion (Acts 6:12).
Syn.: *turbázō* (5182), to trouble; *tarássō* (5015), to disturb; *saleúō* (4531), to incite; *parotrúnō* (3951), to stir up.
Ant.: *hēsucházō* (2270), to be quiet; *eirēnopoiéō* (1517), to make peace; *katastéllō* (2687), to quell.

4788. συγκλείω *sugkleíō*; fut. *sugkleísō*, from *sún* (4862), together, and *kleíō* (2808), to shut up, enclose. To shut up or enclose together, trans. (Luke 5:6; Sept.: Ex 14:3). Figuratively to include together, to deliver over in the same manner, with *eis* (1519), unto (Rom 11:32), where Paul speaks of

Israel who as a nation manifested unbelief in Christ as the Messiah. This speaks of God's omniscience. He knew the reaction of Israel, yet He came unto His people first, but His people did not receive Him (John 1:11). This did not constitute a surprise to the Lord.

Rom 11:32 ought to be viewed with 11:26 where the declaration is made that all Israel shall be saved. As in 11:32 where we have a prophecy which was fulfilled in view of Israel's attitude toward the Lord Jesus in 11:26, we have a yet unfulfilled prediction of Israel's attitude when the Lord shall come again and they shall say, "Blessed is he that cometh in the name of the Lord" (a.t. [Matt 23:39]). The meaning here is that to all those who were imprisoned in unbelief, there has been offered the promise of Christ's mercy and salvation. There is no intimation here of universal salvation.

The same offer of salvation that is made to all Israel is also made to all nations as we see in Matt 23:12–25. With *hupó* (5259), under in Gal 3:22, "The Scripture hath included all under sin" means that sin affected everything: Jews, Gentiles, and nature itself (Rom 8:19–22). Rom 8:23 indicates that God's first provision against this total subjugation under sin was the Law, but it was not a permanent arrangement. It was only until such time as faith in the Lord Jesus Christ would be revealed (cf. Josh 20:5; Ps 78:50; Sept.: Ps 31:9).

4789. συγκληρονόμος *sugklēronómos*; gen. *sugklēronómou*, masc. noun from *sún* (4862), together, and *klēronómos* (2818), an heir, a sharer by lot. One who participates in the same lot, a joint heir (Rom 8:17). In Heb 11:9, it speaks of Isaac and Jacob in their relation to Abraham; in 1 Pet 3:7, of women as being joint heirs with their husbands of the grace of life; in Eph 3:6, of the Gentiles being joint heirs with Israel (see Eph 1:11).

Syn.: *summétochos* (4830), a co-participant; *sugkoinōnós* (4791), a partaker with.

4790. συγκοινωνέω *sugkoinōnéō*; contracted *sugkoinōnṓ*, fut. *sugkoinōnḗsō*, from *sún* (4862), with, and *koinōnéō* (2841), to partake. To participate in something with someone. In the NT, only with a dat. of the thing, as a strengthened form of *koinōnéō*, to have in common (Eph 5:11; Phil 4:14 [cf. 4:15]; Rev 18:4). To be a partaker or sharer together with others, a fellow or joint partaker (Rom 11:17; 1 Cor 9:23; Phil 1:7; Rev 1:9).

Syn.: *summerízomai* (4829), to share jointly.

4791. συγκοινωνός *sugkoinōnós*; gen. *sugkoinōnoú*, masc.-fem. noun from *koinōnós* (2844), a companion, partner. A partaker together with others, a fellow or joint partaker, a sharer with someone (Rom 11:17; 1 Cor 9:23; Phil 1:7). With *en* (1722), in, (Rev 1:9).

Syn.: *summétochos* (4830), a fellow partaker.

4792. συγκομίζω *sugkomízō*; fut. *sugkomísō*, from *sún* (4862), together, and *komízō* (2865), to convey, carry. To gather crops together, bring together, collect as fruits (Sept.: Job 5:26, dead bodies on a field of battle for burning). In the NT, to bear away together a corpse for burial, trans. (Acts 8:2).

Syn.: *apophérō* (399), to carry away.

4793. συγκρίνω *sugkrínō*; fut. *sugkrinṓ*, from *sún* (4862), together, and *krínō* (2919), to judge. To join together, combine, compose. Literally, to compare one thing with another by noting similarities and differences. Comparing spiritual things with spiritual (1 Cor 2:13; Sept.: Gen 40:8, 16, 22; 41:12, 15; Dan 5:12).

4794. συγκύπτω *sugkúptō*; fut. *sugkúpsō*, from *sún* (4862), together, and *kúptō* (2955), to bend, bow. To bend or bow down over, as persons putting their heads together. To be bowed together, to be bent over, intrans. (Luke 13:11; Sept.: Job 9:27).

4795. συγκυρία *sugkuría*; gen. *sugkurías*, fem. noun from *sugkuréō* (n.f.), to coincide, happen together. A happening together, coincidence, accident, chance (Luke 10:31, indicative of coincidence of circumstances).

4796. συγχαίρω *sugchaírō*; fut. *sugcharó*, 2d aor. *sunechárēn*, from *sún* (4862), together, and *chaírō* (5463), to rejoice. To rejoice together, to share in another's joy, with the dat. depending on *sún* (4862), together, in composition (Luke 1:58; 15:6, 9 [in these verses, the translation can be "to congratulate"]; 1 Cor 12:26; 13:6; Phil 2:17, 18; Sept.: Gen 21:6, in the mid.).
Ant.: *sullupéō* (4818), to sorrow or be grieved with someone.

4797. συγχέω *sugchéō* and **συγχύννω** *sugchúnnō*; imperf. *sunécheon* and *sunéchunon*, fut. *sugchúsō*, perf. pass. *sugkéchumai*, aor. pass. *sunechúthēn*, from *sún* (4862), together, and *chéō* (n.f., see *epichéō* [2022]), to pour. Literally, to pour together. Figuratively, to confound, confuse, trans.:
(I) Of an assembly, multitude, to throw into confusion, excite, put in uproar, with the acc. (Acts 21:27); pass. (Acts 19:32; 21:31).
(II) Of the mind, to confound, perplex, a person with whom one disputes, with the acc. (Acts 9:22). Of persons in amazement, consternation (Acts 2:6).
Deriv.: *súgchusis* (4799), confusion.

4798. συγχράομαι *sugchráomai*; contracted *sugchrṓmai*, fut. *sugchrḗsomai*, mid. deponent from *sún* (4862), together with, and *chráomai* (5530), to use, borrow. To use with another, have in common use. To share usage, dealings, communication with someone, with the dat. (John 4:9). This verse states that the Jews had no dealings with the Samaritans, that is, they did not place themselves under any obligation by accepting favors from them.

4799. σύγχυσις *súgchusis*; gen. *sugchúseōs*, fem. noun from *sugchúnnō* (4797), to pour together, to confound by mixing. Confusion, tumult, uproar (Acts 19:29 [cf. Sept.: 1 Sam 14:20]).

4800. συζάω *suzáō*; contracted *suzṓ*, fut. *suzḗsō*, from *sún* (4862), together, or with, and *záō* (2198), to live. To live with someone, to continue to live together with someone, with the dat. expressed or implied (2 Cor 7:3); of eternal life with Christ (Rom 6:8; 2 Tim 2:11).
Syn.: *sunoikéō* (4924), to reside together; *súneimi* (4895), to be together.
Ant.: *sunapothnḗskō* (4880), to die with.

4801. συζευγνύμι *suzeúgnumi*; fut. *suzeúxō*, aor. *sunézeuxa*, from *sún* (4862), together, and *zeúgos* (2201), yoke, pair. To yoke together as animals (Sept.: Ezek 1:11). Figuratively to join together, unite, trans. as husband and wife (Matt 19:6; Mark 10:9).
Deriv.: *súzugos* (4805), yoked together.
Syn.: *proskolláō* (4347), to stick together, join together, glue together.
Ant.: *chōrízō* (5563), to separate.

4802. συζητέω *suzētéō*; contracted *suzētṓ*, fut. *suzētḗsō*, from *sún* (4862), together or together with, and *zētéō* (2212), to seek, inquire. To seek something together. In the NT, figuratively, to seek together, to inquire of one another, to dispute with:
(I) Spoken of several (Mark 9:10); followed by *prós heautoús* (*prós* [4314], to *heautoús* [1438], themselves), to themselves (Luke 22:23); by *prós autoús* (*autoús* [846], them), to them (Mark 1:27).
(II) Generally, to question, reason, dispute with someone; used also in an absolute sense (Mark 12:28; Luke 24:15). With the dat. (Acts 6:9); with *prós* (Acts 9:29). With a dat. following, meaning to question or dispute with (Mark 8:11;

9:14). With an interrogative, followed by *prós* (Mark 9:16).

Deriv.: *suzḗtēsis* (4803), discussion; *suzētētḗs* (4804), a disputer.

Syn.: *dialégomai* (1256), to question, argue, dispute; *dialogízomai* (1260), to reason, discuss; *eperōtáō* (1905), to ask, to question.

Ant.: *sumphōnéō* (4856), to agree; *eunoéō* (2132), to agree.

4803. συζήτησις *suzḗtēsis*; gen. *suzetḗseōs*, fem. noun from *suzētéō* (4802), to dispute, inquire, reason together. Questioning, reasoning, disputation (Acts 15:2, 7; 28:29).

Syn.: *dialogismós* (1261), disputation; *antilogía* (485), dispute.

Ant.: *sumphōnía* (4858), agreement.

4804. συζητητής *suzētētḗs*; gen. *suzētētoú*, masc. noun from *suzētéō* (4802), to dispute, question, inquire. A debater, reasoner, disputant, a sophist (1 Cor 1:20). The rabbis had a house of disputation, a school or academy where matters were discussed or debated.

4805. σύζυγος *súzugos*; gen. *suzúgou*, masc.-fem., neut. *súzugon*, adj. from *suzeúgnumi* (4801), to join together or yoke together, as in marriage. Yoked together. As a subst., a yoke-fellow, figuratively of a spouse, fellow laborer, colleague (Phil 4:3).

Syn.: *súntrophos* (4939), comrade; *sunergós* (4904), a companion in labor; *gunḗ* (1135), wife; *anḗr* (435), husband.

4806. συζωοποιέω *suzōopoiéō*; contracted *suzōopoiō̂*, fut. *suzōopoiḗsō*, from *sún* (4862), together with, and *zōopoiéō* (2227), to make alive, quicken. To make alive or quicken with, as being raised from death to life with Christ; with the dat. (Eph 2:5). With *sún* (4862), together with (Col 2:13).

Ant.: *sunapothnḗskō* (4880), to die with.

4807. συκάμινος *sukáminos*; gen. *sukamínou*, fem. noun. A sycamine or sycamore tree, thought to be a species of the mulberry tree; akin to *sukomōraía* (4809) (Luke 17:6; Sept.: 1 Kgs 10:27; 1 Chr 27:28; Isa 9:10).

4808. συκῆ *sukḗ*; gen. *sukḗs*, fem. noun from *súkon* (4810), fig. A fig tree (Matt 21:19–21; 24:32; Mark 11:13, 20, 21; 13:28; Luke 13:6, 7; 21:29; John 1:48, 50; James 3:12; Rev 6:13; Sept.: Judg 9:10, 11; Prov 27:18).

The fig tree has been cultivated in Palestine from ancient times (Deut 8:8; Isa 34:4), and is also found growing wild. The fruit is pear-shaped and the small, green figs appear before the leaves. At a certain size their interior is filled with minute, white flowers which leads to the common impression that this tree never blossoms. When the leaves have appeared, if there is no fruit among them, the fig tree will be barren for that season (Matt 21:19).

Two types of figs are mentioned in the Bible. One is the early fig of which a few ripen and are gathered in June (Isa 28:4; Hos 9:10; Mic 7:1), but most of this early fruit falls off before it is perfected (Rev 6:13). The second or main crop ordinarily does not ripen until August. These are the "green figs" of Song 2:13. Bethphage means "house of green figs." The sprouting of the fig tree was one of the earliest indications of summer (Song 2:13; Matt 24:32; Luke 21:29, 30), and a failure to bear fruit was a great calamity (Jer 8:13; Joel 1:7, 12; Hab 3:17, 18). A long, dark-colored fig sometimes hangs on the trees all winter.

These various kinds of figs are eaten as they come from the tree and are also dried in clumps or cakes (1 Sam 25:18). They seem to have been a common item of food and to have possessed medicinal properties (2 Kgs 20:7).

The Lord's cursing of the fig tree in Mark 11:14, 21 occurred about the beginning of April when, as Mark states, the time for ripe figs had not come. It seems, then, that Christ should not have sought figs out of season. However, the tree was in leaf and fruit might have been expected. Jesus pronounces a curse upon the tree that it should from that time never bear fruit. Matthew 21:20–22 and Mark 11:20–24 clearly indicate that the purpose of Jesus' action is to give to His disciples an object lesson about the power of faith. Interpretations which find in the fig tree a symbol of apostate Israel or religious hypocrites are unwarranted by the context.

4809. συκομωραία *sukomōraía*, **συκομορέα** *sukomoréa*; gen. *sukomoraías*, fem. noun. from *súkon* (4810), fig, and *móron* (n.f.), berry. A sycamore tree (Luke 19:4). It partakes of the nature of the mulberry tree as to its leaves and the fig tree as to its fruit, which is very much like a fig in its shape and size. This fruit grows neither in clusters nor at the end of the branches, but sticking to the trunk of the tree. Its taste is similar to a wild fig. This tree is common in Egypt and the plains of Palestine. It is more frequently called the sycamine tree (*sukáminos* [4807], sycamore).

4810. σῦκον *súkon*; gen. *súkou*, neut. noun. A fig (Matt 7:16; Mark 11:13; Luke 6:44; James 3:12; Sept.: 2 Kgs 20:7).
Deriv.: *sukḗ* (4808), a fig tree; *sukomōraía* (4809), a sycamore tree; *sukophantéo* (4811), to be an informer.
Syn.: *ólunthos* (3653), an unripe fig which grows in winter and usually falls off in the spring.

4811. συκοφαντέω *sukophantéō*; contracted *sukophantṓ*, fut. *sukophantḗsō*, from *súkon* (4810), fig, and *phaínō* (5316), to show, declare. To inform against, accuse falsely, calumniate. Literally a fig informer, one who watched and informed against persons who, contrary to law, exported figs from Athens. During a time of dearth in Athens, when provisions were scarce, a law was enacted that no figs should be exported out of Attica, the region where Athens is located. This law was not repealed even when a plentiful harvest made the law meaningless and gave occasion for some to accuse those who were caught transgressing the letter of the law. These accusers were called *sukophántai*, accusers of fig trafficking (or as we say in Eng. "sycophants"). By implication, meaning to extort by false accusation, totally defraud (Luke 3:14; 19:8; Sept.: Job 35:9; Ps 119:122; Prov 22:16).
Syn.: *diabállō* (1225), to falsely accuse; *egkaléō* (1458), to bring charge against someone in court; *katēgoréō* (2723), to speak against.
Ant.: *eulogéō* (2127), to speak well of, bless; *eneulogéomai* (1757), to bless, confer benefit on.

4812. συλαγωγέω *sulagōgéō*; contracted *sulagōgṓ*, fut. *sulagōgḗsō*, from *súlon* (n.f.), a prey (from *suláō* [4813], to strip, rob), and *ágō* (71), to carry away. To lead off as prey, carry off as booty, rob, or kidnap. Figuratively, of the destructive effects of false teachers who rob believers of the complete riches available in Christ and revealed in the gospel (Col 2:8).
Syn.: *diarpázō* (1283), to plunder; *harpázō* (726), to seize, snatch away; *suláō* (4813), to rob; *kléptō* (2813), to steal; *aixmalōteúō* (162), to capture; *aixmalōtízō* (163), to make a prisoner, captivate.

4813. συλάω *suláō*; contracted *sulṓ*, fut. *sulḗsō*. To spoil, rob, plunder (2 Cor 11:8).
Deriv.: *hierósulos* (2417), a robber of the temple.
Syn.: *diarpázō* (1283), to plunder; *harpázō* (726), to seize, snatch away; *kléptō* (2813), to steal.

4814. συλλαλέω *sullaléō*; contracted *sullalṓ*, fut. *sullalḗsō*, from *sún* (4862), with, and *laléō* (2980), to talk, speak. To speak or talk with, confer, with the dat. (Mark 9:4; Luke 9:30; 22:4; Sept.: with the dat., Ex 34:35); followed by *metá* (3326), with (Matt 17:3; Acts 25:12);

with *prós allélous* (*prós* [4314], toward; *allélous* [240], each other), towards each other (Luke 4:36).

Syn.: *sunomiléō* (4926), to converse.

4815. συλλαμβάνω *sullambánō*; fut. *sullépsomai*, from *sún* (4862), an intens., or together with, and *lambánō* (2983), to take, receive. To catch hold of, to enclose in the hands, figuratively meaning to comprehend, grasp, seize, collect as scattered troops, clasp to oneself.

(I) Spoken of persons, to take or seize all together, all around, from the idea of clasping together or grasping with the hands, seizing and holding fast to someone or something, stronger than the simple verb *lambánō*.

(A) As of persons taken by authority or force, to seize, apprehend, arrest; with the acc. (Matt 26:55; Mark 14:48; Luke 22:54; John 18:12; Acts 1:16; 12:3). In the mid. (Acts 26:21; Sept.: Josh 8:23; Judg 7:25; 1 Kgs 21:18). In hunting or fishing, to take, catch (Luke 5:9, *ágran* [61], draught or haul [cf. 5:5 where it is *lambánō*]).

(B) Figuratively (of females) to conceive (Luke 1:24); with the acc. *huión* (5207), a son (Luke 1:36); *en gastrí* (*en* [1722], in; *gastrí* [1064], womb), in the womb (Luke 1:31). Also *en tē koilía* (*koilía* [2836], womb) (Luke 2:21; Sept.: Gen 4:1, 17; 19:36). Metaphorically of irregular desire as exciting to sin (James 1:15 [cf. Ps 7:15]).

(II) To take hold with another, to help, aid. In the mid. with the dat. (Luke 5:7; Phil 4:3).

Syn.: *harpázō* (726), to snatch or catch away; *agreúō* (64), to seek in order to catch; *thēreúō* (2340), to hunt or catch wild beasts; *zōgréō* (2221), to take alive; *piázō* (4084), to apprehend; *sunarpázō* (4884), to snatch, seize; *boēthéō* (997), to come to the aid of someone; *sunupourgéō* (4943), to help together, to serve under someone; *sunergéō* (4903), to cooperate.

Ant.: *apolúō* (630), to let go, release; *eleutheróō* (1659), to make free; *rhúomai*

(4506), to rescue from; *sṓzō* (4982), to save.

4816. συλλέγω *sullégō*; fut. *sulléxō*, from *sún* (4862), together, and *légō* (3004), in its original meaning, to gather. To assemble together, gather, collect (Matt 7:16, of fruits and grain; 13:28–30, 40 with tares as the obj.; 13:41, "and they shall gather out of his kingdom"; 13:48, "and gathered the good into vessels"; Luke 6:44; Sept.: Lev 19:9, 10; Ruth 2:3, 7, 15).

Syn.: *sunágō* (4863), to gather or assemble together; *episunágō* (1996), to gather together; *trugáō* (5166), to gather in or to harvest; *súneimi* (4896) and *sunathroízō* (4867), to gather together.

Ant.: *skorpízō* (4650), to scatter; *diaspeírō* (1289), to scatter abroad.

4817. συλλογίζομαι *sullogízomai*; fut. *sullogísomai*, mid. deponent from *sún* (4862), with or together, and *logízomai* (3049), to think. To reason or reckon together, consider, deliberate (Luke 20:5 [cf. Matt 21:25; Mark 11:31; Sept.: Isa 43:18]).

Syn.: *dialogízomai* (1260), to reason; *dialégomai* (1256), to discuss or dispute; *suzētéō* (4802), to discuss, reason together, or argue.

4818. συλλυπέω *sullupéō*; contracted *sullupṓ*, fut. *sullupḗsō*, from *sún* (4862), an intens., and *lupéō* (3076), to afflict, grieve. To grieve together; pass., to be grieved or afflicted for another (Mark 3:5).

Syn.: *sumpathéō* (4834), to feel sympathy with; *sumpáschō* (4841), to experience pain together.

Ant.: *sugchaírō* (4796), to rejoice together; *suneudokéō* (4909), to feel gratified with, have pleasure with.

4819. συμβαίνω *sumbaínō*; fut. *sumbḗsomai*, 2d aor. *sunébēn*, from *sún* (4862), together, or an intens., and *baínō* (n.f., see *apobaínō* [576]), to walk, to come. To walk or happen close together. In the NT, of things or events, to befall concomitantly, to happen together, come to pass. Followed by the dat. of person, to whom (Mark 10:32, "what things should happen unto him"; Acts 3:10; 20:19; 1 Cor 10:11; 1 Pet 4:12; 2 Pet 2:22; Sept.: Gen 42:4, 29). In the part., *tá sumbebēkóta*, events (Luke 24:14; Sept.: Esth 6:13). Impersonal, with the inf. of the principal verb, the inf. clause being strictly the subj. (Acts 21:35, "so it was").

Syn.: *gínomai* (1096), to take place, become, befall.

4820. συμβάλλω *sumbállō*; fut. *sumbalō̃*, from *sún* (4862), together, with, and *bállō* (906), to cast. To contribute, conduce, consider or confer with.

(I) Of things, to throw or put together, with the acc. *lógous* (3056), words, or the like implied, meaning to confer intrans.

(A) Generally with the meaning of to discourse with or dispute, with the dat. (Acts 17:18).

(B) To consult together (Acts 4:15).

(C) To consider, ponder (Luke 2:19).

(D) In the mid, to confer benefit, contribute, help, with the dat. (Acts 18:27).

(II) Of persons (intrans. or with *heautón* [1438], himself, implied), to throw oneself together with another, to encounter, meet with, with the dat.

(A) In a hostile sense (Luke 14:31).

(B) Generally, to meet with (Acts 20:14).

Syn.: *sullaléō* (4814), to speak together; *antilambánomai* (482), to support; *sunantilambánomai* (4878), to cooperate; *boēthéō* (997), to assist; *sunupourgéō* (4943), to be a co-worker; *sunergéō* (4903), to work together, cooperate; *parístēmi* (3936), to stand by, assist; *apantáō* (528), to meet together for the purpose of fighting; *sunantáō* (4876), to meet; *hupantáō* (5221), to meet together in battle.

Ant.: *anakóptō* (348), to hinder; *aphístēmi* (868), to withdraw; *ekklínō* (1578), to avoid; *kōlúō* (2967), to hinder; *periístēmi* (4026), to shun; *sigáō* (4601), keep silent.

4821. συμβασιλεύω *sumbasileúō*; fut. *sumbasileúsō*, from *sún* (4862), together with, and *basileúō* (936), to reign. To reign with someone, be a coregent (1 Cor 4:8; 2 Tim 2:12). To reign with Christ is to participate now and forever in His victory over Satan, sin, and the world (John 12:31; 17:33; Matt 12:24–30; Luke 10:17–20; Rom 5:20, 21; Eph 1:19–22; 2:6; Col 2:15; 1 John 5:4, 5, 18, 19; Rev 1:6; 20:1–6; 22:5).

4822. συμβιβάζω *sumbibázō*; fut. *sumbibásō*, from *sún* (4862), together, and *bibázō* (n.f., see *embibázō* [1688]), to uplift, exalt. To cause to come together, to bring together.

(I) To join or knit together, unite, figuratively of Christians as parts of Christ's spiritual body, the Church, in the pass. (Eph 4:16; Col 2:2, 19).

(II) To put together mentally and hence to infer, to conclude, with *hoti* (3754), that (Acts 16:10). Also to prove, demonstrate, with *hóti* (Acts 9:22). In the NT, with the acc. of person, to teach, instruct (1 Cor 2:16 in allusion to Isa 40:13; Sept.: Ex 4:12; 18:16; Lev 10:11; Deut 4:9; Isa 40:14).

Syn.: *didáskō* (1321), to teach; *katēchéō* (2727), to indoctrinate, catechize, instruct.

4823. συμβουλεύω *sumbouleúō*; fut. *sumbouleúsō*, from *sún* (4862), an intens. or together, and *bouleúō* (1011), to take counsel, decree. To counsel with someone, advise, with the dat. (John 18:14; Rev 3:18; Sept.: Ex 18:19; Jer 38:15). In the mid., spoken of several, to counsel or consult together for evil, to plot (Sept.: 1 Kgs 12:8); followed by *hína* (2443), so that (Matt 26:4; John 11:53); with the inf. (Acts 9:23).

Syn.: *nouthetéō* (3560), to admonish; *parainéō* (3867), to admonish, exhort, recommend, advise; *sunistáō* (4921), to commend; *mēnúō* (3377), to call to mind, intimate, tell.

4824. συμβούλιον *sumboúlion*; gen. *sumboulíou*, neut. noun from *súmboulos* (4825), to counsel.

(I) Counsel, consultation; with *lambánō* (2983), to take or receive counsel, to hold or take a consultation (Matt 12:14; 22:15; 27:1, 7; 28:12). With *poiéō* (4160), to make or take (Mark 3:6; 15:1).

(II) A council, collectively for counselors (Acts 25:12, speaking of persons who sat in public trials with the governor of a province).

Syn.: *sunédrion* (4892), council. The Sanhedrin, which derived its name from this word, was a council.

4825. σύμβουλος *súmboulos*; gen. *sumboúlou*, masc. noun from *sún* (4862), together, and *boulē̂* (1012), counsel. A counselor (Rom 11:34 in allusion to Isa 40:13; Sept.: 2 Sam 15:12; 1 Chr 27:32, 33).

Deriv.: *sumboúlion* (4824), consultation, counsel, council.

Syn.: *nomikós* (3544), lawyer.

4826. Συμεών *Sumeṓn*; masc. proper noun transliterated from the Hebr. *Shimʿʾōn* (8095, OT), a hearing. Simeon, equivalent to Simon (*Símōn* [4613]).

(I) The second son of Jacob, born of Leah; also of the tribe descended from him (Rev 7:7 [cf. Gen 29:33]).

(II) One of the ancestors of Jesus (Luke 3:30).

(III) A pious Jew who took the infant Jesus in his arms and blessed Him in the temple (Luke 2:25, 34). He is supposed by many to be the same as Shammai, and also the same mentioned in the Talmud as the father of Gamaliel.

(IV) Simon Peter, elsewhere Simon (Acts 15:14; 2 Pet 1:1).

(V) A Christian teacher at Antioch surnamed Niger (Acts 13:1).

4827. συμμαθητής *summathētḗs*; gen. *summathētoú*, masc. noun from *sún* (4862), together with, and *mathētḗs* (3101), a disciple. A fellow disciple (John 11:16).

4828. συμμαρτυρέω *summartyréō*; contracted *summartyrō̂*, fut. *summartyrḗsō*, from *sún* (4862), together, with, and *martyréō* (3140), to witness. To witness with another, testify with. With the dat. (Rom 8:16; 9:1; Rev 22:18 [TR]); used in an absolute sense (Rom 2:15).

4829. συμμερίζω *summerízō*; fut. *summerísō*, from *sún* (4862), together with, and *merízō* (3307), to divide. To share with another. In the NT, only in the mid. *summerízomai*, to divide or share with someone, with a dat. (1 Cor 9:13).

Syn.: *koinōnéō* (2841), to have a share of, to share with; *sugkoinōnéō* (4790), to have fellowship with; *metéchō* (3348), to partake of, share in; *antilambánomai* (482), to partake of; *metalambánō* (3335), to be partaker.

4830. συμμέτοχος *summétochos*; gen. *summetóchou*, masc.-fem., neut. *summétochos*, adj. from *sún* (4862), together with, and *métochos* (3353), a partaker. Partaking with, as a subst., a joint partaker (Eph 3:6; 5:7).

Syn.: *koinōnós* (2844), an associate or partner; *sugkoinōnós* (4791), a joint partaker.

4831. συμμιμητής *summimētḗs*; gen. *summimētoú*, masc. noun from *sún* (4862), together with, and *mimētḗs* (3402), an imitator. An imitator of or follower with others, a joint follower (Phil 3:17).

4832. σύμμορφος *súmmorphos*; gen. *summórphou*, masc.-fem., neut. *súmmorphos*, adj. from *sún* (4862), together with, and *morphḗ* (3444), form. In Rom 8:29 it refers to the conformity of children of God "to the image of His Son"; in Phil 3:21 of their physical conformity to His body of glory.

Deriv.: *summorphóō* (4833), becoming conformed.

4833. συμμορφόω *summorphóō*; contracted *summorphṓ*, fut. *summorphṓsō*, from *súmmorphos* (4832), conformed to, conformable. To make of like form with another, conform to. Pass. with the dat., figuratively (Phil 3:10).

    Syn.: *summorphízō* (in some MSS for *summorphóō*); *suschēmatízō* (4964), to fashion alike, to conform to.

4834. συμπαθέω *sumpathéō*; contracted *sumpathṓ*, fut. *sumpathḗsō*, from *sumpathḗs* (4835), sympathizing. With a dat., to sympathize with, be compassionate, have compassion upon (Heb 4:15; 10:34).

    Syn.: *sullupéomai* (the mid. of *sullupéō* [4818]), to experience sorrow with, console; *splagchnízomai* (4697), to feel sympathy, to pity, have compassion.

    Ant.: *miséō* (3404), to hate, detest.

4835. συμπαθής *sumpathḗs*; gen. *sumpathoús*, masc.-fem., neut. *sumpathés*, adj. from *sún* (4862), together or with, and *páthos* (3806), suffering, misfortune. Compassionate, sympathizing (1 Pet 3:8).

    Deriv.: *sumpathéō* (4834), to be compassionate.

4836. συμπαραγίνομαι *sumparagínomai*; fut. *sunparagenḗsomai*, 2d aor. *sumparegenómēn*, from *sún* (4862), together or with, and *paragínomai* (3854), to come, arrive, be present. To stand by someone as a friend and advocate, with the dat. (2 Tim 4:16). Of a multitude, to come together, convene (Luke 23:48).

    Syn.: *sumpáreimi* (4840), to be present with; *sumparaménō* (4839), to remain with; *sunágō* (4863), to come together.

    Ant.: *diaskorpízō* (1287), to scatter; *egkataleípō* (1459), to forsake; *exérchomai* (1831), to depart; *periḯstēmai* (4026), to keep away from, avoid; *skorpízō* (4650), to scatter.

4837. συμπαρακαλέω *sumparakaléō*; contracted *sumparakalṓ*, fut. *sumpara-* *kalésō*, from *sún* (4862), together, and *parakaléō* (3870), to comfort, console. To call for or invite simultaneously, to invoke or exhort with others. In the NT, only in the pass. meaning to be consoled, comforted with others, to receive solace and encouragement in the society of others (Rom 1:12).

4838. συμπαραλαμβάνω *sumparalambánō*; fut. *sunparalḗpsomai*, 2d aor. *sumparélabon*, from *sún* (4862), together with, and *paralambánō* (3880), to take along. To take along with oneself as a companion on a journey, with the acc. (Acts 12:25; 15:37, 38; Gal 2:1; Sept.: Job 1:4).

    Syn.: *sunépomai* (4902), to travel in company with; *sunodeúō* (4922), to journey with.

    Ant.: *apotássomai* (657), to forsake, take leave; *aphíēmi* (863), to leave, lay aside; *egkataleípō* (1459), to leave behind, forsake; *kataleípō* (2641), to abandon, leave behind.

4839. συμπαραμένω *sumparaménō*; fut. *sumparamenṓ*, from *sún* (4862), together with, and *paraménō* (3887), to remain. To remain together, continue with, with a dat. (Phil 1:25[TR]; Sept.: Ps 72:5).

    Syn.: *sumpáreimi* (4840), to be close at hand, be present with.

4840. συμπάρειμι *sumpáreimi*; fut. *sunpareísomai*, from *sún* (4862), with, and *páreimi* (3918), to be present. To be present with, with the dat. (Acts 25:24).

    Syn.: *sumparagínomai* (4836), to come with, be present with someone; *sumparaménō* (4839), to remain together with.

4841. συμπάσχω *sumpáschō*; fut. *sumpeísomai*, from *sún* (4862), together with, and *páschō* (3958), to suffer. To suffer together with (Rom 8:17; 1 Cor 12:26).

4842. συμπέμπω *sumpémpō*; fut. *sumpémpsō*, from *sún* (4862), together with, and *pémpō* (3992), to send. To send with someone, with a dat. (2 Cor 8:22); with *metá* (3326), with, and a gen. (2 Cor 8:18).
Syn.: *sunapostéllō* (4882), to send along with.

4843. συμπεριλαμβάνω *sumperilambánō*; fut. *sumperilépsomai*, 2d aor. *sumperiélabon*, from *sún* (4862), together, at the same time, and *perilambánō* (n.f.), to embrace, which is from *perí* (4012), about, and *lambánō* (2983), to receive, take hold of. To clasp in the arms, to comprehend immediately. To embrace (Acts 20:10).
Syn.: *aspázomai* (782), to welcome or bid farewell by embracing.

4844. συμπίνω *sumpínō*; fut. *sumpíomai*, 2d aor. *sunépion*, from *sún* (4862), together with, and *pínō* (4095), to drink. To drink with someone, with the dat. (Acts 10:41; Sept.: Esth 7:1).
Deriv.: *sumpósion* (4849), a party, a room of guests.

4845. συμπληρόω *sumplēróō*; contracted *sumplērṓ*, fut. *sumplērṓsō*, from *sún* (4862), an intens., and *plēróō* (4137), to fill. To fill to the brim. Used in the pass., to be filled completely, as with water (Luke 8:23 [cf. Mark 4:37]). In the pass., used of time, to be fulfilled or fully come (Luke 9:51; Acts 2:1 [cf. John 7:8]).
Syn.: *katantáō* (2658), to arrive, attain; *pímplēmi* or *pléthō* (4130), to fill up; *gemízō* (1072), to fill full; *empíplēmi* or *emplḗthō* (1705), to fill full; *teleióō* (5048), to complete; *sunteléō* (4931) and *apoteléō* (658), to complete entirely.

4846. συμπνίγω *sumpnígō*; fut. *sumpníxō*, from *sún* (4862), an intens., and *pnígō* (4155), to choke, suffocate. To choke or throttle and thus to suffocate. Figuratively, to overpower, with the acc. (Matt 13:22; Mark 4:7, 19; Luke 8:14).

Figuratively, to crowd, press upon (Luke 8:42 [cf. Mark 5:24]).
Syn.: *sunthlíbō* (4918), to press or throng together; *sunéchō* (4912), to hold or press together; *stenochōréō* (4729), to hem in closely, cramp.
Ant.: *aníēmi* (447), to loose, let up, slacken.

4847. συμπολίτης *sumpolítēs*; gen. *sumpolítou*, masc. noun from *sún* (4862), together with, and *polítēs* (4177), a citizen. A fellow citizen, figuratively of Gentile Christians (Eph 2:19).
Syn.: *sumphulétēs* (4853), fellow citizen, countryman.
Ant.: *allogenés* (241), foreigner, stranger; *allótrios* (245), alien; *allóphulos* (246), one of another tribe or race, foreigner; *xénos* (3581), foreigner, alien, stranger.

4848. συμπορεύομαι *sumporeúomai*; fut. *sumporeúsomai*, from *sún* (4862), together or together with, and *poreúomai* (4198), to go or come. To go together, accompany, with the dat. (Luke 7:11; 14:25; 24:15); with *metá* (3326), with, and the gen. (Sept.: Gen 13:5; 14:24; 18:16). Of a multitude, to come together, assemble (Mark 10:1; Sept.: Job 1:4).
Syn.: *sunérchomai* (4905), to go or come with; *suneisérchomai* (4897), to enter with.

4849. συμπόσιον *sumpósion*; gen. *sumposíou*, neut. noun from *sumpínō* (4844), to drink with someone. A drinking together (Sept.: Esth 7:7, a banquet feast, a banqueting hall). A feast (Mark 6:39, repeated in the pl. *sumpósia sumpósia*, used adv. and distributively meaning by companies or groups).

4850. συμπρεσβύτερος *sumpresbúteros*; gen. *sumpresbutérou*, masc. noun from *sún* (4862), together with, and *presbúteros* (4245), an elder. A fellow elder (1 Pet 5:1). Peter reminds the elders of the dignity of their office that they might not forget their duties (5:2, 3).

4851. συμφέρω *sumphérō*; fut. *sunoísō*, aor. *sunénegka*, from *sún* (4862), together, and *phérō* (5342), to bring. To bring together in one place (Acts 19:19); used in an absolute sense or with a dat. following, to be profitable, advantageous, to contribute or bring together for the benefit of another. Used either personally (1 Cor 6:12; 10:23; 2 Cor 8:10; Sept.: Esth 3:8; Prov 19:10) or impersonally, *sumphérei*, meaning that it is advantageous (Matt 5:29, 30; 18:6; 19:10; John 11:50; 16:7). The neut. part., *tó sumphéron*, advantage, profit, benefit (1 Cor 7:35; 10:33; 12:7; Heb 12:10); pl., *tá sumphéronta*, things profitable (Acts 20:20).

Syn.: *ōpheléō* (5623), to be useful, to benefit; *lusiteléō* (3081), to be advantageous, answer the purpose.

4852. σύμφημι *súmphēmi*; from *sún* (4862), together with, and *phēmí* (5346), to speak. To agree with, to say yes, assent to, with the dat. (Rom 7:16).

Syn.: *sugkatatíthēmi* (4784), to consent; *sumphōnéō* (4856), to agree.

Ant.: *antilégō* (483), to speak against; *suzētéō* (4802), to dispute; *antitássomai* (498), to oppose; *anthístēmi* (436), to oppose, withstand.

4853. συμφυλέτης *sumphulétēs*; gen. *sumphulétou*, masc. noun from *sún* (4862), together with, and *phulétēs* (n.f.), one of the same tribe, which is from *phulḗ* (5443), a race, clan or tribe. One of the same tribe or fraternity. In the NT, generally a fellow citizen, fellow countryman (1 Thess 2:14).

Syn.: *sumpolítes* (4847), fellow citizen.

Ant.: *bárbaros* (915), foreigner, non-Greek; *pároikos* (3941), foreigner, stranger; *xénos* (3581), stranger.

4854. σύμφυτος *súmphutos*; gen. *sumphútou*, masc.-fem., neut. *súmphuton*, adj. from *sumphúō* (4855), to grow together. Planted together, united with, innate (Rom 6:5, oneness with Christ in the likeness of His death, to be explained in accordance with 6:4, 8). It denotes not merely homogeneousness, but a similarity of experience.

4855. συμφύω *sumphúō*; fut. *sumphúsō*, 2d aor. *sunephúēn*, from *sún* (4862), together, and *phúō* (5453), to spring up. To bring forth together, to let spring up or grow together. In the NT, only in the pass., to spring up or grow together (Luke 8:7).

Deriv.: *súmphutos* (4854), planted together.

Syn.: *sunauxánō* (4885), to grow together.

4856. συμφωνέω *sumphōnéō*; contracted *sumphōnṓ*, fut. *sumphōnḗsō*, from *súmphōnos* (4859), be in agreement with. To be in unison, accord, to speak together with another, thus to agree, concur. Intrans., with a dat. expressed or implied:

(I) Generally of what fits or conforms (Luke 5:36).

(II) Of agreement, concurrence (Acts 15:15).

(III) Of a compact, to agree together, followed by *perí* (4012), concerning, with the gen. (Matt 18:19). Pass. with the dat. (Acts 5:9, "how is it that ye have agreed together"; Sept.: 2 Kgs 12:8). Followed by the dat. of person and gen. of price (Matt 20:13); by *metá* (3326), with, and the gen. and *ék* (1537), for, with the gen. of wage (Matt 20:2 the *ek* indicating an intended goal, in this case, one dinar).

Deriv.: *sumphṓnēsis* (4857), the act of agreeing.

Syn.: *sugkatatíthēmi* (4784), to consent.

4857. συμφώνησις *sumphṓnēsis*; gen. *sumphōnḗseōs*, fem. noun from *sumphōnéō* (4856), to agree. Agreement, concord, unison, accord (2 Cor 6:15, concord or agreement).

Ant.: *diákrisis* (1253), disputation; *diastolḗ* (1293), difference.

4858. συμφωνία *sumphōnía*; gen.
sumphōnías, fem. noun from *súmphōnos*
(4859), sounding together, accordant,
harmonious. Symphony, concert of instruments, music.
   Syn.: *húmnos* (5215), hymn, a religious
metrical composition; *psállō* (5567), to
make melody, sing; *psalmós* (5568), a
psalm; *ōdḗ* (5603), a chant.
   Ant.: *akatastasía* (181), tumult;
thorubéō (2350), clamor, noise; *rhoizēdón*
(4500), crash, noise.

4859. σύμφωνος *súmphōnos*; gen.
sumphṓnou, masc.-fem., neut. *súmphōnon*,
adj. also used as a subst. in the neut., *tó*
súmphōnon, from *sún* (4862), together,
and *phōnḗ* (5456), a sound, voice. Sym-
phonious, blending of voices or musical
instruments. Figuratively, consonant, accordant; in the NT, only in the neut. as a
subst., *tó súmphōnon* (1 Cor 7:5, accord,
agreement).
   Deriv.: *asúmphōnos* (800), disagreeing; *sumphōnéō* (4856), to be in accord,
agree; *sumphonía* (4858), symphony.
   Syn.: *homóphrōn* (3675), of the same
mind; *súmpsuchos* (4861), of one soul;
isópsuchos (2473), equal-souled, like-
minded.
   Ant.: *diáphoros* (1313), different;
asúmphōnos (800), not agreeing.

4860. συμψηφίζω *sumpsēphízō*; fut.
sumpsēphísō, from *sún* (4862), together,
and *psēphízō* (5585), to vote, to calculate.
To calculate, compute or reckon together
(Acts 19:19).
   Syn.: *logízomai* (3049), to reckon,
count; *arithméō* (705), to enumerate,
count.

4861. σύμψυχος *súmpsuchos*; gen.
sumpsúchou, masc.-fem., neut. *súm-
psuchon*, adj. from *sún* (4862), together,
and *psuchḗ* (5590), soul. Joined together in soul or sentiment, unanimous (Phil
2:2). It signifies community of life and
love.

   Syn.: *isópsuchos* (2473), like-minded;
súmphōnos (4859), agreeing, of one accord; *homóphrōn* (3675), like-minded.
   Ant.: *asúmphōnos* (800), not agreeing.

4862. σύν *sún*; a prep. governing only
the dat. Together, with, together with,
implying a nearer and closer connection
than the conj. *metá* (3326), with, much as
in Eng. with differs from amid, among.
   (I) Particularly of society, companionship, consort, where one is said to be, do,
suffer with someone, in connection and
company with him. After verbs of sitting,
standing, being or remaining with someone, as *gínomai* (1096), to become (Luke
2:13); *diatríbō* (1304), to remain (Acts
14:28); *hístēmi* (2476), to stand, intrans.
(Acts 2:14; 4:14); *ephístēmi* (2186), to
stand upon, intrans. (Luke 20:1; Acts
23:27); *kathízō* (2523), to sit down (Acts
8:31); *ménō* (3306), remain (Luke 1:56;
24:29; Acts 28:16). With *eínai* (1511), to
be, preceding *sún*, and followed by the
dat., to be with someone, meaning present
with, in company with (Luke 24:44; Phil
1:23; Col 2:5). Followed by *Kuríō*, the
dat. of *Kúrios* (2962), the Lord (1 Thess
4:17). With *eínai* implied (Luke 8:1;
Phil 4:21). As accompanying, following
(Luke 7:12; Acts 13:7; 27:2); as a follower, disciple (Luke 8:38; 22:56; Acts
4:13); as a partisan, to be on one's side
(Acts 14:4). *Hoi sún* followed by *ón* or
óntes ([5607], pres. part. sing. and pl. of
eimí (1510), to be), those with someone,
one's companions, attendants, followers;
fully (Mark 2:26; Acts 22:9). More often
with *ón* or *óntes* implied (Luke 5:9; 9:32,
in later editions; 24:10, 24; Rom 16:14,
15; Gal 1:2; 2:3). Spoken of colleagues
(Acts 5:17, 21; 19:38). After verbs of going, e.g., *érchomai* (2064), to come, or
in its comp. (Luke 24:1; John 21:3; Acts
11:12; 2 Cor 9:4); *apérchomai* (565), to
depart (Acts 5:26); *eisérchomai* (1525),
to enter in (Acts 3:8; 25:23); *exérchomai*
(1831), to go out (John 18:1; Acts 10:23;
14:20; 16:3); *sunérchomai* (4905), to
come together (Acts 21:16); *poreúomai*
(4198), to travel, go (Luke 7:6; Acts

10:20; 23:32; 26:13; 1 Cor 16:4); *eíseimi* (1524), to enter (Acts 21:18); *ekpléō* (1602), to depart by ship (Acts 18:18); *paragínomai* (3854), to come near (Acts 24:24); *sunágomai* (4863), to lead together or come together (Acts 4:27). Generally with neut. and pass. verbs, used like the Eng. "with," where the verb refers to its subj., as in company with others (Matt 26:35; 27:38; Mark 9:4; Luke 2:5; 22:14; 23:32; Acts 1:14, 17 [TR], 22; 3:4; 8:20; 14:5; 15:22; 17:34; 18:8; 20:36; 21:24, 26; 1 Cor 1:2; 11:32; 2 Cor 1:1; Eph 3:18; 4:31; Phil 1:1; 2:22; Col 3:3, 4; 1 Thess 4:17; 5:10). Also with trans. verbs, used like the Eng. "with," where the verb refers either to its obj., as in company with others, or to the subj. (Mark 4:10; Luke 5:19; 19:23; 23:11, 35; Acts 5:1; 10:2; 14:13; 15:22; 21:5; 1 Cor 16:19); to the obj. (Matt 25:27; Mark 8:34; 15:27; Acts 15:25; 23:15; 1 Cor 10:13; 2 Cor 1:21; 4:14; Gal 5:24; Col 3:9; 4:9; 1 Thess 4:14).

(II) Figuratively of connection, association, as arising from similarity of experiences, from a common lot or event, with, in like manner with, like (Rom 6:8; 8:32; 2 Cor 13:4; Gal 3:9, with and like Abraham, by the same acts and in the same manner; Col 2:13, 20; Sept.: with *metá* [3326], with, Ps 106:6; Eccl 2:16).

(III) Of connection arising from possession, the being furnished or instructed with something (1 Cor 15:10, "which was given me" [a.t.], as in 2 Cor 8:19, who is entrusted with this gift; James 1:11).

(IV) Implying a joint effort, cooperation, and thus spoken of a means, instrument, with, through, by virtue of (1 Cor 5:4).

(V) Implying addition, accession, meaning besides, over and above (Luke 24:21, "besides all this").

(VI) In composition *sún* implies:

(A) Company, companionship, association with, together, same as the Eng. con- as a prefix, as in *sunágō* (4863), to lead together, gather; *sunesthíō* (4906), to eat with; *sugkáthēmai* (4775), to sit with.

(B) Completeness of an action, meaning altogether, round about, on every side, wholly, and thus intens. as in *sumplēróō* (4845), to fill up; *sugkalúptō* (4780), to conceal completely.

(VII) Relationship with *metá* (3326), with. In Attic Gr., *sún* meant "including" and "with the aid of" while *metá* simply meant "in company with." *Sún* with the dat. has gradually fallen into misuse as the language developed. It is not used as much as *metá* which is followed by the gen. *Sún* is used 127 times in the NT and of these 75 are in Luke and Acts while *metá* is used 364 times. Though *sún* is used in comp. verbs, very rarely is *metá* used.

It is significant that the closing salutations of the Apostle Paul use *metá* and never *sún* (Rom 16:20, 24; 1 Cor 16:23, 24; 2 Cor 13:11, 14; Gal 6:18; Eph 6:24; Phil 4:23; Col 4:18; 1 Thess 5:28; 2 Thess 3:16, 18; 1 Tim 6:21; 2 Tim 4:22; Titus 3:15; Phile 1:25; Heb 13:25). *Metá* seems to be more appropriate in relating the graces of peace, grace, and love as virtues which accompany believers in the circumstances of life. *Sún* is used to denote a more intimate relationship of Jesus Christ with us, as in the comp. verbs *sustauróō* (4957), to crucify with; *sunapothnḗskō* (4880), to die together or with; *sunegeírō* (4891), to rise up together; *suzáō* (4800), to live with. To illustrate, the criminals punished with Jesus were crucified with (*metá*) Him, i.e., in His company, but not together with (*sún*) Him, i.e., bound up or in union with Him.

(VIII) There are three prep. which are used to indicate the believer's relationship with Christ: *en* (1722), in; *metá*, and *sún*. The inner mystical relationship between the believer and the Lord Jesus Christ is expressed with *en*. We are in Christ (2 Cor 5:17) and as a result of that we are qualitatively new creatures (*kainḗ* [2537], qualitatively new; *ktísis* (2937), creation). When we die as believers we do not cease to be in Christ as we are now in this life (1 Cor 15:18; 1 Thess 4:16). At death we also go to be with (*sún*) Christ. This refers to an individual spatial coexistence and not only our mystical existence in Christ here and now (Phil 1:23; 1 Thess 4:17). Besides this mystical relationship, the Lord is also with (*metá*) us as an obj. reality (Phil 4:9; 2 Thess 3:16).

Syn.: *metá* (3326), with (see VII, VIII); *pará* (3844), near, beside; *homoú* (3674), together.

Ant.: *éxō* (1854), out; *áneu* (427), without; *ektós* (1622), outside, besides, without; *chōrís* (5565), separately, apart from, without; *áter* (817), apart from, without.

4863. συνάγω sunágō; fut. *sunáxō*, from *sún* (4862), with, and *ágō* (71), to lead, assemble, gather together.

(I) Generally of persons or things, with the acc. (Matt 22:10; Luke 15:13; John 6:12; Rev 13:10); with the acc. implied (Matt 13:47; 25:24, 26; John 6:13; Sept.: Num 19:9, 10). Elsewhere with adjuncts: *eis* (1519), into, with the acc. of place (Matt 3:12; 6:26; 13:30; Luke 3:17; John 4:36; 11:52, "in one the children of God," meaning into one family or church); preceded by *poú* (4226), where (Luke 12:17); followed by *metá* (3326), with, and the gen. (Matt 12:30; Luke 11:23).

(II) Of persons, an assembly, multitude, meaning to assemble, convene, gather together.

(A) Act., with the acc. (Matt 2:4; John 11:47; Acts 14:27; 15:30; Sept.: Ex 3:16; 1 Sam 5:11).

(B) Mid. / pass., to be gathered together, assembled, come together (Matt 22:41; 27:17; Mark 2:2; Luke 22:66; Acts 13:44; 15:6; 20:7; 1 Cor 5:4; Rev 19:19; Sept.: Deut 33:5). With adjuncts: preceded by *émprosthen* (1715), before, with the gen. (Matt 25:32); with the acc., meaning at the same place, together (Matt 22:34; Acts 4:26); with *epí* (1909), upon, and the acc., to gather toward (Mark 5:21), against someone (Matt 27:27; Acts 4:27; Sept. Gen 34:30); followed by *eis* and the acc. (Rev 16:14, 16; 20:8); with *eis*, at, and the acc. of place (Matt 26:3; Acts 4:5); with *eis*, in, as final (Matt 18:20, "in my

name," to glorify my name); Rev 19:17, "unto the supper"); with *en* (1722), in, and the dat. of place (Acts 4:31; 11:26); with *metá* and the gen. (Matt 28:12); with *prós* (4314), toward, and the acc., to someone (Matt 13:2; 27:62; Mark 4:1; 6:30; 7:1); with *ekeí* (1563), there (Matt 24:28; Luke 17:37; John 18:2); with *hópou* (3699), where (Matt 26:57; John 20:19); with *hoú* (3757), where (Acts 20:8).

(III) To take into one's house, meaning to give hospitality and protection (Matt 25:35, 38, 43; Sept.: Deut 22:2; Josh 2:18; Judg 19:15, 18).

Deriv.: *episunágō* (1996), to gather together in one place; *sunagōgḗ* (4864), a gathering, synagogue.

Syn.: *sullégō* (4816), to collect or gather up; *trugáō* (5166), to gather in as harvest or vintage; *sunathroízō* (4867), to hoard or gather together; *epathroízō* (1865), to accumulate.

Ant.: *skorpízō* (4650), to scatter, disperse.

4864. συναγωγή sunagōgḗ; gen. *sunagōgḗs*, fem. noun from *sunágō* (4863), to lead together, assemble. A gathering, congregation, synagogue (Sept.; Isa 37:25); of persons (Sept.: Ex 12:3, 19). The congregation of Israel was designated by *sunagōgḗ* or *ekklēsía* (1577), church. As the word was used, it did not imply the natural unity of the people, but a community established in a special way and for a special object. In the NT, *ekklēsía*, church, is used most often as the name for God's Church (i.e, the congregation of the saved). *Sunagōgḗ* is used to designate the fellowship only in Rev 2:9; 3:9 (where the unbelieving Jews as a body are called the "synagogue of Satan"). See also Acts 14:2; 17:5; 18:12. A synagogue was finally designated as the Sabbath assembly of the Jews (Acts 13:14, 15). In James 2:2 a synagogue is used to designate the worshiping assembly of the Jewish Christians. In other places in the NT, it is used as the assembly place of the Jews.

(I) Of a Jewish assembly or congregation, held in the synagogues for prayer, reading the Scriptures, and with certain judicial powers (Matt 10:17; 13:9; Luke 8:41; 12:11; 21:12; Acts 9:2; 13:42, 43; 22:19; 26:11).

(II) Metonymically of a Jewish place of worship, a synagogue, house of assembly. Synagogues appear to have been first introduced during the Babylonian exile when the people were deprived of their usual rites of worship and were accustomed to assemble on the Sabbath to hear portions of the Law read and expounded. After their return from exile, the same custom was continued in Palestine (cf. Neh 8:1ff.).

Assemblies were held in these at first only on the Sabbath and feast days; but subsequently also on the second and fifth days of the week, Mondays and Thursdays. The exercises consisted chiefly in prayers and the public reading of the OT which was expounded from the Hebr. into the vernacular tongue, with suitable exhortation (cf. Luke 4:16ff.; Acts 13:14ff.). The meeting was closed by a short prayer and benediction, to which the assembly responded with "Amen" (Neh 8:6). See Matt 4:23; 6:2, 5; 9:35; 10:17; 12:9; 13:54; 23:6, 34; Mark 1:21, 23, 29, 39; 3:1; 6:2; 12:39; 13:9; Luke 4:15, 16, 20, 28, 33, 38, 44; 6:6; 7:5; 11:43; 13:10; 20:46; John 6:59; 18:20; Acts 9:20; 13:14; 14:1; 15:21; 17:17; 18:4, 7, 19, 26; 19:8; 24:12; *sunagōgḗ tṓn Ioudaíōn* (2453), of the Jews, in Acts 13:5; 17:1, 10; *sunagōgḗ tṓn Libertínōn* (3032), Libertines or freedmen in Acts 6:9.

Originally synagogues would seem not to have differed from the later *proseuchaí* (4335), prayers or prayer chapels, which were erected outside of the cities in the fields, and usually near streams or on the sea shore for the convenience of ablutions. Afterwards they were built in the more elevated parts of every city, and in the larger cities there were several in proportion to the population. In Jerusalem, according to the rabbis, there were not less than 480

or 494 synagogues (doubtless a boastful exaggeration).

(III) Thus synagogue denotes primarily the religious community of Jews (Luke 12:11; Acts 9:2; 26:11). *Sunagōgḗ* was used by the Judeo-Christians but became afterwards the regular term for the Jewish place of worship. Through the Pauline writings, *ekklēsía* became the predominant name for the Christian church.

(IV) In the OT, two different words are used to denote gatherings of the chosen people or their representatives— '*ēdāh* (5712, OT), congregation, and *qāhāl* (6951, OT), assembly. In the Sept., *sunagōgḗ* is the usual translation of '*ēdāh*, while *qāhāl* is commonly rendered *ekklēsía*. By their respective derivations, both *qāhāl* and *ekklēsía* indicate a calling or summoning to a place of meeting. *Qāhāl* and *ekklēsía* are the more sacred terms, denoting the people in relation to Jehovah, especially in public worship. Perhaps for this very reason the less sacred term *sunagōgḗ* was more commonly used by the Jews in the Lord's time and probably influenced the first believers in adopting *ekklēsía* for Christian use. *Sunagōgḗ* quickly went out of use for a Christian assembly (James 2:2), except in sects which were more Jewish than Christian. Due to the growing hostility of the Jews, it came to indicate opposition to the church (Rev 2:9; 3:9). *Ekklēsía*, then, suggests the new people of God, the new Israel.

(V) In Matt 16:18; 18:17, Jesus uses *ekklēsía* (or its Aramaic equivalent) to designate the people of God which He would build with Himself serving as its foundation.

(VI) Paul probably found the word already in use, and outside the Gospels it is very frequent in the NT. We find three uses of the term *ekklēsía*: the general body of believers (Acts 5:11; 9:31; 12:1); the believers in a certain place (1 Thess 1:1; 2 Thess 1:1); an assembly for public worship (1 Cor 11:18; 14:19, 35). It had already become a technical term with strong religious connotations which were partly borrowed from a Jewish ideal, but had been so enriched and transfigured as to indicate a body that was entirely new. The Jewish idea of a chosen people in relation to God received a fuller meaning, and to this was added the ideal of a chosen people in relation to the incarnate and risen Son of God and to the Spirit of God. *Ekklēsía* is nowhere used of heathen religious assemblies.

(VII) A Christian living in isolation from the community of the saints is a contradiction, for every Christian is a member of Christ's body. In reference to the God, Christians are saints (*hágioi* [40]); in reference to one another, they are brothers (*adelphoí* [80]); in reference to Christ, they are members (*mélē* [3196]).

(VIII) In Paul's address to the elders of Miletus (Acts 20:28), we see the old Jewish *sunagōgḗ* in the process of passing into the more distinctly Christian *ekklēsía*. He alludes to Ps 74:2, "Remember thy congregation which thou hast purchased of old," but for the Sept. *sunagōgḗ* he uses *ekklēsía*. Thus in the apostle's hands this passage became one of the channels through which the word *ekklēsía* came to denote God's people in their new and final corporate form.

Deriv.: *aposunágōgos* (656), put out of the synagogue; *archisunágōgos* (752), ruler of the synagogue.

Syn.: *ekklēsía* (1577), church, assembly.

4865. συναγωνίζομαι *sunagōnízomai*; fut. *sunagōnísomai*, from *sún* (4862), together, and *agōnízomai* (75), to strive, contend for victory, as in the public games. To fight in company with, assist or help to fight (Rom 15:30). The word is chosen with reference to the opposers from whom the apostle desired to be delivered (15:31), not like *agōnízomai* (Col 4:12). Neither words are to be thought of as wrestling with God (Gen 32:22–32), but rather a wrestling together against the powers of darkness (Eph 6:12).

Syn.: *sunathléō* (4866), to wrestle in company with, strive together.

Ant.: *antagonízomai* (464), to antagonize.

4866. συναθλέω *sunathléō*; fut. *sunathlṓ*, from *sún* (4862), together or together with and *athléō* (118), to strive. To contend with someone, be on his side; only figuratively, to exert oneself with, to strive with or together, help, aid. With a dat. of the thing following, to strive together for (Phil 1:27); with the dat. of person following, to strive or labor together with (Phil 4:3).

Syn.: *sunagōnízomai* (4865), to help to fight.

Ant.: *antagonízomai* (464), to antagonize.

4867. συναθροίζω *sunathroízō*; fut. *sunathroísō*, from *sún* (4862), together, and *athroízō* (n.f.), to hoard, gather. To gather together. Of persons, to gather together, assemble, with the acc. (Acts 19:25; Sept.: 2 Sam 2:30; 1 Kgs 18:19); in the pass. (Luke 24:33; Acts 12:12; Sept.: 2 Sam 2:25). Also from *athroízō* (n.f.): *epathroízō* (1865), to crowd together.

Syn.: *sunágō* (4863), to gather or bring together; *episunágō* (1996), to gather together into one place; *sullégō* (4816), to collect, gather up or together; *trugáō* (5166), to gather in a harvest.

Ant.: *skorpízō* (4650), to disperse; *dias-korpízō* (1287), to scatter abroad; *diaspeírō* (1289), to sow or scatter abroad.

4868. συναίρω *sunaírō*; fut. *sunarṓ*, from *sún* (4862), together with, and *aírō* (142), to take. To take up with someone the matter of a debt which is owed, to resolve or settle. In the NT, in the pres. inf. *sunaírein* (Matt 18:24); in the aor. inf. *sunárai* (Matt 18:23); in the indic. (Matt 25:19); followed by *lógon* (the acc. of *lógos* [3056], account, word), meaning to take up an account with someone for adjustment, to reckon or compute (Matt 18:23; 25:19).

Syn.: *logízomai* (3049), to calculate, reckon; *sullogízomai* (4817), to reason together, deliberate.

Ant.: *antitássomai* (498), to set one-self against, oppose; *anthístēmi* (436), to stand against, oppose.

4869. συναιχμάλωτος *sunaichmálōtos*; gen. *sunaichmalótou*, masc.-fem., neut. *sunaichmáloton*, adj. from *sún* (4862), together with, and *aichmálōtos* (164), a prisoner of war. Used subst., a fellow prisoner (Rom 16:7; Col 4:10; Phile 1:23).

4870. συνακολουθέω *sunakolouthéō*; contracted *sunakolouthó*, fut. *sunakolouthḗsō*, from *sún* (4862), together, and *akolouthéō* (190), to follow. To go together, to follow with, accompany, with a dat. (Mark 5:37; Luke 23:49).
    Syn.: *propémpō* (4311), to escort, accompany; *sumporeúomai* (4848), to journey together; *sunérchomai* (4905), to go with, accompany; *sunodeúō* (4922), to travel in company with.
    Ant.: *egkataleípō* (1459), to desert, forsake, leave behind; *perileípō* (4035), to survive, remain.

4871. συναλίζω *sunalízō*; fut. *sunalísō*, from *sún* (4862), together, and *halízō* (233), to throng, collect, gather. To gather a throng together, to assemble; in the pass. (Acts 1:4 [cf. 1:6]).
    Syn.: *sunágō* (4863), to assemble; *sunérchomai* (4905), to come together; *episunágō* (1996), to gather together in one place.
    Ant.: *skorpízō* (4650), to scatter.

4872. συναναβαίνω *sunanabaínō*; fut. *sunanabḗsomai*, 2d aor. *sunanébēn*, from *sún* (4862), together with, and *anabaínō* (305) to go up. To go up with someone from a lower to a higher part of a country, with a dat. (Mark 15:41; Acts 13:31; Sept.: Ex 12:38); with *metá* (3326), with (Sept.: Gen 50:9; Ex 33:3).
    Syn.: *sumporeúomai* (4848), to go with; *sunodeúō* (4922), to travel in company with.
    Ant.: *sugkatabaínō* (4782), to descend in company with, to go down with.

4873. συνανάκειμαι *sunanákeimai*; fut. *sunanakeísomai*, from *sún* (4862), together with, and *anákeimai* (345), to recline at a table. To recline with someone at a table, to eat or dine with, with a dat. (Matt 9:10, to sit together to eat; Mark 2:15; Luke 14:10; John 12:2). Part. used as a subst., *hoi sunanakeímenoi*, meaning guests (Matt 14:9; Mark 6:22, 26; Luke 7:49; 14:15).
    Syn.: *sugkáthēmai* (4775), to sit with; *sugkathízō* (4776), to sit together.
    Ant.: *sunegeírō* (4891), to raise, rise up together.

4874. συναναμίγνυμι *sunanamígnumi*; fut. *sunanamíxō*, from *sún* (4862), together or with, and *anamígnumi* (n.f.), to mix together, which is from *aná* (303), on, upon, and *mígnumi* (3396), to mix. To mix together. Pass. or mid, to mingle together, have fellowship or keep company with, with a dat. (1 Cor 5:9, 11; 2 Thess 3:14; Sept.: Hos 7:8).
    Syn.: *koinōnéō* (2841), to share with; *anastréphomai* (390), to have conversation or communication.
    Ant.: *ekklínō* (1578), to avoid, shun; *chōrízomai* (5563), to separate oneself.

4875. συναναπαύω *sunanapaúō*; fut. *sunanapaúsō*, from *sún* (4862), together, with, and *anapaúō* (373), to refresh or take rest. Only occurs in the mid., to refresh oneself or be refreshed with someone, in his company, with the dat. (Rom 15:32).
    Ant.: *sunergéō* (4903), to work together, be a fellow worker.

4876. συναντάω *sunantáō*; fut. *sunantḗsō*, from *sún* (4862), with, and *antáō* (n.f., see *katantáō* [2658]), to meet. To meet with someone, to come together, encounter.
    (I) With the dat. (Luke 9:37; 22:10; Acts 10:25; Heb 7:1, 10; Sept.: Gen 32:1, 17; Num 23:16).
    (II) Figuratively of things or events to happen to someone, befall, with the dat.

(Acts 20:22; Sept.: Eccl 2:14; 9:11, in the mid.).

Deriv.: *sunántēsis* (4877), a meeting with, the act of meeting.

Syn.: *paratugchánō* (3909), to happen to be near or present.

4877. συνάντησις *sunántēsis*; gen. *sunantéseōs*, fem. noun from *sunantáō* (4876), to meet. A meeting with, an encounter. In the NT, only in the phrase *eis sunántēsin* (*eis* [1519], for the purpose of; the acc. *sunántēsin*, used for the inf. *sunantán*, to meet with), for the purpose of meeting together, with a dat. (Matt 8:34; Sept.: Gen 14:17; Ex 18:7).

Syn.: *hupántēsis* (5222), encounter; *apántēsis* (529), a meeting or an official welcome of a newly arrived dignitary.

4878. συναντιλαμβάνομαι *sunantilambánomai* fut. *sunantilépsomai*, from *sún* (4862), together, and *antilambánō* (482), to support, help. Only occurs in the mid., to assist someone, to help, aid, with the dat. (Luke 10:40; Rom 8:26; Sept.: Ex 18:22; Ps 89:22).

Syn.: *boēthéō* (997), to come to the aid of someone; *sunergéō* (4903), to help in work, cooperate.

Ant.: *kōlúō* (2967), to hinder.

4879. συναπάγω *sunapágō*; fut. *sunapáxō*, from *sún* (4862), together, and *apágō* (520), to lead or carry away. To lead off or carry away with someone, with the dat. of person (Sept.: Ex 14:6). In the NT, only in the pass. figuratively, to be led or carried away with something, mostly in a bad sense, meaning to be led astray, with the dat. (Gal 2:13; 2 Pet 3:17); in a good sense (Rom 12:16, not minding high things but led by lowly things, which means cultivating humility).

Syn.: *planáō* (4105), to lead astray; *apoplanáō* (635), to cause to go astray; *apophérō* (667), to carry away; *apatáō* (538), to deceive; *exapatáō* (1818), to beguile completely.

4880. συναποθνήσχω *sunapothnḗskō*; 2d aor. *sunapéthanon*, from *sún* (4862), together, and *apothnḗskō* (599), to die. To die with someone, with a dat. (Mark 14:31; 2 Cor 7:3). Figuratively of dying spiritually with Christ (2 Tim 2:11).

Syn.: *sunapóllumi* (4881), to perish with.

Ant.: *sunegeírō* (4891), to raise up together; *suzáō* (4800), to live with.

4881. συναπόλλυμι *sunapóllumi*; fut. *sunapolésō*, from *sún* (4862), together or with, and *apóllumi* (622), to destroy. To destroy together, with the acc. and dat. (Sept.: Gen 18:23). In the mid. or pass., to be destroyed with someone, perish with others, with the dat. (Heb 11:31; Sept.: Gen 19:15).

Syn.: *sunapothnḗskō* (4880), to die with someone.

4882. συναποστέλλω *sunapostéllō*; fut. *sunapostelṓ*, from *sún* (4862), together or with, and *apostéllō* (649), to send. To send with someone, with the acc. and with the dat. implied (2 Cor 12:18; Sept.: Ex 33:2, 12).

Syn.: *sumpémpō* (4842), to send with.

4883. συναρμολογέω *sunarmologéō*; contracted *sunarmologṓ*, fut. *sunarmologḗsō*, from *sún* (4862), together, and *harmologéō* (n.f.), to join together, which is from *harmós* (719), joint and *lógos* (3056), word, account, reckoning. To fit or frame together. In the pass. (Eph 2:21; 4:16).

Syn.: *sunistáō* (4921), to set together.

Ant.: *lúō* (3089), to loose, set apart; *dialúō* (1262), to dissolve utterly.

4884. συναρπάζω *sunarpázō*; fut. *sunarpásō*, from *sún* (4862), an intens., or together with, and *harpázō* (726), to take, seize. To seize or catch or grasp with great violence. Stronger than the basic verb *harpázō*; the same difference exists between *sullambánō* (4815), to seize with force and violence, and *lambánō* (2983), simply to take. Of persons, a multitude or mob seizing individuals, with the acc. (Acts 6:12; 19:29). Of a demon, violently seizing one possessed (Luke 8:29; Sept.: Prov 6:25). Of things as a ship caught by a tempest, in the pass. (Acts 27:15).

Syn.: *harpázō* (726), to seize.

Ant.: *apolúō* (630), to release, set at liberty.

4885. συναυξάνω *sunauxánō*; fut. *sunauxḗsō*, from *sún* (4862), together with, and *auxánō* (837), to grow with, increase, enlarge. In the NT, in the mid. *sunauxánonai*, intrans., to grow up together (Matt 13:30).

Syn.: *sumphúō* (4855), to grow with.

4886. σύνδεσμος *súndesmos*; gen. *sundésmou*, masc. noun from *sundéō* (4887), to join together. That which binds together, a band, bond. A tendon or ligament of the bones (Col 2:19). Figuratively (Eph 4:3; Col 3:14; Sept.: Dan 5:6, 13). One enslaved by a habit or attitude (Acts 8:23).

4887. συνδέω *sundéō*; fut. *sundḗsō*, from *sún* (4862), together or with, and *déō* (1210), to bind. To bind together or with. In the NT, of persons, to bind together with; in the pass. to be bound or in bonds with someone, with the dat. implied (Heb 13:3), in the part. *sundedeménoi*, fellow prisoners.

Deriv.: *súndesmos* (4886), a band, bond.

4888. συνδοξάζω *sundoxázō*; fut. *sundoxásō*, from *sún* (4862), together, and *doxázō* (1392), to glorify. To glorify together (Rom 8:17).

4889. σύνδουλος *súndoulos*; gen. *sundoúlou*, masc. noun from *sún* (4862), together, and *doúlos* (1401), slave. A fellow slave who is found in the same conditions as another (Matt 18:28, 29, 31, 33; 24:49); a servant of the same Lord (Col 1:7; 4:7; Rev 6:11); used of angels (Rev 19:10; 22:9).

4890. συνδρομή *sundromḗ*; gen. *sundromḗs*, fem. noun from *suntréchō* (4936), to run together. A running together or subscribing to (Acts 21:30).

Ant.: *antíthesis* (477), opposition; *stásis* (4714), controversy, dissension.

4891. συνεγείρω *sunegeírō*; fut. *sunegerṓ*, from *sún* (4862), together, and *egeírō* (1453), to raise. To raise together. In the NT, it occurs only in Eph 2:6 where our being raised up together with Christ is referred to. The revivification by Christ of believers refers to delivery from spiritual death wrought by sin (Rom 6:4, 9). The *sún*, together, in *sunegeírō*, is not to be understood as referring to similarity as though it only meant "like." Rather, it points to a condition or work effected by union with Christ in His resurrection, taking place in and proceeding from it. Baptism, being the sign and seal of salvation, testifies of its work (Rom 6:4). It has a similar meaning in Col 2:12; 3:1. Practically, the meaning coincides with being justified (Rom 4:25; 5:1; Col 2:12, 13).

Ant.: *sunapothnḗskō* (4880), to die with; *suntháptō* (4916), to bury with.

4892. συνέδριον *sunédrion*; gen. *sunedríou*, neut. noun from *súnedros* (n.f.), a counselor. An assembly, council. In the NT, spoken only of Jewish councils.

(I) The Sanhedrin or Sanhedrim, the supreme council of the Jewish nation composed of 70 members (besides the high priest), in imitation of the seventy elders appointed by Moses (Num 11:16ff.). The members were selected from the chief priests, former high priests, and the chief priests or heads of the twenty-four courses or divisions, elders (*presbúteroi* [4245]), and scribes (*grammateís* [1122]) or lawyers (*nomikoí* [3544]). The high priest who was serving at the time acted as ex-officio president. A vice president sat at his right hand. The Sanhedrin dealt with all important matters, both civil and religious, apparently meeting in a hall not far from the temple called by Josephus *boulé* (1012) or *bouleutérion* (it is interesting that parliament in Greece today is called *boulé*). On extraordinary occasions they were sometimes convened in the high priest's palace (Matt 26:3, 57). Under the Romans the right of capital punishment was taken away (John 18:31), though they might aid in carrying a sentence to execution (John 19:6, 16). References to *sunédrion* are in Matt 5:22; 26:59; Mark 14:55; 15:1; John 11:47; Acts 5:21, 27, 34, 41; 22:30; 23:1, 15, 20, 28; 24:20. Some references include the place of meeting, the Sanhedrin as sitting in its hall (Luke 22:66; Acts 4:15; 6:12, 15; 23:6).

(II) A council, tribunal, the smaller tribunals in the cities of Palestine subordinate to the Sanhedrin (cf. Deut 16:18; 2 Chr 19:5). These consisted of twenty-three judges, but Josephus expressly says the number was seven when reference is made to the word "judgment [*krísis* {2920}]" as in Matt 5:21, 22. This refers to crimes that justified the bringing of the accused before these lower courts known as councils (*sunédria*) in the pl. (Matt 10:17; Mark 13:9).

Syn.: *sumboúlion* (4824), consultation or a council.

4893. συνείδησις *suneídēsis*; gen. *suneidéseōs*, fem. noun from *suneídō* (4894), to be conscious of. Conscience, to be one's own witness, one's own conscience coming forward as witness. It denotes an abiding consciousness whose nature it is to bear inner witness to one's own conduct in a moral sense (Titus 1:15). It is self-awareness.

(I) Particularly, a knowing of oneself, consciousness; and hence conscience, that faculty of the soul which distinguishes between right and wrong and prompts one to choose the former and avoid the latter (John 8:9; Rom 2:15; 9:1; 13:5; 1 Cor 10:25, 27, 28, 29; 2 Cor 1:12; 1 Tim 4:2; Titus 1:15; Heb 9:9, 14; 10:2, 22). Used with various adj., e.g., *suneídēsis agathé* (*agathé* [18], intrinsically good),

a good conscience, consciousness of right, rectitude (Acts 23:1; 1 Tim 1:5, 19; 1 Pet 3:16, 21); *suneídēsis kalé* (*kalé* [2570], pragmatically good [Heb 13:18], while *agathé* has also the meaning of choosing what one knows is right, benevolent); *suneídēsis kathará* (*kathará* [2513], clean), a pure conscience (1 Tim 3:9; 2 Tim 1:3, which does not condemn one); *suneídēsis apróskopos* (*apróskopos* [677], inoffensive, not leading into sin), a conscience void of offense (Acts 24:16); *suneídēsis asthenés* (*asthenés* [772], weak, without strength, or in a part. form, *asthenoúsa* [770], to be without strength), a conscience which is weak and hesitant in judging and deciding (1 Cor 8:7, 10, 12); *suneídēsis toú Theoú* (*Theoú* [2316], of God), meaning a conscience toward God, conforming to His will (1 Pet 2:19); *suneídēsis toú eidólou* (*eidólou* [1497], of an idol), meaning a conscience over which the idol has sway, and indicating a weak conscience (1 Cor 8:7).

(II) Used metonymically meaning a person (2 Cor 4:2, to commend oneself to every man; 5:11).

Though not a synonym, the related term *súnesis* (4907), perception, understanding, the ability to understand concepts and see relationships between them, should be distinguished from *suneídēsis*. *Súnesis* is the moral awareness which generally precedes action. However, in the NT there is something of the meaning of *súnesis* in *suneídēsis*. The latter is a moral awareness that springs from and is conditioned by one's knowledge of God and his duties to Him (Rom 1:19, 21, 32; 2:15; 9:1; 2 Cor 1:12; Heb 9:9; 10:2). Accordingly it has the duty of confirming the truth of divine saving revelation designed to meet and satisfy man's religious need (2 Cor 4:2; 5:11; Heb 9:9, 14). Thus conscience is the testimony of the Spirit in man's heart concerning his obligation to God (Acts 23:1; 24:16; 1 Tim 1:5, 19; 3:9; 2 Tim 1:3; Heb 9:9, 14; 10:2). The stain of sin upon the conscience necessitates its purification (Heb 9:14; Heb 10:22).

Syn.: *élegchos* (1650), conviction.

4894. συνείδω *suneídō*; 2d aor. *suneídon*, perf. *súnoida* (but in the pres. sense), from *sún* (4862), together, and *eídō* (1492), to know. To be privy to, to be aware or conscious of, to consider. The word used by Paul in 1 Cor 4:4 is equal to being aware of nothing against oneself.
    Deriv.: *suneídēsis* (4893)
    Ant.: *agnoéō* (50), to be ignorant, not understand.

4895. σύνειμι *súneimi*; fut. *sunésomai*, from *sún* (4862), together, and *eimí* (1510), to be. To be with, with the dat. (Luke 9:18; Acts 22:11).
    Syn.: *sunérchomai* (4905), to come together; *sumparagínomai* (4836), to come together, to stand at one's side.

4896. σύνειμι *súneimi*; from *sún* (4862), together, and *eími* (n.f., see *ápeimi* [549]), to go, come, bring. Only in the part. *suniṓn*, to gather together, convene, bring together. Equal to *suníēmi* (4920), to perceive, understand. Used in an absolute sense (Mark 7:18; Luke 8:4).
    Syn.: *sunágō* (4863), to gather or bring together; *episunágō* (1996), to gather together; *sullégō* (4816), to collect or gather up; *sunathroízō* (4867), to gather together. In a figurative sense of perceiving, understanding: *noéō* (3539), to perceive with the mind; *ginṓskō* (1097), to know experientially; *epístamai* (1987), to know well; *punthánomai* (4441), to understand by searching or inquiring; *gnōrízō* (1107), to make known, to come to know; *manthánō* (3129), understand, learn.
    Ant.: *agnoéō* (50), to be ignorant, not understand.

4897. συνεισέρχομαι *suneisérchomai*; 2d aor. *suneisélthon*, from *sún* (4862), together or with, and *eisérchomai* (1525), to enter in. To go or come in with someone, to enter with, with the dat. (John 18:15). Spoken of a boat, to embark with, with the dat. (John 6:22).

4898. συνέκδημος *sunékdēmos*; gen. *sunekdḗmou*, masc.-fem., neut. *sunék-*dēmon, adj. from *sún* (4862), together or with, and *ékdēmos* (n.f.), one who is absent or a traveler, which is from *ek* (1537), from and *démos* (1218), people, the public. Absent or traveling; as a subst., a fellow traveler in foreign countries (Acts 19:29; 2 Cor 8:19). Also from *ékdēmos* (n.f.): *ekdēméō* (1553), to go away or abroad.
    Syn.: *apódēmos* (590), immigrant, a foreign traveler.

4899. συνεκλεκτός *suneklektós*; fem. *suneklektḗ*, neut. *suneklektón*, adj. from *sún* (4862), together, together with, and *eklektós* (1588), elect, chosen. Chosen with others; as a subst. fellow elect (1 Pet 5:13). There are some who consider *suneklektḗ* to be a reference to the wife of Peter.

4900. συνελαύνω *sunelaúnō*; fut. *sunelásō*, from *sún* (4862), together, together with, and *elaúnō* (1643), to drive. To drive together into one place, of wild beasts or persons. Figuratively, to impel or persuade together, with the acc. (Acts 7:26, with the meaning of to compel).

4901. συνεπιμαρτυρέω *sunepimarturéō*; contracted *sunepimarturṓ*, fut. *sunepimarturḗsō*, from *sún* (4862), together with or at the same time, and *epimarturéō* (1957), to testify or bear witness to. To bear further witness with someone, attest, with the instrument of means (Heb 2:4).
    Ant.: *katamarturéō* (2649), to testify against.

4902. συνέπομαι *sunépomai*; imperf. *suneipómēn*, mid. deponent from *sún* (4862), with, and *hépomai* (n.f.), to follow, accompany. To follow with, accompany, with a dat. (Acts 20:4).
    Syn.: *sunakolouthéō* (4870), to accompany.

4903. συνεργέω *sunergéō*; contracted *sunergṓ*, fut. *sunergḗsō*, from *sunergós* (4904), fellow worker. To work together with someone, cooperate, be a co-worker, fellow laborer (1 Cor 16:16; 2 Cor 6:1). Hence, generally it means to help, aid, with the dat. expressed or implied (Mark 16:20; James 2:22). Of things, to work together for something, cooperate, contribute to an end or a goal, followed by a dat. and *eis* (1519), unto, with the acc. (Rom 8:28).

Syn.: *sullambánō* (4815), to assist; *antilambánomai* (482), to help; *sunantilambánomai* (4878), to have a share in or to assist; *boēthéō* (997), to come to the aid of someone; *sunupourgéō* (4943), to be a co-worker under someone.

Ant.: *argéō* (691), to be idle; *scholázō* (4980), to be at leisure.

4904. συνεργός sunergós; gen. *sunergoú*, masc.-fem., neut. *sunergón*, adj. from *sún* (4862), together with, and *érgon* (2041), work. Fellow laborer or worker, helper. In the NT, spoken only of a co-worker or helper in the Christian work; of Christian teachers with the gen. of person., co-workers of God (1 Cor 3:9). "My co-workers" (a.t.), meaning those of Paul (Rom 16:3, 9, 21; Phil 2:25; 4:3; 1 Thess 3:2; Phile 1:1, 24). With the gen. of the obj. (2 Cor 1:24, meaning co-workers of your joy, laboring together for your happiness). Followed by the dat. (3 John 1:8, co-workers for the sake of truth); by *eis* (1519), unto, with the acc., for or on behalf of (2 Cor 8:23; Col 4:11).

Deriv.: *sunergéō* (4903), to be a fellow worker.

Syn.: *boēthós* (998), a helper.

Ant.: *antídikos* (476), adversary, opponent.

4905. συνέρχομαι sunérchomai; fut. *suneleúsomai*, 2d aor. *sunélthon*, from *sún* (4862), together with or together, and *érchomai* (2064), to come. To go or come with someone, to meet together.

(I) With the dat. of person., to go or come with, accompany (Luke 23:55; John 11:31, 33; Acts 9:39; 10:23, 45; 11:12; 15:38). Also to accompany (Acts 1:21). With *sún* (4862), together, to come

together with someone (Acts 21:16; Sept.: Job 22:4).

(II) Generally and usually, to come together, convene, assemble (Mark 3:20; Luke 5:15; Acts 1:6; 2:6; 10:27; 16:13; 19:32; 21:22; 28:17; 1 Cor 14:26). With the dat. of person., with or to whom (Mark 14:53); with adv. of place such as *hópou* (3699), where (John 18:20), or *entháde* (1759), here (Acts 25:17). As marking result (1 Cor 11:17, 34); with *eis* (1519), unto, with the acc. of place (Acts 5:16); *en* (1722), in, with the dat. (1 Cor 11:18); *epí tó autó* (*epí* [1909], upon; *tó* neut. def. art.; *autó*, the neut. of *autós* [846], same), at the same place (1 Cor 11:20; 14:23); *prós* (4314), toward (Mark 6:33; Sept.: Ex 32:5; 2 Chr 30:13; Jer 3:18; Ezek 33:30; Zech 8:21).

(III) Spoken of conjugal intercourse (Matt 1:18; 1 Cor 7:5).

Syn.: *sunágō* (4863), to assemble, gather together; *episunágō* (1996), to gather together; *sunalízō* (4871), to convene or assemble.

Ant.: *skorpízō* (4650), to scatter; *diaskorpízō* (1287), scatter abroad, disperse; *diaspeírō* (1289), to scatter abroad.

4906. συνεσθίω sunesthíō; 2d aor. *sunéphagon*, from *sún* (4862), together with, and *esthíō* (2068), to eat. To eat with someone, have communion with, dine with, with the dat. (Luke 15:2; 1 Cor 5:11; Gal 2:12; Sept.: Gen 43:32; Ex 18:12; Ps 101:5). Forms of *phágō* occur in Acts 10:41; 11:3.

Syn.: *metalambánō* (3335), to take a part, share; *sumphágō* (4906), to eat with.

4907. σύνεσις súnesis; gen. *sunéseōs*, fem. noun from *suníēmi* (4920), to comprehend, reason out. Comprehension, perception, understanding. The word denotes the ability to understand concepts and see relationships between them (Luke 2:47; 1 Cor 1:19; Eph 3:4; Col 1:9; 2:2; 2 Tim 2:7; Sept.: Ex 31:3; Deut 4:6; Job 15:2; Prov 2:2; Isa 29:14). Metonymically as a faculty of the mind, understanding, put for the mind itself (Mark 12:33).

Syn.: *diánoia* (1271), understanding; *phrḗn* (5424), mind, mental restraint; *phrónesis* (5428), prudence; *sophía* (4678), wisdom.

Ant.: *mōría* (3472), foolishness; *aphrosúnē* (877), senselessness, foolishness, folly.

4908. **συνετός** *sunetós*; fem. *sunetḗ*, neut. *sunetón*, adj. from *suníēmi* (4920), to reason out, perceive, understand. Intelligent, sagacious, discerning. Having *súnesis* (4907), comprehension (Matt 11:25; Luke 10:21; Acts 13:7; 1 Cor 1:19; Sept.: Gen 41:33; 1 Chr 15:22; Prov 28:7; Eccl 9:11; Isa 19:11).
Deriv.: *asúnetos* (801), unwise, without discernment or understanding.
Syn.: *phrónimos* (5429), discreet, prudent; *sophós* (4680), wise.
Ant.: *áphrōn* (878), without reason or mental restraints, foolish; *anóetos* (453), foolish, without understanding; *mōrós* (3474), stupid, foolish; *ánoia* (454), without understanding.

4909. **συνευδοκέω** *suneudokéō*; contracted *suneudokṓ*, fut. *suneuokḗsō*, from *sún* (4862), together with, and *eudokéō* (2106), to think well. To take pleasure with others, hence, to approve, assent to, with the dat. of person (Rom 1:32). Elsewhere with dat. of thing, in or as to which (Luke 11:48; Acts 8:1; 22:20). Followed by the inf., to be like-minded, well-pleased to do something (1 Cor 7:12, 13, which means if both parties in a marriage are mutually pleased).
Syn.: *sugkatatíthēmai* (4784), to consent; *súmphēmi* (4852), to express agreement with.
Ant.: *diïstēmi* (1339), to dissent; *dicházō* (1369), to be at variance; *diaphérō* (1308), to bear apart, to differ.

4910. **συνευωχέω** *suneuōchéō*; contracted *suneuōchṓ*, fut. *suneuōchḗsō*, from *sún* (4862), together with, and *euōchéō* (n.f.), to be well fed, to feast, which is from *eu* (2095), well, and *échō* (2192), to have sustenance. To feast together. In the

mid. / pass., to feast or revel with someone, with the dat. (2 Pet 2:13; Jude 1:12).

4911. **συνεφίστημι** *sunephístēmi*, fut. *sunepistḗsō*, from *sún* (4862), together, and *ephístēmi* (2186), to come upon as either a friend or an enemy, assault. In the NT, only in the 2d aor., *sunepéstēn*, intrans. meaning to assail together, and with *katá* (2596), against (Acts 16:22, made an assault together against them; Sept.: Num 16:3).

4912. **συνέχω** *sunéchō*; fut. *sunéxō*, from *sún* (4862), an intens., and *échō* (2192), to have. To hold fast, to press together; trans.:
(I) Particularly, to plug one's ears (Acts 7:57); the mouth (Sept.: Isa 52:15); of a city besieged (Luke 19:43; Sept.: 1 Sam 23:8); of a crowd, to press together (Luke 8:45); of persons having a prisoner in custody, to hold fast (Luke 22:63).
(II) Figuratively, to constrain, compel, press on, with the acc. (2 Cor 5:14); in the TR, pass. *sunéchomai*, to be in constraint, distressed, perplexed, used in an absolute sense (Luke 12:50; Phil 1:23). With the meaning of to be seized, affected, afflicted, with the dat.; with fear (Luke 8:37); with diseases (Matt 4:24; Luke 4:38; Acts 28:8; Sept. Job 3:24; 31:23). Pass., spoken also of a person held fast, pressed, occupied or the like (Acts 18:5, Paul was compelled or constrained to preach "Jesus Christ, and him crucified").
Deriv.: *sunochḗ* (4928), a holding together, a shutting up of the womb.
Syn.: *thlíbō* (2346), to distress, afflict; *piézō* (4885), to press down together; *anagkázō* (315), to compel; *parabiázō* (3849), to constrain.
Ant.: *apolúō* (630), to release; *eleutheróō* (1659), to set free; *apallássō* (525), to free from, release.

4913. **συνήδομαι** *sunḗdomai*; fut. *sunēsthḗsomai*, pass. deponent from *sún* (4862), with, and *hḗdomai* (n.f.), to be pleased. To joy or rejoice with someone. With the dat. of thing, to delight in something with others (Rom 7:22, "I delight in the law," I am one of those who delight in it). Others attribute to it the meaning of inward satisfaction.

4914. συνήθεια *sunḗtheia*; gen. *sunētheías*, fem. noun from *sunḗthēs* (n.f.), accustomed, common, which is from *sún* (4862), with, and *ḗthos* (2239), a custom. A custom or common practice (John 18:39; 1 Cor 11:16).
Syn.: *ḗthos* (1485), habit, custom, manner; *agōgḗ* (72), manner of life; *anastrophḗ* (391), way of life.

4915. συνηλικιώτης *sunēlikiṓtēs*; gen. *sunēlikiṓtou*, masc. noun from *sún* (4862), together, and *hēlikiṓtēs* (n.f.), one of the same age, which is from *hēlikía* (2244), age. A contemporary or one of the same age (Gal 1:14).
Ant.: *presbúteros* (4245), elder; *neṓteros*, younger.

4916. συνθάπτω *sunthápto*; fut. *sunthápso*, from *sún* (4862), together with, and *tháptō* (2290), to bury. To bury with someone. Burial with Christ refers to participating in His death by virtue of union with Him, with the dat. and pass. (Rom 6:4; Col 2:12).
Ant.: *sunegeírō* (4891), to raise together.

4917. συνθλάω *sunthláō*; fut. *sunthlásō*, from *sún* (4862), together with or an intens., and *thláō* (n.f.), to break or crush. To crush together, dash to pieces. Pass. (Matt 21:44; Luke 20:18; Sept.: Ps 58:7; 107:16; Isa 45:2).
Syn.: *suntríbō* (4937), to shatter, break into pieces by crushing; *sunthrúptō* (4919), to crush, crumble or fragment; *thraúō* (2352), to crush.
Ant.: *katartízō* (2675), to mend, restore; *apokathístēmi* (600) or *apokathistánō*, to restore to a former condition; *sunarmologéō* (4883), to fit or frame together.

4918. συνθλίβω *sunthlíbō*; fut. *sunthlípsō*, from *sún* (4862), an intens., and *thlíbō* (2346), to press. To press together, press closely on all sides as a crowd upon a person, with the acc. (Mark 5:24, 31).
Syn.: *sumpnígō* (4846), to choke, throng; *sunéchō* (4912), to press; *piézō* (4085), to pack or press down.

4919. συνθρύπτω *sunthrúptō*; fut. *sunthrúpsō*, from *sún* (4862), an intens., and *thrúptō* (n.f.), to crumble, crush, break in pieces. To break, crush together into pieces, figuratively to crush the spirit, break the heart, dishearten, take away one's courage (Acts 21:13). Also from *thrúptō* (n.f.): *truphḗ* (5172), delicate living, self-indulgence.
Syn.: *katakláō* (2622), to break or cut into pieces; *suntríbō* (4937), to shatter; *sunthláō* (4917), to crush or break into pieces.
Ant.: *apokathístēmi* (600) or *apokathistánō*, to restore to a former condition; *katartízō* (2675), to mend, restore; *sunarmologéō* (4883), to fit or frame together.

4920. συνίημι *suníēmi*; fut. *sunḗsō*, aor. *sunḗka*, from *sún* (4862), together or together with, and *híēmi* (n.f., see *iós* [2447]), to send or put. To comprehend, understand, perceive.

The comprehending activity of the mind denoted by *suníēmi* entails the assembling of individual facts into an organized whole, as collecting the pieces of a puzzle and putting them together. The mind grasps concepts and sees the proper relationship between them. Such understanding includes the moral and religious awareness of man's heart (Mark 6:52; 8:17; Acts 28:27). The verb is seldom used with an obj. When the word is confined to the sphere of mental perception it means to hear, notice, perceive, recognize, understand, reason things out and make sense.

In the NT, generally to understand, comprehend. Used in an absolute sense (Matt 13:13–15, 19, 23; 15:10; Mark 4:12; 6:52; Luke 8:10; Acts 28:26, 27; Rom 15:21; 2 Cor 10:12, "are not wise," are not men of understanding). Followed by the acc. (Matt 13:51; Luke 2:50; 18:34; 24:45; Eph 5:17; Sept.: Prov 2:5, 9). Followed by *hóti* (3754), that (Matt 16:12; 17:13; Acts 7:25; Sept.: 2 Chr 34:12; Isa 6:9, 10; 43:10). To understand, be wise, in respect to duty toward God to be upright, righteous, godly (Rom 3:11 quoted from Ps 14:2; Sept.: Ps 2:10; Dan 11:35; 12:3).

Deriv.: *súnesis* (4907), understanding; *sunetós* (4908), a person who understands.

Syn.: *epístamai* (1987), to know well; *punthánomai* (4441), to understand as a result of inquiry; *phronéō* (5426), to think, understand; *eídō* (1492), to know intuitively; *ginōskō* (1097), to know; *epiginōskō* (1921), to fully perceive, discern; *diaginōskō* (1231), to know exactly, diagnose; *suneídō* (4894), to know intuitively, be conscious of.

Ant.: *agnoéō* (50), not to know, be ignorant.

4921. **συνίστημι** *sunístēmi* and **συνιστάνω** *sunistánō*, **συνιστάω** *sunistáō*; fut. *sustēsō*, from *sún* (4862), together with, and *hístēmi* (2476), to set, place, stand. Trans., meaning to cause to stand with; intrans., to stand with. *Sunistánō* and *sunistáō* are later forms of *sunístēmi*.

(I) Trans. in the pres., imperf., and aor. act., meaning to cause to stand with, to place together, place with or before someone.

(A) Of persons, to introduce, present to one's acquaintance for favorable notice; hence, to commend, present as worthy, with the acc. (2 Cor 3:1; 10:12, 18). With the acc. and dat. (Rom 16:1; 2 Cor 5:12). With *prós* (4314), toward, followed by the acc (2 Cor 4:2); pass. (2 Cor 12:11).

(B) Figuratively, to set forth with or before someone, to declare, show, make known and conspicuous, with the acc. (Rom 3:5; 5:8; 2 Cor 6:4; Gal 2:18). With

the acc. and inf. (2 Cor 7:11; Sept.: Job 28:23).

(II) Intrans., in the perf. and 2d aor. act., meaning to stand with, together.

(A) Particularly of persons, with a dat. (Luke 9:32; Sept.: 1 Sam 17:26).

(B) Figuratively, from the trans., meaning to join together parts into a whole, to constitute, create, bring into existence. In the NT, intrans. meaning to be constituted, created, to exist (Col 1:17; 2 Pet 3:5).

Deriv.: *sustatikós* (4956), commendatory.

Syn.: *dokimázō* (1381), to prove; *apodeíknumi* (584), to prove by demonstration; *epainéō* (1867), to commend.

Ant.: *anístēmi* (450), to stand against; *katakrínō* (2607), to condemn.

4922. **συνοδεύω** *sunodeúō*; fut. *sunodeúsō*, from *sún* (4862), together with, and *hodeúō* (3593), to journey. To be on the way with someone, to travel or journey with, with the dat. (Acts 9:7).

Syn.: *sumporeúomai* (4848), to travel together; *sunépomai* (4902), to accompany.

Ant.: *egkataleípō* (1459), to leave behind, forsake; *kataleípō* (2641), to leave behind; *aphíēmi* (863), to forsake; *apotássō* (657), to take leave of.

4923. **συνοδία** *sunodía*; gen. *sunodías*, fem. noun from *sún* (4862), together, and *hodós* (3598), a way. A company of travelers, caravan (Luke 2:44).

4924. **συνοικέω** *sunoikéō*; contracted *sunoikō*, fut. *sunoikēsō*, from *sún* (4862), together with, and *oikéō* (3611), to dwell. To dwell with someone, as husband and wife, cohabit (1 Pet 3:7).

4925. **συνοικοδομέω** *sunoikodoméō*; contracted *sunoikodomō*, fut. *sunoikodomēsō*, from *sún* (4862), together, and *oikodoméō* (3618), to build. To build in company with someone. With the dative, in the passive, figuratively to be built together with other Christians into a spiritual temple (Eph 2:22).

Ant.: *kathairéō* (2507), to demolish.

4926. **συνομιλέω** *sunomiléō*; contracted *sunomilô*, fut. *sunomilḗsō*, from *sún* (4862), together with, and *homiléō* (3656), to speak, converse. To converse or talk with, with the dat. (Acts 10:27).

Syn.: *sullaléō* (4814), to converse; *dialégomai* (1256), to discuss.

Ant.: *sigáō* (4601), to keep silent.

4927. **συνομορέω** *sunomoréō*; contracted *sunomorô*, fut. *sunomorḗsō*, from *sún* (4862), together, and *hómoros* (n.f.), bordering, adjoining, which is from *homoú* (3674), together, and *hóros* (n.f.), border. To border together, be contiguous with, with the dat. (Acts 18:7, adjoining).

4928. **συνοχή** *sunochḗ*; gen. *sunochḗs*, fem. noun from *sunéchō* (4912), to constrain, hold together. A holding together, a shutting up of the womb (Sept.: Prov 30:16); used of a besieged city (Sept.: Jer 52:3; Mic 5:1). Figuratively meaning distress, disquiet, anguish (Luke 21:25; 2 Cor 2:4; Sept.: Job 30:3; Ps 25:17).

Syn.: *anágkē* (318), need that causes distress.

Ant.: *anápausis* (372), rest; *ánesis* (425), relief, relaxation.

4929. **συντάσσω** *suntássō*, **συντάττω** *suntáttō*; fut. *suntáxō*, from *sún* (4862), an intens., and *tássō* or *táttō* (5021), to order. To arrange or set in order together. To arrange or set in order, to order, appoint, direct, with the dat. (Matt 26:19; 27:10; Sept.: Gen 18:19; 26:11).

Syn.: *horízō* (3724), to ordain; *anadeíknumi* (322), to appoint, show clearly; *kathístēmi* (2525), to ordain; *cheirotonéō* (5500), to appoint with the hand, vote by a showing of hands.

4930. **συντέλεια** *suntéleia*; gen. *sunteleías*, fem. noun from *sunteléō* (4931), to accomplish. A culmination or completion, the bringing together of an intended purpose. In the NT, used only in the expressions *suntéleia toú aiṓnos*, "the completion of the age," the consummation or accomplishment of its purposes. The word *aiṓn* (165), age, usually translated world, refers to a period of time (Matt 13:39, 40, 49; 24:3; 28:20) and *tṓn aiṓnōn*, means "of the ages" (Heb 9:26; Sept.: Neh 9:31; Jer 4:27; Dan 12:4).

Syn.: *télos* (5056), the end, goal; *éschatos* (2078), last, uttermost.

Ant.: *archḗ* (746), beginning, start.

4931. **συντελέω** *sunteléō*; contracted *suntelô*, fut. *suntelésō*, from *sún* (4862), together or an intens., and *teléō* (5055), to finish. To finish entirely, make an end of (Matt 7:28; Luke 4:13); of time (Luke 4:2; Acts 21:27; Sept.: Gen 2:2; Deut 34:8; 1 Kgs 6:9; Job 36:11); to accomplish, perform (Mark 13:4; Rom 9:28; Sept.: Isa 10:22); to put into effect (Heb 8:8).

Deriv.: *suntéleia* (4930), a finishing, consummation, end.

Syn.: *ekplēróō* (1603), to fulfill; *exartízō* (1822), to fit out, accomplish; *teleióō* (5048), to fulfill a goal or purpose; *gínomai* (1096), to come to pass; *diateléō* (1300), to bring through to an end; *sumplēróō* (4845), to fill completely; *epiteléō* (2005), to complete, accomplish; *plēróō* (4137), to fulfill, complete; *pímplēmi* or *plḗthō* (4130), to fill; *empíplēmi* or *emplḗthō* (1705), to make full, to satisfy; *ekteléō* (1615), to finish out, complete; *apoteléō* (658), to finish, bring to its goal; *poiéō* (4160), to do, fulfill; *katartízō* (2675), to render fit, complete.

4932. **συντέμνω** *suntémnō*; fut. *suntemô*, perf. *suntétmēka*, from *sún* (4862), an intens., and *témnō* (n.f., see *orthotoméō* [3718]), to cut or divide. To cut short, to contract by cutting; of words or actions, to make concise. Figuratively, to decide, determine, decree (Rom 9:28, "For His word He fulfills and He decrees in righteousness, for His word decreed will the Lord execute upon the land" [a.t.] a citation from Isa 10:22, 23 where the Hebr. reads, "Destruction is decreed, bringing in justice as a flood; for a decreed destruction does Jehovah of hosts execute"; Sept.: Isa 28:22; Dan 9:24, 26).

Deriv.: *suntómōs* (4935), concisely, briefly.

Syn.: *kolobóō* (2856), to curtail, shorten; *sustéllō* (4958), to contract, shorten.

Ant.: *parateínō* (3905), to prolong.

4933. **συντηρέω** *suntēréō*; contracted *suntērṓ*, fut. *suntērḗsō*, from *sún* (4862), an intens., and *tēréō* (5083), to guard, keep. To preserve, keep safe, close. In Luke 2:19, to keep carefully (referring to the words of the shepherds); contrast *diatēréō* (1301) in Luke 12:51. In Mark 6:20, used of the protection of John the Baptist from Herodias. In Matt 9:17; Luke 5:38 (in some MSS), used of the preservation of wineskins. See Dan 7:28.

Syn.: *phulássō* (5442), to preserve; *diaphulássō* (1314), to guard carefully; *kratéō* (2902), to hold fast.

Ant.: *anadídōmi* (325), to give up; *apodídōmi* (591), to give away; *katargéō* (2673), to abolish.

4934. **συντίθημι** *suntíthēmi*; fut. *suntithḗsō*, from *sún* (4862), together, and *títhēmi* (5087), to put, place. In the act., to set with or put together, compose. To set or put with a person, deliver to someone. In the NT, only in the mid., *suntíthemai*, to place together, to agree together, covenant with someone, followed by the inf. (Luke 22:5; Acts 23:20); by *hína* (2443), so that (John 9:22; Sept.: Dan 2:9). To assent (Acts 24:9).

Deriv.: *asúnthetos* (802), covenant-breaking, dishonorable, hence faithless.

Syn.: *sumphōnéō* (4856), to agree with; *sugkatatíthēmi* (4784), to consent.

4935. **συντόμως** *suntómōs*; adv. from *suntémnō* (4932), to cut short, execute speedily. Concisely, briefly, in few words (Acts 24:4).

Ant.: *aeí* (104), ever, regularly; the expression *eis tón aiṓna* (*aiṓna*, [165],

age), forever; *eis tó diēnekés* (*diēnekés* [1336], forever), continuously, perpetually; *adialeíptōs* (89), uninterruptedly, without ceasing.

4936. **συντρέχω** *suntréchō*; fut. *suntréxō*, 2d aor. *sunédramon*, from *sún* (4862), together, and *tréchō* (5143), to run. To run together with others, intrans. Figuratively, to fraternize, run around with, be in harmony with (1 Pet 4:4). Of a multitude, to run or flock together (Mark 6:33; Acts 3:11).

Deriv.: *episuntréchō* (1998), to run together to; *sundromḗ* (4890), a running together or subscribing to.

4937. **συντρίβω** *suntríbō*; fut. *suntrípsō*, from *sún* (4862), together or an intens., and *tríbō* (5147), to break, rub. To break, strike against something, crush together, or break in pieces.

(**I**) Particularly (Mark 5:4; 14:3; John 19:36; Rev 2:27; Sept.: Ex 12:46; Lev 6:28; 26:13). Of a reed, to break so as to have a flaw or crack (Matt 12:20, "a crushed reed shall he not break off" [a.t.] quoted from Isa 42:3).

(**II**) Figuratively, to break the strength or power of someone, to crush, weaken, with the acc. (Luke 9:39, weakens him, breaks him down [cf. Mark 9:18 where the word is *xēraínetai* {3583}, dries up]). Of Satan, to break or crush his power (Rom 16:20; Sept.: Josh 10:10; Amos 3:15). In the pass. (Luke 4:18, "the brokenhearted" [cf. Sept.: Ps 34:19; 51:19]).

Deriv.: *súntrimma* (4938), a breaking to pieces, a broken piece.

Syn.: *sunthláō* (4917), to break in pieces; *sunthrúptō* (4919), to weaken, break one's heart; *thraúō* (2352), to shatter, bruise.

Ant.: *katartízō* (2675), to mend, restore; *sunarmologéō* (4883), to fit together; *apokathístēmi* or *apokathistánō* (600), to restore.

4938. **σύντριμμα** *súntrimma*; gen. *suntrímmatos*, neut. noun from *suntríbō* (4937), to break into pieces, crush. A crushing, fracture, breaking to pieces, destruction (Sept.: Lev 21:19; Isa 30:14). Figuratively, destruction, decimation (Rom 3:16 quoted from Isa 59:7; see Isa 22:4; 60:18; Jer 8:21).

Syn.: *apóleia* (684), loss, destruction; *ólethros* (3639), ruin, destruction; *phthorá* (5356), corruption, destruction, ruin; *diaphthorá* (1312), decay, corruption.

Ant.: *apokatástasis* (605), reconstitution, restitution; *anakaínōsis* (342), renovation, renewing; *anástasis* (386), a resurrection, recovery.

4939. σύντροφος *súntrophos*; gen. *suntróphou*, masc.-fem., neut. *súntrophon*, adj. from *suntréphō* (n.f.), to bring up together, which is from *sún* (4862), together with, and *tréphō* (5142), to feed, nourish. Nourished or nursed together. Used as a subst., one brought up or educated with another, a comrade (Acts 13:1).

Syn.: *phílos* (5384), friend; *koinōnós* (2844), companion, friend.

Ant.: *antídikos* (476), adversary; *echthrós* (2190), foe, enemy.

4940. συντυγχάνω *suntugchánō*; fut. *sunteúxomai*, 2d aor. *sunétuchon*, from *sún* (4862), together with, and *tugchánō* (5177), to happen, chance, attain, obtain, gain. To fall in with, meet with, come to or near someone, with the dat. (Luke 8:19).

Syn.: *sunantáō* (4876), to meet with, befall; *apantáō* (528), to encounter, meet; *heurískō* (2147), to find; *entugchánō* (1793), to chance upon, deal with, make intercession; *epitugchánō* (2013), to chance upon, attain, obtain.

4941. Συντύχη *Suntúchē*; gen. *Suntúchēs*, fem. proper noun. Syntyche, meaning fortunate. A female member of the church at Philippi who is exhorted by Paul to be reconciled with *Euodía* ([2136] Phil 4:2). Those who maintain that there was an order of deaconesses in the apostolic church consider these women to be members of it, giving rise to the censure of their differences.

4942. συνυποκρίνομαι *sunupokrínomai*; fut. *sunupokrinoúmai*, mid. deponent from *sún* (4862), together with, and *hupokrínomai* (5271), to feign, pretend. Join in pretending, aor. pass. *sunupekríthēn*, in the mid. sense, to play the hypocrite with someone, to dissemble with, with a dat. (Gal 2:13).

4943. συνυπουργέω *sunupourgéō*; contracted *sunupourgó*, fut. *sunupourgésō*, from *sún* (4862), together, and *hupourgós* (n.f.), rendering service, which is from *hupó* (5259), and *érgō* (n.f.), to work. To serve, or work together under someone, with dat. of manner (2 Cor 1:11).

4944. συνωδίνω *sunōdínō*; fut. *sunōdínō*, from *sún* (4862), together, and *ōdínō* (5605), to be in pain, as a woman in labor. To be in travail together, to bring forth together. Figuratively to be in pain together, spoken in an absolute sense of creation (Rom 8:22).

Syn.: *sustenázō* (4959), to groan together.

Ant.: *sugchaírō* (4796), to rejoice with.

4945. συνωμοσία *sunōmosía*; gen. *sunōmosías*, fem. noun from *sunómnumi* (n.f.), to swear together, which is from *sún* (4862), together, and *omnúō* (3660), to take an oath, swear. A conspiracy (Acts 23:13).

Syn.: *epiboulḗ* (1917), a plot.

4946. Συρακούσαι *Surakoúsai*; gen. *Surakousōn*, fem. pl. proper noun. Syracuse. A noted city in the eastern part of Sicily at which Paul spent three days while on his voyage to Rome (Acts 28:12). It is well situated for commerce, having the best harbor in Sicily.

4947. Συρία *Suría*; gen. *Surías*, fem. proper noun. Syria. The Greek name for the country known to the Jews as Aram.

It may signify the region of Tyre. It included, in a stricter sense, only the highlands of Lebanon and Antilebanon, but in a more extended sense it reached to the Taurus Mountains on the north and across the Euphrates, eastward to the Tigris and the great desert, and westward to Phoenicia and the Mediterranean Sea. It was about 370 miles long and 150 miles wide, and may be called a continuation of Palestine on the north. In the most extended sense, it consisted of Syria of Damascus, Syria of Zobah, and Syria of the Two Rivers (which was nearly the same as Mesopotamia).

Syria was first settled by the Hittites and other Hamitic races. Later, a Semitic element entered it from the southeast under leaders such as Abraham and Chedorlaomer. In early times the country was divided among many petty kings such as those at Damascus, Rehob, Zobah, and Geshur (1 Kgs 10:29; 2 Kgs 7:6). Joshua subdued the country in the region of Hermon and Lebanon (Josh 11:2–18). David conquered the Syrians of Damascus and reduced the country to submission (2 Sam 8; 10:6–19). It continued to be subject to Solomon, but near the close of his reign, an independent kingdom was formed at Damascus (1 Kgs 4:21; 11:23–25).

The kings of Damascus became formidable enemies of Israel and frequently engaged in wars with one or the other of the Israelite nations (1 Kgs 15:18–20; 20; 22; 2 Kgs 6:8–33; 7; 9:14, 15; 10:32, 33; 13:3, 14–25). The attempt of the king of Syria and the king of Israel to overthrow Judah led Ahaz to seek the aid of the king of Assyria, and at the end of the conflict, Syria became a part of the Assyrian Empire.

Syria was ruled by the Babylonians, by the Persians, and was then conquered by Alexander the Great in 333 B.C. At his death it came into possession of one of his generals, Seleucus Nicator, who made Syria the head of a vast kingdom and founded Antioch as its capital (300 B.C.). The country was less prosperous under his successors, the most remarkable of them being Antiochus Epiphanes, a cruel oppressor of the Jews. He plundered the Jewish temple, desecrated the Holy of Holies, and caused a revolt of the Jews under the Hasmonean Princes who gained their independence. The Parthians, under Mithridates I, overran the eastern provinces (164 B.C.), but later Syria was added to the Roman Empire by Pompey (64 B.C.). In the organization under Augustus, Syria became an imperial province of which Antioch was the capital. Several districts, however, retained a degree of independence for some time and took the position of protected states. Damascus was under a governor appointed by Aretas, king of Arabia Petraea, when Paul escaped from there (2 Cor 11:32). Christianity spread in Syria through the preaching of Paul (Acts 15:23, 41; 18:18; 21:3; Gal 1:21).

4948. Σύρος Súros; gen. *Súrou*, masc. noun. Syrian (Luke 4:27).

4949. Συροφοίνισσα Surophoínissa; gen. *Surophoínissas*, fem. proper noun. Syrophenician. A title applied to the woman who sought Jesus to heal her daughter (Mark 7:26), also called a woman of Canaan (Matt 15:22). Syrophenician may denote a mixed race, half Syrian and half Phoenician, or the people in the Phoenician portion of the Roman province of Syria may have been so-called to distinguish them from the Phoenicians of Libya or the Carthaginians.

4950. σύρτις súrtis; gen. *surtéōs*, fem. noun from *súrō* (4951), to draw. A sandbank, shoal or quicksand, so-called because ships running into it are held fast and gradually sink into it—thus becoming a great danger to navigation (Acts 27:17).

4951. σύρω súrō; fut. *surố*. To draw, drag, whether of things (John 21:8; Rev 12:4; Sept.: 2 Sam 17:13) or persons (Acts 8:3; 14:19; 17:6). It involves the notion of violence.

Deriv.: *katasúrō* (2694), to drag down, hale; *súrtis* (4950), a sandbank.

4952. συσπαράσσω *susparássō*, **συσ-παράττω** *susparáttō*; fut. *susparáxō*, from *sún* (4862), together, and *sparássō* (4682), to convulse. To tear or lacerate altogether, completely. Used intens., to convulse altogether, throw into strong spasms, spoken of the effects of demonic possession resembling epilepsy (Luke 9:42).

4953. σύσσημον *sússēmon*; gen. *sussēmou*, neut. noun from *sússēmos* (n.f.), which is from *sún* (4862), together with, and *sēma* (n.f., see *ásēmos* [767]), sign. A concerted sign or token which is agreed upon or communicated to others, a signal (Mark 14:44 [cf. Matt 26:48, *sēmeíon* {4592}, sign, Sept.: Judg 20:40).

4954. σύσσωμος *sússōmos*; gen. *sussómou*, masc.-fem., neut. *sússōmon*, adj. from *sún* (4862), altogether, and *sóma* (4983), body. United in one body, i.e., members of the body of Christ (Eph 3:6). *Sóma* is used elsewhere of the Church.
    Syn.: *adelphós* (80), brother.

4955. συστασιαστής *sustasiastēs*; gen. *sustasiastoú*, masc. noun from *sún* (4862), together with, and *stásis* (4714), insurrection, revolt or riot. A companion in sedition or insurrection, a fellow-insurgent (Mark 15:7).

4956. συστατικός *sustatikós*; fem. *sustatikē*, neut. *sustatikón*, adj. from *sunístēmi* (4921), to commend. Literally placing together, introducing, hence commendatory, referring to a letter of commendation (2 Cor 3:1).

4957. συσταυρόω *sustauróō*; contracted *sustauró*, fut. *sustaurósō*, from *sún* (4862), together with, and *stauróō* (4717), to crucify. To crucify together with, with the dat., whether bodily (Matt 27:44; Mark 15:32; John 19:32) or spiritually by mortifying our worldly and fleshly lusts by the cross of Christ (Rom 6:6; Gal 2:20). In Rom 6:6 the verb is in the pass. *sunestaurōthē*, indicating that the old man was crucified together with Christ so that sin cannot have preeminence in a believer's life.

4958. συστέλλω *sustéllō*; fut. *sustelō*, from *sún* (4862), together, and *stéllō* (4724), to repress, withdraw oneself, contract, shrink. To wrap up, contract.
    (I) To deck together, wrap together, envelop, wind in a garment or robe. Of a dead body rolled up and swathed for burial (Acts 5:6; Sept.: Ezek 29:5).
    (II) To draw together, to contract. Figuratively in the pass., to shrink together, be distressed, anxious. Hence, in 1 Cor 7:29, "the time is full of distress" (a.t.). Others interpret it "the time is short."
    Syn.: *kolobóō* (2856), to curtail, shorten; *sustéllō* (4958), to contract, shorten.
    Ant.: *auxánō* (837), to increase; *parateínō* (3905), to prolong.

4959. συστενάζω *sustenázō*; fut. *sustenáxō*, from *sún* (4862), together, and *stenázō* (4727), to groan. To groan or sigh together, spoken of the creation (Rom 8:22).
    Syn.: *sunéchomai* (4912), to be constrained, afflicted.
    Ant.: *sunédomai* (4913), to rejoice or feel satisfaction with; *sugchaírō* (4796), to rejoice with.

4960. συστοιχέω *sustoichéō*; contracted *sustoichó*, fut. *sustoichésō*, from *sún* (4862), together, and *stoichéō* (4748), to proceed in order. To advance in order together, as soldiers. Figuratively, to correspond to, with the dat. (Gal 4:25).

4961. συστρατιώτης *sustratiótēs*; gen. *sustratiótou*, masc. noun from *sún* (4862), together with, and *stratiótēs* (4757), a soldier. A fellow-soldier, figuratively of Christian teachers, Paul's companions in the labors and dangers of Christian warfare (Phil 2:25; Phile 1:2).

4962. συστρέφω *sustréphō*; fut. *sustrépsō*, from *sún* (4862), together, and *stréphō* (4762), to turn. To revolve or rotate together, to turn, twist, wind together into one bundle, band, or mass; hence, generally to gather together, collect, with the acc. (Acts 28:3; Sept.: Prov 30:4). Of persons, troops (Sept.: Judg 11:3; 12:4).

Deriv.: *sustrophḗ* (4963), an uproar, a riotous crowd.

4963. συστροφή *sustrophḗ*; gen. *sustrophḗs*, fem. noun from *sustréphō* (4962), to roll or collect together into a bundle. A turning or spinning together, as in a whirlwind. A gathering together of people, a multitude, a public tumult (Acts 19:40; Sept.: Judg 14:8) in the sense of conspiracy (Acts 23:12; Sept.: 2 Kgs 15:15; Amos 7:10).

Syn.: *thórubos* (2351), a disturbance, tumult; *tarachḗ* (5016), disturbance, mob, sedition.

4964. συσχηματίζω *suschēmatízō*; fut. *suschēmatísō*, from *sún* (4862), together with, and *schēmatízō* (n.f.), to fashion. To fashion alike, conform to the same pattern outwardly. With a dat. following, to conform to (Rom 12:2 and also 1 Pet 1:14). In Rom 12:2, "be not conformed," *mḗ suschēmatízesthe* (*mḗ* [3361], not, and *suschēmatízesthe* [pres. imper. of *suschēmatízō*]). An expanded rendering might read, "Stop being molded by the external and fleeting fashions of this age, but undergo a deep inner change [*metamorphoústhe* {3339}] by the qualitative renewing [*anakainṓsei* {341}] of your mind." Such a transformation can be wrought only by the Holy Spirit (2 Cor 3:18).

Syn.: *summorphóō* (4833), to conform in one's inner nature and not only in the outer form, as conveyed by *suschēmatízō*.

4965. Συχάρ *Suchár*; indeclinable fem. proper noun. Sychar, meaning drunken (John 4:5). Sychar is another name for Shechem, perhaps applied in derision. See Isa 28:1, 7; Hab 2:15. Whether Sychar occupied precisely the same site as ancient Shechem has been a question of dispute among scholars.

4966. Συχέμ *Suchém*; fem. proper noun transliterated from the Hebr. *Shᵉkhem* (7927, OT), shoulder. Sychem, or Shechem (Acts 7:16). A town in the valley between Mounts Ebal and Gerizim, also called Sichem and Sychar, about thirty-four miles north of Jerusalem and seven miles southeast of Samaria. In later times it was known as Neapolis ("the new city" [a.t.]), and now bears the Arabic name of Nablus. Its sight is unrivaled for beauty in Palestine. The city is mentioned forty-eight times in the Bible.

Its history began 4,000 years ago, when Jerusalem had no existence, extends through Scripture from Abraham to Christ, and continues to the present day. When Abraham came from Chaldea to the land which God would give him, he stopped at the "place of Sichem" (Gen 12:6). Abraham worshiped under the oak which was by Shechem, and there Jacob buried the images brought by Rachel from Padan-Aram. When the latter came from Mesopotamia, Shechem was a Hivite city. Jacob bought from Hamor the parcel of the field which he afterward gave to his son Joseph (Gen 33:18, 19; 48:22; John 4:5). Shechem was captured and the male inhabitants were murdered by Simeon and Levi (Gen 34; 49:5–7). Joseph came from Hebron to Shechem and Dothan seeking his brothers, and he was later buried at Shechem (Gen 37:12–28). A solemn dedicatory service of the whole nation of Israel took place near Shechem (Deut 11:29, 30). Abimelech, a son of Gideon, caused the Shechemites to revolt against the Jews and elect him as king; after a reign of three years, he was expelled, and in revenge destroyed the city and sowed the ground with salt (Judg 9). Shechem was rebuilt, and Rehoboam went there to be crowned, but in consequence of a revolt against him, he fled. The city was fortified by Jeroboam who made it the first seat of the northern kingdom (1 Kgs 12:1–19, 25; 2 Chr chap. 10). Shechemite men were slain by Ishmael, who had previously assassinated the Babylonian-appointed governor of Judah (Jer 41:3, 5). After the captivity, Shechem became the center of Samaritan worship. Jesus visited the region, preached to a woman at Jacob's well, and many from Sychar believed on Him (John 4:5, 39–42). Stephen referred to the sepulchers of the patriarchs at Sychem (Acts 7:16).

4967. σφαγή sphagé; gen. *sphagḗs*, fem. noun from *spházō* (4969), to slay. Slaughter of animals for food or in sacrifice (Acts 8:32 quoted from Isa 53:7; Rom 8:36 quoted from Ps 44:23 [cf. Sept. Zech 11:4]). In James 5:5, like beasts in the day of slaughter, i.e. without care or forethought; Sept.: Jer 12:3.

4968. σφάγιον sphágion; gen. *sphagíou*, neut. noun from *spházō* (4969), to slay. A victim as slaughtered in sacrifice (Acts 7:42 quoted from Amos 5:25).

4969. σφάζω spházō; fut. *spháxō*. To slaughter, kill, slay, trans. of animals for food or sacrifice (Rev 5:6, 9, 12; 13:8 [cf. Isa 53:5]; Sept.: Gen 37:31; 43:15; Ex 22:1; 29:11); of persons, to kill, slay, with the acc. (1 John 3:12; Rev 6:4, 9; 13:3, used of a deadly wound; 18:24; Sept.: Gen 22:10; 2 Kgs 10:7; Isa 57:5).
Deriv.: *kataspházō* (2695), to slaughter, kill; *sphagḗ* (4967), slaughter of animals for food or in sacrifice; *sphágion* (4968), a victim as slaughtered in sacrifice.
Syn.: *kataspházō* (2695), to slaughter, kill; *apokteínō* (615), to kill; *anairéō* (337), to slay; *thúō* (2380), to sacrifice by slaying a victim; *thanatóō* (2289), to kill.
Ant.: *zōogonéō* (2225), to rescue or save from death, live; *zōopoiéō* (2227), to make alive, quicken.

4970. σφόδρα sphódra; adv. from *sphodrós* (n.f.), eager, vehement. Vehemently, greatly, very much (Matt 2:10; 17:6, 23; 18:31; 19:25; 26:22; 27:54; Mark 16:4; Luke 18:23; Acts 6:7; Rev 16:21; Sept.: Gen 17:18, 19 [cf. Jon 4:4, 10]). Equivalent to *sphodrós* (4971), vehemently.
Syn.: *lían* (3029), very, exceedingly; *perissós* (4057), abundantly, more; *perissotérōs* (4056), more exceedingly.
Ant.: *mikrón* (3397), of degree, quantity or time, a little; *olígon* (3641), of time, space, and extent, meaning a while, a little, a short space; *metríos* (3357), moderately, a little.

4971. σφοδρῶς sphodrós; adv. from *sphodrós* (n.f.), equal in meaning to *sphódra* (4970), eager, vehement. Vehemently, greatly, very much (Acts 27:18).

4972. σφραγίζω sphragízō; fut. *sphragísō*, from *sphragís* (4973), seal. To seal, trans.:
(I) To seal, close up and make fast with a seal signet such as letters or books so that they may not be read (Sept.: 1 Kgs 21:8; Isa 29:11; Dan 12:4). Hence, figuratively of lips, to keep in silence, not to make known, with the acc. (Rev 10:4; 22:10; Sept.: Dan 8:26). Generally, to seal or set a seal for the sake of security upon a sepulcher, prison, with the acc. (Matt 27:66; Rev 20:3; Sept.: Song 4:12). Figuratively, to secure to someone, make sure, deliver over safely, in the mid. with the acc. and dat. (Rom 15:28 [cf. Deut 32:34; 2 Kgs 22:4]).
(II) Generally, to set a seal or mark upon a thing as a token of its authenticity or approvedness; used of persons, with the acc. (Rev 7:3); pass. (Rev 7:4–8). More often of decrees or documents, to attest by a seal (Sept.: Esth 8:8, 10; Job 14:17). Hence figuratively, to attest, confirm, establish, with the acc. (John 6:27 [cf. 5:36]), followed by *hóti* (3754), that (John 3:33). So also of Christians whom God attests and confirms by the gift of the

Holy Spirit as the earnest, pledge, or seal of their election to salvation. Mid. with the acc. (2 Cor 1:22); pass. (Eph 1:13; 4:30).

Deriv.: *katasphragízō* (2696), to seal closely.

Syn.: *kleíō* (2808), to shut, close; *asphalízō* (805), to render secure; *sugkleíō* (4788), to enclose, shut up.

Ant.: *anoígō* (455), to open; *dianoígō* (1272), to open up completely; *lúō* (3089), to loose.

4973. σφραγίς sphragís; gen. *sphragídos*, fem. noun.

(I) Particularly an instrument for sealing, a signet, signet-ring (Rev 7:2; Sept.: 1 Kgs 21:8; Song 8:6).

(II) A seal as impressed upon letters or books for the sake of privacy and security (Rev 5:1, 2, 5, 9; 6:1, 3, 5, 7, 9; 8:1). Also a seal impressed as a guarantee of something's genuineness (Rev 9:4); as a motto, inscription (2 Tim 2:19). Figuratively, a promissory token, pledge, proof (Rom 4:11; 1 Cor 9:2).

Deriv.: *sphragízō* (4972), to seal.

Syn.: *sēmeíon* (4592), an indication, sign, token.

4974. σφυρόν sphurón; gen. *sphuroú*, neut. noun. The ankle bone (Acts 3:7). The Greeks called it *sphúron* because the bone resembles a hammer (*sphúra* [n.f.]).

4975. σχεδόν schedón; adv. from *scheín* (n.f.), the 2 aor. inf. of *échō* (2192). Nearly, almost (Acts 13:44; 19:26; Heb 9:22).

4976. σχῆμα schḗma; gen. *schḗmatos*, neut. noun from *scheín* (n.f.), the 2 aor. inf. of *échō* (2192), have. Fashion, external form, appearance (1 Cor 7:31).

The *schḗma* of Phil 2:8 refers to the Lord Jesus' whole outward appearance which bore no difference to that of other men. The phrase "and being found in fashion [*schḗmati* {dat. sing.}] as a man," brings forward the distinction between *schḗma* and *morphḗ* ([3444], form or expression of essence). *Morphḗ* is the necessary and fundamental expression, mode, or form of an object's essence (*hupóstasis* [5287]). *Schḗma* is the fashion, style, or apparent arrangement of an object (yet no less true and real than its form). The deity of Christ in the incarnation is affirmed by the use of the word *morphḗ*. In Phil 2:6, Paul asserts that the Christ of the incarnation was the one who existed in the *morphḗ* of God. It was while in this divine mode of existence that He humbled Himself and assumed the form of a servant (*doúlou* [1401]). The word "took" is *labṓn* (aor. act. part. of *lambánō* [2983]) and the word might be fully translated "having taken on His own initiative and power." The words that follow, *kaí schḗmati euretheís* (*euretheís*, aor. pass. part. of *heurískō* [2147], to find), "and being found in fashion as a man," emphasize the significance of His manifestation to His fellow men. The use of *schḗma* here is not meant to suggest that Christ's humanity was only apparent and not real. Paul could have used *morphḗ* to qualify Christ's humanity. However, the point of the passage is to contrast the pre-incarnate glory of Christ with His incarnate humility and lowliness. Servanthood was the mode of existence which the Son of God assumed and humanity was the receptacle, as it were, into which He poured Himself.

Deriv.: *aschḗmōn* (809), shapeless, uncomely; *euschḗmōn* (2158), comely, well-formed.

4977. σχίζω schízō; fut. *schísō*. To split, rend, divide with violence, trans. Used of wood (Sept.: Gen 22:3; 1 Sam 6:14); rocks (Matt 27:51); the veil of the temple (Matt 27:51; Mark 15:38; Luke 23:45); the heavens (Mark 1:10); a garment (Luke 5:36; John 19:24); a net (John 21:11). See Isa 37:1; 48:21; Zech 14:4. Figuratively, to split into parties, factions, to divide, pass. (Acts 14:4; 23:7).

Deriv.: *schísma* (4978), division, schism.

Syn.: *dicházō* (1369), to set asunder or at variance; *dichotoméō* (1371), to bisect, cut asunder; *diairéō* (1244), to separate, divide; *merízō* (3307), to divide; *apochōrízō* (673), to rend apart; *chōrízō* (5563), to put asunder, separate; *diaspáō* (1288), to sever, pluck asunder, pull in pieces; *dicházō* (1369), to set at variance, divide, alienate.

Ant.: *sumbibázō* (4822), to drive together, compromise; *déō* (1210), to bind; *sundéō* (4887), to bind with; *proskolláō* (4347), to glue to, cleave, join; *sunarmologéō* (4883), to fit together.

4978. σχίσμα *schísma*; gen. *schísmatos*, neut. noun from *schízō* (4977), to split, tear. A schism, division, tear, as in mind or sentiment, and so into factions (Matt 9:16; Mark 2:21; John 7:43; 9:16; 10:19; 1 Cor 1:10; 11:18; 12:25; Sept.: *schismé*, Isa 2:21; Jon 1:7). Contrast *haíresis* (139), heresy, which indicates an opposition to the accepted doctrine or practice, but not a pulling away or a split.

Syn.: *dichostasía* (1370), division, dissension; *haíresis* (139), heresy, sect.

Ant.: *henótēs* (1775), oneness, unanimity, unity.

4979. σχοινίον *schoiníon*; gen. *schoiníou*, neut. noun from *schoínos* (n.f.), bulrush. A cord made of bulrushes, hence generally a cord, rope (John 2:15; Acts 27:32; Sept.: 2 Sam 17:13; 1 Kgs 20:31).

4980. σχολάζω *scholázō*; fut. *scholásō*, from *scholé* (4981), leisure. To have leisure, to be free from labor, vacant, idle (Sept.: Ex 5:8, 17). With the dat., to have leisure for something, to give oneself to something free from other cares and hindrances (1 Cor 7:5). Figuratively of place, to be vacant, empty (Matt 12:44, meaning unoccupied, uninhabited).

Syn.: *anapaúō* (373), to take a rest; *argéō* (691), to be idle; *hēsucházō* (2270), to refrain from labor; *katapaúō* (2664), to settle down, cease, rest.

4981. σχολή *scholé*; gen. *scholés*, fem. noun. Leisure, rest, freedom from labor and business, vacation; later usage and in the NT, a school, a place of learning in leisure where a teacher and his disciples came together and held discussions and disputations (Acts 19:9).

Deriv.: *scholázō* (4980), to have leisure.

4982. σώζω *sózō*; fut. *sósō*, aor. pass. *esóthēn*, perf. pass. *sésōsmai*, from *sōs* (n.f.), safe, delivered. To save, deliver, make whole, preserve safe from danger, loss, destruction. Trans.:

Sózō occurs fifty-four times in the Gospels (not counting Luke 17:33 where *zōogonései* [2225], to rescue from death, is a better attested reading than *sósei* of the TR; nor Matt 18:11, omitted in some MSS). Of the instances where *sózō* is used, fourteen relate to deliverance from disease or demon possession (Matt 9:21, 22; Mark 3:4; 5:23, 28, 34; 6:56; 10:52; Luke 6:9; 8:36, 48, 50; 17:19; 18:42; John 11:12); in twenty instances, the inference is to the rescue of physical life from some impending peril or instant death (Matt 8:25; 14:30; 16:25; 27:40, 42, 49; Mark 8:35; 15:30, 31; Luke 9:24, 56; 23:35, 37, 39; John 12:27); the remaining twenty times, the reference is to spiritual salvation (Matt 1:21; 10:22; 19:25; 24:13, 22; Mark 8:35; 10:26; 13:13, 20; 16:16; Luke 7:50; 8:12; 9:24; 13:23; 18:26; 19:10; John 3:17; 5:34; 10:9; 12:47).

(I) Used particularly of persons (Matt 8:25; 14:30; 24:22; 27:40, 42; Mark 3:4; 13:20; Luke 6:9; Acts 27:20, 31); of the soul (Matt 16:25; Mark 8:35; Luke 9:24; Sept.: Judg 6:15; 1 Sam 10:27; 19:11; 2 Chr 32:14; Job 1:15); followed by *ek* (1537), from, with the gen. to save from, deliver out of (John 12:27; Heb 5:7; Jude 1:5).

(II) Of sick persons, to save from death and (by implication) to heal, restore to health; pass. to be healed, recover (Matt 9:21, 22; Mark 5:23, 28, 34; Luke 7:50;

8:36, 48; John 11:12; Acts 4:9; James 5:15).

(III) Specifically of salvation from eternal death, sin, and the punishment and misery consequent to sin. To save, and (by implication), to give eternal life. Especially of Christ as the Savior, followed by *apó* (575), with the gen. (Matt 1:21; Acts 2:40; Rom 5:9). Of the Lord, to bring someone safely into His kingdom (2 Tim 4:18). Generally (Matt 18:11, "For the Son of man is come to save that which was lost"; Rom 11:14; 1 Cor 1:21; 1 Tim 4:16; Heb 7:25; James 1:21). With *ek* (1537), out of or from death (*thanátou*, the gen. of *thánatos* [2288]; James 5:20). In the pass. (Matt 10:22, "he . . . shall be saved"; 19:25; 24:13; Mark 10:26; 13:13; 16:16; Luke 8:12; 13:23; John 5:34; 10:9; Rom 5:10; 1 Cor 5:5; 1 Tim 2:15). Hence as a part., *hoi sōzómenoi*, those being saved, those who have obtained salvation through Christ and are kept by Him (Acts 2:47; 1 Cor 1:18; 2 Cor 2:15; Rev 21:24).

(IV) The basic meaning of the verb *sōzō* is to rescue from peril, to protect, keep alive. *Sōzō* involves the preservation of life, either physical or spiritual. Whenever the word *sōzō* and its deriv. such as *sōtēría* (4991), salvation, *sōtēr* (4990), savior, and the adj. *sōtērion* (4992), salvation, are used, the context must be considered to determine whether the preservation of physical life (deliverance from physical death, sickness or peril) or spiritual life (deliverance from sin, Satan and hell) is in view.

(V) Salvation of the soul is deliverance from death unto life through Christ (John 6:56; 14:20; Rom 16:7, 11; 1 Cor 1:30; 9:1, 2; 2 Cor 5:17; Eph 2:13) The believing sinner receives the spiritual life of a new nature from God (2 Pet 1:4) and is freed from the power of sin (spiritual death) while having to endure its presence until the resurrection. Deliverance of the body will occur at the resurrection when a entire creation will also be renovated (Rom 8:21–23).

To be saved means to be found. This is the reason why our Lord names *tó*

apolōlós (neut. perf. part. of *apóllumi* [622], to lose), the lost one, as the object of His saving activity (Matt 10:6; 15:24; 18:12–14; Luke 15:4, 6, 8, 24; 19:10). From the figures used, it appears that the Gr. *apóllumi* has in this connection the sense of to miss or be missing, not primarily the sense of destroy or be destroyed. In the parables of Luke 15:1–24, the lost are like sheep gone astray upon the mountains, like the coin slipped out of the hand of the owner and like the prodigal who has left the father's home. A lost condition means estrangement from God, an absence of all the religious, spiritual, and moral relations man is designed to sustain toward his Maker. This lost condition is designated death, for it is the absence of true life (Matt 8:22; Luke 20:38). The salvation of the lost, therefore, is salvation from spiritual death.

(VI) There are two aspects of *apóllumi*. One relates to man's existence and life apart from God, i.e., his experience of futility, meaninglessness, and emptiness. The other relates to man's condition and status apart from God, i.e., his position before God of being condemned, sinful, and doomed to perish. These are joined together in Matt 18:10–14. Here a sinner is compared first to a sheep gone astray and in need of being sought. Jesus reveals the purpose of saving the lost sheep when He says, "Even so it is not the will of your Father which is in heaven, that one of these little ones should perish [*apólētai*]." That which is already lost in the one sense must be diligently sought, lest it should finally and forever be lost. The deliverance from this present *apóleia*, destruction, as well as the final destruction is salvation.

Thus in Mark 16:16, to be saved is the opposite of to be condemned; in John 3:16, 17 it is the opposite of to be judged and to perish; and in John 10:9, 10 it is contrasted to the phrase to destroy. This *apóleia* (destruction), however, and *apóllumi* (to destroy, lose) is equivalent to death, the loss of life. This life is spoken of as *psuché* (5590), soul, or that which represents physical life (Matt 10:39; 16:25; Mark 8:35; Luke 9:24, 25; John 12: 25). Its opposite is to have eternal life (John 3:16; 10:28), or to be raised up at the last day (John 6:39). Thus salvation in its specific spiritual sense is still viewed throughout as a deliverance from death and an introduction into the sphere of spiritual life.

(VII) As the second death (Rev 20:6, 14; 21:8) is essentially an extension and complete experience of present spiritual death, so the resurrection unto life is most essentially an extension and complete experience of present spiritual life. Consequently, future salvation and condemnation are not separate from present salvation and condemnation. The distinction is one if time and not kind. While God's salvation is one whole work, it does take place in stages. One must determine which aspect of salvation (inaugurated or consummated) is in view in any context. The salvation of Luke 7:50, "Thy faith hath saved thee," which Jesus said to the woman who anointed Him, and that of Luke 19:9, of Zacchaeus, "This day is salvation come to this house," and that of 19:10, "The Son of man is come to seek and to save that which was lost," must belong to the present time of our Lord's earthly ministry. Also, in John 12:47, the saving of the world (for which Jesus declares he had come) is a present salvation. In Matt 1:21, since the sins of the people are the evil from which Jesus saves, salvation must be viewed as being present salvation. In other passages, the eschatological context of salvation is equally obvious (as in Matt 10:22; 24:13, "He that endureth to the end shall be saved"). Matt 16:25; Mark 8:35 and Luke 9:24 speak of the finding or saving of life in the future judgment as conditioned by the willingness to sacrifice one's life here. One must not misconstrue this as teaching a kind of synergism. Rather, true faith, which alone brings salvation, bears the fruit of loyalty and love. Therefore the evidence of saving faith is

the willingness to sacrifice one's life for Christ. One may thus refer to the cause of salvation, faith, by speaking of its effect, faithfulness.

(VIII) The context underlying the question of the disciples recorded in Matt 19:25; Mark 10:26 and Luke 18:26, "Then who can be saved?" is eschatological. The question was called forth by the Lord Jesus' declaration that the rich would enter into the kingdom of God with great difficulty, which was in turn brought about by the question of the rich young man, "What good thing shall I do, that I may have eternal life?" "To be saved" means "to enter the kingdom" which means "to inherit eternal life." The qualification of life as eternal, as well as the further context of Peter's question about future rewards and our Lord's answer to it, proved that the whole discussion is eschatological in its scope (Matt 24:22; Mark 13:20, "Except these days had been shortened, no flesh would have been saved" [a.t.]. This statement is best understood as follows: the temptation in these last times will be so severe, that, if their duration had not been kept within certain limits, all men, even the elect, would have fallen away, and so no flesh would have been ultimately saved in the day of judgment).

(IX) In the remainder of the passages, it is difficult to say with certainty whether salvation is future or present. For Matt 18:11 (TR) the reference to the present is supported by Luke 19:10. In Luke 8:12, "lest they should believe and be saved," the eschatological sense would be quite plausible. But the other view may be preferred by the fact that the parables concern the present invisible aspect of the kingdom. In some instances, salvation in its entirety is meant (Luke 13:23, " . . . are there few that be saved.")

In John's Gospel (John 3:16, 17; 4:22; 5:34; 10:9), *sōzō* is used in connection with life to mean eternal life. In the discourses of this Gospel, eternal life, as well as salvation, is both a present possession and a future eschatological possession.

The distinction between the two is temporal and not categorical.

In Acts and the epistles, *sṓzō* predominantly means to rescue and preserve from that spiritual death which is common to all men because of Adam's sin (Rom 5:12). In Acts 4:9; 14:9 *sṓzō* is used for healing from bodily infirmity, and 27:20, 31 refer to deliverance from shipwreck. Jude 1:5 refers to the deliverance from Egypt. Heb 5:7 refers to deliverance from death. The following verses refer to spiritual deliverance: Acts 2:40, 47; 4:12; 11:14; 15:1, 11; 16:30, 31; Rom 5:9, 10; 8:24; 9:27; 10:9, 13; 11:14, 26; 1 Cor 1:18, 21; 3:15; 5:5; 7:16; 9:22; 10:33; 15:2; 2 Cor 2:15; Eph 2:5, 8; 1 Thess 2:16; 2 Thess 2:10; 1 Tim 1:15; 2:4, 15; 4:16; 2 Tim 1:9; 4:18; Titus 3:5; Heb 7:25; James 1:21; 2:14; 4:12; 5:20; 1 Pet 3:21; 4:18; Jude 1:23.

Deriv.: *diasṓzō* (1295), to bring safely through; *sōtḗr* (4990), Savior.

Syn.: *therapeúō* (2323), to care for the sick for the purpose of healing; *iáomai* (2390), to heal both physically and spiritually; *ananḗphō* (366), to return to soberness, recover; *phulássō* (5442), to preserve; *hugiaínō* (5198), to have health; *diasṓzō* (1295), to bring safely through; *dikaióō* (1344), to justify; *anagennáō* (313), to beget again from above.

Ant.: *apóllumi* (622), to destroy, perish; *aphanízō* (853), to banish from; *phtheírō* (5351), to corrupt, destroy; *diaphtheírō* (1311), to perish or corrupt completely; *krínō* (2919), to judge, avenge, punish, condemn; *olothreúō* (3645), to destroy; *exolothreúō* (1842), to utterly destroy; *porthéō* (4199), to ruin by laying waste, destroy.

4983. σῶμα *sṓma*; gen. *sṓmatos*, neut. noun. Body, an organized whole made up of parts and members.

(I) Generally of any material body, as plants (1 Cor 15:37, 38); bodies celestial and terrestrial, the sun, moon, stars (1 Cor 15:40, 41).

(II) Specifically of creatures, living or dead.

(A) Of a human body different from *sárx* (4561), flesh, which word denotes the material body. **(1)** A living body (Matt 5:29, 30; 6:25; 26:12; Mark 5:29; 14:8; Luke 12:22, 23; John 2:21; Rom 1:24; 4:19; 1 Cor 6:13; 15:44; 2 Cor 4:10; 10:10; Col 2:23; Heb 10:5; 1 Pet 2:24). In Col 1:22 the expression "in the body of his flesh [*sárx*]" means in his body incarnate, flesh that forms an organized whole. This is the antithesis of *hē psuchḗ* (5590), the soul (Matt 10:28; Luke 12:4), and *tó pneúma* (4151), the spirit (Rom 8:10; 1 Cor 5:3; 7:34); or where *sṓma*, *psuchḗ* and *pneúma* make a periphrasis for the whole man (1 Thess 5:23). See Sept.: Gen 47:18; Lev 6:10; 14:10; Dan 4:30; 10:6. As the seat of sinful affections and appetites (cf. *sárx* [4561], II, C). See Rom 6:6; 7:23, 24; 8:13; Col 2:11. **(2)** A dead body, corpse, generally (Matt 14:12; 27:52, 58, 59; Luke 23:52, 55; 24:3, 23; John 19:31; Acts 9:40; Jude 1:9). Specifically of the communion bread, as representing the body of Christ crucified for the salvation of man (Matt 26:26; Mark 14:22; Luke 22:19; 1 Cor 10:16; 11:24, 27, 29).

(B) Spoken of living beasts (James 3:3); a dead body of a beast, meaning a carcass (Luke 17:37 [cf. Matt 24:28 where the word *ptṓma* {4430}, corpse, is used]); of victims slain as sacrifices (Heb 13:11 [cf. Ex 29:14; Num 19:3, 5]).

(III) Metonymically referring to the body as the external man, to which is ascribed that which strictly belongs to the person, man, individual; with a gen. of person forming a periphrasis for the person himself (Matt 6:22, "thy whole body" means your whole person [see also 6:23]; Luke 11:34, 36; Rom 12:1, "your bodies," i.e., yourselves [cf. 6:13]; Eph 5:28; Phil 1:20). Used generally and in an absolute sense (1 Cor 6:16 [in antithesis with *tó pneúma*, the spirit, in 6:17]) in allusion to Gen 2:24 where the Sept. has *eis sárka mían* (*eis* [1519], unto; *sárka* [4561], flesh; *mían* [3391], one), one flesh (cf. *sárx* III). Used in an absolute sense (Sept.: Gen 47:12, meaning according to the number of persons). In later usage in NT for a slave, *tá sṓmata*, slaves (Rev 18:13).

(IV) Metaphorically for a body, meaning a whole, aggregate, collective mass, as spoken of the Christian church, the whole body of Christians collectively, of which Christ is the head (Rom 12:5; 1 Cor 10:17; 12:13, 27; Eph 1:23; 2:16; 4:4, 12, 16; 5:23, 30; Col 1:18, 24; 2:19; 3:15).

(V) Figuratively meaning body, substance, reality as opposed *hē skiá* (4639), the shadow or type of future things.

(VI) The Greek philosophers treated the human body with disparagement. For this reason in Homer (and frequently Attic Gr.) *sṓma* meant a dead body, in which sense the word is occasionally used in the Gospels (Matt 14:12; 27:52, 58, 59; Luke 17:37). The usual meaning, however, in the NT and ordinary Gr. usage, is a living body (Matt 6:22; 26:12; Mark 5:29). The NT does not share in the philosophic disparagement of the human body. This is demonstrated by the fact that the Lord Jesus neither practiced nor preached asceticism—"The Son of Man came eating" (Matt 11:19). However, we find Jesus teaching a clear recognition of a duality in human nature—a distinction drawn between body and soul (with the latter referring to man's immaterial part); flesh and spirit (Matt 6:25; 26:41). He emphasizes the antithesis between man's unredeemed body as the lower part of his being, and his soul as the higher part. While He presents the body as a true part of our humanity and does not disparage it, nevertheless He stresses that its value, in its sinful condition, is not to be compared for a moment with that of the spiritual part (Matt 10:28). Those who follow Jesus must be prepared, if need be, to surrender their bodies to the sword and the cross (Matt 23:34); "what shall a man give in exchange for his soul?" (Matt 16:26).

(VII) Jesus associated the resurrection body with the future judgment (Luke 14:14; 20:35; John 5:28, 29).

(VIII) The Lord Jesus as the God-Man possessed a true body as well as a human soul. The Son, eternal, infinite and ever-present with the Father and Holy Spirit, took upon Himself human flesh by the mystical operation of the Holy Spirit, in the womb of the virgin Mary (Matt 1:18 [cf. Gal 4:4]). In due time, according to the laws of human life, He was born at Bethlehem (Luke 2:5, 7). The child thus born was seen in His infancy by the shepherds and the wise men, and when He was eight days old by Simeon and Anna (Luke 2:25, 36). From His conception and birth His body developed in the manner usual to human beings. "The child grew," we are told (Luke 2:40), arrived at "twelve years old," and still "increased in wisdom and stature" (Luke 2:42, 52).

The Lord Jesus possessed a human body similar to ours (except that He did not have a sinful nature [Heb 4:15]). As such He suffered hunger (Matt 4:2); He was wearied with journeying (John 4:6); He experienced pain (Matt 27:26); He underwent death (Matt 27:50). His power of motion, with one exception (Matt 14:25), was limited to that which men in general possess. After death, His body was delivered by Pilate to Joseph of Arimathaea, who wrapped it in a clean linen cloth and laid it in his new tomb (Matt 27:58f.) where it rested until the moment of the resurrection.

(IX) Christ's body after the resurrection appeared to be, in most respects, the same body as before His death. His disciples may have doubted and hesitated at first (Luke 24:16, 37; John 20:14), but they did not fail to recognize Him (Luke 24:31, 52; John 20:16, 20, 28; 21:7, 12; Acts 1:3; 2:32). We find the Lord eating and drinking as a man (Luke 24:43), making use of the natural process of breathing (John 20:22), declaring to His disciples that He had flesh and bones (Luke 24:39), showing them His hands and His feet (Luke 24:40), and giving them the assurance that His body was the identical body which they had seen stretched upon the cross by inviting Thomas, who doubted, to put his finger into the print of the nails and thrust his hand into the wound in His side (John 20:27).

Our Lord's resurrection body, however, was freed from previous material conditions and possessed altogether new capabilities. It is indicated that He could pass at will through material objects (John 20:26); and was not bound as before to the laws of movement (Luke 24:36), visibility (Luke 24:31), or gravitation (Mark 16:19; Luke 24:51). These new powers constituted the difference between His pre-resurrection and His glorified body. It was in His glorified body, thus differentiated, that He ascended into heaven; and in that same glorified body He is to be expected in His final coming (Acts 1:9, 11).

During his earthly post-resurrection life, for forty days He moved along the borders of two worlds. For the sake of His disciples and His future Church, He made use of the natural in order that He might reveal the spiritual. It was one way of revealing to us what our spiritual body (1 Cor 15:44) will be capable of doing. It is in this manner that we must explain His asking for and receiving food (Luke 24:41ff.; Acts 10:41). He did not depend on this food for His bodily support. His purpose in taking it was to convince His disciples that He was still a living man, in body as well as in spirit—that same Jesus who had so often, in past days, partaken with them of their simple meals.

In respect to His body, the risen Jesus now belonged to the same mysterious regions of the invisible world, and it was only when He chose to reveal Himself that His disciples were aware of His presence. It is to be noticed that John describes His appearances as manifestations using the word *phaneróō* (5319), to manifest (John 21:1, 14). He could hide His identity at will and again He could manifest His identity (Mark 16:12, 13; Luke 24:13–35). His resurrection body was a spiritual body, but it had the power of materializing itself to the natural senses, and Jesus made use of this power from time

to time in order to convince His disciples, by the actual evidence of sight, sound and touch, that His victory over death via the resurrection was real.

When this work was accomplished, the Lord parted from His disciples for the last time and ascended to the right hand of the Father where He was appointed Lord and Savior. His lordship encompasses the entire universe in time and space.

In the body of Christ's glory, both Paul and John find the model after which the believer's resurrection body is to be fashioned (Phil 3:21; 1 John 3:2). We will be like our Lord possessing a human body so fully imbued by the spiritual that it will be transformed into a spiritual body (1 Cor 15:42–49).

(X) *Sṓma* is also used in reference to Christ's mystical body, His church (1 Cor 12:12ff. [cf. Rom 12:5]). Paul uses the figure of a body and its members to describe the relationship of Christians to Christ and to one another. Then in 1 Cor 12:27 he definitely applies to the Corinthian church the name *sṓma Christoú*, body of Christ. Every local Christian church, i.e., regenerated believers who have been baptized into the body of Christ, constitutes part of His total universal body. In Eph 1:22, 23; 4:12; Col 1:18, 24 we have the universal Church called the body of Christ, with the def. art. He Himself is presented as the Head of the whole Church which is His body (Eph 5:23, 24; Col 2:19), the head being the vital and organic center of the whole body.

(XI) The word *sṓma* is used symbolically of Christ's body. On the night on which He was betrayed, the Lord Jesus, in instituting the memorial feast of the sacrifice of His body and the shedding of His blood, said of the bread which He took and broke and gave to His disciples, "this is My body" (Matt 26:26; Mark 14:22; Luke 22:19; 1 Cor 11:24). Similarly Paul, in writing to the Corinthians, says of the bread which is broken at the Lord's Supper, "Is it not the communion of the body of Christ?" (1 Cor 10:16). Then in 1 Cor 11:27 he describes the person who eats the memorial bread unworthily as "guilty of the body and blood of the Lord" and says that a man eats and drinks judgment unto himself "if he discern not the body" (a.t. [1 Cor 11:29]). Those who partake of the elements of the Lord's Supper must recognize the reality which they signify.

The Lord Jesus, subsequent to the feeding of the 5,000 (John 6:53–63), gave the discourse on the bread of life (which some interpreters have classified as Eucharistic). It is significant that the word *sṓma* does not occur in this teaching. However, words *sárx* ([4561], flesh) and *haíma* ([129], blood) are used. Furthermore, *sárx* is never employed anywhere in the NT to describe the memorial bread of the Lord's Supper. If Jesus had intended this to be a discourse related to the Lord's Supper, He would most likely have used the word *sṓma*. The spiritual significance of the use of the words flesh and blood in John 6:63 is indicated by 6:63 which states, "It is the spirit that quickeneth, the flesh profiteth nothing: the words that I speak unto you, they are spirit, and they are life." The life that Jesus Christ gives is spiritual and is bestowed through the Holy Spirit. Jesus gave His flesh and shed His blood, and the efficacy of that sacrifice which imparts spiritual life is applied to a believer through the Holy Spirit (John 16:5–15).

Deriv.: *sússōmos* (4954), belonging to the same body, of the same body; *sōmatikós* (4984), corporeal, physical.

Syn.: *chrós* (5559), the surface of a body, especially of a human body; *ptṓma* (4430), a corpse; *kṓlon* (2966), a member of a body; *sárx* (4561), flesh.

Ant.: *pneúma* (4151), spirit; *phántasma* (5326), a phantasm, an appearance, a spectre, apparition; *psuchḗ* (5590), soul.

4984. σωματικός *sōmatikós*; fem. *sōmatikḗ*, neut. *sōmatikón*, adj. from *sṓma* (4983), body. Bodily, corporeal, pertaining to the body (Luke 3:22; 1 Tim 4:8).

Deriv.: *sōmatikṓs* (4985), corporeally, physically, bodily.

Syn.: *sarkikós* (4559), bodily, carnal, fleshly; *sárkinos* (4560), made of flesh;

phusikós (5446), physical, material, natural.

Ant.: *pneumatikós* (4152), spiritual; *psuchikós* (5591), soulish, pertaining to the soul.

4985. σωματικῶς *sōmatikṓs*; adv. from *sōmatikós* (4984), bodily. In a bodily form, substantially, really, truly (Col 2:9).

Ant.: *pneumatikṓs* (4153), spiritually.

4986. Σώπατρος *Sṓpatros*; gen. *Sōpátrou*, masc. proper noun. Sopater, meaning safe father. A Berean who was Paul's companion (Acts 20:4).

4987. σωρεύω *sōreúō*; fut. *sōreúsō*, from *sōrós* (n.f.), heap. To heap, heap up, trans. (Rom 12:20 quoted from Prov 25:22). Also to heap up with something, with a dat., used figuratively (2 Tim 3:6, heaped up with sins, meaning laden, burdened).

Deriv.: *episōreúō* (2002), to heap upon or together.

Syn.: *sunathroízō* (4867), to gather.

4988. Σωσθένης *Sōsthénēs*; gen. *Sōsthénous*, masc. proper noun. Sosthenes, meaning of sound strength. A ruler of the Jewish synagogue at Corinth (Acts 18:17) who replaced Crispus who was excommunicated because he believed the gospel (Acts 18:8). Sosthenes, as the chief ruler of the synagogue, must have also come to believe on the Lord Jesus since Paul in writing to the Corinthians mentions him as "brother" (1 Cor 1:1).

4989. Σωσίπατρος *Sōsípatros*; gen. *Sōsipátrou*, masc. proper noun. Sosipater, meaning preserved father. A native of Berea and a kinsman of Paul (Rom 16:21).

4990. σωτήρ *sōtḗr*; gen. *sōtḗros*, masc. noun from *sṓzō* (4982), to save. A savior, deliverer, preserver, one who saves from danger or destruction and brings into a state of prosperity and happiness (Sept.: Judg 3:9, 15). In Gr. writers, the deliverer and benefactor of an estate. The ancient mythological gods (such as Zeus) were also called *sōtēres* (pl.).

(I) Of God as Savior (Luke 1:47; 1 Tim 1:1; 2:3; 4:10; Titus 1:3; 2:10; 3:4; Jude 1:25; Sept.: Isa 12:2; 17:10; 45:15, 21; Hab 3:18).

(II) Of Jesus as the Messiah, the Savior of men, who saves His people from the guilt and power of sin and from eternal death, from punishment and misery as the consequence of sin, and gives them eternal life and blessedness in His kingdom (Luke 2:11; Acts 5:31; 13:23; Phil 3:20; 2 Pet 1:1, 11; 2:20; 3:2, 18); our Savior (2 Tim 1:10; Titus 1:4; 2:13; 3:6); Savior of the body the Church (Eph 5:23); Savior of the world (John 4:42; 1 John 4:14).

Deriv.: *sōtēria* (4991), salvation; *sōtērion* (4992), the means of salvation

Syn.: *lutrōtēs* (3086), redeemer; *Messías* (3323), Messiah.

Ant.: *olothreutēs* (3644), destroyer; *kritēs* (2923), judge; *apollúōn* (623), destroyer.

4991. σωτηρία *sōtēria*; gen. *sōtērías*, fem. noun from *sōtēr* (4990), a savior, deliverer. Safety, deliverance, preservation from danger or destruction.

(I) Particularly and generally: deliverance from danger (Heb 11:7; Sept.: Ex 14:13; 2 Chr 20:17); deliverance from slavery (Acts 7:25); with *apó* (575), from (Sept.: 2 Sam 15:14); with *ek* (1537), from enemies (Luke 1:71); *kéras* (2768), a horn of salvation, meaning a strong deliverer (Luke 1:69). Hence generally, meaning welfare, prosperity (Phil 1:19; Sept.: Gen 28:21; 44:17; Prov 11:14; Jer 3:23; Hab 3:13; Isa 49:8). By implication victory (Rev 7:10; 12:10; 19:1; Sept.: 1 Sam 14:45; 2 Sam 19:2; 2 Kgs 5:1). In the OT, salvation can mean deliverance from present danger or trouble, or more especially, from defeat in battle (Sept.: Ex 15:2; 1 Sam 10:19; Job 30:15; Prov 11:14). However, it is also deliverance from the future condemnation that Jehovah would rightly bring upon Israel (Ps 53:6; Isa 35:4). Such salvation can also have eschatological connotations (Isa 25:9; 45:17; 46:13; 49:6).

(II) In the NT, salvation is deliverance from sin and its spiritual consequences, involving an attachment to the body of Christ, and admission to eternal life with blessedness in the kingdom of Christ (Luke 1:77; 19:9; John 4:22; Acts 16:17; Rom 1:16; 10:1, 10; 2 Cor 7:10; Phil 1:28; 1 Thess 5:8, 9; 2 Thess 2:13; 2 Tim 2:10; 3:15; Heb 1:14; 2:3, 10; 5:9; 6:9; 9:28; 1 Pet 1:5, 9, 10; Jude 1:3, salvation by a Messiah; Acts 4:12 where the def. art. is used; 13:26; Rom 11:11; 13:11; 2 Cor 1:6; Eph 1:13; Phil 2:12). Metonymically it means a source or bringer of salvation, Savior (Acts 13:47 quoted from Isa 49:6).

(III) The concept of God as the Savior of the individual finds expression throughout the OT (Job 5:15; 22:29; 26:2; Ps 72:4, 13; 109:31; Prov 20:22). Jehovah becomes the Savior of the meek (Ps 76:9; 149:4 [cf. Job 22:29]), and of all that put their trust in Him (Ps 86:2 [cf. 88:1]). David wrote, "This poor man cried, and the Lord heard him, and saved him out of all his troubles" (Ps 34:6). Jehovah saves the upright (Ps 37:39, 40), and such as be of a contrite spirit (Ps 34:18). He hears the cry of them that fear Him and fulfills their desire (Ps 145:19).

This salvation was deliverance not only from the spiritual consequences of sin but from the pollution of sin itself. Such an awareness of the necessity of personal, inner cleansing is expressed in Ps 51: "Create in me a clean heart, O God; and renew a right spirit within me. Cast me not away from thy presence; and take not thy Holy Spirit from me. Restore unto me the joy of thy salvation; and uphold me with thy free spirit" (Ps 51:10–12). Here the salvation for which the Psalmist prays includes deliverance from sin as one of its elements (Ps 39:8; 79:9; 130:7, 8). The prophets Jeremiah and Ezekiel give the clearest expression to the idea of salvation as deliverance from sin (Jer 31:31–34 [cf. 33:8]; Ezek 36:25–29 [cf. 37:28]).

(IV) The crown of this personal salvation is reached in the doctrine of the resurrection. Since the realm of the dead was under God's control, the righteous who had died in distress might still hope after death to see the salvation of God. This hope, which appears in sporadic utterances in Ps 49:15; 73:24, 25, finds a classic expression in Job 19:25–27, "I know that my redeemer liveth." This culminates in the doctrine of individual resurrection, which is found in Isa 26:18, and repeated in Dan 12:1–3.

(V) Thus in the OT we have salvation meaning: (1) Deliverance from present danger or trouble especially from defeat in battle. (2) A preliminary foretaste by the righteous, after death, of the enjoyment of the age to come. It is into a world such as this with concepts of salvation as explained that the Lord Jesus came with His gospel of salvation.

(VI) In the teachings of Jesus the word salvation (sōtēría) is only twice used by Him—in the conversation with Zacchaeus (Luke 19:9) and in the interview with the woman of Samaria (John 4:22).

According to Jesus, to have salvation was to have the kingdom of God within the individual (Luke 17:20, 21). Salvation was thus treated as a present experience. To the sinful woman in the house of Simon, He declares that her faith hath saved her and bids her go in peace (Luke 7:50). To Zacchaeus He says, "This day is salvation come to this house" (Luke 19:9).

Jesus taught that when one possesses His salvation, or eternal life, death brings no interruption in the communion of the individual with God. Abraham, Isaac, and Jacob are even now enjoying the resurrection life with God (Luke 20:37, 38); Lazarus passed at once from this world into Abraham's bosom (Luke 16:22); and to the dying thief on the cross the promise is made that, on that same day, he would be with his Master in paradise (Luke 23:43).

(VII) Salvation, especially as viewed by Paul, is also an eschatological conception. Those Christians who are alive when the rapture occurs, along with the "dead in Christ," will be caught up to meet the Lord in the air (1 Thess 4:17) and freed from the last trace of the flesh which had

hitherto hindered them (Rom 8:23; 1 Cor 15:50–52) and shall enter into the joys of His heavenly kingdom. It is this glorious experience—still in the future—to which Paul refers when he uses salvation as an eschatological term (Rom 13:11).

(VIII) But salvation is not merely deliverance from future punishment; it includes also freedom from sin as a present power. Indeed, it is this present deliverance which alone makes the future possible. Through union with Christ, the believer has become a new creature (2 Cor 5:17). He has died to sin (Rom 6:2), crucified the flesh with the passions and the lusts thereof (Gal 5:24), and entered upon a new spiritual life of righteousness, peace, and joy (Rom 14:17). He is a saved man (Rom 8:24; 1 Cor 1:18; 2 Cor 2:15), reconciled to God (Rom 5:1), claiming and receiving the privileges of a son (Rom 8:14, 15). He rejoices in daily experiences of a Father's grace, knowing how to glory even in tribulations (Rom 5:3), since he has learned that all things work together for good to them that love God (Rom 8:28). He continues to have his conflict with sin, but as he once felt himself to be the slave of the flesh, sold unto sin (Rom 7:14), now he knows himself to be its master. The law of the spirit of life in Christ Jesus has made him free from the law of sin and of death (Rom 8:2). And the day is coming when, through the transformation of his body, he shall be freed from whatever defiling contact with sin still remains (Rom 8:23).

(IX) In the Gospel of John and in 1 John, salvation is a present eschatological and final eschatological experience (John 3:15, 16, 36; 5:24; 6:47; 10:28; 17:2; 1 John 2:18, 28; 3:2; 4:17 [cf. John 5:28; 6:44, 54; 21:22]). The éschaton has begun, it has been inaugurated and eternal life is already the possession of all who believe on Christ. He that hears Christ's word and believes Him that sent Him, "hath eternal life and turneth not into judgment, but hath passed out of death unto life" (a.t. [John 5:24 [cf. 3:36; 5:39, 40; 1 John 4:15; 5:12]). Christ is represented as the bread of life (John 6:48), of which, if a man eat, he shall live forever (John 6:51). He is the resurrection and life (John 11:25), and whosoever believes on Him shall never die (John 11:26 [cf. also the passages which speak of regeneration {e.g., John 3:3; 1 John 3:9; 5:1}]).

Final (or consummated) eschatological salvation is connected with the redemption of the universe. Whatever is hopelessly evil—whether in nature, man, or spirit—shall at last be brought under Christ's feet. No foe will remain to dispute the authority of Christ or mar the glories of His eternal kingdom. The last enemy to be destroyed is death (1 Cor 15:26). Not until then will Christ's saving work be finished, and He restore to the Father the power given to Him, that in the redeemed universe God may be all in all (1 Cor 15:28). In order for saved man to live in a congruous environment, the Lord will create a new earth and a new heaven, in which he will live in peace and righteousness (Rom 8:19–23; Rev 21:1).

Syn.: lútrōsis (3085), a ransoming, redemption; apolútrōsis (629), salvation, ransom in full; sōtérion (4992), the means of salvation.

Ant.: apóleia (684), perdition, loss; katastrophḗ (2692), destruction; ólethros (3639), ruin; phthorá (5356), corruption.

4992. σωτήριος sōtḗrios; gen. sōtēríou, masc.-fem., neut. sōtérion, adj. from sōtḗr (4990), a savior, deliverer. Delivering, saving, bringing salvation. As a subst. deliverance, welfare. When Simeon took the baby Jesus in his arms, he realized that Jesus was the means of salvation and said that his eyes had seen tó sōtérión sou, thy salvation (Luke 2:30). In Luke 3:6, when John the Baptist cited Isaiah's prophecy, "And all flesh shall see the salvation of God [tó sōtérion toú Theoú]," he referred to the Lord Jesus Christ who was the means of the salvation that God was going to bring about. The same is so in Acts 28:28. In Eph 6:17 the helmet of salvation is presented as the means of protection. In all these cases, tó sōtérion is used as an adjectival noun. In Titus 2:11 it is used as an adj. describing grace as sōtérios.

Syn.: lútron (3083), ransom; apolútrōsis (629), redemption, deliverance, salvation; antílutron (487), a redemption price, ransom.

Ant.: apóleia (684), destruction, loss; ólethros (3639), ruin, destruction; kríma (2917), judgment, condemnation; katastrophḗ (2692), destruction; phthorá (5356), corruption, destruction.

4993. σωφρονέω sōphronéō; contracted sōphronṓ, fut. sōphronḗsō, from sṓphrōn (4998), sober-minded. To be of sound mind, intrans. To be sane, in one's right mind (Mark 5:15; Luke 8:35; 2 Cor 5:13). By implication to be sober-minded, to think and act soberly, discreetly, to use sound judgment and moderation, to be self-disciplined (Rom 12:3; Titus 2:6; 1 Pet 4:7).

Syn.: néphō (3525), to be sober.

Ant.: paraphronéō (3912), to act the fool; exístēmi (1839), to be out of one's mind, be insane, be beside oneself; ataktéō (812), to behave in a disorderly manner.

4994. σωφρονίζω sōphronízō; fut. sōphronísō, from sṓphrōn (4998), sober-minded. To discipline, train to think and act soberly, discreetly, and in moderation. To correct, teach, with the acc. and inf. (Titus 2:4).

Deriv.: sōphronismós (4995), encouraging self-control, self-discipline.

4995. σωφρονισμός sōphronismós; gen. sōphronismoú, masc. noun from sōphronízō (4994), to discipline, correct. Self-discipline, sobriety, sound mind, sound judgment (2 Tim 1:7).

4996. σωφρόνως sōphrónōs; adv. from sṓphrōn (4998), sober, of sound mind. With sound mind, rationally, with a sober mind, soberly, moderately (Titus 2:12).

Ant.: asṓtōs (811), dissolutely, riotously, prodigally; atáktōs (814), irregularly, disorderly.

4997. σωφροσύνη *sōphrosúnē*; gen. *sōphrosúnēs*, fem. noun from *sṓphrōn* (4998), of sound mind, sane, temperate. Sober-mindedness, moderation of desires, passions, or conduct (Acts 26:25; 1 Tim 2:9, 15).

Syn.: *phrónēsis* (5428), prudence.

Ant.: *paraphronía* (3913), insanity, foolhardiness; *manía* (3130), mania, madness, craziness; *aphrosúnē* (877), senselessness, foolishness; *ánoia* (454), folly; *asōtía* (810), profligacy.

4998. σώφρων *sṓphrōn*; gen. *sṓphronos*, masc.-fem., neut. *sṓphron*, adj. from *sóos* (n.f.), sound, and *phrḗn* (5424), understanding. Discreet, sober, temperate, of a sound mind (1 Tim 3:2; Titus 1:8; 2:2, 5); self-disciplined in one's freedom, self-restrained in all passions and desires.

T

4999. Ταβέρναι *Tabérnai*; gen. *Tabernón*, pl. fem. noun. Taverns. Part of the name of the Three Taverns, which was a place where some of the brethren came to meet Paul on his journey to Rome, and by their coming the Apostle took fresh courage (Acts 28:13–15). It was on the Appian Way, thirty-three miles southeast from Rome and ten miles from Appii Forum. It may have taken its name from a group of three taverns or places of refreshment for travelers.

5000. Ταβιθά *Tabithá*; indeclinable fem. proper noun transliterated from the Aramaic. Tabitha, meaning gazelle. An exemplary disciple of Christ at Joppa whose deeds of benevolence had greatly endeared her to the people. After she was dead and her body prepared for the grave, she was miraculously restored to life through the instrumentality of Peter (Acts 9:36–40).

5001. τάγμα *tágma*; gen. *tágmatos*, neut. noun from *tássō* (5021), to arrange in an orderly manner. Anything arranged in order or in array such as a body of troops, a band, cohort (Sept.: 2 Sam 23:13). In the NT, order, sequence, or turn (1 Cor 15:23).
    Syn.: *táxis* (5010), regular arrangement, succession.

5002. τακτός *taktós*, fem. *takté*, neut. *taktón*, from *tássō* (5021), to arrange in an orderly manner. Set in order, arranged; only in Acts 12:21, meaning on a fixed or appointed day.
    Ant.: *átaktos* (813), unarranged, unruly; *akatástatos* (182), inconstant, unstable; *astēriktos* (793), unstable, vacillating.

5003. ταλαιπωρέω *talaipōréō*; contracted *talaipōrō̂*, fut. *talaipōrḗsō*, from *talaípōros* (5005), afflicted, wretched, miserable. To endure toil and hardship, be afflicted, distressed, miserable, to lament or mourn. In the NT, used only in James 4:9 metaphorically meaning to endure affliction, distress.
    Deriv.: *talaipōría* (5004), misery.
    Syn.: *kakopathéō* (2553), to suffer hardship; *hupophérō* (5297), to endure, undergo hardship; *páschō* (3958), to suffer; *kataponéō* (2669), to be oppressed with pain; *lupéō* (3076), to grieve, be in heaviness.
    Ant.: *eudokéō* (2106), to take pleasure; *euthuméō* (2114), to be cheerful; *eupsuchéō* (2174), to be in good spirits, be encouraged.

5004. ταλαιπωρία *talaipōría*; gen. *talaipōrías*, fem. noun from *talaipōréō* (5003), to afflict. Affliction, distress, misery (Rom 3:16 quoted from Isa 59:7; James 5:1).
    Syn.: *kákōsis* (2561), affliction, ill-treatment; *thlípsis* (2347), pressure; *básanos* (931), torture, torment; *páthēma* (3804), affliction, suffering.
    Ant.: *eudokía* (2107), satisfaction; *eúnoia* (2133), kindness; *chará* (5479), joy; *agallíasis* (20), gladness, exultation; *euphrosúnē* (2167), merriment, gladness.

5005. ταλαίπωρος *talaípōros*; gen. *talaipórou*, masc.-fem., neut. *talaípōron*, adj. from *tálas* (n.f.), suffering, wretched. Afflicted, wretched, miserable (Rom 7:24, spoken figuratively); suffering from spiritual or emotional misery (Rev 3:17; Sept.: Ps 137:8).
    Deriv.: *talaipōréo* (5003), to endure toil and hardship.
    Syn.: *ptōchós* (4434), poor, helpless; *eleeinós* (1652), pitiable.

5006. ταλαντιαῖος *talantiaíos*; fem. *talantiaía*, neut. *talantiaíon*, adj. from *tálanton* (5007), a weight of measurement, a talent. Weighing a talent, or a talent in weight. A talent was sixty minas, weighing seventy-five pounds or thirty-four kilograms. A mina was fifty shekels with each shekel weighing 0.4 ounces or 0.6 kilograms. Only in Rev 16:21, referring to the weight of the hailstones which will descend from heaven.

5007. τάλαντον *tálanton*; gen. *talántou*, neut. noun from *tláō* (n.f.), to bear. The scale of a balance; pl. *tá tálanta* scales. Later it came to mean something weighed, a weight, and hence a talent as a certain fixed weight for gold and silver. Later it was used as a commercial weight representing different weights. Generally, however, the talent contained sixty minas or 6,000 drachmae. The common Attic talent was generally equal to eighty Roman pounds, but according to others it was equal to fifty-five or fifty-six pounds. The Jewish talent contained 3,000 shekels of the sanctuary (Ex 38:25, 26), equal to 113 pounds and ten ounces. The talent was also used as a denomination for money which was reckoned by weight. Different sums of local currency were attributed to each monetary talent. It is now estimated that a talent was equal to approximately one thousand dollars. Whatever its exact value, in the NT a talent indicates a large sum of money (Matt 18:24; 25:15, 16, 18, 20, 22, 24, 25, 28).

Deriv.: *talantiaíos* (5006), weighing a talent.

5008. ταλιθά *talithá*; transliterated from the Aramaic *ṯᵉlîṯhāh* (not found in the OT). A girl or maiden (Mark 5:41). The Gr. word equivalent to the Aramaic would be *korásion* (2877), damsel.

Syn.: *paidískē* (3814), maid or girl; *paidíon* (3813), a child or servant.

5009. ταμεῖον *tameíon*; gen. *tameíou*, neut. noun from *tamieúō* (n.f.), to collect in one place. A warehouse, a storehouse (Luke 12:24; Sept.: Deut 28:8; Prov 3:10; 24:4). Any place of privacy, a room, closet (Matt 6:6; 24:26; Luke 12:3, where one cannot be easily seen; Sept.: Gen 43:30; 2 Kgs 6:12; Isa 26:20).

5010. τάξις *táxis*; gen. *táxeōs*, fem. noun from *tássō* (5021), to arrange in order. A setting in order; hence, order, arrangement, disposition, especially of troops; an order or rank in a state or in society. In the NT:

(I) Arrangement, disposition, series (Luke 1:8; 1 Cor 14:40, in proper order, orderly). Figuratively, good order, well-regulated life (Col 2:5).

(II) Rank, quality, character, as in the phrase "a priest according to the order of Melchisedeck" (Heb 5:6, 10; 6:20; 7:11, 17, 21; quoted from Ps 110:4) which means a priest of the same order, rank, or quality as Melchizedek. Also Heb 7:11, not according to the order or rank of Aaron.

Syn.: *tágma* (5001), a group of people that has been arranged in an orderly fashion.

Ant.: *akatastasía* (181), instability, confusion; *súgchusis* (4799), confusion.

5011. ταπεινός *tapeinós*; fem. *tapeinḗ*, neut. *tapeinón*, adj. Low, not high, particularly of attitude and social positions.

(I) Of condition or lot, meaning humble, poor, of low degree (Luke 1:52; James 1:9 where it is the opposite of *ploúsios* (4145), wealthy, rich; Sept.: 1 Sam 18:23; Job 12:21).

(II) Of the mind, meaning lowly, humble, modest, including the idea of affliction, depression of mind (2 Cor 10:1 where it means timid, modest, the opposite of *tharrón*, the pres. part. of *tharréō* [2292], to exercise courage, courageous). In the masc. (Rom 12:16). Elsewhere with the accessory idea of piety toward God (James 4:6; 1 Pet 5:5 [in contrast to *huperéphanos* {5244}, proud] quoted from Prov 3:34). See Matt 11:29; 2 Cor

7:6; Sept.: Ps 18:28; 34:19; Isa 11:4; 66:2.

Deriv.: *tapeinóō* (5013), to humble.
Syn.: *eleeinós* (1652), pitiable.

5012. ταπεινοφροσύνη *tapeinophrosúnē*; gen. *tapeinophrosúnēs*, fem. noun from *tapeinóphrōn* (n.f.), lowminded, base, which is from *tapeinós* (5011), lowly, humble. Humility, lowliness of mind, the esteeming of ourselves small, inasmuch as we are so, the correct estimate of ourselves (Acts 20:19; Eph 4:2; Phil 2:3; Col 2:18, 23; 3:12; 1 Pet 5:5). For the sinner *tapeinophrosúnē* involves the confession of his sin and a deep realization of his unworthiness to receive God's marvelous grace.

Syn.: *praǘtēs* (4240), meekness.

Ant.: *alazoneía* (212), pride, boasting, vainglory; *huperēphanía* (5243), haughtiness, considering oneself better than others; *phusíōsis* (5450), disdainful pride.

5013. ταπεινόω *tapeinóō*; contracted *tapeinó*, fut. *tapeinósō*, from *tapeinós* (5011), humble. To humble, bring low:

(I) Particularly (Luke 3:5, "every mountain and hill shall be brought low [made level]," quoted from Isa 40:4).

(II) Figuratively as to condition, circumstances, to bring low, to humble, abase. With the acc. *heautón*, to humble himself, to make himself of low condition, to be poor and needy (Matt 18:4; 2 Cor 11:7). Mid. or pass. (Phil 4:12; Sept.: Prov 13:7; Isa 2:9, 12). In mind, to make humble through disappointment (2 Cor 12:21). In the pass. (Matt 23:12; Luke 14:11; 18:14). With the idea of contrition and penitence toward God (James 4:10; 1 Pet 5:6; Sept.: Isa 5:15; 10:33). See Gen 16:9; Isa 58:3, 5).

Deriv.: *tapeínōsis* (5014), humility.

Syn.: *kataischúnō* (2617), to shame, disgrace, dishonor.

Ant.: *hupsóō* (5312), to exalt, lift up; *megalúnō* (3170), to magnify, enlarge; *epaírō* (1869), to raise up, exalt; *huperaíromai* (5229), to become haughty, exalt oneself, be proud; *huperupsóō*

(5251), to elevate above others, highly exalt; *huperphronéō* (5252), to think too highly of oneself; *tuphóō* (5187), to fill with pride.

5014. ταπείνωσις *tapeínōsis*; gen. *tapeinṓseōs*, fem. noun from *tapeinóō* (5013), to humble, abase. The act of humiliation. In Luke 1:48 the virgin Mary is described as being of *tapeínōsis*, a humble origin or lowly estate. In Acts 8:33, *tapeínōsis* refers to our Lord's humiliation. In Phil 3:21 *tapeínōsis* is translated vile, referring to our present body being a sinful one. See Sept.: 2 Sam 16:12; Ps 136:23. In James 1:10 the rich is made low (*tapeínōsis*) in recognition that his riches can not extend his life or gain the approbation of God.

Syn.: *aischúnē* (152), shame, disgrace; *atimía* (819), indignity, disgrace.

Ant.: *megaleiótēs* (3168), magnificence, majesty; *timḗ* (5092), honor, respect; *dóxa* (1391), glory.

5015. ταράσσω *tarássō*, **ταράττω** *taráttō*; fut. *taráxō*. To stir up, to trouble, agitate. Used trans.:

(I) As agitating water in a pool (John 5:4, 7; Sept.: Ezek 32:2, 13).

(II) Figuratively used of the mind, to stir up, trouble, disturb with various emotions such as fear, put in trepidation. In the pass., to be in trepidation (Matt 2:3; 14:26; Mark 6:50; Luke 1:12; 24:38; 1 Pet 3:14). In Acts 17:8 in the act. and with the acc., to stir up or trouble with questions, meaning to disquiet. Used in the pass. (John 12:27; 13:21; 14:1, 27). John 11:33, "He disturbed himself" (a.t.) in the act. is equal to the pass., "He was troubled in the spirit" in 13:21. It also is used in reference to doubt or perplexity, with the acc. (Acts 15:24), "He perplexed you with his words" (a.t. [Gal 1:7; 5:10]).

Deriv.: *diatarássō* (1298), to disturb greatly; *ektarássō* (1613), to stir up; *tarachḗ* (5016), agitation; *tárachos* (5017), a disturbance.

Syn.: *diegeírō* (1326), to arouse, stir up; *thlíbō* (2346), to afflict; *enochléō* (1776), to vex; *parenochléō* (3926), to harass; *skúllō* (4660), to annoy; *anastatóō* (387), to stir up; *thorubéō* (2350), to make an uproar; *throéō* (2360), to clamor; *thorubéō* (2350), to disturb.

Ant.: *hēsucházō* (2270), to be still; *katastéllō* (2687), to quiet; *eirēneúō* (1514), to bring peace; *eirēnopoiéō* (1517), to make peace.

5016. ταραχή *taraché*; gen. *tarachês*, fem. noun from *tarássō* (5015), to stir or agitate. A stirring up, trouble, agitation. Used of water in a pool (John 5:4); metaphorically of popular excitement meaning commotion or tumult (Mark 13:8).

Syn.: *klúdōn* (2830), a surge of the sea, raging wave; *ánemos* (417), wind; *thúella* (2366), storm, tempest; *laílaps* (2978), a whirlwind, storm, tempest; *sálos* (4535), a billow, wave.

Ant.: *hēsuchía* (2271), quietness, silence; *galénē* (1055), tranquillity, calm; *eirénē* (1515), peace, quietness.

5017. τάραχος *tárachos*; gen. *taráchou*, masc. noun from *tarássō* (5015), to stir or agitate. Stir, commotion, confusion, the same as *ataxía*, without order. In the NT, it means consternation, trepidation resulting from fear (Acts 12:18; Sept.: 1 Sam 5:9), as also resulting from excitement, tumult and contention (Acts 19:23).

5018. Ταρσεύς *Tarseús*; gen. *Tarséōs*, masc. proper noun. A Tarsean, a person from *Tarsós* (5019), Tarsus, a celebrated city of Asia Minor (Acts 9:11; 21:39).

5019. Ταρσός *Tarsós*; gen. *Tarsoú*, fem. noun. Tarsus. Celebrated as the birthplace of the Apostle Paul (Acts 9:11, 30; 11:25; 21:39; 22:3), it was the capital of Cilicia in Asia Minor, and "no mean city." Some writers identify it with Tarshish.

Tarsus was about twelve miles from the Mediterranean and an equal distance to the north of the Taurus Mountains, standing on both banks of the river Cydnus. It possessed a Roman stadium and gymnasium and became famous as the seat of one of the three great universities of the ancient world, ranking next to Athens and Alexandria. The imperial family of Rome selected tutors from Tarsus. Hence the boyhood of the Apostle Paul was passed in a city not only of great commercial importance, but one offering opportunities for secular learning as well.

5020. ταρταρόω *tartaróō*; contracted *tartaró*, fut. *tartarósō*, from *Tártaros* (n.f.), the subterranean abyss of Greek mythology where demigods were punished. It is mentioned in the pseudepigraphal book of Enoch as the place where fallen angels are confined. It is found only in its verbal form in 2 Pet 2:4 meaning to cast into or consign to Tartarus. It is part of the realm of death designated in Scripture as *Shᵉ'ōl* (7585, OT) in the OT and *Hádēs* (86) in the NT. These angels are being held in this netherworld dungeon until the day of final judgment. Peter's usage of this term is not evidence either that Christianity was a syncretistic religion or that Peter himself believed in the pagan myths about Tartarus. Peter has adapted a word and not adopted a theology.

5021. τάσσω *tássō*, **τάττω** *táttō*; fut. *táxō*. To place, set, appoint, arrange, order. In the NT, used figuratively, meaning to set in a certain order, constitute, appoint, used trans.:

(I) Generally with *eis* (1519), unto, and the acc. (1 Cor 16:15, have set or devoted themselves). In the pass. with *eis* (Acts 13:48, "as many as were ordained to eternal life"). Followed by *hupó* (5259), by, with the acc. (Luke 7:8); in an absolute sense (Rom 13:1; Sept.: 2 Kgs 10:24; Job 14:13; Jer 3:19; Ezek 44:14).

(II) To arrange, appoint, with the acc. and dat. (Acts 28:23). Followed by the dat. and inf. (Acts 22:10); with the inf. implied (Matt 28:16; Sept.: 2 Sam 20:5);

followed by the inf. and the acc. (Acts 15:2).

Deriv.: *anatássomai* (392), to compose in an orderly manner; *antitássō* (498), to resist; *apotássō* (657), to set in its proper category away from oneself; *átaktos* (813), disorderly, irregular; *diatássō* (1299), set in order, issue orderly and detailed instructions; *epitássō* (2004), to order; *prostássō* (4367), a specific command for a specific person; *protássō* (4384), to foreordain; *suntássō* (4929), to arrange or set in order together; *tágma* (5001), an order, regular method; *taktós* (5002), arranged, appointed; *táxis* (5010), an arrangement; *hupotássō* (5293), to place under.

Syn.: *títhēmi* (5087), to place, appoint, settle, ordain; *apókeimai* (606), to be reserved, appointed, laid aside for a certain purpose; *diatíthemai* (1303), to set apart, to appoint; *kathístēmi* (2525), to designate, appoint, place.

Ant.: *metatíthēmi* (3346), to transfer, remove.

5022. ταῦρος *taúros*; gen. *taúrou*, masc. noun. A bull, bullock (Matt 22:4; Acts 14:13; Heb 9:13; 10:4; Sept.: Ex 21:28, 29).

Syn.: *boús* (1016), an ox, cow; *móschos* (3448), a young bullock, calf; *dámalis* (1151), a heifer.

5023. ταῦτα *taúta*; neut. pl. (nom. or acc.) of *houtos* (3778), this one. After *kathós* (2531), meaning as (John 8:28); followed by *éte* (2258), you were, meaning such were you (1 Cor 6:11). As, referring to what follows (Luke 18:11). The opposite of *ekeína* (1565), those things, *taúta*, these things, shows proximity. As an adv., with *katá* (2596), according to, meaning after the same manner, thus, so (Luke 6:23, 26; 17:30).

5024. ταυτά *tautá*; composed of *tá* (3588), and *autós* (846), the same. These, these things. It is the same as *tá autá*, the same things (1 Thess 2:14).

Syn.: *tá ídia* (2398), the same things (pl.).

Ant.: *hétera* (2087), different ones (pl.).

5025. ταύταις *taútais*; dat., acc. *taútas*, fem. pl. forms of *houtos* (3778), this one.

5026. ταύτῃ *taútē*; dat, gen. *taútēs*, acc. *taútēn*, fem. sing. forms of *houtos* (3778), this one.

5027. ταφή *taphḗ*; gen. *taphḗs*, fem. noun from *tháptō* (2290), to bury. Burial or place of burial; with the dat. (Matt 27:7, "for burying strangers" [a.t.]; Sept.: Deut 34:6; Eccl 6:3; Ezek 32:23).

Ant.: *anástasis* (386), a raising up, resurrection; *exanástasis* (1815), resurrection out of; *égersis* (1454), a rising up, rousing.

5028. τάφος *táphos*; gen. *táphou*, masc. noun from *tháptō* (2290), to bury. Burial, sepulcher. A burial place, sepulcher (Matt 23:27, 29; 27:61, 64, 66; 28:1). Figuratively (Rom 3:13 quoted from Ps 5:10).

Syn.: *mnḗma* (3418), tomb, monument, grave.

5029. τάχα *tácha*; adv. from *tachús* (5036), prompt, swift. Probably, perhaps (Rom 5:7; Phile 1:15).

Ant.: *alēthḗs* (230), truly, surely; *mén* (3303), indeed, truly.

5030. ταχέως *tachéōs*; adv. from *tachús* (5036), prompt, swift. Quickly, speedily. In the NT, equivalent to soon, shortly, quickly, hastily (1 Cor 4:19; Gal 1:6; Phil 2:19, 24; 2 Tim 4:9; Sept.: Judg 9:48; Isa 8:3). In the sense of hastily (Luke 14:21; 16:6; John 11:31; 2 Thess 2:2; 1 Tim 5:22; Sept.: Prov 25:8).

Syn.: *euthéōs* (2112), straightway, directly, forthwith; *áphnō* (869), suddenly; *exaíphnēs* (1810), suddenly; *exápina* (1819), suddenly, unexpectedly.

5031. ταχινός *tachinós*; fem. *tachinḗ*, neut. *tachinón*, adj. from *tachús* (5036), prompt, swift. Quick, swift (Sept.: Isa 59:7). Figuratively, swift, speedy, near at hand, impending (2 Pet 1:14; 2:1).

Syn.: *aiphnídios* (160), sudden, unexpected.

Ant.: *bradús* (1021), slow; *argós* (692), slow, idle.

5032. τάχιον *táchion*; adv., the neut. of *tachíōn* (n.f.), quicker, more sudden, which is the comparative of *tachús* (5036), prompt, swift. More quickly, more swiftly, more speedily, more suddenly (John 20:4, he outran Peter). Also sooner, the obj. of comparison being everywhere implied, sooner than one expected or intended, more speedily, sooner (John 13:27; 1 Tim 3:14; Heb 13:19, 23).

5033. τάχιστα *táchista*; adv., neut. pl. of *táchistos* (n.f.), quickest, which is the superlative of *tachús* (5036), prompt, swift. Most quickly, most speedily, with the adv. *hōs* (5613), the soonest possible (Acts 17:15).

5034. τάχος *táchos*; gen. *táchous*, neut. noun from *tachús* (5036), prompt, swift. Quickness, swiftness, speed. In the NT, only in a phrase with the prep. *en* (1722), in, used as an adv. meaning quickly, of short duration, speedily, soon, shortly, equivalent to *tachéōs* (5030), suddenly, quickly (Luke 18:8; Acts 25:4; Rom 16:20; Rev 1:1; 22:6, meaning suddenly). Also with the idea of haste (Acts 12:7; 22:18; Sept.: Deut 11:17; Ps 2:12).

Syn.: *spoudḗ* (4710), speed, diligence.

Ant.: *bradútēs* (1022), tardiness, slackness, slow pace.

5035. ταχύ *tachú*; neut. sing. of *tachús* (5036), prompt, swift, used as an adv. Quickly, speedily, with haste (Matt 5:25; 28:7, 8; Mark 16:8 [TR]; John 11:29; Sept.: 2 Sam 17:16); suddenly (Rev 2:5 [TR], 16; 3:11; 11:14; 22:7, 12, 20; Sept.:

Ps 102:3). By implication, carelessly, lightly (Mark 9:39).

5036. ταχύς *tachús*; fem. *tacheía*, neut. *tachú*, adj. Quick, swift, nimble. In the NT, figuratively, quick, swift, with the meaning of ready, prompt (James 1:19; Sept.: Prov 29:20).

Deriv.: *tácha* (5029), quickly, soon; *tachéōs* (5030), quickly, speedily; *tachinós* (5031), quick, swift; *táchos* (5034), quickness, speed.

Ant.: *bradús* (1021), slow, dull; *argós* (692), inactive, idle, slow.

5037. τε *te*; a conj. as an enclitic particle, meaning "and," corresponding to *kaí* (2532), and. In the NT, found chiefly in the writings of Luke and Paul, and in the book of Hebrews; found four times in Matthew (22:10; 23:6 [TR]; 27:48; 28:12); three times in John (2:15; 4:42; 6:18); once in James (3:7); once in Jude (1:6); twice in Rev (1:2; 21:12). In general, *kaí* is used to couple ideas which follow directly and necessarily from what precedes, while *te* is employed generally when something is subjoined which does not thus directly and necessarily follow. *Kaí* connects and *te* annexes. Hence, *te* is the most general of all the copulatives (serving merely to show that the word or words preceding it has some connection with the one or ones following it). The place of *te* is usually after the first word of a clause.

(I) Simply, that is, without other particles where it then serves to annex, as stated above (Matt 28:12; John 4:42; 6:18; Acts 1:15 in a parenthesis; 2:3, 33, 37; 3:10; 4:13, 33; 5:42; 8:1, 3, 6; 12:12; 18:11; 20:11; 23:10; 24:27; 27:20; Rom 2:19; 1 Cor 4:21; Heb 1:3; Jude 1:6). Also repeated as annexing several particulars *te . . . te*, and . . . and (Acts 2:46; 16:11, 12; 24:23; Heb 6:2). Once with the meaning of both / and (Acts 26:16).

(II) Most frequently as strengthening *kaí*, either directly before it as *te kaí* or with one or more words intervening, *te . . . kaí*, implying close connection, not only / but also, both / and. As connecting clauses (Matt 27:48; Luke 24:20; Acts 9:18; 10:2; Heb 6:4); coupling together inf. depending on the same verb (Luke 12:45; Acts 1:1); connecting nouns, for example, *te kaí* (Luke 21:11; Acts 2:9, 10; 26:3; Rom 1:12, 14; 1 Cor 1:2, 30; Heb 2:4; James 3:7); connecting adv. (Acts 24:3; [adj.] Sept.: Job 9:4). Also where one or more words come between *te* and *kaí* or when *kaí* is used more than once (Luke 2:16; 21:11; John 2:15; Acts 1:8; 26:30; Rom 1:16; Phil 1:7; Heb 9:2, 19). Sometimes the word before *te* is also implied after *kaí*, that is, the *te* marks it as belonging equally to both members (Acts 2:43). The same with the art. *hó te*, referring to Peter and James in Acts 1:13; (see Acts 13:1; Rom 1:20); or a relative pron. (Acts 26:22); especially a prep. (Acts 25:23; 28:23). Sometimes two nouns of opposing meaning are connected by *te kaí*, forming then a periphrasis for "all" (Matt 22:10, "both good and bad," meaning all; Acts 24:15; 26:22; Heb 5:14). Rarely *te kaí* is used in the sense of "and also" (Acts 19:27). *Éti* (2089), now, still, yet, with *te kaí*, *éti te kaí*, meaning "and further also" (Acts 21:28); *homoíōs te kaí* (*homoíōs* [3668], likewise; *te kaí*), meaning "and in like manner also" (Rom 1:27). Here *kaí* seems to be used merely to strengthen *te*.

(III) Sometimes *te* corresponds to *dé* (1161), but, in a following clause. The connection then is antithetic and thus emphatic (Acts 19:3, *eípe te prós autoús* . . . *hoi dé eípon*, "And he said unto them, . . . and they said"; 22:8, 10; 22:28).

(IV) With other particles:

(A) *Te gár* (1063), therefore, where *te* simply annexes and *gár* assigns a reason (Rom 1:26; 7:7; Heb 2:11).

(B) *Eán* (1437), if, with *te*, *eán te*, and if; repeated *eán te* . . . *eán te*, whether / or (Rom 14:8). *Eán te gár* (1063) *kaí* (2532), and—*eán te gár kaí*, for though also (2 Cor 10:8). Here the force of *te* cannot be conveyed well in Eng. See *eíte* (1535), III, H, whether / or, as including several particulars.

(C) *Hóte hē te*, *tó te*, that is, the art. (masc. *ho*, fem. *hē*, neut. *tó*), with *te* meaning "and who" (masc., fem., neut.); for example, where *te* merely annexes (Acts 19:12, "and the"; 26:30, "and Bernice"; 27:3, "and the next day"; 27:5, "and . . . over the sea"; Heb 9:1, "and a worldly sanctuary"). Followed by *kaí* after one or more intervening words (Luke 23:12; Acts 5:24, *hó te hiereús kaí* where *hiereús* [2409], priest stands between *hó te* and *kaí* 17:10, 14; 21:25; Rom 1:20, 27; Eph 1:10; Heb 2:11, *hó te gár hagiázōn kaí* Heb 9:2).

Deriv.: *eíte* (1535), and if, ever.

5038. τεῖχος *teíchos*; gen. *teíchous*, neut. noun. A wall, especially of a city (Acts 9:25; 2 Cor 11:33; Heb 11:30; Rev 21:12, 14, 15, 17–19; Sept.: Deut 3:5; Josh 6:5, 20).

Syn.: *toíchos* (5109), a wall, especially of a house.

5039. τεκμήριον *tekmḗrion*; gen. *tekmēríou*, neut. noun from *tekmaíromai* (n.f.), to mark out, which is from *tékmar* (n.f.), a fixed sign, proof, end, limit, goal, token. A fixed sign, certain or sure token, infallible proof (Acts 1:3).

Syn.: *éndeixis* (1732), proof, the act of proving; *éndeigma* (1730), the thing proved; *apódeixis* (585), demonstration, proof.

5040. τεκνίον *tekníon*; gen. *tekníou*, neut. noun, diminutive of *téknon* (5043), child. A little child. Used only figuratively and always in the pl. *teknía*. A term of affection by a teacher to his disciples (John 13:33; Gal 4:19; 1 John 2:1, 12, 28; 3:7, 18; 4:4; 5:21).

Syn.: *gennētós* (1084), one born; *génos* (1085), offspring; *génnēma* (1081), offspring; *paidíon* (3813), young or little child; *paidárion* (3808), a child; *thugátrion* (2365), a young daughter; *korásion* (2877), a maiden, little girl.

Ant.: *goneús* (1118), a parent; *mḗtēr* (3384), mother; *mámmē* (3125), a grandmother; *patḗr* (3962), father; *prógonos*

(4269), ancestor, parent, forefather; *patriárchēs* (3966), a progenitor, patriarch.

5041. τεκνογονέω *teknogonéō*; contracted *teknogonṓ*, fut. *teknogonḗsō*, from *teknogónos* (n.f.), child-bearing, which is from *téknon* (5043), a child, and the obsolete *génō* (n.f.), which has become *gínomai* (1096), to make. To bear children, be the mother of a family. The action represented by this word takes in all the duties of the maternal relationship (1 Tim 5:14).

Deriv.: *teknogonía* (5042), the bearing of children.

Syn.: *gennáō* (1080), to beget, chiefly (not exclusively) used of men, to sire children; *tíktō* (5088) to beget, used of females bearing children; *apokuéō* (616), to give birth to.

5042. τεκνογονία *teknogonía*; gen. *teknogonías*, fem. noun from *teknogonéō* (5041), to bear children. The bearing of children, and thus by implication including all the duties of the maternal relation (1 Tim 2:15, through the faithful performance of her duties as a mother in bringing up her household for God [cf. 1 Tim 5:10]).

5043. τέκνον *téknon*; gen. *téknou*, neut. noun from *tíktō* (5088), to bring forth, bear children. A child, male or female, son or daughter.

(I) Particularly and generally:

(A) Sing., a child (Matt 10:21; Luke 1:7; Rev 12:4). Pl., children (Matt 10:21; Mark 12:19; Luke 7:35; Acts 21:5; Titus 1:6; 2 John 1:4, 13; Sept.: Gen 3:16; 30:1; 33:6, 7).

(B) Specifically of a son, sing. (Matt 21:28; Phil 2:22; Rev 12:5; Sept.: Gen 17:16; 22:7; 48:19). Pl., sons (Matt 21:28; Acts 21:21; Sept.: Esth 9:25).

(II) Pl., *tékna*, children, in a wider sense meaning descendants, posterity (Matt 3:9; Luke 1:17; 3:8; Acts 2:39; Rom 9:7, 8; Gal 4:28, 31; Sept.: Ex 10:2; Josh 14:9; Ps 109:13; Jer 31:17; Zech

10:7, 9). Emphatically it means true children, genuine descendants (John 8:39; 1 Pet 3:6).

(III) Metaphorically of one who is the object of parental love and care, or who yields filial love and reverence toward another.

(A) As a tender term of address, in the voc., equivalent to "my child" or "my son" as from a friend or teacher (Matt 9:2; Mark 2:5; Luke 16:25; Sept.: 1 Sam 3:6, 16).

(B) Generally for a pupil, disciple, the spiritual child of someone (1 Tim 1:18; 2 Tim 1:2; Phile 1:10). Followed by *en kuríō* (*en* [1722], in; *kuríō* [the dat. of *kúrios* {2962}, the Lord]), in the Lord (1 Cor 4:17); by *en pístei* (4102), in the faith (1 Tim 1:2); by *katá pístin* (*katá* [2596], according to; *pístin* [4102], faith), according to the faith (Titus 1:4). In the pl. (1 Cor 4:14; 2 Cor 6:13; 3 John 1:4).

(C) *Tékna toú Theoú* ([2316], God), children of God, means those whom God loves and cherishes as a Father. See also *patḗr* (3962) II, A, B; also *gennáō* (1080), I, A, 2. Also spoken of the Jews (John 11:52 [cf. Sept.: Isa 30:1; Hos 11:1]). Generally of the devout worshipers of God, the righteous, saints, Christians (John 1:12; Rom 8:16, 17, 21; 9:8; Eph 5:1; 1 John 3:1, 2, 10; 5:2; Sept.: Prov 14:27).

(D) *Tékna toú diabólou* (*diabólou* [1228], of the devil), children of the devil, meaning his followers, subjects, in contrast to *tá tékna toú Theoú*, the children of God (1 John 3:10 [cf. 2 Kgs 16:7]).

(IV) On rare occasions, a distinction between *téknon* and *huiós* (5207), son, can be noted. *Huiós* at times refers to a legal heir and thus, by implication, an adult. It seems to underscore the character or maturity of the individual. *Téknon* is a more general designation for offspring and contemplates the individual as one who is parented, one who has been born to another. Nevertheless, because these words often overlap and are used without discrimination, it is unwise to press their semantic difference and make it the basis of an interpretation or doctrine. For example, Jesus is never designated as *téknon* or *téknon Theoú* (gen. of *Theós* [2316], God), Son of God, but always *ho huiós*, the Son, the Son of God or the Son of Man. Some have attributed this to what they perceive to be a real difference between the two words. It is contended that the former points to Christ's origin (speaking of Him as one born of God) and that the latter points to Christ's character or status (speaking of Him as one who possesses God's full likeness or as His heir). However, this is artificial and unnecessary. Still, the absence of the expression *téknon Theoú* would certainly not be due to its theological impropriety. The Scripture bears ample testimony to the eternal generation of the Son. The exclusion of *téknon Theoú* in favor of *huiós Theoú* is doubtless due to the authors' stylistic preferences.

(V) Believers are called both *tékna Theoú*, children of God (John 1:12; Rom 8:16, 17, 21; 9:8; Eph 5:1; 1 John 3:1, 2, 10; 5:2), and *huioí* (5207), sons (Rom 8:14, 19; Gal 3:26; 4:6, 7; Heb 12:7).

Deriv.: *áteknos* (815), childless; *teknotrophéō* (5044), to bring up children; *philóteknos* (5391), loving one's children.

5044. τεκνοτροφέω *teknotrophéō*; contracted *teknotrophṓ*, fut. *teknotrophḗsō*, from *téknon* (5043), child, and *tréphō* (5142), to nourish, bring up. To bring up children, to fulfill the duties of a mother (1 Tim 5:10).

5045. τέκτων *téktōn*; gen. *téktonos*, masc. noun kindred with *teúchō* (n.f.), to fabricate, and *tíktō* (5088), to produce, bear, bring forth. An artificer, especially a worker in wood, a carpenter, joiner (Matt 13:55; Mark 6:3). A craftsman of wood (Sept.: 2 Sam 5:11; 2 Kgs 12:11; Isa 40:20); an artificer of iron (Sept.: 1 Sam 13:19); of brass (Sept.: 1 Kgs 7:14).

Deriv.: *architéktōn* (753), a chief constructor.

Syn.: *technítēs* (5079), an artisan, builder, craftsman; *ktístēs* (2939), a founder, builder, creator.

5046. τέλειος *téleios*; fem. *teleía*, neut. *téleion*, adj. from *télos* (5056), goal, purpose. Finished, that which has reached its end, term, limit; hence, complete, full, wanting in nothing.

(I) Generally (James 1:4, 17, 25; 1 John 4:18 [cf. Heb 9:11]; Sept.: Ex 12:5). Figuratively, in a moral sense, of persons (Matt 5:48 [cf. Luke 6:36]; Matt 19:21; Col 1:28; 4:12; James 1:4; 3:2); the will of God (Rom 12:2; Sept.: Gen 6:9; 1 Kgs 11:4). When used in a moral sense referring to God's expectation of us, it means completely blameless. A "perfect gift" in James 1:17 means one that has all the necessary qualities. In James 1:4, "that ye may be perfect" means that you may keep yourself "unspotted from the world." It has a similar meaning in Matt 5:48; 19:21; Rom 12:2; Col 1:28; 4:12; James 3:2.

(II) Specifically of persons meaning full age, adulthood, full-grown, of persons, meaning full-grown in mind and understanding (1 Cor 14:20); in knowledge of the truth (1 Cor 2:6; Phil 3:15; Heb 5:14); in Christian faith and virtue (Eph 4:13). In the neut. *tó téleion* means the final destination of the believer, that is, heaven (1 Cor 13:10, as contrasted to the full age in knowledge and understanding in 13:11). This image of fully completed growth as contrasted with infancy and childhood underlies the ethical use of *téleioi*, being set over against the babes in Christ (1 Cor 2:6; 14:20; Eph 4:13, 14; Phil 3:15; Heb 5:14).

(III) *Téleios* can be used in a relative or absolute sense (Matt 5:48; 19:21). God's perfection is absolute; man's is relative. The *téleios* is one who has attained moral maturity, the goal for which he was intended, namely, to be a man obedient in Christ.

(IV) *Tó téleion*, perfect, in the neut. means the complete one in contrast with *tó ek mérous* (*ek* [1537], of; *mérous* [3313], a part), that which is in part. *Tó téleion*, therefore, indicates the ultimate goal of heavenly perfection as contrasted with the immediate and merely partial experience of saints on earth (1 Cor 13:10). In 1 John 4:18 *hē teleía agápē* ([26], love), the perfect love, means the love which is mature, not lacking boldness or confidence and therefore not hampered by the insecurity or anxiety which are characteristic of immature love.

(V) Also generally, it means what is renowned or preeminent (Heb 9:11; James 1:25).

Deriv.: *teleiótēs* (5047), completeness, perfection; *teleióō* (5048), to complete, perfect; *teleíōs* (5049), completely, without wavering, to the end.

Syn.: *ártios* (739), fitted, complete, perfect; *plḗrēs* (4134), complete, full; *mestós* (3324), full; *ámemptos* (273), irreproachable, blameless; *áptaistos* (679), not stumbling, without transgression; *holóklēros* (3648), entire, whole. *Téleios* is not to be confused with *anamártētos* (361), without sin or sinless.

Ant.: *endeḗs* (1729), lacking, deficient.

5047. ΤΕΛΕΙΌΤΗΣ *teleiótēs*; gen. *teleiótetos*, fem. noun from *téleios* (5046), perfect, one who reaches a goal. Perfection or perfectness, stressing the realization of an end in view, the state achieved when a goal has been accomplished (Col 3:14; Heb 6:1).

Syn.: *katartismós* (2677), the condition or characteristic of perfection; *plḗrōma* (4138), a filling up, fulfillment, fullness, that which fills or has been filled; *apartismós* (535), completion, finishing; *ékbasis* (1545), the end, result; *holoklēría* (3647), integrity, physical wholeness, perfection, soundness.

Ant.: *hustérēsis* (5304), a falling short.

5048. ΤΕΛΕΙΌΩ *teleióō*; contracted *teleiō̂*, fut. *teleiṓsō*, from *téleios* (5046), complete, mature. To complete, make perfect by reaching the intended goal. Trans.:

(I) Particularly with the meaning to bring to a full end, completion, reaching the intended goal, to finish a work or duty (John 4:34; 5:36; 17:4). In the mid. with the implication of *érgon* (2041), work (Luke 13:32); of a race (*drómon* [1408]) or course (Acts 20:24). In the perf. mid. pass. with *drómon* implied (Phil 3:12, not that I have already completed my course [cf. 20:14 and in *katalambánō* {2638}, to attain, II]; Sept.: 2 Chr 8:16). Of time (Luke 2:43); of prophecy, fulfilled (John 19:28).

(II) Metaphorically meaning to make perfect although not faultless but bringing to a state of completion or fulfillment.

(A) Generally (John 17:23, "that they may be [perfectly or completely united in] one"; 2 Cor 12:9, "my power shows itself perfect in weakness" [a.t.], meaning that it appears as a need arises; James 2:22; 1 John 2:5; 4:12, 17, 18).

(B) In the epistle to the Hebrews, *teleióō* is used in a moral sense meaning to make perfect, to fully cleanse from sin, in contrast to ceremonial cleansing. Moral expiation is the completion or realization of the ceremonial one (Heb 7:19, the Mosaic Law could make no perfect moral expiation [cf. 7:11]; Heb 10:14). Of persons (Heb 9:9) which could never make someone perfect, meaning true moral expiation so as to satisfy the offerer's conscience (Heb 10:1, 14); also to bring to a perfect state of blessedness and glory so as to win and receive the prize (cf. above I); also of Christ as exalted to be head over all things (Heb 2:10; 5:9; 7:28); of saints advanced to glory (Heb 11:40; 12:23).

Teleióō is used of Jesus: Heb 5:9, "and being made perfect, he became the author of eternal salvation unto all them that obey Him." The thought here is not that Jesus suffered from a deficiency of character or nature and that through suffering He underwent moral improvement. Rather, the perfection of Christ concerns His qualification as Savior. The appointed way to Saviorhood followed the path of testing. In the face of even the most pressing hardship and suffering, Jesus remained obedient to His Father. Having successfully endured the trial of life, He was proven fit to be the Savior of God's people.

Teleióō is used of Christians in the following passages:

John 17:23, "I in them, and thou in me, that they may be made perfect [*teteleiōménoi*] in [*eis* {1519}] one [*hén* {1520}]; and that the world may know that thou hast sent me and hast loved them, as thou hast loved me." The aspiration of Jesus' prayer is that believers might be perfectly united. The perfection concerns not personal sanctification *per se*, as though the prayer were that the perfection of individual Christians might occur *en masse*, or in company with one another and not in isolation. The prep. *eis* denotes direction and not position and so does not admit this meaning. Hence, "in one" means "unto oneness" and represents the goal of the perfecting action. The hope is that believers might be in a state of having achieved the unity intended for them; one which reflects the unity between the Father and the Son.

Phil 3:12, "Not as though I have already attained, either were already perfect [*teteleíōmai*]: but I follow after, if that I may apprehend that for which also I am apprehended of Christ Jesus." Here the apostle Paul is referring to his own course of life that it was not always what God expected of him (Rom 7:15–21). By the use of this word, Paul shows that he was not all that God wanted him to be at each instant of his life, but at the end of his life he would reach that goal (Rom 8:23).

Heb 11:40, "God having provided some better thing for us, that they without us should not be made perfect [*teleiōthōsin*]." God's people are one. The saints of the OT and NT share the same hopes and promises of salvation. The writer assures his readers that, therefore, the fulfillment of God's promises

in Christ are now received together by both.

Heb 12:23, "To the general assembly and church of the firstborn, which are written in heaven, and to God the Judge of all, and to the spirits of just men made perfect [*teteleiōménōn*, perf. pass. part.]." The righteous dead are referred to as having been made perfect because they have, like the pioneer of their faith, finished the course of this life and gone on to their heavenly reward.

The verb *teleióō* is used with the following:

Faith: James 2:22, "Seest thou how faith wrought with his works, and by works was faith made perfect [*eteleióthē*]." Here it means faith was fulfilled or made complete by the works of faith or righteousness in the believer.

Love (*agápē* [26]): 1 John 2:5; 4:12, 17, 18 referring to the effectiveness of God's love in the believer demonstrating itself horizontally as it received from above.

Deriv.: *teleíōsis* (5050), the act of completion; *teleiōtḗs* (5051), a completer, perfecter.

Syn.: *suntelḗō* (4931), to complete entirely, finish, fulfill; *plēróō* (4137), to fill, satisfy, execute, finish, accomplish, complete, fulfill; *apotelḗō* (658), to complete entirely, consummate, finish; *sumplēróō* (4845), to fill to the brim, accomplish, fill up, complete.

Ant.: *kolobóō* (2856), to cut off, abridge.

5049. τελείως *teleíōs*; adv. from *téleios* (5046), perfect, complete. Perfectly, entirely, steadfastly, unwaveringly (1 Pet 1:13).

Syn.: *hólōs* (3654), completely, altogether, utterly, by any means; *pántē* (3839), wholly, always.

Ant.: *mólis* (3433), with difficulty, hardly, scarcely; *metríōs* (3357), moderately, slightly, a little; *schedón* (4975), nearly, almost; *mēdamṓs* (3365), by no means, not at all.

5050. **τελείωσις** *teleíōsis*; gen. *teleióseōs*, fem. noun from *teleióō* (5048), to complete. The act of completion, successful effort or fulfillment (Luke 1:45). Also the state or attainment of perfection (Heb 7:11).

Syn.: *holoklēría* (3647), integrity, wholeness, soundness; *suntéleia* (4930), completion, consummation.

5051. **τελειωτής** *teleiōtḗs*; gen. *teleiōtoú*, masc. noun from *teleióō* (5048), to complete. A completer, perfecter, particularly one who reaches a goal so as to win the prize. Used only once in Scripture in Heb 12:2 where Jesus is called the "author [*archēgós* {747}] and finisher [*teleiōtḗs*] of our faith." This expression is commonly understood to mean that Jesus is the creator, sustainer and consummator of faith in the hearts of God's people. However, the context may suggest another interpretation. The phrase "our faith" is actually "the faith" (*tḗs písteōs*, gen. of *pístis* [4102]). While the def. art. can substitute for the poss. pron., It appears in this case to be anaphoric (referring to what has just been discussed or mentioned). The "faith," then, is a term for the course of life dictated by faith. The saints of the OT testify to its power and to the promise of its reward. Jesus is presented as the supreme model of this way of life. Where others failed, He succeeded. By His unerring life of faith, Jesus has made a way to God for those who follow Him. See *archēgós* for further discussion.

Ant.: *archēgós* (747), initiator, author.

5052. **τελεσφορέω** *telesphoréō*; contracted *telesphorṓ*, fut. *telesphorḗsō*, from *télos* (5056), end, goal, perfection, and *phérō* (5342), to bring, bear. To bear to perfection or ripeness, as the seed does the fruit (Luke 8:14 [cf. Matt 13:22]).

5053. **τελευτάω** *teleutáō*; contracted *teleutṓ*, fut. *teleutḗsō*, from *teleutḗ* (5054), death, an end, accomplishment. To end, finish, complete. Intrans. to end. In the NT, intrans. or with *bíon* (979), earthly life, implied, meaning to end one's life, die (Matt 2:19; 9:18; 22:25; Mark 9:44, 46, 48 [cf. Isa 66:24]; Luke 7:2; Acts 2:29; 7:15; Heb 11:22; Sept.: Gen 25:32; 30:1; Prov 11:7). Of a violent death (Matt 15:4; Mark 7:10, "let him die the death," quoted from Ex 21:17, "he shall surely be put to death," or die).

Syn.: *thnḗskō* (2348), to die; *apothnḗskō* (599), to die off; *sunapothnḗskō* (4880), to die with, together.

Ant.: *záō* (2198), to live; *bióō* (980), to live.

5054. **τελευτή** *teleutḗ*; gen. *teleutḗs*, fem. noun from *teléō* (5055), to accomplish or complete something. An end, figurative for death. In Matt 2:15, the end of life, death, decease (Sept.: Gen 27:2; Josh 1:1; Judg 1:1).

Deriv.: *teleutáō* (5053), to end, finish, complete.

Syn.: *thánatos* (2288), death.

Ant.: *zōḗ* (2222), life; *bíos* (979), lifetime, earthly life; *psuchḗ* (5590), soul.

5055. **τελέω** *teléō*; contracted *telṓ*, fut. *telésō*, from *télos* (5056), end, goal. To make an end or to accomplish, to complete something, not merely to end it, but to bring it to perfection or its destined goal, to carry it through. Trans.:

(I) Generally with the acc. (Matt 13:53; 19:1; 26:1; Luke 2:39; 2 Tim 4:7; Rev 11:7; Sept.: Ruth 2:21). In the pass. (Luke 12:50; John 19:28, 30, "it is finished," meaning the whole work of salvation, the purpose for which Jesus came into the world; Rev 10:7; 15:1, 8). See Matt 11:1, "when Jesus had finished commanding" (a.t.). With the part. implied (Matt 10:23, "Ye shall not have finished the cities of Israel" [a.t.], meaning not to have finished fleeing or passing through them). Of time in the pass. meaning to be ended, fulfilled (Rev 20:3, 5, 7).

(II) To accomplish, fulfill, execute fully a rule or law, with the acc. (Rom

2:27; Gal 5:16; James 2:8). Of declarations, prophecy (Luke 18:31; 22:37; Acts 13:29; Rev 17:17; Sept.: Ezra 1:1).

(III) By implication, to pay off or in full, such as taxes, tribute, which is also the meaning of *télos* (5056). A tax, toll, custom (Matt 17:24; Rom 13:6).

Deriv.: *apoteléō* (658), to perfect; *diateléō* (1300), to finish completely; *ekteléō* (1615), to complete fully; *epiteléō* (2005), to complete, finish; *sunteléō* (4931), to finish entirely; *teleutḗ* (5054), and end, death.

Syn.: *sumplēróō* (4845), to fill up completely; *katantáō* (2658), to arrive at, attain; *teleióō* (5048), to complete, accomplish, consecrate, perfect. Although *teléō* and *teleióō* have much the same meaning, to carry through, complete, reach the end, yet between them there is at times a slight difference. *Teléō* signifies the reaching of an end or goal meaning to finish or accomplish a task, to terminate a course (Matt 10:23; 11:1; 13:53; 19:1; 26:1; Acts 13:29; 2 Tim 4:7; James 2:8). *Teleióō*, however, speaks of the continued realization of a purpose throughout the performance of a task. The former word has in view the point of termination. The latter word has in view the entire process. The two verbs are expressive of *télos*, goal, purpose.

Ant.: *árchomai* (756), to begin.

5056. τέλος *télos*; gen. *télous*, neut. noun. An end, term, termination, completion. Particularly only in respect to time.

(I) Generally, with the gen. (Luke 1:33; 1 Cor 10:11; 2 Cor 3:13, unto the end of the transient shining of Moses' countenance [cf. 3:7]; Heb 7:3; 1 Pet 4:7; Sept.: Dan 11:13). With the gen. implied (Matt 10:22; 24:6, the end of all things or this generation [cf. 24:14]; Matt 24:13; Mark 13:7, 13; Luke 21:9, of the completion of the divine plan; John 13:1, of life). To the end of life (1 Cor 1:8; 2 Cor 1:13, *héōs télous* [*héōs* (2193), until]; with *méchri* (3360), as far as, till the end (Heb 3:6, 14); with *áchri* (891), as far as, until the end (Heb 6:11; Rev 2:26). In 1 Cor 15:24,

the end of the work of redemption which is the entrance into heaven, the last or remainder of the dead in Christ. In an absolute sense, with *échō* (2192), to have, to have an end means to be ended, figuratively to be destroyed (Mark 3:26). Adv. in the acc., *tó télos* means finally, at last (1 Pet 3:8). With the prep. *eis* (1519), in, unto the end particularly to the end, continually, perpetually, forever (Luke 18:5; 1 Thess 2:16; Sept.: Job 14:20; Ps 79:5; 103:9).

(II) Figuratively it means end, event, issue, result (Matt 26:58; James 5:11, the issue or event which the Lord gave). Followed by the gen. of person or thing, meaning final lot, ultimate fate (Rom 6:21, 22; 2 Cor 11:15; Phil 3:19; Heb 6:8; 1 Pet 1:9; 4:7, 17; Sept.: Eccl 7:2). Of a declaration, prophecy, accomplishment, fulfillment (Luke 22:37, "have an end," are fulfilled). In 1 Cor 15:24; Heb 7:3, the goal reached, the beginning of a new order of things.

(III) Figuratively meaning the end or final purpose, that to which all the parts tend and in which they terminate, the sum total (1 Tim 1:5).

(IV) Figuratively it means a tax, toll, custom, tribute, particularly what is paid for public purposes for the maintenance of the state (Matt 17:25; Rom 13:7). In another sense among the Greeks, public officers and magistrates were called *tá télē*; hence the Gr. NT term *telṓnēs* (5057), a publican, a collector of taxes.

(V) With the def. neut. art. *tó, télos* usually means end, goal, or the limit, either at which a person or thing ceases to be what he or it had been up to that point or when previous activities ceased (2 Cor 3:13; 1 Pet 4:7). It does not, as is often supposed, mean the extinction, end or termination in time. It simply means the goal reached and conclusion of the activity that went before. For example, when we speak of the end of the war, we speak of victory. When we speak of the *télos andrós* (gen. of *anḗr* [435], man), of man, the end of man, we speak of the full age of man; also used of the ripening of the seed. It denotes not an end of life simply, but of one's activity also. If it simply referred to death, another word, *teleuté* (5054), death, would be used.

(VI) The adv. phrase *eis télos* means "to the last" or to the conclusion of that spoken about, as in John 13:1 where reference is made to Christ's work of love (see Matt 10:22; 24:13; Mark 13:13). It may also mean at last or in the end, finally (Luke 18:5); or completely (1 Thess 2:16).

(VII) In Rom 10:4 it means either termination or goal. Christ is the end of the Law for righteousness to everyone who believes. This means that the Law as a demanded obligation has come to an end because Jesus has fulfilled its demands and imparted His righteousness to those who believe. Christ has freed believers from its tyranny. The standards of righteousness come to us now not from without by imposition, but from within by the Spirit who writes the Law upon our hearts. See Sept.: Eccl 12:13.

(VIII) *Héōs télous* (*héōs* [2193], until) in 2 Cor 1:13 means completely, as contrasted with *apó mérous* (*apó* [575], in); *mérous* ([3313], part), not completely (as in 1:14).

Deriv.: *entéllomai* (1781), to charge, command; *pantelḗs* (3838), complete, whole, entire; *poluteḗs* (4185), very expensive, costly; *téleios* (5046), finished, complete; *telesphoréō* (5052), to bring to an intended perfection or goal; *teléō* (5055), to finish, complete; *telṓnēs* (5057), a reaper of taxes or customs.

Syn.: *péras* (4009), a limit, boundary, uttermost part; *suntéleia* (4930), a completion, consummation, fulfillment; *ékbasis* (1545), end, outcome, result; *ōméga* (5598), the last letter of the Greek alphabet.

Ant.: *archḗ* (746), beginning; *prṓtos* (4413), the first; *aparchḗ* (536), the firstfruits, the beginning or onset; *álpha* (1), the first letter of the Greek alphabet, beginning.

5057. τελώνης *telṓnēs*; gen. *telṓnou*, masc. noun from *télos* (5056), tax, and *ōnéomai* (5608), to buy. A reaper of the taxes or customs, tax-collector, one who pays to the government a certain sum for the privilege of collecting the taxes and customs of a district.

The public revenues of the Greeks and Romans were usually farmed out. Among the latter, the purchasers were chiefly of the equestrian order and were distinguished as being of a higher class because they rode horses, or they were at least persons of wealth and rank like Zacchaeus who is called the chief tax collector (*architelṓnēs* [754] in Luke 19:2). These farmers also had subcontractors or employed agents who collected the taxes and customs at the gates of cities, in seaports, on public ways and bridges. These, too, were called *telṓnai* (pl.), publicans, or *eklégontes* (n.f.), (from *ek* [1537], out of, and *légō* [3004], in its original sense meaning to collect), those who collected out of the people. Such publicans in countries subject to the Roman Empire were the objects of hatred and detestation so that none but persons of worthless character were likely to be found in this employment. They were called *hárpages* (n.f.), extortioners, from *harpagḗ* (724), extortion. Chrysostom calls them *kapélous* (n.f.), hucksters, from *kapēleúō* (2585), to retail, adulterate, take advantage of, corrupt, and *pornoboskoús* (n.f.), shepherds of fornication. They were also called *kólakes* (n.f.), flatterers, from *kolakeía* (2850), flattery.

In the NT, they were toll-gatherers, collectors of customs or public dues and were the objects of bitter hatred and scorn by the Jews. They often associated with the most depraved classes of society (Matt 5:46, 47; 9:9–11; 10:3, Mathew being a publican; Luke 3:12; 5:27, 29; 7:29; 18:10, 11, 13) such as publicans and sinners (Matt 9:10, 11; 11:19; Mark 2:15, 16; Luke 5:30; 7:34; 15:1), Gentile and publican (Matt 18:17), publicans and harlots (Matt 21:31, 32).

Deriv.: *architelṓnēs* (754), a principal tax-collector; *telṓnion* (5058), a custom house, collector's office.

5058. τελώνιον *telṓnion*; gen. *telōníou*, neut. noun from *telṓnēs* (5057), a tax-collector. A toll-house, custom house, collector's office (Matt 9:9; Mark 2:14; Luke 5:27), a place where the publican sat. In the Class. Gr. used in the pl., *tá telṓnia*, indicating the places where the publicans sat.

5059. τέρας *téras*; gen. *tératos*, neut. noun. A wonder or omen. It is often associated with *sēmeíon* (4592), sign, and is usually in the pl. translated "wonders" (Acts 2:19, 22 in the pl. *térata*; Sept.: Joel 2:30). Used of the miracles of Moses (Acts 7:36; Sept.: Ex 7:3; Deut 6:22; 7:19; Jer 32:20); of Christ (John 4:48); of the Apostles and teachers (Acts 2:43; 4:30; 5:12; 6:8; 14:3; 15:12; Rom 15:19; 2 Cor 12:12; Heb 2:4); of false prophets or teachers (Matt 24:24; Mark 13:22; 2 Thess 2:9). These two words refer not to different classes of miracles, but to different aspects of the same miracle. *Téras* is derived from *tēréō* (5083), to keep, watch, connoting that which due to its extraordinary character is apt to be observed and kept in the memory. It is a miracle regarded as startling, imposing or amazing.
Syn.: *dúnamis* (1411), mighty work, miracle; *megaleíos* (3167), something great; *thaumásios* (2297), a miracle; *sēmeíon* (4592), sign; *thaúma* (2295), wonder.

5060. Τέρτιος *Tértios*; gen. *Tertíou*, masc. proper noun. Tertius, meaning the third. Paul's amanuensis to whom he dictated the epistle to the Romans (Rom 16:22).

5061. Τέρτυλλος *Tértullos*; gen. *Tertúllou*, masc. proper noun. Tertullus, a diminutive of Tertius. A lawyer, probably a Roman, who, in consequence of the Jews' lack of familiarity with Roman law, was hired to act as prosecutor in the case of Paul before Felix (Acts 24:1–9).

5062. τεσσαράκοντα *tessarákonta*; indeclinable, used for all genders, cardinal number from *téssares* (5064), four. Forty (Matt 4:2; Mark 1:13; Acts 1:3; Sept.: Gen 5:13; Ex 16:35).
Deriv.: *tessarakontaetḗs* (5063), of forty years.

5063. τεσσαρακονταετής *tessarakontaetḗs*; gen. *tessarakontaetoús*, masc.-fem., neut. *tessarakontaetés*, adj. from *tessarákonta* (5062), forty, and *étos* (2094), year. Of forty years. *Tessarakontaetḗs chrónos* ([5550], year), means the time of forty years (Acts 7:23; 13:18).

5064. τέσσαρες *téssares*; gen. *tessárōn*, masc.-fem., neut. *téssara*, cardinal number. Four (Matt 24:31; Mark 2:3; Acts 10:11; Rev 4:4; Sept.: Gen 2:10; 11:16).
Deriv.: *dekatéssares* (1180), fourteen *tessarákonta* (5062), forty; *tessareskaidékatos* (5065), fourteenth; *tétartos* (5067), the fourth.

5065. τεσσαρεσκαιδέκατος *tessareskaidékatos*; fem. *tessareskaidekátē*, neut. *tessareskaidékaton*, ordinal number from *téssares* (5064), four, *kaí* (2532), and, *dékatos* (1182), a tenth. Fourteenth (Acts 27:27, 33; Sept.: Gen 14:5; Ex 12:6).

5066. τεταρταῖος *tetartaíos*; fem. *tetartaía*, neut. *tetartaíon*, adj. from *tétartos* (5067), fourth. Four days, marking succession of days, used only adv., on the fourth day (John 11:39, "He is now the fourth day dead" [a.t.], four days dead).

5067. τέταρτος *tétartos*; fem. *tetártē*, neut. *tétarton*, ordinal number from *téssares* (5064), four. The fourth (Matt 14:25; Mark 6:48; Acts 10:30; Rev 4:7; 6:7, 8; 8:12; 16:8; 21:19; Sept.: Gen 1:19).

Deriv.: *tetartaíos* (5066), on the fourth day.

5068. τετράγωνος *tetrágōnos*; gen. *tetragōnou*, masc.-fem., neut. *tetrágōnon*, adj. from *tétra* (n.f.), four, and *gōnía* (1137), a corner, angle. Four-cornered, four-square (Rev 21:16; Sept.: Ex 27:1; Ezek 41:21).
Deriv. of *tétra* (n.f.): *tetrakósioi* (5071), four hundred; *tetrámēnon* (5072), of four months; *tetraplóos* (5073), fourfold, quadruple; *tetrápous* (5074), a four-footed animal, quadruped; *tetrárchēs* (5076), a tetrarch; *trápeza* (5132), a table.

5069. τετράδιον *tetrádion*; gen. *tetradíou*, neut. noun, a diminutive of *tetrás* (n.f.), four (Acts 12:4). A quaternion of soldiers or a party consisting of four soldiers, the usual number of a Roman night watch, relieved every three hours (Acts 12:4). A *tetrádion* constituted a *phulákeion* (n.f.), a guard which took care of one *phulakḗ* (5438), a watch of the night consisting of three hours. The Jews and probably the Greeks divided the night into three watches of four hours each (Judg 7:19; Ps 90:6), but after the Jews came under the dominion of the Romans, they changed to four watches of about three hours each. These were numbered as first, second, third, fourth, and were also called *opsé* (3796), eventime or evening; *mesonúktion* (3317), midnight; *alektorophōnía* (219), the cock-crowing; *prōḯ* (4404), early morning (Mark 13:35).

5070. τετρακισχίλιοι *tetrakischílioi*; fem. *tetrakischíliai*, neut. *tetrakischília*, cardinal number from *tetrákis* (n.f.), four times, and *chílioi* (5507), a thousand. Four thousand (Matt 15:38; 16:10; Mark 8:9, 20; Acts 21:38; Sept.: 1 Chr 12:26).

5071. τετρακόσιοι *tetrakósioi*; fem. *tetrakósiai*, neut. *tetrakósia*, cardinal number from *tétra* (n.f., see *tetrágōnos* [5068]), four, and *hekatón* (1540), a

hundred. Four hundred (Acts 5:36; 7:6; 13:20; Gal 3:17; Sept.: Gen 23:15, 16).

5072. τετράμηνον *tetrámēnon*; the neut. of *tetrámēnos*, from *tétra* (n.f., see *tetrágōnos* [5068]), four, and *mḗn* (3376), a month. Of four months (John 4:35), with *chrónos* (5550) understood meaning four months time. In the TR the neut. *tó tetrámēnon* is used in the same sense. See Sept.: Judg 19:2; 20:47.

5073. τετραπλόος *tetraplóos*; contracted *tetraploús*, fem. *tetraplḗ*, neut. *tetraplóon* or *tetraploún*, adj. from *tétra* (n.f., see *tetrágōnos* [5068]), four, and *haplóos* (573), simple, onefold. Fourfold, quadruple (Luke 19:8).

5074. τετράπους *tetrápous*; gen. *tetrápodos*, masc.-fem., neut. *tetrápoun*, adj. from *tétra* (n.f., see *tetrágōnos* [5068]), four, and *poús* (4228) (gen. of *podós* [n.f.], a foot). A four-footed animal, quadruped. In the pl. *tá tetrápoda*, quadrupeds (Acts 10:12; 11:6; Rom 1:23; Sept.: Gen 1:24; Ex 9:9, 10).

5075. τετραρχέω *tetrarchéō*; contracted *tetrarchṓ*, fut. *tetrarchḗsō*, from *tetrárchēs* (5076), tetrarch or a ruler of the fourth of a country. To be a tetrarch, to rule as tetrarch (Luke 3:1).

5076. τετράρχης *tetrárchēs*; gen. *tetrárchou*, masc. noun from *tétra* (n.f., see *tetrágōnos* [5068]), four, and *árchō* (757), to rule. A tetrarch, the ruler of a fourth part of a district or province. Later it became a common title among the Romans for those who governed any part of a province or kingdom subject only to the Roman Emperor. Thus Herod the Great and his brother Phasael were at one time made tetrarchs of Judea by Antony. The former also at his death left half his kingdom to Archaelaus with the title of ethnarch (*ethnárchēs* [1481]), ruler of the nation. He divided the rest between two of his other sons, Herod Antipas and Philip, with the title of tetrarchs

(Josephus Ant. 18.5.1.). Thus Lysanias is said to be tetrarch of Abilene (Luke 3:1). In the NT, spoken only of Herod Antipas (Matt 14:1; Luke 3:19; 9:7; Acts 13:1). Called also *basileús* (935), king (Matt 14:9; Mark 6:14).

Deriv.: *tetrarchéō* (5075), to rule as a tetrarch.

5077. τεφρόω *tephróō*; contracted *tephró*, fut. *tephrṓsō*, from *téphra* (n.f.), ashes. To reduce to ashes, consume, to destroy cities, with the acc. (2 Pet 2:6).

5078. τέχνη *téchne*; gen. *téchnēs*, fem. noun from *tíktō* (5088), to bring forth. An art, trade, craft, skill (Acts 17:29; 18:3; Rev 18:22; Sept.: 1 Kgs 7:14).

Deriv.: *homótechnos* (3673), of the same trade; *technítēs* (5079), an artisan, craftsman.

Syn.: *ergasía* (2039), craft, work.

5079. τεχνίτης *technítēs*; gen. *technítou*, masc. noun from *téchnē* (5078), an art, trade, craft. An artisan, designer, craftsman (Acts 19:24, 38; Rev 18:22; Sept.: Deut 27:15; Jer 10:9). Figuratively of God as the builder and founder of the heavenly Jerusalem (Heb 11:10).

Syn.: *ergátēs* (2040), worker; *ktístēs* (2939), builder, founder, creator.

5080. τήκω *tékō*, fut. *téxō*. To melt, make liquid (Sept.: Nah 1:6). In the NT, pass. *tékomai*, to be melted, melt (2 Pet 3:12; Sept.: Isa 34:4).

Ant.: *stereóō* (4732), to solidify.

5081. τηλαυγῶς *tēlaugós*; adv. from *tēlaugḗs* (n.f.), shining afar or to a distance, resplendent, which is from *téle* (n.f.), afar, and *augḗ* (827), dawn. Radiantly, brightly, clearly, distinctly (Mark 8:25).

Syn.: *lamprós* (2988), brilliantly, brightly, luxuriously; *phanerós* (5320), evidently, manifestly.

5082. τηλικοῦτος *tēlikoútos*; fem. *tēlikaútē*, neut. *tēlikoúto*, demonstrative correlative pron., a strengthened form of *tēlíkos* (n.f.), so great. So vast, so great, so mighty (2 Cor 1:10; Heb 2:3; James 3:4; Rev 16:18).

Syn.: *polús* (4183), much, great; *hikanós* (2425), sufficient, competent, great; *hēlíkos* (2245), how great; *pēlíkos* (4080), how large, great; *pósos* (4214) and *hósos* (3745), how great; *tosoútos* (5118), so great; *lían* (3029), exceeding.

5083. τηρέω *tēréō*; contracted *tēró*, fut. *tērḗsō*, from *tērós* (n.f.), a warden, guard. To keep an eye on, watch, and hence to guard, keep, obey, trans.:

(I) Particularly to watch, observe attentively, keep the eyes fixed upon, with the acc. (Rev 1:3, keeping for the fulfillment of the prophecy; 22:7, 9; Sept.: Eccl 11:4; Prov 23:26). Figuratively, to obey, observe, keep, fulfill a duty, precept, law, custom, or custom meaning to perform watchfully, vigilantly, with the acc. (Matt 19:17; John 14:15, 21; 15:10; 1 Tim 6:14; 1 John 2:3, 4; 3:22, 24; 5:2, 3; Rev 12:17; 14:12); a saying or words (John 8:51, 52, 55; 14:23, 24; 15:20; 17:6; 1 John 2:5; Rev 3:8, 10); the law (Acts 15:5, 24; James 2:10); tradition (Mark 7:9); the Sabbath (John 9:16). Generally with the acc. expressed (Rev 2:26, "he that . . . keepeth my works," meaning the works which I have required. See Matt 23:3; 28:20; Acts 21:25; Rev 3:3; Sept.: generally, Prov 3:1, 21; 8:34).

(II) To keep, guard a prisoner, with the acc. (Matt 27:36, 54; Acts 12:5, 6; 16:23; 24:23; 25:4, 21; 1 John 5:18, is on his guard). Part. (Matt 28:4, "the keepers," guards). Of things such as the clothes (Rev 16:15; Sept.: Song 3:3); of things (Sept.: Song 8:11, 12). Figuratively meaning to keep in safety, preserve, maintain, with the acc. of thing (Eph 4:3; 2 Tim 4:7; Jude 1:6, negatively, deserting their first estate; Sept.: Prov 16:17). Figuratively, with the acc. and adjuncts: of persons (2 Cor 11:9; 1 Tim 5:22; James 1:27); with an adv. (1 Thess 5:23); with the dat. of person (Jude 1:1). Followed by *en* (1722), in, with the dat. of state (John

17:11, 12; Jude 1:21); by *ek* (1537), from, followed by the gen. (John 17:15; Rev 3:10); by *apó* (575), from, followed by the gen. (James 1:27; Sept.: Prov 7:5).

(III) To keep back or in store, reserve, with the acc. (John 2:10; 12:7); with a nom. (2 Pet 2:17; Jude 1:13); with the dat. (1 Pet 1:4 [TR]). Of persons (1 Cor 7:37, to keep a woman at home, unmarried, as opposed to *ekgamízō* [1547], to give in marriage in 7:38; 2 Pet 2:4, 9; 3:7, "unto the day of judgment" [a.t.]; Jude 1:6, "unto the judgment of the great day").

Deriv.: *diatēréō* (1301), watch thoroughly, observe strictly, keep, store up; *paratēréō* (3906), to watch closely, guard; *suntēréō* (4933), keep closely together, conserve, keep, protect, preserve; *tḗrēsis* (5084), watch, custody.

Syn.: *phulássō* (5442), to guard, watch, keep by way of protection, observe, protect; *diaphulássō* (1314), to guard thoroughly; *phrouréō* (5432), to keep with a military guard; *kratéō* (2902), to get possession of, hold fast, keep.

Ant.: *eleutheróō* (1659), to make free, deliver; *apallássō* (525), to release, deliver; *lúō* (3089), to loose.

5084. τήρησις *tḗrēsis*; gen. *tērēseōs*, fem. noun from *tēréō* (5083), to keep watch. Custody, keeping, watching. A prison, hold (Acts 4:3), of the imprisonment of the Apostles (Acts 5:18). A keeping or observance of commandments (1 Cor 7:19).

Syn.: *phulakḗ* (5438), a guarding or guard, prison, hold; *desmōtḗrion* (1201), a place of bonds, prison.

Ant.: *eleuthería* (1657), liberty.

5085. Τιβεριάς *Tiberiás*; gen. *Tiberiádos*, fem. proper noun. Tiberias. A town of Galilee situated on the western bank of the Sea of Galilee which is also called the Sea of Tiberias by John (John 6:1; 21:1). It is only mentioned once In the NT (John 6:23). Although it was an important and busy town in Christ's time, there is no record that He ever visited it. It was a new city then, built by Herod Antipas in A.D. 20–22, and named in honor of the Emperor Tiberius. After Jerusalem was destroyed the Sanhedrin settled in Tiberias, and for many centuries it was one of the most celebrated seats of Jewish learning. The Jewish Mishna (an ancient traditional law) and the Masorah, were compiled here.

5086. Τιβέριος *Tibérios*; gen. *Tiberíou*, masc. proper noun. Tiberius. His full title was Claudius Nero Caesar, known as Tiberius Caesar (Luke 3:1). He was a stepson and successor of Augustus, and was one of the most infamous tyrants of the Empire of Rome. He began well, but quickly degenerated into an oppressive despot. Madness was probably the excuse for his cruelties. His reign began in A.D. 14 and continued during the eventful period of the succeeding twenty-three years until he was murdered by suffocation. All the events of Christ's manhood took place during his reign.

5087. τίθημι *títhēmi*; imperf. *etíthoun* (Matt 5:15; 2 Cor 3:13), fut. *thḗsō*, aor. *éthēka*, perf. *tétheika*. To set, put, place, lay.

(I) Particularly, to set, put, or place a person or thing. In the act. it means to place; under a bushel (*módion* [3426], Matt 5:15; Mark 4:21) or under a bed (*klínē* [2825], Luke 8:16); in a secret place (*kruptḗn* [2926], Luke 11:33). Of a title on the cross (John 19:19); of one's foot upon the sea (Rev 10:2). In the mid. meaning to set or place on one's own behalf, or by one's own order; to put persons in prison (*eis phulakḗn* [*eis* {1519}, into; *phulakḗn* {5438}, prison]) (Acts 12:4); *eis tḗrēsin* (5084), in custody or jail (Acts 4:3); *en phulakḗ* (*en* [1722], in), in prison (Matt 14:3; Acts 5:25; Sept.: Gen 40:3; 41:10). Spoken of food or drink, to set on or out, with the acc. (John 2:10).

(II) More often of things, to set, put, or lay down. To set in the proper place, assign a place (1 Cor 12:18; Sept.: Ex 26:35).

(A) Particularly a foundation (Luke 6:48; 14:29; 1 Cor 3:10, 11; Sept.: Ezra 6:3); a stone, stumbling stone (Rom 9:33; 1 Pet 2:6 quoted from Isa 28:16). See Rom 14:13. Of dead bodies, to lay in a tomb or sepulcher, with the acc. (Mark 15:47; 16:6; Luke 23:53, 55; John 11:34; 19:42; 20:2, 13, 15; Acts 9:37; 13:29; Rev 11:9); with *en* (1722), in, followed by the dat. (Matt 27:60; Mark 6:29; John 19:41; Acts 7:16; Sept. with *en*: Gen 50:26); followed by *epí* (1909), upon, with the gen. (Acts 5:15); *epí* with the acc. (Mark 10:16, "his hands upon them"; 2 Cor 3:13, "a veil over his face"), also with the acc., to bend or bow the knees, to kneel (Mark 15:19; Luke 22:41; Acts 7:60; 9:40; 20:36; 21:5); followed by *enópion* (1799), before, in the sight of, and the gen. (Luke 5:18; Sept.: 1 Sam 10:25 [cf. Ezek 16:18]); by *pará* (3844), by, near, and the dat. (1 Cor 16:2); by *pará* and the acc. (Acts 4:35, 37; 5:2); by *prós* (4314), toward, with the acc. (Acts 3:2); by *hupó* (5259), by, under, and the acc. (1 Cor 15:25 quoted from Ps 110:1). In the sense of to lay off or aside, such as garments (John 13:4).

(B) Figuratively, to lay down one's life (John 10:11, 15, 17, 18; 13:37, 38; 15:13; 1 John 3:16); followed by *epí* (1909), upon, with the acc. (Matt 12:18, "will give [or impart] unto him" [a.t.], quoted from Isa 42:1 where the Sept. has *édōka*, aor. indic. act. of *dídōmi* [1325], to give). In the mid. with *en* (1722), in (2 Cor 5:19, *thémenos*, aor. mid. part. nom., "and has assigned to us" (a.t.) [cf. Sept.: Isa 63:11]); followed by *eis tá óta humṓn* (*hóta* being the acc. pl. of *oús* [3775], ear), "into your ears," meaning to lay up in your ears or let sink in your hearts or minds (Luke 9:44); followed by *eis tḗn kardían* ([2588], heart), to lay to heart, to resolve (Luke 21:14 [cf. Sept.: 1 Sam 9:20; Eccl 7:22]). Followed by *en tḗ kardía*, to lay up in the heart, to resolve in mind, ponder (Luke 1:66; Sept.: 1 Sam 21:13). To resolve, purpose (Acts 5:4; 19:21, "in the spirit" [cf. Sept.: Dan 1:8]).

(C) Figuratively, to set, appoint, constitute, with the same meaning as to make, for example, of time (Acts 1:7, "which the Father has set by virtue of His own authority" [a.t.]). To constitute the lot of someone (*tó méros* [3313], part, portion, allotment), followed by *metá* (3326), with, and the gen. (Matt 24:51; Luke 12:46). Of a decision, decree, law (Acts 27:12, made a decision, decided, determined; Gal 3:19 [in TR *prosetéthē*, was added, from *prostíthēmi* (4369), to add], in later editions, the law was set, made; 1 Cor 9:18, "I may make the gospel of Christ without charge," i.e., free of expense). Of persons (Matt 22:44; Mark 12:36; Luke 20:43; Acts 2:35; Heb 1:13; 10:13, all quoted from Ps 110:1; Acts 20:28; Rom 4:17 quoted from Gen 17:5; 1 Cor 12:28; Heb 1:2; 2 Pet 2:6). In the pass. construction with *eis* (1519), unto, with the relative pron. *hó*, which is used as final (1 Tim 2:7; 2 Tim 1:11). With the acc. and *eis* as predicate (Acts 13:47, "I have appointed thee as a light unto the nations" [a.t.]). See Sept.: Jer 9:11; Isa 42:15; Nah 3:6. Followed by the acc. and *eis* as final in the mid. (1 Thess 5:9, "For God hath not appointed us to wrath"; 1 Tim 1:12); in the pass. (1 Pet 2:8). Followed by the acc. and *hína* (2443), so that (John 15:16).

Deriv.: *anatíthēmi* (394), to put up or before; *apotíthēmi* (659), to put off from oneself; *diatíthemai* (1303), to set apart, dispose, bequest, to appoint a testator; *ektíthēmi* (1620), to expose; *epitíthēmi* (2007), to lay on; *eúthetos* (2111), well placed, proper; *thḗkē* (2336), receptacle; *thēsaurós* (2344), a treasure; *katatíthēmi* (2698), to lay down; *metatíthēmi* (3346), to put in another place, transfer, transport, change, remove; *nomothétēs* (3550), a lawgiver; *nouthetéō* (3560), to admonish; *horothesía* (3734), bound; *paratíthēmi* (3908), to place alongside, present, commit, set before; *peritíthēmi* (4060), to place or put around; *prostíthēmi* (4369), to place additionally, lay beside, annex, add to; *protíthemai* (4388), to place before for oneself, exhibit, propose, purpose; *suntíthemai* (4934), agree, assent, covenant; *huiothesía* (5206) adoption; *hupotíthēmi* (5294), to place under, lay down.

Syn.: *hístēmi* (2476), to make to stand, appoint; *kathístēmi* (2525), to cause to stand, appoint a person to a position, ordain, set down; *tássō* (5021), to place or arrange in order; *apókeimai* (606), to be laid up, reserved, appointed; *cheirotonéō* (5500), to place the hands on, choose by raising of hands, ordain; *procheirízō* (4400), to deliver up, appoint; *horízō* (3724), to mark by a limit, determine, ordain, define; *kathízō* (2523), to seat someone, set, appoint.

Ant.: *metakinéō* (3334), to remove, place elsewhere; *aphairéō* (851), to remove, take away; *exaírō* (1808), to remove, put away; *katargéō* (2673), to abolish, render inactive; *katalúō* (2647), to overthrow.

5088. τίκτω *tíktō*; fut. *téxomai*, 2d aor. *étekon*. To bring forth, bear, bring.
(I) Of females (Matt 1:21, 23, 25; 2:2; Luke 1:31, 57; 2:6, 7, 11; John 16:21; Gal 4:27; Heb 11:11 [TR]; Rev 12:2, 4, 5, 13; Sept.: Gen 3:16; 4:1). Metaphorically of irregular desire as exciting to sin (James 1:15).
(II) Of the earth (Heb 6:7).
Deriv.: *protótokos* (4416), firstborn; *téknon* (5043), a child; *téchne* (5078), an art, trade, craft, skill; *tókos* (5110), a bringing forth, birth.
Syn.: *apokuéō* (616), to bring forth; *gennáō* (1080), to give birth; *phérō* (5342), to bring or bear.

5089. τίλλω *tíllō*; fut. *tilō*. To pull, pluck, pull out or off as ears of grain, with the acc. (Matt 12:1; Mark 2:23; Luke 6:1).
Syn.: *ekrizóō* (1610), to pluck up by the roots.
Ant.: *speírō* (4687), to sow; *phuteúō* (5452), to plant.

5090. Τιμαῖος *Timaíos*; gen. *Timaíou*, masc. proper noun. Timaeus. The father of Bartimaeus (the prefix "bar" in Aramaic standing for "son"), whom Jesus cured of blindness (Mark 10:46).

5091. τιμάω *timáō*; contracted *timō̂*, fut. *timḗsō*, from the *timḗ* (5092), honor, price.
(I) To esteem, honor, reverence, with the acc.
(A) Generally (1 Tim 5:3); especially of parents (Matt 15:4, 6; 19:19; Mark 7:10; 10:19; Luke 18:20; Eph 6:2; Sept.: Ex 20:12; Deut 5:16); everyone, kings (1 Pet 2:17); God and Christ (John 5:23; 8:49); of feigned piety toward God and Christ (Matt 15:8; Mark 7:6 quoted from Isa 29:13; Prov 3:9).
(B) To treat with honor, to bestow special marks of honor and favor upon someone, with the acc. (John 12:26; Acts 28:10).
(II) To prize, to fix a value or price upon something. Pass. and mid. with the acc. (Matt 27:9 [cf. Zech 11:12, 13]; Sept.: Lev 27:8, 12, 14).
Deriv.: *epitimáō* (2008), to rebuke; *tímios* (5093), most honorable.
Syn.: *hēgéomai* (2233), to lead, to esteem; *doxázō* (1392), to glorify, honor.
Ant.: *exouthenéō* (1848), to despise, treat contemptuously; *kataphronéō* (2706), despise; *periphronéō* (4065), to despise; *atimázō* (818), to dishonor; *oligōréō* (3643), to care little for, regard lightly; the expression *logízomai eis oudén* (*logízomai* [3049], to count; *eis* [1519], unto; *oudén* [3762], nothing), to reckon or count as nothing, be made of no account; *apodokimázō* (593), to reject as disapproved.

5092. τιμή *timḗ*; gen. *timḗs*, fem. noun from *tíō* (n.f.), to pay honor, respect.
(I) Honor, respect, reverence, esteem.
(A) Generally as rendered or exhibited towards a person or thing (John 4:44; Rom 12:10; 1 Cor 12:23, 24; Col 2:23; 1 Thess 4:4, meaning reputably; Heb 3:3; 1 Pet 3:7). Vessel unto honor (Rom 9:21; 2 Tim 2:20, 21); as rendered to masters (1 Tim 6:1); to magistrates (Rom 13:7); to Christ (2 Pet 1:17; Rev 5:12, 13); to

God (1 Tim 1:17; 6:16; Rev 4:9, 11; 7:12; 19:1 [TR]; Sept.: Ps 29:1; 96:7; Isa 14:18; Dan 4:27).

(B) Of a state or condition of honor, rank, dignity, joined with *dóxa* (1391), glory (Heb 2:7 quoted from Ps 8:6); as conferred in reward (Rom 2:7, 10; Heb 2:9; 1 Pet 1:7; 2:7). An office of honor (Heb 5:4); glory and honor (Rev 21:24, 26).

(C) Metonymically for honor as a mark or token of favor, reward (Acts 28:10; Sept.: Dan 2:6).

(D) Compensation, remuneration, that which is paid in honor of another's work. In 1 Tim 5:7 "double honor" probably refers to an honorarium or wage.

(II) Value, price (Matt 27:6, 9, price of blood; Acts 4:34; 5:2, 3; 7:16; 19:19; 1 Cor 6:20; 7:23; Sept.: Lev 5:15, 18; 27:2; Job 31:39; Isa 55:1).

Deriv.: *átimos* (820), without fear; *barútimos* (927), valuable, of great price; *éntimos* (1784), honored; *isótimos* (2472), equally precious; *polútimos* (4186), of great price, very precious; *timáō* (5091), to esteem, honor; *tímios* (5093), esteemed, honored.

Syn.: *dóxa* (1391), glory, honor; *kaúchēma* (2745), that in which one glories, reason for boasting; *kléos* (2811), renown; *phémē* (5345), fame; *eusébeia* (2150), respect.

Ant.: *atimía* (819), indignity, dishonor; *asébeia* (763), impiety; *aischúnē* (152), shame, disgrace; *aschēmosúnē* (808), indecency, shame.

5093. τίμιος *tímios*; fem. *timía*, neut. *tímion*, adj. from *timḗ* (5092), to honor. Held in esteem, respected, honored.

(I) Esteemed, honored, honorable (Acts 5:34; Heb 13:4; Sept.: Ps 116:15).

(II) Valued, prized, precious.

(A) Of high price, costly, as a precious stone generally (1 Cor 3:12; Rev 17:4; 18:16; 21:19); pl. *timiótatos* (Rev 18:12; 21:11, "precious"; Sept.: 1 Kgs 10:2; 2 Chr 9:1, 10).

(B) Figuratively meaning precious, dear, desirable (Acts 20:24; James 5:7;

1 Pet 1:7, 19; 2 Pet 1:4; Sept.: Prov 3:15; 8:11).

Deriv.: *timiótēs* (5094), preciousness, costliness.

Syn.: *polutelḗs* (4185), very expensive, of great price, precious; *kalós* (2570), good; *áxios* (514), worthy; *éntimos* (1784), valued, precious, honorable; *sebastós* (4575), venerable; *hieroprepḗs* (2412), reverent; *eulabḗs* (2126), pious, devout; *euthús* (2117), righteous in character; *chrēstós* (5543), good, gracious, kind; *akéraios* (185), blameless.

Ant.: *átimos* (820), dishonored, without honor; *kakós* (2556), bad, evil, wicked; *phaúlos* (5337), depraved; *aischrós* (150), shameful.

5094. τιμιότης *timiótēs*; gen. *timiótētos*, fem. noun from *tímios* (5093), esteemed, honored. Preciousness, costliness. Metonymously as precious things, magnificence, wealthy (Rev 18:19).

5095. Τιμόθεος *Timótheos*; gen. *Timothéou*. Timotheus or Timothy, meaning honoring God; an evangelist and pupil of St. Paul. He was a Lycaonian, a native of either Derbe or Lystra. His father was a Greek Gentile. His mother Eunice was a Jewess of distinguished piety as was also his grandmother Lois (2 Tim 1:5), and by them he was educated early in the Holy Scriptures of the OT (2 Tim 3:15). Paul found him in one of the cities named above, and, being informed of his good standing among the Christians there, selected him as an assistant in his labors. To avoid the complicity of the Jews, he had Timothy undergo the rite of circumcision (Acts 16:1–3). He afterward became the companion of Paul, and it is evident from Paul's epistles that he held him in high esteem. Timothy was left in charge of the church at Ephesus, and that probably when he was quite young, about thirty-five years old (1 Tim 4:12).

Paul wrote two epistles to Timothy, which, along with the one to Titus, are commonly known as the Pastoral Epistles because they predominantly contain directions regarding church work. The first is supposed to have been written about A.D. 64 and contains special instructions concerning the qualifications and duties of different church officers and other persons, and the most affectionate and poignant exhortations to faithfulness. The second epistle was written a year or two later when Paul was in constant expectation of martyrdom (2 Tim 4:6–8) and contains the fatherly counsel of Paul to his son in the Lord. It consists of a variety of injunctions to, and duties of, Christians under trials and temptations and concludes with expressions of a full and triumphant faith in the Lord Jesus Christ and in all the glorious promises made to His true followers.

Timothy was chosen by Paul to be his companion in his journeys and labors in preaching the gospel (Acts 16:1, 3). He appears to have been with Paul at Rome (Heb 13:23), but his later history is unknown. See Acts 16:1; 17:14, 15; 18:5; 19:22; 20:4; 1 Cor 16:10; 2 Cor 1:19; Phil 1:1; 2:19; 1 Thess 1:1; 3:6; 2 Thess 1:1; 1 Tim 6:20; 2 Tim 1:2. In Rom 16:21 Paul calls him his fellow worker; in 2 Cor 1:1; Col 1:1; 1 Thess 3:2; Phile 1:1; Heb 13:23 he is called the brother; in 1 Cor 4:17; 1 Tim 1:18; 2 Tim 1:2 he is called my child.

5096. Τίμων Tímōn; gen. *Tímōnos*, masc. proper noun. Timon, meaning honoring. One of the seven deacons appointed by the Apostles at Jerusalem (Acts 6:5).

5097. τιμωρέω timōréō; contracted *timōrṓ*; fut. *timōrḗsō*, contracted from *timōrós* (n.f.), watching one's honor, which is from *timḗ* (5092), revenge, punishment, and *horáō* (3708), to see, inspect. To vindicate, avenge, punish in behalf of someone (Acts 26:11); pass. (Acts 22:5).

Deriv.: *timōría* (5098), punishment.
Syn.: *kolázō* (2849), to punish; *katakrínō* (2632), to condemn.
Ant.: *stephanóō* (4737), to crown.

5098. τιμωρία timōría; gen. *timōrías*, fem. noun from *timōréō* (5097), to punish. Punishment, only in Heb 10:29. In Class. Gr., the idea of punishment represented by *timōría* was deeply colored by vindictiveness. It is a punishment meant to satisfy a sense of outraged justice, the defense one's honor or that of a violated law.

Syn.: *kólasis* (2851), torment; *epitimía* (2009), penalty, punishment; *ekdíkēsis* (1557), punishment, retribution; *díkē* (1349), justice, the execution of a sentence, punishment.
Ant.: *stéphanos* (4735), a crown, as an award; *dóxa* (1391), glory, honor; *épainos* (1868), a commendation, praise.

5099. τίνω tínō; fut. *tísō*. Originally it meant to honor, value. In the NT, it means to be punished, to suffer, to pay a penalty. With the acc. (2 Thess 1:9).

Deriv.: *apotínō* (661), to pay off, repay.

5100. τὶς tìs; neut. *ti*, gen. *tinós*; enclitic indef. pron. One, someone, a certain one.

(I) Particularly and generally of some person or thing whom one cannot or does not wish to name or specify particularly. It is used in various constructions:

(A) Simply (Matt 12:29, 47; 20:20; Mark 8:4; Luke 8:49; 9:57; 13:6; John 2:25; Acts 5:25, 34). Pl. *tinés* (Mark 14:4; Luke 13:1; 24:1; John 13:29; Rom 3:3; 1 Cor 4:18; 15:12; 1 Tim 6:10, 21; Heb 4:6). Distributively, *tis . . . héteros* (2087), another, followed by *dé* (1161), a continuative particle, meaning one . . . and another (1 Cor 3:4); in the pl. *tinés . . . tinés dé* meaning some . . . and others (Luke 9:7, 8; Phil 1:15).

(B) Joined with a subst. or adj. taken substantively, a certain person or thing, someone or something. After a subst. (Mark 5:25; Luke 8:27; 9:19; 10:31, 38; John 6:7; Acts 5:1; 27:39); pl. (Luke 8:2; 24:22; Acts 9:19; 17:20; 2 Pet 3:16). Also before the subst. or adj. (Matt 18:12; Luke 17:12; John 4:46; Acts 3:2; 9:36; Gal 6:1). Pl. (Luke 13:31; Acts 13:1;

15:2; 27:1; Jude 1:4). Preceded by *heís* (1520), one, meaning someone (Mark 14:51). Joined with names, meaning one by the name of (Mark 15:21; Acts 9:43). By apposition after a name (Luke 10:33); before a name (John 11:1).

(C) Followed by the gen. of class or partition of which *tis* and *tinés* expresses a part (Luke 14:15, "one of them that sat at meat"; 2 Cor 12:17); the expression *heís tis* (*heís* [1520], one), someone (Mark 14:47); pl. (Matt 9:3; 27:47; Mark 2:6; Luke 19:39; Acts 6:9; Rom 11:17; 2 Cor 10:12). With the same meaning, followed by *ek* (1537), from, with the gen. (Luke 12:13, "one of the company"; John 11:49). Pl. with *ek* (Luke 11:15; John 7:25; 9:16; Rom 11:14).

(D) With numerals where it renders the number indef., about, some (Luke 7:19, "about two of His disciples" [a.t.], meaning some two, two or three; Acts 23:23).

(E) Sometimes *tis* or *tinés* is omitted where the sense requires it to be supplied (Mark 2:1; Luke 8:20); before a gen. partitive (Acts 21:16).

(II) Generally meaning someone, somebody, someone or other, in various constructions and uses (cf. above I).

(A) Simply (Matt 8:28; Mark 12:19; Luke 14:8; John 10:28; Acts 19:38; Rom 5:7; James 2:18). The neut. *ti* (Matt 5:23, "something"; Mark 11:13; Luke 22:35; Acts 3:5; James 1:7).

(B) In a similar sense meaning one, someone, for everyone, similar to *hékastos* (1538), each one (John 6:50; Acts 2:45; 11:29; 1 Cor 4:2; Heb 10:28).

(C) Followed by the gen. of class or of partition (cf. I, C [Acts 5:15; 1 Cor 6:1; 2 Thess 3:8]). The neut. *ti* (Acts 4:32; Rom 15:18; Eph 5:27). Also followed by *apó* (575) with a gen. (Luke 16:30); *ek* (1537), out of, from, with the gen. (Heb 3:13; James 2:16).

(D) Preceded by *eán* (1437), if, meaning if someone (Matt 21:3; Mark 11:3; Col 3:13; James 2:14; Rev 22:18); by *eán mé* (3362), unless, meaning unless one (John 3:3, 5; Acts 8:31); by *án* (302),

if, followed by *tis*, meaning if someone, whosoever (John 20:23).

(E) *Eí* (1487), if, followed by *tis*, meaning if someone (1 Pet 4:11). In a hypothetical clause, the simple *tis* is sometimes said to be equivalent to *eí tis*, but not accurately. In 1 Cor 7:18, "Is one called being circumcised" (a.t.), means be it so that one is thus called. See James 5:13, 14.

(F) Sometimes *tis*, someone, is omitted where the sense requires it to be supplied (cf. I, F [Matt 23:9]).

(III) Emphatically meaning somebody, something, some person or thing of weight and importance, some great one.

(A) Simply (Acts 5:36, "saying that he is somebody" [a.t.]). In the neut. (1 Cor 3:7, "nor the one who plants is something" [a.t.], meaning somebody; 1 Cor 8:2; 10:19; Gal 2:6; 6:15).

(B) With an adj. (Acts 8:9; Heb 10:27, "a certain fearful looking for of judgment").

(IV) *Tis* with a subst. or adj. sometimes serves to limit or modify the full meaning, somewhat, in some measure, a kind of (Rom 1:11, 13; 1 Cor 6:11; James 1:18).

(V) Neut. *ti*, adv. or as acc. of manner.

(A) Simply, in, or as to something, in any way (Phil 3:15; Phile 1:18, "if he owes thee anything"). Hence it means perhaps, in the formulae *ei mé ti* (*ei* [1487], if; *mé* [3361], not), unless, perhaps (Luke 9:13) and *eán mé ti* (*eán* [1437], if) (John 5:19).

(B) With another acc. neut. as adv., thus serving to modify it (cf. IV). The meaning in this case is some, somewhat, a little, some little, spoken of time (Acts 5:34); of place or rank (Acts 23:20; 2 Cor 10:8; 11:16; Heb 2:7). Preceded by *méros* (3313), part, meaning in some part, partly (1 Cor 11:18).

5101. τίς *tís*; neut. *tí*, gen. *tínos*, an interrogative pron. Who?, which?, or what? As an interrogative pron. it is always written with the acute accent, and is thus distinguished from *tis* or *ti*, as an indef. pron. See *tis* (5100). The place of *tís* as an interrogative is usually at the beginning of the interrogative clause, or at most after a particle or the like (See I, A, 6).

(**I**) Used in direct questions, usually with the indic. but sometimes with the subjunctive and opt., which then serve to modify its power (See F, G.).

(**A**) With the indic. generally and in various constructions. (**1**) (Matt 3:7; 21:23; Mark 2:7; Luke 10:29; John 1:22, 38; 13:25; Acts 7:27; 19:3, "unto what"; Heb 3:17, 18; Rev 6:17). In the phrase *tí esti toúto* (*esti* [2076], 3d person sing. of *eimí* [1510], to be, is; *toúto* [5127], this), what is this? what means this? (Mark 1:27; 9:10; Eph 4:9). Also with the demonstrative pron. in a contracted clause (Luke 16:2 [cf. John 16:18; Acts 11:17]) for the phrases *tí prós hēmás*, what is this to us? (*prós* [4314], toward, as unto; *hēmás* [2248], us) (Matt 27:4) *tí prós sé*, what is that to you?, see *prós* (4314), toward, for, III, C, 1. The expression *tí / hēmín* (to us) / *emoí* (to me) *kaí soí* (and you) in Matt 8:29; Mark 5:7; Luke 8:28; John 2:4 means what is it to me (us) and thee?, or what have I in common with thee? (cf. 4). (**2**) With a subst. (Matt 5:46; 7:9; Mark 5:9, "what man is there of you?"; Luke 11:11; 14:31; John 2:18, what sign do you show; Rom 6:21; Heb 7:11). With an adj. taken substantively the expression *tí perissón poieíte* (*perissón* [4053], more; *poieíte*, you do, from *poiéō* [4160]), what more do you do? (Matt 5:47). The expression *tí gár kakón epoíēsen* (*gár*, particle meaning therefore; *kakón* [2556], evil; *epoíēsen*, the aor. 3d person sing. of *poiéō* [4160], to do), what therefore evil did he do?, for what evil did he do? (Matt 27:23). (**3**) Followed by the gen. of class or of partition, meaning of which, *tís*, *tínes*, expresses a part (Matt 22:28, "whose wife shall she be of the seven?"; Luke 10:36; Acts 7:52, "which of the prophets?"; Heb 1:5, 13). Followed by *ek* (1537), with gen. partitive, "which of you" (Matt 6:27; John 8:46). (**4**) After *tís*,

the verb *eínai* (1511), to be, exist, is often omitted; *tí emoí kaí soí* "what have I to do with thee?" (John 2:4); *tí soí ónoma*, "What is thy name?" (Mark 5:9; Luke 4:36; Acts 7:49; 10:21; Rom 3:1; 8:31, 34; James 3:13). Also *gínomai* (1096), to become, is often omitted (Matt 26:8; John 21:21). (**5**) In the sing. *tí* as a predicate sometimes refers to a pl. subj. (John 6:9; Acts 17:20 [cf. G]. (**6**) *Tís* is sometimes used after several words in a clause (cf. Matt 6:28; John 6:9; 16:18; Acts 11:17; 19:15; Rom 14:10; Eph 4:9). (**7**) With other particles: *kaí tís* meaning and who?, who then? (Mark 10:26; 2 Cor 2:2; see *kaí* [2532] cf. I, E). *Tís ára* (686), a particle denoting inference, as perhaps, therefore, wherefore, meaning, who then? See *ára* I, B. *Tí gár* means what then? (Rom 3:3; Phil 1:18). See *gár* (1063) I, C. *Tí oún* meaning what therefore? what then?; see *oún* (3767) cf. II, D. *Tí hóti* meaning why?; see *hóti* (3754) I, B. *Diá tí* or *diatí* (*diá* [1223], through; *diatí* [1302], wherefore), on account of what? wherefore? why? *Eis tí* (*eis* [1519], unto) meaning for what? to what end? wherefore? why? (Matt 14:31; Mark 14:4). For Acts 19:3 see A, 1. *Prós* (4314), unto, followed by *tí*, meaning for what? for what reason? wherefore? (John 13:28).

(**B**) The neut. *tí* is used as adv. of interrogation or as an interrogative acc. of manner. (**1**) Wherefore? why? for what cause? equivalent to *diá tí* (Matt 8:26; Mark 11:3; Luke 6:2; John 7:19; Acts 26:14; 1 Cor 10:30; Sept.: Ex 14:15), *tí kaí* ([2532], and, then), meaning why then? (1 Cor 15:29, 30), *tí dé* ([1161], but), meaning but why? expressing surprise (Matt 7:3; Luke 6:41), also and why? continuative (1 Cor 4:7), *tí oún* ([3767], therefore, accordingly), meaning why then? (Matt 17:10; John 1:25), to what end? for what purpose? equal to *eis* (1519), unto, followed by *tí* (Matt 26:65; Gal 3:19). (**2**) As to what? how? in what respect? equal to *katá tí* (*katá* [2596], according to), as to what? (Matt 16:26; 19:20, "as to what do I lack" [a.t.]; Mark 8:36; Luke 9:25). Also equal to in what way? how? (Matt 22:17; Mark 14:63; Acts 26:8; Rom 8:24; 1 Cor 7:16). Also as an intens. meaning how! how greatly! (Matt 7:14 [UBS], "how straight the gate" [a.t.] [*hóti* {3754}, because {TR}]; Luke 12:49; Sept.: Ps 3:2; Song 4:10; 7:7).

(C) Equivalent to *póteros* (4220), an interrogative pron. meaning which of two, where two are spoken about meaning who or which of the two? (Matt 21:31; 27:21 [cf. A, 3]; 23:17, 19; Luke 7:42; 1 Cor 4:21). *Tí gár estin eukopóteron* meaning which of the two is easier? (Matt 9:5).

(D) *Tís* with the indic. through the force of the context sometimes approaches to the sense of *poíos* (4169), meaning of what kind or sort? Of persons (Matt 16:13, "Whom do men say that I the Son of man am?"; Matt 16:15; Mark 8:27, 29; 1 Cor 3:5, "Who then is Paul"; James 4:12). *Tís* followed by *ára* (686), a particle denoting inference, perhaps, therefore (Luke 1:66, "What manner of child shall this be?"; 8:25). Of things (Luke 4:36; 24:17; John 7:36).

(E) Specifically with the indic. fut. *tís* expresses: (1) Deliberation (Matt 11:16, "whereunto shall I liken this generation?"; Mark 6:24; Luke 3:10, 12; 13:18; Acts 4:16). In most of these examples, some MSS have the subjunctive. With the pres. indic. (John 11:47; Acts 21:22). (2) Introducing an idea, shall, may, can (Matt 5:13; Luke 1:18; Acts 8:33; Rom 8:33, 35). (3) Sometimes used where a general truth is to be illustrated by a particular example (Matt 12:11; Luke 11:5 where the subjunctive alternates with the fut.; 14:5).

(F) With the subjunctive implying deliberation with expectation of deliberation (Matt 6:31; 20:32; 27:17, 21, 22; Luke 12:17; 16:3).

(G) Opt. and *án* (302), if, implying uncertainty (Luke 1:62; 6:11; 9:46; John 13:24; Acts 2:12; 5:24; 10:17; 17:18, 20; 21:33).

(II) Indirect, where it is often equivalent to *hóstis* (3748), who, or *hóti*, the neut., meaning what.

(A) With the indic. after verbs of hearing, inquiring, showing, knowing, and the like, in various constructions and uses. (1) Generally (Matt 6:3; 9:13; 10:11; 12:3, 7; 21:16; Mark 14:36; Luke 6:47; 7:39; John 19:24; Acts 21:33; 1 Cor 15:2; Eph 5:10; 1 Pet 1:11; 1 John 3:2). With the subjunctive (Rom 8:27; Eph 3:18; Heb 5:12). In an interrogative (Luke 19:15, that he might know who had gained what). (2) Equivalent to *póteros* (4220), which of two (cf. I, C; Phil 1:22). (3) Equivalent to *poíos* (4169), which one (cf. I, D). See John 10:6; Acts 17:19.

(B) With the subjunctive implying what may or can be done, the possibility (Matt 6:25; 10:19; 15:32; Mark 9:6; Luke 12:5, 11, 29; 17:8; 19:48; Rom 8:26; 1 Pet 5:8); also in an interrogative (Mark 15:24 [cf. A]).

(C) With the opt. after a preceding preterite implying doubt or curiosity (Luke 8:9; 15:26 [cf. I, D, 5]; Luke 18:36; 22:23).

Deriv.: *diatí* (1302), why?, wherefore?

5102. τίτλος *títlos*; gen. *títlou*, masc. noun. A title, a board with an inscription, superscription (John 19:19, 20).

Syn.: *epigraphḗ* (1923), a superscription.

5103. Τίτος *Títos*; gen. *Títou*, masc. proper noun. Titus, a Gentile who was probably converted to Christianity under the preaching of Paul (Titus 1:4). Paul did not subject him to the rite of circumcision, although some have inferred he was strongly urged to do so (Gal 2:3–5). Titus was the companion of Paul in many of his trials and missionary journeys (2 Cor 7:6, 13, 14; 8:6, 16, 23; Gal 2:1, 3) and was entrusted with several important commissions (2 Cor 12:18; 2 Tim 4:10; Titus 1:5). He was sent by Paul to Dalmatia (2 Tim 4:10) and was left in Crete to establish and regulate the churches (Titus 1:5). Tradition relates that he was bishop of Crete, and died there at the age of ninety-two. Paul calls him his brother

(2 Cor 2:13) and wrote an epistle to him instructing regarding the proper discharge of his ministerial offices in Crete, a difficult field due to the character of the inhabitants who were noted for lying, idleness, and gluttony (Titus 1:12). The epistle was probably written from Asia Minor in the year A.D. 65 when Paul was on his way to *Nikópolis* (3533).

5104. τοι *toi*; an enclitic particle. By consequence, consequently, therefore. In comp. forms such as *toigár* or *toigaroún* (5105) with *toi* itself retaining only a confirmatory aspect as indeed, yet. In the NT, only in the comp. *kaítoige* (2544), nevertheless, though (John 4:2); *toigaroún* (5105), consequently (1 Thess 4:8; Heb 12:1); *toínun* (5106), accordingly (Luke 20:25; 1 Cor 9:26; Heb 13:13; James 2:24).

5105. τοιγαροῦν *toigaroún*; composed of *toi* (5104), strengthened by the particles *gár* (1063), therefore, and *oún* (3767), then, therefore. By certain consequence, consequently (1 Thess 4:8; Heb 12:1; Sept.: Job 22:10; 24:22).

5106. τοίνυν *toínun*; composed of *toi* (5104), truly, indeed, strengthened by *nún* (3568), now. Indeed now, yet now, therefore, used where one proceeds with an inference. Usually after one or more words in a clause (Luke 20:25; 1 Cor 9:26; James 2:24 [TR]). More rarely put at the beginning of a clause (Heb 13:13; Sept.: Isa 3:10; 5:13).

5107. τοιόσδε *toiósdē*; fem. *toiáde*, neut. *toióde*, correlative demonstrative pron., a strengthened form of *toíos* (n.f.), such. Of this kind or sort, such, so great (2 Pet 1:17). It has a qualitative force.

5108. τοιοῦτος *toioútos*; fem. *toiaútē*, neut. *toioúto* / *toioúton* (Matt 18:5), correlative demonstrative pron., a strengthened form of *toíos* (n.f.), such. Such as, of this kind or sort. It has a qualitative force.

(I) Generally:

(A) Without an article or corresponding relative pron. (Matt 18:5; Mark 4:33; John 4:23; Acts 16:24; 1 Cor 11:16; James 4:16). With a corresponding relative pron. *hoíos* (3634), such (1 Cor 15:48; 2 Cor 10:11); *hopoíos* (3697), such as (Acts 26:29); *hōs* (5613), as (Phile 1:9).

(B) Preceded by the def. art. *ho*, *hē*, *tó*, masc., fem., neut., the (Matt 19:14, "For of such is the kingdom of heaven"; Mark 9:37; Acts 19:25; Rom 1:32; 1 Cor 5:11; Gal 5:21; 1 Tim 6:5; 3 John 1:8).

(II) By implication, such, so great.

(A) Without the art. or relative pron. (Matt 9:8; Mark 6:2). Neut. pl. *toiaúta*, such things, so great things, meaning good (Luke 9:9; John 9:16); evil (Luke 13:2; Heb 12:3 [fem. sing.]). With a relative pron. corresponding, *hóstis* (3748), who (1 Cor 5:1); *hós* (3739), who (Heb 8:1).

(B) With the art. *ho* in the phrase *ho toioútos*, such a one, such a person, one distinguished. In a good sense (2 Cor 12:2, 3, 5); in a bad sense, "such a fellow" (Acts 22:22; 1 Cor 5:5; 2 Cor 2:6, 7).

5109. τοῖχος *toíchos*; gen. *toíchou*, masc. noun. A wall of a house. To be distinguished from *teíchos* (5038), a wall of a city (Sept. Ex 30:3; Lev 14:37). Used metaphorically, "Thou whited wall" (Acts 23:3)

Deriv.: *mesótoichon* (3320), a partition wall.

5110. τόκος *tókos*; gen. *tókou*, masc. noun from *tíktō* (5088), to bring forth. A bringing forth, birth, offspring. Figuratively, gain from money lent out, interest, usury (Matt 25:27; Luke 19:23; Sept.: Ex 22:25; Lev 25:36, 37).

Syn.: *kérdos* (2771), gain; *ōphéleia* (5622), benefit, profit.

Ant.: *dapánē* (1160), expense, cost; *zēmía* (2209), loss; *apóleia* (684), waste, loss.

5111. τολμάω *tolmáō*; contracted *tolmô*, fut. *tolmēsō*, from *tólma* (n.f.), courage, which is from *tláō* (n.f.), to sustain, support, endure. To have courage, boldness, confidence to do something, to venture, dare. Intrans. with the inf. (Matt 22:46; Mark 12:34; Luke 20:40; John 21:12; Acts 5:13; 7:32; Rom 5:7; 15:18; 1 Cor 6:1; 2 Cor 10:12; Phil 1:14; Jude 1:9; Sept: Esth 7:5). To show oneself bold, to act with boldness, confidence against someone or something (2 Cor 10:2; 11:21).

Deriv.: *apotolmáō* (662), to be very bold; *tolmētḗs* (5113), daring.

Syn.: *tharréō* (2292), to be courageous; *tharséō* (2293), to be courageous.

Ant.: *phríssō* (5425), to shudder, fear, tremble; *trémō* (5141), to tremble; *deiliáō* (1168), to be timid, afraid; *phobéō* (5399), to be afraid.

5112. τολμηρότερον *tolmēróteron*; adv., the comparative of *tolmērós* (n.f.). More boldly, with greater confidence and freedom (Rom 15:15).

5113. τολμητής *tolmētḗs*; gen. *tolmētoú*, masc. noun from *tolmáō* (5111), to dare. A bold, daring or enterprising person. In a bad sense, an audacious or presumptuous person (2 Pet 2:10).

5114. τομώτερος *tomóteros*; adj., the comparative of *tomós* (n.f.), sharp, from *témnō* (n.f., see *orthotoméō* [3718]), to cut. Finer edged, sharper (Heb 4:12).

5115. τόξον *tóxon*; gen. *tóxou*, neut. noun. A bow for shooting arrows (Rev 6:2; Sept.: Gen 27:3; Ps 7:13).

5116. τοπάζιον *topázion*; gen. *topazíou*, neut. noun. The topaz, a transparent precious stone, the color of shining gold, of a fainter green than the emerald but with a yellowish tinge (Rev 21:20; Sept.: Ex 28:17; Ezek 28:13).

5117. τόπος *tópos*; gen. *tópou*, masc. noun. Place.

(I) As occupied or filled by any person or thing, a spot, space, room.

(A) Particularly (Matt 28:6; Mark 16:6; Luke 2:7; 14:9, 10, 22; John 20:7; Acts 7:33; Heb 8:7; Rev 2:5; 6:14; 20:11; Sept. Gen 24:23; 1 Kgs 8:6, 7; Prov 25:6). In Luke 14:9, to give place to someone means to make room. See Rom 12:19; Eph 4:27. Of things, as a place where something is kept such as a sword, meaning a sheath, scabbard (Matt 26:52).

(B) Figuratively, condition, part, character (1 Cor 14:16, "he who fills the place of one unlearned" [a.t.], who is unlearned).

(C) Figuratively, place, opportunity, occasion (Acts 25:16; Rom 15:23; Heb 12:17).

(II) Of a particular place or spot where something is done or takes place (Luke 10:32; 11:1; 19:5; John 4:20; 5:13; 6:23; 10:40; 11:30; 18:2; 19:20, 41; 2 Pet 1:19). Pleonastically (Rom 9:26, "in the place where," meaning simply where, quoted from Hos 2:1; Sept.: Gen 28:16, 17; 35:14; Ruth 3:4).

(III) Of a place in which one dwells, sojourns or belongs; a dwelling place, abode, home (Luke 16:28; John 11:6; 14:2, 3; Acts 1:25; 12:17; Rev 12:6, 8, 14). Of a house, dwelling (Acts 4:31); a temple (Acts 7:49 quoted from Isa 66:1); the temple as the abode of God is called the Holy Place (Matt 24:15; Acts 6:13, 14; 21:28; Sept.: 1 Sam 10:25; 24:23; Ps 24:3; Isa 60:13).

(IV) In a geographical or topographical sense, a place or part of a country, the earth.

(A) Of a definite place or spot in a city, district, country (Matt 27:33; Mark 15:22; Luke 6:17; 22:40; 23:33; John 6:10; 19:13; Acts 27:8, 29, 41; 28:7; Rev 16:16; Sept.: Gen 22:2, 14; 28:19; 29:26; Num 24:11).

(B) Of an inhabited place, a city, village, quarter (Matt 14:35; Luke 4:37; 10:1; Acts 16:3; 27:2). In 1 Cor 1:2, "in every place," everywhere among men (2 Cor 2:14; 1 Thess 1:8; 1 Tim 2:8; Sept.: 2 Chr 34:6).

(C) Of a tract of country as a district, region, desert place (Matt 14:13, 15; Mark

1:35, 45; 6:31, 32, 35; Luke 4:42; 9:10, 12); "through dry places" (Matt 12:43; Luke 11:24); "in divers places" meaning quarters, countries (Matt 24:7; Mark 13:8; Luke 21:11). Also in the sense of a land, country (John 11:48, "our place and nation"). "In this place" (Acts 7:7) in allusion to Gen 15:4 (cf. Heb 11:8).

(D) Figuratively of a place or passage in a book (Luke 4:17).

Deriv.: *átopos* (824), out of place, inconvenient; *entópios* (1786), a resident.

Syn.: *chóra* (5561), a space or territory, country, ground, region, land; *chōríon* (5564), a region; *chōros* (5566), area, place; *periochḗ* (1042), the area around; *méros* (3313), place, part, portion.

5118. τοσοῦτος *tosoútos*; fem. *tosaútē*, neut. *tosoúto/tosoúton*, correlative demonstrative pron., a strengthened form of *tósos* (n.f.), so much. So great, so much.

(I) Of magnitude as an intens., so great (Matt 8:10; 15:33; Luke 7:9; Heb 12:1; Rev 18:17). Pl. neut. *tosaúta*, so many things, benefits. With *hósos* corresponding (Heb 1:4; Rev 18:7; 21:16 [TR]). Of a specific amount meaning so much and no more, so much (Acts 5:8).

(II) Of time meaning so long (John 14:9; Heb 4:7).

(III) Of number meaning so many, so numerous (Matt 15:33; Luke 15:29; John 6:9; 12:37; 21:11; 1 Cor 14:10; Gal 3:4).

Syn.: *pósos* (4214), how great, how much, how many; *tēlikoútos* (5082), so great.

Ant.: *brachús* (1024), short of time, quantity or number; *olígos* (3641), few, somewhat, a while; *suntómōs* (4935), briefly, a few words.

5119. τότε *tóte*; adv. of time. Then, at that time, correlated to *hóte* (3753), when, while, and *póte* (4219), at what time, when.

(I) In general prepositions marking succession, e.g., after *próton* (4412), first (Matt 5:24; 12:29; Mark 3:27; Luke 6:42; John 2:10). With *hótan* (3752), when,

(Luke 11:26; 21:20; John 2:10; 2 Cor 12:10).

(II) Of time past, e.g., with a notation of time preceding, with *hóte* (3753), when (Matt 13:26; 21:1; John 12:16); with *hōs* (5613), as (John 7:10; 11:6); with *metá* (3326), after, with the acc. (John 13:27). After a word denoting time (Acts 27:21; 28:1). As the opposite to *nún* (3568), now (Rom 6:21; Gal 4:8, 9, 29; Heb 12:26); *euthéōs* (2112), immediately, straight away, followed by *tóte*, then, at that time (Acts 17:14). Where the notation of time lies in the context and is often equivalent to thereupon, after that (Matt 2:7, 17; 3:5, 13, meaning after this, 3:15; 4:1; 26:3; John 19:1, 16; Acts 1:12; 10:46, 48; Heb 10:7, 9; Sept.: Gen 13:7; Ezra 4:23, 24). *Apó tóte* (*apó* [575], from), from then, from that time (Matt 4:17; 16:21; 26:16; Luke 16:16; Sept.: Eccl 8:12). With the art. as adj., *ho tóte kósmos* (2889), world, "the then world" (a.t. [2 Pet 3:6]).

(III) Of a time future, e.g., with *hótan* (3752), at the time when (Matt 25:31; Mark 13:14; Luke 5:35; 14:10; 21:20; John 8:28; 1 Cor 13:10; 16:2; 1 Thess 5:3). Meaning then or when (Luke 13:26; 21:27; 1 Cor 4:5; 2 Thess 2:8; Sept.: Ex 12:44, 48).

Syn.: *eíta* (1534), then, moreover; *épeita* (1899), thereafter.

Ant.: *árti* (737), now; *próteron* (4386), previously, before; *prín* (4250), prior.

5120. τοῦ *toú*; the gen. of *tó* (3588), the neut. def. art. Of its. Sometimes used for *toútou* (5127), of this person.

5121. τουναντίον *tounantíon*; from *tó* (3588), the neut. def. art., and *enantíon* (1726), the opposite. In the NT, as an adv., on the contrary, to act contrary to, but not willfully or obstinately so (2 Cor 2:7; Gal 2:7; 1 Pet 3:9).

Syn.: *állōs* (247), otherwise, differently; *hetérōs* (2088), otherwise; *epeí* (1893), otherwise.

Ant.: *homoíōs* (3668), likewise, in like manner; *hōsaútōs* (5615), likewise; *paraplēsíōs* (3898), in like manner.

5122. τοὔνομα *toúnoma*; composed of *tó* (3588), the neut. def. art., and *ónoma* (3686), name. By name (Matt 27:57).

5123. τουτέστι *toutésti*; composed of *toúto* (5124), this one, and *estí*, the 3d person sing. of *eimí* (1510), to be. In other words, equivalent to "which means" and used in explanations as in the TR of Acts 1:19; 19:4; Rom 7:18; 9:8; Phile 1:12; Heb 2:14; 7:5; 9:11; 10:20; 11:16; 13:15; 1 Pet 3:20; Sept.: Job 40:19. In later editions everywhere written separately as *toút' ésti* (Matt 27:46; Mark 7:2; Rom 10:6–8 [TR]).

5124. τοῦτο *toúto*; the neut. (nom. or acc.) sing. of *hoútos* (3778), this one. Used in distribution, *toúto mén . . . toúto dé*, as to this . . . as to that, meaning partly . . . partly (Heb 10:33). In the pl., *taúta* (5023) with the acc. as adv., so, thus, equivalent to *hoútos* (3779), thus; after *kathós* (2531), as (John 8:28). With *hoútos* (3779), thus (Mark 2:8, to be thus, such; 1 Cor 6:11, pl. *taúta* [5023]). Referring to what follows (Luke 18:11).

5125. τούτοις *toútois*; dat. pl. (masc. or neut.) of *hoútos* (3778), this one. To these persons or things which are for further elucidation. Such, then, these.

5126. τοῦτον *toúton*; acc. sing. masc. of *hoútos* (3778), this one. This person, as the obj. of a verb or prep. Him, the same, that, this.

5127. τούτου *toútou*; gen. sing. (masc. or neut.) of *hoútos* (3778), this one. Of this person or thing.

5128. τούτους *toútous*; masc. acc. pl. of *hoútos* (3778), this one. These persons, as the obj. of a verb or prep. Such, them, these.

5129. τούτῳ *toútō*; dat. sing. (masc. or neut.) of *hoútos* (3778), this one. To, in, with, or by this person or thing: hereby, herein, him, one, the same, therein, this.

5130. τούτων *toútōn*; gen. pl. (masc. or neut.) of *hoútos* (3778), this one. Of these persons or things, such, their, these things, they, this sort, those.

5131. τράγος *trágos*; gen. *trágou*, masc. noun. A male goat (Heb 9:12, 13, 19; 10:4; Sept.: Gen 31:10; Num 7:17).
  Syn.: *ériphos* (2056), a kid or goat; *eríphion* (2055), young kid or goat.

5132. τράπεζα *trápeza*; gen. *trapézēs*, fem. noun from *tétra* (n.f., see *tetrágōnos* [5068]), four, and *péza* (n.f., see *pédē* [3976]), a foot. A table:
  (I) Generally the place for setting food or taking meals.
  (A) Particularly (Matt 15:27; Mark 7:28; Luke 16:21; 22:21, 30). Of the table for the shewbread (Heb 9:2; Sept.: Ex 25:23, 27; 26:35). See *próthesis* (4286), shewbread (1 Sam 20:34; 2 Sam 9:7, 10).
  (B) Metonymically for that which is set on a table, food, a meal, banquet (Acts 16:34, meaning he set a table, made ready a meal). See *paratíthēmi* (3908), to put or set before. See also Rom 11:9 quoted from Ps 69:23; 1 Cor 10:21; Sept.: Ps 23:5; Prov 9:2.
  (II) Specifically the table of a money changer, a broker's bench or counter at which he sat in the market or public place, e.g., in the outer court of the temple (Matt 21:12; Mark 11:15; John 2:15). See *kermatistḗs* (2773), a changer of money, and *kollubistḗs* (2855), a coin-dealer. Hence, generally, a broker's office or bank where money is deposited and loaned out (Luke 19:23). The word is used with this meaning in Gr. In Acts 6:2, used metonymically for serving.
  Deriv.: *trapezítēs* (5133), banker, moneychanger, broker.
  Syn.: *brṓma* (1033), food; *trophḗ* (5160), nourishment.

5133. τραπεζίτης *trapezítēs*; gen. *trapezítou*, masc. noun from *trápeza* (5132), table. A moneychanger, broker or banker (Matt 25:27).

5134. τραῦμα *traúma*; gen. *traúmatos*, neut. noun from *titróskō* (n.f.), to wound, hurt. A wound (Luke 10:34; Sept.: Gen 4:23; Isa 1:6).
Deriv.: *traumatízō* (5134), to wound.
Syn.: *plēgḗ* (4127), a blow, stroke, wound.

5135. τραυματίζω *traumatízō*; fut. *traumatísō*, from *traúma* (5134), a wound. To wound, trans. (Luke 20:12; Sept. Song 5:7); pass. part. (Acts 19:16; Sept. Jer 9:1; Ezek 28:23).
Syn.: *plḗssō* (4141), to afflict with calamity, smite; *bláptō* (984), to injure, hurt.
Ant.: *therapeúō* (2323), to relieve, cure, heal; *iáomai* (2390), to heal, make well, cure; *sṓzō* (4982), to save, heal.

5136. τραχηλίζω *trachēlízō*; fut. *trachēlísō*, from *tráchelos* (5137), neck. To expose or lay open. The word was used of the bending back of the neck of wrestlers by their opponent. The bending back of the neck was used also on an animal to be slaughtered for an offering in order to expose the throat; hence, figuratively to lay bare or open, in the pass. part. (Heb 4:13, "opened to sight" [a.t.]). Equivalent to *pephanerōména*, from *phaneróō* (5319), to make manifest.
Syn.: *emphanízō* (1718), to manifest, show; *deiknúō* (1166), to show; *dēlóō* (1213), to declare, show.
Ant.: *krúptō* (2928), to conceal, hide; *apokrúptō* (613), to conceal, keep secret, hide; *egkrúptō* (1470), to conceal in.

5137. τράχηλος *tráchelos*; gen. *trachélou*, masc. noun. The neck (Matt 18:6; Mark 9:42; Luke 15:20; 17:2; Acts 15:10; 20:37, "fell on Paul's neck," meaning embraced him; Rom 16:4, meaning have exposed their lives to peril for his safety [cf. Gen 33:4; 45:14; Deut 10:16; Josh 10:24; Isa 48:4]).
Deriv.: *sklērotráchelos* (4644), stiffnecked; *trachēlízō* (5136), to bend back the neck.

5138. τραχύς *trachús*; fem. *tracheía*, neut. *trachú*, adj. Rough, uneven (Luke 3:5; Acts 27:29 referring to rocks, reefs; Sept.: Isa 40:4; Jer 2:25).
Syn.: *petrṓdēs* (4075), rock-like; *sklērós* (4642), hard, rough.
Ant.: *leíos* (3006), smooth; *malakós* (3120), soft.

5139. Τραχωνῖτις *Trachōnítis*; gen. *Trachōnítidos*. Trachonitis. Rugged or rough. One of the five Roman provinces into which the district northeast of the Jordan was divided in NT times. It lay to the east of Ituraea and Gaulonitis and to the south of Damascus. The Emperor Augustus entrusted it to Herod the Great on the condition that he should clear it of robbers. Herod Philip succeeded to the tetrarchy (Luke 3:1). He died in A.D. 33, and the emperor Caligula bestowed the province of Trachonitis upon Herod Agrippa I. Later it was part of the dominions of Herod Agrippa II, A.D. 53.

5140. τρεῖς *treís*; masc.-fem, neut. *tría*, cardinal number. Three (Matt 12:40; 13:33; 18:20; Sept.: Gen 7:13).
Deriv.: *triákonta* (5144), thirty; *triakósioi* (5145), three hundred; *tríbolos* (5146), three-pointed, three-pronged; *trietía* (5148), three years; *trímēnon* (5150), three months; *trís* (5151), three times; *trístegon* (5152), three-roofed, three-storied; *trítos* (5154), third.

5141. τρέμω *trémō*; only in the pres. and impf., from *tréō* (n.f.), To dread, be terrified, only in indic. and part. to tremble from fear, intrans. (Mark 5:33; Luke 8:47; Acts 9:6; Sept.: Jer 4:24; Dan 5:19; 6:26). To tremble at something, to fear, be afraid, with a part. (2 Pet 2:10, do not tremble or fear speaking evil, "they are not afraid to speak evil"). With the acc. (Sept.: Isa 66:2, 5).
Deriv.: *trómos* (5156), trembling.
Syn.: *seíō* (4579), to shake; *phríssō* (5425), to shudder; *anaseíō* (383), excite, move, stir up; *phobéō* (5399), to fear.

Ant.: *tharréō* (2292), to be courageous, confident.

5142. τρέφω *tréphō*; fut. *thrépsō*. To nourish, feed, nurture. Trans.:
(I) Particularly and generally with the acc. (Matt 6:26; 25:37; Luke 12:24; Acts 12:20; Rev 12:6, 14). To pamper (James 5:5; Sept.: Gen 48:15; 1 Kgs 18:13; Prov 25:21).
(II) To nurture, bring up (Luke 4:16).
Deriv.: *anatréphō* (397), to bring up; *ektréphō* (1625), to nourish, nurture; *thrémma* (2353), cattle, herds; *entréphō* (1789), to nourish up, train up; *teknotrophéō* (5044), to bring up children; *trophḗ* (5160), food, nourishment; *trophós* (5162), a nurse.
Syn.: *bóskō* (1006), to feed, used of shepherds whose primary function is to provide food; *poimaínō* (4165), to shepherd, including complete care and feeding; *chortázō* (5526), to feed providing more than enough to satisfy, to fill; *psōmízō* (5595), to feed with morsels, little by little, to nourish.
Ant.: *nēsteúō* (3522), to abstain from food, fast; *peináō* (3983), to famish.

5143. τρέχω *tréchō*; fut. *thréxomai*, 2d aor. *édramon*. To run, intrans.:
(I) Particularly and generally (Matt 27:48; Mark 5:6; 15:36; Luke 15:20; John 20:2, 4; Sept.: Gen 24:28; 2 Sam 18:19). Followed by *epí* (1909), unto, with the acc. locative (Luke 24:12, "ran unto the sepulcher"; Sept.: Gen 24:20; Joel 2:9); by *eis* (1519), unto, for the purpose of (Rev 9:9); by an inf. showing purpose (Matt 28:8). Of those who run in a stadium or public race (1 Cor 9:24). Figuratively in comparisons drawn from the public races and applied to Christians as expressing strenuous efforts in the Christian life and cause (1 Cor 9:24, 26, lest it be in vain; Gal 2:2; Phil 2:16). With *kalós* (2573), well (Gal 5:7). With the hortatory subjunctive (Heb 12:1, "let us run . . . the race that is set before us"). Of strenuous effort generally (Rom 9:16).

(II) Figuratively of the word of God that may run or spread quickly (2 Thess 3:1; Sept.: Ps 147:15).
Deriv.: *drómos* (1408), course; *eistréchō* (1532), to run in; *katatréchō* (2701), to chase down; *peritréchō* (4063), to run about; *prostréchō* (4370), to run to; *protréchō* (4390), to run before; *suntréchō* (4936), to run with; *trochós* (5164), a runner, wheel; *hupotréchō* (5295), to run under.
Syn.: *hormáō* (3729), to hasten on, rush; *eispēdáō* (1530), to rush or run in; *speúdō* (4692), to speed.
Ant.: *peripatéō* (4043), to walk.

5144. τριάκοντα *triákonta*; used for all genders, cardinal number, from *tría*, the neut. of *treís* (5140), three, and *-konta*, the decimal termination. Thirty (Matt 13:8, 23; 26:15; 27:3, 9; Mark 4:8, 20; Luke 3:23; John 5:5; 6:19; Gal 3:17; Sept.: Gen 5:3, 5, 16).

5145. τριακόσιοι *triakósioi*; fem. *triakósiai*, neut. *triakósia*, cardinal number from *treis* (5140), three, and *hekatón* (1540), a hundred. Three hundred (Mark 14:5; John 12:5; Sept.: Gen 6:15).

5146. τρίβολος *tríbolos*; masc.-fem., neut. *tríbolon*, adj. from *treís* (5140), three, and *bélos* (956), an arrow, dart, or *bolís* (1002), dart. Three-pointed, three-pronged. As a subst., *ho tríbolos*, a crow-foot (so-called because of the crow's group of three talons in front and one backward for balance or grip). Also called a caltrop, a military instrument with four points or prongs—three of them anchoring the ground and the other projecting upward to injure the horses. In the NT, thistles or briers because of their many injurious points or thorns (Matt 7:16; Heb 6:8; Sept.: Gen 3:18; Prov 22:5; Hos 10:8).
Syn.: *ákantha* (173), a brier, thorn; in its figurative sense *skólops* (4647), originally meant something pointed, a stake, something that causes pain and anguish, and in its physical sense it referred to illness.

5147. τρίβος *tríbos*; gen. *tríbou*, fem. noun from *tríbō* (n.f., see *diatríbō* [1304]), to wear away, rub, break in pieces. A beaten pathway, highway (Matt 3:3; Mark 1:3; Luke 3:4, all quoted from Isa 40:3; Sept.: Gen 49:17; Prov 1:15).

Deriv.: *suntríbō* (4937), to break into pieces, crush.

Syn.: *trochiá* (5163), the track of a wheel, path; *hodós* (3598), road, way.

5148. τριετία *trietía*; gen. *trietías*, fem. noun from *treís* (5140), three, and the pl. of *étos* (2094), year. Three years (Acts 20:31).

5149. τρίζω *trízō*; fut. *trísō*, an onomatopoeic sound. To squeak, creak, to grate one's teeth and thus produce a grinding sound. Intrans. spoken chiefly of living things as of the cry or chirping of young birds, the shrieks of women, later of the wheezing or snorting of elephants, the rasp of an iron being filed. In the NT, of the teeth, to grind, gnash, with the acc. (Mark 9:18).

Syn.: *brúchō* (1031), to grind or gnash with the teeth.

5150. τρίμηνον *trímēnon*; adj., the neut. of *trímēnos*, from *treís* (5140), three, and *mḗn* (3376), month. A space of three months (Heb 11:23; Sept.: Gen 38:24; 2 Kgs 24:8).

5151. τρίς *trís*; adv. from *tría*, the neut. of *treís* (5140), three. Thrice, three times (Matt 26:34, 75; Mark 14:30, 72; Luke 22:34, 61; John 13:38; 2 Cor 11:25; 12:8; Sept.: 1 Sam 20:41; 2 Kgs 13:18, 19). With *epí* (1909), upon, preceding *trís*, up to three times (Acts 10:16; 11:10).

Deriv.: *trischílioi* (5153), three thousand.

5152. τρίστεγον *trístegon*; adj., neut. of *trístegos*, from *treís* (5140), three, and *stégē* (4721), a roof. Three-roofed, three-storied, having three floors or stories pertaining to a house or porch. Neut. *tó*

trístegon, the third floor, third story (Acts 20:9).

5153. τρισχίλιοι *trischílioi*; fem. *trischíliai*, neut. *trischília*, cardinal number from *trís* (5151), thrice, and *chílioi* (5507), a thousand. Three thousand (Acts 2:41; Sept.: Ex 32:28).

5154. τρίτος *trítos*; fem. *trítē*, neut. *tríton*, ordinal number from *treís* (5140), three. Third or thirdly.

(**I**) Generally (Matt 20:3, "about the third hour"; 22:26, "the third"; 27:64; Luke 12:38; 20:12; 2 Cor 12:2; Rev 4:7; Sept.: Gen 1:13; 2:14). On the third day (Matt 16:21; Mark 9:31; Luke 13:32); "The third day" (John 2:1).

(**II**) In the neut. with the art. *tó tríton*.

(**A**) As a subst. with *méros* ([3313], part) implied, meaning the third part, followed by the gen. of a whole (Rev 8:7, "the third part of trees," Rev 8:8–12; 9:15, 18; 12:4; Sept.: Num 15:6, 7; 2 Sam 18:2, implied).

(**B**) Adv., the third time, *tó tríton* (Mark 14:41; John 21:17). Simply *tríton* (Luke 23:22; John 21:14; 1 Cor 12:28; 2 Cor 12:14; Sept.: Num 22:28, 32). *Tríton toúto* (5124), this one, this third time (2 Cor 13:1; Sept.: Num 24:10). *Ek trítou* (*ek*, [1537], from; *trítou* [gen.]) as an adv., "the third time" (Matt 26:44).

5155. τρίχινος *tríchinos*; fem. *trichínē*, neut. *tríchinon*, adj. from *thríx* (2359), hair. Made of hair (Rev 6:12; Sept.: Zech 13:4).

5156. τρόμος *trómos*; gen. *trómou*, masc. noun from *trémō* (5141), to tremble. A trembling from fear, terror (Mark 16:8; Sept.: Ex 15:15; Job 4:14; Isa 33:14). Coupled with *phóbos* (5401), fear, fear and trembling, expressing great timidity (1 Cor 2:3) or profound reverence, respect, dread (2 Cor 7:15; Eph 6:5; Phil 2:12 [cf. Sept.: Ps 55:6; Isa 19:16]).

Deriv.: *éntromos* (1790), terrified.

Syn.: *deilía* (1167), fear, timidity; *eulábeia* (2124), reverential awe, dread; *phóbos* (5401), fear.

Ant.: *pepoíthēsis* (4006), confidence; *pístis* (4102), assurance; *galénē* (1055), calm; *thársos* (2294), courage.

5157. τροπή *tropḗ*; gen. *tropḗs*, fem. noun from *trépō* (n.f., see *anatrépō* [396]), to turn. A turning, turning back as of the heavenly bodies in their courses (James 1:17; Sept.: Deut 33:14; Job 38:33).

Syn.: *parallagḗ* (3883), change, variableness, fickleness; *metáthesis* (3331), transposition, change, removing.

5158. τρόπος *trópos*; gen. *trópou*, masc. noun from *trépō* (n.f., see *anatrépō* [396]), to turn. A turning, turn in direction, hence, a general manner, way, mode.

(I) Generally in adv. constructions:

(A) Acc. with *katá* (2596), according to, meaning in the manner of, as even as (Acts 15:11; 27:25, "in every way"; Rom 3:2, "much every way"; 2 Thess 2:3; Sept.: Num 18:7).

(B) Acc. as an adv. *hón trópon* (*hón*, acc. relative pron. of *hós* [3739], in which, with *trópon*) in which manner, as, even as (Matt 23:37; Luke 13:34; Acts 1:11; 7:28; 2 Tim 3:8; Jude 1:7 *tón hómoion trópon* [*hómoios* {3664}, similar], "in the like manner"; Sept.: Gen 26:29; Obad 1:16).

(C) Dat. *pantí trópō* (*pantí* [dat. of *pás* {3956}], every, with *trópō*), in every way (Phil 1:18). With *en pantí trópō* (*en* [1722], in, as; *pantí* [3956], every), in every way (2 Thess 3:16).

(II) Figuratively a turn of mind and life, disposition, manner, mode of thinking or feeling, acting (Heb 13:5).

Deriv.: *polutrópōs* (4187), in many ways, in diverse manners; *tropophoréō* (5159), to be patient with the conduct of others.

Syn.: *anastrophḗ* (391), behavior, conduct; *katástēma* (2688), condition, deportment, behavior.

5159. τροποφορέω *tropophoréō*; contracted *tropophorṓ*, fut. *tropophorḗsō*, from *trópos* (5158), way, manner, and *phoréō* (5409), to bear, endure. To be patient with the difficult or idiosyncratic manners and conduct of others, with the acc. (Acts 13:18 [TR] from Sept.: Deut 1:31).

5160. τροφή *trophḗ*; gen. *trophḗs*, fem. noun from *tréphō* (5142), to feed, eat. Food, nourishment, sustenance (Matt 3:4; 6:25; 24:45; Luke 12:23; John 4:8; Acts 2:46; 9:19; 14:17; 27:33, 34, 36, 38; James 2:15; Sept.: Job 36:31; Ps 104:27; 136:25; Prov 6:8). With the meaning of stipend, hire (Matt 10:10 [cf. Luke 10:7]; 1 Tim 5:18 where *misthós* [3408], wages, hire, reward, pay is used). Figuratively as food for the soul, instruction (Heb 5:12, 14).

Syn.: *sitométrion* (4620), a measured portion of food; *brṓma* (1033), food, meat; *trápeza* (5132), table, used metonymically for the food on the table; *prosphágion* (4371), any meat; *klásma* (2801), a broken piece of bread or other fragment of food; *eidōlóthuton* (1494), meat offered in sacrifice to idols.

5161. Τρόφιμος *Tróphimos*; gen. *Trophímou*, masc. proper noun. Trophimus, meaning foster child. A native of Ephesus (Acts 21:29) and a convert to the faith, probably under Paul's ministry (Acts 20:4). He became one of the apostle's companions and helpers in missionary travels and labors (2 Tim 4:20).

5162. τροφός *trophós*; gen. *trophoú*, masc., fem. noun from *tréphō* (5142), to nourish. A nurse (1 Thess 2:7; Sept.: Gen 35:8; Isa 49:23).

5163. τροχιά *trochiá*; gen. *trochiás*, fem. noun from *trochós* (5164), a wheel. A wheel track, rut. In the NT, in a wider sense, a way, path. Figuratively (Heb 12:13, ways of life and conduct, quoted from Prov 4:26). See Sept.: Prov 2:15; 4:11.

Syn.: *tríbos* (5147), a beaten track; *poreía* (4197), a journey, a way; *hodós* (3598), a way, road.

5164. τροχός *trochós*; gen. *trochoú*, masc. noun from *tréchō* (5143), to run. A runner, something made round for rolling or running, hence, generally a wheel (Sept.: 1 Kgs 7:32), as a potter's wheel for molding. In the NT, figuratively a course as run by a wheel, or perhaps a circular course, circuit (James 3:6, "course of life" [a.t.]).

5165. τρυβλίον *trublíon*; gen. *trublíou*, neut. noun. A dish in which food is brought to the table, a dish or bowl for eating or drinking (Matt 26:23; Mark 14:20; Sept.: Ex 25:28; Num 4:7).
Syn.: *pínax* (4094), a plate; *skeúos* (4632), a vessel, implement.

5166. τρυγάω *trugáō*; contracted *trugṓ*, fut. *trugḗsō*, from *trúgē* (n.f.), the vintage, autumn fruit, ripe fruits or grain, harvest. To gather in ripe fruits or grain, to harvest generally (Sept.: Hos 10:12, 13). Of vintagers, to gather grapes, with the acc. (Luke 6:44; Rev 14:18, 19; Sept.: Deut 24:23; Judg 9:27).
Syn.: *sunágō* (4863), to gather or bring together; *sullégō* (4816), to collect, gather up; *therízō* (2325), to reap; *sugkomízō* (4792), to convey together, collect.
Ant.: *speírō* (4687), to sow; *diaspeírō* (1289), to scatter abroad; *skorpízō* (4650), to scatter abroad.

5167. τρυγών *trugṓn*; gen. *trugónos*, fem. noun from *trúzō* (n.f.), to murmur or coo like a turtledove, a word formed from the sound. A turtledove (Luke 2:24; Sept.: Lev 5:7, 11). A *trugṓn* is noted for its plaintive cooing and affectionate disposition while its syn. *peristerá* figuratively indicates its proverbial harmlessness.
Syn.: *peristerá* (4058), a dove or pigeon.

5168. τρυμαλιά *trumaliá*; gen. *trumaliás*, fem. noun from *trúō* (n.f.), to break or to rub through. A hole, eye of a needle, equal to *trúpēma* (5169), an aperture (Mark 10:25; Luke 18:25; Sept.: Judg 15:11; Jer 13:4; 16:16). Also from *trúō* (n.f.): *trṓgō* (5176), to eat fruits, nuts, raw beans.
Syn.: *opḗ* (3692), hole; *trúpēma* (5169), an aperture, a needle's eye.

5169. τρύπημα *trúpēma*; gen. *trupḗmatos*, neut. noun from *trupáō* (n.f.), to perforate, bore a hole. A hole, as an eye of a needle (Matt 19:24).

5170. Τρύφαινα *Trúphaina*; gen. *Truphaínēs*, fem. proper noun. Tryphena. She and Tryphosa (5173) were two women, possibly twins, of Rome whom Paul commended for their zeal (Rom 16:12).

5171. τρυφάω *trupháō*; contracted *truphṓ*, fut. *truphḗsō*, from *truphḗ* (5172), luxury. To live luxuriously, in pleasure (James 5:5; Sept.: Isa 66:11).
Deriv.: *entrupháō* (1792), to revel luxuriously.
Syn.: *spataláō* (4684), to live in pleasure; *strēniáō* (4763), to live riotously or wantonly.
Ant.: *stenochōréomai* (4729), to be hemmed in, distressed; *egkrateúomai* (1467), to exercise self-restraint; *chrḗrō* (5535), to be in need; *epaitéō* (1871), to beg.

5172. τρυφή *truphḗ*; gen. *truphḗs*, fem. noun from *thrúptō* (n.f.), to break up or enfeeble by luxury which destroys the integrity of body and mind. Delicate living, self-indulgence (Luke 7:25; 2 Pet 2:13; Sept.: Prov 19:10; Song 7:1). Also from *thrúptō* (n.f.): *sunthrúptō* (4919), to break, crush together.
Deriv.: *trupháō* (5171), to live in pleasure.
Syn.: *akrasía* (192), lack of self-restraint, excess; *hēdonḗ* (2237), lust, pleasure.

Ant.: *lúpē* (3077), sadness, grief; *pikría* (4088), bitterness; *stenochōría* (4730), narrowness of room, anguish, distress; *egkráteia* (1466), self-control, continence; *sōphrosúnē* (4997), sobriety, self-control.

5173. Τρυφῶσα *Truphōsa*; gen. *Truphōsēs*, fem. proper noun. Tryphosa. She and Tryphena (5170) were two women of Rome, possibly twins, whom Paul commended for their zeal (Rom 16:12).

5174. Τρωάς *Trōás*; gen. *Trōádos*, fem. proper noun. Troas, a city of Lesser Mysia in the northeastern part of Asia Minor on the seacoast, six miles south of the entrance to the Homeric Troy. Alexandria Troas, as its name implies, owed its origin to Alexander the Great. He chose the site with his usual tasteful discernment, but did not live to cover it with buildings. It had an excellent port and for many centuries was the key port of commerce between Asia and Europe. Paul visited Troas twice, perhaps three times. The first visit was on his second missionary journey. It was from Troas that he sailed to carry the gospel into Europe after the vision of the man of Macedonia occurred (Acts 16:8–11). On his return journey he stopped at Troas for eight days and restored Eutychus to life (Acts 20:5–10). On one visit, he left his cloak and some books there (2 Tim 4:13).

5175. Τρωγύλλιον *Trōgúllion*; gen. *Trōgullíou*, neut. proper noun. Trogyllium, a town and cape on the western coast of Asia Minor between Ephesus and the mouth of the Meander, opposite Samos at the foot of Mount Mycale. Paul spent a night there on his third missionary journey (Acts 20:15).

5176. τρώγω *trṓgō*; fut. *trṓxomai*, 2 aor. *éphagon*, from *trúō* (n.f.), to injure, wear away. To eat fruits, nuts, raw beans, which require crunching with the teeth. Hence, *trōgália* or *trōktá* means fruits, nuts, almonds and the like used as a dessert. In the NT, generally to eat, equal to *esthíō* (2068), to eat as in Matt 24:38, "eating and drinking," feasting, reveling, with *árton* (740), bread in the acc., sing. or pl. (John 13:18 quoted from Ps 41:9). Figuratively (John 6:58) with *sárka* (4561), flesh. See John 6:54, 56, 57. Also from *trúō* (n.f.): *trumaliá* (5168), a hole, eye of a needle.

Syn.: *phágō* (5315), to eat, devour, consume; *geúomai* (1089), to taste; *bibrṓskō* (977), to devour; *korénnumi* (2880), to satiate, satisfy with food; *sunesthíō* (4906), to eat together.

Ant.: *nēsteúō* (3522), to abstain from eating.

5177. τυγχάνω *tugchánō*; fut. *teúxomai*, 2d aor. *étuchon*, perf. *tetúchēka*. To hit, strike, reach a mark or object as by a weapon. Also to fall in with or meet persons casually. Hence in the NT:

(I) Trans., to attain to, obtain, gain, receive (Luke 20:35; Acts 24:2; 26:22; 27:3; 2 Tim 2:10; Heb 8:6; 11:35, in the 2d aor. subjunctive).

(II) Intrans., to happen, to chance.

(A) With *ei* (1487), if, and the impersonal *túchoi*, if it so happens, it may be, perchance, perhaps (1 Cor 14:10; 15:37 where it is equivalent to "for example").

(B) Part. *tuchṓn*, masc., fem. *tuchoúsa*, neut. *tuchón*. **(1)** As an adj., to happen anywhere and at any time, chance, casual, common. Hence, *ou tuchṓn* (*ou* [3756], not), means uncommon, special (Acts 19:11; 28:2). **(2)** Neut. *tuchón* as an adv. meaning it may be, perchance, perhaps (1 Cor 16:6).

(C) After the part. of another verb, *tugchánō* is used in an adv. sense much like the Eng. to happen to be, to chance to be, before a part. In Luke 10:30 the part. *tugchánonta* follows *aphéntes*, the aor. part. of *aphíēmi* (863), to leave, meaning "leaving him happening to be half dead" (a.t.), leaving him, as it were, half dead.

Deriv.: *entugchánō* (1793), to run up against, chance upon, approach, entreat; *epitugchánō* (2013), to light or chance upon, obtain, succeed; *suntugchánō*

(4940), to chance together, meet with; *paratugchánō* (3909), to chance near, meet with.

Syn.: *sunantáō* (4876), to meet with, occur; *apantáō* (528), to encounter, meet; *prosérchomai* (4334), to come near, approach; *katantáō* (2658), to arrive at; *katalambánō* (2638), to seize, apprehend, attain; *phthánō* (5348), to anticipate, to reach; *lambánō* (2983), to obtain; *lagchánō* (2975), to obtain by lot; *ktáomai* (2932), to procure for oneself; *heurískō* (2147), to find.

Ant.: *apophérō* (667), to bear off, carry away; *leípō* (3007), to be absent, leave; *kataleípō* (2641), to leave behind, forsake; *aphíēmi* (863), to leave, let, forsake; *apéchō* (568), to keep away; *eáō* (1439), to let be, permit or leave alone; *apoleípō* (620), to leave behind, forsake; *aphanízō* (853), to cause to disappear, perish, vanish away; *aphístēmi* (868), to depart.

5178. τυμπανίζω *tumpanízō*; fut. *tumpanísō*, from *túmpanon* (n.f.), a drum. To scourge, torture, beat. The *túmpanon*, drum, in the East consisted of a thin wooden rim covered with a membrane with brass bells or rattles hung around it as our tambourine, used chiefly by dancing women (Sept.: Ex 15:20; Judg 11:34). But the *túmpanon* was also an instrument of torture, a wooden frame probably so-called since it resembled a drum on which criminals were bound and beaten to death. The same instrument was called *trochós* (5164), wheel. Hence, *tumpanízō* means to drum, to beat the drum or timbrel. In the NT, to scourge upon the *túmpanon*, to torture, to drum to death, or break upon the wheel (in the pass. in Heb 11:35).

Syn.: *basanízō* (928), to torture; *kakouchéō* (2558), to torment, suffer; *odunáō* (3600), torment; *talaipōréō* (5003), to be miserable, afflicted; *kolázo* (2849) and *timōréō* (5097), to punish; *lumaínomai* (3075), to maltreat, make havoc; *mastízō* (3147), to scourge; *dérō* (1194), to scourge, smite.

5179. τύπος *túpos*; gen. *túpou*, masc. noun from *túptō* (5180), to strike, smite with repeated strokes. A type, i.e., something caused by strokes or blows.

(I) A mark, print, impression (John 20:25).

(II) A figure, form.

(A) Of an image, statue (Acts 7:43 quoted from Amos 5:26).

(B) Of the form, manner, of the style of a letter (Acts 23:25); a doctrine (Rom 6:17).

(C) Figuratively of a person as bearing the form and figure of another, as having a certain resemblance in relations and circumstances (Rom 5:14).

(III) A prototype, pattern.

(A) Particularly of a pattern or model after which something is to be made (Acts 7:44; Heb 8:5 [cf. Ex 25:40]).

(B) Figuratively an example, pattern to be imitated, followed (Phil 3:17; 1 Thess 1:7; 2 Thess 3:9; 1 Tim 4:12; Titus 2:7; 1 Pet 5:3). Hence also for admonition, warning (1 Cor 10:6, 11).

A type as a model of some reality which was yet to appear, a prototype of that which was yet to be developed and evolved, e.g., the ordinances and institutions in the OT were, in their inward essence, types of the NT. The first era serves as a type of the second. However, the outline or archetype or model of some reality which was yet to appear was called *túpos*. A type is different than a symbol. A symbol was an equivalent, a visible sign of what is invisible, e.g., the tares in the parable of the wheat and the tares (Matt 13:24–30; 36–43) are a symbol of the activity of the devil and his agents in one's spiritual life. A symbol is an outward manifestation of something inward, an emblem of what is higher.

Deriv.: *antítupon* (499), that which corresponds to a type, which represents the real thing; *entupóō* (1795), to impress, stamp.

Syn.: *hupotúpōsis* (5296), a sketch, pattern for imitation.

5180. τύπτω *túptō*; fut. *túpsō*. To strike, smite with the hand, stick, or other instrument repeatedly.

(I) Particularly and generally.

(A) To smite in enmity with a stick, club, or the fist, with the acc. of person (Matt 24:49; Luke 12:45; Acts 18:17; 21:32; 23:3; Sept.: Ex 2:11, 13; 21:15); on the cheek (Luke 6:29); on the head (Matt 27:30; Mark 15:19); the face (Luke 22:64); the mouth (Acts 23:2).

(B) Of those who beat upon their chests in strong emotion (Luke 18:13; 23:48).

(C) Figuratively, to smite meaning to punish, inflict evil, afflict with disease, calamity, and spoken only as being done by God, with the acc. (Acts 23:3; Sept.: 2 Sam 24:17; Ezek 7:9).

(II) Figuratively, to strike against, meaning to offend, to wound the conscience of someone (1 Cor 8:12; Sept.: 1 Sam 1:8).

Deriv.: *túpos* (5179), stroke, the impression left by striking, a trace or print.

Syn.: *dérō* (1194), to flay, beat, thrash, strike; *rhabdízō* (4463), to beat with a rod or stick; *patássō* (3960), to hit, strike, with the hand, fist, or weapon; *paíō* (3817), to strike, sting; *plḗssō* (4141), to strike as with a plague; *rhapízō* (4474), to slap, strike.

Ant.: *enagkalízomai* (1723), to embrace; *philéō* (5368), to kiss.

5181. Τύραννος *Túrannos*; gen. *Turánnou*, masc. proper noun. Tyrannus, meaning tyrant. The name of the Greek rhetorician of Ephesus in whose lecture room Paul delivered discourses daily for two years (Acts 19:9). Perhaps Paul and he occupied the same room at different hours. He may have been a convert.

5182. τυρβάζω *turbázō*; fut. *turbásō*, from *túrbē* (n.f.), a crowd, tumult, related to *thórubos* (2351), noise, uproar. To make noise, an uproar, to disturb, stir up. In the NT, figuratively, to disturb in the mind, trouble, make anxious, mid. / pass. (Luke 10:41).

Syn.: *thorubéō* (2350) and *tarássō* (5015), to disturb; *diatarássō* (1298), to agitate greatly; *ektarássō* (1613), to throw into great trouble, agitate; *thlíbō* (2346), to afflict; *enochléō* (1776), to vex; *parenochléō* (3926), to annoy; *skúllō* (4660), to harass, annoy; *anastatóō* (387), to upset, disturb.

Ant.: *hēsucházō* (2270), to be still, quiet; *eirēneúō* (1514), to be at peace; *kopázō* (2869), to relax.

5183. Τύριος *Túrios*; gen. *Turíou*, masc. proper noun. An inhabitant of Tyrus or Tyre, a Tyrian (Acts 12:20).

5184. Τύρος *Túros*; gen. *Túrou*, fem. proper noun. Tyre. In Hebr. *Tsōr* (6865, OT), rock. A celebrated city of Phoenicia on the eastern coast of the Mediterranean Sea, twenty-one miles south of Sidon. The first scriptural mention of Tyre is Josh 19:29. At that time, about 1444 B.C., it was a strong city and was coupled with the Zidonians (Josh 13:6; Isa 23:2, 4, 12; Jer 47:4). The two cities Tyre and Sidon, being only 21 miles apart, were intimately associated. Tyre, under King Hiram, held friendly relations with Israel under David and Solomon. David's census extended to Tyre to embrace the Jews (2 Sam 24:7). The Tyrians furnished the timber for the temple and other great buildings of Jerusalem. The cedars of Lebanon were floated some eighty-five miles from Tyre to Joppa and thence taken to Jerusalem. In NT times, Tyre was a populous and thriving city. Christ referred to it and visited its borders (Matt 11:21, 22; 15:21; Mark 3:8; 7:24, 31; Luke 6:17; 10:13, 14). Paul spent seven days at Tyre (Acts 21:3, 4) which early became the seat of a Christian bishopric.

5185. τυφλός *tuphlós*; fem. *tuphlḗ*, neut. *tuphlón*, adj. from *tuphlóō* (5186), to envelop with smoke, be unable to see clearly. Blind (Matt 9:27, 28; 11:5; 12:22; Luke 7:21, 22; John 9:1ff.; Acts 13:11; Sept.: Lev 19:14; Job 29:15).

Figuratively in respect to the mind as being blind, ignorant, stupid, slow of understanding (Matt 15:14; 23:16, 17, 19, 24, 26; Luke 4:18; John 9:39–41; Rom 2:19; 2 Pet 1:9; Rev 3:17; Sept.: Isa 42:16, 18, 19; 43:8).

Deriv.: *tuphlóō* (5186), to blind.

5186. τυφλόω *tuphlóō*; contracted *tuphlṓ*, fut. *tuphlṓsō*. To blind. In the NT, only figuratively with the acc. (John 12:40; 2 Cor 4:4; 1 John 2:11; Sept.: Isa 42:19).

Syn.: *pōróō* (4456), to harden spiritually.

Ant.: *blépō* (991), to see; *horáō* (3708), to see clearly, perceive; *kathoráō* (2529), to see clearly; *diakrínō* (1252), to discern, discriminate; *theáomai* (2300), to look closely, perceive.

5187. τυφόω *tuphóō*; contracted *tuphṓ*, fut. *tuphṓsō*, from *túphos* (n.f.), smoke. To swell or inflate with pride. In the pass. *tuphóomai*, to be lifted up with pride (1 Tim 3:6; 6:4; 2 Tim 3:4).

Deriv.: *tuphlós* (5185), blind.

Syn.: *hupsēlophronéō* (5309), to be high-minded; *epaíromai* (1869), to exalt self; *huperaíromai* (5229), to become haughty, proud; *phusióō* (5448), to inflate, make proud, puff up; *huperéchō* (5242), to hold oneself above others.

Ant.: *tapeinóō* (5013), to make low, humble.

5188. τύφω *túphō*; fut. *túpsō*. To make a smoke, fume, vapor, to surround or fill with smoke, allow to burn up in smoke slowly and faintly. Pass. / mid. in Matt 12:20 (a smoking wick burning faintly, dimly) quoted from Isa 42:3. In the Sept. *kapnízomai* (n.f.), from *kapnós* (2586), smoke.

5189. τυφωνικός *tuphōnikós*; fem. *tuphōniké*, neut. *tuphōnikón*, adj. from *tuphṓn* (n.f.), a violent, stormy wind or whirlwind. Like a tempest or whirlwind, tempestuous, violent, whirling (Acts 27:14). This is the word from which the Eng. word "typhoon" is derived.

Syn.: *euroklúdōn* (2148), a storm from the east; *thúella* (2366), a hurricane, cyclone, akin to *thumós* (2372), wrath, anger; *cheimṓn* (5494), a winter storm; *laílaps* (2978), a tempest; *ánemos* (417), wind.

Ant.: *eirḗnē* (1515), peace; *galḗnē* (1055), calm; *hēsuchía* (2271), quiet; *eudía* (2105), a clear sky, fine weather.

5190. Τυχικός *Tuchikós*; gen. *Tuchikoú*, masc. proper noun. Tychicus, a companion of Paul (Acts 20:4) and evidently a devoted and faithful disciple (Acts 20:14; Eph 6:21; Col 4:7; 2 Tim 4:12; Titus 3:12).

Υ

5191. ὑακίνθινος huakínthinos; fem. *huakinthínē*, neut. *huakínthinon*, adj. from *huákinthos* (5192), hyacinth. Hyacinthine or jacinth, having the deep blue color of the hyacinth (Rev 9:17; Sept.: Ex 25:5; 26:4).

5192. ὑάκινθος huákinthos, gen. *huakínthou*, masc., fem. noun. The name of a flower which is very fragrant and often of a deep purplish or reddish blue color, the hyacinth. In the NT, the name of a gem or precious stone resembling the color of the flower hyacinth (Rev 21:20).
Deriv.: *huakínthinos* (5191), hyacinthine, having the color of the hyacinth.

5193. ὑάλινος huálinos; fem. *hualínē*, neut. *huálinon*, adj. from *húalos* (5194), glass. Made of glass, glassy, transparent (Rev 4:6, "a sea of glass"; 15:2).

5194. ὕαλος húalos; gen. *huálou*, fem. noun. Something transparent like water, crystal, any transparent stone or gem (Sept.: Job 28:17), glass or crystal. In the NT, glass (Rev 21:18, 21).
Syn.: *krústallos* (2930), crystal; *húalos* (5193), made of glass, glassy, transparent.

5195. ὑβρίζω hubrízō; fut. *hubrísō*, from *húbris* (5196), injury, insult, reproach, arrogance. To act with insolence, wantonness, wicked violence, to treat injuriously. In the NT, with the acc. expressed or implied meaning to act insolently or spitefully toward someone, to treat shamefully, and therefore to injure or to abuse (Matt 22:6; Luke 18:32; Acts 14:5; 1 Thess 2:2; Sept.: 2 Sam 19:43); to reproach (Luke 11:45).
Deriv.: *enubrízō* (1796), to treat with reproach; *hubristḗs* (5197), an insulter.

Syn.: *adikéō* (91), to do an injustice to, to harm, injure; *loidoréō* (3058), to revile, reproach; *blasphēméō* (987), to vilify, blaspheme, defame; *bláptō* (984), to injure, hurt; *lumaínomai* (3075), to insult, make havoc of, mistreat; *kakóō* (2559), to harm, exasperate.
Ant.: *eulogéō* (2127), to speak well of, bless; *eneulogéomai* (1757), to be a blessing to; *timáō* (5091), to honor, value.

5196. ὕβρις húbris; gen. *húbreōs*, fem. noun. Insolence, injurious treatment; in the NT, shown in external acts (2 Cor 12:10; Sept.: Isa 16:6; Nah 2:3). Metonymically injury, harm, damage to a person or property arising from the insolence or violence, even of the sea (Acts 27:10, 21).
Deriv.: *hubrízō* (5195), to treat shamefully, abuse.
Syn.: *loidoría* (3059), railing, reproach; *óneidos* (3681), notoriety, taunt, disgrace; *anaídeia* (335), insolence, impudence; *zēmía* (2209), loss, damage; *adikía* (93), injustice, wrong.
Ant.: *eulogía* (2129), praise; *cháris* (5485), favor, grace; *euergesía* (2108), good deed; *timḗ* (5092), honor.

5197. ὑβριστής hubristḗs; gen. *hubristoú*, masc. noun from *hubrízō* (5195), to act with insolence, and *húbris* (5196), arrogance. An insolent persecutor of others who mistreats them for the pleasure which the affliction of the wrong brings him (Rom 1:30; 1 Tim 1:13; Sept.: Job 40:6; Isa 2:12; 16:6).
Syn.: *loídoros* (3060), reviler.

5198. ὑγιαίνω hugiaínō; fut. *hugianō*, from *hugiḗs* (5199), sound, healthy. To be healthy, sound, physically well (Eng.: hygiene). Intrans.
(I) Particularly (Luke 5:31, those well; 7:10; 3 John 1:2). With the meaning to be

safe and sound (Luke 15:27; Sept.: Gen 29:6; 43:26, 27).

(II) Metaphorically of persons, to be sound in the faith, meaning firm, pure in respect to Christian doctrine and life (Titus 1:13; 2:2). Of doctrine, meaning sound doctrine, i.e., true, pure, uncorrupted (1 Tim 1:10; 6:3; 2 Tim 1:13; 4:3; Titus 1:9; 2:1).

Ant.: *asthenéō* (770), to lose strength, be sick; *échō kakṓs* (*échō* [2192], to have; *kakṓs* [2560], badly), to be ill; *kámnō* (2577), to be weary, to sicken.

5199. ὑγιής *hugiḗs*; gen. *hugioús*, masc.-fem., neut. *hugiés*, adj. Sound, healthy. In the NT, sound, whole, in health (Matt 12:13; 15:31; Mark 3:5; 5:34; Luke 6:10; John 5:4, 6, 9, 11, 14, 15; 7:23; Acts 4:10); of sound speech or doctrine, wholesome, right (Titus 2:8).

Deriv.: *hugiaínō* (5198), to be healthy.

Syn.: *hólos* (3650), whole, healthy.

Ant.: *asthenḗs* (772), without strength, sick; *árrōstos* (732), feeble, sick; *adúnatos* (102), weak.

5200. ὑγρός *hugrós*; fem. *hugrá*, neut. *hugrón*, adj. from *húō* (n.f.), to rain. Watery, wet, moist. Of a tree or plant, sappy, fresh, green. Akin to *húdōr* (5204), water. Homer uses *hugrḗn* for the sea. Also from *húō* (n.f.): *huetós* (5205), rains, rainy season.

Ant.: *xērós* (3584), dry.

5201. ὑδρία *hudría*; gen. *hudrías*, fem. noun from *húdōr* (5204), water. A vessel to hold water, a waterpot (John 2:6, 7). A vessel for drawing and carrying water, a bucket, pail, in the East often of stone or earthenware (John 4:28; Sept.: Gen 24:14).

Syn.: *skeúos* (4632), a vessel, utensil; *aggeíon* (30), a pail, receptacle; *ántlēma* (502), vessel with which to bale or draw; *phiálē* (5357), broad shallow cup, bowl, vial.

5202. ὑδροποτέω *hudropotéō*; contracted *hudropotṓ*, fut. *hudropotḗsō*, from *hudropótēs* (n.f.), a water drinker, which is from *húdōr* (5204), water, and *pínō* (4095), to drink. To drink water (1 Tim 5:23).

5203. ὑδρωπικός *hudrōpikós*; fem. *hudrōpikḗ*, neut. *hudrōpikón*, adj. from *húdrōps* (n.f.), dropsy, which is from *húdōr* (5204), water, and *ōps* (n.f.), face, countenance. Edematous, dropsical, a condition of excessive accumulation of serous fluid in the body (Luke 14:2).

5204. ὕδωρ *húdōr*; gen. *húdatos*, pl. *húdata*, neut. noun from *húō* (n.f.), to rain. Water (Matt 8:32; 17:15). Particularly (Matt 27:24; Mark 9:41; 14:13; Luke 7:44; John 2:7; Rev 16:12; Sept.: Lev 1:9; Judg 4:19). As the instrument of baptism (Matt 3:11, 16; Mark 1:8, 10; Luke 3:16; John 1:26, 31, 33; 3:5; Acts 1:5; 8:36, 38, 39; 10:47; 11:16; 1 John 5:6, 8). See *báptisma* (908), baptism, in its relation to *húdōr*. The watery or serous part of the blood (John 19:34). It denotes the enlivening, refreshing, and comforting influences of the Holy Spirit, whether in His ordinary operations in the hearts of believers (John 4:10, 14 [cf. 6:35]; Rev 21:6; 22:1, 17), or including also His miraculous gifts (John 7:38 [cf. 7:39]). Used in various connections such as running or living (*záō* [2198]) water; of medicinal waters (John 5:3ff.); of flowing waters, as a stream, river (Sept.: Ex 7:15), of a lake or sea such as Tiberias (Matt 8:32; 14:28, 29; Luke 8:24, 25). "Many waters" denote many people or nations (Rev 17:1, 15).

Deriv.: *ánudros* (504), without water; *hudría* (5201), water pot.

5205. ὑετός *huetós*; gen. *huetoú*, masc. noun from *húō* (n.f.), to rain. Rain. In the pl. rains or seasons of rain (Acts 14:17; 28:2; Heb 6:7; James 5:7, 18; Rev 11:6; Sept.: Gen 7:12; Ex 9:33, 34; 2 Sam 1:21; 2 Kgs 3:17).

Syn.: *brochḗ* (1028), rain.
Ant.: *eudía* (2105), fine clear weather.

5206. υἱοθεσία *huiothesía*; gen. *huiothesías*, fem. noun from *huiós* (5207), son, and *títhēmi* (5087), to place. Adoption, receiving into the relationship of a child. In the NT, figuratively meaning adoption, sonship, spoken of the state of those whom God through Christ adopts as His sons and thus makes heirs of His covenanted salvation. See *huiós* (5207) II, B. Of the true Israel, the spiritual descendants of Abraham (Rom 9:4 [cf. 6, 7]), especially of Christians, the followers of the Lord Jesus (elsewhere called *huioí toú Theoú* [2316], of God (Rom 8:14; Gal 3:26 [cf. John 1:12]).

Huiothesía is a technical term used only by Paul five times (Rom 8:15, 23; 9:4; Gal 4:5; Eph 1:5). The word is not found in classical writers although *thetós huiós* (*thetós* [n.f.], placed, set, adopted) is used for an adopted son. Paul in these passages is alluding to a Greek and Roman custom rather than a Hebrew one. Since *huiothesía* was a technical term in Roman law for an act that had specific legal and social effects, there is much probability that Paul had some reference to that in his use of the word. Adoption, when thus legally performed, put a man in every respect in the position of a son by birth to him who had adopted him, so that he possessed the same rights and owed the same obligations. Being a *huiós*, a son, involves the conformity of the child that has the life of God in him to the image, purposes, and interests of God and that spiritual family into which he is born. In eternity there will be a revelation by God which will indicate the measure of this conformity to God (Rom 8:19).

5207. υἱός *huiós*; gen. *huioú*, masc. noun. Son.

(I) Generally.

(A) A male offspring: **(1)** Strictly spoken only of man (Matt 1:21, 25; 7:9; Mark 6:3; 9:17). In Heb 12:8 it is presented emphatically as the opposite of *nóthos* (3541), illegitimate son. Pleonastically *huiós árrēn* ([730], male) (Rev 12:5). See Sept.: Gen 4:16, 24. Spoken of one who fills the place of a son (John 19:26); of an adopted son (Acts 7:21; Heb 11:24 in allusion to Ex 2:10). Often *huiós* is omitted before a gen., the art. remaining in its place (Matt 4:21; 10:2; John 21:15). **(2)** Of the young of animals, "foal of an ass" (Matt 21:5 quoted from Zech 9:9; Sept.: Ps 28:1).

(B) In a wider sense it means a descendant, pl. descendants, posterity; see *téknon* ([5043] cf. II). **(1)** Sing. (Matt 1:1, 20; Luke 19:9). Of the Messiah as descended from the line of David (Matt 22:42, 45; Mark 12:35, 37; Luke 20:41, 44). "Son of David" meaning the Messiah (Matt 9:27; 12:23; 15:22; 20:30, 31; 21:9, 15; Mark 10:47, 48; Luke 18:38, 39 [cf. Sept.: Gen 29:5; Ezra 5:2; Zech 1:1]). **(2)** Pl. (Acts 7:16; Heb 7:5, "sons of Levi," Levites; Sept.: Gen 33:19; Num 26:57); emphatically, the posterity of Abraham, the sons or descendants of Israel, the Israelites (Matt 27:9; Luke 1:16; Acts 5:21; 7:23, 37; Rom 9:27; 2 Cor 3:7, 13; Gal 3:7; Rev 21:12; Sept.: Ex 13:19; 14:2; 16:35; Lev 17:3, 8, 10). **(3)** The Son of Man means Jesus as the Messiah. See *ánthrōpos* (444) IV.

(C) Figuratively of one who is the object of parental love and care or who yields filial love and reverence toward another, a pupil, disciple, follower, the spiritual child of someone (cf. *téknon* [5043] III, B [Heb 2:10; 12:5 quoted from Prov 3:11; 1 Pet 5:13 {cf. Acts 12:12}]). Of the disciples and followers of the Pharisees (Matt 12:27; Luke 11:19; Sept.: 1 Kgs 20:35; 2 Kgs 2:15; Prov 2:1; 3:1; 4:10, 20). For *huiós* versus *huioí toú Theoú*, the son and sons of God (cf. II).

(D) With a gen., the son of something is one connected with, partaking of, or exposed to that thing, often used instead of an adj. (Matt 9:15, sons of the bridal chamber, bridesmen; Mark 2:19; Luke 5:34; see *numphṓn* [3567], bridechamber). Sons of the kingdom means subjects to whom the kingdom's privileges belong (Matt 8:12, spoken of the Jews but also of the true subjects or citizens; 13:38; see in *basileía* [932] III). The sons of the kingdom stand in opposition to the sons of the evil one (*ponēroú* [4190]) meaning subjects of Satan, his followers, imitators (Matt 13:38; Acts 13:10, "son of the devil" [a.t.]). Followed by the gen. implying quality, character, "sons of thunder" (Mark 3:17; see *Boanergés* [993], commotion). "Son of peace" meaning friendly, giving one's benediction, receiving someone hospitably (Luke 10:6). "Sons of the day" (a.t.) meaning enlightened with true knowledge (1 Thess 5:5). "Son of consolation" (Acts 4:36; see *paráklēsis* [{3874} cf. II]). "Sons of light" means enlightened with the true light (Luke 16:8; John 12:36; 1 Thess 5:5, the opposite of sons of this world [*aiṓnos* {165}] or of this age, meaning devoted to the philosophy of this age or this world [Luke 16:8; 20:34]). "Sons of disobedience" (*apeitheías* [543], disobedience) meaning the disobedient (Eph 2:2; 5:6; Col 3:6); and "son of lawlessness" (*anomías* [458]) (a.t. [Sept: Ps 89:23]). Followed by the gen. of that in which one partakes, to which one is exposed, e.g., Luke 20:36, "sons of the resurrection" (a.t.) meaning partakers in it; Acts 3:25, "sons of the prophets and the covenant" (a.t.) meaning to whom the prophecies and the covenant appertain). "Son of perdition" (*apōleías* [684]) meaning devoted to destruction, see *apōleia* (684) II (John 17:12). "Son of hell" (*Géenna* [1067]) meaning deserving everlasting punishment (Matt 23:15 [cf. Sept.: 1 Sam 20:31; 2 Sam 12:5]).

(**II**) Specifically *huiós toú Theoú* (gen. of *Theós* [2316], God) son of God, and *huioí toú Theoú*, sons of God. Spoken of:

(**A**) One who derives his human nature directly from God, and not by ordinary generation: of Adam (Luke 3:38 implied of Jesus [cf. Luke 1:35]).

(**B**) Those whom God loves and cherishes as a father. See *patér* (3962) II, A,

B; and *gennáō* (1080) I, A, 2 (cf. *téknon* [5043] III, C). (**1**) Generally of pious worshipers of God, the righteous, saints, "Blessed are the peacemakers: for they shall be called the sons of God" (Matt 5:9). Of those who are like God in eternal life (Luke 20:36); in disposition, benevolence (Matt 5:45; Luke 6:35, the "sons of the most High" [a.t.]; Sept.: Deut 14:1; Ps 73:15). (**2**) Specifically of the Israelites (Rom 9:26; Sept.: Isa 1:2; 43:6; Jer 3:14); sing. (Ex 4:22, 23; Hos 11:1). (**3**) Of Christians (Rom 8:14, 19; 2 Cor 6:18; Gal 3:26; 4:6, 7; Heb 12:6; Rev 21:7).

(**C**) Jesus Christ as the Son of God, the Son of the Most High (Matt 27:54; Mark 15:39; Luke 1:32 [cf. Mark 5:7; Luke 8:28]). (**1**) In the Jewish sense as the Messiah, the Anointed, the Christ, the expected King of the Jewish nation, constituted of God, and ruling in the world. See *basileía* ([932] cf. III). As joined with *ho Christós* (5547), Christ, in explanation (Matt 16:16, "Thou art the Christ, the Son of the living God"; 26:63; Mark 14:61; Luke 4:41; John 1:49, Thou art the Son of God, thou art the King of Israel [cf. Luke 1:32; John 6:69; 11:27; 20:31]). Matt 2:15 quoted from Hos 11:1, and speaking of Israel, but the evangelist applies it to Christ (Matt 4:3; 8:29; 14:33; 27:40, 43; Mark 3:11; 5:7; Luke 4:3; 8:28; 22:70; John 1:34, 42; 9:35). See Sept.: 2 Sam 7:14; Ps 82:6 (cf. 89:28). (**2**) In the gospel sense as the Messiah, the Savior, the Head of the gospel dispensation; so-called as proceeding and sent forth from God, as partaking of the divine nature and being in intimate union with God the Father. Acts 13:33; Heb 1:5; 5:5, "today have I begotten thee," quoted from Ps 2:7 (cf. *gennáō* [1080] I, A, 2). In *Theós* ([2316], God, cf. II); *lógos* ([3056], word, cf. III); *kúrios* ([2962], lord, cf. II, B, 2); *basileía* ([932], kingdom, cf. III).

(**D**) *Huiós*, when used of Jesus, is not perfectly synonymous with Messiah; it designates the same person, but not in the same respect. Christ is called the Son of God on account of His divine nature (Matt 11:27; Luke 10:22; John 1:14,

18; 10:33–36; Heb 1:5f.; 3:6). The Father and the Son are mentioned together as in most of the above passages (see also Matt 28:19; Mark 13:32; John 5:26; 17:1; 1 John 1:3; 2:22; 4:14; 2 John 1:3, 9). "This is my beloved Son" (Matt 3:17; 17:5); " . . . that he gave his only begotten Son . . . " (John 3:16–18; Rom 1:3, 4, 9; 5:10; 8:3, 29, 32; 1 Cor 1:9; 15:28; 2 Cor 1:19; Gal 1:16; 2:20; Eph 4:13; Col 1:13; 1 Thess 1:10; Heb 1:2; 6:6; 2 Pet 1:17; 1 John 1:7; 5:5; Rev 2:18).

Deriv.: *huiothesía* (5206), adoption.

Syn.: *país* (3816), a child or servant; *paidíon* (3813), a young child; *paidárion* (3808), a lad; *téknon* (5043), a child; *tekníon* (5040), a little child; *népios* (3516), an infant.

Ant.: *patḗr* (3962), father; *goneús* (1118), a parent; *prógonos* (4269), a progenitor, forefather.

5208. ὕλη *húlē*; gen. *húlēs*, fem. noun. The basic material or matter of which all things are formed, especially wood, the forest. In the NT, wood, firewood, fuel (James 3:5).

Syn.: *xúlon* (3586), wood; *ousía* (3776), substance.

Ant.: *pneúma* (4151), spirit; *psuchḗ* (5590), soul; *phántasma* (5326), a phantasm, appearance.

5209. ὑμᾶς *humás*; 2d person personal pron., acc. of *humeís* (5210), you, yourselves. You.

5210. ὑμεῖς *humeís*; 2d person personal pron., nom. pl. of *sú* (4771), you. You, sometimes used as an emphatic meaning yourselves.

Deriv.: *huméteros* (5212), your, yours.

5211. Ὑμέναιος *Huménaios*; gen. *Humenaíou*, masc. proper noun. Hymenaeus, once mentioned with Alexander and once with Philetus. He is first represented as having shipwrecked his faith (1 Tim 1:20), and later as having denied the doctrine of a future resurrection of the body (2 Tim 2:17).

5212. ὑμέτερος *huméteros*; fem. *humetéra*, neut. *huméteron*., poss. pron. from *humeís* (5210), you, yourself, yourselves. Your, yours, referring to that which you have, that which belongs to or pertains to you (John 7:6; 8:17; Acts 27:34; Rom 11:31; Gal 6:13). In Luke 6:20, "yours is the kingdom of God," and in 16:12, "your own," means that which belongs to you or is assured to you. See Sept.: Prov 1:26. It also can mean that which proceeds from you, of which you are the source, cause, occasion (John 15:20; 1 Cor 15:31; 2 Cor 8:8).

Syn.: *sós* (4674), thine.

Ant.: *hēméteros* (2251), our, ours; *emós* (1699), my, mine.

5213. ὑμῖν *humín*; 2d person personal pron., dat. of *humeís* (5210), you. Unto you or with you or by you, sometimes used as an emphatic.

Ant.: *hēmín* (2254), to, for, with, or by us.

5214. ὑμνέω *humnéō*; contracted *humnō̂*, fut. *humnḗsō*, from *húmnos* (5215), hymn. Intrans. meaning to sing a hymn (Matt 26:30; Mark 14:26). Trans. governing an acc., to celebrate or praise with a hymn or hymns, to sing hymns to someone, to praise in song, e.g., God (Acts 16:25; Heb 2:12; Sept.: 2 Chr 29:30; Isa 12:4).

Syn.: *ádō* (103), used always of praise to God; *psállō* (5567), to sing, chant, particularly as accompanying stringed instruments; *eulogéō* (2127), to speak well of, bless; *ainéō* (134), to praise; *epainéō* (1867), to applaud.

Ant.: *kataráomai* (2672), to curse; *blasphēméō* (987), to blaspheme, defame, speak evil; *anathematízō* (332), to curse, bind with an oath.

5215. ὕμνος *húmnos*; gen. *húmnou*, masc. noun. A song or hymn in honor of God. It also came to mean praise to men. Whereas a psalm is the story of man's deliverance or a commemoration of mercies received, a hymn is a magnificat, a declaration of how great someone or something is (Luke 1:46–55, 67–79; Acts 4:24; 16:25). It is a direct address of praise and glory to God. According to Augustine a hymn has three characteristics: It must be sung; it must be praise; it must be to God. The word "hymn" nowhere occurs in the writings of the apostolic fathers because it was used as a praise to heathen deities and thus the early Christians instinctively shrank from it. In Eph 5:19; Col 3:16 it occurs with *psalmós* (5568), psalm, and *hōdḗ* (5603), spiritual song; "a new song;" "the song of Moses" and "of the Lamb" (Rev 5:9; 14:3; 15:3 [cf. Sept.: 2 Chr 7:6; Ps 40:4; Isa 42:10]).

Deriv.: *humnéō* (5214), to sing a hymn.

Syn.: *épainos* (1868), commendable thing, praise; *aínos* (136), praise; *euphēmía* (2162), euphemy, praise, good report; *eulogía* (2129), fair speech, blessing, eulogy.

Ant.: *epitimía* (2009), censure; *momphḗ* (3437), blame; *katára* (2671), curse; *ará* (685), imprecation, curse; *anáthema* (331), a curse, anathema.

5216. ὑμῶν humṓn; 2d person personal pron., gen. of *humeís* (5210), you. Of, from, or concerning you, pl., or in regard to yourselves.

Ant.: *hēmṓn* (2257), of or from us, our, ours.

5217. ὑπάγω hupágō; fut. *hupáxō*, from *hupó* (5259), denoting secrecy, and *ágō* (71), to go. In the NT and later it was used intrans. or with *heautón* (1438) meaning to go away, particularly under cover, out of sight, with stealth. See *ágō* (71), III.

(I) To go, go away, withdraw or depart (Matt 4:10; 5:24). In Matt 26:24; Mark 14:21 it denotes going out of the world, dying (cf. John 13:3, 33). It is used in an absolute sense of persons coming and going (Mark 6:31, 33; John 18:8), also figuratively of persons withdrawing themselves from a teacher or party (John 6:67). As an imper. it is a word

of dismissal (Matt 8:13, 32; 20:14; Mark 7:29; 10:52; Luke 10:3). Once it is used in the inf. in John 11:44. It is used with the word "peace," "go in [*eis* [{519)] peace," Mark 5:34, or with the prep. *en* (1722), in. In Matt 4:10 it expresses aversion, "get thee hence," begone, referring to Satan, or "get thee behind me" (Matt 16:23; Mark 8:33; Luke 4:8). It denotes direction with *eis*, unto, the home (Matt 9:6; Mark 2:11; 5:19; Rev 13:10; 17:8, 11); followed by *prós* (4314), to, with the acc., to the Father (John 7:33; 13:3; 16:5, 10, 16, 17); with *prós tón patéra* (3962), father (John 8:21; 14:28). Similarly followed by *poú* (4226), whither (John 8:14; 12:35; 13:36; 14:5; 16:5). Once of the wind with *poú* (4226), where, whither (John 3:8; 12:35; 1 John 2:11); by *hópou* (3699), where (John 8:21, 22; 13:33, 36; 14:4; Rev 14:4).

(II) It generally refers to go, as to go to a certain place (Matt 26:18; Mark 11:2; 14:13; Luke 19:30; John 7:3; 11:31); to the vineyard (Matt 20:4, 7); to the pool (John 9:7, 11); to land or shore, by ship (John 6:21); with someone (Matt 5:41; Luke 12:58); with *ekeí* (1563), there (John 11:8); with the inf. indicating purpose (John 21:3). Used in an absolute sense (Luke 8:42; 17:14; John 4:16). Whenever *hupágō* precedes, especially in the imper., verbs which imply motion or action, it is to render the expression more full and complete. See *poreúō* (4198), to pass, go, I; *anístēmi* (450), to rise up, II, D. That ye may go and bring forth fruit (John 15:16). Imper. (Matt 5:24; 8:4; 18:15; 19:21; 21:28; 27:65; 28:10; Mark 1:44; 6:38; 10:21; 16:7; Rev 10:8; 16:1).

Syn.: *poreúomai* (4198), to proceed; *proágō* (4254), to go before, usually of locality; *periágō* (4013), to lead about; *anabaínō* (305), to go up; *katabaínō* (2597) and *epidúō* (1931), to go down; *probaínō* (4260), to go farther; *apobaínō* (576), *ápeimi* (548), and *apérchomai* (565), to go away or from; *metabaínō* (3327), to go or pass over from one place to another; *diaperáō* (1276), to pass over or through; *diodeúō* (1353), to journey, travel or pass through; *anachōréō* (402), to depart; *ágō* (71), to bring, lead; *eíseimi* (1524), to go into, enter; *éxeimi* (1826), to go out; *apodēméō* (589), go to another country or go abroad.

Ant.: *érchomai* (2064), to come; *epistréphō* (1994), to return; *paragínomai* (3854), to arrive, come.

5218. ὑπακοή *hupakoḗ*; gen. *hupakoḗs*, fem. noun from *hupakoúō* (5219), to obey, listen to something, hearken. Obedience, compliance (Sept.: 2 Sam 22:36), unknown in Class. Gr. Generally in the NT it refers to the obedience of a slave to a master (Rom 6:16). Elsewhere it always refers to the faith which obeys God's will in a special sense, of relationship and subjection to that which, in the sphere of divine power and revelation, is right (Rom 5:19; Heb 5:8). More especially, it refers to subjection to the saving will of God revealed in Christ and referred to as obedience to the truth (1 Pet 1:22); obedience of faith (Rom 1:5; 16:26); the unquestioning obedience that is demanded by Christ (2 Cor 10:5). The word also stands alone as the manifestation of Christian faith (Rom 15:18; 16:19; 2 Cor 7:15; 10:6; Phile 1:21; 1 Pet 1:2, 14).

Syn.: *hupotagḗ* (5292), subjection.

Ant.: *apeítheia* (543), disobedience; *parakoḗ* (3876), disobedience; *parábasis* (3847), transgression.

5219. ὑπακούω *hupakoúō*; fut. *hupakoúsō*, from *hupó* (5259), and *akoúō* (191), to hear. To hearken, obey.

(I) To listen to something, hearken with stealth, stillness, or attention in order to answer (Acts 12:13).

(II) To yield to a superior command or force (without necessarily being willing).

(A) Of the wind and sea tempest (Matt 8:27; Mark 4:41; Luke 8:25).

(B) Of unclean spirits (Mark 1:27).

(C) Of a sycamine tree (Luke 17:6).

(III) To believe (Acts 6:7; Rom 10:16; 2 Thess 1:8).

(IV) To yield to one's passions giving them the upper hand (Rom 6:12, 16).

(V) To obey God irresistibly (Heb 5:9).

(VI) Of children's obedience to parents (Eph 6:1; Col 3:20).

(VII) Of slaves to their masters (Eph 6:5; Col 3:22).

(VIII) To obey an apostle (Phil 2:12; 2 Thess 3:14).

(IX) Obedience by Abraham (Heb 11:8).

(X) Obedience of Sarah to Abraham (1 Pet 3:6).

(XI) A distinction should be made between the meanings of *hupakoúō* and *hupotássomai* (5293), to place oneself under another, to assume a subordinate position.

(A) *Hupakoúō* is used of the obedience children render to their parents (Eph 6:1; Col 3:20). This refers to an obedience which springs from their sense of duty toward, and dependence on parents.

(B) This same verb is used of the servile obedience rendered by slaves to their masters (Eph 6:5; Col 3:22). They must obey by virtue of their subordinate position.

(C) However, in the NT, when the response of a wife to her husband is in view, it is *hupotássō* (5293) which is most often employed. It means to place under the rank of another, to put in submission. This position is expressed in 1 Tim 2:13: "For Adam was first formed, then Eve. And Adam was not deceived, but the woman being deceived was in the transgression."
(1) The verb *hupotássō* can be used in the act. trans. sense. In such a case it would have a direct obj. and would mean to subdue and place someone in their proper position. In this sense the verb is used in 1 Cor 15:27 where Paul speaks of God the Father at the end time subjugating all things including death and Satan under His feet: "For he hath put all things under his feet." The verb translated "put . . . under" is *hupétaxen* (aor. act. indic. 3d

person sing. of *hupotássō*)in the act. trans. form. Then 15:28 says, "And when all things shall be subdued [*hupotagḗ*, aor. pass. subjunctive 3d person pl.] unto him, then shall the Son also himself be subject [*hupotagḗsetai*, fut. mid. indic. meaning, "the Son will place Himself voluntarily under the Father" {a.t.}] unto him that put all things under him [*hupotáxanti*, aor. act. part. dat. sing., referring to the Father], that God may be all in all." God is presented as the One who subdues everything to Himself at the consummation of the age when Christ's work of redemption is fully realized.

Hupotássō in its act. trans. form is never used of a husband with his wife being the direct obj. Instead the Apostle Paul commands, "Husbands, love your wives, even as Christ also loved the church, and gave himself for it" (Eph 5:25). Loving means discerning your wife's need and meeting it as only you as a husband can meet it. And remember that as the church is imperfect and needs forgiveness, so does your wife. Do not take the role of God in your relationship with your wife. **(2)** The second instance that *hupotássō* is used act. and trans. is in Eph 1:22, "And hath [the Father God] put all things under his [Christ's] feet, and gave him to be the head over all things to the church." This is similar to what the Father is said to do in 1 Cor 15:27, 28. God the Father will subdue all things under Christ the Son and the first-fruits of i.e. Jesus' resurrection (1 Cor 15:20–28). **(3)** The third instance of *hupotássō* in the act. trans. form is in Phil 3:21: "Who [the Lord Jesus Christ] shall change our vile body, that it may be fashioned like unto his glorious body, according to the working whereby he is able even to subdue [*hupotáxai*, aor. act. inf. trans.] all things unto himself." The Father God subdues all things to the Son God. **(4)** The fourth instance is in Heb 2:5, 8: "For unto the angels hath he not put in subjection [*hupétaxen*, act. aor. trans. meaning subdued] the world to come, whereof we speak. . . . Thou hast put all things in subjection [*hupétaxas*, act. aor.

trans.] under his feet. For in that he put all in subjection under him [*hupotáxai*, aor. inf. act. trans.], he left nothing that is not put under him [*anupótakton* (506), unsubdued, used as an adj.]. But now we see not yet all things put under him [*hupotetagména*, perf. pass. part. referring to everything that is yet to be subdued to Christ]."

(D) The mid. form *hupotássomai* is used in Luke 2:51 speaking of the Lord Jesus in His childhood placing Himself under His mother and His stepfather Joseph. "And he went [at age 12] down with them, and came to Nazareth, and was subject [*hupotassómenos*, pres. mid. part.] unto them." This is in keeping with the command given to children to obey their parents as in Eph 6:1: "Children, obey [*hupakoúete*, pres. imper.] your parents in the Lord: for this is right." Even though Lord Jesus stood in a very special relationship with His parents, He was still under their authority. When it comes to a wife's relationship to her husband, it is the mid. form *hupotássomai*, to place oneself under in one's proper position, i.e. used as in Eph 5:22, "Wives, submit yourselves [*hupotássesthe*, pres. mid. imper. 2d person pl.] unto your own husbands, as unto the Lord" (see Col 3:18; Titus 2:5). The only time that *hupakoúō* is used of a wife obeying her husband is 1 Pet 3:6 when Sarah obeyed Abraham. The verb which is used of Sarah's obedience to Abraham is not *hupotássomai* as used in 1 Pet 3:1, 5 to designate the proper attitude of a wife toward her husband, but *hupakoúō*. 1 Pet 3:6 states, "Even as Sarah obeyed [*hupékouse*, aor. act. indic. 3d person sing. of *hupakoúō* {5219}] Abraham, calling him lord [*kúrion* {2962}]." This word in 1 Pet 3:6 concerning Sarah's attitude is a commendation of her as an example to all godly women. And then Peter continues, "whose daughters ye are" or better still, "whose children you become" (a.t.). These faithful wives became children of Sarah by following her example.

Peter is telling these women not to fear the consequences of following the course of action which he has prescribed. They should be confident that God will be with them in their efforts to do what is right regardless of the difficulties they may face in doing so. A woman must do what is good (*agathopoiéō* [15]) and not allow scare tactics to overrule what she knows to be right.

Deriv.: *hupakoḗ* (5218), obedience; *hupḗkoos* (5255), obedient to the will of God.

Syn.: *summorphóomai* (4833), to conform oneself to; *peitharchéō* (3980), to be submitted to a ruler, to hearken, obey one in authority.

Ant.: *apeithéō* (544) and *apistéō* (569), to disbelieve, be disobedient; *parakoúō* (3878), to mishear, neglect to hear, disobey; *anthístēmi* (436), to stand against, oppose; *parabaínō* (3845), to transgress, go contrary to; *epanístamai* (1881), to rise or stand up against, attack; *antidiatíthemai* (475), to set oneself opposite, oppose; *antíkeimai* (480), to lie opposite, be adverse, contrary; *antistrateúomai* (497), to fight or war against.

5220. ὕπανδρος *húpandros*; gen. *hupándrou*, masc.-fem., neut. *húpandron*, adj. from *hupó* (5259), under, and *anḗr* (435), a husband. Under a husband, married. Spoken of a wife (Rom 7:2).

Syn.: *súzugos* (4805), a yokefellow, spouse.

Ant.: *ágamos* (22), unmarried; *chḗra* (5503), a widow.

5221. ὑπαντάω *hupantáō*; contracted *hupantṓ*, fut. *hupantḗsō*, from *hupó* (5259), and *antáō* (n.f., see *katantáō* [2658]), to meet, which is from *antí* (473), opposite. To come opposite someone, happen to meet someone, encounter, meet quietly, happen upon (Matt 8:28; Luke 8:27; John 11:20, 30; 12:18).

Deriv.: *hupántēsis* (5222), an encounter.

Syn.: *paratugchánō* (3909), to happen to be near or present.

Ant.: *ekklínō* (1578), avoid, shun; *periḯstēmi* (4026), stand aloof from; *stéllō* (4724), to withdraw; *hupostéllō* (5288), to avoid, shrink from.

5222. ὑπάντησις *hupántēsis*; gen. *hupantḗseōs*, fem. noun from *hupantáō* (5221), to come opposite someone. Meeting, encounter. In the NT only in the acc. preceded by the prep. *eis* (1519), for the purpose of meeting, followed by the dat. (John 12:13).

Syn.: *sunántēsis* (4877), a meeting with; *apántēsis* (529), a friendly encounter, meeting.

Ant.: *apobolḗ* (580), a casting away; *apóthesis* (595), a putting away; *apostasía* (646), a departure, apostasy; *apostásion* (647), divorcement; *apousía* (666), absence.

5223. ὕπαρξις *húparxis*; gen. *hupárxeōs*, fem. noun from *hupárchō* (5225), to exist. In the NT, the possession belonging to someone, property, goods, substance (Acts 2:45; Heb 10:34; Sept.: 2 Chr 35:7; Prov 18:11; 19:14).

Syn.: *ousía* (3776), substance, property, goods; *bíos* (979), means of livelihood, living; *zōḗ* (2222), life; *hupóstasis* (5287), substance.

Ant.: *aporía* (640), state of need, poverty; *chreía* (5532), need, lack; *anágkē* (318), distress, necessity; *ptōcheía* (4432), poverty, helplessness.

5224. ὑπάρχοντα *hupárchonta*; the pres. part. neut. pl. of *hupárchō* (5225), to exist. Things which someone has, goods, possessions. It is joined either with a dat. (Luke 8:3; Acts 4:32) or with a gen. of person (Matt 19:21; 24:47; 25:14; 11:21; 12:15, 33, 44; 14:33; 16:1; 19:8; 1 Cor 13:3; Heb 10:34; Sept.: Gen 12:5; 31:18; 36:6, 7; 1 Chr 28:1).

Syn.: *bíos* (979), possessions; *skeúos* (4632), goods, vessel; *ploútos* (4149), riches; *ktḗma* (2933), estate; *chōríon* (5564), a plot of ground, possession.

5225. ὑπάρχω *hupárchō*; fut. *hupárxō*, from *hupó* (5259), and *árchō* (757), to begin. To be, live, exist (Luke 7:25; 16:23; 27:34).

(I) Generally and in an absolute sense, to exist (Acts 19:40; 27:21; 28:18; 1 Cor 11:18). Followed by the dat. of person, to be present with someone, implying possession, property (Acts 3:6, "Silver and gold have I none"; 4:37; 28:7; 2 Pet 1:8; Sept.: Job 2:4). The pl. pres. part. *tá hupárchonta* (5224) has the same meaning, used as a subst., things present, in hand, possessions.

(II) To be, the same as *eimí* (1510), to be, logically connecting the subj. and predicate.

(A) With a subst. as predicate (Luke 8:41; 23:50; Acts 2:30; 4:34; 16:3, 20, 37; 17:24, 29; 21:20; 22:3; 1 Cor 11:7; 12:22; Gal 1:14; 2:14; 2 Pet 2:19).

(B) With an adj. as predicate (Luke 9:48; 11:13; 16:14; Acts 3:2; 7:55; 14:8; 27:12; Rom 4:19; 1 Cor 7:26; 2 Cor 8:17; 12:16; James 2:15; 2 Pet 3:11).

(C) As forming a periphrasis for a finite tense of the same verb (Acts 8:16, "only they were baptized").

(D) With an adv. as predicate (Acts 17:27, God, being not far).

(E) With a prep. and its case as predicate. *En* (1722), in, with the dat. where *hupárchei* then implies a being, remaining, living in any state or place. *En* with a dat. of condition (Luke 7:25; 16:23; Acts 5:4; Phil 2:6). *En* with the dat. of place (Acts 10:12; Phil 3:20). *Prós* (4314), toward, with the gen. (Acts 27:34).

Deriv.: *proüpárchō* (4391), to exist before; *húparxis* (5223), being, existence.

Syn.: *gínomai* (1096), to become; *eimí* (1510), to be; *záō* (2198), to live; *anastréphō* (390), to live, behave, conduct one's life.

Ant.: *apothnḗskō* (599), to die off or out; *teleutáō* (5053), to end one's life, die; *thnḗskō* (2348), to die.

5226. ὑπείκω *hupeíkō*; fut. *hupeíxō*, from *hupó* (5259), and *eíkō* (1503), to yield, submit. To submit, surrender, yield, cease to fight. In the NT with the dat. (Heb 13:17, meaning to yield, submit to).

Ant.: *kurieúō* (2961), to rule over; *epitássō* (2004), to order, charge, rule over; *katalambánō* (2638), to seize, possess; *authentéō* (831), to dominate.

5227. ὑπεναντίος *hupenantíos*; fem. *hupenantía*, neut. *hupenantíon*, adj. from *hupó* (5259), and *enantíos* (1727), contrary. Opposed, contrary, adverse, with the idea of stealth, covertness, secretiveness. Used with the dat. (Col 2:14 meaning contrary, adverse). Used as a subst. in the pl. (Heb 10:27 meaning opposers, adversaries; Sept.: Ex 23:27; Lev 26:16; Deut 32:27; Isa 26:11).

Syn.: *antídikos* (476), an opponent, adversary; *suzētētḗs* (4804), a disputant; *asúmphōnos* (800), one who does not agree; *ecthrós* (2190), enemy.

Ant.: *súmphōnos* (4859), one who agrees; *homóphrōn* (3675), one who thinks the same, harmonious; *phílos* (5384), friend.

5228. ὑπέρ *hupér*; prep. governing the gen. and acc. with the primary meaning of over.

(I) With the gen. particularly of place meaning over, above, across or beyond. In the NT, used only figuratively:

(A) Meaning for, in behalf of, for the sake of, in the sense of protection, care, favor, benefit. **(1)** Generally (John 17:19, "for their sakes I sanctify myself"; Acts 21:26; 2 Cor 13:8; Col 1:7; 4:12; Heb 6:20; 13:17). Followed by the gen. of person, "pray for me" (Acts 8:24). After *eúchomai* (2172), to pray (James 5:16); after *proseúchomai* (4336), to pray (Matt 5:44; Luke 6:28; Col 1:9); after *déēsis* (1162), supplication (Rom 10:1; 2 Cor 9:14; Eph 6:18, 19; Phil 1:4); after *proseuchḗ* (4335), prayer (Acts 12:5; Rom 15:30). Generally (1 Tim 2:1, 2).

After verbs implying speaking, pleading, intercession meaning for someone (Acts 26:1; Rom 8:26, 27, 34; Heb 7:25; 9:24). After verbs and nouns implying zeal, care, effort for any person or thing (1 Cor 12:25; 2 Cor 7:7, 12; 8:16; Phil 4:10; Col 4:13). After *eínai* (1511), to be, to be for someone, take his part (Mark 9:40; Luke 9:50; Rom 8:31). Often after words implying suffering on behalf of someone: with the gen. of person (Rom 9:3). With *apothnḗskō* (599), to die (John 11:50–52; Rom 5:6–8; 14:15; 2 Cor 5:14, 15; 1 Thess 5:10); after *apóllumi* (622), to die (John 18:14); after *geúomai thanátou* (*geúomai* [1089], to taste; *thanátou* [2288], of death), to taste of death (Heb 2:9); with *dídōmi* (1325), to give (Luke 22:19; 1 Tim 2:6; Titus 2:14); with *ekchúnō* or *ekchéō* (1632), to pour out, shed, as blood (Luke 22:20); *thúō* (2380), to sacrifice (1 Cor 5:7); *gínomai katára* (*gínomai* [1096], to become; *katára* [2671], a curse), to become a curse (Gal 3:13); *kláō tó sṓma* (*kláō* [2806], to break; *sṓma* [4983], the body), to break the body (1 Cor 11:24); *paradídōmi heautón* (*paradídōmi* [3860], to deliver; *heautón* [1438], himself in the acc.), to deliver him (Rom 8:32; Gal 2:20; Eph 5:2, 25); with *páschō* (3958), to suffer (1 Pet 2:21; 3:18; 4:1); *poiéō* (4160), to make someone to bear sin (2 Cor 5:21); *stauróomai* (4717), to be crucified, in the pass. (1 Cor 1:13); *títhēmi* (5087), to lay down (John 10:11, 15; 13:37, 38; 15:13; 1 John 3:16). Followed by the gen. of thing (John 6:51; Rom 16:4; 2 Cor 12:15). (2) Closely allied to the above is the meaning for, in the stead of someone, in place of (2 Cor 5:20; Eph 6:20).

(B) For, because of, on account of, meaning the aim, purpose or objective of an action and implying the ground, motive, occasion of an action (John 11:4, "for the glory of God" in order to manifest His glory; Acts 5:41, "for his name," for his honor; 9:16; 15:26; 21:13; Rom 1:5; 15:8; 1 Cor 15:3, 29; 2 Cor 1:6; 12:10, 19; Gal 1:4; Eph 3:1, 13; Phil 1:29; Col 1:24; 2 Thess 1:5; Heb 5:1, 3; 7:27; 9:7; 10:12; 3 John 1:7). With

doxázō (1392), to glorify (Rom 15:9); *eucharistéō* (2168), to thank (Rom 1:8; 1 Cor 10:30; 2 Cor 1:11; Eph 1:16; 5:20). Once with God as subj. (Phil 2:13, "for His own good pleasure" [a.t.]).

(C) Over, used with verbs such as speaking meaning upon, about, concerning; to talk over a matter, as to, in respect to, boast about (Rom 9:27; 2 Cor 1:6, 8; 5:12; 7:4, 14; 8:23, 24; 9:2, 3; 12:5, 8; 2 Thess 1:4); with *phronéō* (5426), to think (Phil 1:7); with *erōtáō* (2065), to ask, beg (2 Thess 2:1).

(II) With the acc., particularly of place meaning whither, implying motion or direction meaning over or above a place, beyond.

(A) Implying superiority in rank, dignity, worth (Matt 10:24; Luke 6:40; Eph 1:22; Phile 1:16).

(B) Implying excess above a certain measure or standard and spoken comparatively meaning more than. (1) Generally and simply (Matt 10:37; Acts 26:13; 1 Cor 4:6, "above that which is written," more than that; 10:13; 2 Cor 1:8; 8:3; 12:6; Gal 1:14; Eph 3:20; Phile 1:21; Sept.: 1 Sam 15:22; Ps 19:11). (2) After comparatives (Luke 16:8, "more prudent than the sons of light" [a.t.]; Heb 4:12 [cf. *pará* {3844} III, D]). With a verb (2 Cor 12:13; Sept.: 1 Kgs 19:4). (3) Without case, where it then stands as an adv. meaning more, much, very (2 Cor 11:23). For the adv. forms in the expressions *hupér lían* (3029), exceeding, meaning, either sarcastically or sincerely, superapostles (2 Cor 11:5; 12:11); *hupér ekperissoú* (*ek* [1537], out of; *perissoú* [4053], abundant), more abundantly, far beyond measure, superabundantly (Eph 3:20; 1 Thess 3:10; 5:13).

(III) In composition, *hupér* implies:

(A) Motion or rest over, above, beyond a place, as *huperaíromai* (5229), to exalt oneself; *huperbaínō* (5233), to transcend, overreach; *huperéchō* (5242), to hold oneself above, to excel.

(B) Protection, aid, for or in behalf of, as *huperentugchánō* (5241), to intercede in behalf of.

(C) Exceeding or surpassing, often with the idea of exaggeration, as *huperbállō* (5235), to throw beyond the usual mark, surpass; *huperekteínō* (5239), to overdo, carry too far; *huperperisseúō* (5248), to superabound; *huperauxánō* (5232), to grow extraordinarily; *hupernikáō* (5245), to completely conquer.

Syn.: *pleíōn, pleíon* (4119), more; *mállon* (3123), more, rather; *meízon* (3185), in a greater degree; *meizóteros* (3186), still larger, greater; *meízōn* (3187), greater; *per* (4007), much very, as a suffix; *péran* (4008), beyond, across; *epí* (1909), over, upon; *pró* (4253), above, before; *prós* (4314), pertaining to in respect to, in respect to; *antí* (473), in place of; *perí* (4012), concerning; *ánōthen* (509), from above; *ánō* (507), above; *epánō* (1883), over and on; *huperánō* (5231), far above, over; *perissós* (4053), superior, beyond measure, more; *perissōs* (4057), exceedingly; *perissóteros* (4055), more abundant, greater; *perissóteron* (4054), more abundantly; *perissotérōs* (4056), more abundantly; *lían* (3029), exceeding, great, very; *sphódra* (4970), much, very; *epékeina* (1900), beyond; *pará* (3844), more than; *polús* (4183), much; *pámpolus* (3827), very great, immense.

Ant.: *hupó* (5259), under; *elássōn* (1640), smaller; *hḗssōn* (2276), less, worse; *kátō* (2736), beneath, under; *mikrós* (3398), small; *olígos* (3641), small, short; *brachús* (1024), little, brief; *bradús* (1021), slow; *suntómōs* (4935), briefly; *endeḗs* (1729), lacking; *katóteros* (2737), lower; *enteúthen* (1782), on this side; *entháde* (1759), hither; *eláchistos* (1646), least, smallest; *hupokátō* (5270), under.

5229. ὑπεραίρω *huperaírō*; fut. *huperarō*, from *hupér* (5228), above, or an intens., and *aírō* (142), to lift up. To lift above, elevate, exalt, be conceited, arrogant, insolent. In the NT, only in the mid. *huperaíromai*. Used in an absolute sense in 2 Cor 12:7. Followed by *epí* (1909), upon, and the acc. (2 Thess 2:4).

Syn.: *huperphronéō* (5252), to think too highly, to be vain or proud; *tuphóō*

(5187), to inflate, puff up, lift oneself up with pride; *epaírō* (1869), to raise up, exalt; *huperupsóō* (5251), to elevate above others; *phusióō* (5448), to inflate or puff up with pride.

Ant.: *tapeinóō* (5013), to humble.

5230. ὑπέρακμος *hupérakmos*; gen. *huperákmou*, masc.-fem., neut. *hupérakmon*, adj. from *hupér* (5228), beyond, and *akmḗ* (n.f.), the high point or flower of age, particularly with respect to marriage. Beyond or past the flower of one's age or life, past the usual age for marriage (1 Cor 7:36).

5231. ὑπεράνω *huperánō*; adv. from *hupér* (5228), above, or an intens., and *ánō* (507), up, upwards. Up above, high or far above. Used in an absolute sense (Heb 9:5; Sept.: Ezek 8:2; 11:22). Used of rank or dignity with the gen. (Eph 1:21; 4:10; Sept.: Deut 26:19; 28:1).

Syn.: *anóteros* (511), higher.

Ant.: *hupokátō* (5270), under.

5232. ὑπεραυξάνω *huperauxánō*; fut. *huperauxḗsō*, from *hupér* (5228), an intens., and *auxánō* (837), to increase, grow. To flourish, increase exceedingly or greatly. Used intrans. (2 Thess 1:3).

Syn.: *perisseúō* (4052), to increase, abound; *prokóptō* (4298), to advance; *pleonázō* (4121), to increase, abound; *plēthúnō* (4129), to multiply.

Ant.: *elattóō* (1642), to decrease, make lower, lessen; *husteréō* (5302), to be deficient.

5233. ὑπερβαίνω *huperbaínō*; fut. *huperbḗsomai*, from *hupér* (5228), beyond, and *baínō* (n.f., see *apobaínō* [576]), to go. Intrans., to go or pass over a wall, mountains, with the acc. depending on *hupér* in composition (Sept.: 2 Sam 22:30). Figuratively, to overstep certain limits, to transgress. Used only in 1 Thess 4:6, to go too far, beyond what is right.

Syn.: *parabaínō* (3845), to transgress.

5234. ὑπερβαλλόντως *huperballóntōs*; adv. from *huperbállō* (5235), to excel. Exceedingly, above measure (2 Cor 11:23).

Syn.: *lían* (3029), exceedingly; *sphódra* (4970), exceedingly; *sphodrṓs* (4971), exceedingly; *perissós* (4057), exceedingly; *perissotérōs* (4056), abundantly, exceedingly, more exceedingly; *polús* (4183), greatly; *megálōs* (3171), greatly; *plousíōs* (4146), richly, abundantly.

Ant.: *elássōn* (1640), under, (used adv.); *mikróteros* (3398), less, least; *hḗssōn* (2276), worse, less; *mikrón* (3397), a little, as of distance, quantity, or time; *metríōs* (3357), moderately; *brachús* (1024), short, as of time, distance, or quantity.

5235. ὑπερβάλλω *huperbállō*; fut. *huperbalṓ*, from *hupér* (5228), above, and *bállō* (906), to cast, put. To excel, surpass. In the NT, used only in the pres. part., *huperbállōn*, masc.; *huperbállousa*, fem.; *huperbállon*, neut.; surpassing, exceeding, highly eminent (2 Cor 3:10; 9:14; Eph 1:19; 2:7; 3:19).

Deriv.: *huperballóntōs* (5234), excessively; *huperbolḗ* (5236), excellence.

Syn.: *huperbaínō* (5233), to surpass; *huperéchō* (5242), to excel.

Ant.: *epileípō* (1952), to be insufficient; *husteréō* (5302), to be deficient.

5236. ὑπερβολή *huperbolḗ*; gen. *huperbolḗs*, fem. noun from *huperbállō* (5235), to throw beyond, surpass, (from which is derived the Eng. "hyperbole" meaning an extravagant exaggeration). Abundance (2 Cor 12:7); excellence (2 Cor 4:7). With a prep. in an adv. sense with *katá* (2596), more exceedingly (Rom 7:13; 2 Cor 1:8; 2 Cor 4:17; Gal 1:13). With the meaning of par excellence (1 Cor 12:31, meaning a far better way). With the prep. *eis* (1519), exceeding, exceedingly, in the highest possible degree (2 Cor 4:17).

Syn.: *huperochḗ* (5247), superiority, preeminence.

5237. ὑπερεῖδον *hupereídon*; 2d aor. of *huperoráō* (n.f.), from *hupér* (5228), over, and *eídon* (1492), to see, perceive, which is the 2d aor. of *horáō* (3708), to look. To overlook, to act as if one did not see, to wink at, to bear with. With the acc. (Acts 17:30; Sept.: Lev 20:4).

Syn.: *paratheōréō* (3865), to overlook, disregard; *paríēmi* (3935), to let by; *parérchomai* (3928), to pass over or ignore.

Ant.: *blépō* (991), to observe, heed; *diakrínō* (1252), to discern, distinguish; *horáō* (3708), to behold; *paratēréō* (3906), to note scrupulously, observe, watch; *parakolouthéō* (3877), to trace out, fully know, attend; *theáomai* (2300), to look closely, behold; *theōréō* (2334), to behold, look on, perceive.

5238. ὑπερέκεινα *huperékeina*; adv. from *hupér* (5228), beyond, and *ekeína*, the neut. pl. of *ekeínos* (1565), that one. Beyond; as a subst., that which is beyond, as parts or countries. Governing a gen. (2 Cor 10:16), with the art. *tá* (3588), the, prefixed, meaning in the countries beyond you.

Syn.: *epékeina* (1900), away beyond; *péran* (4008), beyond, farther than; *makrán* (3112), far off; *pórrō* (4206), at a distance, a great way off.

Ant.: *plēsíon* (4139), near; *eggús* (1451), near; *pará* (3844), near; *perí* (4012), around.

5239. ὑπερεκτείνω *huperekteínō*; fut. *huperektenṓ*, from *hupér* (5228), an intens., and *ekteínō* (1614), to put forth, extend. To overdo, carry too far, to extend or stretch out excessively or too far (2 Cor 10:14).

Syn.: *epekteínō* (1901), to stretch forward; *ekpetánnumi* (1600), to stretch forth, extend.

Ant.: *hupostéllō* (5288), to withdraw, draw back; *kolobóō* (2856), to abridge, shorten.

5240. ὑπερεκχύνω *huperekchúnō*, fut. *huperekchúsō*, from *hupér* (5228), over, and *ekchéō /ekchúnō* (1632), to pour out. To run over, overflow, to be poured out over as from a vessel with the meaning to run over, overflow. In the NT, only as a pass. part. *huperekchunnómenon*. Used intrans. (Luke 6:38).
Syn.: *huperpleonázō* (5250), to superabound; *huperperisseúō* (5248), to abound much more.
Ant.: *kenóō* (2758), to make empty.

5241. ὑπερεντυγχάνω *huperentug-chánō*; fut. *huperenteúxomai*, from *hupér* (5228), for, on behalf of, and *entugchánō* (1793), to turn to, appeal. To intercede for or in the behalf of someone, to plead for someone; followed by *hupér*, for, on behalf of, and the gen. (Rom 8:26).
Syn.: *entugchánō* (1793), to make intercession.
Ant.: *egkataleípō* (1459), to forsake, leave behind; *aporphanízō* (642), to forsake completely, leave as an orphan.

5242. ὑπερέχω *huperéchō*; fut. *huper-éxō*, from *hupér* (5228), above, over, and *échō* (2192), to have. Trans., to hold over or extend over something. Intrans., to be over, be prominent, extend over or beyond (Sept.: Ex 26:13; 1 Kgs 8:8). In the NT figuratively meaning to hold one above, superior or better than another.
(I) Generally and particularly with the gen. of person, also with the dat. of manner (Phil 2:3). Followed by the acc. (Phil 4:7). The part. with the neut. art. *tó huperéchon* as a subst. meaning excellence, "super" eminence, equivalent in meaning to *huperoché* (5247), prominence, excellency (Phil 3:8).
(II) To be superior in rank, dignity. In the masc. part. *huperéchōn*, fem. *huperéchousa*, neut. *huperéchon*, meaning superior, higher (Rom 13:1; 1 Pet 2:13).
Deriv.: *huperoché* (5247), prominence, eminence, peak.
Syn.: *diaphérō* (1308), to differ, excel; *perisseúō* (4052), to be abound; *lusiteléō*

(3081), to be better; *huperbállō* (5235), to exceed; *prōteúō* (4409), to be first.
Ant.: *husteréō* (5302), to lag behind.

5243. ὑπερηφανία *huperēphanía*; gen. *huperēphanías*, fem. noun from *huper-éphanos* (5244), proud. Arrogance, pride usually with the ideas of impiety, ungodliness (Mark 7:22; Sept.: Deut 17:12; Ps 31:24; Prov 8:13; Isa 16:6).
Syn.: *alazoneía* (212), the practice of arrogantly displaying or boasting what a person considers himself to be; *kenodoxía* (2754), vain glory; *húbris* (5196), insult, insolence, unrestrained boldness of wrongdoing rather than pride in the strict sense. This is essentially contempt for others evidencing itself by acts of wantonness; an arrogant recklessness as to justice and the feelings of others, willful malice and outrage.
Alazoneía is a sin against truth itself, to think more of oneself in spite of the fact that one knows what the truth is about himself. *Huperēphanía*, on the other hand, is a sin against love (*agápē*) which necessitates the searching for the needs of others and meeting those needs. In 1 John 2:16 we have the expression *hē alazoneía toú bíou*, translated the "pride of life" which is an inflated estimation of the value of our possessions. In this verse, *alazoneía* is not only overestimating the value of possessions, but boasting of their great worth.
There are three words, however, which in the NT refer to boasting, especially by the Apostle Paul. One is *kaucháomai* (2744), to glory, boast, exult, whether in a good sense (Rom 5:2, 3; 1 Cor 1:31) or in a bad sense (1 Cor 4:7; Gal 6:13; Eph 2:9; James 4:16). There are two subst., *kaúchēma* (2745), a boast, the actual boasting, and *kaúchēsis* (2746), the act of boasting. Paul uses the word in a good sense to indicate the legitimate pride which an apostle or Christian may feel as he contemplates the effectiveness of his testimony, ministry, or service in the life and conduct of others (2 Cor 9:3; Phil 2:16). It also expresses the sacred

glorying of God or Christ (1 Cor 1:31; Phil 3:3). This group of words is derived from *auchén* (n.f.), the neck, and refers to one who stretches the neck and holds it up in pride. One may hold his head up because of what he thinks he has made of himself which is *kaúchēsis* in the wrong sense, and thus a sin. The Christian holds his head high because of the indwelling Christ who has made him to be what he is. The recognition of one's position in Christ is reason for glorying, for Christ-centered rejoicing.

Ant.: *tapeinophrosúnē* (5012), humbleness of mind; *tapeínōsis* (5014), humiliation, humbling.

5244. ὑπερήφανος *huperéphanos*; gen. *huperēphánou*, masc.-fem., neut. *huperéphanon*, adj. from *hupér* (5228), over, above, and *phaínō* (5316), to shine, show. Arrogant, proud. Often associated with the rejection of God (Luke 1:51; Rom 1:30; 2 Tim 3:2; James 4:6; 1 Pet 5:5; Sept.: Job 38:15; Ps 94:2; 119:21; 140:6; Isa 2:12; Jer 43:2).

Deriv.: *huperēphanía* (5243), arrogance, pride.

Ant.: *tapeinós* (5011), humble; *semnós* (4586), modest.

For ὑπερλίαν, see ὑπέρ (5228).

5245. ὑπερνικάω *hupernikáō*; contracted *hupernikó*, fut. *hupernikḗsō*, from *hupér* (5228), more, and *nikáō* (3528), to conquer, overcome. To more than conquer, utterly defeat (Rom 8:37).

Syn.: *katakurieúō* (2634), to subjugate, overcome; *authentéō* (831), to dominate, exercise rule over; *basileúō* (936), to rule, be king, reign; *kurieúō* (2961), to have lordship over.

Ant.: *hupeíkō* (5226), to submit.

5246. ὑπέρογκος *hupérogkos*; gen. *huperógkou*, masc.-fem., neut. *hupérogkon*, adj. from *hupér* (5228), over, and *ógkos* (3591), a mass. Oversized, swollen, boastful. In the NT used only figuratively to refer to a bigheaded or boastful person. Used also of language (2 Pet

2:18; Jude 1:16; Sept.: Ex 18:22, 26; Dan 11:36).

Ant.: *mikrós* (3398), small; *eláchistos* (1646), least; *tapeinós* (5011), humble.

5247. ὑπεροχή *huperochḗ*; gen. *huperochḗs*, fem. noun from *huperéchō* (5242), to surpass, be prominent. Prominence, eminence.

(I) Of station, authority, power (1 Tim 2:2).

(II) Generally of things meaning superiority, excellence (1 Cor 2:1).

Syn.: *huperbolḗ* (5236), excellency, exceeding greatness; *prōtokathedría* (4410), preeminence in council, highest or uppermost seat; *prōtoklisía* (4411), a sitting or reclining at preeminence at meals; *prôtos* (4413), foremost, first.

5248. ὑπερπερισσεύω *huperperisseúō*; fut. *huperperisseúsō*, from *hupér* (5228), over, super, and *perisseúō* (4052), to be over and above, exceed. To superabound, abound much more in a comparative sense. Used in an absolute sense (Rom 5:20). Without comparison in the mid. meaning to be made to superabound, to abound greatly or exceedingly in something (as joy), with the dat. (2 Cor 7:4, "I am exceeding joyful").

Syn.: *huperpleonázō* (5250), to abound exceedingly; *huperbállō* (5235), to exceed, excel; *huperéchō* (5242), to surpass.

Ant.: *husteréō* (5302), to come or be behind, be deficient; *elattonéō* (1641), to be less; *leípō* (3007), to be left behind, lack.

5249. ὑπερπερισσῶς *huperperissôs*; adv. from *hupér* (5228), above, more than, and *perissôs* (4057), super abundantly, exceedingly. More than, exceedingly or extreme, "beyond all measure" (Mark 7:37).

Syn.: *huperballóntōs* (5234), beyond measure, exceedingly.

Ant.: *metríōs* (3357), moderately.

5250. ὑπερπλεονάζω *huperpleonázō*; fut. *huperpleonásō*, from *hupér* (5228), above, over, and *pleonázō* (4121), to be more than enough. To superabound, be exceedingly abundant. Intrans. (1 Tim 1:14).

Syn.: *huperbállō* (5235), to exceed, excel; *huperéchō* (5242), to have over, surpass; *huperperisseúō* (5248), to superabound.

Ant.: *hysteréō* (5302), to come or be behind, be deficient; *elattonéō* (1641), to be less; *leípō* (3007), to be left behind, lack.

5251. ὑπερυψόω *huperupsóō*; contracted *huperupsó*, fut. *huperupsósō*, from *hupér* (5228), above, high, and *hupsóō* (5312), to elevate. An intens. meaning to make high above, raise high aloft, to highly exalt; with the acc. (Phil 2:9); in the pass. (Sept.: Ps 97:9 [cf. 37:35]). To highly exalt as in praise (Sept.: Dan 4:34).

Syn.: *huperaíromai* (5229), to become haughty, exalt; *huperbállō* (5235), to surpass, excel; *epaírō* (1869), to lift up, exalt oneself.

Ant.: *tapeinóō* (5013), to make humble, low.

5252. ὑπερφρονέω *huperphronéō*; contracted *huperphronó*, fut. *huperphronésō*, from *hupér* (5228), above, over, and *phronéō* (5426), to think. To think highly, consider something of great importance.

Syn.: *huperaíromai* (5229), to become haughty, exalt oneself; *epaíromai* (1869), to exalt oneself; *huperupsóō* (5251), to highly exalt; *phusióomai* (5448), to be proud, puffed up; *tuphóō* (5187), to lift, be lifted up with pride; *hupsēlophronéō* (5309), high-minded.

Ant.: *tapeinóō* (5013), to humble, be humble (mid.); *hupostéllō* (5288), to be reserved, to shrink from, withdraw.

5253. ὑπερῷον *huperóon*; gen. *huperóou*, neut. noun from *huperóos* (n.f.), upper, over, which is from *hupér* (5228), over, and the adj. suffix *-óios* denoting possession. An upper room or chamber,

the upper part of the house, a sort of guest chamber where company was received and feasts were held, and where at other times they retired for prayer and meditation. In Acts 20:8 the *huperóon* at Troas was on the third floor.

5254. ὑπέχω *hupéchō*; fut. *hupéxō*, from *hupó* (5259), under, and *échō* (2192), to have. Lit. to hold under, meaning to undergo, experience. In the NT with *díkē* (1349), justice, meaning punishment as in Jude 1:7, to pay or suffer punishment.

Syn.: *anéchomai* (430), to suffer, endure; *páschō* (3958), to suffer, bear.

Ant.: *pheúgō* (5343), to run away, escape; *ekpheúgō* (1628), to escape from; *apopheúgō* (668), to flee away from; *diapheúgō* (1309), to flee through, escape through; *apallássomai* (525), to release oneself, be delivered.

5255. ὑπήκοος *hupékoos*; gen. *hupēkóou*, masc.-fem., neut. *hupékoon*, adj. from *hupakoúō* (5219), to submit to, obey. Obedient, as to the will of God (Acts 7:39). As *hupakoúō* it is used of the obedience required in believing (2 Cor 2:9); of Christ in that He was obedient even to death (Phil 2:8; Heb 5:8) shedding His blood for our sins.

Syn.: *eupeithés* (2138), easy to be persuaded, compliant.

Ant.: *apeithés* (545), disobedient; *átaktos* (813), insubordinate, unruly; *anupótaktos* (506), unsubdued, disobedient.

5256. ὑπηρετέω *hupēretéō*; contracted *hupēretó*, fut. *hupēretésō*, from *hupērétēs* (5257), an assistant, attendant. To serve under the direction of someone else, act for someone, minister, serve, subserve. Followed by the dat. (Acts 13:36; 20:34; 24:23).

The idea of service or ministry in the NT is expressed in six groups of Gr. words. They run in triplets, each triplet consisting of a concrete noun, an abstract noun, and a verb, and each could be translated "minister," "ministry," and "to minister." There are various differences among them. These six groups are:

(I) *Diákonos* (1249), a minister, waiter, attendant, servant (applied to a teacher, pastor or deacon); *diakonía* (1248), attendance, aid, service, diaconate, ministry; *diakonéō* (1247), to attend, to wait upon menially or as a host or friend, to act or serve as a Christian deacon or minister.

(II) *Doúlos* (1401), a servant who, however, is related to the master as a slave and who must at all times be subservient; *douleía* (1397), bondage; *douleúō* (1398), to serve as a bondslave.

(III) *Hupērétēs* (5257), an attendant, subordinate, assistant, servant; *hupēresía*, service under the direction of someone (n.f.); *hupēretéō* (5256), to serve as a subordinate, as a sailor on a ship.

(IV) *Látris*, a public servant (n.f.); *latreía* (2999), ministration, as to God, referring to worship that includes service and service that includes worship; *latreúō* (3000), to minister, render religious homage, worship and at the same time serve.

(V) *Leitourgós* (3011), public servant, an official of the church or state; *leitourgía* (3009), a public function as that of a priest from which comes the word "liturgy," a public ministry which includes both worship and service; *leitourgéō* (3008), to be a public servant, perform religious or charitable functions, to minister by worshiping God and serving man.

(VI) *Therápōn* (2324), a menial attendant who shows heart concern; *therapeía* (2322), attendance, domestic service, cure, healing which includes heart and emotional concern; *therapeúō* (2323), to wait upon menially, heal, and at the same time to show concern. This is the word from which the Eng. "therapeutic" is derived.

All of the above words are found in the NT with the exception of *látris*, a hired, menial servant, and *hupēresía*, service under supervision (which, however, occurs in the Sept.).

Different Eng. words translate the same Gr. word, while different Gr. words are sometimes translated by the same Eng. word with the result that the shades of meaning are lost.

The use of a variety of words referring to service reflects the profound view which the early church had of ministry. This set of words highlights the different aspects of Christian service and richly expresses the nature of the ministry and the proper character of those who engage in it. It indicates that ecclesiastical ministry in the primitive church did not lack sophistication or that it was not constructed *ad hoc*. It is apparent that a well-defined and formally structured ministry with recognized offices sprang into existence almost immediately.

Ant.: *proiïstēmi* (4291), to supervise, preside; *árchō* (757), to rule; *hēgéomai* (2233), to lead, command; *episkopéō* (1983), to oversee.

5257. ὑπηρέτης *hupērétēs*; gen. *hupērétou*, masc. noun from *hupó* (5259), under, beneath and *erétēs* (n.f.), a rower. A subordinate, servant, attendant, or assistant in general. The subordinate official who waits to accomplish the commands of his superior. In Class. Gr., a common sailor, as distinguished from *naútēs* (3492), a seaman, sailor. In the NT:

(I) Of those who wait on magistrates or public officials and execute their decrees, a constable or officer, as the attendant on a judge (Matt 5:25). Of the attendants of the Sanhedrin (Matt 26:58; Mark 14:54, 65; John 7:32, 45, 46; 18:3, 12, 18, 22; 19:6; Acts 5:22, 26).

(II) Of the attendant in a synagogue who handed the volume to the reader and returned it to its place (Luke 4:20).

(III) Generally, a minister, attendant, associate in any work (John 18:36; Acts 13:5). Of a minister of the Word of Christ (Luke 1:2; Acts 26:16; 1 Cor 4:1). Luke 1:2 may refer to associates and not to direct ministers of the Word.

Deriv.: *hupēretéō* (5256), to serve under the direction of someone else.

Syn.: *diákonos* (1249), a servant, attendant, minister, deacon; *doúlos* (1401), slave; *leitourgós* (3011), a public servant; *místhios* (3407) or *misthōtós* (3411), one who is hired to do a certain task, a hired servant; *oikétēs* (3610), a menial, domestic servant; *therápōn* (2324), a servant, attendant; *país* (3816), servant.

Ant.: *kúrios* (2962), lord, master; *despótēs* (1203), despot, master, absolute ruler; *megistán* (3175), the greatest, prince, a noble ruling person; *kubernétēs* (2942), a helmsman of a ship, governor, guide, shipmaster.

5258. ὕπνος *húpnos*; gen. *húpnou*, masc. noun. Sleep (Matt 1:24; Luke 9:32; John 11:13; Acts 20:9; Sept.: Gen 28:16; Eccl 5:11). Figuratively of spiritual sleep, sloth (Rom 13:11).

Deriv.: *agrupnéō* (69), to be sleepless; *éxupnos* (1853), out of sleep, a person who is awake.

Syn.: *koímēsis* (2838), sleeping, repose.

Ant.: *agrupnía* (70), sleeplessness.

5259. ὑπό *hupó*; prep. governing the gen. and acc., and in the Gr. Classics also the dat. Under, beneath, through.

(I) With the gen. particularly of place meaning whence, from under, from which something comes forth; of loosing or freeing from under something. Also by, through, from, indicating the subject or agent (especially after pass. and neut. verbs). It is only in this latter sense that *hupó* is used in the NT with the gen.

(A) With pass. verbs with the gen. (Matt 1:22; 2:16; 3:6; 4:1; 5:13; Mark 1:13; 2:3; Luke 5:15; 8:14; 14:8; 21:20; John 10:14; Acts 4:36; 15:4; 23:27; Rom 15:15; 1 Cor 7:25; 2 Cor 1:16; 8:19; Gal 1:11). Followed by the gen. of thing (Matt 8:24; 14:24; Luke 7:24; John 8:9; Acts 2:24; 27:41; Rom 12:21; 1 Cor 10:9; 2 Cor 5:4; James 3:4, 6; 2 Pet 1:17, a voice being sent forth unto Him from or by the radiant glory, by the divine Majesty, from God Himself; 2 Pet 2:7, 17, Jude 1:12; Rev 6:13).

(B) With neut. verbs having a pass. power: after *gínomai* (1096), to become, and *eínai* (1511), to be, meaning to be made, done (*gínomai* in Luke 9:7; 13:17; 23:8; Acts 12:5; 20:3; 26:6; Eph 5:12; with *eínai* in Acts 23:30; 2 Cor 2:6). Also with *páschō* (3958), to suffer something at someone's hand (Matt 17:12; Mark 5:26; 1 Thess 2:14). In the same way after some trans. verbs, where a pass. sense is implied: *lambánō* (2983), to receive from or have been given something by someone (2 Cor 11:24); *hupoménō* (5278), to endure something inflicted upon one (Heb 12:3); *apokteínō* (615), to kill, to cause to be killed by beasts (Rev 6:8).

(II) With the acc. particularly of place meaning from which; of motion or direction meaning under a place; also of place where something is placed to rest under.

(A) Particularly of place, after verbs of motion or direction meaning under, beneath. To place something under a bushel (Matt 5:15; Mark 4:21; Luke 11:33); a bed (Mark 4:21); a roof (Matt 8:8); wings (Matt 23:37; Luke 13:34); the shadow (Mark 4:32); the footstool (James 2:3).

(B) Of place where, after verbs implying a being or remaining under a place or condition, with *eínai*, to be under heaven (Luke 17:24; Acts 2:5; 4:12; Col 1:23); darkness (Jude 1:6); lips (Rom 3:13); the cloud (1 Cor 10:1). Figuratively of what is under the power or authority of any person or thing, generally (Matt 8:9; Luke 7:8; Gal 3:25; 4:2). Followed by the acc. of thing implying state or condition under something (Rom 3:9); the Law (Rom 6:14, 15; 1 Cor 9:20; Gal 4:3–5, 21; 5:18); the curse (Gal 3:10); the yoke (1 Tim 6:1); grace (Rom 6:14, 15). Figuratively of being under the power of something, e.g., sin, the law, the mighty hand of God, under His feet (Rom 7:14; 16:20; 1 Cor 15:25, 27; Gal 3:22, 23; Eph 1:22; 1 Pet 5:6).

(C) Of time, meaning at, during (Acts 5:21).

(III) In composition *hupó* implies:

(A) Place, motion or rest meaning under, beneath, as *hupobállō* (5260), to throw under, implying stealth; *hupodéō* (5265), to bind under one's feet, put on shoes; *hupopódion* (5286), something under the feet, as a footstool.

(B) Subjection, dependence, the state of being under any person or thing as *húpandros* (5220), under a husband or subject to a husband; *hupotássō* (5293), to subordinate.

(C) Succession, being behind or after, as *hupoleípō* (5275), to leave behind, remain; *hupoménō* (5278), to endure.

(D) *Hupó* in composition also implies something done or happening underhandedly, covertly, by stealth, unperceived, without noise or notice; also by degrees: *huponoéō* (5282), to think privately, surmise, conjecture, oppose; *hupopnéō* (5285), to breathe inaudibly (cf. *hupantáō* [5221], to go opposite, quietly; *hupenantíos* [5227], to be contrary or an opponent but covertly).

Syn.: *diá* (1223) which has a variety of meanings. It can mean by, but it expresses personal agency (1 Cor 15:21, *di' anthrṓpou* [444], through the personal agency of man), while *hupó* is more often used of inanimate agencies (Col 2:18, *hupó toú noós* [3563], of the mind), to nonhuman agents (Rev 6:8, *hupó tṓn thēríōn* [2342], the wild beasts), or to personified forces (Luke 7:24, *hupó anémou* [417], wind). *Diá* not only marks personal agency but also the manner of action as intermediate while *hupó* refers to the ultimate or original agency. In Matt 1:22, "which was said by [*hupó*] the Lord" (a.t.), refers to the Lord as the ultimate and original Author of the prophetic Word while *diá* refers to the intermediary, the prophet Isaiah through whom the Lord spoke. The same distinction exists between the prep. *ek* (1537), of, out of, referring to God the Father as the primary origin of everything, and *diá* as the executive agency referring to Jesus Christ (1 Cor 8:6) with regard to the creation and preservation of all things.

Apó (575) refers more to the less immediate and active causation than *hupó* which may refer to immediate and

active causation as in Luke 8:43, *apó etṓn dṓdeka* (*etṓn* [2094], years; *dṓdeka* [1427], twelve). *Apó* refers to the time when she began to be ill, to the less immediate and active causation twelve years before, while *hupó* would refer to the immediate endeavor of attempts at healing. *Hupó* also may refer to the direct origination of an action as in Acts 4:36 referring to Barnabas who was surnamed by [*hupó*] the Apostles indicating directness of action. *Apó* may refer to an external, causal relation, while *hupó* may refer to an internal relation as in Mark 8:31, "that the Son of Man must suffer many things and be rejected by [*apó*] the elders, and the chief priests." In Rev 12:6 *hupó* is used to indicate the occasional cause in that a place was prepared of God for the woman in question. In Rev 9:18 both prep. are used, *hupó* referring to the three plagues as the cause while *ék* is used as the immediate cause of destruction. In James 1:13 it is urged that God should not be viewed even as the ultimate cause of temptation, "Let no man say when he is tempted, I am tempted of [*apó*, the direct cause] God: for God cannot be tempted with evil." James 1:14 says, "But every man is tempted, when he is drawn away of [*hupó*] his own lust," referring to the immediate, internal cause of temptation. James here is referring to the temptations that come as a result of the circumstances and influences that are, since the fall, part of the woof and warp of the world. We live in a sinful environment not because God created that sinful environment, but because man polluted the world with sin according to his free choice. Therefore God cannot be blamed as the cause of our temptation.

Apó and *hupó* stand, however, in many instances as exact' syn. (Luke 7:35; Acts 15:4, 33; 20:9; 2 Cor 7:13).

Pará (3844) with a specific meaning of "by" as an agent, does not replace *hupó* (Acts 22:30). In Luke 1:45 *pará* may allude to the intermediate agency of the angel. *Pará* traces an action back to its point of departure or source, and *hupó* relates an action to its cause.

Apó, *ek*, *pará*, and *hupó* all denote an issuing or proceeding from and are related to the objects to which they refer in varying intimacy of degree, *ek* representing the most intimate connection and *apó* the most remote. Insofar as their intimacy to the object, they stand in the following degree: *ek*, *hupó*, *pará*, *apó* (see Colin Brown, *The New International Dictionary of New Testament Theology.* III:1197–8).

Ant.: *hupér* (5228), over, above; *ánō* (507), above; *antí* (473), against; *epí* (1909), upon; *katá* (2596), against; *sún* (4862), together, with.

5260. ὑποβάλλω *hupobállō*; fut. *hupobalṓ*, from *hupó* (5259), under, and *bállō* (906), to throw, place. To introduce underhandedly, to make a secret agreement, to suborn, put forward by collusion, trans. (Acts 6:11). To suborn in the legal sense is to induce a person to make a false oath, i.e., to commit perjury.

Syn.: *epiorkéō* (1964), to commit perjury, swear a false oath.

Ant.: *alētheúō* (226), to speak the truth.

5261. ὑπογραμμός *hupogrammós*; gen. *hupogrammoú*, masc. noun from *hupográphō* (n.f.), to undersign, from *hupó* (5259), before, and *gráphō* (1125), to write. Used only in biblical and later Class. Gr. meaning a writing copy, pattern, example for imitation (1 Pet 2:21). This subst. is related to *hupográphō* (n.f.), to write under, meaning writing pattern, to teach to write, since the writing copy of the teacher was to be followed by the scholars.

Syn.: *hupódeigma* (5262), an example; *túpos* (5179), a type, model, pattern; *homoíōma* (3667), a form, likeness; *deígma* (1164), a specimen, example.

5262. ὑπόδειγμα *hupódeigma*; gen. *hupodeígmatos*, neut. noun from *hupodeíknumi* (5263), to show, forewarn. An example or pattern to be imitated in action (John 13:15); in suffering (James 5:10); for warning (Heb 4:11). A representation or type (Heb 8:5; 9:23 [cf. 4:11]; 2 Pet 2:6).

Syn.: *hupogrammós* (5261), a copy, pattern, example.

5263. ὑποδείκνυμι *hupodeíknumi*; fut. *hupodeíxō*, from *hupó* (5259), under, and *deiknúō* /*deíknumi* (1166), to show. To show plainly, set before the eyes, exemplify as by words or actions (Luke 6:47; 12:5; Acts 9:16; 20:35; Sept.: 2 Chr 15:3; Esth 2:10); to show, teach, instruct plainly (Matt 3:7; Luke 3:7).

Deriv.: *hupódeigma* (5262), example, pattern.

Syn.: *apodeíknumi* (584), to exhibit, set forth, demonstrate; *dēlóō* (1213), to declare; *sēmaínō* (4591), to signify; *phaneróō* (5319), to render apparent.

Ant.: *krúptō* (2928), to conceal; *apokrúptō* (613), to hide; *kalúptō* (2572), to cover.

5264. ὑποδέχομαι *hupodéchomai*; fut. *hupodéxomai*; mid. deponent from *hupó* (5259), under, and *déchomai* (1209), to receive. To take under one's care, as if placing the hands or arms under a person or thing, to receive hospitably and kindly. In the NT to receive guests hospitably or to welcome, entertain, with the acc. (Luke 10:38; 19:6; Acts 17:7; James 2:25).

Syn.: *apodéchomai* (588), to welcome, receive gladly.

5265. ὑποδέω *hupodéō*; fut. *hupodḗsō*, from *hupó* (5259), under, and *déō* (1210), to bind. To bind under, as sandals under the feet, to put on sandals, slippers, shoes (Mark 6:9; Acts 12:8). Part. followed by the acc. (Eph 6:15).

Deriv.: *hupódēma* (5266), a sandal, shoe.

Ant.: *apobállō* (577), to throw off, cast away; *apekdúomai* (554), to put off; *ekdúō* (1562), to take off; *lúō* (3089), to loose, put off.

5266. ὑπόδημα *hupódēma*; gen. *hupodḗmatos*, neut. noun from *hupodéō* (5265), to bind under. A sandal or shoe (Matt 10:10; Luke 10:4; 15:22; 22:35; Acts 7:33 quoted from Ex 3:5; Deut 25:9; Josh 5:15; Isa 5:27). To unbind someone's sandals (Matt 3:11; Mark 1:7; Luke 3:16; John 1:27; Acts 13:25) is an expression which implies deep humility since this was usually done only by menial servants.

Syn.: *sandálion* (4547), sandal.

5267. ὑπόδικος *hupódikos*; gen. *hupodíkou*, masc.-fem., neut. *hupódikon*, adj. from *hupó* (5259), under, and *díkē* (1349), judgment, justice. Under sentence, condemned, liable, subject to prosecution. It describes one who comes under *díkē*, judgment, and even who is pronounced guilty. *Hupódikos* denotes one who is bound to do or suffer what is imposed for the sake of justice because he has neglected to do what is right. Therefore, it denotes one who is under obligation to make compensation (Rom 3:19).

Syn.: *énochos* (1777), liable, guilty.

Ant.: *anaítios* (338), blameless; *athóos* (121), innocent, not guilty; *eleútheros* (1658), a free person.

5268. ὑποζύγιον *hupozúgion*; gen. *hupozugíou*, neut. noun from *hupó* (5259), under, and *zugós* (2218), a yoke. An animal under a yoke, a beast of burden, such as a donkey (Matt 21:5 quoted from Zech 9:9; 2 Pet 2:16 in allusion to Num 22:28); *hē ónos* (3688), an ass, a female donkey (Sept.: Ex 23:4, 5; Josh 6:21).

5269. ὑποζώννυμι *hupozṓnnumi*; fut. *hupozṓsō*, from *hupó* (5259), under, and *zṓnnumi* (2224), to gird. To undergird. Of persons, to gird under the breast. In the NT used of a ship, to undergird, gird across the keel sides and deck of the ship with chains or cables in order to strengthen it against the waves (Acts 27:17).

5270. ὑποκάτω *hupokátō*; adv. from *hupó* (5259), under, and *kátō* (2736), down. Underneath, spoken of place, with the gen. (Mark 6:11; 7:28; Luke 8:16; John 1:50; Rev 5:3, 13; 6:9; 12:1). Figuratively to put under the feet meaning to subjugate (Heb 2:8; Sept.: 1 Kgs 6:6; Ezek 24:5).

Syn.: *katōtérō* (2736), further under.

Ant.: *huperánō* (5231), above, up, over.

5271. ὑποκρίνομαι *hupokrínomai*; fut. *hupokrinoúmai*, mid. deponent from *hupó* (5259), under, indicating secrecy, and *krínō* (2919), to judge. To pretend, dissemble, dissimulate. Originally syn. with *apokrínomai* (611), to respond, reply. It came further to mean to inquire, distinguish, get under the meaning of dreams, expound and interpret them. Later, it acquired the meaning to represent, act, or impersonate someone as an actor would. It arose from the application of the word in Attic Gr. to persons in a play, and then to people generally who act a part or pretend to be what they are not, to represent oneself as, to simulate, to distinguish oneself. In the NT to pretend, feign. Used in Luke 20:20.

Deriv.: *anupókritos* (505), one without hypocrisy; *sunupokrínomai* (4942), to play the role of a hypocrite together with; *hupókrisis* (5272), hypocrisy; *hupokritḗs* (5273), hypocrite.

Syn.: *prospoiéomai* (4364), to pretend; *epaggéllomai* (1861), to profess something respecting oneself; *metaschēmatízomai* (3345), to disguise oneself.

Ant.: *parrēsiázomai* (3955), to be frank in utterance; *alētheúō* (226), to speak the truth.

5272. ὑπόκρισις *hupókrisis*; gen. *hupokríseōs*, fem. noun from *hupokrínomai* (5271), to pretend. Hypocrisy, dissimulation (Matt 23:28; Mark 12:15; Luke 12:1; Gal 2:13; 1 Tim 4:2; 1 Pet 2:1).

(I) The noun *hupókrisis* was generally used for flattery or evil deception.

Hypocrisy is a thing God cannot tolerate (Job 22:16), and which He is continually exposing (Job 5:13). Idolatry is a form of hypocrisy which keeps a man from being perfect, i.e., wholehearted, with the Lord his God (Deut 18:13). Isaiah's prophecies contain humiliating exposés and scathing denunciations of the religious hypocrisy which was so rampant in his day. Malachi expounds on it extensively as well. All false prophecy was hypocrisy—the saying of the thing that pleased, and not the thing that was true. The person most deceived was the hypocrite himself (Isa 33:14; Job 27:8), but he was also a danger to the society in which he lived (Job 15:34).

(II) In the NT and especially in the synoptics, few sins are so directly denounced as hypocrisy. In John's Gospel it is equated with *pseúdos* (5579), falsehood, lying, which is equally condemned. Our Lord presents this evil as something hidden that one day will be made manifest, a sin which glories in misleading another by smooth flatteries (Matt 22:16). The religious hypocrites of Jesus' day went about in long robes seeking to be reverenced by public salutations, taking honor for granted and cloaking oppressive avarice with long prayers (Mark 12:38–40). Hypocrisy cleanses the outside of the cup and platter while leaving them full of extortion and wickedness. It makes men as hidden tombs, white and shining without but foul within (Luke 11:44).

(III) Hypocrisy is a sin which is exposed by our Lord as no other because it corrupts the conscience averting holiness of life. It substitutes the ceremonial and formal for the personal and practical (Matt 15:6). It uses ecclesiastical rule as a substitute for judgment and the love of God (Luke 11:42). It cannot receive the truth, because its eye is on man and not on God (John 5:44). It makes inquiries not in order to hear the truth, but in order to refute it (John 9:27, 28). It is chained to its error by a confident assurance that it alone is right (John 9:41).

(IV) Direct denunciation is the only way to counter hypocrisy, a foe of all truth. The hypocrite is in a special sense the child of the father of lies (John 8:44). Hypocrisy not being able to live with truth, can defend itself only through the persecution of others (John 8:37). The reason for the vehement denunciation by Christ of the Pharisees in Matt 23 was that sitting in Moses' seat, they showed a spirit in which truth cannot dwell. The Pharisees neither entered the kingdom nor allowed others to enter (Matt 16:3, 4). Hypocrisy stands in opposition to faith as it works to debase the whole man, just as faith works to regenerate him. It takes away the key of knowledge (Luke 11:52).

(V) In the Sermon on the Mount (Matt 5:1ff.) hypocrisy is set in contrast to the kingdom of heaven. To a hypocrite, what is outwardly performed is most important and not what is believed in the heart. The Lord teaches that deliberate care must be taken that one's righteousness be not done for the public eye. Hypocrisy is the opposite of that singleness of eye which fills the whole body with light; it turns the light that is in a man to darkness. Hypocrisy, though attempting to serve two masters, really serves none. It sees splinters in its brother's eye while ignoring beams in its own. It is sheep's clothing without, but a ravening wolf within. As it corrupted Judaism, it was ready to corrupt Christianity, and indeed has made inroads. The Lord treated the publican and the harlot as the lost sheep He had come to seek. For them He opened wide the door of the kingdom. But He knew that the hypocrites could only pretend to enter.

(VI) The ultimate hypocrite presented in Scripture is the Antichrist, the one who stands in place of Christ. He will represent the new hypocrisy. He will come in Christ's name saying, "I am he" (Mark 13:6). He will try to deceive even the elect.

(VII) Hypocrisy can be equated with the blasphemy against the Holy Spirit (Matt 12:22–37; Mark 3:20–30; Luke

12:1–12). Both hypocrisy and the resistance of the conviction of the Holy Spirit are the negation of faith.

Ant.: *eilikríneia* (1505), purity, sincerity; *haplótēs* (572), sincerity.

5273. ὑποκριτής *hupokritḗs*; gen. *hupokritoú*, masc. noun from *hupokrínomai* (5271), to act as a hypocrite. A hypocrite, one who acts pretentiously, a counterfeit, a man who assumes and speaks or acts under a feigned character.

(I) In the Sept. it is used in Job 34:30 to indicate an impiety which lays snares and in Job 36:13 it indicates an impurity of the heart which cherishes an inward bitterness against God.

(II) A dissembler, pretender (Matt 16:3 [TR]; Luke 12:56). Not used in the NT with the Class. meaning, what the Greeks used to call an expounder of dreams, a conjecturer, guesser, diviner.

5274. ὑπολαμβάνω *hupolambánō*; fut. *hupolḗpsomai*, from *hupó* (5259), under, and *lambánō* (2983), to take, receive. To take from someone. Trans.:

(I) Particularly to take or receive from, with the acc. (Acts 1:9).

(II) Figuratively to take up the discourse, continue, and hence to answer, reply. Used in an absolute sense (Luke 10:30; Sept.: Job 2:4; 4:1; 6:1; Dan 3:9).

(III) Figuratively to take up in thought, suppose, think, take it. Used in an absolute sense (Acts 2:15). Followed by *hóti* (3754), that (Luke 7:43; Sept.: Job 25:3).

(IV) To help, aid, support (3 John 1:8).

Syn.: *apokrínomai* (611), to give an answer, begin to speak; *antapokrínomai* (470), to reply against; *apologéomai* (626), to answer by way of making a defense for oneself; *antilégō* (483), to speak against, contradict; *hupodéchomai* (5264), receive under one's roof, give hospitality; *nomízō* (3543), to suppose; *dokéō* (1380), to be of opinion, suppose; *huponoéō* (5282), to suspect, deem, suppose; *oíomai* or *oímai* (3633), to imagine, suppose; *logízomai* (3049), to suppose,

reckon; *hēgéomai* (2233), to reckon, suppose, count.

5275. ὑπολείπω *hupoleípō*; fut. *hupoleípsō*, from *hupó* (5259), and *leípō* (3007), to leave, lack. To leave behind. In the pass. to be left behind, remain (Rom 11:3 quoted from 1 Kgs 19:10, 14; Sept.: Ex 10:19; Judg 7:3).

Syn.: *kataleípō* (2641) and *apoleípō* (620), to leave behind; *hupolambánō* (5277) and *aphíēmi* (863), to leave, bequeath.

5276. ὑπολήνιον *hupolḗnion*; gen. *hupolēníou*, neut. noun from *hupó* (5259), and *lēnós* (3025), a vat. The lower section of a winepress into which the juice of the grapes flowed (Mark 12:1; Sept.: Isa 16:10; Joel 3:13; Hag 2:16).

5277. ὑπολιμπάνω *hupolimpánō*; fut. *hupoleiphthḗsomai*, a late form of *hupoleípō* (5275), to leave behind. To leave behind, trans. (1 Pet 2:21). Found only in the pres. and imperf.

5278. ὑπομένω *hupoménō*; fut. *hupomenṓ*, from *hupó* (5259), under, and *ménō* (3306), to remain. To remain under, i.e., to persevere, endure, sustain, bear up under, suffer, as a load of miseries, adversities, persecutions or provocations with faith (Matt 10:22; 24:13; Mark 13:13; Rom 12:12; 1 Cor 13:7; 2 Tim 2:10, 12; Heb 10:32; 12:2, 3, 7; James 1:12; 5:11; 1 Pet 2:20); to remain privately, stay behind (Luke 2:43; Acts 17:14).

Deriv.: *hupomonḗ* (5281), patience, endurance.

Syn.: *makrothuméō* (3114), to be long-suffering, patient; (Whereas *hupoménō* refers to one's response toward circumstances, denoting perseverance in the face of difficulties, *makrothuméō* refers to one's response toward people, denoting a patient endurance of the faults and even provocations of others without retaliating.); *hupophérō* (5297), to bear, endure; *anéchomai* (430), to put up with; *karteréō* (2594), to be steadfast, patient, to endure; *hupéchō* (5254), to endure; *bastázō* (941), to bear.

Ant.: *aphíēmi* (863), to forsake, let go; *kataleípō* (2641), to leave down, abandon; *egkataleípō* (1459), to leave behind, forsake; *apoleípō* (620), to leave behind, forsake.

5279. ὑπομιμνήσκω *hupomimnḗskō*; fut. *hupomnḗsō*, from *hupó* (5259), under, and *mimnḗskō* (3403), to remind. To remember, perhaps after hints or suggestions, to put in mind of, remind, bring to remembrance.

(**I**) Act. in various constructions: with acc. of person and thing (John 14:26, "shall bring to your remembrance all things" [a.t.]). Followed by the acc. of person with *perí* (4012), concerning; followed by the gen. (2 Pet 1:12); by the acc. of person with the inf. (Titus 3:1); with *hóti* (3754) (Jude 1:5); followed by the acc. of thing such as precepts, duties (2 Tim 2:14); also evil deeds with the idea of censure, reprehension (3 John 1:10).

(**II**) In the mid. meaning to call to mind, recollect, remember, with the gen. (Luke 22:61).

Deriv.: *hupómnēsis* (5280), a reminding, recollection.

Syn.: *hupotíthēmi* (5294), to suggest, put into one's mind; *mnēmoneúō* (3421), to call to mind, remember, always used with an obj.; *anamimnḗskō* (363), to remind, call to one's mind, and in the pass. to call to remembrance; *epanamimnḗskō* (1878), to remind again, put someone in remembrance.

Ant.: *lanthánō* (2990), to be ignorant of; *epilanthánomai* (1950), to forget, neglect; *eklanthánomai* (1585), to forget completely; *agnoéō* (50), to ignore.

5280. ὑπόμνησις *hupómnēsis*; gen. *hupomnḗseōs*, fem. noun from *hupomimnḗskō* (5279), to recall to one's mind. A putting in mind, reminding, remembrance.

(**I**) Putting in mind, by way of remembrance (2 Pet 1:13; 3:1).

(**II**) Recollection, remembrance, remember (2 Tim 1:5).

Syn.: *anámnēsis* (364), recollection, an active exercise of the memory; the act of the recalling of the death of Christ in the celebration of the Eucharist; *mnēmósunon* (3422), a reminder, memorial; *mnḗmē* (3420), memory, remembrance; *mneía* (3417), remembrance, mention.

Ant.: *lḗthē* (3024), forgetfulness; *epilēsmonḗ* (1953), forgetfulness.

5281. ὑπομονή *hupomonḗ*; gen. *hupomonḗs*, fem. noun from *hupoménō* (5278), to persevere, remain under. A bearing up under, patience, endurance as to things or circumstances. This is in contrast to *makrothumía* (3115), long-suffering or endurance toward people. *Hupomonḗ* is associated with hope (1 Thess 1:3) and refers to that quality of character which does not allow one to surrender to circumstances or succumb under trial.

(**I**) Particularly with the gen. of thing borne, as evils (2 Cor 1:6).

(**II**) Generally meaning endurance, patience, perseverance or constancy under suffering in faith and duty. Used in an absolute sense (Luke 8:15; Rom 8:25; 2 Cor 6:4; 12:12; Col 1:11; Heb 10:36; 12:1; James 1:3, 4; 2 Pet 1:6; Rev 2:3); by the gen. of that in or to which one perseveres (Rom 2:7; 1 Thess 1:3; 2 Thess 3:5; Rev 1:9; 3:10). Followed by the gen. of person (Luke 21:19; 2 Thess 1:4; James 5:11; Rev 2:2, 19, the precept of constancy toward God; 13:10; 14:12). Specifically patience as a quality of mind, the bearing of evils and suffering with tranquil mind (Rom 5:3, 4; 15:4, 5, God who bestows patience; 1 Tim 6:11; 2 Tim 3:10; Titus 2:2; Sept.: Ezra 10:2; Ps 9:19).

Syn.: *anochḗ* (463), forbearance, tolerance; *epeíkeia* (1932), clemency, gentleness.

Ant.: *aganáktēsis* (24), indignation; *orgḗ* (3709), anger, wrath; *thumós* (2372), indignation.

5282. ὑπονοέω *huponoéō*; contracted *huponoṓ*, fut. *huponoḗsō*, from *hupó* (5259), under, denoting diminution, and *noéō* (3539), to think. To suppose, theorize, suspect (Acts 13:25; 25:18; 27:27).
Deriv.: *hupónoia* (5283), suspicion, conjecture.
Syn.: *nomízō* (3543), to suppose, consider, think; *dokéō* (1380), to be of opinion, suppose; *hupolambánō* (5274), to suppose; *oíomai* (3633), imagine, suppose; *logízomai* (3049), to reckon; *hēgéomai* (2233), to reckon, suppose; *phronéō* (5426), to think; *krínō* (2919), to judge, reckon; *dialogízomai* (1260), to reason, think.
Ant.: *diastréphomai* (1294), not to know which way to turn; *aporéō* (639), to wonder, doubt, be perplexed.

5283. ὑπόνοια *hupónoia*; gen. *hupónoias*, fem. noun from *huponoéō* (5282), to suspect. Suspicion, surmising, conjecture (1 Tim 6:4).

5284. ὑποπλέω *hupopléō*; fut. *hupopleúsomai*, from *hupó* (5259), under, and *pléō* (4126), to sail. To sail under, to sail under the shelter of an island or shore, followed by the acc. (Acts 27:4, 7).

5285. ὑποπνέω *hupopnéō*; fut. *hupopneúsō*, from *hupó* (5259), under, and *pnéō* (4154), to make a breeze, blow. To blow gently, softly, moderately as of the wind (Acts 27:13).

5286. ὑποπόδιον *hupopódion*; gen. *hupopodíou*, neut. noun from *hupopódios* (n.f.), underfoot, which is from *poús* (4228), foot. A footstool (James 2:3). Used of God whose footstool is the earth (Matt 5:35; Acts 7:49 [cf. Isa 66:1 quoted from Ps 110:1]. See Matt 22:44; Mark 12:36; Luke 20:43; Acts 2:35; Heb 1:13; 10:13; Sept.: Lam 2:1).

5287. ὑπόστασις *hupóstasis*; gen. *hupostáseōs*, fem. noun from *huphístēmi* (n.f.), to place or set under. In general,

that which underlies the apparent, hence, reality, essence, substance; that which is the basis of something, hence, assurance guarantee, confidence (with the obj. sense).
(I) The ground of confidence, assurance, guarantee, or proof; not *fides* but *fiducia* (Heb 3:14, our confidence or first hope in Christ; 1 Tim 5:12 [cf. Heb 10:35]; Heb 11:1, "faith is confidence in the things hoped for" [a.t.], standing in parallel to *élegchos* (1650), certainty, proof, demonstration; Sept.: Ruth 1:12; Ps 39:8; Ezek 19:5).
(II) Metonymically of that quality which leads one to stand under, endure, or undertake something, firmness, boldness, confidence (2 Cor 9:4 [TR]; 11:17, "in this confident boasting" [a.t.], this boldness of boasting).
(III) Substance, what really exists under any appearance, reality, essential nature (Heb 1:3, "the express image" or exact expression of God's essence or being, i.e., of God Himself). Here it approximates *ousía* (3776), existence, substance, and *phúsis* (5449), nature. One must be careful to remember that some Latin Fathers rejected the rendering *substantia* because it was distinct from *essentia* which they felt conveyed unequivocally the notion of *hupóstasis*. However, the word "substance" as used in English is quite suitable since it does not bear the subtle difference of the original Latin.
Syn.: *ousía* (3776), existence, substance; *phúsis* (5449), nature; *élegchos* (1650), certainty, proof, demonstration.
Ant.: *phántasma* (5326), a phantasm or phantom, apparition, something which has no reality; *pneúma* (4151), spirit as lacking corporeal reality.

5288. ὑποστέλλω *hupostéllō*; fut. *hupostelō*, from *hupó* (5259), and *stéllō* (4724), to send or draw. To haul down, lower, referring to a sail, to contract, furl. In the NT with *heautón* (1438), himself, or the mid. *hupostéllomai*, to draw oneself back, out of sight, hence, generally to shrink or draw back, to withdraw oneself, retreat (Gal 2:12; Heb 10:38 quoted from Hab 2:4). With the acc. of thing, to avoid, shun or suppress (Acts 20:20).

Deriv.: *hupostolḗ* (5289), a shrinking or drawing back, apostasy.

Syn.: *hupochōréō* (5298), withdraw oneself.

Ant.: *tharséō* (2293), to exercise courage; *tharréō* (2292), to be bold.

5289. ὑποστολή *hupostolḗ*; gen. *hupostolḗs*, fem. noun from *hupostéllō* (5288), to contract, shrink. A shrinking or drawing back, apostasy, retroversion (Heb 10:39).

Syn.: *apostasía* (646), a departure, defection.

5290. ὑποστρέφω *hupostréphō*; fut. *hupostrépsō*, from *hupó* (5259), and *stréphō* (4762), to turn. To turn from, back, about. In the NT intrans. or with *heautón* (1438), himself, implied meaning to turn back, return. Used in an absolute sense (Mark 14:40; Luke 2:43; 17:18; 23:48, 56; Acts 8:28, "was returning"; Sept.: Josh 2:23). With adjuncts of place with *eis* (1519), to, with the acc. (Luke 1:56; 2:39; 4:14; Gal 1:17). With *eis* with the acc. of state (Acts 13:34); *apó* (575), from, with the gen. (Luke 4:1; Heb 7:1); *ek* (1537), out of, with the gen. (Acts 12:25); *diá* (1223), through, with the gen. (Acts 20:3).

Syn.: *epistréphō* (1994), to turn about, return; *anastréphō* (390), to turn back.

Ant.: *poreúomai* (4198), to go on; *proporeúomai* (4313), to go before; *proágō* (4254), to lead forth; *probaínō* (4260), to go on, advance; *hodoiporéō* (3596), to be on a journey; *anachōréō* (402) and *apochōréō* (672), to depart; *apérchomai* (565), to go away; *apobaínō* (576), to go out; *aphistēmi* (868), to depart.

5291. ὑποστρωννύω *hupostrōnnúō* and **ὑποστρώννυμι** *hupostrṓnnumi*; fut. *hupostrṓsō*, from *hupó* (5259), under, and *strṓnnumi* / *strōnnúō* (4766), to spread, strew. To spread, strew

underneath, trans. (Luke 19:36; Sept.: Isa 58:5).

5292. ὑποταγή *hupotagḗ*; gen. *hupotagḗs*, fem. noun from *hupotássō* (5293), to submit. Subordination, subjection, submission, obedience (2 Cor 9:13; Gal 2:5, "by subjection," so as to submit to them; 1 Tim 2:11; 3:4).

Syn.: *hupakoḗ* (5218), obedience.

Ant.: *apeítheia* (543), disobedience, disbelief; *parakoḗ* (3876), inattention, disobedience; *parábasis* (3847), transgression; *apostasía* (646), departure, apostasy.

5293. ὑποτάσσω *hupotássō*, **ὑποτάττω** *hupotáttō*; fut. *hupotáxō* from *hupó* (5259), and *tássō* (5021), to place in order. To place under in an orderly fashion.

(I) Act., to subjugate, place in submission.

(A) In Rom 8:20, "For the creature was made subject to vanity, not willingly, but by reason of him who hath subjected the same in hope." "Was made subject" is *hupetágē* (aor. pass. indic. 3d person sing. of *hupotássomai*). God is the implied agent of the action of subjugation. The word "creature" is *ktísis* (2937), meaning creation, and by extension creature, which is more particularly expressed in *ktísma* (2938). Reference here is to the whole creation, animate and inanimate. The word *ktísis* in Rom 8:22 is correctly translated "creation" and presented as travailing or being in distress. God made the whole creation including mankind "subject" to vanity because of man's disobedience to God's specific command (Gen 2:16, 17). Man did not believe God's threatened judgment of death as the consequence of disobedience (*parakoḗ* [3876]). Had God not imposed this, He would have proven Himself untrue. God subjugated man and his environment to vanity (*mataiótēs* [3153], futility, aimlessness). Because God alone can give true meaning and lasting purpose to life, autonomous man (*kósmos* [2889], the world of fallen humanity) separated from God in death, is left to define and give purpose to his existence, a task at which he has dismally failed. Apart from God, he has a meaningless existence. Thus the pass. use of the word *hupotássō* is similar to the act. use. God subdues and the creation is subdued. There is not a voluntary acquiescence by the creation. This is clearly expressed with the phrase *ouch hekoúsa* (*ouch*, from *ou* [3756], not; *hekoúsa*, fem. of *hekṓn* [1635], voluntarily, willingly), "not willingly." The second use of *hupotássō* is in the aor. act. part. *hupotáxanta*, the one who subdued. God imposed futility upon creation, but as He did He gave hope. Right from the beginning He planned man's redemption (Rom 8:22, 23) in and through His only begotten Son, Jesus Christ (Gen 3:15; Rom 5:1, 5).

(B) Other instances of the act. voice of *hupotássō*, to subdue: **(1)** 1 Cor 15:27: "For he hath put all things under his feet [*hupétaxen*, aor. act. 3d person sing. referring to forcible subjection]. But when he saith, All things are put under him [*hupotétaktai*, perf. pass. ind. indicating forcible subjugation], it is manifest that he is excepted, which did put all things under him [*hupotáxanti*, aor. act. indic. 3d person, indicating forcible subjugation]." This speaks of Christ (15:24) when in the end He will hand over the kingdom to God the Father. After Christ "has put all things under His feet," He then submits Himself to the Father as the Messiah, having accomplished His task of redemption. **(2)** Phil 3:21: "Who shall change our vile body, that it may be fashioned like unto his glorious body, according to the working whereby he is able even to subdue all things unto himself." The word "subdue" is *hupotáxai* (aor. act. inf.) and indicates the total subjugation of everything including the body of our humiliation (*tapeínōsis* [5014]), a humiliation brought about by our disobedience and fall in and through Adam. **(3)** Heb 2:5: "For not unto the angels hath he put in subjection [*hupétaxen*, aor. act. 3d

person, speaking of God not placing the world under angels, but under His Son] the world to come, whereof we speak." See Heb 2:8 where the act. *hupétaxas* (aor. act. 2d person), *hupotáxai* (aor. act. inf.), and *hupotetagména* (perf. pass. part.) are used.

(II) Mid. *hupotássomai*, to subject oneself, place oneself in submission.

(A) In the relation of a wife to her husband: **(1)** Eph 5:22; Col 3:18; 1 Pet 3:1, 5; Titus 2:5. In these verses the duty of the wife to submit herself to her own husband is clearly enunciated (Gal 3:28; 1 Pet 3:7). Although there is an ontological spiritual equality between men and women, there remain physical, positional and functional differences. There are designated functions for a husband and a wife which man cannot change because God has ordained them. Any endeavor to effect change will bring frustration, vanity, and emptiness (*mataiótēs* [3153] in Rom 8:20). God has made one woman to become a wife to one man, and she is so constituted by God Himself. But this is not due to her being inferior to her husband, for they are both equal before God. It is a willing personal subjection demonstrated in Eph 5:21, "submitting yourselves [*hupotassómenoi*] one to another in the fear of God." The word translated "one to another" is *allélois* (240), in the pl. dat. indicating equality of all concerned. In society all humans, all men and women in various positions of leadership or following and dependence, are equal, yet their functions vary and their responsibilities are diverse. We are all equal before God and the laws of society, and yet we have varying functions and responsibilities. If we accept certain functions under a fellow-human, we must subject ourselves to that individual to accomplish a common goal. So it is with a wife placing herself in the proper and divinely-fitted position under her husband. Only a wife can bear children, and to do this she must subject (*hupotássetai*) herself to her husband. The functions are equally important although different.

And they are different not because we want them to be, but because God made them to be so. (2) 1 Cor 14:34: "Let your women [wives, see XI *gunē* {1135}] keep silence in the churches: for it is not permitted unto them to speak; but they are commanded to be under obedience [*hupotássesthai*, pres. mid. inf.], as also saith the law." If, as some believe, *gunē* has specific reference to wives and not to women in general, then Paul is here ordering the wives in the church to submit themselves to their husbands.

(B) In the relation of Jesus as a child of twelve years of age to his parents, Mary, His mother, and Joseph, His stepfather: "And was subject unto them" (Luke 2:51). The meaning here is identical to *hupakoúō* (5219), to obey, which is the response commanded of children toward their parents (Eph 6:1; Col 3:20).

(C) In relation to the law of God: "Because the carnal mind is enmity against God: for it is not subject [*hupotássetai*, pres. mid. indic. 3d person sing.] to the law of God, neither indeed can be" (Rom 8:7). The law of God is spiritual, and since man is mere flesh (i.e., sinful, fallen), he cannot subject himself to it. The implication is that when man becomes spiritual, he is able to submit himself to God (Rom 8:5). The same attitude holds for a wife. If she recognizes the godly bond of marriage, it is easy for her to submit herself to her husband (*hupotássetai*). The *hupotagē* (5292), submission, is in response to a husband's love and the mystery of the bond of marriage (Eph 5:25, 32).

(D) In relation to the righteousness of God and Israel: "For they [Israel collectively], being ignorant of God's righteousness, and going about to establish their own righteousness, have not submitted themselves [*hupetágēsan*, aor. mid. indic. 3d person pl.] unto the righteousness of God" (Rom 10:3). They did not recognize that God's dealings with them were just and consequently they would not submit themselves to Him.

(E) In relation to government authorities (Rom 13:1, 5; Titus 3:1; 1 Pet 2:13), a Christian must place himself under their authority.

(F) In relation to submitting oneself to a true prophet: "And the spirits of the prophets are subject to the prophets" (1 Cor 14:32). When a person has the spirit of a prophet, discerning what constitutes true prophecy, the declaration of God's revelation, he will yield to other prophets who wish to speak in public worship.

(G) In relation to those ministering (1 Cor 16:15, 16).

(H) In relation to Christ by the Church (Eph 5:24).

(I) In relation to God the Father of spirits by the believers (Heb 12:9; James 4:7).

(J) In relation to masters by servants (Titus 2:9; 1 Pet 2:18).

(K) In relation to the older by the younger (1 Pet 5:5).

(L) In relation to Christ by angels, authorities and powers (1 Pet 3:22).

(III) Pass., to be subjugated without consent or willingness.

In the subjection of demons or evil spirits to the seventy disciples sent out by Jesus (Luke 10:17, 20), these disciples noted to Jesus the power they had over demons saying, "Lord, even the devils [*daimónia* {1140}, demons] are subject unto us through thy name." The verb used is *hupotássetai* (Luke 10:20). This is in the pres. pass. indic. form which indicates that the subjugation of demons or evil spirits was done by force in the name of Christ ("through thy name" [Luke 10:17]). In this sense the pass. form, *hupotássomai*, has the same meaning as *hupakoúō* (5219), to obey, as in Matt 8:27; Mark 1:27 referring to demons; 4:41; Luke 8:25 referring to the storm at sea.

Deriv.: *anupótaktos* (506), unsubdued; *hupotagē* (5292), submission, dependent position.

5294. ὑποτίθημι *hupotíthēmi*; fut. *hupothēsō*, from *hupó* (5259), and *títhēmi*

(5087), to place. To set or put under, lay under, support.

(I) Particularly with the acc. *tón tráchēlon* (5137), neck, to lay down one's neck meaning under the sword or axe of the executioner, to hazard one's life (Rom 16:4).

(II) Mid., *hupotíthemai*, to bring under the mind or notice of someone, suggest, put in mind of, as a teacher or otherwise, with the acc. and dat. (1 Tim 4:6).

Syn.: *hupobállō* (5260), to place under; *hupomimnḗskō* (5279), to suggest to the memory, put in mind.

Ant.: *kurieúō* (2961), to have dominion over; *ekpheúgō* (1628), to escape; *lanthánō* (2990), to escape notice, willfully forget; *epilanthánomai* (1950), to forget, neglect; *eklanthánomai* (1585), to completely forget.

5295. ὑποτρέχω *hupotréchō*; fut. *hupodramoúmai*, 2d aor. *hupédramon*, from *hupó* (5259), under, and *tréchō* (5143), to run. To run under. In the NT to run under the shelter of an island or coast; with the acc. as *hupopléō* (5284), to sail under (Acts 27:16).

5296. ὑποτύπωσις *hupotúpōsis*; gen. *hupotupṓseōs*, fem. noun from *hupotupóō* (n.f.), to draw a sketch or first draft as painters when they begin a picture. A delineation, sketch, concise representation or form (2 Tim 1:13); a pattern, example (1 Tim 1:16).

Syn.: *hupódeigma* (5262), copy, example, pattern; *hupogrammós* (5261), an underwriting, writing copy, example; *eikṓn* (1504), profile, resemblance, image.

5297. ὑποφέρω *hupophérō*; fut. *hupoísō*, aor. *hupénegka*, from *hupó* (5259), under, and *phérō* (5342), to bring, bear. To underpin, bear up from underneath, support, sustain. In the NT figuratively meaning to bear up under, endure evils (1 Cor 10:13; 2 Tim 3:11; 1 Pet 2:19; Sept.: Ps 69:8; Prov 18:14).

Syn.: *bastázō* (941), to support, bear; *anéchomai* (430), to hold up against

or to bear with; *makrothuméō* (3114), to be longsuffering toward people; *hupoménō* (5278), to abide under, endure; *karteréō* (2594), to be steadfast, patient; *kakopathéō* (2553), to suffer evil; *páschō* (3958), to suffer, endure hardness; *hupéchō* (5254), to hold under; *adikéomai* (91), to suffer injustice; *biázomai* (971), to suffer violence.

Ant.: *anapaúō* (373), to refresh, give inner rest; *anapsúchō* (404), to refresh; *katapaúō* (2664), to rest by ceasing from work; *hesucházō* (2270), to rest from labor; *epanapaúomai* (1879), to rest upon; *aníēmi* (447), to let up, loosen, refresh.

5298. ὑποχωρέω *hupochōréō*; contracted *hupochōrṓ*, fut. *hupochōrḗsō*, from *hupó* (5259), under, and *chōréō* (5562), to have, have place, room, to receive. To give place secretly, withdraw oneself under cover without noise or notice. Intrans. with *eis* (1519), to (Luke 9:10, He went aside or withdrew to a desert place); with *en* (1722), in (Luke 5:16; Sept.: Judg 20:37).

Syn.: *hupágō* (5217), to withdraw oneself; *apérchomai* (565), to go away; *anachōréō* (402), to withdraw; *ápeimi* (548), to be away; *apochōréō* (672), to go away from; *apobaínō* (576), to go out; *aphístēmi* (868), to depart; *apáirō* (522), to remove.

Ant.: *epanérchomai* (1880), to come back again; *paragínomai* (3854), to arrive.

5299. ὑπωπιάζω *hupōpiázō*; fut. *hupōpiásō*, from *hupṓpion* (n.f.), the part of the face which is under the eyes, the face, which is from *hupó* (5259), under, and *ōps* (n.f.), eye, face, countenance. To strike under the eyes, beat the face black and blue, give a black eye. In the NT generally to mistreat, trans. spoken of the body, to subject to hardship, mortify (1 Cor 9:27). Figuratively to weary with prayers, entreaties, to tire out someone, with the acc. (Luke 18:5).

Syn.: *kolaphízō* (2852), to strike with clenched hands, box with the fist; *kopiáō*

(2872), to grow weary, feel tired; *kámnō* (2577), to wax weary; *ekkakéō* (1573), to feel faint.

Ant.: *eupsuchéō* (2174), to cause to be encouraged; *parakaléō* (3870), to comfort; *paramuthéomai* (3888), soothe, console, encourage.

5300. ὗς *hús*; gen. *huós*, masc.-fem. noun. A hog, swine, or sow (2 Pet 2:22; Sept.: Deut 14:8).

Syn.: *choíros* (5519), a swine, pig.

5301. ὕσσωπος *hússōpos*; gen. *hussópou*, masc. noun. Hyssop, a low plant or shrub (Sept.: 1 Kgs 4:33). It was also the name among the Jews given to other similar aromatic plants as lavender, and especially origanum, found in great abundance around Mount Sinai. Hyssop was much used in the ritual purifications and sprinklings of the Jews (Sept.: Ex 12:22; Num 19:18; Ps 51:7). In the NT, a stalk or stem of hyssop (John 19:29), equivalent to *kálamos* (2563), a reed (Matt 27:48; Mark 15:36). A bunch of hyssop used for sprinkling (Heb 9:19 [cf. Sept.: Lev 14:4, 6, 49, 51, 52]).

5302. ὑστερέω *hysteréō*; contracted *hysteró*, fut. *hysterḗsō*, from *hústeros* (5306), last. To be last, behind, posterior in place or time. In the NT, figuratively of dignity, condition, strength and the like, to be behind, inferior, to lack. In later usage, also mid. deponent *hysteroúmai*, to lack.

(I) Of dignity, used in an absolute sense, meaning to be the worse (1 Cor 8:8). Followed by the gen. depending on the idea of comparison contained in the verb (2 Cor 11:5, behind the "super" apostles).

(II) Generally meaning to lack, fail.

(A) To fail in something, come short of, miss, not to reach, followed by the gen. expressed or implied (Rom 3:23, "all . . . come short of that glory which is from God" [a.t.], have failed to obtain the divine favor, fall short of the true recog-

nition of God; Heb 4:1). Followed by *apó* (575), from, with the gen. (Heb 12:15).

(B) To want, be without, lack. Followed by the gen. (Luke 22:35); by *en* (1722), in, with the dat. of that in which one is wanting (1 Cor 1:7); by the acc. of thing, meaning as to which (Matt 19:20; Mark 10:21, "what lack I yet?"; Sept.: Ps 23:1; 39:5). Used in an absolute sense, meaning to be in want, suffer need (Luke 15:14; 2 Cor 11:9; Phil 4:12; Heb 11:37).

(C) Intrans. of things, to fail, be lacking, wanting, used in an absolute sense (Matt 19:20; John 2:3).

Deriv.: *hustérēma* (5303), need, want; *hustérēsis* (5304), need.

Syn.: *déomai* (1189), to recognize one's need and beg; *aporéō* (639), to be without means; *leípō* (3007), to fall short, be destitute; *elattonéō* (1641), to have less; *chrḗzō* (5535), to need; *échō anágkēn* (*échō* [2192], to have; *anágkē* [318], need), to have need.

Ant.: *perisseúō* (4052), to abound; *huperperisseúō* (5248) and *huperpleonázō* (5250), to abound exceedingly; *pleonázō* (4121), to superabound; *plēthúnō* (4129), increase, multiply; *huperbállō* (5235), to exceed, excel; *euporéō* (2141), to be well off; *akmázō* (187), to be fully ripe; *gémō* (1073), to be full.

5303. ὑστέρημα *hustérēma*; gen. *hustérēmatos*, neut. noun from *hysteréō* (5302), to lack, fall behind. That which is wanting, want, lack.

(I) Generally following a gen. of thing (Phil 2:30; 1 Cor 16:17 [implied]; Col 1:24, "what is yet lacking of afflictions for Christ" [a.t.]; 1 Thess 3:10; Sept.: Judg 18:10; 19:19, 20; Ps 3:10 [not followed by the gen.]).

(II) Used in an absolute sense or with the gen. of person, meaning want, need, poverty (Mark 12:44 [UBS]; Luke 21:4; 2 Cor 8:13, 14; 9:12; 11:9).

Syn.: *chreía* (5532), need, lack; *hustérēsis* (5304), the act of lacking; *aporía* (640), a state of perplexity, need; *anágkē* (318), need.

Ant.: *hadrótēs* (100), abundance, bountifulness; *perisseía* (4050), superfluity, abundance; *perísseuma* (4051), surplus; *huperochḗ* (5247), prominence; *huperbolḗ* (5236), abundance, that which is beyond measure; *euporía* (2142), abundance of resources; *plēsmonḗ* (4140), a filling up; *plḗrōma* (4138), that which fills up, fullness.

5304. ὑστέρησις *hustérēsis*; gen. *hustGřēseōV*, fem. noun from *husteréō* (5302), to lack. Being in want, need, poverty, the state of being in need (Mark 12:44 [TR]; Phil 4:11).

5305. ὕστερον *hústeron*; adv. from *hústeros* (5306), a later one. Later.
   (I) Followed by the gen. meaning last, after (Matt 22:27; Luke 20:32, last of all; Sept.: Jer 31:19).
   (II) Used in an absolute sense meaning at last, afterwards (Matt 4:2; 21:29, 32, 37; 25:11; 26:60; Mark 16:14; Luke 4:2; John 13:36; Heb 12:11; Sept.: Prov 5:4).

5306. ὕστερος *hústeros*; fem. *hustéra*, neut. *hústeron*, adj. Latter, terminal, last, hindmost. In the NT, only of time. Generally (1 Tim 4:1, "in the latter times," [cf. *éschatos* {2078}, last {see II, B}]; Sept.: 1 Chr 29:29).
   Deriv.: *husteréō* (5302), to be last, behind.
   Syn.: *metépeita* (3347), afterwards; *ópisthen* (3693), following, after.
   Ant.: *próteros* (4387), former; *prṓtos* (4413), first; *archaíos* (744), original, ancient, first descendant; *palaiós* (3820), old, but not necessarily original.

5307. ὑφαντός *huphantós*; fem. *huphantḗ*, neut. *huphantón*, adj. from *huphaínō* (n.f.), to weave. Woven (John 19:23).

5308. ὑψηλός *hupsēlós*; fem. *hupsēlḗ*, neut. *hupsēlón*, adj. from *húpsos* (5311), height, elevation. High, elevated, lofty.
   (I) Particularly of a mountain (Matt 4:8; 17:1; Mark 9:2; Luke 4:5; Rev 21:10; Sept.: Gen 7:19; Isa 2:14; Ezek 20:28);

a wall (Rev 21:12). In the pl., high places, heights, highest heavens (Heb 1:3 [cf. *ouranós* {3772}, IV, B]; Sept.: Ps 93:4; Isa 33:5). In a similar sense, of Christ being made higher than the heavens meaning exalted above the heavens (Heb 7:26 [cf. Eph 4:10]). Symbolically (Acts 13:17, "with a high arm" [a.t.], meaning an arm uplifted as if about to destroy the enemy, thus emblematic of threatening might; Sept.: Ex 6:6; Deut 4:34; Ezek 20:33, 34 [cf. Ex 14:8; Num 33:3]). For the force of the figure see Isa 5:25; 9:11, 12; 14:26.
   (II) Figuratively meaning high, highly esteemed, regarded with pride (Luke 16:15; Rom 12:16, "high things" [a.t.], pride, opposed to *tapeinoís*, dat. pl. of *tapeinós* [5011], low things, implying humility; Sept.: 1 Sam 2:3 [cf. Eccl 7:8; Isa 9:8]).
   Deriv.: *hupsēlophronéō* (5309), to be proud, arrogant.
   Syn.: *húpsistos* (5310), the highest; *ákron* (206), the extremity.
   Ant.: *tapeinós* (5011), base, low; *chamaí* (5476), earthward, on the ground.

5309. ὑψηλοφρονέω *hupsēlophronéō*; contracted *hupsēlophronṓ*, fut. *hupsēlophronḗsō*, from *hupsēlós* (5308), high, and *phronéō* (5426), to think. To be highminded, proud, arrogant. Intrans. (Rom 11:20; 1 Tim 6:17 [cf. Rom 12:16]).
   Syn.: *tuphóō* (5187), to inflate, puff up, be conceited; *huperupsóomai* (5251), to elevate oneself above others; *huperphronéō* (5252), to think oneself highly; *huperéchō* (5242), to hold oneself highly; *huperaíromai* (5229), to be haughty, exalt oneself; *huperbaínō* (5233), to transcend, go beyond; *huperbállō* (5235), to surpass.
   Ant.: *tapeinóō* (5013), to humble.

5310. ὕψιστος *húpsistos*; fem. *hupsístē*, neut. *húpsiston*, adj., the superlative of *húpsos* (5311), height. Highest, most elevated, loftiest.
   (I) In the NT in the neut. pl., *tá húpsista*, the highest places, heights, as used for the highest heavens (cf. *ouranós*

[3772, IV, B]; Matt 21:9; Mark 11:10; Luke 2:14; 19:38; Sept.: Job 16:19; Ps 71:19).

(II) Figuratively, with the def. art., *ho húpsistos*, the Most High, spoken of God as dwelling in the highest heavens and as far exalted above all other things (see *ouranós* [3772, IV]; Mark 5:7; Luke 1:32, 35, 76; 6:35; 8:28; Acts 7:48; 16:17; Heb 7:1; Sept.: Deut 32:8; 2 Sam 22:14; Ps 9:3; 21:8; Dan 4:14, 21; 7:25).

Ant.: *eláchistos* (1646), the least.

5311. ὕψος *húpsos*; gen. *húpsous*, neut. noun from *húpsi* (n.f.), high, aloft. Height, elevation.

(I) Particularly (Rev 21:16; Sept.: Gen 6:15; 1 Sam 17:4). The height on high as used for heaven, meaning the highest heaven, the abode of God (cf. *ouranós* [3772], IV). *Ex húpsous* (*ex* [1537], from), from on high, from God (Luke 1:78; 24:49); *eis húpsos* (*eis* [1519], to), to on high, to God (Eph 4:8 quoted from Ps 68:18; see Ps 18:16; 144:7).

(II) Figuratively, meaning elevation, dignity (Eph 3:18; James 1:9; Sept.: 2 Chr 1:1; 17:12; Job 5:11).

Deriv.: *hupsēlós* (5308), high, lofty; *hupsóō* (5312), to lift up, exalt.

Ant.: *báthos* (899), depth.

5312. ὑψόω *hupsóō*; contracted *hupsó*, fut. *hupsósō*, from *húpsos* (5311), height. To heighten, raise high, elevate, lift up. Trans.:

(I) Particularly of the brazen serpent and also of Jesus on the cross (John 3:14; 8:28; Sept.: of water, Gen 7:17; of a wall, 2 Chr 33:14; of hands, Dan 12:7). Hence Jesus is further said to be lifted up from the earth and exalted to heaven (with allusion to His death on the cross John 12:32, 34); exalted to the right hand of God.

(II) Figuratively to elevate, exalt (Acts 2:33; 5:31 [cf. Heb 7:26]). See Mark 16:19; Heb 1:3; 8:1; 12:2; 1 Pet 3:22.

(A) Generally to raise to a condition of prosperity, dignity, honor (Luke 1:52; Acts 13:17; 2 Cor 11:7; James 4:10; 1 Pet 5:6). In the aor. pass. indic. *hupsōthésetai* (Matt 23:12); fem. aor. pass. part., *hupsōtheisa* (Matt 11:23; Luke 10:15, "exalted to heaven" [a.t.], either in external prosperity or more especially in respect to the privileges of the gospel, as the abode of the Lord Jesus [cf. *Kapernaoúm* {2584}, Capernaum; also *ouranós* {3772, I}; Luke 14:11; 18:14 [see Sept.: Josh 3:7; 1 Kgs 14:7; Job 36:7; Isa 28:29; pass. Num 24:7]).

(B) Reflexively, *hupsóō heautón* (1438), himself, meaning to exalt oneself, be proud, arrogant (Matt 23:12; pass., Luke 14:11; 18:14; Sept.: pass. or mid. 2 Chr 26:16; Ps 131:1; Prov 18:12; Isa 3:16.

Deriv.: *húpsōma* (5313), height; *huperupsóō* (5251), to raise high aloft.

Syn.: *aírō* (142), to lift; *epaírō* (1869), to lift up; *huperaírō* (5229), to exalt exceedingly.

Ant.: *tapeinóō* (5013), to humble.

5313. ὕψωμα *húpsōma*; gen. *hupsómatos*, neut. noun from *hupsóō* (5312), height. Something made high, elevated, a high place, height, elevation (Rom 8:39). Figuratively of a proud adversary, a lofty tower or fortress built up proudly by the enemy (2 Cor 10:5). Pride (Sept.: Job 24:24).

Ant.: *báthos* (899), depth.

5314. φάγος phágos; gen. *phágou*, masc. noun from *phágō* (5315), to eat. A glutton, an excessive or intemperate eater. Used as an accusation against Jesus by His enemies in Matt 11:19, "The Son of man came eating [*esthíōn*, pres. act. part. of *esthíō* {2068}] and drinking [*pínōn*, pres. act. part. of *pínō* {4095}], and they say, Behold a man gluttonous, and a wine bibber [*oinopótēs* {3630}], a friend [*phílos* {5384}] of publicans and sinners." See Luke 7:34. The fact of the matter was that Jesus ate, drank wine, and was sociable without any sacrifice of principle and thus was accused of gluttony, drunkenness, and compromising with the sins of notorious evildoers. In this passage of Matt 11:16–19, the Lord accused His generation of totally misunderstanding John the Baptist who lived sacrificially and managed without that which others felt was necessary. He also accused them of not understanding Himself for His behavior which was socially acceptable.

Ant.: *néstis* (3523), an abstainer from food.

5315. φάγω phágō; fut. *phágomai*, 2d aor. *éphagon*. To eat. Used to supply various tenses for *esthíō* (2068), to eat.

(**I**) To eat (Matt 6:25, 31; 26:17, 26; John 6:31; 1 Cor 11:21; Heb 13:10).

(**II**) To eat away, corrode (James 5:3, where *phágetai* is a 2d fut. mid. 3d person sing. for *phageítai*); also *phágesai* in Luke 17:8 is the 2d person sing. of the same tense for *phágē*, "thou shalt eat."

(**III**) Spiritually to feed by faith and be sustained in a spiritual and eternal life (John 6:50, 51, 53).

Deriv.: *kataphágō* (2719), to devour; *prosphágion* (4371), that which is eaten with bread; *phágos* (5314), glutton.

Syn.: *esthíō* (2068) and *trṓgō* (5176), to eat; *sunesthíō* (4906), to eat together or with; *geúomai* (1089), to taste, eat; *metalambánō* (3335), to participate, eat.

Ant.: *nēsteúō* (3522), to fast; *néphō* (3525), to be discreet, sober; *sōphronéō* (4993), to be of sound mind; *apéchō* (568), to keep oneself away; *pheídomai* (5339), to abstain; *aphístēmi* (868), to desist.

5316. φαίνω phaínō; fut. *phanṓ*, 2d aor. pass. *ephánēn*, from *phṓs* (5457), light. To give light, illuminate.

(**I**) Intrans. to shine or give light, shine forth as a luminous body (2 Pet 1:19; Rev 1:16; 8:12; 21:23; Sept.: Gen 1:17); of spiritual light and truth (John 1:5; 5:35; 1 John 2:8).

(**II**) Trans. in the mid. / pass., *phaínomai*, to appear, be conspicuous, become visible, shine.

(**A**) Strictly with the meaning to shine forth, shine. With *en* (1722), in, indicating place (Rev 18:23). Figuratively (Phil 2:15; Sept.: Isa 60:2).

(**B**) Generally to appear, be seen, followed by the dat. of person expressed or implied. (**1**) Of persons (Matt 1:20; 2:13, 19; Mark 16:9; Sept.: Num 23:3). With a part. or adj. as predicate in the nom. (Matt 6:16, 18; 23:28; 2 Cor 13:7). With the part. implied (Matt 6:5). Used in an absolute sense meaning to appear, make an appearance (Luke 9:8; 1 Pet 4:18). (**2**) Of things (Matt 13:26); an event (Matt 9:33). With the pass. part. and the pl. def. art. *tá phainómena*, things visible, apparent to the senses (Heb 11:3 [with a predicate see I above]; Matt 23:27; Rom 7:13). Especially of things appearing in the sky or air, meaning phenomena (Matt 2:7; 24:27, 30; James 4:14).

(**C**) Figuratively as referring to the mental eye, to appear, seem, followed by the dat. of person with predicate (Mark

14:64); by *enṓpion* (1799), in the face of, before, and the gen. (Luke 24:11).

Deriv.: *anaphaínō* (398), to be shown or appear openly, to show openly; *aphanḗs* (852), hidden, concealed; *áphantos* (855), invisible; *epiphaínō* (2014), to shine over or upon, to give light, in the pass. to appear; *sukophantéō* (4811), to be an informer; *huperḗphanos* (5244), one who is conspicuous; *phanerós* (5318), apparent, manifest; *phanós* (5322), lantern; *phantázō* (5324), to cause to appear.

Syn.: *lámpō* (2989), to shine; *perilámpō* (4034), to shine around; *eklámpō* (1584), to shine forth; *periastráptō* (4015), to shine round about; *astráptō* (797), to shine forth like lightning; *stílbō* (4744), to glitter; *augázō* (826), to irradiate.

Ant.: *krúptō* (2928), to cover, conceal; *katakalúptō* (2619), to cover completely; *kalúptō* (2572), to cover up; *parakalúptō* (3871), to cover with a veil; *sugkalúptō* (4780), to cover together; *lanthánō* (2990), to escape notice; *epikalúptō* (1943), to cover up or over; *perikalúptō* (4028), to cover around.

5317. Φάλεκ Phálek; masc. proper noun transliterated from the Hebr. *Peleg* (6389, OT), division. Peleg (Luke 3:35), the son of Eber and fourth in descent from Shem (see Gen 11:16f.).

5318. φανερός phanerós; fem. *phanerá*, neut. *phanerón*, adj. from *phaínō* (5316), to shine, to make to shine or to cause to appear. Apparent, manifest, plain (Rom 1:19; Gal 5:19; 1 Tim 4:15; 1 John 3:10); with the idea of being known (Matt 12:16; Mark 3:12; 4:22; Luke 8:17; Acts 4:16; 7:13; Phil 1:13); in the sense of being public, open (Matt 6:4, 6, 18 [TR]; 1 Cor 3:13; 11:19; 14:25); eminent (Mark 6:14); to seem to be something, as in the expression *en tṓ phanerṓ* (*en* [1722], in; *tṓ* [3588], the; *phanerṓ*, appearance or outward show) (Rom 2:28).

Deriv.: *phaneróō* (5319), to make manifest or known, show; *phanerṓs* (5320), apparently.

Syn.: *emphanḗs* (1717), manifest; *ékdēlos* (1552), wholly evident, manifest; *gnōstós* (1110), known; *dḗlos* (1212), evident; *pródēlos* (4271), evident, manifest beforehand, clearly evident; *katádēlos* (2612), quite manifest, evident; *éxōthen* (1855), outward; *dēmósios* (1219), public, open.

Ant.: *ádēlos* (82), hidden, uncertain, indistinct; *kruptós* (2927), secret, hidden; *apókruphos* (614), kept hidden, secret; *ésō* (2080), inward; *ésōthen* (2081), inward, within, from within; *aphanḗs* (852), not manifest.

5319. φανερόω phaneróō; contracted *phanerṓ*, fut. *phanerṓsō*, from *phanerós* (5318), manifest, visible, conspicuous. To make apparent, manifest, known, show openly. Trans.:

(I) Of things with the acc. (John 2:11; 1 Cor 4:5; 2 Cor 2:14; Col 4:4; Titus 1:3). With the acc. and dat. (John 17:6; Rom 1:19). In the pass. (Mark 4:22; John 3:21; 9:3; Rom 3:21; 16:26; 2 Cor 7:12; Eph 5:13, "whatever makes manifest is itself light" [a.t.]; 2 Tim 1:10; Heb 9:8; 1 John 3:2; 4:9; Rev 3:18; 15:4). In the body (2 Cor 4:10, 11); with the dat. (Col 1:26; Sept.: Jer 33:6).

(II) Of persons.

(A) Reflexively with *heautón* (acc. of *heautós* [1438]), himself, or the mid. *phaneroúmai*, aor. pass. *ephanerṓthēn* as mid., to manifest oneself, show oneself openly, appear; with the dat. (John 7:4, "show thyself to the world," appear publicly; 21:1). Mid. with *émprosthen* (1715), before, followed by the gen., meaning something or someone (2 Cor 5:10); with the dat. (John 21:14; 1 John 1:2). See Mark 16:12, 14. Used in an absolute sense (Col 3:4; 1 Tim 3:16; Heb 9:26; 1 Pet 1:20; 5:4; 1 John 1:2, Christ as the Source of eternal life; 2:28; 3:2, 5, 8).

(B) In the pass. to be manifested, become or be made manifest, known. With the dat. (John 1:31; 2 Cor 5:11); with *en* (1722), in, with the dat. (John 9:3;

with *hóti* (3754), that (2 Cor 3:3; 1 John 2:19).

Deriv.: *phanérōsis* (5321), manifestation, making known.

Syn.: *gnōrízō* (1107), to make known; *diagnōrízō* (1232), to make fully known, reassert; *anaggéllō* (312) and *apaggéllō* (518), to announce or report; *diaggéllō* (1229), to announce throughout; *kataggéllō* (2605) and *phrázō* (5419), to declare; *dēlóō* (1213), to make plain; *emphanízō* (1718), to declare plainly, make manifest; *apokalúptō* (601), to reveal.

Ant.: *krúptō* (2928), to cover, conceal.

5320. φανερῶς *phaneros*; adv. from *phanerós* (5318), apparent, manifest. Apparently, manifestly, plainly (Acts 10:3). Apparently, openly (Mark 1:45; John 7:10).

Syn.: *parrēsía* (3954), openly, with boldness.

Ant.: *kruphḗ* (2931), secretly; *láthra* (2977), privately, secretly; *kat' idían* (*kat'* [2596], according to; *idían* [2398], alone), privately.

5321. φανέρωσις *phanérōsis*; gen. *phanerōseōs*, fem. noun from *phaneróō* (5319), to make manifest. A manifestation, a making visible or observable (1 Cor 12:7; 2 Cor 4:2).

Syn.: *apokálupsis* (602), revelation.

Ant.: *mustḗrion* (3466), a mystery.

5322. φανός *phanós*; gen. *phanoú*, masc. noun from *phaínō* (5316), to shine. Lantern. It appears in John 18:3 in the pl. with *lampádes* (sing. *lampás* [2985]), translated "torches." *Phanós* was a lantern which showed the way as people traveled at night, but *lampás* was a large and bright burning lamp which distinguished the surrounding elements. When Jesus was arrested, the lanterns were not considered enough, thus brighter, larger torches were brought so that the identity of Jesus Christ might not be mistaken.

The use of *phanós* is functional from *phaínō* (5316), to throw light upon and consequently to make it visible. Its meaning is something that makes things visible. In Class. Gr. writers, it meant a torch made of a vine or twigs to distinguish it from *lúchnos*, a lamp which involved the use of oil.

Syn.: *lúchnos* (3088), a portable lamp usually set on a stand.

5323. Φανουήλ *Phanouḗl*; masc. proper noun transliterated from the Hebr. *P^enū'ēl* (6439, OT), face of God. Phanuel, the father of Anna (Luke 2:36).

5324. φαντάζω *phantázō*; fut. *phantásō*, from *phaínō* (5316), to shine. To cause to appear. The pass. *phantázomai*, to appear, be seen, be visible; the neut. part. as a noun, *tó phantazómenon*, that which appears or appeared, the appearance, sight, found only in Heb 12:21 and meaning that which appeared.

Deriv.: *phantasía* (5325), a show, pomp, splendor; *phántasma* (5326), an apparition.

Syn.: *dokéō* (1380), to recognize, think.

5325. φαντασία *phantasía*; gen. *phantasías*, fem. noun from *phantázō* (5324), to make to appear. An appearing, show, pomp, splendor (Acts 25:23 referring to the splendid show which King Agrippa and his sister Bernice made in the very city where their father had so dreadfully perished for his pride [cf. Acts 12:19, 21–23]; see Sept.: Zech 10:1). The Eng. "fantasy" is derived from this word. See Hab 2:18, 19.

Syn.: *pneúma* (4151), spirit; *skiá* (4639), shadow; *ónar* (3677), dream; *optasía* (3701), vision; *phántasma* (5326), a phantom, apparition; *enúpnion* (1798), dream; *ópsis* (3799), appearance, sight, countenance.

Ant.: *ousía* (3776), substance; *hupóstasis* (5287), essence, substance.

5326. φάντασμα phántasma; gen. *phantásmatos*, neut. noun from *phantázō* (5324), to make to appear. An apparition, a specter, a spirit, or a phantom (Matt 14:26; Mark 6:49).

5327. φάραγξ pháragx; gen. *pháraggos*, fem. noun. A break in the earth, a precipice, a deep and broken valley, a gorge (Luke 3:5 quoted from Isa 40:4; Sept.: Gen 26:17; Deut 2:24; Josh 15:8; Isa 8:7; 22:1).

Syn.: *chásma* (5490), a chasm, gulf; *krēmnós* (2911), precipice, steep place.

Ant.: *pedinós* (3977), level, plain.

5328. Φαραώ Pharaó; masc. proper noun, transliterated from the Hebr. *Parᵉ'ōh* (6547, OT). Pharaoh, the king, a common title of the Egyptian kings down to the time of the Persian invasion, and often used like a proper noun (Acts 7:10, 13, 21; Rom 9:17; Heb 11:24).

5329. Φαρές Pharés; masc. proper noun, transliterated from the Hebr. *Perets* (6557, OT), breach. Phares, one of the sons of Judah by Tamar (Matt 1:3; Luke 3:33 [cf. Gen chap. 38]).

5330. Φαρισαῖος Pharisaíos; gen. *Pharisaíou*, transliterated from the Hebr. A Pharisee.

(I) After the resettling of the Jewish people in Judea on their return from the Babylonian captivity, there were two religious groups among them. One party contented themselves with following only what was written in the Law of Moses. These were called Zadikim, the righteous. The other group added the constitutions and traditions of the elders, as well as other rigorous observances, to the Law and voluntarily complied with them. They were called Chasidim or the pious. From the Zadikim the sects of the Sadducees and Karaites were derived. From the Chasidim were derived the Pharisees and the Essenes.

In I Mac. 2:42, among the persons who joined Mattathias against Antiochus IV (Epiphanes), about 167 B.C., are named the Asideans (*Asidaíoi*), who are described as voluntarily devoted to the law. The Asideans are mentioned also in I Mac. 7:13; II Mac. 14:6.

(II) In the time of our Lord, the Pharisees were the separatists of their day, as well as the principal sect among the Jews. However, *pharisaíos* may have been a title ascribed to the Pharisees by their enemies since the Pharisees called themselves "Haberim" (from the Aramaic word meaning associate).

The Pharisees considered themselves much holier than the common people (Luke 18:11, 12). They wore special garments to distinguish themselves from others.

(III) The principal tenets of the Pharisees were in opposition to those of the Sadducees, and the former group maintained the existence of angels and spirits and the doctrine of the resurrection (Acts 23:8), which the latter party denied (Matt 22:23; Mark 12:18; Luke 20:27). The Pharisees made everything dependent upon God and fate (Josephus, *The Jewish Wars*, ii.8.14). However, they did not deny the role of the human will in affecting events (Josephus, *Antiquities*, xviii.1.3).

(IV) The Pharisees distinguished themselves with their zeal for the traditions of the elders, which they taught was derived from the same fountain as the written Word itself, claiming both to have been delivered to Moses on Mount Sinai (Matt 15:1–6; Mark 7:3–5). See also *parádosis* (3862), tradition, and *éntalma* (1778), a religious precept versus *entolé* (1785), commandment.

(V) In the NT, Jesus is often represented as the one denouncing the great body of the Pharisees for their hypocrisy and profligacy (Matt 23:13ff.; Luke 16:14). Yet there were doubtless exceptions, and some of them appear to have been men of probity and even of genuine piety.

5331. φαρμακεία *pharmakeía*; gen. *pharmakeías*, fem. noun from *phármakon* (n.f.), a drug, which in the Gr. writers is used both for a curative or medicinal drug, and also as a poisonous one. *Pharmakeía* means the occult, sorcery, witchcraft, illicit pharmaceuticals, trance, magical incantation with drugs (Gal 5:20; Rev 9:21; 18:23; Sept.: Ex 7:22; Isa 47:9, 12).

Syn.: *mageía* (3095), magic.

5332. φαρμακεύς *pharmakeús*; gen. *pharmakéōs*, masc. noun from *phármakeúō* (n.f.), to administer a drug. An enchanter with drugs, a sorcerer (Rev 21:8 [TR]).

Syn.: *pharmakós* (5333), a magician, sorcerer, enchanter.

5333. φαρμακός *pharmakós*; gen. *pharmakoú*, masc. noun. A magician, sorcerer, enchanter (Rev 21:8 [UBS]; 22:15; Sept.: Ex 7:11; 9:11; Deut 18:10; Dan 2:2). The same as *pharmakeús* (5332). The noun *pharmakeía* (5331) means the preparing and giving of medicine, and in the NT, sorcery, enchantment.

5334. φάσις *phásis*; gen. *pháseōs*, fem. noun from *phēmí* (5346), to speak, say. Information, used as a legal term and meaning private information on crimes in progress, as in Acts 21:31. This is the word from which the Eng. "phase" is derived.

Syn.: *lógos* (3056), word, information.

5335. φάσκω *pháskō*; imperf. *éphaskon*. Used to supply the imperfect for *phēmí* (5346), to affirm, say. To assert, affirm, say (Acts 24:9; 25:19; Rev 2:2). Followed by inf. (Rom 1:22; Sept.: Gen 26:20).

Syn.: *légō* (3004), to speak; *eréō* (2046), to declare, promise; *laléō* (2980), to utter; *rhéō* (4483), to say, speak, speak of.

Ant.: *sigáō* (4601), to be silent; *siōpáō* (4623), to be mute.

5336. φάτνη *phátnē*; gen. *phátnēs*, fem. noun. A manger or crib at which cattle are fed (Luke 2:7, 12, 16; 13:15; Sept.: Job 39:9; Isa 1:3). In Luke 13:15 it is rendered "stall," as the word is also sometimes used in the Gr. writers. Some ancient writers believe that Jesus was born in a stable formed by nature and not constructed by man. When Joseph found no room to lodge in Bethlehem, he lodged in a certain cave near the village. While they were there, Mary brought forth Christ, and laid Him in a manger.

5337. φαῦλος *phaúlos*; fem. *phaúlē*, neut. *phaúlon*, adj. Vile, evil, wicked, foul, corrupt, good-for-nothing, depraved, worthless, mediocre, unimportant. In the NT, used of evil deeds (John 3:20; 5:29; James 3:16), statements (Titus 2:8). See Sept.: Prov 22:8.

Syn.: *kakós* (2556), bad, *ponērós* (4190), malevolent.

Ant.: *kalós* (2570), good; *agathós* (18), good, benevolent.

5338. φέγγος *phéggos*; gen. *phéggous*, neut. noun. Light or brilliance. Used of the moon or other luminaries of the sky (Matt 24:29; Mark 13:24 [cf. Isa 13:10]; a lamp, Luke 11:33 [TR]; Sept.: for the stars, Joel 2:10; the sun, 2 Sam 23:4).

Syn.: *phōstḗr* (5458), luminary, light, light-giving; *phōtismós* (5462), an illumination, light; *lúchnos* (3088), a portable lamp; *lampás* (2985), a torch.

Ant.: *skotía* (4653) and *skótos* (4655), darkness; *zóphos* (2217), gloom, darkness.

5339. φείδομαι *pheídomai*; fut. *pheísomai*, mid. deponent.

(I) Governing a gen., to spare, treat with tenderness (Acts 20:29; Rom 8:32 [cf. Sept: Gen 22:12]; 1 Cor 7:28; 2 Cor 1:23). To avoid, spare, or refrain.

(II) To spare, as implying forgiveness, either with a gen. following (Rom 11:21; 2 Pet 2:4, 5) or in an absolute sense (2 Cor 13:2).

(III) To forbear, abstain (2 Cor 12:6).

Deriv.: *pheidoménōs* (5340), sparingly, stingily.

Syn.: *anéchomai* (430), to endure, forbear; *apéchomai* (567), to refrain, abstain.

5340. φειδομένως *pheidoménōs*; adv. from *pheídomai* (5339), to spare, forbear. Sparingly, not plentifully (2 Cor 9:6).

Syn.: *metríōs* (3357), moderately, in measure, slightly.

Ant.: *perissós* (4057), exceedingly; *perissotérōs* (4056), more abundantly; *huperperissós* (5249), exceeding abundantly; *huperballóntōs* (5234), above measure; *plousíōs* (4146), richly, abundantly.

5341. φελόνης *phelónēs*, **φαιλόνης** *phailónēs*; gen. *phelónou*, masc. noun. A garment (*énduma* [1742]), although some have thought it to be a case where Paul's books were kept (2 Tim 4:13). The evidence is for the meaning of a cloak, a waistcoat, or an undergarment to protect the body from the wind. We arrive at this meaning since in the same verse the books and the parchments are mentioned.

Syn.: *himátion* (2440), an outer cloak or cape; *himatismós* (2441), clothing, apparel; *chlamús* (5511), a military cloak worn over the *chitón* by emperors, kings, magistrates, military officers; *stolé* (4749), a stately robe or uniform, a long gown worn as mark of dignity; *katastolé* (2689), long robe of dignity; *esthḗs* (2066) and *ésthēsis* (2067), clothing; *énduma* (1742), a garment of any kind; *ependútēs* (1903), an upper or outer garment which sometimes fishermen wore when at work; *phelónēs* (5341), a mantle, traveling robe for protection against stormy weather, overcoat; *peribólaion* (4018), a wrap or cape, a garment thrown around one; *podḗrēs* (4158), an outer garment reaching to the feet; *sképasma* (4629), a covering, raiment.

5342. φέρω *phérō*; fut. *oísō*, aor. *ḗnegka*, aor. pass. *ēnéchthēn*, obsolete form *oíō* (3634a), to bring, carry. To bear, bring.

(I) Particularly to bear as a burden, bear up, have or take upon oneself. In the NT, only figuratively.

(A) To bear up under or with, to endure, e.g., evils, with the acc. (Rom 9:22; Heb 12:20; 13:13; Sept.: Gen 36:7; Deut 1:12; Ezek 34:29; 36:15).

(B) To bear up something, uphold, have in charge, to direct, govern, with the acc. (Heb 1:3; Sept.: Num 11:14; Deut 1:9).

(II) To bear with the idea of motion, bear along or about, carry (Luke 23:26; Sept.: Isa 30:6). In the pass. *phéromai*, to be borne along, as in a ship before the wind, be driven (Acts 27:15, 17). Figuratively to be moved, incited (2 Pet 1:21; Sept.: Job 17:1). In the mid. part., *pheroménēs*, to bear oneself along, move along, rush as a wind (Acts 2:2). Figuratively to go on, advance in teaching (Heb 6:1).

(III) To bear, with the idea of motion to a place, bear hither or thither, to bring.

(A) Used of things, with the acc. expressed or implied. Generally (Mark 6:28; Luke 24:1; John 19:39; Acts 4:34, 37; 5:2; 2 Tim 4:13); followed by *apó* (575), from, partitively (John 21:10). In the pass. (Matt 14:11; Mark 6:27). Also with the dat. of person (Mark 12:15, 16; John 2:8; 4:33); with *hṓde* (5602), hither, as an additive (Matt 14:18); followed by *eis* (1519), unto, with the acc. of place (Rev 21:24, 26; Sept.: 1 Sam 31:12). Spoken of the finger or hand, to reach hither (John 20:27; Sept.: Gen 43:12); with the dat. (Sept.: Gen 27:14, 17). Figuratively of a voice or declaration, in the pass., to be borne, brought, to come (2 Pet 1:17, 18); of good brought to or bestowed on someone, in the pass. with the dat. (1 Pet 1:13); of accusations, charges, to bring forward, present, followed by *katá* (2596), against (John 18:29; Acts 25:7; 2 Pet 2:11); of a doctrine, prophecy, to announce, make known (2 Pet 1:21, "the prophecy"; 2 John 1:10, the doctrine). Of a fact or event as reported or testified, to adduce, show, prove (Heb 9:16, in the pass.).

(B) Used of persons, with the acc., to bear, bring, e.g., the sick (Mark 2:3; Luke 5:18; Acts 5:16); followed by the dat. (Matt 17:17; Mark 7:32; 8:22); with *prós* (4314), toward, and the acc. (Mark 1:32; 9:17, 19, 20). Spoken of any motion to a place not proceeding from the person himself, to bring, lead, with the acc. and *epí* (1909), upon (Mark 15:22); with *hópou* (3699), where (John 21:18); of beasts (Luke 15:23; Acts 14:13; Sept.: Neh 12:27). Used figuratively and in an absolute sense, a way or gate is said to lead somewhere (Acts 12:10).

(IV) To bear as trees or fields bear their fruits, to yield fruit (Mark 4:8; John 12:24; 15:2, 4, 5, 8, 16; Sept.: Ezek 17:8; Joel 2:22).

Deriv.: *anaphérō* (399), to lead or take up, offer up; *apophérō* (667), to carry away; *diaphérō* (1308), to bear through, differ; *eisphérō* (1533), to bring to or into; *ekphérō* (1627), to carry something out, to carry out to burial; *epiphérō* (2018), to bring, carry to, inflict; *thanatēphóros* (2287), deadly; *karpophóros* (2593), fruitful; *kataphérō* (2702), to bring down; *paraphérō* (3911), to bear along, carry off; *periphérō* (4064), to carry about or around; *prosphérō* (4374), to bring to or before, to offer; *prophérō* (4393), bring forth, produce; *sumphérō* (4851), to bear together, contribute; *telesphoréō* (5052), to bring to an intended perfection or goal; *tropophoréō* (5159), mode or style, deportment, character; *hupophérō* (5297), to bear up under, endure; *phoréō* (5409), to have a burden, bear; *phóros* (5411), a tax; *phórtos* (5414), the freight of a ship.

Syn.: *bastázō* (941), to bear, take up, carry; *paréchō* (3930), to offer, furnish, supply; *tíktō* (5088), *apokuéō* (616), and *gennáō* (1080), to bring forth, give birth to, beget.

Ant.: *harpázō* (726), to seize, take; *aphairéō* (851), to take away.

5343. φεύγω *pheúgō*; fut. *pheúxomai*, 2d aor. *éphugon*. To escape, flee from. Particularly and generally.

(I) To flee, to run or move hastily from danger because of fear (Matt 26:56; Mark 5:14; 14:50, 52; 16:8; Luke 8:34; John 10:5, 12, 13; Sept.: Gen 14:10; Jer 50:16). Followed by *ek* (1537), out of, from (Acts 27:30; Sept.: Jer 51:6); by *eis* (1519), with the acc. (Matt 2:13; 10:23; Mark 13:14; Luke 21:21); by *epí* (1909), upon (Matt 24:16; Sept.: Gen 39:12; Ex 14:5; Josh 10:16); with *apó* (575), from (Sept.: Ex 4:8). Poetically, of death fleeing from men with *apó*, from (Rev 9:6). Also of heaven and earth, to flee away, vanish suddenly (Rev 16:20).

(II) To escape danger or punishment (Acts 7:29; Heb 11:34; 12:25).

(III) To flee, avoid, shun, followed by *apó* (575), from, with the gen., to flee, run away from (Matt 3:7; 23:33; Luke 3:7; John 10:5; James 4:7).

(IV) With *apó* (575), from, with an acc. following, to flee from sin, to avoid it earnestly (1 Cor 10:14).

Deriv.: *apopheúgō* (668), to escape; *diapheúgō* (1309), to flee through; *ekpheúgō* (1628), to flee from; *katapheúgō* (2703), to flee away; *phugḗ* (5437), escape.

Syn. with the meaning of depart: *exérchomai* (1831), to depart or escape out of; *chōrízō* (5563), to separate; *apérchomai* (565), to go from; *metabaínō* (3327), to go from one place to another; *apochōréō* (672), to go from; *ekporeúomai* (1607), to go out or come forth; *éxeimi* (1826) and *ekchōréō* (1633), to go out.

Ant.: *ménō* (3306), to remain; *paraménō* (3887), to stay near; *diaménō* (1265), to continue remaining; *kataménō* (2650), to reside; *diatríbō* (1304), to remain; *emménō* (1696), to stay in the same place; *hupoménō* (5278), to remain behind; *prosménō* (4357), to remain in a place.

5344. Φῆλιξ *Phélix*; gen. *Phélikos*, masc. proper noun. Felix, meaning happy. The Roman governor of Judea (A.D. 52–60) was a profligate and cruel man. He was married three times. His third wife was Drusilla, whom he persuaded to leave her husband and marry him. They were residing at Caesarea by the sea when Paul was brought there as a prisoner.

He is especially known for the manner in which he treated the exhortations and warnings of Paul (Acts 24:24–26), who preached before him a most practical sermon, arraigning his crimes and urging upon him the duty of repentance in view of future judgment.

The sermon made an impression for "Felix trembled," but the feeling was transient. He kept the Apostle imprisoned for two years and postponed the inquiry respecting his own salvation until a "convenient season" which, so far as we know, never came. Felix was superceded by Porcius Festus (Acts 24:27) two years after this event and tried at Rome before Nero for misuse of his office. However, he escaped punishment through the intervention of Pallas, the freedman of Claudius and his successor Nero.

5345. φήμη *phémé*; gen. *phémes*, fem. noun from *phēmí* (5346), to speak. A report, rumor, fame (Matt 9:26; Luke 4:14).

Deriv.: *blásphēmos* (989), blasphemous; *eúphēmos* (2163), reputable.

Syn.: *akoé* (189), hearing, report, rumor; *échos* (2279), echo, roar, rumor, sound, fame; *lógos* (3056), word, talk.

5346. φημί *phēmí*; imp. *éphēn*, fut. *phéso*, aor. *éphē*, from the obsolete *pháō* (n.f.), to shine. Particularly to bring to light by speech; generally to say, speak, utter. The other tenses are supplied from *eípon* (2036) and *eréō* (2046), to say.

(I) Generally, usually followed by the words which are spoken (Matt 26:34, 61; Luke 7:44; Acts 8:36; 10:28, 31; Rom 3:8). With the acc. (1 Cor 10:15). As interposed in the middle of a clause quoted, equivalent to I said, he said (Matt 14:8; Acts 23:35; 25:5, 22; 1 Cor 6:16; 2 Cor 10:10; Heb 8:5).

(II) As modified by the context, where the sense often lies not so much in *phēmí* as in the adjuncts.

(A) Before interrogations, meaning to ask, inquire (Matt 27:23; Acts 16:30; 21:37).

(B) Before replies, meaning to answer, reply (Matt 4:7; 13:29; John 1:23; Acts 2:38). With *apokritheís* (aor. part. of *apokrínomai* [611], to answer), "Answering he said" (Matt 8:8; Luke 23:3).

(C) Emphatically, meaning to affirm, assert (1 Cor 7:29; 10:19; 15:50).

Deriv.: *súmphēmi* (4852), to agree with; *phásis* (5334), information; *phémē* (5345), fame, rumor.

Syn.: *diabebaióomai* (1226), to affirm confidently; *diïschurízomai* (1340), to assert vehemently; *homologéō* (3670), to profess, confess; *légō* (3004), to speak; *laléō* (2980), to utter; *phthéggomai* (5350), to enunciate clearly; *apophthéggomai* (669), to speak clearly, articulate, give utterance; *eréō* (2046), to say, speak.

Ant.: *sigáō* (4601), to be silent; *siōpáō* (4623), to hush, keep silence.

5347. Φῆστος *Phéstos*; gen. *Phéstou*, masc. proper noun. Porcius Festus who succeeded Felix in A.D. 60 in the government of Judea (Acts 24:27) and died in A.D. 62. Paul had a hearing before him on various charges and Festus would have released him if Paul had not appealed to the Emperor (Acts 26:32). Josephus characterized him as an efficient ruler, especially because he did his best to rid the country of robbers. See Acts 25:1, 4, 9, 12–14, 22–24; 26:24, 25.

5348. φθάνω *phthánō*; fut. *phthásō*, aor. *éphthasa*. To come suddenly and unexpectedly.

(I) Intrans., to come, come suddenly or before an expectation (Matt 12:28; Luke 11:20; 1 Thess 2:16).

(II) Trans., to anticipate, precede (1 Thess 4:15).

(III) Construed with the prep. *eis* (1519), unto, meaning to come, attain to (Rom 9:31; Phil 3:16).

(IV) Construed with the prep. *áchri* (891), until, meaning to come to or as far as (2 Cor 10:14).

Deriv.: *prophtháno* (4399), anticipate.

Syn.: *parabállo* (3846), to arrive, compare; *katapléo* (2668), to land at, arrive; *paragínomai* (3854), approach, arrive; *katantáo* (2658), to come to, arrive at, attain; *tugcháno* (5177), to chance upon, reach, meet with; *epérchomai* (1904), to come upon; *hḗko* (2240), to arrive, with the emphasis on one's presence; *aphiknéomai* (864), to arrive; *enístēmi* (1764), to be at hand, current; *ephístēmi* (2186), to be at hand, present; *parístēmi* (3936), to stand nearby, be at hand.

Ant.: *apérchomai* (565), to go away.

5349. φθαρτός *phthartós*; fem. *phthartḗ*, neut. *phthartón*, adj. from *phtheíro* (5351), to corrupt. Subject to corruption, corruptible.

An adj. to indicate degenerating man (Rom 1:23, equivalent to *thnētós* [2349], mortal). In this verse, God is called *áphthartos* (862), incorruptible, referring to His eternal essence as Spirit. As such, God cannot be represented by the image of corruptible flesh.

In 1 Cor 9:25, *phthartós* is used in connection with the temporal character of a crown won on this earth. The crown received as a result of winning an earthly race is called corruptible while the crown received in heaven cannot suffer deterioration.

In 1 Cor 15:53, 54, reference is made to the body being mortal. This is not the body of the unbelievers that is referred to, but that of the believers. It indicates that, at the time of salvation, God does not change our bodies to exempt them from the degeneration of age and sickness and finally death. The body of the believer is constituted exactly the same as the body of the unbeliever and is subject to the same laws of corruptibility. These verses, however, provide a clear indication that this characteristic of corruptibility will be changed to one of incorruptibility, a mark of the believer's resurrection body (Rom 8:23), which is glorious even as is Christ's resurrection body (Phil 3:21).

In 1 Pet 1:18, 23, *phthartós* is used of the physical means which cannot bring spiritual salvation. Silver and the seed of the body are called corruptible, which applies to something material. The neg. *áphthartos* (862), incorruptible, refers not to the soul, but to the body of man (1 Cor 15:52).

Syn.: *saprós* (4550), rotten, corrupt.

Ant.: *áphthartos* (862), incorruptible; *akatálutos* (179), indissoluble, permanent; *aiṓnios* (166), eternal; *akéraios* (185), innocent, harmless.

5350. φθέγγομαι *phthéggomai*; fut. *phthégxomai*, mid. deponent. To sound a tone, speak, utter a word (Acts 4:18; 2 Pet 2:16, 18). It is putting sounds together to communicate something to someone else.

Deriv.: *apophthéggomai* (669), to give an opinion or judgment; *phthóggos* (5353), utter a sound, especially of a musical instrument.

Syn.: *laléo* (2980), to utter; *légo* (3004), to speak; *eíro* or *eréo* (2046), to speak, say.

Ant.: *sigáo* (4601), to be silent; *siōpáo* (4623), to keep silence; *phimóo* (5392), to muzzle, put to silence.

5351. φθείρω *phtheíro*; fut. *phtherṓ*, from *phthío* or *phthíno* (n.f.), to waste, pine. To corrupt, destroy. Trans. to destroy, punish with destruction, bring to a worse state (1 Cor 3:17). To corrupt, spoil, vitiate, in a moral or spiritual sense (1 Cor 15:33; Eph 4:22; Jude 1:10; Rev 19:2). To corrupt, with the meaning of to subvert or corrupt opinions (2 Cor 7:2; 11:3; see Sept.: Gen 6:3; Isa 54:16; Jer 13:9). Also from *phthíno* (n.f.): *phthinopōrinós* (5352), whose fruit withered.

Deriv.: *diaptheírō* (1311), to corrupt completely, decay utterly, destroy; *kataphtheírō* (2704), to corrupt fully, destroy utterly, spoil entirely, deprave; *phthartós* (5349), corruptible; *phthorá* (5356), corruption, both physical and spiritual.

Syn.: *épō* (4595), to rot.

Ant.: *phulássō* (5442), to guard; *tēréō* (5083), to preserve; *phrontízō* (5431), to take care of; *suntēréō* (4933), to conserve, preserve, keep.

5352. φθινοπωρινός *phthinopōrinós*; fem. *phthinopōrinē*, neut. *phthinopōrinón*, adj. from *phthínō* (n.f.), to decay, fail, wither, and *opóra* (3703), autumn. Pertaining to the autumn, found only in Jude 1:12. Also from *phthínō* (n.f.): *phtheírō* (5351), to corrupt, destroy.

5353. φθόγγος *phthóggos*; gen. *phthóggou*, masc. noun from *phthéggomai* (5350), to speak, utter a sound, especially of a musical instrument. A voice, sound (Rom 10:18 quoted from Ps 19:5; 1 Cor 14:7). *Phthóggos* is distinguished from *phōnḗ* (5456), voice, in that it denotes a musical sound.

Syn.: *laliá* (2981), speech, dialect; *lógos* (3056), word, expression, reasoning, utterance; *rhḗma* (4487), utterance; *épos* (2031), a word.

Ant.: *sigḗ* (4602), silence; *hēsuchía* (2271), quietness.

5354. φθονέω *phthonéō*; contracted *phthonṓ*, fut. *phthonḗsō*, from *phthónos* (5355), envy. To envy (Gal 5:26).

Syn.: *zēlóō* (2206), to covet, be jealous (1 Cor 13:4).

Ant.: *sugchaírō* (4796), to rejoice with, congratulate.

5355. φθόνος *phthónos*; gen. *phthónou*, masc. noun. Envy, jealousy, pain felt and malignity conceived at the sight of excellence or happiness (Matt 27:18; Mark 15:10; Rom 1:29; Phil 1:15; 1 Tim 6:4;

Titus 3:3; James 4:5). Pl. *phthónoi*, envyings, bursts of envy (Gal 5:21; 1 Pet 2:1). *Phthónos*, unlike *zḗlos* (2205), zeal, is incapable of good and always is used with an evil meaning.

Deriv.: *phthonéō* (5354), to envy.

Ant.: *chará* (5479), joy, delight.

5356. φθορά *phthorá*; gen. *phthorás*, fem. noun from *phtheírō* (5351), to corrupt. Spoiling, corruption, destruction, ruin, decay, generally a fraying or wasting away.

(**I**) Destruction, deterioration, slaughter, change of existing state (2 Pet 2:12).

(**II**) Death, corruption in a natural sense (1 Cor 15:42; Gal 6:8 [cf. Rom 8:21]; Col 2:22; Sept.: Ps 103:4; Jon 2:7); the abstract being put for the concrete, what is corruptible or subject to corruption (1 Cor 15:50).

(**III**) Corruption in a moral or spiritual sense (2 Pet 1:4; 2:19).

Syn.: *apóleia* (684), perdition, destruction; *ólethros* (3639), ruin, destruction; *súntrimma* (4938), a breaking in pieces, shattering, ruin.

Ant.: *aphtharsía* (861), incorruption; *adiaphthoría* (90), incorruptibility, moral and physical soundness.

5357. φιάλη *phiálē*; gen. *phiálēs*, fem. noun. A bowl or basin, a vial with a wide mouth (Rev 5:8; 15:7; 16:1–4, 8, 10, 12, 17; 17:1; 21:9; Sept.: Ex 27:3; Num 7:13f.).

Syn.: *askós* (779), a bag or bottle made of skin; *aggeíon* (30), a vessel.

5358. φιλάγαθος *philágathos*; gen. *philagáthou*, masc.-fem., neut. *philágathon*, adj. from *phílos* (5384), friend, and *agathós* (18), benevolent. Loving and practicing what is good (Titus 1:8). It combines not only the liking to be kind but also the actual doing of good. The word is similar in implication to *eleḗmōn* ([1655], merciful), and *oiktírmōn* ([3629], compassionate) but stands in contradistinction to *philooiktírmōn* (n.f.), one who enjoys sympathetic feelings without necessarily externalizing them in good actions.

Deriv.: *aphilágathos* (865), not loving good.

5359. Φιλαδέλφεια *Philadélpheia*; gen. *Philadelpheías*, fem. proper noun from *philádelphos* (5361), the love of brethren. A city in Lydia of Asia Minor where one of the seven churches of Asia (Rev 1:11; 3:7) was located. Presently part of Turkey known as Allah-Sheryr or city of God.

5360. φιλαδελφία *philadelphía*; gen. *philadelphías*, fem. noun from *philádelphos* (5361), one who loves his brother. Brotherly love. In the NT, used of the love of Christians one to another, brotherly love out of a common spiritual life (Rom 12:10; 1 Thess 4:9; Heb 13:1; 1 Pet 1:22; 2 Pet 1:7).

Syn.: *philanthrōpía* (5363), benevolence, philanthropy; *philía* (5373), friendship; *eúnoia* (2133), kindness, goodwill, benevolence.

5361. φιλάδελφος *philádelphos*; gen. *philadélphou*, masc.-fem., neut. *philádelphon*, adj. from *phílos* (5384), friend, and *adelphós* (80), brother. Loving one's brother, brotherly affectionate. In a wider sense it meant love of one's fellow countrymen. In the strictly Christian sense of loving as brothers. *Philádelphoi* (pl.) sums up the bearing of Christians to each other, and the adj. which follow describe what their behavior should be (1 Pet 3:8).

Deriv.: *Philadélpheia* (5359), Philadelphia; *philadelphía* (5360), brotherly love.

Syn.: *phílos* (5384), friendly; *eúsplagchnos* (2155), compassionate, sympathetic; *philóstorgos* (5387), having natural love.

5362. φίλανδρος *phílandros*; gen. *philándrou*, masc.-fem., neut. *phílandron*, adj. from *phílos* (5384), a friend or loving as a friend, and *anér* (435), a husband. Loving one's husband (Titus 2:4).

5363. φιλανθρωπία *philanthrōpía*; gen. *philanthrōpías*, fem. noun from *philánthrōpos* (n.f.), a lover of mankind, which is from *phílos* (5384), friend, and *ánthrōpos* (444), human being. Human friendship, philanthropy, benevolence, kindness. In the NT, it occurs as a subst. in Acts 28:2, referring to the hospitable reception of the shipwrecked by the Melitans. In Titus 3:4 we have the philanthropy of God as a Savior, which means His work in the salvation of man.

Philanthrōpía, which is transliterated in Eng. as "philanthropy," is that disposition which does not always think of self, but takes thought for the needs and wishes of others. It denotes that apparent and ready goodwill usually manifested in a friendly, considerate demeanor, and (especially in the practice of hospitality) readiness to help, tenderheartedness, cherishing and maintaining fellowship. The philanthropist serves his fellow citizens, protects the oppressed, is mindful of the erring, gentle to the conquered, and self-renouncing in reference to his rights.

Philanthropy does not occur in the list of Christian virtues. This social virtue in the NT is expressed with the words *agápē* (26) and *philadelphía* (5360), brotherly love, which occupy the place of social righteousness. It is actually one further step to nobility from *philanthrōpía* to *philadelphía*, because the latter regards man as a brother while the former considers him only as a fellow human being.

Syn.: *éleos* (1656), compassion, mercy; *oiktirmós* (3628), compassion; *splágchna* (pl. of *splágchon* [4698]) bowels of compassion.

Ant.: *sklērokardía* (4641), hardness of heart; *sklērótēs* (4643), callousness, hardness.

5364. φιλανθρώπως *philanthrṓpōs*; adv. from *philánthrōpos* (n.f.), loving man or mankind. Humanely, philanthropically, with mercy or benevolence (Acts

27:3). Also from *philánthrōpos* (n.f.): *philanthrōpía* (5363), philanthropy.

5365. φιλαργυρία *philarguría*; gen. *philargurías*, fem. noun from *philárguros* (5366), a lover of money. The love of money (1 Tim 6:10; Sept.: Jer 8:10). *Philarguría* may be regarded as a type of *pleonexía* (4124), covetousness.

5366. φιλάργυρος *philárguros*; gen. *philargúrou*, masc.-fem., neut. *philárguron*, adj. from *phílos* (5384), a friend or loving, and *árguros* (696), silver, money. Loving money, avaricious, covetous (Luke 16:14; 2 Tim 3:2).

Deriv.: *aphilárguros* (866), not fond of money; *philarguría* (5365), love of money.

Syn.: *pleonéktēs* (4123), desirous of gain; *phílautos* (5367), selfish.

Ant.: *aphilárguros* (866), not covetous.

5367. φίλαυτος *phílautos*; gen. *philaútou*, masc.-fem., neut. *phílauton*, adj. from *phílos* (5384), loving or friend, and *autós* (846), himself. Self-centered or selfish (2 Tim 3:2). An undue sparing of self with the primary concern that things be easy and pleasant for oneself. The *phílautos* is one who loves his life so much that he seeks ignobly to save it.

5368. φιλέω *philéō*; contracted *philṓ*, fut. *philḗsō*, from *phílos* (5384), loved, dear, friend. To love. Trans.:

(I) Generally with the acc. of person to have affection for someone (Matt 10:37; John 5:20; 11:3, 36; 15:19; 16:27; 20:2; 21:15–17; 1 Cor 16:22; Titus 3:15, with Christian love; Rev 3:19; Sept.: Gen 37:4; Prov 8:17). Of things, to be fond of, to like, with the acc. (Matt 23:6; Luke 20:46; Rev 22:15; Sept.: Prov 29:3). With the idea of overweening fondness (John 12:25; Sept.: Gen 27:4, 9).

(II) Specifically, to kiss, with the acc. (Matt 26:48; Mark 14:44; Luke 22:47; Sept.: Gen 27:26, 27; Ex 18:7).

(III) Followed by the inf. meaning to love to do something (Matt 6:5, they love to pray in public, desire to do it).

Much discussion has arisen concerning the semantic relationship between this word and *agapáō* (25), to love. Of the two, *agapáō* is used predominantly for man's love toward God while *philéō* is rarely used of it. However, *philéō* occurs when the love of the disciples for Jesus is spoken about (John 16:27; 21:15–17; 1 Cor 16:22). Furthermore, God's love to man is spoken of, both *agapáō* and *philéō* are used. It is difficult to find any significance in the pattern of theses words' usages. Some scholars, having drawn hard and fast differences between the words, have imposed these differences upon various texts of Scripture and thereby produced strained and awkward interpretations. Only on occasion do these words bear particular meanings distinct from one another.

Simply stated, to love (*agapáō*) fellow humans means to see or discern what their need is and to meet that need, not according to the object's concept of need, but that of the one who loves. It is in this concept that the saying of Christ in Matt 5:44, "love [*agapáte*] your enemies," can be understood. For a believer, his enemies are his enemies because they are not believers. What he sees is their need of faith and he must do everything that he can to meet that need in their lives in whatever manner. Believers are never told to love their enemies with the word *philéō* because that would mean to have the same interests as they have.

God calls man his friend (*phílos*), as He did Abraham (James 2:23), when man has adopted God's interests as his own, just as Abraham was willing to sacrifice his son even as God did His own.

Deriv.: *phílēma* (5370), a kiss; *kataphiléō* (2705), to kiss affectionately.

Ant.: *miséō* (3404), to hate.

5369. φιλήδονος *philḗdonos*; gen. *philēdónou*, masc.-fem., neut. *philḗdonon*, adj. from *phílos* (5384), friend or loving, and *hēdonē* (2237), pleasure. A lover of pleasure (2 Tim 3:4).

5370. φίλημα *phílēma*; gen. *philēmatos*, neut. noun from *phileó* (5368), to love, befriend, kiss. A kiss, a token of love and friendship (Luke 7:45; 22:48; Rom 16:16; 1 Cor 16:20; 2 Cor 13:12; 1 Thess 5:26; 1 Pet 5:14; Sept.: Prov 27:6).

5371. Φιλήμων *Philēmōn*; gen. *Philēmonos*, masc. proper noun. Philemon, meaning affectionate, a member of the church of Colossae who owed his conversion to the Apostle Paul (Phile 1:19 [cf. Col 4:9]). The epistle in the NT was written by Paul to Philemon on behalf of Onesimus, Philemon's slave who had run away from him. A church met in Philemon's house (Phile 1:2).

5372. Φιλητός *Philētós*; gen. *Philētoú*, masc. proper noun. Philetus, meaning beloved. A Christian named in connection with Hymenaeus (2 Tim 2:17) with whom he held false views regarding the resurrection. They attributed only a spiritual meaning to the resurrection, allegorizing the doctrine and turning it into figure and metaphor.

5373. φιλία *philía*; gen. *philías*, fem. noun from *phileó* (5368), to befriend, love, kiss. Love, friendship, fondness, with the gen. of obj. (James 4:4; Sept.: Prov 10:12; 15:17). In James 4:4, *philía* involves the adopting of the interests of the world to be one's own.

　Syn.: *agápē* (26), love.
　Ant.: *échthra* (2189), enmity.

5374. Φιλιππήσιος *Philippḗsios*; gen. *Philippēsíou*, masc. proper adj. A Philippian, a native of Philippi (Phil 4:15).

5375. Φίλιπποι *Phílippoi*; gen. *Philíppōn*, pl. masc. proper noun. Philippi, a city in Macedonia. Paul and Silas were imprisoned in Philippi on Paul's second missionary journey (Acts 16:9–40; [cf. 1 Thess 2:2]). The Philippian

Church was especially generous to, and beloved by, the Apostle Paul (Phil 4:16; see 2 Cor 8:1–6; 11:9). Paul wrote an epistle to the Philippians (Phil 1:1). From Philippi he wrote his epistles of 1 and 2 Corinthians.

5376. Φίλιππος *Phílippos*; gen. *Philíppou*, masc. proper noun from *phílos* (5384), a friend, and *híppos* (2462), horse. Philip, meaning a lover of horses.
　(I) The Apostle from Bethsaida in Galilee (Matt 10:3; Mark 3:18; Luke 6:14; John 1:43–48; 6:5, 7; 12:21, 22; 14:8, 9; Acts 1:13).
　(II) Philip the Evangelist who was appointed a deacon to serve at tables (Acts 6:5; 21:8). After the death of Stephen he preached the gospel at Samaria (Acts 8:5, 6, 12, 13 [cf. 8:14]) and baptized the Ethiopian treasurer (Acts 8:38 [cf. 8:5ff.]).
　(III) Philip, tetrarch of Batanea, Trachonitis and Auranitis (Luke · 3:1). He was a son of Herod the Great by his wife Cleopatra and the brother of Herod Antipas. At his death his tetrarchy was annexed to Syria. From him the city Caesarea Philippi took its name (Matt 16:13; Mark 8:27).
　(IV) Philip Herod, called by Josephus only Herod, also a son of Herod the Great by Mariamne, the daughter of Simon the high priest. He was the first husband of Herodias and lived a private life, having been disinherited by his father (Matt 14:3; Mark 6:17; Luke 3:19).

5377. φιλόθεος *philótheos*; gen. *philothéou*, masc.-fem., neut. *philótheon*, adj. from *phílos* (5384), a friend or loving, and *Theós* (2316), God. Loving God, a lover of God (2 Tim 3:4).

5378. Φιλόλογος *Philólogos*; gen. *Philológou*, masc. proper noun, from *phílos* (5384), a friend or loving, and *légō* (3004), to say. Philologus, meaning fond of words or a lover of words, talkative. The name of a Christian at Rome to whom Paul sends his greeting (Rom 16:15).

5379. φιλονεικία *philoneikía*; gen. *philoneikías*, fem. noun from *philóneikos* (5380), contentious, a contentious person. A contention, dispute, or more literally, a love of contention (Luke 22:24).

Syn.: *dichostasía* (1370), dissension; *logomachía* (3055), strife of words; *éris* (2054), quarrel, wrangling; *eritheía* (2052), faction, strife; *máchē* (3163), fighting; *pólemos* (4171), war.

Ant.: *eirḗnē* (1515), peace; *katallagḗ* (2643), restoration, reconciliation.

5380. φιλόνεικος *philóneikos*; gen. *philoneíkou*, masc.-fem., neut. *philóneikon*, adj. from *phílos* (5384), a friend or loving, and *neíkos* (n.f.), a contention, dispute, war. Fond of contention or disputing, contentious, a lover of disputation (1 Cor 11:16).

Deriv.: *philoneikía* (5379), a love of contention.

5381. φιλοξενία *philoxenía*; gen. *philoxenías*, fem. noun from *philóxenos* (5382), hospitable. Hospitality or kindness to strangers (Rom 12:13; Heb 13:2).

Syn.: *xenía* (3578), hospitality.

5382. φιλόξενος *philóxenos*; gen. *philoxénou*, masc.-fem., neut. *philóxenon*, adj. from *phílos* (5384), a friend or loving, and *xénos* (3581), a stranger. Hospitable, loving strangers, a friend of, or kind to strangers (1 Tim 3:2; Titus 1:8; 1 Pet 4:9).

Deriv.: *philoxenía* (5381), hospitality or kindness to strangers.

5383. φιλοπρωτεύω *philoprōteúō*; fut. *philoprōteúsō*, from *phílos* (5384), a friend or loving, and *prōteúō* (4409), to be first, preeminent. To love to have preeminence (3 John 1:9).

5384. φίλος *phílos*; fem. *phílē*, neut. *phílon*, adj. Loved, dear, befriended, friendly, kind; as a subst. friend. In the NT a friend (Luke 7:6; 11:5, 6, 8; 12:4; 14:12; 15:6, 29; 16:9; 21:16; 23:12; John

11:11; 15:13–15; 19:12; Acts 10:24; 19:31; 27:3; James 2:23; 4:4; 3 John 1:14; Sept.: Ex 33:11; Job 2:11; Prov 14:20). With the meaning of companion (Matt 11:19; Luke 7:34; John 3:29, a bridesman; Sept.: Dan 2:13, 17, 18; Sept.: Esth 5:10). As a word of courteous address (Luke 14:10). *Tás phílas* (fem. pl.), female friends (Luke 15:9).

Deriv.: *philágathos* (5358), one who practices what is good; *philádelphos* (5361), brotherly love; *phílandros* (5362), loving one's husband *philárguros* (5366), loving money, covetous; *phílautos* (5367), one who loves himself more than he ought; *philéō* (5368), to love; *philḗdonos* (5369), a lover of pleasure; *Phílippos* (5376), Philip, a lover of horses; *philótheos* (5377), a lover of God; *Philólogos* (5378), Philologus, a lover of words; *philóneikos* (5380), a lover of contention; *philóxenos* (5382), hospitable, kind to strangers; *philoprōteúō* (5383), to love preeminence; *philósophos* (5386), a philosopher; *philóstorgos* (5387), family love; *philóteknos* (5388), loving one's children; *philóphrōn* (5391), friendly.

Syn.: *hetaíros* (2083), a comrade, though for selfish reasons.

Ant.: *echthrós* (2190), enemy.

5385. φιλοσοφία *philosophía*; gen. *philosophías*, fem. noun from *philosophéō* (n.f.), which is from *philósophos* (5386), a philosopher, friend of wisdom. Love of wisdom, philosophy, which came to mean the doctrine or tenets of the heathen or Gentile philosophers (Col 2:8 [cf. 2:16]; 1 Tim 6:20). The modern definition of the word must not be read into its use in the Bible. Philosophy, as the study of reality, knowledge, and values, is a profitable and biblically supported endeavor. However, this is not the meaning of the word in Scripture. There it carries a negative connotation and refers to quasi-religious doctrines and speculations (e.g., gnosticism) all of which are irreconcilable with the Christian faith.

5386. φιλόσοφος *philósophos*; gen. *philosóphou*, masc.-fem., neut. *philósophon*, adj. from *phílos* (5384), a friend and *sophía* (4678), wisdom. A friend or lover of wisdom, a philosopher (Acts 17:18). Those who professed the study of wisdom were, among the ancient Greeks, called *sophoí* (4680), wise men; but Pythagoras introduced the more modest name of *philósophos*, a lover of wisdom, and called himself by this title.

5387. φιλόστοργος *philóstorgos*; gen. *philostórgou*, masc.-fem., neut. *philóstorgon*, adj. from *phílos* (5384), a friend, and *storgḗ* (n.f.), a natural family love or tender affection. Loving with that natural affection that characterizes members of the same family (Rom 12:10). Also from *storgḗ* (n.f.): *ástorgos* (794), without family love.
   Ant.: *ástorgos* (794), lacking family affection; *stugētós* (4767), hateful.

5388. φιλότεκνος *philóteknos*; gen. *philotéknou*, masc.-fem., neut. *philóteknon*, adj. from *phílos* (5384), a friend, and *téknon* (5043), a child. Loving one's children (Titus 2:4).

5389. φιλοτιμέομαι *philotiméomai*; contracted *philotimoúmai*, fut. *philotimḗsomai*, mid. deponent from *philótimos* (n.f.), loving or fond of honor, ambitious, which is from *phílos* (5384), a friend, and *timḗ* (5092), honor. To make something an ambition, aspire (Rom 15:20; 2 Cor 5:9; 1 Thess 4:11).

5390. φιλοφρόνως *philophrónōs*; adv. from *philóphrōn* (5391). In a friendly or kind manner, courteously (Acts 28:7). The Greek writers often applied the word particularly to the entertainment of strangers.

5391. φιλόφρων *philóphrōn*; gen. *philóphronos*, masc. fem. adj. from *phílos* (5384), a friend, and *phronéō*

(5426), to think, have a mindset. Friendly, courteous, benign (1 Pet 3:8).
   Deriv.: *philophrónōs* (5390), in a friendly or kind manner.

5392. φιμόω *phimóō*; contracted *phimṓ*, fut. *phimṓsō*, from *phimós* (n.f.), a muzzle for a beast's mouth. To muzzle.
   (I) Trans., to muzzle, as an ox (1 Cor 9:9; 1 Tim 5:18).
   (II) Figuratively to stop the mouth in order to silence (Matt 22:34; 1 Pet 2:15); the aor. pass. *ephimṓthēn*, to be silenced, speechless (Matt 22:12).
   (III) Used by Christ in commanding an evil spirit not to speak through the demoniac (Mark 1:25; Luke 4:35); the raging sea to be still (Mark 4:39, perf. imper. *pephímōso*).
   Syn.: *sigáō* (4601), to keep silence; *siōpáō* (4623), to be silent.
   Ant.: *légō* (3004), to speak.

5393. Φλέγων *Phlégōn*; gen. *phlégontos*, masc. proper noun. Phlegon, meaning flame. A Christian at Rome to whom Paul sent greetings (Rom 16:14).

5394. φλογίζω *phlogízō*; fut. *phlogísō*, from *phlóx* (5395), flame, blaze. To inflame, set on fire (James 3:6, of the tongue representing discord).
   Syn.: *puróō* (4448), to be on fire, hot, burn up; *kaíō* (2545), to set fire to, burn; *katakaíō* (2618), to burn up completely; *ekkaíō* (1572), to inflame, deeply burn; *empíprēmi* or *emprḗthō* (1714), to burn up; *thermaínō* (2328), to heat; *zéō* (2204), to be feverish, hot, and figuratively meaning fervent, earnest; *kaumatízō* (2739), to scorch; *kausóō* (2741), to burn with great heat as of fever.
   Ant.: *psúchō* (5594), to chill, cool; *katapsúchō* (2711), to cool down, refresh; *anapsúchō* (404), to cool off, relieve, refresh; *aníēmi* (447), to let up, slacken, and thus give opportunity to ease off.

5395. φλόξ *phlóx*; gen. *phlogós*, fem. noun from *phlégō* (n.f.), to burn, shine as fire (Sept.: Ex 3:2; Isa 29:6; Joel 1:19).

A bright burning fire or flame (Luke 16:24; Acts 7:30; 2 Thess 1:8; Heb 1:7 quoted from Ps 104:4; Rev 1:14; 2:18; 19:12; Sept.: Isa 30:30). The description of the Son of Man in Rev 1:14 is similar to those found in OT (cf. especially Dan 3:25).

Deriv.: *phlogízō* (5394), to inflame.

Syn.: *púr* (4442), fire; *puretós* (4446), feverish, fever; *purá* (4443), a fire; *púrōsis* (4451), burning, used figuratively for trial; *kaúsis* (2740), the act of burning; *kaúsōn* (2742), burning heat; *kaúma* (2738), the result of burning, the glow or heat produced; *thérmē* (2329), warmth, heat.

Ant.: *psúchos* (5592), cold.

5396. φλυαρέω *phluaréō*; contracted *phluarō*, fut. *phluarḗsō*, from *phlúaros* (5397), talkative. To overflow with talk, chatter, prattle. With an acc. of person, to blabber, chatter, talk in an idle, trifling manner against someone; talking idly or falsely (3 John 1:10).

Syn.: *battologéō* (945), to stutter, talk tediously.

5397. φλύαρος *phlúaros*; gen. *phluárou*, masc.-fem., neut. *plúaron*, adj. from *phlúō* (n.f.), to boil, bubble, as with heat. A tattler, an idle or trifling talker, one who boils over with impertinent talk (1 Tim 5:13).

Deriv.: *phluaréō* (5396), to overflow with talk, chatter.

Syn.: *mataiológos* (3151), a vain, idle talker, wrangler.

Ant.: *sōphrōn* (4998), sober-minded, self-controlled.

5398. φοβερός *phoberós*; fem. *phoberá*, neut. *phoberón*, adj. from *phóbos* (5401), fear. Dreadful, terrible, horrifying (Heb 10:27, 31; 12:21; Sept.: Gen 28:17; Deut 10:17).

Syn.: *deilós* (1169), cowardly; *ékphobos* (1630), thoroughly frightened; *éntromos* (1790), trembling with fear; *émphobos* (1719), alarmed, frightened.

Ant.: *tolmētḗs* (5113), a daring person.

5399. φοβέω *phobéō*; contracted *phobṓ*, fut. *phobḗsō*, from *phóbos* (5401), fear. To put in fear, terrify, frighten. In the Class. Gr., to cause to run away. In the NT, only in the mid. *phobéomai* (contracted *phoboúmai*), aor. pass. *ephobḗthēn* and fut. pass. *phobēthḗsomai*, meaning particularly to become fearful, afraid, terrified.

(I) Particularly and generally in various constructions:

(A) Intrans. and in an absolute sense (Mark 5:36, "Be not afraid"; Luke 1:13, 30; Rom 13:4); in the pl., as a command not to fear (Matt 14:27; Mark 6:50); "they were afraid" (Mark 10:32; 16:8); "he was afraid" (Matt 14:30); "greatly afraid" (a.t. [Matt 17:6; 27:54]); "I shall not be afraid" (a.t. [Sept.: Ps 118:6]). See Gen 15:1; 50:19; Ex 2:14. Followed by the acc. of a cognate noun (1 Pet 3:14, fear not the fear which they would inspire and instigate; see 3:6). Emphatically (Mark 4:41; Luke 2:9).

(B) Trans. with the acc. of person (Matt 10:26; 14:5; Mark 12:12; Luke 20:19; John 9:22; Acts 9:26; Rom 13:3; Gal 2:12; Sept.: Num 21:34; Deut 3:2); followed by the acc. of thing (Heb 11:23, 27; Rev 2:10).

(C) Followed by *apó* (575), from, with a gen., to fear because of something or someone (Matt 10:28; Luke 12:4; Sept.: Lev 26:2; Deut 1:29; Ps 3:5).

(D) Followed by *mḗ* (3361), not, lest (Acts 27:17; see *mḗ* [3361], II). Followed by *mḗpōs* (3381), lest somehow (Acts 27:29; 2 Cor 11:3; 12:20; Gal 4:11, "as to you" [a.t.]). Followed by *mḗpote* (3379), lest at any time (Heb 4:1; Sept.: Gen 32:11).

(E) Followed by the inf., to fear to do something, hesitate (Matt 1:20; 2:22; Mark 9:32; Luke 9:45; Sept.: Gen 19:30; 46:3; Ex 34:30).

(II) Morally, to fear, reverence, honor, with the acc.

(A) Generally (Mark 6:20; Eph 5:33; Sept.: Lev 19:3; Josh 4:14).

(B) In regard to the Lord, meaning to reverence God, to stand in awe of God

(Luke 18:2, 4; 23:40; Col 3:22; 1 Pet 2:17; Sept.: Ex 1:17, 21; Lev 19:14); expressing piety, equivalent to worship, adoration of God (Luke 1:50; Acts 10:22, 35; Rev 11:18; 14:7; 15:4; 19:5); *hoi phoboúmenoi tón Theón* (*hoi* [3588], the; *phoboúmenoi*, pres. mid. part. of *phobéō*, used subst.; *tón* [3588], the; *Theón* [2316], God), those fearing God, referring to proselytes (Acts 13:16, 26). Equal to *sébomai* (4576), to adore, revere, express religious devotion. See Sept.: Deut 4:10, 29; 6:2, 13, 24; 28:58; 1 Sam 12:14.

Deriv.: *ékphobos* (1630), very frightened; *phoberós* (5398), fearful; *phóbētron* (5400), that which causes fear, terror.

Syn.: *sébomai* (4576), to revere; *trémō* (5141), to tremble.

Ant.: *tharréō* (2292), to exercise courage; *tharséō* (2293), to have courage.

5400. φόβητρον *phóbētron*; gen. *phobḗtrou*, neut. noun from *phobéō* (5399), to terrify or frighten, and *phóbos* (5401), fear. A dreadful or terrible sight or appearance (Luke 21:11; Sept.: Isa 19:17).

5401. φόβος *phóbos*; gen. *phóbou*, masc. noun from *phébomai* (n.f.), to flee from. Fear, terror, reverence, respect, honor.
(I) Particularly and generally (Matt 14:26; Luke 1:12; 2:9; 8:37; 21:26; Rom 8:15; 2 Cor 7:5, 11; 1 Tim 5:20; 1 John 4:18; Sept.: Ps 53:5; Jon 1:10, 16). Followed by the gen. of person or thing feared meaning that which inspires fear (Matt 28:4; John 7:13; 19:38; 20:19; Heb 2:15; 1 Pet 3:14; Rev 18:10, 15). Metonymically a terror, object of fear (Rom 13:3; Sept.: Gen 9:2; Deut 11:25; Job 20:25). Including the idea of astonishment, amazement (Matt 28:8; Mark 4:41; Luke 1:65; 5:26; 7:16; Acts 2:43; 5:5, 11; 19:17; Rev 11:11).
(II) In a moral sense, fear, reverence, respect, honor (1 Pet 1:17; 3:2, 15; Sept.: Ps 19:9; 111:10). Of persons (Rom 13:7); of God or Christ, the fear "of God" or the Lord meaning a deep and reverential sense of accountability to God or Christ (Acts 9:31; Rom 3:18; 2 Cor 5:11; 7:1;

Eph 5:21; Sept.: 2 Chr 19:9; Ps 2:11; 36:1; Prov 1:7, 29; 8:13; 9:10; 14:27). The fear of God implied (1 Pet 2:18; Jude 1:23). Intensively, in fear and trembling (1 Cor 2:3; 2 Cor 7:15; Eph 6:5; Phil 2:12).

Deriv.: *émphobos* (1719), afraid; *phobéō* (5399), to terrify, frighten.

Syn.: *deilía* (1167), timidity, fear; *eulábeia* (2124), fear, reverence, piety; *trómos* (5156), trembling.

Ant.: *thársos* (2294), boldness, courage.

5402. Φοίβη *Phoíbē*; gen. *Phoíbēs*, fem. proper noun. Phoebe, meaning radiant. A servant (*diákonos* [1249]) of the church of Cenchrea, commended by Paul who had been a recipient of her kindness (Rom 16:1, 2) to the church of Rome. See *diákonos* (1249) for a discussion as to whether *diákonos* as spoken of her means simply servant or deaconess.

5403. Φοινίκη *Phoiníkē*; gen. *Phoiníkēs*, fem. proper noun from *phoínix* (5404), palm tree. Phoenice or Phoenicia, the narrow coastland stretching along the northeast Mediterranean. It is bordered on the east by the Lebanon mountains and on the southeast by the hills of Galilee. Famous for its commerce, it was a part of OT Canaan. In NT times Phoenicia extended as far south as Dor, sixteen miles south of Tyre. It was thus a narrow ribbon of coastland, being some two hundred miles long at its greatest extent (Acts 11:19; 15:3; 21:2).

5404. φοῖνιξ *phoínix*; gen. *phoínikos*, masc. noun. A palm tree (John 12:13), also a branch of the palm tree (Rev 7:9). The palm grows to be a straight tree with a very stately and beautiful appearance. It was used for ornamentation in eastern architecture. Hence in the outer temple palm trees were engraved on the walls and doors between the coupled cherubs (see 1 Kgs 6:29; Ezek 41:18, 19).

In the higher regions, the palm was rare, and thus it was noted that the prophetess Deborah (Judg 4:5) dwelt under a palm tree which was most likely a land-mark at that time.

The palm is symbolic of righteousness. Ps 92:12 likens the righteous person to a palm tree in that nothing can sway a palm tree from perfect uprightness and neither does it change from season to season.

It must also be mentioned that the palm tree was among the idolatrous emblems of or sacred to the sun. The Delian palm consecrated to Apollo was from very ancient times famous among the Greeks. There were many palm trees at Apollo's temple at Butus in Egypt, and in the temple of Athena there were columns in imitation of palm trees. The symbolism is based upon the permanency of the palm's leaves and their resemblance to the solar rays.

The branches of this tree were also used as emblems of victory, both by believers and idolaters. The reason given for their being considered emblems of victory is the nature of the tree by which it so remarkably resists persistently heavy pressure.

This helps us to understand the importance of the palm branches mentioned in the NT. The multitudes carried them before Christ (John 12:13) in order to express by that object and their actions that which they proclaimed—"Hosanna [which means, save us]: Blessed is the King of Israel [the Messiah] that cometh in the name of the Lord." The saints in Rev 7:9, by bearing palm branches in their hands, were similarly ascribing salvation to their God who sits on the throne and to the Lamb (Rev 7:10).

Deriv.: *Phoiníkē* (5403), Phoenicia.

5405. Φοῖνιξ *Phoínix*; gen. *Phoínikos*, fem. proper noun. Phenice, a harbor of Crete (Acts 27:12).

5406. φονεύς *phoneús*; gen. *phonéōs*, masc. noun from *phoneúō* (5407), to kill. A murderer (Matt 22:7; Acts 3:14; 7:52; 28:4; 1 Pet 4:15; Rev 21:8; 22:15). Two other words also translated murderer have distinctive features:

(I) *Anthrōpoktónos* (443), manslayer.

(II) *Sikários* (4607), an assassin hired to kill somebody. Of the three words, *phoneús* is the most vague.

Syn.: *patralóas* (3964), a murderer of one's father; *mētralóas* (3389), a murderer or striker of his mother.

5407. φονεύω *phoneúō*; fut. *phoneúsō*, from *phónos* (5408), murder. To murder, kill a man unjustly (Matt 5:21; 19:18; 23:31, 35; Mark 10:19; Luke 18:20; Rom 13:9; James 2:11; 4:2; 5:6). See Sept.: Ex 20:15; Deut 4:42; 5:17.

Deriv.: *phoneús* (5406), a murderer.

Syn.: *apokteínō* (615), to kill; *thúō* (2380), to slay as a sacrifice or for food; *diacheirízomai* (1315), to kill with the hand; *spházō* or *spháttō* (4969), to slaughter as in sacrifice or to kill by violence; *thanatóō* (2289), to put to death, mortify.

Ant.: *zōopoiéō* (2227), to make alive; *zōogonéō* (2225), to rescue from death, engender life; *egeírō* (1453), to raise from the dead; *anístēmi* (450), to raise, as from the dead; *exegeírō* (1825), to awaken or resurrect from among; *exanístēmi* (1817), to raise up from among.

5408. φόνος *phónos*; gen. *phónou*, masc. noun from *phénō* (n.f.), to murder. Murder, particularly slaughter, slaying or killing by the sword (Matt 15:19; Mark 7:21; 15:7; Luke 23:19, 25; Acts 9:1; Rom 1:29; Gal 5:21; Heb 11:37; Rev 9:21; see also Ex 17:13; 22:2; Num 21:24; Deut 13:15; 20:13; 22:8; Prov 1:18). Also from *phénō* (n.f.): *prósphatos* (4372), newly killed, fresh meat.

Deriv.: *androphónos* (409), a murderer; *phoneúō* (5407), to murder.

Syn.: *sphagḗ* (4967), slaughter; *kopḗ* (2871), butchery, a cutting to pieces.

5409. φορέω *phoréō*; contracted *phorṓ*, fut. *phorésō*, from *phérō* (5342), to bear, bring. Particularly a frequentative form implying the repetition or continuance of the simple action expressed by *phérō*, to bring, carry, bear. To bear about with or on oneself, to wear. Trans. (Matt 11:8; John 19:5; Rom 13:4; 1 Cor 15:49; James 2:3).

Deriv.:*potamophórētos*(4216),carried away by a flood or stream; *plerophoréō* (4135), to fulfill; *tropophoréō* (5159), to endure another's habits or manner of life.

Syn.: *endúō* (1746), to put on, clothe.

Ant.: *apobállō* (577), to throw off; *ekdúō* (1562), to take off; *apekdúomai* (554), to put off entirely, to divest or strip.

5410. Φόρον *Phóron*; gen. *Phórou*, neut. proper noun formed from the Lat. *forum*. A market place to which things are taken to be sold. Forum, found only as part of the proper noun, Appii Forum, a town about fifty miles from Rome (Acts 28:15).

5411. φόρος *phóros*; gen. *phórou*, masc. noun from *phérō* (5342), to bring. Particularly what is borne, brought; hence a tax or tribute imposed upon persons and their property annually, in distinction from *télos* (5056), toll, which was usually levied on merchandise and travelers (Luke 20:22; 23:2; Rom 13:6, 7; Sept.: Judg 1:30; 2 Sam 20:24).

Syn.: *kênsos* (2778), a poll tax; *dídrachmon* (1323), two (or a double) drachmae, the equivalent of a half-shekel, which was the amount of the tribute in the first century A.D., due from every adult Jew for the maintenance of the temple services; *statḗr* (4715), a standard of value equivalent to *tetrádrachmon* or four drachmae which would pay the temple tax for two persons.

5412. φορτίζω *phortízō*; fut. *phortísō*, from *phórtos* (5414), the freight of a ship. To overload, heavily burden (Matt 11:28; Luke 11:46).

Deriv.: *apophortízomai* (670), to unload.

Syn.: *katabaréō* (2599), to burden; *baréō* (916), to weigh down.

Ant.: *kouphízō* (2893), to make light in weight.

5413. φορτίον *phortíon*; gen. *phortíou*, neut. noun from *phórtos* (5414), a burden, load. A diminutive in form but not in sense. The goods or merchandise carried by a ship, freight, barge (Isa 46:1). Used in the NT only figuratively as the burden of Christ's commandments (Matt 11:30); the burden of ceremonial observances rigorously exacted and increased by human traditions (Matt 23:4; Luke 11:46); the burden of one's own responsibilities and failures (Gal 6:5 [cf. Sept.: Ps 38:4]).

Syn.: *gómos* (1117), the freight of a ship; *gémō* (1073), to be full; *báros* (922), a weight, something pressing on one physically or emotionally either in a bad or good sense. Some critics contend that a contradiction exists in Gal 6 between Paul's injunction that we should bear "one another's burdens" (6:2) and his assertion that "every man shall bear his own burden." (6:5). However, the conflict is only apparent. In 6:2 the word for burden is *báros*, a burden or difficulty. In 6:5 the word for burden is *phortíon*, responsibility. In the first case, Christians are being enjoined to help each other bear up under the vicissitudes of life. In the last case, Christians are told that each person must assume responsibility for his particular (*ídios* [2398], one's own) duties in life; they have no right to shirk their responsibilities or to expect others to perform them.

5414. φόρτος *phórtos*; gen. *phórtou*, masc. noun from *phérō* (5342), to bring or carry. The freight of a ship (Acts 27:10).

Deriv.: *phortíon* (5413), the goods carried by a ship.

Syn.: *báros* (922), weight; *gómos* (1117), the burden or lading of a ship, or merchandise brought by sea. See *phortíon* (5413), burden, for its distinction from *báros* (922), burden.

5415. Φορτουνᾶτος *Phortounátos*; gen. *Phortounátou*, masc. proper noun. Fortunatus, meaning fortunate, a disciple of Corinth of Roman birth or origin, as his name indicates. He visited Paul at Ephesus and returned along with Stephanas and Achaicus and was in charge of Paul's first epistle to the Corinthian church (1 Cor 16:17).

5416. φραγέλλιον *phragéllion*; gen. *phragellíou*, neut. noun from the Lat. *flagellum*. A scourge, whip (John 2:15).
   Deriv.: *phragellóō* (5417), to scourge.
   Syn.: *mástix* (3148), a whip, scourge, metaphorically a plague.

5417. φραγελλόω *phragellóō*; contracted *phragelló*, fut. *phragelósō*, from *phragéllion* (5416), a scourge, whip. To scourge with a whip (Matt 27:26; Mark 15:15) which was a Roman punishment.
   Syn.: *mastigóō* (3146), to scourge; *mastízō* (3147), to scourge or whip.

5418. φραγμός *phragmós*; gen. *phragmoú*, from *phrássō* (5420), to fence. A fence, hedge, a thorn hedge around a vineyard, beside which there was often a wall (Matt 21:33; Mark 12:1 [cf. Isa 5:2, 5]; Luke 14:23, "into the highways and hedges," the narrow ways among the vineyards). Figuratively a partition. Used with, and equivalent to, *mesótoichon* (3320), a middle wall of partition (Eph 2:14: See also Sept.: Num 22:24; Eccl 10:8).
   Syn.: *teíchos* (5038), a wall of a city; *toíchos* (5109), a wall of a house.

5419. φράζω *phrázō*; fut. *phrásō*. To expound, explain (Matt 13:36; 15:15; Sept.: Job 6:24; 12:8).
   Syn.: *exēgéomai* (1834), to make known, declare, explain; *diasaphéō* (1285), to clarify, explain thoroughly; *hermēneúō* (2059), to interpret; *diermēneúō* (1329), to explain thoroughly.

   Ant.: *skotízō* (4654), to darken, obscure; *sugchéō* (4797), to confound.

5420. φράσσω *phrássō*, **φράττω** *phráttō*; fut. *phráxō*. To enclose with a fence, hedge or wall, to block up. Trans. (Sept.: Prov 21:13; Hos 2:6). In the NT only with reference to the mouth, to stop the mouth, silence.
   (I) Particularly, the mouth of wild beasts (Heb 11:33).
   (II) To stop the mouth from speaking, to silence (Rom 3:19).
   (III) To stop or refrain from boasting (2 Cor 11:10).
   Deriv.: *phragmós* (5418), a fence, hedge.
   Syn.: *sunéchō* (4912), to hold fast, confine; *epistomízō* (1993), to muzzle; *phimóō* (5392), to muzzle, put to silence; *sigáō* (4601), to put to silence, to be silent; *siōpáō* (4623), to hush; *chalinagōgéō* (5468), to bridle; *kleíō* (2808), to shut; *katakleíō* (2623), to shut up in confinement.
   Ant.: *anoígō* (455), to open; *eleutheróō* (1659), to make free, deliver.

5421. φρέαρ *phréar*; gen. *phréatos*, neut. noun. A well or pit dug in the earth for water or other purposes (Gen 16:14; 26:15, 18) and thus strictly distinguished from *pēgḗ* (4077), fountain, though a well may also be called a fountain. (See Luke 14:5; John 4:11, 12, and Rev 9:1, 2 figuratively meaning *hádēs* [86], hell). In Ps 55:23, *phréar diaphthorás* (1312), well of corruption.
   Syn.: *bóthunos* (999), pit, ditch, cistern.

5422. φρεναπατάω *phrenapatáō*; contracted *phrenapató*, fut. *phrenapatḗsō*, from *phrḗn* (5424), mind, and *apatáō* (538), to deceive. To deceive. Trans. (Gal 6:3).
   Deriv.: *phrenapátēs* (5423), deceiver.
   Syn.: *planáō* (4105), to cause to stray or wander; *apatáō* (538), to seduce into error, delude; *exapatáō* (1818), to thoroughly seduce into error; *paralogízomai*

(3884), to deceive or beguile by false reasoning; *pagideúō* (3802), to ensnare.

5423. φρεναπάτης *phrenapátēs*; gen. *phrenapátou*, masc. noun from *phrenapatáō* (5422), to deceive the mind. A deceiver, impostor (Titus 1:10).

    Syn.: *dólios* (1386), guileful, deceitful; *plános* (4108), one who diverts others from the right way; *mágos* (3097), sorcerer, magician.

5424. φρήν *phrḗn*; gen. *phrenós*, fem. noun. Literally the diaphragm, that which curbs or restrains. Figuratively, the supposed seat of all mental and emotional activity. In the NT metonymically meaning the mind, intellect, disposition, feelings. Only in 1 Cor 14:20 translated "understanding." See Prov 7:7; 9:4. *Phrénes* was regarded as the seat of intellectual and spiritual activity. It was the diaphragm which determined the strength of the breath and hence also the human spirit and its emotions. It precisely refers to the ability not only to think, but also to control one's thoughts and attitudes. It is the heart as the seat of passions as well as the mind as the seat of mental faculties.

    Deriv.: *áphrōn* (878), a fool; *homóphrōn* (3675), of the same mind; *sṓphrōn* (4998), of sound mind; *phrenapatáō* (5422), to deceive; *phronéō* (5426), to think.

    Syn.: *noús* (3563), mind; *súnesis* (4907), discernment, the ability to understand the relationships between ideas; *diánoia* (1271), intellect, mind.

5425. φρίσσω *phríssō*, φρίττω *phríttō*; fut. *phríxō*. To bristle, to have one's hair stand on end. In the NT, to shudder or quake from fear or aversion (James 2:19, by the demons; Sept.: Dan 7:15).

    Syn.: *trémō* (5141), to tremble; *ptoéō* (4422), to scare and in the mid. *ptoéomai*, to be in trepidation; *tarássomai* (5015), to be troubled; *deiliáō* (1168), to be timid; *phoboúmai* (5399), to be afraid; *seíō* (4579), to shake, tremble.

    Ant.: *parrēsiázomai* (3955), to be confident, bold; *tharséō* (2293), to have courage; *tharréō* (2292), to exercise courage, confidence; *tolmáō* (5111), to have courage, be bold.

5426. φρονέω *phronéō*; contracted *phronṓ*, fut. *phronḗsō*, from *phrḗn* (5424), mind. To think, have a mindset, be minded. The activity represented by this word involves the will, affections, and conscience.

    (I) Generally, to be of an opinion. Followed by the acc. of thing (Acts 28:22; Rom 12:3; 1 Cor 4:6; Gal 5:10; Phil 1:7). With an adv. or adv. phrase (Rom 12:3; 1 Cor 13:11). Of time, to regard, keep (Rom 14:6 [cf. Gal 4:10]).

    (II) To think, to sense mentally, followed by the acc.

    (A) Generally (Phil 2:5, "let the same mind be in you as in Christ" [a.t.]; Phil 3:15). In Rom 12:16, not to think of "high things" (*hupsēlá* [5308]) means not to be proud. In the phrase *tó autó* ([846], the same thing) *phronéō* it means to be of one mind, one accord, to think the same thing. *Tó autó* is the same as *tó hén* (neut. of *heís* [1520], one), to think one and the same thing (Rom 15:5; 2 Cor 13:11; Phil 2:2; 3:16; 4:2).

    (B) To be mindful of, to be devoted to (Matt 16:23; Mark 8:33; Rom 8:5; Phil 3:19; Col 3:2); with *hupér* ([5228], on behalf of, for), to mind, regard, care for (Phil 4:10).

    Deriv.: *kataphronéō* (2706), to despise; *paraphronéō* (3912), to be foolhardy; *periphronéō* (4065), to despise; *huperphronéō* (5252), to be vain, arrogant; *hupsēlophronéō* (5309), to be proud, arrogant *philóphrōn* (5391), friendly; *phrónēma* (5427), thought; *phrónēsis* (5428), thinking; *phrónimos* (5429), thoughtful.

    Syn.: *phrontízō* (5431), to think, consider, be careful; *dokéō* (1380), to think, form an opinion; *hēgéomai* (2233), to think; *noéō* (3539), to perceive, understand; *katanoéō* (2657), to perceive fully, comprehend; *aisthánomai* (143), to perceive, understand; *katalambánō* (2638), to apprehend, comprehend; *oída* (1482), to know intuitively; *suníēmi* (4920), to perceive, understand; *epístamai* (1987), to know well; *punthánomai* (4441), to ascertain; *ginóskō* (1097) and *gnōrízō* (1107), to know experientially; *logízomai* (3049), to reckon, think; *huponoéō* (5282), *nomízō* (3543), and *oíomai* (3633) or *oímai*, to suppose, think; *phaínō* (5316), to appear, think; *enthuméomai* (1760), to reflect, ponder; *krínō* (2919), to judge.

Ant.: *paraphronéō* (3912), to be beside oneself, deranged, a fool; *mōraínō* (3471), to make foolish, and the mid. *mōraínomai*, to become foolish; *paralogízomai* (3884), to delude, deceive; *exístēmi* (1839), to become insane or beside oneself.

5427. φρόνημα *phrónēma*; gen. *phronématos*, neut. noun from *phronéō* (5426), to think, have a mind set. The tendency or inclination of the mind, its bent. It includes the act of the understanding and of the will. Rom 8:6, 7 teaches that the will follows or obeys the dominant interest of the mind. If it is the flesh, then death follows; if it is the Spirit, then life and peace follow. Rom 8:27 refers to the way the Holy Spirit influences our spirits in praying. The suffix -*ma* indicates the result of one's thinking. Contrasted to *phrónēsis* (5428) which indicates mental action and willingness.

Syn.: *diánoia* (1271), the faculty of knowing; *dianóēma* (1270), thought; *noús* (3563), mind, the seat of reflective consciousness; *énnoia* (1771), mind, intent; *nóēma* (3540), thought, design; *gnómē* (1106), opinion, mind; *krísis* (2920), judgment.

Ant.: *agnōsía* (56), lack of knowledge; *ágnoia* (52), ignorance; *agnóēma* (51), a sin committed in ignorance.

5428. φρόνησις *phrónēsis*; gen. *phronéseōs*, fem. noun from *phronéō* (5426), to think, have a mind set. Prudence, good judgment, wisdom. The ability to govern one's own life wisely; a skill and carefulness in dealing with one's own resources.

(I) A wise mode of thinking (Luke 1:17).

(II) Understanding, prudence (Eph 1:8, where it occurs with the noun *sophía* [4678], wisdom; Sept.: 1 Kgs 3:28; 4:29; Prov 1:2; 3:13; 7:4; 8:1).

Syn.: *súnesis* (4907), perception, discernment.

Ant.: *agnōsía* (56), ignorance; *aphrosúnē* (877), senselessness.

5429. φρόνιμος *phrónimos*; fem. *phrónimē*, neut. *phrónimon*, adj. from *phronéō* (5426), to think, have a mindset. Prudent, sensible, practically wise in relationships with others (Matt 7:24; 10:16; 24:45; 25:2, 4, 8, 9; Luke 12:42; 16:8; 1 Cor 10:15; Sept.: 1 Kgs 3:12; Prov 3:7; 14:6; 18:15; Isa 44:25). In an evil sense, thinking oneself to be prudent or wise because of self-complacency (Rom 11:25; 12:16; used ironically in 1 Cor 4:10; 2 Cor 11:19; Sept.: Prov 3:7).

Deriv.: *phronímōs* (5430), prudently.

Syn.: *sunetós* (4908), sagacious, understanding, able to reason; *sóphrōn* (4998), of sound mind; *sophós* (4680), wise.

Ant.: *mōrós* (3474), stupid, foolish, absurd; *asúnetos* (801), without understanding; *anóētos* (453), unintelligent, foolish; *áphrōn* (878), mindless, stupid, foolish.

5430. φρονίμως *phronímōs*; adv. from *phrónimos* (5429), prudent. Prudently. It denotes the wise, prudent and sensible manner in which one conducts himself and his affairs. In Luke 16:8 the word means with advantage, shrewdly.

Syn.: *orthós* (3723), rightly, correctly; *akribós* (199), circumspectly, exactly, diligently; *asphalós* (806), securely, safely; *kalós* (2573), well; *sōphrónōs* (4996), with sound mind.

Ant.: *atáktōs* (814), disorderly; *kakós* (2560), badly.

5431. φροντίζω *phrontízō*; fut. *phrontísō*, from *phrontís* (n.f.), care. To take care, concentrate upon, be careful, solicitous, to consider (Titus 3:8; Sept.: with gen. Ps 40:17).
Syn.: *mélō* (3199), to concern oneself; *merimnáō* (3309), to show anxious care; *phronéō* (5426), to think with concern; *epimeléomai* (1959), to take care of; *episkopéō* (1983), to oversee; *proséchō* (4337), to pay attention, be cautious about, attend, heed.
Ant.: *ameléō* (272), to neglect; *oligōréō* (3643), to have little regard for; *periḯstēmi* (4026), to avoid, shun.

5432. φρουρέω *phrouréō*; contracted *phrourṓ*, fut. *phrourḗsō*, from *phrourós* (n.f.), a sentinel, guard. In the NT and generally followed by the acc., to watch, guard, keep.
(I) To guard, keep with a military guard (2 Cor 11:32).
(II) Figuratively, *phrouréomai*, to be kept or guarded under the law, namely from sin (Gal 3:23).
(III) To keep, guard, preserve spiritually (Phil 4:7; 1 Pet 1:5).
Syn.: *tēréō* (5083), to keep, preserve; *diatēréō* (1301), to preserve carefully or exactly; *suntēréō* (4933), to preserve safely; *phulássō* (5442), to keep, preserve from injury or harm; *diaphulássō* (1314), to keep, preserve carefully; *kratéō* (2902), to hold fast.
Ant.: *kataleípō* (2641), to forsake; *aphíēmi* (863), to send forth, forsake, leave; *egkataleípō* (1459), to leave behind, desert; *ameléō* (272), to neglect; *epilanthánomai* (1950), to forget; *oligōréō* (3643), to give little time or attention.

5433. φρυάσσω *phruássō*, **φρυάττω** *phruáttō*; fut. *phruáxō*, mid./pass. *phruássomai*, kindred to *brúō* (1032), to overflow, pour forth. To make a noise such as snorting, neighing, to be tumultuous, noisy, fierce, to rage (Acts 4:25 quoted from Ps 2:1).

Syn.: *diegeírō* (1326), to arouse; *thumóō* (2373), to enrage; *choláō* (5520), to be angry, choleric; *orgízō* (3710), to become or cause to be exasperated, enraged; *anastatóō* (387), to upset.
Ant.: *eirēneúō* (1514), to be peaceful.

5434. φρύγανον *phrúganon*; gen. *phrugánou*, neut. noun from *phrúgō* (n.f.), to burn. A stick for burning, kindling (Acts 28:3; Sept.: Isa 40:24; 47:14).
Syn.: *xúlon* (3586), timber; *hulē* (5208), wood, fuel.

5435. Φρυγία *Phrugía*; gen. *Phrugías*, fem. proper noun. Phrygia. A province of Asia Minor. Paul crossed this province twice in the course of his missionary journeys. The towns of Antioch in Pisidia (Acts 13:14), Colosse, Hierapolis, Iconium, and Laodicea were situated in greater Phrygia. See Acts 2:10; 16:6; 18:23.

5436. Φύγελλος *Phúgellos*; gen. *Phugéllou*, masc. proper noun. Phygellus, meaning a fugitive. A Christian connected with those in Asia who had turned away from Paul (2 Tim 1:15).

5437. φυγή *phugḗ*; fem. noun from *pheúgō* (5343), to flee. A flight or fleeing (Matt 24:20; Mark 13:18; Sept.: Jer 25:35; 49:23).
Syn.: *éxodos* (1841), exit, exodus.
Ant.: *epistrophḗ* (1995), a return.

5438. φυλακή *phulakḗ*; gen. *phulakḗs*, fem. noun from *phulássō* (5442), to keep.
(I) The act of keeping watch, guarding (Luke 2:8; Sept.: Num 1:53; 3:7, 28).
(II) Metonymically of persons set to watch, a watch, guard or guards (Acts 12:10).
(III) Metonymically, the place where a watch is kept (Sept.: Hab 2:1). In the NT figuratively of Babylon as the dwelling place, station, haunt of demons and unclean birds where they resort and hold

their vigils (Rev 18:2 [cf. Isa 34:11f.; Jer 50:39; 51:37]).

(IV) Of the place where someone is watched, guarded, kept in custody, a prison. Generally (Matt 5:25; 14:3, 10; 18:30; 25:36, 39, 43, 44; Mark 6:17, 40; Luke 3:20; 12:58; 21:12; 22:33; 23:19, 25; John 3:24; Acts 5:19, 22, 25; 8:3; 12:4–6, 17; 16:23, 24, 27, 37, 40; 22:4; 26:10; Rev 2:10). In the sense of imprisonment (2 Cor 6:5; 11:23; Heb 11:36; Sept.: Gen 40:3f.; 42:17; Lev 24:12; 1 Kgs 22:27). Poetically of the bottomless pit, abyss, Tartarus, as the prison of demons and the souls of wicked men (1 Pet 3:19; Rev 20:7 [cf. 2 Pet 2:4; Jude 1:6]). See *tartaróō* (5020), to consign to Tartarus.

(V) Metonymically of time, a watch of the night, a period of the night during which one watch of soldiers kept guard and were then relieved (Matt 14:25; 24:43; Mark 6:48; Luke 12:38). The ancient Jews, and probably the Greeks, divided the night into three watches of four hours each (Sept.: Judg 7:19; Ps 90:4). But after the Jews came under the dominion of the Romans, they made four watches of about three hours each as the Romans had. These were either numbered first, second, third, fourth, and were also called *opsé* (3796), late in the day, after the close of the day, evening; *mesonúktion* (3317), midnight; *alektorophōnía* (219), the time of the cock crowing; *prōḯ* (4404), morning (cf. Mark 13:35). See *tetrádion* (5069), a quaternion or squadron of four Roman soldiers.

Deriv.: *gazophulákion* (1049), a treasury; *phulakízō* (5439), to imprison.

Syn.: *tḗrēsis* (5084), a watching, guarding, imprisonment; *desmōtḗrion* (1201), a prison *koustōdía* (2892), watch, guard; *douleía* (1397), slavery; *desmá* (1199), shackle of a prisoner.

Ant.: *eleuthería* (1657), freedom; *lútrōsis* (3085), deliverance.

5439. **φυλακίζω** *phulakízō*; fut. *phulakísō*, from *phulakḗ* (5438), prison. To imprison (Acts 22:19).

Syn.: *déō* (1210) and *desmeúō* (1195), to bind; *kratéō* (2902), to hold, to rule over; *sunéchō* (4912), to hold fast; *aichmalōtízō* (163), to make captive; *doulóō* (1402), to bring into bondage.

Ant.: *lúō* (3089), to loose, unbind; *eleutheróō* (1659), to liberate; *lutróō* (3084), to redeem.

5440. **φυλακτήριον** *phulaktḗrion*; gen. *phulaktēriou*, neut. noun from *phulássō* (5442), to keep, preserve. Phylacteries were pouches or boxes containing scrolls of parchment on which the Jews wrote certain portions of the Law and bound them on their foreheads and their wrists (Matt 23:5; see Ex 13:8, 9, 11–16; Deut 6:4–9; 11:13–21). They were originally called *phulaktḗria*, places of preservation, because they reminded the Jews to keep the Law. However, the Jews in our Lord's day came to regard them as amulets or charms which would keep or preserve them from evil.

5441. **φύλαξ** *phúlax*; gen. *phúlakos*, masc. noun from *phulássō* (5442), to keep. A keeper, guard, sentinel (Acts 5:23; 12:6, 19; Sept.: Gen 4:9; Isa 62:6).

Deriv.: *desmophúlax* (1200), a prison keeper.

Syn.: *koustōdía* (2892), a Roman sentry; *spekoulátōr* (4688), a lookout officer, bodyguard, an executioner.

5442. **φυλάσσω** *phulássō*, **φυλάττω** *phuláttō*; fut. *phuláxō*. To watch, keep watch.

(I) Intrans. followed by the acc. of the cognate noun (Luke 2:8); passive intrans. (Luke 8:29; Acts 23:35).

(II) Trans. with the acc., to watch, guard, keep:

(A) Persons or things from escape or violence (Luke 8:29; Acts 12:4; 28:16). Followed by *en* (1722), in, and the dat. (Acts 23:35); by the acc. (Luke 11:21; Acts 22:20; Sept.: Gen 2:15; 3:25; 1 Sam 19:11).

(B) Of persons or things kept in safety, to keep, preserve (John 17:12; 2 Pet

2:5; Jude 1:24; Sept.: Ex 23:20; Prov 6:22). Followed by *apó* (575), from, and the gen. (2 Thess 3:3; 1 John 5:21, "keep yourselves from idols"); with the acc. (1 Tim 6:20; 2 Tim 1:14). With *eis hēméran* (*eis* [1519], unto; *hēméran* [2250], day), unto the day (2 Tim 1:12); followed by *eis zōḗn* ([2222], life), "unto life" (John 12:25).

(C) In the mid., to protect oneself, to be on one's guard, to beware of, avoid. In the mid. (Luke 12:15); followed by the acc., to guard against (Acts 21:25; 2 Tim 4:15). Followed by *hína* (2443) and *mḗ* (3361), not, so that not (2 Pet 3:17).

(III) Figuratively, to keep, observe, not to violate, e.g., precepts, laws. With the acc. (Luke 11:28; Acts 7:53; 16:4; 21:24; Rom 2:26; Gal 6:13; 1 Tim 5:21; Sept.: 1 Kgs 11:38; Ps 105:45; Prov 4:4; 6:20; 28:7). In the mid., "all these things have I kept from my youth up" (Matt 19:20; Mark 10:20; Luke 18:21; Sept.: Deut 5:15).

Deriv.: *diaphulássō* (1314), to guard thoroughly, protect; *phulakḗ* (5438), the act of guarding; *phulaktḗrion* (5440), phylactery; *phúlax* (5441), a keeper, guard.

Syn.: *kratéō* (2902), to hold fast; *sunéchō* (4912), to hold together; *sṓzō* (4982), save, preserve; *blépō* (991), to take heed; *proséchō* (4337), to be on guard, to beware; *horáō* (3708), to behold, pay attention to; *epéchō* (1907), to take heed; *skopéō* (4648), to mark, heed, consider; *phrouréō* (5432), to guard; *tēréō* (5083), to watch over, preserve, keep; *diatēréō* (1301), to keep carefully; *suntēréō* (4933), to preserve, keep safe.

Ant.: *lanthánō* (2990), to be unaware; *epilanthánomai* (1950), forget, neglect; *eklanthánomai* (1585), to forget completely; *paradídōmi* (3860), to betray; *eleutheróō* (1659), to make free; *parabaínō* (3845), to transgress; *biázō* (971), to violate; *ameléō* (272), to neglect.

5443. φυλή *phulḗ*; gen. *phulḗs*, fem. noun from *phúlon* (n.f.), race, tribe, class,

which is from *phúō* (5453), to generate, produce. A tribe, race, lineage, kindred.

(I) A nation or people descended from a common ancestor (Matt 24:30, "all the tribes," nations of the earth; Rev 1:7). Pleonastically (Rev 5:9, "out of every kindred, and tongue, and people, and nation," all referring to the same thing; Rev 7:9; 11:9; 13:7; 14:6; Sept.: Gen 12:3).

(II) Specifically, a tribe, clan, spoken of the tribes of Israel as subdivisions of the whole nation (Matt 19:28; Luke 22:30; Sept.: Deut 1:13); "of the tribe of Asher" (Luke 2:36); "of the tribe of Benjamin" (Acts 13:21; Rom 11:1; Phil 3:5). See Heb 7:13, 14; James 1:1; Rev 5:5; 7.

Deriv.: *allóphulos* (246), foreign, alien; *dōdekáphulos* (1429), of twelve tribes.

Syn.: *génos* (1085), generation, kindred, nation, stock; *haíma* (129), blood, kindred; *éthnos* (1484), tribe, nation, people, Gentiles; *rhíza* (4491), root, progenitors; *geneá* (1074), a generation, age, nation; *patriá* (3965), paternal descent, family, kindred, lineage; *genealogía* (1076), genealogy; *laós* (2992), people, nation, tribe.

5444. φύλλον *phúllon*; gen. *phúllou*, neut. noun from *phúō* (5453), to produce, yield. A leaf, as of a tree (Matt 21:19; 24:32; Mark 11:13; 13:28; Rev 22:2; Sept.: Gen 3:8; 8:11; Neh 8:15). Other parts of the tree: *rhíza* (4491), root; *kládos* (2798), branch; *ánthos* (438), flower, blossom; *karpós* (2590), fruit. The word for trunk is *kormós* which does not occur in the NT.

5445. φύραμα *phúrama*; gen. *phurámatos*, neut. noun from *phuráō* (n.f.), to break, dissolve, knead. A mass or lump, as of clay kneaded and thus prepared for use by the potter (Rom 9:21); of kneaded dough (1 Cor 5:6 [cf. 5:7]; Rom 11:16; Gal 5:9). See Sept.: Ex 8:3; 12:34; Num 15:19, 21. See *zúmē* (2219), leaven.

5446. φυσικός *phusikós*; fem. *phusikḗ*, neut. *phusikón*, adj. from *phúsis* (5449), nature. Natural, as established by God in nature (Rom 1:26, 27); like natural or wild beasts, i.e., unreasoning, yielding only to baser instincts (2 Pet 2:12).

Deriv.: *phusikós* (5447), physically or naturally.

Syn.: *psuchikós* (5591), sensual; *sarkikós* (4559), pertaining to the flesh, temporal, carnal, fleshly; *sárkinos* (4560), made of flesh in distinction from *sarkikós* which indicates the desire to do the inclinations of the flesh; *sōmatikós* (4984), bodily.

Ant.: *pneumatikós* (4152), spiritual.

5447. φυσικῶς *phusikós*; adv. from *phusikós* (5446), natural. Naturally, by instinct (Jude 1:10 [cf. 2 Pet 2:12]).

Syn.: *sōmatikós* (4985), corporeally, physically, bodily.

Ant.: *pneumatikós* (4153), spiritually.

5448. φυσιόω *phusióō*; contracted *phusió*, fut. *phusiósō*, from *phusáō* (n.f.), to breathe, blow, inflate. To inflate, blow or puff up. In the NT spoken only figuratively of pride or self-conceit (1 Cor 4:6, 18, 19; 5:2; 8:1; 13:4; Col 2:18). Also from *phusáō* (n.f.): *emphusáō* (1720), to breathe on, blow on.

Deriv.: *phusíōsis* (5450), haughtiness.

Syn.: *tuphóō* (5187), to inflate with pride; *hupsēlophronéō* (5309), to be high-minded; *epaírō* (1869), to exalt; *huperaírō* (5229), to exalt above; *huperupsóō* (5251), to elevate above others; *huperphronéō* (5252), to over esteem, be vain or arrogant.

Ant.: *tapeinóō* (5013), to humble; *hupostéllō* (5288), to withhold from sight, fold under, conceal.

5449. φύσις *phúsis*; gen. *phúseōs*, fem. noun from *phúō* (5453), to bring forth. Nature, natural birth or condition (Rom 2:27; Gal 2:15); natural disposition (Eph 2:3; 2 Pet 1:4). Paul uses the word in Rom 2:14, 15 speaking of the Gentiles who though not having the Law still obey it: "For when the Gentiles, which have not the law, do by nature the things contained in the law, these, having not the law, are a law unto themselves: which show the work of the law written in their hearts." He tells us that they neither possess nor observe the written ceremonial law (cf. 2:25–29), and yet they do by nature (*phúsei*, adv. dat.) the things of the Law, i.e., the great duties of a regenerate life (cf. 2:26, 27). Paul refers not to the unconverted, but to the converted Gentiles and uses the description given prophetically by Jeremiah of the Christian condition (see Jer 31:31–34 [cf. 2 Cor 3:3; Heb 8:6–13; 10:16]). The verbs do (*poiḗ* [4160]), and are (*eisí* [1510]) in Rom 2:14, and show (*endeíknuntai* [1731]) in Rom 2:15 are all in the pres. tense and carry a simple linear force. The pres. tense does not indicate that Paul had in mind only the Gentiles of his day. The subj. mood with *hótan* (3752), whenever, establishes the fact that Paul's words are timeless and universal referring to any such cases. Apart from such cases, however, the past condition of the Gentiles was in general as degenerate and apostate as Paul previously described it (Rom 1:24). Paul continues, then, asking that because some Gentiles who do not have the Law do the things of the Law, will they not be regarded as though they were circumcised (Rom 2:26)? The Apostle asks, "Shall not his uncircumcision be counted for circumcision? And shall not uncircumcision, which is by nature, if it fulfill the law, judge thee, who by the letter and circumcision dost transgress the law? For he is not a Jew which is one outwardly; neither is that circumcision which is outward in the flesh: but he is a Jew which is one inwardly; and circumcision is that of the heart, in the spirit, and not in the letter; whose praise is not of men, but of God" (Rom 2:26b–29). We should compare this passage with the contrast Paul makes between Judaistic teachers and true saints (Phil 3:2, 3), "Beware of dogs, beware of evil workers, beware of the concision: for we are the circumcision, which worship God in the spirit, and rejoice in Christ Jesus, and have no confidence in the flesh."

In examining these passages together, we find strong reason to think that the Gentiles mentioned in Rom 2:14 whose uncircumcision is counted for circumcision (2:26) are the very same sort of persons as those of whom Paul says in Phil 3:3, "We are the circumcision." These are believers.

Phúsis also means nature, essence, essential constitution and properties (Gal 4:8). It also means the constitution and order of God in the natural world (Rom 1:26; 11:21, 24; 1 Cor 11:14). It also refers to species of living creatures (James 3:7).

The statement in 2 Pet 1:4 that Christians have become "partakers of the divine nature" has been grossly misunderstood by some interpreters. God's nature here refers not to His essence but to certain of His attributes, i.e., divine qualities. It is similar to the expression in 1:4 *theías dunámeōs* (*theíos* [2304], divine; *dúnamis* [1411], power), divine power.

Deriv.: *phusikós* (5446), natural, instinctive.

Syn.: *génesis* (1078), generation, nature; *psuchḗ* (5590), soul, the inward disposition of man; *charaktḗr* (5481), likeness, exact image; *éthos* (2239), moral habits, ethics; *hormḗ* (3730), an inward impulse.

5450. φυσίωσις phusíōsis; gen. *phusiōseōs*, fem. noun from *phusióō* (5448), to inflate, blow or puff up through pride. A swelling of pride or ambition, arrogance (2 Cor 12:20).

Syn.: *huperēphanía* (5243), pride, haughtiness; *alazoneía* (212), bragging, boasting; *kenodoxía* (2754), empty glory, vain glory.

Ant.: *tapeinophrosúnē* (5012), lowliness of mind, humility; *tapeínōsis* (5014), humiliation.

5451. φυτεία phuteía; gen. *phuteías*, fem. noun from *phuteúō* (5452), to plant. A planting, the act of planting, or a plant (Matt 15:13) denoting figuratively a religious doctrine.

Syn.: *botánē* (1008), herbage, herb; *láchanon* (3001), a vegetable, herb; *chórtos* (5528), herbage, vegetation, grass.

5452. φυτεύω phuteúō; fut. *phuteúsō*, from *phutón* (n.f.), a plant, which is from *phúō* (5453), to generate, spring up. To plant, to put into the ground in order to grow, to set (Matt 21:33; Mark 12:1; Luke 13:6; 17:6, 28; 20:9; 1 Cor 9:7; Sept.: Gen 9:20; Ps 1:3). To plant figuratively, to establish, authorize teachers or their doctrines (Matt 15:13). To plant the gospel, i.e., to be first to preach it in a place (1 Cor 3:6–8 [cf. 3:10]). Comp. *phuteía* (5451), a plant.

Deriv.: *phuteía* (5451), the act of planting.

Syn.: *phúō* (5453), to generate, bring forth.

Ant.: *therízō* (2325), to reap; *amáō* (270), to reap; *trugáō* (5166), to collect the vintage; *ekrizóō* (1610), to uproot.

5453. φύω phúō; fut. *phúsō*, 2d aor. *éphun*, perf. *péphuka* (as intrans., to be generated, produced). To generate, produce, bring forth, let grow, of plants, fruit, or persons. Usages in the NT:

(I) 2d aor. pass. indic. *ephúēn*, part. *phueís*, to spring up or grow as a plant (Luke 8:6, 8). This form of the aor. is used only by later writers, instead of the earlier word *éphun*.

(II) Act. intrans., to spring up, grow up (Heb 12:15 quoted from Deut 29:18).

Deriv.: *ekphúō* (1631), to produce; *neóphutos* (3504), newly planted, novice; *sumphúō* (4855), to bring forth together; *phúllon* (5444), a leaf; *phúsis* (5449), nature, natural birth or condition.

Syn.: *auxánō* (837), to grow or increase; *gínomai* (1096), to become, to be.

5454. φωλεός phōleós; gen. *phōleoú*, masc. noun. A hole, burrow, a place where animals lurk. Used only in the pl. (Matt 8:20; Luke 9:58).

Syn.: *opḗ* (3692), hole; *spḗlaion* (4693), a grotto, cavern, den, cave.

5455. φωνέω *phōnéō*; fut. *phōnḗsō*, from *phōnḗ* (5456), voice. Intrans. meaning to utter a sound, to call or cry out (Mark 10:49; 15:35; Luke 8:8, 54; 16:24; 23:46; Acts 10:18; Rev 14:18; Sept.: 1 Chr 15:16; Dan 4:11). To crow as a rooster (Matt 26:34, 74, 75; Mark 14:30, 68, 72; Luke 22:34, 60, 61; John 13:38; 18:27); of other birds (Sept.: Isa 38:14; Jer 17:11); of beasts, to cry (Zeph 2:14); of a trumpet (Sept.: Amos 3:6). Trans. with an acc., to call, call for, speak to, address (Matt 20:32; Mark 3:31; 9:35; 10:49; Luke 16:2; 19:15; John 1:48; 4:16; 9:18, 24; 11:28; 18:33; Acts 9:41; 10:7). To call to, speak to with a loud voice, or simply to speak to (John 2:9; Acts 16:28). To call, invite (Luke 14:12). To call, name, denominate (John 13:13). Followed by *ek* (1537), out of, from somewhere (John 12:17 [cf. 11:43]). To call out to someone for help (Matt 27:47; Mark 15:35).

Deriv.: *anaphōnéō* (400), to speak out; *epiphōnéō* (2019), to clamor, shout; *prosphōnéō* (4377), to speak to someone.

Syn.: *kaléō* (2564), to call; *epikaléō* (1941), to call upon; *proskaléomai* (4341), to call to oneself; *prosagoreúomai* (4316), to address, salute by name; *boáō* (994), to raise a cry, cry out; *krázō* (2896), to cry out; *kraugázō* (2905), to make a clamor or outcry.

Ant.: *agnoéō* (50), to ignore; *lanthánō* (2990), to forget; *epilanthánomai* (1950), to forget, neglect; *eklanthánomai* (1585), to forget completely; *sigáō* (4601), to be silent; *siōpáō* (4623), to keep quiet.

5456. φωνή *phōnḗ*; gen. *phōnḗs*, fem. noun from *pháō* (n.f.), to shine. A sound or tone made or given forth. Plutarch calls it "that which brings light upon that which is thought of in the mind." The voice explains the attitude one has for others. It is variably translated: voice (Matt 2:18); sound (John 3:8); noise (Rev

6:1). *Phōnḗ* is the cry of a living being which can be heard by others. It is ascribed to God (Matt 3:17); to men (Matt 3:3); to inanimate objects (1 Cor 14:7) as a trumpet (Matt 24:31 [TR]); the wind (John 3:8); thunder (Rev 6:1). It is distinct from *lógos* (3056), a rational expression of the mind either spoken (*prophorikós* [n.f.], with utterance, as in Dan 7:11) or unspoken (*endiáthetos* [n.f.], remaining with oneself). *Endiáthetos* is equivalent to reason and can only be predicated of men who can think. Therefore, *lógos* is something that only intelligent beings can exercise and it can be either spoken or unspoken. Thus Jesus Christ is called not *phōnḗ*, but *Lógos*, intelligence, the expression of that intelligence in terms that could make us understand what was in the mind of God eternally (John 1:1).

(I) Generally and spoken of things: of a trumpet or other instrument (Matt 24:31; 1 Cor 14:7, 8; Sept.: Ex 19:19; 20:18; Ezek 26:13; Dan 3:5, 7, 10); the wind (John 3:8; Acts 2:6); rushing wings, chariots, waters (Rev 9:9; 14:2; 18:22; 19:6; Sept.: Ezek 1:24; 3:13; 26:10; Nah 3:2); of thunder (Rev 6:1; 14:2; 19:6), voices and thunders *brontaí* ([1027], thunders [cf. Rev 4:5; 8:5; 11:19; Sept.: Ex 19:16; 1 Sam 7:10]); *Phōnḗ rhēmátōn* ([4487], of utterances), the thunders in which the words of the Law were proclaimed (Heb 12:19).

(II) Specifically, the voice or cry of a person.

(A) Particularly and generally as in phrases with verbs of speaking, calling, crying out: *phōnḗ megálē* ([3173], great) "with a loud voice" (Matt 27:46, 50; Mark 5:7; 15:34; Luke 8:28; John 11:43; Acts 8:7; Rev 6:10; Sept.: Job 2:12); *en* ([1722], in) *megálē phōnḗ*, "with a loud voice" (Rev 14:15); *metá* ([3326], with) *megálēs phōnḗs*, "with a loud voice" (Luke 17:15;), with *aphíēmi* ([863], to send forth) *phōnḗn megálēn*, to utter a loud cry, cry with a loud voice (Mark 15:37); *aírō* ([142], to raise) or *epaírō* ([1869], to raise up) *phōnḗn*, to lift up the voice, cry or call aloud (Luke 11:27;

17:13; Acts 2:14; 4:24; 14:11; 22:22); with *epíkeimai* ([1945], to press upon) *megálais phōnaís*, to press upon with loud voices (Luke 23:23); with *gínomai* (1096), to be, where the voice of one speaking is said to come forth (Luke 9:35, 36; Acts 7:31). Followed by *prós* (4314), unto, and the acc. (Acts 10:13). With *phérō* (5342), to bring, in the pass., *phōnḗ phéretai* followed by the dat., *phōnḗs enechtheísēs autṓ*, "when there came such a voice to him" (2 Pet 1:17). Followed by *ek* (1537), out of, with the gen., "there came out of heaven a voice" (a.t. [Matt 3:17; Luke 3:22; John 12:28]); *ek tḗs nephélēs* ([3507], cloud), "out of the cloud" (Mark 9:7; Luke 9:35; Sept.: Isa 66:6); *ek pántōn*, "with one cry from all" (a.t. [Acts 19:34]). Followed by *apó* (575), from, with the gen. (Rev 16:17; Sept.: Zeph 1:10). With the verb *akoúō* (191), to hear, followed by the acc. or gen. meaning to hear a voice (Matt 2:18, pass. preceded by nom.; Luke 1:44; Acts 9:4, 7; Rev 6:6; "I . . . heard behind me a great voice," Rev 1:10). See also Sept.: Gen 3:8, 10; 4:23. Followed by *ek* with the gen., as *ex ouranoú* (3772), "out of heaven" (a.t. [2 Pet 1:18]); "out of the four horns" (a.t. [Rev 9:13]); "out of his mouth" (a.t. [Acts 22:14]). Followed by the gen. of person (Matt 3:3; 12:19; Mark 1:3). "The dead shall hear the voice of the Son of God" (John 5:25); "his voice" in the gen. (John 5:28); "Peter's voice" (Acts 12:14); "the voice of a god" (Acts 12:22); "the voice of the archangel" (1 Thess 4:16). See also Heb 12:26; Rev 5:11; 19:1, "a great voice of the multitude" (a.t.); Rev 19:6. Of the voice of song with the gen. (Rev 18:22); "the voice of the bridegroom and of the bride" (Rev 18:23). With *akoúō* (191), to hear or hear one's voice, it has the meaning of obeying one's voice or obeying the person himself (John 10:16, 27; Heb 3:7, 15; 4:7; Sept.: Gen 3:17). Used figuratively, "to change my voice," meaning to change one's tone, to speak in a different manner and spirit (Gal 4:20).

(B) Metonymically for what is uttered by the voice, a word, saying (Acts 13:27, "the voices of the prophets," for what the prophets said; 24:21).

(C) Metonymically meaning manner of speaking, speech, language, dialect (1 Cor 14:10, 11; Sept.: Gen 11:1).

Deriv.: *alektorophōnía* (219), crowing of a rooster; *áphōnos* (880), voiceless, mute; *kenophōnía* (2757), empty speaking; *súmphōnos* (4859), agreeable, sounding together, harmonious; *phōnéō* (5455), to address, speak.

Syn.: *kraugḗ* (2906), clamor, crying; *ḗchos* (2279), a loud noise, roar, echo, sound; *phthóggos* (5353), utterance, musical note, sound; *laliá* (2981), talk, speech, saying, prattle; *lógos* (3056), word, speech, discourse; *boḗ* (995), cry for help; *thrḗnos* (2355), wailing.

Ant.: *sigḗ* (4602), silence; *hēsuchía* (2271), quietness.

5457. φῶς *phṓs*; gen. *phōtós*, neut. noun from *pháō* (n.f.), to shine. Light. Also from *pháō* (n.f.): *phōnḗ* (5456), to sound.

(I) Particularly and generally:

(A) Of light in itself (2 Cor 4:6, "For God, who commanded the light to shine out of darkness"); raiment (Matt 17:2, "and his raiment was white as the light"; Sept.: Gen 1:3, 4, 18).

(B) As emitted from a luminous body as a lamp, *phṓs lúchnou* ([3088], of a candle), the light of a candle (Luke 8:16; Rev 18:23); of the sun (Rev 22:5; Sept.: Isa 4:5; 30:26; Jer 25:10; of the moon, Ezek 32:7; Hab 3:11).

(C) Of daylight (John 11:9, 10; Sept.: 1 Sam 25:34, 36; Job 3:16) as the opposite of *núx* (3571), night. "Hateth the light" (John 3:20); "to the light" (John 3:21) meaning openly, publicly, opposite of *en tḗ skotía* (4653), "in the darkness" (a.t. [Matt 10:27; Luke 12:3]). In Eph 5:13 it also stands in opposition to *skótos* (4655), darkness, figurative of sin. See Eph 5:11.

(D) Of the dazzling light, splendor or glory which surrounds the throne of God

in which He dwells (1 Tim 6:16; Rev
21:24 [cf. Ps 104:2; Isa 60:1, 19, 20]).
Hence, also as surrounding the Lord Jesus
Christ in His appearances after His ascension (Acts 9:3, 5; 22:6, 9, 11; 26:13); of
angels (Acts 12:7; 2 Cor 11:14); of glorified saints (Col 1:12).

(II) Metonymically, a light, a luminous body.

(A) A lamp or torch (Acts 16:29; Sept.:
Ps 119:105).

(B) A fire (Mark 14:54; Luke 22:56).

(C) Of the heavenly luminaries, the
sun, moon, and stars (James 1:17; Sept.:
Jer 4:23).

(III) Figuratively, meaning moral and
spiritual light and knowledge which enlightens the mind, soul or conscience; including also the idea of moral goodness,
purity and holiness, and of consequent
reward and happiness.

(A) Generally, true knowledge of God
and spiritual things, Christian piety (John
3:19; 8:12; Acts 26:18; Rom 13:12; 2 Cor
6:14; Eph 5:8; 1 John 2:8), true Christians as *huioí* (5207), "sons of light"
(a.t. [Luke 16:8; John 12:36]), and *tékna*
(5043), "children of light" (1 Thess 5:5).
In Eph 5:8, "ye were sometimes darkness, but now are ye light in the Lord,"
means you are enlightened by the Lord.
In 1 John 2:10, "He that loveth his brother abideth [*méno* {3306}] in the light."
As exhibited in the life and teaching of
someone (Matt 5:16, "let your light so
shine before men"; John 5:35; Sept.: Isa
2:5). Where the idea of holiness predominates as of God and those conformed to
Him (1 John 1:5, 7); of peace and happiness (1 Pet 2:9). In Matt 4:16, "the people which sat in darkness saw great light"
quoted from Isa 9:2. See also Acts 26:23;
Sept.: Ps 36:9; Isa 58:8, 10.

(B) Metonymically, a light, the author
or dispenser of moral and spiritual light, a
moral teacher; generally (Rom 2:19). Of
disciplers (Matt 5:14; Acts 13:47 quoted
from Isa 49:6; see also Sept.: Isa 42:6).
Especially of Jesus as the great Teacher and Savior of the world who brought
life and immortality to light in His gospel

(see Luke 2:32; John 1:4, 5, 7–9; 3:19;
8:12; 9:5; 12:35, 36, 46).

(C) "The light that is in thee" (Matt
6:23; Luke 11:35) means the mind, conscience, corresponding to *ho lúchnos*
(3088), candle, light, and *ho ophthalmós*
(3788), the eye.

Deriv.: *phaínō* (5316), to give light
illuminate; *phōstér* (5458), gleam;
phōsphóros (5459), bearing light, morning star; *phōteinós* (5460), bright, radiant;
phōtízō (5461), to shine, make known.

Syn.: *apaúgasma* (541), brightness;
lamprótēs (2987), brilliancy, brightness.

Ant.: *skótos* (4655), darkness; *skotía*
(4653), darkness; *zóphos* (2217), gloom,
blackness, darkness.

5458. φωστήρ *phōstér*; gen. *phōstéros*,
from *phós* (5457), light. A light, light
given. In Class. Gr. a window. In the NT
a luminary, figuratively of a brilliant person who gives light to those about him
(Phil 2:15; Sept.: Gen 1:14, 16). Metonymically, the radiance spoken of the
holy Jerusalem which came from the divine *dóxa* (1391), glory (Rev 21:11).

5459. φωσφόρος *phōsphóros*; gen.
phōsphórou, masc.-fem., neut. *phōs-
phóron*, adj. from *phós* (5457), light, and
phérō (5342), to bring. The day or morning star which is the name that the Greeks
assigned to the planet Venus while passing from its lower to its upper conjunction with the sun, during which time it
appears to the west of the sun and consequently rises before it and ushers in the
light of day. Spiritually it refers to that
clear and comfortable knowledge of and
strong faith in Christ which is the har-
binger of an eternal day in life and blessedness (2 Pet 1:19 [cf. John 3:36; 5:24;
6:40, 47; 11:25, 26; 17:3; Eph 2:17]).

Syn.: *astér* (792), a star, planet, comet;
ástron (798), a constellation consisting of
several stars.

5460. φωτεινός *phōteinós*; fem. *phō-
teiné*, neut. *phōteinón*, adj. from *phós*
(5457), light. Giving light, luminous,

splendid, bright (Matt 17:5); enlightened in a spiritual sense (Matt 6:22; Luke 11:34, 36).

Syn.: *lamprós* (2986), shining, resplendent.

Ant.: *skoteinós* (4652), dark; *mélas* (3189), black; *dusnóētos* (1425), hard to be understood.

5461. φωτίζω *phōtízō*; fut. *phōtísō*, related to *phós* (5457), light. To give light to (Luke 11:36; Rev 18:1; [cf. Rev 21:23; 22:5; Sept.: Isa 60:19]), to enlighten, shine light upon (John 1:9; Eph 1:18; Heb 6:4; 10:32; Sept.: Ps 119:130); to illuminate, make one see or understand (Eph 3:9; Sept.: Judg 13:8; 2 Kgs 12:2; 17:27); to bring to light, make known (1 Cor 4:5; 2 Tim 1:10).

Deriv.: *phōtismós* (5462), a shining, illumination;

Syn.: *anáptō* (381), to enkindle, light; *diaugázō* (1306), to glimmer through, dawn; *exēgéō* (1834), to explain; *hermēneúō* (2059), to interpret; *diermēneúō* (1329), to explain thoroughly, expound; *phaneróō* (5319), to make apparent, show, manifest, declare; *diasaphéō* (1285), to clear thoroughly, declare; *plērophoréō* (4135), to inform fully, completely assure; *apokalúptō* (601), to take off the cover, disclose, reveal; *dēlóō* (1213), to show, declare; *dialaléō* (1255), to declare publicly; *diaphēmízō* (1310), to report thoroughly, spread abroad.

Ant.: *diastréphō* (1294), to distort, misinterpret; *skotízō* (4654), to obscure, darken; *episkiázō* (1982), to overshadow, cast a shade upon.

5462. φωτισμός *phōtismós*; gen. *phōtismoú*, masc. noun from *phōtízō* (5461), to lighten. Illumination, light, a bringing to light. Illumination from the Lord Himself (2 Cor 4:6; Sept.: Ps 27:1; 44:3); the light of the gospel (2 Cor 4:4); daylight or firelight (Sept.: Job 3:9; Ps 78:14).

Syn.: *apaúgasma* (541), effulgence, brightness; *lamprótēs* (2987), brilliancy, brightness.

X

5463. χαίρω chaírō; fut. *charḗsomai* or *chairḗsō* (Luke 1:14; John 16:20, 22; Phil 1:18; Sept.: Hab 1:15; Zech 10:7), 2d aor. *echárēn*. To rejoice, be glad. Intrans.:

(I) Particularly in various constructions:

(A) Used in an absolute sense (Luke 6:23; 15:32; 22:5; 23:8; John 4:36; 8:56; 16:20, 22; Acts 11:23; 13:48; Rom 12:15; 1 Cor 7:30; 2 Cor 7:7; 13:9; Phil 2:17; 3 John 1:3; Rev 19:7; Sept.: Hab 1:15). Followed by *hína* (2443), to the end that (1 Pet 4:13). In the part. *chaírōn*, joying, rejoicing (2 Cor 6:10; Sept.: 1 Kgs 4:20; 8:66). Joined with another verb or part., the part. *chaírōn* may often be rendered joyfully, gladly, (Col 2:5, "joyfully beholding"; Luke 15:5; 19:6, 37; Acts 5:41; 8:39; Sept.: Zech 4:10).

(B) With the cognate noun *chará* (5479), joy, in the acc. intens. (Matt 2:10, "they rejoiced with . . . great joy"; Sept.: Jon 4:6 [cf. 1 Kgs 1:40]). In the dat. (intens., John 3:29, "rejoiceth greatly"); without emphasis in 1 Thess 3:9.

(C) Followed by the dat. of cause, of that in or over which one rejoices (Rom 12:12, "rejoicing in the hope," which is the usual Gr. construction; Sept: Prov 17:19).

(D) Followed by the acc. of cause (Rom 16:19; Phil 2:18, for the same cause also do ye joy).

(E) With a part. in the nom. expressing the occasion of joy; also a frequent construction in Gr. writers (Mark 14:11; John 20:20; Phil 2:28). Once with the part. of a kindred verb intens. (1 Pet 4:13).

(F) Followed by *hóti* (3754), that, marking cause or occasion, meaning that, because (Luke 10:20; John 14:28; Acts 5:41; 2 Cor 7:9, 16; 2 John 1:4; Sept.: Ex 4:31). With the expression *en toútō . . . hóti*, "in this . . . that" (Luke 10:20); *en Kuríō . . . hóti*, "in the Lord . . . that"

(Phil 4:10); *di' humás . . . hóti*, "for your sakes . . . that" (John 11:15).

(G) With a prep. expressing the cause or occasion of joy: *epí* (1909), on, with the dat. See in *epí* (cf. II, C, 3, e; Matt 18:13; Luke 1:14; 13:17; Acts 15:31; 1 Cor 13:6; 16:17; 2 Cor 7:13; Rev 11:10; Sept.: Prov 2:14; Hab 3:18). With *en* (1722), in, with the dat., to rejoice in (Col 1:24). With *en* followed by *toútō hóti*, "in this . . . that" (*toútō* [5129], this, Luke 10:20; Phil 1:18; Sept.: Zech 10:7). Preceded by *en Kuríō*, in the Lord (*kuríō* dat. of *kúrios* [2962]), meaning in union and communion with Him. Followed by *diá* (1223), for, with the acc. (John 3:29); *di' humás hóti*, "for you because" (a.t. [John 11:15]), by *apó* (575), from, with the gen. (2 Cor 2:3 where *chaírein* [inf. pres.], to rejoice, stands in contrast to *lúpēn échō*, "grief I have [*lúpēn*, acc. of *lúpē* {3077}, sorrow; *échō* {2192}, I have]" (a.t. [cf. 3 John 1:4]).

(II) Imper. and inf. as a word of salutation or greeting.

(A) Imper., *chaíre* in the sing. and *chaírete* in the pl. in a personal salutation, meaning Joy to thee! Joy to you! the same as "Hail!" (Matt 5:12; 26:49; 27:29; 28:9; Mark 15:18; Luke 1:28; 6:23; John 19:3; 2 Cor 13:11; 1 Thess 5;16; Phil 3:1; 4:4; *en Kuríō hóti* "in the Lord," Phil 4:10)

(B) In the inf. *chaírein*, particularly with *légō* (3004), I say, *légō chaírein*, to wish joy, to bid, hail, salute (2 John 1:10). Used in an absolute sense in the inf. *chaírein*, meaning greeting, at the beginning of an epistle or address (Acts 15:23; 23:26; James 1:1; Sept.: used in an absolute sense, Isa 48:22; 57:21, equivalent to *rhṓnnumi* [4517], to have health, strength).

Deriv.: *sugchaírō* (4796), to rejoice with; *chará* (5479), joy, delight, gladness; *cháris* (5485), grace.

Syn.: *euphraínō* (2165), to cheer, gladden; *agalliáō* (21), to exult, rejoice greatly; *euarestéō* (2100), to please, gratify entirely, please well; *euphraínō* (2165), to rejoice; *heortázō* (1858), to celebrate; *skirtáō* (4640), to leap for joy; *euthuméō* (2114), to cheer up, make merry; *aréskō* (700), to please; *onínēmi* (3685), to gratify.

Ant.: *lupéō* (3076), to sorrow; *kakopathéō* (2553), to suffer hardship; *talaipōréō* (5003), to endure hardship; *athuméō* (120), to become spiritless, disheartened; *barúnō* (925), to be oppressed, burdened; *adēmonéō* (85), to be in distress; *aganaktéō* (23), to be greatly afflicted.

5464. χάλαζα *chálaza*; gen. *chalázēs*, fem. noun. Hail, precipitation (Rev 8:7; 11:19; 16:21; Sept.: Ex 9:18, 19).
Syn.: *chiṓn* (5510), snow; *krústallos* (2930), ice.
Ant.: *eudía* (2105), good weather.

5465. χαλάω *chaláō*; contracted *chalṓ*, fut. *chalásō*, aor. pass. *echalásthēn*. To loose, relax, let down, as a bed from the roof of a house (Mark 2:4); a net from a boat (Luke 5:4, 5); a boat from a ship (Acts 27:30); a person over a wall (Acts 9:25; pass. 2 Cor 11:33; Sept.: Jer 38:6); the sails of a ship from the mast or even the mast itself, as was usual in ancient ships (Acts 27:17; Sept.: Isa 33:23).
Deriv.: *chalinós* (5469), a bridle.
Syn.: *lúō* (3089), to loose; *aníēmi* (447), to let up, relax, let go, loosen.
Ant.: *déō* (1210), to bind; *sundéō* (4887), to bind together; *sunéchō* (4912), to hold together; *peridéō* (4019), to bind around one; *kratéō* (2902), to hold; *phulássō* (5442), to keep guard; *egeírō* (1453), to lift up, raise, take up.

5466. Χαλδαῖος *Chaldaíos*; gen. *Chaldaíou*, masc. proper noun. A Chaldean, a native of Chaldea (Babylonia). The Chaldeans were a warlike, aggressive people from the mountains of Kurdistan. See Gen 11:28; Jer 24:5; 25:12; Ezek 1:3.

Abraham came out of Ur in Mesopotamia, or the land of the Chaldeans (Acts 7:4).

5467. χαλεπός *chalepós*; fem. *chalepḗ*, neut. *chalepón*, adj. Violent, fierce. Used of demoniacs, wild, difficult (Matt 8:28). Grievous, hard to bear, distressing, referring to the times (2 Tim 3:1).
Syn.: *ágrios* (66), wild; *anḗmeros* (434), not tame, savage; *sklērós* (4642), hard, rough; *barús* (926), grievous, burdensome; *ponērós* (4190), evil, bad, calamitous; *dusbástaktos* (1419), hard to be borne.
Ant.: *kalós* (2570), good; *euprósdektos* (2144), favorable, acceptable; *épios* (2261), mild; *praǘs* (4239), meek; *epieikḗs* (1933), gentle, patient.

5468. χαλιναγωγέω *chalinagōgéō*; contracted *chalinagōgṓ*, fut. *chalinagōgḗsō*, from *chalinós* (5469), a bridle, and *ágō* (71), to lead, direct, govern. To direct or restrain by a bridle. Figuratively, to restrain, govern or control (James 1:26, of the tongue; 3:2, of the body).
Syn.: *anakóptō* (348), to hinder, check.
Ant.: *lúō* (3089), to loose; *apolúō* (630), to release from oneself; *aníēmi* (447), to loose, relax; *eklúō* (1590), to relax; *aphíēmi* (863), to let go; *eleutheróō* (1659), to liberate.

5469. χαλινός *chalinós*; gen. *chaninoú*, masc. noun from *chaláō* (5465), to let go, relax, loosen. A bridle (James 3:3; Rev 14:20; Sept.: 2 Kgs 19:28; Isa 37:29).
Deriv.: *chalinagōgéō* (5468), to direct or restrain by a bridle.

5470. χάλκεος *chálkeos*; contracted *chalkoús*, fem. *chalkéa*, neut. *chálkeon*, adj. from *chalkós* (5475), copper. Made of copper or brass (Rev 9:20; Sept.: Ex 26:11, 37; 2 Sam 22:35).

5471. χαλκεύς *chalkeús*; gen. *chalkéōs*, masc. noun from *chalkós* (5475), copper, brass. A coppersmith, a brazier, any metal worker (2 Tim 4:14; Sept.: Gen 4:22; 2 Chr 24:12).

5472. χαλκηδών *chalkēdṓn*; gen. *chalkēdónos*, masc. noun. The name of a gem, a chalcedony (Rev 21:19). A modern variety of it is the carnelian.

5473. χαλκίον *chalkíon*; gen. *chalkíou*, neut. noun from *chalkós* (5475), copper. A brazen vessel (Mark 7:4).

5474. χαλκολίβανον *chalkolíbanon*; gen. *chalkolibánou*, neut. noun. A type of fine copper or brass (Rev 1:15; 2:18 [cf. Dan 10:6, see also Ezek 1:4, 7, 27; 8:2]).

5475. χαλκός *chalkós*; gen. *chalkoú*, masc. noun. Copper, brass, or any metal (1 Cor 13:1; Rev 18:12 [cf. Gen 4:22; 1 Chr 15:19; Ezra 8:27; Dan 10:6]). Copper or brass money (Matt 10:9). Money in general (cf. *argúrion* [694], silver or money; Mark 6:8; 12:41).
    Deriv.: *chálkeos* (5470), made of copper or brass; *chalkeús* (5471), a coppersmith; *chalkíon* (5473), copper.

5476. χαμαί *chamaí*; adv. On or to the ground (John 9:6; 18:6; Sept.: Job 1:20; Dan 8:12).
    Syn.: *édaphos* (1475), ground; *kátō* (2736), down.
    Ant.: *ánō* (507), high up, upward; *epánō* (1883), above, up.

5477. Χαναάν *Chanaán*; masc. proper noun transliterated from the Hebr. *Keng'an* (3667, OT), low. Canaan (Acts 7:11; 13:19). This was the more ancient name of Palestine. It covers all Palestine west of the Jordan (Num 34:3–12). It referred to "the low lands," in distinction from the highlands of Lebanon and Syria and in contrast to Gilead (Num 33:51; Josh 22:9).
    Deriv.: *Chananaíos* (5478), a Canaanite or Canaanaean.

5478. Χαναναῖος *Chananaíos*; fem. *Chananaía*, neut. *Chananaíon*, adj. from

Chanaán (5477), Canaan. Canaanitish or used subst., Canaanite, a native of Canaan, the name given to the plains of the Jordan and seacoast, contrasting them to the inhabitants of the highlands (Num 13:29; Deut 7:1; Josh 11:3) used then as a general name for the inhabitants of Palestine (Gen 12:6; 24:3; 34:30; Josh 17:12; Judg 1:27ff.). Also specifically of the Phoenicians (Judg 1:32, 33). Simon is called "the Canaanite" (*Kananítēs* [2581] (Matt 10:4; Mark 3:18), otherwise described as Simon *Zēlōtḗs*, the zealot (Luke 6:15; Acts 1:13). The term *zēlōtḗs* (2207) is peculiar to Luke and is the equivalent for the Aramaic Canaanaean, preserved by Matthew and Mark. Each of these equally points out Simon as belonging to the faction of the zealots who were conspicuous for the fierce advocacy of Jewish independence from Rome. He is not to be identified with Simon the brother of Jesus (Matt 13:55). Also a Phoenician woman (Matt 15:22 [cf. Mark 7:26 where she is called *Surophoiníkissa* or *Syrophínissa* {4949}, Syrophenician]). See also Gen 38:2.

5479. χαρά *chará*; gen. *charás*, fem. noun from *chaírō* (5463), to rejoice. Joy, rejoicing, gladness.
    (I) Generally (Matt 2:10; Luke 1:14 where it is joined with *agallíasis* [20], exultation or great joy; 15:7, 10; John 3:29; 15:11; 16:20–22, 24; 17:13; Acts 8:8; 13:52; 15:3; Rom 14:17, "joy in the Holy Ghost," meaning the joy which the Holy Spirit imparts by His influence; 15:13; 2 Cor 1:24; 2:3; 7:4, 13; 8:2; Gal 5:22; Phil 1:25, joy of faith, meaning in and arising from the faith of the gospel; 2:2, 29; 1 Thess 1:6 [cf. Rom 14:17]; 1 Thess 3:9; 2 Tim 1:4; Phile 1:7; James 4:9; 1 Pet 1:8; 1 John 1:4; 2 John 1:12). With *apó* (575), from, and the gen., from or for joy (Matt 13:44; Luke 24:41; Acts 12:14). With *metá* (3326), with, and the gen. meaning with joy, joyfully, rejoicingly (Matt 13:20; 28:8; Mark 4:16; Luke 8:13; 10:17; 24:52; Acts 20:24; Phil 1:4; Col 1:11; Heb 10:34; 13:17; Sept.: 1 Chr

29:22). With *en* (1722), in, and the dat. meaning in joy, joyfully (Rom 15:32).

(II) Metonymically the cause, ground, occasion of joy (Luke 2:10; Phil 4:1; 1 Thess 2:19, 20; James 1:2; 3 John 1:4).

(III) Metonymically meaning enjoyment, fruition of joy, bliss (Matt 25:21, 23, "the bliss prepared for thee of thy Lord" [a.t.]; Heb 12:2).

Syn.: *agallíasis* (20), exultation, exuberant joy; *euphrosúnē* (2167), good cheer, mirth, gladness of heart.

Ant.: *lúpē* (3077), grief, sorrow; *odúnē* (3601), pain, consuming grief; *ōdín* (5604), a birth pang, travail, pain; *pénthos* (3997), mourning, sorrow; *thlípsis* (2347), affliction, tribulation; *pónos* (4192), toil, pain, anguish; *pikría* (4088), bitterness; *kakopátheia* (2552), suffering affliction; *talaipōría* (5004), misery; *stenochōría* (4730), anguish, distress.

5480. χάραγμα *cháragma*; gen. *charágmatos*, neut. noun from *charássō* (n.f., see below), to engrave. An engraving, something graven or sculptured, an impression, mark or symbol.

(I) An engraving or sculptured work such as images or idols (Acts 17:29).

(II) A mark cut in or stamped on, a sign ("the mark of the beast" Rev 13:16, 17; 14:9, 11; 15:2; 16:2; 19:20; 20:4).

Deriv. of *charássō* (n.f.), to carve: *charaktḗr* (5481), something engraved, an impression; *chárax* (5482), a strong stake used in fortification; *chártēs* (5489), paper.

Syn.: *stígma* (4742), mark, brand; *sphragís* (4973), mark, seal, impression.

5481. χαρακτήρ *charaktḗr*; gen. *charaktēros*, masc. noun from *charássō* (n.f., see *cháragma* [5480]), to carve. The *-tḗr* suffix signifies agency, hence the word originally denoted an engraver or engraving tool. Later it meant the impression itself, usually something engraven, cut in, or stamped, a character, letter, mark, sign. This impression with its particular features was considered as the exact representation of the object whose image it bore. In the NT, representation, express image. Occurs only in Heb 1:3 where it is translated "express image," referring to Jesus Christ. Here He is described as the *charaktḗr tḗs hupostáseōs autoú* (*tḗs* [3588], the [gen. fem.]; *hupostáseōs* [5287], essence [gen.]; *autoú* [846], he [gen. masc.]), "the exact image of His [God's] essence" (a.t.). Whatever the divine essence is, Jesus is said to be its perfect expression. The writer of Hebrews thus sets forth a high Christology affirming the deity of Jesus Christ.

Syn.: *eikṓn* (1504), image; *homoíōsis* (3669), likeness; *homoíōma* (3667), likeness.

5482. χάραξ *chárax*; gen. *chárakos*, masc. noun from *charássō* (n.f., see *cháragma* [5480]), to engrave, impress a mark. A strong stake of wood used in ancient fortifications (Luke 19:43; Sept.: Isa 37:33; Ezek 4:2). A type of fence or wall consisting of strong stakes thickly interwoven with boughs or branches of trees, a barricade.

5483. χαρίζομαι *charízomai*; fut. *charísomai*, mid. deponent from *cháris* (5485), grace. To show someone a favor, be kind to. To give or bestow a thing willingly, with the acc. of thing and dat. of person (Luke 7:21; Acts 27:24; Rom 8:32; Phil 2:9); to hand someone over to the authorities (Acts 25:11, 16) or to a mob (Acts 3:14). The most common meaning peculiar to the NT is to pardon, to graciously remit a person's sin (Col 2:13). With the acc. only, *charízomai* means to forgive something (2 Cor 2:10; 12:13); with the dat. only, to forgive someone, be gracious to (Eph 4:32; Col 3:13). 2 Cor 2:7 uses it without any expressed obj. with the meaning to forgive. In Luke 7:42, 43 it means simply to pardon or remit a penalty. In the pass., especially in the aor., *echarísthēn*, and the fut., *charisthḗsomai*, it means to be permitted or granted something (1 Cor 2:12; Phil 1:29; Phile 1:22).

Deriv.: *chárisma* (5486), a gift of grace.

Syn.: *dídōmi* (1325), to give, bestow; *eleutheróō* (1659), to set free, deliver; *rhúomai* (4506), to deliver, rescue; *sṓzō* (4982), to save; *aphíēmi* (863), to send forth, remit; *apolúō* (630), to loose from; *paréchō* (3930), to provide, supply; *dōréō* (1433), to give, make a gift; *chorēgéō* (5524), to supply, give.

Ant.: *kataginṓskō* (2607), to condemn, think ill of; *katadikázō* (2613), to pronounce judgment, condemn; *krínō* (2919), to judge, condemn; *katakrínō* (2632), to judge against, pronounce sentence upon.

5484. χάριν *chárin*; the acc. of *cháris* (5485), grace, favor, gift. On account of, because of, for the sake of (Luke 7:47; Gal 3:19; Eph 3:1, 14; 1 Tim 5:14; Titus 1:5, 11; 1 John 3:12; Jude 1:16).

√ **5485. χάρις** *cháris*; gen. *cháritos*, fem. noun from *chaírō* (5463), to rejoice. Grace, particularly that which causes joy, pleasure, gratification, favor, acceptance, for a kindness granted or desired, a benefit, thanks, gratitude. A favor done without expectation of return; the absolutely free expression of the loving kindness of God to men finding its only motive in the bounty and benevolence of the Giver; unearned and unmerited favor. *Cháris* √ stands in direct antithesis to *érga* (2041), works, the two being mutually exclusive. God's grace affects man's sinfulness and not only forgives the repentant sinner, but brings joy and thankfulness to him. It changes the individual to a new creature without destroying his individuality (2 Cor 5:17; Eph 2:8, 9).

(I) *Cháris*, when received by faith, transforms man and causes him to love and to seek after the righteousness of God. *Cháris* is initially regeneration, the work of the Holy Spirit in which spiritual life is given to man and by which his nature is brought under the dominion of righteousness. The maintenance of this condition requires an unbroken and immense supply of grace. Grace remains constant in, and basic to, a believer's fight without against the devil and his struggle within against sin. Renewal is stimulated and impelled by God's illuminating and strengthening of the soul, and will continue and increase so long as the soul perseveres. God's grace insures that those who have been truly regenerated will persevere until the end of life. This entire work is called sanctification, a work of God "whereby we are renewed in the whole man and are enabled more and more to die daily unto sin and to live unto righteousness" as is stated by the *Westminster Shorter Catechism* (Rom 12:2; 2 Cor 4:16; Eph 4:23; Col 3:10).

(II) Grace may also refer to the external form or manner, particularly of persons meaning gracefulness, elegance. In the NT only of words or discourses as gratefulness, agreeableness, acceptableness (Luke 4:22, "gracious words"; Eph 4:29, "that it may minister grace unto the hearers" meaning what is acceptable; Col 4:6; Sept.: Ps 45:2).

(III) Grace also means disposition, attitude toward another, favor, goodwill, benevolence.

(A) Generally (Luke 2:40, 52; Sept.: Ex 33:12; Acts 2:47, "having favor with all the people"; 4:33; 7:10; Sept.: Gen 39:21). With *heurískō* (2147), to find grace or favor, *pará Theṓ* (*pará* [3844], before; *Theṓ* [2316], God), before God (Luke 1:30); *enṓpion toú Theoú* (*enṓpion* [1799], before, in the presence of; *toú Theoú*, the God), "before God" Acts 7:46; Heb 4:16; followed by *pará* (3844), with, Sept.: Gen 6:9; 18:3; Esth 2:15). With *katatíthēmi* ([2698] followed by the dat.), to place down, deposit or grace with someone, meaning to lay down, or lay up favor with someone, gain favor (Acts 25:9). With the acc. pl. *cháritas*, to be in the good graces of the Jews (Acts 24:27). Metonymically as the object of favor, something acceptable (1 Pet 2:19, 20, "this is well-pleasing to God" [a.t. {cf. Col 3:20; 1 Tim 2:3; 4:5}]).

(B) Of the grace, favor and good-will of God and Christ as exercised to-ward men: where *cháris* is joined with *eirḗnē* (1515), peace, *éleos* (1656), mer-cy, and the like in salutations, including the idea of every kind of favor, blessing, good, as proceeding from God the Fa-ther and the Lord Jesus Christ (Rom 1:7; 1 Cor 1:3; 2 Cor 1:2; Gal 1:3). Also in the introduction to most of the epistles (Eph 1:2; Phil 1:2; Col 1:2; 1 Thess 1:1; 2 Thess 1:2; 1 Tim 1:2; 2 Tim 1:2; Ti-tus 1:4; Phile 1:3; 1 Pet 1:2; 2 Pet 1:2; 2 John 1:3; Rev 1:4). Also the grace of the Lord Jesus Christ in the benedictions at the close of most of the epistles (Rom 16:20, 24; 1 Cor 16:23; 2 Cor 13:14; Gal 6:18). Simply with the def. art. *hē cháris* with equal meaning (Eph 6:24; Col 4:18; 1 Tim 6:21; 2 Tim 4:22; Titus 3:15; Heb 13:25). Used by Christ in Luke 6:32–34, although the KJV translates *cháris* "thank" (the NASB, NKJV, NIV have "credit"); this word marks the difference between unbelievers and believers. Of Christ, generally (Acts 15:11 "through the grace of the Lord Jesus Christ" which indicates effective faith unto salvation (2 Cor 8:9; 1 Tim 1:14). Of God, gen-erally, meaning the gracious feeling of approbation, benignity and love, which God exercises toward any of the human race [cf. II]. Of God's unmerited favor, in the exercise of which He sovereign-ly and efficaciously confers upon sinful men the blessings of salvation. This is to be distinguished from His general good-ness (*chrēstós* [5543], gentle, gracious), by which He shows favor even to the un-thankful and wicked (Luke 6:35) in con-ferring on them common blessings such as the sun (Matt 5:45). "The word of his grace" means the gospel of the grace of God, the good news of God's effec-tive favor (Acts 14:3, 26; 20:24 [cf. Acts 15:40]). "Justified freely by His grace" refers to the forgiveness of sin and rec-onciliation to a holy God (Rom 3:24; 5:2; 1 Cor 15:10; 2 Cor 1:12; 9:14; 12:9; Gal 1:15; Eph 1:6; Heb 2:9; 1 Pet 4:10). With *toú Theoú*, of God, or with the like

implied (Acts 18:27; Rom 4:16; 11:5, 6; 12:6; 2 Thess 2:16; Heb 2:9, "through the gracious counsel of God" [a.t.]; Heb 4:16). With *en* (1722), in, followed by the dat. *en cháriti*, referring to the gift of Je-sus Christ (Rom 5:15; Gal 1:6, the grace of God through Christ).

(C) Specifically of the divine grace and favor as exercised in conferring gifts, graces and benefits on man (2 Cor 4:15; 8:1; James 4:6; 1 Pet 5:5). Partic-ularly as manifested in the benefits be-stowed in and through Christ and His gospel (Acts 13:43; 2 Cor 6:1; Eph 4:7; Phil 1:7; 1 Pet 1:10, 13, "ye all are par-takers of my grace" meaning "fellow par-takers with me in the grace of the gospel" [a.t.]; Heb 12:15; 13:9, "it is good that the heart be made steadfast in grace, not in meats" [a.t.] meaning in the grace of the gospel, the gospel doctrines [cf. Rom 14:15, 17]). Specifically of the grace or gift of the apostleship, the apostolic of-fice (Rom 12:3; 15:15; 1 Cor 3:10; Gal 2:9; Eph 3:2, 8; 2 Tim 2:1); as exhibited in the pardon of sins and admission to the divine kingdom, saving grace; with *toú Theoú*, of God (Rom 5:15; Gal 2:21; Ti-tus 2:11; 37 implied; 1 Pet 3:7 "the grace of life"; 5:12; simply in Rom 1:5; 5:2, 17, 20, 21; 6:1, 14, 15, we are not under law but under grace; Gal 5:4; Eph 2:5, 8, "by grace are you saved"; 1 Pet 1:13); Heb 10:29, "the Spirit of grace," which is the gift and earnest of divine favor.

(IV) Grace, in act and deed, favor con-ferred, a kindness, benefit, benefaction.

(A) Generally (Acts 25:3 in asking a favor against Paul, to be prejudiced against him, that he might be sent forth to Jerusalem; Rom 4:4). Of a gift, alms (1 Cor 16:3; 2 Cor 8:4, 6, 7, 19).

(B) Of the various divine favors, ben-efits, blessings, gifts conferred on man through Christ and His gospel; generally (John 1:14, 16, 17; Acts 11:23; 1 Cor 1:4; 2 Cor 9:8; Col 1:6; 1 Pet 4:10; Jude 1:4).

(C) Metonymically for gratification or joy arising from a favor or benefit re-ceived (2 Cor 1:15; Phile 1:7).

(V) Gratitude, thanks. In the acc. with *échō* (2192), to have. In Luke 17:9, it means that the employer does not owe thanks for an act not outside the realm of the farm worker's job description. In 1 Tim 1:12; 2 Tim 1:3; Heb 12:28, it means to give thanks, which is an acceptable service to God. Followed by *tó Theó* ([2316], God), unto God meaning thanks be unto God (Rom 6:17; 1 Cor 15:57; 2 Cor 2:14; 8:16; 9:15). In the dat. *cháriti* meaning with thanks, thankfully (1 Cor 10:30 *eucharistía* [2169], thankfulness or gratitude). With *en* (1722), in, followed by the dat. *en cháriti* (Col 3:16, singing with thanks, thankfully in worship to the Lord).

Deriv.: *charízomai* (5483), to be kind to; *charitóō* (5487), to grace, highly honor.

Syn.: *euergesía* (2108), a benefit; *apodochḗ* (594), acceptance; *eulogía* (2129), a blessing; *haplótēs* (572), liberality; *eucharistía* (2169), thankfulness, gratitude; *épainos* (1868), praise; *dóron* (1435), a gift; *dōreá* (1431), a free gift; *dórēma* (1434), a favor; *dóma* (1390), a gift; *dósis* (1394), a gift or the act of giving; *chárisma* (5486), a gift, the result of grace, a gift; *áphesis* (859), forgiveness.

Ant.: *krísis* (2920) and *kríma* (2917), judgment, condemnation; *katákrisis* (2633), condemnation, sentencing adversely; *katákrima* (2631), an adverse sentence, condemnation; *timōría* (5097), punishment; *kólasis* (2851), punishment, disciplinary in nature.

5486. χάρισμα chárisma; gen. *charísmatos*, neut. noun from *charízomai* (5483), to show favor. A gift of grace, an undeserved benefit. The suffix -*ma*, indicates the result of grace. Equivalent to *dóron* (1435), gift. In the NT used only of gifts and graces imparted from God, deliverance from peril (2 Cor 1:11); the gift of self-control (1 Cor 7:7); gifts of Christian knowledge, consolation, confidence (Rom 1:11; 1 Cor 1:7); redemption, salvation through Christ (Rom 5:15, 16; 6:23; 11:29). Specifically of the gifts

imparted to the early Christians and particularly to Christian teachers by the Holy Spirit (Rom 12:6; 1 Cor 12:4, 9, 28, 30, 31; 1 Pet 4:10). As communicated with the laying on of hands (1 Tim 4:14; 2 Tim 1:6).

The relationship between the grace of God in Christ Jesus and the gifts which it bestows is indicated in 1 Cor 1:4–7. In 1 Cor 1:4 Paul says, "I thank my God always on your behalf, for the grace of God which is given you by Jesus Christ." What is translated "which is given you" is the fem. aor. pass. part. *tḗ dotheísē* (*tḗ* [3588], the [dat. fem]; *dídōmi* [1325], to give) preceded by the def. art. and would be better translated "which was given to you" (a.t.) referring to the grace of God given in Christ Jesus. Whoever has that grace is not lacking, 1 Cor 1:7 says, in any gift. *Chárisma* is the instantaneous enablement of the Holy Spirit in the life of any believer to exercise a gift for the edification of others.

Syn.: *dóron* (1435), a gift; *dōreá* (1431), a free gift; *dórēma* (1434), a favor, something given; *dóma* (1390), a gift; *dósis* (1394), act of giving; *merismós* (3311), a dividing, distribution of gifts.

Ant.: *kríma* (2917), the sentence pronounced; *katákrima* (2631), condemnation with a subjection to punishment following; *krísis* (2920), the act of judgment; *katákrisis* (2633), the act of condemnation.

5487. χαριτόω charitóō; contracted *charitō̂*, fut. *charitósō*, from *cháris* (5485), grace. To grace, highly honor or greatly favor. In the NT spoken only of the divine favor, as to the virgin Mary in Luke 1:28, *kecharitōménē*, the perf. pass. part. sing. fem. The verb *charitóō* declares the virgin Mary to be highly favored, approved of God to conceive the Son of God through the Holy Spirit. The only other use of *charitóō* is in Eph 1:6 where believers are said to be "accepted in the beloved," i.e., objects of grace. (See *huiothesía* [5206], adoption, occurring in Eph 1:5) In *charitóō* there is not only the impartation of God's grace, but also the adoption into God's family in imparting special favor in distinction to *charízomai* (5483), to give grace, to remit, forgive.

5488. Χαρράν *Charrán*; fem. proper noun transliterated from the Hebr. *Chārān* (2771, OT). Haran. A place in Mesopotamia (Acts 7:2, 4) or Haran, located in Padan-Aram (field of Aram) on the busy caravan route connecting with Nineveh, Ashur, and Babylon in Mesopotamia, and with Damascus, Tyre, and Egyptian cities in the west and south. Haran, like Ur, was the center of the moon god cult.

5489. χάρτης *chártēs*; gen. *chártou*, masc. noun from *charássō* (n.f., see *cháragma* [5480]), to engrave, inscribe. Paper (2 John 1:12), equivalent to papyrus of which paper was made. *Chártēs* is the word from which the Eng. chart, charter, and cartel are derived.

5490. χάσμα *chásma*; gen. *chásmatos*, neut. noun from *chaínō* (n.f.), to gape, open the mouth wide. A gaping or yawning of the mouth, a gulf, chasm (Luke 16:26; Sept.: 2 Sam 18:17).
    Syn.: *bóthunos* (999), pit; *ábussos* (12), abyss, deep, bottomless pit.

5491. χεῖλος *cheílos*; gen. *cheílous*, neut. noun. A lip, pl. *cheílē*, lips (Matt 15:8; Mark 7:6; Rom 3:13 quoted from Ps 140:3, 4, contains a striking allusion to the poison of the asp which, like that of the common viper and other poisonous serpents, is lodged under the upper lip and at the inner end of two hollow fangs with which it bites and through which it infuses its venom). Metonymically, language, dialect, tongue (1 Cor 14:21 in allusion to Isa 28:11; Heb 13:15; 1 Pet 3:10). The lip of the sea means the shore, brink, bank (Heb 11:12; Sept.: Gen 22:17; Ex 7:15 of the river or the sea; 14:31) refers to the edge or shore of the sea. See Sept.: Gen 11:1, 6, 9; Job 2:10; Prov 17:4.

5492. χειμάζω *cheimázō*; fut. *cheimásō*, from *cheíma* (n.f., see *cheimṓn* [5494]), winter-weather, cold frost. To winter, spend the winter. In the mid./pass. form *cheimázomai*, to be tossed with a storm or tempest (Acts 27:18).
    Deriv.: *paracheimázō* (3914), to spend the winter.
    Syn.: *kludōnízomai* (2831), to be tossed by waves.

5493. χείμαρρος *cheímarros*; gen. *cheimárrou*, masc.-fem., neut. *cheímarron*, adj. from *cheíma* (n.f., see *cheimṓn* [5494]), winter-weather, cold frost, and *rhéō* (4482), to flow. Winter-flowing, used as a subst. stream, brook, or torrent so-called because it runs only in the winter or when swollen with rains (John 18:1 [cf. 2 Sam 15:23; 1 Kgs 2:37; 15:13]).
    Syn.: *rhúsis* (4511), a flow of blood; *potamós* (4215), a stream, river; *kataklusmós* (2627), a deluge, flood; *plēmmúra* (4132), flood.
    Ant.: *límnē* (3041), lake.

5494. χειμών *cheimṓn*; gen. *cheimṓnos*, masc. noun from *cheíma* (n.f., see below), winter-weather, cold frost. The winter when rains are poured forth on the earth, hence rain, storm, tempest, storm with rain, foul weather (Matt 16:3; 24:20; Mark 13:18; John 10:22; 2 Tim 4:21). A storm, tempest (Acts 27:20; Sept.: Ezra 10:9; Job 37:6).
    Deriv. of *cheíma* (n.f.), winter-weather, cold frost: *cheimázō* (5492), to spend the winter; *cheímarros* (5493), a stream, brook.
    Syn.: *thúella* (2366), hurricane, cyclone, whirlwind; *seismós* (4578), a tempest or earthquake; *laílaps* (2978), a tempest, storm; *chálaza* (5464), hail.
    Ant.: *eudía* (2105), fair weather.

5495. χείρ *cheír*; gen. *cheirós*, fem. noun. The hand. Originally it meant the whole arm from the shoulder to the end of the fingers (Matt 8:15).

(I) Particularly and generally, as of men (Matt 5:30; 8:15; 12:10; 15:20, "unwashen hands"; Matt 26:23 in allusion to the oriental manner of eating; Matt 27:24; Mark 3:1, 3, 5; Luke 6:1; Acts 3:7; 17:25; 28:3, 4; 1 Cor 4:12; Gal 6:11; Col 4:18; 1 Thess 4:11, "work with your own hands"; Acts 15:23; Phile 1:19; Heb 12:12; James 4:8; 1 John 1:1; Sept.: Gen 22:6; 24:2; Prov 26:15); of angels (Matt 4:6; Luke 4:11; Rev 6:5; 8:4; Sept.: Isa 6:6). In phrases such as *érga* ([2041], works) *cheirōn* followed by the gen., "the works of their own hands" meaning an idol (Acts 7:41; Rev 9:20 referring to evil deeds or conduct); of God, the works of creation (Heb 1:10; 2:7; Sept.: Ps 8:6); with *aírō* (142), to lift, followed by the acc. (Rev 10:5). For other frequent phrases and constructions see *dexiós* (1188), right; *ekteínō* (1614), to stretch forth; *epaírō* (1869), to raise up; *epibállō* (1911), to throw upon, lay; *epíthesis* (1936), laying; *epilambánō* (1949), to seize; *kataseíō* (2678), to sway downward; *kratéō* (2902), to hold, lay hand on; *níptō* (3538), to wash.

Of importance is the expression *tas cheíras epitíthesthai* (pres. act. inf. of *epitíthēmi* [2007], to lay upon), to lay the hands upon. This expression was used as the symbol of healing power, followed by *epí* (1909), upon, with the acc. (Matt 9:18; Mark 8:25; 16:18; Acts 9:17); followed by the dat. (Matt 19:13, 15; Mark 5:23; 6:5; 7:32; 8:23; Luke 4:40; 13:13; Acts 9:12; 28:8). It was also used for benediction, inauguration: followed by *epí* with the acc. (Acts 8:17); followed by the dat. (Acts 6:6; 8:19; 13:3; 19:6; 1 Tim 5:22). The noun *epíthesis* (1936), the placing upon, laying upon or imposition of hands was also used as the emblem through which the Holy Spirit was imparted (Acts 8:18; 1 Tim 4:14; 2 Tim 1:6; Heb 6:2). The verb is also used in Rev 1:17 (TR), "he placed his hand upon me" (a.t.). Those who were chosen to serve as deacons in Acts 6:5, 6 were set apart by the laying on of hands.

In the OT, the imposition of hands was used as a symbol in acts of blessing, of appointment to office, and of dedication to God. Moses laid his hands on Joshua when he set him apart as his successor (Num 27:23; Deut 34:9). Jacob blessed his grandchildren by laying his hands on their heads (Gen 48:14, 17). Imposition of hands was used in dedicating sacrifices (Lev 1:4) and in setting apart Levites (Num 8:10).

Similarly our Lord blessed by laying on of hands (Matt 19:13, 15; Mark 10:13, 16), and used the same symbolic act in healing (Luke 13:13), which shows that it was a well-known practice, as Jesus is asked to lay on hands (Mark 5:23; Luke 4:40). The disciples also used laying on of hands in healing (Mark 16:18; Acts 9:12, 17 referring probably to the restoration of Saul's sight; Acts 28:8). The symbol of laying on of hands therefore had more than one meaning. The Apostles used it when praying for the gift of the Holy Spirit for the baptized (Acts 8:17; 19:6), and also when setting men apart for the ministry. The "laying on of hands" in Heb 6:2 perhaps refers to all the occasions when the symbol was used, or else to confirm an act only. Laying on of hands is explicitly mentioned in Acts 6:6, the Seven; 13:3, mission of Barnabas and Saul; 1 Tim 4:14; 5:22, if that refers to ordination; 2 Tim 1:6, ordination of Timothy.

(II) Anthropomorphically, as if God were man; or of God meaning the powerful hand of God. The hand of God is indicated as an instrument of action and of power and is ascribed strictly to God Himself as also is *ophthalmós* (3788), the eye (Acts 4:28, 30; 7:50; 1 Pet 5:6 [cf. Sept.: Ps 8:6; 104:28; Isa 66:2]). "The hand of the Lord was with him" meaning for help, aid (Luke 1:66; Acts 11:21). "The hand of the Lord is upon thee" meaning for punishment (Acts 13:11; see Sept.: 1 Sam 7:13; 12:15; Ezek 13:9; Amos 1:8).

(III) With a prep. where *cheír*, the hand, is the instrument of action and power. Thus, to the hand is ascribed what strictly belongs to the person himself or to his power (cf. II).

(A) "By the hand" or hands of someone, by his intervention (Mark 6:2; Acts 2:23; 5:12; 7:25; 11:30; 14:3; 19:11; Sept.: Lev 10:11; 1 Kgs 2:25; 12:15; 2 Chr 34:14).

(B) "Into the hands" of someone meaning into his power, with *paradídōmi* (3860), to give over (Matt 17:22; 26:45; Mark 9:31; 14:41; Luke 9:44; 24:7; Acts 21:11; 28:17; Sept.: 1 Sam 23:4, 12, 14; Job 16:12). Also with verbs of committing: *dídōmi* (1325), to give something into the hands (John 13:3); *paratíthēmi* (3908), to deposit, put forth, commit unto the hands (Luke 23:46; Sept.: Gen 42:37); *empíptō* (1706), to fall on or among or into the hands of someone meaning into his power, punishment (Heb 10:31; Sept.: 2 Sam 24:14; 1 Chr 21:13).

(C) With *en* (1722), in, followed by the dat., *en cheirí* (John 3:35; Acts 7:35; Gal 3:19; Sept.: Num 15:23; Josh 2:24; Judg 1:2; 2; 2:14; 6:1; 2 Chr 29:25).

(D) With *ek* (1537), out of, followed by the gen., *ek cheirós*, out of the hand of someone, out of his power, after verbs of freeing, delivering, and the like (Luke 1:71, 74; John 10:28, 29, 39; Acts 12:11; 24:7; Sept.: Gen 32:11; Ex 18:9, 10).

Deriv.: *autócheir* (849), self-handed, doing personally or with one's own hands; *epicheiréō* (2021), to put the hand to, undertake; *cheiragōgós* (5497), one who leads by the hand; *cheirógraphon* (5498), a handwriting, handwritten document; *cheiropoíetos* (5499), made with hands; *cheirotonéō* (5500), to raise the hands, stretch forth the hands, to select or appoint, choose or ordain.

5496. χειραγωγέω *cheiragōgéō*; contracted *cheiragōgó*, fut. *cheiragōgésō*, from *cheiragōgós* (5497), one who leads another by the hand. To lead by the hand (Acts 9:8; 22:11). The Gr. writers used this verb and also the noun *cheiragōgós* (5497), hand leader, particularly when speaking of leading blind persons.

Syn.: *hodēgéō* (3594), to lead, guide; *kateuthúnō* (2720), to direct; *hēgéomai* (2233) and *ágō* (71), to lead; *phérō* (5342), to bring; *periágō* (4013), to lead about.

Ant.: *kataleípō* (2641), to leave behind; *apoleípō* (620), to leave behind; *egkataleípō* (1459), to abandon; *hupolimpánō* (5277), to leave behind; *ekbállō* (1544), to cast out; *apotássō* (657), to withdraw from.

5497. χειραγωγός *cheiragōgós*; gen. *cheiragōgoú*, masc., fem. noun from *cheír* (5495), the hand, and *ágō* (71), to lead. One who leads another by the hand, used by the Gr. writers for those leading the blind (Acts 13:11).

Deriv.: *cheiragōgéō* (5496), to lead by the hand.

Syn.: *hodēgós* (3595), a guide; *kathēgētés* (2519), a guide, teacher.

Ant.: *mathētés* (3101), disciple, follower.

5498. χειρόγραφον *cheirógraphon*; gen. *cheirográphou*, neut. noun from *cheír* (5495), hand, and *gráphō* (1125), to write. Handwriting, record of debt, a note written by the hand which makes one obligated to fulfill what is written (Col 2:14 [cf. Eph 2:15]).

Syn.: *grámma* (1121), letter, document; *epistolé* (1992), an epistle, a letter; *biblíon apostasíou* (*biblíon* [975], book, document; *apostasíou* [647], separation, divorce [gen.]), document of divorce, separation.

5499. χειροποίητος *cheiropoíetos*; gen. *cheiropoiétou*, masc.-fem., neut. *cheiropoíeton*, adj. from *cheír* (5495), hand, and *poiéō* (4160), to make. Made with hands (Mark 14:58; Acts 7:48; 17:24; Eph 2:11; Heb 9:11, 24).

Deriv.: *acheiropoíetos* (886), not made with hands.

5500. χειροτονέω *cheirotonéō*; contracted *cheirotonó*, fut. *cheirotonésō*, from *cheirotónos* (n.f.), stretching out the hands. To elect to an office by lifting up the hand; to choose, vote (2 Cor 8:19); to appoint to an office (Acts 14:23). In the appointment of the elders in Acts 14:23 *cheirotonéō* is used which in later days often meant "to ordain." However, it does not necessarily imply the actual laying on of hands. It means to elect through a show of hands by an assembly, as in 2 Cor 8:19, or to appoint, as by God (Acts 10:41) or man (Acts 14:23).

Deriv.: *procheirontonéō* (4401), to choose beforehand.

Syn.: *tássō* (5021), to assign; *horízō* (3724), to mark out, specify, ordain; *apostéllō* (649), to set apart; *eklégomai* (1586), to chose.

Ant.: *anairéō* (337), to abolish; *katargéō* (2673), to put down, cancel out; *anathematízō* (332), to curse; *paraitéomai* (3868), to depreciate, reject; *aporríptō* (641), to hurl off, reject.

5501. χείρων *cheírōn*; gen. *cheíronos*, masc.-fem., neut. *cheíron*, adj., irregular comparative of *kakós* (2556), bad. Worse, inferior in rank, dignity, goodness, excellence, or condition (Matt 9:16; 12:45; 27:64; Mark 2:21; 5:26; Luke 11:26; 1 Tim 5:8; 2 Tim 3:13; 2 Pet 2:20). More grievous, more severe as spoken of punishment (Heb 10:29 [cf. John 5:14]). Comparative of *kakós* (2556), bad.

Syn.: *elássōn* (1640), less; *hḗssōn* (2276), less, inferior.

Ant.: *kreíssōn* (2908), better; *mállon* (3123), rather, far; *pollṓ* (dat. sing. of *polús* [4183]), much, great; *pollṓ mállon*, much better, very far better.

5502. Χερουβίμ *cheroubím*; or *cheroubeín*, contracted *cheroubín* (Heb 9:5), pl. transliteration of Hebr. *kᵉrūv* (3742, OT). Originally thought to be the bearers of God when He appeared in His glory upon the earth (Ps 18:10). In Ezekiel's vision they carried the throne of God (Ezek 1:11, 22 [cf. 1:19; 10:16ff.]). They are the "wings of the wind" by which God in the thundercloud is borne to the world (Ps 104:3; Isa 19:1). Hence they are the witnesses of His presence. Wherever they are, God is. Representations of them were placed in the tabernacle and temple. In the tabernacle, two golden cherubim stood in the Holy of Holies upon the Mercy Seat (Ex 37:8). They were likewise pictured upon the curtains (Ex 26:1, 31; 36:8, 35). In Solomon's Temple, two colossal figures of the cherubim overlaid with gold stood upon the floor and overshadowed the ark which was between them in the Holy of Holies (1 Kgs 6:27). They were also carved upon the doors, upon all the "walls of the house," and put between representations of palm trees (1 Kgs 6:29, 32, 35; 2 Chr 3:7). They constituted the ornamentation of the temple parts with lions, oxen, and palm trees (1 Kgs 7:29, 36). The cherubim, therefore, testified that God was in the midst of His people.

A second idea which they represent is that they were the watchers of the places where God is. They stand in the service of the invisible and the unapproachable God (cf. Ex 19:9, 16; 24:15).

5503. χήρα *chḗra*; gen. *chḗras*, fem. noun. A widow, a woman who has been bereaved of her husband (Matt 23:14; Mark 12:40, 42, 43; Luke 2:37; 4:25; 7:12; 18:3, 5; 20:47; 21:2, 3; Acts 6:1; 9:39, 41; 1 Cor 7:8; 1 Tim 5:3–5, 9, 11, 16; James 1:27; Sept.: Gen 38:11; Ex 22:22, 24). In Rev 18:7 it is applied figuratively to a city left desolate (cf. Isa 47:8; Lam 1:1). It is the fem. of the adj. *chḗros*, a widow (Luke 4:26). However, the word *chḗros* (masc.), according to the Class. Gr. writers, means not only a widow, but also a bachelor, a man who has never married.

Syn.: *ágamos* (22), unmarried.

Ant.: *húpandros* (5220), a married woman; *gunḗ* (1135), a wife, woman.

5504. χθές *chthés*; adv. of time. Yesterday (John 4:52; Acts 7:28; Sept.: Gen 31:2; 2 Sam 3:17). It also refers to past or former time (Heb 13:8).

Syn.: *pálai* (3819), long ago; *ékpalai* (1597), from of old; *poté* (4218), formerly, in the old time.

Ant.: *aúrion* (839), tomorrow; *hexḗs* (1836), after, following, next; *kathexḗs* (2517), afterward, consecutively; *metépeita* (3347), afterwards, without necessarily indicating an order of events; *hústeron* (5305), later, last, final, afterwards; *eíta* (1534) and *épeita* (1899), afterwards, thereupon.

5505. χιλιάς chiliás; gen. *chiliádos*, fem. noun from *chílioi* (5507), a thousand. One thousand in number, a chiliad (Luke 14:31; Acts 4:4; 1 Cor 10:8; Rev 5:11; 7:4–8; 11:13; 14:1, 3; 21:16; Sept.: Gen 24:60; Ex 12:37). Other numbers: *heís* (1520), one, single; *déka* (1176), ten; *hekatón* (1540), a hundred; *muriás* (3461), ten thousand.

5506. χιλίαρχος chiliárchos; gen. *chiliárchou*, masc. noun from *chílioi* (5507), a thousand, and *árchō* (757), to rule. A military officer who commands a thousand men (Mark 6:21; John 18:12; Acts 25:23 the captain or prefect of the temple, equal to *stratēgós* [4755], a general, captain, the temple warden; Acts 21:31–33, 37; 22:24, 26–29; 23:10, 15, 17–19, 22; 24:7, 22; Rev 6:15; 19:18; Sept.: Deut 1:15; 2 Sam 18:1).

Syn.: *archēgós* (747), leader, prince, author; *stratopedárchēs* (4759), camp commander, commander of the emperor's bodyguard, the captain of the praetorian guard.

5507. χίλιοι chílioi; fem. *chíliai*, neut. *chília*, cardinal number. A thousand (2 Pet 3:8; Rev 11:3; 12:6; 14:20; 20:2–7; Sept.: Gen 20:16). The significance of this numerical term in Rev 20:2–7 is much disputed. On the one hand, there are those who take this to be formally literal and understand it to represent a period of time lasting one-thousand years; they are called chiliasts. Those chiliasts who locate this period after the return of Christ are called premillennialists (a few of whom do not insist on exactly one-thousand years considering the expression to be figurative for a large segment of time). Those chiliasts who locate this period before Christ's return are called postmillennialists (represented by the liberal and the evangelical schools). On the other hand, there are those who take this to be essentially literal and understand the thousand-year reign to represent ideally the present spiritual victory of Christ and His redeemed over this evil world system (Babylon); they are called amillennialists or "nuncmillennialists" [now-millennialists]. The use of the expression "thousand years" itself does not require a formally literal interpretation. The literary genré of the Book of Revelation is apocalyptic and as such uses numbers, places, personages, and its other elements primarily as symbols.

Deriv.: *dischílioi* (1367), two thousand; *eptakischílioi* (2035), seven thousand *pentakischílioi* (4000), five thousand; *tetrakischílioi* (5070), four thousand; *trischílioi* (5153), three thousand; *chiliás* (5505), a thousand in number; *chiliárchos* (5506), captain of a thousand.

5508. Χίος Chíos; gen. *Chíou*, fem. proper noun. Chios, a Greek island west of Smyrna, between Samos and Lesbos (Acts 20:15).

5509. χιτών chitṓn, gen. *chitṓnos*, masc. noun. A close-fitting inner vest, an inner garment (Matt 5:40; John 19:23; Acts 9:39; Jude 1:23). At times two tunics seem to have been worn, probably of different materials for ornament or luxury (Matt 10:10; Mark 6:9; Luke 3:11; 9:3). Hence it is said of the high priest that he rent his clothes (*chitṓnas*) or garments (Mark 14:63 where it is used in the pl.; Sept.: Gen 37:3; 2 Sam 15:32). In Luke 6:29 it is used with *himátion* (2440), an outer cloak as equivalent to *himátia* (Matt 26:65).

Syn.: *himátion* (2440), an outer cloak or cape; *himatismós* (2441), clothing, apparel; *chlamús* (5511), a military cloak worn over the *chitōn* by emperors, kings, magistrates, military officers; *stolē* (4749), a stately robe or uniform, a long gown worn as mark of dignity; *katastolē* (2689), long robe of dignity; *esthēs* (2066) and *ésthēsis* (2067), clothing; *énduma* (1742), a garment of any kind; *ependútēs* (1903), an upper or outer garment which sometimes fishermen wore when at work; *phelónēs* (5341), a mantle, traveling robe for protection against stormy weather, overcoat; *peribólaion* (4018), a wrap or cape, a garment thrown around one; *podērēs* (4158), an outer garment reaching to the feet; *sképasma* (4629), a covering, raiment.

5510. χιών chiōn; gen. *chiónos*, fem. noun. Snow (Matt 28:3; Mark 9:3; Rev 1:14; Sept.: Job 37:6; Isa 1:18; 55:10).
   Syn.: *chálaza* (5464), hail; *brochē* (1028), rain; *huetós* (5205), a shower of rain; *ómbros* (3655), a thunderstorm, shower; *krústallos* (2930), ice, crystal.
   Ant.: *eudía* (2105), fair weather.

5511. χλαμύς chlamús; gen. *chlamúdos*, fem noun. A garment of dignity and office. The purple robe with which our Lord was arrayed in scorn by the mockers in Pilate's judgment hall (Matt 27:28, 31). When put over the shoulders of someone, it was an indication that he was assuming a magistracy. It may have been the cast-off cloak of some high Roman officer which they put over the body of Jesus to mock Him as if He were an official person.
   Syn.: *chitōn* (5509), a tunic, an inner garment.

5512. χλευάζω chleuázō; fut. *chleuásō*, from *chleuē* (n.f.), joke, jest. To mock, scoff, deride in words (Acts 2:13; 17:32).
   Syn.: *empaízō* (1702), to jest, insult, mock; *muktērízō* (3456), turn up the nose at, sneer at, treat with contempt; *ekmuktērízō* (1592), to scoff at.
   Ant.: *eulogéō* (2127), to bless, speak well of; *eneulogéomai* (1757), to bless,

confer blessing upon; *makarízō* (3106), to pronounce blessed; *ainéō* (134), to speak in praise of; *humnéō* (5214), to laud, praise.

5513. χλιαρός chliarós; fem. *chliará*, neut. *chliarón*, adj. from *chliaínō* (n.f.), to warm, make warm. Lukewarm, tepid. In Rev 3:16 the church at Laodicea is likened to lukewarm water, an emetic, something good for little more than inducing vomiting, and is censured for this blighted condition. God expresses His desire that they be cold or hot. This has been frequently misunderstood to mean that God would rather they hate Him or love Him than remain indifferent. However, it would be contradictory for God to rebuke the Laodiceans for not hating Him and to prefer that they recede from indifference to hatred. Rather, hot and cold represent beneficial qualities just as hot water soothes the body and cold water slakes one's thirst. God cannot find any redeeming feature in this church; it is spiritually bankrupt.

5514. Χλόη Chlóē; gen. *Chlóēs*, fem. proper noun. Verdure, tender shoot. Chloe, a female Christian mentioned in 1 Cor 1:11, some of whose household had informed the Apostle Paul of divisions in the Corinthian Church.

5515. χλωρός chlōrós; fem. *chlōrá*, neut. *chlōrón*, adj. from *chlóē* (n.f.), the green herb or grass, akin to fresh, green. Green, as the grass or plants (Mark 6:39; Rev 8:7; 9:4; Sept.: Gen 1:30; 2 Kgs 19:26; Isa 15:6). Pale or yellowish like the grass when dried up in the heat (Rev 6:8).
   Ant.: *xērós* (3584), dry; *ánudros* (504), waterless, dry.

5516. χξς ch x s; the *ch* (chi) standing for 600, the *x* (xi) standing for 60, and the *s* (sigma) standing for 6. 666. An enigmatic number found in Rev 13:18. The number six, being the number of man, may indicate that 666 symbolizes the zenith of man's power. This power is concentrated in the apocalyptic beast of Rev 13:1–8 identified by many as the antichrist (*antíchristos* [500]). According to the Genesis narrative, man was created on the sixth day. His appointed days of labor and toil are six. A Hebrew slave was to serve six years. For six years the land was to be sown. Under the sixth seal, appalling and universal catastrophe upon mankind ensues. As the number seven denotes what is perfect or complete, six, being short of that, signifies human imperfection and toil although a demonstration of human strength. It should also be noted that the image of gold set up by Nebuchadnezzar for his own glorification was sixty cubits long (Dan chap. 3). Daniel 3 can be said to point forward to the even deeper and Satanic evil of Revelation 13 The one foreshadows the other. Thus we might say that this triple six is the fullest, highest development of man under direct satanic control. It is the combination of civil, religious, and political power satanically inspired. It is, so far as man can do it, the complete setting aside of God as the Supreme Ruler. (See Scott, *Exposition of the Revelation of Jesus Christ*. London: Pickering and Inglis Ltd., N.d.)

5517. χοϊκός *choïkós*; fem. *choïkḗ*, neut. *choïkón*, adj. from *chóos* (5522), earth, dust. Earthy, made of earth or dust (1 Cor 15:47–49). Not used in Sept.

    Syn.: *ostrákinos* (3749), of earthenware or clay, earthen; *epígeios* (1919), earthly; *katachthónios* (2709), subterranean.

    Ant.: *ouránios* (3770), heavenly; *epouránios* (2032), pertaining to heaven; *ouranóthen* (3771), from heaven.

5518. χοῖνιξ *choínix*; gen. *choínikos*, fem. noun. A Greek measure for dry things which some consider to be equal to a pint (Rev 6:6) which was considered to be a man's daily allowance just as a dinar, usually translated "penny," was his daily wages.

Other measures: *métron* (3358), a measure, a limited portion; *méros* (3313), a portion; *sáton* (4568), about a peck and a half, three of which make an ephah, a quantity sufficient for a baking; *kóros* (2884), equivalent to ten ephahs, about eleven bushels; *bátos* (943), a liquid measure equivalent to an ephah, containing between eight and nine gallons.

5519. χοῖρος *choíros*; gen. *choírou*, masc.-fem. noun. A hog, and in the pl. swine (Matt 7:6; 8:30–32; Mark 5:11–14, 16; Luke 8:32, 33; 15:15, 16).

    Syn.: *hús* (5300), pig.

5520. χολάω *choláō*; contracted *cholṓ*, fut. *cholḗsō*, from *cholē* (5521), bile. To be bilious, peevish, ill-natured, bitter with, violently angry or incensed at (John 7:23).

    Syn.: *orgízomai* (3710), to be angry; *parorgízomai* (3949), to be aroused to wrath, be provoked; *thumomachéō* (2371), to be extremely angry; *aganaktéō* (23), to be indignant.

    Ant.: *eupsuchéō* (2174), to be of good comfort; *tharséō* (2293), to be of good cheer; *euphraínomai* (2165), to rejoice.

5521. χολή *cholḗ*; gen. *cholḗs*, fem. noun from *chéō* (n.f., see *epichéō* [2022]), to pour. Bile (Matt 27:34). Applied figuratively (Acts 8:23).

    Deriv.: *choláō* (5520), to be bilious, peevish, ill-natured, bitter with.

    Syn.: *pikría* (4088), bitterness.

    Ant.: *epieíkeia* (1932), gentleness; *praütēs* (4240), meekness, clemency; *anochḗ* (463), tolerance, forbearance; *makrothumía* (3115), longsuffering toward people; *hupomonḗ* (5281), patience in regard to things or circumstances; *chrēstótēs* (5544), gentleness, kindness.

5522. χόος *chóos*; contracted *choús*, gen. *choós*, from *chéō* (n.f., see *epichéō* [2022]), to pour. Earth or dust cast upon the head in token of grief or mourning (Rev 18:19 [cf. Josh 7:6; Isa 52:2]). It also refers to dust or dirt flicking onto the feet of travelers. "Shake off the dust" (Mark 6:11).

Deriv.: *choïkós* (5517), earthy, made of earth or dust.

Syn.: *spodós* (4700), ashes; *koniortós* (2868), flying dust.

5523. Χοραζίν *Chorazín*; fem. proper noun. Chorazin, a city in the general vicinity of Bethsaida and Capernaum, near the Sea of Galilee. Chorazin was upbraided by the Lord Jesus for its unbelief in the face of His mighty works and was warned of final destruction (Matt 11:21; Luke 10:13).

5524. χορηγέω *chorēgéō*; contracted *chorēgṓ*, fut. *chorēgḗsō*, from *chorēgós* (n.f.), the leader of the ancient chorus who supplied the chorus at his own expense, which is from *chorós* (5525), the chorus, and *hēgéomai* (2233), to lead. In the NT in general it means to supply or furnish generously, lavishly (2 Cor 9:10; 1 Pet 4:11).

Deriv.: *epichorēgéō* (2023), to fully supply.

Syn.: *paréchō* (3930), to furnish, give, offer; *dídōmi* (1325), to give; *aponémō* (632), to bestow, give; *dōréomai* (1433), to bestow.

Ant.: *aposteréō* (650), to keep back, defraud; *aphairéō* (851), to take away.

5525. χορός *chorós*; gen. *choroú*, masc. noun. A dance or dancing. Used in the OT for David's dancing before the ark (2 Sam 6:14, 16). In the Gr. often used by writers for a company of dancers (Luke 15:25; Sept.: Ex 15:20; Judg 11:34).

5526. χορτάζω *chortázō*; fut. *chortásō*, from *chórtos* (5528), grass. To feed, fill, or satisfy. With food, of persons (Matt 15:33; Mark 8:4; Jer 5:7; Lam 3:15); in the mid./pass. form *chortázomai*, to be fed, satisfied, or filled (Matt 14:20; 15:37; Mark 6:42; 7:27; 8:8; Luke 9:17; 16:21, "to be fed with the crumbs"; John 6:26; Phil 4:12; James 2:16; Rev 19:21, used of fowls; Sept.: Ps 37:19; 104:13;

Lam 3:30); to fill or satisfy with spiritual blessings (Matt 5:6; Luke 6:21).

Deriv.: *chórtasma* (5527), food, sustenance.

Syn.: *plēróō* (4137), to fill up; *pímplēmi* (4130), to fill; *empíplēmi* (1705), to fill full, satisfy; *gemízō* (1072) and *mestóō* (3325), to fill full; *korénnumi* (2880), to satisfy, have enough.

Ant.: *hysteréō* (5302), to lack; *elattonéō* (1641), to have lack; *leípō* (3007), to lack, be destitute; *chrēzō* (5535), to need; *peináō* (3983), to hunger.

5527. χόρτασμα *chórtasma*; gen. *chortásmatos*, neut. noun from *chortázō* (5526), to feed, fill or satiate. Food or provender for cattle (Sept.: Gen 24:25, 32; 42:27; Deut 11:15). Food or sustenance for men (Acts 7:11).

5528. χόρτος *chórtos*, gen. *chórtou*, masc. noun. The grass or herbage of the field in general (Matt 14:19; Mark 6:39; John 6:10; James 1:10, 11; 1 Pet 1:24; Rev 8:7; 9:4). In Matt 6:30; Luke 12:28, *chórtos* includes the lilies of the field of which the Lord had just been speaking. Hay or grass cut down and dried (1 Cor 3:12, applied figuratively to deficient works). The stalk or blade of corn as distinguished from the ear (Matt 13:26; Mark 4:28; Sept.: Gen 2:5; Ps 37:2; Prov 19:12; Isa 40:7, 8).

Deriv.: *chortázō* (5526), to feed, fill or satiate.

5529. Χουζᾶς *Chouzás*; gen. *Chouzá*, masc. proper noun. Chuzas, the steward of Herod (Antipas) whose wife Joanna, after being healed by the Lord (of either possession by an evil spirit or of a disease), became attached to that body of women which accompanied the Lord on His journeys (Luke 8:3).

5530. χράομαι *chráomai*; contracted *chrṓmai*, fut. *chrḗsomai*, mid. deponent of *chráō* (5531), to lend. To use, make use of, make the most of, followed by the dat. of things (Acts 27:17; 1 Cor 7:21, 31; 9:12, 15; 2 Cor 1:17; 3:12; 1 Tim 1:8; 5:23). Of persons meaning to treat well or badly, with the dat. (Acts 27:3; implied 2 Cor 13:10; Sept.: Gen 16:6; 19:8).

Deriv.: *eúchrēstos* (2173), useful; *katachráomai* (2710), to abuse; *sugchráomai* (4798), to share usage with someone; *chrḗma* (5536), something usable as wealth, money; *chrḗsimos* (5539), useful, profitable; *chrḗsis* (5540), use; *chrēstós* (5543), profitable, good for any use.

Syn.: *apaitéō* (523), to demand back.

Ant.: *achreióō* (889), to render useless, become unprofitable, spoil.

5531. χράω *chráō*; contracted *chrṓ*, fut. *chrḗsō*. To lend, furnish as a loan (Luke 11:5); the mid. voice, *chráomai* (5530), to borrow, receive for use.

5532. χρεία *chreía*; gen. *chreías*, fem. noun from *chréos* (n.f.), debt. Also from *chréos* (n.f.): *chreōpheilétēs* (5533), one who owes a debt.

(I) Use, usage, employment, act of using. In the NT metonymically, that in which one is employed, an employment, affair, business (Acts 6:3).

(II) Need, necessity, want.

(A) Generally (Eph 4:29 meaning merciful, needful edification). With *estí* (2076), is, and the gen. (Luke 10:42, "one thing is needful"). With the inf. (Heb 7:11).

(B) Of personal need, necessity, want (Acts 20:34; 28:10, "such things as were necessary"; Rom 12:13; Phil 2:25; 4:16, for one's need or wants; 4:19; Titus 3:14).

(C) Elsewhere only in the phrase *chreían échō* (2192), I have need. **(1)** Generally and followed by the gen. meaning to have need of (Matt 9:12; 21:3; 26:65; Mark 2:17; 11:3; 14:63; Luke 5:31; 9:11; 15:7; 19:31, 34; 22:71; John 13:29; 1 Cor 12:21, 24; Heb 5:12; 10:36; Rev 21:23; 22:5). **(2)** Of personal need, want, with the gen. (Matt 6:8; 1 Thess 4:12; Rev 3:17). Used in an absolute sense, meaning to have need, to be

in need or want (Mark 2:25; Acts 2:45; 4:35; Eph 4:28; 1 John 3:17). Followed by the inf. act. (Matt 14:16; 1 Thess 1:8; 4:9); also the inf. pass. (Matt 3:14; 1 Thess 5:1); by *hína* (2443), so that (John 2:25; 16:30; 1 John 2:27). In the Sept. with the gen. (Prov 18:2; Isa 13:17).

Deriv.: *achreíos* (888), unprofitable; *chrḗzō* (5535), to have need of, want, desire.

Syn.: *anágkē* (318), necessity, need; *hustérēsis* (5304), need; *anagkaíon* (316), necessary, needful; *epánagkes* (1876), necessary; *tó déon*, that which is needful, from *deí* (1163), necessary; *tó prépon* (from *prépō* [4241]), that which is necessary.

5533. χρεωφειλέτης *chreōpheilétēs*; gen. *chreōpheilétou*, masc. noun from *chréos* (n.f.), a loan, debt, and *opheilétēs* (3781), a debtor (Luke 7:41; 16:5). One who owes a debt. Also from *chréos* (n.f.): *chreía* (5532), usage, need.

Ant.: *daneistḗs* (1157), a lender, creditor.

5534. χρή *chrḗ*; an impersonal verb from *chreía* (5532), need, necessity. It is necessary, it needs to be, ought to be; translated "it is becoming" or "it is appropriate" (James 3:10 with the neg. *ou* [3756], not).

5535. χρήζω *chrḗzō*; fut. *chrḗsō*, from *chreía* (5532), need, necessity. Governing a gen., to have need of, want, desire (Matt 6:32; Luke 11:8; 12:30; Rom 16:2).

5536. χρῆμα *chrḗma*; gen. *chrḗmatos*, neut. noun from *chráomai* (5530), to use, need. Something useful or capable of being used. In both the sing. and pl. it means money (Luke 18:24; Acts 4:37; 8:18; 24:26; Sept.: Job 27:17). In Gr. writings it also means thing, matter, business, equal to *prágma* (4229), business, matter, thing, from which is derived *pragmateúomai* (4231), to trade.

Deriv.: *parachrḗma* (3916), at the very moment, immediately; *chrēmatízō* (5537), to manage a business.

Syn.: *argúrion* (694), silver, money; *chalkós* (5475), copper, as used for money; *kérma* (2772), a coin, change; *nómisma* (3546), money; *statḗr* (4715), a coin, equivalent to four drachmae; *drachmaí* (1406), drachmae, the Greek money; *ploútos* (4149), wealth; *porismós* (4200), gain, a means of gain.

Ant.: *ptōcheía* (4432), poverty, destitution, helplessness; *chreía* (5532), need; *aporía* (640), destitution; *anágkē* (318), necessity.

5537. χρηματίζω *chrēmatízō*; fut. *chrēmatísō*, from *chrḗma* (5536), an affair, business. To have a business affair or dealings, manage a business (Sept.: 1 Kgs 18:27), especially in trade and money affairs. In the mid. *chrēmatízomai*, to do good business, make a profit, gain. Of kings and magistrates, to do business publicly, to give audience; to answer as to ambassadors, petitioners, to warn, advise, give a response or decision. Hence in the NT:

(I) Spoken in respect to a divine response, oracle, or declaration, to give response, speak as an oracle, warn from God, used in an absolute sense (Heb 12:25 of Moses who consulted God and delivered to the people the divine response, precepts, warnings, and the like). Used of a prophet (Sept.: Jer 26:2); of God (Sept.: Jer 30:2; 36:4). In the pass. of persons, to receive a divine response, warning, to be warned or admonished of God, used in an absolute sense (Heb 8:5 speaking of Moses); followed by *perí* (4012), concerning, with the gen. (Heb 11:7); with *kat' ónar* (katá [2596], according, in; *ónar* [3677], dream), in a dream (Matt 2:12, 22). Of things, to be given in response, be revealed (Luke 2:26, by the Holy Spirit).

(II) In later Gr. usage it means to do business under someone's name; hence generally, to take or bear a name, to be named, called, constructed with the name in apposition (Acts 11:26, "named [or called] Christians for the first time" [a.t.]; Rom 7:3, "named an adulteress" [a.t.]).

Deriv.: *chrēmatismós* (5538), an oracle, response or decision.

Syn.: *kaléō* (2564), to call; *onomázō* (3687), to name; *eponomázō* (2028), to surname, call; *apokalúptō* (601), to unveil, reveal; *légō* (3004), to say, speak; *laléō* (2980), to say; *eréō* (2046), to utter, speak, say, tell.

5538. χρηματισμός *chrēmatismós*; gen. *chrēmatismoú*, masc. noun from *chrēmatízō* (5537), to do business, utter an oracle, to be warned of God as by an oracle. An oracle, a reply, response or decision (Rom 11:4).

Syn.: *apókrisis* (612), answer; *apókrima* (610), a judicial sentence, answer of God.

5539. χρήσιμος *chrḗsimos*; fem. *chrḗsimē*, neut. *chrḗsimon*, adj. from *chráomai* (5530), to use, need. Useful, profitable (2 Tim 2:14).

Syn.: *eúchrēstos* (2173), useful; *ōphélimos* (5624), useful, profitable; *lusitheleí* (3081), is advantageous, profitable.

Ant.: *áchrēstos* (890), useless, unprofitable; *achreíos* (888), useless; *alusitelḗs* (255), not advantageous; *anōphelḗs* (512), not beneficial or serviceable, unprofitable.

5540. χρῆσις *chrḗsis*; gen. *chrḗseōs*, fem. noun from *chráomai* (5530), to use. Use, the act (usage) or manner (use) of using (Rom 1:26, 27 of the use of the body in sexual intercourse).

5541. χρηστεύομαι *chrēsteúomai*; fut. *chrēsteúsomai*, mid. deponent from *chrēstós* (5543), useful. To be kind, obliging, willing to help or assist (1 Cor 13:4).

Syn.: *parístēmi* (3936), to stand beside; *antilambánomai* (482), to help, be a partaker of, to succor; *boēthéō* (997), to succor, aid; *agathopoiéō* (15), to act beneficially; *agathoergéō* (14), to do good; *euergetéō* (2109), to bestow a benefit, do good; *sumphérō* (4851), to be profitable; *ōpheléō* (5623), to benefit.

Ant.: *bláptō* (984), endanger, hurt, hinder.

5542. χρηστολογία *chrēstología*; gen. *chrēstologías*, fem. noun from *chrēstológos* (n.f.), speaking fairly, from *chrēstós* (5543), kind, obliging, and *légō* (3004), to say. Smooth speaking, eloquent words or speeches (Rom 16:18).

Syn.: *kolakeía* (2850), flattery; *apátē* (539), deceit; *dólos* (1388), subtlety, guile; *plánē* (4106), fraudulence, deceit.

Ant.: *alḗtheia* (225), truth.

5543. χρηστός *chrēstós*; fem. *chrēstḗ*, neut. *chrēstón*, adj. from *chráomai* (5530), to furnish what is needed. Profitable, fit, good for any use.

(I) Of things (Luke 5:39, better for drinking; Sept.: Jer 24:2, 5, good for eating). Figuratively, good, gentle, easy to use or bear; Christ's yoke is *chrēstós*, as having nothing harsh or galling about it (Matt 11:30). In a moral sense, moral, useful, good, virtuous (in the proverb in 1 Cor 15:33 quoted from Menander).

(II) Of persons, useful toward others, hence good-natured, good, gentle, kind (Luke 6:35 of God; Eph 4:32; 1 Pet 2:3); *tó chrēstón* (neut. with the art.), goodness, kindness, equal to *he chrēstótēs* (5544) (Rom 2:4; Sept.: Ps 86:5).

Deriv.: *áchrēstos* (890), unprofitable, useless; *chrēsteúomai* (5541), to be kind, willing to help; *chrēstótēs* (5544), kindness, usefulness.

Syn.: *epieikḗs* (1933), seemly, equitable, fair, forbearing, tolerant; *anexíkakos* (420), one who patiently forbears evil; *ḗpios* (2261), mild, gentle; *kalós* (2570), good; *agathós* (18), benevolent; *akéraios* (185), harmless.

Ant.: *kakós* (2556), bad; *phaúlos* (5337), bad, rotten; *áchrēstos* (890), unprofitable, useless.

5544. χρηστότης *chrēstótēs*; gen. *chrēstótetos*, fem. noun from *chrēstós* (5543), useful, profitable. Benignity,

kindness, usefulness. It often occurs with *philanthrōpía* (5363), philanthropy; *anochḗ* (463), forbearance (Rom 2:4), and is the opposite of *apotomía* (663), severity or cutting something short and quickly (Rom 11:22). *Chrēstótēs* is translated "good" (Rom 3:12); "kindness" (2 Cor 6:6; Eph 2:7; Col 3:12; Titus 3:4); "gentleness" (Gal 5:22). It is the grace which pervades the whole nature, mellowing all which would be been harsh and austere. Thus, wine is *chrēstós* (5543), mellowed with age (Luke 5:39). The word is descriptive of one's disposition and does not necessarily entail acts of goodness as does the word *agathōsúnē* (19), active benignity. *Chrēstótēs* has the harmlessness of the dove but not the wisdom of the serpent which *agathōsúnē* shows in sharpness and rebuke.

Syn.: *epieíkeia* (1932), fairness, moderation, clemency, an active dealing with others involving equity and justice; *praútēs* (4240), meekness; *eupoiḯa* (2140), beneficence, doing that which is good.

Ant.: *pṓrōsis* (4457), callousness, hardness; *kakoḗtheia* (2550), bad character, mischievousness, malignity; *ponēría* (4189), depravity, iniquity.

5545. χρίσμα *chrísma*; gen. *chrísmatos*, neut. noun from *chríō* (5548), to anoint. The anointing (Ex 29:7; 30:25). The specially-prepared anointing oil was called *chrísma hágion* (*hágion* [39], holy). By metonymy used of the Holy Spirit in 1 John 2:20, 27 where it signifies an anointing which had been experienced, a communication and reception of the Spirit (cf. John 16:13). The allusion is to the anointing and consecration of kings and priests (Ex 28:41; 1 Sam 10:1). This was emblematic of a divine spirit descending and abiding upon them from God, as was afterwards the laying on of hands (Deut 34:9). In Dan 9:26 *chrísma* stands for the Anointed One, Christ (*christós* [5547]), as it stands for the Holy Spirit in 1 John 2. *Chrísma* is not merely a figurative name for the Spirit as seen from the expressions *chrísma échete* ("you have an anointing" [a.t.] 2:20) and *elábete* ("you received" [a.t.] 2:27). The word seems chosen on the one hand, to give prominence to what the readers had experienced, and on the other hand, by referring to the OT practice, and especially to Christ, to remind them of their calling and mark (1 Pet 2:5, 9).

5546. Χριστιανός *Christianós*; gen. *Christianoú*, masc. noun from *Christós* (5547), Christ. A name given to the disciples or followers of Christ, first adopted at Antioch. It does not occur in the NT as a name commonly used by Christians themselves (Acts 11:26; 26:28; 1 Pet 4:16). The believers first became known as Christians as an appellation of ridicule.

Syn.: *mathētés* (3101), a learner; *pistós* (4103), faithful (one); *adelphós* (80), a brother; *hágios* (40), a saint.

Ant.: *ápistos* (571), an unbeliever; *ádikos* (94), unjust; *ethnikós* (1482), Gentile, pagan.

5547. Χριστός *Christós*; fem. *christé*, neut. *christón*, adj. from *chríō* (5548), to anoint. Anointed, a term used in the OT applied to everyone anointed with the holy oil, primarily to the high priesthood (Lev 4:5, 16). Also a name applied to others acting as redeemers.

(I) As an appellative and with the art. *ho*, the, *Christós*, Christ, it occurs chiefly in the Gospels and means the Messiah (Mark 15:32, "the King of Israel"; John 1:41; 4:42 "the Christ, the Savior of the world"; Acts 2:36; 9:22; 18:28. Also see Matt 1:17; 2:4; 16:16; Mark 12:35; 13:21; Luke 2:11, 26, "the Christ of the Lord" [a.t.]; 4:41; 23:2; John 1:20, 25; Acts 2:30; 3:18; Rom 8:11; 1 John 2:22; 5:1, 6; Rev 11:15; 12:10; Sept.: Ps 2:2 [cf. Dan 9:25]). Joined with *Iēsoús* (2424), Jesus, *Iēsoús ho Christós*, Jesus the Christ (Acts 5:42; 9:34; 1 Cor 3:11), *Iēsoús Christós* (John 17:3; Acts 2:38; 3:20; 1 John 4:2, 3; 2 John 1:7), *ho Christós Iēsoús*, the Christ Jesus (Acts 17:3; 18:5, 28; 19:4).

(II) As a proper noun, Christ.

(A) Used in an absolute sense, *Christós* or *ho Christós* chiefly in the epistles referring to the Messiah (Rom 5:6, 8; 8:10; 1 Cor 1:12; 3:23; Gal 1:6, 7; 2:20; Eph 4:12; Heb 3:6; 5:5; 1 Pet 1:11; 4:14).

(B) More often joined with *Iēsoús* (Matt 1:16, "Jesus the One called Christ" [a.t.]); *Iēsoús Christós* in the Gospels (Matt 1:1, 18; Mark 1:1; John 1:17; Acts 3:6, "In the name of Jesus Christ"; 4:10; 8:12; 10:36; 28:31; Rom 1:1, 6, 8; 1 Cor 1:1; 5:4). *Christós Iēsoús*, stressing the deity of Christ first and then His humanity only after His resurrection beginning with Acts 19:4 and often in the epistles (Rom 3:24; 8:2, 39; 15:5; 1 Cor 1:2, 30; Gal 3:26; 4:14; Phil 2:5; 3:3, 8; Col 1:4; Heb 3:1). For the use of *ho Kúrios* (2962), the Lord, in connection with the names *Iēsoús* and *Christós*, see *Kúrios* (2962), Lord (cf. II, B, 2).

(C) Other designations attributed to Christ:

(1) The servant of God (*país* [3816], child, servant; Acts 3:13, 26); *tón hágion paída sou* (*hágion* [40], holy; *paída* [3816], child, servant; Acts 4:27, 30). This is a Messianic title of our Lord indicative of humility, submission, vicarious suffering and death (see Acts 8:35; Isa 53:7).

(2) Prince and Savior (*archēgós* [747], chief leader, author or captain; *sōtér* [4990], Savior; Acts 5:31 [cf. Acts 3:15; Heb 2:10; 12:2]). The word *archēgós* reflects the meaning of author or originator as expressed in Acts 3:15, *archēgón tēs zōēs* (*zōēs* [2222], of life), the Originator, Author, and Sustainer of life or the one who inaugurates and controls the Messianic experience of salvation here called *zōē*, life (Isa 60:16).

(3) Son of Man, *ho Huiós toú anthrṓpou* (*Huiós* [5207], son; *anthrṓpou* [444], of man). This expression occurs 81 times in the Gospels, 30 times in Matthew, of which nine passages have direct parallels in both Mark and Luke, four have parallels in Mark only, eight in Luke only, and the remaining nine are peculiar to Matthew. Apart from the Gospels, the term the "Son of Man" is found only in Acts 7:56 (cf. Luke 22:69). In Rev 1:13; 14:14, the expression which is used, though related, is not the same. It is "one [sitting] like unto the son of man" which is a precise reproduction of the phrase in Dan 7:13. With but one exception, the name as found in the Gospels is used only by our Lord Himself. The exception is John 12:34, and even there it is presupposed that Jesus had spoken of Himself as "the Son of Man." The multitude were familiar with the title "the Son of Man." To them it was a designation of the Messiah. Their difficulty was to reconcile Messiahship with exaltation through death. Also throughout the Gospel narratives, there is not a trace that disciples or the wider public were in any wise perplexed by the designation.

The use of the title "the Son of Man" was adopted by our Lord because it was generally understood to refer to the Messiah, but the Messiah was conceived by the Jews as associated with His coming in glory to exercise everlasting rule over the world. The Lord used this expression to make them realize that He had indeed come to rule over the world, but before coming as the Ruler, He had to come as the Sufferer, the Servant who laid down His life for the sins of mankind. (See Matt 25:31 ff; Mark 8:38; 9:9, 12, 31; 10:33; 13:26; 14:21, 41, 62.)

(4) The Son of God, *Huiós toú Theoú* (*huiós* [5207], son; *Theós* [2316], God). Jesus taught that He was the Son of God (Matt 11:27; 24:36; 27:43; Mark 13:32), and therefore the true Messiah, the Lord's anointed. In His native Aramaic, "Abba" or Father, was the mode of address in prayer that came most naturally to His lips, and became a tradition in the worship of the early Christian church (Rom 8:15). The relation claimed by Jesus was a special one, and this is indicated by His use of the expression "My Father" in Matt 11:27; 18:35; 20:23, whereas in Matt 6:32; 10:29 when speaking to the audience, Jesus refers to God as "your Father." More significant still is the designation by Jesus of Himself as the "beloved Son" in the parable of the Vineyard (Mark 12:6), and also by the voice which spoke to Him from heaven at His baptism (Matt 3:16, 17; Mark 1:10, 11; Luke 3:21, 22). Paul "preached Christ . . . , that he is the Son of God" (Acts 9:20). This title is used in its Messianic and official sense, founded on Ps 2:7 (cf. Matt 16:16; John 1:49). Acts 9:22 implies that in Acts 9:20 Paul preached in order to prove that the Son of God is none other than the Christ, the Messiah. See also Mark 8:29; Luke 9:20.

(5) "Son of David" alludes to the Messianic expectation of an anointed Jewish king who would be the deliverer of God's people. The Messianic king was a descendant of David who at the end of the ages would erect His throne. (See Ps 2; 72; 110.)

(6) The Lord, *ho Kúrios* (2962). This was an expression of profound respect. This title, attributed often in antiquity to emperors, was used in a unique sense (Acts 2:36; 10:36). In the Sept., *ho Kúrios* was used for Jehovah (3068, OT). This indeed became the prevailing designation of the Lord Jesus Christ. In the NT, calling upon the name of the Lord Jesus (Acts 9:21 [cf. 9:14; 2:21; 22:16; Rom 10:13; 1 Cor 1:2]) was the same language ascribed to those who worshiped the true God of the OT (cf. Gen 4:26; 12:8; 2 Kgs 5:11). Stephen died "calling upon [the Lord], and saying, Lord Jesus receive my spirit" (Acts 7:59); and Peter posits universal dominion of the same Person—"He is Lord of all" (Acts 10:36).

(7) There are many other ascriptions to the Lord Jesus Christ. One in particular, *monogenés* (3439), unique, the only one of its kind, commonly translated "only begotten" (a name attributed to Him especially by John), is worthy of mention (John 1:14, 18; 3:16, 18; 1 John 4:9).

(III) Metonymically.

(A) Equivalent to *ho lógos toú Christoú* (*lógos* [3056], word), the word of Christ meaning the doctrine of Christ, the gospel (2 Cor 1:19, 21; Eph 4:20).

(B) *Tó sṓma toú Christoú* (*sṓma* [4983], body), the body of Christ meaning the church (1 Cor 12:12).

(C) The salvation of Christ obtained through Him (Gal 3:27; Phil 3:8).

(D) In Christ, see *en* (1722), in, I, C, 1 (cf. *Kuríō* [2962, II, B, 2], Lord).

Deriv.: *antíchristos* (500), one in place of Christ; counterpart and yet antithesis; *Christianós* (5546), Christian; *pseudóchristos* (5580), false Christ.

5548. χρίω *chríō*; fut. *chrísō*. To daub, smear, anoint with oil or ointment, to rub oneself with oil. The practice of anointing is found throughout the biblical record. The following paragraphs discuss its practice and are based upon passages either referring to the concept or employing the key verbs *chríō* or *aleíphō* (218). It was a mark of luxury to use specially scented oils (Amos 6:6) such as those Hezekiah kept in his treasure house (2 Kgs 20:13). The use of ointment was a sign of joy (Prov 27:9), and was discontinued during times of mourning (Dan 10:3); thus Joab instructed the woman of Tekoa to appear unanointed before David (2 Sam 14:2). On the death of Bathsheba's child, David anointed himself to show that his mourning had ended (2 Sam 12:20). The cessation of anointing was to be a mark of God's displeasure if Israel proved rebellious (Deut 28:40; Mic 6:15), and the restoration of the custom was to be a sign of God's returning favor (Isa 61:3). Anointing is used as a symbol of prosperity in Ps 92:10; Eccl 9:8.

Before paying visits of ceremony, the head was anointed. So Naomi told Ruth to anoint herself before visiting Boaz (Ruth 3:3). Oil of myrrh was used for this purpose in the harem of Ahasuerus (Esth 2:12). This must have been a custom in Palestine as Simon's failure to show hospitality in this respect is commented upon by our Lord in Luke 7:46. Mary's anointing of our Lord was according to this custom.

Rubbing with oil was practiced among the Jews in pre-Christian times as well as by the Apostles (Mark 6:13), recommended by James (James 5:14), mentioned in the parable of the Good Samaritan (Luke 10:34), and used as a type of God's forgiving grace when healing the sin-sick soul (Isa 1:6; Ezek 16:9). In Egypt and Palestine the application of ointment and spices to the dead body was customary (Mark 16:1; Luke 23:56; John 19:40). They were externally applied and did not prevent decomposition (John 11:39).

Anointing had the significance of dedication to God. Jacob consecrated the stones at Bethel by pouring oil upon them (Gen 28:18; 35:14), and God recognized the action (Gen 31:13). The tabernacle and its furniture were thus consecrated (Ex 30:26; 40:10; Lev 8:11), and the altar of burnt offering was reconsecrated after the sin offering (Ex 29:36). Other offerings, however, were anointed with oil (Lev 2:1ff.), but no oil was to be poured on the sin offering (Lev 5:11; Num 5:15).

Priests were set apart by anointing. In the case of Aaron and probably all high priests, this was done twice, first by pouring the holy oil on his head after his robing, but before the sacrifice of consecration (Lev 8:12; Ps 133:2), and next by sprinkling after the sacrifice (Lev 8:30). The ordinary priests were only sprinkled with oil after the application of the blood of the sacrifice. Hence the high priest is called the anointed priest (Lev 4:3, 5).

Kings were designated by anointing, such as Saul (1 Sam 10:1) and David (1 Sam 16:13). This act was accompanied by the gift of the Spirit. So when David was anointed, the Spirit descended on him and departed from Saul. Also Hazael was anointed over Syria by God's command (1 Kgs 19:15). Kings thus designated were called the Lord's anointed. David thus speaks of Saul (1 Sam 26:11) and of himself (Ps 2:2). This passage is used by the apostles as prophetic of Christ (Acts 4:26). By anointing, kings were installed into office. David was anointed when made king of Judah and a third time when made king of united Israel (2 Sam 2:4; 5:3).

Anointing also was used metaphorically to mean setting apart for the prophetic office. Elijah was told to anoint Elisha although the actual event is left unrecorded in Scripture (1 Kgs 19:16). In Ps 105:15 the words "anointed" and "prophets" are used as syn. The servant of the Lord says that he is anointed to preach (Isa 61:1), and Christ tells the people of Nazareth that this prophecy is fulfilled in Him (Luke 4:18).

Similarly in a metaphorical sense someone chosen of God is called an anointed one. Thus Israel as a nation is called God's anointed (Ps 84:9; 89:38, 51; Hab 3:13) being promised deliverance on this account (1 Sam 2:10). The name Christ comes from *chríō*, to anoint, equivalent to Messiah. The anointing of Ps 45:7 is taken in Heb 1:9 as prophetic of the Savior's anointing.

Before battle, shields were oiled so that their surfaces might be slippery and shining (Isa 21:5), as was done to the shield of Saul (2 Sam 1:21).

NT uses:

(I) Of Jesus as the Messiah, the anointed King (cf. *Christós* [5547], Christ; Acts 4:27, as a prophet; Luke 4:18 from Isa 61:1). With the acc. (Heb 1:9 quoted from Ps 45:7).

(II) Of Christians as anointed or consecrated, set apart to the service and ministry of Christ and His gospel by the gift of the Holy Spirit (cf. *chrísma* [5545], anointing; 2 Cor 1:21).

Confusion arises in the NT when two distinct words, *chríō* which has a sacred or religious meaning, and *aleíphō* (218), to oil or rub with oil, are translated with the same Eng. word "anoint," without any distinction between the meanings of the words. *Chríō* is consistently translated "anoint" in Luke 4:18; Acts 4:27; 10:38; 2 Cor 1:21; Heb 1:9. *Aleíphō*, which means to besmear, rub, oil, with a mundane, non-sacred meaning, is also translated "anoint" in every instance of its

occurrence (Matt 6:17; Mark 6:13; 16:1; Luke 7:38, 46; John 11:2; 12:3; James 5:14). Since the Eng. translation "anoint" also bears the connotation of sacredness, dedication, and *aleíphō* does not, and since both words are translated by the same word, much confusion has arisen in the exegesis of the passages (especially where *aleíphō* occurs). Because of the distinction that exists between these two words, it is necessary for us to examine the passages where each occurs.

The verb *aleíphō*, meaning to besmear or oil, is found in Matt 6:17: "But thou when thou fastest, anoint [*áleipsai*, the aor. imper. sing. of *aleíphō*] thine head, and wash thy face." The meaning here is evidently that the person who was fasting should use ointment so that his face would look refreshed and not express a sad countenance. The word here has nothing to do with ceremonial anointing. In Mark 6:13, "and they cast out many devils [demons], and anointed [*éleiphon*, the imperf. of *aleíphō*, they were rubbing with oil as a medicinal means] with oil many that were sick, and healed them." Some have argued that because the works performed here were undoubtedly supernatural then the anointing must have been sacral in nature. Two problems hamper this position. First of all, in sacral anointings, the oil is viewed largely as a visible symbol along with which divine activity occurs. No efficacy is attached to the element itself. God works, we might say, supranaturally (above nature) and coordinately with the human action. However, in the case at hand, the application of oil was an instance of a common medical procedure of that day and was looked upon as the immediate agent of healing. That the healings were instantaneous and thoroughly effectual indeed required a special work by God to accelerate the process and exaggerate the results of the oil's healing power. Yet here God's work was not supranatural (above nature) but supernatural (within nature but extending the normal limits) operating through the oil and not simply alongside it. Lastly, the ritual mode in which sacral anointings were usually administered and the mystery in which they were shrouded are conspicuously absent from this scene. The disciples here are not priestly officials performing cultic ritual; they are the representatives of Jesus sent out to proclaim in word and deed the gospel. In fact, the significance of Jesus' circumventing the Levitical body and its work is critical in understanding the import of the disciples' action. Such a gesture was in effect invalidating or treating as obsolete the OT order and signaling the inception of the NT. In this new economy, all men are priests and all things are sacred. In this light, it would be possible to speak of these healings as quasi-sacramental. Nevertheless, the context of the passage and the teaching of Scripture on the subject would not allow one to classify the disciples' deed as strictly sacral. Elsewhere, we see that oil was used for medicinal means as in the parable of the Good Samaritan (Luke 10:34) and also in James 5:14 where "anointing him with oil" is *aleípsantes* (aor. act. part. of *aleíphō*) which means "having rubbed the sick person with oil" (a.t.). The injunction by James is that medicinal means should be applied prior to prayer. It is to be remembered that as priests were to show concern for the body, so also the elders of the local church. In Mark 16:1: "And when the Sabbath was passed, Mary Magdalene, and Mary the mother of James, and Salome, had brought sweet spices, that they might come and anoint [*aleípsosin*, aor. act. subjunctive 3d person pl.] him," which clearly meant the application of ointments and spices to the dead body as was customary in Palestine (Luke 23:56; John 19:40). Such an application of ointment did not have any resurrection power, nor was it meant to prevent decomposition (John 11:39).

However, the distinction between *chríō* and *aleíphō*, while consistently drawn within the NT, is not as clear in the Sept. (Ex 40:15) and especially in patristic writings.

Deriv.: *egchríō* (1472), to anoint, rub in, besmear; *epichríō* (2025), to anoint; *chrísma* (5545), an anointing; *Christós* (5547), Anointed, the Christ.

5549. χρονίζω *chronízō*; fut. *chronísō*, from *chrónos* (5550), time. To while away time, linger, delay, defer, tarry (Matt 24:48; 25:5; Luke 1:21; 12:45; Heb 10:37, where *chronieí* is the fut. 3d person. Attic for *chronísei* Sept.: Gen 34:19; Deut 23:22; Judg 5:28; Dan 9:19; Hab 2:3).

Syn.: *anabállomai* (306), to put off, defer; *bradúnō* (1019), to delay, be slow; *argéō* (691), to delay, linger.

Ant.: *prophthánō* (4399), to get an early start, anticipate; *katalambánō* (2638), to overtake; *speúdō* (4692), to speed, hurry.

5550. χρόνος *chrónos*; gen. *chrónou*, masc. noun. Time. This word perceives time quantitatively as a period measured by the succession of objects and events and denotes the passing of moments. Another word, *kairós* (2540), season, the time of accomplishment, considers time qualitatively as a period characterized by the influence or prevalence of something. *Chrónos* is a period of measured time, not a period of accomplishment as *kairós*. *Chrónos* embraces all possible *kairoí* (pl.), and is often used as the larger and more inclusive term, but not the converse. In the NT:

(I) Time, particularly and generally.

(A) Mark 9:21; Luke 4:5; Acts 7:23; 14:3, 28; 15:33; 18:23; 27:9; Gal 4:4; Heb 11:32; Rev 2:21; 10:6. With the prep.: *diá* (1223), for (Heb 5:12); *ek* (1537), from (Luke 8:27, "from long times" [a.t.]); *en* (1722), in (Acts 1:21, "at all times" [a.t.]; Sept.: Josh 4:24); *epí* (1909), upon (Luke 18:4, "for a time" [a.t.]; Acts 18:20; Rom 7:1; 1 Cor 7:39; Gal 4:1); *metá* (3326), after (Matt 25:19, "after a long time"; Heb 4:7).

(B) In the acc. *chrónon*, sing.; *chrónous*, pl., marking duration, time, how long (Mark 2:19; Luke 20:9; John

5:6; 7:33; 12:35; 14:9; Acts 13:18; 19:22; 20:18; 1 Cor 16:7; Rev 6:11; 20:3; Sept.: Deut 12:19; 22:19; Josh 4:14; Isa 54:7.

(C) Dat. *chrónō*, sing.; *chrónois*, pl., marking time meaning when, in, or during which (Luke 8:29, "oftentimes," in, during, since long time; Acts 8:11; Rom 16:25).

(II) Specifically by the force of adjuncts *chrónos* sometimes stands for a time, season, period, like *kairós* (Acts 1:7; 1 Thess 5:1). Followed by the gen. of event or the like (Matt 2:7; Luke 1:57; Acts 3:21; 7:17; 17:30; 1 Pet 1:17; 4:3); with an adj. pron. (Matt 2:16; 2 Tim 1:9; Titus 1:2; 1 Pet 1:20).

Deriv.: *makrochrónios* (3118), long-lived; *chronízō* (5549), to while away time; *chronotribéō* (5551), to spend time.

Syn.: *hṓra* (5610), hour; *hēméra* (2250), day as referring to a period of time; *diástēma* (1292), an interval, space; *étos* (2094) and *eniautós* (1763), a year; *stigmḗ* (4743), moment.

5551. χρονοτριβέω *chronotribéō*; contracted *chronotribṓ*, fut. *chronotribḗsō*, from *chrónos* (5550), time, and *tríbō* (n.f., see *diatríbō* [1304]), to spend. To spend time (Acts 20:16).

Syn.: *diatríbō* (1304), to abide, tarry; *eukairéō* (2119), to spend one's leisure time; *paraménō* (3887), to remain beside; *kataménō* (2650), to reside; *ménō* (3306), to remain, abide; *diaménō* (1265), to remain constantly.

5552. χρύσεος *chrúseos*; contracted *chrusoús*, fem. *chruséē*, neut. *chrúseon*, adj. from *chrusós* (5557), gold. Golden, made of gold (2 Tim 2:20; Heb 9:4; Rev 1:12, 13, 20; 2:1; 4:4; 5:8; 8:3; 9:13, 20; 14:14; 15:6, 7; 17:4; 21:15; Sept.: Gen 41:42; Ex 3:22).

5553. χρυσίον *chrusíon*; gen. *chrusíou*, neut. noun, the diminutive of *chrusós* (5557), gold. Gold (Heb 9:4 [cf. Rev 21:18, 21]; Sept.: Ex 37:4). 1 Pet 3:3 refers to chains of gold about the neck,

golden earrings, or bracelets of gold on the arms. Money made of gold (Acts 3:6; 20:33 [cf. 1 Pet 1:7, 18]). Spiritually it also denotes the true riches of Christ (Rev 3:18).

5554. χρυσοδακτύλιος *chrusodaktúlios*; gen. *chrusodaktulíou*, masc.-fem., neut. *chrusodaktúlion*, adj. from *chrusós* (5557), gold, and *daktúlios* (1146), a ring for the finger. Having a gold ring or rings on one's fingers (James 2:2).

5555. χρυσόλιθος *chrusólithos*; gen. *chrusolíthou*, masc. noun from *chrusós* (5557), gold, and *líthos* (3037), stone. A chrysolite, a precious stone of a golden color, today known as topaz (Rev 21:20; Sept.: Ex 39:12).

5556. χρυσόπρασος *chrusóprasos*; gen. *chrusoprásou*, masc. noun from *chrusós* (5557), gold, and *práson* (n.f.), a leek. A chrysoprase, a gem having a color which resembles apple green or grass green (Rev 21:20).

5557. χρυσός *chrusós*; gen. *chrusoú*, masc. noun. Gold, a type of precious metal (Matt 2:11; 23:16, 17; Acts 17:29; Rev 9:7 [TR]; 18:12; Sept.: 2 Chr 3:7; Ezra 1:6; Prov 17:3); money of gold (Matt 10:9; James 5:3); golden ornaments (1 Tim 2:9; Rev 17:4; 18:16 [TR]); the precious and weighty truths or doctrines of the gospel; figuratively (1 Cor 3:12). Diminutive, *chrusíon* (5553), gold.

Deriv.: *chrúseos* (5552), made of gold; *chrusodaktúlios* (5554), wearing a golden ring on a finger; *chrusólithos* (5555), gold stone; *chrusóprasos* (5556), a greenish-yellow gem; *chrusóō* (5558), to overlay or adorn with gold.

5558. χρυσόω *chrusóō*; contracted *chrusṓ*, fut. *chrusṓsō*, from *chrusós* (5557), gold. To overlay or adorn with gold (Rev 17:4; 18:16; Sept.: Ex 26:32, 37; 2 Kgs 18:16).

5559. χρώς chrốs; gen. *chrōtós*, masc. noun. The surface of the body, the skin (Acts 19:12, "which had been on his body" [a.t.]; Sept.: Lev 13:2f.). To differentiate from *sōma* (4983), body, *chrōs* refers rather to the surface or skin of the body.

Syn.: *sōma* (4983), body as a whole; *ptōma* (4430), corpse, carcass; *kōlon* (2966), a corpse or a dead body; *dérma* (1192), skin.

Ant.: *psuchē* (5590), soul; *pneúma* (4151), spirit.

5560. χωλός chōlós; fem. *chōlē*, neut. *chōlón*, adj. from *chaláō* (n.f.), to slacken, loosen, let fall, be lame (Matt 11:5; 15:30, 31; 18:8; 21:14; Luke 7:22; 14:13, 21; John 5:3; Acts 3:2; 8:7; 14:8). Lame or infirm in a spiritual sense (Heb 12:13). Maimed (Mark 9:45), the same as *anápēros* (376), crippled (Sept.: Lev 21:18; Deut 15:21).

Syn.: *kullós* (2948), literally rocking about, crippled, maimed.

5561. χώρα chōra; gen. *chōras*, fem. noun from *chōros* (5566), a field or place, usually where cattle range and feed. A country, land, region, province.

(I) Generally (Matt 4:16 [cf. Isa 9:1]).

(A) Particularly (Matt 2:12; Luke 3:1; 15:13–15; 19:12; John 11:54, 55; Acts 8:1; 10:39; 13:49; 16:6; 18:23, "the country of Galatia," the region or province of Galatia; 26:20). Opposite to the sea (Acts 27:27; Sept.: Gen 42:9; 1 Kgs 21:14; Job 1:1).

(B) Metonymically for the inhabitants of a country or region (Mark 1:5; Acts 12:20).

(II) Used with the name of a town or city, meaning a district, territory, around and belonging to that city (Matt 8:28; Mark 5:1; Luke 8:26; implied in Mark 5:10; Luke 2:8).

(III) Specifically referring to the country, the open country, fields as opposed to the city (Luke 21:21 in contrast to Jerusalem in verse 20); as sown, tilled, harvested (Luke 12:16; John 4:35; James 5:4).

Deriv.: *eurúchōros* (2149), spacious; *períchōros* (4066), country round about *stenochōréō* (4729), to hem in closely, cramp, distress; *stenochōría* (4730), narrowness, and figuratively anguish, distress.

Syn.: *agrós* (68), field; *patrís* (3968), nation, country; *gē* (1093), earth, land; *méros* (3313), a part, country; *klíma* (2824), slope, inclination, region; *édaphos* (1475), ground; *tópos* (5117), a spot, space, locality.

Ant.: *thálassa* (2281), sea; *pélagos* (3989), deep sea.

5562. χωρέω chōréō; contracted *chōrō*, fut. *chōrēsō*, from *chōros* (5566). To go from, give space, place, room, give way, yield, or come to some place.

(I) To go away from a place.

(A) Generally, to go, pass, intrans. with *eis* (1519), into (Matt 15:17; used figuratively in 2 Pet 3:9).

(B) To go forward, metaphorically to go well, succeed, have success or progress (John 8:37, "in [or among] you").

(II) Spoken of capacity, to make place or room, take in or receive, hold, contain.

(A) Particularly as a vessel with the acc. of measure (John 2:6). Generally of a place, with the acc. of thing (Mark 2:2; John 21:25); of a vessel (Sept.: 1 Kgs 7:24; 2 Chr 4:5; Gen 13:6).

(B) Figuratively to receive a doctrine, matter, to admit, assent to, with the acc. (Matt 19:11, 12). Also of persons, to receive to one's heart, affection (2 Cor 7:2 in allusion to 2 Cor 6:11–13).

Deriv.: *anachōréō* (402), to withdraw, depart, to go or turn back again; *apochōréō* (672), to depart from; *ekchōréō* (1633), to depart out, leave a place; *hupochōréō* (5298), to go back, retire, withdraw.

Syn.: *prosdéchomai* (4327), to be hospitable; *metabaínō* (3327), to depart; *poreúomai* (4198), to go on one's way; *periéchō* (4023), to enclose, contain; *ágō* (71), to lead, go; *érchomai* (2064), to come; *paragínomai* (3854), to come, be present; *embaínō* (1684), to enter in;

sumperilambánō (4843), to embrace, include; *empíptō* (1706), to fall in among, to include; *egkrúptō* (1470), to conceal in, incorporate with.

Ant.: *apokleíō* (608), to exclude.

5563. χωρίζω *chorízō*; fut. *chōrísō*, from *chōrís* (5565), without. To put apart, separate, sever.

(I) Act. (Matt 19:6; Mark 10:9); followed by *apó* (575), from, with the gen., from something (Rom 8:35, 39). Pass. (Heb 7:26).

. **(II)** Mid. *chōrízomai*, aor. pass. *echōrísthēn*. Mid. meaning to separate oneself, to depart from a person, with *apó* (575), from (1 Cor 7:10, 15). Of a wife (Sept.: Neh 9:2). From a place, to go away, depart, with *apó*, from (Acts 1:4); with *ek* (1537), out of or from (Acts 18:1, 2).

Deriv.: *apochōrízō* (673), to separate off, remove; *diachōrízō* (1316), to separate completely, throughout.

Syn.: *aphorízō* (873), to separate from; *apodiorízō* (592), to separate from; *metaírō* (3332), to remove; *apotíthēmi* (659), to put away from, put off; *exaírō* (1808), to put away from the midst of; *methístēmi* (3179), to remove; *apostréphō* (654), to turn away, remove.

Ant.: *suzeúgnumi* (4801), to yoke together, conjoin; *mígnumi* (3396), to mix, mingle; *suníēmi* (4920), to put together, understand; *sunístēmi* or *sunistáō* (4921), to set together, to constitute, stand with; *sustréphō* (4962), to twist together; *súneimi* (4896), to assemble, gather together; *sugkeránnumi* (4786), to commingle, combine or assimilate, mix with.

5564. χωρίον *chōríon*; gen. *chōríou*, neut. noun, a diminutive of *chóros* (5566), space. A field, a parcel of ground,

a place (Matt 26:36; Mark 14:32; John 4:5; Acts 1:18, 19; 4:34; 5:3, 8; 28:7; Sept.: 1 Chr 27:27).

5565. χωρίς *chōrís*; adv. and prep. As an adverb it means separately, by itself, apart (John 20:7). As a prep. governing a gen. it means:

(I) Separately from, without (Matt 13:34; Mark 4:34; Luke 6:49; John 1:3; Rom 3:21, 28; 4:6; 7:8, 9; 10:14; 1 Cor 4:8; 11:11; Eph 2:12; Phil 2:14; 1 Tim 2:8; 5:21; Phile 1:14; Heb 4:15, "yet without sin," either without having sinned or apart from sin (see II below); 7:7, 20, 21; 9:7, 18, 22, 28; 10:28; 11:6, 40; 12:8, 14; James 2:20, 26).

(II) Besides, exclusive of (Matt 14:21; 15:38; 2 Cor 11:28; Sept.: Gen 46:26; 1 Kgs 5:16). If Heb 4:15 carries this meaning, then the expression "without sin" means "apart from sin [the sinful nature]" and points to the fact that Jesus endured temptation in every point except in an appeal to a fallen nature which He did not possess.

Deriv.: *chorízō* (5563), to put apart, separate.

Syn.: *áneu* (427), without; *áter* (817), without, in the absence of; *ektós* (1622), without, except, besides; *parektós* (3924), except, save, without; *plēn* (4133), except, nevertheless.

Ant.: *sún* (4862), with, together.

5566. χῶρος *chóros*; gen. *chórou*, masc. noun. The northwest or the wind from that direction (Acts 27:12). See the diminutive *choríon* (5564), a field, place.

Deriv.: *chóra* (5561), a country, land, region, province; *chōréō* (5562), to go from, give way.

5567. ψάλλω *psállō*; fut. *psalṓ*, from *psáō* (n.f., see *psēlapháō* [5584]), to touch lightly, twang or snap. To play a stringed instrument or to sing a hymn. Musicians who play upon an instrument were said to pluck the strings (*psálloun chordás* [n.f.]) or simply pluck (*psálloun*). The word came to signify the making of music in any fashion. Because stringed instruments were commonly used both by believers and heathen in singing praises to their respective gods, it meant to sing, sing praises or psalms to God whether with or without instruments (Rom 15:9; 1 Cor 14:15; Eph 5:19; James 5:13; Sept.: Judg 5:3; 2 Sam 22:50; Ps 9:2; 18:49; 30:4; 47:6).

Deriv.: *psalmós* (5568), psalm.

Syn.: *ádō* (103), to sing in praise or honor of someone; *humnéō* (5214), laud in song.

5568. ψαλμός *psalmós*; gen. *psalmoú*, masc. noun from *psállō* (5567), to sing, chant. Originally a touching, and then a touching of the harp or other stringed instruments with the finger or with the plectrum; later known as the instrument itself, and finally it became known as the song sung with musical accompaniment. This latest stage of its meaning was adopted in the Sept. In all probability the psalms of Eph 5:19; Col 3:16 are the inspired Psalms of the Hebrew Canon (Sept.: Ps 95:1. In superscripts, Pss 3; 4; 5). Specifically of the Psalms as a part of the OT (Luke 20:42; 24:44; Acts 1:20; 13:33). The word certainly designates these on all other occasions when it occurs in the NT, with the one possible exception of 1 Cor 14:26. These are the old songs to which new hymns and praises are added (Rev 5:9).

Syn.: *húmnos* (5215), a hymn, religious ode; *ōdḗ* (5603) song of praise.

5569. ψευδάδελφος *pseudádelphos*; gen. *pseudadélphou*, masc. noun from *pseudḗs* (5571), false, and *adelphós* (80), brother. A false brother. In Gal 2:4 it denotes those who had become outwardly members of the Christian church, sharers in its fellowship of life and love, but in reality were not so inwardly. Therefore, they had no right to be counted as brothers. They had the companionship of the brothers but the real kinship of spiritual life was missing (see 2 Cor 11:26).

Ant.: *adelphós* (80), brother.

5570. ψευδαπόστολος *pseudapóstolos*; gen. *pseudapostólou*, masc. noun from *pseudḗs* (5571), false, and *apóstolos* (652), apostle. A false apostle, one who pretends to be an apostle of Christ (2 Cor 11:13).

Ant.: *apóstolos* (652), apostle.

5571. ψευδής *pseudḗs*; gen. *pseudoús*, masc.-fem., neut. *pseudés*, adj. from *pseúdomai* (5574), to lie. False, lying; as a subst. a liar (Acts 6:13; Rev 2:2; Sept.: 1 Kgs 22:22, 23; Prov 12:22; 19:5, 9). In Rev 21:8 the word denotes all those who contrive idolatrous worship and false miracles to deceive men and make them fall into idolatry. See Sept.: Prov 8:7; 28:6.

Deriv.: *apseudḗs* (893), that which cannot lie; *pseudádelphos* (5569), a false brother; *pseudapóstolos* (5570), a false apostle; *pseudodidáskalos* (5572), a false teacher; *pseudológos* (5573), one speaking falsely; *pseudomártus* (5575), a false witness; *pseudomarturéō* (5576), to bear false witness; *pseudomarturía* (5577), false witness; *pseudoprophḗtēs* (5578), a false prophet; *pseudóchristos* (5580), a false Christ; *pseudṓnumos* (5581), falsely named.

Syn.: *nóthos* (3541), illegitimate, spurious; *plastós* (4112), artificial, fictitious, plastic, false; *hupokritḗs* (5273), a hypocrite; *dólios* (1386), guileful, deceitful.

Ant.: *alēthḗs* (227), true, truthful; *alēthinós* (228), real, genuine; *gnḗsios* (1103), genuine; *pistós* (4103), faithful, true, dependable; *eilikrinḗs* (1506), pure, sincere; *ádolos* (97), guileless; *anupókritos* (505), unhypocritical, unfeigned; *apseudḗs* (893), veracious, one who cannot lie.

5572. ψευδοδιδάσκαλος *pseudodidáskalos*; gen. *pseudodidaskálou*, masc. noun from *pseudḗs* (5571), false, and *didáskalos* (1320), a teacher. A false teacher or one who pretends to be a Christian teacher but teaches false doctrine (2 Pet 2:1).

5573. ψευδολόγος *pseudológos*; gen. *pseudológou*, masc.-fem., neut. *pseudológon*, adj. from *pseudḗs* (5571), false, and *légō* (3004), to speak. Lying, as a subst. a speaker of lies or falsehoods, a liar (1 Tim 4:2).

5574. ψεύδομαι *pseúdomai*; fut. *pseúsomai*, mid. deponent of *pseúdō* (n.f.), to cheat, defraud, falsify. To lie, to speak falsely or deceitfully (Matt 5:11; Acts 5:3, 4; Rom 9:1; 2 Cor 11:31; Gal 1:20; Col 3:9; 1 Tim 2:7; Heb 6:18; James 3:14; 1 John 1:6; Rev 3:9; Sept.: Lev 19:11; Deut 33:29; Prov 14:5; Isa 57:11). With a dat. following, to lie to (Acts 5:4; Sept.: Ps 78:36; 89:35).
Deriv.: *pseudḗs* (5571), false; *pseúdos* (5579), lie; *pseúsma* (5582), a falsehood; *pseústēs* (5583), a liar, deceiver.
Syn.: *planáō* (4105), to deceive; *epiorkéō* (1964), to commit perjury.
Ant.: *alētheúō* (226), to speak or act in truth.

5575. ψευδομάρτυς *pseudomártus*; gen. *pseudomárturos*, masc. noun from *pseudḗs* (5571), false, and *mártur* (3144), a witness. A lying or false witness (Matt 26:60; 1 Cor 15:15).

5576. ψευδομαρτυρέω *pseudomarturéō*; contracted *pseudomarturṓ*, fut. *pseudomarturḗsō*, from *pseudḗs* (5571), false, and *márturéō* (3140), to bear witness. To bear false witness. Intrans. (Matt 19:18; Mark 10:19; 14:56, 57; Luke 18:20; Rom 13:9; Sept.: Ex 20:16; Deut 5:20).

5577. ψευδομαρτυρία *pseudomarturía*; gen. *pseudomarturías*, fem. noun from *pseudḗs* (5571), false, and *marturía* (3141), a witness. False witness (Matt 15:19; 26:59).

5578. ψευδοπροφήτης *pseudoprophḗtēs*; gen. *pseudoprophḗtou*, masc. noun from *pseudḗs* (5571), false, and *prophḗtēs* (4396), a prophet. A false prophet, one who falsely assumes the work of a prophet when he pretending to foretell things to come (Matt 24:11, 24; Mark 13:22) or teaching false doctrines in the name of God (Matt 7:15; Luke 6:26; Acts 13:6; 2 Pet 2:1; 1 John 4:1; Rev 16:13; 19:20; 20:10; Sept.: Jer 6:13; Zech 13:2 [cf. *prophḗtēs* {4396}, a prophet]).

5579. ψεῦδος *pseúdos*; gen. *pseúdous*, neut. noun from *pseúdomai* (5574), to lie. A lie, falsehood (John 8:44 [cf. Col 3:9; 2 Thess 2:11; 1 John 2:21, 27]; Sept.: Ps 5:6; Jer 5:2). Lying in general (Eph 4:25). 2 Thess 2:9 refers to false, fictitious, pretended miracles. An idol, a vain or false idol, as used in the Sept.: Isa 44:20. Rev 21:27 refers to making a lie, i.e., making idols and contriving false miracles. See Rev 22:15 (cf. Rom 1:25); Sept.: Hos 7:3; 11:12. Of false gods (Jer 3:10; 13:25).
Syn.: *múthos* (3454), a myth; *dólos* (1388), deceit, guile; *apátē* (539), deceit or deceitfulness; *plánē* (4106), error, wandering; *panourgía* (3834), craftiness.
Ant.: *alḗtheia* (225), truth; *eilikríneia* (1505), sincerity.

5580. ψευδόχριστος *pseudóchristos*; gen. *pseudochrístou*, masc. noun from *pseudés* (5571), false, and *Christós* (5547), Christ. False christ (Matt 24:24; Mark 13:22). The false christ does not necessarily deny the existence of Christ. On the contrary, he builds on the world's expectations of such a person, while he blasphemously appropriates these to himself and affirms that he is the foretold One in whom God's promises and the saint's expectations are fulfilled. He is of the same character as the *antíchristos* (500), antichrist, who opposes the true Christ (1 John 4:3). The *pseudóchristos* affirms himself to be the Christ. Both are against the Christ of God. The final antichrist will also be a pseudochrist as well. He will usurp to himself Christ's offices, presenting himself to the world as the true center of its hopes, the satisfier of all its needs, and the healer of all its ills. He will be a pseudochrist and antichrist in one.

5581. ψευδώνυμος *pseudṓnumos*; gen. *pseudōnúmou*, masc.-fem., neut. *pseudṓnumon*, adj. from *pseudés* (5571), false, and *ónoma* (3686), a name. Falsely named or called (1 Tim 6:20).

5582. ψεῦσμα *pseúsma*; gen. *pseúsmatos*, neut. noun from *pseúdomai* (5574), to lie. A lie, falsehood (Rom 3:7 [cf. Rom 3:3–5]).
Syn.: *múthos* (3454), a myth; *pseúdos* (5579), a falsehood, while *pseúsma* is an acted lie.
Ant.: *alḗtheia* (225), truth; *eilikríneia* (1505), sincerity, purity.

5583. ψεύστης *pseústēs*; gen. *pseústou*, masc. noun from *pseúdomai* (5574), to lie. A liar (John 8:44, 55; Rom 3:4, one false toward God, a wicked person; 1 Tim 1:10; Titus 1:12; 1 John 1:10; 2:4, 22, of those who profess salvation but live and think contrary to Christian truth; 4:20; 5:10). See Sept.: Prov 19:22.

Syn.: *pseudológos* (5573), one telling lies.

5584. ψηλαφάω *psēlapháō*; contracted *psēlaphṓ*, fut. *psēlaphḗsō*, from *psáō* (n.f., see below), to touch lightly. To feel an object or to feel for or after an object (Luke 24:39; Acts 17:27; Heb 12:18; 1 John 1:1; Sept.: Gen 27:12, 21, 22).
Deriv. of *psáō* (n.f.), to touch lightly: *psállō* (5567), to play a stringed instrument; *psḗphos* (5586), a small stone; *psichíon* (5589), a crumb; *psōmíon* (5596), a sop; *psṓchō* (5597), to rub.
Syn.: *háptomai* (680), to touch, cling to, lay hold of; *thiggánō* (2345), to touch by way of inquiry, to handle.

5585. ψηφίζω *psēphízō*; fut. *psēphísō*, from *psḗphos* (5586), a small stone or pebble used particularly by the Greeks and Egyptians in their calculations. To reckon, compute, calculate, figure out (Luke 14:28; Rev 13:18). In the classics also in the mid. meaning to give one's vote, vote for, decree.
Deriv.: *sugkatapsēphizō* (4785), to be reckoned or numbered with; *sumpsēphízō* (4860), to count up, reckon together.
Syn.: *logízomai* (3049), to reckon, count; *sunaírō* (4868), to make a reckoning together.

5586. ψῆφος *psḗphos*; gen. *psḗphou*, fem. noun from *psáō* (n.f., see *psēlapháō* [5584]), to lightly touch. A small stone or pebble. In Rev 2:17, an allusion to the ancient custom among the Greeks of acquitting with a white stone or pebble and condemning with a black one. A vote, suffrage, voice (Acts 26:10).
Deriv.: *psēphízō* (5585), to reckon, compute.
Syn.: *kataphérō* (2702), to cast a vote; *klḗros* (2819), a lot.

5587. ψιθυρισμός *psithurismós*, gen. *psithurismoú*, masc. noun from *psithurízō* (n.f.), to whisper. A whispering, particularly of slander and detraction, hurtful gossip (2 Cor 12:20). Also from *psithurízō* (n.f.): *psithupistḗs* (5588), a whisperer.

Syn.: *pseúdos* (5579), a lie.

5588. ψιθυριστής *psithuristḗs*; gen. *psithuristoú*, masc. noun from *psithurízō* (n.f.), to whisper. A whisperer, a secret slanderer. It is similar to *katálalos* (2637), an accuser, a backbiter who does his slandering openly (Rom 1:29). Also from *psithurízō* (n.f.): *psithurismós* (5587), a whispering.

5589. ψιχίον *psichíon*; gen. *psichíou*, neut. noun, a diminutive of *psíx* (n.f.), a bit, crumb, which is from *psáō* (n.f., see *psēlapháō* [5584]), to crumble. A crumb of bread, meat, or other items of food (Matt 15:27; Mark 7:28; Luke 16:21). Found only in the NT.

5590. ψυχή *psuchḗ*; gen. *psuchḗs*, fem. noun from *psúchō* (5594), to breathe, blow. Soul, that immaterial part of man held in common with animals. One's understanding of this word's relationship to related terms is contingent upon his position regarding biblical anthropology. Dichotomists view man as consisting of two parts (or substances), material and immaterial, with spirit and soul denoting the immaterial and bearing only a functional and not a metaphysical difference. Trichotomists also view man as consisting of two parts (or substances), but with spirit and soul representing in some contexts a real subdivision of the immaterial. This latter view is here adopted. Accordingly, *psuchḗ* is contrasted to *sṓma* (4983), body, and *pneúma* (4151), spirit (1 Thess 5:23). The *psuchḗ*, no less than the *sárx* (4561), flesh, belongs to the lower region of man's being. Sometimes *psuchḗ* stands for the immaterial part of man made up of the soul (*psuchḗ* in the restrictive sense of the life element), and the spirit *pneúma*. However, animals are not said to possess a spirit; this is only in man, giving him the ability to communicate with God. Also breath (Sept.: Gen 1:30; Job 41:12), and in the NT, usually meaning the vital breath, the life element through which the body lives and feels, the principle of life manifested in the breath.

(I) The soul as the vital principle, the animating element in men and animals.

(A) Generally (Luke 12:20; Acts 20:10; Sept.: Gen 35:18; 1 Kgs 17:21). Of beasts (Rev 8:9).

(B) Metonymically, for life itself (Matt 6:25; 20:28; Mark 3:4; 10:45; Luke 6:9; 12:22, 23; 14:26; 21:19; Acts 15:26; 20:24; 27:10, 22; Rom 16:4; Phil 2:30; 1 Thess 2:8; Rev 12:11). To lay down one's life (John 10:11, 15, 17; 13:37, 38; 15:13; 1 John 3:16). To seek one's life (Matt 2:20; Rom 11:3; Sept.: Ex 4:19). Including the idea of life or the spirit, both natural and eternal (Matt 16:26; Mark 8:36, 37 [cf. Luke 9:25]). In antithetic declarations of the Lord Jesus, *psuchḗ* refers not only to natural life, but also to life as continued beyond the grave (Matt 10:39; 16:25; Mark 8:35; Luke 9:24; 17:33; John 12:25). Generally, the soul of man, his spiritual and immortal nature with its higher and lower powers, its rational and natural faculties (Matt 10:28; 2 Cor 1:23; Heb 6:19; 10:39; 13:17; James 1:21; 5:20; 1 Pet 1:9; 2:11, 25; 4:19). Generally the soul (1 Cor 15:45, a living soul in allusion to Gen 2:7; Rev 16:3; Sept.: Gen 1:24; 2:19; 9:10, 12, 15).

(C) Of a departed soul, separate from the body; spoken in Greek mythology of the ghosts inhabiting Hades (Acts 2:27, 31, quoted from Ps 16:10; Rev 6:9; 20:4).

(II) Specifically the soul as the sentient principle, the seat of the senses, desires, affections, appetites, passions, the lower aspect of one's nature. Distinguished in Pythagorean and Platonic philosophy from the higher rational nature, expressed by *noús* (3563), mind, and *pneúma* (4151), spirit belonging to man only. This distinction is also followed by the Sept. and sometimes in the NT (cf. *pneúma* [4151], spirit, II, B). In 1 Thess 5:23 the whole man is indicated as consisting of spirit, soul, and body;

soul and spirit, the immaterial part of man upon which the word of God is operative (Heb 4:12); "my soul . . . and my spirit," the immaterial part of personality with which Mary could magnify the Lord (Luke 1:46, 47). Distinguished from *diánoia* (1271), understanding or mind, because soul is related to the affections (Matt 22:37; Mark 12:30; Luke 10:27). From *súnesis* (4907), the ability to put facts together, knowledge, understanding, intellect (Mark 12:33). Some-times the soul means the mind, feelings (Matt 11:29; Luke 2:35; John 10:24; Acts 14:2, 22; 15:24; Heb 12:3; 1 Pet 1:22; 2 Pet 2:8, 14; Sept.: Ex 23:9; 1 Sam 1:15; Isa 44:19). "With all one's soul" (a.t.) means with his entire affection (Matt 22:37; Mark 12:30, 33; Luke 10:27; Sept.: Deut 26:16; 30:2, 6, 10; 2 Chr 15:15; 31:21); *Ek psuchḗs* (*ek* [1537], out of), "from the soul" (a.t.), meaning heartily (Eph 6:6; Col 3:23). To be of one soul means to be unanimous, united in affection and will (Acts 4:32; Phil 1:27). That which strictly belongs to the person himself, often ascribed to the soul as the seat of the desires, affections, and appetites (Matt 12:18; 26:38; Mark 14:34; Luke 1:46; 12:19; John 12:27; Heb 10:38; 3 John 1:2; Rev 18:14; Sept.: Gen 27:4, 19; Isa 1:14; 33:18).

(III) Metonymically, a soul, a living thing in which is *hē psuchḗ*, life.

(A) More often of a man, a soul, a living person, *pása psuchḗ* (*pás* [3956], every), every soul, every person, everyone (Acts 2:43; 3:23; Rom 13:1). In a periphrasis, *pása psuchḗ anthrṓpou* ([444], man), "every soul of man" meaning every man (Rom 2:9); *psuchás anthrṓpōn*, "souls of men" (a.t. [Luke 9:56 {TR}; simply *psuchḗ*, Sept.: Gen 17:14; Lev 5:1, 2; Deut 24:8]). *Psuchḗ anthrṓpou*, soul of man (Num 19:11, 13). In enumerations (Acts 2:41, "about three thousand souls"; 7:14; 27:37; 1 Pet 3:20; Sept.: Gen 46:15, 18, 26, 27; Ex 1:5; Deut 10:22).

(B) Specifically for a servant, slave (Rev 18:13), probably female slaves in distinction from the preceding *sṓmata*

(4983), bodies (cf. *ánthrōpos* [444], man, I, C, 5); Sept.: Gen 12:5.

Deriv.: *ápsuchos* (895), lifeless, inanimate, without life; *dípsuchos* (1374), two-souled, double minded; *isópsuchos* (2473), like-minded; *oligópsuchos* (3642), little-souled, of little spirit, fainthearted, fearful; *súmpsuchos* (4861), joint-souled, agreeing with one accord; *psuchikós* (5591), natural, physical, pertaining to the animal instinct in man.

Syn.: *kardía* (2588), the heart as the seat of life; *diánoia* (1271), understanding; *zōḗ* (2222), life as a principle; *bíos* (979), possessions of life; *bíōsis* (981), the spending of one's life; *agōgḗ* (72), conduct; *noús* (3563), mind, the seat of reflective consciousness; *pneúma* (4151), spirit, only in man as the means of communication with God while soul is held in common with animals as the consciousness of one's environment.

Ant.: *sṓma* (4983), the body, the material element of man as distinct from the duplex spiritual nature; *sárx* (4561), flesh; *húlē* (5208), matter.

5591. ψυχικός *psuchikós*; fem. *psuchikḗ*, neut. *psuchikón*, adj. from *psuchḗ* (5590), soul, the part of the immaterial life held in common with the animals, as contrasted with spirit (*pneúma* [4151]), only in man, enabling him to communicate with God. Natural, pertaining to the natural as distinguished from the spiritual or glorified nature of man. 1 Cor 15:44 refers to a body *psuchikón*, a body governed by the soul or natural and fallen instinct of man, and a body *pneumatikón* (4152), spiritual, governed by the divine quality in man, the spirit. Rendered as "natural" in 1 Cor 2:14; 15:44, 46 and sensual in James 3:15; Jude 1:19. The term *psuchikós* is not a word of honor even as *sarkikós* (4559), carnal, is not.

Ant.: *pneumatikós* (4152), spiritual.

5592. ψύχος *psúchos*; gen. *psúchous*, neut. noun from *psúchō* (5594), to breathe, blow. Cold (John 18:18; Acts

28:2; 2 Cor 11:27; Sept.: Gen 8:22; Ps 147:4).

Ant.: *kaúsōn* (2742), burning heat; *púrōsis* (4451), burning, conflagration; *purá* (4443), a fire; *púr* (4442), fire; *kaúma* (2738), something scorched, the result of burning; *kaúsis* (2740), burning, the act of burning; *thérmē* (2329), warmth, heat; *puretós* (4446), fever; *púrinos* (4447), flaming, fiery.

5593. ψυχρός *psuchrós*; fem. *psuchrá*, neut. *psuchrón*, adj. from *psúchō* (5594), to breathe, blow. Cold (Matt 10:42). As a metaphor in Rev 3:15, 16, it does not represent spiritual lifelessness or an absence of zeal. Rather, it signifies a good quality and is analogous to one of the two conditions (hot or cold) in which water proves beneficial. That one's life is neither cold nor hot is to say it is devoid of any good quality. See also *chliarós* (5513), lukewarm, tepid.

Ant.: *zestós* (2200), boiling hot; *purrós* (4450), fire-like, fire-colored.

5594. ψύχω *psúchō*; fut. *psúxō*, 2d aor. pass. *epsúgēn*. To breathe, blow, refresh with cool air, or breathe naturally. It is from this verb that *psuchḗ* (5590), soul, is derived. Hence *psuchḗ* is the breath of a living creature, animal life, and *psúchō* in the pass. *psúchomai*, means to be cool, to grow cool or cold in a spiritual sense, as in Christian love (Matt 24:12).

Deriv.: *anapsúchō* (404), to make cool, refresh; *apopsúchō* (674), to be faint of heart; *ekpsúchō* (1634), to expire, die; *katapsúchō* (2711), to cool off; *psuchḗ*

(5590), soul; *psúchos* (5592), cold; *psuchrós* (5593), cool, fresh, chilly.

Ant.: *thermaínō* (2328), to heat, warm; *kaíō* (2545), to be on fire, burn; *kaumatízō* (2739), to burn, scorch; *puróō* (4448), to kindle, inflame, burn, be on fire; *kausóō* (2741), to burn with great heat or fever.

5595. ψωμίζω *psōmízō*; fut. *psōmísō*, from *psōmós* (n.f.), a morsel or piece of food, particularly of bread, which is from *psáō* (n.f.), to break in pieces. To feed by providing food (Rom 12:20; 1 Cor 13:3). To spend in feeding others, to divide, as it were, into mouthfuls for feeding others (1 Cor 13:3). Sept.: Num 11:4; Deut 8:16.

Syn.: *bóskō* (1006), to feed, used of shepherds as they graze their flocks; *tréphō* (5142), to nourish, feed; *chortázō* (5526), to feed, fatten, satiate.

Ant.: *aposteréō* (650), to deprive.

5596. ψωμίον *psōmíon*; gen. *psōmíou*, neut. noun, a diminutive of *psōmós* (n.f.), a sop of bread, which is from *psáō* (n.f., see *psēlapháō* [5584]), to break in pieces. A sop, a piece of food, particularly of bread used for dipping (John 13:26, 27, 30).

Syn.: *ártos* (740), bread; *klásma* (2801), a fragment as of food.

5597. ψώχω *psṓchō*; fut. *psṓxō*, from *psáō* (n.f., see *psēlapháō* [5584]), to crumble, grind. To rub, as ears of corn, in order to force out the grains (Luke 6:1).

Syn.: *aléthō* (229), to grind at the mill; *trízō* (5149), to grind the teeth; *likmáō* (3039), to winnow.

Ω

5598. Ω Ōméga; the last letter of the Gr. alphabet. There is evidence that ōméga was composed of two o's—ómikron-o. Ōméga, being the last letter of the Gr. alphabet, is opposite to *álpha* or *a*, the first letter, and is applied to Christ, as being the end or last (Rev 1:8, 11; 21:6; 22:13).

5599. ὦ Ṓ. As a note of exclamation, O! Oh! before the voc. in a direct address (Matt 15:28; Mark 9:19; Luke 9:41; Acts 18:14; Rom 2:1, 3; 9:20; Gal 3:1; James 3:20; Sept.: Jer 4:10); for addressing (Acts 1:1; 27:21; 1 Tim 6:20); to express admiration (Rom 11:33); in upbraiding or reproving (Matt 17:17; Luke 24:25; Acts 13:10).

5600. ὦ Ṓ; subjunctive of *eimí* (1510), to be. May, might, can, could, would, should, must; also with *ei* (1487), if, whether, that, and its comp., meaning to be.

5601. Ὠβήδ Ōbéd; masc. proper noun transliterated from the Hebr. ʿŌvēd (5744, OT), serving. Obed, the son of Boaz and Ruth, father of Jesse, the father of David (Matt 1:5; Luke 3:22; Sept.: Ruth 4:17, 21, 22; 1 Chr 2:12). Obed lived about 1070 B.C. His name occurs in these four genealogies.

5602. ὧδε hṓde; demonstrative adv. of place.

(I) Hither, to this place, after verbs of motion (Matt 8:29; 14:18; 17:17; 22:12; Mark 11:3; Luke 9:41; 14:21; 19:27; John 6:25; 20:27; Acts 9:21; Rev 4:1; 11:12; Sept.: Ex 3:5; Ruth 2:14), after *héos* (2193), until, *héos hṓde*, until here (Luke 23:5).

(II) Here, in this place (Matt 12:6, 41, 42; 14:8, 17; 16:28; 17:4; 20:6; 24:2; 26:38; 28:6; Mark 6:3, here in our city; 8:4; 9:1, 5; 14:32, 34; 16:6; Luke 4:23; 9:12, 27, 33; 11:31, 32; 22:38; 24:6; John 6:9; 11:21, 32; Acts 9:14, in this city; Heb 7:8 referring to the Mosaic dispensation; 13:14, here on earth; James 2:3; Sept.: Gen 19:12; Num 32:16; Judg 19:9; Ruth 4:1, 2; 2 Kgs 7:3). The opposite of *hṓde . . . hṓde*, here or there (Matt 24:23). *Tá hṓde*, "all things which are done here" (Col 4:9). Figuratively, in this thing (Rev 13:10, 18; 14:12; 17:9).

Syn.: *entháde* (1759), here, hither; *autoú* (847), just here, there; *deúro* (1204), come hither.

Ant.: *ekeí* (1563), there; *ekeíse* (1566), thither; *ekeíthen* (1564), from there, thence.

5603. ᾠδή ōdḗ; gen. *ōdḗs*, fem. noun from *ádō* (103), to sing in praise or honor of someone. Song. The original use of singing among both believers and idolaters was in the confessions and praises of the respective gods. Paul qualifies it in Eph 5:19; Col 3:16 as spiritual songs in association with psalms and hymns, because *ōdḗ* by itself might mean any kind of song, as of battle, harvest, festal, whereas *psalmós* (5568), psalm, from its Hebr. use, and *húmnos* (5215), hymn, from its Gr. use, did not require any such qualifying adj. In Rev 5:9; 14:3 *ōdḗ* is designated as *kainḗ* (2537), qualitatively new; in Rev 15:3 as the *ōdḗ* of Moses as celebrating the deliverance of God's people, and the *ōdḗ* of the Lamb as celebrating redemption by atoning sacrifice (Sept.: Judg 5:12; 1 Kgs 4:32; Ps 42:8).

Syn.: *húmnos* (5215), hymn; *psalmós* (5568), psalm.

5604. ᾠδίν ōdín; gen. *ōdínos*, fem. noun. Pain, sorrow. Used in the sing. when referring to the travail or pain of childbirth (1 Thess 5:3). Used in the pl. when warning of the sorrows that would follow wars, famines and other catastrophes (Matt 24:8; Mark 13:8; Sept.: Job 21:17; Nah 2:10). In Acts 2:24 the *ōdínas thanátou*, the cords or snares of death in allusion to Ps 18:4, 5.

Deriv.: *sunōdínō* (4944), to be in travail together; *ōdínō* (5605), to be in pain, travail.

Syn.: *pónos* (4192), pain of any kind; *lúpē* (3077), sorrow; *móchthos* (3449), labor, travail; *stenochōría* (4730), anguish; *sunochḗ* (4928), pressure, anguish; *thlípsis* (2347), affliction.

Ant.: *hēdonḗ* (2237), pleasure; *chará* (5479), joy; *agallíasis* (20), gladness; *euphrosúnē* (2167), joy, good-mindedness.

5605. ὠδίνω *ōdínō*; fut. *ōdinṓ*, from *ōdín* (5604), labor pain at the birth of a child. Intrans., to be in pain as when a woman is in travail (Gal 4:27; Rev 12:2, in both cases applied spiritually to the Church; see Sept.: Song 8:5; Isa 23:4; 26:18; 66:7, 8); trans. with an acc., to travail in birth of, to be in labor with (Gal 4:19 where Paul applies it in a spiritual sense to himself with respect to the Galatian converts).

Deriv.: *sunōdínō* (4944), to travail together.

Syn.: *tíktō* (5088), to bear, produce, give birth; *basanízō* (928), torture, torment; *skúllō* (4660), to vex, annoy, trouble; *stenochōréō* (4729), to anguish; *kataponéō* (2669), to toil, afflict, oppress.

5606. ὦμος *ṓmos*; gen. *ṓmou*, masc. noun. Shoulder (Matt 23:4; Luke 15:5; Sept.: Gen 21:14; Num 7:9; Isa 9:6; 49:22).

5607. ὤν *ṓn*; fem. *oúsa*, neut. *ón*, pres. part. masc. nom. sing. of *eimí* (1510), to be. Being, it refers to existence. It does not, however, refer to the beginning of that existence. John 1:18 says, "The only begotten Son, which is in the bosom of the Father." What is translated "which is" is the pres. part. *ho ṓn*, the one being. It means the one who has always been with the Father; there was no time when that one began to be with the Father. The Son here is designated as coeternal with the Father. There is, however, the verb *hupárchō* (5225), to be, which we must consider here. When used in the pres. part. as in Phil 2:6 in regard to the person of Jesus Christ, "who, being [*hupárchōn*]" it asserts that Christ's present existence was (and still is) simply a continuation of His preexistence. What He came to be in His incarnation did not involve the giving up of what He was previously, i.e., God. It confirms that the Lord Jesus continued to be, in addition to His assumed manhood, what He always was, namely, Deity. This is what Paul says in Col 2:9, that "in Him dwelleth all the fullness of the Godhead bodily." The part. of *gínomai* ([1096], to be or become) would suggest origin or result and would mean becoming instead of being. For this reason, this word is avoided when speaking of Christ's existence as God. There is a unique expression with *ho ṓn* in the following passages in Rev: 1:4, *ho ṓn kaí ho ḗn kai ho erchómenos*, "which is, and which was, and which is to come." This refers to God the Father. The TR, UBS, and Nestle's texts have the expression *apó* ([575], from) preceding this phrase. Ordinarily after *apó* one would expect the use of the gen. However, here the whole designation stands as indeclinable and is appositional with the gen., either *Theoú* (Majority Text), "of God," or *toú* ([3588] [gen. sing.]), "of the one [i.e. God]," being implied. Whether explicit as *apó Theoú*, "from God," or implicit only with *toú*, "of the one" (with *Theoú* implied), deity is meant, either as God the Father distinctly or the Godhead in whom there is the Father, the Son, and the Holy Spirit. The expression *ho ṓn kaí ho ḗn kaí ho erchómenos*, therefore refers to the timelessness of both God the Father and the Godhead in three persons. The correct translation of the three verbs would be, "the One being" (a.t. [cf. John

1:18 {see above}]), or "the One who has always been" (a.t.), ever existent, without beginning. The second designation with *ho én* is the same as in John 1:1 (three times), 2, 3 (twice), 8, 9, 10, 15 where it is in the imperf. of *eimí*. In these verses, it would be better rendered as "had been," i.e., that there had never been a time when He was not; He was prior to any beginning. The third designation is eschatological and refers to a future occasion when God the Son comes to receive His resurrected and translated saints (Col 3:4; 1 Thess 3:13) and comes in His glory (Matt 25:31ff.). This shows that the triune God is timeless. In Rev 1:4 there is a second *apó* ([575], from) followed by the gen., the seven spirits which refer to the third person of the Trinity, the Holy Spirit (Rev 3:1; 4:5; 5:6). The number seven figuratively stands for perfection and completeness. The third *apó* is in Rev 1:5 followed by the gen. Jesus Christ. For the designation of the Trinity and their respective works see John 16:8–11. In Rev 1:8, the Lord Jesus Christ is speaking and identifying Himself as God in the same expression *ho ṓn kaí ho én kaí ho erchómenos*, "the One who has always been, the One who had been, and the One who is yet coming" (a.t.).

In Rev 11:17 the same expression is repeated in the TR; but in the UBS, the Nestle's text and the Majority Text, only *ho ṓn kaí ho én* is used, omitting *kaí ho erchómenos*.

In Rev 16:5 (UBS) only *ho ṓn kaí ho én* is followed by *hósios* (3741), sacred, holy, referring to the Lord Jesus Christ.

5608. ὠνέομαι ōnéomai; contracted *ōnoúmai*, fut. *ōnḗsomai*, aor. mid. *ōnēsá-mēn*, mid. deponent. To buy, purchase, with acc. and gen. of price (Acts 7:16).

Deriv.: *telṓnēs* (5057), a reaper of taxes or customs.

Syn.: *agorázō* (59), to buy, purchase; *emporeúomai* (1710), to buy and sell or to carry on business.

Ant.: *pōléō* (4453), to sell; *pipráskō* (4097), to sell.

5609. ᾠόν ōón; gen. *ōoú*, neut. noun. An egg (Luke 11:12; Sept.: Deut 22:6; Job 39:14).

5610. ὥρα hṓra; gen. *hṓras*, fem. noun. Hour, a time, season, a definite space or division of time recurring at fixed intervals, as marked by natural or conventional limits. Figuratively, of a season of life, the fresh, full bloom and beauty of youth, the ripeness and vigor of manhood meaning bloom, beauty. In the NT, of shorter intervals, a time, season, hour.

(I) Of the day generally, daytime (Matt 14:15; Mark 6:35; 11:11).

(II) Of a definite part or division of the day, in earlier writers used only of the greater divisions as morning, noon, evening, night. In the NT, an hour, one of the twelve equal parts into which the natural day and also the night were divided, and which of course, were of different lengths at different seasons of the year.

(A) Particularly and generally (Matt 24:36; 25:13; Mark 13:32; Luke 22:59; John 4:52; 11:9; Acts 5:7; 10:30; Rev 9:15). Dat. with *én* (1722), in, of time, when (Matt 8:13; 10:19; 24:50; Luke 12:46; John 4:53). Acc. of time, meaning how long (Matt 26:40; Mark 14:37; Acts 19:34). With a numeral marking the hour of the day, as counted from sunrise (Matt 20:3, 5, 6, 9; 27:45, 46; Mark 15:25, 33, 34; Luke 23:44; John 1:39; 4:6; 19:14; Acts 2:15; 3:1; 10:3, 9, 30). Of the hours of the nights as counted from sunset (Acts 23:23).

(B) Figuratively meaning a short time, a brief interval, in the acc. (Rev 17:12); dat. (Rev 18:10, 17, 19). With *prós* (4314), toward (John 5:35; 2 Cor 7:8; Gal 2:5; 1 Thess 2:17; Phile 1:15).

(III) Metonymically and generally, an hour meaning a time or period as spoken of any definite point or space of time.

(A) With adjuncts such as an adj. or pron. as *apó tḗs hṓras ekeínēs* (*apó* [575], from; *ekeínēs* [gen. fem. of *ekeínos* {1565}, that]), from that hour or that period (Matt 9:22; 15:28; 17:18; John 19:27); with *autḗ* (fem. dat. of *autós*

[846], this one, *autḗ tḗ hṓra*), at this time. Dat. of time, when (Luke 2:38; 24:33; Acts 16:18; 22:13; Sept.: Dan 3:6, 15); with the interrogative *poía* the fem dat. of *poíos* (4169), which (*Poía hṓra* or *hḗ hṓra* [dat. fem. of *hós* {3739}, which], what hour [Matt 24:42, 44; Luke 12:39, 40]); with *en* ([1722], in; *en autḗ tḗ hṓra*), in that same hour (Luke 7:21; 10:21; 12:12; 20:19); with *en ekeínē tḗ hṓra*, at that time (Matt 10:19; 18:1; 26:55; Mark 13:11; Rev 11:13). With *áchri* (891), until, *áchri tḗs árti* ([*árti* {737}, the present]), until the present time (1 Cor 4:11). With *pásan* (3956), every, *pásan hṓran*, every hour meaning all the time (1 Cor 15:30; Sept.: Ex 18:22, 26). With an adv. or relative pron.; *érchetai hṓra hóte* (*érchetai* [2064] the pres. indic. 3d person sing. of *érchomai*, I come; *hóte* [3753], when), there comes an hour when (John 4:21, 23; 5:25; 16:25); followed by *en* and the relative pron. (John 5:28). With *hína* (2443), so that (John 12:23; 13:1; 16:2, 32). With the gen. of thing, to be done or to happen (Sept.: Dan 9:21, *tḗ hṓra toú deípnou* (*deípnou* [gen. sing. of *deípnon* {1173}, dinner, supper]), at the time of the supper or feast (Luke 1:10; 14:17); temptation (Rev 3:10); judgment (Rev 14:7, 15); one's own (time) (Luke 22:14). With the inf. (Rom 13:11; Sept.: Gen 29:7); the gen. of person, one's time, appointed to him in which he is to do or suffer (Luke 22:53; John 16:21), elsewhere of Christ (John 2:4; 7:30; 8:20; 13:1).

(B) Simply meaning the time spoken of or otherwise understood (Matt 26:45; Mark 14:41; John 16:4; 1 John 2:18). Emphatically (John 17:1); by implication meaning time or hour of trial, sorrow, suffering (Mark 14:35; John 12:27).

Deriv.: *hēmiṓrion* (2256), a half hour; *hōraíos* (5611), attractive, comely.

Syn.: *hēméra* (2250), day, the period of natural light; *kairós* (2540), season, time, opportunity; *chrónos* (5550), time duration; *stigmḗ* (4743), instant, moment.

5611. ὡραῖος *hōraíos*; fem. *hōraía*, neut. *hōraíon*, adj. from *hṓra* (5610), hour. Attractive, comely. Figuratively of a virgin ready for marriage. In the NT only figuratively meaning fair, comely, beautiful, spoken of things (Matt 23:27; Rom 10:15; Sept.: Gen 2:9; 3:6). Of persons (Gen 29:17; 39:6); of a gate of the temple (Acts 3:2, 10), the Beautiful Gate supposed by some to have been the large gate leading from the court of the Gentiles to the court of the Israelites over against the eastern side of the temple, otherwise called the Gate of Nicanor. It was described by Josephus as covered with plates of gold and silver, and was very splendid and massive. However, from Acts 3:3, 8, it would seem rather to have been one of the external gates leading from without into the court of the Gentiles in which also was Solomon's porch (Acts 3:11).

Syn.: *kalós* (2570), beautiful, good; *kósmios* (2887), decorous.

Ant.: *aschḗmōn* (809), uncomely.

5612. ὠρύομαι *ōrúomai*; fut. *ōrúsomai*, mid. deponent. To roar or howl, as a lion after his prey (1 Pet 5:8). It is a word derived from the sound of roaring.

Syn.: *mukáomai* (3455), to moo, to low as the cow or ox; in the NT it is used of a lion; *ēchéō* (2278), an onomatopoeia meaning to echo, to sound, resound as the brass or the waves.

5613. ὡς *hōs*; relative adv. from *hós* (3739), who, correlative to *pṓs* (4459), how, in what manner or way. As, so as, how, sometimes equivalent to a conjunction (cf. IV). For *hōs án*, as if, see *án* ([302], cf. II, A, 1, and B, 3).

(I) In comparisons. In Attic writers *hṓsper* (5618), just as, is the prevailing word in this usage.

(A) Particularly, fully, with the corresponding demonstrative adv. as *hoútōs* (3779), thus, or the like, either preceding or following, *hoútōs . . . hōs*, so . . . as (Mark 4:26; John 7:46, so as if; 1 Cor 3:15); *hōs amnós . . . hoútōs*, as . . . so (Acts 8:32 quoted from Isa 53:7; Acts 23:11); *hōs gár . . . oútō* (*gár* [1063], and, but, for, therefore; *oútō* [3779], thus), as therefore, "as . . . so also"; Rom 5:15, 18; 2 Cor 7:14; 11:3; 1 Thess 2:7; 5:2); *ísos . . . hōs*, (*ísos* [2470], similar, equal), the like, similar, equal gift . . . as (Acts 11:17). *Homoíōs kaí hōs* (*homoíōs* [3668], similarly, likewise; *kaí* [2532], and), likewise also as (Luke 17:28); *hōs . . . kaí*, where *hoútōs* ([3779], thus) is strictly implied (cf. *kai* [2532], and, II, B). *Hōs en ouranō͂, kaí epí tēs gēs* (*ouranō͂* [3772], heaven; *gēs* [1063], earth), as in heaven, also on earth (Matt 6:10; Acts 7:51; Gal 1:9). Frequently *hoútos* is omitted and then *hōs* may often be rendered "so as" or simply "as" (Acts 7:37; Rom 4:17; 5:16). Sometimes the whole clause to which *hōs* refers is omitted as in Mark 4:31, "the kingdom of God" is omitted, which, however, occurs in 4:30.

(B) Generally before a noun or adj. in the nom. or acc. meaning as, like as, like (Matt 6:29; 10:25; Mark 1:22; 6:15; Luke 6:10, 40; 21:35; 10:3, 16; 13:43; 28:3; 22:31; John 15:6; Acts 11:5; 1 Cor 3:10; 14:33; Gal 4:12; 1 Thess 5:6; Heb 1:11; Heb 6:19; James 1:10; 1 Pet 2:25; 1 John 1:7; Jude 1:10; Rev 1:14; 8:1, 10; 10:1; 20:8; 22:1; Sept.: Judg 8:18; 1 Sam 25:36). Here, too, the construction is often elliptical, e.g., where a part. belonging to the noun before *hōs* is also implied with the noun after *hōs*, as in Luke 10:18 (cf. Matt 3:16; Mark 1:10). Also where the noun before *hōs* is also implied after it, as in Rev 1:10, "as [the voice] of a trumpet"; 16:3; Sept.: Jer 4:31. Sometimes the noun after *hōs* is implied before it (Rev 6:1, "saying with a voice, as it were, the voice of a thunder" [a.t.]). A noun preceded by *hōs* often denotes something like itself, a person or thing like that which the noun refers to, with the meaning "as it were" (Rev 4:6 [UBS], something like a sea of glass, as it were a sea of glass; 8:8, "as it were a great mountain"; 9:7, "as it were crowns like gold" or as if they were golden crowns; 15:2; Sept.: Dan 10:18); acc. (Rev 19:1 [UBS], a sound like the voice; 9:6).

(II) Implying quality, character, circumstances as known or supposed to exist in any personal thing; something which is matter of belief or opinion, whether true or false.

(A) Before a part. referring to a preceding noun and expressing a quality or circumstance belonging to that noun, either real or supposed, meaning as, as if, as though. **(1)** Before a nom. as referring to a preceding subject (Luke 16:1, as wasting his goods, being so accounted; Acts 23:20, "as though they would inquire"; 28:19, "not as having" [a.t.], meaning not supposing that I have; 1 Cor 4:7; 5:3; 7:25; 2 Cor 6:9, 10; 10:14; 13:2; Col 2:20; 1 Thess 2:4; Heb 11:27; 13:3, 17; James 2:12; Sept.: Gen 27:12). With a part. implied (Eph 6:7; 1 Pet 4:11). **(2)** Before a gen. referring to a preceding noun (Heb 12:27). Elliptically (John 1:14). Often with a gen. absolute (1 Cor 4:18, "they, supposing that I shall not come" [a.t.]; 2 Cor 5:20; 1 Pet 4:12; 2 Pet 1:3). After *prophásei*, the dat. of *próphasis* (4392), pretense (Acts 27:30, as though they would have cast). **(3)** Before a dat. referring to a preceding noun (Acts 3:12; 1 Pet 2:14). **(4)** Before an acc. referring to a preceding object (Acts 23:15; Rom 6:13; 15:15; 2 Cor 10:2; Rev 5:6). **(5)** Once before an inf. apparently with a part. implied or perhaps instead of the part. construction (2 Cor 10:9).

(B) Before a subst. or adj. either as predicate or obj. expressing a quality or circumstance known or supposed to belong to a preceding noun, meaning as, as if, as though. Here the part. *ón* ([5607] masc., *oúsa* fem., *ón* neut.) or the like, may always be supplied, and the construction is then the same as in section II A above. **(1)** Before the nom. as referring to a preceding subject (Rom 3:7, "as though I were a sinner" [a.t.]; 2 Cor 6:4, 8, 10; 11:15; 13:7; Eph 5:1, 8, as it becomes children of the light, as they are supposed to walk; 6:6; Col 3:12, 22; Heb 3:5, 6; James 2:9; 1 Pet 1:14; 2:2, 5, 16; 4:10, 15, 16). Once preceded by *toioútos* (5108), such a one (Phile 1:9, "being such a one as Paul the aged," such a one as you know Paul to be, your aged teacher and friend). **(2)** Before the gen. as referring to a preceding noun (1 Pet 2:12; 3:16 [cf. II, A, 2 in text on word *hōs*]). **(3)** Before the dat. as referring to a preceding noun (1 Cor 3:1, "as unto spiritual"; 10:15; 2 Cor 6:13; Heb 12:5, 7; 1 Pet 2:13; 3:7; 4:19; 2 Pet 1:19), implied (1 Pet 1:19). **(4)** Before the acc. as referring to another object (Matt 14:5; Luke 6:22; 15:19; Rom 1:21; 1 Cor 4:9, 14; 8:7; 2 Cor 11:16; Heb 11:9). Preceded by *hoútōs* (3779), thus, *hoútōs hōs*, thus as (2 Cor 9:5).

(C) Before prep. with their cases in the same manner as before part. (cf. II, A). **(1)** With *diá* (1223), through (2 Thess 2:2); *en* (1722), in (John 7:10; Rom 13:13); *ek* (1537), out of, of (Rom 9:32 [cf. 9:31]; 2 Cor 2:17; 3:5; 1 Pet 4:11); *epí* (1909), upon (Matt 26:55, "as though against a robber" [a.t.]; Gal 3:16). **(2)** Before a prep. implying motion to a place, *hōs* qualifies the force of the prep. meaning as if to, toward, in the direction of, leaving it undetermined whether one arrives at the place or not. Used in the NT only once with *epí* (Acts 17:14, "as toward the sea" [a.t.]).

(D) Before numerals meaning as if it were, about, marking a supposed or conjectural number (Mark 5:13, about two thousand; 8:9; Luke 2:37; 8:42; John 6:19; 21:8; Acts 1:15; 5:7; 19:34; Sept.: Ruth 1:4).

(E) Intens. meaning how! how very! how much! expressing admiration. In the NT only before adj., see below III, C (Rom 10:15, how beautiful the feet; 11:33). Once before the comparative (Acts 17:22, how much more religiously inclined do I behold you than other cities or nations; Sept.: Ps 73:1).

(III) Implying manner before a dependent clause qualifying or defining the action of a preceding verb or one that follows.

(A) Generally, meaning as, according as (Matt 1:24; 8:13; 20:14; Luke 14:22; Rom 12:3; 1 Cor 3:5; Col 2:6; 4:4; Titus 1:5; Rev 9:3; 18:6; 22:12). Once with

hoútō (3779), thus, corresponding (1 Cor 7:17). Here in a somewhat more less restrictive *hōs kaí* ([2532], and), like the relative *hós* (3739), he who, serves as a connective particle (Acts 13:33; 17:28; 22:5; 25:10; Rom 9:25).

(B) Before a minor or parenthetic clause which then serves to modify or restrict the general proposition (Matt 27:65; Mark 4:27; 10:1; Luke 3:23; Acts 2:15; 1 Cor 12:2; 1 Pet 5:12; 2 Pet 3:9; Rev 2:24).

(C) Before a superlative used as an intens. meaning most speedily, as speedily as possible (Acts 17:15).

(IV) Before dependent clauses expressing the obj. or reference of a preceding verb or word, the nature of the action, the circumstances under which it takes place, and so forth, meaning in what way, how, as, often equivalent to a conjunction.

(A) Generally, meaning how, equivalent to *hópōs* (3704), in the manner that. With the aor. indic. (Mark 12:26; Luke 8:47; 23:55; 24:35; Acts 11:16; Rom 11:2; 2 Cor 7:15). Pleonastically (Luke 22:61). Once with *toúto* (5124), this, preceding (Luke 6:3, 4). Also followed by *hóti* (3754), that, meaning how that, *hōs hóti*, as that, to wit that. In the NT subjoined to a noun for fuller explanation, usually regarded as pleonastic, but not so in strictness (2 Cor 5:19; 11:21, "I speak as to the reproach [cast upon us] how that [*hōs hóti*] we are weak, although we were weak" (a.t.); 2 Thess 2:2, "nor by letter . . . as that."

(B) Before an obj. clause in a more restrictive sense meaning how, how that, that, with the indic. equivalent to *hóti*, that (cf. *hóti* [3754] I, C) (Acts 10:28, 38; Rom 1:9; 1 Thess 2:10; 2 Tim 1:3; Sept.: 1 Sam 13:11).

(C) Before a clause expressing end or purpose meaning as that, so that, equivalent to that, to the end that, like *hína* (2443), so that, or *hópōs* (3704), so that. Followed by the inf. expressing the purpose of a preceding verb meaning so as to, in order to (Acts 20:24, "I count not my life dear so that I may finish" [a.t.]; Heb 7:9, "so to speak" [a.t.], "that I may so speak" [a.t.]).

(D) Before a clause expressing result or consequence, so as that, so that, like *hóste* (5620), so to, so that; with the indic. (Heb 3:11; 4:3 quoted from Ps 95:11).

(E) Before a clause expressing a cause or reason meaning as, that, equivalent to since, because, like *epeí* (1893), thereupon, since, because; *hóti* (3754), that (Gal 6:10, "since we now have opportunity" [a.t.]; perhaps Matt 6:12 [cf. Luke 11:4]).

(F) Before a clause implying time, as when, like *epeí* (1893), thereupon. **(1)** Generally meaning when, in that, while. With the indic. (Matt 28:9; Luke 1:41, 44; 4:25; 19:5; John 2:9; Acts 5:24; 28:4). By implication meaning whenever, as often as (Luke 12:58; Sept.: 2 Chr 24:11). Also when, with the indic. (Luke 1:23; 2:15, 39; 11:1; John 4:1; 6:12, 16; Acts 7:23; 10:7; 13:18, 29). Followed by *tóte* (5119), then, at that time (John 7:10). From when, since (Mark 9:21). **(2)** Followed by *án* (302), a particle denoting a supposition, wish, possibility, *hōs án* meaning whensoever, as soon as, with the aor. subjunctive (Rom 15:24 [UBS]; 1 Cor 11:34, as soon as I come; Phil 2:23).

Deriv.: *hōsaútōs* (5615), likewise; *hōseí* (5616), about; *hósper* (5618), just as; *hóste* (5620), therefore.

Syn.: *katá* (2596), according to, as; *katháper* (2509), exactly as; *hoíos* (3739), in the neut. *hoíon*, with a neg., not so, such as; *áchri* (891), until; *méchri* (3360), till (a reference to a space of time).

5614. ὡσαννά *hōsanná*; an interjection. Hosanna! from the Hebr. meaning save now, help now, or save we pray thee. It became a word of common acclamation (Ps 118:25), and later a common form of wishing safety and prosperity, Save and prosper, O Lord (Mark 11:9, 10; John 12:13). With the dat. following, "to the Son of David" (Matt 21:9, 15).

5615. ὡσαύτως *hōsaútōs*; adv. from *hōs* (5613), as, and *aútos* (846), likewise, the same. In the same or like manner, likewise (Matt 20:5; 21:30, 36; 25:17; Mark 12:21; 14:31; Luke 13:3; 20:31; 22:20; Rom 8:26; 1 Cor 11:25; 1 Tim 2:9; 3:8, 11; 5:25; Titus 2:3, 6; Sept.: Deut 12:22; Judg 8:8).

Syn.: *hoútō*, before a consonant, or *hoútōs* (3779) before a vowel, thus, in this manner; *hósper* (5618), exactly like; *homoíōs* (3668), in like manner; *kaí* (2532), and, even, also, likewise; *paraplēsíōs* (3898), similarly, in a similar manner.

Ant.: *állōs* (247), differently; *hetérōs* (2088), differently, otherwise, taking into account the difference between *állos* (243), another of the same kind, and *héteros* (2087), another of a different kind.

5616. ὡσεί *hōseí*; conditional adv. from *hōs* (5613), as, and *ei* (1487), if. As if, as though, followed by the opt. In the NT only before a noun or adj.

(I) In comparisons, as if, as it were, as, like as (cf. *hōs* [5613] I, B) (Matt 9:36; 28:3, 4; Mark 9:26; Luke 22:44; 24:11; Acts 2:3; 6:15; 9:18; Heb 1:12; 11:12; Rev 1:14; Sept.: Job 28:5; 29:25). Elliptically where a part. or inf. belonging to the noun before *hōseí* is also implied with the noun after *hōseí* (Matt 3:16, "as a dove descending" [a.t.]; Mark 1:10; John 1:32; inf. Luke 3:22).

(II) Before words of number and measure, as if, as it were, meaning about, approximately (cf. *hōs* [5613] II, D). Before numerals (Matt 14:21, "about five thousand"; Mark 6:44; Luke 1:56; 3:23; 9:14, 28; 22:59; 23:44; John 4:6; 6:10; 19:14, 39; Acts 2:41; 4:4; 5:36; 10:3; 19:7; Sept.: Judg 3:29). Of measure (Luke 22:41).

5617. Ὡσηέ *Hōsēé*; masc. proper noun transliterated from the Hebr. *Hōshē'a* (1954, OT), God is help. Hosea, the name of the prophet (Rom 9:25). One of the minor prophets who prophesied between 790 and 725 B.C. in the kingdom of Israel. At that time, Israel was under the reign of Jeroboam II and had reached the zenith of its earthly prosperity and was fast ripening for ruin. Hosea was a contemporary of Isaiah.

5618. ὥσπερ hósper; adv. from *hōs* (5613), as, and the emphatic enclitic particle *per* (4007), much. Wholly as, just as, exactly like. In the NT, it is used only in comparisons.

(**I**) It introduces a comparison followed by a corresponding clause with *houtōs* (3779), thus, or the like (Matt 12:40; 13:40; 24:27, 37; Luke 17:24; John 5:21, 26; Rom 5:19, 21; 6:4, 19; 11:30; 1 Cor 11:12; 15:22; 16:1; 2 Cor 1:7; Gal 4:29; Eph 5:24; James 2:26). Once with *houtōs* omitted as inconsequential (Matt 25:14), and in Rom 5:12 suspended by a parenthetic clause (cf. Rom 5:18). In 2 Cor 8:7 used with *kaí* (2532), and.

(**II**) Generally and without *houtōs* (3779), thus, corresponding (Matt 5:48; 6:2, 5, 7, 16; 20:28; 25:32; Luke 18:11; Acts 2:2; 3:17; 11:15; 2 Cor 9:5 [TR]; 1 Thess 5:3; Heb 4:10; 7:27; 9:25; Rev 10:3). In Matt 18:17 it should be translated "just as" (a.t.).

(**III**) After a hypothetical proposition, as asserting or confirming its truth and reality, meaning as indeed (1 Cor 8:5).

Deriv.: *hōspereí* (5619), just as if, as it were.

5619. ὡσπερεί hōspereí; adv. from *hōsper* (5618), exactly like, and *ei* (1487), if. Just as if, as it were (1 Cor 15:8).

Syn.: *hōsaútōs* (5615), likewise; *hōsper* (5618), wholly as.

5620. ὥστε hōste; conj. from *hōs* (5613), as, strengthened by the enclitic particle *te* (5037) which serves to connect more closely a following clause with the preceding one. So that, accordingly, thus. Used also as an adv. like *hōs* (5613), as, used in comparisons and meaning as, like as. In the NT generally used as a conj. meaning so as that, so that, before a clause expressing an event,

result, consequence, whether real or supposed; and followed usually by an inf., but also by the indic.

(**I**) Followed by an inf. with an acc. expressed or implied:

(**A**) Fully preceded by a demonstrative adv. or pron., as *houtō* (3779), thus, *tosoútos* (5108), such (Matt 15:33; Acts 14:1).

(**B**) Simply, without a preceding demonstrative (Matt 8:24, 28; 10:1; 13:54; Mark 1:27, 45; Luke 5:7; Acts 1:19; 16:26; Rom 7:6; 15:19; 1 Cor 5:1; Sept.: Gen 9:15; Josh 10:14).

(**C**) Infrequently instead of an actual result, *hōste* with an inf. serves to mark a purpose, like *hína* (2443) or *hópōs* (3704), so that (Matt 27:1; Luke 9:52).

(**II**) Often used at the beginning of a sentence with the indic. or imper. as an emphatic inferential particle, meaning so that, consequently, therefore, wherefore (Matt 12:12; 23:31; Mark 2:28; 10:8; Rom 7:12; 1 Cor 3:7; 7:38; Gal 3:9, 24). With the imper. (1 Cor 3:21; 15:58; Phil 2:12; 4:1; 1 Thess 4:18; James 1:19; 1 Pet 4:19).

(**III**) Followed by the indic. and preceded by *houtōs* or *houtō* (3779), thus (John 3:16), *houtō* . . . *hōste*. Used simply in Gal 2:13.

Syn.: *oún* (3767), a particle expressing sequence, wherefore, now, then, therefore; *diá* (1223), for (in the acc.), and *toúto*, the neut. of *oútos* (846), this, for this reason; *kathó* (2526), insomuch as, inasmuch as; *eph' hóson* (*epí* [1909], upon; *hóson* [3745], much), inasmuch as; *kath' hóson* (*katá* [2596], inasmuch, according; *hóson*), according to, inasmuch as; *eis tó* (*eis* [1519], unto; *tó*, the neut. def. art.), for the purpose, followed by the inf., insomuch that; *diá toúto* (*diá* [1223], for; *toúto* [5124], this), on account of this; *di' hēn aitían* (*hēn*, the fem. relative pron.; *aitían* [156], reason), for which reason, on account of which; *diá tí* or *diatí* (1302), why, on account of what? or on account of which; *dió* (1352), sometimes *di' hó*, consequently on account of which; *dióper* (1355), on which account;

hóthen (3606), wherefore; *héneka* (1752), because; *tí* (the neut. of *tís* [5101], who, what), what, why; *chárin hoú* (*chárin* [5484], sake; *hoú*, the gen. relative pron.), for the sake of which; *eis tí*, unto what; *ára* (687), therefore, with *ge* (1065), a particle of affirmation; *toigaroún* (5105), wherefore; *eph' hó* from *epí*, upon, and the neut. relative pron. meaning upon which.

5621. ὠτίον ōtíon; gen. *ōtíou*, neut. noun. Ear, the diminutive of *oús* (3775). The ear, metaphorically the capacity to receive truth (Matt 26:51; Mark 14:47; Luke 22:51; John 18:10, 26; Sept.: 1 Sam 9:15; 20:2).

5622. ὠφέλεια ōphéleia; gen. *ōpheleías*, fem. noun from *ōpheléō* (5623), to profit. Increase, profit, advantage (Rom 3:1). Profit, gain (Jude 1:16; Sept.: Job 22:3; Ps 30:9). It primarily denotes assistance, then advantage, benefit, profit.
Syn.: *tó sumphéron* (pres. part. neut. of *sumphérō* [4851]), to help, confer a benefit; *prokopé* (4297), profiting, progress, furtherance; *euergesía* (2108), beneficence; *chrēstótēs* (5544), usefulness, kindness.
Ant.: *mataiótēs* (3153), vanity, uselessness.

5623. ὠφελέω ōpheléō; contracted *ōphelō̂*, fut. *ōphelḗsō*, from *óphelos* (3786), increase, profit. To be useful, profitable, to profit.
(I) Act. absolute: to further, help, profit, be of use. Used in an act. absolute sense (Mark 8:36; Rom 2:25; 1 Cor 14:6; Gal 5:2); with the simple acc. of person (Heb 4:2); with *tí*, the neut. of *tís* (5100), who, *oudén*, the neut. of *oudeís* (3762), none, and *mēdén*, the neut. of *mēdeís* (3367), not a one (Matt 27:24; John 6:63; 12:19; Sept. with the acc.: Prov 10:2; Isa 30:5, 6).
(II) In the mid. / pass. *ōpheléomai*, to be profited, have advantage. Used with

the neut. *tí* (5100), what, *oudén*, nothing, *mēdén*, none, nothing (Matt 16:26; Mark 5:26; Luke 9:25; 1 Cor 13:3). Followed by the prep. *ek* (1537), from, of, with the gen. meaning to be profited of or by someone; with the rel. pron. (Matt 15:5; Mark 7:11; Sept. Jer 2:11); by the prep. *en* (1722), in, and the dat. (Heb 13:9, in which or by which).
Deriv.: *anōphelḗs* (512), unprofitable, unprofitableness; *ōphéleia* (5622), usefulness, benefit, advantage; *ōphélimos* (5624), helpful.
Syn.: *sumphérō* (4851), to be profitable, expedient; *prokóptō* (4298), to advance, profit; *auxánō* (837), to increase or grow; *lusiteléō* (3081), it is better, advantageous; *euergetéō* (2109), to be beneficent; *therapeúō* (2323), to attend to; *hupēretéō* (5256), to minister to.
Ant.: *achreióō* (889), to render useless; *bláptō* (984), to hurt; *zēmióō* (2210), to injure, lose; *katastréphō* (2690), to turn upside down, upset, overthrow; *phtheírō* (5351), to shrivel, wither, spoil, corrupt; *analískō* (355), to use up, destroy, consume; *katastrēniázō* (2691), to revel against; *adikéō* (91), to wrong, hurt, injure, be unjust to.

5624. ὠφέλιμος ōphélimos; gen. *ōphelímou*, masc.-fem., neut. *ōphélimon*, adj. from *ōpheléō* (5623), to be useful, profitable, advantageous. Helpful, profitable, useful. With *prós* (4314), unto, for, and the acc. (1 Tim 4:8; 2 Tim 3:16). With the dat. (Titus 3:8).
Syn.: *chrḗsimos* (5539), useful; *eúchrēstos* (2173), serviceable; *anagkaíos* (316), necessary; *polútimos* (4186), extremely valuable.
Ant.: *anōphelḗs* (512), useless, unprofitable; *alusitelḗs* (255), gainless, unprofitable; *áchrēstos* (890), inefficient, unprofitable; *kenós* (2756), empty, vain; *mátaios* (3152), empty, profitless, vain; *perissós* or *perittós* (4053), superfluous.